THE OXFORD ANTHO
OF ENGLISH LITERATU

Volume II

General Editors: Frank Kermode and John Hollander

VOLUME I
The Middle Ages
through the Eighteenth Century

Medieval English Literature
J. B. TRAPP
Warburg Institute

The Literature of Renaissance England
JOHN HOLLANDER AND FRANK KERMODE

The Restoration and the Eighteenth Century
MARTIN PRICE
Yale University

The Oxford Anthology of English Literature

VOLUME II

1800 to the Present

Romantic Poetry and Prose
HAROLD BLOOM AND LIONEL TRILLING
Yale University   Columbia University

Victorian Prose and Poetry
LIONEL TRILLING AND HAROLD BLOOM

Modern British Literature
FRANK KERMODE AND JOHN HOLLANDER
University College London   Hunter College

NEW YORK
OXFORD UNIVERSITY PRESS
LONDON   TORONTO

Copyright © 1973 by Oxford University Press, Inc.

Library of Congress Catalogue Card Number: 72–92355

printing, last digit: 10 9 8 7

Selections from works by the following authors were made possible by the kind permission of their respective publishers and representatives:

ROMANTIC POETRY AND PROSE

Thomas Lovell Beddoes: The Works of *Thomas Lovell Beddoes*, edited by H. W. Donner, reprinted by permission of Oxford University Press, London.

William Blake: *The Poetry and Prose of William Blake*, by David V. Erdman with commentary by Harold Bloom, copyright © 1965 by David V. Erdman and Harold Bloom; reprinted by permission of Doubleday and Company, Inc.

John Clare: *The Poems of John Clare*, edited with an introduction by J. W. Tibble, copyright © 1935 by J. M. Dent & Sons Ltd.; reprinted by permission of J. M. Dent and Sons Ltd., and E. P. Dutton, Inc. *Selected Poems and Prose of John Clare*, edited by Eric Robinson and Geoffrey Summerfield, copyright © 1967 by Eric Robinson; reprinted by permission of Curtis Brown Ltd., and Oxford University Press, London.

John Keats: *The Letters of John Keats*, edited by Robert Gittings, reprinted by permission of Oxford University Press, London. *The Letters of John Keats*, edited by Hyder Edward Rollins, reprinted by permission of Harvard University Press.

Percy Bysshe Shelley: *"The Triumph of Life": A Critical Study* by Donald H. Reiman, reprinted by permission of The University of Illinois Press.

Dorothy Wordsworth: *The Journals of Dorothy Wordsworth*, edited by Mary Moorman, reprinted by permission of the editor and Oxford University Press, London.

William Wordsworth: "The Ruined Cottage" taken from *William Wordsworth* by Jonathan Wordsworth, reprinted by permission of A. D. Peters and Company.

Printed in the United States of America

VICTORIAN PROSE AND POETRY

Gerard Manley Hopkins: *The Poems of Gerard Manley Hopkins,* fourth edition, edited by W. H. Gardner and N. H. MacKenzie, reprinted by permission of Oxford University Press. Edward Lear: *Teapots and Quails and Other New Nonsenses,* edited by Davison and Hofer, reprinted by permission of John Murray Ltd.

MODERN BRITISH LITERATURE

Kingsley Amis: *A Case of Samples,* reprinted by permission of Curtis Brown Ltd. and Victor Gollancz Ltd.

W. H. Auden: *Collected Shorter Poems, 1927–1957,* poems copyright 1934 (renewed 1962), 1937 (renewed 1965), 1940 (renewed 1968), 1947, 1951, and 1954 by W. H. Auden; *City Without Walls and Other Poems,* copyright © 1966 by W. H. Auden, all reprinted by permission of Random House, Inc., and Faber and Faber Ltd. *Collected Longer Poems,* copyright 1944 by W. H. Auden; *The Collected Poetry of W. H. Auden,* copyright 1934 and renewed 1961 by W. H. Auden; reprinted by permission of Random House, Inc. *For the Time Being* and *The Orators,* reprinted by permission of Faber and Faber Ltd.

Samuel Beckett: *Watt,* reprinted by permission of Grove Press, Inc., all rights reserved, and Calder and Boyars Ltd.

John Betjeman: *Collected Poems,* reprinted by permission of John Murray (Publishers) Ltd. and Houghton Mifflin Co.

Robert Bridges: *The Poetical Works of Robert Bridges,* reprinted by permission of The Clarendon Press, Oxford.

Basil Bunting: *Collected Poems,* reprinted by permission of Fulcrum Press.

Joseph Conrad: *Heart of Darkness,* reprinted by permission of J. M. Dent & Sons Ltd. and The Trustees of the Joseph Conrad Estate.

Donald Davie: *Collected Poems, 1950–1970,* copyright © 1971 by Donald Davie; reprinted by permission of Oxford University Press, Inc., and Routledge & Kegan Paul Ltd.

Walter de la Mare: *The Collected Poems,* reprinted by permission of The Literary Trustees of Walter de la Mare and The Society of Authors as their representative.

T. S. Eliot: *Collected Poems, 1909–1962,* copyright 1936 by Harcourt Brace Jovanovich, Inc.; copyright © 1943, 1963, 1964 by T. S. Eliot; copyright 1971 by Esme Valerie Eliot; *Selected Essays:* New Edition by T. S. Eliot, copyright 1932, 1936, 1950 by Harcourt Brace Jovanovich, Inc.; copyright 1960, 1964 by T. S. Eliot; reprinted by permission of Harcourt Brace Jovanovich, Inc., and Faber and Faber Ltd.

William Empson: *Collected Poems of William Empson,* copyright 1949 by William Empson; reprinted by permission of Harcourt Brace Jovanovich, Inc., and Chatto and Windus Ltd.

E. M. Forster: *Two Cheers for Democracy,* copyright 1939, 1967 by E. M. Forster; reprinted by permission of Harcourt Brace Jovanovich, Inc., and Edward Arnold (Publishers) Ltd.

Robert Graves: *Collected Poems,* copyright © 1955 by Robert Graves; reprinted by permission of Collins-Knowlton-Wing, Inc.

Thom Gunn: *The Sense of Movement,* reprinted by permission of Faber and Faber Ltd.

Thomas Hardy: *The Dynasts,* copyright 1904 by The Macmillan Company, renewed 1931 by Florence E. Hardy; *Collected Poems,* copyright 1925 by The Macmillan Company, renewed 1953 by Lloyds Bank Ltd.; reprinted by permission of The Macmillan Company, New York, the Trustees of the Hardy Estate, The Macmillan Company of Canada Limited, and Macmillan London and Basingstoke.

John Heath-Stubbs: *Selected Poems,* reprinted by permission of Oxford University Press, New York.

Geoffrey Hill: *For the Unfallen,* reprinted by permission of Dufour Editions, Inc., and Andre Deutsch Ltd.

A. E. Housman: From "A Shropshire Lad," Authorised Edition, from *The Collected Poems of A. E. Housman,* copyright 1939, 1940, © 1959 by Holt, Rinehart and Winston, Inc.; copyright © 1967, 1968 by Robert E. Symons; *The Collected Poems of A. E. Housman,* copyright 1922 by Holt, Rinehart and Winston, Inc.; copyright 1936, 1950 by Barclays Bank Limited; copyright © 1964 by Robert E. Symons; reprinted by permission of Holt, Rinehart and Winston, Inc., The Society of Authors as the literary representative of the Estate of A. E. Housman, and Jonathan Cape Ltd.

Ted Hughes: *Wodwo,* copyright © 1961 by Ted Hughes; *Crow,* copyright © 1971 by Ted Hughes; reprinted by permission of Harper & Row, Publishers, Inc., and Faber and Faber Ltd.

Aldous Huxley: "Wordsworth in the Tropics" from *Collected Essays,* copyright 1929, 1957 by Aldous Huxley; reprinted by permission of Harper & Row, Publishers, Inc., Mrs. Laura Huxley, and Chatto and Windus Ltd.

David Jones: *In Parenthesis,* reprinted by permission of Chilmark Press and Faber and Faber Ltd.

James Joyce: *Dubliners,* copyright © 1967 by the Estate of James Joyce; originally published in 1916 by B. W. Huebsch, Inc.; *A Portrait of the Artist as a Young Man,* copyright © 1964 by The

"Michael Robartes and the Dancer," "Easter, 1916," "On a Political Prisoner," "The Second Coming," copyright 1924 by The Macmillan Company, renewed 1952 by Bertha Georgie Yeats; "Sailing to Byzantium," "Ancestral Houses," "Two Songs from a Play," "Leda and the Swan," "Among School Children," copyright 1928 by The Macmillan Company, renewed 1956 by Georgie Yeats; "In Memory of Eva Gore-Booth . . . ," "Coole Park, 1929," "Byzantium," "Crazy Jane Talks with the Bishop," "After Long Silence," "A Last Confession," copyright 1933 by The Macmillan Company, renewed 1961 by Bertha Georgie Yeats; "Meru," copyright 1934 by The Macmillan Company, renewed 1962 by Bertha Georgie Yeats; "Lapis Lazuli," "The Statues," "John Kinsella's Lament for Mrs. Mary Moore," "The Circus Animals' Desertion," "Cuchulian Comforted," copyright 1940 by Georgie Yeats, renewed 1968 by Bertha Georgie Yeats, Michael Butler Yeats and Anne Yeats; in Collected Poems; reprinted by permission of The Macmillan Company, New York, M. B. Yeats, Macmillan & Co. (London), and The Macmillan Company of Canada.

A selection from Picture Show by Siegfried Sassoon is reprinted by permission of G. T. Sassoon.

General Editors' Preface

The purpose of the Oxford Anthology is to provide students with a selective canon of the entire range of English Literature from the beginnings to recent times, with introductory matter and authoritative annotation. Its method is historical, in the broadest sense, and its arrangement, commentary, and notes, both analytic and contextual, have benefited not only from the teaching experience of the several editors, but from a study of the virtues and shortcomings of comparable works. A primary aim has been to avoid the insulation of any one section from the influence of others, and more positively, to allow both student and instructor to come to terms with the manner in which English literature has generated its own history. This aim has been accomplished in several ways.

First, a reorganization of chronological phases has allowed the Tudor and Stuart periods to be unified under the broad heading of the English Renaissance, with two editors collaborating over the whole extended period. Similarly, the nineteenth century has two editors, one for the poetry of the whole period, and one for the prose. This arrangement seemed appropriate in every way, especially since neither of these scholars could be called a narrow specialist in "Romantic" or "Victorian," as these terms are used in semester- or course-labels.

Every contributing editor has worked and taught in at least one period or field outside the one for which he is, in this anthology, principally responsible, and none has ever allowed specialization to reduce his broader commitment to humane studies more largely considered. Thus we were able to plan a work which called for an unusual degree of cross reference and collaboration. During a crucial phase in the preparation of the text, the editors held daily discussions of their work for a period of months. By selection, allusion, comparison, by direction and indirection, we contrived to preserve continuity between epochs, and to illuminate its character. At the same time, the close co-operation of the various editors has precluded the possibility of common surrender to any single dominating literary theory; and the teacher need have no fear that he must prepare to do battle with some critical Hydra showing a head on every page.

The method of selecting text was consistent with these principles. In the eighteenth- and nineteenth-century sections it was our general policy to exclude the novel, for obvious reasons of length; but in the twentieth, where short fiction becomes more prominent and more central, we have included entire works of fiction, or clearly defined parts of them—for example, *Heart of Darkness*, "The Dead," the "Nausicaa" episode of *Ulysses*, and *St. Mawr*. On the other hand we were persuaded, after much reflection, that a different principle must apply in the cases of Spenser and Milton, where we waived the requirement of completeness. To have given the whole of one book—say, the First of *The Faerie Queene*—would have been a solution as easy as it is, no doubt, defensible; but it is asking a great deal of students to see that portion of the poem as an epitome of the rest, which is often so delightfully different; and we decided that we must provide selections from the whole poem, with linking commentary. We did the same for *Paradise Lost* though without abandoning the practice of providing complete texts when this was both possible and desirable; for example, *Comus* is reprinted entire, and so is a lesser-known but still very important masque, Jonson's *Pleasure Reconciled to Virtue*, which is interesting not only in relation to *Comus* but as an illustration of the part poetry can play in political spectacle and—more generally—in the focusing of the moral vision. Minor texts have been chosen for their exemplary force and their beauty, as well as to embody thematic concerns. If the teacher wishes, he or she may work, both within and across periods, with recurrent patterns as large as the conception of the Earthly Paradise, or with sub-genres as small but as fascinating as the Mad Song. It will also be evident from certain patterns of selection—*The Tempest* as the Shakesperean play, the very large amount of Blake, the emphasis given to D. H. Lawrence's poems as well as his fiction—that a genuinely modern taste, rather than an eager modishness, has helped to shape our presentation of the historical canon. It is also hoped that the unusually generous sampling of material in certain sections—notably the Renaissance, eighteenth century, and the Romantics—will allow the teacher to use secondary or minor works, if he so chooses, to highlight these newer concerns or to fill in contextual background.

As for the annotations, the editors have never been afraid to be lively or even speculative. They have consistently tried to avoid usurping the teacher's role, as providing standard or definitive readings might do. On the other hand, the commentary goes beyond merely providing a lowest common denominator of information by suggesting interpretive directions and levels along which the teacher is free to move or not; and of course he always has the freedom to disagree. The editors have been neither prudish nor portentous in their tone, nor have they sought—in the interests of some superficial consistency, but with leaden effect—to efface their personal styles.

Texts have all been based on the best modern editions, which happen quite often to be published by the Oxford University Press. Spelling and punctuation have been modernized throughout, save in three instances: portions of the medieval period, and the texts of Spenser and Blake, two poets whose spelling and punctuation are so far from idiosyncrasies to be silently normalized that they constitute attempts to refashion poetic language. In the medieval section, modern verse translations of *Beowulf* (by C. W. Kennedy) and of *Gawain* (by Brian Stone) have been adopted. Glossaries of literary and historical terms in all periods have been provided, sometimes keyed to the annotations, sometimes supplementing the larger headnotes. These, it will be noticed, seek to illuminate the immediate contexts of the literature of a period rather than to provide a dense précis of its social, political, and economic history. Similarly, the reading lists at the end of each volume are not exhaustive bibliographies; in the happy instance where a teacher finds an extensive bibliography advisable, he or she will want to supply one.

A word about the pictures. They are not to be thought of simply as illustrations, and certainly not as mere decorations, but rather as part of the anthologized material, like the musical examples and the special sections (such as the one on Ovidian mythology in the Renaissance and on the Urban Scene in the eighteenth century). Throughout, the reader is introduced to the relations between poem as speaking picture, and picture as mute poem. Aside from contextual and anecdotal illustration, of which there is indeed a good deal, the pictorial examples allow teachers, or students on their own, to explore some of the interrelations of texts and the visual arts in all periods, whether exemplified in Renaissance emblems or in contemporary illustrations of Victorian poems.

Finally, an inevitable inadequate word of acknowledgment. To the English Department of Dartmouth College the editors are deeply indebted for having so generously and hospitably provided a place in which to work together for a sustained period. The staff of the Dartmouth College Library was extraordinarily helpful and attentive.

All of the editors would like to extend a note of gratitude to the many academics throughout the United States who willingly made suggestions as to what should be included as well as excluded. A special note of thanks to Jim Cox of Dartmouth College and Paul Dolan of the State University of New York at Stony Brook for their challenging and always helpful comments.

And finally to the entire staff of the New York branch of the Oxford University Press who have done more than could be humanly expected in connection with the planning and execution of this book. We would especially like to thank our editor John Wright, as well as Leona Capeless and her staff, Mary Ellen Evans, Patricia Cristol, Joyce Berry, Deborah Zwecher, and Jean Shapiro. An unusual but very deserved note of thanks to the Production people, especially Gerard S. Case and Leslie Phillips and to the designer, Frederick Schneider, whose excellent work speaks for itself.

Frank Kermode
John Hollander

New York
September 1972

Contents

* An asterisk is used to indicate that a work does not appear in its entirety.

Other Romantic Poets, 559

VICTORIAN POETRY, 1177

The Pre-Raphaelite Poets, 1401

Other Victorian Poets, 1476

Poetry of the Nineties, 1493

MODERN BRITISH LITERATURE, 1511

English Literary History in Process, 2168

Romantic Poetry and Prose

Romantic Poetry

Romanticism resists its definers, who can fix neither its characteristics nor its dates. It is a broad movement in the history of European (and American) consciousness, but whether it represented a genuine change in consciousness we still cannot know. In the later seventeenth century, the European Enlightenment or triumph of rationalism was one such change, and marked the end of the last stage of the Renaissance. Just as Romanticism still prevails today, for all the modernist rebellions against it, so it may be that Romanticism is only a very late phase of the Enlightenment against which it vainly rebelled. The spiritual differences between Pope and Blake, large as they are, quite fade away when we compare either writer with a representative current figure like Norman Mailer or Robert Lowell. Milton and Wordsworth, Tennyson and Yeats, contrasted with any of our contemporaries, are Enlightened rationalists, for all believed—as did Pope and Blake—in the power of the mind over the universe of sense. All believed that the poet's mind could make, or be found by, a coherent order in history or nature or society, or some combination thereof. None of them beheld a vision of chaos without believing also that chaos was irrational, and capable therefore of being organized into an intellectual coherence.

In this anthology, English Romanticism, as a historical phase of literature, is taken as extending from Blake's earliest poems (printed in 1783) up to Tennyson's first public volume (1830). These dates are arbitrary and, to some extent, now traditional. Romantic poetry in English does not end with the young, unhappy poets of the 1820's (Clare, Beddoes, Darley) but continues its complex course through Victorian and modern poetry. Yeats is not less Romantic than Blake, or Hardy than Shelley. Nor can we say just where English Romantic poetry, let alone Romantic poetry, begins. English Romanticism, whether rightly or not, saw itself as a Renaissance of the English Renaissance, a return to Spenser, Shakespeare, and Milton, and a repudiation of the literature of Enlightened England. But this return had begun long before Blake's *Poetical Sketches* of 1783. That volume owes most to the poetry of Sensibility—of anguished feeling—that had attempted a return to a pre-Enlightened age some forty years before. Yet we cannot say now that Collins, Gray, Cowper were closer to Milton than Pope was, nor would we quite know what we were talking about if we debated whether Spenser or Milton was the more Romantic poet. In a very broad sense *The Odyssey* is a Romantic poem, or at least much more Romantic than *The Iliad*. What can we mean when we call a poem or a person (or an idea) Romantic?

Plotinus, the third century neoplatonic philosopher, proposed an allegorical reading of the story of Odysseus, in which the seafarer's journey back home was interpreted as the soul's quest back to the Divine Unity. Though various Romantics seem to echo this interpretation of *The Odyssey*, their actual quests took them back not so much to a Christian or neoplatonic homecoming but rather outwards and downwards to a series of individual and glorious defeats. The major Romantic questers, whether we see these as the poets themselves or as the quasi-autobiographical heroes of their poems, are all engaged in the extraordinary enterprise of seeking to re-beget their own selves, as though through the imagination a man might hope to become his own father, or at least his own heroic precursor.

The temptations that haunted Odysseus—Circe and Calypso in particular—become in Romantic poetry the mysterious forms of Nature herself. Wordsworthian Nature, with all her representatives—Lucy, Margaret, the image of the child—is the most complex and positive of these temptations. The idealized heroines of Byron, Shelley, and Keats yield to purgatorial figures—the Moneta of *The Fall of Hyperion* and the "Shape all light" of *The Triumph of Life* being the most memorable. "I loved but woman fell away," the tragic John Clare proclaims, and this is the darker Romantic pattern, lamented by Coleridge and thoroughly analyzed and attacked by Blake. Because the quester demands more love and beauty than nature can give (or than a merely natural man could sustain on receiving), nature is discovered to be inadequate to the Romantic imagination.

Older scholarly views of Romanticism have tended to emphasize the movement's emotional naturalism, its supposed return to feeling, to folk traditions, to stories of the marvelous and supernatural. Romanticism was a health-restoring revival of the instinctual life, in contradistinction to eighteenth-century restraints that sought to sublimate the instincts in the united names of reason and society. Such views are not wrong except as they are inadequate in not going far enough. Romanticism, even in Wordsworth, depends finally upon a fuller sublimation of the instinctual life than had been thought necessary in all the centuries of European thought and feeling. By demanding more of natural love and of sensuous beauty than these could afford, the High Romantics each in turn attained a crisis in the instinctual life that could be overcome only by a yielding up of the instinctual life to a fully self-conscious creative mind. By a profound irony, the most heroic exalters of human emotion became responsible for an enormous sacrifice of instinct upon the altar of imaginative form. Keats delighted in every sensuous experience; yet he admits at last that he cannot unperplex joy from pain, if he is to write poems. Shelley, the Orphic priest of a healing Eros, ends with a vision of judgment in which Eros is much more of a destroyer than a preserver. Romantic love, the legacy of which still torments us all, could not solve the dilemma of the self and the other, any more than Romantic vision could heal the dumbfounding abyss between the subject and the object. Though these were spiritual failures, they tended also to be aesthetic triumphs, for Romantic poetry has the sharp poignance of awakening every reader's own nostalgias for the unending quest after the love and beauty that come to us only imperfectly in our post-Romantic lives.

The discrimination between Romanticisms generally ends in a hopeless jumble, and none will be attempted here. We need a meaning for the term comprehensive enough to make coherent such statements as these: that Ezekiel is a more Romantic prophetic poet than Isaiah; that Emerson and his American descendants, from Whitman to Wallace Stevens and Hart Crane, are Romantic poets; that D. H. Lawrence is a central figure in Romantic tradition. Yet the term's usage must be narrow enough to have a period meaning also. This editor suggests that, as a literary period in England, from the American Rebellion through the First Reform Bill (1832), we speak of a High Romantic Age. Romanticism, as an ageless and recurrent phenomenon, cannot be defined, but the High Romantic, manifest at somewhat varied times in England, America, France, Germany, Italy, can sustain a simple historical definition. It is the literary form of the Revolution, which began in America and the West Indies, flowered in France, and spread from France through space and time into the continuing world upheaval of our century.

The virtual identity between High Romanticism and Revolution marks the French visionary, Jean-Jacques Rousseau, as the central man of Romantic tradition: ". . . it was Rousseau who brought the feeling of irreconcilable enmity to rank and privileges, *above humanity*, home to the bosom of every man—identified it with all the pride of intellect, and with the deepest yearnings of the human heart." To this remark of Hazlitt, one can add that it was Rousseau who completed the process of "inventing" adolescence and also of raising the vision of external nature to an ecstasy. Unfortunately, this ecstasy was a reduction, since it was purchased at the price of estrangement, of making nature wholly other than the human viewer. Ruskin, who consolidated so much of Romantic criticism, calculated the price of this estranging ecstasy as what he called "the pathetic fallacy," the imputation of consciousness to an objective world secretly known to be lifeless. Though himself an inheritor from Wordsworth and Coleridge, Ruskin expressed profound uneasiness as to this characteristic mode of Romantic vision.

For even High Romanticism was divided severely against itself, precisely where it quested most urgently to correct the Enlightenment. It was as dualistic as the empiricists in its actual emphasis on the power of creative mind as contrasted to the phenomenal universe, which widened still further the split between subject and object. Against this involuntary dualism, High Romanticism stressed a doctrine or principle (perhaps more nearly, an analogue) of Organicism. Taking the universe primarily as a process, Romanticism tried to believe that a poem resulted from the same process, one that produced simultaneously a tree, a world, and a work of art. Pater, protesting Coleridge's reliance upon this analogue, observed that it negated each artist's hard struggle, the mind's heroic effort to make something of its own. In twentieth-century criticism Pater's dark prophecy of the negative effects of Organicism has been fulfilled, but in Coleridge and his contemporaries the analogue had a pragmatically liberating effect.

This effect was felt most strongly in the idea (or complex of ideas) that High Romanticism called the Imagination. Though Wordsworth refers to the Imagination as a glorious faculty, neither he nor his major contemporaries considered Imagination as one faculty among many making up the human endowment. Though only Blake overtly denied it was a faculty at all, most of the High Romantics came close to Blake's identification of the Imagination with what he called the Real Man, the unfallen human potential. Bewilderingly as all of these poets used the term, what seems central is a common tendency in them (at their most concentrated and intense) to insist that the Imagination or creative power is autonomous. The implications of this autonomy are still being worked out in modern literature, but each major High Romantic poet either argues or sometimes verges on assuming that the Imagination can both perceive and at least half-create reality and truth, far more reliably than any other mode of apprehension.

The center of High Romantic consciousness is found in each poet's difficult realization of the Sublime, a realization that internalizes the quest-pattern of the ancient literary form of the romance, or marvelous tale, suspended in its context halfway between natural and supernatural realms. Quite narrowly, High Romanticism can be called the internalization of quest-romance, with the poet as quester, a principle of Selfhood (manifested as excessive self-consciousness) his antagonist, and a Muse-figure his goal (frequently shadowy). The goal of the quest from Wordsworth's "Solitary" through Yeats's wandering Oisin is sublimity, but this is a sublimity not easy to distinguish from solipsism, that is, from the sense that all other selves and the external world are unreal compared with the quester's own exalted self-consciousness. This sublimity, unlike the eighteenth-century Sublime, is not a Sublime of great conceptions, before which the self feels small, but rather of a hoped-for potential, in which the private self turns upon infinitude, and so is found by its own greatness.

Quest becomes the journey to re-beget the self, to be one's own father, and the pattern of the poetic career assumes the shapes of the life cycle of what we now call Freudian or Psychological Man. The High Romantic mythology of love, still prevalent among us, deliberately confuses yearnings for a more-than-natural, a Sublime apotheosis, with a purely erotic fulfillment. More than any poetry, before or since, High Romanticism offers a vision of desire as being its own value, with necessarily a counter-version of hell as failed or frustrated desire. Romantic love, as a passion, was hardly the creation of High Romanticism, but to see love as "the sanction which connects not only man with man but with everything that exists," as Shelley phrased it, was to burden love with a hope that no relation could sustain.

Love taken up into the Imagination tended to be the High Romantic formula for apocalypse, the final or total form subsuming the Revolution, which was thus reduced to an omen or a promise. No burden could have been greater for poetry, and High Romanticism, risking everything by its astonishing ambitions, necessarily lost nearly as much as it gained by such aspiration. A vision that was meant to become a continuity became instead a discontinuous recording of Good Moments, whose life was menaced by the tendency to memorialize them even before they had passed. A poetry that had insisted "If not now, when?" became a study of the nostalgias, of the lost childhood of each creator. The preference for the Sublime over the Beautiful, for a wild infinity over an orderly bounded vista, dwindled to an ambivalent concern with the terrors of individual Selfhood. The High Romantic, whether as alternative to or extension of the Enlightened mind, became a failed quest for a widened consciousness. Self-consciousness, conceived as the Romantic antagonist, became the central Romantic characteristic.

But "failure" itself is a dialectical term when applied to the High Romantic enterprise. Matthew Arnold, who believed that the Romantics had "failed" for not knowing enough, nevertheless received his psychological education from Romantic poetry, and could not go on as a creator when he became anti-Romantic. He demonstrated, unintentionally, what all poets in English have demonstrated since. We have been, and still are, in a phase where our poets are Romantic even as once poets were Christian, that is, whether they want to be or not. Wordsworth, with his massive turn to the subjective, changed Western poetry as decisively as Homer had, or as Freud, with his Romantic rationalism, was to change Western psychology.

THE ROMANTIC POETS

Of the six major poets now commonly grouped as the English Romantics, two clearly stand in eminence just after Chaucer, Spenser, Shakespeare, and Milton among all English poets. Blake and Wordsworth have little in common beyond this shared greatness, despite their similar desire to awaken us from the sleep of death, which we call life. Wordsworth insists he will do this by words that speak of nothing more than what we already are, while Blake urges us to cast away everything we are, in the name of what we were and might be again. Whether or not Wordsworth was a poet of Nature, he refused to yield up human nature or the external world, and at least attempted to hallow the commonplace. The human heart by which we live is to him a perpetual cause for thanksgiving, and even the most Sublime of his ecstasies are grounded in ordinary experience. No poet before him—not even Homer or Shakespeare—so exalts the common decencies that bind human beings together.

But, to Blake, the human heart was a hopeless labyrinth of "selfish virtues," and Nature the den of Ulro, the ultimate error nurtured by the fallen understanding. The outward creation, he asserted, was hindrance to him, not action, no part of him. His strenuous enterprise seeks to burn away every context—conceptual, societal, natural—that limits the human from becoming the Divine. Nature, to Wordsworth, was a saving process and a benign Presence. To Blake, Nature's final form is a mythological triple Whore, whom he called Rahab, Vala, Tirzah, or secrecy, illusive beauty, necessity. Though he read Wordsworth with uneasy admiration, Blake saw in Wordsworth the Natural Man rising up against the Spiritual Man continually, and for Blake the Natural Man was at enmity with God. Yet Blake and Wordsworth, as poets, shared the same prime precursor, Milton, and both began with the same hope, that the French Revolution would fulfill Milton's vision of England "rousing herself like a strong man after sleep."

The English government under which Blake and Wordsworth lived was engaged either in Continental warfare or in suppressing internal dissent, or both together, for most of their lives. The London of the last decade of the eighteenth century and the first of the nineteenth is the London shown in Blake's poem of that title in Songs of Experience: a city in which the traditional English liberties of free press, free speech, and the rights of petition and assembly were frequently denied. A country already shaken by war and anarchic economic cycles was beginning to experience the social unrest that had overthrown the French social order, and the English ruling class responded to this challenge by a vicious and largely effective repression.

Voices raised against this repression included Tom Paine, who had to flee for his life to France, where he then nearly lost it again, and a much more significant figure, the philosophical anarchist William Godwin, who was the major English theorist of social revolution. Godwin subsided into a timid silence during the English counter-terror, but his philosophic materialism was crucial for the early Wordsworth and the young Shelley alike, though both poets were to break from Godwin in their mature works.

Behind the materialist vision of Godwin was a consciousness that older modes of thought were dying with the society that had informed them. When Blake was eight years old, in 1765, the steam engine was perfected, and what were to be the images of prophetic labor in Blake's poetry, the hammer and the forge, had their antagonist images prepared for them in the furnaces and mills of another England. In the year of Wordsworth's birth, 1770, we have the ironical juxtaposition of Goldsmith's poem *The Deserted Village*, a sad celebration of an open, pastoral England vanishing into the isolated farm holdings, and wandering laborers, resulting from enclosure. "Nature," insofar as it had an outward, phenomenal, meaning for Pope, was a relaxed word, betokening the gift of God that lay all about him. Wordsworthian nature, the hard, phenomenal otherness that opposes itself to all we have made and marred, takes part of its complex origin from this vast social dislocation.

The real misery in England brought about through these economic and social developments was on a scale unparalleled since the Black Death in the fourteenth century. The French wars, against which all of Blake's prophetic poetry protests with Biblical passion, were typical of many modern wars fought by industrial nations. Enormous profits for the manufacturing classes were accompanied by inflation and food shortages for the mass of people, and victory over Napoleon brought on an enormous economic depression, unemployment, hunger, and more class unrest.

This unrest, which there was no means of channeling into organization or a protest vote, led to giant public meetings, riots, and what was called frame-breaking, a direct attempt to end technological unemployment by the destruction of machines. The government reacted by decreeing that frame-breaking was punishable by death. The climax of popular agitation and government brutality came in August 1819, in the Peterloo Massacre at Manchester, where mounted troops charged a large, orderly group that was meeting to demand parliamentary reform, killing and maiming many of the unarmed protesters. For a moment, England stood at the verge of revolution, but no popular leaders of sufficient force and initiative came forward to organize the indignation of the mass of people, and the moment passed. A similar movement was to come in 1832, at the start of another age, but then revolution was to be averted by the backing-down of Parliament, and its passage of the First Reform Bill that helped to establish the Victorian compromise. So the political energies of the age were not without issue, even in England; yet to idealists of any sort living in England during the first three decades of the nineteenth century it seemed that a new energy had been born into the world and then had died in its infancy. The great English writers of the period reacted to a stagnant situation by withdrawal, as Milton had withdrawn internally before them. In Blake and Wordsworth this internal movement helped create a new kind of poetry; it created modern poetry as we know it.

Coleridge, less clearly in Milton's shadow and so less concerned with the failures of revolutionary energies, did not emulate the Miltonic disillusion as closely as Blake and Wordsworth did. Coleridge suffered the anxiety of Milton's influence more in the passive manner of the poets of Sensibility like Collins and Cowper, than in the active, struggling way of Blake in his *Milton* or Wordsworth in his *Recluse* fragment. Coleridge had a deeper fear of profaning Nature than even Wordsworth had, and this joined itself, in Coleridge, to an inhibition that prevented him, except in fragments, from following Milton into a daemonic Sublime.

With the second generation of major Romantic poets the reaction to the failures of the Revolution are less personal, but the uneasy dialectic of Nature and Imagination, and the struggle with Milton's influence, became yet more complex because of the shadow of Wordsworth's achievement. Shelley, Byron, and Keats each responded very differently to Wordsworth (as they did also to Milton), but their poetry, even the scoffing Byron's, could not get beyond the dilemmas of Wordsworth's humanized Sublime. Shelley's visionary skepticism, Byron's satiric near-nihilism, and Keats's carefully qualified and finally tragic naturalism, all accept as the given a Wordsworthian account of the relations between Nature and poetic consciousness. Shelley emphasized a division in this heightened consciousness, between distrusting head and loving heart, and exported something like such a division into Nature itself. An unwilling dross, a ruin that is love's shadow, stalks every aspiration in Shelley's poetry, but this was Shelley's own reading of Wordsworth's poetry, as the entire Wordsworth-haunted sequence from *Alastor* through to *The Triumph of Life* makes clear. Byron, who bitterly read the "Solitary" of Wordsworth's *The Excursion* as a moralizing portrait of himself, became an obvious if involuntary Wordsworthian in *Childe Harold's Pilgrimage III* and *Manfred*. Where Byron is most himself, in *Don Juan* (acclaimed by Shelley as the greatest poem of the age), he still uneasily continues an argument with the Wordsworthian analysis of the self-destructiveness of the solitary consciousness. Keats, the natural heir of Wordsworth, read more receptively than his two great contemporaries, and so his poetic argument with Wordsworth is deeper and subtler. Wordsworth, with all his sense of imaginative loss, declined to take a tragic view of natural existence. Though Wordsworth's hidden subject is almost always mortality, his poetry frequently evades its own darkest implications. Keats, whose heroic stance evades no difficulties, engages the themes of mortality more directly than any poet but Shakespeare.

The ambition of all the High Romantic poets was to reach and even surpass Milton in epic. Necessarily, this ambition was frustrated, but the large-scale internalized romance, in one form or another, became one of the two prime Romantic achievements. *Milton, Jerusalem, The Prelude, Prometheus Unbound, Don Juan,* and the two *Hyperions;* for all their limitations, these constitute the last full-scale attainments of the Sublime in English poetry. More influential on Victorian and modern poetry, the Romantic lyric achievement surpassed the expectations and even the designs of its makers. The great invention of Coleridge and Wordsworth was the crisis-lyric, by which the poet saved himself for the next poem, and for at least the possibility of a fuller life. Though the High Romantics intended to continue and to extend Milton, the characteristic art of the therapeutic lyric was born instead. When we think of Romantic poetry (or, if our perspective is larger, of modern poetry), we think first of poems like "Resolution and Independence," "Dejection: An Ode," "Ode to the West Wind," "To Autumn." The major paradox of High Romanticism is that its minor mode became its central (and still unsurpassed) legacy.

It is difficult now, when we have seen so many disasters, human and societal, emerge from Romanticism, whether recurrent or High, to arrive at any last judgment upon its values and its achievements. Recurrent romanticism is apparently endemic in human nature; all men and women are questers to some degree. Those who quest beyond reason, beyond societal and familial constraints, who like Shelley go on until they are stopped and never are stopped, stand beyond aesthetic judgment in any case. High Romanticism is, by now, largely an aesthetic phenomenon and invites an aesthetic judgment. Whatever its human cost, the literature of internalized quest, of Promethean aspiration, is the most vitalizing and formidable achievement in the Western arts since the Renaissance.

WILLIAM BLAKE
1757–1827

Blake was born in London on November 28, 1757, into the family of a hosier. He had no formal education, but was apprenticed to an engraver, James Basire. In 1782 he married Catherine Boucher; the marriage was childless, and went through intense difficulties, particularly in early 1793, when Blake complained bitterly of her sexual jealousy, but eventually the relationship became serene and very close. Blake died on a Sunday evening, August 12, 1827, Catherine by his side, and by all accounts he died majestically, a fulfilled and happy man.

There were almost no outward events in Blake's life. He was not a professional poet or man of letters, but earned his living, sometimes very precariously, as an engraver. Insofar as he had any public reputation during his lifetime, it was as a failed, eccentric painter. But some of his lyrics were known and admired by Coleridge and other literary men, and his paintings were valued by some of the better artists of his time. Almost unknown, however, were what are widely (and rightly) now regarded as his most important achievement, a series of visionary poems culminating in three brief or foreshortened epics, works demonstrating probably the greatest conceptual power ever to appear among poets.

Blake, for all his gifts, is not a poet of the eminence of Chaucer, Shakespeare, or Milton, yet he gives his readers not only what can be expected from a great poet, but a profundity of schematized psychological insight comparable to Freud's, and a disciplined intellectual inventiveness comparable to Hegel's. His difficulty for readers, and his unique value, is that he offers even more than that, for he is, as he insisted, a prophet, in the precise sense that Isaiah and Ezekiel (he would have added Milton) are prophetic poets. His poems, which are always poems, are astonishingly ambitious, even for the Romantic Age, into which he survived. They propose nothing less than to teach us how to live, and to explain to us what has made it so hard to live as fully human rather than merely natural beings.

Blake, a self-taught London radical Protestant, was more than deeply read in the King James Bible, and in Milton. In the Talmudic phrase, he had "eaten those books," and they account for all but an insignificant part of his literary tradition, and indeed of his knowledge. Much scholarship has wasted itself, from Yeats to the present moment, in attempting to trace Blake's ideas and images to a large number of arcane traditions. But Blake was a very impatient reader, except of the Bible and Milton, and though he glanced at anything he encountered, he would have snorted at the suggestion that he give serious effort to the study of alchemy, mysticism, theosophy, esoteric forms of neoplatonism, occult "science," latter-day gnosticisms or any of the crankeries that have elicited respectful concentration from some of his scholarly pursuers.

To comprehend Blake, his reader needs to understand how Blake read the Bible and Milton, or as Blake might have said, how to read poetry. For Blake was primarily an intellectual revisionist, even as Nietzsche, Marx, Freud, in the longest perspective, seem most important as revisionists of the European Enlightenment. Blake, like the major Romantics after him, sought to correct the Enlightenment, and not to abolish it. He had no quarrel with reason itself but only with inadequate accounts of reason, and he refused to distinguish between "the intellectual powers" and what he called "the Real Man the Imagination," whose most complete expression was in the arts of poetry and painting. The Bible, whose degree of historical validity was quite irrelevant to Blake, represented for him the Great Code of Art, the total form of what he called the Divine Vision, which he believed to have been so obscured by the nightmare of history as to be all but totally darkened in his own time.

Most of what currently passes for movements of human liberation would have been condemned by Blake as what he bitterly called Druidism, taking the name from what he judged to have been the native British version of natural religion. All of Blake's work is based on a firm distinction between what is imaginative and what is merely natural in us, with the natural rejected, cast out beyond the balance of what Blake termed "contraries." The revolt of youth-as-youth Blake saw as a cyclic self-defeat, the sad destiny of the eternal rebel he called Orc. The revolt of women-as-women (as exemplified in his acquaintance Mary Wollstonecraft) he judged also as doomed to the perpetual failure of natural cycle, for all natural women, like all natural men, were subject to what he named the Female Will, always rampant in nature. The revolt of the heart against the head (as represented by Rousseau) he pungently characterized as "reasoning from the loins in the unreal forms of Beulah's Night," Beulah being a lower paradise of illusory appearances. D. H. Lawrence, a lesser Blake, inveighed against "sex in the head," following Blake's prophecy, but proceeded, like so many since, to reason from the loins, hardly a more humanizing procedure, in Blake's view.

Blake's view was what he himself always termed Vision or Intellectual Vision, which he took ironic care to distinguish from the literalism of the natural eye, and from the chemistry of the natural mind. He saw with the eye of the imagination, and without the aid of artificial paradises of any kind whatsoever. His visions are what Ezekiel and Milton saw, and what he believed all of us could see, by the hard efforts of poetry and painting, or of learning to apprehend the poets and the painters, and so to re-create their worlds after them. He hoped to rescue English culture from what he interpreted as its decadence, by restoring poetry to what it had been in Milton and the Renaissance writers before Milton, and by raising English painting to what it had never been, the spiritual art of Michelangelo and Raphael.

Yet Blake's own genius was curiously divided. As poet and as painter he excels as a caricaturist, an intellectual satirist, and a master of a new kind of vitalizing but ironic parody, which first triumphs in The Marriage of Heaven and Hell. Where he wished most to excel was in the Sublime of Milton and Michelangelo, and here his achievement was only partial, though larger in poetry than in painting. His painting was anachronistic in a somewhat crippling sense, and his failure to understand Rubens and Rembrandt was more self-defeating than it need have been. In his Sublime poetry, he is least successful where he is most directly Miltonic, and rather closer to the highest kind of accomplishment when he is even more Hebraic than Milton is. But there too, his stature is lessened when he is read in direct juxtaposition with the Bible. His own true Sublime comes in another mode, a Northern one, in the tradition of the Icelandic Eddas, and in the less strenuous but still Miltonic eighteenth-century English tradition of James Thomson, Thomas Gray, William Collins, and William Cowper, the poets of Sensibility, as recent scholarly criticism has begun to call them. After Milton, Blake felt closer to Cowper than to any other English poet, and though he read, admired, and (very complexly) protested Wordsworth's poetry, he always was more comfortable with an ode like Gray's "The Progress of Poesy" than with one like "Intimations of Immortality."

The Miltonizing poets of Sensibility failed, in Blake's opinion, because they were not sane enough to overthrow a world view Blake regarded as totally mad, and which he associated with Bacon, Newton, and Locke in metaphysics and with Dryden, Pope, Dr. Johnson, and Sir Joshua Reynolds in the arts. This world view is so savagely caricatured by Blake that we need to be very wary about accepting his version of it as being in any way adequate to those thinkers and artists. But Blake was no more unjust than the Augustan satirists were, from their almost opposite points of departure. Blake was politically of the permanent Left, like Shelley in the next generation, and to him the Augustan trinity of Reason, Nature, and Society was a three-headed beast or triple whore responsible for the sufferings of the lower classes of England, out of whom he had come and with whom he defiantly remained. The Revolution did not come to England, the repression of Pitt did its work well, and Blake learned the joyless wisdom of public timidity. He secretly raged, in his notebooks and his poems, but he accurately said of his outward obedience: "I am hid." When he did speak his mind, he suffered for it, whether in defying patrons or in angrily throwing a soldier out of his garden. The first brought on Jobean trials of poverty for himself and his loyal, suffering wife, and the second brought on him the ordeal of trial for treason (he was acquitted, but the terror of the experience is intense throughout his greatest poem, *Jerusalem*). Too profound a consciousness to accept any easy explanations for the torments of his fellows and himself, Blake prophetically indicted the English conservative cultural tradition in its totality. In his gathering vision all fit together: the theology of the English state church, the political theory of Burke, the deistic natural religion which he believed the church only pretended to oppose, the poetics of Pope and the aesthetics of Reynolds, the philosophy of Locke, the physics of Newton, the morality of Bacon. The aggregate of all this, quite unfairly but wholly unforgettably, Blake fused together as the Accuser of Sin, the spectral torturer of English man, of Albion. His mature poetry became an attempt to identify, with final clarity, this Accuser, in the belief that to know the clear outline of error, particularly within the self, is to make its destruction inevitable.

To achieve this identification, Blake tried several times to organize his vision, so as to tell a comprehensive story of how mankind fell into its present condition, what that condition was, and how mankind was to be freed from all conditions, particularly from the confining context of nature. We begin to apprehend Blake when we realize that for him "human nature" is a wholly unacceptable phrase, an absolute contradiction, or, as he said, "an impossible absurdity." What was human about us, Blake insisted, was the imagination; what was natural about us had to be redeemed by the imagination, or else it would destroy us. The imagination, to Blake, was not a faculty, however glorious, but was the Real Man, the unfallen unity we had been and must become again.

Blake's story is too complex and long for this introduction, and one major aspect of it is sketched in the Headnote to the selection from the epic *The Four Zoas*. But it is crucial, as we begin to read Blake, that we ask why he made his story so difficult for us. Though several major poets since Blake have invented mythologies, and though there are mythopoeic elements in all major poets, Blake's myths are the most formidable and complete in the language. Northrop Frye, probably Blake's best critic, has insisted that Blake's poetic procedures were as central as any poet's, and this may be so; yet the experience of most common readers seems to tell them otherwise. What can be made explicit to the idiot, Blake said, was not worth his care, and so he addressed a sublime allegory to the intellectual powers. But need his address have been so solitary a one? Could he have been more direct and immediate, as apparently he was in his earlier work, or is there convincing inner necessity in his initially strange procedures? Did a voice crying in the wilderness of 1790–1810, the years of his major works, have to cry aloud in so subtly complex a language that it seems always to need translation for even willing auditors?

There are no certain answers, yet one can be ventured, by comparing Blake's poetry to that of his older contemporary, Cowper, and his younger contemporary, Wordsworth. Cowper is so Milton-haunted that he never fully finds his own voice, and so afflicted by a sense of worthlessness and damnation that he scarcely can find his way past fear and trembling. When we read Cowper, if we read acutely and sympathetically, we are very moved, but what moves us is the pathos of Cowper's predicament, and his helplessness at breaking out of it. Blake's was a fierce spirit, akin to the greatest dissenters that the "inner light" tradition of Protestantism has produced among the English. He would not allow himself to be a victim or a latecomer, like the poets of Sensibility before him, and so he resolved to break through every net, external and internal, that had blocked his precursors from joining themselves to Milton's greatness, even the net of Milton himself.

Wordsworth, born thirteen years after Blake, was also a titanic individuality, a consciousness fierce enough not to accept victimization by history and circumstances, or even by Milton, whom he revered quite as much as Cowper and Blake did. But Wordsworth chose another way, not a personal mythology, but a de-mythologizing so radical that it enabled him to create modern poetry, if any single figure can be said to have done so. He is ultimately a more difficult poet than Blake, if "difficult" means problematic, as it should. Once a reader has mastered Blake's initial complexities, he goes on encountering vast profundities, but his way is clear before him. A little way into Wordsworth, the reader begins to encounter enormous and legitimate obscurities and dark passages, whereas Blake gives almost too continuous and directing a light. For Blake is not only more systematic than Wordsworth; he is also far closer than Wordsworth to English Renaissance poetry, and necessarily far less modern, however you want to interpret "modern." It is one of the disturbing paradoxes about Blake that, lifelong rebel though he was, his mature work increasingly seems conservative in the longest perspectives we can achieve. An enemy of the rationalists, he was a great rationalizer; an exploder of the mythologies, he re-mythologized so extensively as to help preserve the cultural life of many phenomena he wished to bury. Though he has been reclaimed for the latest movements of social, political, and artistic revolt from late nineteenth-century England down to this present moment, he is farther away from any and all of us than he is from the Enlightenment he prophesied against.

Blake could or would not do what Hazlitt rightly said Wordsworth had done: begin anew on a *tabula rasa* ("clean slate") of poetry, almost as though none had been written before him. *Jerusalem,* at first reading, may baffle or repel an unprepared contemporary reader, but so does Ezekiel, and so does John Milton. Poetry meant too much to Blake to abandon the main continuities of what it had been; poetry meant a great deal to Wordsworth, but nature meant more. Yet to Blake, nature was hindrance, not action, and so no part of him. He undertook the immense task of his mythologizing so as to begin the preservation of man by the preservation of poetry, in a form still fundamentally recognizable as a major creation of the English Renaissance. Though, in his own terms, he did not fail, and on any terms he became one of the half-dozen or so poets in the language, he did not succeed as Wordsworth was to succeed. Blake became the last epic poet in the old sense of epic. It was left for Wordsworth to become a new kind of poet, one which, perhaps to our sorrow, is necessarily with us still.

The texts reprinted here are from *The Poetry and Prose of William Blake,* edited by David Erdman. Blake's original spelling and punctuation have been preserved to give the reader the full sense of Blake's extraordinary individuality. Blake himself would have sanctioned this refusal to modernize, for most of his poetry was engraved by him in this form.

From Poetical Sketches°

To Spring°

O thou, with dewy locks, who lookest down
Thro' the clear windows of the morning;° turn
Thine angel eyes upon our western isle,
Which in full choir hails thy approach, O Spring!

The hills tell each other, and the list'ning
Vallies hear; all our longing eyes are turned
Up to thy bright pavillions: issue forth,
And let thy holy feet visit our clime.

Poetical Sketches Blake's early poems, written between the ages of twelve and twenty-one, are collected in this, his only conventionally printed volume (1783); like the poets of Sensibility, Blake explicitly imitates Spenser, Shakespeare, and Milton in his first poems, but already these lyrics foreshadow the crucial element in his mature mythology, the coexistence of "states-of-being," even of contrary states, though this is not yet a psychological doctrine, as it will become by 1788–89.

To Spring The first poem in his first book, this will be significantly echoed in Night IX, "The Last Judgment," of *The Four Zoas,* initially intended to be his definitive epic; here it introduces four poems addressed to the seasons, stanzaic but unrhymed, in imitation of James Thomson's blank verse poem *The Seasons,* itself a Miltonic imitation.
clear . . . morning See *The Four Zoas,* Night IX, 120:50, where this is assimilated to Rahab's "window" of Joshua 2:18.

Come o'er the eastern hills,° and let our winds
10 Kiss thy perfumed garments; let us taste
Thy morn and evening breath; scatter thy pearls
Upon our love-sick land that mourns for thee.

O deck her forth with thy fair fingers; pour
Thy soft kisses on her bosom; and put
Thy golden crown upon her languish'd head,
Whose modest tresses were bound up for thee!
1769–77   1783

To the Evening Star°

Thou fair-hair'd angel of the evening,
Now, while the sun rests on the mountains, light
Thy bright torch of love;° thy radiant crown
Put on, and smile upon our evening bed!
Smile on our loves; and, while thou drawest the
Blue curtains of the sky, scatter thy silver dew
On every flower that shuts its sweet eyes
In timely sleep. Let thy west wind sleep on
The lake; speak silence with thy glimmering eyes,
10 And wash the dusk with silver. Soon, full soon,
Dost thou withdraw; then the wolf rages wide,
And the lion glares thro' the dun forest:
The fleeces of our flocks are cover'd with
Thy sacred dew: protect them with thine influence.
1769–77   1783

Song°

How sweet I roam'd from field to field,
    And tasted all the summer's pride,
'Till I the prince of love° beheld,
    Who in the sunny beams did glide!

He shew'd me lilies for my hair,
    And blushing roses for my brow;
He led me through his gardens fair,
    Where all his golden pleasures grow.

---

eastern hills See the Song of Solomon 2:8 ff.
To the Evening Star See Spenser's *Epithalamion*,
ll. 285–95, for Blake's prime source; this poem
is a precursor of the *Songs of Innocence*.
torch of love the Evening Star, Venus

Song The tradition is that Blake wrote this poem
before he was fourteen; it is a precursor of the
Songs of Experience.
prince of love Eros, or Cupid, who usurps the
role of Phoebus, the sun god, and glides down
in Phoebus' chariot

With sweet May dews my wings were wet,
10   And Phoebus fir'd my vocal rage;
He caught me in his silken net,
    And shut me in his golden cage.

He loves to sit and hear me sing,
    Then, laughing, sports and plays with me;
Then stretches out my golden wing,
    And mocks my loss of liberty.
    1769-77   1783

Mad Song°

The wild winds weep,
    And the night is a-cold;
Come hither, Sleep,
    And my griefs infold:
But lo! the morning peeps
    Over the eastern steeps,
And the rustling birds of dawn
The earth do scorn.

Lo! to the vault
10   Of paved heaven,°
With sorrow fraught
    My notes are driven:
They strike the ear of night,
    Make weep the eyes of day;
They make mad the roaring winds,
    And with tempests play.

Like a fiend in a cloud
    With howling woe,
After night I do croud,
20   And with night will go;°
I turn my back to the east,
From whence comforts° have increas'd;
For light doth seize my brain
With frantic pain.°
    1769-77   1783

Mad Song Blake's first intellectual satire, based on the Elizabethan "mad songs" and their later imitations; the singer is being satirized, but so is the mental world he seeks to escape; he can be regarded as a poet of Sensibility like Cowper, whose madness (in Blake's judgment) is an evasion of the burden of prophecy.
paved heaven The singer's heaven is the self-paved "vault" of materialist concepts of space.

After . . . go Crowding after night, the singer seeks to escape a materialist (and self-imposed) concept of time.
comforts a grim humor on Blake's part; the singer cannot bear "comforts"
frantic pain another satiric suggestion that the singer wishes to be more insane than he has managed (so far) to make himself

To the Muses°

Whether on Ida's° shady brow,
  Or in the chambers of the East,
The chambers of the sun, that now
  From antient melody have ceas'd;

Whether in Heav'n ye wander fair,
  Or the green corners of the earth,
Or the blue regions of the air,
  Where the melodious winds have birth;

Whether on chrystal rocks ye rove,
10   Beneath the bosom of the sea
Wand'ring in many a coral grove,
  Fair Nine, forsaking Poetry!

How have you left the antient love
  That bards of old enjoy'd in you!°
The languid strings do scarcely move!
  The sound is forc'd, the notes are few!
1769–77   1783

Songs of Innocence and of Experience

There are twenty-one copies of *Songs of Innocence,* and twenty-seven of the combined work, but no separate copies at all of *Songs of Experience.* Blake therefore was willing to have *Songs of Innocence* read separately (he continued to issue it after he had combined the two groups) but not the contrary work. These are works in illuminated printing, engraved after a process of Blake's own invention, in which he applied words and pictures to copper plates, and then etched surrounding surfaces away. The colors of inks and the tints and washes, some translucent, some opaque, vary from copy to copy.

Together with some early tracts, Blake's *Songs of Innocence* and *The Book of Thel* begin his deliberate canon of engraved works. The first drafts of three of the *Songs of Innocence* are to be found in a satirical context in the early prose fragment *An Island in the Moon,* and satire of a very subtle kind is crucial throughout the combined work, in which Innocence and Experience are so juxtaposed as to demonstrate one another's inadequacies.

The *Songs of Innocence* are indeed "of" and not "about" the state of innocence. There is much critical debate about Blake's Innocence, and little that is definitive can be said about it. The reader should know that the root meaning of innocence is "harmlessness," the derived meanings "guiltlessness"and "freedom from sin." But Blake uses the word to mean "inexperience" as well, which is a very different matter.

To the Muses This is a defiant and confident "lament," employing the diction of Augustan minor verse to mock that verse's failure of inspiration. There are overtones of Milton's *Comus,* ll. 98 ff., and Psalms 19:4–5.
Ida's Mountain in Crete; there is also one of the same name near Troy; both are notable in Greek poetry.
How . . . you you loved Spenser and Milton, and the other bards of Britain, but now you have become faithless

17

As the contrary of Experience, Innocence cannot be reconciled with it within the context of natural existence. Implicit in the contrast between the two states is a distinction Blake made between "unorganized innocence," unable to sustain experience, and an organized kind which could. On the manuscript of *The Four Zoas*, he jotted down: "*Unorganized Innocence: An Impossibility.* Innocence dwells with Wisdom, but never with Ignorance."

Since Innocence and Experience are states of the soul through which we pass, neither is a finality, both are necessary, and neither is wholly preferable to the other. Not only are they satires upon one another, but they exist in a cyclic relation as well. Blake does not intend us to see Innocence as belonging to childhood and Experience to adulthood, which would be not only untrue but also uninteresting.

The relation of the matched pairs of poems, where they exist, does not appear to be schematic, but varies from instance to instance. The matching of "The Divine Image" and "The Human Abstract" seems to be the crucial one, since it shows the widest possibilities of relationship, and demonstrates vividly what readers are too likely to forget, which is that Innocence satirizes Experience just as intensely as it itself is satirized by Experience, and also that any song of either state is also a kind of satire upon itself.

From Songs of Innocence and of Experience

Shewing the Two Contrary States of the Human Soul

Songs of Innocence

1789
The Author & Printer   W Blake

Introduction

Piping down the valleys wild
Piping songs of pleasant glee
On a cloud I saw a child.
And he laughing said to me.

Pipe a song about a Lamb;
So I piped with merry chear,
Piper pipe that song again—
So I piped, he wept to hear.

Drop thy pipe thy happy pipe
10 Sing thy songs of happy chear,
So I sung the same again
While he wept with joy to hear

Piper sit thee down and write
In a book that all may read—
So he vanish'd from my sight.
And I pluck'd a hollow reed.

And I made a rural pen,
And I stain'd° the water clear,
And I wrote my happy songs
20 Every child may joy to hear
1789

The Lamb

Little Lamb who made thee
Dost thou know who made thee
Gave thee life & bid thee feed.
By the stream & o'er the mead;
Gave thee clothing of delight,
Softest clothing wooly bright;
Gave thee such a tender voice,
Making all the vales rejoice!
Little Lamb who made thee
10 Dost thou know who made thee

Little Lamb I'll tell thee,
Little Lamb I'll tell thee!
He is called by thy name,
For he calls himself a Lamb:°
He is meek & he is mild,
He became a little child:
I a child & thou a lamb,
We are called by his name.
Little Lamb God bless thee.
20 Little Lamb God bless thee.
1789

The Little Black Boy°

My mother bore me in the southern wild,
And I am black, but O! my soul is white;°

stain'd as a painter stains, yet the sense including an overtone of "polluted"
Lamb Christ as the Lamb of God
The Little Black Boy The speaker applies his
mother's teachings to the dilemma of his own
condition. Her wisdom is a summary of the beliefs
of the Innocent state of the soul: God is a loving father, nature is a loving mother, and all

children share a brotherhood from nature under
God. Though the voice singing this song is
poignant and admirable, the poem explores
the inadequacy of Innocence to sustain that
voice's idealizations.
And I . . . white The Black Boy has been
taught a pernicious dualism, at once metaphysical and societal.

White as an angel is the English child:
But I am black as if bereav'd° of light.

My mother taught me underneath a tree°
And sitting down before the heat of day,
She took me on her lap and kissed me,
And pointing to the east began to say.

Look on the rising sun: there God does live
10   And gives his light, and gives his heat away.
And flowers and trees and beasts and men receive
Comfort in morning joy in the noon day.

And we are put on earth a little space,
That we may learn to bear the beams of love,
And these black bodies and this sun-burnt face
Is but a cloud, and like a shady grove.

For when our souls have learn'd the heat to bear
The cloud will vanish we shall hear his voice.
Saying: come out from the grove my love & care,
20   And round my golden tent like lambs rejoice.

Thus did my mother say and kissed me,
And thus I say to little English boy.
When I from black and he from white cloud free,°
And round the tent of God like lambs we joy:

Ill shade him from the heat till he can bear,
To lean in joy upon our fathers knee.
And then I'll stand and stroke his silver hair,
And be like him and he will then love me.
                                    1789

The Chimney Sweeper°

When my mother died I was very young,
And my father sold me while yet my tongue,
Could scarcely cry weep weep weep weep.°
So your chimneys I sweep & in soot I sleep.

bereav'd Here "dispossessed" or "divested"; the child has been taught a myth of the Fall of Man.
underneath a tree Any teaching beneath a tree (thus shrouded by nature) is abhorred by Blake, for whom all trees are versions of the Tree of Mystery (see "The Human Abstract").
When I . . . free a line implying all the ambiguities of Innocence
The Chimney Sweeper As in "The Little Black Boy," here an innocent speaker condemns societal and psychic repressiveness without being

aware of the full burden of his own song. The Chimney Sweeper is a charity child sold into commercial bondage by his father and the English church. Here too there is no consciously directed irony on the child's part, but an enormous moral urgency is developed against the forces of exploitation, particularly at their success in conditioning the child's mind and even his dreams.
weep The lisping little children pronounce "sweep" as "weep."

Theres little Tom Dacre, who cried when his head
That curl'd like a lambs back, was shav'd, so I said.
Hush Tom never mind it, for when your head's bare,
You know that the soot cannot spoil your white hair.

10 And so he was quiet, & that very night,
As Tom was a sleeping he had such a sight,
That thousands of sweepers Dick, Joe Ned & Jack
Were all of them lock'd up in coffins of black°

And by came an Angel who had a bright key,
And he open'd the coffins & set them all free.
Then down a green plain leaping laughing they run
And wash in a river and shine in the Sun.

Then naked & white, all their bags left behind,
They rise upon clouds, and sport in the wind.
And the Angel told Tom if he'd be a good boy,
20 He'd have God for his father & never want joy.

And so Tom awoke and we rose in the dark
And got with our bags & our brushes to work.
Tho' the morning was cold, Tom was happy & warm,
So if all do their duty, they need not fear harm.°

                                    1789

The Divine Image°

To Mercy Pity Peace and Love,
All pray in their distress:
And to these virtues of delight
Return their thankfulness.

For Mercy Pity Peace and Love,
Is God our father dear:
And Mercy Pity Peace and Love,
Is Man his child and care.

For Mercy has a human heart
10 Pity, a human face:
And Love, the human form divine,
And Peace, the human dress.

Then every man of every clime,
That prays in his distress,

coffins of black the chimneys, and also the
blackened bodies of the chimney sweepers
So . . . harm Compare the effect of this with
the similar moral tags at the end of "The Little

Black Boy" and the "Holy Thursday" of Innocence.
The Divine Image Note the absence of imagery
in this lyric of abstractions, and compare it to the
contrary of Experience, "The Human Abstract."

Prays to the human form divine
Love Mercy Pity Peace.

And all must love the human form,
In heathen, turk or jew.
Where Mercy, Love & Pity dwell
20   There God is dwelling too.
                    1789

Holy Thursday°

Twas on a Holy Thursday their innocent faces clean
The children walking two & two in red & blue & green
Grey headed beadles walkd before with wands as white as snow°
Till into the high dome of Pauls they like Thames waters flow

O what a multitude they seemd these flowers of London town
Seated in companies they sit with radiance all their own
The hum of multitudes was there but multitudes of lambs°
Thousands of little boys & girls raising their innocent hands

Now like a mighty wind they raise to heaven the voice of song
10   Or like harmonious thunderings the seats of heaven among
Beneath them sit the aged men wise guardians of the poor
Then cherish pity, lest you drive an angel from your door°
1784   1789

Songs of Experience

1794
The Author & Printer   W Blake

Introduction°

Hear the voice of the Bard!
Who Present, Past, & Future sees
Whose ears have heard,

Holy Thursday These are the chimney sweepers again, charity wards of the exploiting church, being led into St. Paul's Cathedral on Ascension Day, the fortieth day after Easter Sunday, on which Christ ascended into Heaven. Their march is regimented, and the poem, depending upon perspective, can be read as either the bitterest or most idyllic of Blake's songs.
as white as snow leprously white, in Blake's symbolism. The beadles are church flunkeys whose "wands" are also disciplinary rods, as well as badges of office.
multitudes of lambs See Joel 3:14, where the

prophet sees "multitudes, multitudes in the valley of decision."
Then cherish . . . door a bitter contrast to Hebrews 13:2: "Be not forgetful to entertain strangers: for thereby some have entertained angels unawares"
Introduction Blake is no more to be identified with the Bard of Experience than he is with the Piper of Innocence, though the Bard speaks for a larger and more urgent component of his imagination, as the deliberate echoings of Jeremiah and Milton here indicate.

The Holy Word,
That walk'd among the ancient trees.°

Calling the lapsed Soul°
And weeping in the evening dew;
That might controll,
The starry pole;
10 And fallen fallen light renew!

O Earth O Earth return!°
Arise from out the dewy grass;
Night is worn,
And the morn
Rises from the slumberous mass.

Turn away no more:
Why wilt thou turn away
The starry floor
The watry shore
20 Is giv'n thee till the break of day.°

1794

Earth's Answer°

Earth rais'd up her head,
From the darkness dread & drear.
Her light fled:
Stony dread!°
And her locks cover'd with grey despair.

Prison'd on watry shore
Starry Jealousy does keep my den
Cold and hoar
Weeping o'er
10 I hear the Father of the ancient men

Selfish father of men
Cruel jealous selfish fear
Can delight
Chain'd in night
The virgins of youth and morning bear?

---

ancient trees See Genesis 3:8.
lapsed Soul This is not Blake's view, but the Bard's.
return See Jeremiah 22:29 and Milton's allusion to this in his *The Ready and Easy Way to Establish a Free Commonwealth.*
break of day Apocalypse, when the "starry floor" and "watry shore" will be swept away
Earth's Answer Like the Earth, mother of Prometheus, in Shelley's *Prometheus Unbound,* Act

I, this Earth is fearful of "Starry Jealousy" or the "Selfish father of men," Shelley's Jupiter or Blake's Urizen-Jehovah. Yet her bitter point against the Bard (and all men) seems justified. Where the Bard blames nature for turning away, nature replies by blaming men, for not freeing love.

Stony dread There is here a suggestion of Medusa, whose glance turned men to stone.

Does spring hide its joy
When buds and blossoms grow?
Does the sower?
Sow by night?
20 Or the plowman in darkness plow?

Break this heavy chain,
That does freeze my bones around°
Selfish! vain,
Eternal bane!
That free Love with bondage bound.
1793   1794

Holy Thursday

Is this a holy thing to see,
In a rich and fruitful land,
Babes reducd to misery,
Fed with cold and usurous hand?

Is that trembling cry a song?
Can it be a song of joy?
And so many children poor?
It is a land of poverty!

And their sun does never shine.
10 And their fields are bleak & bare.
And their ways are fill'd with thorns.
It is eternal winter there.

For where-e'er the sun does shine,
And where-e'er the rain does fall:
Babe can never hunger there,
Nor poverty the mind appall.
1793   1794

The Chimney Sweeper

A little black thing among the snow:
Crying weep, weep, in notes of woe!
Where are thy father & mother? say?
They are both gone up to the church to pray.

Because I was happy upon the heath,
And smil'd among the winters snow:

Break . . . around The chain of jealousy is
derived from the chain used to bind Loki in
the Northern Prose Edda.

They clothed me in the clothes of death,
And taught me to sing the notes of woe.

And because I am happy, & dance & sing,
10 They think they have done me no injury:
And are gone to praise God & his Priest & King
Who make up a heaven of our misery.
1793   1794

The Sick Rose°

O Rose thou art sick.
The invisible worm,
That flies in the night
In the howling storm:

Has found out thy bed
Of crimson joy:
And his dark secret love
Does thy life destroy.
1794

The Tyger°

Tyger Tyger, burning bright,
In the forests of the night;
What immortal hand or eye,
Could frame thy fearful symmetry?

In what distant deeps or skies
Burnt the fire of thine eyes!
On what wings dare he aspire?°
What the hand, dare sieze the fire?°

And what shoulder, & what art,
10 Could twist the sinews of thy heart?

The Sick Rose Note that the Rose's bed is "of crimson joy" *before* the worm finds it out. The bed is concealed, and evidently a place of self-gratification. "Dark secret love" comes and destroys, possibly because a bright open love would have been rejected anyway.

The Tyger This is the most disputed of Blake's lyrics among interpreters. The increasingly rhetorical questions are akin to those asked by God at the end of the Book of Job, and the Tyger is a kind of cousin to the Leviathan and Behemoth with whom God confronts Job. However the poem is interpreted, the reader should be wary of identifying the poem's chanter with Blake, who did not react with awe or fear to any natural phenomenon whatsoever.

Blake probably had considerable satirical in-

tention in this lyric, as a juxtaposition of his verbal description of the Tyger with his illustration seems to suggest. The poem's speaker, though a man of considerable imagination (quite possibly a poet like William Cowper), is at work terrifying himself with a monster of his own creation. Though Blake may mean us to regard the poem's questions as unanswerable, he himself would have answered by saying that the "immortal hand or eye" belonged only to Man, who makes both Tyger and Lamb. In "the forests of the night," or mental darkness, Man makes the Tyger, but in the open vision of day Man makes the Lamb.

On . . . aspire a suggestion of Icarus
What . . . fire a hint of Prometheus

And when thy heart began to beat,
What dread hand? & what dread feet?°

What the hammer? what the chain,
In what furnace was thy brain?
What the anvil? what dread grasp,
Dare its deadly terrors clasp?

When the stars threw down their spears°
And water'd heaven with their tears:
Did he smile his work to see?
20   Did he who made the Lamb make thee?

Tyger, Tyger burning bright,
In the forests of the night:
What immortal hand or eye,
Dare frame thy fearful symmetry?
1793   1794

Ah! Sun-flower°

Ah Sun-flower! weary of time,
Who countest the steps of the Sun:
Seeking after that sweet golden clime
Where the travellers journey is done.

Where the Youth pined away with desire,
And the pale Virgin shrouded in snow:
Arise from their graves and aspire,
Where my Sun-flower wishes to go.
1794

London°

I wander thro' each charter'd° street,
Near where the charter'd Thames does flow.

what dread feet David Erdman notes that "&
what dread feet?" was altered in ink to "formed
thy dread feet" in a late copy; another late
source gives "forged thy dread feet."
When . . . spears The stars, or fallen angels,
never throw down their spears and surrender in
Milton's *Paradise Lost;* in Night V of Blake's
The Four Zoas, Blake clearly associates "The
Tyger" with the Fall of Urizen, who says: "I
call'd the stars around my feet in the night of
councils dark; / The stars threw down their
spears & fled naked away. / We fell."
Ah! Sun-Flower In Blake's poem *Europe,* heaven
is described as "an allegorical abode where
existence hath never come." Blake's Sun-Flower
is weary of time because it is trapped in helio-
tropic bondage, in perpetual cycle, and longs
vainly for such an allegorical abode. The reader
should ask himself whether the three "where"s
of this poem are not the same place.
    Blake is giving his own version here of Ovid's
story of Clytia, who was first loved but then
abandoned by Helius, the sun god. As she still
gazed at him, with yearning, she was meta-
morphosed into a heliotrope or sunflower.
London This greatest of Blake's prophetic lyrics
is based on Ezekiel, and associates London under
Pitt's counter-revolutionary repression with Jerusalem waiting for its destruction. But only the
third stanza centers upon societal repression; the
other three describe every person's all-too-natural
abandonment of his own liberty.
charter'd A bitter, multiple usage; it refers to
"the charter'd rights of Englishmen," curtailed
by Pitt, but also to commercial chartering, and
finally to "natural" chartering (the Thames is
"bound" or chartered between its banks).

And mark in every face I meet
Marks of weakness, marks of woe.°

In every cry of every Man,
In every Infants cry of fear,
In every° voice: in every ban,°
The mind-forg'd manacles I hear

How the Chimney-sweepers cry
10 Every blackning Church appalls,°
And the hapless Soldiers sigh,°
Runs in blood down Palace walls

But most thro' midnight streets I hear
How the youthful Harlots curse
Blasts the new-born Infants tear°
And blights with plagues the Marriage hearse°
1793   1794

The Human Abstract°

Pity would be no more,
If we did not make somebody Poor:
And Mercy no more could be,
If all were as happy as we;

And mutual fear brings peace;
Till the selfish loves increase.
Then Cruelty knits a snare,
And spreads his baits with care.

He sits down with holy fears,
10 And waters the ground with tears:

marks of woe Here, and later in the poem, Blake closely echoes Ezekiel, as he will in the larger structure of his epic *Jerusalem;* see Ezekiel 9:4, where God says: "Go through the midst of the city, through the midst of Jerusalem, and set a mark upon the foreheads of the men that sigh and that cry for all the abominations that be done in the midst thereof."
every The emphasis on "every" should make us wary of a purely societal interpretation; Blake means *natural* fear, which warrants the repetition of "every."
ban the marriage announcement as well as all societal prohibitions
appalls drapes in a pall
sigh Like "cry" in l.9, this derives from Ezekiel 9:4.
new-born Infants tear Newborn infants have no tears until their eyes are moistened by doctor or midwife; Blake attributes a natural fact to the harlot's curse; the other meaning found here by interpreters, that the infant suffers prenatal blindness, caused by the parent's venereal dis-

ease by earlier infection from the harlot, blends into the curse as spell; the curse is a shouted outcry in the street (most of the poem consists of *sounds*) which "blasts" the tear in the sense of scattering it, as if by wind; the harlot ultimately is Nature herself, as we should expect in Blake.
Marriage hearse Blake means that every marriage whatsoever rides in a hearse, rather than in a celebratory coach.
The Human Abstract This contrary poem to "The Divine Image" of Innocence is as much an organic and terrible image as that poem is a deliberately confused tangle of abstractions. All the virtues of "The Divine Image" are revealed here as stemming from the selfishness of the natural heart. "Abstract" is not to be understood in the sense of the Latin *abstractus* ("separated," "drawn apart"), because Blake does not mean that human nature is split in the state of Experience, but probably that we reduce the truly human to a pernicious series of misleading abstractions.

Then Humility takes its root
Underneath his foot.

Soon spreads the dismal shade
Of Mystery over his head;°
And the Catterpiller and Fly,
Feed on the Mystery.

And it bears the fruit of Deceit,
Ruddy and sweet to eat;
And the Raven° his nest has made
20 In its thickest shade.

The Gods of the earth and sea,
Sought thro' Nature to find this Tree°
But their search was all in vain:
There grows one in the Human Brain
1793   1794

To Tirzah°

Whate'er is Born of Mortal Birth,
Must be consumed with the Earth
To rise from Generation° free;
Then what have I to do with thee?°

The Sexes sprung from Shame & Pride
Blow'd in the morn: in evening died
But Mercy changd Death into Sleep;
The Sexes rose to work & weep.°

Thou Mother of my Mortal part°
10 With cruelty didst mould my Heart,

Soon . . . head This is the Tree of Mystery, the Norse Yggdrasil that the god Odin hanged himself upon, in order to gain knowledge of the runes, or riddles of Mystery.
the Raven Odin's emblem, here a scavenger upon humanity's repressed desires
The Gods . . . Tree After Loki, by trickery, arranged for Balder to die by a mistletoe branch, the gods searched through nature to find the tree, so as to restore Balder; Blake's tree is natural enough, but grows in our minds, which have fallen into nature.
To Tirzah This poem, the last of the Songs of Experience, with its illustration showing the raising of the Spiritual Body from death, was added late to the song cycle, perhaps as late as 1805, which makes it one of Blake's final poems, since he wrote little in the last twenty years of his life. The most difficult of the songs, it condenses the entire argument of Blake's work. "To Tirzah" repudiates both Innocence and Experience, for Tirzah presides over both states.
Tirzah was the capital of the Northern king-

dom of Israel, and so the contrary city to the Jerusalem of the Prophets, capital of the Southern kingdom of Judah; the two tribes of the Southern kingdom were redeemed from the captivity, but the ten lost tribes of Tirzah never returned from Babylon; even as Jerusalem is for Blake the Emanation or spiritual freedom of man, so Tirzah is his natural bondage; in Blake's longer poems she turns the spindle of Necessity, so that to defy her is to deny natural religion, but also all natural limitation.
Generation sexual generation, but also Blake's technical name for the state of Experience
what . . . thee Jesus to Mary his mother in John 2:4
The Sexes . . . weep Blake says that the sexual act preceded the Fall, yet sexual division with its present limitations came from a "Shame & Pride" not originally human; the "Mercy" here is Time.
Mortal part Nature is not the mother of Blake's Imagination, his immortal part.

And with false self-deceiving tears,
Didst bind my Nostrils Eyes & Ears.

Didst close my Tongue in senseless clay°
And me to Mortal Life betray:
The Death of Jesus set me free,°
Then what have I to do with thee?
1805   1805

The Book of Thel

This Blakean version of pastoral is an extended Song of Innocence, written in Blake's characteristic long line, the fourteener, and in the genre of the Renaissance mythological epyllion, or brief epic. The pathos of Thel's story is a function of her weakness of will, and her failure to endure the necessary sufferings of the state of Experience is both a failure of desire, and another exposure of the limitations of Innocence. Blake shows her as an unborn being discontented with her paradisal abode, yet not courageous enough to sustain the will to be born. She is an image of Innocence unwilling to carry herself over into the world of Experience, and so she comes to represent a failure in desire. The reader is left free to interpret her failure on many levels, from a thought that does not permit itself to find expression to a love that does not allow itself to be realized by sexual fulfillment.

The Book of Thel°

The Author & Printer   Willm Blake, 1789

PLATE i

Thel's Motto,°
Does the Eagle know what is in the pit?
Or wilt thou go ask the Mole:
Can Wisdom be put in a silver rod?
Or Love in a golden bowl?

senseless clay The "red clay" (literal meaning of "Adam") of the fallen human form; notice that Blake grants nature's power to curtail only four senses, but not the fifth sense, the sexual one of touch.
set me free not from the orthodox notion of original sin, but from the deceits of natural religion
Thel From the Greek for "will" or "wish"; like so many of Blake's names, this is a grim irony as well as a gentle pathos, because Thel fails in will, in the strength of desire.

Motto The source is Ecclesiastes 12:4–7: "and all the daughters of musick shall be brought low; / . . . and fears shall be in the way . . . and desire shall fail: because man goeth to his long home . . . / Or ever the silver cord be loosed, or the golden bowl be broken . . . / Then shall the dust return to the earth as it was. . . ." The Mole is in the pit of Experience, where knowledge of Experience must be sought. Wisdom and Love must be put into a rod and bowl of flesh, the organs of fallen human generation.

PLATE 1

Thel

I

The daughters of Mne Seraphim° led round their sunny flocks,
All but the youngest. she in paleness sought the secret air.
To fade away like morning beauty from her mortal day:

Down by the river of Adona° her soft voice is heard:
And thus her gentle lamentation falls like morning dew.

O life of this our spring! why fades the lotus of the water?
Why fade these children of the spring? born but to smile & fall.
Ah! Thel is like a watry bow, and like a parting cloud,
Like a reflection in a glass. like shadows in the water.
10   Like dreams of infants. like a smile upon an infants face,
Like the doves voice, like transient day, like music in the air;
Ah! gentle may I lay me down, and gentle rest my head.
And gentle sleep the sleep of death. and gentle hear the voice
Of him that walketh in the garden in the evening time.°

The Lilly of the valley breathing in the humble grass
Answer'd the lovely maid and said; I am a watry weed,
And I am very small, and love to dwell in lowly vales;
So weak, the gilded butterfly scarce perches on my head
Yet I am visited from heaven and he that smiles on all.
20   Walks in the valley. and each morn over me spreads his hand
Saying, rejoice thou humble grass, thou new-born lilly flower,
Thou gentle maid of silent valleys. and of modest brooks;
For thou shalt be clothed in light, and fed with morning manna:
Till summers heat melts thee beside the fountains and the springs
To flourish in eternal vales: then why should Thel complain,

PLATE 2

Why should the mistress of the vales of Har, utter a sigh.

She ceasd & smild in tears, then sat down in her silver shrine.

Thel answerd. O thou little virgin of the peaceful valley.
Giving to those that cannot crave, the voiceless, the o'ertired.
Thy breath doth nourish the innocent lamb, he smells thy milky garments,
He crops thy flowers. while thou sittest smiling in his face,
Wiping his mild and meekin mouth from all contagious taints.

Mne Seraphim The Seraphim were the highest order of angels, generally pictured as having the heads of children; in *Tiriel,* an earlier experiment at a mythological brief epic, Blake made Mnetha (a compound of Mnemosyne, or memory, and Athena) the goddess of the vales of Har, or world of the ungenerated. Thel and her sisters are thus angelic daughters of Mnetha,

pastoral shepherdesses more ornamental than functional in their unborn realm.
river of Adona See *Paradise Lost* I.450–52 and Spenser's Garden of Adonis, *The Faerie Queene* III.vi.29.
the voice . . . time See Genesis 3:8; Thel's prison-paradise is thus identical with the Hebraic Garden of Eden.

Thy wine doth purify the golden honey, thy perfume,
Which thou dost scatter on every little blade of grass that springs
10 Revives the milked cow, & tames the fire-breathing steed.
But Thel is like a faint cloud kindled at the rising sun:
I vanish from my pearly throne, and who shall find my place.

Queen of the vales the Lilly answered, ask the tender cloud,
And it shall tell thee why it glitters in the morning sky,
And why it scatters its bright beauty thro' the humid air.
Descend O little cloud & hover before the eyes of Thel.

The Cloud descended, and the Lilly bowd her modest head:
And went to mind her numerous charge among the verdant grass.

PLATE 3
II

O little Cloud the virgin said, I charge thee tell to me,
Why thou complainest not when in one hour thou fade away:
Then we shall seek thee but not find; ah Thel is like to Thee.
I pass away. yet I complain, and no one hears my voice.

The Cloud then shew'd his golden head & his bright form emerg'd,
Hovering and glittering on the air before the face of Thel.

O virgin know'st thou not. our steeds drink of the golden springs
Where Luvah° doth renew his horses: look'st thou on my youth,
And fearest thou because I vanish and am seen no more.
10 Nothing remains; O maid I tell thee, when I pass away,
It is to tenfold life, to love, to peace, and raptures holy:
Unseen descending, weigh my light wings upon balmy flowers;
And court the fair eyed dew. to take me to her shining tent;
The weeping virgin,° trembling kneels before the risen sun,
Till we arise link'd in a golden band, and never part;
But walk united, bearing food to all our tender flowers
Dost thou O little Cloud? I fear that I am not like thee;
For I walk through the vales of Har.° and smell the sweetest flowers;
But I feed not the little flowers: I hear the warbling birds,
20 But I feed not the warbling birds. they fly and seek their food;
But Thel delights in these no more because I fade away,
And all shall say, without a use this shining woman liv'd,
Or did she only live. to be at death the food of worms.

The Cloud reclind upon his airy throne and answer'd thus.

Then if thou art the food of worms. O virgin of the skies,
How great thy use. how great thy blessing; every thing that lives,

---

Luvah the first appearance of one of Blake's
Zoas, the "Giant Forms" or Titans of his comprehensive mythology. In his fallen form Luvah
will be Orc, the fiery rebel of unbridled sexual
energy, but here he is unfallen, and presides
over a world of only infantile sexuality.
weeping virgin the vaporizing half of the water

cycle in nature, from cloud to rain to sea to
cloud again
vales of Har Har is Hebrew for "mountain";
the name also suggests the Miltonic alternate
placing of the earthly paradise in Abyssinia or
Ethiopia.

Lives not alone, nor for itself: fear not and I will call
The weak worm from its lowly bed, and thou shalt hear its voice.
Come forth worm of the silent valley, to thy pensive queen.

30   The helpless worm arose, and sat upon the Lillys leaf,
And the bright Cloud saild on, to find his partner in the vale.

PLATE 4

III

Then Thel astonish'd view'd the Worm upon its dewy bed.

Art thou a Worm? image of weakness. art thou but a Worm?
I see thee like an infant wrapped in the Lillys leaf:
Ah weep not little voice, thou can'st not speak. but thou can'st weep;
Is this a Worm? I see thee lay helpless & naked: weeping,
And none to answer, none to cherish thee with mothers smiles.°

The Clod of Clay heard the Worms voice, & raisd her pitying head;
She bow'd over the weeping infant, and her life exhal'd
In milky fondness, then on Thel she fix'd her humble eyes.

10   O beauty of the vales of Har. we live not for ourselves,
Thou seest me the meanest thing, and so I am indeed;
My bosom of itself is cold. and of itself is dark,

PLATE 5

But he that loves the lowly, pours his oil upon my head.
And kisses me, and binds his nuptial bands around my breast,
And says; Thou mother of my children, I have loved thee.
And I have given thee a crown that none can take away
But how this is sweet maid, I know not, and I cannot know,
I ponder, and I cannot ponder;° yet I live and love.

The daughter of beauty wip'd her pitying tears with her white veil,
And said. Alas! I knew not this, and therefore did I weep:
That God would love a Worm I knew, and punish the evil foot
10   That wilful, bruis'd its helpless form: but that he cherish'd it
With milk and oil. I never knew; and therefore did I weep,
And I complaind in the mild air, because I fade away,
And lay me down in thy cold bed, and leave my shining lot.

Queen of the vales, the matron Clay answerd; I heard thy sighs.
And all thy moans flew o'er my roof. but I have call'd them down:
Wilt thou O Queen enter my house. 'tis given thee to enter,
And to return; fear nothing. enter with thy virgin feet.°

---

mothers smiles An appeal to Thel's repressed
maternal impulses; the worm is emblematic of
sexual generation, but also of death.
cannot ponder The Clod of Clay represents both
the Adamic flesh and the grave, the worm's two
aspects, and so speaks for it; the Clay's puzzlement is a gentle satire upon natural innocence,
which is unorganized and thus ignorant.
virgin feet The feet, for Blake, always represent
visionary stance; here an irony, as only Thel's
feet will cease to be virgin, in her brief encounter with Experience.

PLATE 6

IV

The eternal gates terrific porter lifted the northern bar:°
Thel enter'd in & saw the secrets of the land unknown;
She saw the couches of the dead, & where the fibrous roots
Of every heart on earth infixes deep its restless twists:°
A land of sorrows & of tears where never smile was seen.

She wanderd in the land of clouds thro' valleys dark, listning
Dolours & lamentations: waiting oft beside a dewy grave
She stood in silence. listning to the voices of the ground,
Till to her own grave plot° she came, & there she sat down.
10   And heard this voice of sorrow breathed from the hollow pit.

Why cannot the Ear be closed to its own destruction?
Or the glistning Eye to the poison of a smile!
Why are Eyelids stord with arrows ready drawn,
Where a thousand fighting men in ambush lie?
Or an Eye of gifts & graces, show'ring fruits & coined gold!
Why a Tongue impress'd with honey from every wind?
Why an Ear, a whirlpool fierce to draw creations in?
Why a Nostril wide inhaling terror trembling & affright
Why a tender curb upon the youthful burning boy!
20   Why a little curtain of flesh on the bed of our desire?°

The Virgin started from her seat, & with a shriek.°
Fled back unhinderd° till she came into the vales of Har
      THE END
1789–91   1789–91

The Marriage of Heaven and Hell

This is Blake's manifesto, his declaration of spiritual independence, and his version of what it means to rise in the body at thirty-three, the age at which Christ died. Deliberately, he makes it the entry-way into the canon of his mature work, his highly organized story of how man and the universe got into their present sorry condition,

northern bar See the *Odyssey* XIII. where the Cave of the Naiades or sea nymphs has two entrances, a northern one for men, and a southern one for gods; some scholars see Blake's source here as the neoplatonic philosopher Porphyry's commentary on the Cave of the Nymphs, but Blake is closer to Spenser's double gates and their double-natured porter in the Garden of Adonis (*The Faerie Queene* III.vi.31–32); in his epic *Milton* 26:16–18, Blake identifies his porter as Los the Poetic Genius; Spenser's porter is Old Genius. So the northern gate is the gate for men, not gods, from Innocence to Experience; Thel passes out and then flees back through the northern gate.
every heart . . . twists the naturalized heart,

a labyrinth of jealousy and selfishness
grave plot where Thel would be buried eventually if she accepted natural incarnation; the lament that rises would be her own voice
Why cannot . . . desire The lament's vocabulary is Petrarchan-Elizabethan in its erotic conventions; Thel protests the excessive strength of four senses, but bewails the failure of the fifth, the sexual sense of touch, to be strong enough to have broken through her inhibitions; even in Experience, she would have remained a virgin.
shriek the reverse of a birth shriek, since Thel refuses to be born
unhinderd ironic, since she is choosing "hindrance, not action"

and his prophecy of what should be done by every man who wishes to work free of a merely natural or given condition.

The central element in this prose poem is Blake's presentation of his dialectic, his imaginative but still rational process of arriving at truth through the progression of contraries, opposites which are not negations or denials but partial truths. What makes *The Marriage* initially a little difficult is that its rhetoric of presentation and its complex and experimental literary form embody a dialectical argument, so that the shock value of the work goes beyond its actually quite restrained wisdom. Commenting on Emanuel Swedenborg (Swedish theologian and mystic, 1688–1772) in 1788, Blake wrote, "Good and Evil are here both Good and the two contraries Married"; Blake's contraries replace Swedenborg's "correspondences," which are mutually absorbing categories, identities between the spiritual and natural worlds. By "marriage" Blake means that the contraries are to be reconciled, but are not to absorb or subsume one another. Blake was never a Swedenborgian, but may have believed him to be a fellow visionary, until by reading more of Swedenborg, he came to know better. In another 1788 comment on Swedenborg, Blake wrote, "Heaven and Hell are born Together," meaning that Swedenborg never knew this, since that onetime rebel against Calvinism had embraced the doctrine of Predestination. Blake begins and largely continues as though he were on the "Devil's" or imaginative rebel's side, and certainly he is more in that camp than among "Angels" or the timidly orthodox, but his final stance transcends any upsurge of energy and desire. Just as the states of Innocence and of Experience satirize one another, so the contraries of Devil and Angel satirically reveal one another's limitations.

The Marriage, then, is an intellectual satire, but it is also a qualified prophecy of an apocalypse that may be imminent. Rabelais (whom Blake never read) provides the closest analogue to Blake's tone, with the difference that Blake sees in his contemporary time of troubles the presages of the promised end. Not so much the French Revolution but the English reaction against the spread of revolution is Blake's starting point. The notes below trace his movement from that point to his overt declaration of election as the prophet his bad time requires.

The Marriage of Heaven and Hell

The Argument°

PLATE 2

Rintrah° roars & shakes his fires in the burdend air;
Hungry clouds swag° on the deep

Once meek, and in a perilous path,
The just man kept his course along
The vale of death.

The Argument This introductory lyric obliquely presents the contraries of Devil and Angel as an endlessly unresolved cycle of just man driven out and villain accepted by society.
Rintrah representative of prophetic wrath in Blake's mythology. He is a forerunner, like

Elijah or John the Baptist, and his fury precedes the turning over of a societal and natural cycle, but he himself is only a harbinger, not a redeemer.
swag sway or lurch

Roses are planted where thorns grow.
And on the barren heath
Sing the honey bees.

Then the perilous path was planted:
10   And a river, and a spring
On every cliff and tomb;
And on the bleached bones
Red clay° brought forth.°

Till the villain left the paths of ease,
To walk in perilous paths, and drive
The just man into barren climes.

Now the sneaking serpent walks
In mild humility.
And the just man rages in the wilds
20   Where lions roam.

Rintrah roars & shakes his fires in the burdend air;
Hungry clouds swag on the deep.

PLATE 3
   As a new heaven is begun, and it is now thirty-three years since its advent:
the Eternal Hell revives.° And lo! Swedenborg is the Angel sitting at the
tomb; his writings are the linen clothes folded up.° Now is the dominion of
Edom, & the return of Adam into Paradise; see Isaiah xxxiv & XXXV Chap:°
   Without Contraries is no progression. Attraction and Repulsion, Reason and
Energy, Love and Hate, are necessary to Human existence.
   From these contraries spring what the religious call Good & Evil. Good is
the passive that obeys Reason[.] Evil is the active springing from Energy.
   Good is Heaven. Evil is Hell.°

PLATE 4
   The Voice of the Devil°
   All Bibles or sacred codes. have been the causes of the following Errors.
   1. That Man has two real existing principles Viz: a Body & a Soul.

Red clay literal meaning of the Hebrew "Adam"
Then forth The general source is Exodus 17:1–8.
As . . . revives In Swedenborg's book *Last Judgment,* Blake had read: "The evil are cast into the
hells, and the good elevated into heaven, and thus
that all things are reduced into order, the spiritual equilibrium between good and evil, or between heaven and hell, being thence restored.
. . . This Last Judgment was commenced in the
beginning of the year 1757. . . ." Blake was
born in 1757; writing in 1790, aged thirty-three,
he ironically sees his birth as the contrary to
Swedenborg's pronouncement of a new heaven
of Angelic restraint.
Swedenborg . . . folded up See Matthew 28:
1–7.
XXXV Chap The red man of Edom was identified with Esau, tricked of the inheritance by

his brother Jacob or Israel in Genesis 28:40,
where their father Isaac then prophesies the
eventual dominion of Esau's descendants. Isaiah
63:1–4 amplifies this prophecy by the vision of a
savior coming out of Edom, taken by Christian
exegetes as a foretelling of Christ. Blake associates both these texts with the earlier prophecy in
Isaiah 34 and 35, where the desolate land of
Israel is restored, once the wicked are cut off.
As Blake displaces the prophecy into the situation of 1790, Edom is France, and the red man
will soon be identified as Orc, the Revolution
threatening to cross the English Channel.
Evil is Hell ironical identifications, as Blake
adopts the vocabulary of the Angels
the Devil again an irony of stance, "diabolical" only to the Angels

2. That Energy. calld Evil. is alone from the Body. & that Reason. calld Good. is alone from the Soul.

3. That God will torment Man in Eternity for following his Energies. But the following Contraries to these are True

1. Man has no Body distinct from his Soul for that calld Body is a portion of Soul discernd by the five Senses, the chief inlets of Soul in this age°

2. Energy is the only life and is from the Body and Reason is the bound or outward circumference of Energy.

3. Energy is Eternal Delight

PLATE 5

Those who restrain desire, do so because theirs is weak enough to be restrained; and the restrainer or reason usurps its place & governs the unwilling.

And being restrained it by degrees becomes passive till it is only the shadow of desire.

The history of this is written in Paradise Lost.° & the Governor or Reason is call'd Messiah.

And the original Archangel or possessor of the command of the heavenly host, is calld the Devil or Satan and his children are call'd Sin & Death

But in the Book of Job Miltons Messiah is call'd Satan.°

For this history has been adopted by both parties

It indeed appear'd to Reason as if Desire was cast out, but the Devils account is, that the Messi[PL 6]ah fell. & formed a heaven of what he stole from the Abyss

This is shewn in the Gospel, where he prays to the Father to send the comforter or Desire that Reason may have Ideas to build on, the Jehovah of the Bible being no other than he, who dwells in flaming fire.° Know that after Christs death, he became Jehovah.

But in Milton; the Father is Destiny, the Son, a Ratio° of the five senses. & the Holy-ghost, Vacuum!

Note. The reason Milton wrote in fetters when he wrote of Angels & God, and at liberty when of Devils & Hell, is because he was a true Poet and of the Devils party without knowing it°

A Memorable Fancy°

As I was walking among the fires of hell, delighted with the enjoyments of Genius; which to Angels look like torment and insanity. I collected some of their Proverbs: thinking that as the sayings used in a nation, mark its character,

in this age Though Blake is rejecting the Pauline dualism of body and soul, he does not equate body and soul, as a pure naturalist would; "this age" is fallen, and so the Body is all of the Soul that our shrunken senses can perceive.

The history . . . Paradise Lost This is an aesthetic reading of the poem's design, and not a reading of Milton's intentions; Blake traces the declining movement of creative energy from the active of the early books to the passive of the poem's conclusion, and particularly has in mind the poem's continual denigrations of fallen man's creative powers.

But . . . Satan In the Book of Job, Satan is a moral accuser who torments Job with physical pain; in *Paradise Lost* Christ is instrumental in

carrying the fire of God's wrath down into the abyss, so that Hell is created as a place of moral and physical punishment; so Blake arrives at the equation: Job's Satan is Milton's Messiah.

This . . . fire See John 16:7 for the Comforter or Paraclete, but the reference is probably to John 14:16–17, with "the Spirit of Truth" interpreted by Blake as Desire.

Ratio rationalistic reduction

Note . . . it This means that for a poet *as poet* the energy of human desire cannot be separated from the imagination.

A Memorable Fancy This, and subsequent sections with the same title, are parodies of what Swedenborg called "Memorable Relations," literal-minded reports of his spiritual visions.

so the Proverbs of Hell, shew the nature of Infernal wisdom better than any description of buildings or garments.°

When I came home; on the abyss of the five senses, where a flat sided steep frowns over the present world. I saw a mighty Devil folded in black clouds, hovering on the side of the rock, with cor[PL 7]roding fires he wrote the following sentence now perceived by the minds of men, & read by them on earth.°

> How do you know but ev'ry Bird that cuts the airy way,
> Is an immense world of delight, clos'd by your senses five?°

Proverbs of Hell°

In seed time learn, in harvest teach, in winter enjoy.

Drive your cart and your plow over the bones of the dead.

The road of excess leads to the palace of wisdom.

Prudence is a rich ugly old maid courted by Incapacity.

He who desires but acts not, breeds pestilence.

The cut worm forgives the plow.

Dip him in the river who loves water.

A fool sees not the same tree that a wise man sees.

He whose face gives no light, shall never become a star.

10 Eternity is in love with the productions of time.

The busy bee has no time for sorrow.

The hours of folly are measur'd by the clock, but of wisdom: no clock
    can measure.

All wholsom food is caught without a net or a trap.

Bring out number weight & measure in a year of dearth.

No bird soars too high. if he soars with his own wings.

A dead body. revenges not injuries.

The most sublime act is to set another before you.

If the fool would persist in his folly he would become wise

Folly is the cloke of knavery.

20 Shame is Prides cloke.

PLATE 8

Prisons are built with stones of Law, Brothels with bricks of Religion.

The pride of the peacock is the glory of God.

The lust of the goat is the bounty of God.

any description . . . garments a parody of the Devil's activities in *Paradise Lost* II, after Satan goes off on his voyage through Chaos

I saw . . . earth The "mighty Devil" is Blake at work engraving the *Marriage*, the "corroding fires" are of his satiric art, and the "rock" is our fallen human minds, as we read and study his engraved plates.

How . . . five The couplet the Devil Blake etches is a tribute to Thomas Chatterton, closely following a quatrain from his "The Dethe of Syr Charles Bawdin," ll.133–36: "How dydd I knowe thatt ev'ry darte, / That cutte the airie waie, / Myghte nott fynde passage toe my harte, / And close myne eyes for aie?" Blake's parody of this reminds us of our perceptive limitations.

Proverbs of Hell "Diabolic" or antinomian in their rhetoric, these seventy proverbs depend upon a dialectical definition of an "act," and have been generally misunderstood, particularly in recent years. In his annotations to Johann Kaspar Lavater's (1741–1801) *Aphorisms on Man*, Blake wrote: "As I understand Vice it is a Negative—It does not signify what the laws of Kings and Priests have calld Vice . . . Accident is the omission of act in self and the hindering of act in another, This is Vice but all Act is Virtue. To hinder another is not an act it is the contrary it is a restraint on action both in ourselves and in the person hinderd. for he who hinders another omits his own duty at the time. Murder is Hindering Another. Theft is Hindering Another. Backbiting, Undermining, Circumventing and whatever is Negative is Vice." The reader needs to apply these ideas of act and hindrance to the Proverbs.

The wrath of the lion is the wisdom of God.

The nakedness of woman is the work of God.

Excess of sorrow laughs. Excess of joy weeps.

The roaring of lions, the howling of wolves, the raging of the stormy sea, and
    the destructive sword. are portions of eternity too great for the eye of man.

The fox condemns the trap, not himself.

Joys impregnate. Sorrows bring forth.

30 Let man wear the fell of the lion. woman the fleece of the sheep.

The bird a nest, the spider a web, man friendship.

The selfish smiling fool. & the sullen frowning fool. shall be both
    thought wise. that they may be a rod.

What is now proved was once, only imagin'd.

The rat, the mouse, the fox, the rabbet; watch the roots, the lion, the tyger, the
    horse, the elephant, watch the fruits.

The cistern contains: the fountain overflows

One thought. fills immensity.

Always be ready to speak your mind, and a base man will avoid you.

Every thing possible to be believ'd is an image of truth.

The eagle never lost so much time. as when he submitted to learn of the crow.

PLATE 9

40 The fox provides for himself. but God provides for the lion.

Think in the morning, Act in the noon, Eat in the evening, Sleep in the night.

He who has sufferd you to impose on him knows you.

As the plow follows words, so God rewards prayers.

The tygers of wrath are wiser than the horses of instruction

Expect poison from the standing water.

You never know what is enough unless you know what is more than enough.

Listen to the fools reproach! it is a kingly title!

The eyes of fire, the nostrils of air, the mouth of water, the beard of earth.

The weak in courage is strong in cunning.

50 The apple tree never asks the beech how he shall grow, nor the lion. the horse,
    how he shall take his prey.

The thankful receiver bears a plentiful harvest.

If others had not been foolish, we should be so.

The soul of sweet delight, can never be defil'd,

When thou seest an Eagle, thou seest a portion of Genius. lift up thy head!

As the catterpiller chooses the fairest leaves to lay her eggs on, so the priest
    lays his curse on the fairest joys.

To create a little flower is the labour of ages.

Damn. braces: Bless relaxes.

The best wine is the oldest. the best water the newest.

Prayers plow not! Praises reap not!

60 Joys laugh not! Sorrows weep not!

PLATE 10

The head Sublime, the heart Pathos, the genitals Beauty, the hands & feet
    Proportion.

As the air to a bird or the sea to a fish, so is contempt to the contemptible.

The crow wish'd every thing was black, the owl, that every thing was white.
Exuberance is Beauty.
If the lion was advise'd by the fox. he would be cunning.
Improve[me]nt makes strait roads, but the crooked roads without Improvement,
     are roads of Genius.
Sooner murder an infant in its cradle than nurse unacted desires
Where man is not nature is barren.
Truth can never be told so as to be understood, and not be believ'd.
70   Enough! or Too much

PLATE 11°

The ancient Poets animated all sensible objects with Gods or Geniuses,
calling them by the names and adorning them with the properties of woods,
rivers, mountains, lakes, cities, nations, and whatever their enlarged & numerous
senses could perceive.

And particularly they studied the genius of each city & country. placing it
under its mental deity.

Till a system was formed, which some took advantage of & enslav'd the
vulgar by attempting to realize or abstract the mental deities from their objects;
thus began Priesthood.

Choosing forms of worship from poetic tales.

And at length they pronounced that the Gods had orderd such things.

Thus men forgot that All deities reside in the human breast.

PLATE 12

A Memorable Fancy
The Prophets Isaiah and Ezekiel dined with me, and I asked them how they
dared so roundly to assert. that God spake to them; and whether they did not
think at the time, that they would be misunderstood, & so be the cause of
imposition.

Isaiah answer'd. I saw no God, nor heard any, in a finite organical perception;
but my senses discover'd the infinite in every thing, and as I was then per-
swaded, & remain confirm'd; that the voice of honest indignation is the voice
of God, I cared not for consequences but wrote.

Then I asked: does a firm perswasion that a thing is so, make it so?

He replied. All poets believe that it does, & in ages of imagination this firm
perswasion removed mountains; but many are not capable of a firm perswasion
of any thing.

Then Ezekiel said. The philosophy of the east taught the first principles of
human perception   some nations held one principle for the origin & some another, we of Israel taught that the Poetic Genius (as you now call it) was
the first principle and all the others merely derivative, which was the cause
of our despising the Prisets & Philosophers of other countries, and prophecying
that all Gods [PL 13] would at last be proved to originate in ours & to be the
tributaries of the Poetic Genius, it was this. that our great poet King David
desired so fervently & invokes so patheticly, saying by this he conquers enemies

Plate 11 This section describes the codification
of poetry into scripture, in a little history of
religion.

& governs kingdoms; and we so loved our God. that we cursed in his name all the deities of surrounding nations, and asserted that they had rebelled; from these opinions the vulgar came to think that all nations would at last be subject to the jews.

This said he, like all firm perswasions, is come to pass, for all nations believe the jews code and worship the jews god, and what greater subjection can be

I heard this with some wonder, & must confess my own conviction. After dinner I ask'd Isaiah to favour the world with his lost works, he said none of equal value was lost. Ezekiel said the same of his.

I also asked Isaiah what made him go naked and barefoot three years? he answerd, the same that made our friend Diogenes the Grecian.°

I then asked Ezekiel. why he eat dung, & lay so long on his right & left side? he answerd. the desire of raising other men into a perception of the infinite this the North American tribes practise. & is he honest who resists his genius or conscience. only for the sake of present ease or gratification?°

PLATE 14

The ancient tradition that the world will be consumed in fire at the end of six thousand years is true. as I have heard from Hell.°

For the cherub with his flaming sword is hereby commanded to leave his guard at tree of life, and when he does, the whole creation will be consumed, and appear infinite. and holy whereas it now appears finite & corrupt.°

This will come to pass by an improvement of sensual enjoyment.°

But first the notion that man has a body distinct from his soul, is to be expunged; this I shall do, by printing in the infernal method, by corrosives, which in Hell are salutary and medicinal, melting apparent surfaces away, and displaying the infinite which was hid.°

If the doors of perception were cleansed every thing would appear to man as it is, infinite.

For man has closed himself up, till he sees all things thro' narrow chinks of his cavern.°

PLATE 15

A Memorable Fancy°

I was in a Printing house in Hell & saw the method in which knowledge is transmitted from generation to generation.

I also . . . Grecian See Isaiah 20:3; Diogenes (412–323 B.C.) was a Cynic philosopher, noted for eccentric behavior.
I then . . . gratification See Ezekiel 4:4–12.
The ancient . . . Hell The tradition was hardly ancient, since Blake relies upon later Christian interpretations of II Peter 3:8.
for the . . . corrupt The cherub is from Genesis 3:24, but assimilated to the Covering Cherub of Ezekiel 28:11–16, with whom Blake identified Satan in his poem Milton 9:30–35.
sensual enjoyment the necessary first step for Blake, but only a first step
this I shall do . . . hid Note that Blake refers to his satiric art as poet and visionary art as engraver, and not to mysticism or extraordinary states of consciousness.

cavern our body as it is now
A Memorable Fancy An allegory of artistic creation; it begins with the Dragon or phallic man improving sensual enjoyment, while the Dragons expand our other senses; the Viper of repression seeks to conceal our fallen condition, but the Eagle or portion of Genius defeats the Viper and raises us to infinite potential; the "Eagle like men" are artists; in the fourth chamber appearances are melted down into the stuff of poetry by the Lions who represent archetypes of imagination; in the fifth chamber, which influenced the "golden smithies" of Yeats's "Byzantium," the flood of spirit is broken by forms of art; the metals are then cast into the sixth chamber, where the creative process culminates.

In the first chamber was a Dragon-Man, clearing away the rubbish from a caves mouth; within, a number of Dragons were hollowing the cave,

In the second chamber was a Viper folding round the rock & the cave, and others adorning it with gold silver and precious stones.

In the third chamber was an Eagle with wings and feathers of air, he caused the inside of the cave to be infinite, around were numbers of Eagle like men, who built palaces in the immense cliffs.

In the fourth chamber were Lions of flaming fire raging around & melting the metals into living fluids.

In the fifth chamber were Unnam'd forms, which cast the metals into the expanse.

There they were reciev'd by Men who occupied the sixth chamber, and took the forms of books & were arranged in libraries.

PLATE 16

The Giants who formed this world into its sensual existence and now seem to live in it in chains, are in truth. the causes of its life & the sources of all activity, but the chains are, the cunning of weak and tame minds. which have power to resist energy, according to the proverb, the weak in courage is strong in cunning.

Thus one portion of being, is the Prolific. the other, the Devouring: to the devourer it seems as if the producer was in his chains, but it is not so, he only takes portions of existence and fancies that the whole.

But the Prolific would cease to be Prolific unless the Devourer as a sea received the excess of his delights.°

Some will say, Is not God alone the Prolific? I answer, God only Acts & Is, in existing beings or Men.

These two classes of men are always upon earth, & they should be enemies; whoever tries [PL 17] to reconcile them seeks to destroy existence.

Religion is an endeavour to reconcile the two.

Note. Jesus Christ did not wish to unite but to seperate them, as in the Parable of sheep and goats! & he says I came not to send Peace but a Sword.°

Messiah or Satan or Tempter was formerly thought to be one of the Antediluvians° who are our Energies.

A Memorable Fancy°

An Angel came to me and said   O pitiable foolish young man! O horrible! O dreadful state! consider the hot burning dungeon thou art preparing for thyself to all eternity, to which thou art going in such career.

I said, perhaps you will be willing to shew me my eternal lot & we will contemplate together upon it and see whether your lot or mine is most desirable

Thus one . . . delights The most central passage in *The Marriage*, making clear that Blake goes beyond Devil as well as Angel, and the one passage in *The Marriage* free of all irony; the Devourer is the outer limit of the Prolific, as Freud's ego is of his id, but the Devourer cannot operate independently; the Prolific, unlike Freud's id, is not chaotic, yet needs the Devourer to avoid chaos.

Note . . . Sword For the Parable, see Matthew 25:32–33; Christ's remark is in Matthew 10:34.

Antediluvians the Giant Race before the Flood that only Noah and his family survived

A Memorable Fancy The "stable" is where Jesus was born, the "vault" where he was buried, the "mill" represents rationalistic reduction; the "winding cavern" suits rationalistic metaphysics, and the "void" is nature; Hell, an orthodox illusion, scares away the Angel, allowing Blake the solitude of his own creative vision.

So he took me thro' a stable & thro' a church & down into the church vault at the end of which was a mill: thro' the mill we went, and came to a cave. down the winding cavern we groped our tedious way till a void boundless as a nether sky appeard beneath us. & we held by the roots of trees and hung over this immensity, but I said, if you please we will commit ourselves to this void, and see whether providence is here also, if you will not I will? but he answerd, do not presume O young man but as we here remain behold thy lot which will soon appear when the darkness passes away

So I remaind with him sitting in the twisted [PL 18] root of an oak. he was suspended in a fungus which hung with the head downward into the deep;

By degrees we beheld the infinite Abyss, fiery as the smoke of a burning city; beneath us at an immense distance was the sun, black but shining[;] round it were fiery tracks on which revolv'd vast spiders, crawling after their prey; which flew or rather swum in the finite deep, in the most terrific shapes of animals sprung from corruption. & the air was full of them, & seemd composed of them; these are Devils. and are called Powers of the air, I now asked my companion which was my eternal lot? he said, between the black & white spiders

But now, from between the black & white spiders a cloud and fire burst and rolled thro the deep blackning all beneath, so that the nether deep grew black as a sea & rolled with a terrible noise: beneath us was nothing now to be seen but a black tempest, till looking east between the clouds & the waves, we saw a cataract of blood mixed with fire and not many stones throw from us appeard and sunk again the scaly fold of a monstrous serpent[.] at last to the east, distant about three degrees appeard a fiery crest above the waves[.] slowly it reared like a ridge of golden rocks till we discoverd two globes of crimson fire, from which the sea fled away in clouds of smoke, and now we saw, it was the head of Leviathan, his forehead was divided into streaks of green & purple like those on a tygers forehead:° soon we saw his mouth & red gills hang just above the raging foam tinging the black deep with beams of blood, advancing toward [PL 19] us with all the fury of a spiritual existence.

My friend the Angel climb'd up from his station into the mill; I remain'd alone, & then this appearance was no more, but I found myself sitting on a pleasant bank beside a river by moon light hearing a harper who sung to the harp, & his theme was, The man who never alters his opinion is like standing water, & breeds reptiles of the mind.

But I arose, and sought for the mill, & there I found my Angel, who surprised asked me, how I escaped?

I answerd. All that we saw was owing to your metaphysics: for when you ran away, I found myself on a bank by moonlight hearing a harper, But now we have seen my eternal lot, shall I shew you yours? he laughd at my proposal; but I by force suddenly caught him in my arms, & flew westerly thro' the night, till we were elevated above the earths shadow: then I flung myself with him directly into the body of the sun, here I clothed myself in white, & taking in my hand Swedenborgs volumes sunk from the glorious clime, and passed all the planets till we came to saturn, here I staid to rest & then leap'd into the void, between saturn & the fixed stars.

tygers forehead This confirms the association in "The Tyger" with the Leviathan of Job.

Here said I! is your lot, in this space, if space it may be calld, Soon we saw the stable and the church, & I took him to the altar and open'd the Bible, and lo! it was a deep pit, into which I descended driving the Angel before me, soon we saw seven houses of brick,° one we enterd; in it were a [PL 20] number of monkeys, baboons, & all of that species chaind by the middle, grinning and snatching at one another, but witheld by the shortness of their chains: however I saw that they sometimes grew numerous, and then the weak were caught by the strong and with a grinning aspect, first coupled with & then devourd, by plucking off first one limb and then another till the body was left a helpless trunk. this after grinning & kissing it with seeming fondness they devourd too; and here & there I saw one savourily picking the flesh off of his own tail; as the stench terribly annoyd us both we went into the mill, & I in my hand brought the skeleton of a body, which in the mill was Aristotles Analytics.°

So the Angel said: thy phantasy has imposed upon me & thou oughtest to be ashamed.

I answerd: we impose on one another, & it is but lost time to converse with you whose works are only Analytics

Opposition is true Friendship.

PLATE 21

I have always found that Angels have the vanity to speak of themselves as the only wise; this they do with a confident insolence sprouting from systematic reasoning;

Thus Swedenborg boasts that what he writes is new; tho' it is only the Contents or Index of already publish'd books

A man carried a monkey about for a shew, & because he was a little wiser than the monkey, grew vain, and conciev'd himself as much wiser than seven men. It is so with Swedenborg; he shews the folly of churches & exposes hypocrites, till he imagines that all are religious. & himself the single [PL 22] one on earth that ever broke a net.

Now hear a plain fact: Swedenborg has not written one new truth: Now hear another: he has written all the old falshoods.

And now hear the reason. He conversed with Angels who are all religious, & conversed not with Devils who all hate religion, for he was incapable thro' his conceited notions.

Thus Swedenborgs writings are a recapitulation of all superficial opinions, and an analysis of the more sublime, but no further.

Have now another plain fact: Any man of mechanical talents may from the writings of Paracelsus or Jacob Behmen, produce ten thousand volumes of equal value with Swedenborg's. and from those of Dante or Shakespear, an infinite number.°

seven houses of brick the seven churches in Asia to whom St. John addressed his Revelation
Aristotles Analytics his writings on logic, which contributed to the theological monkey-quarrels the passage satirizes
Have now . . . number It is vital to get this passage right; Paracelsus (Theophrastus Bombastus von Hohenheim, 1493–1541, the subject and title of a Browning poem) was an alchemist; Jacob Behmen (Böhme, 1573–1624) was a theosophist and mystic; scholars delight in trac-

ing their "influence" on Blake, but such scholars show a more exemplary patience with obscurantism than Blake did. This passage insists that the alchemists and theosophists are more imaginative than poor Swedenborg, but then goes on to say that these spiritual amateurs are only candles in sunshine when compared with Dante and Shakespeare, who in turn meant very little to Blake when compared with Milton and the Bible.

But when he has done this, let him not say that he knows better than his master, for he only holds a candle in sunshine.

A Memorable Fancy

Once I saw a Devil in a flame of fire, who arose before an Angel that sat on a cloud. and the Devil utterd these words.

The worship of God is. Honouring his gifts in other men each according to his genius. and loving the [PL 23] greatest men best, those who envy or calumniate great men hate God, for there is no other God.°

The Angel hearing this became almost blue but mastering himself he grew yellow, & at last white pink & smiling, and then replied,

Thou Idolater, is not God One? & is not he visible in Jesus Christ? and has not Jesus Christ given his sanction to the law of ten commandments and are not all other men fools, sinners, & nothings?

The Devil answer'd; bray a fool in a morter with wheat. yet shall not his folly be beaten out of him: if Jesus Christ is the greatest man, you ought to love him in the greatest degree; now hear how he has given his sanction to the law of ten commandments: did he not mock at the sabbath, and so mock the sabbaths God? murder those who were murderd because of him? turn away the law from the woman taken in adultery? steal the labor of others to support him? bear false witness when he omitted making a defence before Pilate? covet when he pray'd for his disciples, and when he bid them shake off the dust of their feet against such as refused to lodge them? I tell you, no virtue can exist without breaking these ten commandments.˙. Jesus was all virtue, and acted from im[PL 24]pulse. not from rules.°

When he had so spoken: I beheld the Angel who stretched out his arms embracing the flame of fire & he was consumed and arose as Elijah.°

Note. This Angel, who is now become a Devil, is my particular friend: we often read the Bible together in its infernal or diabolical sense which the world shall have if they behave well

I have also: The Bible of Hell:° which the world shall have whether they will or no.

One Law for the Lion & Ox is Oppression°
1790–93   1793

Visions of the Daughters of Albion

Like Shelley's *Epipsychidion*, this is a rapturous hymn to free love, but where Shelley will see free love fail because of the incurable solitariness of individuals, Blake sees it as doomed because of what the Blake scholar Peter Fisher called "the failure of the fallen understanding to cope with the organization of desire." Oothoon is defeated

those who envy . . . God This ought not to be confused with the egregious Hero Worship of Carlyle, for "greatest men" here means greatest artists, and no one else.
not from rules Blake's Jesus is an antinomian or rebel against the Moral Law.
Elijah biblical model for Blake's Rintrah

The Bible of Hell the canon of Blake's engraved works, evidently anticipated here
One Law . . . Oppression This accompanies the illustration of Nebuchadnezzar eating grass (Daniel 4:33), which is the final plate of *The Marriage;* see Bromion's questioning use of this in *Visions of the Daughters of Albion* 4:22.

because both her lovers are imaginatively inadequate, and so the poem is essentially a vision of the limitations of male jealousy and of male sexual fearfulness.

Bromion's name is from the Greek "bromios," for "roaring," ordinarily a Dionysiac title, but used ironically here, since Bromion is a puritanical deist with nothing Dionysiac about him. He despises his own lust, and is a rather Dickensian satiric villain, as he roars out his conventional and disgusting morality. Theotormon, Oothoon's wretchedly weak betrothed, is tormented by his absurd notions of god, as his name is meant to indicate. Oothoon's mellifluous name is a variant on the *Oithona* of James MacPherson (Ossian), and satirizes the conventional heroine of that tiresome prose poem, since Oithona prefers death to the dishonor of rape, while Oothoon, after being raped, attempts to choose a more abundant life. Blake's insights here into the psychic origins of sexual jealousy have not been surpassed. Oothoon wishes to offer herself sexually to Theotormon, but is taken forcibly by Bromion. After a brief period in which she accepts the conventional morality which would condemn her as a harlot (for having enjoyed the sexual act, though it was a rape) she rises into an imaginative freedom that Theotormon can neither understand nor accept, and that Bromion understands but rejects out of natural fear.

Visions of the Daughters of Albion°

The Eye sees more than the Heart knows.°

Printed by Will:ᵐ Blake: 1793.

PLATE iii

The Argument°
I loved Theotormon
And I was not ashamed
I trembled in my virgin fears
And I hid in Leutha's vale!
I plucked Leutha's flower,
And I rose up from the vale;
But the terrible thunders tore
My virgin mantle in twain.

PLATE I

Visions
Enslav'd, the Daughters of Albion weep: a trembling lamentation
Upon their mountains; in their valleys. sighs toward America.

Visions of the Daughters of Albion The title's reference is to what the Daughters *see,* since their function throughout is to be a lamenting chorus. Blake elsewhere identifies Albion with the Greek Titan Atlas, which identifies the Daughters with the Hesperides, who live in a last remainder of Lost Atlantis, and there guard a golden apple tree, which in Blake's poem becomes a flower, "the bright Marygold."
The Eye . . . knows vision surpasses the limited awareness of the natural heart
The Argument Spoken by Oothoon, and summarizing the first seventeen lines of what follows, but significantly different in tone; the Argument indicates that Oothoon's initial timidity was due only to sexual inexperience; Leutha will appear in Blake's *Europe* as a sexual temptress, and in his *Milton* as Sin to Blake's version of Milton's Satan; to hide in Leutha's vale is to repress sexuality, and to pluck her flower and rise up from her vale is to achieve the first step in sexual liberation, but the rapist Bromion intervenes.

For the soft soul of America, Oothoon wanderd in woe,
Along the vales of Leutha seeking flowers to comfort her;
And thus she spoke to the bright Marygold of Leutha's vale

    Art thou a flower! art thou a nymph! I see thee now a flower;
    Now nymph! I dare not pluck thee from thy dewy bed?

    The Golden nymph replied; pluck thou my flower Oothoon the mild
    Another flower shall spring, because the soul of sweet delight
10   Can never pass away. she ceas'd & closd her golden shrine.

Then Oothoon pluck'd the flower saying, I pluck thee from thy bed
Sweet flower. and put thee here to glow between my breasts
And thus I turn my face to where my whole soul seeks.

Over the waves she went in wing'd exulting swift delight;
And over Theotormons reign, took her impetuous course.

Bromion rent her with his thunders. on his stormy bed
Lay the faint maid, and soon her woes appalld his thunders hoarse

Bromion spoke. behold this harlot here on Bromions bed,
And let the jealous dolphins sport around the lovely maid;
20 Thy soft American plains are mine, and mine thy north & south:
Stampt with my signet° are the swarthy children of the sun:
They are obedient, they resist not, they obey the scourge:
Their daughters worship terrors and obey the violent:

PLATE 2
Now thou maist marry Bromions harlot, and protect the child
Of Bromions rage, that Oothoon shall put forth in nine moons time

Then storms rent Theotormons limbs; he rolld his waves around.
And folded his black jealous waters round the adulterate pair
Bound back to back in Bromions caves terror & meekness dwell°

At entrance Theotormon sits wearing the threshold hard
With secret tears; beneath him sound like waves on a desart shore
The voice of slaves beneath the sun, and children bought with money.
That shiver in religious caves beneath the burning fires
10 Of lust, that belch incessant from the summits of the earth

Oothoon weeps not: she cannot weep! her tears are locked up;
But she can howl incessant writhing her soft snowy limbs.
And calling Theotormons Eagles to prey upon her flesh.°

signet Bromion is a slave-owner and the signet
is his seal or mark of ownership.
Then storms . . . dwell This is a fantasy of
what Theotormon would like to see.
Oothoon weeps . . . flesh The subtlest passage
in the poem (ll. 11–19); she *begins* by trying
to accept the morality of Bromion and Theotormon, but the psychic actuality of her reaction to sexual experience belies her conventional
acceptance; though she tries to weep, she can't,
and the writhing of her limbs shows that Theotormon ought to save the situation by fulfilling
her sexual desires, and ignoring the rape; his
failure brings about the sado-masochistic substitute gratification of her submission to a Pro-
metheus-like punishment; when she next speaks
in the poem, she will have surmounted all this.

I call with holy voice! kings of the sounding air,
Rend away this defiled bosom that I may reflect.
The image of Theotormon on my pure transparent breast.

The Eagles at her call descend & rend their bleeding prey;
Theotormon severely smiles. her soul reflects the smile;
As the clear spring mudded with feet of beasts grows pure & smiles.

20 The Daughters of Albion hear her woes. & eccho back her sighs.
Why does my Theotormon sit weeping upon the threshold;
And Oothoon hovers by his side, perswading him in vain:
I cry arise O Theotormon for the village dog
Barks at the breaking day. the nightingale has done lamenting.
The lark does rustle in the ripe corn, and the Eagle returns
From nightly prey, and lifts his golden beak to the pure east;
Shaking the dust from his immortal pinions to awake
The sun that sleeps too long. Arise my Theotormon I am pure.
Because the night is gone that clos'd me in its deadly black.
30 They told me that the night & day were all that I could see;
They told me that I had five senses to inclose me up.
And they inclos'd my infinite brain into a narrow circle.
And sunk my heart into the Abyss, a red round globe hot burning
Till all from life I was obliterated and erased.
Instead of morn arises a bright shadow, like an eye
In the eastern cloud: instead of night a sickly charnel house;
That Theotormon hears me not! to him the night and morn
Are both alike: a night of sighs, a morning of fresh tears;

PLATE 3
And none but Bromion can hear my lamentations.

With what sense is it that the chicken shuns the ravenous hawk?
With what sense does the tame pigeon measure out the expanse?
With what sense does the bee form cells? have not the mouse & frog
Eyes and ears and sense of touch? yet are their habitations.
And their pursuits, as different as their forms and as their joys:
Ask the wild ass why he refuses burdens: and the meek camel
Why he loves man: is it because of eye ear mouth or skin
Or breathing nostrils? No. for these the wolf and tyger have.
10 Ask the blind worm the secrets of the grave, and why her spires
Love to curl round the bones of death; and ask the rav'nous snake
Where she gets poison: & the wing'd eagle why he loves the sun
And then tell me the thoughts of man, that have been hid of old.

Silent I hover all the night, and all day could be silent.
If Theotormon once would turn his loved eyes upon me;
How can I be defild when I reflect thy image pure?
Sweetest the fruit that the worm feeds on. & the soul prey'd on by woe
The new wash'd lamb ting'd with the village smoke & the bright swan

By the red earth of our immortal river: I bathe my wings.
20 And I am white and pure to hover round Theotormons breast.

Then Theotormon broke his silence. and he answered.

Tell me what is the night or day to one o'erflowd with woe?
Tell me what is a thought? & of what substance is it made?
Tell me what is a joy? & in what gardens do joys grow?
And in what rivers swim the sorrows? and upon what mountains

PLATE 4

Wave shadows of discontent? and in what houses dwell the wretched
Drunken with woe forgotten. and shut up from cold despair.

Tell me where dwell the thoughts forgotten till thou call them forth
Tell me where dwell the joys of old! & where the ancient loves?
And when will they renew again & the night of oblivion past?
That I might traverse times & spaces far remote and bring
Comforts into a present sorrow and a night of pain
Where goest thou O thought? to what remote land is thy flight?
If thou returnest to the present moment of affliction
10 Wilt thou bring comforts on thy wings. and dews and honey and balm;
Or poison from the desart wilds, from the eyes of the envier.°

Then Bromion said: and shook the cavern with his lamentation

Thou knowest that the ancient trees seen by thine eyes have fruit;
But knowest thou that trees and fruits flourish upon the earth
To gratify senses unknown? trees beasts and birds unknown:
Unknown, not unpercievd, spread in the infinite microscope,
In places yet unvisited by the voyager. and in worlds
Over another kind of seas, and in atmospheres unknown:
Ah! are there other wars, beside the wars of sword and fire!
20 And are there other sorrows, beside the sorrows of poverty!
And are there other joys, beside the joys of riches and ease?
And is there not one law for both the lion and the ox?
And is there not eternal fire, and eternal chains?
To bind the phantoms of existence from eternal life?°

Then Oothoon waited silent all the day. and all the night,

PLATE 5

But when the morn arose, her lamentation renewd,
The Daughters of Albion hear her woes, & eccho back her sighs.

Tell me . . . envier Theotormon lives only in a "present moment of affliction," bound in by the circumference of his sexual envy; Blake's insight is that jealousy stems from an acceptance of a materialist concept of limited time, from the fear that there can never be enough time, which is a fear of death; sexual jealousy is thus death-in-life.
Thou knowest . . . life Bromion, an insane and debased rationalist, is far more complex in his fears; he dreads the potential chaos of experience, and so insists upon the necessity for uniform laws (which, ironically, he is incapable of obeying himself); but notice how intelligent Bromion is in his sickness, for he does not deny the reality of Oothoon's vision (as Theotormon does) but admits that he fears the vision's implications.

O Urizen!° Creator of men! mistaken Demon of heaven:
Thy joys are tears! thy labour vain, to form men to thine image.
How can one joy absorb another? are not different joys
Holy, eternal, infinite! and each joy is a Love.

Does not the great mouth laugh at a gift? & the narrow eyelids mock
At the labour that is above payment, and wilt thou take the ape
For thy councellor? or the dog, for a schoolmaster to thy children?
10 Does he who contemns° poverty, and he who turns with abhorrence
From usury: feel the same passion or are they moved alike?°
How can the giver of gifts experience the delights of the merchant?
How the industrious citizen the pains of the husbandman.
How different far the fat fed hireling with hollow drum;
Who buys whole corn fields into wastes, and sings upon the heath:
How different their eye and ear! how different the world to them!
With what sense does the parson claim the labour of the farmer?
What are his nets & gins° & traps. & how does he surround him
With cold floods of abstraction, and with forests of solitude,
20 To build him castles and high spires. where kings & priests may dwell.
Till she who burns with youth. and knows no fixed lot; is bound
In spells of law to one she loaths: and must she drag the chain
Of life, in weary lust! must chilling murderous thoughts. obscure
The clear heaven of her eternal spring? to bear the wintry rage
Of a harsh terror driv'n to madness, bound to hold a rod
Over her shrinking shoulders all the day; & all the night
To turn the wheel of false desire: and longings that wake her womb
To the abhorred birth of cherubs in the human form
That live a pestilence & die a meteor & are no more.
30 Till the child dwell with one he hates. and do the deed he loaths
And the impure scourge forces his seed into its unripe birth
E'er yet his eyelids can behold the arrows of the day.

Does the whale worship at thy footsteps as the hungry dog?
Or does he scent the mountain prey, because his nostrils wide
Draw in the ocean? does his eye discern the flying cloud
As the ravens eye? or does he measure the expanse like the vulture?
Does the still spider view the cliffs where eagles hide their young?
Or does the fly rejoice. because the harvest is brought in?
Does not the eagle scorn the earth & despise the treasures beneath?
40 But the mole knoweth what is there, & the worm shall tell it thee.
Does not the worm erect a pillar in the mouldering church yard?

PLATE 6
And a palace of eternity in the jaws of the hungry grave
Over his porch these words are written. Take thy bliss O Man!
And sweet shall be thy taste & sweet thy infant joys renew!

Urizen The first appearance of Urizen by name
in Blake's work; his name comes from the Greek
for "to draw with a compass, to circumscribe,"
and echoes the sound and meaning of "horizon,"
based on the same Greek word.

contemns despises
are they moved alike? a profound question
that Blake wants his reader to answer
gins snares

Infancy, fearless, lustful, happy! nestling for delight
In laps of pleasure; Innocence! honest, open, seeking
The vigorous joys of morning light; open to virgin bliss,
Who taught thee modesty, subtil modesty! child of night & sleep
When thou awakest. wilt thou dissemble all thy secret joys
Or wert thou not, awake when all this mystery was disclos'd!
10 Then com'st thou forth a modest virgin knowing to dissemble
With nets found under thy night pillow, to catch virgin joy,
And brand it with the name of whore; & sell it in the night,
In silence. ev'n without a whisper, and in seeming sleep:
Religious dreams and holy vespers, light thy smoky fires:
Once were thy fires lighted by the eyes of honest morn
And does my Theotormon seek this hypocrite modesty!
This knowing, artful, secret, fearful, cautious, trembling hypocrite.
Then is Oothoon a whore indeed! and all the virgin joys
Of life are harlots: and Theotormon is a sick mans dream
20 And Oothoon is the crafty slave of selfish holiness.
But Oothoon is not so, a virgin fill'd with virgin fancies
Open to joy and to delight where ever beauty appears
If in the morning sun I find it: there my eyes are fix'd

PLATE 7
In happy copulation; if in evening mild. wearied with work;
Sit on a bank and draw the pleasures of this free born joy.

 The moment of desire! the moment of desire! The virgin
That pines for man; shall awaken her womb to enormous joys
In the secret shadows of her chamber; the youth shut up from
The lustful joy. shall forget to generate. & create an amorous image
In the shadows of his curtains and in the folds of his silent pillow.
Are not these the places of religion? the rewards of continence?
The self enjoyings of self denial? Why dost thou seek religion?
10 Is it because acts are not lovely, that thou seekest solitude,
Where the horrible darkness is impressed with reflections of desire.

Father of Jealousy. be thou accursed from the earth!
Why hast thou taught my Theotormon this accursed thing?
Till beauty fades from off my shoulders darken'd and cast out,
A solitary shadow wailing on the margin of non-entity.

I cry, Love! Love! Love! happy happy Love! free as the mountain wind!
Can that be Love, that drinks another as a sponge drinks water?
That clouds with jealousy his nights, with weepings all the day:
To spin a web of age around him. grey and hoary dark!
20 Till his eyes sicken at the fruit that hangs before his sight.
Such is self-love that envies all! a creeping skeleton
With lamplike eyes watching around the frozen marriage bed.

But silken nets and traps of adamant will Oothoon spread,
And catch for thee girls of mild silver, or of furious gold;

I'll lie beside thee on a bank & view their wanton play
In lovely copulation bliss on bliss with Theotormon:
Red as the rosy morning, lustful as the first born beam,
Oothoon shall view his dear delight, nor e'er with jealous cloud
Come in the heaven of generous love; nor selfish blightings bring.

30   Does the sun walk in glorious raiment. on the secret floor

PLATE 8
Where the cold miser spreads his gold? or does the bright cloud drop
On his stone threshold? does his eye behold the beam that brings
Expansion to the eye of pity? or will he bind himself
Beside the ox to thy hard furrow? does not that mild beam blot
The bat, the owl, the glowing tyger, and the king of night.
The sea fowl takes the wintry blast. for a cov'ring to her limbs:
And the wild snake, the pestilence to adorn him with gems & gold.
And trees. & birds. & beasts. & men. behold their eternal joy.
Arise you little glancing wings, and sing your infant joy!
10   Arise and drink your bliss, for every thing that lives is holy!

Thus every morning wails Oothoon. but Theotormon sits
Upon the margind ocean conversing with shadows dire.

The Daughters of Albion hear her woes, & eccho back her sighs.
        THE END
1793   1793

America a Prophecy

This is Blake's first poem fully set in his own mythic universe. Throughout Blake's
life and work, the American Revolution counted for much more than the French, not
only because it came first and so seemed the "voice of the morning," but because
Blake wanted to see it as a more genuinely imaginative change in history, and not
just as the organic, cyclic revolution of repressed energies that took place in Europe.
It does not matter that Blake knew too little about American conditions; for him
America was the Golden World of Atlantean symbolism, and the prophetic force of
his poem's hopefulness still endures.

America *a Prophecy*

Lambeth
Printed by William Blake in the year 1793

PLATE 1

Preludium°

The shadowy daughter of Urthona° stood before red Orc.°
When fourteen suns had faintly journey'd o'er his dark abode;
His food she brought in iron baskets, his drink in cups of iron;°
Crown'd with a helmet & dark hair the nameless female stood;
A quiver with its burning stores, a bow like that of night,
When pestilence is shot from heaven; no other arms she need:
Invulnerable tho' naked, save where clouds roll round her loins,
Their awful folds in the dark air; silent she stood as night;
For never from her iron tongue could voice or sound arise;
10 But dumb till that dread day when Orc assay'd his fierce embrace.

Dark virgin; said the hairy youth, thy father stern abhorr'd;
Rivets my tenfold chains while still on high my spirit soars;
Sometimes an eagle screaming in the sky, sometimes a lion,
Stalking upon the mountains, & sometimes a whale I lash
The raging fathomless abyss, anon a serpent folding
Around the pillars of Urthona, and round thy dark limbs,
On the Canadian wilds I fold, feeble my spirit folds.°
For chaind beneath I rend these caverns; when thou bringest food
I howl my joy! and my red eyes seek to behold thy face
20 In vain! these clouds roll to & fro, & hide thee from my sight.

PLATE 2

Silent as despairing love, and strong as jealousy,
The hairy shoulders rend the links, free are the wrists of fire;
Round the terrific loins he siez'd the panting struggling womb;
It joy'd: she put aside her clouds & smiled her first-born smile;
As when a black cloud shews its light'nings to the silent deep.

Preludium This myth-making fantasia gives the primordial prelude to the poem's visionary politics; behind political revolution lurk these tremendous images of sexual bondage and triumphant sexual release; the world shown has come only recently into life, as its emblems indicate: shadows, clouds, darkness, silence, namelessness, all of which cause imprisoned sexuality to attack the female ministering to it; as in all subsequent poetry by Blake, the male personages symbolize humankind, male and female alike; the female figures all represent different aspects of the confining natural context that limits or confines the human.
shadowy daughter of Urthona Nameless in this poem, but later to be called Vala (from "veil," and pronounced like it), the beauty of the visible world; Urthona's name may be formed from "fourth one," whose form "is like the Son of God," and who appears in the burning fiery furnace of Daniel 3:25. In Blake's story, he is

the most important of the Four Zoas, and appears in our fallen world of time as Los the Poetic Genius. In *America,* Urthona is a recently fallen, primitive smith god, like Thor or Vulcan, and his dens imprison energy under Urizen's promptings.
red Orc The fallen form of the Zoa, Luvah; Orc (from *orcus,* Latin for hell, or a hell-like monster, because he seems that to the Angels) is the force of libido, of organic energy, the youth of nature, the Promethean element of fire, and politically the permanent Left; he can make revolutions, and prefigure the apocalypse, but himself cannot bring apocalypse about.
His food . . . iron Blake's naïve notion of an Iron Age; the general atmosphere and appearances suggest the influence of Norse mythology.
Sometimes . . . folds The various animals are emblems of contemporary revolutions in the Western hemisphere.

Soon as she saw the terrible boy then burst the virgin cry.°
I know thee, I have found thee, & I will not let thee go;
Thou art the image of God who dwells in darkness of Africa;°
And thou art fall'n to give me life in regions of dark death.
On my American plains I feel the struggling afflictions
Endur'd by roots that writhe their arms into the nether deep:
I see a serpent in Canada, who courts me to his love;
In Mexico an Eagle, and a Lion in Peru;
I see a Whale in the South-sea, drinking my soul away.°
O what limb rending pains I feel. thy fire & my frost
Mingle in howling pains, in furrows by thy lightnings rent;
This is eternal death; and this the torment long foretold.°

The stern Bard ceas'd, asham'd of his own song; enrag'd he swung
His harp aloft sounding, then dash'd its shining frame against
A ruin'd pillar in glittring fragments; silent he turn'd away,
And wander'd down the vales of Kent in sick & drear lamentings.°

PLATE 3
    A *Prophecy*
The Guardian Prince of Albion° burns in his nightly tent,
Sullen fires across the Atlantic glow to America's shore:
Piercing the souls of warlike men, who rise in silent night,
Washington, Franklin, Paine & Warren, Gates, Hancock & Green;°
Meet on the coast glowing with blood from Albions fiery Prince.

Washington spoke; Friends of America look over the Atlantic sea;
A bended bow is lifted in heaven, & a heavy iron chain
Descends link by link from Albions cliffs across the sea to bind
Brothers & sons of America, till our faces pale and yellow;
Heads deprest, voices weak, eyes downcast, hands work-bruis'd,
Feet bleeding on the sultry sands, and the furrows of the whip
Descend to generations that in future times forget.—

The strong voice ceas'd; for a terrible blast swept over the heaving sea;
The eastern cloud rent; on his cliffs stood Albions wrathful Prince
A dragon form clashing his scales° at midnight he arose,
And flam'd red meteors round the land of Albion beneath[.]
His voice, his locks, his awful shoulders, and his glowing eyes,

virgin cry Nature, barren when not possessed by man, now breaks silence for the first time.
Thou art . . . Africa Blake identified the biblical Egypt with all of Africa, and both with primordial natural religion .
I see . . . away Though embraced by Orc, her father's false teachings prevail in her, and she dreads the emblems of revolt.
This . . . foretold "Eternal death" is Blake's irony, and means generative life, a torment from the unfallen point of view in Eternity; see the opening of "The Mental Traveller."
The stern . . . lamentings The Bard is not

Blake, and is ashamed because the shadowy female is unconverted.
Prince of Albion King George III, also called Albion's Angel; a dragon form even as Pharaoh was called a dragon by Ezekiel
Washington . . . Green all leaders and agitators of the American Revolution
A dragon . . . scales Both Albion's Angel and Orc are dragon forms of death, from one another's perspective; Blake's insight is that there is an Orc-Urizen cycle, in which revolution always transforms itself into the repression it seeks to destroy.

PLATE 4
Appear to the Americans upon the cloudy night.

Solemn heave the Atlantic waves between the gloomy nations,
Swelling, belching from its deeps red clouds & raging Fires!
Albion is sick! America faints! enrag'd the Zenith grew.
As human blood shooting its veins all round the orbed heaven
Red rose the clouds from the Atlantic in vast wheels of blood
And in the red clouds rose a Wonder o'er the Atlantic sea;
Intense! naked! a Human fire fierce glowing, as the wedge
Of iron heated in the furnace; his terrible limbs were fire
10   With myriads of cloudy terrors banners dark & towers
Surrounded; heat but not light° went thro' the murky atmosphere

The King of England looking westward trembles at the vision

PLATE 5
Albions Angel stood beside the Stone of night,° and saw
The terror like a comet, or more like the planet red°
That once inclos'd the terrible wandering comets in its sphere.
Then Mars thou wast our center, & the planets three flew round
Thy crimson disk; so e'er the Sun was rent from thy red sphere;
The Spectre° glowd his horrid length staining the temple long
With beams of blood; & thus a voice came forth, and shook the temple

PLATE 6
The morning comes, the night decays, the watchmen leave their stations;
The grave is burst, the spices shed, the linen wrapped up;°
The bones of death, the cov'ring clay, the sinews shrunk & dry'd.
Reviving shake, inspiring move, breathing! awakening!
Spring like redeemed captives when their bonds & bars are burst;
Let the slave grinding at the mill, run out into the field:
Let him look up into the heavens & laugh in the bright air;
Let the inchained soul shut up in darkness and in sighing,
Whose face has never seen a smile in thirty weary years;
10   Rise and look out, his chains are loose, his dungeon doors are open.
And let his wife and children return from the opressors scourge;
They look behind at every step & believe it is a dream.
Singing. The Sun has left his blackness, & has found a fresher morning
And the fair Moon rejoices in the clear & cloudless night;°
For Empire is no more, and now the Lion & Wolf shall cease.

---

heat but not light See *Paradise Lost* I.62–63.
Stone of Night See the pillows of Jacob in Genesis 28:11; the stone tablets of the Law of Sinai
hover in the background.
planet red Mars. There is no precedent for
Blake's fantastic astronomy here, nor does he
develop it elsewhere.
Spectre Albion's Angel; the word means a phan-

tom; in Blake, the shadow of desire, or withered
form of repression.
The morning . . . wrapped up This image of
Christ's Resurrection echoes *The Marriage;* the
entire speech echoes Oothoon's great chants.
The Sun . . . cloudless night Orc's final lines
will be repeated in Blake's depiction of the Last
Judgment, *The Four Zoas* Night IX, 138:20–21.

PLATE 7

In thunders ends the voice. Then Albions Angel wrathful burnt
Beside the Stone of Night; and like the Eternal Lions howl
In famine & war, reply'd. Art thou not Orc; who serpent-form'd
Stands at the gate of Enitharmon° to devour her children;
Blasphemous Demon, Antichrist, hater of Dignities;
Lover of wild rebellion, and transgresser of Gods Law;
Why dost thou come to Angels eyes in this terrific form?

PLATE 8

The terror answer'd: I am Orc, wreath'd round the accursed tree:°
The times are ended; shadows pass the morning gins° to break;
The fiery joy, that Urizen perverted to ten commands,
What night he led the starry hosts thro' the wide wilderness:°
That stony law I stamp to dust: and scatter religion abroad
To the four winds as a torn book, & none shall gather the leaves;
But they shall rot on desart sands, & consume in bottomless deeps;
To make the desarts blossom, & the deeps shrink to their fountains,
And to renew the fiery joy, and burst the stony roof.
10 That pale religious letchery, seeking Virginity,
May find it in a harlot, and in coarse-clad honesty
The undefil'd tho' ravish'd in her cradle night and morn:
For every thing that lives is holy, life delights in life;
Because the soul of sweet delight can never be defil'd.
Fires inwrap the earthly globe, yet man is not consumd;°
Amidst the lustful fires he walks: his feet become like brass,
His knees and thighs like silver, & his breast and head like gold.°

PLATE 9

Sound! sound! my loud war-trumpets & alarm my Thirteen Angels!°
Loud howls the eternal Wolf! the eternal Lion lashes his tail!
America is darkned; and my punishing Demons terrified
Crouch howling before their caverns deep like skins dry'd in the wind.
They cannot smite the wheat, nor quench the fatness of the earth.
They cannot smite with sorrows, nor subdue the plow and spade.
They cannot wall the city, nor moat round the castle of princes.
They cannot bring the stubbed oak to overgrow the hills.
For terrible men stand on the shores, & in their robes I see
10 Children take shelter from the lightnings, there stands Washington
And Paine and Warren with their foreheads reard toward the east

Enitharmon Queen of Heaven, her name is derived from the Greek for "numberless," as she is
also Blake's Eve, mother of numberless mankind.
accursed tree The Tree of Mystery, which Orc
will climb, in order that he be crucified like
Christ and Odin, so as to become Jehovah or a
repressive god.
gins begins
What night . . . wilderness Orc identifies Urizen with the Jehovah of Exodus.
fire . . . consumd Redeemed man is identi-

fied with the walkers in the furnace; see
Daniel 3:25.
Amidst . . . gold Renovated man is the image
seen in King Nebuchadnezzar's dream, Daniel
2:31–35, but there is a subtle, crucial difference, for Orc's man is one level nearer to
ultimate salvation, since the feet of iron and
clay are now feet of brass, the thighs of brass
are now silver, and the silver breast is now
golden, like the head.
Thirteen Angels the colonies in America

But clouds obscure my aged sight. A vision from afar!
Sound! sound! my loud war-trumpets & alarm my thirteen Angels:
Ah vision from afar! Ah rebel form that rent the ancient
Heavens; Eternal Viper self-renew'd, rolling in clouds
I see thee in thick clouds and darkness on America's shore.
Writhing in pangs of abhorred birth; red flames the crest rebellious
And eyes of death; the harlot womb oft opened in vain
Heaves in enormous circles, now the times are return'd upon thee,
20   Devourer of thy parent, now thy unutterable torment renews.
Sound! sound! my loud war trumpets & alarm my thirteen Angels!
Ah terrible birth! a young one bursting! where is the weeping mouth?
And where the mothers milk? instead those ever-hissing jaws
And parched lips drop with fresh gore; now roll thou in the clouds
Thy mother lays her length outstretch'd upon the shore beneath.
Sound! sound! my loud war-trumpets & alarm my thirteen Angels!
Loud howls the eternal Wolf: the eternal Lion lashes his tail!

PLATE 10

Thus wept the Angel voice & as he wept the terrible blasts
Of trumpets, blew a loud alarm across the Atlantic deep.
No trumpets answer; no reply of clarions or of fifes,
Silent the Colonies remain and refuse the loud alarm.

On those vast shady hills between America & Albions shore;
Now barr'd out by the Atlantic sea: call'd Atlantean hills:°
Because from their bright summits you may pass to the Golden world
An ancient palace, archetype of mighty Emperies,
Rears its immortal pinnacles, built in the forest of God
10   By Ariston° the king of beauty for his stolen bride,

Here on their magic seats the thirteen Angels sat perturb'd
For clouds from the Atlantic hover o'er the solemn roof.

PLATE 11

Fiery the Angels rose, & as they rose deep thunder roll'd
Around their shores: indignant burning with the fires of Orc
And Bostons Angel cried aloud as they flew thro' the dark night.

He cried: Why trembles honesty and like a murderer,
Why seeks he refuge from the frowns of his immortal station!
Must the generous tremble & leave his joy, to the idle: to the pestilence!
That mock him? who commanded this? what God? what Angel!
To keep the gen'rous from experience till the ungenerous
Are unrestraind performers of the energies of nature;
10   Till pity is become a trade, and generosity a science,
That men get rich by, & the sandy desert is giv'n to the strong

Atlantean hills The American Revolution promises to restore Atlantis, the lost, unfallen world.
Ariston Greek name meaning "the best"; Blake's
source is Herodotus VII.61–66; that the bride
is "stolen" is Blake's characteristic hint that the
Greek archetype of Atlantis was stolen from a
Hebrew original; cf. the Preface to Blake's *Jerusalem*.

What God is he, writes laws of peace, & clothes him in a tempest
What pitying Angel lusts for tears, and fans himself with sighs
What crawling villain preaches abstinence & wraps himself
In fat of lambs? no more I follow, no more obedience pay.

PLATE 12

So cried he, rending off his robe° & throwing down his scepter.
In sight of Albions Guardian, and all the thirteen Angels
Rent off their robes to the hungry wind, & threw their golden scepters
Down on the land of America. indignant they descended
Headlong from out their heav'nly heights, descending swift as fires
Over the land; naked & flaming are their lineaments seen
In the deep gloom, by Washington & Paine & Warren they stood
And the flame folded roaring fierce within the pitchy night
Before the Demon red, who burnt towards America,
10 In black smoke thunders and loud winds rejoicing in its terror
Breaking in smoky wreaths from the wild deep, & gath'ring thick
In flames as of a furnace on the land from North to South

PLATE 13

What time the thirteen Governors that England sent convene
In Bernards house;° the flames coverd the land, they rouze they cry
Shaking their mental chains they rush in fury to the sea
To quench their anguish; at the feet of Washington down fall'n
They grovel on the sand and writhing lie, while all
The British soldiers thro' the thirteen states sent up a howl
Of anguish: threw their swords & muskets to the earth & ran
From their encampments and dark castles seeking where to hide
From the grim flames; and from the visions of Orc: in sight
10 Of Albions Angel; who enrag'd his secret clouds open'd
From north to south, and burnt outstretchd on wings of wrath cov'ring
The eastern sky, spreading his awful wings across the heavens;
Beneath him roll'd his num'rous hosts, all Albions Angels camp'd
Darkend the Atlantic mountains & their trumpets shook the valleys
Arm'd with diseases of the earth to cast upon the Abyss,
Their numbers forty millions, must'ring in the eastern sky.

PLATE 14

In the flames stood & view'd the armies drawn out in the sky
Washington Franklin Paine & Warren Allen Gates & Lee:
And heard the voice of Albions Angel give the thunderous command:
His plagues obedient to his voice flew forth out of their clouds
Falling upon America, as a storm to cut them off
As a blight cuts the tender corn when it begins to appear.

rending off his robe Taking off the garment of the Law; the great instance of this in Blake is in Milton's declaration of descent in the poem *Milton* (the declaration is included in this anthology).

Bernards house The Angels become Devils and follow Boston in rebellion; the colonial governor Bernard was recalled from Massachusetts in 1769, but he represents British rule in general.

Dark is the heaven above, & cold & hard the earth beneath;
And as a plague wind fill'd with insects cuts off man & beast;
And as a sea o'erwhelms a land in the day of an earthquake:

10   Fury! rage! madness! in a wind swept through America
And the red flames of Orc that folded roaring fierce around
The angry shores, and the fierce rushing of th'inhabitants together:
The citizens of New-York close their books & lock their chests;
The mariners of Boston drop their anchors and unlade;
The scribe of Pensylvania casts his pen upon the earth;
The builder of Virginia throws his hammer down in fear.

Then had America been lost, o'erwhelm'd by the Atlantic,
And Earth had lost another portion of the infinite,
But all rush together in the night in wrath and raging fire
20   The red fires rag'd! the plagues recoil'd! then rolld they back with fury°

PLATE 15
On Albions Angels; then the Pestilence began in streaks of red
Across the limbs of Albions Guardian, the spotted plague smote Bristols
And the Leprosy Londons Spirits, sickening all their bands:
The millions sent up a howl of anguish and threw off their hammerd mail,°
And cast their swords & spears to earth, & stood a naked multitude.
Albions Guardian writhed in torment on the eastern sky
Pale quivring toward the brain his glimmering eyes, teeth chattering
Howling & shuddering his legs quivering; convuls'd each muscle & sinew
Sick'ning lay Londons Guardian, and the ancient miter'd York°
10   Their heads on snowy hills, their ensigns sick'ning in the sky
The plagues creep on the burning winds driven by flames of Orc,
And by the fierce Americans rushing together in the night
Driven o'er the Guardians of Ireland and Scotland and Wales
They spotted with plagues forsook the frontiers & their banners seard
With fires of hell, deform their ancient heavens with shame & woe.
Hid in his caves the Bard of Albion° felt the enormous plagues.
And a cowl of flesh grew o'er his head & scales on his back & ribs;°
And rough with black scales all his Angels fright their ancient heavens
The doors of marriage are open,° and the Priests in rustling scales
20   Rush into reptile coverts, hiding from the fires of Orc,
That play around the golden roofs in wreaths of fierce desire,
Leaving the females naked and glowing with the lusts of youth

For the female spirits of the dead pining in bonds of religion;
Run from their fetters reddening, & in long drawn arches sitting:

The red . . . fury David Erdman relates this reversal of the plagues onto England's shores to the Great Pestilence of 1348, which followed English aggression upon France; Blake's symbolic point is clear enough in contemporary America.
The millions . . . mail the troops desert

miter'd York the Archbishop, who like the King sickens almost to madness
Bard of Albion the (as usual) undistinguished Poet Laureate, William Whitehead (1715–85)
And a cowl . . . ribs See Paradise Lost X.511 ff., where Satan and his host become reptilian.
The doors . . . open the societal restrictions upon sexuality fall away

They feel the nerves of youth renew, and desires of ancient times,
Over their pale limbs as a vine when the tender grape appears

PLATE 16
Over the hills, the vales, the cities, rage the red flames fierce;
The Heavens melted from north to south; and Urizen who sat
Above all heavens in thunders wrap'd, emerg'd his leprous head
From out his holy shrine, his tears in deluge piteous
Falling into the deep sublime! flag'd with grey-brow'd snows
And thunderous visages, his jealous wings wav'd over the deep;
Weeping in dismal howling woe he dark descended howling
Around the smitten bands, clothed in tears & trembling shudd'ring cold.
His stored snows he poured forth, and his icy magazines
10 He open'd on the deep, and on the Atlantic sea white shiv'ring.
Leprous his limbs, all over white, and hoary was his visage.°
Weeping in dismal howlings before the stern Americans
Hiding the Demon red with clouds & cold mists from the earth;
Till Angels & weak men twelve years° should govern o'er the strong:
And then their end should come, when France reciev'd the Demons light.°

Stiff shudderings shook the heav'nly thrones! France Spain & Italy,
In terror view'd the bands of Albion, and the ancient Guardians
Fainting upon the elements, smitten with their own plagues
They slow advance to shut the five gates of their law-built heaven°
20 Filled with blasting fancies and with mildews of despair
With fierce disease and lust, unable to stem the fires of Orc;
But the five gates were consum'd, & their bolts and hinges melted
And the fierce flames burnt round the heavens & round the abodes of men°
    FINIS
1793   1794

From Blake's Notebook

Never Pain To Tell Thy Love

Never pain to tell thy love
Love that never told can be
For the gentle wind does move
Silently invisibly

I told my love I told my love
I told her all my heart

Leprous . . . visage Urizen is exposed as being leprous and impotent.
twelve years the time span between the American and French Revolutions
Demons light appearance of Orc's revolutionary fire in France
They slow . . . heaven The tyranny of society is founded upon natural law, founded in turn upon the barred gates of the five fallen senses.
And . . . men Flames of desire burn *round* but not yet *through* the five fallen senses; natural tyranny is threatened, but not yet overthrown.

Trembling cold in ghastly fears
Ah she doth depart

Soon as she was gone from me
10 A traveller came by
Silently invisibly
O was no deny
1793?   1863

To Nobodaddy°

Why art thou silent & invisible
Father of Jealousy
Why dost thou hide thyself in clouds
From every searching Eye

Why darkness & obscurity
In all thy words & laws
That none dare eat the fruit but from
The wily serpents jaws
Or is it because Secrecy
10 gains females loud applause
1800–1803   1863

What Is It Men in Women Do Require?

What is it men in women do require?
The lineaments° of Gratified Desire
What is it women do in men require?
The lineaments of Gratified Desire
1800–1803   1863

My Spectre Around Me Night & Day

The Spectre is Blake's term for the isolate Selfhood, the spirit of solipsism that Shelley
(on Peacock's advice) called the *alastor* or self-avenging *daemon*. Each human is
isolated from his bride, which means that everyone is in his Spectre's power. The
bride Blake calls an Emanation, the total form of what any human being creates and
loves. In this frightening lyric from the Notebook, the Spectre "guards" only as a
menace keeping all others from the Self. The Emanation at first has failed to
emanate, and keeps far within the psyche, weeping for a sin which is the Self's
failure to create and love. Throughout the lyric, the speaker is trapped in what Blake
calls the state of Ulro (ultimate error), or single vision, the world of egomania. To

Nobodaddy God the Father is actually no-   **lineaments** features
body's daddy.

break the cycle of frustrated flight and pursuit, in which the elusive Emanation, after venturing out, cannot be embraced, the speaker at last vows to "turn from Female Love." This does not mean that the speaker intends to be ascetic or homosexual, but that he will give up love as what the Female Will understands it to be. The reader needs to remember that Female Will means natural will, and that the poem's speaker can be either a man or a woman, who heroically breaks out of isolation into the prophetic mode of Oothoon, who urged a love that does not seek to drink the beloved up, or absorb the other.

My Spectre Around Me Night & Day

My Spectre around me night & day
Like a Wild beast guards my way
My Emanation far within
Weeps incessantly for my Sin

A Fathomless & boundless deep
There we wander there we weep
On the hungry craving wind
My Spectre follows thee behind

10 He scents thy footsteps in the snow
Wheresoever thou dost go
Thro the wintry hail & rain
When wilt thou return again

Dost thou not in Pride & Scorn
Fill with tempests all my morn
And with jealousies & fears
Fill my pleasant nights with tears

Seven of my sweet loves thy knife
Has bereaved of their life
Their marble tombs I built with tears
20 And with cold & shuddering fears

Seven more loves weep night & day
Round the tombs where my loves lay
And seven more loves attend each night
Around my couch with torches bright

And seven more Loves in my bed
Crown with wine my mournful head
Pitying & forgiving all
Thy transgressions great & small

When wilt thou return & view
30 My loves & them to life renew

When wilt thou return & live
When wilt thou pity as I forgive

Never Never I return
Still for Victory I burn
Living thee alone Ill have
And when dead Ill be thy Grave

Thro the Heaven & Earth & Hell
Thou shalt never never quell
I will fly & thou pursue
40   Night & Morn the flight renew

Till I turn from Female Love
And root up the Infernal Grove
I shall never worthy be
To Step into Eternity

And to end thy cruel mocks
Annihilate thee on the rocks
And another form create
To be subservient to my Fate

Let us agree to give up Love
50   And root up the infernal grove
Then shall we return & see
The worlds of happy Eternity

& Throughout all Eternity
I forgive you you forgive me
As our Dear Redeemer said
This the Wine & this the Bread
1800–1803   1863

Mock on Mock on Voltaire Rousseau

Mock on Mock on Voltaire Rousseau°
Mock on Mock on tis all in vain
You throw the sand against the wind
And the wind blows it back again

And every sand becomes a Gem
Reflected in the beams divine
Blown back they blind the mocking Eye
But still in Israels paths they shine

The Atoms of Democritus°
10   And Newtons Particles of light°

Voltaire Rousseau deists and so (in Blake's view) enemies of imaginative religion
Democritus (460–362 B.C.), Greek philosopher who taught a version of atomic theory
Particles of light corpuscular theory of light, which Blake doubted (with good reason)

Are sands upon the Red sea shore
Where Israels tents do shine so bright
1800–1803   1863

Morning

To find the Western path
Right thro the Gates of Wrath°
I urge my way
Sweet Mercy leads me on
With soft repentant moan
I see the break of day

The war of swords & spears
Melted by dewy tears
Exhales on high
10   The Sun is freed from fears
And with soft grateful tears
Ascends the sky
1803?   1863

When Klopstock England Defied°

When Klopstock England defied
Uprose terrible Blake in his pride
For old Nobodaddy aloft
Farted & Belchd & coughd
Then swore a great oath that made heavn quake
And called aloud to English Blake
Blake was giving his body ease
At Lambeth beneath the poplar trees
From his seat then started he
10   And turnd himself round three times three
The Moon at that sight blushd scarlet red
The stars threw down their cups & fled
And all the devils that were in hell
Answered with a ninefold yell
Klopstock felt the intripled turn
And all his bowels began to churn
And his bowels turned round three times three

To find . . . Wrath This opening couplet is
the epigraph to the American poet Hart Crane's
"The Tunnel," the descent into a subway hell
in his brief epic *The Bridge* (1930).
When Klopstock England Defied Friedrich Gottlieb Klopstock (1724–1803), German poet, whose
religious epic *Messias* was influenced by *Paradise
Lost.* Someone told Blake that Klopstock was
Germany's answer to Milton. This poetic impromptu is Blake's answer to Klopstock, and is
rather more active than anything in *Messias*, a
work renowned for the continuous piety of its
sentiments, and its author's studious genius for
avoiding mere incidents, or anything else that
might have made his poem readable.

And lockd in his soul with a ninefold key
That from his body it neer could be parted
20   Till to the last trumpet it was farted
Then again old Nobodaddy swore
He neer had seen such a thing before
Since Noah was shut in the ark
Since Eve first chose her hell fire spark
Since twas the fashion to go naked
Since the old anything was created
And so feeling he begd him to turn again
And ease poor Klopstocks nine fold pain
From pity then he redend round
30   And the Spell removed unwound
If Blake could do this when he rose up from shite
What might he not do if he sat down to write
1797–99   1965 (in this form)

[Epigrams]

Some people admire the work of a Fool
For its sure to keep your judgment cool
It does not reproach you with want of wit
It is not like a lawyer serving a writ

Her whole Life is an Epigram smack smooth & neatly pend
Plated quite neat to catch applause with a sliding noose at the end

When a Man has Married a Wife
he finds out whether
Her knees & elbows are only
glued together

Grown old in Love from Seven till Seven times Seven
I oft have wished for Hell for Ease from Heaven

The Hebrew Nation did not write it
Avarice & Chastity did shite it

To God

If you have formed a Circle to go into
Go into it yourself & see how you would do

Since all the Riches of this World
May be gifts from the Devil & Earthly Kings
I should suspect that I worshiped the Devil
If I thanked my God for Worldly things

The Mental Traveller

Like "The Crystal Cabinet," this poem exists in a fair copy manuscript that Blake may have intended for engraving. Both poems are highly finished, economical, complex ballads, and seem to be deliberate experiments at telling versions of Blake's myths without using a technical vocabulary or private personages. "The Mental Traveller" foreshadows the entire Orc-Urizen cycle, and is perhaps the bleakest of Blake's comprehensive accounts of fallen existence. Yeats acknowledged its influence upon his mythological book *A Vision*. Few poems in the language do so much so grandly and so grimly in just over a hundred lines.

The poem may be described, briefly, as a report upon a grotesque planet given by a being alien to it, who cannot quite understand the horrors he sees. He describes two cycles moving in opposite directions, and out of phase with one another. The natural cycle (symbolized by the female) is moving backward, the human (symbolized by the male) forward. There are only two personages in the poem, but they move through several phases, and phantoms of earlier phases sometimes linger. The human cycle moves between an infant Orc and an aged, beggared Urizen, and then back again. The natural sequence is Tirzah (Nature-as-Necessity), Vala (Nature-as-Temptress), and Rahab (Nature-as-Destroyer), and then back again.

The Mental Traveller°

I traveld thro' a Land of Men
A Land of Men & Women too°
And heard & saw such dreadful things
As cold Earth wanderers never knew°

For there the Babe is born in joy
That was begotten in dire woe
Just as we Reap in joy the fruit
Which we in bitter tears did sow°

And if the Babe is born a Boy
10 He's given to a Woman Old
Who nails him down upon a rock
Catches his shrieks in cups of gold°

She binds iron thorns around his head
She pierces both his hands & feet°
She cuts his heart out at his side
To make it feel both cold & heat°

The Mental Traveller The speaker is one of Blake's Unfallen Eternals, who descends from a world where "Mental Things alone are Real."
Women too Before the Fall the Zoas were not separate from their Emanations, and each human was both man and woman.
And heard . . . knew Human beings hear and see the horrors of existence, but cannot convert sounds and sights into knowledge; the Mental Traveller can.

for there . . . sow The Traveller sees fallen sexual intercourse as "dire woe" and the pain of fallen birth as "joy"; he compares this to the strife of Eternity, which ensues in reconciliations; Blake's Eternity is a realm of "mental fight," and not a static heaven.
Who nails . . . gold the fate of Loki in the Norse Edda
She binds . . . feet the crucified Christ
She cuts . . . heat the torment of Prometheus

65

Her fingers number every Nerve
Just as a Miser counts his gold
She lives upon his shrieks & cries
20   And she grows young as he grows old

Till he becomes a bleeding youth
And she becomes a Virgin bright
Then he rends up his Manacles
And binds her down for his delight

He plants himself in all her Nerves
Just as a Husbandman his mould
And she becomes his dwelling place
And Garden fruitful seventy fold

An aged Shadow soon he fades
30   Wandring round an Earthly Cot
Full filled all with gems & gold
Which he by industry had got

And these are the gems of the Human Soul
The rubies & pearls of a lovesick eye
The countless gold of the akeing heart
The martyrs groan & the lovers sigh

They are his meat they are his drink
He feeds the Beggar & the Poor
And the wayfaring Traveller
40   For ever open is his door

His grief is their eternal joy
They make the roofs & walls to ring
Till from the fire on the hearth
A little Female Babe° does spring

And she is all of solid fire
And gems & gold that none his hand
Dares stretch to touch her Baby form
Or wrap her in his swaddling-band

But She comes to the Man she loves
50   If young or old or rich or poor
They soon drive out the aged Host°
A Beggar at anothers door

He wanders weeping far away
Untill some other take him in
Oft blind & age-bent sore distrest
Untill he can a Maiden win

Female Babe an infant Rahab or baby whore,
Blake would have commented

aged Host the earlier self, now abandoned by
nature

And to allay his freezing Age
The Poor Man takes her in his arms
The Cottage fades before his sight
60 The Garden & its lovely Charms

The Guests are scatterd thro' the land
For the Eye altering alters all
The Senses roll themselves in fear
And the flat Earth becomes a Ball°

The Stars Sun Moon all shrink away
A desart vast without a bound
And nothing left to eat or drink
And a dark desart all around

The honey of her Infant lips
70 The bread & wine of her sweet smile
The wild game of her roving Eye
Does him to Infancy beguile

For as he eats & drinks he grows
Younger & younger every day
And on the desart wild they both
Wander in terror & dismay

Like the wild Stag she flees away
Her fear plants many a thicket wild
While he pursues her night & day
80 By various arts of Love beguild

By various arts of Love & Hate
Till the wide desart planted oer
With Labyrinths of wayward Love
Where roams the Lion Wolf & Boar

Till he becomes a wayward Babe
And she a weeping Woman Old
Then many a Lover wanders here
The Sun & Stars are nearer rolld°

The trees bring forth sweet Extacy°
90 To all who in the desart roam°
Till many a City there is Built°
And many a pleasant Shepherds home°

But when they find the frowning Babe
Terror strikes thro the region wide

The Senses . . . Ball Blake insisted that to an
imaginative eye, the Earth was flat; to see it as
a Ball rolling through space was to yield to a
dehumanization of our context.
nearer rolld meaning that this is the one opportunity of breaking the cycle, through a humanizing love, but it is not broken

Extacy Generation or Experience
To all . . . roam the Ulro
City there is Built the state of Eden, a city not
a garden
Shepherds home the state of Beulah, a pastoral
garden

They cry the Babe the Babe is Born
And flee away on Every side

For who dare touch the frowning form
His arm is witherd to its root
Lions Boars Wolves all howling flee
100   And every Tree does shed its fruit

And none can touch° that frowning form
Except it be a Woman Old
She nails him down upon the Rock
And all is done as I have told
1803?   1863

The Crystal Cabinet

The Maiden caught me in the Wild
Where I was dancing merrily
She put me into her Cabinet°
And Lockd me up with a golden Key

This Cabinet is formd of Gold
And Pearl & Crystal shining bright
And within it opens into a World
And a little lovely Moony Night°

Another England there I saw
10   Another London with its Tower
Another Thames & other Hills
And another pleasant Surrey Bower

Another Maiden like herself
Translucent lovely shining clear
Threefold each in the other closd°
O what a pleasant trembling fear

O what a smile a threefold Smile
Filld me that like a flame I burnd
I bent to Kiss the lovely Maid
20   And found a Threefold Kiss returnd°

I strove to sieze the inmost Form°
With ardor fierce & hands of flame
But burst the Crystal Cabinet
And like a Weeping Babe became

An none can touch The cycle grows harsher, as
history grinds on; the Babe of the third stanza
could be given to the terrible foster-mother but
now he is more fearsome, and only she can
touch him.
Cabinet quite possibly the vagina
Moony Night the state of Beulah

Threefold . . . closd three mirror-outlines enclosed one within the other
Threefold Kiss returnd cf. *Jerusalem* 70:20–27,
where the Maiden is Rahab the Whore
inmost Form which cannot be grasped in the
phenomenal shimmer-of-appearances that is
Beulah

A weeping Babe upon the wild
And Weeping Woman pale reclind
And in the outward air again
I filld with woes the passing Wind°
1803?   1863

Auguries of Innocence°

To see a World in a Grain of Sand
And a Heaven in a Wild Flower
Hold Infinity in the palm of your hand
And Eternity in an hour

A Robin Red breast in a Cage
Puts all Heaven in a Rage
A dove house filld with doves & Pigeons
Shudders Hell thro all its regions
A dog starvd at his Masters Gate
10   Predicts the ruin of the State
A Horse misusd upon the Road
Calls to Heaven for Human blood
Each outcry of the hunted Hare
A fibre from the Brain does tear
A Skylark wounded in the wing
A Cherubim does cease to sing
The Game Cock clipd & armd for fight°
Does the Rising Sun affright
Every Wolfs & Lions howl
20   Raises from Hell a Human Soul
The wild deer wandring here & there
Keeps the Human Soul from Care
The Lamb misusd breeds Public strife
And yet forgives the Butchers Knife
The Bat that flits at close of Eve
Has left the Brain that wont Believe
The Owl that calls upon the Night
Speaks the Unbelievers fright
He who shall hurt the little Wren
30   Shall never be belovd by Men
He who the Ox to wrath has movd
Shall never be by Woman lovd
The wanton Boy that kills the Fly
Shall feel the Spiders enmity

A weeping . . . Wind compared to the opening
stanza, the speaker has suffered only loss,
through seeking in sexual experience a finality
it cannot afford anyone
Auguries of Innocence The title, which probably

refers only to the opening quatrain, means omens
or divinations, that is, tokens of the state of
Innocence; this is not so much a single poem as
a collection of aphorisms and epigrams.
armd for fight in cockfighting sport

He who torments the Chafers° sprite
Weaves a Bower in endless Night
The Catterpiller on the Leaf
Repeats to thee thy Mothers grief
Kill not the Moth nor Butterfly
40   For the Last Judgment draweth nigh
He who shall train the Horse to War
Shall never pass the Polar Bar
The Beggers Dog & Widows Cat
Feed them & thou wilt grow fat
The Gnat that sings his Summers song
Poison gets from Slanders tongue
The poison of the Snake & Newt
Is the sweat of Envys Foot
The Poison of the Honey Bee
50   Is the Artists Jealousy
The Princes Robes & Beggars Rags
Are Toadstools on the Misers Bags
A truth thats told with bad intent
Beats all the Lies you can invent
It is right it should be so
Man was made for Joy & Woe
And when this we rightly know
Thro the World we safely go
Joy & Woe are woven fine
60   A Clothing for the Soul divine
Under every grief & pine
Runs a joy with silken twine
The Babe is more than swadling Bands
Throughout all these Human Lands
Tools were made & Born were hands
Every Farmer Understands
Every Tear from Every Eye
Becomes a Babe in Eternity
This is caught by Females bright
70   And returnd to its own delight
The Bleat the Bark Bellow & Roar
Are Waves that Beat on Heavens Shore
The Babe that weeps the Rod beneath
Writes Revenge in realms of death
The Beggars Rags fluttering in Air
Does to Rags the Heavens tear
The Soldier armd with Sword & Gun
Palsied strikes the Summers Sun
The poor Mans Farthing is worth more
80   Than all the Gold on Africs Shore

Chafers beetle's

One Mite wrung from the Labrers hands
Shall buy & sell the Misers Lands
Or if protected from on high
Does that whole Nation sell & buy
He who mocks the Infants Faith
Shall be mock'd in Age & Death
He who shall teach the Child to Doubt
The rotting Grave shall neer get out
He who respects the Infants faith
90 Triumphs over Hell & Death
The Childs Toys & the Old Mans Reasons
Are the Fruits of the Two seasons
The Questioner who sits so sly
Shall never know how to Reply
He who replies to words of Doubt
Doth put the Light of Knowledge out
The Strongest Poison ever known
Came from Caesars Laurel Crown
Nought can deform the Human Race
100 Like to the Armours iron brace
When Gold & Gems adorn the Plow
To peaceful Arts shall Envy Bow
A Riddle or the Crickets Cry
Is to Doubt a fit Reply
The Emmets° Inch & Eagles Mile
Make Lame Philosophy to smile
He who Doubts from what he sees
Will never Believe do what you Please
If the Sun & Moon should doubt
110 Theyd immediately Go out
To be in a Passion you Good may do
But no Good if a Passion is in you
The Whore & Gambler by the State
Licencd build that Nations Fate
The Harlots cry from Street to Street
Shall weave Old Englands winding Sheet
The Winners Shout the Losers Curse
Dance before dead Englands Hearse
Every Night & every Morn
120 Some to Misery are Born
Every Morn & every Night
Some are Born to sweet delight
Some are Born to sweet delight
Some are Born to Endless Night
We are led to Believe a Lie
When we see not Thro the Eye

Emmets ant's

Which was Born in a Night to perish in a Night°
When the Soul Slept in Beams of Light
God Appears & God is Light
130   To those poor Souls who dwell in Night
But does a Human Form Display
To those who Dwell in Realms of day
1803?   1863

The Four Zoas

The subtitle of Blake's first epic describes the poem with great precision: *The Torments of Love and Jealousy in the Death and Judgment of Albion the Ancient Man.* Albion is mentioned by Spenser and Milton as the father of the British people, after whom the island is named. Blake's Albion is his version of Milton's Adam, with the enormous difference that unfallen Albion is both Man and God, a vision of all that was. In the pre-existent unity which Blake posits, Albion contained, in a harmony of creative tensions, his own female principle or Emanation, Jerusalem, who represented his freedom from strife or, as Milton would have said, his Christian Liberty. He contained also four sons (or principles, faculties, elements), named Urthona, Urizen, Luvah, and Tharmas.

Blake's source is essential knowledge here, and makes clear how central and traditional a mythic structure is being elaborated. The Bible forbids the Jews to make images of God, but allows one complex image anyway, the vision of the Divine Chariot (*Merkabah* in Hebrew) that opens the book of the prophet Ezekiel. Ezekiel sees what he calls "the wheels and their work," a crystalline fire of swift movement. In the midst of the fire are "four living creatures" that "had the likeness of a man," each with four faces and four wings. These "living creatures" themselves constitute what Blake calls "the Vehicular form of Divinity," the Chariot in which an enthroned Man rides, "and this was the appearance of the likeness of the glory of the Lord." In Revelation 4:6 (based upon Ezekiel), "four beasts full of eyes before and behind" surround God's throne. The New Testament Greek word for these beasts is adapted by Blake for his Zoas or Giant Forms, as he also called them.

Blake's Zoas, in their fallen form, together with their emanations, are in every human being, man and woman alike (Blake's symbolism does *not* suggest that each male among us is possessed by the Four Zoas, and each female by their four emanations). It is a mistake to translate the Giant Forms into allegorical equivalents, though this is by now a very traditional error in the criticism devoted to Blake. Urizen is not intellect, Luvah is not the passions, Tharmas is not the instincts, and Urthona is not the imagination. The Zoas and their emanations are *what they do* in the poetry. But since any reader must begin by translating, and since Freud's psychic cartography is the common mythology we now share, it can be useful to translate (warily) Blake's beings into their very rough Freudian equivalents. In their fallen forms, Los (Urthona) is the ego, the Spectral or Satanic Urizen the superego, the inchoate Tharmas the id, and Orc (Luvah) the libido rising out of the id. Of the fallen emanations, the lost delight in his true function of each Zoa, Enitharmon is

Which . . . Night See Jonah 4:10.

the spatial consciousness of the time-ridden ego, Los; Ahania is the Urizenic super-ego's dread of futurity; Enion is the lost sense of the id's unity with the object-world; and Vala is the troubling, narcissistic beauty of the object-world that the libido vainly seeks to possess.

Given below are two extraordinary biblical chants that conclude Night II of the poem, and the whole of the dazzling fury of Night IX, the last Night and the Apocalypse or Last Judgment.

From The Four Zoas

[Song of Enitharmon°]
Night passd & Enitharmon eer the dawn returnd in bliss
She sang Oer Los reviving him to Life his groans were terrible.
But thus she sang I sieze the sphery harp I strike the strings

At the first Sound the Golden sun arises from the Deep
And shakes his awful hair
60 The Eccho wakes the moon to unbind her silver locks
The golden sun bears on my song
And nine bright spheres of harmony rise round the fiery King°

The joy of woman is the Death of her most best beloved
Who dies for Love of her
In torments of fierce jealousy & pangs of adoration.
The Lovers night bears on my song
And the nine Spheres rejoice beneath my powerful controll

They sing unceasing to the notes of my immortal hand
The solemn silent moon
70 Reverberates the living harmony upon my limbs
The birds & beasts rejoice & play
And every one seeks for his mate to prove his inmost joy

Furious & terrible they sport & rend the nether deeps
The deep lifts up his rugged head
And lost in infinite hum[m]ing wings vanishes with a cry
The fading cry is ever dying
The living voice is ever living in its inmost joy

Arise you little glancing wings & sing your infant joy
Arise & drink your bliss
80 For every thing that lives is holy for the source of life
Descends to be a weeping babe
For the Earthworm renews the moisture of the sandy plain

Song of Enitharmon a triumph-hymn of the Female Will and particularly admired by Yeats **fiery King** the fallen sun as Enitharmon's son, Orc, born of her in fallen nature; nine spheres because in Blake's day only seven planets were known, to which he adds the sun and the moon

Now my left hand I stretch to earth beneath
And strike the terrible string
I wake sweet joy in dens of sorrow & I plant a smile
In forests of affliction
And wake the bubbling springs of life in regions of dark death

O I am weary lay thine hand upon me or I faint
I faint beneath these beams of thine
90 For thou hast touchd my five senses & they answerd thee
Now I am nothing & I sink
And on the bed of silence sleep till thou awakest me

PAGE 35

[Song of Enion°]

I am made to sow the thistle for wheat; the nettle for a nourishing dainty
I have planted a false oath in the earth,° it has brought forth a poison tree
I have chosen the serpent for a councellor & the dog
For a schoolmaster to my children
I have blotted out from light & living the dove & nightingale
And I have caused the earth worm to beg from door to door
I have taught the thief a secret path into the house of the just
I have taught pale artifice to spread his nets upon the morning
My heavens are brass my earth is iron my moon a clod of clay
10 My sun a pestilence burning at noon & a vapour of death in night

What is the price of Experience do men buy it for a song°
Or wisdom for a dance in the street? No it is bought with the price
Of all that a man hath his house his wife his children
Wisdom is sold in the desolate market where none come to buy
And in the witherd field where the farmer plows for bread in vain°

It is an easy thing to triumph in the summers sun
And in the vintage & to sing on the waggon loaded with corn
It is an easy thing to talk of patience to the afflicted
To speak the laws of prudence to the houseless wanderer

PAGE 36

To listen to the hungry ravens cry in wintry season
When the red blood is filld with wine & with the marrow of lambs
It is an easy thing to laugh at wrathful elements
To hear the dog howl at the wintry door, the ox in the slaughter house moan
To see a god on every wind & a blessing on every blast
To hear sounds of love in the thunder storm that destroys our enemies house
To rejoice in the blight that covers his field, & the sickness that cuts off his
    children

Song of Enion The burden of this terrifying
chant is that, in our fallen existence, we can
only be happy by ignoring the torments of all
other beings; the page numbers are Blake's.

I have . . . earth See Zechariah 8:17.
What is . . . song See Job 28:12–13.
Wisdom . . . vain Blake himself is both seller
and farmer.

While our olive & vine sing & laugh round our door & our children bring fruits
    & flowers

Then the groan & the dolor are quite forgotten & the slave grinding at the mill
10 And the captive in chains & the poor in the prison, & the soldier in the field
When the shatterd bone hath laid him groaning among the happier dead

It is an easy thing to rejoice in the tents of prosperity
Thus could I sing & thus rejoice, but it is not so with me!
1796–1807?   1893

Night the Ninth
Being The Last Judgment

This extraordinary final section of *The Four Zoas* is the culmination of the first phase of Blake's rhetorical art, which becomes considerably more chastened and subdued in *Milton* and in *Jerusalem*. The continuous exuberance of violent invention in Night the Ninth is regulated as a series of approaches to Apocalypse, rather than a single outburst of finality, but the intensity and driving energy of the whole Night is remorseless and even awesome, perhaps unmatched in the language.

Blake's starting point in Night IX is not Revelation, though he will weave in a number of significant allusions to the Apocalypse of St. John the Divine (and to St. John's principal source, Ezekiel), but Paul Henri Mallet's *Northern Antiquities,* translated by Bishop Percy from the French. Compare to the opening of Night IX the opening of Mallet's Fable 32, "Of the Twilight of the Gods":

> Then will happen such things as may well be called prodigies. The Wolf FENRIS will devour the Sun. . . . Another monster will carry off the Moon . . . the stars shall fly away and vanish from the heavens; the earth and the mountains shall be seen violently agitated; the trees torn up from the earth by the roots; the tottering hills to tumble headlong from their foundations; all the chains and irons of the prisoners to be broken and dashed in pieces. Then is the Wolf Fenris let loose; the sea rushes impetuously over the earth, because the great Serpent, changed into a Spectre, gains the shore. . . . The great Ash Tree of Ydrasil is shaken: nor is any thing in heaven or earth exempt from fear and danger.

The unique tone of Night IX stems from its displacement of the Hebrew-Christian account of the Last Things into this world of a Northern Apocalypse, where even finality is not quite final. Everything in Blake that belonged emotionally to Orc, despite Blake's dialectical awareness of organic energy's limitations, is allowed its absolute expression for once in Night IX. Though Blake evidently judged Night IX to be a spiritual failure, and rejected its violence and wish-fulfillment by refraining from engraving *The Four Zoas*, the poem remains his most titanic and strenuous attempt at the Sublime, and the culmination of what Martin Price has called the Theater of Mind, the characteristic creation of the eighteenth-century poets of Sensibility.

Night the Ninth
Being The Last Judgment

And Los & Enitharmon builded Jerusalem weeping
Over the Sepulcher & over the Crucified body°
Which to their Phantom Eyes appear'd still in the Sepulcher
But Jesus stood beside them in the Spirit Separating
Their Spirit from their body. Terrified at Non Existence
For such they deemd the death of the body. Los his vegetable hands
Outstretchd his right hand branching out in fibrous Strength
Siezd the Sun. His left hand like dark roots coverd the Moon
And tore them down cracking the heavens across from immense to immense°
10 Then fell the fires of Eternity with loud & shrill
Sound of Loud Trumpet thundering along from heaven to heaven
A mighty sound articulate Awake ye dead & come
To Judgment from the four winds Awake & Come away
Folding like scrolls of the Enormous volume of Heaven & Earth°
With thunderous noise & dreadful shakings rocking to & fro
The heavens are shaken & the Earth removed from its place
The foundations of the Eternal hills discoverd
The thrones of Kings are shaken they have lost their robes & crowns
The poor smite their opressors they awake up to the harvest
20 The naked warriors rush together down to the sea shore
Trembling before the multitudes of slaves now set at liberty
They are become like wintry flocks like forests stripd of leaves
The opressed pursue like the wind there is no room for escape°
The Spectre of Enitharmon let loose on the troubled deep
Waild shrill in the confusion & the Spectre of Urthona

Recievd her in the darkning South their bodies lost they stood
Trembling & weak a faint embrace a fierce desire as when
Two shadows mingle on a wall they wail & shadowy tears
Fell down & shadowy forms of joy mixd with despair & grief

And Los . . . Crucified body At the close of
Night VIII, Blake brings his story to his own
historical moment, with Rahab the Whore triumphing, in the guise of the English state
church sacrificing the sons of England on the
altar of Urizen-as-war god. But Satan divides
against Satan, Rahab begins to waver, and what
Blake saw as the particular spiritual significance
of Deism now emerges. In the exhaustions of
natural religion, Blake sees the decadence of
Babylon begin anew, and at last history is ripe
for the Last Judgment. As Night IX begins,
Los and Enitharmon are in despair, but they
continue their creative labor of building Jerusalem, which means that the crucified body of
Jesus is not still in the sepulcher, as they fear,
but stands beside them, freeing them from
nature. Los, aware that his body is dying
(Blake's subtle indication of the contemporary
low state of the arts, in his opinion) but not
knowing that Jesus actively prepares the resurrection of his body, reaches out in a shudder
of revulsion and begins the Apocalypse by a
frontal attack upon nature. This, on one level,
is the act of Blake in writing Night IX, his
own desperate shudder against the darkness of
the age.

Los his . . . immense As in the Norse Twilight
of the Gods, Apocalypse's first stage attacks
sun and moon, the centers of the universe of
death, the sun that once was unfallen Urizen
and the moon that was unfallen Luvah; though
this attack is inadequate, being only a natural
impulse ("fibrous Strength," "dark roots"), it
begins a more-than-natural movement of release,
since it is the natural reaction of Los the imaginative man.

folding . . . Earth See Revelation 6:14, and its
source in Isaiah 25:3-4.

The opressed . . . escape See Revelation 6:9-10.

Their bodies buried in the ruins of the Universe
Mingled with the confusion. Who shall call them from the Grave°

Rahab & Tirzah wail aloud in the wild flames they give up themselves to
    Consummation

The books of Urizen unroll with dreadful noise the folding Serpent
Of Orc began to Consume in fierce raving fire his fierce flames
10 Issud on all sides gathring strength in animating volumes
Roaming abroad on all the winds raging intense reddening
Into resistless pillars of fire rolling round & round gathering
Strength from the Earths consumd & heavens & all hidden abysses
Wherever the Eagle has Explord or Lion or Tyger trod
Or where the Comets of the night or stars of asterial day
Have shot their arrows or long beamed spears in wrath & fury

And all the while the trumpet sounds from the clotted gore & from the hollow
    den
Start forth the trembling millions into flames of mental fire
Bathing their limbs in the bright visions of Eternity

20 Then like the doves from pillars of Smoke the trembling families
Of women & children throughout every nation under heaven
Cling round the men in bands of twenties & of fifties pale
As snow that falls around a leafless tree upon the green
Their opressors are falln they have Stricken them they awake to life
Yet pale the just man stands erect & looking up to heavn
Trembling & strucken by the Universal stroke the trees unroot
The rocks groan horrible & run about. The mountains &
Their rivers cry with a dismal cry   the cattle gather together
Lowing they kneel before the heavens. the wild beasts of the forests
30 Tremble the Lion shuddering asks the Leopard. Feelest thou
The dread I feel unknown before My voice refuses to roar
And in weak moans I speak to thee This night
Before the mornings dawn the Eagle calld the Vulture
The Raven calld the hawk I heard them from my forests black
Saying Let us go up far for soon I smell upon the wind
A terror coming from the South. The Eagle & Hawk fled away
At dawn & Eer the sun arose the raven & Vulture followd
Let us flee also to the north. They fled. The Sons of Men
Saw them depart in dismal droves. The trumpet sounded loud
40 And all the Sons of Eternity Descended into Beulah

PAGE 119
In the fierce flames the limbs of Mystery lay consuming with howling
And deep despair. Rattling go up the flames around the Synagogue
Of Satan   Loud the Serpent Orc ragd thro his twenty Seven

Recievd . . . Grave A conceptual allegory revitalized; the spectre of Urthona is clock-time, the spectre of Enitharmon "yardstick-space" (Northrop Frye's phrase); they are overthrown together and go down with the ruined wall of nature.

Folds. The tree of Mystery went up in folding flames
Blood issud out in mighty volumes pouring in whirlpools fierce
From out the flood gates of the Sky The Gates are burst down pour
The torrents black upon the Earth the blood pours down incessant
Kings in their palaces lie drownd Shepherds their flocks their tents
Roll down the mountains in black torrents Cities Villages
High spires & Castles drownd in the black deluge Shoal on Shoal
Float the dead carcases of Men & Beasts driven to & fro on waves
Of foaming blood beneath the black incessant Sky till all
Mysterys tyrants are cut off & not one left on Earth

And when all Tyranny was cut off from the face of Earth
Around the Dragon form of Urizen & round his stony form
The flames rolling intense thro the wide Universe
Began to Enter the Holy City° Entring the dismal clouds
In furrowd lightnings break their way the wild flames whirring up
The Bloody Deluge living flames winged with intellect
And Reason round the Earth they march in order flame by flame
From the clotted gore & from the hollow den
Start forth the trembling millions into flames of mental fire
Bathing their Limbs in the bright visions of Eternity

Beyond this Universal Confusion beyond the remotest Pole
Where their vortexes begin to operate there stands
A Horrible rock far in the South° it was forsaken when
Urizen gave the horses of Light into the hands of Luvah
On this rock lay the faded head of the Eternal Man
Enwrapped round with weeds of death pale cold in sorrow & woe
He lifts the blue lamps of his Eyes & cries with heavenly voice
Bowing his head over the consuming Universe he cried

O weakness & O weariness   O war within my members°
My sons exiled from my breast pass to & fro before me
My birds are silent on my hills flocks die beneath my branches
My tents are fallen my trumpets & the sweet sounds of my harp
Is silent on my clouded hills that belch forth storms & fires
My milk of cows & honey of bees & fruit of golden harvest
Are gatherd in the scorching heat & in the driving rain
My robe is turned to confusion & my bright gold to stones
Where once I sat   I weary walk in misery & pain
For from within my witherd breast grown narrow with my woes
The Corn is turnd to thistles & the apples into poison
The birds of song to murderous crows My joys to bitter groans

10
20
30
40

Holy City Golgonooza, Blake's City of Art, the
name based on the Hebrew for "hidden hub or
center"; compare ll. 16–23 to Yeats's "Byzantium," which they influenced.
rock far in the South Not the Rock of Ages,
but the rock where Orc (like Loki or Prometheus) was tortured by Urizen earlier in the
poem; the South is Urizen's abandoned realm
in Eternity; Urizen's move to the North (like
similar directional moves by Milton's Satan and
Isaiah's Lucifer) began his Fall.
within my members Within the Zoas; the tone
of this is Pauline, but its thrust is against all
dualisms, St. Paul's included.

PAGE 120

The voices of children in my tents to cries of helpless infants
And all exiled from the face of light & shine of morning
In this dark world a narrow house I wander up & down
I hear Mystery howling in these flames of Consummation
When shall the Man of future times become as in days of old
O weary life why sit I here & give up all my powers
To indolence to the night of death when indolence & mourning
Sit hovring over my dark threshold. tho I arise look out
And scorn the war within my members yet my heart is weak
10 And my head faint Yet will I look again unto the morning
Whence is this sound of rage of Men drinking each others blood
Drunk with the smoking gore & red but not with nourishing wine

The Eternal Man sat on the Rocks & cried with awful voice

O Prince of Light where art thou   I behold thee not as once
In those Eternal fields in clouds of morning stepping forth
With harps & songs where bright Ahania sang before thy face
And all thy sons & daughters gatherd round my ample table
See you not all this wracking furious confusion
Come forth from slumbers of thy cold abstraction come forth
20 Arise to Eternal births shake off thy cold repose
Schoolmaster of souls great opposer of change arise
That the Eternal worlds may see thy face in peace & joy
That thou dread form of Certainty maist sit in town & village
While little children play around thy feet in gentle awe
Fearing thy frown loving thy smile O Urizen Prince of light

He calld the deep buried his voice & answer none returnd

Then wrath burst round the Eternal Man was wrath again he cried
Arise O stony form of death O dragon of the Deeps°
Lie down before my feet O Dragon let Urizen arise
30 O how couldst thou deform those beautiful proportions
Of life & person for as the Person so is his life proportiond
Let Luvah rage in the dark deep even to Consummation
For if thou feedest not his rage it will subside in peace
But if thou darest obstinate refuse my stern behest
Thy crown & scepter I will sieze & regulate all my members
In stern severity & cast thee out into the indefinite
Where nothing lives, there to wander. & if thou returnst weary
Weeping at the threshold of Existence I will steel my heart
Against thee to Eternity & never recieve thee more
40 Thy self destroying beast formd Science shall be thy eternal lot
My anger against thee is greater than against this Luvah
For war is energy Enslavd but thy religion
The first author of this war & the distracting of honest minds

dragon of the Deeps See Psalms 148:7.

Into confused perturbation & strife & honour & pride
Is a deceit so detestable that I will cast thee out
If thou repentest not & leave thee as a rotten branch to be burnd
With Mystery the Harlot & with Satan for Ever & Ever
Error can never be redeemd in all Eternity
But Sin Even Rahab is redeemd in blood & fury & jealousy
50   That line of blood that stretchd across the windows of the morning
Redeemd from Errors power.° Wake thou dragon of the Deeps

PAGE 121
Urizen wept in the dark deep anxious his Scaly form
To reassume the human & he wept in the dark deep

Saying O that I had never drank the wine nor eat the bread
Of dark mortality nor cast my view into futurity nor turnd
My back darkning the present clouding with a cloud
And building arches high & cities turrets & towers & domes
Whose smoke destroyd the pleasant garden & whose running Kennels
Chokd the bright rivers burdning with my Ships the angry deep
Thro Chaos seeking for delight & in spaces remote
10   Seeking the Eternal which is always present to the wise
Seeking for pleasure which unsought falls round the infants path
And on the fleeces of mild flocks who neither care nor labour
But I the labourer of ages whose unwearied hands
Are thus deformd with hardness with the sword & with the spear
And with the Chisel & the mallet I whose labours vast
Order the nations separating family by family
Alone enjoy not   I alone in misery supreme
Ungratified give all my joy unto this Luvah & Vala
Then Go O dark futurity I will cast thee forth from these
20   Heavens of my brain nor will I look upon futurity more
I cast futurity away & turn my back upon that void
Which I have made for lo futurity is in this moment
Let Orc consume let Tharmas rage let dark Urthona give
All strength to Los & Enitharmon & let Los self cursd
Rend down this fabric as a wall ruind & family extinct
Rage Orc Rage Tharmas Urizen no longer curbs your rage

So Urizen spoke he shook his snows from off his Shoulders & arose
As on a Pyramid of mist his white robes scattering
The fleecy white renewd he shook his aged mantles off
30   Into the fires Then glorious bright Exulting in his joy

But sin . . . power For the "line of blood" see
the "line of scarlet thread" of Joshua 2:18,
interpreted by orthodox Christian tradition as a
sign of Christ's sacrifice, which made Rahab a
prototype of the church. Blake was ironically
happy to accept this interpretation, since his
Rahab is the radical Protestant identification of
the church with Revelation's Scarlet Woman,
the Whore of Babylon. In this passage (ll. 27–
51) Rahab redeems herself from error, the
church's claim to exclusiveness of salvation. Line
50 is a beautiful, deliberate assertion of continuity in Blake's own work, linking this intended
last poem to the first poem in Blake's first book,
"To Spring," l. 2.

He sounding rose into the heavens in naked majesty
In radiant Youth. when Lo like garlands in the Eastern sky
When vocal may comes dancing from the East Ahania came
Exulting in her flight as when a bubble rises up
On to the surface of a lake. Ahania rose in joy
Excess of Joy is worse than grief—her heart beat high her blood
Burst its bright Vessels She fell down dead at the feet of Urizen°
Outstretchd a Smiling corse they buried her in a silent cave
Urizen dropt a tear the Eternal Man Darkend with sorrow

40   The three daughters of Urizen guard Ahanias Death couch
Rising from the confusion in tears & howlings & despair
Calling upon their fathers Name upon their Rivers dark

And the Eternal Man Said Hear my words O Prince of Light

PAGE 122

Behold Jerusalem in whose bosom the Lamb of God
Is seen tho slain before her Gates he self renewd remains
Eternal & I thro him awake from deaths dark vale
The times revolve the time is coming when all these delights
Shall be renewd & all these Elements that now consume
Shall reflourish. Then bright Ahania shall awake from death
A glorious Vision to thine Eyes a Self renewing Vision
The spring. the summer to be thine then sleep the wintry days
In silken garments spun by her own hands against her funeral
10   The winter thou shalt plow & lay thy stores into thy barns
Expecting to receive Ahania in the spring with joy
Immortal thou. Regenerate She & all the lovely Sex°
From her shall learn obedience & prepare for a wintry grave
That spring may see them rise in tenfold joy & sweet delight
Thus shall the male & female live the life of Eternity
Because the Lamb of God Creates himself a bride & wife
That we his Children evermore may live in Jerusalem
Which now descendeth out of heaven a City yet a Woman°
Mother of myriads redeemd & born in her spiritual palaces
20   By a New Spiritual birth Regenerated from Death

Urizen said. I have Erred & my Error remains with me
What Chain encompasses in what Lock is the river of light confind
That issues forth in the morning by measure & the evening by carefulness

Ahania . . . Urizen Ahania, Urizen's emanation, normally represents the intellect's legitimate pleasure in itself, debased in the Fall to the intellect's sado-masochistic self-hatred, or acute self-consciousness. This revival and subsequent apparent "death" of Ahania is a crucial moment in Night IX. Her premature reunion with Urizen represents Blake's warning against self-deception (his own and ours) in an apocalyptic age, when the apparently renovated mind becomes suddenly too joyful at taking pleasure in itself again, a too-easy gratification that cannot precede, but must follow, a terrible struggle toward self-integration.
the lovely Sex Again the reader must remember that this refers to the self-sacrifice of the emanations in the unfallen life of Eden; Blake does *not* mean it to be a paradigm for human female behavior, since it refers to natural forms (in the fallen world) and human creations (in Eternity) and not to human beings at all, female or male.
a City yet a Woman See Revelation 21:2-10,

Where shall we take our stand to view the infinite & unbounded
Or where are human feet for Lo our eyes are in the heavens

He ceasd for rivn link from link the bursting Universe explodes
All things reversd flew from their centers rattling bones
To bones Join,° shaking convulsd the shivering clay breathes
Each speck of dust to the Earths center nestles round & round
30 In pangs of an Eternal Birth in torment & awe & fear
All spirits deceasd let loose from reptile prisons come in shoals
Wild furies from the tygers brain & from the lions Eyes
And from the ox & ass come moping terrors. from the Eagle
And raven numerous as the leaves of autumn   every species
Flock to the trumpet muttring over the sides of the grave & crying
In the fierce wind round heaving rocks & mountains filld with groans
On rifted rocks suspended in the air by inward fires
Many a woful company & many on clouds & waters
Fathers & friends Mothers & Infants Kings & Warriors
40 Priests & chaind Captives met together in a horrible fear
And every one of the dead appears as he had livd before

PAGE 123
And all the marks remain of the slaves scourge & tyrants Crown
And of the Priests oergorged Abdomen & of the merchants thin
Sinewy deception & of the warriors ou[t]braving & thoughtlessness
In lineaments too extended & in bones too strait & long

They shew their wounds they accuse they sieze the opressor howlings began
On the golden palace Songs & joy on the desart the Cold babe
Stands in the furious air he cries the children of six thousand years
Who died in infancy rage furious a mighty multitude rage furious
Naked & pale standing on the expecting air to be deliverd
10 Rend limb from limb the Warrior & the tyrant reuniting in pain
The furious wind still rends around they flee in sluggish effort

They beg they intreat in vain now they Listend not to intreaty
They view the flames red rolling on thro the wide universe
From the dark jaws of death beneath & desolate shores remote
These covering Vaults of heaven & these trembling globes of Earth
One Planet calls to another & one star enquires of another
What flames are these coming from the South what noise what dreadful rout
As of a battle in the heavens hark heard you not the trumpet
As of fierce battle While they spoke the flames come on intense roaring

20 They see him whom they have piercd they wail because of him°
They magnify themselves no more against Jerusalem Nor
Against her little ones the innocent accused before the Judges
Shines with immortal Glory trembling the Judge springs from his throne
Hiding his face in the dust beneath the prisoners feet & saying

rattling . . . Join See Ezekiel 37:7.   **They see . . . him** See Revelation 1:7.

Brother of Jesus what have I done intreat thy lord for me
Perhaps I may be forgiven While he speaks the flames roll on

And after the flames appears the Cloud of the Son of Man°
Descending from Jerusalem with power and great Glory
All nations look up to the Cloud & behold him who was Crucified

30   The Prisoner answers you scourgd my father to death before my face
While I stood bound with cords & heavy chains. your hipocrisy
Shall now avail you nought. So speaking he dashd him with his foot

The Cloud is Blood dazling upon the heavens & in the cloud
Above upon its volumes is beheld a throne & a pavement
Of precious stones. surrounded by twenty four venerable patriarchs°
And these again surrounded by four Wonders of the Almighty
Incomprehensible. pervading all amidst & round about
Fourfold each in the other reflected they are named Life's in Eternity°
Four Starry Universes going forward from Eternity to Eternity
40   And the Falln Man who was arisen upon the Rock of Ages

PAGE 124
Beheld the Vision of God & he arose up from the Rock°
And Urizen arose up with him walking thro the flames
To meet the Lord coming to Judgment but the flames repelld them
Still to the Rock in vain they strove to Enter the Consummation
Together for the Redeemd Man could not enter the Consummation

Then siezd the Sons of Urizen the Plow they polished it°
From rust of ages all its ornaments of Gold & silver & ivory
Reshone across the field immense where all the nations
Darkend like Mould in the divided fallows where the weed
10   Triumphs in its own destruction they took down the harness
From the blue walls of heaven starry jingling ornamented
With beautiful art the study of angels the workmanship of Demons
When Heaven & Hell in Emulation strove in sports of Glory

The noise of rural work resounded thro the heavens of heavens
The horse[s] neigh from the battle the wild bulls from the sultry waste
The tygers from the forests & the lions from the sandy desarts
They Sing they sieze the instruments of harmony they throw away
The spear the bow the gun the mortar they level the fortifications
They beat the iron engines of destruction into wedges°
20   They give them to Urthonas Sons ringing the hammers sound

the Son of Man See Luke 21:27, and Revelation
1:7.
in the cloud . . . patriarchs See Revelation 4:2–4.
Life's in Eternity The Zoas, in Eternity, define
truly what Life is.
And the . . . Rock a crucial moment, like
Prometheus being unbound from his ravine, but
the passage goes on to apply the lessons learned

from the failure of the French Revolution
Then siezd . . . polished it The work of restora-
tion begins in our minds, where the reclaimed
Urizen now assumes his proper place; the mind
must plow up the hell of the physical universe,
in a truly humanistic Harrowing of Hell; see
Revelation 14:15–20.
They beat . . . wedges See Isaiah 2:4.

In dens of death° to forge the spade the mattock & the ax
The heavy roller to break the clods to pass over the nations

The Sons of Urizen Shout Their father rose The Eternal horses
Harnessd They calld to Urizen the heavens moved at their call
The limbs of Urizen shone with ardor. He laid his ha[n]d on the Plow
Thro dismal darkness drave the Plow of ages over Cities
And all their Villages over Mountains & all their Vallies
Over the graves & caverns of the dead   Over the Planets
And over the void Spaces over Sun & moon & star & constellation

30   Then Urizen commanded & they brought the Seed of Men°
The trembling souls of All the Dead stood before Urizen
Weak wailing in the troubled air East west & north & south

PAGE 125

He turnd the horses loose & laid his Plow in the northern corner
Of the wide Universal field. then Stepd forth into the immense

Then he began to sow the seed he girded round his loins
With a bright girdle & his skirt filld with immortal souls
Howling & Wailing fly the souls from Urizens strong hand

For from the hand of Urizen the myriads fall like stars
Into their own appointed places driven back by the winds
The naked warriors rush together down to the sea shores
They are become like wintry flocks like forests stripd of leaves
10   The Kings & Princes of the Earth cry with a feeble cry
Driven on the unproducing sands & on the hardend rocks
And all the while the flames of Orc follow the ventrous feet
Of Urizen & all the while the Trump of Tharmas sounds
Weeping & wailing fly the souls from Urizens strong hand
The daughters of Urizen stand with Cups & measures of foaming wine
Immense upon the heavens with bread & delicate repasts

Then follows the golden harrow in the midst of Mental fires
To ravishing melody of flutes & harps & softest voice
The seed is harrowd in while flames heat the black mould & cause
20   The human harvest to begin Towards the south first sprang
The myriads & in silent fear they look out from their graves

Then Urizen sits down to rest & all his wearied Sons
Take their repose on beds they drink they sing they view the flames
Of Orc in joy they view the human harvest springing up
A time they give to sweet repose till all the harvest is ripe°

---

dens of death Dens of Urthona, the Ulro; this underworld or unconscious must be broken through before Luvah's world of Experience or Generation and the Innocence or Beulah of Tharmas can be reclaimed.

Seed of Men after the plowing, the sowing for the human harvest; see Matthew 13:3–8
A time . . . ripe See Revelation 14:15; Urizen's initial labor has been performed, and his momentary rest permits Ahania now to be truly revived.

And Lo like the harvest Moon Ahania cast off her death clothes°
She folded them up in care in silence & her brightning limbs
Bathd in the clear spring of the rock then from her darksom cave
Issud in majesty divine   Urizen rose up from his couch
On wings of tenfold joy clapping his hands his feet his radiant wings
In the immense as when the Sun dances upon the mountains
A shout of jubilee in lovely notes responding from daughter to daughter
From son to Son as if the Stars beaming innumerable
Thro night should sing soft warbling filling Earth & heaven
And bright Ahania took her seat by Urizen in songs & joy

30

The Eternal Man also sat down upon the Couches of Beulah
Sorrowful that he could not put off his new risen body°
In mental flames the flames refusd they drove him back to Beulah
His body was redeemd to be permanent thro the Mercy Divine

PAGE 126
And now fierce Orc had quite consumd himself in Mental flames°
Expending all his energy against the fuel of fire
The Regenerate Man stoopd his head over the Universe & in
His holy hands recievd the flaming Demon & Demoness of Smoke
And gave them to Urizens hands the Immortal frownd Saying

Luvah & Vala henceforth you are Servants obey & live
You shall forget your former state return O Love in peace
Into your place the place of seed not in the brain or heart
If Gods combine against Man Setting their Dominion above
The Human form Divine. Thrown down from their high Station
In the Eternal heavens of Human Imagination: buried beneath
In dark oblivion with incessant pangs ages on ages
In Enmity & war first weakend then in stern repentance
They must renew their brightness & their disorganizd functions
Again reorganize till they resume the image of the human
Cooperating in the bliss of Man obeying his Will
Servants to the infinite & Eternal of the Human form°

10

Luvah & Vala descended & enterd the Gates of Dark Urthona
And walkd from the hands of Urizen in the shadows of Valas Garden
Where the impressions of Despair & Hope for ever vegetate
In flowers in fruits in fishes birds & beasts & clouds & waters
The land of doubts & shadows sweet delusions unformd hopes
They saw no more the terrible confusion of the wracking universe
They heard not saw not felt not all the terrible confusion

20

And Lo . . . clothes Ahania is one with the
harvest goddess here.
The Eternal . . . body Albion wishes to enter
Eden, the condition of fire, but it is still Millennium, and he must abide in Beulah or redeemed nature for a time.
And now . . . flames The focus moves now
from Urizen and Ahania to Luvah and Vala;

Orc, as natural man, is burned up, and his
eternal forms of Luvah and Vala reappear, the
children of Experience abandoning what D. H.
Lawrence called "sex in the head" and returning
to their generative "place of seed."
If Gods . . . form Ll. 9–17 summarize the moral
of the entire poem.

For in their orbed senses within closd up they wanderd at will
And those upon the Couches viewd them in the dreams of Beulah°
As they reposd from the terrible wide universal harvest
Invisible Luvah in bright clouds hoverd over Valas head
And thus their ancient golden age renewd for Luvah spoke
30   With voice mild from his golden Cloud upon the breath of morning

Come forth O Vala from the grass & from the silent Dew
Rise from the dews of death for the Eternal Man is Risen

She rises among flowers & looks toward the Eastern clearness
She walks yea runs her feet are wingd on the tops of the bending grass
Her garments rejoice in the vocal wind & her hair glistens with dew
She answerd thus Whose voice is this in the voice of the nourishing air
In the spirit of the morning awaking the Soul from its grassy bed

PAGE 127
Where dost thou dwell for it is thee I seek & but for thee
I must have slept Eternally nor have felt the dew of thy morning
Look how the opening dawn advances with vocal harmony
Look how the beams foreshew the rising of some glorious power
The sun is thine he goeth forth in his majestic brightness
O thou creating voice that callest & who shall answer thee

Where dost thou flee O fair one where dost thou seek thy happy place

To yonder brightness there I haste for sure I came from thence
Or I must have slept eternally nor have felt the dew of morning

10   Eternally thou must have slept nor have felt the morning dew
But for yon nourishing sun tis that by which thou art arisen
The birds adore the sun the beasts rise up & play in his beams
And every flower & every leaf rejoices in his light
Then O thou fair one sit thee down for thou art as the grass
Thou risest in the dew of morning & at night art folded up°

Alas am I but as a flower then will I sit me down
Then will I weep then Ill complain & sigh for immortality
And chide my maker thee O Sun that raisedst me to fall

So saying she sat down & wept beneath the apple trees

20   O be thou blotted out thou Sun that raisedst me to trouble
That gavest me a heart to crave & raisedst me thy phantom
To feel thy heat & see thy light & wander here alone
Hopeless if I am like the grass & so shall pass away

Rise sluggish Soul why sitst thou here why dost thou sit & weep
Yon Sun shall wax old & decay but thou shalt ever flourish

Luvah . . . Beulah Ll. 18–26 deliberately echo
The Book of Thel for the renovated Vala is the
contrary to the pathetic Thel, and welcomes
entry into a humanized Generation.
Thou . . . folded up See Psalm 90:6.

The fruit shall ripen & fall down & the flowers consume away
But thou shalt still survive arise O dry thy dewy tears°

Hah! Shall I still survive whence came that sweet & comforting voice
And whence that voice of sorrow O sun thou art nothing now to me
30 Go on thy course rejoicing & let us both rejoice together
I walk among his flocks & hear the bleating of his lambs
O that I could behold his face & follow his pure feet
I walk by the footsteps of his flocks come hither tender flocks
Can you converse with a pure Soul that seeketh for her maker
You answer not then am I set your mistress in this garden
Ill watch you & attend your footsteps you are not like the birds

PAGE 128
That sing & fly in the bright air but you do lick my feet
And let me touch your wooly backs   follow me as I sing
For in my bosom a new song arises to my Lord
Rise up O Sun most glorious minister & light of day
Flow on ye gentle airs & bear the voice of my rejoicing
Wave freshly clear waters flowing around the tender grass
And thou sweet smelling ground put forth thy life in fruits & flowers
Follow me O my flocks & hear me sing my rapturous Song
I will cause my voice to be heard on the clouds that glitter in the sun
10 I will call & who shall answer me   I will sing   who shall reply
For from my pleasant hills behold the living living springs
Running among my green pastures delighting among my trees
I am not here alone my flocks you are my brethren
And you birds that sing & adorn the sky you are my sisters
I sing & you reply to my Song   I rejoice & you are glad
Follow me O my flocks we will now descend into the valley
O how delicious are the grapes flourishing in the Sun
How clear the spring of the rock running among the golden sand
How cool the breezes of the vally & the arms of the branching trees
20 Cover us from the Sun come & let us sit in the Shade
My Luvah here hath placd me in a Sweet & pleasant Land
And given me fruits & pleasant waters & warm hills & cool valleys
Here will I build myself a house & here Ill call on his name
Here Ill return when I am weary & take my pleasant rest

So spoke the Sinless Soul & laid her head on the downy fleece
Of a curld Ram who stretchd himself in sleep beside his mistress
And soft sleep fell upon her eyelids in the silent noon of day

Then Luvah passed by & saw the sinless Soul
And said   Let a pleasant house arise to be the dwelling place
30 Of this immortal Spirit growing in lower Paradise

Where . . . tears Ll. 7–27 echo *The Book of
Thel*, again providing a positive contrary to
Thel's pathos.

He spoke & pillars were builded & walls as white as ivory
The grass she slept upon was pavd with pavement as of pearl
Beneath her rose a downy bed & a cieling coverd all

Vala awoke. When in the pleasant gates of sleep I enterd
I saw my Luvah like a spirit stand in the bright air
Round him stood spirits like me who reard me a bright house
And here I see thee house remain in my most pleasant world

PAGE 129
My Luvah smild I kneeled down he laid his hand on my head
And when he laid his hand upon me from the gates of sleep I came
Into this bodily house to tend my flocks in my pleasant garden

So saying she arose & walked round her beautiful house
And then from her white door she lookd to see her bleating lambs
But her flocks were gone up from beneath the trees into the hills

I see the hand that leadeth me doth also lead my flocks
She went up to her flocks & turned oft to see her shining house
She stopd to drink of the clear spring & eat the grapes & apples
10   She bore the fruits in her lap she gatherd flowers for her bosom
She called to her flocks saying follow me o my flocks

They followd her to the silent vally beneath the spreading trees
And on the rivers margin she ungirded her golden girdle
She stood in the river & viewd herself within the watry glass
And her bright hair was wet with the waters She rose up from the river
And as she rose her Eyes were opend to the world of waters°
She saw Tharmas sitting upon the rocks beside the wavy sea
He strokd the water from his beard & mournd faint thro the summer vales

And Vala stood on the rocks of Tharmas & heard his mournful voice

20   O Enion my weary head is in the bed of death
For weeds of death have wrapd around my limbs in the hoary deeps
I sit in the place of shells & mourn & thou art closd in clouds
When will the time of Clouds be past & the dismal night of Tharmas
Arise O Enion Arise & smile upon my head
As thou dost smile upon the barren mountains and they rejoice
When wilt thou smile on Tharmas O thou bringer of golden day
Arise O Enion arise for Lo I have calmd my seas°

So saying his faint head he laid upon the Oozy rock
And darkness coverd all the deep the light of Enion faded
30   Like a fa[i]nt flame quivering upon the surface of the darkness

My Luvah . . . waters In this beautiful passage
(ll. 1–16), the redeemed Vala surmounts an
Eve-like narcist contemplation of her own
beauty, and by opening her eyes to the world
of waters begins the redemption of Tharmas and
Enion, the mother and father figures of the
world of Innocence; Experience having been
purged, Beulah or Innocence can be recovered.
calmed my seas From having been the harmony
and instinctual unity of the Eternal world,
Tharmas has fallen into the Old Man of the Sea
or voice of Chaos; repenting, he calms his seas,
which means that his emanation, the Earth
Mother, is able to return to him.

Then Vala lifted up her hands to heaven to call on Enion
She calld but none could answer her & the Eccho of her voice returnd

Where is the voice of God that calld me from the silent dew
Where is the Lord of Vala dost thou hide in clefts of the rock°
Why shouldst thou hide thyself from Vala from the soul that wanders desolate

She ceas'd & light beamd round her like the glory of the morning

PAGE 130
And She arose out of the river & girded on her golden girdle

And now her feet step on the grassy bosom of the ground
Among her flocks & she turnd her eyes toward her pleasant house
And saw in the door way beneath the trees two little children playing°
She drew near to her house & her flocks followd her footsteps
The Children clung around her knees she embracd them & wept over them

Thou little Boy art Tharmas & thou bright Girl Enion
How are ye thus renewd & brought into the Gardens of Vala

She embracd them in tears. till the sun descended the western hills
10   And then she enterd her bright house leading her mighty children
And when night came the flocks laid round the house beneath the trees
She laid the Children on the beds which she saw prepard in the house
Then last herself laid down & closd her Eyelids in soft slumbers

And in the morning when the Sun arose in the crystal sky
Vala awoke & calld the children from their gentle slumbers

Awake O Enion awake & let thine innocent Eyes
Enlighten all the Crystal house of Vala awake awake
Awake Tharmas awake awake thou child of dewy tears
Open the orbs of thy blue eyes & smile upon my gardens

20   The Children woke & smild on Vala. she kneeld by the golden couch
She presd them to her bosom & her pearly tears dropd down
O my sweet Children Enion let Tharmas kiss thy Cheek
Why dost thou turn thyself away from his sweet watry eyes
Tharmas henceforth in Valas bosom thou shalt find sweet peace
O bless the lovely eyes of Tharmas & the Eyes of Enion

They rose they went out wandring sometimes together sometimes alone
Why weepest thou Tharmas Child of tears in the bright house of joy
Doth Enion avoid the sight of thy blue heavenly Eyes
And dost thou wander with my lambs & wet their innocent faces
30   With thy bright tears because the steps of Enion are in the gardens
Arise sweet boy & let us follow the path of Enion

clefts of the rock See Song of Solomon 2:14.   the *Songs of Innocence* return as a restored
two little children playing The lost children of   Tharmas and Enion.

So saying they went down into the garden among the fruits
And Enion sang among the flowers that grew among the trees
And Vala said Go Tharmas weep not Go to Enion

PAGE 131

He said O Vala I am sick & all this garden of Pleasure
Swims like a dream before my eyes but the sweet smelling fruit
Revives me to new deaths I fade even like a water lilly
In the suns heat till in the night on the couch of Enion
I drink new life & feel the breath of sleeping Enion
But in the morning she arises to avoid my Eyes
Then my loins fade & in the house I sit me down & weep

Chear up thy Countenance bright boy & go to Enion
Tell her that Vala waits her in the shadows of her garden

10   He went with timid steps & Enion like the ruddy morn
When infant spring appears in swelling buds & opening flowers
Behind her Veil withdraws so Enion turnd her modest head

But Tharmas spoke Vala seeks thee sweet Enion in the shades
Follow the steps of Tharmas, O thou brightness of the gardens
He took her hand reluctant she followd in infant doubts

Thus in Eternal Childhood straying among Valas flocks
In infant sorrow & joy alternate Enion & Tharmas playd
Round Vala in the Gardens of Vala & by her rivers margin

They are the shadows of Tharmas & of Enion in Valas world
20   And the sleepers who rested from their harvest work beheld these visions
Thus were the sleepers entertaind upon the Couches of Beulah

When Luvah & Vala were closd up in their world of shadowy forms
Darkness was all beneath the heavens only a little light
Such as glows out from sleeping spirits appeard in the deeps beneath
As when the wind sweeps over a Corn field the noise of souls
Thro all the immense borne down by Clouds swagging in autumnal heat
Muttering along from heaven to heaven hoarse roll the human forms
Beneath thick clouds dreadful lightnings burst & thunders roll
Down pour the torrent Floods of heaven on all the human harvest
30   Then Urizen sitting at his repose on beds in the bright South
Cried Times are Ended° he Exulted he arose in joy he exulted
He pourd his light & all his Sons & daughters pourd their light
To exhale the spirits of Luvah & Vala thro the atmosphere
And Luvah & Vala saw the Light their spirits were Exhald
In all their ancient innocence the floods depart the clouds
Dissipate or sink into the Seas of Tharmas   Luvah sat
Above on the bright heavens in peace. the Spirits of Men beneath

Times are Ended See Revelation 10:6; Urizen's
role in 131:22–132:1 fulfills Revelation 14:14– 16, as he becomes the joyful reaper of the now
fully prepared harvest.

Cried out to be deliverd & the Spirit of Luvah wept
Over the human harvest & over Vala the sweet wanderer
40 In pain the human harvest wavd in horrible groans of woe°

PAGE 132
The Universal Groan went up the Eternal Man was Darkend

Then Urizen arose & took his Sickle in his hand
There is a brazen sickle & a scythe of iron hid
Deep in the South guarded by a few solitary stars°
This sickle Urizen took the scythe his sons embracd
And went forth & began to reap & all his joyful sons
Reapd the wide Universe & bound in Sheaves a wondrous harvest
They took them into the wide barns with loud rejoicings & triumph
Of flute & harp & drum & trumpet horn & clarion°

10 The feast was spread in the bright South & the Regenerate Man
Sat at the feast rejoicing & the wine of Eternity
Was servd round by the flames of Luvah all Day & all the Night
And when Morning began to dawn upon the distant hills
a whirlwind rose up in the Center & in the Whirlwind a shriek
And in the Shriek a rattling of bones & in the rattling of bones
A dolorous groan & from the dolorous groan in tears
Rose Enion like a gentle light° & Enion spoke saying

O Dreams of Death the human form dissolving companied
By beasts & worms & creeping things & darkness & despair
20 The clouds fall off from my wet brow the dust from my cold limbs
Into the Sea of Tharmas Soon renewd a Golden Moth°
I shall cast off my death clothes & Embrace Tharmas again
For Lo the winter melted away upon the distant hills
And all the black mould sings. She speaks to her infant race her milk
Descends down on the sand. the thirsty sand drinks & rejoices
Wondering to behold the Emmet the Grasshopper the jointed worm
The roots shoot thick thro the solid rocks bursting their way
They cry out in joys of existence. the broad stems
Rear on the mountains stem after stem the scaly newt creeps
30 From the stone & the armed fly springs from the rocky crevice
The spider. The bat burst from the hardend slime crying
To one another What are we & whence is our joy & delight
Lo the little moss begins to spring & the tender weed
Creeps round our secret nest. Flocks brighten the Mountains
Herds throng up the Valley wild beasts fill the forests

groans of woe at not yet being reaped, and so still enduring nature and history
Then Urizen . . . stars To perform his labors as reaper, Urizen dismantles his star world, formerly one of Blake's prime images of tyranny and repression.
This sickle . . . clarion See Revelation 14:14–16.
Rose . . . light Enion's rising is the particular joy of the body's resurrection, in *The Marriage*'s sense of the body's being all of the soul that the five senses can apprehend; Enion's "gentle light" is the body's joy at finding itself whole again.
Golden Moth A butterfly, for which see "Auguries of Innocence," ll. 39–40; as Tharmas humanizes, all instinctual life acquires a human awareness.

Joy thrilld thro all the Furious form of Tharmas humanizing
Mild he Embracd her whom he sought he raisd her thro the heavens
Sounding his trumpet to awake the dead on high he soard
Over the ruind worlds the smoking tomb of the Eternal Prophet°

PAGE 133
The Eternal Man arose He welcomd them to the Feast
The feast was spread in the bright South & the Eternal Man°
Sat at the feast rejoicing & the wine of Eternity
Was servd round by the flames of Luvah all day & all the night

And Many Eternal Men sat at the golden feast to see
The female form now separate They shudderd° at the horrible thing
Not born for the sport and amusement of Man but born to drink up all his
    powers
They wept to see their shadows they said to one another this is Sin
This is the Generative world they rememberd the Days of old

10   And One of the Eternals spoke All was silent at the feast

Man is a Worm wearied with joy he seeks the caves of sleep
Among the Flowers of Beulah in his Selfish cold repose
Forsaking Brotherhood & Universal love in selfish clay
Folding the pure wings of his mind seeking the places dark
Abstracted from the roots of Science then inclosd around
In walls of Gold we cast him like a Seed into the Earth
Till times & spaces have passd over him duly every morn
We visit him covering with a Veil the immortal seed
With windows from the inclement sky we cover him & with walls
20   And hearths protect the Selfish terror till divided all
In families we see our shadows born. & thence we know   ⎫
That Man subsists by Brotherhood & Universal Love   ⎬ Ephesi-
We fall on one anothers necks more closely we embrace   ⎭ ans iii c.
                                                              10 v°

Not for ourselves but for the Eternal family we live
Man liveth not by Self alone but in his brothers face
Each shall behold the Eternal Father & love & joy abound

So spoke the Eternal at the Feast they embracd the New born Man
Calling him Brother image of the Eternal Father. they sat down
At the immortal tables sounding loud their instruments of joy
30   Calling the Morning into Beulah the Eternal Man rejoicd°

tomb . . . Prophet The natural world now
transcended is the tomb of Jesus; Jesus is Los,
and Los is now again Urthona.
The feast . . . the Eternal Man Unfallen Albion's head was in the South, realm of Urizen,
once the zenith, and now the place of celebration in the Apocalypse.
They shudderd because the emanations still retain
separate existence, since the feast is in Beulah,
and the integration of Eden has not yet been
reattained.
Ephesians iii c.10 v An ironical reference, in
part, since the text is: "To the intent that now
unto the principalities and powers in heavenly

places might be known by the church the
manifold wisdom of God," to which compare
Blake's motto to the whole of The Four Zoas,
from Ephesians 6:12: "For we wrestle not
against flesh and blood, but against principalities, against powers, against the rulers of the
darkness of this world, against spiritual wickedness in high places." The juxtaposition of passages reminds the reader that the English state
church is the enemy of Revelation.
Eternal Man rejoicd but he is still in Beulah,
the garden of the South, so the joy is not yet
final.

When Morning dawnd The Eternals rose to labour at the Vintage°
Beneath they saw their sons & daughters wondering inconceivable
At the dark myriads in Shadows in the worlds beneath

The morning dawnd Urizen rose & in his hand the Flail
Sounds on the Floor heard terrible by all beneath the heavens
Dismal loud redounding the nether floor shakes with the sound

PAGE 134
And all Nations were threshed out & the stars threshd from their husks°

Then Tharmas took the Winnowing fan the winnowing wind furious
Above veerd round by the violent whirlwind driven west & south
Tossed the Nations like Chaff into the seas of Tharmas

O Mystery Fierce Tharmas cries Behold thy end is come
Art thou she that made the nations drunk with the cup of Religion°
Go down ye Kings & Councillors & Giant Warriors
Go down into the depths go down & hide yourselves beneath
Go down with horse & Chariots & Trumpets of hoarse war

10   Lo how the Pomp of Mystery goes down into the Caves
Her great men howl & throw the dust & rend their hoary hair
Her delicate women & children shriek upon the bitter wind
Spoild of their beauty their hair rent & their skin shriveld up
Lo darkness covers the long pomp of banners on the wind
And black horses & armed men & miserable bound captives
Where shall the graves recieve them all & where shall be their place
And who shall mourn for Mystery who never loosd her Captives

Let the slave grinding at the mill run out into the field
Let him look up into the heavens & laugh in the bright air
20   Let the inchaind soul shut up in darkness & in sighing
Whose face has never seen a smile in thirty weary years
Rise & look out his chains are loose his dungeon doors are open
And let his wife & children return from the opressors scourge

They look behind at every step & believe it is a dream°
Are these the Slaves that groand along the streets of Mystery
Where are your bonds & task masters are these the prisoners
Where are your chains where are your tears why do you look around
If you are thirsty there is the river go bathe your parched limbs
The good of all the Land is before you for Mystery is no more

30   Then All the Slaves from every Earth in the wide Universe
Sing a New Song° drowning confusion in its happy notes
While the flail of Urizen sounded loud & the winnowing wind of Tharmas

When . . . Vintage This begins with threshing
and winnowing, for which Blake had no precedent in Revelation, but see Matthew 3:12.
And all . . . husks With some variants this is
used by Yeats as the epigraph to the early group
of lyrics he later called "Crossways."

Mystery the Harlot of Revelation 17
Let the slave . . . dream Ll. 18–24 are repeated from America 6:6–12, but note the enlargement of their power in this more comprehensive context.
New Song See Revelation 5:9.

So loud so clear in the wide heavens & the song that they sung was this
Composed by an African Black from the little Earth of Sotha°

Aha Aha how came I here so soon in my sweet native land
How came I here Methinks I am as I was in my youth

PAGE 135
When in my fathers house I sat & heard his chearing voice
Methinks I see his flocks & herds & feel my limbs renewd
And Lo my Brethren in their tents & their little ones around them

The song arose to the Golden feast the Eternal Man rejoicd
Then the Eternal Man said Luvah the Vintage is ripe° arise
The sons of Urizen shall gather the vintage with sharp hooks
And all thy sons O Luvah bear away the families of Earth
I hear the flail of Urizen his barns are full no roo[m]
Remains & in the Vineyards stand the abounding sheaves beneath
10 The falling Grapes that odorous burst upon the winds. Arise
My flocks & herds trample the Corn my cattle browze upon
The ripe Clusters The shepherds shout for Luvah prince of Love
Let the Bulls of Luvah tread the Corn & draw the loaded waggon
Into the Barn while children glean the Ears around the door
Then shall they lift their innocent hands & stroke his furious nose
And he shall lick the little girls white neck & on her head
Scatter the perfume of his breath while from his mountains high
The lion of terror shall come down & bending his bright mane
And couching at their side shall eat from the curld boys white lap
20 His golden food and in the evening sleep before the Door

Attempting to be more than Man We become less said Luvah
As he arose from the bright feast drunk with the wine of ages
His crown of thorns fell from his head he hung his living Lyre
Behind the seat of the Eternal Man & took his way
Sounding the Song of Los descending to the Vineyards bright
His sons arising from the feast with golden baskets follow
A fiery train as when the Sun sings in the ripe vineyards
Then Luvah stood before the wine press all his fiery sons
Brought up the loaded Waggons with shoutings ramping tygers play
30 In the jingling traces furious lions sound the song of joy
To the golden wheels circling upon the pavement of heaven & all
The Villages of Luvah ring the golden tiles of the villages
Reply to violins & tabors to the pipe flute lyre & cymbal
Then fell the Legions of Mystery in maddning confusion
Down Down thro the immense with outcry fury & despair
Into the wine presses of Luvah° howling fell the Clusters
Of human families thro the deep. the wine presses were filld

Sotha Associated in Blake's poem "Africa" (part of *The Song of Los*) with a code of war; the African is now set free from the code.
Vintage is ripe See Revelation 14:17–19.

wine presses of Luvah see Revelation 14:17–19 again; Blake's Vintage is at once a festival of rebirth, the terror of the Napoleonic Wars, and the self-sacrifice of the natural man.

The blood of life flowd plentiful Odors of life arose
All round the heavenly arches & the Odors rose singing this song

PAGE 136
O terrible wine presses of Luvah O caverns of the Grave
How lovely the delights of those risen again from death
O trembling joy excess of joy is like Excess of grief

So sang the Human Odors round the wine presses of Luvah

But in the Wine presses is wailing terror & despair
Forsaken of their Elements they vanish & are no more
No more but a desire of Being a distracted ravening desire
Desiring like the hungry worm & like the gaping grave
They plunge into the Elements the Elements cast them forth
10   Or else consume their shadowy semblance Yet they obstinate
Tho pained to distraction Cry O let us Exist for
This dreadful Non Existence is worse than pains of Eternal Birth
Eternal Death who can Endure. let us consume in fires
In waters stifling or in air corroding or in earth shut up
The Pangs of Eternal birth are better than the Pangs of Eternal Death

How red the sons & daughters of Luvah how they tread the Grapes
Laughing & shouting drunk with odors many fall oerwearied
Drownd in the wine is many a youth & maiden those around
Lay them on skins of tygers or the spotted Leopard or wild Ass
20   Till they revive or bury them in cool Grots making lamentation

But in the Wine Presses the Human Grapes Sing not nor dance
They howl & writhe in shoals of torment in fierce flames consuming
In chains of iron & in dungeons circled with ceaseless fires
In pits & dens & shades of death in shapes of torment & woe
The Plates the Screws and Racks & Saws & cords & fires & floods
The cruel joy of Luvahs daughters lacerating with knives
And whip[s] their Victims & the deadly sports of Luvahs sons

Timbrels & Violins sport round the Wine Presses The little Seed
The Sportive root the Earthworm the small beetle the wise Emmet
30   Dance round the Wine Presses of Luvah. the Centipede is there
The ground Spider with many Eyes the Mole clothed in Velvet
The Earwig armd the tender maggot emblem of Immortality
The Slow Slug the grasshopper that sings & laughs & drinks
The winter comes he folds his slender bones without a murmur
There is the Nettle that stings with soft down & there
The indignant Thistle whose bitterness is bred in his milk
And who lives on the contempt of his neighbour there all the idle weeds
That creep about the obscure places shew their various limbs
Naked in all their beauty dancing round the Wine Presses
40   They Dance around the Dying & they Drink the howl & groan

PAGE 137

They catch the Shrieks in cups of gold they hand them to one another
These are the sports of love & these the sweet delights of amorous play
Tears of the grapes the death sweat of the Cluster the last sigh
Of the mild youth who listens to the luring songs of Luvah

The Eternal Man darkend with Sorrow & a wintry mantle
Coverd the Hills   He said O Tharmas rise & O Urthona

Then Tharmas & Urthona rose from the Golden feast satiated
With Mirth & Joy Urthona limping from his fall on Tharmas leand°
In his right hand his hammer Tharmas held his Shepherds crook
10   Beset with gold gold were the ornaments formd by sons of Urizen

Then Enion & Ahania & Vala & the wife of Dark Urthona
Rose from the feast in joy ascending to their Golden Looms
There the wingd shuttle Sang the spindle & the distaff & the Reel
Rang sweet the praise of industry. Thro all the golden rooms
Heaven rang with winged Exultation   All beneath howld loud
With tenfold rout & desolation roard the Chasms beneath
Where the wide woof flowd down & where the Nations are gatherd together

Tharmas went down to the Wine presses & beheld the sons & daughters
Of Luvah quite exhausted with the Labour & quite filld
20   With new wine, that they began to torment one another and to tread
The weak. Luvah & Vala slept on the floor o'erwearied

Urthona calld his Sons around him Tharmas calld his sons
Numrous. they took the wine they separated the Lees
And Luvah was put for dung on the ground by the Sons of Tharmas & Urthona
They formed heavens of sweetest wo[o]d[s] of gold & silver & ivory
Of glass & precious stones They loaded all the waggons of heaven
And took away the wine of ages with solemn songs & joy

Luvah & Vala woke & all the sons & daughters of Luvah
Awoke they wept to one another & they reascended
30   To the Eternal Man in woe he cast them wailing into
The world of shadows thro the air till winter is over & gone

But the Human Wine stood wondering in all their delightful Expanses
The Elements subside the heavens rolld on with vocal harmony

Then Los who is Urthona rose in all his regenerate power
The Sea that rolld & foamd with darkness & the shadows of death
Vomited out & gave up all° the floods lift up their hands
Singing & shouting to the Man they bow their hoary heads
And murmuring in their channels flow & circle round his feet

on Tharmas leand Blake wisely qualifies his apocalypse, even in this first and most exuberant of its versions; Urthona, though restored, is still a crippled smith god, though no longer a mere Thor or Vulcan, which means the imagination is not yet wholly healed; by leaning on Tharmas, who is once more the human integral or instinctual wholeness, he finds support and can hope.
The Sea . . . gave up all See Revelation 20:13.

PAGE 138

Then Dark Urthona took the Corn out of the Stores of Urizen
He ground it in his rumbling Mills Terrible the distress
Of all the Nations of Earth ground in the Mills of Urthona
In his hand Tharmas takes the Storms. he turns the whirlwind Loose
Upon the wheels the stormy seas howl at his dread command
And Eddying fierce rejoice in the fierce agitation of the wheels
Of Dark Urthona Thunders Earthquakes Fires Water floods
Rejoice to one another loud their voices shake the Abyss
Their dread forms tending the dire mills The grey hoar frost was there
10   And his pale wife the aged Snow they watch over the fires
They build the Ovens of Urthona Nature in darkness groans°
And Men are bound to sullen contemplations in the night
Restless they turn on beds of sorrow. in their inmost brain
Feeling the crushing Wheels they rise they write the bitter words
Of Stern Philosophy & knead the bread of knowledge with tears & groans

Such are the works of Dark Urthona Tharmas sifted the corn
Urthona made the Bread of Ages & he placed it
In golden & in silver baskets in heavens of precious stone
And then took his repose in Winter in the night of Time°

20   The Sun has left his blackness & has found a fresher morning°
And the mild moon rejoices in the clear & cloudless night
And Man walks forth from midst of the fires the evil is all consumd
His eyes behold the Angelic spheres arising night & day
The stars consumd like a lamp blown out & in their stead behold
The Expanding Eyes of Man behold the depths of wondrous worlds

One Earth one sea beneath nor Erring Globes wander but Stars
Of fire rise up nightly from the Ocean & one Sun
Each morning like a New born Man issues with songs & Joy
Calling the Plowman to his Labour & the Shepherd to his rest
30   He walks upon the Eternal Mountains raising his heavenly voice
Conversing with the Animal forms of wisdom night & day
That risen from the Sea of fire renewd walk oer the Earth

For Tharmas brought his flocks upon the hills & in the Vales
Around the Eternal Mans bright tent the little Children play
Among the wooly flocks The hammer of Urthona sounds
In the deep caves beneath his limbs renewd his Lions roar
Around the Furnaces & in Evening sport upon the plains
They raise their faces from the Earth conversing with the Man

How is it we have walkd thro fires & yet are not consumd
40   How is it that all things are changd even as in ancient times

---

Nature in darkness groans For a last time, we are back in the nightmare of history.
Winter in the night of Time the moment poised just before breakthrough

The Sun . . . morning Apocalypse proper begins with this line.

PAGE 139

The Sun arises from his dewy bed & the fresh airs
Play in his smiling beams giving the seeds of life to grow
And the fresh Earth beams forth ten thousand thousand springs of life
Urthona is arisen in his strength no longer now
Divided from Enitharmon no longer the Spectre Los
Where is the Spectre of Prophecy° where the delusive Phantom
Departed & Urthona rises from the ruinous walls
In all his ancient strength to form the golden armour of science
For intellectual War The war of swords departed now

10   The dark Religions are departed & sweet Science reigns°
          END OF THE DREAM

1796–1807?   1893

Milton

Though Blake may have worked at revising *The Four Zoas* as late as 1807, he seems
to have chosen to write a poem or poems to replace it as early as 1800. Some version
of *Milton* existed by 1803, but revision presumably continued until the etching of
the plates in 1809–10 (I am following David Erdman's datings). *Milton* is a deliberately
foreshortened or "brief" epic, on the model of John Milton's *Paradise Regained*, which
itself took the Book of Job as a thematic model.

Both *Paradise Regained* and the Book of Job justify God's ways through dramatic
dialogues, but Blake's *Milton* is a more internalized and autobiographical work, though
the self-portrayal has little to do with either personality or character. Blake is his
own Job, and overcomes a personal Satan by following the example of his great precursor, Milton. The most original element in Blake's poem is that his precursor is the
poem's Sublime hero, not just a moral guide like Virgil in Dante's *Comedy*, or a dark
parody of such a guide like Rousseau in Shelley's *The Triumph of Life*. Discontented
with the extraordinary mythopoeic rival to *Paradise Lost* that he had attempted in *The
Four Zoas,* Blake turned to the spiritual form of John Milton to serve him as an
epic hero. The audacity of such a procedure is astonishing; try to conceive of *Browning: a Poem in 2 Books* by Ezra Pound, or an *Eliot Agonistes* by Robert Lowell. Blake's
success was proportionate to his audacity and, genius aside, can be tracked to his
own enormous need of the work, which is as much a crisis poem as Wordsworth's
The Prelude, but also to Blake's profound and intense relation to John Milton.

Blake's crisis took place at Felpham village in Sussex where he lived from 1800
to 1803 under the patronage of the wealthy William Hayley, minor poet and
biographer of William Cowper. The crisis was double, in Blake's own sense of his
epic vocation, and in an accusation of treason against him made by a soldier named
Schofield. The treason accusation and subsequent trial (Blake was acquitted) play their
part in *Jerusalem;* the crisis in poetic self-confidence is the hidden subject of
Milton, particularly of the first part of Book I of the poem, a "Bard's Song," which
appears to be grounded in a quarrel about Blake's work as artist and poet that occurred between Blake and Hayley. Menaced by these outer circumstances, and by

Spectre of Prophecy Los, as opposed to Urthona, the Zoa of Prophecy
sweet Science reigns not the science of the
deists and empiricists but the totally organized
imaginative knowledge attainable only through
the experience of art

inner doubts, Blake turned to a purgatorial theme of temptation and endurance, and to Milton as a kind of savior.

Yet Blake, from *The Marriage of Heaven and Hell* onward, had sought not only to weather Milton's influence upon him, but to swerve away from Milton by creatively "correcting" his Sublime precursor. Blake's Milton is therefore a marvelously complex figure, and the selections that follow have been chosen to reveal this complexity.

From Milton

a Poem in 2 Books

The Author & Printer W Blake 1804

To Justify the Ways of God to Men°

PLATE 1

Preface

The Stolen and Perverted Writings of Homer & Ovid: of Plato & Cicero. which all Men ought to contemn:° are set up by artifice against the Sublime of the Bible. but when the New Age is at leisure to Pronounce: all will be set right: & those Grand Works of the more ancient & consciously & professedly Inspired Men, will hold their proper rank, & the Daughters of Memory shall become the Daughters of Inspiration. Shakspeare & Milton were both curbd by the general malady & infection from the silly Greek & Latin slaves of the Sword.

Rouze up O Young Men of the New Age! set your foreheads against the ignorant Hirelings! For we have Hirelings in the Camp, the Court & the University: who would if they could, for ever depress Mental & prolong Corporeal War. Painters! on you I call! Sculptors! Architects! Suffer not the fash[i]onable Fools to depress your powers by the prices they pretend to give for contemptible works or the expensive advertizing boasts that they make of such works; believe Christ & his Apostles that there is a Class of Men whose whole delight is in Destroying. We do not want either Greek or Roman Models if we are but just & true to our own Imaginations, those Worlds of Eternity in which we shall live for ever; in Jesus our Lord.

> And did those feet in ancient time.
> Walk upon Englands mountains green:
> And was the holy Lamb of God,
> On Englands pleasant pastures seen!

> And did the Countenance Divine,
> Shine forth upon our clouded hills?
> And was Jerusalem builded here,
> Among these dark Satanic Mills?°

To Justify . . . Men See *Paradise Lost* I.26.
The Stolen . . . contemn See Milton's *Paradise Regained* IV.331–64, where Jesus sets the Hebrew Scriptures over Greek literature, asserting "that rather Greece from us these Arts derived; / Ill imitated."

dark Satanic Mills These are not industrial mills, but mills of the mind; see *Milton* 4:2–3, "where the Starry Mills of Satan / Are built beneath the Earth and Waters," hardly locations for industry.

10
Bring me my Bow of burning gold:
Bring me my Arrows of desire:
Bring me my Spear: O clouds unfold!
Bring me my Chariot of fire!°

I will not cease from Mental Fight,
Nor shall my Sword sleep in my hand:
Till we have built Jerusalem,
In Englands green & pleasant Land.

Would to God that all the Lords people were Prophets.°

Numbers XI. ch 29 v.

PLATE 14
[Milton's Descent°]
10 Then Milton rose up from the heavens of Albion ardorous!°
The whole Assembly wept prophetic, seeing in Miltons face
And in his lineaments divine the shades of Death & Ulro°
He took off the robe of the promise, & ungirded himself from the oath of God

And Milton said, I go to Eternal Death!° The Nations still
Follow after the detestable Gods of Priam;° in pomp
Of warlike selfhood, contradicting and blaspheming.
When will the Resurrection come; to deliver the sleeping body
From corruptibility: O when Lord Jesus wilt thou come?
Tarry no longer; for my soul lies at the gates of death.
20 I will arise and look forth for the morning of the grave.°
I will go down to the sepulcher to see if morning breaks!
I will go down to self annihilation and eternal death,
Lest the Last Judgment come & find me unannihilate
And I be siez'd & giv'n into the hands of my own Selfhood.
The Lamb of God is seen thro' mists & shadows, hov'ring
Over the sepulchers in clouds of Jehovah & winds of Elohim°
A disk of blood, distant; & heav'ns & earth's roll dark between
What do I here before the Judgment? without my Emanation?

Chariot of fire a reference to the vision of Milton in Thomas Gray's Pindaric ode "The Progress of Poesy"
Would . . . Prophets a reproof of Moses to
Joshua, who urged the Lawgiver to silence "un-
authorized" prophets
Milton's Descent These passages are all from
Book I of the poem, the plate and line numbers
being 14:10–17:20, 18:51–19:14, 20:7–21:14.
Then . . . ardorous Unhappy in his own
Heaven, Milton has just heard the Bard's Song,
which turns upon the imaginative realization
that Pity and Love are part of the Human Abstract, and not of the Divine Vision. His poetic
ardor reawakened, he is weary of an unimaginative heaven where he has nothing to do but
walk about "pondring the intricate mazes of
Providence," in parody of his own Fallen Angels. His rising up means that he has decided
to go down from Eternity into time, not as a

mere Mental Traveller, but as the prophet armed
that he was in his heroic life.
Death and Ulro that is, he will descend into
their world, giving up immortality and Eden
Eternal Death our life, from the perspective of
Eternity
Gods of Priam Priam was king of Troy, father
of Hector; in his "Descriptive Catalogue" Blake
said of the "gods of Priam" that they were
"destructive to humanity." Blake's Milton's reference here is to the invocation to Book IX of
Paradise Lost, which attempts to change the
theme of epic from warfare to heroic martyrdom.
But the nations of Europe, England included,
have failed to learn Milton's lesson.
I will . . . grave Milton renews the role of
the disciples who watched at the sepulcher.
The Lamb . . . Elohim Neither clouds nor
winds are anything but negative, natural emblems for Blake, and both serve here to obscure
the Lamb of God.

With the daughters of memory, & not with the daughters of inspiration[?]°
30 I in my Selfhood am that Satan: I am that Evil One!
He is my Spectre! in my obedience to loose him from my Hells
To claim the Hells, my Furnaces,° I go to Eternal Death.
And Milton said. I go to Eternal Death! Eternity shudder'd
For he took the outside course, among the graves of the dead
A mournful shade. Eternity shudderd at the image of eternal death

Then on the verge of Beulah he beheld his own Shadow;
A mournful form double; hermaphroditic: male & female
In one wonderful body. and he enterd into it
In direful pain for the dread shadow, twenty-seven-fold°
40 Reachd to the depths of direst Hell, & thence to Albions land:
Which is this earth of vegetation on which now I write.

The Seven Angels of the Presence° wept over Miltons Shadow!

PLATE 15
As when a man dreams, he reflects not that his body sleeps,
Else he would wake; so seem'd he entering his Shadow: but
With him the Spirits of the Seven Angels of the Presence
Entering; they gave him still perceptions of his Sleeping Body;
Which now arose and walk'd with them in Eden, as an Eighth
Image Divine tho' darken'd; and tho walking as one walks
In sleep; and the Seven comforted and supported him.°

Like as a Polypus° that vegetates beneath the deep!
They saw his Shadow vegetated underneath the Couch
10 Of death: for when he enterd into his Shadow: Himself:
His real and immortal Self: was as appeard to those
Who dwell in immortality, as One sleeping on a couch
Of gold; and those in immortality gave forth their Emanations
Like Females of sweet beauty, to guard round him & to feed
His lips with food of Eden in his cold and dim repose!
But to himself he seemd a wanderer lost in dreary night.

Onwards his Shadow kept its course among the Spectres; call'd
Satan, but swift as lightning passing them, startled the shades

With . . . inspiration See this distinction in
the Preface to the poem; it was implicit already in the boyish "To the Muses."
the Hells, my Furnaces The furnace is the creative mind, going back to Hebrew prophetic
imagery, particularly Daniel 3:19–26; see also
the remarkable "the furnace shall come up at
last" in Christopher Smart's *Jubilate Agno;*
Milton here undoes the "errors" of *Paradise
Lost* and goes to reclaim his cast-out energies
of desire.
twenty-seven-fold The shadow of the cycles of
history; they moved in a lunar twenty-eight-
phase sequence, called Churches by Blake, but
the twenty-eighth is Apocalypse and so does not
belong to the shadow.

The Seven . . . Presence Opposed to the spectral cycle of the Churches are the Seven Angels
or Eyes of God, who impose prophetic order
upon fallen history; they weep because Milton
is re-entering the nightmare of history.
As when . . . supported him Though Milton
goes down into illusion, his spiritual body joins
the Seven Angels as an Eighth walker in Eden
(thus associating Milton's self-sacrifice with
that of Jesus) even as his material body sleep-
walks first in Beulah and then in Generation.
Polypus Greek name for hydra or water snake;
Ovidian emblem of materiality or natural existence

Of Hell beheld him in a trail of light as of a comet
20   That travels into Chaos:° so Milton went guarded within.

The nature of infinity is this: That every thing has its
Own Vortex;° and when once a traveller thro' Eternity
Has passd that Vortex, he percieves it roll backward behind
His path, into a globe itself infolding; like a sun:
Or like a moon, or like a universe of starry majesty,
While he keeps onwards in his wondrous journey on the earth
Or like a human form, a friend with whom he livd benevolent.
As the eye of man views both the east & west encompassing
Its vortex; and the north & south, with all their starry host;
30   Also the rising sun & setting moon he views surrounding
His corn-fields and his valleys of five hundred acres square.
Thus is the earth one infinite plane, and not as apparent
To the weak traveller confin'd beneath the moony shade.
Thus is the heaven a vortex passd already, and the earth
A vortex not yet pass'd by the traveller thro' Eternity.

First Milton saw Albion upon the Rock of Ages,°
Deadly pale outstretchd and snowy cold, storm coverd;
A Giant form of perfect beauty outstretchd on the rock
In solemn death: the Sea of Time & Space thunderd aloud
40   Against the rock, which was inwrapped with the weeds of death
Hovering over the cold bosom, in its vortex Milton bent down
To the bosom of death, what was underneath soon seemd above.°
A cloudy heaven mingled with stormy seas in loudest ruin;
But as a wintry globe descends precipitant thro' Beulah bursting,
With thunders loud, and terrible: so Miltons shadow fell,
Precipitant loud thundring into the Sea of Time & Space.

Then first I saw him in the Zenith as a falling star,
Descending perpendicular, swift as the swallow or swift;°
And on my left foot falling on the tarsus,° enterd there;
50   But from my left foot a black cloud° redounding spread over Europe.

Onwards . . . Chaos Coming down through
the Shadow, Milton seems to be a comet, ironically suggesting the fall of his own Satan.
The nature . . . Vortex A difficult and powerful conceptual image, probably a bitter parody
of the materialist theory of perception of Descartes. The vortex is the whirlpool or eddy of
unfallen consciousness. At its center is any object that unfallen consciousness sees and so creates. Since, in unfallen vision, center and circumference are one, the eternal perceiver is
simultaneously at the apex of his own vision,
and yet able to regard it from a distance. But
Milton, passing into Beulah, forsakes eternity for
time, and so becomes the apex of his own
vision. This objectifies him, and the eternal circumference of his vision rolls up behind him,
solidifying into the globed universe of Newto-
nian and Cartesian perception. But, even in
time, Milton retains his imagination, and can
achieve an approximation of eternal perception
by seeing the object world as human (l. 27)
and so encompass his vortex.

Rock of Ages not in Blake a reference to Matthew 16:18, but the rocky shore that is the
physical universe
Hovering . . . above Milton, emerging into
time and space, sees Man as a fallen giant,
Albion, and enters Albion's heart, again passing
through an apex of vision; he discovers that
fallen Urizen ("cloudy heaven") and fallen
Tharmas ("stormy seas") have usurped that
heart, excluding Orc and Los. The "vortex"
Milton has invaded rolls up behind him, forming a falling globe, again resembling the falling
Satan. Milton will enter Blake by the "left
foot," thus provisionally changing Blake's prophetic stance.
swift a bird outwardly resembling a swallow;
noted for quickness
tarsus The ankle: but there is a pun on Saul of
Tarsus, who became St. Paul.
black cloud Foster Damon identified this as
Puritanism.

Then Milton knew that the Three Heavens of Beulah° were beheld
By him on earth in his bright pilgrimage of sixty years

PLATE 16

PLATE 17
In those three females whom his Wives, & those three whom his Daughters°
Had represented and containd, that they might be resum'd
By giving up of Selfhood: & they distant view'd his journey
In their eternal spheres, now Human, tho' their Bodies remain clos'd
In the dark Ulro till the Judgment: also Milton knew: they and
Himself was Human, tho' now wandering thro Death's Vale
In conflict with those Female forms, which in blood & jealousy
Surrounded him, dividing & uniting without end or number.

He saw the Cruelties of Ulro, and he wrote them down
10 In iron tablets: and his Wives & Daughters names were these
Rahab and Tirzah, & Milcah & Malah & Noah & Hoglah.°
They sat rang'd round him as the rocks of Horeb round the land
Of Canaan:° and they wrote in thunder smoke and fire
His dictate; and his body was the Rock Sinai; that body,
Which was on earth born to corruption: & the six Females
Are Hor & Peor & Bashan & Abarim & Lebanon & Hermon
Seven rocky masses terrible in the Desarts of Midian.°

But Miltons Human Shadow continu'd journeying above
The rocky masses of The Mundane Shell;° in the Lands
20 Of Edom & Aram & Moab & Midian & Amalek.°

. . .

PLATE 18
Urizen emerged from his Rocky Form & from his Snows,

PLATE 19
And he also darkend his brows: freezing dark rocks between
The footsteps. and infixing deep the feet in marble beds:
That Milton labourd with his journey, & his feet bled sore

Three . . . Beulah threefold or sexual vision, hence limited

In . . . Daughters Milton had three wives and three daughters; Blake accepted the bad tradition that Milton lived unhappily with all of them.

Rahab . . . Hoglah Rahab is chief of Milton's emanations; the other wives and daughters were the daughters of the sonless Zelophehad (Numbers 26:33) for whom Moses (reluctantly) legislated a separate female inheritance; Blake interprets this to mean that Milton yielded to his Female Will, with the destructive Rahab presiding over his five fallen senses.

They sat . . . Canaan This is an extraordinary vision of Milton (who by tradition dictated his major poems to his daughters) serving as the

Rock Sinai and dictating the Law to six lesser masses of rock; though this is austerely sublime, it is also satirical.

Hor . . . Midian These are all biblical mountains or high regions; in a burst of visionary geography, Blake places them in the Midian desert, thus associating Milton's errors with the symbolic desert-wanderings of Moses and of Christ in the Temptation.

Mundane Shell the fallen world, in its most illusory aspect, hence merely mundane and, even more merely, a shell

Edom . . . Amalek These are all lands that opposed the Israelites; Blake associates them with Urizen's Mundane Shell, the twenty-seven natural religions, each with its own absurd Heaven and demonic Hell.

Upon the clay now changd to marble; also Urizen rose,
And met him on the shores of Arnon;° & by the streams of the brooks

Silent they met, and silent strove among the streams, of Arnon
Even to Mahanaim,° when with cold hand Urizen stoop'd down
And took up water from the river Jordan: pouring on
To Miltons brain the icy fluid from his broad cold palm.°
10   But Milton took of the red clay of Succoth,° moulding it with care
Between his palms; and filling up the furrows of many years
Beginning at the feet of Urizen, and on the bones
Creating new flesh on the Demon cold, and building him,
As with new clay a Human form in the Valley of Beth Peor.°

. . . .

PLATE 20

. . . Silent Milton stood before
The darkend Urizen; as the sculptor silent stands before
His forming image; he walks round it patient labouring.
10   Thus Milton stood forming bright Urizen, while his Mortal part
Sat frozen in the rock of Horeb: and his Redeemed portion,
Thus form'd the Clay of Urizen; but within that portion
His real Human walkd above in power and majesty
Tho darkend; and the Seven Angels of the Presence attended him.

O how can I with my gross tongue that cleaveth to the dust,
Tell of the Four-fold Man,° in starry numbers fitly orderd
Or how can I with my cold hand of clay! But thou O Lord
Do with me as thou wilt! for I am nothing, and vanity.
If thou chuse to elect a worm, it shall remove the mountains.
20   For that portion namd the Elect:° the Spectrous body of Milton:
Redounding from my left foot into Los's Mundane space,
Brooded over his Body in Horeb against the Resurrection
Preparing it for the Great Consummation;° red the Cherub° on Sinai
Glow'd; but in terrors folded round his clouds of blood.

Now Albions sleeping Humanity began to turn upon his Couch;
Feeling the electric flame of Miltons awful precipitate descent.

Arnon The Arnon river divides the trans-Jordan lands of Israel from Moab; in Numbers 21:14, the Arnon is associated with the Red Sea, and is therefore a River of Error; crossing it, or the Red Sea, is thus a movement from death to life, Moab to Canaan, Urizen to Luvah-Christ. Later in this poem (Plate 38) and in *Jerusalem* 89:25 the Arnon is identified with possessive natural love or the Selfhood's murderous jealousy, the two being the same for Blake. In this passage, Urizen fails to stop Milton by transforming the clay Adamic earth into purgatorial marble, and so Urizen is forced to wrestle Milton, even as Jehovah wrestled Jacob. But Milton is the New Israel, and instead of seeking Urizen's blessing, labors to remake Urizen-Jehovah, and so humanize him.

Mahanaim See Genesis 32:1–2; this is the place where Jacob meets the angels of God.
And took . . . palm a parody of baptism
Succoth See Kings 7:46 and Genesis 33:17.
Beth Peor the burial place of Moses; see Deuteronomy 34:6
Four-fold Man unfallen Albion, both Man and God
Elect Used sardonically; the Elect are the Angels or time-serving orthodox; the Reprobate are the Devils or imaginative rebels; the Redeemed are everyone else, and ironically their name means that they require redemption.
Great Consummation Apocalypse
Cherub the Covering Cherub, in Blake's symbolism the fallen Tharmas; see Genesis 3:24 and, more crucially, Ezekiel 28:14–16

Seest thou the little winged fly, smaller than a grain of sand?
It has a heart like thee; a brain open to heaven & hell,
Withinside wondrous & expansive; its gates are not clos'd,
30 I hope thine are not: hence it clothes itself in rich array;
Hence thou art cloth'd with human beauty O thou mortal man.
Seek not thy heavenly father then beyond the skies:
There Chaos dwells & ancient Night & Og & Anak° old:
For every human heart has gates of brass & bars of adamant,
Which few dare unbar because dread Og & Anak guard the gates
Terrific! and each mortal brain is walld and moated round
Within: and Og & Anak watch here; here is the Seat
Of Satan in its Webs; for in brain and heart and loins
Gates open behind Satans Seat to the City of Golgonooza°
40 Which is the spiritual fourfold London, in the loins of Albion.

Thus Milton fell thro Albions heart, travelling outside of Humanity
Beyond the Stars in Chaos in Caverns of the Mundane Shell.
But many of the Eternals rose up from eternal tables
Drunk with the Spirit, burning round the Couch of death they stood
Looking down into Beulah: wrathful, fill'd with rage!
They rend the heavens round the Watchers in a fiery circle:
And round the Shadowy Eighth: the Eight close up the Couch
Into a tabernacle, and flee with cries down to the Deeps:
Where Los opens his three wide gates, surrounded by raging fires!
50 They soon find their own place & join the Watchers of the Ulro.

Los saw them and a cold pale horror coverd o'er his limbs
Pondering he knew that Rintrah & Palamabron° might depart:
Even as Reuben & as Gad;° gave up himself to tears.
He sat down on his anvil-stock; and leand upon the trough.
Looking into the black water, mingling it with tears.

At last when desperation almost tore his heart in twain
He recollected an old Prophecy in Eden recorded,
And often sung to the loud harp at the immortal feasts
That Milton of the Land of Albion should up ascend
60 Forwards from Ulro from the Vale of Felpham; and set free
Orc from his Chain of Jealousy, he started at the thought

PLATE 21
And down descended into Udan-Adan;° it was night:
And Satan sat sleeping upon his Couch in Udan-Adan:
His Spectre slept, his Shadow woke; when one sleeps th'other wakes.

Og & Anak giants who opposed the Israelites; see Numbers 21:33 and Joshua 11:21
Golgonooza Blake's New Jerusalem of Art or, as he will call it, the "spiritual fourfold London"; very roughly akin to Spenser's Cleopolis, which, however, is an earthly city only
Rintrah & Palamabron sons of Los. Rintrah is the angry "Science of Wrath"; Palamabron the gentle "Science of Pity": both are, or should be, civilizing forces.
Reuben . . . Gad sons of Jacob; see Joshua 22: 9–34. This seems a later attempt by Blake to integrate Milton into the denser biblical symbolism of Jerusalem.
Udan-Adan world of illusive appearances

But Milton entering my Foot; I saw in the nether
Regions of the Imagination; also all men on Earth,
And all in Heaven, saw in the nether regions of the Imagination
In Ulro beneath Beulah, the vast breach of Miltons descent.
But I knew not that it was Milton, for man cannot know
What passes in his members till periods of Space & Time
10   Reveal the secrets of Eternity: for more extensive
Than any other earthly things, are Mans earthly lineaments.

And all this Vegetable World appeard on my left Foot,
As a bright sandal formd immortal of precious stones & gold:
I stooped down & bound it on to walk forward thro' Eternity.°

PLATE 28

      [The World of Los]
But others of the Sons of Los build Moments & Minutes & Hours
And Days & Months & Years & Ages & Periods; wondrous buildings
And every Moment has a Couch of gold for soft repose,
 (A Moment equals a pulsation of the artery)°
And between every two Moments stands a Daughter of Beulah
To feed the Sleepers on their Couches with maternal care.
50   And every Minute has an azure Tent with Silken Veils.
And every Hour has a bright golden Gate carved with skill.
And every Day & Night, has Walls of brass & Gates of adamant,
Shining like precious stones & ornamented with appropriate signs:
And every Month, a silver paved Terrace builded high:
And every Year, invulnerable Barriers with high Towers.
And every Age is Moated deep with Bridges of silver & gold:
And every Seven Ages is Incircled with a Flaming Fire.
Now Seven Ages is amounting to Two Hundred Years
Each has its Guard. each Moment Minute Hour Day Month & Year.
60   All are the work of Fairy hands of the Four Elements
The Guard are Angels of Providence on duty evermore
Every Time less than a pulsation of the artery
Is equal in its period & value to Six Thousand Years.°

PLATE 29
For in this Period the Poets Work is Done: and all the Great
Events of Time start forth & are concievd in such a Period
Within a Moment: a Pulsation of the Artery.

The Sky is an immortal Tent built by the Sons of Los°
And every Space that a Man views around his dwelling-place:

I stooped . . . thro' Eternity a crucial moment,
for in it Blake and Milton become one poet
But others . . . artery Book I of *Milton* ends
with one of Blake's very rare positive (though
qualified) visions of Experience as being in its
best sense the creation of Los and his children;
this passage is a saving vision of time as the
mercy of Eternity *through* the poet's work,

which takes place *in* time, but in its smallest
indivisible unity—the pulsation of an artery.
Six Thousand Years Blake's notion of the historical span between Creation and Apocalypse
The Sky . . . Los The sky is a tent just as
the Israelites moved their tents in their God-
directed wanderings back to their own land.
We move our sky as our divine imagination de-

Standing on his own roof, or in his garden on a mount
Of twenty-five cubits° in height, such space is his Universe;
And on its verge the Sun rises & sets. the Clouds bow
To meet the flat Earth & the Sea in such an orderd Space:
10   The Starry heavens reach no further but here bend and set
On all sides & the two Poles turn on their valves of gold:
And if he move his dwelling-place, his heavens also move.
Wher'eer he goes & all his neighbourhood bewail his loss:
Such are the Spaces called Earth & such its dimension:
As to that false appearance which appears to the reasoner,
As of a Globe rolling thro Voidness, it is a delusion of Ulro
The Microscope knows not of this nor the Telescope. they alter
The ratio of the Spectators Organs but leave Objects untouchd
For every Space larger than a red Globule of Mans blood.
20   Is visionary: and is created by the Hammer of Los
And every Space smaller than a Globule of Mans blood. opens
Into Eternity of which this vegetable Earth is but a shadow:
The red Globule is the unwearied Sun by Los created
To measure Time and Space to mortal Men every morning.

. . .

The Vision of Beulah

This opens Book II of *Milton* and is Blake's most extensive single account of what he called "lower paradise," organized Innocence, the sexual state at its most favorable, and his culmination of pastoral convention. Blake's prime sources for his Beulah were Isaiah and John Bunyan. Isaiah 62:4 reads:

> Thou shalt no more be termed Forsaken; neither shall thy land any more be termed Desolate; but thou shalt be called Hephzibah, and thy land Beulah; for the Lord delighteth in thee, and thy land shall be married.

Bunyan's *The Pilgrim's Progress* reads (with reference to the Song of Solomon 2:10–12, as well as to Isaiah 62:4–12):

> Now I saw in my Dream, that by this time the Pilgrims were got over the Inchanted Ground, and entering into the Country of *Beulah*, whose Air was very sweet and pleasant, the way lying directly through it, they solaced themselves there for a season. . . . Here they were within sight of the City they were going to. . . . For in this Land the shining Ones commonly walked, because it was upon the Borders of Heaven. In this Land also the contract between the Bride and the Bridegroom was renewed. . . .

---

sires, and see as we create. Each loss of a human being literally diminishes the heavens, for all empirical observation is a delusion or an ultimate error, since space as well as time is visionary (*not* subjective). The only irreducibles are the Minute Particulars, the red globule of human blood that is true space, and the pulsation's artery that is true time. To go beyond these, or to reduce them, we would need to open into Eternity, beyond space and time. Finally, the Minute Particulars themselves are the creations of Los, invisible suns within us giving out the pure flame that is life.

cubits A cubit was 18 to 22 inches; 25 cubits comes to about 40 feet, evidently about as high a merely natural aggregate as Blake was willing to tolerate.

Book II of *Milton* centers on the self-purgations of Milton and Ololon, his composite Emanation, and their recovery of Innocence. It begins therefore in Beulah, as that state requires purgation from its own ambiguities. Beulah, for all its attractions, is relatively static, and represents the threefold sexual, and not the fourfold or wholly human. All contraries are equally true in it, and since progression is only by the strife of contraries, *human* existence is not possible in Beulah. In one of Blake's hardest paradoxes, taking us back to the early *Songs,* Beulah is both a higher and a lower state than Generation.

In this passage, Beulah is the loving Mother Nature, but only to its own proper dwellers, its unregenerated Daughters. To the Sons of Eden, like Milton, it can only be a rest.

PLATE 30

[The Vision of Beulah]

There is a place where Contrarieties are equally True
This place is called Beulah, It is a pleasant lovely Shadow
Where no dispute can come. Because of those who Sleep.
Into this place the Sons & Daughters of Ololon° descended
With solemn mourning, into Beulahs moony shades & hills
Weeping for Milton: mute wonder held the Daughters of Beulah
Enraptur'd with affection sweet and mild benevolence

Beulah is evermore Created around Eternity; appearing
To the Inhabitants of Eden, around them on all sides.
10   But Beulah to its Inhabitants appears within each district
As the beloved infant in his mothers bosom round incircled
With arms of love & pity & sweet compassion. But to
The Sons of Eden the moony habitations of Beulah,
Are from Great Eternity a mild & pleasant Rest.

And it is thus Created. Lo the Eternal Great Humanity°
To whom be Glory & Dominion Evermore Amen
Walks among all his awful Family seen in every face
As the breath of the Almighty. such are the words of man to man
In the great Wars of Eternity, in fury of Poetic Inspiration,
20   To build the Universe stupendous: Mental forms Creating

But the Emanations trembled exceedingly, nor could they
Live, because the life of Man was too exceeding unbounded
His joy became terrible to them, they trembled & wept
Crying with one voice. Give us a habitation & a place
In which we may be hidden under the shadow of wings°
For if we who are but for a time, & who pass away in winter

Ololon Sometimes an individual, sometimes a host, she is the goal of Milton's quest, and ironically descends to seek him even as he descends after her, as evidently no one gets to meet a bride or husband of the imagination in Heaven (where the orthodox, after all, say there is no giving or taking in marriage); her name stems from a Greek word for the lamenting out-cry of women to the gods (see the English "ululate").

the Eternal Great Humanity Blake's God

shadow of wings The reference is to the caduceus or winged staff of Hermes; see the commentary of George Sandys to his translation of Ovid's *Metamorphoses* II.

Behold these wonders of Eternity we shall consume
But you O our Fathers & Brothers, remain in Eternity
But grant us a Temporal Habitation. do you speak
30   To us; we will obey your words as you obey Jesus
The Eternal who is blessed for ever & ever. Amen

So spake the lovely Emanations; & there appeard a pleasant
Mild Shadow above: beneath: & on all sides round,

PLATE 31
Into this pleasant Shadow all the weak & weary
Like Women & Children were taken away as on wings
Of dovelike softness, & shadowy habitations prepared for them
But every Man returnd & went still going forward thro'
The Bosom of the Father in Eternity on Eternity
Neither did any lack or fall into Error without
A Shadow to repose in all the Days of Happy Eternity

Into this pleasant Shadow Beulah, all Ololon descended
And when the Daughters of Beulah heard the lamentation
10   All Beulah wept, for they saw the Lord coming in the Clouds.
And the Shadows of Beulah terminate in rocky Albion.
And all Nations wept in affliction Family by Family
Germany wept towards France & Italy: England wept & trembled
Towards America: India rose up from his golden bed:
As one awakend in the night: they saw the Lord coming
In the Clouds of Ololon with Power & Great Glory!

And all the Living Creatures of the Four Elements, wail'd
With bitter wailing: these in the aggregate are named Satan
And Rahab: they know not of Regeneration, but only of Generation
20   The Fairies, Nymphs, Gnomes & Genii of the Four Elements
Unforgiving & unalterable: these cannot be Regenerated
But must be Created, for they know only of Generation
These are the Gods of the Kingdoms of the Earth: in contrarious
And cruel opposition: Element against Element, opposed in War
Not Mental, as the Wars of Eternity, but a Corporeal Strife
In Los's Halls continual labouring in the Furnaces of Golgonooza
Orc howls on the Atlantic: Enitharmon trembles: All Beulah weeps

Thou hearest the Nightingale begin the Song of Spring;°
The Lark sitting upon his earthy bed: just as the morn
30   Appears; listens silent; then springing from the waving Corn-field! loud

Song of Spring This is an expression of the glory of Beulah as seen from the standpoint of Generation, for in Generation any song of Beulah must be a Song of Spring (like Solomon's Song) just as in Eden the songs of Beulah would mean Autumn, while a song of Generation would seem like Spring. Since the "Thou" addressed in this lyric is generative man, ourselves, the poem's subtle beauty depends on the paradox that a lamentation of Beulah sounds to us, necessarily, as a Song of Spring. The Daughters of Beulah (Blake's Muses, insofar as he would tolerate them, but not very brilliant girls) lament the descent of Ololon from Eden through Beulah to Generation. But their tears are spring rain to us, for to us *any* song of the Earthly Paradise seems happy. Blake knew better.

He leads the Choir of Day! trill, trill, trill, trill,
Mounting upon the wings of light into the Great Expanse:
Reecchoing against the lovely blue & shining heavenly Shell:
His little throat labours with inspiration; every feather
On throat & breast & wings vibrates with the effluence Divine
All Nature listens silent to him & the awful Sun
Stands still upon the Mountain looking on this little Bird
With eyes of soft humility, & wonder love & awe.
Then loud from their green covert all the Birds begin their Song
40   The Thrush, the Linnet & the Goldfinch, Robin & the Wren
Awake the Sun from his sweet reverie upon the Mountain:
The Nightingale again assays his song, & thro the day,
And thro the night warbles luxuriant; every Bird of Song
Attending his loud harmony with admiration & love.
This is a Vision of the lamentation of Beulah over Ololon!

Thou percievest the Flowers put forth their precious Odours!
And none can tell how from so small a center comes such sweets
Forgetting that within that Center Eternity expands
Its ever during doors, that Og & Anak fiercely guard[.]
50   First eer the morning breaks joy opens in the flowery bosoms
Joy even to tears, which the Sun rising dries; first the Wild Thyme°
And Meadow-sweet downy & soft waving among the reeds.
Light springing on the air lead the sweet Dance: they wake
The Honeysuckle sleeping on the Oak: the flaunting beauty
Revels along upon the wind; the White-thorn lovely May
Opens her many lovely eyes: listening the Rose still sleeps
None dare to wake her. soon she bursts her crimson curtaind bed
And comes forth in the majestiy of beauty; every Flower:
The Pink, the Jessamine, the Wall-flower, the Carnation
60   The Jonquil, the mild Lilly opes her heavens! every Tree,
And Flower & Herb soon fill the air with an innumerable Dance
Yet all in order sweet & lovely, Men are sick with Love!
Such is a Vision of the lamentation of Beulah over Ololon

PLATE 40
   [Milton's Declaration]
But turning toward Ololon in terrible majesty Milton
Replied.° Obey thou the Words of the Inspired Man
30   All that can be annihilated must be annihilated
That the Children of Jerusalem may be saved from slavery
There is a Negation, & there is a Contrary
The Negation must be destroyd to redeem the Contraries°

Wild Thyme one of Blake's transcendent puns
But . . . Replied This is the poem's great climax, and one of Blake's luminous triumphs of prophetic oratory; Ololon has rejected, as a true poet's loved creation should, natural religion and the Female Will, thus compelling Rahab to

a negative epiphany as the Whore of Revelation; Milton approvingly replies, but urges her to go farther as he now will in self-annihilation.
The Negation . . . Contraries Milton and Ololon must war as creative Contraries in Eden, but these will be the "wars of life."

The Negation is the Spectre; the Reasoning Power in Man
This is a false Body: an Incrustation over my Immortal
Spirit; a Selfhood, which must be put off & annihilated alway
To cleanse the Face of my Spirit by Self-examination.

PLATE 41
To bathe in the Waters of Life; to wash off the Not Human
I come in Self-annihilation & the grandeur of Inspiration
To cast off Rational Demonstration by Faith in the Saviour
To cast off the rotten rags of Memory by Inspiration
To cast off Bacon, Locke & Newton from Albions covering°
To take off his filthy garments, & clothe him with Imagination
To cast aside from Poetry, all that is not Inspiration
That it no longer shall dare to mock with the aspersion of Madness
Cast on the Inspired, by the tame high finisher of paltry Blots,
10 Indefinite, or paltry Rhymes; or paltry Harmonies.
Who creeps into State Government like a catterpiller to destroy
To cast off the idiot Questioner° who is always questioning,
But never capable of answering; who sits with a sly grin
Silent plotting when to question, like a thief in a cave;
Who publishes doubt & calls it knowledge; whose Science is Despair,
Whose pretence to knowledge is Envy, whose whole Science is
To destroy the wisdom of ages to gratify ravenous Envy;
That rages round him like a Wolf day & night without rest
He smiles with condescension; he talks of Benevolence & Virtue
20 And those who act with Benevolence & Virtue, they murder time on time
These are the destroyers of Jerusalem, these are the murderers
Of Jesus, who deny the Faith & mock at Eternal Life!
Who pretend to Poetry that they may destroy Imagination;
By imitation of Natures Images drawn from Remembrance
These are the Sexual Garments, the Abomination of Desolation°
Hiding the Human Lineaments as with an Ark & Curtains
Which Jesus rent:° & now shall wholly purge away with Fire
Till Generation is swallowd up in Regeneration.

·   ·   ·

1800–1809?   1809–10

To cast off . . . covering The imagery of removing false garments goes through the whole
poem; see Yeats's use of this in "Supernatural
Songs."
idiot Questioner the spectre within every man,
Blake included
Abomination of Desolation False or pagan god
placed in the Jerusalem Temple, prototype of
the Antichrist; here, the "Sexual Garments"
meaning what Blake called "Female Love,"
that is, merely natural or selfish, possessive love

as opposed to human love, which Ololon and
Milton now accept; again, this does *not* mean
they are to abandon sexual love-making, a common or vulgar error in much interpretation of
Blake.
Which Jesus rent The "Ark" and "Curtains"
refer to the Holy-of-Holies in the Jerusalem
Temple; Blake means that his Jesus came to
destroy all Mystery, all concealment, as his
heroic Milton has now done, and persuaded
Ololon to do also.

Jerusalem
The Emanation of the Giant Albion

Jerusalem is Blake's definitive poem, his most finished and profound work, but also his most difficult, in form and argument. The three brief excerpts that follow cannot represent it, but are given here because of their own unique values, even ripped from context, and to aid in the apprehension of other Blakean poems and extracts in this volume. The passages in Blake's plate and line numbering are 10:23–65, 45:2–42, 90:67–91:57.

Much of *Jerusalem* turns on a harsh internal conflict between Los-in-Blake and the Spectre of Urthona in Blake, defined as the despair of the imaginative man—and on his own terms he *is always right.* He is a reductionist, who insists always on knowing by knowing the worst, particularly concerning the self and its tribulations with others. His ancestry in Blake's work is complex, but fundamentally he began as a satire upon the poets of Sensibility, a satire all the more moving because it was self-satire, since Blake started as a Bard of Sensibility, and developed into the greatest poet of the group while growing well beyond it. Though we tend now (and rightly, I think) to read and study Blake in the company of other High Romantics, from Wordsworth to Yeats, he himself never lost his passion for William Cowper, who meant more to him than any English poet except Milton; and his deep affinities persisted also with Thomson, Collins, Gray, and Chatterton.

The Spectre of Urthona is not a satire on any particular poet (and certainly least of all on the beloved Cowper) but on a sinister tendency in all men, one to which poets at certain historical moments are peculiarly vulnerable. Yet a particular annotation by Blake is helpful in apprehending the Spectre of Urthona. Reading Spurzheim's *Observations on . . . Insanity,* some time after 1817, Blake jotted down a remarkable observation:

> Cowper came to me and said, o that I were insane always I will never rest. Can you not make me truly insane. I will never rest till I am so. O that in the bosom of God I was hid. You retain health and yet are as mad as any of us all—over us all—mad as a refuge from unbelief—from Bacon, Newton and Locke.

This covers a wide range of Blake's work in its reference, from the early "Mad Song" to the Spectre of Urthona in *Jerusalem.* For the Spectre of Urthona is the anxiety of the imagination itself, fearful that its words can never become deeds, and yet desiring only to continue in that fear. Hating his own separate existence, and yet sensing the danger (and excitation) of every threat that might end separation, the Spectre of Urthona is a personified Dread, and a menace to every one's continued imaginative functioning.

From Jerusalem
The Emanation of the Giant Albion

PLATE 10

[The Spectre of Urthona]

Shuddring the Spectre howls. his howlings terrify the night
He stamps around the Anvil, beating blows of stern despair
He curses Heaven & Earth, Day & Night & Sun & Moon
He curses Forest Spring & River, Desart & sandy Waste
Cities & Nations, Families & Peoples, Tongues & Laws
Driven to desperation by Los's terrors & threatning fears

Los cries, Obey my voice & never deviate from my will
30 And I will be merciful to thee: be thou invisible to all
To whom I make thee invisible, but chief to my own Children°
O Spectre of Urthona: Reason not against their dear approach
Nor them obstruct with thy temptations of doubt & despair[.]
O Shame O strong & mighty Shame I break thy brazen fetters
If thou refuse, thy present torments will seem southern breezes
To what thou shalt endure if thou obey not my great will.

The Spectre answer'd. Art thou not ashamd of those thy Sins
That thou callest thy Children? lo the Law of God commands
That they be offered upon his Altar: O cruelty & torment
40 For thine are also mine! I have kept silent hitherto,
Concerning my chief delight: but thou hast broken silence
Now I will speak my mind! Where is my lovely Enitharmon
O thou my enemy, where is my Great Sin? She is also thine
I said: now is my grief at worst: incapable of being
Surpassed: but every moment it accumulates more & more
It continues accumulating to eternity! the joys of God° advance
For he is Righteous: he is not a Being of Pity & Compassion
He cannot feel Distress: he feeds on Sacrifice & Offering:
Delighting in cries & tears & clothed in holiness & solitude
50 But my griefs advance also, for ever & ever without end
O that I could cease to be! Despair! I am Despair
Created to be the great example of horror & agony: also my
Prayer is vain I called for compassion: compassion mockd[,]
Mercy & pity threw the grave stone over me & with lead
And iron, bound it over me for ever: Life lives on my
Consuming: & the Almighty hath made me his Contrary°
To be all evil, all reversed & for ever dead: knowing

my own **Children** Los's creative acts, but the
Spectre is willing to surrender them, as in relation to any making he is merely a passive instrument, a temporal will opposed to creation.
joys of God The Spectre's God is fallen Urizen,
as the Spectre is the sickness unto death, in despair at the meaninglessness of his own repet-
itive existence, yet dreading to see it end; the

Spectre attacks Los (and of course Blake) cunningly, where any imagination is most vulnerable, in its creative jealousy of its own emanations, its possessive love for what it has made.
his Contrary See Milton's Satan on Mt. Niphates,
Paradise Lost IV.32–113; Spenser's Despair in
The Faerie Queene I.ix is also in the background.

And seeing life, yet living not; how can I then behold
And not tremble; how can I be beheld & not abhorrd

60   So spoke the Spectre shuddring, & dark tears ran down his shadowy face
Which Los wiped off, but comfort none could give! or beam of hope
Yet ceasd he not from labouring at the roarings of his Forge
With iron & brass Building Golgonooza in great contendings
Till his Sons & Daughters came forth from the Furnaces
At the sublime Labours, for Los compelld the invisible Spectre

PLATE 45
   [The Minute Particulars]
Fearing that Albion should turn his back against the Divine Vision
Los took his globe of fire to search the interiors of Albions
Bosom,° in all the terrors of friendship, entering the caves
Of despair & death, to search the tempters out, walking among
Albions rocks & precipices! caves of solitude & dark despair,
And saw every Minute Particular° of Albion degraded & murderd
But saw not by whom; they were hidden within in the minute particulars
Of which they had possessd themselves; and there they take up
10   The articulations of a mans soul, and laughing throw it down
Into the frame, then knock it out upon the plank, & souls are bak'd
In bricks to build the pyramids of Heber & Terah.° But Los
Searchd in vain: closd from the minutia he walkd, difficult.
He came down from Highgate thro Hackney & Holloway towards London
Till he came to old Stratford & thence to Stepney & the Isle
Of Leuthas Dogs, thence thro the narrows of the Rivers side
And saw every minute particular, the jewels of Albion, running down
The kennels of the streets & lanes as if they were abhorrd.
Every Universal Form, was become barren mountains of Moral
20   Virtue:° and every Minute Particular hardend into grains of sand:
And all the tendernesses of the soul cast forth as filth & mire,
Among the winding places of deep contemplation intricate
To where the Tower of London frownd dreadful over Jerusalem:
A building of Luvah builded in Jerusalems eastern gate to be
His secluded Court: thence to Bethlehem where was builded
Dens of despair in the house of bread: enquiring in vain
Of stones and rocks he took his way, for human form was none:
And thus he spoke, looking on Albions City with many tears

Fearing . . . Bosom This introduces a central
passage of the poem, as Los goes within Albion,
questing for evidences of incorruptibility, in
the prophetic faith that he can search out alien
invaders within Albion.
Minute Particular The irreducible individualities
that make up the human; the phrase occurs in
Dr. Johnson's Life of Waller, which Blake had
read.
Heber & Terah Terah was Abraham's father;
Heber was Terah's ancestor, but the name is
also that of the husband of Jael who, in the Song
of Deborah, Judges 5, slays Sisera in his tent.

Blake's immensely grim point is that there are
no alien invaders. The Minute Particulars are
murdered by the Satanic Accusers who are intimate parts of every man, and these Accusers
are like brickmakers who reduce our individual
articulations into the sameness of bricks in the
pyramid of bondage. Since Albion is Israel,
Heber and Terah are his ancestors also, and
Albion, like Sisera, is slain by the Female Will.
Every . . . Virtue a violent protest against
the 18th century's proclivity for making moral
generalizations

What shall I do! what could I do, if I could find these Criminals
30 I could not dare to take vengeance; for all things are so constructed
And builded by the Divine hand, that the sinner shall always escape,
And he who takes vengeance alone is the criminal of Providence;
If I should dare to lay my finger on a grain of sand
In way of vengeance; I punish the already punishd: O whom
Should I pity if I pity not the sinner who is gone astray!
O Albion, if thou takest vengeance; if thou revengest thy wrongs
Thou art for ever lost! What can I do to hinder the Sons
Of Albion from taking vengeance? or how shall I them perswade.
So spoke Los, travelling thro darkness & horrid solitude:
40 And he beheld Jerusalem in Westminster & Marybone,
Among the ruins of the Temple: and Vala who is her Shadow,
Jerusalems Shadow bent northward over the Island white.

PLATE 90
    [The Declaration of Los]

67 But still the thunder of Los peals loud & thus the thunder's cry°
These beautiful Witchcrafts of Albion are gratifyd by Cruelty

PLATE 91
It is easier to forgive an Enemy than to forgive a Friend:
The man who permits you to injure him, deserves your vengeance:°
He also will recieve it; go Spectre! obey my most secret desire:
Which thou knowest without my speaking: Go to these Fiends of Righteousness
Tell them to obey their Humanities, & not pretend Holiness;
When they are murderers: as far as my Hammer & Anvil permit
Go, tell them that the Worship of God, is honouring his gifts
In other men: & loving the greatest men best, each according
To his Genius: which is the Holy Ghost in Man; there is no other
10 God, than that God who is the intellectual fountain of Humanity;°
He who envies or calumniates: which is murder & cruelty,
Murders the Holy-one: Go tell them this & overthrow their cup,
Their bread, their altar-table, their incense & their oath:
Their marriage & their baptism, their burial & consecration:°
I have tried to make friends by corporeal gifts but have only
Made enemies: I never made friends but by spiritual gifts;
By severe contentions of friendship & the burning fire of thought.°
He who would see the Divinity must see him in his Children
One first, in friendship & love; then a Divine Family, & in the midst
20 Jesus will appear; so he who wishes to see a Vision; a perfect Whole

But . . . cry This is the triumph of Los, akin
to Milton's great declaration on Plate 41 of that
poem; Milton's speech was addressed to Ololon
and overheard by Blake, but the speech of Los
is made to the Spectre of Urthona, and is the
utterance of a unified being who is also Blake.
It is . . . your vengeance undoubtedly a reflection on the relationship between Blake and
Hayley (see Headnote to *Milton*)
go, tell . . . Humanity This echoes the fifth
Memorable Fancy in *The Marriage.*
go tell . . . consecration an echo and expansion from Blake's *Milton* when he resolved
to descend
fire of thought Blake's vision of Eden

Must see it in its Minute Particulars;° Organized & not as thou
O Fiend of Righteousness pretendest; thine is a Disorganized
And snowy cloud: brooder of tempests & destructive War.
You smile with pomp & rigor: you talk of benevolence & virtue!
I act with benevolence & Virtue & get murderd time after time:
You accumulate Particulars, & murder by analyzing, that you
May take the aggregate; & you call the aggregate Moral Law:
And you call that Swelld & bloated Form; a Minute Particular.
But General Forms have their vitality in Particulars: & every
30   Particular is a Man; a Divine Member of the Divine Jesus.°

So Los cried at his Anvil in the horrible darkness weeping!°

The Spectre builded stupendous Works, taking the Starry Heavens
Like to a curtain & folding them according to his will
Repeating the Smaragdine Table of Hermes° to draw Los down
Into the Indefinite, refusing to believe without demonstration[.]
Los reads the Stars of Albion! the Spectre reads the Voids
Between the Stars; among the arches of Albions Tomb sublime
Rolling the Sea in rocky paths: forming Leviathan
And Behemoth: the War by Sea enormous & the War
40   By Land astounding: erecting pillars in the deepest Hell,
To reach the heavenly arches; Los beheld undaunted furious
His heavd Hammer; he swung it round & at one blow,
In unpitying ruin driving down the pyramids of pride°
Smiting the Spectre on his Anvil & the integuments° of his Eye
And Ear unbinding in dire pain, with many blows,
Of strict severity self-subduing, & with many tears labouring.

Then he sent forth the Spectre all his pyramids were grains
Of sand & his pillars: dust on the flys wing: & his starry
Heavens; a moth of gold & silver mocking his anxious grasp
50   Thus Los alterd his Spectre & every Ratio of his Reason
He alterd time after time, with dire pain & many tears
Till he had completely divided him into a separate space.°

He who . . . Particulars Both a moral and
an aesthetic argument; to "organize" the Particulars is to attain vision; in the "aggregate"
they disorganize into the Moral Law.
& every . . . Jesus The Minute Particulars,
because they stand for human wholeness and
integrity, stand also for Blake's Jesus.
So . . . weeping Though this speech is masterly and assured, its situation is terrible, as
Los weeps in a darkness just preceding the
advent of Apocalypse.
Smaragdine Table of Hermes The central text
of occult tradition, clearly repudiated (and all
occultism with it) by Blake-Los in this passage.
"Smaragdine" means resembling an emerald or
emerald-green in color, while Hermes here is
the fictive Hermes Trismegistus ("thrice greatest"), supposedly an Ancient Egyptian authority, but the Table is actually a late medieval
forgery with Hellenistic antecedents; the crucial
part of this Table reads: "That which is above
is as that which is below, and that which is
below is as that which is above, to accomplish

the one thing of all things most wonderful."
Yeats cites the Table (or Tablet) approvingly
in his "Supernatural Songs," but Blake dislikes
it for the same reason Yeats approves it, that it
states a correspondence between a suprasensual
"above" and the sensual "below," a "below"
Blake was determined to see burned up, and
upon which he was not willing to build a model
for Eternity. Here it is a magical spell of the
Spectre to trap Los in nature, the "below," and
is rejected as another "rational" mode of demonstration, just another variety of natural religion.
the Spectre . . . pride The Spectre emulates
the God of the Book of Job by confronting Los
with emblems of the sanctified tyranny of nature over man, Leviathan and Behemoth; Los
smashes them also with the hammer of his art.
integuments natural coverings
Thus . . . space The Spectre of Urthona is
finally subdued by breaking up its desperate
continuities, which are mostly temporal; by destroying its repetition-compulsiveness, as we
might say.

Terrified Los sat to behold trembling & weeping & howling
I care not whether a Man is Good or Evil; all that I care
Is whether he is a Wise man or a Fool. Go! put off Holiness
And put on Intellect: or my thundrous Hammer shall drive thee
To wrath which thou condemnest: till thou obey my voice

1804–15?   1815–20?

From The Gates of Paradise°

[Epilogue]

To The Accuser who is
The God of This World°

Truly My Satan thou art but a Dunce
And dost not know the Garment from the Man
Every Harlot was a Virgin once
Nor canst thou ever change Kate into Nan°

Tho thou art Worshipd by the Names Divine
Of Jesus & Jehovah: thou art still
The Son of Morn in weary Nights decline
The lost Travellers Dream under the Hill
1818?   1818?

From [A Vision of the Last Judgment]°

PAGE 70
    For the Year 1810
    Additions to Blake's Catalogue of Pictures &c

    The Last Judgment [will be] when all those are Cast away who trouble
Religion with Questions concerning Good & Evil or Eating of the Tree of
those Knowledges or Reasonings which hinder the Vision of God, turning all
into a Consuming Fire. When Imagination, Art & Science & all Intellectual Gifts,
all the Gifts of the Holy Ghost, are look'd upon as of no use & only Contention
remains to Man, then the Last Judgment begins, & its Vision is seen by the
Imaginative Eye of Every one according to the situation he holds.

PAGE 68
    The Last Judgment is not Fable or Allegory, but Vision. Fable or Allegory
are a totally distinct & inferior kind of Poetry. Vision or Imagination is a

The Gates of Paradise Blake engraved a little
emblem book with this title in 1793; perhaps as
late as 1818 he reissued it, with new text, including this confident "Epilogue."
To . . . World to Satan, in his role as God's
Accusing Angel of the Book of Job, and in his
power as the principle worshiped by the orthodox of this world under the names of Jesus and
Jehovah

Every . . . Nan Even the spouse of Blake's
Satan, Rahab the Harlot (the English state
church), was once a Virgin and will be so again;
Kate (Blake's wife's name) signifies wholesome-
ness and Nan whorishness.
[A Vision of the Last Judgment] a commentary
in the Notebook by Blake upon one of his
major paintings, now unfortunately lost

Representation of what Eternally Exists, Really & Unchangeably. Fable or Allegory is Form'd by the daughters of Memory. Imagination is surrounded by the daughters of Inspiration, who in the aggregate are call'd Jerusalem. Fable is Allegory, but what Critics call The Fable, is Vision itself. The Hebrew Bible & the Gospel of Jesus are not Allegory, but Eternal Vision or Imagination of All that Exists. Note here that Fable or Allegory is seldom without some Vision. Pilgrim's Progress is full of it, the Greek Poets the same; but Allegory & Vision ought to be known as Two Distinct Things, & so call'd for the Sake of Eternal Life. Plato has made Socrates say that Poets & Prophets do not know or Understand what they write or Utter; this is a most Pernicious Falshood. If they do not, pray is an inferior kind to be call'd Knowing? Plato confutes himself.°

PAGES 68–69

The Last Judgment is one of these Stupendous Visions. I have represented it as I saw it; to different People it appears differently as everything else does; for tho' on Earth things seem Permanent, they are less permanent than a Shadow, as we all know too well.

The Nature of Visionary Fancy, or Imagination, is very little Known, & the Eternal nature & permanence of its ever Existent Images is consider'd as less permanent than the things of Vegetative & Generative Nature; yet the Oak dies as well as the Lettuce, but Its Eternal Image & Individuality never dies, but renews by its seed; just so the Imaginative Image returns by the seed of Contemplative Thought; the Writings of the Prophets illustrate these conceptions of the Visionary Fancy by their various sublime & Divine Images as seen in the Worlds of Vision.

PAGES 71–72

. . . Let it here be Noted that the Greek Fables originated in Spiritual Mystery & Real Visions, which are lost & clouded in Fable & Allegory, while the Hebrew Bible & the Greek Gospel are Genuine, Preserv'd by the Saviour's Mercy. The Nature of my Work is Visionary or Imaginative; it is an Endeavour to Restore what the Ancients call'd the Golden Age.

PAGES 82–84

. . . If the Spectator could Enter into these Images in his Imagination, approaching them on the Fiery Chariot of his Contemplative Thought, if he could Enter into Noah's Rainbow or into his bosom, or could make a Friend & Companion of one of these Images of wonder, which always intreats him to leave mortal things (as he must know), then would he arise from his Grave, then would he meet the Lord in the Air & then he would be happy. General Knowledge is Remote Knowledge; it is in Particulars that Wisdom consists & Happiness too. Both in Art & in Life, General Masses are as Much Art as a Pasteboard Man is Human. Every Man has Eyes, Nose & Mouth; this Every Idiot knows, but he who enters into & discriminates most minutely the Manners & Intentions, the Characters in all their branches, is the alone Wise or Sensible Man, & on this discrimination All Art is founded. I intreat, then, that the Spectator will attend to the Hands & Feet, to the Lineaments of the

Plato confutes himself in the dialogue *Ion*

Countenances; they are all descriptive of Character, & not a line is drawn without intention, & that most discriminate & particular. As Poetry admits not a Letter that is Insignificant, so Painting admits not a Grain of Sand or a Blade of Grass Insignificant—much less an Insignificant Blur or Mark.

A Last Judgment is Necessary because Fools flourish. Nations Flourish under Wise Rulers & are depress'd under foolish Rulers; it is the same with Individuals as Nations; works of Art can only be produc'd in Perfection where the Man is either in Affluence or is Above the Care of it. Poverty is the Fool's Rod, which at last is turn'd on his own back; this is A Last Judgment—when Men of Real Art Govern & Pretenders Fall. Some People & not a few Artists have asserted that the Painter of this Picture would not have done so well if he had been properly Encourag'd. Let those who think so, reflect on the State of Nations under Poverty & their incapability of Art; tho' Art is Above Either, the Argument is better for Affluence than Poverty; & tho' he would not have been a greater Artist, yet he would have produc'd Greater works of Art in proportion to his means. A Last Judgment is not for the purpose of making Bad Men better, but for the Purpose of hindering them from opressing the Good with Poverty & Pain by means of Such Vile Arguments & Insinuations.

Around the Throne Heaven is open'd & the Nature of Eternal Things Display'd, All Springing from the Divine Humanity. All beams from him. He is the Bread & the Wine; he is the Water of Life; accordingly on Each Side of the opening Heaven appears an Apostle; that on the Right Represents Baptism, that on the Left Represents the Lord's Supper. All Life consists of these Two, Throwing off Error & Knaves from our company continually & Recieving Truth or Wise Men into our Company continually. He who is out of the Church & opposes it is no less an Agent of Religion than he who is in it; to be an Error & to be Cast out is a part of God's design. No man can Embrace True Art till he has Explor'd & cast out False Art (such is the Nature of Mortal Things), or he will be himself Cast out by those who have Already Embraced True Art. Thus My Picture is a History of Art & Science, the Foundation of Society, Which is Humanity itself. What are all the Gifts of the Spirit but Mental Gifts? Whenever any Individual Rejects Error & Embraces Truth, a Last Judgment passes upon that Individual.

PAGES 90–91
Here they are no longer talking of what is Good & Evil, or of what is Right or Wrong, & puzzling themselves in Satan's Labyrinth,° But are Conversing with Eternal Realities as they Exist in the Human Imagination. We are in a World of Generation & death, & this world we must cast off if we would be Painters such as Rafael, Mich. Angelo & the Ancient Sculptors; if we do not cast off his world we shall be only Venetian Painters, who will be cast off & Lost from Art.

PAGES 91–92
Many suppose that before the Creation All was Solitude & Chaos. This is the most pernicious Idea that can enter the Mind, as it takes away all sublimity from the Bible & Limits All Existence to Creation & to Chaos. To the Time &

Satan's Labyrinth See *Paradise Lost* II.561.

Space fixed by the Corporeal Vegetative Eye, & leaves the Man who entertains such an Idea the habitation of Unbelieving demons. Eternity Exists, and All things in Eternity, Independent of Creation which was an act of Mercy. I have represented those who are in Eternity by some in a Cloud within the Rainbow that Surrounds the Throne; they merely appear as in a Cloud when any thing of Creation, Redemption or Judgment are the Subjects of Contemplation, tho' their Whole Contemplation is concerning these things; the Reason they so appear is The Humiliation of the Reason & doubting Self-hood, & the Giving all up to Inspiration. By this it will be seen that I do not consider either the Just or the Wicked to be in a Supreme State, but to be every one of them States of the Sleep which the Soul may fall into in its deadly dreams of Good & Evil when it leaves Paradise following the Serpent.

PAGE 91

The Greeks represent Chronos or Time as a very Aged Man; this is Fable, but the Real Vision of Time is in Eternal Youth. I have, however, somewhat accomodated my Figure of Time to the common opinion, as I myself am also infected with it & my Visions also infected, & I see Time Aged, alas, too much so.

Allegories are things that Relate to Moral Virtues. Moral Virtues do not Exist; they are Allegories & dissimulations. But Time & Space are Real Beings, a Male & a Female. Time is a Man, Space is a Woman, & her Masculine Portion is Death.

PAGES 86, 90

The Combats of Good & Evil & of Truth & Error which are the same thing is Eating of the Tree of Knowledge. The Combats of Truth & Error is Eating of the Tree of Life; these are not only Universal, but Particular. Each are Personified. There is not an Error but it has a Man for its Agent, that is, it is a Man. There is not a Truth but it has also a Man. Good & Evil are Qualities in Every Man, whether a Good or Evil Man. These are Enemies & destroy one another by every Means in their power, both of deceit & of open Violence. The deist & the Christian are but the Results of these Opposing Natures. Many are deists who would in certain Circumstances have been Christians in outward appearance. Voltaire was one of this number; he was as intolerant as an Inquisitor. Manners make the Man, not Habits. It is the same in Art: by their Works ye shall know them; the Knave who is Converted to Deism & the Knave who is Converted to Christianity is still a Knave, but he himself will not know it, tho' Every body else does. Christ comes, as he came at first, to deliver those who were bound under the Knave, not to deliver the Knave. He Comes to deliver Man, the Accused, & not Satan, the Accuser. We do not find any where that Satan is Accused of Sin; he is only accused of Unbelief & thereby drawing Man into Sin that he may accuse him. Such is the Last Judgment—a deliverance from Satan's Accusation. Satan thinks that Sin is displeasing to God; he ought to know that Nothing is displeasing to God but Unbelief & Eating of the Tree of Knowledge of Good & Evil.

PAGE 87

Men are admitted into Heaven not because they have curbed & govern'd their Passions or have No Passions, but because they have Cultivated their Understandings. The Treasures of Heaven are not Negations of Passion, but

Realities of Intellect, from which all the Passions Emanate Uncurbed in their Eternal Glory. The Fool shall not enter into Heaven let him be ever so Holy. Holiness is not The Price of Enterance into Heaven. Those who are cast out are All Those who, having no Passions of their own because No Intellect, Have spent their lives in Curbing & Governing other People's by the Various arts of Poverty & Cruelty of all kinds. Wo, Wo, Wo to you Hypocrites. Even Murder, the Courts of Justice, more merciful than the Church, are compell'd to allow is not done in Passion, but in Cool Blooded design & Intention.

The Modern Church Crucifies Christ with the Head Downwards.

PAGES 92–95

.   .   .

Thinking as I do that the Creator of this World is a very Cruel Being, & being a Worshipper of Christ, I cannot help saying: 'the Son, O how unlike the Father!' First God Almighty comes with a Thump on the Head. Then Jesus Christ comes with a balm to heal it.

The Last Judgment is an Overwhelming of Bad Art & Science. Mental Things are alone Real; what is call'd Corporeal, Nobody Knows of its Dwelling Place: it is in Fallacy, & its Existence an Imposture. Where is the Existence Out of Mind or Thought? Where is it but in the Mind of a Fool? Some People flatter themselves that there will be No Last Judgment & that Bad Art will be adopted & mixed with Good Art, That Error or Experiment will make a Part of Truth, & they Boast that it is its Foundation; these People flatter themselves: I will not Flatter them. Error is Created. Truth is Eternal. Error, or Creation, will be Burned up, & then, & not till Then, Truth or Eternity will appear. It is Burnt up the Moment Men cease to behold it. I assert for My Self that I do not behold the outward Creation & that to me it is hindrance & not Action; it is as the Dirt upon my feet, No part of Me. 'What,' it will be Question'd, 'When the Sun rises, do you not see a round disk of fire somewhat like a Guinea?' O no, no, I see an Innumerable company of the Heavenly host crying 'Holy, Holy, Holy is the Lord God Almighty.' I question not my Corporeal or Vegetative Eye any more than I would Question a Window concerning a Sight. I look thro' it & not with it.

[END OF A VISION OF THE LAST JUDGMENT]

1810   1810

From The Letters

To Dr. Trusler [1] 23 August 1799

Revd Sir,

I really am sorry that you are fall'n out with the Spiritual World, Especially if I should have to answer for it. I feel very sorry that your Ideas & Mine on Moral Painting differ so much as to have made you angry with my method of Study. If I am wrong, I am wrong in good company. I had hoped your plan

1. John Trusler (1735–1820), an Enlightened clergyman, wrote the words "Blake, dimmed with Superstition," on the margin of this letter.

comprehended All Species of this Art, & Expecially that you would not regret that Species which gives Existence to Every other, namely, Visions of Eternity. You say that I want somebody to Elucidate my Ideas. But you ought to know that What is Grand is necessarily obscure to Weak men. That which can be made Explicit to the Idiot is not worth my care. The wisest of the Ancients consider'd what is not too Explicit as the fittest for Instruction, because it rouzes the faculties to act. I name Moses, Solomon, Esop, Homer, Plato.

But as you have favor'd me with your remarks on my Design, permit me in return to defend it against a mistaken one, which is, That I have supposed Malevolence without a Cause. Is not Merit in one a Cause of Envy in another, & Serenity & Happiness & Beauty a Cause of Malevolence? But Want of Money & the Distress of A Thief can never be alledged as the Cause of his Thieving, for many honest people endure greater hardships with Fortitude. We must therefore seek the Cause elsewhere than in want of Money, for that is the Miser's passion, not the Thief's.

I have therefore proved your Reasonings Ill proportion'd, which you can never prove my figures to be; they are those of Michael Angelo, Rafael & the Antique, & of the best living Models. I percieve that your Eye is perverted by Caricature Prints, which ought not to abound so much as they do. Fun I love, but too much Fun is of all things the most loathsome. Mirth is better than Fun, & Happiness is better than Mirth. I feel that a Man may be happy in This World. And I know that This World Is a World of imagination & Vision. I see Every thing I paint In This World, but Every body does not see alike. To the Eyes of a Miser a Guinea is more beautiful than the Sun, & a bag worn with the use of Money has more beautiful proportions than a Vine filled with Grapes. The tree which moves some to tears of joy is in the Eyes of others only a Green thing that stands in the way. Some See Nature all Ridicule & Deformity, & by these I shall not regulate my proportions; & Some Scarce see Nature at all. But to the Eyes of the Man of Imagination, Nature is Imagination itself. As a man is, So he Sees. As the Eye is formed, such are its Powers. You certainly Mistake, when you say that the Visions of Fancy are not to be found in This World. To Me This World is all One continued Vision of Fancy or Imagination, & I feel Flatter'd when I am told so. What is it sets Homer, Virgil & Milton in so high a rank of Art? Why is the Bible more Entertaining & Instructive than any other book? Is it not because they are addressed to the Imagination, which is Spiritual Sensation, & but mediately to the Understanding or Reason? Such is True Painting, and such was alone valued by the Greeks & the best modern Artists. Consider what Lord Bacon says: 'Sense sends over to Imagination before Reason have judged, & Reason sends over to Imagination before the Decree can be acted.' See Advancem[t] of Learning, Part 2, P. 47 of first Edition.

But I am happy to find a Great Majority of Fellow Mortals who can Elucidate My Visions, & Particularly they have been Elucidated by Children, who have taken a greater delight in contemplating my Pictures than I even hoped. Neither Youth nor Childhood is Folly or Incapacity. Some Children are Fools & so are some Old Men. But There is a vast Majority on the side of Imagination or Spiritual Sensation.

To Engrave after another Painter is infinitely more laborious than to Engrave

one's own Inventions. And of the size you require my price has been Thirty
Guineas, & I cannot afford to do it for less. I had Twelve for the Head I sent you
as a Specimen; but after my own designs I could do at least Six times the quantity of labour in the same time, which will account for the difference of price
as also that Chalk Engraving is at least six times as laborious as Aqua tinta. I
have no objection to Engraving after another Artist. Engraving is the profession
I was apprenticed to, & should never have attempted to live by any thing else,
If orders had not come in for my Designs & Paintings, which I have the
pleasure to tell you are Increasing Every Day. Thus If I am a Painter it is not
to be attributed to Seeking after. But I am contented whether I live by Painting
or Engraving.

I am, Revd Sir, your very obedient servant,

William Blake

13 Hercules Buildings
Lambeth
August 23. 1799

To George Cumberland [1] 12 April 1827

Dear Cumberland,

I have been very near the Gates of Death & have returned very weak & an
Old Man feeble & tottering, but not in Spirit & Life, not in The Real Man The
Imagination which Liveth for Ever. In that I am stronger & stronger as this
Foolish Body decays. I thank you for the Pains you have taken with Poor Job.
I know too well that a great majority of Englishmen are fond of The Indefinite
which they Measure by Newton's Doctrine of the Fluxions of an Atom, A Thing
that does not Exist. These are Politicians & think that Republican Art is Inimical
to their Atom. For a Line or Lineament is not formed by Chance: a Line is a
Line in its Minutest Subdivisions: Strait or Crooked It is Itself & Not Intermeasurable with or by any Thing Else. Such is Job, but since the French Revolution Englishmen are all Intermeasurable One by Another, Certainly a happy
state of Agreement to which I for One do not Agree. God keep me from the
Divinity of Yes & No too, The Yea Nay Creeping Jesus, from supposing Up &
Down to be the same Thing as all Experimentalists must suppose.

You are desirous I know to dispose of some of my Works & to make them
Pleasin[g]. I am obliged to you & to all who do so. But having none remaining
of all that I had Printed I cannot Print more Except at a great loss, for at the
time I printed those things I had a whole House to range in: now I am shut up
in a Corner therefore am forced to ask a Price for them that I scarce expect to
get from a Stranger. I am now Printing a Set of the Songs of Innocence & Experience for a Friend at Ten Guineas which I cannot do under Six Months
consistent with my other Work, so that I have little hope of doing any more of
such things. The Last Work I produced is a Poem Entitled Jerusalem the
Emanation of the Giant Albion, but find that to Print it will Cost my Time the
amount of Twenty Guineas. One I have Finish'd. It contains 100 Plates but it
is not likely that I shall get a Customer for it.[2]

1. Writer on art and one of Blake's patrons.   2. This is the unique colored copy of *Jerusalem*.

As you wish me to send you a list with the Prices of these things they are as follows

	£	s	d
America	6.	6.	0
Europe	6.	6.	0
Visions &c	5.	5.	0
Thel	3.	3.	0
Songs of Inn. & Exp.	10.	10.	0
Urizen	6.	6.	0

The Little Card I will do as soon as Possible but when you Consider that I have been reduced to a Skeleton from which I am slowly recovering you will I hope have Patience with me.

Flaxman [3] is Gone & we must All soon follow, every one to his Own Eternal House, Leaving the Delusive Goddess Nature & her Laws to get into Freedom from all Law of the Members into The Mind, in which every one is King & Priest in his own House. God send it so on Earth as it is in Heaven.

I am, Dear Sir, Yours Affectionately

William Blake

12 April 1827
N 3 Fountain Court Strand

WILLIAM WORDSWORTH
1770–1850

Born near, and raised in, the English Lake District, Wordsworth was left alone with the visible world at an unnaturally early age. Though he had three brothers and a sister, Dorothy, to whom he was closer than ever he would be to anyone else, he still had to sustain the death of his mother when he was just eight, and of his father when he was thirteen. His "family romance" (as Freud would have called it) was primarily with the natural world, surpassingly beautiful in the Lake Country.

From 1787 to 1791 Wordsworth attended St. John's College, Cambridge, where he did nothing particularly remarkable. In the summer of 1790 he went on a walking tour of the Alps and France (see *The Prelude* VI) and observed France at the height of its revolutionary hopefulness, which he shared. He returned to France and lived there for a turbulent year (November 1791–December 1792), during which time he associated himself with the moderate faction of the Revolution, fell in love with Annette Vallon, and fathered their daughter, Caroline. Abandoning both mother and child, and his political friends, he returned to England, to spend five years troubled by guilt and remorse, not only about these near-betrayals, but concerning also his identity as Englishman and as poet. Though the continued presence of Dorothy (she never married) was an essential element in Wordsworth's recovery from this long crisis, the catalyst for his renovation was his best friend, Coleridge, whom he first met early in 1795. Coleridge gave Wordsworth rather more than he took, intellectually and poetically, but in return Wordsworth gave Coleridge something necessary out of his

3. John Flaxman, eminent sculptor and Blake's friend, had died a few months before.

own massive (though still turbulent) emotional strength. Later in 1795 a friend's legacy enabled Wordsworth to free himself from financial burdens. By 1797 Wordsworth had surmounted his crisis, and in the almost-daily company of Coleridge was able to begin upon his mature and characteristic work, first published (anonymously) in 1798 as *Lyrical Ballads, With a Few Other Poems.* The ballads included Coleridge's "The Ancient Mariner," and the other poems included "Tintern Abbey." Historically considered, this remains the most important volume of verse in English since the Renaissance, for it began modern poetry, the poetry of the growing inner self.

The birth of this self had preceded Wordsworth, and is located variously by different intellectual historians. It seems clear that the inner self was a Protestant creation, and that before Luther it was prefigured in Catholic thinkers as diverse as the furious reformer Savonarola and the meditative Thomas à Kempis, who wrote *The Imitation of Christ.* In Luther, though, the inner self achieves the kind of prominence that made a writer like Rousseau possible. As the inner self grew, landscape paradoxically began to enter European literature, for the inner self made landscape visible precisely through a devaluation of everything else that the self would not contain. The outer world moved more outward as the inner self grew more inward, until the estrangement between the two worlds produced the phenomenon of Rousseau's ecstatic nature worship. Confronting what had ceased to be a world in which he shared, Rousseau was moved by love and longing for what he had lost. The next and all-important step in poetry was taken by Wordsworth, who did for literature what Freud was to do for modern psychology, nearly a century later.

The immense burden of Wordsworth's poetry is the contradiction that he understood better than all his followers down to today: self-consciousness is essential for modern poetry, yet self-consciousness is the antagonist of poetry, the demon that needs to be exorcised. Before Wordsworth, poetry had a subject. After Wordsworth, its prevalent subject was the poet's own subjectivity. Before Wordsworth, any poet, professional or amateur, would in some sense *choose a subject* in order to write a poem. After Wordsworth, this is no longer true, and so a new poetry was born.

Hazlitt, in some ways a more acute critic of Wordsworth than Coleridge (because much more detached), reviewed *The Excursion* in 1814, and said of its poet: "He sees all things in himself," and added that his mind was "conversant only with itself and nature." Lecturing on the "living poets" in 1818, Hazlitt emphasized Wordsworth's astonishing originality, and simply observed that the poet "is his own subject." Rightly associating Wordsworth's poetical revolution with the French Revolution, Hazlitt nevertheless added the stern warning that a poet of Wordsworth's school necessarily manifested an "egotism [that] is in some respects a madness." Yet Wordsworth knew this better than Hazlitt did, as "Resolution and Independence" and *The Prelude* show.

What was Wordsworth's "healing power"? How does his best poetry work so as to save not only the poet himself in his own crises, but so as to have been therapeutic for the imagination of so many poets and readers since? Five generations have passed since Wordsworth experienced his Great Decade (1797–1807), and still the attentive and dedicated reader can learn to find in him the human art he teaches better than any poet before or since, including precursors greater than himself (but no successors as yet, of his eminence). The art is simply what Keats, Shelley, Arnold, Emerson, and others called it: *how to feel.* Wordsworth, by a primordial power uncanny in its depths, educates the affective life of his reader. He teaches precisely what he knew he could teach: how to become, within severe limitations, a renovated spirit, free of crippling self-consciousness yet still enjoying the varied gifts of an awakened consciousness. He proposes to observe nature with an eye steadily on the object, and yet not to lose his freedom to the tyranny of the eye, while also preserving the integrity of nature from our profane tendency to practice analysis upon it.

This is the primary Wordsworth of whom Matthew Arnold was the classical critic, the poet "Of blessed consolations in distress, / Of moral strength and intellectual powers, / Of joy in widest commonalty spread—." Arnold superbly located Wordsworth's healing effect in *power*, "the extraordinary power with which Wordsworth feels the joy offered to us in nature, the joy offered to us in the simple primary affections and duties . . . and renders it so as to make us share it." Like Tolstoy at his finest, like the great sages of Judaic and some aspects of Christian tradition, this Wordsworth hallows the commonplace, celebrates the common, human heart by which we live, and the nature that cares for and refreshes that heart.

But there is another Wordsworth, and he is a great poet also, but more problematic and far less heartening. Arnold turned away from the Miltonic, strong, sublime, non-Coleridgean side of Wordsworth, as the critic A. C. Bradley first demonstrated early in the twentieth century. Recent critics have followed Bradley in exploring Wordsworth's uneasiness with nature, his dark sense that nature was a hidden antagonist to the full, Miltonic development of his own imagination. The hidden story of *The Prelude* and of the great crisis poems of 1802 (e.g. "Resolution and Independence" and the "Intimations" ode) is largely concerned with this struggle, and the inability to resolve this conflict between questing self and adherence to nature may be the clue to Wordsworth's rapid, indeed catastrophic decline after 1807, at the very latest.

Certainly the facts of Wordsworth's own mature biography do little to explain his poetic decay. He settled, with Dorothy, late in 1799 at Grasmere, not far from the beloved scenes of his boyhood. Coleridge settled nearby. Wordsworth married, happily, in 1802, but sorrows began to shadow him. His closest brother, John, drowned in 1805; the friendship with the increasingly unhappy Coleridge began to fade, and largely ended in a dreadful quarrel in 1810. Two of his children died in 1812, and the fear of his own mortality, always strong in him, necessarily augmented. He became outwardly well-off, politically a champion of the established order, and eminently orthodox in the Church of England. He iced over.

But the astonishing poems remained, and cannot die. In them, more than any other in the language before or since, we find ourselves, and this "we" is very nearly universal. The great poems do not champion any cause or urge any vision but one: to know ourselves, sincerely, in our own origins and in what we still are. The hiding places of every person's power, Wordsworth insisted, are in his own past, however painful that past might have been. To live life, and not death-in-life, Wordsworth gently but forcefully advises us to find the natural continuities between what we were and what we are. If he himself never quite became what he might have been, that does not matter. Though he himself could not sustain even the strength he attained, that also does not matter. What matters is that his poetry found a way of showing how much a natural man might do for himself, by the hard discipline of holding himself open both to imagination and to nature.

Lines Written in Early Spring

I heard a thousand blended notes,
While in a grove I sate reclined,
In that sweet mood when pleasant thoughts
Bring sad thoughts to the mind.

To her fair works did Nature link
The human soul that through me ran;
And much it grieved my heart to think
What man has made of man.

Through primrose tufts, in that green bower,
10 The periwinkle trailed its wreaths;
And 'tis my faith that every flower
Enjoys the air it breathes.

The birds around me hopped and played,
Their thoughts I cannot measure—
But the least motion which they made,
It seemed a thrill of pleasure.

The budding twigs spread out their fan,
To catch the breezy air;
And I must think, do all I can,
20 That there was pleasure there.

If this belief from heaven be sent,
If such be Nature's holy plan,
Have I not reason to lament
What man has made of man?
1798   1798

Expostulation and Reply

'Why, William, on that old grey stone,
Thus for the length of half a day,
Why, William, sit you thus alone,
And dream your time away?

'Where are your books?—that light bequeathed
To Beings else forlorn and blind!
Up! up! and drink the spirit breathed
From dead men to their kind.

'You look round on your Mother Earth,
10 As if she for no purpose bore you;
As if you were her first-born birth,
And none had lived before you!'

One morning thus, by Esthwaite lake,
When life was sweet, I knew not why,
To me my good friend Matthew spake,
And thus I made reply:

'The eye—it cannot choose but see;
We cannot bid the ear be still;
Our bodies feel, where'er they be,
20   Against or with our will.

'Nor less I deem that there are Powers
Which of themselves our minds impress;
That we can feed this mind of ours
In a wise passiveness.

'Think you, 'mid all this mighty sum
Of things for ever speaking,
That nothing of itself will come,
But we must still be seeking?

'—Then ask not wherefore, here, alone,
30   Conversing as I may,
I sit upon this old grey stone,
And dream my time away.'
1798   1798

The Tables Turned

An Evening Scene on the Same Subject

Up! up! my Friend, and quit your books;
Or surely you'll grow double:
Up! up! my Friend, and clear your looks;
Why all this toil and trouble?

The sun, above the mountain's head,
A freshening lustre mellow
Through all the long green fields has spread,
His first sweet evening yellow.

Books! 'tis a dull and endless strife:
10   Come, hear the woodland linnet,
How sweet his music! on my life,
There's more of wisdom in it.

And hark! how blithe the throstle sings!
He, too, is no mean preacher:
Come forth into the light of things,
Let Nature be your Teacher.

She has a world of ready wealth,
Our minds and hearts to bless—
Spontaneous wisdom breathed by health,
20   Truth breathed by cheerfulness.

One impulse from a vernal wood
May teach you more of man,
Of moral evil and of good,
Than all the sages can.

Sweet is the lore which Nature brings;
Our meddling intellect
Mis-shapes the beauteous forms of things:—
We murder to dissect.

Enough of Science and of Art;
30   Close up those barren leaves;
Come forth, and bring with you a heart
That watches and receives.
1798   1798

To My Sister

It is the first mild day of March:
Each minute sweeter than before,
The redbreast sings from the tall larch
That stands beside our door.

There is a blessing in the air,
Which seems a sense of joy to yield
To the bare trees, and mountains bare,
And grass in the green field.

My Sister! ('tis a wish of mine)
10   Now that our morning meal is done,
Make haste, your morning task resign;
Come forth and feel the sun.

Edward will come with you—and, pray,
Put on with speed your woodland dress,
And bring no book; for this one day
We'll give to idleness.

No joyless forms shall regulate
Our living calendar;
We from today, my Friend, will date
20   The opening of the year.

Love, now a universal birth,
From heart to heart is stealing;

From earth to man, from man to earth:
—It is the hour of feeling.

One moment now may give us more
Than years of toiling reason;
Our minds shall drink at every pore
The spirit of the season.

Some silent laws our hearts will make,
30   Which they shall long obey;
We for the year to come may take
Our temper from today.

And from the blessed power that rolls
About, below, above,
We'll frame the measure of our souls:
They shall be tuned to love.

Then come, my Sister! come, I pray,
With speed put on your woodland dress;
And bring no book: for this one day
40   We'll give to idleness.
1798   1798

The Ruined Cottage

The Tale of Margaret, first published belatedly as Book I of *The Excursion*, exists in several different versions. This one, transcribed by Jonathan Wordsworth in his book *The Music of Humanity* (1968), is by common scholarly agreement now considered the most effective.

   Though the simplicity of Margaret's story is crucial, it is important to note that she is destroyed by excess of hope, and not of sorrow. She stands for something dangerous and poignant in Wordsworth's consciousness, for a preternatural strength of hope that can destroy what is most necessary for continued existence, our ability to come to terms with human loss.

The Ruined Cottage

   First Part

'Twas Summer and the sun was mounted high.
Along the south the uplands feebly glared
Through a pale steam, and all the northern downs,
In clearer air ascending, showed far off
Their surfaces with shadows dappled o'er
Of deep embattled clouds. Far as the sight
Could reach those many shadows lay in spots
Determined and unmoved, with steady beams

Of clear and pleasant sunshine interposed—
10 Pleasant to him who on the soft cool grass
Extends his careless limbs beside the root
Of some huge oak whose agèd branches make
A twilight of their own, a dewy shade
Where the wren warbles while the dreaming man,
Half conscious of that soothing melody,
With sidelong eye looks out upon the scene,
By those impending branches made more soft,
More soft and distant.

                Other lot was mine.
Across a bare wide Common I had toiled
20 With languid feet which by the slippery ground
Were baffled still, and when I stretched myself
On the brown earth my limbs from very heat
Could find no rest, nor my weak arm disperse
The insect host which gathered round my face
And joined their murmurs to the tedious noise
Of seeds of bursting gorse that crackled round.
I rose and turned towards a group of trees
Which midway in that level stood alone;
And thither come at length, beneath a shade
30 Of clustering elms that sprang from the same root
I found a ruined house, four naked walls
That stared upon each other. I looked round
And near the door I saw an agèd Man,
Alone and stretched upon the cottage bench,
An iron-pointed staff lay at his side.
With instantaneous joy I recognized
That pride of nature and of lowly life,
The venerable *Armytage*, a friend
As dear to me as is the setting sun.

40   Two days before
We had been fellow travellers. I knew
That he was in this neighbourhood, and now
Delighted found him here in the cool shade.
He lay, his pack of rustic merchandise
Pillowing his head. I guess he had no thought
Of his way-wandering life. His eyes were shut,
The shadows of the breezy elms above
Dappled his face. With thirsty heat oppressed
At length I hailed him, glad to see his hat
50 Bedewed with waterdrops, as if the brim
Had newly scooped a running stream. He rose
And pointing to a sunflower, bade me climb
The [   ] wall where that same gaudy flower
Looked out upon the road.

It was a plot
Of garden ground now wild, its matted weeds
Marked with the steps of those whom as they passed,
The gooseberry trees that shot in long lank slips,
Or currants hanging from their leafless stems
In scanty strings, had tempted to o'erleap
60   The broken wall. Within that cheerless spot,
Where two tall hedgerows of thick alder boughs
Joined in a damp cold nook, I found a well
Half covered up with willow flowers and grass.
I slaked my thirst and to the shady bench
Returned, and while I stood unbonneted
To catch the motion of the cooler air,
The old Man said, 'I see around me here
Things which you cannot see. We die, my Friend,
Nor we alone, but that which each man loved
70   And prized in his peculiar nook of earth
Dies with him, or is changed, and very soon
Even of the good is no memorial left.
The Poets, in their elegies and songs
Lamenting the departed, call the groves,
They call upon the hills and streams to mourn,
And senseless rocks—nor idly, for they speak
In these their invocations with a voice
Obedient to the strong creative power
Of human passion. Sympathies there are
80   More tranquil, yet perhaps of kindred birth,
That steal upon the meditative mind
And grow with thought. Beside yon spring I stood,
And eyed its waters till we seemed to feel
One sadness, they and I. For them a bond
Of brotherhood is broken; time has been
When every day the touch of human hand
Disturbed their stillness, and they ministered
To human comfort. When I stopped to drink
A spider's web hung to the water's edge,
90   And on the wet and slimy footstone lay
The useless fragment of a wooden bowl.
It moved my very heart.

'The day has been
When I could never pass this road but she
Who lived within these walls, when I appeared,
A daughter's welcome gave me, and I loved her
As my own child. Oh Sir, the good die first,
And they whose hearts are dry as summer dust
Burn to the socket. Many a passenger
Has blessed poor Margaret for her gentle looks

100   When she upheld the cool refreshment drawn
       From that forsaken spring, and no one came
       But he was welcome, no one went away
       But that it seemed she loved him. She is dead,
       The worm is on her cheek, and this poor hut,
       Stripped of its outward garb of household flowers,
       Of rose and sweetbriar, offers to the wind
       A cold bare wall whose earthy top is tricked
       With weeds and the rank spear grass. She is dead,
       And nettles rot and adders sun themselves
110   Where we have sate together while she nursed
       Her infant at her breast. The unshod colt,
       The wandring heifer and the Potter's ass,
       Find shelter now within the chimney wall
       Where I have seen her evening hearthstone blaze
       And through the window spread upon the road
       Its cheerful light. You will forgive me, sir,
       But often on this cottage do I muse
       As on a picture, till my wiser mind
       Sinks, yielding to the foolishness of grief.

120   'She had a husband, an industrious man,
       Sober and steady. I have heard her say
       That he was up and busy at his loom
       In summer ere the mower's scythe had swept
       The dewy grass, and in the early spring
       Ere the last star had vanished. They who passed
       At evening, from behind the garden fence
       Might hear his busy spade, which he would ply
       After his daily work till the daylight
       Was gone, and every leaf and flower were lost
130   In the dark hedges. So they passed their days
       In peace and comfort, and two pretty babes
       Were their best hope next to the God in Heaven.

       'You may remember, now some ten years gone,
       Two blighting seasons when the fields were left
       With half a harvest. It pleased heaven to add
       A worse affliction in the plague of war,
       A happy land was stricken to the heart,
       'Twas a sad time of sorrow and distress.
       A wanderer among the cottages,
140   I with my pack of winter raiment saw
       The hardships of that season. Many rich
       Sunk down as in a dream among the poor,
       And of the poor did many cease to be,
       And their place knew them not. Meanwhile, abridged
       Of daily comforts, gladly reconciled
       To numerous self-denials, Margaret

Went struggling on through those calamitous years
With cheerful hope. But ere the second autumn
A fever seized her husband. In disease
He lingered long, and when his strength returned
He found the little he had stored to meet
The hour of accident, or crippling age,
Was all consumed. As I have said, 'twas now
A time of trouble: shoals of artisans
Were from their daily labour turned away
To hang for bread on parish charity,
They and their wives and children, happier far
Could they have lived as do the little birds
That peck along the hedges, or the kite
That makes her dwelling in the mountain rocks.

'Ill fared it now with Robert, he who dwelt
In this poor cottage. At his door he stood
And whistled many a snatch of merry tunes
That had no mirth in them, or with his knife
Carved uncouth figures on the heads of sticks.
Then idly sought about through every nook
Of house or garden any casual task
Of use or ornament, and with a strange
Amusing but uneasy novelty
He blended where he might the various tasks
Of summer, autumn, winter, and of spring.
But this endured not, his good humour soon
Became a weight in which no pleasure was,
And poverty brought on a petted mood
And a sore temper. Day by day he drooped.
And he would leave his home, and to the town
Without an errand would he turn his steps,
Or wander here and there among the fields.
One while he would speak lightly of his babes
And with a cruel tongue, at other times
He played with them wild freaks of merriment.
And 'twas a piteous thing to see the looks
Of the poor innocent children. "Every smile,"
Said Margaret to me here beneath these trees,
"Made my heart bleed." '

                     At this the old Man paused
And looking up to those enormous elms
He said, ' 'Tis now the hour of deepest noon.
At this still season of repose and peace,
This hour when all things which are not at rest
Are cheerful, while this multitude of flies
Fills all the air with happy melody,

Why should a tear be in an old man's eye?
Why should we thus with an untoward mind,
And in the weakness of humanity,
From natural wisdom turn our hearts away.
To natural comfort shut our eyes and ears.
And, feeding on disquiet, thus disturb
The calm of Nature with our restless thoughts?'

 END OF THE FIRST PART

Second Part

He spake with somewhat of a solemn tone,
200 But when he ended there was in his face
Such easy cheerfulness, a look so mild,
That for a little time it stole away
All recollection, and that simple tale
Passed from my mind like a forgotten sound.
A while on trivial things we held discourse
To me soon tasteless. In my own despite
I thought of that poor woman as of one
Whom I had known and loved. He had rehearsed
Her homely tale with such familiar power,
210 With such an active countenance, an eye
So busy, that the things of which he spake
Seemed present, and, attention now relaxed,
There was a heartfelt chillness in my veins.
I rose, and turning from that breezy shade
Went out into the open air, and stood
To drink the comfort of the warmer sun.
Long time I had not stayed ere, looking round
Upon that tranquil ruin, I returned
And begged of the old man that for my sake
220 He would resume his story.

               He replied,
'It were a wantonness, and would demand
Severe reproof, if we were men whose hearts
Could hold vain dalliance with the misery
Even of the dead, contented thence to draw
A momentary pleasure, never marked
By reason, barren of all future good.
But we have known that there is often found
In mournful thoughts, and always might be found,
A power to virtue friendly; were't not so
230 I am a dreamer among men, indeed
An idle dreamer. 'Tis a common tale
By moving accidents uncharactered,
A tale of silent suffering, hardly clothed
In bodily form, and to the grosser sense

But ill adapted, scarcely palpable
To him who does not think. But at your bidding
I will proceed.

            'While thus it fared with them
To whom this cottage till that hapless year
Had been a blessed home, it was my chance
To travel in a country far remote;
And glad I was when, halting by yon gate
That leads from the green lane, again I saw
These lofty elm trees. Long I did not rest:
With many pleasant thoughts I cheered my way
O'er the flat common. At the door arrived,
I knocked, and when I entered, with the hope
Of usual greeting, Margaret looked at me
A little while, then turned her head away
Speechless, and sitting down upon a chair
Wept bitterly. I wist not what to do,
Or how to speak to her. Poor wretch, at last
She rose from off her seat, and then, oh Sir,
I cannot tell how she pronounced my name.
With fervent love, and with a face of grief
Unutterably helpless, and a look
That seemed to cling upon me, she enquired
If I had seen her husband. As she spake
A strange surprise and fear came to my heart,
Nor had I power to answer ere she told
That he had disappeared—just two months gone.
He left his house: two wretched days had passed,
And on the third by the first break of light,
Within her casement full in view she saw
A purse of gold. "I trembled at the sight,"
Said Margaret, "for I knew it was his hand
That placed it there. And on that very day
By one, a stranger, from my husband sent,
The tidings came that he had joined a troop
Of soldiers going to a distant land.
He left me thus. Poor Man, he had not heart
To take farewell of me, and he feared
That I should follow with my babes, and sink
Beneath the misery of a soldier's life."

'This tale did Margaret tell with many tears,
And when she ended I had little power
To give her comfort, and was glad to take
Such words of hope from her own mouth as served
To cheer us both. But long we had not talked
Ere we built up a pile of better thoughts,
And with a brighter eye she looked around,

As if she had been shedding tears of joy.
We parted. It was then the early spring:
I left her busy with her garden tools,
And well remember, o'er that fence she looked,
And, while I paced along the footway path,
Called out and sent a blessing after me,
With tender cheerfulness, and with a voice
That seemed the very sound of happy thoughts.

'I roved o'er many a hill and many a dale
290 With this my weary load, in heat and cold,
Through many a wood and many an open ground,
In sunshine or in shade, in wet or fair,
Now blithe, now drooping, as it might befall;
My best companions now the driving winds
And now the "trotting brooks" and whispering trees,
And now the music of my own sad steps,
With many a short-lived thought that passed between
And disappeared.

                    'I came this way again
Towards the wane of summer, when the wheat
300 Was yellow, and the soft and bladed grass
Sprang up afresh and o'er the hay field spread
Its tender green. When I had reached the door
I found that she was absent. In the shade,
Where we now sit, I waited her return.
Her cottage in its outward look appeared
As cheerful as before, in any show
Of neatness little changed, but that I thought
The honeysuckle crowded round the door,
And from the wall hung down in heavier tufts,
310 And knots of worthless stonecrop started out
Along the window's edge, and grew like weeds
Against the lower panes. I turned aside
And strolled into her garden. It was changed.
The unprofitable bindweed spread his bells
From side to side, and with unwieldy wreaths
Had dragged the rose from its sustaining wall
And bent it down to earth. The border tufts,
Daisy, and thrift, and lowly camomile,
And thyme, had straggled out into the paths
320 Which they were used to deck.

                    'Ere this an hour
Was wasted. Back I turned my restless steps,
And as I walked before the door it chanced
A stranger passed, and guessing whom I sought,
He said that she was used to ramble far.

The sun was sinking in the west, and now
I sate with sad impatience. From within
Her solitary infant cried aloud.
The spot though fair seemed very desolate,
The longer I remained more desolate;
330 And looking round I saw the cornerstones,
Till then unmarked, on either side the door
With dull red stains discoloured, and stuck o'er
With tufts and hairs of wool, as if the sheep
That feed upon the commons thither came
Familiarly, and found a couching place
Even at her threshold.

      'The house clock struck eight:
I turned and saw her distant a few steps.
Her face was pale and thin, her figure too
Was changed. As she unlocked the door she said,
340 "It grieves me you have waited here so long,
But in good truth I've wandered much of late,
And sometimes, to my shame I speak, have need
Of my best prayers to bring me back again."
While on the board she spread our evening meal,
She told me she had lost her elder child,
That he for months had been a serving boy,
Apprenticed by the parish. "I perceive
You look at me, and you have cause. Today
I have been travelling far, and many days
350 About the fields I wander, knowing this
Only, that what I seek I cannot find.
And so I waste my time: for I am changed,
And to myself," she said, "have done much wrong,
And to this helpless infant. I have slept
Weeping, and weeping I have waked. My tears
Have flowed as if my body were not such
As others are, and I could never die.
But I am now in mind and in my heart
More easy, and I hope," she said, "that heaven
360 Will give me patience to endure the things
Which I behold at home."

      'It would have grieved
Your very soul to see her. Sir, I feel
The story linger in my heart. I fear
'Tis long and tedious, but my spirit clings
To that poor woman. So familiarly
Do I perceive her manner and her look
And presence, and so deeply do I feel
Her goodness, that not seldom in my walks
A momentary trance comes over me,

370   And to myself I seem to muse on one
       By sorrow laid asleep or borne away,
       A human being destined to awake
       To human life, or something very near
       To human life, when he shall come again
       For whom she suffered. Sir, it would have grieved
       Your very soul to see her: evermore
       Her eyelids drooped, her eyes were downward cast,
       And when she at her table gave me food
       She did not look at me. Her voice was low,
380   Her body was subdued. In every act
       Pertaining to her house affairs appeared
       The careless stillness which a thinking mind
       Gives to an idle matter. Still she sighed,
       But yet no motion of the breast was seen,
       No heaving of the heart. While by the fire
       We sate together, sighs came on my ear,
       I knew not how, and hardly whence they came.
       I took my staff, and when I kissed her babe
       The tears stood in her eyes. I left her then
390   With the best hope and comfort I could give:
       She thanked me for my will, but for my hope
       It seemed she did not thank me.

                              'I returned
       And took my rounds along this road again
       Ere on its sunny bank the primrose flower
       Had chronicled the earliest day of spring.
       I found her sad and drooping. She had learned
       No tidings of her husband; if he lived,
       She knew not that he lived; if he were dead,
       She knew not he was dead. She seemed the same
400   In person or appearance, but her house
       Bespoke a sleepy hand of negligence.
       The floor was neither dry nor neat, the hearth
       Was comfortless,
       The windows too were dim, and her few books,
       Which one upon the other heretofore
       Had been piled up against the corner panes
       In seemly order, now with straggling leaves
       Lay scattered here and there, open or shut,
       As they had chanced to fall. Her infant babe
410   Had from its mother caught the trick of grief,
       And sighed among its playthings. Once again
       I turned towards the garden gate, and saw
       More plainly still that poverty and grief
       Were now come nearer to her. The earth was hard,
       With weeds defaced and knots of withered grass;

No ridges there appeared of clear black mould,
No winter greenness. Of her herbs and flowers
It seemed the better part were gnawed away
Or trampled on the earth. A chain of straw,
420   Which had been twisted round the tender stem
Of a young apple tree, lay at its root;
The bark was nibbled round by truant sheep.
Margaret stood near, her infant in her arms,
And, seeing that my eye was on the tree,
She said, "I fear it will be dead and gone
Ere Robert come again."

        'Towards the house
Together we returned, and she enquired
If I had any hope. But for her Babe,
And for her little friendless Boy, she said,
430   She had no wish to live—that she must die
Of sorrow. Yet I saw the idle loom
Still in its place. His Sunday garments hung
Upon the selfsame nail, his very staff
Stood undisturbed behind the door. And when
I passed this way beaten by Autumn winds,
She told me that her little babe was dead,
And she was left alone. That very time,
I yet remember, through the miry lane
She walked with me a mile, when the bare trees
440   Trickled with foggy damps, and in such sort
That any heart had ached to hear her, begged
That wheresoe'r I went I still would ask
For him whom she had lost. We parted then,
Our final parting; for from that time forth
Did many seasons pass ere I returned
Into this tract again.

        'Five tedious years
She lingered in unquiet widowhood,
A wife and widow. Needs must it have been
A sore heart-wasting. I have heard, my friend,
450   That in that broken arbour she would sit
The idle length of half a sabbath day;
There, where you see the toadstool's lazy head;
And when a dog passed by she still would quit
The shade and look abroad. On this old Bench
For hours she sate, and evermore her eye
Was busy in the distance, shaping things
Which made her heart beat quick. Seest thou that path?
The green sward now has broken its gray line—
There to and fro she paced through many a day
460   Of the warm summer, from a belt of flax

That girt her waist, spinning the long-drawn thread
With backward steps. Yet ever as there passed
A man whose garments showed the Soldier's red,
Or crippled Mendicant in Sailor's garb,
The little child who sate to turn the wheel
Ceased from his toil, and she, with faltering voice,
Expecting still to hear her husband's fate,
Made many a fond enquiry; and when they
Whose presence gave no comfort, were gone by,
470 Her heart was still more sad. And by yon gate,
Which bars the traveller's road, she often stood,
And when a stranger horseman came, the latch
Would lift, and in his face look wistfully,
Most happy if from aught discovered there
Of tender feeling she might dare repeat
The same sad question.

    'Meanwhile her poor hut
Sunk to decay; for he was gone, whose hand
At the first nippings of October frost
Closed up each chink, and with fresh bands of straw
480 Chequered the green-grown thatch. And so she lived
Through the long winter, reckless and alone,
Till this reft house, by frost, and thaw, and rain,
Was sapped; and when she slept, the nightly damps
Did chill her breast, and in the stormy day
Her tattered clothes were ruffled by the wind
Even at the side of her own fire. Yet still
She loved this wretched spot, nor would for worlds
Have parted hence; and still that length of road,
And this rude bench, one torturing hope endeared,
490 Fast rooted at her heart. And here, my friend,
In sickness she remained; and here she died,
Last human tenant of these ruined walls.'

The old Man ceased: he saw that I was moved.
From that low bench rising instinctively,
I turned aside in weakness, nor had power
To thank him for the tale which he had told.
I stood, and leaning o'er the garden gate
Reviewed that Woman's sufferings; and it seemed
To comfort me while with a brother's love
500 I blessed her in the impotence of grief.
At length towards the cottage I returned
Fondly, and traced with milder interest,
That secret spirit of humanity
Which, 'mid the calm oblivious tendencies
Of nature, 'mid her plants, her weeds and flowers,
And silent overgrowings, still survived.

The old man seeing this resumed, and said,
'My friend, enough to sorrow have you given,
The purposes of Wisdom ask no more:
510 Be wise and cheerful, and no longer read
The forms of things with an unworthy eye.
She sleeps in the calm earth, and peace is here.
I well remember that those very plumes,
Those weeds, and the high spear grass on that wall,
By mist and silent raindrops silvered o'er,
As once I passed, did to my mind convey
So still an image of tranquillity,
So calm and still, and looked so beautiful
Amid the uneasy thoughts which filled my mind,
520 That what we feel of sorrow and despair
From ruin and from change, and all the grief
The passing shows of being leave behind,
Appeared an idle dream that could not live
Where meditation was. I turned away,
And walked along my road in happiness.'

He ceased. By this the sun declining shot
A slant and mellow radiance, which began
To fall upon us where beneath the trees
We sate on that low bench. And now we felt,
530 Admonished thus, the sweet hour coming on:
A linnet warbled from those lofty elms,
A thrush sang loud, and other melodies
At distance heard, peopled the milder air.
The old man rose and hoisted up his load.
Together casting then a farewell look
Upon those silent walls, we left the shade;
And, ere the stars were visible, attained
A rustic inn, our evening resting place.

     THE END

1797–99   1968

Home at Grasmere

['Prospectus' to *The Excursion*]

These are the final one hundred and seven lines of "Home at Grasmere," Book One of
Part One of the projected epic *The Recluse,* and almost all of that poem ever
written, except for *The Excursion,* which was to be Part Two of three parts. Wordsworth waited sixteen years before publishing these lines, as a "Prospectus" to *The
Excursion* in 1814. *The Prelude* was not part of the design of *The Recluse,* but was
intended as a preparatory poem toward the (hopefully) greater work. Wordsworth, a
little defensively, characterized the relation between the completed but unpublished *Prelude* and the incomplete but partly published *Recluse* as being like the one

that "the ante-chapel has to the body of a gothic church. Continuing this allusion, he may be permitted to add, that his minor Pieces, which have been long before the public, when they shall be properly arranged, will be found by the attentive reader to have such connection with the main work as may give them claim to be likened to the little cells, oratories, and sepulchral recesses, ordinarily included in those edifices."

This fragment, extraordinary in itself as Wordsworth's most defiantly unorthodox manifesto of a naturalistic humanism, is vital also as a central influence upon Keats and Shelley. It provoked Blake to passionate protest, and his comments have been integrated with the notes below.

From Home at Grasmere

['Prospectus' to *The Excursion*]

On Man, on Nature, and on Human Life,
Musing in solitude, I oft perceive
Fair trains of imagery before me rise,
Accompanied by feelings of delight
Pure, or with no unpleasing sadness mixed;
And I am conscious of affecting thoughts
And dear remembrances, whose presence soothes
Or elevates the Mind, intent to weigh
The good and evil of our mortal state.
10 —To these emotions, whencesoe'er they come,
Whether from breath of outward circumstance,
Or from the Soul—an impulse to herself—
I would give utterance in numerous verse.°
Of Truth, of Grandeur, Beauty, Love, and Hope,
And melancholy Fear subdued by Faith;
Of blessed consolations in distress;
Of moral strength, and intellectual Power;
Of joy in widest commonalty spread;
Of the individual Mind that keeps her own
20 Inviolate retirement, subject there
To Conscience only, and the law supreme
Of that Intelligence which governs all,
I sing—'fit audience let me find though few!'°

So prayed, more gaining than he asked, the Bard—
In holiest mood. Urania,° I shall need
Thy guidance, or a greater Muse, if such
Descend to earth or dwell in highest heaven!
For I must tread on shadowy ground, must sink
Deep—and, aloft ascending, breathe in worlds

numerous verse See *Paradise Lost* V.150.   **fit . . . few** *Paradise Lost* VII.31.
Urania See invocation to Bk. VII, *Paradise Lost*.

30   To which the heaven of heavens is but a veil.
   All strength—all terror, single or in bands,
   That ever was put forth in personal form—
   Jehovah—with his thunder, and the choir
   Of shouting Angels, and the empyreal thrones—
   I pass them unalarmed.° Not Chaos, not
   The darkest pit of lowest Erebus,°
   Nor aught of blinder vacancy, scooped out
   By help of dreams—can breed such fear and awe
   As fall upon us often when we look
40   Into our Minds, into the Mind of Man—
   My haunt, and the main region of my song.
   —Beauty—a living Presence of the earth,
   Surpassing the most fair ideal Forms
   Which craft of delicate Spirits hath composed
   From earth's materials—waits upon my steps;
   Pitches her tents before me as I move,
   An hourly neighbour. Paradise, and groves
   Elysian, Fortunate Fields°—like those of old
   Sought in the Atlantic Main—why should they be
50   A history only of departed things,
   Or a mere fiction of what never was?
   For the discerning intellect of Man,
   When wedded to this goodly universe
   In love and holy passion, shall find these
   A simple produce of the common day.
   —I, long before the blissful hour arrives,
   Would chant, in lonely peace, the spousal verse°
   Of this great consummation—and, by words
   Which speak of nothing more than what we are,
60   Would I arouse the sensual from their sleep
   Of Death, and win the vacant and the vain
   To noble raptures; while my voice proclaims
   How exquisitely the individual Mind
   (And the progressive powers perhaps no less
   Of the whole species) to the external World
   Is fitted—and how exquisitely, too—
   Theme this but little heard of among men—
   The external World is fitted to the Mind;°
   And the creation (by no lower name

All strength . . . unalarmed (ll. 31–35) Blake commented: "Solomon when he Married Pharaoh's daughter and became a Convert to the Heathen Mythology Talked exactly in this way of Jehovah as a Very inferior object of Mans Contemplations he also passed him by unalarmed and was permitted, Jehovah dropped a tear and followed him by his Spirit into the Abstract Void it is called the Divine Mercy Satan dwells in it but Mercy does not dwell in him he knows not to Forgive."

Erebus antechamber to Hades
Fortunate Fields the place of the blessed in the afterlife, islands where Achilles is said to have gone, beyond Gibraltar, out in the Atlantic, and sometimes associated (as by Wordsworth here) with lost Atlantis
spousal verse a nuptial song, an epithalamion
The external . . . Mind Blake snapped: "You shall not bring me down to believe such fitting and fitted I know better and Please your Lordship."

70   Can it be called) which they with blended might
      Accomplish—this is our high argument.
      —Such grateful haunts foregoing, if I oft
      Must turn elsewhere—to travel near the tribes
      And fellowships of men, and see ill sights
      Of madding passions mutually inflamed;
      Must hear Humanity in fields and groves
      Pipe solitary anguish; or must hang
      Brooding above the fierce confederate storm
      Of sorrow, barricadoed evermore
80   Within the walls of cities—may these sounds
      Have their authentic comment; that even these
      Hearing, I be not downcast or forlorn!°—
      Descend, prophetic Spirit! that inspirest
      The human Soul of universal earth,
      Dreaming on things to come;° and dost possess
      A metropolitan temple in the hearts
      Of mighty Poets: upon me bestow
      A gift of genuine insight; that my Song
      With starlike virtue in its place may shine,
90   Shedding benignant influence, and secure,
      Itself, from all malevolent effect
      Of those mutations that extend their sway
      Throughout the nether sphere!—And if with this
      I mix more lowly matter; with the thing
      Contemplated, describe the Mind and Man
      Contemplating; and who, and what he was—
      The transitory Being that beheld
      The Vision; when and where, and how he lived—
      Be not this labour useless. If such theme
100   May sort with highest objects, then—dread Power!
      Whose gracious favour is the primal source
      Of all illumination—may my Life
      Express the image of a better time,
      More wise desires, and simpler manners—nurse
      My Heart in genuine freedom—all pure thoughts
      Be with me—so shall thy unfailing love
      Guide, and support, and cheer me to the end!
      1798   1814

—**Such . . . forlorn** (ll. 72–82) Blake underlined "Humanity in fields and groves / Pipe solitary anguish" and then commented on the whole passage: "does not this Fit and is it not Fitting most Exquisitely too but to what not to Mind but to the Vile Body only and to its Laws of Good and Evil and its Enmities against Mind."
things to come Wordsworth's own note cites Shakespeare's Sonnet CVII: ". . . the prophetic soul / Of the wide world dreaming on things to come."

Tintern Abbey

Here, under Coleridge's direct influence, Wordsworth arrives at his myth of memory. Coming again into the presence of a remembered place, he attains a more complete understanding of his poetic self than he enjoyed before. What he persuades himself he has learned is a principle of reciprocity between himself and nature, a mutual generosity, an exchange of his disinterested love for nature's disinterested beauty. In the poet's recognition of this sharing, there comes into being a state of aesthetic contemplation, in which his will ceases to attempt to relate knowledge of the natural world to discursive knowledge of any kind. Nature is a reality to him, one that he will not murder by dissecting.

Yet this great poem is not a celebration, though it would like to be. It is almost a lament. Wordsworth wants the poem to be about renovation, about carrying the past alive into the present, and so being able to live on into the future with a full sense of continuity. "Tintern Abbey" is all the more powerful for breaking away from Wordsworth's intention. The poem's subject, despite the poet, is memory. Is the story he tells himself about memory a visionary lie? Though he is eager to renew his covenant with nature, has he adequate cause to trust that nature will renew her past movements toward him?

The poem does not trust its own answers to these questions. What Emerson, following Coleridge, called the law of compensation, now comes into operation. "Nothing is got for nothing," Emerson grimly observed. Wordsworth now *knows* consciously his love for nature, as he begins to know his bond to other men, but this knowing is darkened by shadows of mortality. An urgency enters the second half of the poem, as the poet begins to press for evidences of continuity with the ardors of his earlier self. Simply, he seeks what in religion is called salvation, but his quest is displaced into a wholly naturalistic context. He knows only nature and his own mind; he remembers when nature gave him a more direct joy than he now has; and farther back there was a time when he knew himself only in union with nature. Desperately, he affirms that nature will not betray him, but the deep reverberations of this seminal poem hint distinctly at how troubled he is.

Lines

Composed a Few Miles Above Tintern Abbey
On Revisiting the Banks of the Wye During a Tour. July 13, 1798°

Five years have passed; five summers, with the length
Of five long winters! and again I hear
These waters, rolling from their mountain-springs
With a soft inland murmur.°—Once again
Do I behold these steep and lofty cliffs,
That on a wild secluded scene impress

Lines . . . July 13, 1798 Wordsworth noted: "I have not ventured to call this Poem an Ode; but it was written with a hope that in the transitions, and the impassioned music of the versification, would be found the principal requisites of that species of composition." The tradition of the Sublime ode hovers in the background throughout, and the thematic connections to the later "Intimations of Immortality" ode should become clearer with each rereading.
soft inland murmur See "Though inland far we be" in the "Intimations" ode, l.162.

Thoughts of more deep seclusion; and connect
The landscape with the quiet of the sky.
The day is come when I again repose

10 Here, under this dark sycamore, and view
These plots of cottage-ground, these orchard-tufts,
Which at this season, with their unripe fruits,
Are clad in one green hue, and lose themselves
'Mid groves and copses. Once again I see
These hedge-rows, hardly hedge-rows, little lines
Of sportive wood run wild: these pastoral farms,
Green to the very door; and wreaths of smoke
Sent up, in silence, from among the trees!
With some uncertain notice, as might seem

20 Of vagrant dwellers in the houseless woods,
Or of some Hermit's cave, where by his fire
The Hermit sits alone.

                  These beauteous forms,
Through a long absence, have not been to me
As is a landscape to a blind man's eye:
But oft, in lonely rooms, and 'mid the din
Of towns and cities, I have owed to them
In hours of weariness, sensations sweet,
Felt in the blood, and felt along the heart;
And passing even into my purer mind,°

30 With tranquil restoration:°—feelings too
Of unremembered pleasure: such, perhaps,
As have no slight or trivial influence
On that best portion of a good man's life,
His little, nameless, unremembered, acts
Of kindness and of love. Nor less, I trust,
To them I may have owed another gift,
Of aspect more sublime; that blessed mood
In which the burthen of the mystery,
In which the heavy and the weary weight

40 Of all this unintelligible world,
Is lightened:—that serene and blessed mood,
In which the affections gently lead us on,—
Until, the breath of this corporeal frame
And even the motion of our human blood
Almost suspended, we are laid asleep
In body, and become a living soul:
While with an eye made quiet by the power
Of harmony, and the deep power of joy,
We see into the life of things.°

purer mind not that the mind is purer than the
heart or blood; he means a purer part or, likelier, state of the mind
tranquil restoration Involved here is the "emotion recollected in tranquillity" of the 1800

Preface to *Lyrical Ballads*, but restoration has
a very strong meaning, almost "renovation."
that serene . . . things (ll. 41–49) Not a
mystical reverie, but an aesthetic state of contemplation is described.

If this

50 Be but a vain belief, yet, oh! how oft—
In darkness and amid the many shapes
Of joyless daylight; when the fretful stir
Unprofitable, and the fever of the world,
Have hung upon the beatings of my heart—
How oft, in spirit, have I turned to thee,
O sylvan Wye! thou wanderer through the woods,
How often has my spirit turned to thee!

And now, with gleams of half-extinguished thought,
With many recognitions dim and faint,
60 And somewhat of a sad perplexity,°
The picture of the mind revives again:
While here I stand, not only with the sense
Of present pleasure, but with pleasing thoughts
That in this moment there is life and food
For future years. And so I dare to hope,
Though changed, no doubt, from what I was when first
I came among these hills; when like a roe
I bounded o'er the mountains, by the sides
Of the deep rivers, and the lonely streams,
70 Wherever nature led: more like a man
Flying from something that he dreads° than one
Who sought the thing he loved. For nature then
(The coarser pleasures of my boyish days,°
And their glad animal movements all gone by)
To me was all in all.°—I cannot paint
What then I was. The sounding cataract
Haunted me like a passion: the tall rock,
The mountain, and the deep and gloomy wood,
Their colours and their forms, were then to me
80 An appetite; a feeling and a love,
That had no need of a remoter charm,
By thought supplied, nor any interest
Unborrowed from the eye.—That time is past,
And all its aching joys are now no more,
And all its dizzy raptures.° Not for this
Faint I, nor mourn nor murmur; other gifts
Have followed; for such loss, I would believe,
Abundant recompense.° For I have learned

sad perplexity There is evidently a felt sense of loss in the contrast between memory and the scene before him; the dark undersong of the poem has begun.
Flying . . . dreads Flying from time; what he dreads is mortality, the poem's hidden subject.
my boyish days his first stage, so much at one with Nature that he was not aware of her
all in all The second stage, when he was aware of Nature and loved her without anxiety, five years before; the third stage is the "now" of the poem, when he is conscious of the possibility

of estrangement both from Nature and from his own former self.
dizzy raptures like "aching joys." This is an ambiguous phrase; "dizzy" and "aching" seek to qualify negatively, yet primarily they testify to the intensity and authenticity of the now past raptures and joys.
other gifts . . . recompense first central verse statement of Wordsworth's great idea of the compensatory imagination, which converts experiential loss into poetic and (Wordsworth desperately insisted) human gain

To look on nature, not as in the hour
90   Of thoughtless youth; but hearing oftentimes
The still, sad music of humanity,
Nor harsh nor grating, though of ample power
To chasten and subdue. And I have felt
A presence that disturbs me with the joy
Of elevated thoughts; a sense sublime
Of something far more deeply interfused,
Whose dwelling is the light of setting suns,
And the round ocean and the living air,
And the blue sky, and in the mind of man:
100   A motion and a spirit, that impels
All thinking things, all objects of all thought,
And rolls through all things. Therefore am I still
A lover of the meadows and the woods,
And mountains; and of all that we behold
From this green earth; of all the mighty world
Of eye, and ear,—both what they half create,°
And what perceive; well pleased to recognize
In nature and the language of the sense
The anchor of my purest thoughts, the nurse,°
110   The guide, the guardian of my heart, and soul
Of all my moral being.
                              Nor perchance,
If I were not thus taught, should I the more
Suffer my genial spirits° to decay:
For thou art with me here upon the banks
Of this fair river; thou my dearest Friend,
My dear, dear Friend;° and in thy voice I catch
The language of my former heart, and read
My former pleasures in the shooting lights
Of thy wild eyes. Oh! yet a little while
120   May I behold in thee what I was once,
My dear, dear Sister! and this prayer I make,°
Knowing that Nature never did betray
The heart that loved her; 'tis her privilege,
Through all the years of this our life, to lead
From joy to joy: for she can so inform
The mind that is within us, so impress

half create crucial and controversial phrase, deliberately echoed in Yeats's "Adam's Curse,"
and itself a conscious echo from Edward Young's
Night Thoughts VI.427, where the human senses
"half create the wondrous world they see." It
may be interpreted as follows: Man half creates
as well as perceives Nature because his senses
are not wholly passive but selective, to a high
degree; Man's choice among what his senses
present to him is a kind of creation, one that
is guided by memory, and that strives to attain
continuity by linking together earlier and later
presences of Nature.
nurse as in the "Intimations" ode, l. 81

genial spirits The source is Milton's Samson
Agonistes, ll. 594–98; the fearful descendant is
Coleridge's "Dejection: An Ode," l. 39.
Friend his sister Dorothy. It is a shock to learn
in l. 114 that she is present in the scene at all;
it is another shock to remember that she was
only a year-and-a-half younger than the poet,
though he reads in her "the language of my
former heart."
this prayer I make Does he ever make it in
this poem? Some critics interpret the prayer as
beginning in l. 134, but that seems a blessing,
not a prayer.

With quietness and beauty, and so feed
With lofty thoughts, that neither evil tongues,
Rash judgments, nor the sneers of selfish men,
130 Nor greetings where no kindness is, nor all
The dreary intercourse of daily life,
Shall e'er prevail against us, or disturb
Our cheerful faith, that all which we behold
Is full of blessings. Therefore let the moon
Shine on thee in thy solitary walk;°
And let the misty mountain-winds be free
To blow against thee: and, in after years,
When these wild ecstasies shall be matured
Into a sober pleasure;° when thy mind
140 Shall be a mansion for all lovely forms,
Thy memory be as a dwelling-place
For all sweet sounds and harmonies; oh! then,
If solitude, or fear, or pain, or grief,
Should be thy portion, with what healing thoughts
Of tender joy wilt thou remember me,
And these my exhortations! Nor, perchance—
If I should be where I no more can hear
Thy voice, nor catch from thy wild eyes these gleams
Of past existence—wilt thou then forget
150 That on the banks of this delightful stream
We stood together; and that I, so long
A worshipper of Nature, hither came
Unwearied in that service: rather say
With warmer love—oh! with far deeper zeal
Of holier love.° Nor wilt thou then forget,
That after many wanderings, many years
Of absence, these steep woods and lofty cliffs,
And this green pastoral landscape, were to me
More dear, both for themselves and for thy sake!
1798   1798

Nutting°

————————It seems a day
(I speak of one from many singled out)
One of those heavenly days that cannot die;

solitary walk The passage is clearly indebted to Coleridge's "Frost at Midnight," written less than a half-year before.
sober pleasure It is difficult to prefer a sober pleasure to a wild ecstasy, but this is Wordsworth's desperate wisdom, for which see again the "Intimations" ode, ll. 196–98.
holier love The displacement of the vocabulary of religious devotion into a naturalistic context

here has been noted by many critics, and made Wordsworth very nervous in later years; so in 1814 he denied that he was ever "a worshipper of Nature," and deprecated "a passionate expression, uttered incautiously in the poem upon the Wye. . . ."
Nutting rejected from *The Prelude,* but akin to the crucial episodes of Bk. I

When, in the eagerness of boyish hope,
I left our cottage-threshold, sallying forth
With a huge wallet o'er my shoulders slung,
A nutting-crook in hand; and turned my steps
Toward some far-distant wood, a Figure quaint,
Tricked out in proud disguise of cast-off weeds
10   Which for that service had been husbanded,
By exhortation of my frugal Dame—
Motley accoutrement, of power to smile
At thorns, and brakes, and brambles,—and, in truth,
More ragged than need was! O'er path-less rocks,
Through beds of matted fern, and tangled thickets,
Forcing my way, I came to one dear nook
Unvisited, where not a broken bough
Drooped with its withered leaves, ungracious sign
Of devastation; but the hazels rose
20   Tall and erect, with tempting clusters hung,
A virgin scene!—A little while I stood,
Breathing with such suppression of the heart
As joy delights in; and, with wise restraint
Voluptuous, fearless of a rival, eyed
The banquet;—or beneath the trees I sate
Among the flowers, and with the flowers I played;
A temper known to those who, after long
And weary expectation, have been blest
With sudden happiness beyond all hope.
30   Perhaps it was a bower beneath whose leaves
The violets of five seasons re-appear
And fade, unseen by any human eye;
Where fairy water-breaks do murmur on
Forever; and I saw the sparkling foam,
And—with my cheek on one of those green stones
That, fleeced with moss, under the shady trees,
Lay round me, scattered like a flock of sheep—
I heard the murmur and the murmuring sound,
In that sweet mood when pleasure loves to pay
40   Tribute to ease; and, of its joy secure,
The heart luxuriates with indifferent things,
Wasting its kindliness on stocks and stones,
And on the vacant air. Then up I rose,
And dragged to earth both branch and bough, with crash
And merciless ravage: and the shady nook
Of hazels, and the green and mossy bower,
Deformed and sullied, patiently gave up
Their quiet being: and, unless I now
Confound my present feelings with the past,
50   Ere from the mutilated bower I turned
Exulting, rich beyond the wealth of kings,

I felt a sense of pain when I beheld
The silent trees, and saw the intruding sky.—
Then, dearest Maiden, move along these shades
In gentleness of heart; with gentle hand
Touch—for there is a spirit in the woods.
1798   1800

The Lucy Poems

These five poems are traditionally grouped, and do seem to create an extraordinary
unity, though Wordsworth himself never printed them as a sequence. Coleridge,
commenting on "A Slumber Did My Spirit Seal," surmised that the poem recorded
a gloomy moment in which Wordsworth experienced a passing fear that Dorothy
might die. The most persuasive modern speculation is that of H. M. Margoliouth, who
identified "Lucy" as Margaret (Peggy) Hutchinson, younger sister of the Mary
whom Wordsworth married, and of the Sara whom Coleridge wished to marry but
could not. Margaret, born in 1772, died in 1796. Margoliouth noted that "I travelled
among unknown men" is a subtle declaration of love for Mary, "beloved not only
for herself but as part of England, not only for herself but as inheriting also Wordsworth's unfulfilled love for her dead sister." This must all remain surmise, as no definitive evidence exists.

Strange Fits of Passion

Strange fits of passion have I known:
And I will dare to tell,
But in the Lover's ear alone,
What once to me befell.

When she I loved looked every day
Fresh as a rose in June,
I to her cottage bent my way,
Beneath an evening-moon.

Upon the moon I fixed my eye,
10   All over the wide lea;
With quickening pace my horse drew nigh
Those paths so dear to me.

And now we reached the orchard-plot;
And, as we climbed the hill,
The sinking moon to Lucy's cot
Came near, and nearer still.

In one of those sweet dreams I slept,
Kind Nature's gentlest boon!
And all the while my eyes I kept
20   On the descending moon.

My horse moved on; hoof after hoof
He raised, and never stopped:
When down behind the cottage roof,
At once, the bright moon dropped.

What fond and wayward thoughts will slide
Into a Lover's head!
'O mercy!' to myself I cried,
'If Lucy should be dead!'
1799   1800

She Dwelt Among the Untrodden Ways

She dwelt among the untrodden ways
   Beside the springs of Dove,°
A Maid whom there were none to praise
   And very few to love:

A violet by a mossy stone
   Half hidden from the eye!
—Fair as a star, when only one
   Is shining in the sky.

She lived unknown, and few could know
   When Lucy ceased to be;
But she is in her grave, and, oh,
   The difference to me!°
1799   1800

Three Years She Grew in Sun and Shower

Three years she grew in sun and shower,°
Then Nature said, 'A lovelier flower
On earth was never sown;
This Child I to myself will take;
She shall be mine, and I will make
A Lady of my own.

'Myself will to my darling be
Both law and impulse: and with me
The Girl, in rock and plain,
In earth and heaven, in glade and bower,
Shall feel an overseeing power
To kindle or restrain.

Dove any of several English streams
The . . . me! a line in which Keats found
"perfect pathos"
Three . . . shower almost certainly means she

lived for three years after the "I" of the poem
fell in love with her, not that she was a three-
year-old child when she died (see the next-to-
the-last stanza).

'She shall be sportive as the fawn
That wild with glee across the lawn
Or up the mountain springs;
And hers shall be the breathing balm,
And hers the silence and the calm
Of mute insensate things.

20 'The floating clouds their state shall lend
To her; for her the willow bend;
Nor shall she fail to see
Even in the motions of the Storm
Grace that shall mould the Maiden's form
By silent sympathy.

'The stars of midnight shall be dear
To her; and she shall lean her ear
In many a secret place
Where rivulets dance their wayward round,
And beauty born of murmuring sound
30 Shall pass into her face.

'And vital feelings of delight
Shall rear her form to stately height,
Her virgin bosom swell;
Such thoughts to Lucy I will give
While she and I together live
Here in this happy dell.'

Thus Nature spake—The work was done—
How soon my Lucy's race was run!
She died, and left to me
40 This heath, this calm, and quiet scene;
The memory of what has been,
And never more will be.
1799   1800

A Slumber Did My Spirit Seal

A slumber did my spirit seal;
    I had no human fears:
She seemed a thing that could not feel
    The touch of earthly years.

No motion has she now, no force;
    She neither hears nor sees;
Rolled round in earth's diurnal° course,
    With rocks, and stones, and trees.
1799   1800

diurnal daily

I Travelled Among Unknown Men

I travelled among unknown men,
　　In lands beyond the sea;
Nor, England! did I know till then
　　What love I bore to thee.

'Tis past, that melancholy dream!
　　Nor will I quit thy shore
A second time; for still I seem
　　To love thee more and more.

Among thy mountains did I feel
10　　The joy of my desire;
And she I cherished turned her wheel
　　Beside an English fire.

Thy mornings showed, thy nights concealed,
　　The bowers where Lucy played;
And thine too is the last green field
　　That Lucy's eyes surveyed.
　1801　　　　　　　　1807

Lucy Gray;

Or, Solitude

Oft I had heard of Lucy Gray:
And, when I crossed the wild,
I chanced to see at break of day
The solitary child.

No mate, no comrade Lucy knew;
She dwelt on a wide moor,
—The sweetest thing that ever grew
Beside a human door!

You yet may spy the fawn at play,
10　The hare upon the green;
But the sweet face of Lucy Gray
Will never more be seen.

'Tonight will be a stormy night—
You to the town must go;
And take a lantern, Child, to light
Your mother through the snow.'

'That, Father! will I gladly do:
'Tis scarcely afternoon—

The minster-clock° has just struck two,
20   And yonder is the moon!'

At this the Father raised his hook,
And snapped a faggot-band;
He plied his work;—and Lucy took
The lantern in her hand.

Not blither is the mountain roe:
With many a wanton stroke
Her feet disperse the powdery snow,
That rises up like smoke.

The storm came on before its time:
30   She wandered up and down;
And many a hill did Lucy climb:
But never reached the town.

The wretched parents all that night
Went shouting far and wide;
But there was neither sound nor sight
To serve them for a guide.

At day-break on a hill they stood
That overlooked the moor;
And thence they saw the bridge of wood,
40   A furlong from their door.

They wept—and, turning homeward, cried,
'In heaven we all shall meet';
—When in the snow the mother spied
The print of Lucy's feet.

Then downwards from the steep hill's edge
They tracked the footmarks small;
And through the broken hawthorn hedge,
And by the long stone-wall;

And then an open field they crossed:
50   The marks were still the same;
They tracked them on, nor ever lost;
And to the bridge they came.

They followed from the snowy bank
Those footmarks, one by one,
Into the middle of the plank;
And further there were none!

—Yet some maintain that to this day
She is a living child;
That you may see sweet Lucy Gray
60   Upon the lonesome wild.

minster-clock church clock

O'er rough and smooth she trips along,
And never looks behind;
And sings a solitary song
That whistles in the wind.
1799   1800

Michael

This is one of Wordsworth's great visions of the dignity of Natural Man, defeated (if at all) neither by circumstance nor by himself, but by the corrupting influence of urban society upon his son. The whole poem, Wordsworth's most beautiful version of pastoral, turns on the idea of covenant, between Michael and Nature, and between Michael and his son. Michael remains true to both covenants, but Nature is more constant than Luke, and the poem ends therefore in profound (though noble) pathos.

Michael

A Pastoral Poem

If from the public way you turn your steps
Up the tumultuous brook of Green-head Ghyll,°
You will suppose that with an upright path
Your feet must struggle; in such bold ascent
The pastoral mountains front you, face to face.
But, courage! for around that boisterous brook
The mountains have all opened out themselves,
And made a hidden valley of their own.
No habitation can be seen; but they
10   Who journey thither find themselves alone
With a few sheep, with rocks and stones, and kites
That overhead are sailing in the sky.
It is in truth an utter solitude;
Nor should I have made mention of this Dell
But for one object which you might pass by,
Might see and notice not. Beside the brook
Appears a straggling heap of unhewn stones!
And to that simple object appertains
A story—unenriched with strange events,
20   Yet not unfit, I deem, for the fireside,
Or for the summer shade. It was the first
Of those domestic tales that spake to me
Of Shepherds, dwellers in the valleys, men
Whom I already loved;—not verily

Ghyll a narrow valley usually wooded and containing a stream. Greenhead is near Wordsworth's house at Grasmere.

For their own sakes, but for the fields and hills
Where was their occupation and abode.
And hence this Tale, while I was yet a Boy
Careless of books, yet having felt the power
Of Nature, by the gentle agency
30   Of natural objects, led me on to feel
For passions that were not my own, and think
(At random and imperfectly indeed)
On man, the heart of man, and human life.
Therefore, although it be a history
Homely and rude, I will relate the same
For the delight of a few natural hearts;
And, with yet fonder feeling, for the sake
Of youthful Poets, who among these hills
Will be my second self when I am gone.°

40   Upon the forest-side in Grasmere Vale
There dwelt a Shepherd, Michael was his name;
An old man, stout of heart, and strong of limb.
His bodily frame had been from youth to age
Of an unusual strength: his mind was keen,
Intense, and frugal, apt for all affairs,
And in his shepherd's calling he was prompt
And watchful more than ordinary men.
Hence had he learned the meaning of all winds,
Of blasts of every tone; and oftentimes,
50   When others heeded not, He heard the South
Make subterraneous music, like the noise
Of bagpipers on distant Highland hills.
The Shepherd, at such warning, of his flock
Bethought him, and he to himself would say,
'The winds are now devising work for me!'
And, truly, at all times, the storm, that drives
The traveller to a shelter, summoned him
Up to the mountains: he had been alone
Amid the heart of many thousand mists,
60   That came to him, and left him, on the heights.
So lived he till his eightieth year was past.
And grossly that man errs, who should suppose
That the green valleys, and the streams and rocks,
Were things indifferent to the Shepherd's thoughts.
Fields, where with cheerful spirits he had breathed
The common air; hills, which with vigorous step
He had so often climbed; which had impressed
So many incidents upon his mind
Of hardship, skill or courage, joy or fear;

And . . . gone a beautiful prophecy, but sad   to recognize the poetic gifts of his best disci-
because unfulfilled; Wordsworth was reluctant   ples: Shelley, Keats, Clare.

70   Which, like a book, preserved the memory
        Of the dumb animals, whom he had saved,
        Had fed or sheltered, linking to such acts
        The certainty of honourable gain;
        Those fields, those hills—what could they less? had laid
        Strong hold on his affections, were to him
        A pleasurable feeling of blind love,
        The pleasure which there is in life itself.

        His days had not been passed in singleness.
        His Helpmate was a comely matron, old—
80   Though younger than himself full twenty years.
        She was a woman of a stirring life,
        Whose heart was in her house: two wheels she had
        Of antique form; this large, for spinning wool;
        That small, for flax; and if one wheel had rest,
        It was because the other was at work.
        The Pair had but one inmate in their house,
        An only Child, who had been born to them
        When Michael, telling o'er his years, began
        To deem that he was old,—in shepherd's phrase,
90   With one foot in the grave. This only Son,
        With two brave sheep-dogs tried in many a storm,
        The one of an inestimable worth,
        Made all their household. I may truly say,
        That they were as a proverb in the vale
        For endless industry. When day was gone,
        And from their occupations out of doors
        The Son and Father were come home, even then,
        Their labour did not cease; unless when all
        Turned to the cleanly supper-board, and there,
100   Each with a mess of pottage and skimmed milk,
        Sat round the basket piled with oaten cakes,
        And their plain home-made cheese. Yet when the meal
        Was ended, Luke (for so the Son was named)
        And his old Father both betook themselves
        To such convenient work as might employ
        Their hands by the fire-side; perhaps to card
        Wool for the Housewife's spindle, or repair
        Some injury done to sickle, flail, or scythe,
        Or other implement of house or field.

110   Down from the ceiling, by the chimney's edge,
        That in our ancient uncouth country style
        With huge and black projection overbrowed
        Large space beneath, as duly as the light
        Of day grew dim the Housewife hung a lamp;
        An aged utensil, which had performed
        Service beyond all others of its kind.

Early at evening did it burn—and late,
Surviving comrade of uncounted hours,
Which, going by from year to year, had found,
120 And left the couple neither gay perhaps
Nor cheerful, yet with objects and with hopes,
Living a life of eager industry.
And now, when Luke had reached his eighteenth year,
There by the light of this old lamp they sate,
Father and Son, while far into the night
The Housewife plied her own peculiar work,
Making the cottage through the silent hours
Murmur as with the sound of summer flies.
This light was famous in its neighbourhood,
130 And was a public symbol of the life
That thrifty Pair had lived.   For, as it chanced,
Their cottage on a plot of rising ground
Stood single, with large prospect, north and south,
High into Easedale, up to Dunmail-Raise,
And westward to the village near the lake;
And from this constant light, so regular,
And so far seen, the House itself, by all
Who dwelt within the limits of the vale,
Both old and young, was named THE EVENING STAR.

140   Thus living on through such a length of years,
The Shepherd, if he loved himself, must needs
Have loved his Helpmate; but to Michael's heart
This son of his old age was yet more dear—
Less from instinctive tenderness, the same
Fond spirit that blindly works in the blood of all—
Than that a child, more than all other gifts
That earth can offer to declining man,
Brings hope with it, and forward-looking thoughts,
And stirrings of inquietude, when they
150 By tendency of nature needs must fail.
Exceeding was the love he bare to him,
His heart and his heart's joy! For often-times
Old Michael, while he was a babe in arms,
Had done him female service, not alone
For pastime and delight, as is the use
Of fathers, but with patient mind enforced
To acts of tenderness; and he had rocked
His cradle, as with a woman's gentle hand.

     And in a later time, ere yet the Boy
160 Had put on boy's attire, did Michael love,
Albeit of a stern unbending mind,
To have the Young-one in his sight, when he
Wrought in the field, or on his shepherd's stool

Sate with a fettered sheep before him stretched
Under the large old oak, that near his door
Stood single, and, from matchless depth of shade,
Chosen for the Shearer's covert from the sun,
Thence in our rustic dialect was called
The CLIPPING° TREE, a name which yet it bears.
170 There, while they two were sitting in the shade,
With others round them, earnest all and blithe,
Would Michael exercise his heart with looks
Of fond correction and reproof bestowed
Upon the Child, if he disturbed the sheep
By catching at their legs, or with his shouts
Scared them, while they lay still beneath the shears.

And when by Heaven's good grace the boy grew up
A healthy Lad, and carried in his cheek
Two steady roses that were five years old;
180 Then Michael from a winter coppice cut
With his own hand a sapling, which he hooped
With iron, making it throughout in all
Due requisites a perfect shepherd's staff,
And gave it to the Boy; wherewith equipt
He as a watchman oftentimes was placed
At gate or gap, to stem or turn the flock;
And, to his office prematurely called,
There stood the urchin, as you will divine,
Something between a hindrance and a help;
190 And for this cause not always, I believe,
Receiving from his Father hire of praise;
Though nought was left undone which staff, or voice,
Or looks, or threatening gestures, could perform.

But soon as Luke, full ten years old, could stand
Against the mountain blasts; and to the heights,
Not fearing toil, nor length of weary ways,
He with his Father daily went, and they
Were as companions, why should I relate
That objects which the Shepherd loved before
200 Were dearer now? that from the Boy there came
Feelings and emanations—things which were
Light to the sun and music to the wind;
And that the old Man's heart seemed born again?

Thus in his Father's sight the Boy grew up:
And now, when he had reached his eighteenth year,
He was his comfort and his daily hope.

Clipping the word used in the North of England for shearing

While in this sort the simple household lived
From day to day, to Michael's ear there came
Distressful tidings. Long before the time
210   Of which I speak, the Shepherd had been bound
In surety for his brother's son, a man
Of an industrious life, and ample means;
But unforeseen misfortunes suddenly
Had pressed upon him; and old Michael now
Was summoned to discharge the forfeiture,
A grievous penalty, but little less
Than half his substance. This unlooked-for claim,
At the first hearing, for a moment took
More hope out of his life than he supposed
220   That any old man ever could have lost.
As soon as he had armed himself with strength
To look his trouble in the face, it seemed
The Shepherd's sole resource to sell at once
A portion of his patrimonial fields.
Such was his first resolve; he thought again,
And his heart failed him. 'Isabel,' said he,
Two evenings after he had heard the news,
'I have been toiling more than seventy years,
And in the open sunshine of God's love
230   Have we all lived; yet if these fields of ours
Should pass into a stranger's hand, I think
That I could not lie quiet in my grave.
Our lot is a hard lot; the sun himself
Has scarcely been more diligent than I;
And I have lived to be a fool at last
To my own family. An evil man
That was, and made an evil choice, if he
Were false to us; and, if he were not false,
There are ten thousand to whom loss like this
240   Had been no sorrow. I forgive him;—but
'Twere better to be dumb than to talk thus.

'When I began, my purpose was to speak
Of remedies and of a cheerful hope.
Our Luke shall leave us, Isabel; the land
Shall not go from us, and it shall be free;
He shall possess it, free as is the wind
That passes over it. We have, thou knowest,
Another kinsman—he will be our friend
In this distress. He is a prosperous man,
250   Thriving in trade—and Luke to him shall go,
And with his kinsman's help and his own thrift
He quickly will repair this loss, and then
He may return to us. If here he stay,

What can be done? Where every one is poor,
What can be gained?'
          At this the old Man paused,
And Isabel sat silent, for her mind
Was busy, looking back into past times.
There's Richard Bateman, thought she to herself,
He was a parish-boy—at the church-door
260   They made a gathering for him, shillings, pence,
And halfpennies, wherewith the neighbours bought
A basket, which they filled with pedlar's wares;
And, with this basket on his arm, the lad
Went up to London, found a master there,
Who, out of many, chose the trusty boy
To go and overlook his merchandise
Beyond the seas; where he grew wondrous rich,
And left estates and monies to the poor,
And, at his birth-place, built a chapel floored
270   With marble, which he sent from foreign lands.
These thoughts, and many others of like sort,
Passed quickly through the mind of Isabel,
And her face brightened. The old Man was glad,
And thus resumed:—'Well, Isabel! this scheme
These two days has been meat and drink to me.
Far more than we have lost is left us yet.
—We have enough—I wish indeed that I
Were younger;—but this hope is a good hope.
Make ready Luke's best garments, of the best
280   Buy for him more, and let us send him forth
Tomorrow, or the next day, or tonight:
—If he *could* go, the Boy should go tonight.'

Here Michael ceased, and to the fields went forth
With a light heart. The Housewife for five days
Was restless morn and night, and all day long
Wrought on with her best fingers to prepare
Things needful for the journey of her son.
But Isabel was glad when Sunday came
To stop her in her work: for, when she lay
290   By Michael's side, she through the last two nights
Heard him, how he was troubled in his sleep:
And when they rose at morning she could see
That all his hopes were gone. That day at noon
She said to Luke, while they two by themselves
Were sitting at the door, 'Thou must not go:
We have no other Child but thee to lose,
None to remember—do not go away,
For if thou leave thy Father he will die.'
The Youth made answer with a jocund voice;

300   And Isabel, when she had told her fears,
    Recovered heart. That evening her best fare
    Did she bring forth, and all together sat
    Like happy people round a Christmas fire.

      With daylight Isabel resumed her work;
    And all the ensuing week the house appeared
    As cheerful as a grove in Spring: at length
    The expected letter from their kinsman came,
    With kind assurances that he would do
    His utmost for the welfare of the Boy;
310   To which, requests were added, that forthwith
    He might be sent to him. Ten times or more
    The letter was read over; Isabel
    Went forth to show it to the neighbours round;
    Nor was there at that time on English land
    A prouder heart than Luke's. When Isabel
    Had to her house returned, the old Man said,
    'He shall depart to-morrow.' To this word
    The Housewife answered, talking much of things
    Which, if at such short notice he should go,
320   Would surely be forgotten. But at length
    She gave consent, and Michael was at ease.

      Near the tumultuous brook of Green-head Ghyll,
    In that deep valley, Michael had designed
    To build a Sheep-fold; and, before he heard
    The tidings of his melancholy loss,
    For this same purpose he had gathered up
    A heap of stones, which by the streamlet's edge
    Lay thrown together, ready for the work.
    With Luke that evening thitherward he walked:
330   And soon as they had reached the place he stopped,
    And thus the old Man spake to him:—'My son,
    To-morrow thou wilt leave me: with full heart
    I look upon thee, for thou art the same
    That wert a promise to me ere thy birth,
    And all thy life hast been my daily joy.
    I will relate to thee some little part
    Of our two histories; 'twill do thee good
    When thou art from me, even if I should touch
    On things thou canst not know of.——After thou
340   First cam'st into the world—as oft befalls
    To new-born infants—thou didst sleep away
    Two days, and blessings from thy Father's tongue
    Then fell upon thee. Day by day passed on,
    And still I loved thee with increasing love.
    Never to living ear came sweeter sounds
    Than when I heard thee by our own fire-side

First uttering, without words, a natural tune;
While thou, a feeding babe, didst in thy joy
Sing at thy Mother's breast. Month followed month,
350   And in the open fields my life was passed
And on the mountains; else I think that thou
Hadst been brought up upon thy Father's knees.
But we were playmates, Luke: among these hills,
As well thou knowest, in us the old and young
Have played together, nor with me didst thou
Lack any pleasure which a boy can know.'
Luke had a manly heart; but at these words
He sobbed aloud. The old Man grasped his hand,
And said, 'Nay, do not take it so—I see
360   That these are things of which I need not speak.
—Even to the utmost I have been to thee
A kind and a good Father: and herein
I but repay a gift which I myself
Received at others' hands; for, though now old
Beyond the common life of man, I still
Remember them who loved me in my youth.
Both of them sleep together: here they lived,
As all their Forefathers had done; and when
At length their time was come, they were not loth
370   To give their bodies to the family mould.
I wished that thou should'st live the life they lived,
But 'tis a long time to look back, my Son,
And see so little gain from threescore years.
These fields were burthened when they came to me;
Till I was forty years of age, not more
Than half of my inheritance was mine.
I toiled and toiled; God blessed me in my work,
And till these three weeks past the land was free.
—It looks as if it never could endure
380   Another Master. Heaven forgive me, Luke,
If I judge ill for thee, but it seems good
That thou shouldst go.'
                              At this the old Man paused;
Then, pointing to the stones near which they stood,
Thus, after a short silence, he resumed:
'This was a work for us; and now, my Son,
It is a work for me. But, lay one stone—
Here, lay it for me, Luke, with thine own hands.
Nay, Boy, be of good hope;—we both may live
To see a better day. At eighty-four
390   I still am strong and hale;—do thou thy part;
I will do mine.—I will begin again
With many tasks that were resigned to thee:
Up to the heights, and in among the storms,

Will I without thee go again, and do
All works which I was wont to do alone,
Before I knew thy face.—Heaven bless thee, Boy!
Thy heart these two weeks has been beating fast
With many hopes; it should be so—yes—yes—
I knew that thou couldst never have a wish
400   To leave me, Luke: thou hast been bound to me
Only by links of love: when thou art gone,
What will be left to us!—But I forget
My purposes. Lay now the corner-stone,
As I requested; and hereafter, Luke,
When thou art gone away, should evil men
Be thy companions, think of me, my Son,
And of this moment; hither turn thy thoughts,
And God will strengthen thee: amid all fear
And all temptation, Luke, I pray that thou
410   May'st bear in mind the life thy Fathers lived,
Who, being innocent, did for that cause
Bestir them in good deeds. Now, fare thee well—
When thou return'st, thou in this place wilt see
A work which is not here: a covenant
'Twill be between us; but, whatever fate
Befall thee, I shall love thee to the last,
And bear thy memory with me to the grave.'

    The Shepherd ended here; and Luke stooped down,
And, as his Father had requested, laid
420   The first stone of the Sheep-fold. At the sight
The old Man's grief broke from him; to his heart
He pressed his Son, he kissed him and wept;
And to the house together they returned.
—Hushed was that House in peace, or seeming peace,
Ere the night fell:—with morrow's dawn the Boy
Began his journey, and when he had reached
The public way, he put on a bold face;
And all the neighbours, as he passed their doors,
Came forth with wishes and with farewell prayers,
430   That followed him till he was out of sight.

    A good report did from their Kinsman come,
Of Luke and his well-doing: and the Boy
Wrote loving letters, full of wondrous news,
Which, as the Housewife phrased it, were throughout
'The prettiest letters that were ever seen.'
Both parents read them with rejoicing hearts.
So, many months passed on: and once again
The Shepherd went about his daily work
With confident and cheerful thoughts; and now
440   Sometimes when he could find a leisure hour

He to that valley took his way, and there
Wrought at the Sheep-fold. Meantime Luke began
To slacken in his duty; and, at length,
He in the dissolute city gave himself
To evil courses: ignominy and shame
Fell on him, so that he was driven at last
To seek a hiding-place beyond the seas.

    There is a comfort in the strength of love;
'Twill make a thing endurable, which else
450   Would overset the brain, or break the heart:
I have conversed with more than one who well
Remember the old Man, and what he was
Years after he had heard this heavy news.
His bodily frame had been from youth to age
Of an unusual strength. Among the rocks
He went, and still looked up to sun and cloud,
And listened to the wind; and, as before,
Performed all kinds of labour for his sheep,
And for the land, his small inheritance.
460   And to that hollow dell from time to time
Did he repair, to build the Fold of which
His flock had need. 'Tis not forgotten yet
The pity which was then in every heart
For the old Man—and 'tis believed by all
That many and many a day he thither went,
And never lifted up a single stone.°

    There, by the Sheep-fold, sometimes was he seen
Sitting alone, or with his faithful Dog,
Then old, beside him, lying at his feet.
470   The length of full seven years, from time to time,
He at the building of this Sheep-fold wrought,
And left the work unfinished when he died.
Three years, or little more, did Isabel
Survive her Husband: at her death the estate
Was sold, and went into a stranger's hand.
The Cottage which was named THE EVENING STAR
Is gone—the ploughshare has been through the ground
On which it stood; great changes have been wrought
In all the neighbourhood:—yet the oak is left
480   That grew beside their door; and the remains
Of the unfinished Sheep-fold may be seen
Beside the boisterous brook of Green-head Ghyll.
1800   1800

And . . . stone Matthew Arnold observed that this line epitomizes Wordsworth's peculiar strength: "Nothing subtle in it, no heightening, no study of poetic style, strictly so called, at all; yet it is expression of the highest and most expressive kind."

My Heart Leaps Up°

My heart leaps up when I behold
   A rainbow in the sky:
So was it when my life began;
So is it now I am a man;
So be it when I shall grow old,
   Or let me die!
The Child is father of the Man;
And I could wish my days to be
Bound each to each by natural piety.°
1802   1807

Resolution and Independence

More even than "Tintern Abbey" and the "Intimations of Immortality" ode, this is the archetype that sets the pattern for the modern crisis-lyric, the poem through and in which a poet saves himself for poetry, and by implication for life. In a secularized epiphany or "privileged moment," as Walter Pater was to call it (Wordsworth's own phrase for it, in *The Prelude*, is "spots of time"), the poet receives the equivalent of a "peculiar grace," a "something given" that redeems the time, that allows renovation to begin. Coleridge in Chapter XXII of his *Biographia Literaria* says: "Indeed this fine poem is *especially* characteristic of the author. There is scarce a defect or excellence in his writings of which it would not present a specimen." Something of the defects can be studied in the mad reflecting-glasses of the poem's two great parodies, Lewis Carroll's "The White Knight's Ballad" and Edward Lear's "Incidents in the Life of My Uncle Arly."

Wordsworth based the poem on an actual meeting with an old leech-gatherer, and wrote a strong commentary on his poetic intentions in a letter written to Sara Hutchinson on June 14, 1802 (while the poem was still being composed). She had disliked the latter part of the draft she had read. Wordsworth defended his poem with considerable passion:

> I describe myself as having been exalted to the highest pitch of delight by the joyousness and beauty of Nature and then as depressed, even in the midst of these beautiful objects, to the lowest dejection and despair. A young Poet in the midst of the happiness of Nature is described as overwhelmed by the thought of the miserable reverses which have befallen the happiest of all men, viz Poets—I think of this till I am so deeply impressed by it, that I consider the manner in which I was rescued from my dejection and despair almost as an interposition of Providence. . . . It is in the character of the old man to tell his story in a manner which an *impatient* reader must necessarily feel as tedious. But Good God! Such a figure, in such a place, a pious self-respecting, miserably infirm old man telling such a tale!

My Heart Leaps Up This is the seed of the "Intimations" ode; after 1815, ll. 7–9 were used as an epigraph to that poem.
natural piety Coleridge approved, and said of this poem that it showed men "that continuity in their self-consciousness, which Nature has made the law of their animal Life." But Blake protested bitterly: "There is no such Thing as Natural Piety Because The Natural Man is at Enmity with God."

Chatterton's "Excellent Ballade of Charitie" gave Wordsworth the poem's metrical form and something of its setting. Hovering in the background is the example of Spenser's *Prothalamion,* with its restoration of the poet's spirits from an initial despondency of self.

Resolution and Independence

I

There was a roaring in the wind all night;
The rain came heavily and fell in floods;
But now the sun is rising calm and bright;
The birds are singing in the distant woods;
Over his own sweet voice the Stock-dove broods;°
The Jay makes answer as the Magpie chatters;
And all the air is filled with pleasant noise of waters.

II

All things that love the sun are out of doors;
The sky rejoices in the morning's birth;
10   The grass is bright with rain-drops;—on the moors
The hare is running races in her mirth;
And with her feet she from the plashy earth
Raises a mist; that, glittering in the sun,
Runs with her all the way, wherever she doth run.

III

I was a Traveller then upon the moor;
I saw the hare that raced about with joy;
I heard the woods and distant waters roar;
Or heard them not, as happy as a boy:
The pleasant season did my heart employ:
20   My old remembrances went from me wholly;
And all the ways of men, so vain and melancholy.

IV

But, as it sometimes chanceth, from the might
Of joy in minds that can no further go,
As high as we have mounted in delight
In our dejection do we sink as low;
To me that morning did it happen so;
And fears and fancies thick upon me came;
Dim sadness—and blind thoughts, I knew not, nor could name.

Over . . . broods In his Preface of 1815 Wordsworth commented upon this line: "The stockdove is said to *coo,* a sound well imitating the note of the bird; but, by the intervention of the metaphor *broods,* the affections are called in by the imagination to assist in marking the manner in which the bird reiterates and prolongs her soft note, as if herself delighting to listen to it. . . ."

V

I heard the sky-lark warbling in the sky;
30 And I bethought me of the playful hare:
Even such a happy Child of earth am I;
Even as these blissful creatures do I fare;
Far from the world I walk, and from all care;
But there may come another day to me—
Solitude, pain of heart, distress, and poverty.

VI

My whole life I have lived in pleasant thought,
As if life's business were a summer mood;
As if all needful things would come unsought
To genial faith, still rich in genial good;
40 But how can He° expect that others should
Build for him, sow for him, and at his call
Love him, who for himself will take no heed at all?

VII

I thought of Chatterton,° the marvellous Boy,
The sleepless Soul that perished in his pride;
Of Him° who walked in glory and in joy
Following his plough, along the mountain-side:
By our own spirits are we deified:
We Poets in our youth begin in gladness;
But thereof come in the end despondency and madness.°

VIII

50 Now, whether it were by peculiar grace,
A leading from above, a something given,
Yet it befell that, in this lonely place,
When I with these untoward thoughts had striven,
Beside a pool bare to the eye of heaven
I saw a Man before me unawares:
The oldest man he seemed that ever wore grey hairs.

IX

As a huge stone is sometimes seen to lie
Couched on the bald top of an eminence;
Wonder to all who do the same espy,
60 By what means it could thither come, and whence;
So that it seems a thing endued with sense:
Like a sea-beast crawled forth, that on a shelf
Of rock or sand reposeth, there to sun itself;

He Coleridge, not just anyone
Chatterton the poet Thomas Chatterton (1752–70), who killed himself at 17. Swinburne particularly admired these two lines about Chatterton.

Him Burns died at 37, desperate and self-ruined.
But . . . madness that is, from the joy itself comes the final madness

X

Such seemed this Man, not all alive nor dead,
Nor all asleep—in his extreme old age:
His body was bent double, feet and head
Coming together in life's pilgrimage;
As if some dire constraint of pain, or rage
Of sickness felt by him in times long past,
70   A more than human weight upon his frame had cast.

XI

Himself he propped, limbs, body, and pale face,
Upon a long grey staff of shaven wood:
And, still as I drew near with gentle pace,
Upon the margin of that moorish flood
Motionless as a cloud the old Man stood,
That heareth not the loud winds when they call;
And moveth all together, if it move at all.

XII

At length, himself unsettling, he the pond
Stirred with his staff, and fixedly did look
80   Upon the muddy water, which he conned,
As if he had been reading in a book:
And now a stranger's privilege I took;
And, drawing to his side, to him did say,
'This morning gives us promise of a glorious day.'

XIII

A gentle answer did the old Man make,
In courteous speech which forth he slowly drew:
And him with further words I thus bespake,
'What occupation do you there pursue?
This is a lonesome place for one like you.'
90   Ere he replied, a flash of mild surprise
Broke from the sable orbs of his yet-vivid eyes.

XIV

His words came feebly, from a feeble chest,
But each in solemn order followed each,
With something of a lofty utterance drest—
Choice word and measured phrase, above the reach
Of ordinary men; a stately speech;
Such as grave Livers do in Scotland use,
Religious men, who give to God and man their dues.

XV

He told, that to these waters he had come
100   To gather leeches,° being old and poor:

leeches still used in early 19th-century medicine,
to let blood to relieve minor illnesses

Employment hazardous and wearisome!
And he had many hardships to endure:
From pond to pond he roamed, from moor to moor;
Housing, with God's good help, by choice or chance;
And in this way he gained an honest maintenance.

XVI

The old Man still stood talking by my side;
But now his voice to me was like a stream
Scarce heard; nor word from word could I divide;
And the whole body of the Man did seem
110   Like one whom I had met with in a dream;
Or like a man from some far region sent,
To give me human strength, by apt admonishment.

XVII

My former thoughts returned: the fear that kills;
And hope that is unwilling to be fed;
Cold, pain, and labour, and all fleshly ills;
And mighty Poets in their misery dead.
—Perplexed, and longing to be comforted,
My question eagerly did I renew,
'How is it that you live, and what is it you do?'

XVIII

120   He with a smile did then his words repeat;
And said that, gathering leeches, far and wide
He travelled; stirring thus about his feet
The waters of the pools where they abide.
'Once I could meet with them on every side;
But they have dwindled long by slow decay;
Yet still I persevere, and find them where I may.'

XIX

While he was talking thus, the lonely place,
The old Man's shape, and speech—all troubled me:
In my mind's eye I seemed to see him pace
130   About the weary moors continually,
Wandering about alone and silently.
While I these thoughts within myself pursued,
He, having made a pause, the same discourse renewed.

XX

And soon with this he other matter blended,
Cheerfully uttered, with demeanour kind,
But stately in the main; and when he ended,
I could have laughed myself to scorn to find
In that decrepit Man so firm a mind.

'God,' said I, 'be my help and stay secure;
140   I'll think of the Leech-gatherer on the lonely moor!'
1802   1807

Composed upon Westminster Bridge, September 3, 1802

Earth has not anything to show more fair:
Dull would he be of soul who could pass by
A sight so touching in its majesty:
This City now doth, like a garment, wear
The beauty of the morning; silent, bare,
Ships, towers, domes, theatres, and temples lie
Open unto the fields, and to the sky;
All bright and glittering in the smokeless air.
Never did sun more beautifully steep
10   In his first splendour, valley, rock, or hill;
Ne'er saw I, never felt, a calm so deep!
The river glideth at his own sweet will:
Dear God! the very houses seem asleep;
And all that mighty heart is lying still!
1802   1807

It Is a Beauteous Evening

It is a beauteous evening, calm and free,
The holy time is quiet as a Nun
Breathless with adoration; the broad sun
Is sinking down in its tranquillity;
The gentleness of heaven broods o'er the Sea:
Listen! the mighty Being° is awake,
And doth with his eternal motion make
A sound like thunder—everlastingly.
Dear Child!° dear Girl! that walkest with me here,
10   If thou appear untouched by solemn thought,
Thy nature is not therefore less divine:
Thou liest in Abraham's bosom° all the year;
And worshippest at the Temple's inner shrine,°
God being with thee when we know it not.
1802   1807

Being the sea, not God
Child almost certainly Caroline, the poet's
daughter by Annette Vallon
Abraham's bosom See Luke 16:22.

inner shrine the Holy of Holies, inner recess
of the Jerusalem Temple, entered by the High
Priest only once a year, on the Day of Atonement

I Wandered Lonely as a Cloud°

I wandered lonely as a cloud
That floats on high o'er vales and hills,
When all at once I saw a crowd,
A host, of golden daffodils;
Beside the lake, beneath the trees,
Fluttering and dancing in the breeze.

Continuous as the stars that shine
And twinkle on the milky way,
They stretched in never-ending line
10 Along the margin of a bay:
Ten thousand saw I at a glance,
Tossing their heads in sprightly dance.

The waves beside them danced; but they
Outdid the sparkling waves in glee;
A poet could not but be gay,
In such a jocund company;
I gazed—and gazed—but little thought
What wealth the show to me had brought:

For oft, when on my couch I lie
20 In vacant or in pensive mood,
They flash upon that inward eye
Which is the bliss of solitude;
And then my heart with pleasure fills,
And dances with the daffodils.
                                    1807

The World Is Too Much with Us

The world is too much with us; late and soon,
Getting and spending, we lay waste our powers:
Little we see in Nature that is ours;
We have given our hearts away, a sordid boon!
This Sea that bares her bosom to the moon;
The winds that will be howling at all hours,
And are up-gathered now like sleeping flowers;
For this, for everything, we are out of tune;
It moves us not.—Great God! I'd rather be
10 A Pagan suckled in a creed outworn;
So might I, standing on this pleasant lea,°

I Wandered Lonely as A Cloud based on a
passage in Dorothy Wordsworth's *Journals*,
April 15, 1802: "I never saw daffodils so beautiful. They grew among the mossy stones about
and about them, some rested their heads upon
these stones as on a pillow for weariness and the
rest tossed and reeled and danced and seemed

as if they verily laughed with the wind that
blew upon them over the lake, they looked so
gay, ever glancing, ever changing."
pleasant lea See Spenser's "Colin Clouts Come
Home Againe," l. 283: "Yet seemed to be a
goodly pleasant lea."

Have glimpses that would make me less forlorn;
Have sight of Proteus rising from the sea;°
Or hear old Triton blow his wreathèd horn.°
1802–4   1807

Ode: Intimations of Immortality from Recollections of Early Childhood

It has been maintained, with justice, that after Milton's *Lycidas* this is the most important shorter poem in the language; certainly it has been one of the most influential upon poets coming after Wordsworth. The Great Ode's effect can be traced in Coleridge, Shelley, Keats, Byron, Clare, Tennyson, Browning, Arnold, Hopkins, Swinburne, and Yeats, among many others, and in American poetry throughout the entire succession that moves between Emerson and Wallace Stevens.

Lionel Trilling succinctly observed that the Ode is not about growing old, but about growing up, with its mingling of painful loss and hard-won gain. Whether, and in what sense, the Ode is also a poem about mortality (rather than about immortality at all) is in perpetual dispute. Wordsworth himself said that "this poem rests entirely upon two recollections of childhood: one that of a splendour in the objects of sense which is passed away; and the other an indisposition to bend to the law of death, as applying to our own particular case." The poet's more general comment on the poem is of great value:

> Two years at least passed between the writing of the first four stanzas and the remaining part. To the attentive and competent reader the whole sufficiently explains itself, but there is no harm in adverting here to particular feelings or *experiences* of my own mind on which the structure of the poem partly rests. Nothing was more difficult for me in childhood than to admit the notion of death as a state applicable to my own being . . . it was not so much from the source of animal vivacity that *my* difficulty came as from a sense of the indomitableness of the spirit within me. I used to brood over the stories of Enoch and Elijah, and almost to persuade myself that, whatever might become of others, I should be translated in something of the same way to heaven. With a feeling congenial to this, I was often unable to think of external things as having external existence, and I communed with all that I saw as something not apart from, but inherent in, my own immaterial nature. Many times while going to school have I grasped at a wall or a tree to recall myself from this abyss of idealism to the reality. At that time I was afraid of such processes. In later periods of life I have deplored, as we have all reason to do, a subjugation of an opposite character, and have rejoiced over the remembrances, as is expressed in the lines, "obstinate questionings," etc. To that dreamlike vividness and splendour which invest objects of sight in childhood, everyone, I believe, if he would look back, could bear testimony. . . .

Though Wordsworth goes on to deny that the Ode argues for the pre-existence of the soul, his denial is ambivalent, since he asserts that there is nothing in the Christian

---

from the sea See *Paradise Lost* III.604: "In various shapes old *Proteus* from the Sea." Homer said that Proteus could assume any shape he wished.
horn See Spenser's "Colin Clouts . . . ," ll. 244–45: "Of them the shepherd which hath charge in chief, / Is *Triton* blowing loud his wreathed horne." Triton, a kind of male mermaid, was generally visualized as playing on a conch shell-trumpet. In identifying the Sea with mythological poetry by Spenser and Milton, Wordsworth opposed their tradition to what he felt was a falling away from Nature, and prepared the way for Keats, whose sonnet "On the Sea" owes much to this sonnet.

revelation to contradict it. Despite scholarly tradition, which has found "sources" for the Ode in Plato's *Phaedrus* and his *Phaedo*, it is well to remember that Wordsworth actually denied any Platonic influence.

Structurally, the Ode is in three parts, with stanzas I through IV stating the problem of Wordsworth's sense of loss, and stanzas V through VIII and IX through XI giving contrary reactions to that sense. Trilling's comment has justly attained a kind of classical status:

> That there should be ambivalence in Wordsworth's response to this diminution is quite natural, and the two answers, that of stanzas V–VIII and that of stanzas IX–XI, comprise both the resistance to and the acceptance of growth. Inevitably we resist change and turn back with passionate nostalgia to the stage we are leaving. Still, we fulfill ourselves by choosing what is painful and difficult and necessary, and we develop by moving toward death. In short, organic development is a hard paradox which Wordsworth is stating in the discrepant answers of the second part of the Ode.

Ode

Intimations of Immortality from Recollections of Early Childhood°

> The Child is father of the Man;
> And I could wish my days to be
> Bound each to each by natural piety.°
>   PAULÒ MAJORA CANAMUS°

I

There was a time when meadow, grove, and stream,
The earth, and every common° sight,
        To me did seem
        Apparelled in celestial light,
The glory and the freshness of a dream.°
It is not now as it hath been of yore;—
        Turn wheresoe'er I may,
        By night or day,
The things which I have seen I now can see no more.

II

10   The Rainbow comes and goes,
        And lovely is the Rose,

Ode . . . Childhood "Intimations" in the title means something very like "signs" or "tokens," and the title therefore suggests that the poem is a searching for evidences, almost a quest for election. The precursor poem, in a deep sense, is the *Lycidas* of Milton, and this ode was intended also primarily to be a dedication to the poet's higher powers, a prologue to the great epic he hoped still to write.
The Child . . . piety the last three lines of "My Heart Leaps Up," reminding us that "bound each to each" means a covenant of continuity with the poet's earlier self

Paulò . . . canamus "Let us sing of somewhat more exalted things," an invocation of the Muses of Sicily (that is, of Pastoral) at the opening of Virgil's *Fourth Eclogue;* Wordsworth is remembering the deliberate echoing of this phrase in l. 17 of *Lycidas:* "Begin, and somewhat loudly sweep the string."
common for Wordsworth, an honorific adjective
The glory . . . dream See the "dreamlike vividness and splendour" in the passage quoted in the Headnote; there is no irony intended here, as dreams to Wordsworth suggest images livelier than those of wakefulness.

The Moon doth with delight
Look round her when the heavens are bare;
     Waters on a starry night
     Are beautiful and fair;
     The sunshine is a glorious birth;°
     But yet I know, where'er I go,
That there hath past away a glory from the earth.

III

Now, while the birds thus sing a joyous song,
    And while the young lambs bound
20   As to the tabor's sound,°
To me alone there came a thought of grief:
A timely utterance gave that thought relief,°
    And I again am strong:
The cataracts blow their trumpets from the steep;
No more shall grief of mine the season wrong;
I hear the Echoes through the mountains throng,
The Winds come to me from the fields of sleep,°
    And all the earth is gay;
30   Land and sea
    Give themselves up to jollity,
    And with the heart of May
    Doth every Beast keep holiday;—
    Thou Child of Joy,
Shout round me, let me hear thy shouts, thou happy Shepherd-boy!

IV

Ye blessèd Creatures, I have heard the call
    Ye to each other make; I see
The heavens laugh with you in your jubilee;
    My heart is at your festival,
40   My head hath its coronal,°
The fulness of your bliss, I feel—I feel it all.
    Oh evil day! if I were sullen°
    While Earth herself is adorning,
    This sweet May-morning,
    And the Children are culling
    On every side,

glorious birth The present tense of stanza II tes-
tifies to the poet's continued vividness of ordinary perception; the loss is real, but is of something extraordinary.
tabor's sound beating of pastoral drum, to
provide rhythm for pipe or flute
A timely . . . relief The "timely utterance"
is presumably a poem; possibly "My Heart
Leaps Up," possibly "Resolution and Independence" (Trilling's suggestion).
The Winds . . . sleep A much-disputed line;
it may mean simply that the poet wakes each

morning with a fresh sense of inspiration.
coronal pastoral garland; see the poignant response of Coleridge in the verse letter to Sara
Hutchinson from which "Dejection: An Ode"
was quarried: "I too will crown me with a
Coronal—" (l. 136)
Oh . . . sullen a Dantesque touch; as in
"Resolution and Independence," Wordsworth
fears the hellish condition he thinks he observes in Coleridge, that of being sullen in the
sweet air

In a thousand valleys far and wide,
    Fresh flowers; while the sun shines warm,
And the Babe leaps up on his Mother's arm:—
50   I hear, I hear, with joy I hear!
    —But there's a Tree, of many, one,°
A single Field which I have looked upon,
Both of them speak of something that is gone:
      The Pansy at my feet
      Doth the same tale repeat:
Whither is fled the visionary gleam?
Where is it now,° the glory and the dream?

      V

Our birth is but a sleep and a forgetting:
The Soul that rises with us, our life's Star,°
60   Hath had elsewhere its setting,
        And cometh from afar:
    Not in entire forgetfulness,
    And not in utter nakedness,
But trailing clouds of glory do we come
      From God, who is our home:
Heaven lies about us in our infancy!
Shades of the prison-house begin to close
      Upon the growing Boy,
        But He
70 Beholds the light, and whence it flows,
      He sees it in his joy;
The Youth, who daily farther from the east
      Must travel, still is Nature's Priest,
      And by the vision splendid
      Is on his way attended;
At length the Man perceives it die away,
And fade into the light of common day.

      VI

Earth fills her lap with pleasures of her own;
Yearnings she hath in her own natural kind,
80 And, even with something of a Mother's mind,
      And no unworthy aim,
    The homely° Nurse doth all she can
To make her Foster-child, her Inmate Man,
      Forget the glories he hath known,
And that imperial palace whence he came.

But . . . one not an archetypal or Platonic tree, but simply a particular tree whose individual appearance Wordsworth had noticed, and now remembers. Blake (according to Crabb Robinson) was deeply moved by ll. 51–57. **Where is it now** not necessarily the same question as "whither is fled" in the line just before
our life's Star not an astrological image, but "the Sun" is not an adequate interpretation
homely archaic sense, familiar or homelike

VII

Behold the Child° among his new-born blisses,
A six years' Darling of a pigmy size!
See, where 'mid work of his own hand he lies,
Fretted° by sallies of his mother's kisses,
90 With light upon him from his father's eyes!
See, at his feet, some little plan or chart,
Some fragment from his dream of human life,
Shaped by himself with newly-learned art;
     A wedding or a festival,
     A mourning or a funeral;
       And this hath now his heart,
       And unto this he frames his song:
         Then will he fit his tongue
To dialogues of business, love, or strife;
100   But it will not be long
       Ere this be thrown aside,
       And with new joy and pride
The little Actor cons another part;
Filling from time to time his 'humorous stage'°
With all the Persons, down to palsied Age,
That Life brings with her in her equipage;
     As if his whole vocation
     Were endless imitation.

VIII

Thou, whose exterior semblance doth belie
110   Thy Soul's immensity;
Thou best Philosopher, who yet dost keep
Thy heritage, thou Eye among the blind,
That, deaf and silent, read'st the eternal deep,
Haunted for ever by the eternal mind,—
     Mighty Prophet! Seer blest!
     On whom those truths do rest,
Which we are toiling all our lives to find,
In darkness lost, the darkness of the grave;
Thou, over whom thy Immortality
120 Broods like the Day, a Master o'er a Slave,
A Presence which is not to be put by;°
Thou little Child, yet glorious in the might
Of heaven-born freedom on thy being's height,
Why with such earnest pains dost thou provoke
The years to bring the inevitable yoke,

Child Hartley Coleridge, who always found a second father in Wordsworth
Fretted vexed, bothered
'humorous stage' from the sonnet dedicating *Musophilus* by Samuel Daniel (1562–1619), one of Wordsworth's acknowledged precursors
A Presence . . . by followed originally by four lines Wordsworth discarded, possibly because Coleridge disliked them so much, but they are a loss from the poem: "To whom the grave / Is but a lonely bed without the sense or sight / Of day or the warm light, / A place of thought where we in waiting lie"

Thus blindly with thy blessedness at strife?
Full soon thy Soul shall have her earthly freight,
And custom lie upon thee with a weight,
Heavy as frost, and deep almost as life!

IX

130
     O joy! that in our embers
     Is something that doth live,
     That nature yet remembers
     What was so fugitive!
The thought of our past years in me doth breed
Perpetual benediction: not indeed
For that which is most worthy to be blest;
Delight and liberty, the simple creed
Of Childhood, whether busy or at rest,
With new-fledged hope still fluttering in his breast:—

140
     Not for these I raise
     The song of thanks and praise;
     But for those obstinate questionings
     Of sense and outward things,
     Fallings from us, vanishings;°
     Blank misgivings of a Creature
Moving about in worlds not realized,°
High instincts before which our mortal Nature
Did tremble like a guilty Thing surprised:
     But for those first affections,

150
     Those shadowy recollections,
     Which, be they what they may,
Are yet the fountain light of all our day,
Are yet a master light of all our seeing;
     Uphold us, cherish, and have power to make
Our noisy years seem moments in the being
Of the eternal Silence: truths that wake,
     To perish never;
Which neither listlessness, nor mad endeavour,
     Nor Man nor Boy,

160
Nor all that is at enmity with joy,
Can utterly abolish or destroy!
     Hence in a season of calm weather
     Though inland far we be,
Our Souls have sight of that immortal sea
     Which brought us hither,
     Can in a moment travel thither,
And see the Children sport upon the shore,
And hear the mighty waters rolling evermore.°

vanishings when external things began to assert an external existence, previously not acknowledged
realized perhaps in the double sense, "made real" and "made conscious of"

And see . . . evermore This vision of the children, and of the immortal sea ("the oceanic sense," as Freud ironically named it), is the prime intimation of immortality in the Ode.

X

Then sing, ye Birds, sing, sing a joyous song!
170   And let the young Lambs bound
     As to the tabor's sound!
We in thought will join your throng,
     Ye that pipe and ye that play,
     Ye that through your hearts today
     Feel the gladness of the May!
What though the radiance which was once so bright
Be now for ever taken from my sight,
     Though nothing can bring back the hour
Of splendour in the grass, of glory in the flower;
180   We will grieve not, rather find
     Strength in what remains behind;
     In the primal sympathy
     Which having been must ever be;
     In the soothing thoughts that spring
     Out of human suffering;
     In the faith that looks through death,
In years that bring the philosophic mind.°

XI

And O, ye Fountains, Meadows, Hills, and Groves,
Forebode not any severing of our loves!
190 Yet in my heart of hearts I feel your might;
I only have relinquished one delight
To live beneath your more habitual sway.
I love the Brooks which down their channels fret,
Even more than when I tripped lightly as they;
The innocent brightness of a new-born Day
     Is lovely yet;
The Clouds that gather round the setting sun
Do take a sober colouring° from an eye
That hath kept watch o'er man's mortality;
200 Another race hath been, and other palms are won.°
Thanks to the human heart by which we live,
Thanks to its tenderness, its joys, and fears,
To me the meanest flower that blows° can give
Thoughts that do often lie too deep for tears.°
1802–4   1807

philosophic mind the reflective or mature mind, not necessarily a metaphysical one
sober colouring the visual equivalent of "the still, sad music" of "Tintern Abbey," l. 91
other . . . won that is, different rewards are given for the contests of maturity as opposed

to the contests of childhood and youth
meanest . . . blows a living flower, however unsightly
too . . . tears thoughts so profound that even mourning cannot express them; a suggestion that joy is ultimately deeper than sorrow

She Was a Phantom of Delight

She° was a Phantom of delight
When first she gleamed upon my sight;
A lovely Apparition, sent
To be a moment's ornament;
Her eyes as stars of Twilight fair;
Like Twilight's, too, her dusky hair;
But all things else about her drawn
From May-time and the cheerful Dawn;
A dancing Shape, an Image gay,
10   To haunt, to startle, and way-lay.

I saw her upon nearer view,
A Spirit, yet a Woman too!
Her household motions light and free,
And steps of virgin-liberty;
A countenance in which did meet
Sweet records, promises as sweet;
A Creature not too bright or good
For human nature's daily food;
For transient sorrows, simple wiles,
20   Praise, blame, love, kisses, tears, and smiles.

And now I see with eye serene
The very pulse of the machine;
A Being breathing thoughtful breath,
A Traveller between life and death;
The reason firm, the temperate will,
Endurance, foresight, strength, and skill;
A perfect Woman, nobly planned,
To warn, to comfort, and command;
And yet a Spirit still, and bright
30   With something of angelic light.
1804   1807

Ode to Duty°

Jam non consilio bonus, sed more eò perductus, ut non tantum
rectè facere possim, sed nisi rectè facere non possim.°

Stern Daughter of the Voice of God!°
O Duty! if that name thou love
Who art a light to guide, a rod

She Mary Hutchinson. Contrast this poem to
Coleridge's "Phantom," a dream poem about
Sara Hutchinson.
Ode to Duty Wordsworth acknowledged that
"this Ode is on the model of Gray's 'Ode to
Adversity,' which is copied from Horace's 'Ode
to Fortune'."
Jam . . . possim taken, with modifications,

from the Roman Stoic moralist Seneca (d. 65
A.D.), and can be translated: "Now I am not
intentionally good, but so led by habit that not
only am I capable of acting rightly, but cannot
act other than rightly."
Voice of God See *Paradise Lost* IX.652–53:
"God so commanded, and left that command /
Sole daughter of his voice."

To check the erring, and reprove;
Thou, who art victory and law
When empty terrors overawe;
From vain temptations dost set free;
And calmest the weary strife of frail humanity!

There are who ask not if thine eye
10   Be on them; who, in love and truth,
Where no misgiving is, rely
Upon the genial sense° of youth;
Glad Hearts! without reproach or blot;
Who do thy work, and know it not:
Oh! if through confidence misplaced
They fail, thy saving arms, dread Power! around them cast.

Serene will be our days and bright,
And happy will our nature be,
When love is an unerring light,
20   And joy its own security.
And they a blissful course may hold
Even now, who, not unwisely bold,
Live in the spirit of this creed;
Yet seek thy firm support, according to their need.

I, loving freedom, and untried;
No sport of every random gust,
Yet being to myself a guide,
Too blindly have reposed my trust:
And oft, when in my heart was heard
30   Thy timely mandate, I deferred
The task, in smoother walks to stray;
But thee I now would serve more strictly, if I may.

Through no disturbance of my soul,
Or strong compunction° in me wrought,
I supplicate for thy control;
But in the quietness of thought:
Me this unchartered freedom tires;
I feel the weight of chance-desires:
My hopes no more must change their name,
40   I long for a repose that ever is the same.°

[Yet not the less would I throughout
Still act according to the voice
Of my own wish; and feel past doubt
That my submissiveness was choice:
Not seeking in the school of pride

---

genial sense vital sense, the primal exuberance
of youth
compunction contrition, or moral uneasiness

I long . . . same "I have sought for a joy
without pain, / For a solid without fluctuation,"
said Blake's Urizen.

For 'precepts over dignified,'°
Denial and restraint I prize
No farther than they breed a second Will more wise.°]

Stern Lawgiver! yet thou dost wear
50   The Godhead's most benignant grace;
Nor know we anything so fair
As is the smile upon thy face:
Flowers laugh before thee on their beds
And fragrance in thy footing treads;
Thou dost preserve the stars from wrong;
And the most ancient heavens, through Thee, are fresh and strong.

To humbler functions, awful Power!
I call thee: I myself commend
Unto thy guidance from this hour;
60   Oh, let my weakness have an end!
Give unto me, made lowly wise,°
The spirit of self-sacrifice;
The confidence of reason° give;
And in the light of truth thy Bondman let me live!
1804   1807

The Solitary Reaper°

Behold her, single in the field,
Yon solitary Highland Lass!
Reaping and singing by herself;
Stop here, or gently pass!
Alone she cuts and binds the grain,
And sings a melancholy strain;
O listen! for the Vale profound
Is overflowing with the sound.

No Nightingale did ever chaunt
10   More welcome notes to weary bands
Of travellers in some shady haunt,
Among Arabian sands:

'precepts over dignified' from Milton's plea for divorce, where he defends the dignity of man from "empty and over dignified precepts"
Yet not . . . wise Wordsworth later excised this stanza, but it is too good to lose, with its powerful notion of "a second Will."
lowly wise See *Paradise Lost* VIII.173–74, where Raphael warns Adam: "Heaven is for thee too high / To know what passes there. Be lowly wise; / Think only what concerns thee and thy being."
reason a moral as well as an analytical faculty, as in its Miltonic usage
The Solitary Reaper Wordsworth acknowledged his debt to his friend Thomas Wilkinson's *Tours to the British Mountains* (not published until 1824), where a sentence reads: "Passed a female who was reaping alone; she sung in Erse as she bended over her sickle; the sweetest human voice I ever heard: her strains were tenderly melancholy, and felt delicious, long after they were heard no more." Notice that Wordsworth's imagination is moved to surmise because he does not know the language in which the Highland girl sings. The best modern analogue, as many critics have noted, is Wallace Stevens's Wordsworthian poem "The Idea of Order at Key West."

A voice so thrilling ne'er was heard
In spring-time from the Cuckoo-bird,
Breaking the silence of the seas
Among the farthest Hebrides.

Will no one tell me what she sings?—
Perhaps the plaintive numbers flow
For old, unhappy, far-off things,
20   And battles long ago:
Or is it some more humble lay,
Familiar matter of today?
Some natural sorrow, loss, or pain,
That has been, and may be again?

Whate'er the theme, the Maiden sang
As if her song could have no ending;
I saw her singing at her work,
And o'er the sickle bending:—
I listened, motionless and still;
30   And, as I mounted up the hill,
The music in my heart I bore,
Long after it was heard no more.
1805   1807

Elegiac Stanzas°

Suggested by A Picture of Peele Castle,° in A Storm, Painted by Sir George Beaumont°

I was thy neighbour once, thou rugged Pile!
Four summer weeks I dwelt in sight of thee:
I saw thee every day; and all the while
Thy Form was sleeping on a glassy sea.

So pure the sky, so quiet was the air!
So like, so very like, was day to day!
Whene'er I looked, thy Image still was there;
It trembled, but it never passed away.

How perfect was the calm! it seemed no sleep;
10   No mood, which season takes away, or brings:
I could have fancied that the mighty Deep
Was even the gentlest of all gentle Things.

Elegiac Stanzas Wordsworth's beloved brother John was drowned by shipwreck on February 5, 1805. This poem was written more than a year later, and does not represent a first shocked reaction of grief, but a deeply considered loss of faith in both nature and the imagination. This loss, on the evidence of Wordsworth's later poetry, was more complex and deeper than the poet himself could realize.
Peele Castle stands on an island near the coast of Lancashire.
Beaumont Wordsworth's friend and patron; a rich amateur artist

Ah! THEN, if mine had been the Painter's hand,
To express what then I saw; and add the gleam,
The light that never was, on sea or land,
The consecration, and the Poet's dream;°

I would have planted thee, thou hoary Pile
Amid a world how different from this!
Beside a sea that could not cease to smile;
20 On tranquil land, beneath a sky of bliss.

Thou shouldst have seemed a treasure-house divine
Of peaceful years; a chronicle of heaven;—
Of all the sunbeams that did ever shine
The very sweetest had to thee been given.

A Picture had it been of lasting ease,
Elysian quiet, without toil or strife;
No motion but the moving tide, a breeze,
Or merely silent Nature's breathing life.

Such, in the fond illusion of my heart,
30 Such Picture would I at that time have made:
And seen the soul of truth in every part,
A steadfast peace that might not be betrayed.

So once it would have been,—'tis so no more;
I have submitted to a new control:°
A power is gone, which nothing can restore;°
A deep distress hath humanised my Soul.°

Not for a moment could I now behold
A smiling sea, and be what I have been:
The feeling of my loss will ne'er be old;
40 This, which I know, I speak with mind serene.°

Then, Beaumont, Friend! who would have been the Friend,
If he had lived, of Him whom I deplore,°
This work of thine I blame not, but commend;
This sea in anger, and that dismal shore.

O 'tis a passionate Work!—yet wise and well,
Well chosen is the spirit that is here;
That Hulk which labours in the deadly swell,
This rueful sky, this pageantry of fear!

And this huge Castle, standing here sublime,
50 I love to see the look with which it braves,

Poet's dream "Dream" has a negative meaning
here, very close to "delusion."
new control not the reciprocal relation with
Nature, but obedience to the moral law
A power . . . restore See the "Intimations"
ode, ll. 177–78.

A deep . . . Soul Before this, joy had humanized Wordsworth's soul.
with mind serene not in the immediate grief of
John's death
deplore mourn

Cased in the unfeeling armour of old time,
The lightning, the fierce wind, and trampling waves.

Farewell, farewell the heart that lives alone,
Housed in a dream, at distance from the Kind!°
Such happiness, wherever it be known,
Is to be pitied; for 'tis surely blind.

But welcome fortitude, and patient cheer,
And frequent sights of what is to be borne!
Such sights, or worse, as are before me here.—
60 Not without hope we suffer and we mourn.
1806   1807

The Prelude

The first version of this internalized romance (see period Headnote) was completed in 1805, but Wordsworth refused to publish the poem, and resented Coleridge's publication of "To William Wordsworth," the poem giving his reactions at having heard Wordsworth read aloud this major work. Wordsworth revised it over several decades, and the 1850 version, published posthumously, is rhetorically superior to the 1805 text, and is the source of the substantial selections that follow. Yet Wordsworth's reasons for declining publication were not stylistic. "The Poem to Coleridge," as he always called it (the title The Prelude was chosen by his widow), is the summation of his earlier self, the central poem of his Great Decade (1797–1807). The poet aged very quickly, and only a double handful of strong poems came out of the second half of his life. Though he would not have accepted such a judgment, something in him was unable to confront his own earlier self. He could not abandon The Prelude, but also he could not live with it as a public presence. Perhaps his sense of survival compelled him to keep the poem to himself, as a talisman against death. With Wordsworth, massive simplicity is usually the accurate formula for understanding; perhaps he just did not want to be reminded, or have others reminded, of how much he had lost.

The Prelude is not a "confessional" poem, as is so much recent verse in America. Its subject is subjectivity, and the poet maps the growth of his consciousness in the faith that he is wholly representative of the best potentialities of mankind. Unlike St. Augustine, whose crises were resolved by the realization he was hardly alone in the universe, but shared it with God as well as with other men, Wordsworth is essentially alone with the universe. If The Prelude is a religious poem, then the religion is not quite Christianity, though it is certainly closer to Christianity than to the natural religion of eighteenth-century England or of Rousseau. The God of The Prelude is neither nature nor Wordsworth's imagination but an unnamed third presence which, at crucial moments, can subsume both. Yet The Prelude is not a quest after that presence, or a quest after nature. It is, like some works of Ruskin and Proust and Beckett after it, a search for lost time, a journey seeking a remembered world. That world belonged to imagination, and Wordsworth finds it again by returning to a perception that was also creation, a way of thinking that was a way of recognition.

Kind mankind

The persistent theme of *The Prelude* is the power of the poet's mind over the universe it inhabits. This power is so great that it could be saved for the discipline of poetry, Wordsworth believed, only because nature worked to subdue and chasten it. Wordsworth feared the strength of his own imagination, and showed himself the terror of such strength in figures like Margaret and the Solitary of *The Excursion*, and in the dream-figure of the Arab in Book V of *The Prelude*. His imagination pressed for autonomy, as against nature, and would have been wholly and dangerously free of nature had Wordsworth yielded to it. He did not, but this did not make him only a nature poet, as *The Prelude* shows throughout. The poem's theme, like that of "Tintern Abbey," is not the humanizing of nature (a more Coleridgean ambition) and not the naturalizing of the human imagination (Arnold's interpretation of Wordsworth). The poet knows he is wholly apart from nature, once he is mature, but he confronts in nature presences from whom he fears (and cannot accept) estrangement. His theme is the tempering of imagination by nature, an educational process that leads to renovation, and to a balanced power of imagining that neither yields to a universe of decay nor seeks (as Blake did) to burn through that universe.

The Prelude

Or, Growth of a Poet's Mind
An Autobiographical Poem

From *Book First*

INTRODUCTION—CHILDHOOD
AND SCHOOL-TIME

O there is blessing in this gentle breeze,
A visitant that while it fans my cheek
Doth seem half-conscious of the joy it brings
From the green fields, and from yon azure sky.°
Whate'er its mission, the soft breeze can come
To none more grateful than to me; escaped
From the vast city, where I long had pined
A discontented sojourner: now free,
Free as a bird to settle where I will.°
10 What dwelling shall receive me? in what vale
Shall be my harbour? underneath what grove
Shall I take up my home? and what clear stream
Shall with its murmur lull me into rest?
The earth is all before me.° With a heart

O there . . . sky (ll. 1–4) Wordsworth said that the poem's opening lines were written extempore as he walked from Bristol to Racedown in 1795; what matters is that the wind rises, and the spirit of the poet rises with it.
Free . . . will Escaping London, where he had lived unhappily for half a year in 1795, the poet celebrates his recovered liberty, to return to nature and compose again (made possible by a legacy).
The earth . . . me a beautiful contrast to poor Adam and Eve in *Paradise Lost* XII.646

Joyous, nor scared at its own liberty,
I look about; and should the chosen guide
Be nothing better than a wandering cloud,
I cannot miss my way.° I breathe again!
Trances of thought and mountings of the mind
20   Come fast upon me: it is shaken off,
That burthen of my own unnatural self,°
The heavy weight of many a weary day
Not mine, and such as were not made for me.
Long months of peace (if such bold word accord
With any promises of human life),
Long months of ease and undisturbed delight
Are mine in prospect; whither shall I turn,
By road or pathway, or through trackless field,
Up hill or down, or shall some floating thing
30   Upon the river point me out my course?

      Dear Liberty! Yet what would it avail
But for a gift that consecrates the joy?
For I, methought, while the sweet breath of heaven
Was blowing on my body, felt within
A correspondent breeze, that gently moved
With quickening virtue, but is now become
A tempest, a redundant energy,
Vexing its own creation.° Thanks to both,
And their congenial powers, that, while they join
40   In breaking up a long-continued frost,
Bring with them vernal promises, the hope
Of active days urged on by flying hours,—
Days of sweet leisure, taxed with patient thought
Abstruse, nor wanting punctual service high,
Matins and vespers of harmonious verse!

      Thus far, O Friend! did I, not used to make
A present joy° the matter of a song,
Pour forth that day my soul in measured strains
That would not be forgotten, and are here
50   Recorded: to the open fields I told
A prophecy: poetic numbers came
Spontaneously to clothe in priestly robe
A renovated spirit singled out,°
Such hope was mine, for holy services.

---

and should . . . way another contrast, to the
pillar of cloud the Israelites followed across the
desert on their way to the Promised Land
it is shaken . . . unnatural self Compare "Tintern Abbey," ll. 37–41, written three years later.
For I . . . creation (ll. 33–38) The breeze
rising within him is like an over-prepared event,
which cannot come off; the wise passivity he
needs is lacking.

A present joy Having defied what he will term
later, in the 1800 Preface to *Lyrical Ballads*,
as the mood in which successful composition
generally begins, he is defeated by "a present
joy."
singled out The sense of election is already
strong here, the spirit already renovated.

My own voice cheered me, and, far more, the mind's
Internal echo of the imperfect sound;
To both I listened, drawing from them both
A cheerful confidence in things to come.

       .   .   .

It was a splendid evening, and my soul
Once more made trial of her strength, nor lacked
Aeolian visitations; but the harp
Was soon defrauded, and the banded host
Of harmony dispersed in straggling sounds,
And lastly utter silence! 'Be it so;
100 Why think of any thing but present good?'°
So, like a home-bound labourer I pursued
My way beneath the mellowing sun, that shed
Mild influence;° nor left in me one wish
Again to bend the Sabbath of that time
To a servile yoke. What need of many words?
A pleasant loitering journey, through three days
Continued, brought me to my hermitage.
I spare to tell of what ensued, the life
In common things—the endless store of things,
110 Rare, or at least so seeming, every day
Found all about me in one neighbourhood—
The self-congratulation, and, from morn
To night, unbroken cheerfulness serene.
But speedily an earnest longing rose
To brace myself to some determined aim,
Reading or thinking; either to lay up
New stores, or rescue from decay the old
By timely interference: and therewith
Came hopes still higher, that with outward life
120 I might endue some airy phantasies
That had been floating loose about for years,
And to such beings temperately deal forth
The many feelings that oppressed my heart.
That hope hath been discouraged; welcome light
Dawns from the east, but dawns to disappear
And mock me with a sky that ripens not
Into a steady morning: if my mind,
Remembering the bold promise of the past,
Would gladly grapple with some noble theme,
130 Vain is her wish; where'er she turns she finds
Impediments from day to day renewed.

       .   .   .

Why . . . good There is no anxiety in this misadventure of redundant inspiration; anxiety will come, overwhelmingly, with the problem of an epic theme, and its hidden burden of the anxiety of influence, Wordsworth's own fear that he may be only a latecomer, arriving after all the stories of poetry have been told.
Mild influence See *Paradise Lost* VII.375.

Sometimes it suits me better to invent
A tale from my own heart, more near akin
To my own passions and habitual thoughts;
Some variegated story, in the main
Lofty, but the unsubstantial structure melts
Before the very sun that brightens it,
Mist into air dissolving! Then a wish,
My best and favourite aspiration, mounts
With yearning toward some philosophic song
230   Of Truth that cherishes our daily life;
With meditations passionate from deep
Recesses in man's heart, immortal verse
Thoughtfully fitted to the Orphean lyre;
But from this awful burthen I full soon
Take refuge and beguile myself with trust
That mellower years will bring a riper mind
And clearer insight. Thus my days are passed
In contradiction; with no skill to part
Vague longing, haply bred by want of power,
240   From paramount impulse not to be withstood,
A timorous capacity from prudence,
From circumspection, infinite delay.
Humility and modest awe themselves
Betray me, serving often for a cloak
To a more subtle selfishness; that now
Locks every function up in blank reserve,
Now dupes me, trusting to an anxious eye
That with intrusive restlessness beats off
Simplicity and self-presented truth.
250   Ah! better far than this, to stray about
Voluptuously through fields and rural walks,
And ask no record of the hours, resigned
To vacant musing, unreproved neglect
Of all things, and deliberate holiday.
Far better never to have heard the name
Of zeal and just ambition, than to live
Baffled and plagued by a mind that every hour
Turns recreant to her task; takes heart again,
Then feels immediately some hollow thought
260   Hang like an interdict upon her hopes.
This is my lot; for either still I find
Some imperfection in the chosen theme,
Or see of absolute accomplishment
Much wanting, so much wanting, in myself,
That I recoil and droop, and seek repose
In listlessness from vain perplexity,
Unprofitably travelling toward the grave,

Like a false steward who hath much received
And renders nothing back.°
                Was it for this
270 That one, the fairest of all rivers, loved
To blend his murmurs with my nurse's song,
And, from his alder shades and rocky falls,
And from his fords and shallows, sent a voice
That flowed along my dreams? For this, didst thou,
O Derwent! winding among grassy holms°
Where I was looking on, a babe in arms,
Make ceaseless music that composed my thoughts
To more than infant softness, giving me
Amid the fretful dwellings of mankind
280 A foretaste, a dim earnest, of the calm
That Nature breathes among the hills and groves.°
When he had left the mountains and received
On his smooth breast the shadow of those towers
That yet survive, a shattered monument
Of feudal sway, the bright blue river passed
Along the margin of our terrace walk;
A tempting playmate whom we dearly loved.
Oh, many a time have I, a five years' child,
In a small mill-race severed from his stream,
290 Made one long bathing of a summer's day;
Basked in the sun, and plunged and basked again
Alternate, all a summer's day, or scoured
The sandy fields, leaping through flowery groves
Of yellow ragwort; or when rock and hill,
The woods, and distant Skiddaw's lofty height,
Were bronzed with deepest radiance, stood alone
Beneath the sky, as if I had been born
On Indian plains, and from my mother's hut
Had run abroad in wantonness, to sport
300 A naked savage, in the thunder shower.

    Fair seed-time had my soul, and I grew up
Fostered alike by beauty and by fear:
Much favoured in my birth-place, and no less
In that beloved Vale to which erelong
We were transplanted—there were we let loose
For sports of wider range. Ere I had told
Ten birth-days, when among the mountain slopes
Frost, and the breath of frosty wind, had snapped
The last autumnal crocus, 'twas my joy

Unprofitably . . . back the starting crisis-point of the poem; almost a death-in-life condition for a strong poet with Wordsworth's ambitions
holms low land at riverside
Was it . . . groves (ll. 269–281) With more-than-Proustian skill, the Derwent River is transformed from an agent of admonishment to the messenger of the poetic theme, the development of the poet's own imagination.

310 With store of springes° o'er my shoulder hung
     To range the open heights where woodcocks run
     Along the smooth green turf. Through half the night,
     Scudding° away from snare to snare, I plied
     That anxious visitation;—moon and stars
     Were shining o'er my head. I was alone,
     And seemed to be a trouble to the peace
     That dwelt among them. Sometimes it befel
     In these night wanderings, that a strong desire
     O'erpowered my better reason, and the bird
320 Which was the captive of another's toil
     Became my prey; and when the deed was done
     I heard among the solitary hills
     Low breathings coming after me, and sounds
     Of undistinguishable motion, steps
     Almost as silent as the turf they trod.

          Nor less when spring had warmed the cultured Vale,
     Roved we as plunderers where the mother-bird
     Had in high places built her lodge; though mean
     Our object and inglorious, yet the end
330 Was not ignoble. Oh! when I have hung
     Above the raven's nest, by knots of grass
     And half-inch fissures in the slippery rock
     But ill sustained, and almost (so it seemed)
     Suspended by the blast that blew amain,
     Shouldering the naked crag, oh, at that time
     While on the perilous ridge I hung alone,
     With what strange utterance did the loud dry wind
     Blow through my ear! the sky seemed not a sky
     Of earth—and with what motion moved the clouds!

340   Dust as we are, the immortal spirit grows
     Like harmony in music; there is a dark
     Inscrutable workmanship that reconciles
     Discordant elements, makes them cling together
     In one society. How strange that all
     The terrors, pains, and early miseries,
     Regrets, vexations, lassitudes interfused
     Within my mind, should e'er have borne a part,
     And that a needful part, in making up
     The calm existence that is mine when I
350 Am worthy of myself! Praise to the end!
     Thanks to the means which Nature deigned to employ;
     Whether her fearless visitings, or those
     That came with soft alarm, like hurtless light
     Opening the peaceful clouds; or she may use

Springes traps or snares   **Scudding** moving hurriedly

Severer interventions, ministry
More palpable, as best might suit her aim.

One summer evening (led by her) I found
A little boat tied to a willow tree
Within a rocky cave, its usual home.
360   Straight I unloosed her chain, and stepping in
Pushed from the shore. It was an act of stealth
And troubled pleasure, nor without the voice
Of mountain-echoes did my boat move on;
Leaving behind her still, on either side,
Small circles glittering idly in the moon,
Until they melted all into one track
Of sparkling light. But now, like one who rows,
Proud of his skill, to reach a chosen point
With an unswerving line, I fixed my view
370   Upon the summit of a craggy ridge,
The horizon's utmost boundary; far above
Was nothing but the stars and the grey sky.
She was an elfin pinnace; lustily
I dipped my oars into the silent lake,
And, as I rose upon the stroke, my boat
Went heaving through the water like a swan;
When, from behind that craggy steep till then
The horizon's bound, a huge peak, black and huge,
As if with voluntary power instinct
380   Upreared its head. I struck and struck again,
And growing still in stature the grim shape
Towered up between me and the stars, and still,
For so it seemed, with purpose of its own
And measured motion like a living thing,
Strode after me. With trembling oars I turned,
And through the silent water stole my way
Back to the covert of the willow tree;
There in her mooring-place I left my bark,—
And through the meadows homeward went, in grave
390   And serious mood; but after I had seen
That spectacle, for many days, my brain
Worked with a dim and undetermined sense
Of unknown modes of being; o'er my thoughts
There hung a darkness, call it solitude
Or blank desertion. No familiar shapes
Remained, no pleasant images of trees,
Of sea or sky, no colours of green fields;
But huge and mighty forms, that do not live
Like living men, moved slowly through the mind
400   By day, and were a trouble to my dreams.

Wisdom and Spirit of the universe!
Thou Soul that art the eternity of thought,
That givest to forms and images a breath
And everlasting motion, not in vain
By day or star-light thus from my first dawn
Of childhood didst thou intertwine for me
The passions that build up our human soul;
Not with the mean and vulgar works of man,
But with high objects, with enduring things—
410   With life and nature, purifying thus
The elements of feeling and of thought,
And sanctifying, by such discipline,
Both pain and fear, until we recognise
A grandeur in the beatings of the heart.
Nor was this fellowship vouchsafed to me
With stinted kindness. In November days,
When vapours rolling down the valley made
A lonely scene more lonesome, among woods,
At noon and 'mid the calm of summer nights,
420   When, by the margin of the trembling lake,
Beneath the gloomy hills homeward I went
In solitude, such intercourse was mine;
Mine was it in the fields both day and night,
And by the waters, all the summer long.

And in the frosty season, when the sun
Was set, and visible for many a mile
The cottage windows blazed through twilight gloom,
I heeded not their summons: happy time
It was indeed for all of us—for me
430   It was a time of rapture! Clear and loud
The village clock tolled six,—I wheeled about,
Proud and exulting like an untired horse
That cares not for his home. All shod with steel,
We hissed along the polished ice in games
Confederate, imitative of the chase
And woodland pleasures,—the resounding horn,
The pack loud chiming, and the hunted hare.
So through the darkness and the cold we flew,
And not a voice was idle; with the din
440   Smitten, the precipices rang aloud;
The leafless trees and every icy crag
Tinkled like iron; while far distant hills
Into the tumult sent an alien sound
Of melancholy not unnoticed, while the stars
Eastward were sparkling clear, and in the west
The orange sky of evening died away.

Not seldom from the uproar I retired
Into a silent bay, or sportively
Glanced sideway, leaving the tumultuous throng,
450   To cut across the reflex of a star
That fled, and, flying still before me, gleamed
Upon the glassy plain; and oftentimes,
When we had given our bodies to the wind,
And all the shadowy banks on either side
Came sweeping through the darkness, spinning still
The rapid line of motion, then at once
Have I, reclining back upon my heels,
Stopped short; yet still the solitary cliffs
Wheeled by me—even as if the earth had rolled
460   With visible motion her diurnal round!
Behind me did they stretch in solemn train,
Feebler and feebler, and I stood and watched
Till all was tranquil as a dreamless sleep.

Ye Presences of Nature in the sky
And on the earth! Ye Visions of the hills!
And Souls of lonely places! can I think
A vulgar hope was yours when ye employed
Such ministry, when ye through many a year
Haunting me thus among my boyish sports,
470   On caves and trees, upon the woods and hills,
Impressed upon all forms the characters
Of danger or desire; and thus did make
The surface of the universal earth
With triumph and delight, with hope and fear,
Work like a sea? . . .

From *Book Second*

SCHOOL-TIME

Those incidental charms which first attached
My heart to rural objects, day by day
200   Grew weaker, and I hasten on to tell
How Nature, intervenient° till this time
And secondary, now at length was sought
For her own sake. But who shall parcel out
His intellect by geometric rules,
Split like a province into round and square?
Who knows the individual hour in which
His habits were first sown, even as a seed?
Who that shall point as with a wand and say
'This portion of the river of my mind
210   Came from yon fountain?' Thou, my Friend!° art one

intervenient something extraneous   Friend Coleridge

More deeply read in thy own thoughts; to thee
Science appears but what in truth she is,
Not as our glory and our absolute boast,
But as a succedaneum,° and a prop
To our infirmity. No officious slave
Art thou of that false secondary power
By which we multiply distinctions, then
Deem that our puny boundaries are things
That we perceive, and not that we have made.
220 To thee, unblinded by these formal arts,
The unity of all hath been revealed,
And thou wilt doubt with me, less aptly skilled
Than many are to range the faculties
In scale and order, class the cabinet
Of their sensations, and in voluble phrase
Run through the history and birth of each
As of a single independent thing.
Hard task, vain hope, to analyse the mind,
If each most obvious and particular thought,
230 Not in a mystical and idle sense,
But in the words of Reason deeply weighed,
Hath no beginning.
                        Blest the infant Babe,
(For with my best conjecture I would trace
Our Being's earthly progress,) blest the Babe,
Nursed in his Mother's arms, who sinks to sleep
Rocked on his Mother's breast; who with his soul
Drinks in the feelings of his Mother's eye!
For him, in one dear Presence, there exists
A virtue which irradiates and exalts
240 Objects through widest intercourse of sense.
No outcast he, bewildered and depressed:
Along his infant veins are interfused
The gravitation and the filial bond
Of nature that connect him with the world.
Is there a flower, to which he points with hand
Too weak to gather it, already love
Drawn from love's purest earthly fount for him
Hath beautified that flower; already shades
Of pity cast from inward tenderness
250 Do fall around him upon aught that bears
Unsightly marks of violence or harm.
Emphatically such a Being lives,
Frail creature as he is, helpless as frail,
An inmate of this active universe.
For feeling has to him imparted power

succedaneum replacement

That through the growing faculties of sense
Doth like an agent of the one great Mind
Create, creator and receiver both,
Working but in alliance with the works
260   Which it beholds.—Such, verily, is the first
Poetic spirit of our human life,
By uniform control of after years,
In most, abated or suppressed; in some,
Through every change of growth and of decay,
Pre-eminent till death.
                          From early days,
Beginning not long after that first time
In which, a Babe, by intercourse of touch
I held mute dialogues with my Mother's heart,
I have endeavoured to display the means
270   Whereby this infant sensibility,
Great birthright of our being, was in me
Augmented and sustained. Yet is a path
More difficult before me; and I fear
That in its broken windings we shall need
The chamois'° sinews, and the eagle's wing:
For now a trouble came into my mind
From unknown causes. I was left alone
Seeking the visible world, nor knowing why.°
The props of my affections were removed,
280   And yet the building stood, as if sustained
By its own spirit! All that I beheld
Was dear, and hence to finer influxes
The mind lay open to a more exact
And close communion. Many are our joys
In youth, but oh! what happiness to live
When every hour brings palpable access
Of knowledge, when all knowledge is delight,
And sorrow is not there! The seasons came,
And every season wheresoe'er I moved
290   Unfolded transitory qualities,
Which, but for this most watchful power of love,
Had been neglected; left a register
Of permanent relations, else unknown.
Hence life, and change, and beauty, solitude
More active even than 'best society'—
Society made sweet as solitude
By silent inobtrusive sympathies,
And gentle agitations of the mind
From manifold distinctions, difference

chamois' an agile, goat-like antelope
nor knowing why The crisis of a lifelong
solipsist (a person for whom external things
lack reality, including a full sense of other
selves) begins to be revealed here.

300   Perceived in things, where, to the unwatchful eye,
No difference is, and hence, from the same source,
Sublimer joy; for I would walk alone,
Under the quiet stars, and at that time
Have felt whate'er there is of power in sound
To breathe an elevated mood, by form
Or image unprofaned; and I would stand,
If the night blackened with a coming storm,
Beneath some rock, listening to notes that are
The ghostly language of the ancient earth,
310   Or make their dim abode in distant winds.
Thence did I drink the visionary power;
And deem not profitless those fleeting moods
Of shadowy exultation: not for this,
That they are kindred to our purer mind
And intellectual life; but that the soul,
Remembering how she felt, but what she felt
Remembering not, retains an obscure sense
Of possible sublimity, whereto
With growing faculties she doth aspire,
320   With faculties still growing, feeling still
That whatsoever point they gain, they yet
Have something to pursue.° . . .

From *Book Fourth*

SUMMER VACATION

It seemed the very garments that I wore
Preyed on my strength, and stopped the quiet stream
Of self-forgetfulness.
                Yes, that heartless chase
Of trivial pleasures was a poor exchange
For books and nature at that early age.
300   'Tis true, some casual knowledge might be gained
Of character or life; but at that time,
Of manners put to school I took small note,
And all my deeper passions lay elsewhere.
For better had it been to exalt the mind
By solitary study, to uphold
Intense desire through meditative peace;
And yet, for chastisement of these regrets,
The memory of one particular hour
Doth here rise up against me. 'Mid a throng
310   Of maids and youths, old men, and matrons staid,
A medley of all tempers, I had passed

but that . . . pursue (ll. 315–22) Compare this
"possible sublimity" with Book VI.608 "and
something evermore about to be."

The night in dancing, gaiety, and mirth,
With din of instruments and shuffling feet,
And glancing forms, and tapers glittering,
And unaimed prattle flying up and down;
Spirits upon the stretch, and here and there
Slight shocks of young love-liking interspersed,
Whose transient pleasure mounted to the head,
And tingled through the veins. Ere we retired,
320   The cock had crowed, and now the eastern sky
Was kindling, not unseen, from humble copse
And open field, through which the pathway wound,
And homeward led my steps. Magnificent
The morning rose, in memorable pomp,
Glorious as e'er I had beheld—in front,
The sea lay laughing at a distance; near,
The solid mountains shone, bright as the clouds,
Grain-tinctured, drenched in empyrean light;
And in the meadows and the lower grounds
330   Was all the sweetness of a common dawn—
Dews, vapours, and the melody of birds,
And labourers going forth to till the fields.°

Ah! need I say, dear Friend! that to the brim
My heart was full; I made no vows, but vows
Were then made for me; bond unknown to me
Was given, that I should be, else sinning greatly,
A dedicated Spirit. On I walked
In thankful blessedness, which yet survives.

. . .

From *Book Fifth*

BOOKS

When Contemplation, like the night-calm felt
Through earth and sky, spreads widely, and sends deep
Into the soul its tranquillizing power,
Even then I sometimes grieve for thee, O Man,
Earth's paramount Creature! not so much for woes
That thou endurest; heavy though that weight be,
Cloud-like it mounts, or touched with light divine
Doth melt away; but for those palms achieved,
Through length of time, by patient exercise
10   Of study and hard thought; there, there, it is
That sadness finds its fuel. Hitherto,
In progress through this Verse, my mind hath looked
Upon the speaking face of earth and heaven

Magnificent . . . fields This moment of moments (ll. 323–32) is revivalistic in its structure, peculiarly Protestant in its temper,
because of the acute sense of election it conveys.

As her prime teacher, intercourse with man
Established by the sovereign Intellect,
Who through that bodily image hath diffused,
As might appear to the eye of fleeting time,
A deathless spirit. Thou also, man! hast wrought,
For commerce of thy nature with herself,
20   Things that aspire to unconquerable life;
And yet we feel—we cannot choose but feel—
That they must perish. Trembling of the heart
It gives, to think that our immortal being
No more shall need such garments; and yet man,
As long as he shall be the child of earth,
Might almost 'weep to have'° what he may lose,
Nor be himself extinguished, but survive,
Abject, depressed, forlorn, disconsolate.
A thought is with me sometimes, and I say,—
30   Should the whole frame of earth by inward throes
Be wrenched, or fire come down from far to scorch
Her pleasant habitations, and dry up
Old Ocean, in his bed left singed and bare,
Yet would the living Presence still subsist
Victorious, and composure would ensue,
And kindlings like the morning—presage sure
Of day returning and of life revived.
But all the meditations of mankind,
Yea, all the adamantine holds of truth
40   By reason built, or passion, which itself
Is highest reason in a soul sublime;
The consecrated works of Bard and Sage,
Sensuous or intellectual, wrought by men,
Twin labourers and heirs of the same hopes;
Where would they be? Oh! why hath not the Mind
Some element to stamp her image on
In nature somewhat nearer to her own?
Why, gifted with such powers to send abroad
Her spirit, must it lodge in shrines so frail?

50   One day, when from my lips a like complaint
Had fallen in presence of a studious friend,
He with a smile made answer, that in truth
'Twas going far to seek disquietude;
But on the front of his reproof confessed
That he himself had oftentimes given way
To kindred hauntings. Whereupon I told,
That once in the stillness of a summer's noon,
While I was seated in a rocky cave

'weep to have' See Shakespeare, Sonnet LXIV,
l. 14.

60 By the sea-side, perusing, so it chanced,
    The famous history of the errant knight
    Recorded by Cervantes, these same thoughts
    Beset me, and to height unusual rose,
    While listlessly I sate, and, having closed
    The book, had turned my eyes toward the wide sea.
    On poetry and geometric truth,
    And their high privilege of lasting life,
    From all internal injury exempt,
    I mused, upon these chiefly: and at length,
    My senses yielding to the sultry air,
70 Sleep seized me, and I passed into a dream.°
    I saw before me stretched a boundless plain
    Of sandy wilderness, all black and void,
    And as I looked around, distress and fear
    Came creeping over me, when at my side,
    Close at my side, an uncouth shape appeared
    Upon a dromedary,° mounted high.
    He seemed an Arab of the Bedouin tribes:
    A lance he bore, and underneath one arm
    A stone, and in the opposite hand, a shell
80 Of a surpassing brightness. At the sight
    Much I rejoiced, not doubting but a guide
    Was present, one who with unerring skill
    Would through the desert lead me; and while yet
    I looked and looked, self-questioned what this freight
    Which the new-comer carried through the waste
    Could mean, the Arab told me that the stone
    (To give it in the language of the dream)
    Was 'Euclid's Elements'; and 'This,' said he,
    'Is something of more worth'; and at the word
90 Stretched forth the shell, so beautiful in shape,
    In colour so resplendent, with command
    That I should hold it to my ear. I did so,
    And heard that instant in an unknown tongue,
    Which yet I understood, articulate sounds,
    A loud prophetic blast of harmony;
    An Ode, in passion uttered, which foretold
    Destruction to the children of the earth
    By deluge, now at hand. No sooner ceased
    The song, than the Arab with calm look declared
100 That all would come to pass of which the voice
    Had given forewarning, and that he himself
    Was going then to bury those two books:
    The one that held acquaintance with the stars,
    And wedded soul to soul in purest bond

Sleep . . . dream not actually Wordsworth's
own dream, but founded on a dream of the
great French philosopher Descartes (1596–1650)
dromedary camel with one hump

Of reason, undisturbed by space or time;
The other that was a god, yea many gods,
Had voices more than all the winds, with power
To exhilarate the spirit, and to soothe,
Through every clime, the heart of human kind.
110 While this was uttering, strange as it may seem,
I wondered not, although I plainly saw
The one to be a stone, the other a shell;
Nor doubted once but that they both were books,
Having a perfect faith in all that passed.
Far stronger, now, grew the desire I felt
To cleave unto this man; but when I prayed
To share his enterprise, he hurried on
Reckless of me: I followed, not unseen,
For oftentimes he cast a backward look,
120 Grasping his twofold treasure.—Lance in rest,°
He rode, I keeping pace with him; and now
He, to my fancy, had become the knight
Whose tale Cervantes tells; yet not the knight,
But was an Arab of the desert too;
Of these was neither, and was both at once.
His countenance, meanwhile, grew more disturbed;
And, looking backwards when he looked, mine eyes
Saw, over half the wilderness diffused,
A bed of glittering light:° I asked the cause:
130 'It is,' said he, 'the waters of the deep
Gathering upon us'; quickening then the pace
Of the unwieldy creature he bestrode,
He left me: I called after him aloud;
He heeded not; but, with his twofold charge
Still in his grasp, before me, full in view,
Went hurrying o'er the illimitable waste,
With the fleet waters of a drowning world
In chase of him; whereat I waked in terror,
And saw the sea before me, and the book,
140 In which I had been reading, at my side.

Full often, taking from the world of sleep
This Arab phantom, which I thus beheld,
This semi-Quixote, I to him have given
A substance, fancied him a living man,
A gentle dweller in the desert, crazed
By love and feeling, and internal thought
Protracted among endless solitudes;
Have shaped him wandering upon this quest!

Lance in rest Previously the Arab held both shell and lance; now, farther along in his saving quest, he holds both shell and stone.
glittering light Wordsworth's consciousness does not fear engulfment, which appears as a kind of glory, but fears instead the black and void sandy wilderness in which the dream began.

Nor have I pitied him; but rather felt
Reverence was due to a being thus employed;
And thought that, in the blind and awful lair
Of such a madness, reason did lie couched.
Enow there are on earth to take in charge
Their wives, their children, and their virgin loves,
Or whatsoever else the heart holds dear;
Enow to stir for these; yea, will I say,
Contemplating in soberness the approach
Of an event so dire, by signs in earth
Or heaven made manifest, that I could share
That maniac's fond anxiety, and go
Upon like errand. Oftentimes at least
Me hath such strong entrancement overcome,
When I have held a volume in my hand,
Poor earthly casket of immortal verse,
Shakespeare, or Milton, labourers divine!

. . .

There was a Boy:° ye knew him well, ye cliffs
And islands of Winander!—many a time
At evening, when the earliest stars began
To move along the edges of the hills,
Rising or setting, would he stand alone
Beneath the trees or by the glimmering lake,
And there, with fingers interwoven, both hands
Pressed closely palm to palm, and to his mouth
Uplifted, he, as through an instrument,
Blew mimic hootings to the silent owls,
That they might answer him; and they would shout
Across the watery vale, and shout again,
Responsive to his call, with quivering peals,
And long halloos and screams, and echoes loud,
Redoubled and redoubled, concourse wild
Of jocund din; and, when a lengthened pause
Of silence came and baffled his best skill,
Then sometimes, in that silence while he hung
Listening, a gentle shock of mild surprise
Has carried far into his heart the voice
Of mountain torrents; or the visible scene
Would enter unawares into his mind,
With all its solemn imagery, its rocks,
Its woods, and that uncertain heaven, received
Into the bosom of the steady lake.°

This Boy was taken from his mates, and died
In childhood, ere he was full twelve years old.

Line numbers: 150, 160, 370, 380, 390

Boy In the first draft the boy is Wordsworth himself.
Its woods . . . lake Coleridge said of ll. 387–

88: "Had I met these lines running wild in the deserts of Arabia, I should have instantly screamed out 'Wordsworth!'"

Fair is the spot, most beautiful the vale
Where he was born; the grassy churchyard hangs
Upon a slope above the village school,
And through that churchyard when my way has led
On summer evenings, I believe that there
A long half hour together I have stood
Mute, looking at the grave in which he lies!
Even now appears before the mind's clear eye
That self-same village church; I see her sit
400   (The thronèd Lady whom erewhile we hailed)
On her green hill, forgetful of this Boy
Who slumbers at her feet,—forgetful, too,
Of all her silent neighbourhood of graves,
And listening only to the gladsome sounds
That, from the rural school ascending, play
Beneath her and about her. May she long
Behold a race of young ones like to those
With whom I herded!—(easily, indeed,
We might have fed upon a fatter soil
410   Of arts and letters—but be that forgiven)—
A race of real children; not too wise,
Too learned, or too good; but wanton, fresh,
And bandied up and down by love and hate;
Not unresentful where self-justified;
Fierce, moody, patient, venturous, modest, shy;
Mad at their sports like withered leaves in winds;
Though doing wrong and suffering, and full oft
Bending beneath our life's mysterious weight
Of pain, and doubt, and fear, yet yielding not
420   In happiness to the happiest upon earth.
Simplicity in habit, truth in speech,
Be these the daily strengtheners of their minds;
May books and Nature be their early joy!
And knowledge, rightly honoured with that name—
Knowledge not purchased by the loss of power!°

430   . . . that very week,
While I was roving up and down alone,
Seeking I knew not what, I chanced to cross
One of those open fields, which, shaped like ears,
Make green peninsulas on Esthwaite's Lake:
Twilight was coming on, yet through the gloom
Appeared distinctly on the opposite shore
A heap of garments, as if left by one
Who might have there been bathing. Long I watched,
But no one owned them; meanwhile the calm lake

Knowledge . . . power a concern central to Wordsworth, since the compensatory imagination verges on a kind of increase in knowledge at the expense of a drain upon experience.

Wordsworth's terms here influenced De Quincey and Shelley, and play their part in Yeats, as in the final question of "Leda and the Swan."

440   Grew dark with all the shadows on its breast,
    And, now and then, a fish up-leaping snapped
    The breathless stillness. The succeeding day,
    Those unclaimed garments telling a plain tale
    Drew to the spot an anxious crowd; some looked
    In passive expectation from the shore,
    While from a boat others hung o'er the deep,
    Sounding with grappling irons and long poles.
    At last, the dead man, 'mid that beauteous scene
    Of trees and hills and water, bolt upright
450   Rose, with his ghastly face, a spectre shape
    Of terror; yet no soul-debasing fear,
    Young as I was, a child not nine years old,
    Possessed me, for my inner eye had seen
    Such sights before, among the shining streams
    Of faery land, the forest of romance.
    Their spirit hallowed the sad spectacle
    With decoration of ideal grace;
    A dignity, a smoothness, like the works
    Of Grecian art, and purest poesy.°

           .   .   .

    A gracious spirit o'er this earth presides,
    And o'er the heart of man: invisibly
    It comes, to works of unreproved delight,
    And tendency benign, directing those
    Who care not, know not, think not what they do.
    The tales that charm away the wakeful night
    In Araby, romances; legends penned
    For solace by dim light of monkish lamps;
    Fictions, for ladies of their love, devised
500   By youthful squires; adventures endless, spun
    By the dismantled warrior in old age,
    Out of the bowels of those very schemes
    In which his youth did first extravagate;
    These spread like day, and something in the shape
    Of these will live till man shall be no more.
    Dumb yearnings, hidden appetites, are ours,
    And *they must* have their food. Our childhood sits,
    Our simple childhood, sits upon a throne
    That hath more power than all the elements.
510   I guess not what this tells of Being past,
    Nor what it augurs of the life to come;
    But so it is, and, in that dubious hour,
    That twilight when we first begin to see
    This dawning earth, to recognise, expect,
    And in the long probation that ensues,

---

yet no . . poesy An extraordinarily difficult
argument is implicit here (ll. 451–59), but the
kernal is the contention that early immersion in
the romance world serves to defend the mind
from too early an exposure to experiential
horrors.

The time of trial, ere we learn to live
In reconcilement with our stinted powers;
To endure this state of meagre vassalage,
Unwilling to forego, confess, submit,
520   Uneasy and unsettled, yoke-fellows
To custom, mettlesome, and not yet tamed
And humbled down; oh! then we feel, we feel,
We know where we have friends. Ye dreamers, then,
Forgers of daring tales! we bless you then,
Impostors, drivellers, dotards, as the ape
Philosophy will call you: *then* we feel
With what, and how great might ye are in league,
Who make our wish, our power, our thought a deed,
An empire, a possession,—ye whom time
530   And seasons serve; all Faculties to whom
Earth crouches, the elements are potter's clay,
Space like a heaven filled up with northern lights,
Here, nowhere, there, and everywhere at once.°

. . .

Here must we pause: this only let me add,
From heart-experience, and in humblest sense
Of modesty, that he, who in his youth
A daily wanderer among woods and fields
With living Nature hath been intimate,
Not only in that raw unpractised time
590   Is stirred to extasy, as others are,
By glittering verse; but further, doth receive,
In measure only dealt out to himself,
Knowledge and increase of enduring joy
From the great Nature that exists in works
Of mighty Poets. Visionary power
Attends the motions of the viewless winds,
Embodied in the mystery of words:
There, darkness makes abode, and all the host
Of shadowy things work endless changes,—there,
600   As in a mansion like their proper home,
Even forms and substances are circumfused
By that transparent veil with light divine,
And, through the turnings intricate of verse,
Present themselves as objects recognised,
In flashes, and with glory not their own.

From *Book Sixth*

CAMBRIDGE AND THE ALPS

When the third summer freed us from restraint,
A youthful friend, he too a mountaineer,

Space . . . once See the opening section of
Wallace Stevens's *The Auroras of Autumn*.

Not slow to share my wishes, took his staff,
And sallying forth, we journeyed side by side,
Bound to the distant Alps. A hardy slight
Did this unprecedented course imply
Of college studies and their set rewards;
Nor had, in truth, the scheme been formed by me
330   Without uneasy forethought of the pain,
The censures, and ill-omening of those
To whom my worldly interests were dear.
But Nature then was sovereign in my mind,
And mighty forms, seizing a youthful fancy,
Had given a charter to irregular hopes.
In any age of uneventful calm
Among the nations, surely would my heart
Have been possessed by similar desire;
But Europe at that time was thrilled with joy,
340   France standing on the top of golden hours,°
And human nature seeming born again.

. . .

                    That very day,
From a bare ridge we also first beheld
Unveiled the summit of Mont Blanc, and grieved
To have a soulless image on the eye
That had usurped upon a living thought
That never more could be. The wondrous Vale
Of Chamouny stretched far below, and soon
530   With its dumb cataracts and streams of ice,
A motionless array of mighty waves,
Five rivers broad and vast, made rich amends,
And reconciled us to realities;
There small birds warble from the leafy trees,
The eagle soars high in the element,
There doth the reaper bind the yellow sheaf,
The maiden spread the haycock in the sun,
While Winter like a well-tamed lion walks,
Descending from the mountain to make sport
540   Among the cottages by beds of flowers.

    Whate'er in this wide circuit we beheld,
Or heard, was fitted to our unripe state
Of intellect and heart. With such a book
Before our eyes, we could not choose but read
Lessons of genuine brotherhood, the plain
And universal reason of mankind,
The truths of young and old. Nor, side by side
Pacing, two social pilgrims, or alone

the top of golden hours See Shakespeare, Sonnet
XVI, l. 5: "Now stand you on the top of happy
hours."

Each with his humour, could we fail to abound
550   In dreams and fictions, pensively composed:
Dejection taken up for pleasure's sake,
And gilded sympathies, the willow wreath,
And sober posies of funereal flowers,
Gathered among those solitudes sublime
From formal gardens of the lady Sorrow,
Did sweeten many a meditative hour.

    Yet still in me with those soft luxuries
Mixed something of stern mood,° an under-thirst
Of vigour seldom utterly allayed.
560   And from that source how different a sadness
Would issue, let one incident make known.
When from the Vallais we had turned, and clomb
Along the Simplon's steep and rugged road,
Following a band of muleteers, we reached
A halting-place, where all together took
Their noon-tide meal. Hastily rose our guide,
Leaving us at the board; awhile we lingered,
Then paced the beaten downward way that led
Right to a rough stream's edge, and there broke off;
570   The only track now visible was one
That from the torrent's further brink held forth
Conspicuous invitation to ascend
A lofty mountain. After brief delay
Crossing the unbridged stream, that road we took,
And clomb with eagerness, till anxious fears
Intruded, for we failed to overtake
Our comrades gone before. By fortunate chance,
While every moment added doubt to doubt,
A peasant met us, from whose mouth we learned
580   That to the spot which had perplexed us first
We must descend, and there should find the road,
Which in the stony channel of the stream
Lay a few steps, and then along its banks;
And, that our future course, all plain to sight,
Was downwards, with the current of that stream.
Loth to believe what we so grieved to hear,
For still we had hopes that pointed to the clouds,
We questioned him again, and yet again;
But every word that from the peasant's lips
590   Came in reply, translated by our feelings,
Ended in this,—*that we had crossed the Alps.*°

---

stern mood Geoffrey Hartman observes: "The
stern mood to which Wordsworth refers can only
be his premonition of spiritual autonomy, of an
independence from sense-experience. . . ."
Loth . . . Alps (ll. 586–91) Hartman: "The
poet recognizes at last that the power he has
looked for in the outside world is really within
and frustrating his search. A shock of recognition
then feeds the very blindness toward the external world which helped to produce that shock."

Imagination—here the Power so called
Through sad incompetence of human speech,
That awful Power rose from the mind's abyss
Like an unfathered vapour that enwraps,
At once, some lonely traveller. I was lost;
Halted without an effort to break through;
But to my conscious soul I now can say—
'I recognise thy glory': in such strength
600   Of usurpation, when the light of sense
Goes out, but with a flash that has revealed
The invisible world, doth greatness make abode,
There harbours; whether we be young or old,
Our destiny, our being's heart and home,
Is with infinitude, and only there;
With hope it is, hope that can never die,
Effort, and expectation, and desire,
And something evermore about to be.
Under such banners militant, the soul
610   Seeks for no trophies, struggles for no spoils
That may attest her prowess, blest in thoughts
That are their own perfection and reward,
Strong in herself and in beatitude
That hides her, like the mighty flood of Nile
Poured from his fount of Abyssinian clouds
To fertilise the whole Egyptian plain.°

The melancholy slackening that ensued
Upon those tidings by the peasant given
Was soon dislodged. Downwards we hurried fast,
620   And, with the half-shaped road which we had missed,
Entered a narrow chasm. The brook and road
Were fellow-travellers in this gloomy strait,
And with them did we journey several hours
At a slow pace. The immeasurable height
Of woods decaying, never to be decayed,
The stationary blasts of waterfalls,
And in the narrow rent at every turn
Winds thwarting winds, bewildered and forlorn,
The torrents shooting from the clear blue sky,
630   The rocks that muttered close upon our ears,
Black drizzling crags that spake by the way-side
As if a voice were in them, the sick sight
And giddy prospect of the raving stream,
The unfettered clouds and region of the Heavens,
Tumult and peace, the darkness and the light—
Were all like workings of one mind, the features

Imagination . . . plain This passage (ll. 592–
616) is a sublime afterthought, nearly fourteen years after the event.

Of the same face, blossoms upon one tree;
Characters of the great Apocalypse,°
The types and symbols of Eternity,
640   Of first, and last, and midst, and without end.°

. . .

From *Book Seventh*

RESIDENCE IN LONDON

        Rise up, thou monstrous ant-hill on the plain
150   Of a too busy world! Before me flow,
Thou endless stream of men and moving things!
Thy every-day appearance, as it strikes—
With wonder heightened, or sublimed by awe—
On strangers, of all ages; the quick dance
Of colours, lights, and forms; the deafening din;
The comers and the goers face to face,
Face after face; the string of dazzling wares,
Shop after shop, with symbols, blazoned names,
And all the tradesman's honours overhead:
160   Here, fronts of houses, like a title-page,
With letters huge inscribed from top to toe,
Stationed above the door, like guardian saints;
There, allegoric shapes, female or male,
Or physiognomies of real men,
Land-warriors, kings, or admirals of the sea,
Boyle,° Shakespeare, Newton, or the attractive head
Of some quack-doctor, famous in his day.

        Meanwhile the roar continues, till at length,
Escaped as from an enemy, we turn
170   Abruptly into some sequestered nook,
Still as a sheltered place when winds blow loud!
At leisure, thence, through tracts of thin resort,
And sights and sounds that come at intervals,
We take our way. A raree-show° is here,
With children gathered round; another street
Presents a company of dancing dogs,
Or dromedary, with an antic pair
Of monkeys on his back; a minstrel band
Of Savoyards; or, single and alone,
180   An English ballad-singer. Private courts,

Apocalypse Revelation, the last book of the New Testament, and also the last act in the Christian drama of history; here natural objects are seen as being at once written words of Revelation and actors in the final drama of redemption.
Of first . . . without end See *Paradise Lost* V.165.

Boyle Robert Boyle, 17th-century physical scientist
raree-show Savoyard pronunciation of rare-show, a show-in-a-box or a peep-show; Savoyards were immigrants from the duchy of Savoy on the border between France and Italy.

Gloomy as coffins, and unsightly lanes
Thrilled by some female vendor's scream, belike
The very shrillest of all London cries,
May then entangle our impatient steps;
Conducted through those labyrinths, unawares,
To privileged regions and inviolate,
Where from their airy lodges studious lawyers
Look out on waters, walks, and gardens green.

. . .

As the black storm upon the mountain top
620 Sets off the sunbeam in the valley, so
That huge fermenting mass of human-kind
Serves as a solemn back-ground, or relief,
To single forms and objects, whence they draw,
For feeling and contemplative regard,
More than inherent liveliness and power.
How oft, amid those overflowing streets,
Have I gone forward with the crowd, and said
Unto myself, 'The face of every one
That passes by me is a mystery!'
630 Thus have I looked, nor ceased to look, oppressed
By thoughts of what and whither, when and how,
Until the shapes before my eyes became
A second-sight procession, such as glides
Over still mountains, or appears in dreams;
And once, far-travelled in such mood, beyond
The reach of common indication, lost
Amid the moving pageant, I was smitten
Abruptly, with the view (a sight not rare)
Of a blind Beggar, who, with upright face,
640 Stood, propped against a wall, upon his chest
Wearing a written paper, to explain
His story, whence he came, and who he was.
Caught by the spectacle my mind turned round
As with the might of waters; an apt type
This label seemed of the utmost we can know,
Both of ourselves and of the universe;
And, on the shape of that unmoving man,
His steadfast face and sightless eyes, I gazed,
As if admonished from another world.°

650 Though reared upon the base of outward things,
Structures like these the excited spirit mainly
Builds for herself; scenes different there are,
Full-formed, that take, with small internal help,
Possession of the faculties,—the peace

And . . . world The blind Beggar belongs to the visionary world of the Leech-gatherer in "Resolution and Independence," for here too "the might of waters" is invoked.

That comes with night; the deep solemnity
Of nature's intermediate hours of rest,
When the great tide of human life stands still;
The business of the day to come, unborn,
Of that gone by, locked up, as in the grave;
660   The blended calmness of the heavens and earth,
Moonlight and stars, and empty streets, and sounds
Unfrequent as in deserts; at late hours
Of winter evenings, when unwholesome rains
Are falling hard, with people yet astir,
The feeble salutation from the voice
Of some unhappy woman, now and then
Heard as we pass, when no one looks about,
Nothing is listened to. But these, I fear,
Are falsely catalogued; things that are, are not,
670   As the mind answers to them, or the heart
Is prompt, or slow, to feel. What say you, then,
To times, when half the city shall break out
Full of one passion, vengeance, rage, or fear?
To executions, to a street on fire,
Mobs, riots, or rejoicings? From these sights
Take one,—that ancient festival, the Fair,
Holden where martyrs suffered in past time,
And named of St. Bartholomew;° there, see
A work completed to our hands, that lays,
680   If any spectacle on earth can do,
The whole creative powers of man asleep!—
For once, the Muse's help will we implore,
And she shall lodge us, wafted on her wings,
Above the press and danger of the crowd,
Upon some showman's platform. What a shock
For eyes and ears! what anarchy and din,
Barbarian and infernal,—a phantasma,°
Monstrous in colour, motion, shape, sight, sound!
Below, the open space, through every nook
690   Of the wide area, twinkles, is alive
With heads; the midway region, and above,
Is thronged with staring pictures and huge scrolls,
Dumb proclamations of the Prodigies;°
With chattering monkeys dangling from their poles,
And children whirling in their roundabouts;°
With those that stretch the neck and strain the eyes,
And crack the voice in rivalship, the crowd
Inviting; with buffoons against buffoons

that ancient . . . St. Bartholomew This fair took
place in Smithfield, where Protestants were
martyred when the Catholic Queen Mary ruled,
from 1553 to 1558.

phantasma illusion
Prodigies wonders; here, freaks
roundabouts merry-go-rounds

Grimacing, writhing, screaming,—him who grinds
700 The hurdy-gurdy, at the fiddle weaves,
Rattles the salt-box, thumps the kettle-drum,
And him who at the trumpet puffs his cheeks,
The silver-collared Negro with his timbrel,
Equestrians, tumblers, women, girls, and boys,
Blue-breeched, pink-vested, with high-towering plumes.
All moveables of wonder, from all parts,
Are here—Albinos, painted Indians, Dwarfs,
The Horse of knowledge, and the learned Pig,
The Stone-eater, the man that swallows fire,
710 Giants, Ventriloquists, the Invisible Girl,
The Bust that speaks and moves its goggling eyes,
The Wax-work, Clock-work, all the marvellous craft
Of modern Merlins, Wild Beasts, Puppet-shows,
All out-o'-the-way, far-fetched, perverted things,
All freaks of nature, all Promethean thoughts
Of man, his dullness, madness, and their feats
All jumbled up together, to compose
A Parliament of Monsters. Tents and Booths
Meanwhile, as if the whole were one vast mill,
720 Are vomiting, receiving on all sides,
Men, Women, three-years Children, Babes in arms.

    Oh, blank confusion! true epitome
Of what the mighty City is herself
To thousands upon thousands of her sons,
Living amid the same perpetual whirl
Of trivial objects, melted and reduced
To one identity, by differences
That have no law, no meaning, and no end—
Oppression, under which even highest minds
730 Must labour, whence the strongest are not free.
But though the picture weary out the eye,
By nature an unmanageable sight,
It is not wholly so to him who looks
In steadiness, who hath among least things
An under-sense of greatest; sees the parts
As parts, but with a feeling of the whole.

       .   .   .

From *Book Eighth*

RETROSPECT

    But lovelier far than this, the paradise
Where I was reared; in Nature's primitive gifts
100 Favoured no less, and more to every sense
Delicious, seeing that the sun and sky,

The elements, and seasons as they change,
Do find a worthy fellow-labourer there—
Man free, man working for himself, with choice
Of time, and place, and object; by his wants,
His comforts, native occupations, cares,
Cheerfully led to individual ends
Or social, and still followed by a train
Unwooed, unthought-of even—simplicity,
110   And beauty, and inevitable grace.

      Yea, when a glimpse of those imperial bowers
Would to a child be transport over-great,
When but a half-hour's roam through such a place
Would leave behind a dance of images,
That shall break in upon his sleep for weeks;
Even then the common haunts of the green earth,
And ordinary interests of man,
Which they embosom, all without regard
As both may seem, are fastening on the heart
120   Insensibly, each with the other's help.
For me, when my affections first were led
From kindred, friends, and playmates, to partake
Love for the human creature's absolute self,
That noticeable kindliness of heart
Sprang out of fountains, there abounding most
Where sovereign Nature dictated the tasks
And occupations which her beauty adorned,
And Shepherds were the men that pleased me first;

      . . . For this he quits his home
At day-spring, and no sooner doth the sun
Begin to strike him with a fire-like heat,
Than he lies down upon some shining rock,
And breakfasts with his dog. When they have stolen,
As is their wont, a pittance from strict time,
240   For rest not needed or exchange of love,
Then from his couch he starts; and now his feet
Crush out a livelier fragrance from the flowers
Of lowly thyme, by Nature's skill enwrought
In the wild turf: the lingering dews of morn
Smoke round him, as from hill to hill he lies,
His staff protending° like a hunter's spear,
Or by its aid leaping from crag to crag,
And o'er the brawling beds of unbridged streams.
Philosophy, methinks, at Fancy's call,
250   Might deign to follow him through what he does
Or sees in his day's march; himself he feels,
In those vast regions where his service lies,

protending stretching out

A freeman, wedded to his life of hope
And hazard, and hard labour interchanged
With that majestic indolence so dear
To native man. A rambling school-boy, thus
I felt his presence in his own domain,
As of a lord and master, or a power,
Or genius, under Nature, under God,
260   Presiding; and severest solitude
Had more commanding looks when he was there.
When up the lonely brooks on rainy days
Angling I went, or trod the trackless hills
By mists bewildered, suddenly mine eyes
Have glanced upon him distant a few steps,
In size a giant, stalking through thick fog,
His sheep like Greenland bears; or, as he stepped
Beyond the boundary line of some hill-shadow,
His form hath flashed upon me, glorified
270   By the deep radiance of the setting sun:
Or him have I descried in distant sky,
A solitary object and sublime,
Above all height! like an aerial cross
Stationed alone upon a spiry rock
Of the Chartreuse,° for worship. Thus was man
Ennobled outwardly before my sight,
And thus my heart was early introduced
To an unconscious love and reverence
Of human nature; hence the human form
280   To me became an index of delight,
Of grace and honour, power and worthiness.
Meanwhile this creature—spiritual almost
As those of books, but more exalted far;
Far more of an imaginative form
Than the gay Corin° of the groves, who lives
For his own fancies, or to dance by the hour,
In coronal, with Phyllis in the midst—
Was, for the purposes of kind, a man
With the most common; husband, father; learned,
290   Could teach, admonish; suffered with the rest
From vice and folly, wretchedness and fear;
Of this I little saw, cared less for it,
But something must have felt.
      Call ye these appearances—
Which I beheld of shepherds in my youth,
This sanctity of Nature given to man—
A shadow, a delusion, ye who pore

Chartreuse the mountains near Grenoble; the Carthusian monks placed crosses on the tops of them

Corin Corin and Phyllis are traditional names in literary pastoral.

On the dead letter, miss the spirit of things;
Whose truth is not a motion or a shape
Instinct with vital functions, but a block
300 Or waxen image which yourselves have made,
And ye adore! But blessed be the God
Of Nature and of Man that this was so;
That men before my inexperienced eyes
Did first present themselves thus purified,
Removed, and to a distance that was fit:

.   .   .

From *Book Tenth*

RESIDENCE IN FRANCE

. . . It pleased me more
To abide in the great City,° where I found
The general air still busy with the stir
Of that first memorable onset made
By a strong levy of humanity
Upon the traffickers in Negro blood;°
250 Effort which, though defeated, had recalled
To notice old forgotten principles,
And through the nation spread a novel heat
Of virtuous feeling. For myself, I own
That this particular strife had wanted power
To rivet my affections; nor did now
Its unsuccessful issue much excite
My sorrow; for I brought with me the faith
That, if France prospered, good men would not long
Pay fruitless worship to humanity,
260 And this most rotten branch of human shame,
Object, so seemed it, of superfluous pains,
Would fall together with its parent tree.
What, then, were my emotions, when in arms
Britain put forth her free-born strength in league,
Oh, pity and shame! with those confederate Powers!°
Not in my single self alone I found,
But in the minds of all ingenuous youth,
Change and subversion from that hour. No shock
Given to my moral nature had I known

great City London. Wordsworth went to France late in 1791, and stayed for one year, intensely sympathizing with the moderate Girondist faction among the revolutionaries, and falling in love (and fathering a daughter) with Annette Vallon; on his return to England, he experienced the double guilt of not sharing the Girondists' fate, when most were executed by the radical Jacobins in the Terror, and of having abandoned his mistress and their daughter.

Of that . . . Negro blood William Wilberforce's bill for abolishing the slave trade passed the House of Commons in April 1792, but was killed in the House of Lords; abolition did not come until 1807.
What . . . Powers On February 11, 1793, England declared war against France, thus joining itself to the most tyrannical European nations in their league against the Revolution.

270   Down to that very moment;° neither lapse
       Nor turn of sentiment that might be named
       A revolution, save at this one time;
       All else was progress on the self-same path
       On which, with a diversity of pace,
       I had been travelling: this a stride at once
       Into another region. As a light
       And pliant harebell, swinging in the breeze
       On some grey rock—its birth-place—so had I
       Wantoned, fast rooted on the ancient tower
280   Of my beloved country, wishing not
       A happier fortune than to wither there:
       Now was I from that pleasant station torn
       And tossed about in whirlwind. I rejoiced,
       Yea, afterwards—truth most painful to record!—
       Exulted, in the triumph of my soul,
       When Englishmen by thousands were o'erthrown,
       Left without glory on the field, or driven,
       Brave hearts! to shameful flight.° It was a grief,—
       Grief call it not, 'twas anything but that,—
290   A conflict of sensations without name,
       Of which *he* only, who may love the sight
       Of a village steeple, as I do, can judge,
       When, in the congregation bending all
       To their great Father, prayers were offered up,
       Or praises for our country's victories;
       And, 'mid the simple worshippers, perchance
       I only, like an uninvited guest
       Whom no one owned, sate silent, shall I add,
       Fed on the day of vengeance yet to come.

                    .   .   .

       It was a lamentable time for man,
       Whether a hope had e'er been his or not;
       A woeful time for them whose hopes survived
       The shock; most woeful for those few who still
       Were flattered, and had trust in human kind:
       They had the deepest feeling of the grief.
390   Meanwhile the Invaders fared as they deserved:
       The Herculean Commonwealth had put forth her arms,
       And throttled with an infant godhead's might
       The snakes about her cradle; that was well,
       And as it should be; yet no cure for them
       Whose souls were sick with pain of what would be
       Hereafter brought in charge against mankind.

No shock . . . moment Not even the failure of
the Revolution affected Wordsworth as strongly
as the English counter-revolutionary crusade;
this holds true for Blake and Coleridge also.

shameful flight retreat of the Duke of York's
army after the battle of Hondshoote, in September 1793

Most melancholy at that time, O Friend!
Were my day-thoughts,—my nights were miserable;
Through months, through years, long after the last beat
400   Of those atrocities,° the hour of sleep
To me came rarely charged with natural gifts,
Such ghastly visions had I of despair
And tyranny, and implements of death;
And innocent victims sinking under fear,
And momentary hope, and worn-out prayer,
Each in his separate cell, or penned in crowds
For sacrifice, and struggling with fond mirth
And levity in dungeons, where the dust
Was laid with tears. Then suddenly the scene
410   Changed, and the unbroken dream entangled me
In long orations, which I strove to plead
Before unjust tribunals,—with a voice
Labouring, a brain confounded, and a sense,
Death-like, of treacherous desertion,° felt
In the last place of refuge—my own soul.

.　　.　　.

From *Book Eleventh*

FRANCE

O pleasant exercise of hope and joy!°
For mighty were the auxiliars which then stood
Upon our side, us who were strong in love!
Bliss was it in that dawn to be alive,
But to be young was very Heaven! O times,
110   In which the meagre, stale, forbidding ways
Of custom, law, and statute, took at once
The attraction of a country in romance!
When Reason seemed the most to assert her rights
When most intent on making of herself
A prime enchantress—to assist the work,
Which then was going forward in her name!
Not favoured spots alone, but the whole Earth,
The beauty wore of promise—that which sets
(As at some moments might not be unfelt
120   Among the bowers of Paradise itself)
The budding rose above the rose full blown.
What temper at the prospect did not wake

those atrocities the Reign of Terror, autumn 1793 to summer 1794
treacherous desertion His guilt is complex here; the manifest element is having abandoned the Girondists, but the latent, stronger anxiety is for having abandoned Annette and his child.

hope and joy This rhapsody (ll. 105–44) on the original prospects of the Revolution should be compared with the concluding passage from "Home at Grasmere" used as the "Prospectus" to *The Excursion*.

To happiness unthought of? The inert
Were roused, and lively natures rapt away!
They who had fed their childhood upon dreams,
The play-fellows of fancy, who had made
All powers of swiftness, subtilty, and strength
Their ministers,—who in lordly wise had stirred
Among the grandest objects of the sense,
And dealt with whatsoever they found there
As if they had within some lurking right
To wield it;—they, too, who of gentle mood
Had watched all gentle motions, and to these
Had fitted their own thoughts, schemers more mild,
And in the region of their peaceful selves;—
Now was it that *both* found, the meek and lofty
Did both find helpers to their hearts' desire,
And stuff at hand, plastic as they could wish,—
Were called upon to exercise their skill,
Not in Utopia,—subterranean fields,—
Or some secreted island, Heaven knows where!
But in the very world, which is the world
Of all of us,—the place where, in the end,
We find our happiness, or not at all!

. . .

But now, become oppressors in their turn,°
Frenchmen had changed a war of self-defence
For one of conquest, losing sight of all
Which they had struggled for: now mounted up,
Openly in the eye of earth and heaven,
The scale of liberty. I read her doom,
With anger vexed, with disappointment sore,
But not dismayed, nor taking to the shame
Of a false prophet. While resentment rose
Striving to hide, what nought could heal, the wounds
Of mortified presumption, I adhered
More firmly to old tenets, and, to prove
Their temper, strained them more; and thus, in heat
Of contest, did opinions every day
Grow into consequence, till round my mind
They clung, as if they were its life, nay more,
The very being of the immortal soul.°

. . .

I summoned my best skill, and toiled, intent
To anatomize the frame of social life,
Yea, the whole body of society

But . . . turn By early 1795, French armies were thrusting deep into Italy, Spain, and Germany.

immortal soul This passage (ll. 206–22) is the start of Wordsworth's *intellectual* crisis, as contrasted to the *poetic* crisis depicted in Book First.

Searched to its heart.° Share with me, Friend! the wish
That some dramatic tale, endued with shapes
Livelier, and flinging out less guarded words
Than suit the work we fashion, might set forth
What then I learned, or think I learned, of truth,
And the errors into which I fell, betrayed
By present objects, and by reasonings false
From their beginnings, inasmuch as drawn
290 Out of a heart that had been turned aside
From Nature's way by outward accidents,
And which was thus confounded, more and more
Misguided, and misguiding. So I fared,
Dragging all precepts, judgments, maxims, creeds,
Like culprits to the bar; calling the mind,
Suspiciously, to establish in plain day
Her titles and her honours; now believing,
Now disbelieving; endlessly perplexed
With impulse, motive, right and wrong, the ground
300 Of obligation, what the rule and whence
The sanction; till, demanding formal *proof*,
And seeking it in every thing, I lost
All feeling of conviction, and, in fine,
Sick, wearied out with contrarieties,
Yielded up moral questions in despair.°

. . .

From *Book Twelfth*

IMAGINATION AND TASTE, HOW IMPAIRED AND RESTORED

In such strange passion, if I may once more
Review the past, I warred against myself—
A bigot to a new idolatry—
Like a cowled monk who hath forsworn the world,
Zealously laboured to cut off my heart
80 From all the sources of her former strength;
And as, by simple waving of a wand,
The wizard instantaneously dissolves
Palace or grove, even so could I unsoul
As readily by syllogistic words
Those mysteries of being which have made,
And shall continue evermore to make,

I summoned . . . heart He falls into the imaginative error of the rationalist analysts of society and human nature, who do not begin and end with the human heart, as his best poetry does.
till, demanding . . . despair (ll. 301–5) the low point of this crisis, from which his former

self, in the shape of Dorothy and his own "spots of time," will save him. Wordsworth is describing the pernicious effects of having become, however briefly, a follower of the intellectual and social theories of William Godwin, the Necessitarian Anarchist philosopher.

Of the whole human race one brotherhood.

    What wonder, then, if, to a mind so far
Perverted, even the visible Universe
90   Fell under the dominion of a taste
Less spiritual, with microscopic view
Was scanned, as I had scanned the moral world?

     .   .   .

I speak in recollection of a time
When the bodily eye, in every stage of life
The most despotic of our senses, gained
130   Such strength in *me* as often held my mind
In absolute dominion.° Gladly here,
Entering upon abstruser argument,
Could I endeavour to unfold the means
Which Nature studiously employs to thwart
This tyranny, summons all the senses each
To counteract the other, and themselves,
And makes them all, and the objects with which all
Are conversant, subservient in their turn
To the great ends of Liberty and Power.
140   But leave we this: enough that my delights
(Such as they were) were sought insatiably.
Vivid the transport, vivid though not profound;
I roamed from hill to hill, from rock to rock,
Still craving combinations of new forms,
New pleasure, wider empire for the sight,
Proud of her own endowments, and rejoiced
To lay the inner faculties asleep.

     .   .   .

In truth, the degradation—howsoe'er
Induced, effect, in whatsoe'er degree,
Of custom that prepares a partial scale
In which the little oft outweighs the great;
Or any other cause that hath been named;
Or lastly, aggravated by the times
And their impassioned sounds, which well might make
200   The milder minstrelsies of rural scenes
Inaudible—was transient; I had known
Too forcibly, too early in my life,
Visitings of imaginative power
For this to last: I shook the habit off
Entirely and forever, and again
In Nature's presence stood, as now I stand,
A sensitive being, a *creative* soul.

I speak . . . dominion (ll. 126–31) He seeks
the power of the mind over the universe of
sense; in his crisis time, he rightly feared en-
slavement to the eye, the ultimate fate of
visionaries when their energies are fled; see,
for instance, Thoreau's later journals.

There are in our existence spots of time,°
That with distinct pre-eminence retain
210   A renovating virtue, whence, depressed
By false opinion and contentious thought,
Or aught of heavier or more deadly weight,
In trivial occupations, and the round
Of ordinary intercourse, our minds
Are nourished and invisibly repaired;
A virtue, by which pleasure is enhanced,
That penetrates, enables us to mount,
When high, more high, and lifts us up when fallen.
This efficacious spirit chiefly lurks
220   Among those passages of life that give
Profoundest knowledge to what point, and how,
The mind is lord and master—outward sense
The obedient servant of her will.° Such moments
Are scattered everywhere, taking their date
From our first childhood. I remember well,
That once, while yet my inexperienced hand
Could scarcely hold a bridle, with proud hopes
I mounted, and we journeyed towards the hills:
An ancient servant of my father's house
230   Was with me, my encourager and guide:
We had not travelled long, ere some mischance
Disjoined me from my comrade; and, through fear
Dismounting, down the rough and stony moor
I led my horse, and, stumbling on, at length
Came to a bottom, where in former times
A murderer had been hung in iron chains.
The gibbet-mast had mouldered down, the bones
And iron case were gone; but on the turf,
Hard by, soon after that fell deed was wrought,
240   Some unknown hand had carved the murderer's name.
The monumental letters were inscribed
In times long past; but still, from year to year,
By superstition of the neighbourhood,
The grass is cleared away, and to this hour
The characters are fresh and visible:
A casual glance had shown them, and I fled,
Faltering and faint, and ignorant of the road:
Then, reascending the bare common, saw
A naked pool that lay beneath the hills,
250   The beacon on the summit, and, more near,
A girl, who bore a pitcher on her head,

---

spots of time The most important conceptual image in *The Prelude;* the "spots of time" are also what might be termed "moments of space," the equivalent of Blake's pulsation of an artery in which the poet's work is done; their function is to enshrine "the spirit of the Past for future restoration" (see ll. 285–86).
her will the creative mind or imagination's will

And seemed with difficult steps to force her way
Against the blowing wind. It was, in truth,
An ordinary sight; but I should need
Colours and words that are unknown to man,
To paint the visionary dreariness
Which, while I looked all round for my lost guide,
Invested moorland waste, and naked pool,
The beacon crowning the lone eminence,
260   The female and her garments vexed and tossed
By the strong wind. When, in the blessed hours
Of early love, the loved one at my side,
I roamed, in daily presence of this scene,
Upon the naked pool and dreary crags,
And on the melancholy beacon fell
A spirit of pleasure and youth's golden gleam;
And think ye not with radiance more sublime
For these remembrances, and for the power
They had left behind? So feeling comes in aid
270   Of feeling, and diversity of strength
Attends us, if but once we have been strong.°
Oh! mystery of man, from what a depth
Proceed thy honours. I am lost, but see
In simple childhood something of the base
On which thy greatness stands; but this I feel,
That from thyself it comes, that thou must give,
Else never canst receive. The days gone by
Return upon me almost from the dawn
Of life: the hiding-places of man's power
280   Open; I would approach them, but they close.
I see by glimpses now; when age comes on,
May scarcely see at all; and I would give,
While yet we may, as far as words can give,
Substance and life to what I feel, enshrining,
Such is my hope, the spirit of the Past
For future restoration.—Yet another
Of these memorials:—
                    One Christmas-time,
On the glad eve of its dear holidays,
Feverish, and tired, and restless, I went forth
290   Into the fields, impatient for the sight
Of those led palfreys that should bear us home;
My brothers and myself. There rose a crag,
That, from the meeting-point of two highways
Ascending, overlooked them both, far stretched;
Thither, uncertain on which road to fix

if . . . strong the kernel of Wordsworth's
faith; his confidence that he began as a strong
poet, a capable imagination

My expectation, thither I repaired,
Scout-like, and gained the summit; 'twas a day
Tempestuous, dark, and wild, and on the grass
I sate half-sheltered by a naked wall;
300   Upon my right hand couched a single sheep,
Upon my left a blasted hawthorn stood;
With those companions at my side, I watched,
Straining my eyes intensely, as the mist
Gave intermitting prospect of the copse
And plain beneath. Ere we to school returned,—
That dreary time,—ere we had been ten days
Sojourners in my father's house, he died,
And I and my three brothers, orphans then,
Followed his body to the grave. The event,
310   With all the sorrow that it brought, appeared
A chastisement; and when I called to mind
That day so lately past, when from the crag
I looked in such anxiety of hope;
With trite reflections of morality,
Yet in the deepest passion, I bowed low
To God, Who thus corrected my desires;
And, afterwards, the wind and sleety rain,
And all the business of the elements,
The single sheep, and the one blasted tree,
320   And the bleak music from that old stone wall,
The noise of wood and water, and the mist
That on the line of each of those two roads
Advanced in such indisputable shapes;
All these were kindred spectacles and sounds
To which I oft repaired, and thence would drink,
As at a fountain; and on winter nights,
Down to this very time, when storm and rain
Beat on my roof, or, haply, at noon-day,
While in a grove I walk, whose lofty trees,
330   Laden with summer's thickest foliage, rock
In a strong wind, some working of the spirit,
Some inward agitations thence are brought,
Whate'er their office, whether to beguile
Thoughts over busy in the course they took,
Or animate an hour of vacant ease.

From *Book Fourteenth*

CONCLUSION

In one of those excursions (may they ne'er
Fade from remembrance!) through the Northern tracts
Of Cambria° ranging with a youthful friend,
Cambria Wales

I left Bethgelert's° huts at couching-time,
And westward took my way, to see the sun
Rise from the top of Snowdon. To the door
Of a rude cottage at the mountain's base
We came, and roused the shepherd who attends
The adventurous stranger's steps, a trusty guide;
Then, cheered by short refreshment, sallied forth.

    It was a close, warm, breezeless summer night,
Wan, dull, and glaring, with a dripping fog
Low-hung and thick that covered all the sky;
But, undiscouraged, we began to climb
The mountain-side. The mist soon girt us round,
And, after ordinary travellers' talk
With our conductor, pensively we sank
Each into commerce with his private thoughts:
Thus did we breast the ascent, and by myself
Was nothing either seen or heard that checked
Those musings or diverted, save that once
The shepherd's lurcher,° who, among the crags,
Had to his joy unearthed a hedgehog, teased
His coiled-up prey with barkings turbulent.
This small adventure, for even such it seemed
In that wild place and at the dead of night,
Being over and forgotten, on we wound
In silence as before. With forehead bent
Earthward, as if in opposition set
Against an enemy, I panted up
With eager pace, and no less eager thoughts.
Thus might we wear a midnight hour away,
Ascending at loose distance each from each,
And I, as chanced, the foremost of the band;
When at my feet the ground appeared to brighten,
And with a step or two seemed brighter still;
Nor was time given to ask or learn the cause,
For instantly a light upon the turf
Fell like a flash, and lo! as I looked up,
The Moon hung naked in a firmament
Of azure without cloud, and at my feet
Rested a silent sea of hoary mist.
A hundred hills their dusky backs upheaved
All over this still ocean; and beyond,
Far, far beyond, the solid vapours stretched,
In headlands, tongues, and promontory shapes,
Into the main Atlantic, that appeared
To dwindle, and give up his majesty,

10

20

30

40

Bethgelert's village near Snowdon, the highest   **lurcher** hunting dog
mountain in Wales

Usurped upon far as the sight could reach.
50   Not so the ethereal vault; encroachment none
Was there, nor loss; only the inferior stars
Had disappeared, or shed a fainter light
In the clear presence of the full-orbed Moon,
Who, from her sovereign elevation, gazed
Upon the billowy ocean, as it lay
All meek and silent, save that through a rift—
Not distant from the shore whereon we stood,
A fixed, abysmal, gloomy, breathing-place—
Mounted the roar of waters, torrents, streams
60   Innumerable, roaring with one voice!
Heard over earth and sea, and, in that hour,
For so it seemed, felt by the starry heavens.

    When into air had partially dissolved
That vision, given to spirits of the night
And three chance human wanderers, in calm thought
Reflected, it appeared to me the type
Of a majestic intellect, its acts
And its possessions, what it has and craves,
What in itself it is, and would become.
70   There I beheld the emblem of a mind
That feeds upon infinity, that broods
Over the dark abyss, intent to hear
Its voices issuing forth to silent light
In one continuous stream; a mind sustained
By recognitions of transcendent power,
In sense conducting to ideal form,
In soul of more than mortal privilege.
One function, above all, of such a mind
Had Nature shadowed there, by putting forth,
80   'Mid circumstances awful and sublime,
That mutual domination which she loves
To exert upon the face of outward things,
So moulded, joined, abstracted, so endowed
With interchangeable supremacy,
That men, least sensitive, see, hear, perceive,
And cannot choose but feel. The power, which all
Acknowledge when thus moved, which Nature thus
To bodily sense exhibits, is the express
Resemblance of that glorious faculty°
90   That higher minds bear with them as their own.
This is the very spirit in which they deal
With the whole compass of the universe:
They from their native selves can send abroad

glorious faculty the higher Reason or poetic
imagination

Kindred mutations; for themselves create
A like existence; and, whene'er it dawns
Created for them, catch it, or are caught
By its inevitable mastery,
Like angels stopped upon the wing by sound
Of harmony from Heaven's remotest spheres.°
100 Them the enduring and the transient both
Serve to exalt; they build up greatest things
From least suggestions; ever on the watch,
Willing to work and to be wrought upon,
They need not extraordinary calls
To rouse them; in a world of life they live,
By sensible impressions not enthralled,
But by their quickening impulse made more prompt
To hold fit converse with the spiritual world,
And with the generations of mankind
110 Spread over time, past, present, and to come,
Age after age, till Time shall be no more.
Such minds are truly from the Deity,
For they are Powers; and hence the highest bliss
That flesh can know is theirs—the consciousness
Of Whom° they are, habitually infused
Through every image and through every thought,
And all affections by communion raised
From earth to heaven, from human to divine;
Hence endless occupation for the Soul,
120 Whether discursive or intuitive;°
Hence cheerfulness for acts of daily life,
Emotions which best foresight need not fear,
Most worthy then of trust when most intense.
Hence, amid ills that vex and wrongs that crush
Our hearts—if here the words of Holy Writ
May with fit reverence be applied—that peace
Which passeth understanding,° that repose
In moral judgments which from this pure source
Must come, or will by man be sought in vain.

.   .   .

430   Oh! yet a few short years of useful life,
And all will be complete, thy° race be run,
Thy monument of glory will be raised;
Then, though (too weak to tread the ways of truth)
This age fall back to old idolatry,

Like angels . . . spheres Frank Kermode noted
Wallace Stevens's debt to this and subsequent
passages in Notes Toward a Supreme Fiction,
"It Must Give Pleasure" VIII.
Whom refers to a composite poetic selfhood,
and not to God
And all . . . intuitive (ll. 117-20) See Paradise

Lost V.483-90 where Raphael discourses to
Adam on the "gradual scale sublimed" which
distinguishes human from angelic faculties, a
passage crucial also for Coleridge's formulation
of the Secondary Imagination.
that peace . . . understanding Philippians 4:7
thy Coleridge's

Though men return to servitude as fast
As the tide ebbs, to ignominy and shame
By nations sink together, we shall still
Find solace—knowing what we have learnt to know,
Rich in true happiness if allowed to be
440 Faithful alike in forwarding a day
Of firmer trust, joint labourers in the work
(Should Providence such grace to us vouchsafe)
Of their deliverance, surely yet to come.
Prophets of Nature, we to them will speak
A lasting inspiration, sanctified
By reason, blest by faith: what we have loved,
Others will love, and we will teach them how;
Instruct them how the mind of man becomes
A thousand times more beautiful than the earth
450 On which he dwells, above this frame of things
(Which, 'mid all revolution in the hopes
And fears of men, doth still remain unchanged)
In beauty exalted, as it is itself
Of quality and fabric more divine.
1799–1805   1850

Surprised by Joy

Surprised by joy—impatient as the Wind
I turned to share the transport—Oh! with whom
But Thee,° deep buried in the silent tomb,
That spot which no vicissitude can find?
Love, faithful love, recalled thee to my mind—
But how could I forget thee? Through what power,
Even for the least division of an hour,
Have I been so beguiled as to be blind
To my most grievous loss!—That thought's return
10 Was the worst pang that sorrow ever bore,
Save one, one only, when I stood forlorn,
Knowing my heart's best treasure was no more;
That neither present time, nor years unborn
Could to my sight that heavenly face restore.
1815

Thee the poet's daughter Catherine, who had
died in June 1812, three years old

Composed upon an Evening of Extraordinary Splendour and Beauty°

I

Had this effulgence disappeared
With flying haste, I might have sent,
Among the speechless clouds, a look
Of blank astonishment;
But 'tis endued with power to stay,
And sanctify one closing day,
That frail Mortality may see—
What is?—ah no, but what *can* be!
Time was when field and watery cove
10   With modulated echoes rang,
While choirs of fervent Angels sang
Their vespers in the grove;
Or, crowning, star-like, each some sovereign height,
Warbled, for heaven above and earth below,
Strains suitable to both.—Such holy rite,
Methinks, if audibly repeated now
From hill or valley, could not move
Sublimer transport, purer love,
Than doth this silent spectacle—the gleam—
20   The shadow—and the peace supreme!

II

No sound is uttered,—but a deep
And solemn harmony pervades
The hollow vale from steep to steep,
And penetrates the glades.
Far-distant images draw nigh,
Called forth by wondrous potency
Of beamy radiance, that imbues
Whate'er it strikes with gem-like hues!
In vision exquisitely clear,
30   Herds range along the mountain side;
And glistening antlers are descried;
And gilded flocks appear.
Thine is the tranquil hour, purpureal Eve!
But long as god-like wish, or hope divine,
Informs my spirit, ne'er can I believe
That this magnificence is wholly thine!
—From worlds not quickened by the sun
A portion of the gift is won;

Composed . . . Beauty Wordsworth's own note to this very poignant poem: "The multiplication of mountain-ridges, described at the commencement of the third stanza of this Ode, as a kind of Jacob's Ladder, leading to Heaven, is produced either by watery vapours, or sunny haze;—in the present instance by the latter cause. Allusions to the Ode, entitled 'Intimations of Immortality,' pervade the last stanza."

An intermingling of Heaven's pomp is spread
40 On grounds which British shepherds tread!

III

And, if there be whom broken ties
Afflict, or injuries assail,
Yon hazy ridges to their eyes
Present a glorious scale,
Climbing suffused with sunny air,
To stop—no record hath told where!
And tempting Fancy to ascend,
And with immortal Spirits blend!
—Wings at my shoulders seem to play;
50 But, rooted here, I stand and gaze
On those bright steps that heavenward raise
Their practicable way.
Come forth, ye drooping old men, look abroad,
And see to what fair countries ye are bound!
And if some traveller, weary of his road,
Hath slept since noon-tide on the grassy ground,
Ye Genii! to his covert speed;
And wake him with such gentle heed
As may attune his soul to meet the dower
60 Bestowed on this transcendent hour!

IV

Such hues from their celestial Urn
Were wont to stream before mine eye,
Where'er it wandered in the morn
Of blissful infancy.
This glimpse of glory, why renewed?
Nay, rather speak with gratitude;
For, if a vestige of those gleams
Survived, 'twas only in my dreams.
Dread Power! whom peace and calmness serve
70 No less than Nature's threatening voice,
If aught unworthy be my choice,
From THEE if I would swerve;
Oh, let Thy grace remind me of the light
Full early lost, and fruitlessly deplored;
Which, at this moment, on my waking sight
Appears to shine, by miracle restored:
My soul, though yet confined to earth,
Rejoices in a second birth!
—'Tis past, the visionary splendour fades;
80 And night approaches with her shades.
    1817   1820

Mutability

From low to high doth dissolution climb,
And sink from high to low, along a scale
Of awful notes, whose concord shall not fail;
A musical but melancholy chime,
Which they can hear who meddle not with crime,
Nor avarice, nor over-anxious care.
Truth fails not; but her outward forms that bear
The longest date do melt like frosty rime,
That in the morning whitened hill and plain
10 And is no more; drop like the tower sublime
Of yesterday, which royally did wear
His crown of weeds, but could not even sustain
Some casual shout that broke the silent air,
Or the unimaginable touch of Time.°
1821   1822

Extempore Effusion upon the Death of James Hogg°

When first, descending from the moorlands,
I saw the Stream of Yarrow° glide
Along a bare and open valley,
The Ettrick Shepherd was my guide.

When last along its banks I wandered,
Through groves that had begun to shed
Their golden leaves upon the pathways,
My steps the Border-minstrel° led.

The mighty Minstrel breathes no longer,
10 'Mid mouldering ruins low he lies;
And death upon the braes° of Yarrow,
Has closed the Shepherd-poet's eyes:

Nor has the rolling year twice measured,
From sign to sign, its stedfast course,
Since every mortal power of Coleridge
Was frozen at its marvellous source;

The rapt One, of the godlike forehead,
The heaven-eyed creature sleeps in earth:°

Or . . . Time Samuel Monk points out that
this alludes to Milton's tract, *Of Education*,
where he mentions the "unimaginable touches"
of music.
James Hogg Scottish poet known as "the Ettrick Shepherd," died November 21, 1835
Yarrow river in southern Scotland

Border-minstrel Sir Walter Scott had died in
1832.
braes hillsides
The rapt . . . earth Coleridge had died in
1834; the two men had been reconciled, but
Wordsworth waited a year before elegizing his
closest friend, as he so movingly does here.

20 And Lamb, the frolic and the gentle,
    Has vanished from his lonely hearth.°

    Like clouds that rake the mountain-summits,
    Or waves that own no curbing hand,
    How fast has brother followed brother,
    From sunshine to the sunless land!

    Yet I, whose lids from infant slumber
    Were earlier raised, remain to hear
    A timid voice, that asks in whispers,
    'Who next will drop and disappear?'

    Our haughty life is crowned with darkness,
30 Like London with its own black wreath,
    On which with thee, O Crabbe!° forth-looking.
    I gazed from Hampstead's breezy heath.

    As if but yesterday departed,
    Thou too art gone before; but why,
    O'er ripe fruit, seasonably gathered,
    Should frail survivors heave a sigh?

    Mourn rather for that holy Spirit,
    Sweet as the spring, as ocean deep;
    For Her° who, ere her summer faded,
40 Has sunk into a breathless sleep.

    No more of old romantic sorrows,
    For slaughtered Youth or love-lorn Maid!
    With sharper grief is Yarrow smitten,
    And Ettrick mourns with her their Poet dead.
    1835   1835

SAMUEL TAYLOR COLERIDGE
1772–1834

Coleridge was the youngest of fourteen children of a country clergyman, a precocious and lonely child, a kind of changeling in his own family. Early a dreamer and
(as he said) a "character," he suffered the loss of his father (who had loved him best)
when he was only nine. At Christ's Hospital in London, soon after his father's death,
he found an excellent school that gave him the intellectual nurture he needed, as well
as a lifelong friend in the future essayist, Charles Lamb. Early a poet, he fell deeply
in love with Mary Evans, a schoolfellow's sister, but nothing came of it.

At Jesus College, Cambridge, Coleridge started well, but temperamentally he was
not suited to academic discipline, and failed of distinction. Fleeing Cambridge, and

And Lamb . . . hearth Charles Lamb also
had died in 1834.
Crabbe George Crabbe had died in 1832.
Her Felicia Hemans, a rather unfortunate poetess, who died at the age of forty-two in 1835;
she was very popular for many decades after-
ward, in America and in England, but is now
remembered only for the splendidly bad lyric
"Casabianca," with its memorable first line:
"The boy stood on the burning deck."

much in debt, he enlisted in the cavalry under the immortal name of Silas Tomkyn Comberbacke, but kept falling off his horse. Though he proved useful to his fellow dragoons at writing love letters, he was good for little else but stable-cleaning, and the cavalry allowed his brothers to buy him out. He returned to Cambridge, but his characteristic guilt impeded academic labor, and when he abandoned Cambridge in 1794 he had no degree.

A penniless young poet, radical in politics, original in religion, he fell in with the then equally radical bard Robert Southey, remembered today as the Conservative Laureate constantly savaged in Byron's satirical verse. Like our contemporary communards, the two poetical youths projected what they named a Pantisocracy. With the right young ladies, and other choice spirits, they would found a communistic agrarian-literary settlement on the banks of the Susquehanna in exotic Pennsylvania. At Southey's urging, Coleridge made a Pantisocratic engagement to the not very brilliant Miss Sara Fricker, whose sister Southey was to marry. Pantisocracy died at birth, and Coleridge in time woke up to find himself unsuitably married, the largest misfortune of his life.

He turned to Wordsworth, whom he had met early in 1795. His poetry influenced Wordsworth's, and helped Wordsworth attain his characteristic mode. It is not too much to say that Coleridge's poetry disappeared into Wordsworth's. We remember *Lyrical Ballads* (1798) as Wordsworth's book; yet about a third of it (in length) was Coleridge's, and "Tintern Abbey," the crown of the volume except for *The Ancient Mariner,* is immensely indebted to Coleridge's "Frost at Midnight." Nor is there much evidence of Wordsworth's admiring or encouraging his friend's poetry; toward *The Ancient Mariner* he was always very grudging, and he was discomfited (but inevitably so) by both "Dejection: An Ode" and "To William Wordsworth." Selfless where Wordsworth's poetry was concerned, Coleridge had to suffer his closest friend's neglect of his own poetic ambitions.

This is not an easy matter to be fair about, since literature necessarily is as much a matter of personality as it is of character. Coleridge, like Keats (and to certain readers, Shelley) is lovable. Byron is at least always fascinating, and Blake in his lonely magnificence is a hero of the imagination. But Wordsworth's personality, like Milton's or Dante's, does not stimulate affection for the poet in the common reader. Coleridge has, as Walter Pater observed, a "peculiar charm"; he seems to lend himself to myths of failure, which is astonishing when the totality of his work is contemplated.

Yet it is his life, and his self-abandonment of his poetic ambitions, that continue to convince us that we ought to find in him parables of the failure of genius. His best poetry was all written in the year and a half in which he saw Wordsworth daily (1797–98); yet even his best poetry, with the single exception of *The Ancient Mariner,* is fragmentary. The pattern of his life is fragmentary also. When he received an annuity from the Wedgwood family, he left Wordsworth and Dorothy to study language and philosophy in Germany (1798–99). Soon after returning, his miserable middle years began, though he was only twenty-seven. He moved near the Wordsworths again, and fell in love, permanently and unhappily, with Sara Hutchinson, whose sister Mary was to become Wordsworth's wife in 1802. His own marriage was hopeless, and his health rapidly deteriorated, perhaps for psychological reasons. To help endure the pain he began to drink laudanum, liquid opium, and thus contracted an addiction he never entirely cast off. In 1804, seeking better health, he went to work in Malta, but returned two years later in the worst condition of his life. Separating from his wife, he moved to London, and began another career as lecturer, general man-of-letters, and periodical editor, while his miseries augmented. The inevitable quarrel with Wordsworth in 1810 was ostensibly reconciled in 1812, but real friendship was not re-established until 1828.

From 1816 on, Coleridge lived in the household of a physician, James Gillman, so as to be able to keep working, and thus avoid total breakdown. Prematurely aged, his poetry over, Coleridge entered into a major last phase as critic and philosopher, upon which his historical importance depends; but this, like his earlier prose achievements, is beyond the scope of an introduction to his poetry. It remains to ask, what was his achievement as a poet, and extraordinary as that was, why did his poetry effectively cease after about 1807? Wordsworth went on with poetry after 1807, but mostly very badly. The few poems Coleridge wrote, from the age of thirty-five on, are powerful but occasional. Did not the poetic will fail in him, since his imaginative powers remained always fresh?

Coleridge's large poetic ambitions included the writing of a philosophic epic on the origin of evil, and a sequence of hymns to the sun, moon, and elements. These high plans died, slowly but definitively, and were replaced by the dream of a philosophic *opus maximum,* a huge work of synthesis that would reconcile German Idealist philosophy with the orthodox truths of Christianity. Though only fragments of this work were ever written, much was done in its place—speculations on theology, political theory, and criticism that had a profound influence on conservative British thought in the Victorian period, and in quite another way on the American Transcendentalism led by Emerson and Theodore Parker.

Coleridge's actual achievement as poet divides into two remarkably diverse groups, remarkable because they are almost simultaneous. The daemonic group, necessarily more famous, is the triad of The Ancient Mariner, Christabel and "Kubla Khan." The conversational group includes the conversation-poems proper, of which "The Eolian Harp" and "Frost at Midnight" are the most important, as well as the irregular ode, "Dejection," and "To William Wordsworth." The late fragments "Limbo" and "Ne Plus Ultra" mark a kind of return to the daemonic mode. To have written only nine poems that really matter, for a poet of Coleridge's gifts, is a sorrow, but the uniqueness of the two groups partly compensates for the slenderness of the canon.

The daemonic poems break through the orthodox censor set up by Coleridge's moral fears of his own imaginative impulses. Unifying the group is a magical quest-pattern which intends as its goal a reconciliation between the poet's self-consciousness and a higher order of being, associated with divine forgiveness, but this reconciliation fortunately lies beyond the border of all these poems. The Mariner attains a state of purgation, but cannot get beyond that process. Christabel is violated by Geraldine, but this too is a purgation, rather than damnation, as her utter innocence is her only flaw. Coleridge himself, in the most piercing moment in his poetry, is tempted to assume the state of an Apollo-rebirth, the youth with flashing eyes and floating hair in "Kubla Khan," but he withdraws from his vision of a poet's paradise, judging it to be only another purgatory.

The conversational group, though so immensely different in mode, speaks more directly of an allied theme: the desire to go home, not to the past, but to what Hart Crane beautifully called "an improved infancy." Each of these poems, like the daemonic group, verges upon a kind of vicarious and purgatorial atonement, in which Coleridge must fail or suffer so that someone he loves may succeed or experience joy. There is a subdued implication that somehow the poet will yet be accepted into a true home this side of the grave, if he can perfect an atonement.

Where Wordsworth, in his primordial power, masters the subjective world, and aids his readers in the difficult art of feeling, Coleridge deliberately courts defeat by subjectivity, and is content to be confessional. But, though he cannot help us to feel, as Wordsworth does, he gives us to understand how deeply felt his own sense of reality is. Though in a way his poetry is a testament of defeat, a yielding to the anxiety of influence, and to the fear of self-glorification, it is one of the most enduringly poignant of such testaments that literature affords us.

Sonnet°

To the River Otter

Dear native Brook!° wild Streamlet of the West!
    How many various-fated years have past,
    What happy and what mournful hours, since last
I skimmed the smooth thin stone along thy breast,
Numbering its light leaps! yet so deep imprest
Sink the sweet scenes of childhood, that mine eyes
    I never shut amid the sunny ray,
But straight with all their tints thy waters rise,
    Thy crossing plank, thy marge with willows grey,
10 And bedded sand that veined with various dyes
Gleamed through thy bright transparence! On my way,
    Visions of Childhood! oft have ye beguiled
Lone manhood's cares, yet waking fondest sighs:
    Ah! that once more I were a careless Child!
    1793?   1796

The Eolian Harp°

COMPOSED AT CLEVEDON, SOMERSETSHIRE°

My pensive Sara! thy soft cheek reclined
Thus on mine arm, most soothing sweet it is
To sit beside our Cot, our Cot o'ergrown
With white-flowered Jasmin, and the broad-leaved Myrtle,
(Meet emblems they of Innocence and Love!)
And watch the clouds, that late were rich with light,

Sonnet See Bowles's "To the River Itchin" for Coleridge's model.
native Brook The Otter ran near Coleridge's birthplace, Ottery St. Mary.
The Eolian Harp from Aeolus, Greek god of the winds; this was an instrument of strings stretched across a sound box; attached to an open window, it produced a quasi-music when

the wind swept over it. For the poets of Sensibility and the Romantics the Harp provided an emblem for inspiration, its natural strength and also its limitations.
Clevedon, Somersetshire place of Coleridge's honeymoon with Sara Fricker. This, grimly and prophetically, was a honeymoon poem.

Slow saddening round, and mark the star of eve
Serenely brilliant (such should Wisdom be)
Shine opposite! How exquisite the scents
10   Snatched from yon bean-field! and the world so hushed!
The stilly murmur of the distant Sea
Tells us of silence.
                        And that simplest Lute,
Placed length-ways in the clasping casement, hark!
How by the desultory breeze caressed,
Like some coy maid half yielding to her lover,
It pours such sweet upbraiding, as must needs
Tempt to repeat the wrong! And now, its strings
Boldlier swept, the long sequacious° notes
Over delicious surges sink and rise,
20   Such a soft floating witchery of sound
As twilight Elfins make, when they at eve
Voyage on gentle gales from Fairy-Land,
Where Melodies round honey-dropping flowers,
Footless and wild, like birds of Paradise,
Nor pause, nor perch, hovering on untamed wing!
O! the one Life within us and abroad,
Which meets all motion and becomes its soul,
A light in sound, a sound-like power in light,
Rhythm in all thought, and joyance everywhere—
30   Methinks, it should have been impossible
Not to love all things in a world so filled;
Where the breeze warbles, and the mute still air
Is Music slumbering on her instrument.°

And thus, my Love! as on the midway slope
Of yonder hill I stretch my limbs at noon,
Whilst through my half-closed eye-lids I behold
The sunbeams dance, like diamonds, on the main,
And tranquil muse upon tranquillity;
Full many a thought uncalled and undetained,
40   And many idle flitting phantasies,
Traverse my indolent and passive brain,
As wild and various as the random gales
That swell and flutter on this subject Lute!
    And what if all of animated nature
Be but organic Harps diversely framed,
That tremble into thought, as o'er them sweeps
Plastic and vast, one intellectual breeze,
At once the Soul of each, and God of all?°

sequacious successive
O . . . instrument Ll. 26–33 are an afterthought, as is the title, both being added in
1817.
At . . . all Influenced by the Idealist philosopher Bishop George Berkeley (1685–1753),
but more daring in speculation; in one manuscript Coleridge added: "Thus *God* would be
the universal Soul,/Mechanized matter as the
organic harps/And each one's Tubes be that,
which each calls I."

But thy more serious eye a mild reproof
50 Darts, O belovèd Woman! nor such thoughts
Dim and unhallowed dost thou not reject,
And biddest me walk humbly with my God.
Meek Daughter in the family of Christ!
Well hast thou said and holily dispraised
These shapings of the unregenerate mind;
Bubbles that glitter as they rise and break
On vain Philosophy's aye-babbling spring.
For never guiltless may I speak of him,
The Incomprehensible! save when with awe
60 I praise him, and with Faith that inly *feels*;
Who with his saving mercies healed me,
A sinful and most miserable man,
Wildered and dark, and gave me to possess
Peace, and this Cot, and thee, heart-honored Maid!
1795   1796

The Rime of the Ancient Mariner°

In Seven Parts

Facile credo, plures esse Naturas invisibiles quam visibiles in rerum univer-
sitate. Sed horum omnium familiam quis nobis enarrabit? et gradus et cogna-
tiones et discrimina et singulorum munera? Quid agunt? quae loca habitant?
Harum rerum notitiam semper ambivit ingenium humanum, nunquam attigit.
Juvat, interea, non diffiteor, quandoque in animo, tanquam in tabula, majoris
et melioris mundi imaginem contemplari: ne mens assuefacta hodiernae vitae
minutiis se contrahat nimis, et tota subsidat in pusillas cogitationes. Sed veritati
interea invigilandum est, modusque servandus, ut certa ab incertis, diem a
nocte, distinguamus.—T. BURNET,° *Archaeol. Phil.* p. 68.

ARGUMENT

How a Ship having passed the Line was driven by storms to the cold Country
towards the South Pole; and how from thence she made her course to the

The Rime of the Ancient Mariner First published in *Lyrical Ballads;* this is the revised
version, to which the marginal glosses were
added in 1816; Coleridge's most helpful comment on the poem was recorded in 1830, in
reply to the celebrated Bluestocking, Mrs. Bar-
bauld, who had objected that the poem lacked
a moral: "I told her that in my own judgment
the poem had too much; and that the only, or
chief fault, if I might say so, was the obtrusion
of the moral sentiment so openly on the reader
as a principle or cause of action in a work of
pure imagination. It ought to have had no more
moral than the *Arabian Nights'* tale of the merchant's sitting down to eat dates by the side of
a well and throwing the shells aside, and lo! a
genie starts up and says he *must* kill the aforesaid merchant *because* one of the date shells
had, it seems, put out the eye of the genie's son."
T. Burnet Thomas Burnet (1635?–1715), English churchman, best known for his mythologizing cosmogony, *The Sacred Theory of the Earth.*
The motto can be rendered: "I easily believe
that there are more invisible than visible beings
in the universe. But who will tell us the families of all these? And the ranks, affinities, differences, and functions of each? What do they do?
Where do they live? The human mind has always circled after knowledge of these things,
but has never attained it. But I do not deny
that it is good sometimes to contemplate in
thought, as in a picture, the image of a greater
and better world; otherwise the mind, habituated to the petty matters of daily life, may contract itself too much, and subside entirely into
trivial thoughts. But meanwhile we must be vigi-
lant for truth, and keep proportion, that we may
distinguish certain from uncertain, day from
night."

tropical Latitude of the Great Pacific Ocean; and of the strange things that befell; and in what manner the Ancyent Marinere came back to his own Country.°

PART I

<table>
<tr><td>An ancient Mariner meeteth three Gallants bidden to a wedding-feast, and detaineth one.</td><td>

It is an ancient Mariner,
And he stoppeth one of three.
'By thy long grey beard and glittering eye,°
Now wherefore stopp'st thou me?

'The Bridegroom's doors are opened wide,
And I am next of kin;
The guests are met, the feast is set:
May'st hear the merry din.'

</td></tr>
</table>

He holds him with his skinny hand,
10   'There was a ship,' quoth he.
'Hold off! unhand me, grey-beard loon!'
Eftsoons° his hand dropped he.

The Wedding-Guest is spellbound by the eye of the old seafaring man, and constrained to hear his tale.

He holds him with his glittering eye—
The Wedding-Guest stood still,
And listens like a three years' child:
The Mariner hath his will.

The Wedding-Guest sat on a stone:
He cannot choose but hear;
And thus spake on that ancient man,
20   The bright-eyed Mariner.

'The ship was cheered, the harbour cleared,
Merrily did we drop
Below the kirk, below the hill,
Below the lighthouse top.

The Mariner tells how the ship sailed southward with a good wind and fair weather, till it reached the line.

'The Sun came up upon the left,
Out of the sea came he!
And he shone bright, and on the right
Went down into the sea.

'Higher and higher every day,
30   Till over the mast at noon—'
The Wedding-Guest here beat his breast,
For he heard the loud bassoon.

How . . . Country This is the Argument in *Lyrical Ballads*, 1798; in the 1800 edition Coleridge inserted: "how the Ancient Mariner cruelly and in contempt of the laws of hospitality killed a sea-bird and how he was followed by many and strange Judgments."

glittering eye The Mariner is a mesmerist or hypnotist, like the vampire Geraldine in *Christabel*.
Eftsoons immediately

The Wedding-Guest heareth the bridal music; but the Mariner continueth his tale.

The bride hath paced into the hall,
  Red as a rose is she;
Nodding their heads before her goes
  The merry minstrelsy.

The Wedding-Guest he beat his breast,
  Yet he cannot choose but hear;
And thus spake on that ancient man,
  The bright-eyed Mariner.

40

The ship driven by a storm toward the south pole.

'And now the STORM-BLAST came, and he
  Was tyrannous and strong:
He struck with his o'ertaking wings,
  And chased us south along.

'With sloping masts and dipping prow,
As who pursued with yell and blow
Still treads the shadow of his foe,
  And forward bends his head,
The ship drove fast, loud roared the blast,
  And southward aye we fled.

50

'And now there came both mist and snow,
  And it grew wondrous cold:
And ice, mast-high, came floating by,
  As green as emerald.

The land of ice, and of fearful sounds where no living thing was to be seen.

'And through the drifts the snowy clifts
  Did send a dismal sheen:
Nor shapes of men nor beasts we ken—
  The ice was all between.

'The ice was here, the ice was there,
  The ice was all around:
It cracked and growled, and roared and howled,
  Like noises in a swound!°

60

Till a great sea-bird, called the Albatross, came through the snow-fog, and was received with great joy and hospitality.

'At length did cross an Albatross,
  Thorough the fog it came;
As if it had been a Christian soul,
  We hailed it in God's name.

'It ate the food it ne'er had eat,
  And round and round it flew.
The ice did split with a thunder-fit;
  The helmsman steered us through!

70

And lo! the Albatross proveth a bird of good omen, and followeth

'And a good south wind sprung up behind;
  The Albatross did follow,
And every day, for food or play,
  Came to the mariner's hollo!

swound swoon

the ship as it
returned
northward
through fog
and floating
ice.

'In mist or cloud, on mast or shroud,°
It perched for vespers nine;
Whiles all the night, through fog-smoke white,
Glimmered the white Moon-shine.'

The ancient
Mariner
inhospitably
killeth the
pious bird of
good omen.

80

'God save thee, ancient Mariner!
From the fiends, that plague thee thus!—
Why lookest thou so?'—With my cross-bow
I shot the ALBATROSS.

PART II

The Sun now rose upon the right:°
Out of the sea came he,
Still hid in mist, and on the left
Went down into the sea.

And the good south wind still blew behind,
But no sweet bird did follow,
Nor any day for food or play
Came to the mariners' hollo!

90

His shipmates
cry out against
the ancient
Mariner, for
killing the
bird of good
luck.

And I had done a hellish thing,
And it would work 'em woe:
For all averred, I had killed the bird
That made the breeze to blow.
Ah wretch! said they, the bird to slay,
That made the breeze to blow!

But when the
fog cleared
off, they
justify the
same, and
thus make
themselves
accomplices
in the crime.

100

Nor dim nor red, like God's own head,
The glorious Sun uprist:
Then all averred, I had killed the bird
That brought the fog and mist.
'Twas right, said they, such birds to slay,
That bring the fog and mist.

The fair breeze
continues;
the ship enters
the Pacific
Ocean, and
sails north-
ward, even
till it reaches
the Line.

The fair breeze blew, the white foam flew,
The furrow followed free;
We were the first that ever burst
Into that silent sea.

110

The ship hath
been suddenly
becalmed.

Down dropped the breeze, the sails dropped down,
'Twas sad as sad could be;
And we did speak only to break
The silence of the sea!

All in a hot and copper sky,
The bloody Sun, at noon,
Right up above the mast did stand,
No bigger than the Moon.

shroud a set of ropes which supports the mast   The Sun . . . right The ship had rounded Cape
Horn and now headed north.

Day after day, day after day,
We stuck, nor breath nor motion;
As idle as a painted ship
Upon a painted ocean.

120 · And the Alba-
tross begins to
be avenged.

Water, water, every where,
And all the boards did shrink;
Water, water, every where,
Nor any drop to drink.

The very deep did rot: O Christ!
That ever this should be!
Yea, slimy things did crawl with legs
Upon the slimy sea.

About, about, in reel and rout
The death-fires° danced at night;
The water, like a witch's oils,
130 · Burnt green, and blue and white.

A Spirit had
followed them;
one of the in-
visible inhabi-
tants of this
planet, neither

And some in dreams assurèd were
Of the Spirit° that plagued us so;
Nine fathom deep he had followed us
From the land of mist and snow.

departed souls nor angels; concerning whom the learned Jew, Josephus, and the Platonic
Constantinopolitan, Michael Psellus, may be consulted. They are very numerous, and there
is no climate or element without one or more.

And every tongue, through utter drought,
Was withered at the root;
We could not speak, no more than if
We had been choked with soot.

140 · The shipmates,
in their sore
distress, would
fain throw the
whole guilt on
the ancient

Ah! well a-day! what evil looks
Had I from old and young!
Instead of the cross, the Albatross
About my neck was hung.

Mariner: in sign whereof they hang the dead sea-bird round his neck.

PART III

There passed a weary time. Each throat
Was parched, and glazed each eye.
A weary time! a weary time!
How glazed each weary eye,

The ancient
Mariner be-
holdeth a sign
in the element
afar off.

When looking westward, I beheld
A something in the sky.

150 ·

At first it seemed a little speck,
And then it seemed a mist;

death-fires electrical effect like lights, called St.
Elmo's fire; by sailors' superstition, they are
death-omens

Spirit a daemon, intermediary between men
and gods

It moved and moved, and took at last
A certain shape, I wist.°

A speck, a mist, a shape, I wist!
And still it neared and neared:
As if it dodged a water-sprite,
It plunged and tacked and veered.

<table>
<tr><td>

At its nearer
approach, it
seemeth him
to be a ship;
and at a dear
ransom he
freeth his
speech from
the bonds of
thirst.
</td><td>

With throats unslaked, with black lips baked
We could nor laugh nor wail;
Through utter drought all dumb we stood!
I bit my arm, I sucked the blood,
And cried, A sail! a sail!
</td></tr>
</table>

160

A flash of joy;

With throats unslaked, with black lips baked
Agape they heard me call:
Gramercy!° they for joy did grin,
And all at once their breath drew in,
As they were drinking all.

And horror
follows. For
can it be a
ship that
comes onward
without wind
or tide?

See! see! (I cried) she tacks no more!
Hither to work us weal;°
Without a breeze, without a tide,
She steadies with upright keel!

170

The western wave was all a-flame.
The day was well nigh done!
Almost upon the western wave
Rested the broad bright Sun;
When that strange shape drove suddenly
Betwixt us and the Sun.

It seemeth
him but the
skeleton of
a ship.

And straight the Sun was flecked with bars,
(Heaven's Mother send us grace!)
As if through a dungeon-grate he peered
With broad and burning face.

180

And its ribs
are seen as
bars on the
face of the
setting Sun.

Alas! (thought I, and my heart beat loud)
How fast she nears and nears!
Are those *her* sails that glance in the Sun,
Like restless gossameres?

The Spectre-
Woman and
her Death-
mate, and no
other on
board the
skeleton ship.

Are those *her* ribs through which the Sun
Did peer, as through a grate?
And is that Woman all her crew?
Is that a DEATH? and are there two?
Is DEATH that woman's mate?

190

Like vessel,
like crew!

Her lips were red, *her* looks were free,
Her locks were yellow as gold:

wist knew   weal good
Gramercy "great thanks" (French, *grand-merci*)

Death and Life-in-Death have diced for the ship's crew, and she (the latter) winneth the ancient Mariner.	Her skin was as white as leprosy, The Night-mare LIFE-IN-DEATH was she, Who thicks man's blood with cold.

The naked hulk alongside came,
And the twain were casting dice;
'The game is done! I've won! I've won!'
Quoth she, and whistles thrice.

200 *No twilight within the courts of the Sun.*

The Sun's rim dips; the stars rush out:
At one stride comes the dark;
With far-heard whisper, o'er the sea,
Off shot the spectre-bark.

At the rising of the Moon,

We listened and looked sideways up!
Fear at my heart, as at a cup,
My life-blood seemed to sip!
The stars were dim, and thick the night,
The steersman's face by his lamp gleamed white;
From the sails the dew did drip—

210

Till clomb above the eastern bar
The hornèd Moon, with one bright star
Within the nether tip.

One after another,

One after one, by the star-dogged Moon,°
Too quick for groan or sigh,
Each turned his face with a ghastly pang,
And cursed me with his eye.

His shipmates drop down dead.

Four times fifty living men,
(And I heard nor sigh nor groan)
With heavy thump, a lifeless lump,
They dropped down one by one.

220 *But Life-in-Death begins her work on the ancient Mariner.*

The souls did from their bodies fly,—
They fled to bliss or woe!
And every soul, it passed me by,
Like the whizz of my cross-bow!

PART IV

The Wedding-Guest feareth that a Spirit is talking to him;

'I fear thee, ancient Mariner!
I fear thy skinny hand!
And thou art long, and lank, and brown,
As is the ribbed sea-sand.

'I fear thee and thy glittering eye,
And thy skinny hand, so brown.'—

230 *But the ancient Mariner assureth*

Fear not, fear not, thou Wedding-Guest!
This body dropped not down.

star-dogged Moon "It is a common superstition among sailors that something evil is about to happen whenever a star dogs the Moon" (Coleridge).

him of his
bodily life, and
proceedeth to
relate his hor-
rible penance.

Alone, alone, all, all alone,
Alone on a wide wide sea!
And never a saint took pity on
My soul in agony.

He despiseth
the creatures
of the calm,

The many men, so beautiful!
And they all dead did lie:
And a thousand thousand slimy things
Lived on; and so did I.

240 And envieth
that *they*
should live,
and so many
lie dead.

I looked upon the rotting sea,
And drew my eyes away;
I looked upon the rotting deck,
And there the dead men lay.

I looked to heaven, and tried to pray;
But or ever a prayer had gusht,
A wicked whisper came, and made
My heart as dry as dust.

250

I closed my lids, and kept them close,
And the balls like pulses beat;
For the sky and the sea, and the sea and the sky
Lay like a load on my weary eye,
And the dead were at my feet.

But the curse
liveth for him
in the eye of
the dead men.

The cold sweat melted from their limbs,
Nor rot nor reek did they:
The look with which they looked on me
Had never passed away.

260

An orphan's curse would drag to hell
A spirit from on high;
But oh! more horrible than that
Is the curse in a dead man's eye!
Seven days, seven nights, I saw that curse,
And yet I could not die.

In his lone-
liness and
fixedness he
yearneth to-
wards the
journeying
Moon, and the
stars that still
sojourn, yet
still move
onward; and
270 every where
the blue sky
belongs to

The moving Moon went up the sky,
And no where did abide:
Softly she was going up,
And a star or two beside—

Her beams bemocked the sultry main,
Like April hoar-frost spread;
But where the ship's huge shadow lay,
The charmèd water burnt alway
A still and awful red.

them, and is their appointed rest, and their native country and their own natural homes,
which they enter unannounced, as lords that are certainly expected and yet there is a
silent joy at their arrival.

By the light
of the Moon he
beholdeth
God's crea-
tures of the
great calm.

Beyond the shadow of the ship,
I watched the water-snakes:
They moved in tracks of shining white,
And when they reared, the elfish light
Fell off in hoary flakes.

Within the shadow of the ship
I watched their rich attire:
Blue, glossy green, and velvet black,
280   They coiled and swam; and every track
Was a flash of golden fire.

Their beauty
and their
happiness.

O happy living things! no tongue
Their beauty might declare:
A spring of love gushed from my heart,

He blesseth
them in his
heart.

And I blessed them unaware:
Sure my kind saint took pity on me,
And I blessed them unaware.

The spell
begins to
break.

290

The self-same moment I could pray;
And from my neck so free
The Albatross fell off, and sank
Like lead into the sea.

PART V

Oh sleep! it is a gentle thing,
Beloved from pole to pole!
To Mary Queen the praise be given!
She sent the gentle sleep from Heaven,
That slid into my soul.

By grace of
the holy
Mother, the
ancient
300   Mariner is
refreshed with
rain.

The silly° buckets on the deck,
That had so long remained,
I dreamt that they were filled with dew;
And when I awoke, it rained.

My lips were wet, my throat was cold,
My garments all were dank;
Sure I had drunken in my dreams,
And still my body drank.

I moved, and could not feel my limbs:
I was so light—almost
I thought that I had died in sleep,
And was a blessèd ghost.

He heareth
310   sounds and
seeth strange
sights and
commotions in
the sky and
the element.

And soon I heard a roaring wind:
It did not come anear;
But with its sound it shook the sails,
That were so thin and sere.

silly in the archaic sense of "simple" or
"homely," perhaps also "blessed"

The upper air burst into life!
And a hundred fire-flags sheen,°
To and fro they were hurried about!
And to and fro, and in and out,
The wan stars danced between.

And the coming wind did roar more loud,
And the sails did sigh like sedge;°
320   And the rain poured down from one black cloud;
The Moon was at its edge.

The thick black cloud was cleft, and still
The Moon was at its side:
Like waters shot from some high crag,
The lightning fell with never a jag,
A river steep and wide.

The bodies of
the ship's crew
are inspired
and the ship
330   moves on;

The loud wind never reached the ship,
Yet now the ship moved on!
Beneath the lightning and the Moon
The dead men gave a groan.

They groaned, they stirred, they all uprose,
Nor spake, nor moved their eyes;
It had been strange, even in a dream,
To have seen those dead men rise.

The helmsman steered, the ship moved on;
Yet never a breeze up-blew;
The mariners all 'gan work the ropes,
Where they were wont to do;
They raised their limbs like lifeless tools—
340   We were a ghastly crew.

The body of my brother's son
Stood by me, knee to knee:
The body and I pulled at one rope,
But he said nought to me.

But not by the
souls of the
men, nor by
daemons of
earth or
middle air, but
by a blessed
troop of
350   angelic spirits,
sent down by
the invocation

'I fear thee, ancient Mariner!'
Be calm, thou Wedding-Guest!
'Twas not those souls that fled in pain,
Which to their corses came again,
But a troop of spirits blest:

For when it dawned—they dropped their arms,
And clustered round the mast;
Sweet sounds rose slowly through their mouths,
And from their bodies passed.

And . . . sheen lights waving as if they were   **sedge** coarse, grassy plant bordering lakes and
flags   streams

of the guar-
dian saint.

Around, around, flew each sweet sound,
Then darted to the Sun;
Slowly the sounds came back again,
Now mixed, now one by one.

Sometimes a-dropping from the sky
I heard the sky-lark sing;

360

Sometimes all little birds that are,
How they seemed to fill the sea and air
With their sweet jargoning!°

And now 'twas like all instruments,
Now like a lonely flute;
And now it is an angel's song,
That makes the heavens be mute.

It ceased; yet still the sails made on
A pleasant noise till noon,
A noise like of a hidden brook

370

In the leafy month of June,
That to the sleeping woods all night
Singeth a quiet tune.

Till noon we quietly sailed on,
Yet never a breeze did breathe:
Slowly and smoothly went the ship,
Moved onward from beneath.

The lonesome
Spirit from
the south-pole
carries on the
ship as far as
the Line, in
obedience to
the angelic
troop, but still
requireth
vengeance.

Under the keel nine fathom deep,
From the land of mist and snow,
The spirit slid: and it was he

380

That made the ship to go.
The sails at noon left off their tune,
And the ship stood still also.

The Sun, right up above the mast,
Had fixed her to the ocean:
But in a minute she 'gan stir,
With a short uneasy motion—
Backwards and forwards half her length
With a short uneasy motion.

Then like a pawing horse let go,
She made a sudden bound:

390

It flung the blood into my head,
And I fell down in a swound.

The Polar
Spirit's fellow-
daemons, the
invisible in-

How long in that same fit I lay,
I have not to declare;
But ere my living life returned,

jargoning archaic sense, "warbling"

I heard and in my soul discerned
Two voices in the air.

'Is it he?' quoth one, 'Is this the man?
By him who died on cross,
With his cruel bow he laid full low
The harmless Albatross.

'The spirit who bideth by himself
In the land of mist and snow,
He loved the bird that loved the man
Who shot him with his bow.'

The other was a softer voice,
As soft as honey-dew:
Quoth he, 'The man hath penance done,
And penance more will do.'

PART VI

FIRST VOICE

'But tell me, tell me! speak again,
Thy soft response renewing—
What makes that ship drive on so fast?
What is the ocean doing?'

SECOND VOICE

'Still as a slave before his lord,
The ocean hath no blast;
His great bright eye most silently
Up to the Moon is cast—

'If he may know which way to go;
For she guides him smooth or grim.
See, brother, see! how graciously
She looketh down on him.'

FIRST VOICE

'But why drives on that ship so fast,
Without or wave or wind?'

SECOND VOICE

'The air is cut away before,
And closes from behind.

'Fly, brother, fly! more high, more high!
Or we shall be belated:
For slow and slow that ship will go,
When the Mariner's trance is abated.'

habitants of the element, take part in his wrong; and two of them relate, one to the other, that penance long and heavy for the ancient Mariner hath been accorded to the Polar Spirit, who returneth southward.

400

410

420

The Mariner hath been cast into a trance; for the angelic power causeth the vessel to drive northward faster than human life could endure.

430

The super-
natural motion
is retarded;
the Mariner
awakes, and
his penance
begins anew.

I woke, and we were sailing on
As in a gentle weather:
'Twas night, calm night, the moon was high;
The dead men stood together.

All stood together on the deck,
For a charnel-dungeon° fitter:
All fixed on me their stony eyes,
That in the Moon did glitter.

440

The pang, the curse, with which they died,
Had never passed away:
I could not draw my eyes from theirs,
Nor turn them up to pray.

The curse is
finally ex-
piated.

And now this spell was snapped: once more
I viewed the ocean green,
And looked far forth, yet little saw
Of what had else been seen—

Like one, that on a lonesome road
Doth walk in fear and dread,
And having once turned round walks on,
And turns no more his head;
Because he knows, a frightful fiend
Doth close behind him tread.

450

But soon there breathed a wind on me,
Nor sound nor motion made:
Its path was not upon the sea,
In ripple or in shade.

It raised my hair, it fanned my cheek
Like a meadow-gale° of spring—
It mingled strangely with my fears,
Yet it felt like a welcoming.

460

Swiftly, swiftly flew the ship,
Yet she sailed softly too:
Sweetly, sweetly blew the breeze—
On me alone it blew.

And the
ancient
Mariner be-
holdeth his
native
country.

Oh! dream of joy! is this indeed
The light-house top I see?
Is this the hill? is this the kirk?
Is this mine own countree?

We drifted o'er the harbour-bar,
And I with sobs did pray—
O let me be awake, my God!
Or let me sleep alway.

470

charnel-dungeon where dead bodies are piled   **meadow-gale** breeze

The harbour-bay was clear as glass,
So smoothly it was strewn!
And on the bay the moonlight lay,
And the shadow of the Moon.

The rock shone bright, the kirk no less,
That stands above the rock:
The moonlight steeped in silentness
The steady weathercock.

480 And the bay was white with silent light,
Till rising from the same,
Full many shapes, that shadows were,
In crimson colours came.

A little distance from the prow
Those crimson shadows were:
I turned my eyes upon the deck—
Oh, Christ! what saw I there!

Each corse lay flat, lifeless and flat,
And, by the holy rood!°
490 A man all light, a seraph-man,
On every corse there stood.

This seraph-band, each waved his hand:
It was a heavenly sight!
They stood as signals to the land,
Each one a lovely light;

This seraph-band, each waved his hand,
No voice did they impart—
No voice; but oh! the silence sank
Like music on my heart.

500 But soon I heard the dash of oars,
I heard the Pilot's cheer;
My head was turned perforce away
And I saw a boat appear.

The Pilot and the Pilot's boy,
I heard them coming fast:
Dear Lord in Heaven! it was a joy
The dead men could not blast.

I saw a third—I heard his voice:
It is the Hermit good!
510 He singeth loud his godly hymns
That he makes in the wood.
He'll shrieve my soul, he'll wash away
The Albatross's blood.

The angelic
spirits leave
the dead
bodies,

And appear in
their own
forms of light.

rood cross

PART VII

The Hermit of
the Wood,

This Hermit good lives in that wood
Which slopes down to the sea.
How loudly his sweet voice he rears!
He loves to talk with marineres
That come from a far countree.

520

He kneels at morn, and noon, and eve—
He hath a cushion plump:
It is the moss that wholly hides
The rotted old oak-stump.

The skiff-boat neared: I heard them talk,
'Why, this is strange, I trow!
Where are those lights so many and fair,
That signal made but now?'

Approacheth
the ship with
wonder.

'Strange, by my faith!' the Hermit said—
'And they answered not our cheer!
The planks looked warped! and see those sails,
How thin they are and sere!
I never saw aught like to them,
Unless perchance it were

530

'Brown skeletons of leaves that lag
My forest-brook along;
'When the ivy-tod° is heavy with snow,
And the owlet whoops to the wolf below,
That eats the she-wolf's young.'

'Dear Lord! it hath a fiendish look—
(The Pilot made reply)
I am a-feared'—'Push on, push on!'
Said the Hermit cheerily.

540

The boat came closer to the ship,
But I nor spake nor stirred;
The boat came close beneath the ship,
And straight a sound was heard.

The ship
suddenly
sinketh.

Under the water it rumbled on,
Still louder and more dread:
It reached the ship, it split the bay;
The ship went down like lead.

550   The ancient
Mariner is
saved in the
Pilot's boat.

Stunned by that loud and dreadful sound,
Which sky and ocean smote,
Like one that hath been seven days drowned
My body lay afloat;

ivy-tod ivy bush

But swift as dreams, myself I found
Within the Pilot's boat.

Upon the whirl, where sank the ship,
The boat spun round and round;
And all was still, save that the hill
Was telling of the sound.

560   I moved my lips—the Pilot shrieked
And fell down in a fit;
The holy Hermit raised his eyes,
And prayed where he did sit.

I took the oars: the Pilot's boy,
Who now doth crazy go,
Laughed loud and long, and all the while
His eyes went to and fro.
'Ha! ha!' quoth he, 'full plain I see,
The Devil knows how to row.'

570   And now, all in my own countree,
I stood on the firm land!
The Hermit stepped forth from the boat,
And scarcely he could stand.

The ancient Mariner earnestly en-treateth the Hermit to shrieve him; and the penance of life falls on
580 *him.*

'O shrieve° me, shrieve me, holy man!'
The Hermit crossed his brow.
'Say quick,' quoth he, 'I bid thee say—
What manner of man art thou?'

Forthwith this frame of mine was wrenched
With a woeful agony,
Which forced me to begin my tale;
And then it left me free.

And ever and anon through out his future life an agony constraineth him to travel from land to land;

Since then, at an uncertain hour,
That agony returns:
And till my ghastly tale is told,
This heart within me burns.

I pass, like night, from land to land;°
I have strange power of speech;
That moment that his face I see,
I know the man that must hear me:
590   To him my tale I teach.

What loud uproar bursts from that door!
The wedding-guests are there:
But in the garden-bower the bride
And bride-maids singing are:

shrieve me hear my confession and give me   **I pass . . . land** like the Wandering Jew, or
absolution   Cain

And hark the little vesper bell,
Which biddeth me to prayer!

O Wedding-Guest! this soul hath been
Alone on a wide wide sea:
So lonely 'twas, that God himself
600   Scarce seemèd there to be.

O sweeter than the marriage-feast,
'Tis sweeter far to me,
To walk together to the kirk
With a goodly company!—

To walk together to the kirk,
And all together pray,
While each to his great Father bends,
Old men, and babes, and loving friends
And youths and maidens gay!

610   *And to teach,*
by his own
example, love
and reverence
to all things
that God made
and loveth.

Farewell, farewell! but this I tell
To thee, thou Wedding-Guest!
He prayeth well, who loveth well
Both man and bird and beast.

He prayeth best, who loveth best
All things both great and small;
For the dear God who loveth us,
He made and loveth all.

The Mariner, whose eye is bright,
Whose beard with age is hoar,
620   Is gone: and now the Wedding-Guest
Turned from the bridegroom's door.

He went like one that hath been stunned,
And is of sense forlorn:
A sadder and a wiser man,
He rose the morrow morn.
1797–98   1798

Kubla Khan:

Or, a Vision in a Dream. A Fragment.

The following fragment is here published at the request of a poet [1] of great and deserved celebrity, and, as far as the Author's own opinions are concerned, rather as a psychological curiosity, than on the ground of any supposed *poetic* merits.

1. Lord Byron.

In the summer of the year 1797, the Author, then in ill health, had retired to a lonely farm-house between Porlock and Linton, on the Exmoor confines of Somerset and Devonshire. In consequence of a slight indisposition, an anodyne had been prescribed, from the effects of which he fell asleep in his chair at the moment that he was reading the following sentence, or words of the same substance, in 'Purchas's Pilgrimage': 'Here the Khan Kubla commanded a palace to be built, and a stately garden thereunto. And thus ten miles of fertile ground were inclosed with a wall.'[2] The Author continued for about three hours in a profound sleep,[3] at least of the external senses, during which time he has the most vivid confidence, that he could not have composed less than from two to three hundred lines; if that indeed can be called composition in which all the images rose up before him as *things*, with a parallel production of the correspondent expressions, without any sensation or consciousness of effort. On awaking he appeared to himself to have a distinct recollection of the whole, and taking his pen, ink, and paper, instantly and eagerly wrote down the lines that are here preserved. At this moment he was unfortunately called out by a person on business from Porlock, and detained by him above an hour, and on his return to his room, found, to his no small surprise and mortification, that though he still retained some vague and dim recollection of the general purport of the vision, yet, with the exception of some eight or ten scattered lines and images, all the rest had passed away like the images on the surface of a stream into which a stone has been cast, but, alas! without the after restoration of the latter!

　　　　　Then all the charm
Is broken—all that phantom-world so fair
Vanishes, and a thousand circlets spread,
And each mis-shape[s] the other. Stay awhile,
Poor youth! who scarcely dar'st lift up thine eyes—
The stream will soon renew its smoothness, soon
The visions will return! And lo, he stays,
And soon the fragments dim of lovely forms
Come trembling back, unite, and now once more
The pool becomes a mirror.
　　[From *The Picture; or, the Lover's Resolution*, ll. 91–100.]

Yet from the still surviving recollections in his mind, the Author has frequently purposed to finish for himself what had been originally, as it were,

2. The correct quotation from Samuel Purchas, *Purchas His Pilgrimage* (1613), is: "In Xamdu did Cublai Can build a stately Palace, encompassing sixteene miles of plaine ground with a wall, wherein are fertile Meddowes, pleasant springs, delightfull Streams, and all sorts of beasts of chase and game, and in the middest thereof a sumptuous house of pleasure, which may be removed from place to place." J. L. Lowes demonstrated that other borrowings from Purchas are important, particularly from the account of Alvadine, the Old Man of the Mountain, who employed his earthly paradise or garden of delights to train the assassins whom he sent against his enemies.
3. In a manuscript note Coleridge confessed that his supposed sleep was actually an opium-induced reverie.

given to him. Σαμερον αδιον ασω [Αὔριον ἄδιον ἄσω 1834]: but the to-morrow is yet to come.

In Xanadu did Kubla Khan
A stately pleasure-dome decree:
Where Alph,° the sacred river, ran
Through caverns measureless to man
    Down to a sunless sea.
So twice five miles of fertile ground
  With walls and towers were girdled round:
And there were gardens bright with sinuous rills,
  Where blossomed many an incense-bearing tree;
10 And here were forests ancient as the hills,
Enfolding sunny spots of greenery.

But oh! that deep romantic chasm which slanted
Down the green hill athwart a cedarn cover!
A savage place! as holy and enchanted
As e'er beneath a waning moon was haunted
By woman wailing for her demon-lover!
And from this chasm, with ceaseless turmoil seething,
As if this earth in fast thick pants were breathing,
A mighty fountain momently was forced:
20 Amid whose swift half-intermitted burst
Huge fragments vaulted like rebounding hail,
Or chaffy grain beneath the thresher's flail:
And 'mid these dancing rocks at once and ever
It flung up momently the sacred river.
Five miles meandering with a mazy motion
Through wood and dale the sacred river ran,
Then reached the caverns measureless to man,
And sank in tumult to a lifeless ocean:
And 'mid this tumult Kubla heard from far
30 Ancestral voices prophesying war!
    The shadow of the dome of pleasure
    Floated midway on the waves;
    Where was heard the mingled measure°
    From the fountain and the caves.
It was a miracle of rare device,
A sunny pleasure-dome with caves of ice!

    A damsel with a dulcimer
    In a vision once I saw:

4. From Theocritus, *Idylls* I.145, "I'll sing to you a sweeter song another day."
5. "I'll sing to you a sweeter song tomorrow."

Alph Scholars agree that Coleridge compounded the first letter of the Greek alphabet, "Alpha," with mythological speculations that the Garden of Eden, where language began, was in Abyssinia, and with memories of the classical river Alpheus, which ran underground.
mingled measure See William Collins's ode "The Passions," l. 64.

It was an Abyssinian maid,
40 And on her dulcimer she played,
Singing of Mount Abora.°
Could I revive within me
Her symphony and song,
To such a deep delight 'twould win me,
That with music loud and long,
I would build that dome in air,
That sunny dome! those caves of ice!
And all who heard should see them there,
And all should cry, Beware! Beware!
50 His flashing eyes, his floating hair!
Weave a circle round him thrice,
And close your eyes with holy dread,
For he on honey-dew hath fed,
And drunk the milk of Paradise.°
1798   1816

Christabel [1]

Preface

The first part of the following poem was written in the year 1797, at Stowey, in the county of Somerset. The second part, after my return from Germany, in the year 1800, at Keswick, Cumberland. It is probable that if the poem had been finished at either of the former periods, or if even the first and second part had been published in the year 1800, the impression of its originality would have been much greater than I dare at present expect. But for this I have only my own indolence to blame. The dates are mentioned for the exclusive purpose of precluding charges of plagiarism or servile imitation from myself. For there is amongst us a set of critics, who seem to hold, that every possible thought and image is traditional; who have no notion that there are such things as fountains in the world, small as well as great; and who would therefore charitably derive every rill they behold flowing, from a perforation made in some other man's tank. I am confident, however, that as far as the present poem is concerned, the celebrated poets [2] whose writings I might be suspected of having imitated,

Mount Abora See *Paradise Lost* IV.280–82: "where *Abassin* Kings their issue Guard, / Mount *Amara*, though this by some supposed / True Paradise under the Ethiop Line."

milk of Paradise See Plato's *Ion* 534 a-b, where a poet's inspiration is compared to the Dionysiac women who receive honey and milk from the rivers of a Muses' paradise.

1. This is perhaps best read as a sequence of fragments, or four poems linked together, only partly by subject, and partly by the theme best described by W. J. Bate as "the open admission of evil by innocence." Coleridge said that the poem was "founded on the notion, that the virtuous of this world save the wicked," and he remarked also that, in composing *Christabel,* he was haunted by lines from Richard Crashaw's "A Hymn to the Name and Honour of the Admirable Saint Teresa": "Since 'tis not to be had at home / She'll travel to a martyrdome. / No home for her confesses she, / But where she may a martyr be." But in the fragments as they stand, there are no indications that Geraldine will be redeemed by the sacrifice (apparently sexual) of Christabel.
2. Sir Walter Scott and Lord Byron.

either in particular passages, or in the tone and the spirit of the whole, would be among the first to vindicate me from the charge, and who, on any striking coincidence, would permit me to address them in this doggerel version of two monkish Latin hexameters.

'Tis mine and it is likewise yours;
But an if this will not do;
Let it be mine, good friend! for I
Am the poorer of the two.

I have only to add that the metre of Christabel is not, properly speaking, irregular, though it may seem so from its being founded on a new principle: namely, that of counting in each line the accents, not the syllables. Though the latter may vary from seven to twelve, yet in each line the accents will be found to be only four. Nevertheless, this occasional variation in number of syllables is not introduced wantonly, or for the mere ends of convenience, but in correspondence with some transition in the nature of the imagery or passion.

PART I

'Tis the middle of night by the castle clock,
And the owls have awakened the crowing cock;
Tu—whit!——Tu—whoo!
And hark, again! the crowing cock,
How drowsily it crew.
Sir Leoline, the Baron rich,
Hath a toothless mastiff bitch;
From her kennel beneath the rock
She maketh answer to the clock,
10   Four for the quarters, and twelve for the hour;
Ever and aye, by shine and shower,
Sixteen short howls, not over loud;
Some say, she sees my lady's shroud.

Is the night chilly and dark?
The night is chilly, but not dark.
The thin grey cloud is spread on high,
It covers but not hides the sky.
The moon is behind, and at the full;
And yet she looks both small and dull.
20   The night is chill, the cloud is grey:
'Tis a month before the month of May,
And the Spring comes slowly up this way.

The lovely lady, Christabel,
Whom her father loves so well,
What makes her in the wood so late,
A furlong from the castle gate?
She had dreams all yesternight
Of her own betrothèd knight;

And she in the midnight wood will pray
30   For the weal° of her lover that's far away.

She stole along, she nothing spoke,
The sighs she heaved were soft and low,
And naught was green upon the oak
But moss and rarest mistletoe:
She kneels beneath the huge oak tree,
And in silence prayeth she.

The lady sprang up suddenly,
The lovely lady, Christabel!
It moaned as near, as near can be,
40   But what it is she cannot tell.—
On the other side it seems to be,
Of the huge, broad-breasted, old oak tree.

The night is chill; the forest bare;
Is it the wind that moaneth bleak?
There is not wind enough in the air
To move away the ringlet curl
From the lovely lady's cheek—
There is not wind enough to twirl
The one red leaf, the last of its clan,
50   That dances as often as dance it can,
Hanging so light, and hanging so high,
On the topmost twig that looks up at the sky.

Hush, beating heart of Christabel!
Jesu, Maria, shield her well!
She folded her arms beneath her cloak,
And stole to the other side of the oak.
          What sees she there?

There she sees a damsel bright,
Dressed in a silken robe of white,
60   That shadowy in the moonlight shone:
The neck that made that white robe wan,
Her stately neck, and arms were bare;
Her blue-veined feet unsandaled were,
And wildly glittered here and there
The gems entangled in her hair.
I guess, 'twas frightful there to see
A lady so richly clad as she—
Beautiful exceedingly!

Mary mother, save me now!
70   (Said Christabel,) And who art thou?

weal welfare

The lady strange made answer meet,
And her voice was faint and sweet:—
Have pity on my sore distress,
I scarce can speak for weariness:
Stretch forth thy hand, and have no fear!
Said Christabel, How camest thou here?
And the lady, whose voice was faint and sweet,
Did thus pursue her answer meet:—

80   My sire is of noble line,
And my name is Geraldine:
Five warriors seized me yestermorn,
Me, even me, a maid forlorn:
They choked my cries with force and fright,
And tied me on a palfrey white.
The palfrey was as fleet as wind,
And they rode furiously behind.

They spurred amain,° their steeds were white:
And once we crossed the shade of night.
As sure as Heaven shall rescue me,
90   I have no thought what men they be;
Nor do I know how long it is
(For I have lain entranced I wis)°
Since one, the tallest of the five,
Took me from the palfrey's back,
A weary woman, scarce alive.
Some muttered words his comrades spoke:
He placed me underneath this oak;
He swore they would return with haste;
Whither they went I cannot tell—
100 I thought I heard, some minutes past,
Sounds as of a castle bell.
Stretch forth thy hand (thus ended she).
And help a wretched maid to flee.

Then Christabel stretched forth her hand,
And comforted fair Geraldine:
O well, bright dame! may you command
The service of Sir Leoline;
And gladly our stout chivalry
Will he send forth and friends withal
110 To guide and guard you safe and free
Home to your noble father's hall.

She rose: and forth with steps they passed
That strove to be, and were not, fast.
Her gracious stars the lady blest,

amain vehemently, exceedingly   **wis** think

And thus spake on sweet Christabel:
All our household are at rest,
The hall as silent as the cell;
Sir Leoline is weak in health,
And may not well awakened be,
120   But we will move as if in stealth,
And I beseech your courtesy,
This night, to share your couch with me.

They crossed the moat, and Christabel
Took the key that fitted well;
A little door she opened straight,
All in the middle of the gate;
The gate that was ironed within and without,
Where an army in battle array had marched out.
The lady sank, belike through pain,
130   And Christabel with might and main
Lifted her up,° a weary weight,
Over the threshold of the gate:
Then the lady rose again,
And moved, as she were not in pain.

So free from danger, free from fear,
They crossed the court: right glad they were.
And Christabel devoutly cried
To the lady by her side,
Praise we the Virgin all divine
140   Who hath rescued thee from thy distress!
Alas, alas! said Geraldine,
I cannot speak for weariness.
So free from danger, free from fear,
They crossed the court: right glad they were.

Outside her kennel, the mastiff old
Lay fast asleep, in moonshine cold.
The mastiff old did not awake,
Yet she an angry moan did make!
And what can ail the mastiff bitch?
150   Never till now she uttered yell
Beneath the eye of Christabel.
Perhaps it is the owlet's scritch:°
For what can ail the mastiff bitch?

They passed the hall, that echoes still,
Pass as lightly as you will!
The brands were flat, the brands were dying,
Amid their own white ashes lying;
But when the lady passed, there came

Lifted her up Evil beings cannot enter without   **scritch** screech
the aid of the innocent.

A tongue of light, a fit of flame;
160 And Christabel saw the lady's eye,
And nothing else saw she thereby,
Save the boss of the shield of Sir Leoline tall,
Which hung in a murky old niche in the wall.
O softly tread, said Christabel,
My father seldom sleepeth well.

Sweet Christabel her feet doth bare,
And jealous of the listening air
They steal their way from stair to stair,
Now in glimmer, and now in gloom,
170 And now they pass the Baron's room,
As still as death, with stifled breath!
And now have reached her chamber door;
And now doth Geraldine press down
The rushes° of the chamber floor.

The moon shines dim in the open air,
And not a moonbeam enters here.
But they without its light can see
The chamber carved so curiously,
Carved with figures strange and sweet,
180 All made out of the carver's brain,
For a lady's chamber meet:
The lamp with twofold silver chain
Is fastened to an angel's feet.

The silver lamp burns dead and dim;
But Christabel the lamp will trim.
She trimmed the lamp, and made it bright,
And left it swinging to and fro,
While Geraldine, in wretched plight,
Sank down upon the floor below.

190 O weary lady, Geraldine,
I pray you, drink this cordial wine!
It is a wine of virtuous powers;
My mother made it of wild flowers.

And will your mother pity me,
Who am a maiden most forlorn?
Christabel answered—Woe is me!
She died the hour that I was born.
I have heard the grey-haired friar tell
How on her death-bed she did say,
200 That she should hear the castle-bell
Strike twelve upon my wedding-day.

rushes spread as floor covering, a general medieval custom

O mother dear! that thou wert here!
I would, said Geraldine, she were!

But soon with altered voice, said she—
'Off, wandering mother! Peak° and pine!
I have power to bid thee flee.'
Alas! what ails poor Geraldine?
Why stares she with unsettled eye?
Can she the bodiless dead espy?
210 And why with hollow voice cries she,
'Off, woman, off! this hour is mine—
Though thou her guardian spirit be,
Off, woman, off! 'tis given to me.'

Then Christabel knelt by the lady's side,
And raised to heaven her eyes so blue—
Alas! said she, this ghastly ride—
Dear lady! it hath wildered you!
The lady wiped her moist cold brow,
And faintly said, ''tis over now!'

220 Again the wild-flower wine she drank:
Her fair large eyes 'gan glitter bright,
And from the floor whereon she sank,
The lofty lady stood upright:
She was most beautiful to see,
Like a lady of a far countree.

And thus the lofty lady spake—
'All they who live in the upper sky,
Do love you, holy Christabel!
And you love them, and for their sake
230 And for the good which me befel,
Even I in my degree will try,
Fair maiden, to requite you well.
But now unrobe yourself; for I
Must pray, ere yet in bed I lie.'

Quoth Christabel, So let it be!
And as the lady bade, did she.
Her gentle limbs did she undress,
And lay down in her loveliness.

But through her brain of weal and woe
240 So many thoughts moved to and fro,
That vain it were her lids to close;
So half-way from the bed she rose,
And on her elbow did recline
To look at the lady Geraldine.

Peak grow thin; see *Macbeth* I.iii.23, where the
witches incant: "dwindle, peak and pine"

Beneath the lamp the lady bowed,
And slowly rolled her eyes around;
Then drawing in her breath aloud,
Like one that shuddered, she unbound
The cincture from beneath her breast:
250　Her silken robe, and inner vest,
Dropped to her feet, and full in view,
Behold! her bosom and half her side——
A sight to dream of, not to tell!
O shield her! shield sweet Christabel!

Yet Geraldine nor speaks nor stirs;
Ah! what a stricken look was hers!
Deep from within she seems half-way
To lift some weight with sick assay,°
And eyes the maid and seeks delay;
260　Then suddenly, as one defied,
Collects herself in scorn and pride,
And lay down by the Maiden's side!—
And in her arms the maid she took,
　　　　Ah wel-a-day!
And with low voice and doleful look
These words did say:
'In the touch of this bosom there worketh a spell,
Which is lord of thy utterance, Christabel!
Thou knowest tonight, and wilt know tomorrow,
270　This mark of my shame, this seal of my sorrow;
　　　　But vainly thou warrest,
　　　　　　For this is alone in
　　　　Thy power to declare,
　　　　　　That in the dim forest
　　　　Thou heardest a low moaning.
And foundest a bright lady, surpassingly fair;
And didst bring her home with thee in love and in charity,
To shield her and shelter her from the damp air.'

THE CONCLUSION TO PART I

It was a lovely sight to see
280　The lady Christabel, when she
Was praying at the old oak tree.
　　　　Amid the jaggèd shadows
　　　　Of mossy leafless boughs,
　　　　Kneeling in the moonlight,
　　　　To make her gentle vows;
Her slender palms together prest,
Heaving sometimes on her breast;
Her face resigned to bliss or bale—

assay attempt

Her face, oh call it fair not pale,
290 And both blue eyes more bright than clear,
Each about to have a tear.

With open eyes (ah woe is me!)
Asleep, and dreaming fearfully,
Fearfully dreaming, yet, I wis,
Dreaming that alone, which is—
O sorrow and shame! Can this be she,
The lady, who knelt at the old oak tree?
And lo! the worker of these harms,
That holds the maiden in her arms,
300 Seems to slumber still and mild,
As a mother with her child.

A star hath set, a star hath risen,
O Geraldine! since arms of thine
Have been the lovely lady's prison.
O Geraldine! one hour was thine—
Thou'st had thy will! By tairn° and rill,
The night-birds all that hour were still.
But now they are jubilant anew,
From cliff and tower, tu—whoo! tu—whoo!
310 Tu—whoo! tu—woo! from wood and fell!°

And see! the lady Christabel
Gathers herself from out her trance;
Her limbs relax, her countenance
Grows sad and soft; the smooth thin lids
Close o'er her eyes; and tears she sheds—
Large tears that leave the lashes bright!
And oft the while she seems to smile
As infants at a sudden light!

Yea, she doth smile, and she doth weep,
320 Like a youthful hermitess,°
Beauteous in a wilderness,
Who, praying always, prays in sleep.
And, if she move unquietly,
Perchance, 'tis but the blood so free
Comes back and tingles in her feet.
No doubt, she hath a vision sweet.
What if her guardian spirit 'twere,
What if she knew her mother near?
But this she knows, in joys and woes,
330 That saints will aid if men will call:
For the blue sky bends over all!
1797   1798

---

tairn mountain pool
fell moor, hill

hermitess perhaps a remembrance of Crashaw's
St. Teresa (see note 1)

PART II

Each matin bell, the Baron saith,
Knells us back to a world of death.
These words Sir Leoline first said,
When he rose and found his lady dead:
These words Sir Leoline will say
Many a morn to his dying day!

And hence the custom and law began
That still at dawn the sacristan,
340   Who duly pulls the heavy bell,
Five and forty beads must tell
Between each stroke—a warning knell,
Which not a soul can choose but hear
From Bratha Head to Wyndermere.°

Saith Bracy the bard, So let it knell!
And let the drowsy sacristan
Still count as slowly as he can!
There is no lack of such, I ween,°
As well fill up the space between.
350   In Langdale Pike° and Witch's Lair,
And Dungeon-ghyll° so foully rent,
With ropes of rock and bells of air
Three sinful sextons' ghosts are pent,
Who all give back, one after t'other,
The death-note to their living brother;
And oft too, by the knell offended,
Just as their one! two! three! is ended,
The devil mocks the doleful tale
With a merry peal from Borodale.

360   The air is still! through mist and cloud
That merry peal comes ringing loud;
And Geraldine shakes off her dread,
And rises lightly from the bed;
Puts on her silken vestments white,
And tricks her hair in lovely plight,°
And nothing doubting of her spell
Awakens the lady Christabel.
'Sleep you, sweet lady Christabel?
I trust that you have rested well.'

370   And Christabel awoke and spied
The same who lay down by her side—
O rather say, the same whom she

Wyndermere The place names in Part II are all
in the Lake Country.
ween believe

Pike peak
ghyll bed of a stream
plight fashion

Raised up beneath the old oak tree!
Nay, fairer yet! and yet more fair!
For she belike hath drunken deep
Of all the blessedness of sleep!
And while she spake, her looks, her air
Such gentle thankfulness declare,
That (so it seemed) her girded vests
380 Grew tight beneath her heaving breasts.
'Sure I have sinned!' said Christabel,
'Now heaven be praised if all be well!'
And in low faltering tones, yet sweet,
Did she the lofty lady greet
With such perplexity of mind
As dreams too lively leave behind.

So quickly she rose, and quickly arrayed
Her maiden limbs, and having prayed
That He, who on the cross did groan,
390 Might wash away her sins unknown,
She forthwith led fair Geraldine
To meet her sire, Sir Leoline.

The lovely maid and the lady tall
Are pacing both into the hall,
And pacing on through page and groom,
Enter the Baron's presence-room.

The Baron rose, and while he prest
His gentle daughter to his breast,
With cheerful wonder in his eyes
400 The lady Geraldine espies,
And gave such welcome to the same,
As might beseem so bright a dame!

But when he heard the lady's tale,
And when she told her father's name,
Why waxed Sir Leoline so pale,
Murmuring o'er the name again,
Lord Roland de Vaux of Tryermaine?

Alas! they had been friends in youth;
But whispering tongues can poison truth;
410 And constancy lives in realms above;
And life is thorny; and youth is vain;
And to be wroth with one we love
Doth work like madness in the brain.
And thus it chanced, as I divine,
With Roland and Sir Leoline.
Each spake words of high disdain
And insult to his heart's best brother:

They parted—ne'er to meet again!
But never either found another
420   To free the hollow heart from paining—
They stood aloof, the scars remaining,
Like cliffs which had been rent asunder;
A dreary sea now flows between;—
But neither heat, nor frost, nor thunder,
Shall wholly do away, I ween,
The marks of that which once hath been.

Sir Leoline, a moment's space,
Stood gazing on the damsel's face:
And the youthful Lord of Tryermaine
430   Came back upon his heart again.

O then the Baron forgot his age,
His noble heart swelled high with rage;
He swore by the wounds in Jesu's side
He would proclaim it far and wide,
With trump and solemn heraldry,
That they, who thus had wronged the dame,
Were base as spotted infamy!
'And if they dare deny the same,
My herald shall appoint a week,
440   And let the recreant traitors seek
My tourney court—that there and then
I may dislodge their reptile souls
From the bodies and forms of men!'
He spake: his eye in lightning rolls!
For the lady was ruthlessly seized; and he kenned°
In the beautiful lady the child of his friend!

And now the tears were on his face,
And fondly in his arms he took
Fair Geraldine, who met the embrace,
450   Prolonging it with joyous look.
Which when she viewed, a vision fell
Upon the soul of Christabel,
The vision of fear, the touch and pain!
She shrunk and shuddered, and saw again—
(Ah, woe is me! Was it for thee,
Thou gentle maid! such sights to see?)

Again she saw that bosom old,
Again she felt that bosom cold,
And drew in her breath with a hissing sound:
460   Whereat the Knight turned wildly round,
And nothing saw, but his own sweet maid
With eyes upraised, as one that prayed.

kenned recognized

The touch, the sight, had passed away,
And in its stead that vision blest,
Which comforted her after-rest
While in the lady's arms she lay,
Had put a rapture in her breast,
And on her lips and o'er her eyes
Spread smiles like light!
                       With new surprise,
470 'What ails then my belovèd child?'
The Baron said—His daughter mild
Made answer, 'All will yet be well!'
I ween, she had no power to tell
Aught else: so mighty was the spell.

Yet he, who saw this Geraldine,
Had deemed her sure a thing divine:
Such sorrow with such grace she blended,
As if she feared she had offended
Sweet Christabel, that gentle maid!
480 And with such lowly tones she prayed
She might be sent without delay
Home to her father's mansion.
                         'Nay!
Nay, by my soul!' said Leoline.
'Ho! Bracy the bard, the charge be thine!
Go thou, with music sweet and loud,
And take two steeds with trappings proud,
And take the youth whom thou lovest best
To bear thy harp, and learn thy song,
And clothe you both in solemn vest,
490 And over the mountains haste along,
Lest wandering folk, that are abroad,
Detain you on the valley road.

'And when he has crossed the Irthing flood,
My merry bard! he hastes, he hastes
Up Knorren Moor, through Halegarth Wood,
And reaches soon that castle good
Which stands and threatens Scotland's wastes.

'Bard Bracy! bard Bracy! your horses are fleet,
Ye must ride up the hall, your music so sweet,
500 More loud than your horses' echoing feet!
And loud and loud to Lord Roland call,
Thy daughter is safe in Langdale hall!
Thy beautiful daughter is safe and free—
Sir Leoline greets thee thus through me!
He bids thee come without delay
With all thy numerous array

And take thy lovely daughter home:
And he will meet thee on the way
With all his numerous array
510   White with their panting palfreys' foam:
And, by mine honour! I will say,
That I repent me of the day
When I spake words of fierce disdain
To Roland de Vaux of Tryermaine!—
—For since that evil hour hath flown,
Many a summer's sun hath shone;
Yet ne'er found I a friend again
Like Roland de Vaux of Tryermaine.'

The lady fell, and clasped his knees,
520   Her face upraised, her eyes o'erflowing;
And Bracy replied, with faltering voice,
His gracious Hail on all bestowing!—
'Thy words, thou sire of Christabel,
Are sweeter than my harp can tell;
Yet might I gain a boon of thee,
This day my journey should not be,
So strange a dream hath come to me,
That I have vowed with music loud
To clear yon wood from thing unblest,
530   Warned by a vision in my rest!
For in my sleep I saw that dove,
That gentle bird, whom thou dost love,
And callest by thy own daughter's name—
Sir Leoline! I saw the same
Fluttering, and uttering fearful moan,
Among the green herbs in the forest alone.
Which when I saw and when I heard,
I wondered what might ail the bird;
For nothing near it could I see,
540   Save the grass and green herbs underneath the old tree.

'And in my dream methought I went
To search out what might there be found;
And what the sweet bird's trouble meant,
That thus lay fluttering on the ground.
I went and peered, and could descry
No cause for her distressful cry;
But yet for her dear lady's sake
I stooped, methought, the dove to take,
When lo! I saw a bright green snake
550   Coiled around its wings and neck.
Green as the herbs on which it couched,
Close by the dove's its head it crouched;
And with the dove it heaves and stirs,

Swelling its neck as she swelled hers!
I woke; it was the midnight hour,
The clock was echoing in the tower;
But though my slumber was gone by,
This dream it would not pass away—
It seems to live upon my eye!
560   And thence I vowed this self-same day
With music strong and saintly song
To wander through the forest bare,
Lest aught unholy loiter there.'

Thus Bracy said: the Baron, the while,
Half-listening heard him with a smile;
Then turned to Lady Geraldine,
His eyes made up of wonder and love;
And said in courtly accents fine,
'Sweet maid, Lord Roland's beauteous dove,
570   With arms more strong than harp or song,
Thy sire and I will crush the snake!'
He kissed her forehead as he spake,
And Geraldine in maiden wise
Casting down her large bright eyes,
With blushing cheek and courtesy fine
She turned her from Sir Leoline;
Softly gathering up her train,
That o'er her right arm fell again;
And folded her arms across her chest,
580   And couched her head upon her breast,
And looked askance at Christabel——
Jesu, Maria, shield her well!

A snake's small eye blinks dull and shy;
And the lady's eyes they shrunk in her head,
Each shrunk up to a serpent's eye,
And with somewhat of malice, and more of dread,
At Christabel she looked askance!—
One moment—and the sight was fled!
But Christabel in dizzy trance
590   Stumbling on the unsteady ground
Shuddered aloud, with a hissing sound;
And Geraldine again turned round,
And like a thing, that sought relief,
Full of wonder and full of grief,
She rolled her large bright eyes divine
Wildly on Sir Leoline.

The maid, alas! her thoughts are gone
She nothing sees—no sight but one!
The maid, devoid of guile and sin,

600   I know not how, in fearful wise,
     So deeply had she drunken in
     That look, those shrunken serpent eyes,
     That all her features were resigned
     To this sole image in her mind:
     And passively did imitate
     That look of dull and treacherous hate!
     And thus she stood, in dizzy trance,
     Still picturing that look askance
     With forced unconscious sympathy
610   Full before her father's view——
     As far as such a look could be
     In eyes so innocent and blue!

     And when the trance was o'er, the maid
     Paused awhile, and inly prayed:
     Then falling at the Baron's feet,
     'By my mother's soul do I entreat
     That thou this woman send away!'
     She said: and more she could not say:
     For what she knew she could not tell,
620   O'er-mastered by the mighty spell.

     Why is thy cheek so wan and wild,
     Sir Leoline? Thy only child
     Lies at thy feet, thy joy, thy pride,
     So fair, so innocent, so mild;
     The same, for whom thy lady died!
     O by the pangs of her dear mother
     Think thou no evil of thy child!
     For her, and thee, and for no other,
     She prayed the moment ere she died:
630   Prayed that the babe for whom she died,
     Might prove her dear lord's joy and pride!
        That prayer her deadly pangs beguiled,
          Sir Leoline!
        And wouldst thou wrong thy only child,
          Her child and thine?

     Within the Baron's heart and brain
     If thoughts, like these, had any share,
     They only swelled his rage and pain,
     And did but work confusion there.
640   His heart was cleft with pain and rage,
     His cheeks they quivered, his eyes were wild,
     Dishonoured thus in his old age;
     Dishonoured by his only child,
     And all his hospitality
     To the wronged daughter of his friend

By more than woman's jealousy
Brought thus to a disgraceful end—
He rolled his eye with stern regard
Upon the gentle minstrel bard,
650   And said in tones abrupt, austere—
'Why, Bracy! dost thou loiter here?
I bade thee hence!' The bard obeyed;
And turning from his own sweet maid,
The agèd knight, Sir Leoline,
Led forth the lady Geraldine!
1797–1800   1816

THE CONCLUSION TO PART II

A little child,° a limber elf,
Singing, dancing to itself,
A fairy thing with red round cheeks,
That always finds, and never seeks,
660   Makes such a vision to the sight
As fills a father's eyes with light;
And pleasures flow in so thick and fast
Upon his heart, that he at last
Must needs express his love's excess
With words of unmeant bitterness.
Perhaps 'tis pretty to force together
Thoughts so all unlike each other;
To mutter and mock a broken charm,
To dally with wrong that does no harm.
670   Perhaps 'tis tender too and pretty
At each wild word to feel within
A sweet recoil of love and pity.
And what, if in a world of sin
(O sorrow and shame should this be true!)
Such giddiness of heart and brain
Comes seldom save from rage and pain,
So talks as it's most used to do.
1801   1816

Frost at Midnight°

The Frost performs its secret ministry,
Unhelped by any wind. The owlet's cry
Came loud—and hark, again! loud as before.
The inmates of my cottage, all at rest,

child Hartley Coleridge
Frost at Midnight This poem, the perfection of
Coleridge's conversation group, is greatly in-
debted to Cowper's *The Task* IV.286–310, "The
Winter Evening"; in turn, it strongly influenced
Wordsworth's "Tintern Abbey," as a compari-
son of the conclusions of the two poems will
show.

Have left me to that solitude, which suits
Abstruser musings: save that at my side
My cradled infant slumbers peacefully.
'Tis calm indeed! so calm, that it disturbs
And vexes meditation with its strange
10   And extreme silentness. Sea, hill, and wood,
This populous village! Sea, and hill, and wood,
With all the numberless goings-on of life,
Inaudible as dreams! the thin blue flame
Lies on my low-burnt fire, and quivers not;
Only that film,° which fluttered on the grate,
Still flutters there, the sole unquiet thing.
Methinks, its motion in this hush of nature
Gives it dim sympathies with me who live,
Making it a companionable form,
20   Whose puny flaps and freaks the idling Spirit
By its own moods interprets, everywhere
Echo or mirror seeking of itself,
And makes a toy of Thought.

                              But O! how oft,
How oft, at school,° with most believing mind,
Presageful, have I grazed upon the bars,
To watch that fluttering *stranger*! and as oft
With unclosed lids, already had I dreamt
Of my sweet birth-place, and the old church-tower,
Whose bells, the poor man's only music, rang
30   From morn to evening, all the hot Fair-day,
So sweetly, that they stirred and haunted me
With a wild pleasure, falling on mine ear
Most like articulate sounds of things to come!
So gazed I, till the soothing things, I dreamt,
Lulled me to sleep, and sleep prolonged my dreams!
And so I brooded all the following morn,
Awed by the stern preceptor's face, mine eye
Fixed with mock study on my swimming book:
Save if the door half opened, and I snatched
40   A hasty glance, and still my heart leaped up,
For still I hoped to see the *stranger's* face,
Townsman, or aunt, or sister more beloved,
My play-mate° when we both were clothed alike!

    Dear Babe, that sleepest cradled by my side,
Whose gentle breathings, heard in this deep calm,
Fill up the interspersèd vacancies

film soot on the grate; Coleridge noted: "In all parts of the Kingdom these films are called *strangers* and supposed to portend the arrival of some absent friend"

school Christ's Hospital, London
play-mate Coleridge's sister Ann

And momentary pauses of the thought!
My babe so beautiful! it thrills my heart
With tender gladness, thus to look at thee,
50   And think that thou shalt learn far other lore,
And in far other scenes! For I was reared
In the great city, pent 'mid cloisters° dim,
And saw nought lovely but the sky and stars.
But *thou*, my babe! shalt wander like a breeze
By lakes and sandy shores, beneath the crags
Of ancient mountain, and beneath the clouds,
Which image in their bulk both lakes and shores
And mountain crags: so shalt thou see and hear
The lovely shapes and sounds intelligible
60   Of that eternal language,° which thy God
Utters, who from eternity doth teach
Himself in all, and all things in himself.
Great universal Teacher! he shall mould
Thy spirit, and by giving make it ask.

Therefore all seasons shall be sweet to thee,
Whether the summer clothe the general earth
With greenness, or the redbreast sit and sing
Betwixt the tufts of snow on the bare branch
Of mossy apple-tree, while the nigh thatch
70   Smokes in the sun-thaw; whether the eave-drops fall
Heard only in the trances of the blast,
Or if the secret ministry of frost
Shall hang them up in silent icicles,
Quietly shining to the quiet Moon.
1798   1798

Dejection: An Ode

This began as a long verse-letter to Sara Hutchinson, whom Coleridge hopelessly loved, and who was soon to become Wordsworth's sister-in-law. The occasion for the letter was Wordsworth's reading aloud to Coleridge of the first four stanzas of the "Intimations of Immortality" ode. When the verse-letter was worked into an ode, many of the direct references to Wordsworth's stanzas were removed, together with all overt references to Sara Hutchinson and Coleridge's unhappy marriage. The person addressed became "William" rather than "Sara" while still in manuscript, then "Edmund" in the first publication of the poem on the very day of Wordsworth's marriage, and finally "Lady" when first included in a book.

The central argument Coleridge conducts with Wordsworth is most crucial in stanza IV, where the origin of joy is located only in the human viewer and not in the external scene.

cloisters of Christ's Hospital   eternal language of natural appearances

Dejection: An Ode

> Late, late yestreen I saw the new Moon,
> With the old Moon in her arms;
> And I fear, I fear, my Master dear!
> We shall have a deadly storm.
> BALLAD OF SIR PATRICK SPENCE

I

Well! If the Bard was weather-wise, who made
   The grand old ballad of Sir Patrick Spence,
   This night, so tranquil now, will not go hence
Unroused by winds, that ply a busier trade
Than those which mould yon cloud in lazy flakes,
Or the dull sobbing draft, that moans and rakes
Upon the strings of this Aeolian lute,
      Which better far were mute.
   For lo! the New-moon winter-bright!
10   And overspread with phantom light,
      (With swimming phantom light o'erspread
      But rimmed and circled by a silver thread)
I see the old Moon in her lap, foretelling
   The coming-on of rain and squally blast.
And oh! that even now the gust were swelling,
   And the slant night-shower driving loud and fast!
Those sounds which oft have raised me, whilst they awed,
      And sent my soul abroad,
Might now perhaps their wonted impulse give,
20 Might startle this dull pain, and make it move and live!

II

A grief without a pang, void, dark, and drear,
   A stifled, drowsy, unimpassioned grief,
   Which finds no natural outlet, no relief,
      In word, or sigh, or tear—
O Lady! in this wan and heartless mood,
To other thoughts by yonder throstle wooed,
   All this long eve, so balmy and serene,
Have I been gazing on the western sky,
   And its peculiar tint of yellow green:
30 And still I gaze—and with how blank an eye!
And those thin clouds above, in flakes and bars,
That give away their motion to the stars;
Those stars, that glide behind them or between,
Now sparkling, now bedimmed, but always seen:
Yon crescent Moon, as fixed as if it grew
In its own cloudless, starless lake of blue;
I see them all so excellently fair,
I see, not feel, how beautiful they are!

III

My genial spirits° fail;
40   And what can these avail
To lift the smothering weight from off my breast?
    It were a vain endeavour,
    Though I should gaze forever
On that green light that lingers in the west:
I may not hope from outward forms to win
The passion and the life, whose fountains are within.

IV

O Lady! we receive but what we give,
And in our life alone does Nature live:
Ours is her wedding garment, ours her shroud!
50   And would we aught behold, of higher worth,
Than that inanimate cold world allowed
To the poor loveless ever-anxious crowd,
    Ah! from the soul itself must issue forth
A light, a glory, a fair luminous cloud
        Enveloping the Earth—
And from the soul itself must there be sent
    A sweet and potent voice, of its own birth,
Of all sweet sounds the life and element!

V

O pure of heart! thou needest not ask of me
60 What this strong music in the soul may be!
What, and wherein it doth exist,
This light, this glory, this fair luminous mist,
This beautiful and beauty-making power.
    Joy, virtuous Lady! Joy that ne'er was given,
Save to the pure, and in their purest hour,
Life, and Life's effluence, cloud at once and shower,
Joy, Lady! is the spirit and the power,
Which, wedding Nature to us, gives in dower
    A new Earth and new Heaven,
70 Undreamt of by the sensual and the proud—
Joy is the sweet voice, Joy the luminous cloud—
        We in ourselves rejoice!
And thence flows all that charms or ear or sight,
    All melodies the echoes of that voice,
All colours a suffusion from that light.

VI

There was a time when, though my path was rough,
    This joy within me dallied with distress,

genial spirits See Milton's *Samson Agonistes*, ll.
594–98, and Wordsworth's "Tintern Abbey,"
l. 113.

And all misfortunes were but as the stuff
   Whence Fancy made me dreams of happiness:
80   For hope grew round me, like the twining vine,
And fruits, and foliage, not my own, seemed mine.
But now afflictions bow me down to earth:
Nor care I that they rob me of my mirth;
     But oh! each visitation
Suspends what nature gave me at my birth,
   My shaping spirit of Imagination.
For not to think of what I needs must feel,
   But to be still and patient, all I can;
And haply by abstruse research to steal
90   From my own nature all the natural man—
   This was my sole resource, my only plan:
Till that which suits a part infects the whole,
And now is almost grown the habit of my soul.

       VII
Hence, viper thoughts, that coil around my mind,
    Reality's dark dream!
I turn from you, and listen to the wind,
   Which long has raved unnoticed. What a scream
Of agony by torture lengthened out
That lute sent forth! Thou Wind, that rav'st without,
100   Bare crag, or mountain tairn,° or blasted tree,
Or pine-grove whither woodman never clomb,
Or lonely house, long held the witches' home,
   Methinks were fitter instruments for thee,
Mad Lutanist! who in this month of showers,
Of dark-brown gardens, and of peeping flowers,
Makest Devils' yule, with worse than wintry song,
The blossoms, buds, and timorous leaves among.
   Thou Actor, perfect in all tragic sounds!
Thou mighty Poet, e'en to frenzy bold!
110   What tellest thou now about?
   'Tis of the rushing of an host in rout,
With groans, of trampled men, with smarting wounds—
At once they groan with pain, and shudder with the cold!
But hush! there is a pause of deepest silence!
   And all that noise, as of a rushing crowd,
With groans, and tremulous shudderings—all is over—
   It tells another tale, with sounds less deep and loud!
    A tale of less affright,
    And tempered with delight,
120 As Otway's self had framed the tender lay,°—

tairn pool
As Otway's . . . lay Thomas Otway (1652–
85), Restoration dramatist, is merely an absurd
cover here; the original manuscript read "William's self" and the reference is clearly to
Wordsworth's "Lucy Gray."

'Tis of a little child
Upon a lonesome wild,
Not far from home, but she hath lost her way:
And now moans low in bitter grief and fear,
And now screams loud, and hopes to make her mother hear.

VIII

'Tis midnight, but small thoughts have I of sleep:
Full seldom may my friend such vigils keep!
Visit her, gentle Sleep! with wings of healing,
   And may this storm be but a mountain-birth,°
130 May all the stars hang bright above her dwelling,
   Silent as though they watched the sleeping Earth!
    With light heart may she rise,
    Gay fancy, cheerful eyes,
Joy lift her spirit, joy attune her voice;
To her may all things live, from pole to pole,
Their life the eddying of her living soul!
  O simple spirit, guided from above,
Dear Lady! friend devoutest of my choice,
Thus mayest thou ever, evermore rejoice.
1802   1802

Phantom°

All look and likeness caught from earth
All accident of kin and birth,
Had passed away. There was no trace
Of aught on that illumined face,
Upraised beneath the rifted stone
But of one spirit all her own;—
She, she herself, and only she,
Shone through her body visibly.
1805   1834

To William Wordsworth

COMPOSED ON THE NIGHT AFTER HIS RECITATION
OF A POEM ON THE GROWTH OF AN INDIVIDUAL MIND°

Friend of the wise! and Teacher of the Good!°

mountain-birth The probable reference is to the famous tag in Horace's *Ars Poetica*, l. 139, where the mountain labors and brings forth a mouse. **Phantom** evidently a description of Sara Hutchinson as she appeared to Coleridge in a dream **Composed . . . Mind** Wordsworth read *The Prelude* aloud to Coleridge (it took some two weeks) when Coleridge returned from Malta, a somewhat broken man, in 1806. Wordsworth asked Coleridge not to publish this poem; Coleridge printed it anyway, at first under the bland title, *To a Gentleman*. After the quarrel between the two friends in 1810, the poem underwent significant revision, but much of it was equivocal from the first, though its tribute to *The Prelude* is still unsurpassed. **Friend . . . Good** In 1807 this first line read, "O Friend! O Teacher! God's great gift to me."

Into my heart have I received that Lay
More than historic, that prophetic Lay
Wherein (high theme by thee first sung aright)
Of the foundations and the building up
Of a Human Spirit thou hast dared to tell
What may be told, to the understanding mind
Revealable; and what within the mind
By vital breathings secret as the soul
10 Of vernal growth, oft quickens in the heart
Thoughts all too deep for words!°—

                        Theme hard as high!
Of smiles spontaneous, and mysterious fears°
(The first-born they of Reason° and twin-birth),
Of tides obedient to external force,
And currents self-determined, as might seem,
 Or by some inner Power; of moments awful,
Now in thy inner life, and now abroad,
When power streamed from thee, and thy soul received
The light reflected, as a light bestowed—
20 Of fancies fair, and milder hours of youth,
Hyblean° murmurs of poetic thought
Industrious in its joy, in vales and glens
Native or outland, lakes and famous hills!
Or on the lonely high-road, when the stars
Were rising; or by secret mountain streams,
The guides and the companions of thy way!

Of more than Fancy, of the Social Sense
Distending wide, and man beloved as man,
Where France in all her towns lay vibrating
30 Like some becalmèd bark beneath the burst
Of Heaven's immediate thunder, when no cloud
Is visible, or shadow on the main.
For thou wert there, thine own brows garlanded,
Amid the tremor of a realm aglow,
Amid a mighty nation jubilant,
When from the general heart of human kind
Hope sprang forth like a full-born Deity!
——Of that dear Hope afflicted and struck down,
So summoned homeward, thenceforth calm and sure
40 From the dread watch-tower of man's absolute self,
With light unwaning on her eyes, to look
Far on—herself a glory to behold,
The Angel of the vision! Then (last strain)

Thoughts . . . words See the last line of the *Intimations of Immortality* ode.
mysterious fears See *The Prelude* I and II.
Reason in the transcendental sense, a higher faculty than the mere Understanding, which deals only with the realm of experience
Hyblean Ancient Hybla, in Sicily, was renowned for its honey.

Of Duty, chosen Laws controlling choice,
Action and joy!—An Orphic° song indeed,
A song divine of high and passionate thoughts
To their own music chaunted!

                    O great Bard!
Ere yet that last strain dying awed the air,
With stedfast eye I viewed thee in the choir
50 Of ever-enduring men. The truly great
Have all one age, and from one visible space
Shed influence! They, both in power and act,
Are permanent, and Time is not with them,
Save as it worketh for them, they in it.
Nor less a sacred roll, than those of old,
And to be placed, as they, with gradual fame
Among the archives of mankind, thy work
Makes audible a linkèd lay of Truth,
Of Truth profound a sweet continuous lay,
60 Not learnt, but native, her own natural notes!
Ah! as I listened with a heart forlorn,
The pulses of my being beat anew:
And even as Life returns upon the drowned,
Life's joy rekindling roused a throng of pains—
Keen pangs of Love, awakening as a babe
Turbulent, with an outcry in the heart;
And fears self-willed, that shunned the eye of Hope;
And Hope that scarce would know itself from Fear;
Sense of past Youth, and Manhood come in vain,
70 And Genius given, and Knowledge won in vain;
And all which I had culled in wood-walks wild,
And all which patient toil had reared, and all,
Commune with thee had opened out—but flowers
Strewed on my corse, and borne upon my bier
In the same coffin, for the self-same grave!

    That way no more! and ill beseems it me,
Who came a welcomer in herald's guise,
Singing of Glory, and Futurity,
To wander back on such unhealthful road,
80 Plucking the poisons of self-harm! And ill
Such intertwine beseems triumphal wreaths
Strewed before thy advancing!

                    Nor do thou,
Sage Bard! impair the memory of that hour,
Of thy communion with my nobler mind°
By pity or grief, already felt too long!

Orphic pertaining to the legendary bard, Or-   nobler mind i.e. nobler in 1798 than in 1807
pheus; hence a synonym for "oracular"

Nor let my words import more blame than needs.
The tumult rose and ceased: for Peace is nigh
Where Wisdom's voice has found a listening heart.
Amid the howl of more than wintry storms,
90   The Halcyon° hears the voice of vernal hours
Already on the wing.

           Eve following eve,
Dear tranquil time, when the sweet sense of Home
Is sweetest! moments for their own sake hailed
And more desired, more precious, for thy song,
In silence listening, like a devout child,
My soul lay passive, by thy various strain
Driven as in surges now beneath the stars,
With momentary stars of my own birth,
Fair constellated foam, still darting off
100   Into the darkness; now a tranquil sea,
Outspread and bright, yet swelling to the moon.

And when—O Friend! my comforter and guide!
Strong in thyself, and powerful to give strength!—
Thy long sustainèd Song finally closed,
And thy deep voice had ceased—yet thou thyself
Wert still before my eyes, and round us both
That happy vision of belovèd faces—
Scarce conscious, and yet conscious of its close
I sate, my being blended in one thought
110   (Thought was it? or aspiration? or resolve?)
Absorbed, yet hanging still upon the sound—
And when I rose, I found myself in prayer.
1807   1817

On Donne's Poetry°

With Donne, whose muse on dromedary° trots,
Wreathe iron pokers into true-love knots;
Rhyme's sturdy cripple, fancy's maze and clue,
Wit's forge and fire-blast, meaning's press and screw.
1818?   1836

Halcyon mythological bird credited with so
calming the ocean as to nest upon it; from the
story of Halcyone, who drowned herself after
finding her husband Ceyx drowned; the gods
changed them into magical birds
On Donne's Poetry Coleridge remarked that "to
read Dryden, Pope, etc., you need only count
syllables; but to read Donne you must measure
Time, and discover the Time of each word by
the sense of the Passion."
dromedary fleet, one-humped camel

Limbo°

The sole true Something—This! In Limbo's Den
It frightens Ghosts, as here Ghosts frighten men.
Thence cross'd unseized—and shall some fated hour
Be pulverised by Demogorgon's° power,
And given as poison to annihilate souls—
Even now it shrinks them—they shrink in as Moles
(Nature's mute monks, live mandrakes° of the ground)
Creep back from Light—then listen for its sound;—
See but to dread, and dread they know not why—
10 The natural alien of their negative eye.

'Tis a strange place, this Limbo!–not a Place,
Yet name it so;—where Time and weary Space
Fettered from flight, with night-mare sense of fleeing,
Strive for their last crepuscular° half-being:—
Lank Space, and scytheless Time with branny hands
Barren and soundless as the measuring sands,
Not marked by flit of Shades,—unmeaning they
As moonlight on the dial of the day!
But that is lovely—looks like Human Time,
20 An Old Man with a steady look sublime,
That stops his earthly task to watch the skies;
But he is blind—a Statue hath such eyes;—
Yet having moonward turned his face by chance,
Gazes the orb with moon-like countenance,
With scant white hairs, with foretop bald and high,
He gazes still,—his eyeless face all eye;—
As 'twere an organ full of silent sight,
His whole face seemeth to rejoice in light!
Lip touching lip, all moveless, bust and limb—
30 He seems to gaze at that which seems to gaze on him!

    No such sweet sights doth Limbo den immure,
Walled round, and made a spirit-jail secure,
By the mere horror of blank Naught-at-all,
Whose circumambience doth these ghosts enthral.
A lurid thought is growthless, dull Privation,
Yet that is but a Purgatory curse;
Hell knows a fear far worse,
A fear—a future state;—'tis positive Negation!
1817   1893

Limbo From one of Coleridge's notebooks, where
it is followed by the fragment "Ne Plus Ultra";
George Ridenour demonstrates both fragments'
debts to Coleridge's earlier "Ode to the Departing Year," and to the theosophical writings of
Jacob Boehme. David Perkins usefully cites
Aphorism XIX from Coleridge's Aids to Reflection: "There is another death, not the mere
negation of life, but its positive opposite." Coleridge's Limbo is evidently not the traditional
one (on Hell's borders, for the virtuous unbap-
tized) but a state on the ambiguous line between what is and what is not, a kind of half-
phantasmagoria or waking nightmare.
Demogorgon's god of the abyss; see the note to
l.207 of Shelley's Prometheus Unbound
mandrakes poisonous plants, whose forked roots
were thought to resemble humans; legend held
that mandrakes shrieked when picked
crepuscular relating to twilight, hence indistinct
or dim

Ne Plus Ultra°

Sole Positive of Night!
Antipathist° of Light!
Fate's only essence! primal scorpion rod°—
The one permitted opposite of God!—
Condensèd blackness and abysmal storm
        Compacted to one sceptre
        Arms the Grasp enorm—
        The Intercepter—
The Substance that still casts the shadow Death!—
10   The Dragon foul and fell—
        The unrevealable,
And hidden one, whose breath
Gives wind and fuel to the fires of Hell!
        Ah! sole despair
        Of both the eternities° in Heaven!
Sole interdict of all-bedewing prayer,
        The all-compassionate!
        Save to the Lampads Seven°
Revealed to none of all the Angelic State,
20   Save to the Lampads Seven,
        That watch the throne of Heaven!
        1826?   1834

To Nature°

It may indeed be phantasy, when I
    Essay to draw from all created things
    Deep, heartfelt, inward joy that closely clings;
And trace in leaves and flowers that round me lie
Lessons of love and earnest piety.
    So let it be; and if the wide world rings
    In mock of this belief, it brings
Nor fear, nor grief, nor vain perplexity.
So will I build my altar in the fields,
10   And the blue sky my fretted dome shall be,
And the sweet fragrance that the wild flower yields
    Shall be the incense I will yield to Thee,
Thee only God! and thou shalt not despise
Even me, the priest of this poor sacrifice.
1820?   1836

Ne Plus Ultra literally, "nothing more beyond,"
here meaning something like "nothing worse
than this condition"
Antipathist natural enemy
scorpion rod the contrary to Aaron's rod, Exodus 7:10–12

both the eternities the two are Divine Love
and Divine Knowledge
Lampads Seven seven lamps of fire burning before the Divine Throne in Revelation 4:5
To Nature This late sonnet is a touching return
to the earlier vision Coleridge had tried to share
with Wordsworth.

Epitaph°

Stop, Christian passer-by!—Stop, child of God,
And read with gentle breast. Beneath this sod
A poet lies, or that which once seemed he.
O, lift one thought in prayer for S. T. C.;
That he who many a year with toil of breath
Found death in life, may here find life in death!
Mercy for praise—to be forgiven for° fame
He asked, and hoped, through Christ. Do thou the same!
1833   1834

GEORGE GORDON, LORD BYRON
1788–1824

Byron's life and personality are at least as fascinating as his poetry. No author before or since has enjoyed and suffered such notoriety, or had a literary and social influence so much out of proportion with his actual imaginative achievement, considerable as that was. Somehow Byron was at once a man of incredible personal beauty, and yet congenitally half-lame and incessantly struggling against a tendency to grow fat. The most brilliant conversationalist of his time, except for the incomparable Coleridge, he glorified solitude and at last attained it. Celebrated as the highest of High Romantics (the only one to attain a European reputation, in part because he does not lose too much by translation, but primarily because of his life), he despised Romanticism, and insisted that English poetry all but died with the death of Pope. A virtual synonym for the greatest of lovers, he was passive toward women, sodomistic, sado-masochistic, fundamentally homosexual, and early disgusted with all sexual experience anyway. Outcast for his incest with his half-sister, he nevertheless seems to have gotten beyond narcissistic self-regard only in relation to her, yet she was in no way remarkable. A radical by the English standards of his day, and an active revolutionary in Italy, he was wholly skeptical as to the benefits of either reform or revolution. Acclaimed to this day as the martyr-hero of the Greek Revolution against the Turks, he despised the modern Greeks even as he financed, trained, and led them in rebellion. Apparently emancipated in religion, he was shocked by his closest friend Shelley's polemic against Christianity, could not rid himself of a Calvinistic temper, and inclined secretly toward Catholicism. A superb athlete and champion swimmer, he had to compel his reluctant, sluggish body to keep up with his restless spirit. To sum up: he was the most antithetical of men, and one of the most self-divided of poets.

Byron's father, widely known as a rakehell, died when the poet was three, leaving him with a neurotic, unstable mother and a governess who both seduced and chastised him. He attended Harrow, and Trinity College, Cambridge, where he had homosexual experience. When his early lyrics, *Hours of Idleness* (1807), were attacked in *The Edinburgh Review*, Byron retaliated in his first satire, *English Bards and Scotch Reviewers* (1809). Returning from a grand tour of Iberia and Greece (1809–11), he published his verse diary, *Childe Harold's Pilgrimage*, Cantos I and II, in 1812, and his

Epitaph not actually written for his own me-   for instead of
morial stone, but intended for the final page of
an edition of his poems

true career began: "I awoke one morning and found myself famous." Enormous success in Regency society followed, including love affairs with Lady Oxford and with Caroline Lamb, who terrorized him to the extent that he sought refuge in marriage with Annabella Milbanke, a virtuous lady much given to mathematical interests, and a very improbable choice on his part. A number of verse tales (*Lara* is the best of them) enjoyed the same popularity as *Childe Harold,* and meanwhile Byron devoted himself also to the left wing of the Whig party. In eloquent speeches to the House of Lords, he urged Catholic Emancipation and defended the "framebreakers," workers who had destroyed machines that had displaced them.

Though a daughter was born to Lady Byron, the marriage soon became insupportable, evidently because of Byron's periodic rages, continued incest with his half-sister, and sodomistic demands on his highly conventional wife. They separated, amid much public scandal, and Byron, after encountering many social snubs, abandoned England for good in April 1816. He went to Geneva, and began his close friendship with Shelley, which lasted unbroken—though with strains—until Shelley drowned in 1822. Under Shelley's influence (and, paradoxically, of Wordsworth's through Shelley) he wrote Canto III of *Childe Harold,* and entered on a new phase of his poetry. Moving to Italy in autumn 1817, he enjoyed an orgiastic season in Venice, involving many scores of women. During this time, he completed the second Romantic phase of his work, writing Canto IV of *Childe Harold* and finishing *Manfred,* which he had begun in Shelley's company. More important, he discovered his true mode in the poem *Beppo,* a light satire in ottava rima that soon led him to begin his masterpiece, *Don Juan.*

From 1819 until he left for Greece in 1823, Byron settled down in a domestic relationship with the Countess Teresa Guiccioli, joining her family in revolutionary plots against the Austrians, and following them to Pisa, where he was again in daily association with Shelley. To this time belong much the largest part of *Don Juan,* the brilliant satire *The Vision of Judgment,* and an effective, apocalyptic drama, *Cain* (a work difficult to represent by excerpts).

Weary of his life, Byron went to Greece to seek a soldier's death at thirty-six, and found it. He found also, though, a last, bitter, frustrated homosexual passion for his Greek page boy Loukas, and his final verses and letters betray profound self-disgust but an unwearied intelligence and quick humor. His death at Missolonghi in April 1824 saved him from middle age, and made his legend imperishable.

If we can put aside the phenomenon of Byronism, which flowered extravagantly all over Europe after so Romantic a death, we are left with two parts of Byron's accomplishment—*Don Juan* and everything else. Of the latter, there is clearly lasting value in a handful of lyrics, in aspects of *Childe Harold* III and IV and of *Manfred,* and major achievement in *Cain* and in *The Vision of Judgment.* But, taken together, this is little compared with *Don Juan,* which only Shelley of Byron's contemporaries judged accurately and adequately, as being something wholly new and yet completely relevant to the Romantic Age.

From English Bards and Scotch Reviewers°

Behold! in various throngs the scribbling crew,
For notice eager, pass in long review:
Each spurs his jaded Pegasus apace,
And rhyme and blank maintain an equal race;
Sonnets on sonnets crowd, and ode on ode;
And Tales of Terror° jostle on the road;
Immeasurable measures move along;
150 For simpering folly loves a varied song,
To strange mysterious dulness still the friend,
Admires the strain she cannot comprehend.
Thus Lays of Minstrels°—may they be the last!—
On half-strung harps whine mournful to the blast.
While mountain spirits prate to river sprites,
That dames may listen to the sound at nights;
And goblin brats, of Gilpin Horner's brood,°
Decoy young border-nobles through the wood,
And skip at every step, Lord knows how high,
160 And frighten foolish babes, the Lord knows why;
While high-born ladies in their magic cell,
Forbidding knights to read who cannot spell,
Dispatch a courier to a wizard's grave,
And fight with honest men to shield a knave.

Next view in state, proud prancing on his roan,
The golden-crested haughty Marmion,°
Now forging scrolls, now foremost in the fight,
Not quite a felon, yet but half a knight,
The gibbet or the field prepared to grace;
170 A mighty mixture of the great and base.
And think'st thou, Scott! by vain conceit perchance,
On public taste to foist thy stale romance,
Though Murray with his Miller° may combine
To yield thy muse just half-a-crown per line?
No! when the sons of song descend to trade,
Their bays are sear, their former laurels fade.
Let such forego the poet's sacred name,
Who rack their brains for lucre, not for fame:
Still for stern Mammon may they toil in vain!
180 And sadly gaze on gold they cannot gain!

English Bards and Scotch Reviewers Byron was
at work on this poem, as *English Bards,* when
his volume of lyrics, *Hours of Idleness,* was savaged (not unjustly) by Lord Brougham in *The
Edinburgh Review* of January 1808. The poem
consequently was enlarged to include *Scotch
Reviewers,* but the portions given here are all
devoted to the older generation of Romantics—
Scott, Southey, Wordsworth, and Coleridge.
Byron later repudiated the poem and had its
fifth edition burned, but could not suppress it.

Tales of Terror refers to the vogue of the
Gothic novel, but particularly to works of Sir
Walter Scott and Matthew Gregory Lewis
(1775–1818), notorious author of *The Monk*
Lays of Minstrels Scott's metrical romance *The
Lay of the Last Minstrel* (1805)
Horner's brood Scott's poem uses the border
legend of Gilpin Horner.
Marmion Scott's long poem of 1808
Murray . . . Miller London publisher

Such be their meed, such still the just reward
Of prostituted muse and hireling bard!
For this we spurn Apollo's venal son,
And bid a long 'good night to Marmion.'°

    These are the themes that claim our plaudits now;
These are the bards to whom the muse must bow;
While Milton, Dryden, Pope, alike forgot,
Resign their hallowed bays to Walter Scott.

    The time has been, when yet the muse was young,
190   When Homer swept the lyre, and Maro° sung,
An epic scarce ten centuries could claim,
While awe-struck nations hailed the magic name:
The work of each immortal bard appears
The single wonder of a thousand years.
Empires have mouldered from the face of earth,
Tongues have expired with those who gave them birth,
Without the glory such a strain can give,
As even in ruin bids the language live.
Not so with us, though minor bards, content,
200   On one great work a life of labour spent:
With eagle pinion soaring to the skies,
Behold the ballad-monger Southey° rise!
To him let Camoëns,° Milton, Tasso° yield,
Whose annual strains, like armies, take the field.
First in the ranks see Joan of Arc° advance,
The scourge of England and the boast of France!
Though burnt by wicked Bedford° for a witch,
Behold her statue placed in glory's niche;
Her fetters burst, and just released from prison,
210   A virgin phoenix from her ashes risen.
Next see tremendous Thalaba° come on,
Arabia's monstrous, wild, and wondrous son;
Domdaniel's dread destroyer,° who o'erthrew
More mad magicians than the world e'er knew.
Immortal hero! all thy foes o'ercome,
For ever reign—the rival of Tom Thumb!°
Since startled metre fled before thy face,
Well wert thou doomed the last of all thy race!

'good . . . Marmion' spoken on Marmion's
death (*Marmion* VI.869)
Maro Virgil
ballad-monger Southey the first of many attacks upon Southey, to culminate in *Don Juan*
and *The Vision of Judgment*
Camoëns Luis de Camoëns (1524–80), Portugal's great poet, wrote the epic *Lusiads*
Tasso Torquato Tasso (1544–95), Italian epic
poet, wrote *Jerusalem Delivered*
Joan of Arc Southey's revolutionary poem on
her was published in 1796.

Bedford Duke of Bedford, English commander,
who burned Joan at the stake
Thalaba Southey's mythological epic *Thalaba
the Destroyer* (1801)
destroyer Thalaba destroys a horde of evil magicians who live in Domdaniel, an undersea
palace.
Tom Thumb *The Tragedy of Tragedies; or, the
Life and Death of Tom Thumb the Great*
(1730), a farce by Henry Fielding

Well might triumphant genii bear thee hence,
220   Illustrious conqueror of common sense!
Now, last and greatest, Madoc° spreads his sails,
Cacique° in Mexico, and prince in Wales;
Tells us strange tales, as other travellers do,
More old than Mandeville's,° and not so true.
Oh! Southey! Southey! cease thy varied song!
A bard may chant too often and too long:
As thou art strong in verse, in mercy, spare!
A fourth, alas! were more than we could bear.
But if, in spite of all the world can say,
230   Thou still wilt verseward plod thy weary way;
If still in Berkley ballads most uncivil,
Thou wilt devote old women to the devil,°
The babe unborn thy dread intent may rue:
'God help thee,' Southey, and thy readers too.

    Next comes the dull disciple of thy school,
That mild apostate from poetic rule,
The simple Wordsworth, framer of a lay
As soft as evening in his favourite May,
Who warns his friend 'to shake off toil and trouble,
240   And quit his books, for fear of growing double';°
Who, both by precept and example, shows
That prose is verse, and verse is merely prose;°
Convincing all, by demonstration plain,
Poetic souls delight in prose insane;
And Christmas stories tortured into rhyme
Contain the essence of the true sublime.
Thus, when he tells the tale of Betty Foy,
The idiot mother of 'an idiot boy';
A moon struck, silly lad, who lost his way,
250   And, like his bard, confounded night with day;
So close on each pathetic part he dwells,
And each adventure so sublimely tells,
That all who view the 'idiot in his glory'
Conceive the bard the hero of the story.°

    Shall gentle Coleridge pass unnoticed here,
To turgid ode and tumid stanza dear?
Though themes of innocence amuse him best,
Yet still obscurity's a welcome guest.
If Inspiration should her aid refuse

Madoc epic by Southey (1805)
Cacique native chief
Mandeville's Sir John Mandeville (died 1372), credited with a famous travel book
devil Southey's ballad, "The Old Woman of Berkeley," a rather good poem about a witch

to shake . . . double from Wordsworth's "The Tables Turned" (1798)
That . . . prose See the Preface to the Second Edition of *Lyrical Ballads* (1800).
That . . . story See Wordsworth's "The Idiot Boy," included in *Lyrical Ballads.*

260   To him who takes a pixy for a muse,°
         Yet none in lofty numbers can surpass
         The bard who soars to elegize an ass.°
         So well the subject suits his noble mind,
         He brays, the laureate of the long-eared kind.
         1807–08   1809

From Lara°

XVII

         In him inexplicably mixed appeared
290   Much to be loved and hated, sought and feared;
         Opinion varying o'er his hidden lot,
         In praise or railing ne'er his name forgot:
         His silence formed a theme for others' prate—
         They guessed—they gazed—they fain would know his fate.
         What had he been? what was he, thus unknown,
         Who walked their world, his lineage only known?
         A hater of his kind? yet some would say,
         With them he could seem gay amidst the gay;
         But owned that smile, if oft observed and near,
300   Waned in its mirth, and withered to a sneer;
         That smile might reach his lip but passed not by,
         None e'er could trace its laughter to his eye:
         Yet there was softness too in his regard,
         At times, a heart as not by nature hard,
         But once perceived, his spirit seemed to chide
         Such weakness as unworthy of its pride,
         And steeled itself, as scorning to redeem
         One doubt from others' half withheld esteem;
         In self-inflicted penance of a breast
310   Which tenderness might once have wrung from rest;
         In vigilance of grief that would compel
         The soul to hate for having loved too well.

XVIII

         There was in him a vital scorn of all:
         As if the worst had fallen which could befall,
         He stood a stranger in this breathing world,
         An erring spirit from another hurled;
         A thing of dark imaginings, that shaped
         By choice the perils he by chance escaped;
         But 'scaped in vain, for in their memory yet

To . . . muse See Coleridge's "Song of the
Pixies" (1796).
The bard . . . ass See Coleridge's unfortunate
poem "To a Young Ass" (1794).
Lara Though this Gothic romance is not of high
poetic interest, the portrait of Lara in these
sections is a remarkable epitome of the High
Romantic hero and a splendid idealized self-
portrait of Byron. The flavor of Milton's Satan
can be tasted throughout.

320 His mind would half exult and half regret.
With more capacity for love than earth
Bestows on most of mortal mould and birth,
His early dreams of good outstripped the truth,
And troubled manhood followed baffled youth;
With thought of years in phantom chase misspent,
And wasted powers for better purpose lent;
And fiery passions that had poured their wrath
In hurried desolation o'er his path,
And left the better feelings all at strife
330 In wild reflection o'er his stormy life;
But haughty still and loth himself to blame,
He called on Nature's self to share the shame,
And charged all faults upon the fleshly form
She gave to clog the soul, and feast the worm;
Till he at last confounded good and ill,
And half mistook for fate the acts of will.
Too high for common selfishness, he could
At times resign his own for others' good,
But not in pity, not because he ought,
340 But in some strange perversity of thought,
That swayed him onward with a secret pride
To do what few or none would do beside;
And this same impulse would, in tempting time,
Mislead his spirit equally to crime;
So much he soared beyond, or sunk beneath,
The men with whom he felt condemned to breathe,
And longed by good or ill to separate
Himself from all who shared his mortal state.
His mind abhorring this had fixed her throne
350 Far from the world, in regions of her own:
Thus coldly passing all that passed below,
His blood in temperate seeming now would flow:
Ah! happier if it ne'er with guilt had glowed,
But ever in that icy smoothness flowed!
'Tis true, with other men their path he walked,
And like the rest in seeming did and talked,
Nor outraged Reason's rules by flaw nor start,
His madness was not of the head, but heart;
And rarely wandered in his speech, or drew
360 His thoughts so forth as to offend the view.

XIX

With all that chilling mystery of mien,
And seeming gladness to remain unseen,
He had (if 'twere not Nature's boon) an art
Of fixing memory on another's heart:
It was not love perchance, nor hate, nor aught

That words can image to express the thought;
But they who saw him did not see in vain,
And once beheld, would ask of him again:
And those to whom he spake remembered well,
370 And on the words, however light, would dwell:
None knew, nor how, nor why, but he entwined
Himself perforce around the hearer's mind;
There he was stamped, in liking, or in hate,
If greeted once; however brief the date
That friendship, pity, or aversion knew,
Still there within the inmost thought he grew.
You could not penetrate his soul, but found,
Despite your wonder, to your own he wound;
His presence haunted still; and from the breast
380 He forced an all unwilling interest:
Vain was the struggle in that mental net,
His spirit seemed to dare you to forget!
1814   1814

Stanzas for Music°

There be none of Beauty's daughters
    With a magic like thee;
And like music on the waters
    Is thy sweet voice to me:
When, as if its sound were causing
The charmed ocean's pausing,
The waves lie still and gleaming,
And the lulled winds seem dreaming.

And the midnight moon is weaving
10   Her bright chain o'er the deep;
Whose breast is gently heaving,
    As an infant's asleep:
So the spirit bows before thee,
To listen and adore thee;
With a full but soft emotion,
Like the swell of Summer's ocean.
1816   1816

Stanzas for Music This rather Shelleyan lyric
traditionally was believed to refer to Claire
Clairmont, but almost certainly refers to John
Edleston, a choirboy who moved the noble lord
rather more than any of "Beauty's daughters."

Childe Harold's Pilgrimage, A Romaunt°

From *Canto the Third*

I

Is thy face like thy mother's, my fair child!
ADA! sole daughter of my house and heart?
When last I saw thy young blue eyes they smiled,
And then we parted,—not as now we part,
But with a hope.°—
                Awaking with a start,
The waters heave around me; and on high
The winds lift up their voices: I depart,
Whither I know not; but the hour's gone by,
When Albion's lessening shores could grieve or glad mine eye.

II

10   Once more upon the waters! yet once more!°
And the waves bound beneath me as a steed
That knows his rider. Welcome to their roar!
Swift be their guidance, wheresoe'er it lead!
Though the strained mast should quiver as a reed,
And the rent canvass fluttering strew the gale,
Still must I on; for I am as a weed,
Flung from the rock on Ocean's foam, to sail
Where'er the surge may sweep, the tempest's breath prevail.

III

In my youth's summer I did sing of One,°
20   The wandering outlaw of his own dark mind;
Again I seize the theme, then but begun,
And bear it with me, as the rushing wind
Bears the cloud onwards: in that Tale I find
The furrows of long thought, and dried-up tears,
Which, ebbing, leave a sterile track behind,
O'er which all heavily the journeying years
Plod the last sands of life,—where not a flower appears.

IV

Since my young days of passion—joy, or pain—
Perchance my heart and harp have lost a string,
30   And both may jar: it may be that in vain
 .   I would essay as I have sung to sing.
Yet, though a dreary strain, to this I cling,

Romaunt romance
When . . . hope Byron had last seen his
daughter, Augusta Ada, when she was just a
month old, in January 1816, when Lady Byron
left him. He now acknowledges that he will

never see the child again (and he did not).
Once . . . more! Byron echoes Henry V's
speech to his soldiers in Shakespeare's *Henry* V
III.i.19.
One Childe Harold, or Byron at twenty-one

So that it wean me from the weary dream
Of selfish grief or gladness—so it fling
Forgetfulness around me—it shall seem
To me, though to none else, a not ungrateful theme.

V

He, who grown aged in this world of woe,
In deeds, not years, piercing the depths of life,
So that no wonder waits him; nor below
40   Can love, or sorrow, fame, ambition, strife,
Cut to his heart again with the keen knife
Of silent, sharp endurance: he can tell
Why thought seeks refuge in lone caves, yet rife
With airy images, and shapes which dwell
Still unimpaired, though old, in the soul's haunted cell.

VI

'Tis to create, and in creating live
A being more intense, that we endow
With form our fancy, gaining as we give
The life we image, even as I do now.
50   What am I? Nothing: but not so art thou,
Soul of my thought! with whom I traverse earth,
Invisible but gazing, as I glow
Mixed with thy spirit, blended with thy birth,
And feeling still with thee in my crushed feelings' dearth.

VII

Yet must I think less wildly:—I *have* thought
Too long and darkly, till my brain became,
In its own eddy boiling and o'erwrought,
A whirling gulf of phantasy and flame:
And thus, untaught in youth my heart to tame,
60   My springs of life were poisoned. 'Tis too late!
Yet am I changed; though still enough the same
In strength to bear what time can not abate,
And feed on bitter fruits without accusing Fate.

VIII

Something too much of this:°—but now 'tis past,
And the spell closes with its silent seal.°
Long absent HAROLD re-appears at last;
He of the breast which fain no more would feel,
Wrung with the wounds which kill not but ne'er heal;
Yet Time, who changes all, had altered him
70   In soul and aspect as in age: years steal

Something . . . this See *Hamlet* III.ii.69.   **silent seal** seal enforcing silence

Fire from the mind as vigour from the limb,
And life's enchanted cup but sparkles near the brim.

IX

His had been quaffed too quickly, and he found
The dregs were wormwood; but he filled again,
And from a purer fount, on holier ground,°
And deemed its spring perpetual; but in vain!
Still round him clung invisibly a chain
Which galled for ever, fettering though unseen,
And heavy though it clanked not; worn with pain,
80   Which pined although it spoke not, and grew keen,
Entering with every step he took through many a scene.

X

Secure in guarded coldness, he had mixed
Again in fancied safety with his kind,
And deemed his spirit now so firmly fixed
And sheathed with an invulnerable mind,
That, if no joy, no sorrow lurked behind;
And he, as one, might 'midst the many stand
Unheeded, searching through the crowd to find
Fit speculation—such as in strange land
90   He found in wonder-works of God and Nature's hand.

XI

But who can view the ripened rose, nor seek
To wear it? who can curiously behold
The smoothness and the sheen of beauty's cheek,
Nor feel the heart can never all grow old?
Who can contemplate Fame through clouds unfold
The star which rises o'er her steep, nor climb?
Harold, once more within the vortex, rolled
On with the giddy circle, chasing Time,
Yet with a nobler aim than in his youth's fond° prime.

XII

100   But soon he knew himself the most unfit
Of men to herd with Man, with whom he held
Little in common; untaught to submit
His thoughts to others, though his soul was quelled
In youth by his own thoughts; still uncompelled,
He would not yield dominion of his mind
To spirits against whom his own rebelled;
Proud though in desolation; which could find
A life within itself, to breathe without mankind.

holier ground Greece, where Byron was to die   **fond** foolish
his heroic death

XIII

Where rose the mountains, there to him were friends;
110   Where rolled the ocean, thereon was his home;
Where a blue sky, and glowing clime, extends,
He had the passion and the power to roam;
The desert, forest, cavern, breaker's foam,
Were unto him companionship; they spake
A mutual language, clearer than the tome
Of his land's tongue, which he would oft forsake
For Nature's pages glassed° by sunbeams on the lake.

XIV

Like the Chaldean,° he could watch the stars,
Till he'had peopled them with beings bright
120   As their own beams; and earth, and earth-born jars,
And human frailties, were forgotten quite:
Could he have kept his spirit to that flight
He had been happy; but this clay will sink
Its spark immortal, envying it the light
To which it mounts, as if to break the link
That keeps us from yon heaven which woos us to its brink.

XV

But in Man's dwellings he became a thing
Restless and worn, and stern and wearisome,
Drooped as a wild-born falcon with clipt wing,
130   To whom the boundless air alone were home:
Then came his fit° again, which to o'ercome,
As eagerly the barred-up bird will beat
His breast and beak against his wiry dome
Till the blood tinge his plumage, so the heat
Of his impeded soul would through his bosom eat.

XVI

Self-exiled Harold wanders forth again,
With nought of hope left, but with less of gloom;
The very knowledge that he lived in vain,
That all was over on this side the tomb,
140   Had made Despair a smilingness assume,
Which, though 'twere wild,—as on the plundered wreck
When mariners would madly meet their doom
With draughts intemperate on the sinking deck,—
Did yet inspire a cheer which he forbore to check.

---

glassed either made like glass or made reflected
Chaldean Babylonian; Babylon was famous for

its astrologers; see Yeats's "Two Songs from a
Play."
Then . . . fit See *Macbeth* III.iv.21.

XVII

Stop!°—for thy tread is on an Empire's dust!
An Earthquake's spoil is sepulchred below!
Is the spot marked with no colossal bust,
Nor column trophied for triumphal show?
None; but the moral's truth tells simpler so,
150 As the ground was before, thus let it be;—
How that red rain hath made the harvest grow!
And is this all the world has gained by thee,
Thou first and last of fields, king-making° Victory?

XVIII

And Harold stands upon this place of skulls,
The grave of France, the deadly Waterloo!
How in an hour the power which gave annuls
Its gifts, transferring fame as fleeting too!
In 'pride of place'° here last the eagle flew,
Then tore with bloody talon the rent plain,
160 Pierced by the shaft of banded nations through;
Ambition's life and labours all were vain;
He wears the shattered links of the world's broken chain.°

XIX

Fit retribution! Gaul° may champ the bit
And foam in fetters;—but is Earth more free?
Did nations combat to make *One* submit;
Or league to teach all kings true sovereignty?
What! shall reviving Thraldom again be
The patched-up idol of enlightened days?°
Shall we, who struck the Lion° down, shall we
170 Pay the Wolf° homage? proffering lowly gaze
And servile knees to thrones? No; *prove*° before ye praise!

XX

If not, o'er one fallen despot boast no more!
In vain fair cheeks were furrowed with hot tears
For Europe's flowers long rooted up before
The trampler of her vineyards; in vain years
Of death, depopulation, bondage, fears,
Have all been borne, and broken by the accord
Of roused-up millions: all that most endears

Stop because we are on the field of Waterloo,
only a year after the battle
king-making making Louis XVIII the King of
France again
'pride of place' highest point of flight, the eagle
being Napoleon, but also see *Macbeth* II.iv.12
He . . . chain at St. Helena, where he was
kept until he died

Gaul Roman name for France
enlightened days a reference to the 18th
century, before the Revolution
Lion Napoleon
Wolf possibly Metternich, or Wellington
prove have it proved to you

Glory, is when the myrtle wreathes a sword
180   Such as Harmodius° drew on Athens' tyrant lord.

XXI

There was a sound of revelry by night,°
And Belgium's Capital had gathered then
Her Beauty and her Chivalry, and bright
The lamps shone o'er fair women and brave men;
A thousand hearts beat happily; and when
Music arose with its voluptuous swell,
Soft eyes looked love to eyes which spake again,
And all went merry as a marriage-bell;—
But hush! hark! a deep sound strikes like a rising knell!

XXII

190   Did ye not hear it?—No; 'twas but the wind,
Or the car rattling o'er the stony street;
On with the dance! let joy be unconfined;
No sleep till morn, when Youth and Pleasure meet
To chase the glowing Hours with flying feet—
But hark!—that heavy sound breaks in once more,
As if the clouds its echo would repeat;
And nearer, clearer, deadlier than before!
Arm! Arm! it is—it is—the cannon's opening roar!

XXIII

Within a windowed niche of that high hall
200   Sate Brunswick's fated chieftain;° he did hear
That sound the first amidst the festival,
And caught its tone with Death's prophetic ear;
And when they smiled because he deemed it near,
His heart more truly knew that peal too well
Which stretched his father on a bloody bier,
And roused the vengeance blood alone could quell:
He rushed into the field, and, foremost fighting, fell.

XXIV

Ah! then and there was hurrying to and fro,
And gathering tears, and tremblings of distress,
210   And cheeks all pale, which but an hour ago
Blushed at the praise of their own loveliness;
And there were sudden partings, such as press
The life from out young hearts, and choking sighs
Which ne'er might be repeated; who could guess

Harmodius who killed the tyrant Hipparchus,
with a dagger hidden in a myrtle branch
There . . . night at the ball given in Brussels by the Duchess of Richmond on the eve of
the battle

chieftain Duke of Brunswick, killed the day
after the ball; his father had died in battle in
1806

If ever more should meet those mutual eyes,
Since upon night so sweet such awful morn could rise!

XXV

And there was mounting in hot haste: the steed,
The mustering squadron, and the clattering car,
When pouring forward with impetuous speed,
220   And swiftly forming in the ranks of war;
And the deep thunder peal on peal afar;
And near, the beat of the alarming drum
Roused up the soldier ere the morning star;
While thronged the citizens with terror dumb,
Or whispering, with white lips—'The foe! They come! they come!'

XXVI

And wild and high the 'Cameron's gathering'° rose!
The war-note of Lochiel,° which Albyn's° hills
Have heard, and heard, too, have her Saxon° foes:—
How in the noon of night that pibroch° thrills,
230   Savage and shrill! But with the breath which fills
Their mountain-pipe, so fill the mountaineers
With the fierce native daring which instils
The stirring memory of a thousand years,
And Evan's, Donald's° fame rings in each clansman's ears!

XXVII

And Ardennes° waves above them her green leaves,
Dewy with nature's tear-drops, as they pass,
Grieving, if aught inanimate e'er grieves,
Over the unreturning brave,—alas!
Ere evening to be trodden like the grass
240   Which now beneath them, but above shall grow
In its next verdure, when this fiery mass
Of living valour, rolling on the foe
And burning with high hope, shall moulder cold and low.

XXVIII

Last noon beheld them full of lusty life,
Last eve in Beauty's circle proudly gay,
The midnight brought the signal-sound of strife,
The morn the marshalling in arms,—the day
Battle's magnificently-stern array!

'Cameron's gathering' war song of the Highland
clan, the Cameronians
Lochiel title of Cameronian chief
Albyn's Gaelic for Scotland
Saxon English
pibroch battle-call of the bagpipes
Evan's, Donald's Sir Evan Cameron, who fought
against Cromwell, and later for James II; Don-

ald Cameron, his descendant, fought for the
Young Pretender, and was wounded at Culloden,
the last stand of the Highlanders as an independent fighting force
Ardennes forest area not actually the site of
this battle; Byron wanted it for its Shakespearean associations (see *As You Like It*)

The thunder-clouds close o'er it, which when rent
250   The earth is covered thick with other clay,
Which her own clay shall cover, heaped and pent,
Rider and horse,—friend, foe,—in one red burial blent!

XLI

If, like a tower upon a headlong rock,
Thou° hadst been made to stand or fall alone,
Such scorn of man had helped to brave the shock;
But men's thoughts were the steps which paved thy throne,
Their admiration thy best weapon shone;
The part of Philip's son° was thine, not then
(Unless aside thy purple had been thrown)
Like stern Diogenes° to mock at men;
For sceptred cynics earth were far too wide a den.

XLII

370   But quiet to quick bosoms is a hell,
And *there* hath been thy bane; there is a fire
And motion of the soul which will not dwell
In its own narrow being, but aspire
Beyond the fitting medium of desire;
And, but once kindled, quenchless evermore,
Preys upon high adventure, nor can tire
Of aught but rest; a fever at the core,
Fatal to him who bears, to all who ever bore.

XLIII

This makes the madmen who have made men mad
380   By their contagion; Conquerors and Kings,
Founders of sects and systems, to whom add
Sophists, Bards, Statesmen, all unquiet things
Which stir too strongly the soul's secret springs,
And are themselves the fools to those they fool;
Envied, yet how unenviable! what stings
Are theirs! One breast laid open were a school
Which would unteach mankind the lust to shine or rule.

XLIV

Their breath is agitation, and their life
A storm whereon they ride, to sink at last;
390   And yet so nursed and bigoted to strife,
That should their days, surviving perils past,
Melt to calm twilight, they feel overcast
With sorrow and supineness, and so die;

Thou Napoleon
Philip's son Alexander the Great

Diogenes Greek Cynic philosopher of Alexander's time

Even as a flame unfed which runs to waste
With its own flickering, or a sword laid by,
Which eats into itself and rusts ingloriously.

XLV

He who ascends to mountain-tops, shall find
The loftiest peaks most wrapt in clouds and snow;
He who surpasses or subdues mankind,
400   Must look down on the hate of those below.
Though high *above* the sun of glory glow,
And far *beneath* the earth and ocean spread,
Round him are icy rocks, and loudly blow
Contending tempests on his naked head,
And thus reward the toils which to those summits led.

. . .

LXXII

680   I live not in myself, but I become
Portion of that around me; and to me
High mountains are a feeling,° but the hum
Of human cities torture: I can see
Nothing to loathe in nature, save to be
A link reluctant in a fleshly chain,
Classed among creatures, when the soul can flee,
And with the sky, the peak, the heaving plain
Of ocean, or the stars, mingle, and not in vain.

LXXIII

And thus I am absorbed, and this is life:
690   I look upon the peopled desert past,
As on a place of agony and strife,
Where, for some sin, to sorrow I was cast,
To act and suffer, but remount at last
With a fresh pinion; which I feel to spring,
Though young, yet waxing vigorous, as the blast
Which it would cope with, on delighted wing,
Spurning the clay-cold bonds which round our being cling.

LXXIV

And when, at length, the mind shall be all free
From what it hates in this degraded form,
700   Reft of its carnal life, save what shall be
Existent happier in the fly and worm,—
When elements to elements conform,
And dust is as it should be, shall I not

I live . . . feeling The Wordsworthian influence, through Shelley, is palpable here; Wordsworth was not pleased.

Feel all I see, less dazzling, but more warm?
The bodiless thought? the Spirit of each spot?
Of which, even now, I share at times the immortal lot?

LXXV

Are not the mountains, waves, and skies, a part
Of me and of my soul, as I of them?
Is not the love of these deep in my heart
710   With a pure passion? should I not contemn
All objects, if compared with these? and stem
A tide of suffering, rather than forego
Such feelings for the hard and worldly phlegm
Of those whose eyes are only turned below,
Gazing upon the ground, with thoughts which dare not glow?

1816   1816

. . .

From *Canto the Fourth*

CXXI

Oh Love! no habitant of earth thou art—
An unseen seraph, we believe in thee,
A faith whose martyrs are the broken heart,
But never yet hath seen, nor e'er shall see
The naked eye, thy form, as it should be;
The mind hath made thee, as it peopled heaven,
Even with its own desiring phantasy,
And to a thought such shape and image given,
As haunts the unquenched soul—parched—wearied—wrung—and riven.

CXXII

1090 Of its own beauty is the mind diseased,
And fevers into false creation:—where,
Where are the forms the sculptor's soul hath seized?—
In him alone. Can Nature show so fair?
Where are the charms and virtues which we dare
Conceive in boyhood and pursue as men,
The unreached Paradise of our despair,
Which o'er-informs the pencil and the pen,
And overpowers the page where it would bloom again?

CXXIII

Who loves, raves—'tis youth's frenzy; but the cure
1100 Is bitterer still; as charm by charm unwinds
Which robed our idols, and we see too sure
Nor worth nor beauty dwells from out the mind's
Ideal shape of such; yet still it binds

The fatal spell, and still it draws us on,
Reaping the whirlwind from the oft-sown winds;°
The stubborn heart, its alchemy begun,
Seems ever near the prize,—wealthiest when most undone.

CXXIV

We wither from our youth, we gasp away—
Sick—sick; unfound the boon—unslaked the thirst,
1110   Though to the last, in verge of our decay,
Some phantom lures, such as we sought at first—
But all too late,—so are we doubly curst.
Love, fame, ambition, avarice—'tis the same,
Each idle—and all ill—and none the worst—
For all are meteors with a different name,
And Death the sable smoke where vanishes the flame.

CXXV

Few—none—find what they love or could have loved,
Though accident, blind contact, and the strong
Necessity of loving, have removed
1120   Antipathies—but to recur, ere long,
Envenomed with irrevocable wrong;
And Circumstance, that unspiritual god
And miscreator, makes and helps along
Our coming evils with a crutch-like rod,
Whose touch turns Hope to dust,—the dust we all have trod.

CXXVI

Our life is a false nature—'tis not in
The harmony of things,—this hard decree,
This uneradicable taint of sin,
This boundless upas, this all-blasting tree°
1130   Whose root is earth, whose leaves and branches be
The skies which rain their plagues on men like dew—
Disease, death, bondage—all the woes we see—
And worse, the woes we see not—which throb through
The immedicable soul, with heart-aches ever new.

.   .   .

CXXXVII

But I have lived, and have not lived in vain:
My mind may lose its force, my blood its fire,
And my frame perish even in conquering pain;
But there is that within me which shall tire
Torture and Time, and breathe when I expire;
1230   Something unearthly which they deem not of,

Reaping . . . winds See Hosea 8:7.
This boundless . . . tree The upas-tree, capable of devastating all vegetation near it, was a
pure product of Romantic visionary botany.

Like the remembered tone of a mute lyre,
  Shall on their softened spirits sink, and move
In hearts all rocky now the late remorse of love.

    CXXXVIII

  The seal is set.—Now welcome, thou dread power!
  Nameless, yet thus omnipotent, which here°
  Walkest in the shadow of the midnight hour
  With a deep awe, yet all distinct from fear;
  Thy haunts are ever where the dead walls rear
  Their ivy mantles, and the solemn scene
1240 Derives from thee a sense so deep and clear
  That we become a part of what has been,
And grow unto the spot, all-seeing but unseen.

            .   .   .

    CLXIII

  And if it be Prometheus stole from Heaven
1460 The fire which we endure, it was repaid
  By him to whom the energy was given
  Which this poetic marble hath arrayed
  With an eternal glory—which, if made
  By human hands, is not of human thought;
  And Time himself hath hallowed it, nor laid
  One ringlet in the dust—nor hath it caught
A tinge of years, but breathes the flame with which 'twas wrought.

    CLXIV

  But where is he, the Pilgrim of my song,
  The being who upheld it through the past?
1470 Methinks he cometh late and tarries long.
  He is no more—these breathings are his last;
  His wanderings done, his visions ebbing fast,
  And he himself as nothing:—if he was
  Aught but a phantasy, and could be classed
  With forms which live and suffer—let that pass—
His shadow fades away into Destruction's mass,

            .   .   .

    CLXXVII

  Oh! that the Desert were my dwelling-place,
  With one fair Spirit° for my minister,
  That I might all forget the human race,
  And, hating no one, love but only her!
  Ye Elements!—in whose ennobling stir
1590 I feel myself exalted—Can ye not

here Rome   Spirit his sister Augusta

Accord me such a being? Do I err
In deeming such inhabit many a spot?
Though with them to converse can rarely be our lot.

CLXXVIII

There is a pleasure in the pathless woods,
There is a rapture on the lonely shore,
There is society where none intrudes,
By the deep Sea, and music in its roar:
I love not Man the less, but Nature more,
From these our interviews, in which I steal
1600 From all I may be, or have been before,
To mingle with the Universe, and feel
What I can ne'er express, yet can not all conceal.

CLXXIX

Roll on, thou deep and dark blue Ocean—roll!
Ten thousand fleets sweep over thee in vain;
Man marks the earth with ruin—his control
Stops with the shore;—upon the watery plain
The wrecks are all thy deed, nor doth remain
A shadow of man's ravage, save his own,
When, for a moment, like a drop of rain,
1610 He sinks into thy depths with bubbling groan,
Without a grave, unknelled, uncoffined, and unknown.

CLXXX

His steps are not upon thy paths,—thy fields
Are not a spoil for him,—thou dost arise
And shake him from thee; the vile strength he wields
For earth's destruction thou dost all despise,
Spurning him from thy bosom to the skies,
And sendest him, shivering in thy playful spray
And howling, to his Gods, where haply lies
His petty hope in some near port or bay,
1620 And dashest him again to earth:—there let him lay.°

CLXXXI

The armaments which thunderstrike the walls
Of rock-built cities, bidding nations quake
And monarchs tremble in their capitals,
The oak leviathans,° whose huge ribs make
Their clay creator the vain title take
Of lord of thee, and arbiter of war,—
These are thy toys, and, as the snowy flake,

---

lay lie. This notorious solecism, quite deliberate on Byron's part, was meant to remind his read-ers that, after all, he was a nobleman who could be aristocratically slapdash.
oak leviathans warships

GEORGE GORDON, LORD BYRON

They melt into thy yeast of waves, which mar
Alike the Armada's pride or spoils of Trafalgàr.°

CLXXXII

1630
Thy shores are empires, changed in all save thee—
Assyria, Greece, Rome, Carthage, what are they?
Thy waters washed them power while they were free,
And many a tyrant since; their shores obey
The stranger, slave, or savage; their decay
Has dried up realms to deserts:—not so thou,
Unchangeable save to thy wild·waves' play;
Time writes no wrinkle on thine azure brow—
Such as creation's dawn beheld, thou rollest now.

CLXXXIII

1640
Thou glorious mirror, where the Almighty's form
Glasses° itself in tempests; in all time,
Calm or convulsed—in breeze, or gale, or storm,
Icing the pole, or in the torrid clime
Dark-heaving;—boundless, endless, and sublime—
The image of Eternity—the throne
Of the Invisible; even from out thy slime
The monsters of the deep are made; each zone
Obeys thee; thou goest forth, dread, fathomless, alone.

CLXXXIV

1650
And I have loved thee, Ocean! and my joy
Of youthful sports was on thy breast to be
Borne, like thy bubbles, onward: from a boy
I wantoned with thy breakers—they to me
Were a delight; and if the freshening sea
Made them a terror—'twas a pleasing fear,
For I was as it were a child of thee,
And trusted to thy billows far and near,
And laid my hand upon thy mane—as I do here.

CLXXXV

1660
My task is done—my song hath ceased—my theme
Has died into an echo; it is fit
The spell should break of this protracted dream.
The torch shall be extinguished which hath lit
My midnight lamp—and what is writ, is writ,—
Would it were worthier! but I am not now
That which I have been—and my visions flit

Trafalgàr Half or more of the Spanish Armada
was lost to bad weather, in 1588; many of the
French ships at the battle of Trafalgar, in 1805,
were similarly lost.
Glasses reflects

Less palpably before me—and the glow
Which in my spirit dwelt is fluttering, faint, and low.

CLXXXVI

Farewell! a word that must be, and hath been—
A sound which makes us linger;—yet—farewell!
Ye! who have traced the Pilgrim to the scene
Which is his last, if in your memories dwell
1670 A thought which once was his, if on ye swell
A single recollection, not in vain
He wore his sandal-shoon and scallop-shell;°
Farewell! with *him* alone may rest the pain,
If such there were—with *you*, the moral of his strain!
1817   1818

Prometheus°

Titan! to whose immortal eyes
    The sufferings of mortality,
    Seen in their sad reality,
Were not as things that gods despise;
What was thy pity's recompense?
A silent suffering, and intense;
The rock, the vulture, and the chain,
All that the proud can feel of pain,
The agony they do not show,
10 The suffocating sense of woe,
    Which speaks but in its loneliness,
And then is jealous lest the sky
Should have a listener, nor will sigh
    Until its voice is echoless.

Titan! to thee the strife was given
    Between the suffering and the will,
    Which torture where they cannot kill;
And the inexorable Heaven,
And the deaf tyranny of Fate,
20 The ruling principle of Hate,
Which for its pleasure doth create
The things it may annihilate,
Refused thee even the boon to die:
The wretched gift eternity
Was thine—and thou hast borne it well.
All that the Thunderer wrung from thee

sandal-shoon and scallop-shell pilgrim's emblems, the sandals for land-journeying, and the scallop shell (usually worn on the hat) for sea-voyaging

Prometheus written in Shelley's company, and partly under his influence, but with a kind of Calvinistic tempering very far from Shelley's spirit

Was but the menace which flung back
On him the torments of thy rack;
The fate thou didst so well foresee,
30 But would not to appease him tell;
And in thy Silence was his Sentence,
And in his Soul a vain repentance,
And evil dread so ill dissembled,
That in his hand the lightnings trembled.

Thy Godlike crime was to be kind,
    To render with thy precepts less
    The sum of human wretchedness,
And strengthen Man with his own mind;
But baffled as thou wert from high,
40 Still in thy patient energy,
In the endurance, and repulse
    Of thine impenetrable Spirit,
Which Earth and Heaven could not convulse,
    A mighty lesson we inherit:
Thou art a symbol and a sign
    To Mortals of their fate and force;
Like thee, Man is in part divine,
    A troubled stream from a pure source;
And Man in portions can foresee
50 His own funereal destiny;
His wretchedness, and his resistance,
And his sad unallied existence:
To which his Spirit may oppose
Itself—and equal to all woes,
    And a firm will, and a deep sense,
Which even in torture can descry
    Its own concentered recompense,
Triumphant where it dares defy,
And making Death a Victory.°
1816   1816

Darkness°

I had a dream, which was not all a dream.
The bright sun was extinguished, and the stars
Did wander darkling in the eternal space,
Rayless, and pathless, and the icy earth
Swung blind and blackening in the moonless air;
Morn came and went—and came, and brought no day,

And making . . . Victory See I Corinthians
15:55, and also the stanzas chanted by Demo-
gorgon that end Shelley's *Prometheus Unbound.*
Darkness This is Byron's version of a prevalent
Romantic nightmare, "The Last Man" theme,
upon which Thomas Campbell and Thomas
Hood wrote poems and Mary Shelley a novel.
"Darkness" profoundly influenced Poe, and
should be compared with his "The City in the
Sea."

And men forgot their passions in the dread
Of this their desolation; and all hearts
Were chilled into a selfish prayer for light:
10 And they did live by watchfires—and the thrones,
The palaces of crowned kings—the huts,
The habitations of all things which dwell,
Were burnt for beacons; cities were consumed,
And men were gathered round their blazing homes
To look once more into each other's face;
Happy were those who dwelt within the eye
Of the volcanos, and their mountain-torch:
A fearful hope was all the world contained;
Forests were set on fire—but hour by hour
20 They fell and faded—and the crackling trunks
Extinguished with a crash—and all was black.
The brows of men by the despairing light
Wore an unearthly aspect, as by fits
The flashes fell upon them; some lay down
And hid their eyes and wept; and some did rest
Their chins upon their clenched hands, and smiled;
And others hurried to and fro, and fed
Their funeral piles with fuel, and looked up
With mad disquietude on the dull sky,
30 The pall of a past world; and then again
With curses cast them down upon the dust,
And gnashed their teeth and howled: the wild birds shrieked
And, terrified, did flutter on the ground,
And flap their useless wings; the wildest brutes
Came tame and tremulous; and vipers crawled
And twined themselves among the multitude,
Hissing, but stingless—they were slain for food.
And War, which for a moment was no more,
Did glut himself again:—a meal was bought
40 With blood, and each sate sullenly apart
Gorging himself in gloom: no love was left;
All earth was but one thought—and that was death
Immediate and inglorious; and the pang
Of famine fed upon all entrails—men
Died, and their bones were tombless as their flesh;
The meagre by the meagre were devoured,
Even dogs assailed their masters, all save one,
And he was faithful to a corse, and kept
The birds and beasts and famished men at bay,
50 Till hunger clung° them, or the dropping dead
Lured their lank jaws; himself sought out no food,
But with a piteous and perpetual moan,
And a quick desolate cry, licking the hand

clung in its original sense of "stuck fast to"

Which answered not with a caress—he died.
The crowd was famished by degrees; but two
Of an enormous city did survive,
And they were enemies: they met beside
The dying embers of an altar-place
Where had been heaped a mass of holy things
60 For an unholy usage; they raked up,
And shivering scraped with their cold skeleton hands
The feeble ashes, and their feeble breath
Blew for a little life, and made a flame
Which was a mockery; then they lifted up
Their eyes as it grew lighter, and beheld
Each other's aspects—saw, and shrieked and died—
Even of their mutual hideousness they died,
Unknowing who he was upon whose brow
Famine had written Fiend. The world was void,
70 The populous and the powerful was a lump,
Seasonless, herbless, treeless, manless, lifeless,
A lump of death—a chaos of hard clay.
The rivers, lakes, and ocean all stood still,
And nothing stirred within their silent depths;
Ships sailorless lay rotting on the sea,
And their masts fell down piecemeal: as they dropped
They slept on the abyss without a surge—
The waves were dead; the tides were in their grave,
The moon, their mistress, had expired before;
80 The winds were withered in the stagnant air,
And the clouds perished; Darkness had no need
Of aid from them—She was the Universe.
1816   1816

From Manfred°

A Dramatic Poem

ACT III, SCENE IV

Interior of the Tower
[MANFRED *alone*]
The stars are forth, the moon above the tops
Of the snow-shining mountains.—Beautiful!
I linger yet with Nature, for the night

Manfred This is the closing scene of Byron's Promethean "dramatic poem," best characterized by Goethe as possessing "the gloomy heat of an unbounded and exuberant despair." Manfred, a Faustian magus, has emulated Byron himself, by the crime of deliberate, knowing incest with his sister, Astarte, who evidently killed herself in remorse. Weary of the human condition, but rejecting immortality and seeking only oblivion, Manfred invokes the preternatural powers, presided over by Arimanes, a kind of Gnostic Satan, or god of nature. He is granted a vision of Astarte, who tells him "tomorrow ends thy earthly ills." On the morrow, an abbot unsuccessfully attempts to reconcile Manfred with the church, but he courteously declines. This last scene, which repudiates the Faust story, as Manfred yields only to himself, then follows.

Hath been to me a more familiar face
Than that of man; and in her starry shade
Of dim and solitary loveliness,
I learned the language of another world.
I do remember me, that in my youth,
When I was wandering,—upon such a night
10 I stood within the Coliseum's wall,
Midst the chief relics of almighty Rome.
The trees which grew along the broken arches
Waved dark in the blue midnight, and the stars
Shone through the rents of ruin; from afar
The watch-dog bayed beyond the Tiber; and
More near from out the Caesars' palace came
The owl's long cry, and, interruptedly,
Of distant sentinels the fitful song
Begun and died upon the gentle wind.
20 Some cypresses beyond the time-worn breach
Appeared to skirt the horizon, yet they stood
Within a bowshot. Where the Caesars dwelt,
And dwell the tuneless birds of night, amidst
A grove which springs through levelled battlements
And twines its roots with the imperial hearths,
Ivy usurps the laurel's place of growth;—
But the gladiators' bloody Circus stands,
A noble wreck in ruinous perfection!
While Caesar's chambers, and the Augustan halls,
30 Grovel on earth in indistinct decay.—
And thou didst shine, thou rolling moon, upon
All this, and cast a wide and tender light,
Which softened down the hoar austerity
Of rugged desolation, and filled up,
As 'twere anew, the gaps of centuries;
Leaving that beautiful which still was so,
And making that which was not, till the place
Became religion, and the heart ran o'er
With silent worship of the great of old,—
40 The dead, but sceptred sovereigns, who still rule
Our spirits from their urns.—
                              'Twas such a night!
'Tis strange that I recall it at this time;
But I have found our thoughts take wildest flight
Even at the moment when they should array
Themselves in pensive order.
        [*Enter the* ABBOT]
    ABBOT   My good lord!
I crave a second grace for this approach;
But yet let not my humble zeal offend
By its abruptness—all it hath of ill
Recoils on me; its good in the effect

50   May light upon your head—could I say *heart*—
     Could I touch *that*, with words or prayers, I should
     Recall a noble spirit which hath wandered
     But is not yet all lost.
         MANFRED   Thou knowest me not;
     My days are numbered, and my deeds recorded:
     Retire, or 'twill be dangerous—Away!
         ABBOT   Thou dost not mean to menace me?
         MANFRED   Not I;
     I simply tell thee peril is at hand,
     And would preserve thee.
         ABBOT   What dost thou mean?
         MANFRED   Look there!
     What dost thou see?
         ABBOT   Nothing.
         MANFRED   Look there, I say,
60   And steadfastly;—now tell me what thou seest.
         ABBOT   That which should shake me—but I fear it not:
     I see a dusk and awful figure rise,
     Like an infernal god, from out the earth;
     His face wrapt in a mantle, and his form
     Robed as with angry clouds: he stands between
     Thyself and me—but I do fear him not.
         MANFRED   Thou hast no cause; he shall not harm thee, but
     His sight may shock thine old limbs into palsy.
     I say to thee—Retire!
         ABBOT   And I reply—
70   Never—till I have battled with this fiend:—
     What doth he here?
         MANFRED   Why—ay—what doth he here?—
     I did not send for him,—he is unbidden.
         ABBOT   Alas! lost mortal! what with guests like these
     Hast thou to do? I tremble for thy sake:
     Why doth he gaze on thee, and thou on him?
     Ah! he unveils his aspect: on his brow
     The thunder-scars are graven;° from his eye
     Glares forth the immortality of hell—
     Avaunt!—
         MANFRED   Pronounce—what is thy mission?
         SPIRIT   Come!
         ABBOT   What art thou, unknown being? answer!—
80   speak!
         SPIRIT   The genius of this mortal.—Come! 'tis time.
         MANFRED   I am prepared for all things, but deny
     The power which summons me. Who sent thee here?
         SPIRIT   Thou'lt know anon—Come! Come!

on his brow . . . graven See *Paradise Lost*
I.600 ff.

MANFRED   I have commanded
Things of an essence greater far than thine,
And striven with thy masters. Get thee hence!
    SPIRIT   Mortal! thine hour is come—Away! I say.
    MANFRED   I knew, and know my hour is come, but not
To render up my soul to such as thee:
90 Away! I'll die as I have lived—alone.
    SPIRIT   Then I must summon up my brethren.—Rise!
        [*Other Spirits rise up*]
    ABBOT   Avaunt! ye evil ones!—Avaunt! I say,—
Ye have no power where piety hath power,
And I do charge ye in the name—
    SPIRIT   Old man!
We know ourselves, our mission, and thine order;
Waste not thy holy words on idle uses,
It were in vain: this man is forfeited.
Once more I summon him—Away! away!
    MANFRED   I do defy ye,—though I feel my soul
100 Is ebbing from me, yet I do defy ye;
Nor will I hence, while I have earthly breath
To breathe my scorn upon ye—earthly strength
To wrestle, though with spirits; what ye take
Shall be ta'en limb by limb.
    SPIRIT   Reluctant mortal!
Is this the Magian who would so pervade
The world invisible, and make himself
Almost our equal?—Can it be that thou
Art thus in love with life? the very life
Which made thee wretched!
    MANFRED   Thou false fiend, thou liest!
110 My life is in its last hour,—*that* I know,
Nor would redeem a moment of that hour.
I do not combat against death, but thee
And thy surrounding angels; my past power
Was purchased by no compact with thy crew,
But by superior science—penance—daring—
And length of watching—strength of mind—and skill
In knowledge of our fathers—when the earth
Saw men and spirits walking side by side
And gave ye no supremacy: I stand
120 Upon my strength—I do defy—deny—
Spurn back, and scorn ye!—
    SPIRIT   But thy many crimes
Have made thee—
    MANFRED   What are they to such as thee?
Must crimes be punished but by other crimes,
And greater criminals?—Back to thy hell!
Thou hast no power upon me, *that* I feel;

Thou never shalt possess me, *that* I know:
What I have done is done; I bear within
A torture which could nothing gain from thine:
The mind which is immortal makes itself
130 Requital for its good or evil thoughts,
Is its own origin of ill and end,
And its own place and time°—its innate sense,
When stripp'd of this mortality, derives
No colour from the fleeting things without,
But is absorbed in sufferance or in joy,
Born from the knowledge of its own desert.
Thou didst not tempt me, and thou couldst not tempt me;
I have not been thy dupe nor am thy prey—
But was my own destroyer, and will be
140 My own hereafter.—Back, ye baffled fiends!
The hand of death is on me—but not yours!
     [*The Demons disappear*]
    ABBOT   Alas! how pale thou art—thy lips are white—
And thy breast heaves—and in thy gasping throat
The accents rattle. Give thy prayers to Heaven—
Pray—albeit but in thought,—but die not thus.
    MANFRED   'Tis over—my dull eyes can fix thee not;
But all things swim around me, and the earth
Heaves as it were beneath me. Fare thee well—
Give me thy hand.
    ABBOT   Cold—cold—even to the heart—
150 But yet one prayer—Alas! how fares it with thee?
    MANFRED   Old man! 'tis not so difficult to die.°
    [MANFRED *expires*]
    ABBOT   He's gone—his soul hath ta'en its earthless flight—
Whither? I dread to think—but he is gone.
1816–17   1817

'So We'll Go No More A-Roving'°

So we'll go no more a-roving
   So late into the night,
Though the heart be still as loving,
   And the moon be still as bright.

The mind . . . time See *Paradise Lost* I.254 ff.
Old . . . die After his publisher, Murray, omitted this line in the first edition, Byron wrote to him angrily: "You have destroyed the whole effect and moral of the poem."

'So We'll . . . A-Roving' part of a letter to Thomas Moore. Its motto might be, from the same letter: "At present I am on the invalid regimen myself."

For the sword outwears its sheath,°
   And the soul wears out the breast,
And the heart must pause to breathe,
   And Love itself have rest.

Though the night was made for loving,
10   And the day returns too soon,
Yet we'll go no more a-roving
   By the light of the moon.
   1817   1830

For . . . sheath the will to make love is stronger than potency, or as Byron also remarks in the letter: "Though I did not dissipate much upon the whole, yet I find 'the sword wearing out the scabbard,' though I have but just turned the corner of twenty-nine."

Don Juan

"This crammed, various creation renders the Romantic view of a world too large in all directions and too complex in its workings to be captured and arranged in any neat system of thought or formal pattern." This description by Alvin Kernan best characterizes the open universe of Byron's great satire, his only work that reflects both the immensity and paradoxes of his own character and personality.

In reading a series of excerpts from Don Juan, we need not feel that we are betraying the poem, which is frankly digressive, unfinished and unfinishable (it would have gone on as long as Byron did), and unified only by the identity of the narrator with the poet himself. Byron is not Don Juan, and indeed Don Juan is scarcely a person, but rather a traditional hero of the picaresque mode, who remains unaltered by experience (no matter how violent) and remarkably passive in most of his love affairs. He is eminently seducible, this being his principal point of resemblance to his creator.

The best comments on the poem, in its own day, after Shelley's (he considered it the great poem of the age, superior to the work of Wordsworth and Goethe), were by Hazlitt, and of course by Byron himself. Hazlitt accurately saw Byron's poetry as the record of "a mind preying upon itself." Despite the poem's infectious vitalism, it masks throughout a thoroughgoing transvaluation of values and perhaps, finally, a hopelessness as to the human condition which is precisely prophetic of much more recent literature. Yet the poem's grand defense is Byron's own: "Confess, confess— you dog," he says to us as readers even as he exclaimed in a letter, "it may be bawdy but is it not good English? It may be profligate but is it not *life*, is it not *the thing*?"

The style, first used by him in the slight but charming Beppo, comes from the comic poets of the Italian Renaissance, Pulci and Boiardo in particular. Byron had been preceded in this adaptation by a contemporary, John Hookham Frere, but far outdoes Frere. In a deeper sense, the poem stems from English tradition, rather than Italian. Its true precursors are Butler, Swift, and Sterne.

Don Juan°

Difficile est propriè communia dicere.
HORACE.°

Dost thou think, because thou art virtuous, there shall be no more cakes
and ale? Yes, by Saint Anne, and ginger shall be hot i' the mouth, too!
Shakespeare, Twelfth Night, or What You Will

Fragment
On the back of the Poet's MS. of Canto I

I would to heaven that I were so much clay,
  As I am blood, bone, marrow, passion, feeling—
Because at least the past were passed away—
  And for the future—(but I write this reeling,
Having got drunk exceedingly today,
  So that I seem to stand upon the ceiling)
I say—the future is a serious matter—
And so—for God's sake—hock and soda-water!°

Dedication°

I

Bob Southey! You're a poet—Poet-laureate,
  And representative of all the race,
Although 'tis true that you turned out a Tory at
  Last,—yours has lately been a common case,—
And now, my Epic Renegade! what are ye at?
  With all the Lakers,° in and out of place?
A nest of tuneful persons, to my eye
Like 'four and twenty Blackbirds in a pye;°

II

'Which pye being opened they began to sing'
  (This old song and new simile holds good),
'A dainty dish to set before the King,'
  Or Regent,° who admires such kind of food;—
And Coleridge, too, has lately taken wing,
  But like a hawk encumbered with his hood,—
Explaining metaphysics to the nation—
I wish he would explain his Explanation.°

10

Don Juan to be pronounced in the English, not
the Spanish, manner
Horace Byron's own translation: " 'Tis no slight
task to write on common things"
hock and soda-water Hock is Rhine wine; the
mixture was a hangover remedy.
Dedication Southey evidently was telling the
story that Byron and Shelley, Mary Godwin and
Claire Clairmont, were involved in a "League
of Incest" in their time together at Geneva;

Don Juan begins the *sparagmos* or tearing apart
of the egregious Southey, which is completed in
The Vision of Judgment.
Lakers the "school" of Wordsworth, Southey,
and Coleridge, all resident in the Lake District
pye Henry James Pye (1745–1813), absurd
Poet Laureate before Southey
Regent Prince Regent, and later George IV
I wish . . . Explanation a reference to the
Biographia Literaria (1817)

III

You, Bob! are rather insolent, you know,
  At being disappointed in your wish
To supersede all warblers here below,
20   And be the only Blackbird in the dish;
And then you overstrain yourself, or so,
  And tumble downward like the flying fish
Gasping on deck, because you soar too high, Bob,
And fall, for lack of moisture quite a-dry, Bob!°

IV

And Wordsworth, in a rather long *Excursion*
  (I think the quarto holds five hundred pages),
Has given a sample from the vasty version
  Of his new system to perplex the sages;
'Tis poetry—at least by his assertion,
30   And may appear so when the dog-star rages—
And he who understands it would be able
To add a story to the Tower of Babel.

V

You—Gentlemen! by dint of long seclusion
  From better company, have kept your own
At Keswick, and, through still continued fusion
  Of one another's minds, at last have grown
To deem as a most logical conclusion,
  That Poesy has wreaths for you alone:
There is a narrowness in such a notion,
40 Which makes me wish you'd change your lakes for ocean.

VI

I would not imitate the petty thought,
  Nor coin my self-love to so base a vice,
For all the glory your conversion brought,
  Since gold alone should not have been its price.
You have your salary; was't for that you wrought?
  And Wordsworth has his place in the Excise.°
You're shabby fellows—true—but poets still,
And duly seated on the immortal hill.

VII

Your bays may hide the baldness of your brows—
50   Perhaps some virtuous blushes;—let them go—

quite a-dry, Bob! The double meaning is that
Southey is both a fish, out of the water, gasping
on deck, and sexually unable to come.
And . . . Excise Byron's cruel note: "Wordsworth's place may be in the Customs—it is, I
think, in that or the Excise—besides another at

Lord Lonsdale's table, where this poetical charlatan and political parasite licks up the crumbs
with a hardened alacrity; the converted Jacobin
having long subsided into the clownish syco-
phant of the worse prejudices of the aristocracy."

To you I envy neither fruit nor boughs—
   And for the fame you would engross below,
The field is universal, and allows
   Scope to all such as feel the inherent glow:
Scott, Rogers, Campbell, Moore, and Crabbe, will try
'Gainst you the question with posterity.

VIII

For me, who, wandering with pedestrian Muses,
   Contend not with you on the wingèd steed,
I wish your fate may yield ye, when she chooses,
60   The fame you envy, and the skill you need;
And recollect a poet nothing loses
   In giving to his brethren their full meed
Of merit, and complaint of present days
Is not the certain path to future praise.

IX

He that reserves his laurels for posterity
   (Who does not often claim the bright reversion)
Has generally no great crop to spare it, he
   Being only injured by his own assertion;
And although here and there some glorious rarity
70   Arise like Titan from the sea's immersion,
The major part of such appellants go
To—God knows where—for no one else can know.

X

If, fallen in evil days on evil tongues,°
   Milton appealed to the Avenger, Time,
If Time, the Avenger, execrates his wrongs,
   And makes the word 'Miltonic' mean *'sublime,'*
He deigned not to belie his soul in songs,
   Nor turn his very talent to a crime;
He did not loathe the Sire to laud the Son,°
80 But closed the tyrant-hater he begun.

XI

Think'st thou, could he—the blind Old Man—arise,
   Like Samuel° from the grave, to freeze once more
The blood of monarchs with his prophecies,
   Or be alive again—again all hoar
With time and trials, and those helpless eyes,
   And heartless daughters—worn—and pale—and poor;

If . . . tongues *Paradise Lost* VII.25–26
He . . . the Son Having despised Charles I,
Milton was courageous enough to go on de-
spising Charles II, in defiance of the Restora-
tion.
Samuel I Samuel 27:13–14

Would *he* adore a sultan? *he* obey
The intellectual eunuch Castlereagh?°

XII

Cold-blooded, smooth-faced, placid miscreant!
90   Dabbling its sleek young hands in Erin's gore,°
And thus for wider carnage taught to pant,
    Transferred to gorge upon a sister shore,
The vulgarest tool that Tyranny could want,
    With just enough of talent, and no more,
To lengthen fetters by another fixed,
And offer poison long already mixed.

XIII

An orator of such set trash of phrase
    Ineffably—legitimately vile,
That even its grossest flatterers dare not praise,
100   Nor foes—all nations—condescend to smile,—
Not even a sprightly blunder's spark can blaze
    From that Ixion° grindstone's ceaseless toil,
That turns and turns to give the world a notion
Of endless torments and perpetual motion.

XIV

A bungler even in its disgusting trade,
    And botching, patching, leaving still behind
Something of which its masters are afraid,
    States to be curbed, and thoughts to be confined,
Conspiracy or Congress to be made—
110   Cobbling at manacles for all mankind—
A tinkering slave-maker, who mends old chains,
With God and man's abhorrence for its gains.

XV

If we may judge of matter by the mind,
    Emasculated to the marrow *It*
Hath but two objects, how to serve, and bind,
    Deeming the chain it wears even men may fit,
Eutropius° of its many masters,—blind
    To worth as freedom, wisdom as to wit,
Fearless—because *no* feeling dwells in ice,
120   Its very courage stagnates to a vice.

Castlereagh Viscount Castlereagh (1769–1822), Foreign Secretary in the right-wing government from 1812 to 1822, hated ferociously by Byron, Shelley, Hunt, and their friends
Erin's gore Castlereagh had repressed an Irish rebellion.

Ixion Ungrateful to Zeus, he was bound to an ever-turning wheel.
Eutropius a eunuch who gained power in the Byzantine empire; see Gibbon's *History of the Decline and Fall of the Roman Empire*, chap. 32.

XVI

Where shall I turn me not to *view* its bonds,
   For I will never *feel* them;—Italy!
Thy late reviving Roman soul desponds
   Beneath the lie this State-thing breathed o'er thee°—
Thy clanking chain, and Erin's yet green wounds,
   Have voices—tongues to cry aloud for me.
Europe has slaves, allies, kings, armies still,
And Southey lives to sing them very ill.

XVII

Meantime, Sir Laureate, I proceed to dedicate,
130   In honest simple verse, this song to you.
And, if in flattering strains I do not predicate,
   'Tis that I still retain my 'buff and blue';°
My politics as yet are all to educate:
   Apostasy's so fashionable, too,
To keep *one* creed's a task grown quite Herculean:
Is it not so, my Tory, Ultra-Julian?°
   VENICE, SEPTEMBER 16, 1818

From *Canto the First*

I

I want a hero: an uncommon want,
   When every year and month sends forth a new one,
Till, after cloying the gazettes with cant,
   The age discovers he is not the true one;
Of such as these I should not care to vaunt,
   I'll therefore take our ancient friend Don Juan—
We all have seen him, in the pantomime,°
Sent to the devil somewhat ere his time.

. . .

V

Brave men were living before Agamemnon
   And since, exceeding valorous and sage,
A good deal like him too, though quite the same none;
   But then they shone not on the poet's page,
And so have been forgotten:—I condemn none,
   But can't find any in the present age
Fit for my poem (that is, for my new one);
40   So, as I said, I'll take my friend Don Juan.

Thy late . . . thee Castlereagh was widely
hated in Italy for selling out the city of Genoa,
after first upholding it.
'buff and blue' Whig party colors, worn by
followers of Charles James Fox, Byron among
them

Ultra-Julian an apostate, like the Roman Emperor Julian
We . . . pantomime The story of Don Juan
had been a popular English pantomime for
some time, showing the great lover as a dupe
and a failure.

VI

Most epic poets plunge 'in medias res'°
  (Horace makes this the heroic turnpike road),
And then your hero tells, whene'er you please,
  What went before—by way of episode,
While seated after dinner at his ease,
  Beside his mistress in some soft abode,
Palace, or garden, paradise, or cavern,
Which serves the happy couple for a tavern.

VII

That is the usual method, but not mine—
50   My way is to begin with the beginning;
The regularity of my design
  Forbids all wandering as the worst of sinning,
And therefore I shall open with a line
  (Although it cost me half an hour in spinning)
Narrating somewhat of Don Juan's father,
And also of his mother, if you'd rather.

. . .

X

His mother was a learnèd lady, famed
  For every branch of every science known—
In every Christian language ever named,
  With virtues equalled by her wit alone:
She made the cleverest people quite ashamed,
  And even the good with inward envy groan,
Finding themselves so very much exceeded
80 In their own way by all the things that she did.

. . .

XVIII

Perfect she was, but as perfection is
  Insipid in this naughty world of ours,
Where our first parents never learned to kiss
140   Till they were exiled from their earlier bowers,
Where all was peace, and innocence, and bliss
  (I wonder how they got through the twelve hours),
Don José, like a lineal son of Eve,
Went plucking various fruit without her leave.

XIX

He was a mortal of the careless kind,
  With no great love for learning, or the learned,
Who chose to go where'er he had a mind,

'in medias res' "into the midst of things,"
from Horace's *Ars Poetica*, l.148

And never dreamed his lady was concerned;
The world, as usual, wickedly inclined
150   To see a kingdom or a house o'erturned
Whispered he had a mistress, some said *two*,
But for domestic quarrels *one* will do.

        .   .   .

        LIV

Young Juan now was sixteen years of age,
    Tall, handsome, slender, but well knit: he seemed
Active, though not so sprightly, as a page;
    And everybody but his mother deemed
430   Him almost man; but she flew in a rage
    And bit her lips (for else she might have screamed)
If any said so, for to be precocious
Was in her eyes a thing the most atrocious.

        LV

Amongst her numerous acquaintance, all
    Selected for discretion and devotion,
There was the Donna Julia, whom to call
    Pretty were but to give a feeble notion
Of many charms in her as natural
    As sweetness to the flower, or salt to ocean,
Her zone to Venus, or his bow to Cupid,
440   (But this last simile is trite and stupid).

        LVI

The darkness of her Oriental eye
    Accorded with her Moorish origin;
(Her blood was not all Spanish, by the by;
    In Spain, you know, this is a sort of sin).
When proud Granada fell, and, forced to fly,
    Boabdil° wept, of Donna Julia's kin
Some went to Africa, some stayed in Spain,
Her great great grandmamma chose to remain.

        .   .   .

        LIX

However this might be, the race went on
    Improving still through every generation,
Until it centred in an only son,
    Who left an only daughter: my narration
May have suggested that this single one
470   Could be but Julia (whom on this occasion

Boabdil last Moorish king of Granada, reported to have wept when his capital fell to
the Spanish in 1491

I shall have much to speak about), and she
Was married, charming, chaste, and twenty-three.

LX

Her eye (I'm very fond of handsome eyes)
    Was large and dark, suppressing half its fire
Until she spoke, then through its soft disguise
    Flashed an expression more of pride than ire
And love than either; and there would arise
    A something in them which was not desire,
But would have been, perhaps, but for the soul
480   Which struggled through and chastened down the whole.

LXI

Her glossy hair was clustered o'er a brow
    Bright with intelligence, and fair, and smooth;
Her eyebrow's shape was like the aerial bow,
    Her cheek all purple with the beam of youth,
Mounting, at times, to a transparent glow,
    As if her veins ran lightning; she, in sooth,
Possessed an air and grace by no means common:
Her stature tall—I hate a dumpy woman.

LXII

Wedded she was some years, and to a man
490   Of fifty, and such husbands are in plenty;
And yet, I think, instead of such a ONE
    'Twere better to have TWO of five-and-twenty,
Especially in countries near the sun:
    And now I think on't, 'mi vien in mente,'°
Ladies even of the most uneasy virtue
Prefer a spouse whose age is short of thirty.

LXIII

'Tis a sad thing, I cannot choose but say,
    And all the fault of that indecent sun,
Who cannot leave alone our helpless clay,
500   But will keep baking, broiling, burning on,
That howsoever people fast and pray,
    The flesh is frail, and so the soul undone:
What men call gallantry, and gods adultery,
Is much more common where the climate's sultry.

LXIV

Happy the nations of the moral North!
    Where all is virtue, and the winter season

'mi vien in mente' "it comes to my mind"

Sends sin, without a rag on, shivering forth
    ('Twas snow that brought St. Anthony to reason);°
Where juries cast up what a wife is worth,
510   By laying whate'er sum, in mulct, they please on
The lover, who must pay a handsome price,
    Because it is a marketable vice.

LXV

Alfonso was the name of Julia's lord,
    A man well looking for his years, and who
Was neither much beloved nor yet abhorred:
    They lived together as most people do,
Suffering each other's foibles by accord,
    And not exactly either *one* or *two*;
Yet he was jealous, though he did not show it,
520 For jealousy dislikes the world to know it.

LXVI

Julia was—yet I never could see why—
    With Donna Inez quite a favourite friend;
Between their tastes there was small sympathy,
    For not a line had Julia ever penned:
Some people whisper (but, no doubt, they lie,
    For malice still imputes some private end)
That Inez had, ere Don Alfonso's marriage,
Forgot with him her very prudent carriage;

LXVII

And that still keeping up the old connexion,
530   Which time had lately rendered much more chaste,
She took his lady also in affection,
    And certainly this course was much the best:
She flattered Julia with her sage protection,
    And complimented Don Alfonso's taste;
And if she could not (who can?) silence scandal,
At least she left it a more slender handle.

LXVIII

I can't tell whether Julia saw the affair
    With other people's eyes, or if her own
Discoveries made, but none could be aware
540   Of this, at least no symptom e'er was shown;
Perhaps she did not know, or did not care,
    Indifferent from the first, or callous grown:
I'm really puzzled what to think or say,
She kept her counsel in so close a way.

'Twas . . . **reason** In a note Byron called this
a "recipe for hot blood in cold weather" and
correctly supposed it was St. Francis "who had
the wife of snow."

LXIX

Juan she saw, and, as a pretty child,
  Caressed him often—such a thing might be
Quite innocently done, and harmless styled,
  When she had twenty years, and thirteen he;
But I am not so sure I should have smiled
550   When he was sixteen, Julia twenty-three;
These few short years make wondrous alterations,
Particularly amongst sun-burnt nations.

LXX

Whate'er the cause might be, they had become
  Changed; for the dame grew distant, the youth shy,
Their looks cast down, their greetings almost dumb,
  And much embarrassment in either eye;
There surely will be little doubt with some
  That Donna Julia knew the reason why,
But as for Juan, he had no more notion
560   Than he who never saw the sea of ocean.

LXXI

Yet Julia's very coldness still was kind,
  And tremulously gentle her small hand
Withdrew itself from his, but left behind
  A little pressure, thrilling, and so bland
And slight, so very slight, that to the mind
  'Twas but a doubt; but ne'er magician's wand
Wrought change with all Armida's fairy art°
Like what this light touch left on Juan's heart.

LXXII

And if she met him, though she smiled no more,
570   She looked a sadness sweeter than her smile,
As if her heart had deeper thoughts in store
  She must not own, but cherished more the while
For that compression in its burning core;
  Even innocence itself has many a wile,
And will not dare to trust itself with truth,
And love is taught hypocrisy from youth.

LXXIII

But passion most dissembles, yet betrays
  Even by its darkness; as the blackest sky
Foretells the heaviest tempest, it displays
580   Its workings through the vainly guarded eye,

Armida's . . . art Armida, a witch in Tasso's
Jerusalem Delivered, enchanted Rinaldo, thus
impeding his crusader's career.

And in whatever aspect it arrays
    Itself, 'tis still the same hypocrisy;
Coldness or anger, even disdain or hate,
Are masks it often wears, and still too late.

LXXIV

Then there were sighs, the deeper for suppression,
    And stolen glances, sweeter for the theft,
And burning blushes, though for no transgression,
    Tremblings when met, and restlessness when left;
All these are little preludes to possession,
590   Of which young passion cannot be bereft,
And merely tend to show how greatly love is
Embarrassed at first starting with a novice.

LXXV

Poor Julia's heart was in an awkward state;
    She felt it going, and resolved to make
The noblest efforts for herself and mate,
    For honour's, pride's, religion's, virtue's sake.
Her resolutions were most truly great,
    And almost might have made a Tarquin° quake:
She prayed the Virgin Mary for her grace,
600   As being the best judge of a lady's case.

LXXVI

She vowed she never would see Juan more,
    And next day paid a visit to his mother,
And looked extremely at the opening door,
    Which, by the Virgin's grace, let in another;
Grateful she was, and yet a little sore—
    Again it opens, it can be no other,
'Tis surely Juan now—No! I'm afraid
That night the Virgin was no further prayed.

LXXVII

She now determined that a virtuous woman
610   Should rather face and overcome temptation,
That flight was base and dastardly, and no man
    Should ever give her heart the least sensation;
That is to say, a thought beyond the common
    Preference, that we must feel upon occasion,
For people who are pleasanter than others,
But then they only seem so many brothers.

Tarquin an early Roman royal family, distinguished by its savagery, as in the rape of Lucrece by one Tarquin

LXXVIII

And even if by chance—and who can tell?
   The devil's so very sly—she should discover
That all within was not so very well,
620   And, if still free, that such or such a lover
Might please perhaps, a virtuous wife can quell
   Such thoughts, and be the better when they're over;
And if the man should ask, 'tis but denial:
I recommend young ladies to make trial.

LXXIX

And then there are such things as love divine,
   Bright and immaculate, unmixed and pure,
Such as the angels think so very fine,
   And matrons, who would be no less secure,
Platonic, perfect, 'just such love as mine':
630   Thus Julia said—and thought so, to be sure;
And so I'd have her think, were I the man
On whom her reveries celestial ran.

LXXX

Such love is innocent, and may exist
   Between young persons without any danger.
A hand may first, and then a lip be kissed;
   For my part, to such doings I'm a stranger,
But *hear* these freedoms form the utmost list
   Of all o'er which such love may be a ranger:
If people go beyond, 'tis quite a crime,
640   But not my fault—I tell them all in time.

LXXXI

Love, then, but love within its proper limits,
   Was Julia's innocent determination
In young Don Juan's favour, and to him its
   Exertion might be useful on occasion;
And, lighted at too pure a shrine to dim its
   Ethereal lustre, with what sweet persuasion
He might be taught, by love and her together—
I really don't know what, nor Julia either.

LXXXII

Fraught with this fine intention, and well fenced
650   In mail of proof—her purity of soul,
She, for the future of her strength convinced,
   And that her honour was a rock, or mole,
Exceeding sagely from that hour dispensed
   With any kind of troublesome control;

But whether Julia to the task was equal
Is that which must be mention'd in the sequel.

LXXXIII

Her plan she deemed both innocent and feasible,
    And, surely, with a stripling of sixteen
Not scandal's fangs could fix on much that's seizable,
660   Or if they did so, satisfied to mean
Nothing but what was good, her breast was peaceable:
    A quiet conscience makes one so serene!
Christians have burnt each other, quite persuaded
That all the Apostles would have done as they did.

LXXXIV

And if in the mean time her husband died,
    But Heaven forbid that such a thought should cross
Her brain, though in a dream! (and then she sighed)
    Never could she survive that common loss;
But just suppose that moment should betide,
670   I only say suppose it—*inter nos*.
(This should be *entre nous,* for Julia thought
In French, but then the rhyme would go for nought.)

LXXXV

I only say, suppose this supposition:
    Juan being then grown up to man's estate
Would fully suit a widow of condition,
    Even seven years hence it would not be too late;
And in the interim (to pursue this vision)
    The mischief, after all, could not be great,
For he would learn the rudiments of love,
680   I mean the seraph way of those above.

          . . .

XC

Young Juan wandered by the glassy brooks,
    Thinking unutterable things; he threw
Himself at length within the leafy nooks
    Where the wild branch of the cork forest grew;
There poets find materials for their books,
    And every now and then we read them through,
So that their plan and prosody are eligible,
720   Unless, like Wordsworth, they prove unintelligible.

XCI

He, Juan (and not Wordsworth), so pursued
    His self-communion with his own high soul,
Until his mighty heart, in its great mood,
    Had mitigated part, though not the whole

Of its disease; he did the best he could
   With things not very subject to control,
And turned, without perceiving his condition,
   Like Coleridge, into a metaphysician.

XCII

He thought about himself, and the whole earth,
730   Of man the wonderful, and of the stars,
And how the deuce they ever could have birth;
   And then he thought of earthquakes, and of wars,
How many miles the moon might have in girth,
   Of air-balloons, and of the many bars
To perfect knowledge of the boundless skies;—
And then he thought of Donna Julia's eyes.

XCIII

In thoughts like these true wisdom may discern
   Longings sublime, and aspirations high,
Which some are born with, but the most part learn
740   To plague themselves withal, they know not why:
'Twas strange that one so young should thus concern
   His brain about the action of the sky;
If *you* think 'twas philosophy that this did,
I can't help thinking puberty assisted.

XCIV

He pored upon the leaves, and on the flowers,
   And heard a voice in all the winds; and then
He thought of wood-nymphs and immortal bowers,
   And how the goddesses came down to men:
He missed the pathway, he forgot the hours,
750   And when he looked upon his watch again,
He found how much old Time had been a winner—
He also found that he had lost his dinner.

. . .

CI

But Inez was so anxious, and so clear
   Of sight, that I must think, on this occasion,
She had some other motive much more near
   For leaving Juan to this new temptation;
But what that motive was, I shan't say here;
   Perhaps to finish Juan's education,
Perhaps to open Don Alfonso's eyes,
In case he thought his wife too great a prize.

CII

It was upon a day, a summer's day;—
810   Summer's indeed a very dangerous season,

And so is spring about the end of May;
   The sun, no doubt, is the prevailing reason;
But whatsoe'er the cause is, one may say,
   And stand convicted of more truth than treason,
That there are months which nature grows more merry in,—
March has its hares, and May must have its heroine.

CIII

'Twas on a summer's day—the sixth of June:—
   I like to be particular in dates,
Not only of the age, and year, but moon;
820   They are a sort of post-house, where the Fates
Change horses, making history change its tune,
   Then spur away o'er empires and o'er states,
Leaving at last not much besides chronology,
Excepting the post-obits° of theology.

CIV

'Twas on the sixth of June, about the hour
   Of half-past six—perhaps still nearer seven—
When Julia sate within as pretty a bower
   As e'er held houri in that heathenish heaven
Described by Mahomet, and Anacreon Moore,°
830   To whom the lyre and laurels have been given,
With all the trophies of triumphant song—
He won them well, and may he wear them long!

CV

She sate, but not alone; I know not well
   How this same interview had taken place,
And even if I knew, I should not tell—
   People should hold their tongues in any case;
No matter how or why the thing befell,
   But there were she and Juan, face to face—
When two such faces are so, 'twould be wise,
840 But very difficult, to shut their eyes.

CVI

How beautiful she looked! her conscious heart
   Glow'd in her cheek, and yet she felt no wrong.
Oh Love! how perfect is thy mystic art,
   Strengthening the weak, and trampling on the strong,
How self-deceitful is the sagest part
   Of mortals whom thy lure hath led along—
The precipice she stood on was immense,
So was her creed in her own innocence.

post-obits sum paid on a person's death
Anacreon Moore Thomas Moore's first publication was a translation of Anacreon (born about
570 B.C.), a witty Greek lyric poet.

CVII

She thought of her own strength, and Juan's youth,
850   And of the folly of all prudish fears,
Victorious virtue, and domestic truth,
    And then of Don Alfonso's fifty years:
I wish these last had not occurred, in sooth,
    Because that number rarely much endears,
And through all climes, the snowy and the sunny,
Sounds ill in love, whate'er it may in money.

CVIII

When people say, 'I've told you *fifty* times.'
    They mean to scold, and very often do;
When poets say, 'I've written *fifty* rhymes,'
860   They make you dread that they'll recite them too;
In gangs of *fifty*, thieves commit their crimes;
    At *fifty* love for love is rare, 'tis true,
But then, no doubt, it equally as true is,
A good deal may be bought for *fifty* Louis.

CIX

Julia had honour, virtue, truth, and love
    For Don Alfonso; and she inly swore,
By all the vows below to powers above,
    She never would disgrace the ring she wore,
Nor leave a wish which wisdom might reprove;
870   And while she pondered this, besides much more,
One hand on Juan's carelessly was thrown,
Quite by mistake—she thought it was her own;

CX

Unconsciously she leaned upon the other,
    Which played within the tangles of her hair;
And to contend with thoughts she could not smother
    She seemed, by the distraction of her air.
'Twas surely very wrong in Juan's mother
    To leave together this imprudent pair,
She who for many years had watched her son so—
880   I'm very certain *mine* would not have done so.

CXI

The hand which still held Juan's, by degrees
    Gently, but palpably confirm'd its grasp,
As if it said, 'Detain me, if you please';
    Yet there's no doubt she only meant to clasp
His fingers with a pure Platonic squeeze;
    She would have shrunk as from a toad, or asp,

Had she imagined such a thing could rouse
A feeling dangerous to a prudent spouse.

CXII

I cannot know what Juan thought of this,
890   But what he did, is much what you would do;
His young lip thanked it with a grateful kiss,
    And then, abashed at its own joy, withdrew
In deep despair, lest he had done amiss,—
    Love is so very timid when 'tis new:
She blushed, and frowned not, but she strove to speak,
And held her tongue, her voice was grown so weak.

CXIII

The sun set, and up rose the yellow moon:
    The devil's in the moon for mischief; they
Who called her CHASTE, methinks, began too soon
900   Their nomenclature; there is not a day,
The longest, not the twenty-first of June,
    Sees half the business in a wicked way
On which three single hours of moonshine smile—
And then she looks so modest all the while.

CXIV

There is a dangerous silence in that hour,
    A stillness, which leaves room for the full soul
To open all itself, without the power
    Of calling wholly back its self-control;
The silver light which, hallowing tree and tower,
910   Sheds beauty and deep softness o'er the whole,
Breathes also to the heart, and o'er it throws
A loving languor, which is not repose.

CXV

And Julia sate with Juan, half embraced
    And half retiring from the glowing arm,
Which trembled like the bosom where 'twas placed;
    Yet still she must have thought there was no harm
Or else 'twere easy to withdraw her waist;
    But then the situation had its charm,
And then—God knows what next—I can't go on;
920   I'm almost sorry that I e'er begun.

CXVI

Oh Plato! Plato! you have paved the way,
    With your confounded fantasies, to more
Immoral conduct by the fancied sway
    Your system feigns o'er the controlless core

Of human hearts, than all the long array
    Of poets and romancers:—You're a bore,
A charlatan, a coxcomb—and have been,
At best, no better than a go-between.

CXVII

And Julia's voice was lost, except in sighs,
930   Until too late for useful conversation;
The tears were gushing from her gentle eyes,
    I wish, indeed, they had not had occasion,
But who, alas! can love, and then be wise?
    Not that remorse did not oppose temptation;
A little still she strove, and much repented,
And whispering 'I will ne'er consent'—consented.

CXVIII

'Tis said that Xerxes offered a reward
    To those who could invent him a new pleasure:
Methinks the requisition's rather hard,
940   And must have cost his majesty a treasure:
For my part, I'm a moderate-minded bard,
    Fond of a little love (which I call leisure);
I care not for new pleasures, as the old
Are quite enough for me, so they but hold.

CXIX

Oh Pleasure! you're indeed a pleasant thing,
    Although one must be damned for you, no doubt:
I make a resolution every spring
    Of reformation, ere the year run out,
But somehow, this my vestal vow takes wing,
950   Yet still, I trust, it may be kept throughout:
I'm very sorry, very much ashamed,
And mean, next winter, to be quite reclaimed.

CXX

Here my chaste Muse a liberty must take—
    Start not! still chaster reader—she'll be nice hence-
Forward, and there is no great cause to quake;
    This liberty is a poetic licence,
Which some irregularity may make
    In the design, and as I have a high sense
Of Aristotle and the Rules, 'tis fit
960   To beg his pardon when I err a bit.

CXXI

This licence is to hope the reader will
    Suppose from June the sixth (the fatal day

Without whose epoch my poetic skill
  For want of facts would all be thrown away),
But keeping Julia and Don Juan still
  In sight, that several months have passed; we'll say
'Twas in November, but I'm not so sure
About the day—the era's more obscure.

CXXII

We'll talk of that anon.—'Tis sweet to hear
970 At midnight on the blue and moonlit deep
The song and oar of Adria's gondolier,°
  By distance mellowed, o'er the waters sweep;
'Tis sweet to see the evening star appear;
  'Tis sweet to listen as the night-winds creep
From leaf to leaf; 'tis sweet to view on high
The rainbow, based on ocean, span the sky.

CXXIII

'Tis sweet to hear the watch-dog's honest bark
  Bay deep-mouthed welcome as we draw near home;
'Tis sweet to know there is an eye will mark
980 Our coming, and look brighter when we come;
'Tis sweet to be awakened by the lark,
  Or lulled by falling waters; sweet the hum
Of bees, the voice of girls, the song of birds,
The lisp of children, and their earliest words.

CXXIV

Sweet is the vintage, when the showering grapes
  In Bacchanal° profusion reel to earth,
Purple and gushing: sweet are our escapes
  From civic revelry to rural mirth;
Sweet to the miser are his glittering heaps,
990 Sweet to the father is his first-born's birth;
Sweet is revenge—especially to women,
Pillage to soldiers, prize-money° to seamen.

CXXV

Sweet is a legacy, and passing sweet
  The unexpected death of some old lady
Or gentleman of seventy years complete,
  Who've made 'us youth'° wait too—too long already
For an estate, or cash, or country seat,
  Still breaking, but with stamina so steady

The song . . . gondolier Venetian gondoliers
sang as they rowed.
Bacchanal wanton
prize-money property captured at sea, and hence

legal booty
'us youth' See Falstaff's "They hate us youth,"
I *Henry IV* II.ii.93.

That all the Israelites are fit to mob its
1000 Next owner for their double-damned post-obits.

CXXVI

'Tis sweet to win, no matter how, one's laurels,
  By blood or ink! 'tis sweet to put an end
To strife; 'tis sometimes sweet to have our quarrels,
  Particularly with a tiresome friend:
Sweet is old wine in bottles, ale in barrels;
  Dear is the helpless creature we defend
Against the world; and dear the schoolboy spot
We ne'er forget, though there we are forgot.

CXXVII

But sweeter still than this, than these, than all,
1010 Is first and passionate love—it stands alone,
Like Adam's recollection of his fall;
  The tree of knowledge has been plucked—all's known—
And life yields nothing further to recall
  Worthy of this ambrosial sin, so shown,
No doubt in fable, as the unforgiven
Fire which Prometheus filched for us from heaven.

CXXVIII

Man's a strange animal, and makes strange use
  Of his own nature, and the various arts,
And likes particularly to produce
1020 Some new experiment to show his parts;
This is the age of oddities let loose,
  Where different talents find their different marts;
You'd best begin with truth, and when you've lost your
Labour, there's a sure market for imposture.

CXXIX

What opposite discoveries we have seen!
  (Signs of true genius, and of empty pockets.)
One makes new noses, one a guillotine,
  One breaks your bones, one sets them in their sockets;
But vaccination certainly has been
1030 A kind antithesis to Congreve's rockets,°
With which the Doctor paid off an old pox,
By borrowing a new one from an ox.

CXXX

Bread has been made (indifferent) from potatoes;
  And galvanism has set some corpses grinning,°

Congreve's rockets a new kind of shell employed in the Battle of Leipzig (1813) **And . . . grinning** Luigi Galvani had experimented with the supposed medical possibilities of electricity; his nephew, one Aldini, attempted to revive a murderer with electricity in 1803, undoubtedly contributing to the mythology culminating in Mary Shelley's novel *Frankenstein.*

But has not answer'd like the apparatus
   Of the Humane Society's beginning,
By which men are unsuffocated gratis:
   What wondrous new machines have late been spinning!
I said the small pox has gone out of late;
1040   Perhaps it may be followed by the great.°

        CXXXI

'Tis said the great came from America;
   Perhaps it may set out on its return,—
The population there so spreads, they say
   'Tis grown high time to thin it in its turn,°
With war, or plague, or famine, any way,
   So that civilisation they may learn;
And which in ravage the more loathsome evil is—
Their real lues,° or our pseudo-syphilis?

        CXXXII

This is the patent age of new inventions
1050   For killing bodies, and for saving souls,
All propagated with the best intentions;
   Sir Humphry Davy's lantern,° by which coals
Are safely mined for in the mode he mentions,
   Tombuctoo travels, voyages to the Poles,
Are ways to benefit mankind, as true,
Perhaps, as shooting them at Waterloo.

      . . .

        CXXXVI

'Twas midnight—Donna Julia was in bed,
   Sleeping, most probably,—when at her door
Arose a clatter might awake the dead,
   If they had never been awoke before,
And that they have been so we all have read,
   And are to be so, at the least, once more;—
The door was fastened, but with voice and fist
First knocks were heard, then 'Madam—Madam—hist!

        CXXXVII

'For God's sake, Madam—Madam—here's my master,
1090   With more than half the city at his back—
Was ever heard of such a curst disaster!
   'Tis not my fault—I kept good watch—Alack!
Do pray undo the bolt a little faster—
   They're on the stair just now, and in a crack

---

the great syphilis, known as the "great pox"   lues syphilis
The population . . . turn the doctrine of   lantern coal miner's safety lamp
Malthus, expounded in 1798

Will all be here; perhaps he yet may fly—
Surely the window's not so *very* high!'

CXXXVIII

By this time Don Alfonso was arrived,
    With torches, friends, and servants in great number;
The major part of them had long been wived,
    And therefore paused not to disturb the slumber
Of any wicked woman, who contrived
    By stealth her husband's temples to encumber:
Examples of this kind are so contagious,
Were *one* not punished, *all* would be outrageous.

CXXXIX

I can't tell how, or why, or what suspicion
    Could enter into Don Alfonso's head;
But for a cavalier of his condition
    It surely was exceedingly ill-bred,
Without a word of previous admonition,
    To hold a levee round his lady's bed,
And summon lackeys, armed with fire and sword,
To prove himself the thing he most abhorred.

CXL

Poor Donna Julia! starting as from sleep
    (Mind—that I do not say—she had not slept),
Began at once to scream, and yawn, and weep;
    Her maid, Antonia, who was an adept,
Contrived to fling the bed-clothes in a heap,
    As if she had just now from out them crept:
I can't tell why she should take all this trouble
To prove her mistress had been sleeping double.

CXLI

But Julia mistress, and Antonia maid,
    Appeared like two poor harmless women, who
Of goblins, but still more of men afraid,
    Had thought one man might be deterred by two,
And therefore side by side were gently laid,
    Until the hours of absence should run through,
And truant husband should return, and say,
'My dear, I was the first who came away.'

CXLII

Now Julia found at length a voice, and cried,
    'In heaven's name, Don Alfonso, what d'ye mean?
Has madness seized you? would that I had died
    Ere such a monster's victim I had been!

What may this midnight violence betide,
    A sudden fit of drunkenness or spleen?
Dare you suspect me, whom the thought would kill?
Search, then, the room!'—Alfonso said, 'I will.'

CXLIII

He searched, *they* searched, and rummaged everywhere,
    Closet and clothes-press, chest and window-seat,
And found much linen, lace, and several pair
1140   Of stockings, slippers, brushes, combs, complete,
With other articles of ladies fair,
    To keep them beautiful, or leave them neat:
Arras they pricked and curtains with their swords,
And wounded several shutters, and some boards.

CXLIV

Under the bed they searched, and there they found—
    No matter what—it was not that they sought;
They opened windows, gazing if the ground
    Had signs or footmarks, but the earth said nought;
And then they stared each other's faces round:
1150   'Tis odd, not one of all these seekers thought,
And seems to me almost a sort of blunder,
Of looking *in* the bed as well as under.

CXLV

During this inquisition Julia's tongue
    Was not asleep—'Yes, search and search,' she cried,
'Insult on insult heap, and wrong on wrong!
    It was for this that I became a bride!
For this in silence I have suffered long
    A husband like Alfonso at my side;
But now I'll bear no more, nor here remain,
1160 If there be law or lawyers in all Spain.

CXLVI

'Yes, Don Alfonso! husband now no more,
    If ever you indeed deserved the name,
Is't worthy of your years?—you have three-score—
    Fifty, or sixty, it is all the same—
Is't wise or fitting, causeless to explore
    For facts against a virtuous woman's fame?
Ungrateful, perjured, barbarous Don Alfonso,
How dare you think your lady would go on so?

CXLVII

'Is it for this I have disdained to hold
1170   The common privileges of my sex?

That I have chosen a confessor so old
    And deaf, that any other it would vex,
And never once he has had cause to scold,
    But found my very innocence perplex
So much, he always doubted I was married—
How sorry you will be when I've miscarried!

CXLVIII

'Was it for this that no Cortejo° e'er
    I yet have chosen from out the youth of Seville?
Is it for this I scarce went anywhere,
1180   Except to bull-fights, mass, play, rout, and revel?
Is it for this, whate'er my suitors were,
    I favoured none—nay, was almost uncivil?
Is it for this that General Count O'Reilly,°
Who took Algiers, declares I used him vilely?

CXLIX

'Did not the Italian Musico Cazzani°
    Sing at my heart six months at least in vain?
Did not his countryman, Count Corniani,°
    Call me the only virtuous wife in Spain?
Were there not also Russians, English, many?
1190   The Count Strongstroganoff I put in pain,
And Lord Mount Coffeehouse, the Irish peer,
Who killed himself for love (with wine) last year.

CL

'Have I not had two bishops at my feet?
    The Duke of Ichar, and Don Fernan Nunez?
And is it thus a faithful wife you treat?
    I wonder in what quarter now the moon is:
I praise your vast forbearance not to beat
    Me also, since the time so opportune is—
Oh, valiant man! with sword drawn and cocked trigger,
1200   Now, tell me, don't you cut a pretty figure?

CLI

'Was it for this you took your sudden journey,
    Under pretence of business indispensable,
With that sublime of rascals your attorney,
    Whom I see standing there, and looking sensible
Of having played the fool? though both I spurn, he
    Deserves the worst, his conduct's less defensible,

Cortejo Byron's note: "The Spanish 'Cortejo' is much the same as the Italian 'Cavalier Servente'" (as Byron was to Teresa Guiccioli). **O'Reilly** As Byron noted, Count O'Reilly "did not take Algiers—but Algiers very nearly took him"; he withdrew in some disorder after a fiasco in 1775. **Cazzani** perhaps playing on *cazzo*, the phallus **Corniani** from *cornuto*, a cuckold

Because, no doubt, 'twas for his dirty fee,
And not from any love to you nor me.

CLII

'If he comes here to take a deposition,
1210   By all means let the gentleman proceed;
You've made the apartment in a fit condition:—
    There's pen and ink for you, sir, when you need—
Let everything be noted with precision,
    I would not you for nothing should be fee'd—
But as my maid's undrest, pray turn your spies out.'
'Oh!' sobbed Antonia, 'I could tear their eyes out.'

CLIII

'There is the closet, there the toilet, there
    The antechamber—search them under, over;
There is the sofa, there the great arm-chair,
1220   The chimney—which would really hold a lover.
I wish to sleep, and beg you will take care
    And make no further noise, till you discover
The secret cavern of this lurking treasure—
And when 'tis found, let me, too, have that pleasure.

CLIV

'And now, Hidalgo!° now that you have thrown
    Doubt upon me, confusion over all,
Pray have the courtesy to make it known
    Who is the man you search for? How d'ye call
Him? what his lineage? let him but be shown—
1230   I hope he's young and handsome—is he tall?
Tell me—and be assured, that since you stain
Mine honour thus, it shall not be in vain.

CLV

'At least, perhaps, he has not sixty years,
    At that age he would be too old for slaughter,
Or for so young a husband's jealous fears—
    (Antonia! let me have a glass of water.)
I am ashamed of having shed these tears,
    They are unworthy of my father's daughter;
My mother dreamed not in my natal hour,
1240   That I should fall into a monster's power.

CLVI

'Perhaps 'tis of Antonia you are jealous,
    You saw that she was sleeping by my side

Hidalgo Spanish gentleman

When you broke in upon us with your fellows:
    Look where you please—we've nothing, sir, to hide;
Only another time, I trust, you'll tell us,
    Or for the sake of decency abide
A moment at the door, that we may be
Dressed to receive so much good company.

CLVII

'And now, sir, I have done, and say no more;
1250   The little I have said may serve to show
The guileless heart in silence may grieve o'er
    The wrongs to whose exposure it is slow:—
I leave you to your conscience as before,
    'Twill one day ask you *why* you used me so?
God grant you feel not then the bitterest grief!
Antonia! where's my pocket-handkerchief?'

CLVIII

She ceased, and turned upon her pillow; pale
    She lay, her dark eyes flashing through their tears,
Like skies that rain and lighten; as a veil,
1260   Waved and o'ershading her wan cheek, appears
Her streaming hair: the black curls strive, but fail,
    To hide the glossy shoulder, which uprears
Its snow through all;—her soft lips lie apart,
And louder than her breathing beats her heart.

CLIX

The Senhor Don Alfonso stood confused;
    Antonia bustled around the ransacked room,
And, turning up her nose, with looks abused
    Her master, and his myrmidons, of whom
Not one, except the attorney, was amused;
1270   He, like Achates,° faithful to the tomb,
So there were quarrels, cared not for the cause,
Knowing they must be settled by the laws.

CLX

With prying snub-nose, and small eyes, he stood,
    Following Antonia's motions here and there,
With such suspicion in his attitude;
    For reputations he had little care;
So that a suit or action were made good,
    Small pity had he for the young and fair,
And ne'er believed in negatives, till these
1280   Were proved by competent false witnesses.

Achates the best friend of Aeneas

CLXI

But Don Alfonso stood with downcast looks,
 And, truth to say, he made a foolish figure;
When, after searching in five hundred nooks,
 And treating a young wife with so much rigour,
He gained no point, except some self-rebukes,
 Added to those his lady with such vigour
Had poured upon him for the last half-hour,
Quick, thick, and heavy—as a thunder-shower.

CLXII

At first he tried to hammer an excuse,
1290 To which the sole reply was tears and sobs,
And indications of hysterics, whose
 Prologue is always certain throes, and throbs,
Gasps, and whatever else the owners choose:
 Alfonso saw his wife, and thought of Job's;°
He saw too, in perspective, her relations,
And then he tried to muster all his patience.

CLXIII

He stood in act to speak, or rather stammer,
 But sage Antonia cut him short before
The anvil of his speech received the hammer,
1300 With 'Pray, sir, leave the room, and say no more,
Or madam dies.'—Alfonso mutter'd, 'D—n her.'
 But nothing else, the time of words was o'er;
He cast a rueful look or two, and did,
He knew not wherefore, that which he was bid.

CLXIV

With him retired his *'posse comitatus*,'°
 The attorney last, who lingered near the door
Reluctantly, still tarrying there as late as
 Antonia let him—not a little sore
At this most strange and unexplained *'hiatus'*
1310 In Don Alfonso's facts, which just now wore
An awkward look; as he revolved the case,
The door was fastened in his legal face.

CLXV

No sooner was it bolted, than—Oh shame!
 Oh sin! Oh sorrow! and Oh womankind!
How can you do such things and keep your fame,
 Unless this world, and t'other too, be blind?

Job's who said to him in his misery "Dost thou   'posse comitatus' company
still retain thine integrity? Curse god, and die"
(Job 2:9)

Nothing so dear as an unfilched good name!
　　But to proceed—for there is more behind:
With much heartfelt reluctance be it said,
1320　Young Juan slipped, half-smothered, from the bed.

CLXVI

He had been hid—I don't pretend to say
　　How, nor can I indeed describe the where—
Young, slender, and packed easily, he lay,
　　No doubt, in little compass, round or square;
But pity him I neither must nor may
　　His suffocation by that pretty pair;
'Twere better, sure, to die so, than be shut
With maudlin Clarence in his Malmsey butt.°

CLXVII

And, secondly, I pity not, because
1330　He had no business to commit a sin,
Forbid by heavenly, fined by human laws,
　　At least 'twas rather early to begin;
But at sixteen the conscience rarely gnaws
　　So much as when we call our old debts in
At sixty years, and draw the accompts of evil,
And find a deuced balance with the devil.

CLXVIII

Of his position I can give no notion:
　　'Tis written in the Hebrew Chronicle,°
How the physicians, leaving pill and potion,
1340　Prescribed, by way of blister, a young belle,
When old King David's blood grew dull in motion,
　　And that the medicine answered very well;
Perhaps 'twas in a different way applied,
For David lived, but Juan nearly died.

CLXIX

What's to be done? Alfonso will be back
　　The moment he has sent his fools away.
Antonia's skill was put upon the rack,
　　But no device could be brought into play—
And how to parry the renewed attack?
1350　Besides, it wanted but few hours of day:
Antonia puzzled; Julia did not speak,
But pressed her bloodless lip to Juan's cheek.

With . . . butt See Shakespeare, *Richard III*　Hebrew Chronicle See I Kings 1:1–3.
I.iv.276.

CLXX

He turned his lip to hers, and with his hand
　　Called back the tangles of her wandering hair;
Even then their love they could not all command,
　　And half forgot their danger and despair:
Antonia's patience now was at a stand—
　　'Come, come, 'tis no time now for fooling there,'
She whispered, in great wrath—'I must deposit
1360　This pretty gentleman within the closet:

CLXXI

'Pray, keep your nonsense for some luckier night—
　　Who can have put my master in this mood?
What will become on't—I'm in such a fright,
　　The devil's in the urchin, and no good—
Is this a time for giggling? this a plight?
　　Why, don't you know that it may end in blood?
You'll lose your life, and I shall lose my place,
My mistress all, for that half-girlish face.

CLXXII

'Had it but been for a stout cavalier
1370　Of twenty-five or thirty—(come, make haste)
But for a child, what piece of work is here!
　　I really, madam, wonder at your taste—
(Come, sir, get in)—my master must be near:
　　There, for the present, at the least, he's fast,
And if we can but till the morning keep
Our counsel—Juan, mind, you must not sleep).'

CLXXIII

Now, Don Alfonso entering, but alone,
　　Closed the oration of the trusty maid:
She loitered, and he told her to be gone,
1380　An order somewhat sullenly obeyed;
However, present remedy was none,
　　And no great good seemed answer'd if she stayed:
Regarding both with slow and sidelong view,
She snuffed the candle, curtsied, and withdrew.

CLXXIV

Alfonso paused a minute—then begun
　　Some strange excuses for his late proceeding;
He would not justify what he had done,
　　To say the best, it was extreme ill-breeding;
But there were ample reasons for it, none
1390　Of which he specified in this his pleading:

His speech was a fine sample, on the whole,
Of rhetoric, which the learned call *'rigmarole.'*

CLXXV

Julia said nought; though all the while there rose
　A ready answer, which at once enables
A matron, who her husband's foible knows,
　By a few timely words to turn the tables,
Which, if it does not silence, still must pose,—
　Even if it should comprise a pack of fables;
'Tis to retort with firmness, and when he
1400　Suspects with *one*, do you reproach with *three*.

CLXXVI

Julia, in fact, had tolerable grounds,—
　Alfonso's loves with Inez were well known;
But whether 'twas that one's own guilt confounds—
　But that can't be, as has been often shown,
A lady with apologies abounds;—
　It might be that her silence sprang alone
From delicacy to Don Juan's ear,
To whom she knew his mother's fame was dear.

CLXXVII

There might be one more motive, which makes two;
1410　Alfonso ne'er to Juan had alluded,—
Mentioned his jealousy, but never who
　Had been the happy lover, he concluded,
Concealed amongst his premises; 'tis true,
　His mind the more o'er this its mystery brooded;
To speak of Inez now were, one may say,
Like throwing Juan in Alfonso's way.

CLXXVIII

A hint, in tender cases, is enough;
　Silence is best, besides there is a *tact*—
(That modern phrase appears to me sad stuff,
1420　But it will serve to keep my verse compact)—
Which keeps, when pushed by questions rather rough,
　A lady always distant from the fact:
The charming creatures lie with such a grace,
There's nothing so becoming to the face.

CLXXIX

They blush, and we believe them; at least I
　Have always done so; 'tis of no great use,
In any case, attempting a reply,
　For then their eloquence grows quite profuse;

And when at length they're out of breath, they sigh,
1430   And cast their languid eyes down, and let loose
A tear or two, and then we make it up;
And then—and then—and then—sit down and sup.

          CLXXX

Alfonso closed his speech, and begged her pardon,
     Which Julia half withheld, and then half granted,
And laid conditions, he thought very hard on,
     Denying several little things he wanted:
He stood like Adam lingering near his garden,
     With useless penitence perplexed and haunted,
Beseeching she no further would refuse,
1440   When, lo! he stumbled o'er a pair of shoes.

          CLXXXI

A pair of shoes!—what then? not much, if they
     Are such as fit with ladies' feet, but these
(No one can tell how much I grieve to say)
     Were masculine; to see them, and to seize,
Was but a moment's act.—Ah! well-a-day!
     My teeth begin to chatter, my veins freeze—
Alfonso first examined well their fashion,
And then flew out into another passion.

          CLXXXII

He left the room for his relinquished sword,
1450   And Julia instant to the closet flew.
'Fly, Juan, fly! for heaven's sake—not a word—
     The door is open—you may yet slip through
The passage you so often have explored—
     Here is the garden-key—Fly—fly—Adieu!
Haste—haste! I hear Alfonso's hurrying feet—
Day has not broke—there's no one in the street.'

          CLXXXIII

None can say that this was not good advice,
     The only mischief was, it came too late;
Of all experience 'tis the usual price,
1460   A sort of income-tax laid on by fate:
Juan had reached the room-door in a trice,
     And might have done so by the garden-gate,
But met Alfonso in his dressing-gown,
Who threatened death—so Juan knocked him down.

          CLXXXIV

Dire was the scuffle, and out went the light;
     Antonia cried out 'Rape!' and Julia 'Fire!'

But not a servant stirred to aid the fight.
    Alfonso, pommelled to his heart's desire,
Swore lustily he'd be revenged this night;
1470   And Juan, too, blasphemed an octave higher;
His blood was up: though young, he was a Tartar,
And not at all disposed to prove a martyr.

      CLXXXV
Alfonso's sword had dropped ere he could draw it,
    And they continued battling hand to hand,
For Juan very luckily ne'er saw it;
    His temper not being under great command,
If at that moment he had chanced to claw it,
    Alfonso's days had not been in the land
Much longer.—Think of husbands', lovers' lives!
1480 And how ye may be doubly widows—wives!

      CLXXXVI
Alfonso grappled to detain the foe,
    And Juan throttled him to get away,
And blood ('twas from the nose) began to flow;
    At last, as they more faintly wrestling lay,
Juan contrived to give an awkward blow,
    And then his only garment quite gave way;
He fled, like Joseph, leaving it; but there,
I doubt, all likeness ends between the pair.°

      CLXXXVII
Lights came at length, and men, and maids, who found
1490   An awkward spectacle their eyes before;
Antonia in hysterics, Julia swooned,
    Alfonso leaning, breathless, by the door;
Some half-torn drapery scattered on the ground,
    Some blood, and several footsteps, but no more:
Juan the gate gained, turned the key about,
And liking not the inside, locked the out.

      CLXXXVIII
Here ends this canto.—Need I sing, or say,
    How Juan, naked, favoured by the night,
Who favours what she should not, found his way,
1500   And reached his home in an unseemly plight?
The pleasant scandal which arose next day,
    The nine days' wonder which was brought to light,
And how Alfonso sued for a divorce,
Were in the English newspapers, of course.

the pair See Genesis 39:12.

CLXXXIX

If you would like to see the whole proceedings,
    The depositions, and the cause at full,
The names of all the witnesses, the pleadings
    Of counsel to nonsuit, or to annul,
There's more than one edition, and the readings
1510   Are various, but they none of them are dull;
The best is that in short-hand ta'en by Gurney,°
Who to Madrid on purpose made a journey.

CXC

But Donna Inez, to divert the train
    Of one of the most circulating scandals
That had for centuries been known in Spain,
    At least since the retirement of the Vandals,
First vowed (and never had she vowed in vain)
    To Virgin Mary several pounds of candles;
And then, by the advice of some old ladies,
1520 She sent her son to be shipped off from Cadiz.

CXCI

She had resolved that he should travel through
    All European climes, by land or sea,
To mend his former morals, and get new,
    Especially in France and Italy
(At least this is the thing most people do).
    Julia was sent into a convent: she
Grieved, but, perhaps, her feelings may be better
Shown in the following copy of her Letter:°—

CXCII

'They tell me 'tis decided; you depart:
1530   'Tis wise—'tis well, but not the less a pain;
I have no further claim on your young heart,
    Mine is the victim, and would be again;
To love too much has been the only art
    I used;—I write in haste, and if a stain
Be on this sheet, 'tis not what it appears;
My eyeballs burn and throb, but have no tears.

CXCIII

'I loved, I love you, for this love have lost
    State, station, heaven, mankind's, my own esteem,
And yet can not regret what it hath cost,
1540   So dear is still the memory of that dream;
Yet, if I name my guilt, 'tis not to boast,

Gurney W. B. Gurney, shorthand trial reporter
her Letter a marvelous document, demonstrating enormous advances in sophistication on
Julia's part, and suggesting that her convent
existence was not particularly repressive

None can deem harshlier of me than I deem:
I trace this scrawl because I cannot rest—
I've nothing to reproach or to request.

CXCIV

'Man's love is of man's life a thing apart,
    'Tis woman's whole existence;° man may range
The court, camp, church, the vessel, and the mart;
    Sword, gown, gain, glory, offer in exchange
Pride, fame, ambition, to fill up his heart,
1550   And few there are whom these cannot estrange;
Men have all these resources, we but one,
To love again, and be again undone.

CXCV

'You will proceed in pleasure, and in pride,
    Beloved and loving many; all is o'er
For me on earth, except some years to hide
    My shame and sorrow deep in my heart's core;
These I could bear, but cannot cast aside
    The passion which still rages as before,—
And so farewell—forgive me, love me—No,
1560 That word is idle now—but let it go.

CXCVI

'My breast has been all weakness, is so yet;
    But still I think I can collect my mind;
My blood still rushes where my spirit's set,
    As roll the waves before the settled wind;
My heart is feminine, nor can forget—
    To all, except one image, madly blind;
So shakes the needle, and so stands the pole,
As vibrates my fond heart to my fixed soul.

CXCVII

'I have no more to say, but linger still,
1570   And dare not set my seal upon this sheet,
And yet I may as well the task fulfil,
    My misery can scarce be more complete:
I had not lived till now, could sorrow kill;
    Death shuns the wretch who fain the blow would meet,
And I must even survive this last adieu,
And bear with life, to love and pray for you!'

CXCVIII

This note was written upon gilt-edged paper
    With a neat little crow-quill, slight and new;

Man's . . . existence lifted by Byron from
the celebrated Madame de Staël, whom he knew

Her small white hand could hardly reach the taper,
1580   It trembled as magnetic needles do,
And yet she did not let one tear escape her;
    The seal a sun-flower; '*Elle vous suit partout*,'°
The motto, cut upon a white cornelian;
The wax was superfine, its hue vermilion.

CXCIX

This was Don Juan's earliest scrape; but whether
    I shall proceed with his adventures is
Dependent on the public altogether;
    We'll see, however, what they say to this,
Their favour in an author's cap's a feather,
1590   And no great mischief's done by their caprice;
And if their approbation we experience,
Perhaps they'll have some more about a year hence.

CC

My poem's epic, and is meant to be
    Divided in twelve books; each book containing,
With love, and war, a heavy gale at sea,
    A list of ships, and captains, and kings reigning,
New characters; the episodes are three:
    A panoramic view of hell's in training,
After the style of Virgil and of Homer,
1600 So that my name of Epic's no misnomer.

CCI

All these things will be specified in time,
    With strict regard to Aristotle's rules,
The *Vade Mecum*° of the true sublime,
    Which makes so many poets, and some fools:
Prose poets like blank-verse, I'm fond of rhyme,
    Good workmen never quarrel with their tools;
I've got new mythological machinery,
And very handsome supernatural scenery.

CCII

There's only one slight difference between
1610   Me and my epic brethren gone before,
And here the advantage is my own, I ween
    (Not that I have not several merits more,
But this will more peculiarly be seen);
    They so embellish, that 'tis quite a bore
Their labyrinth of fables to thread through,
Whereas this story's actually true.

'**Elle vous suit partout**' "she follows you every-   **Vade Mecum** a guidebook, literally "go with
where"   me"

CCIII

If any person doubt it, I appeal
    To history, tradition, and to facts,
To newspapers, whose truth all know and feel,
1620   To plays in five, and operas in three acts;
All these confirm my statement a good deal,
    But that which more completely faith exacts
Is, that myself, and several now in Seville,
Saw Juan's last elopement with the devil.

CCIV

If ever I should condescend to prose,
    I'll write poetical commandments, which
Shall supersede beyond all doubt all those
    That went before; in these I shall enrich
My text with many things that no one knows,
1630   And carry precept to the highest pitch:
I'll call the work 'Longinus o'er a Bottle,
Or, Every Poet his *own* Aristotle.'°

CCV

Thou shalt believe in Milton, Dryden, Pope;
    Thou shalt not set up Wordsworth, Coleridge, Southey;
Because the first is crazed beyond all hope,
    The second drunk,° the third so quaint and mouthy:
With Crabbe it may be difficult to cope,
    And Campbell's Hippocrene is somewhat drouthy:
Thou shalt not steal from Samuel Rogers,° nor
1640 Commit—flirtation with the muse of Moore.

CCVI

Thou shalt not covet Mr. Sotheby's° Muse,
    His Pegasus, nor anything that's his;
Thou shalt not bear false witness like 'the Blues'°—
    (There's one,° at least, is very fond of this);
Thou shalt not write, in short, but what I choose:
    This is true criticism, and you may kiss—
Exactly as you please, or not,—the rod;
But if you don't, I'll lay it on, by G—d!

CCVII

If any person should presume to assert
1650   This story is not moral, first, I pray,

'**Longinus . . . Aristotle**' Aristotle was made
the authority for poetic "rules" by Renaissance
and later critics; the more Romantic Longinus
(3rd century A.D.) was interpreted as authority
for yielding to inspiration
The . . . drunk Coleridge was a heavy brandy
drinker

Samuel Rogers (1763–1855) better known as
a conversationalist than as a poet
Sotheby's William Sotheby (1757–1833), poetic
translator
'**the Blues**' "bluestockings," or literary women
There's one perhaps Lady Byron, or else Caroline Lamb, a cast-off mistress of Byron's

That they will not cry out before they're hurt,
    Then that they'll read it o'er again, and say
(But, doubtless, nobody will be so pert),
    That this is not a moral tale, though gay;
Besides, in Canto Twelfth, I mean to show
The very place where wicked people go.

CCVIII

If, after all, there should be some so blind
    To their own good this warning to despise,
Let by some tortuosity of mind,
1660   Not to believe my verse and their own eyes,
And cry that they 'the moral cannot find,'
    I tell him, if a clergyman, he lies;
Should captains the remark, or critics, make,
They also lie too—under a mistake.

CCIX

The public approbation I expect,
    And beg they'll take my word about the moral,
Which I with their amusement will connect
    (So children cutting teeth receive a coral);
Meantime they'll doubtless please to recollect
1670   My epical pretensions to the laurel:
For fear some prudish readers should grow skittish,
I've bribed my grandmother's review—the British.

CCX

I sent it in a letter to the Editor,
    Who thanked me duly by return of post—
I'm for a handsome article his creditor;
    Yet, if my gentle Muse he please to roast,
And break a promise after having made it her,
    Denying the receipt of what it cost,
And smear his page with gall instead of honey,
1680 All I can say is—that he had the money.

CCXI

I think that with this holy new alliance
    I may ensure the public, and defy
All other magazines of art or science,
    Daily, or monthly, or three monthly; I
Have not essayed to multiply their clients,
    Because they tell me 'twere in vain to try,
And that the Edinburgh Review and Quarterly
Treat a dissenting author very martyrly.

CCXII

'Non ego hoc ferrem calida juventâ
1690   Consule Planco,' Horace said,° and so
Say I; by which quotation there is meant a
    Hint that some six or seven good years ago
(Long ere I dreamt of dating from the Brenta)
    I was most ready to return a blow,
And would not brook at all this sort of thing
In my hot youth—when George the Third was King.

CCXIII

But now at thirty years my hair is grey—
    (I wonder what it will be like at forty?
I thought of a peruke° the other day—)
1700   My heart is not much greener; and, in short, I
Have squandered my whole summer while 'twas May,
    And feel no more the spirit to retort; I
Have spent my life, both interest and principal,
And deem not, what I deemed, my soul invincible.

CCXIV

No more—no more—Oh! never more on me
    The freshness of the heart can fall like dew,
Which out of all the lovely things we see
    Extracts emotions beautiful and new,
Hived in our bosom like the bag of the bee:
1710   Think'st thou the honey with those objects grew?
Alas! 'twas not in them, but in thy power
To double even the sweetness of a flower.

CCXV

No more—no more—Oh! never more, my heart,
    Canst thou be my sole world, my universe!
Once all in all, but now a thing apart,
    Thou canst not be my blessing or my curse:
The illusion's gone for ever, and thou art
    Insensible, I trust, but none the worse,
And in thy stead I've got a deal of judgment,
1720   Though heaven knows how it ever found a lodgment.°

CCXVI

My days of love are over;° me no more
    The charms of maid, wife, and still less of widow,
Can make the fool of which they made before,—

Horace said *Odes* III.xiv: "I should not have borne this in the heat of youth when Plancus was Consul"
peruke wig
lodgment These stanzas (CCXIV, CCXV) are

Byron's version of Wordsworth's "Intimations of Immortality" ode.
My . . . over paraphrase of Horace, *Odes* IV. i.29–32

In short, I must not lead the life I did do;
The credulous hope of mutual minds is o'er,
   The copious use of claret is forbid too,
So for a good old-gentlemanly vice,
I think I must take up with avarice.

CCXVII

Ambition was my idol, which was broken
1730   Before the shrines of Sorrow, and of Pleasure;
And the two last have left me many a token
   O'er which reflection may be made at leisure:
Now, like Friar Bacon's brazen head,° I've spoken,
   'Time is, Time was, Time's past:'—a chymic° treasure
Is glittering youth, which I have spent betimes—
My heart in passion, and my head on rhymes.

CCXVIII

What is the end of fame? 'tis but to fill
   A certain portion of uncertain paper:
Some liken it to climbing up a hill,
1740   Whose summit, like all hills, is lost in vapour;
For this men write, speak, preach, and heroes kill,
   And bards burn what they call their 'midnight taper,'
To have, when the original is dust,
A name, a wretched picture, and worse bust.

CCXIX

What are the hopes of man? Old Egypt's King
   Cheops erected the first pyramid
And largest, thinking it was just the thing
   To keep his memory whole, and mummy hid:
But somebody or other rummaging,
1750   Burglariously broke his coffin's lid:
Let not a monument give you or me hopes,
Since not a pinch of dust remains of Cheops.

CCXX

But, I being fond of true philosophy,
   Say very often to myself, 'Alas!
All things that have been born were born to die,
   And flesh (which Death mows down to hay) is grass;
You've passed your youth not so unpleasantly,
   And if you had it o'er again—'twould pass—
So thank your stars that matters are no worse,
1760 And read your Bible, sir, and mind your purse.'

Now . . . head See Robert Greene's *Friar Bacon*   chymic alchemical
and Friar Bungay IV.i.

CCXXI

But for the present, gentle reader! and
 Still gentler purchaser! the bard—that's I—
Must, with permission, shake you by the hand,
 And so your humble servant, and good-bye!
We meet again, if we should understand
 Each other; and if not, I shall not try
Your patience further than by this short sample—
'Twere well if others followed my example.

CCXXII

'Go, little book, from this my solitude!
1770 I cast thee on the waters—go thy ways!
And if, as I believe, thy vein be good,
 The world will find thee after many days.'°
When Southey's read, and Wordsworth understood,
 I can't help putting in my claim to praise—
The four first rhymes are Southey's, every line:
For God's sake, reader! take them not for mine!
1818   1819

From *Canto the Third*

I

Hail, Muse! *et caetera.*—We left Juan sleeping,
 Pillowed upon a fair and happy breast,
And watched by eyes that never yet knew weeping,
 And loved by a young heart, too deeply blessed
To feel the poison through her spirit creeping,
 Or know who rested there, a foe to rest,
Had soiled the current of her sinless years,
And turned her pure heart's purest blood to tears!

II

Oh, Love! what is it in this world of ours
10 Which makes it fatal to be loved? Ah why
With cypress branches hast thou wreathed thy bowers,
 And made thy best interpreter a sigh?
As those who dote on odours pluck the flowers,
 And place them on their breast—but place to die—
Thus the frail beings we would fondly cherish
Are laid within our bosoms but to perish.

III

In her first passion woman loves her lover,
 In all the others all she loves is love,

'**Go . . . days**' from the last stanza of Southey's
Epilogue to the Lay of the Laureate

Which grows a habit she can ne'er get over,
20 And fits her loosely—like an easy glove,
As you may find, whene'er you like to prove her:
  One man alone at first her heart can move;
She then prefers him in the plural number,
Not finding that the additions much encumber.

   IV
I know not if the fault be men's or theirs;
  But one thing's pretty sure; a woman planted
(Unless at once she plunge for life in prayers)
  After a decent time must be gallanted;
Although, no doubt, her first of love affairs
30 Is that to which her heart is wholly granted;
Yet there are some, they say, who have had *none*,
But those who have ne'er end with only *one*.

   V
'Tis melancholy, and a fearful sign
  Of human frailty, folly, also crime,
That love and marriage rarely can combine,
  Although they both are born in the same clime;
Marriage from love, like vinegar from wine—
  A sad, sour, sober beverage—by time
Is sharpened from its high celestial flavour,
40 Down to a very homely household savour.

   VI
There's something of antipathy, as 'twere,
  Between their present and their future state;
A kind of flattery that's hardly fair
  Is used until the truth arrives too late—
Yet what can people do, except despair?
  The same things change their names at such a rate;
For instance—passion in a lover's glorious,
But in a husband is pronounced uxorious.

   VII
Men grow ashamed of being so very fond;
50 They sometimes also get a little tired
(But that, of course, is rare), and then despond:
  The same things cannot always be admired,
Yet 'tis 'so nominated in the bond,'
  That both are tied till one shall have expired.
Sad thought! to lose the spouse that was adorning
Our days, and put one's servants into mourning.

VIII

There's doubtless something in domestic doings
 Which forms, in fact, true love's antithesis;
Romances paint at full length people's wooings,
60 But only give a bust of marriages;
For no one cares for matrimonial cooings,
 There's nothing wrong in a connubial kiss:
Think you, if Laura had been Petrarch's wife,
He would have written sonnets all his life?

IX

All tragedies are finished by a death,
 All comedies are ended by a marriage;
The future states of both are left to faith,
 For authors fear description might disparage
The worlds to come of both, or fall beneath,
70 And then both worlds would punish their miscarriage;
So leaving each their priest and prayer-book ready,
They say no more of Death or of the Lady.°

X

The only two that in my recollection
 Have sung of heaven and hell, or marriage, are
Dante and Milton, and of both the affection
 Was hapless in their nuptials, for some bar
Of fault or temper ruined the connexion
 (Such things, in fact, it don't ask much to mar);
But Dante's Beatrice and Milton's Eve
80 Were not drawn from their spouses, you conceive.

XI

Some persons say that Dante meant theology
 By Beatrice, and not a mistress—I,
Although my opinion may require apology,
 Deem this a commentator's phantasy,
Unless indeed it was from his own knowledge he
 Decided thus, and showed good reason why;
I think that Dante's more abstruse ecstatics
Meant to personify the mathematics.

. . .

XCI

Milton's the prince of poets—so we say;
 A little heavy, but no less divine:
An independent being in his day—
820 Learned, pious, temperate in love and wine;

They . . . Lady refers to popular ballad
"Death and the Lady"

But his life falling into Johnson's way,
    We're told this great high priest of all the Nine
Was whipped at college—a harsh sire—odd spouse,
    For the first Mrs. Milton left his house.

XCII

All these are, *certes*, entertaining facts,
    Like Shakespeare's stealing deer, Lord Bacon's bribes;
Like Titus' youth, and Caesar's earliest acts;°
    Like Burns (whom Doctor Currie well describes);°
Like Cromwell's pranks;—but although truth exacts
830   These amiable descriptions from the scribes,
As most essential to their hero's story,
They do not much contribute to his glory.

XCIII

All are not moralists, like Southey, when
    He prated to the world of 'Pantisocracy';
Or Wordsworth unexcised, unhired, who then
    Seasoned his pedlar poems with democracy;
Or Coleridge, long before his flighty pen
    Let to the Morning Post its aristocracy;°
When he and Southey, following the same path,
840   Espoused two partners (milliners of Bath).°

XCIV

Such names at present cut a convict figure,
    The very Botany Bay° in moral geography;
Their loyal treason, renegado rigour,
    Are good manure for their more bare biography.
Wordsworth's last quarto, by the way, is bigger
    Than any since the birthday of typography;
A drowsy frowzy poem, called the 'Excursion,'
Writ in a manner which is my aversion.

XCV

He there builds up a formidable dike
850   Between his own and others' intellect;
But Wordsworth's poem, and his followers, like
    Joanna Southcote's Shiloh,° and her sect,
Are things which in this century don't strike
    The public mind,—so few are the elect;

Like . . . acts Suetonious said the Emperor Titus, in his youth, was a forger, and Caesar a torturer.
Like . . . describes A life of Burns published in 1800 by James Currie detailed much scandal about the poet.
Or Coleridge . . . aristocracy In 1800 Coleridge began to write for the *Morning Post.*
When . . . Bath In autumn 1795, Coleridge and Southey married the Fricker sisters, of Bath.
Botany Bay penal colony in Australia
Joanna . . . Shiloh The prophetess Joanna Southcott (1750–1814) insisted she would bear the second Messiah, Shiloh.

And the new births of both their stale virginities
Have proved but dropsies, taken for divinities.

XCVI

But let me to my story: I must own,
    If I have any fault, it is digression—
Leaving my people to proceed alone,
860   While I soliloquize beyond expression;
But these are my addresses from the throne,
    Which put off business to the ensuing session:
Forgetting each omission is a loss to
The world, not quite so great as Ariosto.°

XCVII

I know that what our neighbours call 'longueurs,'°
    (We've not so good a *word*, but have the *thing*,
In that complete perfection which insures
    An epic from Bob Southey every Spring—)
Form not the true temptation which allures
870   The reader; but 'twould not be hard to bring
Some fine examples of the *epopée*,°
To prove its grand ingredient is *ennui*.

XCVIII

We learn from Horace, 'Homer sometimes sleeps';
    We feel without him, Wordsworth sometimes wakes,—
To show with what complacency he creeps,
    With his dear 'Waggoners,' around his lakes.°
He wishes for 'a boat' to sail the deeps—
    Of ocean?—No, of air; and then he makes
Another outcry for 'a little boat,'
880 And drivels seas to set it well afloat.°

XCIX

If he must fain sweep o'er the ethereal plain,
    And Pegasus runs restive in his 'Waggon,'
Could he not beg the loan of Charles's Wain?
    Or pray Medea for a single dragon?°
Or if, too classic for his vulgar brain,
    He feared his neck to venture such a nag on,
And he must needs mount nearer to the moon,
Could not the blockhead ask for a balloon?

Ariosto Ludovico Ariosto (1474–1533) wrote *Orlando Furioso*, greatest of the Italian epic romances.
'longueurs' tediousness
epopée épopée, epic poetry

lakes See Wordsworth's *The Waggoner* (1819).
And . . . afloat See the opening passage of Wordsworth's *Peter Bell*.
Or . . . dragon In the *Medea* of Euripides, she escapes in a chariot pulled by dragons.

C

'Pedlars,' and 'Boats,' and 'Waggons!' Oh! ye shades
890   Of Pope and Dryden, are we come to this?
That trash of such sort not alone evades
    Contempt, but from the bathos' vast abyss
Floats scumlike uppermost, and these Jack Cades°
    Of sense and song above your graves may hiss—
The 'little boatman' and his 'Peter Bell'
Can sneer at him who drew 'Achitophel!'

1819   1821

From *Canto the Fourth*

I

Nothing so difficult as a beginning
    In poesy, unless perhaps the end;
For oftentimes when Pegasus seems winning
    The race, he sprains a wing, and down we tend,
Like Lucifer when hurled from heaven for sinning;
    Our sin the same, and hard as his to mend,
Being pride, which leads the mind to soar too far,
Till our own weakness shows us what we are.

II

But time, which brings all beings to their level,
10   And sharp Adversity, will teach at last
Man,—and, as we would hope,—perhaps the devil,
    That neither of their intellects are vast:
While youth's hot wishes in our red veins revel,
    We know not this—the blood flows on too fast:
But as the torrent widens towards the ocean,
We ponder deeply on each past emotion.

III

As boy, I thought myself a clever fellow,
    And wished that others held the same opinion;
They took it up when my days grew more mellow,
20   And other minds acknowledged my dominion:
Now my sere fancy 'falls into the yellow
    Leaf,'° and Imagination droops her pinion,
And the sad truth which hovers o'er my desk
Turns what was once romantic to burlesque.

IV

And if I laugh at any mortal thing,
    'Tis that I may not weep; and if I weep,

Jack Cades Cade, a Pretender to the throne, led
a rebellion in 1450.

'falls . . . Leaf' See *Macbeth* V.iii.22–23, one
of Byron's favorite passages.

'Tis that our nature cannot always bring
    Itself to apathy, for we must steep
Our hearts first in the depths of Lethe's spring,
30   Ere what we least wish to behold will sleep:
Thetis baptized her mortal son in Styx;
A mortal mother would on Lethe fix.

v

Some have accused me of a strange design
    Against the creed and morals of the land,
And trace it in this poem every line:
    I don't pretend that I quite understand
My own meaning when I would be *very* fine;
    But the fact is that I have nothing planned,
Unless it were to be a moment merry,
40 A novel word in my vocabulary.

vi

To the kind reader of our sober clime
    This way of writing will appear exotic;
Pulci° was sire of the half-serious rhyme,
    Who sang when chivalry was more Quixotic,
And revelled in the fancies of the time,
    True knights, chaste dames, huge giants, kings despotic;
But all these, save the last, being obsolete,
I chose a modern subject as more meet.

1819–20   · · ·   1821

From *Canto the Fifth*

xxx

I wonder if his appetite was good?
    Or, if it were, if also his digestion?
Methinks at meals some odd thoughts might intrude,
    And conscience ask a curious sort of question,
About the right divine how far we should
    Sell flesh and blood. When dinner has oppressed one,
I think it is perhaps the gloomiest hour
240 Which turns up out of the sad twenty-four.

xxxi

Voltaire says 'No;' he tells you that Candide
    Found life most tolerable after meals;
He's wrong—unless man were a pig, indeed,
    Repletion rather adds to what he feels,

Pulci Luigi Pulci (1432–84), Florentine poet whose *Morgante Maggiore* begins the mode that leads to *Don Juan;* Byron translated the first canto of Pulci's poem

Unless he's drunk, and then no doubt he's freed
    From his own brain's oppression while it reels.
Of food I think with Philip's son, or rather
Ammon's (ill pleased with one world and one father°);

XXXII

250
I think with Alexander, that the act
    Of eating, with another act or two,
Makes us feel our mortality in fact
    Redoubled; when a roast and a ragout,
And fish, and soup, by some side dishes backed,
    Can give us either pain or pleasure; who
Would pique himself on intellects, whose use
Depends so much upon the gastric juice?

XXXIII

The other evening ('twas on Friday last)—
    This is a fact, and no poetic fable—
Just as my great coat was about me cast,
260
    My hat and gloves still lying on the table,
I heard a shot—'twas eight o'clock scarce past—
    And, running out as fast as I was able,
I found the military commandant
Stretched in the street, and able scarce to pant.

XXXIV

Poor fellow! for some reason, surely bad,
    They had slain him with five slugs; and left him there
To perish on the pavement: so I had
    Him borne into the house and up the stair,
And stripped, and looked to,—But why should I add
270
    More circumstances? vain was every care;
The man was gone: in some Italian quarrel
Killed by five bullets from an old gun-barrel.

XXXV

I gazed upon him, for I knew him well;
    And though I have seen many corpses, never
Saw one, whom such an accident befell,
    So calm; though pierced through stomach, heart, and liver,
He seemed to sleep,—for you could scarcely tell
    (As he bled inwardly, no hideous river
Of gore divulged the cause) that he was dead:
280
So as I gazed on him, I thought or said—

Of . . . father Plutarch tells us that the god
Ammon, in a serpent's form, begot Alexander
the Great upon King Philip's wife; Plutarch
also says that Alexander felt his supposed
godhood threatened only by sleep and sexual
intercourse.

XXXVI

'Can this be death? then what is life or death?
    Speak!' but he spoke not: 'wake!' but still he slept:— .
'But yesterday, and who had mightier breath?
    A thousand warriors by his word were kept
In awe: he said, as the centurion saith,
    "Go," and he goeth; "come," and forth he stepped.
The trump and bugle till he spake were dumb—
And now nought left him but the muffled drum.'

XXXVII

And they who waited once and worshipped—they
290   With their rough faces thronged about the bed
To gaze once more on the commanding clay
    Which for the last, though not the first, time bled:
And such an end! that he who many a day
    Had faced Napoleon's foes until they fled,—
The foremost in the charge or in the sally,
Should now be butchered in a civic alley.

XXXVIII

The scars of his old wounds were near his new,
    Those honourable scars which brought him fame;
And horrid was the contrast to the view——
300   But let me quit the theme; as such things claim
Perhaps even more attention than is due
    From me: I gazed (as oft I have gazed the same)
To try if I could wrench aught out of death
Which should confirm, or shake, or make a faith;

XXXIX

But it was all a mystery. Here we are,
    And there we go:—but *where?* five bits of lead,
Or three, or two, or one, send very far!
    And is this blood, then, formed but to be shed?
Can every element our elements mar?
310   And air—earth—water—fire live—and we dead?
We, whose minds comprehend all things? No more;
But let us to the story as before.

·   ·   ·

1820   1821

From *Canto the Seventh*

I

O Love! O Glory! what are you who fly
    Around us ever, rarely to alight?
There's not a meteor in the Polar sky

Of such transcendent and more fleeting flight.
Chill, and chained to cold earth, we lift on high
    Our eyes in search of either lovely light;
A thousand and a thousand colours they
Assume, then leave us on our freezing way.

II

And such as they are, such my present tale is,
    A nondescript and ever-varying rhyme,
A versified Aurora Borealis,
    Which flashes o'er a waste and icy clime.
When we know what all are, we must bewail us,
    But ne'ertheless I hope it is no crime
To laugh at *all* things—for I wish to know
What, after *all*, are *all* things—but a *show?*

III

They accuse me—*Me*—the present writer of
    The present poem—of—I know not what—
A tendency to under-rate and scoff
    At human power and virtue, and all that;
And this they say in language rather rough.
    Good God! I wonder what they would be at!
I say no more than hath been said in Dante's
Verse, and by Solomon and by Cervantes;

IV

By Swift, by Machiavel, by Rochefoucault,°
    By Fénelon,° by Luther, and by Plato;
By Tillotson,° and Wesley,° and Rousseau,
    Who knew this life was not worth a potato.
'Tis not their fault, nor mine, if this be so,—
    For my part, I pretend not to be Cato,°
Nor even Diogenes.°—We live and die,
But which is best, you know no more than I.

V

Socrates said, our only knowledge was
    'To know that nothing could be known;' a pleasant
Science enough, which levels to an ass
    Each man of wisdom, future, past, or present.
Newton (that proverb of the mind), alas!
    Declared, with all his grand discoveries recent,

Rochefoucault François, Duke of La Roche-foucauld, 17th-century French secular moralist
Fénelon 17th-century French Quietist and religious moralist
Tillotson John Tillotson, 17th-century English divine and prose stylist
Wesley John Wesley, 18th-century Methodist leader
Cato Cato the Younger (Roman politician, 1st century B.C.), known for his moral uprightness
Diogenes ascetic and Cynic philosopher

That he himself felt only 'like a youth
40 Picking up shells by the great ocean—Truth.'

VI

Ecclesiastes said, 'that all is vanity'—
    Most modern preachers say the same, or show it
By their examples of true Christianity:
    In short, all know, or very soon may know it;
And in this scene of all-confessed inanity,
    By saint, by sage, by preacher, and by poet,
Must I restrain me, through the fear of strife,
From holding up the nothingness of life?

VII

Dogs, or men!—for I flatter you in saying
50   That ye are dogs—your betters far—ye may
Read, or read not, what I am now essaying
    To show ye what ye are in every way.
As little as the moon stops for the baying
    Of wolves, will the bright Muse withdraw one ray
From out her skies—then howl your idle wrath!
While she still silvers o'er your gloomy path.

VIII

'Fierce loves and faithless wars'—I am not sure
    If this be the right reading—'tis no matter;°
The fact's about the same, I am secure;
60   I sing them both, and am about to batter
A town which did a famous siege endure,
    And was beleaguer'd both by land and water
By Souvaroff, or Anglicè Suwarrow,°
Who loved blood as an alderman loves marrow.

1822   1823

From *Canto the Ninth*

LXII

Though somewhat large, exuberant, and truculent,
490   When *wroth*—while *pleased*, she° was as fine a figure
As those who like things rosy, ripe, and succulent,
    Would wish to look on, while they are in vigour.
She could repay each amatory look you lent
    With interest, and in turn was wont with rigour

'**Fierce . . . matter** Byron deliberately reverses
Spenser's "Fierce wars and faithful loves shall
moralize my song," the last line of *The Faerie
Queene's* first stanza.
Suwarrow The Russian general Suvaroff attacked

Ismael, a Danubian Turkish fortress-town, on
November 30, 1790; "Anglicè" means "the
English spelling."
she Catherine the Great, Empress of Russia,
notorious for her intense sexual life

To exact of Cupid's bills the full amount
At sight, nor would permit you to discount.

LXIII

With her the latter, though at times convenient,
    Was not so necessary; for they tell
That she was handsome, and though fierce *looked* lenient,
500   And always used her favourites too well.
If once beyond her boudoir's precincts in ye went,
    Your 'fortune' was in a fair way 'to swell
A man' (as Giles says°); for though she would widow all
Nations, she liked man as an individual.

LXIV

What a strange thing is man! and what a stranger
    Is woman! What a whirlwind is her head,
And what a whirlpool full of depth and danger
    Is all the rest about her! Whether wed,
Or widow, maid, or mother, she can change her
510   Mind like the wind: whatever she has said
Or done, is light to what she'll say or do;—
The oldest thing on record, and yet new!

LXV

Oh Catherine! (for of all interjections,
    To thee both *oh!* and *ah!* belong of right
In love and war) how odd are the connexions
    Of human thoughts, which jostle in their flight!
Just now *yours* were cut out in different sections:
    First Ismail's capture caught your fancy quite;
Next of new knights, the fresh and glorious batch;
520 And *thirdly* he who brought you the despatch!

LXVI

Shakespeare talks of 'the herald Mercury
    New lighted on a heaven-kissing hill:'°
And some such visions crossed her majesty,
    While her young herald knelt before her still.
'Tis very true the hill seemed rather high,
    For a lieutenant to climb up; but skill
Smooth'd even the Simplon's steep,° and by God's blessing,
With youth and health all kisses are 'heaven-kissing.'

Giles says See Philip Massinger's *A New Way To Pay Old Debts* V.i, where Sir Giles Overreach says: "His fortune swells him: 'tis rank, he's married."

Shakespeare . . . hill see *Hamlet* III.iv.58–59 **Simplon's steep** side of mountain pass in Swiss Alps

LXVII

Her majesty looked down, the youth looked up—
530   And so they fell in love;—she with his face,
His grace, his God-knows-what: for Cupid's cup
    With the first draught intoxicates apace,
A quintessential laudanum or 'black drop,'
    Which makes one drunk at once, without the base
Expedient of full bumpers; for the eye
In love drinks all life's fountains (save tears) dry.

LXVIII

He, on the other hand, if not in love,
    Fell into that no less imperious passion,
Self-love—which, when some sort of thing above
540   Ourselves, a singer, dancer, much in fashion,
Or duchess, princess, empress, 'deigns to prove'
    ('Tis Pope's phrase°) a great longing, though a rash one,
For one especial person out of many,
Makes us believe ourselves as good as any.

LXIX

Besides, he was of that delighted age
    Which makes all female ages equal—when
We don't much care with whom we may engage,
    As bold as Daniel in the lions' den,
So that we can our native sun assuage
550   In the next ocean, which may flow just then,
To make a twilight in, just as Sol's heat is
Quenched in the lap of the salt sea, or Thetis.

LXX

And Catherine (we must say thus much for Catherine),
    Though bold and bloody, was the kind of thing
Whose temporary passion was quite flattering,
    Because each lover looked a sort of king,
Made up upon an amatory pattern,
    A royal husband in all save the *ring*—
Which, being the damnedest part of matrimony,
560   Seemed taking out the sting to leave the honey.

LXXI

And when you add to this, her womanhood
    In its meridian, her blue eyes or gray—
(The last, if they have soul, are quite as good,
    Or better, as the best examples say:
Napoleon's, Mary's (queen of Scotland), should

Pope's phrase See *Eloisa to Abelard,* ll. 87–88.

Lend to that colour a transcendent ray;
And Pallas also sanctions the same hue,
Too wise to look through optics black or blue)—

LXXII

Her sweet smile, and her then majestic figure,
570   Her plumpness, her imperial condescension,
Her preference of a boy to men much bigger
   (Fellows whom Messalina's self would pension),
Her prime of life, just now in juicy vigour,
   With other *extras*, which we need not mention,—
All these, or any one of these, explain
Enough to make a stripling very vain.

LXXIII

And that's enough, for love is vanity,
   Selfish in its beginning as its end,
Except where 'tis a mere insanity,
580   A maddening spirit which would strive to blend
Itself with beauty's frail inanity,
   On which the passion's self seems to depend:
And hence some heathenish philosophers
Make love the main-spring of the universe.

LXXIV

Besides Platonic love, besides the love
   Of God, the love of sentiment, the loving
Of faithful pairs—I needs must rhyme with dove,
   That good old steam-boat which keeps verses moving
'Gainst reason—Reason ne'er was hand-and-glove
590   With rhyme, but always leant less to improving
The sound than sense) besides all these pretences
To love, there are those things which words name senses;

LXXV

Those movements, those improvements in our bodies
   Which make all bodies anxious to get out
Of their own sand-pits, to mix with a goddess,
   For such all women are at first no doubt.
How beautiful that moment! and how odd is
   That fever which precedes the languid rout
Of our sensations! What a curious way
600   The whole thing is of clothing souls in clay!

LXXVI

The noblest kind of love is love Platonical,
   To end or to begin with; the next grand
Is that which may be christened love canonical,

Because the clergy take the thing in hand;
The third sort to be noted in our chronicle
    As flourishing in every Christian land,
Is, when chaste matrons to their other ties
Add what may be called *marriage in disguise*.

LXXVII

Well, we won't analyse—our story must
610   Tell for itself: the sovereign was smitten,
Juan much flattered by her love, or lust;—
    I cannot stop to alter words once written,
And the two are so mixed with human dust,
    That he who *names one*, both perchance may hit on:
But in such matters Russia's mighty empress
Behaved no better than a common sempstress.

· · ·

1822   1823

From *Canto the Eleventh*

LIII

Juan knew several languages—as well
    He might—and brought them up with skill, in time
To save his fame with each accomplished belle,
420   Who still regretted that he did not rhyme.
There wanted but this requisite to swell
    His qualities (with them) into sublime:
Lady Fitz-Frisky, and Miss Maevia Mannish,
Both longed extremely to be sung in Spanish.

LIV

However, he did pretty well, and was
    Admitted as an aspirant to all
The coteries, and, as in Banquo's glass,
    At great assemblies or in parties small,
He saw ten thousand living authors pass,
430   That being about their average numeral;
Also the eighty 'greatest living poets,'
As every paltry magazine can show *it's*.

LV

In twice five years the 'greatest living poet,'
    Like to the champion in the fisty ring,
Is called on to support his claim, or show it,
    Although 'tis an imaginary thing.
Even I—albeit I'm sure I did not know it,
    Nor sought of foolscap subjects to be king,—
Was reckoned, a considerable time,
440   The grand Napoleon of the realms of rhyme.

LVI

But Juan was my Moscow,° and Faliero°
  My Leipsic,° and my Mont Saint Jean° seems Cain:°
'La Belle Alliance' of dunces down at zero,
  Now that the Lion's fallen, may rise again:
But I will fall at least as fell my hero;
  Nor reign at all, or as a *monarch* reign;
Or to some lonely isle of gaolers go,
With turncoat Southey for my turnkey Lowe.°

LVII

Sir Walter reigned before me; Moore and Campbell
450 Before and after: but now grown more holy,
The Muses upon Sion's hill must ramble
  With poets almost clergymen, or wholly;
And Pegasus has a psalmodic amble
  Beneath the very Reverend Rowley Powley,°
Who shoes the glorious animal with stilts,
A modern Ancient Pistol°—by the hilts!

.

LVIII

Still he excels that artificial hard
  Labourer in the same vineyard, though the vine
Yields him but vinegar for his reward,—
460 That neutralised dull Dorus of the Nine;
That swarthy Sporus,° neither man nor bard;
  That ox of verse, who *ploughs* for every line:—
Cambyses' roaring Romans beat at least
The howling Hebrews of Cybele's priest.°—

LIX

Then there's my gentle Euphues; who, they say,
  Sets up for being a sort of *moral me;*°
He'll find it rather difficult some day
  To turn out both, or either, it may be.
Some persons think that Coleridge hath the sway;
470 And Wordsworth has supporters, two or three;

But . . . Moscow Paralleling his literary career with Napoleon's military one, Byron dates his decline with the reading public from the publication of Canto I of *Don Juan.*
Faliero *Marino Faliero: An Historical Tragedy,* by Byron
Leipsic "The Battle of the Nations," where Napoleon was defeated in 1813
Mont Saint Jean farmhouse on Waterloo battlefield, symbol of Napoleon's final defeat
Cain Byron's great dramatic poem; much denounced for impiety and incest when it was published in 1821
Lowe Sir Hudson Lowe, captor of Napoleon on St. Helena

Powley the Reverend George Croly, a contemporary poet who had imitated Byron's work
Pistol See I *Henry IV* II.iv.197.
Sporus Pope's satirical name for Lord Hervey in his *Epistle to Dr. Arbuthnot*
That ox . . . priest Henry Hart Milman, Professor of Poetry at Oxford, whom Byron considered a critical enemy, is the "Ox of verse"; Leslie Marchand identifies the roaring Romans as being from Croly's *Cataline* and the howling Hebrews from Milman's *Fall of Jerusalem.*
Then . . . me B. W. Procter, a poet who wrote under the name of "Barry Cornwall"

And that deep-mouthed Boeotian 'Savage Landor'°
Has taken for a swan rogue Southey's gander.

LX

John Keats, who was killed off by one critique,
   Just as he really promised something great,
If not intelligible, without Greek
   Contrived to talk about the Gods of late,
Much as they might have been supposed to speak.°
   Poor fellow! His was an untoward fate;
'Tis strange the mind, that fiery particle,
480   Should let itself be snuffed out by an article.

LXI

The list grows long of live and dead pretenders
   To that which none will gain—or none will know
The conqueror at least; who, ere Time renders
   His last award, will have the long grass grow
Above his burnt-out brain, and sapless cinders.
   If I might augur, I should rate but low
Their chances;—they're too numerous, like the thirty
Mock tyrants, when Rome's annals waxed but dirty.

LXII

This is the literary *lower* empire,
490   Where the praetorian bands take up the matter;—
A 'dreadful trade,' like his who 'gathers samphire,'°
   The insolent soldiery to soothe and flatter,
With the same feelings as you'd coax a vampire.
   Now, were I once at home, and in good satire,
I'd try conclusions with those Janizaries,°
And show them *what* an intellectual war is.

LXIII

I think I know a trick or two, would turn
   Their flanks;—but it is hardly worth my while
With such small gear to give myself concern:
500   Indeed I've not the necessary bile;
My natural temper's really aught but stern,
   And even my Muse's worst reproof's a smile;
And then she drops a brief and modern curtsy,
And glides away, assured she never hurts ye.

Landor The Greeks thought the Boeotians to be savage and stupid; Landor was neither, but had a fierce temper; Landor was also on excellent terms with Southey.
John . . . speak in the great fragment *Hype-* *rion*; this is Byron's first praise for Keats's poetry
A . . . samphire See *King Lear* IV.vi.15.
Janizaries Turkish soldiers, particularly of the Sultan's Guard

LXIV

My Juan, whom I left in deadly peril
　Amongst live poets and blue ladies, passed
With some small profit through that field so sterile,
　Being tired in time, and neither least nor last,
Left it before he had been treated very ill;
　And henceforth found himself more gaily classed
Amongst the higher spirits of the day,
The sun's true son, no vapour, but a ray.

1822　　　　　　　　　　　　　　1823

Stanzas to the Po°

River, that rollest by the ancient walls,
　Where dwells the Lady of my love, when she
Walks by thy brink, and there perchance recalls
　A faint and fleeting memory of me;

What if thy deep and ample stream should be
　A mirror of my heart, where she may read
The thousand thoughts I now betray to thee,
　Wild as thy wave, and headlong as thy speed!

What do I say—a mirror of my heart?
　Are not thy waters sweeping, dark, and strong?
Such as my feelings were and are, thou art;
　And such as thou art were my passions long.

Time may have somewhat tamed them,—not for ever;
　Thou overflowest thy banks, and not for aye
Thy bosom overboils, congenial river!
　Thy floods subside, and mine have sunk away—

But left long wrecks behind: and now again,
　Borne in our old unchanged career, we move:
Thou tendest wildly onwards to the main.
　And I—to loving one I should not love.

The current I behold will sweep beneath
　Her native walls, and murmur at her feet;
Her eyes will look on thee, when she shall breathe
　The twilight air, unharmed by summer's heat.

She will look on thee,—I have looked on thee,
　Full of that thought; and, from that moment, ne'er

Stanzas to the Po This lyric, Byron's most accomplished, echoes the firm diction and grave sweet style of some of Dante's love poems. The poem was written only a few weeks after Byron, aged thirty-one, fell in love with the Countess Teresa Guiccioli, aged nineteen, who had been married only a year or so to the fifty-eight-year-old Count. Briefly separated from Teresa, he wrote the first draft of this poem, in which he struggles not to yield to love.

Thy waters could I dream of, name, or see,
    Without the inseparable sigh for her!

Her bright eyes will be imaged in thy stream,—
30   Yes! they will meet the wave I gaze on now:
Mine cannot witness, even in a dream,
    That happy wave repass me in its flow!

The wave that bears my tears returns no more:
    Will she return by whom that wave shall sweep?—
Both tread thy banks, both wander on thy shore,
    I by thy source, she by the dark-blue deep.

But that which keepeth us apart is not
    Distance, nor depth of wave, nor space of earth,
But the distraction of a various lot,
40   As various as the climates of our birth.

A stranger loves the Lady of the land,
    Born far beyond the mountains, but his blood
Is all meridian,° as if never fanned
    By the black wind that chills the polar flood.

My blood is all meridian; were it not,
    I had not left my clime, nor should I be,
In spite of tortures, ne'er to be forgot,
    A slave again of love,—at least of thee.

'Tis vain to struggle—let me perish young—
50   Live as I lived, and love as I have loved;
To dust if I return, from dust I sprung,
    And then, at least, my heart can ne'er be moved.°
    1819   1824

The Vision of Judgment

This is a satire on Robert Southey, a talented and highly productive man of letters, but generally a bad poet; Byron is quite kind to the deceased monarch George III, who needed kindness, as he had been a miserable failure, and died blind and crazy. Southey, like his friends of genius, Wordsworth and Coleridge, was a political

---

meridian the point at which the sun attains its highest altitude
My blood . . . moved Less than two months later, Byron ceased to hesitate and moved to join Teresa, and then redrafted the last two stanzas:

    My heart is all meridian, were it not
        I had not suffered now, nor should
        I be
    Despite old tortures ne'er to be forgot
        The slave again—Oh! Love! at least
        of thee!

'Tis vain to struggle, I have
    struggled long
To love again no more as once I
    loved,
Oh! Time! why leave this worst of
    earliest Passions strong?
To tear a heart which pants to be
    unmoved?

Revealing as this is, Byron was wise to keep to the first version.

turncoat, but also had accepted appointment as Poet Laureate upon the death of the bad poet Pye in 1813. This was enough for Byron to despise him, but Byron heard in 1817 that Southey was active in spreading scandalous rumors about him. The 1818 Dedication to the First Canto of *Don Juan* began the destruction of Southey; this brilliant poem completed it, and has given poor Southey the only immortality he has.

Southey's *A Vision of Judgment*, as befits an official lament for George III, opens with a preface in which the Laureate attacks "the Satanic School" of rebels and immoralists: Byron, Shelley, and their friends. The Laureate then goes into a trance, and "sees" the King gloriously accepted into Heaven.

The Vision of Judgment

I

Saint Peter sat by the celestial gate:
  His keys were rusty, and the lock was dull,
So little trouble had been given of late;
  Not that the place by any means was full,
But since the Gallic era 'eighty-eight'°
  The devils had ta'en a longer, stronger pull,
And 'a pull altogether,' as they say
At sea—which drew most souls another way.

II

The angels all were singing out of tune,
  And hoarse with having little else to do,
Excepting to wind up the sun and moon,
  Or curb a runaway young star or two,
Or wild colt of a comet, which too soon
  Broke out of bounds o'er the ethereal blue,
Splitting some planet with its playful tail,
As boats are sometimes by a wanton whale.

III

The guardian seraphs had retired on high,
  Finding their charges past all care below;
Terrestrial business filled nought in the sky
  Save the recording angel's black bureau;
Who found, indeed, the facts to multiply
  With such rapidity of vice and woe,
That he had stripped off both his wings in quills,
And yet was in arrear of human ills.

IV

His business so augmented of late years,
  That he was forced, against his will no doubt,

10

20

'eighty-eight' Byron takes 1788 as the start of the French Revolution.

(Just like those cherubs, earthly ministers,)
    For some resource to turn himself about,
And claim the help of his celestial peers,
30   To aid him ere he should be quite worn out
By the increased demand for his remarks;
Six angels and twelve saints were named his clerks.

          V
This was a handsome board—at least for heaven;
    And yet they had even then enough to do,
So many conquerors' cars were daily driven,
    So many kingdoms fitted up anew;
Each day too slew its thousands six or seven,
    Till at the crowning carnage, Waterloo,
They threw their pens down in divine disgust—
40 The page was so besmeared with blood and dust.

          VI
This by the way; 'tis not mine to record
    What angels shrink from: even the very devil
On this occasion his own work abhorred,
    So surfeited with the infernal revel:
Though he himself had sharpened every sword,
    It almost quenched his innate thirst of evil.
(Here Satan's sole good work deserves insertion—
'Tis, that he has both generals in reversion.°)

          VII
Let's skip a few short years of hollow peace,
50   Which peopled earth no better, hell as wont,
And heaven none—they form the tyrant's lease,
    With nothing but new names subscribed upon't;
'Twill one day finish: meantime they increase,
    'With seven heads and ten horns,' and all in front,
Like Saint John's foretold beast; but ours are born
Less formidable in the head than horn.

          VIII
In the first year of freedom's second dawn°
    Died George the Third; although no tyrant, one
Who shielded tyrants, till each sense withdrawn
60   Left him nor mental nor external sun:
A better farmer ne'er brushed dew from lawn,
    A worse king never left a realm undone!
He died—but left his subjects still behind,
One half as mad—and t'other no less blind.

Here . . . reversion Napoleon and Wellington
are marked out for Satan.
second dawn 1820, when George III died, saw

the first revolutionary upsurge since the Congress
of Vienna (1814–15).

IX

He died! his death made no great stir on earth;
   His burial made some pomp; there was profusion
Of velvet, gilding, brass, and no great dearth
   Of aught but tears—save those shed by collusion.
For these things may be bought at their true worth;
70   Of elegy there was the due infusion—
Bought also; and the torches, cloaks, and banners,
Heralds, and relics of old Gothic manners,

X

Formed a sepulchral melodrame. Of all
   The fools who flocked to swell or see the show,
Who cared about the corpse? The funeral
   Made the attraction, and the black the woe.
There throbbed not there a thought which pierced the pall;
   And when the gorgeous coffin was laid low,
It seemed the mockery of hell to fold
80   The rottenness of eighty years in gold.

XI

So mix his body with the dust! It might
   Return to what it *must* far sooner, were
The natural compound left alone to fight
   Its way back into earth, and fire, and air;
But the unnatural balsams merely blight
   What nature made him at his birth, as bare
As the mere million's base unmummied clay—
Yet all his spices but prolong decay.

XII

He's dead—and upper earth with him has done;
90   He's buried; save the undertaker's bill,
Or lapidary° scrawl, the world is gone
   For him, unless he left a German will;°
But where's the proctor who will ask his son?
   In whom his qualities are reigning still,
Except that household virtue, most uncommon,
Of constancy to a bad, ugly woman.

XIII

'God save the king!' It is a large economy
   In God to save the like; but if he will
Be saving, all the better; for not one am I
100   Of those who think damnation better still:
I hardly know too if not quite alone am I

lapidary a polisher of precious stones   III, hid away the will of his father, George I.
a German will George II, grandfather of George

In this small hope of bettering future ill
   By circumscribing, with some slight restriction,
   The eternity of hell's hot jurisdiction.

XIV

I know this is unpopular; I know
   'Tis blasphemous; I know one may be damned
For hoping no one else may e'er be so;
   I know my catechism; I know we're crammed
With the best doctrines till we quite o'erflow;
110   I know that all save England's church have shammed,
And that the other twice two hundred churches
And synagogues have made a *damned* bad purchase.

XV

God help us all! God help me too! I am,
   God knows, as helpless as the devil can wish,
And not a whit more difficult to damn,
   Than is to bring to land a late-hooked fish,
Or to the butcher to purvey the lamb;
   Not that I'm fit for such a noble dish,
As one day will be that immortal fry
120 Of almost everybody born to die.

XVI

Saint Peter sat by the celestial gate,
   And nodded o'er his keys; when, lo! there came
A wondrous noise he had not heard of late—
   A rushing sound of wind, and stream, and flame;
In short, a roar of things extremely great,
   Which would have made aught save a saint exclaim;
But he, with first a start and then a wink,
Said, 'There's another star gone out, I think!'

XVII

But ere he could return to his repose,
130   A cherub flapped his right wing o'er his eyes—
At which St. Peter yawned, and rubbed his nose:
   'Saint porter,' said the angel, 'prithee rise!'
Waving a goodly wing, which glowed, as glows
   An earthly peacock's tail, with heavenly dyes:
To which the saint replied, 'Well, what's the matter?
Is Lucifer come back with all this clatter?'

XVIII

'No,' quoth the cherub; 'George the Third is dead.'
   'And who *is* George the Third?' replied the apostle:
'*What George? what Third?*' 'The king of England,' said

140   The angel. 'Well! he won't find kings to jostle
      Him on his way; but does he wear his head;
          Because the last we saw here had a tustle,°
      And ne'er would have got into heaven's good graces,
      Had he not flung his head in all our faces.°

              XIX
      'He was, if I remember, king of France;
          That head of his, which could not keep a crown
      On earth, yet ventured in my face to advance
          A claim to those of martyrs—like my own:
      If I had had my sword, as I had once
150   When I cut ears off, I had cut him down;
      But having but my *keys*, and not my brand,
      I only knocked his head from out his hand.

              XX
      'And then he set up such a headless howl,
          That all the saints came out and took him in;
      And there he sits by St. Paul, cheek by jowl;
          That fellow Paul—the parvenù! The skin
      Of St. Bartholomew, which makes his cowl
          In heaven, and upon earth redeemed his sin°
      So as to make a martyr, never sped
160   Better than did this weak and wooden head.

              XXI
      'But had it come up here upon its shoulders,
          There would have been a different tale to tell:
      The fellow-feeling in the saint's beholders
          Seems to have acted on them like a spell;
      And so this very foolish head heaven solders
          Back on its trunk: it may be very well,
      And seems the custom here to overthrow
      Whatever has been wisely done below.'

              XXII
      The angel answered, 'Peter! do not pout:
170   The king who comes has head and all entire,
      And never knew much what it was about—
          He did as doth the puppet—by its wire,
      And will be judged like all the rest, no doubt:
          My business and your own is not to inquire
      Into such matters, but to mind our cue—
      Which is to act as we are bid to do.'

---

tustle tussle
Had . . . faces Louis XVI of France, guillotined
in 1793

The skin . . . sin St. Bartholomew was first
skinned alive, and then crucified.

XXIII

While thus they spake, the angelic caravan,
  Arriving like a rush of mighty wind,
Cleaving the fields of space, as doth the swan
  Some silver stream (say Ganges, Nile, or Inde,
Or Thames, or Tweed), and 'midst them an old man
  With an old soul, and both extremely blind,
Halted before the gate, and in his shroud
Seated their fellow-traveller on a cloud.

XXIV

But bringing up the rear of this bright host
  A Spirit of a different aspect waved
His wings, like thunder-clouds above some coast
  Whose barren beach with frequent wrecks is paved;
His brow was like the deep when tempest-tossed;
  Fierce and unfathomable thoughts engraved
Eternal wrath on his immortal face,
And *where* he gazed a gloom pervaded space.

XXV

As he drew near, he gazed upon the gate
  Ne'er to be entered more by him or Sin,
With such a glance of supernatural hate,
  As made Saint Peter wish himself within;
He patterned with his keys at a great rate,
  And sweated through his apostolic skin:
Of course his perspiration was but ichor,°
Or some such other spiritual liquor.

XXVI

The very cherubs huddled all together,
  Like birds when soars the falcon; and they felt
A tingling to the tip of every feather,
  And formed a circle like Orion's belt
Around their poor old charge; who scarce knew whither
  His guards had led him, though they gently dealt
With royal manes (for by many stories,
And true, we learn the angels all are Tories).

XXVII

As things were in this posture, the gate flew
  Asunder, and the flashing of its hinges
Flung over space an universal hue
  Of many-coloured flame, until its tinges
Reached even our speck of earth, and made a new

ichor The gods had ichor, an ethereal liquid,
rather than blood in their veins.

The line numbers 180, 190, 200, 210 appear in the left margin.

Aurora borealis spread its fringes
O'er the North Pole; the same seen, when ice-bound,
By Captain Parry's crew, in 'Melville's Sound.'°

XXVIII

And from the gate thrown open issued beaming
    A beautiful and mighty Thing of Light,
Radiant with glory, like a banner streaming
220   Victorious from some world-o'erthrowing fight:
My poor comparisons must needs be teeming
    With earthly likenesses, for here the night
Of clay obscures our best conceptions, saving
Johanna Southcote,° or Bob Southey raving.

XXIX

'Twas the archangel Michael: all men know
    The make of angels and archangels, since
There's scarce a scribbler has not one to show,
    From the fiends' leader to the angels' prince.
There also are some altar-pieces, though
230   I really can't say that they much evince
One's inner notions of immortal spirits;
But let the connoisseurs explain *their* merits.

XXX

Michael flew forth in glory and in good;
    A goodly work of him from whom all glory
And good arise; the portal past—he stood;
    Before him the young cherubs and saints hoary—
(I say *young*, begging to be understood
    By looks, not years; and should be very sorry
To state, they were not older than St. Peter,
240   But merely that they seemed a little sweeter).

XXXI

The cherubs and the saints bowed down before
    That arch-angelic hierarch, the first
Of essences angelical, who wore
    The aspect of a god; but this ne'er nursed
Pride in his heavenly bosom, in whose core
    No thought, save for his Master's service, durst
Intrude, however glorified and high;
He knew him but the viceroy of the sky.

'Melville's Sound' described by Sir William Edward Parry in his account of his voyages in quest of the Northwest Passage (1819–20)   **Johanna Southcote** Joanna Southcott (1750–1814), authoress of the *Book of Wonders*, a prophetess who expected to bear the Messiah, but died of a brain malady instead

XXXII

He and the sombre silent Spirit met—
250   They knew each other both for good and ill;
Such was their power, that neither could forget
     His former friend and future foe; but still
There was a high, immortal, proud regret
     In either's eye, as if 'twere less their will
Than destiny to make the eternal years
Their date of war, and their 'champ clos'° the spheres.

XXXIII

But here they were in neutral space: we know
     From Job,° that Satan hath the power to pay
A heavenly visit thrice a year or so;
260   And that the 'sons of God,' like those of clay,
Must keep him company; and we might show
     From the same book, in how polite a way
The dialogue is held between the Powers
Of Good and Evil—but 'twould take up hours.

XXXIV

And this is not a theologic tract,
     To prove with Hebrew and with Arabic
If Job be allegory or a fact,
     But a true narrative; and thus I pick
From out the whole but such and such an act
270   As sets aside the slightest thought of trick.
'Tis every tittle true, beyond suspicion,
And accurate as any other vision.

XXXV

The spirits were in neutral space, before
     The gate of heaven; like eastern thresholds is
The place where Death's grand cause is argued o'er,°
     And souls dispatched to that world or to this;
And therefore Michael and the other wore
     A civil aspect: though they did not kiss,
Yet still between his Darkness and his Brightness
280   There passed a mutual glance of great politeness.

XXXVI

The Archangel bowed, not like a modern beau,
     But with a graceful oriental bend,
Pressing one radiant arm just where below
     The heart in good men is supposed to tend.

'champ clos' tournament field, therefore closed off
Job Job 1:2

The spirits . . . o'er Oriental cities frequently debated policy and dealt out justice in their gateways.

He turned as to an equal, not too low,
    But kindly; Satan met his ancient friend
With more hauteur, as might an old Castilian
Poor noble meet a mushroom rich civilian.

XXXVII

He merely bent his diabolic brow
290   An instant; and then raising it, he stood
In act to assert his right or wrong, and show
    Cause why King George by no means could or should
Make out a case to be exempt from woe
    Eternal, more than other kings, endued
With better sense and hearts, whom history mentions,
Who long have 'paved hell with their good intentions.'

XXXVIII

Michael began: 'What wouldst thou with this man,
    Now dead, and brought before the Lord? What ill
Hath he wrought since his mortal race began,
300   That thou canst claim him? Speak! and do thy will,
If it be just: if in this earthly span
    He hath been greatly failing to fulfil
His duties as a king and mortal, say,
And he is thine; if not, let him have way.'

XXXIX

'Michael!' replied the Prince of Air, 'even here,
    Before the Gate of him thou servest, must
I claim my subject: and will make appear
    That as he was my worshipper in dust,
So shall he be in spirit, although dear
310   To thee and thine, because nor wine nor lust
Were of his weaknesses; yet on the throne
He reigned o'er millions to serve me alone.

XL

Look to *our* earth, or rather *mine;* it was,
    Once, more thy master's: but I triumph not
In this poor planet's conquest; nor, alas!
    Need he thou servest envy me my lot:
With all the myriads of bright worlds which pass
    In worship round him, he may have forgot
Yon weak creation of such paltry things:
320   I think few worth damnation save their kings,—

XLI

'And these but as a kind of quit-rent,° to
    Assert my right as lord: and even had

quit-rent feudal arrangement in which small
fixed sum was paid to overlord in lieu of
services due

I such an inclination, 'twere (as you
   Well know) superfluous; they are grown so bad,
That hell has nothing better left to do
   Than leave them to themselves: so much more mad
And evil by their own internal curse,
Heaven cannot make them better, nor I worse.

          XLII
   'Look to the earth, I said, and say again:
330   When this old, blind, mad, helpless, weak, poor worm
Began in youth's first bloom and flush to reign,
   The world and he both wore a different form,
And much of earth and all the watery plain
   Of ocean called him king: through many a storm
His isles had floated on the abyss of time;
For the rough virtues chose them for their clime.

          XLIII
   'He came to his sceptre young; he leaves it old:
   Look to the state in which he found his realm,
And left it; and his annals too behold,
340   How to a minion first he gave the helm;°
How grew upon his heart a thirst for gold,
   The beggar's vice, which can but overwhelm
The meanest hearts; and for the rest, but glance
Thine eye along America and France.

          XLIV
   ' 'Tis true, he was a tool from first to last
   (I have the workmen safe); but as a tool
So let him be consumed. From out the past
   Of ages, since mankind have known the rule
Of monarchs—from the bloody rolls amassed
350   Of sin and slaughter—from the Caesar's school,
Take the worst pupil; and produce a reign
More drenched with gore, more cumbered with the slain.

          XLV
   'He ever warred with freedom and the free:
   Nations as men, home subjects, foreign foes,
So that they uttered the word "Liberty!"
   Found George the Third their first opponent. Whose
History was ever stained as his will be
   With national and individual woes?
I grant his household abstinence; I grant
360   His neutral virtues, which most monarchs want;

How . . . helm The minion was the Earl of
Bute, Prime Minister (1762–63).

XLVI

'I know he was a constant consort; own
　　He was a decent sire, and middling lord.
All this is much, and most upon a throne;
　　As temperance, if at Apicius' board,°
Is more than at an anchorite's supper shown.
　　I grant him all the kindest can accord;
And this was well for him, but not for those
Millions who found him what oppression chose.

XLVII

370
'The New World shook him off; the Old yet groans
　　Beneath what he and his prepared, if not
Completed: he leaves heirs on many thrones
　　To all his vices, without what begot
Compassion for him—his tame virtues; drones
　　Who sleep, or despots who have now forgot
A lesson which shall be re-taught them, wake
Upon the thrones of earth; but let them quake!

XLVIII

'Five millions of the primitive, who hold
　　The faith which makes ye great on earth, implored
A *part* of that vast *all* they held of old,—
380
　　Freedom to worship—not alone your Lord,
Michael, but you, and you, Saint Peter! Cold
　　Must be your souls, if you have not abhorred
The foe to Catholic participation
In all the license of a Christian nation.°

XLIX

'True! he allowed them to pray God; but as
　　A consequence of prayer, refused the law
Which would have placed them upon the same base
　　With those who did not hold the saints in awe.'
But here Saint Peter started from his place,
390
　　And cried, 'You may the prisoner withdraw:
Ere heaven shall ope her portals to this Guelph,°
While I am guard, may I be damned myself!

L

'Sooner will I with Cerberus° exchange
　　My office (and *his* is no sinecure)
Than see this royal Bedlam bigot range

Apicius' board Apicius was a famous epicure
in Augustan Rome.
The foe . . . nation George III had opposed
the enfranchisement of the Catholic Irish.

Guelph family name of House of Hanover, the
line of George III
Cerberus three-headed dog who guarded the
gates of Hades

The azure fields of heaven, of that be sure!'
'Saint!' replied Satan, 'you do well to avenge
    The wrongs he made your satellites endure;
And if to this exchange you should be given,
400   I'll try to coax *our* Cerberus up to heaven.

LI

Here Michael interposed: 'Good saint! and devil!
    Pray, not so fast; you both outrun discretion.
Saint Peter! you were wont to be more civil!
    Satan! excuse this warmth of his expression,
And condescension to the vulgar's level:
    Even saints sometimes forget themselves in session.
Have you got more to say?'—'No.'—'If you please,
I'll trouble you to call your witnesses.'

LII

Then Satan turned and waved his swarthy hand,
410   Which stirred with its electric qualities
Clouds farther off than we can understand,
    Although we find him sometimes in our skies;
Infernal thunder shook both sea and land
    In all the planets, and hell's batteries
Let off the artillery, which Milton mentions°
As one of Satan's most sublime inventions.

LIII

This was a signal unto such damned souls
    As have the privilege of their damnation
Extended far beyond the mere controls
420   Of worlds past, present, or to come; no station
Is theirs particularly in the rolls
    Of hell assigned; but where their inclination
Or business carries them in search of game,
They may range freely—being damned the same.

LIV

They're proud of this—as very well they may,
    It being a sort of knighthood, or gilt key°
Stuck in their loins; or like to an 'entré'
    Up the back stairs, or such free-masonry.
I borrow my comparisons from clay,
430   Being clay myself. Let not those spirits be
Offended with such base low likenesses;
We know their posts are nobler far than these.

Milton mentions *Paradise Lost* VI.484–85   **gilt key** insignia of court officials

LV

When the great signal ran from heaven to hell—
  About ten million times the distance reckoned
From our sun to its earth, as we can tell
  How much time it takes up, even to a second,
For every ray that travels to dispel
  The fogs of London, through which, dimly beaconed,
The weathercocks are gilt some thrice a year,
440   If that the *summer* is not too severe:°—

LVI

I say that I can tell—'twas half a minute:
  I know the solar beams take up more time
Ere, packed up for their journey, they begin it;
  But then their telegraph° is less sublime,
And if they ran a race, they would not win it
  'Gainst Satan's couriers bound for their own clime.
The sun takes up some years for every ray
To reach its goal—the devil not half a day.

LVII

Upon the verge of space, about the size
450   Of half-a-crown, a little speck appeared
(I've seen a something like it in the skies
  In the Aegean, ere a squall); it neared,
And, growing bigger, took another guise;
  Like an aerial ship it tacked, and steered,
Or *was* steered (I am doubtful of the grammar
Of the last phrase, which makes the stanza stammer:—

LVIII

But take your choice); and then it grew a cloud;
  And so it was—a cloud of witnesses.
But such a cloud! No land e'er saw a crowd
460   Of locusts numerous as the heavens saw these;
They shadowed with their myriads space; their loud
  And varied cries were like those of wild geese
(If nations may be likened to a goose),
And realised the phrase of 'hell broke loose.'°

LIX

Here crashed a sturdy oath of stout John Bull,
  Who damned away his eyes as heretofore:
There Paddy brogued 'By Jasus!'—'What's your wull?'
  The temperate Scot exclaimed: the French ghost swore

If . . . severe Byron steals the joke from
Horace Walpole: "The summer has set in with
its usual severity"

telegraph presumably the London-Portsmouth
semaphore
'hell broke loose' *Paradise Lost* IV.918

In certain terms I shan't translate in full,
470   As the first coachman will; and 'midst the war,
The voice of Jonathan° was heard to express,
'*Our* president is going to war, I guess.'

LX

Besides there were the Spaniard, Dutch, and Dane;
        In short, an universal shoal of shades,
From Otaheite's isle° to Salisbury Plain,
        Of all climes and professions, years and trades,
Ready to swear against the good king's reign,
        Bitter as clubs in cards are against spades;
All summoned by this grand 'subpoena,' to
480   Try if kings mayn't be damned like me or you.

LXI

When Michael saw this host, he first grew pale,
        As angels can; next, like Italian twilight,
He turned all colours—as a peacock's tail,
        Or sunset streaming through a Gothic skylight
In some old abbey, or a trout not stale,
        Or distant lightning on the horizon *by* night,
Or a fresh rainbow, or a grand review
Of thirty regiments in red, green, and blue.

LXII

Then he addressed himself to Satan: 'Why—
490   My good old friend, for such I deem you, though
Our different parties make us fight so shy,
        I ne'er mistake you for a *personal* foe;
Our difference is *political,* and I
        Trust that, whatever may occur below,
You know my great respect for you: and this
Makes me regret whate'er you do amiss—

LXIII

'Why, my dear Lucifer, would you abuse
        My call for witnesses? I did not mean
That you should half of earth and hell produce;
500   'Tis even superfluous, since two honest, clean,
True testimonies are enough: we lose
        Our time, nay, our eternity, between
The accusation and defence: if we
Hear both, 'twill stretch our immortality.'

Jonathan that is, the United States, from   **Otaheite's isle** Tahiti
Jonathan Trumbull, American politician (1710–
85)

LXIV

Satan replied, 'To me the matter is
   Indifferent, in a personal point of view:
I can have fifty better souls than this
   With far less trouble than we have gone through
Already; and I merely argued his
510   Late majesty of Britain's case with you
Upon a point of form: you may dispose
   Of him; I've kings enough below, God knows!'

LXV

Thus spoke the Demon (late called 'multifaced'
   By multo-scribbling Southey). 'Then we'll call
One or two persons of the myriads placed
   Around our congress, and dispense with all
The rest,' quoth Michael: 'Who may be so graced
   As to speak first? there's choice enough—who shall
It be?' Then Satan answered, 'There are many;
520   But you may choose Jack Wilkes° as well as any.'

LXVI

A merry, cock-eyed, curious-looking sprite
   Upon the instant started from the throng,
Dressed in a fashion now forgotten quite;
   For all the fashions of the flesh stick long
By people in the next world; where unite
   All the costumes since Adam's, right or wrong,
From Eve's fig-leaf down to the petticoat,
Almost as scanty, of days less remote.

LXVII

The spirit looked around upon the crowds
530   Assembled, and exclaimed, 'My friends of all
The spheres, we shall catch cold amongst these clouds;
   So let's to business: why this general call?
If those are freeholders I see in shrouds,
   And 'tis for an election that they bawl,
Behold a candidate with unturned coat!
Saint Peter, may I count upon your vote?'

LXVIII

'Sir,' replied Michael, 'you mistake; these things
   Are of a former life, and what we do
Above is more august; to judge of kings
540   Is the tribunal met: so now you know.'

Jack Wilkes noted Radical politician and libertine, a leader of the opposition to George III,
who jailed and exiled him, but vainly, as
Wilkes returned to the House of Commons,
vindicated by the populace

'Then I presume those gentlemen with wings,'
    Said Wilkes, 'are cherubs; and that soul below
Looks much like George the Third, but to my mind
A good deal older—Bless me! is he blind?'

LXIX

'He is what you behold him, and his doom
    Depends upon his deeds,' the Angel said.
'If you have aught to arraign in him, the tomb
    Gives license to the humblest beggar's head
To lift itself against the loftiest.'—'Some,'
550   Said Wilkes, 'don't wait to see them laid in lead,
For such a liberty—and I, for one,
Have told them what I thought beneath the sun.'

LXX

'*Above* the sun repeat, then, what thou hast
    To urge against him,' said the Archangel. 'Why,'
Replied the spirit, 'since old scores are past,
    Must I turn evidence? In faith, not I.
Besides, I beat him hollow at the last,°
    With all his Lords and Commons: in the sky
I don't like ripping up old stories, since
560 His conduct was but natural in a prince.

LXXI

'Foolish, no doubt, and wicked, to oppress
    A poor unlucky devil without a shilling;
But then I blame the man himself much less
    Than Bute and Grafton,° and shall be unwilling
To see him punished here for their excess,
    Since they were both damned long ago, and still in
Their place below: for me, I have forgiven,
And vote his "habeas corpus" into heaven.'

LXXII

'Wilkes,' said the Devil, 'I understand all this;
570   You turned to half a courtier ere you died,
And seem to think it would not be amiss
    To grow a whole one on the other side
Of Charon's ferry; you forget that *his*
    Reign is concluded; whatsoe'er betide,
He won't be sovereign more: you've lost your labour
For at the best he will but be your neighbour.

Besides . . . last In 1782 the resolutions expel-   Grafton the Duke of Grafton, like the Earl of
ling Wilkes in 1764 were stricken from the   Bute a minister of George III
Commons journals.

LXXIII

'However, I knew what to think of it,
   When I beheld you in your jesting way
Flitting and whispering round about the spit
580   Where Belial, upon duty for the day,
With Fox's lard° was basting William Pitt,
   His pupil; I knew what to think, I say:
That fellow even in hell breeds farther ills;
I'll have him *gagged*—'twas one of his own bills.

LXXIV

'Call Junius!'° From the crowd a shadow stalked,
   And at the name there was a general squeeze,
So that the very ghosts no longer walked
   In comfort, at their own aerial ease,
But were all rammed, and jammed (but to be balked,
590   As we shall see), and jostled hands and knees,
Like wind compressed and pent within a bladder,
Or like a human colic, which is sadder.

LXXV

The shadow came°—a tall, thin, grey-haired figure,
   That looked as it had been a shade on earth;
Quick in its motions, with an air of vigour,
   But nought to mark its breeding or its birth:
Now it waxed little, then again grew bigger,
   With now an air of gloom, or savage mirth;
But as you gazed upon its features, they
600 Changed every instant—to *what*, none could say.

LXXVI

The more intently the ghosts gazed, the less
   Could they distinguish whose the features were;
The Devil himself seemed puzzled even to guess;
   They varied like a dream—now here, now there;
And several people swore from out the press,
   They knew him perfectly; and one could swear
He was his father: upon which another
Was sure he was his mother's cousin's brother:

LXXVII

Another, that he was a duke, or knight,
610   An orator, a lawyer, or a priest,
A nabob, a man-midwife; but the wight

Fox's lard Charles James Fox, the Whig leader, was rather fat.
Junius pseudonym of eloquent author who satirized George III and the Tories; his title

page had the motto *Stat Nominis Umbra* ("A Shadow Stands for the Name")
The shadow came The reference is to the motto of Junius.

Mysterious changed his countenance at least
As oft as they their minds: though in full sight
  He stood, the puzzle only was increased;
The man was a phantasmagoria in
Himself—he was so volatile and thin.

LXXVIII

The moment that you had pronounced him *one*,
  Presto! his face changed, and he was another;
And when that change was hardly well put on,
620   It varied, till I don't think his own mother
(If that he had a mother) would her son
  Have known, he shifted so from one to t'other;
Till guessing from a pleasure grew a task,
At this epistolary 'Iron Mask.'°

LXXIX

For sometimes he like Cerberus would seem—
  'Three gentlemen at once' (as sagely says
Good Mrs. Malaprop°); then you might deem
  That he was not even *one;* now many rays
Were flashing round him; and now a thick stream
630   Hid him from sight—like fogs on London days:
Now Burke,° now Tooke,° he grew to people's fancies,
And certes often like Sir Philip Francis.°

LXXX

I've an hypothesis—'tis quite my own;
  I never let it out till now, for fear
Of doing people harm about the throne,
  And injuring some minister or peer,
On whom the stigma might perhaps be blown;
  It is—my gentle public, lend thine ear!
'Tis, that what Junius we are wont to call
640 Was *really, truly,* nobody at all.

LXXXI

I don't see wherefore letters should not be
  Written without hands, since we daily view
Them written without heads; and books, we see,
  Are filled as well without the latter too:
And really till we fix on somebody

'Iron Mask' The "Man in the Iron Mask" was imprisoned in the Bastille by Louis XIV; Byron's point is that Junius too remains unknown.
Mrs. Malaprop delightful misuser of words in R. B. Sheridan's comedy, *The Rivals* (1775), hence the term "malapropism." The most splendid of her remarks: "as headstrong as an allegory on the banks of the Nile."
Burke Edmund Burke (1729–97), great Whig orator and author
Tooke John Horne Tooke (1736–1812), another opponent of the American War
Sir Philip Francis (1740–1818) probably was Junius.

For certain sure to claim them as his due,
Their author, like the Niger's mouth,° will bother
The world to say if *there* be mouth or author.

LXXXII

'And who and what art thou?' the Archangel said.
650   'For *that* you may consult my title-page,'
Replied this mighty shadow of a shade:
'If I have kept my secret half an age,
I scarce shall tell it now.'—'Canst thou upbraid,'
    Continued Michael, 'George Rex, or allege
Aught further?' Junius answered, 'You had better
First ask him for *his* answer to my letter:

LXXXIII

'My charges upon record will outlast
    The brass of both his epitaph and tomb.'
'Repent'st thou not,' said Michael, 'of some past
660   Exaggeration? something which may doom
Thyself if false, as him if true? Thou wast
    Too bitter—is it not so?—in thy gloom
Of passion?'—'Passion!' cried the phantom dim,
'I loved my country, and I hated him.

LXXXIV

'What I have written, I have written:° let
    The rest be on his head or mine!' So spoke
Old 'Nominis Umbra;' and while speaking yet,
    Away he melted in celestial smoke.
Then Satan said to Michael, 'Don't forget
670   To call George Washington, and John Horne Tooke,
And Franklin;'—but at this time there was heard
A cry for room, though not a phantom stirred.

LXXXV

At length with jostling, elbowing, and the aid
    Of cherubim appointed to that post,
The devil Asmodeus° to the circle made
    His way, and looked as if his journey cost
Some trouble. When his burden down he laid,
    'What's this?' cried Michael; 'why, 'tis not a ghost?'
'I know it,' quoth the incubus; 'but he
680   Shall be one, if you leave the affair to me.

LXXXVI

'Confound the renegado! I have sprained
    My left wing, he's so heavy; one would think

Niger's mouth allusion to recent explorations in
Africa

What . . . written John 19:22
Asmodeus name for the devil

Some of his works about his neck were chained.
But to the point; while hovering o'er the brink
Of Skiddaw° (where as usual it still rained),
I saw a taper, far below me, wink,
And stooping, caught this fellow at a libel—
No less on history than the Holy Bible.

LXXXVII

'The former is the devil's scripture, and
690   The latter yours, good Michael: so the affair
Belongs to all of us, you understand.
I snatched him up just as you see him there,
And brought him off for sentence out of hand:
I've scarcely been ten minutes in the air—
At least a quarter it can hardly be:
I dare say that his wife is still at tea.'

LXXXVIII

Here Satan said, 'I know this man of old,
And have expected him for some time here;
A sillier fellow you will scarce behold,
700   Or more conceited in his petty sphere:
But surely it was not worth while to fold
Such trash below your wing, Asmodeus dear:
We had the poor wretch safe (without being bored
With carriage) coming of his own accord.

LXXXIX

'But since he's here, let's see what he has done.'
'Done!' cried Asmodeus, 'he anticipates
The very business you are now upon,
And scribbles as if head clerk to the Fates.
Who knows to what his ribaldry may run,
710   When such an ass as this, like Balaam's,° prates?'
'Let's hear,' quoth Michael, 'what he has to say:
You know we're bound to that in every way.'

XC

Now the bard, glad to get an audience, which
By no means often was his case below,
Began to cough, and hawk, and hem, and pitch
His voice into that awful note of woe
To all unhappy hearers within reach
Of poets when the tide of rhyme's in flow;
But stuck fast with his first hexameter,
720   Not one of all whose gouty feet would stir.

Skiddaw mountain in the Lake District; Southey   Balaam's Numbers 22:28
resided near it

XCI

But ere the spavined dactyls could be spurred
   Into recitative, in great dismay
Both cherubim and seraphim were heard
   To murmur loudly through their long array;
And Michael rose ere he could get a word
   Of all his foundered verses under way,
And cried, 'For God's sake stop, my friend! 'twere best—
Non Di, non homines°—you know the rest.'

XCII

A general bustle spread throughout the throng,
   Which seemed to hold all verse in detestation;
The angels had of course enough of song
   When upon service; and the generation
Of ghosts had heard too much in life, not long
   Before, to profit by a new occasion:
The monarch, mute till then, exclaimed, 'What! what!
Pye° come again? No more—no more of that!'

XCIII

The tumult grew; an universal cough
   Convulsed the skies, as during a debate,
When Castlereagh has been up long enough
   (Before he was first minister of state,
I mean—the *slaves hear now*); some cried 'Off, off!'
   As at a farce; till, grown quite desperate,
The bard Saint Peter prayed to interpose
(Himself an author) only for his prose.

XCIV

The varlet was not an ill-favoured knave;
   A good deal like a vulture in the face,
With a hook nose and a hawk's eye, which gave
   A smart and sharper-looking sort of grace
To his whole aspect, which, though rather grave,
   Was by no means so ugly as his case;
But that, indeed, was hopeless as can be,
Quite a poetic felony *'de se.'*°

XCV

Then Michael blew his trump, and stilled the noise
   With one still greater, as is yet the mode
On earth besides; except some grumbling voice,
   Which now and then will make a slight inroad

30

740

750

Non . . . homines Horace's *Ars Poetica,* ll. 372–73, "Neither gods nor men can stand mediocre poets."

Pye Henry James Pye, wretched Laureate before Southey
felony 'de se' suicide

Upon decorous silence, few will twice
   Lift up their lungs when fairly overcrowed;
And now the bard could plead his own bad cause,
760 With all the attitudes of self-applause.

     XCVI

He said—(I only give the heads)—he said,
   He meant no harm in scribbling; 'twas his way
Upon all topics; 'twas, besides, his bread,
   Of which he buttered both sides; 'twould delay
Too long the assembly (he was pleased to dread),
   And take up rather more time than a day,
To name his works—he would but cite a few—
'Wat Tyler'—'Rhymes on Blenheim'—'Waterloo.'

     XCVII

He had written praises of a regicide;°
770   He had written praises of all kings whatever;
He had written for republics far and wide,
   And then against them bitterer than ever:
For pantisocracy he once had cried
   Aloud, a scheme less moral than 'twas clever;
Then grew a hearty anti-jacobin—
Had turned his coat—and would have turned his skin.

     XCVIII

He had sung against all battles, and again
   In their high praise and glory; he had called
Reviewing 'the ungentle craft,'° and then
780   Become as base a critic as e'er crawled—
Fed, paid, and pampered by the very men
   By whom his muse and morals had been mauled:
He had written much blank verse, and blanker prose,
And more of both than anybody knows.

     XCIX

He had written Wesley's life:—here turning round
   To Satan, 'Sir, I'm ready to write yours,
In two octavo volumes, nicely bound,
   With notes and preface, all that most allures
The pious purchaser; and there's no ground
790   For fear, for I can choose my own reviewers:
So let me have the proper documents,
That I may add you to my other saints.'

He . . . regicide Southey wrote a poem praising Henry Marten, one of the judges who commanded the execution of Charles I.

'the ungentle craft' memorable characterization
of reviewers by Southey, in his edition of the
poet Kirke White

C

Satan bowed, and was silent. 'Well, if you,
      With amiable modesty, decline
My offer, what says Michael? There are few
      Whose memoirs could be rendered more divine.
Mine is a pen of all work; not so new
      As it was once, but I would make you shine
800   Like your own trumpet. By the way, my own
      Has more of brass in it, and is as well blown.

CI

'But talking about trumpets, here's my Vision!
      Now you shall judge, all people; yes, you shall
Judge with my judgment, and by my decision
      Be guided who shall enter heaven or fall.
I settle all these things by intuition,
      Times present, past, to come, heaven, hell, and all.
Like King Alfonso.° When I thus see double,
I save the Deity some worlds of trouble.'

CII

He ceased, and drew forth an MS.; and no
810   Persuasion on the part of devils, saints,
Or angels, now could stop the torrent; so
      He read the first three lines of the contents;
But at the fourth, the whole spiritual show
      Had vinished, with variety of scents,
Ambrosial and sulphureous, as they sprang,
Like lightning, off from his 'melodious twang.'°

CIII

Those grand heroics acted as a spell:
      The angels stopped their ears and plied their pinions;
The devils ran howling, deafened, down to hell;
820   The ghosts fled, gibbering, for their own dominions—
(For 'tis not yet decided where they dwell,
      And I leave every man to his opinions);
Michael took refuge in his trump—but, lo!
His teeth were set on edge, he could not blow!

CIV

Saint Peter, who has hitherto been known
      For an impetuous saint, upraised his keys,
And at the fifth line knocked the poet down;
      Who fell like Phaeton,° but more at ease,

Alfonso Byron's note: "King Alfonso, speaking
of the Ptolomean System, said that 'had he been
consulted at the creation of the world, he would
have spared the Maker some absurdities'."
'melodious twang' Byron's note cites John

Aubrey's *Miscellanies* (1696) as speaking of
a ghost that vanished with "a curious perfume,
and most melodious twang."
Phaeton Apollo's son, who fell to destruction
when he usurped the chariot of the sun

Into his lake, for there he did not drown;
830   A different web being by the Destinies
Woven for the Laureate's final wreath, whene'er
Reform shall happen either here or there.

CV

He first sank to the bottom—like his works,
    But soon rose to the surface—like himself;
For all corrupted things are buoyed like corks,
    By their own rottenness, light as an elf,
Or wisp that flits o'er a morass: he lurks,
    It may be, still, like dull books on a shelf,
In his own den, to scrawl some 'Life' or 'Vision,'
840   As Welborn° says—'the devil turn'd precisian.'°

CVI

As for the rest, to come to the conclusion
    Of this true dream, the telescope is gone
Which kept my optics free from all delusion,
    And showed me what I in my turn have shown;
All I saw farther, in the last confusion,
    Was, that King George slipped into heaven for one;
And when the tumult dwindled to a calm,
I left him practising the hundredth psalm.°
1821   1822

On This Day I Complete My Thirty-sixth Year°

'Tis time this heart should be unmoved,°
    Since others it hath ceased to move:
Yet, though I cannot be beloved,
        Still let me love!

My days are in the yellow leaf;°
    The flowers and fruits of love are gone;
The worm, the canker, and the grief
        Are mine alone!

The fire that on my bosom preys
10   Is lone as some volcanic isle;
No torch is kindled at its blaze—
        A funeral pile.

Welborn character in Philip Massinger's drama
A New Way To Pay Old Debts (1633)
precisian Puritan
hundredth psalm See Psalm 100:4: "Enter into
his gates with thanksgiving . . .".
Thirty-sixth Year written at Missolonghi in
Greece, where he was to die three months later,
a martyr of the Greek Revolution against the
Turks
unmoved See the last line of "Stanzas to the
Po."
yellow leaf See Shakespeare's Sonnet LXXIII
and *Macbeth* V.III.21 ff.

The hope, the fear, the jealous care,
   The exalted portion of the pain
And power of love, I cannot share,
     But wear the chain.

But 'tis not *thus*—and 'tis not *here*—
   Such thoughts should shake my soul, nor *now*,
Where glory decks the hero's bier,
20   Or binds his brow.

The sword, the banner, and the field,
   Glory and Greece, around me see!
The Spartan, borne upon his shield,°
     Was not more free.

Awake! (not Greece—she *is* awake!)
   Awake, my spirit! Think through *whom*°
Thy life-blood tracks its parent lake,
     And then strike home!

Tread those reviving passions down,
30   Unworthy manhood!—unto thee
Indifferent should the smile or frown
     Of beauty be.°

If thou regret'st thy youth, *why live?*
   The land of honourable death
Is here:—up to the field, and give
     Away thy breath!

Seek out—less often sought than found—
   A soldier's grave, for thee the best;
Then look around, and choose thy ground,
40   And take thy rest.
    1824   1824

PERCY BYSSHE SHELLEY
1792–1822

Shelley, the most intense and original lyrical poet in the language, was born on August 4, 1792, to a very wealthy family of country gentry in Sussex. His extremely radical religious and political vision came to him very early and led him to rebel against the system at Eton. He was expelled from University College, Oxford, in March 1811, after less than half a year in residence, during which he co-authored and published *The Necessity of Atheism*. Going to London, he met Leigh Hunt, mixed in

The . . . shield Wounded or dead Spartans were honored by being so carried off the battle-field.
whom Byron was descended (through his mother) from the ancient kings of Scotland.

Tread . . . be Byron was in love again, during the closing months of his life, with his page boy Loukas, but evidently this love was not reciprocated.

radical circles, and eloped with Harriet Westbrook, he having just turned nineteen, she being sixteen. With the astonishing rapidity that always characterized his life and his poetry ("I always go on until I am stopped and I never am stopped"), he proceeded to announce himself to the Necessitarian philosopher-reformer William Godwin as a true disciple, journeyed to Ireland to agitate against the English government, poured out pamphlets, was shadowed by royal agents, privately printed the revolutionary poem Queen Mab, fathered a daughter upon Harriet and then abandoned her, again pregnant, to elope with Mary Godwin, the brilliant seventeen-year-old daughter of Godwin and the late woman's liberation pioneer Mary Wollstonecraft.

In the autumn of 1815, fearing imminent death from tuberculosis (which he did not have), he wrote his first considerable poem, Alastor, in a Wordsworthian style but subtly directed against Wordsworth. In May 1816, Shelley left England, and went to Geneva, where his friendship with Byron commenced, and where his genius found its true direction in the composing of the "Hymn to Intellectual Beauty" and "Mont Blanc." Soon after he had returned to England, in the autumn, Harriet drowned herself, freeing him to legalize his union with Mary Godwin. In 1817, the Lord Chancellor Eldon refused Shelley custody of his two children by Harriet, ostensibly on moral grounds. In March 1818, Shelley went into exile to Italy, never to return.

During his four Italian years, in his later twenties (he drowned a month before his thirtieth birthday), Shelley wrote his succession of major poems: Julian and Maddalo, Prometheus Unbound, The Cenci, The Sensitive Plant, The Witch of Atlas, Epipsychidion, Adonais, Hellas, the unfinished death-poem, The Triumph of Life, scores of magnificent lyrics, and the major prose essay, his Defence of Poetry. These years were also crowded with intense friendships, love affairs, revolutionary politics, and continual study and meditation. Personally all but selfless, almost preternaturally benevolent, Shelley was also habitually gentle, urbane, and by all accounts the most lovable of human beings. Byron, a bitter judge of character, said of him after his death that everyone else he knew seemed a beast compared to Shelley. Nevertheless, Shelley was constantly reviled in England as an immoralist and an atheist, an opponent of everything supposedly decent in established society. One prominent English obituary trumpeted: "Shelley the Atheist is dead. Now he knows whether there is a Hell or not."

Shelley's posthumous poetic reputation is the most volatile and hardest-fought-over of the last hundred and fifty years. Eminent modern critics have agreed with one another that he is all but totally worthless, an opinion held in his own time by Charles Lamb, and developed later by Carlyle and Arnold. T. S. Eliot, F. R. Leavis, Allen Tate, and W. H. Auden are typical of the majority view in modern criticism that prevailed until recently. Their Shelley is a confused emotionalist, a bad craftsman, a mock lyrist, a perpetual adolescent.

All this is not even good nonsense. Shelley is a crucial, sometimes the dominant, influence upon Beddoes, Browning, Swinburne, Yeats, Shaw, and Hardy. His emotions are very powerful, but his urbane control more powerful still. He is a superb craftsman, a lyrical poet without rival, and one of the most advanced and mature skeptical intellects ever to write a poem. He is as close to being both an English Pindar and an English Lucretius as anyone has been, and in his greater works challenges both those classical precursors. His poetry clearly does not have universal appeal among literary people; it never had and never will, probably because it is idiosyncratic enough to be menacing. Also, beyond question, the sheer violence of dissent in Shelley's political, religious, and sexual views is going to continue to alienate certain readers. But to the common readers of poetry, where we still have them, Shelley's position seems fixed. He stands as the modern lyrical poet proper, the passionately erotic idealist who attempts to find ultimate values in this world more perpetually than most of us can bear to try, and who goes on questing even though he fails to find what he seeks.

The central form of Shelley's poetry is remorseless quest, for a world where Eros is triumphant always, where desire shall not fail, and a confrontation of life by life is always taking place. Shelley, much scholarly opinion aside, was no Platonist, though he loved Plato's writings. Rather, he was a visionary skeptic, who found he could not reconcile heart and head, and could not bear to deceive either. A passionately religious temperament, Shelley evolved what might be termed a Protestant Orphism as his personal faith, a strenuous prophecy of human renovation in which fallen men would rise to "Man, one harmonious soul of many a soul, / Whose nature is its own divine control, / Where all things flow to all, as rivers to the sea. . . ." As the poet matured, he saw more clearly that this hope could not be realized by reform or revolution (though he always remained on the Left) but must come, if at all, through an overcoming of each natural selfhood by imagination. Though this approximates Blake's faith, the two poets never met, and evidently never read one another (though both personally knew Godwin, and others). Shelley differs from Blake in not systemizing his emergent myth of salvation, for his intellectual skepticism (the true ground of his being) compelled him to doubt profoundly his own idealizations.

There is, despite his own yearnings, an unmistakable pattern of deepening despair in the cycle of Shelley's poetry. From the dead end of *Alastor*, Shelley rose to the highly qualified hope of *Prometheus Unbound*, and then came full circle again to the natural defeat of imaginative quest in *Adonais* and in the unfinished but totally hopeless *The Triumph of Life*, which is not a *Purgatorio* but an *Inferno* (though most Shelley scholars would dispute this). Shelley's heart, when he died, had begun to touch the limits of desire, as his final love lyrics show. A tough but subtle temperament, he had worn himself out, and was ready to depart.

Alastor

The title of Shelley's first major poem was suggested by Thomas Love Peacock after he had read the completed work, and means (according to Peacock) "an evil genius"; "a relentless daemon" or a kind of Nemesis might be closer to Shelley's poem, where the Spirit of Solitude is an implicit being in pursuit of the Poet, but a being that is the solipsistic part of him (his Spectre, Blake would have said). Shelley's Poet is haunted by his own acute self-consciousness, even as he pursues his narcist dream vision of a beloved woman. Shelley's Preface does not blame his Poet, nor does the poem, for the Poet represents the most dangerous but also the most attractive part of Shelley's own mind, the questing element we rightly identify with him. *Alastor* stems directly from Wordsworth's account of the Solitary in *The Excursion*, and had an immense effect upon subsequent nineteenth-century poetry. Keats's *Endymion*, Browning's *Pauline* and *Paracelsus*, Yeats's *The Wanderings of Oisin* and *The Shadowy Waters* (among others) take up Shelley's version of internalized quest romance, which is parodied in our century by Wallace Stevens's *The Comedian as the*

Letter C. The excerpts that follow are meant to indicate the poem's central sequence, the Poet's idealistic but remorselessly self-destructive drive, against all natural limitation or even human obligation, to attain an impossibly complete union with his vision.

From Alastor

or The Spirit of Solitude

Preface

The poem entitled *Alastor* may be considered as allegorical of one of the most interesting situations of the human mind. It represents a youth of uncorrupted feelings and adventurous genius led forth by an imagination inflamed and purified through familiarity with all that is excellent and majestic, to the contemplation of the universe. He drinks deep of the fountains of knowledge, and is still insatiate. The magnificence and beauty of the external world sinks profoundly into the frame of his conceptions, and affords to their modifications a variety not to be exhausted. So long as it is possible for his desires to point towards objects thus infinite and unmeasured, he is joyous, and tranquil, and self-possessed. But the period arrives when these objects cease to suffice. His mind is at length suddenly awakened and thirsts for intercourse with an intelligence similar to itself. He images to himself the Being whom he loves. Conversant with speculations of the sublimest and most perfect natures, the vision in which he embodies his own imaginations unites all of wonderful, or wise, or beautiful, which the poet, the philosopher, or the lover could depicture. The intellectual faculties, the imagination, the functions of sense, have their respective requisitions on the sympathy of corresponding powers in other human beings. The Poet is represented as uniting these requisitions, and attaching them to a single image. He seeks in vain for a prototype of his conception. Blasted by his disappointment, he descends to an untimely grave.

The picture is not barren of instruction to actual men. The Poet's self-centred seclusion was avenged by the furies of an irresistible passion pursuing him to speedy ruin. But that Power° which strikes the luminaries of the world with sudden darkness and extinction, by awakening them to too exquisite a perception of its influences, dooms to a slow and poisonous decay those meaner spirits that dare to abjure its dominion. Their destiny is more abject and inglorious as their delinquency is more contemptible and pernicious. They who, deluded by no generous error, instigated by no sacred thirst of doubtful knowledge, duped by no illustrious superstition, loving nothing on this earth, and cherishing no hopes beyond, yet keep aloof from sympathies with their kind, rejoicing neither in human joy nor mourning with human grief; these, and such as they, have their apportioned curse. They languish, because none feel with them their common nature. They are morally dead. They are neither friends, nor lovers, nor fathers, nor citizens of the world, nor benefactors of their country. Among those who attempt to exist without human sympathy, the pure and tender-

that **Power** the imagination

hearted perish through the intensity and passion of their search after its communities, when the vacancy of their spirit suddenly makes itself felt. All else,
selfish, blind, and torpid, are those unforeseeing multitudes who constitute,
together with their own, the lasting misery and loneliness of the world. Those
who love not their fellow-beings live unfruitful lives, and prepare for their old
age a miserable grave.

> The good die first,
> And those whose hearts are dry as summer dust,
> Burn to the socket!°

DECEMBER 14, 1815

Nondum amabam, et amare amabam, quaerebam quid
amarem, amans amare.°—*Confess. St. August.*

Earth, ocean, air, belovèd brotherhood!°
If our great Mother° has imbued my soul
With aught of natural piety° to feel
Your love, and recompense the boon with mine;
If dewy morn, and odorous noon, and even,
With sunset and its gorgeous ministers,
And solemn midnight's tingling silentness;
If autumn's hollow sighs in the sere wood,
And winter robing with pure snow and crowns
10   Of starry ice the grey grass and bare boughs;
If spring's voluptuous pantings when she breathes
Her first sweet kisses, have been dear to me;
If no bright bird, insect, or gentle beast
I consciously have injured, but still loved
And cherished these my kindred; then forgive
This boast, belovèd brethren, and withdraw
No portion of your wonted favour now!

   Mother of this unfathomable world!
Favour my solemn song, for I have loved
20   Thee ever, and thee only; I have watched
Thy shadow, and the darkness of thy steps,
And my heart ever gazes on the depth
Of thy deep mysteries. I have made my bed
In charnels and on coffins, where black death
Keeps record of the trophies won from thee,
Hoping to still these obstinate questionings°
Of thee and thine, by forcing some lone ghost
Thy messenger, to render up the tale
Of what we are. In lone and silent hours,

The good . . . socket Wordsworth's *The Excursion* I.500–502, slightly modified
Nondum . . . amare "Not yet I loved, and I
loved to love; I sought what I should love,
loving to love"
Earth . . . brotherhood Shelley speaks as the

Promethean element of fire, addressing his
brother-elements as a Muse-principle
Mother Wordsworthian Nature
natural piety from Wordsworth's lyric, "My
Heart Leaps Up," l. 9
obstinate questionings See Wordsworth, "Intimations of Immortality" ode, l. 145

30 When night makes a weird sound of its own stillness,
    Like an inspired and desperate alchemist
    Staking his very life on some dark hope,
    Have I mixed awful talk and asking looks
    With my most innocent love, until strange tears
    Uniting with those breathless kisses, made
    Such magic as compels the charmèd night
    To render up thy charge: . . . and, though ne'er yet
    Thou hast unveiled thy inmost sanctuary,
    Enough from incommunicable dream,
40 And twilight phantasms, and deep noon-day thought,
    Has shone within me, that serenely now
    And moveless, as a long-forgotten lyre°
    Suspended in the solitary dome
    Of some mysterious and deserted fane,
    I wait thy breath, Great Parent, that my strain
    May modulate with murmurs of the air,
    And motions of the forests and the sea,
    And voice of living beings, and woven hymns
    Of night and day, and the deep heart of man.

                    . . .

    When early youth had passed, he left
    His cold fireside and alienated home
    To seek strange truths in undiscovered lands.
    Many a wide waste and tangled wilderness
    Has lured his fearless steps; and he has bought
80 With his sweet voice and eyes, from savage men,
    His rest and food. Nature's most secret steps
    He like her shadow has pursued, where'er
    The red volcano overcanopies
    Its fields of snow and pinnacles of ice
    With burning smoke, or where bitumen lakes
    On black bare pointed islets ever beat
    With sluggish surge, or where the secret caves°
    Rugged and dark, winding among the springs
    Of fire and poison, inaccessible
90 To avarice or pride, their starry domes
    Of diamond and of gold expand above
    Numberless and immeasurable halls,
    Frequent° with crystal column, and clear shrines
    Of pearl, and thrones radiant with chrysolite.
    Nor had that scene of ampler majesty
    Than gems or gold, the varying roof of heaven
    And the green earth lost in his heart its claims
    To love and wonder; he would linger long

---

lyre the Romantic wind-lyre or Aeolian harp   **Frequent** crowded
secret caves the first of several echoes of Cole-
ridge's *Kubla Khan*

In lonesome vales, making the wild his home,
100   Until the doves and squirrels would partake
From his innocuous hand his bloodless food,°
Lured by the gentle meaning of his looks,
And the wild antelope, that starts whene'er
The dry leaf rustles in the brake,° suspend
Her timid steps to gaze upon a form
More graceful than her own.

            .   .   .

140   The Poet wandering on, through Arabie
And Persia, and the wild Carmanian waste,°
And o'er the aerial mountains which pour down
Indus and Oxus from their icy caves,
In joy and exultation held his way;
Till in the vale of Cashmire, far within
Its loneliest dell, where odorous plants entwine
Beneath the hollow rocks a natural bower,
Beside a sparkling rivulet he stretched
His languid limbs. A vision on his sleep
150   There came, a dream of hopes that never yet
Had flushed his cheek. He dreamed a veilèd maid
Sate near him, talking in low solemn tones.
Her voice was like the voice of his own soul
Heard in the calm of thought; its music long,
Like woven sounds of streams and breezes, held
His inmost sense suspended in its web
Of many-coloured woof and shifting hues.
Knowledge and truth and virtue were her theme,
And lofty hopes of divine liberty,
160   Thoughts the most dear to him, and poesy,
Herself a poet. Soon the solemn mood
Of her pure mind kindled through all her frame
A permeating fire: wild numbers then
She raised, with voice stifled in tremulous sobs
Subdued by its own pathos: her fair hands
Were bare alone, sweeping from some strange harp
Strange symphony, and in their branching veins
The eloquent blood told an ineffable tale.
The beating of her heart was heard to fill
170   The pauses of her music, and her breath
Tumultuously accorded with those fits
Of intermitted song. Sudden she rose,
As if her heart impatiently endured
Its bursting burthen: at the sound he turned,
And saw by the warm light of their own life
Her glowing limbs beneath the sinuous veil

---

bloodless food Shelley was a notorious vegetarian

brake thicket
Carmanian waste desert in Persia

Of woven wind, her outspread arms now bare,
Her dark locks floating in the breath of night,
Her beamy bending eyes, her parted lips
180   Outstretched, and pale, and quivering eagerly.
His strong heart sunk and sickened with excess
Of love. He reared his shuddering limbs and quelled
His gasping breath, and spread his arms to meet
Her panting bosom: . . . she drew back a while,
Then, yielding to the irresistible joy,
With frantic gesture and short breathless cry
Folded his frame in her dissolving arms.
Now blackness veiled his dizzy eyes, and night
Involved and swallowed up the vision; sleep,
190   Like a dark flood suspended in its course,
Rolled back its impulse on his vacant brain.

. . .

    At length upon the lone Chorasmian° shore
He paused, a wide and melancholy waste
Of putrid marshes. A strong impulse urged
His steps to the sea-shore. A swan was there,°
Beside a sluggish stream among the reeds.
It rose as he approached, and with strong wings
Scaling the upward sky, bent its bright course
High over the immeasurable main.
280   His eyes pursued its flight.—'Thou hast a home,
Beautiful bird; thou voyagest to thine home,
Where thy sweet mate will twine her downy neck
With thine, and welcome thy return with eyes
Bright in the lustre of their own fond joy.
And what am I that I should linger here,
With voice far sweeter than thy dying notes,
Spirit more vast than thine, frame more attuned
To beauty, wasting these surpassing powers
In the deaf air, to the blind earth, and heaven
290   That echoes not my thoughts?' A gloomy smile
Of desperate hope wrinkled his quivering lips.
For sleep, he knew, kept most relentlessly
Its precious charge, and silent death exposed,
Faithless perhaps as sleep, a shadowy lure,
With doubtful smile mocking its own strange charms.

    Startled by his own thoughts he looked around.
There was no fair fiend near him, not a sight
Or sound of awe but in his own deep mind.
A little shallop floating near the shore
300   Caught the impatient wandering of his gaze.

Chorasmian Aral Sea
A swan was there This passage (ll. 275–90) echoes throughout Yeats's poetry.

It had been long abandoned, for its sides
Gaped wide with many a rift, and its frail joints
Swayed with the undulations of the tide.
A restless impulse urged him to embark
And meet lone Death on the drear ocean's waste;
For well he knew that mighty Shadow loves
The slimy caverns of the populous deep.

    The day was fair and sunny, sea and sky
Drank its inspiring radiance, and the wind
310 Swept strongly from the shore, blackening the waves.
Following his eager soul, the wanderer
Leaped in the boat, he spread his cloak aloft
On the bare mast, and took his lonely seat,
And felt the boat speed o'er the tranquil sea
Like a torn cloud before the hurricane.

       . . .

    When on the threshold of the green recess
The wanderer's footsteps fell, he knew that death
Was on him. Yet a little, ere it fled,
Did he resign his high and holy soul
To images of the majestic past,
630 That paused within his passive being now,
Like winds that bear sweet music, when they breathe
Through some dim latticed chamber. He did place
His pale lean hand upon the rugged trunk
Of the old pine. Upon an ivied stone
Reclined his languid head, his limbs did rest,
Diffused and motionless, on the smooth brink
Of that obscurest chasm;—and thus he lay,
Surrendering to their final impulses
The hovering powers of life. Hope and despair,
640 The torturers, slept; no mortal pain or fear
Marred his repose, the influxes of sense,
And his own being unalloyed by pain,
Yet feebler and more feeble, calmly fed
The stream of thought, till he lay breathing there
At peace, and faintly smiling:—his last sight
Was the great moon, which o'er the western line
Of the wide world her mighty horn suspended,
With whose dun beams inwoven darkness seemed
To mingle. Now upon the jaggèd hills
650 It rests, and still as the divided frame
Of the vast meteor sunk, the Poet's blood,
That ever beat in mystic sympathy
With nature's ebb and flow, grew feebler still:
And when two lessening points of light alone
Gleamed through the darkness, the alternate gasp
Of his faint respiration scarce did stir

The stagnate night:—till the minutest ray
Was quenched, the pulse yet lingered in his heart.
It paused—it fluttered. But when heaven remained
660 Utterly black, the murky shades involved
An image, silent, cold, and motionless,
As their own voiceless earth and vacant air.
Even as a vapour fed with golden beams
That ministered on sunlight, ere the west
Eclipses it, was now that wondrous frame—
No sense, no motion, no divinity—
A fragile lute, on whose harmonious strings
The breath of heaven did wander—a bright stream
Once fed with many-voicèd waves—a dream
670 Of youth, which night and time have quenched for ever,
Still, dark, and dry, and unremembered now.
    O, for Medea's wondrous alchemy,°
Which wheresoe'er it fell made the earth gleam
With bright flowers, and the wintry boughs exhale
From vernal blooms fresh fragrance! O, that God,
Profuse of poisons, would concede the chalice
Which but one living man° has drained, who now,
Vessel of deathless wrath, a slave that feels
No proud exemption in the blighting curse
680 He bears, over the world wanders for ever,
Lone as incarnate death! O, that the dream
Of dark magician in his visioned cave,°
Raking the cinders of a crucible
For life and power, even when his feeble hand
Shakes in its last decay, were the true law
Of this so lovely world! But thou art fled
Like some frail exhalation; which the dawn
Robes in its golden beams,—ah! thou hast fled!
The brave, the gentle, and the beautiful,
690 The child of grace and genius. Heartless things
Are done and said in the world, and many worms
And beasts and men live on, and mighty Earth
From sea and mountain, city and wilderness,
In vesper low or joyous orison,
Lifts still its solemn voice:—but thou art fled—
Thou canst no longer know or love the shapes
Of this phantasmal scene, who have to thee
Been purest ministers, who are, alas!
Now thou art not. Upon those pallid lips
700 So sweet even in their silence, on those eyes
That image sleep in death, upon that form
Yet safe from the worm's outrage, let no tear

Medea's . . . alchemy i.e. she could restore the
dead to life
one living man Ahasuerus, the Wandering Jew,

a late-medieval legend of an eternally condemned outcast, and one of Shelley's heroes
visioned cave cave of visions

Be shed—not even in thought. Nor, when those hues
Are gone, and those divinest lineaments,
Worn by the senseless wind, shall live alone
In the frail pauses of this simple strain,
Let not high verse, mourning the memory
Of that which is no more, or painting's woe
Or sculpture, speak in feeble imagery
710   Their own cold powers. Art and eloquence,
And all the shows o' the world are frail and vain
To weep a loss that turns their lights to shade.
It is a woe too 'deep for tears,'° when all
Is reft at once, when some surpassing Spirit,
Whose light adorned the world around it, leaves
Those who remain behind, not sobs or groans,
The passionate tumult of a clinging hope;
But pale despair and cold tranquillity,
Nature's vast frame, the web of human things,
720   Birth and the grave, that are not as they were.
1815   1816

Hymn to Intellectual° Beauty

I

The awful shadow of some unseen Power
　　Floats though unseen among us,—visiting
　　This various world with as inconstant wing
As summer winds that creep from flower to flower,—
Like moonbeams that behind some piny mountain shower,
　　　　It visits with inconstant glance
　　　　Each human heart and countenance;
Like hues and harmonies of evening,—
　　　　Like clouds in starlight widely spread,—
10   　　　Like memory of music fled,—
　　　　Like aught that for its grace may be
Dear, and yet dearer for its mystery.

II

Spirit of BEAUTY, that dost consecrate
　　With thine own hues all thou dost shine upon
　　Of human thought or form,—where art thou gone?
Why dost thou pass away and leave our state,
This dim vast vale of tears, vacant and desolate?
　　　　Ask why the sunlight not for ever
　　　　Weaves rainbows o'er yon mountain-river,
20   Why aught should fail and fade that once is shown,

'deep for tears' "Intimations" ode, l. 203   Intellectual in its 18-century meaning of "be-
                                                     yond the senses"

Why fear and dream and death and birth
Cast on the daylight of this earth
Such gloom,—why man has such a scope
For love and hate, despondency and hope?

III

No voice° from some sublimer world hath ever
   To sage or poet these responses given—
   Therefore the names of Demon, Ghost, and Heaven,
Remain the records of their vain endeavour,
Frail spells—whose uttered charm might not avail to sever,
30   From all we hear and all we see,
      Doubt, chance, and mutability.
Thy light alone—like mist o'er mountains driven,
     Or music by the night-wind sent
     Through strings of some still instrument,°
     Or moonlight on a midnight stream,
Gives grace and truth to life's unquiet dream.

IV

Love, Hope, and Self-esteem,° like clouds depart
   And come, for some uncertain moments lent.
   Man were immortal, and omnipotent,
40 Didst thou, unknown and awful as thou art,
Keep with thy glorious train firm state within his heart.
     Thou messenger of sympathies,
     That wax and wane in lovers' eyes—
Thou—that to human thought art nourishment,
     Like darkness to a dying flame!
     Depart not as thy shadow came,
     Depart not—lest the grave should be,
Like life and fear, a dark reality.

V

While yet a boy I sought for ghosts, and sped
50   Through many a listening chamber, cave and ruin,
   And starlight wood, with fearful steps pursuing
Hopes of high talk with the departed dead.
I called on poisonous names° with which our youth is fed;
     I was not heard—I saw them not—
     When musing deeply on the lot
Of life, at that sweet time when winds are wooing
     All vital things that wake to bring
     News of birds and blossoming,—
     Sudden, thy shadow fell on me;
60 I shrieked, and clasped my hands in ecstasy!°

No voice Shelley's "atheism"
instrument Aeolian harp
Love . . . Self-esteem Shelley's version of the
three prime Pauline virtues, with Self-esteem
replacing Faith

poisonous names God and Christ
I shrieked . . . ecstasy This line deliberately
adopts the Sibylline stance.

VI

I vowed that I would dedicate my powers
  To thee and thine—have I not kept the vow?
  With beating heart and streaming eyes, even now
I call the phantoms of a thousand hours
Each from his voiceless grave: they have in visioned bowers
    Of studious zeal or love's delight
    Outwatched with me the envious night—
They know that never joy illumed my brow
    Unlinked with hope that thou wouldst free
70   This world from its dark slavery,
    That thou—O awful LOVELINESS,
Wouldst give whate'er these words cannot express.

VII

The day becomes more solemn and serene
  When noon is past—there is a harmony
  In autumn, and a lustre in its sky,
Which through the summer is not heard or seen,
As if it could not be, as if it had not been!°
    Thus let thy power, which like the truth
    Of nature on my passive youth
80 Descended, to my onward life supply
    Its calm—to one who worships thee,
    And every form containing thee,
Whom, SPIRIT fair, thy spells did bind
To fear° himself, and love all human kind.
1816   1817

Mont Blanc°

Lines Written in the Vale of Chamouni

I

The everlasting universe of things°
Flows through the mind,° and rolls its rapid waves,
Now dark—now glittering—now reflecting gloom—

As if . . . been Shelley's version of the "sober colouring" of Wordsworth's "Intimations" ode, l. 198
fear hold in reverence
Mont Blanc in the Swiss Alps, the highest mountain in Europe. This poem is the sister-hymn to Shelley's invocation of the Intellectual Beauty, but where that saluted a transient, though benign, force, this addresses a Power at once constant, indifferent, and removed; the best analogues to Shelley's complex myth-makings here are to be found, not in platonism or in any philosophy contemporary with Shelley, but in various forms of the Gnostic religion,

or heretical Christianity, or in Blake. An illuminating modern analogue is provided by Wallace Stevens's The Auroras of Autumn, where the initially terrifying Northern Lights intimate to the poet his own dangerous imaginative freedom from a naturalistically manifested hidden Power that has no regard for him.
universe of things at once the Arve river and all natural phenomena, in their relation to the adverting mind
mind at once the Ravine of Arve and a universal mind, such as is represented by Prometheus in Shelley's lyrical drama

Now lending splendour, where from secret springs
The source of human thought its tribute brings
Of waters,—with a sound but half its own,
Such as a feeble brook° will oft assume
In the wild woods, among the mountains lone,
Where waterfalls around it leap for ever,
10   Where woods and winds contend, and a vast river
Over its rocks ceaselessly bursts and raves.

II

Thus thou, Ravine of Arve—dark, deep Ravine—
Thou many-coloured, many-voicèd vale,
Over whose pines, and crags, and caverns sail
Fast cloud-shadows and sunbeams: awful scene,
Where Power in likeness of the Arve comes down
From the ice-gulfs that gird his secret throne,°
Bursting through these dark mountains like the flame
Of lightning through the tempest;—thou dost lie,
20   Thy giant brood of pines around thee clinging,
Children of elder time, in whose devotion
The chainless winds still come and ever came
To drink their odours, and their mighty swinging
To hear—an old and solemn harmony;
Thine earthly rainbows stretched across the sweep
Of the aethereal waterfall, whose veil
Robes some unsculptured image; the strange sleep
Which when the voices of the desert fail
Wraps all in its own deep eternity;—
30   Thy caverns echoing to the Arve's commotion,
A loud, lone sound no other sound can tame;
Thou art pervaded with that ceaseless motion,
Thou art the path of that unresting sound—
Dizzy Ravine! and when I gaze on thee
I seem as in a trance sublime and strange
To muse on my own separate fantasy,
My own, my human mind, which passively
Now renders and receives fast influencings,
Holding an unremitting interchange
40   With the clear universe of things around;
One legion of wild thoughts, whose wandering wings
Now float above thy darkness, and now rest
Where that or thou art no unbidden guest,
In the still cave of the witch Poesy,
Seeking among the shadows that pass by
Ghosts of all things that are, some shade of thee,

---

feeble brook like the individual human mind
(see l. 37)

Where Power . . . throne anticipation of Demogorgon, in *Prometheus Unbound*

Some phantom, some faint image; till the breast
From which they fled recalls them, thou art there!°

III

Some say that gleams of a remoter world
50   Visit the soul in sleep,—that death is slumber,
And that its shapes the busy thoughts outnumber
Of those who wake and live.—I look on high;
Has some unknown omnipotence unfurled
The veil of life and death? or do I lie
In dream, and does the mightier world of sleep
Spread far around and inaccessibly
Its circles? For the very spirit fails,
Driven like a homeless cloud from steep to steep
That vanishes among the viewless gales!
60   Far, far above, piercing the infinite sky,
Mont Blanc appears,—still, snowy, and serene—
Its subject mountains their unearthly forms
Pile around it, ice and rock; broad vales between
Of frozen floods, unfathomable deeps,
Blue as the overhanging heaven, that spread
And wind among the accumulated steeps;
A desert peopled by the storms alone,
Save when the eagle brings some hunter's bone,
And the wolf tracks her there—how hideously
70   Its shapes are heaped around! rude, bare, and high,
Ghastly, and scarred, and riven.—Is this the scene
Where the old Earthquake-daemon taught her young
Ruin? Were these their toys? or did a sea
Of fire envelop once this silent snow?
None can reply—all seems eternal now.
The wilderness has a mysterious tongue
Which teaches awful doubt, or faith so mild,
So solemn, so serene, that man may be,
But for such faith, with nature reconciled;°
80   Thou hast a voice, great Mountain, to repeal
Large codes of fraud and woe;° not understood
By all, but which the wise, and great, and good
Interpret, or make felt, or deeply feel.°

IV

The fields, the lakes, the forests, and the streams,
Ocean, and all the living things that dwell

thou art there when the poet ceases to search for an image of the Power, he finds it in the scene that he confronts
that man . . . reconciled Wordsworthian "faith so mild" is an idealism that prevents us from being reconciled with nature's indifference, unlike the Shelleyan "awful doubt"
Large . . . woe The codes of fraud are Chris-

tianity's; the codes of woe are made by the governments of counter-revolutionary Europe.
the wise . . . feel Godwin represents the "wise" who can "interpret"; Wordsworth the "great" who can make the mountain's voice "felt"; Coleridge the "good" who can "deeply feel"; Shelley, as skeptical visionary, stands apart from all three.

Within the daedal° earth; lightning, and rain,
Earthquake, and fiery flood, and hurricane,
The torpor of the year when feeble dreams
Visit the hidden buds, or dreamless sleep
90 Holds every future leaf and flower;—the bound
With which from that detested trance they leap;
The works and ways of man, their death and birth,
And that of him and all that his may be;
All things that move and breathe with toil and sound
Are born and die; revolve, subside, and swell.
Power dwells apart in its tranquillity,
Remote, serene, and inaccessible:
And *this*, the naked countenance of earth,
On which I gaze, even these primaeval mountains
100 Teach the adverting mind. The glaciers creep
Like snakes that watch their prey, from their far fountains,
Slow rolling on; there, many a precipice,
Frost and the Sun in scorn of mortal power
Have piled: dome, pyramid, and pinnacle,
A city of death, distinct with many a tower
And wall impregnable of beaming ice.
Yet not a city, but a flood of ruin
Is there, that from the boundaries of the sky
Rolls its perpetual stream; vast pines are strewing
110 Its destined path, or in the mangled soil
Branchless and shattered stand; the rocks, drawn down
From yon remotest waste, have overthrown
The limits of the dead and living world,
Never to be reclaimed. The dwelling-place
Of insects, beasts, and birds, becomes its spoil
Their food and their retreat for ever gone,
So much of life and joy is lost. The race
Of man flies far in dread; his work and dwelling
Vanish, like smoke before the tempest's stream,
120 And their place is not known. Below, vast caves
Shine in the rushing torrents' restless gleam,
Which from those secret chasms in tumult welling
Meet in the vale, and one majestic River,
The breath and blood of distant lands, for ever
Rolls its loud waters to the ocean-waves,
Breathes its swift vapours to the circling air.°

v

Mont Blanc yet gleams on high:—the power is there,
The still and solemn power of many sights,
And many sounds, and much of life and death.

daedal from Daedalus, great artificer of labyrinths; Shelley uses the word to mean "wonderfully made"

Below . . . air This passage (ll. 120–26)
closely echoes Coleridge's *Kubla Khan*.

130 In the calm darkness of the moonless nights,
    In the lone glare of day, the snows descend
    Upon that Mountain; none beholds them there,
    Nor when the flakes burn in the sinking sun,
    Or the star-beams dart through them:—Winds contend
    Silently there, and heap the snow with breath
    Rapid and strong, but silently! Its home
    The voiceless lightning in these solitudes
    Keeps innocently, and like vapour broods
    Over the snow. The secret Strength of things
140 Which governs thought, and to the infinite dome
    Of Heaven is as a law, inhabits thee!
    And what were thou, and earth, and stars, and sea,
    If to the human mind's imaginings
    Silence and solitude were vacancy?°
    1816   1817

Ozymandias°

    I met a traveller from an antique land
    Who said: Two vast and trunkless legs of stone
    Stand in the desert . . . Near them, on the sand,
    Half sunk, a shattered visage lies, whose frown,
    And wrinkled lip, and sneer of cold command,
    Tell that its sculptor well those passions read
    Which yet survive, stamped on these lifeless things,
    The hand that mocked° them, and the heart that fed:
    And on the pedestal these words appear:
10 'My name is Ozymandias, king of kings:
    Look on my works, ye Mighty, and despair!'
    Nothing beside remains. Round the decay
    Of that colossal wreck, boundless and bare
    The lone and level sands stretch far away.
    1817   1818

And what . . . vacancy What would the Power, or any phenomenon mean in human terms, if our imagination could not create out of silence and solitude? Shelley ends the poem by celebrating the "violence from within," the imagination, in its response to the "violence from without," the "Dizzy Ravine."
Ozymandias another name for Rameses II of Egypt (13th century B.C.), whose colossal tomb at Thebes was in the shape of a male Sphinx. Yeats's "The Second Coming" and Stevens's *Notes Toward a Supreme Fiction* both make use of this sonnet.
mocked Shelley uses this to mean "artistically imitated" as well as "disdained."

From Julian and Maddalo°

A Conversation

I rode one evening with Count Maddalo
Upon the bank of land° which breaks the flow
Of Adria° towards Venice: a bare strand
Of hillocks, heaped from ever-shifting sand,
Matted with thistles and amphibious weeds,
Such as from earth's embrace the salt ooze breeds,
Is this; an uninhabited sea-side,
Which the lone fisher, when his nets are dried,
Abandons; and no other object breaks
10   The waste, but one dwarf tree and some few stakes
Broken and unrepaired, and the tide makes
A narrow space of level sand thereon,
Where 'twas our wont to ride while day went down.
This ride was my delight. I love all waste
And solitary places; where we taste
The pleasure of believing what we see
Is boundless, as we wish our souls to be:
And such was this wide ocean, and this shore
More barren than its billows; and yet more
20   Than all, with a remembered friend I love
To ride as then I rode;—for the winds drove
The living spray along the sunny air
Into our faces; the blue heavens were bare,
Stripped to their depths by the awakening north;
And, from the waves, sound like delight broke forth
Harmonising with solitude, and sent
Into our hearts aereal merriment.
So, as we rode, we talked; and the swift thought,
Winging itself with laughter, lingered not,
30   But flew from brain to brain,—such glee was ours,
Charged with light memories of remembered hours,
None slow enough for sadness: till we came
Homeward, which always makes the spirit tame.
This day had been cheerful but cold, and now
The sun was sinking, and the wind also.
Our talk grew somewhat serious, as may be
Talk interrupted with such raillery
As mocks itself, because it cannot scorn
The thoughts it would extinguish:—'twas forlorn,
40   Yet pleasing, such as once, so poets tell,
The devils held within the dales of Hell

Julian and Maddalo Julian is Shelley, Maddalo is Lord Byron; the poem undoubetdly records actual conversations between them; the poem's landscape and other details deeply influenced Browning, for which see "Two in the Cam-pagna," "Love Among the Ruins," and *Childe Roland to the Dark Tower Came,* in particular. **bank of land** the Lido **Adria** Adriatic sea

Concerning God, freewill and destiny:°
Of all that earth has been or yet may be,
All that vain men imagine or believe,
Or hope can paint or suffering may achieve,
We descanted, and I (for ever still
Is it not wise to make the best of ill?)
Argued against despondency, but pride
Made my companion take the darker side.
50 The sense that he was greater than his kind
Had struck, methinks, his eagle spirit blind
By gazing on its own exceeding light.
Meanwhile the sun paused ere it should alight,
Over the horizon of the mountains;—Oh,
How beautiful is sunset, when the glow
Of Heaven descends upon a land like thee,
Thou Paradise of exiles, Italy!
Thy mountains, seas, and vineyards, and the towers
Of cities they encircle!—it was ours
60 To stand on thee, beholding it: and then,
Just where we had dismounted, the Count's men
Were waiting for us with the gondola.—
As those who pause on some delightful way
Though bent on pleasant pilgrimage, we stood
Looking upon the evening, and the flood
Which lay between the city and the shore,
Paved with the image of the sky . . . the hoar
And aery Alps towards the North appeared
Through mist, an heaven-sustaining bulwark reared
70 Between the East and West; and half the sky
Was roofed with clouds of rich emblazonry
Dark purple at the zenith, which still grew
Down the steep West into a wondrous hue
Brighter than burning gold, even to the rent
Where the swift sun yet paused in his descent
Among the many-folded hills: they were
Those famous Euganean hills, which bear,
As seen from Lido through the harbour piles,
The likeness of a clump of peakèd isles—
80 And then—as if the Earth and Sea had been
Dissolved into one lake of fire, were seen
Those mountains towering as from waves of flame
Around the vaporous sun, from which there came
The inmost purple spirit of light, and made
Their very peaks transparent. 'Ere it fade,'
Said my companion, 'I will show you soon
A better station'—so, o'er the lagune°

'twas forlorn . . . destiny See *Paradise Lost*   lagune lagoon
II.555–69.

1. The Royal Pavilion at Brighton, reconstructed in 1818 by John Nash (1752–1835), a monumental plaything of the Regency period, reflecting a vogue for orientalizing décor on a sizable scale. *The Granger Collection.*

2. The British Museum, London, from a wood engraving of 1844. It was designed by Sir Robert Smirke (1781–1867), and built 1823–47, to house the collections of classical antiquities which had been augmented by such treasures as the Elgin marbles from the Parthenon in Athens. *The Granger Collection.*

3. The illustrations for Homer, Hesiod, and Dante by the sculptor John Flaxman (1775–1826) were notably influential both in England and abroad. *Homer Invoking the Muse* was engraved by Blake himself (1793). *New York Public Library.*

ENGLISH NEOCLASSICAL STYLE

4. *The Furies,* from Dante's *Inferno* IX.46–48: "This is Megaera, on the left; she who weeps on the right is Alecto; Tisiphone is in the middle." This series was engraved by Thomas Pirolli. *New York Public Library.*

5. *The Nightmare*, 1781, by the Swiss-born Henry Fuseli (1741–1825), visionary artist and friend of Blake who anticipated the concerns of Surrealist painting with his interest in dream and derangement. *Frankfurter Goethemuseum.*

6. *Titania, Bottom, and Fairies,* 1793–94, by Fuseli shows a concern not with the pageantry or the dramatic moment in Shakespeare usually rendered by late Victorian narrative painters, but with moments of terror and transformation, like this epitome of *A Midsummer Night's Dream. Kunsthaus,* Zürich.

7. William Blake's Head of Spenser, from a series done in 1800–1801 for the library of William Hayley in Felpham, Sussex. Spenser is shown in a laurel garland, with Queen Elizabeth, as Cynthia, resting in a crescent moon ("Eliza" is inscribed on the medal Spenser wears); on the right, regarding her meditatively, an old man with two stars above him and a shepherd's staff. Nymphs fly about the wreath. The imagery may refer to the April Eclogue of Spenser's *The Shepheardes Calendar*. *City Art Gallery*, Manchester.

8. William Blake in 1807, detail from the portrait by Thomas Phillips (1770–1845). *National Portrait Gallery*, London.

9. Blake, "The Little Black Boy," from *Songs of Innocence and Experience. The Library of Congress*, Rosenwald Collection, Washington, D.C.

10. Blake, "The Tyger," from *Songs of Innocence and Experience.* The Library of Congress, Rosenwald Collection.

11. Blake, *The Ancient of Days;* the painting for the frontispiece to *Europe: a Prophecy,* 1794, shows Urizen bent over the fallen world, marking out its limits with compasses in a complex parody, perhaps, of Proverbs 8:27: "When he set a compass upon the face of the depth." *The Whitworth Art Gallery,* Manchester.

12. Blake, *Newton*, 1795, a color print, showing an absorption in contraction and bounding, parallel to Urizen's, but here set at the bottom of a sea of time and space. *The Tate Gallery*, London.

13. Blake, frontispiece to *Visions of the Daughters of Albion*, showing *left to right*, Bromion, Oothoon, and Theotormon. The scene does not literally occur in the poem but is, rather, Theotormon's vision of what is happening. (See *Visions of the Daughters of Albion*). *The Tate Gallery.*

14. Blake, *Nebuchadnezzar*, 1795, a color print showing the fallen Babylonian king who, "driven from men . . . did eat grass as oxen, and his body was wet with the dew of heaven, till his hairs were grown like eagles' feathers, and his nails like birds' claws" (Daniel 4:33). *The Tate Gallery.*

15. Plate 24 of *The Marriage of Heaven and Hell,* upon which the print above was based. *The Pierpont Morgan Library,* New York.

16. *Satan with Adam and Eve*, 1808, Blake's watercolor illustrating *Paradise Lost*, IX. *Museum of Fine Arts*, Boston.

17. *Pandemonium*, 1824, John Martin's (1789–1854) mezzotint illustration of Book II of *Paradise Lost* showing the Romantic reading of Milton at its most theatrical. *The Metropolitan Museum of Art*, New York, *Harris Brisbane Dick Fund, 1949.*

18. *Manfred on the Jungfrau,* 1837, by John Martin. Byron and the Ossianic poems of Macpherson joined Milton and Shakespeare in providing subjects and images for Romantic painting in England. Here, the tormented hero of Byron's drama is about to fling himself from the Alpine peak:

> . . . Farewell, ye opening heavens!
> Look not upon me thus reproachfully—
> You were not meant for me—Earth! take these atoms!

He is restrained by a chamois hunter behind him. *Birmingham* (England) *Museum and Art Gallery.*

19. *The Valley Thick with Corn,* 1825, brush and pen in sepia. The visionary paintings of Samuel Palmer (1805–81), friend and follower of Blake, were done mostly in Shoreham, Kent, during the painter's youth, and depict a condition of life not unlike Blake's Beulah, rich and moonlit. Unlike Blake's vision of Beulah, however, this is not equivocal: what Blake saw as a necessary but dangerous state of repose from intellectual warfare, Palmer saw as a final good. *Ashmolean Museum,* Oxford.

20. *The Valley with a Bright Cloud,* 1825, brush and pen in sepia. *Ashmolean Museum.*

21. Samuel Palmer, *A Hilly Scene*, c. 1826, water color and tempera. *The Tate Gallery.*

22. Samuel Palmer, *Early Morning*, 1825, brush and pen in sepia. *Ashmolean Museum.*

23. Samuel Palmer, *Shepherds under a Full Moon, c.* 1830, brush and pen in sepia. *Ashmolean Museum.*

24. *The Bellman,* Samuel Palmer's mezzotint done in 1879 (near the end of his life), for Milton's "Il Penseroso":

> Where glowing embers through the room
> Teach light to counterfeit a gloom,
> Far from all resort of mirth
> Save the cricket on the hearth,
> Or the Bellman's drowsy charm,
> To bless the doors from nightly harm.

Museum of Fine Arts, Boston.

25. Samuel Palmer, *The Lonely Tower,* also from "Il Penseroso":

> Or let my Lamp at midnight hour,
> Be seen in some high lonely tower,
> Where I may oft out-watch the Bear . . .

William Butler Yeats in "The Phases of the Moon" celebrated this print and

> . . . the candelight
> From the far tower where Milton's Platonist
> Sat late, or Shelley's visionary prince:
> The lonely light that Samuel Palmer engraved,
> An image of mysterious wisdom won by toil . . .

British Museum.

26. Samuel Palmer, *Coming from Evening Church*, 1830, oil and tempera on canvas. The Tate Gallery.

27. Samuel Palmer, *The Magic Apple Tree*, 1830, watercolor.
Fitzwilliam Museum, Cambridge.

28. Wordsworth in 1805, a drawing by Henry Edridge (1769–1821). *The Granger Collection.*

29. Coleridge in 1814, a portrait by the American Romantic painter Washington Allston (1779–1843). *The Granger Collection.*

30. *Chirk Aqueduct,* 1804, by John Sell Cotman (1782–1842). This watercolor of a newly constructed aqueduct in Yorkshire represents the finest work of one of the greatest English water-colorists. Cotman's bold, almost abstract planes look forward to modern art; in general, his work displays the triumph of a peculiarly English landscape idiom. *Victoria and Albert Museum,* London.

THE VISION OF LANDSCAPE

31. *Stonehenge,* here shown in a storm, by J. M. W. Turner (1775–1851); drawn between 1820 and 1830. *British Museum.*

32. *Stonehenge,* by John Constable, another of the pre-eminent English painters (1776–1837). Along with Turner, Constable dominates the sphere of landscape in early nineteenth-century painting. His scene, penetrated by rainbows, is fully as agitated as Turner's, but in a different mode. *Victoria and Albert Museum.*

33. Mount Snowdon in Wales, c. 1800, painted by John Varley (1778–1842). Compare with Wordsworth's description in *The Prelude*, Bk. XIV. *Walker Art Gallery*, Liverpool.

34. *The Ploughman,* by Edward Calvert (1789–1883), Palmer's friend and associate at Shoreham. The Romantic pastoral vision is of a secondary paradise, with the serpent transfixed, and musical graces dancing on a low rise. *Victoria and Albert Museum.*

35. *The Primitive City,* 1822, Edward Calvert's watercolor, shows imaginative affinities with both Blake and Palmer in its way of generating a mythology of its own. *British Museum.*

36. Shelley in 1819, a portrait by Amelia Curran. *National Portrait Gallery.*

. Keats in 1821, painted in Rome by seph Severn (1783–1879). *National rtrait Gallery.*

38. Lord Byron in 1814, in Albanian costume, painted by Thomas Phillips (1770–1845). *National Portrait Gallery.*

39. J. M. W. Turner (1775–1851), *Slavers Throwing Overboard the Dead and Dying — Typhon Coming On,* 1840. In his Romantic vision Turner sees beyond this manifest attack on the slave-trade (becoming extinct at the time of the painting; the incident suggesting it had probably occurred in 1783). He extends his censure to the whole world of trade, of "getting and spending," and in his own verses accompanying the painting he makes it clear that the typhoon is no mere natural cataclysm:

> Aloft all hands, strike the top-masts and belay;
> You angry setting sun and fierce-edged clouds
> Declare the Typhon's coming.
> Before it sweeps your decks, throw overboard
> The dead and dying—ne'er heed their chains.
> Hope, Hope, fallacious Hope!
> Where is thy market now?

Museum of Fine Arts, Boston.

40. *Rain, Steam and Speed* (The Great Western Railway), by J. M. W. Turner. Exhibited in 1844, this great canvas represents a complex response to the industrial revolution's ability to produce new natural phenomena. That response lies beyond Wordsworth's resolve, in his sonnet of 1835 called "Steamboats, Viaducts, and Railways," that technology

> . . . howsoe'er it mar
> The loveliness of Nature

never

> prove a bar
> To the Mind's gaining that prophetic sense
> Of future change, that point of vision. . . .

For Turner's total vision of a world made of light, the railway does not "mar," but participates. *National Gallery*, London.

We glided; and from that funereal bark
I leaned, and saw the city, and could mark
90 How from their many isles, in evening's gleam,
Its temples and its palaces did seem
Like fabrics of enchantment piled to Heaven.
I was about to speak, when—'We are even
Now at the point I meant,' said Maddalo,
And bade the gondolieri cease to row.
'Look, Julian, on the west, and listen well
If you hear not a deep and heavy bell.'
I looked, and saw between us and the sun
A building on an island; such a one
100 As age to age might add, for uses vile,
A windowless, deformed and dreary pile;
And on the top an open tower, where hung
A bell, which in the radiance swayed and swung;
We could just hear its hoarse and iron tongue:
The broad sun sunk behind it, and it tolled
In strong and black relief.—'What we behold
Shall be the madhouse and its belfry tower,'
Said Maddalo, 'and ever at this hour
Those who may cross the water, hear that bell
110 Which calls the maniacs, each one from his cell,
To vespers.'—'As much skill as need to pray
In thanks or hope for their dark lot have they
To their stern maker,' I replied. 'O ho!
You talk as in years past,' said Maddalo.
''Tis strange men change not. You were ever still
Among Christ's flock a perilous infidel,
A wolf for the meek lambs—if you can't swim
Beware of Providence.'° I looked on him,
But the gay smile had faded in his eye.
120 'And such,'—he cried, 'is our mortality,
And this must be the emblem and the sign
Of what should be eternal and divine!—
And like that black and dreary bell, the soul,
Hung in a heaven-illumined tower, must toll
Our thoughts and our desires to meet below
Round the rent heart and pray—as madmen do
For what? they know not,—till the night of death
As sunset that strange vision, severeth
Our memory from itself, and us from all
130 We sought and yet were baffled.' I recall
The sense of what he said, although I mar
The force of his expressions. The broad star

---

if you . . . Providence Byron was a swimmer of European reputation; Shelley declined to
learn.

Of day meanwhile had sunk behind the hill,
And the black bell became invisible,
And the red tower looked gray, and all between
The churches, ships and palaces were seen
Huddled in gloom;—into the purple sea
The orange hues of heaven sunk silently.
We hardly spoke, and soon the gondola
140 Conveyed me to my lodging by the way.
 The following morn was rainy, cold and dim:
Ere Maddalo arose, I called on him,
And whilst I waited with his child° I played;
A lovelier toy sweet Nature never made,
A serious, subtle, wild, yet gentle being,
Graceful without design and unforeseeing,
With eye—Oh speak not of her eyes!—which seem
Twin mirrors of Italian Heaven, yet gleam
With such deep meaning, as we never see
150 But in the human countenance: with me
She was a special favourite: I had nursed
Her fine and feeble limbs when she came first
To this bleak world; and she yet seemed to know
On second sight her ancient playfellow,
Less changed than she was by six months or so;
For after her first shyness was worn out
We sate there, rolling billiard balls about,
When the Count entered. Salutations past—
'The word you spoke last night might well have cast
160 A darkness on my spirit—if man be
The passive thing you say, I should not see
Much harm in the religions and old saws
(Though I may never own such leaden laws)
Which break a teachless nature to the yoke:
Mine is another faith'—thus much I spoke
And noting he replied not, added: 'See
This lovely child, blithe, innocent and free;
She spends a happy time with little care,
While we to such sick thoughts subjected are
170 As came on you last night—it is our will
That thus enchains us to permitted ill—
We might be otherwise—we might be all
We dream of happy, high, majestical.
Where is the love, beauty, and truth we seek
But in our mind? and if we were not weak
Should we be less in deed than in desire?'
'Ay, if we were not weak—and we aspire

his child Allegra, the natural daughter of Byron and Claire Clairmont, Mary Shelley's foster-sister

How vainly to be strong!' said Maddalo:
'You talk Utopia.' 'It remains to know,'
180 I then rejoined, 'and those who try may find
How strong the chains are which our spirit bind;
Brittle perchance as straw . . . We are assured
Much may be conquered, much may be endured,
Of what degrades and crushes us. We know
That we have power over ourselves to do
And suffer—what, we know not till we try;
But something nobler than to live and die—
So taught those kings of old philosophy
Who reigned, before Religion made men blind;
190 And those who suffer with their suffering kind
Yet feel their faith, religion.'. . .

. . . . .

. . . then we lingered not,
520 Although our argument was quite forgot,
But calling the attendants, went to dine
At Maddalo's; yet neither cheer nor wine
Could give us spirits, for we talked of him°
And nothing else, till daylight made stars dim;
And we agreed his was some dreadful ill
Wrought on him boldly, yet unspeakable,
By a dear friend; some deadly change in love
Of one vowed deeply which he dreamed not of;
For whose sake he, it seemed, had fixed a blot
530 Of falsehood on his mind which flourished not
But in the light of all-beholding truth;
And having stamped this canker on his youth
She had abandoned him—and how much more
Might be his woe, we guessed not—he had store
Of friends and fortune once, as we could guess
From his nice habits and his gentleness;
These were now lost . . . it were a grief indeed
If he had changed one unsustaining reed
For all that such a man might else adorn.
540 The colours of his mind seemed yet unworn;
For the wild language of his grief was high,
Such as in measure were called poetry;
And I remember one remark which then
Maddalo made. He said: 'Most wretched men
Are cradled into poetry by wrong,
They learn in suffering what they teach in song.'
    If I had been an unconnected man
I, from this moment, should have formed some plan

him a nameless mad poet (probably Tasso)
whose confinement is the subject of the middle
part of the poem

Never to leave sweet Venice,—for to me
550 It was delight to ride by the lone sea;
And then, the town is silent—one may write
Or read in gondolas by day or night,
Having the little brazen lamp alight,
Unseen, uninterrupted; books are there,
Pictures, and casts from all those statues fair
Which were twin-born with poetry, and all
We seek in towns, with little to recall
Regrets for the green country. I might sit
In Maddalo's great palace, and his wit
560 And subtle talk would cheer the winter night
And make me know myself, and the firelight
Would flash upon our faces, till the day
Might dawn and make me wonder at my stay:
But I had friends in London too: the chief
Attraction here, was that I sought relief
From the deep tenderness that maniac wrought
Within me—'twas perhaps an idle thought—
But I imagined that if day by day
I watched him, and but seldom went away,
570 And studied all the beatings of his heart
With zeal, as men study some stubborn art
For their own good, and could by patience find
An entrance to the caverns of his mind,
I might reclaim him from his dark estate:
In friendships I had been most fortunate—
Yet never saw I one whom I would call
More willingly my friend; and this was all
Accomplished not; such dreams of baseless good
Oft come and go in crowds or solitude
580 And leave no trace—but what I now designed
Made for long years impression on my mind.
The following morning, urged by my affairs,
I left bright Venice . . .
1818   1824

Prometheus Unbound

The Greek Orphic tradition maintained that the Titans, whom Zeus and the Olympian gods overthrew, were our ancestors. Hesiod said that the name, Titans, meant "punished overreachers." Of these overreachers, Prometheus (whose name means "foresighted," "prophetic") is the most celebrated. Aeschylus, the Athenian tragic dramatist, wrote a trilogy on Prometheus, of which only the first play, Prometheus Bound, survives. In it, Zeus (Shelley's Jupiter) is a tyrant who tortures Prometheus, but the Titan has faults also, being prideful and unrestrained. The surviving fragments of Aeschylus' second play, Prometheus Unbound, indicate that Zeus is reforming himself, as he has partly restored the Titan, and has given up his threats to destroy mankind. He still seeks to induce Prometheus to reveal a fatal secret, known only to the Titan, which will destroy Olympian rule, the secret being that any child Zeus begets upon Thetis, a mortal woman, will rise eventually to destroy his father.

Shelley rejects the outcome of Aeschylus' lost second play, which reconciles Zeus and Prometheus, and which permits Zeus to be warned in time. Shelley's Romantic Prometheus never yields to Jupiter, but he ceases to hate Jupiter, and in doing so begins a process that destroys the High God, whom Shelley regards as being beyond redemption. This process is imaginatively difficult, but is undoubtedly the supreme poetic invention in Shelley's work. To understand it, a reader needs to clarify for himself the curious shape of Shelley's myth in the poem.

As in Blake's The Four Zoas, the postulate is that a unitary Man fell, and separated out into torturing and tortured components, and into male and female forms as well. Jupiter is not an ultimate evil, even though he would like to be; he is too limited, because he has been invented by his victim, Prometheus, and cannot survive long once Prometheus abandons hatred of his own invention. As for Prometheus himself, he is limited also, for though he contains the human imagination and sexual energy, he can only begin the process of freeing imagination and sexuality. To complete it he requires Asia, who is again a limited being. Despite much scholarly interpretation to the contrary, she does not contain a universal Love or what Shelley termed the Intellectual Beauty, though in her apotheosis (at the end of Act II) she momentarily becomes one with these high powers. Mostly she remains subject to nature and can best be thought of as that provisional strength in humanity (much celebrated by Wordsworth) that holds the natural world, even in its dreadfully fallen condition, open to the love and beauty that hover perpetually (according to Shelley) just beyond the range of our senses.

Demogorgon is the lyrical drama's prime difficulty. Unlike the Demogorgon of Spenser, Milton, and Coleridge (see his fragment, "Limbo"), Shelley's daemon is not the pagan god of the abyss, but rather the god of skepticism, of our appalled but honest question: "What can we know?" He is a dialectical entity, who governs the turning-over of historical cycles, resembling in this the Marxist dialectic of history (Engels and Marx greatly admired Shelley's poem). He is also a parody of the descent of the Holy Spirit in some Christian accounts of fallen history. His limitation is what most characterizes him, for he represents the imagelessness of ultimates, like the dread, morally unallied Power behind the ravine in Shelley's Mont Blanc.

Though it is very much a poem of Shelley's own revolutionary age, Prometheus Unbound transcends the limiting context of any particular time, or rather becomes sharply relevant in any new time-of-troubles. Shelley, always a revolutionary temperament, is not teaching quietism or acceptance. But he shows, in agonizing, deeply inward ways, how difficult the path of regeneration is, and how much both the head and the heart need to purge in themselves if and when regeneration is ever to begin.

Prometheus Unbound

A Lyrical Drama in Four Acts

Audisne haec amphiarae, sub terram abdite? [1]

Preface

The Greek tragic writers, in selecting as their subject any portion of their national history or mythology, . employed in their treatment of it a certain arbitrary discretion. They by no means conceived themselves bound to adhere to the common interpretation or to imitate in story as in title their rivals and predecessors. Such a system would have amounted to a resignation of those claims to preference over their competitors which incited the composition. The Agamemnonian story was exhibited on the Athenian theatre with as many variations as dramas.

I have presumed to employ a similar licence. The *Prometheus Unbound* of Aeschylus supposed the reconciliation of Jupiter with his victim as the price of the disclosure of the danger threatened to his empire by the consummation of his marriage with Thetis. Thetis, according to this view of the subject, was given in marriage to Peleus, and Prometheus, by the permission of Jupiter, delivered from his captivity by Hercules. Had I framed my story on this model, I should have done no more than have attempted to restore the lost drama of Aeschylus; an ambition which, if my preference to this mode of treating the subject had incited me to cherish, the recollection of the high comparison such an attempt would challenge might well abate. But, in truth, I was averse from a catastrophe so feeble as that of reconciling the Champion with the Oppressor of mankind. The moral interest of the fable, which is so powerfully sustained by the sufferings and endurance of Prometheus, would be annihilated if we could conceive of him as unsaying his high language and quailing before his successful and perfidious adversary. The only imaginary being resembling in any degree Prometheus, is Satan; and Prometheus is, in my judgement, a more poetical character than Satan, because, in addition to courage, and majesty, and firm and patient opposition to omnipotent force, he is susceptible of being described as exempt from the taints of ambition, envy, revenge, and a desire for personal aggrandisement, which, in the Hero of *Paradise Lost,* interfere with the interest. The character of Satan engenders in the mind a pernicious casuistry which leads us to weigh his faults with his wrongs, and to excuse the former because the latter exceed all measure. In the minds of those who consider that magnificent fiction with a religious feeling it engenders something worse. But Prometheus is, as it were, the type of the highest perfection of moral and intellectual nature, impelled by the purest and the truest motives to the best and noblest ends.

---

1. "Do you hear this, Amphiaraus, in your home beneath the earth?" This verse, by an unknown translator of a lost play by Aeschylus, is quoted in Cicero's *Tusculan Disputations,* as a reproach to a wavering stoic. Amphiaraus, a renowned Seer, was one of the Seven against Thebes, who later became an oracular god in a cave beneath the earth. Shelley's epigraph (perhaps over-subtle) seems directed against Wordsworth and Coleridge, once rebels but now oracular in their piety. They are asked to hear this play, which voices the stoic defiance of Prometheus (and of Shelley).

This Poem was chiefly written upon the mountainous ruins of the Baths of Caracalla,[2] among the flowery glades, and thickets of odoriferous blossoming trees, which are extended in ever winding labyrinths upon its immense platforms and dizzy arches suspended in the air. The bright blue sky of Rome, and the effect of the vigorous awakening spring in that divinest climate, and the new life with which it drenches the spirits even to intoxication, were the inspiration of this drama.

The imagery which I have employed will be found, in many instances, to have been drawn from the operations of the human mind, or from those external actions by which they are expressed. This is unusual in modern poetry, although Dante and Shakespeare are full of instances of the same kind: Dante indeed more than any other poet, and with greater success. But the Greek poets, as writers to whom no resource of awakening the sympathy of their contemporaries was unknown, were in the habitual use of this power; and it is the study of their works (since a higher merit would probably be denied me) to which I am willing that my readers should impute this singularity.

One word is due in candour to the degree in which the study of contemporary writings may have tinged my composition, for such has been a topic of censure with regard to poems far more popular, and indeed more deservedly popular, than mine. It is impossible that any one who inhabits the same age with such writers as those who stand in the foremost ranks of our own, can conscientiously assure himself that his language and tone of thought may not have been modified by the study of the productions of those extraordinary intellects. It is true, that, not the spirit of their genius, but the forms in which it has manifested itself, are due less to the peculiarities of their own minds than to the peculiarity of the moral and intellectual condition of the minds among which they have been produced. Thus a number of writers possess the form, whilst they want the spirit of those whom, it is alleged, they imitate; because the former is the endowment of the age in which they live, and the latter must be the uncommunicated lightning of their own mind.

The peculiar style of intense and comprehensive imagery which distinguishes the modern literature of England, has not been, as a general power, the product of the imitation of any particular writer. The mass of capabilities remains at every period materially the same; the circumstances which awaken it to action perpetually change. If England were divided into forty republics, each equal in population and extent to Athens, there is no reason to suppose but that, under institutions not more perfect than those of Athens, each would produce philosophers and poets equal to those who (if we except Shakespeare) have never been surpassed. We owe the great writers of the golden age of our literature to that fervid awakening of the public mind which shook to dust the oldest and most oppressive form of the Christian religion. We owe Milton to the progress and development of the same spirit: the sacred Milton was, let it ever be remembered, a republican, and a bold inquirer into morals and religion. The great writers of our own age are, we have reason to suppose, the companions and forerunners of some unimagined change in our social condition or the opinions which cement it. The cloud of mind is discharging its

2. Ancient sprawling baths of Rome named for the Emperor Caracalla (188-217 A.D.).

collected lightning, and the equilibrium between institutions and opinions is now restoring, or is about to be restored.

As to imitation, poetry is a mimetic art. It creates, but it creates by combination and representation. Poetical abstractions are beautiful and new, not because the portions of which they are composed had no previous existence in the mind of man or in nature, but because the whole produced by their combination has some intelligible and beautiful analogy with those sources of emotion and thought, and with the contemporary condition of them: one great poet is a masterpiece of nature which another not only ought to study but must study. He might as wisely and as easily determine that his mind should no longer be the mirror of all that is lovely in the visible universe, as exclude from his contemplation the beautiful which exists in the writings of a great contemporary. The pretence of doing it would be a presumption in any but the greatest; the effect, even in him, would be strained, unnatural, and ineffectual. A poet is the combined product of such internal powers as modify the nature of others; and of such external influences as excite and sustain these powers; he is not one, but both. Every man's mind is, in this respect, modified by all the objects of nature and art; by every word and every suggestion which he ever admitted to act upon his consciousness; it is the mirror upon which all forms are reflected, and in which they compose one form. Poets, not otherwise than philosophers, painters, sculptors, and musicians, are, in one sense, the creators, and, in another, the creations, of their age. From this subjection the loftiest do not escape. There is a similarity between Homer and Hesiod, between Aeschylus and Euripides, between Virgil and Horace, between Dante and Petrarch, between Shakespeare and Fletcher, between Dryden and Pope; each has a generic resemblance under which their specific distinctions are arranged. If this similarity be the result of imitation, I am willing to confess that I have imitated.

Let this opportunity be conceded to me of acknowledging that I have, what a Scotch philosopher characteristically terms, 'a passion for reforming the world': what passion incited him to write and publish his book, he omits to explain. For my part I had rather be damned with Plato and Lord Bacon, than go to Heaven with Paley and Malthus.[3] But it is a mistake to suppose that I dedicate my poetical compositions solely to the direct enforcement of reform, or that I consider them in any degree as containing a reasoned system on the theory of human life. Didactic poetry is my abhorrence; nothing can be equally well expressed in prose that is not tedious and supererogatory in verse. My purpose has hitherto been simply to familiarise the highly refined imagination of the more select classes of poetical readers with beautiful idealisms of moral excellence; aware that until the mind can love, and admire, and trust, and hope, and endure, reasoned principles of moral conduct are seeds cast upon the highway of life which the unconscious passenger tramples into dust, although they would bear the harvest of his happiness. Should I live to accomplish what I purpose, that is, produce a systematical history of what

3. William Paley (1743–1805), popular theologian, maintained the case for natural religion, and argued the moral usefulness of Hell. Thomas Robert Malthus (1776–1834), popular economist, demonstrated war, famine, and pestilence to be necessary due to the excess of population growth over food production. Shelley, as a revolutionary reformer, despised both as apologists for things-as-they-are.

appear to me to be the genuine elements of human society, let not the advocates of injustice and superstition flatter themselves that I should take Aeschylus rather than Plato as my model.

The having spoken of myself with unaffected freedom will need little apology with the candid; and let the uncandid consider that they injure me less than their own hearts and minds by misrepresentation. Whatever talents a person may possess to amuse and instruct others, be they ever so inconsiderable, he is yet bound to exert them: if his attempt be ineffectual, let the punishment of an unaccomplished purpose have been sufficient; let none trouble themselves to heap the dust of oblivion upon his efforts; the pile they raise will betray his grave which might otherwise have been unknown.

DRAMATIS PERSONAE

PROMETHEUS	APOLLO	HERCULES
DEMOGORGON	MERCURY	THE PHANTASM OF JUPITER
JUPITER	ASIA ⎱	THE SPIRIT OF THE EARTH
THE EARTH	PANTHEA ⎰ *Oceanides.*	THE SPIRIT OF THE MOON
OCEAN	IONE ⎰	SPIRITS OF THE HOURS

SPIRITS ECHOES FAUNS FURIES

From ACT I

SCENE *A Ravine of Icy Rocks in the Indian Caucasus.* PROMETHEUS *is discovered bound to the Precipice.* PANTHEA *and* IONE *are seated at his feet. Time, night. During the Scene, morning slowly breaks.*

PROMETHEUS   Monarch of Gods and Daemons, and all Spirits
But One,° who throng those bright and rolling worlds
Which Thou and I alone of living things
Behold with sleepless eyes! regard this Earth
Made multitudinous with thy slaves, whom thou
Requitest for knee-worship, prayer, and praise,
And toil, and hecatombs° of broken hearts,
With fear and self-contempt and barren hope.°
Whilst me, who am thy foe, eyeless in hate,
10   Hast thou made reign and triumph, to thy scorn,°
O'er mine own misery and thy vain revenge.
Three thousand years of sleep-unsheltered hours,
And moments aye divided by keen pangs
Till they seemed years, torture and solitude,
Scorn and despair,—these are mine empire:—
More glorious far than that which thou surveyest
From thine unenvied throne, O Mighty God!
Almighty, had I deigned to share the shame
Of thine ill tyranny, and hung not here
20   Nailed to this wall of eagle-baffling mountain,

One probably Demogorgon
hecatombs gigantic sacrifices
With fear . . . hope the negations of the

Shelleyan virtues: love, self-esteem, hope
Whilst me . . . scorn making you (Jupiter) an object of scorn

Black, wintry, dead, unmeasured; without herb,
Insect, or beast, or shape or sound of life.
Ah me! alas, pain, pain ever, forever!

No change, no pause, no hope! Yet I endure.
I ask the Earth, have not the mountains felt?
I ask yon Heaven, the all-beholding Sun,
Has it not seen? The sea, in storm or calm,
Heaven's ever-changing Shadow, spread below,
Have its deaf waves not heard my agony?
30   Ah me! alas, pain, pain ever, forever!

The crawling glaciers pierce me with the spears
Of their moon-freezing crystals, the bright chains
Eat with their burning cold into my bones.
Heaven's wingèd hound, polluting from thy lips
His beak in poison not his own, tears up
My heart;° and shapeless sights come wandering by,
The ghastly people of the realm of dream,
Mocking me: and the Earthquake-fiends are charged
To wrench the rivets from my quivering wounds
40   When the rocks split and close again behind:
While from their loud abysses howling throng
The genii of the storm, urging the rage
Of whirlwind, and afflict me with keen hail.
And yet to me welcome is day and night,
Whether one breaks the hoar frost of the morn,
Or starry, dim, and slow, the other climbs
The leaden-coloured east; for then they lead
The wingless, crawling hours, one among whom
—As some dark Priest hales the reluctant victim
50   Shall drag thee, cruel King, to kiss the blood
From these pale feet, which then might trample thee
If they disdained not such a prostrate slave.
Disdain! Ah no! I pity thee.° What ruin
Will hunt thee undefended through wide Heaven!
How will thy soul, cloven to its depth with terror,
Gape like a hell within! I speak in grief,
Not exultation, for I hate no more,
As then ere misery made me wise. The curse
Once breathed on thee I would recall. Ye Mountains,
60   Whose many-voicèd Echoes, through the mist
Of cataracts, flung the thunder of that spell!
Ye icy Springs, stagnant with wrinkling frost,
Which vibrated to hear me, and then crept
Shuddering through India! Thou serenest Air,

Heaven's . . . heart The vulture perpetually kissed Jupiter, and then proceeded to its daily torture of Prometheus.

I pity thee the turning over of the Promethean cycle

Through which the Sun walks burning without beams!
And ye swift Whirlwinds, who on poisèd wings
Hung mute and moveless o'er yon hushed abyss,
As thunder, louder than your own, made rock
The orbèd world! If then my words had power,
70 Though I am changed so that aught evil wish
Is dead within; although no memory be
Of what is hate, let them not lose it now!
What was that curse? for ye all heard me speak.

· · ·

    PROMETHEUS   Venerable mother!°
All else who live and suffer take from thee
Some comfort; flowers, and fruits, and happy sounds,
And love, though fleeting; these may not be mine.
190 But mine own words, I pray, deny me not.
    THE EARTH   They shall be told. Ere Babylon was dust,
The Magus Zoroaster, my dead child,
Met his own image walking in the garden.°
That apparition, sole of men, he saw.
For know there are two worlds of life and death:
One that which thou beholdest; but the other
Is underneath the grave, where do inhabit
The shadows of all forms that think and live
Till death unite them and they part no more;°
200 Dreams and the light imaginings of men,
And all that faith creates or love desires,
Terrible, strange, sublime and beauteous shapes.
There thou art, and dost hang, a writhing shade,
'Mid whirlwind-peopled mountains; all the gods
Are there, and all the powers of nameless worlds,
Vast, sceptred phantoms; heroes, men, and beasts;
And Demogorgon,° a tremendous gloom;
And he, the supreme Tyrant, on his throne
Of burning gold. Son, one of these shall utter
210 The curse which all remember. Call at will

Venerable mother After the scatterd components of a fallen world have refused to repeat his forgotten curse, the Titan appeals to the Earth, his mother.
Zoroaster . . . garden Zoroaster, a 6th-century B.C. Persian, founded a dualistic religion, as the prophet of Ormazd, spirit of good, against Ahriman (or Ahuramazda), spirit of evil. The story of his meeting his double is Shelley's invention, and repeats the ancient superstition that to meet one's double is to be close to one's death. There is a legend that Shelley met his double a few days before he drowned, and fainted when the double asked him: "How long do you mean to be content?"
Till . . . more an anticipation of the modern German poet R.M. Rilke's myth that we become complete by marrying our own deaths
Demogorgon The most difficult interpretative problem in the poem; late medieval and early Renaissance mythologists made Demogorgon the father of all the Gentile gods, and the original ruler of the Abyss or Chaos, a role he fills in Spenser, Milton, and in Coleridge's "Limbo." In Shelley's poem he is more a dialectic or process of how things happen than he is a personage; he is morally unallied, and thus the god of skepticism, preceptor of our appalling freedom to imagine well or badly. As such, he resembles both the historical dialectic of the Marxists, and the descent of the Holy Spirit in Christian readings of history. He may be a deliberate parody of the Holy Spirit.

Thine own ghost, or the ghost of Jupiter,
Hades or Typhon,° or what mightier Gods
From all-prolific Evil, since thy ruin
Have sprung, and trampled on my prostrate sons.
Ask, and they must reply: so the revenge
Of the Supreme may sweep through vacant shades,
As rainy wind through the abandoned gate
Of a fallen palace.

. . .

PHANTASM OF JUPITER
    Fiend, I defy thee! with a calm, fixed mind,°
        All that thou canst inflict I bid thee do;
    Foul Tyrant both of Gods and Human-kind,
        One only being shalt thou not subdue.
    Rain then thy plagues upon me here,
    Ghastly disease, and frenzying fear;
    And let alternate frost and fire
    Eat into me, and be thine ire
270 Lightning, and cutting hail, and legioned forms
    Of furies, driving by upon the wounding storms,

    Ay, do thy worst. Thou art omnipotent.
        O'er all things but thyself I gave thee power,
    And my own will. Be thy swift mischiefs sent
        To blast mankind, from yon ethereal tower.
    Let thy malignant spirit move
    In darkness over those I love:
    On me and mine I imprecate
    The utmost torture of thy hate;
280 And thus devote to sleepless agony,
    This undeclining head while thou must reign on high.

    But thou, who art the God and Lord: O, thou,
        Who fillest with thy soul this world of woe,
    To whom all things of Earth and Heaven do bow
        In fear and worship: all-prevailing foe!
    I curse thee! let a sufferer's curse
    Clasp thee, his torturer, like remorse;
    Till thine Infinity shall be
    A robe of envenomed agony;°
290 And thine Omnipotence a crown of pain,
    To cling like burning gold round thy dissolving brain.

Hades or Typhon Hades here is Pluto, lord of Hades; Typhon is a monster with many heads, responsible for earthquakes.
mind The mind is that of Prometheus, but the speaker is the Phantasm or shadow-form, the double of Jupiter, uttering a curse of which he

will be the victim, and which Prometheus now seeks vainly to recall.
thine . . . agony the Infinity of Jupiter will torture him even as the shirt of the centaur Nessus tormented Heracles, a suffering that caused Heracles to mount his death-pyre

Heap on thy soul, by virtue of this Curse,
   Ill deeds, then be thou damned, beholding good;°
Both infinite as is the universe,
   And thou, and thy self-torturing solitude.
An awful image of calm power
   Though now thou sittest, let the hour
Come, when thou must appear to be
   That which thou art internally;
300 And after many a false and fruitless crime
Scorn track thy lagging fall through boundless space and time.

PROMETHEUS   Were these my words, O Parent?
THE EARTH   They were thine.
PROMETHEUS   It doth repent me: words are quick and vain;
Grief for awhile is blind, and so was mine.
I wish no living thing to suffer pain.

. . .

FURY   Behold an emblem: those who do endure
Deep wrongs for man, and scorn, and chains, but heap
Thousandfold torment on themselves and him.°
PROMETHEUS   Remit the anguish of that lighted stare;
Close those wan lips; let that thorn-wounded brow
Stream not with blood; it mingles with thy tears!
600 Fix, fix those tortured orbs in peace and death,
So thy sick throes shake not that crucifix,
So those pale fingers play not with thy gore.
O, horrible! Thy name I will not speak,
It hath become a curse.° I see, I see
The wise, the mild, the lofty, and the just,
Whom thy slaves hate for being like to thee,
Some hunted by foul lies from their heart's home,
An early-chosen, late-lamented home;
As hooded ounces° cling to the driven hind;
610 Some linked to corpses in unwholesome cells:
Some—Hear I not the multitude laugh loud?—
Impaled in lingering fire: and mighty realms
Float by my feet, like sea-uprooted isles,
Whose sons are kneaded down in common blood
By the red light of their own burning homes.
FURY   Blood thou canst see, and fire; and canst hear groans;
Worse things, unheard, unseen, remain behind.
PROMETHEUS   Worse?
FURY   In each human heart terror survives

Heap . . . good Prometheus cursed Jupiter as Milton's God cursed Satan, a peculiarly Shelleyan irony; see *Paradise Lost* I.209–20.
Behold . . . him The Furies, sent by Jupiter to torment Prometheus, have given him a vision of the moral failure of the French Revolution; the last and subtlest Fury now demonstrates that the sacrifice of Christ only brought about a new tyranny, historical and institutional Christianity, which has martyred man afresh.
It . . . curse In the sense that societal Christianity has driven out Shelley, Byron, and others for supposed moral offenses, and deprived Shelley of his children by his first marriage.
ounces trained leopards kept hooded until released to hunt down the hind, or deer

The ravin° it has gorged: the loftiest fear
620 All that they would disdain to think were true:
Hypocrisy and custom make their minds
The fanes of many a worship, now outworn.
They dare not devise good for man's estate,
And yet they know not that they do not dare.
The good want power, but to weep barren tears.
The powerful goodness want: worse need for them.
The wise want love; and those who love want wisdom;
And all best things are thus confused to ill.°
Many are strong and rich, and would be just,
630 But live among their suffering fellow-men
As if none felt: they know not what they do.°
    PROMETHEUS Thy words are like a cloud of wingèd snakes;
And yet I pity those they torture not.
    FURY Thou pitiest them? I speak no more!
[*Vanishes*]

·   ·   ·

ACT II
From SCENE IV°   *The Cave of* DEMOGORGON. ASIA *and* PANTHEA.
    PANTHEA What veilèd form sits on that ebon throne?
    ASIA The veil has fallen.
    PANTHEA   I see a mighty darkness
Filling the seat of power, and rays of gloom
Dart round, as light from the meridian sun.
—Ungazed upon and shapeless; neither limb,
Nor form, nor outline; yet we feel it is
A living Spirit.
    DEMOGORGON Ask what thou wouldst know.
    ASIA What canst thou tell?
    DEMOGORGON   All things thou dar'st demand.
    ASIA Who made the living world?
    DEMOGORGON   God.°
    ASIA   Who made all
10 That it contains? thought, passion, reason, will,
Imagination?
    DEMOGORGON God: Almighty God.°
    ASIA Who made that sense which, when the winds of Spring
In rarest visitation, or the voice

---

ravin carrion
The wise . . . ill Compare Yeats's "The Second
Coming," which echoes this passage; the wise
who lack love include Godwin and Shelley's own
revolutionary intelligentsia, while those who love
but lack wisdom include Wordsworth and Coleridge.
they know . . . do See Luke 23:34.
Scene IV Asia, the wife of Prometheus, long
separated from him by Jupiter, has descended to
the oracular cave of Demogorgon, to find out

how and when the overthrow of Jupiter, and her
subsequent reunion with Prometheus, will take
place. In her difficult dialogue with Demogorgon, he is not so much evasive as relatively unknowing; she learns only what she already knows
and is, but this is enough, since the time of
renovation is now.
God not Jupiter, but a figure closer to Prometheus himself
Almighty God the ultimate Power, as in "Mont
Blanc"

Of one beloved heard in youth alone,
Fills the faint eyes with falling tears which dim
The radiant looks of unbewailing flowers,
And leaves this peopled earth a solitude
When it returns no more?°

DEMOGORGON   Merciful God.°

ASIA   And who made terror, madness, crime, remorse,
20 Which from the links of the great chain of things,
To every thought within the mind of man
Sway and drag heavily, and each one reels
Under the load towards the pit of death;
Abandoned hope, and love that turns to hate;
And self-contempt,° bitterer to drink than blood;
Pain, whose unheeded and familiar speech
Is howling, and keen shrieks, day after day;
And Hell, or the sharp fear of Hell?

DEMOGORGON   He reigns.°

ASIA   Utter his name: a world pining in pain
30 Asks but his name: curses shall drag him down.

DEMOGORGON   He reigns.

ASIA   I feel, I know it: who?

DEMOGORGON   He reigns.

ASIA   Who reigns? There was the Heaven and Earth at first,°
And Light and Love; then Saturn, from whose throne
Time fell, an envious shadow: such the state
Of the earth's primal spirits beneath his sway,
As the calm joy of flowers and living leaves
Before the wind or sun has withered them
And semivital worms; but he refused
The birthright of their being, knowledge, power,
40 The skill which wields the elements, the thought
Which pierces this dim universe like light,
Self-empire, and the majesty of love;
For thirst of which they fainted. Then Prometheus
Gave wisdom, which is strength, to Jupiter,   .
And with this law alone, 'Let man be free,'
Clothed him with the dominion of wide Heaven.°
To know nor faith, nor love, nor law; to be
Omnipotent but friendless is to reign;
And Jove now reigned; for on the race of man
50 First famine, and then toil, and then disease,

Who made . . . more Asia's experience recalls
the "Hymn to Intellectual Beauty."
Merciful God the Intellectual Beauty
self-contempt the greatest of vices in Shelley's
moral universe
He reigns Jupiter
at first Asia's complex cosmogony describes (ll.
32–38), as Blake's does, an original Saturnian
or happy and unfallen universe, rather than an

initial chaos, as in the Hebraic account.
Then Prometheus . . . Heaven Saturn, king of
the Titans, refused to give us the equivocal gift
of consciousness, which Prometheus (as in the
poetry of Empedocles, a pre-Socratic philosopher) insisted was necessary for us to be wholly
human; Jupiter, the agent of Prometheus, betrayed him and us, imposing the tyranny of
Heaven.

Strife, wounds, and ghastly death unseen before,
Fell; and the unseasonable seasons drove
With alternating shafts of frost and fire,
Their shelterless, pale tribes to mountain caves:
And in their desert hearts fierce wants he sent,
And mad disquietudes, and shadows idle
Of unreal good, which levied mutual war,
So ruining the lair wherein they raged.
Prometheus saw, and waked the legioned hopes
60   Which sleep within folded Elysian flowers,
Nepenthe, Moly, Amaranth,° fadeless blooms,
That they might hide with thin and rainbow wings
The shape of Death; and Love he sent to bind
The disunited tendrils of that vine
Which bears the wine of life, the human heart;
And he tamed fire which, like some beast of prey,
Most terrible, but lovely, played beneath
The frown of man; and tortured to his will
Iron and gold, the slaves and signs of power,
70   And gems and poisons, and all subtlest forms
Hidden beneath the mountains and the waves.
He gave man speech, and speech created thought,
Which is the measure of the universe;
And Science struck the thrones of earth and heaven,
Which shook, but fell not; and the harmonious mind
Poured itself forth in all-prophetic song;
And music lifted up the listening spirit
Until it walked, exempt from mortal care.
Godlike, o'er the clear billows of sweet sound;
80   And human hands first mimicked and then mocked,
With moulded limbs more lovely than its own,
The human form, till marble grew divine;
And mothers, gazing, drank the love men see
Reflected in their race, behold, and perish.
He told the hidden power of herbs and springs,
And Disease drank and slept. Death grew like sleep.
He taught the implicated orbits woven
Of the wide-wandering stars; and how the sun
Changes his lair, and by what secret spell
90   The pale moon is transformed, when her broad eye
Gazes not on the interlunar sea:
He taught to rule, as life directs the limbs,
The tempest-wingèd chariots of the Ocean,
And the Celt knew the Indian. Cities then
Were built, and through their snow-like columns flowed
The warm winds, and the azure aether shone,

Nepenthe was a drug giving forgetfulness,
Moly a herb to protect against enchantment,
and Amaranth an undying, unfading flower.

And the blue sea and shadowy hills were seen.
Such, the alleviations of his state,
Prometheus gave to man, for which he hangs
100 Withering in destined pain: but who rains down
Evil, the immedicable plague, which, while
Man looks on his creation like a God
And sees that it is glorious, drives him on,
The wreck of his own will, the scorn of earth,
The outcast, the abandoned, the alone?
Not Jove: while yet his frown shook Heaven, ay, when
His adversary from adamantine chains
Cursed him, he trembled like a slave. Declare
Who is his master? Is he too a slave?
110   DEMOGORGON   All spirits are enslaved which serve things evil:
Thou knowest if Jupiter be such or no.
    ASIA   Whom calledst thou God?
    DEMOGORGON   I spoke but as ye speak,
For Jove is the supreme of living things.
    ASIA   Who is the master of the slave?
    DEMOGORGON   If the abysm
Could vomit forth its secrets. . . . But a voice
Is wanting, the deep truth is imageless;°
For what would it avail to bid thee gaze
On the revolving world? What to bid speak
Fate, Time, Occasion, Chance, and Change? To these
120 All things are subject but eternal Love.°
    ASIA   So much I asked before, and my heart gave
The response thou hast given; and of such truths
Each to itself must be the oracle.°
One more demand; and do thou answer me
As mine own soul would answer, did it know
That which I ask. Prometheus shall arise
Henceforth the sun of this rejoicing world:
When shall the destined hour arrive?
    DEMOGORGON   Behold!°
    . . .

From SCENE V   *The Car pauses within a Cloud on the top of a snowy Mountain.*
    VOICE IN THE AIR, *singing*°
        Life of Life! thy lips enkindle
          With their love the breath between them;

deep . . . imageless Demogorgon expresses the central truth of skepticism, that ultimates cannot be known or portrayed.
Love This transcendent love is identical with the Intellectual Beauty, but it is not manifested or represented in the poem, not even by Asia, except in her momentary transfiguration at the end of Act II.
So much . . . oracle She has learned, as F. A. Pottle phrased it, "to give up her demand for an ultimate Personal Evil, to combine an unshak-

able faith that the universe is sound at the core with a realization that, as regards man, Time is radically and incurably evil."
Behold! The chariot of the Hours descends, to take Asia back up to the soon-to-be-transformed world.
singing The Voice in the Air, confronting a transfigured Asia, in her moment-of-moments in which she becomes a kind of heavenly Venus, attempts to image the imageless, and fails, but brilliantly and unforgettably.

50   And thy smiles before they dwindle
    Make the cold air fire; then screen them
In those looks, where whoso gazes
Faints, entangled in their mazes.

Child of Light! thy limbs are burning
    Through the vest which seems to hide them;
As the radiant lines of morning
    Through the clouds ere they divide them;
And this atmosphere divinest
Shrouds thee wheresoe'er thou shinest.

60   Fair are others; none beholds thee,
    But thy voice sounds low and tender
Like the fairest, for it folds thee
    From the sight, that liquid splendour,
And all feel, yet see thee never,
As I feel now, lost forever!

Lamp of Earth! where'er thou movest
    Its dim shapes are clad with brightness,
And the souls of whom thou lovest
    Walk upon the winds with lightness,
70   Till they fail, as I am failing,
Dizzy, lost, yet unbewailing!

ASIA
My soul is an enchanted boat,
Which, like a sleeping swan, doth float
Upon the silver waves of thy sweet singing;
    And thine doth like an angel sit
    Beside a helm conducting it,
Whilst all the winds with melody are ringing.
    It seems to float ever, forever,
    Upon that many-winding river,
80   Between mountains, woods, abysses,
    A paradise of wildernesses!
Till, like one in slumber bound,
Borne to the ocean, I float down, around,
Into a sea profound, of ever-spreading sound:

    Meanwhile thy spirit lifts its pinions
    In music's most serene dominions;
Catching the winds that fan that happy heaven.
    And we sail on, away, afar,
    Without a course, without a star,
90   But, by the instinct of sweet music driven;
    Till through Elysian garden islets
    By thee, most beautiful of pilots,
    Where never mortal pinnace glided,
    The boat of my desire is guided:

Realms where the air we breathe is love,
Which in the winds and on the waves doth move,
Harmonizing this earth with what we feel above.

100
We have passed Age's icy caves,
And Manhood's dark and tossing waves,
And Youth's smooth ocean, smiling to betray:
Beyond the glassy gulfs we flee
Of shadow-peopled Infancy,
Through Death and Birth, to a diviner day;
A paradise of vaulted bowers,
Lit by downward-gazing flowers,
And watery paths that wind between
Wildernesses calm and green,
Peopled by shapes too bright to see,°
And rest, having beheld; somewhat like thee;
110
Which walk upon the sea, and chant melodiously!

END OF THE SECOND ACT

ACT III

SCENE I   *Heaven.* JUPITER *on his Throne;* THETIS *and the other Deities*
assembled.

JUPITER   Ye congregated powers of heaven, who share
The glory and the strength of him ye serve,
Rejoice! henceforth I am omnipotent.
All else had been subdued to me; alone
The soul of man, like unextinguished fire,
Yet burns towards heaven with fierce reproach, and doubt,
And lamentation, and reluctant prayer,
Hurling up insurrection, which might make
Our antique empire insecure, though built
10
On eldest faith, and hell's coeval,° fear;
And though my curses through the pendulous air,
Like snow on herbless peaks, fall flake by flake,
And cling to it; though under my wrath's night
It climbs the crags of life, step after step,
Which wound it, as ice wounds unsandalled feet,
It yet remains supreme o'er misery,
Aspiring, unrepressed, yet soon to fall:
Even now have I begotten a strange wonder,
That fatal child,° the terror of the earth,
20
Who waits but till the destined hour arrive,
Bearing from Demogorgon's vacant throne°

A paradise . . . see (ll. 104–8) She describes,
in her apotheosis, a return to a divine infancy,
like "the Shining Ones" described by John Bunyan or Blake's children of Beulah or Wordsworth's children on the shore in his "Intimations" Ode.
coeval of equal age

fatal child Jupiter's unintentional irony, as Jupiter's son by Thetis will be fatal for him, precisely
because the son is unbegotten
vacant throne another irony; the throne is vacant only because Demogorgon is in the act of
rising up from it

The dreadful might of ever-living limbs
Which clothed that awful spirit unbeheld,
To redescend, and trample out the spark.
Pour forth heaven's wine, Idaean Ganymede,°
And let it fill the Daedal cups like fire,
And from the flower-inwoven soil divine
Ye all-triumphant harmonies arise,
As dew from earth under the twilight stars:
30   Drink! be the nectar circling through your veins
The soul of joy, ye ever-living Gods,
Till exultation burst in one wide voice
Like music from Elysian winds.
     And thou
Ascend beside me, veilèd in the light
Of the desire which makes thee one with me,
Thetis, bright image of eternity!
When thou didst cry, 'Insufferable might!
God! Spare me! I sustain not the quick flames,
The penetrating presence; all my being,
40   Like him whom the Numidian seps° did thaw
Into a dew with poison, is dissolved,°
Sinking through its foundations:' even then
Two mighty spirits, mingling, made a third
Mightier than either, which, unbodied now,
Between us floats, felt, although unbeheld,
Waiting the incarnation, which ascends,
(Hear ye the thunder of the fiery wheels
Griding° the winds?) from Demogorgon's throne.
Victory! victory! Feel'st thou not, O world,
50   The earthquake of his chariot thundering up
Olympus?
[*The Car of the* HOUR *arrives.* DEMOGORGON *descends,
and moves towards the Throne of* JUPITER.]
    Awful shape, what art thou? Speak!
 DEMOGORGON Eternity. Demand no direr name.°
Descend, and follow me down the abyss.
I am thy child, as thou wert Saturn's child;°
Mightier than thee: and we must dwell together
Henceforth in darkness. Lift thy lightnings not.
The tyranny of heaven none may retain,
Or reassume, or hold, succeeding thee:
Yet if thou wilt, as 'tis the destiny
60   Of trodden worms to writhe till they are dead,
Put forth thy might.

Ganymede boy abducted from Mt. Ida to be
Jupiter's cupbearer
seps serpent whose bite caused decomposition
dissolved she could not sustain him, and so
did not conceive

Griding cutting with a strident sound
Eternity . . . name whatever one wishes to call
one's own dialectic or process of doom
child usurper only

JUPITER   Detested prodigy!
Even thus beneath the deep Titanian prisons
I trample thee! thou lingerest?
                         Mercy! mercy!
No pity, no release, no respite! Oh,
That thou wouldst make mine enemy my judge,
Even where he hangs, seared by my long revenge,
On Caucasus! he would not doom me thus.
Gentle, and just, and dreadless, is he not
The monarch of the world? What then art thou?
No refuge! No appeal!
70   Sink with me then,
We two will sink on the wide waves of ruin,
     Even as a vulture and a snake outspent°
Drop, twisted in inextricable fight,
Into a shoreless sea. Let hell unlock
Its mounded oceans of tempestuous fire,
And whelm on them into the bottomless void
This desolated world, and thee, and me,
The conqueror and the conquered, and the wreck
Of that for which they combated.
                              Ai! Ai!°
80   The elements obey me not. I sink
Dizzily down, ever, forever, down.
And, like a cloud, mine enemy above
Darknes my fall with victory! Ai, Ai!

SCENE II   *The Mouth of a great River in the Island Atlantis.* OCEAN *is discovered
reclining near the Shore;* APOLLO *stands beside him.*
     OCEAN   He fell, thou sayest, beneath his conqueror's frown?
     APOLLO   Ay, when the strife was ended which made dim
The orb I rule, and shook the solid stars,
The terrors of his eye illumined heaven
With sanguine light, through the thick ragged skirts
Of the victorious darkness, as he fell:
Like the last glare of day's red agony,
Which, from a rent among the fiery clouds,
Burns far along the tempest-wrinkled deep.
10   OCEAN   He sunk to the abyss? To the dark void?
     APOLLO   Ay, when the strife was ended which made dim
On Caucasus, his thunder-baffled wings
Entangled in the whirlwind, and his eyes
Which gazed on the undazzling sun, now blinded
By the white lightning, while the ponderous hail
Beats on his struggling form, which sinks at length

Even . . . outspent The image of a serpent
wrestling to the death with a vulture or eagle
haunted Shelley, and is crucial in his early
Spenserian epic, *The Revolt of Islam;* for a
modern instance, indebted to Shelley, see the
end of "The Dance" in Hart Crane's *The Bridge.*
Ai! "woe!" in Greek

Prone, and the aereal ice clings over it.

OCEAN   Henceforth the fields of heaven-reflecting sea
Which are my realm, will heave, unstained with blood,
20   Beneath the uplifting winds, like plains of corn
Swayed by the summer air; my streams will flow
Round many-peopled continents, and round
Fortunate isles; and from their glassy thrones
Blue Proteus° and his humid nymphs shall mark
The shadow of fair ships, as mortals see
The floating bark of the light-laden moon
With that white star, its sightless pilot's crest,
Borne down the rapid sunset's ebbing sea;
Tracking their path no more by blood and groans,
30   And desolation, and the mingled voice
Of slavery and command; but by the light
Of wave-reflected flowers, and floating odours,
And music soft, and mild, free, gentle voices,
And sweetest music, such as spirits love.

APOLLO   And I shall gaze not on the deeds which make
My mind obscure with sorrow, as eclipse
Darkens the sphere I guide; but list, I hear
The small, clear, silver lute of the young Spirit
That sits in the morning star.

OCEAN   Thou must away;
40   Thy steeds will pause at even, till when farewell:
The loud deep calls me home even now to feed it
With azure calm out of the emerald urns
Which stand for ever full beside my throne.
Behold the Nereids° under the green sea,
Their wavering limbs borne on the wind-like stream,
Their white arms lifted o'er their streaming hair
With garlands pied and starry sea-flower crowns,
Hastening to grace their mighty sister's joy.
[A sound of waves is heard]
It is the unpastured sea hungering for calm.
Peace, monster; I come now. Farewell.
50   APOLLO   Farewell.

From SCENE III   *Caucasus.*

SPIRIT OF THE EARTH   Mother, I am grown wiser, though a child
Cannot be wise like thee, within this day;
And happier too; happier and wiser both.
Thou knowest that toads, and snakes, and loathly worms,
And venomous and malicious beasts, and boughs
That bore ill berries in the woods, were ever

Proteus an older sea god, a shape-shifter and prophet; if caught and held while he exhausts his changes, he will reveal the future

Nereids fifty sea nymphs, daughters of Nereus, good-natured Old Man of the Sea

An hindrance to my walks o'er the green world:
40   And that, among the haunts of humankind,
Hard-featured men, or with proud, angry looks,
Or cold, staid gait, or false and hollow smiles,
Or the dull sneer of self-loved ignorance,
Or other such foul masks, with which ill thoughts
Hide that fair being whom we spirits call man;
And women too, ugliest of all things evil,
(Though fair, even in a world where thou art fair,
When good and kind, free and sincere like thee),
When false or frowning made me sick at heart
50   To pass them, though they slept, and I unseen.
Well, my path lately lay through a great city
Into the woody hills surrounding it:
A sentinel was sleeping at the gate:
When there was heard a sound, so loud, it shook
The towers amid the moonlight, yet more sweet
Than any voice but thine, sweetest of all;
A long, long sound, as it would never end:
And all the inhabitants leaped suddenly
Out of their rest, and gathered in the streets,
60   Looking in wonder up to Heaven, while yet
The music pealed along. I hid myself
Within a fountain in the public square,
Where I lay like the reflex of the moon
Seen in a wave under green leaves; and soon
Those ugly human shapes and visages
Of which I spoke as having wrought me pain,
Passed floating through the air, and fading still
Into the winds that scattered them; and those
From whom they passed seemed mild and lovely forms
70   After some foul disguise had fallen, and all
Were somewhat changed, and after brief surprise
And greetings of delighted wonder, all
Went to their sleep again:° and when the dawn
Came, wouldst thou think that toads, and snakes, and efts,
Could e'er be beautiful? yet so they were,
And that with little change of shape or hue:
All things had put their evil nature off:
I cannot tell my joy, when o'er a lake
Upon a drooping bough with nightshade twined,
80   I saw two azure halcyons clinging downward
And thinning one bright bunch of amber berries,°
With quick long beaks, and in the deep there lay
Those lovely forms imaged as in a sky;

---

all went . . . again surely the gentlest and   **I saw . . . berries** deadly nightshade is now
most urbane Apocalypse in literature   harmless

So, with my thoughts full of these happy changes,
We meet again, the happiest change of all.

.   .   .

[*The* SPIRIT OF THE HOUR *enters*]
   PROMETHEUS   We feel what thou hast heard and seen: yet speak.
   SPIRIT OF THE HOUR   Soon as the sound had ceased whose thunder filled
The abysses of the sky and the wide earth,
100 There was a change: the impalpable thin air
And the all-circling sunlight were transformed,
As if the sense of love dissolved in them
Had folded itself round the spherèd world.
My vision then grew clear, and I could see
Into the mysteries of the universe:
Dizzy as with delight I floated down,
Winnowing the lightsome air with languid plumes,
My coursers sought their birthplace in the sun,
Where they henceforth will live exempt from toil,
110 Pasturing flowers of vegetable fire;
And where my moonlike car will stand within
A temple, gazed upon by Phidian forms°
Of thee, and Asia, and the Earth, and me,
And you fair nymphs looking the love we feel,—
In memory of the tidings it has borne,—
Beneath a dome fretted with graven flowers,
Poised on twelve columns of resplendent stone,
And open to the bright and liquid sky.
Yoked to it by an amphisbaenic snake°
120 The likeness of those wingèd steeds will mock°
The flight from which they find repose. Alas,
Whither has wandered now my partial tongue
When all remains untold which ye would hear?
As I have said, I floated to the earth:
It was, as it is still, the pain of bliss
To move, to breathe, to be; I wandering went
Among the haunts and dwellings of mankind,
And first was disappointed not to see
Such mighty change as I had felt within
130 Expressed in outward things; but soon I looked,
And behold, thrones were kingless, and men walked
One with the other even as spirits do,
None fawned, none trampled; hate, disdain, or fear,
Self-love or self-contempt, on human brows
No more inscribed, as o'er the gate of hell,
'All hope abandon ye who enter here;'°

Phidian forms Phidias was the greatest of Greek
sculptors (5th century B.C.).
amphisbaenic snake with a head at each end,
and so capable of moving either way

mock "imitate" and perhaps "disdain"
All . . . here See Dante's *Inferno* III, where
this is the inscription over the gate of Hell.

None frowned, none trembled, none with eager fear
Gazed on another's eye of cold command,
Until the subject of a tyrant's will
140 Became, worse fate, the abject of his own,
Which spurred him, like an outspent horse, to death.
None wrought his lips in truth-entangling lines
Which smiled the lie his tongue disdained to speak;
None, with firm sneer, trod out in his own heart
The sparks of love and hope till there remained
Those bitter ashes, a soul self-consumed,
And the wretch crept a vampire among men,
Infecting all with his own hideous ill;
None talked that common, false, cold, hollow talk
150 Which makes the heart deny the *yes* it breathes,
Yet question that unmeant hypocrisy
With such a self-mistrust as has no name.
And women, too, frank, beautiful, and kind
As the free heaven which rains fresh light and dew
On the wide earth, past; gentle radiant forms,
From custom's evil taint exempt and pure;
Speaking the wisdom once they could not think,
Looking emotions once they feared to feel,
And changed to all which once they dared not be,
160 Yet being now, made earth like heaven; nor pride,
Nor jealousy, nor envy, nor ill shame,
The bitterest of those drops of treasured gall,
Spoilt the sweet taste of the nepenthe, love.

Thrones, altars, judgement-seats, and prisons; wherein,
And beside which, by wretched men were borne
Sceptres, tiaras, swords, and chains, and tomes
Of reasoned wrong, glozed on° by ignorance,
Were like those monstrous and barbaric shapes,
The ghosts of a no-more-remembered fame,
170 Which, from their unworn obelisks, look forth
In triumph o'er the palaces and tombs
Of those who were their conquerors: mouldering round,
These imaged to the pride of kings and priests
A dark yet mighty faith, a power as wide
As is the world it wasted, and are now
But an astonishment; even so the tools
And emblems of its last captivity,
Amid the dwellings of the peopled earth,
Stand, not o'erthrown, but unregarded now.
180 And those foul shapes, abhorred by god and man,—
Which, under many a name and many a form
Strange, savage, ghastly, dark and execrable,

glozed on commented on

Were Jupiter, the tyrant of the world;
And which the nations, panic-stricken, served
With blood, and hearts broken by long hope, and love
Dragged to his altars soiled and garlandless,
And slain amid men's unreclaiming tears,
Flattering the thing they feared, which fear was hate,—
Frown, mouldering fast, o'er their abandoned shrines:
190   The painted veil, by those who were, called life,
Which mimicked, as with colours idly spread,
All men believed or hoped, is torn aside;
The loathsome mask has fallen, the man remains
Sceptreless, free, uncircumscribed, but man
Equal, unclassed, tribeless, and nationless,
Exempt from awe, worship, degree, the king
Over himself; just, gentle, wise: but man
Passionless?——no, yet free from guilt or pain,
Which were, for his will made or suffered them,
200   Nor yet exempt, though ruling them like slaves,
From chance, and death, and mutability,
The clogs of that which else might oversoar
The loftiest star of unascended heaven,
Pinnacled dim in the intense inane.°

END OF THE THIRD ACT

From ACT IV°

SCENE   *A Part of the Forest near the Cave of* PROMETHEUS.

PANTHEA   But see where through two openings in the forest
Which hanging branches overcanopy,
And where two runnels of a rivulet,
Between the close moss violet-inwoven,
Have made their path of melody, like sisters
Who part with sighs that they may meet in smiles,
200   Turning their dear disunion to an isle
Of lovely grief, a wood of sweet sad thoughts;
Two visions of strange radiance float upon
The ocean-like enchantment of strong sound,
Which flows intenser, keener, deeper yet
Under the ground and through the windless air.

IONE   I see a chariot like that thinnest boat,°
In which the Mother of the Months° is borne
By ebbing light into her western cave,
When she upsprings from interlunar dreams;

inane formless void of infinite space, a Lucretian concept
Act IV A great afterthought, composed just
after the "Ode to the West Wind," opens with
songs and dances of Spirits and Hours celebrating the New Day; the "two visions of strange
radiance," now described by Panthea and Ione,

Asia's sisters, are the symbolic center of the Act.
boat the old moon in the new moon's arms,
bearing an apocalyptic infant who heralds a
storm of change
Mother . . . Months Diana, the moon, bears
the months.

210   O'er which is curved an orblike canopy
       Of gentle darkness, and the hills and woods,
       Distinctly seen through that dusk aery veil,
       Regard° like shapes in an enchanter's glass;
       Its wheels are solid clouds, azure and gold,
       Such as the genii of the thunderstorm
       Pile on the floor of the illumined sea
       When the sun rushes under it; they roll
       And move and grow as with an inward wind;
       Within it sits a wingèd infant, white°
220   Its countenance, like the whiteness of bright snow,
       Its plumes are as feathers of sunny frost,
       Its limbs gleam white, through the wind-flowing folds
       Of its white robe, woof of ethereal pearl.
       Its hair is white, the brightness of white light
       Scattered in strings; yet its two eyes are heavens
       Of liquid darkness, which the Deity
       Within seems pouring, as a storm is poured
       From jaggèd clouds, out of their arrowy lashes,
       Tempering the cold and radiant air around,
230   With fire that is not brightness; in its hand
       It sways a quivering moonbeam, from whose point
       A guiding power directs the chariot's prow
       Over its wheelèd clouds, which as they roll
       Over the grass, and flowers, and waves, wake sounds,
       Sweet as a singing rain of silver dew.
       PANTHEA   And from the other opening in the wood
       Rushes, with loud and whirlwind harmony,
       A sphere, which is as many thousand spheres,
       Solid as crystal, yet through all its mass
240   Flow, as through empty space, music and light:
       Ten thousand orbs involving and involved,
       Purple and azure, white, and green, and golden,
       Sphere within sphere; and every space between
       Peopled with unimaginable shapes,
       Such as ghosts dream dwell in the lampless deep,
       Yet each inter-transpicuous,° and they whirl
       Over each other with a thousand motions,
       Upon a thousand sightless axles spinning,
       And with the force of self-destroying swiftness,
250   Intensely, slowly, solemnly roll on,
       Kindling with mingled sounds, and many tones,
       Intelligible words and music wild.
       With mighty whirl the multitudinous orb
       Grinds the bright brook into an azure mist

Regard appear   Man in Ezekiel 1:27, and the Son of Man in
Within . . . white based on the Enthroned   Revelation 1:14
                                                   inter-transpicuous inter-transparent

Of elemental subtlety, like light;
And the wild odour of the forest flowers,
The music of the living grass and air,
The emerald light of leaf-entangled beams
Round its intense yet self-conflicting speed,
260   Seem kneaded into one aëreal mass
Which drowns the sense. Within the orb itself,
Pillowed upon its alabaster arms,
Like to a child o'erwearied with sweet toil,
On its own folded wings, and wavy hair,
The Spirit of the Earth is laid asleep,
And you can see its little lips are moving,
Amid the changing light of their own smiles,
Like one who talks of what he loves in dream.°
      IONE   'Tis only mocking the orb's harmony.°
270   PANTHEA   And from a star upon its forehead, shoot,
Like swords of azure fire, or golden spears
With tyrant-quelling myrtle° overtwined,
Embleming heaven and earth united now,
Vast beams like spokes of some invisible wheel
Which whirl as the orb whirls, swifter than thought,
Filling the abyss with sun-like lightenings,
And perpendicular now, and now transverse,
Pierce the dark soil, and as they pierce and pass,
Make bare the secrets of the earth's deep heart;
280   Infinite mines of adamant and gold,
Valueless° stones, and unimagined gems,
And caverns on crystalline columns poised
With vegetable silver overspread;
Wells of unfathomed fire, and water springs
Whence the great sea, even as a child is fed,
Whose vapours clothe earth's monarch mountain-tops
With kingly, ermine snow. The beams flash on
And make appear the melancholy ruins
Of cancelled cycles; anchors, beaks of ships;
290   Planks turned to marble; quivers, helms, and spears,
And gorgon-headed targes,° and the wheels
Of scythèd chariots,° and the emblazonry
Of trophies, standards, and armorial beasts,°
Round which death laughed, sepulchred emblems
Of dead destruction, ruin within ruin!
The wrecks beside of many a city vast,

loves in dream (ll. 236–68) See Ezekiel's vision of "the wheels and their work," Ezekiel 1:16–18, and *Paradise Lost* V.618–25; Shelley describes an earth whirling itself on toward finality.
'Tis . . . harmony an example of Shelley's urbanity in apocalyptic writing: the sleeping infant Spirit mocks the inhuman harmony of its own vehicle
myrtle emblem of love
Valueless beyond value, priceless
targes shields
scythèd chariots war chariots with bladed wheels
armorial beasts heraldic emblems

Whose population which the earth grew over
Was mortal, but not human; see, they lie,
Their monstrous works, and uncouth skeletons,
300   Their statues, homes and fanes; prodigious shapes
Huddled in gray annihilation, split,
Jammed in the hard, black deep; and over these,
The anatomies of unknown wingèd things,
And fishes which were isles of living scale,
And serpents, bony chains, twisted around
The iron crags, or within heaps of dust
To which the tortuous strength of their last pangs
Had crushed the iron crags; and over these
The jaggèd alligator, and the might
310   Of earth-convulsing behemoth,° which once
Were monarch beasts, and on the slimy shores,
And weed-overgrown continents of earth,
Increased and multiplied like summer worms
On an abandoned corpse, till the blue globe°
Wrapped deluge round it like a cloak, and they
Yelled, gasped, and were abolished; or some God
Whose throne was in a comet, passed, and cried,
'Be not!' And like my words they were no more.

            .   .   .

DEMOGORGON

Man, who wert once a despot and a slave;
550   A dupe and a deceiver; a decay;
A traveller from the cradle to the grave
    Through the dim night of this immortal day:°

ALL

Speak: thy strong words may never pass away.

DEMOGORGON

This is the day, which down the void abysm
At the Earth-born's spell° yawns for Heaven's despotism,
    And Conquest is dragged captive through the deep:
Love, from its awful throne of patient power
In the wise heart, from the last giddy hour
    Of dread endurance, from the slippery, steep,
560   And narrow verge of crag-like agony, springs
And folds over the world its healing wings.°

Gentleness, Virtue, Wisdom, and Endurance,
These are the seals of that most firm assurance

---

behemoth The alligator is Shelley's version of Job's Leviathan, who appears with Behemoth (perhaps a mythologized hippopotamus) in Job 40:15–24.
blue globe covered by water
Man . . . day Demogorgon has summoned up the scattered Spirits of the Universe for a final accounting; this quatrain should be compared to

Blake's "To the Accuser Who Is the God of This World" from *The Gates of Paradise*.
spell Prometheus, child of Earth, has made this magic.
And folds . . . wings Love here takes the role of the Christian Holy Spirit as Paraclete or comforter.

Which bars the pit over Destruction's strength;
And if, with infirm hand, Eternity,
Mother of many acts and hours, should free
   The serpent that would clasp her with his length;
These are the spells by which to reassume
An empire o'er the disentangled doom.°

570 To suffer woes which Hope thinks infinite;
To forgive wrongs darker than death or night;
   To defy Power, which seems omnipotent;
To love, and bear; to hope till Hope creates
From its own wreck the thing it contemplates;°
   Neither to change, nor falter, nor repent;
This, like thy glory, Titan, is to be
Good, great and joyous, beautiful and free;
This is alone Life, Joy, Empire, and Victory.
1818–19   1820

England in 1819

An old, mad, blind, despised, and dying king,°—
Princes, the dregs of their dull race,° who flow
Through public scorn,—mud from a muddy spring,—
Rulers who neither see, nor feel, nor know,
But leech-like to their fainting country cling,
Till they drop, blind in blood, without a blow,—
A people starved and stabbed in the untilled field,°—
An army, which liberticide and prey
Makes as a two-edged sword to all who wield,—
10 Golden and sanguine laws which tempt and slay;
Religion Christless, Godless—a book sealed;
A Senate,—Time's worst statute unrepealed,°—
Are graves, from which a glorious Phantom may
Burst, to illumine our tempestuous day.
1819   1839

doom the serpent, Eternity, which may undo the Renewal
to hope . . . contemplates M.H. Abrams, in his *Natural Supernaturalism,* usefully relates Demogorgon's final lyric to Wordsworth's "Prospectus" to *The Excursion,* which speaks "Of blessèd consolations in distress" and like Shelley emphasizes humanistic Hope as a cardinal virtue.
An old . . . king George III, who died the next year; he had been blind and mentally ill for some time. See Byron's *Vision of Judgment.*

Princes . . . race The Prince Regent was neither virtuous nor popular.
stabbed . . . field the "Peterloo Massacre" at Manchester, August 16, 1819, where a peaceful assembly was dispersed by mounted troops, who killed or injured a number of the unarmed protesters. As the assault took place on St. Peter's Field, the public sardonically called it "Peterloo," so as to discredit Wellington's more glorious victory at Waterloo.
Time's . . . unrepealed the law barring Dissenters and Roman Catholics from holding office

Ode to the West Wind

Shelley's supreme lyric was composed simultaneously with Act III of *Prometheus Unbound,* and is close in spirit to the Psalms and the prophetic poetry of the Old Testament. On one level, it is a prophecy of political revolution against the Europe established by the Congress of Vienna in 1815. On another, it attempts to find in natural cycle a harbinger of a human finality beyond cyclic change. Most profoundly, the poem is Jobean, concerned with purgatorial trial and a highly personal yet universal despair, the sense of having failed one's own creative powers. It should be noted that the fourth and fifth sections propose exactly contrary answers to the dilemma implicitly developed in the first three.

The poem's form is a unique amalgam of Dante's *terza rima* and the English or Shakespearean sonnet.

Ode to the West Wind

This poem was conceived and chiefly written in a wood that skirts the Arno, near Florence, and on a day when that tempestuous wind, whose temperature is at once mild and animating, was collecting the vapours which pour down the autumnal rains. They began, as I foresaw, at sunset with a violent tempest of hail and rain, attended by that magnificent thunder and lightning peculiar to the Cisalpine regions.

The phenomenon alluded to at the conclusion of the third stanza is well known to naturalists. The vegetation at the bottom of the sea, of rivers, and of lakes, sympathizes with that of the land in the change of seasons, and is consequently influenced by the winds which announce it.—

I

O wild West Wind,° thou breath of Autumn's being,
Thou, from whose unseen presence the leaves dead
Are driven, like ghosts from an enchanter fleeing,

Yellow, and black, and pale, and hectic red,
Pestilence-stricken multitudes: O thou,
Who chariotest to their dark wintry bed

The wingèd seeds, where they lie cold and low,
Each like a corpse within its grave, until
Thine azure sister of the Spring shall blow

10 Her clarion o'er the dreaming earth, and fill
(Driving sweet buds like flocks to feed in air)
With living hues and odours plain and hill:

Wild Spirit, which art moving everywhere;
Destroyer and preserver; hear, oh, hear!

West Wind Westerly winds rule in the Cisalpine most of the year; Shelley is observing the action of the wind marking the end of summer; another westerly wind ("thine azure sister of the Spring") will mark the end of winter for the western coast of Italy.

II

Thou on whose stream, mid the steep sky's commotion,
Loose clouds like earth's decaying leaves are shed,
Shook from the tangled boughs of Heaven and Ocean,° ·

Angels of rain and lightning: there are spread
On the blue surface of thine aery surge,
20   Like the bright hair uplifted from the head

Of some fierce Maenad,° even from the dim verge
Of the horizon to the zenith's height,
The locks of the approaching storm. Thou dirge

Of the dying year, to which this closing night
Will be the dome of a vast sepulchre,
Vaulted with all thy congregated might

Of vapours, from whose solid atmosphere
Black rain, and fire, and hail will burst: oh, hear!

III

Thou who didst waken from his summer dreams
30   The blue Mediterranean, where he lay,
Lulled by the coil of his crystàlline streams,

Beside a pumice° isle in Baiae's° bay,
And saw in sleep old palaces and towers
Quivering within the wave's intenser day,

All overgrown with azure moss and flowers
So sweet, the sense faints picturing them! Thou
For whose path the Atlantic's level powers

Cleave themselves into chasms, while far below
The sea-blooms and the oozy woods which wear
40   The sapless foliage of the ocean, know

Thy voice, and suddenly grow grey with fear,
And tremble and despoil themselves: oh, hear!

IV

If I were a dead leaf thou mightest bear;
If I were a swift cloud to fly with thee;
A wave to pant beneath thy power, and share

The impulse of thy strength, only less free
Than thou, O uncontrollable! If even
I were as in my boyhood, and could be

Loose . . . Ocean High up is a canopy of solid, relatively stationary clouds; below are smaller, 'loose' clouds driven swiftly along by the wind. Shelley calls the upper stationary cloud-formations the boughs of Heaven and Ocean because it consists of condensed water-vapor drawn up from the ocean by the heat of the sun."—F.A. Pottle
Maenad the "frenzied woman"; Maenads were followers of Dionysus, who tore Orpheus apart
pumice porous, volcanic stone
Baiae's resort near Naples; frequented by Roman emperors

The comrade of thy wanderings over Heaven,
50 As then, when to outstrip thy skiey speed
Scarce seemed a vision; I would ne'er have striven

As thus with thee in prayer in my sore need.
Oh, lift me as a wave, a leaf, a cloud!
I fall upon the thorns of life!° I bleed!

A heavy weight of hours has chained and bowed
One too like thee: tameless, and swift, and proud.

v
Make me thy lyre,° even as the forest is:
What if my leaves are falling like its own!
The tumult of thy mighty harmonies

60 Will take from both a deep, autumnal tone,
Sweet though in sadness. Be thou, Spirit fierce,
My spirit! Be thou me, impetuous one!

Drive my dead thoughts over the universe
Like withered leaves to quicken a new birth!
And, by the incantation of this verse,

Scatter, as from an unextinguished hearth
Ashes and sparks, my words among mankind!
Be through my lips to unawakened earth

The trumpet of a prophecy! O, Wind,
70 If Winter comes, can Spring be far behind?
1819   1820

To a Skylark°

Hail to thee, blithe Spirit!
    Bird thou never wert,
    That from Heaven, or near it,
    Pourest thy full heart
In profuse strains of unpremeditated art.

    Higher still and higher
    From the earth thou springest
    Like a cloud of fire;
    The blue deep thou wingest,
10 And singing still dost soar, and soaring ever singest.

thorns of life a grimly ironic echo of Keats's
Sleep and Poetry, l. 245, which Shelley evidently
judged to be an attack upon him rather than
Byron; there are Jobean overtones
lyre the aeolian harp
To a Skylark This famous lyric, written about
a year after the "Ode to the West Wind," is a
plangent farewell to the theme of the poet's prophetic relation to a Power hidden behind Nature. It is important to keep in mind that the
skylark is already out of sight when this poem
begins; the bird flies too high for visibility, and
can just barely be heard. Throughout the lyric,
Shelley emphasizes his estrangement from the
joy he intuits, and so ecstatically conveys.

In the golden lightning
　Of the sunken sun,
O'er which clouds are brightening,
　Thou dost float and run;
Like an unbodied joy whose race is just begun.

The pale purple even
　Melts around thy flight;
Like a star of Heaven,
　In the broad daylight
20　Thou art unseen, but yet I hear thy shrill delight,

Keen as are the arrows
　Of that silver sphere,°
Whose intense lamp narrows
　In the white dawn clear
Until we hardly see—we feel that it is there.

All the earth and air
　With thy voice is loud,
As, when night is bare,
　From one lonely cloud
30　The moon rains out her beams, and Heaven is overflowed.

What thou art we know not;
　What is most like thee?
From rainbow clouds there flow not
　Drops so bright to see
As from thy presence showers a rain of melody.

Like a Poet hidden
　In the light of thought,
Singing hymns unbidden,
　Till the world is wrought
40　To sympathy with hopes and fears it heeded not:

Like a high-born maiden
　In a palace-tower,
Soothing her love-laden
　Soul in secret hour
With music sweet as love, which overflows her bower:

Like a glow-worm golden
　In a dell of dew,
Scattering unbeholden
　Its aereal hue
50　Among the flowers and grass, which screen it from the view!

Like a rose embowered
　In its own green leaves,

silver sphere the Morning Star

By warm winds deflowered,
   Till the scent it gives
Makes faint with too much sweet those heavy-wingèd thieves:

   Sound of vernal showers
     On the twinkling grass,
   Rain-awakened flowers,
     All that ever was
60 Joyous, and clear, and fresh, thy music doth surpass:

   Teach us, Sprite or Bird,
     What sweet thoughts are thine:
   I have never heard
     Praise of love or wine
That panted forth a flood of rapture so divine.

   Chorus Hymeneal,°
     Or triumphal chant,
   Matched with thine would be all
     But an empty vaunt,
70 A thing wherein we feel there is some hidden want.

   What objects are the fountains
     Of thy happy strain?
   What fields, or waves, or mountains?
     What shapes of sky or plain?
What love of thine own kind? what ignorance of pain?

   With thy clear keen joyance
     Languor cannot be:
   Shadow of annoyance
     Never came near thee:
80 Thou lovest—but ne'er knew love's sad satiety.

   Waking or asleep,
     Thou of death must deem
   Things more true and deep
     Than we mortals dream,
Or how could thy notes flow in such a crystal stream?

   We look before and after,
     And pine for what is not:
   Our sincerest laughter
     With some pain is fraught;
90 Our sweetest songs are those that tell of saddest thought.

   Yet if we could scorn
     Hate, and pride, and fear;
   If we were things born
     Not to shed a tear,
I know not how thy joy we ever should come near.

Hymeneal pertaining to marriage

Better than all measures
  Of delightful sound,
Better than all treasures
  That in books are found,
100 Thy skill to poet were, thou scorner of the ground!

Teach me half the gladness
  That thy brain must know,
Such harmonious madness
  From my lips would flow
The world should listen then—as I am listening now.
1820   1820

From The Sensitive Plant°

CONCLUSION

Whether the Sensitive Plant, or that
Which within its boughs like a Spirit sat,
Ere its outward form had known decay,
Now felt this change, I cannot say.

Whether that Lady's gentle mind,
No longer with the form combined
120 Which scattered love, as stars do light,
Found sadness, where it left delight,

I dare not guess; but in this life
Of error, ignorance, and strife,
Where nothing is, but all things seem,
And we the shadows of the dream,

It is a modest creed, and yet
Pleasant if one considers it,
To own that death itself must be,
Like all the rest, a mockery.

130 That garden sweet, that lady fair,
And all sweet shapes and odours there,
In truth have never passed away:
'Tis we, 'tis ours, are changed; not they.

For love, and beauty, and delight,
There is no death nor change: their might
Exceeds our organs, which endure
No light, being themselves obscure.
1820   1820

The Sensitive Plant These urbane, skeptical, yet still idealistic quatrains are a coda to a poem ostensibly about a mimosa or sensitive plant (the leaves react to darkness, or to touch, by closing together, with an upward movement). The plant, the pastoral Lady who attends it, and the gar- den in which both live are shown in their vision- ary prime, interpenetrated by a mutual love, and then all three are destroyed by winter. The Conclusion questions the reality of this destruc- tion.

Hymn of Apollo

I

The sleepless Hours who watch me as I lie,
  Curtained with star-inwoven tapestries
From the broad moonlight of the sky,
  Fanning the busy dreams from my dim eyes,—
Waken me when their Mother, the grey Dawn,
Tells them that dreams and that the moon is gone.

II

Then I arise, and climbing Heaven's blue dome,
  I walk over the mountains and the waves,
Leaving my robe upon the ocean foam;
10   My footsteps pave the clouds with fire; the caves
Are filled with my bright presence, and the air
Leaves the green Earth to my embraces bare.

III

The sunbeams are my shafts, with which I kill
  Deceit, that loves the night and fears the day;
All men who do or even imagine ill
  Fly me, and from the glory of my ray
Good minds and open actions take new might,
Until diminished by the reign of Night.

IV

I feed the clouds, the rainbows and the flowers
20   With their aethereal colours; the moon's globe
And the pure stars in their eternal bowers
  Are cinctured° with my power as with a robe;
Whatever lamps on Earth or Heaven may shine
Are portions of one power, which is mine.

V

I stand at noon upon the peak of Heaven,
  Then with unwilling steps I wander down
Into the clouds of the Atlantic even;
  For grief that I depart they weep and frown:
What look is more delightful than the smile
30   With which I soothe them from the western isle?

VI

I am the eye with which the Universe
  Beholds itself and knows itself divine;°
All harmony of instrument or verse,

cinctured encompassed, girded   I am . . . divine the highest praise given poetry, even by Shelley

453

All prophecy, all medicine is mine,
All light of art or nature;—to my song
Victory and praise in its own right belong.
1820   1824

The Two Spirits: An Allegory°

FIRST SPIRIT

O thou, who plumed with strong desire
    Wouldst float above the earth, beware!
A Shadow° tracks thy flight of fire—
        Night is coming!
    Bright are the regions of the air,
And among the winds and beams
    It were delight to wander there—
        Night is coming!

SECOND SPIRIT

The deathless stars are bright above;
10   If I would cross the shade of night,°
Within my heart is the lamp of love,°
        And that is day!
And the moon will smile with gentle light
On my golden plumes where'er they move;
    The meteors will linger round my flight,
        And make night day.

FIRST SPIRIT

But if the whirlwinds of darkness waken
    Hail, and lightning, and stormy rain;
See, the bounds of the air are shaken—
        Night is coming!
20   The red swift clouds of the hurricane
Yon declining sun have overtaken,
    The clash of the hail sweeps over the plain—
        Night is coming!

SECOND SPIRIT

I see the light, and I hear the sound;
    I'll sail on the flood of the tempest dark,
With the calm within and the light around
        Which makes night day:
And thou, when the gloom is deep and stark,

The Two Spirits: An Allegory The Second Spirit
represents infinite desire, the First is a Spirit of
repression, of finite limits; more specifically, the
Second Spirit is first love, and the First Spirit
everything that attempts to defeat it.

Shadow the ruin haunting love, or frustration
of desire
shade of night the shadow thrown into the
heavens by our earth
lamp of love the sphere of Venus, the Evening
Star, where earth's shadow ends

30   Look from thy dull earth, slumber-bound,
          My moon-like flight thou then mayst mark
                On high, far away.

      Some say there is a precipice
          Where one vast pine is frozen to ruin
      O'er piles of snow and chasms of ice
                Mid Alpine mountains;
      And that the languid storm pursuing
      That wingèd shape, forever flies
          Round those hoar branches, aye renewing
40   Its aery fountains.°

      Some say when nights are dry and clear,
          And the death-dews sleep on the morass,
      Sweet whispers are heard by the traveller,
                Which make night day:
      And a silver shape like his early love doth pass
      Upborne by her wild and glittering hair,
          And when he awakes on the fragrant grass,
                He finds night day.°
                1820   1824

Epipsychidion

This is Shelley's most original and most rhapsodic poem. The theme, as in Blake's *Visions of the Daughters of Albion,* is the necessity of free love, but Shelley characteristically at last sees love defeated not by societal and individual repressions, but by the separateness that irreparably shadows the human condition. Taking its occasion from Shelley's love affair with Emilia Viviani, which ended badly, the poem emulates Dante by seeking to make Emilia a kind of Beatrice, a guide to a higher, more visionary existence. The title, which means "a work about the soul out of my soul," expresses an intention to universalize this experience of passion.

   The first of these selections, three pungent sermons against the restrictiveness of marriage, is followed by a passage near the poem's conclusion, where desire touches its limits, and gloriously fails.

From Epipsychidion

          [Three Sermons on Free Love]
       Thy° wisdom speaks in me, and bids me dare
      Beacon the rocks on which high hearts are wrecked.
      I never was attached to that great sect,
150   Whose doctrine is, that each one should select

Some . . . fountains This stanza (ll. 33–40) is the First Spirit's vision of the Second Spirit's ruinous fate, a cyclic and frozen pursuit.

Some . . . day (ll. 41–48) The "traveller" sees the shape of early desire in the Second Spirit. **Thy** Emilia's

Out of the crowd a mistress or a friend,
And all the rest, though fair and wise, commend
To cold oblivion, though it is in the code
Of modern morals, and the beaten road
Which those poor slaves with weary footsteps tread,
Who travel to their home among the dead
By the broad highway of the world, and so
With one chained friend, perhaps a jealous foe,
The dreariest and the longest journey° go.

160   True Love in this differs from gold and clay,
That to divide is not to take away.
Love is like understanding, that grows bright,
Gazing on many truths; 'tis like thy light,
Imagination! which from earth and sky,
And from the depths of human fantasy,
As from a thousand prisms and mirrors, fills
The Universe with glorious beams, and kills
Error, the worm, with many a sun-like arrow
Of its reverberated lightning. Narrow
170   The heart that loves, the brain that contemplates,
The life that wears, the spirit that creates
One object, and one form, and builds thereby
A sepulchre° for its eternity.

Mind from its object differs most in this:
Evil from good; misery from happiness;
The baser from the nobler; the impure
And frail, from what is clear and must endure.
If you divide suffering and dross, you may
Diminish till it is consumed away;
180   If you divide pleasure and love and thought,
Each part exceeds the whole; and we know not
How much, while any yet remains unshared,
Of pleasure may be gained, of sorrow spared:
This truth is that deep well, whence sages draw
The unenvied light of hope; the eternal law
By which those live, to whom this world of life
Is as a garden ravaged,° and whose strife
Tills for the promise of a later birth
The wilderness of this Elysian earth.

.   .   .

[The Annihilation of Love]
Let us become the overhanging day,
The living soul of this Elysian isle,
540   Conscious, inseparable, one. Meanwhile
We two will rise, and sit, and walk together,

---

longest journey marriage; used by E. M. Forster   sepulchre marriage
as a title for his novel (1907)   ravaged by marriage

Under the roof of blue Ionian weather,
And wander in the meadows, or ascend
The mossy mountains, where the blue heavens bend
With lightest winds, to touch their paramour;
Or linger, where the pebble-paven shore,
Under the quick, faint kisses of the sea
Trembles and sparkles as with ecstasy,—
Possessing and possessed by all that is
550　Within that calm circumference of bliss,
And by each other, till to love and live
Be one:—or, at the noontide hour, arrive
Where some old cavern hoar seems yet to keep
The moonlight of the expired night asleep,
Through which the awakened day can never peep;
A veil for our seclusion, close as night's,
Where secure sleep may kill thine innocent lights;
Sleep, the fresh dew of languid love, the rain
Whose drops quench kisses till they burn again.
560　And we will talk, until thought's melody
Become too sweet for utterance, and it die
In words, to live again in looks, which dart
With thrilling tone into the voiceless heart,
Harmonizing silence without a sound.
Our breath shall intermix, our bosoms bound,
And our veins beat together; and our lips
With other eloquence than words, eclipse
The soul that burns between them, and the wells
Which boil under our being's inmost cells,
570　The fountains of our deepest life, shall be
Confused in Passion's golden purity,
As mountain-springs under the morning sun.
We shall become the same, we shall be one
Spirit within two frames, oh! wherefore two?
One passion in twin-hearts, which grows and grew,
Till like two meteors of expanding flame,
Those spheres instinct with it become the same,
Touch, mingle, are transfigured; ever still
Burning, yet ever inconsumable:
580　In one another's substance finding food,
Like flames too pure and light and unimbued
To nourish their bright lives with baser prey,
Which point to Heaven and cannot pass away:
One hope within two wills, one will beneath
Two overshadowing minds, one life, one death,
One Heaven, one Hell, one immortality,
And one annihilation . . .
　　1821　　　　　　　1839

Adonais

Adonais is one of the major pastoral elegies, and like the others it both laments a dead poet and speculates darkly on its author's own possible fate. Shelley's poem is unique, partly for the extraneous reason that he mourns a poet of his own stature, John Keats, but largely because of its scope and ambition, which break down the limits of elegy. The last seventeen stanzas of *Adonais* are closer to their descendants, Yeats's "Sailing to Byzantium" and "Byzantium," than to their ancestors: the second-century (B.C.) Hellenic poems, Bion's "Lament of Venus for Adonis" and Moschus' "Lament for Bion," and the great English Renaissance elegies, Spenser's *Astrophel* for Sir Philip Sidney and Milton's *Lycidas* for Edward King. Bion mourns the death of Adonis, god of the vegetative year and lover of Venus. Moschus laments the untimely death of the mourner for Adonis, and the Renaissance elegists follow, though with astonishing departures in Milton's poem. But Shelley, in the last third of his poem, is not mourning at all. He struggles to attain a luminous self-recognition that will prepare him for his own death, which he accurately senses is coming shortly (only a year away), and he strives to secure also some vision of the state of being of poetry itself, in its border relations both to life and to death.

Adonais°

An Elegy on the Death of John Keats, Author of Endymion, Hyperion, Etc.

Ἀστὴρ πρὶν μὲν ἔλαμπες ἐνὶ ζωοῖσιν Ἑῷος·
νῦν δὲ θανὼν λάμπεις Ἕσπερος ἐν φθιμένοις. —PLATO°

I

I weep for Adonais—he is dead!
O, weep for Adonais! though our tears
Thaw not the frost which binds so dear a head!
And thou, sad Hour, selected from all years
To mourn our loss, rouse thy obscure compeers,
And teach them thine own sorrow, say: 'With me
Died Adonais; till the Future dares
Forget the Past, his fate and fame shall be
An echo and a light unto eternity!'

II

10 Where wert thou, mighty Mother,° when he lay,
When thy Son lay, pierced by the shaft which flies
In darkness?° where was lorn Urania

When Adonais died? With veilèd eyes,
'Mid listening Echoes, in her Paradise
She sate, while one, with soft enamoured breath,
Rekindled all the fading melodies,
With which, like flowers that mock the corse beneath,
He had adorned and hid the coming bulk of Death.

III

Oh, weep for Adonais—he is dead!
20   Wake, melancholy Mother, wake and weep!
Yet wherefore? Quench within their burning bed
Thy fiery tears, and let thy loud heart keep
Like his, a mute and uncomplaining sleep;
For he is gone, where all things wise and fair
Descend;—oh, dream not that the amorous Deep
Will yet restore him to the vital air;
Death feeds on his mute voice, and laughs at our despair.

IV

Most musical of mourners, weep again!
Lament anew, Urania!—He died,°
30   Who was the Sire of an immortal strain,
Blind, old, and lonely, when his country's pride,
The priest, the slave, and the liberticide,
Trampled and mocked with many a loathèd rite
Of lust and blood; he went, unterrified,
Into the gulf of death; but his clear Sprite
Yet reigns o'er earth; the third among the sons of light.°

V

Most musical of mourners, weep anew!
Not all to that bright station dared to climb;
And happier they their happiness who knew,
40   Whose tapers yet burn through that night of time
In which suns perished; others more sublime,
Struck by the envious wrath of man or god,
Have sunk, extinct in their refulgent prime;
And some yet live, treading the thorny road,
Which leads, through toil and hate, to Fame's serene abode.°

VI

But now, thy youngest, dearest one, has perished—
The nursling of thy widowhood, who grew,
Like a pale flower by some sad maiden cherished,

He died Milton, Keats's precursor, and father of what Shelley took to be the true tradition of English poetry
sons of light Homer, Dante, Milton: the three greatest Western writers of epic

And some . . . abode Destined for this abode, Shelley believed, were Wordsworth, Byron, and Coleridge.

And fed with true-love tears, instead of dew;
50 Most musical of mourners, weep anew!
Thy extreme hope, the loveliest and the last,
The bloom, whose petals nipped before they blew
Died on the promise of the fruit, is waste;
The broken lily lies—the storm is overpast.

VII

To that high Capital,° where kingly Death
Keeps his pale court in beauty and decay,
He came; and bought, with price of purest breath,
A grave among the eternal.—Come away!
Haste, while the vault of blue Italian day
60 Is yet his fitting charnel-roof! while still
He lies, as if in dewy sleep he lay;
Awake him not! surely he takes his fill
Of deep and liquid rest, forgetful of all ill.

VIII

He will awake no more, oh, never more!—
Within the twilight chamber spreads apace
The shadow of white Death, and at the door
Invisible Corruption waits to trace
His extreme way to her dim dwelling-place;
The eternal Hunger sits, but pity and awe
70 Soothe her pale rage, nor dares she to deface
So fair a prey, till darkness, and the law
Of change, shall o'er his sleep the mortal curtain draw.

IX

Oh, weep for Adonais!—The quick Dreams,
The passion-wingèd Ministers of thought,
Who were his flocks, whom near the living streams
Of his young spirit he fed, and whom he taught
The love which was its music, wander not,—
Wander no more, from kindling brain to brain,
But droop there, whence they sprung; and mourn their lot
80 Round the cold heart, where, after their sweet pain,
They ne'er will gather strength, or find a home again.

X

And one with trembling hands clasps his cold head,
And fans him with her moonlight wings, and cries;
'Our love, our hope, our sorrow, is not dead;
See, on the silken fringe of his faint eyes,
Like dew upon a sleeping flower, there lies

Capital Rome

A tear some Dream has loosened from his brain.'
Lost Angel of a ruined Paradise!
She knew not 'twas her own; as with no stain
90   She faded, like a cloud which had outwept its rain.

XI

One from a lucid urn of starry dew
Washed his light limbs as if embalming them;
Another clipped her profuse locks, and threw
The wreath upon him, like an anadem,°
Which frozen tears instead of pearls begem;
Another in her wilful grief would break
Her bow and wingèd reeds, as if to stem
A greater loss with one which was more weak;
And dull the barbèd fire against his frozen cheek.

XII

100   Another Splendour on his mouth alit,
That mouth, whence it was wont to draw the breath
Which gave it strength to pierce the guarded wit,°
And pass into the panting heart beneath
With lightning and with music: the damp death
Quenched its caress upon his icy lips;
And, as a dying meteor stains a wreath
Of moonlight vapour, which the cold night clips,°
It flushed through his pale limbs, and passed to its eclipse.

XIII

And others came . . . Desires and Adorations,
110   Wingèd Persuasions and veiled Destinies,
Splendours, and Glooms, and glimmering Incarnations
Of hopes and fears, and twilight Phantasies;
And Sorrow, with her family of Sighs,
And Pleasure, blind with tears, led by the gleam
Of her own dying smile instead of eyes,
Came in slow pomp;—the moving pomp might seem
Like pageantry of mist on an autumnal stream.

XIV

All he had loved, and moulded into thought,
From shape, and hue, and odour, and sweet sound,
120   Lamented Adonais. Morning sought
Her eastern watch-tower, and her hair unbound,
Wet with the tears which should adorn the ground,
Dimmed the aereal eyes that kindle day;
Afar the melancholy thunder moaned,

anadem garland   clips embraces
guarded wit defensive minds of potential readers

Pale Ocean in unquiet slumber lay,
And the wild Winds flew round, sobbing in their dismay.

xv

Lost Echo° sits amid the voiceless mountains,
And feeds her grief with his remembered lay,
And will no more reply to winds or fountains,
130   Or amorous birds perched on the young green spray,
Or herdsman's horn, or bell at closing day;
Since she can mimic not his lips, more dear
Than those for whose disdain she pined away
Into a shadow of all sounds:—a drear
Murmur, between their songs, is all the woodmen hear.

xvi

Grief made the young Spring wild, and she threw down
Her kindling buds, as if she Autumn were,
Or they dead leaves; since her delight is flown,
For whom should she have waked the sullen year?
140   To Phoebus was not Hyacinth° so dear
Nor to himself Narcissus,° as to both
Thou, Adonais: wan they stand and sere
Amid the faint companions of their youth,
With dew all turned to tears; odour, to sighing ruth.

xvii

Thy spirit's sister, the lorn nightingale°
Mourns not her mate with such melodious pain;
Not so the eagle, who like thee could scale
Heaven, and could nourish in the sun's domain
Her mighty youth with morning,° doth complain,
150   Soaring and screaming round her empty nest,
As Albion wails for thee: the curse of Cain
Light on his head who pierced thy innocent breast,
And scared the angel soul that was its earthly guest!

xviii

Ah, woe is me! Winter is come and gone,
But grief returns with the revolving year;°
The airs and streams renew their joyous tone;
The ants, the bees, the swallows reappear;
Fresh leaves and flowers deck the dead Seasons' bier;

Echo Echo was a nymph in love with Narcissus, who was in love with himself; consequently, as Shelley says, "she pined away."
Hyacinth a youth beloved by Phoebus Apollo, but accidentally slain by that god, who changed the youth's blood into the flower hyacinth, whose markings were interpreted by the Greeks as "ai ai" ("woe! woe!")

Narcissus as much the flower he became as the self-enamored youth he was
nightingale a reference to Keats's great ode
Not so . . . morning By legend, old eagles regain youth by flying high enough, and thus melting down.
But . . . year Compare l. 472.

The amorous birds now pair in every brake,°
160   And build their mossy homes in field and brere;°
And the green lizard, and the golden snake,
Like unimprisoned flames, out of their trance awake.

XIX

Through wood and stream and field and hill and Ocean
A quickening life from the Earth's heart has burst
As it has ever done, with change and motion,
From the great morning of the world when first
God dawned on Chaos; in its stream immersed,
The lamps of Heaven flash with a softer light;
All baser things pant with life's sacred thirst;
170   Diffuse themselves; and spend in love's delight,
The beauty and the joy of their renewèd might.

XX

The leprous corpse, touched by this spirit tender,
Exhales itself in flowers of gentle breath;
Like incarnations of the stars, when splendour
Is changed to fragrance, they illumine death
And mock the merry worm that wakes beneath;
Nought we know, dies. Shall that alone which knows
Be as a sword consumed before the sheath
By sightless lightning?—the intense atom glows
180 A moment, then is quenched in a most cold repose.

XXI

Alas! that all we loved of him should be,
But for our grief, as if it had not been,
And grief itself be mortal! Woe is me!
Whence are we, and why are we? of what scene
The actors or spectators? Great and mean
Meet massed in death, who lends what life must borrow.
As long as skies are blue, and fields are green,
Evening must usher night, night urge the morrow,
Month follow month with woe, and year wake year to sorrow.

XXII

190 *He* will awake no more, oh, never more!
'Wake thou,' cried Misery, 'childless Mother, rise
Out of thy sleep, and slake, in thy heart's core,
A wound more fierce than his, with tears and sighs.'
And all the Dreams that watched Urania's eyes,
And all the Echoes whom their sister's song
Had held in holy silence, cried: 'Arise!'

brake thicket   **brere** briar

Swift as a Thought by the snake Memory stung,
From her ambrosial rest the fading Splendour sprung.

XXIII

She rose like an autumnal Night, that springs
200   Out of the East, and follows wild and drear
The golden Day, which, on eternal wings,
Even as a ghost abandoning a bier,
Had left the Earth a corpse. Sorrow and fear
So struck, so roused, so rapt Urania;
So saddened round her like an atmosphere
Of stormy mist; so swept her on her way
Even to the mournful place where Adonais lay.

XXIV

Out of her secret Paradise she sped,
Through camps and cities rough with stone, and steel,
210   And human hearts, which to her aery tread
Yielding not, wounded the invisible
Palms of her tender feet where'er they fell:
And barbèd tongues, and thoughts more sharp than they,
Rent the soft Form they never could repel,
Whose sacred blood, like the young tears of May,
Paved with eternal flowers that undeserving way.

XXV

In the death-chamber for a moment Death,
Shamed by the presence of that living Might,
Blushed to annihilation, and the breath
220   Revisited those lips, and Life's pale light
Flashed through those limbs, so late her dear delight.
'Leave me not wild and dread and comfortless,
As silent lightning leaves the starless night!
Leave me not!' cried Urania: her distress
Roused Death: Death rose and smiled, and met her vain caress.

XXVI

'Stay yet awhile! speak to me once again;
Kiss me, so long but as a kiss may live;
And in my heartless breast and burning brain
That word, that kiss, shall all thoughts else survive,
230   With food of saddest memory kept alive,
Now thou art dead, as if it were a part
Of thee, my Adonais! I would give
All that I am to be as thou now art!
But I am chained to Time, and cannot thence depart!

XXVII

'O gentle child, beautiful as thou wert,
Why didst thou leave the trodden paths of men
Too soon, and with weak hands though mighty heart
Dare the unpastured dragon in his den?
Defenceless as thou wert, oh, where was then
240   Wisdom the mirrored shield,° or scorn the spear?
Or hadst thou waited the full cycle, when
Thy spirit should have filled its crescent sphere,°
The monsters of life's waste had fled from thee like deer.

XXVIII

'The herded wolves, bold only to pursue;
The obscene ravens, clamorous o'er the dead;
The vultures° to the conqueror's banner true
Who feed where Desolation first has fed,
And whose wings rain contagion;—how they fled,
When, like Apollo, from his golden bow
250   The Pythian° of the age one arrow sped
And smiled!—The spoilers tempt no second blow,
They fawn on the proud feet that spurn them lying low.

XXIX

'The sun comes forth, and many reptiles spawn;
He sets, and each ephemeral insect then
Is gathered into death without a dawn,
And the immortal stars awake again;
So is it in the world of living men:
A godlike mind soars forth, in its delight
Making earth bare and veiling heaven, and when
260   It sinks, the swarms that dimmed or shared its light
Leave to its kindred lamps the spirit's awful night.'

XXX

Thus ceased she: and the mountain shepherds came,
Their garlands sere, their magic mantles rent;
The Pilgrim of Eternity,° whose fame
Over his living head like Heaven is bent,
An early but enduring monument,
Came, veiling all the lightnings of his song
In sorrow; from her wilds Ierne sent

---

mirrored shield Perseus, given a mirror-shield by Athena, and a sword by Hermes, cut off Medusa's head, by looking at her reflection in the shield; otherwise, she would have turned him into stone.
crescent sphere i.e. full maturity
vultures critics; so also, wolves and ravens

Pythian Apollo Pythius or the Python-slayer; here, Lord Byron, for his *English Bards and Scotch Reviewers*
Pilgrim of Eternity Byron, foremost of the "mountain shepherds" or contemporary poets; the Pilgrim because of *Childe Harold's Pilgrimage*

The sweetest lyrist° of her saddest wrong,
270   And Love taught Grief to fall like music from his tongue.

XXXI

Midst others of less note, came one frail Form,°
A phantom among men; companionless
As the last cloud of an expiring storm
Whose thunder is its knell; he, as I guess,
Had gazed on Nature's naked loveliness,
Actaeon-like, and now he fled astray
With feeble steps o'er the world's wilderness,
And his own thoughts, along that rugged way,
Pursued, like raging hounds, their father and their prey.°

XXXII

280   A pardlike Spirit beautiful and swift°—
A Love in desolation masked;—a Power
Girt round with weakness;—it can scarce uplift
The weight of the superincumbent hour;
It is a dying lamp, a falling shower,
A breaking billow;—even whilst we speak
Is it not broken? On the withering flower
The killing sun smiles brightly: on a cheek
The life can burn in blood, even while the heart may break.

XXXIII

His head was bound with pansies overblown,
290   And faded violets, white, and pied, and blue;
And a light spear topped with a cypress cone,°
Round whose rude shaft dark ivy-tresses grew
Yet dripping with the forest's noonday dew,
Vibrated, as the ever-beating heart
Shook the weak hand that grasped it; of that crew
He came the last, neglected and apart;
A herd-abandoned deer struck by the hunter's dart.

XXXIV

All stood aloof, and at his partial moan
Smiled through their tears; well knew that gentle band
300   Who in another's fate now wept his own,
As in the accents of an unknown land

---

sweetest lyrist Byron's friend Thomas Moore, poet of the *Irish Melodies* (Ierne = Ireland). In fact, both Moore and Byron despised Keats's poetry.
Form not so much Shelley, as his antithetical self, the Poet of *Alastor*.
Actaeon-like . . . prey Actaeon had the misfortune to peep at Diana when she was bathing; she punished him by turning the unfortunate

hunter into a stag, and he was torn to pieces by his own dogs.
A pardlike . . . swift The leopard image suggests Dionysus.
cypress cone Shelley bears the thyrsus or Dionysiac wand, as well as the mourning cypress, the pansies of acute self-consciousness, and other emblems of a poet bound for self-destruction.

He sung new sorrow; sad Urania scanned
The Stranger's mien, and murmured: 'Who art thou?'
He answered not, but with a sudden hand
Made bare his branded and ensanguined brow,
Which was like Cain's° or Christ's—oh! that it should be so!

XXXV

What softer voice is hushed over the dead?
Athwart what brow is that dark mantle thrown?
What form leans sadly o'er the white death-bed,
310 In mockery° of monumental stone,
The heavy heart heaving without a moan?
If it be He, who, gentlest of the wise,°
Taught, soothed, loved, honoured the departed one,
Let me not vex, with inharmonious sighs,
The silence of that heart's accepted sacrifice.

XXXVI

Our Adonais has drunk poison—oh!
What deaf and viperous murderer could crown
Life's early cup with such a draught of woe?
The nameless worm° would now itself disown:
320 It felt, yet could escape, the magic tone
Whose prelude held all envy, hate, and wrong,
But what was howling in one breast alone,
Silent with expectation of the song,
Whose master's hand is cold, whose silver lyre unstrung.

XXXVII

Live thou, whose infamy is not thy fame!
Live! fear no heavier chastisement from me,
Thou noteless blot on a remembered name!
But be thyself, and know thyself to be!
And ever at thy season be thou free
330 To spill the venom when thy fangs o'erflow;
Remorse and Self-contempt shall cling to thee;
Hot Shame shall burn upon thy secret brow,
And like a beaten hound tremble thou shalt—as now.

XXXVIII

Nor let us weep that our delight is fled
Far from these carrion kites that scream below;
He wakes or sleeps with the enduring dead;
Thou canst not soar where he is sitting now.—
Dust to the dust! but the pure spirit shall flow

Cain's perhaps guilt for not having protected
his "brother," Keats
mockery imitation

gentlest . . . wise Leigh Hunt
nameless worm anonymous reviewer

Back to the burning fountain whence it came,
340   A portion of the Eternal, which must glow
Through time and change, unquenchably the same,
Whilst thy cold embers choke the sordid hearth of shame.

XXXIX

Peace, peace! he is not dead, he doth not sleep—
He hath awakened from the dream of life—
'Tis we, who lost in stormy visions, keep
With phantoms an unprofitable strife,
And in mad trance, strike with our spirit's knife
Invulnerable nothings.°—*We* decay
Like corpses in a charnel; fear and grief
350   Convulse us and consume us day by day,
And cold hopes swarm like worms within our living clay.

XL

He has outsoared the shadow of our night;°
Envy and calumny and hate and pain,
And that unrest which men miscall delight,
Can touch him not and torture not again;
From the contagion of the world's slow stain
He is secure, and now can never mourn
A heart grown cold, a head grown gray in vain;
Nor, when the spirit's self has ceased to burn,
360   With sparkless ashes load an unlamented urn.°

XLI

He lives, he wakes—'tis Death is dead, not he;
Mourn not for Adonais.—Thou young Dawn,
Turn all thy dew to splendour, for from thee
The spirit thou lamentest is not gone;
Ye caverns and ye forests, cease to moan!
Cease, ye faint flowers and fountains, and thou Air,
Which like a mourning veil thy scarf hadst thrown
O'er the abandoned Earth, now leave it bare
Even to the joyous stars which smile on its despair!

XLII

370   He is made one with Nature: there is heard
His voice in all her music, from the moan
Of thunder, to the song of night's sweet bird;°
He is a presence to be felt and known
In darkness and in light, from herb and stone,

And in . . . nothings the situation of *Mac-*   an unlamented urn the fate of Wordsworth and
beth II.i.33–34   Coleridge
shadow . . . night shadow cast upward by   sweet bird another reference to Keats's ode
earth into the heavens

Spreading itself where'er that Power may move
Which has withdrawn his being to its own;
Which wields the world with never-wearied love,
Sustains it from beneath, and kindles it above.

XLIII

He is a portion of the loveliness
380   Which once he made more lovely: he doth bear
His part, while the one Spirit's plastic stress°
Sweeps through the dull dense world, compelling there,
All new successions to the forms they wear;
Torturing the unwilling dross° that checks its flight
To its own likeness, as each mass may bear;
And bursting in its beauty and its might
From trees and beasts and men into the Heaven's light.

XLIV

The splendours of the firmament of time
May be eclipsed, but are extinguished not;
390   Like stars° to their appointed height they climb,
And death is a low mist which cannot blot
The brightness it may veil. When lofty thought
Lifts a young heart above its mortal lair,
And love and life contend in it, for what
Shall be its earthly doom, the dead live there
And move like winds of light on dark and stormy air.

XLV

The inheritors of unfulfilled renown
Rose from their thrones, built beyond mortal thought,
Far in the Unapparent. Chatterton°
400   Rose pale,—his solemn agony had not
Yet faded from him; Sidney,° as he fought
And as he fell and as he lived and loved
Sublimely mild, a Spirit without spot,
Arose; and Lucan,° by his death approved:
Oblivion as they rose shrank like a thing reproved.

XLVI

And many more, whose names on Earth are dark,
But whose transmitted effluence cannot die

plastic stress shaping pressure; see Coleridge's
"The Eolian Harp," ll. 46–48
unwilling dross the natural recalcitrance of all
substance to become spirit
Like stars Shelley uses the same image for true
poets in The Triumph of Life.
Chatterton Thomas Chatterton (1752–70); the
agony is from his suicide at seventeen; Shelley
knew that Chatterton was peculiarly important
to Keats.

Sidney Sir Philip Sidney (1554–86) died in
battle at thirty-two.
Lucan Marcus Annaeus Lucanus (39–65 A.D.),
Roman poet remembered for his Pharsalia, on
the Civil Wars, killed himself at twenty-six,
when his participation in a plot against Nero
was revealed; Shelley is saying that his death
was the one good thing about him.

So long as fire outlives the parent spark,
Rose, robed in dazzling immortality.
410 'Thou art become as one of us,' they cry,
'It was for thee yon kingless sphere has long
Swung blind in unascended majesty,
Silent alone amid an Heaven of Song.
Assume thy wingèd throne, thou Vesper° of our throng!'

      XLVII

Who mourns for Adonais? Oh, come forth,
Fond° wretch! and know thyself and him aright.
Clasp with thy panting soul the pendulous° Earth;
As from a centre, dart thy spirit's light
Beyond all worlds, until its spacious might
420 Satiate the void circumference: then shrink
Even to a point within our day and night;
And keep thy heart light lest it make thee sink
When hope has kindled hope, and lured thee to the brink.

      XLVIII

Or go to Rome, which is the sepulchre,
Oh, not of him, but of our joy: 'tis nought
That ages, empires, and religions there
Lie buried in the ravage they have wrought;
For such as he can lend,—they borrow not
Glory from those who made the world their prey;
430 And he is gathered to the kings of thought
Who waged contention with their time's decay,
And of the past are all that cannot pass away.

      XLIX

Go thou to Rome,—at once the Paradise,
The grave, the city, and the wilderness;
And where its wrecks like shattered mountains rise,
And flowering weeds, and fragrant copses dress
The bones of Desolation's nakedness
Pass, till the spirit of the spot shall lead
Thy footsteps to a slope of green access
440 Where, like an infant's smile, over the dead
A light of laughing flowers along the grass is spread;

      L

And gray walls moulder round, on which dull Time
Feeds, like slow fire upon a hoary brand;
And one keen pyramid with wedge sublime,°

Vesper Hesperus, the Evening Star
Fond foolish
pendulous hanging
And one . . . sublime the pyramid-tomb of
the Roman tribune Gaius Cestus, near the Protestant cemetery where Keats was buried (and where Shelley was to be buried)

Pavilioning the dust of him who planned
This refuge for his memory, doth stand
Like flame transformed to marble; and beneath,
A field is spread, on which a newer band
Have pitched in Heaven's smile their camp of death,
450   Welcoming him we lose with scarce extinguished breath.

LI

Here pause: these graves are all too young as yet
To have outgrown the sorrow which consigned
Its charge to each; and if the seal is set,
Here, on one fountain of a mourning mind,°
Break it not thou! too surely shalt thou find
Thine own well full, if thou returnest home,
Of tears and gall. From the world's bitter wind
Seek shelter in the shadow of the tomb.
What Adonais is, why fear we to become?

LII

460   The One remains, the many change and pass;
Heaven's light forever shines, Earth's shadows fly;
Life, like a dome of many-coloured glass,
Stains the white radiance of Eternity,
Until Death tramples it to fragments.—Die,
If thou wouldst be with that which thou dost seek!
Follow where all is fled!—Rome's azure sky,
Flowers, ruins, statues, music, words, are weak
The glory they transfuse with fitting truth to speak.°

LIII

Why linger, why turn back, why shrink, my Heart?
470   Thy hopes are gone before: from all things here
They have departed; thou shouldst now depart!
A light is passed from the revolving year,
And man, and woman; and what still is dear
Attracts to crush, repels to make thee wither.
The soft sky smiles,—the low wind whispers near:
'Tis Adonais calls! oh, hasten thither,
No more let Life divide what Death can join together.

LIV

That Light whose smile kindles the Universe,
That Beauty in which all things work and move,

mourning mind Shelley's three-year-old son
William was buried in the same cemetery a
year and one-half before Keats.
The One . . . speak Though the language here
(ll. 460–68) derives from Platonic tradition, this
famous stanza blends Platonic Idealism with
Shelley's own visionary skepticism. Here the
One or Eternal radiance, and phenomenal life

or the many-colored glass, are opposing realities
(where in a purer Platonism only the Eternal
would be real). Life is a staining, and in some
sense, therefore, a loss, but "stains" here means
coloring, and the colors are identical with
"azure sky, / Flowers, ruins, statues, music,
words," which fall short of Eternal glory yet
are valuable and lovely in themselves.

480   That Benediction which the eclipsing Curse
    Of birth can quench not, that sustaining Love
    Which through the web of being blindly wove
    By man and beast and earth and air and sea,
    Burns bright or dim, as each° are mirrors of
    The fire for which all thirst; now beams on me,
Consuming the last clouds of cold mortality.

       LV
    The breath whose might I have invoked in song°
    Descends on me; my spirit's bark is driven,
    Far from the shore, far from the trembling throng
490   Whose sails were never to the tempest given;
    The massy earth and sphered skies are riven!
    I am borne darkly, fearfully, afar;
    Whilst, burning through the inmost veil of Heaven,
    The soul of Adonais, like a star,
Beacons from the abode where the Eternal are.°
1821   1821

To Night

       I
Swiftly walk o'er the western wave,
    Spirit of Night!
Out of the misty eastern cave,°
Where, all the long and lone daylight,
Thou wovest dreams of joy and fear,
Which make thee terrible and dear,—
    Swift be thy flight!

       II
Wrap thy form in a mantle grey,
    Star-inwrought!
10   Blind with thine hair the eyes of Day;
Kiss her until she be wearied out,
Then wander o'er city, and sea, and land,
Touching all with thine opiate wand—
    Come, long-sought!

       III
When I arose and saw the dawn,
    I sighed for thee;
When light rode high, and the dew was gone,

as each to the degree that each
song in the "Ode to the West Wind"
The soul . . . are Contrast the close of *Lycidas*,
where the dead poet becomes "the Genius of
the shore."

Out . . . cave As the day closes, the first core
of darkness is in the east, and in its relation to
the light of the whole sky, it seems the dark
mouth of a cave.

And noon lay heavy on flower and tree,
And the weary Day turned to his° rest,
20   Lingering like an unloved guest,
       I sighed for thee.

IV

Thy brother Death came, and cried,
       Wouldst thou me?
Thy sweet child Sleep, the filmy-eyed,
Murmured like a noontide bee,
Shall I nestle near thy side?
Wouldst thou me?—And I replied,
       No, not thee!

V

Death will come when thou art dead,
30   Soon, too soon—
Sleep will come when thou art fled;
Of neither would I ask the boon
I ask of thee, belovèd Night—
Swift be thine approaching flight,
       Come soon, soon!
    1821   1824

From Hellas°

CHORUS

1060 The world's great age begins anew,
    The golden years return,
  The earth doth like a snake renew
    Her winter weeds° outworn:
Heaven smiles, and faiths and empires gleam,
Like wrecks of a dissolving dream.

A brighter Hellas rears its mountains
    From waves serener far;
A new Peneus rolls his fountains
    Against the morning star.
1070 Where fairer Tempes° bloom, there sleep
Young Cyclads° on a sunnier deep.

Day . . . his This "Day" is the Sun only, hence male, and not the mythic female "Day" of stanza II.
Hellas A lyrical drama celebrating the Greek rebellion against the Turks in 1821, roughly founded on *The Persians* of Aeschylus. In his own note to this the final Chorus, Shelley indicates a skeptical reserve as to his own prophecy: "It will remind the reader . . . of Isaiah and Virgil, whose ardent spirits overleaping the actual reign of evil which we endure and be-

wail, already saw the possible and perhaps approaching state of society in which the *'lion shall lie down with the lamb.'* . . ." Compare Yeats's "Two Songs from a Play" (the play is *The Resurrection*).
weeds garments
Tempes the vale of Tempe in Thessaly, near Mt. Pelion, where the river Peneus flows; the daughter of Peneus, Daphne, was transformed into the laurel, sacred to Apollo
Cyclads islands in the Aegean

A loftier Argo° cleaves the main,
  Fraught with a later prize;
Another Orpheus sings again,
  And loves, and weeps, and dies.
A new Ulysses leaves once more
Calypso for his native shore.

Oh, write no more the tale of Troy,
  If earth Death's scroll must be!
1080 Nor mix with Laian° rage the joy
  Which dawns upon the free:
Although a subtler Sphinx renew
Riddles of death Thebes never knew.°

Another Athens shall arise,
  And to remoter time
Bequeath, like sunset to the skies,
  The splendour of its prime;
And leave, if nought so bright may live,
All earth can take or Heaven can give.

1090 Saturn and Love their long repose
  Shall burst, more bright and good
Than all who fell, than One° who rose,
  Than many unsubdued:
Not gold, not blood, their altar dowers,
But votive tears and symbol flowers.

Oh, cease! must hate and death return?
  Cease! must men kill and die?
Cease! drain not to its dregs the urn
  Of bitter prophecy.
1100 The world is weary of the past,
Oh, might it die or rest at last!
1821   1822

With a Guitar, To Jane°

Ariel to Miranda:°—Take
This slave of Music, for the sake
Of him who is the slave of thee,

Argo Jason's ship in his quest of the Golden Fleece
Laian Laius was the father of Oedipus.
Although . . . knew The Sphinx of Thebes, overcome by Oedipus, asked riddles of life, particularly of human origins; "a subtler Sphinx" will concern itself with the mystery of human death.
One Identified by Shelley's own note as Christ; "all who fell," he said, were the Gods of Greece,
Asia, and Egypt, while the "many unsubdued" were the surviving religions of China, India, "and the native tribes of America."
Jane Jane Williams, with whom Shelley was in love during the closing months of his life; he drowned with her husband, Edward Williams, in circumstances still mysterious. This poem accompanied the present of a guitar.
Ariel to Miranda characters in Shakespeare's *The Tempest,* as are Ferdinand and Prospero

And teach it all the harmony
In which thou canst, and only thou,
Make the delighted spirit glow,
Till joy denies itself again,
And, too intense, is turned to pain;
For by permission and command
10 Of thine own Prince Ferdinand,°
Poor Ariel sends this silent token
Of more than ever can be spoken;
Your guardian spirit, Ariel, who,
From life to life, must still pursue
Your happiness;—for thus alone
Can Ariel ever find his own.
From Prospero's enchanted cell,
As the mighty verses tell,
To the throne of Naples, he
20 Lit you o'er the trackless sea,
Flitting on, your prow before,
Like a living meteor.
When you die, the silent Moon,
In her interlunar swoon,°
Is not sadder in her cell
Than deserted Ariel.
When you live again on earth,
Like an unseen star of birth,
Ariel guides you o'er the sea
30 Of life from your nativity.
Many changes have been run
Since Ferdinand and you begun
Your course of love, and Ariel still
Has tracked your steps, and served your will;
Now, in humbler, happier lot,
This is all remembered not;
And now, alas! the poor sprite is
Imprisoned, for some fault of his,
In a body like a grave;—
40 From you he only dares to crave,
For his service and his sorrow,
A smile today, a song tomorrow.
The artist who this idol wrought,
To echo all harmonious thought,
Felled a tree, while on the steep
The woods were in their winter sleep,
Rocked in that repose divine
On the wind-swept Apennine;
And dreaming, some of Autumn past,

Ferdinand i.e. Edward Williams   **swoon** time between the old and the new moon

50   And some of Spring approaching fast,
     And some of April buds and showers,
     And some of songs in July bowers,
     And all of love; and so this tree,—
     O that such our death may be!—
     Died in sleep, and felt no pain,
     To live in happier form again:
     From which, beneath Heaven's fairest star,
     The artist wrought this loved Guitar,
     And taught it justly to reply,
60   To all who question skilfully,
     In language gentle as thine own;
     Whispering in enamoured tone
     Sweet oracles of woods and dells,
     And summer winds in sylvan cells;
     For it had learned all harmonies
     Of the plains and of the skies,
     Of the forests and the mountains,
     And the many-voicèd fountains;
     The clearest echoes of the hills,
70   The softest notes of falling rills,
     The melodies of birds and bees,
     The murmuring of summer seas,
     And pattering rain, and breathing dew,
     And airs of evening; and it knew
     That seldom-heard mysterious sound,
     Which, driven on its diurnal round,
     As it floats through boundless day,
     Our world enkindles on its way.—
     All this it knows, but will not tell
80   To those who cannot question well
     The Spirit that inhabits it;
     It talks according to the wit
     Of its companions; and no more
     Is heard than has been felt before,
     By those who tempt it to betray
     These secrets of an elder day:
     But, sweetly as its answers will
     Flatter hands of perfect skill,
     It keeps its highest, holiest tone
90   For our belovèd Jane alone.
     1822   1832

Lines Written in the Bay of Lerici°

She left me at the silent time
When the moon had ceased to climb
The azure path of Heaven's steep,
And like an albatross asleep,
Balanced on her wings of light,
Hovered in the purple night,
Ere she sought her ocean nest
In the chambers of the West.
She left me, and I stayed alone
10 Thinking over every tone
Which, though silent to the ear,
The enchanted heart could hear,
Like notes which die when born, but still
Haunt the echoes of the hill;
And feeling ever—oh, too much!—
The soft vibration of her touch,
As if her gentle hand, even now,
Lightly trembled on my brow;
And thus, although she absent were,
20 Memory gave me all of her
That even Fancy dares to claim:—
Her presence had made weak and tame
All passions, and I lived alone
In the time which is our own;
The past and future were forgot,
As they had been, and would be, not.
But soon, the guardian angel gone,
The daemon° reassumed his throne
In my faint heart. I dare not speak
30 My thoughts, but thus disturbed and weak
I sat and saw the vessels glide
Over the ocean bright and wide,
Like spirit-wingèd chariots sent
O'er some serenest element
For ministrations strange and far;
As if to some Elysian star
Sailed for drink to medicine
Such sweet and bitter pain as mine.
And the wind that winged their flight
40 From the land came fresh and light,
And the scent of wingèd flowers,
And the coolness of the hours
Of dew, and sweet warmth left by day,
Were scattered o'er the twinkling bay.

Lines . . . Lerici another lyric to Jane Williams; Shelley left it untitled

daemon presumably the spirit that dominated
the poet in *Alastor*

And the fisher with his lamp
And spear about the low rocks damp
Crept, and struck the fish which came
To worship the delusive flame.
Too happy they, whose pleasure sought
50   Extinguishes all sense and thought
Of the regret that pleasure leaves,
Destroying life° alone, not peace!
1822   1862

The Triumph of Life

Shelley's last poem, left unfinished when he drowned, manifests a new severity of impulse and extraordinary purgation of style, and yet it is the most despairing poem he wrote, even darker in its implications than *Adonais*. Many readers want to believe that the poem would have ended in some affirmation, had it been completed, but there is little in the poem to encourage such speculation. The poem's best critics, from Hazlitt to Yeats, have seen its sadness, and the extent to which it constitutes a palinode or recantation of Shelley's more positive visions, such as *Prometheus Unbound*. What Yeats called the *antithetical* quest, undertaken against the natural man and his human affections, which Shelley had begun to pursue in *Alastor*, here attains its shattering climax. The best (and most restrained) statement of a more hopeful reading of the poem can be found in M. H. Abrams's *Natural Supernaturalism*.

Shelley's poem takes its tone from Dante's *Purgatorio*, but the action and context of *The Triumph of Life* share more with the *Inferno*. Rousseau, prophet of nature, serving as a surrogate for Wordsworth, enters the poem as Virgil, the guide to Shelley's Dante. But Shelley here is no Pilgrim of the Absolute. What he sees in this magnificent fragment is horror, the defeat of all human integrity by life, our life, which is only a lively death. This vision is not nihilistic, for all its hopelessness, not because anything in the text suggests that Shelley will clamber out of the abyss, but because he will not join the dance, will not be seduced by Nature as his precursor Rousseau was. And yet he stands in the hell of life's triumph, and sees around him all men who have lived save for a sacred few of Athens and Jerusalem, whom he declines to name.

Amid this frightening splendor, two elements stand forth: the chastening of Shelley's idiom and mythic inventiveness, and the provocative distinction between three realms of light—poetry (the stars), nature (the sun), life (the chariot's glare). As nature outshines imagination, so the chariot's horrible splendor outshines Nature. In the fragment's closing passages, Shelley writes his last and most convincing critique of Wordsworthianism. Nature, whether she desires otherwise or not, always does betray the heart that loves her. The "shape all light," Wordsworthian Nature, offers her cup of communion, Rousseau drinks, and his imagination becomes as sand. Shelley, perhaps hours from his death, is at the height of his powers, but gazes out at a universe of death that offers only a parody of his own vitalism.

The text printed here was prepared and edited by Donald H. Reiman and published in 1965 in *Shelley's "The Triumph of Life": A Critical Study*.

life in the same sense as "life" is used in *The
Triumph of Life*

The Triumph of Life°

Swift as a spirit hastening to his task
   Of glory & of good, the Sun sprang forth
Rejoicing in his splendour, & the mask

Of darkness fell from the awakened Earth.°
The smokeless altars of the mountain snows
   Flamed above crimson clouds, & at the birth

Of light, the Ocean's orison arose
   To which the birds tempered their matin lay.°
All flowers in field or forest which unclose

10   Their trembling eyelids to the kiss of day,
Swinging their censers in the element,
   With orient incense lit by the new ray

Burned slow & inconsumably, & sent
   Their odorous sighs up to the smiling air,
And in succession due, did Continent,

Isle, Ocean, & all things that in them wear
The form & character of mortal mould
   Rise as the Sun their father rose, to bear

Their portion of the toil which he of old
20   Took as his own & then imposed on them;°
But I, whom thoughts which must remain untold

Had kept as wakeful as the stars that gem
The cone of night,° now they were laid asleep,
   Stretched my faint limbs beneath the hoary stem

Which an old chestnut flung athwart the steep
   Of a green Apennine: before me fled
The night; behind me rose the day; the Deep

Was at my feet, & Heaven above my head
When a strange trance over my fancy grew
30   Which was not slumber, for the shade it spread

Was so transparent that the scene came through
   As clear as when a veil of light is drawn
O'er evening hills they glimmer; and I knew

The Triumph of Life As in Petrarch's *Triumphs*,
the title means a triumphal procession, but
"Life" ironically means "Death-in-Life," or
everything in life that can triumph over imaginative integrity.
the Sun . . . Earth The Sun is swift *as* a beneficent spirit, but its task here is morally ambiguous; the emotional temper of this opening
resembles the lyric "To Night."

matin lay The religious vocabulary suggests a
Wordsworthian displacement of sacramentalism
into nature worship, but this is a scene from
which Shelley consciously stands apart.
imposed on them As Yeats noted, the Sun here
is something of a despot.
cone of night earth's shadow, which is a cone-
like shape

That I had felt the freshness of that dawn,
  Bathed in the same cold dew my brow & hair
  And sate as thus upon that slope of lawn

Under the self same bough, & heard as there
  The birds, the fountains & the Ocean hold
  Sweet talk in music through the enamoured air.°

40   And then a Vision on my brain was rolled.

_____

As in that trance of wondrous thought I lay
  This was the tenour of my waking dream.
  Methought I sate beside a public way

Thick strewn with summer dust, & a great stream
  Of people there was hurrying to & fro
  Numerous as gnats upon the evening gleam,

All hastening onward, yet none seemed to know
  Whither he went, or whence he came, or why
  He made one of the multitude, yet so

50   Was born amid the crowd as through the sky
  One of the million leaves of summer's bier.°—
  Old age & youth, manhood & infancy,

Mixed in one mighty torrent did appear,
  Some flying from the thing they feared & some
  Seeking the object of another's fear,

And others as with steps towards the tomb
  Pored on the trodden worms that crawled beneath,
  And others mournfully within the gloom

Of their own shadow walked, and called it death . . .
60   And some fled from it as it were a ghost,
  Half fainting in the affliction of vain breath.

But more with motions which each other crost
  Pursued or shunned the shadows the clouds threw
  Or birds within the noonday ether lost,

Upon that path where flowers never grew;
  And weary with vain toil & faint for thirst
  Heard not the fountains whose melodious dew

Out of their mossy cells forever burst
  Nor felt the breeze which from the forest told
70   Of grassy paths, & wood lawns interspersed

_____

enamoured air The vision is recurrent, and en-   summer's bier See the opening of "Ode to the
chanted.   West Wind."

With overarching elms & caverns cold,
   And violet banks where sweet dreams brood, but they
Pursued their serious folly as of old . . . .

And as I gazed methought that in the way
   The throng grew wilder, as the woods of June
When the South wind shakes the extinguished day.—

And a cold glare, intenser than the noon
   But icy cold, obscured with   light
The Sun as he the stars. Like the young moon

80   When on the sunlit limits of the night
   Her white shell trembles amid crimson air
And whilst the sleeping tempest gathers might

Doth, as a herald of its coming, bear
   The ghost of her dead Mother, whose dim form
Bends in dark ether from her infant's chair,°

So came a chariot on the silent storm
   Of its own rushing splendour, and a Shape°
So sate within as one whom years deform

90   Beneath a dusky hood & double cape
   Crouching within the shadow of a tomb,
And o'er what seemed the head, a cloud like crape,

Was bent a dun & faint aetherial gloom
   Tempering the light; upon the chariot's beam
A Janus-visaged Shadow° did assume

The guidance of that wonder-wingèd team.
   The Shapes which drew it in thick lightnings
Were lost:° I heard alone on the air's soft stream

The music of their ever moving wings.
   All the four faces° of that charioteer
100   Had their eyes banded°. . . little profit brings

Speed in the van & blindness in the rear,
   Nor then avail the beams that quench the Sun
Or that his banded eyes could pierce the sphere

Of all that is, has been, or will be done.—
   So ill was the car guided, but it past
With solemn speed majestically on . . .

infant's chair the old moon in the new moon's arms; see the epigraph to Coleridge's "Dejection" and the chariot-vision in *Prometheus Unbound* IV.206–35
Shape Life the Conqueror
Shadow a parody of the cherubim or guiding angels of the divine chariot in Ezekiel, Revelation, Dante, and Milton; "Janus-visaged" because looking before and after (though here seeing nothing), like the Roman god Janus
lost because though a parody of the divine chariot, it is self-propelled as that was
four faces again in parody of Ezekiel's four "living creatures" (Blake's Zoas), each with his four faces
banded probably means blindfolded, whereas Ezekiel and Dante emphasize a plethora of open eyes.

The crowd gave way, & I arose aghast,
  Or seemed to rise, so mighty was the trance,
And saw like clouds upon the thunder blast

110   The million with fierce song and maniac dance
  Raging around; such seemed the jubilee
  As when to greet some conqueror's advance

Imperial Rome poured forth her living sea
  From senatehouse & prison & theatre
When Freedom left those who upon the free

Had bound a yoke which soon they stooped to bear.°
  Nor wanted here the true similitude
  Of a triumphal pageant, for where'er

The chariot rolled a captive multitude
120   Was driven; all those who had grown old in power
Or misery,—all who have their age subdued,

  By action or by suffering, and whose hour
Was drained to its last sand in weal or woe,
  So that the trunk survived both fruit & flower;

All those whose fame or infamy must grow
  Till the great winter lay the form & name
Of their own earth with them forever low,

  All but the sacred few who could not tame
Their spirits to the Conqueror, but as soon
130   As they had touched the world with living flame

Fled back like eagles to their native noon,°
  Or those who put aside the diadem
Of earthly thrones or gems, till the last one

  Were there;—for they of Athens & Jerusalem
Were neither mid the mighty captives seen
  Nor mid the ribald crowd that followed them°

Or fled before . . Now swift, fierce & obscene
  The wild dance maddens in the van, & those
Who lead it, fleet as shadows on the green,

140   Outspeed the chariot & without repose
Mix with each other in tempestuous measure
  To savage music . . . . Wilder as it grows,

Had . . . bear Like the "mind-forged manacles" of Blake's "London," this yoke relies upon
the oppressed and their failure of will.
Fled . . . noon as Keats did in *Adonais*
for they . . . them Since Shelley does not name
Socrates and Jesus, we should grant him his deliberate ambiguity; there are some in the traditions of Athens and Jerusalem who did not yield
to Life, but we are not certain who they were.

They, tortured by the agonizing pleasure,
   Convulsed & on the rapid whirlwinds spun
Of that fierce spirit, whose unholy leisure

   Was soothed by mischief since the world begun,
Throw back their heads & loose their streaming hair,
   And in their dance round her who dims the Sun

Maidens & youths fling their wild arms in air
150   As their feet twinkle; they recede, and now
Bending within each other's atmosphere

   Kindle invisibly; and as they glow
Like moths by light attracted & repelled,
   Oft to new bright destruction come & go.°

Till like two clouds into one vale impelled
   That shake the mountains when their lightnings mingle
And die in rain,—the fiery band which held

   Their natures, snaps . . . ere the shock cease to tingle
One falls and then another in the path
160   Senseless, nor is the desolation single,

Yet ere I can say *where* the chariot hath
   Past over them; nor other trace I find
But as of foam° after the Ocean's wrath

   Is spent upon the desert shore.—Behind,
Old men, and women foully disarrayed
   Shake their grey hair in the insulting wind,

Limp in the dance & strain with limbs decayed
   To reach the car of light which leaves them still
Farther behind & deeper in the shade.

170   But not the less with impotence of will
They wheel, though ghastly shadows interpose
   Round them & round each other, and fulfill

Their work and to the dust whence they arose
   Sink & corruption veils them as they lie
And frost in these performs what fire in those.°

   Struck to the heart by this sad pageantry,
Half to myself I said, 'And what is this?
   Whose shape is that within the car? & why'—

Maidens . . . go Shelley's final vision of sexual love; the contrast with *Epipsychidion* is instructive.
foam the foam of Aphrodite

And frost . . . those Contrast the "frost" of the opening of *Adonais* and the "burning through" fire of its close.

I would have added—'is all here amiss?'
180   But a voice answered . . 'Life' . . . . I turned & knew
(O Heaven have mercy on such wretchedness!)

That what I thought was an old root which grew
To strange distortion out of the hill side
    Was indeed one of that deluded crew,

And that the grass which methought hung so wide
    And white, was but his thin discoloured hair,
And that the holes it vainly sought to hide

Were or had been eyes.°—'If thou canst forbear
To join the dance, which I had well forborne.'
190   Said the grim Feature,° of my thought aware,

'I will now tell that which to this deep scorn
    Led me & my companions, and relate
The progress of the pageant since the morn;

'If thirst of knowledge doth not thus abate,
Follow it even to the night, but I
    Am weary'. . . . Then like one who with the weight

Of his own words is staggered, wearily
    He paused, and ere he could resume, I cried,
'First who art thou?'. . . 'Before thy memory

200   'I feared, loved, hated, suffered, did, & died,
And if the spark with which Heaven lit my spirit
    Earth had with purer nutriment supplied

'Corruption would not now thus much inherit
    Of what was once Rousseau—nor this disguise
Stained that within which still disdains to wear it.°—

'If I have been extinguished, yet there rise
    A thousand beacons from the spark I bore.'°—
'And who are those chained to the car?' 'The Wise,

'The great, the unforgotten: they who wore
210   Mitres & helms & crowns, or wreathes of light,°
Signs of thought's empire over thought; their lore

'Taught them not this—to know themselves; their might
Could not repress the mutiny within,°
    And for the morn of truth they feigned, deep night

---

the holes . . . eyes Rousseau, a great poet (in
Shelley's judgment) and thus one of "heaven's
living eyes," is fearfully ashamed of his loss,
which parallels the blindfolding of the charioteer.
grim Feature See *Paradise Lost* X.279; "Feature" used in the sense of form or shape.
Corruption . . . it The disdain is like that of

Farinata (*Inferno* X.36) and the other heroic
damned in Dante.
spark I bore as one of the founders of Romanticism
wreathes of light The saints too are chained to
the chariot.
mutiny within the unregenerate selfhood

'Caught them ere evening.' 'Who is he with chin
   Upon his breast and hands crost on his chain?'
'The Child of a fierce hour; he sought to win

   'The world, and lost all it did contain
   Of greatness, in its hope destroyed; & more
220   Of fame & peace than Virtue's self can gain

'Without the opportunity which bore
   Him on its eagle's pinion to the peak
From which a thousand climbers have before

   'Fall'n as Napoleon fell.'—I felt my cheek
Alter to see the great form pass away
   Whose grasp had left the giant world so weak

That every pigmy kicked it as it lay—
   And much I grieved to think how power & will
In opposition rule our mortal day—

230   And why God made irreconcilable
Good & the means of good,° and for despair
   I half disdained mine eye's desire to fill

With the spent vision of the times that were
   And scarce have ceased to be . . . 'Dost thou behold,'
Said then my guide, 'those spoilers spoiled, Voltaire,

   'Frederic, & Kant, Catherine, & Leopold,°
Chained hoary anarchs, demagogue & sage
   Whose name the fresh world thinks already old—

'For in the battle Life & they did wage
240   She remained conqueror—I was overcome
By my own heart alone, which neither age

   'Nor tears nor infamy nor now the tomb
Could temper to its object.'°—'Let them pass'—
   I cried—'the world & its mysterious doom

'Is not so much more glorious than it was
   That I desire to worship those who drew
New figures on its false & fragile glass

   'As the old faded.'—'Figures ever new
Rise on the bubble, paint them how you may;
250   We have but thrown, as those before us threw,

God . . . good Shelley's central and most sorrowful insight
Frederic . . . Leopold the "enlightened despots," Frederick the Great of Prussia, Catherine the Great of Russia, and Leopold II of Austria, together with Voltaire, the Enlightenment man of letters, who inspired them to "reforms," and Immanuel Kant, culminating philosopher of the Enlightenment. These make an odd company, but in the view of the emotional naturalist Rousseau they all neglected the heart and its impulses.
For in . . . object (ll. 239–43) The Enlightened fell victim to life; Rousseau fell victim too, but to his heart's infinite desires, which could not temper themselves to any attainable objects.

'Our shadows on it as it past away.
    But mark, how chained to the triumphal chair
The mighty phantoms of an elder day—

    'All that is mortal of great Plato there
Expiates the joy & woe his master knew not,°
That star that ruled his doom was far too fair—

'And Life, where long that flower of Heaven grew not,
    Conquered the heart by love which gold or pain
Or age or sloth or slavery could subdue not—

260   And near   walk the   twain,
    The tutor & his pupil,° whom Dominion
    Followed as tame as vulture in a chain.—

'The world was darkened beneath either pinion
    Of him whom from the flock of conquerors
Fame singled as her thunderbearing minion;

'The other long outlived both woes & wars,
Throned in new thoughts of men, and still had kept
The jealous keys of truth's eternal doors

'If Bacon's spirit°   had not leapt
270   Like lightning out of darkness; he compelled
The Proteus shape of Nature's as it slept

'To wake & to unbar the caves that held
The treasure of the secrets of its reign—
See the great bards of old who inly quelled

'The passions which they sung, as by their strain
    May well be known: their living melody
Tempers its own contagion to the vein

'Of those who are infected with it°—I
Have suffered what I wrote, or viler pain!—

280   'And so my words were seeds of misery—
Even as the deeds of others.'—'Not as theirs,'
    I said—he pointed to a company

In which I recognized amid the heirs
    Of Caesar's crime from him to Constantine,°
The Anarchs old whose force & murderous snares

---

master knew not Socrates was invulnerable to
Eros, but Plato (by legend) experienced passionate homosexual love for a youth named
Aster, whose name means "star" but in English
also a flower (l. 257); see the elegiac epigram
on Aster, attributed to Plato, used by Shelley as
the epigraph to Adonais.
tutor & his pupil Aristotle and Alexander the
Great

Bacon's spirit Francis Bacon (1561–1626),
whose empiricism helped overturn the Aristotelian intellectual authority
infected with it Rousseau, who as a Romantic
suffers what he writes, stands apart from classical writers and their readers.
Constantine 4th-century Roman emperor who
established Christianity as the state religion

Had founded many a sceptre bearing line
And spread the plague of blood & gold abroad,
 And Gregory & John° and men divine

Who rose like shadows between Man & god
290 Till that eclipse, still hanging under Heaven,
 Was worshipped by the world o'er which they strode

For the true Sun it quenched.°—'Their power was given
But to destroy,' replied the leader—'I
 Am one of those who have created, even

'If it be but a world of agony.'—
 'Whence camest thou & whither goest thou?
How did thy course begin,' I said, '& why?

'Mine eyes are sick of this perpetual flow
Of people, & my heart of one sad thought.—
300 Speak.' 'Whence I came, partly I seem to know,

'And how & by what paths I have been brought
 To this dread pass, methinks even thou mayst guess;
Why this should be my mind can compass not;

'Whither the conqueror hurries me still less.
But follow thou, & from spectator turn
 Actor or victim in this wretchedness,

'And what thou wouldst be taught I then may learn
 From thee.—Now listen . . . In the April prime°
When all the forest tops began to burn

310 'With kindling green, touched by the azure clime
Of the young year, I found myself asleep
 Under a mountain which from unknown time

'Had yawned into a cavern high & deep,
 And from it came a gentle rivulet
Whose water like clear air in its calm sweep

'Bent the soft grass & kept for ever wet
The stems of the sweet flowers, and filled the grove
 With sound which all who hear must needs forget

'All pleasure & all pain, all hate & love,
320 Which they had known before that hour of rest:
A sleeping mother then would dream not of

'The only child who died upon her breast
At eventide, a king would mourn no more
 The crown of which his brow was dispossest

Gregory & John Pope Gregory the Great (*c.*
540–604) traditionally is credited with establishing the Papacy as a secular entity; John,
a name frequently assumed by popes

it quenched the "eclipse" of historical, institutionalized Christianity destroys the true God
April prime spring of the year, and second
birth of Rousseau into adolescence and poetry

'When the sun lingered o'er the Ocean floor
    To gild his rival's new prosperity.—
Thou wouldst forget thus vainly to deplore

'Ills, which if ills, can find no cure from thee,
The thought of which no other sleep will quell
330   Nor other music blot from memory—

'So sweet & deep is the oblivious spell.—
    Whether my life had been before that sleep
The Heaven which I imagine, or a Hell

'Like this harsh world in which I wake to weep,
I know not. I arose & for a space
    The scene of woods & waters seemed to keep,

'Though it was now broad day, a gentle trace
    Of light diviner than the common Sun
Sheds on the common Earth,° but all the place

340   'Was filled with many sounds woven into one
Oblivious melody, confusing sense°
    Amid the gliding waves & shadows dun;

'And as I looked the bright omnipresence
    Of morning through the orient cavern flowed,
And the Sun's image radiantly intense

'Burned on the waters of the well that glowed
Like gold, and threaded all the forest maze
    With winding paths of emerald fire—there stood

'Amid the sun, as he amid the blaze
350   Of his own glory, on the vibrating
Floor of the fountain, paved with flashing rays,

'A shape all light,° which with one hand did fling
Dew on the earth, as if she were the Dawn
    Whose invisible rain forever seemed to sing

'A silver music on the mossy lawn,
    And still before her on the dusky grass
Iris her many coloured scarf had drawn.°—

'In her right hand she bore a crystal glass
Mantling with bright Nepenthe;°—the fierce splendour
360   Fell from her as she moved under the mass

common Earth The use of "common" is Wordsworthian, and the remainder of the fragment
deliberately parodies the "Intimations of Immortality" ode.
confusing sense the synesthesia that typifies
Wordsworthian-Coleridgean Imagination
A shape all light Wordsworthian Nature, mask-
ing as the "celestial light" or "glory" of the
"Intimations" ode. Whatever her intentions

(Shelley leaves them ambiguous), her pragmatic
effect upon Rousseau is malevolent.
Iris . . . drawn the rainbow, emblem of the
Wordsworthian covenant with Nature, as in the
epigraph to the "Intimations" ode
Nepenthe drug of forgetfulness; here, what is
forgotten is the Divine Vision or childood intensity of imagination

'Of the deep cavern, & with palms so tender
  Their tread broke not the mirror of its billow,
Glided along the river, and did bend her

  'Head under the dark boughs, till like a willow
Her fair hair swept the bosom of the stream
  That whispered with delight to be their pillow.—

'As one enamoured is upborne in dream
  O'er lily-paven lakes mid silver mist
To wondrous music, so this shape might seem

370   'Partly to tread the waves with feet which kist
The dancing foam, partly to glide along
  The airs that roughened the moist amethyst,

'Or the slant morning beams that fell among
  The trees, or the soft shadows of the trees;
And her feet ever to the ceaseless song

  'Of leaves & winds & waves & birds & bees
And falling drops moved in a measure new
  Yet sweet, as on the summer evening breeze

'Up from the lake a shape of golden dew
380   Between two rocks, athwart the rising moon,
Moves up the east, where eagle never flew.—

  'And still her feet, no less than the sweet tune
To which they moved, seemed as they moved, to blot
  The thoughts of him who gazed on them, & soon

'All that was seemed as if it had been not,
  As if the gazer's mind was strewn beneath
Her feet like embers, & she, thought by thought,

  'Trampled its fires into the dust of death,°
As Day upon the threshold of the east
390   Treads out the lamps of night, until the breath

'Of darkness reillumines even the least
  Of heaven's living eyes°—like day she came,
Making the night a dream; and ere she ceased

  'To move, as one between desire and shame
Suspended, I said—"If, as it doth seem,
  Thou comest from the realm without a name,

' "Into this valley of perpetual dream,
  Shew whence I came, and where I am, and why—
Pass not away upon the passing stream."

---

dust of death the end of Rousseau's greater
vision, as he yields to the Muse of Nature

living eyes the stars, who are the poets, as in
Adonais XLIV

400   ' "Arise and quench thy thirst,"° was her reply.
        And as a shut lily, stricken by the wand
            Of dewy morning's vital alchemy,

        'I rose; and, bending at her sweet command,
            Touched with faint lips the cup she raised,
        And suddenly my brain became as sand

            'Where the first wave had more than half erased
        The track of deer on desert Labrador,
            Whilst the fierce wolf from which they fled amazed

        'Leaves his stamp visibly upon the shore
410   Until the second bursts—so on my sight
        Burst a new Vision never seen before.—

            'And the fair shape waned in the coming light
        As veil by veil the silent splendour drops
            From Lucifer,° amid the chrysolite

        'Of sunrise ere it strike the mountain tops—
            And as the presence of that fairest planet
        Although unseen is felt by one who hopes

            'That his day's path may end as he began it
        In that star's smile, whose light is like the scent
420   Of a jonquil when evening breezes fan it,

        'Or the soft note in which his dear lament
            The Brescian shepherd breathes,° or the caress
        That turned his weary slumber to content.—

            'So knew I in that light's severe excess
        The presence of that shape which on the stream
            Moved, as I moved along the wilderness,

        'More dimly than a day appearing dream,
            The ghost of a forgotten form of sleep,
        A light from Heaven whose half extinguished beam

430   'Through the sick day in which we wake to weep
        Glimmers, forever sought, forever lost.—
            So did that shape its obscure tenour keep

        'Beside my path, as silent as a ghost,
            But the new Vision, and its cold bright car,
        With savage music, stunning music, crost

            'The forest, and as if from some dread war
        Triumphantly returning, the loud million
            Fiercely extolled the fortune of her star.—

"Arise . . . thirst" Her reply is ambiguous, as
he did not understand.
Lucifer the Morning Star, "light-bearer"

Or the . . . breathes national song of Brescia
(northern Italy) which begins, "I am weary of
pasturing the sheep"

'A moving arch of victory the vermilion
440   And green & azure plumes of Iris had
Built high over her wind-winged pavilion,

'And underneath aetherial glory clad
The wilderness, and far before her flew
The tempest of the splendour which forbade

'Shadow to fall from leaf or stone;—the crew
Seemed in that light like atomies° that dance
Within a sunbeam.—Some upon the new

'Embroidery of flowers that did enhance
The grassy vesture of the desert, played,
450   Forgetful of the chariot's swift advance;

'Others stood gazing till within the shade
Of the great mountain its light left them dim.—
Others outspeeded it, and others made

'Circles around it like the clouds that swim
Round the high moon in a bright sea of air,
And more did follow, with exulting hymn,

'The chariot & the captives fettered there,
But all like bubbles on an eddying flood
Fell into the same track at last & were

460   'Borne onward.—I among the multitude
Was swept; me sweetest flowers delayed not long,
Me not the shadow nor the solitude,

'Me not the falling stream's Lethean song,
Me, not the phantom of that early form
Which moved upon its motion,—but among

'The thickest billows of the living storm
I plunged, and bared my bosom to the clime
Of that cold light, whose airs too soon deform.—

'Before the chariot had begun to climb
470   The opposing steep of that mysterious dell,
Behold a wonder worthy of the rhyme

'Of him whom from the lowest depths of Hell
Through every Paradise & through all glory
Love led serene, & who returned to tell

'In words of hate & awe the wondrous story
How all things are transfigured, except Love;°
For deaf as is a sea which wrath makes hoary

atomies bits of dust   Of him . . . Love (ll. 472–76) Dante, pro-
                                        tected by Beatrice's love

'The world can hear not the sweet notes that move
. The sphere whose light is melody to lovers°—
480   A wonder worthy of his rhyme—the grove

'Grew dense with shadows to its inmost covers,
The earth was grey with phantoms, & the air
Was peopled with dim forms, as when there hovers

'A flock of vampire-bats before the glare
Of the tropic sun, bringing ere evening
Strange night upon some Indian isle,—thus were

'Phantoms diffused around, & some did fling
Shadows of shadows, yet unlike themselves,
Behind them, some like eaglets on the wing

490   'Were lost in the white blaze, others like elves
Danced in a thousand unimagined shapes
Upon the sunny streams & grassy shelves;

'And others sate chattering like restless apes
On vulgar paws and voluble like fire.
Some made a cradle of the ermined capes

'Of kingly mantles, some upon the tiar°
Of pontiffs sate like vultures, others played
Within the crown which girt with empire

'A baby's or an idiot's brow, & made
500   Their nests in it; the old anatomies°
Sate hatching their bare brood under the shade

'Of demon wings, and laughed from their dead eyes
To reassume the delegated power
Arrayed in which these worms did monarchize

'Who make this earth their charnel.°—Others more
Humble, like falcons sate upon the fist
Of common men, and round their heads did soar,

'Or like small gnats & flies, as thick as mist
On evening marshes, thronged about the brow
510   Of lawyer, statesman, priest & theorist,

'And others like discoloured flakes of snow
On fairest bosoms & the sunniest hair
Fell, and were melted by the youthful glow

'Which they extinguished; for like tears, they were
A veil to those from whose faint lids they rained
In drops of sorrow.—I became aware

The sphere . . . lovers the sphere of Venus   anatomies skeletons
tiar tiara, crown of the Papacy   charnel cemetery

'Of whence those forms proceeded which thus stained
   The track in which we moved; after brief space
From every form the beauty slowly waned,

520   'From every firmest limb & fairest face
The strength & freshness fell like dust, & left
   The action & the shape without the grace

'Of life; the marble brow of youth was cleft
   With care, and in the eyes where once hope shone
Desire like a lioness bereft

   'Of its last cub, glared ere it died; each one
Of that great crowd sent forth incessantly
   These shadows, numerous as the dead leaves blown

'In Autumn evening from a poplar tree—
530   Each, like himself & like each other were,
At first, but soon distorted, seemed to be

   'Obscure clouds moulded by the casual air;
And of this stuff the car's creative ray°
   Wrought all the busy phantoms that were there

'As the sun shapes the clouds—thus, on the way
   Mask after mask fell from the countenance
And form of all, and long before the day

   'Was old, the joy which waked like Heaven's glance
The sleepers in the oblivious valley, died,
540   And some grew weary of the ghastly dance

'And fell, as I have fallen by the way side,
   Those soonest from whose forms most shadows past
And least of strength & beauty did abide.'—

   'Then, what is Life?' I said . . . the cripple cast
His eye upon the car which now had rolled
   Onward, as if that look must be the last,

And answered . . . . 'Happy those for whom the fold
Of
1822   1824

JOHN KEATS
1795–1821

Keats was born October 31, 1795, in London, the first of four children in the family
of a prosperous coachman. His father died in a riding accident when the future
poet was eight, his mother of tuberculosis when he was fourteen. He grew up, despite

creative ray The terrible bitterness of "creative"
in this context should be noted.

the tubercular inheritance, to be pugnacious and handsome, but stunted in size at five feet. Apprenticed to a surgeon by his dishonest guardian, he went on in 1815 to Guy's Hospital, London, as a medical student. His earliest poetry was mawkish, but "Sleep and Poetry" in 1816 demonstrated a genuine voice rising in him, and consolidated his poetic ambitions.

Haunted, like all his major contemporaries, by the shadow of Milton's splendor, Keats was also both burdened and aided by his perceptive reading of Wordsworth. His long poem *Endymion* rightly seemed a failure even to him, and he probably did not suffer as keenly from its negative reviews as tradition has held. Intellectually, the principal influence upon him was Hazlitt, but, from early 1818 on, his matchless letters show a rugged independence of mind, and a speculative development well in advance of his own poetry. One of the puzzles of Keats's rapid development was that the poet in him did not catch up with the man until the autumn of 1818. In the year between the ages of twenty-three and twenty-four, certainly one of the most fecund ever experienced by any poet, Keats wrote almost all of his major poetry.

Yet this brilliant year was full of sorrows. A summer walking tour, largely in Scotland, ended suddenly in August 1818 with the first signs of the tuberculosis that was to kill him. Autumn 1818, when the glorious year of poetry started, was largely spent nursing his brother Tom, who was dying, with agonizing slowness, of the family disease. In December, Tom died, and soon after Keats fell genuinely in love with Fanny Brawne—a relationship that was never to be fulfilled, as Keats gradually began to realize but naturally could not accept. He worked at his first *Hyperion* fragment, but could not advance in it. In January 1819, surely in tribute to Fanny Brawne, he wrote *The Eve of St. Agnes,* his least tragic major poem. The great self-recognition of his imaginative life began in April, with the composition of "Ode to Psyche" and "La Belle Dame sans Merci." In May, the great odes "On a Grecian Urn," "On Melancholy," and "To a Nightingale" were written. *Lamia,* probably his only poem to be over-rated consistently in our century, began to be drafted in June and July. Culmination came in August–September, with the superb fragment, *The Fall of Hyperion,* and the perfect ode "To Autumn." But with the transition to middle and fuller autumn, an ultimate despair followed all these gifts of the spirit, and effectively ended Keats's poetry.

By February 1820, Keats came to understand that he might have only a year or so to live, and consequently had no hope of marriage to Fanny Brawne. After a terrible half-year, he sailed to Italy in September, on the outside chance of improving his health, but he lingered only until February 23, 1821, when he died in Rome, aged twenty-five years and four months.

Of all nineteenth-century poets who wrote in English, Keats has demonstrated the most universal power to move readers in our own time. His effect upon later nineteenth-century poets was extraordinary, from Thomas Hood through Tennyson, Arnold (an unwilling and even unrecognized case of influence), Hopkins, Rossetti, and Morris, but a vast audience did not come to him until the twentieth century. The modern common reader and literary critic have agreed on Keats, for somewhat different reasons, and his influence is still vital in several major twentieth-century poets, particularly in Wallace Stevens. It seems justified to observe that Keats has the most secure and uncontested reputation of any poet since the Renaissance, an astonishing eminence for a unique but flawed artist who did not live long enough to perfect more than a handful of works.

Even the poet's letters, which were viciously deprecated as "unmanly" during the

Victorian period, enjoy a prestige today second to none in the language. Keats-idolatry is a benign malady, compared with many other literary disorders, and this editor has no desire to deplore it. But why does Keats appear a more timeless phenomenon than his great contemporaries now seem to be? What accounts for the generous over-praise that consistently links him with Shakespeare in modern criticism? Clearly he is the most sympathetic of modern poets, though he does not compare to Blake in conceptual power or to Wordsworth in originality. To define this power of sympathy is to identify what intrinsically belongs to Keats, what could not have come to us without him.

The prime element is Keats's thoroughgoing naturalistic humanism, in him a tough-minded and healthy doctrine very difficult to parallel in any writer since. Here he stemmed from Wordsworth, particularly the poet of *Home at Grasmere* (*The Recluse* fragment), who, by words which speak of nothing more than what we already are, would rouse us from the sleep of death to show us we are at home in a nature fitted to our minds. But Wordsworth's naturalism, his sense that the earth was enough, remained uneasy. Even in "Tintern Abbey" it wavers at the borders of a theophany, as though the visible world threatened to go out with the light of sense, and only infinity remained as an emblem of the deepest truth. From at least the "Ode to Psyche" on, Keats proclaims a more strenuously naturalistic confidence: "I see, and sing, by my own eyes inspired."

Allied to this heroic priesthood of the visible is Keats's extraordinary detachment, a capacity for disinterestedness so rare in a poet of all men as to be especially refreshing. He himself, in the crucial letter of December 21–27, 1817, to his brothers, developed this gift into the difficult but radiant quality "which Shakespeare possessed so enor-mously—I mean *Negative Capability*, that is when man is capable of being in uncer-tainties, Mysteries, doubts, without any irritable reaching after fact and reason—." No better description could be made of the poet-quester of *The Fall of Hyperion*, or of the voice that chants the great odes.

Beyond the uncompromising sense that we are completely physical in a physical world, and the allied realization that we are compelled to imagine more than we can know or understand, there is a third quality in Keats more clearly present than in any other poet since Shakespeare. This is the gift of tragic acceptance, which per-suades us again that Keats was the least solipsistic of poets, the one most able to grasp the individuality and reality of selves totally distinct from his own, and of an outward world that would survive his perception of it. In his final poems he succeeds mirac-ulously in communicating to us what it would be like if we shared this most un-common and most gracious of human gifts.

On First Looking into Chapman's Homer°

Much have I travelled in the realms of gold,
    And many goodly states and kingdoms seen;
    Round many western islands have I been

On First . . . Homer Keats had been reading George Chapman's translation (published be-tween 1598 and 1616) with his friend Charles Cowden Clarke; as he had no Greek, this was Keats's true introduction to the greatest Western poet.

Which bards in fealty to Apollo hold.
Oft of one wide expanse had I been told
  That deep-browed Homer ruled as his demesne;
  Yet did I never breathe its pure serene°
Till I heard Chapman speak out loud and bold:
Then felt I like some watcher of the skies
10   When a new planet swims into his ken;
Or like stout Cortez° when with eagle eyes
  He stared at the Pacific—and all his men
Looked at each other with a wild surmise—
  Silent, upon a peak in Darien.
1816   1816

On the Grasshopper and Cricket°

The poetry of earth is never dead:
  When all the birds are faint with the hot sun,
  And hide in cooling trees, a voice will run
From hedge to hedge about the new-mown mead;
That is the Grasshopper's—he takes the lead
  In summer luxury,—he has never done
  With his delights; for when tired out with fun
He rests at ease beneath some pleasant weed.
The poetry of earth is ceasing never:
10   On a lone winter evening, when the frost
    Has wrought a silence, from the stove there shrills
The Cricket's song, in warmth increasing ever,
  And seems to one in drowsiness half lost,
    The Grasshopper's among some grassy hills.
1816   1817

From Sleep and Poetry°

O for ten years, that I may overwhelm
Myself in poesy; so I may do the deed
That my own soul has to itself decreed.
Then will I pass the countries that I see
100 In long perspective, and continually

---

pure serene clear air; presumably remembered from Coleridge's poem, "Hymn Before Sunrise, in the Vale of Chamouni," l. 72
Cortez a celebrated mistake; it should be Balboa, who discovered the Pacific in 1513
On the Grasshopper and Cricket written in a sonnet competition with Leigh Hunt, who had suggested the subject
Sleep and Poetry Though not a mature work (Keats was barely twenty-one), this is the-

matically a crucial poem in Keats's development, showing both his indebtedness to Wordsworth and his passionate intention to swerve away from that great original, while abiding in a naturalistic humanism still recognizably Wordsworthian; sleep, in the title and throughout, is taken as a mode of half-wakeful consciousness, almost equivalent to the poetic state proper.

Taste their pure fountains. First the realm I'll pass
Of Flora, and old Pan:° sleep in the grass,
Feed upon apples red, and strawberries,
And choose each pleasure that my fancy sees;
Catch the white-handed nymphs in shady places,
To woo sweet kisses from averted faces,—
Play with their fingers, touch their shoulders white
Into a pretty shrinking with a bite
As hard as lips can make it: till agreed,
110 A lovely tale of human life we'll read.
And one will teach a tame dove how it best
May fan the cool air gently o'er my rest;
Another, bending o'er her nimble tread,
Will set a green robe floating round her head,
And still will dance with ever varied ease,
Smiling upon the flowers and the trees:
Another will entice me on, and on
Through almond blossoms and rich cinnamon;
Till in the bosom of a leafy world
120 We rest in silence, like two gems upcurled
In the recesses of a pearly shell.
And can I ever bid these joys farewell?
Yes, I must pass them for a nobler life,
Where I may find the agonies, the strife
Of human hearts:° for lo! I see afar,
O'er sailing the blue cragginess, a car
And steeds with streamy manes—the charioteer
Looks out upon the winds with glorious fear:°
And now the numerous tramplings quiver lightly
130 Along a huge cloud's ridge; and now with sprightly
Wheel downward come they into fresher skies,
Tipped round with silver from the sun's bright eyes.
Still downward with capacious whirl they glide;
And now I see them on the green-hill's side
In breezy rest among the nodding stalks.
The charioteer with wondrous gesture talks
To the trees and mountains; and there soon appear
Shapes of delight, of mystery, and fear,
Passing along before a dusky space
140 Made by some mighty oaks: as they would chase
Some ever-fleeting music on they sweep.
Lo! how they murmur, laugh, and smile, and weep:

Flora . . . Pan Flora was the Roman goddess of flowers; Pan, the Greek god of flocks, shepherds.
hearts The passage, up to this point, is heavily influenced by Wordsworth's *Tintern Abbey*, with its three stages of poetic development: "boyish days," aesthetic response to nature, and sympathy with other mortals.

I see . . . fear This vision of the chariot of imagination, akin to visions in Gray and Shelley, has a distinct tonal coloring of Collins, as Douglas Bush notes; Keats's charioteer, like Collins's, is not so much daemonic himself as a fearful invoker of the daemonic world.

Some with upholden hand and mouth severe;
Some with their faces muffled to the ear
Between their arms; some, clear in youthful bloom,
Go glad and smilingly athwart the gloom;
Some looking back, and some with upward gaze;
Yes, thousands in a thousand different ways
Flit onward—now a lovely wreath of girls
150   Dancing their sleek hair into tangled curls;
And now broad wings. Most awfully intent
The driver of those steeds is forward bent,
And seems to listen: O that I might know
All that he writes with such a hurrying glow.

The visions all are fled—the car is fled
Into the light of heaven, and in their stead
A sense of real things comes doubly strong,
And, like a muddy stream, would bear along
My soul to nothingness: but I will strive
160   Against all doubtings, and will keep alive
The thought of that same chariot, and the strange
Journey it went.

        Is there so small a range
In the present strength of manhood, that the high
Imagination cannot freely fly
As she was wont of old? Prepare her steeds,
Paw up against the light, and do strange deeds
Upon the clouds? Has she not shown us all?
From the clear space of ether, to the small
Breath of new buds unfolding? From the meaning
170   Of Jove's large eye-brow, to the tender greening
Of April meadows? Here her altar shone,
Even in this isle; and who could paragon
The fervid choir that lifted up a noise
Of harmony, to where it aye will poise
Its mighty self of convoluting sound,
Huge as a planet, and like that roll round,
Eternally around a dizzy void?
Ay, in those days the Muses were nigh cloyed
With honours; nor had any other care
180   Than to sing out and sooth their wavy hair.

Could all this be forgotten? Yes, a schism
Nurtured by foppery and barbarism,
Made great Apollo blush for this his land.
Men were thought wise who could not understand
His glories: with a puling infant's force
They swayed about upon a rocking horse,

And thought it Pegasus.° Ah dismal souled!
The winds of heaven blew, the ocean rolled
Its gathering waves—ye felt it not. The blue
190 Bared its eternal bosom, and the dew
Of summer nights collected still to make
The morning precious: beauty was awake!
Why were ye not awake? But ye were dead
To things ye knew not of,—were closely wed
To musty laws lined out with wretched rule
And compass vile: so that ye taught a school
Of dolts to smooth, inlay, and clip, and fit,
Till, like the certain wands of Jacob's wit,°
Their verses tallied. Easy was the task:
200 A thousand handicraftsmen wore the mask
Of Poesy. Ill-fated, impious race!
That blasphemed the bright Lyrist° to his face,
And did not know it,—no, they went about,
Holding a poor, decrepid standard out
Marked with most flimsy mottos, and in large
The name of one Boileau!°

       O ye whose charge
It is to hover round our pleasant hills!
Whose congregated majesty so fills
My boundly reverence, that I cannot trace
210 Your hallowed names, in this unholy place,
So near those common folk; did not their shames
Affright you? Did our old lamenting Thames
Delight you? Did ye never cluster round
Delicious Avon, with a mournful sound,
And weep? Or did ye wholly bid adieu
To regions where no more the laurel grew?
Or did ye stay to give a welcoming
To some lone spirits who could proudly sing
Their youth away, and die?° 'Twas even so:
220 But let me think away those times of woe:
Now 'tis a fairer season; ye have breathed
Rich benedictions o'er us; ye have wreathed
Fresh garlands: for sweet music has been heard
In many places;°—some has been upstirred

They swayed . . . Pegasus This attack on the Popean couplet is derived from William Hazlitt, who said that Pope and Dr. Johnson would have converted Milton's "vaulting Pegasus into a rocking-horse," Pegasus being the steed of the Muses.
Jacob's wit See Genesis 30:31–43; but here, as generally, Keats's biblical allusions come from other poets; see The Merchant of Venice I.iii.85.
Lyrist Apollo

Boileau Nicolas Boileau-Despréaux (1636–1711), French poet and critic, who was probably only a name to Keats, and who was regarded by Leigh Hunt and others as the true founder of "the French school" of English poetry, that is, the neoclassical school of Pope
To some . . . die Thomas Chatterton, the 18th-century poet
places an attempt to particularize the "Romantic Revival" of English poetry

From out its crystal dwelling in a lake,°
By a swan's ebon bill; from a thick brake,
Nested and quiet in a valley mild,
Bubbles a pipe;° fine sounds are floating wild
About the earth: happy are ye and glad.

230   These things are doubtless: yet in truth we've had
Strange thunders from the potency of song;
Mingled indeed with what is sweet and strong,
From majesty: but in clear truth the themes
Are ugly clubs, the Poets Polyphemes
Disturbing the grand sea.° A drainless shower
Of light is poesy; 'tis the supreme of power;
'Tis might half slumbering on its own right arm.°
The very archings of her eye-lids charm
A thousand willing agents to obey,
240   And still she governs with the mildest sway:
But strength alone though of the Muses born
Is like a fallen angel: trees uptorn,
Darkness, and worms, and shrouds, and sepulchres
Delight it; for it feeds upon the burrs,
And thorns of life;° forgetting the great end
Of poesy, that it should be a friend
To sooth the cares, and lift the thoughts of man.°

1816   1817

On the Sea°

It keeps eternal whisperings around
    Desolate shores, and with its mighty swell
    Gluts twice ten thousand Caverns, till the spell
Of Hecate° leaves them their old shadowy sound.
Often 'tis in such gentle temper found,
    That scarcely will the very smallest shell
    Be moved for days from where it sometime fell,
When last the winds of Heaven were unbound.

some . . . lake Wordsworth
from . . . pipe Leigh Hunt; Keats was to
change his mind as to Hunt's poetical eminence.
Poets . . . sea The sea is poetry; the poets,
even Wordsworth and certainly Byron, are
thematically tendentious and have a design
upon us, which they subdue their poems to expressing; such poets are like Homer's blind
Cyclops, Polyphemus, who threw rocks into the
sea at Odysseus, vainly; Wordsworth and Byron
will miss us because they are club-wielders,
thematically obsessed.
'Tis . . . arm Keats's definition of true poetry
as always keeping some of its strength in reserve

thorns of life The "fallen angel" suggests Byron,
but Shelley divined some reference to himself,
and appropriated this phrase with extraordinary
effect in his "Ode to the West Wind," l. 54.
To sooth . . . man This climax of the passage
is Wordsworthian again, in its conception of the
purpose of poetry.
On the Sea See *King Lear* IV.vi.4: "Hark! do
you hear the sea," which Keats said was his
starting point for this sonnet; it seems inescap-
able that the Sea, to Keats, represented primarily the universe of poetry.
Hecate goddess of the netherworld and of witchcraft, and associated by Keats with the moon
goddess governing the tides

Oh ye! who have your eyeballs vexed and tired,
10   Feast them upon the wideness of the Sea;
    Oh ye! whose ears are dinned with uproar rude,
    Or fed too much with cloying melody—
      Sit ye near some old Cavern's Mouth and brood,
Until ye start, as if the sea-nymphs quired!
1817   1848

In Drear-Nighted December

I

In drear-nighted December,
    Too happy, happy tree,
Thy branches ne'er remember
    Their green felicity:
The north cannot undo them
With a sleety whistle through them;
Nor frozen thawings glue them
    From budding at the prime.

II

In drear-nighted December,
10   Too happy, happy brook,
Thy bubblings ne'er remember
    Apollo's summer look;
But with a sweet forgetting,
They stay their crystal fretting,
Never, never petting°
    About the frozen time.

III

Ah! would 'twere so with many
    A gentle girl and boy!
But were there ever any
20   Writhed not of passèd joy?
The feel of not to feel it,
When there is none to heal it,
Nor numbèd sense to steel it,
    Was never said in rhyme.
1817   1829

petting complaining

From Epistle to John Hamilton Reynolds°

O that our dreamings all, of sleep or wake,
Would all their colours from the sunset take:
From something of material sublime,
70   Rather than shadow our own soul's day-time
In the dark void of night. For in the world
We jostle,—but my flag is not unfurled
On the admiral-staff,—and to philosophise
I dare not yet! Oh, never will the prize,
High reason, and the lore of good and ill,
Be my award! Things cannot to the will
Be settled, but they tease us out of thought;°
Or is it that imagination brought
Beyond its proper bound, yet still confined,
80   Lost in a sort of Purgatory blind,
Cannot refer to any standard law
Of either earth or heaven? It is a flaw
In happiness, to see beyond our bourn,—
It forces us in summer skies to mourn,
It spoils the singing of the nightingale.

Dear Reynolds! I have a mysterious tale,
And cannot speak it: the first page I read
Upon a lampit° rock of green sea-weed
Among the breakers; 'twas a quiet eve,
90   The rocks were silent, the wide sea did weave
An untumultuous fringe of silver foam
Along the flat brown sand; I was at home
And should have been most happy,—but I saw
Too far into the sea, where every maw°
The greater on the less feeds evermore.—
But I saw too distinct into the core
Of an eternal fierce destruction,
And so from happiness I far was gone.
Still am I sick of it, and though, today,
100   I've gathered young spring-leaves, and flowers gay
Of periwinkle and wild strawberry,
Still do I that most fierce destruction see,—
The shark at savage prey,—the hawk at pounce,—
The gentle robin, like a pard or ounce,°
Ravening a worm,—Away, ye horrid moods!
Moods of one's mind! You know I hate them well.

Epistle to John Hamilton Reynolds These lines
are from a verse-and-prose letter, March 25,
1818, that Keats wrote to his friend, Reynolds
(1796–1852), a poet now best remembered
for a verse-satire on Wordsworth's poem *Peter
Bell*, which work Shelley also satirized.

tease . . . thought used again in "On a Grecian Urn," l. 44
lampit limpit, mollusk
maw stomach
pard or ounce lynx or leopard

You know I'd sooner be a clapping bell
To some Kamschatkan° missionary church,
Than with these horrid moods be left i' the lurch.—
110   Do you get health—and Tom the same—I'll dance,
And from detested moods in new romance°
Take refuge—Of bad lines a centaine dose
Is sure enough—and so 'here follows prose.'°—
1818   1848

When I Have Fears

When I have fears that I may cease to be
    Before my pen has gleaned my teeming brain,
Before high-piled books, in charactery,°
    Hold like rich garners the full ripened grain;
When I behold, upon the night's starred face,
    Huge cloudy symbols of a high romance,
And think that I may never live to trace
    Their shadows, with the magic hand of chance;
And when I feel, fair creature of an hour,
10   That I shall never look upon thee more,
Never have relish in the faery power
    Of unreflecting love;—then on the shore
Of the wide world I stand alone, and think
Till love and fame to nothingness do sink.
1818   1848

Fragment of an Ode to Maia

Mother of Hermes! and still youthful Maia!°
        May I sing to thee
As thou wast hymned on the shores of Baiae?°
        Or may I woo thee
In earlier Sicilian?° or thy smiles
Seek as they once were sought, in Grecian isles,
By bards who died content on pleasant sward,°
    Leaving great verse unto a little clan?
O, give me their old vigour, and unheard
10   Save of the quiet primrose, and the span
        Of heaven and few ears,

Kamschatkan Kamchatka, in Siberia
new romance presumably refers to a contemplated poem
'here . . . prose' See *Twelfth Night* II.v.154.
charactery writing
Maia mother, by Zeus, of Hermes, god of lucky

finds, shepherds, thieves, and travelers
Baiae Roman colony near Naples
Sicilian in the pastoral mode of the poet Theocritus (d. 260? B.C.)
sward grassy turf

Rounded by thee, my song should die away
      Content as theirs,
Rich in the simple worship of a day.
1818   1848

Hyperion

Rejecting the sentimentality of much of his earlier work, including *Endymion,* Keats wrote *Hyperion* in what he called "a more naked and grecian Manner." Though he had abandoned the fragment by April 1819, and it is undeniably an inconsistent work, few more powerful attempts at the Sublime exist. The view taken of the conflict between Olympians and Titans is an original one, and contrasts strongly with those of Shelley and Byron (see Headnote to *Prometheus Unbound*). In an atmosphere at once strong and cool, *Hyperion* surveys the fallen condition of the Titans without either a Miltonic didactic emphasis or a Shelleyan personalizing self-dramatization. Here is the first triumph of Keats's earlier idea of poetry as a disinterested mode.

The situation in which the poem begins is that difficult moment in myth when the old gods are departing and the new are not yet securely themselves. In particular, Hyperion, Titan of the sun, uneasily abides in heaven, and the young Apollo, down on earth, is "dying into life," becoming the god of poetry. Though an overt march-of-mind moral, of history as necessary progress, is given to Oceanus, displaced god of the sea, there is small reason to believe that he speaks for Keats himself. The poem hesitates at the verge of becoming an allegory of the history of imagination, and this hesitation is one of its strengths.

We can surmise that Keats gave up this first *Hyperion* for two reasons, first that the fragment is so complete in itself that any continuation would have meant redundancy, and second that he either could not or more likely would not maintain the beautiful but strained Miltonic high style of the first two books. The brief fragment of Book III shows a return to the subjective, romance style of *Endymion,* which was to be transformed into the harsh, purgatorial style of *The Fall of Hyperion.* Something vital and open in Keats had begun to discover his own personalizing involvement in this magnificent but abortive epic, and he was too honest to go on. But he had made already the most successful single emulation of Miltonic style and procedure in the Romantic tradition. Even the use throughout of sonorous Titanic names is a return of the Miltonic glory of a Sublime cataloguing.

Hyperion

A Fragment

Book I

Deep in the shady sadness of a vale
Far sunken from the healthy breath of morn,
Far from the fiery noon, and eve's one star,

Sat grey-haired Saturn, quiet as a stone,
Still as the silence round about his lair;
Forest on forest hung about his head
Like cloud on cloud. No stir of air was there,
Not so much life as on a summer's day
Robs not one light seed from the feathered grass,
10   But where the dead leaf fell, there did it rest.
A stream went voiceless by, still deadened more
By reason of his fallen divinity
Spreading a shade: the Naiad° mid her reeds
Pressed her cold finger closer to her lips.

Along the margin-sand large foot-marks went,
No further than to where his feet had stayed,°
And slept there since. Upon the sodden ground
His old right hand lay nerveless, listless, dead,
Unsceptred; and his realmless eyes were closed;
20   While his bowed head seemed listening to the Earth,
His ancient mother, for some comfort yet.

It seemed no force could wake him from his place;
But there came one,° who with a kindred hand
Touched his wide shoulders, after bending low
With reverence, though to one who knew it not.
She was a Goddess of the infant world;
By her in stature the tall Amazon
Had stood a pigmy's height: she would have ta'en
Achilles by the hair and bent his neck;
30   Or with a finger stayed Ixion's wheel.°
Her face was large as that of Memphian sphinx,°
Pedestaled haply in a palace court,
When sages looked to Egypt for their lore.
But oh! how unlike marble was that face:
How beautiful, if sorrow had not made
Sorrow more beautiful than Beauty's self.
There was a listening fear in her regard,
As if calamity had but begun;
As if the vanward clouds of evil days
40   Had spent their malice, and the sullen rear
Was with its stored thunder labouring up.
One hand she pressed upon that aching spot
Where beats the human heart, as if just there,
Though an immortal, she felt cruel pain:
The other upon Saturn's bended neck
She laid, and to the level of his ear

Naiad water nymph
stayed Douglas Bush's emendation for "strayed"
one Thea, Hyperion's wife and sister
Ixion's wheel Ixion's punishment in Hades
was to be bound to a perpetually revolving

wheel because he had dared to love Hera, the
wife of Zeus.
sphinx the Egyptian sphinx at Memphis, not
the Theban one of the Oedipus story

Leaning with parted lips, some words she spake
In solemn tenour and deep organ tone:
Some mourning words, which in our feeble tongue
Would come in these like accents; O how frail
50   To that large utterance of the early Gods!
'Saturn, look up!—though wherefore, poor old King?°
I have no comfort for thee, no not one:
I cannot say, "O wherefore sleepest thou?"
For heaven is parted from thee, and the earth
Knows thee not, thus afflicted, for a God;
And ocean too, with all its solemn noise,
Has from thy sceptre passed; and all the air
Is emptied of thine hoary majesty.
60   Thy thunder, conscious of the new command,
Rumbles reluctant o'er our fallen house;
And thy sharp lightning in unpractised hands
Scorches and burns our once serene domain.
O aching time! O moments big as years!
All as ye pass swell out the monstrous truth,
And press it so upon our weary griefs
That unbelief has not a space to breathe.
Saturn, sleep on:—O thoughtless, why did I
Thus violate thy slumbrous solitude?
70   Why should I ope thy melancholy eyes?
Saturn, sleep on! while at thy feet I weep.'

As when, upon a trancèd summer-night,
Those green-robed senators of mighty woods,
Tall oaks, branch-charmèd by the earnest stars,
Dream, and so dream all night without a stir,
Save from one gradual solitary gust
Which comes upon the silence, and dies off,
As if the ebbing air had but one wave;
So came these words and went; the while in tears
80   She touched her fair large forehead to the ground,
Just where her falling hair might be outspread
A soft and silken mat for Saturn's feet.
One moon, with alteration slow, had shed
Her silver seasons four upon the night,
And still these two were posturèd motionless,
Like natural sculpture in cathedral cavern;
The frozen God still couchant on the earth,
And the sad Goddess weeping at his feet:
Until at length old Saturn lifted up
90   His faded eyes, and saw his kingdom gone,

poor old King The association between Saturn
and Shakespeare's King Lear seems deliberate
throughout.

And all the gloom and sorrow of the place,
And that fair kneeling Goddess; and then spake,
As with a palsied tongue, and while his beard
Shook horrid° with such aspen-malady:
'O tender spouse of gold Hyperion,
Thea, I feel thee ere I see thy face;
Look up, and let me see our doom in it;
Look up, and tell me if this feeble shape
Is Saturn's; tell me, if thou hear'st the voice
100 Of Saturn; tell me, if this wrinkling brow,
Naked and bare of its great diadem,
Peers like the front of Saturn. Who had power
To make me desolate? whence came the strength?
How was it nurtured to such bursting forth,
While Fate seemed strangled in my nervous° grasp?
But it is so; and I am smothered up,
And buried from all godlike exercise
Of influence benign on planets pale,
Of admonitions to the winds and seas,
110 Of peaceful sway above man's harvesting,
And all those acts which Deity supreme
Doth ease its heart of love in.—I am gone
Away from my own bosom: I have left
My strong identity, my real self,
Somewhere between the throne, and where I sit
Here on this spot of earth. Search, Thea, search!
Open thine eyes eterne, and sphere them round
Upon all space: space starred, and lorn of light;
Space regioned with life-air; and barren void;
Spaces of fire, and all the yawn of hell.—
120 Search, Thea, search! and tell me, if thou seest
A certain shape or shadow, making way
With wings or chariot fierce to repossess
A heaven he lost erewhile: it must—it must
Be of ripe progress—Saturn must be King.
Yes, there must be a golden victory;
There must be Gods thrown down, and trumpets blown
Of triumph calm, and hymns of festival
Upon the gold clouds metropolitan,
Voices of soft proclaim, and silver stir
130 Of strings in hollow shells; and there shall be
Beautiful things made new, for the surprise
Of the sky-children; I will give command:
Thea! Thea! Thea! where is Saturn?'

This passion lifted him upon his feet,
And made his hands to struggle in the air,

horrid bristling   **nervous** powerful

His Druid locks° to shake and ooze with sweat,
His eyes to fever out, his voice to cease.
He stood, and heard not Thea's sobbing deep;
140   A little time, and then again he snatched
Utterance thus.—'But cannot I create?
Cannot I form? Cannot I fashion forth
Another world, another universe,
To overbear and crumble this to naught?
Where is another chaos? Where?'—That word
Found way unto Olympus, and made quake
The rebel three.°—Thea was startled up,
And in her bearing was a sort of hope,
As thus she quick-voiced spake, yet full of awe.
.150   'This cheers our fallen house: come to our friends,
O Saturn! come away, and give them heart;
I know the covert, for thence came I hither.'
Thus brief; then with beseeching eyes she went
With backward footing through the shade a space:
He followed, and she turned to lead the way
Through agèd boughs, that yielded like the mist
Which eagles cleave upmounting from their nest.

Meanwhile in other realms big tears were shed,
More sorrow like to this, and such like woe,
160   Too huge for mortal tongue or pen of scribe:
The Titans fierce, self-hid, or prison-bound,
Groaned for the old allegiance once more,
And listened in sharp pain for Saturn's voice.
But one of the whole mammoth-brood still kept
His sovereignty, and rule, and majesty;—
Blazing Hyperion on his orbèd fire
Still sat, still snuffed the incense, teeming up
From man to the sun's God; yet unsecure:
For as among us mortals omens drear
170   Fright and perplex, so also shuddered he—
Not at dog's howl, or gloom-bird's hated screech,
Or the familiar visiting of one
Upon the first toll of his passing-bell,
Or prophesyings of the midnight lamp;
But horrors, portioned to a giant nerve,
Oft made Hyperion ache. His palace bright
Bastioned with pyramids of glowing gold,
And touched with shade of bronzèd obelisks,
Glared a blood-red through all its thousand courts,
180   Arches, and domes, and fiery galleries;

Druid locks Later 18th-century antiquarians attempted to identify the Celtic Druids or pagan priests with the Titans.

rebel three Jupiter, Neptune, Pluto; Saturn's sons by Rhea and rulers respectively of sky, sea, and underworld

And all its curtains of Aurorian° clouds
Flushed angerly: while sometimes eagle's wings,
Unseen before by Gods or wondering men,
Darkened the place; and neighing steeds were heard,
Not heard before by Gods or wondering men.
Also, when he would taste the spicy wreaths
Of incense, breathed aloft from sacred hills,
Instead of sweets, his ample palate took
Savour of poisonous brass and metal sick:
190 And so, when harboured in the sleepy west,
After the full completion of fair day,—
For rest divine upon exalted couch
And slumber in the arms of melody,
He paced away the pleasant hours of ease
With stride colossal, on from hall to hall;
While far within each aisle and deep recess,
His wingèd minions in close clusters stood,
Amazed and full of fear; like anxious men
Who on wide plains gather in panting troops,
200 When earthquakes jar their battlements and towers.
Even now, while Saturn, roused from icy trance,
Went step for step with Thea through the woods,
Hyperion, leaving twilight in the rear,
Came slope upon the threshold of the west;
Then, as was wont, his palace-door flew ope
In smoothest silence, save what solemn tubes,
Blown by the serious Zephyrs, gave of sweet
And wandering sounds, slow-breathèd melodies;
And like a rose in vermeil° tint and shape,
210 In fragrance soft, and coolness to the eye,
That inlet to severe magnificence
Stood full blown, for the God to enter in.

   He entered, but he entered full of wrath;
His flaming robes streamed out beyond his heels,
And gave a roar, as if of earthly fire,
That scared away the meek ethereal Hours°
And made their dove-wings tremble. On he flared,
From stately nave to nave, from vault to vault,
Through bowers of fragrant and enwreathèd light,
220 And diamond-pavèd lustrous long arcades,
Until he reached the great main cupola;
There standing fierce beneath, he stamped his foot,
And from the basement deep to the high towers
Jarred his own golden region; and before
The quavering thunder thereupon had ceased,

Aurorian from Aurora, the dawn goddess
vermeil vermilion

Hours female divinities who presided over the
changes of the seasons

His voice leapt out, despite of godlike curb,
To this result: 'O dreams of day and night!
O monstrous forms! O effigies of pain!
O spectres busy in a cold, cold gloom!
230   O lank-eared Phantoms of black-weeded pools!
Why do I know ye? why have I seen ye? why
Is my eternal essence thus distraught
To see and to behold these horrors new?
Saturn is fallen, am I too to fall?
Am I to leave this haven of my rest,
This cradle of my glory, this soft clime,
This calm luxuriance of blissful light,
These crystalline pavilions, and pure fanes,
Of all my lucent empire? It is left
240   Deserted, void, nor any haunt of mine.
The blaze, the splendour, and the symmetry,
I cannot see—but darkness, death and darkness.
Even here, into my centre of repose,
The shady visions come to domineer,
Insult, and blind, and stifle up my pomp.—
Fall!—No, by Tellus° and her briny robes!
Over the fiery frontier of my realms
I will advance a terrible right arm
Shall scare that infant thunderer, rebel Jove,
250   And bid old Saturn take his throne again.'—
He spake, and ceased, the while a heavier threat
Held struggle with his throat but came not forth;
For as in theatres of crowded men
Hubbub increases more they call out 'Hush!'
So at Hyperion's words the Phantoms pale
Bestirred themselves, thrice horrible and cold;
And from the mirrored level where he stood
A mist arose, as from a scummy marsh.
At this, through all his bulk an agony
260   Crept gradual, from the feet unto the crown,
Like a lithe serpent vast and muscular
Making slow way, with head and neck convulsed
From over-strainèd might. Released, he fled
To the eastern gates, and full six dewy hours
Before the dawn in season due should blush,
He breathed fierce breath against the sleepy portals,
Cleared them of heavy vapours, burst them wide
Suddenly on the ocean's chilly streams.
The planet orb of fire, whereon he rode
270   Each day from east to west the heavens through,
Spun round in sable curtaining of clouds;

Tellus Earth

Not therefore veilèd quite, blindfold, and hid,
But ever and anon the glancing spheres,
Circles, and arcs, and broad-belting colure,°
Glowed through, and wrought upon the muffling dark
Sweet-shapèd lightnings from the nadir deep
Up to the zenith,—hieroglyphics old
Which sages and keen-eyed astrologers
Then living on the earth, with labouring thought
280   Won from the gaze of many centuries:
Now lost, save what we find on remnants huge
Of stone, or marble swart;° their import gone,
Their wisdom long since fled.—Two wings this orb
Possessed for glory, two fair argent° wings,
Ever exalted at the God's approach:
And now, from forth the gloom their plumes immense
Rose, one by one, till all outspreaded were;
While still the dazzling globe maintained eclipse,
Awaiting for Hyperion's command.
290   Fain would he have commanded, fain took throne
And bid the day begin, if but for change.
He might not:—No, though a primeval God:
The sacred seasons might not be disturbed.
Therefore the operations of the dawn
Stayed in their birth, even as here 'tis told.
Those silver wings expanded sisterly,
Eager to sail their orb; the porches wide
Opened upon the dusk demesnes of night;
And the bright Titan, frenzied with new woes,
300   Unused to bend, by hard compulsion bent
His spirit to the sorrow of the time;
And all along a dismal rack of clouds,
Upon the boundaries of day and night,
He stretched himself in grief and radiance faint.
There as he lay, the Heaven with its stars
Looked down on him with pity, and the voice
Of Coelus, from the universal space,
Thus whispered low and solemn in his ear.
'O brightest of my children dear, earth-born
310   And sky-engendered, Son of Mysteries
All unrevealèd even to the powers
Which met at thy creating; at whose joys
And palpitations sweet, and pleasures soft,
I, Coelus, wonder, how they came and whence;
And at the fruits thereof what shapes they be,
Distinct, and visible; symbols divine,

colure a great circle on the celestial sphere   swart dark, dusky
passing through the poles and the equinoxes or   argent silver
solstices

Manifestations of that beauteous life
Diffused unseen throughout eternal space:
Of these new-formed art thou, oh brightest child!
320   Of these, thy brethren and the Goddesses!
There is sad feud among ye, and rebellion
Of son against his sire. I saw him fall,
I saw my first-born° tumbled from his throne!
To me his arms were spread, to me his voice
Found way from forth the thunders round his head!
Pale wox I, and in vapours hid my face.
Art thou, too, near such doom? Vague fear there is:
For I have seen my sons most unlike Gods.
Divine ye were created, and divine
330   In sad demeanour, solemn, undisturbed,
Unruffled, like high Gods, ye lived and ruled:
Now I behold in you fear, hope, and wrath;
Actions of rage and passion; even as
I see them, on the mortal world beneath,
In men who die.—This is the grief, O Son!
Sad sign of ruin, sudden dismay, and fall!
Yet do thou strive; as thou art capable,
As thou canst move about, an evident God;
And canst oppose to each malignant hour
340   Ethereal presence:—I am but a voice;
My life is but the life of winds and tides,
No more than winds and tides can I avail:—
But thou canst.—Be thou therefore in the van
Of circumstance; yea, seize the arrow's barb
Before the tense string murmur.—To the earth!
For there thou wilt find Saturn, and his woes.
Meantime I will keep watch on thy bright sun,
And of thy seasons be a careful nurse.'—
Ere half this region-whisper had come down,
350   Hyperion arose, and on the stars
Lifted his curvèd lids, and kept them wide
Until it ceased; and still he kept them wide:
And still they were the same bright, patient stars.
Then with a slow incline of his broad breast,
Like to a diver in the pearly seas,
Forward he stooped over the airy shore,
And plunged all noiseless into the deep night.

Book II
Just at the self-same beat of Time's wide wings
Hyperion slid into the rustled air,
And Saturn gained with Thea that sad place

first-born Saturn

Where Cybele° and the bruisèd Titans mourned.
It was a den where no insulting light
Could glimmer on their tears; where their own groans
They felt, but heard not, for the solid roar
Of thunderous waterfalls and torrents hoarse,
Pouring a constant bulk, uncertain where.
10 Crag jutting forth to crag, and rocks that seemed
Ever as if just rising from a sleep,
Forehead to forehead held their monstrous horns;
And thus in thousand hugest phantasies
Made a fit roofing to this nest of woe.
Instead of thrones, hard flint they sat upon,
Couches of rugged stone, and slaty ridge
Stubborned with iron. All were not assembled:
Some chained in torture, and some wandering.
Coeus, and Gyges, and Briareus,
20 Typhon, and Dolor, and Porphyrion,°
With many more, the brawniest in assault,
Were pent in regions of laborious breath;
Dungeoned in opaque element, to keep
Their clenchèd teeth still clenched, and all their limbs
Locked up like veins of metal, cramped and screwed;
Without a motion, save of their big hearts
Heaving in pain, and horribly convulsed
With sanguine feverous boiling gurge° of pulse.
Mnemosyne° was straying in the world;
30 Far from her moon had Phoebe° wanderèd;
And many else were free to roam abroad,
But for the main, here found they covert drear.
Scarce images of life, one here, one there,
Lay vast and edgeways; like a dismal cirque°
Of Druid stones, upon a forlorn moor,
When the chill rain begins at shut of eve,
In dull November, and their chancel vault,
The Heaven itself, is blinded throughout night.
Each one kept shroud, nor to his neighbour gave
40 Or word, or look, or action of despair.
Creus was one; his ponderous iron mace
Lay by him, and a shattered rib of rock
Told of his rage, ere he thus sank and pined.
Iapetus another; in his grasp,
A serpent's plashy° neck; its barbèd tongue

Cybele in mythology, wife of Saturn and so
mother of all the other gods
Coeus . . . Porphyrion Coeus is a Titan; Gyges
and Briareus giants with a hundred hands;
Typhon, a monster with a hundred heads;
Dolor (Latin for sorrow), a Titan created by
Keats; Porphyrion, a giant of obscure origins.

gurge whirlpool
Mnemosyne Mother of the Muses, daughter of
Coelus, her name means "Memory."
Phoebe goddess of the moon
cirque circle, ring
plashy splashed with colors

Squeezed from the gorge, and all its uncurled length
Dead; and because the creature could not spit
Its poison in the eyes of conquering Jove.
Next Cottus: prone he lay, chin uppermost,
As though in pain; for still upon the flint
He ground severe his skull, with open mouth
And eyes at horrid working. Nearest him
Asia,° born of most enormous Caf,
Who cost her mother Tellus keener pangs,
Though feminine, than any of her sons:
More thought than woe was in her dusky face,
For she was prophesying of her glory;
And in her wide imagination stood
Palm-shaded temples, and high rival fanes,
By Oxus or in Ganges' sacred isles.
Even as Hope upon her anchor leans,
So leant she, not so fair, upon a tusk
Shed from the broadest of her elephants.
Above her, on a crag's uneasy shelf,
Upon his elbow raised, all prostrate else,
Shadowed Enceladus; once tame and mild
As grazing ox unworried in the meads;
Now tiger-passioned, lion-thoughted, wroth,
He meditated, plotted, and even now
Was hurling mountains in that second war,
Not long delayed, that scared the younger Gods
To hide themselves in forms of beast and bird.
Not far hence Atlas; and beside him prone
Phorcus, the sire of Gorgons.° Neighboured close
Oceanus, and Tethys, in whose lap
Sobbed Clymene° among her tangled hair.
In midst of all lay Themis,° at the feet
Of Ops° the queen all clouded round from sight;
No shape distinguishable, more than when
Thick night confounds the pine-tops with the clouds:
And many else whose names may not be told.
For when the Muse's wings are air-ward spread,
Who shall delay her flight? And she must chaunt°
Of Saturn, and his guide, who now had climbed
With damp and slippery footing from a depth
More horrid still. Above a sombre cliff
Their heads appeared, and up their stature grew

50

60

70

80

Asia in mythology, daughter of the Titans
Oceanus and Tethys
Phorcus . . . Gorgons Phorcus is a sea god; the
Gorgons are his three daughters—Medusa being
the most famous—noted for their snaky locks
and their ability to turn people to stone with
a glance.
Clymene in mythology, daughter of Oceanus and

wife of Iapetus, but Keats seems to mean the
mother of Phaethon, as in Ovid's *Metamorphoses* II
Themis Her name means "Law"; daughter of
Coelus.
Ops another name for Cybele
chaunt chant

Till on the level height their steps found ease:
Then Thea spread abroad her trembling arms
90 Upon the precincts of this nest of pain,
And sidelong fixed her eye on Saturn's face:
There saw she direst strife; the supreme God
At war with all the frailty of grief,
Of rage, of fear, anxiety, revenge,
Remorse, spleen, hope, but most of all despair.
Against these plagues he strove in vain; for Fate
Had poured a mortal oil upon his head,°
A disanointing poison: so that Thea,
Affrighted, kept her still, and let him pass
100 First onwards in, among the fallen tribe.

As with us mortal men, the laden heart
Is persecuted more, and fevered more,
When it is nighing to the mournful house
Where other hearts are sick of the same bruise;
So Saturn, as he walked into the midst,
Felt faint, and would have sunk among the rest,
But that he met Enceladus's eye,
Whose mightiness, and awe of him, at once
Came like an inspiration; and he shouted,
110 'Titans, behold your God!' at which some groaned;
Some started on their feet; some also shouted;
Some wept, some wailed, all bowed with reverence;
And Ops, uplifting her black folded veil,
Showed her pale cheeks, and all her forehead wan,
Her eye-brows thin and jet, and hollow eyes.
There is a roaring in the bleak-grown pines
When Winter lifts his voice; there is a noise
Among immortals when a God gives sign,
With hushing finger, how he means to load
120 His tongue with the full weight of utterless thought,
With thunder, and with music, and with pomp:
Such noise is like the roar of bleak-grown pines:
Which, when it ceases in this mountained world,
No other sound succeeds; but ceasing here,
Among these fallen, Saturn's voice therefrom
Grew up like organ, that begins anew
Its strain, when other harmonies, stopped short,
Leave the dinned air vibrating silverly.
Thus grew it up—'Not in my own sad breast,
130 Which is its own great judge and searcher out,
Can I find reason why ye should be thus:
Not in the legends of the first of days,

for Fate . . . head thus making him human,
and so weaker

Studied from that old spirit-leavèd book
Which starry Uranus with finger bright
Saved from the shores of darkness, when the waves
Low-ebbed still hid it up in shallow gloom;—
And the which book ye know I ever kept
For my firm-based footstool:—Ah, infirm!
Not there, nor in sign, symbol, or portent
140   Of element, earth, water, air, and fire,—
At war, at peace, or inter-quarreling
One against one, or two, or three, or all
Each several one against the other three,
As fire with air loud warring when rain-floods
Drown both, and press them both against earth's face,
Where, finding sulphur, a quadruple wrath
Unhinges the poor world;—not in that strife,
Wherefrom I take strange lore, and read it deep,
Can I find reason why ye should be thus:
150   No, nowhere can unriddle, though I search,
And pore on Nature's universal scroll
Even to swooning, why ye, Divinities,
The first-born of all shaped and palpable Gods,
Should cower beneath what, in comparison,
Is untremendous might. Yet ye are here,
O'erwhelmed, and spurned, and battered, ye are here!
O Titans, shall I say, "Arise!"—Ye groan:
Shall I say "Crouch!"—Ye groan. What can I then?
O Heaven wide! O unseen parent dear!
160   What can I? Tell me, all ye brethren Gods,
How we can war, how engine our great wrath!
O speak your counsel now, for Saturn's ear
Is all a-hungered. Thou, Oceanus,
Ponderest high and deep; and in thy face
I see, astonied,° that severe content
Which comes of thought and musing: give us help!'

So ended Saturn; and the God of the Sea,
Sophist° and sage, from no Athenian grove,°
But cogitation in his watery shades,
170   Arose, with locks not oozy, and began,
In murmurs, which his first-endeavouring tongue
Caught infant-like from the far-foamèd sands.
'O ye, whom wrath consumes! who, passion-stung,
Writhe at defeat, and nurse your agonies!
Shut up your senses, stifle up your ears,
My voice is not a bellows unto ire.

astonied astonished
Sophist probably in a positive sense, as being
wise, yet its negative aspect of rhetorician and

casuist may suggest that Keats had some reservations as to the following speech
Athenian grove Plato's Academy

Yet listen, ye who will, whilst I bring proof
How ye, perforce, must be content to stoop:
And in the proof much comfort will I give,
180   If ye will take that comfort in its truth.
We fall by course of Nature's law, not force
Of thunder, or of Jove. Great Saturn, thou
Hast sifted well the atom-universe;
But for this reason, that thou art the King,
And only blind from sheer supremacy,
One avenue was shaded from thine eyes,
Through which I wandered to eternal truth.
And first, as thou wast not the first of powers,
So art thou not the last; it cannot be:
190   Thou art not the beginning nor the end.
From chaos and parental darkness came
Light, the first fruits of that intestine broil,
That sullen ferment, which for wondrous ends
Was ripening in itself. The ripe hour came,
And with it light, and light, engendering
Upon its own producer, forthwith touched
The whole enormous matter into life.
Upon that very hour, our parentage,
The Heavens, and the Earth, were manifest:
200   Then thou first born, and we the giant race,
Found ourselves ruling new and beauteous realms.
Now comes the pain of truth, to whom 'tis pain;
O folly! for to bear all naked truths,
And to envisage circumstance, all calm,
That is the top of sovereignty. Mark well!
As Heaven and Earth are fairer, fairer far
Than Chaos and blank Darkness, though once chiefs;
And as we show beyond that Heaven and Earth
In form and shape compact and beautiful,
210   In will, in action free, companionship,
And thousand other signs of purer life;
So on our heels a fresh perfection treads,
A power more strong in beauty, born of us
And fated to excel us, as we pass
In glory that old Darkness: nor are we
Thereby more conquered, than by us the rule
Of shapeless Chaos. Say, doth the dull soil
Quarrel with the proud forests it hath fed,
And feedeth still, more comely than itself?
220   Can it deny the chiefdom of green groves?
Or shall the tree be envious of the dove
Because it cooeth, and hath snowy wings
To wander wherewithal and find its joys?
We are such forest-trees, and our fair boughs

Have bred forth, not pale solitary doves,
But eagles golden-feathered, who do tower
Above us in their beauty, and must reign
In right thereof; for 'tis the eternal law
That first in beauty should be first in might:
230   Yea, by that law, another race may drive
Our conquerors to mourn as we do now.
Have ye beheld the young God of the Seas,°
My dispossessor? Have ye seen his face?
Have ye beheld his chariot, foamed along
By noble wingèd creatures he hath made?
I saw him on the calmèd waters scud,°
With such a glow of beauty in his eyes,
That it enforced me to bid sad farewell
To all my empire: farewell sad I took,
240   And hither came, to see how dolorous fate
Had wrought upon ye; and how I might best
Give consolation in this woe extreme.
Receive the truth, and let it be your balm.'

     Whether through pozed° conviction, or disdain,
They guarded silence, when Oceanus
Left murmuring, what deepest thought can tell?
But so it was, none answered for a space,
Save one whom none regarded, Clymene;
And yet she answered not, only complained,
250   With hectic lips, and eyes up-looking mild,
Thus wording timidly among the fierce:
'O Father, I am here the simplest voice,
And all my knowledge is that joy is gone,
And this thing woe crept in among our hearts,
There to remain forever, as I fear:
I would not bode of evil, if I thought
So weak a creature could turn off the help
Which by just right should come of mighty Gods;
Yet let me tell my sorrow, let me tell
260   Of what I heard, and how it made me weep,
And know that we had parted from all hope.
I stood upon a shore, a pleasant shore,
Where a sweet clime was breathèd from a land
Of fragrance, quietness, and trees, and flowers.
Full of calm joy it was, as I of grief;
Too full of joy and soft delicious warmth;
So that I felt a movement in my heart
To chide, and to reproach that solitude
With songs of misery, music of our woes;

God of the Seas Neptune   pozed puzzled
scud move rapidly

270 And sat me down, and took a mouthèd shell
And murmured into it, and made melody—
O melody no more! for while I sang,
And with poor skill let pass into the breeze
The dull shell's echo, from a bowery strand
Just opposite, an island of the sea,
There came enchantment with the shifting wind,
That did both drown and keep alive my ears.
I threw my shell away upon the sand,
And a wave filled it, as my sense was filled
280 With that new blissful golden melody.
A living death was in each gush of sounds,
Each family of rapturous hurried notes,
That fell, one after one, yet all at once,
Like pearl beads dropping sudden from their string:
And then another, then another strain,
Each like a dove leaving its olive perch,
With music winged instead of silent plumes,
To hover round my head, and make me sick
Of joy and grief at once. Grief overcame,
290 And I was stopping up my frantic ears,
When, past all hindrance of my trembling hands,
A voice came sweeter, sweeter than all tune,
And still it cried, "Apollo! young Apollo!
The morning-bright Apollo! young Apollo!"
I fled, it followed me, and cried "Apollo!"
O Father, and O Brethren, had ye felt
Those pains of mine; O Saturn, hadst thou felt,
Ye would not call this too indulgèd tongue
Presumptuous, in thus venturing to be heard.'

300   So far her voice flowed on, like timorous brook
That, lingering along a pebbled coast,
Doth fear to meet the sea: but sea it met,
And shuddered; for the overwhelming voice
Of huge Enceladus swallowed it in wrath:
The ponderous syllables, like sullen waves
In the half-glutted hollows of reef-rocks,
Came booming thus, while still upon his arm
He leaned; not rising, from supreme contempt.
'Or shall we listen to the over-wise,
310 Or to the over-foolish, Giant-Gods?
Not thunderbolt on thunderbolt, till all
That rebel Jove's whole armoury were spent,
Not world on world upon these shoulders piled,
Could agonize me more than baby-words
In midst of this dethronement horrible.
Speak! roar! shout! yell! ye sleepy Titans all.

Do ye forget the blows, the buffets vile?
Are ye not smitten by a youngling arm?
Dost thou forget, sham Monarch of the Waves,
320 Thy scalding in the seas? What, have I roused
Your spleens with so few simple words as these?
O joy! for now I see ye are not lost:
O joy! for now I see a thousand eyes
Wide-glaring for revenge!'—As this he said,
He lifted up his stature vast, and stood,
Still without intermission speaking thus:
'Now ye are flames, I'll tell you how to burn,
And purge the ether of our enemies;
How to feed fierce the crooked stings of fire,
330 And singe away the swollen clouds of Jove,
Stifling that puny essence in its tent.
O let him feel the evil he hath done;
For though I scorn Oceanus's lore,
Much pain have I for more than loss of realms:
The days of peace and slumberous calm are fled;
Those days, all innocent of scathing war,
When all the fair Existences of heaven
Came open-eyed to guess what we would speak:—
That was before our brows were taught to frown,
340 Before our lips knew else but solemn sounds;
That was before we knew the wingèd thing,
Victory, might be lost, or might be won.
And be ye mindful that Hyperion,
Our brightest brother, still is undisgraced—
Hyperion, lo! his radiance is here!'

All eyes were on Enceladus's face,
And they beheld, while still Hyperion's name
Flew from his lips up to the vaulted rocks,
A pallid gleam across his features stern:
350 Not savage, for he saw full many a God
Wroth as himself. He looked upon them all,
And in each face he saw a gleam of light,
But splendider in Saturn's, whose hoar locks
Shone like the bubbling foam about a keel
When the prow sweeps into a midnight cove.
In pale and silver silence they remained,
Till suddenly a splendour, like the morn,
Pervaded all the beetling gloomy steeps,
All the sad spaces of oblivion,
360 And every gulf, and every chasm old,
And every height, and every sullen depth,
Voiceless, or hoarse with loud tormented streams:
And all the everlasting cataracts,

And all the headlong torrents far and near,
Mantled before in darkness and huge shade,
Now saw the light and made it terrible.
It was Hyperion:—a granite peak
His bright feet touched, and there he stayed to view
The misery his brilliance had betrayed
370 To the most hateful seeing of itself.
Golden his hair of short Numidian curl,
Regal his shape majestic, a vast shade
In midst of his own brightness, like the bulk
Of Memnon's image at the set of sun
To one who travels from the dusking East:
Sighs, too, as mournful as that Memnon's harp°
He uttered, while his hands contemplative
He pressed together, and in silence stood.
Despondence seized again the fallen Gods
380 At sight of the dejected King of Day,
And many hid their faces from the light: ʼ
But fierce Enceladus sent forth his eyes
Among the brotherhood; and, at their glare,
Uprose Iapetus, and Creus too,
And Phorcus, sea-born, and together strode
To where he towered on his eminence.
There those four shouted forth old Saturn's name;
Hyperion from the peak loud answered, 'Saturn!'
Saturn sat near the Mother of the Gods,°
390 In whose face was no joy, though all the Gods
Gave from their hollow throats the name of 'Saturn!'

    Book III
Thus in alternate uproar and sad peace,
Amazèd were those Titans utterly.
O leave them, Muse! O leave them to their woes;
For thou art weak to sing such tumults dire:
A solitary sorrow best befits
Thy lips, and antheming a lonely grief.
Leave them, O Muse! for thou anon wilt find
Many a fallen old Divinity
Wandering in vain about bewildered shores.
10 Meantime touch piously the Delphic harp,
And not a wind of heaven but will breathe
In aid soft warble from the Dorian flute;°
For lo! 'tis for the Father of all verse.°
Flush every thing that hath a vermeil hue,

Memnon's harp Memnon, son of Aurora and
Tithonus, was a mythical king of Ethiopia slain
by Achilles; his statue, in the Egyptian city of
Thebes, made mourning sounds when touched
by the rising and setting sun.

Mother of the Gods Cybele
Dorian flute See *Paradise Lost* I.550–51, for
Keats's thematic reference.
Father . . . verse Apollo

Let the rose glow intense and warm the air,
And let the clouds of even and of morn
Float in voluptuous fleeces o'er the hills;
Let the red wine within the goblet boil,
Cold as a bubbling well; let faint-lipped shells,
20 On sands, or in great deeps, vermilion turn
Through all their labyrinths; and let the maid
Blush keenly, as with some warm kiss surprised.
Chief isle of the embowered Cyclades,
Rejoice, O Delos,° with thine olives green,
And poplars, and lawn-shading palms, and beech,
In which the Zephyr breathes the loudest song,
And hazels thick, dark-stemmed beneath the shade:
Apollo is once more the golden theme!
Where was he, when the Giant of the Sun
30 Stood bright, amid the sorrow of his peers?
Together had he left his mother° fair
And his twin-sister° sleeping in their bower,
And in the morning twilight wandered forth
Beside the osiers of a rivulet,
Full ankle-deep in lilies of the vale.
The nightingale had ceased, and a few stars
Were lingering in the heavens, while the thrush
Began calm-throated. Throughout all the isle
There was no covert, no retired cave
40 Unhaunted by the murmurous noise of waves,
Though scarcely heard in many a green recess.
He listened, and he wept, and his bright tears
Went trickling down the golden bow he held.
Thus with half-shut suffusèd eyes he stood,
While from beneath some cumbrous boughs hard by
With solemn step an awful Goddess° came,
And there was purport in her looks for him,
Which he with eager guess began to read
Perplexed, the while melodiously he said:
50 'How cam'st thou over the unfooted sea?
Oh hath that antique mien and robèd form
Moved in these vales invisible till now?
Sure I have heard those vestments sweeping o'er
The fallen leaves, when I have sat alone
In cool mid-forest. Surely I have traced
The rustle of those ample skirts about
These grassy solitudes, and seen the flowers
Lift up their heads, as still the whisper passed.
Goddess! I have beheld those eyes before,

Delos small, sacred island, the birthplace of
Apollo; it is one of a group of islands in the
Aegean known as the Cyclades

mother Leto
twin-sister Diana
Goddess Mnemosyne

60   And their eternal calm, and all that face,
      Or I have dreamed.'—'Yes,' said the supreme shape,
      Thou hast dreamed of me; and awaking up
      Didst find a lyre all golden by thy side,
      Whose strings touched by thy fingers, all the vast
      Unwearied ear of the whole universe
      Listened in pain and pleasure at the birth
      Of such new tuneful wonder. Is't not strange
      That thou shouldst weep, so gifted? Tell me, youth,
      What sorrow thou canst feel; for I am sad
70   When thou dost shed a tear: explain thy griefs
      To one who in this lonely isle hath been
      The watcher of thy sleep and hours of life,
      From the young day when first thy infant hand
      Plucked witless the weak flowers, till thine arm
      Could bend that bow heroic to all times.
      Show thy heart's secret to an ancient Power
      Who hath forsaken old and sacred thrones
      For prophecies of thee, and for the sake
      Of loveliness new born.'—Apollo then,
80   With sudden scrutiny and gloomless eyes,
      Thus answered, while his white melodious throat
      Throbbed with the syllables.—'Mnemosyne!
      Thy name is on my tongue, I know not how;
      Why should I tell thee what thou so well seest?
      Why should I strive to show what from thy lips
      Would come no mystery? For me, dark, dark,
      And painful vile oblivion seals my eyes:
      I strive to search wherefore I am so sad,
      Until a melancholy numbs my limbs;
90   And then upon the grass I sit, and moan,
      Like one who once had wings.—O why should I
      Feel cursed and thwarted, when the liegeless air
      Yields to my step aspirant? Why should I
      Spurn the green turf as hateful to my feet?
      Goddess benign, point forth some unknown thing:
      Are there not other regions than this isle?
      What are the stars? There is the sun, the sun!
      And the most patient brilliance of the moon!
      And stars by thousands! Point me out the way
100   To any one particular beauteous star,
      And I will flit into it with my lyre
      And make its silvery splendour pant with bliss.
      I have heard the cloudy thunder: Where is power?
      Whose hand, whose essence, what divinity
      Makes this alarum in the elements,
      While I here idle listen on the shores
      In fearless yet in aching ignorance?

O tell me, lonely Goddess, by thy harp,
That waileth every morn and eventide,
110 Tell me why thus I rave, about these groves!
Mute thou remainest—mute! Yet I can read
A wondrous lesson in thy silent face:
Knowledge enormous makes a God of me.
Names, deeds, grey legends, dire events, rebellions,
Majesties, sovereign voices, agonies,
Creations and destroyings, all at once
Pour into the wide hollows of my brain,
And deify me, as if some blithe wine
Or bright elixir peerless I had drunk,
120 And so become immortal.'—Thus the God,
While his enkindled eyes, with level glance
Beneath his white soft temples, stedfast kept
Trembling with light upon Mnemosyne.
Soon wild commotions shook him, and made flush
All the immortal fairness of his limbs;
Most like the struggle at the gate of death;
Or liker still to one who should take leave
Of pale immortal death, and with a pang
As hot as death's is chill, with fierce convulse
130 Die into life:° so young Apollo anguished:
His very hair, his golden tresses famed
Kept undulation round his eager neck.
During the pain Mnemosyne upheld
Her arms as one who prophesied.—At length
Apollo shrieked;—and lo! from all his limbs
Celestial   *   *   *   *   *   *   *
*   *   *   *   *   *   *   *

THE END
1818–19   1820

The Eve of St. Agnes°

I

St. Agnes' Eve—Ah, bitter chill it was!
The owl, for all his feathers, was a-cold;
The hare limped trembling through the frozen grass,
And silent was the flock in woolly fold:

Die into life hardly in the Christian or Pauline sense, which is a paradoxical one; probably it means "to become a poet"
The Eve of St. Agnes By superstition, a girl may have a vision of her future husband on St. Agnes's Eve (January 20), if she performs the proper magical rituals. Using the Spenserian stanza, Keats writes a Spenserian version of *Romeo and Juliet,* but with a romantic and happy ending; though St. Agnes is the patroness of virgins, Keats seems happily skeptical in this poem as to her influence.

Numb were the Beadsman's° fingers, while he told
His rosary, and while his frosted breath,
Like pious incense from a censer old,
Seemed taking flight for heaven, without a death,
Past the sweet Virgin's picture, while his prayer he saith.

II

His prayer he saith, this patient, holy man;
Then takes his lamp, and riseth from his knees,
And back returneth, meagre, barefoot, wan,
Along the chapel aisle by slow degrees:
The sculptured dead, on each side, seem to freeze,
Imprisoned in black, purgatorial rails:
Knights, ladies, praying in dumb orat'ries,°
He passeth by; and his weak spirit fails
To think how they may ache in icy hoods and mails.

III

Northward he turneth through a little door,
And scarce three steps, ere Music's golden tongue
Flattered to tears this aged man and poor;
But no—already had his deathbell rung:
The joys of all his life were said and sung:
His was harsh penance on St. Agnes' Eve:
Another way he went, and soon among
Rough ashes sat he for his soul's reprieve,
And all night kept awake, for sinners' sake to grieve.

IV

That ancient Beadsman heard the prelude soft;
And so it chanced, for many a door was wide,
From hurry to and fro. Soon, up aloft,
The silver, snarling trumpets 'gan to chide:
The level chambers, ready with their pride,
Were glowing to receive a thousand guests:
The carvèd angels, ever eager-eyed,
Stared, where upon their heads the cornice rests,
With hair blown back, and wings put cross-wise on their breasts.

V

At length burst in the argent° revelry,
With plume, tiara, and all rich array,
Numerous as shadows haunting faerily
The brain, new stuffed, in youth, with triumphs gay

10

20

30

40

Beadsman's A beadsman was a pauper paid to
pray for one, the reference being to the beads
of his rosary.

orat'ries oratories, chapels
argent silver

Of old romance. These let us wish away,
And turn, sole-thoughted, to one Lady there,
Whose heart had brooded, all that wintry day,
On love, and winged St. Agnes' saintly care,
As she had heard old dames full many times declare.

VI

They told her how, upon St. Agnes' Eve,
Young virgins might have visions of delight,
And soft adorings from their loves receive
Upon the honeyed middle of the night,
If ceremonies due they did aright;
As, supperless to bed they must retire,
And couch supine their beauties, lilly white;
Nor look behind, nor sideways, but require
Of Heaven with upward eyes for all that they desire.

VII

Full of this whim was thoughtful Madeline:
The music, yearning like a God in pain,
She scarcely heard: her maiden eyes divine,
Fixed on the floor, saw many a sweeping train°
Pass by—she heeded not at all: in vain
Came many a tiptoe, amorous cavalier,
And back retired; not cooled by high disdain,
But she saw not: her heart was otherwhere:
She sighed for Agnes' dreams, the sweetest of the year.

VIII

She danced along with vague, regardless eyes,
Anxious her lips, her breathing quick and short:
The hallowed hour was near at hand: she sighs
Amid the timbrels,° and the thronged resort
Of whisperers in anger, or in sport;
'Mid looks of love, defiance, hate, and scorn,
Hoodwinked° with faery fancy; all amort,°
Save to St. Agnes and her lambs unshorn,°
And all the bliss to be before tomorrow morn.

IX

So, purposing each moment to retire,
She lingered still. Meantime, across the moors,
Had come young Porphyro, with heart on fire
For Madeline. Beside the portal doors,

50
60
70

train skirts sweeping the floor
timbrels snare drums
hoodwinked blinded
amort as if dead

unshorn On St. Agnes's Day, two lambs were
offered at the altar during Mass, their wool later
being spun and woven by nuns.

Buttressed from moonlight, stands he, and implores
All saints to give him sight of Madeline,
But for one moment in the tedious hours,
80   That he might gaze and worship all unseen;
Perchance speak, kneel, touch, kiss—in sooth such things have been.

X

He ventures in: let no buzzed whisper tell:
All eyes be muffled, or a hundred swords
Will storm his heart, Love's feverous citadel:
For him, those chambers held barbarian hordes,
Hyena foemen, and hot-blooded lords,
Whose very dogs would execrations howl
Against his lineage: not one breast affords
Him any mercy, in that mansion foul,
90   Save one old beldame,° weak in body and in soul.

XI

Ah, happy chance! the aged creature came,
Shuffling along with ivory-headed wand,
To where he stood, hid from the torch's flame,
Behind a broad hall-pillar, far beyond
The sound of merriment and chorus bland:
He startled her; but soon she knew his face,
And grasped his fingers in her palsied hand,
Saying, 'Mercy, Porphyro! hie thee from this place:
They are all here tonight, the whole blood-thirsty race!

XII

100   'Get hence! get hence! there's dwarfish Hildebrand;
He had a fever late, and in the fit
He cursed thee and thine, both house and land:
Then there's that old Lord Maurice, not a whit
More tame for his grey hairs—Alas me! flit!
Flit like a ghost away.'—'Ah, Gossip dear,
We're safe enough; here in this arm-chair sit,
And tell me how'—'Good Saints! not here, not here;
Follow me, child, or else these stones will be thy bier.'

XIII

He followed through a lowly archèd way,
110   Brushing the cobwebs with his lofty plume,
And as she muttered 'Well-a—well-a-day!'
He found him in a little moonlight room,
Pale, latticed, chill, and silent as a tomb.
'Now tell me where is Madeline,' said he,

beldame old woman, hag

'O tell me, Angela, by the holy loom
  Which none but secret sisterhood may see,
When they St. Agnes' wool are weaving piously.'

XIV

'St. Agnes! Ah! it is St. Agnes' Eve—
  Yet men will murder upon holy days:
120 Thou must hold water in a witch's sieve,°
  And be liege-lord of all the Elves and Fays,
  To venture so: it fills me with amaze
  To see thee, Porphyro!—St. Agnes' Eve!
  God's help! my lady fair the conjuror plays
  This very night: good angels her deceive!
But let me laugh awhile, I've mickle° time to grieve.'

XV

Feebly she laugheth in the languid moon,
  While Porphyro upon her face doth look,
  Like puzzled urchin on an aged crone
130 Who keepeth closed a wondrous riddle-book,
  As spectacled she sits in chimney nook.
  But soon his eyes grew brilliant, when she told
  His lady's purpose; and he scarce could brook
  Tears, at the thought of those enchantments cold,
And Madeline asleep in lap of legends old.

XVI

Sudden a thought came like a full-blown rose,
  Flushing his brow, and in his pained heart
  Made purple riot: then doth he propose
  A stratagem, that makes the beldame start:
140 'A cruel man and impious thou art:
  Sweet lady, let her pray, and sleep, and dream
  Alone with her good angels, far apart
  From wicked men like thee. Go, go!—I deem
Thou canst not surely be the same that thou didst seem.'

XVII

'I will not harm her, by all saints I swear,'
  Quoth Porphyro: 'O may I ne'er find grace
  When my weak voice shall whisper its last prayer,
  If one of her soft ringlets I displace,
  Or look with ruffian passion in her face:
150 Good Angela, believe me by these tears;
  Or I will, even in a moment's space,
  Awake, with horrid shout, my foemen's ears,
And beard them, though they be more fanged than wolves and bears.'

sieve bewitched so as to hold water   **mickle** much

XVIII

'Ah! why wilt thou affright a feeble soul?
A poor, weak, palsy-stricken, churchyard thing,
Whose passing-bell may ere the midnight toll;
Whose prayers for thee, each morn and evening,
Were never missed.'—Thus plaining, doth she bring
A gentler speech from burning Porphyro;
160 So woful, and of such deep sorrowing,
That Angela gives promise she will do
Whatever he shall wish, betide her weal or woe.

XIX

Which was, to lead him, in close secrecy,
Even to Madeline's chamber, and there hide
Him in a closet, of such privacy
That he might see her beauty unespied,
And win perhaps that night a peerless bride,
While legioned faeries paced the coverlet,
And pale enchantment held her sleepy-eyed.
170 Never on such a night have lovers met,
Since Merlin paid his Demon all the monstrous debt.°

XX

'It shall be as thou wishest,' said the Dame:
'All cates° and dainties shall be stored there
Quickly on this feast-night: by the tambour frame°
Her own lute thou wilt see: no time to spare,
For I am slow and feeble, and scarce dare
On such a catering trust my dizzy head.
Wait here, my child, with patience; kneel in prayer
The while: Ah! thou must needs the lady wed,
180 Or may I never leave my grave among the dead.'—

XXI

So saying, she hobbled off with busy fear.
. The lover's endless minutes slowly passed;
The dame returned, and whispered in his ear
To follow her; with aged eyes aghast
From fright of dim espial. Safe at last,
Through many a dusky gallery, they gain
The maiden's chamber, silken, hushed, and chaste;
Where Porphyro took covert, pleased amain.°
His poor guide hurried back with agues in her brain.

Since . . . debt The Demon presumably was
the temptress Vivien, who trapped Merlin after
coaxing his spells from him.
cates delicacies

tambour frame drum-shaped frame for embroidery
amain exceedingly

XXII

190 Her faltering hand upon the balustrade,
Old Angela was feeling for the stair,
When Madeline, St. Agnes' charmèd maid,
Rose, like a missioned spirit, unaware:
With silver taper's light, and pious care,
She turned, and down the aged gossip led
To a safe level matting. Now prepare,
Young Porphyro, for gazing on that bed;
She comes, she comes again, like ring-dove frayed° and fled.

XXIII

Out went the taper as she hurried in;
200 Its little smoke, in pallid moonshine, died:
She closed the door, she panted, all akin
To spirits of the air, and visions wide:
No uttered syllable, or, woe betide!
But to her heart, her heart was voluble,
Paining with eloquence her balmy side;
As though a tongueless nightingale should swell
Her throat in vain, and die, heart-stifled, in her dell.

XXIV

A casement high and triple-arched there was,
All garlanded with carven imag'ries
210 Of fruits, and flowers, and bunches of knot-grass,
And diamonded with panes of quaint device,
Innumerable of stains and splendid dyes,
As are the tiger-moth's deep-damasked wings;
And in the midst, 'mong thousand heraldries,
And twilight saints, and dim emblazonings,
A shielded scutcheon blushed with blood of queens and kings.

XXV

Full on this casement shone the wintry moon,
And threw warm gules° on Madeline's fair breast,
As down she knelt for heaven's grace and boon;
220 Rose-bloom fell on her hands, together pressed,
And on her silver cross soft amethyst,
And on her hair a glory, like a saint:
She seemed a splendid angel, newly dressed,
Save wings, for heaven:—Porphyro grew faint:
She knelt, so pure a thing, so free from mortal taint.

XXVI

Anon his heart revives: her vespers done,
Of all its wreathèd pearls her hair she frees;

frayed frightened   gules the heraldic name for red

Unclasps her warmèd jewels one by one;
Loosens her fragrant bodice; by degrees
230   Her rich attire creeps rustling to her knees:
Half-hidden, like a mermaid in sea-weed,
Pensive awhile she dreams awake, and sees,
In fancy, fair St. Agnes in her bed,
But dares not look behind, or all the charm is fled.

       XXVII
Soon, trembling in her soft and chilly nest,
In sort of wakeful swoon, perplexed she lay,
Until the poppied warmth of sleep oppressed
Her soothèd limbs, and soul fatigued away;
Flown, like a thought, until the morrow-day;
240   Blissfully havened both from joy and pain;
Clasped like a missal where swart Paynims pray;°
Blinded alike from sunshine and from rain,
As though a rose should shut, and be a bud again.

       XXVIII
Stol'n to this paradise, and so entranced,
Porphyro gazed upon her empty dress,
And listened to her breathing, if it chanced
To wake into a slumberous tenderness;
Which when he heard, that minute did he bless,
And breathed himself: then from the closet crept,
250   Noiseless as fear° in a wide wilderness,
And over the hushed carpet, silent, stepped,
And 'tween the curtains peeped, where, lo!—how fast she slept.

       XXIX
Then by the bed-side, where the faded moon
Made a dim, silver twilight, soft he set
A table, and, half anguished, threw thereon
A cloth of woven crimson, gold, and jet:—
O for some drowsy Morphean° amulet!
The boisterous, midnight, festive clarion,
The kettle-drum, and far-heard clarinet,
260   Affray his ears, though but in dying tone:—
The hall door shuts again, and all the noise is gone.

       XXX
And still she slept an azure-lidded sleep,
In blanchèd linen, smooth, and lavendered,
While he from forth the closet brought a heap
Of candied apple, quince, and plum, and gourd;

Clasped . . . pray kept shut as a Christian
prayer book would be where pagans pray

fear frightened person
Morphean pertaining to the god of sleep

With jellies soother° than the creamy curd,
And lucent syrups, tinct° with cinnamon;
Manna and dates, in argosy transferred
From Fez;° and spiced dainties, every one,
270   From silken Samarcand° to cedared Lebanon.

XXXI

These delicates he heaped with glowing hand
On golden dishes and in baskets bright
Of wreathed silver: sumptuous they stand
In the retired quiet of the night,
Filling the chilly room with perfume light.—
'And now, my love, my seraph fair, awake!
Thou art my heaven, and I thine eremite:°
Open thine eyes, for meek St. Agnes' sake,
Or I shall drowse beside thee, so my soul doth ache.'

XXXII

280   Thus whispering, his warm, unnervèd arm
Sank in her pillow. Shaded was her dream
By the dusk curtains:—'twas a midnight charm
Impossible to melt as icèd stream:
The lustrous salvers in the moonlight gleam;
Broad golden fringe upon the carpet lies:
It seemed he never, never could redeem
From such a stedfast spell his lady's eyes;
So mused awhile, entoiled in woofèd° phantasies.

XXXIII

Awakening up, he took her hollow lute,—
290   Tumultuous,—and, in chords that tenderest be,
He played an ancient ditty, long since mute,
In Provence called, 'La belle dame sans merci:'°
Close to her ear touching the melody;—
Wherewith disturbed, she uttered a soft moan:
He ceased—she panted quick—and suddenly
Her blue affrayèd eyes wide open shone:
Upon his knees he sank, pale as smooth-sculptured stone.

XXXIV

Her eyes were open, but she still beheld,
Now wide awake, the vision of her sleep:
300   There was a painful change, that nigh expelled
The blisses of her dream so pure and deep

soother smoother
tinct tinctured
Fez commercial city in northern Morocco
Samarcand today a city in southern Russia, and
still noted for its silks

eremite hermit, usually has religious connotations
woofèd woven
'La belle . . . merci' poem by Alain Chartier,
medieval French poet, as well as a poem by
Keats (see below)

At which fair Madeline began to weep,
And moan forth witless words with many a sigh;
While still her gaze on Porphyro would keep;
Who knelt, with joinèd hands and piteous eye,
Fearing to move or speak, she looked so dreamingly.

XXXV

'Ah, Porphyro!' said she, 'but even now
Thy voice was at sweet tremble in mine ear,
Made tuneable with every sweetest vow;
And those sad eyes were spiritual and clear:
How changed thou art! how pallid, chill, and drear!
Give me that voice again, my Porphyro,
Those looks immortal, those complainings dear!
Oh leave me not in this eternal woe,
For if thou diest, my Love, I know not where to go.'

XXXVI

Beyond a mortal man impassioned far
At these voluptuous accents, he arose,
Ethereal, flushed, and like a throbbing star
Seen mid the sapphire heaven's deep repose;
Into her dream he melted, as the rose
Blendeth its odour with the violet,—
Solution sweet: meantime the frost-wind blows
Like Love's alarum pattering the sharp sleet
Against the window-panes; St. Agnes' moon hath set.

XXXVII

'Tis dark: quick pattereth the flaw-blown° sleet:
'This is no dream, my bride, my Madeline!'
'Tis dark: the icèd gusts still rave and beat:
'No dream, alas! alas! and woe is mine!
Porphyro will leave me here to fade and pine.—
Cruel! what traitor could thee hither bring?
I curse not, for my heart is lost in thine,
Though thou forsakest a deceivèd thing;—
A dove forlorn and lost with sick unprunèd wing.'

XXXVIII

'My Madeline! sweet dreamer! lovely bride!
Say, may I be for aye thy vassal blest?
Thy beauty's shield, heart-shaped and vermeil° dyed?
Ah, silver shrine, here will I take my rest
After so many hours of toil and quest,
A famished pilgrim,—saved by miracle.

310

320

330

---

flaw-blown gust-blown   **vermeil** vermilion

340   Though I have found, I will not rob thy nest
         Saving of thy sweet self; if thou thinkest well
       To trust, fair Madeline, to no rude infidel.

                  XXXIX
         'Hark! 'tis an elfin-storm from faery land,
         Of haggard° seeming, but a boon indeed:
         Arise—arise! the morning is at hand;—
         The bloated wassaillers will never heed:—
         Let us away, my love, with happy speed;
         There are no ears to hear, or eyes to see,—
         Drowned all in Rhenish° and the sleepy mead:°
350   Awake! arise! my love, and fearless be,
       For o'er the southern moors I have a home for thee.'

                  XL
         She hurried at his words, beset with fears,
         For there were sleeping dragons all around,
         At glaring watch, perhaps, with ready spears—
         Down the wide stairs a darkling way they found.—
         In all the house was heard no human sound.
         A chain-drooped lamp was flickering by each door;
         The arras,° rich with horseman, hawk, and hound,
         Fluttered in the besieging wind's uproar;
360   And the long carpets rose along the gusty floor.

                  XLI
         They glide, like phantoms, into the wide hall;
         Like phantoms, to the iron porch, they glide;
         Where lay the Porter, in uneasy sprawl,
         With a huge empty flagon by his side:
         The wakeful bloodhound rose, and shook his hide,
         But his sagacious eye an inmate owns:
         By one, and one, the bolts full easy slide:—
         The chains lie silent on the footworn stones;—
       The key turns, and the door upon its hinges groans.

                  XLII
370   And they are gone: aye, ages long ago
         These lovers fled away into the storm.
         That night the Baron dreamt of many a woe,
         And all his warrior-guests, with shade and form
         Of witch, and demon, and large coffin-worm,
         Were long be-nightmared. Angela the old
         Died palsy-twitched, with meagre face deform;

  haggard wild   **mead** fermented liquor, made of malt and honey
  Rhenish Rhine wine   **arras** tapestry

The Beadsman, after thousand aves° told,
For aye unsought for slept among his ashes cold.
1819   1820

La Belle Dame Sans Merci°

A Ballad

O, what can ail thee, knight-at-arms,
    Alone and palely loitering?
The sedge has withered from the lake,
    And no birds sing.

O, what can ail thee, knight-at-arms,
    So haggard and so woe-begone?
The squirrel's granary is full,
    And the harvest's done.

10 I see a lily on thy brow,
    With anguish moist and fever dew;
And on thy cheeks a fading rose
    Fast withereth too.

I met a lady in the meads,
    Full beautiful—a faery's child,
Her hair was long, her foot was light,
    And her eyes were wild.°

I made a garland for her head,
    And bracelets too, and fragrant zone;°
She looked at me as she did love,
20   And made sweet moan.

I set her on my pacing steed,
    And nothing else saw all day long;
For sidelong would she bend, and sing
    A faery's song.

She found me roots of relish sweet,
    And honey wild, and manna dew,°
And sure in language strange she said—
    'I love thee true.'

She took me to her elfin grot,
30   And there she wept and sighed full sore,

---

aves Hail Marys (Ave Maria)
La Belle Dame Sans Merci The title, which
means "The Beautiful Lady Without Pity," is
taken from a medieval poem by Alain Chartier,
but the lady of this poem is not so much without pity as unable to make herself understood by
the infatuated knight, since they speak different
languages; the poem is complex and perhaps
deliberately confused, since the lady combines
aspects of two absolutely opposing Spenserian
ladies, the whore Duessa and the Faerie Queene
herself.
And . . . wild See Wordsworth's lyric "Her
Eyes Are Wild."
zone girdle
And honey . . . dew See Coleridge's Kubla
Khan, l. 53.

And there I shut her wild wild eyes
  With kisses four.

And there she lullèd me asleep
  And there I dreamed—Ah! woe betide!
The latest dream I ever dreamed
  On the cold hill side.

I saw pale kings and princes too,
  Pale warriors, death-pale were they all;
40 They cried—'La Belle Dame sans Merci
  Hath thee in thrall!'

I saw their starved lips in the gloam,
  With horrid warning gapèd wide,
And I awoke and found me here,
  On the cold hill's side.

And this is why I sojourn here
  Alone and palely loitering,
Though the sedge has withered from the lake,
  And no birds sing.
  1819   1820

On the Sonnet°

If by dull rhymes our English must be chained,
And, like Andromeda,° the Sonnet sweet
Fettered, in spite of painèd loveliness,
Let us find out, if we must be constrained,
Sandals more interwoven and complete
To fit the naked foot of Poesy:
Let us inspect the Lyre, and weigh the stress
Of every chord, and see what may be gained
By ear industrious, and attention meet;
10 Misers of sound and syllable, no less
Than Midas° of his coinage, let us be
Jealous of dead leaves in the bay wreath crown;
So, if we may not let the Muse be free,
She will be bound with garlands of her own.
  1819   1848

Ode to Psyche°

O Goddess! hear these tuneless numbers, wrung
    By sweet enforcement and remembrance dear,
And pardon that thy secrets should be sung
    Even into thine own soft-conchèd° ear:
Surely I dreamt today, or did I see
    The wingèd Psyche with awakened eyes?°
I wandered in a forest thoughtlessly,
    And, on the sudden, fainting with surprise,
Saw two fair creatures, couchèd side by side°
10   In deepest grass, beneath the whispering roof
    Of leaves and trembled blossoms, where there ran
        A brooklet, scarce espied:

'Mid hushed, cool-rooted flowers, fragrant-eyed,
    Blue, silver-white, and budded Tyrian,°
They lay calm-breathing on the bedded grass;
    Their arms embracèd, and their pinions too;
    Their lips touched not, but had not bade adieu,
As if disjoinèd by soft-handed slumber,
And ready still past kisses to outnumber
20   At tender eye-dawn of aurorean love:
        The wingèd boy I knew;
But who wast thou, O happy, happy dove?
        His Psyche true!

O latest born and loveliest vision far
    Of all Olympus' faded hierarchy!
Fairer than Phoebe's° sapphire-regioned star,
    Or Vesper,° amorous glow-worm of the sky;
Fairer than these, though temple thou hast none,
    Nor altar heaped with flowers;
30 Nor virgin-choir to make delicious moan
        Upon the midnight hours;
No voice, no lute, no pipe, no incense sweet
    From chain-swung censer teeming;

Ode to Psyche This first of the great odes (written during the month April 20–May 20, 1819) is addressed to a goddess largely of Keat's own creation. W. J. Bate interprets her as the "inner life," which one could amend to the "inner life-in-love," or the internalized quest turned outward again by the impulse of sharing. The Hellenistic Psyche (for her story see *The Golden Ass* by Apuleius, Latin author of the 2nd century A.D.) was a mortal with whom Cupid or Eros fell in love. Fearing the wrath of his mother Venus, he visited Psyche only in darkness, until the naturally curious girl exposed him by the sudden lighting of a torch (see the poem's last stanza). After separation and suffering, Cupid and Psyche were reunited among the gods, with Psyche made immortal. Keats begins his poem by bringing the reunited lovers down to earth, and proceeds to declare himself Psyche's priest. In this declaration, he writes a manifesto for his imagination, and begins his major poetry. See his journal-letter of February–May 1819, to George and Georgiana Keats.
soft-conchèd shaped like a soft shell
awakened eyes See Spenser's *Amoretti* LXXVII: "Was it a dreame, or did I see it playne . . . ?"
side by side See *Paradise Lost* IV.741, 790.
Tyrian famous purple-blue dye of ancient Tyre; see Browning's poem on Keats, "Popularity"
Phoebe's the moon, Diana
Vesper the Evening Star, Hesperus

537

No shrine, no grove, no oracle, no heat
   Of pale-mouthed prophet dreaming.

O brightest! though too late for antique vows,
   Too, too late for the fond° believing lyre,
When holy were the haunted forest boughs,
   Holy the air, the water, and the fire;
40   Yet even in these days so far retired
      From happy pieties, thy lucent fans,°
   Fluttering among the faint Olympians,
I see, and sing, by my own eyes inspired.
So let me be thy choir, and make a moan
      Upon the midnight hours;
Thy voice, thy lute, thy pipe, thy incense sweet
   From swingèd censer teeming;
Thy shrine, thy grove, thy oracle, thy heat
   Of pale-mouthed prophet dreaming.

50   Yes, I will be thy priest, and build a fane°
   In some untrodden region of my mind,°
Where branchèd thoughts, new grown with pleasant pain,
   Instead of pines shall murmur in the wind:
Far, far around shall those dark-clustered trees
   Fledge the wild-ridgèd mountains steep by steep;
And there by zephyrs, streams, and birds, and bees,
   The moss-lain Dryads° shall be lulled to sleep;
And in the midst of this wide quietness
   A rosy sanctuary will I dress
60   With the wreathed trellis of a working brain,
   With buds, and bells, and stars without a name,
With all the gardener Fancy e'er could feign,
   Who breeding flowers, will never breed the same:
And there shall be for thee all soft delight
   That shadowy thought can win,
A bright torch, and a casement ope° at night,
   To let the warm Love in!
   1819   1820

Ode to a Nightingale

I

My heart aches, and a drowsy numbness pains
   My sense, as though of hemlock° I had drunk,

fond probably has both the older meaning of
"foolish" and the modern one of "affectionate"
fans wings
fane temple
and build . . . mind See Spenser's *Amoretti*
XXII: "Her temple fayre is built within my
mind . . .".

moss-lain Dryads wood nymphs reclining on
banks of moss
casement ope See "To a Nightingale," l. 69.
hemlock poisonous herb, and not the American
tree of that name

Or emptied some dull opiate to the drains
  One minute past, and Lethe-wards° had sunk:
'Tis not through envy of thy happy lot,
  But being too happy in thine happiness,—
    That thou, light-wingèd Dryad° of the trees,
      In some melodious plot
Of beechen green, and shadows numberless,
  10   Singest of summer in full-throated ease.

            II
O, for a draught of vintage! that hath been
  Cooled a long age in the deep-delved earth,
Tasting of Flora° and the country green,
  Dance, and Provençal° song, and sunburnt mirth!
O for a beaker full of the warm South,
  Full of the true, the blushful Hippocrene,°
    With beaded bubbles winking at the brim,
      And purple-stainèd mouth;
That I might drink, and leave the world unseen,
  20   And with thee fade away into the forest dim:

            III
Fade far away, dissolve, and quite forget
  What thou among the leaves hast never known,
The weariness, the fever, and the fret
  Here, where men sit and hear each other groan;
Where palsy shakes a few, sad, last grey hairs,
  Where youth grows pale, and spectre-thin, and dies;°
    Where but to think is to be full of sorrow
      And leaden-eyed despairs,
Where Beauty cannot keep her lustrous eyes,
  30   Or new Love pine at them beyond tomorrow.

            IV
Away! away! for I will fly to thee,
  Not charioted by Bacchus and his pards,°
But on the viewless° wings of Poesy,
  Though the dull brain perplexes and retards:
Already with thee! tender is the night,
  And haply the Queen-Moon is on her throne,
    Clustered around by all her starry Fays;°
      But here there is no light,

Lethe-wards down to the river of forgetfulness in the underworld
Dryad wood nymph
Flora Roman goddess of fertility
Provençal province in southern France associated with the troubadours and the origins of Romantic poetry

Hippocrene fountain of the Muses on Mt. Helicon
Where youth . . . dies Keats's brother Tom died of tuberculosis in December 1818.
pards leopards drawing the chariot of Bacchus, god of intoxication
viewless flying too high to have any view
Fays fairies

Save what from heaven is with the breezes blown
40   Through verdurous glooms and winding mossy ways.

v

I cannot see what flowers are at my feet,
    Nor what soft incense hangs upon the boughs,
But, in embalmèd° darkness, guess each sweet
    Wherewith the seasonable month endows
The grass, the thicket, and the fruit-tree wild;
    White hawthorn, and the pastoral eglantine;
        Fast fading violets covered up in leaves;
            And mid-May's eldest child,
    The coming musk-rose, full of dewy wine,
50   The murmurous haunt of flies on summer eves.

vi

Darkling° I listen; and, for many a time
    I have been half in love with easeful Death,
Called him soft names in many a musèd rhyme,
    To take into the air my quiet breath;
Now more than ever seems it rich to die,
    To cease upon the midnight with no pain,
        While thou art pouring forth thy soul abroad
            In such an ecstasy!
    Still wouldst thou sing, and I have ears in vain—
60   To thy high requiem become a sod.

vii

Thou wast not born for death, immortal Bird!
    No hungry generations tread thee down;
The voice I hear this passing night was heard
    In ancient days by emperor and clown:
Perhaps the self-same song that found a path
    Through the sad heart of Ruth,° when, sick for home,
        She stood in tears amid the alien corn;
            The same that oft-times hath
    Charmed magic casements, opening on the foam
70   Of perilous seas, in faery lands forlorn.

viii

Forlorn! the very word is like a bell
    To toll me back from thee to my sole self!
Adieu! the fancy cannot cheat so well
    As she is famed to do, deceiving elf.

---

embalmèd perfumed
Darkling in the darkness; see *Paradise Lost*
III.39, where the blind Milton compares him-
self to the nightingale that "sings darkling"

Ruth See Ruth 2 in the Bible, but Keats's vision has more in common with Wordsworth's
"The Solitary Reaper."

Adieu! adieu! thy plaintive anthem fades
 Past the near meadows, over the still stream,
  Up the hill-side; and now 'tis buried deep
   In the next valley-glades:
 Was it a vision, or a waking dream?°
80   Fled is that music:—Do I wake or sleep?
   1819   1819

Ode on a Grecian Urn

I

Thou still unravished bride of quietness,
 Thou foster-child of silence and slow time,
Sylvan historian, who canst thus express
 A flowery tale more sweetly than our rhyme:
What leaf-fringed legend haunts about thy shape
 Of deities or mortals, or of both,
  In Tempe° or the dales of Arcady?°
What men or gods are these? What maidens loth?
What mad pursuit? What struggle to escape?
10 What pipes and timbrels? What wild ecstasy?

II

Heard melodies are sweet, but those unheard
 Are sweeter; therefore, ye soft pipes, play on;
Not to the sensual° ear, but, more endeared,
 Pipe to the spirit ditties of no tone:
Fair youth, beneath the trees, thou canst not leave
 Thy song, nor ever can those trees be bare;
  Bold Lover, never, never canst thou kiss,
Though winning near the goal—yet, do not grieve;
 She cannot fade, though thou hast not thy bliss,
20 Forever wilt thou love, and she be fair!

III

Ah, happy, happy boughs! that cannot shed
 Your leaves, nor ever bid the Spring adieu;
And, happy melodist, unwearièd,
 Forever piping songs forever new;
More happy love! more happy, happy love!
 Forever warm and still to be enjoyed,
  Forever panting, and forever young;

---

waking dream Douglas Bush usefully cites Hazlitt's lecture "On Chaucer and Spenser" (which Keats heard delivered): "Spenser was the poet of our waking dreams . . . lulling the senses into a deep oblivion of the jarring noises of the world, from which we have no wish to be ever recalled"
Tempe valley in Thessaly
Arcady a region of ancient Greece, but primarily a vision of the pastoral ideal
sensual sensuous

All breathing human passion far above,
  That leaves a heart high-sorrowful and cloyed,
30   A burning forehead, and a parching tongue.

IV

Who are these coming to the sacrifice?
  To what green altar, O mysterious priest,
Lead'st thou that heifer lowing at the skies,
  And all her silken flanks with garlands dressed?
What little town by river or sea shore,
  Or mountain-built with peaceful citadel,
    Is emptied of this folk, this pious morn?
And, little town, thy streets for evermore
  Will silent be; and not a soul to tell
40   Why thou art desolate, can e'er return.°

V

O Attic° shape! Fair attitude! with brede°
  Of marble men and maidens overwrought,
With forest branches and the trodden weed;
  Thou, silent form, dost tease us out of thought°
As doth eternity: Cold Pastoral!
  When old age shall this generation waste,
    Thou shalt remain, in midst of other woe
Than ours, a friend to man, to whom thou say'st,
  'Beauty is truth, truth beauty,—that is all
50   Ye know on earth, and all ye need to know.'°
    1819   1820

Ode on Melancholy°

I

No, no, go not to Lethe,° neither twist
  Wolf's-bane,° tight-rooted, for its poisonous wine;
Nor suffer thy pale forehead to be kissed
  By nightshade, ruby grape of Proserpine;°

And . . . return The "little town" is not on
the urn, but exists only in the implications of
art.
Attic pertaining to Attica, i.e. Athens
brede embroidery
tease . . . thought as in the "Epistle to John
Hamilton Reynolds" l. 77
Beauty . . . know There has been much critical controversy as to where Keats intended the
quotation to end; I follow Douglas Bush in as-
signing the last two lines to the urn, and not
just the first five words of l. 49.
Ode on Melancholy The ode originally opened
with the following stanza, which Keats later
canceled:

Though you should build a bark of dead men's
      bones,
  And rear a phantom gibbet for a mast,
Stitch creeds together for a sail, with groans
  To fill it out, blood-stainèd and aghast;
Although your rudder be a dragon's tail
  Long severed, yet still hard with agony,
    Your cordage large uprootings from the skull
Of bald Medusa, certes you would fail
  To find the Melancholy—whether she
    Dreameth in any isle of Lethe dull.
Lethe See "To a Nightingale," l. 4.
Wolf's-bane poisonous plant, as is nightshade
Proserpine queen of the underworld; wife of
Pluto

Make not your rosary of yew-berries,°
   Nor let the beetle,° nor the death-moth° be
     Your mournful Psyche,° nor the downy owl
A partner in your sorrow's mysteries;
   For shade to shade will come too drowsily,
10   And drown the wakeful anguish of the soul.

       II

But when the melancholy fit shall fall
   Sudden from heaven like a weeping cloud,
That fosters the droop-headed flowers all,
   And hides the green hill in an April shroud;
Then glut thy sorrow on a morning rose,
   Or on the rainbow of the salt sand-wave,
     Or on the wealth of globèd peonies;
Or if thy mistress some rich anger shows,
   Emprison her soft hand, and let her rave,
20   And feed deep, deep upon her peerless eyes.

       III

She° dwells with Beauty—Beauty that must die;
   And Joy, whose hand is ever at his lips
Bidding adieu; and aching Pleasure nigh,
   Turning to poison while the bee-mouth sips:
Ay, in the very temple of Delight
   Veiled Melancholy has her sovereign shrine,°
     Though seen of none save him whose strenuous tongue
Can burst Joy's grape against his palate fine;
   His soul shall taste the sadness of her might,
30   And be among her cloudy trophies hung.°
    1819   1820

The Fall of Hyperion

This purgatorial fragment is parallel to Shelley's *The Triumph of Life,* in that each poem derives its structure and procedure from Dante (by way of the Cary translation, in Keats's case), each has elements of palinode or recantation, and shows also a new severity of style and firmer discipline of mythopoetic invention. Keats too is writing his vision of judgment, but his vision, though tragic, is not as dark or as deliberately universalizing as Shelley's. Where Shelley passively renders Rousseau's terrifying story, Keats actively confronts his Muse, Moneta, and compels her not only to accept him as a true poet but to modify her harsh and narrow categorizations of

yew-berries associated with mourning
beetle coffin emblem, as Egyptian scarab
death-moth moth with skull-like markings
Psyche the soul, symbolized by the butterfly
She refers both to "thy mistress" and the goddess Melancholy.

shrine See the shrine of Moneta in *The Fall of Hyperion.*
And . . . hung See Shakespeare's Sonnet XXXI: "Hung with the trophies of my lovers gone."

poets and of humanist men of action. He does this not by asserting his own identity, but by finding a truer form in the merged, higher identify of a more humanistic poethood than the world has known.

Incomplete as it is (probably Keats did not go on because he was no longer healthy enough, in spirit or in body), *The Fall of Hyperion* shows the start of a different kind of tragic theme and procedure, one that is founded upon a realization that every credence attending literary and spiritual tradition is now dead. Moneta presides over a ruined shrine of all the dead faiths, and the lesson Keats searches out in her countenance is that tragedy is not enough, though he still desires to be a tragic poet. The burden of history, of the fused but broken splendor of past poetic achievements, is heroically taken on by Keats as a necessary prelude to a new level of achievement he believes he can attain. He did not live to do so, but this fragment persuades us that he was the chosen man to make the attempt.

The Fall of Hyperion

A Dream

Canto I

Fanatics have their dreams, wherewith they weave
A paradise for a sect; the savage too
From forth the loftiest fashion of his sleep
Guesses at Heaven; pity these have not
Traced upon vellum or wild Indian leaf
The shadows of melodious utterance.
But bare of laurel they live, dream, and die;
For Poesy alone can tell her dreams,
With the fine spell of words alone can save
10   Imagination from the sable charm
And dumb enchantment. Who alive can say,
'Thou art no Poet—mayst not tell thy dreams?'
Since every man whose soul is not a clod
Hath visions, and would speak, if he had loved,
And been well nurtured in his mother tongue.
Whether the dream now purposed to rehearse
Be poet's or fanatic's will be known
When this warm scribe my hand is in the grave.

       Methought I stood where trees of every clime,
20   Palm, myrtle, oak, and sycamore, and beech,
With plantain, and spice-blossoms, made a screen;
In neighbourhood of fountains (by the noise
Soft-showering in my ears), and (by the touch
Of scent) not far from roses. Turning round
I saw an arbour with a drooping roof
Of trellis vines, and bells, and larger blooms,°

I saw . . . blooms See "Ode to Psyche," ll.
60–63.

Like floral censers, swinging light in air;
Before its wreathèd doorway, on a mound
Of moss, was spread a feast of summer fruits,
30 Which, nearer seen, seemed refuse of a meal
By angel tasted or our Mother Eve;°
For empty shells were scattered on the grass,
And grape-stalks but half bare, and remnants more,
Sweet-smelling, whose pure kinds I could not know.
Still was more plenty than the fabled horn°
Thrice emptied could pour forth, at banqueting
For Proserpine returned to her own fields,
Where the white heifers low. And appetite
More yearning than on Earth I ever felt
40 Growing within, I ate deliciously;
And, after not long, thirsted, for thereby
Stood a cool vessel of transparent juice
Sipped by the wandered bee, the which I took,
And, pledging all the mortals of the world,
And all the dead whose names are in our lips,°
Drank. That full draught is parent of my theme.
No Asian poppy nor elixir fine
Of the soon-fading jealous Caliphat;°
No poison gendered in close monkish cell,
50 To thin the scarlet conclave° of old men,
Could so have rapt unwilling life away.
Among the fragrant husks and berries crushed,
Upon the grass I struggled hard against
The domineering potion; but in vain:
The cloudy swoon came on, and down I sank,
Like a Silenus° on an antique vase.
How long I slumbered 'tis a chance to guess.
When sense of life returned, I started up
As if with wings; but the fair trees were gone,
60 The mossy mound and arbour were no more:
I looked around upon the carvèd sides
Of an old sanctuary with roof august,
Builded so high, it seemed that filmèd clouds
Might spread beneath, as o'er the stars of heaven;
So old the place was, I remembered none
The like upon the Earth: what I had seen
Of grey cathedrals, buttressed walls, rent towers,
The superannuations of sunk realms,
Or Nature's rocks toiled hard in waves and winds,
70 Seemed but the faulture of decrepit things
To that eternal domèd Monument.—

Eve See *Paradise Lost* V.321–49.
horn cornucopia or horn of plenty, from a goat
whose milk fed the infant Jupiter
And all . . . lips dead poets, still spoken of
Caliphat council of Caliphs, successors to Mo-

hammed's power, notorious for poisoning one
another
scarlet conclave the College of Cardinals
Silenus drunken satyr who instructed Bacchus

Upon the marble at my feet there lay
Store of strange vessels and large draperies,
Which needs had been of dyed asbestos wove,
Or in that place the moth could not corrupt,°
So white the linen, so, in some, distinct
Ran imageries from a sombre loom.
All in a mingled heap confused there lay
Robes, golden tongs, censer and chafing-dish,
80   Girdles, and chains, and holy jewelries.

       Turning from these with awe, once more I raised
My eyes to fathom the space every way;
The embossed roof, the silent massy range
Of columns north and south, ending in mist
Of nothing, then to eastward, where black gates
Were shut against the sunrise evermore.—
Then to the west° I looked, and saw far off
An image, huge of feature as a cloud,
At level of whose feet an altar slept,
90   To be approached on either side by steps,
And marble balustrade, and patient travail
To count with toil the innumerable degrees.
Towards the altar sober-paced I went,
Repressing haste, as too unholy there;
And, coming nearer, saw beside the shrine
One ministering;° and there arose a flame.—
When in mid-May the sickening East wind°
Shifts sudden to the south, the small warm rain
Melts out the frozen incense from all flowers,
100   And fills the air with so much pleasant health
That even the dying man forgets his shroud;—
Even so that lofty sacrificial fire,
Sending forth Maian° incense, spread around
Forgetfulness of everything but bliss,
And clouded all the altar with soft smoke;
From whose white fragrant curtains thus I heard
Language pronounced: 'If thou canst not ascend
These steps,° die on that marble where thou art.
Thy flesh, near cousin to the common dust,
110   Will parch for lack of nutriment—thy bones
Will wither in few years, and vanish so

---

moth . . . corrupt See Matthew 6:19.
west the direction of conclusions, of personal
death
One ministering Moneta, at once Keats's Virgil and his Beatrice; an admonisher (so her
name) who replaces the Mnemosyne of the first
Hyperion
East wind See *Purgatorio* XXV.145 ff.: "And,
as the May breeze, the herald / of the dawn,
blows and is fragrant, / steeped in the odour of

grass and flowers, / so I felt a fanning on the
middle of my brow / and the moving of a wing
/ which brought the fragrance of ambrosia";
this is followed by a blessing upon those "who
hunger always in right measure."
Maian one of the Pleiades or Daughters of
Atlas, and mother of Hermes. For Keats,
"Maian" is almost a synonym for "naturalistic."
steps as in Dante's *Purgatorio* IV, IX, XII–XIII

That not the quickest eye could find a grain
Of what thou now art on that pavement cold.
The sands of thy short life are spent this hour,
And no hand in the universe can turn
Thy hourglass, if these gummed leaves be burnt
Ere thou canst mount up these immortal steps.'
I heard, I looked: two senses both at once,
So fine, so subtle, felt the tyranny
120 Of that fierce threat and the hard task proposed.
Prodigious seemed the toil; the leaves were yet
Burning—when suddenly a palsied chill
Struck from the pavèd level up my limbs,
And was ascending quick to put cold grasp
Upon those streams that pulse beside the throat:
I shrieked, and the sharp anguish of my shriek
Stung my own ears—I strove hard to escape
The numbness; strove to gain the lowest step.
Slow, heavy, deadly was my pace: the cold°
130 Grew stifling, suffocating, at the heart;
And when I clasped my hands I felt them not.
One minute before death, my iced foot touched
The lowest stair; and as it touched, life seemed
To pour in at the toes: I mounted up,
As once fair angels on a ladder° flew
From the green turf to Heaven—'Holy Power,'
Cried I, approaching near the hornèd shrine,
'What am I that should so be saved from death?
What am I that another death come not
140 To choke my utterance sacrilegious, here?'
Then said the veiled shadow—'Thou hast felt
What 'tis to die and live again° before
Thy fated hour, that thou hadst power to do so
Is thy own safety; thou hast dated on
Thy doom.'—'High Prophetess,' said I, 'purge off,
Benign, if so it please thee, my mind's film.'—
'None can usurp this height,' returned that shade,
'But those to whom the miseries of the world
Are misery, and will not let them rest.
150 All else who find a haven in the world,
Where they may thoughtless sleep away their days,
If by a chance into this fane they come,
Rot on the pavement where thou rottedst half.'—
'Are there not thousands in the world,' said I,
Encouraged by the sooth voice of the shade,

cold See *Purgatorio* XXX.97–100.
ladder Jacob's vision; Keats's allusion is probably to *Paradise Lost* III.510–15 rather than to
Genesis 28:12

live again as in *Hyperion* III.130, where Apollo
"dies into life"

'Who love their fellows even to the death,
Who feel the giant agony of the world,
And more, like slaves to poor humanity,
Labour for mortal good? I sure should see
160   Other men here; but I am here alone.'
'Those whom thou spak'st of are no visionaries,'
Rejoined that voice—'They are no dreamers weak,
They seek no wonder but the human face;
No music but a happy-noted voice—
They come not here, they have no thought to come—
And thou art here, for thou art less than they—
What benefit canst thou do, or all thy tribe,
To the great world? Thou art a dreaming thing,
A fever of thyself—think of the Earth;
170   What bliss even in hope is there for thee?
What haven? every creature hath its home;
Every sole man hath days of joy and pain,
Whether his labours be sublime or low—
The pain alone; the joy alone; distinct:
Only the dreamer venoms all his days,
Bearing more woe than all his sins deserve.
Therefore, that happiness be somewhat shared,
Such things as thou art are admitted oft
Into like gardens thou didst pass erewhile,
180   And suffered in these temples: for that cause
Thou standest safe beneath this statue's knees.'
'That I am favoured for unworthiness,
By such propitious parley medicined
In sickness not ignoble, I rejoice,
Aye, and could weep for love of such award.'
So answered I, continuing, 'If it please,
Majestic shadow, tell me: sure not all
Those melodies sung into the World's ear
Are useless: sure a poet is a sage;°
190   A humanist, physician to all men.
That I am none I feel, as vultures feel
They are no birds when eagles are abroad.
What am I then: Thou spakest of my tribe:
What tribe?' The tall shade veiled in drooping white
Then spake, so much more earnest, that the breath
Moved the thin linen folds that drooping hung
About a golden censer from the hand
Pendent—'Art thou not of the dreamer tribe?
The poet and the dreamer are distinct,
200   Diverse, sheer opposite, antipodes.
The one pours out a balm upon the World,

sage as Dante invoked Virgil, *Inferno* I.85

The other vexes it.' Then shouted I
Spite of myself, and with a Pythia's spleen,°
'Apollo! faded! O far flown Apollo!
Where is thy misty pestilence to creep
Into the dwellings, through the door crannies
Of all mock lyrists, large self worshippers
And careless Hectorers in proud bad verse.°
Though I breathe death with them it will be life
210 To see them sprawl before me into graves.
Majestic shadow, tell me where I am,
Whose altar this; for whom this incense curls;
What image this whose face I cannot see,
For the broad marble knees; and who thou art,
Of accent feminine so courteous?'

    Then the tall shade, in drooping linens veiled,
Spoke out, so much more earnest, that her breath
Stirred the thin folds of gauze that drooping hung
About a golden censer from her hand
220 Pendent; and by her voice I knew she shed
Long-treasured tears. 'This temple, sad and lone,
Is all spared from the thunder of a war
Foughten long since by giant hierarchy
Against rebellion: this old image here,
Whose carvèd features wrinkled as he fell,
Is Saturn's; I Moneta, left supreme
Sole Priestess of this desolation,'—
I had no words to answer, for my tongue,
Useless, could find about its roofèd home
230 No syllable of a fit majesty
To make rejoinder to Moneta's mourn.
There was a silence, while the altar's blaze
Was fainting for sweet food: I looked thereon,
And on the pavèd floor, where nigh were piled
Faggots of cinnamon, and many heaps
Of other crispèd spice-wood—then again
I looked upon the altar, and its horns
Whitened with ashes, and its languorous flame,
And then upon the offerings again;
240 And so by turns—till sad Moneta cried,
'The sacrifice is done, but not the less
Will I be kind to thee for thy good will.
My power, which to me is still a curse,
Shall be to thee a wonder; for the scenes
Still swooning vivid through my globèd brain,

---

with . . . spleen with anger like that of the
priestess of Apollo's temple at Delphi
Of all . . . bad verse This appears to be an
attack upon Keats's greatest contemporaries;
"mock lyrists": Shelley; "large self worshippers": Wordsworth; "careless Hectorers": Byron.

With an electral changing misery,
Thou shalt with those dull mortal eyes behold,
Free from all pain, if wonder pain thee not.'
As near as an immortal's spherèd words
250 Could to a mother's soften, were these last:
And yet I had a terror of her robes,
And chiefly of the veils, that from her brow
Hung pale, and curtained her in mysteries,
That made my heart too small to hold its blood.
This saw that Goddess, and with sacred hand
Parted the veils. Then saw I a wan face,°
Not pined by human sorrows, but bright-blanched
By an immortal sickness which kills not;
It works a constant change, which happy death
260 Can put no end to; deathwards progressing
To no death was that visage; it had passed
The lily and the snow; and beyond these
I must not think now, though I saw that face—
But for her eyes I should have fled away.
They held me back, with a benignant light,
Soft mitigated by divinest lids
Half-closed, and visionless entire they seemed
Of all external things;—they saw me not,
But in blank splendour, beamed like the mild moon,
270 Who comforts those she sees not, who knows not
What eyes are upward cast. As I had found
A grain of gold upon a mountain side,
And twinged with avarice strained out my eyes
To search its sullen entrails rich with ore,
So at the view of sad Moneta's brow,
I ached to see what things the hollow brain
Behind enwombèd: what high tragedy
In the dark secret chambers of her skull
Was acting, that could give so dread a stress
280 To her cold lips, and fill with such a light
Her planetary eyes; and touch her voice
With such a sorrow—'Shade of Memory!'—
Cried I, with act adorant at her feet,
'By all the gloom hung round thy fallen house,
By this last temple, by the golden age,
By great Apollo, thy dear Foster Child,
And by thyself, forlorn divinity,
The pale Omega° of a withered race,
Let me behold, according as thou saidst,
290 What in thy brain so ferments to and fro!'

wan face For a possible source, see *Purgatorio*   the ultimate, revealed form, as in Revelation
XXXI.117 ff.   1:8, 11, and *Paradiso* XXVI.19
Omega final letter of Greek alphabet, and so

No sooner had this conjuration passed
My devout lips, than side by side we stood
(Like a stunt bramble by a solemn pine)
Deep in the shady sadness of a vale,°
Far sunken from the healthy breath of morn,
Far from the fiery noon and eve's one star.
Onward I looked beneath the gloomy boughs,
And saw, what first I thought an image huge,
Like to the image pedestaled so high
In Saturn's temple. Then Moneta's voice   300
Came brief upon mine ear—'So Saturn sat
When he had lost his Realms—' whereon there grew
A power within me of enormous ken
To see as a god sees, and take the depth
Of things as nimbly as the outward eye
Can size and shape pervade. The lofty theme
At those few words hung vast before my mind,
With half-unraveled web. I sat myself
Upon an eagle's watch, that I might see,
And seeing ne'er forget. No stir of life   310
Was in this shrouded vale, not so much air
As in the zoning° of a summer's day
Robs not one light seed from the feathered grass,
But where the dead leaf fell there did it rest:
A stream went voiceless by, still deadened more
By reason of the fallen divinity
Spreading more shade; the Naiad 'mid her reeds
Pressed her cold finger closer to her lips.

Along the margin-sand large footmarks went
No farther than to where old Saturn's feet   320
Had rested, and there slept, how long a sleep!
Degraded, cold, upon the sodden ground
His old right hand lay nerveless, listless, dead,
Unsceptred; and his realmless eyes were closed,
While his bowed head seemed listening to the Earth,
His ancient mother, for some comfort yet.

It seemed no force could wake him from his place;
But there came one who, with a kindred hand
Touched his wide shoulders after bending low
With reverence, though to one who knew it not.   330
Then came the grieved voice of Mnemosyne,°
And grieved I hearkened. 'That divinity
Whom thou saw'st step from yon forlornest wood,

Deep . . . vale Keats now returns to the first
Hyperion (this is the very first line), revising
it as he goes on.
zoning moving from zone to zone

Mnemosyne perhaps a mistake for "Moneta,"
or perhaps Keats intended the names to be
alternate, once the story-telling had commenced;
see II.50

And with slow pace approach our fallen King,
Is Thea, softest-natured of our Brood.'
I marked the Goddess in fair statuary
Surpassing wan Moneta by the head,
And in her sorrow nearer woman's tears.
There was a listening fear in her regard,
340   As if calamity had but begun;
As if the vanward clouds of evil days
Had spent their malice, and the sullen rear
Was with its storèd thunder labouring up.
One hand she pressed upon that aching spot
Where beats the human heart, as if just there,
Though an immortal, she felt cruel pain;
The other upon Saturn's bended neck
She laid, and to the level of his hollow ear
Leaning with parted lips, some words she spake
350   In solemn tenor and deep organ tune;
Some mourning words, which in our feeble tongue
Would come in this-like accenting; how frail
To that large utterance of the early Gods!

'Saturn! look up—and for what, poor lost King?
I have no comfort for thee; no not one;
I cannot cry, wherefore thus sleepest thou?
For Heaven is parted from thee, and the Earth
Knows thee not, so afflicted, for a God;
And Ocean too, with all its solemn noise,
360   Has from thy sceptre passed, and all the air
Is emptied of thine hoary majesty:
Thy thunder, captious at the new command,
Rumbles reluctant o'er our fallen house;
And thy sharp lightning, in unpracticed hands,
Scorches and burns our once serene domain.
With such remorseless speed still come new woes,
That unbelief has not a space to breathe.
Saturn! sleep on:—Me thoughtless, why should I
Thus violate thy slumbrous solitude?
370   Why should I ope thy melancholy eyes?
Saturn, sleep on, while at thy feet I weep.'

As when upon a trancèd summer-night
Forests, branch-charmèd by the earnest stars,
Dream, and so dream all night without a noise,
Save from one gradual solitary gust,
Swelling upon the silence; dying off;
As if the ebbing air had but one wave;
So came these words, and went; the while in tears
She pressed her fair large forehead to the earth,
380   Just where her fallen hair might spread in curls,

A soft and silken mat for Saturn's feet.
Long, long those two were postured motionless,
Like sculpture builded-up upon the grave
Of their own power. A long awful time
I looked upon them: still they were the same;
The frozen God still bending to the earth,
And the sad Goddess weeping at his feet,
Moneta silent. Without stay or prop,
But my own weak mortality, I bore
390 The load of this eternal quietude,
The unchanging gloom, and the three fixèd shapes
Ponderous upon my senses, a whole moon.
For by my burning brain I measured sure
Her silver seasons shedded on the night,
And ever day by day methought I grew
More gaunt and ghostly.—Oftentimes I prayed
Intense, that Death would take me from the Vale
And all its burthens—gasping with despair
Of change, hour after hour I cursed myself;
400 Until old Saturn raised his faded eyes,
And looked around and saw his kingdom gone,
And all the gloom and sorrow of the place,
And that fair kneeling Goddess at his feet.
As the moist scent of flowers, and grass, and leaves,
Fills forest dells with a pervading air,
Known to the woodland nostril, so the words
Of Saturn filled the mossy glooms around,
Even to the hollows of time-eaten oaks,
And to the windings of the foxes' hole,
410 With sad low tones, while thus he spake, and sent
Strange musings to the solitary Pan.
'Moan, brethren, moan; for we are swallowed up
And buried from all Godlike exercise
Of influence benign on planets pale,
And peaceful sway above man's harvesting,
And all those acts which Deity supreme
Doth ease its heart of love in. Moan and wail,
Moan, brethren, moan; for lo, the rebel spheres
Spin round, the stars their ancient courses keep,
420 Clouds still with shadowy moisture haunt the earth,
Still suck their fill of light from sun and moon;
Still buds the tree, and still the sea-shores murmur;
There is no death in all the Universe,
No smell of death—there shall be death—Moan, moan,
Moan, Cybele, moan; for thy pernicious Babes
Have changed a god into a shaking Palsy.
Moan, brethren, moan, for I have no strength left,
Weak as the reed—weak—feeble as my voice—

O, O, the pain, the pain of feebleness.
430 Moan, moan, for still I thaw—or give me help;
Throw down those imps, and give me victory.
Let me hear other groans, and trumpets blown
Of triumph calm, and hymns of festival,
From the gold peaks of Heaven's high-pilèd clouds;
Voices of soft proclaim, and silver stir
Of strings in hollow shells; and let there be
Beautiful things made new for the surprise
Of the sky-children.' So he feebly ceased,
With such a poor and sickly sounding pause,
440 Methought I heard some old man of the earth
Bewailing earthly loss; nor could my eyes
And ears act with that pleasant unison of sense
Which marries sweet sound with the grace of form,
And dolorous accent from a tragic harp
With large-limbed visions.—More I scrutinized:
Still fixed he sat beneath the sable trees,
Whose arms spread straggling in wild serpent forms,
With leaves all hushed; his awful presence there
(Now all was silent) gave a deadly lie
450 To what I erewhile heard—only his lips
Trembled amid the white curls of his beard.
They told the truth, though, round, the snowy locks
Hung nobly, as upon the face of heaven
A mid-day fleece of clouds. Thea arose,
And stretched her white arm through the hollow dark,
Pointing some whither: whereat he too rose
Like a vast giant, seen by men at sea
To grow pale from the waves at dull midnight.
They melted from my sight into the woods;
460 Ere I could turn, Moneta cried, 'These twain
Are speeding to the families of grief,
Where roofed in by black rocks they waste, in pain
And darkness, for no hope.'°—And she spake on,
As ye may read who can unwearied pass
Onward from the Antechamber of this dream,
Where even at the open doors awhile
I must delay, and glean my memory
Of her high phrase:—perhaps no further dare.

Canto II
'Mortal, that thou may'st understand aright,
I humanize my sayings to thine ear,
Making comparisons of earthly things;
Or thou might'st better listen to the wind,

no hope See *Inferno* IV.

Whose language is to thee a barren noise,
Though it blows legend-laden through the trees.—
In melancholy realms big tears are shed,
More sorrow like to this, and such like woe,
Too huge for mortal tongue, or pen of scribe.
10   The Titans fierce, self hid or prison bound,
Groan for the old allegiance once more,
Listening in their doom for Saturn's voice.
But one of our whole eagle-brood still keeps
His sovereignty, and rule, and majesty;
Blazing Hyperion on his orbèd fire
Still sits, still snuffs the incense teeming up
From Man to the Sun's God: yet unsecure.
For as upon the earth dire prodigies
Fright and perplex, so also shudders he:
20   Nor at dog's howl or gloom-bird's Even screech,
Or the familiar visitings of one
Upon the first toll of his passing bell:
But horrors, portioned to a giant nerve,
Make great Hyperion ache. His palace bright,
Bastioned with pyramids of glowing gold,
And touched with shade of bronzèd obelisks,
Glares a blood-red through all the thousand courts,
Arches, and domes, and fiery galleries:
And all its curtains of Aurorian clouds
30   Flush angerly; when he would taste the wreaths
Of incense breathed aloft from sacred hills,
Instead of sweets, his ample palate takes
Savour of poisonous brass and metals sick.
Wherefore when harboured in the sleepy West,
After the full completion of fair day,
For rest divine upon exalted couch
And slumber in the arms of melody,
He paces through the pleasant hours of ease
With strides colossal, on from hall to hall;
40   While far within each aisle and deep recess
His wingèd minions in close clusters stand
Amazed, and full of fear; like anxious men,
Who on a wide plain gather in sad troops,
When earthquakes jar their battlements and towers.
Even now, while Saturn, roused from icy trance,
Goes, step for step, with Thea from yon woods,
Hyperion, leaving twilight in the rear,
Is sloping to the threshold of the West.—
Thither we tend.'—Now in clear light I stood,
50   Relieved from the dusk vale. Mnemosyne
Was sitting on a square-edged polished stone,
That in its lucid depth reflected pure ·

Her priestess-garments.—My quick eyes ran on
From stately nave to nave, from vault to vault,
Through bowers of fragrant and enwreathèd light,
And diamond-pavèd lustrous long arcades.
Anon rushed by the bright Hyperion;
His flaming robes streamed out beyond his heels,
And gave a roar, as if of earthly fire,
60   That scared away the meek ethereal hours,
And made their dove-wings tremble. On he flared.
1819   1856

To Autumn°

I

Season of mists and mellow fruitfulness,
    Close bosom-friend of the maturing sun;
Conspiring with him how to load and bless
    With fruit the vines that round the thatch-eves run;
To bend with apples the mossed cottage-trees,°
    And fill all fruit with ripeness to the core;
        To swell the gourd, and plump the hazel shells
With a sweet kernel; to set budding more,
    And still more, later flowers for the bees,
10   Until they think warm days will never cease,
        For Summer has o'er-brimmed their clammy cells.

II

Who hath not seen thee oft amid thy store?
    Sometimes whoever seeks abroad may find
Thee sitting careless on a granary floor,
    Thy hair soft-lifted by the winnowing wind;
Or on a half-reaped furrow sound asleep,
    Drowsed with the fume of poppies, while thy hook
        Spares the next swath and all its twinèd flowers:
And sometimes like a gleaner thou dost keep
20   Steady thy laden head across a brook;
    Or by a cider-press, with patient look,
        Thou watchest the last oozings hours by hours.

To Autumn Two days after writing this ode,
Keats commented upon it in a letter to Reynolds: "How beautiful the season is now—How
fine the air. A temperate sharpness about it.
Really, without joking, chaste weather—Dian
skies—I never lik'd stubble fields so much as
now—Aye better than the chilly green of the
spring. Somehow a stubble plain looks warm—
in the same way that some pictures look warm
—this struck me so much in my Sunday's walk
that I composed upon it."

To bend . . . cottage-trees The line recalls
Chatterton, and Keats in his September 21 letter
to Reynolds says: "I always somehow associate
Chatterton with autumn." See Chatterton's Aella,
ll. 184–85: "When the fair apple, red as even
sky, / Do bend the tree unto the fruitful
ground." In associating Chatterton with autumn,
Keats compelled himself to remember an admired young poet who died before he had gathered in the harvest of his poetry.

III

Where are the songs of Spring? Aye, where are they?
    Think not of them, thou hast thy music too,—
While barred clouds bloom the soft-dying day,
    And touch the stubble-plains with rosy hue;
Then in a wailful choir the small gnats mourn
    Among the river sallows,° borne aloft
        Or sinking as the light wind lives or dies;
30 And full-grown lambs loud bleat from hilly bourn;
    Hedge-crickets sing; and now with treble soft
    The red-breast whistles from a garden-croft;
        And gathering swallows twitter in the skies.
    1819   1820

To———°

What can I do to drive away
Remembrance from my eyes? For they have seen,
Aye, an hour ago, my brilliant Queen!
Touch has a memory. O say, love, say,
What can I do to kill it and be free
In my old liberty?°
When every fair one that I saw was fair,
Enough to catch me in but half a snare,
Not keep me there:
10 When, howe'er poor or particoloured things,
My muse had wings,
And ever ready was to take her course
Whither I bent her force,
Unintellectual, yet divine to me;—
Divine, I say!—What sea-bird o'er the sea
Is a philosopher the while he goes
Winging along where the great water throes?°

    How shall I do
    To get anew
20 Those moulted feathers, and so mount once more
    Above, above
    The reach of fluttering Love,
And make him cower lowly while I soar?

Shall I gulp wine? No, that is vulgarism,
A heresy and schism,
    Foisted into the canon law of love;—
No,—wine is only sweet to happy men;

sallows willows
To——— almost certainly to Fanny Brawne
What can . . . liberty a desperate attempt by
the frustrated lover to free himself from love
throes i.e. is in throes

More dismal cares
Seize on me unawares,—
30 Where shall I learn to get my peace again?
To banish thoughts of that most hateful land,°
Dungeoner of my friends, that wicked strand
Where they were wrecked and live a wreckèd life;
That monstrous region, whose dull rivers pour,
Ever from their sordid urns unto the shore,
Unowned of any weedy-hairèd gods;
Whose winds, all zephyrless, hold scourging rods,
Iced in the great lakes, to afflict mankind;
Whose rank-grown forests, frosted, black, and blind,
40 Would fright a Dryad;° whose harsh herbaged meads
Make lean and lank the starved ox while he feeds;
There flowers have no scent, birds no sweet song,
And great unerring Nature once seems wrong.

O, for some sunny spell
To dissipate the shadows of this hell!
Say they are gone,—with the new dawning light
Steps forth my lady bright!
O, let me once more rest
My soul upon that dazzling breast!
50 Let once again these aching arms be placed,
The tender gaolers of thy waist!
And let me feel that warm breath here and there
To spread a rapture in my very hair,—
O, the sweetness of the pain!
Give me those lips again!
Enough! Enough! it is enough for me
To dream of thee!
1819   1848

Bright Star°

[Written on a Blank Page in Shakespeare's Poems,
facing 'A Lover's Complaint']

Bright star, would I were stedfast as thou art—
    Not in lone splendour hung aloft the night
And watching, with eternal lids° apart,
    Like nature's patient, sleepless Eremite,°

hateful land the United States, where Keats's
brother and sister-in-law were in acute financial distress
Dryad wood nymph
Bright Star Keats copied out this revised version of an earlier sonnet while journeying to
Italy with Severn, possibly on October 1, 1820.
lids In his letter to his brother Tom (June 25–

27, 1818), Keats said that natural scenes in the
Lake Country "refine one's sensual vision into
a sort of north star which can never cease to
be open lidded and stedfast over the wonders
of the great Power."
Eremite hermit (with usually a religious connotation)

The moving waters at their priestlike task
   Of pure ablution° round earth's human shores,
Or gazing on the new soft-fallen mask
   Of snow upon the mountains and the moors—
No—yet still stedfast, still unchangeable,
10   Pillowed upon my fair love's ripening breast,
To feel forever its soft fall and swell,
   Awake forever in a sweet unrest,
Still, still to hear her tender-taken breath,
And so live ever—or else swoon to death.
1819–20   1838

This Living Hand°

This living hand, now warm and capable
Of earnest grasping, would, if it were cold
And in the icy silence of the tomb,
So haunt thy days and chill thy dreaming nights
That thou wouldst wish thine own heart dry of blood
So in my veins red life might stream again,
And thou be conscience-calmed—see here it is—
I hold it towards you.
1819–20   1898

OTHER ROMANTIC POETS

The eleven poets gathered together here were all contemporaries of the six major Romantic poets. One of them, John Clare, is all but a major poet in his own right. At least two others, Landor and Beddoes, wrote perfect poems within the limitations of their chosen modes. The others are both valuable in themselves and important reflectors of the greater poets of the period.

William Lisle Bowles (1762–1850), a clergyman of the Church of England, matters because of his little volume of 1789, *Fourteen Sonnets,* which influenced much of Coleridge's early poetry, and which is discussed in Chapter 1 of Coleridge's *Biographia Literaria.*

Sir Walter Scott (1771–1832) was formerly accounted a major poet, but time has demonstrated that his permanent work was done in the novel (*Ivanhoe, The Heart of Midlothian,* etc.). Born in Edinburgh, he practiced law, and began his literary career as a translator and ballad collector. From 1805 to 1812, when Byron's competing success helped turn him toward prose fiction, Scott wrote a sequence of metrical tales, of which the best are *The Lay of the Last Minstrel, Marmion,* and *The Lady of the Lake.* But his best poems are lyrics like the three given here: ballad-like,

ablution the act of washing clean; associated with religious rites (hence "priestlike")
This Living Hand probably the last lines of poetry that Keats wrote, perhaps as late as January 1820. Though there is a tradition that they were addressed to Fanny Brawne, they would fit more readily into a Romantic drama of the Jacobean mode, like those by Beddoes and Darley.

archaic, restrained, but with undertones of the deeper emotions to be found in Wordsworth and Coleridge.

Walter Savage Landor (1775–1864) is too large a poetic figure to be justly represented here, though the nine poems chosen do show his elegiac powers. A vehement and overwhelming personality whose career spans much of the history of nineteenth-century poetry, he associated both with the major Romantic and the major Victorian writers. His life was a series of lawsuits, controversies, quarrels with parents, wife, children, friends, and strangers, but his art, in the prose *Imaginary Conversations* and in the deliberately classical, epigrammatic poems, is rightly described as "marmoreal." He died in Italy, at ninety, still turbulent in personality, still restrained and disciplined in style.

Thomas Love Peacock (1785–1866), Shelley's close friend and George Meredith's father-in-law, did his best work as comic novelist (*Nightmare Abbey, Headlong Hall, Crotchet Castle*) and in the shrewd essay "The Four Ages of Poetry" that inspired Shelley's rhapsodic "A Defence of Poetry." Self-educated and wealthy, he delayed steady work until he entered the East India Company, with which he remained for the rest of his life. His best verse, like the delightful novels, is on the border between intellectual satire and fantastic comedy.

With **John Clare** (1793–1864) we come to a poet whose range is narrow, but so intense and pure are his best poems that in them he matches the major Romantics. Though in his madness Clare identified himself with Byron, he is a Wordsworthian poet, and a genuine visionary of nature. More than Burns, he was a peasant poet, whose father was a Northamptonshire farm laborer. In 1820 he published *Poems Descriptive of Rural Life and Scenery,* followed by *The Village Minstrel* in 1821, both of which were popular for a brief while. But his success passed, and the strains of supporting his wife and children aggravated schizoid tendencies always present in him. From 1836 until 1841, when he ran off, Clare was confined in a private asylum, a victim of an acute manic-depressive cycle. From 1841 until 1864, when he died, poor Clare lived in the Northampton General Lunatic Asylum, where he continued to write copiously.

The eleven poems and fragments given here are representative of what is best in Clare, from the overt exploration of Wordsworthian-Coleridgean ideas in "Pastoral Poesy" to the astonishing visionary group of Blake-like lyrics. What is unique to Clare is difficult to describe, but unmistakable. Though he lacks Wordsworth's power and Blake's insight, he can write in the modes of both with a freedom from self-consciousness that makes him one of the most direct and decently human poets in the language. And his indeliberate pathos, which might be expected to be an aesthetic liability, is redeemed by his immediacy, and moves us because in its integrity it seems not to need us. A poem like "A Vision" stands beyond the contraries of human existence, and persuades us that Clare himself, for all his life's horror and defeat, knew a final triumph in the spirit.

The remaining poets, like Clare, are in the generation of Keats and Shelley, and led mostly desperate lives, like the greater poets they imitated. **George Darley** (1795–1846), an Anglo-Irishman born and educated in Dublin, came to London to earn his living as a literary hack, writing art and literary reviews for the periodicals, and mathematical textbooks, as well as tragedies in the Jacobean style, like those of Beddoes, Procter, and Wade. Darley's genius was for lyrical poetry, particularly exemplified in the astonishing *Nepenthe,* which takes *Alastor* and *Endymion* as its models.

But Darley was defeated by his own nature; a struggle with his own inversions made him a compulsive stutterer, and augmented a melancholia that carried him to the borders of madness. His relation to the Muse is beautifully summed up by him in what can serve as the epitaph for his entire generation of poets: "He who the Syren's hair would win / Is mostly strangled in the tide."

Hartley Coleridge (1796–1849), first-born son of his illustrious father, spent his life in the shadows of his father and of Wordsworth and Southey, who were almost his foster-fathers. Poor Hartley could fulfill the prophecies of "Frost at Midnight" only ironically, yet the sweetness of his temperament made him a beloved figure in the Lake Country. He drank his way out of his Oxford fellowship, and was a near-alcoholic all his life, but he left behind a few good sonnets as a small extension of the family tradition.

Thomas Hood's life (1799–1845) war still sadder, as Hood had a larger talent to dissipate. Born in London, the son of a Scottish bookseller, Hood became a popular man of lettters, writing in most available forms. Tuberculosis and poverty deadened his poetic ambitions, and turned him from his earlier, Keatsian poetry to the comic verse for which he is now mostly recalled.

With **Thomas Lovell Beddoes** (1803–1849), we return to doomed genius, as with Clare, but Beddoes is a very different poet, closely influenced by Shelley's more de-spairing work. Though less famous than Poe, he is a much better poet than his Ameri-can analogue, for Beddoes achieved mastery in his revival of Gothic morbidities. Born near Bristol, he was the son of a famous eccentric literary physician. At Pembroke College, Oxford, he began to write his peculiar versions of Jacobean tragedy, and lamented the death of Shelley in a radiant outburst of 1822. He proceeded to Germany, where he studied anatomy, in which he became rather grimly learned. Most of his life was spent in Germany and Switzerland, and was occupied by revolutionary ac-tivity, the practice of medicine, and many unhappy homosexual love affairs. In 1829, he made his first attempt at suicide; his last and successful attempt came at Basel, when he was forty-six.

For the last twenty years of his life, Beddoes worked at the composition of his masterpiece, *Death's Jest-Book; or The Fool's Tragedy*, a monumental visionary drama that breaks the confines of its quasi-Jacobean form. Interspersed throughout the play are haunting songs, unlike those even of Shelley, whom Beddoes loved and con-stantly imitated. The deliberate contrast between the unearthly delicacy of tone, and the grotesque vision of death everywhere insinuating itself into life, is the basis of Beddoes's narrow but eminently satisfying lyrical art.

Samuel Palmer (1805–1881), represented in this volume by several of his pictures as well as one visionary lyric, was in his very early work one of Blake's disciples and one of England's best painters. In after years, he aged into a relatively mediocre Victorian landscapist, but the paintings done at Shoreham in his youth are more vivid and successful visual realizations of the lower paradise Blake called Beulah than Blake could manage himself.

Thomas Wade (1805–1875), the last of these poets, is now almost forgotten. Another Jacobean revivalist, and Shelleyan enthusiast, he outlived his brief reputation, but a few of his meditations on sublime scenes recapture something of the Shelleyan intensity of *Alastor* and "Julian and Maddalo."

WILLIAM LISLE BOWLES

To the River Itchin, Near Winton°

Itchin, when I behold thy banks again,
   Thy crumbling margin, and thy silver breast,
   On which the self-same tints still seem to rest,
Why feels my heart the shivering sense of pain?
Is it—that many a summer's day has past
   Since, in life's morn, I caroled on thy side?
   Is it—that oft, since then, my heart has sighed,
As Youth, and Hope's delusive gleams, flew fast?
   Is it—that those, who circled on thy shore,
10   Companions of my youth, now meet no more?
Whate'er the cause, upon thy banks I bend
   Sorrowing, yet feel such solace at my heart,
As at the meeting of some long-lost friend,
   From whom, in happier hours, we wept to part.

1789

SIR WALTER SCOTT

The Dreary Change°

The sun upon the Weirdlaw Hill,
   In Ettrick's vale, is sinking sweet;
The westland wind is hush and still,
   The lake lies sleeping at my feet.
Yet not the landscape to mine eye
   Bears those bright hues that once it bore;
Though evening, with her richest dye,
   Flames o'er the hills of Ettrick's shore.

With listless look along the plain,
10   I see Tweed's silver current glide,
And coldly mark the holy fane
   Of Melrose rise in ruined pride.
The quiet lake, the balmy air,
   The hill, the stream, the tower, the tree,—
Are they still such as once they were?
   Or is the dreary change in me?

Alas, the warped and broken board,
   How can it bear the painter's dye!
The harp of strained and tuneless chord,
20   How to the minstrel's skill reply!

To the River Itchin, Near Winton This and similar sonnets by Bowles provided the model for Coleridge's early "Sonnet: To the River Otter."

The Dreary Change This is Scott's modest equivalent of Wordsworth's "Intimations" ode.

To aching eyes each landscape lowers,
　　To feverish pulse each gale blows chill;
And Araby's or Eden's bowers
　　Were barren as this moorland hill.

　　　　　　　1817

'Proud Maisie'°

Proud Maisie is in the wood,
　　Walking so early;
Sweet Robin sits on the bush,
　　Singing so rarely.

'Tell me, thou bonny bird,
　　When shall I marry me?'
'When six braw° gentlemen
　　Kirkward shall carry ye.'

'Who makes the bridal bed,
10　　Birdie, say truly?'
'The grey-headed sexton
　　That delves the grave duly.

'The glow-worm o'er grave and stone
　　Shall light thee steady.
The owl from the steeple sing,
　　"Welcome, proud lady".'

　　　　　　　1818

The Song of the Reim-kennar°

Stern eagle of the far north-west,
Thou that bearest in thy grasp the thunderbolt,
Thou whose rushing pinions stir ocean to madness,
Thou the destroyer of herds, thou the scatterer of navies,
Amidst the scream of thy rage,
Amidst the rushing of thy onward wings,
Though thy scream be loud as the cry of a perishing nation,
Though the rushing of thy wings be like the roar of ten thousand waves,
Yet hear, in thine ire and thy haste,
10　Hear thou the voice of the Reim-kennar.

Thou hast met the pine-trees of Drontheim,
Their dark-green heads lie prostrate beside their up-rooted stems;

Proud Maisie sung by Madge Wildfire on her deathbed in the novel *The Heart of Midlothian;* it is in the tradition of the mad song
braw fine
Reim-kennar Scott's own pseudo-archaism, formed from Germanic reim (rhyme) and kenner (knower), to mean one of the Norns or Fates skilled in magic rhymes or runic verse; the song is from the novel *The Pirate*

Thou hast met the rider of the ocean,
The tall, the strong bark of the fearless rover,
And she has struck to thee the topsail
That she had not veiled to a royal armada;
Thou hast met the tower that bears its crest among the clouds,
The battled massive tower of the Jarl° of former days,
And the cope-stone of the turret
20   Is lying upon its hospitable hearth;
But thou too shalt stoop, proud compeller of clouds,
When thou hearest the voice of the Reim-kennar.

There are verses that can stop the stag in the forest,
Ay, and when the dark-coloured dog is opening on his track;
There are verses can make the wild hawk pause on the wing,
Like the falcon that wears the hood and the jesses,°
And who knows the shrill whistle of the fowler;
Thou who canst mock at the scream of the drowning mariner,
And the crash of the ravaged forest,
30   And the groan of the overwhelmed crowds,
When the church hath fallen in the moment of prayer,
There are sounds which thou also must list,
When they are chaunted by the voice of the Reim-kennar.

Enough of woe hast thou wrought on the ocean,
The widows wring their hands on the beach;
Enough of woe hast thou wrought on the land,
The husbandman folds his arms in despair;
Cease thou the waving of thy pinions,
Let the ocean repose in her dark strength;
40   Cease thou the flashing of thine eye,
Let the thunderbolt sleep in the armoury of Odin;°
Be thou still at my bidding, viewless racer of the north-western heaven,
Sleep thou at the voice of Norna° the Reim-kennar.

Eagle of the far north-western waters,
Thou hast heard the voice of the Reim-kennar,
Thou hast closed thy wide sails at her bidding,
And folded them in peace by thy side.
My blessing be on thy retiring path;
When thou stoopest from thy place on high,
50   Soft be thy slumbers in the caverns of the unknown ocean,
Rest till destiny shall again awaken thee;
Eagle of the north-west, thou hast heard the voice of the Reim-kennar.
1821?   1822

Jarl an earl   **Odin** Scandinavian god of war
jesses short straps fastened about each leg of a   **Norna** Latinized name of Norn, one of the
falcon   three Fates

WALTER SAVAGE LANDOR

'Lately Our Poets'

Lately our poets loitered in green lanes,
Content to catch the ballads of the plains;°
I fancied I had strength enough to climb
A loftier station at no distant time,
And might securely from intrusion doze
Upon the flowers through which Ilissus° flows.
In those pale olive grounds all voices cease,
And from afar dust fills the paths of Greece.
My slumber broken and my doublet torn,
10   I find the laurel also bears a thorn.

1863

[Rose Aylmer, 1779–1800]°

Ah what avails the sceptred race,°
    Ah what the form divine!
What every virtue, every grace!
    Rose Aylmer, all were thine.
Rose Aylmer, whom these wakeful eyes
    May weep, but never see,
A night of memories and of sighs
    I consecrate to thee.

1806

Dirce

Stand close around, ye Stygian set,°
    With Dirce in one boat conveyed!
Or Charon,° seeing, may forget
    That he is old and she a shade

1831

On His Seventy-fifth Birthday

I strove with none, for none was worth my strife:
    Nature I loved, and next to Nature, Art:
I warmed both hands before the fire of Life;
    It sinks; and I am ready to depart.

1853

the plains a reference to the Lake School of
Wordsworth, Coleridge, and Landor's close
friend Southey
Ilissus river near Athens, mentioned in Plato's
Phaedrus
[Rose Aylmer, 1779–1800] an epitaph for a
young woman, befriended by Landor

sceptred race She was the daughter of a nobleman.
Stygian set the dead being carried across the
river Styx to Hades
Charon ferryman of the dead

Death Stands Above Me

Death stands above me, whispering low
   I know not what into my ear:
Of his strange language all I know
   Is, there is not a world of fear.
                  1853

Poem

I cannot tell, not I, why she
Awhile so gracious, now should be
So grave: I cannot tell you why
The violet hangs its head awry.
It shall be culled,° it shall be worn,
In spite of every sign of scorn,
Dark look, and overhanging thorn.
                  1846

Autumnal Song

Very true, the linnets sing
Sweetest in the leaves of spring:
You have found in all these leaves
That which changes and deceives,
And, to pine by sun or star,
Left them, false ones as they are.
But there be who walk beside
Autumn's, till they all have died,
And who lend a patient ear
10   To low notes from branches sere.°
                  1846

Memory

The Mother of the Muses, we are taught,
Is Memory: she has left me; they remain,
And shake my shoulder, urging me to sing
About the summer days, my loves of old.

---

culled gathered, picked   sere withered, dry

Alas! alas! is all I can reply.
Memory has left with me that name alone,
Harmonious name, which other bards may sing,
But her bright image in my darkest hour
Comes back, in vain comes back, called or uncalled.
10   Forgotten are the names of visitors
Ready to press my hand but yesterday;
Forgotten are the names of earlier friends
Whose genial converse and glad countenance
Are fresh as ever to mine ear and eye;
To these, when I have written and besought
Remembrance of me, the word *Dear* alone
Hangs on the upper verge, and waits in vain.
A blessing wert thou, O oblivion,
If thy stream carried only weeds away,
20   But vernal° and autumnal flowers alike
It hurries down to wither on the strand.

                                          1863

To Wordsworth

Those who have laid the harp aside
     And turned to idler things,
From very restlessness have tried
     The loose and dusty strings,
And, catching back some favourite strain,
Run with it o'er the chords again.

But Memory is not a Muse,
     O Wordsworth! though 'tis said
They all descend from her, and use
10   To haunt her fountain-head:
That other men should work for me
In the rich mines of Poesie,

Pleases me better than the toil
     Of smoothing under hardened hand
With attic emery and oil,
     The shining point for Wisdom's wand,
Like those thou temperest 'mid the rills
Descending from thy native hills.

Without his governance, in vain
20   Manhood is strong, and youth is bold.
If oftentimes the o'erpiled strain

vernal spring

Clogs in the furnace, and grows cold
Beneath his pinions deep and frore,
And swells and melts and flows no more,

That is because the heat beneath
   Pants in its cavern poorly fed.
Life springs not from the couch of Death,
   Nor Muse nor Grace can raise the dead;
Unturned then let the mass remain,
30   Intractable to sun or rain.

A marsh where only flat leaves lie,
And showing but the broken sky,
Too surely is the sweetest lay
That wins the ear and wastes the day,
Where youthful Fancy pouts alone
And lets not Wisdom touch her zone.
He who would build his fame up high,
The rule and plummet must apply,
Nor say, 'I'll do what I have planned,'
40   Before he try if loam or sand
Be still remaining in the place
Delved for each polished pillar's base.
With skilful eye and fit device
Thou raisest every edifice,
Whether in sheltered vale it stand,
Or overlook the Dardan strand,°
Amid the cypresses that mourn
Laodameia's love forlorn.°

We both have run o'er half the space,
50   Listed for mortal's earthly race;
We both have crossed life's fervid line,
And other stars before us shine:
May they be bright and prosperous
As those that have been stars for us!
Our course by Milton's light was sped,
And Shakespeare shining overhead:
Chatting on deck was Dryden too,
The Bacon of the rhyming crew;°
None ever crossed our mystic sea
60   More richly stored with thought than he;
Though never tender nor sublime,
He wrestles with and conquers Time.
To learn my lore on Chaucer's knee,

Dardan strand Trojan shore
Laodameia's . . . forlorn Wordsworth wrote a strong classic poem, "Laodamia" (1814), which ends with the image of trees growing out of the tomb of Laodamia's husband, an emblem of her frustrated love for him; Landor discusses the poem in his "Southey and Porson," one of the *Imaginary Conversations.*
Bacon . . . crew a tribute to Dryden; to be the Sir Francis Bacon among poets is to excel in pithy expressions of prudence and wisdom

I left much prouder company;
Thee gentle Spenser fondly led,
But me he mostly sent to bed.
I wish them every joy above
That highly blessed spirits prove,
Save one: and that too shall be theirs,
70 But after many rolling years,
When 'mid their light thy light appears.
1833   1834

THOMAS LOVE PEACOCK

Song by Mr. Cypress°

There is a fever of the spirit,
  The brand of Cain's unresting doom,
Which in the lone dark souls that bear it
  Glows like the lamp in Tullia's tomb.°
Unlike the lamp, its subtle fire
  Burns, blasts, consumes its cell, the heart.
Till, one by one, hope, joy, desire,
  Like dreams of shadowy smoke depart.

When hope, love, life itself, are only
10 Dust—spectral memories—dead and cold—
The unfed fire burns bright and lonely,
  Like that undying lamp of old:
And by that drear illumination,
  Till time its clay-built home has rent,
Thought broods on feeling's desolation—
  The soul is its own monument.
                                    1818

The War-Song of Dinas Vawr°

The mountain sheep are sweeter,
But the valley sheep are fatter;
We therefore deemed it meeter

Song by Mr. Cypress (from the novel, Nightmare Abbey) a parody of Lord Byron. The fashionably melancholy young Mr. Cypress is about to go into exile, explaining that he has quarreled with his wife, and so is free of any further obligations to his country; he sings this lyric, so good a parody of Childe Harold's Pilgrimage that little in Byron's poem is worthy of it.
Tullia's tomb Cicero's daughter, who died still a young woman. Cicero, in remorse, attempted to make a shrine of her tomb; in the early 16th century a Roman tomb was discovered on the

Appian Way with the embalmed, perfectly preserved body of a young woman, and a lamp; and it was taken, rather dubiously, to be Tullia's tomb.
The War-Song of Dinas Vawr (from the novel, The Misfortunes of Elphin) a minor Welsh king in King Arthur's time. As Peacock observed: this is "the quintessence of all war-songs that ever were written, and the sum and substance of all appetencies, tendencies, and consequences of military."

To carry off the latter,
We made an expedition;
We met a host, and quelled it;
We forced a strong position,
And killed the men who held it.

On Dyfed's° richest valley,
10 Where herds of kine were browsing,
We made a mighty sally,
To furnish our carousing.
Fierce warriors rushed to meet us;
We met them, and o'erthrew them:
They struggled hard to beat us;
But we conquered them, and slew them.

As we drove our prize at leisure.
The king marched forth to catch us;
His rage surpassed all measure,
20 But his people could not match us.
He fled to his hall-pillars;
And, ere our force we led off,
Some sacked his house and cellars,
While others cut his head off.

We there, in strife bewildr'ing,
Spilt blood enough to swim in:
We orphaned many children,
And widowed many women.
The eagles and the ravens
30 We glutted with our foemen;
The heroes and the cravens,
The spearmen and the bowmen.

We brought away from battle,
And much their land bemoaned them,
Two thousand head of cattle.
And the head of him who owned them:
Ednyfed, king of Dyfed,
His head was borne before us;
His wine and beasts supplied our feasts,
40 And his overthrow, our chorus.

                    1829

Dyfed's archaic name for region in Wales

JOHN CLARE

Pastoral Poesy

True poesy is not in words,
    But images that thoughts express,
By which the simplest hearts are stirred
    To elevated happiness.

Mere books would be but useless things
    Where none had taste or mind to read,
Like unknown lands where beauty springs
    And none are there to heed.

But poesy is a language meet,
10   And fields are every one's employ;
The wild flower 'neath the shepherd's feet
    Looks up and gives him joy;

A language that is ever green,
    That feelings unto all impart,
As hawthorn blossoms, soon as seen,
    Give May to every heart.

An image to the mind is brought,
    Where happiness enjoys
An easy thoughtlessness of thought
20   And meets excess of joys.

And such is poesy; its power
    May varied lights employ,
Yet to all minds it gives the dower
    Of self-creating joy.°

And whether it be hill or moor,
    I feel where'er I go
A silence that discourses more
    That any tongue can do.

Unruffled quietness hath made
30   A peace in every place,
And woods are resting in their shade
    Of social loneliness.

The storm, from which the shepherd turns
    To pull his beaver° down,
While he upon the heath sojourns,
    Which autumn pleaches° brown.

---

self-creating joy The poem echoes the dispute between Wordsworth's "Intimations of Immortality" ode and Coleridge's "Dejection: An Ode"; in phrases like this, Clare appears to take Coleridge's side.
beaver hat made of beaver's fur
pleaches bleaches

571

Is music, ay, and more indeed
    To those of musing mind
Who through the yellow woods proceed
40   And listen to the wind.

The poet in his fitful glee
    And fancy's many moods
Meets it as some strange melody,
    A poem of the woods,

And now a harp that flings around
    The music of the wind;
The poet often hears the sound
    When beauty fills the mind.

So would I my own mind employ,
50   And my own heart impress,
That poesy's self's a dwelling joy
    Of humble quietness.
    1824–32   1935

From Signs of Winter

The cat runs races with her tail. The dog
Leaps o'er the orchard hedge and knarls° the grass.
The swine run round and grunt and play with straw,
Snatching out hasty mouthfuls from the stack.
Sudden upon the elm-tree tops the crows
Unceremonious visit pays and croaks,
Then swops away. From mossy barn the owl
Bobs hasty out—wheels round and, scared as soon,
As hastily retires. The ducks grow wild
10 And from the muddy pond fly up and wheel
A circle round the village and soon tired
Plunge in the pond again. The maids in haste
Snatch from the orchard hedge the mizled° clothes
And laughing hurry in to keep them dry.

           · · ·
1832–35   1920

From Badger

When midnight comes a host of dogs and men
Go out and track the badger to his den,
And put a sack within the hole, and lie
Till the old grunting badger passes by.

knarls nibbles   **mizled** wet with drizzle

He comes and hears—they let the strongest loose.
The old fox hears the noise and drops the goose.
The poacher shoots and hurries from the cry,
And the old hare half wounded buzzes by.
They get a forkèd stick to bear him down
10 And clapt the dogs and bare him to the town,
And bait him all the day with many dogs,
And laugh and shout and fright the scampering hogs.
He runs along and bites at all he meets:
They shout and hollo down the noisy streets.

He turns about to face the loud uproar
And drives the rebels to their very door.
The frequent stone is hurled where 'er they go;
When badgers fight, and every one's a foe.
The dogs are clapt and urged to join the fray;
20 The badger turns and drives them all away.
Though scarcely half as big, dimute° and small,
He fights with dogs for hours and beats them all.
The heavy mastiff, savage in the fray,
Lies down and licks his feet and turns away.
The bulldog knows his match and waxes cold,
The badger grins and never leaves his hold.
He drives the crowd and follows at their heels
And bites them through—the drunkard swears and reels.

The frighted women take the boys away,
30 The blackguard laughs and hurries on the fray.
He tries to reach the woods, an awkward race,
But sticks and cudgels quickly stop the chase.
He turns agen and drives the noisy crowd
And beats the many dogs in noises loud.
He drives away and beats them every one,
And then they loose them all and set them on.
He falls as dead and kicked by boys and men,
Then starts and grins and drives the crowd agen;
Till kicked and torn and beaten out he lies
40 And leaves his hold and cackles, groans, and dies.

· · ·

1835–37   1920

To Wordsworth

Wordsworth I love, his books are like the fields,
    Not filled with flowers, but works of human kind;
The pleasant weed a fragrant pleasure yields,

dimute diminished

The briar and broomwood shaken by the wind,
The thorn and bramble o'er the water shoot
     A finer flower than gardens e'er gave birth,
The aged huntsman grubbing up the root—
     I love them all as tenants of the earth:
Where genius is, there often die the seeds;
10   What critics throw away I love the more;
I love to stoop and look among the weeds,
     To find a flower I never knew before;
Wordsworth, go on—a greater poet be;
Merit will live, though parties disagree!
1840–41   1949

[Poem]

I feel I am, I only know I am,
     And plod upon the earth as dull and void:
Earth's prison chilled my body with its dram
     Of dullness, and my soaring thoughts destroyed.
I fled to solitudes from passion's dream,
     But strife pursued—I only know I am.
I was a being created in the race
     Of men, disdaining bounds of place and time,
A spirit that could travel o'er the space
10   Of earth and heaven, like a thought sublime—
Tracing creation, like my Maker free,—
     A soul unshackled—like eternity:
Spurning earth's vain and soul debasing thrall—
But now I only know I am,—that's all.
after 1842   1935

Song [Secret Love]

I hid my love when young while I
Couldn't bear the buzzing of a fly;
I hid my love to my despite
Till I could not bear to look at light:
I dare not gaze upon her face
But left her memory in each place;
Where'er I saw a wild flower lie
I kissed and bade my love good-bye.

I met her in the greenest dells,
10   Where dewdrops pearl the wood bluebells;
The lost breeze kissed her bright blue eye,
The bee kissed and went singing by,

A sunbeam found a passage there,
A gold chain round her neck so fair;
As secret as the wild bee's song
She lay there all the summer long.

I hid my love in field and town
Till e'en the breeze would knock me down;
The bees seemed singing ballads o'er,
20 The fly's buss° turned a lion's roar;
And even silence found a tongue,
To haunt me all the summer long;
The riddle nature could not prove
Was nothing else but secret love.
after 1842   1920

Hesperus°

Hesperus! the day is gone,
Soft falls the silent dew,
A tear is now on many a flower
And heaven lives in you.

Hesperus! the evening mild
Falls round us soft and sweet.
'Tis like the breathings of a child
When day and evening meet.

Hesperus! the closing flower
10 Sleeps on the dewy ground,
While dews fall in a silent shower
And heaven breathes around.

Hesperus! thy twinkling ray
Beams in the blue of heaven,
And tells the traveller on his way
That Earth shall be forgiven!
after 1842   1949

Written in Prison°

I envy e'en the fly its gleams of joy
In the green woods; from being but a boy
Among the vulgar and the lowly bred,
I envied e'en the hare her grassy bed.
Inured to strife and hardship from a child,

buss a kiss, and also a variant of "buzz"   **Prison** when Clare was confined in an asylum
Hesperus the Evening Star

I traced with lonely step the desert wild,
Sighed o'er bird pleasures, but no nest destroyed,
With pleasure felt the singing they enjoyed,
Saw nature smile on all and shed no tears,
10   A slave through ages, though a child in years—
The mockery and scorn of those more old,
An Aesop° in the world's extended fold.
The fly I envy settling in the sun
On the green leaf, and wish my goal was won.
after 1842   1935

The Maid o' the West

In the mountains o' the west
Lives the girl I love the best
With her red rose cheeks and her coal black hair,
Her face is like the rose and her rose breast the lily fair.
In the mountains of the west lives the girl I love the best,
O there's nothing half so sweet as Love, and fair.

In the lands not made of clay
Where the sun ne'er sets away,
But shineth through the midnight bright and fair,
10   I love the lassie best wi' the bright auburn hair,
And she liveth in the land that knoweth no decay,
And the maid I love the best is for ever bright and fair.

The birds sing on the clouds in that eternal land,
Jewels and siller° are they a', and gouden° is the sand.
The sun is one vast world of fire that burneth a' to-day,
And night wi' hells of darkness for ever keeps away.
And dearly I love the queen o' that bright land,
The lily flowers o' woman that meeteth no decay.

Her eyes are springs of light
20   And the blue veins in the white
Of her bosom, may love there
For ever bright and ever fair.
How beautiful she seems to mortal sight,
The white robed maiden with the auburn hair.

And lips of amaranth° and eyes of light
And cheeks the rose of heaven as bright,
Angel of heaven—Maiden o' the West—
She is the maiden that I love the best.

Aesop 6th-century B.C. teller of moralized fables   amaranth imaginary purple flower that never
siller silver   fades
gouden golden

Her very eyes are suns o' living light,
30 And dear I love the lady o' the west.
after 1842   1949

The Peasant Poet

He loved the brook's soft sound,
    The swallow swimming by,
He loved the daisy-covered ground,
    The cloud-bedappled sky.
To him the dismal storm appeared
    The very voice of God;
And when the evening rock was reared
    Stood Moses with his rod.
And everything his eyes surveyed,
10   The insects i' the brake,
Were creatures God Almighty made,
    He loved them for his sake—
A silent man in life's affairs,
    A thinker from a boy,
A peasant in his daily cares,
    A poet in his joy.
        after 1842 1920

Poets Love Nature

Poets love nature, and themselves are love,
The scorn of fools, and mock of idle pride.
The vile in nature worthless deeds approve,
They court the vile and spurn all good beside.
Poets love nature; like the calm of heaven,
Her gifts like heaven's love spread far and wide:
In all her works there are no signs of leaven,
Sorrow abashes from her simple pride.
Her flowers, like pleasures, have their season's birth,
10 And bloom through regions here below;
They are her very scriptures upon earth,
And teach us simple mirth where'er we go.
Even in prison they can solace me,
For where they bloom God is, and I am free.
    after 1842   1873

I Am°

I am: yet what I am none cares or knows;
   My friends forsake me like a memory lost;
I am the self-consumer of my woes—
   They rise and vanish in oblivion's host,
Like shadows in love, frenzied, stifled throes:—
And yet I am, and live—like vapours tost

Into the nothingness of scorn and noise,
   Into the living sea of waking dreams,
Where there is neither sense of life or joys,
10   But the vast shipwreck of my life's esteems;
Even the dearest, that I love the best
Are strange—nay, rather stranger than the rest.

I long for scenes, where man hath never trod,
   A place where woman never smiled or wept
There to abide with my Creator God,
   And sleep as I in childhood sweetly slept,
Untroubling and untroubled where I lie,
The grass below, above, the vaulted sky.
1844?   1865

An Invite to Eternity

Wilt thou go with me, sweet maid
Say, maiden, wilt thou go with me
Through the valley depths of shade,
Of night and dark obscurity,
Where the path hath lost its way,
Where the sun forgets the day,
Where there's nor life nor light to see,
Sweet maiden, wilt thou go with me?

Where stones will turn to flooding streams,
10 Where plains will rise like ocean waves,
Where life will fade like visioned dreams
And mountains darken into caves,
Say, maiden, wilt thou go with me
Through this sad non-identity,
Where parents live and are forgot,
And sisters live and know us not?

Say, maiden, wilt thou go with me
In this strange death of life to be,

I Am perhaps an ironical reflection of Jehovah's "I am That I am," Exodus 3:14; perhaps even a reaction to Coleridge's definition of the Primary Imagination in *Biographia Literaria* XIII

To live in death and be the same
20   Without this life, or home, or name,
At once to be and not to be—
That was and is not—yet to see
Things pass like shadows and the sky
Above, below, around us lie?

The land of shadows wilt thou trace,
And look, nor know each other's face;
The present mixed with reasons gone,
And past and present all as one?
Say, maiden, can thy life be led
30   To join the living with the dead?
Then trace thy footsteps on with me;
We're wed to one eternity.
1844?   1920

A Vision

I lost the love of heaven above,
    I spurned the lust of earth below,
I felt the sweets of fancied love,
    And hell itself my only foe.

I lost earth's joys, but felt the glow
    Of heaven's flame abound in me,
Till loveliness and I did grow
    The bard of immortality.

I loved but woman fell away,
10   I hid me from her faded flame,
I snatched the sun's eternal ray
    And wrote till earth was but a name.

In every language upon earth,
    On every shore, o'er every sea,
I gave my name immortal birth
    And kept my spirit with the free.
1844   1924

Clock-a-Clay°

In the cowslip peeps I lie
Hidden from the buzzing fly,
While green grass beneath me lies
Pearled wi' dew like fishes' eyes.

Clock-a-Clay the ladybird

Here I lie, a clock-a-clay,
Waiting for the time o' day.

While grassy forests quake surprise,
And the wild wind sobs and sighs,
My gold home rocks as like to fall
10   On its pillar green and tall;
When the parting rain drives by
Clock-a-clay keeps warm and dry.

Day by day and night by night
All the week I hide from sight.
In the cowslip peeps I lie,
In rain and dew still warm and dry.
Day and night, and night and day,
Red, black-spotted clock-a-clay.

My home it shakes in wind and shows
20   Pale green pillar topped wi' flowers,
Bending at the wild wind's breath
Till I touch the grass beneath.
Here I live, lone clock-a-clay,
Watching for the time of day.
1848?   1873

Fragment: Language Has Not the Power

Language has not the power to speak what love indites:
The Soul lies buried in the ink that writes.
                    1950

Bird's Nests

'Tis spring, warm glows the south,
Chaffinch carries the moss in his mouth
To filbert hedges all day long,
And charms the poet with his beautiful song;
The wind blows bleak o'er the sedgy fen,
But warm the sun shines by the little wood,
Where the old cow at her leisure chews her cud.
1863   1935

GEORGE DARLEY

It Is Not Beauty I Demand°

It is not Beauty I demand,
    A crystal brow, the moon's despair,
Nor the snow's daughter, a white hand,
    Nor mermaid's yellow pride of hair.

Tell me not of your starry eyes,
    Your lips that seem on roses fed,
Your breasts where Cupid trembling lies,
    Nor sleeps for kissing of his bed.

A bloomy pair of vermeil cheeks,
10   Like Hebe's° in her ruddiest hours,
A breath that softer music speaks
    Than summer winds a-wooing flowers.

These are but gauds; nay, what are lips?
    Coral beneath the ocean-stream,
Whose brink when your adventurer sips
    Full oft he perisheth on them.

And what are cheeks but ensigns oft
    That wave hot youth to fields of blood?
Did Helen's breast though ne'er so soft,
20   Do Greece or Ilium any good?

Eyes can with baleful ardour burn,
    Poison can breath that erst perfumed,
There's many a white hand holds an urn
    With lovers' hearts to dust consumed.

For crystal brows—there's naught within,
    They are but empty cells for pride;
He who the Syren's hair would win
    Is mostly strangled in the tide.°

Give me, instead of beauty's bust,°
30   A tender heart, a loyal mind,
Which with temptation I could trust,
    Yet never linked with error find.

One in whose gentle bosom I
    Could pour my secret heart of woes,

It Is Not Beauty I Demand This stately lyric has something of a 17th-century flavor, though its High Romantic vision of love should have warned the anthologist Francis Turner Palgrave, who included it in *The Golden Treasury* (where it is still so to be found) as a 17th-century lyric, sandwiched in between poems of Milton and Carew under the Palgrave-invented title "The Loveliness of Love."
Hebe's daughter of Zeus and Hera, and herself goddess of youth; she married Heracles
For crystal . . . tide a stanza, glorious in itself, that should have warned Palgrave
beauty's bust possibly a bust of Pallas Athena or of Venus

Like the care-burthened honey-fly
　　That hides his murmurs in the rose.

My earthly comforter! whose love
　　So indefeasible° might be,
That when my spirit won above
40　　Hers could not stay for sympathy.
　　　　　　　　　　　1828

The Phoenix°

I

O blest unfabled Incense Tree,
That burns in glorious Araby,
With red scent chalicing° the air,
Till earth-life grow Elysian there!

Half buried to her flaming breast
In this bright tree, she makes her nest,
Hundred-sunned Phoenix! when she must
Crumble at length to hoary dust!

Her gorgeous death-bed! her rich pyre
10　Burnt up with aromatic fire!
Her urn, sight high from spoiler men!
Her birthplace when self-born again!

The mountainless green wilds among,
Here ends she her unechoing song!
With amber tears and odorous sighs
Mourned by the desert where she dies!

II

Laid like the young fawn mossily
In sun-green vales of Araby,
I woke hard by the Phoenix tree
20　That with shadeless boughs flamed over me;
And upward called by a dumb cry
With moonbroad orbs of wonder, I
Beheld the immortal Bird on high
Glassing the great sun in her eye.
Stedfast she gazed upon his fire,
Still her destroyer and her sire!
As if to his her soul of flame
Had flown already, whence it came;

---

indefeasible not to be forfeited, never to be
voided
The Phoenix (from the long poem *Nepenthe*) a
legendary bird of great size and beauty, which
after hundreds of years would burn up; from its

ashes another Phoenix would arise, or perhaps
the same one. The association with the sun is
traditional and not Darley's invention.
chalicing as in the Eucharist, where the chalice
is the Communion cup

Like those that sit and glare so still,
30 Intense with their death struggle, till
We touch, and curdle at their chill!—
But breathing yet while she doth burn,
    The deathless Daughter of the sun!
Slowly to crimson embers turn
    The beauties of the brightsome one.
O'er the broad nest her silver wings
Shook down their wasteful glitterings;
Her brinded° neck high-arched in air
Like a small rainbow faded there;
40 But brighter glowed her plumy crown
Mouldering to golden ashes down;
With fume of sweet woods, to the skies,
· Pure as a Saint's adoring sighs,
Warm as a prayer in Paradise,
Her life-breath rose in sacrifice!
The while with shrill triumphant tone
Sounding aloud, aloft, alone
Ceaseless her joyful deathwail she
Sang to departing Araby!
50   Deep melancholy wonder drew
Tears from my heartspring at that view;
Like cresset° shedding its last flare
Upon some wistful mariner,
The Bird, fast blending with the sky,
Turned on me her dead-gazing eye
Once—and as surge to shallow spray
Sank down to vapoury dust away!

                III
O, fast her amber blood doth flow
    From the heart-wounded Incense Tree,
60 Fast as earth's deep-embosomed woe
    In silent rivulets to the sea!

Beauty may weep her fair first-born,
    Perchance in as resplendent tears,
Such golden dewdrops bow the corn
    When the stern sickleman appears.

But oh! such perfume to a bower
    Never allured sweet-seeking bee,
As to sip fast that nectarous shower
    A thirstier minstrel drew in me!
                1835

---

brinded streaked or spotted, with tawny color   cresset iron basket with burning light in it

HARTLEY COLERIDGE
Dedicatory Sonnet to S. T. Coleridge

Father, and Bard revered! to whom I owe,
Whate'er it be, my little art of numbers,
Thou, in thy night-watch o'er my cradled slumbers,
Didst meditate the verse that lives to show
(And long shall live, when we alike are low),
Thy prayer how ardent, and thy hope how strong,
That I should learn of Nature's self the song,
The lore which none but Nature's pupils know.

The prayer was heard: I 'wandered like a breeze,'°
By mountain brooks and solitary meres,
And gathered there the shapes and phantasies
Which, mixed with passions of my sadder years,
Composed this book. If good therein there be,
That good, my sire, I dedicate to thee.

1832   1833

THOMAS HOOD
Ode°

Autumn

I

I saw old Autumn in the misty morn
Stand shadowless like Silence, listening
To silence, for no lonely bird would sing
Into his hollow ear from woods forlorn,
Nor lowly hedge nor solitary thorn;
Shaking his languid locks all dewy bright
With tangled gossamer that fell by night,
   Pearling his coronet of golden corn.

II

Where are the songs of Summer?°—With the sun,
Oping the dusky eyelids of the south,
Till shade and silence waken up as one,
And Morning sings with a warm odorous mouth.
Where are the merry birds?—Away, away,
On panting wings through the inclement skies,
    Lest owls should prey

'wandered . . . breeze' See the beautiful prayer in "Frost at Midnight," ll. 54–64.
Ode a deliberate and beautiful elaboration upon, and tribute to, Keats's great ode "To Autumn," with echoes also of the "Ode to Psyche" and "Ode on Melancholy"
songs of Summer See "Where are the songs of Spring?" in "To Autumn," l. 23.

Undazzled at noonday,
And tear with horny beak their lustrous eyes.

III

Where are the blooms of Summer?—In the west,
Blushing their last to the last sunny hours,
20 When the mild Eve by sudden Night is prest
Like tearful Proserpine,° snatched from her flowers
      To a most gloomy breast.
Where is the pride of Summer,—the green prime,—
The many, many leaves all twinkling?—Three
      On the mossed elm; three on the naked lime
Trembling,—and one upon the old oak tree!
      Where is the Dryads' immortality?°
Gone into mournful cypress and dark yew,
Or wearing the long gloomy Winter through
30   In the smooth holly's green eternity.

IV

The squirrel gloats on his accomplished hoard,
The ants have brimmed their garners with ripe grain,
      And honey bees have stored
The sweets of Summer in their luscious cells;
The swallows all have winged across the main;
But here the Autumn melancholy dwells,
And sighs her tearful spells,
Amongst the sunless shadows of the plain.
      Alone, alone,
40   Upon a mossy stone,
She sits and reckons up the dead and gone
With the last leaves for a love-rosary,
Whilst all the withered world looks drearily,
Like a dim picture of the drownèd past
In the hushed mind's mysterious far away,
Doubtful what ghostly thing will steal the last
Into the distance, grey upon the grey.

V

O go and sit with her, and be o'ershaded
Under the languid downfall of her hair:
50 She wears a coronal of flowers faded
Upon her forehead, and a face of care;
There is enough of withered everywhere
To make her bower,—and enough of gloom;
There is enough of sadness to invite,
If only for the rose that died,—whose doom

Proserpine involuntary queen of Hades, ab-   Dryads' immortality See "Ode to Psyche," l. 57.
ducted by Pluto

Is Beauty's,°—she that with the living bloom
Of conscious cheeks most beautifies the light;
There is enough of sorrowing, and quite
Enough of bitter fruits the earth doth bear,—
60   Enough of chilly droppings for her bowl;
Enough of fear and shadowy despair,
To frame her cloudy prison° for the soul!
                                    1822

THOMAS LOVELL BEDDOES

Lines°

Written in a Blank Leaf of the Prometheus Unbound

Write it in gold—a Spirit of the sun,
An Intellect ablaze with heavenly thoughts,
A Soul with all the dews of pathos shining,
Odorous with love, and sweet to silent woe
With the dark glories of concentrate song,
Was sphered in mortal earth. Angelic sounds
Alive with panting thoughts sunned the dim world.
The bright creations of an human heart
Wrought magic in the bosoms of mankind.
10   A flooding summer burst on Poetry;
Of which the crowning sun, the night of beauty,
The dancing showers, the birds whose anthems wild
Note after note unbind the enchanted leaves
Of breaking buds, eve, and the flow of dawn,
Were centred and condensed in his one name
As in a providence—and that was SHELLEY.
1822   1851

Song°

Old Adam, the carrion crow,
  The old crow of Cairo;
He sat in the shower, and let it flow
Under his tail and over his crest;
    And through every feather
    Leaked the wet weather;
And the bough swung under his nest;
For his beak it was heavy with marrow.
  Is that the wind dying? O no;

If . . . Beauty's See "Ode on Melancholy,"
l. 21.
cloudy prison See "Ode on Melancholy," l. 30.
Lines Beddoes wrote this in his copy of Prometheus Unbound when news reached him that
Shelley had drowned.
Song sung by Isbrand, the revenger disguised
as a court jester in the play Death's Jest-Book

10 It's only two devils, that blow
    Through a murderer's bones, to and fro,
        In the ghosts' moonshine.

    Ho! Eve, my grey carrion wife,
        When we have supped on king's marrow,
    Where shall we drink and make merry our life?
    Our nest it is queen Cleopatra's skull,
        'Tis cloven and cracked,
        And battered and hacked,
    But with tears of blue eyes it is full:
20 Let us drink then, my raven of Cairo.
        Is that the wind dying? O no;
    It's only two devils, that blow
    Through a murderer's bones, to and fro,
        In the ghosts' moonshine.
            1825?   1850

The New Cecilia°

    Whoever has heard of St. Gingo°
        Must know that the gipsy
        He married was tipsy
    Every day of her life with old Stingo.°

    And after the death of St. Gingo
        The wonders he did do
        The incredulous widow
    Denied with unladylike lingo:

    'For St. Gingo a fig's and a feather-end!°
10   He no more can work wonder
        Than a clyster-pipe° thunder
    Or I sing a psalm with my nether-end.'

    As she said it, her breakfast beginning on
        A tankard of home-brewed inviting ale,
    Lo! the part she was sitting and sinning on
        Struck the old hundredth° up like a nightingale.

    Loud as psophia° in an American forest or
        The mystic Memnonian marble in
    A desert at daybreak,° that chorister
20   Breathed forth his Aeolian warbling.

Cecilia St. Cecilia was patroness of music.
St. Gingo a saint canonized by Beddoes
Stingo particularly strong ale
feather-end She affirms that the good saint
lacked an adequate member; a "fig" here is a
small, contemptible thing or, as she nastily adds,
a "feather-end."

clyster-pipe an enema
old hundredth Psalm 100, "Make a joyful noise
unto the lord . . . "
psophia a wise bird
The mystic . . . daybreak the statue of Memnon at Thebes, Egypt, which sang in the dawn-
light

That creature seraphic and spherical,
Her firmament,° kept up its clerical
    Thanksgivings, until she did aged die
Cooing and praising and chirping alert in
Her petticoat, swung like a curtain
    Let down o'er the tail of a Tragedy.

Therefore, Ladies, repent and be sedulous°
    In praising your lords, lest, ah! well a day!
Such judgement befall the incredulous
30   And your latter ends melt into melody.
        1829–49   1935

Song of the Stygian Naiades°

> What do you think the mermaids of the Styx were singing as
> I watched them bathing the other day—

I

Proserpine° may pull her flowers,
    Wet with dew or wet with tears,
    Red with anger, pale with fears;
Is it any fault of ours,
If Pluto be an amorous king
    And come home nightly, laden
Underneath his broad bat-wing
    With a gentle earthly maiden?
Is it so, Wind, is it so?
10   All that I and you do know
Is that we saw fly and fix
'Mongst the flowers and reeds of Styx,
            Yesterday,
Where the Furies made their hay
For a bed of tiger cubs,
A great fly of Beelzebub's,°
The bee of hearts, which mortals name
Cupid, Love, and Fie for shame.

II

Proserpine may weep in rage,
20   But ere I and you have done
    Kissing, bathing in the sun,
What I have in yonder cage,
    She shall guess and ask in vain,
Bird or serpent, wild or tame;

firmament here, her fundament
sedulous diligent, here in praising the amorous
powers of saintly husbands
Stygian Naiades river nymphs or mermaids of
Styx, the river of death surrounding Hades

Proserpine involuntary queen of Hades, abducted there by the amorous Pluto
Beelzebub's sometimes the Devil, sometimes
one of his higher subordinates, known as the
lord of the flies

But if Pluto does't again,
It shall sing out loud his shame.
  What hast caught then? What hast caught?
Nothing but a poet's thought,
  Which so light did fall and fix
30   'Mongst the flowers and reeds of Styx,
             Yesterday,
Where the Furies made their hay
For a bed of tiger cubs,
A great fly of Beelzebub's,
The bee of hearts, which mortals name
Cupid, Love, and Fie for shame.
1835?   1851

SAMUEL PALMER

Shoreham: Twilight Time°

And now the trembling light
Glimmers behind the little hills and corn,
Lingering as loth to part; yet part thou must
And though than open day far pleasing more
(Ere yet the fields and pearlèd cups of flowers
    Twinkle in the parting light;)
Thee night shall hide, sweet visionary gleam
That softly lookest through the rising dew;
    Till all like silver bright,
10   The faithful witness, pure and white,
    Shall look o'er yonder grassy hill,
    At this village, safe and still.
All is safe and all is still,
Save what noise the watch-dog makes
Or the shrill cock the silence breaks.
    Now and then—
    And now and then—
    Hark! Once again,
    The wether's° bell
20   To us doth tell
Some little stirring in the fold.
Methinks the lingering dying ray
Of twilight time, doth seem more fair,
And lights the soul up more than day
When wide-spread sultry sunshines are:
Yet all is right and all most fair,
For thou, dear God, has formèd all;
Thou deckest every little flower,

Shoreham: Twilight Time Palmer wrote a few poems and some Virgilian translations; this pastoral lyric is a remarkable description of the world of many of his best paintings, the world his master Blake called Beulah or Innocence. wether's gelded male sheep's

Thou girdest every planet ball,
30   And mark'st when sparrows fall.
    1825   1960

THOMAS WADE

The Winter Shore

A mighty change it is, and ominous
Of mightier, sleeping in Eternity.
The bare cliffs seem half-sinking in the sand,
Heaved high by winter seas; and their white crowns,
Struck by the whirlwinds, shed their hair-like snow
Upon the desolate air. Sullen and black,
Their huge backs rearing far along the waves,
The rocks lie barrenly, which there have lain,
Revealed, or hidden, from immemorial time;
10   And o'er them hangs a sea-weed drapery,
Like some old Triton's° hair, beneath which lurk
Myriads of crowned shell-fish, things whose life,
Like a celled hermit's, seemeth profitless.
Vast slimy masses hardened into stone
Rise smoothly from the surface of the Deep,
Each with a hundred thousand fairy cells
Perforate, like a honeycomb, and, cup-like,
Filled with the sea's salt crystal—the soft beds
Once of so many pebbles, thence divorced
20   By the continual waters, as they grew
Slowly to rock. The bleak shore is o'erspread
With sea-weeds green and sere, curled and dishevelled
As they were mermaids' tresses, wildly torn
For some sea-sorrow. The small mountain-stream,
Swollen to a river, laves the quivering beach,
And flows in many channels to the sea
Between high shingly banks, that shake for ever.
The solitary sea-bird, like a spirit,
Balanced in air upon his crescent wings,
30   Hangs floating in the winds, as he were lord
Of the drear vastness round him, and alone
Natured for such dominion. Spring and Summer
And stored Autumn, of their liveries
Here is no vestige; Winter, tempest-robed,
In gloomy grandeur o'er the hills and seas
Reigneth omnipotent.
    1835

Triton's minor sea god; see Wordsworth's sonnet
"The World Is Too Much with Us"

Romantic Prose

That prose and poetry are of their natures antithetical to each other is an old and stubborn idea. The extremity of their presumed difference is suggested by part of the definition of prose given by the *Oxford English Dictionary:* "Plain, simple, matter of fact (and hence) dull or commonplace, expression, quality, spirit, etc. (The opposite of Poetry.)" It was one of the achievements of the Romantic Movement that it demonstrated that prose need not be restricted to mere practical purposes, that, so far from being necessarily plain, simple, and matter of fact, let alone dull or commonplace, it might be (to quote the *OED*'s definition of one meaning of poetry) "the expression or embodiment of beautiful or elevated thought, imagination, or feeling in language adapted to stir the imagination and emotions." Wordsworth's Preface to *Lyrical Ballads* (see below), which said that between the language of prose and of poetry there was no essential dissimilarity and that prose can be just as poetical as poetry itself, may be thought of as the trumpet which brought down the wall separating the two modes of expression.

Walter Pater, in his essay *Style,* says of what he calls "imaginative prose" that it is the "special art of the modern world." The three great practitioners of the new art, Hazlitt, Lamb, and De Quincey, would have wished to qualify Pater's temporal characterization. They saw themselves as being in a line of descent from a great, though in their time discredited, tradition, and they claimed one or another degree of kinship with the prose masters of the seventeenth century. The lucid rhetoric of the eighteenth century had a greater effect upon the shape of their sentences than is commonly said, but they took their conscious inspiration from the textured and adumbrative style of the writers of an earlier time, from the grave sonorities of John Milton, Jeremy Taylor, and Sir Thomas Browne or from the lighter manner of Izaak Walton and Charles Cotton. Yet of course Pater was right in suggesting that they had brought a new art into being. Of the great trio, De Quincey was the most overtly intentional and theoretical in his conception of prose. He took seriously an idea to which poets had often given a merely conventional utterance, that music is the most affecting and most nearly autonomous of the arts, and envisaged an "impassioned prose" which would rival music in the subtlety of its evocations and the hypnotic power of its cadences. Hazlitt and Lamb were neither so explicit nor so elaborate in their intentions, but their artistry in the medium of prose was scarcely less conscious. They loved it for itself, as poets love verse, and they cherished it as the means by which, to paraphrase Pater, they might express not mere fact but their imaginative sense of fact—fact as they themselves experienced it. They were committed to the personal authority of their vision perhaps even more intensely than were the Romantic poets.

If, as Pater says, "imaginative prose" is indeed to be regarded as "the special art of the modern world," its present status lends support to the idea advanced by some critics and cultural historians that the modern world has come to an end and that we are now in what is coming to be called the "post-modern" era. Imaginative prose was indeed a pre-eminent genre of the nineteenth century, both in its Romantic and in its Victorian phases. The great Victorian practitioners of the art, Carlyle, Ruskin, Newman, Dickens, Arnold (sometimes), and Pater himself, are not in all ways continuous with the Romantic prose writers, but each of them, equally with his predecessors, was concerned to shape a prose that would express not mere fact but his sense of it, what Pater calls "his peculiar intuition of the world." Eventually, however, such prose came to seem less appropriate to serious intellectual and artistic purposes than it had formerly been. After a certain point it becomes impossible to discover in the utterances of any notable literary or intellectual figures a concern with a prose which will be an object of interest in itself because it so well expresses the writer's peculiar intuition of the world in language adapted to stir the imagination and the emotions. This is not to say that we are not responsive to peculiar intuitions of the world or that we resist having our imagination and emotions stirred, but only that, for reasons which are numerous and complex, our culture has decided not to trust or take pleasure in such use of language as avows the writer's conscious purpose of communicating his peculiar intuition and his delight in doing so.

We have, in short, a different relation to the written word than that which prevailed among the Romantics. Not merely the work of the three conscious prose artists, Lamb, Hazlitt and De Quincey, but all the examples of Romantic prose included in this volume, whatever their genre, suggest that their words had been put on paper with a peculiar eagerness and urgency, as if the act of writing, like the act of love, was the happy gratuitous expression of vital existence. Even Wordsworth, who disliked the physical art of writing and avoided prose composition because it had to be carried on with pen in hand, when he got down to it displayed in the undertaking a gusto—to use that word of Hazlitt's so much liked by Keats—which no critic of our day can match. For Keats in his letters or for Dorothy Wordsworth in her journals to describe an experience, he with his brilliance, she with her modest immediacy, is as natural as having the experience, is, indeed, part of having it. For all these writers the written word has what Wordsworth said nature itself had, "a breathing life."

WILLIAM WORDSWORTH
1770–1850

Preface to Lyrical Ballads (1802)

When Wordsworth and Coleridge published *Lyrical Ballads* in 1798, they prefaced it with a brief "Advertisement" written by Wordsworth. This peremptory document puts the reader on notice that the poems he is about to encounter will probably not suit his taste and instructs him how to revise his settled standards of judgment with a view to finding pleasure in the poems, as it is right that he should. He is to understand that the majority of the poems were written as "experiments," the purpose of which is to "ascertain how far the language of conversation in the lower and middle classes of society is adapted to the purpose of poetic pleasure." This being the case, he might wonder whether what he is reading is rightly to be called poetry, for the chances are that he takes the defining characteristic of poetry to be "the gaudiness and inane phraseology of many modern writers." He is advised that he can rescue himself from this ignorant opinion only by recognizing that poetry is a difficult subject and requires much severe thought.

In 1800, when a second edition of *Lyrical Ballads* was called for, Wordsworth developed the position taken in the "Advertisement" to make the famous Preface. He revised and expanded it in 1802, the most notable of his additions being the eloquent passage which describes the nature and function of the poet.

The Preface is less peremptory than the "Advertisement" only because it consents to give reasons for its imperatives. Even so, its voice rings with a confident and uncompromising militancy which is unique in the history of criticism, as if a rebel general were announcing the terms on which he will accept the leadership of the state whose corrupt government he is about to overthrow. Toward the government itself, the poets and critics who have misled the people's taste, it takes the tone of Cromwell to the Rump Parliament: "It is not fit that you should sit here any longer! . . . . you shall now give place to better men." To the misguided people its language is courteous though stern, for truth is truth and not to be paltered with, and the Preface is firm in its intention that, under the new poetic dispensation, the public shall be given, in Cromwell's phrase, "not what they want but what is good for them."

That poetry is good for people is not a new idea, but never before has so much potentiality of beneficence been claimed for it, and with so much moral fervor. One of the elements of the Preface which make it, of all great documents of literary criticism, the most dramatically urgent is its explicit sense of cultural crisis. Like Rousseau before him, Wordsworth is conscious of something new that has come into society which tends to deteriorate the mind, to "blunt its discriminatory powers," "to unfit it for all voluntary exertion," and thus to "reduce it to a state of almost savage torpor." In specifying the "multitude of causes unknown to former times" which lead to this state of affairs—among them the crowding of men in cities and the ennui of urban work which produces a craving for excitement all too readily gratified by sensational news and entertainment—Wordsworth is responding to the early stages of that mass society and mass culture which we recognize as among the defining characteristics of modern life. It is as a countervailing force against the malign effects of this development—they are manifestly political as well as individual and personal—that Wordsworth defines the nature and function of poetry. In his own way he is describing the condition of human existence which nowadays preoccupies our thought under the name of "alienation." The informing idea of Wordsworth's theory of poetry, as of his practice, is that poetry has the power to prevent and reverse modern man's alienation, his estrangement from himself, from his fellow men, and from the universe. To the enforcement of this idea and to the explication of the particular means by which the poet realizes it, the Preface is devoted.

In a letter of 1802, Coleridge says of the Preface that it is "half a child of my own Brain," arising out of conversations between him and Wordsworth which were so frequent "that we could scarcely either of us perhaps positively say, which first started any particular thought." Yet Coleridge goes on to assert that he is "far from going all lengths with Wordsworth," that, indeed, he rather suspects "that somewhere or other there is a radical difference in our theoretical opinions respecting Poetry." What these differences were Coleridge was to make plain fourteen years later in Chapters XVII through XXII of *Biographia Literaria* (see below).

Preface to Lyrical Ballads (1802)

The first volume of these poems has already been submitted to general perusal. It was published, as an experiment, which, I hoped,[1] might be of some use to ascertain, how far, by fitting to metrical arrangement a selection of the real language of men in a state of vivid sensation, that sort of pleasure and that quantity of pleasure may be imparted, which a poet may rationally endeavour to impart.

I had formed no very inaccurate estimate of the probable effect of those poems: I flattered myself that they who should be pleased with them would read them with more than common pleasure: and, on the other hand, I was well aware, that by those who should dislike them they would be read with more than common dislike. The result has differed from my expectation in this only, that I have pleased a greater number, than I ventured to hope I should please.

For the sake of variety, and from a consciousness of my own weakness, I was induced to request the assistance of a friend, who furnished me with the poems of the *Ancient Mariner*, the 'Foster-Mother's Tale,' the *Nightingale*, and the poem entitled *Love*. I should not, however, have requested this assistance, had I not believed that the poems of my friend would in a great measure have the same tendency as my own, and that, though there would be found a difference, there would be found no discordance in the colours of our style; as our opinions on the subject of poetry do almost entirely coincide.

Several of my friends are anxious for the success of these poems from a belief, that, if the views with which they were composed were indeed realized, a class of poetry would be produced, well adapted to interest mankind permanently, and not unimportant in the multiplicity, and in the quality of its moral relations: and on this account they have advised me to prefix a systematic defence of the theory, upon which the poems were written. But I was unwilling to undertake the task, because I knew that on this occasion the reader would look coldly upon my arguments, since I might be suspected of having been principally influenced by the selfish and foolish hope of *reasoning* him into an approbation of these particular poems: and I was still more unwilling to undertake the task, because, adequately to display my opinions, and fully to enforce my arguments, would require a space wholly disproportionate to the nature of a preface. For to treat the subject with the clearness and coherence, of which I believe it susceptible, it would be necessary to give a full account

---

1. Wordsworth speaks as if *Lyrical Ballads* was his alone, a not unjustifiable view since all the poems that were added to the second edition of the volume were his.

of the present state of the public taste in this country, and to determine how far this taste is healthy or depraved; which, again, could not be determined, without pointing out, in what manner language and the human mind act and react on each other, and without retracing the revolutions, not of literature alone, but likewise of society itself. I have therefore altogether declined to enter regularly upon this defence; yet I am sensible, that there would be some impropriety in abruptly obtruding upon the public, without a few words of introduction, poems so materially different from those, upon which general approbation is at present bestowed.

It is supposed, that by the act of writing in verse an author makes a formal engagement that he will gratify certain known habits of association; that he not only thus apprizes the reader that certain classes of ideas and expressions will be found in his book, but that others will be carefully excluded. This exponent or symbol held forth by metrical language must in different eras of literature have excited very different expectations: for example, in the age of Catullus, Terence, and Lucretius and that of Statius or Claudian; [2] and in our own country, in the age of Shakespeare and Beaumont and Fletcher, and that of Donne and Cowley, or Dryden, or Pope. I will not take upon me to determine the exact import of the promise which by the act of writing in verse an author, in the present day, makes to his reader; but I am certain, it will appear to many persons that I have not fulfilled the terms of an engagement thus voluntarily contracted. They who have been accustomed to the gaudiness and inane phraseology of many modern writers, if they persist in reading this book to its conclusion, will, no doubt, frequently have to struggle with feelings of strangeness and awkwardness: they will look round for poetry, and will be induced to inquire by what species of courtesy these attempts can be permitted to assume that title. I hope therefore the reader will not censure me, if I attempt to state what I have proposed to myself to perform; and also (as far as the limits of a preface will permit), to explain some of the chief reasons which have determined me in the choice of my purpose: that at least he may be spared any unpleasant feeling of disappointment, and that I myself may be protected from the most dishonourable accusation which can be brought against an author, namely, that of an indolence which prevents him from endeavouring to ascertain what is his duty, or, when his duty is ascertained, prevents him from performing it.[3]

The principal object, then, which I proposed to myself in these poems was to choose incidents and situations from common life and to relate or describe them, throughout, as far as was possible, in a selection of language really used by men; and, at the same time, to throw over them a certain colouring of imagination, whereby ordinary things should be presented to the mind in an unusual way; and, further, and above all, to make these incidents and situations

2. Wordsworth seems to be saying that the earlier Roman and the earlier English poets used verse less self-consciously than did the poets who came at a later time. An adverse judgment on the later poets is probably, though not necessarily, implied.
3. Wordsworth writes here under the influence of the view, prevalent through the Renaissance and especially strong in the 18th century, that the poet owes it as a "duty" to his audience to satisfy its expectations. Actually, of course, he and Coleridge did much to vitiate the force of this obligation.

interesting by tracing in them, truly though not ostentatiously, the primary laws of our nature: [4] chiefly, as far as regards the manner in which we associate ideas in a state of excitement. Low and rustic life was generally chosen, because in that condition, the essential passions of the heart find a better soil in which they can attain their maturity, are less under restraint, and speak a plainer and more emphatic language; because in that condition of life our elementary feelings co-exist in a state of greater simplicity, and, consequently, may be more accurately contemplated, and more forcibly communicated; because the manners of rural life germinate from those elementary feelings; and, from the necessary character of rural occupations, are more easily comprehended; and are more durable; and lastly, because in that condition the passions of men are incorporated with the beautiful and permanent forms of nature. The language, too, of these men is adopted (purified indeed from what appear to be its real defects, from all lasting and rational causes of dislike or disgust) because such men hourly communicate with the best objects from which the best part of language is originally derived; and because, from their rank in society and the sameness and narrow circle of their intercourse, being less under the influence of social vanity they convey their feelings and notions in simple and unelaborated expressions. Accordingly, such a language, arising out of repeated experience and regular feelings, is a more permanent, and a far more philosophical language, than that which is frequently substituted for it by poets, who think that they are conferring honour upon themselves and their art, in proportion as they separate themselves from the sympathies of men, and indulge in arbitrary and capricious habits of expression, in order to furnish food for fickle tastes, and fickle appetites, of their own creation.[5]

I cannot, however, be insensible of the present outcry against the triviality and meanness both of thought and language, which some of my contemporaries have occasionally introduced into their metrical compositions; and I acknowledge, that this defect, where it exists, is more dishonourable to the writer's own character than false refinement or arbitrary innovation, though I should contend at the same time that it is far less pernicious in the sum of its consequences. From such verses the poems in these volumes will be found distinguished at least by one mark of difference, that each of them has a worthy *purpose*. Not that I mean to say, that I always began to write with a distinct purpose formally conceived; but I believe that my habits of meditation have so formed my feelings, as that my descriptions of such objects as strongly excite those feelings, will be found to carry along with them a *purpose*. If in this opinion I am mistaken, I can have little right to the name of a poet. For all good poetry is the spontaneous overflow of powerful feelings: [6] but

4. Compare Coleridge's account of the undertaking in *Biographia Literaria* XIV and XVII. Note that Wordsworth does not refer to the intention, realized in *The Ancient Mariner*, to write poems that set forth supernatural incidents.
5. "It is worthwhile here to observe, that the affecting parts of Chaucer are almost always expressed in language pure and universally intelligible even to this day" (Wordsworth). See Coleridge's disagreement with Wordsworth on the virtues of the language of low and rustic life, *Biographia Literaria* XVII.
6. It is often erroneously supposed that this famous statement constitutes a *definition* of poetry. Not only does Wordsworth immediately qualify the statement, but from the first he does not mean it to say what poetry *is* but only to suggest what the process of making poetry is.

though this be true, poems to which any value can be attached, were never produced on any variety of subjects but by a man, who being possessed of more than usual organic sensibility, had also thought long and deeply. For our continued influxes of feeling are modified and directed by our thoughts, which are indeed the representatives of all our past feelings; and, as by contemplating the relation of these general representatives to each other we discover what is really important to men, so, by the repetition and continuance of this act, our feelings will be connected with important subjects, till at length, if we be originally possessed of much sensibility, such habits of mind will be produced, that, by obeying blindly and mechanically the impulses of those habits, we shall describe objects, and utter sentiments, of such a nature and in such connection with each other, that the understanding of the being to whom we address ourselves, if he be in a healthful state of association, must necessarily be in some degree enlightened, and his affections ameliorated.

I have said that each of these poems has a purpose. I have also informed my reader what this purpose will be found principally to be: namely to illustrate the manner in which our feelings and ideas are associated in a state of excitement. But, speaking in language somewhat more appropriate, it is to follow the fluxes and refluxes of the mind when agitated by the great and simple affections of our nature. This object I have endeavoured in these short essays to attain by various means; by tracing the maternal passion through many of its more subtle windings, as in the poems of the *Idiot Boy* and the *Mad Mother*; by accompanying the last struggles of a human being, at the approach of death, cleaving in solitude to life and society, as in the poem of the 'Forsaken Indian'; by showing, as in the stanzas entitled 'We Are Seven,' the perplexity and obscurity which in childhood attend our notion of death, or rather our utter inability to admit that notion; or by displaying the strength of fraternal, or to speak more philosophically, of moral attachment when early associated with the great and beautiful objects of nature, as in *The Brothers*; or, as in the incident of 'Simon Lee,' by placing my reader in the way of receiving from ordinary moral sensations another and more salutary impression than we are accustomed to receive from them. It has also been part of my general purpose to attempt to sketch characters under the influence of less impassioned feelings, as in the 'Two April Mornings,' 'The Fountain,' *The Old Man Travelling*, *The Two Thieves*, etc. characters of which the elements are simple, belonging rather to nature than to manners, such as exist now, and will probably always exist, and which from their constitution may be distinctly and profitably contemplated. I will not abuse the indulgence of my reader by dwelling longer upon this subject; but it is proper that I should mention one other circumstance which distinguishes these poems from the popular poetry of the day; it is this, that the feeling therein developed gives importance to the action and situation, and not the action and situation to the feeling. My meaning will be rendered perfectly intelligible by referring my reader to the poems entitled 'Poor Susan' and the 'Childless Father,' particularly to the last stanza of the latter poem.

I will not suffer a sense of false modesty to prevent me from asserting, that I point my reader's attention to this mark of distinction, far less for the sake of these particular poems than from the general importance of the subject. The subject is indeed important! For the human mind is capable of being excited without the application of gross and violent stimulants; and he must have a very faint perception of its beauty and dignity who does not know this, and who does not further know, that one being is elevated above another, in proportion as he possesses this capability. It has therefore appeared to me, that to endeavour to produce or enlarge this capability is one of the best services in which, at any period, a writer can be engaged; but this service, excellent at all times, is especially so at the present day. For a multitude of causes, unknown to former times, are now acting with a combined force to blunt the discriminating powers of the mind, and unfitting it for all voluntary exertion to reduce it to a state of almost savage torpor. The most effective of these causes are the great national events which are daily taking place, and the increasing accumulation of men in cities, where the uniformity of their occupations produces a craving for extraordinary incident, which the rapid communication of intelligence hourly gratifies.[7] To this tendency of life and manners the literature and theatrical exhibitions of the country have conformed themselves. The invaluable works of our elder writers, I had almost said the works of Shakespeare and Milton, are driven into neglect by frantic novels, sickly and stupid German tragedies, and deluges of idle and extravagant stories in verse.[8]—When I think upon this degrading thirst after outrageous stimulation, I am almost ashamed to have spoken of the feeble effort with which I have endeavoured to counteract it; and, reflecting upon the magnitude of the general evil, I should be oppressed with no dishonourable melancholy, had I not a deep impression of certain inherent and indestructible qualities of the human mind, and likewise of certain powers in the great and permanent objects that act upon it which are equally inherent and indestructible; and did I not further add to this impression a belief, that the time is approaching when the evil will be systematically opposed, by men of greater powers, and with far more distinguished success.

Having dwelt thus long on the subjects and aim of these poems, I shall request the reader's permission to apprize him of a few circumstances relating to their *style*, in order, among other reasons, that I may not be censured for not having performed what I never attempted. The reader will find that personifications of abstract ideas rarely occur in these volumes; and, I hope, are utterly rejected as an ordinary device to elevate the style, and raise it above prose.[9] I have proposed to myself to imitate, and, as far as is possible,

7. Although Wordsworth writes out of his own observation of the drastic changes that were taking place in the culture of his time, he probably was confirmed in his anxiety by his reading of Rousseau, one of whose characteristic themes was the loss of personal autonomy that results from urban life and from the proliferation of literature and of organized public opinion. "[T]he rapid communication of intelligence" (i.e. of news) refers to the striking increase in the number of daily newspapers in England in the last quarter of the 18th century.
8. A reference to the "Gothic" novels of terror, of which Horace Walpole's *The Castle of Otranto* (1764) was the prototype; among the best known examples of the genre are Ann Radcliffe's *The Mysteries of Udolpho* (1794) and Matthew Gregory Lewis's *The Monk* (1795). Jane Austen parodied such novels in *Northanger Abbey*. The most notorious of the German sentimental melodramatists was August von Kotzebue (1761–1819); one of his plays, *Lovers' Vows*, figures in Jane Austen's *Mansfield Park*.
9. Personification is a figure of speech which attributes human form and feeling to inanimate objects or abstract ideas, e.g. "Secure from flames, from *Envy's fiercer rages*" (Pope). It was common in the 18th century. For a developed example, see Wordsworth's own "Ode to Duty."

to adopt the very language of men; and assuredly such personifications do not make any natural or regular part of that language. They are, indeed, a figure of speech occasionally prompted by passion, and I have made use of them as such; but I have endeavoured utterly to reject them as a mechanical device of style, or as a family language which writers in metre seem to lay claim to by prescription. I have wished to keep my reader in the company of flesh and blood, persuaded that by so doing I shall interest him. I am, however, well aware that others who pursue a different track may interest him likewise; I do not interfere with their claim, I only wish to prefer a different claim of my own. There will also be found in these volumes little of what is usually called poetic diction; [10] I have taken as much pains to avoid it as others ordinarily take to produce it; this I have done for the reason already alleged, to bring my language near to the language of men, and further, because the pleasure which I have proposed to myself to impart is of a kind very different from that which is supposed by many persons to be the proper object of poetry. I do not know how without being culpably particular I can give my reader a more exact notion of the style in which I wished these poems to be written than by informing him that I have at all times endeavoured to look steadily at my subject, consequently, I hope that there is in these poems little falsehood of description, and that my ideas are expressed in language fitted to their respective importance. Something I must have gained by this practice, as it is friendly to one property of all good poetry, namely, good sense; [11] but it has necessarily cut me off from a large portion of phrases and figures of speech which from father to son have long been regarded as the common inheritance of poets. I have also thought it expedient to restrict myself still further, having abstained from the use of many expressions, in themselves proper and beautiful, but which have been foolishly repeated by bad poets, till such feelings of disgust are connected with them as it is scarcely possible by any art of association to overpower.

If in a poem there should be found a series of lines, or even a single line, in which the language, though naturally arranged and according to the strict laws of metre, does not differ from that of prose, there is a numerous class of critics, who, when they stumble upon these prosaisms as they call them, imagine that they have made a notable discovery, and exult over the poet as over a man ignorant of his own profession. Now these men would establish a canon of criticism which the reader will conclude he must utterly reject, if he wishes to be pleased with these volumes. And it would be a most easy task to prove to him, that not only the language of a large portion of every good poem, even of the most elevated character, must necessarily, except with reference to the metre, in no respect differ from that of good prose, but likewise that some of the most interesting parts of the best poems will be found to be strictly the language of prose, when prose is well written. The truth of this assertion might be demonstrated by innumerable passages from almost all the poetical

10. "Diction" is a neutral word which means simply the choice of words. "Poetic diction" refers to words or phrases which have established themselves as appropriate to poetry, perhaps especially because they are not used in prose or speech.

11. Cf. Coleridge in *Biographia Literaria* IV: "Finally, GOOD SENSE is the BODY of poetic genius."

writings, even of Milton himself. I have not space for much quotation; but, to illustrate the subject in a general manner, I will here adduce a short composition of Gray, who was at the head of those who by their reasonings have attempted to widen the space of separation betwixt prose and metrical composition, and was more than any other man curiously elaborate in the structure of his own poetic diction.[12]

> In vain to me the smiling mornings shine,
> And reddening Phoebus lifts his golden fire:
> The birds in vain their amorous descant join,
> Or cheerful fields resume their green attire:
> These ears alas! for other notes repine;
> *A different object do these eyes require;*
> *My lonely anguish melts no heart but mine;*
> *And in my breast the imperfect joys expire;*
> Yet Morning smiles the busy race to cheer,
> And new-born pleasure brings to happier men;
> The fields to all their wonted tribute bear;
> To warm their little loves the birds complain.
> *I fruitless mourn to him that cannot hear*
> *And weep the more because I weep in vain.*

It will easily be perceived that the only part of this sonnet which is of any value is the lines printed in italics: it is equally obvious, that, except in the rhyme, and in the use of the single word 'fruitless' for fruitlessly, which is so far a defect, the language of these lines does in no respect differ from that of prose.

By the foregoing quotation I have shown that the language of prose may yet be well adapted to poetry; and I have previously asserted that a large portion of the language of every good poem can in no respect differ from that of good prose. I will go further. I do not doubt that it may be safely affirmed, that there neither is, nor can be, any essential ·difference between the language of prose and metrical composition. We are fond of tracing the resemblance between poetry and painting, and, accordingly, we call them sisters: but where shall we find bonds of connection sufficiently strict to typify the affinity betwixt metrical and prose composition? They both speak by and to the same organs; the bodies in which both of them are clothed may be said to be of the same substance, their affections are kindred and almost identical, not necessarily differing even in degree; poetry [13] sheds no tears 'such as Angels weep,' [14] but

---

12. The poem of Thomas Gray's is the "Sonnet on the Death of Richard West." The italics are Wordsworth's. It was in a letter to West, later published, that Gray said that "the language of the age is never the language of poetry."

13. "I here use the word 'poetry' (though against my own judgment) as opposed to the word prose, and synonymous with metrical composition. But much confusion has been introduced into criticism by this contradistinction of poetry and prose, instead of the more philosophical one of poetry and matter of fact, or science. The only strict antithesis to prose is metre; nor is this, in truth, a *strict* antithesis, because lines and passages of metre so naturally occur in writing prose, that it would be scarcely possible to avoid them, even were it desirable." (Wordsworth)

14. *Paradise Lost* I.620.

natural and human tears; she can boast of no celestial ichor [15] that distinguishes her vital juices from those of prose; the same human blood circulates through the veins of them both.

If it be affirmed that rhyme and metrical arrangement of themselves constitute a distinction which overturns what I have been saying on the strict affinity of metrical language with that of prose, and paves the way for other artificial distinctions which the mind voluntarily admits, I answer that the language of such poetry as I am recommending is, as far as is possible, a selection of the language really spoken by men; that this selection, wherever it is made with true taste and feeling, will of itself form a distinction far greater than would at first be imagined, and will entirely separate the composition from the vulgarity and meanness of ordinary life; and, if metre be superadded thereto, I believe that a dissimilitude will be produced altogether sufficient for the gratification of a rational mind. What other distinction would we have? Whence is it to come? And where is it to exist? Not, surely, where the poet speaks through the mouths of his characters: it cannot be necessary here, either for elevation of style, or any of its supposed ornaments: for, if the poet's subject be judiciously chosen, it will naturally, and upon fit occasion, lead him to passions the language of which, if selected truly and judiciously, must necessarily be dignified and variegated, and alive with metaphors and figures. I forbear to speak of an incongruity which would shock the intelligent reader, should the poet interweave any foreign splendour of his own with that which the passion naturally suggests: it is sufficient to say that such addition is unnecessary. And, surely, it is more probable that those passages, which with propriety abound with metaphors and figures, will have their due effect, if, upon other occasions where the passions are of a milder character, the style also be subdued and temperate.

But, as the pleasure which I hope to give by the poems I now present to the reader must depend entirely on just notions upon this subject, and, as it is in itself of the highest importance to our taste and moral feelings, I cannot content myself with these detached remarks. And if, in what I am about to say, it shall appear to some that my labour is unnecessary, and that I am like a man fighting a battle without enemies, I would remind such persons, that, whatever may be the language outwardly holden by men, a practical faith in the opinions which I am wishing to establish is almost unknown. If my conclusions are admitted, and carried as far as they must be carried if admitted at all, our judgments concerning the works of the greatest poets both ancient and modern will be far different from what they are at present, both when we praise, and when we censure: and our moral feelings influencing, and influenced by these judgments will, I believe, be corrected and purified.[16]

Taking up the subject, then, upon general grounds, I ask what is meant by the word poet? What is a poet? To whom does he address himself? And what language is to be expected from him? He is a man speaking to men: a man, it is true, endued with more lively sensibility, more enthusiasm and tenderness, who has a greater knowledge of human nature, and a more comprehensive soul,

15. The ethereal fluid that was said to run, instead of blood, in the veins of the Greek gods.
16. Wordsworth expresses here his consciousness of the revolutionary effect his poetic theory would have upon the taste of future readers.

than are supposed to be common among mankind; a man pleased with his own passions and volitions, and who rejoices more than other men in the spirit of life that is in him; delighting to contemplate similar volitions and passions as manifested in the goings-on of the universe, and habitually impelled to create them where he does not find them. To these qualities he has added a disposition to be affected more than other men by absent things as if they were present; an ability of conjuring up in himself passions, which are indeed far from being the same as those produced by real events, yet (especially in those parts of the general sympathy which are pleasing and delightful) do more nearly resemble the passions produced by real events, than any thing which, from the motions of their own minds merely, other men are accustomed to feel in themselves; whence, and from practice, he has acquired a greater readiness and power in expressing what he thinks and feels, and especially those thoughts and feelings which, by his own choice, or from the structure of his own mind, arise in him without immediate external excitement.

But, whatever portion of this faculty we may suppose even the greatest poet to possess, there cannot be a doubt but that the language which it will suggest to him, must, in liveliness and truth, fall far short of that which is uttered by men in real life, under the actual pressure of those passions, certain shadows of which the poet thus produces, or feels to be produced, in himself. However exalted a notion we would wish to cherish of the character of a poet, it is obvious, that, while he describes and imitates passions, his situation is altogether slavish and mechanical,[17] compared with the freedom and power of real and substantial action and suffering. So that it will be the wish of the poet to bring his feelings near to those of the persons whose feelings he describes, nay, for short spaces of time perhaps, to let himself slip into an entire delusion, and even confound and identify his own feelings with theirs; modifying only the language which is thus suggested to him, by a consideration that he describes for a particular purpose, that of giving pleasure. Here, then, he will apply the principle on which I have so much insisted, namely, that of selection; on this he will depend for removing what would otherwise be painful or disgusting in the passion; he will feel that there is no necessity to trick out or to elevate nature: and, the more industriously he applies this principle, the deeper will be his faith that no words, which his fancy or imagination can suggest, will be to be compared with those which are the emanations of reality and truth.

But it may be said by those who do not object to the general spirit of these remarks, that, as it is impossible for the poet to produce upon all occasions language as exquisitely fitted for the passion as that which the real passion itself suggests, it is proper that he should consider himself as in the situation of a translator, who deems himself justified when he substitutes excellences of another kind for those which are unattainable by him; and endeavours occasionally to surpass his original, in order to make some amends for the general inferiority to which he feels that he must submit. But this would be to encourage idleness and unmanly despair. Further, it is the language of men who

17. Wordsworth is using "mechanical" in the old derogatory sense in which it denoted manual labor and subservience. In a later version of the Preface, Wordsworth altered the phrase to read "in some degree mechanical."

speak of what they do not understand; who talk of poetry as of a matter of amusement and idle pleasure; who will converse with us as gravely about a *taste* for poetry, as they express it, as if it were a thing as indifferent as a taste for rope-dancing, or frontiniac [18] or sherry. Aristotle, I have been told, hath said, that poetry is the most philosophic of all writing: [19] it is so: its object is truth, not individual and local, but general, and operative; not standing upon external testimony, but carried alive into the heart by passion; truth which is its own testimony, which gives strength and divinity to the tribunal to which it appeals, and receives them from the same tribunal. Poetry is the image of man and nature. The obstacles which stand in the way of the fidelity of the biographer and historian, and of their consequent utility, are incalculably greater than those which are to be encountered by the poet who has an adequate notion of the dignity of his art. The poet writes under one restriction only, namely, that of the necessity of giving immediate pleasure to a human being possessed of that information which may be expected from him, not as a lawyer, a physician, a mariner, an astronomer or a natural philosopher, but as a man. Except this one restriction, there is no object standing between the poet and the image of things; between this, and the biographer and historian there are a thousand.

Nor let this necessity of producing immediate pleasure be considered as a degradation of the poet's art.[20] It is far otherwise. It is an acknowledgment of the beauty of the universe, an acknowledgment the more sincere because it is not formal, but indirect; it is a task light and easy to him who looks at the world in the spirit of love: further, it is a homage paid to the native and naked dignity of man, to the grand elementary principle of pleasure, by which he knows, and feels, and lives, and moves. We have no sympathy but what is propagated by pleasure: I would not be misunderstood; but wherever we sympathize with pain it will be found that the sympathy is produced and carried on by subtle combinations with pleasure. We have no knowledge, that is, no general principles drawn from the contemplation of particular facts, but what has been built up by pleasure, and exists in us by pleasure alone. The man of science, the chemist and mathematician, whatever difficulties and disgusts they may have had to struggle with, know and feel this. However painful may be the objects with which the anatomist's knowledge is connected, he feels that his knowledge is pleasure; and where he has no pleasure he has no knowledge. What then does the poet? He considers man and the objects that surround him as acting and reacting upon each other, so as to produce an infinite complexity of pain and pleasure; he considers man in his own nature and in his ordinary life as contemplating this with a certain quantity of immediate knowledge, with certain convictions, intuitions, and deductions which by habit become of the nature of intuitions; he considers him as looking

18. One of the rich sweet wines produced in France, Italy, and Spain from muscat grapes; more commonly called Frontignan.
19. Actually Aristotle, in his *Poetics*, said only that poetry is more philosophical than history. It is a striking comment on the literary culture of the time that Wordsworth had not read this important work of criticism but cites it from hearsay.
20. Wordsworth has in mind what the *Oxford English Dictionary* calls the "unfavourable sense" of the word "pleasure"—"sensuous enjoyment as . . . an end in itself. . . . The indulgence of the appetites."

upon this complex scene of ideas and sensations, and finding every where objects that immediately excite in him sympathies which, from the necessities of his nature, are accompanied by an overbalance of enjoyment.

To this knowledge which all men carry about with them, and to these sympathies in which without any other discipline than that of our daily life we are fitted to take delight, the poet principally directs his attention. He considers man and nature as essentially adapted to each other,[21] and the mind of man as naturally the mirror of the fairest and most interesting qualities of nature. And thus the poet, prompted by this feeling of pleasure which accompanies him through the whole course of his studies, converses with general nature with affections akin to those, which, through labour and length of time, the man of science has raised up in himself, by conversing with those particular parts of nature which are the objects of his studies. The knowledge both of the poet and the man of science is pleasure; but the knowledge of the one cleaves to us as a necessary part of our existence, our natural and unalienable inheritance; the other is a personal and individual acquisition, slow to come to us, and by no habitual and direct sympathy connecting us with our fellow-beings. The man of science seeks truth as a remote and unknown benefactor; he cherishes and loves it in his solitude: the poet, singing a song in which all human beings join with him, rejoices in the presence of truth as our visible friend and hourly companion. Poetry is the breath and finer spirit of all knowledge; it is the impassioned expression which is in the countenance of all science. Emphatically may it be said of the poet, as Shakespeare hath said of man, 'that he looks before and after.' [22] He is the rock of defence of human nature; an upholder and preserver, carrying every where with him relationship and love. In spite of difference of soil and climate, of language and manners, of laws and customs, in spite of things silently gone out of mind and things violently destroyed, the poet binds together by passion and knowledge the vast empire of human society, as it is spread over the whole earth, and over all time. The objects of the poet's thoughts are every where; though the eyes and senses of man are, it is true, his favourite guides, yet he will follow wheresoever he can find an atmosphere of sensation in which to move his wings. Poetry is the first and last of all knowledge—it is as immortal as the heart of man. If the labours of men of science should ever create any material revolution, direct or indirect, in our condition, and in the impressions which we habitually receive, the poet will sleep then no more than at present, but

---

21. In the Preface to *The Excursion* (1814) Wordsworth quotes a passage from his unfinished poem *The Recluse,* in which he gives eloquent expression to the idea that nature and the mind of man are adapted—"fitted"—to each other.

> . . . my voice proclaims
> How exquisitely the individual Mind
> (And the progressive powers perhaps no less
> Of the whole Species) to the external world
> Is fitted: and how exquisitely, too
>   . . .
> The external world is fitted to the mind;
> And the creation (by no lower name
> Can it be called) which they with blended might
> Accomplish . . .

22. *Hamlet* IV.iv.37.

he will be ready to follow the steps of the man of science, not only in those general indirect effects, but he will be at his side, carrying sensation into the midst of the objects of the science itself. The remotest discoveries of the chemist, the botanist, or mineralogist, will be as proper objects of the poet's art as any upon which it can be employed, if the time should ever come when these things shall be familiar to us, and the relations under which they are contemplated by the followers of these respective sciences shall be manifestly and palpably material to us as enjoying and suffering beings. If the time should ever come when what is now called science, thus familiarized to men, shall be ready to put on, as it were, a form of flesh and blood, the poet will lend his divine spirit to aid the transfiguration, and will welcome the being thus produced, as a dear and genuine inmate of the household of man.[23]—It is not, then, to be supposed that any one, who holds that sublime notion of poetry which I have attempted to convey, will break in upon the sanctity and truth of his pictures by transitory and accidental ornaments, and endeavour to excite admiration of himself by arts, the necessity of which must manifestly depend upon the assumed meanness of his subject.

What I have thus far said applies to poetry in general; but especially to those parts of composition where the poet speaks through the mouths of his characters; and upon this point it appears to have such weight that I will conclude, there are few persons, of good sense, who would not allow that the dramatic parts of composition are defective, in proportion as they deviate from the real language of nature, and are coloured by a diction of the poet's own, either peculiar to him as an individual poet, or belonging simply to poets in general, to a body of men who, from the circumstance of their compositions being in metre, it is expected will employ a particular language.

It is not, then, in the dramatic parts of composition that we look for this distinction of language; but still it may be proper and necessary where the poet speaks to us in his own person and character. To this I answer by referring my reader to the description which I have before given of a poet. Among the qualities which I have enumerated as principally conducing to form a poet, is implied nothing differing in kind from other men, but only in degree. The sum of what I have there said is, that the poet is chiefly distinguished from other men by a greater promptness to think and feel without immediate external excitement, and a greater power in expressing such thoughts and feelings as are produced in him in that manner. But these passions and thoughts and feelings are the general passions and thoughts and feelings of men. And with what are they connected? Undoubtedly with our moral sentiments and animal sensations, and with the causes which excite these; with the operations of the elements and the appearances of the visible universe; with storm and sunshine, with the revolutions of the seasons, with cold and heat, with loss of friends and kindred, with injuries and resentments, gratitude and hope, with fear and sorrow. These, and the like, are the sensations and objects which the poet describes, as they are the sensations of other men, and the objects which interest them. The poet thinks and feels in the spirit of the passions of men.

23. Alas, this has not come to pass. Science, so far from being "familiarized to men," has developed to the point where it is beyond the comprehension of most men, including poets.

How, then, can his language differ in any material degree from that of all other men who feel vividly and see clearly? It might be *proved* that it is impossible. But supposing that this were not the case, the poet might then be allowed to use a peculiar language, when expressing his feelings for his own gratification, or that of men like himself. But poets do not write for poets alone, but for men. Unless therefore we are advocates for that admiration which depends upon ignorance, and that pleasure which arises from hearing what we do not understand, the poet must descend from this supposed height, and, in order to excite rational sympathy, he must express himself as other men express themselves. To this it may be added, that while he is only selecting from the real language of men, or, which amounts to the same thing, composing accurately in the spirit of such selection, he is treading upon safe ground, and we know what we are to expect from him. Our feelings are the same with respect to metre; for, as it may be proper to remind the reader, the distinction of metre is regular and uniform, and not like that which is produced by what is usually called poetic diction, arbitrary, and subject to infinite caprices upon which no calculation whatever can be made. In the one case, the reader is utterly at the mercy of the poet respecting what imagery or diction he may choose to connect with the passion, whereas, in the other, the metre obeys certain laws, to which the poet and reader both willingly submit because they are certain, and because no interference is made by them with the passion but such as the concurring testimony of ages has shown to heighten and improve the pleasure which co-exists with it.

It will now be proper to answer an obvious question, namely, why, professing these opinions, have I written in verse? To this, in addition to such answer as is included in what I have already said, I reply in the first place, because, however I may have restricted myself, there is still left open to me what confessedly constitutes the most valuable object of all writing whether in prose or verse, the great and universal passions of men, the most general and interesting of their occupations, and the entire world of nature, from which I am at liberty to supply myself with endless combinations of forms and imagery. Now, supposing for a moment that whatever is interesting in these objects may be as vividly described in prose, why am I to be condemned, if to such description I have endeavoured to superadd the charm which, by the consent of all nations, is acknowledged to exist in metrical language? To this, by such as are unconvinced by what I have already said, it may be answered, that a very small part of the pleasure given by poetry depends upon the metre, and that it is injudicious to write in metre, unless it be accompanied with the other artificial distinctions of style with which metre is usually accompanied, and that by such deviation more will be lost from the shock which will be thereby given to the reader's associations, than will be counterbalanced by any pleasure which he can derive from the general power of numbers. In answer to those who still contend for the necessity of accompanying metre with certain appropriate colours of style in order to the accomplishment of its appropriate end, and who also, in my opinion, greatly underrate the power of metre in itself, it might perhaps, as far as relates to these poems, have been almost sufficient to observe, that poems are extant, written upon more humble subjects, and in a more naked and simple style than I have aimed at, which poems have continued to give pleasure from generation to generation. Now, if nakedness and simplicity be a defect, the fact here mentioned affords a strong presumption that poems somewhat less naked and simple are capable of affording pleasure at the present day; and, what I wished *chiefly* to attempt, at present, was to justify myself for having written under the impression of this belief.

But I might point out various causes why, when the style is manly, and the subject of some importance, words metrically arranged will long continue to impart such a pleasure to mankind as he who is sensible of the extent of that pleasure will be desirous to impart. The end of poetry is to produce excitement in co-existence with an overbalance of pleasure. Now, by the supposition, excitement is an unusual and irregular state of the mind; ideas and feelings do not in that state succeed each other in accustomed order. But, if the words by which this excitement is produced are in themselves powerful, or the images and feelings have an undue proportion of pain connected with them, there is some danger that the excitement may be carried beyond its proper bounds. Now the co-presence of something regular, something to which the mind has been accustomed in various moods and in a less excited state, cannot but have great efficacy in tempering and restraining the passion by an intertexture of ordinary feeling, and of feeling not strictly and necessarily connected with the passion. This is unquestionably true, and hence, though the opinion will at first appear paradoxical, from the tendency of metre to divest language in a certain degree of its reality, and thus to throw a sort of half consciousness of unsubstantial existence over the whole composition, there can be little doubt but that more pathetic situations and sentiments, that is, those which have a greater proportion of pain connected with them, may be endured in metrical composition, especially in rhyme, than in prose. The metre of the old ballads is very artless; yet they contain many passages which would illustrate this opinion, and, I hope, if the following poems be attentively perused, similar instances will be found in them. This opinion may be further illustrated by appealing to the reader's own experience of the reluctance with which he comes to the re-perusal of the distressful parts of *Clarissa Harlowe*, or the *Gamester*.[24] While Shakespeare's writings, in the most pathetic scenes, never act upon us as pathetic beyond the bounds of pleasure—an effect which, in a much greater degree than might at first be imagined, is to be ascribed to small, but continual and regular impulses of pleasurable surprise from the metrical arrangement.—On the other hand (what it must be allowed will much more frequently happen) if the poet's words should be incommensurate with the passion, and inadequate to raise the reader to a height of desirable excitement, then, (unless the poet's choice of his metre has been grossly injudicious) in the feelings of pleasure which the reader has been accustomed to connect with metre in general, and in the feeling, whether cheerful or melancholy, which he has been accustomed to connect with that particular movement of metre, there will be found something which will greatly contribute to impart passion to the words, and to effect the complex end which the poet proposes to himself.

If I had undertaken a systematic defence of the theory upon which these

24. Samuel Richardson's novel *Clarissa* (1747–48) and Edward Moore's play (1753).

poems are written, it would have been my duty to develop the various causes upon which the pleasure received from metrical language depends. Among the chief of these causes is to be reckoned a principle which must be well known to those who have made any of the arts the object of accurate reflection; I mean the pleasure which the mind derives from the perception of similitude in dissimilitude. This principle is the great spring of the activity of our minds, and their chief feeder. From this principle the direction of the sexual appetite, and all the passions connected with it take their origin: it is the life of our ordinary conversation; and upon the accuracy with which similitude in dissimilitude, and dissimilitude in similitude are perceived, depend our taste and our moral feelings. It would not have been a useless employment to have applied this principle to the consideration of metre, and to have shown that metre is hence enabled to afford much pleasure, and to have pointed out in what manner that pleasure is produced. But my limits will not permit me to enter upon this subject, and I must content myself with a general summary.

I have said that poetry is the spontaneous overflow of powerful feelings: it takes its origin from emotion recollected in tranquillity: [25] the emotion is contemplated till by a species of reaction the tranquillity gradually disappears, and an emotion, kindred to that which was before the subject of contemplation, is gradually produced, and does itself actually exist in the mind. In this mood successful composition generally begins, and in a mood similar to this it is carried on; but the emotion, of whatever kind and in whatever degree, from various causes is qualified by various pleasures, so that in describing any passions whatsoever, which are voluntarily described, the mind will upon the whole be in a state of enjoyment. Now, if nature be thus cautious in preserving in a state of enjoyment a being thus employed, the poet ought to profit by the lesson thus held forth to him, and ought especially to take care, that whatever passions he communicates to his reader, those passions, if his reader's mind be sound and vigorous, should always be accompanied with an overbalance of pleasure. Now the music of harmonious metrical language, the sense of difficulty overcome, and the blind association of pleasure which has been previously received from works of rhyme or metre of the same or similar construction, an indistinct perception perpetually renewed of language closely resembling that of real life, and yet, in the circumstance of metre, differing from it so widely, all these imperceptibly make up a complex feeling of delight, which is of the most important use in tempering the painful feeling which will always be found intermingled with powerful descriptions of the deeper passions. This effect is always produced in pathetic and impassioned poetry; while, in lighter compositions, the ease and gracefulness with which the poet manages his numbers are themselves confessedly a principal source of the gratification of the reader. I might perhaps include all which it is *necessary* to say upon this subject by affirming, what few persons will deny, that, of two descriptions, either of passions, manners, or characters, each of them equally well executed, the one in prose and the other in verse, the verse will be read a hundred times where the prose is read once. We see that Pope by the power of verse alone, has contrived to render the plainest common sense interesting, and even fre-

---

25. This statement is often remembered and quoted as if it said that poetry *is* "emotion recollected in tranquillity." See note 6.

quently to invest it with the appearance of passion. In consequence of these convictions I related in metre the tale of *Goody Blake and Harry Gill,* which is one of the rudest of this collection. I wished to draw attention to the truth that the power of the human imagination is sufficient to produce such changes even in our physical nature as might almost appear miraculous. The truth is an important one; the fact (for it is a *fact*) is a valuable illustration of it. And I have the satisfaction of knowing that it has been communicated to many hundreds of people who would never have heard of it, had it not been narrated as a ballad, and in a more impressive metre than is usual in ballads.

Having thus explained a few of the reasons why I have written in verse, and why I have chosen subjects from common life, and endeavoured to bring my language near to the real language of men, if I have been too minute in pleading my own cause, I have at the same time been treating a subject of general interest; and it is for this reason that I request the reader's permission to add a few words with reference solely to these particular poems, and to some defects which will probably be found in them. I am sensible that my associations must have sometimes been particular instead of general, and that, consequently, giving to things a false importance, sometimes from diseased impulses I may have written upon unworthy subjects; but I am less apprehensive on this account, than that my language may frequently have suffered from those arbitrary connexions of feelings and ideas with particular words and phrases, from which no man can altogether protect himself. Hence I have no doubt, that, in some instances, feelings even of the ludicrous may be given to my readers by expressions which appeared to me tender and pathetic. Such faulty expressions, were I convinced they were faulty at present, and that they must necessarily continue to be so, I would willingly take all reasonable pains to correct. But it is dangerous to make these alterations on the simple authority of a few individuals, or even of certain classes of men; for where the understanding of an author is not convinced, or his feelings altered, this cannot be done without great injury to himself: for his own feelings are his stay and support, and, if he sets them aside in one instance, he may be induced to repeat this act till his mind loses all confidence in itself, and becomes utterly debilitated. To this it may be added, that the reader ought never to forget that he is himself exposed to the same errors as the poet, and perhaps in a much greater degree: for there can be no presumption in saying, that it is not probable he will be so well acquainted with the various stages of meaning through which words have passed, or with the fickleness or stability of the relations of particular ideas to each other; and above all, since he is so much less interested in the subject, he may decide lightly and carelessly.

Long as I have detained my reader, I hope he will permit me to caution him against a mode of false criticism which has been applied to poetry in which the language closely resembles that of life and nature. Such verses have been triumphed over in parodies of which Dr. Johnson's stanza is a fair specimen.

> I put my hat upon my head,
> And walked into the Strand,
> And there I met another man
> Whose hat was in his hand.

Immediately under these lines I will place one of the most justly admired stanzas of the 'Babes in the Wood.'

> These pretty Babes with hand in hand
> Went wandering up and down;
> But never more they saw the Man
> Approaching from the Town.

In both these stanzas the words, and the order of the words, in no respect differ from the most unimpassioned conversation. There are words in both, for example, 'the Strand,' and 'the Town,' connected with none but the most familiar ideas; yet the one stanza we admit as admirable, and the other as a fair example of the superlatively contemptible. Whence arises this difference? Not from the metre, not from the language, not from the order of the words; but the *matter* expressed in Dr. Johnson's stanza is contemptible. The proper method of treating trivial and simple verses to which Dr. Johnson's stanza would be a fair parallelism is not to say, this is a bad kind of poetry, or this is not poetry; but this wants sense; it is neither interesting in itself, nor can *lead* to any thing interesting; the images neither originate in that sane state of feeling which arises out of thought, nor can excite thought or feeling in the reader. This is the only sensible manner of dealing with such verses: Why trouble yourself about the species till you have previously decided upon the genus? Why take pains to prove that an ape is not a Newton when it is self-evident that he is not a man?

I have one request to make of my reader, which is, that in judging these poems he would decide by his own feelings genuinely, and not by reflection upon what will probably be the judgment of others. How common is it to hear a person say, 'I myself do not object to this style of composition or this or that expression, but to such an such classes of people it will appear mean or ludicrous.' This mode of criticism, so destructive of all sound unadulterated judgment, is almost universal: I have therefore to request, that the reader would abide independently by his own feelings, and that if he finds himself affected he would not suffer such conjectures to interfere with his pleasure.

If an author by any single composition has impressed us with respect for his talents, it is useful to consider this as affording a presumption, that, on other occasions where we have been displeased, he nevertheless may not have written ill or absurdly; and, further, to give him so much credit for this one composition as may induce us to review what has displeased us with more care than we should otherwise have bestowed upon it. This is not only an act of justice, but in our decisions upon poetry especially, may conduce in a high degree to the improvement of our own taste: for an *accurate* taste in poetry, and in all the other arts, as Sir Joshua Reynolds has observed,[26] is an *acquired* talent, which can only be produced by thought and a long continued intercourse with the best models of composition. This is mentioned, not with so ridiculous a purpose as to prevent the most inexperienced reader from judging for him-

26. The great portrait painter of the 18th century, friend of Johnson, Burke, and Goldsmith. As the first president of the Royal Academy of Arts, he delivered between 1769 and 1790 annual *Discourses* on the principles of art. Wordsworth paraphrases a remark in Discourse XII.

self (I have already said that I wish him to judge for himself), but merely to temper the rashness of decision, and to suggest, that, if poetry be a subject on which much time has not been bestowed, the judgment may be erroneous; and that in many cases it necessarily will be so.

I know that nothing would have so effectually contributed to further the end which I have in view as to have shown of what kind the pleasure is, and how that pleasure is produced, which is confessedly produced by metrical composition essentially different from that which I have here endeavoured to recommend: for the reader will say that he has been pleased by such composition; and what can I do more for him? The power of any art is limited; and he will suspect, that, if I propose to furnish him with new friends, it is only upon condition of his abandoning his old friends. Besides, as I have said, the reader is himself conscious of the pleasure which he has received from such composition, composition to which he has peculiarly attached the endearing name of poetry; and all men feel an habitual gratitude, and something of an honourable bigotry for the objects which have long continued to please them: we not only wish to be pleased, but to be pleased in that particular way in which we have been accustomed to be pleased. There is a host of arguments in these feelings; and I should be the less able to combat them successfully, as I am willing to allow, that, in order entirely to enjoy the poetry which I am recommending, it would be necessary to give up much of what is ordinarily enjoyed. But, would my limits have permitted me to point out how this pleasure is produced, I might have removed many obstacles, and assisted my reader in perceiving that the powers of language are not so limited as he may suppose; and that it is possible that poetry may give other enjoyments, of a purer, more lasting, and more exquisite nature. This part of my subject I have not altogether neglected; but it has been less my present aim to prove, that the interest excited by some other kinds of poetry is less vivid, and less worthy of the nobler powers of the mind, than to offer reasons for presuming, that, if the object which I have proposed to myself were adequately attained, a species of poetry would be produced, which is genuine poetry; in its nature well adapted to interest mankind permanently, and likewise important in the multiplicity and quality of its moral relations.

From what has been said, and from a perusal of the poems, the reader will be able clearly to perceive the object which I have proposed to myself: he will determine how far I have attained this object; and, what is a much more important question, whether it be worth attaining; and upon the decision of these two questions will rest my claim to the approbation of the public.

1800, 1802   1802

DOROTHY WORDSWORTH
1771–1855

The article on Dorothy Wordsworth in an authoritative encyclopedia identifies her as "English writer and diarist." A writer in the most common meaning of the word she was not. She put many words on paper, enough to fill two sizable volumes, but nothing she wrote was intended for publication and she said that she would "detest" setting up as an author. For her *Recollections of a Tour Made in Scotland* (1803) she did indeed have in mind a small audience, "a few friends," but the Grasmere journal, which is the most memorable of all the records of her existence that she made, was intended to be read only by herself and her brother William.

Part of the interest of the journal is of course historical. No other document gives us so intimate a sense of the tone and temper of the first generation of English Romantic poets—not even in their own letters do Wordsworth and Coleridge stand so present before us as they do through Dorothy Wordsworth's loving references to them. And the clues to Wordsworth's creative processes which the journal affords are of decisive significance. But quite apart from its evidential importance, the journal has an inherent value, surely its greatest, as the expression of a rare spirit.

Dorothy, the third of the five Wordsworth children and the only girl, was born in 1771, a year and a half after the birth of William. She was seven years old when their mother died and for the next seventeen years she lived with one or another family of relatives, sometimes happily, sometimes not. William had always had a special place in her affections, as she in his, and for many years they entertained the hope of living together. This was made possible when Wordsworth received the famous bequest from his friend Raisley Calvert; in 1795 the brother and sister set up house together at Racedown in Dorsetshire. *The Prelude* makes plain the therapeutic effect which the reunion with Dorothy had upon Wordsworth's development, how when he was alienated from humanity by his despair over the course taken by the French Revolution, and from nature, and from his vocation as a poet, "the beloved woman" maintained for him "a saving intercourse" with his "true self."

In 1794 Wordsworth had made the acquaintance of Coleridge, who was to be the other salutary influence on his development as a poet, and in 1797 he and Dorothy moved from Racedown to Alfoxden in order to be near this most valued of all their friends. The association was of exceptional closeness; they were, in the phrase attributed to Coleridge, "three persons, but one soul." Dorothy's influence upon Coleridge's intellectual and imaginative life at this time was only less profound than upon her brother's. It was at Alfoxden that Dorothy first undertook to keep a journal, starting in January and ending in May of 1798, and she continued the practice through the first weeks of the visit which she, William, and Coleridge made to Germany in the autumn and part of the winter of 1798–99. In December 1799 Wordsworth and Dorothy realized their long-cherished plan of returning to live in their native Lake District. They established themselves in the little house known as Dove Cottage in the town of Grasmere, in full view of the lovely lake of the same name.

Of the journal that Dorothy kept at Grasmere between May 14, 1800, and January 16, 1803, it seems possible to say that in the whole range of literature no equal number of pages is so crammed and crowded with life. The life of nature is a ceaseless and urgent presence—every budding, flowering, falling, every change of aspect wrought by the process of the seasons or the hours is a vital event to which precise and delighted notice must be given. Yet intense as is Dorothy's response to what her brother called "Nature's breathing life," her consciousness of human life is even more salient and more memorable. The gentry of the neighborhood who make up the Wordsworths' social circle are pretty much taken for granted and are but faintly delineated, but persons lower in the social scale—the working people of the town and most especially the wandering population of the roads—are perceived with an often startling realization of their perdurable solidity and uniqueness. Times were bad and many persons were being displaced from their occupations and homes. Their suffering and their fortitude make one of Wordsworth's great recurrent themes, and one has the sense that before they might be seen in the transcendent momentousness in which they appear in his poems, they had first to be encountered in their immediate actuality by Dorothy.

No least part of the life with which the journal is charged is Dorothy's own passionate existence. It moves, if not toward what can properly be called tragedy, then at least toward great suffering. Of some part of what was to befall her she was inevitably conscious, that she must share her brother's love with another woman. Her feeling for Mary Hutchinson, whom Wordsworth married in 1802, was truly sisterly. But her feeling for her brother was more than that, at any rate more than sisterly feeling is commonly conceived to be, and when we have become aware of this from the tenor of her references to William in the Journal, we cannot read her account of her brother's wedding day without concluding that for her it was a kind of death, the end not of life but of joy. It says much for the strength and largeness of her spirit that it was by no means the end of her tenderness and devotion. For more than thirty years she lived in her brother's household, sharing its joys and sorrows, a cherished and honored figure. But in 1835, presumably as the result of arteriosclerosis, she suffered a drastic physical and mental deterioration which confined her to bed or to a wheelchair and cut her off from human intercourse. It was thus that she, once the most sentient of beings, survived for two decades, outliving her brother by five years.

So that the full flavor of the original may be preserved, the text of our selections from the Grasmere Journals has been taken, without change, from the edition of the Journals prepared by Mary Moorman, published by Oxford University Press in 1971. Miss Moorman worked from the manuscripts of the Grasmere Journals preserved at the Wordsworth Library in Grasmere, and has kept, in virtually every particular, to the punctuation, orthography, and dating of the original.

From The Grasmere Journals
1800–1802

1800

May 14 1800 [*Wednesday*]   Wm and John set off into Yorkshire [1] after dinner at ½ past 2 o'clock, cold pork in their pockets. I left them at the turning of the Low-wood bay under the trees. My heart was so full 'hat I could hardly speak to W. when I gave him a farewell kiss. I sate a long time upon a stone at the margin of the lake, and after a flood of tears my heart was easier. The lake looked to me I knew not why dull and melancholy, and the weltering on the shores seemed a heavy sound. I walked as long as I could amongst the stones of the shore. The wood rich in flowers. A beautiful yellow, palish yellow flower, that looked thick round and double, and smelt very sweet—I

1. To visit Mary Hutchinson, who was to become William's wife in 1802. John is John Wordsworth (1771–1805), William and Dorothy's younger brother.

supposed it was a ranunculus—Crowfoot, the grassy-leaved Rabbit-toothed white flower, strawberries, geranium—scentless violet, anemones two kinds, orchises, primroses. The heck-berry very beautiful, the crab coming out as a low shrub. Met a blind man, driving a very large beautiful Bull and a cow —he walked with two sticks. Came home by Clappersgate. The valley very green, many sweet views up to Rydale head when I could juggle away the fine houses, but they disturbed me even more than when I have been happier. One beautiful view of the Bridge, without Sir Michael's.[2] Sate down very often, though it was cold. I resolved to write a journal of the time till W. and J. return, and I set about keeping my resolve because I will not quarrel with myself, and because I shall give Wm Pleasure by it when he comes home again. At Rydale a woman of the village, stout and well dressed, begged a halfpenny—she had never she said done it before, but these hard times— — Arrived at home with a bad head-ach, set some slips of privett. The evening cold, had a fire—my face now flame-coloured. It is nine o'clock. I shall soon go to bed. A young woman begged at the door—she had come from Manchester on Sunday morn with two shillings and a slip of paper which she supposed a Bank note—it was a cheat. She had buried her husband and three children within a year and a half—all in one grave—burying very dear —paupers all put in one place—20 shillings paid for as much ground as will bury a man—a stone to be put over it or the right will be lost—11/6 each time the ground is opened. Oh! that I had a letter from William!

May 15 Thursday A coldish dull morning—hoed the first row of peas, weeded etc. etc., sat hard to mending till evening. The rain which had threatened all day came on just when I was going to walk.

Friday morning [*16th*] Warm and mild, after a fine night of rain. Transplanted raddishes after breakfast, walked to Mr Gell's [3] with the Books, gathered mosses and plants. The woods extremely beautiful with all autumnal variety and softness. I carried a basket for mosses, and gathered some wild plants. Oh! that we had a book of botany. All flowers now are gay and deliciously sweet. The primrose still pre-eminent among the later flowers of the spring. Foxgloves very tall, with their heads budding. I went forward round the lake at the foot of Loughrigg fell.[4] I was much amused with the business of a pair of stone chats. Their restless voices as they skimmed along the water following each other their shadows under them, and their returning back to the stones on the shore, chirping with the same unwearied voice. Could not cross the water so I went round by the stepping-stones. The morning clear but cloudy, that is the hills were not overhung by mists. After dinner Aggy [5] weeded onions and carrots. I helped for a little—wrote to Mary Hutchinson— washed my head—worked. After tea went to Ambleside [6]—a pleasant cool

2. Rydal Hall, the house of Sir Michael de Fleming.
3. William Gell (1777–1836), an archeologist and topographer; he was knighted in 1803.
4. "Fell" is a North of England word for a hill or a mountain.
5. Agnes Fisher lived with her husband John in a cottage near by. John's sister Mary —called Molly—did housework for the Wordsworths.
6. A walk of about 3 miles.

but not cold evening. Rydale was very beautiful with spear-shaped streaks of polished steel. No letters!—only one newspaper. I returned by Clappersgate Grasmere [7] was very solemn in the last glimpse of twilight it calls home the heart to quietness. I had been very melancholy in my walk back. I had many of my saddest thoughts and I could not keep the tears within me. But when I came to Grasmere I felt that it did me good. I finished my letter to M. H. Ate hasty pudding,[8] and went to bed. As I was going out in the morning I met a half crazy old man. He shewed me a pincushion and begged a pin, afterwards a halfpenny. He began in a kind of indistinct voice in this manner: 'Matthew Jobson's lost a cow. Tom Nichol has two good horses strayed. Jim Jones's cow's brokken her horn, etc. etc.' He went into Aggy's and persuaded her to give him some whey [9] and let him boil some porridge. She declares he ate two quarts.

Saturday [17th] Incessant rain from morning till night. T. Ashburner [10] brought us coals. Worked hard and read Mid-summer Night's Dream, Ballads —sauntered a little in the garden. The Skobby sate quietly in its nest rocked by the winds and beaten by the rain.

Sunday 19th Went to church, slight showers, a cold air. The mountains from this window look much greener and I think the valley is more green than ever. The corn begins to shew itself. The ashes are still bare. Went part of the way home with Miss Simpson.[11] A little girl from Coniston came to beg. She had lain out all night—her step-mother had turned her out of doors. Her father could not stay at home 'She flights so.' Walked to Ambleside in the evening round the lake. The prospect exceedingly beautiful from Loughrigg fell. It was so green, that no eye could be weary of reposing upon it. The most beautiful situation for a house in the field next to Mr Benson's. It threatened rain all the evening but was mild and pleasant. I was overtaken by 2 Cumberland people on the other side of Rydale who complimented me upon my walking. They were going to sell cloth, and odd things which they make themselves in Hawkshead and the neighbourhood. The post was not arrived so I walked thro' the town, past Mrs Taylor's, and met him.[12] Letters from Coleridge and Cottle.[13] John Fisher overtook me on the other side of Rydale. He talked much about the alteration in the times, and observed that in a short time there would be only two ranks of people, the very rich and the very poor, for those who have small estates says he are forced to sell, and all the land goes into one hand. Did not reach home till 10 o'clock.

Monday [19th] Sauntered a good deal in the garden, bound carpets, mended old clothes. Read Timon of Athens. Dried linen. Molly weeded the turnips, John stuck the peas. We had not much sunshine or wind but no rain till about 7 o'clock when we had a slight shower just after I had set out

7. The name of both the lake and the town; here the lake.
8. A porridge of flour and oatmeal boiled with seasonings in watered milk.
9. The watery part of milk not separated from the curds in making cheese.
10. Thomas Ashburner was a neighbor who supplied the Wordsworths with coal from Keswick.
11. Daughter of a clergyman of the district.
12. That is, the post—the postman.
13. Joseph Cottle of Bristol published Lyrical Ballads in 1798.

upon my walk. I did not return but walked up into the Black Quarter.[14] I sauntered a long time among the rocks above the church. The most delightful situation possible for a cottage commanding two distinct views of the vale and of the lake, is among those rocks. I strolled on, gathered mosses, etc. The quietness and still seclusion of the valley affected me even to producing the deepest melancholy. I forced myself from it. The wind rose before I went to bed. No rain—. . .

Tuesday Morning [*20th*]   A fine mild rain. After Breakfast the sky cleared and before the clouds passed from the hills I went to Ambleside. It was a sweet morning. Everything green and overflowing with life, and the streams making a perpetual song with the thrushes and all little birds, not forgetting the Stone chats. The post was not come in. I walked as far as Windermere.[15] and met him there. No letters! no papers. Came home by Clappersgate. I was sadly tired, ate a hasty dinner and had a bad head-ach. Went to bed and slept at least 2 hours. Rain came on in the Evening—Molly washing.

Wednesday [*21st*]   Went often to spread the linen which was bleaching—a rainy day and very wet night.

Thursday [*22nd*]   A very fine day with showers—dried the linen and starched. Drank tea at Mr Simpson's. Brought down Batchelor's Buttons (Rock Ranunculus) and other plants—went part of the way back. A showery, mild evening—all the peas up.

Friday 23rd   Ironing till tea time. So heavy a rain that I could not go for letters—put by the linen, mended stockings etc.

Saturday May 24th   Walked in the morning to Ambleside. I found a letter from Wm and from Mary Hutchinson and Douglass.[16] Returned on the other side of the lakes—wrote to William after dinner, nailed up the beds, worked in the garden, sate in the evening under the trees. I went to bed soon with a bad head-ache. A fine day.

Sunday [*25th*]   A very fine warm day, had no fire. Read Macbeth in the morning, sate under the trees after dinner. Miss Simpson came just as I was going out and she sate with me. I wrote to my Brother Christopher, and sent John Fisher to Ambleside after tea. Miss Simpson and I walked to the foot of the lake—her Brother met us. I went with them nearly home and on my return found a letter from Coleridge and from Charles Lloyd,[17] and three papers.

Monday May 26   A very fine morning, worked in the garden till after 10 when old Mr Simpson came and talked to me till after 12. Molly weeding. Wrote letters to J. H.,[18] Coleridge, C. Ll., and W. I walked towards Rydale and turned aside at my favorite field. The air and the lake were still—one cottage light in the vale, and so much of day left that I could distinguish objects, the woods; trees and houses. Two or three different kinds of Birds

---

14. The name given by the Wordsworths to the locality of Easedale.
15. The head of the lake.
16. Charles Douglas of Jamaica, a barrister, a Cambridge friend of Wordsworth's.
17. For a time the friend of Coleridge and Lamb. At this period he lived in the district, near Clappersgate.
18. Joanna Hutchinson, youngest sister of Mary Hutchinson.

sang at intervals on the opposite shore. I sate till I could hardly drag myself away I grew so sad. 'When pleasant thoughts,' etc. . . .[19]

Tuesday 27th I walked to Ambleside with letters—met the post before I reached Mr Partridge's, one paper, only a letter for Coleridge—I expected a letter from Wm. It was a sweet morning, the ashes in the valley nearly in full leaf but still to be distinguished, quite bare on the higher grounds. I was warm in returning, and becoming cold with sitting in the house—I had a bad head-ach—went to bed after dinner, and lay till after 5—not well after tea. I worked in the garden, but did not walk further. A delightful evening before the Sun set but afterwards it grew colder. Mended stockings etc.

Wednesday [28th] In the morning walked up to the rocks above Jenny Dockeray's sate a long time upon the grass the prospect divinely beautiful. If I had three hundred pounds and could afford to have a bad interest for my money I would buy that estate, and we would build a cottage there to end our days in. I went into her garden and got white and yellow lilies, periwinkle, etc., which I planted. Sate under the trees with my work. No fire in the morning. Worked till between 7 and 8, and then watered the garden, and was about to go up to Mr Simpson's, when Miss S. and her visitors passed the door. I went home with them, a beautiful evening the crescent moon hang-ing above Helm crag.

Thursday [29th] In the morning worked in the garden a little, read King John. Miss Simpson, and Miss Falcon and Mr S. came very early. Went to Mr Gell's boat before tea. We fished upon the lake and amongst us caught 13 Bass. Miss Simpson brought gooseberries *and cream*. Left the water at near nine o'clock, very cold. Went part of the way home with the party.

Friday [30th] In the morning went to Ambleside, forgetting that the post does not come till the evening. How was I grieved when I was so informed. I walked back resolving to go again in the evening. It rained very mildly and sweetly in the morning as I came home, but came on a wet afternoon and evening—but chilly. I caught Mr Olliff's Lad as he was going for letters, he brought me one from Wm and 2 papers. I planted London pride upon the well and many things on the Borders. John sodded the well. As I came past Rydale in the morning I saw a Heron swimming with only its neck out of water—it beat and struggled amongst the water when it flew away and was long in getting loose.

Saturday [31st] A sweet mild rainy morning. Grundy the carpet man called. I paid him 1-10/-. Went to the Blind man's for plants. I got such a load that I was obliged to leave my Basket in the Road and send Molly for it. Planted till after dinner when I was putting up vallances. . . .

Sunday June 1st Rain in the night—a sweet mild morning. Read Ballads; went to church. Singers from Wytheburn. Went part of the way home with Miss Simpson. Walked upon the hill above the house till dinner time—went again to church—a Christening and singing which kept us very late. The pew-side came down with me. Walked with Miss Simpson nearly home. After tea went to Ambleside, round the lakes—a very fine warm evening. I

19. "In that sweet mood when pleasant thoughts / Bring sad thoughts to the mind." Wordsworth, "Lines Written in Early Spring."

lay upon the steep of Loughrigg my heart dissolved in what I saw when I was not startled but re-called from my reverie by a noise as of a child paddling without shoes. I looked up and saw a lamb close to me. It approached nearer and nearer as if to examine me and stood a long time. I did not move. At last it ran past me and went bleating along the pathway seeming to be seeking its mother. I saw a hare in the high road. The post was not come in; waited in the Road till John's apprentice came with a letter from Coleridge and 3 papers. The moon shone upon the water—reached home at 10 o'clock—went to bed immediately. Molly brought Daisies etc. which we planted.

Monday [*2nd*] A cold dry windy morning. I worked in the garden and planted flowers, etc. Sate under the trees after dinner till tea time. John Fisher stuck the peas, Molly weeded and washed. I went to Ambleside after tea, crossed the stepping-stones at the foot of Grasmere and pursued my way on the other side of Rydale and by Clappersgate. I sate a long time to watch the hurrying waves and to hear the regularly irregular sound of the dashing waters. The waves round about the little [Island] seemed like a dance of spirits that rose out of the water, round its small circumference of shore. Inquired about lodgings for Coleridge, and was accompanied by Mrs Nicholson as far as Rydale. This was very kind, but God be thanked I want not society by a moonlight lake—It was near 11 when I reached home. I wrote to Coleridge and went late to bed.

Tuesday [*3rd*] Sent off my letter by the Butcher—a boisterous drying day. I worked in the garden before dinner. Read R[ichar]d Second—was not well after dinner and lay down. Mrs Simpson's grandson brought me some gooseberries. . . . After tea the wind fell. I walked towards Mr Simpson's. Gave the newspapers to the Girl, reached home at 10. No letter, no William—a letter from R[ichar]d [20] to John.

Wednesday [*4th*] A very fine day. I sate out of doors most of the day, wrote to Mr Jackson.[21] Ambleside fair. I walked to the lake-side in the morning, took up plants and sate upon a stone reading Ballads. In the Evening I was watering plants when Mr and Miss Simpson called. I accompanied them home, and we went to the waterfall at the head of the valley. It was very interesting in the Twilight. I brought home lemon thyme and several other plants, and planted them by moonlight. I lingered out of doors in the hope of hearing my Brothers tread.

Thursday [*5th*] I sate out of doors great part of the day and worked in the garden—had a letter from Mr Jackson, and wrote an answer to Coleridge. The little birds busy making love and pecking the blossoms and bits of moss off the trees, they flutter about and about and thrid the trees as I lie under them. Molly went out to tea, I would not go far from home, expecting my Brothers. I rambled on the hill above the house gathered wild thyme and took up roots of wild Columbine. . . .

. . .

Saturday [*7th*] A very warm cloudy morning, threatening to rain. I walked up to Mr Simpson's to gather gooseberries—it was a very fine afternoon. Little

---

20. The eldest of Dorothy's three brothers.
21. About letting his house, Greta Hall, to the Coleridges.

Tommy [22] came down with me, ate gooseberry pudding and drank tea with me. We went up the hill to gather sods and plants and went down to the lake side and took up orchises etc. I watered the garden and weeded. I did not leave home in the expectation of Wm and John, and sitting at work till after 11 o'clock I heard a foot go to the front of the house, turn round, and open the gate. It was William——After our first joy was over, we got some tea. We did not go to bed till 4 o'clock in the morning so he had an opportunity of seeing our improvements. The birds were singing, and all looked fresh, though not day. There was a greyness on earth and sky. We did not rise till near 10 in the morning [Sunday]. . . .

. . .

Tuesday [*10th*]   On Tuesday, May 27th, a very tall woman,[23] tall much beyond the measure of tall women, called at the door. She had on a very long brown cloak, and a very white cap without Bonnet—her face was excessively brown, but it had plainly once been fair. She led a little bare-footed child about 2 years old by the hand and said her husband who was a tinker was gone before with the other children. I gave her a piece of Bread. Afterwards on my road to Ambleside, beside the Bridge at Rydale, I saw her husband sitting by the roadside, his two asses feeding beside him and the two young children at play upon the grass. The man did not beg. I passed on and about ¼ of a mile further I saw two boys before me, one about 10 the other about 8 years old at play chasing a butterfly. They were wild figures, not very ragged, but without shoes and stockings; the hat of the elder was wreathed round with yellow flowers, the younger whose hat was only a rimless crown, had stuck it round with laurel leaves. They continued at play till I drew very near and then they addressed me with the Beggars' cant and the whining voice of sorrow. I said I served your mother this morning. (The Boys were so like the woman who had called at the door that I could not be mistaken.) O! says the elder you could not serve my mother for she's dead and my father's on at the next town—he's a potter. I persisted in my assertion and that I would give them nothing. Says the elder Come, let's away, and away they flew like lightning. They had however sauntered so long in their road that they did not reach Ambleside before me, and I saw them go up to Matthew Harrison's house with their wallet upon the elder's shoulder, and creeping with a Beggar's complaining foot. On my return through Ambleside I met in the street the mother driving her asses; in the two Panniers of one of which were the two little children whom she was chiding and threatening with a wand which she used to drive on her asses, while the little things hung in wantonness over the Pannier's edge. The woman had told me in the morning that she was of Scotland, which her accent fully proved, but that she had lived (I think at Wigton), that they could not keep a house and so they travelled.

. . .

Monday [*16th*]   Wm and I went to Brathay by Little Langdale and Collath and Skelleth. It was a warm mild morning with threatening of rain. The vale

22. Probably a grandson of Mr. Simpson's.
23. This woman and the incident with her sons became the subject of Wordsworth's poem "Beggars."

of Little Langdale looked bare and unlovely. Collath was wild and interesting, from the Peat carts and peat gatherers—the valley all perfumed with the Gale and wild thyme. The woods about the waterfall veined with rich yellow Broom. A succession of delicious views from Skelleth to Brathay. We met near Skelleth a pretty little Boy with a wallet over his shoulder—he came from Hawkshead and was going to 'late' a lock [24] of meal. He spoke gently and without complaint. When I asked him if he got enough to eat he looked surprized and said 'Nay'. He was 7 years old but seemed not more than 5. . . .

Thursday [*19th*]   A very hot morning. W. and I walked up to Mr Simpson's. W. and old Mr S. went to fish in Wytheburn water. I dined with John, and lay under the trees. The afternoon changed from clear to cloudy and to clear again. John and I walked up to the waterfall and to Mr Simpson's, and with Miss Simpson met the fishers. W. caught a pike weighing 4¾ lbs. There was a gloom almost terrible over Grasmere water and vale. A few drops fell but not much rain. No Coleridge whom we fully expected.

Friday [*20th*]   I worked in the garden in the morning. Wm prepared Pea sticks. Threatening for rain but yet it comes not. On Wednesday evening a poor man called, a hatter—he had been long ill, but was now recovered and his wife was lying in of her 4th child. The parish would not help him because he had implements of trade etc. etc. We gave him 6d.

Saturday [*21st*]   In the morning W. and I went to Ambleside to get his tooth drawn, and put in. A fine clear morning but cold. W.'s tooth drawn with very little pain—he slept till 3 o'clock. Young Mr S. drank tea and supped with us then fished in Rydale water and they caught 2 small fishes —W. no bite—John 3. Miss Simpson and 3 children called—I walked with them to Rydale. The evening cold and clear and frosty, but the wind was falling as I returned. I staid at home about an hour and then walked up the hill to Rydale lake. Grasmere looked so beautiful that my heart was almost melted away. It was quite calm only spotted with sparkles of light. The church visible. On our return all distant objects had faded away—all but the hills. The reflection of the light bright sky above Black quarter was very solemn. Mr S. did not go till 12 o'clock.

Sunday [*22nd*]   In the morning W. and I walked towards Rydale and up into the wood but finding it not very pleasant we returned—sauntered in the garden—a showery day. In the evening I planted a honeysuckle round the yew tree. In the evening we walked for letters. No letters: no news of Coleridge. Jimmy Benson came home drunk beside us.

Wednesday [*25th*] [25]   A very rainy day. I made a shoe. Wm and John went to fish in Langdale. In the evening I went above the house, and gathered flowers which I planted, fox-gloves, etc. On Sunday [29 June] Mr and Mrs Coleridge and Hartley came. The day was very warm. We sailed to the foot of Loughrigg. They staid with us three weeks and till the Thursday following, i.e. till the 23 [24th] of July. On the Friday preceding their departure

24. Dialect for "beg a measure."
25. The month is July, the journal having been interrupted by the three-week visit of the Coleridges, briefly summarized in this entry.

we drank tea at the island. The weather very delightful, and on the Sunday
we made a great fire, and drank tea in Bainriggs with the Simpsons. I accompanied Mrs C. to Wytheburne, and returned with W.—to tea at Mr Simpson's—it was excessively hot, but the day after Friday July 24th [25th] still
hotter. All the morning I was engaged in unpacking our Somersetshire goods [26]
and in making pies. The house was a hot oven but yet we could not bake the
pies. I was so weary I could not walk, so I went and sate with Wm in the
orchard. We had a delightful half hour in the warm still evening.

Saturday 25th Still hotter. I sate with W. in the orchard all the morning
and made my shoes. In the afternoon from excessive heat I was ill in the
headach and toothach and went to bed—I was refreshed with washing myself
after I got up, but it was too hot to walk till near dark, and then I sate upon
the wall finishing my shoes.

. . .

Monday morning [28th] Received a letter from Coleridge enclosing one
from Mr Davy [27] about the Lyrical Ballads. Intensely hot. I made pies in the
morning. Wm went into the wood and altered his poems. In the Evening it
was so very warm that I was too much tired to walk.

Tuesday [29th] Still very hot. We gathered peas for dinner. We walked up
in the Evening to find out Hewetson's cottage but it was too dark. I was sick
and weary.

. . .

Thursday [31st] All the morning I was busy copying poems. Gathered
peas, and in the afternoon Coleridge came, very hot, he brought the 2nd
volume of the Anthology.[28] The men went to bathe, and we afterwards sailed
down to Loughrigg. Read poems on the water, and let the boat take its own
course. We walked a long time upon Loughrigg and returned in the grey
twilight. The moon just setting as we reached home.

Friday 1st August In the morning I copied The Brothers.[29] Coleridge and
Wm went down to the lake. They returned and we all went together to
Mary Point [30] where we sate in the breeze and the shade, and read Wm's
poems. Altered The Whirlblast [31] etc. Mr Simpson came to tea and Mr B. Simpson afterwards. We drank tea in the orchard.

Saturday Morning 2nd Wm and Coleridge went to Keswick. John went
with them to Wytheburn and staid all day fishing and brought home 2 small
pikes at night. I accompanied them to Lewthwaite's cottage and on my return
papered Wm's room. I afterwards lay down till tea time and after tea worked
at my shifts in the orchard. A grey evening. About 8 o'clock it gathered for
rain and I had the scatterings of a shower, but afterwards the lake became
of a glassy calmness and all was still. I sate till I could see no longer and
then continued my work in the house.

Sunday Morning 3rd I made pies and stuffed the pike—baked a loaf. Head-

26. Presumably household possessions that had been in storage.
27. Who was to become famous as Sir Humphrey Davy the chemist (1778–1829). He was
a friend of Joseph Cottle.
28. The *Annual Anthology*, edited by Southey.
29. Wordsworth's poem.
30. Named by the Wordsworths for Mary Hutchinson.
31. Wordsworth's poem, written in 1798.

ach after dinner—I lay down. A letter from Wm rouzed me, desiring us to go to Keswick. After writing to Wm we walked as far as Mr Simpson's and ate black cherries. A Heavenly warm evening with scattered clouds upon the hills. There was a vernal greenness upon the grass from the rains of the morning and afternoon. Peas for dinner.

Wednesday 3rd September Coleridge Wm and John went from home to go upon Helvellyn [32] with Mr Simpson. They set out after breakfast. I accompanied them up near the Blacksmith's. A fine coolish morning. I ironed till ½ past three—now very hot. I then went to a funeral at John Dawson's. About 10 men and 4 women. Bread cheese and ale. They talked sensibly and chearfully about common things. The dead person 56 years of age buried by the parish. The coffin was neatly lettered and painted black and covered with a decent cloth. They set the corpse down at the door and while we stood within the threshold the men with their hats off sang with decent and solemn countenances a verse of a funeral psalm. The corpse was then borne down the hill and they sang till they had got past the Town-end. I was affected to tears while we stood in the house, the coffin lying before me. There were no near kindred, no children. When we got out of the dark house the sun was shining and the prospect looked so divinely beautiful as I never saw it. It seemed more sacred than I had ever seen it, and yet more allied to human life. The green fields, neighbours of the churchyard, were as green as possible and with the brightness of the sunshine looked quite gay. I thought she was going to a quiet spot and I could not help weeping very much. When we came to the bridge they began to sing again and stopped during 4 lines before they entered the churchyard. The priest met us—he did not look as a man ought to do on such an occasion—I had seen him half-drunk the day before in a pot-house. Before we came with the corpse one of the company observed he wondered what sort of cue 'our Parson would be in.' N.B. it was the day after the Fair. I had not finished ironing till 7 o'clock. The wind was now high and I did not walk—writing my journal now at 8 o'clock. Wm and John came home at 10 o'clock.

Saturday Morning 13th September William writing his preface [33] did not walk. Jones [34] and Mr Palmer came to tea. We walked with them to Borricks—a lovely evening but the air frosty—worked when I returned home. Wm walked out. John came home from Mr Marshall. Sent back word to Mrs Clarkson.

Sunday Morning 14th Made bread. A sore thumb from a cut. A lovely day —read Boswell in the house in the morning and after dinner under the bright yellow leaves of the orchard. The pear trees a bright yellow, the apple trees green still. A sweet lovely afternoon.

Friday 3rd October Very rainy all the morning. Little Sally learning to mark. Wm walked to Ambleside after dinner. I went with him part of the

32. One of the highest mountains in the Lake District (3118 feet).
33. To the 1800 edition of *Lyrical Ballads*.
34. The Reverend Robert Jones, with whom Wordsworth made his Continental tour in 1790.

way—he talked much about the object of his Essay for the 2nd volume of LB. I returned expecting the Simpsons—they did not come. I should have met Wm but my teeth ached and it was showery and late—he returned after 10. Amos Cottle's [35] death in the Morning Post. . . .

N.B. When Wm and I returned from accompanying Jones we met an old man almost double,[36] he had on a coat thrown over his shoulders above his waistcoat and coat. Under this he carried a bundle and had an apron on and a night cap. His face was interesting. He had dark eyes and a long nose. John who afterwards met him at Wythburn took him for a Jew. He was of Scotch parents but had been born in the army. He had had a wife 'and a good woman and it pleased God to bless us with ten children.' All these were dead but one of whom he had not heard for many years, a sailor. His trade was to gather leeches, but now leeches are scarce and he had not strength for it. He lived by begging and was making his way to Carlisle where he should buy a few godly books to sell. He said leeches were very scarce partly owing to this dry season, but many years they have been scarce—he supposed it owing to their being much sought after, that they did not breed fast, and were of slow growth. Leeches were formerly 2/6 [per] 100; they are now 30/. He had been hurt in driving a cart, his leg broke his body driven over his skull fractured. He felt no pain till he recovered from his first insensibility. 'It was then later in the evening, when the light was just going away.'

Saturday October 4th [1800]   A very rainy, or rather showery and gusty morning for often the sun shines. Thomas Ashburner could not go to Keswick. Read a part of Lamb's play.[37] The language is often very beautiful, but too imitative in particular phrases, words etc. The characters except Margaret's unintelligible, and except Margaret's do not shew themselves in action. Coleridge came in while we were at dinner very wet.—We talked till 12 o'clock. He had sate up all the night before writing Essays for the newspaper.—His youngest child had been very ill in convulsion fits. Exceedingly delighted with the 2nd part of Christabel.

Sunday Morning 5th October   Coleridge read a 2nd time Christabel [38]— we had increasing pleasure. A delicious morning. Wm and I were employed all the morning in writing an addition to the preface. Wm went to bed very ill after working after dinner. Coleridge and I walked to Ambleside after dark with the letter. Returned to tea at 9 o'clock. Wm still in bed and very ill. . . .

Monday [6th]   A rainy day. Coleridge intending to go but did not get off. We walked after dinner to Rydale. After tea read The Pedlar.[39] Determined not to print Christabel with the LB.

Tuesday [7th]   Coleridge went off at 11 o'clock.—I went as far as Mr

---

35. Brother of Joseph Cottle.
36. The original of the leech-gatherer in Wordsworth's great poem *Resolution and Independence.*
37. *John Woodvil*, at this time called *Pride's Cure*. It was rejected for production, and when Lamb published it (at his own expense) it was harshly received by the critics.
38. His never to be finished poem.
39. A long poem begun in 1785; part of it was incorporated in *The Excursion* and part used in the second and third books of *The Prelude*.

Simpson's. . . . I was very ill in the evening at the Simpsons—went to bed —supped there. Returned with Miss S. and Mrs. J.[40]—heavy showers. Found Wm at home. I was still weak and unwell—went to bed immediately.

   Wednesday Morning [*22nd*] We walked to Mr Gell's a very fine morning. Wm composed without much success at the Sheepfold.[41] Coleridge came in to dinner. He had done nothing. We were very merry. C. and I went to look at the prospect from his seat. In the evening Stoddart came in when we were at tea, and after tea Mr and Miss Simpson with large potatoes and plumbs. Wm read after supper, Ruth etc.—Coleridge Christabel.

   1801

   Tuesday [*November*]*10th* Poor C. left us [42] and we came home together. We left Keswick at 2 o'clock and did not arrive at G. till 9 o'clock. Drank tea at John Stanley's very comfortably. I burnt myself with Coleridge's Aquafortis.[43] Mary's feet sore. C. had a sweet day for his ride. Every sight and every sound reminded me of him dear dear fellow—of his many walks to us by day and by night—of all dear things. I was melancholy and could not talk, but at last I eased my heart by weeping—nervous blubbering says William. It is not so. O how many, many reasons have I to be anxious for him.

   Wednesday 11th Baked bread and giblet pie—put books in order— mended stockings. Put aside dearest C.'s letters, and now at about 7 o'clock we are all sitting by a nice fire—W. with his book and a candle and Mary [44] writing to Sara.

   Friday 27th Snow upon the ground thinly scattered. It snowed after we got up and then the sun shone and it was very warm though frosty—now the sun shines sweetly. A woman came who was travelling with her husband —he had been wounded and was going with her to live at Whitehaven. She had been at Ambleside the night before, offered 4d at the Cock for a bed— they sent her to one Harrison's where she and her husband had slept upon the hearth and bought a pennyworth of chips for a fire. Her husband was gone before very lame—'Aye' says she 'I was once an officer's wife I, as you see me now. My first husband married me at Appleby. I had 18£ a year for teaching a school and because I had no fortune his father turned him out of doors. I have been in the West Indies. I lost the use of this Finger just before he died he came to me and said he must bid farewell to his dear children and me. I had a muslin gown on like yours—I seized hold of his coat as he went from me and slipped the joint of my finger. He was shot directly. I came to London and married this man. He was clerk to Judge Chambray, *that man,* that man that's going on the Road now. If he, Judge

<hr />

40. Presumably a married sister of Miss Simpson's.
41. The poem that was to become *Michael*. Wordsworth would seem to have begun it on October 11; the entries for several of the intervening days record his difficulty with its composition.
42. To spend the winter in London.
43. Nitric acid, used for etching.
44. Mary Hutchinson was visiting the Wordsworths. Sara was her sister, the object of Coleridge's affections.

Chambray,[45] had been at Kendal he would [have] given us a guinea or two and made nought of it, for he is very generous.' . . .

. . .

Tuesday 22nd [December]   Still thaw. I washed my head. Wm and I went to Rydale for letters. The road was covered with dirty snow, rough and rather slippery. We had a melancholy letter from C., for he had been very ill, though he was better when he wrote. We walked home almost without speaking. Wm composed a few lines of the Pedlar. We talked about Lamb's Tragedy as we went down the White Moss. We stopped a long time in going to watch a little bird with a salmon coloured breast—a white cross or T upon its wings, and a brownish back with faint stripes. It was pecking the scattered Dung upon the road. It began to peck at the distance of 4 yards from us and advanced nearer and nearer till it came within the length of Wm's stick without any apparent fear of us. As we came up the White Moss we met an old man, who I saw was a beggar by his two bags hanging over his shoulder, but from a half laziness, half indifference and a wanting to *try* him if he would speak I let him pass. He said nothing, and my heart smote me. I turned back and said You are begging? 'Ay,' says he. I gave him a halfpenny. William, judging from his appearance joined in I suppose you were a sailor? 'Ay,' he replied, 'I have been 57 years at sea, 12 of them on board a man-of-war under Sir Hugh Palmer.' Why have you not a pension? 'I have no pension, but I could have got into Greenwich hospital [46] but all my officers are dead.' He was 75 years of age, had a freshish colour in his cheeks, grey hair, a decent hat with a binding round the edge, the hat worn brown and glossy, his shoes were small thin shoes low in the quarters, pretty good. They had belonged to a gentleman. His coat was blue, frock shaped coming over his thighs, it had been joined up at the seams behind with paler blue to let it out, and there were three Bell-shaped patches of darker blue behind where the Buttons had been. His breeches were either of fustian or grey cloth, with strings hanging down, whole and tight; he had a checked shirt on, and a small coloured handkerchief tyed round his neck. His bags were hung over each shoulder and lay on each side of him, below his breast. One was brownish and of coarse stuff, the other was white with meal on the outside, and his blue waistcoat was whitened with meal. In the coarse bag I guessed he put his scraps of meat etc. He walked with a slender stick decently stout, but his legs bowed outwards. We overtook old Fleming [47] at Rydale, leading his little Dutchman-like grandchild along the slippery road. The same pace seemed to be natural to them both, the old man and the little child, and they went hand in hand, the grandfather cautious, yet looking proud of his charge. He had two patches of new cloth at the shoulder blades of his faded claret coloured coat, like eyes at each shoulder, not worn elsewhere. I found Mary at home in her riding-habit all her clothes being put up. We were very sad about Coleridge. Wm walked further. When he came home he cleared a path to the necessary—called me out to see it but before we got there a whole housetop full of snow had fallen from the

45. Sir Alan Chambré; he was known for his benevolence.
46. For distressed sailors.
47. He kept an inn at Rydal.

roof upon the path and it echoed in the ground beneath like a dull beating upon it. . . .

1802

Friday 29th January   William was very unwell. Worn out with his bad night's rest—he went to bed—I read to him to endeavour to make him sleep. Then I came into the other room, and read the 1st Book of Paradise Lost. After dinner we walked to Ambleside. Found Lloyds at Luff's—we stayed and drank tea by ourselves. A heart-rending letter from Coleridge—we were sad as we could be. Wm wrote to him. We talked about Wm's going to London. It was a mild afternoon—there was an unusual softness in the prospects as we went, a rich yellow upon the fields, and a soft grave purple on the waters. When we returned, many stars were out, the clouds were moveless, in the sky soft purple, the Lake of Rydale calm, Jupiter behind, Jupiter at least *we* call him, but William says we always call the largest star Jupiter. When we came home we both wrote to C. I was stupefied.

Saturday January 30th   A cold dark morning. William chopped wood—I brought it in in a basket. A cold wind. Wm slept better but he thinks he looks ill—he is shaving now. . . .

. . .

Tuesday [9th February]   William had slept better. He fell to work, and made himself unwell. We did not walk. A funeral came by of a poor woman who had drowned herself, some say because she was hardly treated by her husband, others that he was a very decent respectable man and *she* but an indifferent wife. However this was she had only been married to him last Whitsuntide and had had very indifferent health ever since. She had got up in the night and drowned herself in the pond. She had requested to be buried beside her mother and so she was brought in a hearse. She was followed by several decent-looking men on horseback, her Sister, Thomas Fleming's wife, in a Chaise, and some others with her, and a cart full of women. Molly says folks thinks o' their mothers. Poor Body *she* has been little thought of by any body else. We did a little of Lessing. I attempted a fable, but my head ached my bones were sore with the cold of the day before and I was downright stupid. We went to bed but not till William had tired himself.

. . .

Friday 12th   A very fine bright, clear, hard frost. William working again. I recopied the Pedlar, but poor William all the time at work. Molly tells me 'What! little Sally's gone to visit at Mr Simpson's. They says she's very smart she's got on a new bed-gown that her Cousin gave her. It's a very bonny one they tell me, but I've not seen it. Sally and me's in Luck.' In the afternoon a poor woman came, *she said* to beg some rags for her husband's leg which had been wounded by a slate from the Roof in the great wind—but she has been used to go a-begging, for she has often come here. Her father lived to the age of 105. She is a woman of strong bones with a complexion that has been beautiful, and remained very fresh last year, but now she looks broken, and her little Boy, a pretty little fellow, and whom I have loved for the sake of Basil,[48] looks thin and pale. I observed this to her. Aye says she we have

48. The son of Wordsworth's friend Basil Montague. He lived with the Wordsworths from 1795 to 1798 and is the child who figures in "Anecdote for Fathers."

all been ill. Our house was unroofed in the storm nearly and *so* we lived in it for more than a week. The Child wears a ragged drab coat and a fur cap, poor little fellow, I think he seems scarcely at all grown since the first time I saw him. William was with me—we met him in a lane going to Skelwith Bridge. He looked very pretty. He was walking lazily in the deep narrow lane, overshadowed with the hedge-rows, his meal poke hung over his shoulder. He said he was going 'a laiting.'[49] He now wears the same coat he had on at that time. Poor creatures! When the woman was gone, I could not help thinking that we are not half thankful enough that we are placed in that condition of life in which we are. We do not so often bless god for this as we wish for this 50£ that 100£ etc. etc. We have not, however to reproach ourselves with ever breathing a murmur. This woman's was but a *common* case.—The snow still lies upon the ground. Just at the closing in of the Day I heard a cart pass the door, and at the same time the dismal sound of a crying Infant. I went to the window and had light enough to see that a man was driving a cart which seemed not to be very full, and that a woman with an infant in her arms was following close behind and a dog close to her. It was a wild and melancholy sight.—William rubbed his Table after candles were lighted, and we sate a long time with the windows unclosed. I almost finished writing The Pedlar, but poor William wore himself and me out with labour. We had an affecting conversation. Went to bed at 12 o'clock.

· · ·

Thursday [4th March]   Before we had quite finished Breakfast Calvert's man brought the horses for Wm.[50] We had a deal to do to shave—pens to make —poems to put in order for writing, to settle the dress pack up etc. The man came before the pens were made and he was obliged to leave me with only two. Since he has left me (at ½ past 11) it is now 2 I have been putting the Drawers into order, laid by his clothes which we had thrown here and there and everywhere, filed two months' newspapers and got my dinner 2 boiled eggs and 2 apple tarts. I have set Molly on to clear the garden a little, and I myself have helped. I transplanted some snowdrops—The Bees are busy— Wm has a nice bright day. It was hard frost in the night. The Robins are singing sweetly. Now for my walk. I *will* be busy, I *will* look well and be well when he comes back to me. O the Darling! Here is one of his bitten apples! I can hardly find in my heart to throw it into the fire. I must wash myself, then off—I walked round the two Lakes crossed the stepping stones at Rydale Foot. State down where we always sit. I was full of thoughts about my darling. Blessings on him. I came home at the foot of our own hill under Loughrigg. They are making sad ravages in the woods. Benson's Wood is going and the wood above the River. The wind has blown down a [?small] fir tree on the Rock that terminates John's path—I suppose the wind of Wednesday night. I read German after my return till tea time. After tea I worked and read the LB, enchanted with the Idiot Boy. Wrote to Wm then went to Bed. It snowed when I went to Bed.

Friday [5th]   First walked in the garden and orchard. A frosty sunny morning. After dinner I gathered mosses in Easedale. I saw before me sitting

49. Begging.
50. To ride to Keswick on a visit to Coleridge.

in the open field upon his Sack of Rags the old Ragman that I know. His coat is of scarlet in a thousand patches. His Breeches knees were untied—the breeches have been given him by some one. He has a round hat pretty good, small crowned but large rimmed. When I came to him he said Is there a brigg yonder that'll carry me ow'r t'watter? He seemed half stupid. When I came home Molly had shook the carpet and cleaned every thing upstairs. When I see her so happy in her work and exulting in her own importance I often think of that affecting expression which she made use of to me one evening lately. Talking of her good luck in being in this house, 'Aye Mistress them 'at's Low laid would have been a proud creature could they but have [seen] where I is now fra what they thought mud [51] be my Doom.'—I was tired when I reached home. I sent Molly Ashburner to Rydale. No letters! I was sadly mortified. I expected one fully from Coleridge. Wrote to William. Read the L B, got into sad thoughts, tried at German but could not go on —Read LB.—Blessings on that Brother of mine! Beautiful new moon over Silver How.

. . .

Sunday Morning [*14th*] William had slept badly—he got up at 9 o'clock, but before he rose he had finished the Beggar Boys—and while we were at Breakfast that is (for I had breakfasted) he, with his Basin of Broth before him untouched and a little plate of Bread and butter he wrote the Poem to a Butterfly! He ate not a morsel, nor put on his stockings but sate with his shirt neck unbuttoned, and his waistcoat open while he did it. The thought first came upon him as we were talking about the pleasure we both always feel at the sight of a Butterfly. I told him that I used to chase them a little but that I was afraid of brushing the dust off their wings, and did not catch them— He told me how they used to kill all the white ones when he went to school because they were frenchmen. Mr Simpson came in just as he was finishing the Poem. After he was gone I wrote it down and the other poems and I read them all over to him. We then called at Mr Olliff's. Mr O. walked with us to within sight of Rydale—the sun shone very pleasantly, yet it was extremely cold. We dined and then Wm went to bed. I lay upon the fur gown before the fire but I could not sleep—I lay there a long time—it is now half past 5 I am going to write letters. . . .—William rose without having slept we sate comfortably by the fire till he began to try to alter the butterfly, and tired himself—he went to bed tired.

Monday Morning [*15th*] We sate reading the poems and I read a little German. Mr Luff came in at one o'clock. He had a long talk with William —he went to Mr Olliff's after dinner and returned to us to tea. During his absence a sailor who was travelling from Liverpool to Whitehaven called he was faint and pale when he knocked at the door, a young Man very well dressed. We sate by the kitchen fire talking with him for 2 hours—he told us [? most] interesting stories of his life. His name was Isaac Chapel—he had been at sea since he was 15 years old. He was by trade a sail-maker. His last voyage was to the Coast of Guinea. He had been on board a slave ship the Captain's name Maxwell where one man had been killed a Boy put to

51. "Might."

lodge with the pigs and was half eaten, one Boy set to watch in the hot sun till he dropped down dead. He had been cast away in North America and had travelled 30 days among the Indians where he had been well treated— He had twice swum from a King's ship in the night and escaped, he said he would rather be in hell than be pressed. He was now going to wait in England to appear against Captain Maxwell. 'O he's a Rascal, Sir, he ought to be put in the papers!' The poor man had not been in bed since Friday Night. He left Liverpool at 2 o'clock on Saturday morning. He had called at a farm house to beg victuals and had been refused. The woman said she would give him nothing. 'Won't you? Then I can't help it.' He was excessively like my Brother John.52. . .

Wednesday [*17th*] William went up into the orchard and finished the Poem. Mrs Luff and Mrs Olliff called I went with Mrs O. to the top of the White Moss—Mr O. met us and I went to their house he offered me manure for the garden. I went and sate with W. and walked backwards and forwards in the orchard till dinner time—he read me his poem. I broiled Beefsteaks. After dinner we made a pillow of my shoulder, I read to him and my Beloved slept. . . .

Friday [*19th*] A very rainy morning. I went up into the lane to collect a few green mosses to make the chimney gay against my darling's return. Poor C! I did not wish for, or expect him it rained so. Mr Luff came in before my dinner. We had a long talk. He left me before 4 o'clock, and about ½ an hour after Coleridge came in. His eyes were a little swollen with the wind. I was much affected with the sight of him—he seemed half stupefied.53 William came in soon after. Coleridge went to bed late, and Wm and I sate up till 4 o'clock. A letter from Sara sent by Mary. They disputed about Ben Jonson. My spirits were agitated very much.

Sunday [*21st*] A showery day. Coleridge and William lay long in bed. We sent up to G. Mackareth's for the horse to go to Keswick but we could not have it. Went with C. to Borwick's where he left us. William was very unwell this evening. We had a sweet and tender conversation. I wrote to Mary and Sara.

Monday [*22nd*] A rainy day. William very poorly. Mr Luff came in after dinner and brought us 2 letters from Sara H. and one from poor Annette. I read Sara's letters while he was here. I finished my letters to M. and S. and wrote to my Br Richard. We talked a good deal about C. and other interesting things. We resolved to see Annette,54 and that Wm should go to Mary. We wrote to Coleridge not to expect us till Thursday or Friday.

52. Also a sailor; in 1805 he perished in the wreck of the ship he commanded.
53. Possibly from the effects of opium. This and the troubled state of Coleridge's relations with his wife might account for Dorothy's agitated spirits.
54. Although Wordsworth's love affair with Annette Vallon, by whom he had a daughter, was not "discovered" until early in the 20th century, it was never a secret in the Wordsworth family, nor, as is apparent, was it hidden from Mary Hutchinson. Wordsworth, in company with Dorothy, went to Calais in August of 1802 to see Annette and the child.

Tuesday [23rd]   A mild morning. William worked at the Cuckow poem.[55] I sewed beside him. After dinner he slept I read German, and at the closing in of day went to sit in the orchard. He came to me, walked backwards and forwards. We talked about C. Wm repeated the poem to me. I left him there and in 20 minutes he came in, rather tired with attempting to write. He is now reading Ben Jonson and I am going to read German it is about 10 o'clock, a quiet night. The fire flutters and the watch ticks I hear nothing else save the Breathing of my Beloved and he now and then pushes his book forward and turns over a leaf. . . . No letter from C. . . .

Friday [26th]   A beautiful morning. William wrote to Annette then worked at the Cuckow. I was ill and in bad spirits—after dinner I sate 2 hours in the orchard. William and I walked together after tea first to the top of White Moss, then to Mr Olliff's. I left Wm and while he was absent wrote out poems. I grew alarmed and went to seek him—I met him at Mr Olliff's. He had been trying without success to alter a passage in Silver How poem [56]—he had written a conclusion just before he went out. While I was getting into bed he wrote the Rainbow.[57]

Saturday [27th]   A divine morning. At Breakfast Wm wrote part of an ode.[58] Mr Olliff sent the dung and Wm went to work in the garden. We sate all day in the orchard.

Thursday 29th [April]   A beautiful morning. The sun shone and all was pleasant. We sent off our parcel to Coleridge by the waggon. Mr Simpson heard the Cuckow today. Before we went out after I had written down the Tinker (which William finished this morning) Luff called. He was very lame, limped into the kitchen—he came on a little Pony. We then went to John's Grove, sate a while at first. Afterwards William lay, and I lay in the trench under the fence—he with his eyes shut and listening to the waterfalls and the Birds. There was no one waterfall above another—it was a sound of waters in the air—the voice of the air. William heard me breathing and rustling now and then but we both lay still, and unseen by one another. He thought that it would be as sweet thus to lie so in the grave, to hear the *peaceful* sounds of the earth and just to know that our dear friends were near. The Lake was still. There was a Boat out. Silver How reflected with delicate purple and yellowish hues as I have seen Spar. Lambs on the island and running races together by the half dozen in the round field near us. The copses green*ish*, hawthorn green. . . .

Saturday May 1st   Rose not till ½ past 8. A heavenly morning. As soon as Breakfast was over we went into the garden and sowed the scarlet beans about the house. It was a clear sky a heavenly morning. I sowed the flowers William helped me. We then went and sate in the orchard till dinner time. It was very hot. William wrote the Celandine.[59] We planned a shed for the sun was

55. "To the Cuckoo."
56. Perhaps *The Firgrove*.
57. "My Heart Leaps Up."
58. "Intimations" Ode, of which "My Heart Leaps Up" became the epigraph.
59. "To the Small Celandine."

too much for us. After dinner we went again to our old resting place in the Hollins under the Rock. We first lay under a holly where we saw nothing but the holly tree and a budding elm mossed with [?] and the sky above our heads. But that holly tree had a beauty about it more than its own, knowing as we did where we were. When the sun had got low enough we went to the Rock shade. Oh the overwhelming beauty of the vale below—greener than green. Two Ravens flew high high in the sky and the sun shone upon their bellys and their wings long after there was none of his light to be seen but a little space on the top of Loughrigg Fell. We went down to tea at 8 o'clock—had lost the poem and returned after tea. The Landscape was fading, sheep and lambs quiet among the Rocks. . . . The sky was perfectly cloudless. N.B. Is it often so? 3 solitary stars in the middle of the blue vault one or two on the points of the high hills. Wm wrote the Celandine 2nd part tonight. Heard the cuckow today this first of May.[60]

Sunday 2nd May   Again a heavenly morning. Letter from Coleridge.

. . .

Sunday Morning May 9th 1802   The air considerably colder today but the sun shone all day. William worked at the Leech gatherer almost incessantly from morning till tea-time. I copied the Leech-gatherer and other poems for Coleridge. I was oppressed and sick at heart for he wearied himself to death. After tea he wrote 2 stanzas in the manner of Thomson's Castle of Indolence,[61] and was tired out. Bad news of Coleridge.

. . .

Monday 31st   I was much better. We sate out all the day. Mary Jameson dined. I wrote out the poem on 'Our Departure'[62] which he seemed to have finished. In the evening Miss Simpson brought us a letter from M. H. and a complimentary and critical letter to W. from John Wilson of Glasgow[63] Post Paid. I went a little way with Miss S. My tooth broke today. They will soon be gone.[64] Let that pass I shall be beloved—I want no more.

. . .

Wednesday 2nd June 1802   In the morning we observed that the scarlet Beans were drooping in the leaves in great numbers owing, we guess, to an insect. We sate a while in the orchard—then we went to the old carpenter's about the hurdles. Yesterday an old man called, a grey-headed man, above 70 years of age. He said he had been a soldier, that his wife and children had died in Jamaica. He had a Beggar's wallet over his shoulders, a coat of shreds and patches altogether of a drab colour—he was tall and though his body was bent he had the look of one used to have been upright. I talked a while to him, and then gave him a piece of cold Bacon and a penny. Said he 'You're a fine woman!' I could not help smiling. I suppose he meant 'You're a kind woman.' Afterwards a woman called travelling to Glasgow. After dinner

60. The editor of the text, Mary Moorman, notes that "this sentence is written in large letters across the page."
61. *The Castle of Indolence,* an allegorical poem in the manner of Spenser, by James Thomson (1700–1748), was published in 1748.
62. "A Farewell."
63. He later wrote under the name of Christopher North and was one of the founders of *Blackwood's Magazine.*
64. She means her teeth.

William was very unwell. We went into Frank's field, crawled up the little glen and planned a seat then went to Mr Olliff's Hollins and sate there— found a beautiful shell-like purple fungus in Frank's field. After tea we walked to Butterlip How and backwards and forwards there. All the young oak tree leaves are dry as powder. A cold south wind portending Rain. After we came in we sate in deep silence at the window—I on a chair and William with his hand on my shoulder. We were deep in Silence and Love, a blessed hour. We drew to the fire before bed-time and ate some Broth for our suppers. . . .

Thursday 17th William had slept well. I took castor oil and lay in bed till 12 o'clock. William injured himself with working a little.—When I got up we sate in the orchard, a sweet mild day. Miss Hudson called. I went with her to the top of the hill. When I came home I found William at work, at-tempting to alter a stanza in the poem on our going for Mary [65] which I convinced him did not need altering. We sate in the house after dinner. In the evening walked on our favourite path. A short letter from Coleridge. William added a little to the Ode he is writing.[66]

Thursday 7th [July] A rainy morning. I paid Thomas Ashburner, and Frank Baty. When I was coming home, a post chaise passed with a little girl behind in a patched ragged red cloak. The child and cloak—Alice Fell's own self.[67] We sate in tranquillity together by the fire in the morning. In the afternoon after we had talked a little, Wm fell asleep, I read the Winter's Tale. Then I went to bed but did not sleep. The Swallows stole in and out of their nest, and sate there *whiles* quite still, *whiles* they sung low for 2 minutes or more at a time just like a muffled Robin. William was looking at the Pedlar when I got up. He arranged it, and after tea I wrote it out—280 lines. In the meantime the evening being fine he carried his coat to the Tailor's and went to George Mackareth's to engage the horse. He came in to me at about ½ past nine pressing me to go out; he had got letters which we were to read out of doors—I was rather unwilling, fearing I could not see to read the letters, but I saw well enough. One was from M. H., a very tender affecting letter, another from Sara to C., from C. to us, and from my B[rothe]r R[ichar]d. The moon was behind. William hurried me out in hopes that I should see her. We walked first to the top of the hill to see Rydale. It was dark and dull but our own vale was very solemn. The shape of Helm Crag was quite distinct, though black. We walked backwards and forwards on the White Moss path there was a sky-like white brightness on the lake. The Wyke Cottage Light at the foot of Silver How. Glowworms out, but not so numerous as last night. O beautiful place! Dear Mary William. The horse is come Friday morning, so I must give over. William is eating his Broth. I must prepare to go. The Swallows I must leave them the well the garden the Roses, all. Dear creatures!!

65. "A Farewell."
66. "Intimations" ode.
67. "Alice Fell; or, Poverty" relates that the poet, traveling by post-chaise, continually hears a cry that he cannot account for; at one of the post stops he discovers that a little girl, poor and orphaned, has been riding behind the chaise and weeping because her ragged cloak was caught in the wheel.

they sang last night after I was in bed—seemed to be singing to one another, just before they settled to rest for the night. Well, I must go. Farewell.— — —

1896, 1904

SAMUEL TAYLOR COLERIDGE
1772–1834

"Through a natural development," André Gide has said, "all great poets eventually become critics." The statement is of course too categorical to be literally true, but that it approaches truth is attested by even a partial roster of the poets whose critical writing is of the highest interest: Dante, Goethe, Schiller, Wordsworth, Shelley, Arnold, Baudelaire, Valéry, Eliot. Of all poets who became critics, none became so wholly and passionately a critic as Coleridge. From his early youth he was deeply engaged by the theory of literature; in his difficult middle years, when his poetic genius had deserted him, he was preoccupied, we might almost say obsessed, with the effort to comprehend and explicate literature in its innermost being, in its essential and ideal nature. To this arduous undertaking he brought a combination of intellectual powers which is perhaps unique in the history of criticism—the boldness and profundity of his philosophic speculation, the precision of his particular observations, and the acuity of his psychological insight have won for him, at least in the English-speaking world, an immense prestige.

Coleridge is not a critic who offers himself to easy comprehension. His concepts are sometimes inherently difficult and they are made the more so by being often formulated in the intellectual idiom of the German philosophers whose seminal thought on aesthetic questions had a decisive influence upon his own. The difficulty is compounded by the circumstance that Coleridge's criticism never achieved a systematic form. Much of it exists as disjointed fragments, unfinished manuscripts, reports which others made of his lectures, notes for and outlines of work to be undertaken. Even *Biographia Literaria* (1817), his best-known work in criticism and the one that comes nearest to being fully composed, is not so much completed as brought to a stop. Yet no one who seriously gives himself to the inchoate canon of Coleridge's criticism is likely to doubt its essential coherence.

It is commonly and correctly said that the idea which informs Coleridge's critical speculation is his conception of the function of literature, or, to use his own word, poetry. This is indeed momentous—nothing less than that of mediating between man and Nature, of confirming and sustaining a mode of perceiving the world which discovers in it, or (what for Coleridge is the same thing) bestows upon it, those attributes which make it responsive and hospitable to man.

This central idea of Coleridge's criticism is given an especially memorable expression in his last great utterance as a poet, *Dejection: An Ode*. The subject of the poem is the painful state into which the poet has fallen in consequence of his being no longer able to exercise what he calls his "shaping spirit of Imagination." It was through the active power of imagination that animation and beauty had been bestowed upon—actually infused into—"that inanimate cold world" which ordinary vision perceives. And the animated world, as if in return for this gift of life made to it by the creative imagination, had confirmed and sustained the imagination in its joyous activity. But now this happy reciprocation of creativity is disastrously at an end. The misfortunes with which the poet has been long afflicted have, he says, incapacitated his imagination, and because he cannot bring it into play to animate the world, the world cannot animate him—"We receive but what we give, / And in our life alone does Nature live." In Coleridge's view the imagination is the presiding faculty or "soul" of literature and as such defines its function. The chief intention of his critical enterprise is to discover the laws by which the imagination operates in carrying on its life-bestowing activity.

That the imagination operates by its own laws is a fundamental assumption of Coleridge's criticism and is the reason for his intense antagonism to the prescriptive criticism of the preceding age. French and English critical theory since the late seventeenth century gave large credence to the idea of "rules"—that is, formulated standards of judgment which were designed to guide the writer toward achieving literary works equal in quality to the admired works of the past. It is true that the tradition of the "rules," which goes back ultimately to Horace's *Ars Poetica*, was from the first quite willing to take account of "genius," to which it gave license to break the rules on due occasion; Pope and Johnson are explicit in their liberality on this score. But the obvious implication of even a permissive formulation of rules is that the work of art is a thing that is *made*, and for a certain purpose, that of satisfying the expectations of the audience. This was a conception of art which Coleridge passionately rejected, as did all the Romanticists—a work of art was not to be thought of as an object consciously contrived, like a mechanical device, with the end in view of gratifying the settled taste of the public, but as an autonomous and living entity, coming into being and growing and developing as a tree does, by the laws of its own nature. If it gives pleasure, as a tree may indeed give pleasure and of the highest kind, this is not its defining purpose, which is, rather, simply to come into being, to fulfill, as it were, the demands of its own nature. Its author does, to be sure, in some sense bring it into being, but in doing so his conscious intention and intellect play but a secondary part. This conception of the process of literary creation as being "organic" rather than "mechanical" was pre-eminently exemplified for Coleridge, as for the Romanticists generally, by Shakespeare. The formulation of the idea of organicism which Coleridge made in the notebook entry given below is its classic expression in English. It will be seen that the idea is salient in Shelley's *Defence of Poetry*.

Biographia Literaria

From *Chapter I*

The discipline of his taste at school—Bowles's sonnets—Comparison between the poets before and since Mr. Pope.

At school I enjoyed the inestimable advantage of a very sensible, though at the same time a very severe master. He [1] early moulded my taste to the preference of Demosthenes to Cicero, of Homer and Theocritus to Virgil, and

---

1. "The Rev. James Bowyer, many years Head Master of the Grammar School, Christ's Hospital" (Coleridge). See below Lamb's account of Bowyer in *Christ's Hospital Five and Thirty Years Ago*.

again of Virgil to Ovid.[2] He habituated me to compare Lucretius (in such extracts as I then read), Terence, and above all the chaster poems of Catullus, not only with the Roman poets of the, so called, silver and brazen ages; but with even those of the Augustan era: and on grounds of plain sense and universal logic to see and assert the superiority of the former in the truth and nativeness, both of their thoughts and diction. At the same time that we were studying the Greek Tragic Poets, he made us read Shakespeare and Milton as lessons: and they were the lessons too, which required most time and trouble to *bring up*, so as to escape his censure. I learnt from him, that Poetry, even that of the loftiest and, seemingly, that of the wildest odes, had a logic of its own, as severe as that of science; and more difficult, because more subtle, more complex, and dependent on more, and more fugitive causes. In the truly great poets, he would say, there is a reason assignable, not only for every word, but for the position of every word; and I will remember that, availing himself of the synonyms to the Homer of Didymus,[3] he made us attempt to show, with regard to each, *why* it would not have answered the same purpose; and *wherein* consisted the peculiar fitness of the word in the original text.

In our own English compositions (at least for the last three years of our school education) he showed no mercy to phrase, metaphor, or image, unsupported by a sound sense, or where the same sense might have been conveyed with equal force and dignity in plainer words. Lute, harp, and lyre, muse, muses, and inspirations, Pegasus, Parnassus, and Hippocrene [4] were all an abomination to him. In fancy I can almost hear him now, exclaiming 'Harp? Harp? Lyre? Pen and ink, boy, you mean! Muse, boy, Muse? Your Nurse's daughter, you mean! Pierian spring? Oh aye! the cloister-pump, I suppose!' Nay, certain introductions, similes, and examples, were placed by name on a list of interdiction. Among the similes, there was, I remember, that of the manchineel fruit,[5] as suiting equally well with too many subjects; in which however it yielded the palm at once to the example of Alexander and Clytus,[6] which was equally good and apt, whatever might be the theme. Was it ambition? Alexander and Clytus!—Flattery? Alexander and Clytus!—Anger? Drunkenness? Pride? Friendship? Ingratitude? Late repentance? Still, still Alexander and Clytus! At length, the praises of agriculture having been exemplified in the sagacious observation, that, had Alexander been holding the plough, he would not have run his friend Clytus through with a spear, this tried and serviceable old friend was banished by public edict in *secula*

2. The particular reasons for the preferences which Coleridge mentions in this and the next sentence need not be gone into—what he is saying in sum is that Bowyer taught him to regard the ancient classics as living literature.

3. Didymus (c. 65 B.C.–10 A.D.) was an Alexandrian literary scholar, author of a commentary on Homer. He was nicknamed *Chalkenteros*, Brazen-guts, because of his relentless industry.

4. Pegasus was the winged horse of the Muses. Parnassus was a mountain in Greece, one of whose two summits was the home of Apollo and the Muses. Hippocrene was the fountain of the Muses on another of their homes, Mount Helicon.

5. The manchineel is a tropical American tree, having poisonous sap and poisonous fruit.

6. Clytus—more usually, Cleitus—was a friend of Alexander's and the brother of his foster mother, and had once in battle saved Alexander's life. Alexander killed him in a moment of drunken rage and was overcome with remorse.

seculorum.[7] I have sometimes ventured to think, that a list of this kind, or an *index expurgatorius* [8] of certain well known and ever returning phrases, both introductory, and transitional, including a large assortment of modest egoisms, and flattering illeisms,[9] &c., &c., might be hung up in our law-courts, and both houses of parliament, with great advantage to the public, as an important saving of national time, an incalculable relief to his Majesty's ministers, but above all, as ensuring the thanks of country attorneys, and their clients, who have private bills to carry through the House.

Be this as it may, there was one custom of our master's, which I cannot pass over in silence, because I think it imitable and worthy of imitation. He would often permit our exercises, under some pretext of want of time, to accumulate, till each lad had four or five to be looked over. Then placing the whole number *abreast* on his desk, he would ask the writer, why this or that sentence might not have found as appropriate a place under this or that other thesis: and if no satisfying answer could be returned, and two faults of the same kind were found in one exercise, the irrevocable verdict followed, the exercise was torn up, and another on the same subject to be produced, in addition to the tasks of the day. The reader will, I trust, excuse this tribute of recollection to a man, whose severities, even now, not seldom furnish the dreams, by which the blind fancy would fain interpret to the mind the painful sensations of distempered sleep; but neither lessen nor dim the deep sense of my moral and intellectual obligations. He sent us to the University excellent Latin and Greek scholars, and tolerable Hebraists. Yet our classical knowledge was the least of the good gifts, which we derived from his zealous and conscientious tutorage. He is now gone to his final reward, full of years, and full of honours, even of those honours, which were dearest to his heart, as gratefully bestowed by that school, and still binding him to the interests of that school, in which he had been himself educated, and to which during his whole life he was a dedicated thing.

From causes, which this is not the place to investigate, no models of past times, however perfect, can have the same vivid effect on the youthful mind, as the productions of contemporary genius. . . . The great works of past ages seem to a young man things of another race, in respect to which his faculties must remain passive and submiss, even as to the stars and mountains. But the writings of a contemporary, perhaps not many years older than himself, surrounded by the same circumstances, and disciplined by the same manners, possess a *reality* for him, and inspire an actual friendship as of a man for a man. His very admiration is the wind which fans and feeds his hope. The poems themselves assume the properties of flesh and blood. To recite, to extol, to contend for them is but the payment of a debt due to one, who exists to receive it.

. . .

I had just entered on my seventeenth year, when the sonnets of Mr. Bowles,[10] twenty in number, and just then published in a quarto pamphlet, were first

7. In perpetuity—for "centuries of centuries."
8. The phrase commonly refers to a list of books that Roman Catholics were once not permitted to read until certain parts were expunged.
9. The excessive use of *he* (Latin: *ille*), especially when meaning oneself.
10. William Lisle Bowles (1762–1850) published *Fourteen Sonnets* in 1789. To Cole-

made known and presented to me, by a schoolfellow who had quitted us for the University, and who, during the whole time that he was in our first form (or in our school language a Grecian [11]) had been my patron and protector. I refer to Dr. Middleton, the truly learned, and every way excellent Bishop of Calcutta. . . .

It was a double pleasure to me, and still remains a tender recollection, that I should have received from a friend so revered the first knowledge of a poet, by whose works, year after year, I was so enthusiastically delighted and inspired. My earliest acquaintances will not have forgotten the undisciplined eagerness and impetuous zeal, with which I laboured to make proselytes, not only of my companions, but of all with whom I conversed, of whatever rank, and in whatever place. As my school finances did not permit me to purchase copies, I made, within less than a year and a half, more than forty transcriptions, as the best presents I could offer to those, who had in any way won my regard. And with almost equal delight did I receive the three or four following publications of the same author.

Though I have seen and known enough of mankind to be well aware, that I shall perhaps stand alone in my creed, and that it will be well, if I subject myself to no worse charge than that of singularity; I am not therefore deterred from avowing, that I regard, and ever have regarded the obligations of intellect among the most sacred of the claims of gratitude. A valuable thought, or a particular train of thoughts, gives me additional pleasure, when I can safely refer and attribute it to the conversation or correspondence of another. My obligations to Mr. Bowles were indeed important, and for radical good. At a very premature age, even before my fifteenth year, I had bewildered myself in metaphysics, and in theological controversy. Nothing else pleased me. History, and particular facts, lost all interest in my mind. Poetry (though for a schoolboy of that age, I was above par in English versification, and had already produced two or three compositions which, I may venture to say, without reference to my age, were somewhat above mediocrity, and which had gained me more credit than the sound, good sense of my old master was at all pleased with), poetry itself, yea, novels and romances, became insipid to me. In my friendless wanderings on our leave-days (for I was an orphan, and had scarcely any connexions in London), highly was I delighted, if any passenger, especially if he were dressed in black,[12] would enter into conversation with me. For I soon found the means of directing it to my favourite subjects

---

ridge they came as a revelation by reason of the simplicity of their diction, their air of sincerity, and their responsiveness to nature. In 1806 Bowles produced an edition of Pope in the preface of which he expressed an adverse view of Pope's style. This involved him in a heated and extended controversy with Pope's admirers, of whom Byron was one of the most ardent.

11. The name given to the gifted older pupils of the school who were being prepared for the university. The numbering of "forms" or classes at Christ's Hospital would seem to have been different from that in use in other English schools; usually the youngest class is the first form.

12. That is, a clergyman. He would be the more willing to enter into conversation with the young Coleridge because, from the uniform of long blue coat and bright yellow stockings, he would identify the youth as a member of the school of Christ's Hospital whose pupils, Charles Lamb tells us, were affectionately regarded by Londoners. The uniform is still sometimes worn by pupils of the school.

> Of providence, fore-knowledge, will, and fate,
> Fixed fate, free will, fore-knowledge absolute,
> And found no end in wandering mazes lost.[13]

This preposterous pursuit was, beyond doubt, injurious both to my natural powers, and to the progress of my education. It would perhaps have been destructive, had it been continued; but from this I was auspiciously withdrawn, partly indeed by an accidental introduction to an amiable family,[14] chiefly however, by the genial influence of a style of poetry, so tender and yet so manly, so natural and real, and yet so dignified and harmonious, as the sonnets etc. of Mr. Bowles! Well were it for me, perhaps, had I never relapsed into the same mental disease; if I had continued to pluck the flower and reap the harvest from the cultivated surface, instead of delving in the unwholesome quicksilver mines of metaphysic depths. But if in after time I have sought a refuge from bodily pain and mismanaged sensibility in abstruse researches, which exercised the strength and subtlety of the understanding without awakening the feelings of the heart; still there was a long and blessed interval, during which my natural faculties were allowed to expand, and my original tendencies to develop themselves: my fancy, and the love of nature, and the sense of beauty in forms and sounds.

The second advantage, which I owe to my early perusal, and admiration of these poems (to which let me add, though known to me at a somewhat later period, the *Lewesdon Hill* of Mr. Crowe [15]), bears more immediately on my present subject. Among those with whom I conversed, there were, of course, very many who had formed their taste, and their notions of poetry, from the writings of Mr. Pope and his followers: or to speak more generally, in that school of French poetry, condensed and invigorated by English understanding, which had predominated from the last century. I was not blind to the merits of this school, yet as from inexperience of the world, and consequent want of sympathy with the general subjects of these poems, they gave me little pleasure, I doubtless undervalued the *kind*, and with the presumption of youth withheld from its masters the legitimate name of poets. I saw that the excellence of this kind consisted in just and acute observations on men and manners in an artificial state of society, as its matter and substance: and in the logic of wit, conveyed in smooth and strong epigrammatic couplets, as its *form*. Even when the subject was addressed to the fancy, or the intellect, as in the *Rape of the Lock*, or the *Essay on Man;* nay, when it was a consecutive narration, as in that astonishing product of matchless talent and ingenuity, Pope's translation of the *Iliad;* still a *point* was looked for at the end of each second line, and the whole was as it were a sorites,[16] or, if I may exchange a logical for a grammatical metaphor, a *conjunction disjunctive*, of epigrams.[17] Meantime

13. *Paradise Lost* II.559–61.
14. The widowed mother and three sisters of a school friend, Tom Evans. Coleridge fell in love with the eldest sister, Mary.
15. William Crowe (1745–1829), a clergyman and scholar, published *Lewesdon Hill* in 1788. It is a long descriptive poem in blank verse and in its day much admired.
16. A series of linked syllogisms.
17. A "conjunction disjunctive" is a grammatical element that both joins part of a sentence and suggests an opposition between them—e.g. *either-or, neither-nor, but-although*.

the matter and diction seemed to me characterized not so much by poetic thoughts, as by thoughts *translated* into the language of poetry. On this last point, I had occasion to render my own thoughts gradually more and more plain to myself, by frequent amicable disputes concerning Darwin's *Botanic Garden*,[18] which, for some years, was greatly extolled, not only by the reading public in general, but even by those, whose genius and natural robustness of understanding enabled them afterwards to act foremost in dissipating these 'painted mists' that occasionally rise from the marshes at the foot of Parnassus. During my first Cambridge vacation, I assisted a friend in a contribution for a literary society in Devonshire: and in this I remember to have compared Darwin's work to the Russian palace of ice, glittering, cold and transitory. In the same essay too, I assigned sundry reasons, chiefly drawn from a comparison of passages in the Latin poets with the original Greek, from which they were borrowed, for the preference of Collins' odes to those of Gray; and of the simile in Shakespeare:

> How like a younker or a prodigal,
> The scarfed bark puts from her native bay,
> Hugged and embraced by the strumpet wind!
> How like the prodigal doth she return,
> With over-weathered ribs and ragged sails,
> Lean, rent, and beggared by the strumpet wind! [19]

to the imitation in *The Bard:*

> Fair laughs the morn, and soft the zephyr blows,
> While proudly riding o'er the azure realm
> In gallant trim the gilded vessel goes,
> YOUTH at the prow and PLEASURE at the helm;
> Regardless of the sweeping whirlwind's sway,
> That hushed in grim repose, expects its evening prey.[20]

(In which, by the bye, the words 'realm' and 'sway' are rhymes dearly purchased.) I preferred the original on the ground, that in the imitation it depended wholly on the compositor's putting, or not putting, a *small capital*, both in this, and in many other passages of the same poet, whether the words should be personifications, or mere abstractions. I mention this, because, in referring various lines in Gray to their original in Shakespeare and Milton, and in the clear perception how completely all the propriety was lost in the transfer, I was, at that early period, led to a conjecture, which, many years afterwards was recalled to me from the same thought having been started in conversation, but far more ably, and developed more fully, by Mr. Wordsworth; namely, that this style of poetry, which I have characterized above, as translations of prose thoughts into poetic language, had been kept up by, if it did not wholly arise

---

18. Erasmus Darwin (1731–1802) was the grandfather of Charles Darwin. *The Botanic Garden* (1789, 1791) is a didactic poem in rhymed couplets on plants and flowers. Some of Erasmus Darwin's scientific views are absurd, some brilliant, and the same can be said of his verse.
19. *The Merchant of Venice* II.vi.14–19.
20. Thomas Gray, *The Bard*, ll. 71–74.

from, the custom of writing Latin verses, and the great importance attached to these exercises, in our public schools. Whatever might have been the case in the fifteenth century, when the use of the Latin tongue was so general among learned men, that Erasmus is said to have forgotten his native language; yet in the present day it is not to be supposed, that a youth can *think* in Latin, or that he can have any other reliance on the force or fitness of his phrases, but the authority of the writer from whence he has adopted them. Consequently he must first prepare his thoughts, and then pick out, from Virgil, Horace, Ovid, or perhaps more compendiously from his *Gradus*,[21] halves and quarters of lines, in which to embody them.

I never object to a certain degree of disputatiousness in a young man from the age of seventeen to that of four or five and twenty, provided I find him always arguing on one side of the question. The controversies, occasioned by my unfeigned zeal for the honour of a favourite contemporary, then known to me only by his works, were of great advantage in the formation and establishment of my taste and critical opinions. In my defence of the lines running into each other, instead of closing at each couplet, and of natural language, neither bookish, nor vulgar, neither redolent of the lamp, nor of the kennel, such as *I will remember thee*; instead of the same thought tricked up in the rag-fair finery of

> ————Thy image on her wing
> Before my Fancy's eye shall Memory bring,

I had continually to adduce the metre and diction of the Greek poets from Homer to Theocritus inclusive; and still more of our elder English poets from Chaucer to Milton. Nor was this all. But as it was my constant reply to authorities brought against me from later poets of great name, that no authority could avail in opposition to Truth, Nature, Logic, and the Laws of Universal Grammar; actuated too by my former passion for metaphysical investigations; I laboured at a solid foundation, on which permanently to ground my opinions, in the component faculties of the human mind itself, and their comparative dignity and importance. According to the faculty or source, from which the pleasure given by any poem or passage was derived, I estimated the merit of such poem or passage. As the result of all my reading and meditation, I abstracted two critical aphorisms, deeming them to comprise the conditions and criteria of poetic style; first, that not the poem which we have *read*, but that to which we *return*, with the greatest pleasure, possesses the genuine power, and claims the name of *essential poetry*. Second, that whatever lines can be translated into other words of the same language, without diminution of their significance, either in sense, or association, or in any worthy feeling, are so far vicious in their diction. Be it however observed, that I excluded from the list of worthy feelings, the pleasure derived from mere novelty in the reader, and the desire of exciting wonderment at his powers in the author. Oftentimes since then, in pursuing French tragedies, I have fancied two marks

21. Short for *Gradus ad Parnassum* (Step to Parnassus). This was a dictionary of Latin poetical phrases once used in English schools to aid pupils in the composition of Latin verse.

of admiration at the end of each line, as hieroglyphics of the author's own admiration at his own cleverness. Our genuine admiration of a great poet is a continuous *undercurrent* of feeling; it is everywhere present, but seldom anywhere as a separate excitement. I was wont boldly to affirm, that it would be scarcely more difficult to push a stone out from the pyramids with the bare hand, than to alter a word, or the position of a word, in Milton or Shakespeare (in their most important works at least) without making the author say something else, or something worse, than he does say. One great distinction, I appeared to myself to see plainly, between, even the characteristic faults of our elder poets, and the false beauty of the moderns. In the former, from Donne to Cowley, we find the most fantastic out-of-the-way thoughts, but in the most pure and genuine mother English; in the latter, the most obvious thoughts, in language the most fantastic and arbitrary. Our faulty elder poets sacrificed the passion and passionate flow of poetry, to the subtleties of intellect, and to the starts of wit; the moderns to the glare and glitter of a perpetual, yet broken and heterogeneous imagery, or rather to an amphibious something, made up, half of image, and half of abstract meaning.[22] The one sacrificed the heart to the head; the other both heart and head to point and drapery . . .

From *Chapter IV*
Mr. Wordsworth's earlier poems—On fancy and imagination—The investigation of the distinction important to the fine arts.

During the last year of my residence at Cambridge, I became acquainted with Mr. Wordsworth's first publication entitled *Descriptive Sketches;* [1] and seldom, if ever, was the emergence of an original poetic genius above the literary horizon more evidently announced. In the form, style, and manner of the whole poem, and in the structure of the particular lines and periods, there is an harshness and acerbity connected and combined with words and images all aglow, which might recall those products of the vegetable world, where gorgeous blossoms rise out of the hard and thorny rind and shell, within which the rich fruit was elaborating. The language was not only peculiar and strong, but at times knotty and contorted, as by its own impatient strength; while the novelty and struggling crowd of images, acting in conjunction with the difficulties of the style, demanded always a greater closeness of attention, than poetry (at all events, than descriptive poetry) has a right to claim. It not seldom therefore justified the complaint of obscurity. In the following extract I have sometimes fancied, that I saw an emblem of the poem itself, and of the author's genius as it was then displayed.

'Tis storm; and hid in mist from hour to hour,
All day the floods a deepening murmur pour;
The sky is veiled, and every cheerful sight:
Dark is the region as with coming night;

22. "I remember a ludicrous instance in the poem of a young tradesman: No more will I endure love's pleasing pain, / Or round my *heart's leg* tie his galling chain." (Coleridge)

1. Published in 1793. The poem sets forth Wordsworth's impressions and emotions on his walking trip through the Alps in the summer of 1790. The same tour is described in a much more impressive way in *The Prelude* VI.

And yet what frequent bursts of overpowering light!
Triumphant on the bosom of the storm,
Glances the fire-clad eagle's wheeling form;
Eastward, in long perspective glittering, shine
The wood-crowned cliffs that o'er the lake recline;
Wide o'er the Alps a hundred streams unfold,
At once to pillars turned that flame with gold;
Behind his sail the peasant strives to shun
The West, that burns like one dilated sun,
Where in a mighty crucible expire
The mountains, glowing hot, like coals of fire.[2]

The poetic Psyche, in its process to full development, undergoes as many changes as its Greek namesake, the butterfly.[3] And it is remarkable how soon genius clears and purifies itself from the faults and errors of its earliest products; faults which, in its earliest compositions, are the more obtrusive and confluent, because as heterogeneous elements, which had only a temporary use, they constitute the very *ferment*, by which themselves are carried off. Or we may compare them to some diseases, which must work on the humours, and be thrown out on the surface, in order to secure the patient from their future recurrence. I was in my twenty-fourth year, when I had the happiness of knowing Mr. Wordsworth personally, and while memory lasts, I shall hardly forget the sudden effect produced on my mind, by his recitation of a manuscript poem, which still remains unpublished, but of which the stanza, and tone of style, were the same as those of the 'Female Vagrant,' as originally printed in the first volume of the *Lyrical Ballads*.[4] There was here no mark of strained thought, or forced diction, no crowd or turbulence of imagery; and, as the poet hath himself well described in his lines 'On Re-visiting the Wye,' manly reflection, and human associations had given both variety, and an additional interest to natural objects, which in the passion and appetite of the first love they had seemed to him neither to need or permit.[5] The occasional obscurities, which had risen from an imperfect control over the resources of his native language, had almost wholly disappeared, together with that worse defect of arbitrary and illogical phrases, at once hackneyed, and fantastic, which hold so distinguished a place in the *technique* of ordinary poetry, and will,

2. *Descriptive Sketches*, ll. 332–47. Coleridge quotes the passage as it appeared in a revised version in 1815.
3. "The fact, that in Greek Psyche is the common name for the soul, and the butterfly, is thus alluded to in the following stanzas from an unpublished poem of the author:
The butterfly the ancient Grecians made
The soul's fair emblem, and its only name—
But of the soul, escaped the slavish trade
Of mortal life! For in this earthly frame
Ours is the reptile's lot, much toil, much blame,
Manifold motions making little speed,
And to deform and kill the things, whereon we feed." (Coleridge)
4. The manuscript poem was *Guilt and Sorrow*, which Wordsworth composed between 1791 and 1794. He revised part of the poem and, under the title "The Female Vagrant," included it in *Lyrical Ballads*.
5. Coleridge refers to *Tintern Abbey*, ll. 72–102.

more or less, alloy the earlier poems of the truest genius, unless the attention has been specifically directed to their worthlessness and incongruity. I did not perceive anything particular in the mere style of the poem alluded to during its recitation, except indeed such difference as was not separable from the thought and manner; and the Spenserian stanza, which always, more or less, recalls to the reader's mind Spenser's own style, would doubtless have authorized, in my then opinion, a more frequent descent to the phrases of ordinary life, than could without an ill effect have been hazarded in the heroic couplet. It was not however the freedom from false taste, whether as to common defects, or to those more properly his own, which made so unusual an impression on my feelings immediately, and subsequently on my judgement. It was the union of deep feeling with profound thought; the fine balance of truth in observing, with the imaginative faculty in modifying the objects observed; and above all the original gift of spreading the tone, the *atmosphere*, and with it the depth and height of the ideal world around forms, incidents, and situations, of which, for the common view, custom had bedimmed all the lustre, had dried up the sparkle and the dew drops. 'To find no contradiction in the union of old and new; to contemplate the Ancient of Days and all his works with feelings as fresh, as if all had then sprang forth at the first creative fiat; characterizes the mind that feels the riddle of the world, and may help to unravel it. To carry on the feelings of childhood into the powers of manhood; to combine the child's sense of wonder and novelty with the appearances, which every day for perhaps forty years had rendered familiar;

> With sun and moon and stars throughout the year,
>   And man and woman; [6]

this is the character and privilege of genius, and one of the marks which distinguish genius from talents. And therefore is it the prime merit of genius and its most unequivocal mode of manifestation, so to represent familiar objects as to awaken in the minds of others a kindred feeling concerning them and that freshness of sensation which is the constant accompaniment of mental, no less than of bodily, convalescence. Who has not a thousand times seen snow fall on water? Who has not watched it with a new feeling, from the time that he has read Burns' comparison of sensual pleasure

> To snow that falls upon a river
>   A moment white—then gone forever! [7]

In poems, equally as in philosophic disquisitions, genius produces the strongest impressions of novelty, while it rescues the most admitted truths from the impotence caused by the very circumstance of their universal admission. 'Truths of all others the most awful and mysterious, yet being at the same time of universal interest, are too often considered as *so* true, that they lose all the life and efficiency of truth, and lie bed-ridden in the dormitory of the soul,

6. Milton, "Sonnet, To Mr. Cyriak Skinner upon His Blindness," somewhat altered.
7. *Tam O'Shanter*, ll. 61–62: "Or like the snow falls in the river— / A moment white, then melts forever."

side by side with the most despised and exploded errors.'—*The Friend*, p. 76, No. 5.[8]

This excellence, which in all Mr. Wordsworth's writings is more or less predominant, and which constitutes the character of his mind, I no sooner felt, than I sought to understand. Repeated meditations led me first to suspect (and a more intimate analysis of the human faculties, their appropriate marks, functions, and effects matured my conjecture into full conviction) that fancy and imagination were two distinct and widely different faculties, instead of being, according to the general belief, either two names with one meaning, or, at furthest, the lower and higher degree of one and the same power. It is not, I own, easy to conceive a more opposite translation of the Greek *phantasia* than the Latin *imaginatio;* but it is equally true that in all societies there exists an instinct of growth, a certain collective, unconscious good sense working progressively to desynonymize those words originally of the same meaning, which the conflux of dialects had supplied to the more homogeneous languages, as the Greek and German: and which the same cause, joined with accidents of translation from original works of different countries, occasion in mixed languages like our own. The first and most important point to be proved is, that two conceptions perfectly distinct are confused under one and the same word, and (this done) to appropriate that word exclusively to one meaning, and the synonym (should there be one) to the other. But if (as will be often the case in the arts and sciences) no synonym exists, we must either invent or borrow a word. In the present instance the appropriation has already begun, and been legitimated in the derivative adjective: Milton had a highly *imaginative,* Cowley a very *fanciful* mind. If therefore I should succeed in establishing the actual existences of two faculties generally different, the nomenclature would be at once determined. To the faculty by which I had characterized Milton, we should confine the term *imagination;* while the other would be contra-distinguished as *fancy.* Now were it once fully ascertained, that this division is no less grounded in nature, than that of delirium from mania, or Otway's

> Lutes, lobsters, seas of milk, and ships of amber,[9]

from Shakespeare's

> What! have his daughters brought him to this pass?[10]

or from the preceding apostrophe to the elements; the theory of the fine arts, and of poetry in particular, could not, I thought, but derive some additional and important light. It would in its immediate effects furnish a torch of guidance to the philosophical critic; and ultimately to the poet himself. In energetic minds, truth soon changes by domestication into power; and from directing in the discrimination and appraisal of the product, becomes influencive

8. *The Friend: A Literary, Moral, and Political Weekly Paper* (of minute circulation) was written and published by Coleridge in 1809–10.
9. Thomas Otway, *Venice Preserved* (1682), V.ii.151. Coleridge is being unkind in the way he quotes the line—absurd as it is, it does not read "Lutes, lobsters . . ." but "Lutes, laurels. . . ."
10. *King Lear* III.iv.65.

in the production. To admire on principle, is the only way to imitate without loss of originality . . .

Chapter XIV
Occasion of the Lyrical Ballads, and the objects originally proposed—Preface to the second edition—The ensuing controversy, its causes and acrimony—Philosophic definitions of a poem and poetry with scholia.[1]

During the first year that Mr. Wordsworth and I were neighbours,[2] our conversations turned frequently on the two cardinal points of poetry, the power of exciting the sympathy of the reader by a faithful adherence to the truth of nature, and the power of giving the interest of novelty by the modifying colours of imagination. The sudden charm, which accidents of light and shade, which moonlight or sunset diffused over a known and familiar landscape, appeared to represent the practicability of combining both. These are the poetry of nature. The thought suggested itself (to which of us I do not recollect) that a series of poems might be composed of two sorts. In the one, the incidents and agents were to be, in part at least, supernatural; and the excellence aimed at was to consist in the interesting of the affections by the dramatic truth of such emotions, as would naturally accompany such situations, supposing them real. And real in *this* sense they have been to every human being who, from whatever source of delusion, has at any time believed himself under supernatural agency. For the second class, subjects were to be chosen from ordinary life; the characters and incidents were to be such, as will be found in every village and its vicinity, where there is a meditative and feeling mind to seek after them, or to notice them, when they present themselves.

In this idea originated the plan of the *Lyrical Ballads;* in which it was agreed, that my endeavours should be directed to persons and characters supernatural, or at least romantic; yet so as to transfer from our inward nature a human interest and a semblance of truth sufficient to procure for these shadows of imagination that willing suspension of disbelief for the moment, which constitutes poetic faith. Mr. Wordsworth, on the other hand, was to propose to himself as his object, to give the charm of novelty to things of every day, and to excite a feeling analogous to the supernatural, by awakening the mind's attention from the lethargy of custom, and directing it to the loveliness and the wonders of the world before us; an inexhaustible treasure, but for which, in consequence of the film of familiarity and selfish solicitude we have eyes, yet see not, ears that hear not, and hearts that neither feel nor understand.[3]

With this view I wrote *The Ancient Mariner,* and was preparing among other poems, 'The Dark Ladie,' and the *Christabel,* in which I should have more nearly realized my ideal, than I had done in my first attempt. But Mr. Wordsworth's industry had proved so much more successful, and the number of his poems so much greater, that my compositions, instead of forming a balance, appeared rather an interpolation of heterogeneous matter. Mr. Wordsworth added two or three poems written in his own character, in the impassioned,

---

1. Plural of *scholium* (Latin), an explanatory note or commentary.
2. In 1797 at Nether Stowey and Alfoxden. See Hazlitt's *My First Acquaintance with Poets.*
3. *Isaiah* 6: 9–10.

lofty, and sustained diction, which is characteristic of his genius.[4] In this form the *Lyrical Ballads* were published; and were presented by him, as an *experiment*,[5] whether subjects, which from their nature rejected the usual ornaments and extra-colloquial style of poems in general, might not be so managed in the language of ordinary life as to produce the pleasureable interest, which it is the peculiar business of poetry to impart. To the second edition he added a preface of considerable length; in which, notwithstanding some passages of apparently a contrary import, he was understood to contend for the extension of this style to poetry of all kinds, and to reject as vicious and indefensible all phrases and forms of style that were not included in what he (unfortunately, I think, adopting an equivocal expression) called the language of *real* life. From this preface, prefixed to poems in which it was impossible to deny the presence of original genius, however mistaken its direction might be deemed, arose the whole long-continued controversy.[6] For from the conjunction of perceived power with supposed heresy I explain the inveteracy and in some instances, I grieve to say, the acrimonious passions, with which the controversy has been conducted by the assailants.

Had Mr. Wordsworth's poems been the silly, the childish things, which they were for a long time described as being; had they been really distinguished from the compositions of other poets merely by meanness of language and inanity of thought; had they indeed contained nothing more than what is found in the parodies and pretended imitations of them; they must have sunk at once, a dead weight, into the slough of oblivion, and have dragged the preface along with them. But year after year increased the number of Mr. Wordsworth's admirers. They were found too not in the lower classes of the reading public, but chiefly among young men of strong sensibility and meditative minds; and their admiration (inflamed perhaps in some degree by opposition) was distinguished by its intensity, I might almost say, by its *religious* fervour. These facts, and the intellectual energy of the author, which was more or less consciously felt, where it was outwardly and even boisterously denied, meeting with sentiments of aversion to his opinions, and of alarm at their consequences, produced an eddy of criticism, which would of itself have borne up the poems by the violence, with which it whirled them round and round. With many parts of this preface, in the sense attributed to them, and which the words undoubtedly seem to authorize, I never concurred; but on the contrary objected to them as erroneous in principle, and as contradictory (in appearance at least) both to other parts of the same preface, and to the author's own practice in the greater number of the poems themselves. Mr. Wordsworth in his recent collection [7] has, I find, degraded this prefatory disquisition to the end of his second volume, to

4. Coleridge means those of Wordsworth's poems, of which *Tintern Abbey* is the preeminent example, which were not among the "experiments" referred to in the next sentence.

5. Wordsworth uses the word in the brief "Advertisement" to the first edition of *Lyrical Ballads* as well as in his Preface to the second edition (1800). The concept of conscious "experiment" in art became of great consequence in the later 19th century, although without reference to Wordsworth.

6. The often acrimonious debate over Wordsworth's theory of the language appropriate to poetry.

7. *Poems*, two volumes, 1815.

be read or not at the reader's choice. But he has not, as far as I can discover, announced any change in his poetic creed. At all events, considering it as the source of a controversy, in which I have been honoured more than I deserve by the frequent conjunction of my name with his, I think it expedient to declare once for all, in what points I coincide with his opinions, and in what points I altogether differ. But in order to render myself intelligible I must previously, in as few words as possible, explain my ideas, first, of a POEM; and secondly, of POETRY itself, in *kind*, and in *essence*.

The office of philosophical *disquisition* consists in just *distinction;* while it is the privilege of the philosopher to preserve himself constantly aware, that distinction is not division. In order to obtain adequate notions of any truth, we must intellectually separate its distinguishable parts; and this is the technical *process* of philosophy. But having so done, we must then restore them in our conceptions to the unity, in which they actually co-exist; and this is the *result* of philosophy. A poem contains the same elements as a prose composition; the difference therefore must consist in a different combination of them, in consequence of a different object being proposed. According to the difference of the object will be the difference of the combination. It is possible, that the object may be merely to facilitate the recollection of any given facts or observations by artificial arrangement; and the composition will be a poem, merely because it is distinguished from prose by metre, or by rhyme, or by both conjointly. In this, the lowest sense, a man might attribute the name of a poem to the well-known enumeration of the days in the several months;

> Thirty days hath September,
> April, June, and November, etc.

and others of the same class and purpose. And as a particular pleasure is found in anticipating the recurrence of sounds and quantities, all compositions that have this charm super-added, whatever be their contents, *may* be entitled poems.

So much for the superficial *form.* A difference of object and contents supplies an additional ground of distinction. The immediate purpose may be the communication of truths; either of truth absolute and demonstrable, as in works of science; or of facts experienced and recorded, as in history. Pleasure, and that of the highest and most permanent kind, may *result* from the *attainment* of the end; but it is not itself the immediate end. In other works the communication of pleasure may be the immediate purpose; and though truth, either moral or intellectual, ought to be the *ultimate* end, yet this will distinguish the character of the author, not the class to which the work belongs. Blest indeed is that state of society, in which the immediate purpose would be baffled by the perversion of the proper ultimate end; in which no charm of diction or imagery could exempt the Bathyllus even of an Anacreon, or the Alexis of Virgil, from disgust and aversion! [8]

But the communication of pleasure may be the immediate object of a work

8. The adverse feelings to which Coleridge refers are those which might be occasioned by the representation of homosexuality. The beauty of the youth Bathyllus is celebrated by Anacreon (6th century B.C.); in Virgil's Second Eclogue the shepherd Corydon loves the young Alexis.

not metrically composed; and that object may have been in a high degree attained, as in novels and romances. Would then the mere superaddition of metre, with or without rhyme, entitle *these* to the name of poems? The answer is, that nothing can permanently please, which does not contain in itself the reason why it is so, and not otherwise. If metre be super-added, all other parts must be made consonant with it. They must be such, as to justify the perpetual and distinct attention to each part, which an exact correspondent recurrence of accent and sound are calculated to excite. The final definition then, so deduced, may be thus worded. A poem is that species of composition, which is opposed to works of science, by proposing for its *immediate* object pleasure, not truth; and from all other species (having *this* object in common with it) it is discriminated by proposing to itself such delight from the *whole,* as is compatible with a distinct gratification from each component *part.*

Controversy is not seldom excited in consequence of the disputants attaching each a different meaning to the same word; and in few instances has this been more striking, than in disputes concerning the present subject. If a man chooses to call every composition a poem, which is rhyme, or measure, or both, I must leave his opinion uncontroverted. The distinction is at least competent to characterize the writer's intention. If it were subjoined, that the whole is likewise entertaining or affecting, as a tale, or as a series of interesting reflections, I of course admit this as another fit ingredient of a poem, and an additional merit. But if the definition sought for be that of a *legitimate* poem, I answer, it must be one, the parts of which mutually support and explain each other; all in their proportion harmonizing with, and supporting the purpose and known influences of metrical arrangement. The philosophic critics of all ages coincide with the ultimate judgement of all countries, in equally denying the praises of a just poem, on the one hand, to a series of striking lines or distichs,[9] each of which, absorbing the whole attention of the reader to itself, disjoins it from its context, and makes it a separate whole, instead of an harmonizing part; and on the other hand, to an unsustained composition, from which the reader collects rapidly the general result, unattracted by the component parts. The reader should be carried forward, not merely or chiefly by the mechanical impulse of curiosity, or by a restless desire to arrive at the final solution; but by the pleasureable activity of mind excited by the attractions of the journey itself. Like the motion of a serpent, which the Egyptians made the emblem of intellectual power; or like the path of sound through the air; at every step he pauses and half recedes, and from the retrogressive movement collects the force which again carries him onward. 'Praecipitandus est, liber *spiritus,*' says Petronius Arbiter most happily.[10] The epithet, *liber,* here balances the preceding verb; and it is not easy to conceive more meaning condensed in fewer words.

But if this should be admitted as a satisfactory character of a poem, we have still to seek for a definition of poetry. The writings of Plato, and Bishop

9. A distich is a group of two lines of verse. The word is used in reference to Greek verse. The English rhymed distich is called a couplet.
10. "The free spirit must be impelled forward." Petronius (d. 66 A.D.), whom Tacitus called *Arbiter Elegantiae* (judge of elegance), was a member of Nero's court and the reputed author of *Satyricon,* a brilliant satirical novel of Roman life.

Taylor, and the *Theoria Sacra* of Burnet,[11] furnish undeniable proofs that poetry of the highest kind may exist without metre, and even without the contra-distinguishing objects of a poem. The first chapter of Isaiah (indeed a very large portion of the whole book) is poetry in the most emphatic sense; yet it would be not less irrational than strange to assert, that pleasure, and not truth, was the immediate object of the prophet. In short, whatever *specific* import we attach to the word, poetry, there will be found involved in it, as a necessary consequence, that a poem of any length neither can be, or ought to be, all poetry. Yet if an harmonious whole is to be produced, the remaining parts must be preserved *in keeping* with the poetry; and this can be no other-wise effected than by such a studied selection and artificial arrangement, as will partake of *one*, though not a *peculiar* property of poetry. And this again can be no other than the property of exciting a more continuous and equal attention than the language of prose aims at, whether colloquial or written.

My own conclusions on the nature of poetry, in the strictest use of the word, have been in part anticipated in the preceding disquisition on the fancy and imagination. What is poetry? is so nearly the same question with, what is a poet? that the answer to the one is involved in the solution of the other. For it is a distinction resulting from the poetic genius itself, which sustains and modifies the images, thoughts, and emotions of the poet's own mind.

The poet, described in *ideal* perfection, brings the whole soul of man into activity, with the subordination of its faculties to each other, according to their relative worth and dignity. He diffuses a tone and spirit of unity, that blends, and (as it were) *fuses*, each into each, by that synthetic and magical power, to which we have exclusively appropriated the name of imagination. This power, first put in action by the will and understanding, and retained under their irremissive, though gentle and unnoticed, controul (*laxis effertur habenis*[12]) reveals itself in the balance or reconciliation of opposite or discord-ant qualities: of sameness, with difference; of the general, with the concrete; the idea, with the image; the individual, with the representative; the sense of novelty and freshness, with old and familiar objects; a more than usual state of emotion, with more than usual order; judgement ever awake and steady self-possession, with enthusiasm and feeling profound or vehement; and while it blends and harmonizes the natural and the artificial, still subordinates art to nature; the manner to the matter; and our admiration of the poet to our sympathy with the poetry. 'Doubtless,' as Sir John Davies observes of the soul (and his words may with slight alteration be applied, and even more appropri-ately, to the poetic IMAGINATION),

> Doubtless this could not be, but that she turns
> Bodies to spirit by sublimation strange,

---

11. Jeremy Taylor (1613–67), the author of *Holy Living* and *Holy Dying*. The chief work of Thomas Burnet (1635–1715) is *Telluris Theoria Sacra,* first composed in Latin and then rendered into English as *The Sacred Theory of the Earth.* The scientific views expressed in the book are fanciful, but Coleridge admired Burnet's prose, as he did the prose of Taylor, for its richness and stately eloquence, qualities that often characterized the work of 17th-century authors but not those of the 18th century, at least until Burke.
12. "Driven with a loose rein."

As fire converts to fire the things it burns,
   As we our food into our nature change.

From their gross matter she abstracts their forms,
   And draws a kind of quintessence from things;
Which to her proper nature she transforms,
   To bear them light on her celestial wings.

Thus does she, when from individual states
   She doth abstract the universal kinds;
Which then re-clothed in divers names and fates
   Steal access through our senses to our minds.[13]

Finally, GOOD SENSE is the BODY of poetic genius, FANCY its DRAPERY, MOTION its LIFE, and IMAGINATION the SOUL that is everywhere, and in each; and forms all into one graceful and intelligent whole.

From *Chapter XVII*

Examination of the tenets peculiar to Mr. Wordsworth—Rustic life (above all, low and rustic life) especially unfavourable to the formation of a human diction —The best parts of language the product of philosophers, not of clowns or shepherds—Poetry essentially ideal and generic—The language of Milton as much the language of real life, yea, incomparably more so than that of the cottager.

As far then as Mr. Wordsworth in his preface contended, and most ably contended, for a reformation in our poetic diction, as far as he has evinced the truth of passion, and the *dramatic* propriety of those figures and metaphors in the original poets, which, stripped of their justifying reasons, and converted into mere artifices of connection or oranament, constitute the characteristic falsity in the poetic style of the moderns; and as far as he has, with equal acuteness and clearness, pointed out the process by which this change was effected, and the resemblances between that state into which the reader's mind is thrown by the pleasureable confusion of thought from an unaccustomed train of words and images; and that state which is induced by the natural language of impassioned feeling; he undertook a useful task, and deserves all praise, both for the attempt and for the execution. The provocations to this remonstrance in behalf of truth and nature were still of perpetual recurrence before and after the publication of this preface. I cannot likewise but add, that the comparison of such poems of merit, as have been given to the public within the last ten or twelve years, with the majority of those produced previously to the appearance of that preface, leave no doubt on my mind, that Mr. Wordsworth is fully justified in believing his efforts to have been by no means ineffectual. Not only in the verses of those who have professed their admiration of his genius, but even of those who have distinguished themselves by hostility to his theory, and depreciation of his writings, are the impressions of his principles plainly visible. It is possible, that with these principles others may have been blended, which are not equally evident; and some which are un-

---

13. Coleridge quotes, with some significant alterations, from *Nosce Teipsum* (Know Thyself), a long poem by Sir John Davies (1569–1626) on the nature of the soul, with emphasis on its immortality.

steady and subvertible from the narrowness or imperfection of their basis. But it is more than possible, that these errors of defect or exaggeration, by kindling and feeding the controversy, may have conduced not only to the wider propagation of the accompanying truths, but that, by their frequent presentation to the mind in an excited state, they may have won for them a more permanent and practical result. A man will borrow a part from his opponent the more easily, if he feels himself justified in continuing to reject a part. While there remain important points in which he can still feel himself in the right, in which he still finds firm footing for continued resistance, he will gradually adopt those opinions, which were the least remote from his own convictions, as not less congruous with his own theory than with that which he reprobates. In like manner with a kind of instinctive prudence, he will abandon by little and little his weakest posts, till at length he seems to forget that they had ever belonged to him, or affects to consider them at most as accidental and 'petty annexments,' the removal of which leaves the citadel unhurt and unendangered.

My own differences from certain supposed parts of Mr. Wordsworth's theory ground themselves on the assumption, that his words had been rightly interpreted, as purporting that the proper diction for poetry in general consists altogether in a language taken, with due exceptions, from the mouths of men in real life, a language which actually constitutes the natural conversation of men under the influence of natural feelings.[1] My objection is, first, that in *any* sense this rule is applicable only to *certain* classes of poetry; secondly, that even to these classes it is not applicable, except in such a sense, as hath never by any one (as far as I know or have read) been denied or doubted; and lastly, that as far as, and in that degree in which it is *practicable*, yet as a *rule* it is useless, if not injurious, and therefore either need not, or ought not to be practised. The poet informs his reader, that he had generally chosen *low and rustic* life; but not *as* low and rustic, or in order to repeat that pleasure of doubtful moral effect, which persons of elevated rank and of superior refinement oftentimes derive from a happy *imitation* of the rude unpolished manners and discourse of their inferiors. For the pleasure so derived may be traced to three exciting causes. The first is the naturalness, in *fact*, of the things represented. The second is the apparent naturalness of the *representation*, as raised and qualified by an imperceptible infusion of the author's own knowledge and talent, which infusion does, indeed, constitute it an *imitation* as distinguished from a mere *copy*. The third cause may be found in the reader's conscious feeling of his superiority awakened by the contrast presented to him; even as for the same purpose the kings and great barons of yore retained sometimes *actual* clowns and fools, but more frequently shrewd and witty fellows in that *character*. These, however, were not Mr. Wordsworth's objects. *He* chose low and rustic life, 'because in that condition the essential passions of the heart find a better soil, in which they can attain their maturity, are less under restraint, and speak a plainer and more emphatic language; because in that condition of life our elementary feelings coexist in a state of greater simplicity, and consequently may be more accurately contemplated, and more forcibly

1. See Preface to *Lyrical Ballads*.

communicated; because the manners of rural life germinate from those elementary feelings; and from the necessary character of rural occupations are more easily comprehended, and are more durable; and lastly, because in that condition the passions of men are incorporated with the beautiful and permanent forms of nature.' [2]

Now it is clear to me, that in the most interesting of the poems, in which the author is more or less dramatic, as *The Brothers, Michael, Ruth, The Mad Mother*, etc., the persons introduced are by no means taken *from low or rustic life* in the common acceptation of those words; and it is not less clear, that the sentiments and language, as far as they can be conceived to have been really transferred from the minds and conversation of such persons, are attributable to causes and circumstances not necessarily connected with 'their occupations and abode.' The thoughts, feelings, language, and manners of the shepherd-farmers in the vales of Cumberland and Westmoreland, as far as they are actually adopted in those poems, may be accounted for from causes, which will and do produce the same results in *every* state of life, whether in town or country. As the two principal I rank that INDEPENDENCE, which raises a man above servitude, or daily toil for the profit of others, yet not above the necessity of industry and a frugal simplicity of domestic life; and the accompanying unambitious, but solid and religious, EDUCATION, which has rendered few books familiar, but the Bible, and the liturgy or hymn book. To this latter cause, indeed, which is so far *accidental,* that it is the blessing of particular countries and a particular age, not the product of particular places or employments, the poet owes the show of probability, that his personages might really feel, think, and talk with any tolerable resemblance to his representation. . . .

It is, moreover, to be considered that to the formation of healthy feelings, and a reflecting mind, *negations* involve impediments not less formidable than sophistication and vicious intermixture. I am convinced, that for the human soul to prosper in rustic life a certain vantage-ground is prerequisite. It is not every man that is likely to be improved by a country life or by country labours. Education, or original sensibility, or both, must pre-exist, if the changes, forms, and incidents of nature are to prove a sufficient stimulant. And where these are not sufficient, the mind contracts and hardens by want of stimulants: and the man becomes selfish, sensual, gross, and hard-hearted. Let the management of the Poor Laws in Liverpool, Manchester, or Bristol be compared with the ordinary dispensation of the poor rates in agricultural villages, where the *farmers* are the overseers and guardians of the poor. If my own experience have not been particularly unfortunate, as well as that of the many respectable country clergymen with whom I have conversed on the subject, the result would engender more than scepticism concerning the desireable influences of low and rustic life in and for itself. Whatever may be concluded on the other side, from the stronger local attachments and enterprising spirit of the Swiss, and other mountaineers, applies to a particular mode of pastoral life, under forms of property that permit and beget manners truly republican, not to rustic life in general, or to the absence of artificial cultivation. On the contrary the mountaineers, whose manners have been so often eulogized, are in general

2. In the Preface.

better educated and greater readers than men of equal rank elsewhere. But where this is not the case, as among the peasantry of North Wales, the ancient mountains, with all their terrors and all their glories, are pictures to the blind, and music to the deaf.

I should not have entered so much into detail upon this passage, but here seems to be the point, to which all the lines of difference converge as to their source and centre. (I mean, as far as, and in whatever respect, my poetic creed *does* differ from the doctrines promulged in this preface.) I adopt with full faith the principle of Aristotle, that poetry as poetry is essentially *ideal,* that it avoids and excludes all *accident;* that its apparent individualities of rank, character, or occupation must be *representative* of a class; and that the *persons* of poetry must be clothed with *generic* attributes, with the *common* attributes of the class: not with such as one gifted individual might *possibly* possess, but such as from his situation it is most probable beforehand that he *would* possess.[3]

Here let me be permitted to remind the reader, that the positions, which I controvert, are contained in the sentences—'a selection of the REAL *language of men';—'the language of these men'* (i.e. men in low and rustic life) '*I propose to myself to imitate, and, as far as is possible, to adopt the very language of men.' 'Between the language of prose and that of metrical composition, there neither is, nor can be any essential difference.'* It is against these exclusively that my opposition is directed.

I object, in the very first instance, to an equivocation in the use of the word 'real.' Every man's language varies, according to the extent of his knowledge, the activity of his faculties, and the depth or quickness of his feelings. Every man's language has, first, its *individualities;* secondly, the common properties of the *class* to which he belongs; and thirdly, words and phrases of *universal* use. The language of Hooker, Bacon, Bishop Taylor, and Burke[4] differs from the common language of the learned class only by the superior number and novelty of the thoughts and relations which they had to convey. The language of Algernon Sidney[5] differs not at all from that, which every well-educated gentleman would wish to write, and (with due allowances for the undeliberateness, and less connected train, of thinking natural and proper to conversation) such as he would wish to talk. Neither one nor the other differ half so much from the general language of cultivated society, as the language of Mr. Wordsworth's homeliest composition differs from that of a common peasant. For 'real' therefore, we must substitute *ordinary,* or *lingua communis.*[6] And this, we have proved, is no more to be found in the phraseology of low and rustic life than

3. "Say not that I am recommending abstractions; for these class-characteristics which constitute the instructiveness of a character, are so modified and particularized in each person of the Shakespearean drama, that life itself does not excite more distinctly that sense of individuality which belongs to real existence. . . ." (Coleridge)
4. The works of the four men whose use of language Coleridge cites as admirable span two centuries—the first part of Richard Hooker's great *Laws of Ecclesiastical Polity* was published in 1593, Edmund Burke's *Reflections on the French Revolution* in 1790.
5. Algernon Sidney (1622?–83) was the grand-nephew of Sir Philip Sidney. His dramatic political life was controlled by his strong republican principles, which he expressed in his posthumous *Discourses Concerning Government* (1698).
6. "The common tongue."

in that of any other class. Omit the peculiarities of each, and the result of course must be common to all. And assuredly the omissions and changes to be made in the language of rustics, before it could be transferred to any species of poem, except the drama or other professed imitation, are at least as numerous and weighty, as would be required in adapting to the same purpose the ordinary language of tradesmen and manufacturers. Not to mention, that the language so highly extolled by Mr. Wordsworth varies in every county, nay in every village, according to the accidental character of the clergyman, the existence or non-existence of schools; or even, perhaps, as the exciseman, publican, or barber, happen to be, or not to be, zealous politicians, and readers of the weekly newspaper *pro bono publico*.[7] Anterior to cultivation, the *lingua communis* of every country, as Dante has well observed,[8] exists everywhere in parts, and nowhere as a whole.

Neither is the case rendered at all more tenable by the addition of the words, *in a state of excitement*. For the nature of a man's words, where he is strongly affected by joy, grief, or anger, must necessarily depend on the number and quality of the general truths, conceptions and images, and of the words expressing them, with which his mind had been previously stored. For the property of passion is not to *create*; but to set in increased activity. At least, whatever new connections of thoughts or images, or (which is equally, if not more than equally, the appropriate effect of strong excitement) whatever generalizations of truth or experience, the heat of passion may produce; yet the terms of their conveyance must have pre-existed in his former conversations, and are only collected and crowded together by the unusual stimulation. It is indeed very possible to adopt in a poem the unmeaning repetitions, habitual phrases, and other blank counters, which an unfurnished or confused understanding interposes at short intervals, in order to keep hold of his subject, which is still slipping from him, and to give him time for recollection; or in mere aid of vacancy, as in the scanty companies of a country stage the same player pops backwards and forwards, in order to prevent the appearance of empty spaces, in the procession of *Macbeth*, or *Henry VIII*. But what assistance to the poet, or ornament to the poem, these can supply, I am at a loss to conjecture. Nothing assuredly can differ either in origin or in mode more widely from the *apparent* tautologies of intense and turbulent feeling, in which the passion is greater and of longer endurance than to be exhausted or satisfied by a single representation of the image or incident exciting it. Such repetitions I admit to be a beauty of the highest kind; as illustrated by Mr. Wordsworth himself from the song of Deborah. '*At her feet he bowed, he fell, he lay down; at her feet he bowed, he fell; where he bowed, there he fell down dead.*'[9]

1817

7. "For the public good."
8. In his essay *De Vulgari Eloquentia* ("On the Speech of the People") Dante puts the case for the use in poetry of colloquial Italian purged of the peculiarities of regional dialects.
9. *Judges* 5:27. Wordsworth cites this passage in a note to *The Thorn* in which he defends the repetitions that mark the poem as being appropriate to a state of heightened feeling.

Organic Form

[In the course of the nineteenth century the idea of the organic nature of the creative process (see Headnote) established itself as an orthodox doctrine of aesthetic thought. Walter Pater, in his comprehensive essay on Coleridge (1866, 1880), comments on it in a cogent way. He gives it his general assent but goes on to remark the paradox that, in insisting on the organic model of artistic creation as against the older classical view that the work of art is *made* by the artist, Coleridge represents the artist as "almost a mechanical agent." Here is the whole of Pater's objection:

> Instead of the most luminous and self-possessed phase of consciousness, the associative act in art or poetry is made to look like some blindly organic process of assimilation. The work of art is likened to a living organism. That expresses truly the sense of self-delighting, independent life which the finished work of art gives us: it hardly figures that process by which such work was produced. Here there is no blind ferment of lifeless elements toward the realization of a type. By exquisite analysis the artist attains clearness of idea; then, through many stages of refining, clearness of expression. He moves slowly over his work, calculating the tenderest tone, and restraining the subtlest curve, never letting hand or fancy move at large, gradually enforcing flaccid spaces to the higher degree of expressiveness. The philosophic critic, at least, will value, even in works of imagination, seemingly the most intuitive, the power of the understanding in them, their logical process of construction, the spectacle of a supreme intellectual dexterity which they afford.

The passage which follows is a notebook entry for one of Coleridge's public lectures on Shakespeare, which he never prepared for publication. The text is that of T. M. Raysor, published in *Coleridge's Shakespearean Criticism*.]

The subject of the present lecture is no less than a question submitted to your understandings, emancipated from national prejudice: Are the plays of Shakespeare works of rude uncultivated genius, in which the splendour of the parts compensates, if aught can compensate, for the barbarous shapelessness and irregularity of the whole? To which not only the French critics, but even his own English admirers, say [yes].[1] Or is the form equally admirable with the matter, the judgement of the great poet not less deserving of our wonder than his genius? Or to repeat the question in other words, is Shakespeare a great dramatic poet on account only of these beauties and excellencies which he possesses in common with the ancients, but with diminished claims to our love and honour to the full extent of his difference from them? Or are these very differences additional proofs of poetic wisdom, at once results and symbols of living power as contrasted with lifeless mechanism, of free and rival originality as contra-distinguished from servile imitation, or more accurately, [from] a blind copying of effects instead of a true imitation of the essential principles? Imagine not I am about to oppose genius to rules. No! the comparative value of these rules is the very cause to be tried. The spirit of poetry, like all other living powers, must of necessity circumscribe itself by rules, were it only to unite power with beauty. It must embody in order to reveal itself; but a living body is of necessity an organized one,—and what is organization, but the

---

1. Coleridge rightly singles out Voltaire as the extreme example of the French critics holding this view; but it is hard to think of an English critic who went so far as to impute to Shakespeare a "barbarous shapelessness."

connection of parts to a whole, so that each part is at once end and means! This is no discovery of criticism; it is a necessity of the human mind—and all nations have felt and obeyed it, in the invention of metre and measured sounds as the vehicle and involucrum [2] of poetry, itself a fellow-growth from the same life, even as the bark is to the tree.

No work of true genius dare want its appropriate form; neither indeed is there any danger of this. As it must not, so neither can it, be lawless! For it is even this that constitutes it genius—the power of acting creatively under laws of its own origination. How then comes it that not only single Zoili,[3] but whole nations have combined in unhesitating condemnation of our great dramatist, as a sort of African nature, fertile in beautiful monsters, as a wild heath where islands of fertility look greener from the surrounding waste, where the loveliest plants now shine out among unsightly weeds and now are choked by their parasitic growth, so intertwined that we cannot disentangle the weed without snapping the flower. In this statement I have had no reference to the vulgar abuse of Voltaire, save as far as his charges are coincident with the decisions of his commentators and (so they tell you) his almost idolatrous admirers. The true ground of the mistake, as has been well remarked by a continental critic,[4] lies in the confounding mechanical regularity with organic form. The form is mechanic when on any given material we impress a pre-determined form, not necessarily arising out of the properties of the material, as when to a mass of wet clay we give whatever shape we wish it to retain when hardened. The organic form, on the other hand, is innate; it shapes as it develops itself from within, and the fullness of its development is one and the same with the perfection of its outward form. Such is the life, such the form. Nature, the prime genial [5] artist, inexhaustible in diverse powers, is equally inexhaustible in forms. Each exterior is the physiognomy of the being within, its true image reflected and thrown out from the concave mirror. And even such is the appropriate excellence of her chosen poet, of our own Shakespeare, himself a nature humanized, a genial understanding directing self-consciously a power and an implicit wisdom deeper than consciousness.

1930

CHARLES LAMB
1775–1834

London was to Charles Lamb what the Lake Country was to his friend William Wordsworth—the beloved place, the scene uniquely appropriate to his spirit. He was not being wholly serious when he said that he had "an almost insurmountable aversion from solitude and rural scenes," but the joking hyperbole expresses the militancy of his

2. Case or envelope, especially around a flower.
3. Zoilus—Zoili is the plural which generalizes him into a type—was a critic of the 4th century B.C. notorious for the bitterness of his attacks on Plato and Homer.
4. This is August Wilhelm von Schlegel, the German critic, from whom Coleridge derived many of his ideas about literature, including the one that he here sets forth.
5. This word was used by the Romanticists—in Germany as well as England—in the sense that connects it with "genius" and suggests generation.

feeling for the town at a time when it was becoming received opinion that sensibility could flourish only in the country.

He was born in the very heart of the metropolis, in the district which was once the ancient walled town and is still called "the City," and in, we might say, its heart's core, the Inner Temple, one of the four curious institutions known as the Inns of Court. Although these are voluntary societies, not chartered by the state, they have in charge the whole of the legal profession of England. They came into being in the fourteenth century and are descended from organizations which combined the functions of trade guilds and law schools. Their buildings, some of which are of great antiquity, are extensive; they include churches, libraries, and dining halls, and they accommodate not only professional offices but also residences.

Lamb's having been born and reared in the Inner Temple suggests the paradox of his social position. His father in his youth had gone into domestic service and although he subsequently rose a little in the social scale by becoming a scrivener, that is, a professional legal copyist, he served his employer, a successful lawyer named Samuel Salt, not only in the capacity of confidential clerk but also as a trusted servant. Lamb's maternal grandmother had been housekeeper to a country family, and his mother was Salt's housekeeper. In a society charged with class feeling one might expect the menial callings of his family to have been a source of distress to a highly conscious young man, but this seems not to have been the case. Lamb writes of his father with affectionate respect as a man of proud and independent spirit and some intellectual attainment; he cherished the memory of his grandmother, and of his mother he said that she was a "perfect gentlewoman."

At the age of seven Lamb was enrolled in the famous school of Christ's Hospital, not far from the Temple. He remained a pupil there until he was fifteen, and his account of his experience is to be read in his great autobiographical essay, *Christ's Hospital Five and Thirty Years Ago* (see below). The friendship with Coleridge that he formed at the school was a strong and lasting one, although it had its vicissitudes. It was through Coleridge that he met Wordsworth, and it says much about Lamb that between him and the craggy and difficult person that Wordsworth became in his later years there was the warmest affection.

After leaving school, Lamb was briefly employed in South Sea House and in 1792 he was appointed to a clerkship in India House, the office of the great private but quasi-official body which, until 1858, had charge of the government of India. He remained a member of the staff for thirty years. In his twenty-second year the event occurred which determined the course of his life. There was in his mother's family a strain of insanity which on one occasion showed itself in Lamb himself. It manifested itself in a terrible way in his sister Mary, who was eleven years his senior: in a fit of rage she mortally stabbed their mother. Lamb was witness to the catastrophe. The authorities did not contemplate criminal prosecution but it seemed likely that Mary would be remanded to a public insane asylum. However, through the intervention of influential friends she was released in the custody of her young brother. There was an older and relatively prosperous brother, but he had cut himself off from the family, and Charles was quite alone in his responsibility, which included the care of his senile father. He placed Mary in a private and decent home where he could visit her and from which he removed her some three years later when her rationality was restored. Henceforward the brother and sister were inseparable, except for the periods (which were frequent) when Mary's reason again gave way; the terrible violence would begin to rise and Mary had to be put under the constraint which she herself would ask for. Lamb's devotion through all his life—he predeceased Mary by thirteen years—was entire. Although his domestic affections were strong, his situation made marriage impossible. No resentment over the sacrifice he was making seems ever to have figured in his feelings for Mary, with whom he lived in a reciprocation of tenderness and admiration. When she was in health she was a person of considerable charm and she was liked and highly regarded by Lamb's many distinguished friends. Although unschooled, she read widely and wrote with simple grace.

It was not until he was in his forties that Lamb began to do the work upon which his fame rests. He had had literary ambitions since early youth, and over the following years he was to make several forays toward fame which were either inconclusive or disastrous. In 1796 he published four sonnets in Coleridge's first volume of poems; to these he added when a second edition of the work appeared in the following year. In 1798 he published a slight volume with his friend Charles Lloyd, which included his well-known and still affecting poem *Old Familiar Faces*. He attempted to write for the theater, but his tragedy *John Woodvil* was rejected for production and damned when it was published (1802), and his comedy *Mr. H.* failed dismally when it was staged—Lamb himself joined in hissing it. In 1807 he and Mary wrote a children's book, *Tales from Shakespeare*, which was to be for many years one of the staples of juvenile literature. The publication of *Specimens of English Dramatic Poets Contemporary with Shakespeare* (1808) brought him a certain small reputation as a critic. In 1820, through the good offices of Hazlitt, he was introduced to the editor of the new *London Magazine*, who invited him to contribute occasional essays. The first of these was a reminiscence of his brief time in South Sea House, in the course of which he made mention of an obscure old clerk called Elia; on a whim he signed the essay with that name. Thereafter it was as Elia—he wanted it pronounced "Ellia"—that Lamb wrote. Of the circumstantial details by which he gave substance to this *persona* of the aging harmless bachelor, some were drawn from his own life, some were invented, some compounded of actuality and invention. Within the next two years he contributed twenty-five essays to the *London Magazine;* in 1823 they were gathered together in a volume, *Essays of Elia,* which, although it did not sell well, established itself in the canon of English prose. A decade later *Last Essays of Elia* appeared; with the exception of one piece, "The Superannuated Man," it is inferior to its predecessor.

The power of the *Elia* essays is of a curious kind and baffles explanation. If one undertakes to name their manifest characteristics, one comes up with a list which, although it might account for the admiration given to the essays in an earlier day, can only suggest that they are bound to alienate contemporary taste. They are sentimental: they cherish emotion for its own sake, and have a special predilection for such emotions as are associated with transience, with the pathos of what once was with us and is now forever gone. They are whimsical: they seize upon trivial subjects and with conscious caprice attribute to them large significance. They are quaint: they are given to proposing the peculiar charm which is presumed to lie in the customs and manners of a distant time and they often affect language that long ago fell into disuse. But then, suddenly, they are none of these things; or if they continue to be, it does not matter. The preciousness and self-consciousness come to seem merely adventitious, and what we are aware of as esssential is a strong, clear intelligence, commanding in its centrality, its courage, its refusal of deception, and its vital irony. So formidable a judge as A. C. Bradley said of Lamb that he was the greatest critic of his age; the estimate is an extravagant one, the more because what might be called the canon of Lamb's actual criticism must be gathered mostly from statements made by the way and would make but a slim volume; yet it may serve to suggest something of the effect that the unexpected authority of Lamb's intelligence might have upon a percipient and responsive reader.

Christ's Hospital Five and Thirty Years Ago

[Christ's Hospital was founded in 1552 by Edward VI, its purpose being to "take out of the streets all the fatherless children and other poor men's children" and to give them shelter, food, and schooling. Later the intention of beneficence was changed, and the children admitted were those of respectable parents in reduced financial circumstances rather than those of the very poor. By the eighteenth century the school was the chief enterprise of the foundation. It was commonly called the Blue Coat School from its uniform, which was completed by knee-breeches and yellow stockings. Until 1902, when it was moved to new buildings in the country, the school was housed in the old Grey Friars (Franciscan) monastery on Newgate Street.

In this reminiscence of his schooldays, Lamb plays a curious game of identities. At the beginning of the essay he speaks of himself in the third person, and the "I" recalls circumstances and feelings which are actually those of Lamb's schoolfellow Coleridge. But as the essay proceeds, the "I" becomes Lamb himself.]

In Mr. Lamb's *Works*,[1] published a year or two since, I find a magnificent eulogy on my old school, such as it was, or now appears to him to have been, between the years 1782 and 1789. It happens, very oddly, that my own standing at Christ's was nearly corresponding with his; and, with all gratitude to him for his enthusiasm for the cloisters, I think he has contrived to bring together whatever can be said in praise of them, dropping all the other side of the argument most ingeniously.

I remember L. at school; and can well recollect that he had some peculiar advantages, which I and others of his school-fellows had not. His friends lived in town, and were near at hand; and he had the privilege of going to see them, almost as often as he wished, through some invidious distinction, which was denied to us. The present worthy sub-treasurer to the Inner Temple[2] can explain how that happened. He had his tea and hot rolls in a morning, while we were battening upon our quarter of a penny loaf—our *crug*[3]—moistened with attenuated small beer, in wooden piggins, smacking of the pitched

1. A collection of Lamb's miscellaneous prose and verse published in 1818. The essay to which he refers was published in the *Gentleman's Magazine* in 1813.
2. This was Randal Norris, a friend of Lamb's father; he took a paternal interest in Charles, who held him in great affection.—The Inner Temple is one of the four societies, called Inns of Court, which license the practice of law in England. The name applies also to the group of buildings, containing offices and residences, in which the society is housed.
3. The word for bread in Christ's Hospital slang.

leathern jack it was poured from.[4] Our Monday's milk porritch,[5] blue and tasteless, and the pease soup of Saturday, coarse and choking, were enriched for him with a slice of 'extraordinary bread and butter,' from the hot-loaf of the Temple. The Wednesday's mess of millet, somewhat less repugnant—(we had three banyan [6] to four meat days in the week)—was endeared to his palate with a lump of double-refined,[7] and a smack of ginger (to make it go down the more glibly) or the fragrant cinnamon. In lieu of our *half-pickled* Sundays, or *quite fresh* boiled beef on Thursdays (strong as *caro equina* [8]), with detestable marigolds floating in the pail to poison the broth—our scanty mutton crags [9] on Fridays—and rather more savoury, but grudging, portions of the same flesh, rotten-roasted or rare, on the Tuesdays (the only dish which excited our appetites, and disappointed our stomachs, in almost equal proportion)—he had his hot plate of roast veal, or the more tempting griskin [10] (exotics unknown to our palates), cooked in the paternal kitchen (a great thing), and brought him daily by his maid or aunt! I remember the good old relative (in whom love forbade pride) squatting down upon some odd stone in a by-nook of the cloisters, disclosing the viands (of higher regale than those cates which the ravens ministered to the Tishbite [11]); and the contending passions of L. at the unfolding. There was love for the bringer; shame for the thing brought, and the manner of its bringing; sympathy for those who were too many to share in it; and, at top of all, hunger (eldest, strongest of the passions!) predominant, breaking down the stony fences of shame, and awkwardness, and a troubling over-consciousness.

I was a poor friendless boy. My parents, and those who should care for me, were far away. Those few acquaintances of theirs, which they could reckon upon being kind to me in the great city, after a little forced notice, which they had the grace to take of me on my first arrival in town, soon grew tired of my holiday visits. They seemed to them to recur too often, though I thought them few enough; and, one after another, they all failed me, and I felt myself alone among six hundred playmates.

O the cruelty of separating a poor lad from his early homestead! The yearnings which I used to have towards it in those unfledged years! How, in my dreams, would my native town (far in the west) come back, with its church, and trees, and faces! How I would wake weeping, and in the anguish of my heart exclaim upon sweet Calne in Wiltshire! [12]

To this late hour of my life, I trace impressions left by the recollection of

4. Small beer is weak beer; a piggin is a small wooden pail with an upright handle, a sort of dipper; leather receptacles for liquids were once common.
5. Porridge; oatmeal.
6. A banian is a member of a Hindu caste which abstains from meat; English sailors used the word to signify a mess at which no meat was served.
7. Sugar.
8. Horse meat.
9. Necks.
10. A pork loin.
11. Cates are dainties. The Tishbite is the prophet Elijah, to whom, at the command of God, ravens brought food when he was in hiding: I Kings 17: 4–6.
12. Under this name Lamb conceals the actual place of Coleridge's home, Ottery St. Mary, in Devonshire.

those friendless holidays. The long warm days of summer never return but they bring with them a gloom from the haunting memory of those *whole-day-leaves*, when, by some strange arrangement, we were turned out, for the live-long day, upon our own hands, whether we had friends to go to, or none. I remember those bathing-excursions to the New-River,[13] which L. recalls with such relish, better, I think, than he can—for he was a home-seeking lad, and did not much care for such water-pastimes:—How merrily we would sally forth into the fields; and strip under the first warmth of the sun; and wanton like young dace [14] in the streams; getting us appetites for noon, which those of us that were pennyless (our scanty morning crust long since exhausted) had not the means of allaying—while the cattle, and the birds, and the fishes, were at feed about us, and we had nothing to satisfy our cravings—the very beauty of the day, and the exercise of the pastime, and the sense of liberty, setting a keener edge upon them!—How faint and languid, finally, we would return, towards nightfall, to our desired morsel, half-rejoicing, half-reluctant, that the hours of our uneasy liberty had expired!

It was worse in the days of winter, to go prowling about the streets object-less—shivering at cold windows of print-shops, to extract a little amusement; or haply, as a last resort, in the hope of a little novelty, to pay a fifty-times repeated visit (where our individual faces should be as well known to the warden as those of his own charges) to the Lions in the Tower—to whose levée,[15] by courtesy immemorial, we had a prescriptive title to admission.

L.'s governor (so we called the patron who presented us to the foundation) [16] lived in a manner under his paternal roof. Any complaint which he had to make was sure of being attended to. This was understood at Christ's, and was an effectual screen to him against the severity of masters, or worse tyranny of the monitors. The oppressions of these young brutes are heart-sickening to call to recollection. I have been called out of my bed, and *waked for the purpose*, in the coldest winter nights—and this not once, but night after night—in my shirt, to receive the discipline of a leathern thong, with eleven other sufferers, because it pleased my callow overseer, when there has been any talking heard after we were gone to bed, to make the six last beds in the dormitory, where the youngest children of us slept, answerable for an offence they neither dared to commit, nor had the power to hinder.—The same execrable tyranny drove the younger part of us from the fires, when our feet were perishing with snow; and, under the cruelest penalties, forbad the indulgence of a drink of water, when we lay in sleepless summer nights, fevered with the season, and the day's sports.

13. A stream brought into London (1609–13) to augment the city's water supply.
14. A minnow-like fish.
15. The Tower of London is a group of buildings, the earliest dating back to William the Conqueror, which has served as fortress, royal residence, and prison for eminent persons accused of crimes against the state. The crown jewels are still kept here but the menagerie is no longer maintained. A levée is the ceremonial reception held by a monarch (here the King of Beasts) upon arising from bed.
16. The substantial citizen who arranged the admission of a boy to Christ's Hospital. In Lamb's case, this was Samuel Salt, his father's employer, a well-known lawyer and member of Parliament. Lamb has described him at length in *Old Benchers of the Inner Temple*.

There was one H——, who, I learned, in after days, was seen expiating some maturer offence in the hulks.[17] (Do I flatter myself in fancying that this might be the planter of that name, who suffered—at Nevis, I think, or St. Kitts,[18]—some few years since? My friend Tobin was the benevolent instrument of bringing him to the gallows.) This petty Nero actually branded a boy, who had offended him, with a red hot iron; and nearly starved forty of us, with exacting contributions, to the one half of our bread, to pamper a young ass, which, incredible as it may seem, with the connivance of the nurse's daughter (a young flame of his) he had contrived to smuggle in, and keep upon the leads of the *ward*, as they called our dormitories. This game went on for better than a week, till the foolish beast, not able to fare well but he must cry roast meat—happier than Caligula's minion,[19] could he have kept his own counsel—but, foolisher, alas! than any of his species in the fables—waxing fat, and kicking, in the fulness of bread, one unlucky minute would needs proclaim his good fortune to the world below; and, laying out his simple throat, blew such a ram's horn blast, as (toppling down the walls of his own Jericho)[20] set concealment any longer at defiance. The client was dismissed, with certain attentions, to Smithfield;[21] but I never understood that the patron underwent any censure on the occasion. This was in the stewardship of L.'s admired Perry.[22]

Under the same *facile* administration, can L. have forgotten the cool impunity with which the nurses used to carry away openly, in open platters, for their own tables, one out of two of every hot joint, which the careful matron had been seeing scrupulously weighed out for our dinners? These things were daily practised in that magnificent apartment, which L. (grown connoisseur since, we presume) praises so highly for the grand paintings 'by Verrio,[23] and others,' with which it is 'hung round and adorned.' But the sight of sleek well-fed blue-coat boys in pictures was, at that time, I believe, little consolatory to him, or us, the living ones, who saw the better part of our provisions carried away before our faces by harpies; and ourselves reduced (with the Trojan in the hall of Dido)

To feed our mind with idle portraiture.[24]

L. has recorded the repugnance of the school to *gags*, or the fat of fresh beef boiled; and sets it down to some superstition. But these unctuous morsels are never grateful to young palates (children are universally fat-haters) and

17. Stationary, demasted ships used as prisons.
18. Islands in the West Indies.
19. The mad Roman emperor Caligula assigned a retinue of slaves to his favorite horse and appointed it consul.
20. The story of how Joshua brought down the walls of Jericho by marching around it with seven priests blowing trumpets is told in Joshua 6: 2–20.
21. A horse and cattle market.
22. In his first essay on the school Lamb writes affectionately of its steward, or superintendent, John Perry.
23. Antonio Verrio was an Italian painter of the 17th century who lived in England and decorated royal residences. Verrio's large picture shows the mathematics students of the school being received by James II.
24. In Bk. I of the *Aeneid*, when Aeneas and his companions reach Dido's city, they see on the wall of the temple to Juno paintings which depict the fall of Troy.

in strong, coarse, boiled meats, *unsalted,* are detestable. A *gag-eater* in our time was equivalent to a *goul,* and held in equal detestation.   —— suffered under the imputation.

——— 'Twas said
He ate strange flesh.[25]

He was observed, after dinner, carefully to gather up the remnants left at his table (not many, nor very choice fragments, you may credit me)—and, in an especial manner, these disreputable morsels, which he would convey away, and secretly stow in the settle that stood at his bed-side. None saw when he ate them. It was rumoured that he privately devoured them in the night. He was watched, but no traces of such midnight practices were discoverable. Some reported, that, on leave-days, he had been seen to carry out of the bounds a large blue check handkerchief, full of something. This then must be the accursed thing. Conjecture next was at work to imagine how he could dispose of it. Some said he sold it to the beggars. This belief generally prevailed. He went about moping. None spake to him. No one would play with him. He was excommunicated; put out of the pale of the school. He was too powerful a boy to be beaten, but he underwent every mode of that negative punishment, which is more grievous than many stripes. Still he persevered. At length he was observed by two of his school-fellows, who were determined to get at the secret, and had traced him one leave-day for that purpose, to enter a large worn-out building, such as there exist specimens of in Chancery-lane, which are let out to various scales of pauperism with open door, and a common staircase. After him they silently slunk in, and followed by stealth up four flights, and saw him tap at a poor wicket, which was opened by an aged woman, meanly clad. Suspicion was now ripened into certainty. The informers had secured their victim. They had him in their toils. Accusation was formally preferred, and retribution most signal was looked for. Mr. Hathaway, the then steward (for this happened a little after my time), with that patient sagacity which tempered all his conduct, determined to investigate the matter, before he proceeded to sentence. The result was, that the supposed mendicants, the receivers or purchasers of the mysterious scraps, turned out to be the parents of ——, an honest couple come to decay,—whom this seasonable supply had, in all probability, saved from mendicancy; and that this young stork, at the expense of his own good name, had all this while been only feeding the old birds!—The governors on this occasion, much to their honour, voted a present relief to the family of ——, and presented him with a silver medal. The lesson which the steward read upon RASH JUDGMENT, on the occasion of publicly delivering the medal to ——, I believe, would not be lost upon his auditory.—I had left school then, but I well remember ——. He was a tall, shambling youth, with a cast in his eye, not at all calculated to conciliate hostile prejudices. I have since seen him carrying a baker's basket. I think I heard he did not do quite so well by himself, as he had done by the old folks.

I was a hypochondriac lad; and the sight of a boy in fetters, upon the day of my first putting on the blue clothes, was not exactly fitted to assuage the natural terrors of initiation. I was of tender years, barely turned of seven;

25. Derived from *Antony and Cleopatra* I.iv.67.

and had only read of such things in books, or seen them but in dreams. I was told he had *run away*. This was the punishment for the first offence.—As a novice I was soon after taken to see the dungeons. These were little, square, Bedlam [25] cells, where a boy could just lie at his length upon straw and a blanket—a mattress, I think, was afterwards substituted—with a peep of light, let in askance, from a prison-orifice at top, barely enough to read by. Here the poor boy was locked in by himself all day, without sight of any but the porter who brought him his bread and water—who *might not speak to him;* —or of the beadle, who came twice a week to call him out to receive his periodical chastisement, which was almost welcome, because it separated him for a brief interval from solitude:—and here he was shut up by himself *of nights*, out of the reach of any sound, to suffer whatever horrors the weak nerves, and superstition incident to his time of life, might subject him to.[26] This was the penalty for the second offence.—Wouldst thou like, reader, to see what became of him in the next degree?

The culprit, who had been a third time an offender, and whose expulsion was at this time deemed irreversible, was brought forth, as at some solemn *auto da fe*,[27] arrayed in uncouth and most appalling attire—all trace of his late 'watchet weeds' [28] carefully affaced, he was exposed in a jacket, resembling those which London lamplighters formerly delighted in, with a cap of the same. The effect of this divestiture was such as the ingenious devisers of it could have anticipated. With his pale and frighted features, it was as if some of those disfigurements in Dante had seized upon him. In this disguisement he was brought into the hall (*L.'s favourite state-room*), where awaited him the whole number of his school-fellows, whose joint lessons and sports he was thenceforth to share no more; the awful presence of the steward, to be seen for the last time; of the executioner beadle, clad in his state robe for the occasion; and of two faces more, of direr import, because never but in these extremities visible. These were governors; two of whom, by choice, or charter, were always accustomed to officiate at these *Ultima Supplicia;* [29] not to mitigate (so at least we understood it), but to enforce the uttermost stripe. Old Bamber Gascoigne, and Peter Aubert, I remember, were colleagues on one occasion, when the beadle turning rather pale, a glass of brandy was ordered to prepare him for the mysteries. The scourging was, after the old Roman fashion, long and stately. The lictor [30] accompanied the criminal quite round the hall. We were generally too faint with attending to the previous disgusting circumstances, to make accurate report with our eyes of the degree of corporal suffering inflicted. Report, of course, gave out the back knotty and livid. After

---

25. Bedlam, corrupted pronunciation of "Bethlehem," i.e. the Hospital of St. Mary of Bethlehem, in London, in which insane persons were confined.
26. "One or two instances of lunacy, or attempted suicide, accordingly, at length convinced the governors of the impolicy of this part of the sentence, and the midnight torture of the spirits was dispensed with. . . ." (Lamb)
27. "Act of faith" (Spanish): the public execution of sentences upon persons condemned by the Inquisition.
28. Clothes of a blue color—the reference is to his school coat.
29. "Extreme punishments."
30. A Roman functionary who walked before a magistrate, carrying a bundle of rods, bound around an axe.

scourging, he was made over, in his *San Benito*,[31] to his friends, if he had any (but commonly such poor runagates were friendless), or to his parish officer, who, to enhance the effect of the scene, had his station allotted to him on the outside of the hall gate.

These solemn pageantries were not played off so often as to spoil the general mirth of the community. We had plenty of exercise and recreation *after* school hours; and, for myself, I must confess, that I was never happier, than *in* them. The Upper and the Lower Grammar Schools were held in the same room; and an imaginary line only divided their bounds. Their character was as different as that of the inhabitants on the two sides of the Pyrennes. The Rev. James Boyer was the Upper Master;[32] but the Rev. Matthew Field presided over that portion of the apartment, of which I had the good fortune to be a member. We lived a life as careless as birds. We talked and did just what we pleased, and nobody molested us. We carried an accidence,[33] or a grammar, for form; but, for any trouble it gave us, we might take two years in getting through the verbs deponent,[34] and another two in forgetting all that we had learned about them. There was now and then the formality of saying a lesson, but if you had not learned it, a brush across the shoulders (just enough to disturb a fly) was the sole remonstrance. Field never used the rod; and in truth he wielded the cane with no great good will—holding it 'like a dancer.' It looked in his hands rather like an emblem than an instrument of authority; and an emblem, too, he was ashamed of. He was a good easy man, that did not care to ruffle his own peace, nor perhaps set any great consideration upon the value of juvenile time. He came among us, now and then, but often stayed away whole days from us; and when he came, it made no difference to us—he had his private room to retire to, the short time he stayed, to be out of the sound of our noise. Our mirth and uproar went on. We had classics of our own, without being beholden to 'insolent Greece or haughty Rome,'[35] that passed current among us—*Peter Wilkins—The Adventures of the Hon. Capt. Robert Boyle—The Fortunate Blue Coat Boy*[36]—and the like. Or we cultivated a turn for mechanic or scientific operations; making little sun-dials of paper; or weaving those ingenious parentheses, called *cat-cradles;* or making dry peas to dance upon the end of a tin pipe; or studying the art military over that laudable game 'French and English,' and a hundred other such devices to pass away the time—mixing the useful with the agreeable—as would have made the souls of Rousseau and John Locke chuckle to have seen us.[37]

Matthew Field belonged to that class of modest divines who affect to mix in equal proportion the *gentleman,* the *scholar,* and the *Christian;* but, I know not how, the first ingredient is generally found to be the predominating dose

31. The garment of yellow sackcloth worn by the condemned person at an *auto da fé.*
32. See Coleridge's account of him (as James Bowyer) in chapter I of *Biographia Literaria* (above).
33. Lists of the declensions of nouns and the conjugation of verbs in Latin or Greek.
34. A verb in Latin or Greek having an active meaning but a passive form.
35. Ben Jonson, "To the Memory of My Beloved Master, William Shakespeare," l. 39.
36. Widely read adventure stories of the day. *Peter Wilkins* is still of considerable interest as an early work of science fiction.
37. In their writings on the education of young children the two philosophers proposed the usefulness of "doing" as a way of learning.

in the composition. He was engaged in gay parties, or with his courtly bow at some episcopal levée, when he should have been attending upon us. He had for many years the classical charge of a hundred children, during the four or five first years of their education; and his very highest form seldom proceeded further than two or three of the introductory fables of Phaedrus.[38] How things were suffered to go on thus, I cannot guess. Boyer, who was the proper person to have remedied these abuses, always affected, perhaps felt, a delicacy in interfering in a province not strictly his own. I have not been without my suspicions, that he was not altogether displeased at the contrast we presented to his end of the school. We were a sort of Helots to his young Spartans.[39] He would sometimes, with ironic deference, send to borrow a rod of the Under Master, and then, with sardonic grin, observe to one of his upper boys, 'how neat and fresh the twigs looked.' While his pale students were battering their brains over Xenophon and Plato, with a silence as deep as that enjoined by the Samite,[40] we were enjoying ourselves at our ease in our little Goshen.[41] We saw a little into the secrets of his discipline, and the prospect did but the more reconcile us to our lot. His thunders rolled innocuous for us; his storms came near, but never touched us; contrary to Gideon's miracle, while all around were drenched, our fleece was dry.[42] His boys turned out the better scholars; we, I suspect, have the advantage in temper. His pupils cannot speak of him without something of terror allaying their gratitude; the remembrance of Field comes back with all the soothing images of indolence, and summer slumbers, and work like play, and innocent idleness, and Elysian exemptions, and life itself a 'playing holiday.'

Thought sufficiently removed from the jurisdiction of Boyer, we were near enough (as I have said) to understand a little of his system. We occasionally heard sounds of the *Ululantes,* and caught glances of Tartarus.[43] B. was a rabid pedant. His English style was cramped to barbarism. His Easter anthems (for his duty obliged him to those periodical flights) were grating as scrannel pipes.[44]—He would laugh, ay, and heartily, but then it must be at Flaccus's quibble about *Rex*—or at the *tristis severitas in vultu,* or *inspicere in patinas,* of Terence—thin jests, which at their first broaching could hardly have had *vis* enough to move a Roman muscle.[45]—He had two wigs, both pedantic, but

38. A Roman author of the reign of Augustus best known for his beast fables, many of which are based on those of Aesop.
39. Helots were the serfs or slaves in Sparta. In order to disgust their sons with drunkenness, the Spartans would exhibit a besotted member of this despised class.
40. The Greek philosopher Pythagoras of Samos, who enjoined his students to silence until they had listened to his lectures for five years.
41. The region of ancient Egypt where the Israelites were allowed to live from the time of Joseph until the Exodus.
42. Actually, in Judges 6:36–40, Gideon asks God for *two* miraculous signs, that his sleeping-fleece be wet when the ground is dry and that it be dry when the ground is wet.
43. Tartarus is the region of Hades where the wicked are punished. The *Ululantes* are those whose cries of pain Aeneas hears on his visit to the underworld in Bk. VI of the *Aeneid.*
44. That is, harsh pipes; see *Lycidas,* l. 124.
45. In the first of his *Satires,* Horace—Quintus Horatius Flaccus—makes play with *Rex* as meaning *king* and as a man's name. In Terence's comedy *Andrea,* a character says of a patent rogue that there is to be seen "a sad severity in his countenance"; in the same

of differing omen. The one serene, smiling, fresh powdered, betokening a mild day. The other, an old discoloured, unkempt, angry caxon,[46] denoting frequent and bloody execution. Woe to the school, when he made his morning appearance in his *passy*, or *passionate wig*. No comet expounded surer.[47]—J. B. had a heavy hand. I have known him double his knotty fist at a poor trembling child (the maternal milk hardly dry upon its lips) with a 'Sirrah, do you presume to set your wits at me?'—Nothing was more common than to see him make a headlong entry into the schoolroom, from his inner recess, or library, and, with turbulent eye, singling out a lad, roar out, 'Od's my life, Sirrah,' (his favourite adjuration) 'I have a great mind to whip you,'—then, with as sudden a retracting impulse, fling back into his lair—and, after a cooling lapse of some minutes (during which all but the culprit had totally forgotten the context) drive headlong out again, piecing out his imperfect sense, as if it had been some Devil's Litany, with the expletory yell—'*and I* WILL, *too*.'—In his gentler moods, when the *rabidus furor* [48] was assuaged, he had resort to an ingenious method, peculiar, for what I have heard, to himself, of whipping the boy, and reading the Debates,[49] at the same time; a paragraph, and a lash between; which in those times, when parliamentary oratory was most at a height and flourishing in these realms, was not calculated to impress the patient with a veneration for the diffuser graces of rhetoric.

Once, and but once, the uplifted rod was known to fall ineffectual from his hand—when droll squinting W—— having been caught putting the inside of the master's desk to a use for which the architect had clearly not designed it, to justify himself, with great simplicity averred, that *he did not know that the thing had been forewarned*. This exquisite irrecognition of any law antecedent to the *oral* or *declaratory*, struck so irresistibly upon the fancy of all who heard it (the pedagogue himself not excepted) that remission was unavoidable.

L. has given credit to B.'s great merits as an instructor. Coleridge, in his literary life,[50] has pronounced a more intelligible and ample encomium on them. The author of the *Country Spectator* [51] doubts not to compare him with the ablest teachers of antiquity. Perhaps we cannot dismiss him better than with the pious ejaculation of C.—when he heard that his old master was on his death-bed—'Poor J.B.!—may all his faults be forgiven; and may he be wafted to bliss by little cherub boys, all head and wings, with no *bottoms* to reproach his sublunary infirmities.'

Under him were many good and sound scholars bred.—First Grecian [52] of

---

author's *Adelphi*, in mockery of a father who has adjured his son to look into men's lives as into a mirror, the comic slave solemnly tells the kitchen force to look into the pans. *Vis* is "force."

46. A kind of wig, especially a shabby one.
47. A comet was once thought to portend disaster.
48. "Mad fury."
49. Reports of the proceedings of Parliament.
50. *Biographia Literaria.*
51. A weekly periodical (1792–93) edited and largely written by Lamb's schoolmate, Thomas Fanshaw Middleton.
52. "Grecians" was the name given to the small group of Christ's Hospital pupils who, by reason of their scholarly abilities, were prepared for the university; they usually went to Cambridge.

my time was Lancelot Pepys Stevens, kindest of boys and men, since Co-grammar-master (and inseparable companion) with Dr. T——e. What an edifying spectacle did this brace of friends present to those who remembered the anti-socialities of their predecessors!—You never met the one by chance in the street without a wonder, which was quickly dissipated by the almost immediate sub-appearance of the other. Generally arm in arm, these kindly coadjutors lightened for each other the toilsome duties of their profession, and when, in advanced age, one found it convenient to retire, the other was not long in discovering that it suited him to lay down the fasces [53] also. Oh, it is pleasant, as it is rare, to find the same arm linked in yours at forty, which at thirteen helped it to turn over the *Cicero De Amicitia*,[54] or some tale of Antique Friendship, which the young heart even then was burning to anticipate!—Co-Grecian with S. was Th——, who has since executed with ability various diplomatic functions at the Northern courts. Th—— was a tall, dark, saturnine youth, sparing of speech, with raven locks.—Thomas Fanshaw Middleton followed him (now Bishop of Calcutta) a scholar and a gentleman in his teens. He has the reputation of an excellent critic; and is author (besides the *Country Spectator*) of a treatise on the Greek Article, against Sharpe.—M. is said to bear his mitre high in India, where the *regni novitas* [55] (I dare say) sufficiently justifies the bearing. A humility quite as primitive as that of Jewel or Hooker [56] might not be exactly fitted to impress the minds of those Anglo-Asiatic diocesans with a reverence for home institutions, and the church which those fathers watered. The manners of M. at school, though firm, were mild, and unassuming.—Next to M. (if not senior to him) was Richards, author of the *Aboriginal Britons*, the most spirited of the Oxford Prize Poems; a pale, studious Grecian.—Then followed poor S——, ill-fated M——! of these the Muse is silent.[57]

> Finding some of Edward's race
> Unhappy, pass their annals by.[58]

Come back into memory, like as thou wert in the day-spring of thy fancies, with hope like a fiery column before thee—the dark pillar not yet turned—Samuel Taylor Coleridge—Logician, Metaphysician, Bard!—How have I seen the casual passer through the Cloisters stand still, entranced with admiration (while he weighed the disproportion between the *speech* and the *garb* of the young Mirandola),[59] to hear thee unfold, in thy deep and sweet intonations, the mysteries of Jamblichus, or Plotinus [60] (for even in those years thou

53. The bundle of rods bound around an axe carried by the lictor (see note 30) before a Roman magistrate as a sign of his authority.
54. Cicero's discourse "On Friendship."
55. "Newness of the reign."
56. Famous ecclesiastics of the 16th century, when the authority of the Roman Church was repudiated in England and the Anglican Church was constituted.
57. Identified by Lamb as Scott, who died in a hospital for the insane, and Maunde, who was expelled from school.
58. Lamb alters Matthew Prior's *Carmen Seculare* (1700) viii.4–5. "Edward's race" because Christ's Hospital had been founded by Edward VI.
59. Pico della Mirandola (1463–94), the brilliant and engaging Italian humanist.
60. Jamblichus—usually Iamblichus—a mystic and neoplatonic philosopher of the 4th century; Plotinus, who flourished a century earlier, is the chief exponent of neoplatonism.

waxedst not pale at such philosophic draughts), or reciting Homer in his Greek, or Pindar——while the walls of the old Grey Friars re-echoed to the accents of the *inspired charity-boy!*—Many were the 'wit-combats,' (to dally awhile with the words of old Fuller,[61]) between him and C. V. Le G——, 'which two I behold like a Spanish great gallion, and an English man of war; Master Coleridge, like the former, was built far higher in learning, solid, but slow in his performance. C. V. L., with the English man of war, lesser in bulk, but lighter in sailing, could turn with all tides, tack about, and take advantage of all winds, by the quickness of his wit and invention.'

Nor shalt thou, their compeer, be quickly forgotten, Allen, with the cordial smile, and still more cordial laugh, with which thou wert wont to make the old Cloisters shake, in thy cognition of some poignant jest of theirs; or the anticipation of some more material, and, peradventure, practical one, of thine own. Extinct are those smiles, with that beautiful countenance, with which (for thou wert the *Nireus formosus* [62] of the school), in the days of thy maturer waggery, thou didst disarm the wrath of infuriated town-damsel, who, incensed by provoking pinch, turning tigress-like round, suddenly converted by thy angel-look, exchanged the half-formed terrible '*bl*——,' for a gentler greeting—'*bless thy handsome face!*'

Next follow two, who ought to be now alive, and the friends of Elia—the junior Le G—— [63] and F——; [64] who impelled, the former by a roving temper, the latter by too quick a sense of neglect—ill capable of enduring the slights poor Sizars [65] are sometimes subject to in our seats of learning—exchanged their Alma Mater for the camp; perishing, one by climate, and one on the plains of Salamanca:—Le G——, sanguine, volatile, sweet-natured; F—— dogged, faithful, anticipative of insult, warm-hearted, with something of the old Roman height about him.

Fine, frank-hearted Fr——,[66] the present master of Hertford, with Marmaduke T——,[67] mildest of Missionaries—and both my good friends still—close the catalogue of Grecians in my time.

1820

The Two Races of Men

The human species, according to the best theory I can form of it, is composed of two distinct races, *the men who borrow,* and *the men who lend*. To these two original diversities may be reduced all those impertinent classifications of Gothic and Celtic tribes, white men, black men, red men. All the dwellers upon earth,

---

61. Thomas Fuller, from whose *Worthies of England* (1662) Lamb takes the description of the "wit-combats" between Shakespeare and Ben Jonson, adapting it to Coleridge and Charles Valentine Le Grice.
62. "Beautiful Nireus." He was one of the Greek warriors who besieged Troy.
63. Samuel Le Grice, a military man who died in the West Indies.
64. Joseph Favell.
65. At Cambridge, a student who receives financial help. He was formerly required to perform certain menial services.
66. Frederick William Franklin.
67. Marmaduke Thompson.

'Parthians, and Medes, and Elamites,'[1] flock hither, and do naturally fall in with one or other of these primary distinctions. The infinite superiority of the former, which I choose to designate as the *great race,* is discernible in their figure, port, and a certain instinctive sovereignty. The latter are born degraded. 'He shall serve his brethren.'[2] There is something in the air of one of this cast, lean and suspicious; contrasting with the open, trusting, generous manners of the other.

Observe who have been the greatest borrowers of all ages—Alcibiades— Falstaff—Sir Richard Steele—our late incomparable Brinsley[3]—what a family likeness in all four!

What a careless, even deportment hath your borrower! what rosy gills! what a beautiful reliance on Providence doth he manifest,—taking no more thought than lilies! What contempt for money,—accounting it (yours and mine especially) no better than dross. What a liberal confounding of those pedantic distinctions of *meum* and *tuum!*[4] or rather, what a noble simplification of language (beyond Tooke),[5] resolving these supposed opposites into one clear, intelligible pronoun adjective!—What near approaches doth he make to the primitive *community,*[6]—to the extent of one half of the principle at least!—

He is the true taxer who 'calleth all the world up to be taxed;'[7] and the distance is as vast between him and *one of us,* as subsisted betwixt the Augustan Majesty and the poorest obolary Jew[8] that paid it tribute-pittance at Jerusalem! —His exactions, too, have such a cheerful, voluntary air! So far removed from your sour parochial or state-gatherers,—those ink-horn varlets, who carry their want of welcome in their faces! He cometh to you with a smile, and troubleth you with no receipt; confining himself to no set season. Every day is his Candlemas, or his Feast of Holy Michael.[9] He applieth the *lene tormentum*[10] of a pleasant look to your purse,—which to that gentle warmth expands her silken leaves, as naturally as the cloak of the traveller, for which sun and wind contended! He is the true Propontic[11] which never ebbeth! The sea which taketh handsomely at each man's hand. In vain the victim, whom he delighteth to honour, struggles with destiny; he is in the net. Lend therefore cheerfully,

---

1. Acts 2:9.
2. Genesis 9:25.
3. Alcibiades, the brilliant, ambitious, dissolute, and traitorous Athenian, friend of Socrates; Falstaff, the most famous of Shakespeare's comic characters (I and II *Henry IV, The Merry Wives of Windsor*); Richard Steele, the essayist and dramatist (1672–1729) was notoriously improvident; Brinsley is Richard Brinsley Sheridan (1751–1816), author of *The Rivals* and *The School for Scandal* who was also notorious for his improvidence.
4. "Mine" and "thine."
5. John Horne Tooke (1736–1812), in addition to being an active political radical, was a well-known philologist who emphasized the importance of studying Gothic and Anglo-Saxon.
6. The Apostles "had all things in common; And sold their possessions and goods, and parted them to all men as every man had need, . . ." Acts 2:44–45.
7. The decree of the Emperor, in Luke 2:1.
8. A Jew who had at least an *obolus,* a small coin.
9. Candlemas and Michaelmas are, respectively, Scottish and English "quarter-days," that is, days on which rents, etc., were to be paid.
10. "The gentle spur." Horace, *Odes* III.21, 13.
11. The sea of Marmora. Doubtless Lamb had in mind Othello's reference to it (III. iii. 453–56).

O man ordained to lend—that thou lose not in the end, with thy worldly penny, the reversion promised.[12] Combine not preposterously in thine own person the penalties of Lazarus and of Dives! [13]—but, when thou seest the proper authority coming, meet it smilingly, as it were half-way. Come, a handsome sacrifice! See how light *he* makes of it! Strain not courtesies with a noble enemy.

Reflections like the foregoing were forced upon my mind by the death of my old friend, Ralph Bigod, Esq.,[14] who departed this life on Wednesday evening; dying, as he had lived, without much trouble. He boasted himself a descendant from mighty ancestors of that name, who heretofore held ducal dignities in this realm. In his actions and sentiments he belied not the stock to which he pretended. Early in life he found himself invested with ample revenues; which, with that noble disinterestedness which I have noticed as inherent in men of the *great race*, he took almost immediate measures entirely to dissipate and bring to nothing: for there is something revolting in the idea of a king holding a private purse; and the thoughts of Bigod were all regal. Thus furnished, by the very act of disfurnishment; getting rid of the cumbersome luggage of riches, more apt (as one sings)

> To slacken virtue, and abate her edge,
> Than prompt her to do aught may merit praise,[15]

he set forth, like some Alexander, upon his great enterprise, 'borrowing and to borrow!' [16]

In his periegesis, or triumphant progress throughout this island, it has been calculated that he laid a tythe part of the inhabitants under contribution. I reject this estimate as greatly exaggerated:—but having had the honour of accompanying my friend, divers times, in his perambulations about this vast city, I own I was greatly struck at first with the prodigious number of faces we met, who claimed a sort of respectful acquaintance with us. He was one day so obliging as to explain the phenomenon. It seems, these were his tributaries; feeders of his exchequer; gentlemen, his good friends (as he was pleased to express himself), to whom he had occasionally been beholden for a loan. Their multitudes did no way disconcert him. He rather took a pride in numbering them; and, with Comus, seemed pleased to be 'stocked with so fair a herd.' [17]

With such sources, it was a wonder how he contrived to keep his treasury always empty. He did it by force of an aphorism, which he had often in his mouth, that 'money kept longer than three days stinks.' So he made use of it while it was fresh. A good part he drank away (for he was an excellent toss-pot), some he gave away, the rest he threw away, literally tossing and hurling it violently from him—as boys do burrs, or as if it had been infectious,—into

12. Proverbs 9:17: "He that hath pity upon the poor lendeth to the Lord; and that which he hath given will he pay him again."
13. Not the Lazarus whom Jesus raised from the dead but the one who begged daily at the gate of the rich man Dives (Luke 16:19).
14. Under this name, Lamb speaks of a friend, John Fenwick.
15. *Paradise Regained* II.455–56.
16. Revelation 6:2.
17. *Comus*, ll. 151–53.

ponds, or ditches, or deep holes,—inscrutable cavities of the earth;—or he would bury it (where he would never seek it again) by a river's side under some bank, which (he would facetiously observe) paid no interest—but out away from him it must go peremptorily, as Hagar's offspring [18] into the wilderness, while it was sweet. He never missed it. The streams were perennial which fed his fisc.[19] When new supplies became necessary, the first person that had the felicity to fall in with him, friend or stranger, was sure to contribute to the deficiency. For Bigod had an *undeniable* way with him. He had a cheerful, open exterior, a quick jovial eye, a bald forehead, just touched with grey (*cana fides*).[20] He anticipated no excuse, and found none. And, waiving for a while my theory as to the *great race,* I would put it to the most untheorising reader, who may at times have disposable coin in his pocket, whether it is not more repugnant to the kindliness of his nature to refuse such a one as I am describing, than to say *no* to a poor petitionary rogue (your bastard borrower), who, by his mumping visnomy,[21] tells you, that he expects nothing better; and, therefore, whose preconceived notions and expectations you do in reality so much less shock in the refusal.

When I think of this man; his fiery glow of heart; his swell of feeling; how magnificent, how *ideal* he was; how great at the midnight hour; and when I compare with him the companions with whom I have associated since, I grudge the saving of a few idle ducats, and think that I am fallen into the society of *lenders,* and *little men.*

To one like Elia, whose treasures are rather cased in leather covers than closed in iron coffers, there is a class of alienators more formidable than that which I have touched upon; I mean your *borrowers of books*—those mutilators of collections, spoilers of the symmetry of shelves, and creators of odd volumes. There is Comberbatch,[22] matchless in his depredations!

That foul gap in the bottom shelf facing you, like a great eye-tooth knocked out—(you are now with me in my little back study in Bloomsbury,[23] reader!) ——with the huge Switzer-like [24] tomes on each side (like the Guildhall giants,[25] in their reformed posture, guardant of nothing) once held the tallest of my folios, *Opera Bonaventurae,* choice and massy divinity, to which its two supporters (school divinity also, but of a lesser calibre,—Bellarmine, and Holy Thomas),[26] showed but as dwarfs,—itself an Ascapart! [27]—*that* Comberbatch

18. Genesis 21. Hagar's son by Abraham was Ishmael. Both were cast out into the wilderness by Abraham.
19. The treasury of a kingdom or a state.
20. Virgil, *Aeneid* I. 292. The phrase means "ancient honor"—by extension, "gray hair."
21. "To mump" is to mumble like a beggar; "visnomy" is an obsolete form of "physiognomy" for which Lamb had a fondness.
22. When Coleridge as a young man enlisted in the Dragoons, he did so, as his old friends knew, under the name of Silas Tomkyn Comberbacke.
23. A district of London. Lamb did not actually live in it.
24. That is, like the Swiss Guards of the French kings and the pope; they were chosen for their stature.
25. Statues in the London Guildhall, which had been moved from their original places.
26. St. Bonaventure, "The Seraphic Doctor," a 13th-century theologian; Bellarmine, St. Robert Bellarmine, 16th-century theologian; Holy Thomas is St. Thomas Aquinas (13th century), one of the most famous theologians of the time.
27. A giant slain by Bevis of Southampton in Michael Drayton's *Polyolbion* (1613–22).

abstracted upon the faith of a theory he holds, which is more easy, I confess, for me to suffer by than to refute, namely, that 'the title to property in a book (my Bonaventure, for instance), is in exact ratio to the claimant's powers of understanding and appreciating the same.' Should he go on acting upon this theory, which of our shelves is safe?

The slight vacuum in the left-hand case—two shelves from the ceiling— scarcely distinguishable but by the quick eye of a loser—was whilom the commodious resting-place of Browne on *Urn Burial*.[28] C. will hardly allege that he knows more about that treatise than I do, who introduced it to him, and was indeed the first (of the moderns) to discover its beauties—but so have I known a foolish lover to praise his mistress in the presence of a rival more qualified to carry her off than himself.—Just below, Dodsley's dramas [29] want their fourth volume, where Vittoria Corombona is! [30] The remainder nine are as distasteful as Priam's refuse sons, when the Fates *borrowed* Hector.[31] Here stood the *Anatomy of Melancholy*,[32] in sober state.—There loitered the *Complete Angler;* [33] quiet as in life, by some stream side.—In yonder nook, John Buncle,[34] a widower-volume, with 'eyes closed,' mourns his ravished mate.

One justice I must do my friend, that if he sometimes, like the sea, sweeps away a treasure, at another time, sea-like, he throws up as rich an equivalent to match it. I have a small under-collection of this nature (my friend's gatherings in his various calls), picked up, he has forgotten at what odd places, and deposited with as little memory as mine. I take in these orphans, the twice-deserted. These proselytes of the gate are welcome as the true Hebrews. There they stand in conjunction; natives, and naturalised. The latter seem as little disposed to inquire out their true lineage as I am.—I charge no warehouse-room for these deodands,[35] nor shall ever put myself to the ungentlemanly trouble of advertising a sale of them to pay expenses.

To lose a volume to C. carries some sense and meaning in it. You are sure that he will make one hearty meal on your viands, if he can give no account of the platter after it. But what moved thee, wayward, spiteful K.,[36] to be so importunate to carry off with thee, in spite of tears and adjurations to thee to forbear, the Letters of that princely woman, the thrice noble Margaret New-

28. Sir Thomas Browne's *Urn Burial,* or *Hydriotaphia,* was published in 1658. Lamb's pride in his "discovery" of this book is justified. His praise of the prose writers of the 17th century was influential in establishing them in modern taste.

29. Robert Dodsley published his *Select Collection of Old Plays* in 1744. The book did much to revive the interest in Elizabethan drama, which was furthered by Lamb's *Specimens of English Dramatic Poets.*

30. That is, Webster's *The White Devil,* of which Vittoria Corombona is the chief female character.

31. Of Priam's fifty sons, the slain Hector was the most cherished.

32. By Robert Burton, published 1621.

33. By Izaak Walton, published 1653, 1655.

34. *The Life of John Buncle, Esq.,* by Thomas Amory. It was published in two volumes, 1756–66. The phrase "widower-volume" is apt because the hero of the novel was a widower seven times.

35. A deodand—"that which is to be given to God." By English law, a thing which having been the immediate cause of a person's death, is forfeited to the Crown to be used for pious purposes. Lamb uses the word inaccurately.

36. James Kenney (1780–1849), a dramatist and a good friend of Lamb's.

castle?[37]—knowing at the time, and knowing that I knew also, thou most assuredly wouldst never turn over one leaf of the illustrious folio:—what but the mere spirit of contradiction, and childish love of getting the better of thy friend?—Then, worst cut of all! to transport it with thee to the Gallican lands[38]

> Unworthy land to harbour such a sweetness,
> A virtue in which all ennobling thoughts dwelt,
> Pure thoughts, kind thoughts, high thoughts, her sex's wonder![39]

—hadst thou not thy play-books, and books of jests and fancies, about thee, to keep thee merry, even as thou keepest all companies with thy quips and mirthful tales?—Child of the Green-room, it was unkindly done of thee. Thy wife, too, that part-French, better-part Englishwoman!—that *she* could fix upon no other treatise to bear away, in kindly token of remembering us, than the works of Fulke Greville, Lord Brook[40]—of which no Frenchman, nor woman of France, Italy, or England, was ever by nature constituted to comprehend a tittle! *Was there not Zimmerman on Solitude?*[41]

Reader, if haply thou art blessed with a moderate collection, be shy of showing it; or if thy heart overfloweth to lend them, lend thy books; but let it be to such a one as S. T. C.—he will return them (generally anticipating the time appointed) with usuary; enriched with annotations, tripling their value. I have had experience. Many are these precious MSS of his—(in *matter* oftentimes, and almost in *quantity* not unfrequently, vying with the originals) —in no very clerkly hand—legible in my Daniel;[42] in old Burton; in Sir Thomas Browne; and those abstruser cogitations of the Greville, now, alas! wandering in Pagan lands.—I counsel thee, shut not thy heart, nor thy library, against S. T. C.[43]

1820

New Year's Eve

[Death was a more immediate element of human life in the early nineteenth century than it was later to be. Its actual occurrence was more likely to be witnessed; its mystery and terror were more present to consciousness. And in the degree that this was so, what religion had to offer in the way of light and comfort was still cherished by many. It is therefore not surprising that Lamb's essay, with its frank avowal of the dread of death and its refusal of the hope of, or desire for, an afterlife, should have

37. Margaret, Duchess of Newcastle (1624?–74), wrote in many genres—the essay, drama, poetry, biography (of her husband), autobiography, and *Sociable Letters*, the book whose loss Lamb laments.
38. France—at this time Kenney lived at Versailles.
39. It is thought that these lines are by Lamb.
40. Sir Fulke Greville, 1st Baron Brooke (1554–1628), was the friend and biographer of Sir Philip Sidney.
41. Johann Georg von Zimmerman (1728–95), a Swiss doctor and writer. His sentimental *On Solitude* (1755; 1785), now forgotten, was translated from German into almost every European language.
42. Samuel Daniel (1562–1619), the poet.
43. Coleridge often referred to himself by his initials.

proved distressing to the sensibilities of some of his contemporary readers, a few of whom, including his friend, the poet Robert Southey, took him to task for his deficiency of religious feeling.]

Every man hath two birthdays: two days at least, in every year, which set him upon revolving the lapse of time, as it affects his mortal duration. The one is that which in an especial manner he termeth *his*. In the gradual desuetude of old observances, this custom of solemnising our proper birthday hath nearly passed away, or is left to children, who reflect nothing at all about the matter, nor understand anything in it beyond cake and orange. But the birth of a New Year is of an interest too wide to be pretermitted by king or cobbler. No one ever regarded the First of January with indifference. It is that from which all date their time, and count upon what is left. It is the nativity of our common Adam.

Of all sound of all bells—(bells, the music nighest bordering upon heaven) —most solemn and touching is the peal which rings out the Old Year. I never hear it without a gathering-up of my mind to a concentration of all the images that have been diffused over the past twelvemonth; all I have done or suffered, performed or neglected, in that regretted time. I begin to know its worth, as when a person dies. It takes a personal colour; nor was it a poetical flight in a contemporary, when he exclaimed—

I saw the skirts of the departing Year.[1]

It is no more than what in sober sadness every one of us seems to be conscious of, in that awful leave-taking. I am sure I felt it, and all felt it with me, last night; though some of my companions affected rather to manifest an exhilaration at the birth of the coming year, than any very tender regrets for the decease of its predecessor. But I am none of those who—

Welcome the coming, speed the parting guest.[2]

I am naturally, beforehand, shy of novelties; new books, new faces, new years,—from some mental twist which makes it difficult in me to face the prospective. I have almost ceased to hope; and am sanguine only in the prospects of other (former) years. I plunge into foregone vision and conclusions. I encounter pell-mell with past disappointments. I am armour-proof against old discouragements. I forgive, or overcome in fancy, old adversaries. I play over again *for love*, as the gamesters phrase it, games for which I once paid so dear. I would scarce now have any of those untoward accidents and events of my life reversed. I would no more alter them than the incidents of some well-contrived novel. Methinks, it is better that I should have pined away seven of my goldenest years, when I was thrall to the fair hair, and fairer eyes, of Alice W———n,[3] than that so passionate a love adventure should be lost. It was better that our family should have missed that legacy, which old

1. From Coleridge's *Ode to the Departing Year* in the version of 1796. In a later version "skirts" becomes "train."
2. Pope's translation of the *Odyssey* XV.84; the line appears also in Pope's Horatian *Satires* II. ii. 160.
3. Winterton, the fictitious name Lamb used to indicate the object of a youthful adoration, Ann Simmons.

Dorrell cheated us of,[4] than that I should have at this moment two thousand pounds *in banco*,[5] and be without the idea of that specious old rogue.

In a degree beneath manhood, it is my infirmity to look back upon those early days. Do I advance a paradox when I say, that, skipping over the intervention of forty years, a man may have leave to love *himself*, without the imputation of self-love?

If I know aught of myself, no one whose mind is introspective—and mine is painfully so—can have a less respect for his present identity than I have for the man Elia. I know him to be light, and vain, and humoursome; a notorious ***;[6] addicted to ***; averse from counsel, neither taking it, nor offering it;—*** besides; a stammering [7] buffoon; what you will; lay it on, and spare not; I subscribe to it all, and much more, than thou canst be willing to lay at his door:—but for the child Elia—that 'other me,' there, in the background—I must take leave to cherish the remembrance of that young master—with as little reference, I protest, to this stupid changeling of five-and-forty, as if it had been a child of some other house, and not of my parents. I can cry over its patient smallpox at five, and rougher medicaments. I can lay its poor fevered head upon the sick pillow at Christ's,[8] and wake with it in surprise at the gentle posture of maternal tenderness hanging over it, that unknown had watched its sleep. I know how it shrank from any the least colour of falsehood.—God help thee, Elia, how art thou changed!—Thou art sophisticated.[9]—I know how honest, how courageous (for a weakling) it was —how religious, how imaginative, how hopeful! From what have I not fallen, if the child I remember was indeed myself,—and not some dissembling guardian, presenting a false identity, to give the rule to my unpractised steps, and regulate the tone of my moral being!

That I am fond of indulging, beyond a hope of sympathy, in such retrospection, may be the symptom of some sickly idiosyncrasy. Or is it owing to another cause: simply, that being without wife or family, I have not learned to project myself enough out of myself; and having no offspring of my own to dally with, I turn back upon memory, and adopt my own early idea, as my heir and favourite? If these speculations seem fantastical to thee, reader —(a busy man, perchance), if I tread out of the way of thy sympathy, and am singularly conceited only, I retire, impenetrable to ridicule, under the phantom cloud of Elia.

The elders, with whom I was brought up, were of a character not likely to let slip the sacred observance of any old institution; and the ringing out of the Old Year was kept by them with circumstances of peculiar ceremony.—In those days the sound of those midnight chimes, though it seemed to raise

---

4. William Dorrell was one of the witnesses to the will of Lamb's father, and Lamb believed that he had engaged in some sharp practice which deprived the Lamb children of their inheritance.
5. "In the bank."
6. Lamb leaves the reader to supply the pejorative words.
7. Lamb's stammer, at its worst in boyhood but continuing all his life, kept him from training for a career as clergyman.
8. Christ's Hospital, Lamb's school.
9. In the old sense of adulterated or weakened, rather than in the sense of being less naïve.

hilarity in all around me, never failed to bring a train of pensive imagery into my fancy. Yet I then scarce conceived what it meant, or thought of it as a reckoning that concerned me. Not childhood alone, but the young man till thirty, never feels practically that he is mortal.[10] He knows it indeed, and, if need were, he could preach a homily on the fragility of life; but he brings it not home to himself, any more than in a hot June we can appropriate to our imagination the freezing days of December. But now, shall I confess a truth? —I feel these audits but too powerfully. I begin to count the probabilities of my duration, and to grudge at the expenditure of moments and shortest periods, like misers' farthings. In proportion as the years both lessen and shorten, I set more count upon their periods, and would fain lay my ineffectual finger upon the spoke of the great wheel. I am not content to pass away 'like a weaver's shuttle.' [11] Those metaphors solace me not, nor sweeten the unpalatable draught of mortality. I care not to be carried with the tide, that smoothly bears human life to eternity; and reluct at the inevitable course of destiny. I am in love with this green earth; the face of town and country; the unspeakable rural solitudes, and the sweet security of streets. I would set up my tabernacle here. I am content to stand still at the age to which I am arrived; I, and my friends: to be no younger, no richer, no handsomer. I do not want to be weaned by age; or drop, like mellow fruit, as they say, into the grave.—Any alteration, on this earth of mine, in diet or in lodging, puzzles and discomposes me. My household-gods plant a terrible fixed foot, and are not rooted up without blood. They do not willingly seek Lavinian shores.[12] A new state of being staggers me.

Sun, and sky, and breeze, and solitary walks, and summer holidays, and the greenness of fields, and the delicious juices of meats and fishes, and society, and the cheerful glass, and candlelight, and fireside conversations, and innocent vanities, and jests, and *irony itself*—do these things go out with life?

Can a ghost laugh, or shake his gaunt sides, when you are pleasant with him?

And you, my midnight darlings, my Folios; must I part with the intense delight of having you (huge armfuls) in my embraces? Must knowledge come to me, if it come at all, by some awkward experiment of intuition, and no longer by this familiar process of reading?

Shall I enjoy friendships there, wanting the smiling indications which point me to them here,—the recognizable face—the 'sweet assurance of a look'? [13]

In winter this intolerable disinclination to dying—to give it its mildest name —does more especially haunt and beset me. In a genial August noon, beneath a sweltering sky, death is almost problematic.[14] At those times do such poor snakes as myself enjoy an immortality. Then we expand and burgeon. Then

10. See Hazlitt's essay *On the Feeling of Immortality in Youth.*
11. Job 7:6: "My days are swifter than a weaver's shuttle."
12. In the *Aeneid,* Aeneas transports his household gods (*penates*) from Troy to Italy, where he founds the town of Lavinium, naming it for his Italian wife Lavinia. Lavinian shores are thus the shores of Italy, attained by the wandering Aeneas on orders from the gods. Lamb is saying he is not inclined so to wander.
13. Adapted from the elegy on Sir Philip Sidney by Matthew Roydon.
14. De Quincey records the opposite feeling—see the passage in *The Confessions of an English Opium Eater* dated June 1819.

we are as strong again, as valiant again, as wise again, and a great deal taller. The blast that nips and shrinks me, puts me in thoughts of death. All things allied to the insubstantial, wait upon that master feeling; cold, numbness, dreams, perplexity; moonlight itself, with its shadowy and spectral appearances, —that cold ghost of the sun, or Phoebus' sickly sister, like that innutritious one denounced in the Canticles: [15]—I am none of her minions—I hold with the Persian.[16]

Whatsoever thwarts, or puts me out of my way, brings death unto my mind. All partial evils, like humours, run into that capital plague-sore.—I have heard some profess an indifference to life. Such hail the end of their existence as a port of refuge; and speak of the grave as of some soft arms, in which they may slumber as on a pillow. Some have wooed death——but out upon thee, I say, thou foul, ugly phantom! I detest, abhor, execrate, and (with Friar John) give thee to six score thousand devils, as in no instance to be excused or tolerated, but shunned as an universal viper; to be branded, proscribed, and spoken evil of! In no way can I be brought to digest thee, thou thin, melancholy *Privation*, or more frightful and confounding *Positive!* [17]

Those antidotes, prescribed against the fear of thee, are altogether frigid and insulting, like thyself. For what satisfaction hath a man, that he shall 'lie down with kings and emperors in death,' [18] who in his lifetime never greatly coveted the society of such bed-fellows?—or, forsooth, that 'so shall the fairest face appear'? [19]—why, to comfort me, must Alice W——n be a goblin? More than all, I conceive disgust at those impertinent and misbecoming familiarities, inscribed upon your ordinary tombstones. Every dead man must take upon himself to be lecturing me with his odious truism, that 'Such as he now is I must shortly be.' Not so shortly, friend, perhaps, as thou imaginest. In the meantime I am alive. I move about. I am worth twenty of thee. Know thy betters! Thy New Years' days are past. I survive, a jolly candidate for 1821. Another cup of wine—and while that turncoat bell, that just now mournfully chanted the obsequies of 1820 departed, with changed notes lustily rings in a successor, let us attune to its peal the song made on a like occasion, by hearty, cheerful Mr. Cotton.[20]

THE NEW YEAR

Hark, the cock crows, and yon bright star
Tells us, the day himself's not far;
And see where, breaking from the night,
He gilds the western hills with light.

---

15. That is, the Song of Songs, also called the Song of Solomon. Presumably the "innutritious one" derives from 8:8: "We have a little sister, and she hath no breasts," but there is no ground for supposing, as Lamb brilliantly does suppose, that this refers to the moon!
16. The ancient Persians worshiped the sun.
17. Lamb is playing with the not uncommon idea that death may not be the absence of life but another, and terrible, form of existence.
18. Job 3:13–14 has "kings and counselors."
19. David Mallet, *William and Margaret* l. 9. In this 18th-century ballad, young Margaret dies and appears in ghostly form to her faithless lover William.
20. Charles Cotton (1630–87). He is remembered chiefly as the author of the dialogue between Piscator and Victor in the second part of Izaak Walton's *Compleat Angler*.

With him old Janus doth appear,
Peeping into the future year,
With such a look as seems to say
The prospect is not good that way.
Thus do we rise ill sights to see,
And 'gainst ourselves to prophesy;
When the prophetic fear of things
A more tormenting mischief brings,
More full of soul-tormenting gall
Than direst mischiefs can befall.
But stay! but stay! methinks my sight,
Better informed by clearer light,
Discerns sereneness in that brow
That all contracted seemed but now.
His reversed face may show distaste,
And frown upon the ills are past;
But that which this way looks is clear,
And smiles upon the New-born Year.
He looks too from a place so high,
The year lies open to his eye;
And all the moments open are
To the exact discoverer.
Yet more and more he smiles upon
The happy revolution.
Why should we then suspect or fear
The influences of a year,
So smiles upon us the first morn,
And speaks us good so soon as born?
Plague on't! the last was ill enough,
This cannot but make better proof;
Or, at the worst, as we brushed through
The last, why so we may this too;
And then the next in reason should
Be superexcellently good:
For the worst ills (we daily see)
Have no more perpetuity
Than the best fortunes that do fall;
Which also bring us wherewithal
Longer their being to support,
Than those do of the other sort:
And who has one good year in three,
And yet repines at destiny,
Appears ungrateful in the case,
And merits not the good he has.
Then let us welcome the New Guest
With lusty brimmers of the best:
Mirth always should Good Fortune meet,
And renders e'en Disaster sweet:

And though the Princess turn her back,
Let us but line ourselves with sack,
We better shall by far hold out,
Till the next year she face about.

How say you, reader—do not these verses smack of the rough magnanimity of the old English vein? Do they not fortify like a cordial; enlarging the heart, and productive of sweet blood, and generous spirits, in the concoction? Where be those puling fears of death, just now expressed or affected?—Passed like a cloud—absorbed in the purging sunlight of clear poetry—clean washed away by a wave of genuine Helicon,[21] your only spa [22] for these hypochondries. And now another cup of the generous! and a merry New Year, and many of them to you all, my masters!

1821

On the Artificial Comedy of the Last Century

[The critical position taken by Lamb in this brilliant essay was attacked—although with sincere protestations of admiration for its author—by Macaulay, who said that its argument was "ingenious" but "altogether sophisticated." "In the name of art, as well as in the name of virtue," he said, "we protest against the principle that the world of pure comedy is one in which no moral enters." And an eminent American critic, the late Joseph Wood Krutch, in his Comedy and Conscience in the Restoration, said that Lamb, in the view he took of Restoration comedy, had been "blinded by its brilliance . . . and [saw] only the wit." Both writers mean to suggest that the comedy of the Restoration represented manners and morals as they really were and should therefore be understood as offering an occasion for moral judgment. But this is to miss Lamb's intention, which has nothing to do with the congruence, or lack of it, between what is actually the moral situation of the society and the representation of it on the stage, but reaches far beyond that to propose one of the possible functions of art. Friedrich von Schiller is the last man in the world to be accused of light-mindedness and he took what is essentially Lamb's position. In his far-ranging work Letters on the Aesthetic Education of Mankind (1795) he says that the "mere play," which is what the experience of art can be and ultimately should be, suggests to man the possibility of his freedom, giving him a taste of what it feels like to overcome the "earnestness of duty and destiny"; it makes the paradigm of man's true being; it teaches him what he must hope to be. "Man," Schiller says, "only plays when he is in the fullest sense of the word a human being, and he is only a human being when he plays." Lamb, in his own unsystematic way, is saying the same thing.]

The artificial comedy, or comedy of manners, is quite extinct on our stage. Congreve and Farquhar [1] show their heads once in seven years only, to be

21. A mountain sacred to the Muses; just below its summit is the spring Hippocrene, whose waters inspire poets.

22. A resort in which a mineral spring of presumed health-giving properties is situated.

1. William Congreve (1670–1729) was the most brilliant practitioner of the Restoration comedy of manners. His masterpiece is The Way of the World (1700). The most admired of the comedies of George Farquhar (1678–1707) is The Beaux' Stratagem (1707).

exploded and put down instantly. The times cannot bear them. Is it for a few wild speeches, an occasional license of dialogue? I think not altogether. The business of their dramatic characters will not stand the moral test. We screw everything up to that. Idle gallantry [2] in a fiction, a dream, the passing pageant of an evening, startles us in the same way as the alarming indications of profligacy in a son or ward in real life should startle a parent or guardian. We have no such middle emotions as dramatic interests left. We see a stage libertine playing his loose pranks of two hours' duration, and of no after consequence, with the severe eyes which inspect real vices with their bearings upon two worlds. We are spectators to a plot or intrigue (not reducible in life to the point of strict morality), and take it all for truth. We substitute a real for a dramatic person, and judge him accordingly. We try him in our courts, from which there is no appeal to the *dramatis personae*, his peers. We have been spoiled with—not sentimental comedy—but a tyrant far more pernicious to our pleasures which has succeeded to it, the exclusive and all-devouring drama of common life; where the moral point is everything; where, instead of the fictitious half-believed personages of the stage (the phantoms of old comedy), we recognize ourselves, our brothers, aunts, kinsfolk, allies, patrons, enemies,—the same as in life,—with an interest in what is going on so hearty and substantial, that we cannot afford our moral judgment, in its deepest and most vital results, to compromise or slumber for a moment. What is *there* transacting, by no modification is made to affect us in any other manner than the same events or characters would do in our relationships of life. We carry our fireside concerns to the theatre with us. We do not go thither like our ancestors, to escape from the pressure of reality, so much as to confirm our experience of it; to make assurance double, and take a bond of fate. We must live our toilsome lives twice over, as it was the mournful privilege of Ulysses to descend twice to the shades.[3] All that neutral ground of character, which stood between vice and virtue; or which in fact was indifferent to neither, where neither properly was called in question; that happy breathing-place from the burthen of a perpetual moral questioning—the sanctuary and quiet Alsatia of hunted casuistry [4]—is broken up and disfranchised, as injurious to the interests of society. The privileges of the place are taken away by law. We dare not dally with images, or names, of wrong. We bark like foolish dogs at shadows. We dread infection from the scenic representation of disorder, and fear a painted pustule. In our anxiety that our morality should not take cold, we wrap it up in a great blanket surtout [5] of precaution against the breeze and sunshine.

I confess for myself that (with no great delinquencies to answer for) I am glad for a season to take an airing beyond the diocese of the strict conscience,

---

2. In the sense not of courage but of sexual adventure.

3. Once, as the *Odyssey* relates, while still a living man, to consult the shade of the prophet Tiresias; a second time when at his death he himself becomes a shade.

4. Lamb uses the word "casuistry" not in its now usual sense of specious reasoning, but in its older sense, in which it denotes the ecclesiastical science of dealing with cases of conscience, of resolving questions of right and wrong. Alsatia was the name given to White-friars, a district of London, which was long a sanctuary for insolvent debtors and criminals.

5. An overcoat.

—not to live always in the precincts of the law courts,—but now and then, for a dream-while or so, to imagine a world with no meddling restrictions—to get into recesses, whither the hunter cannot follow me—

—Secret shades
Of woody Ida's inmost grove,
While yet there was no fear of Jove.[6]

I come back to my cage and my restraint the fresher and more healthy for it. I wear my shackles more contentedly for having respired the breath of an imaginary freedom. I do not know how it is with others, but I feel the better always for the perusal of one of Congreve's—nay, why should I not add even of Wycherley's [7]—comedies. I am the gayer at least for it; and I could never connect those sports of a witty fancy in any shape with any result to be drawn from them to imitation in real life. They are a world of themselves almost as much as fairy land. Take one of their characters, male or female (with few exceptions they are alike), and place it in a modern play, and my virtuous indignation shall rise against the profligate wretch as warmly as the Catos of the pit [8] could desire; because in a modern play I am to judge of the right and the wrong. The standard of *police* is the measure of *political justice*. The atmosphere will blight it; it cannot live here. It has got into a moral world, where it has no business, from which it must needs fall headlong; as dizzy, and incapable of making a stand, as a Swedenborgian bad spirit [9] that has wandered unawares into the sphere of one of his Good Men, or Angels. But in its own world do we feel the creature is so very bad?—The Fainalls and the Mirabels, the Dorimants and the Lady Touchwoods,[10] in their own sphere, do not offend my moral sense; in fact, they do not appeal to it at all. They seem engaged in their proper element. They break through no laws or conscientious restraints. They know of none. They have got out of Christendom into the land— what shall I call it?—of cuckoldry—the Utopia of gallantry, where pleasure is duty, and the manners perfect freedom. It is altogether a speculative scene of things, which has no reference whatever to the world that is. No good person can be justly offended as a spectator, because no good person suffers on the stage. Judged morally, every character in these plays—the few exceptions only are *mistakes*—is alike essentially vain and worthless. The great art of Congreve

6. Milton, "Il Penseroso," ll. 28–30.
7. William Wycherley (1640–1716) is one of the most notable of the Restoration comic dramatists. His best-known plays are *The Country Wife* (1672) and *The Plain Dealer* (1674). Lamb says "even Wycherley" because his comedies, unlike those of Congreve and Farquhar, are savage and cynical in their satire and often coarse in their language.
8. What Americans call the orchestra of a theater the English call the pit. In the 18th century, people of superior social position did not sit there. Marcius Porcius Cato (234–149 B.C.) known as Cato the Elder and Cato the Censor, was the exponent of a stern, "old-Roman" moral rectitude and the implacable enemy of new ways of thought and conduct. His name has become synonymous with harsh judgment.
9. In the theological system of the Swedish scientist, philosopher, and mystic Emmanuel Swedenborg (1688–1772), evil spirits strive to prevent the approximation of God and man, which is the goal of creation.
10. Fainall and Mirabel are characters in Congreve's *The Way of the World;* Dorimant is a character in Sir George Etherege's *The Man of Mode;* Lady Touchwood is a character in Congreve's *The Double Dealer.*

is especially shown in this, that he has entirely excluded from his scenes—some little generosities in the part of Angelica [11] perhaps excepted—not only anything like a faultless character, but any pretensions to goodness or good feelings whatsoever. Whether he did this designedly, or instinctively, the effect is as happy as the design (if design) was bold. I used to wonder at the strange power which his *Way of the World* in particular possesses of interesting you all along in the pursuits of characters, for whom you absolutely care nothing—for you neither hate nor love his personages—and I think it is owing to this very indifference for any, that you endure the whole. He has spread a privation of moral light, I will call it, rather than by the ugly name of palpable darkness, over his creations; and his shadows flit before you without distinction or preference. Had he introduced a good character, a single gush of moral feeling, a revulsion of the judgment to actual life and actual duties, the impertinent Goshen [12] would have only lighted to the discovery of deformities, which now are none, because we think them none.

Translated into real life, the characters of his, and his friend Wycherley's dramas, are profligates and strumpets,—the business of their brief existence, the undivided pursuit of lawless gallantry. No other spring of action, or possible motive of conduct, is recognized; principles which, universally acted upon, must reduce this frame of things to a chaos. But we do them wrong in so translating them. No such effects are produced, in *their* world. When we are among them, we are amongst a chaotic people. We are not to judge them by our usages. No reverend institutions are insulted by their proceedings—for they have none among them. No peace of families is violated—for no family ties exist among them. No purity of the marriage bed is stained—for none is supposed to have a being. No deep affections are disquieted, no holy wedlock bands are snapped asunder—for affection's depth and wedded faith are not of the growth of that soil. There is neither right nor wrong,—gratitude or its opposite,—claim or duty,—paternity or sonship. Of what consequence is it to Virtue, or how is she at all concerned about it, whether Sir Simon or Dapperwit steal away Miss Martha; or who is the father of Lord Froth's or Sir Paul Pliant's children? [13]

The whole is a passing pageant, where we should sit as unconcerned at the issues, for life or death, as at the battle of the frogs and mice. [14] But, like Don Quixote, we take part against the puppets, and quite as impertinently. [15] We dare not contemplate an Atlantis, [16] a scheme, out of which our coxcombical moral sense is for a little transitory ease excluded. We have not the courage

11. The heroine of Congreve's *Love for Love*.

12. Genesis 47:1–4, the part of Egypt which the Pharaoh assigned to the family of Joseph and where the Israelites were allowed to live until they left Egypt; in Exodus 8:22 it is related that the flies sent to plague the Egyptians did not come into Goshen. Hence, a place of refuge; see "Alsatia" in note 4.

13. Sir Simon, Dapperwit, and Martha are characters in Wycherley's *Love in a Wood*; Lord Froth and Sir Paul Pliant are characters in Congreve's *The Double Dealer*.

14. *The Battle of the Frogs and the Mice* is an ancient parody of epic poetry; at one time it was attributed to Homer himself.

15. *Don Quixote* II.xxv. At a puppet play Don Quixote takes literally the plight of the hero and heroine, intervenes in their behalf, and destroys the puppets unfriendly to them.

16. In two of his dialogues, *Timaeus* and *Critias*, Plato speaks of this mythical island, of great extent, which long ago vanished in the sea.

to imagine a state of things for which there is neither reward nor punishment. We cling to the painful necessities of shame and blame. We would indict our very dreams.

Amidst the mortifying circumstances attendant upon growing old, it is something to have seen *The School for Scandal*[17] in its glory. This comedy grew out of Congreve and Wycherley, but gathered some allays of the sentimental comedy which followed theirs. It is impossible that it should be now *acted*, though it continues, at long intervals, to be announced in the bills. Its hero, when Palmer played it at least, was Joseph Surface.[18] When I remember the gay boldness, the graceful solemn plausibility, the measured step, the insinuating voice—to express it in a word—the downright *acted* villany of the part, so different from the pressure of conscious actual wickedness,—the hypocritical assumption of hypocrisy,—which made Jack so deservedly a favourite in that character, I must needs conclude the present generation of playgoers more virtuous than myself, or more dense. I freely confess that he divided the palm with me with his better brother; that, in fact, I liked him quite as well. Not but there are passages,—like that, for instance, where Joseph is made to refuse a pittance to a poor relation,—incongruities which Sheridan was forced upon by the attempt to join the artificial with the sentimental comedy, either of which must destroy the other—but over these obstructions Jack's manner floated him so lightly, that a refusal from him no more shocked you, than the easy compliance of Charles gave you in reality any pleasure; you got over the paltry question as quickly as you could, to get back into the regions of pure comedy, where no cold moral reigns. The highly artificial manner of Palmer in this character counteracted every disagreeable impression which you might have received from the contrast, supposing them real, between the two brothers. You did not believe in Joseph with the same faith with which you believed in Charles. The latter was a pleasant reality, the former a no less pleasant poetical foil to it. The comedy, I have said, is incongruous; a mixture of Congreve with sentimental incompatibilities; the gaiety upon the whole is buoyant; but it required the consummate art of Palmer to reconcile the discordant elements.

A player with Jack's talents, if we had one now, would not dare to do the part in the same manner. He would instinctively avoid every turn which might tend to unrealize,[19] and so to make the character fascinating. He must take his cue from his spectators, who would expect a bad man and a good man as rigidly opposed to each other as the death-beds of those geniuses are contrasted in the prints, which I am sorry to say have disappeared from the windows of my old friend Carrington Bowles,[20] of St. Paul's churchyard

17. By Richard Brinsley Sheridan (1751–1816). First performed in 1777, it has remained one of the most popular comedies in the language.
18. Joseph Surface, of course, is actually the "villain" of the play. John Palmer (1742?–1798) was one of the most gifted and popular comic actors of his time. He played Joseph Surface in the first performance of *The School for Scandal* and was ever after identified with the role. He was himself a quite unprincipled man and his hypocrisy is suggested by his nickname, Jack Plausible.
19. Lamb is saying that the modern actor, unlike Palmer, would play Joseph Surface in a style that would lead us to take his wickedness seriously.
20. Carrington Bowles was a publisher of engravings. These were often of a moralizing character, depicting the consequences of improvidence and wrongdoing as contrasted with those of probity and industry. Lamb greatly admired Hogarth, the pre-eminent practitioner of this artistic genre.

memory—(an exhibition as venerable as the adjacent cathedral, and almost coeval) of the bad and good man at the hour of death; where the ghastly apprehensions of the former,—and truly the grim phantom with his reality of a toasting-fork is not to be despised,—so finely contrast with the meek complacent kissing of the rod,—taking it in like honey and butter,—with which the latter submits to the scythe of the gentle bleeder,[21] Time, who wields his lancet with the apprehensive finger of a popular young ladies' surgeon. What flesh, like loving grass, would not covet to meet half-way the stroke of such a delicate mower?—John Palmer was twice an actor in this exquisite part. He was playing to you all the while that he was playing upon Sir Peter and his lady.[22] You had the first intimation of a sentiment before it was on his lips. His altered voice was meant to you, and you were to suppose that his fictitious co-flutterers on the stage perceived nothing at all of it. What was it to you if that half reality, the husband, was overreached by the puppetry—or the thin thing (Lady Teazle's reputation) was persuaded it was dying of a plethory? The fortunes of Othello and Desdemona were not concerned in it. Poor Jack has passed from the stage of good time, that he did not live to this our age of seriousness. The pleasant old Teazle King,[23] too, is gone in good time. His manner would scarce have passed current in our day. We must love or hate—acquit or condemn—censure or pity—exert our detestable coxcombry of moral judgment upon everything. Joseph Surface, to go down now, must be a downright revolting villain—no compromise—his first appearance must shock and give horror—his specious plausibilities, which the pleasurable faculties of our fathers welcomed with such hearty greetings, knowing that no harm (dramatic harm even) could come, or was meant to come, of them, must inspire a cold and killing aversion. Charles (the real canting person of the scene—for the hypocrisy of Joseph has its ulterior legitimate ends, but his brother's professions of a good heart centre in downright self-satisfaction) must be *loved*, and Joseph *hated*. To balance one disagreeable reality with another, Sir Peter Teazle must be no longer the comic idea of a fretful old bachelor bridegroom, whose teasings (while King acted it) were evidently as much played off at you, as they were meant to concern anybody on the stage,—he must be a real person, capable in law of sustaining an injury—a person towards whom duties are to be acknowledged—the genuine crim. con. [24] antagonist of the villainous seducer Joseph. To realize him more, his sufferings under his unfortunate match must have the downright pungency of life—must (or should) make you not mirthful but uncomfortable, just as the same predicament would move you in a neighbour or old friend.

The delicious scenes which give the play its name and zest, must affect you in the same serious manner as if you heard the reputation of a dear female friend attacked in your real presence. Crabtree and Sir Benjamin [25]—those

21. One who bleeds another person for medical reasons, once a standard procedure in the treatment of certain illnesses.

22. Sir Peter and Lady Teazle in *The School for Scandal.*

23. Thomas King (1730–1805), one of the most admired actors of his day, played innumerable comic roles and was the first Sir Peter Teazle.

24. A common abbreviation of "criminal conversation," i.e. adultery.

25. Characters in *The School for Scandal,* as is Mrs. Candour. Parsons, Dodd, and Miss Pope were accomplished actors of Lamb's day.

poor snakes that live but in the sunshine of your mirth—must be ripened by this hot-bed process of realization into asps or amphisbaenas;[26] and Mrs. Candour—O! frightful!—become a hooded serpent. O! who that remembers Parsons and Dodd—the wasp and butterfly of *The School for Scandal*—in those two characters; and charming natural Miss Pope, the perfect gentlewoman as distinguished from the fine lady of comedy, in this latter part—would forego the true scenic delight—the escape from life—the oblivion of conse-quences—the holiday barring out[27] of the pedant Reflection—those Satur-nalia[28] of two or three brief hours, well won from the world—to sit instead at one of our modern plays—to have his coward conscience (that forsooth must not be left for a moment) stimulated with perpetual appeals—dulled rather, and blunted, as a faculty without repose must be—and his moral vanity pampered with images of notional justice, notional beneficence, lives saved without the spectator's risk, and fortunes given away that cost the author nothing? . . .[29]

1823

Sanity of True Genius

[The idea that the poet is "mad" was given its most famous expression by Plato, in two of whose dialogues, *Phaedrus* and *Ion*, Socrates takes the line that what poets say cannot be construed as making ordinary sense and that their utterances are to be understood as the expression of a "noble madness." The intention of this view is chiefly ironic, a way of proposing the idea that poetry is not under the dominion of the rational intellect; Plato certainly did not mean to say anything more to the dis-credit of poetry than that it is not philosophy. The idea that the poet does not speak in the voice of reason, or, indeed, in his own voice, but is "possessed" or "inspired," associates him with the prophet or the shaman through whom a god or a spirit com-municates, often in language not comprehensible to human intellect. The madness of the poet became part of popular lore—see Shakespeare's "The lunatic, the lover, and the poet" and "The poet's eye in a fine frenzy rolling" (A *Midsummer Night's Dream* V.i.7, 12)—and as such was generally thought to be benign, if it was taken seriously at all. It could, however, be used to belittle the value of poetry in an age which, as Lamb felt, was increasingly concerned with fact and practicality. The question of how far the processes of creative fancies are "abnormal" became salient in the nineteenth century and continues into the twentieth. We may suppose that Lamb felt that he might claim a special authority in dealing with the question—not only did he live intimately with the often realized threat to his sister's reason, but he himself had brief episodes of insanity.]

---

26. A mythological serpent having a head at each end of its body.
27. The act of schoolboys closing a schoolroom to the master. This was once a common prank in English schools.
28. The Roman festival, held at about the time of our Christmas; at that festival moral restraints were relaxed and decorum forgotten.
29. The rest of the essay discusses the abilities of the actor John Kemble, a member of the astonishing family of actors of whom his sister Mrs. Siddons was the greatest.

So far from the position holding true, that great wit (or genius, in our modern way of speaking), has a necessary alliance with insanity,[1] the greatest wits, on the contrary, will ever be found to be the sanest writers. It is impossible for the mind to conceive of a mad Shakspeare. The greatness of wit, by which the poetic talent is here chiefly to be understood, manifests itself in the admirable balance of all the faculties. Madness is the disproportionate straining or excess of any one of them. 'So strong a wit,' says Cowley, speaking of a poetical friend,

> ——did Nature to him frame,
> As all things but his judgment overcame,
> His judgment like the heavenly moon did show,
> Tempering that mighty sea below. [2]

The ground of the mistake is, that men, finding in the raptures of the higher poetry a condition of exaltation, to which they have no parallel in their own experience, besides the spurious resemblance of it in dreams and fevers, impute a state of dreaminess and fever to the poet. But the true poet dreams being awake. He is not possessed by his subject, but has dominion over it. In the groves of Eden he walks familiar as in his native paths. He ascends the empyrean heaven, and is not intoxicated. He treads the burning marl[3] without dismay; he wins his flight without self-loss through realms of chaos 'and old night.'[4] Or if, abandoning himself to that severer chaos of a 'human mind untuned,'[5] he is content awhile to be mad with Lear, or to hate mankind (a sort of madness) with Timon,[6] neither is that madness, nor this misanthropy, so unchecked, but that,—never letting the reins of reason wholly go, while most he seems to do so,—he has his better genius still whispering at his ear, with the good servant Kent suggesting saner counsels,[7] or with the honest steward Flavius[8] recommending kindlier resolutions. Where he seems most to recede from humanity, he will be found the truest to it. From beyond the scope of Nature if he summon possible existences, he subjugates them to the law of her consistency. He is beautifully loyal to that sovereign directress, even when he appears most to betray and desert her. His ideal tribes submit to policy; his very monsters are tamed to his hand, even as that wild sea-brood, shepherded by Proteus.[9] He tames, and he clothes them with attributes of flesh and blood, till they wonder at themselves, like Indian Islanders forced to submit to European vesture. Caliban, the Witches,[10] are as true to the laws

1. Lamb refers to Dryden's famous couplet (in *Absalom and Achitophel* I.164–65) "Great wits are sure to madness near allied, / And thin partitions do their bounds divide."
2. Abraham Cowley (1618–67), *On the Death of Mr. William Harvey*, stanza 13.
3. *Paradise Lost* I.296.
4. *Ibid.* I.543.
5. Probably a reminiscence of *King Lear* IV.vii.16–17: "The untuned and jarring senses, wind up / Of this child-changèd father."
6. Shakespeare, *Timon of Athens.*
7. In *King Lear* Kent braves the anger of the king by urging him not to misunderstand Cordelia; Lear banishes him, but Kent returns in disguise to serve his master.
8. In *Timon of Athens,* the faithful steward of Timon.
9. In Bk. IV of the *Odyssey*, Proteus, an aged prophet who has the power of assuming any form he wishes, is in charge of a herd of seals or sea cows.
10. Caliban, the misshapen monster, Prospero's recalcitrant slave, in *The Tempest.* The witches in *Macbeth* prophesy the tragic hero's destiny.

of their own nature (ours with a difference), as Othello, Hamlet, and Macbeth. Herein the great and the little wits are differenced; that if the latter wander ever so little from nature or actual existence, they lose themselves, and their readers. Their phantoms are lawless; their visions nightmares. They do not create, which implies shaping and consistency. Their imaginations are not active —for to be active is to call something into act and form—but passive, as men in sick dreams. For the supernatural, or something super-added to what we know of nature, they give you the plainly non-natural. And if this were all, and that these mental hallucinations were discoverable only in the treatment of subjects out of nature, or transcending it, the judgment might with some plea be pardoned if it ran riot, and a little wantonized: but even in the describing of real and every day life, that which is before their eyes, one of these lesser wits shall more deviate from nature—show more of that inconsequence, which has a natural alliance with frenzy,—than a great genius in his 'maddest fits,' as Wither [11] somewhere calls them. We appeal to any one that is acquainted with the common run of Lane's novels,[12]—as they existed some twenty or thirty years back,—those scanty intellectual viands of the whole female reading public, till a happier genius arose, and expelled for ever the innutritious phantoms,—whether he has not found his brain more 'betossed,' his memory more puzzled, his sense of when and where more confounded, among the improbable events, the incoherent incidents, the inconsistent characters, or no-characters, of some third-rate love intrigue—where the persons shall be a Lord Glendamour and a Miss Rivers, and the scene only alternate between Bath and Bond-street—a more bewildering dreaminess induced upon him, than he has felt wandering over all the fairy grounds of Spenser. In the productions we refer to, nothing but names and places is familiar; the persons are neither of this world nor of any other conceivable one; an endless string of activities without purpose, of purposes destitute of motive:—we meet phantoms in our known walks; *fantasques* [13] only christened. In the poet we have names which announce fiction; and we have absolutely no place at all, for the things and persons of *The Fairy Queen* prate not of their 'whereabout.' But in their inner nature, and the law of their speech and actions, we are at home and upon acquainted ground. The one turns life into a dream; the other to the wildest dreams gives the sobrieties of every day occurrences. By what subtle art of tracing the mental processes it is effected, we are not philosophers enough to explain, but in that wonderful episode of the cave of Mammon,[14] in which the Money God appears first in the lowest form of a miser, is then a worker of metals, and becomes the god of all the treasures of the world; and has a daughter, Ambition, before whom all the world kneels for favours—

11. George Wither (1588–1667), in addition to being a poet, was a most voluminous Puritan pamphleteer.
12. Lamb is referring to the Minerva Press, which at the turn of the century was notorious for the trashy sentimental novels it issued.
13. "Odd, strange" (French).
14. In Spenser's *The Faerie Queene* II.vii Sir Guyon comes to the cave of Mammon, who, as the Money God (see Matthew 6:24 and Luke 16:9–13) is identified with the figures of Greek mythology, Plutus, god of wealth, and Pluto, ruler of the underworld. Mammon tries to tempt the knight with offers of riches and with marriage to his daughter, Ambition, but wholly without success.

with the Hesperian fruit,[15] the waters of Tantalus,[16] with Pilate washing his hands vainly, but not impertinently, in the same stream [17]—that we should be at one moment in the cave of an old hoarder of treasures, at the next at the forge of the Cyclops,[18] in a palace and yet in hell, all at once, with the shifting mutations of the most rambling dream, and our judgment yet all the time awake, and neither able nor willing to detect the fallacy,—is a proof of that hidden sanity which still guides the poet in his widest seeming-aberrations.

It is not enough to say that the whole episode is a copy of the mind's conceptions in sleep; it is, in some sort—but what a copy! Let the most romantic of us, that has been entertained all night with the spectacle of some wild and magnificent vision, recombine it in the morning, and try it by his waking judgment. That which appeared so shifting, and yet so coherent, while that faculty was passive, when it comes under cool examination, shall appear so reasonless and so unlinked, that we are ashamed to have been so deluded; and to have taken, though but in sleep, a monster for a god. But the transitions in this episode are every whit as violent as in the most extravagant dream, and yet the waking judgment ratifies them.

1833

WILLIAM HAZLITT
1778–1830

Of the three great prose writers of the Romantic period, it is Hazlitt who makes the most immediate appeal to modern taste. Lamb's conscious sentimentality and quaint archaism are likely to delay our perception of his essential cogency and force. And it may require a conscious effort for the modern reader to come to terms with the gorgeous elaborations yielded by De Quincey's theory of an "impassioned prose" which would rival music in its potentiality for depth and grandeur. But Hazlitt's prose is likely to reach us at once—it is all speed, energy, and masculine decisiveness. It is not, certainly, prose as it is now written for expository purposes; it is more arbitrary, more stamped with personality, and, at moments, more eloquent than modern practice encourages. Yet in its characteristic downright middle style, in what might be called its *working* mode, it can serve as at least a partial model for the modern writer, as the prose of Lamb and De Quincey cannot possibly do. Its superb urgency is as much a function of intellect as of artistry. Hazlitt's earliest commitment had been to systematic philosophy, and although he did not achieve much in this line, his years of preoccupation with it may be thought to account in some part for the inspiriting

---

15. The Hesperides—"daughters of evening"—were nymphs who guarded a tree on which grew golden apples.
16. In Hades, Tantalus was set in a pool of water which, whenever he sought to allay the thirst with which he was afflicted, receded from him.
17. Pontius Pilate, the Roman governor of Judaea, who wished to release Jesus but yielded to the importunity of the crowd (John 19:1–16); calling for a basin of water, he symbolically washed his hands of the blood of Jesus (Matthew 27:24). Lamb remarks on the appropriateness of the same water figuring in the punishment of Pilate and of Tantalus.
18. The Cyclops were one-eyed giants. In the *Odyssey* they are shepherds but in Hesiod's *Theogony* they are smiths who forge thunderbolts for Zeus.

purposiveness of his style, its eagerness to reach conclusions, whether about literature or about life.

William Hazlitt was born in 1778, the son of a Unitarian minister of strong libertarian principles. When he was five, his father made a missionary voyage to America, taking his family with him. Of the four years' sojourn in the new nation, first in Philadelphia, then in the environs of Boston, surprisingly little seems to have stayed in Hazlitt's memory, for it is referred to scarcely at all in his mature writing. His later and apparently happy boyhood was spent in the little town of Wem in Shropshire, where his father had a small congregation. In 1793 he was sent to the Unitarian New College at Hackney, a district of London, to prepare for the ministry. He remained there for some three years, a recalcitrant pupil who neglected his prescribed studies to pursue his philosophical interests and who moved ever closer to his eventual repudiation of Christianity. His meeting, in 1798, with Coleridge, who was a great name in Unitarian circles, was decisive in his career, confirming him in his dedication to a life of art and thought (see below, *My First Acquaintance with Poets*) and leading to his entry into the society of the rising poets of his day.

With these friends of his youth Hazlitt was not to continue in happy relations. He was by no means a person of easy and conformable temperament—quite the contrary, indeed, he was touchy and suspicious, and at least in his youth and early middle age his behavior was often heedless and calculated to give offense. But what chiefly accounts for the bitter antagonism which grew up between him and Coleridge and Wordsworth is the unremitting passion of his political opinions. All through his life he maintained a passionate commitment to the radical views which he had first received from his father, while his friends, disenchanted by the developments of the French Revolution, abandoned their youthful hopes, in Hazlitt's eyes an unforgivable apostasy. Yet his bitterness was matched by his critical magnanimity, and in his writings, while deploring their politics, he expressed his strong though discriminating admiration for the genius of Coleridge and Wordsworth. It is pleasant to recall that his friendship with Charles Lamb, who was present at his deathbed, was able to transcend all difficulties and that Keats, who said of Hazlitt's "depth of Taste" that it was one of the few things to rejoice at in the age, found his company nothing but congenial.

Hazlitt's first professional venture was not in literature but in painting. His older brother John was a portraitist of some ability and establishment, and Hazlitt put himself under his instruction. One of William's portraits, of Charles Lamb in the dress of a Venetian senator, is well known and quite striking, but he was doubtless right in the conclusion he came to in 1805 that his abilities were not of an order to justify his hopes of artistic excellence. From this time forward he devoted himself to writing, though not for some years to come did he turn to the work by which he is remembered, which began in 1813 when he became the parliamentary reporter and subsequently the dramatic critic of the *Morning Chronicle*. Of the very large canon of his work a chief part was written for periodical publication, usually in haste under the pressure of deadliness, and it is a cause for wonder how much of it is of high value.

Of Hazlitt's characteristics as a critic perhaps the first to be remarked is his comprehensiveness—in his essays and lectures he covers the whole range of English literature from the age of Elizabeth to his own day. Cognate with this is the catholicity of his taste; his judgments are strict but seldom doctrinaire and partisan, a virtue the more to be praised because it was exercised at a time of warring critical creeds. What he chiefly sought in literature, as in painting, was the quality of "gusto," which he defined and celebrated in one of his most attractive critical essays (see below), and he found it in Pope as well as in Shakespeare. Keats was right to speak of the *depth* rather than of the *breadth* of Hazlitt's taste—his phrase suggests the activity by which Hazlitt sees beneath the merely adventitious attributes of the work of art to discern in its design and in its parts the energies which animate it. This is not to say, however, that Hazlitt is to be called a "profound" critic, as Coleridge commonly is; his particular concern is not to explicate the essential nature of art or its processes but, rather, to point out and validate its achievements.

In the genre of the personal or familiar essay Hazlitt is surely the pre-eminent master in English. This is a literary form which apparently is no longer viable—it ceased to be so, indeed, with the death of its great Romantic practitioners, and although from time to time there have been attempts to revive it, they have met with but faint success. The secret which Montaigne discovered for the world, of speaking colloquially and modestly but unabashedly as "I," seems to have been lost. Hazlitt is not Montaigne's equal—although the comparison is by no means an improper one—but like his greater predecessor (whom he much admired), he commands the curious knack of putting "I" boldly forward, indulging the First Person Singular in all its impulses of self-reference and autobiography, and exactly through the activity of egoism conjuring up considerations in which the ego is forgotten and only the actualities of the moral life are of moment.

My First Acquaintance with Poets

My father was a Dissenting [1] Minister at W——m [2] in Shropshire; and in the year 1798 (the figures that composed that date are to me like the 'dreaded name of Demogorgon') [3] Mr. Coleridge came to Shrewsbury, to succeed Mr. Rowe in the spiritual charge of a Unitarian Congregation there. He did not come till late on the Saturday afternoon before he was to preach; and Mr. Rowe, who himself went down to the coach in a state of anxiety and expectation, to look for the arrival of his successor, could find no one at all answering the description but a round-faced man in a short black coat (like a shooting jacket) which hardly seemed to have been made for him, but who seemed to be talking at a great rate to his fellow-passengers. Mr. Rowe had scarce returned to give an account of his disappointment, when the round-faced man in black entered, and dissipated all doubts on the subject, by beginning to

1. "Dissenters" were those who belonged to any of the English Protestant sects—Presbyterians, Independents, Methodists, Unitarians, etc. They dissented from the doctrines of the established Church of England and did not recognize its temporal authority.

2. Wem. It is difficult to know what degree of anonymity Hazlitt thought he had gained for the little town by the omission of one letter—or why he wanted it!

3. *Paradise Lost* II.964–65. Demogorgon was a terrible deity, the very utterance of whose name was believed to have disastrous effects. See note to Shelley's *Prometheus Unbound*, l. 207. Hazlitt, by the reference to him, means to suggest that the great event of 1798, his meeting with Coleridge and Wordsworth, had the dire consequence of committing him to the literary life.

talk. He did not cease while he stayed; nor has he since, that I know of. He held the good town of Shrewsbury in delightful suspense for three weeks that he remained there, 'fluttering the *proud Salopians* like an eagle in a dove-cote'; [4] and the Welsh mountains that skirt the horizon with their tempestuous confusion, agree to have heard no such mystic sounds since the days of

> High-born Hoel's harp or soft Llewellyn's lay! [5]

As we passed along between W——m and Shrewsbury, and I eyed their blue tops seen through the wintry branches, or the red rustling leaves of the sturdy oak-trees by the roadside, a sound was in my ears as of a Siren's song; I was stunned, startled with it, as from deep sleep; but I had no notion then that I should ever be able to express my admiration to others in motley imagery or quaint allusion, till the light of his genius shone into my soul, like the sun's rays glittering in the puddles of the road. I was at that time dumb, inarticulate, helpless, like a worm by the wayside, crushed, bleeding, lifeless; but now, bursting from the deadly bands that 'bound them,

> With Styx nine times round them,' [6]

my ideas float on winged words, and as they expand their plumes, catch the golden light of other years. My soul has indeed remained in its original bondage, dark, obscure, with longings infinite and unsatisfied; my heart, shut up in the prison-house of this rude clay, has never found, nor will it ever find, a heart to speak to; but that my understanding also did not remain dumb and brutish, or at length found a language to express itself, I owe to Coleridge. But this is not to my purpose.

My father lived ten miles from Shrewsbury, and was in the habit of exchanging visits with Mr. Rowe, and with Mr. Jenkins of Whitchurch (nine miles farther on) according to the custom of Dissenting Ministers in each other's neighbourhood. A line of communication is thus established, by which the flame of civil and religious liberty is kept alive, and nourishes its smouldering fire unquenchable, like the fires in the *Agamemnon* of Aeschylus, placed at different stations, that waited for ten long years to announce with their blazing pyramids the destruction of Troy. Coleridge had agreed to come over to see my father, according to the courtesy of the country, as Mr. Rowe's probable successor; but in the meantime I had gone to hear him preach the Sunday after his arrival. A poet and a philosopher getting up into a Unitarian pulpit to preach the Gospel, was a romance in these degenerate days, a sort of revival of the primitive spirit of Christianity, which was not to be resisted.

It was in January, 1798, that I rose one morning before daylight, to walk ten miles in the mud, and went to hear this celebrated person preach. Never, the longest day I have to live, shall I have such another walk as this cold, raw,

---

4. Hazlitt is playing with a passage in *Coriolanus* (V.vi.114–15) in which a military exploit of the hero is described—for the war-like Volscians he substitutes Salopians, i.e. inhabitants of Salop, an old name for the county of Shropshire; he counts on this to seem mildly comical to his contemporary readers because "salop" or "saloop" was the name of a hot drink made of milk, sugar, and sassafras that was formerly sold in the London streets in the night and early morning.

5. Gray, *The Bard*, l. 28.

6. Pope, *Ode on St. Cecelia's Day*, ll. 90–91.

comfortless one, in the winter of the year 1798. *Il y a des impressions que ni le tems ni les circonstances peuvent effacer. Dusse-je vivre des siècles entiers, le doux tems de ma jeunesse ne peut renaître pour moi, ni s'effacer jamais dans ma mémoire.*[7] When I got there, the organ was playing the hundredth psalm, and, when it was done, Mr. Coleridge rose and gave out his text, 'And he went up into the mountain to pray, HIMSELF, ALONE.'[8] As he gave out his text, his voice 'rose like a steam of rich distilled perfumes,'[9] and when he came to the two last words, which he pronounced loud, deep, and distinct, it seemed to me, who was then young, as if the sounds had echoed from the bottom of the human heart, and as if that prayer might have floated in solemn silence through the universe. The idea of St. John came into mind, 'of one crying in the wilderness, who had his loins girt about, and whose food was locusts and wild honey.'[10] The preacher then launched into his subject, like an eagle dallying with the wind. The sermon was upon peace and war; upon church and state—not their alliance, but their separation[11]—on the spirit of the world and the spirit of Christianity, not as the same, but as opposed to one another. He talked of those who had 'inscribed the cross of Christ on banners dripping with human gore.' He made a poetical and pastoral excursion,—and to show the fatal effects of war, drew a striking contrast between the simple shepherd boy, driving his team afield, or sitting under the hawthorn, piping to his flock, 'as though he should never be old,'[12] and the same poor country-lad, crimped,[13] kidnapped, brought into town, made drunk at an alehouse, turned into a wretched drummer-boy, with his hair sticking on end with powder and pomatum, a long cue at his back, and tricked out in the loathsome finery of the profession of blood.

Such were the notes our once-loved poet sung.[14]

And for myself, I could not have been more delighted if I had heard the music of the spheres. Poetry and Philosophy had met together. Truth and Genius had embraced, under the eye and with the sanction of Religion. This was even beyond my hopes. I returned home well satisfied. The sun that was still labouring pale and wan through the sky, obscured by thick mists, seemed an emblem of the *good cause;* and the cold dank drops of dew that hung half melted on the beard of the thistle, had something genial and refreshing in them; for there was a spirit of hope and youth in all nature, that turned every thing into good. The face of nature had not then the brand of *Jus Divinum*[15] on it:

7. "There are impressions which neither time nor circumstance is able to efface. Were I to live whole centuries, the sweet time of my youth never could be reborn for me, but neither could it ever be erased from my memory." An approximate quotation from Rousseau's enormously popular novel *La Nouvelle Héloïse* (1761), Part VI, Letter 7.

8. Matthew 14:23 and John 6:15.

9. Milton, *Comus*, l. 556.

10. Matthew 3:3–4 and Mark 1:3.

11. Coleridge was later to change his opinion on this score.

12. Sir Philip Sidney, *Arcadia* I.2.

13. Tricked or coerced into military (or naval) service.

14. Pope, "Epistle to Robert, Earl of Oxford," l. 1.

15. "The divine right," i.e. of kings, the doctrine that a king receives his right to rule from God.

Like to that sanguine flower inscribed with woe.[16]

On the Tuesday following, the half-inspired speaker came. I was called down into the room where he was, and went half-hoping, half-afraid. He received me very graciously, and I listened for a long time without uttering a word. I did not suffer in his opinion by my silence. 'For those two hours,' he afterwards was pleased to say, 'he was conversing with W. H.'s forehead!' His appearance was different from what I had anticipated from seeing him before. At a distance, and in the dim light of the chapel, there was to me a strange wildness in his aspect, a dusky obscurity, and I thought him pitted with the smallpox. His complexion was at that time clear, and even bright—

As are the children of yon azure sheen.[17]

His forehead was broad and high, light as if built of ivory, with large projecting eyebrows, and his eyes rolling beneath them like a sea with darkened lustre. 'A certain tender bloom his face o'erspread,'[18] a purple tinge as we see it in the pale thoughtful complexions of the Spanish portrait painters, Murillo and Velasquez. His mouth was gross, voluptuous, open, eloquent; his chin good-humoured and round; but his nose, the rudder of the face, the index of the will, was small, feeble, nothing—like what he has done.[19] It might seem that the genius of his face as from a height surveyed and projected him (with sufficient capacity and huge aspiration) into the world unknown of thought and imagination, with nothing to support or guide his veering purpose, as if Columbus had launched his adventurous course for the New World in a scallop,[20] without oars or compass. So at least I comment on it after the event. Coleridge in his person was rather above the common size, inclining to the corpulent, or like Lord Hamlet, 'somewhat fat and pursy.'[21] His hair (now, alas! grey) was then black and glossy as the raven's, and fell in smooth masses over his forehead. This long pendulous hair is peculiar to enthusiasts, to those whose minds tend heavenward; and is traditionally inseparable (though of a different colour) from the pictures of Christ. It ought to belong, as a character, to all who preach *Christ crucified*, and Coleridge was at that time one of those!

It was curious to observe the contrast between him and my father, who was a veteran in the cause, and then declining into the vale of years. He had been a poor Irish lad, carefully brought up by his parents, and sent to the

16. *Lycidas,* l. 106. The flower is the hyacinth (not, however, the modern flower of that name), which was thought to be marked with the letters *ai,* the Greek cry of woe. Hazlitt is saying that as a young man he thought of nature only as beneficent, not as tyrannical and cruel. See *On the Feeling of Immortality in Youth.*
17. Thomson, *The Castle of Indolence* II.xxxiii.
18. *Ibid.* I.lvii.3: "A certain tender gloom o'erspread his face." It is likely that "bloom" is a misprint for "gloom."
19. The idea that Coleridge accomplished "nothing" was once commonly held. It arose partly from the circumstance that Coleridge projected more works than he completed. But even the list of works published in his lifetime is formidable and the edition of his complete works, including his unfinished manuscripts, will run to many volumes.
20. This would seem to be a miswriting or misprinting of "shallop," a small open sailing boat.
21. Hazlitt's memory has conflated two lines of *Hamlet*—III.iv.153, "For in the fatness of these pursy times," and V.ii.298, "He's fat and scant of breath."

University of Glasgow (where he studied under Adam Smith[22]) to prepare him for his future destination. It was his mother's proudest wish to see her son a Dissenting Minister. So if we look back to past generations (as far as eye can reach) we see the same hopes, fears, wishes, followed by the same disappointments, throbbing in the human heart; and so we may see them (if we look forward) rising up for ever, and disappearing, like vapourish bubbles, in the human breast! After being tossed about from congregation to congregation in the heats of the Unitarian controversy,[23] and squabbles about the American war, he had been relegated to an obscure village, where he was to spend the last thirty years of his life, far from the only converse that he loved, the talk about disputed texts of Scripture and the cause of civil and religious liberty. Here he passed his days, repining but resigned, in the study of the Bible, and the perusal of the Commentators,—huge folios, not easily got through, one of which would outlast a winter! Why did he pore on these from morn to night (with the exception of a walk in the fields or a turn in the garden to gather broccoli-plants or kidney-beans of his own rearing, with no small degree of pride and pleasure)?—Here were 'no figures nor no fantasies,'[24] —neither poetry nor philosophy—nothing to dazzle, nothing to excite modern curiosity; but to his lacklustre eyes there appeared, within the pages of the ponderous, unwieldy, neglected tomes, the sacred name of JEHOVAH in Hebrew capitals: pressed down by the weight of the style, worn to the last fading thinness of the understanding, there were glimpses, glimmering notions of the patriarchal wanderings, with palm trees hovering in the horizon, and processions of camels at the distance of three thousand years; there was Moses with the Burning Bush, the number of the Twelve Tribes, types,[25] shadows, glosses on the law and the prophets; there were discussions (dull enough) on the age of Methuselah, a mighty speculation! there were outlines, rude guesses at the shape of Noah's Ark and of the riches of Solomon's Temple; questions as to the date of the creation, predictions of the end of all things; the great lapses of time, the strange mutations of the globe were unfolded with the voluminous leaf, as it turned over; and though the soul might slumber with an hieroglyphic veil of inscrutable mysteries drawn over it, yet it was in a slumber ill exchanged for all the sharpened realities of sense, wit, fancy, or reason. My father's life was comparatively a dream; but it was a dream of infinity and eternity, of death, the resurrection, and a judgment to come!

No two individuals were ever more unlike than were the host and his guest.

22. Although he is now remembered chiefly for *The Wealth of Nations* (1776), his pioneering work in economic theory, Adam Smith (1723–90) was also renowned as a moral philosopher.

23. Unitarianism is a system of Christian thought which derives its name from its belief in the single personality of God the Father, as against the doctrine that God has a threefold being, Father, Son, and Holy Spirit. It holds Jesus Christ in highest regard as the greatest of spiritual teachers but does not worship Him as divine. Until 1813 Unitarians in England were under threat of the laws against those who denied the Trinity; their struggle for their civil liberties made them sympathetic with radical causes, including that of American independence.

24. Shakespeare, *Julius Caesar* II.i.231.

25. In theology, "types" are the foreshadowings of the Christian dispensation in the events and persons of the Old Testament.

A poet was to my father a sort of nondescript: yet whatever added grace to the Unitarian cause was to him welcome. He could hardly have been more surprised or pleased, if our visitor had worn wings. Indeed, his thoughts had wings; and as the silken sounds rustled round our little wainscoted parlour, my father threw back his spectacles over his forehead, his white hairs mixing with its sanguine hue; and a smile of delight beamed across his rugged cordial face, to think that Truth had found a new ally in Fancy![26] Besides, Coleridge seemed to take considerable notice of me, and that of itself was enough. He talked very familiarly, but agreeably, and glanced over a variety of subjects. At dinner-time he grew more animated, and dilated in a very edifying manner on Mary Wollstonecraft and Mackintosh.[27] The last, he said, he considered (on my father's speaking of his *Vindiciae Gallicae* as a capital performance) as a clever scholastic man—a master of the topics,—or as the ready warehouseman of letters, who knew exactly where to lay his hand on what he wanted, though the goods were not his own. He thought him no match for Burke, either in style or matter. Burke was a metaphysician, Mackintosh a mere logician. Burke was an orator (almost a poet) who reasoned in figures, because he had an eye for nature: Mackintosh, on the other hand, was a rhetorician, who had only an eye to commonplaces. On this I ventured to say that I had always entertained a great opinion of Burke, and that (as far as I could find) the speaking of him with contempt might be made the test of a vulgar democratical mind.[28] This was the first observation I ever made to Coleridge, and he said it was a very just and striking one. I remember the leg of Welsh mutton and the turnips on the table that day had the finest flavour imaginable. Coleridge added that Mackintosh and Tom Wedgwood[29] (of whom, however, he spoke highly) had expressed a very indifferent opinion of his friend Mr. Wordsworth, on which he remarked to them—'He strides on so far before you, that he dwindles in the distance!' Godwin[30] had once boasted to him of having carried on an argument with Mackintosh for three hours with dubious success; Coleridge told him—'If there had been a man of genius in the room, he would have settled the question in five minutes.' He asked me if I had ever seen Mary Wollstonecraft, and I said, I had once for a few moments,

26. "My father was one of those who mistook his talent after all. He used to be very much dissatisfied that I preferred his Letters to his Sermons. The last were forced and dry; the first came naturally from him. For ease, half-plays on words, and a supine, monkish, indolent pleasantry, I have never seen them equalled." (Hazlitt)
27. Mary Wollstonecraft (1759–97) is best known for her *Vindication of the Rights of Women* (1792). She married William Godwin in 1797 and died giving birth to their daughter Mary, who became the second wife of Shelley. Sir James Mackintosh (1765–1832), Scottish writer, lawyer, and civil servant, in 1791 published *Vindiciae Gallicae* (Defense of France) in answer to Edmund Burke's *Reflections on the French Revolution* (1790).
28. In England the words "democracy," "democratic," etc., were likely to be used with a pejorative intention in the early part of the 19th century.
29. The son of Josiah Wedgwood, the founder of the famous English firm of potters. He is sometimes called the first photographer. He was greatly admired by all who knew him, and is remembered for his benefaction to Coleridge.
30. William Godwin (1756–1836) had great influence over two generations of Romantic poets with his *Enquiry Concerning Political Justice* (1793), one of the classics of anarchist theory. He is also remembered for his novels, especially *The Adventures of Caleb Williams* (1794).

and that she seemed to me to turn off Godwin's objections to something she advanced with quite a playful, easy air. He replied, that 'this was only one instance of the ascendancy which people of imagination exercised over those of mere intellect.' He did not rate Godwin very high [31] (this was caprice or prejudice, real or affected) but he had a great idea of Mrs. Wollstonecraft's powers of conversation, none at all of her talent for bookmaking. We talked a little about Holcroft.[32] He had been asked if he was not much struck *with* him, and he said, he thought himself in more danger of being struck *by* him. I complained that he would not let me get on at all, for he required a definition of every the commonest word, exclaiming, 'What do you mean by a *sensation*, Sir? What do you mean by an *idea?*' This, Coleridge said, was barricadoing the road to truth:—it was setting up a turnpike-gate at every step we took. I forget a great number of things, many more than I remember; but the day passed off pleasantly, and the next morning Mr. Coleridge was to return to Shrewsbury. When I came down to breakfast, I found that he had just received a letter from his friend T. Wedgwood, making him an offer of 150 £ a year if he chose to waive his present pursuit, and devote himself entirely to the study of poetry and philosophy. Coleridge seemed to make up his mind to close with this proposal in the act of tying on one of his shoes. It threw an additional damp on his departure. It took the wayward enthusiast quite from us to cast him into Deva's [33] winding vales, or by the shores of old romance. Instead of living at ten miles distance, of being the pastor of a Dissenting congregation at Shrewsbury, he was henceforth to inhabit the Hill of Parnassus, to be a shepherd on the Delectable Mountains.[34] Alas! I knew not the way thither, and felt very little gratitude for Mr. Wedgwood's bounty. I was presently relieved from this dilemma; for Mr. Coleridge, asking for a pen and ink, and going to a table to write something on a bit of card, advanced towards me with undulating step, and giving me the precious document, said that that was his address, *Mr. Coleridge, Nether-Stowey, Somersetshire;* and that he should be glad to see me there in a few weeks' time, and, if I chose, would come half-way to meet me. I was not less surprised than the shepherd boy (this simile is to be found in *Cassandra*[35]) when he sees a thunderbolt fall close at his feet. I stammered out my acknowledgments and acceptance of this

31. "He complained in particular of the presumption of attempting to establish the future immortality of man 'without' (as he said) 'knowing what Death was or what Life was'— and the tone in which he pronounced these two words seemed to convey a complete image of both." (Hazlitt)

32. Thomas Holcroft (1745–1809), the self-educated son of poor parents, became a journalist, dramatist, and novelist and the admired friend of Godwin, Lamb, and Hazlitt, the last of whom edited his interesting *Memoirs*. He was a strong partisan of the French Revolution and in 1794 his radical activities led to his being indicted for high treason; he was, however, discharged without a trial.

33. The Latin name for the river Dee. Hazlitt has in mind l. 54 of *Lycidas,* in which Deva is spoken of as a "wizard stream"—it was reputed to have prophetic powers, like the "old Bards, the famous Druids," spoken of two lines before. The whole passage deals with the profession of poetry.

34. Mount Parnassus in Greek mythology was sacred to Apollo and the Muses. In *Pilgrim's Progress* the Delectable Mountains are reached by Christian and Hopeful after they escape from Doubting Castle and the Giant Despair.

35. An interminable—ten-volume!—romance by Gauthier de Costes de la Calprenède much admired in the 17th century.

offer (I thought Mr. Wedgwood's annuity a trifle to it) as well as I could; and this mighty business being settled, the poet-preacher took leave, and I accompanied him six miles on the road. It was a fine morning in the middle of winter, and he talked the whole way. The scholar in Chaucer is described as going—

Sounding on his way.[36]

So Coleridge went on his. In digressing, in dilating, in passing from subject to subject, he appeared to me to float in air, to slide on ice. He told me in confidence (going along) that he should have preached two sermons before he accepted the situation at Shrewsbury, one on Infant Baptism, the other on the Lord's Supper, showing that he could not administer either, which would have effectually disqualified him for the object in view. I observed that he continually crossed me on the way by shifting from one side of the foot-path to the other. This struck me as an odd movement; but I did not at that time connect it with any instability of purpose or involuntary change of principle, as I have done since. He seemed unable to keep on in a straight line. He spoke slightly of Hume [37] (whose "Essay on Miracles" he said was stolen from an objection started in one of South's sermons—*Credat Judaeus Appella!* [38]). I was not very much pleased at this account of Hume, for I had just been reading, with infinite relish, that completest of all metaphysical *choke-pears*, his *Treatise on Human Nature*, to which the *Essays*, in point of scholastic subtlety and close reasoning, are mere elegant trifling, light summer-reading. Coleridge even denied the excellence of Hume's general style, which I think betrayed a want of taste or candour. He however made me amends by the manner in which he spoke of Berkeley.[39] He dwelt particularly on his *Essay on Vision* as a masterpiece of analytical reasoning. So it undoubtedly is. He was exceedingly angry with Dr. Johnson for striking the stone with his foot, in allusion to this author's Theory of Matter and Spirit, and saying, 'Thus I confute him, Sir.' [40] Coleridge drew a parallel (I don't know how he brought about the connection) between Bishop Berkeley and Tom Paine.[41] He said the one was an instance

36. Hazlitt both misremembers and misunderstands l. 307 of the General Prologue of *The Canterbury Tales*, which reads, "Sounynge in moral vertu was his speche"; "sounynge in" means tending toward, consonant with.
37. David Hume (1711–76), the Scottish philosopher. His skepticism, which had great influence on subsequent philosophical thought, was anathema to Coleridge.
38. The Latin phrase ("let the Jew Apella believe it"—i.e. I do not) is from Horace, *Satires* I.100. Dr. Robert South (1634–1716) was a noted English ecclesiastic.
39. George Berkeley (1685–1753), Bishop of Cloyne in Ireland, was one of the most influential philosophers of his time. Coleridge found his "idealistic" position very congenial.
40. The incident is one of the famous episodes in Boswell's *Life of Johnson*. "After we came out of the church, we stood talking for some time together of Bishop Berkeley's ingenious sophistry to prove the non-existence of matter, and that everything in the universe is merely ideal. I observed, that though we are satisfied that the doctrine is not true, it is impossible to refute it. I shall never forget the alacrity with which Johnson answered, striking his foot with mighty force against a large stone, till he rebounded from it, 'I refute it *thus*'" (1763). Dr. Johnson's "refutation" made plain his failure to understand what Berkeley was saying.
41. Thomas Paine (1737–1809), the political radical who supported and participated in both the American and the French revolutions. He is the author of *Common Sense* (1776) and *The Rights of Man* (1791–92).

of a subtle, the other of an acute mind, than which no two things could be more distinct. The one was a shop-boy's quality, the other the characteristic of a philosopher. He considered Bishop Butler [42] as a true philosopher, a profound and conscientious thinker, a genuine reader of nature and of his own mind. He did not speak of his *Analogy,* but of his *Sermons at the Rolls' Chapel,* of which I had never heard. Coleridge somehow always contrived to prefer the *unknown* to the *known.* In this instance he was right. The *Analogy* is a tissue of sophistry, of wire-drawn, theological special-pleading; the *Sermons* (with the Preface to them) are in a fine vein of deep, matured reflection, a candid appeal to our observation of human nature, without pedantry and without bias. I told Coleridge I had written a few remarks, and was sometimes foolish enough to believe that I had made a discovery on the same subject (the *Natural Disinterestedness of the Human Mind* [43])—and I tried to explain my view of it to Coleridge, who listened with great willingness, but I did not succeed in making myself understood. I sat down to the task shortly afterwards for the twentieth time, got new pens and paper, determined to make clear work of it, wrote a few meagre sentences in the skeleton-style of a mathematical demonstration, stopped half-way down the second page; and, after trying in vain to pump up any words, images, motions, apprehensions, facts, or observations, from that gulf of abstraction in which I had plunged myself for four or five years preceding, gave up the attempt as labour in vain, and shed tears of helpless despondency on the blank unfinished paper. I can write fast enough now. Am I better than I was then? Oh no! One truth discovered, one pang of regret at not being able to express it, is better than all the fluency and flippancy in the world. Would that I could go back to what I then was! Why can we not revive past times as we can revisit old places? If I had the quaint Muse of Sir Philip Sidney to assist me, I would write a *Sonnet to the Road between W—m and Shrewsbury,* and immortalize every step of it by some fond enigmatical conceit. I would swear that the very milestones had ears, and that Harmer-hill stooped with all its pines, to listen to a poet, as he passed! I remember but one other topic of discourse in this walk. He mentioned Paley,[44] praised the naturalness and clearness of his style, but condemned his sentiments, thought him a mere time-serving casuist, and said that 'the fact of his work on Moral and Political Philosophy being made a text-book in our Universities was a disgrace to the national character.' We parted at the six-mile stone; and I returned homeward pensive but much pleased. I had met with unexpected notice from a person, whom I believed to have been prejudiced against me. 'Kind and affable to me had been his condescension, and should

---

42. Joseph Butler (1692–1752), the moral philosopher and divine whose famous work, *The Analogy of Religion, Natural and Revealed, to the Course and Constitution of Nature,* once had great authority as a defense of the probability of revealed religion.

43. "Disinterestedness" means the state of being free of bias and self-interest. Hazlitt published the work to which he refers under the title *An Essay on the Principles of Human Action* (1805).

44. William Paley (1743–1805), theologian and philosopher, whose *View of the Evidences of Christianity,* a rationalistic defense of religion, was celebrated in its day. It was at Cambridge that his *Principles of Moral Political Philosophy* became a textbook upon its publication in 1785.

be honoured ever with suitable regard.'[45] He was the first poet I had known, and he certainly answered to that inspired name. I had heard a great deal of his powers of conversation, and was not disappointed. In fact, I never met with any thing at all like them, either before or since. I could easily credit the accounts which were circulated of his holding forth to a large party of ladies and gentlemen, an evening or two before, on the Berkeleian Theory, when he made the whole material universe look like a transparency of fine words; and another story (which I believe he has somewhere told himself) of his being asked to a party at Birmingham, of his smoking tobacco and going to sleep after dinner on a sofa, where the company found him to their no small surprise, which was increased to wonder when he started up of a sudden, and rubbing his eyes, looked about him, and launched into a three-hours' description of the third heaven, of which he had had a dream, very different from Mr. Southey's *Vision of Judgment,* and also from that other *Vision of Judgment,* [46] which Mr. Murray, the Secretary of the Bridge-street Junto,[47] has taken into his especial keeping!

On my way back, I had a sound in my ears, it was the voice of Fancy: I had a light before me, it was the face of Poetry. The one still lingers there, the other has not quitted my side! Coleridge in truth met me half-way on the ground of philosophy, or I should not have been won over to his imaginative creed. I had an uneasy, pleasurable sensation all the time, till I was to visit him. During those months the chill breath of winter gave me a welcoming; the vernal air was balm and inspiration to me. The golden sunsets, the silver star of evening, lighted me on my way to new hopes and prospects. *I was to visit Coleridge in the spring.* This circumstance was never absent from my thoughts, and mingled with all my feelings. I wrote to him at the time proposed, and received an answer postponing my intended visit for a week or two, but very cordially urging me to complete my promise then. This delay did not damp, but rather increased my ardour. In the meantime, I went to Llangollen Vale,[48] by way of initiating myself in the mysteries of natural scenery; and I must say I was enchanted with it. I had been reading Coleridge's description of England in his fine *Ode on the Departing Year,* and I applied it, *con amore,*[49] to the objects before me. That valley was to me (in a manner) the

45. At the end of Bk. VIII of *Paradise Lost* Adam says to the angel Raphael, "Gentle to me and affable hath been / Thy condescension and shall be honoured ever / With suitable regard."

46. Robert Southey's *A Vision of Judgment* (1821) describes in a sanctimonious way the reception in heaven of the unhappy George III. In the preface to the poem Southey refers to the "lewdness and impiety" of Byron, who responded with his own *The Vision of Judgment* (1822), a parody of Southey's and a satire on the late king and his government.

47. Byron's *The Vision of Judgment* appeared in the first issue of the *Liberal,* a periodical edited by Leigh Hunt and published by his brother John. It made a great scandal and the prosecution of John Hunt was initiated by Charles Murray of Bridge Street, an officer of the Constitutional Association, on the ground that he had published "a gross, impious, and slanderous" libel on George III "calculated to destroy the comfort and happiness of his present majesty."

48. In Wales, some forty miles from Wem.

49. "With love," warmly.

cradle of a new existence: in the river that winds through it, my spirit was baptised in the waters of Helicon! [50]

I returned home, and soon after set out on my journey with unworn heart and untried feet. My way lay through Worcester and Gloucester, and by Upton, where I thought of Tom Jones and the adventure of the muff.[51] I remember getting completely wet through one day, and stopping at an inn (I think it was at Tewkesbury) where I sat up all night to read *Paul and Virginia*.[52] Sweet were the showers in early youth that drenched my body, and sweet the drops of pity that fell upon the books I read! I recollect a remark of Coleridge's upon this very book, that nothing could shew the gross indelicacy of French manners and the entire corruption of their imagination more strongly than the behaviour of the heroine in the last fatal scene, who turns away from a person on board the sinking vessel, that offers to save her life, because he has thrown off his clothes to assist him in swimming. Was this a time to think of such a circumstance? I once hinted to Wordsworth, as we were sailing in his boat on Grasmere lake, that I thought he had borrowed the idea of his *Poems on the Naming of Places* from the local inscriptions of the same kind in *Paul and Virginia*. He did not own the obligation, and stated some distinction without a difference, in defence of his claim to originality. Any the slightest variation would be sufficient for this purpose in his mind; for whatever *he* added or omitted would inevitably be worth all that any one else had done, and contain the marrow of the sentiment. I was still two days before the time fixed for my arrival, for I had taken care to set out early enough. I stopped these two days at Bridgewater, and when I was tired of sauntering on the banks of its muddy river, returned to the inn, and read *Camilla*.[53] So have I loitered my life away, reading books, looking at pictures, going to plays, hearing, thinking, writing on what pleased me best. I have wanted only one thing to make me happy; but wanting that, have wanted everything!

I arrived, and was well received. The country about Nether Stowey is beautiful, green and hilly, and near the seashore. I saw it but the other day, after an interval of twenty years, from a hill near Taunton. How was the map of my life spread out before me, as the map of the country lay at my feet! In the afternoon, Coleridge took me over to All-Foxden,[54] a romantic old family-mansion of the St. Aubins, where Wordsworth lived. It was then in the possession of a friend of the poet's who gave him the free use of it.[55] Somehow that period (the time just after the French Revolution) was not a time when *nothing was given for nothing*. The mind opened, and a softness might be perceived coming over the heart of individuals, beneath 'the scales that fence' our self-interest. Wordsworth himself was from home, but his sister kept house,

50. A mountain which the ancient Greeks thought of as one of the homes of the Muses, the other being Parnassus.
51. Henry Fielding, *The History of Tom Jones, A Foundling* (1749), X.v–vi.
52. An enormously popular novel of young love in an Edenic setting (1787) by Bernadin de Saint-Pierre.
53. *Camilla; or, A Picture of Youth* (1796) is a novel by Fanny Burney.
54. Hazlitt's spelling of Alfoxden.
55. Actually Wordsworth paid a rental of £23 for the year of his occupancy.

and set before us a frugal repast; and we had free access to her brother's poems, the *Lyrical Ballads*, which were still in manuscript, or in the form of *Sybilline Leaves*.[56] I dipped into a few of these with great satisfaction, and with the faith of a novice. I slept that night in an old room with blue hangings, and covered with the round-faced family-portraits of the age of George I and II, and from the wooded declivity of the adjoining part that overlooked my window, at the dawn of day, could

———hear the loud stag speak.[57]

In the outset of life (and particularly at this time I felt it so) our imagination has a body to it. We are in a state between sleeping and waking, and have indistinct but glorious glimpses of strange shapes, and there is always something to come better than what we see. As in our dreams the fulness of the blood gives warmth and reality to the coinage of the brain, so in youth our ideas are clothed, and fed, and pampered with our good spirits; we breathe thick with thoughtless happiness, the weight of future years presses on the strong pulses of the heart, and we repose with undisturbed faith in truth and good. As we advance, we exhaust our fund of enjoyment and of hope. We are no longer wrapped in *lamb's-wool*, lulled in Elysium. As we taste the pleasures of life, their spirit evaporates, the sense palls; and nothing is left but the phantoms, the lifeless shadows of what *has been!*

That morning, as soon as breakfast was over, we strolled out into the park, and seating ourselves on the trunk of an old ash-tree that stretched along the ground, Coleridge read aloud with a sonorous and musical voice, the ballad of *Betty Foy*.[58] I was not critically or sceptically inclined. I saw touches of truth and nature, and took the rest for granted. But in the *Thorn*, the *Mad Mother*, and the *Complaint of a Poor Indian Woman*, I felt that deeper power and pathos which have been since acknowledged,

In spite of pride, in erring reason's spite,[59]

as the characteristics of this author; and the sense of a new style and a new spirit in poetry came over me. It had to me something of the effect that arises from the turning up of the fresh soil, or of the first welcome breath of Spring,

While yet the trembling year is unconfirmed.[60]

Coleridge and myself walked back to Stowey that evening, and his voice sounded high

Of Providence, foreknowledge, will, and fate,
Fixed fate, free-will, foreknowledge absolute,[61]

56. Although the two poets worked closely together on their early poems and although *Lyrical Ballads* was a joint enterprise, it is difficult to know what Hazlitt means by Wordsworth's poems being "in the form of *Sybilline Leaves*," which was the title of Coleridge's volume of 1817. A sibyl—the more usual spelling—was a prophetess thought by the Greeks and Romans to be inspired by Apollo.
57. Ben Jonson, "To Sir Robert Wroth," l. 22.
58. Wordsworth's *The Idiot Boy*. It was included in *Lyrical Ballads*, as were the other poems mentioned in the paragraph.
59. Pope, *An Essay on Man* I.293.
60. Thomson, *The Seasons*, Spring, l. 18.
61. *Paradise Lost* II.559–60.

nt from that of some later critics! Whatever might be thought of the poem, 'his ace was as a book where men might read strange matters,' [68] and he announced he fate of his hero in prophetic tones. There is a *chaunt* in the recitation both of Coleridge and Wordsworth, which acts as a spell upon the hearer, and disarms the judgment. Perhaps they have deceived themselves by making habitual use of this ambiguous accompaniment. Coleridge's manner is more full, animated, and varied; Wordsworth's more equable, sustained, and internal. The one might be termed more *dramatic,* the other more *lyrical.* Coleridge has told me that he himself liked to compose in walking over uneven ground, or breaking through the straggling branches of a copse-wood; whereas Wordsworth always wrote (if he could) walking up and down a straight gravel-walk, or in some spot where the continuity of his verse met with no collateral interruption. Returning that same evening, I got into a metaphysical argument with Wordsworth, while Coleridge was explaining the different notes of the nightingale to his sister, in which we neither of us succeeded in making ourselves perfectly clear and intelligible. Thus I passed three weeks at Nether Stowey and in the neighbourhood, generally devoting the afternoons to a delightful chat in an arbour made of bark by the poet's friend Tom Poole,[69] sitting under two fine elm-trees, and listening to the bees humming round us, while we quaffed our flip.[70] It was agreed, among other things, that we should make a jaunt down the Bristol-Channel, as far as Linton. We set off together on foot, Coleridge, John Chester, and I. This Chester was a native of Nether Stowey, one of those who were attracted to Coleridge's discourse as flies are to honey, or bees in swarming-time to the sound of a brass pan. He 'followed in the chase, like a dog who hunts, not like one that made up the cry.' [71] He had on a brown cloth coat, boots, and corduroy breeches, was low in stature, bowlegged, had a drag in his walk like a drover, which he assisted by a hazel switch, and kept on a sort of trot by the side of Coleridge, like a running footman by a state coach, that he might not lose a syllable or sound that fell from Coleridge's lips. He told me his private opinion, that Coleridge was a wonderful man. He scarcely opened his lips, much less offered an opinion the whole way: yet of the three, had I to choose during that journey, I would be John Chester. He afterwards followed Coleridge into Germany, where the Kantean philosophers were puzzled how to bring him under any of their categories. When he sat down at table with his idol, John's felicity was complete; Sir Walter Scott's, or Mr. Blackwood's, when they sat down at the same table with the King, was not more so.[72] We passed Dunster on our right, a small town between the brow of a hill and the sea. I remember eyeing it wistfully as it lay below us: contrasted with the woody scene around, it looked as clear, as pure, as *embrowned* and ideal as any landscape I have

8. *Macbeth* I.v.63–64.

9. Thomas Poole (1765–1837), for many years Coleridge's friend and benefactor. The son of a rough tanner who refused him proper schooling, he acquired an education by his own efforts and won the regard and affection of many distinguished persons.

0. A mixed drink, variously made, usually containing beaten eggs.

1. Based on *Othello* II.iii.369–70.

2. William Blackwood, publisher of *Blackwood's Magazine,* and Sir Walter Scott were staunch Tories. Hazlitt probably refers to their attendance at the banquet given to George IV in Edinburgh in 1822.

as we passed through echoing grove, by fairy stream or waterfall, gleam
the summer moonlight! He lamented that Wordsworth was not prone e
to believe in the traditional superstitions of the place, and that there
something corporeal, a *matter-of-fact-ness,* a clinging to the palpable, or
to the petty, in his poetry, in consequence. His genius was not a spir
descended to him through the air; it sprung out of the ground like a
or unfolded itself from a green spray, on which the goldfinch sang. H
however (if I remember right), that this objection must be confined
descriptive pieces, that his philosophic poetry had a grand and comprel
spirit in it, so that his soul seemed to inhabit the universe like a palac
to discover truth by intuition, rather than by deduction. The next day `
worth arrived from Bristol at Coleridge's cottage. I think I see him nc
answered in some degree to his friend's description of him, but was
gaunt and Don Quixote-like. He was quaintly dressed (according to the c
of that unconstrained period) in a brown fustian [62] jacket and striped
loons. There was something of a roll, a lounge in his gait, not unlike h
Peter Bell.[63] There was a severe, worn pressure of thought about his t
a fire in his eye (as if he saw something in objects more than the o
appearance), an intense high narrow forehead, a Roman nose, cheeks fu
by strong purpose and feeling, and a convulsive inclination to laughtei
the mouth, a good deal at variance with the solemn, stately expression of
of his face. Chantrey's [64] bust wants the marking traits; but he was teaz
making it regular and heavy: Haydon's [65] head of him, introduced ii
Entrance of Christ into Jerusalem, is the most like his drooping we
thought and expression. He sat down and talked very naturally and freel
a mixture of clear gushing accents in his voice, a deep guttural intonation
strong tincture of the northern *burr,* like the crust on wine. He instantl
to make havoc of the half of a Cheshire cheese on the table, and said tr
antly that 'his marriage with experience had not been so unproduc
Mr. Southey's in teaching him a knowledge of the good things of this l
had been to see the *Castle Spectre* by Monk Lewis, while at Bristol, a
scribed it very well.[66] He said 'it fitted the taste of the audience like a
This *ad captandum* [67] merit was however by no means a recommendatic
according to the severe principles of the new school, which reject rath
court popular effect. Wordsworth, looking out of the low, latticed windov
'How beautifully the sun sets on that yellow bank!' I thought within
'With what eyes these poets see nature!' and ever after, when I saw the
stream upon the objects facing it, conceived I had made a discovery, or t
Mr. Wordsworth for having made one for me! We went over to All-
again the day following, and Wordsworth read us the story of Peter Bel
open air; and the comment made upon it by his face and voice was very

62. A coarse sturdy cloth made of cotton and flax.
63. Of the poem of that name.
64. Sir Francis Chantrey (1781–1841), a portrait sculptor well known in his d
65. Benjamin Robert Haydon (1786–1846) exhibited this huge painting in 1
contained portraits not only of Wordsworth but also of Keats and Hazlitt.
66. Matthew Gregory Lewis (1775–1818) derived his nickname of Monk from his
novel of "Gothic" terror, *The Monk* (1795).
67. Designed to capture the fancy of the audience.

seen since, of Gaspar Poussin's or Domenichino's.[73] We had a long day's march
—(our feet kept time to the echoes of Coleridge's tongue)—through Minehead
and by the Blue Anchor, and on to Linton, which we did not reach till near
midnight, and where we had some difficulty in making a lodgment. We however
knocked the people of the house up at last, and we were repaid for our apprehensions and fatigue by some excellent rashers of fried bacon and eggs. The
view in coming along had been splendid. We walked for miles and miles on dark
brown heaths overlooking the Channel, with the Welsh hills beyond, and at
times descended into little sheltered valleys close by the seaside, with a smug-
gler's face scowling by us, and then had to ascend conical hills with a path winding up through a coppice to a barren top, like a monk's shaven crown, from one
of which I pointed out to Coleridge's notice the bare masts of a vessel on the
very edge of the horizon and within the red-orbed disk of the setting sun, like
his own spectre-ship in the *Ancient Mariner*. At Linton the character of the
seacoast becomes more marked and rugged. There is a place called the *Valley
of Rocks* (I suspect this was only the poetical name for it) bedded among
precipices overhanging the sea, with rocky caverns beneath, into which the
waves dash, and where the sea-gull for ever wheels its screaming flight. On
the tops of these are huge stones thrown transverse, as if an earthquake had
tossed them there, and behind these is a fretwork of perpendicular rocks,
something like the *Giant's Causeway*.[74] A thunder-storm came on while we
were at the inn, and Coleridge was running out bare-headed to enjoy the
commotion of the elements in the *Valley of Rocks*, but as if in spite, the clouds
only muttered a few angry sounds, and let fall a few refreshing drops. Coleridge told me that he and Wordsworth were to have made this place the
scene of a prose-tale, which was to have been in the manner of, but far
superior to, the *Death of Abel*, but they relinquished the design.[75] In the
morning of the second day, we breakfasted luxuriously in an old-fashioned
parlour, on tea, toast, eggs, and honey, in the very sight of the beehives from
which it had been taken, and a garden full of thyme and wild flowers that
had produced it. On this occasion Coleridge spoke of Virgil's Georgics, but
not well. I do not think he had much feeling for the classical or elegant. It was
in this room that we found a little worn-out copy of the *Seasons*,[76] lying in
a window-seat, on which Coleridge exclaimed, 'That is true fame!' He said
Thomson was a great poet, rather than a good one; his style was as meretri-
cious as his thoughts were natural. He spoke of Cowper as the best modern
poet. He said the *Lyrical Ballads* were an experiment about to be tried by
him and Wordsworth, to see how far the public taste would endure poetry
written in a more natural and simple style than had hitherto been attempted;
totally discarding the artifices of poetical diction, and making use only of

73. Gaspar Poussin (1613–75), whose real name was Gaspar Dughet, was the brother-in-
law and pupil of the more famous Nicolas Poussin; his landscapes were popular in the
18th century. Il Domenichino is Domenico Zampieri (1581–1641), a well-known Italian
painter.
74. A celebrated formation of basaltic columns extending into the sea on the north coast
of Ireland.
75. The *Death of Abel* (1758), by the Swiss poet and painter Salomon Gessner, was
once very popular. The abandoned tale was *The Wanderings of Cain*.
76. By James Thomson (1726–30).

such words as had probably been common in the most ordinary language since the days of Henry II.[77] Some comparison was introduced between Shakespeare and Milton. He said 'he hardly knew which to prefer. Shakespeare appeared to him a mere stripling in the art; he was as tall and as strong, with infinitely more activity than Milton, but he never appeared to have come to man's estate; or if he had, he would not have been a man, but a monster.' He spoke with contempt of Gray, and with intolerance of Pope. He did not like the versification of the latter. He observed that 'the ears of these couplet-writers might be charged with having short memories, that could not retain the harmony of whole passages.' He thought little of Junius [78] as a writer; he had a dislike of Dr. Johnson; and a much higher opinion of Burke as an orator and politician, than of Fox or Pitt.[79] He however thought him very inferior in richness of style and imagery to some of our elder prose-writers, particularly Jeremy Taylor.[80] He liked Richardson, but not Fielding; [81] nor could I get him to enter into the merits of *Caleb Williams*.[82] In short, he was profound and discriminating with respect to those authors whom he liked, and where he gave his judgment fair play; capricious, perverse, and prejudiced in his antipathies and distastes. We loitered on the 'ribbed sea-sands,' [83] in such talk as this, a whole morning, and I recollect met with a curious seaweed, of which John Chester told us the country name! A fisherman gave Coleridge an account of a boy that had been drowned the day before, and that they had tried to save him at the risk of their own lives. He said 'he did not know how it was that they ventured, but, Sir, we have a *nature* towards one another.' This expression, Coleridge remarked to me, was a fine illustration of that theory of disinterestedness which I (in common with Butler) had adopted. I broached to him an argument of mine to prove that *likeness* was not mere association of ideas. I said that the mark in the sand put one in mind of a man's foot, not because it was part of a former impression of a man's foot (for it was quite new) but because it was like the shape of a man's foot. He assented to the justness of this distinction (which I have explained at length elsewhere, for the benefit of the curious) and John Chester listened; not from any interest

77. See Wordsworth's Preface to *Lyrical Ballads*.
78. The anonymous author of a famous series of political pamphlets (1769–72) which attacked the government of George III. His identity has never been established.
79. Charles James Fox (1749–1806), one of the most brilliant and fascinating figures in English political history, defended many liberal and radical causes, including American independence and the French Revolution. He was devoted to gambling only more than to literature; he admired Wordsworth, with whom he corresponded. William Pitt (1759–1806), called "the Younger Pitt" to distinguish him from his equally famous father, became prime minister in 1783 and held office until 1801. In many respects his policies were liberal.
80. In large part because of the beauty of his prose, Taylor is one of the best-remembered of the divines of the 17th century. His most admired works are *Holy Living* (1650) and *Holy Dying* (1651).
81. Samuel Richardson (1689–1761) and Henry Fielding (1707–54) are the two pre-eminent English novelists of the 18th century. The latter began his career by parodying the former. In the 18th and early 19th century their relative merits were commonly debated. Coleridge, for once, is in agreement with Dr. Johnson, who also preferred Richardson to Fielding.
82. A novel by William Godwin, 1794.
83. *The Rime of the Ancient Mariner*, l. 237.

in the subject, but because he was astonished that I should be able to suggest anything to Coleridge that he did not already know. We returned on the third morning, and Coleridge remarked the silent cottage-smoke curling up the valleys where, a few evenings before, we had seen the lights gleaming through the dark.

In a day or two after we arrived at Stowey, we set out, I on my return home, and he for Germany. It was a Sunday morning, and he was to preach that day for Dr. Toulmin of Taunton. I asked him if he had prepared anything for the occasion? He said he had not even thought of the text, but should as soon as we parted. I did not go to hear him,—this was a fault,—but we met in the evening at Bridgewater. The next day we had a long day's walk to Bristol, and sat down, I recollect, by a well-side on the road, to cool ourselves and satisfy our thirst, when Coleridge repeated to me some descriptive lines from his tragedy of *Remorse;* which I must say became his mouth and that occasion better than they, some years after, did Mr. Elliston's and the Drury-lane boards,[84]—

> Oh memory! shield me from the world's poor strife,
> And give those scenes thine everlasting life.

I saw no more of him for a year or two, during which period he had been wandering in the Hartz Forest in Germany; and his return was cometary, meteorous, unlike his setting out. It was not till some time after that I knew his friends Lamb and Southey. The last always appears to me (as I first saw him) with a commonplace book [85] under his arm, and the first with a *bon-mot* in his mouth. It was at Godwin's that I met him with Holcroft and Coleridge, where they were disputing fiercely which was the best—*Man as he was, or man as he is to be.* 'Give me,' says Lamb, 'man as he is *not* to be.' This saying was the beginning of a friendship between us, which I believe still continues. —Enough of this for the present.

> But there is matter for another rhyme,
> And I to this may add a second tale.[86]

1823

On the Feeling of Immortality in Youth

Life is a pure flame, and we live by an invisible sun within us.
SIR THOMAS BROWNE [1]

No young man believes he shall ever die. It was a saying of my brother's,[2] and a fine one. There is a feeling of Eternity in youth, which makes us amends for every thing. To be young is to be as one of the Immortal Gods. One half

---

84. Robert William Elliston (1774–1831) was one of the best-known actors of the day, much admired by Charles Lamb. *Remorse* was produced at the Drury Lane Theatre in 1813.
84. A notebook in which one enters passages from one's reading for later reference.
86. Wordsworth, *Hart-Leap Well,* ll. 95–96.
1. Sir Thomas Browne, *Hydriotaphia* or *Urn Burial* V.
2. John Hazlitt, a year older than William, had studied under Sir Joshua Reynolds and had some success as a portrait painter.

of time indeed is flown—the other half remains in store for us with all its countless treasures; for there is no line drawn, and we see no limit to our hopes and wishes. We make the coming age our own.——

> The vast, the unbounded prospect lies before us.[3]

Death, old age, are words without a meaning, that pass by us like the idle air which we regard not. Others may have undergone, or may still be liable to them—we 'bear a charmed life,'[4] which laughs to scorn all such sickly fancies. As in setting out on a delightful journey, we strain our eager gaze forward——

> Bidding the lovely scenes at distance hail,[5]

—and see no end to the landscape, new objects presenting themselves as we advance; so, in the commencement of life, we set no bounds to our inclinations, nor to the unrestricted opportunities of gratifying them. We have as yet found no obstacle, no disposition to flag; and it seems that we can go on so forever. We look round in a new world, full of life, and motion, and ceaseless progress; and feel in ourselves all the vigour and spirit to keep pace with it, and do not foresee from any present symptoms how we shall be left behind in the natural course of things, decline into old age, and drop into the grave. It is the simplicity, and as it were *abstractedness* of our feelings in youth, that (so to speak) identifies us with nature, and (our experience being slight and our passions strong) deludes us into a belief of being immortal like it. Our short-lived connexion with existence, we fondly flatter ourselves, is an indissoluble and lasting union—a honeymoon that knows neither coldness, jar, nor separation. As infants smile and sleep, we are rocked in the cradle of our wayward fancies, and lulled into security by the roar of the universe around us—we quaff the cup of life with eager haste without draining it, instead of which it only overflows the more—objects press around us, filling the mind with their magnitude and with the throng of desires that wait upon them, so that we have no room for the thoughts of death. From that plenitude of our being, we cannot change all at once to dust and ashes, we cannot imagine 'this sensible, warm motion, to become a kneaded clod'[6]—we are too much dazzled by the brightness of the waking dream around us to look into the darkness of the tomb. We no more see our end than our beginning: the one is lost in oblivion and vacancy, as the other is hid from us by the crowd and hurry of approaching events. Or the grim shadow is seen lingering in the horizon, which we are doomed never to overtake, or whose last, faint, glimmering outline touches upon Heaven and translates us to the skies! Nor would the hold that life has taken of us permit us to detach our thoughts from present objects and pursuits, even if we would. What is there more opposed to health, than sickness; to strength and beauty, than decay and dissolution; to the active search of knowledge than mere oblivion? Or is there none of the usual advantage to bar the

3. Addison, *Cato* V.i.13. Hazlitt misquotes; the line is "The wide, the unbounded prospect lies before us."
4. *Macbeth* V.viii.12.
5. Collins, "The Passions," l. 32.
6. *Measure for Measure* III.i.119–20.

approach of Death, and mock his idle threats; Hope supplies their place, and draws a veil over the abrupt termination of all our cherished schemes. While the spirit of youth remains unimpaired, ere the 'wine of life is drank up,' [7] we are like people intoxicated or in a fever, who are hurried away by the violence of their own sensations: it is only as present objects begin to pall upon the sense, as we have been disappointed in our favourite pursuits, cut off from our closest ties, that passion loosens its hold upon the breast, that we by degrees become weaned from the world, and allow ourselves to contemplate, 'as in a glass, darkly,' [8] the possibility of parting with it for good. The example of others, the voice of experience, has no effect upon us whatever. Casualties we must avoid: the slow and deliberate advances of age we can play at *hide-and-seek* with. We think ourselves too lusty and too nimble for that blear-eyed decrepit old gentleman to catch us. Like the foolish fat scullion, in Sterne, when she hears that Master Bobby is dead, our only reflection is—'So am not I!' [9] The idea of death, instead of staggering our confidence, rather seems to strengthen and enhance our possession and our enjoyment of life. Others may fall around us like leaves, or be mowed down like flowers by the scythe of Time: these are but tropes and figures [10] to the unreflecting ears and overweening presumption of youth. It is not till we see the flowers of Love, Hope, and Joy, withering around us, and our own pleasures cut up by the roots, that we bring the moral home to ourselves, that we abate something of the wanton extravagance of our pretensions, or that the emptiness and dreariness of the prospect before us reconciles us to the stillness of the grave!

> Life! thou strange thing, that hast a power to feel
> Thou art, and to perceive that others are.[11]

Well might the poet begin his indignant invective against an art, whose professed object is its destruction, with this animated apostrophe to life. Life is indeed a strange gift, and its privileges are most miraculous. Nor is it singular that when the splendid boon is first granted us, our gratitude, our admiration, and our delight should prevent us from reflecting our own nothingness, or from thinking it will ever be recalled. Our first and strongest impressions are taken from the mighty scene that is opened to us, and we very innocently transfer its durability as well as magnificence to ourselves. So newly found, we cannot make up our minds to parting with it yet and at least put off that consideration to an indefinite term. Like a clown [12] at a fair, we are full of amazement and rapture, and have no thoughts of going home, or that it will soon be night. We know our existence only from external objects, and we measure it by them.

7. Hazlitt doubtless has in mind *Macbeth* II.iii.94: "The wine of life is drawn."
8. I *Corinthians* 13:12. "For now we see through a glass, darkly." Hazlitt's tampering with the King James text makes its sense more apparent, for the "glass" is a mirror, which, in modern idiom, we see "in" rather than "through."
9. *Tristram Shandy* V.vii.
10. A "trope" is the use of a word in a sense different from that which it usually has, a "figure" of speech.
11. "Fawcett's *Art of War,* a poem, 1794" (Hazlitt). Joseph Fawcett (1758?–1804) was a dissenting minister of liberal political views who achieved considerable fame as a preacher in London. He was a friend of Hazlitt's.
12. In the old meaning of the word—a rustic and naïve person.

We can never be satisfied with gazing; and nature will still want us to look on and applaud. Otherwise, the sumptuous entertainment, 'the feast of reason and the flow of soul,' [13] to which we were invited, seems little better than a mockery and a cruel insult. We do not go from a play till the scene is ended, and the lights are ready to be extinguished. But the fair face of things still shines on; shall we be called away, before the curtain falls, or ere we have scarce had a glimpse of what is going on? Like children, our stepmother Nature holds us up to see the raree-show [14] of the universe; and then, as if life were a burthen to support, lets us instantly down again. Yet in that short interval, what 'brave sublunary things' [15] does not the spectacle unfold; like a bubble, at one minute reflecting the universe, and the next, shook to air!—To see the golden sun and the azure sky, the outstretched ocean, to walk upon the green earth, and to be lord of a thousand creatures, to look down giddy precipices or over distant flowery vales, to see the world spread out under one's finger in a map, to bring the stars near, to view the smallest insects in a microscope, to read history, and witness the revolutions of empires and the succession of generations, to hear of the glory of Sidon and Tyre, of Babylon and Susa, as of a faded pageant, and to say all these were, and are now nothing, to think that we exist in such a point of time, and in such a corner of space, to be at once spectators and a part of the moving scene, to watch the return of the seasons, of spring and autumn, to hear—

> The stockdove plain amid the forest deep,
> That drowsy rustles to the sighing gale [16]

—to traverse desert wildernesses, to listen to the midnight choir, to visit lighted halls, or plunge into the dungeon's gloom, or sit in crowded theatres and see life itself mocked, to feel heat and cold, pleasure and pain, right and wrong, truth and falsehood, to study the works of art and refine the sense of beauty to agony, to worship fame and to dream of immortality, to have read Shakespeare and belong to the same species as Sir Isaac Newton; [17] to be and to do all this, and then in a moment to be nothing, to have it all snatched from one like a juggler's ball or a phantasmagoria; there is something revolting and incredible to sense in the transition, and no wonder that, aided by youth and warm blood, and the flush of enthusiasm, the mind contrives for a long time to reject it with disdain and loathing as a monstrous and improbable fiction, like a monkey on a house-top, that is loath, amidst its fine discoveries and specious antics, to be tumbled headlong into the street, and crushed to atoms, the sport and laughter of the multitude!

13. Pope, *Imitations of Horace,* Satire I, l. 128.
14. A street show.
15. Michael Drayton, "To My Most Dearly-loved Friend, Henry Reynolds, Esquire, of Poets and Poesy," l. 106. Drayton's actual phrase is "brave *translunary* things."
16. Thomson, *The Castle of Indolence* I.33–34.
17. At this point Hazlitt appends a long footnote about a contemptuous comment on Newton which Lady Mary Wortley Montagu (1689–1762) makes in one of her letters, which are famous for their vivacity and wit. He deals severely with this, is led to remark on similar arrogant judgments of Lady Mary's, and goes on to denounce the contempt with which, he says, the aristocracy regards writers of genius who are of lowly social origin.

The change, from the commencement to the close of life, appears like a fable, after it has taken place; how should we treat it otherwise than as a chimera before it has come to pass? There are some things that happened so long ago, places or persons we have formerly seen, of which such dim traces remain, we hardly know whether it was sleeping or waking they occurred; they are like dreams within the dream of life, a mist, a film before the eye of memory, which, as we try to recall them more distinctly, elude our notice altogether. It is but natural that the lone interval that we thus look back upon, should have appeared long and endless in prospect. There are others so distinct and fresh, they seem but of yesterday—their very vividness might be deemed a pledge of their permanence. Then, however far back our impressions may go, we find others still older (for our years are multiplied in youth); descriptions of scenes that we had read, and people before our time, Priam [18] and the Trojan war; and even then, Nestor [19] was old and dwelt delighted on his youth, and spoke of the race of heroes that were no more;—what wonder that, seeing this long line of being pictured in our minds, and reviving as it were in us, we should give ourselves involuntary credit for an indeterminate period of existence? In the Cathedral at Peterborough there is a monument to Mary, Queen of Scots, at which I used to gaze when a boy, while the events of the period, all that had happened since, passed in review before me. If all this mass of feeling and imagination could be crowded into a moment's compass, what might not the whole of life be supposed to contain? We are heirs of the past; we count upon the future as our natural reversion. Besides, there are some of our early impressions so exquisitely tempered, it appears that they must always last—nothing can add to or take away from their sweetness and purity—the first breath of spring, the hyacinth dipped in the dew, the mild lustre of the evening-star, the rainbow after a storm—while we have the full enjoyment of these, we must be young; and what can ever alter us in this respect? Truth, friendship, love, books, are also proof against the canker of time; and while we live, but for them, we can never grow old. We take out a new lease of existence from the objects on which we set our affections, and become abstracted, impassive, immortal in them. We cannot conceive how certain sentiments should ever decay or grow cold in our breasts; and, consequently, to maintain them in their first youthful glow and vigour, the flame of life must continue to burn as bright as ever, or rather, they are the fuel that feed the sacred lamp, that kindle 'the purple light of love,' [20] and spread a golden cloud around our heads! Again, we not only flourish and survive in our affections (in which we will not listen to the possibility of a change, any more than we foresee the wrinkles on the brow of a mistress), but we have a farther guarantee against the thoughts of death in our favourite studies and pursuits, and in their continual advance. Art we know is long; life, we feel, should be so too. We see no end of the difficulties we have to encounter: perfection is slow of attainment, and we must have time to accomplish it in. Rubens [21]

18. Priam was the aged king of Troy when that city was sacked by the Greeks.
19. Nestor was the oldest of the Greek generals who besieged Troy and was esteemed the wisest.
20. Gray, *The Progress of Poesy*, l. 41.
21. Peter Paul Rubens (1577–1640), the great Flemish painter.

complained that when he had just learnt his art, he was snatched away from it: we trust we shall be more fortunate! A wrinkle in an old head takes whole days to finish it properly: but to catch 'the Raphael grace, the Guido air,' [22] no limit should be put to our endeavours. What a prospect for the future! What a task we have entered upon! and shall we be arrested in the middle of it? We do not reckon our time thus employed lost, or our pains thrown away, or our progress slow—we do not droop or grow tired, but 'gain new vigour at our endless task'; [23]—and shall Time grudge us the opportunity to finish what we have auspiciously begun, and have formed a sort of compact with nature to achieve? The fame of the great names we look up to is also imperishable; and shall not we, who contemplate it with such intense yearnings, imbibe a portion of ethereal fire, the *divinae particula aurae*,[24] which nothing can extinguish? I remember to have looked at a print of Rembrandt for hours together, without being conscious of the flight of time, trying to resolve it into its component parts, to connect its strong and sharp gradations, to learn the secret of its reflected lights, and found neither satiety nor pause in the prosecution of my studies. The print over which I was poring would last long enough; why should the idea in my mind, which was finer, more impalpable, perish before it? At this, I redoubled the ardour of my pursuit, and by the very subtlety and refinement of my inquiries, seemed to bespeak for them an exemption from corruption and the rude grasp of Death.[25]

Objects, on our first acquaintance with them, have that singleness and integrity of impression that it seems as if nothing could destroy or obliterate them, so firmly are they stamped and rivetted on the brain. We repose on them with a sort of voluptuous indolence, in full faith and boundless confidence. We are absorbed in the present moment, or return to the same point—idling away a great deal of time in youth, thinking we have enough and to spare. There is often a local feeling in the air, which is as fixed as if it were of marble; we loiter in dim cloisters, losing ourselves in thought and in their glimmering arches; a winding road before us seems as long as the journey of life, and as full of events. Time and experience dissipate this illusion; and by reducing them to detail, circumscribe the limits of our expectations. It is only as the pageant of life passes by and the masques turn their backs upon us, that we see through the deception, or believe that the train will have an end. In many cases, the slow progress and monotonous texture of our lives, before we mingle with the world and are embroiled in its affairs, has a tendency to aid the same feeling. We have a difficulty, when left to ourselves, and without the resource of books or some more lively pursuit, to 'beguile the slow and creeping hours of time,' [26] and argue that if it moves on always at this tedious snail's-pace, it can never come to an end. We are willing to skip over certain portions of it that separate us from favourite objects, that irritate ourselves at the unnecessary delay. The young are prodigal of life from

22. Pope, *Epistle to Mr. Jervas,* 1. 36. Raphael (1483–1520) is the famous Italian painter; Guido is Guido Reni (1575–1642), also an Italian painter.
23. Cowper, *Charity,* l. 104.
24. "Parts of the divine breath."
25. "Is it not this that frequently keeps artists alive so long, *viz.,* the constant occupation of their minds with vivid images, with little of the *wear-and-tear* of the body?" (Hazlitt)
26. *As You Like It* II.vii.112.

a superabundance of it; the old are tenacious on the same score, because they have little left, and cannot enjoy even what remains of it.

For my part, I set out in life with the French Revolution, and that event had considerable influence on my early feelings, as on those of others.[27] Youth was then doubly such. It was the dawn on a new era, a new impulse had been given to men's minds, and the sun of Liberty rose upon the sun of Life in the same day, and both were proud to run their race together. Little did I dream, while my first hopes and wishes went hand in hand with those of the human race, that long before my eyes should close, that dawn would be over-cast, and set once more in the night of despotism—'total eclipse!'[28] Happy that I did not. I felt for years, and during the best part of my existence, *heart-whole* in that cause, and triumphed in the triumphs over the enemies of man! At that time, while the fairest aspirations of the human mind seemed about to be realized, ere the image of man was defaced and his breast mangled in scorn, philosophy took a higher, poetry could afford a deeper range. At that time, to read *The Robbers*[29] was indeed delicious, and to hear

> From the dungeon of the tower time-rent,
> That fearful voice, a famished father's cry,[30]

could be borne only amidst the fulness of hope, the crash of the fall of the strongholds of power, and the exulting sounds of the march of human freedom. What feelings the death-scene in *Don Carlos*[31] sent into the soul! In that head-long career of lofty enthusiasm, and the joyous opening of the prospects of the world and our own, the thought of death crossing it, smote doubly cold upon the mind; there was a stifling sense of oppression and confinement, an impatience of our present knowledge, a desire to grasp the whole of our exist-ence in one strong embrace, to sound the mystery of life and death, and in order to put an end to the agony of doubt and dread, to burst through our prison-house, and confront the King of Terrors in his grisly palace!—— As I was writing out this passage, my miniature-picture when a child lay on the mantle-piece, and I took it out of the case to look at it. I could perceive few traces of myself in it; but there was the same placid brow, the dimpled mouth, the same timid, inquisitive glance as ever. But its careless smile did not seem to reproach me with having become a recreant to the sentiments that were then sown in my mind, or with having written a sentence that could call up a blush in this image of ingenuous youth!

27. In 1789, when the French Revolution began, Hazlitt was a boy of eleven. For what the French Revolution might mean to young people of the day, see Wordsworth, *The Prelude* VI.342–408 and IX, X, and XI. Wordsworth, like Hazlitt, speaks of the Revolu-tion as a "dawn": "Bliss was it in that dawn to be alive, / But to be young was very Heaven!" (IX.108–9; see the lines that follow for an account of the promise of the renovation of all of life that the Revolution seemed to hold out).
28. Milton, *Samson Agonistes* I.79. The phrase occurs in the famous passage of Samson's lament over his blindness which begins, "O dark, dark, dark, amid the blaze of noon, / Ir-recoverably dark, total eclipse / Without all hope of day!"
29. *The Robbers* (1782), a play by Friedrich Schiller (1759–1805), the import of which is socially radical although not revolutionary.
30. Coleridge, "Sonnet to Schiller," ll. 3–4.
31. *Don Carlos* (1787), a play by Schiller of libertarian tendency. It is the basis of Verdi's opera *Don Carlo* (1867).

'That time is past with all its giddy raptures.'[32] Since the future was barred to my progress, I have turned for consolation to the past, gathering up the fragments of my early recollections, and putting them into a form that might live. It is thus, that when we find our personal and substantial identity vanishing from us, we strive to gain a reflected and substituted one in our thoughts: we do not like to perish wholly, and wish to bequeath our names at least to posterity. As long as we can keep alive our cherished thoughts and nearest interests in the minds of others, we do not appear to have retired altogether from the stage, we still occupy a place in the estimation of mankind, [and] exercise a powerful influence over them, and it is only our bodies that are trampled into dust or dispersed to air. Our darling speculations still find favour and encouragement, and we make as good a figure in the eyes of our descendants, nay, perhaps, a better than we did in our lifetime. This is one point gained; the demands of our self-love are so far satisfied. Besides, if by the proofs of intellectual superiority we survive ourselves in this world, by exemplary virtue or unblemished faith, we are taught to ensure an interest in another and a higher state of being, and to anticipate at the same time the applauses of men and angels.

> Even from the tomb the voice of nature cries;
> Even in our ashes live their wonted fires.[33]

As we advance in life, we acquire a keener sense of the value of time. Nothing else, indeed, seems of any consequence; and we become misers in this respect. We try to arrest its few last tottering steps, and to make it linger on the brink of the grave. We can never leave off wondering how that which has ever been should cease to be, and would still live on, that we may wonder at our own shadow, and when 'all the life of life is flown,'[34] dwell on the retrospect of the past. This is accompanied by a mechanical tenaciousness of whatever we possess, by a distrust and a sense of fallacious hollowness in all we see. Instead of the full, pulpy feeling of youth, every thing is flat and insipid. The world is a painted witch, that puts us off with false shows and tempting appearances. The ease, the jocund gaiety, the unsuspecting security of youth are fled: nor can we, without flying in the face of common sense,

> From the last dregs of life, hope to receive
> What its first sprightly runnings could not give.[35]

If we can slip out of the world without notice or mischance, can tamper with bodily infirmity, and frame our minds to the becoming composure of *still-life*,[36] before we sink into total insensibility, it is as much as we ought to expect. We do not in the regular course of nature die all at once: we have mouldered away gradually long before; faculty after faculty, attachment after attachment,

---

32. Wordsworth, *Tintern Abbey*, ll. 83–85: "That time is past, / And all its aching joys are now no more, / And all its dizzy raptures."
33. Gray, *Elegy in a Country Churchyard*, ll. 91–92.
34. Burns, "Lament for James, Earl of Glencairn," vi.
35. Dryden, *Aurengzebe* IV.i.41–42.
36. In painting, the representation of inanimate objects. Hazlitt no doubt had in mind the rather grim French phrase for this—*nature morte*.

we are torn from ourselves piecemeal while living; year after year takes some-thing from us; and death only consigns the last remnant of what we were to the grave. The revulsion is not so great, and a quiet *euthanasia* [37] is a wind-ing-up of the plot, that is not out of reason or nature.

That we should thus in a manner outlive ourselves, and dwindle impercepti-bly into nothing, is not surprising, when even in our prime the strongest im-pressions leave so little traces of themselves behind, and the last object is driven out by the succeeding one. How little effect is produced on us at any time by the books we have read, the scenes we have witnessed, the sufferings we have gone through! Think only of the variety of feelings we experience in reading an interesting romance, or being present at a fine play—what beauty, what sublimity, what soothing, what heart-rending emotions! You would suppose these would last for ever, or at least subdue the mind to a correspondent tone and harmony—while we turn over the page, while the scene is passing before us, it seems as if nothing could ever after shake our resolution that 'treason domestic, foreign levy, nothing could touch us farther!' [38] The first splash of mud we get, on entering the street, the first pettifogging shop-keeper that cheats us out of twopence, and the whole vanishes clean out of our remembrance, and we become the idle prey of the most petty and annoy-ing circumstances. The mind soars by an effort to the grand and lofty: it is at home in the grovelling, the disagreeable, and the little. This happens in the height and heyday of our existence, when novelty gives a stronger impulse to the blood and takes a faster hold of the brain (I have known the impression on coming out of a gallery of pictures then last half a day)—as we grow old, we become more feeble and querulous, every object 'reverbs its own hollow-ness,' [39] and both worlds are not enough to satisfy the peevish importunity and extravagant presumption of our desires! There are a few superior, happy beings, who are born with a temper exempt from every trifling annoyance. This spirit sits serene and smiling as in its native skies, and a divine harmony (whether heard or not) plays around them. This is to be at peace. Without this, it is in vain to fly into deserts, or to build a hermitage on the top of rocks, if regret and ill-humour follow us there: and with this, it is needless to make the experiment. The only true retirement is that of the heart; the only true leisure is the repose of the passions. To such persons it makes little difference whether they are young or old; and they die as they have lived, with graceful resignation.

1827   1836 / 1850

On Gusto

Gusto in art is power or passion defining any object.—It is not so difficult to explain this term in what relates to expression (of which it may be said to be the highest degree) as in what relates to things without expression, to the

37. An easy and painless death. Hazlitt does not use the word as it is commonly used today, to mean such a death induced for merciful reasons.
38. *Macbeth* III.ii.24–26.
39. *King Lear* I.i.154.

natural appearances of objects, as mere colour or form. In one sense, however, there is hardly any object entirely devoid of expression, without some character of power belonging to it, some precise association with pleasure or pain: and it is in giving this truth of character from the truth of feeling, whether in the highest or the lowest degree, but always in the highest degree of which the subject is capable, that gusto consists.

There is a gusto in the colouring of Titian.[1] Not only do his heads seem to think—his bodies seem to feel. This is what the Italians mean by the *morbidezza* [2] of his flesh-colour. It seems sensitive and alive all over; not merely to have the look and texture of flesh, but the feeling in itself. For example, the limbs of his female figures have a luxurious softness and delicacy, which appears conscious of the pleasure of the beholder. As the objects themselves in nature would produce an impression on the sense, distinct from every other object, and having something divine in it, which the heart owns and the imagination consecrates, the objects in the picture preserve the same impression, absolute, unimpaired, stamped with all the truth of passion, the pride of the eye, and the charm of beauty. Rubens [3] makes his flesh-colour like flowers; Albano's [4] is like ivory; Titian's is like flesh, and like nothing else. It is as different from that of other painters, as the skin is from a piece of white or red drapery thrown over it. The blood circulates here and there, the blue veins just appear, the rest is distinguished throughout only by that sort of tingling sensation to the eye, which the body feels within itself. This is gusto.—Vandyke's [5] flesh-colour, though it has great truth and purity, wants gusto. It has not the internal character, the living principle in it. It is a smooth surface, not a warm, moving mass. It is painted without passion, with indifference. The hand only has been concerned. The impression slides off from the eye, and does not, like the tones of Titian's pencil, leave a sting behind it in the mind of the spectator. The eye does not acquire a taste or appetite for what it sees. In a word, gusto in painting is where the impression made on one sense excites by affinity those of another.

Michael Angelo's [6] forms are full of gusto. They everywhere obtrude the sense of power upon the eye. His limbs convey an idea of muscular strength, of moral grandeur, and even of intellectual dignity: they are firm, commanding, broad, and massy, capable of executing with ease the determined purposes of the will. His faces have no other expression than his figures, conscious power and capacity. They appear only to think what they shall do, and to know that they can do it. This is what is meant by saying that his style is hard and masculine. It is the reverse of Correggio's,[7] which is effeminate. That is, the

1. The name by which the great Venetian painter Tiziano Vecellio (1490?–1576) is commonly known among English-speaking people.
2. Softness, delicacy.
3. Peter Paul Rubens (1577–1640), great Flemish painter; his pictures are notable for their exuberance.
4. Francesco Albani (1578–1660), a painter of the school of Bologna.
5. Sir Anthony Van Dyck (1599–1641), Flemish portraitist, pupil of Rubens. He settled in England in 1632.
6. Michelangelo Buonarroti (1475–1564), Italian painter, sculptor, and architect, generally regarded as the greatest figure of the Italian Renaissance.
7. Antonio Allegri da Correggio (c. 1494–1534), one of the eminent Italian painters of his day.

gusto of Michael Angelo consists in expressing energy of will without proportionable sensibility, Correggio's in expressing exquisite sensibility without
energy of will. In Correggio's faces as well as figures we see neither bones
nor muscles, but then what a soul is there, full of sweetness and of grace—
pure, playful, soft, angelical! There is sentiment enough in a hand painted by
Correggio to set up a school of history painters. Whenever we look at the hands
of Correggio's women or of Raphael's,[8] we always wish to touch them.

Again, Titian's landscapes have a prodigious gusto, both in the colouring
and forms. We shall never forget one that we saw many years ago in the
Orleans Gallery [9] of Acteon hunting.[10] It had a brown, mellow, autumnal look.
The sky was of the colour of stone. The winds seemed to sing through the
rustling branches of the trees, and already you might hear the twanging of
bows resound through the tangled mazes of the wood. Mr. West,[11] we understand, has this landscape. He will know if this description of it is just. The
landscape background of the St. Peter Martyr [12] is another well-known instance
of the power of this great painter to give a romantic interest and an appropriate
character to the objects of his pencil, where every circumstance adds to the
effect of the scene,—the bold trunks of the tall forest trees, the trailing ground
plants, with that cold convent spire rising in the distance, amidst the blue
sapphire mountains and the golden sky.

Rubens has a great deal of gusto in his Fauns and Satyrs, and in all that
expresses motion, but in nothing else. Rembrandt [13] has it in everything; everything in his pictures has a tangible character. If he puts a diamond in the ear
of a Burgomaster's wife, it is of the first water; and his furs and stuffs are
proof against a Russian winter. Raphael's gusto was only in expression; he had
no idea of the character of anything but the human form. The dryness and
poverty of his style in other respects is a phenomenon in the art. His trees are
like sprigs of grass stuck in a book of botanical specimens. Was it that
Raphael never had time to go beyond the walls of Rome? That he was always
in the streets, at church, or in the bath? He was not one of the Society of
Arcadians.[14]

Claude's [15] landscapes, perfect as they are, want gusto. This is not easy to
explain. They are perfect abstractions of the visible images of things; they speak
the visible language of nature truly. They resemble a mirror or microscope. To

8. Raffaello Santi (1483–1520) stands with Leonardo da Vinci and Michelangelo as one
of the pre-eminent figures of Italian Renaissance art.
9. An exhibition of paintings of the old Italian masters, most of them from the collection
of the Duke of Orleans, which was held in London in 1798–99.
10. The painting is generally called *Diana and Actaeon*.
11. Benjamin West (1738–1820), English historical painter born in America; in 1792
he succeeded Sir Joshua Reynolds as president of the Royal Academy.
12. Hazlitt saw this painting by Titian at the Louvre in 1802. It was destroyed by fire in
1867 after it had been restored to Venice.
13. Rembrandt van Rijn (1606–69), the greatest of the Dutch painters.
14. "Raphael not only could not paint a landscape; he could not paint people in a landscape. He could not have painted the heads or the figures, or even the dresses of the St.
Peter Martyr. His figures have always an *in-door* look, that is, a set, determined, voluntary,
dramatic character, arising from their own passions, or a watchfulness of those of others,
and want that wild uncertainty of expression, which is connected with the accidents of
nature and the changes of the elements. He has nothing *romantic* about him." (Hazlitt)
15. Claude Gellée, called Claude Lorrain (1600–1682), French landscape painter.

the eye only they are more perfect than any other landscapes that ever were or will be painted; they give more of nature, as cognizable by one sense alone; but they lay an equal stress on all visible impressions; they do not interpret one sense by another; they do not distinguish the character of different objects as we are taught, and can only be taught, to distinguish them by their effect on the different senses. That is, his eye wanted imagination: it did not strongly sympathize with his other faculties. He saw the atmosphere, but he did not feel it. He painted the trunk of a tree or a rock in the foreground as smooth—with as complete an abstraction of the gross, tangible impression, as any other part of the picture; his trees are perfectly beautiful, but quite immovable; they have a look of enchantment. In short, his landscapes are unequalled imitations of nature, released from its subjection to the elements,—as if all objects were become a delightful fairy vision, and the eye had rarefied and refined away the other senses.

The gusto in the Greek statues is of a very singular kind. The sense of perfect form nearly occupies the whole mind, and hardly suffers it to dwell on any other feeling. It seems enough for them *to be*, without acting or suffering. Their forms are ideal, spiritual. Their beauty is power. By their beauty they are raised above the frailties of pain or passion; by their beauty they are deified.

The infinite quantity of dramatic invention in Shakespeare takes from his gusto. The power he delights to show is not intense, but discursive. He never insists on any thing as much as he might, except a quibble. Milton has great gusto. He repeats his blow twice; grapples with and exhausts his subject. His imagination has a double relish of its objects, an inveterate attachment to the things he describes, and to the words describing them.—

> Or where Chineses drive
> With sails and wind their *cany* waggons *light*.[16]

> . . . . .
> Wild above rule or art, *enormous* bliss.[17]

There is a gusto in Pope's compliments, in Dryden's satires, and Prior's tales; and among prose-writers, Boccaccio and Rabelais had the most of it. We will only mention one other work which appears to us to be full of gusto, and that is the *Beggar's Opera*.[18] If it is not, we are altogether mistaken in our notions on this delicate subject.

1816

THOMAS DE QUINCEY
1785–1859

Thomas De Quincey was born in Manchester, the son of a prosperous merchant of some literary cultivation and of a mother whom he was to describe as intellectually distinguished. De Quincey's father died when Thomas was seven, leaving the large

16. *Paradise Lost* III.438–39.
17. *Ibid.* V.297.
18. By John Gay (1685–1732). It was produced in 1728 and was an extraordinary success.

family in easy financial circumstances. Despite the poor quality of the schools he attended, the boy early acquired an exceptional command of the classical languages—his skill in writing Latin verse was prodigious and by the age of fifteen he could not only write Greek but also speak it fluently. His precocity was intellectual as well as scholastic; he formed friendships with several adults of notable intelligence and learning, read enormously, and resolved upon a life of literary and philosophical pursuits. In 1801 he was sent by his guardians to the Manchester Grammar School, where the quality of instruction was good but the care of the pupils so negligent and the daily routine so oppressively dull that young De Quincey fell into a low state of spirits and health. Unable to prevail upon his guardians to remove him from the school, he ran away in July of 1802, a month before his seventeenth birthday. He went first to Wales, where he delighted in the mountain scenery and, through a chance acquaintance, was introduced to German literature, and then traveled to London.

The London experience was a momentous one and De Quincey has immortalized it in the first part of his *Confessions of an English Opium-Eater.* His small stock of money was soon exhausted and his hopes of raising a loan against his financial expectations when he should come of age were frustrated. A disreputable lawyer in the employ of the money-lenders with whom he negotiated gave him permission to sleep in an untenanted, unfurnished, and unheated house, an accommodation he shared with a miserable child, a ten-year-old girl of unknown parentage. All the clothes he had were on his back and he went hungry for days. It was at this time of self-elected and quite extreme privation that De Quincey made the acquaintance of the young woman who was to play a significant part in his emotional life. Ann, his senior by a year or two, was a prostitute for whom he conceived a tender and presumably unerotic affection, which she reciprocated—as he recalled with undying gratitude, when he once fainted on the street from hunger, she spent her last sixpence for a glass of wine to revive him. This precious relationship ended abruptly. Having been given a sum of money by a friend of his family whom he met by chance, De Quincey took coach for Eton to visit a friend, a young lord, who he hoped would stand as security for a loan; when he returned to London after a few days, Ann was not at the appointed meeting place and was nowhere to be found. De Quincey never saw her again, except in the dreams which soon became the most significant part of his life.

Just how his reconciliation with his guardians came about De Quincey does not make clear, but we next see him at Worcester College, Oxford. The university made but little impression on him and he left without taking a degree. He kept to himself and gave much of his time to studying Hebrew and enlarging his knowledge of German literature. During his Oxford residence, while on a visit to London, he made the step which decided the course of his life and the bent of his genius. To allay a severe toothache and neuralgia, on the advice of a friend he took his first opium.

In the early nineteenth century, opium was far from being a forbidden drug. Laudanum, which is opium dissolved in alcohol, was the standard pain-reliever of the day, to be bought without prescription at any chemist's shop; it was taken as casually as we now take aspirin and it was commonly given to children. Pellets of opium might also be freely bought; in bad times the drug in this form was in common use by the poor to allay the pangs of hunger. The number of eminent and respectable people who habitually used it, with or without extreme deleterious effects, was considerable. Yet it cannot be said that its use was regarded wholly with indifference, as the case of Coleridge makes plain; his extreme addiction dismayed his friends and filled him with intense guilt. De Quincey, who was more nearly in control of his addiction than Coleridge, was consciously ambivalent in his attitude toward the drug. He candidly describes the "pains of opium" and he knows its dangers, but he took opium not only as he was coerced by his addiction but also with some degree of free will. He was aware that his use of the drug diminished certain of his mental processes and curtailed his power of sustained work, but he believed that it was the source of his best artistic effects. The dreams or dream-like states which it produced were his most cherished forms of experience, and he prized even those that terrified him.

In 1807 De Quincey made the acquaintance of Coleridge, whom he had long admired, and subsequently that of Wordsworth; and in 1809 he settled at Dove Cottage in Grasmere, which the Wordsworths had given up two years before. He lived twelve years in the Lake District, married a local farmer's daughter who had been his mistress and borne him a child, and became confirmed in his addiction. His relationship with the Wordsworths was for a time very close, but deteriorated into acrimony on both sides. In 1821 he left the Lake Country and settled in London. His inherited income had been much curtailed by unfortunate investment and he now undertook to support himself and his growing family by periodical writing. His beginning was auspicious—in the first year of his residence in London he published Confessions of an English Opium-Eater in the London Magazine to great acclaim, which was augmented when the work was brought out as a volume in 1822. Although never exactly a popular author, his work from then on was always in demand. In 1828 he removed from London to Edinburgh, where he lived the rest of his life. His mode of existence was disordered and vagrant and by preference solitary, yet he was an affectionate husband and father, and his personal charm and enchanting conversation made his company much sought after.

Virtually the whole of the large canon of De Quincey's work consists of his contributions to monthly or quarterly journals. Only a small proportion of it is of enduring value. Financial necessity forced him turn his hand to a great variety of subjects, for his erudition was vast and curious, and although brilliant passages occur in most of his all too discursive articles on history, metaphysics, political economy, and literature, in the main these writings are the hackwork of genius. Yet De Quincey never surrendered his ideal of himself as the subtle psychologist and the conscious artist and he fully realized it in a part of his work which, though small in proportion to the whole, is yet in itself quite considerable in extent. His best powers are evoked by the occasions in which he recollects his own experience of persons, of books, most especially of dreams. To the explication of what he called the "germinal principles of the dream" he devoted the best efforts of his often profound intelligence. It was these principles which directed his conception of an "impassioned prose" which, deriving its rhetoric from Milton, Sir Thomas Browne, and Jeremy Taylor, should have the complexity, the power, and the autonomy of music itself. This was not De Quincey's only prose mode (in the best of his narrative or expository writing he could be relatively literal and explicit), but it is the one by which he set highest store, as do his admirers. It is the mode of the unfinished Suspiria de Profundis (Sighs from the Depths)—of which "Levana and Our Ladies of Sorrows" (see below) is a part—and De Quincey was probably right in saying that this was his masterpiece.

Confessions of an English Opium-Eater

In 1856 De Quincey undertook to revise the *Confessions of an English Opium-Eater* for a collected edition of his work that was being prepared. In the process he quadrupled the length of the original text. Although doubtless he added some things of value, most admirers of his work prefer the first version, finding it more direct and immediate and closer to the actuality of the experiences described, and it is from this version that the following selection is taken.

The substance of the first of the *Confessions'* three sections has been suggested in the Headnote on De Quincey; it is called "Preliminary Confessions" and opium does not figure in it; perhaps its chief purpose is to acquaint the reader with Ann, the dear lost friend (see below, the dream of June 1819). The second section, "The Pleasures of Opium," describes the sensations of heightened perception and significance which for De Quincey were the drug's chief charm. The selected passage is from "The Pains of Opium," which concludes the book.

From Confessions of an English Opium-Eater

The Pains of Opium

. . . I now pass to what is the main subject of these latter confessions, to the history and journal of what took place in my dreams; for these were the immediate and proximate cause of my acutest suffering.

The first notice I had of any important change going on in this part of my physical economy, was from the re-awakening of a state of eye generally incident to childhood, or exalted states of irritability. I know not whether my reader is aware that many children, perhaps most, have a power of painting, as it were, upon the darkness, all sorts of phantoms; in some, that power is simply a mechanic affection of the eye; others have a voluntary, or a semi-voluntary power to dismiss or to summon them; or, as a child once said to me when I questioned him on this matter, 'I can tell them to go, and they go; but sometimes they come when I don't tell them to come.' Whereupon I told him that he had almost as unlimited command over apparitions as a Roman centurion [1] over his soldiers.—In the middle of 1817, I think it was, that this faculty became positively distressing to me: at night, when I lay awake in bed, vast processions passed along in mournful pomp; friezes of never-ending stories, that to my feelings were as sad and solemn as if they were stories drawn from times before Oedipus or Priam—before Tyre—before Memphis.[2] And, at the same time, a corresponding change took place in my dreams; a theatre seemed suddenly opened and lighted up within my brain, which presented nightly spectacles of more than earthly splendour. And the four following facts may be mentioned, as noticeable at this time:

1. That, as the creative state of the eye increased, a sympathy seemed to arise between the waking and the dreaming states of the brain in one point— that whatsoever I happened to call up and to trace by a voluntary act upon the

1. An officer of the Roman army commanding a century, i.e. a group of 100 men.
2. Oedipus was king of Thebes, Priam king of Troy; Tyre was the great city of Phoenicia; Memphis became the capital of Egypt after the fall of Thebes.

darkness was very apt to transfer itself to my dreams; so that I feared to exercise this faculty; for, as Midas [3] turned all things to gold, that yet baffled his hopes and defrauded his human desires, so whatsoever things capable of being visually represented I did but think of in the darkness, immediately shaped themselves into phantoms of the eye; and, by a process apparently no less inevitable, when thus once traced in faint and visionary colours, like writings in sympathetic ink,[4] they were drawn out by the fierce chemistry of my dreams, into insufferable splendour that fretted my heart.

2. For this, and all other changes in my dreams, were accompanied by deep-seated anxiety and gloomy melancholy, such as are wholly incommunicable by words. I seemed every night to descend, not metaphorically, but literally to descend, into chasms and sunless abysses, depths below depths, from which it seemed hopeless that I could ever reascend. Nor did I, by waking, feel that I *had* reascended. This I do not dwell upon; because the state of gloom which attended these gorgeous spectacles, amounting at least to utter darkness, as of some suicidal despondency, cannot be approached by words.

3. The sense of space, and in the end, the sense of time, were both powerfully affected. Buildings, landscapes, etc. were exhibited in proportions so vast as the bodily eye is not fitted to receive. Space swelled, and was amplified to an extent of unutterable infinity. This, however, did not disturb me so much as the vast expansion of time; I sometimes seemed to have lived for 70 or 100 years in one night; nay, sometimes had feelings representative of a millennium passed in that time, or, however, of a duration far beyond the limits of any human experience.

4. The minutest incidents of childhood, or forgotten scenes of later years, were often revived: I could not be said to recollect them; for if I had been told of them when waking, I should not have been able to acknowledge them as parts of my past experience. But placed as they were before me, in dreams like intuitions, and clothed in all their evanescent circumstances and accompanying feelings, I *recognized* them instantaneously. I was once told by a near relative of mine, that having in her childhood fallen into a river, and being on the very verge of death but for the critical assistance which reached her, she saw in a moment her whole life, in its minutest incidents, arrayed before her simultaneously as in a mirror; and she had a faculty developed as suddenly for comprehending the whole and every part. This, from some opium experiences of mine, I can believe; I have, indeed, seen the same thing asserted twice in modern books, and accompanied by a remark which I am convinced is true; viz. that the dread book of account,[5] which the Scriptures speak of, is, in fact, the mind itself of each individual. Of this at least feel assured, that there is no such thing as *forgetting* possible to the mind; a thousand accidents may, and will interpose a veil between our present consciousness and the secret inscriptions on the mind; accidents of the same sort will also rend away this veil; but alike, whether veiled or unveiled, the inscription remains for ever; just as the stars seem to withdraw before the common light of day, whereas, in fact, we all know

3. When Dionysus offered to gratify any wish that Midas might make, this legendary king asked that everything he touched be turned to gold; to his dismay, he found that this applied to food, as well as everything else.
4. Ink that is invisible until treated by a chemical or by heat.
5. Revelation 20:12.

that it is the light which is drawn over them as a veil—and that they are waiting to be revealed when the obscuring daylight shall have withdrawn.

Having noticed these four facts as memorably distinguishing my dreams from those of health, I shall now cite a case illustrative of the first fact; and shall then cite any others that I remember, either in their chronological order, or any other that may give them more effect as pictures to the reader.

I had been in youth, and even since, for occasional amusement, a great reader of Livy,[6] whom, I confess, that I prefer, both for style and matter, to any other of the Roman historians; and I had often felt as most solemn and appalling sounds, and most emphatically representative of the majesty of the Roman people, the two words so often occurring in Livy—*Consul Romanus;*[7] especially when the consul is introduced in his military character. I mean to say, that the words king —sultan—regent, &c. or any other titles of those who embody in their own persons the collective majesty of a great people, had less power over my reverential feelings. I had also, though no great reader of history, made myself minutely and critically familiar with one period of English history, viz. the period of the Parliamentary War, having been attracted by the moral grandeur of some who figured in that day, and by the many interesting memoirs which survive those unquiet times. Both these parts of my lighter reading, having furnished me often with matter of reflection, now furnished me with matter for my dreams. Often I used to see, after painting upon the blank darkness a sort of rehearsal whilst waking, a crowd of ladies, and perhaps a festival, and dances. And I heard it said, or I said to myself, 'These are English ladies from the unhappy times of Charles I. These are the wives and the daughters of those who met in peace, and sat at the same tables, and were allied by marriage or by blood; and yet, after a certain day in August, 1642,[8] never smiled upon each other again, nor met but in the field of battle; and at Marston Moor, at Newbury, or at Naseby,[9] cut asunder all ties of love by the cruel sabre, and washed away in blood the memory of ancient friendship.' —The ladies danced, and looked as lovely as the court of George IV.[10] Yet I knew, even in my dream, that they had been in the grave for nearly two centuries.—This pageant would suddenly dissolve: and, at a clapping of hands, would be heard the heart-quaking sound of *Consul Romanus:* and immediately came 'sweeping by,'[11] in gorgeous paludaments,[12] Paulus or Marius,[13] girt round by a company of centurions, with the crimson tunic hoisted on a spear,[14] and followed by the *alalagmos*[15] of the Roman legions.

6. Titus Livius (59 B.C.–17 A.D.) wrote an enormous history of Rome; of its 142 books, only 35 have survived.
7. "Roman consul." Under the Republic the consul was the supreme civil and military magistrate of Rome.
8. On August 22 the royal standard was raised at Nottingham and the Civil War began, ending in the deposition and beheading of Charles I.
9. Battles in the Civil War in which the Royalist forces met defeat.
10. The monarch at the time De Quincey was writing.
11. Milton, "Il Penseroso," l. 98: "In scepter'd pall come sweeping by."
12. *Paludamentum:* a military cloak worn by a general.
13. Lucius Paulus (b. 230 B.C.), conqueror of Macedonia, and Gaius Marius (b. 157 B.C.), victor over the invading Germans. Their triumphs were celebrated with great pomp.
14. Token of victory.
15. A loud noise (Greek)—that of the Roman war cry.

Many years ago, when I was looking over Piranesi's [16] *Antiquities of Rome,* Mr. Coleridge, who was standing by, described to me a set of plates by that artist, called his *Dreams,* and which record the scenery of his own visions during the delirium of a fever: some of them (I describe only from memory of Mr. Coleridge's account) representing vast Gothic halls: on the floor of which stood all sorts of engines and machinery, wheels, cables, pulleys, levers, catapults, etc. etc. expressive of enormous power put forth, and resistance overcome. Creeping along the sides of the walls, you perceived a staircase; and upon it, groping his way upwards, was Piranesi himself: follow the stairs a little further, and you perceive it come to a sudden abrupt termination, without any balustrade, and allowing no step onwards to him who had reached the extremity, except into the depths below. Whatever is to become of poor Piranesi, you suppose, at least, that his labours must in some way terminate here. But raise your eyes, and behold a second flight of stairs still higher: on which again Piranesi is perceived, but this time standing on the very brink of the abyss. Again elevate your eye, and a still more aerial flight of stairs is beheld: and again is poor Piranesi busy on his aspiring labours: and so on, until the unfinished stairs and Piranesi both are lost in the upper gloom of the hall.—With the same power of endless growth and self-reproduction did my architecture proceed in dreams. In the early stage of my malady, the splendours of my dreams were indeed chiefly architectural: and I beheld such pomp of cities and palaces as was never yet beheld by the waking eye, unless in the clouds. From a great modern poet [17] I cite part of a passage which describes, as an appearance actually beheld in the clouds, what in many of its circumstances I saw frequently in sleep:

> The appearance, instantaneously disclosed,
> Was of a mighty city—boldly say
> A wilderness of building, sinking far
> And self-withdrawn into a wondrous depth,
> Far sinking into splendour—without end!
> Fabric it seemed of diamond, and of gold,
> With alabaster domes, and silver spires,
> And blazing terrace upon terrace, high
> Uplifted; here, serene pavilions bright
> In avenues disposed; there towers begirt
> With battlements that on their restless fronts
> Bore stars—illumination of all gems!
> By earthly nature had the effect been wrought
> Upon the dark materials of the storm
> Now pacified: on them, and on the coves,
> And mountain-steeps and summits, whereunto

16. Giovanni Battista Piranesi (1720–78) was an engraver who produced innumerable representations of the ancient monuments of Rome. None of the books he published bears the title *Dreams,* but in 1750 he brought out two volumes of prints which depicted not actual buildings but fanciful structures, disturbingly dream-like in their quality and not the less so because of the precision of their detail. One of the volumes, *Carceri,* was devoted to the representation of fantasies of vast prisons.
17. Wordsworth. The passage is from *The Excursion* II.834–51.

> The vapours had receded,—taking there
> Their station under a cerulean sky, etc. etc.

The sublime circumstance—'battlements that on their *restless* fronts bore stars,'—might have been copied from my architectural dreams, for it often occurred.—We hear it reported of Dryden, and of Fuseli [18] in modern times, that they thought proper to eat raw meat for the sake of obtaining splendid dreams: how much better for such a purpose to have eaten opium, which yet I do not remember that any poet is recorded to have done, except the dramatist Shadwell: [19] and in ancient days, Homer is, I think, rightly reputed to have known the virtues of opium.[20]

To my architecture succeeded dreams of lakes and silvery expanses of water: —these haunted me so much that I feared, though possibly it will appear ludicrous to a medical man, that some dropsical [21] state or tendency of the brain might thus be making itself, to use a metaphysical word, *objective;* and the sentient organ *project* itself as its own object.—For two months I suffered greatly in my head—a part of my bodily structure which had hitherto been so clear from all touch or taint of weakness, physically, I mean, that I used to say of it, as the last Lord Orford [22] said of his stomach, that it seemed likely to survive the rest of my person.—Till now I had never felt a headache even, or any the slightest pain, except rheumatic pains caused by my own folly. However, I got over this attack, though it must have been verging on something very dangerous.

The waters now changed their character,—from translucent lakes, shining like mirrors, they now became seas and oceans. And now came a tremendous change, which, unfolding itself slowly like a scroll, through many months, promised an abiding torment; and, in fact, it never left me until the winding up of my case. Hitherto the human face had mixed often in my dreams, but not despotically, nor with any special power of tormenting. But now that which I have called the tyranny of the human face began to unfold itself. Perhaps some part of my London life might be answerable for this. Be that as it may, now it was that upon the rocking waters of the ocean the human face began to appear: the sea appeared paved with innumerable faces, upturned to the heavens: faces, imploring, wrathful, despairing, surged upwards by thousands, by myriads, by generations, by centuries:—my agitation was infinite,—my mind tossed—and surged with the ocean.

May, 1818. The Malay [23] has been a fearful enemy for months. I have been every night, through his means, transported into Asiatic scenes. I know not

18. Henry Fuseli (1741–1825), a Swiss-born English painter. Many of his pictures are the representation of dreams or dream-like scenes.
19. Thomas Shadwell (1642?–92), dramatist and poet, satirized by Dryden in *The Medal* and *Mac Flecknoe.*
20. In the *Odyssey* IV.220–21 Homer speaks feelingly of a drug—the lotos—that quiets pain and anger and brings forgetfulness of every sorrow.
21. Dropsy is a pathological accumulation of fluid in the tissues and cavities of the body.
22. This was Horace Walpole (1717–97), author of *The Castle of Otranto* (1764).
23. Earlier in his narrative, De Quincey relates that "one day a Malay knocked at my door." He was at that time living in the Lake Country. The man was wholly pacific but his aspect—"small, fierce, restless eyes, thin lips, slavish postures"—was disturbing. He

whether others share in my feelings on this point; but I have often thought that if I were compelled to forego England, and to live in China, and among Chinese manners and modes of life and scenery, I should go mad. The causes of my horror lie deep; and some of them must be common to others. Southern Asia, in general, is the seat of awful images and associations. As the cradle of the human race, it would alone have a dim and reverential feeling connected with it. But there are other reasons. No man can pretend that the wild, barbarous, and capricious superstitions of Africa, or of savage tribes elsewhere, affect him in the way that he is affected by the ancient, monumental, cruel, and elaborate religions of Indostan, etc. The mere antiquity of Asiatic things, of their institutions, histories, modes of faith, etc. is so impressive, that to me the vast age of the race and name overpowers the sense of youth in the individual. A young Chinese seems to me an antediluvian man renewed. Even Englishmen, though not bred in any knowledge of such institutions, cannot but shudder at the mystic sublimity of *castes* [24] that have flowed apart, and refused to mix, through such immemorial tracts of time; nor can any man fail to be awed by the names of the Ganges or the Euphrates. It contributes much to these feelings that southern Asia is, and has been for thousands of years, the part of the earth most swarming with human life; the great *officina gentium*.[25] Man is a weed in those regions. The vast empires also, into which the enormous population of Asia has always been cast, give a further sublimity to the feelings associated with all Oriental names or images. In China, over and above what it has in common with the rest of southern Asia, I am terrified by the modes of life, by the manners, and the barrier of utter abhorrence, and want of sympathy, placed between us by feelings deeper than I can analyse. I could sooner live with lunatics, or brute animals. All this, and much more than I can say, or have time to say, the reader must enter into before he can comprehend the unimaginable horror which these dreams of Oriental imagery, and mythological tortures, impressed upon me. Under the connecting feeling of tropical heat and vertical sun-lights, I brought together all creatures, birds, beasts, reptiles, all trees and plants, usages and appearances, that are found in all tropical regions, and assembled them together in China or Indostan. From kindred feelings, I soon brought Egypt and all her gods under the same law. I was stared at, hooted at, grinned at, chattered at, by monkeys, by paroquets, by cockatoos. I ran into pagodas: and was fixed for centuries at the summit, or in secret rooms; I was the idol; I was the priest; I was worshipped; I was sacrificed. I fled from the wrath of Brama [26] through all the forests of Asia: Vishnu hated me: Seeva laid wait for me. I came

---

spoke no English and communication with him was not possible. De Quincey gave him a large piece of opium; the man bolted down the whole of it, went on his way, and was never heard from again. But, as De Quincey says, he "festered afterwards upon my dreams, and brought other Malays with him, worse than himself, that ran 'a-muck' at me and led me into a world of troubles."

24. Hindu society is divided into four hereditary classes, sharply divided from each other by restrictions on professions and marriage. The system, although less rigorous than formerly, still prevails.

25. "Workshop of the nations."

26. In the religion of the Brahmins, Brahma is the creative power, Vishnu the preserving power, Siva the destructive power.

suddenly upon Isis and Osiris: [27] I had done a deed, they said, which the ibis and the crocodile trembled at. I was buried for a thousand years in stone coffins, with mummies and sphinxes, in narrow chambers at the heart of eternal pyramids. I was kissed, with cancerous kisses, by crocodiles; and laid, confounded with all unutterable slimy things, amongst reeds and Nilotic mud.

I thus give the reader some slight abstraction of my Oriental dreams, which always filled me with such amazement at the monstrous scenery, that horror seemed absorbed, for a while, in sheer astonishment. Sooner or later, came a reflux of feeling that swallowed up the astonishment, and left me, not so much in terror, as in hatred and abomination of what I saw. Over every form, and threat, and punishment, and dim sightless incarceration, brooded a sense of eternity and infinity that drove me into an oppression as of madness. Into these dreams only, it was, with one or two slight exceptions, that any circumstances of physical horror entered. All before had been moral and spiritual terrors. But here the main agents were ugly birds, or snakes, or crocodiles; especially the last. The cursed crocodile became to me the object of more horror than almost all the rest. I was compelled to live with him; and (as was always the case almost in my dreams) for centuries. I escaped sometimes, and found myself in Chinese houses, with cane tables, etc. All the feet of the tables, sofas, etc. soon became instinct with life: the abominable head of the crocodile, and his leering eyes, looked out at me, multiplied into a thousand repetitions: and I stood loathing and fascinated. And so often did this hideous reptile haunt my dreams, that many times the very same dream was broken up in the very same way: I heard gentle voices speaking to me (I hear everything when I am sleeping); and instantly I awoke: it was broad noon; and my children were standing, hand in hand, at my bedside; come to show me their coloured shoes, or new frocks, or to let me see them dressed for going out. I protest that so awful was the transition from the damned crocodile, and the other unutterable monsters and abortions of my dreams, to the sight of innocent *human* natures and of infancy, that, in the mighty and sudden revulsion of mind, I wept, and could not forbear it, as I kissed their faces.

June, 1819. I have had occasion to remark, at various periods of my life, that the deaths of those whom we love, and indeed the contemplation of death generally, is (*caeteris paribus*) [28] more affecting in summer than in any other season of the year. And the reasons are these three, I think: first, that the visible heavens in summer appear far higher, more distant, and (if such a solecism [29] may be excused) more infinite; the clouds, by which chiefly the eye expounds the distance of the blue pavilion stretched over our heads, are in summer more voluminous, massed, and accumulated in far grander and more towering piles: secondly, the light and the appearances of the declining and the setting sun are much more fitted to be types and characters of the Infinite: and, thirdly, which is the main reason, the exuberant and riotous

27. Isis is the Egyptian goddess of fertility, sister and wife of Osiris, the god who, by annually dying and returning to life, personifies the self-renewing power of nature.
28. "Other things being equal."
29. The solecism, or impropriety of language, is the phrase "more infinite," since "infinite" cannot be qualified with respect to degree.

prodigality of life naturally forces the mind more powerfully upon the antagonist thought of death, and the wintry sterility of the grave. For it may be observed, generally, that wherever two thoughts stand related to each other by a law of antagonism, and exist, as it were, by mutual repulsion, they are apt to suggest each other. On these accounts it is that I find it impossible to banish the thought of death when I am walking alone in the endless days of summer; and any particular death, if not more affecting, at least haunts my mind more obstinately and besiegingly in that season. Perhaps this cause, and a slight incident which I omit, might have been the immediate occasions of the following dream; to which, however, a predisposition must always have existed in my mind; but having been once roused, it never left me, and split into a thousand fantastic varieties, which often suddenly reunited, and composed again the original dream.

I thought that it was a Sunday morning in May, that it was Easter Sunday, and as yet very early in the morning. I was standing, as it seemed to me, at the door of my own cottage. Right before me lay the very scene which could really be commanded from that situation, but exalted, as was usual, and solemnized by the power of dreams. There were the same mountains, and the same lovely valley at their feet; but the mountains were raised to more than Alpine height, and there was interspace far larger between them of meadows and forest lawns; the hedges were rich with white roses; and no living creature was to be seen, excepting that in the green churchyard there were cattle tranquilly reposing upon the verdant graves, and particularly round about the grave of a child whom I had tenderly loved, just as I had really beheld them, a little before sunrise in the same summer, when that child died.[30] I gazed upon the well-known scene, and I said aloud (as I thought) to myself, 'It yet wants much of sunrise; and it is Easter Sunday; and that is the day on which they celebrate the first-fruits of resurrection. I will walk abroad; old griefs shall be forgotten today; for the air is cool and still, and the hills are high, and stretch away to heaven; and the forest-glades are as quiet as the churchyard; and, with the dew I can wash the fever from my forehead, and then I shall be unhappy no longer.' And I turned, as if to open my garden gate; and immediately I saw upon the left a scene far different; but which yet the power of dreams had reconciled into harmony with the other. The scene was an Oriental one; and there also it was Easter Sunday, and very early in the morning. And at a vast distance were visible, as a stain upon the horizon, the domes and cupolas of a great city—an image or faint abstraction, caught perhaps in childhood from some picture of Jerusalem. And not a bow-shot from me, upon a stone, and shaded by Judean palms, there sat a woman; and I looked; and it was—Ann! She fixed her eyes upon me earnestly; and I said to her at length: 'So then I have found you at last.' I waited: but she answered me not a word. Her face was the same as when I saw it last, and yet again how different! Seventeen years ago, when the lamp-light fell upon her face, as for the last time I kissed her lips (lips, Ann, that to me were not polluted), her eyes were streaming with tears: the tears were now wiped away; she seemed more beautiful than she was at that time, but in all other

30. The child was little Kate Wordsworth. De Quincey described his feelings about her death in one of his essays.

points the same, and not older. Her looks were tranquil, but with unusual solemnity of expression; and I now gazed upon her with some awe, but suddenly her countenance grew dim, and, turning to the mountains, I perceived vapours rolling between us; in a moment, all had vanished; thick darkness came on; and, in the twinkling of an eye, I was far away from mountains, and by lamplight in Oxford-street, walking again with Ann—just as we walked seventeen years before, when we were both children.

As a final specimen, I cite one of a different character, from 1820.

The dream commenced with a music which now I often heard in dreams—a music of preparation and of awakening suspense; a music like the opening of the Coronation Anthem,[31] and which, like *that,* gave the feeling of a vast march—of infinite cavalcades filing off—and the tread of innumerable armies. The morning was come of a mighty day—a day of crisis and of final hope for human nature, then suffering some mysterious eclipse, and labouring in some dread extremity. Somewhere, I knew not where—somehow, I knew not how —by some beings, I knew not whom—a battle, a strife, an agony, was conducting,—was evolving like a great drama, or piece of music; with which my sympathy was the more insupportable from my confusion as to its place, its cause, its nature, and its possible issue. I, as is usual in dreams (where, of necessity, we make ourselves central to every movement), had the power, and yet had not the power, to decide it. I had the power, if I could raise myself, to will it; and yet again had not the power, for the weight of twenty Atlantics was upon me, or the oppression of inexpiable guilt. 'Deeper than ever plummet sounded,'[32] I lay inactive. Then, like a chorus, the passion deepened. Some greater interest was at stake; some mightier cause than ever yet the sword had pleaded, or trumpet had proclaimed. Then came sudden alarms: hurryings to and fro: trepidations of innumerable fugitives, I knew not whether from the good cause or the bad: darkness and lights: tempest and human faces: and at last, with the sense that all was lost, female forms, and the features that were worth all the world to me, and but a moment allowed,—and clasped hands, and heart-breaking partings, and then—everlasting farewells! and with a sigh, such as the caves of hell sighed when the incestuous mother uttered the abhorred name of death, the sound was reverberated—everlasting farewells! and again, and yet again reverberated—everlasting farewells!

And I awoke in struggles, and cried aloud—'I will sleep no more!'[33]

But I am now called upon to wind up a narrative which has already extended to an unreasonable length. Within more spacious limits, the materials which I have used might have been better unfolded; and much which I have not used might have been added with effect. Perhaps, however, enough has been given. It now remains that I should say something of the way in which this conflict of horrors was finally brought to its crisis. The reader is already aware (form a passage near the beginning of the introduction to the first part) that the opium-eater has, in some way or other, 'unwound, almost to its final links,

31. Written by G. F. Handel (1685–1759) for the coronation of George II in 1727.
32. *The Tempest* III.iii.101.
33. *Macbeth* II.ii.35–43.

the accursed chain which bound him.' By what means? To have narrated this, according to the original intention, would have far exceeded the space which can now be allowed. It is fortunate, as such a cogent reason exists for abridging it, that I should, on a maturer view of the case, have been exceedingly unwilling to injure, by any such unaffecting details, the impression of the history itself, as an appeal to the prudence and the conscience of the yet unconfirmed opium-eater—or even, though a very inferior consideration, to injure its effect as a composition. The interest of the judicious reader will not attach itself chiefly to the subject of the fascinating spells, but to the fascinating power. Not the opium-eater, but the opium, is the true hero of the tale; and the legitimate centre on which the interest revolves. The object was to display the marvellous agency of opium, whether for pleasure or for pain: if that is done, the action of the piece has closed.

However, as some people, in spite of all laws to the contrary, will persist in asking what became of the opium-eater, and in what state he now is, I answer for him thus: The reader is aware that opium had long ceased to found its empire on spells of pleasure; it was solely by the tortures connected with the attempt to abjure it, that it kept its hold. Yet, as other tortures, no less it may be thought, attended the non-abjuration of such a tyrant, a choice only of evils was left; and *that* might as well have been adopted, which, however terrific in itself, held out a prospect of final restoration to happiness. This appears true; but good logic gave the author no strength to act upon it. However, a crisis arrived for the author's life, and a crisis for other objects still dearer to him—and which will always be far dearer to him than his life, even now that it is again a happy one.—I saw that I must die if I continued the opium: I determined, therefore, if that should be required, to die in throwing it off. How much I was at that time taking I cannot say; for the opium which I used had been purchased for me by a friend who afterwards refused to let me pay him; so that I could not ascertain even what quantity I had used within the year. I apprehend, however, that I took it very irregularly: and that I varied from about fifty or sixty grains, to 150 a day. My first task was to reduce it to forty, to thirty, and, as fast as I could, to twelve grains.

I triumphed: but think not, reader, that therefore my sufferings were ended; nor think of me as of one sitting in a *dejected* state. Think of me as of one, even when four months had passed, still agitated, writhing, throbbing, palpitating, shattered; and much, perhaps, in the situation of him who has been racked, as I collect the torments of that state from the affecting account of them left by the most innocent sufferer of the times of James I.[34] Meantime, I derived no benefit from any medicine, except one prescribed to me by an Edinburgh surgeon of great eminence, viz. ammoniated tincture of valerian. Medical account, therefore, of my emancipation I have not much to give: and even that little, as managed by a man so ignorant of medicine as myself, would probably tend only to mislead. At all events, it would be misplaced in this situation. The moral of the narrative is addressed to the opium-eater; and therefore, of necessity, limited in its application. If he is taught to fear and tremble, enough

34. "William Lithgow [1582–1645?]: His book (Travels, &c.) is ill and pedantically written; but the account of his own sufferings on the rack at Malaga is overpoweringly affecting." (De Quincey)

has been effected. But he may say, that the issue of my case is at least a proof that opium, after a seventeen years' use, and an eight years' abuse of its powers, may still be renounced: and that *he* may chance to bring to the task greater energy than I did, or that with a stronger constitution than mine he may obtain the same results with less. This may be true: I would not presume to measure the efforts of other men by my own: I heartily wish him more energy: I wish him the same success. Nevertheless, I had motives external to myself which he may unfortunately want: and these supplied me with conscientious supports which mere personal interests might fail to supply to a mind debilitated by opium.

Lord Bacon conjectures that it may be as painful to be born as to die: I think it probable: and, during the whole period of diminishing the opium, I had the torments of a man passing out of one mode of existence into another. The issue was not death, but a sort of physical regeneration: and I may add, that ever since, at intervals, I have had a restoration of more than youthful spirits, though under the pressure of difficulties, which, in a less happy state of mind, I should have called misfortunes.

One memorial of my former condition still remains: my dreams are not yet perfectly calm: the dread swell and agitation of the storm have not wholly subsided: the legions that encamped in them are drawing off, but not all departed: my sleep is still tumultuous, and, like the gates of Paradise to our first parents when looking back from afar, it is still, in the tremendous line of Milton—

With dreadful faces thronged and fiery arms.[35]

1821   1821

On the Knocking at the Gate in "Macbeth"

[When Macbeth has stabbed King Duncan and his two attendants, and Lady Macbeth carries back to the chamber the grooms' bloody daggers which her husband has inadvertently brought out with him, a knocking at the castle gate is heard. It is repeated three more times before the guilty couple leaves the stage. The knocking continues, growing louder; a drunken porter eventually makes his appearance on the empty stage and in his own good time, after some grimly comic soliloquizing, opens the gate to Macduff and Lennox. The scene has a unique force which De Quincey was the first to remark. It is interesting to note that he makes no reference to the porter's soliloquy and his subsequent dialogue with Macduff, now generally thought very striking but which Coleridge found disgusting and believed could not have been written by Shakespeare. The last paragraph of the famous essay is an extreme example of the Romantic view of Shakespeare as transcending the limits of mere art, as being identical with nature itself.]

From my boyish days I had always felt a great perplexity on one point in *Macbeth*. It was this: the knocking at the gate which succeeds to the murder of Duncan produced to my feelings an effect for which I never could account.

35. *Paradise Lost* XII.644.

The effect was that it reflected back upon the murderer a peculiar awfulness and a depth of solemnity; yet, however obstinately I endeavoured with my understanding to comprehend this, for many years I never could see *why* it should produce such an effect.

Here I pause for one moment, to exhort the reader never to pay any attention to his understanding [1] when it stands in opposition to any other faculty of his mind. The mere understanding, however useful and indispensable, is the meanest faculty in the human mind, and the most to be distrusted; and yet the great majority of people trust to nothing else—which may do for ordinary life, but not for philosophical purposes. Of this out of ten thousand instances that I might produce I will cite one. Ask of any person whatsoever who is not previously prepared for the demand by a knowledge of the perspective to draw in the rudest way the commonest appearance which depends upon the laws of that science—as, for instance, to represent the effect of two walls standing at right angles to each other, or the appearance of the houses on each side of a street as seen by a person looking down the street from one extremity. Now, in all cases, unless the person has happened to observe in pictures how it is that artists produce these effects, he will be utterly unable to make the smallest approximation to it. Yet why? For he has actually seen the effect every day of his life. The reason is that he allows his understanding to overrule his eyes. His understanding, which includes no intuitive knowledge of the laws of vision, can furnish him with no reason why a line which is known and can be proved to be a horizontal line should not *appear* a horizontal line: a line that made any angle with the perpendicular less than a right angle would seem to him to indicate that his houses were all tumbling down together. Accordingly, he makes the line of his houses a horizontal line, and fails, of course, to produce the effect demanded. Here, then, is one instance out of many in which not only the understanding is allowed to overrule the eyes, but where the understanding is positively allowed to obliterate the eyes, as it were; for not only does the man believe the evidence of his understanding in opposition to that of his eyes, but (what is monstrous) the idiot is not aware that his eyes ever gave such evidence. He does not know that he has seen (and therefore *quoad* [2] his consciousness has *not* seen) that which he *has* seen every day of his life.

But to return from this digression. My understanding could furnish no reason why the knocking at the gate in *Macbeth* should produce any effect, direct or reflected. In fact, my understanding said positively that it could *not* produce any effect. But I knew better; I felt that it did; and I waited and clung to the problem until further knowledge should enable me to solve it. At length, in 1812, Mr. Williams made his *début* on the stage of Ratcliffe Highway, and

1. De Quincey means to use this word in the special sense which was initiated by the German philosopher Immanuel Kant (1724–1804), who distinguished between understanding (*Verstand*) and reason (*Vernunft*). He conceived *reason* to be the highest faculty of the mind; it is the power by which the mind synthesizes into unity the concepts provided by the understanding or intellect. It is thus the *creative* faculty; "the mere understanding," as De Quincey calls it, is but mechanical and subordinate. Actually, De Quincey, although he has Kant's distinction in mind, is using the word in a much more limited sense than Kant intended.
2. "So far."

executed those unparalleled murders which have procured for him such a brilliant and undying reputation.[3] On which murders, by the way, I must observe that in one respect they have had an ill effect, by making the connoisseur in murder very fastidious in his taste, and dissatisfied by anything that has been since done in that line. All other murders look pale by the deep crimson of his; and, as an amateur [4] once said to me in a querulous tone, 'There has been absolutely nothing *doing* since his time, or nothing that's worth speaking of.' But this is wrong; for it is unreasonable to expect all men to be great artists, and born with the genius of Mr. Williams. Now, it will be remembered that in the first of these murders (that of the Marrs) the same incident (of a knocking at the door soon after the work of extermination was complete) did actually occur which the genius of Shakespeare has invented; and all good judges, and the most eminent dilettanti,[5] acknowledged the felicity of Shakespeare's suggestion as soon as it was actually realized. Here, then, was a fresh proof that I was right in relying on my own feeling, in opposition to my understanding; and I again set myself to study the problem. At length I solved it to my own satisfaction; and my solution is this: murder, in ordinary cases, where the sympathy is wholly directed to the case of the murdered person, is an incident of coarse and vulgar horror; and for this reason—that it flings the interest exclusively upon the natural but ignoble instinct by which we cleave to life: an instinct which, as being indispensable to the primal law of self-preservation, is the same in kind (though different in degree) amongst all living creatures. This instinct, therefore, because it annihilates all distinctions, and degrades the greatest of men to the level of 'the poor beetle that we tread on,' [6] exhibits human nature in its most abject and humiliating attitude. Such an attitude would little suit the purposes of the poet. What then must he do? He must throw the interest on the murderer. Our sympathy must be with *him* (of course I mean a sympathy of comprehension, a sympathy by which we enter into his feelings, and are made to understand them—not a sympathy of pity or approbation).[7] In the murdered person, all strife of thought, all flux and reflux of passion and of purpose, are crushed by one overwhelming

3. In the winter of 1811–12, in Ratcliffe Highway, a depressed nautical neighborhood, John Williams, a sailor, murdered the members of two households—that of the Marrs (four persons) and that of the Williamsons (three persons). He was apprehended and committed suicide in prison. The tone of whimsically ironic admiration in which De Quincey speaks of his terrible exploit is developed in the essays *On Murder Considered as One of the Fine Arts*, to which is appended a Postcript giving a detailed account of Williams's crimes.

4. In its early sense: a lover of a fine art.

5. Not in the modern sense of those who practice an art without commitment, but lovers of art, connoisseurs.

6. *Measure for Measure* III.i.79.

7. "It seems almost ludicrous to guard and explain my use of a word in a situation where it would naturally explain itself. But it has become necessary to do so, in consequence of the unscholar-like use of the word sympathy, at present so general, by which, instead of taking it in its proper sense, as the act of reproducing in our minds the feelings of another. whether for hatred, indignation, love, pity, or approbation, it is made a mere synonym of the word *pity*; and hence, instead of saying 'sympathy *with* another,' many writers adopt the monstrous barbarism of 'sympathy *for* another.'" (De Quincey)

panic; the fear of instant death smites him 'with its petrific mace.' [8] But in the murderer, such a murderer as a poet will condescend to, there must be raging some great storm of passion—jealousy, ambition, vengeance, hatred—which will create a hell within him; and into this hell we are to look.

In *Macbeth*, for the sake of gratifying his own enormous and teeming faculty of creation, Shakespeare has introduced two murderers: and, as usual in his hands, they are remarkably discriminated: but—though in Macbeth the strife of mind is greater than in his wife, the tiger spirit not so awake, and his feelings caught chiefly by contagion from her—yet, as both were finally involved in the guilt of murder, the murderous mind of necessity is finally to be presumed in both. This was to be expressed; and, on its own account, as well as to make it a more proportionable antagonist to the unoffending nature of their victim, 'the gracious Duncan,' [9] and adequately to expound 'the deep damnation of his taking off,' [10] this was to be expressed with peculiar energy. We were to be made to feel that the human nature—*i.e.* the divine nature of love and mercy, spread through the hearts of all creatures, and seldom utterly withdrawn from man—was gone, vanished, extinct, and that the fiendish nature had taken its place. And, as this effect is marvellously accomplished in the *dialogues* and *soliloquies* themselves, so it is finally consummated by the expedient under consideration; and it is to this that I now solicit the reader's attention. If the reader has ever witnessed a wife, daughter, or sister in a fainting fit, he may chance to have observed that the most affecting moment in such a spectacle is *that* in which a sigh and a stirring announce the recommencement of suspended life. Or, if the reader has ever been present in a vast metropolis on the day when some great national idol was carried in funeral pomp to his grave, and, chancing to walk near the course through which it passed, has felt powerfully, in the silence and desertion of the streets, and in the stagnation of ordinary business, the deep interest which at that moment was possessing the heart of man—if all at once he should hear the death-like stillness broken up by the sound of wheels rattling away from the scene, and making known that the transitory vision was dissolved, he will be aware that at no moment was his sense of the complete suspension and pause in ordinary human concerns so full and affecting as at that moment when the suspension ceases, and the goings-on of human life are suddenly resumed. All action in any direction is best expounded, measured, and made apprehensible, by reaction. Now, apply this to the case in *Macbeth*. Here, as I have said, the retiring of the human heart and the entrance of the fiendish heart was to be expressed and made sensible. Another world has stepped in; and the murderers are taken out of the region of human things, human purposes, human desires. They are transfigured: Lady Macbeth is 'unsexed'; [11] Macbeth has forgot that he was born of woman; both are conformed to the image of devils; and the world of devils is suddenly revealed. But how shall this be conveyed and made palpable?

8. *Paradise Lost* X.294. Petrific: having the power to turn to stone.
9. *Macbeth* III.i.65.
10. *Macbeth* I.vii.20.
11. *Macbeth* I.v.41. Lady Macbeth asks the spirits "that tend on mortal thoughts" to "unsex" her, that is, take away all her womanly feelings so that she can carry out the assassination of King Duncan.

In order that a new world may step in, this world must for a time disappear. The murderers and the murder must be insulated—cut off by an immeasurable gulf from the ordinary tide and succession of human affairs—locked up and sequestered in some deep recess; we must be made sensible that the world of ordinary life is suddenly arrested, laid asleep, tranced, racked into a dread armistice; time must be annihilated, relation to things without abolished; and all must pass self-withdrawn into a deep syncope [12] and suspension of earthly passion. Hence it is that, when the deed is done, when the work of darkness is perfect, then the world of darkness passes away like a pageantry in the clouds: the knocking at the gate is heard, and it makes known audibly that the reaction has commenced; the human has made its reflux upon the fiendish; the pulses of life are beginning to beat again; and the re-establishment of the goings-on of the world in which we live first makes us profoundly sensible of the awful parenthesis that had suspended them.

O mighty poet! Thy works are not as those of other men, simply and merely great works of art, but are also like the phenomena of nature, like the sun and the sea, the stars and the flowers, like frost and snow, rain and dew, hail-storm and thunder, which are to be studied with entire submission of our own faculties, and in the perfect faith that in them there can be no too much or too little, nothing useless or inert, but that, the farther we press in our discoveries, the more we shall see proofs of design and self-supporting arrangement where the careless eye had seen nothing but accident!

1823   1823

Levana and Our Ladies of Sorrow

Oftentimes at Oxford I saw Levana in my dreams. I knew her by her Roman symbols. Who is Levana? Reader, that do not pretend to have leisure for very much scholarship, you will not be angry with me for telling you. Levana was the Roman goddess that performed for the newborn infant the earliest office of ennobling kindness—typical, by its mode, of that grandeur which belongs to man everywhere, and of that benignity in powers invisible which even in Pagan worlds sometimes descends to sustain it. At the very moment of birth, just as the infant tasted for the first time the atmosphere of our troubled planet, it was laid on the ground. *That* might bear different interpretations.[1] But immediately, lest so grand a creature should grovel there for more than one instant, either the paternal hand, as proxy for the goddess Levana, or some near kinsman, as proxy for the father, raised it upright, bade it look erect as the king of all this world, and presented its forehead to the stars, saying, perhaps, in his heart, 'Behold what is greater than yourselves!' This symbolic act represented the function of Levana. And that mysterious lady, who never revealed her face (except to me in dreams), but always acted by delegation, had her name from the Latin verb (as still it is the Italian verb) *levare*, to raise aloft.

12. The word is used here in the now rare sense of a pause, a cessation.

1. De Quincey probably has in mind the mythological story of the giant Antaeus, who was made stronger by contact with his mother, the Earth.

This is the explanation of Levana. And hence it has arisen that some people have understood by Levana the tutelary power that controls the education of the nursery. She, that would not suffer at his birth even a prefigurative or mimic degradation for her awful [2] ward, far less could be supposed to suffer the real degradation attaching to the non-development of his powers. She therefore watches over human education. Now, the word *edŭco*, with the penultimate short, was derived (by a process often exemplified in the crystallization of languages) from the word *edūco*, with the penultimate long. Whatsoever *educes*, or develops, *educates*. By the education of Levana, therefore, is meant, not the poor machinery that moves by spelling-books and grammars, but by that mighty system of central forces hidden in the deep bosom of human life, which by passion, by strife, by temptation, by the energies of resistance, works forever upon children, resting not day or night, any more than the mighty wheel of day and night themselves, whose moments, like restless spokes, are glimmering forever as they revolve.

If, then, *these* are the ministries by which Levana works, how profoundly must she reverence the agencies of grief! But you, reader, think that children generally are not liable to grief such as mine. There are two senses in the word *generally*—the sense of Euclid, where it means *universally* (or in the whole extent of the *genus*), and a foolish sense of this word, where it means *usually*. Now, I am far from saying that children universally are capable of grief like mine. But there are more than you ever heard of who die of grief in this island of ours. I will tell you a common case. The rules of Eton require that a boy on the *foundation* [3] should be there twelve years: he is superannuated at eighteen; consequently he must come at six. Children torn away from mothers and sisters at that age not unfrequently die. I speak of what I know. The complaint is not entered by the registrar as grief; but *that* it is. Grief of that sort, and at that age, has killed more than ever have been counted amongst its martyrs.

Therefore it is that Levana often communes with the powers that shake man's heart; therefore it is that she dotes upon grief. 'These ladies,' said I softly to myself, on seeing the ministers [4] with whom Levana was conversing, 'these are the Sorrows; and they are three in number: as the *Graces* [5] are three, who dress man's life with beauty; the *Parcae* [6] are three, who weave the dark arras [7] of man's life in their mysterious loom always with colours sad in part, sometimes angry with tragic crimson and black; the *Furies* [8] are three, who visit with retributions called from the other side of the grave offences that walk upon this; and once even the *Muses* were but three,[9] who fit the harp, the trumpet, or the lute, to the great burdens of man's impassioned creations.

2. "Awful" not because of his great power but because of his painful destiny.
3. A boy who receives his schooling free of cost.
4. "Minister" in the sense of a person who serves as an agent for another.
5. Greek goddesses personifying charm and beauty.
6. The Latin name for the Fates. They were represented as weaving the fabric of a man's life.
7. Tapestry.
8. Spirits of the underworld who wreaked vengeance upon those who transgressed against the laws, especially those pertaining to the family.
9. Greek female deities of the arts, traditionally nine in number.

These are the Sorrows; all three of whom I know.' That last words I say now; but in Oxford I said, 'one of whom I know, and the others too surely I *shall* know.' For already, in my fervent youth, I saw (dimly relieved upon the dark background of my dreams) the imperfect lineaments of the awful Sisters.

These Sisters—by what name shall we call them? If I say simply 'The Sorrows,' there will be a chance of mistaking the term; it might be understood of individual sorrow—separate cases of sorrow—whereas I want a term expressing the mighty abstractions that incarnate themselves in all individual sufferings of man's heart, and I wish to have these abstractions presented as impersonations, that is, as clothed with human attributes of life, and with functions pointing to flesh. Let us call them, therefore, *Our Ladies of Sorrow.*

I know them thoroughly, and have walked in all their kingdoms. Three sisters they are, of one mysterious household; and their paths are wide apart; but of their dominion there is no end. Them I saw often conversing with Levana, and sometimes about myself. Do they talk, then? O no! Mighty phantoms like these disdain the infirmities of language. They may utter voices through the organs of man when they dwell in human hearts, but amongst themselves is no voice nor sound; eternal silence reigns in *their* kingdoms. They spoke not as they talked with Levana, they whispered not; they sang not; though oftentimes methought they *might* have sung: for I upon earth had heard their mysteries oftentimes deciphered by harp and timbrel, by dulcimer and organ. Like God, whose servants they are, they utter their pleasure not by sounds that perish, or by words that go astray, but by signs in heaven, by changes on earth, by pulses in secret rivers, heraldries painted on darkness, and hieroglyphics written on the tablets of the brain. *They* wheeled in mazes; *I* spelled the steps. *They* telegraphed [10] from afar; *I* read the signals. *They* conspired together; and on the mirrors of darkness *my* eye traced the plots. *Theirs* were the symbols; *mine* are the words.

What is it the Sisters are? What is it that they do? Let me describe their form and their presence, if form it were that still fluctuated in its outline, or presence it were that forever advanced to the front or forever receded amongst shades.

The eldest of the three is named *Mater Lachrymarum,* Our Lady of Tears. She it is that night and day raves and moans, calling for vanished faces. She stood in Rama, where a voice was heard of lamentation—Rachel weeping for her children, and refusing to be comforted.[11] She it was that stood in Bethlehem on the night when Herod's sword swept its nurseries of Innocents, and the little feet were stiffened forever which, heard at times as they trotted along floors overhead, woke pulses of love in household hearts that were not unmarked in heaven. Her eyes are sweet and subtle, wild and sleepy, by turns; oftentimes rising to the clouds, oftentimes challenging the heavens. She wears a diadem

10. Although the word was used for signaling by semaphore, De Quincey probably had in mind the electric telegraph, which was invented in 1844, the year before this essay was written.

11. In Matthew 2, in the account of the massacre of the Innocents, the verse in Jeremiah 31:15 about Rachel weeping for her children is quoted. Rama was Rachel's burying place. Herod ("the Great"), King of Judaea, ordered the slaughter of all male children less than two years old in order that the infant Jesus should be destroyed.

round her head. And I knew by childish memories that she could go abroad upon the winds, when she heard the sobbing of litanies, or the thundering of organs, and when she beheld the mustering of summer clouds. This Sister, the elder, it is that carries keys more than papal [12] at her girdle, which open every cottage and every palace. She, to my knowledge, sat all last summer by the bedside of the blind beggar, him that so often and so gladly I talked with, whose pious daughter, eight years old, with the sunny countenance, resisted the temptations of play and village mirth, to travel all day long on dusty roads with her afflicted father. For this did God send her a great reward. In the spring time of the year, and whilst yet her own spring was budding, He recalled her to himself. But her blind father mourns for ever over *her*: still he dreams at midnight that the little guiding hand is locked within his own; and still he wakens to a darkness that is *now* within a second and a deeper darkness. This *Mater Lachrymarum* also has been sitting all this winter of 1844–5 within the bedchamber of the Czar,[13] bringing before his eyes a daughter (not less pious) that vanished to God not less suddenly, and left behind her a darkness not less profound. By the power of the keys it is that Our Lady of Tears glides, a ghostly intruder, into the chambers of sleepless men, sleepless women, sleepless children, from Ganges to the Nile, from Nile to Mississippi. And her, because she is the first-born of her house, and has the widest empire, let us honour with the title of 'Madonna.' [14]

The second Sister is called *Mater Suspiriorum*, Our Lady of Sighs. She never scales the clouds, nor walks abroad upon the winds. She wears no diadem. And her eyes, if they were ever seen, would be neither sweet nor subtle; no man could read their story; they would be found filled with perishing dreams, and with wrecks of forgotten delirium. But she raises not her eyes; her head, on which sits a dilapidated turban, droops forever, forever fastens on the dust. She weeps not. She groans not. But she sighs inaudibly at intervals. Her sister, Madonna, is oftentimes stormy and frantic, raging in the highest against heaven, and demanding back her darlings. But Our Lady of Sighs never clamours, never defies, dreams not of rebellious aspirations. She is humble to abjectness. Hers is the meekness that belongs to the hopeless. Murmur she may, but it is in her sleep. Whisper she may, but it is to herself in the twilight. Mutter she does at times, but it is in solitary places that are desolate as she is desolate, in ruined cities, and when the sun has gone down to his rest. This Sister is the visitor of the Pariah,[15] of the Jew,[16] of the bondsman to the oar in the Mediterranean galleys;[17] of the English criminal in Norfolk Island,[18] blotted out from the books of remembrance in sweet far-off England; of the baffled penitent reverting his eyes forever upon a solitary grave, which to him seems the altar overthrown of some past and bloody sacrifice, on which altar

---

12. In Matthew 16:19 Jesus says to Peter that he will give him the keys to the kingdom of heaven; the authority of the pope, which descends from Peter, is symbolized by keys.
13. The tyrannical Nicholas I (1796–1855), whose daughter Alexandra died when she was nineteen.
14. "My lady"—a term of respect formerly used in Italy in addressing a married woman.
15. A member of a low caste in India. Although they are not outside the caste system and are not even of the lowest caste, the word in English has come to mean an outcast.
16. In England Jews did not enjoy full civil rights until 1858.
17. Ships propelled by oars as well as sails; criminals were condemned to service in them.
18. An island in the South Pacific belonging to Australia, once a penal colony.

no oblations [19] can now be availing, whether towards pardon that he might implore, or towards reparation that he might attempt. Every slave that at noon-day looks up to the tropical sun with timid reproach, as he points with one hand to the earth, our general mother, but for *him* a stepmother, as he points with the other hand to the Bible, our general teacher, but against *him* sealed and sequestered; every woman sitting in darkness, without love to shelter her head, or hope to illumine her solitude, because the heaven-born instincts kindling in her nature germs of holy affections, which God implanted in her womanly bosom, having been stifled by social necessities, now burn sullenly to waste, like sepulchral lamps amongst the ancients; every nun defrauded of her unreturning Maytime by wicked kinsman, whom God will judge; every captive in every dungeon; all that are betrayed, and all that are rejected; outcasts by traditionary law, and children of *hereditary* disgrace: all these walk with Our Lady of Sighs. She also carries a key; but she needs it little. For her kingdom is chiefly amongst the tents of Shem,[20] and the houseless vagrant of every clime. Yet in the very highest ranks of man she finds chapels of her own; and even in glorious England there are some that, to the world, carry their heads as proudly as the reindeer, who yet secretly have received her mark upon their foreheads.

But the third Sister, who is also the youngest——! Hush! whisper whilst we talk of *her!* Her kingdom is not large, or else no flesh should live; but within that kingdom all power is hers. Her head, turreted like that of Cybele,[21] rises almost beyond the reach of sight. She droops not; and her eyes, rising so high, *might* be hidden by distance. But, being what they are, they cannot be hidden: through the treble veil of crape which she wears the fierce light of a blazing misery, that rests not for matins or for vespers, for noon of day or noon of night, for ebbing or for flowing tide, may be read from the very ground. She is the defier of God. She also is the mother of lunacies, and the suggestress of suicides. Deep lie the roots of her power; but narrow is the nation that she rules. For she can approach only those in whom a profound nature has been upheaved by central convulsions; in whom the heart trembles and the brain rocks under conspiracies of tempest from without and tempest from within. Madonna moves with uncertain steps, fast or slow, but still with tragic grace. Our Lady of Sighs creeps timidly and stealthily. But this youngest Sister moves with incalculable motions, bounding, and with tiger's leaps. She carries no key; for, though coming rarely amongst men, she storms all doors at which she is permitted to enter at all. And *her* name is *Mater Tenebrarum* —Our Lady of Darkness.

These were the *Semnai Theai* or Sublime Goddesses, these were the *Eumenides* or Gracious Ladies [22] (so called by antiquity in shuddering propitiation), of my Oxford dreams. Madonna spoke. She spoke by her mysterious hand. Touching my head, she beckoned to Our Lady of Sighs; and *what* she spoke, translated out of the signs which (except in dreams) no man reads, was this:

19. The act of offering something to a deity.
20. The oldest of the sons of Noah. God regarded him with favor. To "dwell in the tents of Shem" (Genesis 9:27) is a phrase of uncertain implication but it is often taken to mean, as here, to live unhappily among strangers.
21. A goddess of contradictory attributes, at once beneficent and terrible; the crown in which she is often represented is in the shape of a city's walls.
22. The Furies, fierce and terrifying in their appearance, were called by this name to propitiate them.

'Lo! here is he whom in childhood I dedicated to my altars. This is he that once I made my darling. Him I led astray, him I beguiled; and from heaven I stole away his young heart to mine. Through me did he become idolatrous; and through me it was, by languishing desires, that he worshipped the worm, and prayed to the wormy grave. Holy was the grave to him; lovely was its darkness; saintly its corruption. Him, this young idolater, I have seasoned for thee, dear gentle Sister of Sighs! Do thou take him now to *thy* heart, and season him for our dreadful sister. And thou,' turning to the *Mater Tenebrarum*, she said, 'wicked sister, that temptest and hatest, do thou take him from *her*. See that thy sceptre lie heavy on his head. Suffer not woman and her tenderness to sit near him in his darkness. Banish the frailties of hope; wither the relenting of love; scorch the fountains of tears; curse him as only *thou* canst curse. So shall he be accomplished in the furnace; so shall he see the things that ought *not* to be seen, sights that are abominable, and secrets that are unutterable. So shall he read elder truths, sad truths, grand truths, fearful truths. So shall he rise again *before* he dies. And so shall our commission be accomplished which from God we had—to plague his heart until we had unfolded the capacities of his spirit.'[23]

1845   1845

The Literature of Knowledge and the Literature of Power[1]

What is it that we mean by *literature?* Popularly, and amongst the thoughtless, it is held to include everything that is printed in a book. Little logic is required to disturb *that* definition. The most thoughtless person is easily made aware that in the idea of *literature* one essential element is some relation to a general and common interest of man—so that what applies only to a local, or professional, or merely personal interest, even though presenting itself in the shape of a book, will not belong to literature. So far the definition is easily narrowed; and it is as easily expanded. For not only is much that takes a station in books not literature; but inversely, much that really *is* literature never reaches a station in books. The weekly sermons of Christendom, that vast pulpit literature which acts so extensively upon the popular mind—to warn, to uphold, to renew, to comfort, to alarm—does not attain the sanctuary of libraries in the ten-thousandth part of its extent. The drama again—as, for instance, the finest of Shakespeare's plays in England, and all leading Athenian plays in the noontide of the Attic stage—operated as a literature on the public mind, and were (according to the strictest letter of that term) *published* through the audiences that witnessed[2] their representation some time before they were published as

23. See Keats's letter of February 14–May 3, 1819 on the world as a "Vale of Soul-making."

1. Originally part of a long essay on Pope, this discourse has achieved an independent existence.
2. "Charles I, for example, when Prince of Wales, and many others in his father's court, gained their known familiarity with Shakespeare not through the original quartos so slenderly diffused, nor through the first folio of 1625, but through the court representation of his chief dramas at Whitehall." (De Quincey)

things to be read; and they were published in this scenical mode of publication with much more effect than they could have had as books during ages of costly copying or of costly printing.

Books, therefore, do not suggest an idea coextensive and interchangeable with the idea of literature; since much literature, scenic, forensic, or didactic (as from lecturers and public orators), may never come into books, and much that *does* come into books may connect itself with no literary interest. But a far more important correction, applicable to the common vague idea of literature, is to be sought not so much in a better definition of literature as in a sharper distinction of the two functions which it fulfils. In that great social organ which, collectively, we call literature, there may be distinguished two separate offices that may blend and often *do* so, but capable, severally, of a severe insulation, and naturally fitted for reciprocal repulsion. There is, first, the Literature of *Knowledge;* and, secondly, the Literature of *Power.* The function of the first is —to *teach;* the function of the second is—to *move:* the first is a rudder; the second, an oar or a sail. The first speaks to the *mere* discursive understanding; the second speaks ultimately, it may happen, to the higher understanding or reason, but always *through* affections of pleasure and sympathy. Remotely, it may travel towards an object seated in what Lord Bacon calls *dry* light; [3] but, proximately, it does and must operate—else it ceases to be a Literature of *Power* —on and through that *humid* light which clothes itself in the mists and glittering *iris* [4] of human passions, desires, and genial emotions. Men have so little reflected on the higher functions of literature as to find it a paradox if one should describe it as a mean or subordinate purpose of books to give information. But this is a paradox only in the sense which makes it honourable to be paradoxical. Whenever we talk in ordinary language of seeking information or gaining knowledge, we understand the words as connected with something of absolute novelty. But it is the grandeur of all truth which *can* occupy a very high place in human interests that it is never absolutely novel to the meanest of minds: it exists eternally by way of germ or latent principle in the lowest as in the highest, needing to be developed, but never to be planted. To be capable of transplantation is the immediate criterion of a truth that ranges on a lower scale. Besides which, there is a rarer thing than truth—namely, *power*, or deep sympathy with truth. What is the effect, for instance, upon society, of children? By the pity, by the tenderness, and by the peculiar modes of admiration, which connect themselves with the helplessness, with the innocence, and with the simplicity of children, not only are the primal affections strengthened and continually renewed, but the qualities which are dearest in the sight of heaven—the frailty, for instance, which appeals to forbearance, the innocence which symbolizes the heavenly, and the simplicity which is most alien from the worldly—are kept up in perpetual remembrance, and their ideals are continually refreshed. A purpose of the same nature is answered by the higher literature, viz. the Literature of Power. What do you learn from *Paradise Lost?* Nothing at all. What do you learn from a cookery-book? Something new, something that you did not know before, in every paragraph. But

3. In *Novum Organum, Aphorisms concerning the Interpretation of Nature and the Kingdom of Man*, Aphorism 49.
4. Rainbow.

would you therefore put the wretched cookery-book on a higher level of estimation than the divine poem? What you owe to Milton is not any knowledge, of which a million separate items are still but a million of advancing steps on the same earthly level; what you owe is *power*—that is, exercise and expansion to your own latent capacity of sympathy with the infinite, where every pulse and each separate influx is a step upwards, a step ascending as upon a Jacob's ladder [5] from earth to mysterious altitudes above the earth. *All* the steps of knowledge, from first to last, carry you further on the same plane, but could never raise you one foot above your ancient level of earth: whereas the very *first* step in power is a flight—is an ascending movement into another element where earth is forgotten.

Were it not that human sensibilities are ventilated and continually called out into exercise by the great phenomena of infancy, or of real life as it moves through chance and change, or of literature as it re-combines these elements in the mimicries of poetry, romance, etc., it is certain that, like any animal power or muscular energy falling into disuse, all such sensibilities would gradually droop and dwindle. It is in relation to these great *moral* capacities of man that the Literature of Power, as contradistinguished from that of knowledge, lives and has its field of action. It is concerned with what is highest in man; for the Scriptures themselves never condescended to deal by suggestion or co-operation with the mere discursive understanding: when speaking of man in his intellectual capacity, the Scriptures speak not of the understanding, but of *'the understanding heart'* [6]—making the heart, *i.e.* the great *intuitive* (or non-discursive) organ, to be the interchangeable formula for man in his highest state of capacity for the infinite. Tragedy, romance, fairy tale, or epopee,[7] all alike restore to man's mind the ideals of justice, of hope, of truth, of mercy, of retribution, which else (left to the support of daily life in its realities) would languish for want of sufficient illustration. What is meant, for instance, by *poetic justice?*—It does not mean a justice that differs by its object from the ordinary justice of human jurisprudence; for then it must be confessedly a very bad kind of justice; but it means a justice that differs from common forensic justice by the degree in which it *attains* its object, a justice that is more omnipotent over its own ends, as dealing—not with the refractory elements of earthly life, but with the elements of its own creation, and with materials flexible to its own purest preconceptions. It is certain that, were it not for the Literature of Power, these ideals would often remain amongst us as mere arid notional forms; whereas, by the creative forces of man put forth in literature, they gain a vernal life of restoration, and germinate into vital activities. The commonest novel, by moving in alliance with human fears and hopes, with human instincts of wrong and right, sustains and quickens those affections. Calling them into action, it rescues them from torpor. And hence the pre-eminency over all authors that merely *teach* of the meanest that *moves*, or that teaches, if at all, indirectly *by* moving. The very highest work that has ever existed in the Literature of Knowledge is but a *provisional* work: a book upon trial and sufferance, and *quamdiu bene se gesserit*.[8] Let its teaching be

5. In Genesis 28:12 Jacob dreams of a ladder to heaven with angels going up and down it.
6. In I Kings 3:12 God says to Solomon, "I have given thee . . . an understanding heart."
7. Epic poetry.
8. "So long as it conducts itself well."

even partially revised, let it be but expanded—nay, even let its teaching be but placed in a better order—and instantly it is superseded. Whereas the feeblest works in the Literature of Power, surviving at all, survive as finished and unalterable amongst men. For instance, the *Principia* of Sir Issac Newton was a book *militant* on earth from the first. In all stages of its progress it would have to fight for its existence: first, as regards absolute truth; secondly, when that combat was over, as regards its form or mode of presenting the truth. And as soon as a Laplace,[9] or anybody else, builds higher upon the foundations laid by this book, effectually he throws it out of the sunshine into decay and darkness; by weapons won from this book he superannuates and destroys this book, so that soon the name of Newton remains as a mere *nominis umbra*,[10] but his book, as a living power, has transmigrated into other forms. Now, on the contrary, the *Iliad,* the *Prometheus* of Aeschylus, the *Othello* or *King Lear,* the *Hamlet* or *Macbeth,* and the *Paradise Lost,* are not militant, but triumphant for ever as long as the languages exist in which they speak or can be taught to speak. They never *can* transmigrate into new incarnations. To reproduce *these* in new forms, or variations, even if in some things they should be improved, would be to plagiarize. A good steam-engine is properly superseded by a better. But one lovely pastoral valley is not superseded by another, nor a statue of Praxiteles [11] by a statue of Michael Angelo.[12] These things are separated not by imparity, but by disparity. They are not thought of as unequal under the same standard, but as different in *kind,* and, if otherwise equal, as equal under a different standard. Human works of immortal beauty and works of nature in one respect stand on the same footing: they never absolutely repeat each other, never approach so near as not to differ; and they differ not as better and worse, or simply by more and less: they differ by undecipherable and incommunicable differences, that cannot be caught by mimicries, that cannot be reflected in the mirror of copies, that cannot become ponderable in the scales of vulgar comparison.

All works in this class, as opposed to those in the Literature of Knowledge, first, work by far deeper agencies, and, secondly, are more permanent; in the strictest sense they are κτήματα ἐς ἀεί:[13] and what evil they do, or what good they do, is commensurate with the national language, sometimes long after the nation has departed. At this hour, five hundred years since their creation, the tales of Chaucer, never equalled on this earth for their tenderness, and for life of picturesqueness, are read familiarly by many in the charming language of their natal day, and by others in the modernizations of Dryden, of Pope, and Wordsworth. . . .

All the Literature of Knowledge builds only ground-nests, that are swept away by floods, or confounded by the plough; but the Literature of Power builds nests in aerial altitudes of temples sacred from violation, or of forests inaccessible to fraud. *This* is a great prerogative of the *power* literature; and it is a greater which lies in the mode of its influence. The *knowledge* literature, like the

9. The great French mathematician and astronomer (1749–1827). Among his many notable achievements is the hypothesis of the nebular origin of the solar system.
10. "Shadow of a name." It is of course not true that this is what Newton's name has become.
11. Greek sculptor of the 4th century B.C.
12. Italian sculptor, painter, architect, and poet (1475–1574).
13. "Eternal possessions."

fashion of this world, passeth away. An encyclopaedia is its abstract; and, in this respect, it may be taken for its speaking symbol—that before one generation has passed an encyclopaedia is superannuated; for it speaks through the dead memory and unimpassioned understanding, which have not the repose of higher faculties, but are continually enlarging and varying their phylacteries.[14] But all literature properly so called—literature κατ' ἐξοχην[15]—for the very same reason that it is so much more durable than the Literature of Knowledge, is (and by the very same proportion it is) more intense and electrically searching in its impressions. The directions in which the tragedy of this planet has trained our human feelings to play, and the combinations into which the poetry of this planet has thrown our human passions of love and hatred, of admiration and contempt, exercise a power for bad or good over human life that cannot be contemplated, when stretching through many generations, without a sentiment allied to awe. And of this let every one be assured—that he owes to the impassioned books which he has read many a thousand more of emotions than he can consciously trace back to them. Dim by their origination, these emotions yet arise in him, and mould him through life, like forgotten incidents of his childhood.

1848   1848

PERCY BYSSHE SHELLEY
1792–1822

A Defence of Poetry

One of the salient characteristics of Romantic thought is the largeness of the claims it made for the power and beneficence of art and, most especially, of poetry. As religion lost its authority with the educated classes, poetry came increasingly to be seen as the basis and guarantor of the spiritual and moral life. This tendency is exemplified by Wordsworth's Preface to the second edition of *Lyrical Ballads* (see above), which assigns to poetry a function more decisive and far-reaching than had ever before been conceived. Yet bold as are the assertions of the power of poetry which the Preface makes, they fall short of those advanced by Shelley in the impassioned eloquence of *A Defence of Poetry*.

The occasion of Shelley's essay was the publication in 1821 of Thomas Love Peacock's *The Four Ages of Poetry*. Peacock was one of Shelley's warmest and most devoted friends despite—or because of—the dissimilarity of the two men in almost every point of temperament. Although manifestly attracted by the ideas and emotions of the Romanticists, Peacock loved the way of the conventional world and set high store by the worldly virtues of amenity, moderation, and good sense. His ambivalence in this regard is perhaps best exemplified by the good nature which informs the caricature he drew of Shelley in *Nightmare Abbey*, one of the five delightful satirical novels he wrote between 1816 and 1861. The same division of mind is to be seen in

14. Phylacteries are small leather boxes containing strips of parchment on which are written passages in Hebrew from the books of Deuteronomy and Exodus; orthodox Jewish men strap one to the forehead, the other to the left arm, during morning prayers.
15. "Pre-eminently."

The Four Ages of Poetry. The avowed intention of the essay is to demonstrate that poetry, of its nature, must inevitably decline with the progress of civilization and that in an age of rationality, such as the nineteenth century, it can only be an anachronism which is both barbaric and absurd. Peacock was dealing with a question which was seriously entertained by many people at the time, as it still is—since poetry takes its rise in the modes of thought which are characteristic of relatively primitive societies, must not the development of more rational and practical modes of thought make poetry an unnatural and inappropriate form of expression? That the answer to the question might be affirmative was suggested by the theory and practice of contemporary poets themselves, by Wordsworth, for example, who in his Preface and in many of his poems seeks to reinstitute primitive modes of thought and the language consonant with them. Yet although Peacock is exploiting an entirely serious idea, he does not do so with entire seriousness. By one device or another, by the jocosity of his tone or by the extravagance of his formulations, he signals that his argument is not to be taken literally, that his assault upon poetry is made chiefly as a spoof. He does indeed mean to mock what he takes to be the extravagant claims for poetry made by the Romanticists, but when he frames his denunciation of their absurdity and vanity, his intention is not to give comfort to the Philistine enemies of poetry but, rather, to tease the poets themselves, taking license to do so from his sense of familial connection with them.

And Shelley must surely have understood something of the humorous character of the essay, for he gave no sign of being shocked or grieved by Peacock's profane handling of the thing that in all the world he himself held most sacred. At the same time, however, he took with quite ultimate seriousness such part of Peacock's argument as might be thought substantive and replied to it in a polemic which undertook to say that poery, so far from being deteriorated and made powerless by the advance of civilization, is actually the decisive and even the sole agent of civilization.

Deeply moving as the essay unquestionably is, it cannot be of material help to us when we try to think about poetry with some degree of particularity. This is so because, as Shelley uses the word, "poetry" does not denote, as it commonly does, the *corpus* of all known poems, or of all known poems that are to be admired, or of these together with all poems yet to be written and admired. For Shelley, "poetry" is a concept or an entity which has its existence apart from and anterior to any actual poem; it may be, although it need not be, embodied in an actual poem, and it may also be embodied in any human creation whatsoever which is beneficent. Shelley is explicit in saying that a poet is anyone who contributes to civilization—poets are not only those who make actual poems, and not only the practitioners of the arts of music, architecture, painting, and sculpture, but also "the institutors of laws, and the founders of civil society and the inventors of the arts of life, and the teachers." Poetry is not a mode of expression but that which is to be expressed—it is possible for Shelley to speak of drama as being admirable "so long as it continues to express poetry." And that which is to be expressed, in whatever human activity, is the harmonious and eternal order of life, the Beauty and Truth which, in Platonic fashion, are conceived to be pre-existent to their expression.

Shelley does recognize that poetry may be spoken of not only in what he calls a "universal sense" but also in what he calls a "restricted sense." Yet when he uses the word in this latter sense and speaks of actual poems, his interest is likely to be confined to those, such as Homer's, Dante's, Milton's, and Shakespeare's, which he understands to be pointing toward that supernal reality which is poetry in the "universal sense." Of actual poems which have a reference less transcendent he takes no account.

One statement that Shelley makes in *A Defence of Poetry* deserves particular consideration, that in which he speaks in quite specific terms of the part that is played in the moral life by the faculty of imagination, which he represents as a form of love. "The great secret of morals," he says, "is love; or a going out of our own nature, and an identification of ourselves with the beautiful which exists in thought, action, or person, not our own. A man to be greatly good, must imagine intensely and comprehensively; he must put himself in the place of another and of many others; the pains and pleasures of his species must become his own. The great instrument of moral good is the imagination; and poetry [in the "restricted sense"] administers to the effect by acting on the cause." This formulates beautifully and precisely the rationale of the nineteenth-century faith in the moral influence of art, which still has power over us in the face of all the dubieties that have grown up around it.

From A Defence of Poetry

According to one mode of regarding those two classes of mental action, which are called reason and imagination, the former may be considered as mind contemplating the relations borne by one thought to another, however produced; and the latter, as mind acting upon those thoughts so as to colour them with its own light, and composing from them, as from elements, other thoughts, each containing within itself the principle of its own integrity. The one [1] is the τò ποιειν,[2] or the principle of synthesis, and has for its objects those forms which are common to universal nature and existence itself; the other is the τò λογιζειν,[3] or principle of analysis, and its action regards the relations of things, simply as relations; considering thoughts, not in their integral unity, but as the algebraical representations which conduct to certain general results. Reason is the enumeration of quantities already known; imagination is the perception of the value of those quantities, both separately and as a whole. Reason respects the differences, and imagination the similitudes of things. Reason is to imagination as the instrument to the agent, as the body to the spirit, as the shadow to the substance.

Poetry, in a general sense, may be defined to be 'the expression of the imagination': and poetry is connate [4] with the origin of man. . . .

In the youth of the world, men dance and sing and imitate natural objects, observing [5] in these actions, as in all others, a certain rhythm or order. And, although all men observe a similar, they observe not the same order, in the motions of the dance, in the melody of the song, in the combinations of lan-

1. Shelley inverts the order in which, in the preceding sentence, he has mentioned and described the two classes of mental action. "The one" is imagination, "the other" is reason.
2. "Making."
3. "Reasoning."
4. Born at the same time.
5. Not in the sense of "perceive" but in the sense of "adhere to" or "comply with," e.g. "observe the law."

guage, in the series of their imitations of natural objects. For there is a certain order or rhythm belonging to each of these classes of mimetic representation, from which the hearer and the spectator receive an intenser and purer pleasure than from any other: the sense of an approximation to this order has been called taste [6] by modern writers. Every man in the infancy of art, observes an order which approximates more or less closely to that from which his highest delight results: but the diversity is not sufficiently marked, as that its grada- tions should be sensible, except in those instances where the predominance of this faculty of approximation to the beautiful (for so we may be permitted to name the relation betwen this highest pleasure and its cause) is very great. Those in whom it [7] exists in excess are poets, in the most universal sense of the word; and the pleasure resulting from the manner in which they express the influence of society or nature upon their own minds, communicates itself to others, and gathers a sort of re-duplication from that community. Their lan- guage is vitally metaphorical; [8] that is, it marks the before unapprehended relations of things and perpetuates their apprehension, until the words which represent them, become, through time, signs for portions or classes of thoughts instead of pictures of integral thoughts; and then if no new poets should arise to create afresh the associations which have been thus disorganized, language will be dead to all the nobler purposes of human intercourse. These similitudes or relations are finely said by Lord Bacon to be 'the same footsteps of nature impressed upon the various subjects of the world' [9]—and he considers the faculty which perceives them as the storehouse of axioms common to all knowl- edge. In the infancy of society every author is necessarily a poet, because language itself is poetry; and to be a poet is to apprehend the true and the beautiful, in a word, the good which exists in the relation, subsisting, first between existence and perception, and secondly between perception and expression. Every original language near to its source is in itself the chaos of a cyclic poem: [10] the copiousness of lexicography [11] and the distinctions of grammar are the works of a later age, and are merely the catalogue and the form of the creations of poetry.

But poets, or those who imagine and express this indestructible order, are not only the authors of language and of music, of the dance and architecture,

6. Although it no longer figures much in aesthetic theory, the concept of "taste," the faculty by which the virtues of a work of art are intuitively perceived and accurately judged, was of great moment in the critical thought of the 18th century and continued to have force through the 19th. Shelley speaks of it here as the faculty which responds to instances of archetypal beauty.
7. That is, "this faculty of approximation to the beautiful."
8. Shelley touches here upon the formation of abstract words from concrete ones and the tendency to forget their concrete origin. For example, "spirit" and "inspiration" derive from the Latin word *spiritus*, meaning breath, the breath of a god; the poet who asks for inspiration—see Shelley's "Ode to the West Wind"—asks that the breath of the god enter into him and give him its powers.
9. *"De Augment. Scient.* Cap. 1, lib. iii" (Shelley). The reference is to *De Augmentis Scientiarum* (Concerning the Enlargement of the Sciences) which has an expanded version of *The Advancement of Learning.*
10. A group of poems dealing with the same hero or event, e.g. the Arthurian cycle, the Trojan cycle.
11. Dictionary-making.

and statuary, and painting; they are the institutors of laws, and the founders
of civil society, and the inventors of the arts of life, and the teachers, who
draw into a certain propinquity with the beautiful and the true, that partial
apprehension of the agencies of the invisible world which is called religion.[12]
Hence all original religions are allegorical, or susceptible of allegory, and, like
Janus,[13] have a double face of false and true. Poets, according to the circumstances of the age and nation in which they appeared, were called, in the
earlier epochs of the world, legislators, or prophets: [14] a poet essentially comprises and unites both these characters. For he not only beholds intensely the
present as it is, and discovers those laws according to which present things
ought to be ordered, but he beholds the future in the present, and his thoughts
are the germs of the flower and the fruit of latest time. Not that I assert poets
to be prophets in the gross sense of the word, or that they can foretell the
form as surely as they foreknow the spirit of events: such is the pretence
of superstition, which would make poetry an attribute of prophecy, rather
than prophecy an attribute of poetry. A poet participates in the eternal, the
infinite, and the one; as far as relates to his conceptions, time and place
and number are not. The grammatical forms which express the moods of time,
and the difference of persons, and the distinction of place, are convertible
with respect to the highest poetry without injuring it as poetry; and the
choruses of Aeschylus, and the book of Job, and Dante's Paradise, would afford,
more than any other writings, examples of this fact, if the limits of this essay
did not forbid citation. The creations of sculpture, painting, and music, are
illustrations still more decisive.

. . . .

A poem is the image of life expressed in its eternal truth. There is this
difference between a story [15] and a poem, that a story is a catalogue of detached facts, which have no other bond of connexion than time, place, circumstance, cause and effect; the other is the creation of actions according to the
unchangeable forms of human nature, as existing in the mind of the creator,
which is itself the image of all other minds. The one is partial, and applies
only to a definite period of time, and a certain combination of events which
can never again recur; the other is universal, and contains within itself the
germ of a relation to whatever motives or actions have place in the possible
varieties of human nature. Time, which destroys the beauty and the use of the
story of particular facts, stripped of the poetry which should invest them,
augments that of poetry, and for ever develops new and wonderful applications of the eternal truth which it contains. Hence epitomes [16] have been
called the moths of just history; they eat out the poetry of it. The story of

---

12. Although Shelley had a strong animus against established religion, his belief in an
invisible world and in the power of its agencies was intensely held.
13. A Roman god of gates and doorways, represented as having two faces looking in
opposite directions. January is named for him.
14. Shelley is referring to the double meaning of the Latin word *vates*, both "prophet"
and "poet."
15. As his definition of it makes plain, Shelley is using the word "story" in a curiously
limited sense.
16. Abstracts or synopses.

particular facts is as a mirror which obscures and distorts that which should be beautiful: poetry is a mirror which makes beautiful that which is distorted.

The parts of a composition may be poetical, without the composition as a whole being a poem. A single sentence may be considered as a whole, though it be found in a series of unassimilated portions; a single word even may be a spark of inextinguishable thought. And thus all the great historians, Herodotus, Plutarch, Livy, were poets; and although the plan of these writers, espectially that of Livy, restrained them from developing this faculty in its highest degree, they make copious and ample amends for their subjection, by filling all the interstices of their subject with living images.

Having determined what is poetry, and who are poets, let us proceed to estimate its effects upon society.

Poetry is ever accompanied with pleasure: all spirits on which it falls open themselves to receive the wisdom which is mingled with its delight. In the infancy of the world, neither poets themselves nor their auditors are fully aware of the excellence of poetry: for it acts in a divine and unapprehended manner, beyond and above consciousness; and it is reserved for future generations to contemplate and measure the mighty cause and effect in all the strength and splendour of their union. Even in modern times, no living poet ever arrived at the fullness of his fame; the jury which sits in judgment upon a poet, belonging as he does to all time, must be composed of his peers: it must be empanelled by Time from the selectest of the wise of many generations. A Poet is a nightingale, who sits in darkness and sings to cheer its own solitude with sweet sounds; his auditors are as men entranced by the melody of an unseen musician, who feel that they are moved and softened, yet know not whence or why. The poems of Homer and his contemporaries were the delight of infant Greece; they were the elements of that social system which is the column upon which all succeeding civilization has reposed. Homer embodied the ideal perfection of his age in human character; nor can we doubt that those who read his verses were awakened to an ambition of becoming like to Achilles, Hector, and Ulysses: the truth and beauty of friendship, patriotism, and persevering devotion to an object,[17] were unveiled to the depths in these immortal creations: the sentiments of the auditors must have been refined and enlarged by a sympathy with such great and lovely impersonations, until from admiring they imitated, and from imitation they identified themselves with the objects of their admiration. Nor let it be objected, that these characters are remote from moral perfection, and that they can by no means be considered as edifying patterns for general imitation. Every epoch, under names more or less specious, has deified its peculiar errors; revenge is the naked idol of the worship of a semi-barbarous age; and self-deceit is the veiled image of unknown evil, before which luxury and satiety lie prostrate. But a poet considers the vices of his contemporaries as the temporary dress in which his creations must be arrayed, and which cover without concealing the eternal proportions of their beauty. An epic or dramatic personage is understood to wear them around his soul, as he may the ancient armour or the modern uniform around his body; whilst it is

17. Achilles' friendship with Patroclus, Hector's unremitting concern for Troy, Ulysses' intention to return to his home and family.

easy to conceive a dress more graceful than either. The beauty of the internal nature cannot be so far concealed by its accidental vesture, but that the spirit of its form shall communicate itself to the very disguise, and indicate the shape it hides from the manner in which it is worn. A majestic form and graceful motions will express themselves through the most barbarous and tasteless costume. Few poets of the highest class have chosen to exhibit the beauty of their conceptions in its naked truth and splendour; and it is doubtful whether the alloy of costume, habit, etc., be not necessary to temper this planetary music for mortal ears.

The whole objection, however, of the immorality of poetry [18] rests upon a misconception of the manner in which poetry acts to produce the moral improvement of man. Ethical science [19] arranges the elements which poetry has created, and propounds schemes and proposes examples of civil and domestic life: nor is it for want of admirable doctrines that men hate, and despise, and censure, and deceive, and subjugate one another. But poetry acts in another and diviner manner. It awakens and enlarges the mind itself by rendering it the receptacle of a thousand unapprehended combinations of thought. Poetry lifts the veil from the hidden beauty of the world, and makes familiar objects be as if they were not familiar; it reproduces [20] all that it represents, and the impersonations clothed in its Elysian [21] lights stand thenceforward in the minds of those who have once contemplated them, as memorials of that gentle and exalted content [22] which extends itself over all thoughts and actions with which it coexists. The great secret of morals is love; or a going out of our own nature, and an identification of ourselves with the beautiful which exists in thought, action, or person, not our own. A man, to be greatly good, must imagine intensely and comprehensively; he must put himself in the place of another and of many others; the pains and pleasures of his species must become his own.[23] The great instrument of moral good is the imagination; and poetry administers to the effect by acting upon the cause. Poetry enlarges the circumference of the imagination by replenishing it with thoughts of ever new delight, which have the power of attracting and assimilating to their own nature all other thoughts, and which form new intervals and interstices whose void for ever craves fresh food. Poetry strengthens that faculty which is the organ of the moral nature of man, in the same manner as exercise strengthens a limb. A poet therefore would do ill to embody his own conceptions of right and wrong, which are usually those of his place and time, in his poetical creations, which participate in neither. By this assumption of the inferior office of interpreting the effect, in which perhaps after all he might acquit himself but

18. The reference is to Plato's *Republic* which proposes that poets be debarred from the perfect state because of the "immorality" that their representations of human conduct are said to foster.
19. That is, moral philosophy. The word "science" did not yet have its present limited meaning.
20. In the sense of "to bring again into material existence," to create or form anew.
21. Elysium is the abode of the blessed after death.
22. With the accent on the second syllable: although we still use the word as an adjective ("Are you content?"), as a noun it has become obsolete, replaced by "contentment."
23. See, in De Quincey's essay *On the Knocking at the Gate in "Macbeth,"* his footnote (note 7) on the word "sympathy."

imperfectly, he would resign the glory in a participation in the cause. There was little danger that Homer, or any of the eternal poets, should have so far misunderstood themselves as to have abdicated this throne of their widest dominion. Those in whom the poetical faculty, though great, is less intense, as Euripides, Lucan, Tasso, Spenser, have frequently affected a moral aim,[24] and the effect of their poetry is diminished in exact proportion to the degree in which they compel us to advert to this purpose.

[A passage is omitted in which Shelley speaks of the rise of the drama in Athens and of drama in general.]

. . . The author of the *Four Ages of Poetry* has prudently omitted to dispute on the effect of the drama upon life and manners. For, if I know the Knight by the device [25] of his shield, I have only to inscribe Philoctetes or Agamemnon or Othello [26] upon mine to put to flight the giant sophisms which have enchanted him, as the mirror of intolerable light though on the arm of one of the weakest of the Paladines [27] could blind and scatter whole armies of necromancers and pagans. The connexion of scenic exhibitions with the improvement or corruption of the manners of men, has been universally recognized: in other words, the presence or absence of poetry in its most perfect and universal form, has been found to be connected with good and evil in conduct and habit. The corruption which has been imputed to the drama as an effect,[28] begins, when the poetry employed in its constitution ends: I appeal to the history of manners [29] whether the gradations of the growth of the one and the decline of the other have not corresponded with an exactness equal to any other example of moral cause and effect.

The drama at Athens, or wheresoever else it may have approached to its perfection, coexisted with the moral and intellectual greatness of the age. The tragedies of the Athenian poets are as mirrors in which the spectator beholds himself, under a thin disguise of circumstance, stripped of all but that ideal perfection and energy which every one feels to be the internal type of all that he loves, admires, and would become. The imagination is enlarged by a sympathy with pains and passions so mighty, that they distend in their conception the capacity of that by which they are conceived; the good affections are strengthened by pity, indignation, terror and sorrow; [30] and an exalted

24. Shelley's point is that an explicit and didactic morality diminishes the possible moral influence of a work by limiting the activity of the reader's imagination. See Keats's letter on "Negative Capability."
25. A symbol or motto on the shield of a knight to identify him.
26. Respectively, the heroes of Sophocles' *Philoctetes,* of Aeschylus' *Agamemnon,* and of Shakespeare's *Othello.*
27. In the cycle of the Charlemagne legends, the twelve peers who accompanied the king; by extension, a heroic champion, a paragon of chivalry.
28. Shelley doubtless has chiefly in mind the attitude of the Puritans to the theater, of which a late expression was Jeremy Collier's *Short View of the Immorality and Profaneness of the English Stage* (1698), but he may also be thinking of the *Letter to M. d'Alembert on the Theatre* (1758), the work in which Rousseau, whom Shelley greatly admired, imputed to the theater a bad influence on morality.
29. In the sense not of etiquette but of the prevailing mode of conduct of a society.
30. Aristotle said in his *Poetics* that tragedy arouses in the spectator the emotions of pity and terror.

calm [31] is prolonged from the satiety of this high exercise of them into the tumult of familiar life: even crime is disarmed of half its horror and all its contagion by being represented as the fatal consequence of the unfathomable agencies of nature; error is thus divested of its wilfulness; men can no longer cherish it as the creation of their choice. In a drama of the highest order there is little food for censure or hatred; it teaches rather self-knowledge and self-respect. Neither the eye nor the mind can see itself, unless reflected upon that which it resembles. The drama, so long as it continues to express poetry,[32] is as a prismatic and many-sided mirror, which collects the brightest rays of human nature and divides and reproduces them from the simplicity of these elementary forms, and touches them with majesty and beauty, and multiplies all that it reflects, and endows it with the power of propagating its like wherever it may fall.

But in periods of the decay of social life, the drama sympathizes with that decay. Tragedy becomes a cold imitation of the form of the great masterpieces of antiquity, divested of all harmonious accompaniment of the kindred arts; and often the very form misunderstood, or a weak attempt to teach certain doctrines, which the writer considers as moral truths; and which are usually no more than specious flatteries of some gross vice or weakness, with which the author, in common with his auditors, are infected. Hence what has been called the classical and domestic drama. Addison's *Cato* is a specimen of the one; [33] and would it were not superfluous to cite examples of the other! [34] To such purposes poetry cannot be made subservient. Poetry is a sword of lightning, ever unsheathed, which consumes the scabbard that would contain it. And thus we observe that all dramatic writings of this nature are unimaginative in a singular degree; they affect sentiment and passion, which, divested of imagination, are other names for caprice and appetite. The period in our own history of the grossest degradation of the drama is the reign of Charles II, when all forms in which poetry had been accustomed to be expressed became hymns to the triumph of kingly power over liberty and virtue. Milton stood alone illuminating an age unworthy of him. At such periods the calculating principle pervades all the forms of dramatic exhibition, and poetry ceases to be expressed upon them. Comedy loses its ideal universality: wit succeeds to humour; we laugh from self complacency and triumph, instead of pleasure; malignity, sarcasm and contempt, succeed to sympathetic merriment; we hardly laugh, but we smile.[35] Obscenity, which is ever blasphemy against the divine beauty in life, becomes, from the very veil which it assumes, more active if less disgusting: it is a monster for which the corruption of society for ever brings forth new food, which it devours in secret.

31. By this phrase Shelley refers to Aristotle's idea of *catharsis*, the condition of mind that tragedy ideally induces by arousing pity and terror, which, after being experienced, leave the spectator in a state of equilibrium.
32. Here Shelley speaks of poetry not as an activity but as achieved knowledge.
33. Produced in 1713, *Cato* was a great popular success but has become the type of the "correct" and dull classical tragedy.
34. The kind of drama that developed early in the 18th century in reaction to Restoration comedy; written from a middle-class point of view, it set store by a simple prudential morality.
35. For a more favorable view of Restoration comedy, see Lamb's essay *On the Artificial Comedy of the Last Century.*

The drama being that form under which a greater number of modes of expression of poetry are susceptible of being combined than any other, the connexion of poetry and social good is more observable in the drama than in whatever other form. And it is indisputable that the highest perfection of human society has ever corresponded with the highest dramatic excellence; and that the corruption or the extinction of the drama in a nation where it has once flourished, is a mark of a corruption of manners, and an extinction of the energies which sustain the soul of social life. But, as Machiavelli says of political institutions, that life may be preserved and renewed, if men should arise capable of bringing back the drama to its principles.[36] And this is true with respect to poetry in its most extended sense; all language institution and form, require not only to be produced but to be sustained: the office and character of a poet participates in the divine nature as regards providence, no less than as regards creation.

[A passage is omitted in which Shelley takes a general survey of the course of literature up to Dante.]

The poetry of Dante may be considered as the bridge thrown over the stream of time, which unites the modern and ancient world. The distorted notions of invisible things which Dante and his rival Milton have idealized, are merely the mask and the mantle in which these great poets walk through eternity enveloped and disguised. It is a difficult question to determine how far they were conscious of the distinction which must have subsisted in their minds between their own creeds and that of the people. Dante at least appears to wish to mark the full extent of it by placing Riphaeus,[37] whom Virgil calls *justissimus unus,* in Paradise, and observing a most heretical caprice in his distribution of rewards and punishments. And Milton's poem contains within itself a philosophical refutation of that system, of which, by a strange and natural antithesis, it has been a chief popular support. Nothing can exceed the energy and magnificence of the character of Satan as expressed in *Paradise Lost.*[38] It is a mistake to suppose that he could ever have been intended for the popular personification of evil. Implacable hate, patient cunning and a sleepless refinement of device to inflict the extremest anguish on an enemy, these things are evil; and, although venial in a slave, are not to be forgiven in a tyrant; although redeemed by much that ennobles his defeat in one subdued, are marked by all that dishonours his conquest in the victor. Milton's Devil as a moral being is as far superior to his God, as one who perseveres in some

36. All the great Romantic writers were intensely interested in the theater, and hoped for the development of a drama comparable to that of the Elizabethan Age. All the poets among them wrote for the stage, usually without either popular or literary success— although Shelley's own tragedy, *The Cenci,* is in many respects a remarkable work.

37. Riphaeus is the warrior Virgil calls most just among the Trojans, *Aeneid* II. 426.

38. See Blake's "Note" in *The Marriage of Heaven and Hell:* "The reason Milton wrote in fetters when he wrote of Angels and God, and at liberty when of devils and Hell, is because he was a true poet, and of the devil's party without knowing it." Satan as the archetype of the heroic rebel was of great interest in the Romantic period. In the Preface to *Prometheus Unbound,* Shelley neutralizes the view of Satan he expresses in *The Defence of Poetry.* "The character of Satan," he says, "engenders in the mind a pernicious casuistry which leads us to weigh his faults with his wrongs, and to excuse the former because the latter exceed all measure." He offers Prometheus as a preferable—a "more poetical"—example of the heroic rebel.

purpose which he has conceived to be excellent in spite of adversity and torture, is to one who in the cold security of undoubted triumph inflicts the most horrible revenge upon his enemy, not from any mistaken notion of inducing him to repent of a perseverance in enmity, but with the alleged design of exasperating him to deserve new torments.[39] Milton has so far violated the popular creed (if this shall be judged to be a violation) as to have alleged no superiority of moral virtue to his God over his Devil. And this bold neglect of a direct moral purpose is the most decisive proof of the supremacy of Milton's genius. He mingled as it were the elements of human nature as colours upon a single pallet, and arranged them in the composition of his great picture according to the laws of epic truth; that is, according to the laws of that principle by which a series of actions of the external universe and of intelligent and ethical beings is calculated to excite the sympathy of succeeding generations of mankind. The *Divina Commedia* and *Paradise Lost* have conferred upon modern mythology a systematic form; and when change and time shall have added one more superstition to the mass of those which have arisen and decayed upon the earth, commentators will be learnedly employed in elucidating the religion of ancestral Europe, only not utterly forgotten because it will have been stamped with the eternity of genius.

Homer was the first and Dante the second epic poet: that is, the second poet, the series of whose creations bore a defined and intelligible relation to the knowledge and sentiment and religion and political conditions of the age in which he lived, and of the ages which followed it: developing itself in correspondence with their development. For Lucretius had limed the wings of his swift spirit in the dregs of the sensible world; [40] and Virgil, with a modesty which ill became his genius, had affected the fame of an imitator, even whilst he created anew all that he copied; [41] and none among the flock of Mock-birds, though their notes were sweet, Apollonius Rhodius, Quintus Calaber Smyrnetheus, Nonnus, Lucan, Statius, or Claudian,[42] have sought even to fulfil a single condition of epic truth. Milton was the third epic poet. For if the title of epic in its highest sense be refused to the *Aeneid,* still less can it be conceded to the *Orlando Furioso,*[43] the *Gerusalemme Liberata,*[44] the *Lusiad,*[45] or the *Faerie Queene.*

39. In *Paradise Lost.* Perhaps the sexual torments of the rebel angels are implied.
40. Lime is a sticky substance made from holly bark, smeared on trees to catch birds. Lucretius, the Roman philosophical poet (94?–55 B.C.), in his long poem *De Rerum Natura* (On the Nature of Things), undertook to liberate mankind from religious superstition and the fear of death; to this end he reasoned that all things exist by their own mechanical laws and are not in the control of supernatural powers, good or bad. Shelley, while admiring him, would naturally be distressed by his denial of spirit and also by his famous attack on love.
41. Virgil based the *Aeneid* on elements of both the *Iliad* and the *Odyssey.*
42. Greek and Roman poets from the 3rd century B.C. to the 4th century A.D. who wrote long narrative poems.
43. "Orlando Mad," a very popular epic poem by Lodovico Ariosto (1474–1533), first published in 1516 and in an expanded version in 1532.
44. "Jerusalem Delivered," an epic poem by Torquato Tasso (1581), no less popular than *Orlando Furioso.*
45. Usually in the plural The *Lusiads,* or *Lusiadas* (1572), an epic poem by Luis de Camoëns. It relates the great deeds of Lusians—Portuguese—of all ages but chiefly those of the explorer Vasco da Gama.

Dante and Milton were both deeply penetrated with the ancient religion of the civilized world; and its spirit exists in their poetry probably in the same proportion as its forms survived in the unreformed worship of modern Europe. The one preceded and the other followed the Reformation at almost equal intervals. Dante was the first religious reformer, and Luther surpassed him rather in the rudeness and acrimony, than in the boldness of his censures of papal usurpation. Dante was the first awakener of entranced Europe; he created a language, in itself music and persuasion, out of a chaos of inharmonious barbarisms. He was the congregator of those great spirits who presided over the resurrection of learning; the Lucifer of that starry flock which in the thirteenth century shone forth from republican Italy, as from a heaven, into the darkness of the benighted world. His very words are instinct with spirit; each is as a spark, a burning atom of inextinguishable thought; and many yet lie covered in the ashes of their birth, and pregnant with a lightning which has yet found no conductor. All high poetry is infinite; it is as the first acorn, which contained all oaks potentially. Veil after veil may be undrawn, and the inmost naked beauty of the meaning never exposed. A great poem is a fountain forever overflowing with the waters of wisdom and delight; and after one person and one age has exhausted all its divine effluence which their peculiar relations enable them to share, another and yet another succeeds, and new relations are ever developed, the source of an unforeseen and an unconceived delight.

The age immediately succeeding to that of Dante, Petrarch,[46] and Boccaccio,[47] was characterized by a revival of painting, sculpture, music, and architecture. Chaucer caught the sacred inspiration, and the superstructure of English literature is based upon the materials of Italian invention.

But let us not be betrayed from a defence into a critical history of poetry and its influence on society. Be it enough to have pointed out the effects of poets, in the large and true sense of the word, upon their own and all succeeding times, and to revert to the partial instances cited as illustrations of an opinion the reverse of that attempted to be established by the author of *The Four Ages of Poetry*.

But poets have been challenged to resign the civic crown to reasoners and mechanists on another plea. It is admitted that the exercise of the imagination is most delightful, but it is alleged, that that of reason is more useful. Let us examine as the grounds of this distinction, what is here meant by utility. Pleasure or good, in a general sense, is that which the consciousness of a sensitive and intelligent being seeks, and in which, when found, it acquiesces. There are two modes or degrees of pleasure, one durable, universal and permanent; the other transitory and particular. Utility may either express the means of producing the former or the latter. In the former sense, whatever strengthens and purifies the affections, enlarges the imagination, and adds spirit to sense, is useful. But the meaning in which the author of *The Four Ages of Poetry* seems to have employed the word utility is the narrower one

---

46. Francesco Petrarca (1304–74), Italian poet and scholar, a moving spirit of the Renaissance.
47. Giovanni Boccaccio (1313?–75), a close friend of Petrarch, and, like him, an influential humanist. The author of many works of scholarship and literature, he is now remembered chiefly for the tales of his *Decameron*.

of banishing the importunity of the wants of our animal nature, the surrounding men with security of life, the dispersing the grosser delusions of superstition, and the conciliating such a degree of mutual forbearance among men as may consist with the motives of personal advantage.[48]

Undoubtedly the promoters of utility, in this limited sense, have their appointed office in society. They follow the footsteps of poets, and copy the sketches of their creations into the book of common life. They make space, and give time. Their exertions are of the highest value, so long as they confine their administration of the concerns of the inferior powers of our nature within the limits due to the superior ones. But whilst the sceptic destroys gross superstitions, let him spare to deface, as some of the French writers [49] have defaced, the eternal truths charactered upon the imaginations of men. Whilst the mechanist abridges, and the political economist combines, labour, let them beware that their speculations, for want of correspondence with those first principles which belong to the imagination, do not tend, as they have in modern England, to exasperate at once the extremes of luxury and want. They have exemplified the saying, 'To him that hath, more shall be given; and from him that hath not, the little that he hath shall be taken away.' [50] The rich have become richer, and the poor have become poorer; and the vessel of the state is driven between the Scylla and Charybdis [51] of anarchy and despotism. Such are the effects which must ever flow from an unmitigated exercise of the calculating faculty.

It is difficult to define pleasure in its highest sense; the definition involving a number of apparent paradoxes. For, from an inexplicable defect of harmony in the constitution of human nature, the pain of the inferior is frequently connected with the pleasures of the superior portions of our being. Sorrow, terror, anguish, despair itself, are often the chosen expressions of an approximation to the highest good. Our sympathy in tragic fiction depends on this principle; tragedy delights by affording a shadow of the pleasure which exists in pain.[52] This is the source also of the melancholy which is inseparable from the sweetest melody. The pleasure that is in sorrow is sweeter than the pleasure of pleasure itself. And hence the saying, 'It is better to go to the house of mourning, than to the house of mirth.' [53] Not that this highest species of pleasure is necessarily linked with pain. The delight of love and friendship, the ecstasy of the admiration of nature, the joy of the perception and still more of the creation of poetry is often wholly unalloyed.

The production and assurance of pleasure in this highest sense is true utility. Those who produce and preserve this pleasure are poets or poetical philosophers.

48. At least in its early development, Utilitarianism defended competition and "free enterprise." J.S. Mill modified this position.
49. Voltaire most especially. See note 55 below.
50. Matthew 25:29.
51. In Greek mythology, two monsters stationed on either side of the narrow strait between Italy and Sicily. The phrase means two equal dangers, the avoidance of one of them leading to the other.
52. Shelley here touches briefly though pointedly upon the question that Keats tries to solve in his Letter of December 21, 1817—why we find pleasure in tragedy.
53. Ecclesiastes 7:2.

The exertions of Locke, Hume, Gibbon, Voltaire, Rousseau,[54] and their disciples, in favour of oppressed and deluded humanity, are entitled to the gratitude of mankind. Yet it is easy to calculate the degree of moral and intellectual improvement which the world would have exhibited, had they never lived. A little more nonsense would have been talked for a century or two; and perhaps a few more men, women, and children, burnt as heretics. We might not at this moment have been congratulating each other on the abolition of the Inquisition in Spain.[55] But it exceeds all imagination to conceive what would have been the moral condition of the world if neither Dante, Petrarch, Boccaccio, Chaucer, Shakespeare, Calderon, Lord Bacon, nor Milton, had ever existed; if Raphael and Michael Angelo had never been born; if the Hebrew poetry had never been translated; if a revival of the study of Greek literature had never taken place; if no monuments of ancient sculpture had been handed down to us; and if the poetry of the religion of the ancient world had been extinguished together with its belief. The human mind could never, except by the intervention of these excitements, have been awakened to the invention of the grosser sciences, and that application of analytical reasoning to the aberrations of society, which it is now attempted to exalt over the direct expression of the inventive and creative faculty itself.

We have more moral, political and historical wisdom, than we know how to reduce into practice; we have more scientific and economical knowledge than can be accommodated to the just distribution of the produce which it multiplies. The poetry in these systems of thought, is concealed by the accumulation of facts and calculating processes. There is no want of knowledge respecting what is wisest and best in morals, government, and political economy, or at least, what is wiser and better than what men now practise and endure. But we let 'I dare not wait upon I would, like the poor cat in the adage.'[56] We want the creative faculty to imagine that which we know; we want the generous impulse to act that which we imagine; we want the poetry of life: our calculations have outrun conception; we have eaten more than we can digest. The cultivation of those sciences which have enlarged the limits of the empire of man over the external world, has, for want of the poetical faculty, proportionally circumscribed those of the internal world; and man, having enslaved the elements, remains himself a slave. To what but a cultivation of the mechanical arts in a degree disproportioned to the presence of the creative faculty, which is the basis of all knowledge, is to be attributed the abuse of all invention for abridging and combining labour, to the exasperation of the inequality of mankind?[57] From what other cause has it arisen that these inventions which should have lightened, have added a weight to the curse imposed on Adam? Thus poetry, and the principle of self, of which money is the visible incarnation, are the God and Mammon of the world.

54. "I follow the classification by the author of *The Four Ages of Poetry;* but he was essentially a poet. The others, even Voltaire, were mere reasoners." (Shelley)
55. Shelley refers to its temporary abolition by the Liberal Revolution of 1820. The Inquisition was not permanently abolished until 1834.
56. *Macbeth* I.vii.44–45.
57. Shelley refers to the seeming paradox that the "labor-saving" inventions of the Industrial Revolution, so far from lightening the labor of the working classes, had made it heavier.

The functions of the poetical faculty are twofold; by one it creates new materials for knowledge, and power and pleasure; by the other it engenders in the mind a desire to reproduce and arrange them according to a certain rhythm and order which may be called the beautiful and the good. The cultivation of poetry is never more to be desired than at periods when, from an excess of the selfish and calculating principle, the accumulation of the materials of external life exceed the quantity of the power of assimilating them to the internal laws of human nature. The body has then become too unwieldy for that which animates it.

Poetry is indeed something divine. It is at once the centre and circumference of knowledge; it is that which comprehends all science, and that to which all science must be referred. It is at the same time the root and blossom of all other systems of thought; it is that from which all spring, and that which adorns all; and that which, if blighted, denies the fruit and the seed, and withholds from the barren world the nourishment and the succession of the scions of the tree of life. It is the perfect and consummate surface and bloom of things; it is as the odour and the colour of the rose to the texture of the elements which compose it, as the form and the splendour of unfaded beauty to the secrets of anatomy and corruption. What were virtue, love, patriotism, friendship—what were the scenery of this beautiful universe which we inhabit; what were our consolations on this side of the grave, and what were our aspirations beyond it, if poetry did not ascend to bring light and fire from those eternal regions where the owl-winged faculty of calculation dare not ever soar? Poetry is not like reasoning, a power to be exerted according to the determination of the will. A man cannot say, 'I will compose poetry.' The greatest poet even cannot say it: for the mind in creation is as a fading coal, which some invisible influence, like an inconstant wind, awakens to transitory brightness: this power arises from within, like the colour of a flower which fades and changes as it is developed, and the conscious portions of our natures are unprophetic either of its approach or its departure. Could this influence be durable in its original purity and force, it is impossible to predict the greatness of the results; but when composition begins, inspiration is already on the decline, and the most glorious poetry that has ever been communicated to the world is probably a feeble shadow of the original conception of the poet.[58] I appeal to the great poets of the present day, whether it be not an error to assert that the finest passages of poetry are produced by labour and study. The toil and the delay recommended by critics, can be justly interpreted to mean no more than a careful observation of the inspired moments, and an artificial connexion of the spaces between their suggestions by the intertexture of conventional expressions; a necessity only imposed by the limitedness of the poetical faculty itself. For Milton conceived the *Paradise Lost* as a whole before he executed it in portions. We have his own authority also for the Muse having 'dictated' to him the 'unpremeditated song,' and let this be an answer to those who would allege the fifty-six various readings of the first line of the *Orlando Furioso*.[59] Compositions so produced are to poetry what mosaic is to painting.

58. This was perhaps Shelley's own experience, yet many writers find that their best inspirations come in the course of composition.
59. Ariosto was given to much revision and correction of his work.

This instinct and intuition of the poetical faculty is still more observable in the plastic and pictorial arts; a great statue or picture grows under the power of the artist as a child in the mother's womb; and the very mind which directs the hands in formation is incapable of accounting to itself for the origin, the gradations, or the media of the process.[60]

Poetry is the record of the best and happiest moments of the happiest and best minds. We are aware of evanescent visitations of thought and feeling sometimes associated with place or person, sometimes regarding our own mind alone, and always arising unforeseen and departing unbidden, but elevating and delightful beyond all expression: so that even in the desire and the regret they leave, there cannot but be pleasure, participating as it does in the nature of its object. It is as it were the interpenetration of a diviner nature through our own; but its footsteps are like those of a wind over a sea, which the coming calm erases, and whose traces remain only, as on the wrinkled sand which paves it. These and corresponding conditions of being are experienced principally by those of the most delicate sensibility and the most enlarged imagination; and the state of mind produced by them is at war with every base desire. The enthusiasm of virtue, love, patriotism, and friendship, is essentially linked with these emotions; and whilst they last, self appears as what it is, an atom to a universe. Poets are not only subject to these experiences as spirits of the most refined organization, but they can colour all that they combine with the evanescent hues of this ethereal world; a word, or a trait in the representation of a scene or a passion, will touch the enchanted chord, and reanimate, in those who have ever experienced these emotions, the sleeping, the cold, the buried image of the past. Poetry thus makes immortal all that is best and most beautiful in the world; it arrests the vanishing apparitions which haunt the interlunations of life, and veiling them, or in language or in form, sends them forth among mankind, bearing sweet news of kindred joy to those with whom their sisters abide—abide, because there is no portal of expression from the caverns of the spirit which they inhabit into the universe of things. Poetry redeems from decay the visitations of the divinity in Man.

Poetry turns all things to loveliness; it exalts the beauty of that which is most beautiful, and it adds beauty to that which is most deformed; it marries exultation and horror, grief and pleasure, eternity and change; it subdues to union under its light yoke, all irreconcilable things. It transmutes all that it touches, and every form moving within the radiance of its presence is changed by wondrous sympathy to an incarnation of the spirit which it breathes; its secret alchemy turns to potable gold [61] the poisonous waters which flow from death through life; it strips the veil of familiarity from the world, and lays bare the naked and sleeping beauty, which is the spirit of its forms.

60. Shelley's emphasis on the unconscious nature of the creative process is in accord with what Coleridge says about the "organic" nature of art. This view, though doubtless basically right, is stated perhaps too categorically—Pater's comment, which is quoted in the Headnote to Coleridge's statement of organicism (see Organic Form above) applies as well to Shelley's insistence on the unconscious.

61. It was believed that gold, the "noblest" metal, would have sovereign powers if it could be made drinkable.

All things exist as they are perceived; at least in relation to the percipient. 'The mind is its own place, and of itself can make a Heaven of Hell, a Hell of Heaven.' [62] But poetry defeats the curse which binds us to be subjected to the accident of surrounding impressions. And whether it spreads its own figured curtain, or withdraws life's dark veil from before the scene of things, it equally creates for us a being within our being. It makes us the inhabitants of a world to which the familiar world is a chaos. It reproduces the common Universe of which we are portions and percipients, and it purges from our inward sight the film of familiarity which obscures from us the wonder of our being. It compels us to feel that which we perceive, and to imagine that which we know. It creates anew the universe, after it has been annihilated in our minds by the recurrence of impressions blunted by reiteration. It justifies that bold and true word of Tasso: *Non merita nome di creatore, se non Iddio ed il Poeta.*[63]

A poet, as he is the author to others of the highest wisdom, pleasure, virtue and glory, so he ought personally to be the happiest, the best, the wisest, and the most illustrious of men. As to his glory, let Time be challenged to declare whether the fame of any other institutor of human life be comparable to that of a poet. That he is the wisest, the happiest, and the best, inasmuch as he is a poet, is equally incontrovertible: the greatest poets have been men of the most spotless virtue, of the most consummate prudence, and, if we could look into the interior of their lives, the most fortunate of men: and the exceptions, as they regard those who possessed the imaginative faculty in a high yet inferior degree, will be found on consideration to confirm rather than destroy the rule. Let us for a moment stoop to the arbitration of popular breath, and usurping and uniting in our own persons the incompatible characters of accuser, witness, judge and executioner, let us without trial, testimony, or form, determine that certain motives of those who are 'there sitting where we dare not soar,' [64] are reprehensible. Let us assume that Homer was a drunkard, that Virgil was a flatterer, that Horace was a coward, that Tasso was a madman, that Lord Bacon was a peculator, that Raphael was a libertine, that Spenser was a poet laureate.[65] It is inconsistent with this division of our subject to cite living poets, but posterity has done ample justice to the great names now referred to. Their errors have been weighed and found to have been dust in the balance; if their sins were as scarlet, they are now white as snow: [66] they have been washed in the blood of the mediator and the redeemer, Time. Observe in what a ludicrous chaos the imputations of real or fictitious crime have been confused in the contemporary calumnies against poetry and poets;

---

62. *Paradise Lost* I.254–55.
63. "No one deserves the name of creator save only God and the poet." Shelley's calling this statement "bold" serves to remind us that the word "create" (and its derivatives) was not yet in common use in reference to art—"making" implies a pre-existent material out of which the thing is formed, whereas "creation" implies that the thing is brought into being *ex nihilo,* out of nothing, which was once thought to be what God alone could do.
64. *Paradise Lost* IV.829.
65. All these accusations were made against these persons; some of them are true. In speaking further on of the "contemporary calumnies against . . . poets," Shelley means the scandals from which he and Byron suffered.
66. Isaiah 1:18.

consider how little is, as it appears—or appears, as it is; look to your own motives, and judge not, lest ye be judged.

Poetry, as has been said, in this respect differs from logic, that it is not subject to the control of the active powers of the mind, and that its birth and recurrence has no necessary connexion with consciousness or will. It is presumptuous to determine that these are the necessary conditions of all mental causation, when mental effects are experienced insusceptible of being referred to them. The frequent recurrence of the poetical power, it is obvious to suppose, may produce in the mind an habit of order and harmony correlative with its own nature and with its effects upon other minds. But in the intervals of inspiration, and they may be frequent without being durable, a poet becomes a man, and is abandoned to the sudden reflux of the influences under which others habitually live. But as he is more delicately organized than other men, and sensible to pain and pleasure, both his own and that of others, in a degree unknown to them, he will avoid the one and pursue the other with an ardour proportioned to this difference. And he renders himself obnoxious [67] to calumny, when he neglects to observe the circumstances under which these objects of universal pursuit and flight have disguised themselves in one another's garments.

But there is nothing necessarily evil in this error, and thus cruelty, envy, revenge, avarice, and the passions purely evil, have never formed any portion of the popular imputations on the lives of poets.

I have thought it most favourable to the cause of truth to set down these remarks according to the order in which they were suggested to my mind, by a consideration of the subject itself, instead of following that of the treatise that excited me to make them public.[68] Thus although devoid of the formality of a polemical reply; if the view they contain be just, they will be found to involve a refutation of the doctrines of *The Four Ages of Poetry*, so far at least as regards the first division of the subject. I can readily conjecture what should have moved the gall of the learned and intelligent author of that paper; I confess myself, like him, unwilling to be stunned by the Theseids [69] of the hoarse Codri of the day. Bavius and Maevius undoubtedly are, as they ever were, insufferable persons. But it belongs to a philosophical critic to distinguish rather than confound.

The first part of these remarks [70] has related to poetry in its elements and principles; and it has been shown, as well as the narrow limits assigned them would permit, that what is called poetry, in a restricted sense, has a common source with all other forms of order and of beauty, according to which the materials of human life are susceptible of being arranged, and which is poetry in an universal sense.

67. The word is used here in a now obsolete sense: exposed to harm or injury.
68. Actually *The Defence* was not made public in Shelley's lifetime; it was first published in 1840.
69. Epic poems about Theseus. Codrus (plural: Codri) was a poet mocked by Virgil, Horace, and Juvenal, the last of whom ascribes to him a tragedy about Theseus; he may be fictitious. Bavius and Maevius were poetasters contemptuously mentioned by Virgil (*Eclogues* III); the latter was also the object of Horace's scorn.
70. Shelley meant this *Defence* to be only the first part of a longer essay, which he meant to continue but did not.

The second part will have for its object an application of these principles to the present state of the cultivation of poetry, and a defence of the attempt to idealize the modern forms of manners and opinions, and compel them into a subordination to the imaginative and creative faculty. For the literature of England, an energetic development of which has ever preceded or accompanied a great and free development of the national will, has arisen as it were from a new birth. In spite of the low-thoughted envy which would undervalue contemporary merit, our own will be a memorable age in intellectual achievements, and we live among such philosophers and poets as surpass beyond comparison any who have appeared since the last national struggle for civil and religious liberty.[71] The most unfailing herald, companion, and follower of the awakening of a great people to work a beneficial change in opinion or institution, is poetry. At such periods there is an accumulation of the power of communicating and receiving intense and impassioned conceptions respecting man and nature. The persons in whom this power resides, may often as far as regards many portions of their nature, have little apparent correspondence with that spirit of good of which they are the ministers. But even whilst they deny and abjure, they are yet compelled to serve, the power which is seated upon the throne of their own soul. It is impossible to read the compositions of the most celebrated writers of the present day without being startled with the electric life which burns within their words. They measure the circumference and sound the depths of human nature with a comprehensive and all-penetrating spirit, and they are themselves perhaps the most sincerely astonished at its manifestations; for it is less their spirit than the spirit of the age.[72] Poets are the hierophants [73] of an unapprehended inspiration; the mirrors of the gigantic shadows which futurity casts upon the present; the words which express what they understand not; the trumpets which sing to battle, and feel not what they inspire; the influence which is moved not, but moves. Poets are the unacknowledged legislators of the world.

1821   1840

JOHN KEATS
1795–1821
Letters

When Matthew Arnold wrote his essay on Keats in 1880 the question to which he chiefly addressed himself was whether Keats was something more than an "enchantingly sensuous" poet, whether there might be found in his work such intellectual and moral elements as would permit him to be thought of as a great poet, or, since he had died so young, as having been potentially a great poet. Arnold answered the question in the affirmative. Yet despite his eloquence and his authority, the prevailing view

71. The 17th-century parliamentary movement which resulted in the deposition of Charles I.
72. The idea that a historical period has a unique character and particular intentions, of which individual men are the unconscious agents, was gaining currency at that time.
73. Priests who expound sacred mysteries.

of Keats as a wholly sensuous poet continued in force for quite half a century. It remained possible for Sidney Colvin, one of his biographers and editors, to say of Keats that he had "a mind constitutionally inapt for abstract thinking." Colvin went even farther—"Keats," he said, "had no mind." As late as 1930 it could come as a revelation to so perceptive a reader as George Santayana that Keats really did have a mind. Writing to J. Middleton Murry, the English critic whose *Studies in Keats* did much to change the older view of the poet, Santayana said that Keats had always been a "personal favourite" of his and that what he had been attracted by was exactly the absence of any intellectual or moral depth, "a certain frank sensuality or youth-fulness . . . a certain plebeian innocence of great human interests: I called him the *Cockney Genius*, and thought him luscious rather than intellectual." Santayana goes on: "I see now [i.e. after reading Murry's book] how wrong that was and that he was really intuitively contemplative."

No one now is likely to read Keats as Santayana read him before his enlightenment and as he was chiefly read for a century. The intensity of his concern with "great human interests" is now taken for granted, as is its complexity and profundity. In this radical revision of the image of Keats his letters have played a decisive part. All that is now seen in the poetry was of course there to be seen from the beginning. But it is understandable that the enchanting sensuousness and the frank sensuality should have captivated the first attention and interest of readers, and that, being in them-selves powerful and significant traits, they should have seemed definitive of the poetry. It was Keats's letters, as they became more available and better known over the years, that made the first characterization of his poetry eventually untenable. Arnold, arguing his view that Keats is a poet of intellectual and moral weight, draws his evidence scarcely at all from the poetry itself; it is the letters that he relies on to make his point. He detested the letters to Fanny Brawne and deplored their having been published, but upon the letters that Keats wrote to his friends and family touching upon art and life he grounded his claims for the poet's profound seriousness.

With the passing years Keats's letters have quite outgrown their earlier validating function. They no longer exist as documents which derive their value from the light they throw on the temperament and intellect of the writer, but in their own right. Indeed, so high do they stand in the admiration and affection of many readers, that critics sometimes feel it necessary to caution against thinking of Keats primarily as the writer of the letters rather than as the writer of the poems. The admonition is proper enough, yet it would seem to have become the case that the poems and the letters exist in happy symbiosis, that they now together make up the canon of Keats. The poems must certainly come first in our thought. But that this needs to be said suggests the difference between our response to the poems and our response to the letters. The poems, even when they are of the highest interest, are seldom perfect, and although, especially when taken together, they quite transcend their imperfections, our response to them is necessarily mediated by complex considerations. The letters are always perfect in their genre, and our response to them is immediate and personal.

Perhaps in our day it requires some effort to think of letters as constituting a genre. Less and less does correspondence play a part in personal relations, the exchange of letters between persons in some intimate connection with each other and concerned to convey the information that intimacy permits, and requires: the casual happenings of the day, gossip, reflections on large matters and small, the news of plans, of troubles, of griefs, of joys. It seems pretty certain that the later twentieth century will have produced a relatively small body of significant collected letters as compared with preceding centuries, beginning with the seventeenth, when letters may be said to have been first thought of as a genre. In the eighteenth century the posthumous collection and publication of the letters of notable persons, especially literary figures, became increasingly common practice. That so many letters were preserved suggests the high store that was set upon them not merely for reasons of sentiment, as personal memorabilia, but because of the intrinsic value they were thought to have.

Not all the criteria of literary excellence bear upon the genre of the letter. Indeed, an especial interest and a chief charm of the form is felt to lie in the opportunity it gives for evading the conventions of public communication. Good letters, it is felt, are those which are free from self-consciousness, which claim their right to be spontaneous and immediate, and even, if the mood dictates and the occasion allows, casual or willful. Yet some of the conventional standards of literary excellence do indeed apply, of which substantiality of subject matter, cogency of observation and reasoning, and sincerity and force of utterance are salient. Judged by these diverse criteria, Keats's letters are pre-eminent in the genre, even unique. No other letters communicate so fully their author's temperament as his do, or display so bold an energy of mind in the confrontation of the problems of art and existence, or move so freely from the trivial to the transcendent and back again, or convey so clearly the actuality of the writer's relation to the person he is writing to, or to himself.

It has become the laudable custom to print Keats's letters in the closest possible approximation to the way he wrote them, that is, without any editorial revision of his spelling and punctuation and with his stricken-out but still legible phrases preserved.

From Letters

To Benjamin Bailey,[1] November 22, 1817

My dear Bailey,

. . . I wish you knew all that I think about Genius and the Heart—and yet I think you are thoroughly acquainted with my innermost breast in that respect or you could not have known me even thus long and still hold me worthy to be your dear friend. In passing however I must say of one thing that has pressed upon me lately and encreased my Humility and capability of submission and that is this truth—Men of Genius are great as certain ethereal Chemicals operating on the Mass of neutral intellect—by [*for* but] they have not any individuality, any determined Character.[2] I would call the top and head of those who have a proper self Men of Power—

But I am running my head into a Subject which I am certain I could not do justice to under five years s[t]udy and 3 vols octavo—and moreover long to be talking about the Imagination— . . . O I wish I was as certain of the end of

1. A close friend of Keats's, who had recently visited him in Oxford, where Bailey was an undergraduate; it was on this visit that Keats composed the third book of *Endymion*. 2. For the development of this idea, see the letter to Richard Woodhouse, October 27, 1818.

all your troubles as that of your momentary start about the authenticity of the Imagination. I am certain of nothing but of the holiness of the Heart's affections and the truth of Imagination—What the imagination seizes as Beauty must be truth [3]—whether it existed before or not—for I have the same Idea of all our Passions as of Love they are all in their sublime, creative of essential Beauty— In a Word, you may know my favorite Speculation by my first Book and the little song I sent in my last [4]—which is a representation from the fancy of the probable mode of operating in these Matters—The Imagination may be compared to Adam's dream [5]—he awoke and found it truth. I am the more zealous in this affair, because I have never yet been able to perceive how any thing can be known for truth by consequitive reasoning—and yet it must be—Can it be that even the greatest Philosopher ever arrived at his goal without putting aside numerous objections—However it may be, O for a Life of Sensations rather than of Thoughts! It is 'a Vision in the form of Youth' a Shadow of reality to come—and this consideration has further conv[i]nced me for it has come as auxiliary to another favorite Speculation of mine, that we shall enjoy ourselves here after by having what we called happiness on Earth repeated in a finer tone and so repeated [6]—And yet such a fate can only befall those who delight in sensation rather than hunger as you do after Truth—Adam's dream will do here and seems to be a conviction that Imagination and its empyreal reflection is the same as human Life and its spiritual repetition. But as I was saying—the simple imaginative Mind may have its rewards in the repeti[ti]on of its own silent Working coming continually on the spirit with a fine suddenness—to compare great things with small—have you never by being surprised with an old Melody —in a delicious place—by a delicious voice, fe[l]t over again your very speculations and surmises at the time it first operated on your soul—do you not remember forming to yourself the singer's face more beautiful that [for than] it was possible and yet with the elevation of the Moment you did not think so— even then you were mounted on the Wings of Imagination so high—that the Prototype must be here after—that delicious face you will see—What a time! I am continually running away from the subject—sure this cannot be exactly the case with a complex Mind—one that is imaginative and at the same time careful of its fruits—who would exist partly on sensation partly on thought— to whom it is necessary that years should bring the philosophic Mind [7]—such an one I consider your's and therefore it is necessary to your eternal Happiness that you not only ~~have~~ drink this old Wine of Heaven which I shall call the redigestion of our most ethereal Musings on Earth; but also increase in knowledge and know all things. I am glad to hear you are in a fair Way for Easter—you will soon get through your unpleasant reading and then!—but the world is full of

3. See the last lines of "Ode on a Grecian Urn."
4. In a letter to Bailey some weeks earlier Keats had included the song "O Sorrow" from *Endymion* IV.
5. *Paradise Lost* VIII.452–90. Adam dreams of Eve and upon awaking finds her present before him.
6. A recurrent idea in Keats's poems is that through certain intense experiences of pleasure man might achieve a kind of divinity, an unconditioned existence which in *Endymion* I.779, he speaks of as "a fellowship with essence." It is this that he suggests by the "finer tone."
7. Wordsworth, the *Intimations of Immortality* Ode, l. 187. Keats loved to repeat this poem.

troubles and I have not much reason to think myself pestered with many—
I think Jane or Marianne [8] has a better opinion of me than I deserve—for really
and truly I do not think my Brothers illness connected with mine—you know
more of the real Cause than they do—nor have I any chance of being rack'd
as you have been—you perhaps at one time thought there was such a thing as
Worldly Happiness to be arrived at, at certain periods of time marked out—you
have of necessity from your disposition been thus led away—I scarcely remember counting upon any Happiness—I look not for it if it be not in the present
hour—nothing startles me beyond the Moment. The setting sun will always set
me to rights—or if a Sparrow come before my Window I take part in its exist-
ince and pick about the Gravel. The first thing that strikes me on hea[r]ing a
Misfortune having befalled another is this. 'Well it cannot be helped.—he will
have the pleasure of trying the resources of his spirit; [9] and I beg now my dear
Bailey that hereafter should you observe any thing cold in me not to but [for
put] it to the account of heartlessness but abstraction—for I assure you I sometimes feel not the influence of a Passion or Affection during a whole week—and
so long this sometimes continues I begin to suspect myself and the genuiness of
my feelings at other times—thinking them a few barren Tragedy-tears—My
Brother Tom is much improved—he is going to Devonshire—whither I shall
follow him— . . .

Your affectionate friend
John Keats

To George and Tom Keats, December 21, 27 (?), 1817

[In this letter Keats sets forth his doctrine of "Negative Capability," which has captivated the attention of critics and has often been explicated, although by no one so
well as by Keats himself. The intellectual attitude he describes and praises is actually
not difficult to comprehend, but perhaps it can be realized somewhat more sharply
if we bring to mind the response we make to tragedy. When, for example, Macbeth
comes to its end, we are not concerned about determining the extent of Macbeth's
evil-doing, or the justness of his doom, or the pitfalls of ambition. Although our moral
sensibilities have been deeply engaged, we do not make moral judgments at all. On
the contrary: we find, perhaps to our surprise, that our hearts in some fashion go out
to Macbeth; we separate him from his wickedness. We feel that the events we have
witnessed do indeed convey a significance, one that is beyond any practical moral
conclusion, but we cannot formulate what it is, and with this "half knowledge" we
"remain content"; we find ourselves in "uncertainties, mysteries, doubts" and take
pleasure in being there. Keats's formulation of Negative Capability, with its rejection

---

8. Jane and Marianne were sisters of Keats's close friend John Hamilton Reynolds, to
whom many of the letters are addressed. Keats's brother Tom was ill of tuberculosis,
from which he died on December 1, 1818. The "real cause" of Keats's illness was once
thought to be a venereal infection. W. J. Bate, Keats's most authoritative biographer, rejects
this. Bailey has been "rack'd" by the pains of an unhappy love affair.
9. Keats develops the implications of this attitude in the famous "Vale of Soul-Making"
passage in his letter to George and Georgiana Keats, February 14–May 3, 1819.

of "any irritable reaching after fact and reason," is an instance of the Romantic hostility toward that subordinate faculty of the mind which the German philosopher Immanuel Kant (1724–1804) called *Verstand,* generally translated as "understanding." See the first paragraph of Shelley's *A Defence of Poetry* and the second paragraph of De Quincey's *On the Knocking at the Gate in "Macbeth."*]

My dear Brothers
I must crave your pardon for not having written ere this & & I saw Kean [10] return to the public in Richard III, & finely he did it, & at the request of Reynolds I went to criticise his Luke in Riches [11]—the critique is in todays champion, which I send you with the Examiner in which you will find very proper lamentation on the obsoletion of christmas Gambols & pastimes: but it was mixed up with so much egotism of that drivelling nature that pleasure is entirely lost.[12]. . . I have had two very pleasant evenings with Dilke [13] yesterday & today; & am at this moment just come from him & feel in the humour to go on with this, began in the morning, & from which he came to fetch me. I spent Friday evening with Wells [14] & went the next morning to see *Death on the Pale horse.* It is a wonderful picture, when West's [15] age is considered; But there is nothing to be intense upon; no women one feels mad to kiss; no face swelling into reality. the excellence of every Art is its intensity, capable of making all disagreeables evaporate, from their being in close relationship with Beauty & Truth—Examine King Lear [16] & you will find this examplified throughout; but in this picture we have unpleasantness without any momentous depth of speculation excited, in which to bury its repulsiveness— The picture is larger than Christ rejected—I dined with Haydon [17] the sunday after you left, & had a very pleasant day, I dined too (for I have been out too much lately) with Horace Smith & met his two brothers with Hill & Kingston & one Du Bois,[18] they only served to convince me, how superior humour is to wit in respect to enjoyment—These men say things which make one start,

10. Edmund Kean, the great actor (1787–1833), especially notable for his performances of Shakespeare's tragic heroes.
11. That is, in his performance of Luke Traffic in Sir J. B. Burges's *Riches.*
12. Keats's review appeared in *The Champion* of December 21. The *Examiner* essay on Christmas about which Keats is so severe was by Leigh Hunt (see note 26).
13. Charles Wentworth Dilke (1789–1864) was a close friend of Keats. He achieved reputation as an essayist and editor. The house in Hampstead in which Keats lived with Charles Armitage Brown was part of a two-family structure, of which Dilke owned the other half. The house is now the Keats Museum.
14. Charles Jeremiah Wells (1800–1879), a poet, was a friend of Tom Keats. He played an elaborate hoax on Tom by fabricating letters from a fictitious lady; Keats never forgave him for this.
15. Benjamin West (1738–1820), American by birth, president of the Royal Academy of Art. *Christ Rejected,* mentioned farther on, is another of his paintings.
16. See the sonnet on *King Lear* in the letter following, in which Keats takes a rather more complex view of the effect of "disagreeables."
17. Benjamin Robert Haydon (1786–1846), a painter of note whose pictures were often of inordinate size. Several of Keats's letters are addressed to him. Disappointed in his ambitions, he committed suicide. His *Autobiography* is of considerable interest.
18. Horace, James, and Leonard Smith. The first two were notable wits and are remembered for their volume of parodies, *Rejected Addresses.* Thomas Hill, a book collector; John Kingston, a civil servant; Edward Dubois, an essayist and editor.

without making one feel, they are all alike; their manners are alike; they all know fashionables; they have a mannerism in their very eating & drinking, in their mere handling a Decanter—They talked of Kean & his low company —Would I were with that company instead of yours said I to myself! I know such like acquaintance will never do for me & yet I am going to Reynolds, on wednesday—Brown [19] & Dilke walked with me & back from the Christmas pantomime. I had not a dispute but a disquisition with Dilke, on various subjects; several things dovetailed in my mind, & at once it struck me, what quality went to form a Man of Achievement especially in Literature & which Shakespeare posessed so enormously—I mean *Negative Capability*, that is when man is capable of being in uncertainties, Mysteries, doubts, without any irritable reaching after fact & reason—Coleridge, for instance,[20] would let go by a fine isolated verisimilitude caught from the Penetralium [21] of mystery, from being incapable of remaining content with half knowledge. This pursued through Volumes would perhaps take us no further than this, that with a great poet the sense of Beauty overcomes every other consideration, or rather obliterates all consideration.

Shelley's poem is out & there are words about its being objected too, as much as Queen Mab was.[22] Poor Shelley I think he has his Quota of good qualities, in sooth la!! Write soon to your most sincere friend & affectionate Brother

John

To George and Tom Keats, January 23, 24, 1818

My dear Brothers.

I was thinking what hindered me from writing so long, for I have many things to say to you & know not where to begin. It shall be upon a thing most interesting to you my Poem. Well! I have given the 1st book to Taylor; [23] he seemed more than satisfied with it, & to my surprise proposed publishing it in Quarto if Haydon would make a drawing of some event therein, for a Frontispeice. I called on Haydon, he said he would do anything I liked, but said he would rather paint a finished picture, from it, which he seems eager to do; this in a year or two will be a glorious thing for us; & it will be, for Haydon is struck with the 1st Book. I left Haydon & the next day received a letter from him, proposing to make, as he says, with all his might, a finished chalk sketch of my head, to be engraved in the first style & put at the head of my Poem,

19. Charles Armitage Brown, a close friend of Keats. See note 13.
20. Keats had but little knowledge of the philosophical tendency of Coleridge and erred grievously in choosing it as a bad example. Of Dilke, in whose company the idea of Negative Capability had occurred to him, he later said, "Dilke was a man who cannot feel he has a personal identity unless he has made up his Mind about everything. . . . Dilke will never come at a truth as long as he lives; because he is always trying at it."
21. *Penetralia:* the innermost parts of a building, especially a temple. The word is not used in the singular, as Keats uses it, getting the form wrong; it should be *penetrale*.
22. *Laon and Cythna*, later entitled *The Revolt of Islam*. The publishers were distressed over its theme of incest between brother and sister, and Shelley was forced to revise it. *Queen Mab* (1813), written when Shelley was eighteen, is an attack on virtually every institution of society.
23. The first book of *Endymion*. John Taylor (1781–1864), senior partner of Taylor and Hessey, Keats's second publishers. He was an intelligent and feeling man and his dealings with Keats were honorable and kind.

saying at the same time he had never done the thing for any human being, & that it must have considerable effect as he will put the name to it—I begin today to copy my 2nd Book 'thus far into the bowels of the Land' 24—You shall hear whether it will be Quarto or non Quarto, picture or non Picture. Leigh Hunt I showed my 1st Book to, he allows it not much merit as a whole; says it is unnatural & made ten objections to it in the mere skimming over.25 He says the conversation is unnatural & too high-flown for the Brother & Sister. Says it should be simple forgetting do ye mind, that they are both overshadowed by a Supernatural Power, & of force could not speak like Franchesca in the Rimini.26 He must first prove that Caliban's poetry is unnatural,—This with me completely overturns his objections—the fact is he & Shelley are hurt & perhaps justly, at my not having showed them the affair officiously & from several hints I have had they appear much disposed to dissect & anatomize, any trip or slip I may have made.—But whose afraid Ay! Tom! demme if I am. I went last tuesday, an hour too late, to Hazlitt's Lecture on poetry, got there just as they were coming out . . . —I think a little change has taken place in my intellect lately—I cannot bear to be uninterested or unemployed, I, who for so long a time, have been addicted to passiveness—Nothing is finer for the purposes of great productions, than a very gradual ripening of the intellectual powers—As an instance of this—observe—I sat down yesterday to read King Lear once again the thing appeared to demand the prologue of a Sonnet, I wrote it & began to read—(I know you would like to see it)

'On sitting down to King Lear once Again'
O golden tongued Romance with serene Lute!
Fair plumed syren! Queen! if [of] far away!
Leave melodizing on this wintry day,
Shut up thine olden volume & be mute.
Adieu! for once again the fierce dispute,
Betwixt Hell torment & impassioned Clay
Must I burn through; once more assay
The bitter sweet of this Shakespeareian fruit
Chief Poet! & ye clouds of Albion.
Begettors of our deep eternal theme,
When I am through the old oak forest gone
Let me not wander in a barren dream
But when I am consumed with the Fire
Give me new Phoenix-wings to fly at my desire

So you see I am getting at it, with a sort of determination & strength, though verily I do not feel it at this moment . . .

My dear Brothers Your very affectionate Brother
John

24. *Richard III* V.ii.3.
25. Leigh Hunt (1784–1859), poet, essayist, and publicist, was one of the earliest of Keats's literary friends. It was he who first published Keats's poems, in his paper the *Examiner*. Keats began by admiring Hunt's poetry and fell under the influence of its easy "naturalness"—actually a colloquial looseness of expression—but later became alienated from it and rather impatient with the poet himself.
26. Hunt's *The Story of Rimini* (1816).

To John Hamilton Reynolds,[27] February 3, 1818

My dear Reynolds,

I thank you for your dish of Filberts—Would I could get a basket of them by way of desert every day for the sum of two pence [28]—Would we were a sort of ethereal Pigs, & turn'd loose to feed upon spiritual Mast & Acorns—which would be merely being a squirrel & feed upon filberts. for what is a squirrel but an airy pig, or a filbert but a sort of archangelical acorn. . . . It may be said that we ought to read our Contemporaries. that Wordsworth &c should have their due from us. but for the sake of a few fine imaginative or domestic passages, are we to be bullied into a certain Philosophy engendered in the whims of an Egotist [29]—Every man has his speculations, but every man does not brood and peacock over them till he makes a false coinage and deceives himself—Many a man can travel to the very bourne of Heaven, and yet want confidence to put down his halfseeing. Sancho will invent a Journey heavenward as well as any body.[30] We hate poetry that has a palpable design upon us—and if we do not agree, seems to put its hand in its breeches pocket. Poetry should be great & unobtrusive, a thing which enters into one's soul, and does not startle it or amaze it with itself but with its subject.—How beautiful are the retired flowers! how would they lose their beauty were they to throng into the highway crying out, 'admire me I am a violet! dote upon me I am a primrose!' Modern poets differ from the Elizabethans in this. Each of the moderns like an Elector of Hanover governs his petty state, & knows how many straws are swept daily from the Causeways in all his dominions & has a continual itching that all the Housewives should have their coppers well scoured: the antients were Emperors of vast Provinces, they had only heard of the remote ones and scarcely cared to visit them.—I will cut all this—I will have no more of Wordsworth or Hunt in particular—Why should we be of the tribe of Manasseh when we can wander with Esau? [31] why should we kick against the Pricks,[32] when we can walk on Roses? Why should we be owls, when we

27. John Hamilton Reynolds (1794–1852), one of Keats's warmest friends, was at this time a clerk in an insurance office but studied law and practiced as a solicitor. He was devoted to literature and had a gift for comic verse. His tombstone identifies him as "The Friend of Keats."

28. Keats is referring to two sonnets by Reynolds on Robin Hood sent by the twopenny post.

29. Keats held Wordsworth in the highest admiration and submitted to his influence in many ways. Yet no poet moves toward his own style and purposes—his own identity—without some dissatisfaction with the predecessors who have shown him the way. Although Keats further on in this letter speaks of Wordsworth and Leigh Hunt in the same breath and the same tone, he of course discriminated between them. Doubtless in the adverse things he says here about Wordsworth, Keats has much in mind the moralizing tone of The Excursion (1814), but his objections go beyond this.

30. In Don Quixote II.xli, Sancho Panza, the mad knight's literal-minded squire, having been hoaxed into believing that he has made a sky-journey on a magical wooden horse, gives a full account of the heavenly wonders he has seen.

31. In Genesis 48:17–20, Jacob, blessing his two grandsons by Joseph, says that the tribe descending from Manasseh will be of less account than the tribe of Ephraim. Keats makes Manasseh the type of respectable mediocrity. Esau, the free-ranging hunter, loses his birthright and also the blessing of his father Isaac to his prudent, scheming brother Jacob (Genesis 25:29–34 and 27).

32. Acts 9:5.

can be Eagles? Why be teased with 'nice Eyed wagtails,' [33] when we have in sight 'the Cherub Contemplation'? [34]—Why with Wordsworths 'Matthew with a bough of wilding in his hand' [35] when we can have Jacques 'under an oak [36] &c'—The secret of the Bough of Wilding will run through your head faster than I can write it—Old Matthew spoke to him some years ago on some nothing, & because he happens in an Evening Walk to imagine the figure of the old man—he must stamp it down in black & white, and it is henceforth sacred—I don't mean to deny Wordsworth's grandeur & Hunt's merit, but I mean to say we need not be teazed with grandeur & merit—when we can have them uncontaminated & unobtrusive. Let us have the old Poets, & robin Hood Your letter and its sonnets gave me more pleasure than will the 4th Book of Childe Harold [37] & the whole of any body's life & opinions. In return for your dish of filberts, I have gathered a few Catkins,[38] I hope they'll look pretty.
[Keats here copies two of Hunt's poems, *Robin Hood* and *Lines on the Mermaid Tavern*.]

Y^r sincere friend and Coscribbler
John Keats

To John Hamilton Reynolds, February 19, 1818

My dear Reynolds,
I have an idea that a Man might pass a very pleasant life in this manner— let him on any certain day read a certain Page of full Poesy or distilled Prose and let him wander with it, and muse upon it, and reflect from it, and bring home to it, and prophesy upon it, and dream upon it—until it becomes stale— but when will it do so? Never—When Man has arrived at a certain ripeness in intellect any one grand and spiritual passage serves him as a starting post towards all 'the two-and thirty Pallaces' [39] How happy is such a 'voyage of conception,' what delicious diligent Indolence! A doze upon a Sofa does not hinder it, and a nap upon Clover engenders ethereal finger-pointings—the prattle of a child gives it wings, and the converse of middle age a strength to beat them—a strain of musick conducts to 'an odd angle of the Isle' [40] and when the leaves whisper it puts a 'girdle round the earth.' [41] Nor will this sparing touch of noble Books be any irreverence to their Writers—for perhaps the honors paid by Man to Man are trifles in comparison to the Benefit done by great Works to the 'Spirit and pulse of good,' [42] by their mere passive existence. Memory should not be called knowledge—Many have original Minds who do not think it—they are led away by Custom—Now it appears to me that almost

33. From Hunt's *The Nymphs* II.170.
34. Milton, *Il Penseroso*, l.54.
35. "The Two April Mornings" (one of Wordsworth's most moving poems, as Keats in a less irritable moment must surely have known). "Wilding" is the wild apple tree.
36. In *As You Like It* the melancholy Jaques is described sitting "under an oak" philosophizing over the fate of a wounded stag.
37. The last canto of Byron's poem was soon to appear.
38. A scaly spike of blossoms, as of the birch and willow.
39. In Buddhist doctrine.
40. *The Tempest* I.ii.223.
41. *Midsummer Night's Dream* II.i.175.
42. Wordsworth, *The Old Cumberland Beggar*. l. 77.

any Man may like the Spider spin from his own inwards his own airy Citadel
—the points of leaves and twigs on which the Spider begins her work are few
and she fills the Air with a beautiful circuiting: man should be content with
as few points to tip with the fine Webb of his Soul and weave a tapestry
empyrean—full of Symbols for his spiritual eye, of softness for his spiritual
touch, of space for his wandering of distinctness for his Luxury—But the
Minds of Mortals are so different and bent on such diverse Journeys that it
may at first appear impossible for any common taste and fellowship to exist
between two or three under these suppositions—It is however quite the contrary
—Minds would leave each other in contrary directions, traverse each other
in Numberless points, and all [for at] last greet each other at the Journeys
end—A old Man and a child would talk together and the old Man be led on
his Path, and the child left thinking—Man should not dispute or assert but
whisper results to his neighbour, and thus by every germ of Spirit sucking the
Sap from mould ethereal every human might become great, and Humanity
instead of being a wide heath of Furse and Briars with here and there a remote
Oak or Pine, would become a grand democracy of Forest Trees. It has been an
old Comparison for our urging on—the Bee hive—however it seems to me that
we should rather be the flower than the Bee—for it is a false notion that more
is gained by receiving than giving—no the receiver and the giver are equal
in their benefits—The f[l]ower I doubt not receives a fair guerdon from the
Bee—its leaves blush deeper in the next spring—and who shall say between
Man and Woman which is the most delighted? [43] Now it is more noble to sit
like Jove that [for than] to fly like Mercury—let us not therefore go hurrying
about and collecting honey-bee like, buzzing here and there impatiently from a
knowledge of what is to be arrived at: but let us open our leaves like a flower
and be passive and receptive—budding patiently under the eye of Apollo and
taking hints from every noble insect that favors us with a visit—sap will be
given us for Meat and dew for drink—I was led into these thoughts, my dear
Reynolds, by the beauty of the morning operating on a sense of Idleness—I
have not read any Books—the Morning said I was right—I had no Idea but
of the Morning and the Thrush said I was right—seeming to say—

O thou whose face hath felt the Winter's wind;
  Whose eye has seen the Snow clouds hung in Mist
And the black-elm tops 'mong the freezing Stars
To thee the Spring will be a harvest-time—
O thou whose only book has been the light
Of supreme darkness which thou feddest on
Night after night, when Phœbus was away
To thee the Spring shall be a tripple morn—
O fret not after knowledge—I have none
And yet my song comes native with the warmth

43. That is, in the sexual act. The prophet Tiresias had been both a man and a woman.
When Zeus and Hera asked him to settle a dispute on this point, he said that woman
had the most pleasure. This made Hera so angry that she blinded him; Zeus in recompense
gave him the gift of prophecy.

O fret not after knowledge—I have none
And yet the Evening listens—He who saddens
At thought of Idleness cannot be idle,
And he's awake who thinks himself asleep.

Now I am sensible all this is a mere sophistication, however it may neighbour
to any truths, to excuse my own indolence—so I will not deceive myself that
Man should be equal with jove—but think himself very well off as a sort of
scullion-Mercury or even a humble Bee—It is not [*for* no] matter whether I
am right or wrong either one way or another, if there is sufficient to lift a little
time from your Shoulders.

Your affectionate friend
John Keats

To John Taylor, February 27, 1818

My dear Taylor,
Your alteration strikes me as being a great improvement [44]—. . . I am extremely indebted to you for this attention and also for your after admonitions—
It is a sorry thing for me that any one should have to overcome Prejudices
in reading my Verses—that affects me more than any hypercriticism on any
particular Passage. In *Endymion* I have most likely but moved into the Go-cart
from the leading strings. In Poetry I have a few Axioms, and you will see how
far I am from their Centre. 1st I think Poetry should surprise by a fine excess
and not by Singularity—it should strike the Reader as a wording of his own
highest thoughts, and appear almost a Remembrance—2nd Its touches of Beauty
should never be half way therby making the reader breathless instead of content: the rise, the progress, the setting of imagery should like the Sun come
natural natural too him—shine over him and set soberly although in magnificence leaving him in the Luxury of twilight—but it is easier to think what
Poetry should be than to write it—and this leads me on to another axiom.
That if Poetry comes not as naturally as the Leaves to a tree it had better not
come at all. However it may be with me I cannot help looking into new
countries with 'O for a Muse of fire to ascend!' [45]—If Endymion serves me as
a Pioneer perhaps I ought to be content. I have great reason to be content,
for thank God I can read and perhaps understand Shakspeare to his depths,
and I have I am sure many friends, who, if I fail, will attribute any change
in my Life and Temper to Humbleness rather than to Pride—to a cowering
under the Wings of great Poets rather than to a Bitterness that I am not
appreciated. I am anxious to get Endymion printed that I may forget it and
proceed. . . .

Your sincere and obligd friend
John Keats

P.S. You shall have a sho[r]t *Preface* in good time—

44. Taylor, as Keats's publisher, made corrections in the punctuation of *Endymion*.
45. An approximate quotation of the first line of the Prologue of *Henry V*. Despite what
the thrush said in the 19 February letter to Reynolds (see above, p. 772), it is plain
that Keats *did* fret after knowledge. The letter following expresses the same desire with
especial eloquence.

To John Taylor, April 24, 1818

My dear Taylor,

I think I Did very wrong to leave you to all the trouble of Endymion—but I could not help it then—another time I shall be more bent to all sort of troubles and disagreeables—Young Men for some time have an idea that such a thing as happiness is to be had and therefore are extremely impatient under any unpleasant restraining—in time however, of such stuff is the world about them, they know better and instead of striving from Uneasiness greet it as an habitual sensation, a pannier which is to weigh upon them through life.

And in proportion to my disgust at the task is my sense of your kindness & anxiety—the book pleased me much—it is very free from faults; and although there are one or two words I should wish replaced, I see in many places an improvement greatly to the purpose—

. . . I was purposing to travel over the north this Summer—there is but one thing to prevent me—I know nothing I have read nothing and I mean to follow Solomon's directions of 'get Wisdom—get understanding' [46]—I find cavalier days are gone by. I find that I can have no enjoyment in the World but continual drinking of Knowledge—I find there is no worthy pursuit but the idea of doing some good for the world—some do it with their society— some with their wit—some with their benevolence—some with a sort of power of conferring pleasure and good humour on all they meet and in a thousand ways all equally dutiful to the command of Great Nature—there is but one way for me—the road lies th[r]ough application study and thought. I will pursue it and to that end purpose retiring for some years. I have been hovering for some time between an exquisite sense of the luxurious and a love for Philosophy—were I calculated for the former I should be glad—but as I am not I shall turn all my soul to the latter. My Brother Tom is getting better and I hope I shall see both him and Reynolds well before I retire from the World. I shall see you soon and have some talk about what Books I shall take with me—

Your very sincere friend
John Keats

To John Hamilton Reynolds, May 3, 1818

My dear Reynolds.

What I complain of is that I have been in so an uneasy a state of Mind as not to be fit to write to an invalid. I cannot write to any length under a dis-guised feeling. I should have loaded you with an addition of gloom, which I am sure you do not want. I am now thank God in a humour to give you a good groats worth—for Tom, after a Night without a Wink of sleep, and overburdened with fever, has got up after a refreshing day sleep and is better than he has been for a long time; and you I trust have been again round the Common without any effect but refreshment. . . .—Were I to study physic or rather Medicine again,[47]—I feel it would not make the least difference in my Poetry; when the Mind is in its infancy a Bias is in reality a Bias, but when

46. Proverbs 4:5.
47. Keats was a Licentiate of the Society of Apothecaries, and as such might treat patients. In a letter of 1819 to George and Georgiana Keats he says that he thinks of going to Edinburgh "to study for a physician," presumably to take the more advanced degree of Doctor of Medicine.

we have acquired more strength, a Bias becomes no Bias. Every department of knowledge we see excellent and calculated towards a great whole. I am so convinced of this, that I am glad at not having given away my medical Books, which I shall again look over to keep alive the little I know thitherwards; and moreover intend through you and Rice to become a sort of Pip-civilian.[48] An extensive knowledge is needful to thinking people—it takes away the heat and fever; and helps, by widening speculation, to ease the Burden of the Mystery: [49] a thing I begin to understand a little, and which weighed upon you in the most gloomy and true sentence in your Letter. The difference of high Sensations with and without knowledge appears to me this—in the latter case we are falling continually ten thousand fathoms deep [50] and being blown up again without wings and with all [the] horror of a bare shoulderd Creature— in the former case, our shoulders are fledge,[51] and we go thro' the same air and space without fear. . . .

You may be anxious to know for fact to what sentence in your Letter I allude. You say 'I fear there is little chance of any thing else in this life.' You seem by that to have been going through with a more painful and acute zest the same labyrinth that I have—I have come to the same conclusion thus far. My Branchings out therefrom have been numerous: one of them is the consideration of Wordsworth's genius and as a help, in the manner of gold being the meridian Line of worldly wealth,—how he differs from Milton.—And here I have nothing but surmises, from an uncertainty whether Miltons apparently less anxiety for Humanity proceeds from his seeing further or no than Wordsworth: And whether Wordsworth has in truth epic passion, and martyrs himself to the human heart, the main region of his song [52]—In regard to his genius alone—we find what he says true as far as we have experienced and we can judge no further but by larger experience—for axioms in philosophy are not axioms until they are proved upon our pulses: We read fine ————things but never feel them to thee full until we have gone the same step as the Author.—I know this is not plain; you will know exactly my meaning when I say, that now I shall relish Hamlet more than I ever have done —Or, better—You are sensible no man can set down Venery [53] as a bestial or joyless thing until he is sick of it and therefore all philosophizing on it would be mere wording. Until we are sick, we understand not;—in fine, as Byron says, 'Knowledge is Sorrow'; [54] and I go on to say that 'Sorrow is Wisdom'—and further for aught we can know for certainty! 'Wisdom is folly'— So you see how I have run away from Wordsworth, and Milton. . . .

48. An amateur lawyer. James Rice, the friend of whom Keats said that he was "the most sensible and ever wise man" he knew, was a lawyer.
49. Wordsworth, *Tintern Abbey*, l. 38. This poem is salient in Keats's mind in this letter, both in his discussion of Wordsworth himself and in his speculations about the nature of human existence; from Wordsworth's account of the stages of his own mental and emotional development, Keats derives the idea of the "Chambers" of human life, discussed later in this letter.
50. *Paradise Lost* II.934; III.267.
51. That is, without wings.
52. A quotation from the fragment of *The Recluse* which Wordsworth had cited in the Preface to *The Excursion*.
53. The pursuit of sexual activity.
54. *Manfred* I.i.10. Actually, "Sorrow is knowledge."

. . .—I will return to Wordsworth—whether or no he has an extended vision or a circumscribed grandeur—whether he is an eagle in his nest, or on the wing—And to be more explicit and to show you how tall I stand by the giant, I will put down a simile of human life as far as I now perceive it; that is, to the point to which I say we both have arrived at—' Well—I compare human life to a large Mansion of Many Apartments, two of which I can only describe, the doors of the rest being as yet shut upon me—The first we step into we call the infant or thoughtless Chamber, in which we remain as long as we do not think—We remain there a long while, and notwithstanding the doors of the second Chamber remain wide open, showing a bright appearance, we care not to hasten to it; but are at length imperceptibly impelled by the awakening of the thinking principle—within us—we no sooner get into the second Chamber, which I shall call the Chamber of Maiden-Thought,[55] than we become intoxicated with the light and the atmosphere, we see nothing but pleasant wonders, and think of delaying there for ever in delight: However among the effects this breathing is father of is that tremendous one of sharpening one's vision into the heart and nature of Man—of convincing ones nerves that the World is full of Misery and Heartbreak, Pain, Sickness and oppression —whereby This Chamber of Maiden Thought becomes gradually darken'd and at the same time on all sides of it many doors are set open—but all dark —all leading to dark passages—We see not the ballance of good and evil. We are in a Mist—*We* are now in that state—We feel the 'burden of the Mystery,' To this point was Wordsworth come, as far as I can conceive when he wrote 'Tintern Abbey' and it seems to me that his Genius is explorative of those dark Passages. Now if we live, and go on thinking, we too shall explore them. he is a Genius and superior [to] us, in so far as he can, more than we, make discoveries, and shed a light in them—Here I must think Wordsworth is deeper than Milton—though I think it has depended more upon the general and gregarious advance of intellect, than individual greatness of Mind—From the Paradise Lost and the other Works of Milton, I hope it is not too presuming, even between ourselves to say, his Philosophy, human and divine, may be tolerably understood by one not much advanced in years, In his time englishmen were just emancipated from a great superstition—and Men had got hold of certain points and resting places in reasoning which were too newly born to be doubted, and too much opposed by the Mass of Europe not to be thought etherial and authentically divine—who could gainsay his ideas on virtue, vice, and Chastity in Comus, just at the time of the dismissal of Cod-pieces [56] and a hundred other disgraces? who would not rest satisfied with his hintings at good and evil in the Paradise Lost, when just free from the inquisition and burrning in Smithfield? [57] The Reformation produced such immediate and great benefits, that Protestantism was considered under the immediate eye of heaven, and its own remaining Dogmas and superstitions, then, as it were, regenerated, constituted those resting places and seeming sure points of Reasoning—from

55. "Maiden" in the sense of first, as in "maiden voyage," "maiden speech," or in the sense of untried, as in "maiden knight." The Chamber of Maiden-Thought corresponds to the stage of existence described by Wordsworth in *Tintern Abbey,* ll. 67–83.
56. A pouch, often elaborately ornamented, at the crotch of the close-fitting breeches worn by men from the 15th to the 17th centuries.
57. The open space outside the walls of the City of London where heretics were burned in the 16th century.

that I have mentioned, Milton, whatever he may have thought in the sequel, appears to have been content with these by his writings—He did not think into the human heart, as Wordsworth has done—Yet Milton as a Philosopher, had sure as great powers as Wordsworth—What is then to be inferr'd? O many things—It proves there is really a grand march of intellect—, It proves that a mighty providence subdues the mightiest Minds to the service of the time being, whether it be in human Knowledge or Religion. After all there is certainly something real in the World . . . Tom has spit a leetle blood this afternoon, and that is rather a damper—but I know—the truth is there is something real in the World Your third Chamber of Life shall be a lucky and a gentle one—stored with the wine of love—and the Bread of Friendship—. . . .

> Your affectionate friend
> John Keats

To Richard Woodhouse,[58] October 27, 1818

My dear Woodhouse,
Your Letter gave me a great satisfaction; more on account of its friendliness, than any relish of that matter in it which is accounted so acceptable in the 'genus irritabile' [59] The best answer I can give you is in a clerklike manner to make some observations on two principle points, which seem to point like indices into the midst of the whole pro and con, about genius, and views and atchievements and ambition and cœtera. 1st As to the poetical Character itself, (I mean that sort of which, if I am any thing, I am a Member; that sort distinguished from the wordsworthian or egotistical sublime; [60] which is a thing per se and stands alone) it is not itself—it has no self—it is every thing and nothing—It has no character [61]—it enjoys light and shade; it lives in gusto,[62] be it foul or fair, high or low, rich or poor, mean or elevated—It has as much delight in conceiving an Iago as an Imogen.[63] What shocks the virtuous philosop[h]er, delights the camelion Poet. It does no harm from its relish of the dark side of things any more than from its taste for the bright one; because they both end in speculation.[64] A Poet is the most unpoetical of any thing in existence; because he has no Identity [65]—he is continually in for [? informing]

---

58. Woodhouse, seven years older than Keats, was a barrister and the literary adviser to Keats's publishers, Taylor and Hessey. He was educated at Eton and was a good classicist and philologist. To his scholarly habits we owe the preservation of the early versions of Keats's poems.
59. "Irritable tribe"—of poets, so called by Horace, *Epistles* II.ii.102.
60. This striking phrase has established itself as the perfect description of one characteristic mode of Wordsworth's poetry.
61. When Keats says that "the poetical Character . . . has no character," he is playing with two meanings of a word of many meanings—character as the sum of the traits of poets of a class, and character as a strongly defined personal identity. But the reference is clearly to William Collins's allegorical figure in his "Ode on the Poetical Character."
62. See Hazlitt's essay "On Gusto."
63. The devilish villain of Shakespeare's *Othello* and the angelic heroine of his *Cymbeline*.
64. That is, not in action.
65. The paradox is that the poet, who has no identity, makes poems which, if they are truly poems, i.e. good poems, are so because they are themselves and cannot, as the poet can (see what Keats goes on to say), be "annihilated" by other identities. See the following letter, in which Keats makes personal identity, acquired through the experience of pain, the crowning achievement of human life.

—and filling some other Body—The Sun, the Moon, the Sea and Men and Women who are creatures of impulse are poetical and have about them an unchangeable attribute—the poet has none; no identity—he is certainly the most unpoetical of all God's Creatures. If then he has no self, and if I am a Poet, where is the Wonder that I should say I would right write no more? Might I not at that very instant [have] been cogitating on the Characters of saturn and Ops? [66] It is a wretched thing to confess; but is a very fact that not one word I ever utter can be taken for granted as an opinion growing out of my identical nature—how can it, when I have no nature? When I am in a room with People if I ever am free from speculating on creations of my own brain, then not myself goes home to myself: but the identity of every one in the room begins to [for so] to press upon me that, I am in a very little time an [ni]hilated—not only among Men; it would be the same in a Nursery of children: I know not whether I make myself wholly understood: I hope enough so to let you see that no dependence is to be placed on what I said that day.

In the second place I will speak of my views, and of the life I purpose to myself—I am ambitious of doing the world some good: if I should be spared that may be the work of maturer years—in the interval I will assay to reach to as high a summit in Poetry as the nerve bestowed upon me will suffer. The faint conceptions I have of Poems to come brings the blood frequently into my forehead—All I hope is that I may not lose all interest in human affairs —that the solitary indifference I feel for applause even from the finest Spirits, will not blunt any acuteness of vision I may have. I do not think it will—I feel assured I should write from the mere yearning and fondness I have for the Beautiful even if my night's labours should be burnt every morning and no eye ever shine upon them. But even now I am perhaps not speaking from myself; but from some character in whose soul I now live. I am sure however that this next sentence is from myself. I feel your anxiety, good opinion and friendliness in the highest degree, and am

Your's most sincerely
John Keats

To George and Georgiana [67] Keats, October 14–31, 1818

My dear George;
. . . Notwithstand your Happiness and your recommendation I hope I shall never marry. Though the most beautiful Creature were waiting for me at the end of a Journey or a Walk; though the carpet were of Silk, the Curtains of the morning Clouds; the chairs and Sofa stuffed with Cygnet's [68] down; the food

66. Characters in Hyperion, Keats's unfinished poem which he was working on at this time and which he left unfinished for reasons given in note 89.
67. George Keats married Georgiana Wylie in 1818 and with her emigrated to America, settling in Louisville, Kentucky. After numerous vicissitudes, he prospered for a time and became prominent in the life of the town, but ended in bankruptcy in 1841, the year of his death. Because the mail service between England and America was still disorganized and infrequent, Keats sent his letters to his brother and sister-in-law by private arrangements and he kept on writing a letter until such arrangements could be made; the letter following this one was composed over nearly three months.
68. A cygnet is a young swan.

Manna,[69] the Wine beyond Claret,[70] the Window opening on Winander mere,[71] I should not feel—or rather my Happiness would not be so fine, as [*corrected from* and] my Solitude is sublime. Then instead of what I have described, there is a Sublimity to welcome me home—The roaring of the wind is my wife and the Stars through the windowpane are my Children. The mighty abstract Idea I have of Beauty in all things stifles the more divided and minute domestic happiness—an amiable wife and sweet Children I contemplate as a part of that Bea[u]ty. but I must have a thousand of those beautiful particles to fill up my heart. I feel more and more every day, as my imagination strengthens, that I do not live in this world alone but in a thousand worlds—No sooner am I alone than shapes of epic greatness are stationed around me, and serve my Spirit the office of which is equivalent to a king's body guard—then 'Tragedy, with scepter'd pall, comes sweeping by' [72] According to my state of mind I am with Achilles shouting in the Trenches or with Theocritus in the Vales of Sicily.[73] Or I throw [*corrected from* through] my whole being into Triolus and repeating those lines, 'I wander, like a lost soul upon the stygian Banks staying for waftage,' [74] I melt into the air with a voluptuousness so delicate that I am content to be alone—These things combined with the opinion I have of the generallity of women—who appear to me as children to whom I would rather give a Sugar Plum than my time, form a barrier against Matrimony which I rejoice in. I have written this that you might see I have my share of the highest pleasures and that though I may choose to pass my days alone I shall be no Solitary. You see therre is nothing spleenical [75] in all this. The only thing that can ever affect me personally for more than one short passing day, is any doubt about my powers for poetry—I seldom have any, and I look with hope to the nighing time when I shall have none. I am as happy as a Man can be—that is in myself I should be happy if Tom was well, and I knew you were passing pleasant days—Then I should be most enviable—with the yearning Passion I have for the beautiful, connected and made one with the ambition of my intellect. Th[i]nk of my Pleasure in Solitude, in comparison of my commerce with the world—there I am a child—there they do not know me not even my most intimate acquaintance—I give into their feelings as though I were refraining from irritating [a] little child—Some think me middling, others silly, others foolish—every one thinks he sees my weak side against my will; when in truth it is with my will—I am content to be thought all this because I have in my own breast so great a resource. This is one great reason why they like me so; because they can all show to advantage in a room, and eclipse from a certain tact one who is reckoned to be a good Poet—I hope I am not here playing

69. The food miraculously provided for the Israelites during their flight from Egypt.
70. Keats's favorite wine.
71. Winander, in Wordsworth's Lake District and celebrated by the poet, is too large to be called a "mere," which means a small lake or pond.
72. Milton, *Il Penseroso*, ll. 97–98.
73. Achilles, the fiercest of the Greek captains who besieged Troy, is the central figure of the *Iliad*. Theocritus (*c.* 300–*c.* 260 B.C.) is the founder of the tradition of bucolic or pastoral poetry, which takes for its subjects the lives and loves of rustics, usually herdsmen.
74. Shakespeare, *Troilus and Cressida* III.ii.8–10.
75. The spleen was once considered to be the organ from which melancholy and ill humor arose. The usual adjectival form is "splenetic" or "spleenful."

tricks 'to make the angels weep': I think not: for I have not the least contempt for my species; and though it may sound paradoxical: my greatest elevations of soul leaves me every time more humbled—Enough of this—though in your Love for me you will not think it enough. . . . Tom is rather more easy than he has been: but is still so nervous that I can not speak to him of these Matters [76]—indeed it is the care I have had to keep his Mind aloof from feelings too acute that has made this Letter so short a one—I did not like to write before him a Letter he knew was to reach your hands—I cannot even now ask him for any Message—his heart speaks to you—Be as happy as you can. Think of me and for my sake be cheerful. Believe me my dear Brother and sister

Your anxious and affectionate Brother
John

This day is my Birth day—. . .

To George and Georgiana Keats, February 14–May 3, 1819

My dear Brother & Sister—How is it we have not heard from you from the Settlement yet? The Letters must surely have miscarried—I am in expectation every day. . . .

. . . .

A Man's life of any worth is a continual allegory—and very few eyes can see the Mystery of his life—a life like the scriptures, figurative—which such people can no more make out than they can the hebrew Bible. Lord Byron cuts a figure—but he is not figurative—Shakspeare led a life of Allegory; his works are the comments on it. . . .

. . . I have this moment received a note from Haslam [77] in which he expects the death of his Father who has been for some time in a state of insensibility—his mother bears up he says very well—I shall go to twon [for town] tommorrow to see him. This is the world—thus we cannot expect to give way many hours to pleasure—Circumstances are like Clouds continually gathering and bursting—While we are laughing the seed of some trouble is put into the wide arable land of events [78]—while we are laughing it sprouts is [for it] grows and suddenly bears a poison fruit which we must pluck—Even so we have leisure to reason on the misfortunes of our friends; our own touch us too nearly for words. Very few men have ever arrived at a complete disinterestedness of Mind: very few have been influenced by a pure desire of the benefit of

---

76. In a preceding passage which has been omitted Keats refers to the George Keatses' expectation of a child. It is characteristic of his imaginative tact that he does not speak to Tom of a nephew or niece Tom could have no hope of ever seeing. Tom died just a month later.

77. William Haslam (1795–1851), "a most kind and obliging and constant friend," as Keats called him, was in business in London.

78. This striking phrase, and what immediately follows it, may have had their unconscious origin in the famous passage from Milton's *Areopagitica:* "Good and evil we know in the field of this world grow up together and almost inseparably, and the knowledge of good is so involved and interwoven with the knowledge of evil . . . that those confused seeds which were imposed on Psyche as an incessant labor to cull out and sort asunder, were not more intermixed. It was from out the rind of one apple tasted, that the knowledge of good and evil, as two twins cleaving together, leaped forth into the world."

others—in the greater part of the Benefactors of & to Humanity some mere-tricious motive has sullied their greatness—some melodramatic scenery has facinated them—From the manner in which I feel Haslam's misfortune I perceive how far I am from any humble standard of disinterestedness—Yet this feeling ought to be carried to its highest pitch, as there is no fear of its ever injuring society—which it would do I fear pushed to an extremity—For in wild nature the Hawk would loose his Breakfast of Robins and the Robin his of Worms The Lion must starve as well as the swallow—The greater part of Men make their way with the same instinctiveness, the same unwandering eye from their purposes, the same animal eagerness as the Hawk—The Hawk wants a Mate, so does the Man—look at them both they set about it and pro-cure on[e] in the same manner—They want both a nest and they both set about one in the same manner—they get their food in the same manner—The noble animal Man for his amusement smokes his pipe—the Hawk balances about the Clouds—that is the only difference of their leisures. This it is that makes the Amusement of Life—to a speculative Mind. I go among the Fields and catch a glimpse of a stoat [79] or a fieldmouse peeping out of the withered grass—the creature hath a purpose and its eyes are bright with it—I go amongst the buildings of a city and I see a Man hurrying along—to what? The Creature has a purpose and his eyes are bright with it. But then as Words-worth says, 'We have all one human heart' [80]—there is an ellectric fire in human nature tending to purify—so that among these human creature[s] there is continully some birth of new heroism—The pity is that we must wonder at it: as we should at finding a pearl in rubbish—I have no doubt that thousands of people never heard of have had hearts comp[l]etely disinterested: I can remember but two—Socrates and Jesus—their Histories evince it—What I heard a little time ago, Taylor [81] observe with respect to Socrates, may be said of Jesus—That he was so great a man that though he transmitted no writing of his own to posterity, we have his Mind and his sayings and his greatness handed to us by others. It is to be lamented that the history of the latter was written and revised by Men interested in the pious frauds of Religion. Yet through all this I see his splendour. Even here though I myself am pursueing the same instinctive course as the veriest human animal you can think of—I am however young writing at random—straining at particles of light in the midst of a great darkness—without knowing the bearing of any one assertion of any one opinion. Yet may I not in this be free from sin? May there not be superior beings amused with any graceful, though instinctive attitude my mind m[a]y fall into, as I am entertained with the alertness of a Stoat or the anxiety of a Deer? Though a quarrel in the streets is a thing to be hated, the energies displayed in it are fine; the commonest Man shows a grace in his quarrel—By a superior being our reasoning[s] may take the same tone—though erroneous they may be fine—This is the very thing in which consists poetry; and if so it is not so fine a thing as philosophy—For the same reason that an eagle is

---

79. Actually, the ermine in its dark-furred phase. The word is often erroneously used to denote the common weasel.
80. *The Old Cumberland Beggar*, l. 153.
81. John Taylor, Keats's publisher.

not so fine a thing as a truth—Give me this credit—Do you not think I strive
—to know myself? Give me this credit—and you will not think that on my
own accou[n]t I repeat Milton's lines

> How charming is divine Philosophy
> Not harsh and crabbed as dull fools suppose
> But musical as is Apollo's lute [82]—

No—no for myself—feeling grateful as I do to have got into a state of mind
to relish them properly—Nothing ever becomes real till it is experienced—
Even a Proverb is no proverb to you till your Life has illustrated it—I am
ever affraid that your anxiety for me will lead you to fear for the violence of
my temperament continually smothered down: for that reason I did not intend
to have sent you the following sonnet [83]—but look over the two last pages and
ask yourselves whether I have not that in me which will well bear the buffets
of the world. . . .

The common cognomen of this world among the misguided and superstitious
is 'a vale of tears' from which we are to be redeemed by a certain arbitary
interposition of God and taken to Heaven—What a little circumscribe[d]
straightened notion! Call the world if you Please 'The vale of Soul-making'
Then you will find out the use of the world (I am speaking now in the highest
terms [84] for human nature admitting it to be immortal which I will here take
for granted for the purpose of showing a thought which has struck me concerning it) I say 'Soul making' Soul as distinguished from an Intelligence—
There may be intelligences or sparks of the divinity in millions—but they are
not Souls the till they acquire identities, till each one is personally itself.
I[n]telligences are atoms of perception—they know and they see and they are
pure, in short they are God—how then are Souls to be made? How then are
these sparks which are God to have identity given them—so as ever to possess
a bliss peculiar to each ones individual existence? How, but by the medium of
a world like this? This point I sincerely wish to consider because I think it a
grander system of salvation than the chrystain religion—or rather it is a system
of Spirit-creation—This is effected by three grand materials acting the one
upon the other for a series of years—These three Materials are the *Intelligence*
—the *human heart* (as distinguished from intelligence or Mind) and the *World*
or *Elemental space* suited for the proper action of *Mind and Heart* on each
other for the purpose of forming the *Soul* or *Intelligence destined to possess the
sense of Identity.* I can scarcely express what I but dimly perceive—and yet
I think I perceive it—that you may judge the more clearly I will put it in the
most homely form possible—I will call the *world* a School instituted for the
purpose of teaching little children to read—I will call the *human heart* the

---

82. Milton, *Comus*, ll. 475–77.
83. "Why Did I Laugh To-Night?" After copying the sonnet, Keats writes, "I went to
bed, and enjoyed an uninterrupted sleep. Sane I went to bed and sane I arose."
84. Perhaps Keats makes this stipulation because it occurs to him that the idea of the
developmental effect of suffering cannot, in ordinary compassion, be thought to apply to
those who, by reason of the circumstances of their lives and natures, are only passive to
experience. His doctrine, that is, is for persons who are so circumstanced that they can
think of their selves as material out of which something significant can be made.

horn Book [85] used in that School—and I will call the *Child able to read, the Soul* made from that *school* and its *hornbook*. Do you not see how necessary a World of Pains and troubles is to school an Intelligence and make it a soul? A Place where the heart must feel and suffer in a thousand diverse ways! Not merely is the Heart a Hornbook, It is the Minds Bible, it is the Minds experience, it is the teat from which the Mind or intelligence sucks its identity [86]—As various as the Lives of Men are—so various become their souls, and thus does God make individual beings, Souls, Identical Souls of the sparks of his own essence—This appears to me a faint sketch of a system of Salvation which does not affront our reason and humanity—I am convinced that many difficulties which christians labour under would vanish before it—There is one wh[i]ch even now Strikes me—the Salvation of Children—In them the Spark or intelligence returns to God without any identity—it having had no time to learn of, and be altered by, the heart—or seat of the human Passions—It is pretty generally suspected that the chr[i]stian scheme has been coppied from the ancient persian and greek Philosophers. Why may they not have made this simple thing even more simple for common apprehension by introducing Mediators and Personages in the same manner as in the hethen mythology abstractions are personified—Seriously I think it probable that this System of Soul-making—may have been the Parent of all the more palpable and personal Schemes of Redemption, among the Zoroastrians the Christians and the Hindoos. For as one part of the human species must have their carved Jupiter; so another part must have the palpable and named Mediator and saviour, their Christ their Oromanes and their Vishnu [87]—If what I have said should not be plain enough, as I fear it may not be, I will but [*for* put] you in the place where I began in this series of thoughts—I mean, I began by seeing how man was formed by circumstances—and what are circumstances?—but touchstones of his heart—? and what are touch stones?—but proovings of his heartt?—and what are proovings of his heart but fortifiers or alterers of his nature? and what is his altered nature but his soul?—and what was his soul before it came into the world and had These provings and alterations and perfectionings?—An intelligence—without Identity—and how is this Identity to be made? Through the medium of the Heart? And how is the heart to become this Medium but in a world of Circumstances?—There now I think what with Poetry and Theology you may thank your Stars that my pen is not very long winded. . . .

. . . This is the 3[d] of May & every thing is in delightful forwardness; the violets are not withered, before the peeping of the first rose; You must let me know every thing, how parcels go & come, what papers you have, & what Newspapers you want, & other things—God bless you my dear Brother & Sister

Your ever Affectionate Brother

John Keats

---

85. Children formerly learned to read from a primer consisting of a single page mounted on wood and protected by a sheet of transparent horn.
86. Images drawn from eating and drinking are salient in Keats's thought.
87. Oromanes is a version of Ahriman, in the Zoroastrian religion the principle of evil, which is combatted by Ormazd, the principle of good. In Hinduism, Vishnu, the Preserver, is the Supreme Spirit.

To George and Georgiana Keats, September 21, 1819

My dear George,

. . . In the course of a few months I shall be as good an Italian Scholar as I am a french one—I am reading Ariosto [88] at present: not manageing more than six or eight stanzas at a time. When I have done this language so as to be able to read it tolerably well—I shall set myself to get complete in latin and there my learning must stop. I do not think of venturing upon Greek. I would not go even so far if I were not persuaded of the power the knowlege of any language gives one. the fact is I like to be acquainted with foreign languages. It is besides a nice way of filling up intervals &c Also the reading of Dante in [*for* is] well worth the while. And in latin there is a fund of curious literature of the middle ages—The Works of many great Men Aretine and Sanazarius and Machievel [89]—I shall never become attach'd to a foreign idiom so as to put it into my writings. The Paradise lost though so fine in itself is a curruption of our Language—it should be kept as it is unique—a curiosity. a beautiful and grand Curiosity. The most remarkable Production of the world —A northern dialect accommodating itself to greek and latin inversions and intonations. The purest english I think—or what ought to be the purest—is Chatterton's [90]—The Language had existed long enough to be entirely uncorrupted of Chaucer's gallicisms and still the old words are used—Chatterton's language is entirely northern—I prefer the native music of it to Milton's cut by feet I have but lately stood on my guard against Milton. Life to him would be death to me. Miltonic verse cannot be written but it [*for* in] the vein of art —I wish to devote myself to another sensation.[91] . . .

Your affectionate and anxious brother

John Keats

To Percy Bysshe Shelley, August 16, 1820

[On July 27, 1819, Shelley wrote to Keats from Pisa saying that he had heard of Keats's bad health, cautioning him against the rigors of an English winter, and extending to him a cordial invitation to come to Pisa to live with the Shelleys. He went on to say that he had lately read *Endymion* again "and ever with a new sense of the treasures of poetry it contains, though treasures poured forth with indistinct

---

88. Ludovico Ariosto (1474–1533), Italian poet, author of the epic poem *Orlando Furioso* (Orlando Mad), 1516, expanded version, 1532.

89. Pietro Aretino (1492–1556), Italian author noted for the audacity of his satire. Jacopo Sannazaro (1458–1530), Italian poet; his *Arcadia* had a direct influence on Sir Philip Sidney's work of the same name. Niccòlo Machiavelli (1469–1527), Italian statesman and political theorist.

90. Thomas Chatterton (1752–70), poetic prodigy, whose pseudo-medieval poems have survived their discovery as fabrications. In despair at his poverty, Chatterton poisoned himself at age 17.

91. Keats made the same comparison between the language of Chatterton and Milton in a letter to Reynolds written the same day. He goes on to say that he has given up *Hyperion*—"There were too many Miltonic inversions in it—Miltonic verse cannot be written but in an artful or rather artist's humour. I wish to give myself to other sensations. English ought to be kept up."

profusion." Then, having spoken of his request to his publisher to send Keats copies of *Prometheus Unbound* and *The Cenci,* he says, "In poetry I have sought to avoid system and mannerism; I wish those who excel me in genius would pursue the same plan." Shelley, Keats's senior by three years, had advantages of social position and education that Keats could not but be conscious of, and, for all his difficulties, he was better established as a poet than Keats, who, in a few references to Shelley in his letters, shows a certain touchiness about him. In his reply to the letter, Keats takes courteous account of the kindness of the invitation and the praise, but seems to see a hint of condescension in Shelley's advice and replies with advice of his own which is not less to the point for having been occasioned by pride.]

My dear Shelley,

I am very much gratified that you, in a foreign country, and with a mind almost over occupied, should write to me in the strain of the Letter beside me. If I do not take advantage of your invitation it will be prevented by a circumstance I have very much at heart to prophesy—There is no doubt that an english winter would put an end to me, and do so in a lingering hateful manner, therefore I must either voyage or journey to Italy as a soldier marches up to a battery. My nerves at present are the worst part of me, yet they feel soothed when I think that come what extreme may, I shall not be destined to remain in one spot long enough to take a hatred of any four particular bed-posts. I am glad you take any pleasure in my poor Poem;—which I would willingly take the trouble to unwrite, if possible, did I care so much as I have done about Reputation. I received a copy of the Cenci, as from yourself from Hunt. There is only one part of it I am judge of; the Poetry, and dramatic effect, which by many spirits now a days is considered the mammon. A modern work it is said must have a purpose,[92] which may be the God—*an artist* must serve Mammon —he must have 'self concentration' selfishness perhaps. You I am sure will forgive me for sincerely remarking that you might curb your magnanimity and be more of an artist, and 'load every rift' of your subject with ore [93] The thought of such discipline must fall like cold chains upon you, who perhaps never sat with your wings furl'd for six Months together. And is not this extraordina[r]y talk for the winter of Endymion? whose mind was like a pack of scattered cards—I am pick'd up and sorted to a pip.[94] My Imagination is a Monastry and I am its Monk—you must explain my metap^cs [*for* metaphysics] to yourself. I am in expectation of Prometheus every day. Could I have my own wish for its interest effected you would have it still in manuscript—or be but now putting an end to the second act. I remember you advising me not to publish my first-blights, on Hampstead heath—I am returning advice upon your hands. Most of the Poems in the volume I send you have been written above two years, and would never have been publish'd but from a hope of gain; so you see I am inclined enough to take your advice now. I must exp[r]ess once more my deep sense of your kindness, adding my sincere thanks and respects for Mrs Shelley. In the hope of soon seeing you (I) remain

most sincerely (yours,)
John Keats

92. The statement was made by Wordsworth in his Preface to *Lyrical Ballads.*
93. *The Faerie Queene* II.vii.28, l. 5.
94. The marking on a playing card.

To Charles Brown, November 30, 1820 [95]

Rome. 30 November 1820

My dear Brown,

'Tis the most difficult thing in the world to me to write a letter. My stomach continues so bad, that I feel it worse on opening any book,—yet I am much better than I was in Quarantine. Then I am afraid to encounter the proing and conning of any thing interesting to me in England. I have an habitual feeling of my real life having past, and that I am leading a posthumous existence. God knows how it would have been—but it appears to me—however, I will not speak of that subject. I must have been at Bedhampton nearly at the time you were writing to me from Chichester—how unfortunate—and to pass on the river too! There was my star predominant! I cannot answer any thing in your letter, which followed me from Naples to Rome, because I am afraid to look it over again. I am so weak (in mind) that I cannot bear the sight of any hand writing of a friend I love so much as I do you. Yet I ride the little horse, —and, at my worst, even in Quarantine, summoned up more puns, in a sort of desperation, in one week than in any year of my life. There is one thought enough to kill me—I have been well, healthy, alert &c, walking with her— and now—the knowledge of contrast, feeling for light and shade, all that information (primitive sense) necessary for a poem are great enemies to the recovery of the stomach. There, you rogue, I put you to the torture,—but you must bring your philosophy to bear—as I do mine, really—or how should I be able to live? Dr Clarke is very attentive to me; he says, there is very little the matter with my lungs, but my stomach, he says, is very bad. I am well disappointed in hearing good news from George,—for it runs in my head we shall all die young. I have not written to x x x x x [96] yet, which he must think very neglectful; being anxious to send him a good account of my health, I have delayed it from week to week. If I recover, I will do all in my power to correct the mistakes made during sickness; and if I should not, all my faults will be forgiven. I shall write to x x x to-morrow, or next day. I will write to x x x x x in the middle of next week. Severn is very well, though he leads so dull a life with me. Remember me to all friends, and tell x x x x I should not have left London without taking leave of him, but from being so low in body and mind. Write to George as soon as you receive this, and tell him how I am, as far as you can guess;—and also a note to my sister—who walks about my imagination like a ghost—she is so like Tom. I can scarcely bid you good bye even in a letter. I always made an awkward bow.

God bless you!

John Keats

95. In a hopeless effort to recover his health, Keats sailed for Italy on September 17, 1820, in the care of one of his friends, Joseph Severn, an artist. They arrived in Rome in mid-November. After great suffering, Keats died on February 23, 1821. This is his last known letter.

96. This letter exists only in a copy and the copyist has thus represented the names of four friends to whom Keats refers. They are probably Haslam, Dilke, Woodhouse, and Reynolds.

Victorian Prose and Poetry

Victorian Prose

It has become common practice, almost the rule, to begin a summary account of the Victorian Age by noting the dramatic improvement in its reputation over relatively recent years. In the early decades of the twentieth century the word Victorian was not likely to be used except pejoratively, in condescension or contempt—perhaps never to such an extent had a new epoch defined itself by its explicit and passionate rejection of its predecessor. Victorianism was understood to be the sum of all that stood in the way of what the new age regarded as its own best characteristics, such freedom as is implied by mobility, such truth as follows from candor. No past age had ever been so precisely conceived as an entity with a personality and a conscious will which it sought to impose upon the human spirit and which had to be resisted. The essence of this gross historical monster was known to be an insensate devotion to respectability, with all that this suggests of compromise and conformity, of conceal-ment and dissembling. The classic statement of the view was Lytton Strachey's *Eminent Victorians*, published in 1918 to great acclaim, which undertook to "shoot a sudden revealing searchlight into obscure recesses, hitherto undivined," the implica-tion being that the Victorian Age was a vast hypocrisy, from whose face the mask was now at last to be torn.

Doubtless the change in this view was largely spontaneous, the result of the natural tendency of any cultural and historical animus to diminish in intensity and, in the process of time, to yield to curiosity about its object, then to a patronizing affection, and, at last, to serious interest and admiration. In the case of Victorian culture this development was reinforced by the uncertainties that began to overtake the spirit of the new age, leading it to perceive in the past age what it was beginning to confront in itself, the anomalies and contradictions which mark any cultural epoch and which, while they constitute its failure, are also the measure of its accomplishment. Viewed thus soberly and with the sympathy which arises from shared defeats, the Victorian Age came to seem very close to our own and to be, in some part, of its achievement, exemplary and enviable.

But one element of the earlier conception of the Victorian Age which has remained unaltered is the impression it makes of being an entity. And, indeed, this is how the age thought of itself. As we make acquaintance with its literature, we cannot but feel that no national epoch was ever so aware of its existence as this one, so filled with the sense of having a particular destiny, even of being charged with a unique mission. This national and cultural self-consciousness, which presents itself as a principle of integration overriding all social and political differences, even those that were extreme, is in large part to be accounted for by the pre-eminent power of England through the latter two-thirds of the nineteenth century. The English navy dominated the seas, gave England a decisive role in world affairs, and made possible the rule of the farthest-flung empire known to history, a hegemony which was dramatized in 1897 when Victoria, the queen of this relatively small island nation, at the Jubilee which celebrated the sixtieth year of her reign and made the occasion for an outpouring of the loyalty and devotion of her subjects, took the title of Empress of India.

The power of British arms, made fully manifest earlier in the century at the battles of Trafalgar and Waterloo, was sustained by British wealth. It was in England that the Industrial Revolution was furthest advanced; the English superiority in manufacture and trade was not effectually challenged until the end of the century. The new economic dispensation brought its characteristic problems, and in the degree that industrial growth was rapid these were distressing, yet the necessity of confronting them had the effect of enhancing Victorian England's consciousness of a peculiar destiny and mission, of confirming the epoch's sense of being different from all periods that had gone before it and being perhaps not really continuous with them. Nothing so much shaped the identity of the Victorian Age as its consciousness of being *modern*.

In this, of course, the Victorian period was continuing a defining trait of the preceding cultural epoch of the nineteenth century, which also was marked by a lively awareness of what Hazlitt called, using the phrase as the title of one of his books, The Spirit of the Age. The difference between the self-consciousness of the Romantic period and that of the Victorian period is chiefly quantitative—in the later period there were more people whose sense of life was decisively conditioned by their perception that the age was an entity about which quite precise predications could be made, as Carlyle made them in two memorable essays, one of which is called *Signs of the Times*, the other *Characteristics*. A simple index of the increase in the number of persons who shared in this consciousness of modernity is the proliferation through the Victorian epoch of the kind of periodical which took this set of mind for granted and served its interests. The Romantic Age had seen the establishment of great organs of opinion—*The Edinburgh Review, The Quarterly Review, Blackwood's Magazine*—which undertook to deal with problems, issues, and tendencies, doing so in a partisan spirit, to be sure, but with a show, by no means always false, of learning and serious thought. In the Victorian period such journals became far more numerous—*The Westminster Review, Fraser's Magazine, The Cornhill Magazine, Macmillan's Magazine, The Fortnightly Review, The Saturday Review, The Athenaeum, The Pall Mall Gazette* are especially memorable—and the size of their audiences grew. Nothing quite comparable to them now exists in either England or the United States. They were not directed to what later came to be called an "intellectual" or "highbrow" audience, although much of what they published would nowadays be thought appropriate to such an audience, but to a category of readers which their editors would have characterized simply as "thoughtful."

To read the files of these journals, or, what is a more likely experience, to read the best-remembered work of the great prose writers of the age, much of which made its first appearance in their pages, is to recognize not only the self-consciousness of the

Victorian period but also how strong a sense of community in his audience and with his audience a writer of the time could count upon. Such judgments are of course relative and this one must not be understood as intending to minimize the extent of the divisions of opinion that did of course exist. Yet we have only to listen to the voices of the great Victorian writers as they addressed their audience to appreciate the assumption they were able to make—that they were speaking to people who, in the face of all differences, knew that they had much in common, who were there to be spoken to. The intonations of direct address, of men speaking to men, is perhaps most explicit in the novelists of the day; in one degree or another, Dickens, Thackeray, Trollope, and George Eliot thought of themselves as directly confronting the reader, telling their stories with a due concern for his interest, comfort, and moral welfare. This show of companionly regard waned with the century and came eventually to be thought old-fashioned; it was replaced by an attitude which pretends to deny the actual presence of the reader or makes it but an inessential part of the act of narration—it is as though the reader is being permitted to overhear the speaker if he has a mind to. But for the Victorian novelist the reader was a personal presence, as the novelist was a personal presence for the reader.

This trust in the reciprocal relationship of reader and writer is characteristic of all the great prose of the Victorian period; it is a *speaking* prose. Its voices are various in their intonations, some being reminiscent of the pulpit, some of the floor of the House of Commons, some of an Oxford lecture hall or senior common room, but all are charged with the confidence that they will be listened to and that what they are talking about lies within every hearer's experience and comprehension. They talk much about here and now, about England and English life, and they count on their readers to believe that there really is an English nation, with particular problems to confront and decisions to make, and with a definable destiny to pursue. There has never been an American writer who could make a similar assumption—from the beginning America has been too vast to permit it. And although even at the present time the sense of community is probably greater in England than in America, no English writer can any longer make such an assumption.

To us today the rapport that existed between the writer and his audience seems one of the most remarkable and engaging aspects of the Victorian epoch. In an age of commanding public figures, none were more established in esteem and affection than writers. Dickens was admired and loved as no writer had been before or has been since. Carlyle and Ruskin sometimes taxed the patience of their readers but they came to be held almost in awe, as sacred repositories of truth. Newman was sourly regarded for many years after his conversion to Catholicism, but upon the publication of his autobiography, *Apologia Pro Vita Sua,* the tide of English feeling turned and he became the object of an almost tender regard. The instances can be multiplied to include virtually every important literary figure of the age.

If this responsiveness to literary and intellectual genius is indeed a salient characteristic of Victorian England, what conclusions may be drawn from it about the English people and national life? That the people were of an unusual sensitivity and profoundly committed to spiritual values? That the national life was being shaped by the powers of imagination and reason? At such proposals the admired writers of the age would have gaped in amazement. The audience to which they addressed themselves were members of the middle class, that great and growing middle class of nineteenth-century England whose dominant position in the nation was the wonder of Europe. This was the class which had made England the "workshop of Europe," an achievement which scarcely argued the likelihood that a spiritual ideal would have dominion over it, and the writers never wearied in their denunciation of its benighted condition and of the gross materialism of its interests. It was the class of which Matthew Arnold said that it was "drugged with business" and to which he gave the name of Philistines, the enemies of the Chosen People, of those who lived by the light of thought and beauty. Carlyle held it chiefly to blame for the social chaos of England and for the injustice and misery which so widely prevailed. Ruskin and William Morris scolded it for the moral obtuseness of which its style of life was an expression—it was the middle class, they said, that had made the cities of England dirty and ugly and their own homes ugly and vulgar. Dickens was remorseless in his mockery of its complacency and self-righteousness and in his reprobation of the unfeeling hardness of its self-concern.

If the middle class is properly to be described in this harsh fashion, surely it is a paradox or an anomaly that the national culture which this class dominated should have given so hearty a response to writers for whom the indictment of the failings of the middle class was a chief part of their enterprise. The contradiction can be quite easily resolved: a first step in that direction is to realize the sheer size of the middle class and the consequent variety of its component elements. Defined in its middling position by the working class below it and the aristocracy above it, the middle class ranged from shopkeepers and small businessmen through the owners of factories of one size or another to entrepreneurs and bankers, and it included members of the professions, whose increasing number was an important feature of Victorian life. The class was so little homogeneous in point of economic establishment that it commonly was, and might well continue to be, referred to in the plural—the middle *classes*, among which are to be distinguished a lower-middle, a middle-middle, and an upper-middle class, each marked by its own mode of life, social ambitions, and cultural standards. There was no discernible difference between the life style of the upper-middle class and the aristocracy, and association between the two was much freer than on the Continent. William Morris was the son of a successful stockbroker, yet his nineteenth-century biographer frequently refers to him as an "aristocrat." What made for this easy interfusion of classes was the English social category of "gentleman," which the great French social theorist Tocqueville found so remarkable and to which he ascribed the stability of English society in contrast to the periodic revolutions of the French; membership in the loose but significant order of gentlemen did not depend upon a man's birth and blood but upon his manners and mode of life. As compared with the affluent freedom of the upper-middle class, the existence of the lower-middle class was exiguous and precarious, yet by contrast with that of the working class it was privileged, and as such was a status which was cherished.

Given this much diversity within the middle class itself, it is not surprising that many of its individual members should themselves turn a questioning eye upon its ethos and seek to repudiate or meliorate those unamiable traits that were commonly ascribed to it. It is, after all, only within certain limits that the characteristics of his class determine the character of an individual. Thus, a certain James Ruskin rose from respectable but humble origins to become a prosperous wine merchant; he lived according to a religious creed of the rigorous simplistic kind which was often said to limit the intellectual and emotional range of the middle-class man but which in his case was tempered by a taste for books, paintings, and landscape, and this he indulged as he became more affluent. His son John was reared in all the strictness of the Protestant ethic, but he was not discouraged from indulging in his passion for the things for which his father had a taste and from them he derived the principles upon which he was to base his assault on English life as the middle class had shaped it. Those who read what John Ruskin wrote and, in one way or another, responded to what he said and held him in honor for having said it, were, like him, members of the middle class who had attained to a degree of freedom from this class ethos.

In the development of critical self-awareness in the middle class, an element of its historical tradition played a decisive part. The Victorian middle class was often said to be impervious to ideas at a time when ideas were coming to rule the world. Matthew Arnold made this a chief article of his indictment of the Philistine mentality and explained it as a legacy of the middle-class Puritanism of the seventeenth century, which he characterized as having been indifferent to ideas and preoccupied with right-doing according to an unexamined code of conduct. In point of fact, however, Puritanism, although certainly moralistic, was also, in its great day, highly intellectual; it brought to bear a current of ideas upon the established conceptions of society and the polity. Such intellectual activity was natural in an energetic class bent on power. And if in the years after the Puritan revolution it had abated, at least in that part of the middle class which was in the Puritan line of descent, now that the middle class was in a new stage of its progress toward power there was reason for it to be revived.

But however mistaken Arnold may have been in his understanding of the Puritan tradition, clearly he was right in the emphasis he put upon the predominantly Protestant character of the English middle class in its middle and lower reaches— upon, that is, its attitude of nonconformism or dissent vis-à-vis the established Church of England. Arnold will nevertheless have misled us if he is understood to be saying that the dissenting form of Christian faith was the sole, or even the most forceful, religious influence upon the culture of the age. The passionate intensity of the dissenting sects, of which he makes much, argues the continuing, even if diminishing, strength of the Church of England and its centrality in the cultural life of the nation.

Nothing is more difficult than to represent the religious situation of England in the nineteenth century. It is charged with contradiction. Any account of it must begin with the great religious revival of the eighteenth century which is associated with the name of John Wesley. This resulted not only in the foundation of the Methodist Movement as a powerful new dissenting sect, but also in the formation within the Church of England of the influential party of Evangelicism, which laid stress on personal conversion and on a pious rectitude of life and did much to overcome the worldliness and negligence of the clergy and the indifference of the laity. The effect of the revival upon the tone of English life in the nineteenth century was decisive; to it may be traced the high value set upon sobriety and respectability as the appropriate mien of a god-fearing people. Yet Emerson in his *English Traits*, which was published in 1856 and based on two extended visits in 1833 and 1847–48, says explicitly and without qualification that the English do not believe in God. In the course of the book he recurs again and again to what is for him the most admirable of all the traits of the English nation, its sincerity. These are people, he says, who insist that the truth be told whatever its consequences may be; for themselves and for others this is their first requirement, the thing they most respect. In only one department of life do they abrogate sincerity—they have no actual religious belief, and therefore, Emerson says, nothing is "so odious as the polite bows to God" which they are always making in their books and newspapers.

A judgment of the accuracy of Emerson's observation must be a divided one. It is both true and not true. As we look backward, it is plain to see that even before the second half of the nineteenth century the English were on the way to their present indifference to religion. The working class had for a considerable time been alienated from the Church of England and was becoming increasingly disaffected from the dissenters. Among the educated class an actual and conscious personal faith was becoming ever rarer. Yet though this was so, there was abundant reason to conclude that England was a religious nation. Nothing engaged public attention more readily than religious questions. The Oxford Movement was the effort on the part of a few learned and pious men to strengthen Christian faith and the Church of England by reviving doctrines and modes of observance which had fallen into disuse; no undertaking could have been more recondite, yet it came to have the status of a scandal, so eagerly was it followed and talked about, so conscious were people of its implications for the national life. The attempt of the church to discipline Bishop Colenso for questioning the plausibility of certain statements of the Bible—most notoriously the dimensions of Noah's ark, which, if it was of the stated size, could not have housed all that many animals—made a *cause célèbre*, one of several of similar kind.

It is true that every educated person understood the force of the intellectual tendencies that were putting religious faith at issue. Personal crises of faith were common. But the suffering they were presumed to entail was the measure of the high store still accorded a settled and assured belief: it was the more precious because it might at any time be called upon to undergo the ordeal of doubt or because it had done so and survived. As late as 1888 the reading public could be shocked, or at least titillated, because the saintly young clergyman who was the hero of Mrs. Humphry Ward's popular novel, *Robert Elsmere,* felt constrained by intellectual honesty to repudiate every supernatural element of his faith and to formulate on his deathbed a creed which could scarcely be considered religious at all, consisting as it did of nothing more than the imperative of social and moral effort. The great Gladstone himself took time from his parliamentary duties to review the book at enormous length.

Yet Emerson was of course right in his judgment of the state of English religion. Much of what passed for belief was mere habit of imagination. And this was becoming ever more difficult to maintain—less and less did it seem possible for the imagination to be at ease with the ancient picture of the universe that was essential to the literal plausibility of the Christian story. The traditional iconography of religion, whether it figured over the altar or in the mind, inevitably came to seem anachronistic, made so by the remorseless progress of science in establishing the scarcely imaginable vastness of the universe and the immutability of its laws. The universe depicted by science could not accommodate, except perhaps in some abstract and therefore not immediate and compelling form, a conception of man's destiny such as was described by Creation, the Fall, the giving of the Law, Judgment, and Redemption.

Sigmund Freud has said that the belief that the universe is purposive "stands or falls with the religious system." This is true, and nothing in the loss of religious belief was more painful than to be required to regard the universe as being without purpose, which is to say, without coherence, without meaning. When that happened, it might seem that the very foundation of the mind had been shaken, that reason was threatened with overthrow. It was thus that Carlyle experienced his discovery of the purposelessness of the universe—his despair brought him to the verge of insanity, as did Tennyson's in a like situation. The dark night of nihilism was a common event in the lives of thoughtful men of the nineteenth century.

Yet the Victorians did not easily surrender their hope of shoring up their faith in the purposiveness of the universe after the religious system had fallen. Carlyle, by an impassioned exercise of will, discovered the "open secret" that the universe, despite all appearances to the contrary, was a spiritual entity, by which he meant that it was capable of having an intention in which man was implicated. Tennyson, in In Memoriam, struggled through the bleakness of nihilism into which his perception of the manifest fortuitousness of life had cast him and reached a faith in an inherent universal purpose. All that Matthew Arnold permitted to be postulated of God was a certain—alas, not very decisive—tendency toward the establishment of moral good: God, he said, is "the power not ourselves that makes for righteousness." And although science seemed ever more strictly to deny that the attributes of spirit were to be found in the universe, there was one scientific development which might be thought ambiguous in this respect. The idea of evolution—which was current and influential long before the publication of Darwin's Origin of Species in 1859 dramatized and popularized it—did of course contribute to the doubt that man had his origins in, and his nature from, the special purpose of a divine creator, but at the same time it licensed the speculation that the universe was not wholly accidental, that in the development of forms of life from simplicity to complexity, from lower to higher, there was manifested an inherent end in view, presumably beneficent. In the late years of the nineteenth century this speculation was formulated (notably by the French philosopher Henri Bergson) in the idea of a goal-directed "life force." It gained a certain currency among the educated classes, and in the early years of the twentieth century it was popularized by the writings of H. G. Wells and Bernard Shaw. The implication was that the "life force" had the attributes of spirit and that it might even be thought of as Divine. It was an idea too abstract to win authority over either the heart or the mind.

Yet if the Victorians failed in their effort to sustain the hegemony of spirit in the cosmos, they achieved a quite impressive degree of success in another venture on behalf of spirit—their formulation of the possibility of its being established in and realized through society. Hegel, in his Philosophy of History, characterized the modern age, the epoch beginning with the Renaissance, by its accelerating commitment to what he called "secular spirituality." He meant by this that the Christian idea that the actual, quotidian world is antithetical to spirit and to the hope of spiritual perfection was giving way to the idea that it is exactly in the world and through the activities required by the world that the spiritual destiny of mankind is fulfilled. The energies of aspiration which were once directed to the supernal goal proposed by Christianity were transferred to the temporal scene, to the development of the human spirit in history. That development was conceived in terms of the defining attribute of spirit, which is freedom—the ability to transcend the limiting conditions of material existence and to achieve autonomy and self-determination.

The central issue of Victorian culture was whether society was to be regarded as a spiritual entity or as a material and mechanical entity. This question, it may be said, was prompted by the existence and condition of the working class.

In recent years a number of social historians have undertaken to show that the life of the working class in England in the nineteenth century was in fact not so terrible as it was represented to be, not only by Friedrich Engels in his famous *Condition of the Working Class in England in 1844* (1845) but also by academic scholars who did not share Engels's radical political bias. However cogent such revisionist arguments may be, they must obviously pertain only to the historical "long view" of the question; they can have little bearing upon what sensitive observers at the time responded to as the immediate social actuality. Doubtless we can uncover circumstances which in some degree qualify the many appalling accounts of working-class distress; and there are indeed tendencies to be discerned which, as they developed through the century, resulted in a notable melioration of working-class life. But these considerations can in no substantial way alter our understanding of the momentous situation which the Victorians confronted, especially in the early years of their epoch. Whatever in point of statistical precision was happening to real wages over this or that decade, or whatever the extent to which the diet of workers was becoming more varied, what inevitably comes home to us in indication of the condition of the working class are such gross and bulking facts as that in a particular month of a particular year, March of 1842, in consequence of an extended crisis in the economy, the official count of paupers in England and Wales stood at 1,429,089.

It was to this disaster that Carlyle responded by writing *Past and Present,* dashing it off in a white heat in two months of 1843. Expectably enough, among the emotions which inform the book compassion plays a large part, as well as bitterness over the deficiency of compassion which permitted so much distress to go without substantial relief. But the ruling emotion of *Past and Present* is neither of these but indignation at the way in which the social organization was viewed by those who held power in England. Carlyle has his quarrel with the aristocratic class but the chief objects of his anger and contempt are the middle class and the social theory that rationalized its practice—its absolute belief in the immutable operation of the given economic system, its never-to-be-questioned assumption that the economy is continuous with nature itself and that its processes are governed by "laws" which are as sternly indifferent to human preference and will as are the scientifically verifiable laws of nature. Although the human consequences of the operation of the laws of economics might be deplored by persons of good will, they were regarded by the middle class as so fixed that any attempt to interfere with them could only invite catastrophe. The doctrine of laissez-faire, of letting the processes of economics work themselves out, was sacrosanct. The law of supply and demand, by which prices and wages are governed, was as intractable as the law of gravity.

It needed a quite extreme degree of deprivation and suffering in the population to persuade even large-minded men to question such a view of the social organization. And perhaps it ought to be remarked that even these people directed their criticism not against the established form of society, with its extremes of privilege and deprivation, but only against the opinion that society, as established, was ineluctably bound by economic law and that it could not implement such intentions as it might have to prevent the suffering of multitudes of its members. Their judgment did not impute blame to the established and traditional form of English society, which is to say, to its class structure. Far from being concerned with social equality, Carlyle was committed to a firm class system. And this in general was the tendency of Victorian

criticism of the existing society. Matthew Arnold did indeed speak eloquently of a time when class differences would no longer exist; he was nevertheless content to accept them in the present. In his later years William Morris became a Marxist and envisaged a perfect equality among men, but up to that point he took class for granted as an inexpugnable condition of social life. As for Ruskin, who incurred the imputation of madness—of literal insanity—for having attacked the economic doctrine of laissez-faire, he was wholly conservative in the matter of differences of class status. The relation of master and servant, of higher and lower, these had been confirmed as a natural propriety by ancient traditions, including that of religion, and despite the fact that English society might permit considerably more social mobility than societies on the Continent, the idea of class, defined by differences in mode of life, manner, and personal temperament, was deep in the English grain (and still is) to an extent which it is often difficult for an American to understand.

Actually, in fact, the traditional relation of master and servant, of superior and inferior, which under feudalism had made the pattern of a whole society, was often taken as the criterion by which the relations that had come to prevail under the industrial dispensation were to be judged. What distressed Carlyle, and Ruskin after him, was that the social theory of the nineteenth century no longer considered the relation between higher and lower as a human and personal one, involving reciprocal obligations. By the factory owner the worker was regarded and dealt with not as if he were a fellow being, even though of a different social order, but as an abstract unit of the work force; between him and his employer the only tie was what Carlyle called the "cash-nexus": he was paid his wages, whose amount was determined by the iron law which applied to that transaction, often so little as to make his existence marginal, even problematical, and if the operation of cognate laws brought it about that there was no work, then there were no wages; the cash-nexus was broken without ado. Granted that in human terms this was to be regretted, the overriding logic of the prevailing conception of society, which had nothing to do with human terms, argued that it was necessary and inevitable, that society could no longer function in any other way. The machine had not only brought about a new method of production which had changed the nature of work and the traditional modes of life; it had also imposed itself as the model of what society is and must be, precluding from the social arrangement all possibility of mind, intention, and will.

On nothing so much do the Victorian writers agree as that the machine principle, the manifest antithesis to spirit, was corrupting the life of England. Its grossest, most readily observable effect was the dehumanization of the worker, who had become a mere element of the process of production, an object, raw material to be used at need, his cost as a source of energy reckoned in no different way than that of coal. But the dehumanizing influence of the machine principle extended well beyond this one class, and how far it went is suggested by Emerson in *English Traits*. Speaking of the admirable freedom of English life and the permission it gives to the expression of individuality, suddenly, without transition or any awareness that he is contradicting himself, Emerson says:

> Machinery has been applied to all work and carried to such perfection that little is left for the men but to mind the engines and feed the furnaces. But the machines require punctual service, and as they never tire they prove too much for their tenders. Mines, forges, mills, breweries, railroads, steam-pump, steam-plow, drill of regiments, drill of police, rule of court and shop-rule are

operated to give a mechanical regularity to all the habit and action of men. A terrible machine has possessed itself of the ground, the air, the men and women, and hardly even thought is free.

Emerson wrote in 1856, when life was far less mechanized than now, yet his sense of the—at least implicit—threat of the machine, even in a society which he characterized by the large measure of individual liberty it granted, was this drastic. His view was in accord with that of the Victorian writers. Between the condition of the working class and that of the privileged or even relatively privileged classes the difference was so great and so apparent as to lead Disraeli to make his often-quoted statement that England was not one nation but two. Yet the Victorian social critics make it their constant theme that the privileged classes, most especially the middle class, are equally in thrall to machinery—they too, although in subtler and less manifest ways than the working class, have suffered a disastrous curtailment of freedom and a diminution of spirit. Among Dickens's many representations of the deteriorated humanity of the commercial middle class, the character of Mr. Podsnap in *Our Mutual Friend* is doubtless the most memorable. From the name of this person Dickens derived the word (which came into common use) to denote the sum of typical middle-class attitudes, Podsnappery. Here is part of the famous first account of Mr. Podsnap:

> Mr. Podsnap's world was not a very large world, morally; no, nor even geographically: seeing that although his business was sustained upon commerce with other countries, he considered other countries, with that important reservation, a mistake, and of their manners and customs would conclusively observe, "Not English!" when, PRESTO! with a flourish of the arm, and a flush of the face, they were swept away. Elsewise, the world got up at eight, shaved close at a quarter-past, breakfasted at nine, went to the City at ten, came home at half-past five, and dined at seven. Mr. Podsnap's notions of the Arts in their integrity might have been stated thus. Literature; large print, respectively descriptive of getting up at eight, shaving close at a quarter-past, breakfasting at nine, going to the City at ten, coming home at half-past five, and dining at seven. Painting and Sculpture; models and portraits representing Professors of getting up at eight, shaving close at a quarter-past, breakfasting at nine, going to the City at ten, coming home at half-past five, and dining at seven. Music; a respectable performance (without variations) on stringed and wind instruments, sedately expressive of getting up at eight, shaving close at a quarter-past, breakfasting at nine, going to the City at ten, coming home at half-past five, and dining at seven. Nothing else to be permitted to those same vagrants the Arts, on pain of excommunication. Nothing else To Be—anywhere!

The connection that Dickens makes between the mechanical regularity of Mr. Podsnap's daily routine and his small-minded, egotistical view of art exemplifies a salient tendency of the Victorians' criticism of their society. In the resistance offered to the de-spiritualization of which the machine was both the agent and the metaphor, art played a decisive part. It may be said, indeed, that never before had art been assigned so large a function. This was nothing less than to supply the place of religion as the guide to life and as the guarantor and evidence of man's spiritual nature.

The view of art and its function which was held by the great Victorian critics descends in its essential characteristics from the Romantics. Coleridge had represented poetry as being the mediator between man and the universe, by which he meant

that the imagination, the chief faculty of poetry, served to transform the "inanimate cold world" of ordinary, quotidian perception into a living entity which, as it were in grateful reciprocation of this gift of life, sustains and enhances man's spiritual powers. Shelley had said that it was not the prescriptions of moralizing religion that made the true basis of the ethical life but, rather, the exercise of the imagination as it was brought into activity by poetry. In the succeeding period Matthew Arnold expressed strong reservations about the English Romantic Movement as a whole and was far from being in sympathy with the intellectual temperament of either Coleridge or Shelley, yet in effect he echoed their view of the power and function of art when, in his essay *The Study of Poetry* (see below), he said that "the future of poetry is immense" and gave as his ground for his prediction the failure of the religion of his time to engage the imagination as religion had done in the past. The purport of his essay is that poetry, in what he represents to be its highest development, can generate the large emotions, the confidence in a spiritual destiny, and the sense of the cosmic significance of human existence which were once exclusively associated with religion. In the intellectual generations after Arnold's there was less emphasis upon those qualities of art which might make it seem cognate with religion, but for Walter Pater and Oscar Wilde the experience of art and what followed from it in the way of heightened perception and emotion were in effect the justification of human existence.

Another, less transcendent, function which the Victorian writers assigned to art is summarized in a famous phrase of Arnold's. "Poetry," Arnold said, "is the criticism of life," by which he meant that poetry, which may be taken to stand for art in general, is the paradigm or model of what life ideally should be and is not. The intention and ability of art to impose order upon multiplicity, to achieve the beauty and significance of coherence, proposes the right conduct of public life. And the power of sympathy and compassion that characterizes art, its responsiveness to nature and man, proposes the right development of the personal life. Increasingly, under the influence of Ruskin and the most notable of his disciples, William Morris, the enterprise of art came to be one of the most readily available criteria in the judgment of Victorian life. The motives of the artist, his dedication to his work for its own sake, were set in opposition to the Mr. Podsnaps of the world, which were those of pecuniary gain and what that brought in the way of power and social advancement. The nature of his work, the gratification he found in its autonomous, self-sufficing purpose, stood in striking antithesis both to the alienated labor forced upon the working classes and the alienated occupations of the more advantaged. We in our time are more circumspect than the great Victorian critics of society in the credence we give to the idea that art has a redemptive and liberating power, yet some vestigial faith in it does remain with us and we still, if a little wryly, shape our conception of the good life according to the paradigm of art.

THOMAS CARLYLE
1795–1881

The career of Thomas Carlyle, at least up to its climax of achievement, may be thought of as a paradigm of English intellectual culture in the Victorian Age. The gifted peasant boy was bred up in the rigor of the Calvinist creed and destined by his family to become a minister of a church which was legendary for the piety and steadfastness of its members. In his university days he experienced an attenuation of his personal faith and found it ever more uncertain that he had a religious calling and, before many years had passed, his developing skepticism brought him to the point of entire unbelief. Yet the whole tendency of his thought in his characteristically best work was directed toward realizing for himself and enforcing upon the world a new form of belief which, by an act of inspired translation, he derived from the one he had repudiated—a secular spirituality which, in its demands upon faith and conduct and in the positive significance it assigned to life, was to be no less imperative than the religion in which he had been reared.

Carlyle was born in 1795 in the little town of Ecclefechan in Dumfrieshire, in the south of Scotland, the eldest of the nine children of a small farmer and stone-mason. It was from the "bold, glowing," and strikingly metaphorical speech of his father that he derived the outrageous boldness of his own style. From both parents in their confrontation of a necessitous life he learned the lesson of duty performed not as an imposed routine but as an expression of reverence for the divine Taskmaster of the stern but sustaining Calvinist creed. When he was eleven, the opportunities for schooling being limited in Ecclefechan, he was sent to the more populous town of Annan, where he lodged with an aunt and attended the local academy. There he was well grounded in mathematics and French and acquired some Latin and a very little Greek. In 1809 he went to Edinburgh to enter the university, making the hundred-mile journey from Ecclefechan on foot; he was fourteen, which at the time was the usual age of beginning students. His life at Edinburgh was penurious, largely solitary, and intellectually not gratifying, but he gave himself to mathematics and distinguished himself in that discipline and took advantage of the libraries of the city to read enormously and in every direction.

When he was nineteen, he returned to his old school at Annan as mathematical tutor, and two years later, in 1816, was appointed to a tutorship at a new school in the larger town of Kirkcaldy. It was while Carlyle was in Kirkcaldy that he read Hume and Gibbon and came to understand that he no longer believed as a Christian. A career in divinity being now at last out of the question and teaching being a hated blind alley, he went to Edinburgh in 1819 with a view to settling upon a profession. He thought of becoming a scientist or an engineer and for a short time undertook the study of law, but the *métier* upon which he finally settled was the precarious one of literary journalism. In one field of literature he became uniquely expert: his reading of Madame de Staël's *Germany* (1813) aroused his interest in German thought; he mastered the language and found in this different and brilliant culture the basis of the affirmation he was eventually to make against the desperate state of mind which had been induced by his skepticism.

The Edinburgh years were a black time for Carlyle. As a consequence of his loss of belief in its divine governance, the universe presented itself to him as a mere mechanism, and human life as devoid of all value and meaning. The despair in which the experience of nothingness issued threatened his sanity and even his life. This distress came to crisis in 1822, presumably in the way that Carlyle has described in the most memorable passage in all his work, the chapter of *Sartor Resartus* called "The Everlasting No" (see below), and it was fully transcended in the affirmation set forth in the chapter called "The Everlasting Yea" (see below), in which, by an act of the imaginative will, he conceived the universe to be not a mere mechanical construct but a spiritual entity, with its own intentions which, although they are but implicit, are yet discernible and give interpretable signs of their being at one with man's best hopes.

In 1822 Carlyle became a tutor in the wealthy Buller family, a post which gave him the opportunity to see something of the great world, including London, which he visited for the first time at the age of twenty-nine, and sufficient leisure to pursue his own work, which was becoming ever surer of its direction. In 1823–24 he published (anonymously in the *London Magazine*) his life of Schiller and in 1824 his translation of Goethe's novel of personal growth and development, *Wilhelm Meister's Apprenticeship*. Most of his writing at this time dealt with the achievements of German authors, by all of whom secular spirituality—the phrase is Hegel's—was taken for granted; without reference to the Christian God and giving no credence to the Christian cosmology, they understood man's life to be a spiritual undertaking which was no less exigent and no less momentous than it had been thought to be under the religious dispensation.

In 1827 Carlyle made his famous marriage with Jane Baillie Welsh, a young woman who was his superior in social position and his equal not, certainly, in genius but in intellectual vivacity and independence. The year following, the couple took up residence in a farmhouse at Craigenputtock, a property of Jane Carlyle's parents. The locality was not only isolated but dreary, and the six years spent there put a strain on the marriage, for Jane loved the pleasures of society; yet it was at this time that Carlyle began to make his name with the essays he contributed to the English journals and it was to Craigenputtock that Emerson journeyed to pay his respects in 1833 on his first visit to England.

In that year Carlyle decided to try his fortunes in London. He brought with him the manuscript of *Sartor Resartus* (written in 1830–31), for which he had hitherto failed to find a publisher. Its acceptance by *Fraser's Magazine* gave him the hope of an auspicious start, which, however, was dashed by the vehement dislike with which the difficult and eccentric work was met on all sides upon its publication in 1833–34. (It was, however, a resounding success in America when Emerson arranged for its publication in 1836.) In the two years following, Carlyle devoted himself to the research for and the composition of the work that was to establish him as one of the leading literary personages of his time and place, *The French Revolution*. Its success was delayed by the appalling accident that befell the manuscript of the first volume—Carlyle gave it to his friend John Stuart Mill to read and criticize, and Mill's housemaid, thinking it waste paper, burned it; Carlyle, after a night of anguish, dauntlessly resolved to rewrite the volume. When the work was completed in 1837 Carlyle said to his wife that he was ready to tell the world: "You have not had for a hundred years any book that comes more direct and flamingly from the heart of man." Many of the best minds of England thought this to be so and gave their assent to the passionate lesson it imparted with an unparalleled dramatic force, that a modern society characterized by falsehood, conventionality, and indifference will incur the terrible justice of a bloody end.

Over the next four years Carlyle's literary output took chiefly the form of lectures, of which he gave four series, the most notable being *Heroes and Hero-Worship, and the Heroic in History* of 1841, in which, against the rising tendency to interpret the development of nations and of civilization itself in terms of general and abstract causes, he set his intensely held view that the decisive element in all cultural achievement is the individual person of genius.

In 1843, being at the time at work on his life of Cromwell, he interrupted that project at the behest of his ever-growing concern with the "Condition of England Question" to write—in two months—the brilliant anatomy of English social and political life *Past and Present*. None of Carlyle's works touching upon the nature of man's life in community is more stirring in its representation of the anomalies and injustices of English society in its commitment to the principles of materialism and laissez-faire. Yet it is in this remarkable book that, while seeking to press upon the complacent classes the realization of the truth that we are all members of each other, he crystallizes his doubt that all men in their membership of each other can get done what needs to be done for the common good and reinforces his belief that authority and power must be invested in the hands of only a few.

From this point on, Carlyle's speculative powers coarsened. His dismay at disorder became a hatred of process—what needed to be done had to be done at once, by fiat, at command. He thought more and more in terms of salvation by absolute monarchs like Frederick the Great whose biography he wrote (published in 1865) and whom he did not think he had belittled when he said that this sovereign's appropriate surrogate was the army drill-sergeant. In 1867, as the Second Reform Bill was about to be passed, he published his intemperate essay *Shooting Niagara, and After?* in which he proclaimed that the extension of the franchise would inevitably bring chaos and ruin to England.

Thereafter, although he was to live for thirteen years longer, he was silent, partly in disgust and despair, partly by reason of a physical infirmity which made the act of writing difficult and eventually impossible. His wife died in 1866 and his grief was the heavier because of his guilt over the sorrow he had caused her by his curiously flagrant neglect of her in her last years. He lived chiefly in lonely seclusion although held in the highest honor—those who did not acknowledge him to be a seer still did not fail to understand that he was a genius. At his death in 1881, the Dean of Westminster offered burial in the Abbey, but Carlyle had left instructions that he be buried beside his parents in the Ecclefechan churchyard, without religious rites of any kind.

Sartor Resartus

When *Sartor Resartus* had gone through a few numbers of *Fraser's Magazine* (1833–34), one of the old subscribers expressed the judgment passed upon the work by most of its early readers when he wrote to the editor threatening cancellation if there was "any more of that damned stuff." We must not be too quick to scorn this blunt gentleman. If he was bewildered, there was reason for him to be, he was meant to be; if he had difficulty in comprehension, that was according to plan; if he thought the language outlandish, not even really English, so he was meant to think. *Sartor Resartus* is an outrageous book and if one is to get on with it, one must consent to be outraged. It is a work in the mode of the grotesque; it is willful, eccentric, intentionally putting stumbling blocks in the way of the reader's under-standing. By turns it is mock-solemn and truly solemn, comic and sentimental, ironic and passionate. It levies on many genres and is by turns a treatise on sociology, a discourse on philosophy, a sentimental novel, a series of sermons, a satire on pedantic scholarship, a biography, a cryptic autobiography. Its very language confounds expec-tation, only reluctantly consents to be English, and proclaims itself as never com-fortable unless it is in close touch with German. In its teasing arbitrariness *Sartor Resartus* is in the line of descent from Rabelais's *Gargantua and Pantagruel* and Sterne's *Tristram Shandy;* it draws on the elaborate ironic humor of Jean Paul Richter's tales. And it was not for nothing that in his university days Carlyle was nicknamed "Jonathan" and "the Dean"—there is much of Swift in the book and the famous garment of *The Tale of a Tub* had a decisive part in its first conception.

The Latin phrase that is its title means "the tailor retailored" or "the tailor reclothed." The metaphor of clothing has two distinct references. One is to the ma-terial world, which is the garment of indwelling spirit. The other is to human institu-tions which clothe the spirit of man in its communal existence. In the former use of the metaphor, both the spirit and the garment are essentially immutable. In the latter use, the spirit is variable and the garments which invest it may become outgrown or go out of fashion and must from time to time be discarded for new ones.

The work purports to be an account of a treatise on the Philosophy of Clothes by a scholar who once held the professorial chair of Things-in-General at the German University of Weissnichtwo, which is to say Know-not-where. The account is given by an English writer, who refers to himself as the Editor; in his youth he visited Weissnichtwo and here made the acquaintance of the Professor. In his enterprise he receives the assistance of the Professor's closest friend and associate, a worthy man named Heuschrecke (Scarecrow), who sends him masses of manuscripts found among the Professor's effects, some of them autobiographical.

This material became available not through the Professor's death but through his mysterious disappearance; it is suggested that some day he will return as mysteriously as he vanished. The name of the Professor is Diogenes Teufelsdröckh: Diogenes means "born of God," Teufelsdröckh is "devil's dung." The conjunction of the two names proposes the dual nature of man.

Book I consists of the Editor's paraphrase of Teufelsdröckh's extrapolation of the clothes metaphor and this is resumed in the third and last book, which ends with the news of the mysterious disappearance. Book II is devoted to the biography of Teufelsdröckh, beginning with a mysterious and reverend stranger bringing him, a new-born infant in a basket, to an aged and worthy couple in the little town of Entefuhl (Duck Puddle) and putting him in their charge. In the basket are gold coins and other indications of the exalted—by which is implied the divine—lineage of the child. It cannot fail to be seen that the legendary account of the child's developing sense of himself and the world is based upon Carlyle's own experience. After his university days the young Teufelsdröckh becomes a tutor in a noble family and falls in love with the daughter of the house, Blumine. His hope of ever winning his beloved is frustrated by the difference in their social positions and also by Blumine's having fallen in love with his English friend, Towgood. After a period of wandering over the world, seeking surcease from his sorrow over his loss, Teufels-dröckh undergoes, as Carlyle did, the metaphysical crisis which is the climax of the book.

In written German all nouns are capitalized, and it is one of the idiosyncrasies of Carlyle's style that he approximates this practice.

From Sartor Resartus

The Everlasting No [1]

Under the strange nebulous envelopment, wherein our Professor has now shrouded himself, no doubt but his spiritual nature is nevertheless progressive, and growing: for how can the 'Son of Time,' in any case, stand still? We behold him, through those dim years, in a state of crisis, of transition: his mad Pilgrimings, and general solution into aimless Discontinuity, what is all this but a mad Fermentation; wherefrom, the fiercer it is, the clearer product will one day evolve itself?

Such transitions are ever full of pain: thus the Eagle when he moults is sickly; and, to attain his new beak, must harshly dash-off the old one upon rocks. What Stoicism soever our Wanderer, in his individual acts and motions, may affect, it is clear that there is a hot fever of anarchy and misery raging within; coruscations of which flash out: as, indeed, how could there be other? Have we not seen him disappointed, bemocked of Destiny, through long years? All that the young heart might desire and pray for has been denied; nay, as in the last worst instance, offered and then snatched away. Ever an 'excellent Passivity'; but of useful, reasonable Activity, essential to the former as Food to Hunger, nothing granted: till at length, in this wild Pilgrimage, he must forcibly seize for himself an Activity, though useless, unreasonable. Alas, his cup of bitterness, which had been filling drop by drop, ever since that first 'ruddy morning' in the Hinterschlag Gymnasium,[2] was at the very lip; and then with that poison-drop, of the Towgood-and-Blumine [3] business, it runs-over, and even hisses-over in a deluge of foam.

He himself says once, with more justice than originality: 'Man is, properly speaking, based upon Hope, he has no other possession but Hope; this world of his is emphatically the Place of Hope.' What, then, was our Professor's possession? We see him, for the present, quite shut-out from Hope; looking not into the golden orient, but vaguely all round into a dim copper firmament, pregnant with earthquake and tornado.

Alas, shut-out from Hope, in a deeper sense than we yet dream of! For, as he wanders wearisomely through this world, he has now lost all tidings of another and higher.[4] Full of religion, or at least of religiosity,[5] as our Friend has since exhibited himself, he hides not that, in those days, he was wholly

1. This selection is from Bk. II, Chap. VII.
2. A Gymnasium is a German classical secondary school. The name of this one is Behind-beat.
3. The immediate cause of Teufelsdröckh's despair is the loss of Blumine, the girl he loved, to his English friend Towgood.
4. Presumably under the influence of rationalism he has lost his religious faith.
5. Carlyle probably intends this word to mean a disposition to be religious. It now has the pejorative meaning of an excessive or affected piety.

irreligious: 'Doubt had darkened into Unbelief,' says he; 'shade after shade goes grimly over your soul, till you have the fixed, starless, Tartarean[6] black.' To such readers as have reflected, what can be called reflecting, on man's life, and happily discovered, in contradiction to much Profit-and-loss Philosophy,[7] speculative and practical, that Soul is *not* synonymous with Stomach; who understand, therefore, in our Friend's words, 'that, for man's well-being, Faith is properly the one thing needful; how, with it, Martyrs, otherwise weak, can cheerfully endure the shame and the cross; and without it, worldlings puke-up their sick existence, by suicide, in the midst of luxury': to such it will be clear that, for a pure moral nature, the loss of his religious Belief was the loss of everything. Unhappy young man! All wounds, the crush of long-continued Destitution, the stab of false Friendship and of false Love, all wounds in thy so genial heart, would have healed again, had not its life-warmth been withdrawn. Well might he exclaim, in his wild way: 'Is there no God, then; but at best an absentee God, sitting idle, ever since the first Sabbath, at the outside of his Universe, and *seeing* it go?[8] Has the word Duty no meaning;[9] is what we call Duty no divine Messenger and Guide, but a false earthly Fantasm, made-up of Desire and Fear, of emanations from the Gallows and from Dr. Graham's Celestial-Bed?[10] Happiness of an approving Conscience! Did not Paul of Tarsus, whom admiring men have since named Saint, feel that *he* was "the chief of sinners";[11] and Nero of Rome, jocund in spirit (*wohlgemuth*), spend much of his time in fiddling? Foolish Word-monger and Motive-grinder, who in thy Logic-mill hast an earthly mechanism for the Godlike itself, and wouldst fain grind me out Virtue from the husks of Pleasure,—I tell thee, Nay! To the unregenerate Prometheus Vinctus[12] of a man, it is ever the bitterest aggravation of his wretchedness that he is conscious of Virtue, that he feels himself the victim not of suffering only, but of injustice. What then? Is the heroic inspiration we name Virtue but some Passion; some bubble of the blood, bubbling in the direction others *profit* by? I know not: only this I know, If what thou namest Happiness be our true aim, then are we all astray. With Stupidity and sound Digestion man may front much. But what, in these dull unimaginative days, are the terrors of Conscience to the diseases of the Liver! Not on Morality, but on Cookery, let us build our stronghold: there brandishing our frying-pan, as censer, let us offer sweet incense to the Devil, and live at ease on the fat things *he* has provided for his Elect!'

Thus has the bewildered Wanderer to stand, as so many have done, shouting

6. Tartarus was the innermost region of Hades in the *Iliad*.

7. A reference to the ethical theory of Utilitarianism, which proposed that the desirability of an action could be determined by a calculation of the degree of pleasure or of pain it would give rise to.

8. A summary of the Deist conception of the relation of God to the universe—once the universe had been brought into being and set in motion, God had no involvement with it.

9. In the mechanical universe of the Deists there is no inherent moral law—the God of that universe makes no demands upon mankind.

10. James Graham (1745–94), a famous quack doctor, invented a bed which he claimed cured sterility.

11. I Timothy 1:15.

12. Prometheus Bound; the title of Aeschylus' play in which the rebellious Titan, chained to a rock by command of Zeus, defies his tormentor.

question after question into the Sibyl-cave of Destiny, and receive no Answer but an Echo. It is all a grim Desert, this once-fair world of his; wherein is heard only the howling of wild-beasts, or the shrieks of despairing, hate-filled men; and no Pillar of Cloud by day, and no Pillar of Fire by night, any longer guides the Pilgrim. To such length has the spirit of Inquiry carried him. 'But what boots it (*was thut's*)?' cries he: 'it is but the common lot in this era. Not having come to spiritual majority prior to the *Siècle de Louis Quinze*,[13] and not being born purely a Loghead (*Dummkopf*), thou hadst no other outlook. The whole world is, like thee, sold to Unbelief; their old Temples of the Godhead, which for long have not been rainproof, crumble down; and men ask now. Where is the Godhead; our eyes never saw him?'

Pitiful enough were it, for all these wild utterances, to call our Diogenes wicked. Unprofitable servants as we all are, perhaps at no era of his life was he more decisively the Servant of Goodness, the Servant of God, than even now when doubting God's existence. 'One circumstance I note,' says he: 'after all the nameless woe that Inquiry, which for me, what it is not always, was genuine Love of Truth, had wrought me, I nevertheless still loved Truth, and would bate no jot of my allegiance to her. "Truth!" I cried, "though the Heavens crush me for following her: no Falsehood! though a whole celestial Lubberland[14] were the price of Apostasy." In conduct it was the same. Had a divine Messenger from the clouds, or miraculous Handwriting on the wall, convincingly proclaimed to me *This thou shalt do*, with what passionate readiness, as I often thought, would I have done it, had it been leaping into the infernal Fire. Thus, in spite of all Motive-grinders, and Mechanical Profit-and-Loss Philosophies, with the sick ophthalmia and hallucination they had brought on, was the Infinite nature of Duty[15] still dimly present to me: living without God in the world, of God's light I was not utterly bereft; if my as yet sealed eyes, with their unspeakable longing, could nowhere see Him, nevertheless in my heart He was present, and His heaven-written Law still stood legible and sacred there.'

Meanwhile, under all these tribulations, and temporal and spiritual destitutions, what must the Wanderer, in his silent soul, have endured! 'The painfullest feeling,' writes he, 'is that of your own Feebleness (*Unkraft*); ever, as the English Milton says, to be weak is the true misery.[16] And yet of your Strength there is and can be no clear feeling, save by what you have prospered in, by what you have done. Between vague wavering Capability and fixed indubitable Performance, what a difference! A certain inarticulate Self-consciousness dwells dimly in us; which only our Works can render articulate and decisively discernible. Our Works are the mirror wherein the spirit first sees its natural lineaments. Hence, too, the folly of that impossible Precept, *Know thyself*;[17] till it be translated into this partially possible one, *Know what thou canst work-at*.

13. "The century of Louis XV"; Carlyle has in mind Voltaire's historical work of that name, which gives an account of the development of the Age of Reason, which Carlyle detested.
14. An imaginary land of plenty and laziness.
15. Infinite in the sense of being absolute, by implication divine.
16. *Paradise Lost* I.157: "To be weak is miserable."
17. This maxim was inscribed on the temple of Apollo at Delphi.

'But for me, so strangely unprosperous had I been, the net-result of my Workings amounted as yet simply to—Nothing. How then could I believe in my Strength, when there was as yet no mirror to see it in? Ever did this agitating, yet, as I now perceive, quite frivolous question, remain to me insoluble: Hast thou a certain Faculty, a certain Worth, such even as the most have not; or art thou the completest Dullard of these modern times? Alas! the fearful Unbelief is unbelief in yourself; and how could I believe? Had not my first, last Faith in myself, when even to me the Heavens seemed laid open, and I dared to love, been all-too cruelly belied? The speculative Mystery of Life grew ever more mysterious to me: neither in the practical Mystery [18] had I made the slightest progress, but been everywhere buffeted, foiled, and contemptuously cast-out. A feeble unit in the middle of a threatening Infinitude, I seemed to have nothing given me but eyes, whereby to discern my own wretchedness. Invisible yet impenetrable walls, as of Enchantment, divided me from all living: was there, in the wide world, any true bosom I could press trustfully to mine? O Heaven, No, there was none! I kept a lock upon my lips: why should I speak much with that shifting variety of so-called Friends, in whose withered, vain and too-hungry souls Friendship was but an incredible tradition? In such cases, your resource is to talk little, and that little mostly from the Newspapers. Now when I look back, it was a strange isolation I then lived in. Then men and women around me, even speaking with me, were but Figures; I had, practically, forgotten that they were alive, that they were not merely automatic. In midst of their crowded streets and assemblages, I walked solitary; and (except as it was my own heart, not another's, that I kept devouring) savage also, as the tiger in his jungle. Some comfort it would have been, could I, like a Faust, have fancied myself tempted and tormented of the Devil; for a Hell, as I imagine, without Life, though only diabolic Life, were more frightful: but in our age of Down-pulling and Disbelief, the very Devil has been pulled down, you cannot so much as believe in a Devil.[19] To me the Universe was all void of Life, of Purpose, of Volition, even of Hostility: it was one huge, dead, immeasurable Steam-engine, rolling on, in its dead indifference, to grind me limb from limb. O, the vast, gloomy, solitary Golgotha,[20] and Mill of Death! Why was the Living banished thither companionless, conscious? Why, if there is no Devil; nay, unless the Devil is your God?'

A prey incessantly to such corrosions, might not, moreover, as the worst aggravation to them, the iron constitution even of a Teufelsdröckh threaten to fail? We conjecture that he has known sickness; and, in spite of his locomotive habits, perhaps sickness of the chronic sort. Hear this, for example: 'How beautiful to die of broken-heart, on Paper! [21] Quite another thing in practice; every window of your Feeling, even of your Intellect, as it were, begrimed and mud-bespattered, so that no pure ray can enter; a whole Drug-

---

18. Carlyle is playing with two meanings of "mystery"—in his second use of the word it signifies a trade or a craft.
19. That is, even positive evil is preferred by Teufelsdröckh to a mechanical universe.
20. Calvary, where Christ was crucified; literally, "Place of Skulls."
21. A satiric allusion to the emulation of the emotions of the despairing heroes of novels of the late 18th and early 19th centuries, of whom Goethe's Werther was the first.

shop in your inwards; the fordone soul drowning slowly in quagmires of Disgust!'

Putting all which external and internal miseries together, may we not find in the following sentences, quite in our Professor's still vein, significance enough? 'From Suicide a certain aftershine (*Nachschein*) of Christianity withheld me: perhaps also a certain indolence of character; for, was not that a remedy I had at any time within reach? Often, however, was there a question present to me: Should some one now, at the turning of that corner, blow thee suddenly out of Space, into the other World, or other No-World, by pistol-shot,—how were it? On which ground, too, I have often, in sea-storms and sieged cities and other death-scenes, exhibited an imperturbability, which passed, falsely enough, for courage.'

'So had it lasted,' concludes the Wanderer, 'so had it lasted, as in bitter protracted Death-agony, through long years. The heart within me, unvisited by any heavenly dewdrop, was smouldering in sulphurous, slow-consuming fire. Almost since earliest memory I had shed no tear; or once only when I, murmuring half-audibly, recited Faust's Deathsong, that wild *Selig der den er im Siegesglanze findet* (Happy whom *he* finds in Battle's splendour),[22] and thought that of this last Friend even I was not forsaken, that Destiny itself could not doom me not to die. Having no hope, neither had I any definite fear, were it of Man or of Devil: nay, I often felt as if it might be solacing, could the Arch-Devil himself, though in Tartarean terrors, but rise to me, that I might tell him a little of my mind. And yet, strangely enough, I lived in a continual, indefinite, pining fear, tremulous, pusillanimous, apprehensive of I knew not what: it seemed as if all things in the Heavens above and the Earth beneath would hurt me; as if the Heavens and the Earth were but boundless jaws of a devouring monster, wherein I, palpitating, waited to be devoured.

'Full of such humour, and perhaps the miserablest man in the whole French Capital or Suburbs, was I, one sultry Dog-day,[23] after much perambulation, toiling along the dirty little *Rue Saint-Thomas de l'Enfer*,[24] among civic rubbish enough, in a close atmosphere, and over pavements hot as Nebuchadnezzar's Furnace;[25] whereby doubtless my spirits were little cheered; when, all at once, there rose a Thought in me, and I asked myself: "What *art* thou afraid of? Wherefore, like a coward, dost thou forever pip and whimper, and go cowering and trembling? Despicable biped! what is the sum-total of the worst that lies before thee? Death? Well, Death; and say the pangs of Tophet[26] too, and all that the Devil and Man may, will or can do against thee! Hast thou not a heart; canst thou not suffer whatsoever it be; and, as a Child of Freedom, though outcast, trample Tophet itself under thy feet, while it consumes thee? Let it come, then; I will meet it and defy it!" And as I so thought, there rushed like a stream of fire over my whole soul; and I shook base Fear

22. Adapted from Goethe's *Faust* I. iv. 1573–76.
23. The dog-days are the hot, sultry period between mid-July and September, so called because the "dog-star" Sirius rises and sets with the sun. They are thought to be unwholesome for body and mind.
24. The street's name is St. Thomas-in-Hell. By this use of his own Christian name, Carlyle invites us to guess that Teufelsdröckh's experience was his own.
25. Daniel 3:19.
26. Hell.

away from me forever. I was strong, of unknown strength; a spirit, almost a god. Ever from that time, the temper of my misery was changed: not Fear or whining Sorrow was it, but Indignation and grim fire-eyed Defiance.

'Thus had the EVERLASTING NO [27] (*das ewige Nein*) pealed authoritatively through all the recesses of my Being, of my ME; and then was it that my whole ME stood up, in native God-created majesty, and with emphasis recorded its Protest. Such a Protest, the most important transaction in Life, may that same Indignation and Defiance, in a psychological point of view, be fitly called. The Everlasting No had said: "Behold, thou art fatherless, outcast, and the Universe is mine (the Devil's)"; to which my whole Me now made answer: "*I* am not thine, but Free, and forever hate thee!"

'It is from this hour that I incline to date my Spiritual New-birth, or Baphometic [28] Fire-baptism; perhaps I directly thereupon began to be a Man.'

[The chapter following "The Everlasting No" is called "The Centre of Indifference." It recounts how Teufelsdröckh, after having passed his crisis, investigates the world in an objective way, looking for some sign of spirituality in human institutions. His bitter, life-denying state of feeling has been overcome, but nothing of a positive kind has come to take its place. He lives in a condition of neutral feeling, enduring life rather than living it.]

The Everlasting Yea [1]

'Temptations in the Wilderness!' [2] exclaims Teufelsdröckh: 'Have we not all to be tried with such? Not so easily can the old Adam,[3] lodged in us by birth, be dispossessed. Our Life is compassed round with Necessity; yet is the meaning of Life itself no other than Freedom, than Voluntary Force: thus have we a warfare; in the beginning, especially, a hard-fought battle. For the God-given mandate, *Work thou in Welldoing*, lies mysteriously written, in Promethean Prophetic Characters, in our hearts; and leaves us no rest, night or day, till it be deciphered and obeyed; till it burn forth, in our conduct, a visible, acted Gospel of Freedom. And as the clay-given [4] mandate, *Eat thou and be filled*, at the same time persuasively proclaims itself through every nerve,—must not there be a confusion, a contest, before the better Influence can become the upper?

'To me nothing seems more natural than that the Son of Man, when such God-given mandate first prophetically stirs within him, and the Clay must

27. There is the chance of at least momentary misunderstanding here—the Everlasting No is spoken *to* Teufelsdröckh, not *by* him. His great moment is his defiance and negation of it. That it is called Everlasting suggests Carlyle's awareness that it is inherent in the nature of life, that it cannot be overcome by reason but only by will.

28. Devilish. Baphomet was the idol or symbolic figure which the Knights Templars were said to worship when they were accused of being infidels. The name may be a corruption of Mahomet.

1. From Bk. II, Chap. IX.
2. The allusion is to the temptation of Christ by Satan, Matthew 4:1.
3. Colossians 3:9. The "old Adam" is man unregenerate. Adam is the Hebrew word for man.
4. In the second of the two versions of the creation of man in Genesis, Adam is moulded by God of clay.

now be vanquished, or vanquish,—should be carried of the spirit into grim Solitudes, and there fronting the Tempter do grimmest battle with him; defiantly setting him at naught, till he yield and fly. Name it as we choose: with or without visible Devil, whether in the natural Desert of rocks and sands, or in the populous Desert of selfishness and baseness,—to such Temptation are we all called. Unhappy if we are not! Unhappy if we are but Half-men, in whom that divine handwriting has never blazed forth, all-subduing, in true sun-splendour; but quivers dubiously amid meaner lights: or smoulders, in dull pain, in darkness, under earthly vapours!—Our Wilderness is the wide World in an Atheistic Century; our Forty Days are long years of suffering and fasting: nevertheless, to these also comes an end. Yes, to me also was given, if not Victory, yet the consciousness of Battle, and the resolve to persevere therein while life or faculty is left. To me also, entangled in the enchanted forests, demon-peopled, doleful of sight and of sound, it was given, after weariest wanderings, to work out my way into the higher sunlit slopes— of that Mountain which has no summit, or whose summit is in Heaven only!'

He says elsewhere, under a less ambitious figure; as figures are, once for all, natural to him: 'Has not thy Life been that of most sufficient men (*tüchtigen Männer*) thou hast known in this generation? An outflush of foolish young Enthusiasm, like the first fallow-crop, wherein are as many weeds as valuable herbs: this all parched away, under the Droughts of practical and spiritual Un-belief, as Disappointment, in thought and act, often-repeated gave rise to Doubt, and Doubt gradually settled into Denial! If I have had a second-crop, and now see the perennial green-sward, and sit under umbrageous cedars, which defy all Drought (and Doubt); herein too, be the Heavens praised, I am not without examples, and even exemplars.'

So that, for Teufelsdröckh also, there has been a 'glorious revolution':[5] these mad shadow-hunting and shadow-hunted Pilgrimings of his were but some purifying 'Temptation in the Wilderness,' before his Apostolic work (such as it was) could begin; which Temptation is now happily over, and the Devil once more worsted! Was 'that high moment in the *Rue de l'Enfer*,' then, properly the turning-point of the battle; when the Fiend said, *Worship me or be torn in shreds;* and was answered valiantly with an *Apage, Satana?*[6]— Singular Teufelsdröckh, would thou hadst told thy singular story in plain words! But it is fruitless to look there, in those Paper-bags,[7] for such. Nothing but innuendoes, figurative crotchets: a typical Shadow, fitfully wavering, prophetico-satiric; no clear logical Picture. 'How paint to the sensual eye,' asks he once, 'what passes in the Holy-of-Holies of Man's Soul; in what words, known to these profane times, speak even afar-off of the unspeakable?' We ask in turn: Why perplex these times, profane as they are, with needless obscurity, by omission and by commission? Not mystical only is our Professor, but whimsical; and involves himself, now more than ever, in eye-bewildering *chiaroscuro*.[8] Successive glimpses, here faithfully imparted, our more gifted readers must endeavour to combine for their own behoof.

5. The phrase commonly used to describe the deposition of King James II in 1688.
6. "Get thee hence, Satan," Matthew 4:8–10.
7. Teufelsdröckh kept his autobiographical manuscripts in six paper bags.
8. Light and shade (in painting).

He says: 'The hot Harmattan-wind[9] had raged itself out; its howl went silent within me; and the long-deafened soul could now hear. I paused in my wild wanderings; and sat me down to wait, and consider; for it was as if the hour of change drew nigh. I seemed to surrender, to renounce utterly, and say: Fly, then, false shadows of Hope; I will chase you no more, I will believe you no more. And ye too, haggard spectres of Fear, I care not for you; ye too are all shadows and a lie. Let me rest here: for I am way-weary and life-weary; I will rest here, were it but to die: to die or to live is alike to me; alike insignificant.'—And again: 'Here, then, as I lay in that CENTRE OF INDIF-FERENCE; cast, doubtless by benignant upper Influence, into a healing sleep, the heavy dreams rolled gradually away, and I awoke to a new Heaven and a new Earth.[10] The first preliminary moral Act, Annihilation of Self (*Selbst-tödtung*), had been happily accomplished; and my mind's eyes were now unsealed, and its hands ungyved.'[11]

Might we not also conjecture that the following passage refers to his Locality, during this same 'healing sleep'; that his Pilgrim-staff lies cast aside here, on 'the high table-land'; and indeed that the repose is already taking wholesome effect on him? If it were not that the tone, in some parts, has more of riancy, even of levity, than we could have expected! However, in Teufelsdröckh, there is always the strangest Dualism: light dancing, with guitar-music, will be going on in the fore-court, while by fits from within comes the faint whimpering of woe and wail. We transcribe the piece entire:

'Beautiful it was to sit there, as in my skyey Tent, musing and meditating; on the high table-land, in front of the Mountains; over me, as roof, the azure Dome, and around me, for walls, four azure-flowing curtains,—namely, of the Four azure winds, on whose bottom-fringes also I have seen gilding. And then to fancy the fair Castles that stood sheltered in these Mountain hollows; with their green flower-lawns, and white dames and damosels, lovely enough: or better still, the straw-roofed Cottages, wherein stood many a Mother baking bread, with her children round her:—all hidden and protectingly folded-up in the valley-folds; yet there and alive, as sure as if I beheld them. Or to see, as well as fancy, the nine Towns and Villages, that lay round my mountain-seat, which, in still weather, were wont to speak to me (by their steeple-bells) with metal tongue; and, in almost all weather, proclaimed their vitality by repeated Smoke-clouds; whereon, as on a culinary horologe,[12] I might read the hour of the day. For it was the smoke of cookery, as kind housewives at morning, mid-day, eventide, were boiling their husbands' kettles; and ever a blue pillar rose up into the air, successively or simultaneously, from each of the nine, saying, as plainly as smoke could say: Such and such a meal is getting ready here. Not uninteresting! For you have the whole Borough, with all its love-makings and scandal-mongeries, contentions and contentments, as in miniature, and could cover it all with your hat.—If, in my wide Wayfarings, I had learned to look into the business of the World in its details, here perhaps

9. A hot, dry, dusty wind that blows from the Sahara.
10. Revelation 21:1.
11. Unshackled.
12. Clock.

was the place for combining it into general propositions, and deducing inferences therefrom.

'Often also could I see the black Tempest marching in anger through the Distance: round some Schreckhorn,[13] as yet grim-blue, would the eddying vapour gather, and there tumultuously eddy, and flow down like a mad witch's hair; till, after a space, it vanished, and, in the clear sunbeam, your Schreckhorn stood smiling grim-white, for the vapour had held snow. How thou fermentest and elaboratest, in thy great fermenting-vat and laboratory of an Atmosphere, of a World, O Nature!—Or what is Nature? Ha! why do I not name thee GOD? Art not thou the "Living Garment of God"?[14] O Heavens, is it, in very deed, HE, then, that ever speaks through thee; that lives and loves in thee, that lives and loves in me?

'Fore-shadows, call them rather fore-splendours, of that Truth, and Beginning of Truths, fell mysteriously over my soul. Sweeter than Dayspring to the Shipwrecked in Nova Zembla; ah, like the mother's voice to her little child that strays bewildered, weeping, in unknown tumults; like soft streamings of celestial music to my too-exasperated heart, came that Evangel. The Universe is not dead and demoniacal, a charnel-house with spectres; but godlike, and my Father's!

'With other eyes, too, could I now look upon my fellow man; with an infinite Love, an infinite Pity. Poor, wandering, wayward man! Art thou not tried, and beaten with stripes, even as I am? Ever, whether thou bear the royal mantle or the beggar's gabardine, art thou not so weary, so heavy-laden; and thy Bed of Rest is but a Grave. O my Brother, my Brother, why cannot I shelter thee in my bosom, and wipe away all tears from thy eyes! [15] Truly, the din of many-voiced Life, which, in this solitude, with the mind's organ, I could hear, was no longer a maddening discord, but a melting one; like inarticulate cries, and sobbings of a dumb creature, which in the ear of Heaven are prayers. The poor Earth, with her poor joys, was now my needy Mother, not my cruel Stepdame; Man, with his so mad Wants and so mean Endeavours, had become the dearer to me; and even for his sufferings and his sins, I now first named him Brother. Thus was I standing in the porch of that "Sanctuary of Sorrow"; [16] by strange, steep ways had I too been guided thither; and ere long its sacred gates would open, and the "Divine Depth of Sorrow" lie disclosed to me.'

The Professor says, he here first got eye on the Knot that had been strangling him, and straightway could unfasten it, and was free. 'A vain interminable controversy,' writes he, 'touching what is at present called Origin of Evil, or some such thing, arises in every soul, since the beginning of the world; and in every soul, that would pass from idle Suffering into actual Endeavouring, must first be put an end to. The most, in our time, have to go content with a simple, incomplete enough Suppression of this controversy; to a few some Solution of it is indispensable. In every new era, too, such

13. "Peak of Terror," in the Bernese Alps, Switzerland.
14. But if so, surely not identical with the being that wears it!
15. See Revelation 21:4.
16. The phrase is derived from Goethe's novel *Wilhelm Meister's Apprenticeship*, which Carlyle translated.

Solution comes-out in different terms; and ever the Solution of the last era has become obsolete, and is found unserviceable. For it is man's nature to change his Dialect from century to century; he cannot help it though he would. The authentic *Church-Catechism* of our present century has not yet fallen into my hands: meanwhile, for my own private behoof, I attempt to elucidate the matter so. Man's Unhappiness, as I construe, comes of his Greatness; it is because there is an Infinite in him, which with all his cunning he cannot quite bury under the Finite.[17] Will the whole Finance Ministers and Uphol-sterers and Confectioners of modern Europe undertake, in joint-stock company, to make one Shoeblack HAPPY? They cannot accomplish it, above an hour or two; for the Shoeblack also has a Soul quite other than his Stomach; and would require, if you consider it, for his permanent satisfaction and saturation, simply this allotment, no more, and no less: *God's infinite Universe altogether to him-self,* therein to enjoy infinitely, and fill every wish as fast as it rose. Oceans of Hochheimer,[18] a Throat like that of Ophiuchus:[19] speak not of them; to the infinite Shoeblack they are as nothing. No sooner is your ocean filled, than he grumbles that it might have been of better vintage. Try him with half of a Universe, of an Omnipotence, he sets to quarrelling with the proprietor of the other half, and declares himself the most maltreated of men.—Always there is a black spot in our sunshine: it is even as I said, the *Shadow of Ourselves.*

'But the whim we have of Happiness is somewhat thus. By certain valuations, and averages, of our own striking, we come upon some sort of average terrestrial lot; this we fancy belongs to us by nature, and of indefeasible right. It is simple payment of our wages, of our deserts; requires neither thanks nor complaint; only such *overplus* as there may be do we account Happiness; any *deficit* again is Misery. Now consider that we have the valuation of our own deserts ourselves, and what a fund of Self-conceit there is in each of us,—do you wonder that the balance should so often dip the wrong way, and many a Blockhead cry: See there, what a payment; was ever worthy gentleman so used!—I tell thee, Blockhead, it all comes of thy Vanity; of what thou *fanciest* those same deserts of thine to be. Fancy that thou deservest to be hanged (as is most likely), thou wilt feel it happiness to be only shot: fancy that thou deservest to be hanged in a hair-halter, it will be a luxury to die in hemp.

'So true is it, what I then say, that *the Fraction of Life can be increased in value not so much by increasing your Numerator as by lessening your Denom-inator.* Nay, unless my Algebra deceive me, *Unity* itself divided by *Zero* will give *Infinity.* Make thy claim of wages of zero, then; thou hast the world under thy feet. Well did the Wisest of our time write: "It is only with Renuncia-tion (*Entsagen*) that Life, properly speaking, can be said to begin." [20]

'I asked myself: What is this that, ever since earliest years, thou hast been fretting and fuming, and lamenting and self-tormenting, on account of? Say it in a word: is it not because thou art not HAPPY? Because the THOU (sweet gentleman) is not sufficiently honoured, nourished, soft-bedded, and lov-ingly cared for? Foolish soul! What Act of Legislature was there that *thou*

17. This idea was central to the thought of the great *Pensées* of Pascal.
18. A Rhine wine from the district of Hochheim.
19. The serpent which is held by a man in the constellation Serpentarius.
20. Goethe in *Wilhelm Meister's Apprenticeship.*

shouldst be Happy? A little while ago thou hadst no right to *be* at all. What if thou wert born and predestined not to be Happy, but to be Unhappy! Art thou nothing other than a Vulture, then, that fliest through the Universe seeking after somewhat to *eat;* and shrieking dolefully because carrion enough is not given thee? Close thy *Byron;* open thy *Goethe.*' [21]

'*Es leuchtet mir ein,* I see a glimpse of it!' [22] cries he elsewhere: 'there is in man a HIGHER than Love of Happiness: he can do without Happiness, and instead thereof find Blessedness! Was it not to preach-forth this same HIGHER than sages and martyrs, the Poet and the Priest, in all times, have spoken and suffered; bearing testimony, through life and through death, of the Godlike that is in Man, and how in the Godlike only has he Strength and Freedom? Which God-inspired Doctrine art thou also honoured to be taught; O Heavens! and broken with manifold merciful Afflictions, even till thou become contrite, and learn it! O, thank thy Destiny for these; thankfully bear what yet remain: thou hadst need of them; the Self in thee needed to be annihilated. By benignant fever-paroxysms is Life rooting out the deep-seated chronic Disease, and triumphs over Death. On the roaring billows of Time, thou art not engulfed, but borne aloft into the azure of Eternity. Love not Pleasure; love God.[23] This is the EVERLASTING YEA, wherein all contradiction is solved: wherein whoso walks and works, it is well with him.'

And again: 'Small is it that thou canst trample the Earth with its injuries under thy feet, as old Greek Zeno [24] trained thee: thou canst love the Earth while it injures thee, and even because it injures thee; for this a Greater than Zeno was needed, and he too was sent.[25] Knowest thou that "*Worship of Sorrow*"? The Temple thereof, founded some eighteen centuries ago, now lies in ruins, overgrown with jungle, the habitation of doleful creatures: nevertheless, venture forward; in a low crypt, arched out of falling fragments, thou findest the Altar still there, and its sacred Lamp perennially burning.'

Without pretending to comment on which strange utterances, the Editor will only remark, that there lies beside them much of a still more questionable character; unsuited to the general apprehension; nay wherein he himself does not see his way. Nebulous disquisitions on Religion, yet not without bursts of splendour; on the 'perennial continuance of Inspiration'; on Prophecy; that there are 'true Priests, as well as Baal-Priests,[26] in our own day': with more of the like sort. We select some fractions, by way of finish to this farrago.[27]

---

21. By this famous and often-quoted injunction Carlyle means that one should turn from the egoistic mode of apprehending the world which emphasizes the limitations that are put upon man's powers and pleasures and turn to a more objective, less egoistic view which leads to the acceptance of life's conditions and the practical dealing with them.

22. Said by Wilhelm Meister.

23. II Timothy 3:4: "Traitors, needy, high-minded, lovers of pleasure more than lovers of God."

24. Stoic philosopher, 3rd century B.C. Zeno lived to be 98. One day, coming from his school, he fell and broke a finger, whereupon he struck the earth, exclaiming, "I am coming, why do you call me?" and immediately went home and committed suicide.

25. Christ. "The Worship of Sorrow"—the phrase is derived from Goethe—is Christianity, which in its established form ("the Temple") is now ruined, although its essence is to be cherished.

26. Baal is a generic name for false gods.

27. Conglomeration; random mixture.

'Cease, my much-respected Herr von Voltaire,' [28] thus apostrophises the Professor: 'shut thy sweet voice; for the task appointed thee seems finished. Sufficiently hast thou demonstrated this proposition, considerable or otherwise: That the Mythus [29] of the Christian Religion looks not in the eighteenth century as it did in the eighth. Alas, were thy six-and-thirty quartos, and the six-and-thirty thousand other quartos and folios, and flying sheets or reams, printed before and since on the same subject, all needed to convince us of so little! But what next? Wilt thou help us to embody the divine Spirit of that Religion in a new Mythus, in a new vehicle and vesture, that our Souls, otherwise too like perishing, may live? What! thou hast no faculty in that kind? Only a torch for burning, no hammer for building? Take our thanks, then, and——thyself away.

'Meanwhile what are antiquated Mythuses to me? Or is the God present, felt in my own heart, a thing which Herr von Voltaire will dispute out of me; or dispute into me? To the *"Worship of Sorrow"* ascribe what origin and genesis thou pleasest, *has* not that Worship originated, and been generated; is it not *here?* Feel it in thy heart, and then say whether it is of God! This is Belief; all else is Opinion,—for which latter whoso will let him worry and be worried.'

'Neither,' observes he elsewhere, 'shall ye tear-out one another's eyes, struggling over "Plenary Inspiration," [30] and suchlike: try rather to get a little even Partial Inspiration, each of you for himself. One Bible I know, of whose Plenary Inspiration doubt is not so much as possible; nay with my own eyes I saw the God's-Hand writing it: thereof all other Bibles are but leaves,—say, in Picture-Writing to assist the weaker faculty.' [31]

Or, to give the wearied reader relief, and bring it to an end, let him take the following perhaps more intelligible passage:

'To me, in this our life,' says the Professor, 'which is an internecine warfare with the Time-spirit, other warfare seems questionable. Hast thou in any way a Contention with thy brother, I advise thee, think well what the meaning thereof is. If thou gauge it to the bottom, it is simply this: "Fellow, see! thou art taking more than thy share of Happiness in the world, something from *my* share: which, by the Heavens, thou shalt not; nay I will fight thee rather."— Alas, and the whole lot to be divided is such a beggarly matter, truly a "feast of shells," [32] for the substance has been spilled out: not enough to quench one Appetite; and the collective human species clutching at them!—Can we not, in all such cases, rather say: "Take it, thou too-ravenous individual; take that pitiful additional fraction of a share, which I reckoned mine, but which thou so wantest; take it with a blessing: would to Heaven I had enough for thee!"— If Fichte's *Wissenschaftslehre* [33] be, "to a certain extent, Applied Christianity,"

28. For Carlyle, Voltaire (1694–1778) often figures as the leader of the movement of skeptical rationalism and therefore as the chief enemy of the spiritual life.
29. Myth, in the sense of a story that explains. The old mythus of Christianity, Carlyle is saying, is doubtless, as Voltaire undertook to show, no longer acceptable, but the essence of Christianity is still precious and can be arrayed in the "clothes" of a new mythus.
30. The doctrine that the Bible is divinely inspired and is literally true in all its statements.
31. Carlyle probably means that the universe is the truly inspired Bible.
32. Empty egg shells; the allusion is obscure.
33. Johann Gottlieb Fichte (1762–1814) published *The Doctrine of Knowledge* in 1794. The quoted description of it was made by Novalis (1772–1801), the German mystical poet.

surely to a still greater extent, so is this. We have here not a Whole Duty of Man,[34] yet a Half Duty, namely the Passive half: could we but do it, as we can demonstrate it!

'But indeed Conviction, were it never so excellent, is worthless till it convert itself into Conduct. Nay properly Conviction is not possible till then; inasmuch as all Speculation is by nature endless, formless, a vortex amid vortices: only by a felt indubitable certainty of Experience does it find any centre to revolve round, and so fashion itself into a system. Most true is it, as a wise man teaches us, that "Doubt of any sort cannot be removed except by Action." [35] On which ground, too, let him who gropes painfully in darkness or uncertain light, and prays vehemently that the dawn may ripen into day, lay this other precept well to heart, which to me was of invaluable service: *"Do the Duty which lies nearest thee,"* [36] which thou knowest to be a Duty! Thy second Duty will already have become clearer.

'May we not say, however, that the hour of Spiritual Enfranchisement is even this: When your Ideal World, wherein the whole man has been dimly struggling and inexpressibly languishing to work, becomes revealed, and thrown open; and you discover, with amazement enough, like the Lothario in *Wilhelm Meister,* that your "America is here or nowhere"? [37] The Situation that has not its Duty, its Ideal, was never yet occupied by man. Yes here, in this poor, miserable, hampered, despicable Actual, wherein thou even now standest, here or nowhere is thy Ideal: work it out therefrom; and working, believe, live, be free. Fool! the Ideal is in thyself, the impediment too is in thyself: thy Condition is but the stuff thou art to shape that same Ideal out of: what matters whether such stuff of this sort or that, so the Form thou give it be heroic, be poetic? O thou that pinest in the imprisonment of the Actual, and criest bitterly to the gods for a kingdom wherein to rule and create, know this of a truth: the thing thou seekest is already with thee, "here or nowhere," couldst thou only see!

'But it is with man's Soul as it was with Nature: the beginning of Creation is—Light.[38] Till the eye have vision, the whole members are in bonds.[39] Divine moment, when over the tempest-tost Soul, as once over the wild-weltering Chaos, it is spoken: Let there be Light! Ever to the greatest that has felt such moment, is it not miraculous and God-announcing; even as, under simpler figures, to the simplest and least. The mad primeval Discord is hushed; the rudely-jumbled conflicting elements bind themselves in to separate Firmaments: deep silent rock-foundations are built beneath; and the skyey vault with its everlasting Luminaries above: instead of a dark wasteful Chaos, we have a blooming, fertile, heaven-encompassed World.

'I too could now say to myself: Be no longer a Chaos, but a World, or even Worldkin. Produce! Produce! Were it but the pitifullest infinitesimal fraction

34. *The Whole Duty of Man* was an enormously popular devotional book of unknown authorship published in 1658.
35. Goethe, in *Wilhelm Meister's Apprenticeship.*
36. *Ibid.*
37. America figures in this statement as the land of promise, where the ideal may be realized.
38. See Genesis 1:3.
39. Derived from Matthew 6:22–23.

of a Product, produce it, in God's name! 'Tis the utmost thou hast in thee: out with it, then. Up, up! Whatsoever thy hand findeth to do, do it with thy whole might. Work while it is called To-day; for the Night cometh, wherein no man can work.'[40]

Natural Supernaturalism [1]

It is in his stupendous Section, headed *Natural Supernaturalism,* that the Professor first becomes a Seer; and, after long effort, such as we have witnessed, finally subdues under his feet this refractory Clothes-Philosophy, and takes victorious possession thereof. Phantasms enough he has had to struggle with; 'Cloth-webs and Cobwebs,' of Imperial Mantles, Superannuated Symbols, and what not: yet still did he courageously pierce through. Nay, worst of all, two quite mysterious, world-embracing Phantasms, TIME and SPACE, have ever hovered round him, perplexing and bewildering: but with these also he now resolutely grapples, these also he victoriously rends asunder. In a word, he has looked fixedly on Existence, till, one after the other, its earthly hulls and garnitures have all melted away; and now, to his rapt vision, the interior celestial Holy of Holies lies disclosed.

Here, therefore, properly it is that the Philosophy of Clothes attains to Transcendentalism; this last leap, can we but clear it, takes us safe into the promised land, where *Palingenesia,*[2] in all senses, may be considered as beginning. 'Courage, then!' may our Diogenes exclaim, with better right than Diogenes the First [3] once did. This stupendous Section we, after long painful meditation, have found not to be unintelligible; but, on the contrary, to grow clear, nay radiant, and all-illuminating. Let the reader, turning on it what utmost force of speculative intellect is in him, do his part; as we, by judicious selection and adjustment, shall study to do ours:

'Deep has been, and is, the significance of Miracles,' thus quietly begins the Professor; 'far deeper perhaps than we imagine. Meanwhile, the question of questions were: What specially is a Miracle? To that Dutch King of Siam, an icicle had been a miracle; [4] whoso had carried with him an air-pump, and vial of vitriolic ether, might have worked a miracle.[5] To my Horse, again, who unhappily is still more unscientific, do not I work a miracle, and magical "*Open*

40. See Ecclesiastes 9:10 and John 9:4.

1. From Bk. III, Chap. VIII. The paradox of the title of this chapter may be said to summarize the doctrine of *Sartor Resartus,* that the universe is not to be defined by its merely material existence, that its processes are not mechanical. Rather is it a living thing, by implication endowed with purpose and will, which, though they are higher than man's, and inscrutable, are yet cognate with man's own purpose and will. Thus conceived, the universe is a perpetual wonder, which is to say a "miracle." It is not, as Deism taught, a universe contrived by God, who thereafter stands apart from his creation; God is present in the universe, whose "natural" laws are therefore "supernatural."

2. Rebirth.

3. The Cynic philosopher whose legend is that he lived in a tub and went about in daylight with a lantern seeking an honest man. The story is told of him that, as a boring lecture was nearing its end, he cried to his neighbors in the audience, "Courage! I see land."

4. He is referred to in the section on miracles in Hume's *Inquiry Concerning Human Understanding* (1751).

5. *I.e.,* making ice.

sesame!" [6] every time I please to pay twopence, and open for him an impassable *Schlagbaum*, or shut Turnpike?

'"But is not a real Miracle simply a violation of the Laws of Nature?" ask several. Whom I answer by this new question: What are the Laws of Nature? To me perhaps the rising of one from the dead were no violation of these Laws, but a confirmation; were some far deeper Law, now first penetrated into, and by Spiritual Force, even as the rest have all been, brought to bear on us with its Material Force.

'Here too may some inquire, not without astonishment: On what ground shall one, that can make Iron swim,[7] come and declare that therefore he can teach Religion? To us, truly, of the Nineteenth Century, such declaration were inept enough; which nevertheless to our fathers, of the First Century, was full of meaning.

'"But is it not the deepest Law of Nature that she be constant?" cries an illuminated class: "Is not the Machine of the Universe fixed to move by unalterable rules?" Probable enough, good friends: nay I, too, must believe that the God, whom ancient inspired men assert to be "without variableness or shadow of turning," [8] does indeed never change; that Nature, that the Universe, which no one whom it so pleases can be prevented from calling a Machine, does move by the most unalterable rules. And now of you, too, I make the old inquiry: What those same unalterable rules, forming the complete Statute-Book of Nature, may possibly be?

'They stand written in our Works of Science, say you; in the accumulated records of Man's Experience?—Was Man with his Experience present at the Creation, then, to see how it all went on? Have any deepest scientific individuals yet dived-down to the foundations of the Universe, and gauged everything there? Did the Maker take them into His counsel; that they read His ground-plan of the incomprehensible All; and can say, This stands marked therein, and no more than this? Alas, not in anywise! These scientific individuals have been nowhere but where we also are; have seen some hand-breadths deeper than we see into the Deep that is infinite, without bottom as without shore.

'Laplace's [9] Book on the Stars, wherein he exhibits that certain Planets, with their Satellites, gyrate round our worthy Sun, at a rate and in a course, which, by greatest good fortune, he and the like of him have succeeded in detecting,— is to me as precious as to another. But is this what thou namest "Mechanism of the Heavens," and "System of the World"; this, wherein Sirius and the Pleiades, and all Herschel's [10] Fifteen-thousand Suns per minute, being left out, some paltry handful of Moons, and inert Balls, had been—looked at, nicknamed, and

---

6. The magical formula for opening the door of the cave in the story of Ali Baba and the Forty Thieves in *The Arabian Nights*. Sesame is a seed commonly used in the Near East for food and oil.

7. See II Kings 6:6, where Elisha makes an axe-head swim.

8. See James 1:17.

9. The Marquis Pierre Simon de Laplace (1749–1827), the great French astronomer and mathematician, author of *Exposition du système du monde* (1796), the famous conclusion to which is the "Book on the Stars" to which Carlyle refers, and of *Mécanique céleste* (1799–1825), called by Carlyle "Mechanism of the Heavens."

10. Sir William Herschel (1738–1822), English astronomer of German birth who discovered a large number of celestial bodies.

marked in the Zodiacal Way-bill; so that we can now prate of their Whereabout; their How, their Why, their What, being hid from us, as in the signless Inane?

'System of Nature! To the wisest man, wide as is his vision, Nature remains of quite *infinite* depth, of quite infinite expansion; and all Experience thereof limits itself to some few computed centuries and measured square-miles. The course of Nature's phases, on this our little fraction of a Planet, is partially known to us: but who knows what deeper courses these depend on; what infinitely larger Cycle (of causes) our little Epicycle [11] revolves on? To the Minnow every cranny and pebble, and quality and accident, of its little native Creek may have become familiar: but does the Minnow understand the Ocean Tides and periodic Currents, the Trade-winds, and Monsoons, and Moon's Eclipses; by all which the condition of its little Creek is regulated, and may, from time to time (*un*miraculously enough), be quite overset and reversed? Such a Minnow is Man; his Creek this Planet Earth; his Ocean the immeasurable All; his Monsoons and periodic Currents the mysterious Course of Providence through Æons of Æons.

'We speak of the Volume of Nature: and truly a Volume it is,—whose Author and Writer is God. To read it! Dost thou, does man, so much as well know the Alphabet thereof? With its Words, Sentences, and grand descriptive Pages, poetical and philosophical, spread out through Solar Systems, and Thousands of Years, we shall not try thee. It is a Volume written in celestial hieroglyphs, in the true Sacred-writing; of which even Prophets are happy that they can read here a line and there a line. As for your Institutes, and Academies of Science, they strive bravely; and, from amid the thick-crowded, inextricably intertwisted hieroglyphic writing, pick-out, by dextrous combination, some Letters in the vulgar Character, and therefrom put together this and the other economic Recipe, of high avail in Practice. That Nature is more than some boundless Volume of such Recipes, or huge, well-nigh inexhaustible Domestic-Cookery Book, of which the whole secret will in this manner one day evolve itself, the fewest dream.

'Custom,' continues the Professor, 'doth make dotards of us all.[12] Consider well, thou wilt find that Custom is the greatest of Weavers; and weaves air-raiment for all the Spirits of the Universe; whereby indeed these dwell with us visibly, as ministering servants, in our houses and workshops; but their spiritual nature becomes, to the most, forever hidden. Philosophy complains that Custom has hoodwinked us, from the first; that we do everything by Custom, even Believe by it; that our very Axioms, let us boast of Free-thinking as we may, are oftenest simply such Beliefs as we have never heard questioned. Nay, what is Philosophy throughout but a continual battle against Custom; an ever-renewed effort to *transcend* the sphere of blind Custom, and so become Transcendental?

'Innumerable are the illusions and legerdemain-tricks of Custom: but of all these, perhaps the cleverest is her knack of persuading us that the Miraculous, by simple repetition, ceases to be Miraculous. True, it is by this means we

11. In the Ptolemaic system of astronomy a small circle whose center moves on the circumference of a larger circle at whose center is the earth.
12. See *Hamlet* III.i.83: "Thus conscience doth make cowards of us all."

live; for man must work as well as wonder: and herein is Custom so far a kind nurse, guiding him to his true benefit. But she is a fond foolish nurse, or rather we are false foolish nurslings, when, in our resting and reflecting hours, we prolong the same deception. Am I to view the Stupendous with stupid indifference, because I have seen it twice, or two-hundred, or two-million times? There is no reason in Nature or in Art why I should: unless, indeed, I am a mere Work-Machine, for whom the divine gift of Thought were no other than the terrestrial gift of Steam is to the Steam-engine; a power whereby Cotton might be spun, and money and money's worth realised.

'Notable enough too, here as elsewhere, wilt thou find the potency of Names; [13] which indeed are but one kind of such custom-woven, wonder-hiding Garments. Witchcraft, and all manner of Spectre-work, and Demonology, we have now named Madness and Diseases of the Nerves. Seldom reflecting that still the new question comes upon us: What is Madness, what are Nerves? Ever, as before, does Madness remain a mysterious-terrific, altogether *infernal* boiling-up of the Nether Chaotic Deep, through this fair-painted Vision of Creation, which swims thereon, which we name the Real.[14] Was Luther's Picture of the Devil [15] less a Reality, whether it were formed within the bodily eye, or without it? In every the wisest Soul lies a whole world of internal Madness, an authentic Demon Empire; out of which, indeed, his world of Wisdom has been creatively built together, and now rests there, as on its dark foundations does a habitable flowery Earth-rind.

'But deepest of all illusory Appearances, for hiding Wonder, as for many other ends, are your two grand fundamental world-enveloping Appearances, SPACE and TIME.[16] These, as spun and woven for us from before Birth itself, to clothe our celestial ME for dwelling here, and yet to blind it,—lie all-embracing, as the universal canvas, or warp and woof, whereby all minor Illusions, in this Phantasm Existence, weave and paint themselves. In vain, while here on Earth, shall you endeavour to strip them off; you can, at best, but rend them asunder for moments, and look through.

'Fortunatus [17] had a wishing Hat, which when he put on, and wished himself Anywhere, behold he was There. By this means had Fortunatus triumphed over Space, he had annihilated Space; for him there was no Where, but all was Here. Were a Hatter to establish himself, in the Wahngasse of Weissnich-two,[18] and make felts of this sort for all mankind, what a world we should have of it! Still stranger, should, on the opposite side of the street, another Hatter establish himself; and as his fellow-craftsman made Space-annihilating Hats, make Time-annihilating! Of both would I purchase, were it with my last

13. Carlyle refers to the primitive belief that if one knows the name of a person or deity, one can exercise a degree of power over him.
14. This view of the *significance* of madness, although in accord with an established poetic belief, was at odds with the prevailing psychiatry.
15. When the Devil appeared to him as he was translating the Bible, Luther hurled his leaden inkstand at the Tempter.
16. Carlyle writes here under the influence of Immanuel Kant (1724–1804), who, in his *Critique of Pure Reason* (1781), advanced the idea that space and time are forms of perception characteristic of the human mind, not in themselves "realities."
17. The hero of a medieval legend. The magic hat was stolen from the Sultan of Cairo.
18. Folly Alley of the University of Know-not-where.

groschen; [19] but chiefly of this latter. To clap-on your felt, and, simply by wishing that you were Any*where*, straightway to be *There!* Next to clap-on your
other felt, and, simply by wishing that you were Any*when*, straightway to be
Then! This were indeed the grander: shooting at will from the Fire-Creation of
the World to its Fire-Consummation; here historically present in the First
Century, conversing face to face with Paul and Seneca; [20] there prophetically
in the Thirty-first, conversing also face to face with other Pauls and Senecas,
who as yet stand hidden in the depth of that late Time!

'Or thinkest thou it were impossible, unimaginable? Is the Past annihilated,
then, or only past; is the Future non-extant, or only future? Those mystic
faculties of thine, Memory and Hope, already answer: already through those
mystic avenues, thou the Earth-blinded summonest both Past and Future, and
communest with them, though as yet darkly, and with mute beckonings. The
curtains of Yesterday drop down, the curtains of To-morrow roll up; but
Yesterday and To-morrow both *are*. Pierce through the Time-element, glance
into the Eternal. Believe what thou findest written in the sanctuaries of Man's
Soul, even as all Thinkers, in all ages, have devoutly read it there: that Time
and Space are not God, but creations of God; that with God as it is a universal
HERE, so is it an everlasting NOW.

'And seest thou therein any glimpse of IMMORTALITY?—O Heaven! Is the
white Tomb of our Loved One, who died from our arms, and had to be left
behind us there, which rises in the distance, like a pale, mournfully receding
Milestone, to tell how many toilsome uncheered miles we have journeyed on
alone,—but a pale spectral Illusion! [21] Is the lost Friend still mysteriously Here,
even as we are Here mysteriously, with God!—Know of a truth that only the
Time-shadows have perished, or are perishable; that the real Being of whatever
was, and whatever is, and whatever will be, *is* even now and forever. This,
should it unhappily seem new, thou mayest ponder at thy leisure; for the next
twenty years, or the next twenty centuries: believe it thou must; understand
it thou canst not.

'That the Thought-forms, Space and Time, wherein, once for all, we are
sent into this Earth to live, should condition and determine our whole Practical
reasonings, conceptions, and imagings or imaginings,—seems altogether fit, just,
and unavoidable. But that they should, furthermore, usurp such sway over
pure spiritual Meditation, and blind us to the wonder everywhere lying close
on us, seems nowise so. Admit Space and Time to their due rank as Forms of
Thought; nay even, if thou wilt, to their quite undue rank of Realities: and
consider, then, with thyself how their thin disguises hide from us the brightest
God-effulgences! Thus, were it not miraculous, could I stretch forth my hand
and clutch the Sun? Yet thou seest me daily stretch forth my hand and therewith clutch many a thing, and swing it hither and thither. Art thou a grown
baby, then, to fancy that the Miracle lies in miles of distance, or in pounds

19. A very small German coin.
20. There was once an unfounded belief that Seneca, the Roman poet and Stoic philosopher, met or corresponded with St. Paul.
21. In the loss of faith in the supernatural elements of Christianity nothing was harder
for the Victorians to bear than the negation of personal immortality, the thought that after
death they would not be reunited with their loved ones. See Tennyson's *In Memoriam*.

avoirdupois of weight; and not to see that the true inexplicable God-revealing Miracle lies in this, that I can stretch forth my hand at all; that I have free Force to clutch aught therewith? Innumerable other of this sort are the deceptions, and wonder-hiding stupefactions, which Space practises on us.

'Still worse is it with regard to Time. Your grand anti-magician, and universal wonder-hider, is this same lying Time. Had we but the Time-annihilating Hat, to put on for once only, we should see ourselves in a World of Miracles, wherein all fabled or authentic Thaumaturgy, and feats of Magic, were outdone. But unhappily we have not such a Hat; and man, poor fool that he is, can seldom and scantily help himself without one.

'Were it not wonderful, for instance, had Orpheus, or Amphion,[22] built the walls of Thebes by the mere sound of his Lyre? Yet tell me, Who built these walls of Weissnichtwo; summoning-out all the sandstone rocks, to dance along from the *Steinbruch* [23] (now a huge Troglodyte [24] Chasm, with frightful green-mantled pools); and shape themselves into Doric and Ionic pillars, squared ashlar houses and noble streets? Was it not the still higher Orpheus, or Orpheuses, who, in past centuries, by the divine Music of Wisdom, succeeded in civilising Man? Our highest Orpheus [25] walked in Judea, eighteen hundred years ago: his sphere-melody, flowing in wild native tones, took captive the ravished souls of men; and, being of a truth sphere-melody, still flows and sounds, though now with thousandfold Accompaniments, and rich symphonies, through all our hearts; and modulates, and divinely leads them. Is that a wonder, which happens in two hours; and does it cease to be wonderful if happening in two-million? Not only was Thebes built by the music of an Orpheus; but without the music of some inspired Orpheus was no city ever built, no work that man glories-in ever done.

'Sweep away the Illusion of Time; glance, if thou hast eyes, from the near moving-cause to its far-distant Mover: The stroke that came transmitted through a whole galaxy of elastic balls, was it less a stroke than if the last ball only had been struck, and sent flying? O, could I (with the Time-annihilating Hat) transport thee direct from the Beginnings to the Endings, how were thy eye-sight unsealed, and thy heart set flaming in the Light-sea of celestial wonder! Then sawest thou that this fair Universe, were it in the meanest province thereof, is in very deed the star-domed City of God; [26] that through every star, through every grass-blade, and most through every Living Soul, the glory of a present God still beams. But Nature, which is the Time-vesture of God, and reveals Him to the wise, hides Him from the foolish.

'Again, could anything be more miraculous than an actual authentic Ghost? The English Johnson longed, all his life, to see one; but could not, though he went to Cock Lane,[27] and thence to the church-vaults, and tapped-on coffins.

22. Orpheus was a son of Apollo whose music tamed wild beasts. Amphion was a son of Zeus; his lyre was given to him by Hermes and with its magic he could move stones.
23. Quarry.
24. A prehistoric cave-dweller.
25. Christ.
26. The name of St. Augustine's long treatise.
27. The Cock Lane ghost was very famous in its day, 1762. It made noises at 33 Cock Lane, Smithfield. Upon investigation, in which Dr. Johnson took part, it was discovered to be an imposition practiced by the family who tenanted the house.

Foolish Doctor! Did he never, with the mind's eye as well as with the body's, look round him into that full tide of human Life he so loved; did he never so much as look into Himself? The good Doctor was a Ghost, as actual and authentic as heart could wish; well-nigh a million of Ghosts were travelling the streets by his side. Once more I say, sweep away the illusion of Time; compress the threescore years into three minutes: what else was he, what else are we? Are we not Spirits, that are shaped into a body, into an Appearance; and that fade-away again into air and Invisibility? This is no metaphor, it is a simple scientific *fact:* we start out of Nothingness, take figure, and are Apparitions; round us, as round the veriest spectre, is Eternity; and to Eternity minutes are as years and æons. Come there not tones of Love and Faith, as from celestial harp-strings, like the Song of beatified Souls? And again, do not we squeak and jibber [28] (in our discordant, screech-owlish debatings and recriminatings); and glide bodeful, and feeble, and fearful; or uproar (*poltern*), and revel in our mad Dance of the Dead,—till the scent of the morning air summons us to our still Home; and dreamy Night becomes awake and Day? Where now is Alexander of Macedon: does the steel Host, that yelled in fierce battle-shouts at Issus and Arbela,[29] remain behind him; or have they all vanished utterly, even as perturbed Goblins must? Napoleon too, and his Moscow Retreats and Austerlitz Campaigns! [30] Was it all other than the veriest Spectre-hunt; which has now, with its howling tumult that made Night hideous, flitted away?— Ghosts! There are nigh a thousand-million walking the Earth openly at noontide; some half-hundred have vanished from it, some half-hundred have arisen in it, ere thy watch ticks once.

'O Heaven, it is mysterious, it is awful to consider that we not only carry each a future Ghost within him; but are, in very deed, Ghosts! These Limbs, whence had we them; this stormy Force; this life-blood with its burning Passion? They are dust and shadow; [31] a Shadow-system gathered round our ME; wherein, through some moments or years, the Divine Essence is to be revealed in the Flesh. That warrior on his strong war-horse, fire flashes through his eyes; force dwells in his arm and heart: but warrior and war-horse are a vision; a revealed Force, nothing more. Stately they tread the Earth, as if it were a firm substance: fool! the earth is but a film; it cracks in twain, and warrior and war-horse sink beyond plummet's sounding.[32] Plummet's? Fantasy herself will not follow them. A little while ago, they were not; a little while, and they are not, their very ashes are not.

'So has it been from the beginning, so will it be to the end. Generation after generation takes to itself the Form of a Body; and forth-issuing from Cimmerian [33] Night, on Heaven's mission APPEARS. What Force and Fire is in

28. *Hamlet* I.i.116. The subject of ghosts raises further echoes of the first act of *Hamlet* as the chapter moves to its conclusion.

29. Towns where Alexander defeated Darius and brought about the downfall of the Persian empire.

30. At Austerlitz (1805) Napoleon defeated the combined armies of Austria and Russia.

31. Carlyle translates Horace's phrase "Pulvis et umbra sumus," *Odes* IV.vii.16.

32. A reference to *The Tempest* V.i.56. A plummet is the weight on the end of a line to measure the depth of water.

33. The Cimmerians were a legendary tribe who lived in a land of endless gloom near Hades.

each he expends: one grinding in the mill of Industry; one hunter-like climbing the giddy Alpine heights of Science; one madly dashed in pieces on the rocks of Strife, in war with his fellow:—and then the Heaven-sent is recalled; his earthly Vesture falls away, and soon even to Sense becomes a vanished Shadow. Thus, like some wild-flaming, wild-thundering train of Heaven's Artillery, does this mysterious MANKIND thunder and flame, in long-drawn, quick-succeeding grandeur, through the unknown Deep. Thus, like a God-created, fire-breathing Spirit-host, we emerge from the Inane; haste stormfully across the astonished Earth; then plunge again into the Inane. Earth's mountains are levelled, and her seas filled up, in our passage: can the Earth, which is but dead and a vision, resist Spirits which have reality and are alive? On the hardest adamant some footprint of us is stamped-in; the last Rear of the host will read traces of the earliest Van. But whence?—O Heaven, whither? Sense knows not; Faith knows not; only that it is through Mystery to Mystery, from God and to God.

> We *are such stuff*
> As Dreams are made of, and our little Life
> Is rounded with a sleep! [34]

1833–34   1838

On Heroes, Hero-Worship, and the Heroic in History

From *The Hero as Poet. Dante; Shakespeare* [1]

The Hero as Divinity, the Hero as Prophet, are productions of old ages; not to be repeated in the new. They presuppose a certain rudeness of conception, which the progress of mere scientific knowledge puts an end to. There needs to be, as it were, a world vacant, or almost vacant of scientific forms, if men in their loving wonder are to fancy their fellow-man either a god or one speaking with the voice of a god. Divinity and Prophet are past. We are now to see our Hero in the less ambitious, but also less questionable, character of Poet; a character which does not pass. The Poet is a heroic figure belonging to all ages; whom all ages possess, when once he is produced, whom the newest age as the oldest may produce;—and will produce, always when Nature pleases. Let Nature send a Hero-soul; in no age is it other than possible that he may be shaped into a Poet.

Hero, Prophet, Poet,—many different names, in different times and places, do we give to Great Men; according to varieties we note in them, according to the sphere in which they have displayed themselves! We might give many more names, on this same principle. I will remark again, however, as a fact not unimportant to be understood, that the different *sphere* constitutes the grand origin of such distinction; that the Hero can be Poet, Prophet, King, Priest or what you will, according to the kind of world he finds himself born

---

34. *The Tempest* IV.i.156–58. Shakespeare says "Dreams are made *on*."

1. This excerpt is from Lecture III given May 12, 1840; the part of the lecture that deals at length with Dante has been omitted.

into. I confess, I have no notion of a truly great man that could not be *all* sorts of men. The Poet who could merely sit on a chair, and compose stanzas, would never make a stanza worth much. He could not sing the Heroic warrior, unless he himself were at least a Heroic warrior too. I fancy there is in him the Politician, the Thinker, Legislator, Philosopher;—in one or the other degree, he could have been, he is all these. So too I cannot understand how a Mirabeau,[2] with that great glowing heart, with the fire that was in it, with the bursting tears that were in it, could not have written verses, tragedies, poems, touched all hearts in that way, had his course of life and education led him thitherward. The grand fundamental character is that of Great Man; that the man be great. Napoleon has words in him which are like Austerlitz Battles.[3] Louis Fourteenth's Marshals are a kind of poetical men withal; the things Turenne[4] says are full of sagacity and geniality, like sayings of Samuel Johnson. The great heart, the clear deep-seeing eye: there it lies; no man whatever, in what province soever, can prosper at all without these. Petrarch and Boccaccio[5] did diplomatic messages, it seems, quite well: one can easily believe it; they had done things a little harder than these! Burns, a gifted song-writer, might have made a still better Mirabeau. Shakespeare,—one knows not what *he* could not have made, in the supreme degree.

True, there are aptitudes of Nature too. Nature does not make all great men, more than all other men, in the self-same mould. Varieties of aptitude doubtless; but infinitely more of circumstance; and far oftenest it is the *latter* only that are looked to. But it is as with common men in the learning of trades. You take any man, as yet a vague capability of a man, who could be any kind of craftsman; and make him into a smith, a carpenter, a mason: he is then and thenceforth that and nothing else. And if, as Addison complains,[6] you sometimes see a street-porter staggering under his load on spindle-shanks, and near at hand a tailor with the frame of a Samson handling a bit of cloth and small Whitechapel[7] needle,—it cannot be considered that aptitude of Nature alone has been consulted here either!—The Great Man also, to what shall he be bound apprentice? Given your Hero, is he to become Conqueror, King, Philosopher, Poet? It is an inexplicably complex controversial-calculation between the world and him! He will read the world and its laws; the world with its laws will be there to be read. What the world, on *this* matter, shall permit and bid is, as we said, the most important fact about the world.—

Poet and Prophet differ greatly in our loose modern notions of them. In some old languages, again, the titles are synonymous; *Vates*[8] means both Prophet and

2. The brilliant French statesman and orator (1749–91). Of all the leaders of the French Revolution he was the one whom Carlyle most admired.

3. At the battle of Austerlitz (1805), Napoleon defeated the combined armies of Austria and Russia. Napoleon's utterances on mankind, statecraft, and even literature are often memorable.

4. One of the sage and genial things said by this great general (1611–75) was, "God is always on the side of the strongest battalions."

5. Petrarch (1304–74), the great Italian poet and humanist, and Boccaccio (1313–75), the Italian scholar and writer of tales.

6. Joseph Addison (1672–1719), English essayist. He makes the complaint Carlyle refers to in the *Spectator*, No. 307 (February 1712).

7. A poor district of London.

8. The Latin *vates* originally meant soothsayer or seer and came later to mean also poet.

Poet: and indeed at all times, Prophet and Poet, well understood, have much kindred of meaning. Fundamentally indeed they are still the same; in this most important respect especially, That they have penetrated both of them into the sacred mystery of the Universe; what Goethe calls 'the open secret.' [9] 'Which is the great secret?' asks one.—'The *open* secret,'—open to all, seen by almost none! That divine mystery, which lies everywhere in all Beings, 'the Divine Idea of the World, that which lies at the bottom of Appearance,' as Fichte styles it; [10] of which all Appearance, from the starry sky to the grass of the field, but especially the Appearance of Man and his work, is but the *vesture*, the embodiment that renders it visible. This divine mystery *is* in all times and in all places; veritably is. In most times and places it is greatly overlooked; and the Universe, definable always in one or the other dialect, as the realised Thought of God, is considered a trivial, inert, commonplace matter,—as if, says the Satirist,[11] it were a dead thing, which some upholsterer had put together! It could do no good, at present, to *speak* much about this; but it is a pity for every one of us if we do not know it, live ever in the knowledge of it. Really a most mournful pity;—a failure to live at all, if we live otherwise!

But now, I say, whoever may forget this divine mystery, the *Vates*, whether Prophet or Poet, has penetrated into it; is a man sent hither to make it more impressively known to us. That always is his message; he is to reveal that to us,— that sacred mystery which he more than others lives ever present with. While others forget it, he knows it;—I might say, he has been driven to know it; without consent asked of *him*, he finds himself living in it, bound to live in it. Once more, here is no Hearsay, but a direct Insight and Belief; this man too could not help being a sincere man! Whosoever may live in the shows of things, it is for him a necessity of nature to live in the very fact of things. A man, once more, in earnest with the Universe, though all others were but toying with it. He is a *Vates*, first of all, in virtue of being sincere.[12] So far Poet and Prophet, participators in the 'open secret,' are one.

With respect to their distinction again: The *Vates* Prophet, we might say, has seized that sacred mystery rather on the moral side, as Good and Evil, Duty and Prohibition; the *Vates* Poet on what the Germans call the æsthetic side, as Beautiful, and the like. The one we may call a revealer of what we are to do, the other of what we are to love. But indeed these two provinces run into one another, and cannot be disjoined. The Prophet too has his eye on what we are to love: how else shall he know what it is we are to do? The highest Voice ever heard on this earth said withal, 'Consider the lilies of the field; they toil not, neither do they spin: yet Solomon in all his glory was not arrayed like one of these.' [13] A glance, that, into the deepest deep of

9. Carlyle often recurred to this statement of Goethe's, made in his *Maxims and Reflections*. An open secret is a matter that is ostensibly secret but actualy known to all. This open secret is that the universe is informed by spirit.

10. Johann Gottlieb Fichte (1762–1814), German philosopher and political thinker. The passage quoted is from *The Nature of the Scholar* (1805).

11. Carlyle himself. See "Natural Supernaturalism" in *Sartor Resartus*, above.

12. As Emerson remarked in his *English Traits*, the Victorians set great conscious store by the quality of sincerity (which is doubtless why the French said the English were hypocrites). On the value of sincerity Carlyle was the most articulate of the Victorians.

13. Matthew 6:28–29.

Beauty. 'The lilies of the field,'—dressed finer than earthly princes, springing-up there in the humble furrow-field; a beautiful *eye* looking-out on you, from the great inner Sea of Beauty! How could the rude Earth make these, if her Essence, rugged as she looks and is, were not inwardly Beauty? In this point of view, too, a saying of Goethe's, which has staggered several, may have meaning: 'The Beautiful,' he intimates, 'is higher than the Good: the Beautiful includes in it the Good.' The *true* Beautiful; which however, I have said some-where,[14] 'differs from the *false* as Heaven does from Vauxhall!' [15] So much for the distinction and identity of Poet and Prophet.—

In ancient and also in modern periods we find a few Poets who are accounted perfect; whom it were a kind of treason to find fault with. This is noteworthy; this is right: yet in strictness it is only an illusion. At bottom, clearly enough, there is no perfect Poet! A vein of Poetry exists in the hearts of all men; no man is made altogether of Poetry. We are all poets when we *read* a poem well. The 'imagination that shudders at the Hell of Dante,' [16] is not that the same faculty, weaker in degree, as Dante's own? No one but Shakespeare can embody, out of *Saxo Grammaticus*, [17] the story of Hamlet as Shakespeare did: but every one models some kind of story out of it; every one embodies it better or worse. We need not spend time in defining. Where there is no specific difference, as between round and square, all definition must be more or less arbitrary. A man that has *so* much more of the poetic element developed in him as to have become noticeable, will be called Poet by his neighbours. World-Poets too, those whom we are to take for perfect Poets, are settled by critics in the same way. One who rises *so* far above the general level of Poets will, to such and such critics, seem a Universal Poet; as he ought to do. And yet it is, and must be, an arbitrary distinction. All Poets, all men, have some touches of the Universal; no man is wholly made of that. Most Poets are very soon for-gotten: but not the noblest Shakespeare or Homer of them can be remembered *forever;*—a day comes when he too is not!

Nevertheless, you will say, there must be a difference between true Poetry and true Speech not poetical: what is the difference? On this point many things have been written, especially by late German Critics, some of which are not very intelligible at first. They say, for example, that the Poet has an *infinitude* in him; communicates an *Unendlichkeit*, a certain character of 'infinitude,' to whatsoever he delineates. This, though not very precise, yet on so vague a matter is worth remembering: if well meditated, some meaning will gradually be found in it. For my own part, I find considerable meaning in the old vulgar distinction of Poetry being *metrical*,[18] having music in it, being a Song. Truly, if pressed to give a definition, one might say this as soon as anything else: If your delineation be authentically *musical*, musical, not in word only, but in heart and substance, in all the thoughts and utterances

14. In his essay on Diderot.
15. A public garden on the Thames in London, in which evening entertainment of various kinds was provided. It was opened in 1661 and closed in 1859.
16. Carlyle quotes from his own essay on Burns.
17. The Danish historian of the 13th century whose *Gesta Danorum* tells the story of Hamlet.
18. On the relation of meter to the essential nature of poetry, see Wordsworth, Preface to *Lyrical Ballads*, and Coleridge, *Biographia Literaria*, Chap. XIV.

of it, in the whole conception of it, then it will be poetical; if not, not.—
Musical: how much lies in that! A *musical* thought is one spoken by a mind
that has penetrated into the inmost heart of the thing; detected the inmost
mystery of it, namely the *melody* that lies hidden in it; the inward harmony
of coherence which is its soul, whereby it exists, and has a right to be, here
in this world. All inmost things, we may say, are melodious; naturally utter
themselves in Song. The meaning of Song goes deep. Who is there that, in
logical words, can express the effect music has on us? A kind of inarticulate
unfathomable speech, which leads us to the edge of the Infinite, and lets us
for moments gaze into that!

Nay all speech, even the commonest speech, has something of song in it:
not a parish in the world but has its parish-accent;—the rhythm or *tune* to
which the people there *sing* what they have to say! Accent is a kind of
chanting; all men have accent of their own,—though they only *notice* that of
others. Observe too how all passionate language does of itself become musical,
—with a finer music than the mere accent; the speech of a man even in
zealous anger becomes a chant, a song. All deep things are Song. It seems
somehow the very central essence of us, Song; as if all the rest were but
wrappages and hulls! The primal element of us; of us, and of all things. The
Greeks fabled of Sphere-Harmonies; it was the feeling they had of the inner
structure of Nature; that the soul of all her voices and utterances was perfect
music. Poetry, therefore, we will call *musical Thought*. The Poet is he who
thinks in that manner. At bottom, it turns still on power of intellect; it is a
man's sincerity and depth of vision that makes him a Poet. See deep enough,
and you see musically; the heart of Nature *being* everywhere music, if you
can only reach it.

The *Vates* Poet, with his melodious Apocalypse of Nature, seems to hold a
poor rank among us, in comparison with the *Vates* Prophet; his function, and
our esteem of him for his function, alike slight. The Hero taken as Divinity;
the Hero taken as Prophet; then next the Hero taken only as Poet: does it
not look as if our estimate of the Great Man, epoch after epoch, were continually diminishing? We take him first for a god, then for one god-inspired;
and now, in the next stage of it, his most miraculous word gains from us only
the recognition that he is a Poet, beautiful verse-maker, man of genius, or
suchlike!—It looks so; but I persuade myself that intrinsically it is not so.
If we consider well, it will perhaps appear that in man still there is the *same*
altogether peculiar admiration for the Heroic Gift, by what name soever
called, that there at any time was.

I should say, if we do not now reckon a Great Man literally divine, it is
that our notions of God, of the supreme unattainable Fountain of Splendour,
Wisdom and Heroism, are ever rising *higher;* not altogether that our reverence
for these qualities, as manifested in our like, is getting lower. This is worth
taking thought of. Sceptical Dilettantism,[19] the curse of these ages, a curse
which will not last forever, does indeed in this the highest province of human

---

19. A dilettante is a dabbler in the arts. By dilettantism Carlyle means a general lack of
intellectual and moral seriousness.

things, as in all provinces, make sad work; and our reverence for great men, all crippled, blinded, paralytic as it is, comes out in poor plight, hardly recognisable. Men worship the shows of great men; the most disbelieve that there is any reality of great men to worship. The dreariest, fatallest faith; believing which, one would literally despair of human things. Nevertheless look, for example, at Napoleon! A Corsican lieutenant of artillery; that is the show of *him:* yet is he not obeyed, *worshipped* after his sort, as all the Tiaraed and Diademed [20] of the world put together could not be? High Duchesses, and ostlers [21] of inns, gather round the Scottish rustic, Burns;—a strange feeling dwelling in each that they had never heard a man like this; that, on the whole, this is the man! In the secret heart of these people it still dimly reveals itself, though there is no accredited way of uttering it at present, that this rustic, with his black brows and flashing sun-eyes, and strange words moving laughter and tears, is of a dignity far beyond all others, incommensurable with all others. Do not we feel it so? But now, were Dilettantism, Scepticism, Triviality, and all that sorrowful brood, cast-out of us,—as, by God's blessing, they shall one day be; were faith in the shows of things entirely swept-out, replaced by clear faith in the *things,* so that a man acted on the impulse of that only, and counted the other non-extant; what a new livelier feeling towards this Burns were it!

Nay here in these pages, such as they are, have we not two mere Poets, if not deified, yet we may say beatified? Shakespeare and Dante are Saints of Poetry; really, if we will think of it, *canonised,* so that it is impiety to meddle with them. The unguided instinct of the world, working across all these perverse impediments, has arrived at such result. Dante and Shakespeare are a peculiar Two. They dwell apart, in a kind of royal solitude; none equal, none second to them: in the general feeling of the world, a certain transcendentalism, a glory as of complete perfection, invests these two. They *are* canonised, though no Pope or Cardinals took hand in doing it! Such, in spite of every perverting influence, in the most unheroic times, is still our indestructible reverence for heroism.—We will look a little at these Two, the Poet Dante and the Poet Shakespeare: what little it is permitted us to say here of the Hero as Poet will most fitly arrange itself in that fashion. . . .

As Dante, the Italian man, was sent into our world to embody musically the Religion of the Middle Ages, the Religion of our Modern Europe, its Inner Life; so Shakespeare, we may say, embodies for us the Outer Life of our Europe as developed then, its chivalries, courtesies, humours, ambitions, what practical way of thinking, acting, looking at the world, men then had. As in Homer we may still construe Old Greece; so in Shakespeare and Dante, after thousands of years, what our modern Europe was, in Faith and in Practice, will still be legible. Dante has given us the Faith or soul; Shakespeare, in a not less noble way, has given us the Practice or body. This latter also we were

20. That is, the elite and powerful. A tiara is a jewelled headdress worn by women on formal occasions; a diadem is a royal headdress.
21. An ostler (or hostler) was the man who took charge of horses at an inn.

to have: a man was sent for it, the man Shakespeare. Just when that chivalry way of life had reached its last finish, and was on the point of breaking down into slow or swift dissolution, as we now see it everywhere, this other sovereign Poet, with his seeing eye, with his perennial singing voice, was sent to take note of it, to give long-enduring record of it. Two fit men: Dante, deep, fierce as the central fire of the world; Shakespeare, wide, placid, far-seeing, as the Sun, the upper light of the world. Italy produced the one world-voice; we English had the honour of producing the other.

Curious enough how, as it were by mere accident, this man came to us. I think always, so great, quiet, complete and self-sufficing is this Shakespeare, had the Warwickshire Squire [22] not prosecuted him for deer-stealing, we had perhaps never heard of him as a Poet! The woods and skies, the rustic Life of Man in Stratford there, had been enough for this man! But indeed that strange outbudding of our whole English Existence, which we call the Elizabethan Era, did not it too come as of its own accord? The 'Tree Igdrasil' [23] buds and withers by its own laws,—too deep for our scanning. Yet it does bud and wither, and every bough and leaf of it is there, by fixed eternal laws; not a Sir Thomas Lucy but comes at the hour fit for him. Curious, I say, and not sufficiently considered: how everything does coöperate with all; not a leaf rotting on the highway but is indissoluble portion of solar and stellar systems; no thought, word or act of man but has sprung withal out of all men, and works sooner or later, recognisably or irrecognisably, on all men! It is all a Tree: circulation of sap and influences, mutual communication of every minutest leaf with the lowest talon of a root, with every other greatest and minutest portion of the whole. The Tree Igdrasil, that has its roots down in the Kingdoms of Hela [24] and Death, and whose boughs overspread the highest Heaven!—

In some sense it may be said that this glorious Elizabethan Era with its Shakespeare, as the outcome and flowerage of all which had preceded it, is itself attributable to the Catholicism of the Middle Ages. The Christian Faith, which was the theme of Dante's Song, had produced this Practical Life which Shakespeare was to sing. For Religion then, as it now and always is, was the soul of Practice; the primary vital fact in men's life. And remark here, as rather curious, that Middle-Age Catholicism was abolished, so far as Acts of Parliament could abolish it, before Shakespeare, the noblest product of it, made his appearance.[25] He did make his appearance nevertheless. Nature at her own time, with Catholicism or what else might be necessary, sent him forth; taking small thought of Acts of Parliament. King-Henrys, Queen-Elizabeths [26] go their way; and Nature too goes hers. Acts of Parliament, on

---

22. He is named below—the Sir Thomas Lucy who is said to have prosecuted Shakespeare for deer-stealing and to be the original of the Justice Shallow of II *Henry IV* and *The Merry Wives of Windsor*.

23. In Northern mythology Igdrasil (or Yggdrasil) is the "world tree" which represents all living nature; it supports heaven and connects heaven, earth, and hell.

24. Hela (or Hel) was the daughter of the malevolent god Loki. She was the queen of the dead and the lower regions and lived under the roots of the tree Igdrasil.

25. In 1534.

26. The Tudor monarchs instrumental in suppressing Catholicism in England.

the whole, are small, notwithstanding the noise they make. What Act of Parliament, debate at St. Stephen's,[27] on the hustings [28] or elsewhere, was it that brought this Shakespeare into being? No dining at Freemasons' Tavern, opening subscription-lists, selling of shares, and infinite other jangling and true or false endeavouring! This Elizabethan Era, and all its nobleness and blessedness, came without proclamation, preparation of ours. Priceless Shakespeare was the free gift of Nature; given altogether silently;—received altogether silently, as if it had been a thing of little account. And yet, very literally, it is a priceless thing. One should look at that side of matters too.

Of this Shakespeare of ours, perhaps the opinion one sometimes hears a little idolatrously expressed is, in fact, the right one; I think the best judgment not of this country only, but of Europe at large, is slowly pointing to the conclusion, That Shakespeare is the chief of all Poets hitherto; the greatest intellect who, in our recorded world, has left record of himself in the way of Literature. On the whole, I know not such a power of vision, such a faculty of thought, if we take all the characters of it, in any other man. Such a calmness of depth; placid joyous strength; all things imaged in that great soul of his so true and clear, as in a tranquil unfathomable sea! It has been said, that in the constructing of Shakespeare's Dramas there is, apart from all other 'faculties' as they are called, an understanding manifested, equal to that in Bacon's *Novum Organum*.[29] That is true; and it is not a truth that strikes every one. It would become more apparent if we tried, any of us for himself, how, out of Shakespeare's dramatic materials, *we* could fashion such a result! The built house seems all so fit,—everyway as it should be, as if it came there by its own law and the nature of things,—we forget the rude disorderly quarry it was shaped from. The very perfection of the house, as if Nature herself had made it, hides the builder's merit. Perfect, more perfect than any other man, we may call Shakespeare in this: he discerns, knows as by instinct, what condition he works under, what his materials are, what his own force and its relation to them is. It is not a transitory glance of insight that will suffice; it is deliberate illumination of the whole matter; it is a calmly *seeing* eye; a great intellect, in short. How a man, of some wide thing that he has witnessed, will construct a narrative, what kind of picture and delineation he will give of it,—is the best measure you could get of what intellect is in the man. Which circumstance is vital and shall stand prominent; which unessential, fit to be suppressed; where is the true *beginning*, the true sequence and ending? To find out this, you task the whole force of insight that is in the man. He must *understand* the thing; according to the depth of his understanding, will the fitness of his answers be. You will try him so. Does like join itself to like; does the spirit of method stir in that confusion, so that its embroilment becomes order? Can the man say, *Fiat lux*, Let there be

27. In the reign of Edward VI, St. Stephen's Chapel, Westminster, was assigned to the use of Parliament. The House of Commons continued to sit here until 1834, when the chapel was destroyed by fire.

28. A platform from which political candidates address the voters; political campaigning in general. The word is not in use in America.

29. The treatise (1620) in which Francis Bacon undertook to describe the intellectual method by which man could extend his dominion over nature.

light; [30] and out of chaos make a world? Precisely as there is *light* in himself, will he accomplish this.

Or indeed we may say again, it is in what I called Portrait-painting, delineating of men and things, especially of men, that Shakespeare is great. All the greatness of the man comes out decisively here. It is unexampled, I think, that calm creative perspicacity of Shakespeare. The thing he looks at reveals not this or that face of it, but its inmost heart, and generic secret: it dissolves itself as in light before him, so that he discerns the perfect structure of it. Creative, we said: poetic creation, what is this too but *seeing* the thing sufficiently? The *word* that will describe the thing, follows of itself from such clear intense sight of the thing. And is not Shakespeare's *morality*, his valour, candour, tolerance, truthfulness; his whole victorious strength and greatness, which can triumph over such obstructions, visible there too? Great as the world! No *twisted*, poor convex-concave mirror, reflecting all objects with its own convexities and concavities; a perfectly *level* mirror;—that is to say withal, if we will understand it, a man justly related to all things and men, a good man. It is truly a lordly spectacle how this great soul takes-in all kinds of men and objects, a Falstaff, an Othello, a Juliet, a Coriolanus; sets them all forth to us in their round completeness; loving, just, the equal brother of all. *Novum Organum,* and all the intellect you will find in Bacon, is of a quite secondary order; earthly, material, poor in comparison with this. Among modern men, one finds, in strictness, almost nothing of the same rank. Goethe alone, since the days of Shakespeare, reminds me of it. Of him too you say that he *saw* the object; you may say what he himself says of Shakespeare: 'His characters are like watches with dial-plates of transparent crystal; they show you the hour like others, and the inward mechanism also is all visible.'

The seeing eye! It is this that discloses the inner harmony of things; what Nature meant, what musical idea Nature has wrapped-up in these often rough embodiments. Something she did mean. To the seeing eye that something were discernible. Are they base, miserable things? You can laugh over them, you can weep over them; you can in some way or other genially relate yourself to them;—you can, at lowest, hold your peace about them, turn away your own and others' face from them, till the hour come for practically exterminating and extinguishing them! At bottom, it is the Poet's first gift, as it is all men's, that he have intellect enough. He will be a Poet if he have: a Poet in word; or failing that, perhaps still better, a Poet in act. Whether he write at all; and if so, whether in prose or in verse, will depend on accidents: who knows on what extremely trivial accidents,—perhaps on his having had a singing-master, on his being taught to sing in his boyhood! But the faculty which enables him to discern the inner heart of things, and the harmony that dwells there (for whatsoever exists has a harmony in the heart of it, or it would not hold together and exist), is not the result of habits or accidents, but the gift of Nature herself; the primary outfit for a Heroic Man in what sort soever. To the Poet, as to every other, we say first of all, *See.* If you cannot do that, it is of no use to keep stringing rhymes together, jingling sensibilities against each other, and *name* yourself a Poet; there is no hope for you. If you can,

30. Genesis 1:3.

there is, in prose or verse, in action or speculation, all manner of hope. The crabbed old Schoolmaster used to ask, when they brought him a new pupil, 'But are ye sure he's *not a dunce?*' [31] Why, really one might ask the same thing, in regard to every man proposed for whatsoever function; and consider it as the one inquiry needful: Are ye sure he's not a dunce? There is, in this world, no other entirely fatal person.

For, in fact, I say the degree of vision that dwells in a man is a correct measure of the man. If called to define Shakespeare's faculty, I should say superiority of Intellect, and think I had included all under that. What indeed are faculties? We talk of faculties as if they were distinct, things separable; as if a man had intellect, imagination, fancy, &c., as he has hands, feet and arms. That is a capital error. Then again, we hear of a man's 'intellectual nature,' and of his 'moral nature,' as if these again were divisible, and existed apart. Necessities of language do perhaps prescribe such forms of utterance; we must speak, I am aware, in that way, if we are to speak at all. But words ought not to harden into things for us. It seems to me, our apprehension of this matter is, for the most part, radically falsified thereby. We ought to know withal, and to keep for ever in mind, that these divisions are at bottom but *names;* that man's spiritual nature, the vital Force which dwells in him, is essentially one and indivisible; that what we call imagination, fancy, understanding, and so forth, are but different figures of the same Power of Insight, all indissolubly connected with each other, physiognomically related; that if we knew one of them, we might know all of them. Morality itself, what we call the moral quality of a man, what is this but another *side* of the one vital Force whereby he is and works? All that a man does is physiognomical of him. You may see how a man would fight, by the way in which he sings; his courage, or want of courage, is visible in the word he utters, in the opinion he has formed, no less than in the stroke he strikes. He is *one;* and preaches the same Self abroad in all these ways.

Without hands a man might have feet, and could still walk: but, consider it,—without morality, intellect were impossible for him; a thoroughly immoral *man* could not know anything at all! To know a thing, what we can call knowing, a man must first *love* the thing, sympathise with it: that is, be *virtuously* related to it. If he have not the justice to put down his own selfishness at every turn, the courage to stand by the dangerous-true at every turn, how shall he know? His virtues, all of them, will lie recorded in his knowledge. Nature, with her truth, remains to the bad, to the selfish and the pusillanimous forever a sealed book: what such can know of Nature is mean, superficial, small; for the uses of the day merely.—But does not the very Fox know something of Nature? Exactly so: it knows where the geese lodge! The human Reynard,[32] very frequent everywhere in the world, what more does he know but this and the like of this? Nay, it should be considered, too, that if the Fox had not a certain vulpine [33] *morality*, he could not even know where the geese were, or get at the geese! If he spent his time in splenetic atrabiliar [34]

---

31. This schoolmaster was known to Carlyle in his boyhood.
32. The name under which a fox figures in several satirical beast-fables of the Middle Ages.
33. Of or pertaining to a fox (from *vulpes,* Latin for fox).
34. Splenetic: ill-humored, peevish; atrabiliar: inclined to melancholy, surly.

reflections on his own misery, his ill usage by Nature, Fortune and other Foxes, and so forth; and had not courage, promptitude, practicality, and other suitable vulpine gifts and graces, he would catch no geese. We may say of the Fox too, that his morality and insight are of the same dimensions; different faces of the same internal unity of vulpine life!—These things are worth stating; for the contrary of them acts with manifold very baleful perversion, in this time: what limitations, modifications they require, your own candour will supply.

If I say, therefore, that Shakespeare is the greatest of Intellects, I have said all concerning him. But there is more in Shakespeare's intellect than we have yet seen. It is what I call an unconscious intellect; there is more virtue in it than he himself is aware of. Novalis beautifully remarks of him, that those Dramas of his are Products of Nature too, deep as Nature herself. I find a great truth in this saying. Shakespeare's Art is not Artifice; the noblest worth of it is not there by plan or precontrivance.[35] It grows-up from the deeps of Nature, through this noble sincere soul, who is a voice of Nature. The latest generations of men will find new meanings in Shakespeare, new elucidations of their own human being; 'new harmonies with the infinite structure of the Universe; concurrences with later ideas, affinities with the higher powers and senses of man.' This well deserves meditating. It is Nature's highest reward to a true simple great soul, that he get thus to be *a part of herself.* Such a man's works, whatsoever he with utmost conscious exertion and forethought shall accomplish, grow up withal *unconsciously*,[36] from the unknown deeps in him;—as the oak-tree grows from the Earth's bosom, as the mountains and waters shape themselves; with a symmetry grounded on Nature's own laws, conformable to all Truth whatsoever. How much in Shakespeare lies hid; his sorrows, his silent struggles known to himself; much that was not known at all, not speakable at all; like *roots,* like sap and forces working underground! Speech is great; but Silence is greater.[37]

Withal the joyful tranquillity of this man is notable. I will not blame Dante for his misery: it is as battle without victory; but true battle,—the first, indispensable thing. Yet I call Shakespeare greater than Dante, in that he fought truly, and did conquer. Doubt it not, he had his own sorrows: those *Sonnets* of his will even testify expressly in what deep waters he had waded, and swum struggling for his life;—as what man like him ever failed to have to do? It seems to me a heedless notion, our common one, that he sat like a bird on the bough; and sang forth, free and offhand, never knowing the troubles of other men. Not so; with no man is it so. How could a man travel forward from rustic deer-poaching to such tragedy-writing, and not fall-in with sorrows by the way? Or, still better, how could a man delineate a Hamlet, a Coriolanus, a Macbeth, so many suffering heroic hearts, if his own heroic heart had never suffered?—And now, in contrast with all this, observe his

35. See Coleridge on Shakespeare and the organic nature of his art.
36. For the unconsciousness of artistic creation, see Shelley, *A Defence of Poetry.* Carlyle set great store by the idea that the mind was at its best and most likely to approach truth when it was not aware of its processes.
37. It is a common joke about Carlyle that no one has uttered so many words about silence as he.

mirthfulness, his genuine overflowing love of laughter! You would say, in no point does he *exaggerate* but only in laughter. Fiery objurgations, words that pierce and burn, are to be found in Shakespeare; yet he is always in measure here; never what Johnson would remark as a specially 'good hater.' [38] But his laughter seems to pour from him in floods; he heaps all manner of ridiculous nicknames on the butt he is bantering, tumbles and tosses him in all sorts of horse-play; you would say, with his whole heart laughs. And then, if not always the finest, it is always a genial laughter. Not at mere weakness, at misery or poverty; never. No man who *can* laugh, what we call laughing, will laugh at these things. It is some poor character only *desiring* to laugh, and have the credit of wit, that does so. Laughter means sympathy; good laughter is not 'the crackling of thorns under the pot.' [39] Even at stupidity and pretension this Shakespeare does not laugh otherwise than genially. Dogberry and Verges [40] tickle our very hearts; and we dismiss them covered with explosions of laughter: but we like the poor fellows only the better for our laughing; and hope they will get on well there, and continue Presidents of the City-watch. [41] Such laughter, like sunshine on the deep sea, is very beautiful to me.

.   .   .

. . . His [Shakespeare's] works are so many windows, through which we see a glimpse of the world that was in him. All his works seem, comparatively speaking, cursory, imperfect, written under cramping circumstances; giving only here and there a note of the full utterance of the man. Passages there are that come upon you like splendour out of Heaven; bursts of radiance, illuminating the very heart of the thing: you say, 'That is *true,* spoken once and forever; wheresoever and whensoever there is an open human soul, that will be recognised as true!' Such bursts, however, make us feel that the surrounding matter is not radiant; that it is, in part, temporary, conventional. Alas, Shakespeare had to write for the Globe Play-house: his great soul had to crush itself, as it could, into that and no other mould. It was with him, then, as it is with us all. No man works save under conditions. The sculptor cannot set his own free Thought before us; but his Thought as he could translate it into the stone that was given, with the tools that were given. *Disjecta membra* [42] are all that we find of any Poet, or of any man.

Whoever looks intelligently at this Shakespeare may recognise that he too was a *Prophet,* in his way; of an insight analogous to the Prophetic, though he took it up in another strain. Nature seemed to this man also divine; *un*speakable, deep as Tophet,[43] high as Heaven: 'We are such stuff as Dreams

38. The remark, made by Johnson about his friend Richard Bathurst, was recorded by Mrs. Thrale in her *Anecdotes of the Late Samuel Johnson* (1786).
39. Ecclesiastes 6:6.
40. Comic characters in *Much Ado About Nothing.*
41. Dogberry and Verges are both members of the watch, or police force, of the city of Messina.
42. "Scattered parts."
43. Hebrew word for hell.

are made of!' [44] That scroll in Westminster Abbey,[45] which few read with understanding, is of the depth of any seer. But the man sang; did not preach, except musically. We called Dante the melodious Priest of Middle-Age Catholicism. May we not call Shakespeare the still more melodious Priest of a *true* Catholicism, the 'Universal Church' of the Future and of all times? No narrow superstition, harsh asceticism, intolerance, fanatical fierceness or perversion: a Revelation, so far as it goes, that such a thousandfold hidden beauty and divineness dwells in all Nature; which let all men worship as they can! We may say without offence, that there rises a kind of universal Psalm out of this Shakespeare too; not unfit to make itself heard among the still more sacred Psalms. Not in disharmony with these, if we understood them, but in harmony! —I cannot call this Shakespeare a 'Sceptic,' as some do; his indifference to the creeds and theological quarrels of his time misleading them. No: neither unpatriotic, though he says little about his Patriotism; nor sceptic, though he says little about his Faith. Such 'indifference' was the fruit of his greatness withal: his whole heart was in his own grand sphere of worship (we may call it such): these other controversies, vitally important to other men, were not vital to him.

But call it worship, call it what you will, is it not a right glorious thing, and set of things, this that Shakespeare has brought us? For myself, I feel that there is actually a kind of sacredness in the fact of such a man being sent into this Earth. Is he not an eye to us all; a blessed heaven-sent Bringer of Light? —And, at bottom, was it not perhaps far better that this Shakespeare, everyway an unconscious man, was *conscious* of no Heavenly message? He did not feel, like Mahomet, because he saw into those internal Splendours, that he specially was the 'Prophet of God': and was he not greater than Mahomet in that? Greater; and also, if we compute strictly, as we did in Dante's case, more successful. It was intrinsically an error that notion of Mahomet's, of his supreme Prophethood: and has come down to us inextricably involved in error to this day; dragging along with it such a coil of fables, impurities, intolerances, as makes it a questionable step for me here and now to say, as I have done, that Mahomet was a true Speaker at all, and not rather an ambitious charlatan, perversity and simulacrum; no Speaker, but a Babbler! Even in Arabia, as I compute, Mahomet will have exhausted himself and become obsolete, while this Shakespeare, this Dante may still be young;—while this Shakespeare may still pretend to be a Priest of Mankind, of Arabia as of other places, for unlimited periods to come!

Compared with any speaker or singer one knows, even with Æschylus or Homer, why should he not, for veracity and universality, last like them? He is *sincere* as they; reaches deep down like them, to the universal and perennial. But as for Mahomet, I think it had been better for him *not* to be so conscious! Alas, poor Mahomet; all that he was *conscious* of was a mere error; a futility

---

44. *The Tempest* IV.i.157. Here, as in his quotation of the passage at the end of the "Natural Supernaturalism" chapter of *Sartor Resartus,* Carlyle substitutes "made of" for Shakespeare's "made on."

45. Carlyle refers to the statue, designed by William Kent, which is part of the memorial to Shakespeare set up in the Poets' Corner of Westminster Abbey in 1741. The line just quoted is inscribed on the scroll that Shakespeare holds.

and triviality,—as indeed such ever is. The truly great in him too was the unconscious: that he was a wild Arab lion of the desert, and did speak-out with that great thunder-voice of his, not by words which he *thought* to be great, but by actions, by feelings, by a history which *were* great! His Koran [46] has become a stupid piece of prolix absurdity; we do not believe, like him, that God wrote that! The Great Man here too, as always, is a Force of Nature: whatsoever is truly great in him springs-up from the *in*articulate deeps.

Well: this is our poor Warwickshire Peasant, who rose to be Manager of a Playhouse, so that he could live without begging; whom the Earl of Southampton [47] cast some kind glances on; whom Sir Thomas Lucy, many thanks to him, was for sending to the Treadmill! [48] We did not account him a god, like Odin, while he dwelt with us;—on which point there were much to be said. But I will say rather, or repeat: In spite of the sad state Hero-worship now lies in, consider what this Shakespeare has actually become among us. Which Englishman we ever made, in this land of ours, which million of Englishmen, would we not give-up rather than the Stratford Peasant? There is no regiment of highest Dignitaries that we would sell him for. He is the grandest thing we have yet done. For our honour among foreign nations, as an ornament to our English Household, what item is there that we would not surrender rather than him? Consider now, if they asked us, Will you give-up your Indian Empire or your Shakespeare, you English; never have had any Indian Empire, or never have had any Shakespeare? Really it were a grave question. Official persons would answer doubtless in official language; but we, for our part too, should not we be forced to answer: Indian Empire, or no Indian Empire; we cannot do without Shakespeare! Indian Empire will go, at any rate, some day; but this Shakespeare does not go, he lasts forever with us; we cannot give-up our Shakespeare!

Nay, apart from spiritualities; and considering him merely as a real, marketable, tangibly-useful possession. England, before long, this Island of ours, will hold but a small fraction of the English: in America, in New Holland, east and west to the very Antipodes, there will be a Saxondom covering great spaces of the Globe. And now, what is it that can keep all these together into virtually one Nation, so that they do not fall-out and fight, but live at peace, in brotherlike intercourse, helping one another? This is justly regarded as the greatest practical problem, the thing all manner of sovereignties and governments are here to accomplish: what is it that will accomplish this? Acts of Parliament, administrative prime-ministers cannot. America is parted from us, so far as Parliament could part it. Call it not fantastic, for there is much reality in it: Here, I say, is an English King, whom no time or chance, Parliament or combination of Parliaments, can dethrone! This King Shakespeare, does not he shine, in crowned sovereignty, over us all, as the noblest, gentlest, yet strongest of rallying-signs; *in*destructible; really more valuable in that point of view than any other means or appliance whatsoever? We can fancy

46. The Bible of Mohammedans. It is considered to be the Word of God communicated directly to Mohammed.
47. Henry Wriothesley, 3rd Earl of Southampton (1573–1624), was Shakespeare's patron.
48. A mill worked by persons who tread on steps on the periphery of a large wheel having a horizontal axis. It was once used in prisons, but not in Shakespeare's day.

him as radiant aloft over all the Nations of Englishmen, a thousand years hence. From Paramatta, from New York, wheresoever, under what sort of Parish-Constable soever, English men and women are, they will say to one another: 'Yes, this Shakespeare is ours; we produced him, we speak and think by him; we are of one blood and kind with him.' The most common-sense politician, too, if he pleases, may think of that.

Yes, truly, it is a great thing for a Nation that it get an articulate voice; that it produce a man who will speak-forth melodiously what the heart of it means! Italy, for example, poor Italy lies dismembered, scattered asunder, not appearing in any protocol or treaty as a unity at all; yet the noble Italy is actually *one:* Italy produced its Dante; Italy can speak! The Czar of all the Russias, he is strong, with so many bayonets, Cossacks [49] and cannons; and does a great feat in keeping such a tract of Earth politically together; but he cannot yet speak. Something great in him, but it is a dumb greatness. He has had no voice of genius, to be heard of all men and times. He must learn to speak. He is a great dumb monster hitherto. His cannons and Cossacks will all have rusted into nonentity, while that Dante's voice is still audible. The Nation that has a Dante is bound together as no dumb Russia can be.—We must here end what we had to say of the *Hero-Poet.*

1840   1841

Past and Present

In 1837 English industry entered a period of depression which was to continue for some years to come. Unemployment was general and the wages of those who did still have work were often inadequate to meet the costs of the barest necessities. The gravity of the crisis is made plain by the official count of paupers in England and Wales for March 1842—1,429,089, or one out of every eleven persons in the population. Carlyle, in the intensity of his distress over the suffering of the working class, found it impossible to continue work on his life of Cromwell, and in December of 1842 he laid it aside to write *Past and Present,* which he did at incredible speed, finishing it in two months. It was published in April 1843. Perhaps no book of the Victorian Age had so direct, immediate, and proliferating an influence. Its effect is to be seen in—to choose but a few examples—Disraeli's *Sybil* (1845), one of the first novels to represent the actualities of factory life; in Kingsley's *Alton Locke* (1850), which depicts the dreadful conditions of London sweatshops; in Mrs. Gaskell's two remarkable novels of working-class life, *Mary Barton* (1848) and *North and South* (1855); in Ruskin's concern with the iniquitous effects of laissez-faire economics— it is not too much to say that it changed the nature of English upper-class sensibility, and ultimately the course of English social and political policy.

Past and Present is divided into four books, of which the first, third, and fourth deal with the present, the second with the past. Book I is devoted to a description of the condition of England and to an account of the ignoble state of thought and feeling to which it may be ascribed. Book II presents a brilliant paradigm of how

---

49. A people of the southern part of Russia, notable for their skill as horsemen; they served as cavalrymen and were used against rebellious elements of the population.

PAST AND PRESENT   839

social heedlessness and disorganization are to be dealt with. It is based on the chronicle of a monk, Jocelin by name, a member of the monastery of St. Edmundsbury at the end of the twelfth century. This work, which had been published by the Camden Society in 1840, tells of the disarray into which the affairs of the monastery had fallen through the incompetence of its old abbot, of how the monks choose as their new abbot one of their number, Brother Samson, and of how he labors to restore the community to order and prosperity, succeeding in this purpose through his firmness of faith, his unremitting effort, and his clear-sighted practicality, not least through his readiness to impose his will upon the captious and self-seeking members of his little polity. Books III and IV draw out for the contemporary crisis the lessons of this moving achievement of seven centuries before.

From Past and Present

Labour [1]

For there is a perennial nobleness, and even sacredness, in Work.[2] Were he never so benighted, forgetful of his high calling, there is always hope in a man that actually and earnestly works: in Idleness alone is there perpetual despair. Work, never so Mammonish,[3] mean, *is* in communication with Nature; the real desire to get Work done will itself lead one more and more to truth, to Nature's appointments and regulations, which are truth.

The latest Gospel in this world is, Know thy work and do it. 'Know thyself': [4] long enough has that poor 'self' of thine tormented thee; thou wilt never get to

1. The selections from *Past and Present* are Chaps. XI, XII, and XIII from Bk. III.

2. One of the notable cultural phenomena of the 19th century was the revision of certain traditional attitudes toward work. In Judaeo-Christian thought work was one of the punitive consequences of the sin of Adam—"In the sweat of thy face shalt thou eat bread." Among the upper classes the view long prevailed that work was inappropriate to a fully developed man, a gentleman. It was in the order of things for him to bear arms and serve the state; physical labor and the routines of work were degrading to him. This aspect of the aristocratic ethos was rationalized in the Renaissance, sometimes with reference to the philosophic support provided by the views of Plato. (See, below, the opening paragraphs of Matthew Arnold's *Literature and Science*.) Yet it was in the Renaissance that the feeling about work began to change, partly by reason of the growing prestige of art and science, partly by reason of the opposition offered to the aristocratic ethos by that of the middle class. Yet even so late as the early years of the 19th century, Carlyle could think it necessary to press upon the English upper classes the practical necessity as well as the spiritual value of work. To understand why this should be so we must not only recognize the continuing force of the old aristocratic ethos, the credence still given to the idea that there were many things a gentleman could not do and still be a gentleman, but also the paucity of the occupations available to young men at the time. Apart from the army and navy and the church, the only really honorable profession was the law; politics needed a solid income; medicine was not yet a calling for the well-born; architecture was suspect; engineering was likely to be thought only for the Scotch; journalism was distinctly low; the academic posts were few in number; the so-called "helping professions" had not yet been invented. In these circumstances it is not surprising that although work would of course be a necessity, it was, as an ideal, in a quite ambiguous state.

3. The god of riches and worldliness. See Luke 16:13: "Ye cannot serve God and Mammon."

4. See, above, *Sartor Resartus*, "The Everlasting No," note 17.

'know' it, I believe! Think it not thy business, this of knowing thyself; thou art an unknowable individual: know what thou canst work at; and work at it, like a Hercules! [5] That will be thy better plan.

It has been written, 'an endless significance lies in Work'; [6] a man perfects himself by working. Foul jungles are cleared away, fair seedfields rise instead, and stately cities; and withal the man himself first ceases to be a jungle and foul unwholesome desert thereby. Consider how, even in the meanest sorts of Labour, the whole soul of a man is composed into a kind of real harmony, the instant he sets himself to work! [7] Doubt, Desire, Sorrow, Remorse, Indignation, Despair itself, all these like helldogs lie beleaguering the soul of the poor day-worker, as of every man: but he bends himself with free valour against his task, and all these are stilled, all these shrink murmuring far off into their caves. The man is now a man. The blessed glow of Labour in him, is it not as purifying fire, wherein all poison is burnt up, and of sour smoke itself there is made bright blessed flame!

Destiny, on the whole, has no other way of cultivating us. A formless Chaos, once set it *revolving*, grows round and ever rounder; ranges itself, by mere force of gravity, into strata, spherical courses; is no longer a Chaos, but a round compacted World. What would become of the Earth, did she cease to revolve? In the poor old Earth, so long as she revolves, all inequalities, irregularities disperse themselves; all irregularities are incessantly becoming regular. Hast thou looked on the Potter's wheel,—one of the venerablest objects; old as the Prophet Ezekiel and far older? [8] Rude lumps of clay, how they spin themselves up, by mere quick whirling, into beautiful circular dishes. And fancy the most assiduous Potter, but without his wheel; reduced to make dishes, or rather amorphous botches, by mere kneading and baking! Even such a Potter were Destiny, with a human soul that would rest and lie at ease, that would not work and spin! Of an idle unrevolving man the kindest Destiny, like the most assiduous Potter without wheel, can bake and knead nothing other than a botch; let her spend on him what expensive colouring, what gilding and enamelling she will, he is but a botch. Not a dish; no, a bulging, kneaded, crooked, shambling, squint-cornered, amorphous botch,—a mere enamelled vessel of dishonour! Let the idle think of this.

Blessed is he who has found his work; let him ask no other blessedness. He

5. Like Hercules, that is, not in strength but in the execution of the tasks—the Twelve Labors—that were imposed upon him.
6. Carlyle is doubtless referring to one of Goethe's many statements about the psychic and spiritual value of work. Even his Werther, the type of brooding subjectivism which Carlyle seeks to discredit, speaks in praise of work.
7. One may readily agree with Carlyle on the salutary emotional effects of work and yet feel that he is heedless in the way he develops this idea. It is surely to be doubted that the "meanest kind" of work induces a "real harmony" in the soul of the worker, that a man becomes "a man" when he is required, as he is by many kinds of work, to function like a machine. On Carlyle's behalf, however, it is to be said that he had before his eyes the consequences of unemployment, of many men suffering the disintegrating effects of having no occupation at all.
8. It is a little difficult to understand why Carlyle conceives of work as essentially a *circular* activity, which gives form to the soul as, by their circular movement, the primeval gases were shaped into the heavenly bodies and as the pot is given its form on the potter's wheel.

has a work, a life-purpose; he has found it, and will follow it! How, as a free-flowing channel, dug and torn by noble force through the sour mud-swamp of one's existence, like an ever-deepening river there, it runs and flows;—draining-off the sour festering water, gradually from the root of the remotest grass-blade; making, instead of pestilential swamp, a green fruitful meadow with its clear-flowing stream. How blessed for the meadow itself, let the stream and *its* value be great or small! Labour is Life: from the inmost heart of the Worker rises his god-given Force, the sacred celestial Life-essence breathed into him by Almighty God; from his inmost heart awakens him to all nobleness,—to all knowledge, 'self-knowledge' and much else, so soon as Work fitly begins. Knowledge? The knowledge that will hold good in working, cleave thou to that; for Nature herself accredits that, says Yea to that. Properly thou hast no other knowledge but what thou hast got by working: the rest is yet all a hypothesis of knowledge; a thing to be argued of in schools, a thing floating in the clouds, in endless logic-vortices, till we try it and fix it. 'Doubt, of whatever kind, can be ended by Action alone.'

And again, hast thou valued Patience, Courage, Perseverance, Openness to light; readiness to own thyself mistaken, to do better next time? All these, all virtues, in wrestling with the dim brute Powers of Fact, in ordering of thy fellows in such wrestle, there and elsewhere not at all, thou wilt continually learn. Set down a brave Sir Christopher [9] in the middle of black ruined Stone-heaps, of foolish unarchitectural Bishops, redtape Officials, idle Nell-Gwyn Defenders of the Faith; [10] and see whether he will ever raise a Paul's Cathedral out of all that, yea or no! Rough, rude, contradictory are all things and persons, from the mutinous masons and Irish hodmen, up to the idle Nell-Gwyn Defenders, to blustering redtape Officials, foolish unarchitectural Bishops. All these things and persons are there not for Christopher's sake and his Cathedral's; they are there for their own sake mainly! Christopher will have to conquer and constrain all these,—if he be able. All these are against him. Equitable Nature herself, who carries her mathematics and architectonics not on the face of her, but deep in the hidden heart of her,—Nature herself is but partially for him; will be wholly against him, if he constrain her not! His very money, where is it to come from? The pious munificence of England lies far-scattered, distant, unable to speak, and say, 'I am here';—must be spoken to before it can speak. Pious munificence, and all help, is so silent, invisible like the gods; impediment, contradictions manifold are so loud and near! O brave Sir Christopher, trust thou in those notwithstanding, and front all these; understand all these; by valiant patience, noble effort, insight, by man's strength, vanquish and compel all these,—and, on the whole, strike down victoriously the last topstone of

9. Sir Christopher Wren (1632–1723), the best known of English architects, who, after the great Fire of London in 1666 was put in charge of the reconstruction of innumerable churches and public buildings. His most famous work is St. Paul's Cathedral, where he is buried; the tablet marking his grave is inscribed *Si monumentam requiris, circumpice* (If you seek his monument, look around you).
10. A reference to Charles II, one of whose mistresses was the actress Nell Gwynn. The title "Defender of the Faith" was first given to Henry VIII by the pope in 1521; it continued to be used by English monarchs despite the break with Rome.

that Paul's Edifice; thy monument for certain centuries, the stamp 'Great Man' impressed very legibly on Portland-stone [11] there!—

Yes, all manner of help, and pious response from Men or Nature, is always what we call silent; cannot speak or come to light, till it be seen, till it be spoken to. Every noble work is at first 'impossible.' In very truth, for every noble work the possibilities will lie diffused through Immensity; inarticulate, undiscoverable except to faith. Like Gideon [12] thou shalt spread out thy fleece at the door of thy tent; see whether under the wide arch of Heaven there be any bounteous moisture, or none. Thy heart and life-purpose shall be as a miraculous Gideon's fleece, spread out in silent appeal to Heaven: and from the kind Immensities, what from the poor unkind Localities and town and country Parishes there never could, blessed dew-moisture to suffice thee shall have fallen!

Work is of a religious nature:—work is of a *brave* nature; which it is the aim of all religion to be. All work of man is as the swimmer's: a waste ocean threatens to devour him; if he front it not bravely, it will keep its word. By incessant wise defiance of it, lusty rebuke and buffet of it, behold how it loyally supports him, bears him as its conqueror along. 'It is so,' says Goethe, 'with all things that man undertakes in this world.' [13]

Brave Sea-captain, Norse Sea-King—Columbus, my hero, royalest Sea-king of all! it is no friendly environment this of thine, in the waste deep waters; around thee mutinous discouraged souls, behind thee disgrace and ruin, before thee the unpenetrated veil of Night. Brother, these wild water-mountains, bounding from their deep bases (ten miles deep, I am told), are not entirely there on thy behalf! Meseems *they* have other work than floating thee forward: —and the huge Winds, that sweep from Ursa Major [14] to the Tropics and Equators, dancing their giant-waltz through the kingdoms of Chaos and Immensity, they care little about filling rightly or filling wrongly the small shoulder-of-mutton sails in this cockle-skiff of thine! Thou art not among articulate-speaking friends, my brother; thou art among immeasurable dumb monsters, tumbling, howling wide as the world here. Secret, far off, invisible to all hearts but thine, there lies a help in them: see how thou wilt get at that. Patiently thou wilt wait till the mad Southwester spend itself, saving thyself by dextrous science of defence, the while: valiantly, with swift decision, wilt thou strike in, when the favouring East, the Possible, springs up. Mutiny of men thou wilt sternly repress; weakness, despondency, thou wilt cheerily encourage: thou wilt swallow down complaint, unreason, weariness, weakness of others and thyself; —how much wilt thou swallow down! There shall be a depth of Silence in thee, deeper than this Sea, which is but ten miles deep: a Silence unsoundable; known to God only. Thou shalt be a Great man. Yes, my World-Soldier, thou of

11. Limestone from the Isle of Portland off the coast of Dorsetshire.
12. Judges 6:37. Gideon asks God for a sign of his favorable intentions toward the Israelites: "Behold, I will put a fleece of wool in the floor; and if the dew be on the fleece only, and it is dry upon all the earth beside then I shall know that thou wilt save Israel by mine hand, as thou hast said."
13. A summary of a passage in *Wilhelm Meister's Apprenticeship.*
14. The constellation of the Great Bear.

the World Marine-service,—thou wilt have to be *greater* than this tumultuous unmeasured World here round thee is: thou, in thy strong soul, as with wrestler's arms, shalt embrace it, harness it down; and make it bear thee on,—to new Americas, or whither God wills!

Reward

'Religion,' I said; for, properly speaking, all true Work is Religion: and whatsoever Religion is not Work may go and dwell among the Brahmins, Antinomians, Spinning Dervishes,[1] or where it will; with me it shall have no harbour. Admirable was that of the old Monks, '*Laborare est Orare*, Work is Worship.'

Older than all preached Gospels was this unpreached, inarticulate, but ineradicable, forever-enduring Gospel: Work, and therein have wellbeing. Man, Son of Earth and of Heaven, lies there not, in the innermost heart of thee, a Spirit of active Method, a Force for Work;—and burns like a painfully-smouldering fire, giving thee no rest till thou unfold it, till thou write it down in beneficent Facts around thee! What is immethodic, waste, thou shalt make methodic, regulated, arable; obedient and productive to thee. Wheresoever thou findest Disorder, there is thy eternal enemy; attack him swiftly, subdue him; make Order of him, the subject not of Chaos, but of Intelligence, Divinity and Thee! The thistle that grows in thy path, dig it out, that a blade of useful grass, a drop of nourishing milk, may grow there instead. The waste cotton-shrub, gather its waste white down, spin it, weave it; that, in place of idle litter, there may be folded webs, and the naked skin of man be covered.

But above all, where thou findest Ignorance, Stupidity, Brute-mindedness,— yes, there, with or without Church-tithes [2] and Shovel-hat,[3] with or without Talfourd-Mahon Copyrights,[4] or were it with mere dungeons and gibbets and crosses, attack it, I say; smite it wisely, unweariedly, and rest not while thou livest and it lives; but smite, smite, in the name of God! The Highest God, as I understand it, does audibly so command thee; still audibly, if thou have ears to hear. He, even He, with his *unspoken* voice, awfuler than any Sinai thunders or syllabled speech of Whirlwinds; for the SILENCE of deep Eternities, of Worlds from beyond the morning-stars, does it not speak to thee? The unborn Ages; the old Graves, with their long-mouldering dust, the very tears that wetted it now all dry,—do not these speak to thee, what ear hath not heard? The deep Death-kingdoms, the Stars in their never-resting courses, all Space and all Time, proclaim it to thee in continual silent admonition. Thou too, if ever man should,

---

1. Brahmins: members of the highest caste of Hindus. Antinomians: members of a Christian sect that holds that faith alone, as against good works, is necessary to salvation. Spinning (or whirling) Dervishes: members of one of several Moslem sects that achieve ecstasy by chanting religious formulas and doing whirling dances.
2. Taxes paid for the support of the established church.
3. A stiff, broad-brimmed, low-crowned hat, turned up at the sides, formerly worn by English clergymen.
4. The Copyright Act of 1842 was passed largely through the efforts of Sir Thomas Noon Talfourd and Lord Philip Stanhope. Carlyle's reference to the new law would seem to intend the (not quite cogent) suggestion that the copyright doesn't exempt stupid books from attack.

shalt work while it is called Today. For the Night cometh, wherein no man can work.[5]

All true Work is sacred; in all true Work, were it but true hand-labour, there is something of divineness. Labour, wide as the Earth, has its summit in Heaven. Sweat of the brow; and up from that to sweat of the brain, sweat of the heart; which includes all Kepler calculations, Newton meditations,[6] all Sciences, all spoken Epics, all acted Heroisms, Martyrdoms,—up to that 'Agony of bloody sweat,'[7] which all men have called divine! O brother, if this is not 'worship,' then I say, the more pity for worship; for this is the noblest thing yet discovered under God's sky. Who art thou that complainest of thy life of toil? Complain not. Look up, my wearied brother; see thy fellow Workmen there, in God's Eternity; surviving there, they alone surviving: sacred Band of the Immortals, celestial Bodyguard of the Empire of Mankind. Even in the weak Human Memory they survive so long, as saints, as heroes, as gods; they alone surviving; peopling, they alone, the unmeasured solitudes of Time! To thee Heaven, though severe, is *not* unkind; Heaven is kind,—as a noble Mother; as that Spartan Mother, saying while she gave her son his shield, 'With it, my son, or upon it!'[8] Thou too shalt return *home* in honour; to thy far-distant Home, in honour; doubt it not,—if in the battle thou keep thy shield! Thou, in the Eternities and deepest Death-kingdoms, art not an alien; thou everywhere art a denizen! Complain not; the very Spartans did not *complain*.

And who art thou that braggest of thy life of Idleness; complacently showest thy bright gilt equipages; sumptuous cushions; appliances for folding of the hands to mere sleep? Looking up, looking down, around, behind or before, discernest thou, if it be not in Mayfair[9] alone, any *idle* hero, saint, god, or even devil? Not a vestige of one. In the Heavens, in the Earth, in the Waters under the Earth, is none like unto thee. Thou art an original figure in this Creation; a denizen in Mayfair alone, in this extraordinary Century or Half-Century alone! One monster there is in the world: the idle man. What is his 'Religion'? That Nature is a Phantasm, where cunning beggary or thievery may sometimes find good victual. That God is a lie; and that Man and his Life are a lie.—Alas, alas, who of us *is* there that can say, I have worked? The faithfulest of us are unprofitable servants;[10] the faithfulest of us know that best. The faithfulest of us may say, with sad and true old Samuel,[11] 'Much of my life has been trifled away!' But he that has, and except 'on public occasions' professes to have, no function but that of going idle in a graceful or graceless manner; and of begetting sons to go idle; and to address Chief Spinners and Diggers, who at

5. See, above, *Sartor Resartus*, "The Everlasting Yea," note 40.
6. Johann Kepler (1571–1630), German astronomer; Sir Isaac Newton (1642–1727), English astronomer.
7. Luke 22:44.
8. For the Spartans, to lose one's shield in battle was the ultimate disgrace.
9. In the 19th century the most fashionable part of London. The name became synonymous with fashionable society. See, below, Oscar Wilde, *The Importance of Being Earnest*.
10. See Luke 17:10.
11. Dr. Samuel Johnson, who often reproached himself for bad habits of work. Boswell mentions this in referring to one of Johnson's *Meditations*, written on his 55th birthday: "I have done nothing. The need of doing, therefore, is pressing since the time of doing is short."

least *are* spinning and digging, 'Ye scandalous persons who produce too much' —My Corn-Law friends,[12] on what imaginary still richer Eldorados, and true iron-spikes with law of gravitation, are ye rushing!

As to the Wages of Work there might innumerable things be said; there will and must yet innumerable things be said and spoken, in St. Stephen's and out of St. Stephen's;[13] and gradually not a few things be ascertained and written, on Law-parchment, concerning this very matter:—'Fair day's-wages for a fair day's-work' is the most unrefusable demand! Money-wages 'to the extent of keeping your worker alive that he may work more'; these, unless you mean to dismiss him straightway out of this world, are indispensable alike to the noblest Worker and to the least noble!

One thing only I will say here, in special reference to the former class, the noble and noblest; but throwing light on all the other classes and their arrangements of this difficult matter: The 'wages' of every noble Work do yet lie in Heaven or else Nowhere. Not in Bank-of-England bills, in Owen's Labour-bank,[14] or any the most improved establishment of banking and money-changing, needest thou, heroic soul, present thy account of earnings. Human banks and labour-banks know thee not; or know thee after generations and centuries have passed away, and thou art clean gone from 'rewarding,'—all manner of bank-drafts, shop-tills, and Downing-street Exchequers [15] lying very invisible, so far from thee! Nay, at bottom, dost thou need any reward? Was it thy aim and life-purpose to be filled with good things for thy heroism; to have a life of pomp and ease, and be what men call 'happy,' in this world, or in any other world? I answer for thee deliberately, No. The whole spiritual secret of the new epoch lies in this, that thou canst answer for thyself, with thy whole clearness of head and heart, deliberately, No!

My brother, the brave man has to give his Life away. Give it, I advise thee;— thou dost not expect to *sell* thy Life in an adequate manner? What price, for example, would content thee? The just price of thy LIFE to thee,—why, God's entire Creation to thyself, the whole Universe of Space, the whole Eternity of Time, and what they hold: that is the price which would content thee; that, and if thou wilt be candid, nothing short of that! It is thy all; and for it thou wouldst have all. Thou art an unreasonable mortal;—or rather thou art a poor *infinite* mortal, who, in thy narrow clay-prison here, *seemest* so unreasonable! Thou wilt never sell thy Life, or any part of thy Life, in a satisfactory manner. Give it, like a royal heart; let the price be Nothing: thou *hast* then, in a certain sense, got All for it! The heroic man,—and is not every man, God be thanked, a

12. The Corn Laws, restricting the importation of breadstuffs in order to maintain the price of domestic wheat, were the subject of fierce controversy in the early 19th century. They were repealed in 1846 in consequence of the wide distress in England and the Irish famine of 1845.

13. Until it burned down in 1834 St. Stephen's Chapel in Westminster was where the House of Commons met.

14. In 1832 the socialist reformer Robert Owen (1771–1858) formed the Equitable Labour Exchange. In transactions with the Exchange "Labour notes" were used as currency, prices being calculated on the basis of the cost of raw material and the time expended on the manufacture of the article.

15. The official residence of the chancellor of the exchequer, like that of the prime minister, is in Downing Street.

potential hero?—has to do so, in all times and circumstances. In the most heroic age, as in the most unheroic, he will have to say, as Burns said proudly and humbly of his little Scottish Songs, little dewdrops of Celestial Melody in an age when so much was unmelodious: 'By Heaven, they shall either be invaluable or of no value; I do not need your guineas for them!' [16] It is an element which should, and must, enter deeply into all settlements of wages here below. They never will be 'satisfactory' otherwise; they cannot, O Mammon Gospel, they never can! Money for my little piece of work 'to the extent that will allow me to keep working'; yes, this,—unless you mean that I shall go my ways *before* the work is all taken out of me: but as to 'wages'—!—

On the whole, we do entirely agree with those old Monks, *Laborare est Orare*. In a thousand senses, from one end of it to the other, true Work *is* Worship. He that works, whatsoever be his work, he bodies forth the form of Things Unseen; a small Poet every Worker is. The idea, were it but of his poor Delf Platter, how much more of his Epic Poem, is as yet 'seen,' half-seen, only by himself; to all others it is a thing unseen, impossible; to Nature herself it is a thing unseen, a thing which never hitherto was;—very 'impossible,' for it is as yet a No-thing! The Unseen Powers had need to watch over such a man; he works in and for the Unseen. Alas, if he look to the Seen Powers only, he may as well quit the business; his No-thing will never rightly issue as a Thing, but as a Deceptivity, a Sham-thing,—which it had better not do!

Thy No-thing of an Intended Poem, O Poet who hast looked merely to reviewers, copyrights, booksellers, popularities, behold it has not yet become a Thing; for the truth is not in it! Though printed, hotpressed,[17] reviewed, celebrated, sold to the twentieth edition: what is all that? The Thing, in philosophical uncommercial language, is still a No-thing, mostly semblance and deception of the sight;—benign Oblivion incessantly gnawing at it, impatient till Chaos, to which it belongs, do reabsorb it!—

He who takes not counsel of the Unseen and Silent, from him will never come real visibility and speech. Thou must descend to the *Mothers*,[18] to the *Manes*,[19] and Hercules-like [20] long suffer and labour there, wouldst thou emerge with victory into the sunlight. As in battle and the shock of war,—for is not this a battle?—thou too shalt fear no pain or death, shalt love no ease or life; the voice of festive Lubberlands,[21] the noise of greedy Acheron [22] shall alike lie silent under thy victorious feet. Thy work, like Dante's, shall 'make thee lean for many years.' [23] The world and its wages, its criticisms, counsels, helps, impediments, shall be as a waste ocean-flood; the chaos through which thou art to swim and sail. Not the waste waves and their weedy gulf-streams, shalt thou

16. Burns wrote to this effect in a letter of September 16, 1792.
17. Hotpressing was a process to make paper glossy.
18. The Mothers are mysterious figures in Part II of Goethe's *Faust* inhabiting a shadowy realm which Faust visits. They seem to have a connection with the Platonic conception of Ideas—they have in charge the forms that existence may take.
19. The spirits of the dead (Latin).
20. See note 5.
21. Lubberland is a mythical place of plenty and laziness.
22. The river of Hades, the infernal region; also Hades itself.
23. Opening lines of Dante's *Paradise* XXV.

take for guidance: thy star alone,—'*Se tu segui tua stella!*' [24] Thy star alone, now clear-beaming over Chaos, nay now by fits gone out, disastrously eclipsed: this only shalt thou strive to follow. O, it is a business, as I fancy, that of weltering your way through Chaos and the murk of Hell! Green-eyed dragons watching you, three-headed Cerberuses,[25]—not without sympathy of *their* sort! '*Eccovi l' uom ch' è stato all' Inferno.*' [26] For in fine, as Poet Dryden says, you do walk hand in hand with sheer Madness, all the way,[27]—who is by no means pleasant company! You look fixedly into Madness, and *her* undiscovered, boundless, bottomless Night-empire; that you may extort new Wisdom out of it, as an Eurydice from Tartarus.[28] The higher the Wisdom, the closer was its neighbourhood and kindred with mere Insanity; literally so;—and thou wilt, with a speechless feeling, observe how highest Wisdom, struggling up into this world, has oftentimes carried such tinctures and adhesions of Insanity still cleaving to it hither!

All Works, each in their degree, are a making of Madness sane;—truly enough a religious operation; which cannot be carried on without religion. You have not work otherwise; you have eye-service, greedy grasping of wages, swift and ever swifter manufacture of semblances to get hold of wages. Instead of better felt-hats to cover your head, you have bigger lath-and-plaster hats set travelling the streets on wheels. Instead of heavenly and earthly Guidance for the souls of men, you have 'Black or White Surplice' Controversies,[29] stuffed hair-and-leather Popes; [30]—terrestrial *Law-wards*,[31] Lords and Law-bringers, 'organising Labour' in these years, by passing Corn-Laws. With all which, alas, this distracted Earth is now full, nigh to bursting. Semblances most smooth to the touch and eye; most accursed, nevertheless, to body and soul. Semblances, be they of Sham-woven Cloth or of Dilettante Legislation, which are *not* real wool or substance, but Devil's-dust, accursed of God and man! No man has

24. Dante, *Inferno* VI. Said by Ulysses to Dante when Ulysses explains why he undertook his last fatal voyage.
25. The monstrous dog guarding the gates of Hades. One of the tasks of Hercules was to bring him to earth and take him back again.
26. "Behold the man who has been in Hell." According to Boccaccio, this was said of Dante by the people of Florence.
27. A reference to Dryden's line "Great wits are sure to madness near allied," *Absolom and Achitophel*, l. 163.
28. When his wife Eurydice died and descended to Hades (Tartarus), the great musician Orpheus, by means of the magic of his song, was able to follow her and prevail upon Pluto, the king of the underworld, to permit her to return to life.
29. A reference to the revived interest in ecclesiastical ceremony, including the use by clergymen of a variety of vestments in church services. The Oxford Movement (1833–45) was itself not much concerned with this question, but its emphasis upon tradition and the continuity of the Anglican Church with the Roman Catholic did much to stimulate the ceremonial tendency among the members of the so-called High Church party.
30. An earlier chapter of *Past and Present* (Bk. III, Chap. I, "Phenomena") relates an incident in which the pope, being afflicted with rheumatism, cannot happily follow the custom of kneeling as he rides through the streets blessing the people on the feast day of Corpus Christi; his cardinals consult and order the construction of a kneeling figure within which the pope can sit comfortably, only his face and hands being visible.
31. The etymology is Old English: *hlaf*, bread, loaf + *weard*, keeper, ward. See, below, the etymology of "lady."

worked, or can work, except religiously; not even the poor day-labourer, the weaver of your coat, the sewer of your shoes. All men, if they work not as in a Great Taskmaster's eye,[32] will work wrong, work unhappily for themselves and you.

Industrial work, still under bondage to Mammon, the rational soul of it not yet awakened, is a tragic spectacle. Men in the rapidest motion and self-motion; restless, with convulsive energy, as if driven by Galvanism,[33] as if possessed by a Devil; tearing asunder mountains,—to no purpose, for Mammonism is always Midas-eared! [34] This is sad, on the face of it. Yet courage: the beneficent Destinies, kind in their sternness, are apprising us that this cannot continue. Labour is not a devil, even while encased in Mammonism; Labour is ever an imprisoned god, writhing unconsciously or consciously to escape out of Mammonism! Plugson of Undershot,[35] like Taillefer of Normandy,[36] wants victory; how much happier will even Plugson be to have a Chivalrous victory than a Chactaw [37] one! The unredeemed ugliness is that of a slothful People. Show me a People energetically busy; heaving, struggling, all shoulders at the wheel; their heart pulsing, every muscle swelling, with man's energy and will;—I show you a People of whom great good is already predicable; to whom all manner of good is yet certain, if their energy endure. By very working, they will learn; they have, Antæus-like,[38] their foot on Mother Fact: how can they but learn?

The vulgarest Plugson of a Master-Worker, who can command Workers, and get work out of them, is already a considerable man. Blessed and thrice-blessed symptoms I discern of Master-Workers who are not vulgar men; who are Nobles, and begin to feel that they must act as such: all speed to these, they are England's hope at present! But in this Plugson himself, conscious of almost no nobleness whatever, how much is there! Not without man's faculty, insight, courage, hard energy, is this rugged figure. His words none of the wisest; but his actings cannot be altogether foolish. Think, how were it, stoodst thou suddenly in his shoes! He has to command a thousand men. And not imaginary commanding; no, it is real, incessantly practical. The evil passions of so many men (with the Devil in them, as in all of us) he has to vanquish; by manifold force of speech and of silence, to repress or evade. What a force of silence, to

32. A phrase from Milton's sonnet "How Soon Hath Time."
33. That is, electricity. Luigi Galvani (1737–98) was the discoverer of electricity produced by chemical action.
34. The unfortunate King Midas, when asked to judge a musical contest between Apollo and Pan, preferred Pan, whereupon Apollo gave him ass's ears.
35. Plugson is the generic name which, earlier in *Past and Present*, Carlyle has given to manufacturers. The place name "of Undershot" is mockingly assigned to him for two reasons: because his factory is powered by undershot water-wheels, that is, wheels moved by water passing under them; and because he has the unthinking tenacity of the English bulldog, which has "undershot" jaws.
36. Taillefer was the minstrel who sang the *Song of Roland* to the army of William the Conqueror before the Battle of Hastings. The point of the comparison is to suggest that the archaic mode of military heroism and the modern mode of industrial enterprise have something in common.
37. Choctaw—generically, "wild Indian," savage.
38. In Greek mythology, a gigantic wrestler, son of Earth, who, whenever he was thrown, gained renewed strength from contact with his mother. Hercules conquered him by lifting him in the air and squeezing him to death.

say nothing of the others, is in Plugson! For these his thousand men he has to provide raw-material, machinery, arrangement, houseroom; and ever at the week's end, wages by due sale. No Civil-List,[39] or Goulburn-Baring Budget [40] has he to fall back upon, for paying of his regiment; he has to pick his supplies from the confused face of the whole Earth and Contemporaneous History, by his dexterity alone. There will be dry eyes if he fail to do it!—He exclaims, at present, 'black in the face,' near strangled with Dilettante Legislation; 'Let me have elbow-room, throat-room, and I will not fail! No, I will spin yet, and conquer like a giant: what "sinews of war" lie in me, untold resources towards the Conquest of this Planet, if instead of hanging me, you husband them, and help me!'—My indomitable friend, it is *true;* and thou shalt and must be helped.

This is not a man I would kill and strangle by Corn-Laws, even if I could! No, I would fling my Corn-Laws and Shot-belts[41] to the Devil; and try to help this man. I would teach him, by noble precept and low-precept, by noble example most of all, that Mammonism was not the essence of his or of my station in God's Universe; but the adscititious excrescence of it; the gross, terrene, godless embodiment of it; which would have to become, more or less, a godlike one. By noble *real* legislation, by true *noble's*-work, by unwearied, valiant, and were it wageless effort, in my Parliament and in my Parish, I would aid, constrain, encourage him to effect more or less this blessed change. I should know that it would have to be effected; that unless it were in some measure effected, he and I and all of us, I first and soonest of all, were doomed to perdition! [42]—Effected it will be; unless it were a Demon that made this Universe; which I, for my own part, do at no moment, under no form, in the least believe.

May it please your Serene Highnesses, your Majesties, Lordships and Lawwardships, the proper Epic of this world is not now 'Arms and the Man'; [43] how much less, 'Shirt-frills and the Man': no, it is now 'Tools and the Man': that, henceforth to all time, is now our Epic;—and you, first of all others, I think, were wise to take note of that!

Democracy

If the Serene Highnesses and Majesties do not take note of that, then, as I perceive, *that* will take note of itself! The time for levity, insincerity, and idle babble and play-acting, in all kinds, is gone by; it is a serious, grave time. Old long-vexed questions, not yet solved in logical words or parliamentary laws, are fast solving themselves in facts, somewhat unblessed to behold! This largest of questions, this question of Work and Wages, which ought, had we heeded

39. The account of the appropriation made by Parliament for the support of the royal family. Until 1901 this included the pensions to individuals that were in the royal bounty.
40. Sir Francis Thornhill Baring was chancellor of the exchequer from 1839 to 1841; he was succeeded in the office by Henry Goulburn, 1841–46.
41. The belt that transmits power from the undershot wheel to the machine.
42. Carlyle proceeds to give this instruction to Plugson in Bk. IV, Chap. IV, of *Past and Present*. The chapter is entitled "Captains of Industry"; its theme is that the members of the manufacturing class must conceive of themselves as leaders of an industrial army, having the sense of responsibility appropriate to such a function and an authority deriving from this responsibility.
43. The opening line of the *Aeneid:* "Arma virumque cano" (Arms and the man I sing).

Heaven's voice, to have begun two generations ago or more, cannot be delayed longer without hearing Earth's voice. 'Labour' will verily need to be somewhat 'organised,' as they say,—God knows with what difficulty. Man will actually need to have his debts and earnings a little better paid by man; which, let Parliaments speak of them or be silent of them, are eternally his due from man, and cannot, without penalty and at length not without death-penalty, be withheld. How much ought to cease among us straightway; how much ought to begin straightway, while the hours yet are!

Truly they are strange results to which this of leaving all to 'Cash'; of quietly shutting-up the God's Temple, and gradually opening wide-open the Mammon's Temple, with 'Laissez-faire, and Every man for himself,'—have led us in these days! We have Upper, speaking Classes, who indeed do 'speak' as never man spake before; the withered flimsiness, the godless baseness and barrenness of whose Speech might of itself indicate what kind of Doing and practical Governing went on under it! For speech is the gaseous element out of which most kinds of Practice and Performance, especially all kinds of moral Performance, condense themselves, and take shape; as the one is, so will the other be. Descending, accordingly, into the Dumb Class in its Stockport Cellars and Poor-Law Bastilles,[1] have we not to announce that they also are hitherto unexampled in the History of Adam's Posterity?

Life was never a May-game for men: in all times the lot of the dumb millions born to toil was defaced with manifold sufferings, injustices, heavy burdens, avoidable and unavoidable; not play at all, but hard work that made the sinews sore and the heart sore. As bond-slaves, *villani, bordarii, sochemanni*,[2] nay indeed as dukes, earls and kings, men were oftentimes made weary of their life; and had to say, in the sweat of their brow and of their soul, Behold, it is not sport, it is grim earnest, and our back can bear no more! Who knows not what massacrings and harryings there have been; grinding, long-continuing, unbearable injustices,—till the heart had to rise in madness. . . .

And yet I will venture to believe that in no time, since the beginnings of Society, was the lot of those same dumb millions of toilers so entirely unbearable as it is even in the days now passing over us. It is not to die, or even to die of hunger, that makes a man wretched; many men have died; all men must die,—the last exit of us all is in a Fire-Chariot of Pain. But it is to live miserable we know not why; to work sore and yet gain nothing; to be heart-worn, weary, yet isolated, unrelated, girt-in with a cold universal Laissez-faire: it is to die slowly all our life long, imprisoned in a deaf, dead, Infinite Injustice, as in the accursed iron belly of a Phalaris' Bull![3] This is and remains forever intolerable to all men whom God has made. Do we wonder at French Revolutions, Chartisms, Revolts of Three Days? The times, if we will consider them, are really unexampled.

1. The homes for the indigent established by the Poor Laws were called Bastilles after the famous prison in Paris whose destruction by the mob in 1789 was the symbolic beginning of the French Revolution.
2. Names for the lowest classes in the feudal system.
3. Phalaris, an ancient tyrant, punished criminals by putting them into a brazen bull which was heated by fire.

Never before did I hear of an Irish Widow reduced to 'prove her sisterhood by dying of typhus-fever and infecting seventeen persons,'—saying in such undeniable way, 'You *see* I was your sister!'[4] Sisterhood, brotherhood, was often forgotten; but not till the rise of these ultimate Mammon and Shotbelt Gospels did I ever see it so expressly denied. If no pious Lord or *Law-ward* would remember it, always some pious Lady (*'Hlaf-dig,'* Benefactress, *'Loaf-giveress,'* they say she is,—blessings on her beautiful heart!) was there, with mild mother-voice and hand, to remember it; some pious thoughtful *Elder,* what we now call 'Prester,' *Presbyter* or 'Priest,' was there to put all men in mind of it, in the name of the God who had made all.

Not even in Black Dahomey[5] was it ever, I think, forgotten to the typhus-fever length. Mungo Park,[6] resourceless, had sunk down to die under the Negro Village-Tree, a horrible White object in the eyes of all. But in the poor Black Woman, and her daughter who stood aghast at him, whose earthly wealth and funded capital consisted of one small calabash[7] of rice, there lived a heart richer than *Laissez-faire:* they, with a royal munificence, boiled their rice for him; they sang all night to him, spinning assiduous on their cotton distaffs, as he lay to sleep: 'Let us pity the poor white man; no mother has he to fetch him milk, no sister to grind him corn!' Thou poor black Noble One,—thou *Lady* too: did not a God make thee too; was there not in thee too something of a God!—

Gurth, born thrall of Cedric the Saxon,[8] has been greatly pitied by Dryas-dust[9] and others. Gurth, with the brass collar round his neck, tending Cedric's pigs in the glades of the wood, is not what I call an exemplar of human felicity: but Gurth, with the sky above him, with the free air and tinted boscage and umbrage[10] round him, and in him at least the certainty of supper and social lodging when he came home; Gurth to me seems happy, in comparison with many a Lancashire and Buckinghamshire[11] man of these days, not born thrall of anybody! Gurth's brass collar did not gall him: Cedric *deserved* to be his master. The pigs were Cedric's, but Gurth too would get his parings of them. Gurth had the inexpressible satisfaction of feeling himself related indissolubly, though in a rude brass-collar way, to his fellow-mortals in this Earth. He had

---

4. In the chapter of *Past and Present* called "Mammonism," Carlyle relates the case of an Irish widow whom no one would help in her destitution; she died of typhus, having infected seventeen persons in her vicinity, all of whom died. In refusing to help her, her neighbors had said in effect " 'No; impossible; thou art no sister of ours.' But she proves her sisterhood; her typhus-fever kills *them;* they actually were her brothers, though denying it. Had human creature ever to go lower for a proof?"

5. Nation of West Africa; its inhabitants at one time practiced human sacrifice and cannibalism.

6. Mungo Park (1771–1806), Scottish surgeon and famous African explorer. He died in a conflict with the natives.

7. A hollow gourd used as a dish.

8. In Scott's *Ivanhoe* Cedric the Saxon is a well-to-do farmer and Gurth is his thrall or serf.

9. Dryasdust is the fictitious stuffy antiquarian whom Sir Walter Scott addresses in the prefaces to some of his novels. Carlyle frequently uses the name to refer to pedantic scholars generally.

10. Thickets and shade.

11. Industrial counties of England.

superiors, inferiors, equals.—Gurth is now 'emancipated' long since; has what we call 'Liberty.' Liberty, I am told, is a divine thing. Liberty when it becomes the 'Liberty to die by starvation' is not so divine!

Liberty? The true liberty of a man, you would say, consisted in his finding out, or being forced to find out the right path, and to walk thereon. To learn, or to be taught, what work he actually was able for; and then by permission, persuasion, and even compulsion, to set about doing of the same! That is his true blessedness, honour, 'liberty' and maximum of wellbeing: if liberty be not that, I for one have small care about liberty. You do not allow a palpable madman to leap over precipices; you violate his liberty, you that are wise; and keep him, were it in strait-waistcoats, away from the precipices! Every stupid, every cowardly and foolish man is but a less palpable madman: his true liberty were that a wiser man, that any and every wiser man, could, by brass collars, or in whatever milder or sharper way, lay hold of him when he was going wrong, and order and compel him to go a little righter. O, if thou really art my *Senior*, Seigneur, my *Elder*, Presbyter or Priest,—if thou art in very deed my *Wiser*, may a beneficent instinct lead and impel thee to 'conquer' me, to command me! If thou do know better than I what is good and right, I conjure thee in the name of God, force me to do it; were it by never such brass collars, whips and handcuffs, leave me not to walk over precipices! That I have been called, by all the Newspapers, a 'free man' will avail me little, if my pilgrimage have ended in death and wreck. O that the Newspapers had called me slave, coward, fool, or what it pleased their sweet voices to name me, and I had attained not death, but life!—Liberty requires new definitions.

A conscious abhorrence and intolerance of Folly, of Baseness, Stupidity, Poltroonery and all that brood of things, dwells deep in some men: still deeper in others an *un*conscious abhorrence and intolerance, clothed moreover by the beneficent Supreme Powers in what stout appetites, energies, egoisms so-called, are suitable to it;—these latter are your Conquerors, Romans, Normans, Russians, Indo-English; Founders of what we call Aristocracies. Which indeed have they not the most 'divine right' to found;—being themselves very truly "Αριστοι,[12] Bravest, Best; and conquering generally a confused rabble of Worst, or at lowest, clearly enough, of Worse? I think their divine right, tried, with affirmatory verdict, in the greatest Law-Court [13] known to me, was good! A class of men who are dreadfully exclaimed against by Dryasdust; of whom nevertheless beneficent Nature has oftentimes had need; and may, alas, again have need.

When, across the hundredfold poor scepticisms, trivialisms and constitutional cobwebberies of Dryasdust, you catch any glimpse of a William the Conqueror, a Tancred of Hauteville [14] or suchlike,—do you not discern veritably some rude outline of a true God-made King; whom not the Champion of England cased in tin, but all Nature and the Universe were calling to the throne? It is absolutely necessary that he get thither. Nature does not mean her poor Saxon children to perish, of obesity, stupor or other malady, as yet: a stern Ruler and Line of Rulers therefore is called in,—a stern but most beneficent *perpetual*

12. Aristoi.
13. That is, the law court of history.
14. A Norman hero of the First Crusade.

House-Surgeon is by Nature herself called in, and even the appropriate *fees* are provided for him! Dryasdust talks lamentably about Hereward[15] and the Fen Counties;[16] fate of Earl Waltheof;[17] Yorkshire and the North reduced to ashes: all which is undoubtedly lamentable. But even Dryasdust apprises me of one fact: 'A child, in this William's reign, might have carried a purse of gold from end to end of England.' My erudite friend, it is a fact which outweighs a thousand! Sweep away thy constitutional, sentimental and other cobwebberies; look eye to eye, if thou still have any eye, in the face of this big burly William Bastard[18] thou wilt see a fellow of most flashing discernment, of most strong lion-heart;—in whom, as it were, within a frame of oak and iron, the gods have planted the soul of 'a man of genius'! Dost thou call that nothing? I call it an immense thing!—Rage enough was in this Willelmus Conquæstor,[19] rage enough for his occasions;—and yet the essential element of him, as of all such men, is not scorching *fire*, but shining illuminative *light*. Fire and light are strangely interchangeable; nay, at bottom, I have found them different forms of the same most godlike 'elementary substance' in our world: a thing worth stating in these days. The essential element of this Conquæstor is, first of all, the most sun-eyed perception of what *is* really what on this God's-Earth;—which, thou wilt find, does mean at bottom 'Justice,' and 'Virtues' not a few: *Conformity* to what the Maker has seen good to make; that, I suppose, will mean Justice and a Virtue or two?—

Dost thou think Willelmus Conquæstor would have tolerated ten years' jargon, one hour's jargon, on the propriety of killing Cotton-manufacturers by partridge Corn-Laws?[20] I fancy, this was not the man to knock out of his night's-rest with nothing but a noisy bedlamism in your mouth! 'Assist us still better to bush the partridges; strangle Plugson who spins the shirts?'—'*Par la Splendeur de Dieu!*'[21]—Dost thou think Willelmus Conquæstor, in this new time, with Steamengine Captains of Industry[22] on one hand of him, and Joe-Manton Captains of Idleness[23] on the other, would have doubted which *was* really the BEST; which did deserve strangling, and which not?

I have a certain indestructible regard for Willelmus Conquæstor. A resident House-Surgeon, provided by Nature for her beloved English People, and even furnished with the requisite fees, as I said; for he by no means felt himself doing Nature's work, this Willelmus, but his own work exclusively! And his own work withal it was; informed '*par la Splendeur de Dieu.*'—I say, it is necessary to get the work out of such a man, however harsh that be! When a

15. Hereward the Wake was a Saxon of the 11th century who resisted the Normans.
16. Lincolnshire and adjacent counties, so called because of their marshy districts; it was here that Hereward's uprisings took place.
17. Earl of Northumberland (d. 1076), suspected by William the Conqueror of having sought the aid of the Danish fleet; he was executed and came later to be regarded as an English martyr.
18. William the Conqueror was of illegitimate birth.
19. Carlyle's Latin for William the Conqueror.
20. "Partridge Corn-Laws" because they are supported by the aristocracy, whose addiction to sports, including the shooting of game birds, Carlyle often mocked.
21. By the glory of God!
22. See note 42 to the section captioned "Reward" (above).
23. Joe Manton was the celebrated maker of fine shotguns. Carlyle had earlier characterized the idle aristocracy by its admiration of his products.

world, not yet doomed for death, is rushing down to ever-deeper Baseness and Confusion, it is a dire necessity of Nature's to bring in her ARISTOCRACIES, her BEST, even by forcible methods. When their descendants or representatives cease entirely to *be* the Best, Nature's poor world will very soon rush down again to Baseness; and it becomes a dire necessity of Nature's to cast them out. Hence French Revolutions, Five-point Charters,[24] Democracies, and a mournful list of *Etceteras,* in these our afflicted times.

To what extent Democracy has now reached, how it advances irresistible with ominous, ever-increasing speed, he that will open his eyes on any province of human affairs may discern. Democracy is everywhere the inexorable demand of these ages, swiftly fulfilling itself. From the thunder of Napoleon battles, to the jabbering of Open-vestry in St. Mary Axe,[25] all things announce Democracy. A distinguished man, whom some of my readers will hear again with pleasure, thus writes to me what in these days he notes from the Wahngasse of Weissnichtwo, where our London fashions seem to be in full vogue. Let us hear the Herr Teufelsdröckh again,[26] were it but the smallest word!

'Democracy, which means despair of finding any Heroes to govern you, and contented putting-up with the want of them,—alas, thou too, *mein Lieber,*[27] seest well how close it is of kin to *Atheism,* and other sad *Isms:* he who discovers no God whatever, how shall he discover Heroes, the visible Temples of God?—Strange enough meanwhile it is, to observe with what thoughtlessness, here in our rigidly Conservative Country, men rush into Democracy with full cry. Beyond doubt, his Excellenz the Titular-Herr Ritter Kauderwälsch von Pferdefuss-Quacksalber,[28] he our distinguished Conservative Premier himself, and all but the thicker-headed of his Party, discern Democracy to be inevitable as death, and are even desperate of delaying it much!

'You cannot walk the streets without beholding Democracy announce itself: the very Tailor has become, if not properly Sansculottic,[29] which to him would be ruinous, yet a Tailor unconsciously symbolising, and prophesying with his scissors, the reign of Equality. What now is our fashionable coat? A thing of superfinest texture, of deeply meditated cut; with Malines-lace [30] cuffs; quilted

24. The "People's Charter" from which the Chartist Movement derived its name had actually six points, all having to do with the rationalizing and equalizing of the suffrage. The movement came into prominence in 1838 and disappeared by 1850. With the exception of the one about annual parliaments, all its "points" are now in force.
25. A reference to the tendency in the administration of the temporal affairs of the Church of England to allow the parishioners who paid rates to express their opinions.
26. Carlyle is not quoting from *Sartor Resartus.* These are presumably newly discovered utterances of Teufelsdröckh.
27. My dear friend.
28. Translated: Mr. Knight Gibberish Horsefoot-Quackdoctor. Sir Robert Peel was the Conservative prime minister who had repealed the Corn Laws and, despite his party affiliation, did much to advance the cause of democracy in England.
29. "Sans culottes" (without breeches) was the name given by the aristocrats to the members of the extreme republican party in the days just before the French Revolution; these radicals had refused to wear the short breeches and silk stockings characteristic of aristocratic dress and adopted instead the loose trousers of the working class. Carlyle in this paragraph and the next is taking account of the change that was taking place in men's fashions, in which the upper classes were giving up their relatively bright and elaborate clothes for the dark suits that tend to make all men seem equal and alike.
30. Lace made in the Belgian town of Malines.

with gold; so that a man can carry, without difficulty, an estate of land on his back? *Keineswegs,* By no manner of means! The Sumptuary Laws [31] have fallen into such a state of desuetude as was never before seen. Our fashionable coat is an amphibium between barn-sack and drayman's doublet. The cloth of it is studiously coarse; the colour a speckled soot-black or rust-brown gray; the nearest approach to a Peasant's. And for shape,—thou shouldst see it! The last consummation of the year now passing over us is definable as Three Bags; a big bag for the body, two small bags for the arms, and by way of collar a hem! The first Antique Cheruscan [32] who, of felt-cloth or bear's-hide, with bone or metal needle, set about making himself a coat, before Tailors had yet awakened out of Nothing,—did not he make it even so? A loose wide poke for body, with two holes to let out the arms; this was his original coat: to which holes it was soon visible that two small loose pokes, or sleeves, easily appended, would be an improvement.

'Thus has the Tailor-art, so to speak, overset itself, like most other things; changed its centre-of-gravity; whirled suddenly over from zenith to nadir. Your Stulz,[33] with huge somerset,[34] vaults from his high shopboard down to the depths of primal savagery,—carrying much along with him! For I will invite thee to reflect that the Tailor, as topmost ultimate froth of Human Society, is indeed swift-passing, evanescent, slippery to decipher; yet significant of much, nay of all. Topmost evanescent froth, he is churned-up from the very lees, and from all intermediate regions of the liquor. The general outcome he, visible to the eye, of what men aimed to do, and were obliged and enabled to do, in this one public department of symbolising themselves to each other by covering of their skins. A smack of all Human Life lies in the Tailor: its wild struggles towards beauty, dignity, freedom, victory; and how, hemmed-in by Sedan and Huddersfield [35] by Nescience, Dulness, Prurience,[36] and other sad necessities and laws of Nature, it has attained just to this: Gray savagery of Three Sacks with a hem!

'When the very Tailor verges towards Sansculottism, is it not ominous? The last Divinity of poor mankind dethroning himself; sinking *his* taper too, flame downmost, like the Genius of Sleep or of Death; admonitory that Tailor time shall be no more!—For, little as one could advise Sumptuary Laws at the present epoch, yet nothing is clearer than that where ranks do actually exist, strict division of costumes will also be enforced; that if we ever have a new Hierarchy and Aristocracy, acknowledged veritably as such, for which I daily pray Heaven, the Tailor will reawaken; and be, by volunteering and appointment, consciously and unconsciously, a safeguard of that same.'—Certain farther observations, from the same invaluable pen, on our never-ending changes of mode, our 'perpetual nomadic and even ape-like appetite for change and mere change' in all the equipments of our existence, and the 'fatal

31. Laws regulating dress, diet, etc.
32. An ancient German tribe.
33. A fashionable tailor.
34. Somersault.
35. Towns, one French, one English, devoted to the weaving of woolen goods.
36. Carlyle is not using this word in its present-day sexual sense, but in its quite literal original sense of *itching*—the result of wearing wool!

revolutionary character' thereby manifested, we suppress for the present. It may be admitted that Democracy, in all meanings of the word, is in full career; irresistible by any Ritter Kauderwälsch or other Son of Adam, as times go. 'Liberty' is a thing men are determined to have.

But truly, as I had to remark in the mean while, 'the liberty of not being oppressed by your fellow man' is an indispensable, yet one of the most insignificant fractional parts of Human Liberty. No man oppresses thee, can bid thee fetch or carry, come or go, without reason shown. True; from all men thou art emancipated: but from Thyself and from the Devil—? No man, wiser, unwiser, can make thee come or go: but thy own futilities, bewilderments, thy false appetites for Money, Windsor Georges [37] and suchlike? No man oppresses thee, O free and independent Franchiser: but does not this stupid Porter-pot [38] oppress thee? No Son of Adam can bid thee come or go; but this absurd Pot of Heavy-wet,[39] this can and does! Thou art the thrall not of Cedric the Saxon, but of thy own brutal appetites and this scoured dish of liquor. And thou pratest of thy 'liberty'? Thou entire blockhead!

Heavy-wet and gin: alas, these are not the only kinds of thraldom. Thou who walkest in a vain show, looking out with ornamental dilettante sniff and serene supremacy at all Life and all Death; and amblest jauntily; perking up thy poor talk into crotchets, thy poor conduct into fatuous somnambulisms;— and art as an 'enchanted Ape' under God's sky, where thou mightest have been a man, had proper Schoolmasters and Conquerors, and Constables with cat-o'-nine tails, been vouchsafed thee; dost thou call that 'liberty'? Or your unreposing Mammon-worshipper again, driven, as if by Galvanisms, by Devils and Fixed-Ideas, who rises early and sits late, chasing the impossible; straining every faculty to 'fill himself with the east wind,'—how merciful were it, could you, by mild persuasion, or by the severest tyranny so-called, check him in his mad path, and turn him into a wiser one! All painful tyranny, in that case again, were but mild 'surgery'; the pain of it cheap, as health and life, instead of galvanism and fixed-idea, are cheap at any price.

Sure enough, of all paths a man could strike into, there *is*, at any given moment, a *best path* for every man; a thing which, here and now, it were of all things *wisest* for him to do;—which could he be but led or driven to do, he were then doing 'like a man,' as we phrase it; all men and gods agreeing with him, the whole Universe virtually exclaiming Well-done to him! His success, in such case, were complete; his felicity a maximum. This path, to find this path and walk in it, is the one thing needful for him. Whatsoever forwards him in that, let it come to him even in the shape of blows and spurnings, is liberty: whatsoever hinders him, were it ward-motes,[40] open-vestries, pollbooths, tremendous cheers, rivers of heavy-wet, is slavery.

The notion that a man's liberty consists in giving his vote at election-hustings, and saying, 'Behold, now I too have my twenty-thousandth part of a Talker in our National Palaver; will not all the gods be good to me?'—is one of the pleasantest! Nature nevertheless is kind at present; and puts it into the heads

37. A reference to royalty and its pomp.
38. Porter is a dark strong beer.
39. Slang term for strong beer.
40. Meeting of the citizens of a ward, a section of the city.

of many, almost of all. The liberty especially which has to purchase itself by social isolation, and each man standing separate from the other, having 'no business with him' but a cash-account: this is such a liberty as the Earth seldom saw;—as the Earth will not long put up with, recommend it how you may. This liberty turns out, before it have long continued in action, with all men flinging up their caps round it, to be, for the Working Millions a liberty to die by want of food; for the Idle Thousands and Units, alas, a still more fatal liberty to live in want of work; to have no earnest duty to do in this God's-World any more. What becomes of a man in such predicament? Earth's Laws are silent; and Heaven's speak in a voice which is not heard. No work, and the ineradicable need of work, give rise to new very wondrous life-philosophies, new very wondrous life-practices! Dilettantism, Pococurantism,[41] Beau-Brummelism,[42] with perhaps an occasional half-mad, protesting burst of Byronism, establish themselves. . . .

. . . England will either learn to reverence its Heroes, and discriminate them from its Sham-Heroes and Valets and gaslighted Histrios; [43] and to prize them as the audible God's-voice, amid all inane jargons and temporary market-cries, and say to them with heart-loyalty, 'Be ye King and Priest, and Gospel and Guidance for us': or else England will continue to worship new and ever-new forms of Quackhood,—and so, with what resiliences and reboundings matters little, go down to the Father of Quacks! Can I dread such things of England? Wretched, thick-eyed, gross-hearted mortals, why will ye worship lies, and 'Stuffed Clothes-suits created by the ninth-parts of men'! It is not your purses that suffer; your farm-rents, your commerces, your mill-revenues, loud as ye lament over these; no, it is not these alone, but a far deeper than these: it is your souls that lie dead, crushed down under despicable Night-mares, Atheisms, Brain-fumes; and are not souls at all, but mere succedanea[44] for *salt* to keep your bodies and their appetites from putrefying! Your cotton-spinning and thrice-miraculous mechanism, what is this too, by itself, but a larger kind of Animalism? Spiders can spin, Beavers can build and show con-trivance; the Ant lays-up accumulation of capital, and has, for aught I know, a Bank of Antland. If there is no soul in man higher than all that, did it reach to sailing on the cloud-rack, and spinning sea-sand; then I say, man is but an animal, a more cunning kind of brute: he has no soul, but only a succeda-neum for salt. Whereupon, seeing himself to be truly of the beasts that perish, he ought to admit it, I think;—and also straightway universally to kill himself; and so, in a manlike manner at least *end*, and wave these brute-worlds *his* dignified farewell!—

1843   1843

41. *Pococurante* is an Italian expression for a person who is indifferent or unconcerned.
42. George Bryan Brummel (1778–1840), generally called Beau Brummel, was the famous dandy and leader of London fashion.
43. Stage actors.
44. Substitutes.

JOHN STUART MILL
1806–1873

The boyhood of John Stuart Mill makes one of the great legends of the nineteenth century. We read it sometimes as a fairy story, a tale of wonder which is about wonder itself and how the young hero achieved the ability to experience it, and sometimes as a myth, an explanation of one of the mysteries of human existence. Inevitably we read it in the light of another great nineteenth-century story of boyhood, Wordsworth's *Prelude*. The account of his rearing that Mill gives in his *Autobiography* (1873) is, we might say, a sort of *Anti-Prelude,* and it is a commonplace of the comparison to recall that Wordsworth, in the course of celebrating the fortunate lack of supervision and constraint which characterized his own upbringing, contrasts it with a newfangled systematic education, designed to produce a model boy, which closely approximates the one which Mill in fact received.

Mill was born in 1806, the eldest child of James Mill, who, far more than fathers commonly are, was his son's fate. The elder Mill was the son of a poor Scotch shoemaker and of a mother who, having resolved that he was to distinguish himself, subordinated the life of the family to that end. Trained for the ministry at the University of Edinburgh, James Mill seems to have alienated the rural congregations by his intense intellectuality, and, failing to secure a pulpit, went to London to try his fortune as a journalist. He achieved some success as an editor of and a contributor to Conservative journals, although his actual opinions were radical. At the age of thirty-five he formed a close association with Jeremy Bentham, the father of the Utilitarian philosophy, the ethical doctrine, still of wide influence, which holds that actions are good in proportion to their "utility," by which is meant the extent of the happiness they promote, the criterion of public acts being "the greatest happiness of the greatest number." Bentham was then sixty, a man of considerable means and famous throughout the world for his works on jurisprudence. Under the protection of Bentham's position and financial benevolence, James Mill felt free to express his radicalism, while Bentham, for his part, was led by Mill to understand that his hopes for reform could be realized only through political agitation. But the two men did not anticipate anything like a rapid realization of their projects for the revision of society, and as they thought of the future they felt some anxiety over how their ideas would be carried forward after their deaths. Young disciples were needed who would be properly trained in the Benthamite doctrine. As the first of these they chose James Mill's son, John Stuart. He was then three years old.

In the education devised by the two friends and administered by the father of the pupil, there was no intention of making a prodigy, only of going about the pedagogical job in the most efficient way possible. The pupil himself was later to say that he had brought no special aptitude to the project, that the result that had been achieved with him could have been achieved with any child. This is surely not true—his natural endowment was unquestionably of a superior kind, like that of the younger Pitt, an accomplished classical scholar before he was ten, or that of Macaulay, who compiled a universal history before he was eight. But these examples of precocious mental power will suggest that Mill's was neither unique nor out of the course of nature. At any rate, at the age of three he was introduced to Greek by a rational and humane method which excluded grammatical rules. He read *Aesop's Fables,* moved on to Xenophon, thence to Herodotus; at the age of seven he was reading Plato's dialogues, which he later said was not a wise choice since he was not yet up to comprehending them. He began Latin at eight and almost at once was reading Cicero. His father carried him through arithmetic, geometry, and algebra, but not being himself grounded in mathematics beyond that point, turned him loose to master trigonometry, conic sections, calculus, and the higher mathematics on his own.

He read widely in history for pleasure and out of natural curiosity; at the age of six and a half he wrote a fifteen-hundred word summary of the history of Rome. He was instructed in logic, both ancient and modern, and a considerable amount of speculative philosophy. He was introduced to economics at twelve, receiving instruction from his father and having as one of his set tasks making a summary of the treatise of his father's friend David Ricardo. In addition to pursuing his own studies, he was required to be responsible for the instruction of his younger sisters and brothers. Outside the family circle, in which, actually, there was for him no intimacy, he knew no one of his own age. His sole form of exercise was going on walks with his father.

When he was fourteen, his father's tuition ceased. Mill judged that it had brought him to the point of knowledge and intellectual competence which young men educated in the conventional way reached at twenty-one; he meant, of course, those who were gifted and earnest in their studies, but even so, he surely underestimated how far he had gone.

The sequel was disastrous. But when Mill relates what he calls "the crisis in his mental history" to the education he had received, he is at pains to discriminate among those elements of the system which were harmful and those which were not. He does not deplore the rigorousness of the pedagogy, or the substance of most of what he had learned. Such blame as he imputes—he does not do so eagerly: he is what the education made him and he gives no indication of not being essentially content with himself—falls only upon the quality or tone of the instruction, upon its excess of abstractness, ultimately upon the temperament of the teacher. For James Mill was a harsh, sharp-tongued man, much given to irony, a mode of expression by which children are peculiarly hurt and confused; nor was his acerbity tempered by moments of affection. What is more, as Mill made explicit in a passage deleted from the published version of the *Autobiography*, he received no affection from his mother and gave her none; in the *Autobiography* she is never mentioned. Mrs. Mill had no pretensions to intellect and was not educated; she was the harassed mother of nine, and doubtless she was the less able to respond warmly to her children, especially her eldest son, because she had come to be held in contempt by her husband. It was a household of gloom and lovelessness and its effect on Mill was for a while extreme. That he transcended the deprivation of his childhood, that he discovered and asserted the importance of the affections and became a large-minded, generous-spirited, and, in his own way, affectionate man, makes the engaging point of his story.

The trouble that was in store for him was not quick to manifest itself. When his studies with his father were at an end in 1820, Mill spent a happy year in France, half of it in the family of Sir Samuel Bentham, Jeremy's brother. Lady Bentham especially had a worldly, humanizing influence upon him; he was a personally propossessing youth, actually quite handsome, and his hostess undertook to put him on the way to being a gentleman, seeing to it that he had clothes that fitted, and lessons in fencing, singing, and the piano, and that he learned to bear the interruption of his compulsive routine of study for the sake of frivolous pleasures. Upon his return to England he undertook the study of psychology and read Roman law with the eminent jurist John Austin, and considered and rejected a career at the bar. In 1818 his father had published his monumental *History of India,* which led in the following year to his appointment to the staff of India House, which had in charge the administration of India. In 1823 John followed him into that office as a clerk. The post permitted him sufficient leisure to pursue his intellectual interests. He became an adherent and exponent of Bentham's ideas. He studied the history of the French Revolution with a view to writing about it, contributed to the *Westminster Review,* the new organ of the growing Benthamite or "philosophical radical" group, and met with the most gifted young men of his day in one or another debating or discussion society.

His life, as he says at the beginning of the chapter of the *Autobiography* in which he describes the famous crisis, was, at the age of twenty-one, as fulfilled and happy as he could wish. How the darkness fell and the manner in which the day broke again may be read in his own words. He emerged from the crisis with a changed view of man and of the nature of human existence, to which he later gave classic expression in the pair of essays he published in the *Westminster Review,* one on Bentham in 1838, the other on Coleridge in 1840. He represents these antithetical figures as exemplary of the two dominant intellectual tendencies of the age, the one rational, practical, and radical, the other imaginative, spiritual, and conservative; intending to keep them in balance as constituting the two elements of a valuable dialectic, he cannot keep it from being discerned that it is to Coleridge that his greater sympathy goes.

In 1830 Mill made the acquaintance of Harriet Taylor, an attractive, spirited, and intellectually energetic young woman who was the wife of a wealthy London merchant, a good man whom she had once seemed to love and still regarded with affection and respect. Mill and Harriet Taylor fell in love, avowed their love, and could do nothing decisive about it. Mrs. Taylor was the mother of three children to whom she was devoted, and in any case divorce in those days was virtually impossible. The husband, though grieved, behaved with uncommon magnanimity. Until his death Mrs. Taylor and Mill were in intimate relation with each other, although not sexually, out of regard for Mr. Taylor. The arrangement made enough scandal to cause pain to all the parties to it and to lead to Mill's rather bitter withdrawal from society. Mr. Taylor died in 1849 and Mill and his widow married in 1851. Despite the tendency of writers about Mill to conclude that his estimate of Mrs. Taylor's intellectual powers was extravagant, there can be no doubt that they were of a high order, and although Mill may have credited her with a greater part in the conception and execution of his own work than the facts warrant, she unquestionably exercised a very considerable influence upon his thought. She was, for example, the effectual author of one chapter, on the development of the working-class character, in *Principles of Political Economy,* and it was at her insistence that Mill deleted from that work his arguments against the feasibility of socialism, an act which was the portent of his later increasingly favorable view of socialism.

The range of Mill's intellectual activities was exceptional and in two major disciplines his authority was pre-eminent for many decades. His *System of Logic,* begun when he was twenty-four, was published in 1843 and was at once adopted as the official textbook of the subject at Oxford and subsequently at Cambridge, and sold widely to the general public. Its chapters on the logic of the moral sciences owes something to the French thinker Auguste Comte, although the developed political theory of Comte's positive philosophy was to horrify Mill by its authoritatianism. *The Principles of Political Economy* was equally successful when it appeared in 1848. Dickens hated it and Ruskin wrote *Unto This Last* against it, but the public exhausted thirty-two editions of the work in fifty years.

In 1858 the East India Company was dissolved by act of Parliament and Mill retired on a handsome pension. His wife died in that same year and he was inconsolable, although he stoically sought what surcease could be found in work. In 1859 he published *On Liberty*, generally regarded as the classic statement of the rights of the individual in relation both to constituted government and to public opinion. *Representative Government*, which advocated proportional representation as essential to the maintenance of true democracy, appeared in 1861. In 1865 he was elected to parliament for Westminster despite his refusal to canvass or to commit himself to making the interests of his constituency his first concern; he took an active part in the debates including those on the Reform Bill of 1867 and made the first proposal ever offered to a legislative body on behalf of the rights of women; despite some buffoonery it was listened to with general respect and won a surprising number of votes. He was defeated in the general election of 1868 and retired to Avignon, where his wife was buried. His last work published in his lifetime was *The Subjection of Women* (1869), written eight years earlier, which was received in most quarters with a quite extraordinary antagonism, although it delighted and heartened a small minority. The constant companion of Mill's last years was his stepdaughter Helen Taylor, who was with him when he died in Avignon in 1873.

What Is Poetry?

Poetry was not wholly neglected in Mill's famous education. His father set him to reading the English poets because, as he explained, through some quirk of the human intellect, ideas expressed in verse commanded a readier credence than those in prose. This view seems to us a fantastic one, yet it was in accord with the received Utilitarian conception of poetry as formulated by Bentham himself, who held that the poet practiced one of the arts of persuasion, undertaking to stimulate the passions and excite the prejudices of his readers to the end of making the worse appear appear the better reason. Perhaps nothing in John Stuart Mill's life was as momentous as the discovery, which he so movingly describes in his account of his mental crisis, that poetry spoke to the innermost part of his being. He may have been what he says he was an "unpoetical nature," but he became one of the best readers of poetry of his time; it was he who, of all English critics, was quickest to perceive the genius of Tennyson and to respond to the stern pathos of Alfred de Vigny. In this brief essay he undertakes to refute the idea upon which the Utilitarian denigration of poetry is based, that, like oratory, it is directed to a public audience with a view to forming opinion through the subversion of rational judgment.

What Is Poetry?

It has often been asked, What is Poetry? And many and various are the answers which have been returned. The vulgarest of all—one with which no person possessed of the faculties to which Poetry addresses itself can ever have been satisfied—is that which confounds poetry with metrical composition: [1] yet to this wretched mockery of a definition, many have been led back, by the failure of all their attempts to find any other that would distinguish what they have been accustomed to call poetry, from much which they have known only under other names.

That, however, the word 'poetry' imports something quite peculiar in its nature, something which may exist in what is called prose as well as in verse, something which does not even require the instrument of words, but can speak through the other audible symbols called musical sounds, and even through the visible ones which are the language of sculpture, painting, and architecture; all this, we believe, is and must be felt, though perhaps indistinctly, by all upon whom poetry in any of its shapes produces any impression beyond that of tickling the ear. The distinction between poetry and what is not poetry, whether explained or not, is felt to be fundamental: and where every one feels a difference, a difference there must be. All other appearances may be fallacious, but the appearance of a difference is a real difference. Appearances too, like other things, must have a cause, and that which can cause anything, even an illusion, must be a reality. And hence, while a half-philosophy disdains the classifications and distinctions indicated by popular language, philosophy carried to its highest point frames new ones, but rarely sets aside the old, content with correcting and regularizing them. It cuts fresh channels for thought, but does not fill up such as it finds ready-made; it traces, on the contrary, more deeply, broadly, and distinctly, those into which the current has spontaneously flowed.

Let us then attempt, in the way of modest inquiry, not to coerce and confine nature within the bounds of an arbitrary definition, but rather to find the boundaries which she herself has set, and erect a barrier round them; not calling mankind to account for having misapplied the word 'poetry,' but attempting to clear up the conception which they already attach to it, and to bring forward as a distinct principle that which, as a vague feeling, has really guided them in their employment of the term.

The object of poetry is confessedly to act upon the emotions; and therein is poetry sufficiently distinguished from what Wordsworth affirms to be its logical opposite, namely, not prose, but matter of fact or science.[2] The one addresses itself to the belief, the other to the feelings. The one does its work by convincing or persuading, the other by moving. The one acts by presenting a proposition to the understanding, the other by offering interesting objects of contemplation to the sensibilities.

This, however, leaves us very far from a definition of poetry. This distinguishes it from one thing, but we are bound to distinguish it from everything. To bring thoughts or images before the mind for the purpose of acting upon

1. On this erroneous conception see Wordsworth, Preface to *Lyrical Ballads*.
2. *Ibid.*

the emotions, does not belong to poetry alone. It is equally the province (for example) of the novelist: and yet the faculty of the poet and that of the novelist are as distinct as any other two faculties; as the faculties of the novelist and of the orator, or of the poet and the metaphysician. The two characters may be united, as characters the most disparate may; but they have no natural connexion.

Many of the greatest poems are in the form of fictitious narratives, and in almost all good serious fictions there is true poetry. But there is a radical distinction between the interest felt in a story as such, and the interest excited by poetry; for the one is derived from incident, the other from the representation of feeling. In one, the source of the emotion excited is the exhibition of a state or states of human sensibility; in the other, of a series of states of mere outward circumstances. Now, all minds are capable of being affected more or less by representations of the latter kind, and all, or almost all, by those of the former; yet the two sources of interest correspond to two distinct, and (as respects their greatest development) mutually exclusive, characters of mind.

At what age is the passion for a story, for almost any kind of story, merely as a story, the most intense? In childhood. But that also is the age at which poetry, even of the simplest description, is least relished and least understood; [3] because the feelings with which it is especially conversant are yet undeveloped, and not having been even in the slightest degree experienced, cannot be sympathized with. In what stage of the progress of society, again, is storytelling most valued, and the story-teller in greatest request and honour?—In a rude state like that of the Tartars and Arabs at this day, and of almost all nations in the earliest ages. But in this state of society there is little poetry except ballads, which are mostly narrative, that is, essentially stories, and derive their principal interest from the incidents. Considered as poetry, they are of the lowest and most elementary kind: the feelings depicted, or rather indicated, are the simplest our nature has; such joys and griefs as the immediate pressure of some outward event excites in rude minds, which live wholly immersed in outward things, and have never, either from choice or a force they could not resist, turned themselves to the contemplation of the world within. Passing now from childhood, and from the childhood of society, to the grown-up men and women of this most grown-up and unchildlike age—the minds and hearts of greatest depth and elevation are commonly those which take greatest delight in poetry; the shallowest and emptiest, on the contrary, are, at all events, not those least addicted to novel-reading.[4] This accords, too, with all analogous experience of human nature. The sort of persons whom not merely in books, but in their lives, we find perpetually engaged in hunting for excitement from without, are invariably those who do not possess, either in the vigour of their intellectual powers or in the depth of their sensibilities, that which would

3. There are theorists of pedagogy who would refuse to accept this statement.
4. For a considerable part of the 19th century, the novel, despite its great exemplars of the 18th century, was still likely to be regarded with a certain condescension and even disdain. Matthew Arnold, for example, pays it no heed, and it is not until Pater—see his *Romanticism*—that it is dealt with as the coeval of poetry. Mill, of course, here has chiefly in mind novels that have no pretensions to literary excellence.

enable them to find ample excitement nearer home. The most idle and frivolous persons take a natural delight in fictitious narrative; the excitement it affords is of the kind which comes from without. Such persons are rarely lovers of poetry, though they may fancy themselves so, because they relish novels in verse. But poetry, which is the delineation of the deeper and more secret workings of human emotion, is interesting only to those to whom it recalls what they have felt, or whose imagination it stirs up to conceive what they could feel, or what they might have been able to feel, had their outward circumstances been different.

Poetry, when it is really such, is truth; and fiction also, if it is good for anything, is truth: but they are different truths. The truth of poetry is to paint the human soul truly: the truth of fiction is to give a true picture of life. The two kinds of knowledge are different, and come by different ways, come mostly to different persons. Great poets are often proverbially ignorant of life. What they know has come by observation of themselves; they have found within them one highly delicate and sensitive specimen of human nature, on which the laws of emotion are written in large characters, such as can be read off without much study. Other knowledge of mankind, such as comes to men of the world by outward experience, is not indispensable to them as poets: but to the novelist such knowledge is all in all; he has to describe outward things, not the inward man; actions and events, not feelings; [5] and it will not do for him to be numbered among those who, as Madame Roland said of Brissot,[6] know man but not *men.*

All this is no bar to the possibility of combining both elements, poetry and narrative or incident, in the same work, and calling it either a novel or a poem; but so may red and white combine on the same human features, or on the same canvas. There is one order of composition which requires the union of poetry and incident, each in its highest kind—the dramatic. Even there the two elements are perfectly distinguishable, and may exist of unequal quality, and in the most various proportion. The incidents of a dramatic poem may be scanty and ineffective, though the delineation of passion and character may be of the highest order; as in Goethe's admirable *Torquato Tasso;* [7] or again, the story as a mere story may be well got up for effect, as is the case with some of the most trashy productions of the Minerva press: [8] It may even be, what those are not, a coherent and probable series of events, though there be scarcely a feeling exhibited which is not represented falsely, or in a manner absolutely commonplace. The combination of the two excellencies is what renders Shakespeare so generally acceptable, each sort of readers finding in him what is suitable to their faculties. To the many he is great as a story-teller, to the few as a poet.

5. The statement must be thought a curious one in the light of the chief concern of two great novels of the 18th century, Richardson's *Clarissa* and Rousseau's *La Nouvelle Héloïse.*
6. Jean-Pierre Brissot was a journalist and a figure of note in the Girondin party of the French Revolution. He was the friend of Madame Roland, one of the most brilliant personalities of the time. She made the comment on him in her *Mémoires.*
7. Written in 1790 and based on the life of the 16th-century Italian poet.
8. Established at the end of the 18th century and notorious for the extravagantly sentimental and improbable novels it issued.

In limiting poetry to the delineation of states of feeling, and denying the name where nothing is delineated but outward objects, we may be thought to have done what we promised to avoid—to have not found, but made a definition, in opposition to the usage of language, since it is established by common consent that there is a poetry called descriptive. We deny the charge. Description is not poetry because there is descriptive poetry, no more than science is poetry because there is such a thing as a didactic poem.[9] But an object which admits of being described, or a truth which may fill a place in a scientific treatise, may also furnish an occasion for the generation of poetry, which we thereupon choose to call descriptive or didactic. The poetry is not in the object itself, nor in the scientific truth itself, but in the state of mind in which the one and the other may be contemplated. The mere delineation of the dimensions and colours of external objects is not poetry, no more than a geometrical ground-plan of St. Peter's or Westminster Abbey is painting. Descriptive poetry consists, no doubt, in description, but in description of things as they appear, not as they are; and it paints them not in their bare and natural lineaments, but seen through the medium and arrayed in the colours of the imagination set in action by the feelings. If a poet describes a lion, he does not describe him as a naturalist would, nor even as a traveller would, who was intent upon stating the truth, the whole truth, and nothing but the truth. He describes him by imagery, that is, by suggesting the most striking likenesses and contrasts which might occur to a mind contemplating the lion, in the state of awe, wonder, or terror, which the spectacle naturally excites, or is, on the occasion, supposed to excite. Now this is describing the lion professedly, but the state of excitement of the spectator really. The lion may be described falsely or with exaggeration, and the poetry be all the better; but if the human emotion be not painted with scrupulous truth, the poetry is bad poetry, *i.e.* is not poetry at all, but a failure.

Thus far our progress towards a clear view of the essentials of poetry has brought us very close to the last two attempts at a definition of poetry which we happen to have seen in print, both of them by poets and men of genius. The one is by Ebenezer Elliott, the author of *Corn-Law Rhymes*,[10] and other poems of still greater merit. 'Poetry,' says he, 'is impassioned truth.' The other is by a writer in *Blackwood's Magazine*, and comes, we think, still nearer the mark. He defines poetry, 'man's thoughts tinged by his feelings.' There is in either definition a near approximation to what we are in search of. Every truth which a human being can enunciate, every thought, even every outward impression, which can enter into his consciousness, may become poetry when shown through any impassioned medium, when invested with the colouring of joy, or grief, or pity, or affection, or admiration, or reverence, or awe, or even hatred or terror: and, unless so coloured, nothing, be it as interesting as it may, is poetry. But both these definitions fail to discriminate between poetry

9. In its literal sense "didactic" means simply "intended to instruct." The pejorative connotation it has acquired is in large part due to the reversal of taste which led to the rejection of the poetry of the 18th century written with a view to instruction. Pope's *Essay on Criticism* is a didactic poem of a high order.
10. In the Preface to this volume of poems (1831) which had as their theme the iniquity of the high import duty on wheat.

and eloquence. Eloquence, as well as poetry, is impassioned truth; eloquence, as well as poetry, is thoughts coloured by the feelings. Yet common apprehension and philosophic criticism alike recognise a distinction between the two: there is much that every one would call eloquence, which no one would think of classing as poetry. A question will sometimes arise, whether some particular author is a poet; and those who maintain the negative commonly allow, that though not a poet, he is a highly eloquent writer. The distinction between poetry and eloquence appears to us to be equally fundamental with the distinction between poetry and narrative, or between poetry and description, while it is still farther from having been satisfactorily cleared up than either of the others.

Poetry and eloquence are both alike the expression or utterance of feeling. But if we may be excused the antithesis, we should say that eloquence is *heard*, poetry is *over*heard. Eloquence supposes an audience; the peculiarity of poetry appears to us to lie in the poet's utter unconsciousness of a listener.[11] Poetry is feeling confessing itself to itself, in moments of solitude, and embodying itself in symbols which are the nearest possible representations of the feeling in the exact shape in which it exists in the poet's mind. Eloquence is feeling pouring itself out to other minds, courting their sympathy, or endeavouring to influence their belief or move them to passion or to action.

All poetry is of the nature of soliloquy. It may be said that poetry which is printed on hot-pressed paper [12] and sold at a bookseller's shop, is a soliloquy in full dress, and on the stage. It is so; but there is nothing absurd in the idea of such a mode of soliloquizing. What we have said to ourselves, we may tell to others afterwards; what we have said or done in solitude, we may voluntarily reproduce when we know that other eyes are upon us. But no trace of consciousness that any eyes are upon us must be visible in the work itself. The actor knows that there is an audience present; but if he act as though he knew it, he acts ill. A poet may write poetry not only with the intention of printing it, but for the express purpose of being paid for it; that it should *be* poetry, being written under such influences, is less probable; not, however, impossible; but no otherwise possible than if he can succeed in excluding from his work every vestige of such lookings-forth into the outward and every-day world, and can express his emotions exactly as he has felt them in solitude, or as he is conscious that he should feel them though they were to remain for ever unuttered, or (at the lowest) as he knows that others feel them in similar circumstances of solitude. But when he turns round and addresses himself to another person; when the act of utterance is not itself the end, but a means to an end,—viz. by the feelings he himself expresses, to work upon the feelings, or upon the belief, or the will, of another,—when the expression of his emotions, or of his thoughts tinged by his emotions, is tinged also by that purpose, by that desire of making an impression upon another mind, then it ceases to be poetry, and becomes eloquence.

Poetry, accordingly, is the natural fruit of solitude and meditation; elo-

11. But see the statement with which Wordsworth begins his definition of the poet in the Preface to *Lyrical Ballads*: "To whom does he address himself? . . . He is a man speaking to men." Farther on in the essay Mill qualifies the formulation he makes here.
12. Paper processed to be glossy.

quence, of intercourse with the world. The persons who have most feeling of their own, if intellectual culture has given them a language in which to express it, have the highest faculty of poetry; those who best understand the feelings of others, are the most eloquent. The persons, and the nations, who commonly excel in poetry, are those whose character and tastes render them least dependent upon the applause, or sympathy, or concurrence of the world in general. Those to whom that applause, that sympathy, that concurrence are most necessary, generally excel most in eloquence. And hence, perhaps, the French, who are the least poetical of all great and intellectual nations,[13] are among the most eloquent: the French, also, being the most sociable, the vainest, and the least self-dependent.

If the above be, as we believe, the true theory of the distinction commonly admitted between eloquence and poetry; or even though it be not so, yet if, as we cannot doubt, the distinction above stated be a real *bonâ fide* [14] distinction, it will be found to hold, not merely in the language of words, but in all other language, and to intersect the whole domain of art.

Take, for example, music: we shall find in that art, so peculiarly the expression of passion, two perfectly distinct styles; one of which may be called the poetry, the other the oratory of music. This difference, being seized, would put an end to much musical sectarianism. There has been much contention whether the music of the modern Italian school, that of Rossini [15] and his successors, be impassioned or not. Without doubt, the passion it expresses is not the musing, meditative tenderness, or pathos, or grief of Mozart or Beethoven. Yet it is passion, but garrulous passion—the passion which pours itself into other ears; and therein the better calculated for dramatic effect, having a natural adaptation for dialogue. Mozart also is great in musical oratory; but his most touching compositions are in the opposite style—that of soliloquy. Who can imagine 'Dove sono' [16] *heard?* We imagine it *over*heard.

Purely pathetic music commonly partakes of soliloquy. The soul is absorbed in its distress, and though there may be bystanders, it is not thinking of them. When the mind is looking within, and not without, its state does not often or rapidly vary; and hence the even, uninterrupted flow, approaching almost to monotony, which a good reader, or a good singer, will give to words or music of a pensive or melancholy cast. But grief taking the form of a prayer, or of a complaint, becomes oratorical; no longer low, and even, and subdued, it assumes a more emphatic rhythm, a more rapidly returning accent; instead of a few slow equal notes, following one after another at regular intervals, it crowds note upon note, and often assumes a hurry and bustle like joy. Those who are familiar with some of the best of Rossini's serious compositions,[17] such as the air 'Tu che i miseri conforti,' in the opera of *Tancredi*,[18] or the duet 'Ebben per

13. This settled opinion of the English through the 19th century has been largely overcome.
14. "In good faith."
15. Gioachino Antonio Rossini (1792–1868), Italian operatic composer of enormous popularity.
16. "Where are fled?"—the aria in Act III of Mozart's *The Marriage of Figaro*, in which the Countess sings of her vanished moments of happiness.
17. "Serious" as against his brilliant comic operas, which include *The Barber of Seville*.
18. "You who comfort the miserable." *Tancredi*, produced in 1813, was Rossini's first opera.

mia memoria,' in *La Gazza Ladra*,[19] will at once understand and feel our meaning. Both are highly tragic and passionate; the passion of both is that of oratory, not poetry. The like may be said of that most moving invocation in Beethoven's *Fidelio*—

> Komm, Hoffnung, lass das letzte Stern
> Der Müde nicht erbleichen; [20]

in which Madame Schröder-Devrient [21] exhibited such consummate powers of pathetic expression. How different from Winter's beautiful 'Paga fui,' [22] the very soul of melancholy exhaling itself in solitude; fuller of meaning, and, therefore, more profoundly poetical than the words for which it was composed —for it seems to express not simple melancholy, but the melancholy of remorse.

If, from vocal music, we now pass to instrumental, we may have a specimen of musical oratory in any fine military symphony or march: while the poetry of music seems to have attained its consummation in Beethoven's Overture to *Egmont*,[23] so wonderful in its mixed expression of grandeur and melancholy.

In the arts which speak to the eye, the same distinctions will be found to hold, not only between poetry and oratory, but between poetry, oratory, narrative, and simple imitation or description.

Pure description is exemplified in a mere portrait or a mere landscape—productions of art, it is true, but of the mechanical rather than of the fine arts, being works of simple imitation, not creation. We say, a mere portrait, or a mere landscape, because it is possible for a portrait or a landscape, without ceasing to be such, to be also a picture; like Turner's [24] landscapes, and the great portraits by Titian or Vandyke.[25]

Whatever in painting or sculpture expresses human feeling—or character, which is only a certain state of feeling grown habitual—may be called, according to circumstances, the poetry, or the eloquence, of the painter's or the sculptor's art: the poetry, if the feeling declares itself by such signs as escape from us when we are unconscious of being seen; the oratory, if the signs are those we use for the purpose of voluntary communication.

The narrative style answers to what is called historical painting, which it is the fashion among connoisseurs to treat as the climax of the pictorial art.[26] That it is the most difficult branch of the art we do not doubt, because, in its perfection, it includes the perfection of all the other branches: as in like manner an epic poem, though in so far as it is epic (*i.e.* narrative) it is not poetry at

19. "So I do remember." *La Gazza Landra* (The Thieving Magpie) was produced in 1817.
20. "Come, Hope, let not the weary one's last star go out." *Fidelio* was produced in 1805.
21. A highly gifted German soprano, especially admired for her singing of the role of Leonore in *Fidelio*, for which Beethoven himself praised her. Mill would have heard her when she sang the part in the London production of the opera in 1832, the year before he wrote this essay.
22. "I have been contented," in *Il Ratto di Proserpina* (The Rape of Proserpine) by Peter von Winter, produced in London in 1804.
23. It was composed in 1811, as part of a suite of incidental music for Goethe's play.
24. J. M. W. Turner (1775–1851), the great English landscape painter.
25. Tiziano Vecelli (*c.* 1477–1576), the greatest master of the Venetian school of painting; his portraits are superb. Sir Anthony Vandyke (1599–1641), Flemish painter, influenced by Titian; he settled in England in 1632.
26. Historical painting continued to be an important genre through the 19th century.

all, is yet esteemed the greatest effort of poetic genius, because there is no kind whatever of poetry which may not appropriately find a place in it. But an historical picture as such, that is, as the representation of an incident, must necessarily, as it seems to us, be poor and ineffective. The narrative powers of painting are extremely limited. Scarcely any picture, scarcely even any series of pictures, tells its own story without the aid of an interpreter. But it is the single figures which, to us, are the great charm even of an historical picture. It is in these that the power of the art is really seen. In the attempt to narrate, visible and permanent signs are too far behind the fugitive audible ones, which follow so fast one after another, while the faces and figures in a narrative picture, even though they be Titian's, stand still. Who would not prefer one Virgin and Child of Raphael, to all the pictures which Rubens,[27] with his fat, frouzy Dutch Venuses, ever painted?[28] Though Rubens, besides excelling almost every one in his mastery over the mechanical parts of his art, often shows real genius in *grouping* his figures, the peculiar problem of historical painting. But then, who, except a mere student of drawing and colouring, ever cared to look twice at any of the figures themselves? The power of painting lies in poetry, of which Rubens had not the slightest tincture—not in narrative, wherein he might have excelled.

The single figures, however, in an historical picture, are rather the eloquence of painting than the poetry: they mostly (unless they are quite out of place in the picture) express the feelings of one person as modified by the presence of others. Accordingly the minds whose bent leads them rather to eloquence than to poetry, rush to historical painting. The French painters, for instance, seldom attempt, because they could make nothing of, single heads, like those glorious ones of the Italian masters, with which they might feed themselves day after day in their own Louvre. They must all be historical; and they are, almost to a man, attitudinizers. If we wished to give any young artist the most impressive warning our imagination could devise against that kind of vice in the pictorial, which corresponds to rant in the histrionic art, we would advise him to walk once up and once down the gallery of the Luxembourg.[29] Every figure in French painting or statuary seems to be showing itself off before spectators: they are not poetical, but in the worst style of corrupted eloquence.

1833   1833, 1859

From On Liberty

Of Individuality, as One of the Elements of Well-being[1]

Such being the reasons which make it imperative that human beings should be free to form opinions and to express their opinions without reserve; and such

27. Peter Paul Rubens (1577–1640), Flemish painter, generally accounted the greatest exponent of baroque art in northern Europe.
28. Many!
29. A palace in Paris. The interior is sumptuously decorated with statues and historical and allegorical paintings of little merit.

1. This is Chap. III.

the baneful consequences to the intellectual, and through that to the moral nature of man, unless this liberty is either conceded or asserted in spite of prohibition; let us next examine whether the same reasons do not require that men should be free to act upon their opinions—to carry these out in their lives without hindrance, either physical or moral, from their fellow men, so long as it is at their own risk and peril. This last proviso is of course indispensable. No one pretends that actions should be as free as opinions. On the contrary, even opinions lose their immunity when the circumstances in which they are expressed are such as to constitute their expression a positive instigation to some mischievous act. An opinion that corn dealers are starvers of the poor, or that private property is robbery, ought to be unmolested when simply circulated through the press, but may justly incur punishment when delivered orally to an excited mob assembled before the house of a corn dealer, or when handed about among the same mob in the form of a placard. Acts, of whatever kind, which without justifiable cause do harm to others may be, and in the more important cases absolutely require to be, controlled by the unfavorable sentiments, and, when needful, by the active interference of mankind. The liberty of the individual must be thus far limited; he must not make himself a nuisance to other people. But if he refrains from molesting others in what concerns them, and merely acts according to his own inclination and judgment in things which concern himself, the same reasons which show that opinion should be free prove also that he should be allowed, without molestation, to carry his opinions into practice at his own cost. That mankind are not infallible; that their truths, for the most part, are only half-truths; that unity of opinion, unless resulting from the fullest and freest comparison of opposite opinions, is not desirable, and diversity not an evil, but a good, until mankind are much more capable than at present of recognizing all sides of the truth, are principles applicable to men's modes of action not less than to their opinions. As it is useful that while mankind are imperfect there should be different opinions, so it is that there should be different experiments of living; that free scope should be given to varieties of character, short of injury to others; and that the worth of different modes of life should be proved practically, when anyone thinks fit to try them. It is desirable, in short, that in things which do not primarily concern others individuality should assert itself. Where not the person's own character but the traditions of customs of other people are the rule of conduct, there is wanting one of the principal ingredients of human happiness, and quite the chief ingredient of individual and social progress.

In maintaining this principle, the greatest difficulty to be encountered does not lie in the appreciation of means toward an acknowledged end, but in the indifference of persons in general to the end itself. If it were felt that the free development of individuality is one of the leading essentials of well-being; that it is not only a co-ordinate element with all that is designated by the terms civilization, instruction, education, culture, but is itself a necessary part and condition of all those things, there would be no danger that liberty should be undervalued, and the adjustment of the boundaries between it and social control would present no extraordinary difficulty. But the evil is that individual spontaneity is hardly recognized by the common modes of thinking as having any intrinsic worth, or deserving any regard on its own account. The majority, being satisfied with the ways of mankind as they now are (for it is they who make them what they are), cannot comprehend why those ways should not be good enough for everybody; and what is more, spontaneity forms no part of the ideal of the majority of moral and social reformers, but is rather looked on with jealousy, as a troublesome and perhaps rebellious obstruction to the general acceptance of what these reformers, in their own judgment, think would be best for mankind. Few persons, out of Germany, even comprehend the meaning of the doctrine which Wilhelm von Humboldt,[2] so eminent both as a *savant* and as a politician, made the text of a treatise—that 'the end of man, or that which is prescribed by the eternal or immutable dictates of reason, and not suggested by vague and transient desires, is the highest and most harmonious development of his powers to a complete and consistent whole'; that, therefore, the object 'toward which every human being must ceaselessly direct his efforts, and on which especially those who design to influence their fellow men must ever keep their eyes, is the individuality of power and development'; that for this there are two requisites, 'freedom, and variety of situations'; and that from the union of these arise 'individual vigour and manifold diversity,' which combine themselves in 'originality.'

Little, however, as people are accustomed to a doctrine like that of von Humboldt, and surprising as it may be to them to find so high a value attached to individuality, the question, one must nevertheless think, can only be one of degree. No one's idea of excellence in conduct is that people should do absolutely nothing but copy one another. No one would assert that people ought not to put into their mode of life, and into the conduct of their concerns, any impress whatever of their own judgment or of their own individual character. On the other hand, it would be absurd to pretend that people ought to live as if nothing whatever had been known in the world before they came into it; as if experience had as yet done nothing toward showing that one mode of existence, or of conduct, is preferable to another. Nobody denies that people should be so taught and trained in youth as to know and benefit by the ascertained results of human experience. But it is the privilege and proper condition of a human being, arrived at the maturity of his faculties, to use and interpret experience in his own way. It is for him to find out what part of recorded experience is properly applicable to his own circumstances and character. The traditions and customs of other people are, to a certain extent, evidence of what their experience has taught *them*—presumptive evidence, and as such, have a claim to his deference: but, in the first place, their experience may be too narrow, or they may have not interpreted it rightly. Secondly, their interpretation of experience may be correct, but unsuitable to him. Customs are made for customary circumstances and customary characters; and his circumstances or his character may be uncustomary. Thirdly, though the customs be both good as customs and suitable to him, yet to conform to custom merely *as* custom does not educate or develop in him any of the qualities which are the distinctive endowment of a human being. The human faculties of perception,

2. Karl Wilhelm von Humboldt (1767–1835), German statesman and philologist, friend of Schiller and Goethe. The work to which Mill refers was written in 1792, published posthumously (1851), and translated into English in 1854 as *The Sphere and Duties of Government*.

judgment, discriminative feeling, mental activity, and even moral preference are exercised only in making a choice. He who does anything because it is the custom makes no choice. He gains no practice either in discerning or in desiring what is best. The mental and moral, like the muscular, powers are improved only by being used. The faculties are called into no exercise by doing a thing merely because others do it, no more than by believing a thing only because others believe it. If the grounds of an opinion are not conclusive to the person's own reason, his reason cannot be strengthened, but is likely to be weakened, by his adopting it: and if the inducements to an act are not such as are consentaneous to his own feelings and character (where affection, or the rights of others, are not concerned), it is so much done toward rendering his feelings and character inert and torpid instead of active and energetic.

He who lets the world, or his own portion of it, choose his plan of life for him has no need of any other faculty than the ape-like one of imitation. He who chooses his plan for himself employs all his faculties. He must use observation to see, reasoning and judgment to foresee, activity to gather materials for decision, discrimination to decide, and when he has decided, firmness and self-control to hold to his deliberate decision. And these qualities he requires and exercises exactly in proportion as the part of his conduct which he determines according to his own judgment and feelings is a large one. It is possible that he might be guided in some good path, and kept out of harm's way, without any of these things. But what will be his comparative worth as a human being? It really is of importance, not only what men do, but also what manner of men they are that do it. Among the works of man which human life is rightly employed in perfecting and beautifying, the first in importance surely is man himself. Supposing it were possible to get houses built, corn grown, battles fought, causes tried, and even churches erected and prayers said by machinery —by automatons in human form—it would be a considerable loss to exchange for these automatons even the men and women who at present inhabit the more civilized parts of the world, and who assuredly are but starved specimens of what nature can and will produce. Human nature is not a machine to be built after a model, and set to do exactly the work prescribed for it, but a tree, which requires to grow and develop itself on all sides, according to the tendency of the inward forces which make it a living thing.

It will probably be conceded that it is desirable people should exercise their understandings, and that of intelligent following of custom, or even occasionally an intelligent deviation from custom, is better than a blind and simply mechanical adhesion to it. To a certain extent it is admitted that our understanding should be our own; but there is not the same willingness to admit that our desires and impulses should be our own likewise, or that to possess impulses of our own, and of any strength, is anything but a peril and a snare. Yet desires and impulses are as much a part of a perfect human being as beliefs and restraints; and strong impulses are only perilous when not properly balanced, when one set of aims and inclinations is developed into strength, while others, which ought to coexist with them, remain weak and inactive. It is not because men's desires are strong that they act ill; it is because their consciences are weak. There is no natural connection between strong impulses and a weak conscience. The natural connection is the other way. To say that one person's desires and feelings are stronger and more various than those of another is merely to say that he has more of the raw material of human nature and is therefore capable, perhaps of more evil, but certainly of more good. Strong impulses are but another name for energy. Energy may be turned to bad uses; but more good may always be made of an energetic nature than of an indolent and impassive one. Those who have most natural feeling are always those whose cultivated feelings may be made the strongest. The same strong susceptibilities which make the personal impulses vivid and powerful are also the source from whence are generated the most passionate love of virtue and the sternest self-control. It is through the cultivation of these that society both does its duty and protects its interests, not by rejecting the stuff of which heroes are made, because it knows not how to make them. A person whose desires and impulses are his own—are the expression of his own nature, as it has been developed and modified by his own culture—is said to have a character. One whose desires and impulses are not his own has no character, no more than a steam engine has a character. If, in addition to being his own, his impulses are strong and are under the government of a strong will, he has an energetic character. Whoever thinks that individuality of desires and impulses should not be encouraged to unfold itself must maintain that society has no need of strong natures—is not the better for containing many persons who have much character—and that a high general average of energy is not desirable.

In some early states of society, these forces might be, and were, too much ahead of the power which society then possessed of disciplining and controlling them. There has been a time when the element of spontaneity and individuality was in excess, and the social principle had a hard struggle with it. The difficulty then was to induce men of strong bodies or minds to pay obedience to any rules which required them to control their impulses. To overcome this difficulty, law and discipline, like the Popes struggling against the Emperors, asserted a power over the whole man, claiming to control all his life in order to control his character—which society had not found any other sufficient means of binding. But society has now fairly got the better of individuality; and the danger which threatens human nature is not the excess, but the deficiency, of personal impulses and preferences. Things are vastly changed since the passions of those who were strong by station or by personal endowment were in a state of habitual rebellion against laws and ordinances, and required to be rigorously chained up to enable the persons within their reach to enjoy any particle of security. In our times, from the highest class of society down to the lowest, everyone lives as under the eye of a hostile and dreaded censorship. Not only in what concerns others, but in what concerns only themselves, the individual or the family do not ask themselves, what do I prefer? or, what would suit my character and disposition? or, what would allow the best and highest in me to have fair play and enable it to grow and thrive? They ask themselves, what is suitable to my position? what is usually done by persons of my station and pecuniary circumstances? or (worse still) what is usually done by persons of a station and circumstances superior to mine? I do not mean that they choose what is customary in preference to what suits their own inclination. It does not occur to them to have any inclination except for what is customary. Thus the mind itself is bowed to the yoke: even in what people do for pleasure, conformity is the first thing thought of; they like in crowds; they exercise choice only among things commonly done; peculiarity of taste, eccentricity of conduct are shunned equally with crimes, until by dint of not following their own nature they have no nature to follow: their human capacities are withered and starved; they become incapable of any strong wishes or native pleasures, and are generally without either opinions or feelings of home growth, or properly their own. Now is this, or is it not, the desirable condition of human nature?

It is so, on the Calvinistic theory. According to that, the one great offense of man is self-will. All the good of which humanity is capable is comprised in obedience. You have no choice; thus you must do, and no otherwise: 'Whatever is not a duty is a sin.' Human nature being radically corrupt, there is no redemption for anyone until human nature is killed within him. To one holding this theory of life, crushing out any of the human faculties, capacities, and susceptibilities is no evil: man needs no capacity but that of surrendering himself to the will of God; and if he uses any of his faculties for any other purpose but to do that supposed will more effectually, he is better without them. This is the theory of Calvinism; and it is held, in a mitigated form, by many who do not consider themselves Calvinists; the mitigation consisting in giving a less ascetic interpretation to the alleged will of God, asserting it to be his will that mankind should gratify some of their inclinations, of course not in the manner they themselves prefer, but in the way of obedience, that is, in a way prescribed to them by authority, and, therefore, by the necessary condition of the case, the same for all.

In some such insidious form there is at present a strong tendency to this narrow theory of life, and to the pinched and hidebound type of human character which it patronizes. Many persons, no doubt, sincerely think that human beings thus cramped and dwarfed are as their Maker designed them to be, just as many have thought that trees are a much finer thing when clipped into pollards,[3] or cut out into figures of animals,[4] than as nature made them. But if it be any part of religion to believe that man was made by a good Being, it is more consistent with that faith to believe that this Being gave all human faculties that they might be cultivated and unfolded, not rooted out and consumed, and that he takes delight in every nearer approach made by his creatures to the ideal conception embodied in them, every increase in any of their capabilities of comprehension, of action, or of enjoyment. There is a different type of human excellence from the Calvinistic: a conception of humanity as having its nature bestowed on it for other purposes than merely to be abnegated. 'Pagan self-assertion' is one of the elements of human worth, as well as 'Christian self-denial.'[5] There is a Greek ideal of self-development, which the Platonic and Christian ideal of self-government blends with, but does not supersede.

3. A tree whose top branches are cut back to the trunk so that it will produce a thick growth of new shoots.
4. Frequently done in elaborate gardens of the 18th and 19th centuries.
5. "Sterling's *Essays*." (Mill). John Sterling (1806–44) was a friend of Mill and Carlyle; the latter wrote his biography.

It may be better to be a John Knox [6] than an Alcibiades,[7] but it is better to be a Pericles [8] than either; nor would a Pericles, if we had one in these days, be without anything good which belonged to John Knox.

It is not by wearing down into uniformity all that is individual in themselves, but by cultivating it and calling it forth, within the limits imposed by the rights and interests of others, that human beings become a noble and beautiful object of contemplation; and as the works partake the character of those who do them, by the same process human life also becomes rich, diversified, and animating, furnishing more abundant aliment to high thoughts and elevating feelings, and strengthening the tie which binds every individual to the race, by making the race infinitely better worth belonging to. In proportion to the development of his individuality, each person becomes more valuable to himself, and is, therefore, capable of being more valuable to others. There is a greater fullness of life about his own existence, and when there is more life in the units there is more in the mass which is composed of them. As much compression as is necessary to prevent the stronger specimens of human nature from encroaching on the rights of others cannot be dispensed with; but for this there is ample compensation even in the point of view of human development. The means of development which the individual loses by being prevented from gratifying his inclinations to the injury of others are chiefly obtained at the expense of the development of other people. And even to himself there is a full equivalent in the better development of the social part of his nature, rendered possible by the restraint put upon the selfish part. To be held to rigid rules of justice for the sake of others develops the feelings and capacities which have the good of others for their object. But to be restrained in things not affecting their good, by their mere displeasure, develops nothing valuable except such force of character as may unfold itself in resisting the restraint. If acquiesced in, it dulls and blunts the whole nature. To give any fair play to the nature of each, it is essential that different persons should be allowed to lead different lives. In proportion as this latitude has been exercised in any age has that age been noteworthy to posterity. Even despotism does not produce its worst effects so long as individuality exists under it; and whatever crushes individuality is despotism, by whatever name it may be called and whether it professes to be enforcing the will of God or the injunctions of men.

Having said that the individuality is the same thing with development, and that it is only the cultivation of individuality which produces, or can produce, well-developed human beings, I might here close the argument; for what more or better can be said of any condition of human affairs than that it brings human beings themselves nearer to the best thing they can be? Or what worse can be said of any obstruction to good than that it prevents this? Doubtless, however, these considerations will not suffice to convince those who most need convincing; and it is necessary further to show that these developed human beings are

6. John Knox (1505–72), Scottish religious reformer, associate of Calvin. He often serves as the prototype of rigorous Puritan morality.
7. Alcibiades (c. 450–404 B.C.), the brilliant and profligate Athenian politician and general.
8. Pericles (c. 500–429 B.C.), the chief and best-remembered Athenian statesman of his day, often cited as the prototype of enlightened civic virtue.

of some use to the undeveloped—to point out to those who do not desire liberty, and would not avail themselves of it, that they may be in some intelligible manner rewarded for allowing other people to make use of it without hindrance.

In the first place, then, I would suggest that they might possibly learn something from them. It will not be denied by anybody that originality is a valuable element in human affairs. There is always need of persons not only to discover new truths and point out when what were once truths are true no longer, but also to commence new practices and set the example of more enlightened conduct and better taste and sense in human life. This cannot well be gainsaid by anybody who does not believe that the world has already attained perfection in all its ways and practices. It is true that this benefit is not capable of being rendered by everybody alike; there are but few persons, in comparison with the whole of mankind, whose experiments, if adopted by others, would be likely to be any improvement on established practice. But these few are the salt of the earth; without them, human life would become a stagnant pool. Not only is it they who introduce good things which did not before exist; it is they who keep the life in those which already exist. If there were nothing new to be done, would human intellect cease to be necessary? Would it be a reason why those who do the old things should forget why they are done, and do them like cattle, not like human beings? There is only too great a tendency in the best beliefs and practices to degenerate into the mechanical; and unless there were a succession of persons whose ever-recurring originality prevents the grounds of those beliefs and practices from becoming merely traditional, such dead matter would not resist the smallest shock from anything really alive, and there would be no reason why civilization should not die out, as in the Byzantine Empire. Persons of genius, it is true, are, and are always likely to be, a small minority; but in order to have them, it is necessary to preserve the soil in which they grow. Genius can only breathe freely in an *atmosphere* of freedom. Persons of genius are, *ex vi termini*,[9] more individual than any other people—less capable, consequently, of fitting themselves, without hurtful compression, into any of the small number of moulds which society provides in order to save its members the trouble of forming their own character. If from timidity they consent to be forced into one of these moulds, and to let all that part of themselves which cannot expand under the pressure remain unexpanded, society will be little the better for their genius. If they are of a strong character and break their fetters, they become a mark for the society which has not succeeded in reducing them to commonplace, to point out with solemn warning as 'wild,' 'erratic,' and the like—much as if one should complain of the Niagara river for not flowing smoothly between its banks like a Dutch canal.

I insist thus emphatically on the importance of genius and the necessity of allowing it to unfold itself freely both in thought and in practice, being well aware that no one will deny the position in theory, but knowing also that almost everyone, in reality, is totally indifferent to it. People think genius a fine thing if it enables a man to write an exciting poem or paint a picture. But in its true sense, that of originality in thought and action, though no one says that it is not a thing to be admired, nearly all, at heart, think that they can do very

9. By definition; literally "by the force of the term."

well without it. Unhappily this is too natural to be wondered at. Originality is the one thing which unoriginal minds cannot feel the use of. They cannot see what it is to do for them: how should they? If they could see what it would do for them, it would not be originality. The first service which originality has to render them is that of opening their eyes: which being once fully done, they would have a chance of being themselves original. Meanwhile, recollecting that nothing was ever done which someone was not the first to do, and that all good things which exist are the fruits of originality, let them be modest enough to believe that there is something still left for it to accomplish, and assure themselves that they are more in need of originality, the less they are conscious of the want.

In sober truth, whatever homage may be professed, or even paid, to real or supposed mental superiority, the general tendency of things throughout the world is to render mediocrity the ascendant power among mankind. In ancient history, in the Middle Ages, and in a diminishing degree through the long transition from feudality to the present time, the individual was a power in himself; and if he had either great talents or a high social position, he was a considerable power. At present individuals are lost in the crowd. In politics it is almost a triviality to say that public opinion now rules the world. The only power deserving the name is that of masses, and of governments while they make themselves the organ of the tendencies and instincts of masses. This is as true in the moral and social relations of private life as in public transactions. Those whose opinions go by the name of public opinion are not always the same sort of public: in America, they are the whole white population; in England, chiefly the middle class. But they are always a mass, that is to say, collective mediocrity. And what is a still greater novelty, the mass do not now take their opinions from dignitaries in Church or State, from ostensible leaders, or from books. Their thinking is done for them by men much like themselves, addressing them or speaking in their name, on the spur of the moment, through the newspapers. I am not complaining of all this. I do not assert that anything better is compatible, as a general rule, with the present low state of the human mind. But that does not hinder the government of mediocrity from being mediocre government. No government by a democracy or a numerous aristocracy, either in its political acts or in the opinions, qualities, and tone of mind which it fosters, ever did or could rise above mediocrity except in so far as the sovereign Many have let themselves be guided (which in their best times they always have done) by the counsels and influence of a more highly gifted and instructed *one* or *few*. The initiation of all wise or noble things comes and must come from individuals; generally at first from some one individual. The honour and glory of the average man is that he is capable of following that initiative; that he can respond internally to wise and noble things, and be led to them with his eyes open. I am not countenancing the sort of 'hero-worship'[10] which applauds the strong man of genius for forcibly seizing on the government of the world and making it do his bidding in spite of itself. All he can claim is freedom to point out the way. The power of compelling others into it

10. A reference to Carlyle's *On Heroes, Hero-Worship, and the Heroic in History* (1841). See above.

is not only inconsistent with the freedom and development of all the rest, but corrupting to the strong man himself. It does seem, however, that when the opinions of masses of merely average men are everywhere become or becoming the dominant power, the counterpoise and corrective to that tendency would be the more and more pronounced individuality of those who stand on the higher eminences of thought. It is in these circumstances most especially that exceptional individuals, instead of being deterred, should be encouraged in acting differently from the mass. In other times there was no advantage in their doing so, unless they acted not only differently but better. In this age, the mere example of nonconformity, the mere refusal to bend the knee to custom, is itself a service. Precisely because the tyranny of opinion is such as to make eccentricity a reproach, it is desirable, in order to break through that tyranny, that people should be eccentric. Eccentricity has always abounded when and where strength of character has abounded; and the amount of eccentricity in a society has generally been proportional the amount of genius, mental vigour, and moral courage it contained. That so few now dare to be eccentric marks the chief danger of the time.

I have said that it is important to give the freest scope possible to uncustomary things, in order that it may in time appear which of these are fit to be converted into customs. But independence of action and disregard of custom are not solely deserving of encouragement for the chance they afford that better modes of action, and customs more worthy of general adoption, may be struck out; nor is it only persons of decided mental superiority who have a just claim to carry on their lives in their own way. There is no reason that all human existence should be constructed on some one or some small number of patterns. If a person possesses any tolerable amount of common sense and experience, his own mode of laying out his existence is the best, not because it is the best in itself, but because it is his own mode. Human beings are not like sheep; and even sheep are not undistinguishably alike. A man cannot get a coat or a pair of boots to fit him unless they are either made to his measure or he has a whole warehouseful to choose from; and is it easier to fit him with a life than with a coat, or are human beings more like one another in their whole physical and spiritual conformation than in the shape of their feet? If it were only that people have diversities of taste, that is reason enough for not attempting to shape them all after one model. But different persons also require different conditions for their spiritual development; and can no more exist healthily in the same moral than all the variety of plants can in the same physical, atmosphere and climate. The same things which are helps to one person toward the cultivation of his higher nature are hindrances to another. The same mode of life is a healthy excitement to one, keeping all his faculties of action and enjoyment in their best order, while to another it is a distracting burden which suspends or crushes all internal life. Such are the differences among human beings in their sources of pleasure, their susceptibilities of pain, and the operation on them of different physical and moral agencies that, unless there is a corresponding diversity in their modes of life, they neither obtain their fair share of happiness, nor grow up to the mental, moral, and aesthetic stature of which their nature is capable. . . .

There is one characteristic of the present direction of public opinion peculiarly calculated to make it intolerant of any marked demonstration of individuality. The general average of mankind are not only moderate in intellect, but also moderate in inclinations; they have no tastes or wishes strong enough to incline them to do anything unusual, and they consequently do not understand those who have, and class all such with the wild and intemperate whom they are accustomed to look down upon. Now, in addition to this fact which is general, we have only to suppose that a strong movement has set in toward the improvement of morals, and it is evident what we have to expect. In these days such a movement has set in; much has actually been effected in the way of increased regularity of conduct and discouragement of excesses; and there is a philanthropic spirit abroad for the exercise of which there is no more inviting field than the moral and prudential improvement of our fellow creatures. These tendencies of the times cause the public to be more disposed than at most former periods to prescribe general rules of conduct and endeavour to make everyone conform to the approved standard. And that standard, express or tacit, is to desire nothing strongly. Its ideal of character is to be without any marked character—to maim by compression, like a Chinese lady's foot,[11] every part of human nature which stands out prominently and tends to make the person markedly dissimilar in outline to commonplace humanity.

As is usually the case with ideals which exclude one-half of what is desirable, the present standard of approbation produces only an inferior imitation of the other half. Instead of great energies guided by vigourous reason and strong feelings strongly controlled by a conscientious will, its result is weak feelings and weak energies, which therefore can be kept in outward conformity to rule without any strength either of will or of reason. Already energetic characters on any large scale are becoming merely traditional.[12] There is now scarcely any outlet for energy in this country except business. The energy expended in this may still be regarded as considerable. What little is left from that employment is expended on some hobby, which may be a useful, even a philanthropic, hobby, but is always some one thing, and generally a thing of small dimensions. The greatness of England is now all collective; individually small, we only appear capable of anything great by our habit of combining; and with this our moral and religious philanthropists are perfectly contented. But it was men of another stamp than this that made England what it has been; and men of another stamp will be needed to prevent its decline.

The despotism of custom is everywhere the standing hindrance to human advancement, being in unceasing antagonism to that disposition to aim at something better than customary, which is called, according to circumstances, the spirit of liberty, or that of progress or improvement. The spirit of improvement is not always a spirit of liberty, for it may aim at forcing improvements on an unwilling people; and the spirit of liberty, in so far as it resists such attempts, may ally itself locally and temporarily with the opponents of improvement; but the only unfailing and permanent source of improvement is liberty, since by it there are as many possible independent centers of improve-

---

11. It was once the custom to bind the feet of Chinese girl children of the aristocratic class to keep them small; this resulted in deformity and in difficulty in walking.

12. The fear that personal and national energy would be lost is characteristic of the Victorian Age.

ment as there are individuals. The progressive principle, however, in either shape, whether as the love of liberty or of improvement, is antagonistic to the sway of custom, involving at least emancipation from that yoke; and the contest between the two constitutes the chief interest of the history of mankind. The greater part of the world has, properly speaking, no history, because the despotism of Custom is complete. This is the case over the whole East. Custom is there, in all things, the final appeal; justice and right mean conformity to custom; the argument of custom no one, unless some tyrant intoxicated with power, thinks of resisting. And we see the result. Those nations must once have had originality; they did not start out of the ground populous, lettered, and versed in many of the arts of life; they made themselves all this, and were then the greatest and most powerful nations of the world. What are they now? The subjects or dependents of tribes whose forefathers wandered in the forests when theirs had magnificent palaces and gorgeous temples, but over whom custom exercised only a divided rule with liberty and progress. A people, it appears, may be progressive for a certain length of time, and then stop: when does it stop? When it ceases to possess individuality. If a similar change should befall the nations of Europe, it will not be in exactly the same shape: the despotism of custom with which these nations are threatened is not precisely stationariness. It proscribes singularity, but it does not preclude change, provided all change together. We have discarded the fixed costumes of our forefathers; everyone must still dress like other people, but the fashion may change once or twice a year. We thus take care that when there is a change, it shall be for change's sake, and not from any idea of beauty or convenience; for the same idea of beauty or convenience would not strike all the world at the same moment, and be simultaneously thrown aside by all at another moment. But we are progressive as well as changeable: we continually make new inventions in mechanical things, and keep them until they are again superseded by better; we are eager for improvement in politics, in education, even in morals, though in this last our idea of improvement chiefly consists in persuading or forcing other people to be as good as ourselves. It is not progress that we object to; on the contrary, we flatter ourselves that we are the most progressive people who ever lived. It is individuality that we war against: we should think we had done wonders if we had made ourselves all alike, forgetting that the unlikeness of one person to another is generally the first thing which draws the attention of either to the imperfection of his own type and the superiority of another, or the possibility, by combining the advantages of both, of producing something better than either. We have a warning example in China—a nation of much talent and, in some respects, even wisdom, owing to the rare good fortune of having been provided at an early period with a particularly good set of customs, the work, in some measure, of men to whom even the most enlightened European must accord, under certain limitations, the title of sages and philosophers. They are remarkable, too, in the excellence of their apparatus for impressing, as far as possible, the best wisdom they possess upon every mind in the community, and securing that those who have appropriated most of it shall occupy the posts of honour and power. Surely the people who did this have discovered the secret of human progressiveness and must have kept themselves steadily at the head of the movement of the world.

On the contrary, they have become stationary—have remained so for thousands of years; and if they are ever to be further improved, it must be by foreigners. They have succeeded beyond all hope in what English philanthropists are so industriously working at—in making a people all alike, all governing their thoughts and conduct by the same maxims and rules; and these are the fruits. The modern *régime* of public opinion is, in an unorganized form, what the Chinese educational and political systems are in an organized; and unless individuality shall be able successfully to assert itself against this yoke, Europe, notwithstanding its noble antecedents and its professed Christianity, will tend to become another China.

What is it that has hitherto preserved Europe from this lot? What has made the European family of nations an improving, instead of a stationary, portion of mankind? Not any superior excellence in them, which, when it exists, exists as the effect, not as the cause, but their remarkable diversity of character and culture. Individuals, classes, nations have been extremely unlike one another: they have struck out a great variety of paths, each leading to something valuable; and although at every period those who travelled in different paths have been intolerant of one another, and each would have thought it an excellent thing if all the rest could have been compelled to travel his road, their attempts to thwart each other's development have rarely had any permanent success, and each has in time endured to receive the good which the others have offered. Europe is, in my judgment, wholly indebted to this plurality of paths for its progressive and many-sided development. But it already begins to possess this benefit in a considerably less degree. It is decidely advancing toward the Chinese ideal of making all people alike. M. de Tocqueville,[13] in his last important work, remarks how much more the Frenchmen of the present day resemble one another than did those even of the last generation. The same remark might be made of Englishmen in a far greater degree. In a passage already quoted from Wilhelm von Humboldt, he points out two things as necessary conditions of human development—because necessary to render people unlike one another—namely, freedom and variety of situations. The second of these two conditions is in this country every day diminishing. The circumstances which surround different classes and individuals, and shape their characters, are daily becoming more assimilated. Formerly, different ranks, different neighbourhoods, different trades and professions lived in what might be called different worlds; at present, to a great degree in the same. Comparatively speaking, they now read the same things, listen to the same things, see the same things, go to the same places, have their hopes and fears directed to the same objects, have the same rights and liberties, and the same means of asserting them. Great as are the differences of position which remain, they are nothing to those which have ceased. And the assimilation is still proceeding. All the political changes of the age promote it, since they all tend

13. Alexis de Tocqueville (1805–59), the great historian and social theorist, published the first volume of his brilliant *Democracy in America* in 1835, the second in 1840. He predicted the eventual triumph of democratic principles throughout the world, a development which he regarded with ambivalence. His views had great influence on Mill. The work to which Mill refers is *L'Ancien Régime*, an investigation into the causes of the French Revolution.

to raise the low and to lower the high. Every extension of education promotes it, because education brings people under common influences and gives them access to the general stock of facts and sentiments. Improvement in the means of communication promotes it, by bringing the inhabitants of distant places into personal contact, and keeping up a rapid flow of changes of residence between one place and another. The increase of commerce and manufactures promotes it, by diffusing more widely the advantages of easy circumstances and opening all objects of ambition, even the highest, to general competition, whereby the desire of rising becomes no longer the character of a particular class, but of all classes. A more powerful agency than even all these, in bringing about a general similarity among mankind, is the complete establishment, in this and other free countries, of the ascendancy of public opinion in the State. As the various social eminences which enabled persons entrenched on them to disregard the opinion of the multitude gradually become levelled; as the very idea of resisting the will of the public, when it is positively known that they have a will, disappears more and more from the minds of practical politicians, there ceases to be any social support for nonconformity—any substantive power in society which, itself opposed to the ascendancy of numbers, is interested in taking under its protection opinions and tendencies at variance with those of the public.

The combination of all these causes forms so great a mass of influences hostile to individuality that it is not easy to see how it can stand its ground. It will do so with increasing difficulty unless the intelligent part of the public can be made to feel its value—to see that it is good there should be differences, even though not for the better, even though, as it may appear to them, some should be for the worse. If the claims of individuality are ever to be asserted, the time is now while much is still wanting to complete the enforced assimilation. It is only in the earlier stages that any stand can be successfully made against the encroachment. The demand that all other people shall resemble ourselves grows by what it feeds on. If resistance waits till life is reduced *nearly* to one uniform type, all deviations from that type will come to be considered impious, immoral, even monstrous and contrary to nature. Mankind speedily become unable to conceive diversity when they have been for some time unaccustomed to see it.

1854   1859

From On the Subjection of Women

[On the Equality of the Sexes]

. . . If it be said that the doctrine of the equality of the sexes rests only on theory, it must be remembered that the contrary doctrine also has only theory to rest upon. All that is proved in its favour by direct experience, is that mankind have been able to exist under it, and to attain the degree of improvement and prosperity which we now see; but whether that prosperity has been attained sooner, or is now greater, than it would have been under the other system, experience does not say. On the other hand, experience does say, that every step in improvement has been so invariably accompanied by a step made in raising the social position of women, that historians and philosophers have been led to adopt their elevation or debasement as on the whole the surest test and most correct measure of the civilization of a people or an age. Through all the progressive period of human history, the condition of women has been approaching nearer to equality with men. This does not of itself prove that the assimilation must go on to complete equality; but it assuredly affords some presumption that such is the case.

Neither does it avail anything to say that the *nature* of the two sexes adapts them to their present functions and position, and renders these appropriate to them. Standing on the ground of common sense and the constitution of the human mind, I deny that any one knows, or can know, the nature of the two sexes, as long as they have only been seen in their present relation to one another. If men had ever been found in society without women, or women without men, or if there had been a society of men and women in which the women were not under the control of the men, something might have been positively known about the mental and moral differences which may be inherent in the nature of each. What is now called the nature of women is an eminently artificial thing—the result of forced repression in some directions, unnatural stimulation in others. It may be asserted without scruple, that no other class of dependents have had their character so entirely distorted from its natural proportions by their relation with their masters; for, if conquered and slave races have been, in some respects, more forcibly repressed, whatever in them has not been crushed down by an iron heel has generally been let alone, and if left with any liberty of development, it has developed itself according to its own laws; but in the case of women, a hot-house and stove cultivation has always been carried on of some of the capabilities of their nature, for the benefit and pleasure of their masters. . . .

Hence, in regard to that most difficult question, what are the natural differences between the two sexes—a subject on which it is impossible in the present state of society to obtain complete and correct knowledge—while almost everybody dogmatizes upon it, almost all neglect and make light of the only means by which any partial insight can be obtained into it. This is an analytic study of the most important department of psychology, the laws of the influence of circumstances on character. For, however great and apparently ineradicable the moral and intellectual differences between men and women might be, the evidence of their being natural differences could only be negative. Those only could be inferred to be natural which could not possibly be artificial—the residuum, after deducting every characteristic of either sex which can admit of being explained from education or external circumstances. The profoundest knowledge of the laws of the formation of character is indispensable to entitle any one to affirm even that there is any difference, much more what the difference is, between the two sexes considered as moral and rational beings; and since no one, as yet, has that knowledge (for there is hardly any subject which, in proportion to its importance, has been so little studied), no one is thus far entitled to any positive opinion on the subject. Conjectures are all that can at present be made; conjectures more or less probable, according as more or less authorized by such knowledge as we yet have of the laws of psychology, as applied to the formation of character.

Even the preliminary knowledge, what the differences between the sexes now are, apart from all question as to how they are made what they are, is still in the crudest and most incomplete state. Medical practitioners and physiologists have ascertained, to some extent, the differences in bodily constitution; and this is an important element to the psychologist: but hardly any medical practitioner is a psychologist. Respecting the mental characteristics of women; their observations are of no more worth than those of common men. It is a subject on which nothing final can be known, so long as those who alone can really know it, women themselves, have given but little testimony, and that little, mostly suborned. It is easy to know stupid women. Stupidity is much the same all the world over. A stupid person's notions and feelings may confidently be inferred from those which prevail in the circle by which the person is surrounded. Not so with those whose opinions and feelings are an emanation from their own nature and faculties. It is only a man here and there who has any tolerable knowledge of the character even of the women of his own family. I do not mean, of their capabilities; these nobody knows, not even themselves, because most of them have never been called out. I mean their actually existing thoughts and feelings. . . .

. . . It is but of yesterday that women have either been qualified by literary accomplishments, or permitted by society, to tell anything to the general public. As yet very few of them dare tell anything, which men, on whom their literary success depends, are unwilling to hear. Let us remember in what manner, up to a very recent time, the expression, even by a male author, of uncustomary opinions, or what are deemed eccentric feelings, usually was, and in some degree still is, received; and we may form some faint conception under what impediments a woman, who is brought up to think custom and opinion her sovereign rule, attempts to express in books anything drawn from the depths of her own nature. The greatest woman who has left writings behind her sufficient to give her an eminent rank in the literature of her country, thought it necessary to prefix as a motto to her boldest work, "Un homme peut braver l'opinion; une femme doit s'y soumettre." [1] The greater part of what women write about women is mere sycophancy to men. In the case of unmarried women, much of it seems only intended to increase their chance of a husband. Many, both married and unmarried, overstep the mark, and inculcate a servility beyond what is desired or relished by any man, except the very vulgarest. But this not so often the case as, even at a quite late period, it still was. Literary women are becoming more freespoken, and more willing to express their real sentiments. Unfortunately, in this country especially, they

1. A man is able to defy opinion, a woman should submit herself to it. "Title page of Mme de Staël's *Delphine*" (Mill). Mme de Staël, the daughter of Jacques Necker, the great Swiss financier who became Louis XVI's chief minister, was a gifted and vivacious intellectual and liberal hated and persecuted by Napoleon. In 1800 she published a study of the relation of literature to social institutions; in 1810 she published her account of the artistic and philosophical culture of Germany; both are still of great interest. *Delphine* (1802) is a novel in letters; its heroine has been called the first "modern woman" in French fiction.

are themselves such artificial products, that their sentiments are compounded of a small element of individual observation and consciousness, and a very large one of acquired associations. This will be less and less the case, but it will remain true to a great extent, as long as social institutions do not admit the same free development of originality in women which is possible to men. When that time comes, and not before, we shall see, and not merely hear, as much as it is necessary to know of the nature of women, and the adaptation of other things to it. . . .

1861   1869

Autobiography

From *A Crisis in My Mental History. One Stage Onward* [1]

For some years after this time I wrote very little, and nothing regularly, for publication: and great were the advantages which I derived from the intermission. It was of no common importance to me, at this period, to be able to digest and mature my thoughts for my own mind only, without any immediate call for giving them out in print. Had I gone on writing, it would have much disturbed the important transformation in my opinions and character, which took place during those years. The origin of this transformation, or at least the process by which I was prepared for it, can only be explained by turning some distance back.

From the winter of 1821, when I first read Bentham, and especially from the commencement of the *Westminster Review*, I had what might truly be called an object in life; to be a reformer of the world. My conception of my own happiness was entirely identified with this object. The personal sympathies I wished for were those of fellow labourers in this enterprise. I endeavoured to pick up as many flowers as I could by the way; but as a serious and permanent personal satisfaction to rest upon, my whole reliance was placed on this: and I was accustomed to felicitate myself on the certainty of a happy life which I enjoyed, through placing my happiness in something durable and distant, in which some progress might be always making, while it could never be exhausted by complete attainment. This did very well for several years, during which the general improvement going on in the world and the idea of myself as engaged with others in struggling to promote it, seemed enough to fill up an interesting and animated existence. But the time came when I awakened from this as from a dream. It was in the autumn of 1826. I was in a dull state of nerves, such as everybody is occasionally liable to; unsusceptible to enjoyment or pleasurable excitement; one of those moods when what is pleasure at other times, becomes insipid or indifferent; the state, I should think, in which converts to Methodism usually are, when smitten by their first 'conviction of sin.' In this frame of mind it occurred to me to put the question directly to myself, 'Suppose that all your objects in life were realized; that all the changes in institutions and opinions which you are looking

1. From Chap. V.

forward to, could be completely effected at this very instant: would this be a great joy and happiness to you?' And an irrepressible self-consciousness distinctly answered, 'No!' At this my heart sank within me: the whole foundation on which my life was constructed fell down. All my happiness was to have been found in the continual pursuit of this end. The end had ceased to charm, and how could there ever again be any interest in the means? I seemed to have nothing left to live for.

At first I hoped that the cloud would pass away of itself; but it did not. A night's sleep, the sovereign remedy for the smaller vexations of life, had no effect on it. I awoke to a renewed consciousness of the woful fact. I carried it with me into all companies, into all occupations. Hardly anything had power to cause me even a few minutes oblivion of it. For some months the cloud seemed to grow thicker and thicker. The lines in Coleridge's 'Dejection'—I was not then acquainted with them—exactly describe my case:

> A grief without a pang, void, dark and drear,
> A drowsy, stifled, unimpassioned grief,
> Which finds no natural outlet or relief
> In word, or sigh, or tear.[2]

In vain I sought relief from my favourite books; those memorials of past nobleness and greatness, from which I had always hitherto drawn strength and animation. I read them now without feeling, or with the accustomed feeling *minus* all its charm; and I became persuaded, that my love of mankind, and of excellence for its own sake, had worn itself out. I sought no comfort by speaking to others of what I felt. If I had loved any one sufficiently to make confiding my griefs a necessity, I should not have been in the condition I was. I felt, too, that mine was not an interesting, or in any way respectable distress. There was nothing in it to attract sympathy. Advice, if I had known where to seek it, would have been most precious. The words of Macbeth to the physician often occurred to my thoughts.[3] But there was no one on whom I could build the faintest hope of such assistance. My father, to whom it would have been natural to me to have recourse in any practical difficulties, was the last person to whom, in such a case as this, I looked for help. Everything convinced me that he had no knowledge of any such mental state as I was suffering from, and that even if he could be made to understand it, he was not the physician who could heal it. My education, which was wholly his work, had been conducted without any regard to the possibility of its ending in this result; and I saw no use in giving him the pain of thinking that his plans had failed, when the failure was probably irremediable, and at all events, beyond the power of *his* remedies. Of other friends, I had at that time none to whom I had any hope of making my condition intelligible. It was however abundantly intelligible to myself; and the more I dwelt upon it, the more hopeless it appeared.

My course of study had led me to believe, that all mental and moral feelings

2. "Dejection: An Ode," ll. 21–24.
3. "Canst thou not minister to a mind diseas'd . . . ?" V.iii.40–45.

and qualities, whether of a good or of a bad kind, were the results of association; [4] that we love one thing and hate another, take pleasure in one sort of action or contemplation, and pain in another sort, through the clinging of pleasurable or painful ideas to those things, from the effect of education or of experience. As a corollary from this, I had always heard it maintained by my father, and was myself convinced, that the object of education should be to form the strongest possible associations of the salutary class; associations of pleasure with all things beneficial to the great whole, and of pain with all things hurtful to it. This doctrine appeared inexpugnable; but it now seemed to me on retrospect, that my teachers [5] had occupied themselves but superficially with the means of forming and keeping up these salutary associations. They seemed to have trusted altogether to the old familiar instruments, praise and blame, reward and punishment. Now I did not doubt that by these means, begun early and applied unremittingly, intense associations of pain and pleasure, especially of pain, might be created, and might produce desires and aversions capable of lasting undiminished to the end of life. But there must always be something artificial and casual in associations thus produced. The pains and pleasures thus forcibly associated with things, are not connected with them by any natural tie; and it is therefore, I thought, essential to the durability of these associations, that they should have become so intense and inveterate as to be practically indissoluble, before the habitual exercise of the power of analysis had commenced. For I now saw, or thought I saw, what I had always before received with incredulity—that the habit of analysis has a tendency to wear away the feelings: as indeed it has when no other mental habit is cultivated, and the analysing spirit remains without its natural complements and correctives. The very excellence of analysis (I argued) is that it tends to weaken and undermine whatever is the result of prejudice; that it enables us mentally to separate ideas which have only casually clung together: and no associations whatever could ultimately resist this dissolving force, were it not that we owe to analysis our clearest knowledge of the permanent sequences in nature; the real connexions between Things, not dependent on our will and feelings; natural laws, by virtue of which, in many cases, one thing is inseparable from another in fact; which laws, in proportion as they are clearly perceived and imaginatively realized, cause our ideas of things which are always joined together in Nature, to cohere more and more closely in our thoughts. Analytic habits may thus even strengthen the associations between causes and effects, means and ends, but tend altogether to weaken

4. The doctrine of the Association of Ideas, which dominated English psychology in the later 18th and early 19th century and played an important part in the thought of Coleridge and Wordsworth, has an ancient provenance, going back to Plato and Aristotle. But it was David Hume who developed it in the form in which it was received and carried forward by David Hartley and James Mill. It proposes that mental experiences which occur together or in close connection with each other tend to cohere in such a way that when any one of them is subsequently presented to the mind, the others will accompany it. Behaviorism, with its idea of the susceptibility of the mind to "conditioning" and its implication that the mind is essentially a complex of such imposed experiences, is a modern version of the Associationist School.

5. Mill may have put the word in the plural because he included Bentham among his teachers. But he probably means to refer to the authors of books on psychology.

those which are, to speak familiarly, a *mere* matter of feeling. They are there-fore (I thought) favourable to prudence and clearsightedness, but a perpetual worm at the root both of the passions and of the virtues; and above all, fear-fully undermine all desires, and all pleasures, which are the effects of associa-tion, that is, according to the theory I held, all except the purely physical and organic; of the entire insufficiency of which to make life desirable, no one had a stronger conviction than I had. These were the laws of human nature by which, as it seemed to me, I had been brought to my present state. All those to whom I looked up, were of opinion that the pleasure of sympathy with human beings, and the feelings which made the good of others, and espe-cially of mankind on a large scale, the object of existence, were the greatest and surest sources of happiness. Of the truth of this I was convinced, but to know that a feeling would make me happy if I had it, did not give me the feeling. My education, I thought, had failed to create these feelings in sufficient strength to resist the dissolving influence of analysis, while the whole course of my intellectual cultivation had made precocious and premature analysis the inveterate habit of my mind. I was thus, as I said to myself, left stranded at the commencement of my voyage, with a well equipped ship and a rudder, but no sail; without any real desire for the ends which I had been so carefully fitted out to work for: no delight in virtue or the general good, but also just as little in anything else. The fountains of vanity and ambition seemed to have dried up within me, as completely as those of benevolence. I had had (as I reflected) some gratification of vanity at too early an age: I had obtained some distinction, and felt myself of some importance, before the desire of distinction and of importance had grown into a passion: and little as it was which I had attained, yet having been attained too early, like all pleasures enjoyed too soon, it had made me *blasé* and indifferent to the pursuit. Thus neither selfish nor unselfish pleasures were pleasures to me. And there seemed no power in nature sufficient to begin the formation of my character anew, and create in a mind now irretrievably analytic, fresh associations of pleasure with any of the objects of human desire.

These were the thoughts which mingled with the dry heavy dejection of the melancholy winter of 1826–7. During this time I was not incapable of my usual occupations. I went on with them mechanically, by the mere force of habit. I had been so drilled in a certain sort of mental exercise, that I could still carry it on when all the spirit had gone out of it. I even composed and spoke several speeches at the debating society,[6] how, or with what degree of success I know not. Of four years continual speaking at that society, this is the only year of which I remember next to nothing. Two lines of Coleridge, in whom alone of all writers I have found a true description of what I felt, were often in my thoughts, not at this time (for I had never read them), but in a later period of the same mental malady:

> Work without hope draws nectar in a sieve,
> And hope without an object cannot live.[7]

6. This was the Speculative Society which Mill and a group of brilliant young men from Oxford and Cambridge founded in 1825.
7. Coleridge, "Work Without Hope," ll. 13–14.

In all probability my case was by no means so peculiar as I fancied it, and I doubt not that many others have passed through a similar state; but the idiosyncrasies of my education had given to the general phenomenon a special character, which made it seem the natural effect of causes that it was hardly possible for time to remove. I frequently asked myself, if I could, or if I was bound to go on living, when life must be passed in this manner. I generally answered to myself, that I did not think I could possibly bear it beyond a year. When, however, not more than half that duration of time had elapsed, a small ray of light broke in upon my gloom. I was reading, accidentally, Marmontel's Memoirs,[8] and came to the passage which relates his father's death, the distressed position of the family, and the sudden inspiration by which he, then a mere boy, felt and made them feel that he would be everything to them—would supply the place of all that they had lost. A vivid conception of the scene and its feelings came over me, and I was moved to tears. From this moment my burthen grew lighter. The oppression of the thought that all feeling was dead within me, was gone. I was no longer hopeless: I was not a stock or a stone. I had still, it seemed, some of the material out of which all worth of character, and all capacity for happiness, are made. Relieved from my ever present sense of irremediable wretchedness, I gradually found that the ordinary incidents of life could again give me some pleasure; that I could again find enjoyment, not intense, but sufficient for cheerfulness, in sunshine and sky, in books, in conversation, in public affairs; and that there was, once more, excitement, though of a moderate kind, in exerting myself for my opinions, and for the public good. Thus the cloud gradually drew off, and I again enjoyed life: and though I had several relapses, some of which lasted many months, I never again was as miserable as I had been.

The experiences of this period had two very marked effects on my opinions and character. In the first place, they led me to adopt a theory of life, very unlike that on which I had before acted, and having much in common with what at that time I certainly had never heard of, the anti-self-consciousness theory of Carlyle.[9] I never, indeed, wavered in the conviction that happiness is the test of all rules of conduct, and the end of life. But I now thought that this end was only to be attained by not making it the direct end. Those only are happy (I thought) who have their minds fixed on some object other than their own happiness; on the happiness of others, on the improvement of mankind, even on some art or pursuit, followed not as a means, but as itself an ideal end. Aiming thus at something else, they find happiness by the way. The enjoyments of life (such was now my theory) are sufficient to make it a pleasant thing, when they are taken en passant,[10] without being made a prin-

8. Jean-François Marmontel (1723–99), French man of letters and contributor to the Encyclopédie. His Mémoires d'un père appeared in 1804. In view both of Mill's ambivalent relation to his father and of his sense of separation from the rest of the family—his relations with his brothers and sisters were never warm and later became hostile, and in the Autobiography he makes not a single reference to his mother—the episode that made the occasion of his tears is significant indeed.
9. In his essay Characteristics and in Sartor Resartus, especially the chapter "The Everlasting Yea."
10. "In passing."

cipal object. Once make them so, and they are immediately felt to be insufficient. They will not bear a scrutinizing examination. Ask yourself whether you are happy, and you cease to be so. The only chance is to treat, not happiness, but some end external to it, as the purpose of life. Let your self-consciousness, your scrutiny, your self-interrogation, exhaust themselves on that; and if otherwise fortunately circumstanced you will inhale happiness with the air you breathe, without dwelling on it or thinking about it, without either forestalling it in imagination, or putting it to flight by fatal questioning. This theory now became the basis of my philosophy of life. And I still hold to it as the best theory for all those who have but a moderate degree of sensibility and of capacity for enjoyment, that is, for the great majority of mankind.[11]

The other important change which my opinions at this time underwent, was that I, for the first time, gave its proper place, among the prime necessities of human well-being, to the internal culture of the individual. I ceased to attach almost exclusive importance to the ordering of outward circumstances, and the training of the human being for speculation and for action. I had now learnt by experience that the passive susceptibilities needed to be cultivated as well as the active capacities, and required to be nourished and enriched as well as guided. I did not, for an instant, lose sight of, or undervalue, that part of the truth which I had seen before; I never turned recreant to intellectual culture, or ceased to consider the power and practice of analysis as an essential condition both of individual and of social improvement. But I thought that it had consequences which required to be corrected, by joining other kinds of cultivation with it. The maintenance of a due balance among the faculties, now seemed to me of primary importance. The cultivation of the feelings became one of the cardinal points in my ethical and philosophical creed. And my thoughts and inclinations turned in an increasing degree towards whatever seemed capable of being instrumental to that object.

I now began to find meaning in the things which I had read or heard about the importance of poetry and art as instruments of human culture. But it was some time longer before I began to know this by personal experience. The only one of the imaginative arts in which I had from childhood taken great pleasure, was music; the best effect of which (and in this it surpasses perhaps every other art) consists in exciting enthusiasm; in winding up to a high pitch those feelings of an elevated kind which are already in the character, but to which this excitement gives a glow and a fervour, which though transitory at its utmost height, is precious for sustaining them at other times. This effect of music I had often experienced; but, like all my pleasurable susceptibilities, it was suspended during the gloomy period. I had sought relief again and again from this quarter, but found none. After the tide had turned, and I was in process of recovery, I had been helped forward by music, but in a much less elevated manner. I at this time first became acquainted with Weber's *Oberon*,[12] and the extreme pleasure which I drew from its delicious melodies

11. Compare the counsel given in this paragraph with that of "The Everlasting Yea."
12. The last opera of Carl Maria Friedrich Ernst von Weber (1786–1826) was written for production in London, its libretto based on Wieland's *Oberon*. Its production in 1826 was a great success.

did me good, by showing me a source of pleasure to which I was as susceptible as ever. The good however was much impaired by the thought, that the pleasure of music (as is quite true of such pleasure as this was, that of mere tune) fades with familiarity, and requires either to be revived by intermittence, or fed by continual novelty. And it is very characteristic both of my then state, and of the general tone of my mind at this period of my life, that I was seriously tormented by the thought of the exhaustibility of musical combinations. The octave consists only of five tones and two semitones, which can be put together in only a limited number of ways, of which but a small proportion are beautiful: most of these, it seemed to me, must have been already discovered, and there could not be room for a long succession of Mozarts and Webers, to strike out as these had done, entirely new and surpassingly rich veins of musical beauty. This source of anxiety may perhaps be thought to resemble that of the philosophers of Laputa, who feared lest the sun should be burnt out.[13] It was, however, connected with the best feature in my character, and the only good point to be found in my very unromantic and in no way honourable distress. For though my dejection, honestly looked at, could not be called other than egotistical, produced by the ruin, as I thought, of my fabric of happiness, yet the destiny of mankind in general was ever in my thoughts, and could not be separated from my own. I felt that the flaw in my life, must be a flaw in life itself; that the question was, whether, if the reformers of society and government could succeed in their objects, and every person in the community were free and in a state of physical comfort, the pleasures of life, being no longer kept up by struggle and privation, would cease to be pleasures. And I felt that unless I could see my way to some better hope than this for human happiness in general, my dejection must continue; but that if I could see such an outlet, I should then look on the world with pleasure; content as far as I was myself concerned, with any fair share of the general lot.

This state of my thoughts and feelings made the fact of my reading Wordsworth for the first time (in the autumn of 1828) an important event in my life. I took up the collection of his poems from curiosity, with no expectation of mental relief from it, though I had before resorted to poetry with that hope. In the worst period of my depression I had read through the whole of Byron (then new to me) to try whether a poet, whose peculiar department was supposed to be that of the intenser feelings, could rouse any feeling in me. As might be expected, I got no good from this reading, but the reverse. The poet's state of mind was too like my own. His was the lament of a man who had worn out all pleasures, and who seemed to think that life, to all who possess the good things of it, must necessarily be the vapid uninteresting thing which I found it. His Harold and Manfred[14] had the same burthen on them which I had; and I was not in a frame of mind to derive any comfort from the vehement sensual passion of his Giaours, or the sullenness of his Laras.[15] But while Byron was exactly what did not suit my condition, Wordsworth was exactly what did. I had looked into The Excursion two or three years before,

---

13. Swift's *Gulliver's Travels* III.ii.
14. The heroes of Byron's *Childe Harold's Pilgrimage* (1812, 1816, 1818) and *Manfred* (1817).
15. *The Giaour* was published in 1813, *Lara*, its sequel, in 1814.

and found little in it; and should probably have found as little, had I read it at this time. But the miscellaneous poems, in the two-volume edition of 1815 [16] (to which little of value was added in the latter part of the author's life), proved to be the precise thing for my mental wants at that particular juncture.

In the first place, these poems addressed themselves powerfully to one of the strongest of my pleasurable susceptibilities, the love of rural objects and natural scenery; to which I had been indebted not only for much of the pleasure of my life, but quite recently for relief from one of my longest relapses into depression. In this power of rural beauty over me, there was a foundation laid for taking pleasure in Wordsworth's poetry; the more so, as his scenery lies mostly among mountains, which, owing to my early Pyrenean excursion, were my ideal of natural beauty.[17] But Wordsworth would never have had any great effect on me, if he had merely placed before me beautiful pictures of natural scenery. Scott does this still better than Wordsworth, and a very second-rate landscape does it more effectually than any poet. What made Wordsworth's poems a medicine for my state of mind, was that they expressed, not mere outward beauty, but states of feeling, and of thought coloured by feeling, under the excitement of beauty.[18] They seemed to be the very culture of the feelings, which I was in quest of.[19] In them I seemed to draw from a source of inward joy, of sympathetic and imaginative pleasure, which could be shared in by all human beings; which had no connexion with struggle or imperfection, but would be made richer by every improvement in the physical or social condition of mankind. From them I seemed to learn what would be the perennial sources of happiness, when all the greater evils of life shall have been removed. And I felt myself at once better and happier as I came under their influence. There have certainly been, even in our own age, greater poets than Wordsworth; but poetry of deeper and loftier feeling could not have done for me at that time what his did. I needed to be made to feel that there was real, permanent happiness in tranquil contemplation. Wordsworth taught me this, not only without turning away from, but with a greatly increased interest in, the common feelings and common destiny of human beings. And the delight which these poems gave me, proved that with culture of this sort, there was nothing to dread from the most confirmed habit of analysis. At the conclusion of the Poems came the famous Ode, falsely called Platonic,[20] 'Intimations of Immortality': in which, along with more than his usual sweetness of melody and rhythm, and along with the two passages of grand imagery but bad philosophy so often quoted, I found that he too had had similar experience to mine; that he also had felt that the first freshness of youthful enjoyment of life was not lasting; but that he had sought for compensation, and found it, in the way in which he was now teaching me to find it. The result was that I

---

16. The first collected edition of Wordsworth's poems.
17. In 1820–21 Mill lived in France in the home of Samuel Bentham, brother of Jeremy, and, with Sir Samuel and his wife, visited the Pyrenees.
18. This is Wordsworth's own doctrine, expressed in the Preface to *Lyrical Ballads*.
19. See Matthew Arnold, *Memorial Verses*, for a comparison of Byron and Wordsworth. Arnold characterizes Wordsworth, as Mill does, by his power to "make us feel."
20. Wordsworth in a note to the Ode denied that its informing idea derives from Plato's doctrine of pre-natal existence and consciousness.

gradually, but completely, emerged from my habitual depression, and was never again subject to it. I long continued to value Wordsworth less according to his intrinsic merits, than by the measure of what he had done for me. Compared with the greatest poets, he may be said to be the poet of unpoetical natures, possessed of quiet and contemplative tastes. But unpoetical natures are precisely those which require poetic cultivation. This cultivation Wordsworth is much more fitted to give, than poets who are intrinsically far more poets than he.

It so fell out that the merits of Wordsworth were the occasion of my first public declaration of my new way of thinking, and separation from those of my habitual companions who had not undergone a similar change. The person with whom at that time I was most in the habit of comparing notes on such subjects was Roebuck,[21] and I induced him to read Wordsworth, in whom he also at first seemed to find much to admire: but I, like most Wordsworthians, threw myself into strong antagonism to Byron, both as a poet and as to his influence on the character. Roebuck, all whose instincts were those of action and struggle, had, on the contrary, a strong relish and great admiration of Byron, whose writings he regarded as the poetry of human life, while Wordsworth's, according to him, was that of flowers and butterflies. We agreed to have the fight out at our Debating Society, where we accordingly discussed for two evenings the comparative merits of Byron and Wordsworth, propounding and illustrating by long recitations our respective theories of poetry: Sterling [22] also, in a brilliant speech, putting forward his particular theory. This was the first debate on any weighty subject in which Roebuck and I had been on opposite sides. The schism between us widened from this time more and more, though we continued for some years longer to be companions. In the beginning, our chief divergence related to the cultivation of the feelings. Roebuck was in many respects very different from the vulgar notion of a Benthamite or Utilitarian. He was a lover of poetry and of most of the fine arts. He took great pleasure in music, in dramatic performances, especially in painting, and himself drew and designed landscapes with great facility and beauty. But he never could be made to see that these things have any value as aids in the formation of character. Personally, instead of being, as Benthamites are supposed to be, void of feeling, he had very quick and strong sensibilities. But, like most Englishmen who have feelings, he found his feelings stand very much in his way. He was much more susceptible to the painful sympathies than to the pleasurable, and looking for his happiness elsewhere, he wished that his feelings should be deadened rather than quickened. And in truth the English character, and English social circumstances, make it so seldom possible to derive happiness from the exercise of the sympathies, that it is not wonderful if they count for little in an Englishman's scheme of life. In most other countries the paramount importance of the sympathies as a constituent of individual happiness is an axiom, taken for granted rather than needing any

21. John Arthur Roebuck (1801–79) became a politician of radical views, although in later life he often took reactionary positions. Mill viewed his career with dismay and in an early draft of the Autobiography expressed his disapproval at length.
22. John Sterling (1806–44) was a friend and disciple of Coleridge and Mill. Carlyle wrote his biography.

formal statement; but most English thinkers almost seem to regard them as
necessary evils, required for keeping men's actions benevolent and compassionate. Roebuck was, or appeared to be, this kind of Englishman. He saw
little good in any cultivation of the feelings, and none at all in cultivating
them through the imagination, which he thought was only cultivating illusions.
It was in vain I urged on him that the imaginative emotion which an idea
when vividly conceived excites in us, is not an illusion but a fact, as real as
any of the other qualities of objects; and far from implying anything erroneous
and delusive in our mental apprehension of the object, is quite consistent with
the most accurate knowledge and most perfect practical recognition of all its
physical and intellectual laws and relations. The intensest feeling of the beauty
of a cloud lighted by the setting sun, is no hindrance to my knowing that the
cloud is vapour of water, subject to all the laws of vapours in a state of
suspension; and I am just as likely to allow for, and act on, these physical
laws whenever there is occasion to do so, as if I had been incapable of perceiving any distinction between beauty and ugliness. . . .

1861, 1871   1873

JOHN HENRY CARDINAL NEWMAN
1801–1890

With the exception of John Stuart Mill, all the great prose writers of the Victorian
Age whose work is represented in this volume were reared in one or another form
of Christian belief. All set store by the cardinal Christian virtues of faith, hope, and
charity. All were dedicated to what they would have agreed to call the life of the
spirit. Yet only one man among them, John Henry Newman, lived and died an
actual believer, giving assent not alone with his heart to Christian sentiment but
also with his mind to Christian doctrine, making faith as it was confirmed by reason
the very substance of his life.

It must be said at once that, except by reason of his genius, Newman was not
singular among his fellow-countrymen at large. Throughout his lifetime religion was
of vital importance to the English, not only as a public issue capable of arousing
intense feelings but also as a power, although doubtless an ever less manifested
one, in the lives of individuals. But for members of the intellectual class, although
they might hold religion in elegiac esteem and be tenacious of its "values," it was
not a living, imperative presence. It still touched but it did not shape their lives.
It did not command their observance in acts of devotion nor their intellectual assent
to its formularies of belief. Among the class of intellectuals, Newman stood pre-
eminent for his intellectual abilities; none surpassed him in mental power; none
equaled him in subtlety of thought. Yet to doctrines that his notable contemporaries
could not suppose to come within the range of credibility he not only gave his eager
assent but based upon that assent his hope of salvation.

Newman's life in religion began early in his temporal life. He was born in London
in 1801, the eldest son of a banker. He was a quiet, meditative boy, even more
responsive than children usually are to stories of wonder; reading the Arabian Nights,
he wished their marvels were true. He records that his mind ran on unknown

influences, magical powers, and talismans. He thought that life might be a dream and he an angel "and all this world a deception." The "mistrust of the reality of material phenomena"—Wordsworth in *Ode: Intimations of Immortality* and in his note on that poem speaks eloquently of the part that such a dubiety played in his childhood, and indeed it is not an uncommon experience of children—stayed with him all his life and was a decisive element of his thought. At the age of fifteen, when he was a pupil at a private school in Ealing, near London, through the influence of one of the masters he read certain books of Calvinist tendency which led him to conceive of the existence of God as equal in self-evidence with his own. Such actually Calvinist doctrine as established itself in his mind he later repudiated, but the clear knowledge of God's existence never left him. It was at this time, he tells us, that he understood it to be the will of God that he live a celibate life.

He entered Trinity College, Oxford, in 1817, a reserved, shy, and solitary youth. Although he was an earnest student, he did not take his degree with high honors. Yet his actual abilities were patent enough to win for him in 1822 the prized election to a fellowship at Oriel, at that time the most distinguished intellectually of the Oxford colleges. It was at Oriel that the course of his religious life was to be set, although not immediately. The college had among its Fellows a group of churchmen of formidable dialectical skill with whom Newman was in closest association. This group, which came to be known as the "Noetics"—the word derives from the Greek word that means "pertaining to the intellect"—was relatively liberal in the views it held on the relation of church and state, and, without being in any sense heterodox, inclined to criticize traditional orthodoxies. From its members Newman learned to be precise in his reasoning and, as he says, to "prefer intellectual excellence to moral." In time, however, the rationalism of the Noetics lost its hold upon him and he began to move toward friends, also members of Oriel, whose religious thought was of an opposite tendency; among these Hurrell Froude, Edward Pusey, and John Keble are the most eminent. It was Froude who first led him to question the idea that the Anglican Church was, in its ideal conception, essentially and necessarily Protestant rather than Catholic.

In 1824 Newman took holy orders; he was appointed public tutor at Oriel in 1826 and vicar of the University Church of St. Mary's in 1828. In 1832 he resigned the Oriel tutorship, for he insisted, against the views of the provost of the college, that it was a post of "substantially religious nature" which required that he seek to affect the moral and spiritual lives of his pupils. This will suggest the growing intensity and intransigence of his religious character. His account of the Mediterranean tour he made with Froude in 1832 is charged with the impassioned consciousness that England was on the point of religious crisis. A serious and prolonged illness on the tour strengthened his feeling that he was called to do battle for the faith, and he returned home in 1833 with the sense of mission burning within him.

At this time, it must be clear, Newman felt no attraction to Catholicism. When he had been in Rome, what he saw of Catholicism had only repelled him. His concern was solely with the fortunes of the Church of England, which did indeed seem to be at a low ebb. A Whig parliament had already abolished several unneeded bishoprics of the English Church in Ireland and now seemed on the point of proceeding to the disestablishment of the Church of England. In 1833, a few days after Newman's return from the Continent, John Keble preached on "National Apostasy" in St. Mary's before the judges of assize and denounced the interference of Parliament with the church. According to orthodox Anglican doctrine, the bishops were in direct line of succession from the Apostles, and the basis of Keble's charge of apostasy was that the temporal power had presumed to negate the spiritual authority thus derived. The famous sermon is commonly regarded as the inauguration of the Oxford Movement, which undertook to combat the rationalistic and liberal tendencies manifesting themselves in religious thought, of which the Noetic group was but a special instance, and to establish as a ground of renewed faith that part of the Anglican tradition which might be identified as antedating its Protestantism.

It was not a project likely to win wide support in the nation. The immediate occasion to which the Oxford Movement responded was the political expression of a state of thought and feeling to which the Protestant tradition of individual judgment and sectarianism contributed equally with the liberal rationalism which verged upon indifference or even hostility to religion. This state of the national mind the members of the Oxford Movement sought to reverse. They repelled the imputation of any wish to bring the Church of England to Roman Catholicism, insisting that they wished to take the *via media,* the middle way, between the Protestant and the Catholic views of tradition and authority, as a new basis of piety. The long-standing antipathy of the English to Catholicism was still strong and the *via media* proposed much too close an approximation to the ancient church they had been taught to fear. The prospect of a renewed piety could not engage the interest of nonconformists, who were quite content with their own state of religious feeling; nor that of conservative churchmen, who set piety below propriety; nor that of liberals of rationalistic bent, the less so because the basis of piety was to be a recognition of ancient tradition and the intellectual authority of the church.

The adherents of the Movement carried on their campaign for the renovation of the conception of the church in a series of *Tracts for the Times*—whence their name of Tractarians—which, despite their often formidable erudition, were widely bought. Religious dispute was of the very essence of English history; the Oxford Movement revived old and interesting feelings, and even had the charm of a scandal. Yet the Movement, however far its echoes may have reached, was in the end limited in its effect to an ecclesiastical and predominantly academic group, chiefly centered in Oxford. Here the emotions and ideas which had their rise in 1833 continued in force for some decades, playing an important and often decisive part in the lives of many members of the university, undergraduates as well as dons.

The Newman of the Oxford Movement was not the Newman of the early Oxford days; the shy young man had become a leader of great charismatic power. Even before 1833 he was generally regarded as one of the most influential teachers in the university; his spiritual dedication and the assiduity with which he carried out his duties as a tutor evoked from his pupils a profound admiration and loyalty. His Sunday afternoon sermons at St. Mary's became famous and formed the rationale of the new religious mode. He was in charge of the publication of *Tracts for the Times.* He drew men to him and exercised great influence upon them. Many of his personal adherents, he was distressed to see, found it impossible to stay in the *via media* and moved toward Rome, and he was greatly troubled about what his own direction must be when he discovered that there was reason to believe that the Anglican position was analogous to that of certain groups condemned as heretical by the ancient church, whose authority Anglicanism was presumed to acknowledge.

In 1841, in the famous Tract 90, he ventured upon the direct controversion of the conventional Anglican position on the Thirty-Nine Articles, which formulate the doctrine of the Church of England. The Articles, Newman said, had been intended as safeguards not against the doctrines of the Catholic Church but against the possible errors of communicants of the Church of England. The view was a tenable one but it provoked a scandalized outcry. At the request of his bishop, Newman broke off the publication of the Tracts, but he knew that his days as an Anglican were numbered. In the next year he retired to Littlemore, a hamlet near Oxford which was part of St. Mary's parish, and here he and a few friends lived in quasi-monastic retirement. It was at this time that he wrote The Development of Christian Doctrine in which he argued that because the church is a living organism, its doctrine is perpetually in growth and has as much authority in its later phases as Protestants concede it to have had in its primitive days. In 1845 his long travail of spirit was ended when he was received into the Roman Catholic Church.

The nature of the intellectual process which led to Newman's decision and which ruled his religious life from beginning to end is likely to be remote from the sympathetic comprehension of most people in our day. This is not to say that religious belief, even though its attenuation is taken for granted throughout the West, is beyond ready understanding. Faith in the existence of a deity and con-formity to a mode of conduct and of sensibility that follows from that faith are recognized forms of experience and on the whole they are treated with respect even by those who reject them. What is nowadays difficult to comprehend is the elaborate and rigorous system of predications by which Newman set such store, predications not about the existence of the deity—that was for Newman a fact of experience—but about the nature of the universe created by the deity, about the mysteries through which his nature and his will were to be apprehended, about his true ecclesiastical surrogate on earth, about the authority of the Catholic Church, its creeds, doctrines, dogmas. It is with the last of these, the precise formulations of particular beliefs, that the contemporary difficulty is greatest. If we give credence to the validity of religious faith, we can go on to understand a preference for one religious communion as against another, a choice of forms of belief, of which one more than another gratifies personal temperament or intellectual or moral predilec-tion. But to direct, as Newman did, a natively powerful and highly trained intellect and a vast historical scholarship to the demonstration that, for a multitude of irrefutable reasons, one church rather than another is the sole guardian of truth and the single gateway to salvation—of this enterprise the modern mind (and increas-ingly, we may say, even the modern Catholic mind) is pretty sure to be impatient.

Yet thus it was that men once thought about their faith and it is a common dis-covery that if one lends oneself to Newman's process of religious reasoning with the natural sympathy of the historic imagination, one finds that it speaks with a startling immediacy and cogency. As one critic has described the experience of reading Newman, "the challenge that he offers to one's assumptions is so lively and so real, his sense of the world is so subtle and coherent, and his psychological perception is so complex and shrewd that any reader who takes pleasure in endan-gering his own fixed ideas must be grateful for the exhilaration that Newman can give."

In 1846 Newman went to Rome and was ordained in the Catholic Church. He was given the degree of Doctor of Divinity, but not much more than this in the way of welcome, for the Italian hierarchy regarded this Englishman's theological writings with suspicion, and long continued to do so. He joined the semi-monastic, chiefly pedagogical Congregation of the Oratory, founded in Florence in the sixteenth century by Saint Philip Neri, and returned to England as head of the Oratory at Egbaston, near Birmingham. His life in most of its outward aspects was not a happy one. By his conversion he sacrificed all his Oxford friendships; many Anglicans regarded him as a traitor not only to the English Church but virtually to England itself. The converts from Anglicanism with whom he was associated—their number was quite considerable—were inclined to extreme views as to the authority of the church and the pope and tended to regard his moderation in this matter, especially his belief that the laity should have a part in the intellectual life of the church and that questions of belief should be openly dealt with, as evidence of tepidity. In 1852 he was made rector-elect of the proposed Catholic University in Dublin, for which he had the high hopes expressed in his famous lectures on *The Idea of a University* (1852). Although these discourses put themselves in opposition to the view that theology is not a science and therefore should not be part of a university curriculum, they are generally held to constitute a peculiarly cogent and eloquent defense of liberal education. During his years in Dublin he made good progress toward his goal, but his admirable plans were brought to naught by indifference and small-minded jealousies and in 1856 he resigned the post, in which in fact he had never been confirmed. In 1857 Cardinal Wiseman informed him of the desire of the Catholic bishops of England that he undertake a new translation of the Bible, but when Newman eagerly got the project under way at the Oratory, Wiseman withdrew his support from it. He was made editor of a liberal Catholic magazine, *The Rambler,* but he had scarcely begun the work when his bishop required him to resign. His unpopularity with his co-religionists became almost proverbial.

In 1863 Charles Kingsley, an Anglican divine widely known as a novelist and historian of extreme anti-Catholic views, made a public statement which impugned Newman's integrity as a priest and his honor as an English gentleman. How Newman responded to this slur by writing his most widely read book, *Apologia Pro Vita Sua,* and how warmly the English public responded to it are related below in the Headnote to Chapter V of the *Apologia.* It was in the new atmosphere created by the *Apologia* that he wrote and published what may well be the most brilliant of his works, *An Essay in Aid of a Grammar of Assent* (1870), and republished his early Anglican works (1877). In 1878 he was greatly touched when Protestant Oxford made its peace with him and he was elected to an honorary fellowship in his old college, Trinity. In 1879 he was made a cardinal of his church. He died in 1890.

From The Tamworth Reading Room [1]

Secular Knowledge Not a Principle of Action

People say to me, that it is but a dream to suppose that Christianity should regain the organic power in human society which once it possessed. I cannot help that; I never said it could. I am not a politician; I am proposing no

1. In 1840, Sir Robert Peel (1788–1850), "the most liberal of conservatives and the most conservative of liberals," soon to be prime minister for a second time, made a gift of a library and reading room to the town of Tamworth, which he represented in Parliament.

measures, but exposing a fallacy, and resisting a pretence. Let Benthamism [2] reign, if men have no aspirations; but do not tell them to be romantic, and then solace them with glory; do not attempt by philosophy what once was done by religion. The ascendency of Faith may be impracticable, but the reign of Knowledge is incomprehensible. The problem for statesmen of this age is how to educate the masses, and literature and science cannot give the solution.

Not so deems Sir Robert Peel; his firm belief and hope is, 'that an increased sagacity will administer to an exalted faith; that it will make men not merely believe in the cold doctrines of Natural Religion, but that it will so prepare and temper the spirit and understanding, that they will be better qualified to comprehend the great scheme of human redemption.' He certainly thinks that scientific pursuits have some considerable power of impressing religion upon the mind of the multitude. I think not, and will now say why.

Science gives us the grounds or premises from which religious truths are to be inferred; but it does not set about inferring them, much less does it reach the inference;—that is not its province. It brings before us phenomena, and it leaves us, if we will, to call them works of design, wisdom, or benevolence; and further still, if we will, to proceed to confess an Intelligent Creator. We have to take its facts, and to give them a meaning, and to draw our own conclusions from them. First comes Knowledge, then a view, then reasoning, and then belief. This is why Science has so little of a religious tendency; deductions have no power of persuasion. The heart is commonly reached, not through the reason, but through the imagination, by means of direct impressions, by the testimony of facts and events, by history, by description. Persons influence us, voices melt us, looks subdue us, deeds inflame us. Many a man will live and die upon a dogma: no man will be a martyr for a conclusion.[3] A conclusion is but an opinion; it is not a thing which *is*, but which *we are 'certain about'*; and it has often been observed, that we never say we are certain without implying that we doubt. To say that a thing *must* be, is to admit that it *may not* be. No one, I say, will die for his own calculations; he dies for realities. This is why a literary religion is so little to be depended upon; it looks well in fair weather, but its doctrines are opinions, and, when called to suffer for them, it slips them between its folios, or burns them at its hearth. And this again is the secret of the distrust and raillery with which moralists have been so commonly visited. They say and do not. Why? Because they are contemplating the fitness of things, and they live by the square, when they should be realizing their high maxims in the concrete. Now Sir Robert thinks better of natural history, chemistry, and astronomy, than of such ethics; but they too, what are they more than

His address at the opening of the institution expressed the current optimistic view of the good effects of secular education upon the working classes. Newman made the address the occasion for a series of seven letters or discourses, published in 1841 in the *Times* and signed "Catholicus," in which he examined the claims put forward for secular education as a decisive force for social good.

2. The philosophical position deriving from the writings of Jeremy Bentham (1748–1832); Utilitarianism, the ethical doctrine which holds that actions are to be judged by their "utility," that is to say, by the extent to which they promote the happiness of mankind.

3. This sentence and the third following, which reiterates the sense of this one, are perhaps more frequently quoted than anything Newman wrote. As well as brief utterances can, they propose what Newman meant by "faith."

divinity *in posse?*[4] He protests against 'controversial divinity':[5] is *inferential* much better?

I have no confidence, then, in philosophers who cannot help being religious, and are Christians by implication. They sit at home, and reach forward to distances which astonish us; but they hit without grasping, and are sometimes as confident about shadows as about realities. They have worked out by a calculation the lie of a country which they never saw, and mapped it by means of a gazetteer; and like blind men, though they can put a stranger on his way, they cannot walk straight themselves, and do not feel it quite their business to walk at all.

Logic makes but a sorry rhetoric with the multitude; first shoot round corners, and you may not despair of converting by a syllogism. Tell men to gain notions of a Creator from His works, and, if they were to set about it (which nobody does), they would be jaded and wearied by the labyrinth they were tracing. Their minds would be gorged and surfeited by the logical operation. Logicians are more set upon concluding rightly, than on right conclusions. They cannot see the end for the process. Few men have that power of mind which may hold fast and firmly a variety of thoughts. We ridicule 'men of one idea'; but a great many of us are born to be such, and we should be happier if we knew it. To most men argument makes the point in hand only more doubtful, and considerably less impressive. After all, man is *not* a reasoning animal; he is a seeing, feeling, contemplating, acting animal. He is influenced by what is direct and precise. It is very well to freshen our impressions and convictions from physics, but to create them we must go elsewhere. Sir Robert Peel 'never can think it possible that a mind can be so constituted, that, after being familiarized with the wonderful discoveries which have been made in every part of experimental science, it can retire from such contemplations without more enlarged conceptions of God's providence, and a higher reverence for His name.' If he speaks of religious minds, he perpetrates a truism; if of irreligious, he insinuates a paradox.

Life is not long enough for a religion of inferences; we shall never have done beginning, if we determine to begin with proof. We shall ever be laying our foundations; we shall turn theology into evidences, and divines into textuaries. We shall never get at our first principles. Resolve to believe nothing, and you must prove your proofs and analyze your elements, sinking further and further, and finding 'in the lowest depth a lower deep,' till you come to the broad bosom of scepticism. I would rather be bound to defend the reasonableness of assuming that Christianity is true, than to demonstrate a moral governance from the physical world. Life is for action. If we insist on proofs for everything, we shall never come to action: to act you must assume, and that assumption is faith.

4. Potentially.
5. In his fifth letter, "Secular Knowledge Not a Principle of Social Unity," Newman had said that there was nothing wrong with religious views' being expressed controversially. "Christianity," he said, "is a faith, faith implies a doctrine, a doctrine proposition, propositions yes or no, yes or no differences. Differences, then, are the natural attendants on Christianity, and you cannot have Christianity and not have differences." He would not have admitted that there was any contradiction between this state of affairs and the sentences commented on in note 3 above.

Let no one suppose that in saying this I am maintaining that all proofs are equally difficult, and all propositions equally debatable. Some assumptions are greater than others, and some doctrines involve postulates larger than others, and more numerous. I only say that impressions lead to action, and that reasonings lead from it. Knowledge of premisses, and inferences upon them,—this is not to *live*. It is very well as a matter of liberal curiosity and of philosophy to analyze our modes of thought; but let this come second, and when there is leisure for it, and then our examinations will in many ways even be subservient to action. But if we commence with scientific knowledge and argumentative proof, or lay any great stress upon it as the basis of personal Christianity, or attempt to make man moral and religious by Libraries and Museums, let us in consistency take chemists for our cooks, and mineralogists for our masons.

Now I wish to state all this as matter of fact, to be judged by the candid testimony of any persons whatever. Why we are so constituted that Faith, not Knowledge or Argument, is our principle of action, is a question with which I have nothing to do; but I think it is a fact, and if it be such, we must resign ourselves to it as best we may, unless we take refuge in the intolerable paradox, that the mass of men are created for nothing, and are meant to leave life as they entered it. So well has this practically been understood in all ages of the world, that no Religion has yet been a Religion of physics or of philosophy. It has ever been synonymous with Revelation. It never has been a deduction from what we know: it has ever been an assertion of what we are to believe. It has never lived in a conclusion; it has never been a message, or a history, or a vision. No legislator or priest ever dreamed of educating our moral nature by science or by argument. There is no difference here between true Religions and pretended. Moses was instructed, not to reason from the creation, but to work miracles. Christianity is a history supernatural, and almost scenic: it tells us what its Author is, by telling us what He has done. I have no wish at all to speak otherwise than respectfully of conscientious Dissenters, but I have heard it said by those who were not their enemies, and who had known much of their preaching, that they had often heard narrow-minded and bigoted clergymen, and often Dissenting ministers of a far more intellectual cast; but that Dissenting teaching came to nothing,—that it was dissipated in thoughts which had no point, and inquiries which converged to no centre, that it ended as it began, and sent away its hearers as it found them;—whereas the instruction in the Church, with all its defects and mistakes, comes to some end, for it started from some beginning. Such is the difference between the dogmatism of faith and the speculations of logic.

Lord Brougham himself, as we have already seen, has recognized the force of this principle. He has not left his philosophical religion to argument; he has committed it to the keeping of the imagination. Why should he depict a great republic of letters, and an intellectual Pantheon, but that he feels that instances and patterns, not logical reasonings, are the living conclusions which alone have a hold over the affections, or can form the character?

1841   1841

From Discourses to Mixed Congregations [1]

Faith and Private Judgment

When we consider the beauty, the majesty, the completeness, the resources, the consolations, of the Catholic Religion, it may strike us with wonder, my brethren, that it does not convert the multitude of those who come in its way. Perhaps you have felt this surprise yourselves; especially those of you who have been recently converted, and can compare it, from experience, with those religions which the millions of this country choose instead of it. You know from experience how barren, unmeaning, and baseless those religions are; what poor attractions they have, and how little they have to say for themselves. Multitudes, indeed, are of no religion at all; and you may not be surprised that those who cannot even bear the thought of God, should not feel drawn to His Church; numbers, too, hear very little about Catholicism, or a great deal of abuse and calumny against it, and you may not be surprised that they do not all at once become Catholics; but what may fairly surprise those who enjoy the fulness of Catholic blessings is, that those who see the Church ever so distantly, who see even gleams or the faint lustre of her majesty, nevertheless should not be so far attracted by what they see as to seek to see more,—should not at least put themselves in the way to be led on to the Truth, which of course is not ordinarily recognised in its Divine authority except by degrees. Moses, when he saw the burning bush, turned aside to see 'that great sight'; [2] Nathaniel, though he thought no good could come out of Nazareth, at least followed Philip to Christ, when Philip said to him, 'Come and see'; [3] but the multitudes about us see and hear, in some measure, surely,—many in ample measure,—and yet are not persuaded thereby to see and hear more, are not moved to act upon their knowledge. Seeing they see not, and hearing they hear not; they are contented to remain as they are; they are not drawn to inquire, or at least not drawn on to embrace.

Many explanations may be given of this difficulty; I will proceed to suggest to you one, which will sound like a truism, but yet has a meaning in it. Men do not become Catholics, because they have not faith. Now you may ask me, how this is saying more than that men do not believe the Catholic Church *because* they do not believe it; which is saying nothing at all. Our Lord, for instance, says, 'He who cometh to Me shall not hunger, and he who believeth in Me shall never thirst'; [4]—to believe then and to come are the same thing. If they had faith, of course they would join the Church, for the very meaning, the very exercise of faith, is joining the Church. But I mean something more than this: faith is a state of mind, it is a particular mode of thinking and acting, which is exercised, always indeed towards God, but in very various ways. Now I mean

1. In 1846, Newman went to Rome, where he was ordained a priest of the Catholic Church. In 1847 he returned to England and in Birmingham he established the Oratory (see Head-note) where the rest of his life was spent. It was at this time that he delivered *Discourses to Mixed Congregations*, his first sermons as a Catholic. This selection is Discourse X.
2. Exodus 3:3.
3. John 1:45–46.
4. John 4:14. Like many of Newman's quotations from the Bible, this does not conform exactly to the text of the King James version. Newman often quoted from memory and sometimes he had in mind the (Catholic) Douay-Rheims version.

to say, that the multitude of men in this country have not this habit or character of mind. We could conceive, for instance, their believing in their own religions, even if they did not believe in the Church; this would be faith, though a faith improperly directed; but they do not believe even their own religions; they do not believe in anything at all. It is a definite defect in their minds: as we might say that a person had not the virtue of meekness, or of liberality, or of prudence, quite independently of this or that exercise of the virtue, so there is such a religious virtue as faith, and there is such a defect as the absence of it. Now I mean to say that the great mass of men in this country have not this particular virtue called faith, have not this virtue at all. As a man might be without eyes or without hands, so they are without faith; it is a distinct want or fault in their soul; and what I say is, that *since* they have not this faculty of religious belief, no wonder they do not embrace that, which cannot really be embraced without it. They do not believe any teaching at all in any true sense; and therefore they do not believe the Church in particular.

Now, in the first place, what is faith? it is assenting to a doctrine as true, which we do not see, which we cannot prove, because God says it is true, who cannot lie. And further than this, since God says it is true, not with His own voice, but by the voice of His messengers, it is assenting to what man says, not simply viewed as a man, but to what he is commissioned to declare, as a messenger, prophet, or ambassador from God. In the ordinary course of this world we account things true either because we see them, or because we can perceive that they follow and are deducible from what we do see; that is, we gain truth by sight or by reason, not by faith. You will say indeed, that we accept a number of things which we cannot prove or see, on the word of others; certainly, but then we accept what they say only as the word of man; and we have not commonly that absolute and unreserved confidence in them, which nothing can shake. We know that man is open to mistake, and we are always glad to find some confirmation of what he says, from other quarters, in any important matter; or we receive his information with negligence and unconcern, as something of little consequence, as a matter of opinion; or, if we act upon it, it is as a matter of prudence, thinking it best and safest to do so. We take his word for what it is worth, and we use it either according to our necessity, or its probability. We keep the decision in our own hands, and reserve to ourselves the right of re-opening the question whenever we please. This is very different from Divine faith; he who believes that God is true, and that this is His word, which He has committed to man, has no doubt at all. He is as certain that the doctrine taught is true, as that God is true; and he is certain, *because* God is true, *because* God has spoken, not because he sees its truth or can prove its truth. That is, faith has two peculiarities;—it is most certain, decided, positive, immovable in its assent, and it gives this assent not because it sees with eye, or sees with the reason, but because it receives the tidings from one who comes from God.

This is what faith was in the time of the Apostles, as no one can deny; and what it was then, it must be now, else it ceases to be the same thing. I say, it certainly was this in the Apostles' time, for you know they preached to the world that Christ was the Son of God, that He was born of a Virgin, that He had ascended on high, that He would come again to judge all, the living and the dead. Could the world see all this? could it prove it? how then were men to receive it? why did so many embrace it? on the word of the Apostles, who were, as their powers showed, messengers from God. Men were told to submit their reason to a living authority. Moreover, whatever an Apostle said, his converts were bound to believe; when they entered the Church, they entered it in order to learn. The Church was their teacher; they did not come to argue, to examine, to pick and choose, but to accept whatever was put before them. No one doubts, no one can doubt this, of those primitive times. A Christian was bound to take without doubting all that the Apostles declared to be revealed; if the Apostles spoke, he had to yield an internal assent of his mind; it would not be enough to keep silence, it would not be enough not to oppose: it was not allowable to credit in a measure; it was not allowable to doubt. No; if a convert had his own private thoughts of what was said, and only kept them to himself, if he made some secret opposition to the teaching, if he waited for further proof before he believed it, this would be a proof that he did not think the Apostles were sent from God to reveal His will; it would be a proof that he did not in any true sense believe at all. Immediate, implicit submission of the mind was, in the lifetime of the Apostles, the only, the necessary token of faith; then there was no room whatever for what is now called private judgment. No one could say: 'I will choose my religion for myself, I will believe this, I will not believe that; I will pledge myself to nothing; I will believe just as long as I please, and no longer; what I believe to-day I will reject to-morrow, if I choose. I will believe what the Apostles have as yet said, but I will not believe what they shall say in time to come.' No; either the Apostles were from God, or they were not; if they were, everything that they preached was to be believed by their hearers; if they were not, there was nothing for their hearers to believe. To believe a little, to believe more or less, was impossible; it contradicted the very notion of believing: if one part was to be believed, every part was to be believed; it was an absurdity to believe one thing and not another; for the word of the Apostles, which made the one true, made the other true too; they were nothing in themselves, they were all things, they were an infallible authority, as coming from God. The world had either to become Christian, or to let it alone; there was no room for private tastes and fancies, no room for private judgment.

Now surely this is quite clear from the nature of the case; but is also clear from the words of Scripture. 'We give thanks to God,' says St. Paul, 'without ceasing, because when ye had received from us the word of hearing, which is of God, ye received it, not as the word of men, but (as it is indeed) the Word of God.' [5] Here you see St. Paul expresses what I have said above; that the Word comes from God, that it is spoken by men, that it must be received, not as man's word, but as God's word. So in another place he says: 'He who despiseth these things, despiseth not man, but God, who hath also given in us His Holy Spirit.' [6] Our Saviour had made a like declaration already: 'He that heareth you, heareth Me; and he that despiseth you, despiseth Me; and he that despiseth Me, despiseth Him that sent Me.' [7] Accordingly, St. Peter on the day

5. I Thessalonians 2:13.
6. I Thessalonians 4:8.
7. Luke 10:16.

of Pentecost said: 'Men of Israel, *hear* these words, God hath raised up this Jesus, whereof *we* are *witnesses*. Let all the house of Israel *know most certainly* that God hath made this Jesus, whom you have crucified, both Lord and Christ.' [8] At another time he said: 'We ought to obey God, rather than man; we are *witnesses* of these things, and so *is the Holy Ghost,* whom God has given to all who obey Him.' [9] And again: 'He commanded us to preach to the people, and to testify that it is He (Jesus) who hath been appointed by God to be the Judge of the living and of the dead.' [10] And you know that the persistent declaration of the first preachers was: 'Believe and thou shalt be saved': they do not say, 'prove our doctrine by your own reason,' nor 'wait till you see before you believe'; but, 'believe without seeing and without proving, because our word is not our own, but God's word.' Men might indeed use their reason in inquiring into the pretensions of the Apostles; they might inquire whether or not they did miracles; they might inquire whether they were predicted in the Old Testament as coming from God; but when they had ascertained this fairly in whatever way, they were to take all the Apostles said for granted without proof; they were to exercise their faith, they were to be saved by hearing. Hence, as you perhaps observed, St. Paul significantly calls the revealed doctrine 'the word of hearing,' in the passage I quoted; men came to hear, to accept, to obey, not to criticise what was said; and in accordance with this he asks elsewhere: 'How shall they believe Him, whom they have not heard? and how shall they hear without a preacher? Faith cometh by hearing, and hearing by the word of Christ.' [11]

Now, my dear brethren, consider, are not these two states or acts of mind quite distinct from each other;—to believe simply what a living authority tells you, and to take a book, such as Scripture, and to use it as you please, to master it, that is, to make yourself the master of it, to interpret it for yourself, and to admit just what you choose to see in it, and nothing more? Are not these two procedures distinct in this, that in the former you submit, in the latter you judge? At this moment I am not asking you which is the better, I am not asking whether this or that is practicable now, but are they not two ways of taking up a doctrine, and not one? is not submission quite contrary to judging? Now, is it not certain that faith in the time of the Apostles consisted in submitting? and is it not certain that it did not consist in judging for one's self. It is in vain to say that the man who judges from the Apostles' writings, does submit to those writings in the first instance, and therefore has faith in them; else why should he refer to them at all? There is, I repeat, an essential difference between the act of submitting to a living oracle, and to his written words; in the former case there is no appeal from the speaker, in the latter the final decision remains with the reader. Consider how different is the confidence with which you report another's words in his presence and in his absence. If he be absent, you boldly say that he holds so and so, or said so and so; but let him come into the room in the midst of the conversation, and your tone is immediately changed. It is then, 'I *think* I have heard you say something *like* this,

8. Acts 10:34–43.
9. Acts 5:32.
10. Acts 10:42.
11. Romans 10:14–17.

or what I *took* to be this'; or you modify considerably the statement or the fact to which you originally pledged him, dropping one-half of it for safety sake, or retrenching the most startling portions of it; and then after all you wait with some anxiety to see whether he will accept any portion of it at all. The same sort of process takes place in the case of the written document of a person now dead. I can fancy a man magisterially expounding St. Paul's Epistle to the Galatians or to the Ephesians, who would be better content with the writer's absence than his sudden re-appearance among us; lest the Apostle should take his own meaning out of his commentator's hands and explain it for himself. In a word, though he says he has faith in St. Paul's writings, he confessedly has no faith in St. Paul; and though he may speak much about truth as found in Scripture, he has no wish at all to be like one of these Christians whose names and deeds occur in it.

I think I may assume that this virtue, which was exercised by the first Christians, is not known at all among Protestants now; or at least if there are instances of it, it is exercised towards those, I mean their own teachers and divines, who expressly disclaim that they are fit objects of it, and who exhort their people to judge for themselves. Protestants, generally speaking, have not faith, in the primitive meaning of that word; this is clear from what I have been saying, and here is a confirmation of it. If men believed now as they did in the times of the Apostles, they could not doubt nor change. No one can doubt whether a word spoken by God is to be believed; of course it is; whereas any one, who is modest and humble, may easily be brought to doubt of his own inferences and deductions. Since men now-a-days deduce from Scripture, in-stead of believing a teacher, you may expect to see them waver about; they will feel the force of their own deductions more strongly at one time than at another, they will change their minds about them, or perhaps deny them altogether; whereas this cannot be, while a man has faith, that is, belief that what a preacher says to him comes from God. This is what St. Paul especially insists on, telling us that Apostles, prophets, evangelists, pastors, and teachers, are given us that 'we may all attain to unity of faith,' and, on the contrary, in order 'that we be *not* as children tossed to and fro, and carried about by every gale of doctrine.' [12] Now, in matter of fact, do not men in this day change about in their religious opinions without any limit? Is not this, then, a proof that they have not that faith which the Apostles demanded of their converts? If they had faith, they would not change. Once believe that God has spoken, and you are sure He cannot unsay what He has already said; He cannot deceive; He cannot change; you have received it once for all; you will believe it ever.

Such is the only rational, consistent account of faith; but so far are Protestants from professing it, that they laugh at the very notion of it. They laugh at the notion itself of men pinning their faith (as they express themselves) upon Pope or Council; they think it simply superstitious and narrow-minded, to profess to believe just what the Church believes, and to assent to whatever she will say in time to come on matters of doctrine. That is, they laugh at the bare notion of doing what Christians undeniably did in the time of the Apostles. Observe, they do not merely ask whether the Catholic Church has a claim to teach, has

12. Ephesians 4:14.

authority, has the gifts;—this is a reasonable question;—no, they think that the very state of mind which such a claim involves in those who admit it, namely, the disposition to accept without reserve or question, that *this* is slavish. They call it priestcraft to insist on this surrender of the reason, and superstition to make it. That is, they quarrel with the very state of mind which all Christians had in the age of the Apostles; nor is there any doubt (who will deny it?) that those who thus boast of not being led blindfold, of judging for themselves, of believing just as much and just as little as they please, of hating dictation, and so forth, would have found it an extreme difficulty to hang on the lips of the Apostles, had they lived at their date, or rather would have simply resisted the sacrifice of their own liberty of thought, would have thought life eternal too dearly purchased at such a price, and would have died in their unbelief. And they would have defended themselves on the plea that it was absurd and childish to ask them to believe without proof, to bid them give up their education, and their intelligence, and their science, and in spite of all those difficulties which reason and sense find in the Christian doctrine, in spite of its mysteriousness, its obscurity, its strangeness, its unacceptableness, its severity, to require them to surrender themselves to the teaching of a few unlettered Galilæans, or a learned indeed but fanatical Pharisee. This is what they would have said then; and if so, is it wonderful they do not become Catholics now? The simple account of their remaining as they are, is, that they lack one thing,—they have not faith; it is a state of mind, it is a virtue, which they do not recognise to be praiseworthy, which they do not aim at possessing.

What they feel now, my brethren, is just what both Jew and Greek felt before them in the time of the Apostles, and what the natural man has felt ever since. The great and wise men of the day looked down upon faith, then as now, as if it were unworthy the dignity of human nature: 'See your vocation, brethren, that there are not,' among you, 'many wise according to the flesh, not many mighty, not many noble; but the foolish things of the world hath God chosen to confound the strong, and the mean things of the world, and the things that are contemptible, hath God chosen, and things that are not, that He might destroy the things that are, that no flesh might glory in His sight.' [13] Hence the same Apostle speaks of 'the foolishness of preaching.' Similar to this is what our Lord had said in His prayer to the Father: 'I thank Thee, Father, Lord of heaven and earth, because thou hast hid these things from the wise and prudent, and hast revealed them unto little ones.' [14] Now, is it not plain that men of this day have just inherited the feelings and traditions of these falsely wise and fatally prudent persons in our Lord's day? They have the same obstruction in their hearts to entering the Catholic Church, which Pharisees and Sophists had before them; it goes against them to believe her doctrine, not so much for want of evidence that she is from God, as because, if so, they shall have to submit their minds to living men, who have not their own cultivation or depth of intellect, and because they must receive a number of doctrines, whether they will or no, which are strange to their imagination and difficult to their reason. The very characteristic of the Catholic teaching and of the Catholic

13. I Corinthians 1:26–29.
14. Matthew 11:25.

teacher is to them a preliminary objection to their becoming Catholics, so great, as to throw into the shade any argument however strong, which is producible in behalf of the mission of those teachers and the origin of that teaching. In short, they have not faith.

They have not in them the principle of faith; and I repeat, it is nothing to the purpose to urge that at least they firmly believe Scripture to be the Word of God. In truth, it is much to be feared that their acceptance of Scripture itself is nothing better than a prejudice or inveterate feeling impressed on them when they were children. A proof of it is this; that, while they profess to be so shocked at Catholic miracles, and are not slow to call them 'lying wonders,' they have no difficulty at all about Scripture narratives, which are quite as difficult to the reason as any miracles recorded in the history of the Saints. I have heard on the contrary of Catholics who have been startled at first reading in Scripture the narratives of the ark in the deluge, of the tower of Babel, of Balaam and Balac, of the Israelites' flight from Egypt and entrance into the promised land, and of Esau's and Saul's rejection; which the bulk of Protestants receive without any effort of mind. How, then, do these Catholics accept them? by faith. They say, 'God is true, and every man a liar.' How come Protestants so easily to receive them? by faith? Nay, I conceive that in most cases there is no submission of the reason at all; simply they are so familiar with the passages in question, that the narrative presents no difficulties to their imagination; they have nothing to overcome. If, however, they *are* led to contemplate these passages in themselves, and to try them in the balance of probability, and to begin to question about them, as will happen when their intellect is cultivated, then there is nothing to bring them back to their former habitual or mechanical belief; they know nothing of submitting to authority, that is, they know nothing of faith; for they have no authority to submit to. They either remain in a state of doubt without any great trouble of mind, or they go on to ripen into utter disbelief on the subjects in question, though they may say nothing about it. Neither before they doubt, nor when they doubt, is there any token of the presence in them of a power subjecting reason to the Word of God. No; what looks like faith, is a mere hereditary persuasion, not a personal principle; it is a habit which they have learned in the nursery, which has never changed into anything higher, and which is scattered and disappears, like a mist, before the light, such as it is, of reason. If, however, there are Protestants, who are not in one or other of these two states, either of credulity or of doubt, but who firmly believe in spite of all difficulties, they certainly have some claim to be considered under the influence of faith; but there is nothing to show that such persons, where they are found, are not in the way to become Catholics, and perhaps they are already called so by their friends, showing in their own examples the logical, indisputable connexion which exists between possessing faith and joining the Church.

If, then, faith be now the same faculty of mind, the same sort of habit or act, which it was in the days of the Apostles, I have made good what I set about showing. But it must be the same; it cannot mean two things; the Word cannot have changed its meaning. Either say that faith is not necessary now at all, or take it to be what the Apostles meant by it, but do not say that you have it, and then show me something quite different, which you have put in the place of it.

In the Apostles' days the peculiarity of faith was submission to a living authority; this is what made it so distinctive; this is what made it an act of submission at all; this is what destroyed private judgment in matters of religion. If you will not look out for a living authority, and will bargain for private judgment, then say at once that you have not Apostolic faith. And in fact you have it not; the bulk of this nation has it not; confess you have it not; and then confess that this is the reason why you are not Catholics. You are not Catholics because you have not faith. Why do not blind men see the sun? because they have no eyes; in like manner it is vain to discourse upon the beauty, the sanctity, the sublimity of the Catholic doctrine and worship, where men have no faith to accept it as Divine. They may confess its beauty, sublimity, and sanctity, without believing it; they may acknowledge that the Catholic religion is noble and majestic; they may be struck with its wisdom, they may admire its adaptation to human nature, they may be penetrated by its tender and winning bearing, they may be awed by its consistency. But to commit themselves to it, that is another matter; to choose it for their portion, to say with the favoured Moabitess, 'Whithersoever thou shalt go, I will go! and where thou shalt dwell, I will dwell; thy people shall be my people, and thy God my God,' [15] this is the language of faith. A man may revere, a man may extol, who has no tendency whatever to obey, no notion whatever of professing. And this often happens in fact: men are respectful to the Catholic religion; they acknowledge its services to mankind, they encourage it and its professors; they like to know them, they are interested in hearing of their movements, but they are not, and never will be Catholics. They will die as they have lived, out of the Church, because they have not possessed themselves of that faculty by which the Church is to be approached. Catholics who have not studied them or human nature, will wonder they remain where they are; nay, they themselves, alas for them! will sometimes lament they cannot become Catholics. They will feel so intimately the blessedness of being a Catholic, that they will cry out, 'Oh, what would I give to be a Catholic! Oh, that I could believe what I admire! but I do not, and I can no more believe merely because I wish to do so, than I can leap over a mountain. I should be much happier were I a Catholic; but I am not; it is no use deceiving myself; I am what I am; I revere, I cannot accept.'

Oh, deplorable state! deplorable because it is utterly and absolutely their own fault, and because such great stress is laid in Scripture, as they know, on the necessity of faith for salvation. Faith is there made the foundation and commencement of all acceptable obedience. It is described as the 'argument' or 'proof of things not seen'; by faith men have understood that God is, that He made the world, that He is a rewarder of those who seek Him, that the flood was coming, that their Saviour was to be born. 'Without faith it is impossible to please God'; 'by faith we stand'; 'by faith we walk'; 'by faith we overcome the world.' When our Lord gave to the Apostles their commission to preach all over the world, He continued, 'He that believeth and is baptised, shall be saved; but he that believeth not, shall be condemned.' [16] And He declared to

15. Ruth 1:16–17.
16. Mark 16:16.

Nicodemus, 'He that believeth in the Son, is not judged; but he that doth not believe is already judged, because he believeth not in the Name of the Only-begotten Son of God.' [17] He said to the Pharisees, 'If you believe not that I am He, ye shall die in your sins.' [18] To the Jews, 'Ye believe not, because ye are not of My sheep.' [19] And you may recollect that before His miracles, He commonly demands faith of the supplicant: 'All things are possible,' He says, 'to him that believeth'; [20] and we find in one place, 'He could not do any miracle,' on account of the unbelief of the inhabitants.

Has faith changed its meaning, or is it less necessary now? Is it not still what it was in the Apostles' day, the very characteristic of Christianity, the special instrument of renovation, the first disposition for justification, one out of the three theological virtues? God might have renewed us by other means, by sight, by reason, by love, but He has chosen to 'purify our hearts by faith'; it has been His will to select an instrument which the world despises, but which is of immense power. He preferred it, in His infinite wisdom, to every other; and if men have it not, they have not the very element and rudiment, out of which are formed, on which are built, the Saints and Servants of God. And they have it not; they are living, they are dying, without the hopes, without the aids of the Gospel, because, in spite of so much that is good in them, in spite of their sense of duty, their tenderness of conscience on many points, their benevolence, their uprightness, their generosity, they are under the dominion (I must say it) of a proud fiend; they have this stout spirit within them, they determine to be their own masters in matters of thought, about which they know so little; they consider their own reason better than any one's else; they will not admit that any one comes from God who contradicts their own view of truth. What! is none their equal in wisdom anywhere? is there none other whose word is to be taken on religion? is there none to wrest from them their ultimate appeal to themselves? Have they in no possible way the occasion or opportunity of faith? Is it a virtue, which, in consequence of their transcendent sagacity, their pre-rogative of omniscience, they must give up hope of exercising? If the pretensions of the Catholic Church do not satisfy them, let them go somewhere else, if they can. If they are so fastidious that they cannot trust her as the oracle of God, let them find another more certainly from Him than the House of His own institution, which has ever been called by His name, has ever maintained the same claims, has ever taught one substance of doctrine, and has triumphed over those who preached any other. Since Apostolic faith was in the beginning reliance on man's word, as being God's word, since what faith was then such it is now, since faith is necessary for salvation, let them attempt to exercise it towards another, if they will not accept the Bride of the Lamb. Let them, if they can, put faith in some of those religions which have lasted a whole two or three centuries in a corner of the earth. Let them stake their eternal prospects on kings and nobles and parliaments and soldiery, let them take some mere fiction of the law, or abortion of the schools, or idol of a populace, or upstart of a crisis, or oracle of lecture-rooms, as the prophet of God. Alas! they are

17. John 3:18.
18. John 8:21, 24.
19. John 10:26.
20. Mark 9:23.

hardly bestead if they must possess a virtue, which they have no means of exercising,—if they must make an act of faith, they know not on whom, and know not why!

What thanks ought we to render to Almighty God, my dear brethren, that He has made us what we are! It is a matter of grace. There are, to be sure, many cogent arguments to lead one to join the Catholic Church, but they do not force the will. We may know them, and not be moved to act upon them. We may be convinced without being persuaded. The two things are quite distinct from each other, seeing you ought to believe, and believing; reason, if left to itself, will bring you to the conclusion that you have sufficient grounds for believing, but belief is the gift of grace. You are then what you are, not from any excellence or merit of your own, but by the grace of God who has chosen you to believe. You might have been as the barbarian of Africa, or the freethinker of Europe, with grace sufficient to condemn you, because it had not furthered your salvation. You might have had strong inspirations of grace and have resisted them, and then additional grace might not have been given to overcome your resistance. God gives not the same measure of grace to all. Has He not visited you with over-abundant grace? and was it not necessary for your hard hearts to receive more than other people? Praise and bless Him continually for the benefit; do not forget, as time goes on, that it is of grace; do not pride yourselves upon it; pray ever not to lose it; and do your best to make others partakers of it.

And you, my brethren, also, if such be present, who are not as yet Catholics, but who by your coming hither seem to show your interest in our teaching, and you wish to know more about it, you too remember, that though you may not yet have faith in the Church, still God has brought you into the way of obtaining it. You are under the influence of His grace; He has brought you a step on your journey; He wishes to bring you further, He wishes to bestow on you the fulness of His blessings, and to make you Catholics. You are still in your sins; probably you are laden with the guilt of many years, the accumulated guilt of many a deep, mortal offence, which no contrition has washed away, and to which no Sacrament has been applied. You at present are troubled with an uneasy conscience, a dissatisfied reason, an unclean heart, and a divided will; you need to be converted. Yet now the first suggestions of grace are working in your souls, and are to issue in pardon for the past and sanctity for the future. God is moving you to acts of faith, hope, love, hatred of sin, repentance; do not disappoint Him, do not thwart Him, concur with Him, obey Him. You look up, and you see, as it were, a great mountain to be scaled; you say, 'How can I possibly find a path over these giant obstacles, which I find in the way of my becoming Catholic? I do not comprehend this doctrine, and I am pained at that; a third seems impossible; I never can be familiar with one practice, I am afraid of another; it is one maze and discomfort to me, and I am led to sink down in despair.' Say not so, my dear brethren, look up in hope, trust in Him who calls you forward. 'Who art thou, O great mountain, before Zorobabel? but a plain.' [21] He will lead you forward step by step, as He has led forward many a one before you. He will make the crooked straight and the

21. Zechariah 4:7.

rough plain. He will turn the streams, and dry up the rivers, which lie in your path. 'He shall strengthen your feet like harts' feet, and set you up on high places. He shall widen your steps under you, and your tread shall not be weakened.' [22] 'There is no God like the God of the righteous; He that mounts the heaven is thy Helper; by His mighty working the clouds disperse; His dwelling is above, and underneath are the everlasting arms; He shall cast out the enemy from before thee, and shall say, Crumble away.' [23] 'The young shall faint, and youths shall fall; but they that hope in the Lord shall be new-fledged in strength, they shall take feathers like eagles, they shall run and not labour, they shall walk and not faint.' [24]

1849   1849

The Idea of a University [1]

From Knowledge Viewed in Relation to Professional Skill

I

I have been insisting, in my two preceding Discourses, first, on the cultivation of the intellect, as an end which may reasonably be pursued for its own sake; and next, on the nature of that cultivation, or what that cultivation consists in. Truth of whatever kind is the proper object of the intellect; its cultivation then lies in fitting it to apprehend and contemplate truth. Now the intellect in its present state, with exceptions which need not here be specified, does not discern truth intuitively, or as a whole. We know, not by a direct and simple vision, not at a glance, but, as it were, by piecemeal and accumulation, by a mental process, by going round an object, by the comparison, the combination, the mutual correction, the continual adaptation, of many partial notions, by the employment, concentration, and joint action of many faculties and exercises of mind. Such a union and concert of the intellectual powers, such an enlargement and development, such a comprehensiveness, is necessarily a matter of training. And again, such a training is a matter of rule; it is not mere application, however exemplary, which introduces the mind to truth, nor the reading many books, nor the getting up many subjects, nor the witnessing many experiments, nor the attending many lectures. All this is short of enough; a man may have done it all, yet be lingering in the vestibule of knowledge:—he may not realize what his mouth utters; he may not see with his mental eye what confronts him; he may have no grasp of things as they are; or at least he may have no power at all of advancing one step forward of himself, in consequence of what he has already acquired, no power of discriminating between truth and false-

22. Psalms 18:33.
23. Deuteronomy 33:26–27.
24. Isaiah 11:30–31.

1. The nine discourses which comprise *The Idea of a University* were delivered in Dublin in 1852. (The one presented here is from Discourse VII.) Their purpose was to define for the Irish clergy and laity the principles by which a projected Catholic university in Ireland should be shaped. In 1854 Newman, at the invitation of the Irish bishops, went to Dublin as rector of the new institution. For a variety of reasons, the enterprise failed, and after four unhappy years Newman returned to Birmingham.

hood, of sifting out the grains of truth from the mass, of arranging things according to their real value, and, if I may use the phrase, of building up ideas. Such a power is the result of a scientific formation of mind; it is an acquired faculty of judgment, of clear-sightedness, of sagacity, of wisdom, of philosophical reach of mind, and of intellectual self-possession and repose,— qualities which do not come of mere acquirement. The bodily eye, the organ for apprehending material objects, is provided by nature; the eye of the mind, of which the object is truth, is the work of discipline and habit.

This process of training, by which the intellect, instead of being formed or sacrificed to some particular or accidental purpose, some specific trade or profession, or study or science, is disciplined for its own sake, for the perception of its own proper object, and for its own highest culture, is called Liberal Education; and though there is no one in whom it is carried as far as is conceivable, or whose intellect would be a pattern of what intellects should be made, yet there is scarcely any one but may gain an idea of what real training is, and at least look towards it, and make its true scope and result, not something else, his standard of excellence; and numbers there are who may submit themselves to it, and secure it to themselves in good measure. And to set forth the right standard, and to train according to it, and to help forward all students towards it according to their various capacities, this I conceive to be the business of a University.

II

Now this is what some great men are very slow to allow; they insist that Education should be confined to some particular and narrow end, and should issue in some definite work, which can be weighed and measured. They argue as if every thing, as well as every person, had its price; and that where there has been a great outlay, they have a right to expect a return in kind. This they call making Education and Instruction 'useful,' and 'Utility' becomes their watchword. With a fundamental principle of this nature, they very naturally go on to ask, what there is to show for the expense of a University; what is the real worth in the market of the article called 'a Liberal Education,' on the supposition that it does not teach us definitely how to advance our manufactures, or to improve our lands, or to better our civil economy; or again, if it does not at once make this man a lawyer, that an engineer, and that a surgeon; or at least if it does not lead to discoveries in chemistry, astronomy, geology, magnetism, and science of every kind.

. . . .

V

. . . Let us take 'useful,' as Locke [2] takes it, in its proper and popular sense, and then we enter upon a large field of thought, to which I cannot do justice in one discourse, though today's is all the space that I can give to it. I say, let

2. John Locke (1632–1704), the English philosopher; his *On Education* urged that emphasis be put on practical subjects. Newman has been dealing with an attack on Oxford education, particularly on classical studies, which had been made a generation before by a group of writers in the *Edinburgh Review*. He identifies Locke as the originator of the ideas advanced by the Edinburgh group and undertakes to deal with the great man rather than with his followers.

us take 'useful' to mean, not what is simply good, but what *tends* to good, or is the *instrument* of good; and in this sense also, Gentlemen, I will show you how a liberal education is truly and fully a useful, though it be not a professional, education. 'Good' indeed means one thing, and 'useful' means another; but I lay it down as a principle, which will save us a great deal of anxiety, that, though the useful is not always good, the good is always useful. Good is not only good, but reproductive of good; this is one of its attributes; nothing is excellent, beautiful, perfect, desirable for its own sake, but it overflows, and spreads the likeness of itself all around it. Good is prolific; it is not only good to the eye, but to the taste; it not only attracts us, but it communicates itself; it excites first our admiration and love, then our desire and our gratitude, and that, in proportion to its intenseness and fulness in particular instances. A great good will impart great good. If then the intellect is so excellent a portion of us, and its cultivation so excellent, it is not only beautiful, perfect, admirable, and noble in itself, but in a true and high sense it must be useful to the possessor and to all around him; not useful in any low, mechanical, mercantile sense, but as diffusing good, or as a blessing, or a gift, or power, or a treasure, first to the owner, then through him to the world, I say then, if a liberal education be good, it must necessarily be useful too.

VI

You will see what I mean by the parallel of bodily health. Health is a good in itself, though nothing came of it, and is especially worth seeking and cherishing; yet, after all, the blessings which attend its presence are so great, while they are so close to it and so redound back upon it and encircle it, that we never think of it except as useful as well as good, and praise and prize it for what it does, as well as for what it is, though at the same time we cannot point out any definite and distinct work or production which it can be said to effect. And so as regards intellectual culture, I am far from denying utility in this large sense as the end of education, when I lay it down that the culture of the intellect is a good in itself and its own end; I do not exclude from the idea of intellectual culture what it cannot but be, from the very nature of things; I only deny that we must be able to point out, before we have any right to call it useful, some art, or business, or profession, or trade, or work, as resulting from it, and as its real and complete end. The parallel is exact: as the body may be sacrificed to some manual or other toil, whether moderate or oppressive, so may the intellect be devoted to some specific profession; and I do not call *this* the culture of the intellect. Again, as some member or organ of the body may be inordinately used and developed, so may memory, or imagination, or the reasoning faculty; and *this* again is not intellectual culture. On the other hand, as the body may be tended, cherished, and exercised with a simple view to its general health, so may the intellect also be generally exercised in order to its perfect state; and this *is* its cultivation.

Again, as health ought to precede labour of the body, and as a man in health can do what an unhealthy man cannot do, and as of this health the properties are strength, energy, agility, graceful carriage and action, manual dexterity, and endurance of fatigue, so in like manner general culture of mind is the best aid to professional and scientific study, and educated men can do what illiterate cannot; and the man who has learned to think and to reason and to compare and to discriminate and to analyze, who has refined his taste, and formed his judgment, and sharpened his mental vision, will not indeed at once be a lawyer, or a pleader, or an orator, or a statesman, or a physician, or a good landlord, or a man of business, or a soldier, or an engineer, or a chemist, or a geologist, or an antiquarian, but he will be placed in that state of intellect in which he can take up any one of the sciences or callings I have referred to, or any other for which he has a taste or special talent, with an ease, a grace, a versatility, and a success, to which another is a stranger. In this sense then, and as yet I have said but a very few words on a large subject, mental culture is emphatically *useful*.

If then I am arguing, and shall argue, against professional or scientific knowledge as the sufficient end of a university education, let me not be supposed, Gentlemen, to be disrespectful towards particular studies, or arts, or vocations, and those who are engaged in them. In saying that law or medicine is not the end of a university course, I do not mean to imply that the university does not teach law or medicine. What indeed can it teach at all, if it does not teach something particular? It teaches *all* knowledge by teaching all *branches* of knowledge, and in no other way. I do but say that there will be this distinction as regards a professor of law, or of medicine, or of geology, or of political economy, in a university and out of it, that out of a university he is in danger of being absorbed and narrowed by his pursuit, and of giving lectures which are the lectures of nothing more than a lawyer, physician, geologist, or political economist; whereas in a university he will just know where he and his science stand, he has come to it, as it were, from a height, he has taken a survey of all knowledge, he is kept from extravagance by the very rivalry of other studies, he has gained from them a special illumination and largeness of mind and freedom and self-possession, and he treats his own in consequence with a philosophy and a resource, which belongs not to the study itself, but to his liberal education.

This then is how I should solve the fallacy, for so I must call it, by which Locke and his disciples would frighten us from cultivating the intellect, under the notion that no education is useful which does not teach us some temporal calling, or some mechanical art, or some physical secret. I say that a cultivated intellect, because it is a good in itself, brings with it a power and a grace to every work and occupation which it undertakes, and enables us to be more useful, and to a greater number. There is a duty we owe to human society as such, to the state to which we belong, to the sphere in which we move, to the individuals towards whom we are variously related, and whom we successively encounter in life; and that philosophical or liberal education, as I have called it, which is the proper function of a University, if it refuses the foremost place to professional interests, does but postpone them to the formation of the citizen, and, while it subserves the larger interests of philanthropy, prepares also for the successful prosecution of those merely personal objects, which at first sight it seems to disparage.

. . .

X

But I must bring these extracts to an end.[3] To-day I have confined myself to saying that that training of the intellect, which is best for the individual himself, best enables him to discharge his duties to society. The Philosopher, indeed, and the man of the world differ in their very notion, but the methods, by which they are respectively formed, are pretty much the same. The Philosopher has the same command of matters of thought, which the true citizen and gentleman has of matters of business and conduct. If then a practical end must be assigned to a University course, I say it is that of training good members of society. Its art is the art of social life, and its end is fitness for the world. It neither confines its views to particular professions on the one hand, nor creates heroes or inspires genius on the other. Works indeed of genius fall under no art; heroic minds come under no rule; a University is not a birthplace of poets or of immortal authors, of founders of schools, leaders of colonies, or conquerors of nations. It does not promise a generation of Aristotles or Newtons, of Napoleons or Washingtons, of Raphaels or Shakespeares, though such miracles of nature it has before now contained within its precincts. Nor is it content on the other hand with forming the critic or the experimentalist, the economist or the engineer, though such too it includes within its scope. But a University training is the great ordinary means to a great but ordinary end; it aims at raising the intellectual tone of society, at cultivating the public mind, at purifying the national taste, at supplying true principles to popular enthusiasm and fixed aims to popular aspiration, at giving enlargement and sobriety to the ideas of the age, at facilitating the exercise of political power, and refining the intercourse of private life. It is the education which gives a man a clear conscious view of his own opinions and judgments, a truth in developing them, an eloquence in expressing them and a force in urging them. It teaches him to see things as they are, to go right to the point, to disentangle a skein of thought, to detect what is sophistical, and to discard what is irrelevant. It prepares him to fill any post with credit, and to master any subject with facility. It shows him how to accommodate himself to others, how to throw himself into their state of mind, hcw to bring before them his own, how to influence them, how to come to an understanding with them, how to bear with them. He is at home in any society, he has common ground with every class; he knows when to speak and when to be silent; he is able to converse, he is able to listen; he can ask a question pertinently, and gain a lesson seasonably, when he has nothing to impart himself; he is ever ready, yet never in the way; he is a pleasant companion, and a comrade you can depend upon; he knows when to be serious and when to trifle, and he has a sure tact which enables him to trifle with gracefulness and to be serious with effect. He has the repose of a mind which lives in itself, while it lives in the world, and which has resources for its happiness at home when it cannot go abroad. He has a gift which serves him in public, and supports him in retirement, without which good fortune is but vulgar, and with which failure and disappointment have a charm. The art

3. Sections 8 and 9 consist largely of quotations from the article in the *Quarterly Review* (1810) in which John Davison defended Oxford from the Edinburgh writers.

which tends to make a man all this, is in the object which it pursues as useful as the art of wealth or the art of health, though it is less susceptible of method, and less tangible, less certain, less complete in its result.

1852   1852, 1859, 1873

Apologia Pro Vita Sua

Newman's autobiography, *Apologia Pro Vita Sua* (Defense [or explanation, not "apology"] of His Life), was composed under circumstances whose drama is of the essence of the work itself. In the January 1864 issue of *Macmillan's Magazine* Charles Kingsley published a long review of J. A. Froude's intensely Protestant *History of England,* in the course of which he attacked several aspects of Catholicism, including the church's attitude toward truth. "Truth for its own sake," Kingsley said, "had never been a virtue with the Roman clergy." And he went on: "Father Newman informs us that it need not, and on the whole ought not be; that cunning is the weapon which Heaven has given to the Saints. . . ."

Kingsley is an engaging figure and in his day he was both popular and influential. An Anglican clergyman, he had taken an active part in movements to secure justice for the working classes; he was Professor of History at Cambridge and the author of novels, poems, and popular works of science which were widely read and which are still of no small charm. His intellect has been characterized as "rough but manly" and he would not have disliked the description; in matters of religion his views were simple, directed more to conduct than to faith, and strongly opposed to Catholicism, which he thought of as un-English.

To the slur on his personal probity and on that of his church, Newman responded with spirit. He called for a retraction and an apology. These Kingsley offered, but in a form that Newman could not possibly consider adequate. Newman replied to the accusation of untruthfulness in a pamphlet which included the letters that had passed between the two men. Although Newman was at the time far from popular, it was generally thought that he was in the right of the matter. Had the affair ended here, the *Apologia* might never have been written, but Kingsley rejoined to Newman's pamphlet with one of his own, an illogical and intensely bitter attack. Within a matter of days, Newman began the *Apologia,* which, by unremitting labor, he completed in three months. It was first issued in an unusual fashion, in weekly parts as it came from his pen. Its reception was all that he might have hoped for. The English intellectual public was almost completely won over to Newman's side and took this isolated, virtually exiled, man to its heart as a great *English* figure, which was what Kingsley had tried to show he was not. It was just this effect that Newman had hoped for—not that he personally should be vindicated in his Englishness, of which truth-telling was an element, but that it should be freely granted that there was nothing in the belief of Catholics that made inappropriate their full participation in the national life.

For many years the crucial chapter of the *Apologia* was felt to be Chapter IV, "History of My Religious Opinions from 1841 to 1845," in which Newman relates the agonized steps by which he came to the realization that he could no longer continue his commitment to the Anglican Church but had to turn to Catholicism. That chapter is indeed of great importance in the understanding of Newman (and the religious life of England at the time), yet for the contemporary reader its detailed account of the particularities of doctrine will seem less immediate than the passionate account which Newman gives in Chapter V of the nature of the faith in which he came to rest.

Apologia Pro Vita Sua

From *Position of My Mind Since 1845* [1]

From the time that I became a Catholic, of course I have no further history of my religious opinions to narrate. In saying this, I do not mean to say that my mind has been idle, or that I have given up thinking on theological subjects; but that I have had no variations to record, and have had no anxiety of heart whatever. I have been in perfect peace and contentment; I never have had one doubt. I was not conscious to myself, on my conversion, of any change, intellectual or moral, wrought in my mind. I was not conscious of firmer faith in the fundamental truths of Revelation, or of more self-command; I had not more fervour; but it was like coming into port after a rough sea; and my happiness on that score remains to this day without interruption.

Nor had I any trouble about receiving those additional articles,[2] which are not found in the Anglican Creed. Some of them I believed already, but not any one of them was a trial to me. I made a profession of them upon my reception with the greatest ease, and I have the same ease in believing them now. I am far of course from denying that every article of the Christian Creed, whether as held by Catholics or by Protestants, is beset with intellectual difficulties; and it is simple fact, that, for myself, I cannot answer those difficulties. Many persons are very sensitive of the difficulties of Religion; I am as sensitive of them as any one; but I have never been able to see a connexion between apprehending those difficulties, however keenly, and multiplying them to any extent, and on the other hand doubting the doctrines to which they are attached. Ten thousand difficulties do not make one doubt, as I understand the subject; difficulty and doubt are incommensurate. There of course may be difficulties in the evidence; but I am speaking of difficulties intrinsic to the doctrines themselves, or to their relations with each other. A man may be annoyed that he cannot work out a mathematical problem, of which the answer is or is not given to him, without doubting that it admits of an answer, or that a certain particular answer is the true one. Of all points of faith, the being of a God is, to my own apprehension, encompassed with most difficulty, and yet borne in upon our minds with most power.

People say that the doctrine of Transubstantiation [3] is difficult to believe;

---

1. This is from Chap. V.
2. Doctrinal statements issued by a church.
3. The doctrine holds that at the consecration of the elements of the Eucharist, i.e. the bread and wine of the Holy Communion, the whole substance of the bread and of the wine is changed into the body and blood of Christ. This is also known as the doctrine of the Real Presence.

I did not believe the doctrine till I was a Catholic. I had no difficulty in believing it, as soon as I believed that the Catholic Roman Church was the oracle of God, and that she had declared this doctrine to be part of the original revelation. It is difficult, impossible, to imagine, I grant;—but how is it difficult to believe? Yet Macaulay thought it so difficult to believe,[4] that he had need of a believer in it of talents as eminent as Sir Thomas More,[5] before he could bring himself to conceive that the Catholics of an enlightened age could resist 'the overwhelming force of the argument against it.' 'Sir Thomas More,' he says, 'is one of the choice specimens of wisdom and virtue; and the doctrine of transubstantiation is a kind of proof charge. A faith which stands that test, will stand any test.' But for myself, I cannot indeed prove it, I cannot tell *how* it is; but I say, 'Why should it not be? What's to hinder it? What do I know of substance or matter? just as much as the greatest philosophers, and that is nothing at all';—so much is this the case, that there is a rising school of philosophy now, which considers phenomena to constitute the whole of our knowledge in physics.[6] The Catholic doctrine leaves phenomena alone. It does not say that the phenomena go; on the contrary, it says that they remain; nor does it say that the same phenomena are in several places at once. It deals with what no one on earth knows any thing about, the material substances themselves. And, in like manner, of that majestic Article of the Anglican as well as of the Catholic Creed,—the doctrine of the Trinity in Unity.[7] What do I know of the Essence [8] of the Divine Being? I know that my abstract idea of three is simply incompatible with my idea of one; but when I come to the question of concrete fact, I have no means of proving that there is not a sense in which one and three can equally be predicated of the Incommunicable God.

But I am going to take upon myself the responsibility of more than the mere Creed of the Church; as the parties accusing me are determined I shall do. They say, that now, in that I am a Catholic, though I may not have offences of my own against honesty [9] to answer for, yet, at least, I am answerable for the offences of others, of my co-religionists, of my brother priests, of the Church herself. I am quite willing to accept the responsibility; and, as I have been able, as I trust, by means of a few words, to dissipate, in the minds of all those who do not begin with disbelieving me, the suspicion with which so many Protestants start, in forming their judgment of Catholics, viz. that our Creed is actually set up in inevitable superstition and hypocrisy, as the original sin of Catholicism; so now I will proceed, as before, identifying myself with the Church and vindicating it,—not of course denying the enormous mass of sin and error which exists of necessity in that world-wide multiform Communion,—

4. Thomas Babington Macaulay (1800–1859), famous historian and essayist, expressed this view in his essay on von Ranke's *History of the Popes*.

5. Sir Thomas More (1478–1535), the great humanist, author of *Utopia*, was Lord Chancellor to Henry VIII. He was executed for his religious beliefs. In 1935 he was canonized by Pope Pius XI.

6. Perhaps a reference to the empiricism of J. S. Mill.

7. The triune nature of God—the Father, the Son, and the Holy Spirit—considered as coequal, coeternal, and indivisible.

8. Essence comprises the permanent phases of being, those which define the nature of an entity. The doctrine of the Trinity is held by the church to be a mystery.

9. See the Headnote to this work.

but going to the proof of this one point, that its system is in no sense dishonest, and that therefore the upholders and teachers of that system, as such, have a claim to be acquitted in their own persons of that odious imputation.

Starting then with the being of a God, (which, as I have said, is as certain to me as the certainty of my own existence, though when I try to put the grounds of that certainty into logical shape I find a difficulty in doing so in mood and figure to my satisfaction,) I look out of myself into the world of men, and there I see a sight which fills me with unspeakable distress. The world seems simply to give the lie to that great truth, of which my whole being is so full; and the effect upon me is, in consequence, as a matter of necessity, as confusing as if it denied that I am in existence myself. If I looked into a mirror, and did not see my face, I should have the sort of feeling which actually comes upon me, when I look into this living busy world, and see no reflexion of its Creator. This is, to me, one of those great difficulties of this absolute primary truth, to which I referred just now. Were it not for this voice, speaking so clearly in my conscience and my heart, I should be an atheist, or a pantheist, or a polytheist when I looked into the world. I am speaking for myself only; and I am far from denying the real force of the arguments in proof of a God, drawn from the general facts of human society and the course of history, but these do not warm me or enlighten me; they do not take away the winter of my desolation, or make the buds unfold and the leaves grow within me, and my moral being rejoice. The sight of the world is nothing else than the prophet's scroll, full of 'lamentations, and mourning, and woe.' [10]

To consider the world in its length and breadth, its various history, the many races of man, their starts, their fortunes, their mutual alienation, their conflicts; and then their ways, habits, governments, forms of worship; their enterprises, their aimless courses, their random achievements and acquirements, the impotent conclusion of long-standing facts, the tokens so faint and broken of a superintending design, the blind evolution of what turn out to be great powers or truths, the progress of things, as if from unreasoning elements, not towards final causes, the greatness and littleness of man, his far-reaching aims, his short duration, the curtain hung over his futurity, the disappointments of life, the defeat of good, the success of evil, physical pain, mental anguish, the prevalence and intensity of sin, the pervading idolatries, the corruptions, the dreary hopeless irreligion, that condition of the whole race, so fearfully yet exactly described in the Apostle's words, 'having no hope and without God in the world,' [11]—all this is a vision to dizzy and appal; and inflicts upon the mind the sense of a profound mystery, which is absolutely beyond human solution.

What shall be said to this heart-piercing, reason-bewildering fact? I can only answer, that either there is no Creator, or this living society of men is in a true sense discarded from His presence. Did I see a boy of good make and mind, with the tokens on him of a refined nature, cast upon the world without provision, unable to say whence he came, his birth-place or his family connexions, I should conclude that there was some mystery connected with his history, and that he was one, of whom, from one cause or other, his parents were ashamed.

10. Ezekiel 2:9–10.
11. Ephesians 2:12.

Thus only should I be able to account for the contrast between the promise and the condition of his being. And so I argue about the world;—*if* there be a God, *since* there is a God, the human race is implicated in some terrible aboriginal calamity. It is out of joint with the purposes of its Creator. This is a fact as true as the fact of its existence; and thus the doctrine of what is theologically called original sin becomes to me almost as certain as that the world exists, and as the existence of God.

And now, supposing it were the blessed and loving will of the Creator to interfere in this anarchical condition of things, what are we to suppose would be the methods which might be necessarily or naturally involved in His purpose of mercy? Since the world is in so abnormal a state, surely it would be no surprise to me, if the interposition were of necessity equally extraordinary—or what is called miraculous. But that subject does not directly come into the scope of my present remarks. Miracles as evidence, involve a process of reason, or an argument; and of course I am thinking of some mode of interference which does not immediately run into argument. I am rather asking what must be the face-to-face antagonist, by which to withstand and baffle the fierce energy of passion and the all-corroding, all-dissolving scepticism of the intellect in religious inquiries? I have no intention at all of denying, that truth is the real object of our reason, and that, if it does not attain to truth, either the premiss or the process is in fault; but I am not speaking here of right reason,[12] but of reason as it acts in fact and concretely in fallen man. I know that even the un-aided reason, when correctly exercised, leads to a belief in God, in the immortality of the soul, and in a future retribution; but I am considering the faculty of reason actually and historically; and in this point of view, I do not think I am wrong in saying that its tendency is towards a simple unbelief in matters of religion. No truth, however sacred, can stand against it, in the long run;[13] and hence it is that in the pagan world, when our Lord came, the last traces of the religious knowledge of former times were all but disappearing from those portions of the world in which the intellect had been active and had had a career.

And in these latter days, in like manner, outside the Catholic Church things are tending,—with far greater rapidity than in that old time from the circumstance of the age,—to atheism in one shape or other. What a scene, what a prospect, does the whole of Europe present at this day! and not only Europe, but every government and every civilization through the world, which is under the influence of the European mind! Especially, for it most concerns us, how sorrowful, in the view of religion, even taken in its most elementary, most attenuated form, is the spectacle presented to us by the educated intellect of England, France, and Germany! Lovers of their country and of their race, religious men, external to the Catholic Church, have attempted various expedients to arrest fierce wilful human nature in its onward course, and to bring it into subjection. The necessity of some form of religion for the interests of humanity, has been generally acknowledged: but where was the concrete representative of things invisible, which would have the force and the toughness necessary to

12. That is, reason in its ideal exercise.
13. Here Newman states with an audacious simplicity the natural antagonism of reason to faith and its power to destroy faith—if faith submits to the destruction.

be a breakwater against the deluge? Three centuries ago the establishment of religion, material, legal, and social, was generally adopted as the best expedient for the purpose, in those countries which separated from the Catholic Church; and for a long time it was successful; but now the crevices of those establishments are admitting the enemy. Thirty years ago, education was relied upon: [14] ten years ago there was a hope that wars would cease for ever, under the influence of commercial enterprise and the reign of the useful and fine arts; [15] but will any one venture to say there is any thing any where on this earth, which will afford a fulcrum for us, whereby to keep the earth from moving onwards?

The judgment, which experience passes whether on establishments [16] or on education, as a means of maintaining religious truth in this anarchical world, must be extended even to Scripture, though Scripture be divine.[17] Experience proves surely that the Bible does not answer a purpose for which it was never intended. It may be accidentally the means of the conversion of individuals; but a book, after all, cannot make a stand against the wild living intellect of man,[18] and in this day it begins to testify, as regards its own structure and contents, to the power of that universal solvent, which is so successfully acting upon religious establishments.

Supposing then it to be the Will of the Creator to interfere in human affairs, and to make provisions for retaining in the world a knowledge of Himself, so definite and distinct as to be proof against the energy of human scepticism, in such a case,—I am far from saying that there was no other way,—but there is nothing to surprise the mind, if He should think fit to introduce a power into the world, invested with the prerogative of infallibility in religious matters. Such a provision would be a direct, immediate, active, and prompt means of withstanding the difficulty; it would be an instrument suited to the need; and, when I find that this is the very claim of the Catholic Church, not only do I feel no difficulty in admitting the idea, but there is a fitness in it, which recommends it to my mind. And thus I am brought to speak of the Church's infallibility, as a provision, adapted by the mercy of the Creator, to preserve religion in the world, and to restrain that freedom of thought, which of course in itself is one of the greatest of our natural gifts, and to rescue it from its own suicidal excesses. And let it be observed that, neither here nor in what follows, shall I have occasion to speak directly of Revelation in its subject-matter, but in reference to the sanction which it gives to truths which may be known independently of it,—as it bears upon the defence of natural religion.[19] I

---

14. See, above, the selection from *The Tamworth Reading Room*, the series of articles Newman published in 1841 dealing with the optimism over the spread of popular education.

15. Perhaps a reference to the expectations aroused by the international representation of manufactured goods at the Great Exhibition of 1851.

16. That is, religious organizations.

17. Newman affirms the Catholic view that the Bible, literally read and interpreted only according to the reader's own lights, cannot be a reliable guide to belief.

18. One of Newman's most memorable phrases and a decisive clue to the ground of his ecclesiastical views.

19. Religion derived from human reason and experience apart from revelation and supernatural evidence.

say, that a power, possessed of infallibility in religious teaching, is happily adapted to be a working instrument, in the course of human affairs, for smiting hard and throwing back the immense energy of the aggressive, capricious, untrustworthy intellect:—and in saying this, as in the other things that I have to say, it must still be recollected that I am all along bearing in mind my main purpose, which is a defence of myself.

I am defending myself here from a plausible charge brought against Catholics, as will be seen better as I proceed. The charge is this:—that I, as a Catholic, not only make profession to hold doctrines which I cannot possibly believe in my heart, but that I also believe in the existence of a power on earth, which at its own will imposes upon men any new set of *credenda*,[20] when it pleases, by a claim to infallibility; in consequence, that my own thoughts are not my own property; that I cannot tell that to-morrow I may not have to give up what I hold to-day, and that the necessary effect of such a condition of mind must be a degrading bondage, or a bitter inward rebellion relieving itself in secret infidelity, or the necessity of ignoring the whole subject of religion in a sort of disgust, and of mechanically saying every thing that the Church says, and leaving to others the defence of it. As then I have above spoken of the relation of my mind towards the Catholic Creed, so now I shall speak of the attitude which it takes up in the view of the Church's infallibility.

And first, the initial doctrine of the infallible teacher must be an emphatic protest against the existing state of mankind. Man had rebelled against his Maker. It was this that caused the divine interposition: and to proclaim it must be the first act of the divinely-accredited messenger. The Church must denounce rebellion as of all possible evils the greatest. She must have no terms with it; if she would be true to her Master, she must ban and anathematize it. This is the meaning of a statement of mine which has furnished matter for one of those special accusations to which I am at present replying: I have, however, no fault at all to confess in regard to it; I have nothing to withdraw, and in consequence I here deliberately repeat it. I said, "The Catholic Church holds it better for the sun and moon to drop from heaven, for the earth to fail, and for all the many millions on it to die of starvation in extremest agony, as far as temporal affliction goes, than that one soul, I will not say, should be lost, but should commit one single venial sin, should tell one wilful untruth, or should steal one poor farthing without excuse.'[21] I think the principle here enunciated to be the mere preamble in the formal credentials of the Catholic Church, as an Act of Parliament might begin with a 'Whereas.' It is because of the intensity of the evil which has possession of mankind, that a suitable antagonist has been provided against it; and the initial act of that divinely-commissioned power is of course to deliver her challenge and to defy the enemy. Such a preamble then gives a meaning to her position in the world, and an interpretation to her whole course of teaching and action.

In like manner she has ever put forth, with most energetic distinctness, those other great elementary truths, which either are an explanation of her mission

20. "Things that are to be believed."
21. The statement had been made in Newman's *On Certain Difficulties of Anglicans* (1851) and cited against him by Kingsley.

or give a character to her work. She does not teach that human nature is irreclaimable, else wherefore should she be sent? not, that it is to be shattered and reversed, but to be extricated, purified, and restored; not, that it is a mere mass of hopeless evil, but that it has the promise upon it of great things, and even now, in its present state of disorder and excess, has a virtue and a praise proper to itself. But in the next place she knows and she preaches that such a restoration, as she aims at effecting in it, must be brought about, not simply through certain outward provisions of preaching and teaching, even though they be her own, but from an inward spiritual power or grace imparted directly from above, and of which she is the channel. She has it in charge to rescue human nature from its misery, but not simply by restoring it on its own level, but by lifting it up to a higher level than its own. She recognizes in it real moral excellence though degraded, but she cannot set it free from earth except by exalting it towards heaven. It was for this end that a renovating grace was put into her hands; and therefore from the nature of the gift, as well as from the reasonableness of the case, she goes on, as a further point, to insist, that all true conversion must begin with the first springs of thought, and to teach that each individual man must be in his own person one whole and perfect temple of God, while he is also one of the living stones which build up a visible religious community. And thus the distinctions between nature and grace,[22] and between outward and inward religion, become two further articles in what I have called the preamble of her divine commission.

Such truths as these she vigorously reiterates, and pertinaciously inflicts upon mankind; as to such she observes no half-measures, no economical reserve, no delicacy or prudence. 'Ye must be born again,'[23] is the simple, direct form of words which she uses after her Divine Master: 'your whole nature must be re-born; your passions, and your affections, and your aims, and your conscience, and your will, must all be bathed in a new element, and reconsecrated to your Maker,—and, the last not the least, your intellect.' It was for repeating these points of her teaching in my own way, that certain passages of one of my Volumes have been brought into the general accusation which has been made against my religious opinions. The writer [24] has said that I was demented if I believed, and unprincipled if I did not believe, in my own statement, that a lazy, ragged, filthy, story-telling beggar-woman, if chaste, sober, cheerful, and religious, had a prospect of heaven, such as was absolutely closed to an accomplished statesman, or lawyer, or noble, be he ever so just, upright, generous, honourable, and conscientious, unless he had also some portion of the divine Christian graces;—yet I should have thought myself defended from criticism by the words which our Lord used to the chief priests, 'The publicans and harlots go into the kingdom of God before you.' And I was subjected again to the same alternative of imputations, for having ventured to say that consent to an unchaste wish was indefinitely more henious than any lie viewed apart from its causes, its motives, and its consequences: though a lie, viewed under the limitation of these conditions, is a random utterance, an almost outward act,

---

22. One of the *Discourses Addressed to Mixed Congregations* (1849) deals with these distinctions.
23. John 3:7.
24. He was Samuel Wilberforce (1805–73), Bishop of Oxford, later of Winchester.

not directly from the heart, however disgraceful and despicable it may be, however prejudicial to the social contract, however deserving of public reprobation; whereas we have the express words of our Lord to the doctrine that 'whoso looketh on a woman to lust after her, hath committed adultery with her already in his heart.' [25] On the strength of these texts, I have surely as much right to believe in these doctrines which have caused so much surprise, as to believe in original sin, or that there is a supernatural revelation, or that a Divine Person suffered, or that punishment is eternal.

Passing now from what I have called the preamble of that grant of power, which is made to the Church, to that power itself, Infallibility,[26] I premise two brief remarks:—1. on the one hand, I am not here determining any thing about the essential seat of that power, because that is a question doctrinal, not historical and practical; 2. nor, on the other hand, am I extending the direct subject-matter, over which that power of Infallibility has jurisdiction, beyond religious opinion:—and now as to the power itself.

This power, viewed in its fulness, is as tremendous as the giant evil which has called for it. It claims, when brought into exercise but in the legitimate manner, for otherwise of course it is but quiescent, to know for certain the very meaning of every portion of that Divine Message in detail, which was committed by our Lord to His Apostles. It claims to know its own limits, and to decide what it can determine absolutely and what it cannot. It claims, moreover, to have a hold upon statements not directly religious, so far as this,—to determine whether they indirectly relate to religion, and, according to its own definitive judgment, to pronounce whether or not, in a particular case, they are simply consistent with revealed truth. It claims to decide magisterially, whether as within its own province or not, that such and such statements are or are not prejudicial to the *Depositum* [27] of faith, in their spirit or in their consequences, and to allow them, or condemn and forbid them, accordingly. It claims to impose silence at will on any matters, or controversies, of doctrine, which on its own *ipse dixit*,[28] it pronounces to be dangerous, or inexpedient, or inopportune. It claims that, whatever may be the judgment of Catholics upon such acts, these acts should be received by them with those outward marks of reverence, submission, and loyalty, which Englishmen, for instance, pay to the presence of their sovereign, without expressing any criticism on them on the ground that in their matter they are inexpedient, or in their manner violent or harsh. And lastly, it claims to have the right of inflicting spiritual punishment, of cutting off from the ordinary channels of the divine life, and of simply excommunicating, those who refuse to submit themselves to its formal declarations. Such is the infallibility lodged in the Catholic Church, viewed in the concrete, as clothed and surrounded by the appendages of its high sov-

25. Matthew 5:27.
26. The doctrine of the infallibility of the church—that it cannot err in teaching revealed truth—is of great antiquity. The doctrine of the infallibility of the pope was promulgated at the Vatican Council of 1870 after much, and often bitter, debate within the Catholic fold. It holds that when the pope speaks *ex cathedra*—that is, in his character of head of the church and in virtue of his apostolic authority—what he lays down concerning faith and morals—these matters alone—is binding to all communicants.
27. "That which is laid down."
28. "He himself said it."

ereignty: it is, to repeat what I said above, a supereminent prodigious power sent upon earth to encounter and master a giant evil.

And now, having thus described it, I profess my own absolute submission to its claim. I believe the whole revealed dogma as taught by the Apostles, as committed by the Apostles to the Church, and as declared by the Church to me. I receive it, as it is infallibly interpreted by the authority to whom it is thus committed, and (implicitly) as it shall be, in like manner, further interpreted by that same authority till the end of time. I submit, moreover, to the universally received traditions of the Church, in which lies the matter of those new dogmatic definitions which are from time to time made, and which in all times are the clothing and the illustration of the Catholic dogma as already defined. And I submit myself to those other decisions of the Holy See, theological or not, through the organs which it has itself appointed, which, waiving the question of their infallibility, on the lowest ground come to me with a claim to be accepted and obeyed. Also, I consider that, gradually and in the course of ages, Catholic inquiry has taken certain definite shapes, and has thrown itself into the form of a science, with a method and a phraseology of its own, under the intellectual handling of great minds, such as St. Athanasius, St. Augustine, and St. Thomas; and I feel no temptation at all to break in pieces the great legacy of thought thus committed to us for these latter days.

All this being considered as the profession which I make *ex animo*,[29] as for myself, so also on the part of the Catholic body, as far as I know it, it will at first sight be said that the restless intellect of our common humanity is utterly weighed down, to the repression of all independent effort and action whatever, so that, if this is to be the mode of bringing it into order, it is brought into order only to be destroyed. But this is far from the result, far from what I conceive to be the intention of that high Providence who has provided a great remedy for a great evil,—far from borne out by the history of the conflict between Infallibility and Reason in the past, and the prospect of it in the future. The energy of the human intellect 'does from opposition grow'; it thrives and is joyous, with a tough elastic strength, under the terrible blows of the divinely-fashioned weapon, and is never so much itself as when it has lately been over-thrown. It is the custom with Protestant writers to consider that, whereas there are two great principles in action in the history of religion, Authority and Private Judgment, they have all the Private Judgment to themselves, and we have the full inheritance and the superincumbent oppression of Authority. But this is not so; it is the vast Catholic body itself, and it only, which affords an arena for both combatants in that awful, never-dying duel. It is necessary for the very life of religion, viewed in its large operations and its history, that the warfare should be incessantly carried on. Every exercise of Infallibility is brought out into act by an intense and varied operation of the Reason, both as its ally and as its opponent, and provokes again, when it has done its work, a re-action of Reason against it; and, as in a civil polity the State exists and endures by means of the rivalry and collision, the encroachments and defeats of its constituent parts, so in like manner Catholic Christendom is no simple exhibition of religious absolutism, but presents a continuous picture of Authority

29. "From my own soul."

and Private Judgment alternately advancing and retreating as the ebb and flow of the tide;—it is a vast assemblage of human beings with wilful intellects and wild passions, brought together into one by the beauty and the Majesty of a Superhuman Power,—into what may be called a large reformatory or training-school, not as if into a hospital or into a prison, not in order to be sent to bed, not to be buried alive, but (if I may change my metaphor) brought together as if into some moral factory,[30] for the melting, refining, and moulding, by an incessant, noisy process, of the raw material of human nature, so excellent, so dangerous, so capable of divine purposes.

St. Paul says in one place that his Apostolical power is given him to edification, and not to destruction. There can be no better account of the Infallibility of the Church. It is a supply for a need, and it does not go beyond that need. Its object is, and its effect also, not to enfeeble the freedom or vigour of human thought in religious speculation, but to resist and control its extravagance. What have been its great works? All of them in the distinct province of theology:—to put down Arianism, Eutychianism, Pelagianism, Manichæism, Lutheranism, Jansenism.[31] Such is the broad result of its action in the past;—and now as to the securities which are given us that so it ever will act in time to come.

First, Infallibility cannot act outside of a definite circle of thought, and it must in all its decisions, or *definitions*, as they are called, profess to be keeping within it. The great truths of the moral law, of natural religion, and of Apostolical faith, are both its boundary and its foundation. It must not go beyond them, and it must ever appeal to them. Both its subject-matter, and its articles in that subject-matter, are fixed. And it must ever profess to be guided by Scripture and by tradition. It must refer to the particular Apostolic truth which it is enforcing, or (what is called) *defining*. Nothing, then, can be presented to me, in time to come, as part of the faith, but what I ought already to have received, and hitherto have been kept from receiving (if so) merely because it has not been brought home to me. Nothing can be imposed upon me different in kind from what I hold already,—much less contrary to it. The new truth which is promulgated, if it is to be called new, must be at least homogeneous, cognate, implicit, viewed relatively to the old truth. It must be what I may even have guessed, or wished, to be included in the Apostolic revelation; and at least it will be of such a character, that my thoughts readily concur in it or coalesce with it, as soon as I hear it. Perhaps I and others actually have always believed it, and the only question which is now decided in my behalf, is, that I have henceforth the satisfaction of having to believe, that I have only been holding all along what the Apostles held before me.

Let me take the doctrine which Protestants consider our greatest difficulty, that of the Immaculate Conception.[32] Here I entreat the reader to recollect my

30. Newman's exquisite literary tact surely fails him here in these images of the world as a "large reformatory or training school" and as a "moral factory." The image of the world as a hospital, originated by Newman, is used to great effect by T. S. Eliot in the lyric in "East Coker" which begins "The wounded surgeon plies the steel. . . ."
31. Heresies from the 5th century to the 17th.
32. The doctrine that the soul of the Virgin Mary was, from its first existence, free of the stain of original sin. It is often confused with the doctrine of the Virgin birth.

main drift, which is this. I have no difficulty in receiving the doctrine; and that, because it so intimately harmonizes with that circle of recognized dogmatic truths, into which it has been recently received;—but if *I* have no difficulty, why may not another have no difficulty also? why may not a hundred? a thousand? Now I am sure that Catholics in general have not any intellectual difficulty at all on the subject of the Immaculate Conception; and that there is no reason why they should. Priests have no difficulty. You tell me that they *ought* to have a difficulty;—but they have not. Be large-minded enough to believe, that men may reason and feel very differently from yourselves; how is it that men, when left to themselves, fall into such various forms of religion, except that there are various types of mind among them, very distinct from each other? From my testimony then about myself, if you believe it, judge of others also who are Catholics: we do not find the difficulties which you do in the doctrines which we hold; we have no intellectual difficulty in that doctrine in particular, which you call a novelty of this day. We priests need not be hypocrites, though we be called upon to believe in the Immaculate Conception. To that large class of minds, who believe in Christianity after our manner,—in the particular temper, spirit, and light, (whatever word is used,) in which Catholics believe it,—there is no burden at all in holding that the Blessed Virgin was conceived without original sin; indeed, it is a simple fact to say, that Catholics have not come to believe it because it is defined, but that it was defined because they believed it.

So far from the definition in 1854 [33] being a tyrannical infliction on the Catholic world, it was received every where on its promulgation with the greatest enthusiasm. It was in consequence of the unanimous petition, presented from all parts of the Church to the Holy See, in behalf of an *ex cathedra* declaration that the doctrine was Apostolic, that it was declared so to be. I never heard of one Catholic having difficulties in receiving the doctrine, whose faith on other grounds was not already suspicious. Of course there were grave and good men, who were made anxious by the doubt whether it could be formally proved to be Apostolical either by Scripture or tradition, and who accordingly, though believing it themselves, did not see how it could be defined by authority and imposed upon all Catholics as a matter of faith; but this is another matter. The point in question is, whether the doctrine is a burden. I believe it to be none. So far from it being so, I sincerely think that St. Bernard and St. Thomas, who scrupled at it in their day,[34] had they lived into this, would have rejoiced to accept it for its own sake. Their difficulty, as I view it, consisted in matters of words, ideas, and arguments. They thought the doctrine inconsistent with other doctrines; and those who defended it in that age had not that precision in their view of it, which has been attained by means of the long disputes of the centuries which followed. And in this want of precision lay the difference of opinion, and the controversy.

Now the instance which I have been taking suggests another remark; the

33. In this year Pope Pius IX defined the doctrine of the Immaculate Conception.
34. St. Bernard of Clairvaux (1090–1153) and St. Thomas Aquinas (1225–74) both opposed the doctrine of the Immaculate Conception. They were more or less at one in holding the view that the Virgin was not conceived without the stain of original sin but was purified before birth.

number of those (so called) new doctrines will not oppress us, if it takes eight centuries to promulgate even one of them. Such is about the length of time through which the preparation has been carried on for the definition of the Immaculate Conception. This of course is an extraordinary case; but it is difficult to say what is ordinary, considering how few are the formal occasions on which the voice of Infallibility has been solemnly lifted up. It is to the Pope in Ecumenical Council that we look, as to the normal seat of Infallibility: now there have been only eighteen such Councils since Christianity was,—an average of one to a century,—and of these Councils some passed no doctrinal decree at all, others were employed on only one, and many of them were concerned with only elementary points of the Creed. . . .

Now I will go on in fairness to say what I think *is* the great trial to the Reason, when confronted with that august prerogative of the Catholic Church, of which I have been speaking. I enlarged just now upon the concrete shape and circumstances, under which pure infallible authority presents itself to the Catholic. That authority has the prerogative of an indirect jurisdiction on subject-matters which lie beyond its own proper limits, and it most reasonably has such a jurisdiction. It could not act in its own province, unless it had a right to act out of it. It could not properly defend religious truth, without claiming for that truth what may be called its *pomœria;* [35] or, to take another illustration, without acting as we act, as a nation, in claiming as our own, not only the land on which we live, but what are called British waters. The Catholic Church claims, not only to judge infallibly on religious questions, but to animadvert on opinions in secular matters which bear upon religion, on matters of philosophy, of science, of literature, of history, and it demands our submission to her claim. It claims to censure books, to silence authors, and to forbid discussions. In this province, taken as a whole, it does not so much speak doctrinally, as enforce measures of discipline. It must of course be obeyed without a word, and perhaps in process of time it will tacitly recede from its own injunctions. In such cases the question of faith does not come in at all; for what is matter of faith is true for all times, and never can be unsaid. Nor does it at all follow, because there is a gift of infallibility in the Catholic Church, that therefore the parties who are in possession of it are in all their proceedings infallible. 'O, it is excellent,' says the poet, 'to have a giant's strength, but tyrannous, to use it like a giant.' [36] I think history supplies us with instances in the Church, where legitimate power has been harshly used. To make such admission is no more than saying that the divine treasure, in the words of the Apostle, is 'in earthen vessels'; [37] nor does it follow that the substance of the acts of the ruling power is not right and expedient, because its manner may have been faulty. Such high authorities act by means of instruments; we know how such instruments claim for themselves the name of their principals, who thus get the credit of faults which really are not theirs. But granting all this to an extent greater than can with any show of reason be imputed to the ruling power in the Church, what difficulty is there in the fact of this want of prudence or moderation more than can be urged, with far

35. Limits or boundaries.
36. *Measure for Measure* II.ii.107–9.
37. II Corinthians 4:7.

greater justice, against Protestant communities and institutions? What is there in it to make us hypocrites, if it has not that effect upon Protestants? We are called upon, not to profess any thing, but to submit and be silent, as Protestant Churchmen have before now obeyed the royal command to abstain from certain theological questions. Such injunctions as I have been contemplaing are laid merely upon our actions, not upon our thoughts. How, for instance, does it tend to make a man a hypocrite, to be forbidden to publish a libel? his thoughts are as free as before: authoritative prohibitions may tease and irritate, but they have no bearing whatever upon the exercise of reason.

So much at first sight; but I will go on to say further, that, in spite of all that the most hostile critic may urge about the encroachments or severities of high ecclesiastics, in times past, in the use of their power, I think that the event has shown after all, that they were mainly in the right, and that those whom they were hard upon were mainly in the wrong. . . . In reading ecclesiastical history, when I was an Anglican, it used to be forcibly brought home to me, how the initial error of what afterwards became heresy was the urging forward some truth against the prohibition of authority at an unseasonable time. There is a time for every thing, and many a man desires a reformation of an abuse, or the fuller development of a doctrine, or the adoption of a particular policy, but forgets to ask himself whether the right time for it is come: and, knowing that there is no one who will be doing any thing towards its accomplishment in his own lifetime unless he does it himself, he will not listen to the voice of authority, and he spoils a good work in his own century, in order that another man, as yet unborn, may not have the opportunity of bringing it happily to perfection in the next. He may seem to the world to be nothing else than a bold champion for the truth and a martyr to free opinion, when he is just one of those persons whom the competent authority ought to silence; and, though the case may not fall within that subject-matter in which that authority is infallible, or the formal conditions of the exercise of that gift may be wanting, it is clearly the duty of authority to act vigorously in the case. Yet its act will go down to posterity as an instance of a tyrannical interference with private judgment, and of the silencing of a reformer, and of a base love of corruption or error; and it will show still less to advantage, if the ruling power happens in its proceedings to evince any defect of prudence or consideration. And all those who take the part of that ruling authority will be considered as time-servers, or indifferent to the cause of uprightness and truth; while, on the other hand, the said authority may be accidentally supported by a violent ultra party, which exalts opinions into dogmas, and has it principally at heart to destroy every school of thought but its own.

Such a state of things may be provoking and discouraging at the time, in the case of two classes of persons; of moderate men who wish to make differences in religious opinion as little as they fairly can be made; and of such as keenly perceive, and are honestly eager to remedy, existing evils,—evils, of which divines in this or that foreign country know nothing at all, and which even at home, where they exist, it is not every one who has the means of estimating. This is a state of things both of past time and of the present. We live in a wonderful age; the enlargement of the circle of secular knowledge just now is simply a bewilderment, and the more so, because it has the promise of continuing, and that with greater rapidity, and more signal results. Now these discoveries, certain or probable, have in matter of fact an indirect bearing upon religious opinions, and the question arises how are the respective claims of revelation and of natural science to be adjusted. Few minds in earnest can remain at ease without some sort of rational grounds for their religious belief; to reconcile theory and fact is almost an instinct of the mind. When then a flood of facts, ascertained or suspected, comes pouring in upon us, with a multitude of others in prospect, all believers in Revelation, be they Catholic or not, are roused to consider their bearing upon themselves, both for the honour of God, and from tenderness for those many souls who, in consequence of the confident tone of the schools of secular knowledge, are in danger of being led away into a bottomless liberalism of thought.

I am not going to criticize here that vast body of men, in the mass, who at this time would profess to be liberals in religion; and who look towards the discoveries of the age, certain or in progress, as their informants, direct or indirect, as to what they shall think about the unseen and the future. The Liberalism [38] which gives a colour to society now, is very different from that character of thought which bore the name thirty or forty years ago. Now it is scarcely a party; it is the educated lay world. When I was young, I knew the word first as giving name to a periodical, set up by Lord Byron and others.[39] Now, as then, I have no sympathy with the philosophy of Byron. Afterwards, Liberalism was the badge of a theological school, of a dry and repulsive character,[40] not very dangerous in itself, though dangerous as opening the door to evils which it did not itself either anticipate or comprehend. At present it is nothing else than that deep, plausible scepticism, of which I spoke above, as being the development of human reason, as practically exercised by the natural man.

The Liberal religionsts of this day are a very mixed body, and therefore I am not intending to speak against them. There may be, and doubtless is, in the hearts of some or many of them a real antipathy or anger against revealed truth, which it is distressing to think of. Again; in many men of science or literature there may be an animosity arising from almost a personal feeling; it being a matter of party, a point of honour, the excitement of a game, or a satisfaction to the soreness or annoyance occasioned by the acrimony or narrowness of apologists for religion, to prove that Christianity or that Scripture is untrustworthy. Many scientific and literary men, on the other hand, go on, I am confident, in a straightforward impartial way, in their own province and on their own line of thought, without any disturbance from religious difficulties in themselves, or any wish at all to give pain to others by the result of their investigations. It would ill become me, as if I were afraid of truth of any kind, to blame those who pursue secular facts, by means of the reason which God has given them, to their logical conclusions: or to be angry with science, because religion is bound in duty to take cognizance of its teaching. But putting these particular classes of men aside, as having no special call on the sympathy of

38. See *Liberalism,* below.

39. *The Liberal* was founded in 1822 by Byron, Shelley, and Leigh Hunt. Four numbers appeared.

40. A reference to the rationalistic theology of the Anglican prelate Richard Whately (1787–1863) and his followers, called Noetics (see the Headnote to Newman).

the Catholic, of course he does most deeply enter into the feelings of a fourth and large class of men, in the educated portions of society, of religious and sincere minds, who are simply perplexed,—frightened or rendered desperate, as the case may be,—by the utter confusion into which late discoveries or speculations have thrown their most elementary ideas of religion. Who does not feel for such men? who can have one unkind thought of them? I take up in their behalf St. Augustine's beautiful words, 'Illi in vos sæviant,' &c.[41] 'Let them be fierce with you who have no experience of the difficulty with which error is discriminated from truth, and the way of life is found amid the illusions of the world.' How many a Catholic has in his thoughts followed such men, many of them so good, so true, so noble! how often has the wish risen in his heart that some one from among his own people should come forward as the champion of revealed truth against its opponents! Various persons, Catholic and Protestant, have asked me to do so myself; but I had several strong difficulties in the way. One of the greatest is this, that at the moment it is so difficult to say precisely what it is that is to be encountered and overthrown. I am far from denying that scientific knowledge is really growing, but it is by fits and starts; hypotheses rise and fall; it is difficult to anticipate which of them will keep their ground, and what the state of knowledge in relation to them will be from year to year. In this condition of things, it has seemed to me to be very undignified for a Catholic to commit himself to the work of chasing what might turn out to be phantoms, and, in behalf of some special objections, to be ingenious in devising a theory, which, before it was completed, might have to give place to some theory newer still, from the fact that those former objections had already come to nought under the uprising of others. It seemed to be specially a time, in which Christians had a call to be patient, in which they had no other way of helping those who were alarmed, than that of exhorting them to have a little faith and fortitude, and to 'beware,' as the poet says, 'of dangerous steps.' [42] This seemed so clear to me, the more I thought of the matter, as to make me surmise, that, if I attempted what had so little promise in it, I should find that the highest Catholic Authority was against the attempt, and that I should have spent my time and my thought, in doing what either it would be imprudent to bring before the public at all, or what, did I do so, would only complicate matters further which were already complicated, without my interference, more than enough. And I interpret recent acts of that authority as fulfilling my expectation; I interpret them as tying the hands of a controversialist, such as I should be, and teaching us that true wisdom, which Moses inculcated on his people, when the Egyptians were pursuing them, 'Fear ye not, stand still; the Lord shall fight for you, and ye shall hold your peace.' [43] And so far from finding a difficulty in obeying in this case, I have cause to be thankful and to rejoice to have so clear a direction in a matter of difficulty.

But if we would ascertain with correctness the real course of a principle, we must look at it at a certain distance, and as history represents it to us. Nothing carried on by human instruments, but has its irregularities, and affords ground for criticism, when minutely scrutinized in matters of detail. I have been speak-

41. Newman's translation follows.
42. William Cowper (1731–1800), *The Needless Alarm*, ll. 132–33.
43. Exodus 14:13–14.

ing of that aspect of the action of an infallible authority, which is most open
to invidious criticism from those who view it from without; I have tried to be
fair, in estimating what can be said to its disadvantage, as witnessed at a particular time in the Catholic Church, and now I wish its adversaries to be
equally fair in their judgment upon its historical character. Can, then, the
infallible authority, with any show of reason, be said in fact to have destroyed
the energy of the Catholic intellect? Let it be observed, I have not here to speak
of any conflict which ecclesiastical authority has had with science, for this
simple reason, that conflict there has been none; and that, because the secular
sciences, as they now exist, are a novelty in the world, and there has been no
time yet for a history of relations between theology and these new methods of
knowledge, and indeed the Church may be said to have kept clear of them,
as is proved by the constantly cited case of Galileo.[44] Here 'exceptio probat
regulam': [45] for it is the one stock argument. Again, I have not to speak of any
relations of the Church to the new sciences, because my simple question all
along has been whether the assumption of infallibility by the proper authority
is adapted to make me a hypocrite, and till that authority passes decrees on
pure physical subjects and calls on me to subscribe them, (which it never will
do, because it has not the power,) it has no tendency to interfere by any of its
acts with my private judgment on those points. The simple question is, whether
authority has so acted upon the reason of individuals, that they can have no
opinion of their own, and have but an alternative of slavish superstition or
secret rebellion of heart; and I think the whole history of theology puts an
absolute negative upon such a supposition. . . .

There is only one other subject, which I think it necessary to introduce here,
as bearing upon the vague suspicions which are attached in this country to
the Catholic Priesthood. It is one of which my accusers have before now said
much,—the charge of reserve and economy.[46] They found it in no slight degree

44. Galileo Galilei (1564–1642), the great physicist and astronomer, was a strong proponent of the Copernican theory, which his researches had done much to confirm and
develop. In 1616 the church condemned the Copernican theory as being against Scripture
and heretical, and affirmed the Ptolemaic theory. When Galileo continued to teach the
Copernican theory despite his having promised not to do so, he was threatened with
torture and abjured his doctrine. Although Newman had once defended the principle on
which the church had acted in this instance, he here admits that the church had been
mistaken, although exceptionally.
45. "The exception proves the rule."
46. The idea of "reserve or economy" was central to the occasion of the Apologia, Kingsley
having said in effect that this idea, recognized and approved by the Catholic Church, put
Newman, as a Catholic priest, in an ambiguous relation to truth-telling. It was perhaps
inevitable that the idea should be misunderstood, as the Oxford English Dictionary makes
clear in its exceptionally full definition of and comment on the theological sense of
"economy": "a. The judicious handling of doctrine, i.e. the preservation of it in such a
manner as to suit the needs or to conciliate the prejudices of the persons addressed. b. This
sense has been (by misapprehension or word-play) often treated as an application of [the
sense of the word which denotes careful management of resources so as to make them go
as far as possible]. Hence the phrase economy (as if 'cautious or sparing use') of truth."
The OED goes on to comment on the polemical use of the word, doing so with particular
reference to Newman: "Newman's history of the Arians (1833) contained a section on the
use of 'the Economy' by the [Church] Fathers. The word was eagerly caught up by
popular writers and used contemptuously, as if it were a euphemistic name for dishonest
evasion; in this sense it is still frequently met with. . . ."

on what I have said on the subject in my History of the Arians, and in a note upon one of my Sermons in which I refer to it. The principle of Reserve is also advocated by an admirable writer in two numbers of the Tracts for the Times,[47] and of these I was the Editor.

Now, as to the Economy itself, it is founded upon the words of our Lord, 'Cast not your pearls before swine'; and it was observed by the early Christians more or less, in their intercourse with the heathen populations among whom they lived. In the midst of the abominable idolatries and impurities of that fearful time, the Rule of the Economy was an imperative duty. But that rule, at least as I have explained and recommended it, in anything that I have written, did not go beyond (1) the concealing the truth when we could do so without deceit, (2) stating it only partially, and (3) representing it under the nearest form possible to a learner or inquirer, when he could not possibly understand it exactly. I conceive that to draw Angels with wings is an instance of the third of these economical modes; and to avoid the question, 'Do Christians believe in a Trinity?' by answering, 'They believe in only one God,' would be an instance of the second. As to the first, it is hardly an Economy, but comes under what is called the 'Disciplina Arcani.'[48] The second and third economical modes Clement calls *lying;* meaning that a partial truth is in some sense a lie, as is also a representative truth. And this, I think, is about the long and the short of the ground of the accusation which has been so violently urged against me, as being a patron of the Economy.

Of late years I have come to think, as I believe most writers do, that Clement meant more than I have said. I used to think he used the word 'lie' as an hyperbole, but I now believe that he, as other early Fathers, thought that, under certain circumstances, it was lawful to tell a lie. This doctrine I never maintained, though I used to think, as I do now, that the theory of the subject is surrounded with considerable difficulty; and it is not strange that I should say so, considering that great English writers declare without hesitation that in certain extreme cases, as to save life, honour, or even property, a lie is allowable. And thus I am brought to the direct question of truth, and of the truthfulness of Catholic priests generally in their dealings with the world, as bearing on the general question of their honesty, and of their internal belief in their religious professions.

It would answer no purpose, and it would be departing from the line of writing which I have been observing all along, if I entered into any formal discussion on this question; what I shall do here, as I have done in the foregoing pages, is to give my own testimony on the matter in question, and there to leave it. Now first I will say, that, when I became a Catholic, nothing struck me more at once than the English out-spoken manner of the Priests. It was the same at Oscott, at Old Hall Green, at Ushaw;[49] there was nothing of that smoothness, or mannerism, which is commonly imputed to them, and they

---

47. *Tracts for the Times* were published from 1833 to 1841 by the members of the Oxford Movement. The two Tracts referred to are 80 and 87 by Isaac Williams.

48. *Arcanum,* Latin, a mystery or secret. The phrase refers to concealing the doctrines of the church in time of persecution.

49. Catholic seminaries.

were more natural and unaffected than many an Anglican clergyman. The many years, which have passed since, have only confirmed my first impression. I have ever found it in the priests of this Diocese; did I wish to point out a straightforward Englishman, I should instance the Bishop, who has, to our great benefit, for so many years presided over it.

And next, I was struck, when I had more opportunity of judging of the Priests, by the simple faith in the Catholic Creed and system, of which they always gave evidence, and which they never seemed to feel, in any sense at all, to be a burden. And now that I have been in the Church nineteen years, I cannot recollect hearing of a single instance in England of an infidel priest. Of course there are men from time to time, who leave the Catholic Church for another religion, but I am speaking of cases, when a man keeps a fair outside to the world and is a hollow hypocrite in his heart.

I wonder that the self-devotion of our priests does not strike a Protestant in this point of view. What do they gain by professing a Creed, in which, if their enemies are to be credited, they really do not believe? What is their reward for committing themselves to a life of self-restraint and toil, and perhaps to a premature and miserable death? The Irish fever cut off between Liverpool and Leeds thirty priests and more, young men in the flower of their days, old men who seemed entitled to some quiet time after their long toil. There was a bishop cut off in the North; but what had a man of his ecclesiastical rank to do with the drudgery and danger of sick calls, except that Christian faith and charity constrained him? Priests volunteered for the dangerous service. It was the same with them on the first coming of the cholera, that mysterious awe-inspiring infliction. If they did not heartily believe in the Creed of the Church, then I will say that the remark of the Apostle had its fullest illustration:—'If in this life only we have hope in Christ, we are of all men most miserable.' What could support a set of hypocrites in the presence of a deadly disorder, one of them following another in long order up the forlorn hope, and one after another perishing? And such, I may say, in its substance, is every Mission-Priest's life. He is ever ready to sacrifice himself for his people. Night and day, sick or well himself, in all weathers, off he is, on the news of a sick call. The fact of a parishioner dying without the Sacraments through his fault is terrible to him; why terrible, if he has not a deep absolute faith, which he acts upon with a free service? Protestants admire this, when they see it; but they do not seem to see as clearly, that it excludes the very notion of hypocrisy.

Sometimes, when they reflect upon it, it leads them to remark on the wonderful discipline of the Catholic priesthood; they say that no Church has so well ordered a clergy, and that in that respect it surpasses their own; they wish they could have such exact discipline among themselves. But is it an excellence which can be purchased? is it a phenomenon which depends on nothing else than itself, or is it an effect which has a cause? You cannot buy devotion at a price. 'It hath never been heard of in the land of Chanaan, neither hath it been seen in Theman. The children of Agar, the merchants of Meran, none of these have known its way." [50] What then is that wonderful charm,

50. Baruch 3:22–23.

which makes a thousand men act all in one way, and infuses a prompt obedience to rule, as if they were under some stern military compulsion? How difficult to find an answer, unless you will allow the obvious one, that they believe intensely what they profess!

[Newman continues his exposition of "reserve and economy" by adducing cognate ideas drawn from the writings of admired English Protestants—Jeremy Taylor, Milton, Paley, Johnson.]

And now, if Protestants wish to know what our real teaching is, as on other subjects, so on that of lying, let them look, not at our books of casuistry, but at our catechisms. Works on pathology do not give the best insight into the form and the harmony of the human frame; and, as it is with the body, so is it with the mind. The Catechism of the Council of Trent was drawn up for the express purpose of providing preachers with subjects for their Sermons; and, as my whole work has been a defence of myself, I may here say that I rarely preach a Sermon, but I go to this beautiful and complete Catechism to get both my matter and my doctrine. There we find the following notices about the duty of Veracity:—

[Newman cites eleven paragraphs from *The Catechism by Decree of the Holy Council of Trent.*]

To one other authority I appeal on this subject, which commands from me attention of a special kind, for it is the teaching of a Father. It will serve to bring my work to a conclusion.

'St. Philip,' says the Roman Oratorian who wrote his Life, 'had a particular dislike of affectation both in himself and others, in speaking, in dressing, or in any thing else.

'He avoided all ceremony which savoured of worldly compliment, and always showed himself a great stickler for Christian simplicity in every thing; so that, when he had to deal with men of worldly prudence, he did not very readily accommodate himself to them.

'And he avoided, as much as possible, having anything to do with *two-faced persons*, who did not go simply and straightforwardly to work in their transactions.

'*As for liars, he could not endure them*, and he was *continually reminding* his spiritual children, *to avoid them as they would a pestilence.*'

These are the principles on which I have acted before I was a Catholic; these are the principles which, I trust, will be my stay and guidance to the end.

I have closed this history of myself with St. Philip's name upon St. Philip's feast-day; and, having done so, to whom can I more suitably offer it, as a memorial of affection and gratitude, than to St. Philip's sons, my dearest brothers of this House, the Priests of the Birmingham Oratory, Ambrose St. John, Henry Austin Mills, Henry Bittleston, Edward Caswall, William Paine Neville, and Henry Ignatius Dudley Ryder? who have been so faithful to me; who have been so sensitive of my needs; who have been so indulgent to my failings; who have carried me through so many trials; who have grudged no sacrifice, if I asked for it; who have been so cheerful under discouragements of my causing; who have done so many good works, and let me have the credit of them;—with whom I have lived so long, with whom I hope to die.

And to you especially, dear Ambrose St. John; [51] whom God gave me, when He took every one else away; who are the link between my old life and my new; who have now for twenty-one years been so devoted to me, so patient, so zealous, so tender; who have let me lean so hard upon you; who have watched me so narrowly; who have never thought of yourself, if I was in question.

And in you I gather up and bear in memory those familiar affectionate companions and counsellors, who in Oxford were given to me, one after another, to be my daily solace and relief; and all those others, of great name and high example, who were my thorough friends, and showed me true attachment in times long past; and also those many younger men, whether I knew them or not, who have never been disloyal to me by word or deed; and of all these, thus various in their relations to me, those more especially who have since joined the Catholic Church.

And I earnestly pray for this whole company, with a hope against hope, that all of us, who once were so united, and so happy in our union, may even now be brought at length, by the Power of the Divine Will, into One Fold and under One Shepherd.

1864   1864, 1865

Liberalism [1]

I have been asked to explain more fully what it is I mean by 'Liberalism,' because merely to call it the Anti-dogmatic Principle is to tell very little about it. . . .

Whenever men are able to act at all, there is the chance of extreme and intemperate action; and therefore, when there is exercise of mind, there is the chance of wayward or mistaken exercise. Liberty of thought is in itself a good; but it gives an opening to false liberty. Now by Liberalism I mean false liberty of thought, or the exercise of thought upon matters, in which, from the constitution of the human mind, thought cannot be brought to any successful issue, and therefore is out of place. Among such matters are first principles of whatever kind; and of these the most sacred and momentous are especially to be reckoned the truths of Revelation. Liberalism then is the mistake of subjecting to human judgment those revealed doctrines which are in their nature beyond and independent of it, and of claiming to determine on intrinsic grounds the truth and value of propositions which rest for their reception simply on the external authority of the Divine Word.

. . .

51. Ambrose St. John (1815–75) had been attached to Newman since 1843. He was a considerable scholar, a student of German biblical criticism. Newman, according to directions left by him, was buried in the same grave with St. John.

1. When Newman published the *Apologia* as a volume in 1865, he added several "Notes," amounting to brief essays, in which he dealt at fuller length with matters touched on in the text. Of these the note on Liberalism is the first. In its entirety, it gives an account of the development of the Liberal tendency in the thought of Newman's Anglican opponents at Oxford. Nothing could better suggest the distance at which Newman stood from the dominant tendency of English life in his time.

I conclude this notice of Liberalism in Oxford, and the party which was antagonistic to it,[2] with some propositions in detail, which, as a member of the latter, and together with the High Church, I earnestly denounced and abjured.

1. No religious tenet is important, unless reason shows it to be so.

> Therefore, e.g. the doctrine of the Athanasian Creed [3] is not to be insisted on, unless it tends to convert the soul; and the doctrine of the Atonement [4] is to be insisted on, if it does convert the soul,

2. No one can believe what he does not understand.

> Therefore, e.g. there are no mysteries in true religion.

3. No theological doctrine is any thing more than an opinion which happens to be held by bodies of men.

> Therefore, e.g. no creed, as such, is necessary for salvation.

4. It is dishonest in a man to make an act of faith in what he has not had brought home to him by actual proof.

> Therefore, e.g. the mass of men ought not absolutely to believe in the divine authority of the Bible.

5. It is immoral in a man to believe more than he can spontaneously receive as being congenial to his moral and mental nature.

> Therefore, e.g. a given individual is not bound to believe in eternal punishment.

6. No revealed doctrines or precepts may reasonably stand in the way of scientific conclusions.

> Therefore, e.g. Political Economy may reverse our Lord's declarations about poverty and riches, or a system of Ethics may teach that the highest condition of body is ordinarily essential to the highest state of mind.

7. Christianity is necessarily modified by the growth of civilization, and the exigencies of times.

> Therefore, e.g. the Catholic priesthood, though necessary in the Middle Ages, may be superseded now.

8. There is a system of religion more simply true than Christianity as it has ever been received.

2. Newman's own party, that of the Tractarians.
3. The Anglican coolness to the Athanasian Creed is a response to its statement that the doctrines it affirms—among them that of the Trinity—must be believed at the risk of damnation.
4. That is, "at-one-ment"—man's reconciliation with God through the sacrificial death of Christ.

Therefore, e.g. we may advance that Christianity is the 'corn of wheat' which has been dead for 1800 years, but at length will bear fruit; and that Mahometanism is the manly religion, and existing Christianity the womanish.

9. There is a right of Private Judgment: that is, there is no existing authority on earth competent to interfere with the liberty of individuals in reasoning and judging for themselves about the Bible and its contents, as they severally please.

Therefore, e.g. religious establishments requiring subscriptions are Anti-christian.

10. There are rights of conscience such, that every one may lawfully advance a claim to profess and teach what is false and wrong in matters, religious, social, and moral, provided that to his private conscience it seems absolutely true and right.

Therefore, e.g. individuals have a right to preach and practise fornication and polygamy.

11. There is no such thing as a national or state conscience.

Therefore, e.g. no judgments can fall upon a sinful or infidel nation.

12. The civil power has no positive duty, in a normal state of things, to maintain religious truth.

Therefore, e.g. blasphemy and sabbath-breaking are not rightly punishable by law.

13. Utility and expedience are the measure of political duty.

Therefore, e.g. no punishment may be enacted, on the ground that God commands it: e.g. on the text, 'Whoso sheddeth man's blood, by man shall his blood be shed.' [5]

14. The Civil Power may dispose of Church property without sacrilege.

Therefore, e.g. Henry VIII committed no sin in his spoliations.[6]

15. The Civil Power has the right of ecclesiastical jurisdiction and administration.

Therefore, e.g. Parliament may impose articles of faith on the Church or suppress Dioceses.[7]

16. It is lawful to rise in arms against legitimate princes.

Therefore, e.g. the Puritans in the 17th century, and the French in the 18th, were justifiable in their Rebellion and Revolution respectively.

5. Genesis 9:6.
6. In abolishing the monasteries.
7. In 1833, Parliament, on Liberal principles, disestablished 10 bishoprics of the Anglican Church in Ireland. This act outraged the proponents of the autonomy of the church and led to their organizing an intellectual opposition to the Liberal conception of the church which came to be known as the Oxford Movement.

17. The people are the legitimate source of power.

Therefore, e.g. Universal Suffrage is among the natural rights of man.

18. Virtue is the child of knowledge, and vice of ignorance.

Therefore, e.g. education, periodical literature, railroad travelling, ventilation, drainage, and the arts of life, when fully carried out, serve to make a population moral and happy.

All of these propositions, and many others too, were familiar to me thirty years ago, as in the number of the tenets of Liberalism, and, while I gave into none of them except No. 12, and perhaps No. 11, and partly No. 1, before I began to publish, so afterwards I wrote against most of them in some part or other of my Anglican works. . . .

I need hardly say that the above Note is mainly historical. How far the Liberal party of 1830–40 really held the above eighteen Theses, which I attributed to them, and how far and in what sense I should oppose those Theses now, could scarcely be explained without a separate Dissertation.

1864   1864, 1865

JOHN RUSKIN
1819–1900

In 1909 the Italian poet Emilio Marinetti issued his famous *Futurist Manifesto*. This flamboyant document, which totally repudiated the past and peremptorily demanded that art dedicate itself to an authentically modern sensibility based on recognition of the beauty and vitality of the machine, is generally regarded as the charter of Aesthetic Modernism, even of those movements of art upon which the Futurist principles had no direct influence. Some three years after the publication of the *Manifesto*, Marinetti gave a lecture in London on the Futurist program and in the course of it put a question to his audience which, he made plain, was crucial to any hope they might have of aesthetic salvation: "When, then," he asked in impatient disdain, "When, then, will you disencumber yourselves of the lymphatic ideology of your deplorable Ruskin?"

The question was shocking in its impiousness and it was doubtless heard with an appalled relief. By 1912 the educated English public was fatigued with Ruskin—he had said so much and had said it for so long, ever since 1843. By the pertinacity, passion, and brilliance of his teaching he had shaped the minds of three intellectual generations in their relation to art. No one had ever made art so momentous; in every sentence he wrote about it was the urgently communicated belief that created objects had a decisive bearing upon the moral and spiritual life and that one's preferences in pictures or buildings, or even household utensils, were indicative of one's relation to oneself, one's fellow men, and the universe. The theorists and practitioners of the new movements certainly held art to be no less momentous than Ruskin said it was, but, however diverse their aesthetic principles might be, they were at one in saying that such moral considerations as Ruskin adduced were irrelevant to the aesthetic experience, and, indeed, qualified art's chief claim to momentousness, its autonomy. Marinetti's English audience may not have been ready to accept the full challenge of the new art, but they had been prepared by their fellow countrymen Walter Pater and Oscar Wilde to acknowledge a growing impatience with Ruskin's overtly moralizing tone and with his insistence upon the necessity of maintaining a sensibility which was consonant with religious faith even while admitting that religion as a system of belief was not tenable. It was just this sensibility that they found burdensome and in the assault that Marinetti made upon "their" Ruskin, which went to extremes of irreverence in its explanation of just why he was "deplorable," they heard the promise of liberation from it.

Given the extent and authority of Ruskin's influence, the revolt against it was inevitable. But with the passing decades it becomes ever more apparent by how much Ruskin transcends the conception of his work which made it a piously received doctrine in the Victorian Age and a burden in the early twentieth century. An evangelical anxiety over the moral and spiritual effect of art is indeed an essential part of Ruskin's thought, to be dealt with by each cultural generation after its own fashion. (One might venture the guess that at the present time it will enlist rather more sympathy than it did a quarter-century ago.) There is this much reason to deplore it, that for some readers—both those too easily reassured and those too easily distressed by moral discourse—it has the effect of obscuring those aspects of Ruskin's criticism that are not specifically moral, for example, his investigations into the formal or purely aesthetic elements of art which, so far from being in opposition to such ideas of modern theory as are vital and liberating, actually formulated them before they were given polemical expression in the articles of modernist faith. It is hard to point to any other body of criticism which is equal to Ruskin's in the range of its interests, in the multitudinousness and precision of its perceptions, in the cogency of the questions it raises, in the courage with which it tests and contradicts its own conclusions.

But if one can, so to speak, provisionally deplore Ruskin's moral impulse as it operates in his art criticism, one recognizes it as definitive of the imagination which informs his great work in social criticism. Taking together what he achieved in the two genres, one may well recognize in Ruskin the pre-eminent intellectual genius of Victorian England.

He was born in London in 1819, the only child of a middle-aged Scottish couple of strict evangelical principles and increasing affluence; his father was a wine merchant, specializing in sherry. The boy's natural precocity was emphasized and developed by the rigorously supervised solitude in which he was reared. He was a destined child, intended for the evangelical clergy, eventually for a bishopric. He was instructed early in reading, in music, in drawing. He was required to learn by heart long chapters of the Bible as well as to read it through aloud from beginning to end about once every year. His father, despite the strictness of his religious views, had a quite considerable feeling for artistic culture; he collected pictures and it was his custom to read aloud every evening from Walter Scott's novels. When John was four, his father began the practice of taking his wife and son with him on the annual tours he made to visit the great country houses whose cellars he supplied; Ruskin was thus early given his first experiences of architecture and landscape, as well as of the collections of paintings which many of the great houses could boast. When he was fourteen he was given a copy of the illustrated edition of Samuel Rogers's *Italy*. The poem itself had but little significance for him; the illustrations of J. M. W. Turner were decisive in his life. For one thing, his pleasure in the pictures, shared by his father, was so great that, at his mother's suggestion, it was resolved that the family should go to see for themselves the scenes depicted; thus began the long series of Continental tours—made in considerable style, in a traveling carriage and with servants in attendance—that Ruskin went on with his parents; it was thus that he acquired his extensive knowledge of the works of art of many cities. An equally important effect of the gift was that it inaugurated the passionate devotion to the work of Turner which was to be at the center of Ruskin's intellectual life for many years.

After a desultory but adequate schooling, largely under private tuition, Ruskin entered Christ Church, Oxford, in 1837. His experience of Oxford was pleasant but cool and remote—doubtless in part because his mother, anxious over his health, had taken up residence in the town and because Ruskin spent every evening with her—and it was interrupted by frequent tours with his parents and once by what seemed the serious threat of tuberculosis. He won the Newdigate Poetry Prize in 1839 but the degree he took in 1841 was undistinguished.

In his engaging autobiography, *Praeterita* (Foreshadowings), Ruskin comments wryly on the snobbery that had led his father to choose for him the most socially elite college of the university. "His ideal for my future," Ruskin says, ". . . was that I should enter at college into the best society, take all the prizes every year, and a double first to finish with; marry Lady Clara Vere de Vere; write poetry as good as Byron's, only pious; preach sermons as good as Bossuet's, only Protestant; be made at forty Bishop of Winchester, and at fifty Primate of England." These expectations the son proceeded to disappoint, but it must be said for the elder Ruskin that, although he long grieved over the unachieved bishopric, he took a measure of satisfaction in the enterprise to which his son then addressed himself and may even be said to have advanced it. Ruskin undertook to write a book in which Turner would be defended and canonized; his father had his own degree of admiration for the painter and was a cautious collector of his minor work. In 1843, when Ruskin published *Modern Painters* (by "A Graduate of Oxford"), Turner was seventy and had long been famous and honored. But Turner's bold later style distressed conventional taste and in response to an attack upon him Ruskin proposed to lay down the principles by which Turner was properly to be judged. The full title of the work will suggest its ambitious range and its uncompromising didacticism: *Modern Painters: Their Superiority in the Art of Landscape Painting to All the Ancient Masters Proved by Examples of the True, the Beautiful, and the Intellectual from the Works of Modern Artists, Especially from Those of J. M. W. Turner, Esq., R.A.* The book was not warmly received by painters, not even by Turner, a transcendent genius but a curmudgeonly man. The public, however, was delighted by the lucidity and eloquence of the prose in which its vigorous judgments were expressed.

In 1845, when he was twenty-six, Ruskin made his first tour alone, which is to say with his valet and a courier but without his parents. It was on this journey, undertaken to forward Volume II of *Modern Painters* (1846), that he became aware of the insufficiency of his knowledge of Italian painting and undertook to revise for a second edition of Volume I (1846) the judgments he had passed upon it. In 1848 he married a distant cousin, Euphemia Gray. The marriage was in every way disastrous. It had been arranged by the parents of the bride and groom; it was never consummated, and in 1854 it was annulled when Effie fell in love with Ruskin's friend, the Pre-Raphaelite painter John Everett Millais.

Suspending work on *Modern Painters*, Ruskin began the study of the cathedrals of Normandy and in 1849 brought out *The Seven Lamps of Architecture*, of which Kenneth Clark has said that, in the history of taste, it is perhaps the most influential book ever published. The work is equally charged with exquisite aesthetic sensibility and stern moral prescription; its peculiar achievement is that it succeeds in bringing its two energies into accord with each other. The thesis of the work is that greatness in art is dependent upon and is the index of the cognate quality in the life of the community that produces it; this quality in its ideality is defined by the "lamps" of Sacrifice, Truth, Power, Beauty, Life, Memory, and Obedience.

The Stones of Venice (1851, 1853) further developed and refined Ruskin's characteristic interpretation of particular works of art in terms of the moral assumptions, social forms, and technology out of which they had come. One chapter of this work, "The Nature of Gothic" (see below) had from the first an exceptional appeal and an incalculable influence on both the aesthetic and social thought of the age.

After 1854, art criticism began to take a second place in Ruskin's painfully intense intellectual life. Questions of social justice pressed ever more urgently upon him and in 1860 his distressed concern led him to make an assault upon the economic basis of English society through an attempt to discredit the method and assumptions of political economy. In four essays published in the *Cornhill Magazine*, collected as *Unto This Last* (see below), Ruskin undertook to controvert the virtually universal belief that the economic arrangements of a nation come into being in the course of nature, that they are to be viewed with the detached objectivity which science brings to bear upon the physical processes of nature, and that no more than the physical processes of nature are they susceptible to moral judgment or interference. He cogently argued the inefficiency as well as the inhumanity of the system which was taken for granted by the political economists, of whom John Stuart Mill was at the time the most authoritative, and proposed a substitute derived from the ethics of three traditional institutions, the household, the learned professions (medicine and law), and the army, none of which sanctioned unchecked competition and the exclusive motive of economic self-interest. Such was the outcry against this view, which is now given ready assent and even a degree of implementation, that Thackeray, who edited the *Cornhill*, was obliged to discontinue the series. The same response was given to the essays of 1862–63 in *Fraser's Magazine* later collected as *Munera Pulveris* (Money of the Dust).

Ruskin's father died in 1864; his mother lived until 1870 and supervised much of her son's life until her death. In 1863 Ruskin showed the initial signs of mental illness and these appeared with increasing intensity during the thirty-five years of life still before him. They were exacerbated over the course of the next few years by his unhappy love for a young girl whom he wished to marry, by the deaths of dear friends, and by acute distress over the realization that his Christian faith had left him. His work from that time on is likely to be touched by eccentricity, but for the most part it shows but little falling off in essential cogency; the beautiful *Praeterita*, composed between 1885 and 1889, is the last work of his genius. His illness was of an intermittent kind and in his periods of health he worked with his characteristic energy. Such was the regard in which he eventually came to be held after the opprobrium that met his economic writings had abated that, although for reasons of health he had resigned the Slade Professorship of Art at Oxford to which he had been elected in 1869, he was called to the chair again in 1883. By the time of his death the considerable fortune left him by his father had been dispersed in his philanthropic enterprises; he founded the Guild of St. George to encourage the return to agricultural life, began several enlightened industrial enterprises, and undertook to instruct the young gentlemen of Oxford in the dignity of labor by supervising their construction of a road—one of the young gentlemen was Oscar Wilde.

Ruskin died in 1900 at Brantwood, his home on Lake Coniston in the Lake District. It may well be that the person for whom his death had most meaning was a young Frenchman to be known to fame as Marcel Proust. Proust had first heard about Ruskin in his student days and when he was in his mid-twenties he developed a passion for this English author whose language he could read only with difficulty. He was to translate into French two of Ruskin's books, *The Bible of Amiens* and *Sesame and Lilies* (1904, 1906), and through Ruskin he was to find, as his biographer G. D. Painter puts it, his salvation—after a period of desiccated feeling, his reading of Ruskin had reaffirmed for him the value of life and shown him his mission as an artist. On the news of Ruskin's death he said to a friend, "My grief is healthy and full of consolations, for I realize what a trivial thing death is, when I see how intensely this dead man lives, and how I admire and listen to his words, and seek to understand and obey him. . . ." And at the end of his essay on Ruskin (1900) he used of his master the words that Ruskin had used of Turner: "It is through these eyes, now closed for ever in the grave, that unborn generations will look upon nature."

From Modern Painters

Of the Real Nature of Greatness of Style [1]

I doubt not that the reader was ill-satisfied with the conclusion arrived at in the last chapter.[2] That 'great art' is art which represents what is beautiful and good, may not seem a very profound discovery; and the main question may be thought to have been all the time lost sight of, namely, 'What is beautiful, and what is good?' No; those are not the main, at least not the first questions; on the contrary, our subject becomes at once opened and simplified as soon as we have left those the *only* questions. For observe, our present task, accord-

1. This selection is Chap. 3 of Vol. II, Part IV.
2. The chapter is entitled "Of Realization." It follows the chapter "Of the Received Opinions Touching the 'Grand Style,'" in which Ruskin undertakes to refute the canons of taste formulated by the famous painter Sir Joshua Reynolds in the presidential discourses which he delivered at the Royal Academy of Art between 1769 and 1790. (They had aroused the scorn which William Blake expresses in the marginal comments to the collected *Discourses*.) The conclusion arrived at in "Of Realization" is that "true criticism of art never can consist in the mere application of rules; it can be just only when it is founded on quick sympathy with the innumerable instincts and changeful efforts of human nature, chastened and guided by unchanging love of all things that God has created to be beautiful and pronounced good."

ing to our old plan, is merely to investigate the relative degrees of the *beautiful* in the art of different masters; and it is an encouragement to be convinced, first of all, that what is lovely will also be great, and what is pleasing, noble. Nor is the conclusion so much a matter of course as it at first appears, for, surprising as the statement may seem, all the confusion into which Reynolds has plunged both himself and his readers, in the essay we have been examining, results primarily from a doubt in his own mind *as to the existence of beauty at all.* In the next paper I alluded to, No. 82 (which needs not, however, to be examined at so great length), he calmly attributes the whole influence of beauty to custom, saying, that 'he has no doubt, if we were more used to deformity than to beauty, deformity would then lose the idea now annexed to it, and take that of beauty; as if the whole world should agree that Yes and No should change their meanings; Yes would then deny, and No would affirm!'

The world does, indeed, succeed—oftener than is, perhaps, altogether well for the world—in making Yes mean No, and No mean Yes. But the world has never succeeded, nor ever will, in making itself delight in black clouds more than in blue sky, or love the dark earth better than the rose that grows from it. Happily for mankind, beauty and ugliness are as positive in their nature as physical pain and pleasure, as light and darkness, or as life and death; and though they may be denied or misunderstood in many fantastic ways, the most subtle reasoner will at last find that colour and sweetness are still attractive to him, and that no logic will enable him to think the rainbow sombre, or the violet scentless. But the theory that beauty was merely a result of custom was very common in Johnson's time. Goldsmith has, I think, expressed it with more force and wit than any other writer, in various passages of the *Citizen of the World.*[3] And it was, indeed, a curious retribution of the folly of the world of art, which for some three centuries had given itself recklessly to the pursuit of beauty, that at last it should be led to deny the very existence of what it had so morbidly and passionately sought. It was as if a child should leave its home to pursue the rainbow, and then, breathless and hopeless, declare that it did not exist. Nor is the lesson less useful which may be gained in observing the adoption of such a theory by Reynolds himself. It shows how completely an artist may be unconscious of the principles of his own work, and how he may be led by instinct to *do* all that is right, while he is misled by false logic to *say* all that is wrong. For nearly every word that Reynolds wrote was contrary to his own practice; he seems to have been born to teach all error by his precept, and all excellence by his example; he enforced with his lips generalization and idealism, while with his pencil he was tracing the patterns of the dresses of the belles of his day; [4] he exhorted his pupils to attend only to the invariable,

---

3. Oliver Goldsmith (1730–74) published a series of *Chinese Letters* in a London periodical in the course of 1760 which were collected as *The Citizen of the World* in 1762. They purport to be written by a philosophical Chinese living in London. In one of his letters he says that the women of England are unendurably ugly judged by the standards of China—they have feet ten inches long "and teeth of a most odious whiteness."

4. The chief theme of Reynolds's lectures was the "grand style" as it was to be achieved in what was said to be the highest genre of art, historical painting. Reynolds's own great achievement was not in this genre but in his entrancing portraits, chiefly of women.

while he himself was occupied in distinguishing every variation of womanly temper; and he denied the existence of the beautiful, at the same instant that he arrested it as it passed, and perpetuated it for ever.

But we must not quit the subject here. However inconsistently or dimly expressed, there is, indeed, some truth in that commonly accepted distinction between high and low art. That a thing should be beautiful is not enough; there is, as we said in the outset, a higher and lower range of beauty, and some ground for separating into various and unequal ranks painters who have, nevertheless, each in his several way, represented something that was beautiful or good.

Nor, if we would, can we get rid of this conviction. We have at all times some instinctive sense that the function of one painter is greater than that of another, even supposing each equally successful in his own way; and we feel that, if it were possible to conquer prejudice, and do away with the iniquities of personal feeling, and the insufficiencies of limited knowledge, we should all agree in this estimate, and be able to place each painter in his right rank, measuring them by a true scale of nobleness. We feel that the men in the higher classes of the scale would be, in the full sense of the word, Great,—men whom one would give much to see the faces of but for an instant; and that those in the lower classes of the scale (though none were admitted but who had true merit of some kind) would be very small men, not greatly exciting either reverence or curiosity. And with this fixed instinct in our minds, we permit our teachers daily to exhort their pupils to the cultivation of 'great art,'—neither they nor we having any very clear notion as to what the greatness consists in: but sometimes inclining to think it must depend on the space of the canvas, and that art on a scale of six feet by ten is something spiritually separated from that on a scale of three feet by five;—sometimes holding it to consist in painting the nude body, rather than the body decently clothed;—sometimes being convinced that it is connected with the study of past history, and that the art is only great which represents what the painter never saw, and about which he knows nothing;—and sometimes being firmly persuaded that it consists in generally finding fault with, and endeavouring to mend, whatsoever the Divine wisdom has made. All which various errors, having yet some notes and atoms of truth in the make of each of them, deserve some attentive analysis, for they come under that general law,—that 'the corruption of the best is the worst.' [5] There are not *worse* errors going than these four; and yet the truth they contain, and the instinct which urges many to preach them, are at the root of all healthy growth in art. We ruin one young painter after another by telling him to follow great art, without knowing ourselves what greatness is; and yet the feeling that it verily *is* something, and that there are depths and breadths, shallows and narrows, in the matter, is all that we have to look to, if we would ever make our art serviceable to ourselves or others. To follow art for the sake of being a great man, and therefore to cast about continually for some means of achieving position or attracting admiration, is the surest way of ending in total extinction. And yet it is only by honest reverence for art itself, and by great self-respect in the practice of it, that it can be rescued from dilettantism,

5. An English proverb, derived from the Latin "*Corruptio optimi pessima*."

raised to approved honourableness, and brought to the proper work it has to accomplish in the service of man.

Let us therefore look into the facts of the thing, not with any metaphysical, or otherwise vain and troublesome effort at acuteness, but in a plain way; for the facts themselves are plain enough, and may be plainly stated, only the difficulty is, that out of these facts, right and left, the different forms of mis-apprehension branch into grievous complexity, and branch so far and wide, that if once we try to follow them, they will lead us quite from our mark into other separate, though not less interesting discussions. The best way will be, therefore, I think, to sketch out at once in this chapter, the different characters which really constitute 'greatness' of style, and to indicate the principal directions of the outbranching misapprehensions of them; then, in the succeeding chapters, to take up in succession those which need more talk about them, and follow out at leisure whatever inquiries they may suggest.

I. *Choice of Noble Subject.*—Greatness of style consists, then: first, in the habitual choice of subjects of thought which involve wide interests and pro-found passions, as opposed to those which involve narrow interests and slight passions. The style is greater or less in exact proportion to the nobleness of the interests and passions involved in the subject. The habitual choice of sacred subjects, such as the Nativity, Transfiguration, Crucifixion (if the choice be sincere), implies that the painter has a natural disposition to dwell on the highest thoughts of which humanity is capable; it constitutes him so far forth a painter of the highest order, as, for instance, Leonardo, in his painting of the Last Supper: he who delights in representing the acts or meditations of great men, as, for instance, Raphael painting the School of Athens,[6] is, so far forth, a painter of the second order: he who represents the passions and events of ordinary life, of the third. And in this ordinary life, he who represents deep thoughts and sorrows, as, for instance, Hunt, in his Claudio and Isabella,[7] and such other works, is of the highest rank in his sphere; and he who represents the slight malignities and passions of the drawing-room, as, for instance, Leslie,[8] of the second rank; he who represents the sports of boys, or simplicities of clowns, as Webster or Teniers,[9] of the third rank; and he who represents brutalities and vices (for delight in them, and not for rebuke of them), of no rank at all, or rather of a negative rank, holding a certain order in the abyss.

The reader will, I hope, understand how much importance is to be attached

6. Raffaello Santi (1483–1520), the Italian painter who stands with Michelangelo and Leonardo as pre-eminent in his age. His most popular paintings are his Madonnas, but he also worked on a grander scale in his historical paintings. The *School of Athens* is one of four frescoes in the Vatican.

7. William Holman Hunt (1827–1910) was, with John Everett Millais and Dante Gabriel Rossetti, one of the initiators of the Pre-Raphaelite Movement (see note 14). The painting Ruskin refers to represents the scene in Shakespeare's *Measure for Measure* in which the chaste Isabella is urged by her brother Claudio to accept the bargain Angelo has offered her, that she give herself to him in exchange for his sparing Claudio's life.

8. Charles Robert Leslie (1794–1859), English painter, American by birth, very popular in his day. His pictures usually represent scenes, mostly humorous, from famous novels and plays.

9. Thomas Webster (1800–1886) specialized in scenes of school life. David Teniers, the younger (1610–90), the Flemish painter known for his realistic portrayal of daily life, including low life.

to the sentence in the first parenthesis, 'if the choice be sincere'; for choice of subject is, of course, only available as a criterion of the rank of the painter, when it is made from the heart. Indeed, in the lower orders of painting, the choice is always made from such a heart as the painter has; for his selection of the brawls of peasants or sports of children can, of course, proceed only from the fact that he has more sympathy with such brawls or pastimes than with nobler subjects. But the choice of the higher kind of subjects is often insincere; and may, therefore, afford no real criterion of the painter's rank. The greater number of men who have lately painted religious or heroic subjects have done so in mere ambition, because they had been taught that it was a good thing to be a 'high art' painter; and the fact is that in nine cases out of ten, the so-called historical or 'high art' painter is a person infinitely inferior to the painter of flowers or still life. He is, in modern times, nearly always a man who has great vanity without pictorial capacity, and differs from the landscape or fruit painter merely in misunderstanding and over-estimating his own powers. He mistakes his vanity for inspiration, his ambition for greatness of soul, and takes pleasure in what he calls 'the ideal,' merely because he has neither humility nor capacity enough to comprehend the real.

But also observe, it is not enough even that the choice be sincere. It must also be wise. It happens very often that a man of weak intellect, sincerely desiring to do what is good and useful, will devote himself to high art subjects because he thinks them the only ones on which time and toil can be usefully spent, or, sometimes, because they are really the only ones he has pleasure in contemplating. But not having intellect enough to enter into the minds of truly great men, or to imagine great events as they really happened, he cannot become a great painter; he degrades the subjects he intended to honour, and his work is more utterly thrown away, and his rank as an artist in reality lower, than if he had devoted himself to the imitation of the simplest objects of natural history. The works of Overbeck [10] are a most notable instance of this form of error.

It must also be remembered, that in nearly all the great periods of art the choice of subject has not been left to the painter. His employer,—abbot, baron, or monarch,—determined for him whether he should earn his bread by making cloisters bright with choirs of saints, painting coats of arms on leaves of romances, or decorating presence chambers with complimentary mythology; and his own personal feelings are ascertainable only by watching, in the themes assigned to him, what are the points in which he seems to take most pleasure. Thus, in the prolonged ranges of varied subjects with which Benozzo Gozzoli [11] decorated the cloisters of Pisa, it is easy to see that love of simple domestic incident, sweet landscape, and glittering ornament, prevails slightly over the solemn elements of religious feeling, which, nevertheless, the spirit of the age

10. Johann Friedrich Overbeck (1789–1869), the painter who undertook to revive Christian art in his native Germany. He turned for his inspiration to Raphael and established a small brotherhood of like-minded artists, the so-called "Nazarenes," dedicated to an ascetic, pious, and laborious life of producing "noble" paintings of sacred subjects. They were precursors of the English Pre-Raphaelites (see note 14). Overbeck's own work is not greatly esteemed by reason of its dryness and pedantry.

11. Italian painter (1420–97).

instilled into him in such measure as to form a very lovely and noble mind, though still one of the second order. In the work of Orcagna,[12] an intense solemnity and energy in the sublimest groups of his figures, fading away as he touches inferior subjects, indicates that his home was among the archangels, and his rank among the first of the sons of men; while Correggio,[13] in the side-long grace, artificial smiles, and purple languors of his saints, indicates the inferior instinct which would have guided his choice in quite other directions, had it not been for the fashion of the age, and the need of the day.

It will follow, of course, from the above considerations, that the choice which characterizes the school of high art is seen as much in the treatment of a subject as in its selection, and that the expression of the thoughts of the persons repre-sented will always be the first thing considered by the painter who worthily enters that highest school. For the artist who sincerely chooses the noblest sub-ject will also choose chiefly to represent what makes that subject noble, namely, the various heroism or other noble emotions of the persons represented. If, instead of this, the artist seeks only to make his picture agreeable by the composition of its masses and colours, or by any other merely pictorial merit, as fine drawing of limbs, it is evident, not only that any other subject would have answered his purpose as well, but that he is unfit to approach the subject he has chosen, because he cannot enter into its deepest meaning, and therefore cannot in reality have chosen it for that meaning. Nevertheless, while the expression is always to be the first thing considered, all other merits must be added to the utmost of the painter's power; for until he can both colour and draw beautifully he has no business to consider himself a painter at all, far less to attempt the noblest subjects of painting; and, when he has once possessed himself of these powers, he will naturally and fitly employ them to deepen and perfect the impression made by the sentiment of his subject.

The perfect unison of expression, as the painter's main purpose, with the full and natural exertion of his pictorial power in the details of the work, is found only in the old Pre-Raphaelite periods, and in the modern Pre-Raphaelite school.[14] In the works of Giotto,[15] Angelico.[16] Orcagna, John

12. Andrea di Cione, Italian painter, sculptor, worker in mosaic, architect (c. 1308–c. 1368).

13. Antonio Allegri da Correggio, Italian painter (1494–1534), famous for the brilliance and gusto of his execution and for the uniqueness of his style and vision. Ruskin's adverse opinion of his work does not generally prevail.

14. The Pre-Raphaelite Movement in England was but a single instance, though the most famous one, of a desire on the part of European painters to escape from what they had come to think of as the commonplace of virtuosity, of the highly developed techniques of representation that descended from the High Renaissance (see note 10). The members of the Pre-Raphaelite Brotherhood—the P.R.B., as it was called—sought for a directness and simplicity of representation which, as they thought, put them in the line of the painters before Raphael, before, that is, the achievements of Renaissance knowledge and technique made the elemental piety of a painting of less account than its powers of complex repre-sentation. Much of the early Pre-Raphaelite work undertook to be hard and dry, but with the passage of time it began to show a degree of sumptuousness; this is especially true of Rossetti, Millais, and Burne-Jones.

15. Giotto (c. 1266–1337), a Florentine, is the most admired painter of the period before the Renaissance. He was also an architect of great attainments.

16. Fra Angelico (1387–1455), Italian painter, a friar of the Dominican order. He is

Bellini,[17] and one or two more, these two conditions of high art are entirely fulfilled, so far as the knowledge of those days enabled them to be fulfilled; and in the modern Pre-Raphaelite school they are fulfilled nearly to the uttermost. Hunt's *Light of the World,*[18] is, I believe, the most perfect instance of expressional purpose with technical power, which the world has yet produced.

Now in the Post-Raphaelite period of ancient art, and in the spurious high art of modern times, two broad forms of error divide the schools; the one consisting in (A) the superseding of expression by technical excellence, and the other in (B) the superseding of technical excellence by expression.

A. Superseding expression by technical excellence.—This takes place most frankly, and therefore most innocently, in the work of the Venetians. They very nearly ignore expression altogether, directing their aim exclusively to the rendering of external truths of colour and form. Paul Veronese [19] will make the Magdalene wash the feet of Christ with a countenance as absolutely unmoved as that of any ordinary servant bringing a ewer to her master, and will introduce the supper at Emmaus [20] as a background to the portraits of two children playing with a dog. Of the wrongness or rightness of such a proceeding we shall reason in another place; at present we have to note it merely as displacing the Venetian work from the highest or expressional rank of art. But the error is generally made in a more subtle and dangerous way. The artist deceives himself into the idea that he is doing all he can to elevate his subject by treating it under rules of art, introducing into it accurate science, and collecting for it the beauties of (so-called) ideal form; whereas he may, in reality, be all the while sacrificing his subject to his own vanity or pleasure, and losing truth, nobleness, and impressiveness for the sake of delightful lines or creditable pedantries.

B. Superseding technical excellence by expression.—This is usually done under the influence of another kind of vanity. The artist desires that men should think he has an elevated soul, affects to despise the ordinary excellence of art, contemplates with separated egotism the course of his own imaginations or sensations, and refuses to look at the real facts round about him, in order that he may adore at leisure the shadow of himself. He lives in an element of what he calls tender emotions and lofty aspirations; which are, in fact,

celebrated for the lyric grace and delicacy of his work. He was admired by the Pre-Raphaelites because he did not respond to the scientific naturalism which was influential in his day.

17. Giovanni Bellini (c. 1430–1516), Venetian painter, the son of Iacopo Bellini and brother of Gentile Bellini. To his two great pupils, Giorgione and Titian, he passed on his concern with light and color which was to be characteristic of the Venetian school of painting in contrast to the Florentine emphasis upon form.

18. In 1854 Hunt, who was a man of intense religious feeling, painted this picture, which is an allegorical representation of Christ knocking on the door of the human soul. Ruskin's admiration of it was shared by many and it may well have been, through reproductions, the best known picture in England in the later 19th century. It is now a byword for sentimentality and dull execution.

19. Paolo Veronese (1528–88), Venetian painter. His indifference to the religious content of his ostensibly religious paintings once got him into trouble with the Inquisition, which charged that he had left the Magdalene out of a Scriptural scene to which her presence was essential and had introduced dogs, buffoons, dwarfs, and German soldiers.

20. Luke 24:13.

nothing more than very ordinary weaknesses or instincts, contemplated through a mist of pride. A large range of modern German art comes under this head.

A more interesting and respectable form of this error is fallen into by some truly earnest men, who, finding their powers not adequate to the attainment of great artistical excellence, but adequate to rendering, up to a certain point, the expression of the human countenance, devote themselves to that object alone, abandoning effort in other directions, and executing the accessories of their pictures feebly or carelessly. With these are associated another group of philosophical painters, who suppose the artistical merits of other parts *adverse* to the expression, as drawing the spectator's attention away from it, and who paint in grey colour, and imperfect light and shade, by way of enforcing the purity of their conceptions. Both these classes of conscientious but narrow-minded artists labour under the same grievous mistake of imagining that wilful fallacy can ever be either pardonable or helpful. They forget that colour, if used at all, must be either true or false, and that what *they* call chastity, dignity, and reserve is, to the eye of any person accustomed to nature, pure, bold, and impertinent falsehood. It does not in the eyes of any soundly minded man, exalt the expression of a female face that the cheeks should be painted of the colour of clay, nor does it in the least enhance his reverence for a saint to find the scenery around him deprived, by his presence, of sunshine. It is an important consolation, however, to reflect that no artist ever fell into any of these last three errors (under head B) who had really the capacity of becoming a great painter. No man ever despised colour who could produce it; and the error of these sentimentalists and philosophers is not so much in the choice of their manner of painting, as in supposing themselves capable of painting at all. Some of them might have made efficient sculptors, but the greater number had their mission in some other sphere than that of art, and would have found, in works of practical charity, better employment for their gentleness and sentimentalism, than in denying to human beauty its colour, and to natural scenery its light; in depriving heaven of its blue, and earth of its bloom, valour of its glow, and modesty of its blush.

II. *Love of Beauty.*—The second characteristic of the great school of art is, that it introduces in the conception of its subject as much beauty as is possible, consistently with truth.[21]

---

21. "As here, for the first time, I am obliged to use the terms Truth and Beauty in a kind of opposition, I must therefore stop for a moment to state clearly the relation of these two qualities of art; and to protest against the vulgar and foolish habit of confusing truth and beauty with each other. People with shallow powers of thought, desiring to flatter themselves with the sensation of having attained profundity, are continually doing the most serious mischief by introducing confusion into plain matters, and then valuing themselves on being confounded. Nothing is more common than to hear people who desire to be thought philosophical, declare that 'beauty is truth,' and 'truth is beauty.' I would most earnestly beg every sensible person who hears such an assertion made, to nip the germinating philosopher in his ambiguous bud; and beg him, if he really believes his own assertion, never henceforward to use two words for the same thing. The fact is, truth and beauty are entirely distinct, though often related, things. One is a property of statements, the other of objects. The statement that two and two make four is true, but it is neither beautiful nor ugly, for it is invisible; a rose is lovely, but it is neither true nor false, for it is silent. That which shows nothing cannot be fair, and that which asserts nothing cannot be false. Even

For instance, in any subject consisting of a number of figures, it will make as many of those figures beautiful as the faithful representation of humanity will admit. It will not deny the facts of ugliness or decrepitude, or relative inferiority and superiority of feature as necessarily manifested in a crowd, but it will, so far as it is in its power, seek for and dwell upon the fairest forms, and in all things insist on the beauty that is in them, not on the ugliness. In this respect, schools of art become higher in exact proportion to the degree in which they apprehend and love the beautiful. Thus, Angelico, intensely loving all spiritual beauty, will be of the highest rank; and Paul Veronese and Correggio, intensely loving physical and corporeal beauty, of the second rank; and Albert Dürer,[22] Rubens,[23] and in general the Northern artists, apparently insensible to beauty, and caring only for truth, whether shapely or not, of the third rank;[24] and Teniers and Salvator, Caravaggio,[25] and other such wor-

---

the ordinary use of the words false and true, as applied to artificial and real things, is inaccurate. An artificial rose is not a 'false' rose, it is not a rose at all. The falseness is in the person who states, or induces the belief, that it *is* a rose.

"Now, therefore, in things concerning art, the words true and false are only to be rightly used while the picture is considered as a statement of facts. The painter asserts that this which he has painted is the form of a dog, a man, or a tree. If it be *not* the form of a dog, a man, or a tree, the painter's statement is false; and, therefore, we justly speak of a false line, or false colour; not that any lines or colours can in themselves be false, but they become so when they convey a statement that they resemble something which they do *not* resemble. But the beauty of the lines or colours is wholly independent of any such statement. They may be beautiful lines, though quite inaccurate, and ugly lines though quite faithful. A picture may be frightfully ugly, which represents with fidelity some base circumstance of daily life; and a painted window may be exquisitely beautiful, which represents men with eagles' faces, and dogs with blue heads and crimson tails (though, by the way, this is not in the strict sense *false* art, as we shall see hereafter, inasmuch as it means no assertion that men ever *had* eagles' faces). If this were not so, it would be impossible to sacrifice truth to beauty; for to attain the one would always be to attain the other. But, unfortunately, this sacrifice is exceedingly possible, and it is chiefly this which characterizes the false schools of high art, so far as high art consists in the pursuit of beauty. For although truth and beauty are independent of each other, it does not follow that we are at liberty to pursue whichever we please. They are indeed separable, but it is wrong to separate them; they are to be sought together in the order of their worthiness; that is to say, truth first, and beauty afterwards. High art differs from low art in possessing an excess of beauty in addition to its truth, not in possessing excess of beauty inconsistent with truth." (Ruskin)

Ruskin, in dealing with the idea of the equivalence of truth and beauty, does not refer to Keats's famous statement of it at the end of "Ode on a Grecian Urn," perhaps because he perceived that Keats had in mind something more complex than the common formulation he is here dealing with.

22. Albrecht Dürer (1471–1528), the great German painter and engraver. In his last years he wrote theoretical works on geometry and perspective and anatomy.

23. Peter Paul Rubens (1577–1640), Flemish painter, generally accounted the greatest exemplar in northern Europe of the dramatic, exuberant style known as baroque.

24. An art critic of today of whatever school of thought could receive this judgment of Dürer and Rubens only in wide-eyed amazement.

25. Salvator Rosa (1615–73), Neapolitan painter, is celebrated for his wild, often savage, scenes which are peopled with shepherds, sailors, and soldiers; he has not a touch of "nobility." Caravaggio (1569–1609) took a principled stand against idealism and painted biblical scenes in a harshly realistic manner, using crude peasant faces as his models and dramatizing them with extreme contrasts of light and shadow. Ruskin goes so far in his condemnation of these men as to assign them, in the last phrase of the paragraph, to the forces of Hell.

shippers of the depraved, of no rank, or as we said before, of a certain order in the abyss.

The corruption of the schools of high art, so far as this particular quality is concerned, consists in the sacrifice of truth to beauty. Great art dwells on all that is beautiful; but false art omits or changes all that is ugly. Great art accepts Nature as she is, but directs the eyes and thoughts to what is most perfect in her; false art saves itself the trouble of direction by removing or altering whatever it thinks objectionable. The evil results of which proceeding are twofold.

First. That beauty deprived of its proper foils and adjuncts ceases to be *Evil first, that* enjoyed as beauty, just as light deprived of all shadow ceases *we lose the true* to be enjoyed as light. A white canvas cannot produce an *force of beauty.* effect of sunshine; the painter must darken it in some places before he can make it look luminous in others; nor can an uninterrupted succession of beauty produce the true effect of beauty; it must be foiled by inferiority before its own power can be developed. Nature has for the most part mingled her inferior and noble elements as she mingles sunshine with shade, giving due use and influence to both, and the painter who chooses to remove the shadow, perishes in the burning desert he has created. The truly high and beautiful art of Angelico is continually refreshed and strengthened by his frank portraiture of the most ordinary features of his brother monks and of the recorded peculiarities of ungainly sanctity; but the modern German and Raphaelesque schools lose all honour and nobleness in barber-like admiration of handsome faces, and have, in fact, no real faith except in straight noses, and curled hair. Paul Veronese opposes the dwarf to the soldier, and the negress to the queen; Shakespeare places Caliban beside Miranda, and Autolycus beside Perdita; [26] but the vulgar idealist withdraws his beauty to the safety of the saloon, [27] and his innocence to the seclusion of the cloister; he pretends that he does this in delicacy of choice and purity of sentiment, while in truth he has neither courage to front the monster, nor wit enough to furnish the knave.

It is only by the habit of representing faithfully all things, that we can truly *Evil second,—* learn what is beautiful, and what is not. The ugliest objects *we lose the true* contain some element of beauty; and in all it is an element *quantity of* peculiar to themselves, which cannot be separated from their *beauty.* ugliness, but must either be enjoyed together with it or not at all. The more a painter accepts nature as he finds it, the more unexpected beauty he discovers in what he at first despised; but once let him arrogate the right of rejection, and he will gradually contract his circle of enjoyment, until what he supposed to be nobleness of selection ends in narrowness of perception. Dwelling perpetually upon one class of ideas, his art becomes at once monstrous and morbid; until at last he cannot faithfully represent even what he

26. Caliban is the misshapen savage slave to Prospero in *The Tempest;* Miranda is Prospero's lovely daughter; in *The Winter's Tale* Autolycus is a ragged, pilfering peddler, Perdita the exquisite shepherdess, actually a princess.

27. Saloon: a large room for receiving people or displaying pictures. Its use to mean a drinking place has led to the substitution of the original French *salon* for its anglicized form. "Vulgar idealist" is a striking phrase for an important idea; it might be turned on many of the Pre-Raphaelite works that Ruskin admired, most especially *The Light of the World.*

chooses to retain; his discrimination contracts into darkness, and his fastidiousness fades into fatuity.

High art, therefore, consists neither in altering, nor in improving nature; but in seeking throughout nature for 'whatsoever things are lovely, and whatsoever things are pure';[28] in loving these, in displaying to the utmost of the painter's power such loveliness as is in them, and directing the thoughts of others to them by winning art or gentle emphasis. Of the degree in which this can be done, and in which it may be permitted to gather together, without falsifying, the finest forms or thoughts, so as to create a sort of perfect vision, we shall have to speak hereafter: at present, it is enough to remember that art (*cæteris paribus*)[29] is great in exact proportion to the love of beauty shown by the painter, provided that love of beauty forfeit no atom of truth.

III. *Sincerity.*—The next[30] characteristic of great art is that it includes the largest possible quantity of Truth in the most perfect possible harmony. If it were possible for art to give all the truths of nature it ought to do it. But this is not possible. Choice must always be made of some facts which *can* be represented, from among others which must be passed by in silence, or even, in some respects, misrepresented. The inferior artist chooses unimportant and scattered truths; the great artist chooses the most necessary first, and afterwards the most consistent with these, so as to obtain the greatest possible and most harmonious *sum.* For instance, Rembrandt[31] always chooses to represent the exact force with which the light on the most illumined part of an object is opposed to its obscurer portions. In order to obtain this, in most cases, not very important truth, he sacrifices the light and colour of five-sixths of his picture, and the expression of every character of objects which depends on tenderness of shape or tint. But he obtains his single truth, and what picturesque and forcible expression is dependent upon it, with magnificent skill and subtlety. Veronese, on the contrary, chooses to represent the great relations of visible things to each other, to the heaven above, and to the earth beneath[32] them. He holds it more important to show how a figure stands relieved from delicate air, or marble wall; how as a red, or purple, or white figure, it separates itself, in clear discernibility, from things not red, nor purple, nor white; how infinite daylight shines round it; how innumerable veils of faint shadow invest it; how its blackness and darkness are, in the excess of their nature, just as limited and local as its intensity of light; all this, I say, he feels to be more important than showing merely the exact *measure* of the spark of sunshine that gleams on a dagger-hilt, or glows on a jewel. All this, moreover, he feels to be harmonious,— capable of being joined in one great system of spacious truth. And with inevitable watchfulness, inestimable subtlety, he unites all this in tenderest balance, noting in each hair's-breadth of colour, not merely what its rightness or wrongness is in itself, but what its relation is to every other on his canvas; restraining, for truth's sake, his exhaustless energy, reining back, for truth's

28. Philippians 4:8.
29. "Other things being equal."
30. "I name them in order of *increasing,* not decreasing importance." (Ruskin)
31. Rembrandt van Rijn (1606–69), the greatest of Dutch painters.
32. Exodus 20:4.

sake, his fiery strength; veiling, before truth, the vanity of brightness; penetrating, for truth, the discouragement of gloom; ruling his restless invention
with a rod of iron; pardoning no error, no thoughtlessness, no forgetfulness;
and subduing all his powers, impulses, and imaginations, to the arbitrament of
a merciless justice, and the obedience of an incorruptible verity.

I give this instance with respect to colour and shade: but, in the whole field
of art, the difference between the great and inferior artists is of the same kind,
and may be determined at once by the question, which of them conveys the
largest sum of truth?

It follows from this principle, that in general all *great* drawing is *distinct*

Corollary 1st:
Great art is
generally dis-
tinct.

drawing; for truths which are rendered indistinctly might, for
the most part, as well not be rendered at all. There are, indeed,
certain facts of mystery, and facts of indistinctness, in all objects, which must have their proper place in the general harmony, and the reader will presently find me, when we come to that part of our
investigation, telling him that all good drawing must in some sort be *indistinct*.
We may, however, understand this apparent contradiction, by reflecting that
the highest knowledge always involves a more advanced perception of the fields
of the unknown; and, therefore, it may most truly be said, that to know anything well involves a profound sensation of ignorance, while yet it is equally
true that good and noble knowledge is distinguished from vain and useless
knowledge chiefly by its clearness and distinctness, and by the vigorous consciousness of what is known and what is not.

So in art. The best drawing involves a wonderful perception and expression
of indistinctness; and yet all noble drawing is separated from the ignoble by
its distinctness, by its fine expression and firm assertion of *Something;* whereas
the bad drawing, without either firmness or fineness, expresses and asserts
Nothing. The first thing, therefore, to be looked for as a sign of noble art, is a
clear consciousness of what is drawn and what is not; the bold statement, and
frank confession—'*This I know*,' '*that* I know not'; and, generally speaking, all
haste, slurring, obscurity, indecision, are signs of low art, and all calmness,
distinctness, luminousness, and positiveness, of high art.

It follows, secondly, from this principle, that as the great painter is always

Corollary 2nd:
Great art is
generally
large in masses
and in scale.

attending to the sum and harmony of his truths rather than
to one or the other of any group, a quality of Grasp is visible
in his work, like the power of a great reasoner over his subject, or a great poet over his conception, manifesting itself
very often in missing out certain details or less truths (which, though good in
themselves, he finds are in the way of others), and in a sweeping manner of
getting the beginnings and ends of things shown at once, and the squares and
depths rather than the surfaces: hence, on the whole, a habit of looking at
large masses rather than small ones; and even a physical largeness of handling,
and love of working, if possible, on a large scale; and various other qualities,
more or less imperfectly expressed by such technical terms as breadth, massing,
unity, boldness, etc., all of which are, indeed, great qualities, when they mean
breadth of truth, weight of truth, unity of truth, and courageous assertion of
truth; but which have all their correlative errors and mockeries, almost uni-

versally mistaken for them,—the breadth which has no contents, the weight which has no value, the unity which plots deception, and the boldness which faces out fallacy.

And it is to be noted especially respecting largeness of scale, that though for the most part it is characteristic of the more powerful masters, they have both more invention wherewith to fill space (as Ghirlandajo wished that he might paint all the walls of Florence) [33] and, often, an impetuosity of mind which makes them like free play for hand and arm (besides that they usually desire to paint everything in the foreground of their picture of the natural size), yet, as this largeness of scale involves the placing of the picture at a considerable distance from the eye, and this distance involves the loss of many delicate details, and especially of the subtle lines of expression in features, it follows that the masters of refined detail and human expression are apt to prefer a small scale to work upon; so that the chief masterpieces of expression which the world possesses are small pictures by Angelico, in which the figures are rarely more than six or seven inches high; in the best works of Raphael and Leonardo the figures are almost always less than life, and the best works of Turner do not exceed the size of 18 inches by 12.

As its greatness depends on the sum of truth, and this sum of truth can

Corollary 3rd: Great art is always delicate. always be increased by delicacy of handling, it follows that all great art must have this delicacy to the utmost possible degree. This rule is infallible and inflexible. All coarse work is the sign of low art. Only, it is to be remembered, that coarseness must be estimated by the distance from the eye; it being necessary to consult this distance, when great, by laying on touches which appear coarse when seen near; but which, so far from being coarse, are, in reality, more delicate in a master's work than the finest close handling, for they involve a calculation of result, and are laid on with a subtlety of sense precisely correspondent to that with which a good archer draws his bow; the spectator seeing in the action nothing but the strain of the strong arm, while there is in reality, in the finger and eye, an ineffably delicate estimate of distance, and touch on the arrow plume. And, indeed, this delicacy is generally quite perceptible to those who know what the truth is, for strokes by Tintoret [34] or Paul Veronese, which were done in an instant, and look to an ignorant spectator merely like a violent dash of loaded colour (and are, as such, imitated by blundering artists), are, in fact, modulated by the brush and finger to that degree of delicacy that no single grain of the colour could be taken from the touch without injury; and little golden particles of it, not the size of a gnat's head, have important share and function in the balances of light in a picture perhaps fifty feet long. Nearly *every* other rule applicable to art has some exception but this. This has absolutely none. All great art is delicate art, and all coarse art is bad art. Nay, even, to a certain extent, all *bold* art is bad art; for boldness is not the proper word to apply to the courage and swiftness of a great master, based on knowledge, and coupled with fear and love. There is as much difference between the

33. Vasari, in his *Lives of the Painters* (1550), records the expression of this wish by Ghirlandaio, the Florentine painter (1483–1561).
34. The brilliant Venetian painter, generally called Tintoretto (1518–94). Ruskin alludes to the rapidity with which he executed his work; it led to his being nicknamed *Il Furioso*.

boldness of the true and the false masters, as there is between the courage of a sure woman and the shamelessness of a lost one.[35]

IV. *Invention.*—The last characteristic of great art is that it must be inventive, that is, be produced by the imagination. In this respect, it must precisely fulfil the definition already given of poetry; and not only present grounds for noble emotion, but furnish these grounds by *imaginative power.* Hence there is at once a great bar fixed between the two schools of Lower and Higher art. The lower merely copies what is set before it, whether in portrait, landscape, or still-life; the higher either entirely imagines its subject, or arranges the materials presented to it, so as to manifest the imaginative power in all the three phases which have been already explained in the second volume.

And this was the truth which was confusedly present in Reynolds's mind when he spoke, as above quoted,[36] of the difference between Historical and Poetical Painting. *Every relation of the plain facts which the painter saw is* proper *historical* painting. If those facts are unimportant (as that he saw a gambler quarrel with another gambler, or a sot [37] enjoying himself with another sot), then the history is trivial; if the facts are important (as that he saw such and such a great man look thus, or act thus, at such a time), then the history is noble: in each case perfect truth of narrative being supposed, otherwise the whole thing is worthless, being neither history nor poetry, but plain falsehood. And farther, as greater or less elegance and precision are manifested in the relation or painting of the incidents, the merit of the work varies; so that, what with difference of subject, and what with difference of treatment, historical painting falls or rises in changeful eminence, from Dutch trivialities [38] to a Velasquez [39] portrait, just as historical talking or writing varies in eminence, from an old woman's story-telling up to Herodotus.[40] Besides which, certain operations of the imagination come into play inevitably, here and there, so as to touch the history with some light of poetry, that is, with some light shot forth of the narrator's mind, or brought out by the way he has put the accidents together: and wherever the imagination has thus had anything to do with the matter at all (and it must be somewhat cold work where it has not), then, the confines of the lower and higher schools touching each other, the work is coloured by both; but there is no reason why, therefore, we should in the least confuse the historical and poetical characters, any more than that we should confuse blue with crimson, because they may overlap each other, and produce purple.

Now, historical or simply narrative art is very precious in its proper place

35. Ruskin uses an established Victorian phrase for a woman who has committed a sexual transgression. That he should have instituted this comparison between two kinds of artists and two kinds of women is indicative of the nature of the Victorian sexual ethos.
36. In the chapter on the "grand style," Ruskin quotes Reynolds to the effect that in the grand—or historical—style, minute attention to detail should be avoided. "To mingle the Dutch [i.e. detailed] with the Italian school is to join contraries, which cannot subsist together, and which destroy the efficacy of each other." (Reynolds)
37. Drunkard.
38. Dutch painting characteristically represented the details of daily life, often naturalistically but sometimes in a heightened and "poetic" way.
39. Velasquez (1599–1660), the great Spanish painter.
40. Herodotus, Greek historian of the 4th century B.C., called the Father of History.

and way, but it is never *great* art until the poetical or imaginative power touches it; and in proportion to the stronger manifestation of this power, it becomes greater and greater, while the highest art is purely imaginative, all its materials being wrought into their form by invention; and it differs, therefore, from the simple historical painting, exactly as Wordsworth's stanza, above quoted, differs from Saussure's plain narrative of the parallel fact; [41] and the imaginative painter differs from the historical painter in the manner that Wordsworth differs from Saussure.

Farther, imaginative art always *includes* historical art; so that, strictly speaking, according to the analogy above used, we meet with the pure blue, and with the crimson ruling the blue and changing it into kingly purple, but not with the pure crimson: for all imagination must deal with the knowledge it has before accumulated; it never produces anything but by combination or contemplation. Creation, in the full sense, is impossible to it. And the mode in which the historical faculties are included by it is often quite simple, and easily seen. Thus, in Hunt's great poetical picture of *The Light of the World*, the whole thought and arrangement of the picture being imaginative, the several details of it are wrought out with simple portraiture; the ivy, the jewels, the creeping plants, and the moonlight being calmly studied or remembered from the things themselves. But of all these special ways in which the invention works with plain facts, we shall have to treat farther afterwards.

And now, finally, since this poetical power includes the historical, if we glance back to the other qualities required in great art, and put all together, we find that the sum of them is simply the sum of all the powers of man. For as (1) the choice of the high subject involves all conditions of right moral choice, and as (2) the love of beauty involves all conditions of right admiration, and as (3) the grasp of truth involves all strength of sense, evenness of judgment, and honesty of purpose, and as (4) the poetical power involves all swiftness of invention, and accuracy of historical memory, the sum of all these powers is the sum of the human soul. Hence we see why the word "Great" is used of this art. It is literally great. It compasses and calls forth the entire human spirit, whereas any other kind of art, being more or less small or narrow, compasses and calls forth only *part* of the human spirit. Hence the idea of its magnitude is a literal and just one, the art being simply less or greater in proportion to the number of faculties it exercises and addresses. And this is the ultimate meaning of the definition I gave of it long ago, as containing the 'greatest number of the greatest ideas.' [42]

Such, then, being the characters required in order to constitute high art, if the reader will think over them a little, and over the various ways in which they may be falsely assumed, he will easily perceive how spacious and dangerous a field of discussion they open to the ambitious critic, and of error to

41. In a footnote to a passage in the chapter on the "grand style" Ruskin quotes a passage from Wordsworth's "The Affliction of Margaret" and a passage of similar import from Saussure's prose narrative of his actual travels *Voyages dans les Alpes*. (Horace Bénédict de Saussure (1740–99), known for his scientific studies of the plants and weather of the Alps.) The first, he says, is poetry because it is invented or made by the writer; the second is not poetry, however affecting it is, but true utterance.
42. In Vol. II of *Modern Painters*.

the ambitious artist; he will see how difficult it must be, either to distinguish what is truly great art from the mockeries of it, or to rank the real artists in anything like a progressive system of greater and less. For it will have been observed that the various qualities which form greatness are partly inconsistent with each other (as some virtues are, docility and firmness for instance), and partly independent of each other; and the fact is, that artists differ not more by mere capacity, than by the component *elements* of their capacity, each possessing in very different proportions the several attributes of greatness; so that, classed by one kind of merit, as, for instance, purity of expression, Angelico will stand highest; classed by another, sincerity of manner, Veronese will stand highest; classed by another, love of beauty, Leonardo will stand highest; and so on: hence arise continual disputes and misunderstandings among those who think that high art must always be one and the same, and that great artists ought to unite all great attributes in an equal degree.

In one of the exquisitely finished tales of Marmontel,[43] a company of critics are received at dinner by the hero of the story, an old gentleman, somewhat vain of his *acquired* taste, and his niece, by whose incorrigible *natural* taste he is seriously disturbed and tormented. During the entertainment, 'On parcourut tous les genres de littérature, et pour donner plus d'essor à l'érudition et à la critique, on mit sur le tapis cette question toute neuve, sçavoir, lequel méritoit la préférence de Corneille ou de Racine. L'on disoit même là-dessus les plus belles choses du monde, lorsque la petite nièce, qui n'avoit pas dit un mot, s'avisa de demander naïvement lequel des deux fruits, de l'orange ou de la pêche, avoit le goût le plus exquis et méritoit le plus d'éloges. Son oncle rougit de sa simplicité, et les convives baissèrent tous les yeux sans daigner répondre à cette bêtise. Ma nièce, dit Fintac, à votre âge, il faut sçavoir écouter, et se taire.' [44]

I cannot close this chapter with shorter or better advice to the reader, than merely, whenever he hears discussions about the relative merits of great masters, to remember the young lady's question. It is, indeed, true that there *is* a relative merit, that a peach is nobler than a hawthorn berry, and still more a hawthorn berry than a bead of the nightshade; but in each rank of fruits, as in each rank of masters, one is endowed with one virtue, and another with another; their glory is their dissimilarity, and they who propose to themselves in the training of an artist that he should unite the colouring of Tintoret, the finish of Albert Dürer, and the tenderness of Correggio, are no wiser than a horticulturist would be, who made it the object of his labour to produce a fruit

43. Jean-François Marmontel (1723–99), French man of letters and contributor to the *Encyclopédie*. It was a passage in his *Memoirs of a Father* that so greatly helped John Stuart Mill in his great emotional crisis.

44. Ruskin quotes from "The Connoisseur," one of the *Moral Tales*, published in book form in 1761 and in 1789–92. "They ran through all the literary genres and to give more play to erudition and criticism they raised what was an entirely new question, namely, who deserved the preference, Corneille or Racine. On this subject they said the finest things in the world, when the little niece who had not yet said a word, took it into her head to ask simply which of two fruits, the orange or the peach, had the more exquisite taste and deserved the greater praise. Her uncle blushed at her naïveté and the guests all dropped their eyes at this lapse from good sense. 'Niece,' said Fintac, 'at your age, one should listen and be silent.' "

which should unite in itself the lusciousness of the grape, the crispness of the nut, and the fragrance of the pine.

And from these considerations one most important practical corollary is to be deduced, with the good help of Mademoiselle Agathe's simile, namely, that the greatness or smallness of a man is, in the most conclusive sense, determined for him at his birth, as strictly as it is determined for a fruit whether it is to be a currant or an apricot. Education, favourable circumstances, resolution, and industry can do much; in a certain sense they do *everything;* that is to say, they determine whether the poor apricot shall fall in the form of a green bead, blighted by the east wind, and be trodden under foot, or whether it shall expand into tender pride, and sweet brightness of golden velvet. But apricot out of currant,—great man out of small,—did never yet art or effort make; and, in a general way, men have their excellence nearly fixed for them when they are born; a little cramped and frost-bitten on one side, a little sun-burnt and fortune-spotted on the other, they reach, between good and evil chances, such size and taste as generally belong to the men of their calibre, and, the small in their serviceable bunches, the great in their golden isolation, have, these no cause for regret, nor those for disdain.

Therefore it is, that every system of teaching is false which holds forth 'great art' as in any wise to be taught to students, or even to be aimed at by them. Great art is precisely that which never was, nor will be taught, it is pre-eminently and finally the expression of the spirits of great men; so that the only wholesome teaching is that which simply endeavours to fix those characters of nobleness in the pupils' mind, of which it seems easily susceptible; and without holding out to him, as a possible or even probable result, that he should ever paint like Titian, or carve like Michael Angelo, enforces upon him the manifest possibility, and assured duty, of endeavouring to draw in a manner at least honest and intelligible; and cultivates in him those general charities of heart, sincerities of thought, and graces of habit which are likely to lead him, throughout life, to prefer openness to affectation, realities to shadows, and beauty to corruption.

1856   1856

The Stones of Venice

From *The Nature of Gothic* [1]

. . . I shall endeavour . . . to give the reader in this chapter an idea, at once broad and definite, of the true nature of *Gothic* architecture, properly so called; not of that of Venice only, but of universal Gothic: for it will be one of the most interesting parts of our subsequent inquiry, to find out how far Venetian architecture reached the universal or perfect type of Gothic, and how far it either fell short of it, or assumed foreign and independent forms.

The principal difficulty in doing this arises from the fact that every building of the Gothic period differs in some important respect from every other; and

1. From Chap. 6 of Vol. II.

many include features which, if they occurred in other buildings, would not be considered Gothic at all; so that all we have to reason upon is merely, if I may be allowed so to express it, a greater or less degree of *Gothicness* in each building we examine. And it is this Gothicness,—the character which, according as it is found more or less in a building, makes it more or less Gothic,—of which I want to define the nature; and I feel the same kind of difficulty in doing so which would be encountered by any one who undertook to explain, for instance, the nature of Redness, without any actually red thing to point to, but only orange and purple things. Suppose he had only a piece of heather and a dead oak-leaf to do it with. He might say, the colour which is mixed with the yellow in this oak-leaf, and with the blue in this heather, would be red, if you had it separate; but it would be difficult, nevertheless, to make the abstraction perfectly intelligible: and it is so in a far greater degree to make the abstraction of the Gothic character intelligible, because that character itself is made up of many mingled ideas, and can consist only in their union. That is to say, pointed arches do not constitute Gothic, nor vaulted roofs, nor flying buttresses, nor grotesque sculptures; but all or some of these things, and many other things with them, when they come together so as to have life. . . .

. . . We shall find that Gothic architecture has external forms, and internal elements. Its elements are certain mental tendencies of the builders, legibly expressed in it; as fancifulness, love of variety, love of richness, and such others. Its external forms are pointed arches, vaulted roofs, &c. And unless both the elements and the forms are there, we have no right to call the style Gothic. It is not enough that it has the Form, if it have not also the power and life. It is not enough that it has the Power, if it have not the form. We must therefore inquire into each of these characters successively; and determine first, what is the Mental Expression, and secondly, what the Material Form, of Gothic architecture, properly so called. . . .

I believe, then, that the characteristic or moral elements of Gothic are the following, placed in the order of their importance:

1. Savageness.	4. Grotesqueness.
2. Changefulness.	5. Rigidity.
3. Naturalism.	6. Redundance.

These characters are here expressed as belonging to the building; as belonging to the builder, they would be expressed thus:—1. Savageness, or Rudeness. 2. Love of Change. 3. Love of Nature. 4. Disturbed Imagination. 5. Obstinacy. 6. Generosity. And I repeat, that the withdrawal of any one, or any two, will not at once destroy the Gothic character of a building, but the removal of a majority of them will. I shall proceed to examine them in their order.

1. *Savageness.* I am not sure when the word 'Gothic' was first generically applied to the architecture of the North; [2] but I presume that, whatever the

2. The first use of the word in description of architecture was probably by Giorgio Vasari, a pupil of Michelangelo. Writing in the 16th century, he spoke of the architectural monuments of the Middle Ages as having been built by the Goths, meaning the German barbarians hostile to Rome, and described the buildings as being a clutter of spires and grotesque ornament, lacking all sense of form and beauty. The word "Gothic" came to be applied to all "rude" art. "All that has nothing of the Ancient gust [i.e. the classic taste]," said Dryden in 1695, "is called a barbarous or Gothique manner."

date of its original usage, it was intended to imply reproach, and express the barbaric character of the nations among whom that architecture arose. It never implied that they were literally of Gothic lineage, far less that their architecture had been originally invented by the Goths themselves; but it did imply that they and their buildings together exhibited a degree of sternness and rudeness, which, in contradistinction to the character of Southern and Eastern nations, appeared like a perpetual reflection of the contrast between the Goth and the Roman in their first encounter. And when that fallen Roman, in the utmost impotence of his luxury, and insolence of his guilt, became the model for the imitation of civilised Europe, at the close of the so-called Dark ages,[3] the word Gothic became a term of unmitigated contempt, not unmixed with aversion. From that contempt, by the exertion of the antiquaries and architects of this century, Gothic architecture has been sufficiently vindicated;[4] and perhaps some among us, in our admiration of the magnificent science of its structure, and sacredness of its expression, might desire that the term of ancient reproach should be withdrawn, and some other, of more apparent honourableness, adopted in its place. There is no chance, as there is no need, of such a substitution. As far as the epithet was used scornfully, it was used falsely; but there is no reproach in the word, rightly understood; on the contrary, there is a profound truth, which the instinct of mankind almost unconsciously recognises. It is true, greatly and deeply true, that the architecture of the North is rude and wild; but it is not true, that, for this reason, we are to condemn it, or despise. Far otherwise: I believe it is in this very character that it deserves our profoundest reverence. . . .

If, however, the savageness of Gothic architecture, merely as an expression of its origin among Northern nations, may be considered, in some sort, a noble character, it possesses a high nobility still, when considered as an index, not of climate, but of religious principle.

In the 13th and 14th paragraphs of Chapter XXI of the first volume of this work, it was noticed that the systems of architectural ornament, properly so called, might be divided into three:—1. Servile ornament, in which the execution or power of the inferior workman is entirely subjected to the intellect of the higher;—2. Constitutional ornament, in which the executive inferior power is, to a certain point, emancipated and independent, having a will of its own, yet confessing its inferiority and rendering obedience to higher powers;—and 3. Revolutionary ornament, in which no executive inferiority is admitted at all. I must here explain the nature of these divisions at somewhat greater length.

3. The "Dark ages" was once a common way of referring to the medieval period. It has long gone out of use, even for the earliest centuries of the epoch.
4. Gothic architecture began to be admired in the 18th century; the most famous example of the new taste is the house which Horace Walpole built at Strawberry Hill in 1747, which was designed as "a little Gothic castle." In the early 19th century the so-called Gothic Revival gathered momentum; the new Houses of Parliament, begun in 1840, were in the Gothic style, which became, indeed, one of the accepted modes of Victorian architecture —to Ruskin's dismay, because he judged it to be used conventionally, without feeling, and commonly with machine-made elements. Within recent years his judgment has been questioned and Victorian Gothic has many admirers among architects and historians of architecture.

Of Servile ornament, the principal schools are the Greek, Ninevite,[5] and Egyptian; but their servility is of different kinds. The Greek master-workman was far advanced in knowledge and power above the Assyrian or Egyptian. Neither he nor those for whom he worked could endure the appearance of imperfection in anything; and, therefore, what ornament he appointed to be done by those beneath him was composed of mere geometrical forms,—balls, ridges, and perfectly symmetrical foliage,—which could be executed with absolute precision by line and rule, and were as perfect in their way, when completed, as his own figure sculpture. The Assyrian and Egyptian, on the contrary, less cognisant of accurate form in anything, were content to allow their figure sculpture to be executed by inferior workmen, but lowered the method of its treatment to a standard which every workman could reach, and then trained him by discipline so rigid, that there was no chance of his falling beneath the standard appointed. The Greek gave to the lower workman no subject which he could not perfectly execute. The Assyrian gave him subjects which he could only execute imperfectly, but fixed a legal standard for his imperfection. The workman was, in both systems, a slave.[6]

But in the mediæval, or especially Christian, system of ornament, this slavery is done away with altogether; Christianity having recognised, in small things as well as great, the individual value of every soul. But it not only recognises its value; it confesses its imperfection, in only bestowing dignity upon the acknowledgment of unworthiness. That admission of lost power and fallen nature, which the Greek or Ninevite felt to be intensely painful, and, as far as might be, altogether refused, the Christian makes daily and hourly, contemplating the fact of it without fear, as tending, in the end, to God's greater glory. Therefore, to every spirit which Christianity summons to her service, her exhortation is: Do what you can, and confess frankly what you are unable to do; neither let your effort be shortened for fear of failure, nor your confession silenced for fear of shame. And it is, perhaps, the principal admirableness of the Gothic schools of architecture, that they thus receive the results of the labour of inferior minds; and out of fragments full of imperfection, and betraying that imperfection in every touch, indulgently raise up a stately and unaccusable whole.

But the modern English mind has this much in common with that of the Greek, that it intensely desires, in all things, the utmost completion or perfection compatible with their nature. This is a noble character in the abstract, but becomes ignoble when it causes us to forget the relative dignities of that nature itself, and to prefer the perfectness of the lower nature to the imperfection of the higher; not considering that as, judged by such a rule, all the brute animals would be preferable to man, because more perfect in their functions and kind,

5. Nineveh was the capital city of the Assyrian empire.
6. "The third kind of ornament, the Renaissance, is that in which the inferior detail becomes principal, the executor of every minor portion being required to exhibit skill and possess knowledge as great as that which is possessed by the master of the design; and in the endeavour to endow him with this skill and knowledge, his own original power is overwhelmed, and the whole building becomes a wearisome exhibition of well-educated imbecility. . . ." (Ruskin)

and yet are always held inferior to him, so also in the works of man, those which are more perfect in their kind are always inferior to those which are, in their nature, liable to more faults and shortcomings. For the finer the nature, the more flaws it will show through the clearness of it; and it is a law of this universe, that the best things shall be seldomest seen in their best form. The wild grass grows well and strongly, one year with another; but the wheat is, according to the greater nobleness of its nature, liable to the bitterer blight. And therefore, while in all things that we see, or do, we are to desire perfection, and strive for it, we are nevertheless not to set the meaner thing, in its narrow accomplishment, above the nobler thing, in its mighty progress; not to esteem smooth minuteness above shattered majesty; not to prefer mean victory to honourable defeat; not to lower the level of our aim, that we may, the more surely enjoy the complacency of success. . . . . Now, in the make and nature of every man, however rude or simple, whom we employ in manual labour, there are some powers for better things: some tardy imagination, torpid capacity of emotion, tottering steps of thought, there are, even at the worst; and in most cases it is all our own fault that they *are* tardy or torpid. But they cannot be strengthened, unless we are content to take them in their feebleness, and unless we prize and honour them in their imperfection above the best and most perfect manual skill. And this is what we have to do with all our labourers; to look for the *thoughtful* part of them, and get that out of them, whatever we lose for it, whatever faults and errors we are obliged to take with it. For the best that is in them cannot manifest itself, but in company with much error. Understand this clearly: You can teach a man to draw a straight line, and to cut one; to strike a curved line, and to carve it; and to copy and carve any number of given lines or forms, with admirable speed and perfect precision; and you find his work perfect of its kind: but if you ask him to think about any of those forms, to consider if he cannot find any better in his own head, he stops; his execution becomes hesitating; he thinks, and ten to one he thinks wrong; ten to one he makes a mistake in the first touch he gives to his work as a thinking being. But you have made a man of him for all that. He was only a machine before, an animated tool.

And observe, you are put to stern choice in this matter. You must either make a tool of the creature, or a man of him. You cannot make both. Men were not intended to work with the accuracy of tools, to be precise and perfect in all their actions. If you will have that precision out of them, and make their fingers measure degrees like cog-wheels, and their arms strike curves like compasses, you must unhumanise them. All the energy of their spirits must be given to make cogs and compasses of themselves. All their attention and strength must go to the accomplishment of the mean act. The eye of the soul must be bent upon the finger-point, and the soul's force must fill all the invisible nerves that guide it, ten hours a day, that it may not err from its steely precision, and so soul and sight be worn away, and the whole human being be lost at last—a heap of sawdust, so far as its intellectual work in this world is concerned; saved only by its Heart, which cannot go into the form of cogs and compasses, but expands, after the ten hours are over, into fireside humanity. On the other hand, if you will make a man of the working creature, you cannot make a tool. Let him but begin to imagine, to think, to try to do anything worth doing; and the engine-turned precision is lost at once. Out come all his roughness, all his dulness, all his incapability; shame upon shame, failure upon failure, pause after pause: but out comes the whole majesty of him also; and we know the height of it only, when we see the clouds settling upon him. And, whether the clouds be bright or dark, there will be transfiguration behind and within them.

And now, reader, look round this English room of yours, about which you have been proud so often, because the work of it was so good and strong, and the ornaments of it so finished. Examine again all those accurate mouldings, and perfect polishings, and unerring adjustments of the seasoned wood and tempered steel. Many a time you have exulted over them, and thought how great England was, because her slightest work was done so thoroughly. Alas! if read rightly, these perfectnesses are signs of a slavery in our England a thousand times more bitter and more degrading than that of the scourged African, or helot [7] Greek. Men may be beaten, chained, tormented, yoked like cattle, slaughtered like summer flies, and yet remain in one sense, and the best sense, free. But to smother their souls within them, to blight and hew into rotting pollards [8] the suckling branches of their human intelligence, to make the flesh and skin which, after the worm's work on it, is to see God,[9] into leathern thongs to yoke machinery with,—this it is to be slave-masters indeed; and there might be more freedom in England, though her feudal lords' lightest words were worth men's lives, and though the blood of the vexed husbandman dropped in the furrows of her fields, than there is while the animation of her multitudes is sent like fuel to feed the factory smoke, and the strength of them is given daily to be wasted into the fineness of a web, or racked into the exactness of a line.

And, on the other hand, go forth again to gaze upon the old cathedral front, where you have smiled so often at the fantastic ignorance of the old sculptors: examine once more those ugly goblins, and formless monsters, and stern statues, anatomiless and rigid; but do not mock at them, for they are signs of the life and liberty of every workman who struck the stone; a freedom of thought, and rank in scale of being, such as no laws, no charters, no charities can secure; but which it must be the first aim of all Europe at this day to regain for her children.

Let me not be thought to speak wildly or extravagantly. It is verily this degradation of the operative into a machine, which, more than any other evil of the times, is leading the mass of the nations everywhere into vain, incoherent, destructive struggling for a freedom of which they cannot explain the nature to themselves. Their universal outcry against wealth, and against nobility, is not forced from them either by the pressure of famine, or the sting of mortified pride. These do much, and have done much in all ages; but the foundations of society were never yet shaken as they are at this day. It is not that men are ill fed, but that they have no pleasure in the work by which they make their bread, and therefore look to wealth as the only means of pleasure. It is

7. A serf in ancient Sparta.
8. A tree whose top branches have been cut back to the trunk so that it will produce a thick growth of new shoots. The practice of pollarding, common in France, is usually spoken of with dislike in England. It is not clear why these pollards should rot.
9. Ruskin's rhetoric has got out of hand here—it can scarcely be "flesh and skin" that will "see God," not even after the grave worms have finished with them.

not that men are pained by the scorn of the upper classes, but they cannot endure their own; for they feel that the kind of labour to which they are condemned is verily a degrading one, and makes them less than men. . . .

We have much studied and much perfected, of late, the great civilised invention of the division of labour; only we give it a false name. It is not, truly speaking, the labour that is divided; but the men:—Divided into mere segments of men—broken into small fragments and crumbs of life; so that all the little piece of intelligence that is left in a man is not enough to make a pin, or a nail, but exhausts itself in making the point of a pin, or the head of a nail. Now it is a good and desirable thing, truly, to make many pins in a day; but if we could only see with what crystal sand their points were polished,—sand of human soul, much to be magnified before it can be discerned for what it is, —we should think there might be some loss in it also. And the great cry that rises from all our manufacturing cities, louder than their furnace blast, is all in very deed for this,—that we manufacture everything there except men; we blanch cotton, and strengthen steel, and refine sugar, and shape pottery; but to brighten, to strengthen, to refine, or to form a single living spirit, never enters into our estimate of advantages. And all the evil to which that cry is urging our myriads can be met only in one way: not by teaching nor preaching, for to teach them is but to show them their misery, and to preach to them, if we do nothing more than preach, is to mock at it. It can be met only by a right understanding, on the part of all classes, of what kinds of labour are good for men, raising them, and making them happy; by a determined sacrifice of such convenience, or beauty, or cheapness as is to be got only by the degradation of the workman; and by equally determined demand for the products and results of healthy and ennobling labour.

And how, it will be asked, are these products to be recognised, and this demand to be regulated? Easily: by the observance of three broad and simple rules:

1. Never encourage the manufacture of any article not absolutely necessary, in the production of which *Invention* has no share.

2. Never demand an exact finish for its own sake, but only for some practical or noble end.

3. Never encourage imitation or copying of any kind, except for the sake of preserving record of great works.

The second of these principles is the only one which directly rises out of the consideration of our immediate subject; but I shall briefly explain the meaning and extent of the first also, reserving the enforcement of the third for another place.

1. Never encourage the manufacture of anything not necessary, in the production of which invention has no share.

For instance. Glass beads are utterly unnecessary, and there is no design or thought employed in their manufacture. They are formed by first drawing out the glass into rods; these rods are chopped up into fragments of the size of beads by the human hand, and the fragments are then rounded in the furnace. The men who chop up the rods sit at their work all day, their hands vibrating with a perpetual and exquisitely timed palsy, and the beads dropping beneath their vibration like hail. Neither they, nor the men who draw out the rods or fuse the fragments, have the smallest occasion for the use of any single human faculty; and every young lady, therefore, who buys glass beads is engaged in the slave-trade, and in a much more cruel one than that which we have so long been endeavouring to put down.

But glass cups and vessels may become the subjects of exquisite invention; and if in buying these we pay for the invention, that is to say for the beautiful form, or colour, or engraving, and not for mere finish of execution, we are doing good to humanity. . . .

. . . Our modern glass is exquisitely clear in its substance, true in its form, accurate in its cutting. We are proud of this. We ought to be ashamed of it. The old Venice glass was muddy, inaccurate in all its forms, and clumsily cut, if at all. And the old Venetian was justly proud of it. For there is this difference between the English and Venetian workman, that the former thinks only of accurately matching his patterns, and getting his curves perfectly true and his edges perfectly sharp, and becomes a mere machine for rounding curves and sharpening edges, while the old Venetian cared not a whit whether his edges were sharp or not, but he invented a new design for every glass that he made, and never moulded a handle or a lip without a new fancy in it. And therefore, though some Venetian glass is ugly and clumsy enough, when made by clumsy and uninventive workmen, other Venetian glass is so lovely in its forms that no price is too great for it; and we never see the same form in it twice. Now you cannot have the finish and the varied form too. If the workman is thinking about his edges, he cannot be thinking of his design; if of his design, he cannot think of his edges. Choose whether you will pay for the lovely form or the perfect finish, and choose at the same moment whether you will make the worker a man or a grindstone.

Nay, but the reader interrupts me,—'If the workman can design beautifully, I would not have him kept at the furnace. Let him be taken away and made a gentleman, and have a studio, and design his glass there, and I will have it blown and cut for him by common workmen, and so I will have my design and my finish too.'. . .

. . . How wide the separation is between original and second-hand execution, I shall endeavour to show elsewhere; it is not so much to our purpose here as to mark the other and more fatal error of despising manual labour when governed by intellect; for it is no less fatal an error to despise it when thus regulated by intellect, than to value it for its own sake. We are always in these days endeavouring to separate the two; we want one man to be always thinking, and another to be always working, and we call one a gentleman, and the other an operative; whereas the workman ought often to be thinking, and the thinker often to be working, and both should be gentlemen, in the best sense. As it is, we make both ungentle, the one envying, the other despising, his brother; and the mass of society is made up of morbid thinkers, and miserable workers. Now it is only by labour that thought can be made healthy, and only by thought that labour can be made happy; and the two cannot be separated with impunity. It would be well if all of us were good handicraftsmen in some kind, and the dishonour of manual labour done away with altogether; so that though there should still be a trenchant distinction of race between nobles and commoners, there should not, among the latter, be a trenchant distinction of employment, as between idle and working men, or between men of liberal and illiberal professions. All professions should be liberal, and there should be less pride felt in peculiarity of employment, and more in excellence of achievement. . . .

. . . Hitherto I have used the words imperfect and perfect merely to distinguish between work grossly unskilful, and work executed with average precision and science; and I have been pleading that any degree of unskillfulness should be admitted, so only that the labourer's mind had room for expression. But, accurately speaking, no good work whatever can be perfect, and *the demand for perfection is always a sign of a misunderstanding of the ends of art.*

. . . Imperfection is in some sort essential to all that we know of life. It is the sign of life in a mortal body, that is to say, of a state of progress and change. Nothing that lives is, or can be, rigidly perfect; part of it is decaying, part nascent. The foxglove blossom,—a third part bud, a third part past, a third part in full bloom,—is a type of the life of this world. And in all things that live there are certain irregularities and deficiencies which are not only signs of life, but sources of beauty. No human face is exactly the same in its lines on each side, no leaf perfect in its lobes, no branch in its symmetry. All admit irregularity as they imply change; and to banish imperfection is to destroy expression, to check exertion, to paralyse vitality. All things are literally better, lovelier, and more beloved for the imperfections which have been divinely appointed, that the law of human life may be Effort, and the law of human judgment, Mercy.

Accept this then for a universal law, that neither architecture nor any other noble work of man can be good unless it be imperfect; and let us be prepared for the otherwise strange fact, which we shall discern clearly as we approach the period of the Renaissance, that the first cause of the fall of the arts of Europe was a relentless requirement of perfection, incapable alike either of being silenced by veneration for greatness, or softened into forgiveness of simplicity.

Thus far then of the Rudeness or Savageness, which is the first mental element of Gothic architecture. It is an element in many other healthy architectures also, as in Byzantine and Romanesque; but true Gothic cannot exist without it.

The second mental element above named was CHANGEFULNESS, or Variety.

I have already enforced the allowing independent operation to the inferior workman, simply as a duty *to him*, and as ennobling the architecture by rendering it more Christian. We have now to consider what reward we obtain for the performance of this duty, namely, the perpetual variety of every feature of the building.

Wherever the workman is utterly enslaved, the parts of the building must of course be absolutely like each other; for the perfection of his execution can only be reached by exercising him in doing one thing, and giving him nothing else to do. . . .

How much the beholder gains from the liberty of the labourer may perhaps be questioned in England, where one of the strongest instincts in nearly every mind is that Love of Order which makes us desire that our house windows should pair like our carriage horses, and allows us to yield our faith unhesitat-

ingly to architectural theories which fix a form for everything, and forbid
variation from it. I would not impeach love of order: it is one of the most
useful elements of the English mind; it helps us in our commerce and in all
purely practical matters; and it is in many cases one of the foundation stones
of morality. Only do not let us suppose that love of order is love of art. It is
true that order, in its highest sense, is one of the necessities of art, just as time
is a necessity of music; but love of order has no more to do with our right
enjoyment of architecture or painting, than love of punctuality with the appreciation of an opera. . . .

Let us then understand at once, that change or variety is as much a necessity to the human heart and brain in buildings as in books; that there is no
merit, though there is some occasional use, in monotony; and that we must no
more expect to derive either pleasure or profit from an architecture whose
ornaments are of one pattern, and whose pillars are of one proportion, than
we should out of a universe in which the clouds were all of one shape, and
the trees all of one size.

And this we confess in deeds, though not in words. All the pleasure which
the people of the nineteenth century take in art, is in pictures, sculpture,
minor objects of virtù,[10] or mediæval architecture, which we enjoy under the
term picturesque: no pleasure is taken anywhere in modern buildings, and we
find all men of true feeling delighting to escape out of modern cities into
natural scenery: hence, as I shall hereafter show, that peculiar love of landscape
which is characteristic of the age. . . .

I must now refer for a moment, before we quit the consideration of this,
the second mental element of Gothic, to the opening of the third chapter of
the 'Seven Lamps of Architecture,' in which the distinction was drawn between
man gathering and man governing; between his acceptance of the sources of
delight from nature, and his development of authoritative or imaginative power
in their arrangement: for the two mental elements, not only of Gothic, but of
all good architecture, which we have just been examining, belong to it, and are
admirable in it, chiefly as it is, more than any other subject of art, the work
of man, and the expression of the average power of man. A picture or poem
is often little more than a feeble utterance of man's admiration of something
out of himself; but architecture approaches more to a creation of his own, born
of his necessities, and expressive of his nature. It is also, in some sort, the
work of the whole race, while the picture or statue are the work of one only,
in most cases more highly gifted than his fellows. And therefore we may expect
that the first two elements of good architecture should be expressive of some
great truths commonly belonging to the whole race, and necessary to be understood or felt by them in all their work that they do under the sun. And observe
what they are: the confession of Imperfection, and the confession of Desire of
Change. The building of the bird and the bee need not express anything like
this. It is perfect and unchanging. But just because we are something better
than birds or bees, or building must confess that we have not reached the
perfection we can imagine, and cannot rest in the condition we have attained.
If we pretend to have reached either perfection or satisfaction, we have de-

10. Objects of beauty or interest such as a collector would wish to possess.

graded ourselves and our work. God's work only may express that; but ours may never have that sentence written upon it,—'And behold, it was very good.' And, observe again, it is not merely as it renders the edifice a book of various knowledge, or a mine of precious thought, that variety is essential to its nobleness. The vital principle is not the love of *Knowledge,* but the love of *Change.* It is that strange *disquietude* of the Gothic spirit that is its greatness; that restlessness of the dreaming mind, that wanders hither and thither among the niches, and flickers feverishly around the pinnacles, and frets and fades in labyrinthine knots and shadows along wall and roof, and yet is not satisfied, nor shall be satisfied. The Greek could stay in his triglyph furrow, and be at peace; but the work of the Gothic heart is fretwork still, and it can neither rest in, nor from, its labour, but must pass on, sleeplessly, until its love of change shall be pacified for ever in the change that must come alike on them that wake and them that sleep.

The third constituent element of the Gothic mind was stated to be NATURALISM; that is to say, the love of natural objects for their own sake, and the effort to represent them frankly, unconstrained by artistical laws. . . .

We are to remember, in the first place, that the arrangement of colours and lines is an art analogous to the composition of music, and entirely independent of the representation of facts. Good colouring does not necessarily convey the image of anything but itself. It consists in certain proportions and arrangements of rays of light, but not in likenesses to anything. A few touches of certain greys and purples laid by a master's hand on white paper, will be good colouring; as more touches are added beside them, we may find out that they were intended to represent a dove's neck, and we may praise, as the drawing advances, the perfect imitation of the dove's neck. But the good colouring does not consist in that imitation, but in the abstract qualities and relations of the grey and purple.

In like manner, as soon as a great sculptor begins to shape his work out of the block, we shall see that its lines are nobly arranged, and of noble character. We may not have the slightest idea for what the forms are intended, whether they are of man or beast, of vegetation or drapery. Their likeness to anything does not affect their nobleness. They are magnificent forms, and that is all we need care to know of them, in order to say whether the workman is a good or bad sculptor.

Now the noblest art is an exact unison of the abstract value, with the imitative power, of forms, and colours. It is the noblest composition, used to express the noblest facts. But the human mind cannot in general unite the two perfections: it either pursues the fact to the neglect of the composition, or pursues the composition to the neglect of the fact.

And it is intended by the Deity that it *should* do this; the best art is not always wanted. Facts are often wanted without art, as in a geological diagram; and art often without facts, as in a Turkey carpet. And most men have been made capable of giving either one or the other, but not both; only one or two, the very highest, can give both.

Observe then. Men are universally divided, as respects their artistical qualifications, into three great classes; a right, a left, and a centre. On the right side are the men of facts, on the left the men of design,[11] in the centre the men of both.

The three classes of course pass into each other by imperceptible gradations. The men of facts are hardly ever altogether without powers of design; the men of design are always in some measure cognisant of facts; and as each class possesses more or less of the powers of the opposite one, it approaches to the character of the central class. Few men, even in that central rank, are so exactly throned on the summit of the crest that they cannot be perceived to incline in the least one way or the other, embracing both horizons with their glance. Now each of these classes has, as I above said, a healthy function in the world, and correlative diseases or unhealthy functions; and, when the work of either of them is seen in its morbid condition, we are apt to find fault with the class of workmen, instead of finding fault only with the particular abuse which has perverted their action. . . .

. . . The Gothic builders were of that central class which unites fact with design; but . . . the part of the work which was more especially their own was the truthfulness. Their power of artistical invention or arrangement was not greater than that of Romanesque and Byzantine workmen: by those workmen they were taught the principles, and from them received their models, of design; but to the ornamental feeling and rich fancy of the Byzantine the Gothic builder added a love of *fact* which is never found in the South. Both Greek and Roman used conventional foliage in their ornament, passing into something that was not foliage at all, knotting itself into strange cup-like buds or clusters, and growing out of lifeless rods instead of stems; the Gothic sculptor received these types, at first, as things that ought to be, just as we have a second time received them; but he could not rest in them. He saw there was no veracity in them, no knowledge, no vitality. Do what he would, he could not help liking the true leaves better; and cautiously, a little at a time, he put more of nature into his work, until at last it was all true, retaining, nevertheless, every valuable character of the original well-disciplined and designed arrangement.

There is, however, one direction in which the Naturalism of the Gothic workmen is peculiarly manifested; and this direction is even more characteristic of the school than the Naturalism itself; I mean their peculiar fondness for the forms of Vegetation. In rendering the various circumstances of daily life, Egyptian and Ninevite sculpture is as frank and as diffuse as the Gothic. From the highest pomps of state or triumphs of battle, to the most trivial domestic arts and amusements, all is taken advantage of to fill the field of granite with the perpetual interest of a crowded drama; and the early Lombardic and Romanesque sculpture is equally copious in its description of the familiar circumstances of war and the chase. But in all the scenes portrayed by the workmen of these nations, vegetation occurs only as an explanatory accessary; the reed is introduced to mark the course of the river, or the tree to mark the covert of the wild beast, or the ambush of the enemy, but there is no especial interest

11. "Design is used in this place as expressive of the power to arrange lines and colours nobly. By facts I mean facts perceived by the eye and the mind, not facts accumulated by knowledge. . . ." (Ruskin)

in the forms of the vegetation strong enough to induce them to make it a subject of separate and accurate study. Again, among the nations who followed the arts of design exclusively, the forms of foliage introduced were meagre and general, and their real intricacy and life were neither admired nor expressed. But to the Gothic workman the living foliage became a subject of intense affection, and he struggled to render all its characters with as much accuracy as was compatible with the laws of his design and the nature of his material, not unfrequently tempted in his enthusiasm to transgress the one and disguise the other.

. . . In that careful distinction of species, and richness of delicate and undisturbed organisation, which characterise the Gothic design, there is the history of rural and thoughtful life, influenced by habitual tenderness, and devoted to subtle inquiry; and every discriminating and delicate touch of the chisel, as it rounds the petal or guides the branch, is a prophecy of the development of the entire body of the natural sciences, beginning with that of medicine, of the recovery of literature, and the establishment of the most necessary principles of domestic wisdom and national peace.

I have before alluded to the strange and vain supposition, that the original conception of Gothic architecture had been derived from vegetation,—from the symmetry of avenues, and the interlacing of branches. It is a supposition which never could have existed for a moment in the mind of any person acquainted with early Gothic; but, however idle as a theory, it is most valuable as a testimony to the character of the perfected style. It is precisely because the reverse of this theory is the fact, because the Gothic did not arise out of, but developed itself into, a resemblance to vegetation, that this resemblance is so instructive as an indication of the temper of the builders. It was no chance suggestion of the form of an arch from the bending of a bough, but a gradual and continual discovery of a beauty in natural forms which could be more and more perfectly transferred into those of stone, that influenced at once the heart of the people, and the form of the edifice. The Gothic architecture arose in massy and mountainous strength, axe-hewn, and iron-bound, block heaved upon block by the monk's enthusiasm and the soldier's force; and cramped and stanchioned into such weight of grisly wall, as might bury the anchoret in darkness, and beat back the utmost storm of battle, suffering but by the same narrow crosslet the passing of the sunbeam, or of the arrow. Gradually, as that monkish enthusiasm became more thoughtful, and as the sound of war became more and more intermittent beyond the gates of the convent or the keep, the stony pillar grew slender and the vaulted roof grew light, till they had wreathed themselves into the semblance of the summer woods at their fairest, and of the dead field-flowers, long trodden down in blood, sweet monumental statues were set to bloom for ever, beneath the porch of the temple, or the canopy of the tomb.

The fourth essential element of the Gothic mind was above stated to be the sense of the GROTESQUE; but I shall defer the endeavour to define this most curious and subtle character until we have occasion to examine one of the divisions of the Renaissance schools, which was morbidly influenced by it (Vol. III, Chap. III). It is the less necessary to insist upon it here, because every reader familiar with Gothic architecture must understand what I mean, and will, I believe, have no hesitation in admitting that the tendency to delight in fantastic and ludicrous, as well as in sublime, images, is a universal instinct of the Gothic imagination.

The fifth element above named was RIGIDITY; and this character I must endeavour carefully to define, for neither the word I have used, nor any other that I can think of, will express it accurately. For I mean, not merely stable, but *active* rigidity; the peculiar energy which gives tension to movement, and stiffness to resistance, which makes the fiercest lightning forked rather than curved, and the stoutest oak-branch angular rather than bending, and is as much seen in the quivering of the lance as in the glittering of the icicle.

I have before had occasion (Vol. I, Chapter XIII, § VII) to note some manifestations of this energy or fixedness; but it must be still more attentively considered here, as it shows itself throughout the whole structure and decoration of Gothic work. Egyptian and Greek buildings stand, for the most part, by their own weight and mass, one stone passively incumbent on another: but in the Gothic vaults and traceries there is a stiffness analogous to that of the bones of a limb, or fibres of a tree; an elastic tension and communication of force from part to part, and also a studious expression of this throughout every visible line of the building. And, in like manner, the Greek and Egyptian ornament is either mere surface engraving, as if the face of the wall had been stamped with a seal, or its lines are flowing, lithe, and luxuriant; in either case, there is no expression of energy in the framework of the ornament itself. But the Gothic ornament stands out in prickly independence, and frosty fortitude, jutting into crockets, and freezing into pinnacles; here starting up into a monster, there germinating into a blossom; anon knitting itself into a branch, alternately thorny, bossy, and bristly, or writhed into every form of nervous entanglement; but, even when most graceful, never for an instant languid, always quickset; erring, if at all, ever on the side of brusquerie.

The feelings or habits in the workman which give rise to this character in the work, are more complicated and various than those indicated by any other sculptural expression hitherto named. There is, first, the habit of hard and rapid working; the industry of the tribes of the North, quickened by the coldness of the climate, and giving an expression of sharp energy to all they do (as above noted, Vol. I, Chap. XIII, § VII), as opposed to the languor of the Southern tribes, however much of fire there may be in the heart of that languor, for lava itself may flow languidly. There is also the habit of finding enjoyment in the signs of cold, which is never found, I believe, in the inhabitants of countries south of the Alps. Cold is to them an unredeemed evil, to be suffered, and forgotten as soon as may be; but the long winter of the North forces the Goth (I mean the Englishman, Frenchman, Dane, or German), if he would lead a happy life at all, to find sources of happiness in foul weather as well as fair, and to rejoice in the leafless as well as in the shady forest. And this we do with all our hearts; finding perhaps nearly as much contentment by the Christmas fire as in the summer sunshine, and gaining health and strength on the ice-fields of winter, as well as among the meadows of spring. So that there is nothing adverse or painful to our feelings in the cramped and stiffened structure of vegetation checked by cold. . . .

There are many subtle sympathies and affections which join to confirm the Gothic mind in this peculiar choice of subject; and when we add to the influence of these, the necessities consequent upon the employment of a rougher material, compelling the workman to seek for vigour of effect, rather than refinement of texture or accuracy of form, we have direct and manifest causes for much of the difference between the Northern and Southern cast of conception: but there are indirect causes holding a far more important place in the Gothic heart, though less immediate in their influence on design. Strength of will, independence of character, resoluteness of purpose, impatience of undue control, and that general tendency to set the individual reason against authority, and the individual deed against destiny, which, in the Northern tribes, has opposed itself throughout all ages to the languid submission, in the Southern, of thought to tradition, and purpose to fatality, are all more or less traceable in the rigid lines, vigorous and various masses, and daringly projecting and independent structure of the Northern Gothic ornament: while the opposite feelings are in like manner legible in the graceful and softly guided waves and wreathed bands, in which Southern decoration is constantly disposed; in its tendency to lose its independence, and fuse itself into the surface of the masses upon which it is traced; and in the expression seen so often, in the arrangement of those masses themselves, of an abandonment of their strength to an inevitable necessity, or a listless repose.

There is virtue in the measure, and error in the excess, of both these characters of mind, and in both of the styles which they have created; the best architecture, and the best temper, are those which unite them both; and this fifth impulse of the Gothic heart is therefore that which needs most caution in its indulgence. It is more definitely Gothic than any other, but the best Gothic building is not that which is *most* Gothic: it can hardly be too frank in its confession of rudeness, hardly too rich in its changefulness, hardly too faithful in its naturalism; but it may go too far in its rigidity, and, like the great Puritan spirit in its extreme, lose itself either in frivolity of division, or perversity of purpose. It actually did so in its later times; but it is gladdening to remember that in its utmost nobleness, the very temper which has been thought most adverse to it, the Protestant spirit of self-dependence and inquiry, was expressed in its every line. Faith and aspiration there were, in every Christian ecclesiastical building, from the first century to the fifteenth; but the moral habits to which England in this age owes the kind of greatness that she has,—the habits of philosophical investigation, of accurate thought, of domestic seclusion and independence, of stern self-reliance, and sincere upright searching into religious truth,—were only traceable in the features which were the distinctive creation of the Gothic schools, in the veined foliage, and thorny fretwork, and shadowy niche, and buttressed pier, and fearless height of subtle pinnacle and crested tower, sent like an 'unperplexed question up to Heaven.' [12]

Last, because the least essential, of the constituent elements of this noble school, was placed that of REDUNDANCE,—the uncalculating bestowal of the wealth of its labour. There is, indeed, much Gothic, and that of the best period, in which this element is hardly traceable, and which depends for its

---

12. "See the beautiful description of Florence in Elizabeth Browning's *Casa Guidi Windows*, which is not only a noble poem, but the only book I have seen which, favouring the Liberal cause in Italy, gives a just account of the incapacities of the modern Italian." (Ruskin)

effect almost exclusively on loveliness of simple design and grace of uninvolved proportion: still, in the most characteristic buildings, a certain portion of their effect depends upon accumulation of ornament; and many of those which have most influence on the minds of men, have attained it by means of this attribute alone. And although, by careful study of the school, it is possible to arrive at a condition of taste which shall be better contented by a few perfect lines than by a whole façade covered with fretwork, the building which only satisfies such a taste is not to be considered the best. For the very first requirement of Gothic architecture being, as we saw above, that it shall both admit the aid, and appeal to the admiration, of the rudest as well as the most refined minds, the richness of the work is, paradoxical as the statement may appear, a part of its humility. No architecture is so haughty as that which is simple; which refuses to address the eye, except in a few clear and forceful lines; which implies, in offering so little to our regards, that all it has offered is perfect; and disdains, either by the complexity of the attractiveness of its features, to embarrass our investigation, or betray us into delight. That humility, which is the very life of the Gothic school, is shown not only in the imperfection, but in the accumulation, of ornament. The inferior rank of the workman is often shown as much in the richness, as the roughness, of his work; and if the co-operation of every hand, and the sympathy of every heart, are to be received, we must be content to allow the redundance which disguises the failure of the feeble, and wins the regard of the inattentive. There are, however, far nobler interests mingling, in the Gothic heart, with the rude love of decorative accumulation: a magnificent enthusiasm, which feels as if it never could do enough to reach the fulness of its ideal; an unselfishness of sacrifice, which would rather cast fruitless labour before the altar than stand idle in the market; [13] and, finally, a profound sympathy with the fulness and wealth of the material universe, rising out of that Naturalism whose operation we have already endeavoured to define. . . .

We have now, I believe, obtained a view approaching to completeness of the various moral or imaginative elements which composed the inner spirit of Gothic architecture. . . .

1852   1853

From Unto This Last [1]

The Roots of Honour

Among the delusions which at different periods have possessed themselves of the minds of large masses of the human race, perhaps the most curious— certainly the least creditable—is the modern *soi-disant* [2] science of political

13. Matthew 20:3.

1. The title derives from Jesus' parable of the vineyard, in which the workers who had been hired earliest, and had therefore worked most, protest because they are paid no more than those who had been hired latest and worked least. To them the master of the vineyard said: "Take that thine is, and go thy way: I will give unto this last, even as unto thee." Matthew 20:4.

2. Self-styled, so-called.

economy, based on the idea that an advantageous code of social action may be determined irrespectively of the influence of social affection.

Of course, as in the instances of alchemy, astrology, witchcraft, and other such popular creeds, political economy has a plausible idea at the root of it. 'The social affections,' says the economist, 'are accidental and disturbing elements in human nature; but avarice and the desire of progress are constant elements. Let us eliminate the inconstants, and, considering the human being merely as a covetous machine, examine by what laws of labour, purchase, and sale, the greatest accumulative result in wealth is attainable. Those laws once determined, it will be for each individual afterwards to introduce as much of the disturbing affectionate element as he chooses, and to determine for himself the result on the new conditions supposed.'

This would be a perfectly logical and successful method of analysis, if the accidentals afterwards to be introduced were of the same nature as the powers first examined. Supposing a body in motion to be influenced by constant and inconstant forces, it is usually the simplest way of examining its course to trace it first under the persistent conditions, and afterwards introduce the causes of variation. But the disturbing elements in the social problem are not of the same nature as the constant ones; they alter the essence of the creature under examination the moment they are added; they operate, not mathematically, but chemically. introducing conditions which render all our previous knowledge unavailable. We made learned experiments upon pure nitrogen, and have convinced ourselves that it is a very manageable gas: but behold! the thing which we have practically to deal with is its chloride; and this, the moment we touch it on our established principles, sends us and our apparatus through the ceiling.

Observe, I neither impugn nor doubt the conclusions of the science, if its terms are accepted. I am simply uninterested in them, as I should be in those of a science of gymnastics which assumed that men had no skeletons. It might be shown, on that supposition, that it would be advantageous to roll the students up into pellets, flatten them into cakes, or stretch them into cables; and that when these results were effected, the re-insertion of the skeleton would be attended with various inconveniences to their constitution. The reasoning might be admirable, the conclusions true, and the science deficient only in applicability. Modern political economy stands on a precisely similar basis. Assuming, not that the human being has no skeleton, but that it is all skeleton, it founds an ossifiant theory of progress on this negation of a soul; and having shown the utmost that may be made of bones, and constructed a number of interesting geometrical figures with death's-heads and humeri, successfully proves the inconvenience of the reappearance of a soul among these corpuscular structures. I do not deny the truth of this theory: I simply deny its applicability to the present phase of the world.

This inapplicability has been curiously manifested during the embarrassment caused by the late strikes of our workmen. Here occurs one of the simplest cases, in a pertinent and positive form, of the first vital problem which political economy has to deal with (the relation between employer and employed); and at a severe crisis, when lives in multitudes, and wealth in masses, are at stake, the political economists are helpless—practically mute; no demonstrable solution of the difficulty can be given by them, such as may convince or calm the opposing parties. Obstinately the masters take one view of the matter; obstinately the operatives another; and no political science can set them at one.

It would be strange if it could, it being not by 'science' of any kind that men were ever intended to be set at one. Disputant after disputant vainly strives to show that the interests of the masters are, or are not, antagonistic to those of the men: none of the pleaders ever seeming to remember that it does not absolutely or always follow that the persons must be antagonistic because their interests are. If there is only a crust of bread in the house, and mother and children are starving, their interests are not the same. If the mother eats it, the children want it; if the children eat it, the mother must go hungry to her work. Yet it does not necessarily follow that there will be 'antagonism' between them, that they will fight for the crust, and that the mother, being strongest, will get it, and eat it. Neither, in any other case, whatever the relations of the persons may be, can it be assumed for certain that, because their interests are diverse, they must necessarily regard each other with hostility, and use violence or cunning to obtain the advantage.

Even if this were so, and it were as just as it is convenient to consider men as actuated by no other moral influences than those which affect rats or swine, the logical conditions of the question are still indeterminable. It can never be shown generally either that the interests of master and labourer are alike, or that they are opposed; for, according to circumstances, they may be either. It is, indeed, always the interest of both that the work should be rightly done, and a just price obtained for it; but, in the division of profits, the gain of the one may or may not be the loss of the other. It is not the master's interest to pay wages so low as to leave the men sickly and depressed, nor the workman's interest to be paid high wages if the smallness of the master's profit hinders him from enlarging his business, or conducting it in a safe and liberal way. A stoker ought not to desire high pay if the company is too poor to keep the engine-wheels in repair.

And the varieties of circumstance which influence these reciprocal interests are so endless, that all endeavour to deduce rules of action from balance of expediency is in vain. And it is meant to be in vain. For no human actions ever were intended by the Maker of men to be guided by balances of expediency, but by balances of justice. He has therefore rendered all endeavours to determine expediency futile for evermore. No man ever knew, or can know, what will be the ultimate result to himself, or to others, of any given line of conduct. But every man may know, and most of us do know, what is a just and unjust act. And all of us may know also, that the consequences of justice will be ultimately the best possible, both to others and ourselves, though we can neither say what *is* best, nor how it is likely to come to pass.

I have said balances of justice, meaning, in the term justice, to include affection,—such affection as one man *owes* to another. All right relations between master and operative,[3] and all their best interests, ultimately depend on these.

We shall find the best and simplest illustration of the relations of master and operative in the position of domestic servants.[4]

3. An industrial worker.
4. It should be realized that virtually all of Ruskin's middle-class readers, even those of

We will suppose that the master of a household desires only to get as much work out of his servants as he can, at the rate of wages he gives. He never allows them to be idle; feeds them as poorly and lodges them as ill as they will endure, and in all things pushes his requirements to the exact point beyond which he cannot go without forcing the servant to leave him. In doing this, there is no violation on his part of what is commonly called 'justice.' He agrees with the domestic for his whole time and service, and takes them;—the limits of hardship in treatment being fixed by the practice of other masters in his neighbourhood; that is to say, by the current rate of wages for domestic labour. If the servant can get a better place, he is free to take one, and the master can only tell what is the real market value of his labour, by requiring as much as he will give.

This is the politico-economical view of the case, according to the doctors of that science; who assert that by this procedure the greatest average of work will be obtained from the servant, and therefore, the greatest benefit to the community, and through the community, by reversion, to the servant himself.

That, however, is not so. It would be so if the servant were an engine of which the motive power was steam, magnetism, gravitation, or any other agent of calculable force. But he being, on the contrary, an engine whose motive power is a Soul, the force of this very peculiar agent, as an unknown quantity, enters into all the political economist's equations, without his knowledge, and falsifies every one of their results. The largest quality of work will not be done by this curious engine for pay, or under pressure, or by help of any kind of fuel which may be supplied by the chaldron. It will be done only when the motive force, that is to say, the will or spirit of the creature, is brought to its greatest strength by its own proper fuel; namely, by the affections.

It may indeed happen, and does happen often, that if the master is a man of sense and energy, a large quantity of material work may be done under mechanical pressure, enforced by strong will and guided by wise method; also it may happen, and does happen often, that if the master is indolent and weak (however good-natured), a very small quantity of work, and that bad, may be produced by the servant's undirected strength, and contemptuous gratitude. But the universal law of the matter is that, assuming any given quantity of energy and sense in master and servant, the greatest material result obtainable by them will be, not through antagonism to each other, but through affection for each other; and that if the master, instead of endeavouring to get as much work as possible from the servant, seeks rather to render his appointed and necessary work beneficial to him, and to forward his interests in all just and wholesome ways, the real amount of work ultimately done, or good rendered, by the person so cared for, will indeed be the greatest possible.

Observe, I say, 'of good rendered,' for a servant's work is not necessarily or always the best thing he can give his master. But good of all kinds, whether in material service, in protective watchfulness of his master's interest and credit, or in joyful readiness to seize unexpected and irregular occasions of help.

---

quite modest means, would have had at least one domestic servant; a fairly affluent family might have three or four. The servants invariably lived in the house, generally in cramped quarters. The relations of servants to their employers—known always as "master" and "mistress"—was a matter of lively interest for humorists.

Nor is this one whit less generally true because indulgence will be frequently abused, and kindness met with ingratitude. For the servant who, gently treated, is ungrateful, treated ungently, will be revengeful; and the man who is dishonest to a liberal master will be injurious to an unjust one.

In any case, and with any person, this unselfish treatment will produce the most effective return. Observe, I am here considering the affections wholly as a motive power; not at all as things in themselves desirable or noble, or in any other way abstractedly good. I look at them simply as an anomalous force, rendering every one of the ordinary political economist's calculations nugatory; while, even if he desired to introduce this new element into his estimates, he has no power of dealing with it; for the affections only become a true motive power when they ignore every other motive and condition of political economy. Treat the servant kindly, with the idea of turning his gratitude to account, and you will get, as you deserve, no gratitude, nor any value for your kindness; but treat him kindly without any economical purpose, and all economical purposes will be answered; in this, as in all other matters, whosoever will save his life shall lose it, whoso loses it shall find it.[5]

The next clearest and simplest example of relation between master and operative is that which exists between the commander of a regiment and his men.

Supposing the officer only desires to apply the rules of discipline so as, with least trouble to himself, to make the regiment most effective, he will not be able, by any rules, or administration of rules, on this selfish principle, to develop the full strength of his subordinates. If a man of sense and firmness, he may, as in the former instance, produce a better result than would be obtained by the irregular kindness of a weak officer; but let the sense and firmness be the same in both cases, and assuredly the officer who has the most direct personal relations with his men, the most care for their interests, and the most value for their lives, will develop their effective strength, through their affection for

5. "The difference between the two modes of treatment, and between their effective material results, may be seen very accurately by a comparison of the relations of Esther and Charlie in *Bleak House,* with those of Miss Brass and the Marchioness in *Master Humphrey's Clock.*

"The essential value and truth of Dickens's writings have been unwisely lost sight of by many thoughtful persons, merely because he presents his truth with some colour of caricature. Unwisely, because Dickens's caricature, though often gross, is never mistaken. Allowing for his manner of telling them, the things he tells us are always true. I wish that he could think it right to limit his brilliant exaggeration to works written only for public amusement: and when he takes up a subject of high national importance, such as that which he handled in *Hard Times,* that he would use severer and more accurate analysis. The usefulness of that work (to my mind, in several respects, the greatest he has written) is with many persons seriously diminished because Mr. Bounderby is a dramatic monster, instead of a characteristic example of a worldly master; and Stephen Blackpool a dramatic perfection, instead of a characteristic example of an honest workman. But let us not lose the use of Dickens's wit and insight, because he chooses to speak in a circle of stage fire. He is entirely right in his main drift and purpose in every book he has written; and all of them, but especially *Hard Times,* should be studied with close and earnest care by persons interested in social questions. They will find much that is partial, and, because partial, apparently unjust; but if they examine all the evidence on the other side, which Dickens seems to overlook, it will appear, after all their trouble, that his view was the finally right one, grossly and sharply told." (Ruskin) his own person, and trust in his character, to a degree wholly unattainable by other means. The law applies still more stringently as the numbers concerned are larger; a charge may often be successful, though the men dislike their officers; a battle has rarely been won, unless they loved their general.

Passing from these simple examples to the more complicated relations existing between a manufacturer and his workmen, we are met first by certain curious difficulties, resulting, apparently, from a harder and colder state of moral elements. It is easy to imagine an enthusiastic affection existing among soldiers for the colonel. Not so easy to imagine an enthusiastic affection among cotton-spinners for the proprietor of the mill. A body of men associated for purposes of robbery (as a Highland clan in ancient times) shall be animated by perfect affection, and every member of it be ready to lay down his life for the life of his chief.[6] But a band of men associated for purposes of legal production and accumulation is usually animated, it appears, by no such emotions, and none of them are in anywise willing to give his life for the life of his chief. Not only are we met by this apparent anomaly, in moral matters, but by others connected with it, in administration of system. For a servant or a soldier is engaged at a definite rate of wages, for a definite period; but a workman at a rate of wages variable according to the demand for labour, and with the risk of being at any time thrown out of his situation by chances of trade. Now, as, under these contingencies, no action of the affections can take place, but only an explosive action of *dis*affections, two points offer themselves for consideration in the matter.

The first—How far the rate of wages may be so regulated as not to vary with the demand for labour.

The second—How far it is possible that bodies of workmen may be engaged and maintained at such fixed rate of wages (whatever the state of trade may be), without enlarging or diminishing their number, so as to give them permanent interest in the establishment with which they are connected, like that of the domestic servants in an old family, or an *esprit de corps*, like that of the soldiers in a crack regiment.

The first question is, I say, how far it may be possible to fix the rate of wages irrespectively of the demand for labour.

Perhaps one of the most curious facts in the history of human error is the denial by the common political economist of the possibility of thus regulating wages; while, for all the important, and much of the unimportant, labour on the earth, wages are already so regulated.

We do not sell our prime-ministership by Dutch auction; [7] nor, on the decease of a bishop, whatever may be the general advantages of simony [8] do we (yet) offer his diocese to the clergyman who will take the episcopacy at the lowest contract. We (with exquisite sagacity of political economy!) do indeed

6. Ruskin could count on his audience's familiarity with an affecting instance of such loyalty in Sir Walter Scott's widely read first novel, *Waverley* (1814).
7. An auction in which the property is offered at a high price, then at gradually lowered prices until someone buys it.
8. The buying or selling of ecclesiastical offices.

sell commissions, but not openly, generalships: [9] sic, we do not inquire for a physician who takes less than a guinea; litigious,[10] we never think of reducing six-and-eightpence to four-and-sixpence; caught in a shower, we do not canvass the cabmen, to find one who values his driving at less than sixpence a mile.

It is true that in all these cases there is, and in every conceivable case there must be, ultimate reference to the presumed difficulty of the work, or number of candidates for the office. If it were thought that the labour necessary to make a good physician would be gone through by a sufficient number of students with the prospect of only half-guinea fees, public consent would soon withdraw the unnecessary half-guinea. In this ultimate sense, the price of labour is indeed always regulated by the demand for it; but so far as the practical and immediate administration of the matter is regarded, the best labour always has been, and is, as *all* labour ought to be, paid by an invariable standard.

'What!' the reader, perhaps, answers amazedly: 'pay good and bad workmen alike?'

Certainly. The difference between one prelate's sermons and his successor's,— or between one physician's opinion and another's,—is far greater, as respects the qualities of mind involved, and far more important in result to you personally, than the difference between good and bad laying of bricks (though that is greater than most people suppose). Yet you pay with equal fee, contentedly, the good and bad workmen upon your soul, and the good and bad workmen upon your body; much more may you pay, contentedly, with equal fees, the good and bad workmen upon your house.

'Nay, but I choose my physician and (?) my clergyman, thus indicating my sense of the quality of their work.' By all means, also, choose your brick-layer; that is the proper reward of the good workman, to be 'chosen.' The natural and right system respecting all labour is, that it should be paid at a fixed rate, but the good workman employed, and the bad workman unemployed. The false, unnatural, and destructive system is when the bad workman is allowed to offer his work at half-price, and either take the place of the good, or force him by his competition to work for an inadequate sum.

This equality of wages, then, being the first object towards which we have to discover the directest available road; the second is, as above stated, that of maintaining constant numbers of workmen in employment, whatever may be the accidental demand for the article they produce.

I believe the sudden and extensive inequalities of demand which necessarily arise in the mercantile operations of an active nation, constitute the only essential difficulty which has to be overcome in a just organization of labour. The subject opens into too many branches to admit of being investigated in a paper of this kind; but the following general facts bearing on it may be noted.

The wages which enable any workman to live are necessarily higher, if his work is liable to intermission, than if it is assured and continuous; and however severe the struggle for work may become, the general law will always hold,

9. It was not until 1871 that the old (and entirely legal) practice of buying and selling army commissions was abolished; however, generalships, as Ruskin indicates, could be secured only by promotion.
10. When we have it in mind to go to law against someone.

that men must get more daily pay if, on the average, they can only calculate on work three days a week, than they would require if they were sure of work six days a week. Supposing that a man cannot live on less than a shilling a day, his seven shillings he must get, either for three days' violent work, or six days' deliberate work. The tendency of all modern mercantile operations is to throw both wages and trade into the form of a lottery, and to make the workman's pay depend on intermittent exertion, and the principal's profit on dexterously used chance.

In what partial degree, I repeat, this may be necessary, in consequence of the activities of modern trade, I do not here investigate; contenting myself with the fact, that in its fatallest aspects it is assuredly unnecessary, and results merely from love of gambling on the part of the masters, and from ignorance and sensuality in the men. The masters cannot bear to let any opportunity of gain escape them, and frantically rush at every gap and breach in the walls of Fortune, raging to be rich, and affronting, with impatient covetousness, every risk of ruin; while the men prefer three days of violent labour, and three days of drunkenness, to six days of moderate work and wise rest. There is no way in which a principal, who really desires to help his workmen, may do it more effectually than by checking these disorderly habits both in himself and them; keeping his own business operations on a scale which will enable him to pursue them securely, not yielding to temptations of precarious gain; and, at the same time, leading his workmen into regular habits of labour and life, either by inducing them rather to take low wages in the form of a fixed salary, than high wages, subject to the chance of their being thrown out of work; or, if this be impossible, by discouraging the system of violent exertion for nominally high day wages, and leading the men to take lower pay for more regular labour.

In effecting any radical changes of this kind, doubtless there would be great inconvenience and loss incurred by all the originators of movement. That which can be done with perfect convenience and without loss, is not always the thing that most needs to be done, or which we are most imperatively required to do.

I have already alluded to the difference hitherto existing between regiments of men associated for purposes of violence, and for purposes of manufacture; in that the former appear capable of self-sacrifice—the latter, not; which singular fact is the real reason of the general lowness of estimate in which the profession of commerce is held, as compared with that of arms. Philosophically, it does not, at first sight, appear reasonable (many writers have endeavoured to prove it unreasonable) that a peaceable and rational person, whose trade is buying and selling, should be held in less honour than an unpeaceable and often irrational person, whose trade is slaying. Nevertheless, the consent of mankind has always, in spite of the philosophers, given precedence to the soldier.

And this is right.

For the soldier's trade, verily and essentially, is not slaying, but being slain. This, without well knowing its own meaning, the world honours it for. A bravo's trade is slaying; but the world has never respected bravos more than merchants: the reason it honours the soldier is, because he holds his life at the service of the State. Reckless he may be—fond of pleasure or of adventure—

all kinds of bye-motives and mean impulses may have determined the choice of his profession, and may affect (to all appearance exclusively) his daily conduct in it; but our estimate of him is based on this ultimate fact—of which we are well assured—that, put him in a fortress breach, with all the pleasures of the world behind him, and only death and his duty in front of him, he will keep his face to the front; and he knows that this choice may be put to him at any moment, and has beforehand taken his part—virtually takes such part continually—does, in reality, die daily.

Not less is the respect we pay to the lawyer and physician, founded ultimately on their self-sacrifice. Whatever the learning or acuteness of a great lawyer, our chief respect for him depends on our belief that, set in a judge's seat, he will strive to judge justly, come of it what may. Could we suppose that he would take bribes, and use his acuteness and legal knowledge to give plausibility to iniquitous decisions, no degree of intellect would win for him our respect. Nothing will win it, short of our tacit conviction, that in all important acts of his life justice is first with him; his own interest, second.

In the case of a physician, the ground of the honour we render him is clearer still. Whatever his science, we should shrink from him in horror if we found him regard his patients merely as subjects to experiment upon; much more, if we found that, receiving bribes from persons interested in their deaths, he was using his best skill to give poison in the mask of medicine.

Finally, the principle holds with utmost clearness as it respects clergymen. No goodness of disposition will excuse want of science in a physician or of shrewdness in an advocate; but a clergyman, even though his power of intellect be small, is respected on the presumed ground of his unselfishness and serviceableness.

Now there can be no question but that the tact, foresight, decision, and other mental powers, required for the successful management of a large mercantile concern, if not such as could be compared with those of a great lawyer, general, or divine, would at least match the general conditions of mind required in the subordinate officers of a ship, or of a regiment, or in the curate of a country parish. If, therefore, all the efficient members of the so-called liberal professions are still, somehow, in public estimate of honour, preferred before the head of a commercial firm, the reason must lie deeper than in the measurement of their several powers of mind.

And the essential reason for such preference will be found to lie in the fact that the merchant is presumed to act always selfishly. His work may be very necessary to the community; but the motive of it is understood to be wholly personal. The merchant's first object in all his dealings must be (the public believe) to get as much for himself, and leave as little to his neighbour (or customer) as possible. Enforcing this upon him, by political statute, as the necessary principle of his action; recommending it to him on all occasions, and themselves reciprocally adopting it; proclaiming vociferously, for law of the universe, that a buyer's function is to cheapen, and a seller's to cheat,—the public, nevertheless, involuntarily condemn the man of commerce for his compliance wtih their own statement, and stamp him for ever as belonging to an inferior grade of human personality.

This they will find, eventually, they must give up doing. They must not cease to condemn selfishness; but they will have to discover a kind of commerce which is not exclusively selfish. Or, rather, they will have to discover that there never was, or can be, any other kind of commerce; that this which they have called commerce was not commerce at all, but cozening; and that a true merchant differs as much from a merchant according to laws of modern political economy, as the hero of the *Excursion* from Autolycus.[11] They will find that commerce is an occupation which gentlemen will every day see more need to engage in, rather than in the businesses of talking to men, or slaying them: that, in true commerce, as in true preaching, or true fighting, it is necessary to admit the idea of occasional voluntary loss;—that sixpences have to be lost, as well as lives, under a sense of duty; that the market may have its martyrdoms as well as the pulpit; and trade its heroisms, as well as war.

May have—in the final issue, must have—and only has not had yet, because men of heroic temper have always been misguided in their youth into other fields, not recognizing what is in our days, perhaps, the most important of all fields; so that, while many a zealous person loses his life in trying to teach the form of a gospel, very few will lose a hundred pounds in showing the practice of one.

The fact is, that people never have had clearly explained to them the true functions of a merchant with respect to other people. I should like the reader to be very clear about this.

Five great intellectual professions, relating to daily necessities of life, have hitherto existed—three exist necessarily, in every civilized nation:

The Soldier's profession is to *defend* it.

The Pastor's, to *teach* it.

The Physician's, to *keep it in health*.

The Lawyer's, to *enforce justice* in it.

The Merchant's, to *provide* for it.

And the duty of all these men is, on due occasion, to *die* for it.

'On due occasion,' namely:—

The Soldier, rather than leave his post in battle.

The Physician, rather than leave his post in plague.

The Pastor, rather than teach Falsehood.

The Lawyer, rather than countenance Injustice.

The Merchant—What is *his* 'due occasion' of death?

It is the main question for the merchant, as for all of us. For, truly, the man who does not know when to die, does not know how to live.

Observe, the merchant's function (or manufacturer's, for in the broad sense in which it is here used the word must be understood to include both) is to provide for the nation. It is no more his function to get profit for himself out of that provision than it is a clergyman's function to get his stipend. The stipend is a due and necessary adjunct, but not the object, of his life, if he be a true clergyman, any more than his fee (or *honorarium*) is the object of life to a true physician. Neither is his fee the object of life to a true merchant. All three, if true men, have a work to be done irrespective of fee—to be done even at

11. The former, in Wordsworth's poem, is a peddler of the highest probity and benevolence; the latter, in Shakespeare's *The Winter's Tale,* is a peddler who prefers pilfering to selling.

any cost, or for quite the contrary of fee; the pastor's function being to teach, the physician's to heal, and the merchant's, as I have said, to provide. That is to say, he has to understand to their very root the qualities of the thing he deals in, and the means of obtaining or producing it; and he has to apply all his sagacity and energy to the producing or obtaining it in perfect state, and distributing it at the cheapest possible price where it is most needed.

And because the production or obtaining of any commodity involves necessarily the agency of many lives and hands, the merchant becomes in the course of his business the master and governor of large masses of men in a more direct, though less confessed way, than a military officer or pastor; so that on him falls, in great part, the responsibility for the kind of life they lead: and it becomes his duty, not only to be always considering how to produce what he sells in the purest and cheapest forms, but how to make the various employments involved in the production, or transference of it, most beneficial to the men employed.

And as into these two functions, requiring for their right exercise the highest intelligence, as well as patience, kindness, and tact, the merchant is bound to put all his energy, so for their just discharge he is bound, as soldier or physician is bound, to give up, if need be, his life, in such way as it may be demanded of him. Two main points he has in his providing function to maintain: first, his engagements (faithfulness to engagements being the real root of all possibilities in commerce); and, secondly, the perfectness and purity of the thing provided; so that, rather than fail in any engagement, or consent to any deterioration, adulteration, or unjust and exorbitant price of that which he provides, he is bound to meet fearlessly any form of distress, poverty, or labour, which may, through maintenance of these points, come upon him.

Again: in his office as governor of the men employed by him, the merchant or manufacturer is invested with a distinctly paternal authority and responsibility. In most cases, a youth entering a commercial establishment is withdrawn altogether from home influence; his master must become his father, else he has, for practical and constant help, no father at hand: in all cases the master's authority, together with the general tone and atmosphere of his business, and the character of the men with whom the youth is compelled in the course of it to associate, have more immediate and pressing weight than the home influence, and will usually neutralize it either for good or evil; so that the only means which the master has of doing justice to the men employed by him is to ask himself sternly whether he is dealing with such subordinate as he would with his own son, if compelled by circumstances to take such a position.

Supposing the captain of a frigate saw it right, or were by any chance obliged, to place his own son in the position of a common sailor; as he would then treat his son, he is bound always to treat every one of the men under him. So, also, supposing the master of a manufactory saw it right, or were by any chance obliged, to place his own son in the position of an ordinary workman; as he would then treat his son, he is bound always to treat every one of his men. This is the only effective, true, or practical RULE which can be given on this point of political economy.

And as the captain of a ship is bound to be the last man to leave his ship in case of wreck, and to share his last crust with the sailors in case of famine, so the manufacturer, in any commercial crisis or distress, is bound to take the suffering of it with his men, and even to take more of it for himself than he allows his men to feel; as a father would in a famine, shipwreck, or battle, sacrifice himself for his son.

All which sounds very strange: the only real strangeness in the matter being, nevertheless, that it should so sound. For all this is true, and that not partially nor theoretically, but everlastingly and practically: all other doctrine than this respecting matters political being false in premises, absurd in deduction, and impossible in practice, consistently with any progressive state of national life; all the life which we now possess as a nation showing itself in the resolute denial and scorn, by a few strong minds and faithful hearts, of the economic principles taught to our multitudes, which principles, so far as accepted, lead straight to national destruction. Respecting the modes and forms of destruction to which they lead, and, on the other hand, respecting the farther practical working of true polity, I hope to reason further in a following paper.

1860   1860

MATTHEW ARNOLD
1822–1888

Matthew Arnold's life in literature falls into two parts, the division being marked by the Preface to the *Poems* of 1853 (see below). It cannot quite be said that this striking essay signalizes the end of Arnold's career as a poet; some of the poems he was still to write are among his most memorable. But after 1853 it is as a critic rather than as a poet that Arnold stands before the world.

It may be thought an open question whether, if Arnold had written nothing but poetry, he would be as well established a poet as in fact he is, at least in literary history, if not in the highest esteem of strict criticism. He was never accounted a great poet, yet his poems had in his own day, and for a considerable time thereafter, an appeal which was disproportionate to their aesthetic success. They spoke with a personal immediacy to a small, influential class of persons who were conscious of the peculiar pathos of modern existence, and perhaps they seemed the more immediate because they were less fully achieved as works of art than they might have been. In a later day, when cultural melancholy has come to seem an archaic emotion and when aesthetic judgment has become more exigent, the claims that can be made for Arnold's poetry probably cannot be large, and sometimes—not always—it seems fair to say that Arnold is not essentially a poet at all, not *naturally* a poet, as, say, Keats and Shelley and Tennyson are naturally poets even when they are at their least impressive. Yet his poems are never less than memorable; they command attention and respect—and, often, affection—as the record of what was felt about the modern world by the man who became Matthew Arnold the critic, who, putting aside the pathos of nostalgia and self-pity which make the essence of his poems, addressed himself to the modern world with an energy that still communicates itself.

The Preface to the *Poems* of 1853 is, we might say, a manifesto against nostalgia and self-pity. It is commonly characterized as anti-Romantic, a belated rearguard skirmish in defense of classicism. The description is accurate but academic. Despite appearances to the contrary, Arnold is really as little interested in a theory of literature called classicism as was Aristotle, to whose *Poetics* he resorted for the informing idea of the Preface. Like Aristotle, his interest in what literature should be is controlled by his conception of what a man should be, not only in himself, for the sake of his own well-being as an individual, but also in relation to the polity, in order to function properly as a citizen. Aristotle's theory of tragedy proposes the idea that tragedy, if it is successful, has a salutary, even a therapeutic, effect: it rids the mind of two oppressive and incapacitating emotions, pity and terror, and establishes the condition in which the mind may perceive and decide as it ideally should. It is not pity and terror that Arnold identifies as the impediments to the health and right conduct of the mind but, rather, doubt—the mind's sense of being divided within itself and of engaging in a dialogue with itself that comes to no resolution in decision and action. The Preface undertakes to explain why Arnold, in collecting into one volume the poems of his two earlier volumes, *The Strayed Reveller, and Other Poems* (1849) and *Empedocles on Etna, and Other Poems* (1852), was omitting the long title poem of the second. The poem had as its protagonist the ancient Greek philosopher who, according to legend, ended his life by flinging himself into the crater of the volcano. The greater part of the poem consists of Empedocles' rehearsal of the reasons, both metaphysical and political, why his life has come to seem of no worth to him and best brought to its end. Such a poem, Arnold says, does not give the reader the kind of joy which it is the function of art to give and which tragedy—it is one of the riddles of the human heart that this is so—does pre-eminently give. The poem fails to give joy not because it represents a sad or painful situation but because it represents a situation in which "a continuous state of mental distress is prolonged, unrelieved by incident, hope, or resistance; in which there is everything to be endured, nothing to be done." It can serve only to enervate, immobilize, and depress the spirits of the reader. At a later time Arnold restored *Empedocles on Etna* to the canon of his work, but at this time it was his belief that it should be sacrificed for, we may say, the good of the polity.

Arnold's commitment to a career in criticism was confirmed by his election to the Professorship of Poetry at Oxford in 1857. He was the first layman to occupy the chair and the first to lecture in English rather than in Latin. At the end of the five-year term he was re-elected. This was a considerable honor but it did not bring Arnold into the quiet and presumed detachment of university life. Although the Oxford Professor of Poetry is obliged to give public lectures, he does not instruct or supervise students and is not required to be in residence except intermittently; during his incumbency of the professorship Arnold continued in his duties as an inspector of elementary schools. This post, to which he had been appointed in 1849, was an onerous one, entailing much travel in uncomfortable trains, sojourns in gloomy hotels, interviewing principals and teachers, examining pupils, reading their papers far into the night, dealing with committees, thinking about the purposes of that strange new enterprise, the education of the population at large, and the means by which this was best to be achieved. Among the great writers of the Victorian Age, Arnold's experience of the modern world was unique in its immediacy and abrasiveness. We may suppose that it had a decisive part in shaping the chief preoccupation of his criticism, which was the definition of the quality of mind best able to take action to cope with the difficulties of modern life.

It was to this concern that Arnold addressed himself in his inaugural lecture at

Oxford, *On the Modern Element in Literature* (published in 1869). As in the 1853 Preface, his emphasis falls on the *effect* that literature produces. To be called great, he says, a work of literature must be both "adequate" and "fortifying." The adequacy of a work is its intellectual wholeness and cogency, its power of making the world accessible to comprehension; the fortifying quality of a work is its power of giving to the reader the energy and courage needed to confront the asperities and confusions of the modern world. In his lectures *On Translating Homer* (1861) he identifies the defining traits of Homer's style as being *rapidity, plainness,* and *directness*—of diction and syntax and also of thought—and *nobility,* and it is manifest that in thus characterizing Homer's style he is adumbrating the qualities he wished to see established in English life. This exposition of the "grand style" Homer exemplifies proposes implicitly the possibility that the national character might come to be marked by the "grand style"—Homer serves as a criterion by which Arnold makes his judgment of the class that increasingly determined the quality of the English rational life, the middle class; it was a class he was later to characterize as being "drugged with business," small in its aims, petty in its conception of the world.

In 1859 Arnold began to be involved with popular education at a higher level than formerly; he was charged with the investigation of the schools of France, and later of Germany, Switzerland, and Italy, and he set forth his findings in reports and essays which had considerable influence on the shaping of national policy, although his views of what constitutes a truly democratic system of education went well beyond what the government was prepared to put into effect. In 1865 he published his epoch-making volume *Essays in Criticism.*

No sooner has the epithet been used than it seems a strange one—*Essays in Criticism* does not have the look and feel of an epoch-making book. The essays that make up the volume had all appeared previously in periodicals and several had been lectures given by Arnold at Oxford. Their subjects are not related to each other in any obvious sense, and at least some of them must seem of only marginal inherent importance. And the tone of the essays, though certainly serious, is not momentous; as compared with the tone of Carlyle's or Ruskin's, it is curiously modest. It manifestly does not seek to dominate the reader but, rather, to put him at ease so that he may the more readily perceive for himself the ideational object that is being presented to him. The title of the volume is in accord with its time; it now seems commonplace enough but Arnold chose it with care: these are *essays,* "in the old sense of the word *Essay,*" that is to say, they are attempts, specimens; they are essays *in* criticism, by which Arnold meant to put emphasis on the idea of criticism as a procedure rather than as what the etymology of the word proposes, the passing of judgment. It is the process which makes right judgment possible—criticism is the effort "to see the object as in itself it really is."

If we seek the explanation of the pre-eminence of Arnold's criticism and why he is often described as virtually the founding father of modern criticism in the English-speaking world, one decisive factor is the tone of his critical writing, its representation of criticism as a procedure by which accurate perception is to be gained and in which the reader is invited to take part, on, as it were, equal terms with the critic. Coleridge may be thought a greater critic than Arnold in the sense of being more intellectually ambitious and more complex, comprehensive, and systematic, and the perceptivity of two of Arnold's contemporaries, Carlyle and Ruskin, especially the latter, is of the highest order, yet it is Arnold who naturalized criticism as a modern intellectual mode and institutionalized it by defining its function and thus, by implication, its ideal operation as well.

Another reason for Arnold's special eminence in criticism is the extent to which his conception of the critical enterprise goes beyond specifically literary criticism. On a first reading of *The Function of Criticism at the Present Time* the question might well arise whether Arnold has any concern at all with literary criticism, for everything he says about criticism has reference to the part it might play in the practical world. But it is exactly through his conception of the possible range of the critical enterprise that Arnold brought literary criticism to its present high status in the intellectual life.

If Arnold's conception of criticism puts its first emphasis upon the procedure through which accuracy of perception is achieved, it by no means suggests that judgment is not of its essence. In another defining statement Arnold says that criticism is "a disinterested endeavour to learn and propagate the best that is known and thought in the world."

The word "disinterested" requires comment. One of the misfortunes that has overtaken the English language in our time is that this word is commonly interchanged with "uninterested." Traditionally the words have very different meanings. To be "uninterested" means that one's attention is not engaged by the matter at hand, that one is indifferent, unconcerned. To be "disinterested" means that one has nothing personally to gain from the matter at hand, that one deals with it in an impartial, unbiased, and unselfish way. Careful writers still distinguish between the two words. If they say of a judge that he is uninterested in the case before him, they mean to impute blame; if they say that he has ruled in the case in a disinterested way, they intend praise.

At a time when the latent conflict of class interests had become manifest and threatened to grow in intensity, Arnold entertained the hope, perhaps doomed to be a forlorn one, that from the critical spirit, of which disinterestedness is an essential quality, there might derive not only an ideal of disinterestedness in political life but also a principle by which that ideal could be made practicable. The last of his Oxford lectures was to be the first chapter of *Culture and Anarchy*, the work in which he sought to discover this principle. (When it was given as a lecture in June 1867, it was called *Culture and Its Enemies* and this was its title as a chapter in the first edition of the book [1869]; in the second edition [1875] it was called *Sweetness and Light*.)

The "anarchy" which Arnold had in mind was of no extreme kind. In the agitation that preceded the passing of the Reform Bill of 1867, which gave the suffrage to the urban working class, there had indeed been public disorders, and Arnold remarks upon them at length. But he did not envisage anything like the breakdown of all political authority in England; by anarchy he meant the absence of any cohering principle of political life by which not merely social peace but grace of life might be attained. The principle by which anarchy is to be overcome he calls "culture."

The sense in which Arnold uses this word is peculiar to him. He does not use it, as anthropologists and sociologists later came to do, to refer to the totality of a society's institutions, beliefs, arts, and modes of behavior. Nor does he use it in the more restricted sense in which it signifies the general intellectual and artistic activity of a society. Arnold's "culture" is to be understood as an elaboration of his conception of criticism—it is the ideal response to the fact that the world in modern times is moved by ideas to an extent never known before and that the welfare of humanity and of any particular nation depends upon bringing the power of intelligence, of imaginative reason, to bear upon social and political life.

In his exploration of how this is to be done and of what stands in the way of its being done, Arnold identifies two opposing dispositions of the human mind, to which he gives the names "Hebraism" and "Hellenism." Hebraism is the disposition to religious faith and to strictness of conscience, to the single-minded conception of what is true and righteous, and to the determination to make it prevail. Hellenism is the disposition to intelligence, to setting store by ideas, to the flexibility of mind that permits the testing of ideas and the withdrawal from them should they not meet the test. In themselves, Arnold says, the two dispositions are equally necessary to human development. What at any given historical moment make the predominance of one preferable to that of the other are the circumstances which at that time prevail. For the present situation of England, Arnold feels that it is not Hebraism that is needed—of Hebraism there is more than enough: the sincere but narrow religious and moral feeling of the middle class, in direct line of descent from the Puritan revolution of the seventeenth century, is the dominant tone of English life. What is needed is the free play of mind which is characteristic of Hellenism. The activity of imaginative reason, based upon "the best that has been known and thought in the world," and having its own kind of religious and moral intention, that of making "reason and the will of God prevail," is what Arnold means by culture.

It is to the Hellenic openness and flexibility of mind which culture fosters that Arnold looks for the acceptance of the idea of the state, which alone, he believes, can hold out to English political life the hope of coherence and peace. To this idea, Arnold says, the middle class is sure to respond with the antagonism of an old and settled conviction, understandably so, because in its rise to its present power it had to overcome the restrictions put upon both its economic enterprise and its liberty of conscience by the state as it was constituted in former times. But culture envisages a state which of its nature cannot oppress or discriminate against any class; while representing all the classes, the newly enfranchised working class as well as the middle class and the aristocracy, it will be above all classes and thus able to deal with each in a disinterested way. Nothing could be easier, surely, than to object that in a society in which classes are defined by their relative economic advantages the state will not be—cannot be—disinterested in an absolute way. Yet in this century the English state has of course become substantially what Arnold wished it would be. Even when all the still existing class antagonisms and acrimonies have been taken into account, it must be said that England has achieved a far firmer national unity than might ever have been thought possible from an inspection of its class structure.

Arnold's poetry still makes its appeal. His criticism is still central in the tradition, its position there attested to if only by the frequency with which its particular judgments are disputed a century after they were made. His political writings still are pertinent. But the religious writings to which he chiefly gave himself between 1870 and 1877 no longer command attention. The issue to which they address themselves has ceased to be a vital one. These works—they include St. Paul and Protestantism (1870), Literature and Dogma (1873), and God and the Bible (1875)—were written out of Arnold's residual but still positive feeling for religion. When Arnold said of culture that it had for its function the task of making "reason and the will of God prevail," he was not lightly using a pious phrase. He did believe in God, although not in a way that an average religious countryman of his would have understood. The purpose of his writings about religion was to purge religious belief of its traditional supernaturalism and the intellectual constructs that were based upon it, which must eventually distress a modern mind and alienate it from religion itself. In Arnold's view, the essence of religion was simply a faith in the moral order of the universe; about that order no specific predications could be made. Religion was to be defined as "morality touched with emotion"; God was to be no more precisely conceived than as "the power not ourselves that makes for righteousness"; the Bible was to be read as "literature" rather than as "dogma"—literature of the most moving kind, still communicating, in concepts and language not ours but nevertheless to be readily understood and deeply felt if properly read, the truths of the moral life. In their own day Arnold's religious writings were widely popular among educated people who rejected much in traditional religion but who yet were reluctant to abandon all faith; with the disappearance of the situation that brought them into being, their interest is to be found only in the often brilliant imaginative sympathy with which Arnold speaks of the religious modes of the past.

Arnold's mature life was a quiet one and perhaps it is to be called happy, although it was touched by the deep sadness of the death of three of his sons. One of the engaging aspects of his temperament is that, although he felt and spoke of the tragic seriousness of life and the necessity of meeting it with fortitude and dutifulness, he loved gaiety and indeed believed that there was no surer sign of the health both of persons and societies. In 1883 he went on an extended lecture tour of America and made a second visit in 1886; in the same year he resigned his post as inspector of schools. He died suddenly of heart failure in 1888.

From First Edition of *Poems*

Preface

In two small volumes of Poems, published anonymously, one in 1849, the other in 1852,[1] many of the poems which compose the present volume have already appeared. The rest are now published for the first time.

I have, in the present collection, omitted the poem from which the volume published in 1852 took its title.[2] I have done so, not because the subject of it was a Sicilian Greek born between two and three thousand years ago, although many persons would think this a sufficient reason. Neither have I done so because I had, in my own opinion, failed in the delineation which I intended to effect. I intended to delineate the feelings of one of the last of the Greek religious philosophers, one of the family of Orpheus and Musæus,[3] having

---

1. *The Strayed Reveller, and Other Poems* and *Empedocles on Etna, and Other Poems.* On their title pages the only indication of authorship was "By A."

2. Empedocles (*c*.493–*c*.433 B.C.), Sicilian philosopher, scientist, poet, orator, statesman, and miracle worker.

3. Mythic singers, whose music had supernatural power. Of the two, Orpheus is the more clearly defined in legend; the poems attributed to him were the basis of the religious cult of Orphism.

survived his fellows, living on into a time when the habits of Greek thought and feeling had begun fast to change, character to dwindle, the influence of the Sophists [4] to prevail. Into the feelings of a man so situated there entered much that we are accustomed to consider as exclusively modern; how much, the fragments of Empedocles himself which remain to us are sufficient at least to indicate. What those who are familiar only with the great monuments of early Greek genius suppose to be its exclusive characteristics, have disappeared: the calm, the cheerfulness, the disinterested objectivity have disappeared; the dialogue of the mind with itself has commenced; modern problems have presented themselves; we hear already the doubts, we witness the discouragement, of Hamlet and of Faust.

The representation of such a man's feelings must be interesting, if consistently drawn. We all naturally take pleasure, says Aristotle, in any imitation or representation whatever: [5] this is the basis of our love of poetry; and we take pleasure in them, he adds, because all knowledge is naturally agreeable to us; not to the philosopher only, but to mankind at large. Every representation, therefore, which is consistently drawn may be supposed to be interesting, inasmuch as it gratifies this natural interest in knowledge of all kinds. What is *not* interesting, is that which does not add to our knowledge of any kind; that which is vaguely conceived and loosely drawn; a representation which is general, indeterminate, and faint, instead of being particular, precise, and firm.

Any accurate representation may therefore be expected to be interesting; but, if the representation be a poetical one, more than this is demanded. It is demanded, not only that it shall interest, but also that it shall inspirit and rejoice the reader; that it shall convey a charm, and infuse delight. For the Muses, as Hesiod [6] says, were born that they might be 'a forgetfulness of evils, and a truce from cares': and it is not enough that the poet should add to the knowledge of men, it is required of him also that he should add to their happiness. 'All art,' says Schiller, 'is dedicated to Joy, and there is no higher and no more serious problem, than how to make men happy. The right art is that alone, which creates the highest enjoyment.' [7]

A poetical work, therefore, is not yet justified when it has been shown to be an accurate, and therefore interesting representation; it has to be shown also that it is a representation from which men can derive enjoyment. In presence of the most tragic circumstances, represented in a work of art, the feeling of enjoyment, as is well known, may still subsist; the representation of the most utter calamity, of the liveliest anguish, is not sufficient to destroy it; the more tragic the situation, the deeper becomes the enjoyment; and the situation is more tragic in proportion as it becomes more terrible.

What then are the situations, from the representation of which, though accurate, no poetical enjoyment can be derived? They are those in which the

4. Literally "wise men," but the term came to be used pejoratively of professional teachers who instructed in one or another intellectual discipline not for its own sake but as a means of getting on in life.
5. In the *Poetics* I, II, IV, VII, XIV.
6. *Theogony* (Genealogy of the Gods) 52–56. Hesiod lived in the 8th century B.C.
7. Friedrich Schiller (1759–1805) in his preface to *The Bride of Messina* (1803), which discusses the use of the chorus in tragedy.

suffering finds no vent in action; in which a continuous state of mental distress is prolonged, unrelieved by incident, hope, or resistance; in which there is everything to be endured, nothing to be done. In such situations there is inevitably something morbid, in the description of them something monotonous. When they occur in actual life, they are painful, not tragic; the representation of them in poetry is painful also.

To this class of situations, poetically faulty as it appears to me, that of Empedocles, as I have endeavoured to represent him, belongs; and I have therefore excluded the poem from the present collection.

And why, it may be asked, have I entered into this explanation respecting a matter so unimportant as the admission or exclusion of the poem in question? I have done so, because I was anxious to avow that the sole reason for its exclusion was that which has been stated above; and that it has not been excluded in deference to the opinion which many critics of the present day appear to entertain against subjects chosen from distant times and countries: against the choice, in short, of any subjects but modern ones.

'The poet,' it is said,[8] and by an intelligent critic, 'the poet who would really fix the public attention must leave the exhausted past, and draw his subjects from matters of present import, and *therefore* both of interest and novelty.'

Now this view I believe to be completely false. It is worth examining, inasmuch as it is a fair sample of a class of critical dicta everywhere current at the present day, having a philosophical form and air, but no real basis in fact; and which are calculated to vitiate the judgment of readers of poetry, while they exert, so far as they are adopted, a misleading influence on the practice of those who make it.

What are the eternal objects of poetry, among all nations, and at all times? They are actions; human actions;[9] possessing an inherent interest in themselves, and which are to be communicated in an interesting manner by the art of the poet. Vainly will the latter imagine that he has everything in his own power; that he can make an intrinsically inferior action equally delightful with a more excellent one by his treatment of it. He may indeed compel us to admire his skill, but his work will possess, within itself, an incurable defect.

The poet, then, has in the first place to select an excellent action; and what actions are the most excellent? Those, certainly, which most powerfully appeal to the great primary human affections: to those elementary feelings which subsist permanently in the race, and which are independent of time. These feelings are permanent and the same; that which interests them is permanent and the same also. The modernness or antiquity of an action, therefore, has nothing to do with its fitness for poetical representation; this depends upon its inherent qualities. To the elementary part of our nature, to our passions, that which is great and passionate is eternally interesting; and interesting solely in proportion to its greatness and to its passion. A great human action of a thousand years ago is more interesting to it than a smaller human action

8. "In the *Spectator* of April 2, 1853. The words quoted were not used with reference to poems of mine." (Arnold) The emphasis of "therefore" was supplied by Arnold. The "intelligent critic" was R. S. Rintoul, the editor of *The Spectator*.
9. Aristotle says so in *Poetics* VI, IX, X.

of to-day, even though upon the representation of this last the most consummate skill may have been expended, and though it has the advantage of appealing by its modern language, familiar manners, and contemporary allusions, to all our transient feelings and interests. These, however, have no right to demand of a poetical work that it shall satisfy them; their claims are to be directed elsewhere. Poetical works belong to the domain of our permanent passions; let them interest these, and the voice of all subordinate claims upon them is at once silenced.

Achilles, Prometheus, Clytemnestra, Dido,—what modern poem presents personages as interesting, even to us moderns, as these personages of an 'exhausted past'? We have the domestic epic dealing with the details of modern life which pass daily under our eyes; [10] we have poems representing modern personages in contact with the problems of modern life, moral, intellectual, and social; these works have been produced by poets the most distinguished of their nation and time; yet I fearlessly assert that *Hermann and Dorothea, Childe Harold, Jocelyn, The Excursion,*[11] leave the reader cold in comparison with the effect produced upon him by the latter books of the *Iliad,* by the *Oresteia,* or by the episode of Dido. And why is this? Simply because in the three last-named cases the action is greater, the personages nobler, the situations more intense: and this is the true basis of the interest in a poetical work, and this alone.

It may be urged, however, that past actions may be interesting in themselves, but that they are not to be adopted by the modern poet, because it is impossible for him to have them clearly present to his own mind, and he cannot therefore feel them deeply, nor represent them forcibly. But this is not necessarily the case. The externals of a past action, indeed, he cannot know with the precision of a contemporary; but his business is with its essentials. The outward man of Oedipus or of Macbeth, the houses in which they lived, the ceremonies of their courts, he cannot accurately figure to himself; but neither do they essentially concern him. His business is with their inward man; with their feelings and behaviour in certain tragic situations, which engage their passions as men; these have in them nothing local and casual; they are as accessible to the modern poet as to a contemporary.

The date of an action, then, signifies nothing: the action itself, its selection and construction, this is what is all-important. This the Greeks understood far more clearly than we do. The radical difference between their poetical theory and ours consists, as it appears to me, in this: that, with them, the poetical character of the action in itself, and the conduct of it, was the first consideration; with us, attention is fixed mainly on the value of the separate thoughts and images which occur in the treatment of an action. They regarded the whole; we regard the parts. With them, the action predominated over the expression of it; with us, the expression predominates over the action. Not that they failed in expression, or were inattentive to it; on the contrary, they are the highest models of expression, the unapproached masters of the *grand*

10. Arnold may have had in mind *The Bothie of Taber-na-Fuosich* (1848), by his close friend Arthur Hugh Clough, which tells in hexameters, the epic meter, the love story of a young Oxford radical; or Alexander Smith's *A Life Drama* (1853).
11. Long poems by Goethe, Byron, Lamartine, and Wordsworth.

style.[12] But their expression is so excellent because it is so admirably kept in its right degree of prominence; because it is so simple and so well subordinated; because it draws its force directly from the pregnancy of the matter which it conveys. For what reason was the Greek tragic poet confined to so limited a range of subjects? Because there are so few actions which unite in themselves, in the highest degree, the conditions of excellence: and it was not thought that on any but an excellent subject could an excellent poem be constructed. A few actions, therefore, eminently adapted for tragedy, maintained almost exclusive possession of the Greek tragic stage. Their significance appeared inexhaustible; they were as permanent problems, perpetually offered to the genius of every fresh poet. This too is the reason of what appears to us moderns a certain baldness of expression in Greek tragedy; of the triviality with which we often reproach the remarks of the chorus, where it takes part in the dialogue: that the action itself, the situation of Orestes, or Merope, or Alcmæon,[13] was to stand the central point of interest, unforgotten, absorbing, principal; that no accessories were for a moment to distract the spectator's attention from this; that the tone of the parts was to be perpetually kept down, in order not to impair the grandiose effect of the whole. The terrible old mythic story on which the drama was founded stood, before he entered the theatre, traced in its bare outlines upon the spectator's mind; it stood in his memory, as a group of statuary, faintly seen, at the end of a long and dark vista: then came the poet, embodying outlines, developing situations, not a word wasted, not a sentiment capriciously thrown in: stroke upon stroke, the drama proceeded: the light deepened upon the group; more and more it revealed itself to the riveted gaze of the spectator: until at last, when the final words were spoken, it stood before him in broad sunlight, a model of immortal beauty.

This was what a Greek critic demanded; this was what a Greek poet endeavoured to effect. It signified nothing to what time an action belonged. We do not find that the *Persæ* [14] occupied a particularly high rank among the dramas of Æschylus, because it represented a matter of contemporary interest; this was not what a cultivated Athenian required. He required that the permanent elements of his nature should be moved; and dramas of which the action, though taken from a long-distant mythic time, yet was calculated to accomplish this in a higher degree than that of the *Persæ*, stood higher in his estimation accordingly. The Greeks felt, no doubt, with their exquisite sagacity of taste, that an action of present times was too near them, too much mixed up

12. In 1861 Arnold gave his series of lectures *On Translating Homer*, in the course of which he discusses the conception of the "grand style" in art and implies that its cultivation has certain good intellectual and social consequences. The grand style arises, he says, "when a noble nature, poetically gifted, treats with simplicity or with severity a serious subject."

13. Orestes took vengeance on his mother, Clytemnestra, for the murder of his father, Agamemnon; he figures in tragedies by Aeschylus, Sophocles, and Euripides. Merope, the widow of a murdered king, is married by force to the murderer; her story is the subject of plays by Euripides, Voltaire, and others, including Arnold himself, whose *Merope* appeared in 1858. Alcmaeon was the subject of several lost Greek tragedies; like Orestes, he avenged his father by slaying his mother.

14. *The Persians*, produced in 472 B.C., dealt with events of the recent invasion of Greece by the Persians.

with what was accidental and passing, to form a sufficiently grand, detached, and self-subsistent object for a tragic poem. Such objects belonged to the domain of the comic poet, and of the lighter kinds of poetry. For the more serious kinds, for *pragmatic* poetry, to use an excellent expression of Polybius,[15] they were more difficult and severe in the range of subjects which they permitted. Their theory and practice alike, the admirable treatise of Aristotle, and the unrivalled works of their poets, exclaim with a thousand tongues—'All depends upon the subject; choose a fitting action, penetrate yourself with the feeling of its situations; this done, everything else will follow.'

But for all kinds of poetry alike there was one point on which they were rigidly exacting: the adaptability of the subject to the kind of poetry selected, and the careful construction of the poem.

How different a way of thinking from this is ours! We can hardly at the present day understand what Menander[16] meant, when he told a man who enquired as to the progress of his comedy that he had finished it, not having yet written a single line, because he had constructed the action of it in his mind. A modern critic would have assured him that the merit of his piece depended on the brilliant things which arose under his pen as he went along. We have poems which seem to exist merely for the sake of single lines and passages; not for the sake of producing any total impression. We have critics who seem to direct their attention merely to detached expressions, to the language about the action, not to the action itself. I verily think that the majority of them do not in their hearts believe that there is such a thing as a total impression to be derived from a poem at all, or to be demanded from a poet; they think the term a commonplace of metaphysical criticism. They will permit the poet to select any action he pleases, and to suffer that action to go as it will, provided he gratifies them with occasional bursts of fine writing, and with a shower of isolated thoughts and images. That is, they permit him to leave their poetical sense ungratified, provided that he gratifies their rhetorical sense and their curiosity. Of his neglecting to gratify these, there is little danger. He needs rather to be warned against the danger of attempting to gratify these alone; he needs rather to be perpetually reminded to prefer his action to everything else; so to treat this, as to permit its inherent excellences to develop themselves, without interruption from the intrusion of his personal peculiarities; most fortunate, when he most entirely succeeds in effacing himself, and in enabling a noble action to subsist as it did in nature.

But the modern critic not only permits a false practice; he absolutely prescribes false aims.—'A true allegory of the state of one's own mind in a representative history,' the poet is told, 'is perhaps the highest thing that one can attempt in the way of poetry.'[17] And accordingly he attempts it. An allegory of the state of one's own mind, the highest problem of an art which imitates actions! No assuredly, it is not, it never can be so: no great poetical work has ever been produced with such an aim. *Faust* itself, in which something of the

15. Greek historian of Rome (202?–125 B.C.). "Pragmatic" would seem to mean "serious," in the sense of being committed to establishing the relation of cause and effect in human affairs.
16. Greek comic dramatist (342–292 B.C.).
17. Arnold quotes from an article in the *North British Review*, XIX (August 1853), p. 180.

kind is attempted, wonderful passages as it contains, and in spite of the unsurpassed beauty of the scenes which relate to Margaret, *Faust* itself, judged as a whole, and judged strictly as a poetical work, is defective: its illustrious author, the greatest poet of modern times, the greatest critic of all times, would have been the first to acknowledge it; he only defended his work, indeed, by asserting it to be 'something incommensurable.' [18]

The confusion of the present times is great, the multitude of voices counselling different things bewildering, the number of existing works capable of attracting a young writer's attention and of becoming his models, immense. What he wants is a hand to guide him through the confusion, a voice to prescribe to him the aim which he should keep in view, and to explain to him that the value of the literary works which offer themselves to his attention is relative to their power of helping him forward on his road towards this aim. Such a guide the English writer at the present day will nowhere find. Failing this, all that can be looked for, all indeed that can be desired, is, that his attention should be fixed on excellent models; that he may reproduce, at any rate, something of their excellence, by penetrating himself with their works and by catching their spirit, if he cannot be taught to produce what is excellent independently.

Foremost among these models for the English writer stands Shakespeare: a name the greatest perhaps of all poetical names; a name never to be mentioned without reverence. I will venture, however, to express a doubt, whether the influence of his works, excellent and fruitful for the readers of poetry, for the great majority, has been of unmixed advantage to the writers of it.[19] Shakespeare indeed chose excellent subjects; the world could afford no better than Macbeth, or Romeo and Juliet, or Othello; he had no theory respecting the necessity of choosing subjects of present import, or the paramount interest attaching to allegories of the state of one's own mind; like all great poets, he knew well what constituted a poetical action; like them, wherever he found such an action, he took it; like them, too, he found his best in past times. But to these general characteristics of all great poets he added a special one of his own; a gift, namely, of happy, abundant, and ingenious expression, eminent and unrivalled: so eminent as irresistibly to strike the attention first in him, and even to throw into comparative shade his other excellences as a poet. Here has been the mischief. These other excellences were his fundamental excellences *as a poet;* what distinguishes the artist from the mere amateur, says Goethe, is *Architectonicè* in the highest sense; [20] that power of execution, which creates, forms, and constitutes: not the profoundness of single thoughts, not the richness of imagery, not the abundance of illustration. But these attractive accessories of a poetical work being more easily seized than the spirit of the whole,

18. J. Eckermann, *Conversations with Goethe,* January 3, 1830.
19. By this date Shakespeare had become virtually sacrosanct in England, in large part through the expressed adoration of the Romantic writers, and for Arnold to suggest that anything but good could follow from emulating him in any way was an act of some courage—see what he says about Hallam's comment on Shakespeare farther on—and likely to be thought a perversity. Arnold's letters to his friend Clough continually express his sense of the danger of modern English poets' basing themselves on the "multitudinousness" of the Elizabethans, "those d_____d Elizabethan poets."
20. Goethe, *Concerning the So-called Dilettantism* (1799).

and these accessories being possessed by Shakespeare in an unequalled degree, a young writer having recourse to Shakespeare as his model runs great risk of being vanquished and absorbed by them, and, in consequence, of reproducing, according to the measure of his power, these, and these alone. Of this preponderating quality of Shakespeare's genius, accordingly, almost the whole of modern English poetry has, it appears to me, felt the influence. To the exclusive attention on the part of his imitators to this it is in a great degree owing, that of the majority of modern poetical works the details alone are valuable, the composition worthless. In reading them one is perpetually reminded of that terrible sentence on a modern French poet:—*Il dit tout ce qu'il veut, mais malheureusement il n'a rien à dire.*[21]

Let me give an instance of what I mean. I will take it from the works of the very chief among those who seem to have been formed in the school of Shakespeare: of one whose exquisite genius and pathetic death render him for ever interesting. I will take the poem of *Isabella, or the Pot of Basil,* by Keats. I choose this rather than the *Endymion,* because the latter work (which a modern critic has classed with the *Fairy Queen!*),[22] although undoubtedly there blows through it the breath of genius, is yet as a whole so utterly incoherent, as not strictly to merit the name of a poem at all. The poem of *Isabella,* then, is a perfect treasure-house of graceful and felicitous words and images: almost in every stanza there occurs one of those vivid and picturesque turns of expression, by which the object is made to flash upon the eye of the mind, and which thrill the reader with a sudden delight. This one short poem contains, perhaps, a greater number of happy single expressions which one could quote than all the extant tragedies of Sophocles. But the action, the story? The action in itself is an excellent one; but so feebly is it conceived by the poet, so loosely constructed, that the effect produced by it, in and for itself, is absolutely null. Let the reader, after he has finished the poem of Keats, turn to the same story in the *Decameron:*[23] he will then feel how pregnant and interesting the same action has become in the hands of a great artist, who above all things delineates his object; who subordinates expression to that which it is designed to express.

I have said that the imitators of Shakespeare, fixing their attention on his wonderful gift of expression, have directed their imitation to this, neglecting his other excellences. These excellences, the fundamental excellences of poetical art, Shakespeare no doubt possessed them,—possessed many of them in a splendid degree; but it may perhaps be doubted whether even he himself did not sometimes give scope to his faculty of expression to the prejudice of a higher poetical duty. For we must never forget that Shakespeare is the great poet he is from his skill in discerning and firmly conceiving an excellent action, from his power of intensely feeling a situation, of intimately associating himself with a character; not from his gift of expression, which rather even leads him astray, degenerating sometimes into a fondness for curiosity of expression, into an irritability of fancy, which seems to make it impossible for him to say a

21. "He says all that he wishes to, but unhappily he has nothing to say." This is thought to have been said of Théophile Gautier (1811–72).
22. In the same issue of the *North British Review* in which Arnold had come on the sentence about "a true allegory of the state of one's own mind."
23. Of Boccaccio, 4th day, 5th tale.

thing plainly, even when the press of the action demands the very directest language, or its level character the very simplest. Mr. Hallam,[24] than whom it is impossible to find a saner and more judicious critic, has had the courage (for at the present day it needs courage) to remark, how extremely and faultily difficult Shakespeare's language often is. It is so: you may find main scenes in some of his greatest tragedies, *King Lear* for instance, where the language is so artificial, so curiously tortured, and so difficult, that every speech has to be read two or three times before its meaning can be comprehended. This over-curiousness of expression is indeed but the excessive employment of a wonderful gift,—of the power of saying a thing in a happier way than any other man; nevertheless, it is carried so far that one understands what M. Guizot [25] meant, when he said that Shakespeare appears in his language to have tried all styles except that of simplicity. He has not the severe and scrupulous self-restraint of the ancients, partly, no doubt, because he had a far less cultivated and exacting audience. He has indeed a far wider range than they had, a far richer fertility of thought; in this respect he rises above them. In his strong conception of his subject, in the genuine way in which he is penetrated with it, he resembles them, and is unlike the moderns. But in the accurate limitation of it, the conscientious rejection of superfluities, the simple and rigorous development of it from the first line of his work to the last, he falls below them, and comes nearer to the moderns. In his chief works, besides what he has of his own, he has the elementary soundness of the ancients; he has their important action and their large and broad manner; but he has not their purity of method. He is therefore a less safe model; for what he has of his own is personal, and inseparable from his own rich nature; it may be imitated and exaggerated, it cannot be learned or applied as an art. He is above all suggestive; more valuable, therefore, to young writers as men than as artists. But clearness of arrangement, rigour of development, simplicity of style,—these may to a certain extent be learned; and these may, I am convinced, be learned best from the ancients, who, although infinitely less suggestive than Shakespeare, are thus, to the artist, more instructive.

What then, it will be asked, are the ancients to be our sole models? the ancients with their comparatively narrow range of experience, and their widely different circumstances? Not, certainly, that which is narrow in the ancients, nor that in which we can no longer sympathise. An action like the action of the *Antigone* of Sophocles, which turns upon the conflict between the heroine's duty to her brother's corpse and that to the laws of her country, is no longer one in which it is possible that we should feel a deep interest.[26] I am speaking too, it will be remembered, not of the best sources of intellectual stimulus for the general reader, but of the best models of instruction for the individual writer. This last may certainly learn of the ancients, better than

24. Henry Hallam (1777–1859), historian, father of Arthur Hallam, Tennyson's dear friend; the remark is made in his *Introduction to the Literature of Europe* (1838–39) III.91–92.
25. F. P. G. Guizot (1787–1874), French statesman and historian. He discusses Shakespeare's sonnets in *Shakespeare et son temps* (1852), p. 114.
26. Arnold is surely mistaken about this. The interest of *Antigone* transcends the archaic particularities of situation and proves to be quite compelling to the modern reader.

anywhere else, three things which it is vitally important for him to know:—the all-importance of the choice of a subject; the necessity of accurate construction; and the subordinate character of expression. He will learn from them how unspeakably superior is the effect of the one moral impression left by a great action treated as a whole, to the effect produced by the most striking single thought or by the happiest image. As he penetrates into the spirit of the great classical works, as he becomes gradually aware of their intense significance, their noble simplicity, and their calm pathos, he will be convinced that it is this effect, unity and profoundness of moral impression, at which the ancient poets aimed; that it is this which constitutes the grandeur of their works, and which makes them immortal. He will desire to direct his own efforts towards producing the same effect. Above all, he will deliver himself from the jargon of modern criticism, and escape the danger of producing poetical works conceived in the spirit of the passing time, and which partake of its transitoriness.

The present age makes great claims upon us: we owe it service, it will not be satisfied without our admiration. I know not how it is, but their commerce with the ancients appears to me to produce, in those who constantly practise it, a steadying and composing effect upon their judgment, not of literary works only, but of men and events in general. They are like persons who have had a very weighty and impressive experience: they are more truly than others under the empire of facts, and more independent of the language current among those with whom they live. They wish neither to applaud nor to revile their age; they wish to know what it is, what it can give them, and whether this is what they want. What they want, they know very well; they want to educe and cultivate what is best and noblest in themselves; they know, too, that this is no easy task—χαλεπόν, as Pittacus said, χαλεπὸν ἐσθλὸν ἔμμεναι[27]— and they ask themselves sincerely whether their age and its literature can assist them in the attempt. If they are endeavouring to practise any art, they remember the plain and simple proceedings of the old artists, who attained their grand results by penetrating themselves with some noble and significant action, not by inflating themselves with a belief in the pre-eminent importance and greatness of their own times. They do not talk of their mission, nor of interpreting their age, nor of the coming poet; all this, they know, is the mere delirium of vanity; their business is not to praise their age, but to afford to the men who live in it the highest pleasure which they are capable of feeling. If asked to afford this by means of subjects drawn from the age itself, they ask what special fitness the present age has for supplying them. They are told that it is an era of progress, an age commissioned to carry out the great ideas of industrial development and social amelioration. They reply that with all this they can do nothing; that the elements they need for the exercise of their art are great actions, calculated powerfully and delightfully to affect what is permanent in the human soul; that so far as the present age can supply such actions, they will gladly make use of them; but that an age wanting in moral grandeur can with difficulty supply such, and an age of spiritual discomfort with difficulty be powerfully and delightfully affected by them.

27. "It is hard to achieve excellence." Pittacus (*c.*650–510 B.C.), a statesman and one of the so-called Seven Sages of Greece. He seems to have been much admired for his "favorite sayings," all of which are crashing platitudes.

A host of voices will indignantly rejoin that the present age is inferior to the past neither in moral grandeur nor in spiritual health. He who possesses the discipline I speak of will content himself with remembering the judgments passed upon the present age, in this respect, by the men of strongest head and widest culture whom it has produced; by Goethe and by Niebuhr.[28] It will be sufficient for him that he knows the opinions held by these two great men respecting the present age and its literature; and that he feels assured in his own mind that their aims and demands upon life were such as he would wish, at any rate, his own to be; and their judgment as to what is impeding and disabling such as he may safely follow. He will not, however, maintain a hostile attitude towards the false pretensions of his age: he will content himself with not being overwhelmed by them. He will esteem himself fortunate if he can succeed in banishing from his mind all feelings of contradiction, and irritation, and impatience; in order to delight himself with the contemplation of some noble action of a heroic time, and to enable others, through his representation of it, to delight in it also.

I am far indeed from making any claim, for myself, that I possess this discipline; or for the following poems, that they breathe its spirit. But I say, that in the sincere endeavour to learn and practise, amid the bewildering confusion of our times, what is sound and true in poetical art, I seemed to myself to find the only sure guidance, the only solid footing, among the ancients. They, at any rate, knew what they wanted in art, and we do not. It is this uncertainty which is disheartening, and not hostile criticism. How often have I felt this when reading words of disparagement or of cavil: that it is the uncertainty as to what is really to be aimed at which makes our difficulty, not the dissatisfaction of the critic, who himself suffers from the same uncertainty! *Non me tua fervida terrent Dicta; . . . Dii me terrent, et Jupiter hostis.*[29]

Two kinds of *dilettanti,*[30] says Goethe, there are in poetry: he who neglects the indispensable mechanical part, and thinks he has done enough if he shows spirituality and feeling; and he who seeks to arrive at poetry merely by mechanism, in which he can acquire an artisan's readiness, and is without soul and matter. And he adds, that the first does most harm to art, and the last to himself. If we must be *dilettanti:* if it is impossible for us, under the circumstances amidst which we live, to think clearly, to feel nobly, and to delineate firmly: if we cannot attain to the mastery of the great artists;—let us, at least, have so much respect for our art as to prefer it to ourselves. Let us not bewilder our successors; let us transmit to them the practice of poetry, with its boundaries and wholesome regulative laws, under which excellent works may again, perhaps, at some future time, be produced, not yet fallen into oblivion through our neglect, not yet condemned and cancelled by the influence of their eternal enemy, caprice.

1853   1853

28. Barthold Georg Niebuhr (1776–1831), a gifted German historian of Rome, influential in England.
29. Virgil, *Aeneid* XII.894–95. "Your hot words do not frighten me; . . . What frightens me is the gods and the enmity of Jupiter."
30. See note 20 above.

From The Function of Criticism at the Present Time

Many objections have been made to a proposition which, in some remarks of mine on translating Homer,[1] I ventured to put forth; a proposition about criticism, and its importance at the present day. I said: 'Of the literature of France and Germany, as of the intellect of Europe in general, the main effort, for now many years, has been a critical effort; the endeavour, in all branches of knowledge, theology, philosophy, history, art, science, to see the object as in itself it really is.' I added, that owing to the operation in English literature of certain causes, 'almost the last thing for which one would come to English literature is just that very thing which now Europe most desires,—criticism'; and that the power and value of English literature was thereby impaired. More than one rejoinder declared that the importance I here assigned to criticism was excessive, and asserted the inherent superiority of the creative effort of the human spirit over its critical effort. And the other day, having been led by Mr. Shairp's excellent notice of Wordsworth [2] to turn again to his biography, I found, in the words of this great man, whom I, for one, must always listen to with the profoundest respect,[3] a sentence passed on the critic's business, which seems to justify every possible disparagement of it. Wordsworth says in one of his letters:—

'The writers in these publications' (the Reviews), 'while they prosecute their inglorious employment, can not be supposed to be in a state of mind very favourable for being affected by the finer influences of a thing so pure as genuine poetry.'

And a trustworthy reporter of his conversation quotes a more elaborate judgment to the same effect:—

'Wordsworth holds the critical power very low, infinitely lower than the inventive; and he said to-day that if the quantity of time consumed in writing critiques on the works of others were given to original composition, of whatever kind it might be, it would be much better employed; it would make a man find out sooner his own level, and it would do infinitely less mischief. A false or malicious criticism may do much injury to the minds of others; a stupid invention, either in prose or verse, is quite harmless.'

It is almost too much to expect of poor human nature, that a man capable of producing some effect in one line of literature, should, for the greater good of society, voluntarily doom himself to impotence and obscurity in another. Still less is this to be expected from men addicted to the composition of the 'false or malicious criticism' of which Wordsworth speaks. However, everybody would admit that a false or malicious criticism had better never have been written. Everybody, too, would be willing to admit, as a general proposition, that the critical faculty is lower than the inventive. But is it true that criticism is really, in itself, a baneful and injurious employment; is it true that all time given to

1. The conclusion of Lecture II of *On Translating Homer* (1861).
2. John Campbell Shairp (1819–85), a Scottish academic and man of letters, was a college-mate of Arnold's. His essay on Wordsworth appeared in the *North British Review*, XLI (August 1864).
3. A personal piety and affection played its part in Arnold's feeling for Wordsworth; the Arnold and Wordsworth families were neighbors in the Lake District, where the Arnolds had their summer home, and Wordsworth took an interest in Matthew as a boy and a young man.

writing critiques on the works of others would be much better employed if it were given to original composition, of whatever kind this may be? Is it true that Johnson had better have gone on producing more *Irenes* instead of writing his *Lives of the Poets;*[4] nay, is it certain that Wordsworth himself was better employed in making his Ecclesiastical Sonnets[5] than when he made his celebrated Preface,[6] so full of criticism, and criticism of the works of others? Wordsworth was himself a great critic, and it is to be sincerely regretted that he has not left us more criticism; Goethe was one of the greatest of critics,[7] and we may sincerely congratulate ourselves that he has left us so much criticism. Without wasting time over the exaggeration which Wordsworth's judgment on criticism clearly contains, or over an attempt to trace the causes,—not difficult, I think, to be traced,[8]—which may have led Wordsworth to this exaggeration, a critic may with advantage seize an occasion for trying his own conscience, and for asking himself of what real service at any given moment the practice of criticism either is or may be made to his own mind and spirit, and to the minds and spirits of others.

The critical power is of lower rank than the creative. True; but in assenting to this proposition, one or two things are to be kept in mind. It is undeniable that the exercise of a creative power, that a free creative activity, is the highest function of man; it is proved to be so by man's finding in it his true happiness. But it is undeniable, also, that men may have the sense of exercising this free creative activity in other ways than in producing great works of literature or art; if it were not so, all but a very few men would be shut out from the true happiness of all men. They may have it in well-doing, they may have it in learning, they may have it even in criticising. This is one thing to be kept in mind. Another is, that the exercise of the creative power in the production of great works of literature or art, however high this exercise of it may rank, is not at all epochs and under all conditions possible; and that therefore labour may be vainly spent in attempting it, which might with more fruit be used in preparing for it, in rendering it possible. This creative power works with elements, with materials; what if it has not those materials, those elements, ready for its use? In that case it must surely wait till they are ready. Now, in literature, —I will limit myself to literature, for it is about literature that the question arises,—the elements with which the creative power works are ideas; the best ideas, on every matter which literature touches, current at the time. At any rate we may lay it down as certain that in modern literature no manifestation of the creative power not working with these can be very important or fruitful. And I say *current* at the time, not merely accessible at the time; for creative literary genius does not principally show itself in discovering new ideas, that is rather the business of the philosopher. The grand work of literary genius is a work of synthesis and exposition, not of analysis and discovery; its gift lies in

4. Dr. Johnson's tragedy *Irene* (1749) is a dull work; his *Lives of the Poets* (1779–81) a continuing delight.
5. This sonnet sequence on the history of the Church of England (1821–22) is among the least rewarding of Wordsworth's works.
6. To the 1800 edition of *Lyrical Ballads,* expanded in 1802.
7. In the Preface to the *Poems* of 1853, Arnold rates him the very greatest of critics.
8. That is, to resentment of the harsh treatment he received from critics.

the faculty of being happily inspired by a certain intellectual and spiritual atmosphere, by a certain order of ideas, when it finds itself in them; of dealing divinely with these ideas, presenting them in the most effective and attractive combinations,—making beautiful works with them, in short. But it must have the atmosphere, it must find itself amidst the order of ideas, in order to work freely; and these it is not so easy to command. This is why great creative epochs in literature are so rare, this is why there is so much that is unsatisfactory in the productions of many men of real genius; because for the creation of a master-work of literature two powers must concur, the power of the man and the power of the moment, and the man is not enough without the moment; [9] the creative power has, for its happy exercise, appointed elements, and those elements are not in its own control.

Nay, they are more within the control of the critical power. It is the business of the critical power, as I said in the words already quoted, 'in all branches of knowledge, theology, philosophy, history, art, science, to see the object as in itself it really is.' Thus it tends, at last, to make an intellectual situation of which the creative power can profitably avail itself. It tends to establish an order of ideas, if not absolutely true, yet true by comparison with that which it displaces; to make the best ideas prevail. Presently these new ideas reach society, the touch of truth is the touch of life, and there is a stir and growth everywhere; out of this stir and growth come the creative epochs of literature.

Or, to narrow our range, and quit these considerations of the general march of genius and of society,—considerations which are apt to become too abstract and impalpable,—every one can see that a poet, for instance, ought to know life and the world before dealing with them in poetry; and life and the world being in modern times very complex things, the creation of a modern poet, to be worth much, implies a great critical effort behind it; else it must be a comparatively poor, barren, and short-lived affair. This is why Byron's poetry had so little endurance in it,[10] and Goethe's so much; both Byron and Goethe had a great productive power, but Goethe's was nourished by a great critical effort providing the true materials for it, and Byron's was not; Goethe knew life and the world, the poet's necessary subjects, much more comprehensively and thoroughly than Byron. He knew a great deal more of them, and he knew them much more as they really are.

It has long seemed to me that the burst of creative activity in our literature, through the first quarter of this century, had about it in fact something premature; and that from this cause its productions are doomed, most of them, in spite of the sanguine hopes which accompanied and do still accompany them, to prove hardly more lasting than the productions of far less splendid epochs. And this prematureness comes from its having proceeded without having its proper data, without sufficient materials to work with. In other words, the English poetry of the first quarter of this century, with plenty of energy, plenty of creative force, did not know enough. This makes Byron so empty a matter,

9. Arnold here shows the influence of Hippolyte Taine (1828–23), whose *Histoire de la littérature anglaise* had appeared in 1863. Taine was concerned to formulate a sort of natural history of culture; in it the idea of "the moment" at which a historical or cultural figure emerges plays an important part.
10. Still and all, it manages to keep going!

Shelley so incoherent, Wordsworth even, profound as he is, yet so wanting in completeness and variety. Wordsworth cared little for books, and disparaged Goethe. I admire Wordsworth, as he is, so much that I cannot wish him different; and it is vain, no doubt, to imagine such a man different from what he is, to suppose that he *could* have been different. But surely the one thing wanting to make Wordsworth an even greater poet than he is,—his thought richer, and his influence of wider application,—was that he should have read more books, among them, no doubt, those of that Goethe whom he disparaged without reading him.

But to speak of books and reading may easily lead to a misunderstanding here. It was not really books and reading that lacked to our poetry at this epoch; Shelley had plenty of reading, Coleridge had immense reading. Pindar[11] and Sophocles—as we all say so glibly, and often with so little discernment of the real import of what we are saying—had not many books; Shakespeare was no deep reader. True; but in the Greece of Pindar and Sophocles, in the England of Shakespeare, the poet lived in a current of ideas in the highest degree animating and nourishing to the creative power; society was, in the fullest measure, permeated by fresh thought, intelligent and alive. And this state of things is the true basis for the creative power's exercise, in this it finds its data, its materials, truly ready for its hand; all the books and reading in the world are only valuable as they are helps to this. Even when this does not actually exist, books and reading may enable a man to construct a kind of semblance of it in his own mind, a world of knowledge and intelligence in which he may live and work. This is by no means an equivalent to the artist for the nationally diffused life and thought of the epochs of Sophocles or Shakespeare; but, besides that it may be a means of preparation for such epochs, it does really constitute, if many share in it, a quickening and sustaining atmosphere of great value. Such an atmosphere the many-sided learning and the long and widely-combined critical effort of Germany formed for Goethe, when he lived and worked. There was no national glow of life and thought there as in the Athens of Pericles or the England of Elizabeth. That was the poet's weakness. But there was a sort of equivalent for it in the complete culture and unfettered thinking of a large body of Germans. That was his strength. In the England of the first quarter of this century there was neither a national glow of life and thought, such as we had in the age of Elizabeth, nor yet a culture and a force of learning and criticism such as were to be found in Germany. Therefore the creative power of poetry wanted, for success in the highest sense, materials and a basis; a thorough interpretation of the world was necessarily denied to it.

At first sight it seems strange that out of the immense stir of the French Revolution and its age should not have come a crop of works of genius equal to that which came out of the stir of the great productive time of Greece, or out of that of the Renascence, with its powerful episode the Reformation. But the truth is that the stir of the French Revolution took a character which essentially distinguished it from such movements as these. These were, in the main, disinterestedly[12] intellectual and spiritual movements; movements in

11. Pindar (518–438 B.C.), Greek lyric poet of great genius.
12. The word "disinterested" is of crucial importance in this essay. See the comment on it in the Headnote to Arnold above.

which the human spirit looked for its satisfaction in itself and in the increased play of its own activity. The French Revolution took a political, practical character. The movement which went on in France under the old *régime,* from 1700 to 1789, was far more really akin than that of the Revolution itself to the movement of the Renascence; the France of Voltaire and Rousseau told far more powerfully upon the mind of Europe than the France of the Revolution. Goethe reproached this last expressly with having 'thrown quiet culture back.' Nay, and the true key to how much in our Byron, even in our Wordsworth, is this!—that they had their source in a great movement of feeling, not in a great movement of mind. The French Revolution, however,—that object of so much blind love and so much blind hatred,—found undoubtedly its motive-power in the intelligence of men, and not in their practical sense; this is what distinguishes it from the English Revolution of Charles the First's time. This is what makes it a more spiritual event than our Revolution, an event of much more powerful and world-wide interest, though practically less successful; it appeals to an order of ideas which are universal, certain, permanent. 1789 asked of a thing, Is it rational? 1642 asked of a thing, Is it legal? or, when it went furthest, Is it according to conscience? This is the English fashion, a fashion to be treated, within its own sphere, with the highest respect; for its success, within its own sphere, has been prodigious. But what is law in one place is not law in another; what is law here to-day is not law even here tomorrow; and as for conscience, what is binding on one man's conscience is not binding on another's. The old woman who threw her stool at the head of the surpliced minister in St. Giles's Church at Edinburgh obeyed an impulse to which millions of the human race may be permitted to remain strangers.[13] But the prescriptions of reason are absolute, unchanging, of universal validity; *to count by tens is the easiest way of counting*—that is a proposition of which every one, from here to the Antipodes, feels the force; at least I should say so if we did not live in a country where it is not impossible that any morning we may find a letter in the *Times* declaring that a decimal coinage is an absurdity.[14] That a whole nation should have been penetrated with an enthusiasm for pure reason and with an ardent zeal for making its prescriptions triumph, is a very remarkable thing, when we consider how little of mind, or anything so worthy and quickening as mind, comes into the motives which alone, in general, impel great masses of men. In spite of the extravagant direction given to this enthusiasm, in spite of the crimes and follies in which it lost itself, the French Revolution derives from the force, truth, and universality of the ideas which it took for its law, and from the passion with which it could inspire a multitude for these ideas, a unique and still living power; it is—it will probably long remain—the greatest, the most animating event in history. And as no sincere passion for the things of the mind, even though it turn out in many respects an unfortunate passion, is ever quite thrown away and quite barren of good,

13. When Charles I prescribed a new church service for Scotland in 1637, riots broke out; according to tradition, they began with the incident Arnold refers to.
14. A decimal coinage went into effect in Britain in 1971 after having been discussed for more than a century. In 1863 a bill proposing a decimal system was introduced into Parliament and defeated. One of Trollope's novels, *The Prime Minister* (1875), teases the idea as a harmless eccentricity.

France has reaped from hers one fruit—the natural and legitimate fruit, though not precisely the grand fruit she expected: she is the country in Europe where *the people* is most alive.

But the mania for giving an immediate political and practical application to all these fine ideas of the reason was fatal. Here an Englishman is in his element: on this theme we can all go on for hours. And all we are in the habit of saying on it has undoubtedly a great deal of truth. Ideas cannot be too much prized in and for themselves, cannot be too much lived with; but to transport them abruptly into the world of politics and practice, violently to revolutionise this world to their bidding,—that is quite another thing. There is the world of ideas and there is the world of practice; the French are often for suppressing the one and the English the other; but neither is to be suppressed. A member of the House of Commons said to me the other day: 'That a thing is an anomaly, I consider to be no objection to it whatever.' I venture to think he was wrong; that a thing is an anomaly *is* an objection to it, but absolutely and in the sphere of ideas: it is not necessarily, under such and such circumstances, or at such and such a moment, an objection to it in the sphere of politics and practice. Joubert [15] has said beautifully: 'C'est la force et le droit qui règlent toutes choses dans le monde; la force en attendant le droit.' (Force and right are the governors of this world; force till right is ready.) *Force till right is ready;* and till right is ready, force,[16] the existing order of things, is justified, is the legitimate ruler. But right is something moral, and implies inward recognition, free assent of the will; we are not ready for right,—*right,* so far as we are concerned, *is not ready,*—until we have attained this sense of seeing it and willing it. The way in which for us it may change and transform force, the existing order of things, and become, in its turn, the legitimate ruler of the world, should depend on the way in which, when our time comes, we see it and will it. Therefore for other people enamoured of their own newly discerned right, to attempt to impose it upon us as ours, and violently to substitute their right for our force, is an act of tyranny, and to be resisted. It sets at nought the second great half of our maximum, *force till right is ready.* This was the grand error of the French Revolution; and its movement of ideas, by quitting the intellectual sphere and rushing furiously into the political sphere, ran, indeed, a prodigious and memorable course, but produced no such intellectual fruit as the movement of ideas of the Renascence, and created, in opposition to itself, what I may call an *epoch of concentration.* The great force of that epoch of concentration was England; and the great voice of that epoch of concentration was Burke.[17] It is the fashion to treat Burke's writings on the French Revolution as superannuated and conquered by the event; as the eloquent but unphilosophical tirades of bigotry and prejudice. I will not deny that they are often disfigured by the violence and passion of the moment, and that in some directions Burke's view

15. Joseph Joubert (1754–1824), French essayist to whom Arnold devotes one of the *Essays in Criticism.*

16. Arnold here boldly confronts the fact that the element of force is implicit in what we call government.

17. Edmund Burke (1729–97), one of England's most notable statesmen and political philosophers, opposed the French Revolution in his brilliant and eloquent *Reflections on the French Revolution* (1790).

was bounded, and his observation therefore at fault. But on the whole, and for those who can make the needful corrections, what distinguishes these writings is their profound, permanent, fruitful, philosophical truth. They contain the true philosophy of an epoch of concentration, dissipate the heavy atmosphere which its own nature is apt to engender round it, and make its resistance rational instead of mechanical.

But Burke is so great because, almost alone in England, he brings thought to bear upon politics, he saturates politics with thought. It is his accident that his ideas were at the service of an epoch of concentration, not of an epoch of expansion; it is his characteristic that he so lived by ideas, and had such a source of them welling up within him, that he could float even an epoch of concentration and English Tory politics with them. It does not hurt him that Dr. Price [18] and the Liberals were enraged with him; it does not even hurt him that George the Third and the Tories were enchanted with him. His greatness is that he lived in a world which neither English Liberalism nor English Toryism is apt to enter;—the world of ideas, not the world of catchwords and party habits. So far is it from being really true of him that he 'to party gave up what was meant for mankind,' [19] that at the very end of his fierce struggle with the French Revolution, after all his invectives against its false pretensions, hollowness, and madness, with his sincere conviction of its mischievousness, he can close a memorandum on the best means of combating it, some of the last pages he ever wrote,[20]—the *Thoughts on French Affairs*, in December 1791,—with these striking words:—

'The evil is stated, in my opinion, as it exists. The remedy must be where power, wisdom, and information, I hope, are more united with good intentions than they can be with me. I have done with this subject, I believe, for ever. It has given me many anxious moments for the last two years. *If a great change is to be made in human affairs, the minds of men will be fitted to it; the general opinions and feelings will draw that way. Every fear, every hope will forward it; and then they who persist in opposing this mighty current in human affairs, will appear rather to resist the decrees of Providence itself, than the mere designs of men. They will not be resolute and firm, but perverse and obstinate.*'

That return of Burke upon himself has always seemed to me one of the finest things in English literature, or indeed in any literature. That is what I call living by ideas: when one side of a question has long had your earnest support, when all your feelings are engaged, when you hear all round you no language but one, when your party talks this language like a steam-engine and can imagine no other,—still to be able to think, still to be irresistibly carried, if so it be, by the current of thought to the opposite side of the question, and, like Balaam, to be unable to speak anything *but what the Lord has put in your mouth*.[21] I

---

18. Richard Price, D.D. (1723–91), was a nonconformist minister, a writer on moral philosophy, and a vocal partisan of the French Revolution. Burke singles him out for attack in the *Reflections*.

19. Said by Oliver Goldsmith of his friend Burke in his poem *Retaliation* (1774).

20. Arnold is in error here—the pages are not the last Burke ever wrote; in 1796 he published *Letter to a Noble Lord* and *Letters on a Regicide Peace*, in which he voiced his relentless condemnation of the Revolution.

21. Numbers 22, 23. The point of the story is that Balaam blessed the Israelites although he had been sent by his king to curse them.

know nothing more striking, and I must add that I know nothing more un-English.

For the Englishman in general is like my friend the Member of Parliament, and believes, point-blank, that for a thing to be an anomaly is absolutely no objection to it whatever. He is like the Lord Auckland [22] of Burke's day, who, in a memorandum on the French Revolution, talks of 'certain miscreants, assuming the name of philosophers, who have presumed themselves capable of establishing a new system of society.' The Englishman has been called a political animal, and he values what is political and practical so much that ideas easily become objects of dislike in his eyes, and thinkers 'miscreants,' because ideas and thinkers have rashly meddled with politics and practice. This would be all very well if the dislike and neglect confined themselves to ideas transported out of their own sphere, and meddling rashly with practice; but they are inevitably extended to ideas as such, and to the whole life of intelligence; practice is everything, a free play of the mind is nothing. The notion of the free play of the mind upon all subjects being a pleasure in itself, being an object of desire, being an essential provider of elements without which a nation's spirit, whatever compensations it may have for them, must, in the long run, die of inanition, hardly enters into an Englishman's thoughts. It is noticeable that the word *curiosity*, which in other languages is used in a good sense, to mean, as a high and fine quality of man's nature, just this disinterested love of a free play of the mind on all subjects, for its own sake,—it is noticeable, I say, that this word has in our language no sense of the kind, no sense but a rather bad and disparaging one.[23] But criticism, real criticism, is essentially the exercise of this very quality. It obeys an instinct prompting it to try to know the best that is known and thought in the world, irrespectively of practice, politics, and everything of the kind; and to value knowledge and thought as they approach this best, without the intrusion of any other considerations whatever. This is an instinct for which there is, I think, little original sympathy in the practical English nature, and what there was of it has undergone a long benumbing period of blight and suppression in the epoch of concentration which followed the French Revolution.

But epochs of concentration cannot well endure for ever; epochs of expansion, in the due course of things, follow them. Such an epoch of expansion seems to be opening in this country. In the first place all danger of a hostile forcible pressure of foreign ideas upon our practice has long disappeared; like the traveller in the fable, therefore, we begin to wear our cloak a little more loosely.[24] Then, with a long peace, the ideas of Europe steal gradually and amicably in, and mingle, though in infinitesimally small quantities at a time, with our own notions. Then, too, in spite of all that is said about the absorbing and brutalising influence of our passionate material progress, it

22. William Eden, first Baron Auckland (1744–1814), was ambassador to The Hague during the French Revolution.

23. That is, personal inquisitiveness, intrusiveness into the affairs of others. Arnold speaks at fuller length of the English attitude toward the word in *Culture and Anarchy*. Pater in his essay *Romanticism* (see below) makes curiosity one of the elements of good modern literature.

24. Referring to Aesop's fable of the contest between the wind and the sun to see which could first make a traveler take off his cloak.

seems to me indisputable that this progress is likely, though not certain, to lead in the end to an apparition of intellectual life; and that man, after he has made himself perfectly comfortable and has now to determine what to do with himself next, may begin to remember that he has a mind, and that the mind may be made the source of great pleasure. I grant it is mainly the privilege of faith, at present, to discern this end to our railways, our business, and our fortune-making; but we shall see if, here as elsewhere, faith is not in the end the true prophet. Our ease, our travelling, and our unbounded liberty to hold just as hard and securely as we please to the practice to which our notions have given birth, all tend to beget an inclination to deal a little more freely with these notions themselves, to canvass them a little, to penetrate a little into their real nature. Flutterings of curiosity, in the foreign sense of the word, appear amongst us, and it is in these that criticism must look to find its account. Criticism first; a time of true creative activity, perhaps,—which, as I have said, must inevitably be preceded amongst us by a time of criticism,—hereafter, when criticism has done its work.

It is of the last importance that English criticism should clearly discern what rule for its course, in order to avail itself of the field now opening to it, and to produce fruit for the future, it ought to take. The rule may be summed up in one word,—*disinterestedness*. And how is criticism to show disinterestedness? By keeping aloof from what is called 'the practical view of things'; by resolutely following the law of its own nature, which is to be a free play of the mind on all subjects which it touches. By steadily refusing to lend itself to any of those ulterior, political, practical considerations about ideas, which plenty of people will be sure to attach to them, which perhaps ought often to be attached to them, which in this country at any rate are certain to be attached to them quite sufficiently, but which criticism has really nothing to do with. Its business is, as I have said, simply to know the best that is known and thought in the world, and by in its turn making this known, to create a current of true and fresh ideas. Its business is to do this with inflexible honesty, with due ability; but its business is to do no more, and to leave alone all questions of practical consequences and applications, questions which will never fail to have due prominence given to them. Else criticism, besides being really false to its own nature, merely continues in the old rut which it has hitherto followed in this country, and will certainly miss the chance now given to it. For what is at present the bane of criticism in this country? It is that practical considerations cling to it and stifle it. It subserves interests not its own. Our organs of criticism are organs of men and parties having practical ends to serve, and with them those practical ends are the first thing and the play of mind the second; so much play of mind as is compatible with the prosecution of those practical ends is all that is wanted. An organ like the *Revue des Deux Mondes*,[25] having for its main function to understand and utter the best that is known and thought in the world, existing, it may be said, as just an organ for a free play of the mind, we have not. But we have the *Edinburgh Review*, existing as an organ of the old Whigs, and for as much

25. Founded in 1829; it was especially notable for its literary and philosophical contributions. It ceased publication in 1944.

play of the mind as may suit its being that; we have the *Quarterly Review,* existing as an organ of the Tories, and for as much play of mind as may suit its being that; we have the *British Quarterly Review,* existing as an organ of the political Dissenters,[26] and for as much play of mind as may suit its being that; we have the *Times,* existing as an organ of the common, satisfied, well-to-do Englishman, and for as much play of m/nd as may suit its being that. And so on through all the various fractions, political and religious, of our society; every fraction has, as such, its organ of criticism, but the notion of combining all fractions in the common pleasure of a free disinterested play of mind meets with no favour. Directly this play of mind wants to have more scope, and to forget the pressure of practical considerations a little, it is checked, it is made to feel the chain. We saw this the other day in the extinction, so much to be regretted, of the *Home and Foreign Review.*[27] Perhaps in no organ of criticism in this country was there so much knowledge, so much play of mind; but these could not save it. The *Dublin Review* subordinates play of mind to the practical business of English and Irish Catholicism, and lives. It must needs be that men should act in sects and parties, that each of these sects and parties should have its organ, and should make this organ subserve the interests of its action; but it would be well, too, that there should be a criticism, not the minister of these interests, not their enemy, but absolutely and entirely independent of them. No other criticism will ever attain any real authority or make any real way towards its end,—the creating a current of true and fresh ideas.

It is because criticism has so little kept in the pure intellectual sphere, has so little detached itself from practice, has been so directly polemical and controversial, that it has so ill accomplished, in this country, its best spiritual work; which is to keep man from a self-satisfaction which is retarding and vulgarising, to lead him towards perfection, by making his mind dwell upon what is excellent in itself, and the absolute beauty and fitness of things. A polemical practical criticism makes men blind even to the ideal imperfection of their practice, makes them willingly assert its ideal perfection, in order the better to secure it against attack; and clearly this is narrowing and baneful for them. If they were reassured on the practical side, speculative considerations of ideal perfection they might be brought to entertain, and their spiritual horizon would thus gradually widen. Sir Charles Adderley [28] says to the Warwickshire farmers:—

'Talk of the improvement of breed! Why, the race we ourselves represent, the men and women, the old Anglo-Saxon race, are the best breed in the whole world. . . . The absence of a too enervating climate, too unclouded skies, and a too luxurious nature, has produced so vigorous a race of people, and has rendered us so superior to all the world.'

Mr. Roebuck [29] says to the Sheffield cutlers:—

26. Members of religious sects opposed to the Church of England and expressing their opposition politically.
27. Published in London 1862–64.
28. A Conservative politician (1814–1905) who inherited a great estate in Warwickshire.
29. John Arthur Roebuck (1801–79) was an aggressively radical politician who sometimes took anomalous reactionary positions.

'I look around me and ask what is the state of England? Is not property safe? Is not every man able to say what he likes? Can you not walk from one end of England to the other in perfect security? I ask you whether, the world over or in past history, there is anything like it? Nothing. I pray that our unrivalled happiness may last.'

Now obviously there is a peril for poor human nature in words and thoughts of such exuberant self-satisfaction, until we find ourselves safe in the streets of the Celestial City.

> Das wenige verschwindet leicht dem Blicke
> Der vorwärts sieht, wie viel noch übrig bleibt—

says Goethe; [30] 'the little that is done seems nothing when we look forward and see how much we have yet to do.' Clearly this is a better line of reflection for weak humanity, so long as it remains on this earthly field of labour and trial.

But neither Sir Charles Adderley nor Mr. Roebuck is by nature inaccessible to considerations of this sort. They only lose sight of them owing to the controversial life we all lead, and the practical form which all speculation takes with us. They have in view opponents whose aim is not ideal, but practical; and in their zeal to uphold their own practice against these innovators, they go so far as even to attribute to this practice an ideal perfection. Somebody has been wanting to introduce a six-pound franchise,[31] or to abolish church-rates,[32] or to collect agricultural statistics by force, or to diminish local self-government. How natural, in reply to such proposals, very likely improper or ill-timed, to go a little beyond the mark, and to say stoutly, 'Such a race of people as we stand, so superior to all the world! The old Anglo-Saxon race, the best breed in the whole world! I pray that our unrivalled happiness may last! I ask you whether, the world over or in past history, there is anything like it?' And so long as criticism answers this dithyramb by insisting that the old Anglo-Saxon race would be still more superior to all others if it had no church-rates, or that our unrivalled happiness would last yet longer with a six-pound franchise, so long will the strain, 'The best breed in the whole world!' swell louder and louder, everything ideal and refining will be lost out of sight, and both the assailed and their critics will remain in a sphere, to say the truth, perfectly unvital, a sphere in which spiritual progression is impossible. But let criticism leave church-rates and the franchise alone, and in the most candid spirit, without a single lurking thought of practical innovation, confront with our dithyramb this paragraph on which I stumbled in a newspaper immediately after reading Mr. Roebuck:—

'A shocking child murder has just been committed at Nottingham. A girl named Wragg left the workhouse there on Saturday morning with her young illegitimate child. The child was soon afterwards found dead on Mapperly Hills, having been strangled. Wragg is in custody.'

Nothing but that; but, in juxtaposition with the absolute eulogies of Sir

30. In *Iphigenie auf Tauris* I.ii.91–92.
31. A proposal to liberalize suffrage by giving the vote to anyone who owned land or buildings worth a rent of £6 a year.
32. Taxes imposed on behalf of the Church of England.

Charles Adderley and Mr. Roebuck, how eloquent, how suggestive are those few lines! 'Our old Anglo-Saxon breed, the best in the whole world!'—how much that is harsh and ill-favoured there is in this best! *Wragg!* If we are to talk of ideal perfection, of 'the best in the whole world,' has any one reflected what a touch of grossness in our race, what an original shortcoming in the more delicate spiritual perceptions, is shown by the natural growth amongst us of such hideous names,—Higginbottom, Stiggins, Bugg! In Ionia and Attica [33] they were luckier in this respect than 'the best race in the world'; by the Ilissus [34] there was no Wragg, poor thing! And 'our unrivalled happiness';—what an element of grimness, bareness, and hideousness mixes with it and blurs it; the workhouse, the dismal Mapperly Hills,[35]—how dismal those who have seen them will remember;—the gloom, the smoke, the cold, the strangled illegitimate child! 'I ask you whether, the world over or in past history, there is anything like it?' Perhaps not, one is inclined to answer; but at any rate, in that case, the world is [not] very much to be pitied. And the final touch,—short, bleak, and inhuman: *Wragg is in custody.* The sex lost in the confusion of our unrivalled happiness; or (shall I say?) the superfluous Christian name lopped off by the straightforward vigour of our old Anglo-Saxon breed! There is profit for the spirit in such contrasts as this; criticism serves the cause of perfection by establishing them. By eluding sterile conflict, by refusing to remain in the sphere where alone narrow and relative conceptions have any worth and validity, criticism may diminish its momentary importance, but only in this way has it a chance of gaining admittance for those wider and more perfect conceptions to which all its duty is really owed. Mr. Roebuck will have a poor opinion of an adversary who replies to his defiant songs of triumph only by murmuring under his breath, *Wragg is in custody;* but in no other way will these songs of triumph be induced gradually to moderate themselves, to get rid of what in them is excessive and offensive, and to fall into a softer and truer key.

It will be said that it is a very subtle and indirect action which I am thus prescribing for criticism, and that, by embracing in this manner the Indian virtue of detachment [36] and abandoning the sphere of practical life, it condemns itself to a slow and obscure work. Slow and obscure it may be, but it is the only proper work of criticism. The mass of mankind will never have any ardent zeal for seeing things as they are; very inadequate ideas will always satisfy them. On these inadequate ideas reposes, and must repose, the general practice of the world. That is as much as saying that whoever sets himself to see things as they are will find himself one of a very small circle; but it is only by this small circle resolutely doing its own work that adequate ideas will ever get current at all. The rush and roar of practical life will always have a dizzying and attracting effect upon the most collected spectator, and tend to draw him into its vortex; most of all will this be the case where that life is so powerful as it is in England. But it is only by remaining collected, and refusing to lend himself to the point of view of the practical man, that the critic can do the

33. Districts of Greece.
34. A river near Athens.
35. The coal-mining environs of Nottingham.
36. Reference to the Buddhist ideal of disengagement from worldly activity.

practical man any service; and it is only by the greatest sincerity in pursuing his own course, and by at last convincing even the practical man of his sincerity, that he can escape misunderstandings which perpetually threaten him.

For the practical man is not apt for fine distinctions, and yet in these distinctions truth and the highest culture greatly find their account. But it is not easy to lead a practical man,—unless you reassure him as to your practical intentions, you have no chance of leading him,—to see that a thing which he has always been used to look at from one side only, which he greatly values, and which, looked at from that side, quite deserves, perhaps, all the prizing and admiring which he bestows upon it,—that this thing, looked at from another side, may appear much less beneficent and beautiful, and yet retain all its claims to our practical allegiance. Where shall we find language innocent enough, how shall we make the spotless purity of our intentions evident enough, to enable us to say to the political Englishman that the British Constitution itself, which, seen from the practical side, looks such a magnificent organ of progress and virtue, seen from the speculative side,—with its compromises, its love of facts, its horror of theory, its studied avoidance of clear thoughts,— that, seen from this side, our august Constitution sometimes looks,—forgive me, shade of Lord Somers! [37]—a colossal machine for the manufacture of Philistines? [38] How is Cobbett [39] to say this and not be misunderstood, blackened as he is with the smoke of a lifelong conflict in the field of political practice? how is Mr. Carlyle to say it and not be misunderstood, after his furious raid into this field with his *Latter-day Pamphlets?* how is Mr. Ruskin, after his pugnacious political economy? [40] I say, the critic must keep out of the region of immediate practice in the political, social, humanitarian sphere, if he wants to make a beginning for that more free speculative treatment of things, which may perhaps one day make its benefits felt even in this sphere, but in a natural and thence irresistible manner.

Do what he will, however, the critic will still remain exposed to frequent misunderstandings, and nowhere so much as in this country. For here people are particularly indisposed even to comprehend that without this free disinterested treatment of things, truth and the highest culture are out of the question. So immersed are they in practical life, so accustomed to take all their notions from this life and its processes, that they are apt to think that truth and culture themselves can be reached by the processes of this life, and that it is an impertinent singularity to think of reaching them in any other. 'We are all *terræ filii,*'[41] cries their eloquent advocate; 'all Philistines together.

37. John Somers, Baron Somers (1651–1716), eminent constitutional lawyer who, after the abdication of James II, presided over the commission that drafted the Bill of Rights.
38. Arnold's name for the middle classes in their resistance to reason and culture. The Philistines were neighbors and enemies of the people of Israel, the "children of light"; for their deplorable conduct, see Judges and Milton's *Samson Agonistes.* Arnold, in his essay on Heinrich Heine, refers to Heine's use of the word in the sense he himself was to establish in the language by his frequent iteration of it.
39. William Cobbett (1762–1835), the famous political journalist and pamphleteer, a passionate fighter for reform and democracy.
40. In *Unto This Last* (1860–62). With these essays, Ruskin turned from art criticism to economics. The first essays appeared in *Cornhill Magazine* and made such a scandal by the heterodoxy of their views that the series was discontinued.
41. "Sons of the earth."

Away with the notion of proceeding by any other course than the course dear to the Philistines; let us have a social movement, let us organise and combine a party to pursue truth and new thought, let us call it *the liberal party,* and let us all stick to each other, and back each other up. Let us have no nonsense about independent criticism, and intellectual delicacy, and the few and the many. Don't let us trouble ourselves about foreign thought; we shall invent the whole thing for ourselves as we go along. If one of us speaks well, applaud him; if one of us speaks ill, applaud him too; we are all in the same movement, we are all liberals, we are all in pursuit of truth.' In this way the pursuit of truth becomes really a social, practical, pleasurable affair, almost requiring a chairman, a secretary, and advertisements; with the excitement of an occasional scandal, with a little resistance to give the happy sense of difficulty overcome; but, in general, plenty of bustle and very little thought. To act is so easy, as Goethe says; to think is so hard! It is true that the critic has many temptations to go with the stream, to make one of the party movement, one of these *terræ filii;* it seems ungracious to refuse to be a *terræ filius,* when so many excellent people are; but the critic's duty is to refuse, or, if resistance is vain, at least to cry with Obermann: *Périssons en résistant.*[42]

[At this point Arnold digresses from the main line of his argument to cite examples of "bustle and very little thought" in the religious life of England. This excursion of three long paragraphs, crowded with topical allusions, has lost interest with the passage of time and has been omitted.]

For criticism, these are elementary laws; but they never can be popular, and in this country they have been very little followed, and one meets with immense obstacles in following them. That is a reason for asserting them again and again. Criticism must maintain its independence of the practical spirit and its aims. Even with well-meant efforts of the practical spirit it must express dissatisfaction, if in the sphere of the ideal they seem impoverishing and limiting. It must not hurry on to the goal because of its practical importance. It must be patient, and know how to wait; and flexible, and know how to attach itself to things and how to withdraw from them. It must be apt to study and praise elements that for the fulness of spiritual perfection are wanted, even though they belong to a power which in the practical sphere may be maleficent. It must be apt to discern the spiritual shortcomings or illusions of powers that in the practical sphere may be beneficent. And this without any notion of favouring or injuring, in the practical sphere, one power or the other; without any notion of playing off, in this sphere, one power against the other. When one looks, for instance, at the English Divorce Court,—an institution which perhaps has its practical conveniences, but which in the ideal sphere is so hideous; an institution which neither makes divorce impossible

42. "Let us die resisting." Obermann is the writer of the letters which make up the novel—if that is what it is to be called—to which he gives his name. It was published in 1804, the work of Etienne Pivert de Senancour (1770–1846), and in its day was famous and influential. Over many years, Obermann, who lives in isolation in a Swiss Alpine valley, writes to a friend describing his melancholy sense of the emptiness of life, his inability to engage in any purposeful activity. Arnold was among the many young men who found in the book the confirmation of their own feeling of alienation from the modern world; he celebrates it in an early poem, *Stanzas in Memory of the Author of "Obermann,"* and in a late one, *Obermann Once More.*

nor makes it decent, which allows a man to get rid of his wife, or a wife of her husband, but makes them drag one another first, for the public edification, through a mire of unutterable infamy,—when one looks at this charming institution, I say, with its crowded trials, its newspaper reports, and its money compensations, this institution in which the gross unregenerate British Philistine has indeed stamped an image of himself,—one may be permitted to find the marriage theory of Catholicism refreshing and elevating. Or when Protestantism, in virtue of its supposed rational and intellectual origin, gives the law to criticism too magisterially, criticism may and must remind it that its pretensions, in this respect, are illusive and do it harm; that the Reformation was a moral rather than an intellectual event; that Luther's theory of grace no more exactly reflects the mind of the spirit than Bossuet's philosophy of history reflects it; [43] and that there is no more antecedent probability of the Bishop of Durham's stock of ideas being agreeable to perfect reason than of Pope Pius the Ninth's.[44] But criticism will not on that account forget the achievements of Protestantism in the practical and moral sphere; nor that, even in the intellectual sphere, Protestantism, though in a blind and stumbling manner, carried forward the Renascence, while Catholicism threw itself violently across its path.

I lately heard a man of thought and energy contrasting the want of ardour and movement which he now found amongst young men in this country with what he remembered in his own youth, twenty years ago. 'What reformers we were then!' he exclaimed; 'what a zeal we had! how we canvassed every institution in Church and State, and were prepared to remodel them all on first principles!' He was inclined to regret, as a spiritual flagging, the lull which he saw. I am disposed rather to regard it as a pause in which the turn to a new mode of spiritual progress is being accomplished. Everything was long seen, by the young and ardent amongst us, in inseparable connection with politics and practical life. We have pretty well exhausted the benefits of seeing things in this connection, we have got all that can be got by so seeing them. Let us try a more disinterested mode of seeing them; let us betake ourselves more to the serener life of the mind and spirit. This life, too, may have its excesses and dangers; but they are not for us at present. Let us think of quietly enlarging our stock of true and fresh ideas, and not, as soon as we get an idea or half an idea, be running out with it into the street, and trying to make it rule there. Our ideas will, in the end, shape the world all the better for maturing a little. Perhaps in fifty years' time it will in the English House of Commons be an objection to an institution that it is an anomaly, and my friend the Member of Parliament will shudder in his grave. But let us in the meanwhile rather endeavour that in twenty years' time it may, in English literature, be an objection to a proposition that it is absurd. That will be a

---

43. Jacques Bénigne Bossuet (1627–1704), French bishop famous as a preacher, moralist, and religious polemicist, advanced the view that historical events were providential, designed for the establishment of Christianity and particularly of the Roman Catholic Church.
44. He was pope from 1846 to 1878; his "stock of ideas" is set over against those of the Bishop of the Church of England.

change so vast, that the imagination almost fails to grasp it. *Ab integro sæclo-rum nascitur ordo.*[45]

If I have insisted so much on the course which criticism must take where politics and religion are concerned, it is because, where these burning matters are in question, it is most likely to go astray. I have wished, above all, to insist on the attitude which criticism should adopt towards things in general; on its right tone and temper of mind. But then comes another question as to the subject-matter which literary criticism should most seek. Here, in general, its course is determined for it by the idea which is the law of its being; the idea of a disinterested endeavour to learn and propagate the best that is known and thought in the world, and thus to establish a current of fresh and true ideas. By the very nature of things, as England is not all the world, much of the best that is known and thought in the world cannot be of English growth, must be foreign; by the nature of things, again, it is just this that we are least likely to know, while English thought is streaming in upon us from all sides, and takes excellent care that we shall not be ignorant of its existence. The English critic of literature, therefore, must dwell much on foreign thought, and with particular heed on any part of it, which, while significant and fruitful in itself, is for any reason specially likely to escape him. Again, judging is often spoken of as the critic's one business, and so in some sense it is; but the judgment which almost insensibly forms itself in a fair and clear mind, along with fresh knowledge, is the valuable one; and thus knowledge, and ever fresh knowledge, must be the critic's great concern for himself. And it is by com-municating fresh knowledge, and letting his own judgment pass along with it,—but insensibly, and in the second place, not the first, as a sort of companion and clue, not as an abstract law-giver,—that the critic will generally do most good to his readers. Sometimes, no doubt, for the sake of establishing an author's place in literature, and his relation to a central standard (and if this is not done, how are we to get at our *best in the world?*) criticism may have to deal with a subject-matter so familiar that fresh knowledge is out of the question, and then it must be all judgment; an enunciation and detailed appli-cation of principles. Here the great safeguard is never to let oneself become abstract, always to retain an intimate and lively consciousness of the truth of what one is saying, and, the moment this fails us, to be sure that something is wrong. Still, under all circumstances, this mere judgment and application of principles is, in itself, not the most satisfactory work to the critics; like mathe-matics, it is tautological, and cannot well give us, like fresh learning, the sense of creative activity.

But stop, some one will say; all this talk is of no practical use to us what-ever; this criticism of yours is not what we have in our minds when we speak of criticism; when we speak of critics and criticism, we mean critics and criti-cism of the current English literature of the day; when you offer to tell criticism its function, it is to this criticism that we expect you to address yourself. I am sorry for it, for I am afraid I must disappoint these expectations. I am bound by my own definition of criticism: *a disinterested endeavour to learn and*

45. "From the renewal of the ages is order born." Virgil, *Eclogues* IV.5.

propagate the best that is known and thought in the world. How much of current English literature comes into this 'best that is known and thought in the world'? Not very much, I fear; certainly less, at this moment, than of the current literature of France or Germany. Well, then, am I to alter my definition of criticism, in order to meet the requirements of a number of practising English critics, who, after all, are free in their choice of a business? That would be making criticism lend itself just to one of those alien practical considerations, which, I have said, are so fatal to it. One may say, indeed, to those who have to deal with the mass—so much better disregarded—of current English literature, that they may at all events endeavour, in dealing with this, to try it, so far as they can, by the standard of the best that is known and thought in the world; one may say, that to get anywhere near this standard, every critic should try and possess one great literature, at least, besides his own; and the more unlike his own, the better. But, after all, the criticism I am really concerned with,—the criticism which alone can much help us for the future, the criticism which, throughout Europe, is at the present day meant, when so much stress is laid on the importance of criticism and the critical spirit,—is a criticism which regards Europe as being, for intellectual and spiritual purposes, one great confederation, bound to a joint action and working to a common result; and whose members have, for their proper outfit, a knowledge of Greek, Roman, and Eastern antiquity, and of one another. Special, local, and temporary advantages being put out of account, that modern nation will in the intellectual and spiritual sphere make most progress, which most thoroughly carries out this programme. And what is that but saying that we too, all of us, as individuals, the more thoroughly we carry it out, shall make the more progress?

There is so much inviting us!—what are we to take? what will nourish us in growth towards perfection? That is the question which, with the immense field of life and of literature lying before him, the critic has to answer; for himself first, and afterwards for others. In this idea of the critic's business the essays brought together in the following pages [46] have had their origin; in this idea, widely different as are their subjects, they have, perhaps, their unity.

I conclude with what I said at the beginning: to have the sense of creative activity is the great happiness and the great proof of being alive, and it is not denied to criticism to have it; but then criticism must be sincere, simple, flexible, ardent, ever widening its knowledge. Then it may have, in no contemptible measure, a joyful sense of creative activity; a sense which a man of insight and conscience will prefer to what he might derive from a poor, starved, fragmentary, inadequate creation. And at some epochs no other creation is possible.

Still, in full measure, the sense of creative activity belongs only to genuine creation; in literature we must never forget that. But what true man of letters ever can forget it? It is no such common matter for a gifted nature to come into possession of a current of true and living ideas, and to produce amidst the inspiration of them, that we are likely to underrate it. The epochs of Æschylus and Shakespeare make us feel their pre-eminence. In an epoch like

46. The essay served as the introduction to *Essays in Criticism.*

those is, no doubt, the true life of literature; there is the promised land, towards which criticism can only beckon. That promised land it will not be ours to enter, and we shall die in the wilderness: but to have desired to enter it, to have saluted it from afar, is already, perhaps, the best distinction among contemporaries; it will certainly be the best title to esteem with posterity.

1864   1864, 1865

The Study of Poetry

Of *The Study of Poetry,* the most ambitious and famous of Arnold's late critical essays, T. S. Eliot said that it is "a classic in English criticism; so much is said in so little space, with such economy and with such authority." The praise has the more force, and an especial interest, as coming from a writer who, both as critic and as poet, put himself in opposition to every canon of taste the essay proposes. In this opposition Eliot is not alone—in our time *The Study of Poetry* exists in the aura of the controversy it provokes. It is challenged in its first premise, that poetry has a "future" which is "immense," that it confronts "high destinies" of which it must be worthy.

Whatever store contemporary critics and poets set upon poetry—and they are intransigent in affirming its everlasting importance—they do not envision its existence to be thus grandiose. They are not likely to accept the condition that Arnold makes for the realization of its potentialities, in effect that it speaks with that largeness of utterance, chiefly about the tragic aspects of life, which will make its voice cognate with that of religion in its emotive aspects. It is this that constitutes Arnold's criterion of greatness in poetry. But the taste and theory of our time are much less concerned with greatness than Arnold was, or at least they are less certain than he was that the word should imply chiefly largeness or grandness of spirit. Our age is drawn rather to such qualities as suggest the personal authenticity of the poetic voice and these, it feels, do not readily consort with the solemnity of greatness. Arnold's roster of English poets is judged strangely incomplete in its silent omissions—it takes no heed, for example, of Donne, Marvell, Herbert, and Vaughan—and culpable in its explicit exclusion of Dryden and Pope, who are held not to be poets at all. But when all possible objections to the essay have been made, it stands as what Eliot says it is, a classic of English criticism. It is that, many will feel, exactly in the degree that we are led to dispute it. The value of a work of literary criticism is not to be measured by the readiness or warmth of assent we give to its judgments but by its ability to induce us to think directly and immediately about literature. Of *The Study of Poetry* it can be said that, Dr. Johnson on *Lycidas* alone excepted, no work of criticism so well instructs us by the disagreement it arouses.

From The Study of Poetry

'The future of poetry is immense, because in poetry, where it is worthy of its high destinies, our race, as time goes on, will find an ever surer and surer stay. There is not a creed which is not shaken, not an accredited dogma which is not shown to be questionable, not a received tradition which does not threaten to dissolve. Our religion has materialised itself in the fact, in the supposed fact; it has attached its emotion to the fact, and now the fact is failing it. But for poetry the idea is everything; the rest is a world of illusion, of divine illusion. Poetry attaches its emotion to the idea; the idea *is* the fact. The strongest part of our religion to-day is its unconscious poetry.'[1]

Let me be permitted to quote these words of my own, as uttering the thought which should, in my opinion, go with us and govern us in all our study of poetry. In the present work[2] it is the course of one great contributory stream to the world-river of poetry that we are invited to follow. We are here invited to trace the stream of English poetry. But whether we set ourselves, as here, to follow only one of the several streams that make the mighty river of poetry, or whether we seek to know them all, our governing thought should be the same. We should conceive of poetry worthily, and more highly than it has been the custom to conceive of it. We should conceive of it as capable of higher uses, and called to higher destinies, than those which in general men have assigned to it hitherto. More and more mankind will discover that we have to turn to poetry to interpret life for us, to console us, to sustain us. Without poetry, our science will appear incomplete; and most of what now passes with us for religion and philosophy will be replaced by poetry. Science, I say, will appear incomplete without it. For finely and truly does Wordsworth call poetry 'the impassioned expression which is in the countenance of all science'; and what is a countenance without its expression? Again, Wordsworth finely and truly calls poetry 'the breath and finer spirit of all knowledge': our religion, parading evidences such as those on which the popular mind relies now;[3] our philosophy, pluming itself on its reasonings about causation and finite and infinite being; what are they but the shadows and dreams and false shows of knowledge? The day will come when we shall wonder at ourselves for having trusted to them, for having taken them seriously; and the more we perceive their hollowness, the more we shall prize 'the breath and finer spirit of knowledge' offered to us by poetry.

But if we conceive thus highly of the destinies of poetry, we must also set our standard for poetry high, since poetry, to be capable of fulfilling such high destinies, must be poetry of a high order of excellence. We must accustom ourselves to a high standard and to a strict judgment. Sainte-Beuve[4] relates that

1. Arnold quotes a slightly abbreviated version of the paragraph which concludes the introduction he had written for an ephemeral book called *The Hundred Greatest Men* (1879).
2. Arnold refers to the comprehensive anthology *The English Poets,* to which his essay serves as the introduction.
3. Arnold here recurs to the idea, already touched on in the opening paragraph, which was at the center of the criticism of English religious life he had been making over the previous decade—that the basis of popular faith was the literal interpretation of the Bible, specifically the credence given to miracles; this, he held, could not possibly maintain itself in the face of developing science, and unless English Protestantism found a more spiritual ground for belief, it would have none at all.
4. Charles-Augustin Sainte-Beuve (1804–69), the French critic for whom Arnold often expressed high respect.

Napoleon one day said, when somebody was spoken of in his presence as a charlatan: 'Charlatan as much as you please; but where is there *not* charlatanism?'—'Yes,' answers Sainte-Beuve, 'in politics, in the art of governing mankind, that is perhaps true. But in the order of thought, in art, the glory, the eternal honour is that charlatanism shall find no entrance; herein lies the inviolableness of that noble portion of man's being.' It is admirably said, and let us hold fast to it. In poetry, which is thought and art in one, it is the glory, the eternal honour, that charlatanism shall find no entrance; that this noble sphere be kept inviolate and inviolable. Charlatanism is for confusing or obliterating the distinctions between excellent and inferior, sound and unsound or only half-sound, true and untrue or only half-true. It is charlatanism, conscious or unconscious, whenever we confuse or obliterate these. And in poetry, more than anywhere else, it is unpermissible to confuse or obliterate them. For in poetry the distinction between excellent and inferior, sound and unsound or only half-sound, true and untrue or only half-true, is of paramount importance. It is of paramount importance because of the high destinies of poetry. In poetry, as a criticism of life [5] under the conditions fixed for such a criticism by the laws of poetic truth and poetic beauty, the spirit of our race will find, we have said, as time goes on and as other helps fail, its consolation and stay. But the consolation and stay will be of power in proportion to the power of the criticism of life. And the criticism of life will be of power in proportion as the poetry conveying it is excellent rather than inferior, sound rather than unsound or half-sound, true rather than untrue or half-true.

The best poetry is what we want; the best poetry will be found to have a power of forming, sustaining, and delighting us, as nothing else can. A clearer, deeper sense of the best in poetry, and of the strength and joy to be drawn from it, is the most precious benefit which we can gather from a poetical collection such as the present. And yet in the very nature and conduct of such a collection there is inevitably something which tends to obscure in us the consciousness of what our benefit should be, and to distract us from the pursuit of it. We should therefore steadily set it before our minds at the outset, and should compel ourselves to revert constantly to the thought of it as we proceed.

Yes; constantly, in reading poetry, a sense for the best, the really excellent, and of the strength and joy to be drawn from it, should be present in our minds and should govern our estimate of what we read. But this real estimate, the only true one, is liable to be superseded, if we are not watchful, by two other kinds of estimate, the historic estimate and the personal estimate, both of which are fallacious. A poet or a poem may count to us historically, they may count to us on grounds personal to ourselves, and they may count to us really. They may count to us historically. The course of development of a

5. No phrase of Arnold's is more often quoted or more often objected to than this one. Among the objections that of T. S. Eliot is probably the best known—Eliot said that as a definition of poetry the phrase must seem "frigid to anyone who has felt the full surprise and elevation of a new experience of poetry." To which the reply might be made that Arnold meant—at least in part—that it is exactly the full surprise and elevation of a new experience of poetry that constitutes a criticism of life, of life as it is all too habitually lived.

nation's language, thought, and poetry, is profoundly interesting; and by regarding a poet's work as a stage in this course of development we may easily bring ourselves to make it of more importance as poetry than in itself it really is, we may come to use a language of quite exaggerated praise in criticising it; in short, to overrate it. So arises in our poetic judgments the fallacy caused by the estimate which we may call historic. Then, again, a poet or a poem may count to us on grounds personal to ourselves. Our personal affinities, likings, and circumstances have great power to sway our estimate of this or that poet's work, and to make us attach more importance to it as poetry than in itself it really possesses, because to us it is, or has been, of high importance. Here also we overrate the object of our interest, and apply to it a language of praise which is quite exaggerated. And thus we get the source of a second fallacy in our poetic judgments—the fallacy caused by an estimate which we may call personal.

Both fallacies are natural. It is evident how naturally the study of the history and development of a poetry may incline a man to pause over reputations and works once conspicuous but now obscure, and to quarrel with a careless public for skipping, in obedience to mere tradition and habit, from one famous name or work in its national poetry to another, ignorant of what it misses, and of the reason for keeping what it keeps, and of the whole process of growth in its poetry. The French have become diligent students of their own early poetry, which they long neglected; the study makes many of them dissatisfied with their so-called classical poetry, the court-tragedy of the seventeenth century, a poetry which Pellisson [6] long ago reproached with its want of the true poetic stamp, with its *politesse stérile et rampante*,[7] but which nevertheless has reigned in France as absolutely as if it had been the perfection of classical poetry indeed. The dissatisfaction is natural; yet a lively and accomplished critic, M. Charles d'Héricault, the editor of Clément Marot,[8] goes too far when he says that 'the cloud of glory playing round a classic is a mist as dangerous to the future of a literature as it is intolerable for the purposes of history.' 'It hinders,' he goes on, 'it hinders us from seeing more than one single point, the culminating and exceptional point; the summary, fictitious and arbitrary, of a thought and of a work. It substitutes a halo for a physiognomy, it puts a statue where there was once a man, and, hiding from us all trace of the labour, the attempts, the weaknesses, the failures, it claims not study but veneration; it does not show us how the thing is done, it imposes upon us a model. Above all, for the historian this creation of classic personages is inadmissible; for it withdraws the poet from his time, from his proper life, it breaks historical relationships, it blinds criticism by conventional admiration, and renders the investigation of literary origins unacceptable. It gives us a human personage no longer, but a God seated immovable amidst His perfect

---

6. Paul Pellisson (1624–93), French man of letters. His history of the French Academy was praised by Sainte-Beuve.

7. "Sterile and truckling urbanity." (In French the word "rampant" means just the opposite of what it means in English.)

8. A witty and graceful poet (1496–1544), whose work had some influence on English poets of the 16th century, including Spenser. Héricault's edition of Marot's poems appeared from 1868 to 1872.

work, like Jupiter on Olympus; and hardly will it be possible for the young student, to whom such work is exhibited at such a distance from him, to believe that it did not issue ready made from that divine head.'

All this is brilliantly and tellingly said, but we must plead for a distinction. Everything depends on the reality of a poet's classic character. If he is a dubious classic, let us sift him; if he is a false classic, let us explode him. But if he is a real classic, if his work belongs to the class of the very best (for this is the true and right meaning of the word *classic, classical*), then the great thing for us is to feel and enjoy his work as deeply as ever we can, and to appreciate the wide difference between it and all work which has not the same high character. This is what is salutary, this is what is formative; this is the great benefit to be got from the study of poetry. Everything which interferes with it, which hinders it, is injurious. True, we must read our classic with open eyes, and not with eyes blinded with superstition; we must perceive when his work comes short, when it drops out of the class of the very best, and we must rate it, in such cases, at its proper value. But the use of this negative criticism is not in itself, it is entirely in its enabling us to have a clearer sense and a deeper enjoyment of what is truly excellent. To trace the labour, the attempts, the weaknesses, the failures of a genuine classic, to acquaint oneself with his time and his life and his historical relationships, is mere literary dilettantism unless it has that clear sense and deeper enjoyment for its end. It may be said that the more we know about a classic the better we shall enjoy him; and, if we lived as long as Methuselah [9] and had all of us heads of perfect clearness and wills of perfect steadfastness, this might be true in fact as it is plausible in theory. But the case here is much the same as the case with the Greek and Latin studies of our schoolboys. The elaborate philological groundwork which we require them to lay is in theory an admirable preparation for appreciating the Greek and Latin authors worthily. The more thoroughly we lay the groundwork, the better we shall be able, it may be said, to enjoy the authors. True, if time were not so short, and schoolboys' wits not so soon tired and their power of attention exhausted; only, as it is, the elaborate philological preparation goes on, but the authors are little known and less enjoyed. So with the investigator of 'historic origins' in poetry. He ought to enjoy the true classic all the better for his investigations; he often is distracted from the enjoyment of the best, and with the less good he overbusies himself, and is prone to overrate it in proportion to the trouble which it has cost him.

The idea of tracing historic origins and historical relationships cannot be absent from a compilation like the present. And naturally the poets to be exhibited in it will be assigned to those persons for exhibition who are known to prize them highly, rather than to those who have no special inclination towards them. Moreover, the very occupation with an author, and the business of exhibiting him, disposes us to affirm and amplify his importance. In the present work, therefore, we are sure of frequent temptation to adopt the historic estimate, or the personal estimate, and to forget the real estimate; which latter, nevertheless, we must employ if we are to make poetry yield us

9. Genesis 5:27 says 969 years.

its full benefit. So high is that benefit, the benefit of clearly feeling and of deeply enjoying the really excellent, the truly classic in poetry, that we do well, I say, to set it fixedly before our minds as our object in studying poets and poetry, and to make the desire of attaining it the one principle to which, as the *Imitation* [10] says, whatever we may read or come to know, we always return. *Cum multa legeris et cognoveris, ad unum semper oportet redire principium.* [11]

The historic estimate is likely in especial to affect our judgment and our language when we are dealing with ancient poets; the personal estimate when we are dealing with poets our contemporaries, or at any rate modern. The exaggerations due to the historic estimate are not in themselves, perhaps, of very much gravity. Their report hardly enters the general ear; probably they do not always impose even on the literary men who adopt them. But they lead to a dangerous abuse of language. So we hear Caedmon,[12] amongst our own poets, compared to Milton. I have already noticed the enthusiasm of one accomplished French critic for 'historic origins.' Another eminent French critic, M. Vitet,[13] comments upon that famous document of the early poetry of his nation, the *Chanson de Roland.*[14] It is indeed a most interesting document. The *joculator* or *jongleur* [15] Taillefer, who was with William the Conqueror's army at Hastings, marched before the Norman troops, so said the tradition, singing 'of Charlemagne and of Roland and of Oliver, and of the vassals who died at Roncevaux'; and it is suggested that in the *Chanson de Roland* by one Turoldus or Théroulde,[16] a poem preserved in a manuscript of the twelfth century in the Bodleian Library at Oxford, we have certainly the matter, perhaps even some of the words, of the chant which Taillefer sang. The poem has vigour and freshness; it is not without pathos. But M. Vitet is not satisfied with seeing in it a document of some poetic value, and of very high historic and linguistic value; he sees in it a grand and beautiful work, a monument of epic genius. In its general design he finds the grandiose conception, in its details he finds the constant union of simplicity with greatness, which are the marks, he truly says, of the genuine epic, and distinguish it from the artificial epic of literary ages. One thinks of Homer; this is the sort of praise which is given to Homer, and justly given. Higher praise there cannot well be, and it is the praise due to epic poetry of the highest order only, and to no other. Let us try, then, the *Chanson de Roland* at its best. Roland, mortally wounded, lay himself down under a pine-tree, with his face turned towards Spain and the enemy:—

10. *The Imitation of Christ* by Thomas à Kempis (1380–1471), a devotional work once of great influence.
11. "When you have read and learned many things, you ought always return to the one principle." III.xliii.2.
12. Cædmon, who lived in the 7th century, wrote an Old English poem on the events of Genesis which Milton treated in *Paradise Lost;* hence the comparison.
13. Ludovic Vitet (1802–73), French politician and man of letters.
14. An epic poem of the 11th century. Its climactic episode is the courageous effort of Roland and Oliver, the two leaders of the rearguard of Charlemagne's army, to hold the pass of Roncevaux (Roncevalles) against the Saracens.
15. Minstrel.
16. It is not known exactly who this person is; he may have been the author of the poem, or the author of its source, or merely its scribe.

> De plusurs choses à remembrer li prist,
> De tantes teres cume li bers cunquist,
> De dulce France, des humes de sun lign,
> De Carlemagne sun seignor ki l'nurrit.[17]

That is primitive work, I repeat, with an undeniable poetic quality of its own. It deserves such praise, and such praise is sufficient for it. But now turn to Homer:—

> "Ὢς φάτο· τοὺς δ' ἤδη κατέχεν φυσίζοος αἶα
> ἐν Λακεδαίμονι αὖθι, φίλῃ ἐν πατρίδι γαίῃ.[18]

We are here in another world, another order of poetry altogether; here is rightly due such supreme praise as that which M. Vitet gives to the *Chanson de Roland*. If our words are to have any meaning, if our judgments are to have any solidity, we must not heap that supreme praise upon poetry of an order immeasurably inferior.

Indeed there can be no more useful help for discovering what poetry belongs to the class of the truly excellent, and can therefore do us most good, than to have always in one's mind lines and expressions of the great masters, and to apply them as a touchstone to other poetry. Of course we are not to require this other poetry to resemble them; it may be very dissimilar. But if we have any tact we shall find them, when we have lodged them well in our minds, an infallible touchstone [19] for detecting the presence or absence of high poetic quality, and also the degree of this quality, in all other poetry which we may place beside them. Short passages, even single lines, will serve our turn quite sufficiently. Take the two lines which I have just quoted from Homer, the poet's comment on Helen's mention of her brothers;—or take his

> Ἄ δειλώ, τί σφῶϊ δόμεν Πηλῆϊ ἄνακτι
> θνητῷ; ὑμεῖς δ' ἐστὸν ἀγήρω τ' ἀθανάτω τε.
> ἦ ἵνα δυστήνοισι μετ' ἀνδράσιν ἄλγε' ἔχητον; [20]

the address of Zeus to the horses of Peleus;—or take finally this

> Καὶ σέ, γέρον, τὸ πρὶν μὲν ἀκούομεν ὄλβιον εἶναι·[21]

the words of Achilles to Priam, a suppliant before him. Take that incomparable line and a half of Dante, Ugolino's tremendous words:—

17. " 'Then began he to call many things to remembrance,—all the lands which his valour conquered, and pleasant France, and the men of his lineage, and Charlemagne his liege lord who nourished him.'—*Chanson de Roland* iii.939–42." (Arnold)

18. " 'So said she; they long since in Earth's soft arms were reposing, / There, in their own dear land, their fatherland, Lacedaemon.'—*Iliad* iii.243–44. (translated by Dr. Hawtrey)." (Arnold)

19. A touchstone is a hard black stone formerly used to test the quality of gold or silver by comparing the streak which is left on the stone by the metal being tested with that left by the standard alloy.

20. " 'Ah, unhappy pair, why gave we you to King Peleus, to a mortal? but ye are without old age, and immortal. Was it that with men born to misery ye might have sorrow?' *Iliad* xvii.443–45." (Arnold) Peleus was the father of Achilles.

21. " 'Nay, and thou too, old man, in former days wast, as we hear, happy.'—*Iliad* xxiv.543." (Arnold) Priam has come to Achilles to beg the return of the corpse of his son Hector, whom Achilles has slain.

> Io no piangeva; sì dentro impietrai.
> Piangevan elli . . .[22]

take the lovely words of Beatrice to Virgil—

> Io son fatta da Dio, sua mercè, tale,
> Che la vostra miseria non mi tange,
> Nè fiamma d' esto incendio non m' assale . . .[23]

take the simple, but perfect, single line—

> In la sua volontade è nostra pace.[24]

Take of Shakespeare a line or two of Henry the Fourth's expostulation with sleep—

> Wilt thou upon the high and giddy mast
> Seal up the ship-boy's eyes, and rock his brains
> In cradle of the rude imperious surge . . .[25]

and take, as well, Hamlet's dying request to Horatio—

> If thou didst ever hold me in thy heart,
> Absent thee from felicity awhile,
> And in this harsh world draw thy breath in pain
> To tell my story . . .[26]

Take of Milton that Miltonic passage—

> Darken'd so, yet shone
> Above them all the archangel; but his face
> Deep scars of thunder had intrench'd, and care
> Sat on his faded cheek . . .[27]

add two such lines as—

> And courage never to submit or yield
> And what is else not to be overcome . . .[28]

and finish with the exquisite close to the loss of Proserpine, the loss

> . . . which cost Ceres all that pain
> To seek her through the world.[29]

These few lines, if we have tact and can use them, are enough even of themselves to keep clear and sound our judgments about poetry, to save us from fallacious estimates of it, to conduct us to a real estimate.

22. " 'I wailed not, so of stone grew I within;—*they* wailed.' *Inferno* xxxiii.39–40." (Arnold)
23. " 'Of such sort hath God, thanked be His mercy, made me, that your misery toucheth me not, neither doth the flame of His fire strike me.'—*Inferno* ii.91–93." (Arnold)
24. " 'In His will is our peace.'—*Paradiso* iii.85." (Arnold)
25. II *Henry IV* III.i.18–20.
26. *Hamlet* V.ii.357–60.
27. *Paradise Lost* I.599–602.
28. *Ibid.* IV.108–9.
29. *Ibid.* IV.271–72.

The specimens I have quoted differ widely from one another, but they have in common this: the possession of the very highest poetical quality. If we are thoroughly penetrated by their power, we shall find that we have acquired a sense enabling us, whatever poetry may be laid before us, to feel the degree in which a high poetical quality is present or wanting there. Critics give themselves great labour to draw out what in the abstract constitutes the characters of a high quality of poetry. It is much better simply to have recourse to concrete examples;—to take specimens of poetry of the high, the very highest, quality, and to say: The characters of a high quality of poetry are what is expressed *there*. They are far better recognised by being felt in the verse of the master, than by being perused in the prose of the critic. Nevertheless if we are urgently pressed to give some critical account of them, we may safely, perhaps, venture on laying down, not indeed how and why the characters arise, but where and in what they arise. They are in the matter and substance of the poetry, and they are in its manner and style. Both of these, the substance and matter on the one hand, the style and manner on the other, have a mark, an accent, of high beauty, worth, and power. But if we are asked to define this mark and accent in the abstract, our answer must be: No, for we should thereby be darkening the question, not clearing it. The mark and accent are as given by the substance and matter of that poetry, by the style and manner of that poetry, and of all other poetry which is akin to it in quality.

Only one thing we may add as to the substance and matter of poetry, guiding ourselves by Aristotle's profound observation that the superiority of poetry over history consists in its possessing a higher truth and a higher seriousness (φιλοσοφώτερον καὶ σπουδαιότερον).[30] Let us add, therefore, to what we have said, this: that the substance and matter of the best poetry acquire their special character from possessing, in an eminent degree, truth and seriousness. We may add yet further what is in itself evident, that to the style and manner of the best poetry their special character, their accent, is given by their diction, and, even yet more, by their movement. And though we distinguish between the two characters, the two accents, of superiority, yet they are nevertheless vitally connected one with the other. The superior character of truth and seriousness, in the matter and substance of the best poetry, is inseparable from the superiority of diction and movement marking its style and manner. The two superiorities are closely related, and are in steadfast proportion one to the other. So far as high poetic truth and seriousness are wanting to a poet's matter and substance, so far also, we may be sure, will a high poetic stamp of diction and movement be wanting to his style and manner. In proportion as this high stamp of diction and movement, again, is absent from a poet's style and manner, we shall find, also, that high poetic truth and seriousness are absent from his substance and matter.

So stated, these are but dry generalities; their whole force lies in their application. And I could wish every student of poetry to make the application of them for himself. Made by himself, the application would impress itself upon his mind far more deeply than made by me. Neither will my limits allow me

---

30. *Poetics* IX. Poetry is more philosophical and serious than history because history relates what has been, but poetry relates what might be: the generality of poetry makes it superior to the particularity of history.

to make any full application of the generalities above propounded; but in the hope of bringing out, at any rate, some significance in them, and of establishing an important principle more firmly by their means, I will, in the space which remains to me, follow rapidly from the commencement the course of our English poetry with them in my view.

Once more I return to the early poetry of France, with which our own poetry, in its origins,[31] is indissolubly connected. In the twelfth and thirteenth centuries, that seed-time of all modern language and literature, the poetry of France had a clear predominance in Europe. Of the two divisions of that poetry, its productions in the *langue d'oil* and its productions in the *langue d'oc*,[32] the poetry of the *langue d'oc,* of southern France, of the troubadours, is of importance because of its effect on Italian literature;—the first literature of modern Europe to strike the true and grand note, and to bring forth, as in Dante and Petrarch it brought forth, classics. But the predominance of French poetry in Europe, during the twelfth and thirteenth centuries, is due to its poetry of the *langue d'oil,* the poetry of northern France and of the tongue which is now the French language. In the twelfth century the bloom of this romance-poetry was earlier and stronger in England, at the court of our Anglo-Norman kings, than in France itself. But it was a bloom of French poetry; and as our native poetry formed itself, it formed itself out of this. The romance-poems which took possession of the heart and imagination of Europe in the twelfth and thirteenth centuries are French; 'they are,' as Southey [33] justly says, 'the pride of French literature, nor have we anything which can be placed in competition with them.' Themes were supplied from all quarters; but the romance-setting which was common to them all, and which gained the ear of Europe, was French. This constituted for the French poetry, literature, and language, at the height of the Middle Age, an unchallenged predominance. The Italian Brunetto Latini,[34] the master of Dante, wrote his *Treasure* in French because, he says, 'la parleure en est plus délitable et plus commune à toutes gens.' [35] In the same century, the thirteenth, the French romance-writer, Christian of Troyes,[36] formulates the claims, in chivalry and letters, of France, his native country, as follows:—

> Or vous ert par ce livre apris,
> Que Gresse ot de chevalerie
> Le premier los et de clergie;
> Puis vint chevalerie à Rome,
> Et de la clergie la some,
> Qui ore est en France venue.

31. Arnold takes no account of the long tradition of Old English poetry.
32. *Oil* (*oui*) and *oc* both mean "yes," the former in the northern dialect of French, the latter in the southern dialect. It is from the *langue d'oil* that modern French descends.
33. Robert Southey (1774–1843), appointed Poet Laureate in 1813, the butt of Byron's "The Vision of Judgment."
34. 13th-century Italian scholar and philosopher.
35. "French speech is pleasanter and more in use among all peoples."
36. Actually Chrétien de Troyes flourished in the second half of the 12th century. He was one of the great literary figures of his age. The quotation that follows is from the opening of his *Cligès*.

Diex doinst qu'ele i soit retenue,
Et que li lius li abelisse
Tant que de France n'isse
L'onor qui s'i est arestée!

'Now by this book you will learn that first Greece had the renown for chivalry and letters: then chivalry and the primacy in letters passed to Rome, and now it is come to France. God grant it may be kept there; and that the place may please it so well, that the honour which has come to make stay in France may never depart thence!'

Yet it is now all gone, this French romance-poetry, of which the weight of substance and the power of style are not unfairly represented by this extract from Christian of Troyes. Only by means of the historic estimate can we persuade ourselves now to think that any of it is of poetical importance.

But in the fourteenth century there comes an Englishman nourished on this poetry, taught his trade by this poetry, getting words, rhyme, metre from this poetry; for even of that stanza which the Italians used, and which Chaucer derived immediately from the Italians, the basis and suggestion was probably given in France. Chaucer (I have already named him) fascinated his contemporaries, but so too did Christian of Troyes and Wolfram of Eschenbach.[37] Chaucer's power of fascination, however, is enduring; his poetical importance does not need the assistance of the historic estimate; it is real. He is a genuine source of joy and strength, which is flowing still for us and will flow always. He will be read, as time goes on, far more generally than he is read now. His language is a cause of difficulty for us; but so also, and I think in quite as great a degree, is the language of Burns. In Chaucer's case, as in that of Burns, it is a difficulty to be unhesitatingly accepted and overcome.

If we ask ourselves wherein consists the immense superiority of Chaucer's poetry over the romance-poetry—why it is that in passing from this to Chaucer we suddenly feel ourselves to be in another world, we shall find that his superiority is both in the substance of his poetry and in the style of his poetry. His superiority in substance is given by his large, free, simple, clear yet kindly view of human life,—so unlike the total want, in the romance-poets, of all intelligent command of it. Chaucer has not their helplessness; he has gained the power to survey the world from a central, a truly human point of view. We have only to call to mind the Prologue to *The Canterbury Tales*. The right comment upon it is Dryden's: 'It is sufficient to say, according to the proverb, that *here is God's plenty*.' And again: 'He is a perpetual fountain of good sense.'[38] It is by a large, free, sound representation of things, that poetry, this high criticism of life, has truth of substance; and Chaucer's poetry has truth of substance.

Of his style and manner, if we think first of the romance-poetry and then of Chaucer's divine liquidness of diction, his divine fluidity of movement, it is difficult to speak temperately. They are irresistible, and justify all the rapture with which his successors speak of his 'gold dew-drops of speech.'[39] Johnson

37. A German poet of the 12th century, perhaps best known for his *Parzival*. He is a major character in Wagner's opera *Tannhäuser*.
38. Both sentences are from Dryden's Preface to his *Fables* (1700).
39. John Lydgate (*c.*1370–*c.*1451) says this in his poem *The Life of Our Lady*.

misses the point entirely when he finds fault with Dryden for ascribing to Chaucer the first refinement of our numbers, and says that Gower also can show smooth numbers and easy rhymes.[40] The refinement of our numbers means something far more than this. A nation may have versifiers with smooth numbers and easy rhymes, and yet may have no real poetry at all. Chaucer is the father of our splendid English poetry; he is our 'well of English undefiled,'[41] because by the lovely charm of his diction, the lovely charm of his movement, he makes an epoch and founds a tradition. In Spenser, Shakespeare, Milton, Keats, we can follow the tradition of the liquid diction, the fluid movement, of Chaucer; at one time it is his liquid diction of which in these poets we feel the virtue, and at another time it is his fluid movement. And the virtue is irresistible.

Bounded as is my space, I must yet find room for an example of Chaucer's virtue, as I have given examples to show the virtue of the great classics. I feel disposed to say that a single line is enough to show the charm of Chaucer's verse; that merely one line like this—

> O martyr souded in virginitee! [42]

has a virtue of manner and movement such as we shall not find in all the verse of romance-poetry;—but this is saying nothing. The virtue is such as we shall not find, perhaps, in all English poetry, outside the poets whom I have named as the special inheritors of Chaucer's tradition. A single line, however, is too little if we have not the strain of Chaucer's verse well in our memory; let us take a stanza. It is from *The Prioress's Tale*, the story of the Christian child murdered in a Jewery—

> My throte is cut unto my nekke-bone
> Saidè this child, and as by way of kinde
> I should have deyd, yea, longè time agone;
> But Jesu Christ, as ye in bookès finde,
> Will that his glory last and be in minde,
> And for the worship of his mother dere
> Yet may I sing *O Alma* [43] loud and clere.

Wordsworth has modernised this Tale, and to feel how delicate and evanescent is the charm of verse, we have only to read Wordsworth's first three lines of this stanza after Chaucer's—

> My throat is cut unto the bone, I trow,
> Said this young child, and by the law of kind
> I should have died, yea, many hours ago.

The charm is departed. It is often said that the power of liquidness and fluidity in Chaucer's verse was dependent upon a free, a licentious dealing with lan-

---

40. John Gower (c.1325–1408), poet and friend of Chaucer; Johnson makes the claim for Gower's refinement in *Idler*, No. 72.
41. Spenser thus praised Chaucer in *The Faerie Queene* IV.ii.32.
42. *The Prioress's Tale*, l. 127. "The French *soudé*: soldered, fixed fast." (Arnold) Actually Chaucer wrote "souded to."
43. The hymn *Alma Redemptoris Mater* (O Gracious Mother of the Redeemer).

guage, such as is now impossible; upon a liberty, such as Burns too enjoyed, of making words like *neck, bird,* into a dissyllable by adding to them, and words like *cause, rhyme,* into a dissyllable by sounding the *e* mute. It is true that Chaucer's fluidity is conjoined with this liberty, and is admirably served by it; but we ought not to say that it was dependent upon it. It was dependent upon his talent. Other poets with a like liberty do not attain to the fluidity of Chaucer; Burns himself does not attain to it. Poets, again, who have a talent akin to Chaucer's, such as Shakespeare or Keats, have known how to attain to his fluidity without the like liberty.

And yet Chaucer is not one of the great classics. His poetry transcends and effaces, easily and without effort, all the romance-poetry of Catholic Christendom; it transcends and effaces all the English poetry contemporary with it; it transcends and effaces all the English poetry subsequent to it down to the age of Elizabeth. Of such avail is poetic truth of substance, in its natural and necessary union with poetic truth of style. And yet, I say, Chaucer is not one of the great classics. He has not their accent. What is wanting to him is suggested by the mere mention of the name of the first great classic of Christendom, the immortal poet who died eighty years before Chaucer,—Dante. The accent of such verse as

> In la sua volontade è nostra pace . . .[44]

is altogether beyond Chaucer's reach; we praise him, but we feel that this accent is out of the question for him. It may be said that it was necessarily out of the reach of any poet in the England of that stage of growth. Possibly; but we are to adopt a real, not a historic, estimate of poetry. However we may account for its absence, something is wanting, then, to the poetry of Chaucer, which poetry must have before it can be placed in the glorious class of the best. And there is no doubt what that something is. It is the σπουδαιότης,[45] the high and excellent seriousness, which Aristotle assigns as one of the grand virtues of poetry. The substance of Chaucer's poetry, his view of things and his criticism of life, has largeness, freedom, shrewdness, benignity; but it has not this high seriousness. Homer's criticism of life has it, Dante's has it, Shakespeare's has it. It is this chiefly which gives to our spirits what they can rest upon; and with the increasing demands of our modern ages upon poetry, this virtue of giving us what we can rest upon will be more and more highly esteemed. A voice from the slums of Paris, fifty or sixty years after Chaucer, the voice of poor Villon [46] out of his life of riot and crime, has at its happy moments (as, for instance, in the last stanza of *La Belle Heaulmière* [47]) more of this

---

44. "In His will is our peace."
45. The word may be transliterated as "spoudaiotes."
46. François Villon (1431–?), French poet and brawler, who, after long neglect, came to be admired in the 19th century. Swinburne translated the poem of which Arnold speaks.
47. "The name *Heaulmière* is said to be derived from a headdress (helm) worn as a mark by courtesans. In Villon's ballad, a poor old creature of this class laments her days of youth and beauty. The last stanza of the ballad runs thus—Ainsi le bon temps regretons / Entre nous, pauvres vieilles sottes. / Assises bas, à croppetons, / Tout en ung tas comme pelottes; / A petit feu de chenevottes / Tost allumées, tost estainctes. / Et jadis fusmes si mognottes! / Ainsi en prend à maintz et maintes.—Thus amongst ourselves we regret the good time, poor silly old things, low-seated on our heels, all in a heap like so many balls,

important poetic virtue of seriousness than all the productions of Chaucer. But its apparition in Villon, and in men like Villon is fitful; the greatness of the great poets, the power of their criticism of life, is that their virtue is sustained.

To our praise, therefore, of Chaucer as a poet there must be this limitation; he lacks the high seriousness of the great classics, and therewith an important part of their virtue. Still, the main fact for us to bear in mind about Chaucer is his sterling value according to that real estimate which we firmly adopted for all poets. He has poetic truth of substance, though he has not high poetic seriousness, and corresponding to his truth of substance he has an exquisite virtue of style and manner. With him is born our real poetry.

For my present purpose I need not dwell on our Elizabethan poetry, or on the continuation and close of this poetry in Milton. We all of us profess to be agreed in the estimate of this poetry; we all of us recognise it as great poetry, our greatest, and Shakespeare and Milton as our poetical classics. The real estimate,[48] here, has universal currency. With the next age of our poetry divergency and difficulty begin. An historic estimate of that poetry has established itself; and the question is, whether it will be found to coincide with the real estimate.

The age of Dryden, together with our whole eighteenth century which followed it, sincerely believed itself to have produced poetical classics of its own, and even to have made advance, in poetry, beyond all its predecessors. Dryden regards as not seriously disputable the opinion 'that the sweetness of English verse was never understood or practised by our fathers.' [49] Cowley could see nothing at all in Chaucer's poetry.[50] Dryden heartily admired, and, as we have seen, praised its matter admirably; but of its exquisite manner and movement all he can find to say is that 'there is the rude sweetness of a Scotch tune in it, which is natural and pleasing, though not perfect.' [51] Addison, wishing to praise Chaucer's numbers, compares them with Dryden's own.[52] And all through the eighteenth century, and down even into our own times, the stereotyped phrase of approbation for good verse found in our early poetry has been, that it even approached the verse of Dryden, Addison, Pope, and Johnson.

Are Dryden and Pope poetical classics? Is the historic estimate, which represents them as such, and which has been so long established that it cannot easily give way, the real estimate? Wordsworth and Coleridge, as is well known, denied it; but the authority of Wordsworth and Coleridge does not weigh much with the young generation, and there are many signs to show that the eighteenth century and its judgments are coming into favour again. Are the favourite poets of the eighteenth century classics?

It is impossible within my present limits to discuss the question fully. And what man of letters would not shrink from seeming to dispose dictatorially of

by a little fire of hemp-stalks, soon lighted, soon spent. And once we were such darlings! So fares it with many and many a one." (Arnold)
48. By "real estimate" Arnold means the estimate which is made of the intrinsic quality of the work, without reference to the personal or historical considerations he has spoken of earlier.
49. Preface to the *Fables*.
50. Dryden cites this opinion, *ibid*.
51. *Ibid*.
52. In *An Account of the Greatest English Poets*.

the claims of two men who are, at any rate, such masters in letters as Dryden and Pope; two men of such admirable talent, both of them, and one of them, Dryden, a man, on all sides, of such energetic and genial power? And yet, if we are to gain the full benefit from poetry, we must have the real estimate of it. I cast about for some mode of arriving, in the present case, at such an estimate without offence. And perhaps the best way is to begin, as it is easy to begin, with cordial praise.

When we find Chapman,[53] the Elizabethan translator of Homer, expressing himself in his preface thus: 'Though truth in her very nakedness sits in so deep a pit, that from Gades to Aurora and Ganges few eyes can sound her, I hope yet those few here will so discover and confirm that, the date being out of her darkness in this morning of our poet, he shall now gird his temples with the sun,'—we pronounce that such a prose is intolerable. When we find Milton writing: 'And long it was not after, when I was confirmed in this opinion, that he, who would not be frustrate of his hope to write well hereafter in laudable things, ought himself to be a true poem,'[54]—we pronounce that such a prose has its own grandeur, but that it is obsolete and inconvenient. But when we find Dryden telling us: 'What Virgil wrote in the vigour of his age, in plenty and at ease, I have undertaken to translate in my declining years; struggling with wants, oppressed with sickness, curbed in my genius, liable to be misconstrued in all I write,'[55]—then we exclaim that here at last we have the true English prose, a prose such as we would all gladly use if we only knew how. Yet Dryden was Milton's contemporary.

But after the Restoration the time had come when our nation felt the imperious need of a fit prose. So, too, the time had likewise come when our nation felt the imperious need of freeing itself from the absorbing preoccupation which religion in the Puritan age had exercised. It was impossible that this freedom should be brought about without some negative excess, without some neglect and impairment of the religious life of the soul; and the spiritual history of the eighteenth century shows us that the freedom was not achieved without them. Still, the freedom was achieved; the preoccupation, an undoubtedly baneful and retarding one if it had continued, was got rid of. And as with religion amongst us at that period, so it was also with letters. A fit prose was a necessity; but it was impossible that a fit prose should establish itself amongst us without some touch of frost to the imaginative life of the soul. The needful qualities for a fit prose are regularity, uniformity, precision, balance. The men of letters, whose destiny it may be to bring their nation to the attainment of a fit prose, must of necessity, whether they work in prose or in verse, give a predominating, and almost exclusive attention to the qualities of regularity, uniformity, precision, balance. But an almost exclusive attention to these qualities involves some repression and silencing of poetry.

We are to regard Dryden as the puissant and glorious founder, Pope as the splendid high priest, of our age of prose and reason, of our excellent and

53. George Chapman (1559?–1634?), playwright and translator; Arnold quotes from the commentary after his translation of Book I of the *Iliad*.
54. From *An Apology for Smectymnuus*.
55. From "Postcript to the Reader"—Dryden's translation of Virgil (1697).

indispensable eighteenth century. For the purposes of their mission and destiny their poetry, like their prose, is admirable. Do you ask me whether Dryden's verse, take it almost where you will, is not good?

> A milk-white Hind, immortal and unchanged,
> Fed on the lawns and in the forest ranged.[56]

I answer: Admirable for the purposes of the inaugurator of an age of prose and reason. Do you ask me whether Pope's verse, take it almost where you will, is not good?

> To Hounslow Heath I point, and Banstead Down;
> Thence comes your mutton, and these chicks my own.[57]

I answer: Admirable for the purposes of the high priest of an age of prose and reason. But do you ask me whether such verse proceeds from men with an adequate poetic criticism of life, from men whose criticism of life has a high seriousness, or even, without that high seriousness, has poetic largeness, freedom, insight, benignity? Do you ask me whether the application of ideas to life in the verse of these men, often a powerful application, no doubt, is a powerful *poetic* application? Do you ask me whether the poetry of these men has either the matter or the inseparable manner of such an adequate poetic criticism; whether it has the accent of

> Absent thee from felicity awhile . . .

or of

> And what is else not to be overcome . . .

or of

> O martyr souded in virginitee!

I answer: It has not and cannot have them; it is the poetry of the builders of an age of prose and reason. Though they may write in verse, though they may in a certain sense be masters of the art of versification, Dryden and Pope are not classics of our poetry, they are classics of our prose.

Gray is our poetical classic of that literature and age; the position of Gray is singular, and demands a word of notice here. He has not the volume or the power of poets who, coming in times more favourable, have attained to an independent criticism of life. But he lived with the great poets, he lived, above all, with the Greeks, through perpetually studying and enjoying them; and he caught their poetic point of view for regarding life, caught their poetic manner. The point of view and the manner are not self-sprung in him, he caught them of others; and he had not the free and abundant use of them. But whereas Addison and Pope never had the use of them, Gray had the use of them at times. He is the scantiest and frailest of classics in our poetry, but he is a classic.

And now, after Gray, we are met, as we draw towards the end of the eighteenth century, we are met by the great name of Burns. We enter now on

---

56. The opening lines of *The Hind and the Panther*.
57. *Imitations of Horace* II.2.143–44. Certainly Arnold has not done justice to Pope's powers by his choice of this couplet!

times where the personal estimate of poets begins to be rife, and where the real estimate of them is not reached without difficulty. But in spite of the disturbing pressures of personal partiality, of national partiality, let us try to reach a real estimate of the poetry of Burns.

By his English poetry Burns in general belongs to the eighteenth century, and has little importance for us.

> Mark ruffian Violence, distain'd with crimes,
> Rousing elate in these degenerate times;
> View unsuspecting Innocence a prey,
> As guileful Fraud points out the erring way;
> While subtle Litigation's pliant tongue
> The life-blood equal sucks of Right and Wrong! [58]

Evidently this is not the real Burns, or his name and fame would have disappeared long ago. Nor is Clarinda's love-poet, Sylvander,[59] the real Burns either. But he tells us himself: 'These English songs gravel me to death. I have not the command of the language that I have of my native tongue. In fact, I think that my ideas are more barren in English than in Scotch. I have been at *Duncan Gray* to dress it in English, but all I can do is desperately stupid.' [60] We English turn naturally, in Burns, to the poems in our own language, because we can read them easily; but in those poems we have not the real Burns.

The real Burns is of course in his Scotch poems. Let us boldly say that of this poetry, a poetry dealing perpetually with Scotch drink, Scotch religion, and Scotch manners, a Scotchman's estimate is apt to be personal. A Scotchman is used to this world of Scotch drink, Scotch religion, and Scotch manners; he has a tenderness for it; he meets its poet half way. In this tender mood he reads pieces like the *Holy Fair* or *Halloween*. But this world of Scotch drink, Scotch religion, and Scotch manners is against a poet, not for him, when it is not a partial countryman who reads him; for in itself it is not a beautiful world, and no one can deny that it is of advantage to a poet to deal with a beautiful world. Burns's world of Scotch drink, Scotch religion, and Scotch manners, is often a harsh, a sordid, a repulsive world; even the world of his *Cottar's Saturday Night* is not a beautiful world. No doubt a poet's criticism of life may have such truth and power that it triumphs over its world and delights us. Burns may triumph over this world, often he does triumph over his world, but let us observe how and where. Burns is the first case we have had where the bias of the personal estimate tends to mislead; let us look at him closely—he can bear it.

Many of his admirers will tell us that we have Burns, convivial, genuine, delightful, here—

> Leeze me on drink! it gies us mair
>   Than either school or college;
> It kindles wit, it waukens lair,
>   It pangs us fou o' knowledge.

58. "On the Death of Lord Dundas," ll. 25–30.
59. Under this affected pastoral name Burns carried on a correspondence with a Mrs. Maclehose, whom he styled Clarinda.
60. In a letter of October 19, 1794.

> Be't whisky gill or penny wheep
>   Or ony stronger potion,
> It never fails, on drinking deep,
>   To kittle up our notion
>   By night or day.[61]

There is a great deal of that sort of thing in Burns, and it is unsatisfactory, not because it is bacchanalian poetry, but because it has not that accent of sincerity which bacchanalian poetry, to do it justice, very often has. There is something in it of bravado, something which makes us feel that we have not the man speaking to us with his real voice; something, therefore, poetically unsound.

With still more confidence, will his admirers tell us that we have the genuine Burns, the great poet, when his strain asserts the independence, equality, dignity, of men, as in the famous song *For a' that and a' that*—

> A prince can mak' a belted knight,
>   A marquis, duke, and a' that;
> But an honest man's aboon his might,
>   Guid faith he mauna fa' that!
>   For a' that, and a' that,
>   Their dignities, and a' that,
>   The pith o' sense, and pride o' worth,
>   Are higher rank than a' that.

Here they find his grand, genuine touches; and still more, when this puissant genius, who so often set morality at defiance, falls moralising—

> The sacred lowe o' weel-placed love
>   Luxuriantly indulge it;
> But never tempt th' illicit rove,
>   Tho' naething should divulge it:
>   I waive the quantum o' the sin,
>   The hazard o' concealing,
>   But och! it hardens a' within,
>   And petrifies the feeling.[62]

Or in a higher strain—

> Who made the heart, 'tis He alone
>   Decidedly can try us;
> He knows each chord, its various tone;
>   Each spring, its various bias.
> Then at the balance let's be mute,
>   We never can adjust it;
> What's *done* we partly may compute,
>   But know not what's resisted.[63]

61. "The Holy Fair," ll. 163–71.
62. "Epistle to a Young Friend," ll. 41–48.
63. "Address to the Unco Guid," ll. 57–64.

Or in a better strain yet, a strain, his admirers will say, unsurpassable—

> To make a happy fire-side clime
>   To weans and wife,
> That's the true pathos and sublime
>   Of human life.[64]

There is criticism of life for you, the admirers of Burns will say to us; there is the application of ideas to life! There is, undoubtedly. The doctrine of the last-quoted lines coincides almost exactly with what was the aim and end, Xenophon tells us,[65] of all the teaching of Socrates. And the application is a powerful one; made by a man of vigorous understanding, and (need I say?) a master of language.

But for supreme poetical success more is required than the powerful application of ideas to life; it must be an application under the conditions fixed by the laws of poetic truth and poetic beauty. Those laws fix as an essential condition, in the poet's treatment of such matters as are here in question, high seriousness;—the high seriousness which comes from absolute sincerity. The accent of high seriousness, born of absolute sincerity, is what gives to such verse as

> In la sua volontade è nostra pace . . .

to such criticism of life as Dante's, its power. Is this accent felt in the passages which I have been quoting from Burns? Surely not; surely, if our sense is quick, we must perceive that we have not in those passages a voice from the very inmost soul of the genuine Burns; he is not speaking to us from these depths, he is more or less preaching. And the compensation for admiring such passages less, from missing the perfect poetic accent in them, will be that we shall admire more the poetry where that accent is found.

No; Burns, like Chaucer, comes short of the high seriousness of the great classics, and the virtue of matter and manner which goes with that high seriousness is wanting to his work. At moments he touches it in a profound and passionate melancholy, as in those four immortal lines taken by Byron as a motto for The Bride of Abydos, but which have in them a depth of poetic quality such as resides in no verse of Byron's own—

> Had we never loved sae kindly,
> Had we never loved sae blindly,
> Never met, or never parted,
> We had ne'er been broken-hearted.

But a whole poem of that quality Burns cannot make; the rest, in the Farewell to Nancy,[66] is verbiage.

We arrive best at the real estimate of Burns, I think, by conceiving his work as having truth of matter and truth of manner, but not the accent or

64. "Epistle to Dr. Blacklock," ll. 51–54.
65. In Memorabilia IV.iv. Xenophon (c.427–c.354) was a Greek historian and essayist best known for the Anabasis.
66. The poem is also called "Ae Fond Kiss." Arnold quotes ll. 13–16.

the poetic virtue of the highest masters. His genuine criticism of life, when the sheer poet in him speaks, is ironic; it is not—

> Thou Power Supreme, whose mighty scheme
>   These woes of mine fulfil,
> Here firm I rest, they must be best
>   Because they are Thy will! [67]

It is far rather: *Whistle owre the lave o't!* Yet we may say of him as of Chaucer, that of life and the world, as they come before him, his view is large, free, shrewd, benignant,—truly poetic, therefore; and his manner of rendering what he sees is to match. But we must note, at the same time, his great difference from Chaucer. The freedom of Chaucer is heightened, in Burns, by a fiery, reckless energy; the benignity of Chaucer deepens, in Burns, into an overwhelming sense of the pathos of things;—of the pathos of human nature, the pathos, also, of non-human nature. Instead of the fluidity of Chaucer's manner, the manner of Burns has spring, bounding swiftness. Burns is by far the greater force, though he has perhaps less charm. The world of Chaucer is fairer, richer, more significant than that of Burns; but when the largeness and freedom of Burns get full sweep, as in *Tam o' Shanter*, or still more in that puissant and splendid production, *The Folly Beggars*, his world may be what it will, his poetic genius triumphs over it. In the world of *The Folly Beggars* there is more than hideousness and squalor, there is bestiality; yet the piece is a superb poetic success. It has a breadth, truth, and power which make the famous scene in Auerbach's Cellar, of Goethe's *Faust*,[68] seem artificial and tame beside it, and which are only matched by Shakespeare and Aristophanes.

Here, where his largeness and freedom serve him so admirably, and also in those poems and songs where to shrewdness he adds infinite archness and wit, and to benignity infinite pathos, where his manner is flawless, and a perfect poetic whole is the result,—in things like the address to the mouse whose home he had ruined, in things like *Duncan Gray, Tam Glen, Whistle and I'll Come To You My Lad, Auld Lang Syne* (this list might be made much longer)—here we have the genuine Burns, of whom the real estimate must be high indeed. Not a classic, nor with the excellent σπουδαιότης [69] of the great classics, nor with a verse rising to a criticism of life and a virtue like theirs; but a poet with thorough truth of substance and an answering truth of style, giving us a poetry sound to the core. We all of us have a leaning towards the pathetic, and may be inclined perhaps to prize Burns most for his touches of piercing, sometimes almost intolerable, pathos; for verse like—

> We twa hae paidl't i' the burn
>   From mornin' sun till dine;
> But seas between us braid hae roar'd
>   Sin auld lang syne . . .[70]

67. "Winter: A Dirge," ll. 17–20.
68. As his first act, after his compact with Mephistopheles, Faust visits a wine cellar and engages in riotous horseplay with a group of drunken students.
69. "High seriousness."
70. "Auld Lang Syne," ll. 17–20.

where he is as lovely as he is sound. But perhaps it is by the perfection of soundness of his lighter and archer masterpieces that he is poetically most wholesome for us. For the votary misled by a personal estimate of Shelley, as so many of us have been, are, and will be,—of that beautiful spirit building his many-coloured haze of words and images

> Pinnacled dim in the intense inane—[71]

no contact can be wholesomer than the contact with Burns at his archest and soundest. Side by side with the

> On the brink of the night and the morning
>> My coursers are wont to respire,
> But the Earth has just whispered a warning
>> That their flight must be swifter than fire . . .[72]

of *Prometheus Unbound,* how salutary, how very salutary, to place this from *Tam Glen*—

> My minnie does constantly deave me
>> And bids me beware o' young men;
> They flatter, she says, to deceive me;
>> But wha can think sae o' Tam Glen?

But we enter on burning ground as we approach the poetry of times so near to us—poetry like that of Byron, Shelley, and Wordsworth—of which the estimates are so often not only personal, but personal with passion. For my purpose, it is enough to have taken the single case of Burns, the first poet we come to of whose work the estimate formed is evidently apt to be personal, and to have suggested how we may proceed, using the poetry of the great classics as a sort of touchstone, to correct this estimate, as we had previously corrected by the same means the historic estimate where we met with it. A collection like the present, with its succession of celebrated names and celebrated poems, offers a good opportunity to us for resolutely endeavouring to make our estimates of poetry real. I have sought to point out a method which will help us in making them so, and to exhibit it in use so far as to put any one who likes in a way of applying it for himself.

At any rate the end to which the method and the estimate are designed to lead, and from leading to which, if they do lead to it, they get their whole value,—the benefit of being able clearly to feel and deeply to enjoy the best, the truly classic, in poetry,—is an end, let me say it once more at parting, of supreme importance. We are often told that an era is opening in which we are to see multitudes of a common sort of readers, and masses of a common

71. Shelley, *Prometheus Unbound* III.iv.204.
72. *Ibid.* II.v.1–4. In his essay on Shelley, included in *Essays in Criticism, Second Series,* Arnold says of Shelley's poetry, "Let no one suppose that a want of humour and a self-delusion such as Shelley's have no effect upon a man's poetry. The man Shelley, in very truth, is not entirely sane, and Shelley's poetry is not entirely sane either. The Shelley of actual life is a vision of beauty and radiance, indeed, but availing nothing, effecting nothing. And in poetry, no less than in life, he is a beautiful and ineffectual angel beating in the void his luminous wings in vain."

sort of literature; that such readers do not want and could not relish anything better than such literature, and that to provide it is becoming a vast and profitable industry. Even if good literature entirely lost currency with the world, it would still be abundantly worthwhile to continue to enjoy it by oneself. But it never will lose currency with the world, in spite of momentary appearances; it never will lose supremacy. Currency and supremacy are insured to it, not indeed by the world's deliberate and conscious choice, but by something far deeper,—by the instinct of self-preservation in humanity.

1880   1880, 1888

Literature and Science

Arnold's reputation in the United States developed slowly, but by the end of the 1870's it was firmly established. In 1883, moved by the financial considerations of his approaching retirement from his post in the Education Office, Arnold agreed to make a lecture tour of America. Like that of Oscar Wilde in the previous year, it was a strenuous experience, not the least because of the ambivalence with which the lecturer was regarded. In the later nineteenth century, Americans were avid for what they had learned from Arnold to call "culture," which they presumed to have its source in Europe, particularly in England. At the same time, they were intent upon making it plain that they would accept no condescension from those who brought the precious commodity from across the ocean. Arnold certainly had no intention of condescending, for he was the most courteous of men, but he was, after all, coming to speak the Word, his English manners were thought odd and "superior," and the opinions he had expressed about American life, while not censorious, had not been exactly flattering; there was in consequence a considerable amount of ragging in the press and a constant chatter of defensive gossip about his manner on the platform, his voice, his whiskers, his ruddy complexion, his eye-glass, the cut of his trousers. Through it all Arnold maintained his good humor and good sense and by the end of his visit he had won almost all hearts. He, for his part, took home a better opinion of American life than the one he had brought with him.

He had prepared for the tour a repertory of three lectures, all being on matters likely to engage American interest. One was on Emerson, the nation's pre-eminent writer, who had died the year before. Another, Numbers; or the Majority and the Remnant, was a consideration of the role of intellect in a democracy. The third was Literature and Science, which he had given as the Rede Lecture at Cambridge University in 1881 and revised with his American audiences in mind. All three lectures were published in Discourses in America (1885).

So far as Literature and Science is controversial, it is a reply to the address Science and Culture, which T. H. Huxley had delivered in 1880 on the occasion of the opening of the Science College at Birmingham. This institution had been endowed by Sir Josiah Mason, a wealthy manufacturer of humble origin, who had stipulated in the trust that no provision be made at the college for "mere literary instruction and education." Had Huxley been consulted on this point, he would almost certainly have urged against it, for he was a man of wide cultivation, responsive to literature, and firmly of the opinion that literature was of value in the education of scientists. But he was, Darwin excepted, the best-known English scientist of his time, the chief proponent of the scientific outlook, and he had ample reason to feel that the neglect of science by the English educational system constituted an intellectual scandal. Whatever his private reservations about Mason's exclusion of literature from the college may have been, he consented to accept and defend it publicly because it redressed the grievance of science at being kept from its proper place in the intellectual life of the nation. He characterized the culpable national attitude to science by reference to the definition of culture that Arnold had put forward. He did not quarrel with Arnold's general conception of culture, of which criticism is the essence; on the contrary, he expressed himself as being in hearty accord with it. But he objected to it in the one respect that it assumes that "the best that has been thought and said in the world" consists chiefly, if not exclusively, of literature. Science is given no part in it. In advancing science to a place in the body of knowledge and thought with which culture works, Huxley is at pains to say that he is concerned only with the enlarging intellectual effect of scientific study, not at all with the utilitarian application of science to industry. And he goes on to suggest that science has potentially as much bearing upon the practical moral life of society as Arnold says literature has: the laws of social existence no less than those of nature are susceptible of being known through the methods of science.

Huxley was wholly justified in his protest of the insensate indifference to science on the part of those who had charge of the educational system of England, and his claims for the critical and cultural importance of the scientific mode of thought are obviously cogent. Yet Arnold was right in perceiving that his lecture, though temperate and rational in itself, was a portent of the modern tendency to belittle the educational value of humane letters; and it is to this threat that his own lecture eloquently responds.

From Literature and Science

Practical people talk with a smile of Plato and of his absolute ideas; [1] and it is impossible to deny that Plato's ideas do often seem unpractical and impracticable, and especially when one views them in connection with the life of a great work-a-day world like the United States. The necessary staple of the life of such a world Plato regards with disdain; handicraft and trade and the working professions he regards with disdain; but what becomes of the life of an industrial modern community if you take handicraft and trade and the working professions out of it? The base mechanic arts and handicrafts, says Plato, bring about a natural weakness in the principle of excellence in a man, so that he cannot govern the ignoble growths in him, but nurses them, and cannot understand fostering any other. Those who exercise such arts and trades, as they have their bodies, he says, marred by their vulgar businesses,

1. For Plato ideas are "absolute" in the sense that they are the essential "forms" or archetypes of things—of material objects, of institutions, of virtues—and remain constant through all the changes which take place in those things as they are apparent to man's senses and intellect. He conceived ideas, thus defined, to have their existence not in the mind but in a realm of their own.

so they have their souls, too, bowed and broken by them. And if one of these uncomely people has a mind to seek self-culture and philosophy, Plato compares him to a bald little tinker, who has scraped together money, and has got his release from service, and has had a bath, and bought a new coat, and is rigged out like a bridegroom about to marry the daughter of his master who has fallen into poor and helpless estate.[2]

Nor do the working professions fare any better than trade at the hands of Plato. He draws for us an inimitable picture of the working lawyer, and of his life of bondage; he shows how this bondage from his youth up has stunted and warped him, and made him small and crooked of soul, encompassing him with difficulties which he is not man enough to rely on justice and truth as means to encounter, but has recourse, for help out of them, to falsehood and wrong. And so, says Plato, this poor creature is bent and broken, and grows up from boy to man without a particle of soundness in him, although exceedingly smart and clever in his own esteem.[3]

One cannot refuse to admire the artist who draws these pictures. But we say to ourselves that his ideas show the influence of a primitive and obsolete order of things, when the warrior caste and the priestly caste were alone in honour, and the humble work of the world was done by slaves. We have now changed all that; the modern majesty consists in work, as Emerson declares; [4] and in work, we may add, principally of such plain and dusty kind as the work of cultivators of the ground, handicraftsmen, men of trade and business, men of the working professions. Above all is this true in a great industrious community such as that of the United States.

Now education, many people go on to say, is still mainly governed by the ideas of men like Plato, who lived when the warrior caste and the priestly or philosophical class were alone in honour, and the really useful part of the community were slaves. It is an education fitted for persons of leisure in such a community. This education passed from Greece and Rome to the feudal communities of Europe, where also the warrior caste and the priestly caste were alone held in honour, and where the really useful and working part of the community, though not nominally slaves as in the pagan world, were practically not much better off than slaves, and not more seriously regarded. And how absurd it is, people end by saying, to inflict this education upon an industrious modern community, where very few indeed are persons of leisure, and the mass to be considered has not leisure, but is bound, for its own great good, and for the great good of the world at large, to plain labour and to industrial pursuits, and the education in question tends necessarily to make men dissatisfied with these pursuits and unfitted for them!

That is what is said. So far I must defend Plato, as to plead that his view of education and studies is in the general, as it seems to me, sound enough, and fitted for all sorts and conditions of men, whatever their pursuits may be. 'An intelligent man,' says Plato, 'will prize those studies which result in his soul getting soberness, righteousness, and wisdom, and will less value the

2. *Republic* VI.ix.
3. *Theatatus* 172–73.
4. *Literary Ethics.* "Feudalism and Orientalism had long enough thought it majestic to do nothing: the modern majesty consists in work."

others.'[5] I cannot consider *that* a bad description of the aim of education, and of the motives which should govern us in the choice of studies, whether we are preparing ourselves for a hereditary seat in the English House of Lords or for the pork trade in Chicago.

Still I admit that Plato's world was not ours, that his scorn of trade and handicraft is fantastic, that he had no conception of a great industrial community such as that of the United States, and that such a community must and will shape its education to suit its own needs. If the usual education handed down to it from the past does not suit it, it will certainly before long drop this and try another. The usual education in the past has been mainly literary. The question is whether the studies which were long supposed to be the best for all of us are practically the best now; whether others are not better. The tyranny of the past, many think, weighs on us injuriously in the predominance given to letters in education. The question is raised whether, to meet the needs of our modern life, the predominance ought not now to pass from letters to science; and naturally the question is nowhere raised with more energy than here in the United States. The design of abasing what is called 'mere literary instruction and education,' and of exalting what is called 'sound, extensive, and practical scientific knowledge,' is, in this intensely modern world of the United States, even more perhaps than in Europe, a very popular design, and makes great and rapid progress.

I am going to ask whether the present movement for ousting letters from their old predominance in education, and for transferring the predominance in education to the natural sciences, whether this brisk and flourishing movement ought to prevail, and whether it is likely that in the end it really will prevail. An objection may be raised which I will anticipate. My own studies have been almost wholly in letters, and my visits to the field of the natural sciences have been very slight and inadequate, although those sciences have always strongly moved my curiosity. A man of letters, it will perhaps be said, is not competent to discuss the comparative merits of letters and natural science as means of education. To this objection I reply, first of all, that his incompetence, if he attempts the discussion but is really incompetent for it, will be abundantly visible; nobody will be taken in; he will have plenty of sharp observers and critics to save mankind from that danger. But the line I am going to follow is, as you will soon discover, so extremely simple, that perhaps it may be followed without failure even by one who for a more ambitious line of discussion would be quite incompetent.

Some of you may possibly remember a phrase of mine which has been the object of a good deal of comment; an observation to the effect that in our culture, the aim being *to know ourselves and the world,* we have, as the means to this end, *to know the best which has been thought and said in the world.*[6] A man of science, who is also an excellent writer and the very prince of debaters, Professor Huxley, in a discourse at the opening of Sir Josiah Mason's college at Birmingham,[7] laying hold of this phrase, expanded it by quoting

5. *Republic* IX.xiii.
6. See *The Function of Criticism at the Present Time,* fourth paragraph from the end.
7. Thomas Henry Huxley (1825–95), the famous English biologist, defender of Darwin's theory of evolution, and popularizer of science. The lecture, *Science and Culture,* was

some more words of mine, which are these: 'The civilised world is to be regarded as now being, for intellectual and spiritual purposes, one great confederation, bound to a joint action and working to a common result; and whose members have for their proper outfit a knowledge of Greek, Roman, and Eastern antiquity, and of one another. Special local and temporary advantages being put out of account, that modern nation will in the intellectual and spiritual sphere make most progress, which most thoroughly carries out this programme.'

Now on my phrase, thus enlarged, Professor Huxley remarks that when I speak of the above-mentioned knowledge as enabling us to know ourselves and the world, I assert *literature* to contain the materials which suffice for thus making us know ourselves and the world. But it is not by any means clear, says he, that after having learnt all which ancient and modern literatures have to tell us, we have laid a sufficiently broad and deep foundation for that criticism of life, that knowledge of ourselves and the world, which constitutes culture. On the contrary, Professor Huxley declares that he finds himself 'wholly unable to admit that either nations or individuals will really advance, if their outfit draws nothing from the stores of physical science. An army without weapons of precision, and with no particular base of operations, might more hopefully enter upon a campaign on the Rhine, than a man, devoid of a knowledge of what physical science has done in the last century, upon a criticism of life.'

This shows how needful it is for those who are to discuss any matter together, to have a common understanding as to the sense of the terms they employ,—how needful, and how difficult. What Professor Huxley says, implies just the reproach which is so often brought against the study of *belles lettres*,[8] as they are called: that the study is an elegant one, but slight and ineffectual; a smattering of Greek and Latin and other ornamental things, of little use for any one whose object is to get at truth, and to be a practical man. So, too, M. Renan [9] talks of the 'superficial humanism' of a school-course which treats us as if we were all going to be poets, writers, preachers, orators, and he opposes this humanism to positive science, or the critical search after truth. And there is always a tendency in those who are remonstrating against the predominance of letters in education, to understand by letters *belles lettres*, and by *belles lettres* a superficial humanism, the opposite of science or true knowledge.

But when we talk of knowing Greek and Roman antiquity, for instance, which is the knowledge people have called the humanities, I for my part mean a knowledge which is something more than a superficial humanism, mainly decorative. 'I call all teaching *scientific*,' says Wolf, the critic of

delivered in 1880. Arnold and Huxley were warm friends; Arnold's niece married Huxley's son.

8. This French phrase, in common use in English, originally denoted literature regarded in its aesthetic aspect, in contradistinction to informative or dialectical writings; it was analogous to the still-current English phrase, "fine arts." But with the passage of time it came to have an adverse or at least condescending connotation, suggesting literature without dignity or force, and the English word "belletristic" is distinctly pejorative. Arnold, of course, uses it in its original meaning.

9. Ernest Renan (1823–92), the influential French critic and historian of religion.

Homer,[10] 'which is systematically laid out and followed up to its original sources. For example: a knowledge of classical antiquity is scientific when the remains of classical antiquity are correctly studied in the original languages.' There can be no doubt that Wolf is perfectly right; that all learning is scientific which is systematically laid out and followed up to its original sources, and that a genuine humanism is scientific.

When I speak of knowing Greek and Roman antiquity, therefore, as a help to knowing ourselves and the world, I mean more than a knowledge of so much vocabulary, so much grammar, so many portions of authors in the Greek and Latin languages. I mean knowing the Greeks and Romans, and their life and genius, and what they were and did in the world; what we get from them, and what is its value. That, at least, is the ideal; and when we talk of endeavouring to know Greek and Roman antiquity, as a help to knowing ourselves and the world, we mean endeavouring so to know them as to satisfy this ideal, however much we may still fall short of it.

The same also as to knowing our own and other modern nations, with the like aim of getting to understand ourselves and the world. To know the best that has been thought and said by the modern nations, is to know, says Professor Huxley, 'only what modern *literatures* have to tell us; it is the criticism of life contained in modern literature.' And yet 'the distinctive character of our times,' he urges, 'lies in the vast and constantly increasing part which is played by natural knowledge.' And how, therefore, can a man, devoid of knowledge of what physical science has done in the last century, enter hopefully upon a criticism of modern life?

Let us, I say, be agreed about the meaning of the terms we are using. I talk of knowing the best which has been thought and uttered in the world; Professor Huxley says this means knowing *literature*. Literature is a large word; it may mean everything written with letters or printed in a book. Euclid's *Elements* and Newton's *Principia* are thus literature. All knowledge that reaches us through books is literature. But by literature Professor Huxley means *belles lettres*. He means to make me say, that knowing the best which has been thought and said by the modern nations is knowing their *belles lettres* and no more. And this is no sufficient equipment, he argues, for a criticism of modern life. But as I do not mean, by knowing ancient Rome, knowing merely more or less of Latin *belles lettres,* and taking no account of Rome's military, and political, and legal, and administrative work in the world; and as, by knowing ancient Greece, I understand knowing her as the giver of Greek art, and the guide to a free and right use of reason and to scientific method, and the founder of our mathematics and physics and astronomy and biology,—I understand knowing her as all this, and not merely knowing certain Greek poems, and histories, and treatises, and speeches,—so as to the knowledge of modern nations also. By knowing modern nations, I mean not merely knowing their *belles lettres*, but knowing also what has been done by such men as Copernicus, Galileo, Newton, Darwin. 'Our ancestors learned,' says Professor Huxley, 'that the earth is the centre of the visible universe, and that man is the cynosure of things terrestrial; and more especially

10. Friedrich August Wolf (1759–1824), German philologist and Homeric scholar. It was he who proposed the idea that the Homeric poems were not by a single author.

was it inculcated that the course of nature had no fixed order, but that it could be, and constantly was, altered.' But for us now, continues Professor Huxley, 'the notions of the beginning and the end of the world entertained by our forefathers are no longer credible. It is very certain that the earth is not the chief body in the material universe, and that the world is not subordinated to man's use. It is even more certain that nature is the expression of a definite order, with which nothing interferes.' 'And yet,' he cries, 'the purely classical education advocated by the representatives of the humanists in our day gives no inkling of all this!'

In due place and time I will just touch upon that vexed question of classical education; but at present the question is as to what is meant by knowing the best which modern nations have thought and said. It is not knowing their *belles lettres* merely which is meant. To know Italian *belles lettres* is not to know Italy, and to know English *belles lettres* is not to know England. Into knowing Italy and England there comes a great deal more, Galileo and Newton, amongst it. The reproach of being a superficial humanism, a tincture of *belles lettres*, may attach rightly enough to some other disciplines; but to the particular discipline recommended when I proposed knowing the best that has been thought and said in the world, it does not apply. In that best I certainly include what in modern times has been thought and said by the great observers and knowers of nature.

There is, therefore, really no question between Professor Huxley and me as to whether knowing the great results of the modern scientific study of nature is not required as a part of our culture, as well as knowing the products of literature and art. But to follow the processes by which those results are reached, ought, say the friends of physical science, to be made the staple of education for the bulk of mankind. And here there does arise a question between those whom Professor Huxley calls with playful sarcasm 'the Levites of culture,' and those whom the poor humanist is sometimes apt to regard as its Nebuchadnezzars.[11]

The great results of the scientific investigation of nature we are agreed upon knowing, but how much of our study are we bound to give to the processes by which those results are reached? The results have their visible bearing on human life. But all the processes, too, all the items of fact, by which those results are reached and established, are interesting. All knowledge is interesting to a wise man, and the knowledge of nature is interesting to all men. It is very interesting to know, that, from the albuminous white of the egg, the chick in the egg gets the materials for its flesh, bones, blood, and feathers; while, from the fatty yolk of the egg, it gets the heat and energy which enable it at length to break its shell and begin the world. It is less interesting, perhaps, but still it is interesting, to know that when a taper burns, the wax is converted into carbonic acid and water. Moreover, it is quite true that the habit of dealing with facts, which is given by the study of nature, is, as the friends of physical science praise it for being, an excellent discipline. The appeal, in the study of nature, is constantly to observation and experiment;

11. The Levites were in charge of the ceremonial observances of the Temple in Jerusalem. Nebuchadnezzar was the Babylonian king who captured Jerusalem. The humanists, Arnold understands Huxley to be saying, are bound by ritual tradition and are tyrannical.

not only is it said that the thing is so, but we can be made to see that it is so. Not only does a man tell us that when a taper burns the wax is converted into carbonic acid and water, as a man may tell us, if he likes, that Charon is punting his ferry-boat on the river Styx, or that Victor Hugo is a sublime poet, or Mr. Gladstone the most admirable of statesmen; but we are made to see that the conversion into carbonic acid and water does actually happen. This reality of natural knowledge it is, which makes the friends of physical science contrast it, as a knowledge of things, with the humanist's knowledge, which is, say they, a knowledge of words. And hence Professor Huxley is moved to lay it down that, 'for the purpose of attaining real culture, an exclusively scientific education is at least as effectual as an exclusively literary education.' And a certain President of the Section for Mechanical Science in the British Association is, in Scripture phrase, 'very bold,' and declares that if a man, in his mental training, 'has substituted literature and history for natural science, he has chosen the less useful alternative.' But whether we go these lengths or not, we must all admit that in natural science the habit gained of dealing with facts is a most valuable discipline, and that every one should have some experience of it.

More than this, however, is demanded by the reformers. It is proposed to make the training in natural science the main part of education, for the great majority of mankind at any rate. And here, I confess, I part company with the friends of physical science, with whom up to this point I have been agreeing. In differing from them, however, I wish to proceed with the utmost caution and diffidence. The smallness of my own acquaintance with the disciplines of natural science is ever before my mind, and I am fearful of doing these disciplines an injustice. The ability and pugnacity of the partisans of natural science makes them formidable persons to contradict. The tone of tentative inquiry, which befits a being of dim faculties and bounded knowledge, is the tone I would wish to take and not to depart from. At present it seems to me, that those who are for giving to natural knowledge, as they call it, the chief place in the education of the majority of mankind, leave one important thing out of their account: the constitution of human nature. But I put this forward on the strength of some facts not at all recondite, very far from it; facts capable of being stated in the simplest possible fashion, and to which, if I so state them, the man of science will, I am sure, be willing to allow their due weight.

Deny the facts altogether, I think, he hardly can. He can hardly deny, that when we set ourselves to enumerate the powers which go to the building up of human life, and say that they are the power of conduct, the power of intellect and knowledge, the power of beauty, and the power of social life and manners,—he can hardly deny that this scheme, though drawn in rough and plain lines enough, and not pretending to scientific exactness, does yet give a fairly true representation of the matter. Human nature is built up by these powers; we have the need for them all. When we have rightly met and adjusted the claims of them all, we shall then be in a fair way for getting soberness and righteousness, with wisdom. This is evident enough, and the friends of physical science would admit it.

But perhaps they may not have sufficiently observed another thing: namely, that the several powers just mentioned are not isolated, but there is, in the generality of mankind, a perpetual tendency to relate them one to another in divers ways. With one such way of relating them I am particularly concerned now. Following our instinct for intellect and knowledge, we acquire pieces of knowledge; and presently, in the generality of men, there arises the desire to relate these pieces of knowledge to our sense for conduct, to our sense for beauty,—and there is weariness and dissatisfaction if the desire is baulked. Now in this desire lies, I think, the strength of that hold which letters have upon us.

All knowledge is, as I said just now, interesting; and even items of knowledge which from the nature of the case cannot well be related, but must stand isolated in our thoughts, have their interest. Even lists of exceptions have their interest. If we are studying Greek accents, it is interesting to know that *pais* and *pas,* and some other monosyllables of the same form of declension, do not take the circumflex upon the last syllable of the genitive plural, but vary, in this respect, from the common rule. If we are studying physiology, it is interesting to know that the pulmonary artery carries dark blood and the pulmonary vein carries bright blood, departing in this respect from the common rule for the division of labour between the veins and the arteries. But every one knows how we seek naturally to combine the pieces of our knowledge together, to bring them under general rules, to relate them to principles; and how unsatisfactory and tiresome it would be to go on for ever learning lists of exceptions, or accumulating items of fact which must stand isolated.

Well, that same need of relating our knowledge, which operates here within the sphere of our knowledge itself, we shall find operating, also, outside that sphere. We experience, as we go on learning and knowing,—the vast majority of us experience,—the need of relating what we have learnt and known to the sense which we have in us for conduct, to the sense which we have in us for beauty.

A certain Greek prophetess of Mantineia in Arcadia, Diotima by name,[12] once explained to the philosopher Socrates that love, and impulse, and bent of all kinds, is, in fact, nothing else but the desire in men that good should for ever be present to them. This desire for good, Diotima assured Socrates, is our fundamental desire, of which fundamental desire every impulse in us is only some one particular form. And therefore this fundamental desire it is, I suppose,—this desire in men that good should be for ever present to them,— which acts in us when we feel the impulse for relating our knowledge to our sense for conduct and to our sense for beauty. At any rate, with men in general the instinct exists. Such is human nature. And the instinct, it will be admitted, is innocent, and human nature is preserved by our following the lead of its innocent instincts. Therefore, in seeking to gratify this instinct in question, we are following the instinct of self-preservation in humanity.

But, no doubt, some kinds of knowledge cannot be made to directly serve the instinct in question, cannot be directly related to the sense for beauty, to the sense for conduct. These are instrument-knowledges; they lead on to other knowledges, which can. A man who passes his life in instrument-knowledges

---

12. In Plato's *Symposium* Socrates speaks of this woman as his great teacher.

is a specialist. They may be invaluable as instruments to something beyond, for those who have the gift thus to employ them; and they may be disciplines in themselves wherein it is useful for every one to have some schooling. But it is inconceivable that the generality of men should pass all their mental life with Greek accents or with formal logic. My friend Professor Sylvester,[13] who is one of the first mathematicians in the world, holds transcendental doctrines as to the virtue of mathematics, but those doctrines are not for common men. In the very Senate House and heart of our English Cambridge [14] I once ventured, though not without an apology for my profaneness, to hazard the opinion that for the majority of mankind a little of mathematics, even, goes a long way. Of course this is quite consistent with their being of immense importance as an instrument to something else; but it is the few who have the aptitude for thus using them, not the bulk of mankind.

The natural sciences do not, however, stand on the same footing with these instrument-knowledges. Experience shows us that the generality of men will find more interest in learning that, when a taper burns, the wax is converted into carbonic acid and water, or in learning the explanation of the phenomenon of dew, or in learning how the circulation of the blood is carried on, than they find in learning that the genitive plural of *pais* and *pas* does not take the circumflex on the termination. And one piece of natural knowledge is added to another, and others are added to that, and at last we come to propositions so interesting as Mr. Darwin's famous proposition that 'our ancestor was a hairy quadruped furnished with a tail and pointed ears, probably arboreal in his habits.' [15] Or we come to propositions of such reach and magnitude as those which Professor Huxley delivers, when he says that the notions of our forefathers about the beginning and the end of the world were all wrong, and that nature is the expression of a definite order with which nothing interferes.

Interesting, indeed, these results of science are, important they are, and we should all of us be acquainted with them. But what I now wish you to mark is, that we are still, when they are propounded to us and we receive them, we are still in the sphere of intellect and knowledge. And for the generality of men there will be found, I say, to arise, when they have duly taken in the proposition that their ancestor was 'a hairy quadruped furnished with a tail and pointed ears, probably arboreal in his habits,' there will be found to arise an invincible desire to relate this proposition to the sense in us for conduct, and to the sense in us for beauty. But this the men of science will not do for us, and will hardly even profess to do. They will give us other pieces of knowledge, other facts, about other animals and their ancestors, or about plants, or about stones, or about stars; and they may finally bring us to those great 'general conceptions of the universe, which are forced upon us all,' says Professor Huxley, 'by the progress of physical science.' But still it will be

13. James Joseph Sylvester (1814–97), the great English mathematician, taught at the new Johns Hopkins University in Baltimore from 1876 to 1884, when he accepted a professorship at Oxford. His striking abilities raised mathematics in America to a new level. He was an accomplished classicist and published verse translations of Horace.
14. Mathematics had long been a pre-eminent study at Cambridge University. See *The Prelude* VI.115–41 and X.304–9 for the charm that the discipline had for Wordsworth.
15. Charles Darwin, *The Descent of Man* (1871) II.CL.xxi.

knowledge only which they give us; knowledge not put for us into relation with our sense for conduct, our sense for beauty, and touched with emotion by being so put; not thus put for us, and therefore, to the majority of mankind, after a certain while, unsatisfying, wearying.

Not to the born naturalist, I admit. But what do we mean by a born naturalist? We mean a man in whom the zeal for observing nature is so uncommonly strong and eminent, that it marks him off from the bulk of mankind. Such a man will pass his life happily in collecting natural knowledge and reasoning upon it, and will ask for nothing, or hardly anything, more. I have heard it said that the sagacious and admirable naturalist whom we lost not very long ago, Mr. Darwin, once owned to a friend that for his part he did not experience the necessity for two things which most men find so necessary to them,—religion and poetry; science and the domestic affections, he thought, were enough. To a born naturalist, I can well understand that this should seem so. So absorbing is his occupation with nature, so strong his love for his occupation, that he goes on acquiring natural knowledge and reasoning upon it, and has little time or inclination for thinking about getting it related to the desire in man for conduct, the desire in man for beauty. He relates it to them for himself as he goes along, so far as he feels the need; and he draws from the domestic affections all the additional solace necessary. But then Darwins are extremely rare. Another great and admirable master of natural knowledge, Faraday, was a Sandemanian.[16] That is to say, he related his knowledge to his instinct for conduct and to his instinct for beauty, by the aid of that respectable Scottish secretary, Robert Sandeman. And so strong, in general, is the demand of religion and poetry to have their share in a man, to associate themselves with his knowing, and to relieve and rejoice it, that, probably, for one man amongst us with the disposition to do as Darwin did in this respect, there are at least fifty with the disposition to do as Faraday.

Education lays hold upon us, in fact, by satisfying this demand. Professor Huxley holds up to scorn mediaeval education, with its neglect of the knowledge of nature, its poverty even of literary studies, its formal logic devoted to 'showing how and why that which the Church said was true must be true.' But the great mediaeval Universities were not brought into being, we may be sure, by the zeal for giving a jejune and contemptible education. Kings have been their nursing fathers, and queens have been their nursing mothers, but not for this. The mediæval Universities came into being, because the supposed knowledge, delivered by Scripture and the Church, so deeply engaged men's hearts, by so simply, easily, and powerfully relating itself to their desire for conduct, their desire for beauty. All other knowledge was dominated by this supposed knowledge and was subordinated to it, because of the surpassing strength of the hold which it gained upon the affections of men, by allying itself profoundly with their sense for conduct, their sense for beauty.

But now, says Professor Huxley, conceptions of the universe fatal to the notions held by our forefathers have been forced upon us by physical science.

16. Michael Faraday (1791–1867), the great English chemist and physicist. The Sandemanians were a Protestant sect deriving their name from the Robert Sandeman mentioned by Arnold below.

Grant to him that they are thus fatal, that the new conceptions must and will soon become current everywhere, and that every one will finally perceive them to be fatal to the beliefs of our forefathers. The need of humane letters, as they are truly called, because they serve the paramount desire in men that good should be for ever present to them,—the need of humane letters, to establish a relation between the new conceptions, and our instinct for beauty, our instinct for conduct, is only the more visible. The Middle Age could do without humane letters, as it could do without the study of nature, because its supposed knowledge was made to engage its emotions so powerfully. Grant that the supposed knowledge disappears, its power of being made to engage the emotions will of course disappear along with it,—but the emotions themselves, and their claim to be engaged and satisfied, will remain. Now if we find by experience that humane letters have an undeniable power of engaging the emotions, the importance of humane letters in a man's training becomes not less, but greater, in proportion to the success of modern science in extirpating what it calls 'mediaeval thinking.'

Have humane letters, then, have poetry and eloquence, the power here attributed to them of engaging the emotions, and do they exercise it? And if they have it and exercise it, *how* do they exercise it, so as to exert an influence upon man's sense for conduct, his sense for beauty? Finally, even if they both can and do exert an influence upon the senses in question, how are they to relate to them the results,—the modern results,—of natural science? All these questions may be asked. First, have poetry and eloquence the power of calling out the emotions? The appeal is to experience. Experience shows that for the vast majority of men, for mankind in general, they have the power. Next do they exercise it? They do. But then, *how* do they exercise it so as to affect man's sense for conduct, his sense for beauty? And this is perhaps a case for applying the Preacher's words: 'Though a man labour to seek it out, yet he shall not find it; yea, farther, though a wise man think to know it, yet shall he not be able to find it.' [17] Why should it be one thing, in its effect upon the emotions, to say, 'Patience is a virtue,' and quite another thing, in its effect upon the emotions, to say with Homer,

τλητὸν γὰρ Μοῖραι θυμὸν θέσαν ἀνθρώποισιν— [18]

'for an enduring heart have the destinies appointed to the children of men'? Why should it be one thing, in its effect upon the emotions, to say with the philosopher Spinoza, *Felicitas in eo consistit quod homo suum esse conservare potest*—'Man's happiness consists in his being able to preserve his own essence,' [19] and quite another thing, in its effect upon the emotions, to say with the Gospel, 'What is a man advantaged, if he gain the whole world, and lose himself, forfeit himself?' [20] How does this difference of effect arise? I cannot tell, and I am not much concerned to know; the important thing is that it does arise, and that we can profit by it. But how, finally, are poetry and eloquence

17. "Ecclesiastes viii.17." (Arnold)
18. "*Iliad* xxiv.49." (Arnold)
19. Spinoza, *Ethics* IV.xviii.
20. Luke 9:25.

to exercise the power of relating the modern results of natural science to man's instinct for conduct, his instinct for beauty? And here again I answer that I do not know *how* they will exercise it, but that they can and will exercise it I am sure. I do not mean that modern philosophical poets and modern philosophical moralists are to come and relate for us, in express terms, the results of modern scientific research to our instinct for conduct, our instinct for beauty. But I mean that we shall find, as a matter of experience, if we know the best that has been thought and uttered in the world, we shall find that the art and poetry and eloquence of men who lived, perhaps, long ago, who had the most limited natural knowledge, who had the most erroneous conceptions about many important matters, we shall find that this art, and poetry, and eloquence, have in fact not only the power of refreshing and delighting us, they have also the power,—such is the strength and worth, in essentials, of their authors' criticism of life,—they have a fortifying, and elevating, and quickening, and suggestive power, capable of wonderfully helping us to relate the results of modern science to our need for conduct, our need for beauty. Homer's conceptions of the physical universe were, I imagine, grotesque; but really, under the shock of hearing from modern science that 'the world is not subordinated to man's use, and that man is not the cynosure of things terrestrial,' I could, for my own part, desire no better comfort than Homer's line which I quoted just now,

τλητὸν γὰρ Μοῖραι θυμὸν θέσαν ἀνθρώποισιν—

'for an enduring heart have the destinies appointed to the children of men!'

And the more that men's minds are cleared, the more that the results of science are frankly accepted, the more that poetry and eloquence come to be received and studied as what in truth they really are,—the criticism of life by gifted men, alive and active with extraordinary power at an unusual number of points;—so much the more will the value of humane letters, and of art also, which is an utterance having a like kind of power with theirs, be felt and acknowledged, and their place in education be secured.

Let us therefore, all of us, avoid indeed as much as possible any invidious comparison between the merits of humane letters, as means of education, and the merits of the natural sciences. But when some President of a Section for Mechanical Science insists on making the comparison, and tells us that 'he who in his training has substituted literature and history for natural science has chosen the less useful alternative,' let us make answer to him that the student of humane letters only, will, at least, know also the great general conceptions brought in by modern physical science; for science, as Professor Huxley says, forces them upon us all. But the student of the natural sciences only, will, by our very hypothesis, know nothing of humane letters; not to mention that in setting himself to be perpetually accumulating natural knowledge, he sets himself to do what only specialists have in general the gift for doing genially. And so he will probably be unsatisfied, or at any rate incomplete, and even more incomplete than the student of humane letters only.

I once mentioned in a school-report, how a young man in one of our English training colleges having to paraphrase the passage in *Macbeth* beginning,

Can'st thou not minister to a mind diseased? [21]

turned this line into, 'Can you not wait upon the lunatic?' And I remarked what a curious state of things it would be, if every pupil of our national schools knew, let us say, that the moon is two thousand one hundred and sixty miles in diameter, and thought at the same time that a good paraphrase for

Can'st thou not minister to a mind diseased?

was, 'Can you not wait upon the lunatic?' If one is driven to choose, I think I would rather have a young person ignorant about the moon's diameter, but aware that 'Can you not wait upon the lunatic?' is bad, than a young person whose education had been such as to manage things the other way.

Or to go higher than the pupils of our national schools. I have in my mind's eye a member of our British Parliament who comes to travel here in America, who afterwards relates his travels, and who shows a really masterly knowledge of the geology of this great country and of its mining capabilities, but who ends by gravely suggesting that the United States should borrow a prince from our Royal Family, and should make him their king, and should create a House of Lords of great landed proprietors after the pattern of ours; and then America, he thinks, would have her future happily and perfectly secured. Surely, in this case, the President of the Section for Mechanical Science would himself hardly say that our member of Parliament, by concentrating himself upon geology and mineralogy, and so on, and not attending to literature and history, had 'chosen the more useful alternative.'

If then there is to be separation and option between humane letters on the one hand, and the natural sciences on the other, the great majority of mankind, all who have not exceptional and overpowering aptitudes for the study of nature, would do well, I cannot but think, to choose to be educated in humane letters rather than in the natural sciences. Letters will call out their being at more points, will make them live more.

I said that before I ended I would just touch on the question of classical education, and I will keep my word. Even if literature is to retain a large place in our education, yet Latin and Greek, say the friends of progress, will certainly have to go. Greek is the grand offender in the eyes of these gentlemen. The attackers of the established course of study think that against Greek, at any rate, they have irresistible arguments. Literature may perhaps be needed in education, they say; but why on earth should it be Greek literature? Why not French or German? Nay, 'has not an Englishman models in his own literature of every kind of excellence?' [22] As before, it is not on any weak pleadings of my own that I rely for convincing the gainsayers; it is on the constitution of human nature itself, and on the instinct of self-preservation in humanity. The instinct for beauty is set in human nature, as surely as the instinct for knowledge is set there, or the instinct for conduct. If the instinct for beauty is served by Greek literature and art as it is served by no other literature and art, we may trust to the instinct of self-preservation in humanity for keeping Greek as part

21. *Macbeth* V.iii.40.
22. Huxley, *Science and Culture.*

of our culture. We may trust to it for even making the study of Greek more prevalent than it is now. Greek will come, I hope, some day to be studied more rationally than at present; but it will be increasingly studied as men increasingly feel the need in them for beauty, and how powerfully Greek art and Greek literature can serve this need. Women will again study Greek, as Lady Jane Grey did; [23] I believe that in that chain of forts, with which the fair host of the Amazons are now engirdling our English universities, I find that here in America, in colleges like Smith College in Massachusetts, and Vassar College in the State of New York, and in the happy families of the mixed universities out West, they are studying it already.[24]

Defuit una mihi symmetria prisca,—'The antique symmetry was the one thing wanting to me,' said Leonardo da Vinci; and he was an Italian. I will not presume to speak for the Americans, but I am sure that, in the Englishman, the want of this admirable symmetry of the Greeks is a thousand times more great and crying than in any italian. The results of the want show themselves most glaringly, perhaps, in our architecture, but they show themselves, also, in all our art. *Fit details strictly combined, in view of a large general result nobly conceived;* that is just the beautiful *symmetria prisca* of the Greeks, and it is just where we English fail, where all our art fails. Striking ideas we have, and well-executed details we have; but that high symmetry which, with satisfying and delightful effect, combines them, we seldom or never have. The glorious beauty of the Acropolis at Athens did not come from single fine things stuck about on that hill, a statue here, a gateway there;—no, it arose from all things being perfectly combined for a supreme total effect. What must not an Englishman feel about our deficiencies in this respect, as the sense for beauty, whereof this symmetry is an essential element, awakens and strengthens within him! what will not one day be his respect and desire for Greece and its *symmetria prisca*, when the scales drop from his eyes as he walks the London streets, and he sees such a lesson in meanness as the Strand,[25] for instance, in its true deformity! But here we are coming to our friend Mr. Ruskin's province,[26] and I will not intrude upon it, for he is its very sufficient guardian.

And so we at last find, it seems, we find flowing in favour of the humanities the natural and necessary stream of things, which seemed against them when we started. The 'hairy quadruped furnished with a tail and pointed ears, probably arboreal in his habits,' this good fellow carried hidden in his nature, apparently, something destined to develop into a necessity for humane letters. Nay, more; we seem finally to be even led to the further conclusion that our hairy ancestor carried in his nature, also, a necessity for Greek.

And therefore, to say the truth, I cannot really think that humane letters

---

23. Lady Jane Grey (*c.* 1537–54) was the great-granddaughter of Henry VII. She was proclaimed Queen of England in 1553 but was deposed and beheaded. She was reputed to be an excellent Greek scholar.
24. Higher education for women and coeducation had an earlier start in America than in England.
25. The Strand is one of the busiest and most important streets of London. Its name is derived from the fact that it once skirted the river Thames. Its aspect is considerably better now than it was in Arnold's day.
26. That is, the criticism of architecture.

are in much actual danger of being thrust out from their leading place in education, in spite of the array of authorities against them at this moment. So long as human nature is what it is, their attractions will remain irresistible. As with Greek, so with letters generally: they will some day come, we may hope, to be studied more rationally, but they will not lose their place. What will happen will rather be that there will be crowded into education other matters besides, far too many; there will be, perhaps, a period of unsettlement and confusion and false tendency; but letters will not in the end lose their leading place. If they lose it for a time, they will get it back again. We shall be brought back to them by our wants and aspirations. And a poor humanist may possess his soul in patience, neither strive nor cry, admit the energy and brilliancy of the partisans of physical science, and their present favour with the public, to be far greater than his own, and still have a happy faith that the nature of things works silently on behalf of the studies which he loves, and that, while we shall all have to acquaint ourselves with the great results reached by modern science, and to give ourselves as much training in its disciplines as we can conveniently carry, yet the majority of men will always require humane letters; and so much the more, as they have the more and the greater results of science to relate to the need in man for conduct, and to the need in him for beauty.

1881, 1883   1882, 1885

T. H. HUXLEY
1825–1895

It may be thought an amusing small curiosity of Victorian intellectual history that when John Henry Newman was a pupil at the private school at Ealing where he had the decisive experience of his life, the self-evidence of God's existence, one of his masters—he is known to have held the young Newman in the highest regard—was the father of T. H. Huxley, among whose claims to fame is the fact that he coined the word "agnostic." It was a word that many Victorians found useful to describe their position as to the existence of God: while disclaiming atheism, it signifies that no predication of either the existence or the non-existence of the Deity can be made on the basis of knowledge.

As Newman dedicated his life to the defense and advancement of religion, especially those of its elements which were transcendent and supernatural, and conceived one of its chief enemies to be the animus and error of the modern scientific imagination, so Huxley was committed to the defense and advancement of science, whose leading antagonist he identified as organized religion. A scientist of great ability, Huxley in time turned from research; although his achievement in that line was considerable, he is now remembered chiefly for his effectiveness as an educator of the public, for having been in his day the pre-eminent exponent of the scientific spirit. As he says in the autobiographical essay he wrote in 1889, he subordinated his ambition for scientific fame to other ends: "to the popularisation of science; to the development and organisation of scientific education; to the endless series of battles over evolution; and to untiring opposition to that ecclesiastical spirit, that clericalism, which in England, as everywhere else, and to whatever denomination it may belong, is the deadly enemy of science."

Thomas Henry Huxley was born at Ealing in 1825. He set store by the first of his Christian names, that of the doubting disciple of Christ, as being indicative of his intellectual temper, although he records of his early childhood a strong identification with the aristocratic vicar of the parish, which led to his preaching to his mother's maids one Sunday morning, his pinafore turned wrong side forward to represent a surplice. His time of systematic education was as short as it was unpleasant. The Ealing school, excellent in Newman's day and for a time thereafter, deteriorated on the death of its headmaster. In 1835, when his son was ten, the elder Huxley gave up teaching and returned to his native Coventry to become manager of a bank. After that, Thomas had no formal instruction. But he read widely in every direction, with a special appetite for science and logical and metaphysical speculation. He held the works of Carlyle in especial admiration and under their influence began to teach himself German. He later went on to the study of French and Italian. In 1841, he undertook the study of medicine, became an assistant to a doctor in one of the poor sections of London, then apprenticed himself to one of his brothers-in-law, attended medical lectures at Sydenham College, and won a Free Scholarship to Charing Cross Hospital. (It is worth relating that the elder Huxley applied to his former pupil, Newman, to support his son's candidacy, and although Huxley's biographer does not say so, we may suppose the request was granted.) In 1845 Huxley took his Bachelor of Medicine degree at the University of London. Through his own enterprise he secured an appointment in the medical service of the navy and was posted to a naval hospital and subsequently to the *Rattlesnake,* a frigate which was being prepared for a long cruise of survey and exploration in Australian and East India waters, to the special end of bringing back an account of the geography, geology, and natural history of New Guinea. For four years the young assistant-surgeon of the ship was unremitting in his researches, carried out with inadequate equipment, chiefly into the physiology of marine animals. (His journal of the cruise was published in 1935.) He sent back numerous scientific articles, some of which were published before his return in 1850; in 1851, on the strength of his paper on the structure of the Medusae (jellyfish), he was elected Fellow of the Royal Society, a coveted honor, and in the following year was awarded the Society's Royal Medal. Despite this signal recognition, he had difficulty in finding a salaried position, but he continued his research and began to be known as a lecturer and writer whose lucidity and charm of presentation could make any scientific subject comprehensible to virtually anyone. By 1854 his posts were numerous; he was Lecturer in Natural History in the Royal School of Mines, Naturalist to the Geological Survey, and Lecturer in Comparative Anatomy at St. Thomas's Hospital; the next year he married the young lady to whom he had become engaged on his visit to Australia. His researches at this period dealt with invertebrates, vertebrates, and plants, and during a visit to Switzerland he undertook the study of the action of glaciers. He was instrumental in the establishment of two important scientific journals, the *Natural History Review* and *Nature.*

In 1859 Charles Darwin published his epoch-making *Origin of Species,* which Huxley reviewed for the London *Times.* Evolution was of course not a new idea for the Victorians. In one or another formulation, the theory that the universe had not been brought into being by a special act of creation but that it and its inhabitants, including man himself, had evolved from more primitive forms, had for some time disquieted the religious imagination; the depth of the distress it could cause is classically exemplified by Tennyson's *In Memoriam*, begun in 1833 and published in 1850. But *The Origin of Species* gave a new force to the idea, partly because it specified by its theory of natural selection the means by which biological evolution proceeds, and it was greeted with a vociferous anger which had its roots in the fear that the supernatural basis of religion stood threatened as never before. Huxley, who had rejected the idea of evolution until Darwin's book convinced him of its truth, was drawn into the great national debate that followed—Darwin himself could not be drawn into controversy—and became the pre-eminent polemicist of the evolutionists.

The most famous, and certainly to him most gratifying, moment of Huxley's career as "Darwin's bulldog," came in the exchange between Bishop Wilberforce and him at the meeting of the British Association at Oxford in 1860. The bishop, who had recently attacked Darwin in an elegant but ignorant article, rose to speak in the discussion period and went on for half an hour ridiculing Darwin and Huxley, his line being that there was really no such thing as evolution. "Then, turning to his antagonist with a smiling insolence, he begged to know, was it through his grandfather or grandmother that he claimed his descent from a monkey?" At this, Huxley said to his neighbor, "The Lord hath delivered him into mine hands," rose to answer the bishop, and concluded his statement by saying that "he was not ashamed to have a monkey for his ancestor; but he would be ashamed to be connected with a man who used great gifts to obscure the truth." (There are many different versions of Huxley's precise words, but all agree as to their purport and the effect they produced in the crowded hall, of elation on the part of the pro-Darwinists, of bitterness on the part of the chiefly clerical anti-Darwinists.)

By 1863, although he continued his researches, Huxley's energies, which were inexhaustible despite his frequent ill-health, were increasingly devoted to science as a cultural issue, as the basis of intellectual and even moral virtue. Huxley became, among other things, a leading theorist of education, and one of his later lectures, *Science and Culture* (1880), was the occasion for Matthew Arnold's *Literature and Science* (see above). His insistence that science had to play a larger part in education than it did was based on intellectual rather than utilitarian grounds; the humanistic bent that had led him from Carlyle to Goethe was permanent, and, despite what might be inferred from Arnold's reply, he had no doubt that literature had to be salient in any effectual system of education. This dedicated exponent of the intellectual value of science undertook the study of Greek in his fifties and made it a first requirement in the training of a scientist that he learn to write well.

The honors that came to Huxley in the course of his life were innumerable, and the responsibilities he assumed were equally beyond count. At one time or another he was president of virtually every scientific association of importance; he served on no less than ten Royal Commissions; he was elected to the first London school board. In 1871 he published his *Manual of the Anatomy of Vertebrated Animals*, which remained a standard text at least until the end of the century. His lectures and essays on scientific subjects, which evinced an ever-growing readiness to bring scientific facts and principles to bear upon the problems of ethics and politics, appeared at frequent intervals and were eagerly read. In 1876 he visited America to give an address on university education at the newly founded Johns Hopkins University and stayed on to lecture through the next year. His health had broken down in 1872; it failed again in 1884 and he gave up his salaried posts to retire on a generous government allowance; yet he carried on the activity which he had come to think of as the one to which he had been peculiarly called, that of offering a ceaseless resistance to the ecclesiastical spirit in its continuing, if ever less sanguine, attacks upon science. He died in 1895.

His grandson Aldous Huxley, before undertaking the career as a novelist which brought him fame, intended to be a biologist but was prevented by an eye disease. Sir Julian Huxley, the elder brother of Aldous, is a biologist of great eminence. Andrew Huxley, the half-brother of Aldous and Julian, was awarded the Nobel Prize in 1963 for his work in physiology.

On the Physical Basis of Life [1]

In order to make the title of this discourse generally intelligible, I have translated the term 'Protoplasm,' which is the scientific name of the substance of which I am about to speak, by the words 'the physical basis of life.' [2] I suppose that, to many, the idea that there is such a thing as a physical basis, or matter, of life may be novel—so widely spread is the conception of life as a something which works through matter, but is independent of it; and even those who are aware that matter and life are inseparably connected, may not be prepared for the conclusion plainly suggested by the phrase, 'the physical basis or matter of life,' that there is some one kind of matter which is common to all living beings, and that their endless diversities are bound together by a physical, as well as an ideal, unity. In fact, when first apprehended, such a doctrine as this appears almost shocking to common sense.

What, truly, can seem to be more obviously different from one another, in faculty, in form, and in substance, than the various kinds of living beings? What community of faculty can there be between the brightly-coloured lichen,[3] which so nearly resembles a mere mineral incrustation of the bare rock on which it grows, and the painter, to whom it is instinct with beauty, or the botanist, whom it feeds with knowledge?

Again, think of the microscopic fungus—a mere infinitesimal ovoid particle, which finds space and duration enough to multiply into countless millions in the body of a living fly; and then of the wealth of foliage, the luxuriance of flower and fruit, which lies between this bald sketch of a plant and the giant pine of California, towering to the dimensions of a cathedral spire, or the Indian fig, which covers acres with its profound shadow, and endures while nations and empires come and go around its vast circumference. Or, turning

1. This lecture was delivered in 1868 to an Edinburgh audience. When Huxley reprinted it in his collected works in 1892, he remarked in an appended note, "I cannot say I have ever had to complain of lack of hostile criticism; but the preceding essay has come in for more than its fair share of that commodity. . . ."
2. The word is compounded of two Greek elements, proto, first in time, earliest, primitive, + plasma, moulded thing, figure, form. It was introduced into biological terminology in 1846, by the German scientist H. von Mohl.
3. Pronounced lī-ken. Any of numerous plants consisting of a fungus in combination with certain green algae. It forms a crust-like growth on rocks or tree trunks.

to the other half of the world of life, picture to yourselves the great Finner whale,[4] hugest of beasts that live, or have lived, disporting his eighty or ninety feet of bone, muscle, and blubber, with easy roll, among waves in which the stoutest ship that ever left dockyard would flounder hopelessly; and contrast him with the invisible animalcules—mere gelatinous specks, multitudes of which could, in fact, dance upon the point of a needle with the same ease as the angels of the Schoolmen could,[5] in imagination. With these images before your minds, you may well ask, what community of form, or structure, is there between the animalcule and the whale; or between the fungus and the fig-tree? And, a fortiori,[6] between all four?

Finally, if we regard substance, or material composition, what hidden bond can connect the flower which a girl wears in her hair and the blood which courses through her youthful veins; or, what is there in common between the dense and resisting mass of the oak, or the strong fabric of the tortoise, and those broad disks of glassy jelly which may be seen pulsating through the waters of a calm sea, but which drain away to mere films in the hand which raises them out of their element?

Such objections as these must, I think, arise in the mind of every one who ponders, for the first time, upon the conception of a single physical basis of life underlying all the diversities of vital existence; but I propose to demonstrate to you that, notwithstanding these apparent difficulties, a threefold unity—namely, a unity of power or faculty, a unity of form, and a unity of substantial composition—does pervade the whole living world.

No very abstruse argumentation is needed, in the first place to prove that the powers, or faculties, of all kinds of living matter, diverse as they may be in degree, are substantially similar in kind.

Goethe has condensed a survey of all powers of mankind into the well-known epigram:—

Warum treibt sich das Volk so und schreit? Es will sich ernähren
Kinder zeugen, und die nähren so gut es vermag.
. . .
Weiter bringt es kein Mensch, stell' er sich wie er auch will.[7]

In physiological language this means that all the multifarious and complicated activities of man are comprehensible under three categories. Either they are immediately directed towards the maintenance and development of the body, or they effect transitory changes in the relative positions of parts of the body, or they tend towards the continuance of the species. Even those manifestations of intellect, of feeling, and of will, which we rightly name the higher faculties, are not excluded from this classification, inasmuch as to every one

4. A whale of elongated shape having a small back fin. Some specimens are even larger than Huxley says, running to a length of over 100 feet.
5. The Schoolmen, or Scholastics as they are also called, were the theological philosophers of the Middle Ages. They were subtle and powerful reasoners, but they did often engage in speculations like the famous one Huxley cites, which to us seem fantastic.
6. "For a stronger reason; all the more."
7. "Why do the people push each other and shout? They want to sustain themselves / Beget children, and sustain them as well as possible. / . . . . Further than that no man can advance, however hard he may try." Goethe, Venetian Epigrams 10.

but the subject of them, they are known only as transitory changes in the relative positions of parts of the body. Speech, gesture, and every other form of human action are, in the long run, resolvable into muscular contraction, and muscular contraction is but a transitory change in the relative positions of the parts of a muscle. But the scheme which is large enough to embrace the activities of the highest form of life, covers all those of the lower creatures. The lowest plant, or animalcule, feeds, grows, and reproduces its kind. In addition, all animals manifest those transitory changes of form which we class under irritability and contractility; and, it is more than probable, that when the vegetable world is thoroughly explored, we shall find all plants in possession of the same powers, at one time or other of their existence.

I am not now alluding to such phenomena, at once rare and conspicuous, as those exhibited by the leaflets of the sensitive plants, or the stamens of the barberry, but to much more widely spread, and at the same time, more subtle and hidden, manifestations of vegetable contractility. You are doubtless aware that the common nettle owes its stinging property to the innumerable stiff and needle-like, though exquisitely delicate, hairs which cover its surface. Each stinging-needle tapers from a broad base to a slender summit, which, though rounded at the end, is of such microscopic fineness that it readily penetrates, and breaks off in, the skin. The whole hair consists of a very delicate outer case of wood, closely applied to the inner surface of which is a layer of semi-fluid matter, full of innumerable granules of extreme minuteness. This semi-fluid lining is protoplasm, which thus constitutes a kind of bag, full of a limpid liquid, and roughly corresponding in form with the interior of the hair which it fills. When viewed with a sufficiently high magnifying power, the protoplasmic layer of the nettle hair is seen to be in a condition of unceasing activity. Local contractions of the whole thickness of its substance pass slowly and gradually from point to point, and give rise to the appearance of progressive waves, just as the bending of successive stalks of corn by a breeze produces the apparent billows of a corn-field.

But, in addition to these movements, and independently of them, the granules are driven, in relatively rapid streams, through channels in the protoplasm which seem to have a considerable amount of persistence. Most commonly, the currents in adjacent parts of the protoplasm take similar directions; and, thus, there is a general stream up one side of the hair and down the other. But this does not prevent the existence of partial currents which take different routes; and sometimes trains of granules may be seen coursing swiftly in opposite directions within a twenty-thousandth of an inch of one another; while, occasionally, opposite streams come into direct collision, and, after a longer or shorter struggle, one predominates. The cause of these currents seems to lie in contractions of the protoplasm which bounds the channels in which they flow, but which are so minute that the best microscopes show only their effects, and not themselves.

The spectacle afforded by the wonderful energies prisoned within the compass of the microscopic hair of a plant, which we commonly regard as a merely passive organism, is not easily forgotten by one who has watched its display, continued hour after hour, without pause or sign of weakening. The possible complexity of many other organic forms, seemingly as simple as the protoplasm of the nettle, dawns upon one; and the comparison of such a protoplasm to a body with an internal circulation, which has been put forward by an eminent physiologist, loses much of its startling character. Currents similar to those of the hairs of the nettle have been observed in a great multitude of very different plants, and weighty authorities have suggested that they probably occur, in more or less perfection, in all young vegetable cells. If such be the case, the wonderful noonday silence of a tropical forest is, after all, due only to the dulness of our hearing; and could our ears catch the murmur of these tiny Maelstroms,[8] as they whirl in the innumerable myriads of living cells which constitute each tree, we should be stunned, as with the roar of a great city.

Among the lower plants, it is the rule rather than the exception, that contractility should be still more openly manifested at some periods of their existence. The protoplasm of *Algae* and *Fungi* becomes, under many circumstances, partially, or completely, freed from its woody case, and exhibits movements of its whole mass, or is propelled by the contractility of one, or more, hair-like prolongations of its body, which are called vibratile cilia. And, so far as the conditions of the manifestation of the phenomena of contractility have yet been studied, they are the same for the plant as for the animal. Heat and electric shocks influence both, and in the same way, though it may be in different degrees. It is by no means my intention to suggest that there is no difference in faculty between the lowest plant and the highest, or between plants and animals. But the difference between the powers of the lowest plant, or animal, and those of the highest, is one of degree, not of kind, and depends, as Milne-Edwards [9] long ago so well pointed out, upon the extent to which the principle of the division of labour is carried out in the living economy. In the lowest organism all parts are competent to perform all functions, and one and the same portion of protoplasm may successfully take on the function of feeding, moving, or reproducing apparatus. In the highest, on the contrary, a great number of parts combine to perform each function, each part doing its allotted share of the work with great accuracy and efficiency, but being useless for any other purpose.

On the other hand, notwithstanding all the fundamental resemblances which exist between the powers of the protoplasm in plants and in animals, they present a striking difference (to which I shall advert more at length presently), in the fact that plants can manufacture fresh protoplasm out of mineral compounds, whereas animals are obliged to procure it ready made, and hence, in the long run, depend upon plants. Upon what condition this difference in the powers of the two great divisions of the world of life depends, nothing is at present known.

With such qualifications as arise out of the last-mentioned fact, it may be truly said that the acts of all living things are fundamentally one. Is any such unity predicable of their forms? Let us seek in easily verified facts for a reply to this question. If a drop of blood be drawn by pricking one's finger, and viewed with proper precautions, and under a sufficiently high microscopic

8. Whirlpools of extraordinary size and violence. Specifically, as a proper noun, a famous whirlpool off the northwest coast of Norway.
9. Henry Milne-Edwards (1800–1885), eminent French zoologist, the son of an Englishman.

power, there will be seen, among the innumerable multitude of little, circular, discoidal bodies, or corpuscles, which float in it and give it its colour, a comparatively small number of colourless corpuscles, of somewhat larger size and very irregular shape. If the drop of blood be kept at the temperature of the body, these colourless corpuscles will be seen to exhibit a marvellous activity, changing their forms with great rapidity, drawing in and thrusting out prolongations of their substance, and creeping about as if they were independent organisms.

The substance which is thus active is a mass of protoplasm, and its activity differs in detail, rather than in principle, from that of the protoplasm of the nettle. Under sundry circumstances the corpuscle dies and becomes distended into a round mass, in the midst of which is seen a smaller spherical body, which existed, but was more or less hidden, in the living corpuscle, and is called its *nucleus*. Corpuscles of essentially similar structure are to be found in the skin, in the lining of the mouth, and scattered through the whole framework of the body. Nay, more; in the earliest condition of the human organism, in that state in which it has but just become distinguishable from the egg in which it arises, it is nothing but an aggregation of such corpuscles, and every organ of the body was, once, no more than such an aggregation.

Thus a nucleated mass of protoplasm turns out to be what may be termed the structural unit of the human body. As a matter of fact, the body, in its earliest state, is a mere multiple of such units; and in its perfect condition, it is a multiple of such units, variously modified.

But does the formula which expresses the essential structural character of the highest animal cover all the rest, as the statement of its powers and faculties covered that of all others? Very nearly. Beast and fowl, reptile and fish, mollusk, worm, and polype, are all composed of structural units of the same character, namely, masses of protoplasm with a nucleus. There are sundry very low animals, each of which, structurally, is a mere colourless blood-corpuscle, leading an independent life. But, at the very bottom of the animal scale, even this simplicity becomes simplified, and all the phenomena of life are manifested by a particle of protoplasm without a nucleus. Nor are such organisms insignificant by reason of their want of complexity. It is a fair question whether the protoplasm of those simplest forms of life, which people an immense extent of the bottom of the sea, would not outweigh that of all the higher living beings which inhabit the land put together. And in ancient times, no less than at the present day, such living beings as these have been the greatest of rock builders.

What has been said of the animal world is no less true of plants. Imbedded in the protoplasm at the broad, or attached, end of the nettle hair, there lies a spheroidal nucleus. Careful examination further proves that the whole substance of the nettle is made up of a repetition of such masses of nucleated protoplasm, each contained in a wooden case, which is modified in form, sometimes into a woody fibre, sometimes, into a duct or spiral vessel, sometimes into a pollen grain, or an ovule. Traced back to its earliest state, the nettle arises as the man does, in a particle of nucleated protoplasm. And in the lowest plants, as in the lowest animals, a single mass of such protoplasm may constitute the whole plant, or the protoplasm may exist without a nucleus.

Under these circumstances it may well be asked, how is one mass of non-nucleated protoplasm to be distinguished from another? why call one 'plant' and the other 'animal'?

The only reply is that, so far as form is concerned, plants and animals are not separable, and that, in many cases, it is a mere matter of convention whether we call a given organism an animal or a plant. There is a living body called *Aethalium septicum*, which appears upon decaying vegetable substances, and, in one of its forms, is common upon the surfaces of tan-pits.[10] In this condition it is, to all intents and purposes, a fungus, and formerly was always regarded as such; but the remarkable investigations of De Bary [11] have shown that, in another condition, the *Aethalium* is an actively locomotive creature, and takes in solid matters, upon which, apparently, it feeds, thus exhibiting the most characteristic feature of animality. Is this a plant; or is it an animal? Is it both; or is it neither? Some decide in favour of the last supposition, and establish an intermediate kingdom, a sort of biological No Man's Land for all these questionable forms. But, as it is admittedly impossible to draw any distinct boundary line between this no man's land and the vegetable world on the one hand, or the animal, on the other, it appears to me that this proceeding merely doubles the difficulty which, before, was single.

Protoplasm, simple or nucleated, is the formal basis of all life. It is the clay of the potter: which, bake it and paint it as he will, remains clay, separated by artifice, and not by nature, from the commonest brick or sun-dried clod.

Thus it becomes clear that all living powers are cognate, and that all living forms are fundamentally of one character. The researches of the chemist have revealed a no less striking uniformity of material composition in living matter.

In perfect strictness, it is true that chemical investigation can tell us little or nothing, directly, of the composition of living matter, inasmuch as such matter must needs die in the act of analysis,—and upon this very obvious ground, objections, which I confess seem to me to be somewhat frivolous, have been raised to the drawing of any conclusions whatever respecting the composition of actually living matter, from that of the dead matter of life, which alone is accessible to us. But objectors of this class do not seem to reflect that it is also, in strictness, true that we know nothing about the composition of any body whatever, as it is. The statement that a crystal of calc-spar [12] consists of carbonate of lime, is quite true, if we only mean that, by appropriate processes, it may be resolved into carbonic acid and quicklime. If you pass the same carbonic acid over the very quicklime thus obtained, you will obtain carbonate of lime again; but it will not be calc-spar, nor anything like it. Can it, therefore, be said that chemical analysis teaches nothing about the chemical composition of calc-spar? Such a statement would be absurd; but it is hardly more so than the talk one occasionally hears about the uselessness of applying the results of chemical analysis to the living bodies which have yielded them.

One fact, at any rate, is out of reach of such refinements, and this is, that all the forms of protoplasm which have yet been examined contain the four elements, carbon, hydrogen, oxygen, and nitrogen, in very complex union, and that they

10. Where hides are converted into leather by the application of tanning.
11. Heinrich Anton de Bary (1831–88), German botanist. He was the founder of modern mycology, the study of fungi.
12. Calc-spar is calcite, the basic constituent of limestone, marble, and chalk.

behave similarly towards several reagents. To this complex combination, the nature of which has never been determined with exactness, the name of Protein [13] has been applied. And if we use this term with such caution as may properly arise out of our comparative ignorance of the things for which it stands, it may be truly said, that all protoplasm is proteinaceous, or, as the white, or albumen, of an egg is one of the commonest examples of a nearly pure protein matter, we may say that all living matter is more or less albuminoid.

Perhaps it would not yet be safe to say that all forms of protoplasm are affected by the direct action of electric shocks; and yet the number of cases in which the contraction of protoplasm is shown to be affected by this agency increases every day.

Nor can it be affirmed with perfect confidence, that all forms of protoplasm are liable to undergo that peculiar coagulation at a temperature of $40°$–$50°$ centigrade, which has been called 'heat-stiffening,' though Kühne's [14] beautiful researches have proved this occurrence to take place in so many and such diverse living beings, that it is hardly rash to expect that the law holds good for all.

Enough has, perhaps, been said to prove the existence of a general uniformity in the character of the protoplasm, or physical basis, of life, in whatever group of living beings it may be studied. But it will be understood that this general uniformity by no means excludes any amount of special modifications of the fundamental substance. The mineral, carbonate of lime, assumes an immense diversity of characters, though no one doubts that, under all these Protean [15] changes, it is one and the same thing.

And now, what is the ultimate fate, and what the origin, of the matter of life?

Is it, as some of the older naturalists supposed, diffused throughout the universe in molecules, which are indestructible and unchangeable in themselves; but, in endless transmigration, unite in innumerable permutations, into the diversified forms of life we know? Or, is the matter of life composed of ordinary matter, differing from it only in the manner in which its atoms are aggregated? Is it built up of ordinary matter, and again resolved into ordinary matter when its work is done?

Modern science does not hesitate a moment between these alternatives. Physiology writes over the portals of life—

Debemur morti nos nostraque,[16]

with a profounder meaning than the Roman poet attached to that melancholy line. Under whatever disguise it takes refuge, whether fungus or oak, worm or man, the living protoplasm not only ultimately dies and is resolved into its mineral and lifeless constituents, but is always dying, and, strange as the paradox may sound, could not live unless it died.

13. This word was first used in 1838 by the French scientist Mulder. It was intended to denote the primary substance of the body (see note 2, on protoplasm).
14. Willy Kühne (1817–1900), German physiologist who worked on the physiology of muscle and nerve and on the chemistry of digestion.
15. In Greek mythology Proteus was a minor sea god, who had the power to take any shape he chose in order to avoid answering questions.
16. "We owe ourselves and all that is ours to death." Horace, Ars Poetica I.63.

In the wonderful story of the 'Peau de Chagrin,' [17] the hero becomes possessed of a magical wild ass' skin, which yields him the means of gratifying all his wishes. But its surface represents the duration of the proprietor's life; and for every satisfied desire the skin shrinks in proportion to the intensity of fruition, until at length life and the last handbreadth of the *peau de chagrin* disappear with the gratification of a last wish.

Balzac's studies had led him over a wide range of thought and speculation, and his shadowing forth of physiological truth in this strange story may have been intentional. At any rate, the matter of life is a veritable *peau de chagrin,* and for every vital act it is somewhat the smaller. All work implies waste, and the work of life results, directly or indirectly, in the waste of protoplasm.

Every word uttered by a speaker costs him some physical loss; and, in the strictest sense, he burns that others may have light—so much eloquence, so much of his body resolved into carbonic acid, water, and urea. It is clear that this process of expenditure cannot go on for ever. But, happily, the protoplasmic *peau de chagrin* differs from Balzac's in its capacity of being repaired, and brought back to its full size, after every exertion.

For example, this present lecture, whatever its intellectual worth to you, has a certain physical value to me, which is, conceivably, expressible by the number of grains of protoplasm and other bodily substance wasted in maintaining my vital processes during its delivery. My *peau de chagrin* will be distinctly smaller at the end of the discourse than it was at the beginning. By and by, I shall probably have recourse to the substance commonly called mutton, for the purpose of stretching it back to its original size. Now this mutton was once the living protoplasm, more or less modified, of another animal—a sheep. As I shall eat it, it is the same matter altered, not only by death, but by exposure to sundry artificial operations in the process of cooking.

But these changes, whatever be their extent, have not rendered it incompetent to resume its old functions as matter of life. A singular inward laboratory, which I possess, will dissolve a certain portion of the modified protoplasm; the solution so formed will pass into my veins; and the subtle influences to which it will then be subjected will convert the dead protoplasm into living protoplasm, and transubstantiate sheep into man.

Nor is this all. If digestion were a thing to be trifled with, I might sup upon lobster, and the matter of life of the crustacean would undergo the same wonderful metamorphosis into humanity. And were I to return to my own place by sea, and undergo shipwreck, the crustacean might, and probably would, return the compliment and demonstrate our common nature by turning my protoplasm into living lobster. Or, if nothing better were to be had, I might supply my wants with mere bread, and I should find the protoplasm of the wheat-plant to be convertible into man, with no more trouble than that of the sheep, and with far less, I fancy, than that of the lobster.

Hence it appears to be a matter of no great moment what animal, or what plant, I lay under contribution for protoplasm, and the fact speaks volumes for the general identity of that substance in all living beings. I share this

17. "Skin of the Wild Ass." The novel by Honoré de Balzac (1799–1850) was published in 1834.

catholicity of assimilation with other animals, all of which, so far as we know, could thrive equally well on the protoplasm of any of their fellows, or of any plant; but here the assimilative powers of the animal world cease. A solution of smelling-salts in water, with an infinitesimal proportion of some other saline matters, contains all the elementary bodies which enter into the composition of protoplasm; but, as I need hardly say, a hogshead of that fluid would not keep a hungry man from starving, nor would it save any animal whatever from a like fate. An animal cannot make protoplasm, but must take it ready-made from some other animal, or some plant—the animal's highest feat of constructive chemistry being to convert dead protoplasm into that living matter of life which is appropriate to itself.

Therefore, in seeking for the origin of protoplasm, we must eventually turn to the vegetable world. A fluid containing carbonic acid, water, and nitrogenous salts, which offers such a Barmecide feast [18] to the animal, is a table richly spread to multitudes of plants; and, with a due supply of only such materials, many a plant will not only maintain itself in vigour, but grow and multiply until it has increased a million-fold, or a million million-fold, the quantity of protoplasm which it originally possessed; in this way building up the matter of life, to an indefinite extent, from the common matter of the universe.

Thus, the animal can only raise the complex substance of dead protoplasm to the higher power, as one may say, of living protoplasm; while the plant can raise the less complex substances—carbonic acid, water, and nitrogenous salts—to the same stage of living protoplasm, if not to the same level. But the plant also has its limitations. Some of the fungi, for example, appear to need higher compounds to start with; and no known plant can live upon the uncompounded elements of protoplasm. A plant supplied with pure carbon, hydrogen, oxygen, and nitrogen, phosphorus, sulphur, and the like, would as infallibly die as the animal in his bath of smelling-salts, though it would be surrounded by all the constituents of protoplasm. Nor, indeed, need the process of simplification of vegetable food be carried so far as this, in order to arrive at the limit of the plant's thaumaturgy.[19] Let water, carbonic acid, and all the other needful constituents be supplied except nitrogenous salts, and an ordinary plant will still be unable to manufacture protoplasm.

Thus the matter of life, so far as we know it (and we have no right to speculate on any other), breaks up, in consequence of that continual death which is the condition of its manifesting vitality, into carbonic acid, water, and nitrogenous compounds, which certainly possess no properties but those of ordinary matter. And out of these same forms of ordinary matter, and from none which are simpler, the vegetable world builds up all the protoplasm which keeps the animal world a-going. Plants are the accumulators of the power which animals distribute and disperse.

But it will be observed, that the existence of the matter of life depends on the pre-existence of certain compounds; namely, carbonic acid, water, and certain nitrogenous bodies. Withdraw any one of these three from the world,

18. An illusion of abundance; from the name of an 8th-century Persian family, one of whom, in a story in the *Arabian Nights*, served a beggar a feast of empty dishes.
19. Magic.

and all vital phenomena come to an end. They are as necessary to the protoplasm of the plant, as the protoplasm of the plant is to that of the animal.
Carbon, hydrogen, oxygen, and nitrogen are all lifeless bodies. Of these, carbon
and oxygen unite in certain proportions and under certain conditions, to give
rise to carbonic acid; hydrogen and oxygen produce water; nitrogen and other
elements give rise to nitrogenous salts. These new compounds, like the elementary bodies of which they are composed, are lifeless. But when they are brought
together, under certain conditions, they give rise to the still more complex
body, protoplasm, and this protoplasm exhibits the phenomena of life.

I see no break in this series of steps in molecular complication, and I am
unable to understand why the language which is applicable to any one term
of the series may not be used to any of the others. We think fit to call different
kinds of matter carbon, oxygen, hydrogen, and nitrogen, and to speak of the
various powers and activities of these substances as the properties of the
matter of which they are composed.

When hydrogen and oxygen are mixed in a certain proportion, and an
electric spark is passed through them, they disappear, and a quantity of water,
equal in weight to the sum of their weights, appears in their place. There is
not the slightest parity between the passive and active powers of the water
and those of the oxygen and hydrogen which have given rise to it. At 32°
Fahrenheit, and far below that temperature, oxygen and hydrogen are elastic
gaseous bodies, whose particles tend to rush away from one another with great
force. Water, at the same temperature, is a strong though brittle solid, whose
particles tend to cohere into definite geometrical shapes, and sometimes build
up frosty imitations of the most complex forms of vegetable foliage.

Nevertheless we call these, and many other strange phenomena, the properties of the water, and we do not hesitate to believe that, in some way or
another, they result from the properties of the component elements of the
water. We do not assume that a something called 'aquosity'[20] entered into and
took possession of the oxidated hydrogen as soon as it was formed, and then
guided the aqueous particles to their places in the facets of the crystal, or
amongst the leaflets of the hoarfrost. On the contrary, we live in the hope
and in the faith that, by the advance of molecular physics, we shall by and
by be able to see our way as clearly from the constituents of water to the
properties of water, as we are now able to deduce the operations of a watch
from the form of its parts and the manner in which they are put together.

Is the case in any way changed when carbonic acid, water, and nitrogenous
salts disappear, and in their place, under the influence of pre-existing living
protoplasm, an equivalent weight of the matter of life makes its appearance?

It is true that there is no sort of parity between the properties of the components and the properties of the resultant, but neither was there in the case
of the water. It is also true that what I have spoken of as the influence of
pre-existing living matter is something quite unintelligible; but does anybody
quite comprehend the *modus operandi*[21] of an electric spark, which traverses
a mixture of oxygen and hydrogen?

What justification is there, then, for the assumption of the existence in the

20. Huxley makes up this word from the Latin for water, *aqua:* "waterness."
21. "The way in which it works."

living matter of a something which has no representative, or correlative, in the not living matter which gave rise to it? What better philosophical status has 'vitality' than 'aquosity'? And why should 'vitality' hope for a better fate than the other 'itys' which have disappeared since Martinus Scriblerus [22] accounted for the operation of the meat-jack by its inherent 'meat roasting quality,' [23] and scorned the 'materialism' of those who explained the turning of the spit by a certain mechanism worked by the draught of the chimney.

If scientific language is to possess a definite and constant signification whenever it is employed, it seems to me that we are logically bound to apply to the protoplasm, or physical basis of life, the same conceptions as those which are held to be legitimate elsewhere. If the phenomena exhibited by water are its properties, so are those presented by protoplasm, living or dead, its properties.

If the properties of water may be properly said to result from the nature and disposition of its component molecules, I can find no intelligible ground for refusing to say that the properties of protoplasm result from the nature and disposition of its molecules.

But I bid you beware that, in accepting these conclusions, you are placing your feet on the first rung of a ladder which, in most people's estimation, is the reverse of Jacob's,[24] and leads to the antipodes of heaven. It may seem a small thing to admit that the dull vital actions of a fungus, or a foraminifer,[25] are the properties of their protoplasm, and are the direct results of the nature of the matter of which they are composed. But if, as I have endeavoured to prove to you, their protoplasm is essentially identical with, and most readily converted into, that of any animal, I can discover no logical halting-place between the admission that such is the case, and the further concession that all vital action may, with equal propriety, be said to be the result of the molecular forces of the protoplasm which displays it. And if so, it must be true, in the same sense and to the same extent, that the thoughts to which I am now giving utterance, and your thoughts regarding them, are the expression of molecular changes in that matter of life which is the source of our other vital phenomena.

Past experience leads me to be tolerably certain that, when the propositions I have just placed before you are accessible to public comment and criticism, they will be condemned by many zealous persons, and perhaps by some few of the wise and thoughtful. I should not wonder if 'gross and brutal materialism' were the mildest phrase applied to them in certain quarters. And, most undoubtedly, the terms of the propositions are distinctly materialistic. Nevertheless two things are certain; the one, that I hold the statements to be substantially true; the other, that I, individually, am no materialist, but, on the contrary, believe materialism to involve grave philosophical error.

22. Martinus Scriblerus was a pedantic character invented by Arbuthnot, Pope, and Swift who amused themselves by writing his memoirs. A meat-jack is a clockwork device to keep a roast on a spit turning before an open fire.
23. The most famous example of this kind of explanation occurs in Molière's comedy *The Imaginary Invalid,* in which a physician says that opium puts one to sleep because of its "dormitive quality."
24. In Genesis 28:12 Jacob dreams of a ladder ascending to heaven.
25. Unicellular micro-organism.

This union of materialistic terminology with the repudiation of materialistic philosophy I share with some of the most thoughtful men with whom I am acquainted. And, when I first undertook to deliver the present discourse, it appeared to me to be a fitting opportunity to explain how such a union is not only consistent with, but necessitated by, sound logic. I purposed to lead you through the territory of vital phenomena to the materialistic slough in which you find yourselves now plunged, and then to point out to you the sole path by which, in my judgment, extrication is possible.

An occurrence of which I was unaware until my arrival here last night renders this line of argument singularly opportune. I found in your papers the eloquent address 'On the Limits of Philosophical Inquiry,' which a distinguished prelate of the English Church delivered before the members of the Philosophical Institution on the previous day. My argument, also, turns upon this very point of the limits of philosophical inquiry; and I cannot bring out my own views better than by contrasting them with those so plainly and, in the main, fairly stated by the Archbishop of York.

But I may be permitted to make a preliminary comment upon an occurrence that greatly astonished me. Applying the name of the 'New Philosophy' to that estimate of the limits of philosophical inquiry which I, in common with many other men of science, hold to be just, the Archbishop opens his address by identifying this 'New Philosophy' with the Positive Philosophy of M. Comte [26] (of whom he speaks as its 'founder'); and then proceeds to attack that philosopher and his doctrines vigorously.

Now, so far as I am concerned, the most reverend prelate might dialectically hew M. Comte in pieces, as a modern Agag,[27] and I should not attempt to stay his hand. In so far as my study of what specially characterises the Positive Philosophy has led me, I find therein little or nothing of any scientific value, and a great deal which is as thoroughly antagonistic to the very essence of science as anything in ultramontane [28] Catholicism. In fact, M. Comte's philosophy, in practice, might be compendiously described as Catholicism *minus* Christianity.

But what has Comtism to do with the 'New Philosophy,' as the Archbishop defines it in the following passage?

Let me briefly remind you of the leading principles of this new philosophy.

26. Auguste Comte (1798–1857), the French social philosopher. His principal work is his *Cours de philosophie positive* (1830–42) in which he proposed the idea that there are three historical stages of knowledge: the theological; the metaphysical; and the positive, i.e. the form of knowledge which takes account only of positive facts and observable phenomena. He applied to society the methods of observation and reasoning characteristic of the sciences and was in effect the founder of the modern discipline of sociology. Huxley's famous characterization of his philosophy as "Catholicism *minus* Christianity" refers to his later effort to construct a religion in which the worship of Humanity was substituted for the worship of God and to contrive an elaborate system of sacraments and prayers. Comte had considerable influence in England, most notably on John Stuart Mill.
27. I Samuel 15:33. Agag was an Amalekite king whom Samuel commanded Saul to slay. Saul spared his life but Samuel hewed him in pieces.
28. "Beyond the mountain"—that is, supporting the authority of the pope as against the authority of the national church.

All knowledge is experience of facts acquired by the senses. The traditions of older philosophies have obscured our experience by mixing with it much that the senses cannot observe, and until these additions are discarded our knowledge is impure. Thus metaphysics tell us that one fact which we observe is a cause, and another is the effect of that cause; but, upon a rigid analysis, we find that our senses observe nothing of cause or effect: they observe, first, that one fact succeeds another, and, after some opportunity, that this fact has never failed to follow —that for cause and effect we should substitute invariable succession. An older philosophy teaches us to define an object by distinguishing its essential from its accidental qualities: but experience knows nothing of essential and accidental; she sees only that certain marks attach to an object, and, after many observations, that some of them attach invariably whilst others may at times be absent. . . . As all knowledge is relative, the notion of anything being necessary must be banished with other traditions. [29]

There is much here that expresses the spirit of the 'New Philosophy,' if by that term be meant the spirit of modern science; but I cannot but marvel that the assembled wisdom and learning of Edinburgh should have utttered no sign of dissent, when Comte was declared to be the founder of these doctrines. No one will accuse Scotchmen of habitually forgetting their great countrymen; but it was enough to make David Hume [30] turn in his grave, that here, almost within ear-shot of his house, an instructed audience should have listened, without a murmur, while his most characteristic doctrines were attributed to a French writer of fifty years later date, in whose dreary and verbose pages we miss alike the vigour of thought and the exquisite clearness of style of the man whom I make bold to term the most acute thinker of the eighteenth century—even though that century produced Kant.

But I did not come to Scotland to vindicate the honour of one of the greatest men she has ever produced. My business is to point out to you that the only way of escape out of the 'crass materialism' in which we just now landed, is the adoption and strict working-out of the very principles which the Archbishop holds up to reprobation.

Let us suppose that knowledge is absolute, and not relative, and therefore, that our conception of matter represents that which it really is. Let us suppose, further, that we do know more of cause and effect than a certain definite order of succession among facts, and that we have a knowledge of the necessity of that succession—and hence, of necessary laws—and I, for my part, do not see what escape there is from utter materialism and necessarianism. For it is obvious that our knowledge of what we call the material world is, to begin with, at least as certain and definite as that of the spiritual world, and that our acquaintance with law is of as old a date as our knowledge of spontaneity. Further, I take it to be demonstrable that it is utterly impossible to prove that anything whatever may not be the effect of a material and necessary cause,

29. *"The Limits of Philosophical Inquiry,* pp. 4 and 5." (Huxley)
30. David Hume (1711–76), the great Scottish philosopher. Huxley wrote an admirable brief life of Hume for the English Men of Letters Series (1878).

and that human logic is equally incompetent to prove that any act is really spontaneous. A really spontaneous act is one which, by the assumption, has no cause; and the attempt to prove such a negative as this is, on the face of the matter, absurd. And while it is thus a philosophical impossibility to demonstrate that any given phenomenon is not the effect of a material cause, any one who is acquainted with the history of science will admit, that its progress has, in all ages, meant, and now, more than ever, means, the extension of the province of what we call matter and causation, and the concomitant gradual banishment from all regions of human thought of what we call spirit and spontaneity.

I have endeavoured, in the first part of this discourse, to give you a conception of the direction towards which modern physiology is tending; and I ask you, what is the difference between the conception of life as the product of a certain disposition of material molecules, and the old notion of an Archaeus [31] governing and directing blind matter within each living body, except this— that here, as elsewhere, matter and law have devoured spirit and spontaneity? And as surely as every future grows out of past and present, so will the physiology of the future gradually extend the realm of matter and law until it is co-extensive with knowledge, with feeling, and with action.

The consciousness of this great truth weighs like a nightmare, I believe, upon many of the best minds of these days. They watch what they conceive to be the progress of materialism, in such fear and powerless anger as a savage feels, when, during an eclipse, the great shadow creeps over the face of the sun. The advancing tide of matter threatens to drown their souls; the tightening grasp of law impedes their freedom; they are alarmed lest man's moral nature be debased by the increase of his wisdom.

If the 'New Philosophy' be worthy of the reprobation with which it is visited, I confess their fears seem to me to be well founded. While, on the contrary, could David Hume be consulted, I think he would smile at their perplexities, and chide them for doing even as the heathen, and falling down in terror before the hideous idols their own hands have raised.

For, after all, what do we know of this terrible 'matter,' except as a name for the unknown and hypothetical cause of states of our own consciousness? And what do we know of that 'spirit' over whose threatened extinction by matter a great lamentation is arising, like that which was heard at the death of Pan,[32] except that it is also a name for an unknown and hypothetical cause, or condition, of states of consciousness? In other words, matter and spirit are but names for the imaginary substrata of groups of natural phenomena.

And what is the dire necessity and 'iron' law under which men groan? Truly, most gratuitously invented bugbears. I suppose if there be an 'iron' law, it is that of gravitation; and if there be a physical necessity, it is that a stone, unsupported, must fall to the ground. But what is all we really know, and can know, about the latter phenomena? Simply, that, in all human experience, stones have fallen to the ground under these conditions; that we have not the

---

31. In the chemical and alchemical thought of Paracelsus (1453–1541), the action of every chemical was said to be under the control of a particular spirit, its Archaeus.
32. Plutarch, *Moralia, Why the Oracles Cease to Give Answers.*

smallest reason for believing that any stone so circumstanced will not fall to the ground; and that we have, on the contrary, every reason to believe that it will so fall. It is very convenient to indicate that all the conditions of belief have been fulfilled in this case, by calling the statement that unsupported stones will fall to the ground, 'a law of Nature.' But when, as commonly happens, we change *will* into *must*, we introduce an idea of necessity which most assuredly does not lie in the observed facts, and has no warranty that I can discover elsewhere. For my part, I utterly repudiate and anathematise the intruder. Fact I know; and Law I know; but what is this Necessity, save an empty shadow of my own mind's throwing?

But, if it is certain that we can have no knowledge of the nature of either matter or spirit, and that the notion of necessity is something illegitimately thrust into the perfectly legitimate conception of law, the materialistic position that there is nothing in the world but matter, force, and necessity, is as utterly devoid of justification as the most baseless of theological dogmas. The fundamental doctrines of materialism, like those of spiritualism, and most other 'isms,' lie outside 'the limits of philosophical inquiry,' and David Hume's great service to humanity is his irrefragable demonstration of what these limits are. Hume called himself a sceptic, and therefore others cannot be blamed if they apply the same title to him; but that does not alter the fact that the name, with its existing implications, does him gross injustice.

If a man asks me what the politics of the inhabitants of the moon are, and I reply that I do not know; that neither I, nor any one else, has any means of knowing; and that, under these circumstances, I decline to trouble myself about the subject at all, I do not think he has any right to call me a sceptic. On the contrary, in replying thus, I conceive that I am simply honest and truthful, and show a proper regard for the economy of time. So Hume's strong and subtle intellect takes up a great many problems about which we are naturally curious, and shows us that they are essentially questions of lunar politics, in their essence incapable of being answered, and therefore not worth the attention of men who have work to do in the world. And he thus ends one of his essays:—

> If we take in hand any volume of Divinity, or school metaphysics, for instance, let us ask, *Does it contain any abstract reasoning concerning quantity or number?* No. *Does it contain any experimental reasoning concerning matter of fact and existence?* No. Commit it then to the flames; for it can contain nothing but sophistry and illusion.[33]

Permit me to enforce this most wise advice. Why trouble ourselves about matters of which, however important they may be, we do know nothing, and can know nothing? We live in a world which is full of misery and ignorance, and the plain duty of each and all of us is to try to make the little corner he can influence somewhat less miserable and somewhat less ignorant than it was before he entered it. To do this effectually it is necessary to be fully possessed of only two beliefs: the first, that the order of Nature is ascertainable

33. "Hume's Essay 'Of the Academical or Sceptical Philosophy,' in the *Inquiry Concerning the Human Understanding.*—[Many critics of this passage seem to forget that the subject-matter of Ethics and Aesthetics consists of matters of fact and existence.—1892]." (Huxley)

by our faculties to an extent which is practically unlimited; the second, that our volition [34] counts for something as a condition of the course of events.

Each of these beliefs can be verified experimentally, as often as we like to try. Each, therefore, stands upon the strongest foundation upon which any belief can rest, and forms one of our highest truths. If we find that the ascertainment of the order of nature is facilitated by using one terminology, or one set of symbols, rather than another, it is our clear duty to use the former; and no harm can accrue, so long as we bear in mind, that we are dealing merely with terms and symbols.

In itself it is of little moment whether we express the phenomena of matter in terms of spirit; or the phenomena of spirit in terms of matter: matter may be regarded as a form of thought, thought may be regarded as a property of matter—each statement has a certain relative truth. But with a view to the progress of science, the materialistic terminology is in every way to be preferred. For it connects thought with the other phenomena of the universe, and suggests inquiry into the nature of those physical conditions, or concomitants of thought, which are more or less accessible to us, and a knowledge of which may, in future, help us to exercise the same kind of control over the world of thought, as we already possess in respect of the material world; whereas, the alternative, or spiritualistic, terminology is utterly barren, and leads to nothing but obscurity and confusion of ideas.

Thus there can be little doubt, that the further science advances, the more extensively and consistently will all the phenomena of Nature be represented by materialistic formulae and symbols.

But the man of science, who, forgetting the limits of philosophical inquiry, slides from these formulae and symbols into what is commonly understood by materialism, seems to me to place himself on a level with the mathematician, who should mistake the x's and y's with which he works his problems, for real entities—and with this further disadvantage, as compared with the mathematician, that the blunders of the latter are of no practical consequence, while the errors of systematic materialism may paralyse the energies and destroy the beauty of a life.

1868   1868, 1892

WILLIAM MORRIS

1834–1896

The profound admiration and affection in which William Morris was held by two famous men of the generation after his own will suggest the peculiar power and charm of his genius. William Butler Yeats and Bernard Shaw are legendary in their dissimilarity. The former celebrated an archaic class-bound social structure which alone, he believed, made it possible for life to be instinctual, significant, and beautiful; the latter was in his day the exemplary exponent of the rational reorganization of

34. "Or, to speak more accurately, the physical state of which volition is the expression.— [1892]." (Huxley)

society. Disparate as they were in their hopes for life and art, both men acknowledged Morris as master. By Morris's vision of the archaic cultures of northern Europe, in which beauty and authenticity were in perfect union, Yeats in his youth was encouraged in his own dream of heroic existence; Morris was, he said, "my chief of men." In the socialism which was the passionate concern of Morris's late years, Shaw found confirmation of his own impulse toward a radical revision of social forms and ideals.

Morris was born in 1834, at Walthamstow, a town near London and adjacent to the beautiful Epping Forest. His father was a stockbroker of considerable and increasing wealth, who, when William was six, moved his family to Woodford Hall, a stately Georgian mansion virtually within the forest. Here William, after a delicate and threatened infancy, lived an outdoor life and developed the feeling for the primeval nature of the ancient world which was to mark his poetry. In the shaping of his imagination Scott's Waverley novels played a decisive part—he had read all of them by the time he was seven—as doubtless did the suit of toy armor in which he rode his pony over his father's acres. In 1847 his father died and William was sent away to school, the newly founded Marlborough College. He took but little pleasure in school life and kept mostly to himself, but he delighted in the pre-Celtic, Roman, and medieval antiquities of the district and became absorbed in the books on archaeology and ecclesiastical architecture with which the school's library happened to be well stocked; he later said that he learned as a schoolboy all that was to be known about English Gothic.

Under the influence of a devout sister, Morris decided upon a career in the church and with this goal in view he entered Exeter College, Oxford, in 1853. It was here that, early in his first year, he formed his intimate and lifelong friendship with Edward Burne-Jones, later to be, with Dante Gabriel Rossetti and John Everett Millais, one of the notable members of the Pre-Raphaelite group of painters; at the time of their meeting, Burne-Jones, like Morris, planned to take holy orders. The year of Morris's coming to Oxford was the year of the publication of Ruskin's *Stones of Venice*, and the famous chapter, "The Nature of Gothic" (see above), offered a new creed which eventually was to set at naught such inclination to the church as Morris had. For a time Newman and the Oxford Movement—or some approximate notion thereof—meant much to Morris and his friends as offering an ideal of dedication and community which would rescue them from the commonplaceness and complacency of English life. Yet if Newman touched the imagination of these young men, Tennyson commanded it, and it was under the spell of Tennyson that Morris tried his hand at poetry. Nothing is more characteristic of him than the remark he made when his first efforts in this line of work were admired by his friends: "Well," he said, "if this is poetry, it is very easy to write." (For comment on his poetry, see above, p. 617f.)

In 1855, on a tour in France, Morris and Burne-Jones came simultaneously to the realization that it was impossible for them to proceed to holy orders and that they must instead dedicate themselves to art, Burne-Jones as a painter, Morris as an architect. So far as can be discerned, once Morris had made his decision, religion was for him a dead issue, and the influence of its idiom is not to be traced in his prose, as it so readily is in the prose of Carlyle, Ruskin, and Arnold. Morris apprenticed himself to an Oxford firm of architects, which later moved to London, where Morris lived with Burne-Jones and studied painting at night. Painting proved to make a stronger claim upon him than the study of the practical aspects of architecture and he withdrew from his apprenticeship at the end of the first year. Yet painting no more than architecture was to be Morris's true métier, which, however, was soon to make itself known to him. He and Burne-Jones were under the necessity of furnishing their quarters and they were repelled by the ugliness and vulgar sham of the domestic goods offered in the shops. Morris met the situation by drafting designs, more or less medieval in feeling, for tables, chairs, and wardrobes, and a carpenter was engaged to execute them. With this enterprise Morris was launched upon his unique career in what he was to call the "lesser arts," those arts with whose products men are in touch every moment of their daily lives and by which —so Morris believed—their sensibilities, ultimately their conceptions of who and what they are, which is to say their very souls, are conditioned and controlled.

Morris married in 1859, and the building of his home, the famous Red House, gave impetus to his work as a designer. He and his friend Philip Webb, the architect of the house, designed the hangings, the wallpapers, the furniture, virtually every appurtenance of the house except the Persian rugs and the china. Two years later Morris set up as a professional decorator. With a group of friends including Webb, Rossetti, and Burne-Jones he organized the firm generally known as Morris and Company. As a business it grew increasingly business-like and in time was successful; when, in 1881, the Throne and Reception rooms of St. James's Palace were to be redecorated, the commission went to Morris and Company. But although Morris kept his eye on the ledgers, and the more closely as his considerable inherited fortune began to diminish, the company was his continuing act of social and moral criticism, his silent ceaseless commentary on the crassness of English taste, ultimately upon the machine civilization which, he believed, had corrupted the English character and made the root and ground of the dullness and ugliness of English lives. His fabrics and his wallpapers—perhaps these especially—were to recall the English to a delight in growing things, in clear true color, in lightness and grace, and in the discernible touch of an actual craftsman's conceiving mind and competent hand.

In 1876, when he was forty-two, Morris's commentary on English life ceased to be a silent one. In letters and conversations he had long been articulate about his social views, and now he became public and political. Moved by the threat of war with Russia over the Turkish question, he joined the Eastern Question Society, served as its treasurer, and, in the following year, on his own account wrote a manifesto, *To the Working-men of England,* in which he denounced the sentiment for war as the expression of the interests of the aristocratic class, which he went on to characterize as being contemptuously antagonistic to every aspiration of the working class.

Many years before, Morris had signalized his alienation from the upper classes by his careless dress, his pipe, his beard, and his tousled hair (from which came the nickname of his Oxford days, Topsy), and his refusal to dine out. Now, although he was ineluctably the gentleman and even, by brevet at least, the imperious aristocrat, his commitment was increasingly to the workers, not only as members of the class that suffered most under a plutocratic system but also as the potential agents of change. It was at this time that he began his public lectures on the decorative arts, the first of which eventually bore the title *The Lesser Arts.* He described art as the type or paradigm of all work that is appropriate to human beings and emphasized the "lesser" quality of the decorative arts, as against the "high" exigent art of the great creative geniuses, in order to put art, or activities cognate with art, within the reach of the generality of mankind. He was far indeed from agreeing with Carlyle's view (see above, the chapter of *Past and Present* called "Labour") that any work at all was in some degree salutary and humanizing; he held with Ruskin that enforced work, exhausting work, trivial work, mechanical work, work of which the worker does not know the meaning, was exactly dehumanizing. The way in which art could increase man's sense of his community and further his happiness was central to his thought, as the titles of his lectures suggest: *Art and Democracy, Art Under Plutocracy, Hopes and Fears for Art.*

With the passage of the years this interest in the quality of human existence was matched by his concern with the practical means by which that quality might be realized. In 1883 Morris joined the Democratic Federation and, when it became the Social Democratic Federation, accepted membership on its executive board. He read Marx's *Capital* (in French), declared himself a socialist, and became an active public lecturer on socialism. His life was now committed to the multifarious activities of radical politics, the acrimonious deliberations of committees, the debates in dingy meeting halls, the editing of agitational journals, and participation in mass protests. Yet he found time for his own work—for his Utopian novels, *The Dream of John Ball* (1886) and the entrancing *News from Nowhere* (1890); for his verse translations of the *Odyssey* (1887) and of *Beowulf* (1895); for the series of prose romances (the first was *The House of the Wolfings* in 1888), of which Yeats said that they were "so great a joy that they were the only books I was ever to read slowly that I might not come quickly to the end"; for his lecture on tapestry weaving and his weaving of the *Adoration of the Magi* tapestry for Exeter College Chapel; and for the setting up of the Kelmscott Press to manufacture beautiful books, and for designing the typefaces, ornaments, and formats. One of the first publications of the Press was Ruskin's "The Nature of Gothic," with a preface by Morris; its most ambitious undertaking was its edition of Chaucer (long one of Morris's best-loved authors), with illustrations by Burne-Jones and decorative designs by Morris (1896). This great labor was his last. This man of inexhaustible energies began to fail, doubtless as a consequence of the severe attack of rheumatic fever he had suffered in 1864, with its sporadic recurrences over the years. But his physician said after his death in 1896 that what he had died of was "simply being William Morris, and having done more work than most ten men."

The Beauty of Life

This is the text of a lecture which Morris delivered before the Birmingham Society of Arts and School of Design on February 19, 1880. It represents Morris's social thought at the mid-point of its development. It summarizes his passionate dissatisfaction with the look and tone of English life, to the revision of which his efforts as a designer had been directed for a quarter-century. And it points forward to the decision which he made some three years later, after a reading of Marx's *Capital*, to commit himself to socialism. His concern with the condition of the working class was to become more central to his purposes and more specifically political, but at this point in his life it was already intense.

The Beauty of Life

'—propter vitam vivendi perdere causas.'

JUVENAL [1]

I stand before you this evening weighted with a disadvantage that I did not feel last year—I have little fresh to tell you; I can somewhat enlarge on what I said then; here and there I may make bold to give you a practical suggestion, or I may put what I have to say in a way which will be clearer to some of you perhaps; but my message is really the same as it was when I first had the pleasure of meeting you.

It is true that if all were going smoothly with art, or at all events so smoothly that there were but a few malcontents in the world, you might listen with some pleasure, and perhaps advantage, to the talk of an old hand in the craft concerning ways of work, the snares that beset success, and the shortest road to it, to a tale of workshop receipts [2] and the like: that would be a pleasant talk surely between friends and fellow-workmen: but it seems to me as if it were not for us as yet; nay, maybe we may live long and find no time fit for such restful talk as the cheerful histories of the hopes and fears of our workshops: anyhow to-night I cannot do it, but must once again call the faithful of art to a battle wider and more distracting than that kindly struggle with nature, to which all true craftsmen are born; which is both the building-up and the wearing-away of their lives.

As I look round on this assemblage, and think of all that it represents, I cannot choose but be moved to the soul by the troubles of the life of civilized man, and the hope that thrusts itself through them; I cannot refrain from giving you once again the message with which, as it seems, some chance-hap has charged me: that message is, in short, to call on you to face the latest danger which civilization is threatened with, a danger of her own breeding: that men in struggling towards the complete attainment of all the luxuries of life for the strongest portion of their race should deprive their whole race of all the beauty of life: a danger that the strongest and wisest of mankind, in striving to attain to a complete mastery over Nature, should destroy her simplest and widest-spread gifts, and thereby enslave simple people to them, and themselves to themselves, and so at last drag the world into a second barbarism more ignoble, and a thousandfold more hopeless, than the first.

Now of you who are listening to me, there are some, I feel sure, who have received this message, and taken it to heart, and are day by day fighting the battle that it calls on you to fight: to you I can say nothing but that if any word I speak discourage you, I shall heartily wish I had never spoken at all: but to be shown the enemy, and the castle we have got to storm, is not to be bidden to run from him; nor am I telling you to sit down deedless in the desert because between you and the promised land lies many a trouble, and death itself maybe: the hope before you you know, and nothing that I can say can take it away from you; but friend may with advantage cry out

1. "—and for the sake of life to sacrifice life's only end." This line is preceded by one which says, "Deem it to be the summit of impiety to prefer existence to honor." *Satires* viii. 83.

2. A "receipt" is the same as a "recipe," which is now the preferred word: a formula for preparing a dish in cookery or a pharmacological prescription.

to friend in the battle that a stroke is coming from this side or that: take my hasty words in that sense, I beg of you.

But I think there will be others of you in whom vague discontent is stirring: who are oppressed by the life that surrounds you; confused and troubled by that oppression, and not knowing on which side to seek a remedy, though you are fain to do so: well, we, who have gone further into those troubles, believe that we can help you: true we cannot at once take your trouble from you; nay, we may at first rather add to it; but we can tell you what we think of the way out of it; and then amidst the many things you will have to do to set yourselves and others fairly on that way, you will many days, nay most days, forget your trouble in thinking of the good that lies beyond it, for which you are working.

But, again, there are others amongst you (and to speak plainly, I daresay they are the majority), who are not by any means troubled by doubt of the road the world is going, nor excited by any hope of its bettering that road: to them the cause of civilization is simple and even commonplace: wonder, hope, and fear no longer hang about it; it has become to us like the rising and setting of the sun; it cannot err, and we have no call to meddle with it, either to complain of its course, or to try to direct it.

There is a ground of reason and wisdom in that way of looking at the matter: surely the world will go on its ways, thrust forward by impulses which we cannot understand or sway: but as it grows in strength for the journey, its necessary food is the life and aspirations of *all* of us: and we discontented strugglers with what at times seems the hurrying blindness of civilization, no less than those who see nothing but smooth, unvarying progress in it, are bred of civilization also, and shall be used up to further it in some way or other, I doubt not: and it may be of some service to those who think themselves the only loyal subjects of progress to hear of our existence, since their not hearing of it would not make an end of it: it may set them a-thinking not unprofitably to hear of burdens that they do not help to bear, but which are nevertheless real and weighty enough to some of their fellow-men, who are helping, even as they are, to form the civilization that is to be.

The danger that the present course of civilization will destroy the beauty of life—these are hard words, and I wish I could mend them, but I cannot, while I speak what I believe to be the truth.

That the beauty of life is a thing of no moment, I suppose few people would venture to assert, and yet most civilized people act as if it were of none, and in so doing are wronging both themselves and those that are to come after them; for that beauty, which is what is meant by *art*, using the word in its widest sense, is, I contend, no mere accident to human life, which people can take or leave as they choose, but a positive necessity of life, if we are to live as nature meant us to; that is, unless we are content to be less than men.

Now I ask you, as I have been asking myself this long while, what proportion of the population in civilized countries has any share at all in that necessity of life?

I say that the answer which must be made to that question justifies my fear that modern civilization is on the road to trample out all the beauty of life, and to make us less than men.

Now if there should be any here who will say: It was always so; there always was a mass of rough ignorance that knew and cared nothing about art; I answer first, that if that be the case, then it was always wrong, and we, as soon as we have become conscious of that wrong, are bound to set it right if we can.

But moreover, strange to say, and in spite of all the suffering that the world has wantonly made for itself, and has in all ages so persistently clung to, as if it were a good and holy thing, this wrong of the mass of men being regardless of art was *not* always so.

So much is now known of the periods of art that have left abundant examples of their work behind them, that we can judge of the art of all periods by comparing these with the remains of times of which less has been left us; and we cannot fail to come to the conclusion that down to very recent days everything that the hand of man touched was more or less beautiful: so that in those days all people who made anything shared in art, as well as all people who used the things so made: that is, *all* people shared in art.

But some people may say: And was that to be wished for? would not this universal spreading of art stop progress in other matters, hinder the work of the world? Would it not make us unmanly?[3] or if not that, would it not be intrusive, and push out other things necessary also for men to study?

Well, I have claimed a necessary place for art, a natural place, and it would be in the very essence of it, that it would apply its own rules of order and fitness to the general ways of life: it seems to me, therefore, that people who are over-anxious of the outward expression of beauty becoming too great a force among the other forces of life, would, if they had had the making of the external world, have been afraid of making an ear of wheat beautiful, lest it should not have been good to eat.

But indeed there seems no chance of art becoming universal, unless on the terms that it shall have little self-consciousness, and for the most part be done with little effort;[4] so that the rough work of the world would be as little hindered by it, as the work of external nature is by the beauty of all her forms and moods: this was the case in the times that I have been speaking of: of art which was made by conscious effort, the result of the individual striving towards perfect expression of their thoughts by men very specially gifted, there was perhaps no more than there is now, except in very wonderful and short periods; though I believe that even for such men the struggle to produce beauty was not so bitter as it now is. But if there were not more great thinkers than there are now, there was a countless multitude of happy workers whose work did express, and could not choose but express, some original thought, and was consequently both interesting and beautiful: now there is certainly no chance of the more individual art becoming common, and either wearying

3. The idea that a concern with art might be a graceful characteristic of women but was not appropriate to the masculine temperament was prevalent among the middle and upper classes in the Victorian period.

4. Morris is proposing here a conception of art which goes counter to the one that prevailed in his time. It is not the art of the genius-artist, the product of his "great brains and miraculously gifted hands," controlled by his ambitions and his exigent ideals, and by his urge to dominate the minds of men, but a much more modest art, the art of the craftsman (who once had been called an artist), naturally manifesting itself in the things of everyday life.

us by its over-abundance, or by noisy self-assertion preventing highly cultivated men taking their due part in the other work of the world; it is too difficult to do: it will be always but the blossom of all the half-conscious work below it, the fulfilment of the shortcomings of less complete minds: but it will waste much of its power, and have much less influence on men's minds, unless it be surrounded by abundance of that commoner work, in which all men once shared, and which, I say, will, when art has really awakened, be done so easily and constantly, that it will stand in no man's way to hinder him from doing what he will, good or evil. And as, on the one hand, I believe that art made by the people and for the people as a joy both to the maker and the user would further progress in other matters rather than hinder it, so also I firmly believe that that higher art produced only by great brains and miraculously gifted hands cannot exist without it: I believe that the present state of things in which it does exist, while popular art is, let us say, asleep or sick, is a transitional state, which must end at last either in utter defeat or utter victory for the arts.

For whereas all works of craftsmanship were once beautiful, unwittingly or not, they are now divided into two kinds, works of art and non-works of art: now nothing made by man's hand can be indifferent: it must be either beautiful and elevating, or ugly and degrading; and those things that are without art are so aggressively; [5] they wound it by their existence, and they are now so much in the majority that the works of art we are obliged to set ourselves to seek for, whereas the other things are the ordinary companions of our everyday life; so that if those who cultivate art intellectually were inclined never so much to wrap themselves in their special gifts and their high cultivation, and so live happily, apart from other men, and despising them, they could not do so: they are as it were living in an enemy's country; at every turn there is something lying in wait to offend and vex their nicer sense and educated eyes: they must share in the general discomfort—and I am glad of it.

So the matter stands: from the first dawn of history till quite modern times, Art, which Nature meant to solace all, fulfilled its purpose; all men shared in it: that was what made life romantic, as people call it, in those days—that and not robber-barons and inaccessible kings with their hierarchy of serving-nobles and other such rubbish: but art grew and grew, saw empires sicken and sickened with them; grew hale again, and haler, and grew so great at last that she seemed in good truth to have conquered everything, and laid the material world under foot. Then came a change at a period of the greatest life and hope in many ways that Europe had known till then: a time of so much and such varied hope that people call it the time of the New Birth: [6] as far as the arts are concerned I deny it that title; rather it seems to me that the great men who lived and glorified the practice of art in those days, were the fruit of the old,

---

5. The ugliness of Victorian domestic objects and architecture—all the more striking by comparison with what had been produced in England only a few years before—was to become proverbial among educated English people, largely through Morris's influence. The passage of time has in some degree abated the harshness of the judgment that was made up through the early years of the 20th century, and it is now possible to find charm in the things that Morris condemned, but although they are often valued as quaint or "interesting" or "amusing," no one is likely to find them beautiful.

6. That is, the Renaissance, a period of which Morris took a dim view.

not the seed of the new order of things: but a stirring and hopeful time it was, and many things were newborn then which have since brought forth fruit enough: and it is strange and perplexing that from those days forward the lapse of time, which, through plenteous confusion and failure, has on the whole been steadily destroying privilege and exclusiveness in other matters, has delivered up art to be the exclusive privilege of a few, and has taken from the people their birthright; while both wronged and wrongers have been wholly unconscious of what they were doing.

Wholly unconscious—yes, but we are no longer so: there lies the sting of it, and there also the hope.

When the brightness of the so-called Renaissance faded, and it faded very suddenly, a deadly chill fell upon the arts: that New-birth mostly meant looking back to past times, wherein the men of those days thought they saw a perfection of art, which to their minds was different in kind, and not in degree only, from the ruder suggestive art of their own fathers: this perfection they were ambitious to imitate, this alone seemed to be art to them, the rest was childishness: so wonderful was their energy, their success so great, that no doubt to commonplace minds among them, though surely not to the great masters, that perfection seemed to be gained: and, perfection being gained, what are you to do?—you can go no further, you must aim at standing still—which you cannot do.[7]

Art by no means stood still in those latter days of the Renaissance, but took the downward road with terrible swiftness, and tumbled down at the bottom of the hill, where as if bewitched it lay long in great content, believing itself to be the art of Michael Angelo, while it was the art of men whom nobody remembers but those who want to sell their pictures.[8]

Thus it fared with the more individual forms of art. As to the art of the people; in countries and places where the greater art had flourished most, it went step by step on the downward path with that: in more out-of-the-way places, England for instance, it still felt the influence of the life of its earlier and happy days, and in a way lived on a while; but its life was so feeble, and, so to say, illogical, that it could not resist any change in external circumstances, still less could it give birth to anything new; and before this century began, its last flicker had died out. Still, while it was living, in whatever dotage, it did imply something going on in those matters of daily use that we have been thinking of, and doubtless satisfied some cravings for beauty: and when it was dead, for a long time people did not know it, or what had taken its place, crept so to

7. Morris describes in an admirably succinct way the rationale of the impulse to classicism. It is not so much the wish to "stand still" that he is condemning as what he suggests is anterior to it, the restless wish for perfection. Ready as Morris surely was to respond to "greatness" in art, he maintained an attitude of suspicion toward the urgency that characterized it, seeing in this, we might say, an analogue with the commercial competitiveness he denounced. His social ideal of the artist was based on what he conceived to be the function and practice of art in primitive, or relatively primitive, societies, in which, to use the formulation of another of his essays, art "is always part of things intended primarily for the service of the body" rather than of the mind.

8. Just which post-Renaissance artists Morris believes to have been rightly assigned to oblivion he does not say, but the chances are that many of them are now considered to be of high interest.

say into its dead body—that pretence of art, to wit, which is done with machines,[9] though sometimes the machines are called men, and doubtless are so out of working hours: nevertheless long before it was quite dead it had fallen so low that the whole subject was usually treated with the utmost contempt by every one who had any pretence of being a sensible man, and in short the whole civilized world had forgotten that there had ever been an art *made by the people for the people as a joy for the maker and the user.*

But now it seems to me that the very suddenness of the change ought to comfort us, to make us look upon this break in the continuity of the golden chain as an accident only, that itself cannot last: for think how many thousand years it may be since that primaeval man graved with a flint splinter on a bone the story of the mammoth he had seen, or told us of the slow uplifting of the heavily-horned heads of the reindeer that he stalked: think I say of the space of time from then till the dimming of the brightness of the Italian Renaissance! Whereas from that time till popular art died unnoticed and despised among ourselves is just but two hundred years.

Strange too, that very death is contemporaneous with new-birth of something at all events; for out of all despair sprang a new time of hope lighted by the torch of the French Revolution: and things that have languished with the languishing of art, rose afresh and surely heralded its new birth: in good earnest poetry was born again, and the English Language, which under the hands of sycophantic verse-makers had been reduced to a miserable jargon, whose meaning, if it have a meaning, cannot be made out without translation,[10] flowed clear, pure, and simple, along with the music of Blake and Coleridge: take those names, the earliest in date among ourselves, as a type of the change that has happened in literature since the time of George II.[11]

With that literature in which romance, that is to say humanity,[12] was re-born, there sprang up also a feeling for the romance of external nature, which is surely strong in us now, joined with a longing to know something real of the lives of those who have gone before us; of these feelings united you will find the broadest expression in the pages of Walter Scott: it is curious as showing how sometimes one art will lag behind another in a revival, that the man who wrote the exquisite and wholly unfettered naturalism of *The Heart of Midlothian,*[13] for instance, thought himself continually bound to seem to feel ashamed

9. The Great Exhibition of 1851 put special emphasis on the triumph of invention in the making of decorative domestic objects by machine.
10. Morris is referring to the poetry of the 18th century, which had generally fallen into low repute in the Victorian period under the influence of the Romantic critics (see Wordsworth's Preface to *Lyrical Ballads*) and poets (see Keats's *Sleep and Poetry*). Matthew Arnold's *Study of Poetry* rates Dryden and Pope as not really poets at all. Morris had but little sympathy for the 18th century in general, not even for its admirable domestic arts.
11. That Morris does not include Wordsworth among the early Romanticists will suggest his dislike of that poet. Blake was not widely known at the time—Arnold does not mention him in *The Study of Poetry*—but William Rossetti, the brother of Morris's friend, Dante Gabriel Rossetti, was a great enthusiast of Blake's and collected his manuscripts.
12. The engaging downright simplicity of this statement is characteristic of Morris.
13. One of the best of Scott's novels, published 1818. Scott's representations of medieval life and of the tribal ethos of the Scottish highlands would naturally win a warm response from Morris. Although Scott might hàve been "ashamed" of loving Gothic architecture—the name was intended to be a pejorative one, pointing to the "rudeness" and "roughness" of

of, and to excuse himself for, his love of Gothic Architecture: he felt that it was romantic, and he knew that it gave him pleasure, but somehow he had not found out that it was art, having been taught in many ways that nothing could be art that was not done by a named man under academical rules.

I need not perhaps dwell much on what of change has been since: you know well that one of the master-arts, the art of painting, has been revolutionized. I have a genuine difficulty in speaking to you of men who are my own personal friends, nay, my masters: still, since I cannot quite say nothing of them I must say the plain truth, which is this: never in the whole history of art did any set of men come nearer to the feat of making something out of nothing than that little knot of painters who have raised English art from what it was when as a boy I used to go to the Royal Academy Exhibition, to what it is now.[14]

It would be ungracious indeed for me who have been so much taught by him that I cannot help feeling continually as I speak that I am echoing his words, to leave out the name of John Ruskin [15] from an account of what has happened since the tide, as we hope, began to turn in the direction of art. True it is, that his unequalled style of English and his wonderful eloquence would, whatever its subject-matter, have gained him some sort of a hearing in a time that has not lost its relish for literature; but surely the influence that he has exercised over cultivated people must be the result of that style and that eloquence expressing what was already stirring in men's minds; he could not have written what he has done unless people were in some sort ready for it; any more than those painters could have begun their crusade against the dulness and incompetency that was the rule in their art thirty years ago unless they had some hope that they would one day move people to understand them.

Well, we find that the gains since the turning-point of the tide are these: that there are some few artists who have, as it were, caught up the golden chain dropped two hundred years ago, and that there are a few highly cultivated people who can understand them; and that beyond these there is a vague feeling abroad among people of the same degree, of discontent at the ignoble ugliness that surrounds them.

That seems to me to mark the advance that we have made since the last of popular art came to an end amongst us, and I do not say, considering where we then were, that it is not a great advance, for it comes to this, that though the battle is still to win, there are those who are ready for the battle.

Indeed it would be a strange shame for this age if it were not so: for as every age of the world has its own troubles to confuse it, and its own follies to cumber it, so has each its own work to do, pointed out to it by unfailing signs of the times; and it is unmanly and stupid for the children of any age to say: We will not set our hands to the work; we did not make the troubles, we will

the style—it should be remembered that the interest in the Gothic goes back to the middle of the 18th century: Horace Walpole's famous Strawberry Hill, "a little Gothic castle," was begun in 1747.

14. Morris has in mind the group of painters known as the Pre-Raphaelite Brotherhood, to whom he was very close. See Ruskin, *Modern Painters*, note 14.

15. Ruskin, whose influence on Morris is of course decisive, was a strong partisan of the Pre-Raphaelites.

not weary ourselves seeking a remedy for them: so heaping up for their sons a heavier load than they can lift without such struggles as will wound and cripple them sorely. Not thus our fathers served us, who, working late and early, left us at last that seething mass of people so terribly alive and energetic, that we call modern Europe; not thus those served us, who have made for us these present days, so fruitful of change and wondering expectation.

The century that is now beginning to draw to an end, if people were to take to nicknaming centuries, would be called the Century of Commerce; and I do not think I undervalue the work that it has done: it has broken down many a prejudice and taught many a lesson that the world has been hitherto slow to learn: it has made it possible for many a man to live free, who would in other times have been a slave, body or soul, or both: if it has not quite spread peace and justice through the world, as at the end of its first half we fondly hoped it would, it has at least stirred up in many fresh cravings for peace and justice: its work has been good and plenteous, but much of it was roughly done, as needs was; recklessness has commonly gone with its energy, blindness too often with its haste: so that perhaps it may be work enough for the next century to repair the blunders of that recklessness, to clear away the rubbish which that hurried work has piled up; nay even we in the second half of its last quarter may do something towards setting its house in order.

You, of this great and famous town, for instance, which has had so much to do with the Century of Commerce,[16] your gains are obvious to all men, but the price you have paid for them is obvious to many—surely to yourselves most of all: I do not say that they are not worth the price; I know that England and the world could very ill afford to exchange the Birmingham of to-day for the Birmingham of the year 1700: but surely if what you have gained be more than a mockery, you cannot stop at those gains, or even go on always piling up similar ones. Nothing can make me believe that the present condition of your Black Country [17] yonder is an unchangeable necessity of your life and position: such miseries as this were begun and carried on in pure thoughtlessness, and a hundredth part of the energy that was spent in creating them would get rid of them: I do think if we were not all of us too prone to acquiesce in the base byword 'after me the deluge,' [18] it would soon be something more than an idle dream to hope that your pleasant midland hills and fields might begin to become pleasant again in some way or other, even without depopulating them; or that those once lovely valleys of Yorkshire in the 'heavy woollen district,' with their sweeping hill-sides and noble rivers, should not need the stroke of ruin to make them once more delightful abodes of men, instead of the dog-holes that the Century of Commerce has made them.

Well, people will not take the trouble or spend the money necessary to begin-ning this sort of reforms, because they do not feel the evils they live amongst,

---

16. Early in the 19th century Birmingham became one of the two leading manufacturing cities of England, the other being Manchester. It produces metal-work of all kinds.
17. The name by which the Midland districts of South Staffordshire and North Warwick-shire are known because of the grime from the coal and iron mines and industry.
18. Madame de Pompadour (1721–64), the mistress of Louis XV, said this—actually, "After us the deluge"—although it is commonly attributed to the king himself. The deluge she envisaged was political.

because they have degraded themselves into something less than men; they are unmanly because they have ceased to have their due share of art.[19]

For again I say that therein rich people have defrauded themselves as well as the poor: you will see a refined and highly educated man nowadays, who has been to Italy and Egypt and where not, who can talk learnedly enough (and fantastically enough sometimes) about art, and who has at his fingers' ends abundant lore concerning the art and literature of past days, sitting down without signs of discomfort in a house, that with all its surroundings is just brutally vulgar and hideous: all his education has not done more for him than that.

The truth is, that in art, and in other things besides, the laboured education of a few will not raise even those few above the reach of the evils that beset the ignorance of the great mass of the population: the brutality of which such a huge stock has been accumulated lower down will often show without much peeling through the selfish refinement of those who have let it accumulate. The lack of art, or rather the murder of art, that curses our streets from the sordidness of the surroundings of the lower classes, has its exact counterpart in the dulness and vulgarity of those of the middle classes, and the double-distilled dulness, and scarcely less vulgarity of those of the upper classes.

I say this is as it should be; it is just and fair as far as it goes; and moreover the rich with their leisure are the more like to move if they feel the pinch themselves.

But how shall they and we, and all of us, move? What is the remedy?

What remedy can there be for the blunders of civilization but further civilization? You do not by any accident think that we have gone as far in that direction as it is possible to go, do you?—even in England, I mean?

When some changes have come to pass, that perhaps will be speedier than most people think, doubtless education will both grow in quality and in quantity; so that it may be, that as the nineteenth century is to be called the Century of Commerce, the twentieth may be called the Century of Education. But that education does not end when people leave school is now a mere commonplace; and how then can you really educate men who lead the life of machines, who only think for the few hours during which they are not at work, who in short spend almost their whole lives in doing work which is not proper for developing them body and mind in some worthy way? You cannot educate, you cannot civilize men, unless you can give them a share in art.[20]

Yes, and it is hard indeed as things go to give most men that share; for they do not miss it, or ask for it, and it is impossible as things are that they should either miss or ask for it. Nevertheless everything has a beginning, and many great things have had very small ones; and since, as I have said, these ideas are already abroad in more than one form, we must not be too much discouraged at the seemingly boundless weight we have to lift.

After all, we are only bound to play our own parts, and do our own share of the lifting; and as in no case that share can be great, so also in all cases it is called for, it is necessary. Therefore let us work and faint not; remembering

19. Morris here boldly inverts the view that a concern with art is unmanly (see note 3).
20. Morris means an *active* share, the actual making of art, not the passive "consumption" of it.

that though it be natural, and therefore excusable, amidst doubtful times to feel doubts of success oppress us at whiles, yet not to crush those doubts, and work as if we had them not, is simple cowardice, which is unforgivable. No man has any right to say that all has been done for nothing, that all the faithful unwearying strife of those that have gone before us shall lead us nowhither; that mankind will but go round and round in a circle for ever: no man has a right to say that, and then get up morning after morning to eat his victuals and sleep a-nights, all the while making other people toil to keep his worthless life a-going.

Be sure that some way or other will be found out of the tangle, even when things seem most tangled, and be no less sure that some use will then have come of our work, if it has been faithful, and therefore unsparingly careful and thoughtful.

So once more I say, if in any matters civilization has gone astray, the remedy lies not in standing still, but in more complete civilization.

Now whatever discussion there may be about that often used and often misused word, I believe all who hear me will agree with me in believing from their hearts, and not merely in saying in conventional phrase, that the civilization which does not carry the whole people with it is doomed to fall, and give place to one which at least aims at doing so.

We talk of the civilization of the ancient peoples, of the classical times: well, civilized they were no doubt, some of their folk at least: an Athenian citizen for instance led a simple, dignified, almost perfect life; [21] but there were draw-backs to happiness perhaps in the lives of his slaves: and the civilization of the ancients was founded on slavery.

Indeed, that ancient society did give a model to the world, and showed us for ever what blessings are freedom of life and thought, self-restraint and a generous education: all those blessings the ancient free peoples set forth to the world—and kept them to themselves.

Therefore [22] no tyrant was too base, no pretext too hollow, for enslaving the grandsons of the men of Salamis [23] and Thermopylae: [24] therefore did the descendants of those stern and self-restrained Romans, who were ready to give up everything, and life as the least of things, to the glory of their commonweal, produce monsters of license and reckless folly. Therefore did a little knot of Galilean peasants [25] overthrow the Roman Empire.

Ancient civilization was chained to slavery and exclusiveness, and it fell; the barbarism that took its place has delivered us from slavery and grown into

21. The virtual perfection of Athenian life was often adduced in Victorian England as a criterion by which English life was to be judged, but a reading of Thucydides or Aristo-phanes or Plato will suggest that the city had its measure of deplorable traits.
22. That is, because the Athenians did not induce other nations to adopt their ideals. Morris has in mind the tendency of the Greeks to look down on other peoples as barbarians.
23. It was at Salamis that the Greeks won their decisive naval victory over the invading Persians in 480 B.C.
24. At the mountain pass of Thermopylae the Greeks were defeated, but the rear-guard action of Leonidas with a small Spartan force, holding the pass to the death against the Persian army, had an inspiring effect on morale. The battle of Salamis took place subsequently.
25. That is, Christians. Morris's attribution of causation seems rather captious.

modern civilization; and that in its turn has before it the choice of never-ceasing growth, or destruction by that which has in it the seeds of higher growth.

There is an ugly word for a dreadful fact, which I must make bold to use— the residuum: that word since the time I first saw it used,[26] has had a terrible significance to me, and I have felt from my heart that if this residuum were a necessary part of modern civilization, as some people openly, and many more tacitly, assume that it is, then this civilization carries with it the poison that shall one day destroy it, even as its elder sister did: if civilization is to go no further than this, it had better not have gone so far: if it does not aim at getting rid of this misery and giving some share in the happiness and dignity of life to *all* the people that it has created, and which it spends such unwearying energy in creating, it is simply an organized injustice, a mere instrument for oppression, so much the worse than that which has gone before it, as its pretensions are higher, its slavery subtler, its mastery harder to overthrow, because supported by such a dense mass of commonplace well-being and comfort.

Surely this cannot be: surely there is a distinct feeling abroad of this injustice: so that if the residuum still clogs all the efforts of modern civilization to rise above mere population-breeding and money-making, the difficulty of dealing with it is the legacy, first of the ages of violence and almost conscious brutal injustice, and next of the ages of thoughtlessness, of hurry and blindness; surely all those who think at all of the future of the world are at work in one way or other in striving to rid it of this shame.

That to my mind is the meaning of what we call National Education, which we have begun, and which is doubtless already bearing its fruits, and will bear greater, when all people are educated, not according to the money which they or their parents possess, but according to the capacity of their minds.[27]

What effect that will have upon the future of the arts I cannot say, but one would surely think a very great effect; for it will enable people to see clearly many things which are now as completely hidden from them as if they were blind in body and idiotic in mind: and this, I say, will act not only upon those who most directly feel the evils of ignorance, but also upon those who feel them indirectly—upon us, the educated: the great wave of rising intelligence, rife with so many natural desires and aspirations, will carry all classes along with it, and force us all to see that many things which we have been used to look upon as necessary and eternal evils are merely the accidental and temporary growths of past stupidity, and can be escaped from by due effort and the exercise of courage, goodwill, and forethought.

And among those evils, I do, and must always, believe will fall that one which last year I told you that I accounted the greatest of all evils, the heaviest of all slaveries; that evil of the greater part of the population being engaged for by far the most part of their lives in work, which at the best cannot interest

26. He first saw it used in *Culture and Anarchy,* in Arnold's discussion of the three English social classes. After describing the aristocracy, to which he gives the name Barbarians, and the middle classes, which he called the Philistines, Arnold speaks of the working class— "to this vast residuum," he says, "we may with great propriety give the name of Populace." 27. Although the matter has been in constant debate in England for over a century, and although many adjustments have been made, the educational opportunities available to the working class are still more strictly limited than in the United States.

them, or develop their best faculties, and at the worst (and that is the commonest, too) is mere unmitigated slavish toil, only to be wrung out of them by the sternest compulsion, a toil which they shirk all they can—small blame to them.[28] And this toil degrades them into less than men: and they will some day come to know it, and cry out to be made men again, and art only can do it, and redeem them from this slavery; and I say once more that this is her highest and most glorious end and aim; and it is in her struggle to attain to it that she will most surely purify herself, and quicken her own aspirations towards perfection.

But we—in the meantime we must not sit waiting for obvious signs of these later and glorious days to show themselves on earth, and in the heavens, but rather turn to the commonplace, and maybe often dull work of fitting ourselves in detail to take part in them if we should live to see one of them; or in doing our best to make the path smooth for their coming, if we are to die before they are here.

What, therefore, can we do, to guard traditions of time past that we may not one day have to begin anew from the beginning with none to teach us? What are we to do, that we may take heed to, and spread the decencies of life, so that at the least we may have a field where it will be possible for art to grow when men begin to long for it: what finally can we do, each of us, to cherish some germ of art, so that it may meet with others, and spread and grow little by little into the thing that we need?

Now I cannot pretend to think that the first of these duties is a matter of indifference to you, after my experience of the enthusiastic meeting that I had the honour of addressing here last autumn on the subject of the (so called) restoration of St. Mark's at Venice; [29] you thought, and most justly thought, it seems to me, that the subject was of such moment to art in general, that it was a simple and obvious thing for men who were anxious on the matter to address themselves to those who had the decision of it in their hands; even though the former were called Englishmen, and the latter Italians; for you felt that the name of lovers of art would cover those differences: if you had any misgivings, you remembered that there was but one such building in the world, and that it was worth while risking a breach of etiquette, if any words of ours could do anything towards saving it; well, the Italians were, some of them, very naturally, though surely unreasonably, irritated, for a time, and in some of their prints they bade us look at home; that was no argument in favour of the wisdom of wantonly rebuilding St. Mark's façade: but certainly those of us who have not yet looked at home in this matter had better do so speedily, late and over late though it be: for though we have no golden-pictured interiors like St. Mark's Church at home, we still have many buildings which are both

28. The idea that work of any kind "degrades" man affronted a piety of the time which had received confirmation from Carlyle, whose doctrine of the value of work made no distinction between kinds of work.

29. The great cathedral. The enterprise of "restoring" the architectural monuments of the past, which often involved not merely the replacement of damaged elements but also the revision of the existing plan of the building, had been frequently denounced by Ruskin and was resented by serious lovers of art. In 1877 Morris founded the Society for the Protection of Ancient Buildings, known as "Anti-Scrape."

works of ancient art and monuments of history: and just think what is happening to them, and note, since we profess to recognize their value, how helpless art is in the Century of Commerce!

In the first place, many and many a beautiful and ancient building is being destroyed all over civilized Europe as well as in England, because it is supposed to interfere with the convenience of the citizens, while a little forethought might save it without trenching on that convenience; but even apart from that, I say that if we are not prepared to put up with a little inconvenience in our lifetimes for the sake of preserving a monument of art which will elevate and educate, not only ourselves, but our sons, and our sons' sons, it is vain and idle of us to talk about art—or education either. Brutality must be bred of such brutality.

The same thing may be said about enlarging, or otherwise altering for convenience's sake, old buildings still in use for something like their original purposes: in almost all such cases it is really nothing more than a question of a little money for a new site: and then a new building can be built exactly fitted for the uses it is needed for, with such art about it as our own days can furnish; while the old monument is left to tell its tale of change and progress, to hold out example and warning to us in the practice of the arts: and thus the convenience of the public, the progress of modern art, and the cause of education, are all furthered at once at the cost of a little money.

Surely if it be worth while troubling ourselves about the works of art of to-day, of which any amount almost can be done, since we are yet alive, it is worth while spending a little care, forethought, and money in preserving the art of bygone ages, of which (woe worth the while!) so little is left, and of which we can never have any more, whatever goodhap the world may attain to.

No man who consents to the destruction or the mutilation of an ancient building has any right to pretend that he cares about art; or has any excuse to plead in defence of his crime against civilization and progress, save sheer brutal ignorance.

But before I leave this subject I must say a word or two about the curious invention of our own days called Restoration, a method of dealing with works of bygone days which, though not so degrading in its spirit as downright destruction, is nevertheless little better in its results on the condition of those works of art; it is obvious that I have no time to argue the question out to-night, so I will only make these assertions:

That ancient buildings, being both works of art and monuments of history, must obviously be treated with great care and delicacy: that the imitative art of to-day is not, and cannot be the same thing as ancient art, and cannot replace it; and that therefore if we superimpose this work on the old, we destroy it both as art and as a record of history: lastly, that the natural weathering of the surface of a building is beautiful, and its loss disastrous.

Now the restorers hold the exact contrary of all this: they think that any clever architect to-day can deal off-hand successfully with the ancient work; that while all things else have changed about us since (say) the thirteenth century, art has not changed, and that our workmen can turn out work identical with that of the thirteenth century; and, lastly, that the weather-beaten surface of an ancient building is worthless, and to be got rid of wherever possible.

You see the question is difficult to argue, because there seem to be no common grounds between the restorers and the anti-restorers: I appeal therefore to the public, and bid them note, that though our opinions may be wrong, the action we advise is not rash: let the question be shelved awhile: if, as we are always pressing on people, due care be taken of these monuments, so that they shall not fall into disrepair, they will be always there to 'restore' whenever people think proper and when we are proved wrong; but if it should turn out that we are right, how can the 'restored' buildings be restored? I beg of you therefore to let the question be shelved, till art has so advanced among us, that we can deal authoritatively with it, till there is no longer any doubt about the matter.

Surely these monuments of our art and history, which, whatever the lawyers may say, belong not to a coterie, or to a rich man here and there, but to the nation at large, are worth this delay: surely the last relics of the life of the 'famous men and our fathers that begat us' [30] may justly claim of us the exercise of a little patience.

It will give us trouble no doubt, all this care of our possessions: but there is more trouble to come; for I must now speak of something else, of possessions which should be common to all of us, of the green grass, and the leaves, and the waters, of the very light and air of heaven, which the Century of Commerce has been too busy to pay any heed to. And first let me remind you that I am supposing every one here present professes to care about art.

Well, there are some rich men among us whom we oddly enough call manufacturers, by which we mean capitalists who pay other men to organize manufacturers; these gentlemen, many of whom buy pictures and profess to care about art, burn a deal of coal: there is an Act in existence which was passed to prevent them sometimes and in some places from pouring a dense cloud of smoke over the world, and, to my thinking, a very lame and partial Act it is: but nothing hinders these lovers of art from being a law to themselves, and making it a point of honour with them to minimize the smoke nuisance as far as their own works are concerned; and if they don't do so, when mere money, and even a very little of that, is what it will cost them, I say that their love of art is a mere pretence: how can you care about the image of a landscape when you show by your deeds that you don't care for the landscape itself? or what right have you to shut yourself up with beautiful form and colour when you make it impossible for other people to have any share in these things?

Well, and as to the Smoke Act itself: I don't know what heed you pay to it in Birmingham,[31] but I have seen myself what heed is paid to it in other places; Bradford for instance: though close by them at Saltaire [32] they have an

30. Ecclesiasticus 44:1.

31. "Since perhaps some people may read these words who are not of Birmingham, I ought to say that it was authoritatively explained at the meeting to which I addressed these words, that in Birmingham the law is strictly enforced." (Morris) The English have had quite striking success with smoke control—London, for example, no longer has its once-famous "pea-soup" fogs which sometimes were so black as to make movement through the streets impossible.

32. The model town founded by Sir Titus Salt on the river Aire, near Bradford in Yorkshire. Salt was an ingenious textile manufacturer of progressive and benevolent views. The enormous factory at Saltaire—opened 1853—was thoughtfully designed with a view to the safety and comfort of the workers.

example which I should have thought might have shamed them; for the huge chimney there which serves the acres of weaving and spinning sheds of Sir Titus Salt and his brothers is as guiltless of smoke as an ordinary kitchen chimney. Or Manchester: a gentleman of that city told me that the Smoke Act was a mere dead letter there: well, they buy pictures in Manchester and profess to wish to further the arts: but you see it must be idle pretence as far as their rich people are concerned: they only want to talk about it, and have themselves talked of.

I don't know what you are doing about this matter here; but you must forgive my saying, that unless you are beginning to think of some way of dealing with it, you are not beginning yet to pave your way to success in the arts.

Well, I have spoken of a huge nuisance, which is a type of the worst nuisances of what an ill-tempered man might be excused for calling the Century of Nuisances, rather than the Century of Commerce. I will now leave it to the consciences of the rich and influential among us, and speak of a minor nuisance which it is in the power of every one of us to abate, and which, small as it is, is so vexatious, that if I can prevail on a score of you to take heed to it by what I am saying, I shall think my evening's work a good one. Sandwich-papers I mean—of course you laugh: but come now, don't you, civilized as you are in Birmingham, leave them all about the Lickey hills [33] and your public gardens and the like? If you don't I really scarcely know with what words to praise you. When we Londoners go to enjoy ourselves at Hampton Court,[34] for instance, we take special good care to let everybody know that we have had something to eat: so that the park just outside the gates (and a beautiful place it is) looks as if it had been snowing dirty paper. I really think you might promise me one and all who are here present to have done with this sluttish habit, which is the type of many another in its way, just as the smoke nuisance is. I mean such things as scrawling one's name on monuments, tearing down tree boughs, and the like.

I suppose 'tis early days in the revival of the arts to express one's disgust at the daily increasing hideousness of the posters with which all our towns are daubed. Still we ought to be disgusted at such horrors, and I think make up our minds never to buy any of the articles so advertised. I can't believe they can be worth much if they need all that shouting to sell them.

Again, I must ask what do you do with the trees on a site that is going to be built over? do you try to save them, to adapt your houses at all to them? do you understand what treasures they are in a town or a suburb? or what a relief they will be to the hideous dog-holes which (forgive me!) you are probably going to build in their places? I ask this anxiously, and with grief in my soul, for in London and its suburbs we always [35] begin by clearing a site till it is as

33. Rural area on the outskirts of Birmingham.
34. Formerly a royal residence, on the Thames, some 12 miles from the center of London. When it and the park surrounding it were opened to the public, it became a favorite holiday spot for Londoners.
35. "Not *quite* always: in the little colony at Bedford Park, Chiswick, as many trees have been left as possible, to the boundless advantage of its quaint and pretty architecture." (Morris) Bedford Park was a model village in a London suburb built in the Georgian style by Norman Shaw, an architect who was influential in leading English taste away from Victorian domestic design. Yeats, who lived there in his boyhood, says, "For years Bedford Park was a romantic excitement."

bare as the pavement: I really think that almost anybody would have been shocked, if I could have shown him some of the trees that have been wantonly murdered in the suburb in which I live (Hammersmith to wit [36]), amongst them some of those magnificent cedars, for which we along the river used to be famous once.

But here again see how helpless those are who care about art or nature amidst the hurry of the Century of Commerce.

Pray dc not forget, that any one who cuts down a tree wantonly or carelessly, especially in a great town or its suburbs, need make no pretence of caring about art.

What else can we do to help to educate ourselves and others in the path of art, to be on the road to attaining an *Art made by the people and for the people as a joy to the maker and the user?*

Why, having got to understand something of what art was, having got to look upon its ancient monuments as friends that can tell us something of times bygone, and whose faces we do not wish to alter, even though they be worn by time and grief: having got to spend money and trouble upon matters of decency, great and little; having made it clear that we really do care about nature even in the suburbs of a big town—having got so far, we shall begin to think of the houses in which we live.

For I must tell you that unless you are resolved to have good and rational architecture, it is, once again, useless your thinking about art at all.

I have spoken of the popular arts, but they might all be summed up in that one word Architecture; they are all parts of that great whole, and the art of house-building begins it all: if we did not know how to dye or to weave; if we had neither gold, nor silver, nor silk; and no pigments to paint with, but half-a-dozen ochres and umbers,[37] we might yet frame a worthy art that would lead to everything, if we had but timber, stone, and life, and a few cutting tools to make these common things not only shelter us from wind and weather, but also express the thoughts and aspirations that stir in us.

Architecture would lead us to all the arts, as it did with earlier men: but if we despise it and take no note of how we are housed, the other arts will have a hard time of it indeed.

Now I do not think the greatest of optimists would deny that, taking us one and all, we are at present housed in a perfectly shameful way, and since the greatest part of us have to live in houses already built for us, it must be admitted that it is rather hard to know what to do, beyond waiting till they tumble about our ears.

Only we must not lay the fault upon the builders, as some people seem inclined to do: they are our very humble servants, and will build what we ask for; remember, that rich men are not obliged to live in ugly houses, and yet you see they do; which the builders may be well excused for taking as a sign of what is wanted.

Well, the point is, we must do what we can, and make people understand what we want them to do for us, by letting them see what we do for ourselves.

---

36. In Kelmscott House, named after his country home, Kelmscott Manor.
37. Ochre: orange-yellow, in various intensities. Umber: brown, in various shades.

Hitherto, judging us by that standard, the builders may well say, that we want the pretence of a thing rather than the thing itself; that we want a show of petty luxury if we are unrich, a show of insulting stupidity if we are rich: and they are quite clear that as a rule we want to get something that shall look as if it cost twice as much as it really did.[38]

You cannot have Architecture on those terms: simplicity and solidity are the very first requisites of it: just think if it is not so: How we please ourselves with an old building by thinking of all the generations of men that have passed through it! do we not remember how it has received their joy, and borne their sorrow, and not even their folly has left sourness upon it? it still looks as kind to us as it did to them. And the converse of this we ought to feel when we look at a newly-built house if it were as it should be: we should feel a pleasure in thinking how he who had built it had left a piece of his soul behind him to greet the new-comers one after another long and long after he was gone:— but what sentiment can an ordinary modern house move in us, or what thought—save a hope that we may speedily forget its base ugliness?

But if you ask me how we are to pay for this solidity and extra expense, that seems to me a reasonable question; for you must dismiss at once as a delusion the hope that has been sometimes cherished, that you can have a building which is a work of art, and is therefore above all things properly built, at the same price as a building which only pretends to be this: never forget when people talk about cheap art in general, by the way, that all art costs time, trouble, and thought, and that money is only a counter to represent these things.

However, I must try to answer the question I have supposed put, how are we to pay for decent houses?

It seems to me that, by a great piece of good luck, the way to pay for them is by doing that which alone can produce popular art among us: living a simpler life, I mean. Once more I say that the greatest foe to art is luxury, art cannot live in its atmosphere.[39]

When you hear of the luxuries of the ancients, you must remember that they were not like our luxuries, they were rather indulgence in pieces of extravagant folly than what we to-day call luxury; which perhaps you would rather call comfort: well, I accept the word, and say that a Greek or Roman of the luxurious time would stare astonished could he be brought back again and shown the comforts of a well-to-do middle-class house.

But some, I know, think that the attainment of these very comforts is what makes the difference between civilization and uncivilization, that they are the essence of civilization. Is it so indeed? Farewell my hope then!—I had thought that civilization meant the attainment of peace and order and freedom, of goodwill between man and man, of the love of truth and the hatred of injustice, and by consequence the attainment of the good life which these things breed, a life free from craven fear, but full of incident: that was what I thought it

38. This desire had become especially salient as a condition of taste in the Victorian period and it was the conscious purpose of manufacturers of household goods to make them look *expensive.*
39. When, in the next paragraph, Morris equates luxury with comfort, he means an ostentation of comfort that denied its actuality.

meant, not more stuffed chairs and more cushions, and more carpets and gas, and more dainty meat and drink—and therewithal more and sharper differences between class and class.

If that be what it is, I for my part wish I were well out of it, and living in a tent in the Persian desert, or a turf hut on the Iceland hill-side. But however it be, and I think my view is the true view, I tell you that art abhors that side of civilization, she cannot breathe in the houses that lie under its stuffy slavery.[40]

Believe me, if we want art to begin at home, as it must, we must clear our houses of troublesome superfluities that are for ever in our way: conventional comforts that are no real comforts, and do but make work for servants and doctors: if you want a golden rule that will fit everybody, this is it:

Have nothing in your houses that you do not know to be useful, or believe to be beautiful.

And if we apply that rule strictly, we shall in the first place show the builders and such-like servants of the public what we really want, we shall create a demand for real art, as the phrase goes; and in the second place, we shall surely have more money to pay for decent houses.

Perhaps it will not try your patience too much if I lay before you my idea of the fittings necessary to the sitting-room of a healthy person: a room, I mean, which he would not have to cook in much, or sleep in generally, or in which he would not have to do any very litter-making manual work.[41]

First a book-case with a great many books in it: next a table that will keep steady when you write or work at it: then several chairs that you can move, and a bench that you can sit or lie upon: next a cupboard with drawers: next, unless either the book-case or the cupboard be very beautiful with painting or carving, you will want pictures or engravings, such as you can afford, only not stopgaps,[42] but real works of art on the wall; or else the wall itself must be ornamented with some beautiful and restful pattern: we shall also want a vase or two to put flowers in, which latter you must have sometimes, especially if you live in a town. Then there will be the fireplace of course, which in our climate is bound to be the chief object in the room.

That is all we shall want, especially if the floor be good; if it be not, as, by the way, in a modern house it is pretty certain not to be, I admit that a small carpet which can be bundled out of the room in two minutes will be useful, and we must also take care that it is beautiful, or it will annoy us terribly.

Now unless we are musical, and need a piano (in which case, as far as beauty is concerned, we are in a bad way),[43] that is quite all we want: and

40. Yeats recalls an occasion in which Morris spoke in dispraise even of the houses decorated by himself. "Do you suppose I like that kind of house? I would like a house like a big barn, where one ate in one corner, cooked in another corner, slept in the third corner, and in the fourth received one's friends." What Morris is protesting against is the restless *clutter* of the Victorian home.

41. Morris's audience being chiefly students or practitioners of art, such specifications have point; we may be sure that in the sitting room of a businessman no cooking or manual work was done.

42. Presumably reproductions.

43. The 19th-century domestic piano was pretty sure to be heavy-legged, over-decorated, and gloomy-looking.

we can add very little to these necessaries without troubling ourselves and hindering our work, our thought, and our rest.

If these things were done at the least cost for which they could be done well and solidly, they ought not to cost much; and they are so few, that those that could afford to have them at all, could afford to spend some trouble to get them fitting and beautiful: and all those who care about art ought to take great trouble to do so, and to take care that there be no sham art amongst them, nothing that it has degraded a man to make or sell. And I feel sure, that if all who care about art were to take this pains, it would make a great impression upon the public.

This simplicity you may make as costly as you please or can, on the other hand: you may hang your walls with tapestry instead of whitewash or paper; or you may cover them with mosaic, or have them frescoed by a great painter: all this is not luxury, if it be done for beauty's sake, and not for show: it does not break our golden rule: *Have nothing in your houses which you do not know to be useful or believe to be beautiful.*

All art starts from this simplicity; and the higher the art rises, the greater the simplicity. I have been speaking of the fittings of a dwelling-house—a place in which we eat and drink, and pass familiar hours; but when you come to places which people want to make more specially beautiful because of the solemnity or dignity of their uses, they will be simpler still, and have little in them save the bare walls made as beautiful as may be. St. Mark's at Venice has very little furniture in it, much less than most Roman Catholic churches: its lovely and stately mother St. Sophia of Constantinople had less still, even when it was a Christian church: [44] but we need not go either to Venice or Stamboul [45] to take note of that: go into one of our own mighty Gothic naves (do any of you remember the first time you did so?) and note how the huge free space satisfies and elevates you, even now when window and wall are stripped of ornament: then think of the meaning of simplicity and absence of encumbering gew-gaws.

Now after all, for us who are learning art, it is not far to seek what is the surest way to further it; that which most breeds art is art; every piece of work that we do which is well done, is so much help to the cause; every piece of pretence and half-heartedness is so much hurt to it. Most of you who take to the practice of art can find out in no very long time whether you have any gifts for it or not: if you have not, throw the thing up, or you will have a wretched time of it yourselves, and will be damaging the cause by laborious pretence: but if you have gifts of any kind, you are happy indeed beyond most men; for your pleasure is always with you, nor can you be intemperate in the enjoyment of it, and as you use it, it does not lessen, but grows: if you are by chance weary of it at night, you get up in the morning eager for it; or if perhaps in the morning it seems folly to you for a while, yet presently, when your hand has been moving a little in its wonted way, fresh hope has sprung up beneath it and you are happy again. While others are getting through the day like plants thrust into the earth, which cannot turn this way

44. It is also known as Hagia Sophia, Greek for "the holy wisdom." It became a mosque when the Turks captured Constantinople in 1453.
45. Constantinople.

or that but as the wind blows them, you know what you want, and your will is on the alert to find it, and you, whatever happens, whether it be joy or grief, are at least alive.

Now when I spoke to you last year, after I had sat down I was half afraid that I had on some point said too much, that I had spoken too bitterly in my eagerness; that a rash word might have discouraged some of you; I was very far from meaning that: what I wanted to do, what I want to do to-night is to put definitely before you a cause for which to strive.

That cause is the Democracy of Art, the ennobling of daily and common work, which will one day put hope and pleasure in the place of fear and pain, as the forces which move men to labour and keep the world a-going.

If I have enlisted any one in that cause, rash as my words may have been, or feeble as they may have been, they have done more good than harm; nor do I believe that any words of mine can discourage any who have joined that cause or are ready to do so: their way is too clear before them for that, and every one of us can help the cause whether he be great or little.

I know indeed that men, wearied by the pettiness of the details of the strife, their patience tried by hope deferred, will at whiles, excusably enough, turn back in their hearts to other days, when if the issues were not clearer, the means of trying them were simpler; when, so stirring were the times, one might even have atoned for many a blunder and backsliding by visibly dying for the cause. To have breasted the Spanish pikes at Leyden,[46] to have drawn sword with Oliver:[47] that may well seem to us at times amidst the tangles of to-day a happy fate: for a man to be able to say, I have lived like a fool, but now I will cast away fooling for an hour, and die like a man—there is something in that certainly: and yet 'tis clear that few men can be so lucky as to die for a cause, without having first of all lived for it. And as this is the most that can be asked from the greatest man that follows a cause, so it is the least that can be taken from the smallest.

So to us who have a Cause at heart, our highest ambition and our simplest duty are one and the same thing: for the most part we shall be too busy doing the work that lies ready to our hands, to let impatience for visibly great prog-ress vex us much; but surely since we are servants of a Cause, hope must be ever with us, and sometimes perhaps it will so quicken our vision that it will outrun the slow lapse of time, and show us the victorious days when millions of those who now sit in darkness [48] will be enlightened by an *Art made by the people and for the people, a joy to the maker and the user.*
1880   1880

46. The inhabitants of the town defended it from the Spaniards in 1574.
47. The friend and comrade-in-arms who died with Roland defending the pass at Ronces-valles (Roncevaux) for Charlemagne.
48. Psalms 108:11.

WALTER PATER
1839–1894

When Oscar Wilde entered Magdalen College, Oxford, in 1874, one of the books he read in his first term was Walter Pater's *Studies in the History of the Renaissance*, published in the year before. Twenty-three years later he referred to *The Renaissance*—so the work was re-titled in its second edition—as "that book which had such a strange influence over my life." The reference was made in the remarkable document which goes under the name of *De Profundis* (Out of the Depths), the immensely long autobiographical letter which Wilde wrote to Lord Alfred Douglas shortly before the end of the prison term to which he had been sentenced after having been tried and found guilty of homosexual practices. Wilde does not further characterize *The Renaissance*; he does not say specifically what its influence was nor why it was "strange." But a famous circumstance of the publication of Pater's volume might tempt us to suppose that Wilde meant to implicate the book in his tragic fate: in its second edition Pater omitted the Conclusion because, as he explained when he restored it in the third edition, he "conceived it might possibly mislead some of the young men into whose hands it might fall. On the whole, I have thought it best to reprint it here, with some slight changes which bring it closer to my original meaning. . . ." (Included here is the 1888 version of the Conclusion.) He had in mind the explicit denial which the Conclusion makes that there is any meaning or any imperative of duty inherent in the universe.

Pater really had not overestimated the subversive potential of the essay. When it speaks of the uncertainty and the tragic brevity of human life, its silence as to religion is absolute—and eloquent: the implication is clear that for men of intelligence and sensibility religion is no longer a possible option. And when it does offer a way of confronting the darkness and cold that encompasses man's short day, it is not a high moral commitment that it proposes, not a noble altruism, or duty, or work, but a complex and urgent hedonism, the "getting of as many pulsations as possible into the given time." The young men into whose hands the book fell, may not have been "misled" by the Conclusion, but it confirmed the natural hedonism of their youth, and Pater, who had no inclination to moral radicalism, feared that his essay, in urging them to cultivate the "ecstasy" of art, might rationalize and license their seeking "success in life" through other forms of ecstasy as well. In later essays Pater considerably qualified the definition of the function of art, which he makes in the Conclusion.

This view had been advanced by Pater not as a philosophic position to be argued but as a self-evident truth which was the basis of his claim that art is of ultimate importance if the emptiness of the universe is to be filled and we are not to live in blank despair. And what he feared, of course, was that this doctrine might mislead young men into moral nihilism. But Wilde did not think that he had fallen into moral nihilism, nor had he. We may count on it that he regarded *The Renaissance* as having exerted its "strange influence" not upon his personal conduct but, rather, upon his cultural situation. Pater's book had effectually set at naught the authority of the theory of art which hitherto had the highest sanction among the enlightened —Ruskin's, in which all aesthetic considerations were directed toward a principle of morality which the universe, deprived of an imaginable and definable divinity, still somehow required and professed. Without engaging Ruskin directly, *The Renais-*

sance swept this doctrine aside, and in doing so brought to an end the once-powerful moral mystique of Victorian high culture and opened the way into the uncharted freedom of a new cultural epoch, which is to say a new way—a strange way—of being human.

It must seem an anomaly that a cultural act so drastic should be laid at the door of the man who was the author of *The Renaissance*. No mode of existence could be more demure, more retired from the world and remote from the controversies and debates by which culture proceeds than that of Walter Horatio Pater, Fellow of Brasenose College, Oxford. He was born in 1839, in a district of East London, the son of a physician, a lapsed Catholic probably of Dutch descent, who, shortly after Walter's birth, moved his family to Enfield, in Middlesex. Not much is known of the particulars of Pater's childhood beyond his pleasure in a game of ecclesiastical ceremonial in improvised vestments, but we doubtless derive an accurate sense of his inner life from certain quasi-autobiographical writings in which, in a manner that we would now call Proustian and that may indeed have had some influence on Proust's own manner, he describes the extreme intensity and subtlety with which he perceived and imagined the world. The quality of the sensibility described in these hushed, elaborate evocations of the past is suggested by the passage in the best of them, *The Child in the House*, in which he speaks of his preoccupation with the interfusion of death and beauty, a theme which may be thought to lie at the heart of his aesthetic doctrine: "With this desire of physical beauty mingled itself early the fear of death—the fear of death intensified by the desire of beauty."

At the age of fourteen Pater entered King's School in Canterbury and, expectably enough, was at odds with school life. His attraction to the idea of religion—the idea rather than the actuality—would seem to have been enhanced by his delight in the great cathedral which overshadowed his school and by an acquaintance he formed with the famous Oxford religious figure John Keble. His dubious involvement with religion continued through his second year at Oxford where, although he had lost his faith, he would have proceeded to take holy orders had not some of his serious-minded friends informed the bishop of the postulant's deficient state of belief.

He entered Queen's College in 1858 and found congenial friends there. He read widely in modern literature and traveled several times to Germany; he was an assiduous student and, although he took his degree with only second-class honors, he was an excellent classical scholar. In 1864 he was made a Probationary Fellow of Brasenose College on the basis of his knowledge of German philosophy and in the following year an Actual Fellow.

A tour of Italy in 1865–66 confirmed him in his growing admiration of the Renaissance. The new enthusiasm was coincident with his responsiveness to the Aesthetic Movement, which sought to take art out of its traditional relation to morality and to find its justification only in the fulfillment of its purely aesthetic intentions. In 1873 he collected the essays on Renaissance figures which he had published in periodicals in the intervening years, adding a few new pieces and the Preface and Conclusion (the last had in fact been composed before any of the essays), and brought out *Studies in the History of the Renaissance*. The work established his reputation in the great world, especially among young men, but it had the effect of separating him from most of Oxford. The very name of the book was capable of arousing suspicion and resistance in some quarters, for although henceforward the Renaissance was to gain an ever greater hold on the English imagination, it was not at that time in good odor. Ruskin had long taken every opportunity to denounce it as the epoch which had departed from the faith, sincerity, and organicism of the medieval period in order to cultivate technique, technology, and an egoistic individualism, and William Morris was to carry on this judgment. Benjamin Jowett, Pater's admired teacher of his undergraduate days and by now Master of Balliol College and an influential figure in university councils, was displeased by the tendency of The Renaissance and when, in 1874, Pater had reason to expect that the Proctorship, a university post at the disposal of his own college, would be given to him, Jowett effectually opposed the appointment.

Form this point on until his death in Oxford in 1894 Pater's biography is chiefly a record of his publications. He lived with his sisters at Oxford and, in their company, traveled abroad in the long vacations. In 1880 he gave up his teaching at Brasenose so that he might have more time for writing, but he retained his fellowship. From 1885 to 1893 he resided in London for part of each year and took pleasure in the social life of the city. The range of his interests was wide; in addition to the Renaissance, the periods from which he chose the subjects of his essays were ancient Greece, seventeenth-century England, English and French romanticism, and, remarkable in a critic whose roots were deep in academic life, the literature of his own day. Most of his books are, like The Renaissance, collections of essays published in periodicals—Imaginary Portraits (1887), Appreciations (1889), Plato and Platonism (1894), and the posthumous Miscellaneous Studies (1895), and Essays from the "Guardian" (1901). An important exception is his novel, or, as it is sometimes called, philosophical romance, Marius the Epicurean (1885), the story of the life of a young Roman in the time of the Antonine emperors, who experiences a variety of philosophical and spiritual influences, is drawn to the personal and moral qualities of the early Christian community, and sacrifices his own life to preserve that of a Christian friend.

Pater's prose is the subject of frequent comment, usually censorious of its tendency toward elaborateness and self-consciousness, even toward a hieratic solemnity. But although it doubtless deserves to be sometimes faulted on these grounds, it must also be admired for its latent and frequently manifest energy and for its superb precision of statement.

From The Renaissance

Preface

Many attempts have been made by writers on art and poetry to define beauty in the abstract, to express it in the most general terms, to find a universal formula for it.[1] The value of these attempts has most often been in the suggestive and penetrating things said by the way. Such discussions help us very

1. Pater refers here to what is called "aesthetics," or the philosophy, or theory, of art, which in the 18th century was especially concerned with the concept of beauty. His point is that he is not concerned with such large abstractions, but, rather, with particular works of art. He calls his enterprise "aesthetic criticism," by which he means no more than "criticism," the purposes of which he specifies. The word "aesthetic" derives from the Greek word that means simply sense-perception. It came into vogue after Pater's use of it and was often intended pejoratively: an "aesthete" was a young man who set too much store by art, to the detriment of his masculinity.

little to enjoy what has been well done in art or poetry, to discriminate between what is more and what is less excellent in them, or to use words like
beauty, excellence, art, poetry, with a more precise meaning than they would
otherwise have. Beauty, like all other qualities presented to human experience,
is relative; and the definition of it becomes unmeaning and useless in proportion
to its abstractness. To define beauty, not in the most abstract, but in the most
concrete terms possible, to find, not a universal formula for it, but the formula
which expresses most adequately this or that special manifestation of it, is the
aim of the true student of aesthetics.

'To see the object as in itself it really is,'[2] has been justly said to be the
aim of all true criticism whatever; and in aesthetic criticism the first step
towards seeing one's object as it really is, is to know one's own impression as
it really is, to discriminate it, to realise it distinctly. The objects with which
aesthetic criticism deals—music, poetry, artistic and accomplished forms of
human life—are indeed receptacles of so many powers or forces: they possess,
like the products of nature, so many virtues or qualities. What is this song
or picture, this engaging personality presented in life or in a book, to *me*?[3]
What effect does it really produce on me? Does it give me pleasure? and if
so, what sort or degree of pleasure? How is my nature modified by its presence,
and under its influence? The answers to these questions are the original facts
with which the aesthetic critic has to do; and, as in the study of light, of
morals, of number, one must realise such primary data for oneself, or not
at all. And he who experiences these impressions strongly, and drives directly
at the discrimination and analysis of them, has no need to trouble himself
with the abstract question what beauty is in itself, or what its exact relation
to truth or experience—metaphysical questions, as unprofitable as metaphysical
questions elsewhere. He may pass them all by as being, answerable or not, of
no interest to him.

The aesthetic critic, then, regards all the objects with which he has to do,
all works of art, and the fairer forms of nature and human life, as powers or
forces producing pleasurable sensations, each of a more or less peculiar or
unique kind. This influence he feels, and wishes to explain, analysing it, and
reducing it to its elements. To him, the picture, the landscape, the engaging
personality in life or in a book, *La Gioconda*,[4] the hills of Carrara,[5] Pico of
Mirandola,[6] are valuable for their virtues,[7] as we say, in speaking of a herb,
a wine, a gem; for the property each has of affecting one with a special, a

2. See Matthew Arnold, the first paragraph of *The Function of Criticism at the Present
Time.*

3. Pater is echoing Arnold, who, in his essay *Heinrich Heine* says of Goethe that his
"profound, imperturbable naturalism is absolutely fatal to all routine thinking; he puts the
standard, once and for all, inside every man, instead of outside him; when he is told,
such a thing must be so . . . . he answers with Olympian politeness, 'But *is* it so? is it so
to *me*?' "

4. Known also as *Mona Lisa*, the famous portrait by Leonardo da Vinci. Pater's description of it in his essay on Leonardo in *The Renaissance* is often quoted.

5. A town in Tuscany, Italy, famous for its quarries of white marble.

6. Giovanni Pico, Count of Mirandola (1463–94), Italian philosopher of vast learning.
He is the subject of one of the essays of *The Renaissance.*

7. Efficacious quality.

unique, impression of pleasure. Our education becomes complete in proportion as our susceptibility to these impressions increases in depth and variety. And the function of the aesthetic critic is to distinguish, analyse, and separate from its adjuncts, the virtue by which a picture, a landscape, a fair personality in life or in a book, produces this special impression of beauty or pleasure, to indicate what the source of that impression is, and under what conditions it is experienced. His end is reached when he has disengaged that virtue, and noted it, as a chemist notes some natural element, for himself and others; and the rule for those who would reach this end is stated with great exactness in the words of a recent critic of Sainte-Beuve:—*De se borner à connaître de près les belles choses, et à s'en nourrir en exquis amateurs, en humanistes accomplis.*[8]

What is important, then, is not that the critic should possess a correct abstract definition of beauty for the intellect, but a certain kind of temperament, the power of being deeply moved by the presence of beautiful objects. He will remember always that beauty exists in many forms. To him all periods, types, schools of taste, are in themselves equal. In all ages there have been some excellent workmen, and some excellent work done. The question he asks is always:—In whom did the stir, the genius, the sentiment of the period find itself? where was the receptacle of its refinement, its elevation, its taste? 'The ages are all equal,' says William Blake, 'but genius is always above its age.'[9]

Often it will require great nicety to disengage this virtue from the commoner elements with which it may be found in combination. Few artists, not Goethe or Byron even, work quite cleanly, casting off all *débris*, and leaving us only what the heat of their imagination has wholly fused and transformed. Take, for instance, the writings of Wordsworth. The heat of his genius, entering into the substance of his work, has crystallised a part, but only a part, of it; and in that great mass of verse there is much which might well be forgotten.[10] But scattered up and down it, sometimes fusing and transforming entire compositions, like the Stanzas on *Resolution and Independence*, and the Ode on the *Recollections of Childhood*,[11] sometimes, as if at random, depositing a fine crystal here or there, in a matter it does not wholly search through and transform, we trace the action of his unique, incommunicable faculty, that strange, mystical sense of a life in natural things, and of man's life as a part of nature, drawing strength and colour and character from local influences, from the hills and streams, and from natural sights and sounds. Well! that is the *virtue*, the active principle in Wordsworth's poetry; and then the function of the critic of Wordsworth is to follow up that active principle, to disengage it, to mark the degree in which it penetrates his verse.

8. "To limit themselves to knowing beautiful things at first hand, and to develop themselves as sensitive lovers of art, as accomplished humanists."
9. From Blake's *Annotations to the Works of Sir Joshua Reynolds*, Discourse III, p. 71: "Ages are All Equal. But Genius is Always Above The Age."
10. Pater is in accord with Arnold who, in the introduction to his volume of selections of Wordsworth's poems, said that the best had to be "disengaged from the quantity of inferior work which now obscures them."
11. *Ode: Intimations of Immortality from Recollections of Early Childhood.*

The subjects of the following studies are taken from the history of the *Renaissance*,[12] and touch what I think the chief points in that complex, many-sided movement. I have explained in the first of them what I understand by the word, giving it a much wider scope than was intended by those who originally used it to denote only that revival of classical antiquity in the fifteenth century which was but one of many results of a general excitement and enlightening of the human mind, of which the great aim and achievements of what, as Christian art, is often falsely opposed to the Renaissance, were another result. This outbreak of the human spirit may be traced far into the Middle Age [13] itself, with its qualities already clearly pronounced, the care for physical beauty, the worship of the body, the breaking down of those limits which the religious system of the Middle Age imposed on the heart and the imagination. I have taken as an example of this movement, this earlier Renaissance within the Middle Age itself, and as an expression of its qualities, two little compositions in early French; not because they constitute the best possible expression of them, but because they help the unity of my series, inasmuch as the Renaissance ends also in France, in French poetry, in a phase of which the writings of Joachim du Bellay [14] are in many ways the most perfect illustration; the Renaissance thus putting forth in France an aftermath, a wonderful later growth, the products of which have to the full that subtle and delicate sweetness which belongs to a refined and comely decadence; just as its earliest phases have the freshness which belongs to all periods of growth in art, the charm of *ascêsis*,[15] of the austere and serious girding of the loins in youth.

But it is in Italy, in the fifteenth century, that the interest of the Renaissance mainly lies,—in that solemn fifteenth century which can hardly be studied too much, not merely for its positive results in the things of the intellect and the imagination, its concrete works of art, its special and prominent personalities, with their profound aesthetic charm, but for its general spirit and character, for the ethical qualities of which it is a consummate type.

The various forms of intellectual activity which together make up the culture of an age, move for the most part from different starting-points, and by unconnected roads. As products of the same generation they partake indeed of a common character, and unconsciously illustrate each other; but of the producers themselves, each group is solitary, gaining what advantage or disadvantage there may be in intellectual isolation. Art and poetry, philosophy and the religious life, and that other life of refined pleasure and action in the open places of the world, are each of them confined to its own circle of ideas, and those who prosecute either [16] of them are generally little curious of the thoughts of others. There come, however, from time to time, eras of more

---

12. This word, which is French for "rebirth," came into use in England in the mid-19th century to denote the great revival of arts and letters, under the influence of classical models, which began in Italy in the 14th century and continued through the 16th century. Pater thought of it as beginning in France at the end of the 12th century.
13. More usually, the Middle Ages.
14. French poet (1524–60), the subject of an essay in *The Renaissance*.
15. In his essay *Style*, Pater makes this Greek word equivalent with "self-restraint, a skilful economy of means."
16. If Pater were writing now, he would say "any one of them," but "either" was in his day sometimes used to refer to more than two objects or persons.

favourable conditions, in which the thoughts of men draw nearer together than is their wont, and the many interests of the intellectual world combine in one complete type of general culture. The fifteenth century in Italy is one of these happier eras; and what is sometimes said of the age of Pericles is true of that of Lorenzo: [17]—it is an age productive in personalities, many-sided, centralised, complete. Here, artists and philosophers and those whom the action of the world has elevated and made keen, do not live in isolation, but breathe a common air, and catch light and heat from each other's thoughts. There is a spirit of general elevation and enlightenment in which all alike communicate. It is the unity of this spirit which gives unity to all the various products of the Renaissance; and it is to this intimate alliance with mind, this participation in the best thoughts which that age produced, that the art of Italy in the fifteenth century owes much of its grave dignity and influence.

I have added an essay on Winckelmann,[18] as not incongruous with the studies which precede it, because Winckelmann, coming in the eighteenth century, really belongs in spirit to an earlier age. By his enthusiasm for the things of the intellect and the imagination for their own sake, by his Hellenism, his life-long struggle to attain to the Greek spirit, he is in sympathy with the humanists of an earlier century. He is the last fruit of the Renaissance, and explains in a striking way its motive and tendencies.

1873   1873

Conclusion

Λέγει που Ἡράκλειτος ὅτι πάντα χωρεῖ καὶ οὐδὲν μένει[1]

To regard all things and principles of things as inconstant modes or fashions has more and more become the tendency of modern thought. Let us begin with that which is without—our physical life. Fix upon it in one of its more exquisite intervals, the moment, for instance, of delicious recoil from the flood of water in summer heat.[2] What is the whole physical life in that moment but a combination of natural elements to which science gives their names? But these elements, phosphorus and lime and delicate fibres, are present not in the human body alone: we detect them in places most remote from it. Our physical life is a perpetual motion of them—the passage of the blood, the wasting and repairing of the lenses of the eye, the modification of the tissues of the brain by every ray of light and sound—processes which science reduces to simpler and more elementary forces. Like the elements of which we are

17. Pericles, the great statesman of Athens in the 5th century B.C., under whose rule the city achieved its pre-eminence in art. Lorenzo de Medici (1449–92), prince of Florence, was not only a patron of the arts but himself a poet and scholar.
18. Johann Joachim Winckelmann (1717–68), the German classical scholar who did much to establish the idea of the flawless perfection of Greek art.

1. "Heracleitus says, 'All things give way; nothing remains.'" Plato, Cratylus 402 A, Pater's translation. Heraclitus was a Greek philosopher of about 500 B.C. At the heart of his thought was the doctrine of perpetual flux; he held fire to be the basis of all material exist-ence. The sense of flux, of the impermanence of things, which Pater in his opening sentence says is characteristic of the 19th centuryy, may be thought of as a consequence of the great acceleration of historical and scientific research, both of which emphasized the idea of process and change.
2. What Pater asks us to consider is simply what it feels like to plunge into a cool stream on a hot day!

composed, the action of these forces extends beyond us; it rusts iron and ripens corn. Far out on every side of us those elements are broadcast, driven by many forces; and birth and gesture and death and the springing of violets from the grave are but a few out of ten thousand resultant combinations. That clear, perpetual outline of face and limb is but an image of ours, under which we group them—a design in a web, the actual threads of which pass out beyond it. This at least of flame-like our life has, that it is but the concurrence, renewed from moment to moment, of forces parting sooner or later on their ways.

Or if we begin with the inward world of thought and feeling, the whirlpool is still more rapid, the flame more eager and devouring. There it is no longer the gradual darkening of the eye and fading of colour from the wall,—the movement of the shore-side, where the water flows down indeed, though in apparent rest,—but the race of the mid-stream, a drift of momentary acts of sight and passion and thought. At first sight experience seems to bury us under a flood of external objects, pressing upon us with a sharp and importunate reality, calling us out of ourselves in a thousand forms of action. But when reflexion begins to act upon those objects they are dissipated under its influence; the cohesive force seems suspended like a trick of magic; each object is loosed into a group of impressions—colour, odour, texture—in the mind of the observer.[3] And if we continue to dwell in thought on this world, not of objects in the solidity with which language invests them, but of impressions unstable, flickering, inconsistent, which burn and are extinguished with our consciousness of them, it contracts still further; the whole scope of observation is dwarfed to the narrow chamber of the individual mind. Experience, already reduced to a swarm of impressions, is ringed round for each one of us by that thick wall of personality through which no real voice has ever pierced on its way to us, or from us to that which we can only conjecture to be without. Every one of those impressions is the impression of the individual in his isolation, each mind keeping as a solitary prisoner its own dream of a world.[4] Analysis goes a step farther still, and assures us that those impressions of the individual mind to which, for each one of us, experience dwindles down, are in perpetual flight; that each of them is limited by time, and that as time is infinitely divisible, each of them is infinitely divisible also; all that is actual in it being a single moment, gone while we try to apprehend it, of which it may ever be more truly said that it has ceased to be than that it is. To such a tremulous wisp constantly re-forming itself on the stream, to a single sharp impression, with a sense in it, a relic more or less fleeting, of such moments gone by, what is real in our life fines itself down. It is with this movement, with the passage and dissolution of impressions, images, sensations, that analysis leaves off—that continual vanishing away, that strange, perpetual weaving and unweaving of ourselves.[5]

3. The idea which Pater is advancing here is that it is only through habit and convention that the influx of multitudinous sense-impressions which we momently experience cohere into significance.

4. Pater here touches upon "solipsism," the idea that the self is the only thing that can be known as a reality.

5. That is, the continuity and actuality of the self is to be thought of not as something given and ineluctable but as the consequence of choice and will.

Philosophiren, says Novalis, *ist dephlegmatisiren, vivificiren.*[6] The service of philosophy, of speculative culture, towards the human spirit is to rouse, to startle it into sharp and eager observation. Every moment some form grows perfect in hand or face; some tone on the hills or the sea is choicer than the rest; some mood of passion or insight or intellectual excitement is irresistibly real and attractive for us,—for that moment only. Not the fruit of experience, but experience itself, is the end. A counted number of pulses only is given to us of a variegated, dramatic life. How may we see in them all that is to be seen in them by the finest senses? How shall we pass most swiftly from point to point, and be present always at the focus where the greatest number of vital forces unite in their purest energy?

To burn always with this hard, gemlike flame,[7] to maintain this ecstasy, is success in life. In a sense it might even be said that our failure is to form habits: for, after all, habit is relative to a stereotyped world, and meantime it is only the roughness of the eye that makes any two persons, things, situations, seem alike. While all melts under our feet, we may well catch at any exquisite passion, or any contribution to knowledge that seems by a lifted horizon to set the spirit free for a moment, or any stirring of the senses, strange dyes, strange colours, and curious odours, or work of the artist's hands, or the face of one's friend. Not to discriminate every moment some passionate attitude in those about us, and in the brilliancy of their gifts some tragic dividing of forces on their ways, is, on this short day of frost and sun, to sleep before evening. With this sense of the splendour of our experience and of its awful brevity, gathering all we are into one desperate effort to see and touch, we shall hardly have time to make theories about the things we see and touch. What we have to do is to be for ever curiously testing new opinions and courting new impressions, never acquiescing in a facile orthodoxy of Comte, or of Hegel,[8] or of our own. Philosophical theories or ideas, as points of view, instruments of criticism, may help us to gather up what might otherwise pass unregarded by us. 'Philosophy is the microscope of thought.' [9] The theory or idea or system which requires of us the sacrifice of any part of this experience, in consideration of some interest into which we cannot enter, or some abstract theory we have not identified with ourselves, or what is only conventional, has no real claim upon us.

One of the most beautiful passages in the writings of Rousseau is that in the sixth book of the *Confessions,* where he describes the awakening in him of the literary sense. An undefinable taint of death had always clung about him, and now in early manhood he believed himself smitten by mortal disease. He asked himself how he might make as much as possible of the interval that remained; and he was not biassed by anything in his previous life when he decided that it must be by intellectual excitement, which he found just then in the clear,

6. "To philosophize is to cast off sluggishness, to make oneself alive." Novalis is the penname of Friedrich Leopold von Hardenberg (1772–1801), one of the leading spirits of German Romanticism.
7. This famous phrase refers to Heraclitus' idea that the principle of life is fire.
8. Auguste Comte (1798–1857) and Georg Wilhelm Friedrich Hegel (1770–1831). Pater refers to the two philosophers, one French, one German, not to express disagreement with the substance of their thought but to oppose the static condition of the mind which follows from acquiescence in any systematic representation of life.
9. Victor Hugo, *Les Misérables* II.2.

fresh writings of Voltaire.[10] Well! we are all *condamnés,* as Victor Hugo says: we are all under sentence of death but with a sort of indefinite reprieve—*les hommes sont tous condamnés à mort avec des sursis indéfinis:* we have an interval, and then our place knows us no more. Some spend this interval in listlessness, some in high passions, the wisest, at least among 'the children of this world,' [11] in art and song. For our one chance lies in expanding that interval, in getting as many pulsations as possible into the given time. Great passions may give us this quickened sense of life, ecstasy and sorrow of love, the various forms of enthusiastic activity, disinterested or otherwise, which come naturally to many of us. Only be sure it is passion—that it does yield you this fruit of a quickened, multiplied consciousness. Of this wisdom, the poetic passion, the desire of beauty, the love of art for art's sake, has most; for art comes to you professing frankly to give nothing but the highest quality to your moments as they pass, and simply for those moments' sake.

1873   1873, 1888

Romanticism [1]

αἴνει δὲ παλαιὸν μὲν οἶνον, ἄνθεα δ' ὕμνων νεωτέρων[2]

The words, *classical* and *romantic,* although, like many other critical expressions, sometimes abused by those who have understood them too vaguely or too absolutely, yet define two real tendencies in the history of art and literature. Used in an exaggerated sense, to express a greater opposition between those tendencies than really exists, they have at times tended to divide people of taste into opposite camps. But in that *House Beautiful,*[3] which the creative minds of all generations—the artists and those who have treated life in the spirit of art—are always building together, for the refreshment of the human spirit, these oppositions cease; and the *Interpreter* [4] of the *House Beautiful,* the true aesthetic critic,[5] uses these divisions, only so far as they enable him to enter into the peculiarities of the objects with which he has to do. The term *classical,* fixed, as it is, to a well-defined literature, and a well-defined group in art, is clear, indeed; but then it has often been used in a hard, and merely

---

10. The "just then" is important to Pater's point, for if at this moment Rousseau delighted in Voltaire's writings, at a later stage of his development he attacked them fiercely.
11. Luke 16:8, ". . . for the children of this world are in their generation wiser than the children of light."

1. This essay first appeared, under its present title, in *Macmillan's Magazine,* November 1876. In 1889, when Pater collected a group of his critical writings to make the volume *Appreciations,* he placed this essay last, although it had been composed before most of the others, and called it "Postscript," seeming by this to suggest that it formulates the principles upon which the preceding critical judgments were made. The cordiality with which it receives works in a large variety of modes, its readiness to overlook extravagances so long as the work is charged with "energy" and "curiosity," are in striking contrast with the strictness of the criteria Matthew Arnold uses in *The Study of Poetry.*
2. "When you praise the wine that is old, praise also the flowers of song that are new." Pindar, *Olympian Odes* IX.48–49.
3. In Bunyan's *Pilgrim's Progress,* the palace in which Christian rests from his journey and has sight of the Delectable Mountains.
4. At the Interpreter's House many significances are disclosed to Christian by its master.
5. See note 1· to the Preface to *The Renaissance.*

scholastic sense, by the praisers of what is old and accustomed, at the expense of what is new, by critics who would never have discovered for themselves the charm of any work, whether new or old, who value what is old, in art or literature, for its accessories, and chiefly for the conventional authority that has gathered about it—people who would never really have been made glad by any Venus fresh-risen from the sea, and who praise the Venus of old Greece and Rome, only because they fancy her grown now into something staid and tame.

And as the term, *classical,* has been used in a too absolute, and therefore in a misleading sense, so the term, *romantic,* has been used much too vaguely, in various accidental senses. The sense in which Scott is called a romantic writer is chiefly this; that, in opposition to the literary tradition of the last century, he loved strange adventure, and sought it in the Middle Age.[6] Much later,[7] in a Yorkshire village, the spirit of romanticism bore a more really characteristic fruit in the work of a young girl, Emily Brontë, the romance of *Wuthering Heights;* the figures of Hareton Earnshaw, of Catherine Linton, and of Heathcliffe—tearing open Catherine's grave, removing one side of her coffin, that he may really lie beside her in death—figures so passionate, yet woven on a background of delicately beautiful, moorland scenery, being typical examples of that spirit. In Germany, again, that spirit is shown less in Tieck,[8] its professional representative, than in Meinhold,[9] the author of *Sidonia the Sorceress* and the *Amber-Witch.* In Germany and France, within the last hundred years, the term has been used to describe a particular school of writers; [10] and, consequently, when Heine [11] criticises the *Romantic School* in Germany—that movement which culminated in Goethe's *Goetz von Berlichingen;* [12] or when Théophile Gautier [13] criticises the romantic movement in France, where, indeed, it bore its most characteristic fruits, and its play is hardly yet over where, by a certain audacity, or *bizarrerie* [14] of motive, united with faultless literary execution, it still shows itself in imaginative literature, they use the word, with an exact

6. Doubtless Pater suggests that Scott is not essentially a Romantic writer because he has in mind Scott's conservative temperament and his strong sense of fact.
7. Not so *very* much later—Scott's first novel, *Waverley,* appeared in 1814, his last in 1832; *Wuthering Heights* appeared in 1847.
8. Johann Ludwig Tieck (1773–1853) was not only a novelist in the Romantic mode but also a propagandist for it.
9. Wilhelm Meinhold (1797–1851). When *The Amber Witch* was published in 1843, it was thought to be an authentic chronicle from the 17th century.
10. Pater means that German and French literary historians and critics do not conceive of Romanticism as a tendency of art that manifests itself in various ways and degrees in various times and places but, rather, as the defining quality of a particular group of artists.
11. Heinrich Heine (1797–1856), the German poet and critic, perhaps the wittiest man of his time, was himself of the Romantic school, in the sense that Pater speaks of. His book about it appeared in 1836.
12. Goethe wrote this play in 1773. Its title is the name of its hero, an actual German knight devoted to an ideal of justice. Its form is Shakespearean, its language colloquial prose.
13. French poet, novelist, and critic (1811–72), in his early youth a passionate propagandist for Romanticism in its extreme manifestations, later devoted to the ideal of formal precision. He was one of the proponents of the doctrine of "art for art's sake" (*l'art pour l'art*), to which Pater gives expression in the Conclusion to *The Renaissance.* His unfinished *History of Romanticism* appeared in 1874.
14. Oddness, extravagance.

sense of special artistic qualities, indeed; but use it, nevertheless, with a limited application to the manifestation of those qualities at a particular period. But the romantic spirit is, in reality, an ever-present, an enduring principle, in the artistic temperament; and the qualities of thought and style which that, and other similar uses of the word *romantic* really indicate, are indeed but symptoms of a very continuous and widely working influence.

Though the words *classical* and *romantic*, then, have acquired an almost technical meaning, in application to certain developments of German and French taste, yet this is but one variation of an old opposition, which may be traced from the very beginning of the formation of European art and literature. From the first formation of anything like a standard of taste in these things, the restless curiosity of their more eager lovers necessarily made itself felt, in the craving for new motives, new subjects of interest, new modifications of style. Hence, the opposition between the classicists and the romanticists— between the adherents, in the culture of beauty, of the principles of liberty, and authority, respectively—of strength, and order or what the Greeks called κοσμιότης.[15]

Sainte-Beuve,[16] in the third volume of the *Causeries du Lundi*, has discussed the question, *What is meant by a classic?* It was a question he was well fitted to answer, having himself lived through many phases of taste, and having been in earlier life an enthusiastic member of the romantic school: he was also a great master of that sort of 'philosophy of literature,' which delights in tracing traditions in it, and the way in which various phases of thought and sentiment maintain themselves, through successive modifications, from epoch to epoch. His aim, then, is to give the word *classic* a wider and, as he says, a more generous sense than it commonly bears, to make it expressly *grandiose et flottant;* [17] and, in doing this, he develops, in a masterly manner, those qualities of measure, purity, temperance, of which it is the especial function of classical art and literature, whatever meaning, narrower or wider, we attach to the term, to take care.

The charm, therefore, of what is classical, in art or literature, is that of the well-known tale, to which we can, nevertheless, listen over and over again, because it is told so well. To the absolute beauty of its artistic form, is added the accidental, tranquil, charm of familiarity. There are times, indeed, at which these charms fail to work on our spirits at all, because they fail to excite us. 'Romanticism,' says Stendhal,[18] 'is the art of presenting to people the literary works which, in the actual state of their habits and beliefs, are capable of giving them the greatest possible pleasure; *classicism*, on the contrary, of pre-

---

15. Orderly behavior (kosmiótes).
16. Charles-Augustin Sainte-Beuve (1804–69) is generally accounted the pre-eminent French critic of the mid-19th century. His series of critical essays *Causeries du Lundi* (Monday Chats), appeared in Parisian newspapers between 1849 and 1869. Pater refers to the fact that Sainte-Beuve's later attitude to the Romantics was at least skeptical and often antagonistic.
17. Imposing and not rigid.
18. The pseudonym of Henri Beyle (1783–1842). Now accounted one of the great novelists of the 19th century, he was ignored in France until the century's end and scarcely heard of in England. Pater quotes from his *Racine and Shakespeare* (1823, 1825), originally two pamphlets in defense of Romanticism.

senting them with that which gave the greatest possible pleasure to their grandfathers.' But then, beneath all changes of habits and beliefs, our love of that mere abstract proportion—of music—which what is classical in literature possesses, still maintains itself in the best of us, and what pleased our grandparents may at least tranquillise us. The 'classic' comes to us out of the cool and quiet of other times, as the measure of what a long experience has shown will at least never displease us. And in the classical literature of Greece and Rome, as in the classics of the last century, the essentially classical element is that quality of order in beauty, which they possess, indeed, in a pre-eminent degree, and which impresses some minds to the exclusion of everything else in them.

It is the addition of strangeness to beauty, that constitutes the romantic character in art; [19] and the desire of beauty being a fixed element in every artistic organisation, it is the addition of curiosity to this desire of beauty, that constitutes the romantic temper. Curiosity and the desire of beauty, have each their place in art, as in all true criticism. When one's curiosity is deficient, when one is not eager enough for new impressions, and new pleasures, one is liable to value mere academical proprieties too highly, to be satisfied with worn-out or conventional types, with the insipid ornament of Racine,[20] or the prettiness of that later Greek sculpture, which passed so long for true Hellenic work; [21] to miss those places where the handiwork of nature, or of the artist, has been most cunning; to find the most stimulating products of art a mere irritation. And when one's curiosity is in excess, when it overbalances the desire of beauty, then one is liable to value in works of art what is inartistic in them; to be satisfied with what is exaggerated in art, with productions like some of those of the romantic school in Germany; not to distinguish, jealously enough, between what is admirably done, and what is done not quite so well, in the writings, for instance, of Jean Paul.[22] And if I had to give instances of these defects, then I should say, that Pope, in common with the age of literature to which he belonged, had too little curiosity, so that there is always a certain insipidity in the effect of his work, exquisite as it is; and, coming down to our own time, that Balzac had an excess of curiosity—curiosity not duly tempered with the desire of beauty.

But, however falsely those two tendencies may be opposed by critics, or exaggerated by artists themselves, they are tendencies really at work at all times in art, moulding it, with the balance sometimes a little on one side, sometimes a little on the other, generating, respectively, as the balance inclines on this side or that, two principles, two traditions, in art, and in literature so far as it partakes of the spirit of art. If there is a great overbalance of curiosity, then, we have the grotesque in art: if the union of strangeness and beauty, under very difficult and complex conditions, be a successful one, if the union

19. The definition has become famous, almost proverbial.
20. The prevailing 19th-century English opinion of this poet, whom the French so much admire.
21. In part through the influence of Winckelmann; see note 18 to the Preface to *The Renaissance*.
22. Jean Paul Friedrich Richter (1763–1825), German humorous novelist and aesthetic theorist, wrote under his first two Christian names.

be entire, then the resultant beauty is very exquisite, very attractive. With a passionate care for beauty, the romantic spirit refuses to have it, unless the condition of strangeness be first fulfilled. Its desire is for a beauty born of unlikely elements, by a profound alchemy, by a difficult initiation, by the charm which wrings it even out of terrible things; and a trace of distortion, of the grotesque, may perhaps linger, as an additional element of expression, about its ultimate grace. Its eager, excited spirit will have strength, the grotesque, first of all—the trees shrieking as you tear off the leaves; [23] for Jean Valjean,[24] the long years of convict life; for Redgauntlet,[25] the quicksands of Solway Moss; then, incorporate with this strangeness, and intensified by restraint, as much sweetness, as much beauty, as is compatible with that. *Énergique, frais, et dispos*—these, according to Sainte-Beuve, are the characteristics of a genuine classic—*les ouvrages anciens ne sont pas classiques parce qu'ils sont vieux, mais parce qu'ils sont énergiques, frais, et dispos.*[26] Energy, freshness, intelligent and masterly disposition:—these are characteristics of Victor Hugo when his alchemy is complete, in certain figures, like Marius and Cosette,[27] in certain scenes, like that in the opening of *Les Travailleurs de la Mer*,[28] where Déruchette writes the name of *Gilliatt* in the snow, on Christmas morning; but always there is a certain note of strangeness discernible there, as well.

The essential elements, then, of the romantic spirit are curiosity and the love of beauty; and it is only as an illustration of these qualities, that it seeks the Middle Age, because, in the over-charged atmosphere of the Middle Age, there are unworked sources of romantic effect, of a strange beauty, to be won, by strong imagination, out of things unlikely or remote.

Few, probably, now read Madame de Staël's *De l'Allemagne*,[29] though it has its interest, the interest which never quite fades out of work really touched with the enthusiasm of the spiritual adventurer, the pioneer in culture. It was published in 1810, to introduce to French readers a new school of writers— the romantic school, from beyond the Rhine; and it was followed, twenty-three years later, by Heine's *Romantische Schule*, as at once a supplement and a correction. Both these books, then, connect romanticism with Germany, with the names especially of Goethe and Tieck; and, to many English readers, the idea of romanticism is still inseparably connected with Germany—that Germany which, in its quaint old towns, under the spire of Strasburg or the towers of Heidelberg, was always listening in rapt inaction to the melodious, fascinating voices of the Middle Age, and which, now that it has got Strasburg

23. This happens in the *Aeneid* III.19–72.
24. The hero of Victor Hugo's *Les Misérables*.
25. A chief character of the novel by Scott that bears his name.
26. "Ancient works are classics not because they are old but because they are energetic, fresh, and well shaped."
27. Characters—young lovers—in *Les Misérables*.
28. *Toilers of the Sea*.
29. Mme de Staël (1766–1817), born Anne-Louise-Germaine Necker (her father was chief minister to Louis XVI), was famous as a liberal and an intellectual. Her book in praise of Germany and its culture, *De l'Allemagne*, was first published in Paris in 1810. All copies were confiscated and destroyed and the author was exiled. One of its chapters is devoted to a comparison of Classic and Romantic poetry.

back again,[30] has, I suppose, almost ceased to exist. But neither Germany, with its Goethe and Tieck, nor England, with its Byron and Scott, is nearly so representative of the romantic temper as France, with Murger,[31] and Gautier, and Victor Hugo. It is in French literature that its most characteristic expression is to be found; and that, as most closely derivative, historically, from such peculiar conditions, as ever reinforce it to the utmost.

For, although temperament has much to do with the generation of the romantic spirit, and although this spirit, with its curiosity, its thirst for a curious beauty, may be always traceable in excellent art (traceable even in Sophocles) yet still, in a limited sense, it may be said to be a product of special epochs. Outbreaks of this spirit, that is, come naturally with particular periods —times, when, in men's approaches towards art and poetry, curiosity may be noticed to take the lead, when men come to art and poetry, with a deep thirst for intellectual excitement, after a long *ennui*, or in reaction against the strain of outward, practical things: in the later Middle Age, for instance; so that medieval poetry, centering in Dante, is often opposed to Greek and Roman poetry, as romantic poetry to the classical. What the romanticism of Dante is, may be estimated, if we compare the lines in which Virgil describes the hazelwood, from whose broken twigs flows the blood of Polydorus, not without the expression of a real shudder at the ghastly incident, with the whole canto of the *Inferno*, into which Dante has expanded them, beautifying and softening it, meanwhile, by a sentiment of profound pity.[32] And it is especially in that period of intellectual disturbance, immediately preceding Dante, amid which the romance languages define themselves at last, that this temper is manifested. Here, in the literature of Provence, the very name of *romanticism* is stamped with its true signification: [33] here we have indeed a romantic world, grotesque even, in the strength of its passions, almost insane in its curious expression of them, drawing all things into its sphere, making the birds, nay! lifeless things, its voices and messengers, yet so penetrated with the desire for beauty and sweetness, that it begets a wholly new species of poetry, in which the *Renaissance* may be said to begin. The last century was pre-eminently a classical age, an age in which, for art and literature, the element of a comely order was in the ascendant; which, passing away, left a hard battle to be fought between the classical and the romantic school. Yet, it is in the heart of this century, of Goldsmith and Stothard, of Watteau and the *Siècle de Louis XIV* [34] —in one of its central, if not most characteristic figures, in Rousseau—that the modern or French romanticism really originates. But, what in the eighteenth century is but an exceptional phenomenon, breaking through its fair reserve

30. Strasbourg, the capital of Alsace-Lorraine, was annexed by the French in 1681 and won back by the Germans in the Franco-Prussian War of 1870.
31. Henri Murger (1822–51) wrote novels of a sentimental kind.
32. Canto XIII.
33. Pater refers to the love poetry composed in the 12th century by the troubadours, the poets of this southern province of France.
34. By his reference to Oliver Goldsmith (1730–74) the English writer, to Thomas Stothard (1755–1834) the English painter, to Jean-Antoine Watteau (1684–1721) the French painter, and to Voltaire's history of the age of Louis XIV, Pater does not mean to say that they represent the essence of classicism but, rather, that they point toward romanticism.

and discretion only at rare intervals, is the habitual guise of the nineteenth, breaking through it perpetually, with a feverishness, and incomprehensible straining and excitement, which all experience to some degree, but yearning also, in the genuine children of the romantic school, to be *énergique, frais, et dispos*—for those qualities of energy, freshness, comely order; and often, in Murger, in Gautier, in Victor Hugo, for instance, with singular felicity attaining them.

It is in the terrible tragedy of Rousseau, in fact, that French romanticism, with much else, begins: reading his *Confessions* we seem actually to assist at the birth of this new, strong spirit in the French mind. The wildness which has shocked so many, and the fascination which has influenced almost every one, in the squalid, yet eloquent figure, we see and hear so clearly in that book, wandering under the apple-blossoms and among the vines of Neuchâtel or Vevey [35] actually give it the quality of a very successful romantic invention. His strangeness or distortion, his profound subjectivity, his passionateness— the *cor laceratum* [36]—Rousseau makes all men in love with these. *Je ne suis fait comme aucun de ceux que j'ai sus. Mais si je ne vaux pas mieux, au moins je suis autre.*—'I am not made like any one else I have ever known: yet, if I am not better, at least I am different.' These words, from the first page of the *Confessions*, anticipate all the Werthers, Renés, Obermanns,[37] of the last hundred years. For Rousseau did but anticipate a trouble in the spirit of the whole world; and thirty years afterwards, what in him was a peculiarity, became part of the general consciousness. A storm was coming: Rousseau, with others, felt it in the air, and they helped to bring it down: they introduced a disturbing element into French literature, then so trim and formal, like our own literature of the age of Queen Anne.

In 1815 the storm had come and gone, but had left, in the spirit of 'young France,' the *ennui* of an immense disillusion. In the last chapter of Edgar Quinet's *Révolution Française*,[38] a work itself full of irony, of disillusion, he distinguishes two books, Senancour's *Obermann* and Chateaubriand's *Génie du Christianisme*,[39] as characteristic of the first decade of the present century. In those two books we detect already the disease and the cure—in *Obermann* the irony, refined into a plaintive philosophy of 'indifference'—in Chateaubriand's *Génie du Christianisme*, the refuge from a tarnished actual present, a present of disillusion, into a world of strength and beauty in the Middle Age, as at an earlier period—in *René* and *Atala* [40]—into the free play of them in savage life. It is to minds in this spiritual situation, weary of the present, but

---

35. Towns in Switzerland associated with Rousseau.
36. The "torn heart."
37. These are all suffering young men, the heroes of, respectively, Goethe's *The Sorrows of Young Werther* (1774), Chateaubriand's *René* (1802), and Etienne Pivert de Senancour's *Obermann* (1804). All these stories were widely read and had large influence on the mode of feeling of their time.
38. Published in 1865.
39. *The Genius of Christianity,* 1802. *René* was part of this work although later it was published separately.
40. A tale of an American-Indian girl who becomes a Christian and dies in a struggle between love and her faith. Like *René, Atala* is part of the *Genius of Christianity,* although it was first published separately in 1801.

yearning for the spectacle of beauty and strength, that the works of French romanticism appeal. They set a positive value on the intense, the exceptional; and a certain distortion is sometimes noticeable in them, as in conceptions like Victor Hugo's *Quasimodo,* or *Gwynplaine,*[41] something of a terrible grotesque, of the *macabre,* as the French themselves call it; though always combined with perfect literary execution, as in Gautier's *La Morte Amoureuse,*[42] or the scene of the 'maimed' burial-rites of the player, dead of the frost, in his *Capitaine Fracasse*—true 'flowers of the yew.' It becomes grim humour in Victor Hugo's combat of Gilliatt with the devil-fish,[43] or the incident, with all its ghastly comedy drawn out at length, of the great gun detached from its fastenings on shipboard, in *Quatre-Vingt-Treize* [44] (perhaps the most terrible of all the accidents that can happen by sea) and in the entire episode, in that book, of the *Convention.*[45] Not less surely does it reach a genuine pathos; for the habit of noting and distinguishing one's own most intimate passages of sentiment makes one sympathetic, begetting, as it must, the power of entering, by all sorts of finer ways, into the intimate recesses of other minds; so that pity is another quality of romanticism, both Victor Hugo and Gautier being great lovers of animals, and charming writers about them, and Murger being unrivalled in the pathos of his *Scènes de la Vie de Jeunesse.*[46] Penetrating so finely into all situations which appeal to pity, above all, into the special or exceptional phases of such feeling, the romantic humour is not afraid of the quaintness or singularity of its circumstances or expression, pity, indeed, being of the essence of humour; so that Victor Hugo does but turn his romanticism into practice, in his hunger and thirst after practical *Justice!*—a justice which shall no longer wrong children, or animals, for instance, by ignoring in a stupid, mere breadth of view, minute facts about them. Yet the romanticists are antinomian,[47] too, sometimes, because the love of energy and beauty, of distinction in passion, tended naturally to become a little *bizarre,* plunging into the Middle Age, into the secrets of old Italian story. *Are we in the Inferno?*—we are tempted to ask, wondering at something malign in so much beauty. For over all a care for the refreshment of the human spirit by fine art manifests itself, a predominant sense of literary charm, so that, in their search for the secret of exquisite expression, the romantic school went back to the forgotten world of early French poetry, and literature itself became the most delicate of the arts—like 'goldsmith's work,' says Sainte-Beuve, of Bertrand's *Gaspard de la Nuit* [48]—

---

41. The hunchback in *Notre Dame* and the facially deformed boy in *The Man Who Laughs.*
42. Théophile Gautier's *La Morte amoureuse* (1857) is a collection of stories of the supernatural.
43. In *Toilers of the Sea.*
44. Pater refers to the episode in *Ninety-three* in which a great gun, having broken its lashings, rolls on its wheeled carriage with every slightest movement of the ship, endangering the lives of the crew and the ship itself.
45. *Ninety-three* is about the year 1793, in which the Reign of Terror took place.
46. Murger's *Scènes de la vie de jeunesse* (1851) is a collection of short stories on social themes.
47. Opposed to the claims of moral law.
48. Louis Bertrand (1807–41) is known for this one work, written in 1830, published in 1842; it is a series of prose poems, touched with fantasy and in feeling not unlike some of De Quincey's work.

and that peculiarly French gift, the gift of exquisite speech, *argute loqui*,[49] attained in them a perfection which it had never seen before.

Stendhal, a writer whom I have already quoted, and of whom English readers might well know much more than they do, stands between the earlier and later growths of the romantic spirit. His novels are rich in romantic quality; and his other writings—partly criticism, partly personal reminiscences—are a very curious and interesting illustration of the needs out of which romanticism arose. In his book on *Racine and Shakespeare*, Stendhal argues that all good art was romantic in its day; and this is perhaps true in Stendhal's sense. That little treatise, full of 'dry light' [50] and fertile ideas, was published in the year 1823, and its object is to defend an entire independence and liberty in the choice and treatment of subject, both in art and literature, against those who upheld the exclusive authority of precedent. In pleading the cause of romanticism, therefore, it is the novelty, both of form and of motive, in writings like the *Hernani* of Victor Hugo (which soon followed it,[51] raising a storm of criticism) that he is chiefly concerned to justify. To be interesting and really stimulating, to keep us from yawning even, art and literature must follow the subtle movements of that nimbly-shifting *Time-Spirit*, or *Zeit-Geist*, understood by French not less than by German criticism, which is always modifying men's taste, as it modifies their manners and their pleasures. This, he contends, is what all great workmen had always understood. Dante, Shakespeare, Molière, had exercised an absolute independence in their choice of subject and treatment. To turn always with that ever-changing spirit, yet to retain the flavour of what was admirably done in past generations, in the classics, as we say—is the problem of true romanticism. 'Dante,' he observes, 'was pre-eminently the romantic poet. He adored Virgil, yet he wrote the *Divine Comedy*, with the episode of Ugolino,[52] which is as unlike the *Aeneid* as can possibly be. And those who thus obey the fundamental principle of romanticism, one by one become classical, and are joined to that ever-increasing common league, formed by men of all countries, to approach nearer and nearer to perfection.'

Romanticism, then, although it has its epochs, is in its essential characteristics rather a spirit which shows itself at all times, in various degrees, in individual workmen and their work, and the amount of which criticism has to estimate in them taken one by one, than the peculiarity of a time or a school. Depending on the varying proportion of curiosity and the desire of beauty, natural tendencies of the artistic spirit at all times, it must always be partly a matter of individual temperament. The eighteenth century in England has been regarded as almost exclusively a classical period; yet William Blake, a type of so much which breaks through what are conventionally thought the influences of that century, is still a noticeable phenomenon in it, and the reaction in favour of

49. "To speak impressively."
50. "The most perfect soul, says Heracleitus, is a dry light. . . ." Plutarch, *Romulus*.
51. In 1830. This play broke all the traditional conventions and its first two performances were riotous partisan occasions in which the applause of the romanticists triumphed over the denunciatory shouts of the traditionalists.
52. Ugolino, Count of Pisa, conspired with the Archbishop Ruggiero to betray Pisa. Ruggiero turned on him and imprisoned him with his four sons until they starved to death. In *Inferno*, Canto XXXIII, Ugolino is shown frozen in the ice of the ninth circle and gnawing on the head of Ruggiero.

naturalism in poetry begins in that century, early. There are, thus, the born romanticists and the born classicists. There are the born classicists who start with *form,* to whose minds the comeliness of the old, immemorial, well-recognised types in art and literature, have revealed themselves impressively; who will entertain no matter which will not go easily and flexibly into them; whose work aspires only to be a variation upon, or study from, the older masters. ' 'Tis art's decline, my son!' [53] they are always saying, to the progressive element in their own generation; to those who care for that which in fifty years' time every one will be caring for. On the other hand, there are the born romanticists, who start with an original, untried *matter,* still in fusion; who conceive this vividly, and hold by it as the essence of their work; who, by the very vividness and heat of their conception, purge away, sooner or later, all that is not organically appropriate to it, till the whole effect adjusts itself in clear, orderly, proportionate form; which form, after a very little time, becomes classical in its turn.

The romantic or classical character of a picture, a poem, a literary work, depends, then, on the balance of certain qualities in it; and in this sense, a very real distinction may be drawn between good classical and good romantic work. But all critical terms are relative; and there is at least a valuable suggestion in that theory of Stendhal's, that all good art was romantic in its day. In the beauties of Homer and Pheidias, quiet as they now seem, there must have been, for those who confronted them for the first time, excitement and surprise, the sudden, unforeseen satisfaction of the desire of beauty. Yet the *Odyssey,* with its marvellous adventure, is more romantic than the *Iliad,* which nevertheless contains, among many other romantic episodes, that of the immortal horses of Achilles, who weep at the death of Patroclus. Aeschylus is more romantic than Sophocles, whose *Philoctetes,* were it written now, might figure, for the strangeness of its motive and the perfectness of its execution, as typically romantic; [54] while, of Euripides, it may be said, that his method in writing his plays is to sacrifice readily almost everything else, so that he may attain the fulness of a single romantic effect. These two tendencies, indeed, might be applied as a measure or standard, all through Greek and Roman art and poetry, with very illuminating results; and for an analyst of the romantic principle in art, no exercise would be more profitable, than to walk through the collection of classical antiquities at the Louvre, or the British Museum, or to examine some representative collection of Greek coins, and note how the element of curiosity, of the love of strangeness, insinuates itself into classical design, and record the effects of the romantic spirit there, the traces of struggle, of the grotesque even, though overbalanced here by sweetness; as in the sculpture of Chartres and Rheims,[55] the real sweetness of mind in the sculptor is often overbalanced by the grotesque, by the rudeness of his strength.

53. Browning, *Fra Lippo Lippi,* l. 233.
54. Philoctetes, a Greek hero, is bitten by a serpent on his way to Troy. His wound gives off a terrible stench and his comrades abandon him on the island of Lemnos. Here he lives in pain and solitude for ten years, hating his former friends. When it is disclosed to the Greeks that they can never take Troy without the bow and arrows of Heracles, which are in the possession of Philoctetes, they seek him out and appeal for his help.
55. That is, of the cathedrals of these towns.

Classicism, then, means for Stendhal, for that younger enthusiastic band of French writers whose unconscious method he formulated into principles, the reign of what is pedantic, conventional, and narrowly academical in art; for him, all good art is romantic. To Sainte-Beuve, who understands the term in a more liberal sense, it is the characteristic of certain epochs, of certain spirits in every epoch, not given to the exercise of original imagination, but rather to the working out of refinements of manner on some authorised matter; and who bring to their perfection, in this way, the elements of sanity, of order and beauty in manner. In general criticism, again, it means the spirit of Greece and Rome, of some phases in literature and art that may seem of equal authority with Greece and Rome, the age of Louis the Fourteenth, the age of Johnson; [56] though this is at best an uncritical use of the term, because in Greek and Roman work there are typical examples of the romantic spirit. But explain the terms as we may, in application to particular epochs, there are these two elements always recognisable; united in perfect art—in Sophocles, in Dante, in the highest work of Goethe, though not always absolutely balanced there; and these two elements may be not inappropriately termed the classical and romantic tendencies.

Material for the artist, motives of inspiration, are not yet exhausted: our curious, complex, aspiring age still abounds in subjects for aesthetic manipulation by the literary as well as by other forms of art. For the literary art, at all events, the problem just now is, to induce order upon the contorted, proportionless accumulation of our knowledge and experience, our science and history, our hopes and disillusion, and, in effecting this, to do consciously what has been done hitherto for the most part too unconsciously, to write our English language as the Latins wrote theirs, as the French write, as scholars should write. Appealing, as he may, to precedent in this matter, the scholar will still remember that if 'the style is the man' it is also the age: that the nineteenth century too will be found to have had its style, justified by necessity—a style very different, alike from the baldness of an impossible 'Queen Anne' revival, and an incorrect, incondite [57] exuberance, after the mode of Elizabeth: [58] that we can only return to either at the price of an impoverishment of form or matter, or both, although, an intellectually rich age such as ours being necessarily an eclectic one, we may well cultivate some of the excellences of literary types so different as those: that in literature as in other matters it is well to unite as many diverse elements as may be: that the individual writer or artist, certainly, is to be estimated by the number of graces he combines, and his power of interpenetrating them in a given work. To discriminate schools, of art, of literature, is, of course, part of the obvious business of literary criticism: but, in the work of literary production, it is easy to be overmuch occupied concerning them. For, in truth, the legitimate contention is, not of one age or school of literary art against another, but of all successive schools alike, against the stupidity which is dead to the substance, and the vulgarity which is dead to form.

1876   1876, 1889

56. Louis XIV of France, 1643–1715; Dr. Samuel Johnson, 1709–84.
57. Crude.
58. Pater speaks pejoratively of efforts to reconstitute the taste and style of bygone epochs.

SAMUEL BUTLER
1835–1902

Reputation came to Samuel Butler only belatedly. Of the books published in his life-time only *Erewhon* (1872) had any degree of success, and although in his later years he did attract a coterie of admirers, of whom Bernard Shaw was the most notable, his pertinacious assaults on the orthodoxies of the age went largely unnoticed by the public. It was not until the publication of his posthumous and only novel in 1903 that he began to be known both as a writer of formidable abilities and as a figure of decisive importance in the cultural history of the English nineteenth century.

If any one book may be thought to signalize the end of the Victorian ethos, it is surely *The Way of All Flesh*. Patently autobiographical in almost all its essential details, it is a remorseless indictment of the institution of the family and as such an assault on the palladium of English piety. No sentiment had a more tenacious hold upon the English than that family life was the crown of personal existence and the source of personal and national virtue. Butler represents the family as the condition of servitude of the individual spirit—home is jail and parents are not merely turnkeys but torturers. Through its violation of a primal sanctity *The Way of All Flesh* became the rallying point for the new generation of the early twentieth century and brought Butler's other writings into general notice and regard.

Samuel Butler was born in 1835 at Langar Rectory, near Bingham in Nottingham-shire. His father was the Reverend Thomas Butler, son of the Dr. Samuel Butler who had been headmaster of Shrewsbury School and Bishop of Lichfield and Coventry. The Butlers were well-to-do—money was a constant presence and issue in the family—and in 1843 they undertook a European tour with their young son, which, in its Italian phase, exercised a decisive effect upon his notion of the quality that life ought rightly to have, that is, quite unlike the quality of English life. In 1848 Samuel entered the school over which his grandfather had once ruled and in 1854 went up to Cambridge as a member of the college his family traditionally attended, St. John's. His father destined him for the church and for several years he acquiesced in the paternal decision, but doubts began to assail him, specifically over the question of infant baptism, and led to an angry exchange of views with his father. Having no hope that his parents would further his ambition to become a painter, Butler emigrated to New Zealand in 1859. His father provided a considerable capital sum for investment in a sheep farm. This venture prospered and yielded the com-petence which made Butler at least temporarily independent of his family and free to pursue his professional inclinations. It was while he was in New Zealand that he made his first start in literature with an account of his experiences as an immigrant, published in 1863 as *A First Year in Canterbury Settlement,* and with a witty specula-tive fantasy published in a New Zealand newspaper, *Darwin Among the Machines,* which was to figure as a memorable part of *Erewhon.*

Returning to England in 1864, Butler settled himself in chambers in Clifford's Inn, which was to be his residence for the rest of his life, and devoted himself to the study of painting. His native gifts were not great and he met with no success, but it was not until 1877 that he confronted the fact that his artistic ambitions were not to be realized and at last surrendered them. In 1870–71 he diverted some of his time and energy from painting to the composition of *Erewhon,* which was published anonymously, although a second edition revealed the identity of the author. His mother died in 1873 and his father was at pains to inform him that her death had been brought about by sorrow over the heterodox views her son had expressed.

Erewhon is a brilliant and engaging book. The name of Swift is often invoked in praise of its satire, and the comparison is not extravagant so far as it bears upon the ingenuity of the work. But of the moral passion of *Gulliver* there is no trace. This doubtless accounts for some part of the charm of the book, which does not force our feelings beyond the cool pleasures to be found in the intelligent, condescending perception of how anomalous and absurd are the institutions of respectable life. It also accounts for the book's falling short of greatness. But this judgment must seem captious and ungrateful when we consider the force of the wit that conceived, as a way of describing the attitude of the English to their established religion, the Erewhonic institution of Musical Banks which issue a currency that everyone must possess although no one will accept it in actual trade; or the imagination that levied upon Plato for the Erewhonian myth of the unborn and the elaborate legal arrangements to which it gave rise (see below); or the brilliance of the fantasy that proposed a state of affairs in which all machines must be destroyed because in their evolution they developed the ability to take over the functions of men.

In 1873 Butler began work on *The Way of All Flesh*, which was to occupy him all his life, but he was diffident of his powers as a novelist, and put the book aside to write *Life and Habit*, the first of the works of speculative biology in which he undertook to discredit the Darwinian theory of evolution. Butler was by no means inclined to reject the fact of evolution—on the contrary—but he was dismayed by the implications of Darwin's way of explaining how it came about. To say that evolution was determined by one process only, that of natural selection, the survival of the fittest, was, in Butler's view, to settle for mere mechanism as the ruling principle of life and to ignore the part played in biological existence, especially that of humans, by mind, intention, and will.

Butler was the less likely to win agreement for his own evolutionary theories because they were all frankly speculative and dialectical, based on avowedly subjective observation and not at all on scientific research. Science might be suffering persecution at the hands of the ecclesiastical spirit, as Huxley said it was, but science had established its own strict orthodoxy and had no wish to be disturbed in it. Butler did, of course, find a redoubtable disciple in Bernard Shaw, who gave entire credence to Butler's evolutionary ideas and embodied them in his enormous play, *Back to Methusaleh*. And although the tendency of scientific thought since Darwin's day does not actually confirm Butler's views, there are eminent scientists who find point in them. Butler followed *Life and Habit* with *Evolution, Old and New* (1879), *Unconscious Memory* (1880), and *Luck, or Cunning, as a Main Means of Organic Modification?* (1887), all of which were silently snubbed by the scientists.

It was about this time that he turned his ambitions to music, and in 1886 his *Narcissus: A Cantata in the Handelian Form* was performed. Shaw, who is to be relied on in his judgment of music, took but a dim view of this composition, and believed it to be, together with Butler's insistence that Handel was immeasurably greater than any other musician who ever composed, including Bach, one of the "dilettante weaknesses" that characterized the latter half of Butler's life. Shaw's crossness with Butler's later concerns is not unjustified. His translations of the *Iliad* and the *Odyssey* into colloquial English prose (1898, 1900) are pleasant; *The Authoress of the Odyssey* (1897), which argues seriously the thesis proposed by its title, carries some weight; but none of these works, let alone *Shakespeare's Sonnets Reconsidered* (1899) which, though not wholly without point, is chiefly crotchety, is of commanding interest. But in 1901 Butler published the last work of his lifetime, *Erewhon Revisited*, in which the narrator-protagonist of *Erewhon* returns to find that he has become the divine person of a new religion. It is a first-rate satire, and the deep feeling with which on occasion it is strangely touched is most moving. Butler died a year after its publication.

From Erewhon [1]

Birth Formulae

I heard what follows not from Arowhena,[2] but from Mr. Nosnibor [3] and some of the gentlemen who occasionally dined at the house; they told me that the Erewhonians believe in pre-existence; and not only this (of which I will write more fully in the next chapter), but they believe that it is of their own free act and deed in a previous state that they come to be born into this world at all. They hold that the unborn are perpetually plaguing and tormenting the married of both sexes, fluttering about them incessantly, and giving them no peace either of mind or body until they have consented to take them under their protection. If this were not so (this at least is what they urge), it would be a monstrous freedom for one man to take with another, to say that he should undergo the chances and changes of this mortal life without any option in the matter. No man would have any right to get married at all, inasmuch as he can never tell what frightful misery his doing so may entail forcibly upon a being who cannot be unhappy as long as he does not exist. They feel this so strongly that they are resolved to shift the blame on to other shoulders; and have fashioned a long mythology as to the world in which the unborn people live, and what they do, and the arts and machinations to which they have recourse in order to get themselves into our own world. But of this more anon; what I would relate here is their manner of dealing with those who do come.

It is a distinguishing peculiarity of the Erewhonians that when they profess themselves to be quite certain about any matter, and avow it as a base on which they are to build a system of practice, they seldom quite believe in it.[4] If they smell a rat about the precincts of a cherished institution, they will always stop their noses to it if they can.

This is what most of them did in this matter of the unborn, for I cannot (and never could) think that they seriously believed in their mythology concerning pre-existence; they did and they did not; they did not know themselves what they believed; all they did know was that it was a disease not to believe as they did. The only thing of which they were quite sure was that it was the

1. Anagram of "nowhere." The following selections are Chaps. 18 and 19.
2. Arowhena is the Erewhonian young woman with whom the traveler falls in love; she instructs him in the customs and beliefs of her people.
3. The father of Arowhena. His name, which is Robinson spelled backward, was chosen to suggest that he is a "typical" respectable Erewhonian.
4. Butler is commenting, of course, on the state of religious belief in 19th-century England.

pestering of the unborn which caused them to be brought into this world, and that they would not have been here if they would have only let peaceable people alone.

It would be hard to disprove this position, and they might have a good case if they would only leave it as it stands. But this they will not do; they must have assurance doubly sure; they must have the written word of the child itself as soon as it is born, giving the parents indemnity from all responsibility on the score of its birth, and asserting its own pre-existence. They have therefore devised something which they call a birth formula—a document which varies in words according to the caution of parents, but is much the same practically in all cases; for it has been the business of the Erewhonian lawyers during many ages to exercise their skill in perfecting it and providing for every contingency.

These formulae are printed on common paper at a moderate cost for the poor; but the rich have them written on parchment and handsomely bound, so that the getting up of a person's birth formula is a test of his social position. They commence by setting forth, That whereas A. B.[5] was a member of the kingdom of the unborn, where he was well provided for in every way, and had no cause of discontent, etc., etc., he did of his own wanton depravity and restlessness conceive a desire to enter into this present world; that thereon having taken the necessary steps as set forth in laws of the unborn kingdom, he did with malice aforethought set himself to plague and pester two unfortunate people who had never wronged him, and who were quite contented and happy until he conceived this base design against their peace; for which wrong he now humbly entreats their pardon.

He acknowledges that he is responsible for all physical blemishes and deficiencies which may render him answerable to the laws of his country; that his parents have nothing whatever to do with any of these things; and that they have a right to kill him at once if they be so minded, though he entreats them to show their marvellous goodness and clemency by sparing his life. If they will do this, he promises to be their most obedient and abject creature during his earlier years, and indeed all his life, unless they should see fit in their abundant generosity to remit some portion of his service hereafter. And so the formula continues, going sometimes into very minute details, according to the fancies of family lawyers, who will not make it any shorter than they can help.

The deed being thus prepared, on the third or fourth day after the birth of the child, or as they call it, the 'final importunity,' the friends gather together, and there is a feast held, where they are all very melancholy—as a general rule, I believe, quite truly so—and make presents to the father and mother of the child in order to console them for the injury which has just been done them by the unborn.

By-and-by the child himself is brought down by his nurse, and the company begin to rail upon him, upbraiding him for his impertinence, and asking him what amends he proposes to make for the wrong that he has committed, and how he can look for care and nourishment from those who have perhaps already

5. The form used in framing legal documents to indicate that an actual name is to be supplied.

1. Tennyson in 1857; the photograph by Lewis Carroll. *The Granger Collection.*

2. Tennyson in 1880. *The Granger Collection.*

3. Browning at forty-three, by Dante Gabriel Rossetti (1828–82). The inscription reads "October 1855." *The Granger Collection.*

4. Browning, c. 1880. *The Granger Collection.*

5. Matthew Arnold.
The Granger Collection.

6. John Henry Cardinal Newman.
The Granger Collection.

I

II

7. *Past and Present,* by Augustus Egg, R.A. (1816–63). This sequence of three paintings, completed in 1858, deals with the highly sentimentalized Victorian theme of the fallen woman, here shown in a bourgeois version of the more dynamic and mythologically powerful Rossettian prostitute. The adulteress is an upper middle-class mother; her infidelity is discovered in picture **I**, while her daughters are only distracted from building their house of cards (such is the instability of the family when threatened by sexual passion) by their mother's collapse. The paintings on the wall are of the Expulsion from Eden and of a shipwreck. Pictures **II** and **III** (now a decade later, in the present) are supposed to be simultaneous (note the configuration of moon and cloud), showing the motherless and miserable girls and, elsewhere in London by a bridge near the Strand, the fallen mother as she clutches to her unwarming bosom a young child, another mark of her infamy. The "reading" of the narrative and emblems in pictures like this and Holman Hunt's *The Awakened Conscience* was frequently aided, in exhibitions, by descriptive catalogues and commentary. *The Tate Gallery,* London.

III

8. The painting by Henry Wallis (1830–1916) usually known as *The Death of Chatterton* (1856) enshrines in a typical literary canvas of its age the Romantic myth of the Dead Young Poet. Wallis painted it in the attic in which Thomas Chatterton actually poisoned himself. Incidentally, Wallis's model was his friend George Meredith, with whose wife (Thomas Love Peacock's daughter) the painter ran off two years later—an event occasioning some of the sonnets of Meredith's *Modern Love* (which are rather better than Wallis's painting). *The Tate Gallery.*

VICTORIAN NARRATIVE PAINTING

9. The young Queen Victoria
in her Coronation Robes,
by Sir George Hayter (1792–1871).
National Portrait Gallery, London.

10. The Albert Memorial, in Kensington Gardens, a perfect example of High Victorian neo-Gothic, designed by Sir George Gilbert Scott (1811–78) and completed in 1872, eleven years after the Prince Consort's death. Surrounding the central portrait are allegorical figures of Agriculture, Commerce, and Engineering, the four continents, and a frieze representing the greatest poets, artists, and musicians of the world. The only inscription is the word "Albert." *British Tourist Authority.*

11. *The Derby Day. The Tate Gallery.*

12. *The Railway Station. Royal Holloway College, University of London.*

OFFICIAL VICTORIAN TASTE

These two celebrated Academy pictures by William Powell Frith, R.A. (1819–1909), represent the attitude toward narrative detail dear to the middle-class aesthetic. *The Derby Day* was exhibited in 1858, and *The Railway Station,* in 1862. Frith boasted that his painting was free of "Pre-Raphaelite taint."

13. The Houses of Parliament (1836–67), by Sir Charles Barry (1795–1860) and A. W. N. Pugin (1812–52). *BOAC.*

14. Eaton Hall, Cheshire (1867–80), brings to a private house the self-assured grossness of a High Victorian railway station. *Country Life*, London.

15. The Crystal Palace (1851), designed by Sir Joseph Paxton (1803–65). The Great Exhibition Building in Hyde Park was the largest building erected of cast iron and glass up to that time. It was thematic of the Great Exhibition of 1851. *The Museum of Modern Art, New York.*

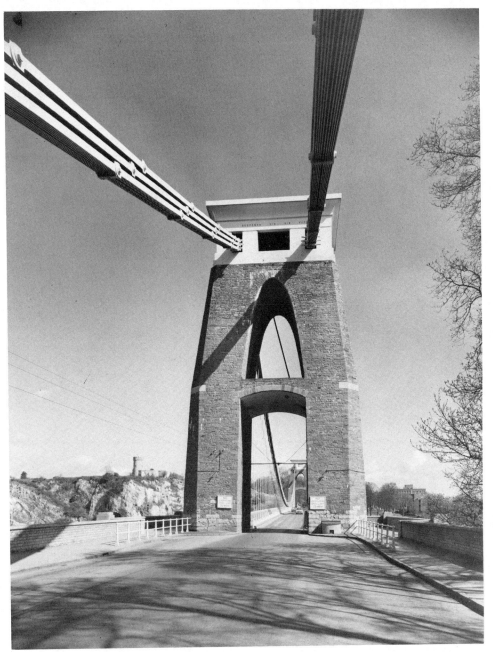

16. The Clifton Suspension Bridge, Bristol (1836), by Isambard Kingdom Brunel (1806–59), represents the kind of Victorian industrial designing whose beauty remains bright to even the most historically intolerant modern eye. *A. F. Kersting.*

17. *Dante Gabriel Rossetti,* a portrait by William Holman Hunt (1827–1910), done around the time in 1848 when Rossetti, Hunt, John Everett Millais, and others had formed the Pre-Raphaelite Brotherhood. The movement brought to illustrative painting not so much the influence of Italian Renaissance art as the attempted transcription of the visionary light and detail in the poetry of Keats, Tennyson, and Rossetti himself. Ford Madox Brown was affiliated with the brotherhood, though never a member, and Sir Edward Coley Burne-Jones and William Morris were more closely associated with Rossetti after the 1850's, by which time the group had dissolved. *City Art Gallery,* Manchester.

18. *Mariana.*   She only said, 'My life is dreary,
He cometh not,' she said;
She said, 'I am aweary, aweary,
I would that I were dead.'

Sir John Everett Millais's (1829–96) painting of Tennyson's protagonist (1851) concentrates on her wasting sexuality rather than on the more complex imagery of the poem's later stanzas (see "Mariana in the Moated Grange." *Courtesy Lord Sherfield (Photo Sydney W. Newberry).*

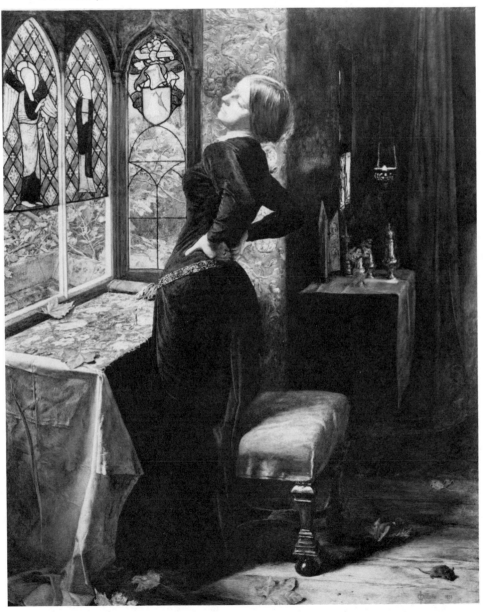

19. Dante Gabriel Rossetti, *Found* (begun 1853, never completed). This painting used as models the painter Ford Madox Brown and Fanny Cornforth, a former prostitute who was Rossetti's mistress and whom he frequently depicted. The anecdote represents a young cattle drover coming to a market town and finding his youthful love literally, and figuratively, a "fallen" woman. Rossetti wrote the following sonnet to accompany the painting:

'There is a budding morrow in midnight' —
So sang our Keats, our English nightingale.
And here, as lamps across the bridge turn pale
In London's smokeless resurrection-light
Dark breaks to dawn. But o'er the deadly blight
Of love deflowered and sorrow of none avail
Which makes this man gasp and this woman quail,
Can day from darkness ever again take flight?
Ah! gave not these two hearts their mutual pledge,
Under one mantle sheltered 'neath the hedge
In gloaming courtship? And O God! today
He only knows he holds her—but what part
Can life now take? She cries in her locked heart,
'Leave me—I do not know you—go away!'

The Samuel and Mary R. Bancroft Collection, Delaware Art Museum, Wilmington.

20. John Ruskin, a portrait by Sir John Everett Millais, finished in 1854. *Christie, Manson, and Woods,* London.

21. *The Last of England.* Ford Madox Brown (1821–93), one of the first of the Pre-Raphaelites, painted this contrary vision of Victorian England in 1855. The couple staring at the receding shore are portraits of Brown and his wife; the subject of emigration was suggested by the departure of the sculptor Thomas Woolner to Australia three years earlier. Though forced (as in the words of Brown's sonnet accompanying the picture) to listen to

> Low ribaldry from sots, and share rough cheer
> With rudely-nurtur'd men, . . .

nevertheless

> She grips his listless hand and clasps her child,
> Through rainbow tears she sees a sunnier gleam,
> She cannot see a void where he will be.

Birmingham (England) *Museum and Art Gallery.*

22. *Work,* Ford Madox Brown's vision of Victorian social consciousness (1852–68), representing a view halfway up Heath Street, in Hampstead, London, where excavations force a diversion of traffic. The manual laborers in the central group are, in Brown's words, "the outward and visible type of Work"; on the right stand two of the "brain workers, who, seeming to be idle, work, and are the cause of well-ordained work and happiness in others—sages, such as in ancient Greece published their opinions in the market square." These are, in fact, portraits: of Carlyle (the hatted one), whose "Produce! Produce!" underlies many of the picture's ideas, and the Rev. Frederick Denison Maurice (1803–72), founder of a working men's college, where Ruskin and his followers taught drawing. Brown's own sonnet on the painting reflects this higher Victorian view of work as sublimated eros:

> Work, which beads the brow and tans the flesh
> Of lusty manhood, casting out its devils,
> By whose weird art transmuting poor man's evils
> Their bed seems down, their one dish ever fresh.

City Art Gallery, Manchester.

23. *Autumn Leaves* (dated 1856), by Sir John Everett Millais. The painting's narrative elements, such as the range of human meditative responses to natural symbols indicated in the children's various expressions, are triumphantly fulfilled in the imagery of the trees receding into the twilight, dwindling in perspective like past moments. Millais was quoted as having remarked of the odor of burning leaves, "To me nothing brings back sweeter memories of days that are gone; it is the incense offered by departing summer to the sky . . .". The scene is a twilit one. *City Art Gallery,* Manchester.

24. *The Awakened Conscience,* by William Holman Hunt (1827–1910); exhibited 1854. This moment catches the response of the "kept" woman to an old song: the music on the piano is Thomas Moore's "Oft, in the Stilly Night" in which

> Fond Memory brings the light
> Of other days around me.

She is recalling her home and her own other purer days and, in the painter's own words, "breaking away from her gilded cage with a startled holy resolve, while her shallow companion still sings on, ignorantly intensifying her repentant purpose." Hunt wrote that he had been thinking of a text from Proverbs 25:20: "As he that taketh away a garment in cold weather, so is he that singeth songs to a heavy heart." The picture is crowded with emblematic details: the cat under the table toying with its captured bird, the glove on the floor "flung aside" (like a cast-off mistress), the music on the floor (it is a setting of Tennyson's recent "Tears, Idle Tears"; as Ruskin commented, even "the very hem of the poor girl's dress . . . has a story in it, if we think how soon its pure whiteness may be soiled with dust and rain, her outcast feet failing in the street." *Birmingham Museum and Art Gallery.*

25. Rossetti's *Lady Lilith* (1864):

> And subtly of herself contemplative,
> Draws men to watch the bright web she can weave,
> Till heart and body and life are in its hold.

The text is from *The House of Life,* Sonnet LXXVIII; the model was Fanny Cornforth. *The Samuel and Mary R. Bancroft Collection, Delaware Art Museum.*

26. *Astarte Syriaca*, Rossetti's 1877 painting of Jane (Mrs. William) Morris as the primal goddess. His own sonnet expounds her identity:

Mystery: lo! between the sun and moon
Astarte of the Syrians: Venus Queen
Ere Aphrodite was. In silver sheen
Her twofold girdle clasps the infinite boon
Of bliss whereof the heaven and earth commune:
And from her neck's inclining flower-stem lean
Love-freighted lips and absolute eyes that wean
The pulse of hearts to the spheres' dominant tune.

Torch-bearing, her sweet ministers compel
All thrones of light beyond the sky and sea
The witnesses of Beauty's face to be:
That face, of Love's all-penetrating spell
Amulet, talisman, and oracle,—
Betwixt the sun and moon a mystery.

City Art Gallery, Manchester.

"Around her, lovers, newly
"Mid deathless love's a
Spake evermore among
Their rapturous new n

First Sketch for background of picture"
1876

27. *The Blessed Damozel:* a preliminary sketch for the background of Rossetti's own illustrative painting (1876), embellishing the lines:

> Around her, lovers, newly met
> 'Mid deathless love's acclaims,
> Spoke evermore among themselves
> Their rapturous new names.

See "The Blessed Damozel," ll. 37–40, rather different in the published text. *Fogg Art Museum, Harvard University, Grenville L. Winthrop Bequest.*

28. *The Golden Stairs* (1880), by Sir Edward Coley Burne-Jones (1833–98) who, influenced by Rossetti, Morris, and Ruskin, continued Pre-Raphaelite traditions later into the century, both in strictly illustrative painting and graphics, and in invented mythologies such as are embodied in the present picture, which provides its own text. The almost spooky repetition of facial type is a convention with him, and that face itself, as well as the treatment of drapery, comes from Rossetti. *The Tate Gallery.*

29. One of his famous floral wallpapers. *A. F. Kersting.*

30. An opened spread from the so-called Kelmscott Chaucer (1896), Morris's triumph of neo-medieval book production. The woodcuts were by Burne-Jones. *Spencer Collection, New York Public Library.*

31. Thomas Carlyle, by James McNeill Whistler (1834–1903); The American expatriate painter's study, characteristically entitled *Arrangement in Grey and Black No. 2 (No. 1 was the famous portrait of the artist's mother)*, was completed in 1873. *Glasgow Art Gallery and Museum.*

32. *The Lady of Shalott.* Holman Hunt worked on this—one of two versions of his illustrative painting of Tennyson's poem—between 1890 and 1905, completing it a half-century after he had helped to found the Pre-Raphaelite Brotherhood. *City Art Gallery,* Manchester.

33. Illustration by Aubrey Beardsley (1872–92) of the climactic moment in Oscar Wilde's *Salome* (1894). Here the heroine kisses the severed head of John the Baptist.

34. Aubrey Beardsley's own bookplate.

35. Walter Pater.
The Granger Collection.

36. Gerard Manley Hopkins.
The Granger Collection.

been injured by the unborn on some ten or twelve occasions; for they say of people with large families, that they have suffered terrible injuries from the unborn; till at last, when this has been carried far enough, some one suggests the formula, which is brought out and solemnly read to the child by the family straightener.[6] This gentleman is always invited on these occasions, for the very fact of intrusion into a peaceful family shows a depravity on the part of the child which requires his professional services.

On being teased by the reading and tweaked by the nurse, the child will commonly begin to cry, which is reckoned a good sign, as showing a consciousness of guilt. He is thereon asked, Does he assent to the formula? on which, as he still continues crying and can obviously make no answer, some one of the friends comes forward and undertakes to sign the document on his behalf, feeling sure (so he says) that the child would do it if he only knew how, and that he will release the present signer from his engagement on arriving at maturity. The friend then inscribes the signature of the child at the foot of the parchment, which is held to bind the child as much as though he had signed it himself.

Even this, however, does not fully content them, for they feel a little uneasy until they have got the child's own signature after all. So when he is about fourteen, these good people partly bribe him by promises of greater liberty and good things, and partly intimidate him through their great power of making themselves actively unpleasant to him, so that though there is a show of freedom made, there is really none; they also use the offices of the teachers in the Colleges of Unreason,[7] till at last, in one way or another, they take very good care that he shall sign the paper by which he professes to have been a free agent in coming into the world, and to take all the responsibility of having done so on to his own shoulders. And yet, though this document is obviously the most important which anyone can sign in his whole life, they will have him do so at an age when neither they nor the law will for many a year allow anyone else to bind him to the smallest obligation, no matter how righteously he may owe it, because they hold him too young to know what he is about, and do not consider it fair that he should commit himself to anything that may prejudice him in after years.

I own that all this seemed rather hard, and not of a piece with the many admirable institutions existing among them. I once ventured to say a part of what I thought about it to one of the Professors of Unreason. I did it very tenderly, but his justification of the system was quite out of my comprehension. I remember asking him whether he did not think it would do harm to a lad's principles, by weakening his sense of the sanctity of his word and of truth generally, that he should be led into entering upon a solemn declaration as to the truth of things about which all that he can certainly know is that he knows

6. Among the Erewhonians physical illness is considered to be a crime; it brings severe punishment and disgrace. But moral lapses are dealt with as indispositions over which the "patient" has no control. The persons who are trained to cure those who suffer from immorality are called straighteners.
7. Under this name Butler represents the universities of Oxford and Cambridge and the part they play in rationalizing the customs and unexamined assumptions of respectable English society.

nothing—whether, in fact, the teachers who so led him, or who taught anything as a certainty of which they were themselves uncertain, were not earning their living by impairing the truth-sense of their pupils (a delicate organization mostly), and by vitiating one of their most sacred instincts.

The Professor, who was a delightful person, seemed greatly surprised at the view which I took, but it had no influence with him whatsoever. No one, he answered, expected that the boy either would or could know all that he said he knew; but the world was full of compromises; and there was hardly any affirmation which would bear being interpreted literally. Human language was too gross a vehicle of thought—thought being incapable of absolute translation. He added, that as there can be no translation from one language into another which shall not scant the meaning somewhat, or enlarge upon it, so there is no language which can render thought without a jarring and a harshness somewhere—and so forth; all of which seemed to come to this in the end, that it was the custom of the country, and that the Erewhonians were a conservative people; that the boy would have to begin compromising sooner or later, and this was part of his education in the art. It was perhaps to be regretted that compromise should be as necessary as it was; still it was necessary, and the sooner the boy got to understand it the better for himself. But they never tell this to the boy.

From the book of their mythology about the unborn I made the extracts which will form the following chapter.

The World of the Unborn [8]

Having waded through many chapters . . . I came at last to the unborn themselves, and found that they were held to be souls pure and simple, having no actual bodies, but living in a sort of gaseous yet more or less anthropomorphic existence, like that of a ghost; they have thus neither flesh nor blood nor warmth. Nevertheless they are supposed to have local habitations and cities wherein they dwell, though these are as unsubstantial as their inhabitants; they are even thought to eat and drink some thin ambrosial sustenance, and generally to be capable of doing whatever mankind can do, only after a visionary ghostly fashion as in a dream. On the other hand, as long as they remain where they are they never die—the only form of death in the unborn world being the leaving it for our own. They are believed to be extremely numerous, far more so than mankind. They arrive from unknown planets, full grown, in large batches at a time; but they can only leave the unborn world by taking the steps necessary for their arrival here—which is, in fact, by suicide.

They ought to be an exceedingly happy people, for they have no extremes of good or ill fortune; never marrying, but living in a state much like that fabled by the poets as the primitive condition of mankind. In spite of this, however, they are incessantly complaining; they know that we in this world have bodies, and indeed they know everything else about us, for they move among us whithersoever they will, and can read our thoughts, as well as survey our actions at pleasure. One would think that this should be enough for them;

8. Butler's conception of the world of the unborn owes much to Plato's myth of human pre-existence as narrated in the *Republic*.

and most of them are indeed alive to the desperate risk which they will run by indulging themselves in that body with 'sensible warm motion' which they so much desire; nevertheless, there are some to whom the *ennui* of a disembodied existence is so intolerable that they will venture anything for a change; so they resolve to quit. The conditions which they must accept are so uncertain, that none but the most foolish of the unborn will consent to them; and it is from these, and these only, that our own ranks are recruited.

When they have finally made up their minds to leave, they must go before the magistrate of the nearest town, and sign an affidavit of their desire to quit their then existence. On their having done this, the magistrate reads them the conditions which they must accept, and which are so long that I can only extract some of the principal points, which are mainly the following:—

First, they must take a potion which will destroy their memory and a sense of identity; they must go into the world helpless, and without a will of their own; they must draw lots for their dispositions before they go, and take them, such as they are, for better or worse—neither are they to be allowed any choice in the matter of the body which they so much desire; they are simply allotted by chance, and without appeal, to two people whom it is their business to find and pester until they adopt them. Who these are to be, whether rich or poor, kind or unkind, healthy or diseased, there is no knowing; they have, in fact, to entrust themselves for many years to the care of those for whose good constitution and good sense they have no sort of guarantee.

It is curious to read the lectures which the wiser heads give to those who are meditating a change. They talk with them as we talk with a spendthrift, and with about as much success.

'To be born,' they say, 'is a felony—it is a capital crime, for which sentence may be executed at any moment after the commission of the offence. You may perhaps happen to live for some seventy or eighty years, but what is that, compared with the eternity you now enjoy? And even though the sentence were commuted, and you were allowed to live on for ever, you would in time become so terribly weary of life that execution would be the greatest mercy to you.

'Consider the infinite risk; to be born of wicked parents and trained in vice! to be born of silly parents, and trained to unrealities! of parents who regard you as a sort of chattel or property, belonging more to them than to yourself! Again, you may draw utterly unsympathetic parents, who will never be able to understand you, and who will do their best to thwart you (as a hen when she has hatched a duckling), and then call you ungrateful because you do not love them; or, again, you may draw parents who look upon you as a thing to be cowed while it is still young, lest it should give them trouble hereafter by having wishes and feelings of its own.

'In later life, when you have been finally allowed to pass muster as a full member of the world, you will yourself become liable to the pesterings of the unborn—and a very happy life you may be led in consequence! For we solicit so strongly that a few only—nor these the best—can refuse us; and yet not to refuse is much the same as going into partnership with half a dozen different people about whom one can know absolutely nothing beforehand—not even whether one is going into partnership with men or women, nor with how many of either. Delude not yourself with thinking that you will be wiser than your parents. You may be an age in advance of those whom you have pestered, but unless you are one of the great ones you will still be an age behind those who will in their turn pester you.

'Imagine what it must be to have an unborn quartered upon you, who is of an entirely different temperament and disposition to your own; nay, half a dozen such, who will not love you though you have stinted yourself in a thousand ways to provide for their comfort and well-being,—who will forget all your self-sacrifice, and of whom you may never be sure that they are not bearing a grudge against you for errors of judgment into which you may have fallen, though you had hoped that such had been long since atoned for. Ingratitude such as this is not uncommon, yet fancy what it must be to bear! It is hard upon the duckling to have been hatched by a hen, but is it not also hard upon the hen to have hatched the duckling?

'Consider it again, we pray you, not for our sake but for your own. Your initial character you must draw by lot; but whatever it is, it can only come to a tolerably successful development after long training; remember that over that training you will have no control. It is possible, and even probable, that whatever you may get in after life which is of real pleasure and service to you, will have to be won in spite of, rather than by the help of, those whom you are now about to pester, and that you will only win your freedom after years of a painful struggle in which it will be hard to say whether you have suffered most injury, or inflicted it.

'Remember also, that if you go into the world you will have free will; that you will be obliged to have it; that there is no escaping it; that you will be fettered to it during your whole life, and must on every occasion do that which on the whole seems best to you at any given time, no matter whether you are right or wrong in choosing it. Your mind will be a balance for considerations, and your action will go with the heavier scale. How it shall fall will depend upon the kind of scales which you may have drawn at birth, the bias which they will have obtained by use, and the weight of the immediate considerations. If the scales were good to start with, and if they have not been outrageously tampered with in childhood, and if the combinations into which you enter are average ones, you may come off well; but there are too many "ifs" in this, and with the failure of any one of them your misery is assured. Reflect on this, and remember that should the ill come upon you, you will have yourself to thank, for it is your own choice to be born, and there is no compulsion in the matter.

'Not that we deny the existence of pleasures among mankind; there is a certain show of sundry phases of contentment which may even amount to very considerable happiness; but mark how they are distributed over a man's life, belonging, all the keenest of them, to the fore part, and few indeed to the after. Can there be any pleasure worth purchasing with the miseries of a decrepit age? If you are good, strong, and handsome, you have a fine fortune indeed at twenty, but how much of it will be left at sixty? For you must live on your capital; there is no investing your powers so that you may get a small annuity of life for ever; you must eat up your principal bit by bit, and be tortured by seeing it grow continually smaller and smaller, even though you happen to escape being rudely robbed of it by crime or casualty.

'Remember, too, that there never yet was a man of forty who would not come back into the world of the unborn if he could do so with decency and honour. Being in the world he will as a general rule stay till he is forced to go; but do you think that he would consent to be born again, and re-live his life, if he had the offer of doing so? Do not think it. If he could so alter the past as that he should never have come into being at all, do you not think that he would do it very gladly?

'What was it that one of their own poets meant, if it was not this, when he cried out upon the day in which he was born, and the night in which it was said there is a man child conceived? "For now," he says, "I should have lain still and been quiet, I should have slept; then had I been at rest with kings and counsellors of the earth, which built desolate places for themselves; or which princes that had gold, who filled their houses with silver; or as an hidden untimely birth, I had not been; as infants which never saw light. There the wicked cease from troubling, and there the weary are at rest." Be very sure that the guilt of being born carries this punishment at times to all men; but how can they ask for pity, or complain of any mischief that may befall them, having entered open-eyed into the snare?

'One word more and we have done. If any faint remembrance, as of a dream, flit in some puzzled moment across your brain, and you shall feel that the potion which is to be given you shall not have done its work, and the memory of this existence which you are leaving endeavours vainly to return; we say in such a moment, when you clutch at the dream but it eludes your grasp, and you watch it, as Orpheus watched Eurydice, gliding back again into the twilight kingdom, fly—fly—if you can remember the advice—to the haven of your present and immediate duty, taking shelter incessantly in the work which you have in hand. This much you may perhaps recall; and this, if you will imprint it deeply upon your every faculty, will be most likely to bring you safely and honourably home through the trials that are before you.' 9

This is the fashion in which they reason with those who would be for leaving them, but it is seldom that they do much good, for none but the unquiet and unreasonable ever think of being born, and those who are foolish enough to think of it are generally foolish enough to do it. Finding, therefore, that they can do no more, the friends follow weeping to the court-house of the chief magistrate, where the one who wishes to be born declares solemnly and openly that he accepts the conditions attached to his decision. On this he is presented with a potion, which immediately destroys his memory and sense of identity, and dissipates the thin gaseous tenement which he has inhabited; he becomes a bare vital principle, not to be perceived by human senses, nor to be by any chemical test appreciated. He has but one instinct, which is that he is to go to such and such a place, where he will find two persons whom he is to importune till they consent to undertake him; but whether he is to find these persons among the race of Chowbok 10 or the Erewhonians themselves is not for him to choose.

1863–65, 1870–71   1872

9. "The myth above alluded to exists in Erewhon with changed names, and considerable modification. I have taken the liberty of referring to the story as familiar to ourselves." (Butler)
10. Chowbok is the New Zealand aborigine who tells the traveler of the existence of Erewhon and guides him to it.

OSCAR WILDE
1854–1900

Oscar Wilde first came into public view as a sort of intellectual mountebank and buffoon, the brilliant publicity agent for his own charm and talent and for certain ideas about art and life calculated to affront, confound, and enthrall the respectable. Then he flamed across the literary firmament with works which no one was disposed to call great but which all the world took pleasure in. At the height of his triumph —three of his plays were running in London at the time—disaster befell him: he was indicted for homosexual practices, found guilty, and sentenced to two years at hard labor; he emerged from prison a broken man, bereft of position, hope, and talent. He died solitary and destitute in a shabby hotel in Paris.

Inevitably such a career puts difficulties in the way of judging the work of the man who pursued it. But these have diminished with the passing of the years—less and less do the extravagances of Wilde's self-dramatization and the pathos of what may fairly be called his martyrdom obscure his quite momentous significance as a writer.

Wilde was born in Dublin in 1854 of parents scarcely less flamboyant than he was to become. His father was Sir William Wilde, a successful physician specializing in ophthalmology. Of diminutive stature, almost a dwarf, Sir William was notorious for his personal untidiness, even uncleanliness—a Dublin quip explained the blackness of his fingernails by his having scratched himself—and for his many love affairs, one of which ended in lawsuit and tremendous scandal. Lady Wilde was as strikingly large for a woman as her husband was small for a man. As a young girl she had been handsome, something of a revolutionary, and, under the name of "Speranza," had published a volume of poems. In her later years she was clever, erudite, and eccentric, and her *salon* in Dublin had a kind of tatty fame.

At the age of ten Oscar—his full name was Oscar Fingal O'Flahertie Wills Wilde— entered Portora Royal School (the closest approximation in Ireland to an English public school), after which he spent three years at Trinity College, Dublin, before winning a scholarship to Magdalen College, Oxford, in 1874. In his schooldays he had discovered a talent for blithe insolence which gained him attention, some hostility, and a good deal of admiration, and this mode of wit, which was to be his characteristic style in maturity, he cultivated to good effect at Oxford. He dressed flamboyantly and collected porcelain; and when a band of hearty college mates, outraged by his affectations, undertook to break up his rooms, he threw one of their number down the stairs and invited them to a brandy party. At the university his intense admiration went to two men, John Ruskin, who was lecturing as Slade Professor of Art, and Walter Pater. So great was his reverence for Ruskin that he joined the undergraduate work-party Ruskin had organized to build a road between two villages as a way of instructing upper-class young men in the dignity of labor. It was Pater, however, who was to have both the more immediate and the more permanent effect upon Wilde, that "strange influence" on his life of which Wilde spoke near his life's end. (See above, Headnote to Walter Pater.)

In 1875 Wilde traveled in Italy with John Mahaffy, his former teacher at Trinity College, a distinguished classical scholar, and in 1877, went with the same companion on a tour of Greece which confirmed him in his growing preference for Greek as against medieval culture; the spirit of Greece, he was often to say, was essentially the modern spirit. Wilde's powers as a classicist were very considerable; despite the dandaical affectations that marked his life as an undergraduate, he took his degree in 1878 with the highest honors. In the year of his graduation he won the Newdigate Prize for his poem—it is not very good—*Ravenna.*

In 1879 Wilde went to live in London. Within two years he was so much a figure in the public eye that he was invited on a lecture tour of the United States which lasted a full year. The eminence and authority to which he attained before the age of twenty-seven were not the consequence of any literary achievement—his *Poems,* published in 1881, were not highly regarded—but rather of the nature of English upper-class society at the time and Wilde's brilliant manipulation of it. The segment of the aristocracy that lived the life of fashion made a cohesive group whose goings-on as reported in the press were of consummate interest to the general public. Through friendships formed at Oxford, Wilde had entry to this society and entranced it by his wit and insolence and also, we may suppose, by his genuine sweetness of temper. To these new friends he carried the "aesthetic" doctrine, compounded of ideas derived from the Pre-Raphaelites, William Morris, and Pater, its substance being that the justification of life was the enjoyment of beauty rather than the performance of duty, that the highest beauty was to be found in art, which ought to manifest its power in all the accoutrements of material existence. The doctrine that Wilde preached had implications of a truly serious kind which a sympathetic reading of his work makes manifest, but at the time it was likely to be received as not much more than an elevated theory of interior decoration and dress. Yet even if it was no more than that, it spoke of a new age and a new kind of sensibility to people who were beginning to be receptive to the charm of the new—the excited response to Wilde may be thought of as the inauguration of a phase of culture in which art and theories about art had great authority and in which they bestowed a kind of social-spiritual prestige. Wilde's intellectual masters had habituated the public to the premises of the "aesthetic" doctrine, and now the middle classes hearkened eagerly to the reports which reached them of a new campaign in the crusade for beauty being waged by this curious young man. The gossip columns retailed his witty paradoxes; *Punch,* the humorous magazine that delighted and reassured the middle classes, caricatured him and his creed. In 1881 Gilbert and Sullivan produced *Patience; or, Bunthorne's Bride,* counting on everyone to recognize that Bunthorne in his velvet knee-breeches was Oscar Wilde giving instruction on how to go about being aesthetic.

> Though the Philistines may jostle, you will rank as an apostle in the high aesthetic line,
> If you walk down Piccadilly with a poppy or a lily in your medieval hand.

Wilde carried the aesthetic word to the farthest reaches of America, was inevitably mocked for his affectations of manner and dress but also was rather liked, and returned in 1883 not much the richer for his labors. In that year he married a beautiful, gentle, and quite unassuming young woman and established their domestic life in a house decorated according to the right principles; their first son was born in 1885, their second in 1886. Wilde was for a time enchanted by family life but inevitably it failed to hold him; inevitably it could not stand against his homosexuality and his impulse toward the raffish and the seamy.

Wilde's first notable achievement as a writer was his novel *The Picture of Dorian*

Gray (1890), which is based upon the ingenious idea of a portrait upon which the passing years work their ravages while the beautiful young man who is the subject of the picture remains to all appearances gloriously young; its salient intention is to celebrate the life that is devoted to the pleasures of the senses and of art, of a hedonistic program pertinaciously carried out in disregard of all the sanctions of morality and even of sentiment. The book, in which the homosexuality of the protagonist is patent though not explicit, created a scandal. Yet the conclusion of the novel is nothing if not moral and even grim in its disclosure of the ugliness, corruption, emptiness, and despair that lie beneath the surface of the mode of existence that has been made to seem so desirable. For all its faults of tone and style, The Picture of Dorian Gray is a significant and memorable work and perhaps in nothing so much as its Preface, which consists of a series of epigrams intended to shock by their insolence. The Preface is brief enough to be quoted entire:

> The artist is the creator of beautiful things.
> To reveal art and conceal the artist is art's aim.
> The critic is he who can translate into another manner or a new material his impression of beautiful things.
> The highest, as the lowest, form of criticism is a mode of autobiography.
> Those who find ugly meanings in beautiful things are corrupt without being charming. This is a fault.
> Those who find beautiful meanings in beautiful things are the cultivated. For these there is hope.
> They are the elect to whom beautiful things mean only Beauty.
> There is no such thing as a moral or an immoral book. Books are well written, or badly written. That is all.
> The nineteenth century dislike of Realism is the rage of Caliban seeing his own face in a glass.
> The nineteenth century dislike of Romanticism is the rage of Caliban not seeing his own face in a glass.
> The moral life of man forms part of the subject-matter of the artist, but the morality of art consists in the perfect use of an imperfect medium. No artist desires to prove anything. Even things that are true can be proved.
> No artist has ethical sympathies. An ethical sympathy in an artist is an unpardonable mannerism of style.
> No artist is ever morbid. The artist can express everything.
> Thought and language are to the artist instruments of an art.
> Vice and virtue are to the artist materials for an art.
> From the point of view of form, the type of all the arts is the art of the musician. From the point of view of feeling, the actor's craft is the type.
> All art is at once surface and symbol.
> Those who go beneath the surface do so at their peril.
> It is the spectator, and not life, that art really mirrors.
> Diversity of opinion about a work of art shows that the work is new, complex, and vital.
> When critics disagree the artist is in accord with himself.
> We can forgive a man for making a useful thing as long as he does not admire it. The only excuse for making a useless thing is that one admires it intensely.
> All art is quite useless.

The substance of this manifesto, which Wilde was to develop in his essays of the next few years, is scarcely unique with him; it represents a dominant tendency in the artistic theory of that time and of some decades to come, derived in essence from, among other French writers, Baudelaire and Flaubert, and perhaps ultimately from William Blake, or so he leads us to think when in the last paragraph of De Profundis, the long terrible letter he wrote in jail to review and explain his life, he says, "Time and space, succession and extension are merely accidental conditions of Thought. The Imagination can transcend them, and move in a free sphere of ideal existences. Things, also, are in their essence what we choose to make them. A thing *is,* according to the mode in which one looks at it. 'Where others,' says Blake, 'see but the Dawn coming over the hill, I see the sons of God shouting for joy.' " (*A Vision of the Last Judgment.* Wilde quotes from memory and approximately.) If we accept that Wilde in some part of his thought is in the line of Blake, we can the better understand the impulse that led this worshiper of artifice and elegance to follow *The Picture of Dorian Gray* with *The Soul of Man Under Socialism.*

In 1892 Wilde had his first great success in the theater with *Lady Windermere's Fan,* which was followed by *A Woman of No Importance* (produced in 1893) and *An Ideal Husband* (produced in 1895). Apart from the epigrammatic wit which often marks the dialogue, these plays are quite conventional and even in their own time might have seemed old-fashioned. Yet they hold the stage tenaciously, surprising generation after generation of theater-goers by their vitality. By the vitality of Wilde's last play, *The Importance of Being Earnest* (see below), no one is ever surprised, for it is by common consent one of the masterpieces of comedy.

In 1891 Wilde had formed his association with Lord Alfred Douglas, the young man who became the chief—although not the only—object of his affections. Douglas's father, from whom he and other members of his family were estranged, was the Marquess of Queensbury, a man eccentric to the verge of insanity who conceived it to be his paternal duty to rescue his son from Wilde's influence, and to this end carried on a campaign of social threat against Wilde. Wilde, after enduring this for some time, decided on the most imprudent course possible—he sued Queensbury for criminal libel. The trial went disastrously against him. Queensbury was acquitted, and on the ground of what the trial had brought to light Wilde was arrested. At the first of two trials the jury disagreed, but at the second found him guilty. He was given a maximum sentence of two years in prison at hard labor. Upon his release in 1897 he assumed the name Sebastian Melmoth—Sebastian to recall the martyr transfixed by arrows and also to commemorate the arrows printed on a convict's garb, Melmoth after the one famous diabolical hero of the novel *Melmoth the Wanderer* by his great-uncle, Charles Maturin—and departed for the Continent, where he spent the three desolate years yet remaining to him.

The Importance of Being Earnest

In the long debate that once went on over whether Oscar Wilde was a writer and cultural figure of high significance or nothing but a showy mediocrity, one of his works was likely to rise above the battle to be acknowledged as perfect of its kind. Likely but not certain: Bernard Shaw, in his day the wittiest of Wilde's admirers, was uncompromising in his dislike of *The Importance of Being Earnest,* giving it as his reason that the play did not "touch" him and that it lacked "reality"—it does not lead us to believe in its humanity, Shaw said, and therefore "we are thrown back on the daintiness and force of its wit."

Which of course is exactly where Wilde wanted us to be thrown. Humanity was not what he aspired to—"It is by a butterfly for butterflies," he said of the play, and presumably it is *about* butterflies too. And the prevailing opinion is that one of the best possible ways of passing a few hours is as a butterfly, concerned—if that can be the word—with the goings-on of butterflies.

The *Importance of Being Earnest* is often praised in superlative terms: the best comedy in the language. But then, because *As You Like It* and *A Midsummer Night's Dream* are also comedies, defining qualifications are introduced: the best comedy of manners, the best artificial comedy. But as soon as the category is made thus precise, two great rivals spring up to make their claim, *The Way of the World* and *The School for Scandal,* and if these are true examples of the comedy of manners or of artificial comedy, then we cannot be sure that *The Importance of Being Earnest* ought to be classed with them. And a recollection of Charles Lamb's great essay, "On the Artificial Comedy of the Last Century," strengthens that dubiety.

Some considerable part of the charm of Wilde's play is the same as that of Congreve's and Sheridan's, as Lamb defines it. Lamb's point about artificial comedy is that it provides a holiday from that particularly oppressive response to reality, moral judgment. It presents conduct which is habitually the object of moral judgment, but in such a way as to have us understand that moral judgment need not be exercised on it. It liberates us from the necessities of practicality—it invites us to *play.* Lamb makes the point that the part of Joseph Surface in *The School for Scandal* must be performed not so as to represent an evil person but so as to represent an actor playing the part of an evil person. Evil is present on the stage but our pleasure comes from seeing that it is not real evil, only histrionic evil. So in *The Way of the World* the style of the play absolves us of any need to take account of the low principles that are rampant in it. But in *The Importance of Being Earnest* there is not only no real evil but also no shadow of evil, and no principles of any kind, no more than there would be in a flotilla of butterflies. The comedies that Lamb discusses give us license to suspend the operation of moral judgment. *The Importance of Being Earnest* gives us license to believe that moral judgment has not yet been invented, and probably never will be; there is no need for it.

It is surely of significance that the most actual and intense emotions of the play are generated by cucumber sandwiches and muffins, by cake or no cake, by sugar in tea, or no sugar in tea—these persons who gobble and make such a fuss about what they gobble or do not gobble are still in the nursery. That lofty asperity which they speak to each other gives them pleasure because it mimics the lofty asperity of their nurses or governesses. When they speak of marrying and giving in marriage we know that for them there is no such thing, that they inhabit the paradise of childhood, which everyone in the audience has lost. The play is the perfect realization of innocence, of harmlessness. This is a world in which it is impossible to hurt or be hurt.

It is also, of course, the world of nonsense, that curious invention of the English of the nineteenth century, of Lewis Carroll and Edward Lear, and (though he is of a lower order) W. S. Gilbert, from whom Wilde borrowed to good effect: that baby in the suitcase is sheer Gilbert. One of the mysteries of art, perhaps as impenetrable as why tragedy gives pleasure, is why nonsense commands so fascinated an attention, and why, when it succeeds, it makes more than sense.

The Importance of Being Earnest

CHARACTERS

JOHN WORTHING, J.P.   LADY BRACKNELL
ALGERNON MONCRIEFF   HON. GWENDOLEN FAIRFAX
REV. CANON CHASUBLE, D.D.   CECILY CARDEW
MERRIMAN, *butler*   MISS PRISM, *governess*
LANE, *manservant*

THE SCENES OF THE PLAY

ACT I   Algernon Moncrieff's Flat in Half-Moon Street, W.
ACT II The Garden at the Manor House, Woolton.
ACT III Drawing-Room of the Manor House, Woolton.

Time—The Present.
Place—London.

ACT I

Scene—*Morning-room in* ALGERNON's *flat in Half-Moon Street.*[1] *The room is luxuriously and artistically furnished. The sound of a piano is heard in the adjoining room.*

LANE *is arranging afternoon tea on the table, and after the music has ceased,* ALGERNON *enters.*

ALGERNON   Did you hear what I was playing, Lane?

LANE   I didn't think it polite to listen, sir.

ALGERNON   I'm sorry for that, for your sake. I don't play accurately—anyone can play accurately—but I play with wonderful expression. As far as the piano is concerned, sentiment is my forte. I keep science for Life.

LANE   Yes, sir.

ALGERNON   And, speaking of the science of Life, have you got the cucumber sandwiches cut for Lady Bracknell?

LANE   Yes, sir.

[*Hands them on a salver*]

ALGERNON [*Inspects them, takes two, and sits down on the sofa*]   Oh! . . . by the way, Lane, I see from your book [2] that on Thursday night, when Lord Shoreman and Mr. Worthing were dining with me, eight bottles of champagne are entered as having been consumed.

LANE   Yes, sir; eight bottles and a pint.

ALGERNON   Why is it that at a bachelor's establishment the servants invariably drink the champagne? I ask merely for information.

LANE   I attribute it to the superior quality of the wine, sir. I have often

---

1. "Flat" is the usual word in England for what Americans call an "apartment." An "apartment house" is called a "block of flats." The degree of luxury of Algernon's flat is suggested by the fact that it has a "morning room," which implies that there is yet another and more formal general room, the drawing room. Half-Moon Street is in Mayfair, at that time the most fashionable part of London.
2. His cellar-book, in which he records the purchase and use of wine.

observed that in married households the champagne is rarely of a first-rate brand.

ALGERNON   Good Heavens! Is marriage so demoralizing as that?

LANE   I believe it *is* a very pleasant state, sir. I have had very little experience of it myself up to the present. I have only been married once. That was in consequence of a misunderstanding between myself and a young person.

ALGERNON   [*Languidly*]   I don't know that I am much interested in your family life, Lane.

LANE   No, sir; it is not a very interesting subject. I never think of it myself.

ALGERNON   Very natural, I am sure. That will do, Lane, thank you.

LANE   Thank you, sir. [LANE *goes out*]

ALGERNON   Lane's views on marriage seem somewhat lax. Really, if the lower orders don't set us a good example, what on earth is the use of them? They seem, as a class, to have absolutely no sense of moral responsibility.[3] [*Enter* LANE]

LANE   Mr. Ernest Worthing.
[*Enter* JACK. LANE *goes out.*]

ALGERNON   How are you, my dear Ernest? What brings you up to town?

JACK   Oh, pleasure, pleasure! What else should bring one anywhere? Eating as usual, I see, Algy!

ALGERNON   [*Stiffly*]   I believe it is customary in good society to take some slight refreshment at five o'clock. Where have you been since last Thursday?

JACK   [*Sitting down on the sofa*]   In the country.

ALGERNON   What on earth do you do there?

JACK   [*Pulling off his gloves*][4]   When one is in town one amuses oneself. When one is in the country one amuses other people. It is excessively boring.

ALGERNON   And who are the people you amuse?

JACK   [*Airily*]   Oh, neighbours, neighbours.

ALGERNON   Got nice neighbours in your part of Shropshire?

JACK   Perfectly horrid! Never speak to one of them.

ALGERNON   How immensely you must amuse them! [*Goes over and takes sandwich*] By the way, Shropshire is your county, is it not?

JACK   Eh? Shropshire? Yes, of course. Hallo! Why all these cups? Why cucumber sandwiches? Why such reckless extravagance in one so young? Who is coming to tea?

ALGERNON   Oh! merely Aunt Augusta and Gwendolen.

JACK   How perfectly delightful!

ALGERNON   Yes, that is all very well; but I am afraid Aunt Augusta won't quite approve of your being here.

JACK   May I ask why?

ALGERNON   My dear fellow, the way you flirt with Gwendolen is perfectly disgraceful. It is almost as bad as the way Gwendolen flirts with you.

3. Wilde touches on the frequently reiterated piety about the upper classes having a responsibility to serve as an example of conduct to the "lower orders."
4. At this time a gentleman wore gloves not for warmth—the season, as we learn from the garden setting of Act II, is summer—but for elegance and as a mark of his social position. Jack doesn't pull off his gloves until he is about to tackle the cucumber sandwiches.

JACK   I am in love with Gwendolen. I have come up to town expressly to propose to her.

ALGERNON   I thought you had come up for pleasure? . . . I call that business.

JACK   How utterly unromantic you are!

ALGERNON   I really don't see anything romantic in proposing. It is very romantic to be in love. But there is nothing romantic about a definite proposal. Why, one may be accepted. One usually is, I believe. Then the excitement is all over. The very essence of romance is uncertainty. If ever I get married, I'll certainly try to forget the fact.

JACK   I have no doubt about that, dear Algy. The Divorce Court was specially invented for people whose memories are so curiously constituted.

ALGERNON   Oh! there is no use speculating on that subject. Divorces are made in Heaven——[JACK *puts out his hand to take a sandwich.* ALGERNON *at once interferes.*] Please don't touch the cucumber sandwiches. They are ordered specially for Aunt Augusta. [*Takes one and eats it*]

JACK   Well, you have been eating them all the time.

ALGERNON   That is quite a different matter. She is my aunt. [*Takes plate from below*] Have some bread and butter. The bread and butter is for Gwendolen. Gwendolen is devoted to bread and butter.

JACK   [*Advancing to table and helping himself*]   And very good bread and butter it is too.

ALGERNON   Well, my dear fellow, you need not eat as if you were going to eat it all. You behave as if you were married to her already. You are not married to her already, and I don't think you ever will be.

JACK   Why on earth do you say that?

ALGERNON   Well, in the first place girls never marry the men they flirt with. Girls don't think it right.

JACK   Oh, that is nonsense!

ALGERNON   It isn't. It is a great truth. It accounts for the extraordinary number of bachelors that one sees all over the place. In the second place, I don't give my consent.

JACK   Your consent!

ALGERNON   My dear fellow, Gwendolen is my first cousin. And before I allow you to marry her, you will have to clear up the whole question of Cecily. [*Rings bell*]

JACK   Cecily! What on earth do you mean? What do you mean, Algy, by Cecily? I don't know anyone of the name of Cecily.
[*Enter* LANE]

ALGERNON   Bring me that cigarette case Mr. Worthing left in the smoking-room the last time he dined here.

LANE   Yes, sir. [LANE *goes out*]

JACK   Do you mean to say you have had my cigarette case all this time? I wish to goodness you had let me know. I have been writing frantic letters to Scotland Yard [5] about it. I was very nearly offering a large reward.

ALGERNON   Well, I wish you would offer one. I happen to be more than usually hard up.

5. The headquarters of the London metropolitan police.

JACK   There is no good offering a large reward now that the thing is found. [*Enter* LANE *with the cigarette case on a salver.* ALGERNON *takes it at once.* LANE *goes out.*]

ALGERNON   I think that is rather mean of you, Ernest, I must say. [*Opens case and examines it*] However, it makes no matter, for, now that I look at the inscription inside, I find that the thing isn't yours after all.

JACK   Of course it's mine. [*Moving to him*] You have seen me with it a hundred times, and you have no right whatsoever to read what is written inside. It is a very ungentlemanly thing to read a private cigarette case.

ALGERNON   Oh! it is absurd to have a hard-and-fast rule about what one should read and what one shouldn't. More than half of modern culture depends on what one shouldn't read.

JACK   I am quite aware of the fact, and I don't propose to discuss modern culture. It isn't the sort of thing one should talk of in private. I simply want my cigarette case back.

ALGERNON   Yes; but this isn't your cigarette case. This cigarette case is a present from someone of the name of Cecily, and you said you didn't know anyone of that name.

JACK   Well, if you want to know, Cecily happens to be my aunt.

ALGERNON   Your aunt!

JACK   Yes. Charming old lady she is, too. Lives at Tunbridge Wells.[6] Just give it back to me, Algy.

ALGERNON   [*Retreating to back of sofa*]   But why does she call herself little Cecily if she is your aunt and lives at Tunbridge Wells? [*Reading*] 'From little Cecily with her fondest love.'

JACK   [*Moving to sofa and kneeling upon it*]   My dear fellow, what on earth is there in that? Some aunts are tall, some aunts are not tall. That is a matter that surely an aunt may be allowed to decide for herself. You seem to think that every aunt should be exactly like your aunt! That is absurd! For Heaven's sake give me back my cigarette case. [*Follows* ALGERNON *round the room*]

ALGERNON   Yes. But why does your aunt call you her uncle? 'From little Cecily, with her fondest love to her dear Uncle Jack.' There is no objection, I admit, to an aunt being a small aunt, but why an aunt, no matter what her size may be, should call her own nephew her uncle, I can't quite make out. Besides, your name isn't Jack at all; it is Ernest.

JACK   It isn't Ernest; it's Jack.

ALGERNON   You have always told me it was Ernest. I have introduced you to everyone as Ernest. You answer to the name of Ernest. You look as if your name was Ernest. You are the most earnest looking person I ever saw in my life. It is perfectly absurd your saying that your name isn't Ernest. It's on your cards. Here is one of them [*Taking it from case*) 'Mr. Ernest Worthing, B 4, The Albany.'[7] I'll keep this as a proof

---

6. In the 18th century a gay and fashionable resort, at this time quiet and respectable.
7. The name of this large block of flats has, since the days of the Regency, carried great social prestige by reason of the elegance of its accommodations and the social distinction of its tenants.

your name is Ernest if ever you attempt to deny it to me, or to Gwendolen, or to anyone else. [*Puts the card in his pocket*]

JACK   Well, my name is Ernest in town and Jack in the country, and the cigarette case was given to me in the country.

ALGERNON   Yes, but that does not account for the fact that your small Aunt Cecily, who lives at Tunbridge Wells, calls you her dear uncle. Come, old boy, you had much better have the thing out at once.

JACK   My dear Algy, you talk exactly as if you were a dentist. It is very vulgar to talk like a dentist when one isn't a dentist. It produces a false impression.

ALGERNON   Well, that is exactly what dentists always do. Now, go on! Tell me the whole thing. I may mention that I have always suspected you of being a confirmed and secret Bunburyist; and I am quite sure of it now.

JACK   Bunburyist? What on earth do you mean by a Bunburyist?

ALGERNON   I'll reveal to you the meaning of that incomparable expression as soon as you are kind enough to inform me why you are Ernest in town and Jack in the country.

JACK   Well, produce my cigarette case first.

ALGERNON   Here it is. [*Hands cigarette case*] Now produce your explanation, and pray make it improbable. [*Sits on sofa*]

JACK   My dear fellow, there is nothing improbable about my explanation at all. In fact it's perfectly ordinary. Old Mr. Thomas Cardew, who adopted me when I was a little boy, made me in his will guardian to his grand-daughter, Miss Cecily Cardew. Cecily, who addresses me as her uncle from motives of respect that you could not possibly appreciate, lives at my place in the country under the charge of her admirable governess, Miss Prism.

ALGERNON   Where is that place in the country, by the way?

JACK   That is nothing to you, dear boy. You are not going to be invited. . . . I may tell you candidly that the place is not in Shropshire.

ALGERNON   I suspected that, my dear fellow! I have Bunburyed all over Shropshire on two separate occasions. Now, go on. Why are you Ernest in town and Jack in the country?

JACK   My dear Algy, I don't know whether you will be able to understand my real motives. You are hardly serious enough. When one is placed in the position of guardian, one has to adopt a very high moral tone on all subjects. It's one's duty to do so. And as a high moral tone can hardly be said to conduce very much to either one's health or one's happiness, in order to get up to town I have always pretended to have a younger brother of the name of Ernest, who lives in the Albany, and gets into the most dreadful scrapes. That, my dear Algy, is the whole truth pure and simple.

ALGERNON   The truth is rarely pure and never simple. Modern life would be very tedious if it were either, and modern literature a complete impossibility!

JACK   That wouldn't be at all a bad thing.

ALGERNON   Literary criticism is not your forte, my dear fellow. Don't try it.

You should leave that to people who haven't been at a University. They do it so well in the daily papers. What you really are is a Bunburyist. I was quite right in saying you were a Bunburyist. You are one of the most advanced Bunburyists I know.

JACK   What on earth do you mean?

ALGERNON   You have invented a very useful younger brother called Ernest, in order that you may be able to come up to town as often as you like. I have invented an invaluable permanent invalid called Bunbury, in order that I may be able to go down into the country whenever I choose. Bunbury is perfectly invaluable. If it wasn't for Bunbury's extraordinary bad health, for instance, I wouldn't be able to dine with you at Willis's to-night, for I have been really engaged to Aunt Augusta for more than a week.

JACK   I haven't asked you to dine with me anywhere to-night.

ALGERNON   I know. You are absurdly careless about sending out invitations. It is very foolish of you. Nothing annoys people so much as not receiving invitations.

JACK   You had much better dine with your Aunt Augusta.

ALGERNON   I haven't the smallest intention of doing anything of the kind. To begin with, I dined there on Monday, and once a week is quite enough to dine with one's own relations. In the second place, whenever I do dine there I am always treated as a member of the family, and sent down with either no woman at all, or two. In the third place, I know perfectly well whom she will place me next to, to-night. She will place me next Mary Farquhar, who always flirts with her own husband across the dinner-table. That is not very pleasant. Indeed, it is not even decent . . . and that sort of thing is enormously on the increase. The amount of women in London who flirt with their own husbands is perfectly scandalous. It looks so bad. It is simply washing one's clean linen in public. Besides, now that I know you to be a confirmed Bunburyist I naturally want to talk to you about Bunburying. I want to tell you the rules.

JACK   I'm not a Bunburyist at all. If Gwendolen accepts me, I am going to kill my brother, indeed I think I'll kill him in any case. Cecily is a little too much interested in him. It is rather a bore. So I am going to get rid of Ernest. And I strongly advise you to do the same with Mr. . . . with your invalid friend who has the absurd name.

ALGERNON   Nothing will induce me to part with Bunbury, and if you ever get married, which seems to me extremely problematic, you will be very glad to know Bunbury. A man who marries without knowing Bunbury has a very tedious time of it.

JACK   That is nonsense. If I marry a charming girl like Gwendolen, and she is the only girl I ever saw in my life that I would marry, I certainly won't want to know Bunbury.

ALGERNON   Then your wife will. You don't seem to realize, that in married life three is company and two is none.

JACK   [Sententiously]   That, my dear young friend, is the theory that the corrupt French Drama has been propounding for the last fifty years.

ALGERNON   Yes; and that the happy English home has proved in half the time.

JACK   For heaven's sake, don't try to be cynical. It's perfectly easy to be cynical.

ALGERNON   My dear fellow, it isn't easy to be anything now-a-days. There's such a lot of beastly competition about. [*The sound of an electric bell* [8] *is heard*] Ah! that must be Aunt Augusta. Only relatives, or creditors, ever ring in that Wagnerian manner. Now, if I get her out of the way for ten minutes, so that you can have an opportunity for proposing to Gwendolen, may I dine with you to-night at Willis's?

JACK   I suppose so, if you want to.

ALGERNON   Yes, but you must be serious about it. I hate people who are not serious about meals. It is so shallow of them.

[*Enter* LANE]

LANE   Lady Bracknell [9] and Miss Fairfax.

[ALGERNON *goes forward to meet them. Enter* LADY BRACKNELL *and* GWENDOLEN]

LADY BRACKNELL   Good afternoon, dear Algernon, I hope you are behaving very well.

ALGERNON   I'm feeling very well, Aunt Augusta.

LADY BRACKNELL   That's not quite the same thing. In fact the two things rarely go together. [*Sees* JACK *and bows to him with icy coldness*]

ALGERNON   [*To* GWENDOLEN]   Dear me, you are smart! [10]

GWENDOLEN   I am always smart! Aren't I, Mr. Worthing?

JACK   You're quite perfect, Miss Fairfax.

GWENDOLEN   Oh! I hope I am not that. It would leave no room for developments, and I intend to develop in many directions. [GWENDOLEN *and* JACK *sit down together in the corner*]

LADY BRACKNELL   I'm sorry if we are a little late, Algernon, but I was obliged to call on dear Lady Harbury. I hadn't been there since her poor husband's death. I never saw a woman so altered; she looks quite twenty years younger. And now I'll have a cup of tea, and one of those nice cucumber sandwiches you promised me.

ALGERNON   Certainly, Aunt Augusta. [*Goes over to tea-table*]

LADY BRACKNELL   Won't you come and sit here, Gwendolen?

GWENDOLEN   Thanks, mamma,[11] I'm quite comfortable where I am.

ALGERNON   [*Picking up empty plate in horror*]   Good heavens! Lane! Why are there no cucumber sandwiches? I ordered them specially.

LANE   [*Gravely*]   There were no cucumbers in the market this morning, sir. I went down twice.

ALGERNON   No cucumbers!

LANE   No, sir. Not even for ready money.

8. The specification of this detail suggests that Algernon's flat was nothing if not *modern!*
9. Pronounced with the accent on the first syllable.
10. In England this word is used only to denote an attractively trim appearance or a high degree of fashionableness.
11. This was the accepted way in which a young woman of the upper classes would address or refer to her mother. It is pronounced with the accent put strongly on the second syllable, the first *a* scarcely sounded.

ALGERNON   That will do, Lane, thank you.

LANE   Thank you, sir. [*Goes out*]

ALGERNON   I am greatly distressed, Aunt Augusta, about there being no cucumbers, not even for ready money.

LADY BRACKNELL   It really makes no matter, Algernon. I had some crumpets [12] with Lady Harbury, who seems to me to be living entirely for pleasure now.

ALGERNON   I hear her hair has turned quite gold from grief.

LADY BRACKNELL   It certainly has changed its colour. From what cause I, of course, cannot say. [ALGERNON *crosses and hands tea*] Thank you. I've quite a treat for you to-night, Algernon. I am going to send you down with Mary Farquhar. She is such a nice woman, and so attentive to her husband. It's delightful to watch them.

ALGERNON   I am afraid, Aunt Augusta, I shall have to give up the pleasure of dining with you to-night after all.

LADY BRACKNELL   [*Frowning*]   I hope not, Algernon. It would put my table completely out.[13] Your uncle would have to dine upstairs. Fortunately he is accustomed to that.

ALGERNON   It is a great bore, and, I need hardly say, a terrible disappointment to me, but the fact is I have just had a telegram to say that my poor friend Bunbury is very ill again. [*Exchanges glances with* JACK] They seem to think I should be with him.

LADY BRACKNELL   It is very strange. This Mr. Bunbury seems to suffer from curiously bad health.

ALGERNON   Yes; poor Bunbury is a dreadful invalid.

LADY BRACKNELL   Well, I must say, Algernon, that I think it is high time that Mr. Bunbury made up his mind whether he was going to live or to die. This shilly-shallying with the question is absurd. Nor do I in any way approve of the modern sympathy with invalids. I consider it morbid. Illness of any kind is hardly a thing to be encouraged in others. Health is the primary duty of life. I am always telling that to your poor uncle, but he never seems to take much notice . . . as far as any improvement in his ailments goes. I should be much obliged if you would ask Mr. Bunbury, from me, to be kind enough not to have a relapse on Saturday, for I rely on you to arrange my music for me.[14] It is my last reception and one wants something that will encourage conversation,[15] particularly at the end of the season when everyone has practically said whatever they had to say, which, in most cases, was probably not much.

ALGERNON   I'll speak to Bunbury, Aunt Augusta, if he is still conscious, and I think I can promise you he'll be all right by Saturday. Of course the music is a great difficulty. You see, if one plays good music, people don't listen, and if one plays bad music people don't talk. But I'll run

12. A sort of muffin, usually toasted and heavily buttered.
13. She means the proper seating arrangement of her guests.
14. That is, prepare the program of what is to be played at her musical evening.
15. This makes the established joke that the English upper classes are likely to talk while music is being played at private homes.

over the programme I've drawn out, if you will kindly come into the next room for a moment.

LADY BRACKNELL   Thank you, Algernon. It is very thoughtful of you. [*Rising, and following* ALGERNON] I'm sure the programme will be delightful, after a few expurgations. French songs I cannot possibly allow. People always seem to think that they are improper, and either look shocked, which is vulgar, or laugh, which is worse. But German sounds a thoroughly respectable language, and indeed, I believe is so. Gwendolen, you will accompany me.

GWENDOLEN   Certainly, mamma.

[LADY BRACKNELL *and* ALGERNON *go into the music room,* GWENDOLEN *remains behind*]

JACK   Charming day it has been, Miss Fairfax.

GWENDOLEN   Pray don't talk to me about the weather, Mr. Worthing. Whenever people talk to me about the weather, I always feel quite certain that they mean something else. And that makes me so nervous.

JACK   I do mean something else.

GWENDOLEN   I thought so. In fact, I am never wrong.

JACK   And I would like to be allowed to take advantage of Lady Bracknell's temporary absence . . .

GWENDOLEN   I would certainly advise you to do so. Mamma has a way of coming back suddenly into a room that I have often had to speak to her about.

JACK [*Nervously*]   Miss Fairfax, ever since I met you I have admired you more than any girl . . . I have ever met since . . . I met you.

GWENDOLEN   Yes, I am quite aware of the fact. And I often wish that in public, at any rate, you had been more demonstrative. For me you have always had an irresistible fascination. Even before I met you I was far from indifferent to you. [JACK *looks at her in amazement*] We live, as I hope you know, Mr. Worthing, in an age of ideals. The fact is constantly mentioned in the more expensive monthly magazines, and has reached the provincial pulpits I am told: and my ideal has always been to love some one of the name of Ernest. There is something in that name that inspires absolute confidence. The moment Algernon first mentioned to me that he had a friend called Ernest, I knew I was destined to love you.

JACK   You really love me, Gwendolen?

GWENDOLEN   Passionately!

JACK   Darling! You don't know how happy you've made me.

GWENDOLEN   My own Ernest!

JACK   But you don't really mean to say that you couldn't love me if my name wasn't Ernest?

GWENDOLEN   But your name is Ernest.

JACK   Yes, I know it is. But supposing it was something else? Do you mean to say you couldn't love me then?

GWENDOLEN [*Glibly*]   Ah! that is clearly a metaphysical speculation, and like most metaphysical speculations has very little reference at all to the actual facts of real life, as we know them.

JACK   Personally, darling, to speak quite candidly, I don't much care about the name of Ernest . . . I don't think the name suits me at all.

GWENDOLEN   It suits you perfectly. It is a divine name. It has a music of its own. It produces vibrations.

JACK   Well, really, Gwendolen, I must say that I think there are lots of other much nicer names. I think Jack, for instance, a charming name.

GWENDOLEN   Jack? . . . No, there is very little music in the name Jack, if any at all, indeed. It does not thrill. It produces absolutely no vibrations. . . . I have known several Jacks, and they all, without exception, were more than usually plain. Besides, Jack is a notorious domesticity for John! And I pity any woman who is married to a man called John. She would probably never be allowed to know the entrancing pleasure of a single moment's solitude. The only really safe name is Ernest.

JACK   Gwendolen, I must get christened at once—I mean we must get married at once. There is no time to be lost.

GWENDOLEN   Married, Mr. Worthing?

JACK [*Astounded*]   Well . . . surely. You know that I love you, and you led me to believe, Miss Fairfax, that you were not absolutely indifferent to me.

GWENDOLEN   I adore you. But you haven't proposed to me yet. Nothing has been said at all about marriage. The subject has not even been touched on.

JACK   Well . . . may I propose to you now?

GWENDOLEN   I think it would be an admirable opportunity. And to spare you any possible disappointment, Mr. Worthing, I think it only fair to tell you quite frankly beforehand that I am fully determined to accept you.

JACK   Gwendolen!

GWENDOLEN   Yes, Mr. Worthing, what have you got to say to me?

JACK   You know what I have got to say to you.

GWENDOLEN   Yes, but you don't say it.

JACK   Gwendolen, will you marry me? [*Goes on his knees* 16]

GWENDOLEN   Of course I will, darling. How long you have been about it! I am afraid you have had very little experience in how to propose.

JACK   My own one, I have never loved anyone in the world but you.

GWENDOLEN   Yes, but men often propose for practice. I know my brother Gerald does. All my girl-friends tell me so. What wonderfully blue eyes you have, Ernest! They are quite, quite, blue. I hope you will always look at me just like that, especially when there are other people present. [*Enter* LADY BRACKNELL]

LADY BRACKNELL   Mr. Worthing! Rise, sir, from this semi-recumbent posture. It is most indecorous.

GWENDOLEN   Mamma! [*He tries to rise; she restrains him.*] I must beg you to retire. This is no place for you. Besides, Mr. Worthing has not quite finished yet.

16. The idea that when a young man proposes marriage he kneels before his beloved was sustained by the stage and by the drawings in humorous magazines. There is little likelihood that this was an actual practice.

LADY BRACKNELL   Finished what, may I ask?

GWENDOLEN   I am engaged to Mr. Worthing, mamma. [*They rise together*]

LADY BRACKNELL   Pardon me, you are not engaged to anyone. When you do become engaged to some one, I, or your father, should his health permit him, will inform you of the fact. An engagement should come on a young girl as a surprise, pleasant or unpleasant, as the case may be. It is hardly a matter that she could be allowed to arrange for herself. . . . And now I have a few questions to put to you, Mr. Worthing. While I am making these inquiries, you, Gwendolen, will wait for me below in the carriage.

GWENDOLEN [*Reproachfully*]   Mamma!

LADY BRACKNELL   In the carriage, Gwendolen!

[GWENDOLEN *goes to the door. She and* JACK *blow kisses to each other behind* LADY BRACKNELL's *back.* LADY BRACKNELL *looks vaguely about as if she could not understand what the noise was. Finally turns round.*] Gwendolen, the carriage!

GWENDOLEN   Yes, mamma. [*Goes out, looking back at* JACK]

LADY BRACKNELL [*Sitting down*]   You can take a seat, Mr. Worthing. [*Looks in her pocket for note-book and pencil*]

JACK   Thank you, Lady Bracknell, I prefer standing.

LADY BRACKNELL [*Pencil and note-book in hand*]   I feel bound to tell you that you are not down on my list of eligible young men, although I have the same list as the dear Duchess of Bolton has. We work together, in fact. However, I am quite ready to enter your name, should your answers be what a really affectionate mother requires. Do you smoke?

JACK   Well, yes, I must admit I smoke.

LADY BRACKNELL   I am glad to hear it. A man should always have an occupation of some kind. There are far too many idle men in London as it is. How old are you?

JACK   Twenty-nine.

LADY BRACKNELL   A very good age to be married at. I have always been of opinion that a man who desires to get married should know either everything or nothing. Which do you know?

JACK [*After some hesitation*]   I know nothing, Lady Bracknell.

LADY BRACKNELL   I am pleased to hear it. I do not approve of anything that tampers with natural ignorance. Ignorance is like a delicate exotic fruit; touch it and the bloom is gone. The whole theory of modern education is radically unsound. Fortunately in England, at any rate, education produces no effect whatsoever. If it did, it would prove a serious danger to the upper classes, and probably lead to acts of violence in Grosvenor Square.[17] What is your income?

JACK   Between seven and eight thousand a year.

LADY BRACKNELL [*Makes a note in her book*]   In land, or in investments?

JACK   In investments, chiefly.

LADY BRACKNELL   That is satisfactory. What between the duties expected of one during one's lifetime, and the duties exacted from one after one's

---

17. An especially elegant residential square.

death, land has ceased to be either a profit or a pleasure. It gives one position, and prevents one from keeping it up. That's all that can be said about land.[18]

JACK   I have a country house with some land, of course, attached to it, about fifteen hundred acres, I believe; but I don't depend on that for my real income. In fact, as far as I can make out, the poachers are the only people who make anything out of it.

LADY BRACKNELL   A country house! How many bedrooms? Well, that point can be cleared up afterwards. You have a town house, I hope? A girl with a simple, unspoiled nature, like Gwendolen, could hardly be expected to reside in the country.

JACK   Well, I own a house in Belgrave Square, but it is let by the year to Lady Bloxham. Of course, I can get it back whenever I like, at six months' notice.

LADY BRACKNELL   Lady Bloxham? I don't know her.

JACK   Oh, she goes about very little. She is a lady considerably advanced in years.

LADY BRACKNELL   Ah, now-a-days that is no guarantee of respectability of character. What number in Belgrave Square?

JACK   149.

LADY BRACKNELL   [Shaking her head]   The unfashionable side. I thought there was something. However, that could easily be altered.

JACK   Do you mean the fashion, or the side?

LADY BRACKNELL   [Sternly]   Both, if necessary, I presume. What are your politics?

JACK   Well, I am afraid I really have none. I am a Liberal Unionist.[19]

LADY BRACKNELL   Oh, they count as Tories. They dine with us. Or come in the evening, at any rate. Now to minor matters. Are your parents living?

JACK   I have lost both my parents.

LADY BRACKNELL   Both? . . . That seems like carelessness. Who was your father? He was evidently a man of some wealth. Was he born in what the Radical papers call the purple of commerce, or did he rise from the ranks of the aristocracy?

JACK   I am afraid I really don't know. The fact is, Lady Bracknell, I said I had lost my parents. It would be nearer the truth to say that my parents seem to have lost me . . . I don't actually know who I am by birth. I was . . . well, I was found.

LADY BRACKNELL   Found!

JACK   The late Mr. Thomas Cardew, an old gentleman of a very charitable and kindly disposition, found me, and gave me the name of Worthing, because he happened to have a first-class ticket for Worthing in his pocket at the time. Worthing is a place in Sussex. It is a seaside resort.

18. Lady Bracknell outrages an important English piety. Owning land and living on it for at least part of the year was thought to confer a degree of social distinction, and it was common practice among men who had succeeded in business to buy country estates, even though they were ever less likely to yield any profit.
19. A reference to the efforts of Gladstone, the prime minister, to secure Home Rule for Wilde's native Ireland.

LADY BRACKNELL   Where did the charitable gentleman who had a first-class ticket for this seaside resort find you?

JACK [*Gravely*]   In a hand-bag.

LADY BRACKNELL   A hand-bag?

JACK [*Very seriously*]   Yes, Lady Bracknell. I was in a hand-bag—a somewhat large, black leather hand-bag, with handles to it—an ordinary hand-bag in fact.

LADY BRACKNELL   In what locality did this Mr. James, or Thomas, Cardew come across this ordinary hand-bag?

JACK   In the cloak-room at Victoria Station. It was given to him in mistake for his own.

LADY BRACKNELL   The cloak-room at Victoria Station?

JACK   Yes. The Brighton line.

LADY BRACKNELL   The line is immaterial. Mr. Worthing, I confess I feel somewhat bewildered by what you have just told me. To be born, or at any rate bred, in a hand-bag, whether it had handles or not, seems to me to display a contempt for the ordinary decencies of family life that remind one of the worst excesses of the French Revolution. And I presume you know what that unfortunate movement led to? As for the particular locality in which the hand-bag was found, a cloak-room at a railway station might serve to conceal a social indiscretion—has probably, indeed, been used for that purpose before now—but it could hardly be regarded as an assured basis for a recognized position in good society.

JACK   May I ask you then what you would advise me to do? I need hardly say I would do anything in the world to ensure Gwendolen's happiness.

LADY BRACKNELL   I would strongly advise you, Mr. Worthing, to try and acquire some relations as soon as possible, and to make a definite effort to produce at any rate one parent, of either sex, before the season is quite over.

JACK   Well, I don't see how I could possibly manage to do that. I can produce the hand-bag at any moment. It is in my dressing-room at home. I really think that should satisfy you, Lady Bracknell.

LADY BRACKNELL   Me, sir! What has it to do with me? You can hardly imagine that I and Lord Bracknell would dream of allowing our only daughter— a girl brought up with the utmost care—to marry into a cloak-room, and form an alliance with a parcel? Good morning, Mr. Worthing!

[LADY BRACKNELL *sweeps out in majestic indignation*]

JACK   Good morning! [ALGERNON, *from the other room, strikes up the Wedding March.* JACK *looks perfectly furious, and goes to the door.*] For goodness' sake don't play that ghastly tune, Algy! How idiotic you are!

[*The music stops, and* ALGERNON *enters cheerily*]

ALGERNON   Didn't it go off all right, old boy? You don't mean to say Gwendolen refused you? I know it is a way she has. She is always refusing people. I think it is most ill-natured of her.

JACK   Oh, Gwendolen is as right as a trivet.[20] As far as she is concerned, we

---

20. A proverbial expression (which sounds odd coming from Jack). A trivet is a three-legged stand used for supporting cooking vessels in a fireplace.

are engaged. Her mother is perfectly unbearable. Never met such a Gorgon . . . I don't really know what a Gorgon is like, but I am quite sure that Lady Bracknell is one.[21] In any case, she is a monster, without being a myth, which is rather unfair. . . . I beg your pardon, Algy, I suppose I shouldn't talk about your own aunt in that way before you.

ALGERNON   My dear boy, I love hearing my relations abused. It is the only thing that makes me put up with them at all. Relations are simply a tedious pack of people, who haven't got the remotest knowledge of how to live, nor the smallest instinct about when to die.

JACK   Oh, that is nonsense!

ALGERNON   It isn't!

JACK   Well, I won't argue about the matter. You always want to argue about things.

ALGERNON   That is exactly what things were originally made for.

JACK   Upon my word, if I thought that, I'd shoot myself . . . [A pause] You don't think there is any chance of Gwendolen becoming like her mother in about a hundred and fifty years, do you Algy?

ALGERNON   All women become like their mothers. That is their tragedy. No man does. That's his.

JACK   Is that clever?

ALGERNON   It is perfectly phrased! and quite as true as any observation in civilized life should be.

JACK   I am sick to death of cleverness. Everybody is clever now-a-days. You can't go anywhere without meeting clever people. The thing has become an absolute public nuisance. I wish to goodness we had a few fools left.

ALGERNON   We have.

JACK   I should extremely like to meet them. What do they talk about?

ALGERNON   The fools? Oh! about the clever people, of course.

JACK   What fools!

ALGERNON   By the way, did you tell Gwendolen the truth about your being Ernest in town, and Jack in the country?

JACK   [In a very patronising manner]   My dear fellow, the truth isn't quite the sort of thing one tells to a nice, sweet, refined girl. What extraordinary ideas you have about the way to behave to a woman!

ALGERNON   The only way to behave to a woman is to make love to her, if she is pretty, and to someone else if she is plain.

JACK   Oh, that is nonsense.

ALGERNON   What about your brother? What about the profligate Ernest?

JACK   Oh, before the end of the week I shall have got rid of him. I'll say he died in Paris of apoplexy. Lots of people die of apoplexy, quite suddenly, don't they?

ALGERNON   Yes, but it's hereditary, my dear fellow. It's a sort of thing that runs in families. You had much better say a severe chill.

JACK   You are sure a severe chill isn't hereditary, or anything of that kind?

21. It is hard to believe that Jack could have gone to school without learning that a Gorgon was one of three sister-monsters, the chief one, Medusa, having a round, ugly face, snakes for hair, sometimes a beard, and eyes that could turn people to stone.

ALGERNON   Of course it isn't!

JACK   Very well, then. My poor brother Ernest is carried off suddenly in Paris, by a severe chill. That gets rid of him.

ALGERNON   But I thought you said that . . . Miss Cardew was a little too much interested in your poor brother Ernest? Won't she feel his loss a good deal?

JACK   Oh, that is all right. Cecily is not a silly, romantic girl, I am glad to say. She has got a capital appetite, goes long walks, and pays no attention at all to her lessons.

ALGERNON   I would rather like to see Cecily.

JACK   I will take very good care you never do. She is excessively pretty, and she is only just eighteen.

ALGERNON   Have you told Gwendolen yet that you have an excessively pretty ward who is only just eighteen?

JACK   Oh! One doesn't blurt these things out to people. Cecily and Gwendolen are perfectly certain to be extremely great friends. I'll bet you anything you like that half an hour after they have met, they will be calling each other sister.

ALGERNON   Women only do that when they have called each other a lot of other things first. Now, my dear boy, if we want to get a good table at Willis's, we really must go and dress.[22] Do you know it is nearly seven?

JACK   [Irritably]   Oh! it always is nearly seven.

ALGERNON   Well, I'm hungry.

JACK   I never knew you when you weren't. . . .

ALGERNON   What shall we do after dinner? Go to a theatre?

JACK   Oh no! I loathe listening.

ALGERNON   Well, let us go to the Club?

JACK   Oh, no! I hate talking.

ALGERNON   Well, we might trot round to the Empire [23] at ten?

JACK   Oh, no! I can't bear looking at things. It is so silly.

ALGERNON   Well, what shall we do?

JACK   Nothing!

ALGERNON   It is awfully hard work doing nothing. However, I don't mind hard work where there is no definite object of any kind.

[Enter LANE]

LANE   Miss Fairfax.

[Enter GWENDOLEN. LANE goes out.]

ALGERNON   Gwendolen, upon my word!

GWENDOLEN   Algy, kindly turn your back. I have something very particular to say to Mr. Worthing.

ALGERNON   Really, Gwendolen, I don't think I can allow this at all.

GWENDOLEN   Algy, you always adopt a strictly immoral attitude towards life. You are not quite old enough to do that. [ALGERNON retires to the fireplace]

---

22. He means in a tailcoat with white tie. The dinner jacket with black tie did not come into use until almost a quarter-century later.

23. A music hall, i.e. a vaudeville theater.

JACK   My own darling!

GWENDOLEN   Ernest, we may never be married. From the expression on mamma's face I fear we never shall. Few parents now-a-days pay any regard to what their children say to them. The old-fashioned respect for the young is fast dying out. Whatever influence I ever had over mamma, I lost at the age of three. But although she may prevent us from becoming man and wife, and I may marry someone else, and marry often, nothing that she can possibly do can alter my eternal devotion to you.

JACK   Dear Gwendolen!

GWENDOLEN   The story of your romantic origin, as related to me by mamma, with unpleasing comments, has naturally stirred the deeper fibres of my nature. Your Christian name has an irresistible fascination. The simplicity of your character makes you exquisitely incomprehensible to me. Your town address at the Albany I have. What is your address in the country?

JACK   The Manor House, Woolton, Hertfordshire.

[ALGERNON, *who has been carefully listening, smiles to himself, and writes the address on his shirt-cuff.*[24] *Then picks up the Railway Guide.*]

GWENDOLEN   There is a good postal service, I suppose? It may be necessary to do something desperate. That, of course, will require serious consideration. I will communicate with you daily.

JACK   My own one!

GWENDOLEN   How long do you remain in town?

JACK   Till Monday.

GWENDOLEN   Good! Algy, you may turn round now.

ALGERNON   Thanks, I've turned round already.

GWENDOLEN   You may also ring the bell.

JACK   You will let me see you to your carriage, my own darling?

GWENDOLEN   Certainly.

JACK [*To* LANE, *who now enters*]   I will see Miss Fairfax out.

LANE   Yes, sir. [JACK *and* GWENDOLEN *go off.* LANE *presents several letters on a salver to* ALGERNON. *It is to be surmised that they are bills, as* ALGERNON *after looking at the envelopes, tears them up.*]

ALGERNON   A glass of sherry, Lane.

LANE   Yes, sir.

ALGERNON   To-morrow, Lane, I'm going Bunburying.

LANE   Yes, sir.

ALGERNON   I shall probably not be back till Monday. You can put up my dress clothes, my smoking jacket,[25] and all the Bunbury suits . . .

LANE   Yes, sir [*Handing sherry*]

ALGERNON   I hope to-morrow will be a fine day, Lane.

LANE   It never is, sir.

24. The cuffs of gentlemen's shirts were starched stiff and were commonly used for jotting down memoranda.

25. This would be a short jacket of silk or velvet, probably quilted, which a gentleman wore in place of his dress coat when he foregathered with other male guests at a country-house weekend to smoke (in the smoking room) before going to bed.

ALGERNON   Lane, you're a perfect pessimist.

LANE   I do my best to give satisfaction, sir.

[*Enter* JACK. LANE *goes off.*]

JACK   There's a sensible, intellectual girl! the only girl I ever cared for in my life. [ALGERNON *is laughing immoderately*] What on earth are you so amused at?

ALGERNON   Oh, I'm a little anxious about poor Bunbury, that is all.

JACK   If you don't take care, your friend Bunbury will get you into a serious scrape some day.

ALGERNON   I love scrapes. They are the only things that are never serious.

JACK   Oh, that's nonsense, Algy. You never talk anything but nonsense.

ALGERNON   Nobody ever does.

[JACK *looks indignantly at him, and leaves the room.* ALGERNON *lights a cigarette, reads his shirt-cuff, and smiles.*]

ACT-DROP

ACT II

Scene—*Garden at the Manor House. A flight of gray stone steps leads up to the house. The garden, an old-fashioned one, full of roses. Time of year, July. Basket chairs, and a table covered with books, are set under a large yew tree.* MISS PRISM [1] *discovered seated at the table.* CECILY *is at the back watering flowers.*

MISS PRISM [*Calling*]   Cecily, Cecily! Surely such a utilitarian occupation as the watering of flowers is rather Moulton's duty than yours? Especially at a moment when intellectual pleasures await you. Your German grammar is on the table. Pray open it at page fifteen. We will repeat yesterday's lesson.

CECILY [*Coming over very slowly*]   But I don't like German. It isn't at all a becoming language. I know perfectly well that I look quite plain after my German lesson.

MISS PRISM   Child, you know how anxious your guardian is that you should improve yourself in every way. He laid particular stress on your German, as he was leaving for town yesterday. Indeed, he always lays stress on your German when he is leaving for town.

CECILY   Dear Uncle Jack is so very serious! Sometimes he is so serious that I think he cannot be quite well.

MISS PRISM [*Drawing herself up*]   Your guardian enjoys the best of health, and his gravity of demeanour is especially to be commended in one so comparatively young as he is. I know no one who has a higher sense of duty and responsibility.

CECILY   I suppose that is why he often looks a little bored when we three are together.

1. Miss Prism's name is chosen with reference to the phrase "prunes and prisms," in common use to denote the proprieties taught to young ladies. It derives from a famous statement of Mrs. General, the snobbish governess in Dickens's *Little Dorrit,* who explains to her charge that there are certain words that give a "pretty form" to the lips. "Papa, potatoes, poultry, prunes and prisms are all very good words for the lips; especially prunes and prisms."

MISS PRISM   Cecily! I am surprised at you. Mr. Worthing has many troubles in his life. Idle merriment and triviality would be out of place in his conversation. You must remember his constant anxiety about that unfortunate young man, his brother.

CECILY   I wish Uncle Jack would allow that unfortunate young man, his brother, to come down here sometimes. We might have a good influence over him, Miss Prism. I am sure you certainly would. You know German, and geology, and things of that kind influence a man very much. [CECILY *begins to write in her diary*]

MISS PRISM   [*Shaking her head*]   I do not think that even I could produce any effect on a character that according to his own brother's admission is irretrievably weak and vacillating. Indeed I am not sure that I would desire to reclaim him. I am not in favour of this modern mania for turning bad people into good people at a moment's notice. As a man sows so let him reap. You must put away your diary, Cecily. I really don't see why you should keep a diary at all.

CECILY   I keep a diary in order to enter the wonderful secrets of my life. If I didn't write them down I should probably forget all about them.

MISS PRISM   Memory, my dear Cecily, is the diary that we all carry about with us.

CECILY   Yes, but it usually chronicles the things that have never happened, and couldn't possibly have happened. I believe that Memory is responsible for nearly all the three-volume novels that Mudie [2] sends us.

MISS PRISM   Do not speak slightingly of the three-volume novel, Cecily. I wrote one myself in earlier days.

CECILY   Did you really, Miss Prism? How wonderfully clever you are! I hope it did not end happily? I don't like novels that end happily. They depress me so much.

MISS PRISM   The good ended happily, and the bad unhappily. That is what Fiction means.

CECILY   I suppose so. But it seems very unfair. And was your novel ever published?

MISS PRISM   Alas! no. The manuscript unfortunately was abandoned. I use the word in the sense of lost or mislaid. [3] To your work, child, these speculations are profitless.

CECILY   [*Smiling*]   But I see dear Dr. Chasuble coming up through the garden.

MISS PRISM   [*Rising and advancing*]   Dr. Chasuble! This is indeed a pleasure. [*Enter* CANON CHASUBLE [4]]

CHASUBLE   And how are we this morning? Miss Prism, you are, I trust, well?

CECILY   Miss Prism has just been complaining of a slight headache. I think it

---

2. Mudie's was the great commercial lending-library in London. The name was synonymous with sentimental novels.

3. Rather than in the sense (once more common than now) of immoral and shameless.

4. He is Dr. Chasuble because he is a Doctor of Divinity. He is Canon Chasuble because he is connected with a cathedral as a member of the bishop's counsel. He is Chasuble because Wilde thought it would be convenient and amusing to suggest his character by naming him after an ecclesiastical vestment: he is what he wears.

would do her so much good to have a short stroll with you in the park,[5] Dr. Chasuble.

MISS PRISM   Cecily, I have not mentioned anything about a headache.

CECILY   No, dear Miss Prism, I know that, but I felt instinctively that you had a headache. Indeed I was thinking about that, and not about my German lesson, when the Rector came in.

CHASUBLE   I hope, Cecily, you are not inattentive.

CECILY   Oh, I am afraid I am.

CHASUBLE   That is strange. Were I fortunate enough to be Miss Prism's pupil, I would hang upon her lips. [MISS PRISM *glares*] I spoke metaphorically. —My metaphor was drawn from bees. Ahem! Mr. Worthing, I suppose, has not returned from town yet?

MISS PRISM   We do not expect him till Monday afternoon.

CHASUBLE   Ah yes, he usually likes to spend his Sunday in London. He is not one of those whose sole aim is enjoyment, as, by all accounts, that unfortunate young man, his brother, seems to be. But I must not disturb Egeria[6] and her pupil any longer.

MISS PRISM   Egeria? My name is Lætitia, Doctor.

CHASUBLE   [*Bowing*]   A classical allusion merely, drawn from the Pagan authors. I shall see you both no doubt at Evensong.[7]

MISS PRISM   I think, dear Doctor, I will have a stroll with you. I find I have a headache after all, and a walk might do it good.

CHASUBLE   With pleasure, Miss Prism, with pleasure. We might go as far as the schools and back.

MISS PRISM   That would be delightful. Cecily, you will read your Political Economy in my absence. The chapter on the Fall of the Rupee[8] you may omit. It is somewhat too sensational. Even these metallic problems have their melodramatic side.

[*Goes down the garden with* DR. CHASUBLE]

CECILY   [*Picks up books and throws them back on table*]   Horrid Political Economy! Horrid Geography! Horrid, horrid German!

[*Enter* MERRIMAN *with a card on a salver*]

MERRIMAN   Mr. Ernest Worthing has just driven over from the station. He has brought his luggage with him.

CECILY   [*Takes the card and reads it*]   'Mr. Ernest Worthing, B 4 The Albany, W.' Uncle Jack's brother! Did you tell him Mr. Worthing was in town?

MERRIMAN   Yes, Miss. He seemed very much disappointed. I mentioned that you and Miss Prism were in the garden. He said he was anxious to speak to you privately for a moment.

CECILY   Ask Mr. Ernest Worthing to come here. I suppose you had better talk to the housekeeper about a room for him.

---

5. The grounds of the estate.

6. A Roman goddess of fountains, birth, and prophecy. She was said to be the consort and counselor of Numa, a legendary king of Rome renowned for his wisdom.

7. Evening prayer in the Anglican Church.

8. The rupee is the basic monetary unit of India. At a time when India was an important part of the Empire, its fall on the money market—which was frequent—was of considerable consequence, especially to those retired Englishmen who had been in the civil or military services in India and who, on retirement, lived in England on a pension paid in rupees.

MERRIMAN   Yes, Miss.

[MERRIMAN *goes off*]

CECILY   I have never met any really wicked person before. I feel rather frightened. I am so afraid he will look just like everyone else.

[*Enter* ALGERNON, *very gay and debonair*]

He does!

ALGERNON [*Raising his hat*]   You are my little cousin Cecily, I'm sure.

CECILY   You are under some strange mistake. I am not little. In fact, I believe I am more than usually tall for my age. [ALGERNON *is rather taken aback*] But I am your cousin Cecily. You, I see from your card, are Uncle Jack's brother, my cousin Ernest, my wicked cousin Ernest.

ALGERNON   Oh! I am not really wicked at all, cousin Cecily. You musn't think that I am wicked.

CECILY   If you are not, then you have certainly been deceiving us all in a very inexcusable manner. I hope you have not been leading a double life, pretending to be wicked and being really good all the time. That would be hypocrisy.

ALGERNON [*Looks at her in amazement*]   Oh! of course I have been rather reckless.

CECILY   I am glad to hear it.

ALGERNON   In fact, now you mention the subject, I have been very bad in my own small way.

CECILY   I don't think you should be so proud of that, though I am sure it must have been very pleasant.

ALGERNON   It is much pleasanter being here with you.

CECILY   I can't understand how you are here at all. Uncle Jack won't be back till Monday afternoon.

ALGERNON   That is a great disappointment. I am obliged to go up by the first train on Monday morning. I have a business appointment that I am anxious . . . to miss.

CECILY   Couldn't you miss it anywhere but in London?

ALGERNON   No: the appointment is in London.

CECILY   Well, I know, of course, how important it is not to keep a business engagement, if one wants to retain any sense of the beauty of life, but still I think you had better wait till Uncle Jack arrives. I know he wants to speak to you about your emigrating.

ALGERNON   About my what?

CECILY   Your emigrating. He has gone up to buy your outfit.

ALGERNON   I certainly wouldn't let Jack buy my outfit. He has no taste in neckties at all.

CECILY   I don't think you will require neckties. Uncle Jack is sending you to Australia.

ALGERNON   Australia! I'd sooner die.

CECILY   Well, he said at dinner on Wednesday night, that you would have to choose between this world, the next world, and Australia.

ALGERNON   Oh, well! The accounts I have received of Australia and the next world, are not particularly encouraging. This world is good enough for me, cousin Cecily.

CECILY   Yes, but are you good enough for it?

ALGERNON   I'm afraid I'm not that. That is why I want you to reform me. You might make that your mission, if you don't mind, cousin Cecily.

CECILY   I'm afraid I've no time, this afternoon.

ALGERNON   Well, would you mind my reforming myself this afternoon?

CECILY   It is rather Quixotic of you. But I think you should try.

ALGERNON   I will. I feel better already.

CECILY   You are looking a little worse.

ALGERNON   That is because I am hungry.

CECILY   How thoughtless of me. I should have remembered that when one is going to lead an entirely new life, one requires regular and wholesome meals. Won't you come in?

ALGERNON   Thank you. Might I have a buttonhole[9] first? I never have any appetite unless I have a buttonhole first.

CECILY   A Maréchal Niel?[10] [*Picks up scissors*]

ALGERNON   No, I'd sooner have a pink rose.

CECILY   Why? [*Cuts a flower*]

ALGERNON   Because you are like a pink rose, cousin Cecily.

CECILY   I don't think it can be right for you to talk to me like that. Miss Prism never says such things to me.

ALGERNON   Then Miss Prism is a short-sighted old lady. [CECILY *puts the rose in his buttonhole*] You are the prettiest girl I ever saw.

CECILY   Miss Prism says that all good looks are a snare.

ALGERNON   They are a snare that every sensible man would like to be caught in.

CECILY   Oh! I don't think I would care to catch a sensible man. I shouldn't know what to talk to him about.

[*They pass into the house.* MISS PRISM *and* DR. CHASUBLE *return.*]

MISS PRISM   You are too much alone, dear Dr. Chasuble. You should get married. A misanthrope I can understand—a womanthrope, never!

CHASUBLE [*With a scholar's shudder*[11]]   Believe me, I do not deserve so neologistic a phrase. The precept as well as the practice of the Primitive Church was distinctly against matrimony.

MISS PRISM [*Sententiously*]   That is obviously the reason why the Primitive Church has not lasted up to the present day. And you do not seem to realize, dear Doctor, that by persistently remaining single, a man converts himself into a permanent public temptation. Men should be more careful; this very celibacy leads weaker vessels astray.

CHASUBLE   But is a man not equally attractive when married?

MISS PRISM   No married man is ever attractive except to his wife.

CHASUBLE   And often, I've been told, not even to her.

MISS PRISM   That depends on the intellectual sympathies of the woman. Matu-

---

9. The word used in England for a *boutonnière*, a flower or small nosegay in the buttonhole of a man's lapel. The practice of wearing them was quite common and Wilde's were famous for their flamboyance.

10. The name of a yellow rose.

11. At her not knowing that a hater of women is a misogynist and her making a new word— a neologism—by combining an English and a Greek element.

rity can always be depended on. Ripeness can be trusted. Young women are green. [DR. CHASUBLE *starts*] I spoke horticulturally. My metaphor was drawn from fruits. But where is Cecily?

CHASUBLE   Perhaps she followed us to the schools.

[*Enter* JACK *slowly from the back of the garden. He is dressed in the deepest mourning, with crape hat-band and black gloves.*[12]]

MISS PRISM   Mr. Worthing!

CHASUBLE   Mr. Worthing?

MISS PRISM   This is indeed a surprise. We did not look for you till Monday afternoon.

JACK [*Shakes* MISS PRISM's *hand in a tragic manner*]   I have returned sooner than I expected. Dr. Chasuble, I hope you are well?

CHASUBLE   Dear Mr. Worthing, I trust this garb of woe does not betoken some terrible calamity?

JACK   My brother.

MISS PRISM   More shameful debts and extravagance?

CHASUBLE   Still leading his life of pleasure?

JACK [*Shaking his head*]   Dead!

CHASUBLE   Your brother Ernest dead?

JACK   Quite dead.

MISS PRISM   What a lesson for him! I trust he will profit by it.

CHASUBLE   Mr. Worthing, I offer you my sincere condolence. You have at least the consolation of knowing that you were always the most generous and forgiving of brothers.

JACK   Poor Ernest! He had many faults, but it is a sad, sad blow.

CHASUBLE   Very sad indeed. Were you with him at the end?

JACK   No. He died abroad; in Paris, in fact. I had a telegram last night from the manager of the Grand Hotel.

CHASUBLE   Was the cause of death mentioned?

JACK   A severe chill, it seems.

MISS PRISM   As a man sows, so shall he reap.

CHASUBLE [*Raising his hand*]   Charity, dear Miss Prism, charity! None of us are perfect. I myself am peculiarly susceptible to draughts. Will the interment take place here?

JACK   No. He seemed to have expressed a desire to be buried in Paris.

CHASUBLE   In Paris! [*Shakes his head*] I fear that hardly points to any very serious state of mind at the last. You would no doubt wish me to make some slight allusion to this tragic domestic affliction next Sunday. [JACK *presses his hand convulsively*] My sermon on the meaning of the manna [13] in the wilderness can be adapted to almost any occasion, joyful, or, as in the present case, distressing. [*All sigh*] I have preached it at harvest celebrations, christenings, confirmations, on days of humiliation and

---

12. The wearing of black clothing in token of mourning was a custom once rigorously observed by both men and women. The hat around which Jack has bound a wide band of black crape is a "high" hat, silk and black. He wears a black frock coat, coming down almost to his knees; his trousers are black. Black also are his necktie, his gloves, his walking stick, and of course his shoes, and his handkerchief has a wide border of black.

13. The food miraculously provided for the Israelites after their flight from Egypt.

festal days. The last time I delivered it was in the Cathedral, as a charity sermon on behalf of the Society for the Prevention of Discontent among the Upper Orders. The Bishop, who was present, was much struck by some of the analogies I drew.

JACK   Ah! that reminds me, you mentioned christenings I think, Dr. Chasuble? I suppose you know how to christen all right? [DR. CHASUBLE *looks astounded*] I mean, of course, you are continually christening, aren't you?

MISS PRISM   It is, I regret to say, one of the Rector's most constant duties in this parish. I have often spoken to the poorer classes on the subject. But they don't seem to know what thrift is.

CHASUBLE   But is there any particular infant in whom you are interested, Mr. Worthing? Your brother was, I believe, unmarried, was he not?

JACK   Oh, yes.

MISS PRISM   [*Bitterly*]   People who live entirely for pleasure usually are.

JACK   But it is not for any child, dear Doctor. I am very fond of children. No! the fact is, I would like to be christened myself, this afternoon, if you have nothing better to do.

CHASUBLE   But surely, Mr. Worthing, you have been christened already?

JACK   I don't remember anything about it.

CHASUBLE   But have you any grave doubts on the subject?

JACK   I certainly intend to have. Of course, I don't know if the thing would bother you in any way, or if you think I am a little too old now.

CHASUBLE   Not at all. The sprinkling, and, indeed, the immersion of adults is a perfectly canonical practice.

JACK   Immersion!

CHASUBLE   You need have no apprehensions. Sprinkling is all that is necessary, or indeed I think advisable. Our weather is so changeable. At what hour would you wish the ceremony performed?

JACK   Oh, I might trot round about five if that would suit you.

CHASUBLE   Perfectly, perfectly! In fact I have two similar ceremonies to perform at that time. A case of twins that occurred recently in one of the outlying cottages on your own estate. Poor Jenkins the carter, a most hard-working man.

JACK   Oh! I don't see much fun in being christened along with other babies. It would be childish. Would half-past five do?

CHASUBLE   Admirably! Admirably! [*Takes out watch*] And now, dear Mr. Worthing, I will not intrude any longer into a house of sorrow. I would merely beg you not to be too much bowed down by grief. What seem to us bitter trials are often blessings in disguise.

MISS PRISM   This seems to me a blessing of an extremely obvious kind.

[*Enter* CECILY *from the house*]

CECILY   Uncle Jack! Oh, I am pleased to see you back. But what horrid clothes you have got on! Do go and change them.

MISS PRISM   Cecily!

CHASUBLE   My child! my child!

[CECILY *goes towards* JACK; *he kisses her brow in a melancholy manner.*]

CECILY   What is the matter, Uncle Jack? Do look happy! You look as if you had toothache, and I have got such a surprise for you. Who do you think is in the dining-room? Your brother!

JACK   Who?

CECILY   Your brother Ernest. He arrived about half an hour ago.

JACK   What nonsense! I haven't got a brother.

CECILY   Oh, don't say that. However badly he may have behaved to you in the past he is still your brother. You couldn't be so heartless as to disown him. I'll tell him to come out. And you will shake hands with him, won't you, Uncle Jack? [*Runs back into the house*]

CHASUBLE   These are very joyful tidings.

MISS PRISM   After we had all been resigned to his loss, his sudden return seems to me peculiarly distressing.

JACK   My brother is in the dining-room? I don't know what it all means. I think it is perfectly absurd.

[*Enter* ALGERNON *and* CECILY *hand in hand. They come slowly up to* JACK.]

JACK   Good heavens! [*Motions* ALGERNON *away*]

ALGERNON   Brother John, I have come down from town to tell you that I am very sorry for all the trouble I have given you, and that I intend to lead a better life in the future. [JACK *glares at him and does not take his hand*]

CECILY   Uncle Jack, you are not going to refuse your own brother's hand?

JACK   Nothing will induce me to take his hand. I think his coming down here disgraceful. He knows perfectly well why.

CECILY   Uncle Jack, do be nice. There is some good in everyone. Ernest has just been telling me about his poor invalid friend Mr. Bunbury, whom he goes to visit so often. And surely there must be much good in one who is kind to an invalid, and leaves the pleasures of London to sit by a bed of pain.

JACK   Oh! he has been talking about Bunbury, has he?

CECILY   Yes, he has told me all about poor Mr. Bunbury, and his terrible state of health.

JACK   Bunbury! Well, I won't have him talk to you about Bunbury or about anything else. It is enough to drive one perfectly frantic.

ALGERNON   Of course I admit that the faults were all on my side. But I must say that I think that brother John's coldness to me is peculiarly painful. I expected a more enthusiastic welcome, especially considering it is the first time I have come here.

CECILY   Uncle Jack, if you don't shake hands with Ernest I will never forgive you.

JACK   Never forgive me?

CECILY   Never, never, never!

JACK   Well, this is the last time I shall ever do it. [*Shakes hand with* ALGERNON *and glares*]

CHASUBLE   It's pleasant, is it not, to see so perfect a reconciliation? I think we might leave the two brothers together.

MISS PRISM   Cecily, you will come with us.

CECILY   Certainly, Miss Prism. My little task of reconciliation is over.

CHASUBLE   You have done a beautiful action to-day, dear child.

MISS PRISM   We must not be premature in our judgments.

CECILY   I feel very happy. [*They all go off*]

JACK   You young scoundrel, Algy, you must get out of this place as soon as possible. I don't allow any Bunburying here.

[*Enter* MERRIMAN]

MERRIMAN   I have put Mr. Ernest's things in the room next to yours, sir. I suppose that is all right?

JACK   What?

MERRIMAN   Mr. Ernest's luggage, sir. I have unpacked it and put it in the room next to your own.

JACK   His luggage?

MERRIMAN   Yes, sir. Three portmanteaus,[14] a dressing-case,[15] two hat-boxes, and a large luncheon-basket.

ALGERNON   I am afraid I can't stay more than a week this time.

JACK   Merriman, order the dog-cart [16] at once. Mr. Ernest has been suddenly called back to town.

MERRIMAN   Yes, sir. [*Goes back into the house*]

ALGERNON   What a fearful liar you are, Jack. I have not been called back to town at all.

JACK   Yes, you have.

ALGERNON   I haven't heard anyone call me.

JACK   Your duty as a gentlemen calls you back.

ALGERNON   My duty as a gentleman has never interfered with my pleasures in the smallest degree.

JACK   I can quite understand that.

ALGERNON   Well, Cecily is a darling.

JACK   You are not to talk of Miss Cardew like that. I don't like it.

ALGERNON   Well, I don't like your clothes. You look perfectly ridiculous in them. Why on earth don't you go up and change? It is perfectly childish to be in deep mourning for a man who is actually staying for a whole week with you in your house as a guest. I call it grotesque.

JACK   You are certainly not staying with me for a whole week as a guest or anything else. You have got to leave . . . by the four-five train.

ALGERNON   I certainly won't leave you so long as you are in mourning. It would be most unfriendly. If I were in mourning you would stay with me, I suppose. I should think it very unkind if you didn't.

JACK   Well, will you go if I change my clothes?

ALGERNON   Yes, if you are not too long. I never saw anybody take so long to dress, and with such little result.

JACK   Well, at any rate, that is better than being always over-dressed as you are.

ALGERNON   If I am occasionally a little over-dressed, I make up for it by being always immensely over-educated.

JACK   Your vanity is ridiculous, your conduct an outrage, and your presence

14. Large leather suitcases.
15. A traveling case fitted with toilet articles.
16. A cart drawn by one horse and accommodating two persons sitting back to back.

in my garden utterly absurd. However, you have got to catch the four-five, and I hope you will have a pleasant journey back to town. This Bunburying, as you call it, has not been a great success for you. [*Goes into the house*]

ALGERNON   I think it has been a great success. I'm in love with Cecily, and that is everything.

[*Enter* CECILY *at the back of the garden. She picks up the can and begins to water the flowers.*]

But I must see her before I go, and make arrangements for another Bunbury. Ah, there she is.

CECILY   Oh, I merely came back to water the roses. I thought you were with Uncle Jack.

ALGERNON   He's gone to order the dog-cart for me.

CECILY   Oh, is he going to take you for a nice drive?

ALGERNON   He's going to send me away.

CECILY   Then have we got to part?

ALGERNON   I am afraid so. It's a very painful parting.

CECILY   It is always painful to part from people whom one has known for a very brief space of time. The absence of old friends one can endure with equanimity. But even a momentary separation from anyone to whom one has just been introduced is almost unbearable.

ALGERNON   Thank you.

[*Enter* MERRIMAN]

MERRIMAN   The dog-cart is at the door, sir. [ALGERNON *looks appealingly at* CECILY]

CECILY   It can wait, Merriman . . . for . . . five minutes.

MERRIMAN   Yes, Miss. [*Exit* MERRIMAN]

ALGERNON   I hope, Cecily, I shall not offend you if I state quite frankly and openly that you seem to me to be in every way the visible personification of absolute perfection.

CECILY   I think your frankness does you great credit, Ernest. If you will allow me I will copy your remarks into my diary. [*Goes over to table and begins writing in diary*]

ALGERNON   Do you really keep a diary? I'd give anything to look at it. May I?

CECILY   Oh, no. [*Puts her hand over it*] You see, it is simply a very young girl's record of her own thoughts and impressions, and consequently meant for publication. When it appears in volume form I hope you will order a copy. But pray, Ernest, don't stop. I delight in taking down from dictation. I have reached 'absolute perfection.' You can go on. I am quite ready for more.

ALGERNON   [*Somewhat taken aback*] Ahem! Ahem!

CECILY   Oh, don't cough, Ernest. When one is dictating one should speak fluently and not cough. Besides, I don't know how to spell a cough. [*Writes as* ALGERNON *speaks*]

ALGERNON   [*Speaking very rapidly*] Cecily, ever since I first looked upon your wonderful and incomparable beauty, I have dared to love you wildly, passionately, devotedly, hopelessly.

CECILY   I don't think that you should tell me that you love me wildly, passionately, devotedly, hopelessly. Hopelessly doesn't seem to make much sense, does it?

ALGERNON   Cecily!

[*Enter* MERRIMAN]

MERRIMAN   The dog-cart is waiting, sir.

ALGERNON   Tell it to come round next week, at the same hour.

MERRIMAN [*Looks at* CECILY, *who makes no sign*]   Yes, sir. [MERRIMAN *retires*]

CECILY   Uncle Jack would be very much annoyed if he knew you were staying on till next week, at the same hour.

ALGERNON   Oh, I don't care about Jack. I don't care for anybody in the whole world but you. I love you, Cecily. You will marry me, won't you?

CECILY   You silly boy! Of course. Why, we have been engaged for the last three months.

ALGERNON   For the last three months?

CECILY   Yes, it will be exactly three months on Thursday.

ALGERNON   But how did we become engaged?

CECILY   Well, ever since dear Uncle Jack first confessed to us that he had a younger brother who was very wicked and bad, you of course have formed the chief topic of conversation between myself and Miss Prism. And of course a man who is much talked about is always very attractive. One feels there must be something in him after all. I daresay it was foolish of me, but I fell in love with you, Ernest.

ALGERNON   Darling! And when was the engagement actually settled?

CECILY   On the 4th of February last. Worn out by your entire ignorance of my existence, I determined to end the matter one way or the other, and after a long struggle with myself I accepted you under this dear old tree here. The next day I bought this little ring in your name, and this is the little bangle [17] with the true lovers' knot I promised you always to wear.

ALGERNON   Did I give you this? It's very pretty, isn't it?

CECILY   Yes, you've wonderfully good taste, Ernest. It's the excuse I've always given for your leading such a bad life. And this is the box in which I keep all your dear letters. [*Kneels at table, opens box, and produces letters tied up with blue ribbon*]

ALGERNON   My letters! But my own sweet Cecily, I have never written you any letters.

CECILY   You need hardly remind me of that, Ernest. I remember only too well that I was forced to write your letters for you. I wrote always three times a week, and sometimes oftener.

ALGERNON   Oh, do let me read them, Cecily?

CECILY   Oh, I couldn't possibly. They would make you far too conceited. [*Replaces box*] The three you wrote me after I had broken off the engagement are so beautiful, and so badly spelled, that even now I can hardly read them without crying a little.

ALGERNON   But was our engagement ever broken off?

CECILY   Of course it was. On the 22nd of last March. You can see the entry

---

17. A rigid bracelet, usually with no clasp.

if you like. [*Shows diary*] 'To-day I broke off my engagement with Ernest. I feel it is better to do so. The weather still continues charming.'

ALGERNON   But why on earth did you break it off? What had I done? I had done nothing at all. Cecily, I am very much hurt indeed to hear you broke it off. Particularly when the weather was so charming.

CECILY   It would hardly have been a really serious engagement if it hadn't been broken off at least once. But I forgave you before the week was out.

ALGERNON   [*Crossing to her, and kneeling*]   What a perfect angel you are, Cecily.

CECILY   You dear romantic boy. [*He kisses her, she puts her fingers through his hair*] I hope your hair curls naturally, does it?

ALGERNON   Yes, darling, with a little help from others.

CECILY   I am so glad.

ALGERNON   You'll never break off our engagement again, Cecily?

CECILY   I don't think I could break it off now that I have actually met you. Besides, of course, there is the question of your name.

ALGERNON   Yes, of course. [*Nervously*]

CECILY   You must not laugh at me, darling, but it had always been a girlish dream of mine to love some one whose name was Ernest. [ALGERNON *rises,* CECILY *also*] There is something in that name that seems to inspire absolute confidence. I pity any poor married woman whose husband is not called Ernest.

ALGERNON   But, my dear child, do you mean to say you could not love me if I had some other name?

CECILY   But what name?

ALGERNON   Oh, any name you like—Algernon—for instance . . .

CECILY   But I don't like the name of Algernon.

ALGERNON   Well, my own dear, sweet, loving little darling, I really can't see why you should object to the name of Algernon. It is not at all a bad name. In fact, it is rather an aristocratic name. Half of the chaps who get into the Bankruptcy Court are called Algernon. But seriously, Cecily . . . [*Moving to her*] . . . if my name was Algy, couldn't you love me?

CECILY   [*Rising*]   I might respect you, Ernest, I might admire your character, but I fear that I should not be able to give you my undivided attention.

ALGERNON   Ahem! Cecily! [*Picking up hat*] Your Rector here is, I suppose, thoroughly experienced in the practice of all the rites and ceremonials of the Church?

CECILY   Oh yes. Dr. Chasuble is a most learned man. He has never written a single book, so you can imagine how much he knows.

ALGERNON   I must see him at once on a most important christening—I mean on most important business.

CECILY   Oh!

ALGERNON   I shan't be away more than half an hour.

CECILY   Considering that we have been engaged since February the 14th, and that I only met you to-day for the first time, I think it is rather hard that you should leave me for so long a period as half an hour. Couldn't you make it twenty minutes?

ALGERNON   I'll be back in no time.

[*Kisses her and rushes down the garden*]

CECILY   What an impetuous boy he is! I like his hair so much. I must enter his proposal in my diary.

[*Enter* MERRIMAN]

MERRIMAN   A Miss Fairfax has just called to see Mr. Worthing. On very important business Miss Fairfax states.

CECILY   Isn't Mr. Worthing in his library?

MERRIMAN   Mr. Worthing went over in the direction of the Rectory some time ago.

CECILY   Pray ask the lady to come out here; Mr. Worthing is sure to be back soon. And you can bring tea.

MERRIMAN   Yes, Miss. [*Goes out*]

CECILY   Miss Fairfax! I suppose one of the many good elderly women who are associated with Uncle Jack in some of his philanthropic work in London. I don't quite like women who are interested in philanthropic work. I think it is so forward of them.

[*Enter* MERRIMAN]

MERRIMAN   Miss Fairfax.

[*Enter* GWENDOLEN. *Exit* MERRIMAN.]

CECILY   [*Advancing to meet her*]   Pray let me introduce myself to you. My name is Cecily Cardew.

GWENDOLEN   Cecily Cardew? [*Moving to her and shaking hands*] What a very sweet name! Something tells me that we are going to be great friends. I like you already more than I can say. My first impressions of people are never wrong.

CECILY   How nice of you to like me so much after we have known each other such a comparatively short time. Pray sit down.

GWENDOLEN   [*Still standing up*]   I may call you Cecily, may I not?

CECILY   With pleasure!

GWENDOLEN   And you will always call me Gwendolen, won't you.

CECILY   If you wish.

GWENDOLEN   Then that is all quite settled, is it not?

CECILY   I hope so. [*A pause. They both sit down together.*]

GWENDOLEN   Perhaps this might be a favorable opportunity for my mentioning who I am. My father is Lord Bracknell. You have never heard of papa, I suppose?

CECILY   I don't think so.

GWENDOLEN   Outside the family circle, papa, I am glad to say, is entirely unknown. I think that is quite as it should be. The home seems to me to be the proper sphere for the man. And certainly once a man begins to neglect his domestic duties he becomes painfully effeminate, does he not? And I don't like that. It makes men so very attractive. Cecily, mamma, whose views on education are remarkably strict, has brought me up to be extremely short-sighted; it is part of her system; so do you mind my looking at you through my glasses?

CECILY   Oh! not at all, Gwendolen. I am very fond of being looked at.

GWENDOLEN [*After examining* CECILY *carefully through a lorgnette* [18]]   You are here on a short visit I suppose.

CECILY   Oh no! I live here.

GWENDOLEN [*Severely*]   Really? Your mother, no doubt, or some female relative of advanced years, resides here also?

CECILY   Oh no! I have no mother, nor, in fact, any relations.

GWENDOLEN   Indeed?

CECILY   My dear guardian, with the assistance of Miss Prism, has the arduous task of looking after me.

GWENDOLEN   Your guardian?

CECILY   Yes, I am Mr. Worthing's ward.

GWENDOLEN   Oh! It is strange he never mentioned to me that he had a ward. How secretive of him! He grows more interesting hourly. I am not sure, however, that the news inspires me with feelings of unmixed delight. [*Rising and going to her*] I am very fond of you, Cecily; I have liked you ever since I met you! But I am bound to state that now that I know that you are Mr. Worthing's ward, I cannot help expressing a wish you were—well just a little older than you seem to be—and not quite so very alluring in appearance. In fact, if I may speak candidly——

CECILY   Pray do! I think that whenever one has anything unpleasant to say, one should always be quite candid.

GWENDOLEN   Well, to speak with perfect candour, Cecily, I wish that you were fully forty-two, and more than usually plain for your age. Ernest has a strong upright nature. He is the very soul of truth and honour. Disloyalty would be as impossible to him as deception. But even men of the noblest possible moral character are extremely susceptible to the influence of the physical charms of others. Modern, no less than Ancient History, supplies us with many most painful examples of what I refer to. If it were not so, indeed, History would be quite unreadable.

CECILY   I beg your pardon, Gwendolen, did you say Ernest?

GWENDOLEN   Yes.

CECILY   Oh, but it is not Mr. Ernest Worthing who is my guardian. It is his brother—his elder brother.

GWENDOLEN [*Sitting down again*]   Ernest never mentioned to me that he had a brother.

CECILY   I am sorry to say they have not been on good terms for a long time.

GWENDOLEN   Ah! that accounts for it. And now that I think of it I have never heard any man mention his brother. The subject seems distasteful to most men. Cecily, you have lifted a load from my mind. I was growing almost anxious. It would have been terrible if any cloud had come across a friendship like ours, would it not? Of course you are quite, quite sure that it is not Mr. Ernest Worthing who is your guardian?

CECILY   Quite sure. [*A pause*] In fact, I am going to be his.

GWENDOLEN [*Enquiringly*]   I beg your pardon?

CECILY [*Rather shy and confidingly*]   Dearest Gwendolen, there is no reason

---

18. Eyeglasses with a short handle. They were likely to be used by older women and suggested haughty condescension, which makes Gwendolen's use of them amusing.

why I should make a secret of it to you. Our little county newspaper is sure to chronicle the fact next week. Mr. Ernest Worthing and I are engaged to be married.

GWENDOLEN [*Quite politely, rising*]   My darling Cecily, I think there must be some slight error. Mr. Ernest Worthing is engaged to me. The announcement will appear in the 'Morning Post' on Saturday at the latest.

CECILY [*Very politely, rising*]   I am afraid you must be under some misconception. Ernest proposed to me exactly ten minutes ago. [*Shows diary*]

GWENDOLEN [*Examines diary through her lorgnette carefully*]   It is certainly very curious, for he asked me to be his wife yesterday afternoon at 5.30. If you would care to verify the incident, pray do so. [*Produces diary of her own*] I never travel without my diary. One should always have something sensational to read in the train. I am so sorry, dear Cecily, if it is any disappointment to you, but I am afraid *I* have the prior claim.

CECILY   It would distress me more than I can tell you, dear Gwendolen, if it caused you any mental or physical anguish, but I feel bound to point out that since Ernest proposed to you he clearly has changed his mind.

GWENDOLEN [*Meditatively*]   If the poor fellow has been entrapped into any foolish promise I shall consider it my duty to rescue him at once, and with a firm hand.

CECILY [*Thoughtfully and sadly*]   Whatever unfortunate entanglement my dear boy may have got into, I will never reproach him with it after we are married.

GWENDOLEN   Do you allude to me, Miss Cardew, as an entanglement? You are presumptuous. On an occasion of this kind it becomes more than a moral duty to speak one's mind. It becomes a pleasure.

CECILY   Do you suggest, Miss Fairfax, that I entrapped Ernest into an engagement? How dare you? This is no time for wearing the shallow mask of manners. When I see a spade I call it a spade.

GWENDOLEN [*Satirically*]   I am glad to say that I have never seen a spade. It is obvious that our social spheres have been widely different.

[*Enter* MERRIMAN, *followed by the footman. He carries a salver, table cloth, and plate stand.* CECILY *is about to retort. The presence of the servants exercises a restraining influence, under which both girls chafe.*]

MERRIMAN   Shall I lay tea here as usual, Miss?

CECILY [*Sternly, in a calm voice*]   Yes, as usual. [MERRIMAN *begins to clear and lay cloth. A long pause.* CECILY *and* GWENDOLEN *glare at each other.*]

GWENDOLEN   Are there many interesting walks in the vicinity, Miss Cardew?

CECILY   Oh! yes! a great many. From the top of one of the hills quite close one can see five counties.

GWENDOLEN   Five counties! I don't think I should like that. I hate crowds.

CECILY [*Sweetly*]   I suppose that is why you live in town? [GWENDOLEN *bites her lip, and beats her foot nervously with her parasol*]

GWENDOLEN [*Looking round*]   Quite a well-kept garden this is, Miss Cardew.

CECILY   So glad you like it, Miss Fairfax.

GWENDOLEN   I had no idea there were any flowers in the country.

CECILY   Oh, flowers are as common here, Miss Fairfax, as people are in London.

GWENDOLEN   Personally I cannot understand how anybody manages to exist in the country, if anybody who is anybody does. The country always bores me to death.

CECILY   Ah! This is what the newspapers call agricultural depression, is it not? I believe the aristocracy are suffering very much from it just at present. It is almost an epidemic amongst them, I have been told. May I offer you some tea, Miss Fairfax?

GWENDOLEN   [*With elaborate politeness*]   Thank you. [*Aside*] Detestable girl! But I require tea!

CECILY   [*Sweetly*]   Sugar?

GWENDOLEN   [*Superciliously*]   No, thank you. Sugar is not fashionable any more. [CECILY *looks angrily at her, takes up the tongs and puts four lumps of sugar into the cup*]

CECILY   [*Severely*]   Cake or bread and butter?

GWENDOLEN   [*In a bored manner*]   Bread and butter, please. Cake is rarely seen at the best houses nowadays.

CECILY   [*Cuts a very large slice of cake, and puts it on the tray*]   Hand that to Miss Fairfax.

[MERRIMAN *does so, and goes out with footman.* GWENDOLEN *drinks the tea and makes a grimace. Puts down cup at once, reaches out her hand to the bread and butter, looks at it, and finds it is cake. Rises in indignation.*]

GWENDOLEN   You have filled my tea with lumps of sugar, and though I asked most distinctly for bread and butter, you have given me cake. I am known for the gentleness of my disposition, and the extraordinary sweetness of my nature, but I warn you, Miss Cardew, you may go too far.

CECILY   [*Rising*]   To save my poor, innocent, trusting boy from the machinations of any other girl there are no lengths to which I would not go.

GWENDOLEN   From the moment I saw you I distrusted you. I felt that you were false and deceitful. I am never deceived in such matters. My first impressions of people are invariably right.

CECILY   It seems to me, Miss Fairfax, that I am trespassing on your valuable time. No doubt you have many other calls of a similar character to make in the neighbourhood.

[*Enter* JACK]

GWENDOLEN   [*Catching sight of him*]   Ernest! My own Ernest!

JACK   Gwendolen! Darling! [*Offers to kiss her*]

GWENDOLEN   [*Drawing back*]   A moment! May I ask if you are engaged to be married to this young lady? [*Points to* CECILY]

JACK   [*Laughing*]   To dear little Cecily! Of course not! What could have put such an idea into your pretty little head?

GWENDOLEN   Thank you. You may. [*Offers her cheek*]

CECILY   [*Very sweetly*]   I knew there must be some misunderstanding, Miss Fairfax. The gentleman whose arm is at present around your waist is my dear guardian, Mr. John Worthing.

GWENDOLEN   I beg your pardon?

CECILY   This is Uncle Jack.

GWENDOLEN [*Receding*]   Jack! Oh!

[*Enter* ALGERNON]

CECILY   Here is Ernest.

ALGERNON [*Goes straight over to* CECILY *without noticing anyone else*]   My own love! [*Offers to kiss her*]

CECILY [*Drawing back*]   A moment, Ernest! May I ask you—are you engaged to be married to this young lady?

ALGERNON [*Looking round*]   To what young lady? Good heavens! Gwendolen!

CECILY   Yes! to good heavens, Gwendolen, I mean to Gwendolen.

ALGERNON [*Laughing*]   Of course not! What could have put such an idea into your pretty little head?

CECILY   Thank you. [*Presenting her cheek to be kissed*] You may. [ALGERNON *kisses her*]

GWENDOLEN   I felt there was some slight error, Miss Cardew. The gentleman who is now embracing you is my cousin, Mr. Algernon Moncrieff.[19]

CECILY [*Breaking away from* ALGERNON]   Algernon Moncrieff! Oh! [*The two girls move towards each other and put their arms round each other's waist as if for protection*]

CECILY   Are you called Algernon?

ALGERNON   I cannot deny it.

CECILY   Oh!

GWENDOLEN   Is your name really John?

JACK [*Standing rather proudly*]   I could deny it if I liked. I could deny anything if I liked. But my name certainly is John. It has been John for years.

CECILY [*To* GWENDOLEN]   A gross deception has been practised on both of us.

GWENDOLEN   My poor wounded Cecily!

CECILY   My sweet wronged Gwendolen!

GWENDOLEN [*Slowly and seriously*]   You will call me sister, will you not? [*They embrace.* JACK *and* ALGERNON *groan and walk up and down.*]

CECILY [*Rather brightly*]   There is just one question I would like to be allowed to ask my guardian.

GWENDOLEN   An admirable idea! Mr. Worthing, there is just one question I would like to be permitted to put to you. Where is your brother Ernest? We are both engaged to be married to your brother Ernest, so it is a matter of some importance to us to know where your brother Ernest is at present.

JACK [*Slowly and hesitatingly*]   Gwendolen—Cecily—it is very painful for me to be forced to speak the truth. It is the first time in my life that I have ever been reduced to such a painful position, and I am really quite inexperienced in doing anything of the kind. However, I will tell you quite frankly that I have no brother Ernest. I have no brother at all. I never had a brother in my life, and I certainly have not the smallest intention of ever having one in the future.

CECILY [*Surprised*]   No brother at all?

JACK [*Cheerily*]   None!

19. Pronounced Mon*creef.*

GWENDOLEN [*Severely*]   Had you never a brother of any kind?

JACK [*Pleasantly*]   Never. Not even of any kind.

GWENDOLEN   I am afraid it is quite clear, Cecily, that neither of us is engaged to be married to anyone.

CECILY   It is not a very pleasant position for a young girl suddenly to find herself in. Is it?

GWENDOLEN   Let us go into the house. They will hardly venture to come after us there.

CECILY   No, men are so cowardly, aren't they?

[*They retire into the house with scornful looks*]

JACK   This ghastly state of things is what you call Bunburying, I suppose?

ALGERNON   Yes, and a perfectly wonderful Bunbury it is. The most wonderful Bunbury I have ever had in my life.

JACK   Well, you've no right whatsoever to Bunbury here.

ALGERNON   That is absurd. One has a right to Bunbury anywhere one chooses. Every serious Bunburyist knows that.

JACK   Serious Bunburyist! Good heavens!

ALGERNON   Well, one must be serious about something, if one wants to have any amusement in life. I happen to be serious about Bunburying. What on earth you are serious about I haven't got the remotest idea. About everything, I should fancy. You have such an absolutely trivial nature.

JACK   Well, the only small satisfaction I have in the whole of this wretched business is that your friend Bunbury is quite exploded. You won't be able to run down to the country quite so often as you used to do, dear Algy. And a very good thing too.

ALGERNON   Your brother is a little off colour, isn't he, dear Jack? You won't be able to disappear to London quite so frequently as your wicked custom was. And not a bad thing either.

JACK   As for your conduct towards Miss Cardew, I must say that your taking in a sweet, simple, innocent girl like that is quite inexcusable. To say nothing of the fact that she is my ward.

ALGERNON   I can see no possible defence at all for your deceiving a brilliant, clever, thoroughly experienced young lady like Miss Fairfax. To say nothing of the fact that she is my cousin.

JACK   I wanted to be engaged to Gwendolen, that is all. I love her.

ALGERNON   Well, I simply wanted to be engaged to Cecily. I adore her.

JACK   There is certainly no chance of your marrying Miss Cardew.

ALGERNON   I don't think there is much likelihood, Jack, of you and Miss Fairfax being united.

JACK   Well, that is no business of yours.

ALGERNON   If it was my business, I wouldn't talk about it. [*Begins to eat muffins*] It is very vulgar to talk about one's business. Only people like stockbrokers do that, and then merely at dinner parties.

JACK   How can you sit there, calmly eating muffins when we are in this horrible trouble, I can't make out. You seem to me to be perfectly heartless.

ALGERNON   Well, I can't eat muffins in an agitated manner. The butter would probably get on my cuffs. One should always eat muffins quite calmly. It is the only way to eat them.

JACK   I say it's perfectly heartless your eating muffins at all, under the circumstances.

ALGERNON   When I am in trouble, eating is the only thing that consoles me. Indeed, when I am in really great trouble, as anyone who knows me intimately will tell you, I refuse everything except food and drink. At the present moment I am eating muffins because I am unhappy. Besides, I am particularly fond of muffins. [*Rising*]

JACK   [*Rising*]   Well, that is no reason why you should eat them all in that greedy way. [*Takes muffins from* ALGERNON]

ALGERNON   [*Offering tea-cake*]   I wish you would have tea-cake instead. I don't like tea-cake.

JACK   Good heavens! I suppose a man may eat his own muffins in his own garden.

ALGERNON   But you have just said it was perfectly heartless to eat muffins.

JACK   I said it was perfectly heartless of you, under the circumstances. That is a very different thing.

ALGERNON   That may be. But the muffins are the same. [*He seizes the muffin-dish from* JACK]

JACK   Algy, I wish to goodness you would go.

ALGERNON   You can't possibly ask me to go without having some dinner. It's absurd. I never go without my dinner. No one ever does, except vegetarians and people like that. Besides I have just made arrangements with Dr. Chasuble to be christened at a quarter to six under the name of Ernest.

JACK   My dear fellow, the sooner you give up that nonsense the better. I made arrangements this morning with Dr. Chasuble to be christened myself at 5.30, and I naturally will take the name of Ernest. Gwendolen would wish it. We can't both be christened Ernest. It's absurd. Besides, I have a perfect right to be christened if I like. There is no evidence at all that I ever have been christened by anybody. I should think it extremely probable I never was, and so does Dr. Chasuble. It is entirely different in your case. You have been christened already.

ALGERNON   Yes, but I have not been christened for years.

JACK   Yes, but you have been christened. That is the important thing.

ALGERNON   Quite so. So I know my constitution can stand it. If you are not quite sure about your ever having been christened, I must say I think it rather dangerous your venturing on it now. It might make you very unwell. You can hardly have forgotten that someone very closely connected with you was very nearly carried off this week in Paris by a severe chill.

JACK   Yes, but you said yourself that a severe chill was not hereditary.

ALGERNON   It usen't to be, I know—but I daresay it is now. Science is always making wonderful improvements in things.

JACK   [*Picking up the muffin-dish*]   Oh, that is nonsense; you are always talking nonsense.

ALGERNON   Jack, you are at the muffins again! I wish you wouldn't. There are only two left. [*Takes them*] I told you I was particularly fond of muffins.

JACK   But I hate tea-cake.

ALGERNON   Why on earth then do you allow tea-cake to be served up for your guests? What ideas you have of hospitality!

JACK   Algernon! I have already told you to go. I don't want you here. Why don't you go!

ALGERNON   I haven't quite finished my tea yet! and there is still one muffin left. [JACK *groans, and sinks into a chair.* ALGERNON *continues eating.*]
ACT-DROP

ACT III

Scene—*Morning-room at the Manor House.*

GWENDOLEN *and* CECILY *are at the window, looking out into the garden.*

GWENDOLEN   The fact that they did not follow us at once into the house, as anyone else would have done, seems to me to show that they have some sense of shame left.

CECILY   They have been eating muffins. That looks like repentance.

GWENDOLEN   [*After a pause*]   They don't seem to notice us at all. Couldn't you cough?

CECILY   But I haven't a cough.

GWENDOLEN   They're looking at us. What effrontery!

CECILY   They're approaching. That's very forward of them.

GWENDOLEN   Let us preserve a dignified silence.

CECILY   Certainly. It's the only thing to do now.

[*Enter* JACK *followed by* ALGERNON. *They whistle some dreadful popular air from a British Opera* 1]

GWENDOLEN   This dignified silence seems to produce an unpleasant effect.

CECILY   A most distasteful one.

GWENDOLEN   But we will not be the first to speak.

CECILY   Certainly not.

GWENDOLEN   Mr. Worthing, I have something very particular to ask you. Much depends on your reply.

CECILY   Gwendolen, your common sense is invaluable. Mr. Moncrieff, kindly answer me the following question. Why did you pretend to be my guardian's brother?

ALGERNON   In order that I might have an opportunity of meeting you.

CECILY   [*To* GWENDOLEN]   That certainly seems a satisfactory explanation, does it not?

GWENDOLEN   Yes, dear, if you can believe him.

CECILY   I don't. But that does not affect the wonderful beauty of his answer.

GWENDOLEN   True. In matters of grave importance, style, not sincerity is the vital·thing. Mr. Worthing, what explanation can you offer to me for pretending to have a brother? Was it in order that you might have an opportunity of coming up to town to see me as often as possible?

JACK   Can you doubt it, Miss Fairfax?

GWENDOLEN   I have the gravest doubts upon the subject. But I intend to crush

1. This may be a swipe at Gilbert and Sullivan, who had caricatured Wilde as Bunthorne in *Patience* (1881).

them. This is not the moment for German scepticism.[2] [*Moving to* CECILY] Their explanations appear to be quite satisfactoory, especially Mr. Worthing's. That seems to me to have the stamp of truth upon it.

CECILY   I am more than content with what Mr. Moncrieff said. His voice alone inspires one with absolute credulity.

GWENDOLEN   Then you think we should forgive them?

CECILY   Yes. I mean no.

GWENDOLEN   True! I had forgotten. There are principles at stake that one cannot surrender. Which of us should tell them? The task is not a pleasant one.

CECILY   Could we not both speak at the same time?

GWENDOLEN   An excellent idea! I nearly always speak at the same time as other people. Will you take the time from me?

CECILY   Certainly. [GWENDOLEN *beats time with uplifted finger*]

GWENDOLEN and CECILY [*Speaking together*]   Your Christian names are still an insuperable barrier. That is all!

JACK and ALGERNON [*Speaking together*]   Our Christian names! Is that all? But we are going to be christened this afternoon.

GWENDOLEN [*To* JACK]   For my sake you are prepared to do this terrible thing?

JACK   I am.

CECILY [*To* ALGERNON]   To please me you are ready to face this fearful ordeal?

ALGERNON   I am!

GWENDOLEN   How absurd to talk of the equality of the sexes! Where questions of self-sacrifice are concerned, men are infinitely beyond us.

JACK   We are. [*Clasps hands with* ALGERNON]

CECILY   They have moments of physical courage of which we women know absolutely nothing.

GWENDOLEN [*To* JACK]   Darling!

ALGERNON [*To* CECILY]   Darling! [*They fall into each other's arms*]
    [*Enter* MERRIMAN. *When he enters he coughs loudly, seeing the situation.*]

MERRIMAN   Ahem! Ahem! Lady Bracknell!

JACK   Good heavens!
    [*Enter* LADY BRACKNELL. *The couples separate in alarm. Exit* MERRIMAN.]

LADY BRACKNELL   Gwendolen! What does this mean?

GWENDOLEN   Merely that I am engaged to be married to Mr. Worthing, mamma.

LADY BRACKNELL   Come here. Sit down. Sit down immediately. Hesitation of any kind is a sign of mental decay in the young, of physical weakness in the old. [*Turns to* JACK] Apprised, sir, of my daughter's sudden flight by her trusty maid, whose confidence I purchased by means of a small coin, I followed her at once by a luggage train. Her unhappy father is, I am glad to say, under the impression that she is attending a more than usually lengthy lecture by the University Extension Scheme [3] on

2. She seems to have been reading Immanuel Kant, who undertook to show that there could be no proof of the existence of God.

3. Courses given by university professors to members of the general public.

the Influence of a permanent income on Thought. I do not propose to undeceive him. Indeed I have never undeceived him on any question. I would consider it wrong. But of course, you will clearly understand that all communication between yourself and my daughter must cease immediately from this moment. On this point, as indeed on all points, I am firm.

JACK I am engaged to be married to Gwendolen, Lady Bracknell!

LADY BRACKNELL You are nothing of the kind, sir. And now, as regards Algernon! . . . Algernon!

ALGERNON Yes, Aunt Augusta.

LADY BRACKNELL May I ask if it is in this house that your invalid friend Mr. Bunbury resides?

ALGERNON [Stammering] Oh! No! Bunbury doesn't live here. Bunbury is somewhere else at present. In fact, Bunbury is dead.

LADY BRACKNELL Dead! When did Mr. Bunbury die? His death must have been extremely sudden.

ALGERNON [Airily] Oh! I killed Bunbury this afternoon. I mean poor Bunbury died this afternoon.

LADY BRACKNELL What did he die of?

ALGERNON Bunbury? Oh, he was quite exploded.

LADY BRACKNELL Exploded! Was he the victim of a revolutionary outrage? I was not aware that Mr. Bunbury was interested in social legislation. If so, he is well punished for his morbidity.

ALGERNON My dear Aunt Augusta, I mean he was found out! The doctors found out that Bunbury could not live, that is what I mean—so Bunbury died.

LADY BRACKNELL He seems to have had great confidence in the opinion of his physicians. I am glad, however, that he made up his mind at the last to some definite course of action, and acted under proper medical advice. And now that we have finally got rid of this Mr. Bunbury, may I ask, Mr. Worthing, who is that young person whose hand my nephew Algernon is now holding in what seems to me a peculiarly unnecessary manner?

JACK That lady is Miss Cecily Cardew, my ward. [LADY BRACKNELL bows coldly to CECILY]

ALGERNON I am engaged to be married to Cecily, Aunt Augusta.

LADY BRACKNELL I beg your pardon?

CECILY Mr. Moncrieff and I are engaged to be married, Lady Bracknell.

LADY BRACKNELL [With a shiver, crossing to the sofa and sitting down] I do not know whether there is anything peculiarly exciting in the air of this particular part of Hertfordshire, but the number of engagements that go on seems to me considerably above the proper average that statistics have laid down for our guidance. I think some preliminary enquiry on my part would not be out of place. Mr. Worthing, is Miss Cardew at all connected with any of the larger railway stations in London? I merely desire information. Until yesterday I had no idea that there were any families or persons whose origin was a Terminus. [JACK looks perfectly furious, but restrains himself]

JACK [*In a clear, cold voice*]   Miss Cardew is the granddaughter of the late Mr. Thomas Cardew of 149, Belgrave Square, S.W.; Gervase Park, Dorking, Surrey; and the Sporran, Fifeshire, N.B.[4]

LADY BRACKNELL   That sounds not unsatisfactory. Three addresses always inspire confidence, even in tradesmen. But what proof have I of their authenticity?

JACK   I have carefully preserved the Court Guides of the period. They are open to your inspection, Lady Bracknell.

LADY BRACKNELL [*Grimly*]   I have known strange errors in that publication.

JACK   Miss Cardew's family solicitors are Messrs. Markby, Markby, and Markby.

LADY BRACKNELL   Markby, Markby, and Markby! A firm of the very highest position in their profession. Indeed I am told that one of the Mr. Markbys is occasionally to be seen at dinner parties. So far I am satisfied.

JACK [*Very irritably*]   How extremely kind of you, Lady Bracknell! I have also in my possession, you will be pleased to hear, certificates of Miss Cardew's birth, baptism, whooping cough, registration, vaccination, confirmation, and the measles; both the German and the English variety.

LADY BRACKNELL   Ah! A life crowded with incident, I see; though perhaps somewhat too exciting for a young girl. I am not myself in favour of premature experiences. [*Rises, looks at her watch*] Gwendolen! the time approaches for our departure. We have not a moment to lose. As a matter of form, Mr. Worthing, I had better ask you if Miss Cardew has any little fortune?

JACK   Oh! about a hundred and thirty thousand pounds in the Funds. That is all. Good-bye, Lady Bracknell. So pleased to have seen you.

LADY BRACKNELL [*Sitting down again*]   A moment, Mr. Worthing. A hundred and thirty thousand pounds! And in the Funds! Miss Cardew seems to me a most attractive young lady, now that I look at her. Few girls of the present day have any really solid qualities, any of the qualities that last, and improve with time. We live, I regret to say, in an age of surfaces. [*To* CECILY] Come over here, dear. [CECILY *goes across*] Pretty child! your dress is sadly simple, and your hair seems almost as Nature might have left it. But we can soon alter all that. A thoroughly experienced French maid produces a really marvellous result in a very brief space of time. I remember recommending one to young Lady Lancing, and after three months her own husband did not know her.

JACK [*Aside*]   And after six months nobody knew her.[5]

LADY BRACKNELL [*Glares at* JACK *for a few moments. Then bends, with a practised smile, to* CECILY.]   Kindly turn round, sweet child. [CECILY *turns completely round*] No, the side view is what I want. [CECILY *presents her profile*] Yes, quite as I expected. There are distinct social possibilities in your profile. The two weak points in our age are its want of principle and its want of profile. The chin a little higher, dear. Style

---

4. Presumably North Britain, a way of referring to Scotland not much liked by the Scots.
5. She had become so "fast" that she was not received in respectable society.

largely depends on the way the chin is worn. They are worn very high, just at present. Algernon!

ALGERNON   Yes, Aunt Augusta!

LADY BRACKNELL   There are distinct social possibilities in Miss Cardew's profile.

ALGERNON   Cecily is the sweetest, dearest, prettiest girl in the whole world. And I don't care twopence about social possibilities.

LADY BRACKNELL   Never speak disrespectfully of Society, Algernon. Only people who can't get into it do that. [*To* CECILY] Dear child, of course you know that Algernon has nothing but his debts to depend upon. But I do not approve of mercenary marriages. When I married Lord Bracknell I had no fortune of any kind. But I never dreamed for a moment of allowing that to stand in my way. Well, I suppose I must give my consent.

ALGERNON   Thank you, Aunt Augusta.

LADY BRACKNELL   Cecily, you may kiss me!

CECILY [*Kisses her*]   Thank you, Lady Bracknell.

LADY BRACKNELL   You may also address me as Aunt Augusta for the future.

CECILY   Thank you, Aunt Augusta.

LADY BRACKNELL   The marriage, I think, had better take place quite soon.

ALGERNON   Thank you, Aunt Augusta.

CECILY   Thank you, Aunt Augusta.

LADY BRACKNELL   To speak frankly, I am not in favour of long engagements. They give people the opportunity of finding out each other's character before marriage, which I think is never advisable.

JACK   I beg your pardon for interrupting you, Lady Bracknell, but this engagement is quite out of the question. I am Miss Cardew's guardian, and she cannot marry without my consent until she comes of age. That consent I absolutely decline to give.

LADY BRACKNELL   Upon what grounds, may I ask? Algernon is an extremely, I may almost say an ostentatiously, eligible young man. He has nothing, but he looks everything. What more can one desire?

JACK   It pains me very much to have to speak frankly to you, Lady Bracknell, about your nephew, but the fact is that I do not approve at all of his moral character. I suspect him of being untruthful. [ALGERNON *and* CECILY *look at him in indignant amazement*]

LADY BRACKNELL   Untruthful! My nephew Algernon? Impossible! He is an Oxonian.[6]

JACK   I fear there can be no possible doubt about the matter. This afternoon, during my temporary absence in London on an important question of romance, he obtained admission to my house by means of the false pretence of being my brother. Under an assumed name he drank, I've just been informed by my butler, an entire pint bottle of my Perrier-Jouet, Brut, '89; a wine I was specially reserving for myself. Continuing his disgraceful deception, he succeeded in the course of the afternoon in alienating the affections of my only ward. He subsequently stayed to

6. A graduate of Oxford. The line is perhaps the only failure in the play.

tea, and devoured every single muffin. And what makes his conduct all the more heartless is, that he was perfectly well aware from the first that I have no brother, that I never had a brother, and that I don't intend to have a brother, not even of any kind. I distinctly told him so myself yesterday afternoon.

LADY BRACKNELL   Ahem! Mr. Worthing, after careful consideration I have decided entirely to overlook my nephew's conduct to you.

JACK   That is very generous of you, Lady Bracknell. My own decision, however, is unalterable. I decline to give my consent.

LADY BRACKNELL   [*To* CECILY]   Come here, sweet child. [CECILY *goes over*] How old are you, dear?

CECILY   Well, I am really only eighteen, but I always admit to twenty when I go to evening parties.

LADY BRACKNELL   You are perfectly right in making some slight alteration. Indeed, no woman should ever be quite accurate about her age. It looks so calculating. . . . [*In a meditative manner*] Eighteen, but admitting to twenty at evening parties. Well, it will not be very long before you are of age and free from the restraints of tutelage. So I don't think your guardian's consent is, after all, a matter of any importance.

JACK   Pray excuse me, Lady Bracknell, for interrupting you again, but it is only fair to tell you that according to the terms of her grandfather's will Miss Cardew does not come legally of age till she is thirty-five.

LADY BRACKNELL   That does not seem to me to be a grave objection. Thirty-five is a very attractive age. London society is full of women of the very highest birth who have, of their own free choice, remained thirty-five for years. Lady Dumbleton is an instance in point. To my own knowledge she has been thirty-five ever since she arrived at the age of forty, which was many years ago now. I see no reason why our dear Cecily should not be even still more attractive at the age you mention than she is at present. There will be a large accumulation of property.

CECILY   Algy, could you wait for me till I was thirty-five?

ALGERNON   Of course I could, Cecily. You know I could.

CECILY   Yes, I felt it instinctively, but I couldn't wait all that time. I hate waiting even five minutes for anybody. It always makes me rather cross. I am not punctual myself, I know, but I do like punctuality in others, and waiting, even to be married, is quite out of the question.

ALGERNON   Then what is to be done, Cecily?

CECILY   I don't know, Mr. Moncrieff.

LADY BRACKNELL   My dear Mr. Worthing, as Miss Cardew states positively that she cannot wait till she is thirty-five—a remark which I am bound to says seems to me to show a somewhat impatient nature—I would beg of you to reconsider your decision.

JACK   But my dear Lady Bracknell, the matter is entirely in your own hands. The moment you consent to my marriage with Gwendolen, I will most gladly allow your nephew to form an alliance with my ward.

LADY BRACKNELL   [*Rising and drawing herself up*]   You must be quite aware that what you propose is out of the question.

JACK   Then a passionate celibacy is all that any of us can look forward to.

LADY BRACKNELL   That is not the destiny I propose for Gwendolen. Algernon, of course, can choose for himself. [*Pulls out her watch*] Come dear; [GWENDOLEN *rises*] we have already missed five, if not six, trains. To miss any more might expose us to comment on the platform.

[*Enter* DR. CHASUBLE]

CHASUBLE   Everything is quite ready for the christenings.

LADY BRACKNELL   The christenings, sir! Is not that somewhat premature?

CHASUBLE [*Looking rather puzzled, and pointing to* JACK *and* ALGERNON]   Both these gentlemen have expressed a desire for immediate baptism.

LADY BRACKNELL   At their age? The idea is grotesque and irreligious! Algernon, I forbid you to be baptised. I will not hear of such excesses. Lord Bracknell would be highly displeased if he learned that that was the way in which you wasted your time and money.

CHASUBLE   Am I to understand then that there are to be no christenings at all this afternoon?

JACK   I don't think that, as things are now, it would be of much practical value to either of us, Dr. Chasuble.

CHASUBLE   I am grieved to hear such sentiments from you, Mr. Worthing. They savour of the heretical views of the Anabaptists,[7] views that I have completely refuted in four of my unpublished sermons. However, as your present mood seems to be one peculiarly secular, I will return to the church at once. Indeed, I have just been informed by the pew-opener that for the last hour and a half Miss Prism has been waiting for me in the vestry.

LADY BRACKNELL [*Starting*]   Miss Prism! Did I hear you mention a Miss Prism?

CHASUBLE   Yes, Lady Bracknell. I am on my way to join her.

LADY BRACKNELL   Pray allow me to detain you for a moment. This matter may prove to be one of vital importance to Lord Bracknell and myself. Is this Miss Prism a female of repellent aspect, remotely connected with education?

CHASUBLE [*Somewhat indignantly*]   She is the most cultivated of ladies, and the very picture of respectability.

LADY BRACKNELL   It is obviously the same person. May I ask what position she holds in your household?

CHASUBLE [*Severely*]   I am a celibate, madam.

JACK [*Interposing*]   Miss Prism, Lady Bracknell, has been for the last three years Miss Cardew's esteemed governess and valued companion.

LADY BRACKNELL   In spite of what I hear of her, I must see her at once. Let her be sent for.

CHASUBLE [*Looking off*]   She approaches; she is nigh.

[*Enter* MISS PRISM *hurriedly*]

MISS PRISM   I was told you expected me in the vestry, dear Canon. I have been waiting for you there for an hour and three-quarters. [*Catches sight of*

7. This Reformation sect held that only adult baptism was valid, which doesn't bring their view into accord with Jack's present position.

LADY BRACKNELL, *who has fixed her with a stony glare.* MISS PRISM *grows pale and quails. She looks anxiously round as if desirous to escape.*]

LADY BRACKNELL [*In a severe, judicial voice*]   Prism! [MISS PRISM *bows her head in shame*] Come here, Prism! [MISS PRISM *approaches in a humble manner*] Prism! Where is that baby? [*General consternation. The Canon starts back in horror.* ALGERNON *and* JACK *pretend to be anxious to shield* CECILY *and* GWENDOLEN *from hearing the details of a terrible public scandal.*] Twenty-eight years ago, Prism, you left Lord Brack-nell's house, Number 104, Upper Grosvenor Street, in charge of a perambulator that contained a baby, of the male sex. You never returned. A few weeks later, through the elaborate investigations of the Metro-politan police, the perambulator was discover at midnight, standing by itself in a remote corner of Bayswater. It contained the manuscript of a three-volume novel of more than usually revolting sentimentality. [MISS PRISM *starts in involuntary indignation*] But the baby was not there! [*Everyone looks at* MISS PRISM] Prism: Where is that baby? [*A pause*]

MISS PRISM   Lady Bracknell, I admit with shame that I do not know. I only wish I did. The plain facts of the case are these. On the morning of the day you mention, a day that is for ever branded on my memory, I pre-pared as usual to take the baby out in its perambulator. I had also with me a somewhat old, but capacious hand-bag in which I had intended to place the manuscript of a work of fiction that I had written during my few unoccupied hours. In a moment of mental abstraction, for which I never can forgive myself, I deposited the mansucript in the bassinette, and placed the baby in the hand-bag.

JACK [*Who has been listening attentively*]   But where did you deposit the hand-bag?

MISS PRISM   Do not ask me, Mr. Worthing.

JACK   Miss Prism, this is a matter of no small importance to me. I insist on knowing where you deposited the hand-bag that contained that infant.

MISS PRISM   I left it in the cloak room of one of the larger railway stations in London.

JACK   What railway station?

MISS PRISM [*Quite crushed*]   Victoria. The Brighton line. [*Sinks into a chair*]

JACK   I must retire to my room for a moment. Gwendolen, wait here for me.

GWENDOLEN   If you are not too long, I will wait here for you all my life.

   [*Exit* JACK *in great excitement*]

CHASUBLE   What do you think this means, Lady Bracknell?

LADY BRACKNELL   I dare not even suspect, Dr. Chasuble. I need hardly tell you that in families of high position strange coincidences are not sup-posed to occur. They are hardly considered the thing.

   [*Noises heard overhead as if someone was throwing trunks about. Everyone looks up.*]

CECILY   Uncle Jack seems strangely agitated.

CHASUBLE   Your guardian has a very emotional nature.

LADY BRACKNELL   This noise is extremely unpleasant. It sounds as if he was having an argument. I dislike arguments of any kind. They are always vulgar, and often convincing.

CHASUBLE [*Looking up*]   It has stopped now. [*The noise is redoubled*]

LADY BRACKNELL   I wish he would arrive at some conclusion.

GWENDOLEN   This suspense is terrible. I hope it will last.

[*Enter* JACK *with a hand-bag of black leather in his hand*]

JACK [*Rushing over to* MISS PRISM]   Is this the hand-bag, Miss Prism? Examine it carefully before you speak. The happiness of more than one life depends on your answer.

MISS PRISM [*Calmly*]   It seems to be mine. Yes, here is the injury it received through the upsetting of a Gower Street omnibus in younger and happier days. Here is the stain on the lining caused by the explosion of a temperance beverage, an incident that occurred at Leamington. And here, on the lock, are my initials. I had forgotten that in an extravagant mood I had had them placed there. The bag is undoubtedly mine. I am delighted to have it so unexpectedly restored to me. It has been a great inconvenience being without it all these years.

JACK [*In a pathetic voice*]   Miss Prism, more is restored to you than this handbag. I was the baby you placed in it.

MISS PRISM [*Amazed*]   You?

JACK [*Embracing her*]   Yes . . . mother!

MISS PRISM [*Recoiling in indignant astonishment*]   Mr. Worthing! I am unmarried!

JACK   Unmarried! I do not deny that is a serious blow. But after all, who has the right to cast a stone against one who has suffered? Cannot repentance wipe out an act of folly? Why should there be one law for men, and another for women? Mother, I forgive you. [*Tries to embrace her again*]

MISS PRISM [*Still more indignant*]   Mr. Worthing, there is some error. [*Pointing to* LADY BRACKNELL] There is the lady who can tell you who you really are.

JACK [*After a pause*]   Lady Bracknell, I hate to seem inquisitive, but would you kindly inform me who I am?

LADY BRACKNELL   I am afraid that the news I have to give you will not altogether please you. You are the son of my poor sister, Mrs. Moncrieff, and consequently Algernon's elder brother.

JACK   Algy's elder brother! Then I have a brother after all. I knew I had a brother! I always said I had a brother! Cecily,—how could you have ever doubted that I had a brother. [*Seizes hold of* ALGERNON] Dr. Chasuble, my unfortunate brother. Miss Prism, my unfortunate brother. Gwendolen, my unfortunate brother. Algy, you young scoundrel, you will have to treat me with more respect in the future. You have never behaved to me like a brother in all your life.

ALGERNON   Well, not till to-day, old boy, I admit. I did my best, however, though I was out of practice. [*Shakes hands*]

GWENDOLEN [*To* JACK]   My own! But what own are you? What is your Christian name, now that you have become someone else?

JACK   Good heavens! . . . I had quite forgotten that point. Your decision on the subject of my name is irrevocable, I suppose?

GWENDOLEN   I never change, except in my affections.

CECILY   What a noble nature you have, Gwendolen!

JACK   Then the question had better be cleared up at once. Aunt Augusta, a moment. At the time when Miss Prism left me in the hand-bag, had I been christened already?

LADY BRACKNELL   Every luxury that money could buy, including christening, had been lavished on you by your fond and doting parents.

JACK   Then I was christened! That is settled. Now, what name was I given? Let me know the worst.

LADY BRACKNELL   Being the eldest son you were naturally christened after your father.

JACK   [*Irritably*]   Yes, but what was my father's Christian name?

LADY BRACKNELL   [*Meditatively*]   I cannot at the present moment recall what the General's Christian name was. But I have no doubt he had one. He was eccentric, I admit. But only in later years. And that was the result of the Indian climate, and marriage, and indigestion, and other things of that kind.

JACK   Algy! Can't you recollect what our father's Christian name was?

ALGERNON   My dear boy, we were never even on speaking terms. He died before I was a year old.

JACK   His name would appear in the Army Lists of the period, I suppose, Aunt Augusta?

LADY BRACKNELL   The General was essentially a man of peace, except in his domestic life. But I have no doubt his name would appear in any military directory.

JACK   The Army Lists of the last forty years are here. These delightful records should have been my constant study [*Rushes to bookcase and tears the books out*] M. Generals . . . Mallam, Maxbohm[8] Magley, what ghastly names they have—Markby, Migsby, Moss, Moncrieff! Lieutenant 1840, Captain, Lieutenant-Colonel, Colonel, General 1869, Christian names, Ernest John [*Puts book very quietly down and speaks quite calmly*] I always told you, Gwendolen, my name was Ernest, didn't I? Well, it is Ernest after all. I mean it naturally is Ernest.

LADY BRACKNELL   Yes, I remember that the General was called Ernest. I knew I had some particular reason for disliking the name.

GWENDOLEN   Ernest! My own Ernest! I felt from the first that you could have no other name!

JACK   Gwendolen, it is a terrible thing for a man to find out suddenly that all his life he has been speaking nothing but the truth. Can you forgive me?

GWENDOLEN   I can. For I feel that you are sure to change.

JACK   My own one!

CHASUBLE   [*To* MISS PRISM]   Lætitia! [*Embraces her*]

MISS PRISM   [*Enthusiastically*]   Frederick! At last!

---

8. Wilde contrived this name to tease Max Beerbohm (1875–1956), later to be known as essayist, parodist, dramatic critic, caricaturist.

ALGERNON   Cecily! [*Embraces her*] At last!

JACK   Gwendolen! [*Embraces her*] At last!

LADY BRACKNELL   My nephew, you seem to be displaying signs of triviality.

JACK   On the contrary, Aunt Augusta, I've now realized for the first time in my life the vital Importance of Being Earnest.

TABLEAU [9]

CURTAIN

1894   1895, 1899

9. French for "picture," designation for the stage device in which all the actors in a scene stand motionless in postures they have taken.

Victorian Poetry

Walter Pater, the great critic whose marvelous sensibility we do a kind of violence by naming it Decadent, remarked in his essay on "Style" (in Appreciations, 1889) that imaginative prose was "the special art of the modern world." Pater had a certain self-interest here, since he had burned his early poems (supposedly for being too religious, but probably also because they were bad) and had devoted his life to writing imaginative prose. Yet Pater had strong impersonal grounds for his assertion, and gave two in particular: "the chaotic variety and complexity" of the modern world's interests, unsuitable for "the restraint proper to verse form, so that the most characteristic verse of the nineteenth century has been lawless verse," and "an all-pervading naturalism" also unsuitable for verse, since verse is more "ambitious" than prose.

Whether the nineteenth-century novel and nonfictional prose of England represent a larger achievement than its verse is highly disputable. What is increasingly certain is that nineteenth-century English poetry is one of the world's major imaginative achievements, almost comparable to the poetry of the English Renaissance. No poet of the absolute eminence of Spenser, Shakespeare, or Milton composed in England during the nineteenth century, but the six major High Romantics—Blake, Wordsworth, Coleridge, Byron, Shelley, Keats—and the somewhat less titanic six major Victorians —Tennyson, Browning, Arnold, Rossetti, Swinburne, and Hopkins—present an extraordinary variety and intensity, not matched by twentieth-century poetry in English, not even by Hardy, Yeats, Stevens. Perhaps only Blake and Wordsworth stand near Chaucer and the greater Renaissance poets, but all of these creators have survived the sorrows of literary fashion, and will go on surviving. More centrally, led by Wordsworth, these poets created "modern poetry," as becomes steadily more apparent with each year that twentieth-century literary Modernism recedes into history.

Victorian poetry, in the perspective made possible by nearly a century's passage, is essentially a continuation of Romantic poetry into the third and fourth generations. If Yeats was right in believing that he and his friends who came to their dark maturity in the 'Nineties were "the Last Romantics," then English Romanticism lasted for five generations: Blake, Wordsworth, and Coleridge (born 1757–72); Byron, Shelley, Keats (born 1788–95); Tennyson and Browning (born 1809–12); Arnold, Rossetti, Morris, Swinburne, Hardy, and Hopkins (born 1822–44), and finally Yeats (born 1865). To trace this main continuity (as broken by highly deliberate attempts at discontinuity) is to sketch also a miniature of the development of modern poetic consciousness.

What allies all the principal Victorian poets is their imaginative, stylistic, and procedural indebtedness to either Keats or Shelley. The division is, Keats: Tennyson, Arnold, Rossetti, Morris, and Hopkins; Shelley: Browning, Swinburne, Hardy, and Yeats. The same complex pattern of influence that dominated the Romantics is at work here also; Blake and Wordsworth struggled with the shadow of Milton, yet the younger Romantics had to wrestle a composite precursor, Milton and Wordsworth. The younger Victorians tended to engage a parent compounded of Keats and Tennyson, or of Shelley and Browning. Pre-Raphaelite poetry is at once a consolidation of the Keats-Tennyson tradition of sensuous naturalism, and a curiously subverting phantasmagoric rebellion against it. But this is still only part of the immense labyrinth of poetic influence in the nineteenth century. Except for Rossetti and Swinburne, who are overt Romantic ideologists, every important Victorian poet attempted, in very diverse ways, to break away from the High Romantic erotic quest. Arnold's explicit (but equivocal) classicism, his dismissal as "morbidity" of everything Romantic except for Wordsworth's most direct nature poetry, is the best known of these swerves away from the precursors, but all the others swerved more subtly (and more successfully).

Shelley and Keats owed to Wordsworth an example he himself wished to repudiate, the self-conscious quester of *The Excursion,* the melancholy Solitary, of whom the Byron of *Childe Harold's Pilgrimage* III and IV was an indeliberate parody. The Victorian poets owed to Shelley and Keats examples provided by the tragic brevity of their lives, and the contrast they (and Byron) afforded to Wordsworth, who had outlived his own imaginative energies. Even Tennyson and Browning had a deep uneasiness at finding themselves accepted, eventually, as public sages, lest they should awaken to discover they shared Wordsworth's fate. The prophetic burden of Romantic poetry was assumed by the Victorian prose seers: Carlyle, Newman, Mill, Ruskin, the later Arnold, the later Morris, and Pater, a displacement which reduced both the ambitions and the risks of Victorian verse. This may account for a curious effect created by every Victorian poet except Swinburne, a sense that they never delivered the whole of their Word. Even the outspoken Browning rightly doubted that he had given his full report to God:

> We may learn from the biography whether his spirit invariably saw and spoke from the last height to which it had attained. An absolute vision is not for this world, but we are permitted a continual approximation to it, every degree of which in the individual, provided it exceed the attainment of the masses, must procure him a clear advantage. Did the poet ever attain to a higher platform than where he rested and exhibited a result? Did he know more than he spoke of?

This is from Browning's essay on his precursor, Shelley, and is meant to be answered: "No," for Shelley, more than any other, continually was permitted an approximation to an absolute vision. As applied to himself, these crucial questions assume a positive answer, and Browning confronts his own relative failure. But Tennyson, the other great poetic imagination of the age, also knew more of a vision than he allowed himself to render. Hopkins, who had both a genius for sensuous apprehension and an immense capacity for language, each almost of Keatsian dimension, scarcely allowed himself to realize the full individuality of his own vision. The largest unanswered question about the major Victorian poets is: why could they neither sustain nor wish to sustain a High Romantic confidence in the autonomy of their own imaginations, when they were sons of Keats and of Shelley who more than any poets except Blake shared a confidence in the imagination's freedom and priority?

The simpler answers here are not adequate, and reduce finally to Pater's historical explanation; the "all-pervading naturalism," as the century advanced, negated high poetic ambitions. Yeats, a Paterian in his prose and in his ideology, agreed and fought back with an all-pervading supernaturalism, free from any orthodox associations. Yet Blake (though Yeats declined to see this) was no more a supernaturalist than he was a naturalist, nor was the skeptical Shelley, Yeats's other poetic father. Scholars rely too much on reductive versions of Pater's argument, and dwell long on Victorian advances in geology, evolutionary theory, and social analysis. Doubtless these were all factors in the Victorian refusal to see that the imagination insists upon being indulged, whatever the pressures of an age's realities. The profound religious uncertainties of the middle and later nineteenth century did constitute the largest force in the violence from without that pressed in upon the poetic mind. But the question remains: why was the answering violence from within the embattled poetic consciousness as subdued as it rapidly became? In what hope did Tennyson and Browning, let alone Arnold and Hopkins, abide when they turned aside from the full intensities of the Romantic quest?

If we glance at the programmatic Victorian Romantics of the Pre-Raphaelite grouping, we will find that there the larger vision was abandoned also, because the sense of the personal predicament of the poet-as-man had become even more acute than it was for Shelley. Swinburne, the most ambitious of these late Romantics, could write a poem like *Hertha* only by excluding himself from the poem's situation, but in spite of his artistry his personal pathology drifted back into the poem's undersong. No Victorian poet, not even Browning, showed the full range of the Romantic audacity that could allow Blake, Wordsworth, and Shelley (more skeptically and unsteadily) to believe that they represented the Divine Vision for their time, or that made possible Keats's and Byron's emphasis on the central, potentially universal significance of their own intellectual and sensuous experience.

Arnold and the principal Pre-Raphaelites, like the younger Romantics, were not Christians, and followed the logic of Romantic tradition by displacing the hopes of Protestantism into cultural (and largely poetic) contexts. Tennyson, very dubiously, remained a vague kind of Christian universalist. Browning, by temperament and belief, is one of the most vehement Protestants in the language, while Hopkins courageously but hopelessly attempted to convert his Paterian temperament to the demands of a Catholic devotional poetry. Arnold, in turning away both from Christianity and Romanticism, found he could not continue as a poet. The answer to the earlier question seems to be that the major Victorian poets modified or abandoned their early Romanticism in order to trust (however faintly) in an even larger and more traditional hope, the Christian humanism that had helped to sustain the young Milton. Whether the hope had even a minimal basis in reality we may doubt, but who can argue against hope? Where Victorian poetry still moves us most is where it exceeds us in hope.

ALFRED, LORD TENNYSON

1809–1892

Tennyson, in some respects the most accomplished artist of all English poets since Pope, was born and raised at Somersby in Lincolnshire, where his father was rector. Two of his elder brothers, Frederick and Charles, were also poets of talent. Himself a natural poet, he began writing at five, and continued his juvenile production until he entered Trinity College, Cambridge, in 1827, where he fell in love with Arthur Henry Hallam, who became the true Muse of all Tennyson's mature work. The friendship between the two was the most important experience of Tennyson's life, and if it had a repressed sexual element, neither Tennyson nor Hallam (nor anyone else) seems ever to have been aware of this. Under Hallam's guidance (he had remarkable critical talents), Tennyson became a Keatsian poet, which despite later development he always remained.

In 1827, together with his brothers Frederick and Charles, Tennyson published the mistitled *Poems by Two Brothers*, but his first real book was *Poems, Chiefly Lyrical* in 1830, followed by *Poems* late in 1832. Both volumes received some negative reviews, and the oversensitive poet did not appear again before the British public until 1842, when he attained a just fame and financial rewards unknown since Byron, by bringing out *Poems* in two volumes. But, between 1830 and 1842, the decisive events of Tennyson's life occurred. His father died in 1831, and subsequently he left Cambridge without taking his degree. On September 15, 1833, Arthur Hallam died suddenly at twenty-two, in Vienna, of a brain seizure. Tennyson had met Emily Sellwood and reached an understanding with her as early as 1830; they became engaged in 1838, but did not marry until 1850. Biographers explain this twenty-year delay as financial in nature, but that seems mildly preposterous. Tennyson would not marry until then, and surely it is significant that his marriage took place only after the first publication (anonymous) of *In Memoriam*, his completed sequence of elegies for Hallam.

In 1850 Tennyson followed Wordsworth as Poet Laureate, and henceforth he was an English institution, whether he wrote well or badly. From 1853 on, he lived in great comfort on an estate on the Isle of Wight, cultivating his close friendships with the other luminaries of the age, cared for faithfully by Mrs. Tennyson, who also bore him two sons, Hallam and Lionel. In 1884, he accepted a barony, having declined the offer twice previously. His reputation remained high until his death in 1892, declined in the earlier twentieth century, and is rightly very high again today. In retrospect, his life had one event only, and that was the terrible experience of losing Hallam. It is hardly an overstatement to say that most of his best poetry, quite aside from *In Memoriam*, is elegiac in nature, and the subject of the sense of loss is always Hallam. "Ulysses," "Tithonus," *Morte d'Arthur*, "Tears, Idle Tears," much of *Idylls of the King*, the late *Merlin and the Gleam*, all mourn Hallam (sometimes obliquely), just as the living Hallam directly inspired the best poems of the 1830 and 1832 volumes. This matter hardly can be overemphasized in considering Tennyson's poetry. He became, in his best poetry after 1833, the perfect model of a poet who is a bereaved lover, and the largest clues we can have to the strength of his poetry lie in its relationship to Hallam. In a sense, Hallam represented Romanticism to Tennyson, and it seems clear that the later Tennyson would have been more of a High Romantic and less of a societal spokesman if Hallam had lived.

Hallam reviewed Tennyson's *Poems, Chiefly Lyrical* in 1831, and characterized his friend's poetry as belonging to the Romantic school of Keats and Shelley as opposed to that of Wordsworth. Yeats, who said that Hallam's review was crucial for his own early work, usefully summarized Hallam's distinction between the two schools: "Keats and Shelley, unlike Wordsworth, intermixed into their poetry no elements from the general thought, but wrote out of the impression made by the world upon their delicate senses." Yeats was remembering one of Hallam's most acute sentences about Keats and Shelley: "So vivid was the delight attending the simple exertions of eye and ear, that it became mingled more and more with trains of active thought, and tended to absorb their whole being into the energy of sense." This is the particular poetic strength of the young Tennyson under Hallam's influence (1828–33), who is genuinely a poet of sensation, and the necessary link between the Keats of *The Eve of St. Agnes* and the great Odes, and the Pre-Raphaelite and Aesthetic poets later in the century. While Hallam lived, and when he wrote in memory of Hallam, Tennyson did not mix into his poetry "elements from the general thought" without taking that thought up into the highly original context of his own imagination. He kept before him a crucial admonition of Hallam's, also included in the invaluable review of 1830: "That delicate sense of fitness which grows with the growth of artist feelings, and strengthens with their strength, until it acquires a celerity and weight of decision hardly inferior to the correspondent judgments of conscience, is weakened by every indulgence of heterogeneous aspirations, however pure they may be, however lofty, however suitable to human nature." Tennyson forgot this too often, particularly after 1850, and perhaps he delayed his marriage and consequent domestication and institutionalization because something in him accurately feared that he would forget it.

Tennyson, like Coleridge but very unlike Keats, always feared his own imagination, and distrusted its tendency to assert autonomy. Hallam's gift to Tennyson, his liberating virtue, was to give the poet enough confidence in the value of his own imagination to allow him to indulge it, for a time. The best early poems—"Mariana," *The Lady of Shalott, The Palace of Art, The Lotos-Eaters* (all except the magical *The Hesperides*)—manifest an uneasiness at their own Spenserian-Keatsian luxuriance, but in all of them the poetry is at work celebrating itself, so that as readers we believe the song and not the singer. What stays with us is the embowered, self-delighting consciousness in the sensuous prison-paradise, and not the societal censor that disapproves of such delight. If we follow a distinction of D. H. Lawrence's, and say that a daemon wrote what is most valuable in Tennyson's early poems, we can add that this daemon, fortunately, never vanished entirely from the later poetry, so long as Hallam continued to haunt it.

Yet this is only part of the truth, even about what is most valuable in Tennyson's poetry. He wrote in praise of Virgil and (very powerfully) in unfair dispraise of Lucretius, because he was at peace with the Virgilian strain in his own poetry, and feared the Lucretian, which he knew secretly he possessed also. This Epicurean tendency, which was to triumph in Pater, in much of Yeats, and in some of Yeats's friends of the 'Nineties, made no intellectual appeal to Tennyson, yet moved him deep within. *In Memoriam* is so troubled by the materialistic metaphysical implications of Victorian geology because Tennyson's imagination responded naturally and even buoyantly to speculations which his moral intellect could not tolerate.

If Tennyson is something of a poetic split personality, this does not make his work less interesting, nor does it affect his work where it is strongest, in style, by which more than diction and metric is meant. Tennyson's style, the most flawless in English poetry after Milton's and Pope's, is itself a sensibility, a means of apprehending both the internal and the external world. Intuitively, Tennyson understood what poetry was, argument that could not be separated from song, gesture, dance, and the rhythms of a unique but representative individual's breath-soul. Browning and Yeats, and the High Romantics before Tennyson, were all more powerful and original conceptualizers than Tennyson, and all of them mastered a great style, but none of them wrote so well so consistently as he did. A reader who knows no Latin and so cannot read Virgil has lost a great deal, but it is Tennyson's triumph that any such reader can remedy the loss by reading Tennyson, who richly sustains the comparison.

Mariana°

Mariana in the moated grange
(*Measure for Measure*)

With blackest moss the flower-plots
   Were thickly crusted, one and all:
The rusted nails fell from the knots
   That held the pear to the gable-wall.
The broken sheds looked sad and strange:
   Unlifted was the clinking latch;
   Weeded and worn the ancient thatch
Upon the lonely moated grange.
      She only said, 'My life is dreary,
10   He cometh not,' she said;
      She said, 'I am aweary, aweary,
      I would that I were dead!'

Her tears fell with the dews at even;
   Her tears fell ere the dews were dried;
She could not look on the sweet heaven,
   Either at morn or eventide.
After the flitting of the bats,
   When thickest dark did trance° the sky,
   She drew her casement-curtain by,
20 And glanced athwart the glooming flats.
      She only said, 'The night is dreary,
      He cometh not,' she said;
      She said, 'I am aweary, aweary,
      I would that I were dead!'

Upon the middle of the night,
   Waking she heard the night-fowl crow:
The cock sung out an hour ere light:
   From the dark fen the oxen's low

Mariana In Shakespeare's *Measure for Measure* III.i.212 ff., she waits, dejectedly, in an isolated farmhouse or grange for her faithless lover. But the heroine of Keats's *Isabella* is more in Tennyson's mind; see stanzas XXX to XXXIV of Keats's poem.
trance throw into a trance

Came to her: without hope of change,
30 In sleep she seemed to walk forlorn,
 Till cold winds woke the gray-eyed morn
About the lonely moated grange.
  She only said, 'The day is dreary,
   He cometh not,' she said;
  She said, 'I am aweary, aweary,
   I would that I were dead!'

About a stone-cast from the wall
 A sluice with blackened waters slept,
And o'er it many, round and small,
40 The clustered marish-mosses° crept.
Hard by a poplar shook alway,
 All silver-green with gnarlèd bark:
 For leagues no other tree did mark
The level waste, the rounding gray.
  She only said, 'My life is dreary,
   He cometh not,' she said;
  She said, 'I am aweary, aweary,
   I would that I were dead!'

And ever when the moon was low,
50 And the shrill winds were up and away,
In the white curtain, to and fro,
 She saw the gusty shadow sway.
But when the moon was very low,
 And wild winds bound within their cell,
 The shadow of the poplar fell
Upon her bed, across her brow.
  She only said, 'The night is dreary,
   He cometh not,' she said;
  She said, 'I am aweary, aweary,
60   I would that I were dead!'

All day within the dreamy house,
 The doors upon their hinges creaked;
The blue fly sung in the pane; the mouse
 Behind the mouldering wainscot shrieked,
Or from the crevice peered about.
 Old faces glimmered through the doors,
 Old footsteps trod the upper floors,
Old voices called her from without.
  She only said, 'My life is dreary,
70   He cometh not,' she said;
  She said, 'I am aweary, aweary,
   I would that I were dead!'

marish-mosses marsh-moss lumps floating on the surface of the floodgate-dammed water

The sparrow's chirrup on the roof,
   The slow clock ticking, and the sound
Which to the wooing wind aloof
   The poplar made, did all confound
Her sense; but most she loathed the hour
   When the thick-moted sunbeam lay
   Athwart the chambers, and the day
80 Was sloping toward his western bower.
      Then, said she, 'I am very dreary,
         He will not come,' she said;
      She wept, 'I am aweary, aweary,
         Oh God, that I were dead!'
              1830

The Kraken

Below the thunders of the upper deep;
Far, far beneath in the abysmal sea,
His ancient, dreamless, uninvaded sleep
The Kraken° sleepeth: faintest sunlights flee
About his shadowy sides: above him swell
Huge sponges of millennial growth and height;
And far away into the sickly light,
From many a wondrous grot and secret cell
Unnumbered and enormous polypi°
10 Winnow with giant arms the slumbering green.
There hath he lain for ages and will lie
Battening upon huge seaworms in his sleep,
Until the latter fire° shall heat the deep;
Then once by man and angels to be seen,
In roaring he shall rise and on the surface die.
              1830

The Lady of Shalott°

PART I

On either side the river lie
Long fields of barley and of rye,
That clothe the wold° and meet the sky;
And through the field the road runs by
   To many-towered Camelot;°
And up and down the people go,

Kraken fabulous sea-monster
polypi hydras, perhaps watersnakes
latter fire Apocalypse; see Revelation 8:8–9, and
13:1
The Lady of Shalott This poem helped form the
style of Pre-Raphaelite poetry and that of Poe.

Shalott is a variant of Astolat, which makes the
Lady "the lily maid of Astolat," Elaine, and
the poem a prefiguration of "Lancelot and
Elaine" in Tennyson's Arthurian cycle.
wold a rolling plain
Camelot mythical capital of Arthur's kingdom

Gazing where the lilies blow°
Round an island there below,
   The island of Shalott.

10 Willows whiten,° aspens quiver,
Little breezes dusk and shiver
Through the wave that runs for ever
By the island in the river
   Flowing down to Camelot.
Four gray walls, and four gray towers,
Overlook a space of flowers,
And the silent isle imbowers
   The Lady of Shalott.

By the margin, willow-veiled,
20 Slide the heavy barges trailed
By slow horses; and unhailed
The shallop° flitteth silken-sailed
   Skimming down to Camelot:
But who hath seen her wave her hand?
Or at the casement seen her stand?
Or is she known in all the land,
   The Lady of Shalott?

Only reapers, reaping early
In among the bearded barley,
30 Hear a song that echoes cheerly
From the river winding clearly,
   Down to towered Camelot:
And by the moon the reaper weary,
Piling sheaves in uplands airy,
Listening, whispers ' 'Tis the fairy
   Lady of Shalott.'

     PART II
There she weaves by night and day
A magic web with colours gay.
She has heard a whisper say,
40 A curse is on her if she stay
   To look down to Camelot.
She knows not what the curse may be,
And so she weaveth steadily,
And little other care hath she,
   The Lady of Shalott.

And moving through a mirror clear°
That hangs before her all the year,

blow blossom
Willows whiten The white undersides of willow
leaves are turned up by the wind.

shallop small, open boat
a mirror clear See Britomart's mirror in *The*
Faerie Queene III. ii.

Shadows of the world appear.
There she sees the highway near
50   Winding down to Camelot:
There the river eddy whirls,
And there the surly village-churls,
And the red cloaks of market girls,
       Pass onward from Shalott.

Sometimes a troop of damsels glad,
An abbot on an ambling pad,°
Sometimes a curly shepherd-lad,
Or long-haired page in crimson clad,
       Goes by to towered Camelot;
60 And sometimes through the mirror blue
The knights come riding two and two:
She hath no loyal knight and true,
       The Lady of Shalott.

But in her web she still delights
To weave the mirror's magic sights,
For often through the silent nights
A funeral, with plumes and lights
       And music, went to Camelot:
Or when the moon was overhead,
70 Came two young lovers lately wed;
'I am half sick of shadows,' said
       The Lady of Shalott.

PART III

A bow-shot from her bower-eaves,
He rode between the barley-sheaves,
The sun came dazzling through the leaves,
And flamed upon the brazen greaves°
       Of bold Sir Lancelot.
A red-cross knight° for ever kneeled
To a lady in his shield,
80 That sparkled on the yellow field,
       Beside remote Shalott.

The gemmy bridle glittered free,
Like to some branch of stars we see
Hung in the golden Galaxy.°
The bridle bells rang merrily
       As he rode down to Camelot:
And from his blazoned baldric° slung

pad gentle, easy-paced horse
greaves shin-armor
red-cross knight not usually Lancelot's emblem, and so may refer to Spenser's St. George of *The Faerie Queene* I

Galaxy the Milky Way
blazoned baldric heraldic shoulder belt, to hold up a bugle

A mighty silver bugle hung,
And as he rode his armour rung,
90   Beside remote Shalott.

All in the blue unclouded weather
Thick-jewelled shone the saddle-leather,
The helmet and the helmet-feather
Burned like one burning flame together,
    As he rode down to Camelot.
As often through the purple night,
Below the starry clusters bright,
Some bearded meteor, trailing light,
    Moves over still Shalott.

100 His broad clear brow in sunlight glowed;
On burnished hooves his war-horse trode;
From underneath his helmet flowed
His coal-black curls as on he rode,
    As he rode down to Camelot.
From the bank and from the river
He flashed into the crystal mirror,
'Tirra lirra,' by the river
    Sang Sir Lancelot.

She left the web, she left the loom,
110 She made three paces through the room,
She saw the water-lily bloom,
She saw the helmet and the plume,
    She looked down to Camelot.
Out flew the web and floated wide;
The mirror cracked from side to side;
'The curse is come upon me,' cried
    The Lady of Shalott.

PART IV

In the stormy east-wind straining,
The pale yellow woods were waning,
120 The broad stream in his banks complaining.
Heavily the low sky raining
    Over towered Camelot;
Down she came and found a boat
Beneath a willow left afloat,
And round about the prow she wrote
    The Lady of Shalott.

And down the river's dim expanse
Like some bold seer in a trance,
Seeing all his own mischance—
130 With a glassy countenance
    Did she look to Camelot.

And at the closing of the day
She loosed the chain, and down she lay;
The broad stream bore her far away,
    The Lady of Shalott.

Lying, robed in snowy white
That loosely flew to left and right—
The leaves upon her falling light—
Through the noises of the night
140   She floated down to Camelot:
And as the boat-head wound along
The willowy hills and fields among,
They heard her singing her last song,
    The Lady of Shalott.

Heard a carol, mournful, holy,
Chanted loudly, chanted lowly,
Till her blood was frozen slowly,
And her eyes were darkened wholly,
    Turned to towered Camelot.
150   For ere she reached upon the tide
The first house by the water-side,
Singing in her song she died,
    The Lady of Shalott.

Under tower and balcony,
By garden-wall and gallery,
A gleaming shape she floated by,
Dead-pale between the houses high,
    Silent into Camelot.
Out upon the wharfs they came,
160   Knight and burgher, lord and dame,
And round the prow they read her name,
    The Lady of Shalott.

Who is this? and what is here?
And in the lighted palace near
Died the sound of royal cheer;
And they crossed themselves for fear,
    All the knights at Camelot:
But Lancelot mused a little space;
He said, 'She has a lovely face;
170   God in his mercy lend her grace,
    The Lady of Shalott.'
        1832

The Hesperides°

Hesperus and his daughters three,
That sing about the golden tree.
Comus [982–83]°

The Northwind fallen, in the newstarrèd night
Zidonian Hanno,° voyaging beyond
The hoary promontory of Soloë
Past Thymiaterion, in calmèd bays,
Between the southern and the western Horn,
Heard neither warbling of the nightingale,
Nor melody o' the Lybian lotusflute
Blown seaward from the shore; but from a slope
That ran bloombright into the Atlantic blue,
10 Beneath a highland leaning down a weight
Of cliffs, and zoned below with cedarshade,
Came voices, like the voices in a dream,
Continuous, till he reached the outer sea.

SONG°

I

The golden apple, the golden apple, the hallowed fruit,
Guard it well, guard it warily,
Singing airily,
Standing about the charmèd root.
Round about all is mute,
As the snowfield on the mountain-peaks,
20 As the sandfield at the mountain-foot.
Crocodiles in briny creeks
Sleep and stir not: all is mute.
If ye sing not, if ye make false measure,
We shall lose eternal pleasure,
Worth eternal want of rest.
Laugh not loudly: watch the treasure
Of the wisdom of the west.
In a corner wisdom whispers. Five and three

The Hesperides This, one of Tennyson's master-pieces, was rejected by the censorious superego in the poet, who declined to reprint it after 1833. G. R. Stange points out its strong affinities to Shelley and Keats, and to the aesthetics of Hallam; on this reading the poem itself is a "Garden of Art," akin to what Tennyson sought to reject in his poem *The Palace of Art*. Some of the implications of *The Hesperides* would have delighted Blake, who wrote his own version of this myth in *Visions of the Daughters of Albion*.
Comus In Milton's poem, there is a marvelous description (ll. 976–91) of the gardens from which the Attendant Spirit descends, a more religious version of Spenser's Gardens of Adonis. Though his starting point is Milton's *Comus*, the young Tennyson returns to something of

Spenser's freedom in singing of the Lower Paradise.
Hanno Taken from a passage in the *Periplus* of Hanno, Carthaginian voyager in the 5th century B.C. The places referred to are on the west coast of Africa.
Song Sung by the Daughters of Hesperus, who with a dragon guard the golden fruit of the Western Isles, until Heracles kills the dragon, and bears away the fruit. Tennyson's surprising invention is that the Daughters sing continuously, so as to create an enchantment so unbroken that the fruit becomes unattainable. Perhaps this means that poetry of this pure, rapturous, incantatory kind is as much of paradise as we can know, but it may also imply that such ravishment by poetry keeps us in our fallen condition.

(Let it not be preached abroad) make an awful mystery.°
30 For the blossom unto threefold music° bloweth;
    Evermore it is born anew;
    And the sap to threefold music floweth,
    From the root
    Drawn in the dark,
    Up to the fruit,
    Creeping under the fragrant bark,
    Liquid gold, honeysweet, through and through.
    Keen-eyed Sisters, singing airily,
    Looking warily
40 Every way,
    Guard the apple night and day,
    Lest one from the East come and take it away.

                        II

    Father Hesper, Father Hesper, watch, watch, ever and aye,
    Looking under silver hair with a silver eye.°
    Father, twinkle not thy steadfast sight;
    Kingdoms lapse, and climates change, and races die;
    Honour comes with mystery;
    Hoarded wisdom brings delight.
    Number, tell them over and number
50 How many the mystic fruittree holds,
    Lest the redcombed dragon slumber
    Rolled together in purple folds.
    Look to him, father, lest he wink, and the golden
        apple be stolen away,
    For his ancient heart is drunk with overwatchings night and day,
    Round about the hallowed fruittree curled—
    Sing away, sing aloud evermore in the wind, without stop,
    Lest his scalèd eyelid drop,
    For he is older than the world.
    If he waken, we waken,
60 Rapidly levelling eager eyes.
    If he sleep, we sleep,
    Dropping the eyelid over the eyes.
    If the golden apple be taken
    The world will be overwise.
    Five links, a golden chain, are we,
    Hesper, the dragon, and sisters three,
    Bound about the golden tree.

---

mystery Why the number 8 should be a mystery has been explained by several scholars
(Stange, Paden, Bush, Ricks) as having reference to several Romantic mythologists (G. S.
Faber, Edward Davies, Jacob Bryant, the last
two of whom influenced Blake's similar number
symbolism); Stange's identification of the "five"

as the five senses, and the "three" as a natural
unity-in-multiplicity is in the spirit of these
mythologists.
threefold music the highest that natural sexual
song can attain, as in Blake and the mythologists
silver eye presumably Hesperus as the Western,
or Evening, Star

III

Father Hesper, Father Hesper, watch, watch, night and day,
Lest the old wound of the world be healèd,°
70 The glory unsealèd,
The golden apple stolen away,
And the ancient secret revealèd.
Look from west to east along:
Father, old Himala weakens, Caucasus is bold and strong.
Wandering waters unto wandering waters call;
Let them clash together, foam and fall.
Out of watchings, out of wiles,
Comes the bliss of secret smiles.
All things are not told to all.
80 Half-round the mantling night is drawn,
Purplefringèd with even and dawn.
Hesper hateth Phosphor,° evening hateth morn.

IV

Every flower and every fruit the redolent breath
Of this warm seawind ripeneth,
Arching the billow in his sleep;
But the landwind wandereth,
Broken by the highland-steep,
Two streams upon the violet deep:
For the western sun and the western star,
90 And the low west wind, breathing afar,
The end of day and beginning of night
Make the apple holy and bright;
Holy and bright, round and full, bright and blest,
Mellowed in a land of rest;
Watch it warily day and night;
All good things are in the west.
Till midnoon the cool east light
Is shut out by the round of the tall hillbrow;
But when the fullfaced sunset yellowly
100 Stays on the flowering arch of the bough,
The luscious fruitage clustereth mellowly,
Goldenkernelled, goldencored,
Sunset-ripened above on the tree.
The world is wasted with fire and sword,
But the apple of gold hangs over the sea.
Five links, a golden chain, are we,
Hesper, the dragon, and sisters three,
Daughters three,
Bound about

be healèd Ricks gives the likely reference as
Revelation 13:3.
Phosphor Lucifer, the Morning Star; i.e., the
planet Venus when visible before sunrise,
called Hesperus at its evening appearance

110   All round about
       The gnarlèd bole of the charmèd tree.
       The golden apple, the golden apple, the hallowed fruit,
       Guard it well, guard it warily,
       Watch it warily,
       Singing airily,
       Standing about the charmèd root.
                                    1832

The Lotos-Eaters°

'Courage!' he° said, and pointed toward the land,
'This mounting wave will roll us shoreward soon.'
In the afternoon they came unto a land
In which it seemèd always afternoon.
All round the coast the languid air did swoon,
Breathing like one that hath a weary dream.
Full-faced above the valley stood the moon;
And like a downward smoke, the slender stream
Along the cliff to fall and pause and fall did seem.

10   A land of streams! some, like a downward smoke,
      Slow-dropping veils of thinnest lawn,° did go;
      And some through wavering lights and shadows broke,
      Rolling a slumbrous sheet of foam below.
      They saw the gleaming river seaward flow
      From the inner land: far off, three mountain-tops,
      Three silent pinnacles of agèd snow,
      Stood sunset-flushed: and, dewed with showery drops,
      Up-clomb the shadowy pine above the woven copse.

      The charmèd sunset lingered low adown
20   In the red West: through mountain clefts the dale
      Was seen far inland, and the yellow down
      Bordered with palm, and many a winding vale
      And meadow, set with slender galingale;°
      A land where all things always seemed the same!
      And round about the keel with faces pale,
      Dark faces pale against that rosy flame,
      The mild-eyed melancholy Lotos-eaters came.

The Lotos-Eaters In Homer's *Odyssey* IX.82 ff.,
Odysseus tells Alcinous the story of how, after
sailing from Troy, he and his men were driven
by the winds to the coast of Africa, where the
Lotos-Eaters lived: "Now it never entered the
heads of these natives to kill my friends; what
they did was to give them some lotos to taste,
and as soon as each had eaten the honeyed
fruit of the plant, all thoughts of reporting to
us or escaping were banished from his mind."
But Tennyson's poem is more Spenserian than
Homeric, with the first five stanzas being written
in Spenserian stanzas, and the "Choric Song"
recalling the Cave of Morpheus in *The Faerie
Queene* I.i.39–41.
he Odysseus
lawn cotton fabric
galingale aromatic herb

Branches they bore of that enchanted stem,
Laden with flower and fruit, whereof they gave
30 To each, but whoso did receive of them,
And taste, to him the gushing of the wave
Far far away did seem to mourn and rave
On alien shores; and if his fellow spake,
His voice was thin, as voices from the grave;
And deep-asleep he seemed, yet all awake,
And music in his ears his beating heart did make.

They sat them down upon the yellow sand,
Between the sun and moon upon the shore;
And sweet it was to dream of Fatherland,
40 Of child, and wife, and slave; but evermore
Most weary seemed the sea, weary the oar,
Weary the wandering fields of barren foam.
Then some one said, 'We will return no more;'
And all at once they sang, 'Our island home°
Is far beyond the wave; we will no longer roam.'

         CHORIC SONG
            I
There is sweet music here that softer falls
Than petals from blown roses on the grass,
Or night-dews on still waters between walls
Of shadowy granite, in a gleaming pass;
50 Music that gentlier on the spirit lies,
Than tired eyelids upon tired eyes;
Music that brings sweet sleep down from the blissful skies.
Here are cool mosses deep,
And through the moss the ivies creep,
And in the stream the long-leaved flowers weep,
And from the craggy ledge the poppy hangs in sleep.

            II
Why are we weighed upon with heaviness,
And utterly consumed with sharp distress,
While all things else have rest from weariness?
60 All things have rest: why should we toil alone,
We only toil, who are the first of things,
And make perpetual moan,
Still from one sorrow to another thrown:
Nor ever fold our wings,
And cease from wanderings,
Nor steep our brows in slumber's holy balm;
Nor harken what the inner spirit sings,

island home Ithaca

'There is no joy but calm!'
Why should we only toil, the roof and crown of things?

III

70   Lo! in the middle of the wood,
The folded leaf is wooed from out the bud
With winds upon the branch, and there
Grows green and broad, and takes no care,
Sun-steeped at noon, and in the moon
Nightly dew-fed; and turning yellow
Falls, and floats adown the air.
Lo! sweetened with the summer light,
The full-juiced apple, waxing over-mellow,
Drops in a silent autumn night.
80   All its allotted length of days,
The flower ripens in its place,
Ripens and fades, and falls, and hath no toil,
Fast-rooted in the fruitful soil.

IV

Hateful is the dark-blue sky,
Vaulted o'er the dark-blue sea.
Death is the end of life; ah, why
Should life all labour be?
Let us alone. Time driveth onward fast,
And in a little while our lips are dumb.
90   Let us alone. What is it that will last?
All things are taken from us, and become
Portions and parcels of the dreadful Past.
Let us alone. What pleasure can we have
To war with evil? Is there any peace
In ever climbing up the climbing wave?
All things have rest, and ripen toward the grave
In silence; ripen, fall and cease:
Give us long rest or death, dark death, or dreamful ease.

V

How sweet it were, hearing the downward stream,
100   With half-shut eyes ever to seem
Falling asleep in a half-dream!
To dream and dream, like yonder amber light,
Which will not leave the myrrh-bush on the height;
To hear each other's whispered speech;
Eating the Lotos day by day,
To watch the crisping ripples on the beach,
And tender curving lines of creamy spray;
To lend our hearts and spirits wholly
To the influence of mild-minded melancholy;

110 To muse and brood and live again in memory,
With those old faces of our infancy
Heaped over with a mound of grass,
Two handfuls of white dust, shut in an urn of brass!

VI

Dear is the memory of our wedded lives,
And dear the last embraces of our wives
And their warm tears: but all hath suffered change:
For surely now our household hearths are cold:
Our sons inherit us: our looks are strange:
And we should come like ghosts to trouble joy.
120 Or else the island princes over-bold
Have eat our substance, and the minstrel sings
Before them of the ten years' war in Troy,
And our great deeds, as half-forgotten things.
Is there confusion in the little isle?
Let what is broken so remain.
The Gods are hard to reconcile:
'Tis hard to settle order once again.
There *is* confusion worse than death,
Trouble on trouble, pain on pain,
130 Long labour unto agèd breath,
Sore task to hearts worn out by many wars
And eyes grown dim with gazing on the pilot-stars.

VII

But, propped on beds of amaranth and moly,°
How sweet (while warm airs lull us, blowing lowly)
With half-dropped eyelid still,
Beneath a heaven dark and holy,
To watch the long bright river drawing slowly
His waters from the purple hill—
To hear the dewy echoes calling
140 From cave to cave through the thick-twinèd vine—
To watch the emerald-coloured water falling
Through many a woven acanthus°-wreath divine!
Only to hear and see the far-off sparkling brine,
Only to hear were sweet, stretched out beneath the pine.

VIII

The Lotos blooms below the barren peak:
The Lotos blows by every winding creek:
All day the wind breathes low with mellower tone:
Through every hollow cave and alley lone

amaranth mythical unfading flower; moly herb   in the *Odyssey* X, to protect him from the en-
of occult power, given by Hermes to Odysseus   chantress Circe
acanthus sacred herb

Round and round the spicy downs the yellow Lotos-dust is blown.
150   We have had enough of action, and of motion we,
Rolled to starboard, rolled to larboard, when the surge was seething free,
Where the wallowing monster spouted his foam-fountains in the sea.
Let us swear an oath, and keep it with an equal mind,
In the hollow Lotos-land to live and lie reclined
On the hills like Gods° together, careless of mankind.
For they lie beside their nectar, and the bolts are hurled
Far below them in the valleys, and the clouds are lightly curled
Round their golden houses, girdled with the gleaming world:
Where they smile in secret, looking over wasted lands,
Blight and famine, plague and earthquake, roaring
160   deeps and fiery sands,
Clanging fights, and flaming towns, and sinking ships,
and praying hands.
But they smile, they find a music centred in a doleful song
Steaming up, a lamentation and an ancient tale of wrong,
Like a tale of little meaning though the words are strong;
Chanted from an ill-used race of men that cleave the soil,
Sow the seed, and reap the harvest with enduring toil,
Storing yearly little dues of wheat, and wine and oil;
Till they perish and they suffer—some, 'tis whispered—down in hell
Suffer endless anguish, others in Elysian valleys° dwell,
170   Resting weary limbs at last on beds of asphodel.
Surely, surely, slumber is more sweet than toil, the shore
Than labour in the deep mid-ocean, wind and wave and oar;
Oh rest ye, brother mariners, we will not wander more.
1830–32   1832

The Eagle

FRAGMENT

He clasps the crag with crookèd hands;
Close to the sun in lonely lands,
Ringed with the azure world, he stands.

The wrinkled sea beneath him crawls;
He watches from his mountain walls,
And like a thunderbolt he falls.

1851

like Gods These are the Epicurean gods as seen
by Lucretius, in *De Rerum Natura* IV. 724 ff.,
V. 83 ff., VI. 58 ff.
Elysian valleys The Elysian Fields (one Greek
version of Paradise) were covered with asphodel, which may have been the narcissus, not the
daffodil or English asphodel.

St. Simeon Stylites°

Although I be the basest of mankind,
From scalp to sole one slough and crust of sin,
Unfit for earth, unfit for heaven, scarce meet
For troops of devils, mad with blasphemy,
I will not cease to grasp the hope I hold
Of saintdom, and to clamour, mourn and sob,
Battering the gates of heaven with storms of prayer,
Have mercy, Lord, and take away my sin.

    Let this avail, just, dreadful, mighty God,
10 This not be all in vain, that thrice ten years,
Thrice multiplied by superhuman pangs,
In hungers and in thirsts, fevers and cold,
In coughs, aches, stitches, ulcerous throes and cramps,
A sign betwixt the meadow and the cloud,
Patient on this tall pillar I have borne
Rain, wind, frost, heat, hail, damp, and sleet, and snow;
And I had hoped that ere this period closed
Thou wouldst have caught me up into thy rest,
Denying not these weather-beaten limbs
20 The meed° of saints, the white robe and the palm.

    O take the meaning, Lord: I do not breathe,
Not whisper, any murmur of complaint.
Pain heaped ten-hundred-fold to this, were still
Less burthen, by ten-hundred-fold, to bear,
Then were those lead-like tons of sin that crushed
My spirit flat before thee.
              O Lord, Lord,
Thou knowest I bore this better at the first,
For I was strong and hale of body then;
And though my teeth, which now are dropped away,
30 Would chatter with the cold, and all my beard
Was tagged with icy fringes in the moon,
I drowned the whoopings of the owl with sound
Of pious hymns and psalms, and sometimes saw
An angel stand and watch me, as I sang.
Now am I feeble grown; my end draws nigh;
I hope my end draws nigh: half deaf I am,
So that I scarce can hear the people hum

St. Simeon Stylites Stylites is from the Greek for "pillar." St. Simeon (390–459) was notorious for his ascetic severities. At the age of 30, he mounted a pillar and lived upon it for 30 years without condescending to come down at all. The pillar eventually was built up to 60 feet in height, with a railing around the top, and a ladder by which the holy man's disciples were enabled to bring him sustenance. St. Simeon preached regularly from his pillar to large and adoring audiences. Tennyson's source is partly Gibbon's *Decline and Fall of the Roman Empire* IV. 320, where the saint is given the treatment he merits, a treatment completed in Tennyson's dramatic monologue, which Browning admired enormously.
meed reward; the white robe and the palm are promised to the saints in heaven in Revelation 7:9

About the column's base, and almost blind,
And scarce can recognize the fields I know;
40 And both my thighs are rotted with the dew;
Yet cease I not to clamour and to cry,
While my stiff spine can hold my weary head,
Till all my limbs drop piecemeal from the stone,
Have mercy, mercy: take away my sin.

O Jesus, if thou wilt not save my soul,
Who may be saved?° who is it may be saved?
Who may be made a saint, if I fail here?
Show me the man hath suffered more than I.
For did not all thy martyrs die one death?
50 For either they were stoned, or crucified,
Or burned in fire, or boiled in oil, or sawn
In twain beneath the ribs; but I die here
Today, and whole years long, a life of death.
Bear witness, if I could have found a way
(And heedfully I sifted all my thought)
More slowly-painful to subdue this home
Of sin, my flesh, which I despise and hate,
I had not stinted practice, O my God.

For not alone this pillar-punishment,
60 Not this alone I bore: but while I lived
In the white convent down the valley there,
For many weeks about my loins I wore
The rope that haled the buckets from the well,
Twisted as tight as I could knot the noose;
And spake not of it to a single soul,
Until the ulcer, eating through my skin,
Betrayed my secret penance, so that all
My brethren marvelled greatly. More than this
I bore, whereof, O God, thou knowest all.

70 Three winters, that my soul might grow to thee,
I lived up there on yonder mountain side.
My right leg chained into the crag, I lay
Pent in a roofless close of ragged stones;
Inswathed sometimes in wandering mist, and twice
Blacked with thy branding thunder, and sometimes
Sucking the damps for drink, and eating not,
Except the spare chance-gift of those that came
To touch my body and be healed, and live:
And they say then that I worked miracles,
80 Whereof my fame is loud amongst mankind,
Cured lameness, palsies, cancers. Thou, O God,

Who may be saved? See Matthew 19:25.

Knowest alone whether this was or no.
Have mercy, mercy! cover all my sin.°

    Then, that I might be more alone with thee,
Three years I lived upon a pillar, high
Six cubits,° and three years on one of twelve;
And twice three years I crouched on one that rose
Twenty by measure; last of all, I grew
Twice ten long weary weary years to this,
90   That numbers forty cubits from the soil.

    I think that I have borne as much as this—
Or else I dream—and for so long a time,
If I may measure time by yon slow light,
And this high dial,° which my sorrow crowns—
So much—even so.
              And yet I know not well,
For that the evil ones come here, and say,
'Fall down, O Simeon; thou hast suffered long
For ages and for ages!' then they prate
Of penances I cannot have gone through,
100 Perplexing me with lies; and oft I fall,
Maybe for months, in such blind lethargies
That Heaven, and Earth, and Time are choked.
           But yet
Bethink thee, Lord, while thou and all the saints
Enjoy themselves in heaven, and men on earth
House in the shade of comfortable roofs,
Sit with their wives by fires, eat wholesome food,
And wear warm clothes, and even beasts have stalls,
I, 'tween the spring and downfall of the light,
Bow down one thousand and two hundred times,
110 To Christ, the Virgin Mother, and the saints;
Or in the night, after a little sleep,
I wake: the chill stars sparkle; I am wet
With drenching dews, or stiff with crackling frost.
I wear an undressed goatskin on my back;
A grazing iron collar grinds my neck;
And in my weak, lean arms I lift the cross,
And strive and wrestle with thee till I die:
O mercy, mercy! wash away my sin.

    O Lord, thou knowest what a man I am;
120 A sinful man, conceived and born in sin:
'Tis their own doing; this is none of mine;
Lay it not to me. Am I to blame for this,

cover all my sin See Psalms 85:2.
six cubits Since a cubit was about 18 inches, the
saint measures the height of his piety as having

augmented from about 9 feet to its culminating 60.
high dial The pillar and saint together make a
sundial.

That here come those that worship me? Ha! ha!
They think that I am somewhat. What am I?
The silly people take me for a saint,
And bring me offerings of fruit and flowers:
And I, in truth (thou wilt bear witness here)
Have all in all endured as much, and more
Than many just and holy men, whose names
130 Are registered and calendared for saints.

    Good people, you do ill to kneel to me.
What is it I can have done to merit this?
I am a sinner viler than you all.
It may be I have wrought some miracles,
And cured some halt and mained; but what of that?
It may be, no one, even among the saints,
May match his pains with mine; but what of that?
Yet do not rise; for you may look on me,
And in your looking you may kneel to God.
140 Speak! is there any of you halt or maimed?
I think you know I have some power with Heaven
From my long penance: let him speak his wish.

    Yes, I can heal him. Power goes forth from me.
They say that they are healed. Ah, hark! they shout
'St. Simeon Stylites.' Why, if so,
God reaps a harvest in me. O my soul,
God reaps a harvest in thee. If this be,
Can I work miracles and not be saved?
This is not told of any. They were saints.
It cannot be but that I shall be saved;
150 Yea, crowned, a saint. They shout, 'Behold a saint!'
And lower voices saint me from above.
Courage, St. Simeon! This dull chrysalis°
Cracks into shining wings, and hope ere death
Spreads more and more and more, that God hath now
Sponged and made blank of crimeful record all
My mortal archives.
          O my sons, my sons,
I, Simeon of the pillar, by surname
Stylites, among men; I, Simeon,
160 The watcher on the column till the end;
I, Simeon, whose brain the sunshine bakes;
I, whose bald brows in silent hours become
Unnaturally hoar with rime, do now
From my high nest of penance here proclaim
That Pontius and Iscariot° by my side

chrysalis The holy man compares himself to the cocoon of a butterfly.
Pontius and Iscariot Pontius Pilate, Roman governor of Judea during the career of Jesus; Judas Iscariot, the betrayer of Jesus

Showed like fair seraphs. On the coals I lay,
A vessel full of sin: all hell beneath
Made me boil over. Devils plucked my sleeve,
Abaddon and Asmodeus° caught at me.
170   I smote them with the cross; they swarmed again.
In bed like monstrous apes they crushed my chest:
They flapped my light out as I read: I saw
Their faces grow between me and my book;
With colt-like whinny and with hoggish whine
They burst my prayer. Yet this way was left,
And by this way I 'scaped them. Mortify
Your flesh, like me, with scourges and with thorns;
Smite, shrink not, spare not. If it may be, fast
Whole Lents, and pray. I hardly, with slow steps,
180   With slow, faint steps, and much exceeding pain,
Have scrambled past those pits of fire, that still
Sing in mine ears. But yield not me the praise:
God only through his bounty hath thought fit,
Among the powers and princes of this world,
To make me an example to mankind,
Which few can reach to. Yet I do not say
But that a time may come—yea, even now,
Now, now, his footsteps smite the threshold stairs
Of life—I say, that time is at the doors
190   When you may worship me without reproach;
For I will leave my relics in your land,
And you may carve a shrine about my dust,
And burn a fragrant lamp before my bones,
When I am gathered to the glorious saints.

While I spake then, a sting of shrewdest pain
Ran shrivelling through me, and a cloudlike change,
In passing, with a grosser film made thick
These heavy, horny eyes. The end! the end!
Surely the end! What's here? a shape, a shade,
200   A flash of light. Is that the angel there
That holds a crown? Come, blessèd brother, come.
I know thy glittering face. I waited long;
My brows are ready. What! deny it now?
Nay, draw, draw, draw nigh. So I clutch it. Christ!
'Tis gone: 'tis here again; the crown! the crown!
So now 'tis fitted on and grows to me,
And from it melt the dews of Paradise,
Sweet! sweet! spikenard, and balm, and frankincense.
Ah! let me not be fooled, sweet saints: I trust
210   That I am whole, and clean, and meet for Heaven.

Abaddon and Asmodeus Abaddon was the Angel   is an evil spirit in Tobit 3:8.
of Destruction; see Revelation 9:11. Asmodeus

Speak, if there be a priest, a man of God,
Among you there, and let him presently
Approach, and lean a ladder on the shaft,
And climbing up into my airy home,
Deliver me the blessèd sacrament;
For by the warning of the Holy Ghost,
I prophesy that I shall die tonight,
A quarter before twelve.
                    But thou, O Lord,
Aid all this foolish people; let them take
220   Example, pattern: lead them to thy light.
1833   1842

Ulysses

This subtle, equivocal dramatic monologue was written in the autumn of 1833, when
Tennyson's despairing grief for Hallam was most oppressive. Retrospectively, the poet
insisted that it stated his "feeling about the need of going forward, and braving the
struggle of life perhaps more simply than anything in *In Memoriam*." Yet the poem
is founded more upon the evil counselor Ulysses of Dante's *Inferno* XXVI (whom
nevertheless Dante in some sense admired) than on the hero of the prophecy of
Tiresias in the *Odyssey* (XI.100–37). Dante's Trojan sympathies stem from his nationality and from his guide Virgil, who sang the flight of Aeneas from fallen Troy, and that
hero's subsequent founding of Rome. In the *Inferno,* Ulysses goes forth again on a
last voyage, to "explore the world, and search the ways of life,/Man's evil and his
virtue" (Cary's translation, which Tennyson probably used); when the Ithacans' ship
comes to the Pillars of Hercules, "the boundaries not to be o'erstepped by man,"
the wily Ulysses urges his "small faithful band/That yet cleaved to me" to attempt a
breakthrough into forbidden realms: "Ye were not formed to live the life of brutes,/But
virtue to pursue and knowledge high." His followers obey him, and are washed down
with Ulysses in the forbidden gulfs when they sight the Mount of Purgatory. Though
Tennyson apparently takes, in contrast to Dante, a High Romantic view of Ulysses as
an indomitable quester animated by heroic humanism and a sustained drive for
knowledge, the poem persistently qualifies our admiration for its speaker. He appears
to lack a capacity for loving other human beings, scorns his son's sense of responsibility, and in his closing lines echoes the defiant Satan of Milton's *Paradise Lost* I–II.

Ulysses

It little profits that an idle king,°
By this still hearth, among these barren crags,
Matched with an agèd wife, I mete and dole

---

idle king In Dante, Ulysses sets out for the west
after leaving Circe. Significantly, Tennyson has
him return home first, experience boredom, and
then quest forth again.

Unequal° laws unto a savage race,
That hoard, and sleep, and feed, and know not me.

I cannot rest from travel: I will drink
Life to the lees: all times I have enjoyed
Greatly, have suffered greatly, both with those
That loved me, and alone; on shore, and when
10 Through scudding drifts the rainy Hyades°
Vexed the dim sea: I am become a name;
For always roaming with a hungry heart
Much have I seen and known; cities of men
And manners, climates, councils, governments,
Myself not least, but honoured of them all;
And drunk delight of battle with my peers,
Far on the ringing plains of windy Troy.
I am a part of all that I have met;
Yet all experience is an arch wherethrough
20 Gleams that untravelled world, whose margin fades
For ever and for ever when I move.
How dull it is to pause, to make an end,
To rust unburnished, not to shine in use!
As though to breathe were life. Life piled on life
Were all too little, and of one to me
Little remains: but every hour is saved
From that eternal silence, something more,
A bringer of new things; and vile it were
For some three suns° to store and hoard myself,
30 And this grey spirit yearning in desire
To follow knowledge like a sinking star,
Beyond the utmost bound of human thought.

    This is my son, mine own Telemachus,
To whom I leave the sceptre and the isle—
Well-loved of me, discerning to fulfil
This labour, by slow prudence to make mild
A rugged people, and through soft degrees
Subdue them to the useful and the good.
Most blameless is he, centred in the sphere
40 Of common duties, decent not to fail
In offices of tenderness, and pay
Meet adoration to my household gods,
When I am gone. He works his work, I mine.

    There lies the port; the vessel puffs her sail:
There gloom the dark broad seas. My mariners,

Unequal Possibly "unjust," but more likely reflecting a still "savage" society. Notice that when talking to himself, Ulysses calls his subjects "savage" (l. 4) but shifts to "rugged" (l. 37) when he speaks out loud.

rainy Hyades 5 stars in the head of the constellation Taurus; their name, "the rainy ones," stems from the fact that their simultaneous rise with the sun heralded the spring rains
three suns three years

Souls that have toiled, and wrought, and thought with me—
That ever with a frolic welcome took
The thunder and the sunshine, and opposed
Free hearts, free foreheads—you and I are old;
50 Old age hath yet his honour and his toil;
Death closes all:° but something ere the end,
Some work of noble note, may yet be done,
Not unbecoming men that strove with Gods.
The lights begin to twinkle from the rocks:
The long day wanes: the slow moon climbs: the deep
Moans round with many voices. Come, my friends,
'Tis not too late to seek a newer world.
Push off, and sitting well in order smite
The sounding furrows; for my purpose holds
60 To sail beyond the sunset, and the baths
Of all the western stars, until I die.
It may be that the gulfs will wash us down:
It may be we shall touch the Happy Isles,°
And see the great Achilles,° whom we knew.
Though much is taken, much abides; and though
We are not now that strength which in old days
Moved earth and heaven; that which we are, we are;
One equal temper of heroic hearts,
Made weak by time and fate, but strong in will
70 To strive, to seek, to find, and not to yield.°
1833   1842

Tithonus°

The woods decay, the woods decay and fall,
The vapours weep their burthen to the ground,
Man comes and tills the field and lies beneath,
And after many a summer dies the swan.
Me only cruel immortality

Death closes all Unlike Tennyson, this Ulysses does not believe in immortality.
Happy Isles the Isles of the Blessed or the Elysian Fields, abode of heroes after death, and lying beyond the Strait of Gibraltar
Achilles hero of the Greeks, scourge of the Trojans, and perhaps in some sense Hallam
not to yield Compare Satan, in his first speech, *Paradise Lost* I.84–124, particularly: "And courage never to submit or yield: / And what is else not to be overcome?"
Tithonus Written originally, in shorter form, as a pendant to *Ulysses* in autumn 1833, and expressing obliquely again the poet's deep grief at continuing in life without Hallam. Tennyson took the story from the Homeric *Hymn to Aphrodite;* Tithonus, beloved of the goddess of

the dawn, Eos or Aurora, received eternal life but not perpetual youth. His withered body was at last transformed into a grasshopper. Profoundly Virgilian in tone, *Tithonus* echoes several Romantic poets in its equivocal lament for a dehumanizing immortality. Whatever Tennyson's intentions, it is notable that this dramatic monologue, like *Ulysses,* gives us a speaker evidently incapable of ever having loved anyone. Though his situation is extreme, Tithonus nevertheless shows no affection for Aurora, who continues to love him, as he can recognize. Mingled with his desire to die is a still profound capacity for aesthetic as opposed to emotional experience. Compare the song, "Tears, Idle Tears."

Consumes: I wither slowly in thine arms,°
Here at the quiet limit of the world,
A white-haired shadow roaming like a dream
The ever-silent spaces of the East,
10 Far-folded mists, and gleaming halls of morn.

   Alas! for this grey shadow, once a man—
So glorious in his beauty and thy choice,
Who madest him thy chosen, that he seemed
To his great heart none other than a God!
I asked thee, 'Give me immortality.'
Then didst thou grant mine asking with a smile,
Like wealthy men who care not how they give.
But thy strong Hours° indignant worked their wills,
And beat me down and marred and wasted me,
20 And though they could not end me, left me maimed
To dwell in presence of immortal youth,°
Immortal age beside immortal youth,
And all I was, in ashes. Can thy love,
Thy beauty, make amends, though even now,
Close over us, the silver star,° thy guide,
Shines in those tremulous eyes that fill with tears
To hear me? Let me go: take back thy gift:
Why should a man desire in any way
To vary from the kindly° race of men,
30 Or pass beyond the goal of ordinance°
Where all should pause, as is most meet for all?

   A soft air fans the cloud apart; there comes
A glimpse of that dark world where I was born.
Once more the old mysterious glimmer steals
From thy pure brows, and from thy shoulders pure,
And bosom beating with a heart renewed.
Thy cheek begins to redden through the gloom,
Thy sweet eyes brighten slowly close to mine,
Ere yet they blind the stars, and the wild team°
40 Which love thee, yearning for thy yoke, arise,
And shake the darkness from their loosened manes,
And beat the twilight into flakes of fire.

   Lo! ever thus thou growest beautiful
In silence, then before thine answer given
Departest, and thy tears are on my cheek.

thine arms Aurora's
Hours Like the Hours in Shelley's *Prometheus Unbound*, these companions of the dawn goddess are responsible for birth, maturation, and decay and are indignant that they cannot destroy Tithonus.

immortal youth Aurora, since she is a goddess
silver star the Morning Star, Venus
kindly human, one's own kind
goal of ordinance fixed limit
team Aurora's chariot and horses, which each morning carry her from Ocean to Olympus

Why wilt thou ever scare me with thy tears,
And make me tremble lest a saying learnt,
In days far-off, on that dark earth, be true?
'The Gods themselves cannot recall their gifts.'

50   Ay me! aye me! with what another heart
In days far-off, and with what other eyes
I used to watch—if I be he that watched—
The lucid outline forming round thee; saw
The dim curls kindle into sunny rings;
Changed with thy mystic change, and felt my blood
Glow with the glow that slowly crimsoned all
Thy presence and thy portals, while I lay,
Mouth, forehead, eyelids, growing dewy-warm
With kisses balmier than half-opening buds
60   Of April, and could hear the lips that kissed
Whispering I knew not what of wild and sweet,
Like that strange song I heard Apollo sing,°
While Ilion like a mist rose into towers.

Yet hold me not for ever in thine East:
How can my nature longer mix with thine?
Coldly thy rosy shadows bathe me, cold
Are all thy lights, and cold my wrinkled feet
Upon thy glimmering thresholds, when the steam
Floats up from those dim fields about the homes
70   Of happy men that have the power to die,
And grassy barrows° of the happier dead.
Release me, and restore me to the ground;
Thou seest all things, thou wilt see my grave:
Thou wilt renew thy beauty morn by morn;
I earth in earth forget these empty courts,
And thee returning on thy silver wheels.
1833, 1859   1860

Morte d'Arthur°

So all day long the noise of battle° rolled
Among the mountains by the winter sea;
Until King Arthur's table, man by man,

Apollo sing Troy (Ilion) was built by Apollo's music
barrows burial mounds
Morte d'Arthur This is Tennyson's first major Arthurian poem, a direct reaction to Hallam's death, and the best poem in *Idylls of the King*, where it is included in full, but rather spoiled by the inadequate passages which surround it. If Tennyson closely follows Malory's *Morte*

Darthur XXI.3–5, his tone has little in common with Malory's. Essentially, this is a mythologizing earlier version of *In Memoriam*, as well as a successful attempt at a lament in the sublime mode.
battle the last, apocalyptic battle between Arthur and the traitors led by his nephew Modred

Had fallen in Lyonnesse° about their Lord,
King Arthur: then, because his wound was deep,
The bold Sir Bedivere uplifted him,
Sir Bedivere, the last of all his knights,
And bore him to a chapel nigh the field,
A broken chancel° with a broken cross,
10 That stood on a dark strait of barren land.
On one side lay the Ocean, and on one
Lay a great water, and the moon was full.

    Then spake King Arthur to Sir Bedivere:
'The sequel of today unsolders all
The goodliest fellowship of famous knights
Whereof this world holds record. Such a sleep
They sleep—the men I loved. I think that we
Shall never more, at any future time,
Delight our souls with talk of knightly deeds,
20 Walking about the gardens and the halls
Of Camelot, as in the days that were.
I perish by this people which I made,—
Though Merlin sware that I should come again
To rule once more—but let what will be, be,
I am so deeply smitten through the helm
That without help I cannot last till morn.
Thou therefore take my brand Excalibur,
Which was my pride: for thou rememberest how
In those old days, one summer noon, an arm
30 Rose up from out the bosom of the lake,
Clothed in white samite,° mystic, wonderful,
Holding the sword—and how I rowed across
And took it, and have worn it, like a king:
And, wheresoever I am sung or told
In aftertime, this also shall be known:
But now delay not: take Excalibur,
And fling him far into the middle mere:°
Watch what thou seest, and lightly bring me word.'

    To him replied the bold Sir Bedivere:
40 'It is not meet, Sir King, to leave thee thus,
Aidless, alone, and smitten through the helm.
A little thing may harm a wounded man.
Yet I thy hest will all perform at full,
Watch what I see, and lightly° bring thee word.'

    So saying, from the ruined shrine he stepped
And in the moon athwart the place of tombs,

Where lay the mighty bones of ancient men,
Old knights, and over them the sea-wind sang
Shrill, chill, with flakes of foam. He, stepping down
50   By zig-zag paths, and juts of pointed rock,
Came on the shining levels of the lake.

There drew he forth the brand Excalibur,
And o'er him, drawing it, the winter moon,
Brightening the skirts of a long cloud, ran forth
And sparkled keen with frost against the hilt:
For all the haft twinkled with diamond sparks,
Myriads of topaz-lights, and jacinth-work°
Of subtlest jewellery. He gazed so long
That both his eyes were dazzled, as he stood,
60   This way and that dividing the swift mind,°
In act to throw: but at the last it seemed
Better to leave Excalibur concealed
There in the many-knotted waterflags,
That whistled stiff and dry about the marge.
So strode he back slow to the wounded King.

Then spake King Arthur to Sir Bedivere:
'Hast thou performed my mission which I gave?
What is it thou hast seen? or what hast heard?'

And answer made the bold Sir Bedivere:
'I heard the ripple washing in the reeds,
And the wild water lapping on the crag.'

To whom replied King Arthur, faint and pale:
'Thou hast betrayed thy nature and thy name,
Not rendering true answer, as beseemed
Thy fealty, nor like a noble knight:
For surer sign had followed, either hand,
Or voice, or else a motion of the mere.
This is a shameful thing for men to lie.
Yet now, I charge thee, quickly go again
80   As thou art lief° and dear, and do the thing
I bad thee, watch, and lightly bring me word.'

Then went Sir Bedivere the second time
Across the ridge, and paced beside the mere,
Counting the dewy pebbles, fixed in thought;
But when he saw the wonder of the hilt,
How curiously and strangely chased,° he smote
His palms together, and he cried aloud,

'And if indeed I cast the brand away,
Surely a precious thing, one worthy note,

jacinth-work gemmed
swift mind See Virgil's *Aeneid* IV.285.

lief beloved
chased engraved

90   Should thus be lost for ever from the earth,
     Which might have pleased the eyes of many men.
     What good should follow this, if this were done?
     What harm, undone? deep harm to disobey,
     Seeing obedience is the bond of rule.
     Were it well to obey then, if a king demand
     An act unprofitable, against himself?
     The King is sick, and knows not what he does.
     What record, or what relic of my lord
     Should be to aftertime, but empty breath
100 And rumours of a doubt? but were this kept,
     Stored in some treasure-house of mighty kings,
     Some one might show it at a joust of arms,
     Saying, "King Arthur's sword, Excalibur,
     Wrought by the lonely maiden of the Lake.
     Nine years she wrought it, sitting in the deeps
     Upon the hidden bases of the hills."
     So might some old man speak in the aftertime
     To all the people, winning reverence.
     But now much honour and much fame were lost.'

110   So spake he, clouded with his own conceit,°
     And hid Excalibur the second time,
     And so strode back slow to the wounded King.

       Then spoke King Arthur, breathing heavily:
     'What is it thou hast seen? or what hast heard?'

       And answer made the bold Sir Bedivere:
     'I heard the water lapping on the crag,
     And the long ripple washing in the reeds.'

       To whom replied King Arthur, much in wrath:
     'Ah, miserable and unkind, untrue,
120 Unknightly, traitor-hearted! Woe is me!
     Authority forgets a dying king,
     Laid widowed of the power in his eye
     That bowed the will. I see thee what thou art,
     For thou, the latest-left of all my knights,
     In whom should meet the offices of all,
     Thou wouldst betray me for the precious hilt;
     Either from lust of gold, or like a girl
     Valuing the giddy pleasure of the eyes.
     Yet, for a man may fail in duty twice,
130 And the third time may prosper, get thee hence:
     But, if thou spare to fling Excalibur,
     I will arise and slay thee with my hands.'

conceit notion

Then quickly rose Sir Bedivere, and ran,
And, leaping down the ridges lightly, plunged
Among the bulrush-beds, and clutched the sword,
And strongly wheeled and threw it. The great brand
Made lightnings in the splendour of the moon,
And flashing round and round, and whirled in an arch,
Shot like a streamer° of the northern morn,
140   Seen where the moving isles of winter shock
By night,° with noises of the northern sea.
So flashed and fell the brand Excalibur:
But ere he dipped the surface, rose an arm
Clothed in white samite, mystic, wonderful,
And caught him by the hilt, and brandished him
Three times, and drew him under in the mere.
And lightly went the other to the King.

Then spoke King Arthur, drawing thicker breath:
'Now see I by thine eyes that this is done.
150   Speak out: what is it thou hast heard, or seen?'

And answer made the bold Sir Bedivere:
'Sir King, I closed mine eyelids, lest the gems
Should blind my purpose, for I never saw,
Nor shall see, here or elsewhere, till I die,
Not though I live three lives of mortal men,
So great a miracle as yonder hilt.
Then with both hands I flung him, wheeling him;
But when I looked again, behold an arm,
Clothed in white samite, mystic, wonderful,
160   That caught him by the hilt, and brandished him
Three times, and drew him under in the mere.'

And answer made King Arthur, breathing hard:
'My end draws nigh; 'tis time that I were gone.
Make broad thy shoulders to receive my weight,
And bear me to the margin; yet I fear
My wound hath taken cold, and I shall die.'

So saying, from the pavement he half rose,
Slowly, with pain, reclining on his arm,
And looking wistfully with wide blue eyes
170   As in a picture. Him Sir Bedivere
Remorsefully regarded through his tears,
And would have spoken, but he found not words,
Then took with care, and kneeling on one knee,
O'er both his shoulders drew the languid hands,
And rising bore him through the place of tombs.

streamer aurora borealis or northern lights
moving isles . . . night icebergs colliding in
the darkness

But, as he walked, King Arthur panted hard,
Like one that feels a nightmare on his bed
When all the house is mute. So sighed the King,
Muttering and murmuring at his ear, 'Quick, quick!
180 I fear it is too late, and I shall die.'
But the other swiftly strode from ridge to ridge,
Clothed with his breath, and looking, as he walked,
Larger than human on the frozen hills.
He heard the deep behind him, and a cry
Before. His own thought drove him, like a goad.
Dry° clashed his harness in the icy caves
And barren chasms, and all to left and right
The bare black cliff clanged round him, as he based
His feet on juts of slippery crag that rang
190 Sharp-smitten with the dint of armèd heels—
And on a sudden, lo! the level lake,
And the long glories of the winter moon.

Then saw they how there hove a dusky barge,
Dark as a funeral scarf from stem to stern,
Beneath them; and descending they were ware
That all the decks were dense with stately forms
Black-stoled, black-hooded, like a dream—by these
Three Queens° with crowns of gold—and from them rose
A cry that shivered to the tingling stars,
200 And, as it were one voice, an agony
Of lamentation, like a wind, that shrills
All night in a waste land, where no one comes,
Or hath come, since the making of the world.

Then murmured Arthur, 'Place me in the barge,'
And to the barge they came. There those three Queens
Put forth their hands, and took the King, and wept.
But she, that rose the tallest of them all
And fairest, laid his head upon her lap,
And loosed the shattered casque, and chafed his hands,
210 And called him by his name, complaining° loud,
And dropping bitter tears against his brow
Striped with dark blood: for all his face was white
And colourless, and like the withered moon
Smote by the fresh beam of the springing east;
And all his greaves and cuisses dashed with drops°
Of onset; and the light and lustrous curls—
That made his forehead like a rising sun
High from the dais-throne—were parched with dust;

Dry harshly
Three Queens Tennyson compared them to the
Three Graces, but asserted their significance
was larger.

complaining lamenting
greaves and cuisses . . . drops his thigh- and
leg-armour, bloody from the battle

Or, clotted into points and hanging loose,
220 Mixed with the knightly growth that fringed his lips.
So like a shattered column lay the King;
Not like that Arthur who, with lance in rest,
From spur to plume a star of tournament,
Shot through the lists at Camelot, and charged
Before the eyes of ladies and of kings.

Then loudly cried the bold Sir Bedivere,
'Ah! my Lord Arthur, whither shall I go?
Where shall I hide my forehead and my eyes?
For now I see the true old times are dead,
230 When every morning brought a noble chance,
And every chance brought out a noble knight.
Such times have been not since the light that led°
The holy Elders with the gift of myrrh.
But now the whole ROUND TABLE is dissolved
Which was an image of the mighty world;
And I, the last, go forth companionless,
And the days darken round me, and the years,
Among new men, strange faces, other minds.'

And slowly answered Arthur from the barge:
240 'The old order changeth, yielding place to new,
And God fulfils Himself in many ways,
Lest one good custom should corrupt the world.
Comfort thyself: what comfort is in me?
I have lived my life, and that which I have done
May He within Himself make pure! but thou,
If thou shouldst never see my face again,
Pray for my soul. More things are wrought by prayer
Than this world dreams of. Wherefore, let thy voice
Rise like a fountain for me night and day.
250 For what are men better than sheep or goats
That nourish a blind life within the brain,
If, knowing God, they lift not hands of prayer
Both for themselves and those who call them friend?
For so the whole round earth is every way
Bound by gold chains° about the feet of God.
But now farewell. I am going a long way
With these thou seest—if indeed I go—
(For all my mind is clouded with a doubt)
To the island-valley of Avilion;°
260 Where falls not hail, or rain, or any snow,°
Nor ever wind blows loudly; but it lies

light that led star that guided the Three Kings
to Christ's birthplace in Bethlehem
gold chains See *Paradise Lost* II.1051.
Avilion Avalon, Celtic version of the Isles of
the Blessed

or any snow See Lucretius, *De Rerum Natura*
III.18, and Tennyson's poem *Lucretius*, ll. 104–
10.

Deep-meadowed, happy, fair with orchard-lawns
And bowery hollows crowned with summer sea,
Where I will heal me of my grievous wound.'

So said he, and the barge with oar and sail
Moved from the brink, like some full-breasted swan
That, fluting a wild carol ere her death,
Ruffles her pure cold plume, and takes the flood
With swarthy webs. Long stood Sir Bedivere
270 Revolving many memories, till the hull
Looked one black dot against the verge of dawn,
And on the mere the wailing died away.
1833–34   1842

Locksley Hall°

Comrades,° leave me here a little, while as yet 'tis early morn:
Leave me here, and when you want me, sound upon the bugle-horn.

'Tis the place, and all around it, as of old, the curlews call,
Dreary gleams° about the moorland flying over Locksley Hall;

Locksley Hall, that in the distance overlooks the sandy tracts,
And the hollow ocean-ridges roaring into cataracts.

Many a night from yonder ivied casement, ere I went to rest,
Did I look on great Orion° sloping slowly to the west.

Many a night I saw the Pleiads,° rising through the mellow shade,
10   Glitter like a swarm of fire-flies tangled in a silver braid.

Here about the beach I wandered, nourishing a youth sublime
With the fairy tales of science, and the long result of time;

When the centuries behind me like a fruitful land reposed;
When I clung to all the present for the promise that it closed:

When I dipped into the future far as human eye could see;
Saw the Vision of the world, and all the wonder that would be.—

In the spring a fuller crimson comes upon the robin's breast;
In the spring the wanton lapwing° gets himself another crest;

Locksley Hall This popular poem may have its origin in Tennyson's early, unhappy love for Rosa Baring, who made an arranged marriage. The 8-stress trochaic couplets effectively convey the tone of a ranting young man, who is the precursor of the morbid youth of sensibility who speaks throughout the more accomplished *Maud.*
Comrades There is a suggestion, here and at the poem's close, that the speaker and his friends are outward-bound soldiers.
Dreary gleams "the flying gleams of light across a dreary moorland" (Tennyson)
Orion constellation of winter sky, named for mythical hunter
Pleiads seven stars within constellation Taurus, named for the daughters of Atlas pursued by Orion
lapwing crested plover

In the spring a livelier iris° changes on the burnished dove;
20   In the spring a young man's fancy lightly turns to thoughts of love.

Then her cheek was pale and thinner than should be for one so young,
And her eyes on all my motions with a mute observance hung.

And I said, 'My cousin Amy, speak, and speak the truth to me,
Trust me, cousin, all the current of my being sets to thee.'

On her pallid cheek and forehead came a colour and a light,
As I have seen the rosy red flushing in the northern night.

And she turned—her bosom shaken with a sudden storm of sighs—
All the spirit deeply dawning in the dark of hazel eyes—

Saying, 'I have hid my feelings, fearing they should do me wrong;
30   Saying, 'Dost thou love me, cousin?' weeping, 'I have loved thee long.'

Love took up the glass of Time, and turned it in his glowing hands;
Every moment, lightly shaken, ran itself in golden sands.

Love took up the harp of Life, and smote on all the chords with might;
Smote the chord of Self, that, trembling, passed in music out of sight.

Many a morning on the moorland did we hear the copses ring,
And her whisper thronged my pulses with the fulness of the spring.

Many an evening by the waters did we watch the stately ships,
And our spirits rushed together at the touching of the lips.

O my cousin, shallow-hearted! O my Amy, mine no more!
40   O the dreary, dreary moorland! O the barren, barren shore!

Falser than all fancy fathoms,° falser than all songs have sung,
Puppet to a father's threat, and servile to a shrewish tongue!

Is it well to wish thee happy?—having known me—to decline
On a range of lower feelings and a narrower heart than mine!

Yet it shall be: thou shalt lower to his level day by day,
What is fine within thee growing coarse to sympathize with clay.

As the husband is, the wife is: thou art mated with a clown,
And the grossness of his nature will have weight to drag thee down.

He will hold thee, when his passion shall have spent its novel force,
50   Something better than his dog, a little dearer than his horse.

What is this? his eyes are heavy: think not they are glazed with wine.
Go to him: it is thy duty: kiss him: take his hand in thine.

It may be my lord is weary, that his brain is overwrought:
Soothe him with thy finer fancies, touch him with thy lighter thought.

iris iridescent coloring on the dove's throat,   fancy fathoms imagination realizes; i.e. Amy is
which brightens in the mating season   falser than his imagination can realize

He will answer to the purpose, easy things to understand—
Better thou wert dead before me, though I slew thee with my hand!

Better thou and I were lying, hidden from the heart's disgrace,
Rolled in one another's arms, and silent in a last embrace.

Cursèd be the social wants that sin against the strength of youth!
60   Cursèd be the social lies that warp us from the living truth!

Cursèd be the sickly forms that err from honest Nature's rule!
Cursèd be the gold that gilds the straitened forehead of the fool!

Well—'tis well that I should bluster!—Hadst thou less unworthy proved—
Would to God—for I had loved thee more than ever wife was loved.

Am I mad, that I should cherish that which bears but bitter fruit?
I will pluck it from my bosom, though my heart be at the root.

Never, though my mortal summers to such length of years should come
As the many-wintered crow° that leads the clanging rookery home.

Where is comfort? in division of the records of the mind?
70   Can I part her from herself, and love her, as I knew her, kind?

I remember one that perished: sweetly did she speak and move:
Such a one do I remember, whom to look at was to love.

Can I think of her as dead, and love her for the love she bore?
No—she never loved me truly: love is love for evermore.

Comfort? comfort scorned of devils! this is truth the poet° sings,
That a sorrow's crown of sorrow is remembering happier things.

Drug thy memories, lest thou learn it, lest thy heart be put to proof,
In the dead unhappy night, and when the rain is on the roof.

Like a dog, he° hunts in dreams, and thou art staring at the wall,
80   Where the dying night-lamp flickers, and the shadows rise and fall.

Then a hand shall pass before thee, pointing to his drunken sleep,
To thy widowed marriage-pillows, to the tears that thou wilt weep.

Thou shalt hear the 'Never, never,' whispered by the phantom years,
And a song from out the distance in the ringing of thine ears;

And an eye shall vex thee, looking ancient kindness on thy pain.
Turn thee, turn thee on thy pillow: get thee to thy rest again.

Nay, but Nature brings thee solace; for a tender voice will cry.
'Tis a purer life than thine; a lip to drain thy trouble dry.

Baby lips will laugh me down: my latest rival brings thee rest.
90   Baby fingers, waxen touches, press me from the mother's breast.

crow the rook, reputed to live to a great age   joy, when misery is at hand."
the poet Dante; see the *Inferno* V.121, "There   he Amy's husband
is no greater grief than to remember days of

O, the child too clothes the father with a dearness not his due.
Half is thine and half is his: it will be worthy of the two.

O, I see thee old and formal, fitted to thy petty part,
With a little hoard of maxims preaching down a daughter's heart.

'They were dangerous guides the feelings—she herself was not exempt—
Truly, she herself had suffered'—Perish in thy self-contempt!

Overlive it—lower yet—be happy! wherefore should I care?
I myself must mix with action, lest I wither by despair.

What is that which I should turn to, lighting upon days like these?
100   Every door is barred with gold, and opens but to golden keys.

Every gate is thronged with suitors, all the markets overflow.
I have but an angry fancy: what is that which I should do?

I had been content to perish, falling on the foeman's ground,
When the ranks are rolled in vapour, and the winds are laid with sound.

But the jingling of the guinea helps the hurt that Honour feels,
And the nations do but murmur, snarling at each other's heels.

Can I but relive in sadness? I will turn that earlier page.
Hide me from my deep emotion, O thou wondrous Mother-Age!

Make me feel the wild pulsation that I felt before the strife,
110   When I heard my days before me, and the tumult of my life;

Yearning for the large excitement that the coming years would yield,
Eager-hearted as a boy when first he leaves his father's field,

And at night along the dusky highway near and nearer drawn,
Sees in heaven the light of London flaring like a dreary dawn;

And his spirit leaps within him to be gone before him then,
Underneath the light he looks at, in among the throngs of men:

Men, my brothers, men the workers, ever reaping something new:
That which they have done but earnest of the things that they shall do:

For I dipped into the future, far as human eye could see,
120   Saw the Vision of the world, and all the wonder that would be;

Saw the heavens fill with commerce, argosies of magic sails,°
Pilots of the purple twilight, dropping down with costly bales;

Heard the heavens fill with shouting, and there rained a ghastly dew
From the nations' airy navies grappling in the central blue;

Far along the world-wide whisper of the south-wind rushing warm,
With the standards of the peoples plunging through the thunder-storm;

Till the war-drum throbbed no longer, and the battle-flags were furled
In the Parliament of man, the Federation of the world.

magic sails balloons

There the common sense of most shall hold a fretful realm in awe,
130   And the kindly earth shall slumber, lapped in universal law.

So I triumphed ere my passion sweeping through me left me dry,
Left me with the palsied heart, and left me with the jaundiced eye;

Eye, to which all order festers, all things here are out of joint:
Science moves, but slowly slowly, creeping on from point to point:

Slowly comes a hungry people, as a lion creeping nigher,
Glares at one that nods and winks behind a slowly-dying fire.

Yet I doubt not through the ages one increasing purpose runs,
And the thoughts of men are widened with the process of the suns.°

What is that to him that reaps not harvest of his youthful joys,
140   Though the deep heart of existence beat for ever like a boy's?

Knowledge comes, but wisdom lingers, and I linger on the shore,
And the individual withers, and the world is more and more.

Knowledge comes, but wisdom lingers, and he bears a laden breast,
Full of sad experience, moving toward the stillness of his rest.

Hark, my merry comrades call me, sounding on the bugle-horn,
They to whom my foolish passion were a target for their scorn:

Shall it not be scorn to me to harp on such a mouldered string?
I am shamed through all my nature to have loved so slight a thing.

Weakness to be wroth with weakness! woman's pleasure, woman's pain—
150   Nature made them blinder motions° bounded in a shallower brain:

Woman is the lesser man, and all thy passions, matched with mine,
Are as moonlight unto sunlight, and as water unto wine—

Here at least, where nature sickens, nothing. Ah, for some retreat
Deep in yonder shining Orient, where my life began to beat;

Where in wild Mahratta°-battle fell my father evil-starred;—
I was left a trampled orphan, and a selfish uncle's ward.

Or to burst all links of habit—there to wander far away,
On from island unto island at the gateways of the day.

Larger constellations burning, mellow moons and happy skies,
160   Breadths of tropic shade and palms in cluster, knots of Paradise.

Never comes the trader, never floats an European flag,
Slides the bird o'er lustrous woodland, swings the trailer° from the crag;

Droops the heavy-blossomed bower, hangs the heavy-fruited tree—
Summer isles of Eden lying in dark-purple spheres of sea.

suns years
motions affective impulses
Mahratta tribe in central India that fought the

British repeatedly in the early 19th century
trailer trailing vine

There methinks would be enjoyment more than in this march of mind,°
In the steamship, in the railway, in the thoughts that shake mankind.

There the passions cramped no longer shall have scope and breathing space;
I will take some savage woman, she shall rear my dusky race.

170 Iron jointed, supple-sinewed, they shall dive, and they shall run,
Catch the wild goat by the hair, and hurl their lances in the sun;

Whistle back the parrot's call, and leap the rainbows of the brooks,
Not with blinded eyesight poring over miserable books—

Fool, again the dream, the fancy! but I *know* my words are wild,
But I count the grey barbarian lower than the Christian child.

I, to herd with narrow foreheads, vacant of our glorious gains,
Like a beast with lower pleasures, like a beast with lower pains!

Mated with a squalid savage—what to me were sun or clime?
I the heir of all the ages, in the foremost files of time—

180 I that rather held it better men should perish one by one,
Than that earth should stand at gaze like Joshua's moon° in Ajalon!

Not in vain the distance beacons.° Forward let us range,
Let the great world spin for ever down the ringing grooves° of change.

Through the shadow of the globe we sweep into the younger day:
Better fifty years of Europe than a cycle of Cathay.°

Mother-Age (for mine I knew not) help me as when life begun:
Rift the hills, and roll the waters, flash the lightnings, weigh the Sun.

O, I see the crescent promise of my spirit hath not set.
Ancient founts of inspiration well through all my fancy yet.

190 Howsoever these things be, a long farewell to Locksley Hall!
Now for me the woods may wither, now for me the roof-tree fall.

Comes a vapour from the margin, blackening over heath and holt,
Cramming all the blast before it, in its breast a thunderbolt.

Let it fall on Locksley Hall, with rain or hail, or fire or snow;
For the mighty wind arises, roaring seaward, and I go.

1842

---

march of mind technological progress, particularly in the 1840's
Joshua's moon Joshua 10:11–12; needing time to complete a victory, Joshua was permitted by God to order the sun and moon to stand still.
beacons shines like a beacon light

ringing grooves a famous mistake, made after the poet's first ride on the steam railroad, whose wheels he thought ran in a groove
Cathay European name for northern China, during the Middle Ages

The Vision of Sin°

I

I had a vision when the night was late:
A youth came riding toward a palace-gate.
He rode a horse with wings,° that would have flown,
But that his heavy rider° kept him down.
And from the palace came a child of sin,
And took him by the curls, and led him in,
Where sat a company with heated eyes,
Expecting when a fountain should arise:
As sleepy light upon their brows and lips—
10 As when the sun, a crescent of eclipse,
Dreams over lake and lawn, and isles and capes—
Suffused them, sitting, lying, languid shapes,
By heaps of gourds, and skins of wine, and piles of grapes.

II

Then methought I heard a mellow sound,
Gathering up from all the lower ground;
Narrowing in to where they sat assembled
Low voluptuous music winding trembled,
Woven in circles: they that heard it sighed,
Panted hand-in-hand with faces pale,
20 Swung themselves, and in low tones replied;
Till the fountain spouted, showering wide
Sleet of diamond-drift and pearly hail;
Then the music touched the gates and died;
Rose again from where it seemed to fail,
Stormed in orbs of song, a growing gale;
Till thronging in and in, to where they waited,
As 'twere a hundred-throated nightingale,
The strong tempestuous treble throbbed and palpitated;
Ran into its giddiest whirl of sound,
30 Caught the sparkles, and in circles,
Purple gauzes, golden hazes, liquid mazes,
Flung the torrent rainbow round:
Then they started from their places,
Moved with violence, changed in hue,
Caught each other with wild grimaces,
Half-invisible to the view,
Wheeling with precipitate paces
To the melody, till they flew,

The Vision of Sin Tennyson had a special fondness for this vivid dream-vision, and summarized it: "This describes the soul of a youth who has given himself up to pleasure and Epicureanism. He at length is worn out and wrapped in the mists of satiety. Afterwards he grows into a cynical old man afflicted with the 'curse of nature,' and joining in the Feast of Death. Then we see the landscape which symbolizes God, Law and the future life."

horse with wings Pegasus
heavy rider the body

Hair, and eyes, and limbs, and faces,
40 Twisted hard in fierce embraces,
Like to Furies, like to Graces,°
Dashed together in blinding dew:
Till, killed with some luxurious agony,
The nerve-dissolving melody
Fluttered headlong from the sky.

III

And then I looked up toward a mountain-tract,
That girt the region with high cliff and lawn:
I saw that every morning, far withdrawn
Beyond the darkness and the cataract,
50 God made Himself an awful rose of dawn,
Unheeded: and detaching, fold by fold,
From those still heights, and, slowly drawing near,
A vapour heavy, hueless, formless, cold,
Came floating on for many a month and year,
Unheeded: and I thought I would have spoken,
And warned that madman ere it grew too late:
But, as in dreams, I could not. Mine was broken,
When that cold vapour touched the palace gate,
And linked again. I saw within my head
60 A grey and gap-toothed man as lean as death,
Who slowly rode across a withered heath,
And lighted at a ruined inn, and said:

IV

'Wrinkled ostler,° grim and thin!
Here is custom come your way;
Take my brute, and lead him in,
Stuff his ribs with mouldy hay.

'Bitter barmaid, waning fast!
See that sheets are on my bed;
What! the flower of life is past:
70   It is long before you wed.

'Slip-shod waiter, lank and sour,
At the Dragon° on the heath!
Let us have a quiet hour,
Let us hob-and-nob with Death.

'I am old, but let me drink;
Bring me spices, bring me wine;

Furies . . . Graces The three Furies (or Eu-   ostler stableman, groom
menides) were avenging goddesses, fearful to   Dragon a tavern
behold; the three Graces, in contrast, were
goddesses of beauty.

I remember, when I think,
      That my youth was half divine.

'Wine is good for shrivelled lips,
80   When a blanket wraps the day,
When the rotten woodland drips,
      And the leaf is stamped in clay.

'Sit thee down, and have no shame,
      Cheek by jowl, and knee by knee:
What care I for any name?
      What for order or degree?

'Let me screw thee up a peg:
      Let me loose thy tongue with wine:
Callest thou that thing a leg?
90   Which is thinnest? thine or mine?

'Thou shalt not be saved by works:
      Thou hast been a sinner too:
Ruined trunks on withered forks,
      Empty scarecrows, I and you!

'Fill the cup, and fill the can:
      Have a rouse° before the morn:
Every moment dies a man,
      Every moment one is born.

'We are men of ruined blood;
100   Therefore comes it we are wise.
Fish are we that love the mud,
      Rising to no fancy-flies.

'Name and fame! to fly sublime
      Through the courts, the camps, the schools,
Is to be the ball of Time,
      Bandied by the hands of fools.

'Friendship!—to be two in one—
      Let the ranting liar pack!
Well I know, when I am gone,
110   How she mouths behind my back.

'Virtue!—to be good and just—
      Every heart, when sifted well,
Is a clot of warmer dust,
      Mixed with cunning sparks of hell.

'O! we two as well can look
      Whited thought and cleanly life
As the priest, above his book
      Leering at his neighbour's wife.

rouse drinking bout

'Fill the cup, and fill the can:
120 Have a rouse before the morn:
  Every moment dies a man,
   Every moment one is born.

'Drink, and let the parties rave:
  They are filled with idle spleen;
  Rising, falling, like a wave,
   For they know not what they mean.

'He that roars for liberty
  Faster binds a tyrant's power;
  And the tyrant's cruel glee
130 Forces on the freer hour.

'Fill the can, and fill the cup:
  All the windy ways of men
  Are but dust that rises up,
   And is lightly laid again.

'Greet her with applausive breath,
  Freedom, gaily doth she tread;
  In her right a civic wreath,
   In her left a human head.

'No, I love not what is new;
140 She is of an ancient house:
  And I think we know the hue°
   Of that cap upon her brows.

'Let her go! her thirst she slakes
  Where the bloody conduit runs,
  Then her sweetest meal she makes
   On the first-born of her sons.

'Drink to lofty hopes that cool°—
  Visions of a perfect State:
  Drink we, last, the public fool,
150 Frantic love and frantic hate.

'Chant me now some wicked stave,°
  Till thy drooping courage rise,
  And the glow-worm of the grave
   Glimmer in thy rheumy eyes.

'Fear not thou to loose thy tongue;
  Set thy hoary fancies free;
  What is loathsome to the young
   Savours well to thee and me.

hue blood-red cap of allegorical figure of Liberty, representing the French Revolution and its ensuing terror
hopes that cool Tennyson may be thinking of Coleridge and Wordsworth, disillusioned partisans of the Revolution.
stave song

'Change, reverting to the years,
160   When thy nerves could understand
What there is in loving tears,
      And the warmth of hand in hand.

'Tell me tales of thy first love—
      April hopes, the fools of chance;
Till the graves begin to move,
      And the dead begin to dance.

'Fill the can, and fill the cup:
      All the windy ways of men
Are but dust that rises up,
170   And is lightly laid again.

'Trooping from their mouldy dens
      The chap-fallen° circle spreads:
Welcome, fellow-citizens,
      Hollow hearts and empty heads!

'You are bones, and what of that?
      Every face, however full,
Padded round with flesh and fat,
      Is but modelled on a skull.

'Death is king, and Vivat Rex!°
180   Tread a measure on the stones,
Madam—if I know your sex,
      From the fashion of your bones.

'No, I cannot praise the fire
      In your eye—nor yet your lip:
All the more do I admire
      Joints of cunning workmanship.

'Lo! God's likeness—the ground-plan—
      Neither modelled, glazed, nor framed:
Buss° me, thou rough sketch of man,
190   Far too naked to be shamed!

'Drink to Fortune, drink to Chance,
      While we keep a little breath!
Drink to heavy Ignorance!
      Hob-and-nob with brother Death!

'Thou art mazed, the night is long,
      And the longer night is near:
What! I am not all as wrong
      As a bitter jest is dear.

chap-fallen disconsolate   buss kiss
Vivat Rex long live the king

'Youthful hopes, by scores, to all,
200   When the locks are crisp and curled;
Unto me my maudlin gall
      And my mockeries of the world.

'Fill the cup, and fill the can:
      Mingle madness, mingle scorn!
Dregs of life, and lees of man:
      Yet we will not die forlorn.'

                    v

The voice grew faint: there came a further change:
Once more uprose the mystic mountain-range:
Below were men and horses pierced with worms,
210 And slowly quickening into lower forms;
By shards and scurf of salt, and scum of dross,
Old plash of rains, and refuse patched with moss.
Then some one spake: 'Behold! it was a crime
Of sense avenged by sense that wore with time.'
Another said: 'The crime of sense became
The crime of malice, and is equal blame.'
And one: 'He had not wholly quenched his power;
A little grain of conscience made him sour.'
At last I heard a voice upon the slope
220 Cry to the summit, 'Is there any hope?'
To which an answer pealed from that high land,
But in a tongue no man could understand;
And on the glimmering limit far withdrawn
God made Himself an awful rose of dawn.°
1835-39   1842

Songs from The Princess

The Splendour Falls

The splendour falls on castle walls
      And snowy summits old in story:
The long light shakes across the lakes,
      And the wild cataract leaps in glory.
Blow, bugle, blow, set the wild echoes flying,
Blow, bugle; answer, echoes, dying, dying, dying.

O hark, O hear! how thin and clear,
      And thinner, clearer, farther going!
O sweet and far from cliff and scar
10   The horns of Elfland° faintly blowing!
Blow, let us hear the purple glens replying:

rose of dawn See Keats's *Hyperion* I.203–12.   Elfland fairyland; the lyric's setting is Ireland

Blow, bugle; answer, echoes, dying, dying, dying.
  O love, they die in yon rich sky,
    They faint on hill or field or river:
  Our echoes roll from soul to soul,
    And grow for ever and for ever.°
Blow, bugle, blow, set the wild echoes flying,
And answer, echoes, answer, dying, dying, dying.

1850

Tears, Idle Tears°

'Tears, idle tears, I know not what they mean,
Tears from the depth of some divine despair
Rise in the heart, and gather to the eyes,
In looking on the happy Autumn-fields,
And thinking of the days that are no more.

'Fresh as the first beam glittering on a sail,
That brings our friends up from the underworld,
Sad as the last which reddens over one
That sinks with all we love below the verge;
So sad, so fresh, the days that are no more.

'Ah, sad and strange as in dark summer dawns
The earliest pipe of half-awakened birds°
To dying ears, when unto dying eyes
The casement slowly grows a glimmering square;
So sad, so strange, the days that are no more.

'Dear as remembered kisses after death,
And sweet as those by hopeless fancy feigned
On lips that are for others; deep as love,
Deep as first love, and wild with all regret;
O Death in Life, the days that are no more.

1847

Come Down, O Maid°

'Come down, O maid, from yonder mountain height:
What pleasure lives in height (the shepherd sang)
In height and cold, the splendour of the hills?
But cease to move so near the Heavens, and cease
To glide a sunbeam by the blasted Pine,

Our echoes . . . for ever our echoes of one
another are not illusive, but all others are
Tears, Idle Tears This Virgilian lyric is another lament for Hallam, written at Tintern
Abbey, and echoing the *Intimations* Ode as well
as *Tintern Abbey*.

half-awakened birds Compare Wallace Stevens's
Sunday Morning IV.1–5.
Come Down, O Maid title taken from Theoc-
ritus, *Idylls* XI.

To sit a star upon the sparkling spire;
And come, for Love is of the valley, come,
For Love is of the valley, come thou down
And find him; by the happy threshold, he,
10 Or hand in hand with Plenty in the maize,
Or red with spirted purple of the vats,
Or foxlike in the vine°; nor cares to walk
With Death and Morning on the silver horns,°
Nor wilt thou snare him in the white ravine,
Nor find him dropped upon the firths of ice,
That huddling slant in furrow-cloven falls
To roll the torrent out of dusky doors:
But follow; let the torrent dance thee down
To find him in the valley; let the wild
20 Lean-headed Eagles yelp alone, and leave
The monstrous ledges there to slope, and spill
Their thousand wreaths of dangling water-smoke,
That like a broken purpose waste in air:
So waste not thou; but come; for all the vales
Await thee; azure pillars° of the hearth
Arise to thee; the children call, and I
Thy shepherd pipe, and sweet is every sound,
Sweeter thy voice, but every sound is sweet;
Myriads of rivulets hurrying through the lawn,
30 The moan of doves in immemorial elms,
And murmuring of innumerable bees.'°

                                    1847

In Memoriam A. H. H.

This is Tennyson's central poem, and as much the characteristic poem of its time as
Eliot's *The Waste Land* was of the 'twenties and 'thirties of this century. "It happens
now and then that a poet by some strange accident expresses the mood of his generation, at the same time that he is expressing a mood of his own which is quite remote
from that of his generation." Eliot shrewdly links *In Memoriam* with *The Waste Land*
in this remark. Both—despite all critical blindness—seem to this editor to be poems
of repressed passions, presumably of a man for a man. Eliot notes again, in Tennyson,
"emotion so deeply suppressed, even from himself, as to tend rather towards the
blackest melancholia." Neo-orthodox critics of both ages have made both poems
celebrations of the necessity for Christianity, but neither of these poems (discontinuous
sequences both), is very convincing when it argues, implicitly or explicitly, against
modern doubt and materialism. Both poems are violently personal, eccentric, High
Romantic at the core, and the quest in each is yet another version of what Yeats
called "the antithetical" and accurately traced back to Shelley's *Alastor*.

A. C. Bradley has given the best account of the structure of *In Memoriam*. Following Tennyson's own statement that the poem's divisions are made by the Christmas sections (XXVIII, LXXVIII, CIV), Bradley sees the poem as a three-year cycle (though written, of course, over many other years). The turning-point, in Bradley's view, is the second Christmas poem, LXXVIII, after which deeper sorrow has passed. This editor would urge attention to sections XCV and CIII, as being not only the best poems in the sequence, but as establishing the deeper enterprise of Tennyson's imagination in the poem. Section XCV is Tennyson's extreme version of Wordsworth's "Intimations" Ode, while section CIII is a variation upon the concluding love voyage of Shelley's *Epipsychidion*. Also remarkable is the apotheosis of Hallam in sections CXXVI to CXXX, a version of the transfiguration of Keats in the closing stanzas of *Adonais*, and about as Christian in its vision as Shelley's poem was.

From In Memoriam A. H. H.

Obiit MDCCCXXXIII

[PROLOGUE]°

Strong Son of God, immortal Love,°
    Whom we, that have not seen thy face,
    By faith, and faith alone, embrace,
Believing where we cannot prove;

Thine are these orbs of light and shade;°
    Thou madest Life in man and brute;
    Thou madest Death; and lo, thy foot
Is on the skull which thou hast made.

Thou wilt not leave us in the dust:
10   Thou madest man, he knows not why,
    He thinks he was not made to die;
And thou hast made him: thou art just.°

Thou seemest human and divine,
    The highest, holiest manhood, thou:
    Our wills are ours, we know not how;
Our wills are ours, to make them thine.

Our little systems° have their day;
    They have their day and cease to be:
    They are but broken lights of thee,
20   And thou, O Lord, art more than they.

[Prologue] written last (1849) and far more orthodox in its religious statement than anything else in the poem; thus, where Wordsworth, Shelley, and Keats are the strongest influences upon the rest of the poem, George Herbert is an overwhelming influence upon the "Prologue"
immortal Love See the opening stanza of George Herbert's "Love"; Tennyson gave I John 4 as a reference.
light and shade earth and the planets, always half in light and half in shadow, half in life and half in death
Thou wilt . . . thou art just See George Herbert's "The Discharge."
systems of thought

We have but faith: we cannot know;
   For knowledge is of things we see;
   And yet we trust it comes from thee,
A beam in darkness: let it grow.

Let knowledge grow from more to more,
   But more of reverence in us dwell;
   That mind and soul, according well,
May make one music as before,°

But vaster. We are fools and slight;
30   We mock thee when we do not fear:
   But help thy foolish ones to bear;
Help thy vain worlds to bear thy light.°

Forgive what seemed my sin in me;
   What seemed my worth since I began;
   For merit lives from man to man,
And not from man, O Lord, to thee.

Forgive my grief for one removed,
   Thy creature, whom I found so fair.
   I trust he lives in thee, and there
40   I find him worthier to be loved.

Forgive these wild and wandering cries,
   Confusions of a wasted° youth;
   Forgive them where they fail in truth,
And in thy wisdom make me wise.
                  1849

         I

I held it truth, with him who sings°
   To one clear harp in divers tones,
   That men may rise on stepping-stones
Of their dead selves to higher things.

But who shall so forecast the years
   And find in loss a gain to match?
   Or reach a hand through time to catch
The far-off interest° of tears?

Let Love clasp Grief lest both be drowned,
10   Let darkness keep her raven gloss:
   Ah, sweeter to be drunk with loss,
To dance with death, to beat the ground,

Than that the victor Hours should scorn
   The long result of love, and boast,

---

as before before supposed increases in knowledge destroyed their harmony
thy light the light that is the knowledge of God
wasted desolated, not thrown away

him who sings Goethe, probably as interpreted
by Carlyle
interest as on a loan, the recompense for use

'Behold the man that loved and lost,
But all he was is overworn.'

II

Old Yew, which graspest at the stones
    That name the under-lying dead,
    Thy fibres net the dreamless head,
Thy roots are wrapped about the bones.°

The seasons bring the flower again,
    And bring the firstling to the flock;
    And in the dusk of thee, the clock
Beats out the little lives of men.

O not for thee the glow, the bloom,
    Who changest not in any gale,
    Nor branding summer suns avail
To touch thy thousand years of gloom:

And gazing on thee, sullen tree,
    Sick for thy stubborn hardihood,
    I seem to fail from out my blood
And grow incorporate into thee.

III

O Sorrow, cruel fellowship,
    O Priestess in the vaults of Death,
    O sweet and bitter in a breath,
What whispers from thy lying lip?

'The stars,' she whispers, 'blindly run;
    A web is woven across the sky;
    From out waste places comes a cry,
And murmurs from the dying sun:°

'And all the phantom, Nature, stands—
    With all the music in her tone,
    A hollow echo of my own,—
A hollow form with empty hands.'

And shall I take a thing so blind,
    Embrace her as my natural good;
    Or crush her, like a vice of blood,
Upon the threshold of the mind?

       . . .

V

I sometimes hold it half a sin
    To put in words the grief I feel;

Thy roots . . . bones See Job 8:17.
dying sun Tennyson's doubt here is due to the now long-discredited nebular hypothesis, which asserted that the earth was a fiery discharge from the sun (CXVIII.9).

For words, like Nature, half reveal
And half conceal the Soul within.

But, for the unquiet heart and brain,
    A use in measured language lies;
    The sad mechanic exercise,
Like dull narcotics, numbing pain.

In words, like weeds,° I'll wrap me o'er,
    Like coarsest clothes against the cold:
    But that large grief which these enfold
Is given in outline and no more.

.   .   .

VII

Dark house,° by which once more I stand
    Here in the long unlovely street,
    Doors, where my heart was used to beat
So quickly, waiting for a hand,

A hand that can be clasped no more—
    Behold me, for I cannot sleep,
    And like a guilty thing° I creep
At earliest morning to the door.

He is not here; but far away
    The noise of life begins again,
    And ghastly through the drizzling rain
On the bald street breaks the blank day.

.   .   .

IX

Fair ship,° that from the Italian shore
    Sailest the placid ocean-plains
    With my lost Arthur's loved remains,
Spread thy full wings, and waft him o'er.

So draw him home to those that mourn
    In vain; a favourable speed
    Ruffle thy mirrored mast, and lead
Through prosperous floods his holy urn.

All night no ruder air perplex
    Thy sliding keel, till Phosphor,° bright
    As our pure love, through early light
Shall glimmer on the dewy decks.

weeds garments
Dark house the Hallam house, 67 Wimpole
Street, London
guilty thing See Wordsworth's *Intimations*

Ode IX.19 and *Hamlet* I.i.148.
Fair ship bringing home Hallam's corpse
Phosphor "star of dawn" (Tennyson)

Sphere all your lights around, above;
   Sleep, gentle heavens, before the prow;
   Sleep, gentle winds, as he sleeps now,
My friend, the brother of my love;

My Arthur, whom I shall not see
   Till all my widowed race be run;
   Dear as the mother to the son,
20 More than my brothers are to me.

      . . .

XV

Tonight the winds begin to rise
   And roar from yonder dropping day:
   The last red leaf° is whirled away,
The rooks are blown about the skies;

The forest cracked, the waters curled,
   The cattle huddled on the lea;
   And wildly dashed on tower and tree
The sunbeam strikes along the world:

And but for fancies, which aver
10   That all thy motions° gently pass
   Athwart a plane of molten glass,°
I scarce could brook the strain and stir

That makes the barren branches loud;
   And but for fear it is not so,
   The wild unrest that lives in woe
Would dote and pore on yonder cloud

That rises upward always higher,
   And onward drags a labouring breast,
   And topples round the dreary west,
20 A looming bastion fringed with fire.

      . . .

XXI

I sing to him that rests below,°
   And, since the grasses round me wave,
   I take the grasses of the grave,
And make them pipes whereon to blow.

The traveller hears me now and then,
   And sometimes harshly will he speak:
   'This fellow would make weakness weak,
And melt the waxen hearts of men.'

---

last red leaf See Coleridge's *Christabel*, ll. 49–
50.
motions of the ship

molton glass See Job 37:18 and Revelation 15:2.
rests below set at Clevedon, Hallam's burial
place

Another answers, 'Let him be,
10   He loves to make parade of pain,
        That with his piping he may gain
The praise that comes to constancy.'

A third is wroth: 'Is this an hour
        For private sorrow's barren song,
        When more and more the people throng
The chairs and thrones of civil power?°

'A time to sicken and to swoon,
        When Science reaches forth her arms
        To feel from world to world, and charms
20 Her secret from the latest moon?'°

Behold, ye speak an idle thing:
        Ye never knew the sacred dust:
        I do but sing because I must,
And pipe but as the linnets sing:°

And one is glad; her note is gay,
        For now her little ones have ranged;
        And one is sad: her note is changed,
Because her brood is stolen away.

                · · ·

              XXIV
And was the day of my delight
        As pure and perfect as I say?
        The very source and fount of Day
Is dashed with wandering isles of night.°

If all was good and fair we met,
        This earth had been the Paradise
        It never looked to human eyes
Since our first Sun arose and set.

And is it that the haze of grief
10   Makes former gladness loom so great?
        The lowness of the present state,
That sets the past in this relief?

Or that the past will always win
        A glory from its being far;
        And orb into the perfect star
We saw not, when we moved therein?°

                · · ·

---

the people . . . civil power the Chartist Movement and, ultimately, the French Revolution
latest moon perhaps the discovery of Neptune
and its moon in 1846
linnets sing See the "Harper's Song" in Goethe's

Wilhelm Meister's Travels II, XI.
isles of night sun-spots
Or that the past . . . moved therein the imperfections seen up close vanish in the distance

XXVII

I envy not in any moods
  The captive void of noble rage,
  The linnet born within the cage,
That never knew the summer woods:

I envy not the beast that takes
  His license in the field of time,
  Unfettered by the sense of crime,
To whom a conscience never wakes;

Nor, what may count itself as blest,
10 The heart that never plighted troth
  But stagnates in the weeds of sloth;
Nor any want-begotten rest.

I hold it true, whate'er befall;
  I feel it, when I sorrow most;
  'Tis better to have loved and lost
Than never to have loved at all.

XXVIII°

The time draws near the birth of Christ:
  The moon is hid; the night is still;
  The Christmas bells from hill to hill
Answer each other in the mist.

Four voices of four hamlets round,
  From far and near, on mead and moor,
  Swell out and fail, as if a door
Were shut between me and the sound:

Each voice four° changes on the wind,
10 That now dilate, and now decrease,
  Peace and goodwill, goodwill and peace,
Peace and goodwill, to all mankind.

This year I slept and woke with pain,
  I almost wished no more to wake,
  And that my hold on life would break
Before I heard those bells again:

But they my troubled spirit rule,
  For they controlled me when a boy;
  They bring me sorrow touched with joy,
20 The merry merry bells of Yule.

. . .

XXVIII This begins the poem's second movement, and was one of the first sections written.
Each voice four Each church has four bells.

XXX

With trembling fingers did we weave
   The holly round the Christmas hearth;
   A rainy cloud possessed the earth,
And sadly fell our Christmas-eve.

At our old pastimes in the hall
   We gambolled, making vain pretence
   Of gladness, with an awful sense
Of one mute Shadow° watching all.

10   We paused: the winds were in the beech:
   We heard them sweep the winter land;
   And in a circle hand-in-hand
Sat silent, looking each at each.

Then echo-like our voices rang;
   We sung, though every eye was dim,
   A merry song we sang with him
Last year: impetuously we sang:

We ceased: a gentler feeling crept
   Upon us: surely rest is meet:
   'They rest,' we said, 'their sleep is sweet,'
20   And silence followed, and we wept.

Our voices took a higher range;
   Once more we sang: 'They do not die
   Nor lose their mortal sympathy,
Nor change to us, although they change;

'Rapt from the fickle and the frail
   With gathered power, yet the same,°
   Pierces the keen seraphic flame
From orb to orb, from veil to veil.'

Rise, happy morn, rise, holy morn,
30   Draw forth the cheerful day from night:
   O Father, touch the east, and light
The light that shone when Hope was born.°

     XXXI

When Lazarus left his charnel-cave,°
   And home to Mary's house returned,
   Was this demanded—if he yearned
To hear her weeping by his grave?

'Where wert thou, brother, those four days?'
   There lives no record of reply,

mute Shadow Hallam
yet the same the soul survives unchanged
Hope was born overtly a reference to the birth
of Christ, but the stanza derives from *Adonais*,
particularly its final lines
charnel-cave See John 11:32–44.

Which telling what it is to die
Had surely added praise to praise.

From every house the neighbours met,
10   The streets were filled with joyful sound,
    A solemn gladness even crowned
The purple brows of Olivet.°

Behold a man raised up by Christ!
    The rest remaineth unrevealed;
    He told it not; or something sealed
The lips of that Evangelist.°

. . .

      XXXIV
My own dim life should teach me this,
    That life shall live for evermore,
    Else earth is darkness at the core,
And dust and ashes all that is;

This round of green, this orb of flame,
    Fantastic beauty; such as lurks
    In some wild Poet, when he works
Without a conscience or an aim.°

What then were God to such as I?
10   'Twere hardly worth my while to choose
    Of things all mortal, or to use
A little patience ere I die;

'Twere best at once to sink to peace,
    Like birds the charming serpent draws,
    To drop head-foremost in the jaws
Of vacant darkness and to cease.

      XXXV
Yet if some voice that man could trust
    Should murmur from the narrow house,
    'The cheeks drop in; the body bows;
Man dies: nor is there hope in dust:'

Might I not say? 'Yet even here,
    But for one hour, O Love, I strive
    To keep so sweet a thing alive:'
But I should turn mine ears and hear

The moanings of the homeless sea,
10   The sound of streams that swift or slow

Olivet high hill near Jerusalem
Evangelist St. John, who alone tells the story
(John 11:1–45)
when he works . . . or an aim Yet Hallam had

countenanced this, almost urged it, and certainly
the poet in Tennyson had felt the temptation;
the reference may be to Thomas Lovell Beddoes.

Draw down Aeonian hills,° and sow
  The dust of continents to be;

And Love would answer with a sigh,
  'The sound of that forgetful shore°
  Will change my sweetness more and more,
Half-dead to know that I shall die.'

O me, what profits it to put
  An idle case? If Death were seen
  At first as Death, Love had not been,
20 Or been in narrowest working shut,

Mere fellowship of sluggish moods,
  Or in his coarsest Satyr-shape
  Had bruised the herb and crushed the grape,
And basked and battened° in the woods.

XXXVI
Though truths in manhood darkly join,
  Deep-seated in our mystic frame,
  We yield all blessing to the name
Of Him that made them current coin;

For Wisdom dealt with mortal powers,
  Where truth in closest words shall fail,
  When truth embodied in a tale
Shall enter in at lowly doors.

And so the Word° had breath, and wrought
10 With human hands the creed of creeds
  In loveliness of perfect deeds,
More strong than all poetic thought;

Which he may read that binds the sheaf,
  Or builds the house, or digs the grave,
  And those wild eyes° that watch the wave
In roarings round the coral reef.

XXXVII
Urania° speaks with darkened brow:
  'Thou pratest here where thou art least;
  This faith has many a purer priest,
And many an abler voice than thou.

'Go down beside thy native rill,
  On thy Parnassus set thy feet,

Aeonian hills hills that have lasted whole eons or geological ages
forgetful shore shore of the river Lethe
basked and battened fed grossly like a beast
the Word Tennyson said that he meant the Logos (Christ, the divine Word) of St. John.

wild eyes According to Tennyson, this meant the Pacific Islanders, then undergoing the unhappy process of being introduced to Christian civilization.
Urania Muse of heavenly poetry, in Milton's invocation to Book VII, *Paradise Lost*

And hear thy laurel whisper sweet
About the ledges of the hill.'

And my Melpomene° replies,
    A touch of shame upon her cheek:
    'I am not worthy even to speak
Of thy prevailing mysteries;

'For I am but an earthly Muse,
    And owning but a little art
    To lull with song an aching heart,
And render human love his dues;

'But brooding on the dear one dead,
    And all he said of things divine,
    (And dear to me as sacred wine
To dying lips is all he said),

'I murmured, as I came along,
    Of comfort clasped in truth revealed;
    And loitered in the master's field,
And darkened sanctities with song.'

                .   ,   .

            XLIX
From art, from nature, from the schools,°
    Let random influences glance,
    Like light in many a shivered lance
That breaks about the dappled pools:

The lightest wave of thought shall lisp,
    The fancy's tenderest eddy wreathe,
    The slightest air of song shall breathe
To make the sullen surface crisp.°

And look thy look, and go thy way,
    But blame not thou the winds that make
    The seeming-wanton ripple break,
The tender-pencilled shadow play.

Beneath all fancied hopes and fears
    Ay me, the sorrow deepens down,
    Whose muffled motions blindly drown
The bases of my life in tears.

            L
Be near me when my light is low,
    When the blood creeps, and the nerves prick
    And tingle; and the heart is sick,
And all the wheels of Being slow.

Melpomene ordinarily Muse of tragedy, here   **the schools** of philosophy
evidently of elegy   **crisp** ripple

Be near me when the sensuous frame
  Is racked with pangs that conquer trust;
  And Time, a maniac scattering dust,
And Life, a Fury slinging flame.

Be near me when my faith is dry,
  And men the flies of latter spring,
  That lay their eggs, and sting and sing°
And weave their petty cells and die.

Be near me when I fade away,
  To point the term of human strife,
  And on the low dark verge of life
The twilight of eternal day.

LI

Do we indeed desire the dead
  Should still be near us at our side?
  Is there no baseness we would hide?
No inner vileness that we dread?

Shall he for whose applause I strove,
  I had such reverence for his blame,
  See with clear eye some hidden shame
And I be lessened in his love?

I wrong the grave with fears untrue:
  Shall love be blamed for want of faith?
  There must be wisdom with great Death:
The dead shall look me through and through.

Be near us when we climb or fall:
  Ye watch, like God, the rolling hours
  With larger other eyes than ours,
To make allowance for us all.

    . . .

LIV

Oh yet we trust that somehow good
  Will be the final goal of ill,
  To pangs of nature, sins of will,
Defects of doubt, and taints of blood;

That nothing walks with aimless feet;
  That not one life shall be destroyed,
  Or cast as rubbish to the void,
When God hath made the pile complete;

That not a worm is cloven in vain;
  That not a moth with vain desire

10 (line marker for "And men the flies of latter spring")
10 (line marker for "Shall love be blamed for want of faith?")
10 (line marker for "That not a moth with vain desire")

sting and sing See Pope's *Epistle to Dr. Ar-*
buthnot, ll. 309–10.

Is shrivelled in a fruitless fire,
Or but subserves another's gain.

Behold, we know not anything;
    I can but trust that good shall fall
    At last—far off°—at last, to all,
And every winter change to spring.

So runs my dream: but what am I?
    An infant crying in the night:
    An infant crying for the light:
20 And with no language but a cry.

LV

The wish, that of the living whole
    No life may fail beyond the grave,
    Derives it not from what we have
The likest God within the soul?

Are God and Nature then at strife,
    That Nature lends such evil dreams?
    So careful of the type she seems,
So careless of the single life;°

That I, considering everywhere
10   Her secret meaning in her deeds,
    And finding that of fifty seeds
She often brings but one to bear,

I falter where I firmly trod,
    And falling with my weight of cares
    Upon the great world's altar-stairs
That slope through darkness up to God,

I stretch lame hands of faith, and grope,
    And gather dust and chaff, and call
    To what I feel is Lord of all,
20 And faintly trust the larger hope.°

LVI

'So careful of the type?' but no.
    From scarpèd° cliff and quarried stone
    She cries, 'A thousand types are gone:
I care for nothing, all shall go.

---

far off See the next to the last line of the poem.
single life nature is not interested in any kind
of individual immortality. This and the next
section precede Darwin's *Origin of Species* by
nine years, and probably derive from Charles
Lyell's books on geology of the 1830's.
larger hope the hope "that the whole human

race would through, perhaps, ages of suffering,
be at length purified and saved" (Tennyson)
scarpèd cut away vertically, exposing strata,
which revealed fossils of extinct species, thus
demonstrating the so-called "supersession of
types"

'Thou makest thine appeal to me:
    I bring to life, I bring to death:
    The spirit does but mean the breath:
I know no more.' And he, shall he,

Man, her last work, who seemed so fair,
10   Such splendid purpose in his eyes,
    Who rolled the psalm to wintry skies,
Who built him fanes° of fruitless prayer,

Who trusted God was love indeed
    And love Creation's final law—
    Though Nature, red in tooth and claw
With ravine, shrieked against his creed—

Who loved, who suffered countless ills,
    Who battled for the True, the Just,
    Be blown about the desert dust,
20   Or sealed within the iron hills?°

No more? A monster then, a dream,
    A discord. Dragons of the prime,°
    That tare° each other in their slime,
Were mellow music matched with him.

O life as futile, then, as frail!
    O for thy voice to soothe and bless!
    What hope of answer, or redress?
Behind the veil, behind the veil.

                .   .   .

                LXVII
When on my bed the moonlight falls,
    I know that in thy place of rest°
    By that broad water of the west,
There comes a glory on the walls;

Thy marble bright in dark appears,
    As slowly steals a silver flame
    Along the letters of thy name,
And o'er the number of thy years.

The mystic glory swims away;
10   From off my bed the moonlight dies;
    And closing eaves of wearied eyes
I sleep till dusk is dipped in grey:

And then I know the mist is drawn
    A lucid veil from coast to coast,

fanes temples   tare tore
iron hills like fossils   place of rest Hallam's grave
Dragons of the prime prehistoric monsters

And in the dark church like a ghost
Thy tablet glimmers to the dawn.

. . .

LXXVII

What hope is here for modern rhyme
   To him, who turns a musing eye
   On songs, and deeds, and lives, that lie
Foreshortened in the tract of time?

These mortal lullabies of pain
   May bind a book, may line a box,
   May serve to curl a maiden's locks;
Or when a thousand moons shall wane

A man upon a stall may find,
   And, passing, turn the page that tells
   A grief, then changed to something else,
Sung by a long-forgotten mind.

But what of that? My darkened ways
   Shall ring with music all the same;
   To breathe my loss is more than fame,
To utter love more sweet than praise.

LXXVIII

Again at Christmas° did we weave
   The holly round the Christmas hearth;
   The silent snow possessed the earth,
And calmly fell our Christmas-eve:

The yule-clog° sparkled keen with frost,
   No wing of wind the region swept,
   But over all things brooding slept
The quiet sense of something lost.

As in the winters left behind,
   Again our ancient games had place,
   The mimic picture's breathing grace,°
And dance and song and hoodman-blind.°

Who showed a token of distress?
   No single tear, no mark of pain:
   O sorrow, then can sorrow wane?
O grief, can grief be changed to less?

O last regret, regret can die!
   No—mixed with all this mystic frame,

Christmas second Christmas Eve after the death, and the start of a third movement in the poem, essentially one of consolation

yule-clog log burned on Christmas Eve
breathing grace only games, but they are alive
hoodman-blind blindman's buff

Her deep relations are the same,
20 But with long use her tears are dry.

LXXIX

'More than my brothers are to me,'—
Let this not vex thee, noble heart!°
I know thee of what force thou art
To hold the costliest love in fee.°

But thou and I are one in kind,
As moulded like in Nature's mint;
And hill and wood and field did print
The same sweet forms in either mind.

For us the same cold streamlet curled
10 Through all his eddying coves; the same
All winds that roam the twilight came
In whispers of the beauteous world.

At one dear knee we proffered vows,
One lesson from one book we learned,
Ere childhood's flaxen ringlet turned
To black and brown on kindred brows.

And so my wealth resembles thine,
But he was rich where I was poor,
And he supplied my want the more
20 As his unlikeness fitted mine.

. . . .

XCV°

By night we lingered on the lawn,
For underfoot the herb was dry;
And genial warmth; and o'er the sky
The silvery haze of summer drawn;

And calm that let the tapers burn
Unwavering: not a cricket chirred:
The brook alone far-off was heard,
And on the board the fluttering urn:°

And bats went round in fragrant skies,
10 And wheeled or lit the filmy shapes°
That haunt the dusk, with ermine capes
And woolly breasts and beaded eyes;

---

noble heart Tennyson's brother Charles, also a
poet
in fee absolute possession
XCV This and CIII are surely the two greatest
sections of the poem, but although that is a
Shelleyan and Promethean dream-vision, this

section of epiphany and near-trance is deeply
Wordsworthian, the renewal of "a spot of time."
urn tea-urn, fluttering because of the flame
under it
filmy shapes ermine moths

While now we sang old songs that pealed
  From knoll to knoll, where, couched at ease,
  The white kine glimmered, and the trees
Laid their dark arms about the field.

But when those others, one by one,
  Withdrew themselves from me and night,
  And in the house light after light
20 Went out, and I was all alone,

A hunger seized my heart; I read
  Of that glad year° which once had been,
  In those fallen leaves which kept their green,
The noble letters of the dead:

And strangely on the silence broke
  The silent-speaking words, and strange
  Was love's dumb cry defying change
To test his worth; and strangely spoke

The faith, the vigour, bold to dwell
30 On doubts that drive the coward back,
  And keen through wordy snares to track
Suggestion to her inmost cell.

So word by word, and line by line,°
  The dead man touched me from the past,
  And all at once it seemed at last
The living soul was flashed on mine,

And mine in this was wound, and whirled
  About empyreal heights of thought,
  And came on that which is, and caught
40 The deep pulsations of the world,

Aeonian music° measuring out
  The steps of Time—the shocks of Chance—
  The blows of Death. At length my trance
Was cancelled, stricken through with doubt.

Vague words! but ah, how hard to frame
  In matter-moulded forms of speech,
  Or even for intellect to reach
Through memory that which I became:

Till now the doubtful dusk revealed
50 The knolls once more where, couched at ease,
  The white kine glimmered, and the trees
Laid their dark arms about the field:

---

glad year probably a particular year of their
love, but unidentified
line by line See Isaiah 28: 13.

Aeonian music music transcending space and
time, by returning to a deeper space, and eternal
time

And sucked from out the distant gloom
   A breeze began to tremble o'er
   The large leaves of the sycamore,
And fluctuate all the still perfume,

And gathering freshlier overhead,
   Rocked the full-foliaged elms, and swung
   The heavy-folded rose, and flung
60 The lilies to and fro, and said

'The dawn, the dawn,' and died away;
   And East and West, without a breath,
   Mixed their dim lights, like life and death,
To broaden into boundless day.°

     . . .

CIII

On that last night before we went
   From out the doors where I was bred,
   I dreamed a vision of the dead,°
Which left my after-morn content.

Methought I dwelt within a hall,
   And maidens° with me: distant hills
   From hidden summits° fed with rills
A river sliding by the wall.

The hall with harp and carol rang.
10 They sang of what is wise and good
   And graceful. In the centre stood
A statue veiled,° to which they sang;

And which, though veiled, was known to me,
   The shape of him I loved, and love
   For ever: then flew in a dove
And brought a summons from the sea:

And when they learnt that I must go
   They wept and wailed, but led the way
   To where a little shallop° lay
20 At anchor in the flood below;

And on by many a level mead,
   And shadowing bluff that made the banks,

The dawn . . . boundless day the wind of inspiration rises, announcing the dawn, and then
dies away; in that moment of stillness, gazing
at the West, the direction of death, Tennyson
sees the reflection of the sunrise in the East
vision of the dead the other climax of the
poem, wholly visionary and with no moral sanction, the ultimate (and wholly revealing) wish-
fulfillment in the poem
maidens the Muses

summits the divine
statue veiled Hallam, about to be resurrected,
like Hermione in Shakespeare's *The Winter's
Tale*
shallop boat. The symbolism of the boat of
death and resurrection goes back to Shelley's
Alastor, and figures in *The Lady of Shalott*,
Monte d'Arthur, and "Crossing the Bar"; a
modern parallel is Lawrence's "Ship of Death."

We glided winding under ranks
Of iris, and the golden reed;

And still as vaster grew the shore
    And rolled the floods in grander space,
    The maidens gathered strength and grace
And presence, lordlier than before;

And I myself, who sat apart
30   And watched them, waxed in every limb;
    I felt the thews of Anakim,°
The pulses of a Titan's heart;°

As one would sing the death of war,
    And one would chant the history
    Of that great race, which is to be,°
And one the shaping of a star;

Until the forward-creeping tides
    Began to foam, and we to draw
    From deep to deep, to where we saw
40 A great ship lift her shining sides.

The man we loved was there on deck,
    But thrice as large as man he bent
    To greet us. Up the side I went,
And fell in silence on his neck:

Whereat those maidens with one mind
    Bewailed their lot; I did them wrong:
    'We served thee here,' they said, 'so long,
And wilt thou leave us now behind?'°

So rapt I was, they could not win
50   An answer from my lips, but he
    Replying, 'Enter likewise ye
And go with us': they entered in.

And while the wind began to sweep
    A music out of sheet and shroud,
    We steered her toward a crimson cloud
That landlike slept along the deep.

CIV

The time draws near the birth of Christ;°
    The moon is hid, the night is still;
    A single church below the hill
Is pealing, folded in the mist.

Anakim the giants of Deuteronomy 2:10 and
Numbers 13:33; "thews" are sinews or muscles
Titan's heart Prometheus, whose heart was
tortured, but then redeemed
is to be in another evolutionary turn

And wilt . . . behind the Muses' fear of being
abandoned, as Hallam so clearly is Tennyson's
Muse
birth of Christ third Christmas since the death,
and start of the poem's last movement

A single peal of bells below,
   That wakens at this hour of rest
   A single murmur in the breast,
That these are not the bells I know.

Like strangers' voices here they sound,
10   In lands where not a memory strays,
   Nor landmark breathes of other days,
But all is new unhallowed ground.

      CV

Tonight ungathered let us leave
   This laurel, let this holly stand:
   We live within the stranger's land,
And strangely falls our Christmas-eve.

Our father's dust is left alone
   And silent under other snows:°
   There in due time the woodbine blows,
The violet comes, but we are gone.

No more shall wayward grief abuse
10   The genial hour with mask and mime;
   For change of place, like growth of time,
Has broke the bond of dying use.

Let cares that petty shadows cast,
   By which our lives are chiefly proved,
   A little spare the night I loved,
And hold it solemn to the past.

But let no footstep beat the floor,
   Nor bowl of wassail° mantle warm;
   For who would keep an ancient form
20 Through which the spirit breathes no more?

Be neither song, nor game, nor feast;
   Nor harp be touched, nor flute be blown;
   No dance, no motion, save alone
What lightens in the lucid east

Of rising worlds° by yonder wood.
   Long sleeps the summer in the seed;
   Run out your measured arcs, and lead
The closing cycle rich in good.

      CVI

Ring out, wild bells, to the wild sky,
   The flying cloud, the frosty light:

other snows The poet moved to Epping Forest
in 1837; his father was buried in Somersby,
their former home, in 1831.

wassail spiced wine causing the face to glow
rising worlds rising planets

The year is dying in the night;
Ring out, wild bells, and let him die.

Ring out the old, ring in the new,
    Ring, happy bells, across the snow:
    The year is going, let him go;
Ring out the false, ring in the true.

Ring out the grief that saps the mind,
10   For those that here we see no more;
    Ring out the feud of rich and poor,
Ring in redress to all mankind.

Ring out a slowly dying cause,
    And ancient forms of party strife;
    Ring in the nobler modes of life,
With sweeter manners, purer laws.

Ring out the want, the care, the sin,
    The faithless coldness of the times;
    Ring out, ring out my mournful rhymes,
20 But ring the fuller minstrel in.

Ring out false pride in place and blood,
    The civic slander and the spite;
    Ring in the love of truth and right,
Ring in the common love of good.

Ring out old shapes of foul disease;
    Ring out the narrowing lust of gold;
    Ring out the thousand wars of old,
Ring in the thousand years of peace.°

Ring in the valiant man and free,
30   The larger heart, the kindlier hand;
    Ring out the darkness of the land,
Ring in the Christ that is to be.°

· · ·

CXVIII
Contemplate all this work of Time,°
    The giant labouring in his youth;
    Nor dream of human love and truth,
As dying Nature's earth and lime;°

But trust that those we call the dead
Are breathers of an ampler day°

thousand years of peace (ll. 27–28) See Revelation 20:2–4.
Christ that is to be a vision of a broader, future
Christianity, free of sects and creeds
work of Time influenced by Lyell again

Nor dream . . . earth and lime what is valuable in us is not perishable
ampler day See Virgil, *Aeneid* VI.640, where
the phrase is "largior aether."

For ever nobler ends. They say,°
The solid earth whereon we tread

In tracts of fluent heat° began,
10 And grew to seeming-random forms,
  The seeming prey of cyclic storms,°
Till at the last arose the man;

Who throve and branched from clime to clime,
  The herald of a higher race,
  And of himself in higher place,
If so he type° this work of time

Within himself, from more to more;
  Or, crowned with attributes of woe
  Like glories, move his course, and show
20 That life is not as idle ore,

But iron dug from central gloom,
  And heated hot with burning fears,
  And dipped in baths of hissing tears,
And battered with the shocks of doom

To shape and use. Arise and fly
  The reeling Faun,° the sensual feast;
  Move upward, working out the beast,
And let the ape and tiger die.°

. . .

CXX

I trust I have not wasted breath:
  I think we are not wholly brain,
  Magnetic mockeries;° not in vain,
Like Paul with beasts, I fought with Death;°

Not only cunning casts in clay:
  Let Science prove we are, and then
  What matters Science unto men,°
At least to me? I would not stay.

Let him, the wiser man who springs
10 Hereafter, up from childhood shape
  His action like the greater ape,
But I was *born* to other things.

. . .

They say Lyell and other geologists
fluent heat the nebular hypothesis of Laplace
that the earth is a fiery discharge from the sun
cyclic storms disasters that will come again, as
they came before
type emulate; thus man's growth shows all
growth in time
reeling Faun half-man, half-goat, drunken and
lustful
ape and tiger die This does not deny our evo-

lutionary heritage, but insists that we must
transcend it.
Magnetic mockeries as though our brains were
electromagnetic mechanisms
fought with Death See I Corinthians 15:32,
where St. Paul says: "If after the manner of
men I have fought with beasts at Ephesus, what
advantageth it me, if the dead rise not?"
What . . . unto men if we are mechanisms

CXXIII

There rolls the deep where grew the tree.
O earth, what changes° hast thou seen!
There where the long street roars, hath been
The stillness of the central sea.

The hills are shadows, and they flow
From form to form, and nothing stands;
They melt like mist, the solid lands,
Like clouds they shape themselves and go.

But in my spirit will I dwell,
10   And dream my dream, and hold it true;
For though my lips may breathe adieu,
I cannot think the thing farewell.

CXXIV

That which we dare invoke to bless;
Our dearest faith; our ghastliest doubt;
He, They, One, All; within, without;
The Power in darkness whom we guess;°

I found Him not in world or sun,°
Or eagle's wing, or insect's eye;
Nor through the questions men may try,
The petty cobwebs we have spun:

If e'er when faith had fallen asleep,
10   I heard a voice 'believe no more'
And heard an ever-breaking shore
That tumbled in the Godless deep;

A warmth within the breast would melt
The freezing reason's colder part,
And like a man in wrath the heart
Stood up and answered 'I have felt.'

No, like a child in doubt and fear:
But that blind clamour made me wise;
Then was I as a child that cries,
20   But, crying, knows his father near;

And what I am beheld again
What is, and no man understands;
And out of darkness came the hands
That reach through nature, moulding men.

. . .

---

changes Geology demonstrates that oceans replace continents and continents oceans, or so
Tennyson thought.
Our dearest faith . . . whom we guess God,
however expressed, is found equally by our faith
or our doubt.
world or sun God may be present in nature, but
Tennyson did not find him there.

CXXVII

And all is well, though faith and form
   Be sundered in the night of fear;
   Well roars the storm to those that hear
A deeper voice across the storm,

Proclaiming social truth shall spread,
   And justice, even though thrice again°
   The red fool-fury of the Seine
Should pile her barricades with dead.

But ill for him that wears a crown,
10   And him, the lazar, in his rags:
   They tremble, the sustaining crags;
The spires of ice are toppled down,

And molten up, and roar in flood;
   The fortress crashes from on high,
   The brute earth lightens to the sky,
And the great Aeon° sinks in blood,

And compassed by the fires of Hell;
   While thou, dear spirit, happy star,
   O'erlook'st the tumult from afar,
20 And smilest, knowing all is well.

     . . .

CXXIX

Dear friend, far off, my lost desire,
   So far, so near in woe and weal;
   O loved the most, when most I feel
There is a lower and a higher;

Known and unknown; human, divine;
   Sweet human hand and lips and eye;
   Dear heavenly friend that canst not die,
Mine, mine, for ever, ever mine;

Strange friend, past, present, and to be;
10   Loved deeplier, darklier understood;
   Behold, I dream a dream of good,
And mingle all the world with thee.

CXXX

Thy voice is on the rolling air;
   I hear thee where the waters run;
   Thou standest in the rising sun,
And in the setting thou art fair.

---

thrice again probably a reference to the three-
day revolution of July 1830 which overthrew

Charles X, last of the French Bourbon monarchs
Aeon huge period of time

What art thou then? I cannot guess;
　　But though I seem in star and flower
　　To feel thee some diffusive power,
　　I do not therefore love thee less:

My love involves the love before;
10　　My love is vaster passion now;
　　Though mixed with God and Nature thou,
　　I seem to love thee more and more.

Far off thou art, but ever nigh;
　　I have thee still, and I rejoice;
　　I prosper, circled with thy voice;
　　I shall not lose thee though I die.

CXXXI

O living will° that shalt endure
　　When all that seems shall suffer shock,
　　Rise in the spiritual rock,°
Flow through our deeds and make them pure,

That we may lift from out of dust
　　A voice as unto him that hears,
　　A cry above the conquered years
To one that with us works, and trust,

With faith that comes of self-control,
10　　The truths that never can be proved
　　Until we close with all we loved,
And all we flow from, soul in soul.

_____

[EPILOGUE]°

O true and tried, so well and long,
　　Demand not thou a marriage lay;
　　In that it is thy marriage day
Is music more than any song.

. . .

And touch with shade the bridal doors,
　　With tender gloom the roof, the wall;
　　And breaking let the splendour fall
120　To spangle all the happy shores

By which they rest, and ocean sounds,
　　And, star and system rolling past,
　　A soul shall draw from out the vast
And strike his being into bounds,

---

will Tennyson said he meant free will.
spiritual rock See I Corinthians 10:4.

[Epilogue] This is a marriage song for one of
the poet's sisters.

And, moved through life of lower phase,
  Result in man, be born and think,
  And act and love, a closer link
Betwixt us and the crowning race

Of those that, eye to eye, shall look
¹³⁰ On knowledge; under whose command
  Is Earth and Earth's, and in their hand
Is Nature like an open book;

No longer half-akin to brute,
  For all we thought and loved and did,
  And hoped, and suffered, is but seed
Of what in them is flower and fruit;

Whereof the man,° that with me trod
  This planet, was a noble type
  Appearing ere the times were ripe,
¹⁴⁰That friend of mine who lives in God,

That God, which ever lives and loves,
  One God, one law, one element,
  And one far-off divine event,
To which the whole creation moves.
1833–50   1850

Maud

Maud, published during the Crimean war against Russia, which its final section (printed here) absurdly glorifies, was subtitled "A Monodrama" because all of it is acted out by only one speaker, a young man of intensely morbid, indeed paranoid, sensibility. The nameless young man is a kind of parody of Tennyson himself, and so compensates for his monomania by the fascination of his perceptions and the continuous eloquence of his language. He is a stunted Byronic figure, and the poem is more a *Manfred*-in-little than the "little *Hamlet*" Tennyson liked to think it.

The direct stimulus for *Maud* seems to have been the challenge (illusory) of the "Spasmodic" poets, Byronic revivalists of the 1850's, particularly Alexander Smith's *A Life Drama* and Sydney Dobell's *Balder*. There is not enough genuine story in *Maud* to bear lengthy summary. The four selections given below convey, in turn: the height of the young man's passion for Maud, his grief at having lost her, his consequent madness, and his return to sanity and proportion as he goes off virtuously to slaughter Russians.

the man Hallam raised to the Divine, as a
Newer Adam than Christ

Maud: A Monodrama

From *Part I*

XXII

I

850 Come into the garden, Maud,
    For the black bat, night, has flown,
Come into the garden, Maud,
    I am here at the gate alone;
And the woodbine spices are wafted abroad,
    And the musk of the rose is blown.

II

For a breeze of morning moves,
    And the planet of Love° is on high,
Beginning to faint in the light that she loves
    On a bed of daffodil sky,
860 To faint in the light of the sun she loves,
    To faint in his light, and to die.

III

All night have the roses heard
    The flute, violin, bassoon;
All night has the casement jessamine stirred
    To the dancers dancing in tune;
Till a silence fell with the waking bird,
    And a hush with the setting moon.

IV

I said to the lily, 'There is but one
    With whom she has heart to be gay.
870 When will the dancers leave her alone?
    She is weary of dance and play.'
Now half to the setting moon are gone,
    And half to the rising day;
Low on the sand and loud on the stone
    The last wheel echoes away.

V

I said to the rose, 'The brief night goes
    In babble and revel and wine.
O young lord-lover, what sighs are those,
    For one that will never be thine?
880 But mine, but mine,' so I swore to the rose,
    'For ever and ever, mine.'

planet of Love Venus, the Morning Star

VI

And the soul of the rose went into my blood,
    As the music clashed in the hall;
And long by the garden lake I stood,
    For I heard your rivulet fall
From the lake to the meadow and on to the wood,
    Our wood, that is dearer than all;

VII

From the meadow your walks have left so sweet
    That whenever a March-wind sighs
890 He sets the jewel-print of your feet
    In violets blue as your eyes,
To the woody hollows in which we meet
    And the valleys of Paradise.

VIII

The slender acacia would not shake
    One long milk-bloom on the tree;
The white lake-blossom fell into the lake
    As the pimpernel° dozed on the lea;
But the rose was awake all night for your sake,
    Knowing your promise to me;
900 The lilies and roses were all awake,
    They sighed for the dawn and thee.

IX

Queen rose of the rosebud garden of girls,
    Come hither, the dances are done,
In gloss of satin and glimmer of pearls,
    Queen lily and rose in one;
Shine out, little head, sunning over with curls,
    To the flowers, and be their sun.

X

There has fallen a splendid tear
    From the passion-flower at the gate.
910 She is coming, my dove, my dear;
    She is coming, my life, my fate;
The red rose cries, 'She is near, she is near;'
    And the white rose weeps, 'She is late;'
The larkspur listens, 'I hear, I hear;'
    And the lily whispers, 'I wait.'

pimpernel a flower that seems to go to sleep in
wet weather

XI

She is coming, my own, my sweet;
  Were it ever so airy a tread,
My heart would hear her and beat,
  Were it earth in an earthy bed;
920 My dust would hear her and beat,
    Had I lain for a century dead;
  Would start and tremble under her feet,
    And blossom in purple and red.

. . .

From *Part II*

IV

I

O that 'twere possible
After long grief and pain
To find the arms of my true love
Round me once again!°

II

When I was wont to meet her
In the silent woody places
By the home that gave me birth,
We stood tranced in long embraces
Mixed with kisses sweeter sweeter
150 Than anything on earth.

III

A shadow flits before me,
Not thou, but like to thee:
Ah Christ, that it were possible
For one short hour to see
The souls we loved, that they might tell us
What and where they be.

. . .

V

I

Dead, long dead,°
240 Long dead!
And my heart is a handful of dust,°
And the wheels go over my head,°
And my bones are shaken with pain,
For into a shallow grave they are thrust,

O that . . . once again Compare this stanza to
the little medieval lyric, "Western Wind."
long dead The young man is now insane and
confined, and has the fantasy that he is dead.
a handful of dust See Eliot's *Waste Land* I.30.
over my head a fantasy of burial

Only a yard beneath the street,
And the hoofs of the horses beat, beat,
The hoofs of the horses beat,
Beat into my scalp and my brain,
With never an end to the stream of passing feet,
250 Driving, hurrying, marrying, burying,
Clamour and rumble, and ringing and clatter,
And here beneath it is all as bad,
For I thought the dead had peace, but it is not so;
To have no peace in the grave, is that not sad?
But up and down and to and fro,
Ever about me the dead men go;°
And then to hear a dead man chatter
Is enough to drive one mad.

II

Wretchedest age, since Time began,
260 They cannot even bury a man;
And though we paid our tithes in the days that are gone,
Not a bell was rung, not a prayer was read;
It is that which makes us loud in the world of the dead;
There is none that does his work, not one;
A touch of their office might have sufficed,
But the churchmen fain would kill their church,
As the churches have killed their Christ.°

. . .

From *Part III*

vi°

I

My life has crept so long on a broken wing°
Through cells of madness, haunts of horror and fear,
That I come to be grateful at last for a little thing:
My mood is changed, for it fell at a time of year
When the face of night is fair on the dewy downs,
And the shining daffodil dies, and the Charioteer°
And starry Gemini hang like glorious crowns
Over Orion's grave low down in the west,°
That like a silent lightning under the stars
10 She seemed to divide in a dream from a band of the blest,
And spoke of a hope for the world in the coming wars°

---

the dead men go the other inmates of the madhouse
killed their Christ with formalism and commerce
VI Section numbering for Part III carries on
from Part II.
on a broken wing He is sane again.
Charioteer constellation Auriga

And starry . . . in the west The Gemini (Castor
and Pollux) are in the southern hemisphere;
the season is spring, so Orion is low in the west
because it is a winter constellation.
She seemed . . . coming wars Maud, as a
phantasm, appears to him and champions the
war against Russia.

'And in that hope, dear soul, let trouble have rest,
Knowing I tarry for thee,' and pointed to Mars
As he glowed like a ruddy shield on the Lion's breast.°

II

And it was but a dream, yet it yielded a dear delight
To have looked, though but in a dream, upon eyes so fair,
That had been in a weary world my one thing bright;
And it was but a dream, yet it lightened my despair
When I thought that a war would arise in defense of the right,
20 That an iron tyranny° now should bend or cease,
The glory of manhood stand on his ancient height,
Nor Britain's one sole God be the millionaire:
No more shall commerce be all in all, and Peace
Pipe on her pastoral hillock a languid note,
And watch her harvest ripen, her herd increase,
Nor the cannon-bullet rust on a slothful shore,
And the cobweb woven across the cannon's throat
Shall shake its threaded tears in the wind no more.

III

And as months ran on and rumour of battle grew,
30 'It is time, it is time, O passionate heart,' said I
(For I cleaved to a cause that I felt to be pure and true),
'It is time, O passionate heart and morbid eye,
That old hysterical mock-disease should die.'
And I stood on a giant deck° and mixed my breath
With a loyal people shouting a battle cry,
Till I saw the dreary phantom arise and fly
Far into the North, and battle, and seas of death.°

IV

Let it go or stay, so I wake to the higher aims
Of a land that has lost for a little her lust of gold,
40 And love of a peace that was full of wrongs and shames,
Horrible, hateful, monstrous, not to be told;
And hail once more to the banner of battle unrolled!
Though many a light shall darken, and many shall weep
For those that are crushed in the clash of jarring claims,
Yet God's just wrath shall be wreaked on a giant liar;°
And many a darkness into the light shall leap,
And shine in the sudden making of splendid names,
And noble thought be freer under the sun,

Lion's breast northern hemisphere constellation, symbolizing England; Mars, then in the constellation of the Lion, signifies war
iron tyranny Czarist Russia
giant deck On a troop transport going to the Crimea he finds solidarity with other soldiers.

Till I saw . . . seas of death He rids himself at last of Maud's haunting presence, thanks to his war fever.
giant liar the Czar of Russia, Nicholas I, no more or less a liar than the English rulers and statesmen

And the heart of a people beat with one desire;
50 For the peace, that I deemed no peace, is over and done,
And now by the side of the Black and the Baltic deep,
And deathful-grinning mouths of the fortress, flames
The blood-red blossom of war with a heart of fire.

v

Let it flame or fade, and the war roll down like a wind,
We have proved we have hearts in a cause, we are noble still,
And myself have awaked, as it seems, to the better mind;
It is better to fight for the good than to rail at the ill;
I have felt with my native land, I am one with my kind,
I embrace the purpose of God, and the doom assigned.
1854–55   1855

From Idylls of the King
[VIVIEN'S SONG]°

But now the wholesome music of the wood
Was dumbed by one from out the hall of Mark,
A damsel-errant, warbling, as she rode
The woodland alleys, Vivien, with her Squire.

'The fire of Heaven has killed the barren cold,
And kindled all the plain and all the wold.
The new leaf ever pushes off the old.
The fire of Heaven is not the flame of Hell.

'Old priest, who mumbled worship in your quire—
10 Old monk and nun, ye scorn the world's desire,
Yet in your frosty cells ye feel the fire!
The fire of Heaven is not the flame of Hell.

'The fire of Heaven is on the dusty ways.
The wayside blossoms open to the blaze.
The whole wood-world is one full peal of praise.
The fire of Heaven is not the flame of Hell.

'The fire of Heaven is lord of all things good,
And starve not thou this fire within thy blood,
But follow Vivien through the fiery flood!
20 The fire of Heaven is not the flame of Hell!'

[Vivien's Song] from *Balin and Balan* (ll. 430–53). This savage and splendid hymn to Eros by Vivien, the evil King Mark's creature who will destroy Merlin, is one of the last outbursts of Tennyson's daemon. It is given here for its excellence and its contrast to Percivale's quest from *The Holy Grail*. Whereas Percivale is meant to illustrate the subtler force that overthrows Arthurian civilization, an overspiritualized ascetic impulse, Vivien embodies the other, more primal force, the body's lust.

Then turning to her Squire 'This fire of Heaven,
This old sun-worship, boy, will rise again,
And beat the cross to earth, and break the King
And all his Table.'. . .
1873   1885

[Percivale's Quest]

This is the most powerful sustained passage in *Idylls of the King*, though Tennyson
himself did not think so, and clearly rated it below the Protestant speech of Arthur
at the close of *The Holy Grail*. But, though he made Percivale, Tennyson would
not wholly understand him. In Percivale's phantasmagoric quest that wastes the land
he traverses, we are given a rival to Browning's *Childe Roland to the Dark Tower
Came*, another parable of a dangerous thwarted poetic consciousness burning its
way through nature and through other selves. Like Childe Roland, Percivale is a
direct descendant of Wordsworth's *Solitary* and the remorseless "Poet" of Shelley's
Alastor. Percivale, as Tennyson uneasily did not acknowledge, represents not so much
an ascetic Catholic consciousness (Tennyson's intention) as he does the antithetical,
dangerous element in Tennyson's poetic mind, a desire to put aside everything that
is not purely the solipsistic celebration of the self's own sublimity. Percivale seeks to
re-beget himself in questing after the Holy Grail, for him (though not for Galahad)
only another version of Childe Roland's Dark Tower.

[PERCIVALE'S QUEST]°

'But when the next day brake from under ground—
O brother, had you known our Camelot,
340   Built by old kings, age after age, so old
The King himself had fears that it would fall,
So strange, and rich, and dim; for where the roofs
Tottered toward each other in the sky,
Met foreheads all along the street of those
Who watched us pass; and lower, and where the long
Rich galleries, lady-laden, weighed the necks
Of dragons clinging to the crazy walls,
Thicker than drops from thunder, showers of flowers
Fell as we past; and men and boys astride
350   On wyvern,° lion, dragon, griffin,° swan,

[Percivale's Quest] from *The Holy Grail* (ll.
338–565). Percivale, called "the Pure," has
given up his knighthood and become a monk.
Soon before his death, he tells the story of the
Holy Grail to a kindly, practical-minded fellow
monk, Ambrosius. In medieval English legend,
the Holy Grail was believed to be the dish in
which Joseph of Arimathea preserved the blood
of the crucified Christ. Alternately, it was held
to be the cup used for sacramental wine at the
Passover service that was the Last Supper. In
Percivale's narration, we have reached the moment after miracle; the Holy Grail has manifested itself in a vision to the Round Table,
when Arthur was absent. To the King's sensible
horror, his knights vow to quest after it.
wyvern two-legged dragon
griffin half-eagle, half-lion

At all the corners, named us each by name,
Calling "God speed!" but in the ways below
The knights and ladies wept, and rich and poor
Wept, and the King himself could hardly speak
For grief, and all in middle street the Queen,
Who rode by Lancelot, wailed and shrieked aloud,
"This madness has come on us for our sins."
So to the Gate of the three Queens° we came,
Where Arthur's wars are rendered mystically,
360   And thence departed every one his way.

'And I was lifted up in heart, and thought
Of all my late-shown prowess in the lists,°
How my strong lance had beaten down the knights,
So many and famous names; and never yet
Had heaven appeared so blue, nor earth so green,
For all my blood danced in me, and I knew
That I should light upon the Holy Grail.

'Thereafter, the dark warning of our King,
That most of us would follow wandering fires,
370   Came like a driving gloom across my mind.
Then every evil word I had spoken once,
And every evil thought I had thought of old,
And every evil deed I ever did,
Awoke and cried, "This Quest is not for thee."
And lifting up mine eyes, I found myself
Alone, and in a land of sand and thorns,
And I was thirsty even unto death;
And I, too, cried, "This Quest is not for thee."

'And on I rode, and when I thought my thirst
380   Would slay me, saw deep lawns, and then a brook,
With one sharp rapid, where the crisping white
Played ever back upon the sloping wave,
And took both ear and eye; and o'er the brook
Were apple-trees, and apples by the brook
Fallen, and on the lawns. "I will rest here,"
I said, "I am not worthy of the Quest;"
But even while I drank the brook, and ate
The goodly apples, all these things at once
Fell into dust, and I was left alone,
390   And thirsting, in a land of sand and thorns.

'And then behold a woman at a door
Spinning; and fair the house whereby she sat,
And kind the woman's eyes and innocent,
And all her bearing gracious; and she rose
Opening her arms to meet me, as who should say,

the three Queens who take the dead Arthur to   **lists** i.e. in combat
Avalon in *Morte d'Arthur*

"Rest here;" but when I touched her, lo! she, too,
Fell into dust and nothing, and the house
Became no better than a broken shed,
And in it a dead babe; and also this
400   Fell into dust, and I was left alone.

'And on I rode, and greater was my thirst.
Then flashed a yellow gleam across the world,
And where it smote the plowshare in the field,
The plowman left his plowing, and fell down
Before it; where it glittered on her pail,
The milkmaid left her milking, and fell down
Before it, and I know not why, but thought
"The sun is rising," though the sun had risen.
Then was I ware of one that on me moved
410   In golden armour with a crown of gold
About a casque all jewels; and his horse
In golden armour jewelled everywhere:
And on the splendour came, flashing me blind;
And seemed to me the Lord of all the world,
Being so huge. But when I thought he meant
To crush me, moving on me, lo! he, too,
Opened his arms to embrace me as he came,
And up I went and touched him, and he, too,
Fell into dust, and I was left alone
420   And wearying in a land of sand and thorns.

'And I rode on and found a mighty hill,
And on the top, a city walled: the spires
Pricked with incredible pinnacles into heaven.
And by the gateway stirred a crowd; and these
Cried to me climbing, "Welcome, Percivale!
Thou mightiest and thou purest among men!"
And glad was I and clomb, but found at top
No man, nor any voice. And thence I past
Far through a ruinous city, and I saw
430   That man had once dwelt there; but there I found
Only one man of an exceeding age.
"Where is that goodly company," said I,
"That so cried out upon me?" and he had
Scarce any voice to answer, and yet gasped,
"Whence and what art thou?" and even as he spoke
Fell into dust, and disappeared, and I
Was left alone once more, and cried in grief,
"Lo, if I find the Holy Grail itself
And touch it, it will crumble into dust."

440   'And thence I dropped into a lowly vale,
Low as the hill was high, and where the vale
Was lowest, found a chapel, and thereby

A holy hermit in a hermitage,
To whom I told my phantoms, and he said:

   ' "O son, thou hast not true humility,
The highest virtue, mother of them all;
For when the Lord of all things made Himself
Naked of glory for His mortal change,
'Take thou my robe,' she° said, 'for all is thine,'
450   And all her form shone forth with sudden light
So that the angels were amazed, and she
Followed Him down, and like a flying star°
Led on the grey-haired wisdom of the east;
But her thou hast not known: for what is this
Thou thoughtest of thy prowess and thy sins?
Thou hast not lost thyself to save thyself
As Galahad." When the hermit made an end,
In silver armour suddenly Galahad shone
Before us, and against the chapel door
460   Laid lance, and entered, and we knelt in prayer.
And there the hermit slaked my burning thirst,
And at the sacring° of the mass I saw
The holy elements alone; but he,
"Saw ye no more? I, Galahad, saw the Grail,
The Holy Grail, descend upon the shrine:
I saw the fiery face as of a child
That smote itself into the bread, and went;
And hither am I come; and never yet
Hath what thy sister taught me first to see,
470   This Holy Thing, failed from my side, nor come
Covered, but moving with me night and day,
Fainter by day, but always in the night
Blood-red, and sliding down the blackened marsh
Blood-red, and on the naked mountain top
Blood-red, and in the sleeping mere below
Blood-red. And in the strength of this I rode,
Shattering all evil customs everywhere,
And past through Pagan realms, and made them mine,
And clashed with Pagan hordes, and bore them down,
480   And broke through all, and in the strength of this
Come victor. But my time is hard at hand,
And hence I go; and one will crown me king
Far in the spiritual city; and come thou, too,
For thou shalt see the vision when I go."

   'While thus he spake, his eye, dwelling on mine,
Drew me, with power upon me, till I grew

---

she Humility
flying star of Bethlehem

sacring consecration that transforms bread and
wine into Christ's flesh and blood

One with him, to believe as he believed.
Then, when the day began to wane, we went.

'There rose a hill that none but man could climb,
490 Scarred with a hundred wintry water-courses—
Storm at the top, and when we gained it, storm
Round us and death; for every moment glanced
His silver arms and gloomed: so quick and thick
The lightnings here and there to left and right
Struck, till the dry old trunks about us, dead,
Yea, rotten with a hundred years of death,
Sprang into fire: and at the base we found
On either hand, as far as eye could see,
A great black swamp and of an evil smell,
500 Part black, part whitened with the bones of men,
Not to be crossed, save that some ancient king
Had built a way, where, linked with many a bridge,
A thousand piers ran into the great Sea.
And Galahad fled along them bridge by bridge,
And every bridge as quickly as he crossed
Sprang into fire and vanished, though I yearned
To follow; and thrice above him all the heavens
Opened and blazed with thunder such as seemed
Shoutings of all the sons of God:° and first
510 At once I saw him far on the great Sea,
In silver-shining armour starry-clear;
And o'er his head the Holy Vessel hung
Clothed in white samite° or a luminous cloud.
And with exceeding swiftness ran the boat,
If boat it were—I saw not whence it came.
And when the heavens opened and blazed again
Roaring, I saw him like a silver star—
And had he set the sail, or had the boat
Become a living creature clad with wings?
520 And o'er his head the Holy Vessel hung
Redder than any rose, a joy to me,
For now I knew the veil had been withdrawn.
Then in a moment when they blazed again
Opening, I saw the least of little stars
Down on the waste, and straight beyond the star
I saw the spiritual city and all her spires°
And gateways in a glory like one pearl—
No larger, though the goal of all the saints—
Strike from the sea; and from the star there shot
530 A rose-red sparkle to the city, and there
Dwelt, and I knew it was the Holy Grail,

Opened . . . sons of God See Job 38:7.   **spiritual city . . . spires** See Revelation 21:2.
samite silk shot with gold

Which never eyes on earth again shall see.
Then fell the floods of heaven drowning the deep.
And how my feet recrossed the deathful ridge
No memory in me lives; but that I touched
The chapel-doors at dawn I know; and thence
Taking my war-horse from the holy man,
Glad that no phantom vexed me more, returned
To whence I came, the gate of Arthur's wars.'

540 'O brother,' asked Ambrosius,—'for in sooth
These ancient books—and they would win thee—teem,
Only I find not there this Holy Grail,
With miracles and marvels like to these,
Not all unlike; which oftentime I read,
Who read but on my breviary° with ease,
Till my head swims; and then go forth and pass
Down to the little thorpe° that lies so close,
And almost plastered like a martin's nest
To these old walls—and mingle with our folk;
550 And knowing every honest face of theirs
As well as ever shepherd knew his sheep,
And every homely secret in their hearts,
Delight myself with gossip and old wives,
And ills and aches, and teethings, lyings-in,
And mirthful sayings, children of the place,
That have no meaning half a league away:
Or lulling random squabbles when they rise,
Chafferings and chatterings at the market-cross,°
Rejoice, small man, in this small world of mine,
560 Yea, even in their hens and in their eggs—
O brother, saving this Sir Galahad,
Came ye on none but phantoms in your quest,
No man, no woman?'

           Then Sir Percivale:
'All men, to one so bound by such a vow,
And women were as phantoms. . . .'
1868   1869

breviary book of Scripture readings recited daily   **thorpe** small town
by priests and monks   **market-cross** cross in the marketplace

Lucretius°

Lucilia, wedded to Lucretius, found
Her master cold; for when the morning flush
Of passion and the first embrace had died
Between them, though he loved her none the less,
Yet often when the woman heard his foot
Return from pacings in the field, and ran
To greet him with a kiss, the master took
Small notice, or austerely, for—his mind
Half buried in some weightier argument,
10 Or fancy-borne perhaps upon the rise
And long roll of the Hexameter° he passed
To turn and ponder those three hundred scrolls
Left by the Teacher,° whom he held divine.
She brooked it not; but wrathful, petulant,
Dreaming some rival, sought and found a witch
Who brewed the philtre which had power, they said,
To lead an errant passion home again.
And this, at times, she mingled with his drink,
And this destroyed him; for the wicked broth
20 Confused the chemic labour of the blood,
And tickling the brute brain within the man's
Made havoc among those tender cells, and checked
His power to shape: he loathed himself; and once
After a tempest woke upon a morn
That mocked him with returning calm, and cried:

'Storm in the night! for thrice I heard the rain
Rushing; and once the flash of a thunderbolt—
Methought I never saw so fierce a fork—
Struck out the streaming mountain-side, and showed
30 A riotous confluence of watercourses
Blanching and billowing in a hollow of it,
Where all but yester-eve was dusty-dry.

'Storm, and what dreams, ye holy Gods, what dreams!
For thrice I wakened after dreams. Perchance

Lucretius This profoundly ambivalent poem is at once Tennyson's sincere tribute to the Roman poet and Epicurean philosopher Titus Lucretius Carus (98–55 B.C.), author of the great discursive poem *De Rerum Natura* (*On the Nature of the Universe*), and also a savagely unfair attack upon philosophic materialism and its supposed moral consequences. Tennyson's unusual rhetorical violence here, the daring of his imagery, the controlled hysteria of his moral outrage, suggest how deeply the Lucretian materialism tempted him. The poem's characteristics may also reflect his defensive reaction to Swinburne's *Poems and Ballads* of 1866, or even to the increasing challenge presented by Browning's mastery of extreme personalities and grotesque situations.

Hexameter meter in which *De Rerum Natura* is written
Teacher Epicurus (341–270 B.C.), Greek founder of the Epicurean philosophy, a common-sense rationalism based on an atomic theory of matter. Epicureanism rejected the immortality of the soul and Divine Providence, affirming instead the joy of natural existence and the reality of appearances. The gods exist for Epicurus and Lucretius, but only as remote examples of happiness, incapable of any influence upon this world, and perfectly indifferent to our fate. Yet Epicurus and Lucretius teach free will, through the image of the *clinamen* or "swerve" of the atoms away from natural necessity.

We do but recollect the dreams that come
Just ere the waking: terrible! for it seemed
A void was made in Nature; all her bonds
Cracked; and I saw the flaring atom-streams°
And torrents of her myriad universe,
40   Ruining along the illimitable inane,
Fly on to clash together again, and make
Another and another frame of things
For ever: that was mine, my dream, I knew it—
Of and belonging to me, as the dog
With inward yelp and restless forefoot plies
His function of the woodland: but the next!
I thought that all the blood by Sylla° shed
Came driving rainlike down again on earth,
And where it dashed the reddening meadow, sprang
50   No dragon warriors from Cadmean teeth,°
For these I thought my dream would show to me,
But girls, Hetairai,° curious in their art,
Hired animalisms, vile as those that made
The mulberry-faced Dictator's° orgies worse
Than aught they fable of the quiet Gods.
And hands they mixed, and yelled and round me drove
In narrowing circles till I yelled again
Half-suffocated, and sprang up, and saw—
Was it the first beam of my latest day?

60   'Then, then, from utter gloom stood out the breasts,
The breasts of Helen,° and hoveringly a sword
Now over and now under, now direct,
Pointed itself to pierce, but sank down shamed
At all that beauty; and as I stared, a fire,
The fire that left a roofless Ilion,
Shot out of them, and scorched me that I woke.

'Is this thy vengeance, holy Venus, thine,
Because I would not one of thine own doves,
Not even a rose, were offered to thee? thine,
70   Forgetful how my rich procemion° makes
Thy glory fly along the Italian field,
In lays that will outlast thy Deity?

flaring atom-streams Closely following *De Rerum
Natura*, here as elsewhere in the poem, Tennyson gives an epitome of the Lucretian vision of
atomic creation and subsequent reduction to
chaos.
Sylla Sulla, dictator of Rome, 82–79 B.C.
Cadmean teeth Cadmus, founder of Thebes, is
reputed to have sown dragon's teeth in the
earth, after which armed men were harvested
from it.

Hetairai whores
mulberry-faced Dictator's that of Sulla, notorious for his sexual excesses
Helen of Troy, whose allurements caused the
Trojan war
procemion proem, introduction. In the introduction to his poem, Lucretius had celebrated
Venus rationally, as the principle of life.

'Deity? nay, thy worshippers. My tongue
Trips, or I speak profanely. Which of these
Angers thee most, or angers thee at all?
Not if thou be'st of those who, far aloof
From envy, hate and pity, and spite and scorn,
Live the great life which all our greatest fain
Would follow, centred in eternal calm.

80   'Nay, if thou canst, O Goddess, like ourselves
Touch, and be touched, then would I cry to thee
To kiss thy Mavors,° roll thy tender arms
Round him, and keep him from the lust of blood
That makes a steaming slaughter-house of Rome.

'Ay, but I meant not thee; I meant not her,
Whom all the pines of Ida° shook to see
Slide from that quiet heaven of hers, and tempt
The Trojan,° while his neat-herds were abroad;
Nor her that o'er her wounded hunter° wept
90   Her Deity false in human-amorous tears;
Nor whom her beardless apple-arbiter°
Decided fairest. Rather, O ye Gods,
Poet-like, as the great Sicilian° called
Calliope° to grace his golden verse—
Ay, and this Kypris° also—did I take
That popular name of thine to shadow forth
The all-generating powers and genial heat
Of Nature, when she strikes through the thick blood
Of cattle, and light is large, and lambs are glad
100   Nosing the mother's udder, and the bird
Makes his heart voice amid the blaze of flowers:
Which things appear the work of mighty Gods.

'The Gods! and if I go *my* work is left
Unfinished—*if* I go. The Gods, who haunt
The lucid interspace of world and world,
Where never creeps a cloud, or moves a wind,
Nor ever falls the least white star of snow,
Nor ever lowest roll of thunder moans,
Nor sound of human sorrow mounts to mar
110   Their sacred everlasting calm! and such,
Not all so fine, nor so divine a calm,
Not such, nor all unlike it, man may gain
Letting his own life go. The Gods, the Gods!

Mavors Mars
Ida mountain near Troy
The Trojan Anchises, who begot Aeneas upon Venus
wounded hunter Adonis, beautiful youth beloved of Venus; he died of a boar-wound
apple-arbiter Paris
great Sicilian Empedocles the poet-philosopher
Calliope Muse of epic poetry
Kypris Cyprus, sacred to Venus

If all be atoms, how then should the Gods
Being atomic not be dissoluble,
Not follow the great law? My master° held
That Gods there are, for all men so believe.
I pressed my footsteps into his, and meant
Surely to lead my Memmius° in a train
120   Of flowery clauses onward to the proof
That Gods there are, and deathless. Meant? I meant?
I have forgotten what I meant: my mind
Stumbles, and all my faculties are lamed.

   'Look where another of our Gods, the Sun,
Apollo, Delius, or of older use
All-seeing Hyperion°—what you will—
Has mounted yonder; since he never sware,
Except his wrath were wreaked on wretched man,
That he would only shine among the dead
130   Hereafter; tales! for never yet on earth
Could dead flesh creep, or bits of roasting ox
Moan round the spit—nor knows he what he sees;
King of the East although he seem, and girt
With song and flame and fragrance, slowly lifts
His golden feet on those empurpled stairs
That climb into the windy halls of heaven:
And here he glances on an eye new-born,
And gets for greeting but a wail of pain;
And here he stays upon a freezing orb
140   That fain would gaze upon him to the last;
And here upon a yellow eyelid fallen
And closed by those who mourn a friend in vain,
Not thankful that his troubles are no more.
And me, although his fire is on my face
Blinding, he sees not, nor at all can tell
Whether I mean this day to end myself,
Or lend an ear to Plato° where he says,
That men like soldiers may not quit the post
Allotted by the Gods: but he that holds
150   The Gods are careless, wherefore need he care
Greatly for them, nor rather plunge at once,
Being troubled, wholly out of sight, and sink
Past earthquake—ay, and gout and stone, that break
Body toward death, and palsy, death-in-life,
And wretched age—and worst disease of all,
These prodigies of myriad nakednesses,
And twisted shapes of lust, unspeakable,
Abominable, strangers at my hearth

master Epicurus
Memmius C. Memmius Gemellus, man of letters to whom Lucretius dedicated his poem

Hyperion like Apollo and Delius, a name for
the sun god
Plato See *Phaedo* VI.

Not welcome, harpies miring every dish,
160 The phantom husks of something foully done,
And fleeting through the boundless universe,
And blasting the long quiet of my breast
With animal heat and dire insanity?

'How should the mind, except it loved them, clasp
These idols to herself? or do they fly
Now thinner, and now thicker, like the flakes
In a fall of snow, and so press in, perforce
Of multitude, as crowds that in an hour
Of civic tumult jam the doors, and bear
170 The keepers down, and throng, their rags and they
The basest, far into that council-hall
Where sit the best and stateliest of the land?

'Can I not fling this horror off me again,
Seeing with how great ease Nature can smile,
Balmier and nobler from her bath of storm,
At random ravage? and how easily
The mountain there has cast his cloudy slough,
Now towering o'er him in serenest air,
A mountain o'er a mountain,—ay, and within
180 All hollow as the hopes and fears of men?

'But who was he, that in the garden snared
Picus and Faunus,° rustic Gods? a tale
To laugh at—more to laugh at in myself—
For look! what is it? there? yon arbutus
Totters; a noiseless riot underneath
Strikes through the wood, sets all the tops quivering—
The mountain quickens into Nymph and Faun;
And here an Oread°—how the sun delights
To glance and shift about her slippery sides,
190 And rosy knees and supple roundedness,
And budded bosom-peaks—who this way runs
Before the rest—A satyr,° a satyr, see,
Follows; but him I proved impossible;°
Twy-natured° is no nature: yet he draws
Nearer and nearer, and I scan him now
Beastlier than any phantom of his kind
That ever butted his rough brother-brute
For lust or lusty blood or provender:
I hate, abhor, spit, sicken at him; and she
200 Loathes him as well; such a precipitate heel,

Picus and Faunus rural gods of early Rome; satyr half-goat, half-man; an emblem of sexual
trapped by King Numa, and compelled to give lust
up their secrets impossible Lucretius had argued that rational
Oread mountain nymph nature could not create such creatures.
Twy-natured two-natured

Fledged as it were with Mercury's ankle-wing,
Whirls her to me: but will she fling herself,
Shameless upon me? Catch her, goat-foot: nay,
Hide, hide them, million-myrtled wilderness,
And cavern-shadowing laurels, hide! do I wish—
What?—that the bush were leafless? or to whelm
All of them in one massacre? O ye Gods,
I know you careless, yet, behold, to you
From childly wont and ancient use I call—
210   I thought I lived securely as yourselves—
No lewdness, narrowing envy, monkey-spite,
No madness of ambition, avarice, none:
No larger feast than under plane or pine
With neighbours laid along the grass, to take
Only such cups as left us friendly-warm,
Affirming each his own philosophy—
Nothing to mar the sober majesties
Of settled, sweet, Epicurean life.
But now it seems some unseen monster lays
220   His vast and filthy hands upon my will,
Wrenching it backward into his; and spoils
My bliss in being; and it was not great;
For save when shutting reasons up in rhythm,
Or Heliconian° honey in living words,
To make a truth less harsh, I often grew
Tired of so much within our little life,
Or of so little in our little life—
Poor little life that toddles half an hour
Crowned with a flower or two, and there an end—
230   And since the nobler pleasure seems to fade,
Why should I, beastlike as I find myself,
Not manlike end myself?—our privilege—
What beast has heart to do it? And what man,
What Roman would be dragged in triumph thus?
Not I; not he, who bears one name with her°
Whose death-blow struck the dateless doom of kings,
When, brooking not the Tarquin in her veins,
She made her blood in sight of Collatine
And all his peers, flushing the guiltless air,
240   Spout from the maiden fountain in her heart.
And from it sprang the Commonwealth, which breaks
As I am breaking now!

                    'And therefore now
Let her, that is the womb and tomb of all,°
Great Nature, take, and forcing far apart

Heliconian pertaining to Helicon, sacred mountain of the Muses
her Lucretia, raped by Sextus, son of King

Tarquin; see Shakespeare's *Rape of Lucrece*
womb and tomb of all Nature: see *Paradise Lost*
II.911

Those blind beginnings that have made me man,
Dash them anew together at her will
Through all her cycles—into man once more,
Or beast or bird or fish, or opulent flower:
But till this cosmic order everywhere
250 Shattered into one earthquake in one day
Cracks all to pieces,—and that hour perhaps
Is not so far when momentary man
Shall seem no more a something to himself,
But he, his hopes and hates, his homes and fanes,°
And even his bones long laid within the grave,
The very sides of the grave itself shall pass,
Vanishing, atom and void, atom and void,
Into the unseen for ever,—till that hour,
My golden work in which I told a truth
260 That stays the rolling Ixionian wheel,°
And numbs the Fury's ringlet-snake, and plucks
The mortal soul from out immortal hell,
Shall stand: ay, surely: then it fails at last
And perishes as I must; for O Thou,
Passionless bride, divine Tranquillity,
Yearned after by the wisest of the wise,
Who fail to find thee, being as thou art
Without one pleasure and without one pain,
Howbeit I know thou surely must be mine
270 Or soon or late, yet out of season, thus
I woo thee roughly, for thou carest not
How roughly men may woo thee so they win—
Thus—thus: the soul flies out and dies in the air.'

With that he drove the knife into his side:
She° heard him raging, heard him fall; ran in,
Beat breast, tore hair, cried out upon herself
As having failed in duty to him, shrieked
That she but meant to win him back, fell on him,
Clasped, kissed him, wailed: he answered, 'Care not thou!
280 Thy duty? What is duty? Fare thee well!'
1865–68   1868

fanes temples
Ixionian wheel Ixion, as punishment for his
sexual attempt at Hera, was bound by Zeus to
an eternally revolving wheel in the netherworld.

She Lucilia, Lucretius' wife, who in dubious
Christian chronicles was said to have driven
him insane by a love potion, thus causing his
suicide

To Virgil°

Written at the Request of the Mantuans for
the Nineteenth Centenary of Virgil's Death°

I

Roman Virgil, thou that singest
    Ilion's lofty temples robed in fire,
Ilion falling, Rome arising,
    wars, and filial faith, and Dido's pyre;°

II

Landscape-lover, lord of language
    more than he that sang the Works and Days,°
All the chosen coin of fancy
    flashing out from many a golden phrase;

III

Thou that singest wheat and woodland,
10   tilth and vineyard, hive and horse and herd;°
All the charm of all the Muses
    often flowering in a lonely word;

IV

Poet of the happy Tityrus°
    piping underneath his beechen bowers;
Poet of the poet-satyr
    whom the laughing shepherd bound with flowers;°

V

Chanter of the Pollio, glorying
    in the blissful years again to be,
Summers of the snakeless meadow,
20   unlaborious earth and oarless sea;°

VI

Thou that seest Universal
    Nature moved by Universal Mind;°

Virgil Born on a farm near Mantua in 70 B.C., died in 19 B.C. Tennyson knew himself to be the most Virgilian of English poets, so that in describing his precursor here, he also described himself.
Virgil's Death The sub-title is inaccurate, as the occasion for the poem, a request from the Virgilian Academy of Mantua, came in 1882.
Dido's pyre. The first stanza celebrates the principal incidents and themes of the *Aeneid*. Ilion is Troy, and poor Dido, Queen of Carthage, immolated herself upon a pyre when the prig Aeneas abandoned her.
Works and Days didactic epic by Hesiod, 8th

century B.C. Greek poet, who influenced Virgil's *Georgics* even as Homer influenced the *Aeneid*
Thou . . . herd This stanza refers to the *Georgics*, Virgil's best poem.
Tityrus See Virgil's *Eclogue* I.
poet-satyr . . . flowers in *Eclogue* VI
Chanter . . . oarless sea description of *Eclogue* IV, called the Pollio because it mentions C. Asinius Pollio, Virgil's patron. The poem, Virgil's most famous, celebrates Augustus as a kind of Messiah, and by later Christian readers (Dante included) was read as a vision of Christ's birth.
Universal Mind See *Aeneid* VI.727.

Thou majestic in thy sadness
    at the doubtful doom of human kind;°

VII

Light among the vanished ages;
    star that gildest yet this phantom shore;
Golden branch amid the shadows,°
    kings and realms that pass to rise no more;

VIII

Now thy Forum° roars no longer,
30   fallen every purple Cæsar's dome—
Though thine ocean-roll of rhythm
    sound for ever of Imperial Rome—

IX

Now the Rome of slaves hath perished,
    and the Rome of freemen holds her place,°
I, from out the Northern Island
    sundered once from all the human race,°

X

I salute thee, Mantovano,°
    I that loved thee since my day began,
Wielder of the stateliest measure°
40   ever moulded by the lips of man.
    1882   1882

Merlin and The Gleam°

I

O young Mariner,°
You from the haven
Under the sea-cliff,
You that are watching
The grey Magician
With eyes of wonder,
I am Merlin,

human kind See *Aeneid* I.462.
Golden . . . shadows See *Aeneid* VI.208; here Virgil himself becomes, in Tennyson's praise, the golden bough that keeps us safe in the underworld.
Forum assembly place of Rome
holds her place Rome joined the Republic of Italy in 1870.
human race See *Eclogue* I.66.
Mantovano Mantuan; Dante so addresses Virgil in *Purgatorio* VI.74

measure the Latin hexameter, the effect of which this poem vainly tries to give by a trochaic meter
Merlin and The Gleam A much better poem than the famous but stale "Crossing the Bar," this is Tennyson's true farewell to his art. Like Emerson in his "Merlin," Tennyson identifies himself with the prophetic bard. For the "gleam" see Wordsworth's *Intimations* Ode.
young Mariner a young poet setting out

And *I* am dying,
I am Merlin
10 Who follow The Gleam.

II

Mighty the Wizard°
Who found me at sunrise
Sleeping, and woke me
And learned me Magic!
Great the Master,
And sweet the Magic,
When over the valley,
In early summers,
Over the mountain,
20 On human faces,
And all around me,
Moving to melody,
Floated The Gleam.°

III

Once at the croak of a Raven° who crossed it,
A barbarous people,
Blind to the magic,
And deaf to the melody,
Snarled at and cursed me.
A demon vexed me,°
30 The light retreated,
The landskip darkened,
The melody deadened,°
The Master whispered
'Follow The Gleam.'

IV

Then to the melody,
Over a wilderness
Gliding, and glancing at
Elf of the woodland,
Gnome of the cavern,
40 Griffin and Giant,
And dancing of Fairies
In desolate hollows,
And wraiths of the mountain,
And rolling of dragons

Wizard Tennyson's precursor, a composite figure made up of his poetic father, Keats, and
poetic grandfather, Wordsworth; hardly Scott,
as some critics have said
Floated The Gleam Tennyson's early poetry,
the volumes of 1830 and 1832

Raven John Wilson ("Christopher North"), who
reviewed Tennyson savagely in 1833
demon vexed me John Lockhart, who also reviewed Tennyson harshly in 1833
melody deadened Tennyson's poetic "silence"
from 1833 to 1842

By warble of water,
Or cataract music
Of falling torrents,
Flitted The Gleam.°

V

Down from the mountain
50 And over the level,
And streaming and shining on
Silent river,
Silvery willow,
Pasture and plowland,
Innocent maidens,
Garrulous children,
Homestead and harvest,
Reaper and gleaner,
And rough-ruddy faces
60 Of lowly labour,
Slided The Gleam°—

VI

Then, with a melody
Stronger and statelier,
Led me at length
To the city and palace
Of Arthur the king;
Touched at the golden
Cross of the churches,
Flashed on the Tournament,
70 Flickered and bickered
From helmet to helmet,
And last on the forehead
Of Arthur the blameless
Rested The Gleam.°

VII

Clouds and darkness
Closed upon Camelot;
Arthur had vanished
I knew not whither,
The king who loved me,
80 And cannot die;°
For out of the darkness
Silent and slowly

Flitted The Gleam Stanza refers to the volumes
he published in 1842.
Slided The Gleam the English idylls, also
printed in 1842

Rested The Gleam the first group of Arthurian
idylls, published in 1859
cannot die a break in chronology, going back
to Hallam's death in 1833

The Gleam, that had waned to a wintry glimmer
On icy fallow
And faded forest,
Drew to the valley
Named of the shadow,
And slowly brightening
Out of the glimmer,
90   And slowly moving again to a melody
Yearningly tender,
Fell on the shadow,
No longer a shadow,
But clothed with The Gleam.°

VIII
And broader and brighter
The Gleam flying onward,
Wed to the melody,
Sang through the world;°
And slower and fainter,
100   Old and weary,
But eager to follow,
I saw, whenever
In passing it glanced upon
Hamlet or city,
That under the Crosses
The dead man's garden,
The mortal hillock,
Would break into blossom;
And so to the land's
110   Last limit I came—
And can no longer,
But die rejoicing,
For through the Magic
Of Him the Mighty,
Who taught me in childhood,
There on the border
Of boundless Ocean,
And all but in Heaven
Hovers The Gleam.°

IX
120   Not of the sunlight,
Not of the moonlight,

clothed with The Gleam *In Memoriam*
Sang through the world his later poetry, including *Maud*
Hovers The Gleam Not only the gleam but the
association of childhood with "the border / Of
boundless Ocean" suggests Wordsworth's *Intimations* Ode.

Not of the starlight!°
O young Mariner,
Down to the haven,
Call your companions,
Launch your vessel,
And crowd your canvas,
And, ere it vanishes
Over the margin,
130   After it, follow it,
Follow The Gleam.
1889   1889

Crossing the Bar°

Sunset and evening star,
    And one clear call for me!
And may there be no moaning of the bar,
    When I put out to sea,

But such a tide as moving seems asleep,
    Too full for sound and foam,
When that which drew from out the boundless deep
    Turns again home.

Twilight and evening bell,
10   And after that the dark!
And may there be no sadness of farewell,
    When I embark;

For though from out our bourne° of Time and Place
    The flood may bear me far,
I hope to see my Pilot face to face°
    When I have crossed the bar.
1889   1889

the starlight Tennyson may be distinguishing his more supernatural and mystical Gleam from the natural "sunlight" of Wordsworth, "moonlight" of Keats, and "starlight" of Shelley.
Crossing the Bar A few days before his death, Tennyson directed that this lyric conclude all editions of his work; the "bar" is a sand-bar at the harbor's mouth, but also the barrier between different realms of being. This is an immensely popular poem, but some critics find it simplistic and confused.
bourne boundary or limit
The flood . . . face to face Tennyson rather lamely said that the Pilot "has been on board all the while, but in the dark I have not seen him." (Actually, pilots leave the boats they guide once the harbor-bar is passed.) More tiresomely, he added that the Pilot was that "Divine and Unseen Who is always guiding us," not the most imaginative of his notions.

ROBERT BROWNING
1812–1889

Browning was born on May 7, 1812, in Camberwell, an outlying district of London, the first-born child of his well-to-do parents. Though the senior Robert Browning worked for the Bank of England, his interests were strongly scholarly and artistic, and his son grew up among the six thousand volumes of a carefully selected and thoroughly used library. Browning's mother, of Scottish and German descent, was an evangelical Protestant, and her dissenting religious views, though in altered form, were always to remain vital in Browning's consciousness.

Educated largely at home after fourteen, Browning set his heart early on being a poet, and prevailed, for against the strong wills of his parents he relied stubbornly upon the preternatural power of his own will. Unusually attached to his mother, Browning partly overcame his own Oedipal anxieties in regard to her, but the intense struggle was probably responsible for some of the stranger patterns in his life and his poetry. In 1826, when he was fourteen, he was given a small, pirated edition of Shelley's lyrics, and the major influence upon his poetry began, quite violently. Under the first impact of Shelley's spirit, Browning renounced his mother's religion. In a veiled form, Browning's first important poem, *Pauline*, based on Shelley's *Alastor*, told the story of the ensuing conflict, and the lasting shame of the boy's defeat. His attachment for his mother proved immediately more compelling than his need for his own integrity, and he yielded. Something fundamental in him was never to forget.

Pauline sold no copies, but the young John Stuart Mill read a review copy, and Mill's written comments reached and affected Browning. Mill, an authority on self-consciousness, saw clearly that *Pauline* only pretended to purge the young poet of that state, and that Browning was free neither of Shelleyanism nor of the psychological consequences of having yielded up his rebellion against society, religion, and parents. Attempting to work out of his conflicts, Browning wrote two more verse romances in the Shelleyan mode, *Paracelsus* (1835) and *Sordello* (1840). Neither is wholly successful, yet each is a remarkable work, but difficult, particularly *Sordello*, which baffled whoever read it. The subjective quest had led Browning into a puzzle of history mixed with personal reflections that is repeated by his poetic disciple, Ezra Pound, in the *Cantos*. Between 1840 and 1842, when *Dramatic Lyrics* appeared, by a process still concealed from his critics Browning accomplished a remarkable transfiguration of his Shelleyan heritage, and emerged with his characteristic and triumphant form, the dramatic monologue.

In 1844 Browning revisited Italy, and for the first time seems to have decided it was the proper context for his vision. He returned to England more lonely and intense than ever, and began in January 1845 a correspondence with the invalid poetess Elizabeth Barrett. This famous and complex courtship continued for almost two years, as the thirty-three-year-old Browning attempted to win over the thirty-nine-year-old poetess. The lovers did not meet until May 1845, and a close reading of the correspondence is both fascinating and troubling, as Browning wavered continually, desiring the lady, but wishing her to be the stronger and make the final decision. On September 19, 1846, by some small miracle, these two immense self-hoods somehow managed to elope together to Italy.

The Brownings' life together was reasonably happy, though it had its hidden difficulties, and some open conflicts. Unfortunately, it lasted only fifteen years, until Mrs. Browning suddenly died on June 29, 1861, in Florence, where they had lived for many years. Browning was left with a son, born in 1849, the year also of his mother's death, which affected him almost as deeply as his wife's, twelve years later. For many reasons, including his wariness at yielding up his new freedom but also because in a way he had become the prisoner of his own myth of perfect married love, Browning never remarried, but he became a social lion both in London and in Italy, and experienced some passionate involvements. His wariness fell away once, in 1869, when he proposed marriage to Lady Ashburton, but he was rejected (rather painfully, for him).

When Browning had fallen in love with Elizabeth Barrett, she had enjoyed a more considerable poetical reputation than he did, despite the *Dramatic Lyrics* of 1842 and the *Dramatic Romances* of 1845. Indeed, throughout even the 1850's, Browning was better known as a husband than as a poet. But in 1855 Browning published his first masterpiece, the fifty magnificent monologues of the two-volume *Men and Women*, and though only a few discerning poets and critics at first realized his achievement, the book's fame grew steadily over a decade. In 1864, *Dramatis Personae*, a collection almost as powerful, appeared, to be followed by his culminating work and second masterpiece, the long poem *The Ring and the Book*, in 1868. After that, and until his death, Browning at last achieved an audience and critical reputation almost equal to Tennyson's. Though he published copiously for the next twenty years, he never again equalled his greatest imaginings. There are, however, some remarkable lyrics in his last volume, *Asolando: Fancies and Facts*, published in London on December 12, 1889, the day that Browning died in Venice, at the house of his son.

Browning, in this editor's judgment, is the most considerable poet in English since the major Romantics, surpassing his great contemporary rival Tennyson, and the principal twentieth-century poets, including even Yeats, Hardy, and Wallace Stevens, let alone the various fashionable modernists whose reputations are now rightly in rapid decline. But Browning is a very difficult poet, notoriously badly served by criticism, and rather badly served also by his own accounts of what he was doing as a poet. His public statements and letters, his conversational asides, and the implicit polemic of his one important essay (inevitably on Shelley) all work together to emphasize the dramatic and objective elements in his poetry. Thus, his essay on Shelley implicitly claims kinship for himself with Shakespeare, classified as the supreme objective poet, as against Shelley, who is judged (with reverence) the outstanding example of the subjective poet. In the advertisement to the original *Dramatic Lyrics* of 1842, Browning insisted that the poems were, "though for the most part Lyric in expression, always Dramatic in principle, and so many utterances of so many imaginary persons, not mine." This insistence he maintained until the end.

Clearly, Browning himself could not *be* the varied group that included Johannes Agricola, the tomb-ordering Bishop, Fra Lippo Lippi, Childe Roland, Andrea del Sarto, Cleon, Abt Vogler, Caliban, the Pope of *The Ring and the Book*, and dozens more, but just as clearly his relation to them is *not* that of Shakespeare to Antony, Lear, Hamlet, Falstaff, Prospero, and the rest, or of Chaucer to his fellow pilgrims. Browning's form is dramatic, but his imaginative procedure is not. His company of ruined questers, imperfect poets, self-sabotaged artists, failed lovers, inspired fanatics, charlatans, monomaniacs, and self-deceiving confidence men all have a certain family resemblance, and they outweigh finally the other groups among his creations. We harm Browning by comparing his work to Shakespeare's or Chaucer's, not only because his range and depth of characterization are narrow and shallow compared with theirs, but because his poems are neither dramatic nor monologues, but something else. They are not dramatic, but lyrical and subjective, despite their coverings and gestures, and they are not monologues, but antiphons in which many voices speak, including several that belong to Browning himself. Browning, in his uncanny greatness, was a kind of psychological atomist, like Blake, Balzac, Proust, Kafka, Lawrence, Yeats, and some other modern innovators. In his work, older conceptions of personality disappear, and a more incoherent individual continuity is allowed to express the truths of actual existence. Whether Browning ever understood how wide the chasm between his own inner and outer selves had become, his art constantly explores the multiplicity of selves that inhabit apparently single, unitary personalities, some of them not at all unlike some of his own. Each of his men and women is at least several men and women, and his lovers learn that we can never embrace any one person at a time, but only the whole of an incoherence, the cluster of voices and beings that jostles in any separate self.

Browning had swerved away from the remorseless, questing, lyrical art of Shelley, where the poet seeks to fulfill desire by associating desire with the Intellectual Beauty that manifests itself just beyond the range of the senses. In Browning's vision the family resemblance to Shelley remains very strong, for all of his beings suffer from a quester's temperament, are self-deceived, and seek a sensuous fulfillment, yet manage all too frequently to turn aside from any fulfillment as being inadequate to the contradictory desires of their own crowded selves.

The uniqueness of Browning's art might have dismayed him, if he could see it in the perspective of a hundred years after, for he meant his speakers to give us their involuntary self-revelations, and just as strongly he did *not* mean them to give us his. Yet when you read your way into his world, precisely his largest gift to you is his involuntary unfolding of one of the largest, most enigmatic, and most multi-personed literary and human selves you can hope to encounter. In a brilliant monologue by the contemporary poet Richard Howard, "November, 1889," Browning is made to observe: "I am not interested in art, but in the obstacles to art." His poems, obsessed with those obstacles, do more to remove them than any others of the last century.

From Pauline°

A Fragment of a Confession

Thou wilt remember. Thou art not more dear
Than song was once to me; and I ne'er sung
But as one entering bright halls where all

Pauline Browning's first published poem, printed at his own expense in March 1833. The young poet making the confession is himself; "Pauline" probably was Eliza Flower, nine years older than Browning; it is unlikely that he was in love with her, as his heart, at this stage, was pretty well taken up by a triad of his mother, Shelley, and, as John Stuart Mill observed, mostly himself.

Will rise and shout for him: sure I must own
80   That I am fallen, having chosen gifts
Distinct from theirs—that I am sad and fain
Would give up all to be but where I was,
Not high as I had been if faithful found,
But low and weak yet full of hope, and sure
Of goodness as of life—that I would lose
All this gay mastery of mind, to sit
Once more with them, trusting in truth and love
And with an aim—not being what I am.

Oh Pauline, I am ruined who believed
90   That though my soul had floated from its sphere
Of wild dominion into the dim orb
Of self—that it was strong and free as ever!
It has conformed itself to that dim orb,
Reflecting all its shades and shapes, and now
Must stay where it alone can be adored.
I have felt this in dreams—in dreams in which
I seemed the fate from which I fled; I felt
A strange delight in causing my decay.
I was a fiend in darkness chained for ever
100   Within some ocean-cave; and ages rolled,
Till through the cleft rock, like a moonbeam, came
A white swan° to remain with me; and ages
Rolled, yet I tired not of my first free joy
In gazing on the peace of its pure wings:
And then I said 'It is most fair to me,
Yet its soft wings must sure have suffered change
From the thick darkness, sure its eyes are dim,
Its silver pinions must be cramped and numbed
With sleeping ages here; it cannot leave me,
110   For it would seem, in light beside its kind,
Withered, though here to me most beautiful.'
And then I was a young witch whose blue eyes,
As she stood naked by the river springs,
Drew down a god: I watched his radiant form
Growing less radiant, and it gladdened me;
Till one morn, as he sat in the sunshine
Upon my knees, singing to me of heaven,
He turned to look at me, ere I could lose
The grin with which I viewed his perishing:
120   And he shrieked and departed and sat long
By his deserted throne, but sunk at last
Murmuring, as I kissed his lips and curled
Around him, 'I am still a god—to thee.'

white swan See Shelley's *Alastor*, ll. 275–90.

Still I can lay my soul bare in its fall,
Since all the wandering and all the weakness
Will be a saddest comment on the song:
And if, that done, I can be young again,
I will give up all gained, as willingly
As one gives up a charm which shuts him out
130   From hope or part or care in human kind.
As life wanes, all its care and strife and toil
Seem strangely valueless, while the old trees
Which grew by our youth's home, the waving mass
Of climbing plants heavy with bloom and dew,
The morning swallows with their songs like words,
All these seem clear and only worth our thoughts:
So, aught connected with my early life,
My rude songs or my wild imaginings,
How I look on them—most distinct amid
140   The fever and the stir of after years!

I ne'er had ventured e'en to hope for this,
Had not the glow I felt at His award,°
Assured me all was not extinct within:
His whom all honour, whose renown springs up
Like sunlight which will visit all the world,
So that e'en they who sneered at him at first,
Come out to it, as some dark spider crawls
From his foul nest which some lit torch invades,
Yet spinning still new films for his retreat.
150   Thou didst smile, poet, but can we forgive?

Sun-treader, life and light be thine for ever!
Thou art gone from us; years go by and spring
Gladdens and the young earth is beautiful,
Yet thy songs come not, other bards arise,
But none like thee: they stand, thy majesties,
Like mighty works which tell some spirit there
Hath sat regardless of neglect and scorn,
Till, its long task completed, it hath risen
And left us, never to return, and all
160   Rush in to peer and praise when all in vain.
The air seems bright with thy past presence yet,
But thou art still for me as thou hast been
When I have stood with thee as on a throne
With all thy dim creations gathered round
Like mountains, and I felt of mould like them,
And with them creatures of my own were mixed,
Like things half-lived, catching and giving life.
But thou art still for me who have adored

His award Shelley's

Though single, panting but to hear thy name
170 Which I believed a spell to me alone,
Scarce deeming thou wast as a star to men!
As one should worship long a sacred spring
Scarce worth a moth's flitting, which long grasses cross,
And one small tree embowers droopingly—
Joying to see some wandering insect won
To live in its few rushes, or some locust
To pasture on its boughs, or some wild bird
Stoop for its freshness from the trackless air:
And then should find it but the fountain-head
180 Long lost, of some great river washing towns
And towers, and seeing old woods which will live
But by its banks untrod of human foot,
Which, when the great sun sinks, lie quivering
In light as some thing lieth half of life
Before God's foot, waiting a wondrous change;
Then girt with rocks which seek to turn or stay
Its course in vain, for it does ever spread
Like a sea's arm as it goes rolling on,
Being the pulse of some great country—so
190 Wast thou to me, and art thou to the world!
And I, perchance, half feel a strange regret
That I am not what I have been to thee:
Like a girl one has silently loved long
In her first loneliness in some retreat,
When, late emerged, all gaze and glow to view
Her fresh eyes and soft hair and lips which bloom
Like a mountain berry: doubtless it is sweet
To see her thus adored, but there have been
Moments when all the world was in our praise,
200 Sweeter than any pride of after hours.
Yet, sun-treader, all hail! From my heart's heart
I bid thee hail! E'en in my wildest dreams,
I proudly feel I would have thrown to dust
The wreaths of fame which seemed o'erhanging me,
To see thee for a moment as thou art.

And if thou livest, if thou lovest, spirit!
Remember me who set this final seal
To wandering thought—that one so pure as thou
Could never die. Remember me who flung
210 All honour from my soul,° yet paused and said
'There is one spark of love remaining yet,
For I have nought in common with him, shapes
Which followed him avoid me, and foul forms

flung . . . my soul when he renounced Shelley
and re-embraced religion, so as to be reconciled with his mother

Seek me, which ne'er could fasten on his mind;
And though I feel how low I am to him,
Yet I aim not even to catch a tone
Of harmonies he called profusely up;
So, one gleam still remains, although the last.'
Remember me who praise thee e'en with tears,
220 For never more shall I walk calm with thee;
Thy sweet imaginings are as an air,
A melody some wondrous singer sings,
Which, though it haunt men oft in the still eve,
They dream not to essay; yet it no less
But more is honoured. I was thine in shame,
And now when all thy proud renown is out,
I am a watcher whose eyes have grown dim
With looking for some star which breaks on him
Altered and worn and weak and full of tears.

1832–33   1833

Johannes Agricola in Meditation°

There's heaven above, and night by night
    I look right through its gorgeous roof;
No suns and moons though e'er so bright
    Avail to stop me; splendour-proof
    I keep the broods of stars aloof:
For I intend to get to God,
    For 'tis to God I speed so fast,
For in God's breast, my own abode,°
    Those shoals of dazzling glory, passed,
10   I lay my spirit down at last.
I lie where I have always lain,
    God smiles as he has always smiled;
Ere suns and moons could wax and wane,
    Ere stars were thundergirt, or piled
    The heavens, God thought on me his child;
Ordained a life for me, arrayed
    Its circumstances every one
To the minutest; ay, God said
    This head this hand should rest upon

Johannes Agricola in Meditation This vehement poem, one of the earliest of Browning's dramatic monologues, first appeared together with *Porphyria's Lover* under the common title *Madhouse Cells.* Johannes Agricola (1492–1566) broke away from Luther to found the sect of Antinomians. Browning quoted this description of the Antinomians: "they say that good works do not further, nor evil works hinder salvation; that the child of God cannot sin, that God never chastiseth him, that murder, drunkenness, etc. are sins in the wicked but not in him, that child of grace, being once assured of salvation, afterwards never doubteth. . . ." Whether Agricola is mad, or merely very dangerous, his zest and vigor manifest a genuine imaginative energy, though twisted askew.
abode because he is persuaded of his election

20 Thus, ere he fashioned star or sun.
  And having thus created me,
   Thus rooted me, he bade me grow,
   Guiltless for ever, like a tree
    That buds and blooms, nor seeks to know
    The law by which it prospers so:
  But sure that thought and word and deed
   All go to swell his love for me,
  Me, made because that love had need
   Of something irreversibly
30   Pledged solely its content to be.
  Yes, yes, a tree which must ascend,
   No poison-gourd° foredoomed to stoop!
  I have God's warrant, could I blend
   All hideous sin, as in a cup,
   To drink the mingled venoms up;
  Secure my nature will convert
   The draught to blossoming gladness fast:
  While sweet dews turn to the gourd's hurt,
   And bloat, and while they bloat it, blast,
40   As from the first its lot was cast.
  For as I lie, smiled on, full-fed
   By unexhausted° power to bless,
  I gaze below on hell's fierce bed,
   And those its waves of flame oppress,
   Swarming in ghastly wretchedness;
  Whose life on earth aspired to be
   One altar-smoke, so pure!—to win
  If not love like God's love for me,
   At least to keep his anger in;
50   And all their striving turned to sin.
  Priest, doctor, hermit, monk grown white
   With prayer, the broken-hearted nun,
  The martyr, the wan acolyte,°
   The incense-swinging child,—undone
   Before God fashioned star or sun!
  God, whom I praise; how could I praise,
   If such as I might understand,
  Make out and reckon on his ways,
   And bargain for his love, and stand,
60   Paying a price, at his right hand?
  1834   1836

poison-gourd a figure for the damned   acolyte priest's attendant in celebrating Mass
unexhausted inexhaustible

Soliloquy of the Spanish Cloister°

I

Gr-rr—there go, my heart's abhorrence!
    Water your damned flower-pots, do!
If hate killed men, Brother Lawrence,
    God's blood,° would not mine kill you!
What? your myrtle-bush wants trimming?
    Oh, that rose has prior claims—
Needs its leaden vase filled brimming?
    Hell dry you up with its flames!

II

At the meal we sit together:
10   *Salve tibi!°* I must hear
Wise talk of the kind of weather,
    Sort of season, time of year:
Not a plenteous cork-crop: scarcely
    Dare we hope oak-galls,° I doubt:
What's the Latin name for 'parsley'?
    What's the Greek name for Swine's Snout?

III

Whew! We'll have our platter burnished,
    Laid with care on our own shelf!
With a fire-new spoon we're furnished,
20   And a goblet for ourself,
Rinsed like something sacrificial
    Ere 'tis fit to touch our chaps°—
Marked with L. for our initial!
    (He-he! There his lily snaps!)

IV

Saint, forsooth! While brown Dolores
    Squats outside the Convent bank
With Sanchicha, telling stories,
    Steeping tresses in the tank,
Blue-black, lustrous, thick like horsehairs,
30   —Can't I see his dead eye glow,
Bright as 'twere a Barbary corsair's?°
    (That is, if he'd let it show!)

Soliloquy of the Spanish Cloister In one sense, this madly humorous monologue resembles Tennyson's *St. Simeon Stylites,* and simply reflects Browning's extreme Protestant prejudices. But, in a finer sense, the zestful hatred felt by the unnamed speaker for the sincerely pious and good-natured Brother Lawrence is curiously infectious, because of its shocking exuberance. Not that we share the hatred as hatred, or come to like the oddly hypocritical yet still credulous Spanish monk, but we enjoy his daemonic intensity, his remorseless verve.
God's blood oath based on the doctrine of transubstantiation (in the Mass the wine is transformed into the blood of Jesus Christ)
Salve tibi! hail to thee; here and in ll. 13–15, the speaker bitterly quotes Lawrence's good-natured salutation and conversation
oak-galls disease of oak-leaves, valuable as source of tannic acid for ink-making
chaps lips
Barbary corsair's northern African pirate's

V

When he finishes refection,
   Knife and fork he never lays
Cross-wise, to my recollection,
   As do I, in Jesu's praise.
I the Trinity illustrate,°
   Drinking watered orange-pulp—
In three sips the Arian° frustrate;
40   While he drains his at one gulp.

VI

Oh, those melons? If he's able
   We're to have a feast! so nice!
One goes to the Abbot's table,
   All of us get each a slice.
How go on your flowers? None double?
   Not one fruit-sort can you spy?
Strange!—And I, too, at such trouble,
   Keep them close-nipped on the sly!

VII

There's a great text in Galatians,°
50   Once you trip on it, entails
Twenty-nine distinct damnations,
   One sure, if another fails:
If I trip him just a-dying,
   Sure of heaven as sure can be,
Spin him round and send him flying
   Off to hell, a Manichee?°

VIII

Or, my scrofulous° French novel
   On grey paper with blunt type!
Simply glance at it, you grovel
60   Hand and foot in Belial's gripe:°
If I double down its pages
   At the woeful° sixteenth print,
When he gathers his greengages,
   Ope a sieve and slip it in't?

illustrate by my crossing of eating utensils
Arian follower of 4th-century heresy that
denied the Trinity
Galatians The text must be Galatians 5:19–21,
which confines itself, however, to a mere 17
damnations, not all of them quite distinct; the
Monk adds 12 in the pardonable enthusiasm of
his faith.
Manichee follower of radically dualistic heresy,
of the 4th century and later. The joke is that
the speaker himself has an inverted Manichean
temperament.
scrofulous morally corrupt, from scrofula, an
enlarging and degenerating disease of the
lymphatic glands
Belial's gripe grip of Belial, a name for the
Devil
woeful deplorable

IX

Or, there's Satan!—one might venture
  Pledge one's soul to him, yet leave
Such a flaw in the indenture
  As he'd miss till, past retrieve,
Blasted lay that rose-acacia
70 We're so proud of! *Hy, Zy, Hine* . . .°
  'St, there's Vespers!° *Plena gratiâ*
  Ave, Virgo!° Gr-r-r—you swine!
  1839   1842

My Last Duchess

FERRARA°

That's my last Duchess° painted on the wall,
Looking as if she were alive. I call
That piece a wonder, now: Frà Pandolf's hands
Worked busily a day, and there she stands.
Will't please you sit and look at her? I said
'Fra Pandolf' by design, for never read
Strangers like you that pictured countenance,
The depth and passion of its earnest glance,
But to myself they turned (since none puts by
10 The curtain I have drawn for you, but I)
And seemed as they would ask me, if they durst,
How such a glance came there; so, not the first
Are you to turn and ask thus. Sir, 'twas not
Her husband's presence only, called that spot
Of joy into the Duchess' cheek: perhaps
Frà Pandolf chanced to say 'Her mantle laps
Over my lady's wrist too much,' or 'Paint
Must never hope to reproduce the faint
Half-flush that dies along her throat:' such stuff
20 Was courtesy, she thought, and cause enough
For calling up that spot of joy. She had
A heart—how shall I say?—too soon made glad,
Too easily impressed; she liked whate'er
She looked on, and her looks went everywhere.
Sir, 'twas all one! My favour at her breast,
The dropping of the daylight in the West,
The bough of cherries some officious fool
Broke in the orchard for her, the white mule

Hy, Zy, Hine personal curse directed against
Lawrence, possibly based on popular Satanism
there's Vespers bell signaling evening prayers
Plena . . . Virgo! Hail Virgin, full of grace
Ferrara Alfonso II of the House of Este, Duke
of Ferrara, was negotiating (in 1564) for the
niece of the Count of Tyrol.
last Duchess The unfortunate lady died in 1561,
at the age of 17, and was believed to have
been poisoned.

She rode with round the terrace—all and each
30 Would draw from her alike the approving speech,
Or blush, at least. She thanked men,—good! but thanked
Somehow—I know not how—as if she ranked
My gift of a nine-hundred-years-old name
With anybody's gift. Who'd stoop to blame
This sort of trifling? Even had you skill
In speech—(which I have not)—to make your will
Quite clear to such an one, and say, 'Just this
Or that in you disgusts me; here you miss,
Or there exceed the mark'—and if she let
40 Herself be lessoned so, nor plainly set
Her wits to yours, forsooth, and made excuse,
—E'en then would be some stooping; and I choose
Never to stoop. Oh sir, she smiled, no doubt,
Whene'er I passed her; but who passed without
Much the same smile? This grew; I gave commands;
Then all smiles stopped together. There she stands
As if alive. Will't please you rise? We'll meet
The company below, then. I repeat,
The Count your master's known munificence
50 Is ample warrant that no just pretence
Of mine for dowry will be disallowed;
Though his fair daughter's self, as I avowed
At starting, is my object. Nay, we'll go
Together down, sir. Notice Neptune, though,
Taming a sea-horse, thought a rarity,
Which Claus of Innsbruck° cast in bronze for me!
1842   1842

The Bishop Orders His Tomb°
at Saint Praxed's Church°

Rome, 15—
Vanity, saith° the preacher, vanity!
Draw round my bed: is Anselm° keeping back?
Nephews—sons mine°. . . ah, God, I know not! Well—

Claus of Innsbruck an imaginary sculptor
The Bishop Orders His Tomb . . . This brilliant poem may be regarded as Browning's response to the challenge of Tennyson's *St. Simeon Stylites*, a dramatic monologue Browning acknowledged as "perfect." The Bishop, Gandolf, and everything else central to the poem are all entirely Browning's own creations, yet Ruskin (in *Modern Painters* IV.380) in 1856 was justified in saying: "I know of no other piece of modern English, prose or poetry, in which there is so much told, as in these lines, of the Renaissance spirit,—its worldliness, inconsistency, pride, hypocrisy, ignorance of itself, love of art, of luxury, and of good Latin. It is nearly all that I have said of the central Renaissance in thirty pages of *The Stones of Venice*, put into as many lines, Browning's also being the antecedent work."
St. Praxed's Church Roman church of St. Praxedes, 2nd-century martyred virgin
Vanity saith in Ecclesiastes 1:2 (*Koheleth,* or the preacher)
Anselm probably the bishop's first-born natural son
sons mine At the moment of death, the bishop can acknowledge that his "nephews" are actually his sons.

She, men would have to be your mother once,
Old Gandolf envied me, so fair she was!
What's done is done, and she is dead beside,
Dead long ago, and I am Bishop since,
And as she died so must we die ourselves,
And thence ye may perceive the world's a dream.
10   Life, how and what is it? As here I lie
In this state-chamber, dying by degrees,
Hours and long hours in the dead night, I ask
'Do I live, am I dead?' Peace, peace seems all.
Saint Praxed's ever was the church for peace;
And so, about this tomb of mine. I fought
With tooth and nail to save my niche, ye know:
—Old Gandolf cozened me, despite my care;
Shrewd was that snatch from out the corner South
He graced his carrion with, God curse the same!
20   Yet still my niche is not so cramped but thence
One sees the pulpit o' the epistle-side,°
And somewhat of the choir, those silent seats,
And up into the aery dome where live
The angels, and a sunbeam's sure to lurk:
And I shall fill my slab of basalt there,
And 'neath my tabernacle° take my rest,
With those nine columns round me, two and two,
The odd one at my feet where Anselm stands:
Peach-blossom marble all, the rare, the ripe
30   As fresh-poured red wine of a mighty pulse.°
—Old Gandolf with his paltry onion-stone,°
Put me where I may look at him! True peach,
Rosy and flawless: how I earned the prize!
Draw close: that conflagration of my church
—What then? So much was saved if aught were missed!
My sons, ye would not be my death? Go dig
The white-grape vineyard where the oil-press stood,
Drop water gently till the surface sink,
And if ye find . . . Ah God, I know not, I! . . .
40   Bedded in store of rotten fig-leaves soft,
And corded up in a tight olive-frail,
Some lump, ah God, of *lapis lazuli*,°
Big as a Jew's head° cut off at the nape,
Blue as a vein o'er the Madonna's breast . . .
Sons, all have I bequeathed you, villas, all,
That brave Frascati° villa with its bath,
So, let the blue lump poise between my knees,

epistle-side right side as one faces the altar;
gospel-side on the left
tabernacle canopy above the tomb
pulse grape's pulp

onion-stone poor marble, colored like an onion
and peeling like it
lapis lazuli blue stone, semi-precious
head John the Baptist's
Frascati elegant Roman suburb

Like God the Father's globe on both his hands
Ye worship in the Jesu Church° so gay,
50 For Gandolf shall not choose but see and burst!
Swift as a weaver's shuttle° fleet our years:
Man goeth to the grave, and where is he?
Did I say basalt for my slab, sons? Black—
'Twas ever antique-black° I meant! How else
Shall ye contrast my frieze to come beneath?
The bas-relief in bronze ye promised me,
Those Pans and Nymphs ye wot of, and perchance
Some tripod,° thyrsus,°, with a vase or so
The Saviour at his sermon on the mount,
60 Saint Praxed in a glory, and one Pan
Ready to twitch the Nymph's last garment off,
And Moses with the tables°. . . but I know
Ye mark me not! What do they whisper thee,
Child of my bowels, Anselm? Ah, ye hope
To revel down my villas while I gasp
Bricked o'er with beggar's mouldy travertine°
Which Gandolf from his tomb-top chuckles at!
Nay, boys, ye love me—all of jasper,° then!
'Tis jasper ye stand pledged to, lest I grieve
70 My bath must needs be left behind, alas!
One block, pure green as a pistachio-nut,
There's plenty jasper somewhere in the world—
And have I not Saint Praxed's ear to pray
Horses for ye, and brown Greek manuscripts,
And mistresses with great smooth marbly limbs?
—That's if ye carve my epitaph aright,
Choice Latin, picked phrase, Tully's° every word,
No gaudy ware like Gandolf's second line—
Tully, my masters? Ulpian° serves his need!
80 And then how I shall lie through centuries,
And hear the blessed mutter of the mass,
And see God made and eaten° all day long,
And feel the steady candle-flame, and taste
Good strong thick stupefying incense-smoke!
For as I lie here, hours of the dead night,
Dying in state and by such slow degrees,
I fold my arms as if they clasped a crook,°
And stretch my feet forth straight as stone can point,

Jesu Church *Il Gesù*, a Jesuit church in Rome
shuttle Job 7:6: "My days are swifter than a weaver's shuttle, and are spent without hope."
antique-black "neroantico," beautiful black stone
tripod three-legged stool used by oracle of Apollo at Delphi
thyrsus staff decorated with ivy or wine branches, carried by Dionysus and his Votaries
tables tablets of the Law, carried down from

Sinai by Moses; see Exodus 32:15
travertine light yellow limestone
jasper quartz
Tully Marcus Tullius Cicero (106–43 B.C.), the orator whose style set the standard for good Latin prose
Ulpian Domitius Ulpianus (170–228 A.D.), late Roman jurist notorious for his bad prose
God . . . eaten in the ceremony of the Mass
crook bishop's crozier or staff

And let the bedclothes, for a mortcloth°, drop
90   Into great laps and folds of sculptor's-work:
And as yon tapers dwindle, and strange thoughts
Grow, with a certain humming in my ears,
About the life before I lived this life,
And this life too, popes, cardinals and priests,
Saint Praxed° at his sermon on the mount,
Your tall pale mother with her talking eyes,
And new-found agate urns as fresh as day,
And marble's language, Latin pure, discreet,
—Aha, ELUCESCEBAT° quoth our friend?
100 No Tully, said I, Ulpian at the best!
Evil and brief hath been my pilgrimage.°
All *lapis*, all, sons! Else I give the Pope
My villas! Will ye ever eat my heart?
Ever your eyes were as a lizard's quick,
They glitter like your mother's for my soul,
Or ye would heighten my impoverished frieze,
Piece out its starved design, and fill my vase
With grapes, and add a vizor° and a Term,°
And to the tripod ye would tie a lynx°
110 That in his struggle throws the thyrsus down,
To comfort me on my entablature
Whereon I am to lie till I must ask
'Do I live, am I dead?' There, leave me, there!
For ye have stabbed me with ingratitude
To death—ye wish it—God, ye wish it! Stone—
Gritstone,° a-crumble! Clammy squares which sweat
As if the corpse they keep were oozing through—
And no more *lapis* to delight the world!
Well go! I bless ye. Fewer tapers there,
120 But in a row: and, going, turn your backs
—Ay, like departing altar-ministrants,
And leave me in my church, the church for peace,
That I may watch at leisure if he leers—
Old Gandolf, at me, from his onion-stone,
As still he envied me, so fair she was!
1844   1845

---

mortcloth funeral pall
Saint Praxed The bishop is close to death, and
mistakenly attributes the Sermon on the Mount
to her instead of Christ.
ELUCESCEBAT "he was illustrious," an example
of bad, decadent Latin, whereas Cicero would
have written: "elucebat"
pilgrimage Jacob to Pharaoh, in Genesis 47:9:
". . . few and evil have the days of the years
of my life been, and have not attained unto

the days of the years of the life of my fathers
in the days of their pilgrimage." Jacob, as the
Bishop knew, was gracefully boasting, being
130 at the time.
vizor . . . Term a mask and a bust terminat-
ing in a pillar or pedestal (like representations
of the Roman god Terminus)
lynx Dionysus was accompanied by lynxes.
Gritstone poor sandstone

Love Among the Ruins°

I

Where the quiet-coloured end of evening smiles,
    Miles and miles
On the solitary pastures where our sheep
    Half-asleep
Tinkle homeward through the twilight, stray or stop
    As they crop—
Was the site once of a city great and gay,
    (So they say)
Of our country's very capital, its prince
10   Ages since
Held his court in, gathered councils, wielding far
    Peace or war.

II

Now,—the country does not even boast a tree,
    As you see,
To distinguish slopes of verdure, certain rills
    From the hills
Intersect and give a name to, (else they run
    Into one)
Where the domed and daring palace shot its spires
20   Up like fires
O'er the hundred-gated circuit of a wall
    Bounding all,
Made of marble, men might march on nor be pressed,
    Twelve abreast.

III

And such plenty and perfection, see, of grass
    Never was!
Such a carpet as, this summer time, o'erspreads
    And embeds
Every vestige of the city, guessed alone,
30   Stock or stone—
Where a multitude of men breathed joy and woe
    Long ago;
Lust of glory pricked their hearts up, dread of shame
    Struck them tame;
And that glory and that shame alike, the gold
    Bought and sold.

Love . . . Ruins evidently more of an ancient Near Eastern city, like Babylon or Nineveh, than an Italian city, though the poem's setting presumably is Italian. The poem was written the day after *Childe Roland,* and one can see similarities in the poems' landscapes.

IV

Now,—the single little turret that remains
    On the plains,
By the caper° overrooted, by the gourd°
40   Overscored,
While the patching houseleek's° head of blossom winks
    Through the chinks—
Marks the basement whence a tower in ancient time
    Sprang sublime,
And a burning ring, all round, the chariots traced
    As they raced,
And the monarch and his minions and his dames
    Viewed the games.

V

And I know, while thus the quiet-coloured eve
50   Smiles to leave
To their folding, all our many-tinkling fleece
    In such peace,
And the slopes and rills in undistinguished grey
    Melt away—
That a girl with eager eyes and yellow hair
    Waits me there
In the turret whence the charioteers caught soul
    For the goal,
When the king looked, where she looks now, breathless, dumb
60   Till I come.

VI

But he looked upon the city, every side,
    Far and wide,
All the mountains topped with temples, all the glades'
    Colonnades,
All the causeys,° bridges, aqueducts,—and then,
    All the men!
When I do come, she will speak not, she will stand,
    Either hand
On my shoulder, give her eyes the first embrace
70   Of my face,
Ere we rush, ere we extinguish sight and speech
    Each on each.

VII

In one year they sent a million fighters forth
    South and North,

caper a prickly bush
gourd the fruit of a climbing plant

houseleek's small plant, with petals giving
clustered effect
causeys raised roads

And they built their gods a brazen pillar high
    As the sky,
Yet reserved a thousand chariots in full force—
    Gold, of course.
Oh heart! oh blood that freezes, blood that burns!
80   Earth's returns
For whole centuries of folly, noise and sin!
    Shut them in,
With their triumphs and their glories and the rest!
    Love is best!
1852   1855

Fra Lippo Lippi°

I am poor brother Lippo, by your leave!
You need not clap your torches to my face.
Zooks,° what's to blame? you think you see a monk!
What, 'tis past midnight, and you go the rounds,
And here you catch me at an alley's end
Where sportive ladies leave their doors ajar?
The Carmine's my cloister: hunt it up,
Do,—harry out, if you must show your zeal,
Whatever rat, there, haps on his wrong hole,
10 And nip each softling of a wee white mouse,
Weke, weke, that's crept to keep him company!
Aha, you know your betters? Then, you'll take
Your hand away that's fiddling on my throat,
And please to know me likewise. Who am I?
Why, one, sir, who is lodging with a friend
Three streets off—he's a certain . . . how d'ye call?
Master—a . . . Cosimo of the Medici,°
In the house that caps the corner. Boh! you were best!
Remember and tell me, the day you're hanged,
20 How you affected such a gullet's-gripe!
But you, sir, it concerns you that your knaves
Pick up a manner nor discredit you:
Zooks, are we pilchards,° that they sweep the streets
And count fair prize what comes into their net?
He's Judas to a tittle, that man is!
Just such a face! Why, sir, you make amends.
Lord, I'm not angry! Bid your hangdogs go

Fra Lippo Lippi (1406–69), Florentine painter
and libertine Carmelite friar, was a superb
(though not innovative, contrary to Browning's
judgment) naturalistic artist, in the manner of
his teacher, Masaccio. Browning was anxious
to portray Lippi as an artist of originality,
since the poem totally identifies his own art
with Lippi's.

Zooks the oath "Gadzooks," the meaning of
which is obscure
Cosimo of the Medici (1389–1464), renowned
as art patron, politician, financier, ruler of
Florence
pilchards small fish

Drink out this quarter-florin° to the health
Of the munificent House that harbours me
30   (And many more beside, lads! more beside!)
And all's come square again. I'd like his face—
His, elbowing on his comrade in the door
With the pike and lantern,—for the slave that holds
John Baptist's head° a-dangle by the hair
With one hand ('Look you, now,' as who should say)
And his weapon in the other, yet unwiped!
It's not your chance to have a bit of chalk,
A wood-coal or the like? or you should see!
Yes, I'm the painter, since you style me so.
40   What, brother Lippo's doings, up and down,
You know them and they take you? like enough!
I saw the proper twinkle in your eye—
'Tell you, I liked your looks at very first.
Let's sit and set things straight now, hip to haunch.
Here's spring come, and the nights one makes up bands
To roam the town and sing out carnival,
And I've been three weeks shut within my mew,
A-painting for the great man, saints and saints
And saints again. I could not paint all night—
50   Ouf! I leaned out of window for fresh air.
There came a hurry of feet and little feet,
A sweep of lute-strings, laughs, and whifts of song,—
Flower o' the broom,°
Take away love, and our earth is a tomb!
Flower o' the quince,
I let Lisa go, and what good in life since?
Flower o' the thyme—and so on. Round they went.
Scarce had they turned the corner when a titter
Like the skipping of rabbits by moonlight,—three slim shapes,
60   And a face that looked up . . . zooks, sir, flesh and blood,
That's all I'm made of! Into shreds it went,
Curtain and counterpane and coverlet,
All the bed furniture—a dozen knots,
There was a ladder! Down I let myself,
Hands and feet, scrambling somehow, and so dropped,
And after them. I came up with the fun
Hard by St. Laurence,° hail fellow, well met.—
Flower o' the rose,
If I've been merry, what matter who knows?
70   And so as I was stealing back again
To get to bed and have a bit of sleep

---

quarter-florin coin of Florence
for the slave . . . head Matthew 14:1–12
Flower o' the broom This and the other flower-
songs that the cheerful Lippi keeps humming

to himself are meant to suggest the *Stornelli,*
a popular kind of folk song in Italy.
Laurence church of San Lorenzo

Ere I rise up to-morrow and go work
On Jerome° knocking at his poor old breast
With his great round stone to subdue the flesh,
You snap me of the sudden. Ah, I see!
Though your eye twinkles still, you shake your head—
Mine's shaved,—a monk, you say—the sting's in that!
If Master Cosimo announced himself,
Mum's the word naturally; but a monk!
80   Come, what am I a beast for? tell us, now!
I was a baby when my mother died
And father died and left me in the street.
I starved there, God knows how, a year or two
On fig-skins, melon-parings, rinds and shucks,
Refuse and rubbish. One fine frosty day,
My stomach being empty as your hat,
The wind doubled me up and down I went.
Old Aunt Lapaccia° trussed me with one hand,
(Its fellow was a stinger as I knew)
90   And so along the wall, over the bridge,
By the straight cut to the convent. Six words there,
While I stood munching my first bread that month:
'So, boy, you're minded,' quoth the good fat father
Wiping his own mouth, 'twas refection-time,°—
To quit this very miserable world?
Will you renounce' . . . 'the mouthful of bread?' thought I;
By no means! Brief, they made a monk of me;
I did renounce the world, its pride and greed,
Palace, farm, villa, shop and banking-house,
100 Trash, such as these poor devils of Medici
Have given their hearts to—all at eight years old.
Well, sir, I found in time, you may be sure,
'Twas not for nothing—the good bellyful,
The warm serge and the rope that goes all round,
And day-long blessed idleness beside!
'Let's see what the urchin's fit for'—that came next.
Not overmuch their way, I must confess.
Such a to-do! they tried me with their books:
Lord, they'd have taught me Latin in pure waste!
110 *Flower o' the clove,*
All the Latin I construe is, 'amo' I love!
But, mind you, when a boy starves in the streets
Eight years together, as my fortune was,
Watching folk's faces to know who will fling
The bit of half-stripped grape-bunch he desires,
And who will curse or kick him for his pains,—

Jerome saint (340–420), renowned for learning and ascetic zeal; never painted by Lippi,
for splendidly obvious reasons

Lapaccia Lippi's foster mother until he joined
the Carmelites
refection-time mealtime

Which gentleman processional° and fine,
Holding a candle to the Sacrament,
Will wink and let him lift a plate and catch
120   The droppings of the wax to sell again,
Or holla for the Eight° and have him whipped,—
How say I?—nay, which dog bites, which lets drop
His bone from the heap of offal in the street,—
Why, soul and sense of him grow sharp alike,
He learns the look of things, and none the less
For admonition from the hunger-pinch.
I had a store of such remarks, be sure,
Which, after I found leisure, turned to use.
I drew men's faces on my copy-books,
130   Scrawled them within the antiphonary's marge,°
Joined legs and arms to the long music-notes,
Found eyes and nose and chin for A's and B's,
And made a string of pictures of the world
Betwixt the ins and outs of verb and noun,
On the wall, the bench, the door. The monks looked black.
'Nay,' quoth the Prior, 'turn him out, d'ye say?
In no wise. Lose a crow and catch a lark.
What if at last we get our man of parts,
We Carmelites,° like those Camaldolese°
140   And Preaching Friars,° to do our church up fine
And put the front on it that ought to be!'
And hereupon he bade me daub away.
Thank you! my head being crammed, the walls a blank,
Never was such prompt disemburdening.
First, every sort of monk, the black and white,
I drew them, fat and lean: then, folk at church,
From good old gossips waiting to confess
Their cribs° of barrel-droppings, candle-ends,—
To the breathless fellow at the altar-foot,
150   Fresh from his murder, safe and sitting there
With the little children round him in a row
Of admiration, half for his beard and half
For that white anger of his victim's son
Shaking a fist at him with one fierce arm,
Signing himself with the other because of Christ
(Whose sad face on the cross sees only this
After the passion of a thousand years)
Till some poor girl, her apron o'er her head,
(Which the intense eyes looked through) came at eve
160   On tiptoe, said a word, dropped in a loaf,

processional garbed for marching in religious parade
Eight magistrates governing Florence
marge margins of books used by choir boys

Carmelites monks of order of Mount Carmel
Camaldolese rival Florentine religious order
Preaching Friars Dominicans
cribs small thefts

Her pair of earrings and a bunch of flowers
(The brute took growling), prayed, and so was gone.
I painted all, then cried, ' 'Tis ask and have;
Choose, for more's ready!—laid the ladder flat,
And showed my covered bit of cloister-wall.
The monks closed in a circle and praised loud
Till checked, taught what to see and not to see,
Being simple bodies,—'That's the very man!
Look at the boy who stoops to pat the dog!
170 That woman's like the Prior's niece° who comes
To care about his asthma: it's the life!'
But there my triumph's straw-fire flared and funked;°
Their betters took their turn to see and say:
The Prior and the learnèd pull a face
And stopped all that in no time. 'How? what's here?
Quite from the mark of painting, bless us all!
Faces, arms, legs and bodies like the true
As much as pea and pea! it's devil's-game!
Your business is not to catch men with show,
180 With homage to the perishable clay,
But lift them over it, ignore it all,
Make them forget there's such a thing as flesh.
Your business is to paint the souls of men—
Man's soul, and it's a fire, smoke . . . no, it's not . . .
It's vapour done up like a new-born babe—
(In that shape when you die it leaves your mouth)
It's . . . well, what matters talking, it's the soul!
Give us no more of body than shows soul!
Here's Giotto,° with his Saint a-praising God,
190 That sets up praising,—why not stop with him?
Why put all thoughts of praise out of our head
With wonder at lines, colours, and what not?
Paint the soul, never mind the legs and arms!
Rub all out, try at it a second time.
Oh, that white smallish female with the breasts,
She's just my niece . . . Herodias,° I would say,—
Who went and danced and got men's heads cut off!
Have it all out!' Now, is this sense, I ask?
A fine way to paint soul, by painting body
200 So ill, the eye can't stop there, must go further
And can't fare worse! Thus, yellow does for white
When what you put for yellow's simply black,
And any sort of meaning looks intense

Prior's niece probably the Prior's natural daughter
funked gone up in smoke
Giotto Giotto di Bondone (1276–1337), founder of school of painting against which

Masaccio (and Lippi) rebelled as being over-spiritualized
Herodias, Herod's sister-in-law; mother of Salome who demanded and got John the Baptist's head as payment for her dance before Herod

When all beside itself means and looks nought.
Why can't a painter lift each foot in turn,
Left foot and right foot, go a double step,
Make his flesh liker and his soul more like,
Both in their order? Take the prettiest face,
The Prior's niece . . . patron-saint—is it so pretty
210 You can't discover if it means hope, fear,
Sorrow or joy? won't beauty go with these?
Suppose I've made her eyes all right and blue,
Can't I take breath and try to add life's flash,
And then add soul and heighten them threefold?
Or say there's beauty with no soul at all—
(I never saw it—put the case the same—)
If you get simple beauty and nought else,
You get about the best thing God invents:
That's somewhat: and you'll find the soul you have missed,
220 Within yourself, when you return him thanks.
'Rub all out!' Well, well, there's my life, in short,
And so the thing has gone on ever since.
I'm grown a man no doubt, I've broken bounds:
You should not take a fellow eight years old
And make him swear to never kiss the girls.
I'm my own master, paint now as I please—
Having a friend, you see, in the Corner-house!°
Lord, it's fast holding by the rings in front—
Those great rings serve more purposes than just
230 To plant a flag in, or tie up a horse!
And yet the old schooling sticks, the old grave eyes
Are peeping o'er my shoulder as I work,
The heads shake still—'It's art's decline, my son!
You're not of the true painters, great and old;
Brother Angelico's° the man, you'll find;
Brother Lorenzo° stands his single peer:
Fag on at flesh, you'll never make the third!'
Flower o' the pine,
You keep your mistr . . . manners, and I'll stick to mine!
240 I'm not the third, then: bless us, they must know!
Don't you think they're the likeliest to know,
They with their Latin? So, I swallow my rage,
Clench my teeth, suck my lips in tight, and paint
To please them—sometimes do and sometimes don't;
For, doing most, there's pretty sure to come
A turn, some warm eve finds me at my saints—
A laugh, a cry, the business of the world—

Corner-house palace of the Medici
Angelico Fra Angelico (1387–1455), major
painter of the school of Giotto; renowned for
his piety

Lorenzo Lorenzo Monaco (1370–1425), school
of Giotto

(*Flower o' the peach,*
Death for us all, and his own life for each!)
250 And my whole soul revolves, the cup runs over,
The world and life's too big to pass for a dream,
And I do these wild things in sheer despite,
And play the fooleries you catch me at,
In pure rage! The old mill-horse, out at grass
After hard years, throws up his stiff heels so,
Although the miller does not preach to him
The only good of grass is to make chaff.
What would men have? Do they like grass or no—
May they or mayn't they? all I want's the thing
260 Settled for ever one way. As it is,
You tell too many lies and hurt yourself:
You don't like what you only like too much,
You do like what, if given you at your word,
You find abundantly detestable.
For me, I think I speak as I was taught;
I always see the garden and God there
A-making man's wife: and, my lesson learned,
The value and significance of flesh,
I can't unlearn ten minutes afterwards.

270   You understand me: I'm a beast, I know.
But see, now—why, I see as certainly
As that the morning-star's about to shine,
What will hap some day. We've a youngster here
Comes to our convent, studies what I do,
Slouches and stares and lets no atom drop:
His name is Guidi°—he'll not mind the monks—
They call him Hulking Tom, he lets them talk—
He picks my practice up—he'll paint apace,
I hope so—though I never live so long,
280 I know what's sure to follow. You be judge!
You speak no Latin more than I, belike,
However, you're my man, you've seen the world
—The beauty and the wonder and the power,
The shapes of things, their colours, lights and shades,
Changes, surprises,—and God made it all!
—For what? Do you feel thankful, ay or no,
For this fair town's face, yonder river's line,
The mountain round it and the sky above,
Much more the figures of man, woman, child,
290 These are the frame to? What's it all about?
To be passed over, despised? or dwelt upon,
Wondered at? oh, this last of course!—you say.

Guidi Tommaso Guidi (1401–28), known as
Masaccio, translatable as "Hulking Tom" or
"Big Tom"

But why not do as well as say,—paint these
Just as they are, careless what comes of it?
God's works—paint anyone, and count it crime
To let a truth slip. Don't object, 'His works
Are here already; nature is complete:
Suppose you reproduce her—(which you can't)
There's no advantage! you must beat her, then.'
300   For, don't you mark? we're made so that we love
First when we see them painted, things we have passed
Perhaps a hundred times nor cared to see;
And so they are better, painted—better to us,
Which is the same thing. Art was given for that;
God uses us to help each other so,
Lending our minds out. Have you noticed, now,
Your cullion's° hanging face? A bit of chalk,
And trust me but you should, though! How much more,
If I drew higher things with the same truth!
310   That were to take the Prior's pulpit-place,
Interpret God to all of you! Oh, oh,
It makes me mad to see what men shall do
And we in our graves! This world's no blot for us,
Nor blank; it means intensely, and means good:
To find its meaning is my meat and drink.
'Ay, but you don't so instigate to prayer!'
Strikes in the Prior: 'when your meaning's plain
It does not say to folk—remember matins,
Or, mind you fast next Friday!' Why, for this
320   What need of art at all? A skull and bones,
Two bits of stick nailed crosswise, or, what's best,
A bell to chime the hour with, does as well.
I painted a Saint Laurence° six months since
At Prato,° splashed the fresco in fine style:
'How looks my painting, now the scaffold's down?'
I ask a brother: 'Hugely,' he returns—
'Already not one phiz of your three slaves
Who turn the Deacon off his toasted side,
But's scratched and prodded to our heart's content,
330   The pious people have so eased their own
With coming to say prayers there in a rage:
We get on fast to see the bricks beneath.
Expect another job this time next year,
For piety and religion grow in the crowd—
Your painting serves its purpose!' Hang the fools!
—That is—you'll not mistake an idle word
Spoke in a huff by a poor monk, God wot,

cullion's base or vile man   Prato near Florence
Laurence martyr-saint roasted on a grid-iron
in 258

Tasting the air this spicy night which turns
The unaccustomed head like Chianti° wine!
340 Oh, the church knows! don't misreport me, now!
It's natural a poor monk out of bounds
Should have his apt word to excuse himself:
And hearken how I plot to make amends.
I have bethought me: I shall paint a piece
. . . There's for you! Give me six months, then go, see
Something in Sant' Ambrogio's!° Bless the nuns!
They want a cast o' my office° I shall paint
God in the midst, Madonna and her babe,
Ringed by a bowery flowery angel-brood,
350 Lilies and vestments and white faces, sweet
As puff on puff of grated orris-root°
When ladies crowd to Church at midsummer.
And then in the front, of course a saint or two—
Saint John, because he saves the Florentines,
  Saint Ambrose, who puts down in black and white
The convent's friends and gives them a long day,
And Job, I must have him there past mistake,
The man of Uz° (and Us without the z,
Painters who need his patience). Well, all these
360 Secured at their devotion, up shall come
Out of a corner when you least expect,
As one by a dark stair into a great light,   ⌐
Music and talking, who but Lippo! I!—
Mazed, motionless and moonstruck—I'm the man!
Back I shrink—what is this I see and hear?
I, caught up with my monk's things by mistake,
My old serge gown and rope that goes all round,
I; in this presence, this pure company!
Where's a hole, where's a corner for escape?
370 Then steps a sweet angelic slip of a thing
Forward, puts out a soft palm—'Not so fast!'
—Addresses the celestial presence, 'nay—
He made you and devised you, after all,
Though he's none of you! Could Saint John° there draw—
His camel-hair make up a painting-brush?
We come to brother Lippo for all that,
Iste perfecit opus!° So, all smile—
I shuffle sideways with my blushing face
Under the cover of a hundred wings
380 Thrown like a spread of kirtles° when you're gay

Chianti region south of Florence, still famous
for its wine
Sant' Ambrogio's nuns' convent
cast o' my office sample of my work
orris-root iris-root made into perfume

Uz Job's birthplace
John Mark 1:6: "And John was clothed with
camel's hair"
Iste . . . opus This man made the work
kirtles dresses

And play hot cockles,° all the doors being shut,
Till, wholly unexpected, in there pops
The hothead husband! Thus I scuttle off
To some safe bench behind, not letting go
The palm of her, the little lily thing
That spoke the good word for me in the nick,
Like the Prior's niece . . . Saint Lucy°, I would say.
And so all's saved for me, and for the church
A pretty picture gained. Go, six months hence!
390   Your hand, sir, and good-bye: no lights, no lights!
The street's hushed, and I know my own way back,
Don't fear me! There's the grey beginning. Zooks!
1853   1855

A Toccata of Galuppi's°

I

Oh Galuppi, Baldassaro, this is very sad to find!
I can hardly misconceive you; it would prove me deaf and blind;
But although I take your meaning, 'tis with such a heavy mind!

II

Here you come with your old music, and here's all the good it brings.
What, they lived once thus at Venice where the merchants were the kings,
Where Saint Mark's° is, where the Doges° used to wed the sea with rings?°

III

Ay, because the sea's the street there; and 'tis arched by . . . what you call
. . . Shylock's bridge° with houses on it, where they kept the carnival:
I was never out of England°—it's as if I saw it all.

IV

10   Did young people take their pleasure when the sea was warm in May?
Balls and masks begun at midnight, burning ever to mid-day,
When they made up fresh adventures for the morrow, do you say?

hot cockles sexual variant on game of blind-man's buff
Saint Lucy Prior's "niece" who served as model
A Toccata of Galuppi's Baldassare Galuppi (1706–85), Venetian composer, organist at St. Mark's, and renowned in his own day for his light operas. A *toccata* or "touch piece" resembles improvisation in its spirit and movement, and is meant to show off the performer's technique, even as this poem demonstrates Browning's uncanny skill at mingling several voices with their rival tones.

St. Mark's cathedral of Venice
Doges Venice's chief magistrate was called the Doge
rings From Ascension Day, 1000 A.D. on, for several centuries, the Doge annually officiated at the marriage of the Adriatic (as bride) to Venice, by ceremonially tossing a ring into the sea, thus symbolizing Venice's domination of the waters.
bridge the Rialto, spanning the Grand Canal
England Browning's way of making clear that he is not this monologue's speaker

V

Was a lady such a lady, cheeks so round and lips so red,—
On her neck the small face buoyant, like a bell-flower on its bed,
O'er the breast's superb abundance where a man might base his head?

VI

Well, and it was graceful of them—they'd break talk off and afford
—She, to bite her mask's black velvet—he, to finger on his sword,
While you sat and played Toccatas, stately at the clavichord?°

VII

What? Those lesser thirds so plaintive, sixths diminished, sigh on sigh,
20   Told them something? Those suspensions, those solutions—'Must we die?'
Those commiserating sevenths°—'Life might last! we can but try!'

VIII

'Were you happy?'—'Yes.'—'And are you still as happy?'—'Yes. And you?'
—'Then, more kisses!'—'Did I stop them, when a million seemed so few?'
Hark, the dominant's persistence till it must be answered to!

IX

So, an octave struck the answer. Oh, they praised you, I dare say!
'Brave Galuppi! that was music! good alike at grave and gay!
I can always leave off talking when I hear a master play!'

X

Then they left you for their pleasure: till in due time, one by one,
Some with lives that came to nothing, some with deeds as well undone,
30   Death stepped tacitly and took them where they never see the sun.

XI

But when I sit down to reason, think to take my stand nor swerve,
While I triumph o'er a secret wrung from nature's close reserve,°
In you come with your cold music till I creep through every nerve.

XII

Yes, you, like a ghostly cricket, creaking where a house was burned:
'Dust and ashes, dead and done with, Venice spent what Venice earned.
The soul, doubtless, is immortal—where a soul can be discerned.

XIII

'Yours for instance: you know physics, something of geology,
Mathematics are your pastime; souls shall rise in their degree;
Butterflies may dread extinction,—you'll not die, it cannot be!

clavichord stringed keyboard instrument; precursor of the piano
sevenths The intervals, and the other musical terms employed, are brilliantly explained by Browning's own implicit comments.
But when . . . reserve The speaker may be a scientist or metaphysician, or simply a cultivated man actively interested in the advances of 19th-century science; either way he tries to abide in an intellectual compromise that seeks natural evidences for immortality, but Galuppi and his public knew better in one way, and Browning (whose faith transcends mere nature) in another.

XIV

40   'As for Venice and her people, merely born to bloom and drop,
Here on earth they bore their fruitage, mirth and folly were the crop:
What of soul was left, I wonder, when the kissing had to stop?

XV

'Dust and ashes!' So you creak it, and I want the heart to scold.
Dear dead women, with such hair, too—what's become of all the gold
Used to hang and brush their bosoms? I feel chilly and grown old.
1847   1855

By the Fire-side

I

How well I know what I mean to do
    When the long dark autumn-evenings come
And where, my soul, is thy pleasant hue?
    With the music of all thy voices, dumb
In life's November too!

II

I shall be found by the fire, suppose,
    O'er a great wise book as beseemeth age,
While the shutters flap as the cross-wind blows
    And I turn the page, and I turn the page,
10   Not verse now, only prose!

III

Till the young ones whisper, finger on lip,
    'There he is at it, deep in Greek:
Now then, or never, out we slip
    To cut from the hazels by the creek
A mainmast for our ship!'

IV

I shall be at it indeed, my friends:
    Greek puts already on either side
Such a branch-work forth as soon extends
    To a vista opening far and wide,
20   And I pass out where it ends.

V

The outside-frame like your hazel-trees:
    But the inside-archway widens fast,
And a rarer sort succeeds to these,
    And we slope to Italy at last
And youth, by green degrees.

VI

I follow wherever I am led,
   Knowing so well the leader's hand:
Oh woman-country, wooed not wed,
   Loved all the more by earth's male-lands,
30   Laid to their hearts instead!

VII

Look at the ruined chapel again
   Half-way up in the Alpine gorge!
Is that a tower, I point you plain,
   Or is it a mill, or an iron-forge
Breaks solitude in vain?

VIII

A turn, and we stand in the heart of things;
   The woods are round us, heaped and dim;
From slab to slab how it slips and springs,
   The thread of water single and slim,
40   Through the ravage some torrent brings!

IX

Does it feed the little lake below?
   That speck of white just on its marge
Is Pella;° see, in the evening glow,
   How sharp the silver spear-heads charge
When Alp meets heaven in snow!

X

On our other side is the straight-up rock;
   And a path is kept 'twixt the gorge and it
By boulder-stones where lichens mock
   The marks on a moth, and small ferns fit
50   Their teeth to the polished block.

XI

Oh the sense of the yellow mountain flowers,
   And thorny balls, each three in one,
The chestnuts throw on our path in showers!
   For the drop of the woodland fruit's begun,
These early November hours,

XII

That crimson the creeper's leaf across
   Like a splash of blood, intense, abrupt,

Pella a high peak

O'er a shield else gold from rim to boss,
   And lay it for show on the fairy-cupped
60 Elf-needled mat of moss,

XIII

By the rose-flesh mushrooms, undivulged
   Last evening—nay, in today's first dew
Yon sudden coral nipple bulged,
   Where a freaked fawn-coloured flaky crew
Of toadstools peep indulged.

XIV

And yonder, at foot of the fronting ridge
   That takes the turn to a range beyond,
Is the chapel reached by the one-arched bridge
   Where the water is stopped in a stagnant pond
70 Danced over by the midge.

XV

The chapel and bridge are of stone alike,
   Blackish-grey and mostly wet;
Cut hemp-stalks steep in the narrow dyke.
   See here again, how the lichens fret
And the roots of the ivy strike!

XVI

Poor little place, where its one priest comes
   On a festa-day, if he comes at all,
To the dozen folk from their scattered homes,
   Gathered within that precinct small
80 By the dozen ways one roams—

XVII

To drop from the charcoal-burners' huts,
   Or climb from the hemp-dressers' low shed,
Leave the grange where the woodman stores his nuts,
   Or the wattled cote where the fowlers spread
Their gear on the rock's bare juts.

XVIII

It has some pretension too, this front,
   With its bit of fresco half-moon-wise
Set over the porch, Art's early wont:
   'Tis John in the Desert,° I surmise,
90 But has borne the weather's brunt—

John . . . Desert Saint John the Evangelist died   religious poem, *A Death in the Desert.*
in the desert; see Browning's harsh but strong

XIX

Not from the fault of the builder, though,
    For a pent-house properly projects
Where three carved beams make a certain show,
    Dating—good thought of our architect's—
'Five, six, nine, he lets you know.

XX

And all day long a bird sings there,
    And a stray sheep drinks at the pond at times;
The place is silent and aware;
    It has had its scenes, its joys and crimes,
100 But that is its own affair.

XXI

My perfect wife, my Leonor,°
    Oh heart, my own, oh eyes, mine too,
Whom else could I dare look backward for,
    With whom beside should I dare pursue
The path grey heads abhor?

XXII

For it leads to a crag's sheer edge with them;
    Youth, flowery all the way, there stops—
Not they; age threatens and they contemn,
    Till they reach the gulf wherein youth drops,
110 One inch from life's safe hem!

XXIII

With me, youth led . . . I will speak now,
    No longer watch you as you sit
Reading by fire-light, that great brow
    And the spirit-small hand propping it,
Mutely, my heart knows how—

XXIV

When, if I think but deep enough,
    You are wont to answer, prompt as rhyme;
And you, too, find without rebuff
    Response your soul seeks many a time
120 Piercing its fine flesh-stuff.

XXV

My own, confirm me! If I tread
    This path back, is it not in pride

Leonor affectionate name for Mrs. Browning,
based on Leonora of *Fidelio*, Beethoven's opera

To think how little I dreamed it led
   To an age so blest that, by its side,
Youth seems the waste instead?

XXVI

My own, see where the years conduct!
   At first, 'twas something our two souls
Should mix as mists do; each is sucked
   Into each now: on, the new stream rolls,
130   Whatever rocks obstruct.

XXVII

Think, when our one soul understands
   The great Word° which makes all things new,
When earth breaks up and heaven expands,
   How will the change strike me and you
In the house not made with hands?

XXVIII

Oh I must feel your brain prompt mine,
   Your heart anticipate my heart,
You must be just before, in fine,
   See and make me see, for your part,
140   New depths of the divine!

XXIX

But who could have expected this
   When we two drew together first
Just for the obvious human bliss,
   To satisfy life's daily thirst
With a thing men seldom miss?

XXX

Come back with me to the first of all,
   Let us lean and love it over again,
Let us now forget and now recall,
   Break the rosary in a pearly rain,
150   And gather what we let fall!

XXXI

What did I say?—that a small bird sings
   All day long, save when a brown pair
Of hawks from the wood float with wide wings
   Strained to a bell: 'gainst noon-day glare
You count the streaks and rings.

---

great Word . . . new Revelation 21:5: "Behold, I make all things new"

XXXII

But at afternoon or almost eve
    'Tis better; then the silence grows
To that degree, you half believe
    It must get rid of what it knows,
160 Its bosom does so heave.

XXXIII

Hither we walked then, side by side,
    Arm in arm and cheek to cheek,
And still I questioned or replied,
    While my heart, convulsed to really speak,
Lay choking in its pride.

XXXIV

Silent the crumbling bridge we cross,
    And pity and praise the chapel sweet,
And care about the fresco's loss,
    And wish for our souls a like retreat,
170 And wonder at the moss.

XXXV

Stoop and kneel on the settle under,
    Look through the window's grated square:
Nothing to see! For fear of plunder,
    The cross is down and the altar bare,
As if thieves don't fear thunder.

XXXVI

We stoop and look in through the grate,
    See the little porch and rustic door,
Read duly the dead builder's date;
    Then cross the bridge that we crossed before,
180 Take the path again—but wait!

XXXVII

Oh moment, one and infinite!
    The water slips o'er stock and stone;
The West is tender, hardly bright:
    How grey at once is the evening grown—
One star, its chrysolite!°

XXXVIII

We two stood there with never a third,
    But each by each, as each knew well:
The sights we saw and the sounds we heard,
    The lights and the shades made up a spell
190 Till the trouble grew and stirred.

chrysolite green semi-precious stone

XXXIX

Oh, the little more, and how much it is!
  And the little less, and what worlds away!
How a sound shall quicken content to bliss,
  Or a breath suspend the blood's best play,
And life be a proof of this!

XL

Had she willed it, still had stood the screen
  So light, so sure, 'twixt my love and her:
I could fix her face with a guard between,
  And find her soul as when friends confer,
200 Friends—lovers that might have been.

XLI

For my heart had a touch of the woodland-time,
  Wanting to sleep now over its best.
Shake the whole tree in the summer-prime,
  But bring to the last leaf no such test!
'Hold the last fast!' runs the rhyme.

XLII

For a chance to make your little much,
  To gain a lover and lose a friend,
Venture the tree and a myriad such,
  When nothing you mar but the year can mend:
210 But a last leaf—fear to touch!

XLIII

Yet should it unfasten itself and fall
  Eddying down till it find your face
At some slight wind—best chance of all!
  Be your heart henceforth its dwelling-place
You trembled to forestall!

XLIV

Worth how well, those dark grey eyes,
  That hair so dark and dear, how worth
That a man should strive and agonize,
  And taste a veriest hell on earth
220 For the hope of such a prize!

XLV

You might have turned and tried a man,
  Set him a space to weary and wear,
And prove which suited more your plan,
  His best of hope or his worst despair,
Yet end as he began.

XLVI

But you spared me this, like the heart you are,
   And filled my empty heart at a word.
If two lives join, there is oft a scar,
   They are one and one, with a shadowy third;
230 One near one is too far.

XLVII

A moment after, and hands unseen
   Were hanging the night around us fast;
But we knew that a bar was broken between
   Life and life: we were mixed at last
In spite of the mortal screen.

XLVIII

The forests had done it; there they stood;
   We caught for a moment the powers at play:
They had mingled us so, for once and good,
   Their work was done—we might go or stay,
240 They relapsed to their ancient mood.

XLIX

How the world is made for each of us!
   How all we perceive and know in it
Tends to some moment's product thus,
   When a soul declares itself—to wit,
By its fruit, the thing it does!

L

Be hate that fruit or love that fruit,
   It forwards the general deed of man,
And each of the Many helps to recruit
   The life of the race by a general plan;
250 Each living his own, to boot.

LI

I am named and known by that moment's feat;
   There took my station and degree;
So grew my own small life complete,
   As nature obtained her best of me—
One born to love you, sweet!

LII

And to watch you sink by the fire-side now
   Back again, as you mutely sit
Musing by fire-light, that great brow
   And the spirit-small hand propping it,
260 Yonder, my heart knows how!

LIII

So, earth has gained by one man the more,
  And the gain of earth must be heaven's gain too;
And the whole is well worth thinking o'er
  When autumn comes: which I mean to do
One day, as I said before.
1853   1855

'Childe Roland to the Dark Tower Came'

This nightmare poem, according to Browning, had no overt allegorical purpose, but the phantasmagoria is so powerful as to invite many allegorizings. W.C. DeVane traced much of the landscape to one chapter of a book Browning had memorized as a boy, Gerard de Lairesse's *The Art of Painting in All Its Branches*. The chapter's title, "Of Things Deformed and Broken," might be a motto to the poem. However the poem is interpreted, its universal appeal seems to center upon its vision of a willfully ruined quester, whose own strength of imagination has become a deforming and breaking agent, and who calls into question the meaningfulness of all premeditated human action. The relation of Childe Roland to his band of brothers, the questers who failed one by one before him, may suggest the relation of Browning to his own poetic precursors, and prefigures the relation between the hero and the cowards in Yeats's death poem, *Cuchulain Comforted*.

The title is taken from Shakespeare's *King Lear* (III.iv.173). A "childe" is a well-born youth who is still a candidate for knighthood.

'Childe Roland to the Dark Tower Came'

(See Edgar's Song in *Lear*)

I

My first thought was, he lied in every word,
  That hoary cripple, with malicious eye
  Askance to watch the working of his lie
On mine, and mouth scarce able to afford
Suppression of the glee, that pursed and scored
  Its edge, at one more victim gained thereby.

II

What else should he be set for, with his staff?
  What, save to waylay with his lies, ensnare
  All travellers who might find him posted there,
And ask the road? I guessed what skull-like laugh
Would break, what crutch 'gin° write my epitaph
  For pastime in the dusty thoroughfare,

'gin begin to

III

If at his counsel I should turn aside
  Into that ominous tract which, all agree,
  Hides the Dark Tower. Yet acquiescingly
I did turn as he pointed: neither pride
Nor hope rekindling at the end descried,
  So much as gladness that some end might be.

IV

For, what with my whole world-wide wandering,
20   What with my search drawn out through years, my hope
  Dwindled into a ghost not fit to cope
With that obstreperous joy success would bring,—
I hardly tried now to rebuke the spring
  My heart made, finding failure in its scope.

V

As when a sick man very near to death
  Seems dead indeed, and feels begin and end
  The tears and takes the farewell of each friend,
And hears one bid the other go, draw breath
  Freelier outside, ('since all is o'er,' he saith,
30   'And the blow fallen no grieving can amend');

VI

While some discuss if near the other graves
  Be room enough for this, and when a day
  Suits best for carrying the corpse away,
With care about the banners, scarves and staves:
And still the man hears all, and only craves
  He may not shame such tender love and stay.

VII

Thus, I had so long suffered in this quest,
  Heard failure prophesied so oft, been writ
  So many times among 'The Band'—to wit,
40   The knights who to the Dark Tower's search addressed
Their steps—that just to fail as they, seemed best,
  And all the doubt was now—should I be fit?

VIII

So, quiet as despair, I turned from him,
  That hateful cripple, out of his highway
  Into the path he pointed. All the day
Had been a dreary one at best, and dim
Was settling to its close, yet shot one grim
  Red leer to see the plain catch its estray.°

estray potential victim who has strayed

IX

For mark! no sooner was I fairly found
50   Pledged to the plain, after a pace or two,
    Than, pausing to throw backward a last view
O'er the safe road, 'twas gone; grey plain all round:
Nothing but plain to the horizon's bound.
    I might go on; nought else remained to do.

X

So, on I went. I think I never saw
    Such starved ignoble nature; nothing throve:
    For flowers—as well expect a cedar grove!
But cockle, spurge,° according to their law
Might propagate their kind, with none to awe,
60   You'd think; a burr had been a treasure-trove.

XI

No! penury, inertness and grimace,
    In some strange sort, were the land's portion. 'See
    Or shut your eyes,' said Nature peevishly,
'It nothing skills: I cannot help my case:
'Tis the Last Judgment's fire must cure this place,
    Calcine° its clods and set my prisoners free.'

XII

If there pushed any ragged thistle-stalk
    Above its mates, the head was chopped; the bents°
    Were jealous else. What made those holes and rents
70   In the dock's harsh swarth leaves, bruised as to baulk
All hope of greenness? 'tis a brute must walk
    Pashing° their life out, with a brute's intents.

XIII

As for the grass, it grew as scant as hair
    In leprosy; thin dry blades pricked the mud
    Which underneath looked kneaded up with blood.
One stiff blind horse, his every bone a-stare,
Stood stupefied, however he came there:
    Thrust out past service from the devil's stud!

XIV

Alive? he might be dead for aught I know,
80   With that red gaunt and colloped° neck a-strain,
    And shut eyes underneath the rusty mane;
Seldom went such grotesqueness with such woe;

cockle, spurge weeds
Calcine melt to a powder
bents very coarse grasses

Pashing trampling down
colloped ridged

I never saw a brute I hated so;
   He must be wicked to deserve such pain.

      xv

I shut my eyes and turned them on my heart.
   As a man calls for wine before he fights,
   I asked one draught of earlier, happier sights,
Ere fitly I could hope to play my part.
Think first, fight afterwards—the soldier's art:
90   One taste of the old time sets all to rights.

      xvi

Not it! I fancied Cuthbert's reddening face
   Beneath its garniture of curly gold,
   Dear fellow, till I almost felt him fold
An arm in mine to fix me to the place,
That way he used. Alas, one night's disgrace!
   Out went my heart's new fire and left it cold.

      xvii

Giles then, the soul of honour—there he stands
   Frank as ten years ago when knighted first.
   What honest men should dare (he said) he durst.
100 Good—but the scene shifts—faugh! what hangman-hands
Pin to his breast a parchment? his own bands
   Read it. Poor traitor, spit upon and curst!

      xviii

Better this present than a past like that;
   Back therefore to my darkening path again!
   No sound, no sight as far as eye could strain.
Will the night send a howlet or a bat?
I asked: when something on the dismal flat
   Came to arrest my thoughts and change their train.

      xix

A sudden little river crossed my path
110 As unexpected as a serpent comes.
   No sluggish tide congenial to the glooms;
This, as it frothed by, might have been a bath
For the fiend's glowing hoof—to see the wrath
   Of its black eddy bespate° with flakes and spumes.

      xx

So petty yet so spiteful! All along,
   Low scrubby alders kneeled down over it;
   Drenched willows flung them headlong in a fit

bespate bespattered

Of mute despair, a suicidal throng:
The river which had done them all the wrong,
120   Whate'er that was, rolled by, deterred no whit.

XXI

Which, while I forded,—good saints, how I feared
    To set my foot upon a dead man's cheek,
    Each step, or feel the spear I thrust to seek
For hollows, tangled in his hair or beard!
—It may have been a water-rat I speared,
    But, ugh! it sounded like a baby's shriek.

XXII

Glad was I when I reached the other bank.
    Now for a better country. Vain presage!
    Who were the strugglers, what war did they wage,
130   Whose savage trample thus could pad the dank
Soil to a plash? Toads in a poisoned tank,
    Or wild cats in a red-hot iron cage—

XXIII

The fight must so have seemed in that fell cirque.
    What penned them there, with all the plain to choose?
    No foot-print leading to the horrid mews,
None out of it. Mad brewage set to work
Their brains, no doubt, like galley-slaves the Turk
    Pits for his pastime, Christians against Jews.

XXIV

And more than that—a furlong on—why, there!
140   What bad use was that engine for, that wheel,
    Or brake, not wheel—that harrow fit to reel
Men's bodies out like silk? with all the air
Of Tophet's° tool, on earth left unaware,
    Or brought to sharpen its rusty teeth of steel.

XXV

Then came a bit of stubbed ground, once a wood,
    Next a marsh, it would seem, and now mere earth
    Desperate and done with; (so a fool finds mirth,
Makes a thing and then mars it, till his mood
Changes and off he goes!) within a rood°—
150   Bog, clay and rubble, sand and stark black dearth.

XXVI

Now blotches rankling, coloured gay and grim,
    Now patches where some leanness of the soil's

Tophet's Hebrew for Hell   **rood** quarter-acre

Broke into moss or substances like boils;
Then came some palsied oak, a cleft in him
Like a distorted mouth that splits its rim
   Gaping at death, and dies while it recoils.

XXVII

And just as far as ever from the end!
   Nought in the distance but the evening, nought
   To point my footstep further! At the thought,
160   A great black bird, Apollyon's° bosom-friend,
   Sailed past, nor beat his wide wing dragon-penned°
   That brushed my cap—perchance the guide I sought.

XXVIII

For, looking up, aware I somehow grew,
   'Spite of the dusk, the plain had given place
   All round to mountains—with such name to grace
Mere ugly heights and heaps now stolen in view.
   How thus they had surprised me,—solve it, you!
   How to get from them was no clearer case.

XXIX

Yet half I seemed to recognize some trick
170   Of mischief happened to me, God knows when—
   In a bad dream perhaps. Here ended, then,
Progress this way. When, in the very nick
Of giving up, one time more, came a click
   As when a trap shuts—you're inside the den!

XXX

Burningly it came on me all at once,
   This was the place! those two hills on the right,
   Crouched like two bulls locked horn in horn in fight;
While to the left, a tall scalped mountain . . . Dunce,
Dotard, a-dozing at the very nonce,
180   After a life spent training for the sight!

XXXI

What in the midst lay but the Tower itself?
   The round squat turret, blind as the fool's heart,
   Built of brown stone, without a counterpart
In the whole world. The tempest's mocking elf
Points to the shipman thus the unseen shelf
   He strikes on, only when the timbers start.

Apollyon Revelation 9:11: "an angel of the   **dragon-penned** dragon-winged
bottomless pit, ... Apollyon"

XXXII

Not see? because of night perhaps?—why, day
   Came back again for that! before it left,
   The dying sunset kindled through a cleft:
190 The hills, like giants at a hunting, lay,
Chin upon hand, to see the game at bay,—
'Now stab and end the creature—to the heft!'

XXXIII

Not hear? when noise was everywhere! it tolled
   Increasing like a bell. Names in my ears
   Of all the lost adventurers my peers,—
How such a one was strong, and such was bold,
And such was fortunate, yet each of old
Lost, lost! one moment knelled the woe of years.

XXXIV

There they stood, ranged along the hill-sides, met
200   To view the last of me, a living frame
   For one more picture! in a sheet of flame
I saw them and I knew them all. And yet
Dauntless the slug-horn° to my lips I set,
   And blew. '*Childe Roland to the Dark Tower came.*'
  1852   1855

How It Strikes a Contemporary°

I only knew one poet in my life:
And this, or something like it, was his way.

   You saw go up and down Valladolid,°
A man of mark, to know next time you saw.
His very serviceable suit of black
Was courtly once and conscientious still,
And many might have worn it, though none did:
The cloak, that somewhat shone and showed the threads,
Had purpose, and the ruff, significance.
10 He walked and tapped the pavement with his cane,

slug-horn a word appearing only in the 18th-century poet Chatterton; his mistake of an archaic spelling of "slogan" to mean a "trumpet"
How It Strikes a Contemporary This poem's imaginary "poet of Valladolid" represents Browning himself, primarily in his imaginative stance, but Browning increasingly (after his wife's death) was to become a fiercely socializing man-about-town. When Browning wrote this poem, he was preparing his essay on Shelley, and rereading both Shelley and Shakespeare. Behind "How It Strikes . . ." are Shelley's suggestion that "poets are the un-acknowledged legislators of the world" and King Lear's "As if we were God's spies." A few years after writing this poem, Browning wrote to Ruskin, "A poet's affair is with God, to whom he is accountable, and of whom is his reward. . . ." Like Browning, the apparently lighthearted "poet of Valladolid" beholds the world and mankind "in their actual state of perfection in imperfection" ("Essay on Shelley") and understands that (as Wallace Stevens liked to observe) the imperfect is our paradise.
Valladolid city in north-central Spain, where presumably Browning had never been

Scenting the world, looking it full in face,
An old dog, bald and blindish, at his heels.
They turned up, now, the alley by the church,
That leads nowhither; now, they breathed themselves°
On the main promenade just at the wrong time:
You'd come upon his scrutinizing hat,
Making a peaked shade blacker than itself
Against the single window spared some house
Intact yet with its mouldered Moorish work,—
20 Or else surprise the ferrel° of his stick
Trying the mortar's temper 'tween the chinks
Of some new shop a-building, French and fine.
He stood and watched the cobbler at his trade,
The man who slices lemons into drink,
The coffee-roaster's brazier, and the boys
That volunteer to help him turn its winch.
He glanced o'er books on stalls with half an eye,
And fly-leaf ballads on the vendor's string,
And broad-edge bold-print posters by the wall.
30 He took such cognizance of men and things,
If any beat a horse, you felt he saw;
If any cursed a woman, he took note;
Yet stared at nobody,—you stared at him,
And found, less to your pleasure than surprise,
He seemed to know you and expect as much.
So, next time that a neighbour's tongue was loosed,
It marked the shameful and notorious fact,
We had among us, not so much a spy,
As a recording chief-inquisitor,
40 The town's true master if the town but knew!
We merely kept a governor for form,
While this man walked about and took account
Of all thought, said and acted, then went home,
And wrote it fully to our Lord the King°
Who has an itch to know things, he knows why,
And reads them in his bedroom of a night.
Oh, you might smile! there wanted not a touch,
A tang of . . . well, it was not wholly ease
As back into your mind the man's look came.
50 Stricken in years a little,—such a brow
His eyes had to live under!—clear as flint
On either side the formidable nose
Curved, cut and coloured like an eagle's claw.
Had he to do with A.'s surprising fate?
When altogether old B. disappeared
And young C. got his mistress,—was't our friend,

breathed themselves walked to take the air   King ultimately, God
ferrel metal point

His letter to the King, that did it all?
What paid the bloodless man for so much pains?
Our Lord the King has favourites manifold,
60   And shifts his ministry some once a month;
Our city gets new governors at whiles,—
But never word or sign, that I could hear,
Notified to this man about the streets
The King's approval of those letters conned
The last thing duly at the dead of night.
Did the man love his office? Frowned our Lord,
Exhorting when none heard—'Beseech me not!
Too far above my people,—beneath me!
I set the watch,—how should the people know?
70   Forget them, keep me all the more in mind!'
Was some such understanding 'twixt the two?

    I found no truth in one report at least—
That if you tracked him to his home, down lanes
Beyond the Jewry,° and as clean to pace,
You found he ate his supper in a room
Blazing with lights, four Titians° on the wall,
And twenty naked girls to change his plate!
Poor man, he lived another kind of life
In that new stuccoed third house by the bridge,
80   Fresh-painted, rather smart than otherwise!
The whole street might o'erlook him as he sat,
Leg crossing leg, one foot on the dog's back,
Playing a decent cribbage with his maid
(Jacynth, you're sure her name was) o'er the cheese
And fruit, three red halves of starved winter-pears,
Or treat of radishes in April. Nine,
Ten, struck the church clock, straight to bed went he.

    My father, like the man of sense he was,
Would point him out to me a dozen times;
90   ' 'St—'St,' he'd whisper, 'the Corregidor!'°
I had been used to think that personage
Was one with lacquered breeches, lustrous belt,
And feathers like a forest in his hat,
Who blew a trumpet and proclaimed the news,
Announced the bull-fights, gave each church its turn,
And memorized the miracle in vogue!
He had a great observance from us boys;
We were in error; that was not the man.

    I'd like now, yet had haply been afraid,
100   To have just looked, when this man came to die,

Jewry Jewish quarter of the city   **Corregidor** chief magistrate
Titians paintings by Titian, Venetian (1477–1576)

And seen who lined the clean gay garret-sides
And stood about the neat low truckle-bed,°
With the heavenly manner of relieving guard.
Here had been, mark, the general-in-chief,
Through a whole campaign of the world's life and death,
Doing the King's work all the dim day long,
In his old coat and up to knees in mud,
Smoked like a herring, dining on a crust,—
And, now the day was won, relieved at once!
110 No further show or need for that old coat,
You are sure, for one thing! Bless us, all the while
How sprucely we are dressed out, you and I!
A second, and the angels alter that.
Well, I could never write a verse,—could you?
Let's to the Prado° and make the most of time.
1851–52   1855

Master Hugues of Saxe-Gotha°

I

Hist, but a word, fair and soft!
    Forth and be judged, Master Hugues!
Answer the question I've put you so oft:—
    What do you mean by your mountainous fugues?°
See, we're alone in the loft,—

II

I, the poor organist here,
    Hugues, the composer of note,
Dead though, and done with, this many a year:
    Let's have a colloquy, something to quote,
10   Make the world prick up its ear!

III

See, the church empties apace:
    Fast they extinguish the lights.
Hallo there, sacristan!° Five minutes' grace!
    Here's a crank pedal wants setting to rights,
Baulks one of holding the base.

truckle-bed trundle-bed
Prado the principal street of the city
Master Hugues of Saxe-Gotha Master Hugues
is an imaginary composer, a cumbersome imitator of Bach, who came from Saxe-Gotha. But
the poem is scarcely interested in him. What
it reveals, unforgettably, is the questing imagination of the "poor organist" who indeed does
"carry the moon" in his pocket.

fugues The root meaning is "flight"; a musical
form in which successive voices take up a
melody, each voice entering before its predecessor has completed the melody; frequently
intricate development ensues, concluded by a
return to the original key.
sacristan church custodian

IV

See, our huge house of the sounds,
  Hushing its hundreds at once,
Bids the last loiterer back to his bounds!
  —O you may challenge them, not a response
20 Get the church-saints on their rounds!

V

(Saints go their rounds, who shall doubt?
  —March, with the moon to admire,
Up nave, down chancel, turn transept about,
  Supervise all betwixt pavement and spire,
Put rats and mice to the rout—

VI

Aloys and Jurien and Just°—
  Order things back to their place,
Have a sharp eye lest the candlesticks rust,
  Rub the church-plate, darn the sacrament-lace,
30 Clear the desk-velvet of dust.)

VII

Here's your book, younger folks shelve!
  Played I not off-hand and runningly,
Just now, your masterpiece, hard number twelve?
  Here's what should strike, could one handle it cunningly:
Help the axe, give it a helve!°

VIII

Page after page as I played,
  Every bar's rest, where one wipes
Sweat from one's brow, I looked up and surveyed,
  O'er my three claviers,° yon forest of pipes
40 Whence you still peeped in the shade.

IX

Sure you were wishful to speak?
  You, with brow ruled like a score,
Yes, and eyes buried in pits on each cheek,
  Like two great breves,° as they wrote them of yore,
Each side that bar, your straight beak!

X

Sure you said—'Good, the mere notes!
  Still, couldst thou take my intent,

Aloys . . . Just patron saints
helve handle
claviers here, banked keyboards

breves longest notes in the score, indicated by
square marks

Know what procured me our Company's votes—
   A master were lauded and sciolists shent,°
50 Parted the sheep from the goats!'

XI

Well then, speak up, never flinch!
   Quick, ere my candle's a snuff
—Burnt, do you see? to its uttermost inch—
   I believe in you, but that's not enough:
Give my conviction a clinch!

XII

First you deliver your phrase
   —Nothing propound, that I see,
Fit in itself for much blame or much praise—
   Answered no less, where no answer needs be:
60 Off start the Two on their ways.

XIII

Straight must a Third interpose,
   Volunteer needlessly help;
In strikes a Fourth, a Fifth thrusts in his nose,
   So the cry's open, the kennel's a-yelp,
Argument's hot to the close.

XIV

One dissertates, he is candid;
   Two must discept,°—has distinguished;
Three helps the couple, if ever yet man did;
   Four protests; Five makes a dart at the thing wished:
70 Back to One, goes the case bandied.

XV

One says his say with a difference;
   More of expounding, explaining!
All now is wrangle, abuse, and vociferance;
   Now there's a truce, all's subdued, self-restraining;
Five, though, stands out all the stiffer hence.

XVI

One is incisive, corrosive;
   Two retorts, nettled, curt, crepitant;
Three makes rejoinder, expansive, explosive;
   Four overbears them all, strident and strepitant:
80 Five . . . O Danaides, O Sieve!°

---

sciolists shent scholarly pretenders shamed
discept differ
Sieve The Danaides, daughters of Danaus, slew
their bridegrooms on their wedding night, and
were condemned eternally to Tartarus, where
they pour water through a sieve.

XVII

Now, they ply axes and crowbars;
    Now, they prick pins at a tissue
Fine as a skein of the casuist Escobar's°
    Worked on the bone of a lie. To what issue?
    Where is our gain at the Two-bars?

XVIII

Est fuga, volvitur rota.°
    On we drift: where looms the dim port?
One, Two, Three, Four, Five, contribute their quota;
    Something is gained, if one caught but the import—
90   Show it us, Hugues of Saxe-Gotha!

XIX

What with affirming, denying,
    Holding, risposting,° subjoining,
All's like . . . it's like . . . for an instance I'm trying . . .
    There! See our roof, its gilt moulding and groining
    Under those spider-webs lying!

XX

So your fugue broadens and thickens,
    Greatens and deepens and lengthens,
Till we exclaim—'But where's music, the dickens?
    Blot ye the gold, while your spider-web strengthens
100   —Blacked to the stoutest of tickens?'°

XXI

I for man's effort am zealous:
    Prove me such censure unfounded!
Seems it surprising a lover grows jealous—
    Hopes 'twas for something, his organ-pipes sounded,
    Tiring three boys at the bellows?

XXII

Is it your moral of Life?
    Such a web, simple and subtle,
Weave we on earth here in impotent strife,
    Backward and forward each throwing his shuttle,
110   Death ending all with a knife?

XXIII

Over our heads truth and nature—
    Still our life's zigzags and dodges,

Escobar's Escobar y Mendoza (1589–1669),
Jesuit writer
Est fuga, volvitur rota It is a flight, the wheel
revolves.

risposting delivering a counter-stroke
tickens mattress ticking

Ins and outs, weaving a new legislature—
   God's gold just shining its last where that lodges,
Palled beneath man's usurpature.

XXIV

So we o'ershroud stars and roses,
   Cherub and trophy and garland;
Nothings grow something which quietly closes
   Heaven's earnest eye: not a glimpse of the far land
120   Gets through our comments and glozes.

XXV

Ah but traditions, inventions,
   (Say we and make up a visage)
So many men with such various intentions,
   Down the past ages, must know more than this age!
Leave we the web its dimensions!

XXVI

Who thinks Hugues wrote for the deaf,
   Proved a mere mountain in labour?
Better submit; try again; what's the clef?°
   'Faith, 'tis no trifle for pipe and for tabor°—
130   Four flats, the minor in F.

XXVII

Friend, your fugue taxes the finger:
   Learning it once, who would lose it?
Yet all the while a misgiving will linger,
   Truth's golden o'er us although we refuse it—
Nature, through cobwebs we string her.

XXVIII

Hugues! I advise *meâ pœnâ*°
   (Counterpoint glares like a Gorgon°)
Bid One, Two, Three, Four, Five, clear the arena!
   Say the word, straight I unstop the full-organ,
140   Blare out the *mode Palestrina.*°

XXIX

While in the roof, if I'm right there,
   . . . Lo you, the wick in the socket!
Hallo, you sacristan, show us a light there!
   Down it dips, gone like a rocket.

clef pitch indication
tabor small drum
meâ pœnâ at my risk
Gorgon one of three snaky-locked ladies whose
glance turned men to stone

mode Palestrina the manner of the great Italian
composer Palestrina (1524–94), who rebelled
against the decadence of compositional artifices
and intricacies, and restored a gracious simplicity to contrapuntal music

What, you want, do you, to come unawares,
Sweeping the church up for first morning-prayers,
And find a poor devil has ended his cares
At the foot of your rotten-runged rat-riddled stairs?
    Do I carry the moon in my pocket?
    1852–53   1855

Memorabilia°

I

Ah, did you once see Shelley plain,
    And did he stop and speak to you,
And did you speak to him again?
    How strange it seems and new!

II

But you were living before that,
    And also you are living after;
And the memory I started at—
    My starting moves your laughter.

III

I crossed a moor, with a name of its own
    And a certain use in the world no doubt,
Yet a hand's-breadth of it shines alone
    'Mid the blank miles round about:

IV

For there I picked up on the heather
    And there I put inside my breast
A moulted feather, an eagle-feather!
    Well, I forget the rest.
    1851   1855

Andrea del Sarto

Andrea, the son of a Florentine tailor (hence "del Sarto"), lived from 1486 until 1531, when he died of the plague, deserted by his wife and by everyone else. Vasari, who was Browning's major source for Andrea's life (see *The Lives of the Most Eminent Painters, Sculptors and Architects*), and who had been Andrea's pupil, sums up the mingled glory and sorrow of this painter:

Memorabilia The title, which means "things worth remembering," hardly conveys the importance of this little poem for the understanding of Browning's relation to Shelley, his prime precursor. A friend recorded Browning as saying "with characteristic vehemence: 'I was one day in the shop of Hodgson, the well-known London bookseller, when a stranger . . . spoke of something that Shelley had once said to him. Suddenly the stranger paused, and burst into laughter as he observed me staring at him with blanched face; and,' the poet continued, 'I still vividly remember how strangely the presence of a man who had seen and spoken with Shelley affected me.'"

. . . that truly excellent Andrea del Sarto, in whom art and nature combined to show all that may be done in painting, when design, colouring and invention unite in one and the same person. Had this master possessed a somewhat bolder and more elevated mind; had he been as much distinguished for higher qualifications as he was for genius and depth of judgment in the art he practiced, he would beyond all doubt, have been without an equal. But there was a certain timidity of mind, a sort of diffidence and want of force in his nature, which rendered it impossible that those evidences of ardour and animation, which are proper to the more exalted character, should ever appear in him; nor did he at any time display one particle of that elevation which, could it have been added to the advantages wherewith he was endowed, would have rendered him a truly divine painter: wherefore the works of Andrea are wanting in those ornaments of grandeur, richness, and force, which appear so conspicuously in those of many other masters.

In this deep study of a deliberate artistic self-crippling, Browning gives us a dramatic speaker who has arranged cunningly his own ruin. Andrea has chosen a wife who he knows will betray him, and an existence which must compromise his own vision as a painter. Fearing to fail by attempting greatness, Andrea is content to have been his own knowing parody of what he might have been.

Andrea del Sarto

(Called 'The Faultless Painter')

But do not let us quarrel any more,
No, my Lucrezia; bear with me for once:
Sit down and all shall happen as you wish.
You turn your face, but does it bring your heart?
I'll work then for your friend's friend, never fear,
Treat his own subject after his own way,
Fix his own time, accept too his own price,
And shut the money into this small hand
When next it takes mine. Will it? tenderly?
Oh, I'll content him,—but tomorrow, Love!
I often am much wearier than you think,
This evening more than usual, and it seems
As if—forgive now—should you let me sit
Here by the window with your hand in mine
And look a half-hour forth on Fiesole,°
Both of one mind, as married people use,
Quietly, quietly the evening through,
I might get up tomorrow to my work
Cheerful and fresh as ever. Let us try.
Tomorrow, how you shall be glad for this!
Your soft hand is a woman of itself,
And mine the man's bared breast she curls inside.
Don't count the time lost, neither; you must serve
For each of the five pictures we require:

Fiesole town on hill outside Florence

It saves a model. So! keep looking so—
My serpentining beauty, rounds on rounds!
—How could you ever prick those perfect ears,
Even to put the pearl there! oh, so sweet—
My face, my moon, my everybody's moon,
30   Which everybody looks on and calls his,
And, I suppose, is looked on by in turn,
While she looks—no one's: very dear, no less.
You smile? why, there's my picture ready made,
There's what we painters call our harmony!
A common greyness silvers everything,—
All in a twilight, you and I alike
—You, at the point of your first pride in me
(That's gone you know),—but I, at every point;
My youth, my hope, my art, being all toned down
40   To yonder sober pleasant Fiesole.
There's the bell clinking from the chapel-top;
That length of convent-wall across the way
Holds the trees safer, huddled more inside;
The last monk leaves the garden; days decrease,
And autumn grows, autumn in everything.
Eh? the whole seems to fall into a shape
As if I saw alike my work and self
And all that I was born to be and do,
A twilight-piece. Love, we are in God's hand.
50   How strange now, looks the life he makes us lead;
So free we seem, so fettered fast we are!
I feel he laid the fetter: let it lie!
This chamber for example—turn your head—
All that's behind us! You don't understand
Nor care to understand about my art,
But you can hear at least when people speak:
And that cartoon,° the second from the door
—It is the thing, Love! so such things should be—
Behold Madonna!—I am bold to say.
60   I can do with my pencil what I know,
What I see, what at bottom of my heart
I wish for, if I ever wish so deep—
Do easily, too—when I say, perfectly,
I do not boast, perhaps: yourself are judge,
Who listened to the Legate's° talk last week,
And just as much they used to say in France.
At any rate 'tis easy, all of it!
No sketches first, no studies, that's long past:
I do what many dream of, all their lives,
70   —Dream? strive to do, and agonize to do,

cartoon drawing preliminary to a fresco   **Legate's** papal representative

And fail in doing. I could count twenty such
On twice your fingers, and not leave this town,
Who strive—you don't know how the others strive
To paint a little thing like that you smeared
Carelessly passing with your robes afloat,—
Yet do much less, so much less, Someone° says,
(I know his name, no matter)—so much less!
Well, less is more, Lucrezia: I am judged.
There burns a truer light of God in them.
80 In their vexed beating stuffed and stopped-up brain,
Heart, or whate'er else, than goes on to prompt
This low-pulsed forthright craftsman's hand of mine.
Their works drop groundward, but themselves, I know,
Reach many a time a heaven that's shut to me,
Enter and take their place there sure enough,
Though they come back and cannot tell the world.
My works are nearer heaven, but I sit here.
The sudden blood of these men! at a word—
Praise them, it boils, or blame them, it boils too.
90 I, painting from myself and to myself,
Know what I do, am unmoved by men's blame
Or their praise either. Somebody remarks
Morello's outline° there is wrongly traced,
His hue mistaken; what of that? or else,
Rightly traced and well ordered; what of that?
Speak as they please, what does the mountain care?
Ah, but a man's reach should exceed his grasp,
Or what's a heaven for? All is silver-grey
Placid and perfect with my art: the worse!
100 I know both what I want and what might gain,
And yet how profitless to know, to sigh
'Had I been two, another and myself,
Our head would have o'erlooked the world!' No doubt.
Yonder's a work now, of that famous youth
The Urbinate° who died five years ago.
('Tis copied, George Vasari sent it me.)
Well, I can fancy how he did it all,
Pouring his soul, with kings and popes to see,
Reaching, that heaven might so replenish him,
110 Above and through his art—for it gives way;
That arm is wrongly put—and there again—
A fault to pardon in the drawing's lines,
Its body, so to speak; its soul is right,
He means right—that, a child may understand.
Still, what an arm! and I could alter it:

Someone Michelangelo Buonarotti (1475–1564)

Morello's outline a mountain in the Apennines, north of Florence

Urbinate Raphael (1483–1520), born in Urbino

But all the play, the insight and the stretch—
Out of me, out of me! And wherefore out?
Had you enjoined them on me, given me soul,
We might have risen to Rafael, I and you!
120 Nay, Love, you did give all I asked, I think—
More than I merit, yes, by many times.
But had you—oh, with the same perfect brow,
And perfect eyes, and more than perfect mouth,
And the low voice my soul hears, as a bird
The fowler's pipe, and follows to the snare—
Had you, with these the same, but brought a mind!
Some women do so. Had the mouth there urged
'God and the glory! never care for gain.
The present by the future, what is that?
130 Live for fame, side by side with Agnolo!°
Rafael is waiting: up to God, all three!'
I might have done it for you. So it seems:
Perhaps not. All is as God over-rules.
Besides, incentives come from the soul's self;
The rest avail not. Why do I need you?
What wife had Rafael, or has Agnolo?
In this world, who can do a thing, will not;
And who would do it, cannot, I perceive:
Yet the will's somewhat—somewhat, too, the power—
140 And thus we half-men struggle. At the end,
God, I conclude, compensates, punishes.
'Tis safer for me, if the award be strict,
That I am something underrated here,
Poor this long while, despised, to speak the truth.
I dared not, do you know, leave home all day,
For fear of chancing on the Paris lords.
The best is when they pass and look aside;
But they speak sometimes; I must bear it all.
Well may they speak! That Francis,° that first time,
150 And that long festal year at Fontainebleau!
I surely then could sometimes leave the ground,
Put on the glory, Rafael's daily wear,
· In that humane great monarch's golden look,—
One finger in his beard or twisted curl
Over his mouth's good mark that made the smile,
One arm about my shoulder, round my neck,
The jingle of his gold chain in my ear,
I painting proudly with his breath on me,
All his court round him, seeing with his eyes,
160 Such frank French eyes, and such a fire of souls
Profuse, my hand kept plying by those hearts,—

Agnolo Michelangelo   **Francis** King Francis I of France (1494–1547),
whose money Andrea had embezzled

And, best of all, this, this, this face beyond,
This in the background, waiting on my work,
To crown the issue with a last reward!
A good time, was it not, my kingly days?
And had you not grown restless . . . but I know—
'Tis done and past; 'twas right, my instinct said;
Too live the life grew, golden and not grey,
And I'm the weak-eyed bat no sun should tempt
170   Out of the grange° whose four walls make his world.
How could it end in any other way?
You called me, and I came home to your heart.
The triumph was—to reach and stay there; since
I reached it ere the triumph, what is lost?
Let my hands frame your face in your hair's gold,
You beautiful Lucrezia that are mine!
'Rafael did this, Andrea painted that;
The Roman's° is the better when you pray,
But still the other's Virgin was his wife—'
180   Men will excuse me. I am glad to judge
Both pictures in your presence; clearer grows
My better fortune, I resolve to think.
For, do you know, Lucrezia, as God lives,
Said one day Agnolo, his very self,
To Rafael . . . I have known it all these years . . .
(When the young man was flaming out his thoughts
Upon a palace-wall for Rome to see,
Too lifted up in heart because of it)
'Friend, there's a certain sorry little scrub
190   Goes up and down our Florence, none cares how,
Who, were he set to plan and execute
As you are, pricked on by your popes and kings,
Would bring the sweat into that brow of yours!'
To Rafael's!—And indeed the arm is wrong.
I hardly dare . . . yet, only you to see,
Give the chalk here—quick, thus the line should go!
Ay, but the soul! he's Rafael! rub it out!
Still, all I care for, if he spoke the truth,
(What he? why, who but Michel Agnolo?
200   Do you forget already words like those?)
If really there was such a chance, so lost,—
Is, whether you're—not grateful—but more pleased.
Well, let me think so. And you smile indeed!
This hour has been an hour! Another smile?
If you would sit thus by me every night
I should work better, do you comprehend?
I mean that I should earn more, give you more.

grange barn   **Roman's** Raphael's

See, it is settled dusk now; there's a star;
Morello's gone, the watch-lights show the wall,
210   The cue-owls° speak the name we call them by.
Come from the window, love,—come in, at last,
Inside the melancholy little house
We built to be so gay with. God is just.
King Francis may forgive me: oft at nights
When I look up from painting, eyes tired out,
The walls become illumined, brick from brick
Distinct, instead of mortar, fierce bright gold,
That gold of his I did cement them with!
Let us but love each other. Must you go?
220   That Cousin° here again? he waits outside?
Must see you—you, and not with me? Those loans?
More gaming debts to pay? you smiled for that?
Well, let smiles buy me! have you more to spend?
While hand and eye and something of a heart
Are left me, work's my ware, and what's it worth?
I'll pay my fancy. Only let me sit
The grey remainder of the evening out,
Idle, you call it, and muse perfectly
How I could paint, were I but back in France,
230   One picture, just one more—the Virgin's face,
Not yours this time! I want you at my side
To hear them—that is, Michel Agnolo—
Judge all I do and tell you of its worth.
Will you? Tomorrow, satisfy your friend.
I take the subjects for his corridor,
Finish the portrait out of hand—there, there,
And throw him in another thing or two
If he demurs; the whole should prove enough
To pay for this same Cousin's freak. Beside,
240   What's better and what's all I care about,
Get you the thirteen scudi° for the ruff!
Love, does that please you? Ah, but what does he,
The Cousin! what does he to please you more?

I am grown peaceful as old age tonight.
I regret little, I would change still less.
Since there my past life lies, why alter it?
The very wrong to Francis!—it is true
I took his coin, was tempted and complied,
And built this house and sinned, and all is said.
250   My father and my mother died of want.°
Well, had I riches of my own? you see
How one gets rich! Let each one bear his lot.

---

cue-owls little owls
Cousin an evasive term for Lucretia's lover
scudi Italian coins

father . . . want Vasari charges Andrea with
neglecting his parents

They were born poor, lived poor, and poor they died:
And I have laboured somewhat in my time
And not been paid profusely. Some good son
Paint my two hundred pictures—let him try!
No doubt, there's something strikes a balance. Yes,
You loved me quite enough, it seems tonight.
This must suffice me here. What would one have?
260   In heaven, perhaps, new chances, one more chance—
Four great walls in the New Jerusalem,°
Meted on each side by the angel's reed,
For Leonard,° Rafael, Agnolo and me
To cover—the three first without a wife,
While I have mine! So—still they overcome
Because there's still Lucrezia,—as I choose.

Again the Cousin's whistle! Go, my Love.
1853   1855

Cleon°

'As certain also of your own poets have said'°—

Cleon the poet (from the sprinkled isles,°
Lily on lily, that o'erlace the sea,
And laugh their pride when the light wave lisps
    'Greece')—
To Protus in his Tyranny:° much health!

They give thy letter to me, even now:
I read and seem as if I heard thee speak.
The master of thy galley still unlades
Gift after gift; they block my court at last
And pile themselves along its portico
10   Royal with sunset,° like a thought of thee:
And one white she-slave from the group dispersed
Of black and white slaves (like the chequer-work
Pavement, at once my nation's work and gift,

New Jerusalem as in Revelation 21:10–21
Leonard Leonardo da Vinci (1452–1519)
Cleon This dramatic monologue of an imaginary Greek poet contemporary with St. Paul's ministry (50 A.D. or so) combines two characteristic kinds of Browning's poems, since it both expresses his own very personal religious synthesis (though only by indirection) and takes its place also in the great sequence of involuntary total self-revelations of failed questers, sometimes relatively inadequate artists and musicians, sometimes charlatans. Cleon, though no charlatan, betrays a deep inner doubt as to his own artistic eminence, for he is more an absorber of culture than a maker of it, and clearly a more considerable critic of

the arts than an artist. Created by Browning in response to Arnold's *Empedocles on Etna*, in some sense he is a kind of Hellenic Matthew Arnold.
As certain . . . have said St. Paul to the Athenian philosophers, Acts 17:28: "For in him [God] we live, and move, and have our being; as certain also of your own poets have said, for we are also his offspring"
sprinkled isles the Sporades, near Crete
Tyranny Protus, an imaginary king or tyrant; "tyranny" simply means a small kingdom, and has no pejorative overtone here
sunset sunset gives a purple (thus royal) tinge to the marble

Now covered with this settle-down of doves),
One lyric woman, in her crocus vest
Woven of sea-wools, with her two white hands
Commends to me the strainer and the cup
Thy lip hath bettered ere it blesses mine.

    Well-counselled, king, in thy munificence!
20 For so shall men remark, in such an act
Of love for him whose song gives life its joy,
Thy recognition of the use of life;
Nor call thy spirit barely adequate
To help on life in straight ways, broad enough
For vulgar souls, by ruling and the rest.
Thou, in the daily building of thy tower,°—
Whether in fierce and sudden spasms of toil,
Or through dim lulls of unapparent growth,
Or when the general work 'mid good acclaim
30 Climbed with the eye to cheer the architect,—
Didst ne'er engage in work for mere work's sake—
Hadst ever in thy heart the luring hope
Of some eventual rest a-top of it,
Whence, all the tumult of the building hushed,
Thou first of men mightst look out to the East:°
The vulgar saw thy tower, thou sawest the sun.
For this, I promise on thy festival
To pour libation,° looking o'er the sea,
Making this slave narrate thy fortunes, speak
Thy great words, and describe thy royal face—
40 Wishing thee wholly where Zeus lives the most,
Within the eventual element of calm.

    Thy letter's first requirement meets me here.
It is as thou hast heard: in one short life
I, Cleon, have effected all those things
Thou wonderingly dost enumerate.
That epos on thy hundred plates of gold°
Is mine,—and also mine the little chant,
So sure to rise from every fishing-bark
50 When, lights at prow, the seamen haul their net.
The image of the sun-god on the phare,°
Men turn from the sun's self to see, is mine;
The Pœcile,° o'er-storied its whole length,
As thou didst hear, with painting, is mine too.

tower the monument Protus is building as a symbol of his reign; Cleon uses it as a symbol of poetic achievement, reflecting Shelley's influence upon Browning
East symbolizing the devotion of Protus to Phoebus Apollo, the sun god, but the land of Christ lies to the east also
libation wine poured to the gods

gold Protus has honored Cleon by donating 100 golden tablets upon which Cleon's epic poem has been engraved
phare lighthouse
Pœcile name of portico (Painted Porch) in marketplace of ancient Athens, adorned with frescoes of the battle of Marathon

I know the true proportions of a man
And woman also, not observed before;
And I have written three books on the soul,
Proving absurd all written hitherto,
And putting us to ignorance again.
60 For music,—why, I have combined the moods,°
Inventing one. In brief, all arts are mine;
Thus much the people know and recognize,
Throughout our seventeen islands. Marvel not.
We of these latter days, with greater mind
Then our forerunners, since more composite,
Look not so great, beside their simple way,
To a judge who only sees one way at once,
One mind-point and no other at a time,—
Compares the small part of a man of us
70 With some whole man of the heroic age,
Great in his way—not ours, nor meant for ours.
And ours is greater, had we skill to know:
For, what we call this life of men on earth,
This sequence of the soul's achievements here
Being, as I find much reason to conceive,
Intended to be viewed eventually
As a great whole, not analyzed to parts,
But each part having reference to all,—
How shall a certain part, pronounced complete,
80 Endure effacement by another part?
Was the thing done?—then, what's to do again?
See, in the chequered pavement opposite,
Suppose the artist made a perfect rhomb,
And next a lozenge, then a trapezoid°—
He did not overlay them, superimpose
The new upon the old and blot it out,
But laid them on a level in his work,
Making at last a picture; there it lies.
So, first the perfect separate forms were made,
90 The portions of mankind; and after, so,
Occurred the combination of the same.
For where had been a progress, otherwise?
Mankind, made up of all the single men,—
In such a synthesis the labour ends.
Now mark me! those divine men of old time
Have reached, thou sayest well, each at one point
The outside verge that rounds our faculty;
And where they reached, who can do more than reach?
It takes but little water just to touch

moods musical modes or scales
rhomb trapezoid A rhomb is a non-right-angled
semi-square; a lozenge is a figure shaped like a
diamond; a trapezoid is a figure with four sides,
none parallel to another.

100 At some one point the inside of a sphere,
And, as we turn the sphere, touch all the rest
In due succession: but the finer air
Which not so palpably nor obviously,
Though no less universally, can touch
The whole circumference of that emptied sphere,
Fills it more fully than the water did;
Holds thrice the weight of water in itself
Resolved into a subtler element.
And yet the vulgar call the sphere first full
110 Up to the visible height—and after, void;
Not knowing air's more hidden properties.
And thus our soul, misknown, cries out to Zeus
To vindicate his purpose in our life:
Why stay we on the earth unless to grow?
Long since, I imaged, wrote the fiction out,
That he or other god descended here
And, once for all, showed simultaneously
What, in its nature, never can be shown,
Piecemeal or in succession;—showed, I say,
120 The worth both absolute and relative
Of all his children from the birth of time,
His instruments for all appointed work.
I now go on to image,—might we hear
The judgment which should give the due to each,
Show where the labour lay and where the ease,
And prove Zeus' self, the latent everywhere!
This is a dream:—but no dream, let us hope,
That years and days, the summers and the springs,
Follow each other with unwaning powers.
130 The grapes which dye thy wine are richer far,
Through culture, than the wild wealth of the rock;
The suave plum than the savage-tasted drupe;°
The pastured honey-bee drops choicer sweet;
The flowers turn double, and the leaves turn flowers;
That young and tender crescent-moon, thy slave,
Sleeping above her robe as buoyed by clouds,
Refines upon the women of my youth.
What, and the soul alone deteriorates?
I have not chanted verse like Homer, no—
140 Nor swept string like Terpander,° no—nor carved
And painted men like Phidias° and his friend:
I am not great as they are, point by point.
But I have entered into sympathy

---

drupe wild plum
Terpander active about 650 B.C., poet and
musician who worked in Sparta, reputed to
have set Homer to lyre music

Phidias 500–432 B.C., sculpted the Parthenon
statues; his "friend" was probably Polygnotus,
who helped to decorate the Painted Porch

With these four, running these into one soul,
Who, separate, ignored each other's art.
Say, is it nothing that I know them all?
The wild flower was the larger; I have dashed
Rose-blood upon its petals, pricked its cup's
Honey with wine, and driven its seed to fruit,
150   And show a better flower if not so large:
I stand myself. Refer this to the gods
Whose gift alone it is! which, shall I dare
(All pride apart) upon the absurd pretext
That such a gift by chance lay in my hand,
Discourse of lightly or depreciate?
It might have fallen to another's hand: what then?
I pass too surely: let at least truth stay!

    And next, of what thou followest on to ask.
This being with me as I declare, O king,
160   My works, in all these varicoloured kinds,
So done by me, accepted so by men—
Thou askest, if (my soul thus in men's hearts)
I must not be accounted to attain
The very crown and proper end of life?
Inquiring thence how, now life closeth up,
I face death with success in my right hand:
Whether I fear death less than dost thyself
The fortunate of men? 'For' (writest thou)
'Thou leavest much behind, while I leave nought.
170   Thy life stays in the poems men shall sing,
The pictures men shall study; while my life,
Complete and whole now in its power and joy,
Dies altogether with my brain and arm,
Is lost indeed; since, what survives myself?
The brazen statue to o'erlook my grave,
Set on the promontory which I named.
And that—some supple courtier of my heir
Shall use its robed and sceptred arm, perhaps,
To fix the rope to, which best drags it down.
180   I go then: triumph thou, who dost not go!'

    Nay, thou art worthy of hearing my whole mind.
Is this apparent, when thou turn'st to muse
Upon the scheme of earth and man in chief,
That admiration grows as knowledge grows?
That imperfection means perfection hid,
Reserved in part, to grace the after-time?
If, in the morning of philosophy,
Ere aught had been recorded, nay perceived,
Thou, with the light now in thee, couldst have looked
190   On all earth's tenantry, from worm to bird,

Ere man, her last, appeared upon the stage—
Thou wouldst have seen them perfect, and deduced
The perfectness of others yet unseen.
Conceding which,—had Zeus then questioned thee
'Shall I go on a step, improve on this,
Do more for visible creatures than is done?'
Thou wouldst have answered, 'Ay, by making each
Grow conscious in himself—by that alone.
All's perfect else: the shell sucks fast the rock,
200   The fish strikes through the sea, the snake both swims
And slides, forth range the beasts, the birds take flight,
Till life's mechanics can no further go—
And all this joy in natural life is put
Like fire from off thy finger into each,
So exquisitely perfect is the same.
But 'tis pure fire, and they mere matter are;
It has them, not they it: and so I choose
For man, thy last premeditated work
(If I might add a glory to the scheme)
210   That a third thing should stand apart from both,
A quality arise within his soul,
Which, intro-active, made to supervise
And feel the force it has, may view itself,
And so be happy.' Man might live at first
The animal life: but is there nothing more?
In due time, let him critically learn
How he lives; and, the more he gets to know
Of his own life's adaptabilities,
The more joy-giving will his life become.
220   Thus man, who hath this quality, is best.

But thou, king, hadst more reasonably said:
'Let progress end at once,—man make no step
Beyond the natural man, the better beast,
Using his senses, not the sense of sense.'°
In man there's failure, only since he left
The lower and inconscious forms of life.
We called it an advance, the rendering plain
Man's spirit might grow conscious of man's life,
And, by new lore so added to the old,
230   Take each step higher over the brute's head.
This grew the only life, the pleasure-house,
Watch-tower° and treasure-fortress of the soul,
Which whole surrounding flats of natural life
Seemed only fit to yield subsistence to;
A tower that crowns a country. But alas,

---

sense of sense consciousness of consciousness
Watch-tower point of survey of the higher
consciousness, an image going back to Isaiah,
and prevalent in Coleridge and Shelley

The soul now climbs it just to perish there!
For thence we have discovered ('tis no dream—
We know this, which we had not else perceived)
That there's a world of capability
240 For joy, spread round about us, meant for us,
Inviting us; and still the soul craves all,
And still the flesh replies, 'Take no jot more
Than ere thou clombst the tower to look abroad!
Nay, so much less as that fatigue has brought
Deduction to it.' We struggle, fain to enlarge
Our bounded physical recipiency,
Increase our power, supply fresh oil to life,
Repair the waste of age and sickness: no,
It skills not!° life's inadequate to joy,
250 As the soul sees joy, tempting life to take.
They praise a fountain in my garden here
Wherein a Naiad° sends the water-bow
Thin from her tube; she smiles to see it rise.
What if I told her, it is just a thread
From that great river which the hills shut up,
And mock her with my leave to take the same?
The artificer has given her one small tube
Past power to widen or exchange—what boots
To know she might spout oceans if she could?
260 She cannot lift beyond her first thin thread:
And so a man can use but a man's joy
While he sees God's. Is it for Zeus to boast,
'See, man, how happy I live, and despair—
That I may be still happier—for thy use!'
If this were so, we could not thank our lord,
As hearts beat on to doing: 'tis not so—
Malice it is not. Is it carelessness?
Still, no. If care—where is the sign? I ask,
And get no answer, and agree in sum,
270 O king, with thy profound discouragement,
Who seest the wider but to sigh the more.
Most progress is most failure: thou sayest well.

The last point now:—thou dost except a case—
Holding joy not impossible to one
With artist-gifts—to such a man as I
Who leave behind me living works indeed;
For, such a poem, such a painting lives.
What? dost thou verily trip upon a word,
Confound the accurate view of what joy is
280 (Caught somewhat clearer by my eyes than thine)
With feeling joy? confound the knowing how

skills not does not suffice   **Naiad** nymph

And showing how to live (my faculty)
With actually living?—Otherwise
Where is the artist's vantage o'er the king?
Because in my great epos I display
How divers men young, strong, fair, wise, can act—
Is this as though I acted? if I paint,
Carve the young Phœbus,° am I therefore young?
Methinks I'm older that I bowed myself
290 The many years of pain that taught me art!
Indeed, to know is something, and to prove
How all this beauty might be enjoyed, is more:
But, knowing nought, to enjoy is something too.
Yon rower, with the moulded muscles there,
Lowering the sail, is nearer it than I.
I can write love-odes: thy fair slave's an ode.
I get to sing of love, when grown too grey
For being beloved: she turns to that young man
The muscles all a-ripple on his back.
300 I know the joy of kingship: well, thou art king!

     'But,' sayest thou—(and I marvel, I repeat,
To find thee trip on such a mere word) 'what
Thou writest, paintest, stays; that does not die:
Sappho° survives, because we sing her songs,
And Æschylus,° because we read his plays!'
Why, if they live still, let them come and take
Thy slave in my despite, drink from thy cup,
Speak in my place. Thou diest while I survive?
Say rather that my fate is deadlier still,
310 In this, that every day my sense of joy
Grows more acute, my soul (intensified
In power and insight) more enlarged, more keen;
While every day my hairs fall more and more,
My hand shakes, and the heavy years increase—
The horror quickening still from year to year,
The consummation coming past escape
When I shall know most, and yet least enjoy—
When all my works wherein I prove my worth,
Being present still to mock me in men's mouths,
320 Alive still, in the praise of such as thou,
I, I the feeling, thinking, acting man,
The man who loved his life so over-much,
Sleep in my urn. It is so horrible,
I dare at times imagine to my need
Some future state revealed to us by Zeus,

Phœbus The young Apollo traditionally symbolizes the perpetual youth of poetry, as in
Keats's *Hyperion.*
Sappho (born c. 610 B.C.) greatest lyric poet
of Greece, whose work survives only in fragments
Æschylus (525–456 B.C.) greatest of the Greek
tragic dramatists

Unlimited in capability
For joy, as this is in desire for joy,
—To seek which, the joy-hunger forces us:
That, stung by straitness of our life, made strait
330   On purpose to make prized the life at large—
Freed by the throbbing impulse we call death,
We burst there as the worm into the fly,
Who, while a worm still, wants° his wings. But no!
Zeus has not yet revealed it;° and alas,
He must have done so, were it possible!

Live long and happy, and in that thought die:
Glad for what was! Farewell. And for the rest,
I cannot tell thy messenger aright
Where to deliver what he bears of thine
340   To one called Paulus;° we have heard his fame
Indeed, if Christus be not one with him—
I know not, nor am troubled much to know.
Thou canst not think a mere barbarian Jew
As Paulus proves to be, one circumcised,°
Hath access to a secret shut from us?
Thou wrongest our philosophy, O king,
In stooping to inquire of such an one,
As if his answer could impose at all!
He writeth, doth he? well, and he may write.
350   Oh, the Jew findeth scholars! certain slaves
Who touched on this same isle, preached him and Christ;
And (as I gathered from a bystander)
Their doctrine could be held by no sane man.
1854   1855

Popularity

I

Stand still, true poet that you are!
    I know you; let me try and draw you.
Some night you'll fail us: when afar
    You rise, remember one man saw you,
Knew you, and named a star!

II

My star, God's glow-worm! Why extend
    That loving hand of his which leads you,
Yet locks you safe from end to end
    Of this dark world, unless he needs you,
10   Just saves your light to spend?

wants lacks
revealed it Immortality, in the Olympian faith,
was granted only by special dispensation.

Paulus Saint Paul, Saul of Tarsus
circumcised Jewish mark of the Covenant

III

His clenched hand shall unclose at last,
  I know, and let out all the beauty:
My poet holds the future fast,
  Accepts the coming ages' duty,
Their present for this past.

IV

That day, the earth's feast-master's brow
  Shall clear, to God the chalice raising;
'Others give best at first, but thou
  Forever set'st our table praising,
20 Keep'st the good wine till now!'°

V

Meantime, I'll draw you as you stand,
  With few or none to watch and wonder:
I'll say—a fisher, on the sand
  By Tyre° the old, his ocean-plunder,
A netful, brought to land.

VI

Who has not heard how Tyrian shells
  Enclosed the blue, that dye of dyes
Whereof one drop worked miracles,
  And coloured like Astarte's° eyes
30 Raw silk the merchant sells?

VII

And each bystander of them all
  Could criticize, and quote tradition
How depths of blue sublimed some pall
  —To get which, pricked a king's ambition;
Worth sceptre, crown and ball.

VIII

Yet there's the dye, in that rough mesh,
  The sea has only just o'erwhispered!
Live whelks, each lip's beard dripping fresh,
  As if they still the water's lisp heard
40 Through foam the rock-weeds thresh.

IX

Enough to furnish Solomon°
  Such hangings for his cedar-house,

Keep'st . . . now See John 2:1–10.
Tyre great Phoenician trading port; the purple
or blue Tyrian-dyed cloths became the European emblems of royalty

Astarte's goddess of the Gentile Semites; worshiped in Tyre, and associated with the Morning Star (Venus)
Solomon See I Kings 6–7.

That, when gold-robed he took the throne
  In that abyss of blue, the Spouse
Might swear his presence shone

X

Most like the centre-spike of gold
  Which burns deep in the blue-bell's womb,
What time, with ardours manifold,
  The bee goes singing to her groom,
50 Drunken and overbold.

XI

Mere conchs! not fit for warp or woof!
  Till cunning come to pound and squeeze
And clarify,—refine to proof
  The liquor filtered by degrees,
While the world stands aloof.

XII

And there's the extract, flasked and fine,
  And priced and saleable at last!
And Hobbs, Nobbs, Stokes and Nokes° combine
  To paint the future from the past,
60 Put blue into their line.

XIII

Hobbs hints blue,—straight he turtle eats:
  Nobbs prints blue,—claret crowns his cup:
Nokes outdares Stokes in azure feats,—
  Both gorge. Who fished the murex° up?
What porridge had John Keats?
1854   1855

The Heretic's Tragedy°

A Middle-Age Interlude°

Rosa mundi; seu, fulcite me floribus.° A conceit° of Master Gysbrecht,
canon-regular of Saint Jodocus-by-the-bar, Ypres city. Cantuque, *Vir-*

Hobbs . . . and Nokes this may refer to Rossetti, Morris, and Keats's other Pre-Raphaelite followers
murex the mussel that is the source of Tyrian purple dye
The Heretic's Tragedy Jacques du Bourg-Molay (called "John" in this poem) was the last Grand Master of the Knights Templars, originally a crusading order, but later essentially a supra-national political and financial organization. Philip IV of France repressed the order, con-

fiscated its funds, and burned Molay at the stake in 1314, on the evidently false charges of heresy, simony, and sodomy. Dante, in his *Purgatorio*, maintains the innocence of the Templars.
Interlude short play, here a farce
Rosa mundi . . . floribus "Rose of the world support me with flowers" (Song of Solomon 2:5)
conceit invention

gilius.° And hath often been sung at hock-tide° and Festivals. Gavisus eram, *Jessides.*°

(It would seem to be a glimpse from the burning of Jacques du Bourg-Molay, at Paris, A.D. 1314; as distorted by the refraction from Flemish brain to brain, during the course of a couple of centuries.)

I

PREADMONISHETH THE ABBOT DEODÆT

The Lord, we look to once for all,
  Is the Lord we should look at, all at once:
He knows not to vary, saith Saint Paul,
  Nor the shadow of turning, for the nonce.
See him no other than as he is!
  Give both the infinitudes their due—
Infinite mercy, but, I wis,
  As infinite a justice too.
    [*Organ: plagal-cadence.*°
  As infinite a justice too.

II

ONE SINGETH

10 John, Master of the Temple of God,
  Falling to sin the Unknown Sin,
What he bought of Emperor Aldabrod,
  He sold it to Sultan Saladin:°
Till, caught by Pope Clement,° a-buzzing there,
  Hornet-prince of the mad wasps' hive,
And clipped of his wings in Paris square,
  They bring him now to be burned alive.

    [*And wanteth there grace of lute or clavicithern,*°
    ye shall say to confirm him who singeth—

We bring John now to be burned alive.

III

In the midst is a goodly gallows built;
20   'Twixt fork and fork, a stake is stuck;
But first they set divers tumbrils° a-tilt,
  Make a trench all round with the city muck;

Inside they pile log upon log, good store;
   Faggots no few, blocks great and small,
Reach a man's mid-thigh, no less, no more,—
   For they mean he should roast in the sight of all.

     CHORUS
We mean he should roast in the sight of all.

     IV
Good sappy bavins° that kindle forthwith;
   Billets that blaze substantial and slow;
30 Pine-stump split deftly, dry as pith;
   Larch-heart that chars to a chalk-white glow:
Then up they hoist me John in a chafe,
   Sling him fast like a hog to scorch,
Spit in his face, then leap back safe,
   Sing 'Laudes'° and bid clap-to the torch.

     CHORUS
   Laus Deo°—who bids clap-to the torch.

     V
John of the Temple, whose fame so bragged,
   Is burning alive in Paris square!
How can he curse, if his mouth is gagged?
40   Or wriggle his neck, with a collar there?
Or heave his chest, which a band goes round?
   Or threat with his fist, since his arms are spliced?
Or kick with his feet, now his legs are bound?
   —Thinks John, I will call upon Jesus Christ.
     [*Here one crosseth himself.*

     VI
Jesus Christ—John had bought and sold,
   Jesus Christ—John had eaten and drunk;
To him, the Flesh meant silver and gold.
   (*Salvâ reverentiâ.*)°
Now it was, 'Saviour, bountiful lamb,
50   I have roasted thee Turks, though men roast me!
See thy servant, the plight wherein I am!
   Art thou a saviour? Save thou me!'

     CHORUS
   'Tis John the mocker cries, 'Save thou me!'

     VII
Who maketh God's menace an idle word?
   —Saith, it no more means what it proclaims,

---

bavins bundles of brushwood for kindling
Laudes the seven Psalms of praise
Laus Deo Praise be to God

Salvâ reverentiâ (literally "a saving reverence")
direction to genuflect to the body of Christ
("Flesh") in the Eucharist

Than a damsel's threat to her wanton bird?—
    For she too prattles of ugly names.
—Saith, he knoweth but one thing,—what he knows?
    That God is good and the rest is breath;
60 Why else is the same styled Sharon's rose?°
    Once a rose, ever a rose, he saith.

      CHORUS
    O, John shall yet find a rose, he saith!

      VIII
Alack, there be roses and roses, John!
    Some, honied of taste like your leman's° tongue:
Some, bitter; for why? (roast gaily on!)
    Their tree struck root in devil's dung.
When Paul once reasoned of righteousness
    And of temperance and of judgment to come,
Good Felix° trembled, he could no less:
70   John, snickering, crooked his wicked thumb.

      CHORUS
    What cometh to John of the wicked thumb?

      IX
Ha ha, John plucketh now at his rose
    To rid himself of a sorrow at heart!
Lo,—petal on petal, fierce rays unclose;
    Anther° on anther, sharp spikes outstart;
And with blood for dew, the bosom boils;
    And a gust of sulphur is all its smell;
And lo, he is horribly in the toils
    Of a coal-black giant flower of hell!

      CHORUS
80 What maketh heaven, That maketh hell.

      X
So, as John called now, through the fire amain,°
    On the Name, he had cursed with, all his life—
To the Person, he bought and sold again—
    For the Face, with his daily buffets rife—
Feature by feature It took its place:
    And his voice, like a mad dog's choking bark,
At the steady whole of the Judge's face—
    Died. Forth John's soul flared into the dark.

Sharon's rose "I am the rose of Sharon, and the lily of the valleys" (Song of Solomon 2:1) **leman** mistress

Felix Felix Antonius, Roman governor of Judea (51–60 A.D.); see Acts 24:25 **Anther** part of the flower containing the pollen **amain** vehemently

SUBJOINETH THE ABBOT DEODAET
God help all poor souls lost in the dark!
1852   1855

Two in the Campagna°

I

I wonder do you feel to-day
　　As I have felt since, hand in hand,
We sat down on the grass, to stray
　　In spirit better through the land,
This morn of Rome and May?

II

For me, I touched a thought, I know,
　　Has tantalized me many times,
(Like turns of thread the spiders throw
　　Mocking across our path) for rhymes
10　To catch at and let go.

III

Help me to hold it! First it left
　　The yellowing fennel, run to seed
There, branching from the brickwork's cleft,
　　Some old tomb's ruin: yonder weed
Took up the floating weft,°

IV

Where one small orange cup amassed
　　Five beetles,—blind and green they grope
Among the honey-meal: and last,
　　Everywhere on the grassy slope
20　I traced it. Hold it fast!

V

The champaign° with its endless fleece
　　Of feathery grasses everywhere!
Silence and passion, joy and peace,
　　An everlasting wash of air—
Rome's ghost° since her decease.

VI

Such life here, through such lengths of hours,
　　Such miracles performed in play,

Campagna the *Campagna di Roma*, large, open
countryside around the city; contains many ruins
weft weaver's cross-threads

champaign open field
ghost ruins of old cities

Such primal naked forms of flowers,
     Such letting nature have her way
30   While heaven looks from its towers!

          VII

How say you? Let us, O my dove,
     Let us be unashamed of soul,
As earth lies bare to heaven above!
     How is it under our control
To love or not to love?

          VIII

I would that you were all to me,
     You that are just so much, no more.
Nor yours nor mine, nor slave nor free!
     Where does the fault lie? What the core
40   O' the wound, since wound must be?

          IX

I would I could adopt your will,
     See with your eyes, and set my heart
Beating by yours, and drink my fill
     At your soul's springs,—your part my part
In life, for good and ill.

          X

No. I yearn upward, touch you close,
     Then stand away. I kiss your cheek,
Catch your soul's warmth,—I pluck the rose
     And love it more than tongue can speak—
50   Then the good minute° goes.

          XI

Already how am I so far
     Out of that minute? Must I go
Still like the thistle-ball°, no bar,
     Onward, whenever light winds blow,
Fixed° by no friendly star?

          XII

Just when I seemed about to learn!
     Where is the thread now? Off again!
The old trick! Only I discern—
     Infinite passion, and the pain
60   Of finite hearts that yearn.
1854   1855

good minute one of Browning's central phrases;   thistle-ball driven, as it is, by the wind
his version of the Romantic epiphany or priv-   fixed guided
ileged moment, here of complete communion
between lovers

Abt Vogler

Georg Joseph Vogler (1749–1814), whose title of "Abt" (Abbé, Father) was honorary, is remembered today as the teacher of the composers Weber and Meyerbeer, and as the speaker of this poem. Vogler, known as an extraordinary extemporizer, particularly upon the organ, was also reputed to be a charlatan, a pious fraud, and perhaps he belongs in Browning's company of failed artists, self-ruined questers, and grand mountebanks. The poem *seems* to celebrate his spirituality, but there are profound demoniac elements revealed by it as well. What the poem's parenthetical subtitle calls the "instrument of his own invention," an "orchestrion" or small portable organ, had the charming knack of sounding superb only when he played upon it but, like the other organs he built, sounding inadequate when played upon by others.

Abt Vogler

(after he has been extemporizing upon
the musical instrument of his invention)

I

Would that the structure brave, the manifold music I build,
  Bidding my organ obey, calling its keys to their work,
Claiming each slave of the sound, at a touch, as when Solomon° willed
  Armies of angels that soar, legions of demons that lurk,
Man, brute, reptile, fly,—alien of end and of aim,
  Adverse, each from the other heaven-high, hell-deep removed,—
Should rush into sight at once as he named the ineffable Name,
  And pile him a palace straight, to pleasure the princess he loved!

II

Would it might tarry like his, the beautiful building of mine,
10   This which my keys in a crowd pressed and importuned to raise!
Ah, one and all, how they helped, would dispart° now and now combine,
  Zealous to hasten the work, heighten their master his praise!
And one would bury his brow with a blind plunge down to hell,
  Burrow awhile and build, broad on the roots of things,
Then up again swim into sight, having based me my palace well,
  Founded it, fearless of flame, flat on the nether springs.

III

And another would mount and march, like the excellent minion he was,
  Ay, another and yet another, one crowd but with many a crest,
Raising my rampired walls of gold as transparent as glass,

Solomon There is a tradition that Solomon had a magical seal bearing the "ineffable Name" of God, by means of which he could command angels and demons.
dispart separate

20   Eager to do and die, yield each his place to the rest:
For higher still and higher (as a runner tips with fire,
   When a great illumination surprises a festal night—
Outlining round and round Rome's dome from space to spire)
   Up, the pinnacled glory reached, and the pride of my soul was in sight.

       IV

In sight? Not half! for it seemed, it was certain, to match man's birth,
   Nature in turn conceived, obeying an impulse as I;
And the emulous heaven yearned down, made effort to reach the earth,
   As the earth had done her best, in my passion, to scale the sky:
Novel splendours burst forth, grew familiar and dwelt with mine,
30   Not a point nor peak but found and fixed its wandering star;
Meteor-moons, balls of blaze: and they did not pale nor pine,
   For earth had attained to heaven, there was no more near nor far.

       V

Nay more; for there wanted not who walked in the glare and glow,
   Presences plain in the place; or, fresh from the Protoplast,°
Furnished for ages to come, when a kindlier wind should blow,
   Lured now to begin and live, in a house to their liking at last;
Or else the wonderful Dead who have passed through the body and gone,
   But were back once more to breathe in an old world worth their new:
What never had been, was now; what was, as it shall be anon;
40   And what is,—shall I say, matched both? for I was made perfect too.

       VI

All through my keys that gave their sounds to a wish of my soul,
   All through my soul that praised as its wish flowed visibly forth,
All through music and me! For think, had I painted the whole,
   Why, there it had stood, to see, nor the process so wonder-worth:
Had I written the same, made verse—still, effect proceeds from cause,
   Ye know why the forms are fair, ye hear how the tale is told;
It is all triumphant art, but art in obedience to laws,
   Painter and poet are proud in the artist-list enrolled:—

       VII

But here is the finger of God, a flash of the will that can,
50   Existent behind all laws, that made them and, lo, they are!
And I know not if, save in this, such gift be allowed to man,
   That out of three sounds he frame, not a fourth sound, but a star.
Consider it well: each tone of our scale in itself is nought;
   It is everywhere in the world—loud, soft, and all is said:
Give it to me to use! I mix it with two in my thought:
   And, there! Ye have heard and seen: consider and bow the head!

Protoplast basic protoplasm, or substance of
life (rather like the beings of Phase 1 in Yeats's
A Vision)

VIII

Well, it is gone at last, the palace of music I reared;
   Gone! and the good tears start, the praises that come too slow;
For one is assured at first, one scarce can say that he feared,
60   That he even gave it a thought, the gone thing was to go.
Never to be again! But many more of the kind
   As good, nay, better perchance: is this your comfort to me?
To me, who must be saved because I cling with my mind
   To the same, same self, same love, same God: ay, what was, shall be.

IX

Therefore to whom turn I but to thee, the ineffable Name?
   Builder and maker, thou, of houses not made with hands!°
What, have fear of change from thee who art ever the same?
   Doubt that thy power can fill the heart that thy power expands?
There shall never be one lost good! What was, shall live as before;
70   The evil is null, is nought, is silence implying sound;
What was good shall be good, with, for evil, so much good more;
   On the earth the broken arcs; in the heaven, a perfect round.

X

All we have willed or hoped or dreamed of good shall exist;
   Not its semblance, but itself; no beauty, nor good, nor power
Whose voice has gone forth, but each survives for the melodist
   When eternity affirms the conception of an hour.
The high that proved too high, the heroic for earth too hard,
   The passion that left the ground to lose itself in the sky,
Are music sent up to God by the lover and the bard;
80   Enough that he heard it once: we shall hear it by-and-by.

XI

And what is our failure here but a triumph's evidence
   For the fulness of the days? Have we withered or agonized?
Why else was the pause prolonged but that singing might issue thence?
   Why rushed the discords in but that harmony should be prized?
Sorrow is hard to bear, and doubt is slow to clear,
   Each sufferer says his say, his scheme of the weal and woe:
But God has a few of us whom he whispers in the ear;
   The rest may reason and welcome: 'tis we musicians know.

XII

Well, it is earth with me; silence resumes her reign:
90   I will be patient and proud, and soberly acquiesce.
Give me the keys. I feel for the common chord° again,
   Sliding by semitones, till I sink to the minor,—yes,

---

houses . . . hands See II Corinthians 5:1.
chord Vogler descends to the common chord,
that is, our earth, to end in the "natural" key,
C Major, where there are no sharps or flats,
"The C Major of this life" in l. 96.

And I blunt it into a ninth, and I stand on alien ground,
  Surveying awhile the heights I rolled from into the deep;
Which, hark, I have dared and done,° for my resting-place is found,
  The C Major of this life: so, now I will try to sleep.

                               1864

Caliban upon Setebos

This masterpiece of grotesque imagination can be read as being primarily an intellectual satire upon anthropomorphic theology, but the correctness of such a reading is
uncertain. The poem may reflect the influence upon Browning's own theology of
the American Transcendentalist Theodore Parker, who with Emerson had led a spiritual revolt against Boston Unitarianism. Parker, before meeting Browning in December 1859, was reading Darwin's *Origin of Species,* which had only just been published.
Parker's deliberate humanizing of God, mingled with new notions of evolution, evidently caused Browning to remember Shakespeare's Caliban in *The Tempest,* and
led to the writing of this poem. C. R. Tracy suggests that Caliban's evolving theology,
in Browning's poem, is a much less sophisticated version of Browning's humanization
of Jesus, rather than just a satire upon natural theology or, as some have said, upon the
Calvinist doctrine of predestination.

Caliban upon Setebos;°
or Natural Theology° in the Island

    'Thou thoughtest that I was altogether such a one as thyself.'°

['Will° sprawl, now that the heat of day is best,
Flat on his belly in the pit's much mire,
With elbows wide, fists clenched to prop his chin.
And, while he kicks both feet in the cool slush,
And feels about his spine small eft-things° course,
Run in and out each arm, and make him laugh:
And while above his head a pompion-plant,°
Coating the cave-top as a brow its eye,
Creeps down to touch and tickle hair and beard,
And now a flower drops with a bee inside,
And now a fruit to snap at, catch and crunch,—

10

dared and done an echo of the closing line of
Christopher Smart's *A Song to David:* "Determined, dared and done"
Setebos In *The Tempest,* Caliban's mother, the
witch Sycorax, worships Setebos as her god.
Natural Theology the attempt to demonstrate
God's existence and his nature by arguing back
to Him from his creation, as opposed to revealed
theology, handed down by God

Thou thoughtest . . . thyself so God says to
the wicked in Psalms 50:21
'Will he will, that is, Caliban will. In the
bracketed passages that begin and end the
poem, Caliban is meditating; he does not speak
out till l. 24; his shifts between third and first
person have not been shown to follow any incontrovertible pattern.
eft-things perhaps lizards
pompion-plant a sort of pumpkin vine

He looks out o'er yon sea which sunbeams cross
And recross till they weave a spider-web
(Meshes of fire, some great fish breaks at times)
And talks to his own self, howe'er he please,
Touching that other, whom his dam° called God.
Because to talk about Him,° vexes—ha,
Could He but know! and time to vex is now,
When talk is safer than in winter-time.
20 Moreover Prosper and Miranda sleep
In confidence he drudges at their task,
And it is good to cheat the pair, and gibe,
Letting the rank tongue blossom into speech.]

Setebos, Setebos, and Setebos!
'Thinketh, He dwelleth in the cold o' the moon.

'Thinketh, He made it, with the sun to match,
But not the stars; the stars came otherwise;
Only made clouds, winds, meteors, such as that:
Also this isle, what lives and grows thereon,
30 And snaky sea which rounds and ends the same.

'Thinketh, it came of being ill at ease:
He hated that He cannot change His cold,
Nor cure its ache. 'Hath spied an icy fish
That longed to 'scape the rock-stream where she lived,
And thaw herself within the lukewarm brine
O' the lazy sea her stream thrusts far amid,
A crystal spike 'twixt two warm walls of wave;
Only, she ever sickened, found repulse
At the other kind of water, not her life,
40 (Green-dense and dim-delicious, bred o' the sun)
Flounced back from bliss she was not born to breathe,
And in her old bounds buried her despair,
Hating and loving warmth alike: so He.

'Thinketh, He made thereat the sun, this isle,
Trees and the fowls here, beast and creeping thing.
Yon otter, sleek-wet, black, lithe as a leech;
Yon auk, one fire-eye in a ball of foam,
That floats and feeds; a certain badger brown
He hath watched hunt with that slant white-wedge eye
50 By moonlight; and the pie° with the long tongue
That pricks deep into oakwarts for a worm,
And says a plain word when she finds her prize,
But will not eat the ants; the ants themselves
That build a wall of seeds and settled stalks
About their hole—He made all these and more,

dam his mother, Sycorax   pie magpie
Him refers throughout to Setebos

Made all we see, and us, in spite: how else?
He could not, Himself, make a second self
To be His mate; as well have made Himself:
He would not make what he mislikes or slights,
60   An eyesore to Him, or not worth His pains:
But did, in envy, listlessness or sport,
Make what Himself would fain, in a manner, be—
Weaker in most points, stronger in a few,
Worthy, and yet mere playthings all the while,
Things He admires and mocks too,—that is it.
Because, so brave, so better though they be,
It nothing skills if He begin to plague.
Look now, I melt a gourd-fruit into mash,
Add honeycomb and pods, I have perceived,
70   Which bite like finches when they bill and kiss,—
Then, when froth rises bladdery,° drink up all,
Quick, quick, till maggots scamper through my brain;
Last, throw me on my back in the seeded thyme,
And wanton, wishing I were born a bird.
Put case, unable to be what I wish,
I yet could make a live bird out of clay:
Would not I take clay, pinch my Caliban
Able to fly?—for, there, see, he hath wings,
And great comb like the hoopoe's° to admire,
80   And there, a sting to do his foes offence,
There, and I will that he begin to live,
Fly to yon rock-top, nip me off the horns
Of grigs° high up that make the merry din,
Saucy through their veined wings, and mind me not.
In which feat, if his leg snapped, brittle clay,
And he lay stupid-like,—why, I should laugh;
And if he, spying me, should fall to weep,
Beseech me to be good, repair his wrong,
Bid his poor leg smart less or grow again,—
90   Well, as the chance were, this might take or else
Not take my fancy: I might hear his cry,
And give the mankin three sound legs for one,
Or pluck the other off, leave him like an egg,
And lessoned he was mine and merely clay.
Were this no pleasure, lying in the thyme,
Drinking the mash, with brain become alive,
Making and marring clay at will? So He.
'Thinketh, such shows nor right nor wrong in Him,
Nor kind, nor cruel: He is strong and Lord.
100   'Am strong myself compared to yonder crabs
That march now from the mountain to the sea,

bladdery the bubbles of his fermenting mash rise like bladders

hoopoe's brightly colored, great crested bird

grigs grasshoppers

'Let twenty pass, and stone the twenty-first,
Loving not, hating not, just choosing so.
'Say, the first straggler that boasts purple spots
Shall join the file, one pincer twisted off;
'Say, this bruised fellow shall receive a worm,
And two worms he whose nippers end in red;
As it likes me each time, I do: so He.

Well then, 'supposeth He is good in the main,
110   Placable if His mind and ways were guessed,
But rougher than His handiwork, be sure!
Oh, He hath made things worthier than Himself,
And envieth that, so helped, such things do more
Than He who made them! What consoles but this?
That they, unless through Him, do nought at all,
And must submit: what other use in things?
'Hath cut a pipe of pithless elder-joint
That, blown through, gives exact the scream o' the jay
When from her wing you twitch the feathers blue:
120   Sound this, and little birds that hate the jay
Flock within stone's throw, glad their foe is hurt:
Put case such pipe could prattle and boast forsooth
'I catch the birds, I am the crafty thing,
I make the cry my maker cannot make
With his great round mouth; he must blow through mine!'
Would not I smash it with my foot? So He.

But wherefore rough, why cold and ill at ease?
Aha, that is a question! Ask, for that,
What knows,—the something over Setebos
130   That made Him, or He, may be, found and fought,
Worsted, drove off and did to nothing, perchance.
There may be something quiet o'er His head,
Out of His reach, that feels nor joy nor grief,
Since both derive from weakness in some way.
I joy because the quails come; would not joy
Could I bring quails here when I have a mind:
This Quiet,° all it hath a mind to, doth.
'Esteemeth stars the outposts of its couch,
But never spends much thought nor care that way.
140   It may look up, work up,—the worse for those
It works on! 'Careth but for Setebos
The many-handed as a cuttle-fish,
Who, making Himself feared through what He does,
Looks up, first, and perceives he cannot soar
To what is quiet and hath happy life;
Next looks down here, and out of very spite

Quiet the Deity beyond Setebos, a kind of
Transcendental Oversoul

Makes this a bauble-world to ape yon real,
These good things to match those as hips° do grapes.
'Tis solace making baubles, ay, and sport.
150 Himself peeped late, eyed Prosper at his books
Careless and lofty, lord now of the isle:
Vexed, 'stiched a book of broad leaves, arrow-shaped,
Wrote thereon, he knows what, prodigious words;
Has peeled a wand and called it by a name;
Weareth at whiles for an enchanter's robe
The eyed skin of a supple oncelot;°
And hath an ounce° sleeker than youngling mole,
A four-legged serpent he makes cower and couch,
Now snarl, now hold its breath and mind his eye,
160 And saith she is Miranda and my wife:
'Keeps for his Ariel a tall pouch-bill crane
He bids go wade for fish and straight disgorge;
Also a sea-beast, lumpish, which he snared,
Blinded the eyes of, and brought somewhat tame,
And split its toe-webs, and now pens the drudge
In a hole o' the rock and calls him Caliban;
A bitter heart that bides its time and bites.
'Plays thus at being Prosper in a way,
Taketh his mirth with make-believes: so He.

170 His dam held that the Quiet made all things
Which Setebos vexed only: 'holds not so.
Who made them weak, meant weakness He might vex.
Had He meant other, while His hand was in,
Why not make horny eyes no thorn could prick,
Or plate my scalp with bone against the snow,
Or overscale my flesh 'neath joint and joint,
Like an orc's° armour? Ay,—so spoil His sport!
He is the One now: only He doth all.

'Saith, He may like, perchance, what profits Him.
180 Ay, himself loves what does him good; but why?
'Gets good no otherwise. This blinded beast
Loves whoso places flesh-meat on his nose,
But, had he eyes, would want no help, but hate
Or love, just as it liked him: He hath eyes.
Also it pleaseth Setebos to work,
Use all His hands, and exercise much craft,
By no means for the love of what is worked.
'Tasteth, himself, no finer good in the world
When all goes right, in this safe summer-time,
190 And he wants little, hungers, aches not much,
Than trying what to do with wit and strength.

hips berries   **ounce** another kind of leopard
oncelot ocelot or leopard   **orc** sea monster

'Falls to make something: 'piled yon pile of turfs,
And squared and stuck there squares of soft white chalk,
And, with a fish-tooth, scratched a moon on each,
And set up endwise certain spikes of tree,
And crowned the whole with a sloth's skull a-top,
Found dead in the woods, too hard for one to kill.
No use at all in the work, for work's sole sake;
'Shall some day knock it down again: so He.

200 'Saith He is terrible: watch His feats in proof!
One hurricane will spoil six good months' hope.
He hath a spite against me, that I know,
Just as He favours Prosper, who knows why?
So it is, all the same, as well I find.
'Wove wattles° half the winter, fenced them firm
With stone and stake to stop she-tortoises
Crawling to lay their eggs here: well, one wave,
Feeling the foot of Him upon its neck,
Gaped as a snake does, lolled out its large tongue,
210 And licked the whole labour flat: so much for spite.
'Saw a ball flame down late (yonder it lies)
Where, half an hour before, I slept in the shade:
Often they scatter sparkles: there is force!
'Dug up a newt He may have envied once
And turned to stone, shut up inside a stone.
Please Him and hinder this?—What Prosper does?
Aha, if He would tell me how! Not He!
There is the sport: discover how or die!
All need not die, for of the things o' the isle
220 Some flee afar, some dive, some run up trees;
Those at His mercy,—why, they please Him most
When . . . when . . . well, never try the same way twice!
Repeat what act has pleased, He may grow wroth.
You must not know His ways, and play Him off,
Sure of the issue. 'Doth the like himself:
'Spareth a squirrel that it nothing fears
But steals the nut from underneath my thumb,
And when I threat, bites stoutly in defence:
'Spareth an urchin° that contrariwise,
230 Curls up into a ball, pretending death
For fright at my approach: the two ways please.
But what would move my choler more than this,
That either creature counted on its life
Tomorrow and next day and all days to come,
Saying, forsooth, in the inmost of its heart,
'Because he did so yesterday with me,
And otherwise with such another brute,

wattles twigs   **urchin** hedgehog

So must he do henceforth and always.'—Ay?
Would teach the reasoning couple what 'must' means!
240   'Doth as he likes, or wherefore Lord? So He.

'Conceiveth all things will continue thus,
And we shall have to live in fear of Him
So long as He lives, keeps His strength: no change,
If He have done His best, make no new world
To please Him more, so leave off watching this,—
If He surprise not even the Quiet's self
Some strange day,—or, suppose, grow into it
As grubs grow butterflies: else, here are we,
And there is He, and nowhere help at all.
250   'Believeth with the life, the pain shall stop.
His dam held different, that after death
He both plagued enemies and feasted friends:
Idly! He doth His worst in this our life,
Giving just respite lest we die through pain,
Saving last pain for worst,—with which, an end.
Meanwhile, the best way to escape His ire
Is, not to seem too happy. 'Sees, himself,
Yonder two flies, with purple films and pink,
Bask on the pompion-bell above: kills both.
260   'Sees two black painful beetles roll their ball
On head and tail as if to save their lives:
Moves them the stick away they strive to clear.

Even so, 'would have Him misconceive, suppose
This Caliban strives hard and ails no less,
And always, above all else, envies Him;
Wherefore he mainly dances on dark nights,
Moans in the sun, gets under holes to laugh,
And never speaks his mind save housed as now:
Outside, 'groans, curses. If He caught me here,
270   O'erheard this speech, and asked 'What chucklest at?'
'Would, to appease Him, cut a finger off,
Or of my three kid yearlings burn the best,
Or let the toothsome apples rot on tree,
Or push my tame beast for the orc to taste:
While myself lit a fire, and made a song
And sung it, *'What I hate, be consecrate*
To celebrate Thee and Thy state, no mate
For Thee; what see for envy in poor me?'
Hoping the while, since evils sometimes mend,
280   Warts rub away and sores are cured with slime,
That some strange day, will either the Quiet catch
And conquer Setebos, or likelier He
Decrepit may doze, doze, as good as die.

[What, what? A curtain o'er the world at once!

Crickets stop hissing; not a bird—or, yes,
There scuds His raven that has told Him all!
It was fool's play, this prattling! Ha! The wind
Shoulders the pillared dust, death's house o' the move,
And fast invading fires begin! White blaze—
290 A tree's head snaps—and there, there, there, there, there,
His thunder follows! Fool to gibe at Him!
Lo! 'Lieth flat and loveth Setebos!
'Maketh his teeth meet through his upper lip,
Will let those quails fly, will not eat this month
One little mess of whelks, so he may 'scape!]
1859–60   1864

Thamuris Marching°

Thamuris marching—lyre and song of Thrace—
(Perpend the first, the worst of woes that were
Allotted lyre and song, ye poet-race!)

Thamuris from Oichalia,° feasted there
By kingly Eurutos of late, now bound
For Dorion at the uprise broad and bare

Of Mount Pangaios (ore with earth enwound
Glittered beneath his footstep)—marching gay
And glad, Thessalia through, came, robed and crowned,

10 From triumph on to triumph, mid a ray
Of early morn—came, saw and knew the spot
Assigned him for his worst of woes, that day.

Balura°—happier while its name was not—
Met him, but nowise menaced; slipped aside,
Obsequious river to pursue its lot

Of solacing the valley—say, some wide
Thick busy human cluster, house and home,
Embanked for peace, or thrift that thanks the tide.

Thamuris, marching, laughed 'Each flake of foam'
20 (As sparklingly the ripple raced him by)
'Mocks slower clouds adrift in the blue dome!'

Thamuris Marching This song, excerpted from a late long poem, *Aristophanes' Apology* (ll. 104–80), was one of Browning's favorite pieces for reading aloud. It is perhaps the most direct expression of High Romanticism in the Victorian period, and a demonstration of how abiding the Shelleyan influence was in Browning. Homer (*Iliad* 2.594 ff.) told the story of Thamyris, a Thracian bard, who in his pride boasted that he would win a poetic contest even if the Muses themselves opposed him. The Muses defeated him, punished him by blindness, and then made him forget his poetic skill. In Browning's song, Thamyris is shown in his human glory, marching courageously toward his doomed contest with the Muses.
Oichalia This and the other Greek place names are merely here for local color.
Balura The river Balyra (from the Greek for "cast away") received its name because Thamyris, after he was blinded, threw his lyre into it.

For Autumn was the season; red the sky
Held morn's conclusive signet of the sun
To break the mists up, bid them blaze and die.

Morn had the mastery as, one by one
All pomps produced themselves along the tract
From earth's far ending to near Heaven begun.

Was there a ravaged tree? it laughed compact
With gold, a leaf-ball crisp, high-brandished now,
30   Tempting to onset frost which late attacked.

Was there a wizened shrub, a starveling bough,
A fleecy thistle filched from by the wind,
A weed, Pan's trampling hoof would disallow?

Each, with a glory and a rapture twined
About it, joined the rush of air and light
And force: the world was of one joyous mind.

Say not the birds flew! they forebore their right—
Swam, reveling onward in the roll of things.
Say not the beasts' mirth bounded! that was flight—

40   How could the creatures leap, no lift of wings?
Such earth's community of purpose, such
The ease of earth's fulfilled imaginings—

So did the near and far appear to touch
In the moment's transport—that an interchange
Of function, far with near, seemed scarce too much;

And had the rooted plant aspired to range
With the snake's license, while the insect yearned
To glow fixed as the flower, it were not strange—

No more than if the fluttery treetop turned
50   To actual music, sang itself aloft;
Or if the wind, impassioned chantress, earned

The right to soar embodied in some soft
Fine form all fit for cloud-companionship,
And, blissful, once touched beauty chased so oft.

Thamuris, marching, let no fancy slip
Born of the fiery transport; lyre and song
Were his, to smite with hand and launch from lip—

Peerless recorded, since the list grew long
Of poets (saith Homeros) free to stand
60   Pedestaled mid the Muses' temple-throng,

A statued service, laureled, lyre in hand,
(Ay, for we see them)—Thamuris of Thrace
Predominating foremost of the band.

Therefore the morn-ray that enriched his face,
If it gave lambent chill, took flame again
From flush of pride; he saw, he knew the place.

What wind arrived with all the rhythms from plain,
Hill, dale, and that rough wildwood interspersed?
Compounding these to one consummate strain,

70   It reached him, music; but his own outburst
Of victory concluded the account,
And that grew song which was mere music erst.

'Be my Parnassos, thou Pangaian mount!
And turn thee, river, nameless hitherto!
Famed shalt thou vie with famed Pieria's fount!°

'Here I await the end of this ado:
Which wins—Earth's poet or the Heavenly Muse.'

1874   1875

Prologue
From Asolando°

PROLOGUE

'The Poet's age is sad: for why?
    In youth, the natural world could show
No common object but his eye
    At once involved with alien glow—
His own soul's iris-bow.°

'And now a flower is just a flower:
    Man, bird, beast are but beast, bird, man—
Simply themselves, uncinct° by dower
    Of dyes which, when life's day began,
10 Round each in glory ran.'°

Friend, did you need an optic glass,
    Which were your choice? A lens to drape
In ruby, emerald, chrysopras,°
    Each object—or reveal its shape
Clear outlined, past escape,

The naked very thing?—so clear
    That, when you had the chance to gaze,

fount place of the Muses
Asolando Browning's last volume, which was published in London on the same day that he died in Venice. The title refers to Asolo, a village near Venice that was a sacred place for the poet. The "Prologue," a powerful variation upon Wordsworth's "Intimations" Ode, goes back 50 years to the first time Browning saw Asolo. But where Wordsworth somberly weighs gain against loss, the fierce spirit of Browning

burns through all loss into a last transcendence.
iris-bow rainbow
uncinct not surrounded
The Poet's . . . glory ran The first two stanzas are spoken by what Blake would have called Browning's "Idiot Questioner," either an aspect of Browning himself, or a well-meaning but obtuse interlocutor.
chrysopras apple-green chalcedony, a precious stone

You found its inmost self appear
   Through outer seeming—truth ablaze,
20 Not falsehood's fancy-haze?

How many a year, my Asolo,
   Since—one step just from sea to land—
I found you, loved yet feared you so—
   For natural objects seemed to stand
Palpably fire-clothed! No—

No mastery of mine o'er these!
   Terror with beauty, like the Bush°
Burning but unconsumed. Bend knees,
   Drop eyes to earthward! Language? Tush!
30 Silence 'tis awe decrees.

And now? The lambent flame is—where?
   Lost from the naked world: earth, sky,
Hill, vale, tree, flower,—Italia's rare
   O'er-running beauty crowds the eye—
But flame? The Bush is bare.

Hill, vale, tree, flower—they stand distinct,
   Nature to know and name. What then?
A Voice spoke thence which straight unlinked
   Fancy from fact: see, all's in ken:°
40 Has once my eyelid winked?

No, for the purged ear apprehends
   Earth's import, not the eye late dazed:
The Voice said 'Call my works thy friends!
   At Nature dost thou shrink amazed?
God is it who transcends.'°
1889   1889

Bad Dreams   III°

This was my dream! I saw a Forest
   Old as the earth, no track nor trace
Of unmade man. Thou, Soul, explorest—
   Though in a trembling rapture—space
Immeasurable! Shrubs, turned trees,
Trees that touch heaven, support its frieze
Studded with sun and moon and star:

Bush See Exodus 3:2, the manifestation of
Jehovah to Moses in the burning bush.
ken knowledge, apprehension, perhaps here sight
transcends goes beyond, but the word is charged
here with extraordinary meaning, for this is
God's ultimate relation to nature
Bad Dreams III This is the third of a sequence
of four nightmare poems depicting the break-up
of a marriage (something like Meredith's *Mod-*

ern Love), developed here as phantasmagoria.
In this poem the man dreams, seeing first a vision of wild nature; then of a city of art, and
then a horror of nature and art devouring one
another. In some way he identifies himself with
the forest of nature, his wife with the city of
art, and their marriage with the mutual destruction.

While—oh, the enormous growths that bar
Mine eye from penetrating past
10   Their tangled twine where lurks—nay, lives
Royally lone, some brute-type cast
    In the rough, time cancels, man forgives.

On, Soul! I saw a lucid City°
Of architectural device
    Every way perfect. Pause for pity,
    Lightning! Nor leave a cicatrice°
On those bright marbles, dome and spire,
Structures palatial,—streets which mire
Dares not defile, paved all too fine
20 For human footstep's smirch, not thine—
Proud solitary traverser,
    My Soul, of silent lengths of way—
With what ecstatic dread, aver,
    Lest life start sanctioned by thy stay!

Ah, but the last sight was the hideous!
    A City, yes,—a Forest, true,—
But each devouring each. Perfidious
    Snake-plants had strangled what I knew
Was a pavilion once: each oak
30 Held on his horns some spoil he broke
By surreptitiously beneath
Upthrusting: pavements, as with teeth,
Griped huge weed widening crack and split
    In squares and circles stone-work erst.
Oh, Nature—good! Oh, Art—no whit
    Less worthy! Both in one—accurst!
    1888   1889

MATTHEW ARNOLD
1822–1888

Arnold is a Romantic poet who did not wish to be one, an impossible conflict which maimed his poetic talent, and caused him finally to abandon poetry for literary criticism and prose prophecy. From the middle 1850's on, Arnold was primarily a prose writer, and so this introductory note will take him only up to that time.

Arnold was born on December 24, 1822, the eldest son of the formidable Dr. Thomas Arnold, who from 1828 on was to be Headmaster of Rugby School. Dr. Arnold, a historian of some limited distinction, was a Protestant moralist of the rationalizing kind. His son did well at Rugby, but alarmed Dr. Arnold with a defensive

On, Soul . . . City Compare this stanza with   **cicatrice** the scar of a healed wound
Yeats's "Byzantium," which also excludes the
fury and the mire of human veins.

posture of continuous gaiety, which became a mock-dandyism at Balliol College, Oxford, where his closest friend was the poet Arthur Hugh Clough. After a fellowship at Oriel College, Oxford, Arnold went to London in 1847, as private secretary to a high official. In September 1848, holidaying in Switzerland, he fell in love with the "Marguerite" of his early poems, which were published in 1849 as The Strayed Reveller, and Other Poems. By 1850, at the latest, he had given up "Marguerite" (evidently because of his own prudery) and fell more properly in love with a judge's daughter, whom he married in 1851, after being appointed an Inspector of Schools.

In 1852 Arnold published his principal poem, the ambitious and uneasy Empedocles on Etna. When he brought his Poems together in 1853, he excluded Empedocles, explaining in the volume's famous anti-Romantic "Preface" that passive suffering was not a fit theme for poetry. When in 1857, he was elected Professor of Poetry at Oxford, almost all his best poetry had been written. Thus, his next poem, Merope. A Tragedy, published in 1858, is rather bad, and the outstanding poems of his last volume, New Poems (1867), were composed many years before. Whatever his achievement as a critic of literature, society, religion, his work as a poet may not merit the reputation it has continued to hold in the twentieth century. Arnold is, at his best, a very good but highly derivative poet, unlike Tennyson, Browning, Hopkins, Swinburne, and Rossetti, all of whom individualized their voices. As with Tennyson, Hopkins, and Rossetti, Arnold's dominant precursor was Keats, but this is an unhappy puzzle, since Arnold (unlike the others) professed not to admire Keats, while writing his own elegiac poems in a diction, meter, imagistic procedure, that are embarrassingly close to Keats (any reader who believes that this judgment is too harsh ought to experiment immediately by reading side-by-side the odes of Keats and Arnold's "The Scholar-Gypsy" or "Thyrsis"). Tennyson, Hopkins, and D. G. Rossetti retain distinctive Keatsian elements in their mature styles, but these elements are subdued to larger effects. But Arnold in "The Scholar-Gypsy," his best poem of some length, uses the language and movement of Keats even though the effect is irrelevant to his poem's theme. With few exceptions, Arnold's poems are seriously flawed, and yet few critics have been bothered by this; some even have argued that Arnold's faults make him more direct.

Still, it is not a mean distinction to have written lyrics as strong as the famous "To Marguerite—Continued" and "Dover Beach" or a meditative poem as insightful as "The Buried Life." Arnold got into his poetry what Tennyson and Browning scarcely needed (but absorbed anyway), the main march of mind in his time. His frequently dry tone and flatness of statement may not have been, as he happily believed, evidences of classicism, but of a lack of poetic exuberance, a failure in the vitality of his language. But much abides in his work, and he is usefully prophetic also of the anti-Romantic "Modernism" of our time, so much of which, like Arnold, has turned out to be Romantic in spite of itself.

The Strayed Reveller

Used as the title poem in Arnold's first book, this is his poetic manifesto, comparable to Keats's "Sleep and Poetry," but attempting to rebel against Keats's, Shelley's, and Byron's imaginative stances. Arnold himself is the strayed reveller, the youth who

carries himself as a Regency dandy but who bides his time, sojourning only provisionally with Circe. The bards of Romanticism, the reveller's precursors, purchase their
intense power through the loss of objective knowledge, and what little knowledge
they have through the loss of moral power. To avoid their fate, the reveller or new
poet goes to Circe, goddess of forgetfulness, and is able to observe "without pain,
without labour." When he is strong enough, he will go forth to make his own, hopefully different kind of poetry out of "the bright procession / Of eddying forms."
Though Arnold (like all young poets) partly deceived himself, "The Strayed Reveller"
is a classic statement of the dilemma of young poets seeking to evade the many (and
crippling) anxieties of influence that are endemic in Romantic tradition.

The Strayed Reveller

The portico of Circe's palace.° Evening

A YOUTH   CIRCE

THE YOUTH
Faster, faster,
O Circe, Goddess,
Let the wild, thronging train,
The bright procession
Of eddying forms,
Sweep through my soul!

Thou standest, smiling
Down on me! thy right arm,
Leaned up against the column there,
10   Props thy soft cheek;
Thy left holds, hanging loosely,
The deep cup, ivy-cinctured,°
I held but now.

Is it, then, evening
So soon? I see, the night-dews,
Clustered in thick beads, dim
The agate brooch-stones
On thy white shoulder;
The cool night-wind, too,
20   Blows through the portico,
Stirs thy hair, Goddess,
Waves thy white robe!

CIRCE
Whence art thou, sleeper?

Circe's palace The setting is from Homer's   **ivy-cinctured** circled by ivy
Odyssey X.210–13.

THE YOUTH

When the white dawn first
Through the rough fir-planks
Of my hut, by the chestnuts,
Up at the valley-head,
Came breaking, Goddess!
I sprang up, I threw round me
30 My dappled fawn-skin;°
Passing out, from the wet turf,
Where they° lay, by the hut door,
I snatched up my vine-crown, my fir-staff,
All drenched in dew—
Came swift down to join
The rout° early gathered
In the town, round the temple,
Iacchus' white fane°
On yonder hill.
40 Quick I passed, following
The wood-cutters' cart-track
Down the dark valley;—I saw
On my left, through the beeches,
Thy palace, Goddess,
Smokeless, empty!
Trembling, I entered; beheld
The court all silent,
The lions sleeping,
On the altar this bowl.
50 I drank, Goddess!
And sank down here, sleeping,
On the steps of thy portico.

CIRCE

Foolish boy! Why tremblest thou?
Thou lovest it, then, my wine?
Wouldst more of it? See, how glows,
Through the delicate, flushed marble,
The red, creaming liquor,
Strown with dark seeds!
Drink, then! I chide thee not,
60 Deny thee not my bowl.
Come, stretch forth thy hand, then—so!
Drink—drink again!

THE YOUTH

Thanks, gracious one!
Ah, the sweet fumes again!

---

fawn-skin costume of a Dionysiac reveller
they the followers of Ulysses
rout Dionysiac or Bacchic orgiastic procession

Iacchus' white fane temple of Iacchus, a god
of the Eleusinian mysteries, but Arnold confuses
him with Bacchus

More soft, ah me,
More subtle-winding
Than Pan's flute-music!°
Faint—faint! Ah me,
Again the sweet sleep!

CIRCE

70 Hist! Thou—within there!
Come forth, Ulysses!
Art tired with hunting?
While we range the woodland,
See what the day brings.

ULYSSES

Ever new magic!
Hast thou then lured hither,
Wonderful Goddess, by thy art,
The young, languid-eyed Ampelus,°
Iacchus' darling—
80 Or some youth beloved of Pan,
Of Pan and the Nymphs?
That he sits, bending downward
His white, delicate neck
To the ivy-wreathed marge°
Of thy cup; the bright, glancing vine-leaves
That crown his hair,
Falling forward, mingling
With the dark ivy-plants—
His fawn-skin, half untied,
90 Smeared with red wine-stains? Who is he,
That he sits, overweighed
By fumes of wine and sleep,
So late, in thy portico?
What youth, Goddess,—what guest
Of Gods or mortals?

CIRCE

Hist! he wakes!
I lured him not hither, Ulysses.
Nay, ask him!

THE YOUTH

Who speaks? Ah, who comes forth
100 To thy side, Goddess, from within?
How shall I name him?
This spare, dark-featured,

Pan's flute music here the pastoral verse of the   Ampelus a satyr whom Dionysus loved
younger Romantics, particularly Keats's *Endy-*   marge brim
mion and his "Ode on a Grecian Urn"

Quick-eyed stranger?
Ah, and I see too
His sailor's bonnet,
His short coat, travel-tarnished
With one arm bare!—
Art thou not he, whom fame
This long time rumours
110 The favoured guest of Circe, brought by the waves?
Art thou he, stranger?
The wise Ulysses,
Laertes' son?

ULYSSES

I am Ulysses.
And thou, too, sleeper?
Thy voice is sweet.
It may be thou hast followed
Through the islands some divine bard,°
By age taught many things,
120 Age and the Muses;
And heard him delighting
The chiefs and people
In the banquet, and learned his songs,
Of Gods and Heroes,
Of war and arts,
And peopled cities,
Inland, or built
By the grey sea.—If so, then hail!
I honour and welcome thee.

THE YOUTH

130 The Gods are happy.
They turn on all sides
Their shining eyes,
And see below them
The earth and men.

They see Tiresias°
Sitting, staff in hand,
On the warm, grassy
Asopus bank,
His robe drawn over

some divine bard a precursor poet
Tiresias Seer of Thebes, possessor of the Oedipal truth. He experienced sexual love both as a woman and a man, but he made his usual mistake of scrupulously telling the truth when Zeus and Hera insisted he judge whether women or men received more pleasure from copulation. After he confirmed the argument of Zeus, that women were more gratified, Hera blinded him, on the outrageous grounds that he was telling secrets. Zeus made what amends he could, granting Tiresias the powers of a seer, and stretching out his life to seven times the normal span. Tennyson wrote a powerful late poem on Tiresias, who also helps define the hidden homosexual theme of Eliot's *Waste Land*. Arnold brings him in because of his confrontation with Ulysses in Hades.

140   His old, sightless head,
      Revolving inly
      The doom of Thebes.

      They see the Centaurs°
      In the upper glens
      Of Pelion, in the streams,
      Where red-berried ashes fringe
      The clear-brown shallow pools,
      With streaming flanks, and heads
      Reared proudly, snuffing
150   The mountain wind.

      They see the Indian°
      Drifting, knife in hand,
      His frail boat moored to
      A floating isle thick-matted
      With large-leaved, low-creeping melon-plants,
      And the dark cucumber.
      He reaps, and stows them,
      Drifting—drifting;—round him,
      Round his green harvest-plot,
160   Flow the cool lake-waves,
      The mountains ring them.

      They see the Scythian°
      On the wide steppe, unharnessing
      His wheeled house at noon.
      He tethers his beast down, and makes his meal—
      Mares' milk, and bread
      Baked on the embers;—all around
      The boundless, waving grass-plains stretch, thick-starred
      With saffron and the yellow hollyhock
170   And flag-leaved iris-flowers.
      Sitting in his cart
      He makes his meal; before him, for long miles,
      Alive with bright green lizards,
      And the springing bustard-fowl,
      The track, a straight black line,
      Furrows the rich soil; here and there
      Clusters of lonely mounds
      Topped with rough-hewn,
      Grey, rain-bleared statues, overpeer
180   The sunny waste.

Centaurs savages—half-man, half-horse—who live on Mt. Pelion in Thessaly
Indian Lines 151–61 and 181–200 take their details from *Travels into Bokhara* (1834) by Sir Alexander Burnes, one of Arnold's favorite substitutes for actual experience.

Scythian barbarian people who came down into Greece from what is now southern Russia; their shamanism deeply affected pre-Socratic poet-philosophers like Empedocles

They see the ferry
On the broad, clay-laden
Lone Chorasmian° stream;—thereon,
With snort and strain,
Two horses, strongly swimming, tow
The ferry-boat, with woven ropes
To either bow
Firm harnessed by the mane; a chief,
With shout and shaken spear,
190   Stands at the prow, and guides them; but astern
The cowering merchants, in long robes,
Sit pale beside their wealth
Of silk-bales and of balsam-drops,
Of gold and ivory,
Of turquoise-earth and amethyst,
Jasper and chalcedony,°
And milk-barred onyx-stones.
The loaded boat swings groaning
In the yellow eddies;
200   The Gods behold them.
They see the Heroes
Sitting in the dark ship
On the foamless, long-heaving
Violet sea,
At sunset nearing
The Happy Islands.°

    These things, Ulysses,
The wise bards also
Behold and sing.
210   But oh, what labour!
O prince, what pain!

They too can see
Tiresias;—but the Gods,
Who give them vision,
Added this law:
That they should bear too
His groping blindness,
His dark foreboding,
His scorned white hairs;
220   Bear Hera's anger
Through a life lengthened
To seven ages.

They see the Centaurs
On Pelion;—then they feel,

Chorasmian Oxus River, south of Aral Sea; the locale is crucial in Shelley's *Alastor,* one of the hidden influences on "The Strayed Reveller" chalcedony transparent precious stone

Happy Islands Isles of the Blessed, where Achilles went after death, beyond Gibraltar, where Ulysses was at last to be destroyed

They too, the maddening wine
Swell their large veins to bursting; in wild pain
They feel the biting spears
Of the grim Lapithæ,° and Theseus, drive,
Drive crashing through their bones; they feel
230 High on a jutting rock in the red stream
Alcmena's dreadful son°
Ply his bow;—such a price
The Gods exact for songs:
To become what we sing.°

They see the Indian
On his mountain lake; but squalls
Make their skiff reel, and worms
In the unkind spring have gnawn
Their melon-harvest to the heart.—They see
240 The Scythian; but long frosts
Parch them in winter-time on the bare steppe,
Till they too fade like grass; they crawl
Like shadows forth in spring.

They see the merchants
On the Oxus stream;—but care
Must visit first them too, and make them pale.
Whether, through whirling sand,
A cloud of desert robber-horse have burst
Upon their caravan; or greedy kings,
250 In the walled cities the way passes through,
Crushed them with tolls; or fever-airs,
On some great river's marge,
Mown them down, far from home.

They see the Heroes
Near harbour;—but they share
Their lives, and former violent toil in Thebes,
Seven-gated Thebes, or Troy;
Or where the echoing oars
Of Argo° first
260 Startled the unknown sea.

The old Silenus°
Came, lolling in the sunshine,
From the dewy forest-coverts,
This way, at noon.

Lapithæ neighbors of the Centaurs, whom they
invited to a wedding feast, but the lustful Centaurs tried to carry off the King's bride; in a
subsequent battle, King Theseus of Athens
fought for the Lapithae
Alcmena's dreadful son Heracles, another opponent of the Centaurs
become what we sing See Rousseau in Shelley's
The Triumph of Life, ll. 279–80: "I/Have suf-

fered what I wrote, or viler pain!"; and Byron-
as-Maddalo in Shelley's *Julian and Maddalo*,
ll. 544–46: "Most wretched men/Are cradled
into poetry by wrong,/They learn in suffering
what they teach in song"
Argo Jason's ship in the quest for the Golden
Fleece
Silenus wisest and deepest-drinking of the
satyrs, teacher of the boy Dionysus

Sitting by me, while his Fauns
Down at the water-side
Sprinkled and smoothed
His drooping garland,
He told me these things.

270 But I, Ulysses,
Sitting on the warm steps,
Looking over the valley,
All day long, have seen,
Without pain, without labour,
Sometimes a wild-haired Mænad°—
Sometimes a Faun with torches—
And sometimes, for a moment,
Passing through the dark stems
Flowing-robed, the beloved,
280 The desired, the divine,
Beloved Iacchus.

Ah, cool night-wind, tremulous stars!
Ah, glimmering water,
Fitful earth-murmur,
Dreaming woods!
Ah, golden-haired, strangely smiling Goddess,
And thou, proved, much enduring,
Wave-tossed Wanderer!
Who can stand still?
290 Ye fade, ye swim, ye waver before me—
The cup again!

Faster, faster,
O Circe, Goddess,
Let the wild, thronging train,
The bright procession
Of eddying forms,
Sweep through my soul!
1847–48   1849

To Marguerite—Continued°

Yes! in the sea of life enisled,°
With echoing straits between us thrown,
Dotting the shoreless watery wild,
We mortal millions live *alone*.

Mænad frenzied female follower of Dionysus
To Marguerite . . . This is not so much a
tragic love poem, as it is Arnold's self-justifica-
tion for having denied love, and a moving but
lame attempt to assign the cause of his own
erotic failure to Necessity, the "God" of l. 22.
enisled cut off as though on an island

The islands feel the enclasping flow,
And then their endless bounds they know.

But when the moon their hollows lights,
And they are swept by balms of spring,
And in their glens, on starry nights,
10   The nightingales divinely sing;
And lovely notes, from shore to shore,
Across the sounds and channels pour—

Oh! then a longing like despair
Is to their farthest caverns sent;
For surely once, they feel, we were
Parts of a single continent!
Now round us spreads the watery plain—
Oh might our marges meet again!

Who ordered, that their longing's fire
20   Should be, as soon as kindled, cooled?
Who renders vain their deep desire?—
A God, a God their severance ruled!
And bade betwixt their shores to be
The unplumbed, salt, estranging sea.
1849   1852

Courage°

True, we must tame our rebel will:
True, we must bow to Nature's law:
Must bear in silence many an ill;
Must learn to wait, renounce, withdraw.°

Yet now, when boldest wills give place,
When Fate and Circumstance are strong,
And in their rush the human race
Are swept, like huddling sheep, along;

Those sterner spirits let me prize,
10   Who, though the tendence of the whole
They less than us might recognize,
Kept, more than us, their strength of soul.

Yes, be the second Cato° praised!
Not that he took the course to die—
But that, when 'gainst himself he raised
His arm, he raised it dauntlessly.

Courage This is Arnold's own comment on the irresolution of his conduct in his love affair with Marguerite; the longing for Byronic strength is extraordinarily revealing.
Must learn . . . withdraw reflecting the prob-
able moral influence of Carlyle and (through him) of Goethe
Cato Stoic descendant of the first Cato; he committed suicide (46 B.C.) to spite Caesar's desire to take him captive

And, Byron! let us dare admire,
If not thy fierce and turbid song,
Yet that, in anguish, doubt, desire,
20 Thy fiery courage still was strong.°

The sun that on thy tossing pain
Did with such cold derision shine,
He crushed thee not with his disdain—
He had his glow, and thou hadst thine.

Our bane, disguise it as we may,
Is weakness, is a faltering course.
Oh that past times could give our day,
Joined to its clearness, of their force!
1849   1852

From Empedocles on Etna

[SONG OF CALLICLES]°

CALLICLES *from below*
Through the black, rushing smoke-bursts,
Thick breaks the red flame;
All Etna heaves fiercely
420 Her forest-clothed frame.

Not here, O Apollo!
Are haunts meet for thee.
But, where Helicon° breaks down
In cliff to the sea,

Where the moon-silvered inlets
Send far their light voice
Up the still vale of Thisbe,°
O speed, and rejoice!

On the sward at the cliff-top
430 Lie strewn the white flocks,
On the cliff-side the pigeons
Roost deep in the rocks.

In the moonlight the shepherds,
Soft lulled by the rills,

And, Byron . . . strong See the description of
Byron in Arnold's "Memorial Verses."
[Song of Callicles] This lyric concludes the dramatic poem *Empedocles on Etna*, whose theme
is the inadequacy of the modern world to sustain the classical poetic imagination. Empedocles, Greek poet-philosopher who lived in
Sicily about 440 B.C., is Arnold's Byronic hero,
who dies because of excessive self-consciousness,
and who is afflicted by his acute sense of being
a spiritual latecomer, alive after the proper context for his work has vanished. The strangely
exultant but still despairing Empedocles has
just destroyed himself by plunging into the volcano's crater. His harp player, Callicles (whose
name is derived from a Greek word for beauty),
survives him to sing this triumphal Keatsian
song of the Muses, which derives many of its
details from Hesiod's *Theogony*, ll. 1–39.
Helicon Boetian mountain of the Muses
Thisbe town between Helicon and Gulf of
Corinth

Lie wrapped in their blankets
Asleep on the hills.

—What forms are these coming
So white through the gloom?
What garments out-glistening
440 The gold-flowered broom?

What sweet-breathing presence
Out-perfumes the thyme?
What voices enrapture
The night's balmy prime?—

'Tis Apollo comes leading
His choir, the Nine.
—The leader is fairest,
But all are divine.

They are lost in the hollows!
450 They stream up again!
What seeks on this mountain
The glorified train?—

They bathe on this mountain,
In the spring by their road;
Then on to Olympus,
Their endless abode.

—Whose praise do they mention?
Of what is it told?—
What will be for ever;
460 What was from of old.

First hymn they the Father
Of all things; and then,
The rest of immortals,
The action of men.

The day in his hotness,
The strife with the palm;
The night in her silence,
The stars in their calm.
1849–52   1852

Memorial Verses

April, 1850°

Goethe in Weimar sleeps, and Greece,
Long since, saw Byron's struggle cease.°

April, 1850 Wordsworth died on April 23, 1850.
Goethe . . . cease Byron died in Greece in 1824; notice that Arnold could not conceive of Byron as "sleeping," like the dead sage Goethe, but only as having ceased in his intense struggle.

But one such death remained to come;
The last poetic voice is dumb°—
We stand today by Wordsworth's tomb.

When Byron's eyes were shut in death,
We bowed our head and held our breath.
He taught us little; but our soul
Had *felt* him like the thunder's roll.
10   With shivering heart the strife we saw
Of passion with eternal law;
And yet with reverential awe
We watched the fount of fiery life
Which served for that Titanic strife.°
    When Goethe's death was told, we said:
Sunk, then, is Europe's sagest head.
Physician of the iron age,°
Goethe has done his pilgrimage.
He took the suffering human race,
20   He read each wound, each weakness clear;
And struck his finger on the place,
And said: *Thou ailest here, and here!*
He looked on Europe's dying hour°
Of fitful dream and feverish power;
His eye plunged down the weltering strife,
The turmoil of expiring life—
He said: *The end is everywhere,
Art still has truth, take refuge there!*
And he was happy, if to know
30   Causes of things, and far below
His feet to see the lurid flow
Of terror, and insane distress,
And headlong fate, be happiness.°

And Wordsworth!—Ah, pale ghosts, rejoice!
For never has such soothing voice
Been to your shadowy world conveyed,°
Since erst, at morn, some wandering shade
Heard the clear song of Orpheus come
Through Hades,° and the mournful gloom.
40   Wordsworth has gone from us—and ye,°
Ah, may ye feel his voice as we!
He too upon a wintry clime
Had fallen—on this iron time

is dumb hardly a compliment to Tennyson and Browning, among others
Titanic strife the battle between the Promethean Byron and the moral law; an internalized battle, and so the more impressive
iron age classical way of describing an age in acute decline
dying hour the end of the European Enlightenment, and the advent of revolution and Romanticism
happiness Lines 29–33 are a fairly close trans-

lation of Virgil (*Georgics* II. 480–82), where Virgil is brooding about Lucretius. Arnold is therefore casting himself as Virgil in relation to Wordsworth or Goethe as Lucretius.
conveyed Wordsworth has gone to Hades, rather than any version of a Christian heaven; an impressive touch on Arnold's part.
Orpheus . . . Hades when Orpheus descended in the vain attempt to bring back his wife, Eurydice
ye inhabitants of Hades

Of doubts, disputes, distractions, fears.
He found us when the age had bound
Our souls in its benumbing round;
He spoke, and loosed our heart in tears.
He laid us as we lay at birth
On the cool flowery lap of earth,
50   Smiles broke from us and we had ease;
The hills were round us, and the breeze
Went o'er the sun-lit fields again;
Our foreheads felt the wind and rain.
Our youth returned; for there was shed
On spirits that had long been dead,
Spirits dried up and closely furled,
The freshness of the early world.

Ah! since dark days still bring to light
Man's prudence and man's fiery might,
60   Time may restore us in his course
Goethe's sage mind and Byron's force;
But where will Europe's latter hour
Again find Wordsworth's healing power?
Others will teach us how to dare,
And against fear our breast to steel;
Others will strengthen us to bear—
But who, ah! who, will make us feel?
The cloud of mortal destiny,
Others will front it fearlessly—
70   But who, like him, will put it by?

Keep fresh the grass upon his grave
O Rotha,° with thy living wave!
Sing him thy best! for few or none
Hears thy voice right, now he is gone.
1850   1850

Dover Beach°

The sea is calm tonight.
The tide is full, the moon lies fair
Upon the straits;—on the French coast the light
Gleams and is gone; the cliffs of England stand,

---

put it by a subtle tribute to Wordsworth's
"Intimations" Ode
Rotha the river that flows close to Grasmere
churchyard, where Wordsworth was buried
Dover Beach Arnold's most famous poem, presumably because it is believed to convey a universal sorrow of his time, this nevertheless has
some flaws. Though it cannot be dated with any
certainty, it may go back as far as 1848, and
reflect not only the European revolutions of
that year, but Arnold's anguish about Mar-

guerite. Whatever its date, a troubled reader,
however justly admiring, can wonder whether
the poem earns the transition between its last
two stanzas. As in the great lyric to Marguerite,
Arnold is rather too ready to ascribe his own
failure of nerve, erotically speaking, to a larger
crisis in the history of culture. For a wry contemporary comment on this fascinating poem,
see Anthony Hecht's poem, "The Dover Bitch,"
which rewrites Arnold from the young lady's
point of view.

Glimmering and vast, out in the tranquil bay.
Come to the window, sweet is the night-air!

Only, from the long line of spray
Where the sea meets the moon-blanched land,
Listen! you hear the grating roar
10   Of pebbles which the waves draw back, and fling,
At their return, up the high strand,
Begin, and cease, and then again begin,
With tremulous cadence slow, and bring
The eternal note of sadness in.

Sophocles long ago°
Heard it on the Ægæan, and it brought
Into his mind the turbid ebb and flow
Of human misery; we
Find also in the sound a thought,
20   Hearing it by this distant northern sea.

The Sea of Faith
Was once, too, at the full, and round earth's shore
Lay like the folds of a bright girdle furled.°
But now I only hear
Its melancholy, long, withdrawing roar,
Retreating, to the breath
Of the night-wind, down the vast edges drear
And naked shingles of the world.

Ah, love, let us be true
30   To one another! for the world, which seems
To lie before us like a land of dreams,
So various, so beautiful, so new,
Hath really neither joy, nor love, nor light,
Nor certitude, nor peace, nor help for pain;
And we are here as on a darkling plain
Swept with confused alarms of struggle and flight,
Where ignorant armies clash by night.°
?1848   1867

Sophocles long ago Though Arnold preferred
Sophocles to the other Greek dramatists, one
can suspect that "Sophocles" here is a mask
for the palpable indebtedness to Wordsworth,
rather like the pseudo-reference to Otway in
Coleridge's "Dejection: An Ode." Every passage
scholars have cited from Sophocles is absurdly
far from Arnold's lines, but the Wordsworth
of "Tintern Abbey," the "Intimations" Ode,
and the sonnets of 1802 is very close. Arnold,
like Wordsworth, is hearing "the still, sad music
of humanity,/Nor harsh nor grating, though of
ample power/To chasten and subdue."
bright girdle furled a difficult line; to be construed only by excessive ingenuity
clash by night Possibly an echo of a passage in
a poem by his friend Clough, but the ultimate
source, as all scholars have said, is almost cer-

tainly the account by the Athenian historian
Thucydides of the battle of Epipolae, between
the Syracusans and the Athenians. In the translation of Thucydides by Arnold's father, the
soldiers "see before them the form of the object but . . . mistrust their knowing who was
friend and who was foe." The Loeb translation,
with greater clarity, gives: "seeing before them
the vision of a person but mistrusting their recognition of their own friends. . . ." If the
poem was written in 1848 or 1849, then Arnold
is manifesting a very ambiguous attitude toward
the third wave of the European revolution, but
tradition has solved this problem by deciding
that the passage is a characterization of the entire Victorian Age, or even of the modern world
in general.

The Buried Life°

Light flows our war° of mocking words, and yet,
Behold, with tears mine eyes are wet!°
I feel a nameless sadness o'er me roll.°
Yes, yes, we know that we can jest,
We know, we know that we can smile!
But there's a something in this breast,
To which thy light words bring no rest,
And thy gay smiles no anodyne.°
Give me thy hand, and hush awhile,°
10 And turn those limpid eyes on mine,
And let me read there, love! thy inmost soul.

Alas! is even love too weak
To unlock the heart, and let it speak?
Are even lovers powerless to reveal
To one another what indeed they feel?
I knew the mass of men concealed
Their thoughts, for fear that if revealed
They would by other men be met
With blank indifference, or with blame reproved;
20 I knew they lived and moved
Tricked in disguises, alien to the rest
Of men, and alien to themselves—and yet
The same heart beats in every human breast!

But we, my love!—doth a like spell benumb
Our hearts, our voices?—must we too be dumb?
Ah! well for us, if even we,
Even for a moment, can get free
Our heart, and have our lips unchained;
For that which seals them hath been deep-ordained!
30 Fate, which foresaw
How frivolous a baby man would be—
By what distractions he would be possessed,
How he would pour himself in every strife,
And well-nigh change his own identity—
That it might keep from his capricious play

The Buried Life Again difficult to date, this most profound of Arnold's poems belongs to the 1848–52 period, and is closely related to the Marguerite poems and to "Dover Beach" (particularly if that is a Marguerite poem also). The parent poem is Keats's "Ode on Melancholy," but there are clear debts also to Wordsworth, and perhaps even to Tennyson. Of all Arnold's poems, this is the most authentic attempt to exorcise the demons of self-consciousness, and not merely to exploit them.
our war Evidently refers to banter between Marguerite and the poet, and yet suddenly he finds himself in tears.

are wet perhaps a reference to Tennyson's "Tears, Idle Tears" (from *The Princess*, 1847), but the resemblance may exist because Keats and Wordsworth inform both poems
I feel . . . roll See Wordsworth's "Resolution and Independence," l. 28.
anodyne pain-killing drug
hush awhile Marguerite was much more vivacious than Arnold, whose lightness of spirit was always a mask; ll. 9–11 clearly stem from Keats's "Ode on Melancholy," ll. 19–20, but Keats's peculiar sense of "melancholy" as a heightened, oxymoronic, creative sense of consciousness pervades Arnold's entire poem.

His genuine self, and force him to obey
Even in his own despite his being's law,
Bade through the deep recesses of our breast
The unregarded river of our life
40 Pursue with indiscernible flow its way;
And that we should not see
The buried stream, and seem to be
Eddying at large in blind uncertainty,
Though driving on with it eternally.

But often, in the world's most crowded streets,
But often, in the din of strife,°
There rises an unspeakable desire°
After the knowledge of our buried life;
A thirst to spend our fire and restless force
50 In tracking out our true, original course;
A longing to inquire
Into the mystery of this heart which beats
So wild, so deep in us—to know
Whence our lives come and where they go.
And many a man in his own breast then delves,
But deep enough, alas! none ever mines.
And we have been on many thousand lines,
And we have shown, on each, spirit and power;
But hardly have we, for one little hour,
60 Been on our own line, have we been ourselves—
Hardly had skill to utter one of all
The nameless feelings that course through our breast,
But they course on for ever unexpressed.

And long we try in vain to speak and act
Our hidden self, and what we say and do
Is eloquent, is well—but 'tis not true!
And then we will no more be racked
With inward striving, and demand
Of all the thousand nothings of the hour
70 Their stupefying° power;
Ah yes, and they benumb us at our call!°
Yet still, from time to time, vague and forlorn,
From the soul's subterranean depth upborne
As from an infinitely distant land,
Come airs, and floating echoes, and convey
A melancholy° into all our day.

Only—but this is rare—
When a belovéd hand is laid in ours,
When, jaded with the rush and glare

---

din of strife See "Tintern Abbey," ll. 25–26.   at our call when we call them
unspeakable desire See *Paradise Lost* III.662–63. melancholy but in the Keatsian, rich sense; not
stupefying to deaden our sense of being lost   the ordinary one

80   Of the interminable hours,
       Our eyes can in another's eyes read clear,
       When our world-deafened ear
       Is by the tones of a loved voice caressed—
       A bolt is shot back somewhere in our breast,
       And a lost pulse of feeling stirs again.
       The eye sinks inward, and the heart lies plain,
       And what we mean, we say, and what we would, we know.
       A man becomes aware of his life's flow,
       And hears its winding murmur; and he sees
90   The meadows where it glides, the sun, the breeze.

       And there arrives a lull in the hot race
       Wherein he doth for ever chase
       That flying and elusive shadow, rest.
       An air of coolness plays upon his face,
       And an unwonted calm pervades his breast.
       And then he thinks he knows
       The hills where his life rose,
       And the sea where it goes.°
1848–52   1852

Stanzas from the Grande Chartreuse

This rugged and impressive poem triumphs over its own confusions, and by any standards is one of Arnold's finest. The central confusion is that the monastery which is his ostensible subject has not much to do with Arnold's theme, and indeed he cares so little for the Grande Chartreuse in itself that he cannot be bothered to get the procedures of the Carthusians right. They are so irrelevant to the modern world's problems, in his view, that he cannot be interested in them. As Tinker and Lowry note in their *Commentary,* in his mind's eye Arnold sees not the Chartreuse, but St. Mary's at Oxford, the church of Newman. The rejection, in the poem, is of the Oxford Movement, but also of the Protestantism in which Arnold was reared, and (most powerfully, because most ambivalently) of High Romanticism, particularly of the Prometheans Byron and Shelley. What is most moving and disarming about the poem is Arnold's candor in telling us he has nothing to install in the place of the ideologies he is compelled to reject. This distinguishes the poem's argument from the aggressiveness of Carlyle, with whom nevertheless it shares many attitudes. Though Arnold speaks of a more fortunate age that may come, his heart, in this poem, remains a handful of dust.

where it goes The general imagery of the "Intimations" Ode is at work here.

Stanzas from the Grande Chartreuse

Through Alpine meadows soft-suffused
With rain, where thick the crocus blows,°
Past the dark forges long disused,
The mule-track from Saint Laurent° goes.
The bridge is crossed, and slow we ride,
Through forest, up the mountainside.

The autumnal evening darkens round,
The wind is up, and drives the rain;
While, hark! far down, with strangled sound
10   Doth the Dead Guier's stream° complain,
Where that wet smoke, among the woods,
Over his boiling cauldron broods.

Swift rush the spectral vapours white
Past limestone scars° with ragged pines,
Showing—then blotting from our sight!—
Halt—through the cloud-drift something shines!
High in the valley, wet and drear,
The huts of Courrerie° appear.

Strike leftward! cries our guide; and higher
20   Mounts up the stony forest-way.
At last the encircling trees retire;
Look! through the showery twilight grey
What pointed roofs are these advance?—
A palace of the Kings of France?

Approach, for what we seek is here!
Alight, and sparely sup, and wait
For rest in this outbuilding near;°
Then cross the sward and reach that gate.
Knock; pass the wicket! Thou art come
30   To the Carthusians' world-famed home.°

The silent courts, where night and day
Into their stone-carved basins cold
The splashing icy fountains play—
The humid corridors behold!
Where, ghostlike in the deepening night,
Cowled forms brush by in gleaming white.

The chapel, where no organ's peal
Invests the stern and naked prayer—

blows blossoms
Saint Laurent a village near the monastery
stream Guier's Mort River
scars cliffs
Courrerie a village near by
outbuilding near guesthouse
Carthusians' world-famed home On September

7, 1851, soon after they married, Arnold and
his wife visited La Grande Chartreuse, the
Carthusian monastery near Grenoble, France.
The Carthusians were renowned for their strict
discipline, and the superb liqueur that they
produced, for commercial purposes.

With penitential cries they kneel
40 And wrestle; rising then, with bare°
And white uplifted faces stand,
Passing the Host from hand to hand;°

Each takes, and then his visage wan
Is buried in his cowl once more.
The cells!—the suffering Son of Man
Upon the wall—the knee-worn floor—
And where they sleep, that wooden bed,
Which shall their coffin be, when dead!°

The library, where tract and tome
50 Not to feed priestly pride are there,
To hymn the conquering march of Rome,°
Nor yet to amuse, as ours are!
They paint of souls the inner strife,
Their drops of blood, their death in life.

The garden, overgrown—yet mild,
See, fragrant herbs are flowering there!
Strong children of the Alpine wild
Whose culture is the brethren's care;
Of human tasks their only one,
60 And cheerful works beneath the sun.°

Those halls, too, destined to contain
Each its own pilgrim-host of old,
From England, Germany, or Spain—
All are before me! I behold
The House, the Brotherhood austere!
—And what am I, that I am here?

For rigorous teachers seized my youth,°
And purged its faith,° and trimmed its fire,
Showed me the high, white star of Truth,
70 There bade me gaze, and there aspire.
Even now their whispers pierce the gloom:
What dost thou in this living tomb?

Forgive me, masters of the mind!
At whose behest I long ago
So much unlearnt, so much resigned—
I come not here to be your foe!

bare unhooded
hand to hand The Host is *not* passed from
hand to hand, and visitors weren't allowed at
Mass anyway; Arnold was being very careless
indeed.
when dead More carelessness; Carthusians are
buried on planks of wood, but *not* on their
wooden beds.

march of Rome victories in history of the
Roman Catholic Church
the sun This stanza refers to the manufacture
of Chartreuse liqueur.
seized my youth probably refers to his father,
Dr. Thomas Arnold, but may mean also the
writings of Goethe and Carlyle
purged its faith of irrational elements

I seek these anchorites,° not in ruth,°
To curse and to deny your truth:

Not as their friend, or child, I speak!
80 But as, on some far northern strand,
Thinking of his own Gods, a Greek
In pity and mournful awe might stand
Before some fallen Runic stone°—
For both were faiths, and both are gone.

Wandering between two worlds, one dead,
The other powerless to be born,
With nowhere yet to rest my head,°
Like these, on earth I wait forlorn.
Their faith, my tears, the world deride—
90 I come to shed them at their side.

Oh, hide me in your gloom profound,
Ye solemn seats of holy pain!
Take me, cowled forms, and fence me round,
Till I possess my soul again;
Till free my thoughts before me roll,
Not chafed by hourly false control!

For the world cries your faith is now
But a dead time's exploded dream;
My melancholy, sciolists° say,
100 Is a passed mode, an outworn theme—
As if the world had ever had
A faith, or sciolists been sad!

Ah, if it *be* passed, take away,
At least, the restlessness, the pain;
Be man henceforth no more a prey
To these out-dated stings again!
The nobleness of grief is gone—
Ah, leave us not the fret alone!

But—if you cannot give us ease—
110 Last of the race of them who grieve
Here leave us to die out with these
Last of the people who believe!

anchorites monks
ruth penitence
Runic stone northern stone inscribed with letters
of earliest Teutonic alphabet. As an emancipated Greek might feel a vain regret both for
his own dead faith and the dead northern religion, so Arnold studies the nostalgias of his
father's Protestantism and the Carthusians'
Catholicism, knowing them both to be gone
forever.

rest my head Notice the "yet," in which there
is some wan hope, and perhaps a touch of the
outcast prophet, with its possibly unconscious
echo of Matthew 8:20: "The foxes have holes,
and the birds of the air have nests; but the
Son of man hath not where to lay his head."
sciolists superficial pretenders to knowledge;
academic impostors

Silent, while years engrave° the brow;
Silent—the best are silent now.°

Achilles ponders in his tent,°
The kings of modern thought are dumb;°
Silent they are, though not content,
And wait to see the future come.
They have the grief men had of yore,
120 But they contend and cry no more.

Our fathers° watered with their tears
This sea of time whereon we sail,
Their voices were in all men's ears
Who passed within their puissant hail.
Still the same ocean round us raves,
But we stand mute, and watch the waves.

For what availed it, all the noise
And outcry of the former men?—
Say, have their sons achieved more joys,
130 Say, is life lighter now than then?
The sufferers died, they left their pain—
The pangs which tortured them remain.

What helps it now, that Byron bore,
With haughty scorn which mocked the smart,
Through Europe to the Ætolian shore°
The pageant of his bleeding heart?
That thousands counted every groan,
And Europe made his woe her own?°

What boots it, Shelley! that the breeze
140 Carried thy lovely wail away,
Musical through Italian trees
Which fringe thy soft blue Spezzian bay?
Inheritors of thy distress
Have restless hearts one throb the less?°

---

engrave make the brow furrowed
silent now a puzzling line, since the early
1850's hardly was a time when the best were
silent (see Yeats's "The Second Coming," ll.
7–8, where this combines with a passage from
Shelley's *Prometheus Unbound*)
in his tent Scholars generally say this is Newman, but Dwight Culler pungently remarks that
"Newman would not have been called 'Achilles'
in 1851–52 when he was in process of being
sued for libel by a defrocked priest named
Achilli." Culler plausibly suggests Carlyle as
Achilles.
are dumb Probably the "kings of modern
thought" are poets, since Arnold is indebted to
Shelley's *Adonais*, ll. 430–31, where the "kings

of thought/Who waged contention with their
time's decay" are the poets to whom Keats is
gathered after his death.
fathers the Romantic poets
Ætolian shore region in Greece where Byron
died a hero's death
woe her own probably a reference to *Childe
Harold's Pilgrimage*
throb the less Shelley drowned in the Bay of
Spezzia; his poetry is not recognizable from
this stanza, or from anything else that Arnold
ever said about it; whatever Shelley wished
to do for his readers, he was not trying to
make their hearts less restless, since he was
always a dedicated revolutionary agitator.

Or are we easier, to have read,
O Obermann!° the sad, stern page,
Which tells us how thou hidd'st thy head
From the fierce tempest of thine age
In the lone brakes of Fontainebleau,°
150   Or chalets near the Alpine snow?

Ye slumber in your silent grave!—
The world, which for an idle day
Grace to your mood of sadness gave,
Long since hath flung her weeds° away.
The eternal trifler breaks your spell;
But we—we learnt your lore too well!

Years hence, perhaps, may dawn an age,
More fortunate, alas! than we,
Which without hardness will be sage,
160   And gay without frivolity.
Sons of the world, oh, speed those years;
But, while we wait, allow our tears!

Allow them! We admire with awe
The exulting thunder of your race;
You give the universe your law,
Your triumph over time and space!
Your pride of life, your tireless powers,
We laud them, but they are not ours.

We are like children reared in shade
170   Beneath some old-world abbey wall,
Forgotten in a forest-glade,
And secret from the eyes of all.
Deep, deep the greenwood round them waves,
Their abbey, and its close° of graves!

But, where the road runs near the stream,
Oft through the trees they catch a glance
Of passing troops in the sun's beam—
Pennon, and plume, and flashing lance!
Forth to the world those soldiers fare,
180   To life, to cities, and to war!

And through the wood, another way,
Faint bugle-notes from far are borne,
Where hunters gather, staghounds bay,
Round some fair forest-lodge at morn.

Obermann Etienne Pivert de Senancour (1770–
1846), French moralist, wrote *Obermann*, a
series of letters reflecting on nature and the
soul. One of Arnold's favorite books (he wrote
an essay and two poems about it), *Obermann*
is a severe, melancholy (and rather boring)
work, and tempted Arnold with a *persona* he
fortunately did not adopt.
Fontainebleau where Senancour died, near
Paris
weeds mourning clothes
close enclosure

Gay dames are there, in sylvan green;
Laughter and cries—those notes between!

The banners flashing through the trees
Make their blood dance and chain their eyes;
That bugle-music on the breeze
190   Arrests them with a charmed surprise.
Banner by turns and bugle woo:
Ye shy recluses, follow too!

O children, what do ye reply?—
'Action and pleasure, will ye roam
Through these secluded dells to cry
And call us?—but too late ye come!
Too late for us your call ye blow,
Whose bent was taken long ago.

'Long since we pace this shadowed nave;
200   We watch those yellow tapers shine,
Emblems of hope over the grave,
In the high altar's depth divine;
The organ carries to our ear
Its accents of another sphere.°

'Fenced early in this cloistral round
Of reverie, of shade, of prayer,
How should we grow in other ground?
How can we flower in foreign air?
—Pass, banners, pass, and bugles, cease;
210   And leave our desert° to its peace!'
1851–55   1855

The Scholar-Gipsy

Arnold based this pastoral on a passage from Joseph Glanvil's *Vanity of Dogmatizing*
(1661), which he condensed so as to make it an introduction to the poem:

> There was very lately a lad in the University of Oxford, who was by his
> poverty forced to leave his studies there; and at last to join himself to a
> company of vagabond gypsies. Among these extravagant people, by the in-
> sinuating subtility of his carriage, he quickly got so much of their love and
> esteem as that they discovered to him their mystery. After he had been a
> pretty while exercised in the trade, there chanced to ride by a couple of
> scholars, who had formerly been of his acquaintance. They quickly spied out
> their old friend among the gypsies; and he gave them an account of the
> necessity which drove him to that kind of life, and told them that the people
> he went with were not such impostors as they were taken for, but that they
> had a traditional kind of learning among them, and could do wonders by
> the power of imagination, their fancy binding that of others: that himself had

sphere As Carthusians did not have organs,   **desert** in the voice-in-the-wilderness sense
Arnold clearly is thinking of the Oxford Move-
ment and other ritualists.

learned much of their art, and when he had compassed the whole secret, he
intended, he said, to leave their company, and give the world an account of
what he had learned.

The Scholar-Gipsy

Go, for they call you, shepherd,° from the hill;
  Go, shepherd, and untie the wattled cotes!°
  No longer leave thy wistful flock unfed,
  Nor let thy bawling fellows° rack their throats,
  Nor the cropped herbage shoot another head.
    But when the fields are still,°
  And the tired men and dogs all gone to rest,
  And only the white sheep are sometimes seen
  Cross and recross the strips of moon-blanched green,
10 Come, shepherd, and again begin the quest!°

Here, where the reaper was at work of late—
  In this high field's dark corner, where he leaves
  His coat, his basket, and his earthen cruse,°
  And in the sun all morning binds the sheaves,
  Then here, at noon, comes back his stores to use—
    Here will I sit and wait,
  While to my ear from uplands far away
  The bleating of the folded° flocks is borne,
  With distant cries of reapers in the corn°—
20 All the live murmur of a summer's day.

Screened is this nook o'er the high, half-reaped field,
  And here till sun-down, shepherd! will I be.
  Through the thick corn the scarlet poppies peep,
  And round green roots and yellowing stalks I see
  Pale pink convolvulus° in tendrils creep;
    And air-swept lindens yield
  Their scent, and rustle down their perfumed showers
  Of bloom on the bent grass where I am laid,
  And bower me from the August sun with shade;
30 And the eye travels down to Oxford's towers.

shepherd probably his friend, the poet Clough
wattled cotes sheepfolds constructed of twigs
bawling fellows the bleating sheep he tends.
Arnold's irony is savage, as it will be later in
this poem in the barely hidden attack upon
Tennyson's *In Memoriam*, for which see ll.
182–91.
fields are still when revolutionary social agitation is momentarily over, freeing Clough for
the more Arnoldian activities of contemplation
and writing reflective verse

the quest presumably for the Scholar-Gipsy
and his art, but that is a rather inadequate
emblem for what Arnold means, which is nothing less than the whole of his enterprise, personal and cultural
cruse water jar
folded properly enclosed
corn wheat or other grain, in England
convolvulus morning-glory

And near me on the grass lies Glanvil's book—
Come, let me read the oft-read tale again!
The story of the Oxford scholar poor,
Of pregnant parts° and quick inventive brain,
Who, tired of knocking at preferment's door,
One summermorn forsook
His friends, and went to learn the gipsy-lore,
And roamed the world with that wild brotherhood,
And came, as most men deemed, to little good,
40   But came to Oxford and his friends no more.

But once, years after, in the country-lanes,
Two scholars, whom at college erst he knew,
Met him, and of his way of life enquired;
Whereat he answered that the gipsy-crew,
His mates, had arts to rule as they desired
The workings of men's brains.
And they can bind them to what thoughts they will.
'And I,' he said, 'the secret of their art,
When fully learned, will to the world impart;
50   But it needs heaven-sent moments for this skill.'

This said, he left them, and returned no more.—
But rumours hung about the countryside,
That the lost Scholar long was seen to stray,
Seen by rare glimpses, pensive and tongue-tied,
In hat of antique shape, and cloak of grey,
The same the gipsies wore.
Shepherds had met him on the Hurst° in spring;
At some lone alehouse in the Berkshire moors,°
On the warm ingle-bench,° the smock-frocked boors°
60   Had found him seated at their entering,

But, 'mid their drink and clatter, he would fly.
And I myself seem half to know thy looks,
And put the shepherds, wanderer! on thy trace;
And boys who in lone wheatfields scare the rooks
I ask if thou hast passed their quiet place;
Or in my boat I lie
Moored to the cool bank in the summer-heats,
'Mid wide grass meadows which the sunshine fills,
And watch the warm, green-muffled Cumner hills,
70   And wonder if thou haunt'st their shy retreats.

For most, I know, thou lov'st retired ground!
Thee at the ferry Oxford riders blithe,

pregnant parts promising intellectual gifts
Hurst hill near Oxford
Berkshire moors south of Oxford

ingle-bench chimney nook bench
smock-frocked boors smock-attired farm workers

Returning home on summer-nights, have met
Crossing the stripling Thames° at Bab-lock-hithe,°
Trailing in the cool stream thy fingers wet,
    As the punt's rope chops round;
And leaning backward in a pensive dream,
And fostering in thy lap a heap of flowers
Plucked in shy fields and distant Wychwood° bowers,
80   And thine eyes resting on the moonlit stream.

And then they land, and thou art seen no more!—
Maidens, who from the distant hamlets come
To dance around the Fyfield elm° in May,
Oft through the darkening fields have seen thee roam,
    Or cross a stile into the public way.
    Oft thou hast given them store
Of flowers—the frail-leafed, white anemony,
Dark bluebells drenched with dews of summer eves,
And purple orchises with spotted leaves—
90   But none hath words she can report of thee.

And, above Godstow Bridge,° when hay-time's here
In June, and many a scythe in sunshine flames,
Men who through those wide fields of breezy grass
Where black-winged swallows haunt the glittering Thames,
    To bathe in the abandoned lasher° pass,
    Have often passed thee near
Sitting upon the river bank o'ergrown;
Marked thine outlandish garb, thy figure spare,
Thy dark vague eyes, and soft abstracted air—
100   But, when they came from bathing, thou wast gone!

At some lone homestead in the Cumner hills,
Where at her open door the housewife darns,
Thou hast been seen, or hanging on a gate
To watch the threshers in the mossy barns.
    Children, who early range these slopes and late
    For cresses from the rills,
Have known thee eying, all an April-day,
The springing pastures and the feeding kine;
And marked thee, when the stars come out and shine,
110   Through the long dewy grass move slow away.

In autumn, on the skirts of Bagley Wood°—
Where most the gipsies by the turf-edged way
Pitch their smoked tents, and every bush you see
With scarlet patches tagged and shreds of grey,

stripling Thames Thames near Oxford is just a
stream.
Bab-lock-hithe Thames ferry near village of
Cumner
Wychwood wood ten miles north of Oxford

Fyfield elm At Fyfield, near Oxford, an elm tree
served as a Maypole for festivities on May 1.
Godstow Bridge near Oxford, over Thames
lasher pool formed below dam
Bagley Wood three miles south of Oxford

Above the forest-ground called Thessaly°—
   The blackbird, picking food,
Sees thee, nor stops his meal, nor fears at all;
So often has he known thee past him stray,
Rapt, twirling in thy hand a withered spray,
120   And waiting for the spark from heaven to fall.

And once, in winter, on the causeway chill
   Where home through flooded fields foot-travellers go,
Have I not passed thee on the wooden bridge,
Wrapped in thy cloak and battling with the snow,
   Thy face toward Hinksey° and its wintry ridge?
   And thou hast climbed the hill,
And gained the white brow of the Cumner range;
Turned once to watch, while thick the snowflakes fall.
   The line of festal light in Christ-Church hall°—
130   Then sought thy straw in some sequestered grange.

But what—I dream! Two hundred years are flown
   Since first thy story ran through Oxford halls,
And the grave Glanvil did the tale inscribe
That thou wert wandered from the studious walls
   To learn strange arts, and join a gipsy-tribe;
   And thou from earth art gone
Long since, and in some quiet churchyard laid—
   Some country-nook, where o'er thy unknown grave
Tall grasses and white flowering nettles wave,
140   Under a dark, red-fruited yew-tree's shade.

—No, no, thou hast not felt the lapse of hours!
For what wears out the life of mortal men?
   'Tis that from change to change their being rolls;
'Tis that repeated shocks, again, again,
   Exhaust the energy of strongest souls
   And numb the elastic powers.
Till having used our nerves with bliss and teen,°
   And tired upon a thousand schemes our wit,
   To the just-pausing Genius° we remit
150   Our worn-out life, and are—what we have been.

Thou hast not lived, why should'st thou perish, so?
   Thou hadst *one* aim, *one* business, *one* desire;
Else wert thou long since numbered with the dead!
Else hadst thou spent, like other men, thy fire!
   The generations of thy peers are fled,
   And we ourselves shall go;

Thessaly Oxford men called a spot near Bagley
Wood by this name
Hinksey village south of Oxford
Christ-Church hall dining hall of an Oxford
college

teen sorrow
just-pausing Genius a transcendental entity
which pauses only momentarily for our individual demises

But thou possessest an immortal lot,
   And we imagine thee exempt from age
   And living as thou livest on Glanvil's page,
160 Because thou hadst—what we, alas! have not.

For early didst thou leave the world, with powers
   Fresh, undiverted to the world without,
     Firm to their mark, not spent on other things;
   Free from the sick fatigue, the languid doubt,
     Which much to have tried, in much been baffled, brings.
       O life unlike to ours!
   Who fluctuate idly without term or scope,
Of whom each strives, nor knows for what he strives,
   And each half lives a hundred different lives;
170 Who wait like thee, but not, like thee, in hope.

Thou waitest for the spark from heaven! and we,
   Light half-believers of our casual creeds,
     Who never deeply felt, not clearly willed,
   Whose insight never has borne fruit in deeds,
     Whose vague resolves never have been fulfilled;
       For whom each year we see
Breeds new beginnings, disappointments new;
   Who hesitate and falter life away,
   And lose tomorrow the ground won today—
180 Ah! do not we, wanderer! await it too?

Yes, we await it!—but it still delays,
   And then we suffer! and amongst us one,°
     Who most has suffered, takes dejectedly
   His seat upon the intellectual throne;
     And all his store of sad experience he
       Lays bare of wretched days;
Tells us his misery's birth and growth and signs,
   And how the dying spark of hope was fed,
   And how the breast was soothed, and how the head,
190 And all his hourly varied anodynes.

This for our wisest!° and we others pine,
   And wish the long unhappy dream would end,
     And waive all claim to bliss, and try to bear;
   With close-lipped patience for our only friend,
     Sad patience, too near neighbour to despair—
       But none has hope like thine!
Thou through the fields and through the woods dost stray,
   Roaming the countryside, a truant boy,

---

one a barely disguised ironic portrait of Tenny-son's performance in the elegies for Hallam, *In Memoriam*. To cover his savagery, Arnold insisted he meant Goethe, but it is Tennyson nevertheless.
wisest an irony: Arnold did not find much wis-dom in Tennyson's poetry

Nursing thy project in unclouded joy,
200   And every doubt long blown by time away.

O born in days when wits were fresh and clear,
    And life ran gaily as the sparkling Thames;
        Before this strange disease of modern life,
    With its sick hurry, its divided aims,
        Its heads o'ertaxed, its palsied hearts, was rife—
            Fly hence, our contact fear!
        Still fly, plunge deeper in the bowering wood!
        Averse, as Dido did with gesture stern
        From her false friend's approach in Hades turn,°
210   Wave us away, and keep thy solitude!

Still nursing the unconquerable hope,
    Still clutching the inviolable shade,
        With a free, onward impulse brushing through,
    By night, the silvered branches of the glade—
        Far on the forest-skirts, where none pursue.
            On some mild pastoral slope
        Emerge, and resting on the moonlit pales°
        Freshen thy flowers as in former years
        With dew, or listen with enchanted ears,
220   From the dark dingles,° to the nightingales!

But fly our paths, our feverish contact fly!
    For strong the infection of our mental strife,
        Which, though it gives no bliss, yet spoils for rest;
    And we should win thee from thy own fair life,
        Like us distracted, and like us unblest.
            Soon, soon thy cheer would die,
        Thy hopes grow timorous, and unfixed thy powers,
        And thy clear aims be cross and shifting made;
        And then thy glad perennial youth would fade,
230   Fade, and grow old at last, and die like ours.

Then fly our greetings, fly our speech and smiles!
    —As some grave Tyrian trader, from the sea,
        Descried at sunrise an emerging prow
    Lifting the cool-haired creepers stealthily,
        The fringes of a southward-facing brow
            Among the Ægæan isles;
        And saw the merry Grecian coaster come,
        Freighted with amber grapes, and Chian° wine,
        Green, bursting figs, and tunnies steeped in brine—
240   And knew the intruders on his ancient home,

Hades turn See Virgil's *Aeneid* VI.450–71,
where Dido will not speak to Aeneas when
they encounter each other, during his descent
to Avernus.

pales fences
dingles valleys
Chian from Greek island of Chios

The young light-hearted masters of the waves—
   And snatched his rudder, and shook out more sail;
     And day and night held on indignantly
   O'er the blue Midland waters with the gale,
     Betwixt the Syrtes° and soft Sicily,
       To where the Atlantic raves
   Outside the western straits; and unbent sails
     There, where down cloudy cliffs, through sheets of foam,
     Shy traffickers, the dark Iberians come;
250   And on the beach undid his corded bales.
    1852–53   1853

Philomela°

Hark! ah, the nightingale—
   The tawny-throated!
Hark, from that moonlit cedar what a burst!
What triumph! hark!—what pain!
O wanderer from a Grecian shore,
Still, after many years, in distant lands,
Still nourishing in thy bewildered brain
That wild, unquenched, deep-sunken, old-world pain—
Say, will it never heal?
10 And can this fragrant lawn
With its cool trees, and night,
And the sweet, tranquil Thames,
And moonshine, and the dew,
To thy racked heart and brain
Afford no balm?
Dost thou tonight behold,
Here, through the moonlight on this English grass,
The unfriendly palace in the Thracian wild?
Dost thou again peruse
20 With hot cheeks and seared eyes
The too clear web,° and thy dumb sister's shame?°

Syrtes Gulf of Sidra, on north coast of Africa
Philomela In Greek myth, she was the sister
of Procne, wife of King Tereus of Thrace,
who raped her and tore out her tongue to conceal his outrage. Philomela revealed the horror to her sister by weaving the story into a
tapestry; in revenge, Procne killed her son
Itys and served his cooked flesh to his father.
Tereus, this crime made known, attempted to
kill both sisters, but all were transformed into
birds, Procne into the nightingale (to become
the unusual bird mourning her lost son), Philomela into the swallow, and Tereus into the
crested hoopoe. Ovid's Latin version of the
story, followed by most Renaissance and later
writers, makes Philomela the nightingale, dra-

matically restoring song to the mute raped
sister. Arnold seems to have got mixed up in
this poem: up through line 19 he is consistently
following the Ovidian version, but in lines 20–
21 he is clearly referring to Procne. Had he
entitled the poem "Procne" or "The Nightingale" Arnold might have simply been using
the Greek version. (Swinburne wrote a powerful poem "Itylus," and the story is also used in
Eliot's *Waste Land*.)
web the tapestry
shame In some sense, Philomela's humiliation
is greater in the inability to protest her ravishment itself, for Arnold's poem has as its hidden
theme the fear of not being able to go on
writing poetry.

Dost thou once more assay
Thy flight, and feel come over thee,
Poor fugitive, the feathery change
Once more, and once more seem to make resound
With love and hate, triumph and agony,
Lone Daulis,° and the high Cephissian vale?°
Listen, Eugenia°—
How thick the bursts come crowding through the leaves!
30   —Again—thou hearest?
Eternal passion!
Eternal pain!
1852–53   1853

Palladium°

Set where the upper streams of Simois° flow
Was the Palladium, high 'mid rock and wood;
And Hector was in Ilium, far below,
And fought, and saw it not—but there it stood!

It stood, and sun and moonshine rained their light
On the pure columns of its glen-built hall.
Backward and forward rolled the waves of fight
Round Troy—but while this stood, Troy could not fall.

So, in its lovely moonlight, lives the soul.
10   Mountains surround it, and sweet virgin air;
Cold plashing, past it, crystal waters roll;
We visit it by moments, ah, too rare!

We shall renew the battle in the plain
Tomorrow;—red with blood will Xanthus° be;
Hector and Ajax will be there again,
Helen will come upon the wall to see.

Then we shall rust in shade, or shine in strife,
And fluctuate 'twixt blind hopes and blind despairs,
And fancy that we put forth all our life,
20   And never know how with the soul it fares.

Daulis town in Phocis, the region occupied by the kingdom of Thrace
Cephissian vale valley of the River Cephisus, running through Phocis
Eugenia Arnold's companion is not identified; her name means "well born."
Palladium This genuinely classical lyric is the one perfect exemplification by Arnold of the kind of poetry he called for in his "Preface" of 1853, and is his one successful poem that stands outside the main traditions of English Romanticism; Gray and Landor have something of this stoic quality and this cool splendor. The Palladium was a wooden image of Pallas Athena, kept in Troy as a magic talisman for the city's survival.
Simois river running near Troy (Ilium)
Xanthus a river near the battlefield outside Troy

Still doth the soul, from its lone fastness high,
Upon our life a ruling effluence send.
And when it fails, fight as we will, we die;
And while it lasts, we cannot wholly end.
?1864   1867

Growing Old°

What is it to grow old?
Is it to lose the glory of the form,
The lustre of the eye?
Is it for beauty to forego her wreath?
—Yes, but not this alone.

Is it to feel our strength—
Not our bloom only, but our strength—decay?
Is it to feel each limb
Grow stiffer, every function less exact,
10   Each nerve more loosely strung?

Yes, this, and more; but not
Ah, 'tis not what in youth we dreamed 'twould be!
'Tis not to have our life
Mellowed and softened as with sunset-glow,
A golden day's decline.

'Tis not to see the world
As from a height, with rapt prophetic eyes,
And heart profoundly stirred;
And weep, and feel the fulness of the past,
20   The years that are no more.°

It is to spend long days
And not once feel that we were ever young;
It is to add, immured
In the hot prison of the present, month
To month with weary pain.

It is to suffer this,
And feel but half, and feebly, what we feel.
Deep in our hidden heart
Festers the dull remembrance of a change,
30   But no emotion—none.

It is—last stage of all—

Growing Old This seems an ironic reply both to Browning ("Rabbi Ben Ezra") and to Wordsworth's consoling reflections upon old age.   **no more** an echo, without irony, of Tennyson's "Tears, Idle Tears"

When we are frozen up within, and quite
The phantom of ourselves,
To hear the world applaud the hollow ghost
Which blamed the living man.
                    1867

The Last Word°

Creep into thy narrow bed,°
Creep, and let no more be said!
Vain thy onset! all stands fast.
Thou thyself must break at last.

Let the long contention cease!
Geese are swans, and swans are geese.
Let them have it how they will!
Thou art tired; best be still.

They out-talked thee, hissed thee, tore thee?
10   Better men fared thus before thee;
Fired their ringing shot and passed,
Hotly charged—and sank at last.

Charge once more, then, and be dumb!
Let the victors, when they come,
When the forts of folly fall,
Find thy body by the wall!
                    1867

From Bacchanalia; or, The New Age

II

The epoch ends, the world is still.
The age has talked and worked its fill—
The famous orators have shone,
The famous poets sung and gone,
The famous men of war have fought,
The famous speculators thought,
The famous players, sculptors, wrought,
The famous painters filled their wall,
The famous critics judged it all.
10   The combatants are parted now—
Uphung the spear, unbent the bow,

The Last Word a bitter reaction to the cam-   narrow bed the tomb
paign for the Reform Bill of 1867, widely ex-
tending the vote

The puissant crowned, the weak laid low.
And in the after-silence sweet,
Now strifes are hushed, our ears doth meet,
Ascending pure, the bell-like fame
Of this or that down-trodden name,
Delicate spirits, pushed away
In the hot press of the noon-day.
And o'er the plain, where the dead age
20 Did its now silent warfare wage—
O'er that wide plain, now wrapt in gloom,
Where many a splendour finds its tomb,
Many spent fames and fallen mights—
The one or two immortal lights
Rise slowly up into the sky
To shine there everlastingly,
Like stars over the bounding hill.
The epoch ends, the world is still.

    Thundering and bursting
30   In torrents, in waves—
    Carolling and shouting
    Over tombs, amid graves—
    See! on the cumbered plain
    Clearing a stage,
    Scattering the past about,
    Comes the new age.
    Bards make new poems,
    Thinkers new schools,
    Statesmen new systems,
40   Critics new rules.
    New things begin again;
    Life is their prize;
    Earth with their deeds they fill,
    Fill with their cries.

    Poet, what ails thee, then?
    Say, why so mute?
    Forth with thy praising voice!
    Forth with thy flute!
    Loiterer! why sittest thou
50   Sunk in thy dream?
    Tempts not the bright new age?
    Shines not its stream?
    Look, ah, what genius,
    Art, science, wit!
    Soldiers like Cæsar,
    Statesmen like Pitt!
    Sculptors like Phidias,
    Raphaels in shoals,

60
    Poets like Shakespeare—
    Beautiful souls!
    See, on their glowing cheeks
    Heavenly the flush!
    —Ah, so the silence was!
    So was the hush!

The world but feels the present's spell,
The poet feels the past as well;
Whatever men have done, might do,
Whatever thought, might think it too.

                1867

THE PRE-RAPHAELITE POETS

As a literary term, "Pre-Raphaelite" is almost meaningless, yet it survives because we need some name for the cluster of poets who are the overt Romantics among the Victorians. Most accurately, Pre-Raphaelite poetry was written by Dante Gabriel Rossetti and his circle, to which we can add other figures for convenience, such as FitzGerald because Rossetti "discovered" and popularized his version of *The Rubáiyát*, Patmore because he published in the Pre-Raphaelite magazine, *The Germ*, and Meredith because his poetry has deep affinities with Rossetti's. Christina Rossetti is here for obvious reasons, though her devotional verse has not much in common with her brother's poetry. Rossetti himself and Morris are the Pre-Raphaelite poets proper; Swinburne is Shelleyan where they are Keatsian, and their characteristic mode of hard-edged phantasmagoria has little to do with his high rhetoric and polemical zeal. Still, insofar as Swinburne had a home in any poetic school of his age, it was here.

Pre-Raphaelitism started as a Brotherhood of young painters, in September 1848, the founders being William Holman Hunt, John Everett Millais (later to elope with Ruskin's neglected wife), and Rossetti. Unhappy (with reason) at mid-century, they sought to change the nature of English painting. Not so much Raphael, but his imitators, had to be rejected, in favor of the example of Pre-Raphaelite artists, the freshness of Gozzoli (c. 1421–97) and other Pisan painters. Like many schools of art, their watchword was the ambiguous "Back to nature!"—which always turns out to mean something rather different. Painters, sculptors, and critics rallied to the three young founders, and a highly confused nonmovement had begun. About the only common characteristic of English Pre-Raphaelite painting was its obsession with naturalistic detail, rendered so artificially as to make it not natural but phantasmagoric. Essentially, Pre-Raphaelite painting failed (with a few brilliant exceptions) but the poetry associated with it did not, because the poetry was the legitimate continuation of a central Romantic current, the daemonic element in Coleridge's poetry and the main achievement of Keats (to some extent, as it had been modified in early Tennyson).

In the mid-'fifties, at Oxford, William Morris and the painter Edward Burne-Jones became Rossetti's disciples, and moved to London to join him. Also at Oxford, in 1857, Swinburne met Rossetti through Morris and Burne-Jones and began a close, long friendship with the group. Through Swinburne's critical writings (rather than his High Romantic verse) the ideas of the movement, greatly altered, helped produce

Pater and the characteristic theory of English Aestheticism, resulting in Oscar Wilde, Aubrey Beardsley, the poetry of the 'Nineties, and the early work of Yeats.

Dante Gabriel Rossetti (1828–82), though out of favor in our time, seems to this editor the best poet of the Victorian period, after Browning and Tennyson, surpassing Arnold and even Hopkins and Swinburne (greatly undervalued as Swinburne now is). Space does not permit including his lyrical masterpiece, *The Stream's Secret*, but the selection given does include a fair representation of his lyrics, and ten sonnets from his other major work, *The House of Life*.

Rossetti was born in London on May 12, 1828, the son of a Neapolitan refugee scholar and a half-English mother. Educated as an artist, and thinking of himself primarily as a painter, his literary culture was narrow but intense, owing most to Keats for English style, and to Dante and other early Italian poets for thematic procedures. His translations from Dante and allied poets are the finest of their kind in English, particularly the sestina given here. His own poetry suffered from the turbulence and irregularity of his life. He could not bear criticism, personal or artistic, and could be described, not unfairly, as a monomaniac, frequently drugged on his characteristic mixture of chloral and whiskey.

Rossetti married his model, the beautiful Elizabeth Siddal, in 1860, after an affair lasting nearly a decade. The marriage was unhappy, and Mrs. Rossetti killed herself after less than two years. Her contrite husband buried his manuscripts with her, and had to exhume them in 1869, when he was preparing his first volume of *Poems* (1870).

In 1857, three years before marrying Elizabeth Siddal, Rossetti had met the other two women in his life, Fanny Cornforth, with whom he lived after the death of Elizabeth, and Jane Burden, who married William Morris in April 1859. The difficult relation between Mrs. Morris and Rossetti was long-lasting, and helped to derange his already overwrought sensibility. Rossetti, when attacked in 1871 by Robert Buchanan (with Swinburne and Morris as fellow victims) as leader of "The Fleshly School of Poetry," reacted with the beginnings of a ghastly persecution mania, which continued until his death on April 14, 1882.

Rossetti is a difficult poet, not only because his art is deliberately committed to sustaining an intensity that precludes mere action, but because the intensity almost invariably is one of baffled passion. Though Rossetti's master was Keats, he was rightly associated with Shelley by Yeats, who observed that the genius of both poets "can hardly stir but to the rejection of Nature." Shelley, though skeptically accepting a pragmatic dualism of heart and head, quested for a monistic Absolute, but one of his own curious invention, neither Platonic nor Christian. Rossetti, a convinced sensualist, writes a naturalistic poetry that yet rejects natural forms, which is almost an impossibility. His lyrics and sonnets are set in a world that is at once phantasmagoria and nature, giving the effect of an artificial nature. His Blessed Damozel leans down to him from a Heaven where a woman's hair glistens "along her back . . . yellow like ripe corn." It is impossible, amid the forests and fountains in *The House of Life*, to decide whether we stand in the remembered natural world, or in some purgatorial realm heavier and more naturally luxurious than nature could ever have been. Rossetti's symbolic world is oppressive to the spirit, but this oppressiveness is his poetry's unique strength. He gives us neither a vision of nature, as Keats did, nor of a second nature, as Shelley rendered, but a surrealistic or fantastic blend of both, and since all are damned in his mixed realm, he gives us also a wholly oblique, and finally nihilistic, vision of judgment in which we cannot be saved through sensual fulfillment, and yet achieve no lasting release without it.

George Meredith (1828–1909), though deeply affected by Rossetti, is by contrast a more refreshing, more simply naturalistic poet, though of lesser achievement. Never a popular novelist, and still not a poet who has attracted critics, let alone a public, Meredith nevertheless was a master in both mediums. At least three of his novels are still vital—*The Ordeal of Richard Feverel* (1859), *The Egoist* (1879), *Diana of the Crossways* (1885), as are two of his major poetic works—"Love in the Valley" (1851) and the sequence *Modern Love* (1862).

Meredith was born on February 12, 1828, in Portsmouth, to a family of naval tailors. He had little formal education, gave up an early attempt to study law, and earned his living as a literary journalist and publisher's reader. His early poetry (*Poems*, 1851) had no success, and his marriage to Thomas Love Peacock's daughter Mary ended in 1858 after nine bad years, to be commemorated in *Modern Love*. He then attempted to share a house in London with Rossetti and Swinburne, a quixotic adventure from which he was rescued by his happy second marriage, in 1864. In his later years, as his literary reputation slowly grew, he worked out his own difficult version of a Wordsworthian natural religion. He died on May 18, 1909, still resolute and independent despite years of ill health.

Meredith's poetry is rugged going, because of his Rossetti-like clusters of detail, but he is rhythmically persuasive, open, and passionate compared with Rossetti. He lacks Rossetti's convincing originality, and can sound too much like Rossetti, like Wordsworth, like Keats, but his stature as poet deserves more from criticism than he has as yet received.

Christina Georgina Rossetti (1830–94), two years younger than her brother, was born in London on December 5, 1830. Educated at home, she composed poetry from an early age, but did not publish her first book until the appearance of *Goblin Market and Other Poems* in 1862. Primarily a devotional poet (except for the powerful *Goblin Market*, too long to include here), she does not sustain comparison with Emily Dickinson, her American contemporary, but can be judged superior to any other woman who wrote poetry in English before the twentieth century.

Having twice declined marriage because of Anglican religious scruples (in 1850 and in 1866), and suffering ill health from middle age on, she gave herself over to a life of seclusion, emphasizing good works and religious meditation. Her poems are as intense as her brother's, but much simpler, being wholly orthodox in their sharp dualism of nature and spirit. Though she lacks dramatic juxtaposition, in which Hopkins abounds, her curious literal-mindedness produces a wholly original kind of devotional poetry, astonishing historically because it gives the effect of being free from self-consciousness—and this in the later 19th century.

William Morris (1834–96), though he wrote a more diffuse poetry than the other Pre-Raphaelites, is a much better poet than his current reputation would suggest. Morris is remembered today more for his personality, energies, Socialist politics, and vision of the arts (in which he followed Ruskin) than for either his verse or prose romances, which is a pity.

Morris was born March 24, 1834, into the family of a wealthy discount broker. After private study, he entered Exeter College, Oxford, where he met Burne-Jones the painter, and the two together became disciples and friends of Rossetti. In 1855, Morris began to write romances in both poetry and prose, which he continued doing, but on and off, throughout the next forty, heroically busy, years of his life. After graduating from Oxford, in 1855, he studied both architecture and painting, and published a superb volume of Pre-Raphaelite poems in The Defence of Guenevere (1858). The next year he married Rossetti's beloved Jane Burden, and abandoned poetry for seven years, during which he founded a company whose intent was to reform all the decorative arts of England: furniture, wallpaper, windows, glassware, tapestries, carpets, tiles, and nearly everything else. Morris himself did much of the work, both in designing and manufacturing, and later he triumphantly extended his craftsmanship to the art of bookmaking.

He returned to poetry with the looser, less Pre-Raphaelite than quasi-Chaucerian, narratives of The Life and Death of Jason (1867) and The Earthly Paradise (1868–70). A further phase of his poetry, probably his strongest as narrative alone, came with interest in Icelandic literature, resulting in his translation of the Volsunga Saga and his original Sigurd the Volsung (1876).

In the 1880's, Morris's Socialism became very active, in organizing, lecturing, and agitating, and resulted in the Socialistic prose romances The Dream of John Ball (1888) and News from Nowhere (1890). In his last literary phase, until his death in 1896, Morris wrote a series of visionary prose romances, which profoundly influenced Yeats, particularly The Well at the World's End, which inspired Yeats's fine play At the Hawk's Well.

The first four poems by Morris below are from The Defence of Guenevere, followed by one lyric from The Life and Death of Jason and a defining "Apology" from The Earthly Paradise. They show Morris at his best, except for the powerful Sigurd the Volsung, which is hard to represent by excerpts. Morris derives from a whole series of major 19th-century poets—Keats, Tennyson, Browning, and Rossetti—but his directness, detachment in depicting savagery, and ability to convey swiftly the effect of violent action are entirely his own, and still unique in the language (a comparison with Robinson Jeffers is not to the American poet's advantage). Medieval poems by Morris are utterly unlike Tennyson's; the blood shed in them is not word painting, and the freedom from intrusive moral judgments is absolute. Morris is one of the very few poets ever who can be criticized for not being ambitious enough. His poems demonstrate more genius than he was willing to concentrate. If his interests had been fewer, his poetry would have sprawled less, and meant more, but he valued his other enterprises at least as much as he cared for his poetry.

Algernon Charles Swinburne (1837–1909), a major lyrical poet now almost totally neglected, was born in London on April 6, 1837, son of an admiral and an earl's daughter. Raised on the Isle of Wight, Swinburne grew up obsessed with the sea (as Whitman did, and for much the same psychic reasons). After attending Eton and Balliol College, Oxford, Swinburne moved to London without taking a degree. A sado-masochist, at times a semi-alcoholic, and his health always uncertain, Swinburne cannot be said to have lived a happy life. But his genius was prodigal, from his best earlier poetry, Atalanta in Calydon (1865) and Poems and Ballads, First Series (1866), through his critical studies of Blake (1868), Shakespeare (1880), Victor Hugo

(1886), and Ben Jonson (1889), on to the superb late lyrics of *Poems and Ballads, Third Series* (1889), and *A Channel Passage* (1904). Politically, religiously, and critically, Swinburne followed in the path of Shelley, supporting Mazzini and Italian liberation, prophesying against institutional and historical Christianity, and celebrating the main Romantic tradition of nineteenth-century literature. Unfortunately, Swinburne's psycho-sexual nature was arrested in development, and his devotion to the Marquis de Sade cannot be accounted one of his prime imaginative virtues. Worn out by the time he was forty-two, he spent his last thirty years at a villa in Putney, nursed by Theodore Watts-Dunton, a solicitor with literary ambitions. Swinburne died at Putney, on April 10, 1909, and was buried on the Isle of Wight.

Though he never wholly swerved away from Shelley's influence, Swinburne is an astonishingly original stylist, absurdly deprecated in a critical age that remains afraid of high rhetoric. His faults are too obvious to be interesting; his splendors are not so obvious as they at first may seem. His deliberate self-parodies, like "Poeta Loquitur," leave his negative critics no work to do, but they have gone on anyway, parodying Swinburne's parodies of himself. Swinburne was very nearly a great critic, though usually a touch too enthusiastic and overwrought; and his best poems, like *Hertha* and the elegy for Baudelaire, are intellectually more powerful than any Victorian poetry except Browning's. Yet the case for Swinburne is finally not to be based upon the power of the philosophical materialism of his poetic mind, authentic as that is, for here he compares poorly with his master, Shelley. The prime virtue of Swinburne's poetry, in the context that matters, of 19th-century verse, is the element of significant variety that it introduces. Faced by the problem of every new poet in the Romantic, that is to say, Modern tradition, Swinburne radically made it new, and wrote a poetry that does extend the circumference of literary experience.

Coventry Patmore (1823–96), remembered today mostly because of his friendships with Hopkins, Tennyson, and the Pre-Raphaelites, is one of the most neglected of good poets in the Victorian period, and would be more fully represented here if space permitted. Born in 1823, he was a spoiled child, and never entirely grew up. He married in 1847, and celebrated his connubial bliss in the dreadful but very popular long poem, *The Angel in the House* (1854–62). Mrs. Patmore died in 1862, and under the influence of his second wife, whom he married in 1864, he converted to Roman Catholicism. His good poems are the odes of *The Unknown Eros* (1877), of which one is given here. His complex, distasteful but compelling blend of sexuality and mystical religion is also manifested in the posthumously published prose aphorisms and essays. He died in 1896, largely forgotten, yet he has attracted a small but steady audience since.

DANTE GABRIEL ROSSETTI

The Blessed Damozel°

The blessed damozel leaned out
   From the gold bar of heaven;
Her eyes were deeper than the depth
   Of waters stilled at even;°
She had three lilies° in her hand,
   And the stars in her hair were seven.°

Her robe, ungirt from clasp to hem,
   No wrought flowers did adorn,
But a white rose° of Mary's gift,
10   For service meetly° worn;
Her hair that lay along her back
   Was yellow like ripe corn.°

Herseemed she scarce had been a day
   One of God's choristers;
The wonder was not yet quite gone
   From that still look of hers;
Albeit, to them she left, her day
   Had counted as ten years.

(To one, it is ten years of years.
20   . . . Yet now, and in this place,
Surely she leaned o'er me—her hair
   Fell all about my face. . . .
Nothing: the autumn-fall of leaves.
   The whole year sets apace.)

It was the rampart of God's house
   That she was standing on;
By God built over the sheer depth
   The which is Space begun;
So high, that looking downward thence
30   She scarce could see the sun.

It lies in Heaven, across the flood
   Of ether, as a bridge.
Beneath, the tides of day and night
   With flame and darkness ridge
The void, as low as where this earth
   Spins like a fretful midge.

Damozel form of "damsel," a young virgin.
Rossetti related his poem to Poe's bad poem,
"The Raven," but with little reason. The
Book of Revelation and Dante are likelier
sources and analogues, though Rossetti's tone
has little in common with either.
even evening
three lilies possibly an allusion to the Trinity

seven See Revelation 1:16, where Jesus "had
in his right hand seven stars," and Revelation
12:1, where a woman wears a crown of stars,
though they number twelve.
white rose for purity
meetly suitably
corn wheat

Around her, lovers, newly met
   'Mid deathless love's acclaims,
Spoke evermore among themselves
40   Their heart-remembered names;
And the souls mounting up to God
   Went by her like thin flames.

And still she bowed herself and stooped
   Out of the circling charm;
Until her bosom must have made
   The bar she leaned on warm,
And the lilies lay as if asleep
   Along her bended arm.

From the fixed place of Heaven she saw
50   Time like a pulse shake fierce
Through all the worlds. Her gaze still strove
   Within the gulf to pierce
Its path; and now she spoke as when
   The stars sang in their spheres.

The sun was gone now; the curled moon
   Was like a little feather
Fluttering far down the gulf; and now
   She spoke through the still weather.
Her voice was like the voice the stars
60   Had when they sang together.

(Ah sweet! Even now, in that bird's song,
   Strove not her accents there,
Fain to be hearkened? When those bells
   Possessed the mid-day air,
Strove not her steps to reach my side
   Down all the echoing stair?)°

'I wish that he were come to me,
   For he will come,' she said.
'Have I not prayed in Heaven?—on earth,
70   Lord, Lord, has he not prayed?
Are not two prayers a perfect strength?
   And shall I feel afraid?

'When round his head the aureole clings,
   And he is clothed in white,
I'll take his hand and go with him
   To the deep wells of light;
As unto a stream we will step down,
   And bathe there in God's sight.

echoing stair the sounds from a purgatorial
stair

'We two will stand beside that shrine,
80　　Occult, withheld, untrod,
Whose lamps are stirred continually
　　With prayer sent up to God;
And see our old prayers, granted, melt
　　Each like a little cloud.

'We two will lie in the shadow of
　　That living mystic tree°
Within whose secret growth the Dove°
　　Is sometimes felt to be,
While every leaf that His plumes touch
90　　Saith His Name audibly.

'And I myself will teach to him,
　　I myself, lying so,
The songs I sing here; which his voice
　　Shall pause in, hushed and slow,
And find some knowledge at each pause,
　　Or some new thing to know.'

(Alas! We two, we two, thou say'st!
　　Yea, one wast thou with me
That once of old. But shall God lift
100　　To endless unity
The soul whose likeness with thy soul
　　Was but its love for thee?)

'We two,' she said, 'will seek the groves
　　Where the lady Mary is,
With her five handmaidens, whose names
　　Are five sweet symphonies,
Cecily, Gertrude, Magdalen,
　　Margaret and Rosalys.

'Circlewise sit they, with bound locks
110　　And foreheads garlanded;
Into the fine cloth white like flame
　　Weaving the golden thread,
To fashion the birth-robes for them
　　Who are just born, being dead.

'He shall fear, haply, and be dumb:
　　Then will I lay my cheek
To his, and tell about our love,
　　Not once abashed or weak:
And the dear Mother will approve
120　　My pride, and let me speak.

mystic **tree** See Revelation 22:2 for "the tree　　**Dove** the Holy Spirit
of life."

'Herself shall bring us, hand in hand,
  To Him round whom all souls
Kneel, the clear-ranged unnumbered heads
  Bowed with their aureoles:
And angels meeting us shall sing
  To their citherns and citoles.°

'There will I ask of Christ the Lord
  Thus much for him and me:—
Only to live as once on earth
130 With Love,—only to be,
As then awhile, for ever now
  Together, I and he.'

She gazed and listened and then said,
  Less sad of speech than mild,—
'All this is when he comes.' She ceased.
  The light thrilled towards her, filled
With angels in strong level flight.
  Her eyes prayed, and she smiled.

(I saw her smile.) But soon their path
140 Was vague in distant spheres:
And then she cast her arms along
  The golden barriers,
And laid her face between her hands,
  And wept. (I heard her tears.)
  1847   1850

The Woodspurge

The wind flapped loose, the wind was still,
Shaken out dead from tree and hill:
I had walked on at the wind's will,—
I sat now, for the wind was still.

Between my knees my forehead was,—
My lips, drawn in, said not Alas!
My hair was over in the grass,
My naked ears heard the day pass.

My eyes, wide open, had the run
10 Of some ten weeds to fix upon;
Among those few, out of the sun,
The woodspurge flowered, three cups in one.

From perfect grief there need not be
Wisdom or even memory:

citherns and citoles medieval stringed instruments

One thing then learnt remains to me,—
That woodspurge has a cup of three.°
1856   1870

Sestina (after Dante)

Of the Lady Pietra degli Scrovigni°

To the dim light and the large circle of shade
I have clomb, and to the whitening of the hills,
There where we see no colour in the grass.
Natheless my longing loses not its green,
It has so taken root in the hard stone
Which talks and hears as though it were a lady.

Utterly frozen is this youthful lady,
Even as the snow that lies within the shade;
For she is no more moved than is the stone
10   By the sweet season which makes warm the hills
And alters them afresh from white to green,
Covering their sides again with flowers and grass.

When on her hair she sets a crown of grass
The thought has no more room for other lady,
Because she weaves the yellow with the green
So well that Love sits down there in the shade,—
Love who has shut me in among low hills
Faster than between walls of granite-stone.

She is more bright than is a precious stone;
20   The wound she gives may not be healed with grass:
I therefore have fled far o'er plains and hills
For refuge from so dangerous a lady;
But from her sunshine nothing can give shade,—
Not any hill, nor wall, nor summer-green.

A while ago, I saw her dressed in green,—
So fair, she might have wakened in a stone
This love which I do feel even for her shade;
And therefore, as one woos a graceful lady,
I wooed her in a field that was all grass
30   Girdled about with very lofty hills.

a cup of three The best comment on this subtle poem is Jerome McGann's: "When the three-in-one detail is completely freed of its possible religious connotations we suddenly realize the enormous relevance of the flower's unsymbolic fact. At that time and in that place this poet gained a measure of relief from a simple act of observation. . . ." There is no better instance of Rossetti's polemical naturalism, which is at the center of the Pre-Raphaelite vision. Pietra degli Scrovigni The hard-hearted lady addressed by Dante in this, the most powerful of his "stony rimes" (the root meaning of "Pietra" is stone). No more successful version of anything by Dante exists in English, and here, more than anywhere else, Rossetti achieves his individual version of the Grand Style.

Yet shall the streams turn back and climb the hills
Before Love's flame in this damp wood and green
Burn, as it burns within a youthful lady,
For my sake, who would sleep away in stone
My life, or feed like beasts upon the grass,
Only to see her garments cast a shade.

How dark soe'er the hills throw out their shade,
Under her summer-green the beautiful lady
Covers it, like a stone covered in grass.

                              1861

Sudden Light

        I have been here before,
            But when or how I cannot tell:
        I know the grass beyond the door,
            The sweet keen smell,
The sighing sound, the lights around the shore.

        You have been mine before,—
            How long ago I may not know:
        But just when at that swallow's soar
            Your neck turned so,
10 Some veil did fall,—I knew it all of yore.

        Then, now,—perchance again! . . .
            O round mine eyes your tresses shake!
        Shall we not lie as we have lain
            Thus for Love's sake,
And sleep, and wake, yet never break the chain?
                              1870

The Sea-Limits

Consider the sea's listless chime:
        Time's self it is, made audible,—
        The murmur of the earth's own shell.
Secret continuance sublime
        Is the sea's end: our sight may pass
        No furlong further. Since time was,
This sound hath told the lapse of time.

        No quiet, which is death's,—it hath
        The mournfulness of ancient life,
10   Enduring always at dull strife.
        As the world's heart of rest and wrath,

Its painful pulse is in the sands.
Last utterly, the whole sky stands,
Grey and not known, along its path.

Listen alone beside the sea,
   Listen alone among the woods;
   Those voices of twin solitudes
Shall have one sound alike to thee:
   Hark where the murmurs of thronged men
20   Surge and sink back and surge again,—
Still the one voice of wave and tree.

Gather a shell from the strown beach
   And listen at its lips: they sigh
   The same desire and mystery,
The echo of the whole sea's speech.
   And all mankind is thus at heart
   Not anything but what thou art:
And Earth, Sea, Man, are all in each.
1849   1850

From The House of Life: A Sonnet Sequence

The title may be taken from astrology, the first of whose twelve "houses" is called "the house of Life," but more likely only the architectural sense of "house" is intended. Whether there is actually a sequence here, despite Rossetti's subtitle, is disputable. Three women are involved or are addressed throughout the sonnets. The first is the poet's wife, Elizabeth Siddal, who killed herself in 1862, and in whose grave he buried his manuscripts as an act of penance (but dug them out in 1869). She appears as Beata Beatrix, a version of Dante's Blessed Beatrice. The wife of William Morris, the beautiful Jane, appears as a composite goddess, Proserpine-Pandora, while Rossetti's housekeeper, Fanny Cornforth, enters as Lilith. But, though the major loves and sorrows of Rossetti's life are always in view, the sonnets are scarcely biographical, and have in common only their verse form and their author.

SONNETS XLIX, L, LI, LII

Willowwood°

XLIX

I sat with Love upon a woodside well,
   Leaning across the water, I and he;
   Nor ever did he speak nor looked at me,
But touched his lute wherein was audible
The certain secret thing he had to tell:

Willowwood willows symbolize grief; Willowwood is a forest of grief enclosing a fountain
of lost love

Only our mirrored eyes met silently
  In the low wave; and that sound came to be
The passionate voice I knew; and my tears fell.

And at their fall, his eyes beneath grew° hers;
10   And with his foot and with his wing-feathers
He swept the spring that watered my heart's drouth.
Then the dark ripples spread to waving hair,
  And as I stooped, her own lips rising there
Bubbled with brimming kisses at my mouth.°

L

And now Love sang: but his was such a song,
  So meshed with half-remembrance hard to free,
  As souls disused in death's sterility°
May sing when the new birthday tarries long.°
And I was made aware of a dumb throng°
  That stood aloof, one form by every tree,
  All mournful forms, for each was I or she,
The shades of those our days that had no tongue.°

They looked on us, and knew us and were known;
10   While fast together, alive from the abyss,
  Clung the soul-wrung implacable close kiss;
And pity of self through all made broken moan
Which said, 'For once, for once, for once alone!'
  And still Love sang, and what he sang was this:—

LI

'O ye, all ye that walk in Willowwood,
  That walk with hollow faces burning white;
What fathom-depth of soul-struck widowhood,°
  What long, what longer hours, one lifelong night,
Ere ye again, who so in vain have wooed
  Your last hope lost, who so in vain invite
Your lips to that their unforgotten food,
  Ere ye, ere ye again shall see the light!

'Alas! the bitter banks in Willowwood,
10   With tear-spurge° wan, with blood-wort° burning red:
Alas! if ever such a pillow could
  Steep deep the soul in sleep till she were dead,—

---

grew transformed into
at my mouth Rossetti's own reading: "The
sonnet describes a dream or trance of divided
love momentarily re-united by the longing
fancy; and in the imagery of the dream, the
face of the beloved rises through deep waters
to kiss the lover."
death's sterility the souls will be reincarnated,
but still abide in death
tarries long yet still is expected

dumb throng the wasted days when love went
undeclared
no tongue in contrast to the reflected kiss in
l. 11
widowhood not actually widowhood, but a
state like it
tear-spurge See "The Woodspurge"; here Rossetti's coinage combines anguish and the forlorn weed.
blood-wort red-veined dock; here the plant is
emblematic of suffering

Better all life forget her than this thing,
That Willowwood should hold her wandering!'

LII

So sang he: and as meeting rose and rose
  Together cling through the wind's wellaway°
  Nor change at once, yet near the end of day
The leaves drop loosened where the heart-stain glows,—
So when the song died did the kiss unclose;
  And her face fell back drowned, and was as grey
  As its grey eyes; and if it ever may
Meet mine again I know not if Love knows.

Only I know that I leaned low and drank
A long draught from the water where she sank,
  Her breath and all her tears and all her soul:
And as I leaned, I know I felt Love's face
Pressed on my neck with moan of pity and grace,
  Till both our heads were in his aureole.°
1868   1869

SONNET LXIV

Ardour and Memory

The cuckoo-throb, the heartbeat of the Spring;
  The rosebud's blush that leaves it as it grows
  Into the full-eyed fair unblushing rose;
The summer clouds that visit every wing
With fires of sunrise and of sunsetting;
  The furtive flickering streams to light re-born
  'Mid airs new-fledged and valorous lusts of morn,
While all the daughters of the daybreak sing:—

These ardour loves, and memory: and when flown
All joys, and through dark forest-boughs in flight
  The wind swoops onward brandishing the light,
Even yet the rose-tree's verdure left alone
Will flush all ruddy though the rose be gone;
  With ditties and with dirges infinite.
1879   1881

wellaway lamentation   aureole nimbus or halo

Autumn Idleness

This sunlight shames November where he grieves
  In dead red leaves, and will not let him shun
  The day, though bough with bough be over-run.
But with a blessing every glade receives
High salutation; while from hillock-eaves
  The deer gaze calling, dappled white and dun,
  As if, being foresters of old, the sun
Had marked them with the shade of forest-leaves.

Here dawn today unveiled her magic glass;°
10 Here noon now gives the thirst and takes the dew;
Till eve bring rest when other good things pass.
  And here the lost hours the lost hours renew
While I still lead my shadow o'er the grass,
  Nor know, for longing, that which I should do.
1850   1870

Body's Beauty°

Of Adam's first wife, Lilith, it is told
  (The witch he loved before the gift of Eve,)
  That, ere the snake's, her sweet tongue could deceive,
And her enchanted hair was the first gold.
And still she sits, young while the earth is old,
  And, subtly of herself contemplative,
  Draws men to watch the bright web° she can weave,
Till heart and body and life are in its hold.

The rose and poppy are her flowers;° for where
10 Is he not found, O Lilith, whom shed scent
And soft-shed kisses and soft sleep shall snare?
  Lo! as that youth's eyes burned at thine, so went
  Thy spell through him, and left his straight neck bent
And round his heart one strangling golden hair.
1867   1868

magic glass frost as a reflector of light
Body's Beauty first entitled "Lilith," and is a
description of Rossetti's painting of her (Fanny
Cornforth); by Hebrew oral tradition, Lilith
was Adam's wicked first wife

bright web her yellow hair
her flowers The rose is emblematic of sexual
passion; the poppy of a swooning away to
death.

Barren Spring

Once more the changed year's turning wheel returns:
    And as a girl sails balanced in the wind,°
    And now before and now again behind
Stoops as it swoops, with cheek that laughs and burns,—
So Spring comes merry towards me here, but earns
    No answering smile from me, whose life is twined
    With the dead boughs that winter still must bind,
And whom today the Spring no more concerns.

Behold, this crocus is a withering flame;
10   This snowdrop, snow; this apple-blossom's part
    To breed the fruit that breeds the serpent's art.°
Nay, for these Spring-flowers, turn thy face from them,
Now stay till on the year's last lily-stem
    The white cup shrivels round the golden heart.
    1870   1870

A Superscription°

Look in my face; my name is Might-have-been;
    I am also called No-more, Too-late, Farewell;
    Unto thine ear I hold the dead-sea shell
Cast up thy Life's foam-fretted feet between;°
Unto thine eyes the glass° where that is seen
    Which had Life's form and Love's, but by my spell
    Is now a shaken shadow intolerable,
Of ultimate things unuttered the frail screen.

Mark me, how still I am! But should there dart
10   One moment through thy soul the soft surprise
    Of that winged Peace which lulls the breath of sighs,—
Then shalt thou see me smile, and turn apart
Thy visage to mine ambush at thy heart
    Sleepless with cold commemorative eyes.
    1869   1869

in the wind probably on a swing
serpent's art as in Genesis 3
Superscription one message written on top of
another; here one love engraved atop another

between He stands in the sea, just beyond the
water's edge.
glass a demonic mirror

The One Hope

When vain desire at last and vain regret
   Go hand in hand to death, and all is vain,
   What shall assuage the unforgotten pain
And teach the unforgetful to forget?
Shall Peace be still a sunk stream long unmet,—
   Or may the soul at once in a green plain
   Stoop through the spray of some sweet life-fountain
And cull the dew-drenched flowering amulet?°

Ah! When the wan soul in that golden air
10   Between the scriptured petals° softly blown
   Peers breathless for the gift of grace unknown,—
Ah! let none other alien spell soe'er
But only the one Hope's one name be there,—
   Not less nor more, but even that word alone.
1870?   1870

The Orchard-Pit

A FRAGMENT

Piled deep below the screening apple branch
   They lie with bitter° apples in their hands:
And some are only ancient bones that blanch,
And some had ships that last year's wind did launch,
   And some were yesterday the lords of lands.

In the soft dell, among the apple trees,
   High up above the hidden pit she stands,°
And there forever sings, who gave to these,
That lie below, her magic hour of ease,
10   And those her apples holden in their hands.

This in my dreams is shown me; and her hair
   Crosses my lips and draws my burning breath;
Her song spreads golden wings upon the air,
Life's eyes are gleaming from her forehead fair,
   And from her breasts the ravishing eyes of Death.°

Men say to me that sleep hath many dreams,
   Yet I knew never but this dream alone:

amulet a charm worn against danger; here it
is a flower
scriptured petals of the amulet-flower; as in
the story of Hyacinthus, the petals carry the
letters of lamentation αιαι (alas, alas)
bitter Printed text has "bitter" but Rossetti
may have used "bitten," which makes better
sense.

she stands This sinister Belle Dame or sorceress
appears to be Proserpina, Queen of Hell, and
probably was identified by Rossetti with Jane
Morris.
eyes of Death By popular superstition, vampire women had eyes in their breasts.

There, from a dried-up channel, once the stream's,
The glen slopes up; even such in sleep it seems
20   As to my waking sight the place well known.

My love I call her, and she loves me well:
    But I love her as in the maelstrom's cup
The whirled stone loves the leaf inseparable
That clings to it round all the circling swell,
    And that the same last eddy swallows up.
1869   1886

GEORGE MEREDITH

Love in the Valley

Under yonder beech-tree single on the green-sward,
    Couched with her arms behind her golden head,
Knees and tresses folded to slip and ripple idly,
    Lies my young love sleeping in the shade.
Had I the heart to slide an arm beneath her,
    Press her parting lips as her waist I gather slow,
Waking in amazement she could not but embrace me:
    Then would she hold me and never let me go?

Shy as the squirrel and wayward as the swallow,
10   Swift as the swallow along the river's light
Circleting the surface to meet his mirrored winglets,
    Fleeter she seems in her stay than in her flight.
Shy as the squirrel that leaps among the pine-tops,
    Wayward as the swallow overhead at set of sun,
She whom I love is hard to catch and conquer,
    Hard, but O the glory of the winning were she won!

When her mother tends her before the laughing mirror,
    Tying up her laces,° looping up her hair,
Often she thinks, were this wild thing wedded,
20   More love should I have, and much less care.
When her mother tends her before the lighted mirror,
    Loosening her laces, combing down her curls,
Often she thinks, were this wild thing wedded,
    I should miss but one for many boys and girls.

Heartless she is as the shadow in the meadows
    Flying to the hills on a blue and breezy noon.
No, she is athirst and drinking up her wonder:

laces presumably of her bodice

Earth to her is young as the slip of the new moon.
Deals she an unkindness, 'tis but her rapid measure,
30   Even as in a dance; and her smile can heal no less:
Like the swinging May-cloud that pelts the flowers with hailstones
Off a sunny border, she was made to bruise and bless.

Lovely are the curves of the white owl sweeping
Wavy in the dusk lit by one large star.
Lone on the fir-branch, his rattle-note unvaried,
Brooding o'er the gloom, spins the brown eve-jar.°
Darker grows the valley, more and more forgetting:
So were it with me if forgetting could be willed.
Tell the grassy hollow that holds the bubbling well-spring,
40   Tell it to forget the source that keeps it filled.

Stepping down the hill with her fair companions,
Arm in arm, all against the raying West,°
Boldly she sings, to the merry tune she marches,
Brave in her shape, and sweeter unpossessed.
Sweeter, for she is what my heart first awaking
Whispered the world was; morning light is she.
Love that so desires would fain keep her changeless;
Fain would fling the net, and fain have her free.

Happy happy time, when the white star hovers
50   Low over dim fields fresh with bloomy dew,
Near the face of dawn, that draws athwart the darkness,
Threading it with colour, like yewberries the yew.
Thicker crowd the shades as the grave East deepens
Glowing, and with crimson a long cloud swells.
Maiden still the morn is; and strange she is, and secret;
Strange her eyes; her cheeks are cold as cold sea-shells.

Sunrays, leaning on our southern hills and lighting
Wild cloud-mountains that drag the hills along,
Oft ends the day of your shifting brilliant laughter
60   Chill as a dull face frowning on a song.
Ay, but shows the South-West a ripple-feathered bosom
Blown to silver while the clouds are shaken and ascend
Scaling the mid-heavens as they stream, there comes a sunset
Rich, deep like love in beauty without end.

When at dawn she sighs, and like an infant to the window
Turns grave eyes craving light, released from dreams,
Beautiful she looks, like a white water-lily
Bursting out of bud in havens of the streams.
When from bed she rises clothed from neck to ankle
70   In her long nightgown sweet as boughs of May,

eve-jar whippoorwill   raying West sunset

Beautiful she looks, like a tall garden lily
   Pure from the night, and splendid for the day.

Mother of the dews, dark eye-lashed twilight,
   Low-lidded twilight, o'er the valley's brim,
Rounding on thy breast sings the dew-delighted skylark,
   Clear as though the dewdrops had their voice in him.
Hidden where the rose-flush drinks the rayless planet,°
   Fountain-full he pours the spraying fountain-showers.
Let me hear her laughter, I would have her ever
80   Cool as dew in twilight, the lark above the flowers.

All the girls are out with their baskets for the primrose;
   Up lanes, woods through, they troop in joyful bands.
My sweet leads: she knows not why, but now she loiters,
   Eyes the bent anemones, and hangs her hands.
Such a look will tell that the violets are peeping,
   Coming the rose: and unaware a cry
Springs in her bosom for odours and for colour,
   Covert and the nightingale; she knows not why.

Kerchiefed head and chin she darts between her tulips,
90   Streaming like a willow grey in arrowy rain:
Some bend beaten cheek to gravel, and their angel
   She will be; she lifts them, and on she speeds again.
Black the driving raincloud breasts the iron gateway:
   She is forth to cheer a neighbour lacking mirth.
So when sky and grass met rolling dumb for thunder
   Saw I once a white dove, sole light of earth.

Prim little scholars are the flowers of her garden,
   Trained to stand in rows, and asking if they please.
I might love them well but for loving more the wild ones:
100   O my wild ones! they tell me more than these.
You, my wild one, you tell of honied field-rose,
   Violet, blushing eglantine in life; and even as they,
They by the wayside are earnest of your goodness,
   You are of life's, on the banks that line the way.

Peering at her chamber the white crowns the red rose,
   Jasmine winds the porch with stars two and three.
Parted is the window; she sleeps; the starry jasmine
   Breathes a falling breath that carries thoughts of me,
Sweeter unpossessed, have I said of her my sweetest?
110   Not while she sleeps: while she sleeps the jasmine breathes,
Luring her to love; she sleeps; the starry jasmine
   Bears me to her pillow under white rose-wreaths.

Yellow with birdfoot-trefoil° are the grass-glades;
   Yellow with cinquefoil° of the dew-grey leaf;

---

rayless planet Evening Star
birdfoot-trefoil three-lobed flower

cinquefoil plant with five-lobed leaves

Yellow with stonecrop; the moss-mounds are yellow;
  Blue-necked the wheat sways, yellowing to the sheaf.
Green-yellow burst from the copse the laughing yaffle;°
  Sharp as a sickle is the edge of shade and shine:
Earth in her heart laughs looking at the heavens,
120 Thinking of the harvest: I look and think of mine.

This I may know: her dressing and undressing
  Such a change of light shows as when the skies in sport
Shift from cloud to moonlight; or edging over thunder
  Slips a ray of sun; or sweeping into port
White sails furl; or on the ocean borders
  White sails lean along the waves leaping green.
Visions of her shower before me, but from eyesight
  Guarded she would be like the sun were she seen.

Front door and back of the mossed old farmhouse
130 Open with the morn, and in a breezy link°
Freshly sparkles garden to stripe-shadowed orchard,
  Green across a rill where on sand the minnows wink.
Busy in the grass the early sun of summer
  Swarms, and the blackbird's mellow fluting notes
Call my darling up with round and roguish challenge:
  Quaintest, richest carol of all the singing throats!

Cool was the woodside; cool as her white dairy
  Keeping sweet the cream pan; and there the boys from school,
Cricketing below, rushed brown and red with sunshine;
140 O the dark translucence of the deep-eyed cool!
Spying from the farm, herself she fetched a pitcher
  Full of milk, and tilted for each in turn the beak.
Then a little fellow, mouth up and on tiptoe,
  Said, 'I will kiss you'; she laughed and leaned her cheek.

Doves of the fir-wood walling high our red roof
  Through the long noon coo, crooning through the coo.
Loose droop the leaves, and down the sleepy roadway
  Sometimes pipes a chaffinch; loose droops the blue.
Cows flap a slow tail knee-deep in the river,
150 Breathless, given up to sun and gnat and fly.
Nowhere is she seen; and if I see her nowhere,
  Lightning may come, straight rains and tiger sky.

O the golden sheaf, the rustling treasure-armful!
  O the nutbrown tresses nodding interlaced!
O the treasure-tresses one another over
  Nodding! O the girdle slack about the waist!
Slain are the poppies that shot their random scarlet
  Quick amid the wheatears: wound about the waist,

yaffle green woodpecker   link river ground, near a bend

Gathered, see the brides of Earth one blush of ripeness!
160   O the nutbrown tresses nodding interlaced!

Large and smoky red the sun's cold disk drops,
    Clipped by naked hills, on violet shaded snow:
Eastward large and still lights up a bower of moonrise,
    Whence at her leisure steps the moon aglow.
Nightlong on black print-branches our beech-tree
    Gazes in this whiteness; nightlong could I.
Here may life on death or death on life be painted.
    Let me clasp her soul to know she cannot die!

Gossips count her faults: they scour a narrow chamber
170   Where there is no window, read not heaven or her.
'When she was a tiny,' one aged woman quavers,
    Plucks at my heart and leads me by the ear.
Faults she had once as she learnt to run and tumbled:
    Faults of feature some see, beauty not complete.
Yet, good gossips, beauty that makes holy
    Earth and air, may have faults from head to feet.

Hither she comes; she comes to me; she lingers,
    Deepens her brown eyebrows, while in new surprise
High rise the lashes in wonder of a stranger;
180   Yet am I the light and living of her eyes.
Something friends have told her fills her heart to brimming,
    Nets her in her blushes, and wounds her, and tames.—
Sure of her haven, O like a dove alighting,
    Arms up, she dropped: our souls were in our names.

Soon will she lie like a white frost sunrise.
    Yellow oats and brown wheat, barley pale as rye,
Long since your sheaves have yielded to the thresher,
    Felt the girdle loosened, seen the tresses fly.
Soon will she lie like a blood-red sunset.
190   Swift with the tomorrow, green-winged Spring!
Sing from the South-West, bring her back the truants,
    Nightingale and swallow, song and dipping wing.

Soft new beech-leaves, up to beamy April
    Spreading bough on bough a primrose mountain, you
Lucid in the moon, raise lilies to the skyfields,
    Youngest green transfused in silver shining through:
Fairer than the lily, than the wild white cherry:
    Fair as in image my seraph love appears
Borne to me by dreams when dawn is at my eyelids:
200   Fair as in the flesh she swims to me on tears.

Could I find a place to be alone with heaven,
    I would speak my heart out: heaven is my need.
Every woodland tree is flushing like the dogwood,

Flashing like the whitebeam,° swaying like the reed.
Flushing like the dogwood crimson in October;
    Streaming like the flag-reed South-West blown;
Flashing as in gusts the sudden-lighted whitebeam:
    All seem to know what is for heaven alone.
1851   1878

From Modern Love°

I

By this he knew she wept with waking eyes:
That, at his hand's light quiver by her head,
The strange low sobs that shook their common bed,
Were called into her with a sharp surprise,
And strangled mute, like little gaping snakes,
Dreadfully venomous to him. She lay
Stone-still, and the long darkness flowed away
With muffled pulses. Then, as midnight makes
Her giant heart of Memory and Tears
Drink the pale drug of silence, and so beat
Sleep's heavy measure, they from head to feet
Were moveless, looking through their dead black years,
By vain regret scrawled over the blank wall.
Like sculptured effigies° they might be seen
Upon their marriage-tomb, the sword between;°
Each wishing for the sword that severs all.°

XLVII

We saw the swallows gathering in the sky,
And in the osier-isle° we heard them noise.
We had not to look back on summer joys,
Or forward to a summer of bright dye:
But in the largeness of the evening earth
Our spirits grew as we went side by side.
The hour became her husband and my bride.
Love that had robbed us so, thus blessed our dearth!
The pilgrims of the year°waxed very loud
In multitudinous chatterings, as the flood
Full brown came from the West, and like pale blood
Expanded to the upper crimson cloud.

10 (line 11)
10 (line 26)

---

whitebeam leaves white on nether-side
Modern Love This is a tight sequence of fifty
16-line sonnet-like poems presenting a highly
fictionalized account of Meredith's first marriage, which ended badly enough, but not with
his wife's suicide, as happens here. (From 1849
until 1858, when she eloped with an indifferent
artist, Meredith was married to the daughter of
Thomas Love Peacock.) Given here are the
first poem and the last four of the sequence.
sculptured effigies as on medieval tombs
sword between image of their sexual failure;
based on the romance tradition of lovers sleeping with a sword between them, to symbolize
continued chastity
severs all this sword is death
osier-isle group of willow trees
pilgrims of the year the swallows migrating

Love, that had robbed us of immortal things,
This little moment mercifully gave,
Where I have seen across the twilight wave
The swan sail with her young beneath her wings.

      XLVIII

Their sense is with their senses all mixed in,
Destroyed by subtleties these women are!
More brain, O Lord, more brain! or we shall mar
Utterly this fair garden we might win.
Behold! I looked for peace, and thought it near.
Our inmost hearts had opened, each to each.
We drank the pure daylight of honest speech.
Alas! that was the fatal draught, I fear.
For when of my lost Lady came the word,
This woman, O this agony of flesh!
Jealous devotion bade her break the mesh,
That I might seek that other like a bird.
I do adore the nobleness! despise
The act! She has gone forth, I know not where.
Will the hard world my sentience° of her share?
I feel the truth; so let the world surmise.

      XLIX

He found her by the ocean's moaning verge,
Nor any wicked change in her discerned;
And she believed his old love had returned,
Which was her exultation, and her scourge.
She took his hand, and walked with him, and seemed
The wife he sought, though shadow-like and dry.
She had one terror, lest her heart should sigh,
And tell her loudly she no longer dreamed.
She dared not say, 'This is my breast: look in.'
But there's a strength to help the desperate weak.
That night he learned how silence best can speak
The awful things when Pity pleads for Sin.
About the middle of the night her call
Was heard, and he came wondering to the bed.
'Now kiss me, dear! it may be, now!' she said.
Lethe° had passed those lips, and he knew all.

      L

Thus piteously Love closed what he begat:
The union of this ever-diverse pair!
These two were rapid falcons in a snare,
Condemned to do the flitting of the bat.

---

sentience consciousness   Lethe river in Hades whose water caused forgetfulness

Lovers beneath the singing sky of May,
They wandered once; clear as the dew on flowers:
But they fed not on the advancing hours:
Their hearts held cravings for the buried day.
Then each applied to each that fatal knife,
Deep questioning, which probes to endless dole.°
Ah, what a dusty answer gets the soul
When hot for certainties in this our life!—
In tragic hints here see what evermore
Moves dark as yonder midnight ocean's force,
Thundering like ramping hosts of warrior horse,
To throw that faint thin line upon the shore!
1862   1892

A Ballad of Past Meridian°

Last night returning from my twilight walk
I met the grey mist Death, whose eyeless brow
Was bent on me, and from his hand of chalk
He reached me flowers as from a withered bough.
O Death, what bitter nosegays givest thou!

Death said, 'I gather,' and pursued his way.
Another stood by me, a shape in stone,
Sword-hacked and iron-stained, with breasts of clay,
And metal veins that sometimes fiery shone.
O Life, how naked and how hard when known!

Life said, 'As thou hast carved me, such am I.'
Then Memory, like the nightjar on the pine,
And sightless Hope, a woodlark in night sky,
Joined notes of Death and Life till night's decline.
Of Death, of Life, those inwound notes are mine.
1876

Lucifer in Starlight

On a starred night Prince Lucifer uprose.
Tired of his dark dominion swung the fiend
Above the rolling ball in cloud part screened,
Where sinners hugged their spectre of repose.
Poor prey to his hot fit of pride were those.
And now upon his western wing he leaned,
Now his huge bulk o'er Afric's sands careened,

---

dole anguish
Past Meridian past the period of a person's greatest elevation (see Wallace Stevens's "Le

Monocle de Mon Oncle" II.9: "No spring can follow past meridian," where "meridian" is forty)

Now the black planet° shadowed Arctic snows.
Soaring through wider zones that pricked his scars°
10 With memory of the old revolt from Awe,
He reached a middle height, and at the stars,
Which are the brain of heaven, he looked, and sank.
 Around the ancient track marched, rank on rank,
The army of unalterable law.

1883

CHRISTINA ROSSETTI

Song

When I am dead, my dearest,
  Sing no sad songs for me;
Plant thou no roses at my head,
  Nor shady cypress tree:°
Be the green grass above me
  With showers and dewdrops wet:
And if thou wilt, remember,
  And if thou wilt, forget.

I shall not see the shadows,
10 I shall not feel the rain;
I shall not hear the nightingale
  Sing on as if in pain:
And dreaming through the twilight
  That doth not rise nor set,
Haply° I may remember,
  And haply may forget.

1848   1862

Rest

O Earth, lie heavily upon her eyes;
  Seal her sweet eyes weary of watching, Earth;
  Lie close around her; leave no room for mirth
With its harsh laughter, nor for sound of sighs.
She hath no questions, she hath no replies,
  Hushed in and curtained with a blessed dearth
  Of all that irked her from the hour of birth;
With stillness that is almost Paradise.
Darkness more clear than noonday holdeth her,

---

black planet Though "Lucifer," the Morning   cypress tree emblematic of mourning
Star, means "light bearer," this is fallen Lucifer.   Haply perhaps
scars See *Paradise Lost* I.601.

10   Silence more musical than any song;
     Even her very heart has ceased to stir:
     Until the morning of Eternity
     Her rest shall not begin nor end, but be;
         And when she wakes she will not think it long.
         1844   1862

Remember

Remember me when I am gone away,
    Gone far away into the silent land;
    When you can no more hold me by the hand,
Nor I half turn to go yet turning stay.
Remember me when no more day by day
    You tell me of our future that you planned:
    Only remember me; you understand
It will be late to counsel then or pray.
Yet if you should forget me for a while
10   And afterwards remember, do not grieve:
    For if the darkness and corruption leave
    A vestige of the thoughts that once I had,
Better by far you should forget and smile
    Than that you should remember and be sad.
    1849   1862

Echo

Come to me in the silence of the night;
    Come in the speaking silence of a dream;
Come with soft rounded cheeks and eyes as bright
        As sunlight on a stream;
            Come back in tears,
O memory, hope, love of finished years.

O dream how sweet, too sweet, too bitter sweet,
    Whose wakening should have been in Paradise,
Where souls brimfull of love abide and meet;
10   Where thirsting longing eyes
            Watch the slow door
That opening, letting in, lets out no more.

Yet come to me in dreams, that I may live
    My very life again though cold in death:
Come back to me in dreams, that I may give
        Pulse for pulse, breath for breath:
            Speak low, lean low,
As long ago, my love, how long ago.
1854   1862

A Birthday

My heart is like a singing bird
   Whose nest is in a watered shoot:°
My heart is like an apple-tree
   Whose boughs are bent with thickset fruit;
My heart is like a rainbow shell
   That paddles in a halcyon° sea;
My heart is gladder than all these
   Because my love is come to me.

Raise me a dais of silk and down;
10   Hang it with vair° and purple dyes;
Carve it in doves and pomegranates,
   And peacocks with a hundred eyes;
Work it in gold and silver grapes,
   In leaves and silver fleurs-de-lys;°
Because the birthday of my life
   Is come, my love is come to me.
1857   1862

Up-Hill

Does the road wind up-hill all the way?
   Yes, to the very end.
Will the day's journey take the whole long day?
   From morn to night, my friend.

But is there for the night a resting-place?
   A roof for when the silow dark hours begin.
May not the darkness hide it from my face?
   You cannot miss that inn.

Shall I meet other wayfarers at night?
10   Those who have gone before.
Then must I knock, or call when just in sight?
   They will not keep you standing at that door.

Shall I find comfort, travel-sore and weak?
   Of labour you shall find the sum.
Will there be beds for me and all who seek?
   Yea, beds for all who come.
1858   1862

shoot fresh growth
halcyon placid

vair heraldic gray squirrel fur
fleurs-de-lys heraldic lilies

Passing Away°

Passing away, saith the World, passing away:
Chances, beauty, and youth, sapped day by day:
Thy life never continueth in one stay.
Is the eye waxen dim, is the dark hair changing to grey
That hath won neither laurel nor bay?°
I shall clothe myself in Spring and bud in May:
Thou, root-stricken, shalt not rebuild thy decay
On my bosom for aye.
Then I answered: Yea.

10   Passing away, saith my Soul, passing away:
With its burden of fear and hope, of labour and play,
Hearken what the past doth witness and say:
Rust in thy gold, a moth is in thine array,
A canker is in thy bud, thy leaf must decay.
A midnight, at cockcrow, at morning, one certain day
Lo the Bridegroom shall come and shall not delay;°
Watch thou and pray.
Then I answered: Yea.

Passing away, saith my God, passing away:
20   Winter passeth° after the long delay:
New grapes on the vine, new figs on the tender spray,
Turtle calleth turtle in Heaven's May.
Though I tarry, wait for Me, trust Me, watch and pray:
Arise, come away, night is past and lo it is day,
My love, My sister, My spouse, thou shalt hear Me say.
Then I answered: Yea.
1860   1862

WILLIAM MORRIS

The Haystack in the Floods°

Had she come all the way for this,
To part at last without a kiss?

Passing Away This virtuoso lyric on one rhyme is a farewell to the poetess's twenties, being written on the last day of a decade, and a study toward a farewell to all worldliness.
neither laurel nor bay At this time she was scarcely recognized as a poet.
shall not delay a beautiful use of Christ's parable of the wise and foolish virgins; see Matthew 25:1–13
Winter passeth This and most of the stanza closely echo Song of Solomon 2:11–13.
The Haystack in the Floods The story here is Morris's own invention, but the circumstances are strictly historical. Morris sets the poem in the late autumn of 1356 in southern France after the battle of Poictiers, fought in Septem-
ber, in which the English badly defeated the French. Sir Robert de Marny, an English commander, with his mistress, a French woman Jehane, and a small band of men are ambushed by Godmar and a group of French partisans. In the tangled treacheries of this direct, brutal, and wonderfully detached poem, Godmar earlier had served the English, and then betrayed them, and Jehane may have been Godmar's mistress and then left him for Robert. In the action of the poem, Robert's band proceeds to betray him and joins Godmar, leaving Jehane the only decision of honor, when she, at the highest price, refuses a last betrayal.

Yea, had she borne the dirt and rain
That her own eyes might see him slain
Beside the haystack in the floods?

Along the dripping leafless woods,
The stirrup touching either shoe,
She rode astride as troopers do;
With kirtle kilted to her knee,°
10   To which the mud splashed wretchedly;
And the wet dripped from every tree
Upon her head and heavy hair,
And on her eyelids broad and fair;
The tears and rain ran down her face.
By fits and starts they rode apace,
And very often was his place
Far off from her; he had to ride
Ahead, to see what might betide
When the roads crossed; and sometimes, when
20   There rose a murmuring from his men,
Had to turn back with promises;
Ah me! she had but little ease;
And often for pure doubt and dread
She sobbed, made giddy in the head
By the swift riding; while, for cold,
Her slender fingers scarce could hold
The wet reins; yea, and scarcely, too,
She felt the foot within her shoe
Against the stirrup: all for this,
30   To part at last without a kiss
Beside the haystack in the floods.

For when they neared that old soaked hay,
They saw across the only way
That Judas, Godmar, and the three
Red running lions dismally
Grinned from his pennon,° under which
In one straight line along the ditch,
They counted thirty heads.
                              So then,
While Robert turned round to his men,
40   She saw at once the wretched end,
And, stooping down, tried hard to rend
Her coif° the wrong way from her head,
And hid her eyes; while Robert said:
'Nay, love, 'tis scarcely two to one,
At Poictiers° where we made them run

kirtle . . . her knee skirts tucked up to the
knee
from his pennon The lions are the emblem on
Godmar's banner.

coif head covering; she reverses it to cover
her eyes
Poictiers 6500 English mauled 16,000 French
at Poictiers.

So fast—why, sweet my love, good cheer.
The Gascon frontier° is so near,
Nought after this.'

But, 'O,' she said,
'My God! my God! I have to tread
50 The long way back without you; then
The court at Paris; those six men;°
The gratings of the Chatelet;°
The swift Seine on some rainy day
Like this, and people standing by,
And laughing, while my weak hands try
To recollect how strong men swim.°
All this, or else a life with him,
For which I should be damned at last.
Would God that this next hour were past!'

60 He answered not, but cried his cry,
'St. George for Marny!'° cheerily;
And laid his hand upon her rein.
Alas! no man of all his train
Gave back that cheery cry again;
And, while for rage his thumb beat fast
Upon his sword-hilts, some one cast
About his neck a kerchief long,
And bound him.

Then they went along
70 To Godmar; who said: 'Now, Jehane,
Your lover's life is on the wane
So fast, that, if this very hour
You yield not as my paramour,
He will not see the rain leave off—
Nay, keep your tongue from gibe and scoff,
Sir Robert, or I slay you now.'

She laid her hand upon her brow,
Then gazed upon the palm, as though
She thought her forehead bled, and—'No!'
She said, and turned her head away,
80 As there were nothing else to say,
And everything were settled: red
Grew Godmar's face from chin to head:
'Jehane, on yonder hill there stands

Gascon frontier Gascony was English territory
(now part of southwestern France).
six men judges in Paris who will put Jehane
on trial
Chatelet prison bars of Parisian dungeon
men swim As a traitress, she will be condemned
to the "trial" of a witch. She will be tossed
into the River Seine; if she drowns, then she
is innocent, but if she survives by swimming,
she will be burned alive as having received the
Devil's aid. The only other possibility, as she
says, is Godmar, but (to her) he is a fate
worse than drowning or burning.
St. George for Marny! St. George is the patron
saint of England.

My castle, guarding well my lands:
What hinders me from taking you,
And doing that I list to do
To your fair wilful body, while
Your knight lies dead?'
                          A wicked smile
Wrinkled her face, her lips grew thin,
90   A long way out she thrust her chin:
'You know that I should strangle you
While you were sleeping; or bite through
Your throat, by God's help—ah!' she said,
'Lord Jesus, pity your poor maid!
For in such wise they hem me in,
I cannot choose but sin and sin,
Whatever happens: yet I think
They could not make me eat or drink,
And so should I just reach my rest.'
100   'Nay, if you do not my behest,
O Jehane! though I love you well,'
Said Godmar, 'would I fail to tell
All that I know?' 'Foul lies,' she said.
'Eh? lies my Jehane? by God's head,
At Paris folks would deem them true!
Do you know, Jehane, they cry for you:
"Jehane the brown! Jehane the brown!
Give us Jehane to burn or drown!"—
Eh—gag me Robert!°—sweet my friend,
110   This were indeed a piteous end
For those long fingers, and long feet,
And long neck, and smooth shoulders sweet,
An end that few men would forget
That saw it—So, an hour yet:
Consider, Jehane, which to take
Of life or death!'
                    So, scarce awake,
Dismounting, did she leave that place,
And totter some yards: with her face
Turned upward to the sky she lay,
120   Her head on a wet heap of hay,
And fell asleep: and while she slept,
And did not dream, the minutes crept
Round to the twelve again; but she,
Being waked at last, sighed quietly,
And strangely childlike came, and said:
'I will not.' Straightway Godmar's head,

gag me Robert! Godmar orders Robert's own
men to gag him, so as to prepare him for execution.

As though it hung on strong wires, turned
Most sharply round, and his face burned.

For Robert—both his eyes were dry,
130   He could not weep, but gloomily
He seemed to watch the rain; yea, too,
His lips were firm; he tried once more
To touch her lips; she reached out, sore
And vain desire so tortured them,
The poor grey lips, and now the hem
Of his sleeve brushed them.
                                    With a start
Up Godmar rose, thrust them apart;
From Robert's throat he loosed the bands
Of silk and mail; with empty hands
140   Held out, she stood and gazed, and saw
The long bright blade without a flaw
Glide out from Godmar's sheath, his hand
From Robert's throat he loosed the bands
Back Robert's head; she saw him send
The thin steel down; the blow told well,
Right backward the knight Robert fell,
And moaned as dogs do, being half dead,
Unwitting, as I deem: so then
Godmar turned grinning to his men,
150   Who ran, some five or six, and beat
His head to pieces at their feet.

Then Godmar turned again and said:
'So, Jehane, the first fitte° is read!
Take note, my lady, that your way
Lies backward to the Chatelet!'
She shook her head and gazed awhile
At her cold hands with a rueful smile,
As though this thing had made her mad.

This was the parting that they had
Beside the haystack in the floods.
                    1858

Near Avalon°

A ship with shields before the sun,
Six maidens round the mast,
A red-gold crown on every one,
A green gown on the last.

first fitte first part of a story
Avalon the Celtic version of the Isles of the
Blessed, where Arthur sojourned in his ap-
parent death, and from which he will return

The fluttering green banners there
Are wrought with ladies' heads most fair,
And a portraiture of Guenevere
The middle of each sail doth bear.

A ship with sails before the wind,
10   And round the helm six knights,
Their heaumes° are on, whereby, half blind,
They pass by many sights.

The tattered scarlet banners there,
Right soon will leave the spear-heads bare,
Those six knights sorrowfully bear
In all their heaumes some yellow hair.°
                            1858

Summer Dawn

Pray but one prayer for me 'twixt thy closed lips,
    Think but one thought of me up in the stars.
The summer night waneth, the morning light slips,
    Faint and grey 'twixt the leaves of the aspen, betwixt the cloud-bars,
That are patiently waiting there for the dawn:
    Patient and colourless, though Heaven's gold
Waits to float through them along with the sun.
Far out in the meadows, above the young corn,°
    The heavy elms wait, and restless and cold
10   The uneasy wind rises; the roses are dun;°
Through the long twilight they pray for the dawn.
Round the lone house in the midst of the corn.
    Speak but one word to me over the corn,
    Over the tender, bowed locks° of the corn.
1856   1858

Riding Together

For many, many days together
    The wind blew steady from the East;
For many days hot grew the weather,
    About the time of our Lady's Feast.°

For many days we rode together,
    Yet met we neither friend nor foe;

heaumes helmets
yellow hair pledges of their ladies; the heroines
of romance are generally blondes, the tempt-
resses brunettes
corn wheat

dun brownish gray in color
bowed locks because of the wind, like a person
kneeling
our Lady's Feast Feast of the Annunciation,
March 25

Hotter and clearer grew the weather,
   Steadily did the East wind blow.

We saw the trees in the hot, bright weather,
10 Clear-cut, with shadows very black,
   As freely we rode on together
      With helms unlaced and bridles slack.

And often as we rode together,
   We, looking down the green-banked stream,
Saw flowers in the sunny weather,
      And saw the bubble-making bream.°

And in the night lay down together,
   And hung above our heads the rood,°
Or watched night-long in the dewy weather,
20   The while the moon did watch the wood.

Our spears stood bright and thick together,
   Straight out the banners streamed behind,
As we galloped on in the sunny weather,
      With faces turned towards the wind.

Down sank our threescore spears together,°
   As thick we saw the pagans ride;
His eager face in the clear fresh weather,
      Shone out that last time by my side.

Up the sweep of the bridge we dashed together,
30   It rocked to the crash of the meeting spears,
Down rained the buds of the dear spring weather,
      The elm-tree flowers fell like tears.

There, as we rolled and writhed together,
   I threw my arms above my head,
For close by my side in the lovely weather,
      I saw him reel and fall back dead.

I and the slayer met together,
   He wanted the death-stroke there in his place,
With thoughts of death, in the lovely weather,
40   Gapingly mazed° at my maddened face.

Madly I fought as we fought together;
   In vain: the little Christian band
The pagans drowned, as in stormy weather
      The river drowns low-lying land.

They bound my blood-stained hands together,
   They bound his corpse to nod by my side:

---

bream a fish
rood cross
together The sixty Crusaders prepare for battle.

Gapingly mazed His antagonist, astonished at the knight's ferocity, lets his mouth hang open.

Then on we rode, in the bright March weather,
　　With clash of cymbals did we ride.

We ride no more, no more together;
50　　My prison-bars are thick and strong,
　I take no heed of any weather,
　　The sweet Saints grant I live not long.
　　1856   1858

A Garden by the Sea

I know a little garden-close,°
Set thick with lily and red rose,
Where I would wander if I might
From dewy dawn to dewy night,
And have one with me wandering.

And though within it no birds sing,
And though no pillared house is there,
And though the apple-boughs are bare
Of fruit and blossom, would to God
10　Her feet upon the green grass trod,
And I beheld them as before.

There comes a murmur from the shore,
And in the place two fair streams are,
Drawn from the purple hills afar,
Drawn down unto the restless sea:
Dark hills whose heath-bloom feeds no bee,
Dark shore no ship has ever seen,
Tormented by the billows green
Whose murmur comes unceasingly
20　Unto the place for which I cry.

For which I cry both day and night,
For which I let slip all delight,
Whereby I grow both deaf and blind,
Careless to win, unskilled to find,
And quick to loose what all men seek.
Yet tottering as I am and weak,
Still have I left a little breath
To seek within the jaws of death
An entrance to that happy place,
30　To seek the unforgotten face,
Once seen, once kissed, once reft° from me
Anigh the murmuring of the sea.
1867   1891

---

garden-close an enclosed garden　　　　　　**reft** robbed

From The Earthly Paradise

APOLOGY°

Of Heaven or Hell I have no power to sing,°
I cannot ease the burden of your fears,
Or make quick-coming death a little thing,
Or bring again the pleasure of past years,
Nor for my words shall ye forget your tears,
Or hope again for aught that I can say,
The idle° singer of an empty day.

But rather, when aweary of your mirth,
From full hearts still unsatisfied ye sigh,
And, feeling kindly unto all the earth,
Grudge every minute as it passes by,
Made the more mindful that the sweet days die—
Remember me a little then I pray,
The idle singer of an empty day.

The heavy trouble, the bewildering care
That weighs us down who live and earn our bread,
These idle verses have no power to bear;
So let me sing of names rememberèd,°
Because they, living not, can ne'er be dead,
Or long time take their memory quite away
From us poor singers of an empty day.

Dreamer of dreams, born out of my due time,
Why should I strive to set the crooked straight?
Let it suffice me that my murmuring rhyme
Beats with light wing against the ivory gate,°
Telling a tale not too importunate°
To those who in the sleepy region stay,
Lulled by the singer of an empty day.

Folk say, a wizard to a northern king°
At Christmas-tide such wondrous things did show,
That through one window men beheld the spring,
And through another saw the summer glow,
And through a third the fruited vines a-row,
While still, unheard, but in its wonted way,
Piped the drear wind of that December day.

So with this Earthly Paradise it is,
If ye will read aright, and pardon me,

10

20

30

Apology a defense of Morris's poetic stance, of
art for the sake of art, despite Morris's convinced and active Socialism
no power to sing unlike Dante or Milton
idle in the sense of pleasantly idle
names rememberèd in mythology or familiar
literature

ivory gate In Homer and Virgil, true dreams
emerge through the gates of horn, and false
ones through the gates of ivory.
importunate pressing
northern king possibly a reference to a legend
of Dr. Faustus

Who strive to build a shadowy isle of bliss
Midmost the beating of the steely sea,
40   Where tossed about all hearts of men must be;
Whose ravening monsters mighty men shall slay,
Not the poor singer of an empty day.

1868

ALGERNON CHARLES SWINBURNE

Atalanta in Calydon

This dramatic poem, Swinburne's finest work, follows closely a number of Greek models for its form, but takes its story mostly from Ovid (*Metamorphoses* VIII. 260 ff.). The choruses are the great strength of the poem, and the two most important are given below.

Althaea, queen of Calydon, pregnant with Meleager, dreams that she gives birth to a burning brand. When the child is born, the Fates prophesy he will die when the brand already in the fire is consumed. Althaea snatches the brand from the fire, puts it out, and then conceals it. After Meleager grows up to be a heroic warrior, the goddess Artemis, patroness of the hunt and of chastity, becomes angry with his father, for not sacrificing to her. She sends a boar, which makes the land of Calydon desolate. Among the Greek heroes who assemble to hunt the boar is the maiden Atalanta of Arcadia, whose life is consecrated to Artemis. The goddess therefore allows her follower the honor of slaying the boar. Althaea's two brothers, shamed by a woman's triumph, intervene against Atalanta, but are killed by their nephew Meleager, who has fallen in love with the maiden. Althaea, in revenge, throws the hidden brand into the fire, thus destroying her son.

The first chorus given here is the first of the play, and is sung by maidens as an invocation to Artemis, before the hunt. The second, Swinburne's most audacious anti-religious work, sums up the poem's dark theme, which is the utter hopelessness of human existence since all human desire is, by its nature, self-destructive, a condition for which the chorus holds the divine world responsible.

From Atalanta in Calydon

CHORUS

When the hounds of spring are on winter's traces,
   The mother of months° in meadow or plain
Fills the shadows and windy places
   With lisp of leaves and ripple of rain;
And the brown bright nightingale amorous
70   Is half assuaged for Itylus,°

mother of months Artemis is also goddess of the moon, and so presides over the monthly cycle.

Itylus the diminutive of Itys, the son of Procne, the nightingale (see notes to Matthew Arnold's "Philomela")

For the Thracian° ships and the foreign faces,
    The tongueless vigil, and all the pain.

Come with bows bent° and with emptying of quivers,
    Maiden most perfect, lady of light,
With a noise of winds and many rivers,
    With a clamour of waters, and with might;
Bind on thy sandals, O thou most fleet,°
Over the splendour and speed of thy feet;
For the faint east quickens, the wan west shivers,
80   Round the feet of the day and the feet of the night.

Where shall we find her, how shall we sing to her,
    Fold our hands round her knees, and cling?
O that man's heart were as fire and could spring to her,
    Fire, or the strength of the streams that spring!
For the stars and the winds are unto her
As raiment, as songs of the harp-player;
For the risen stars and the fallen cling to her,
    And the southwest-wind and the west-wind sing.

For winter's rains and ruins are over,
90   And all the season of snows and sins;
The days dividing lover and lover,
    The light that loses,° the night that wins;
And time remembered is grief forgotten,
And frosts are slain and flowers begotten,
And in green underwood and cover
    Blossom by blossom the spring begins.

The full streams feed on flower of rushes,
    Ripe grasses trammel a travelling foot,
The faint fresh flame of the young year flushes
100   From leaf to flower and flower to fruit;
And fruit and leaf are as gold and fire,
And the oat° is heard above the lyre,
And the hoofèd heel of a satyr crushes
    The chestnut-husk at the chestnut-root.

And Pan by noon and Bacchus by night,
    Fleeter of foot than the fleet-foot kid,
Follows with dancing and fills with delight
    The Maenad and the Bassarid;°
And soft as lips that laugh and hide
110   The laughing leaves of the trees divide,
And screen from seeing and leave in sight
    The god pursuing, the maiden hid.

Thracian the locus of horror in the Procne-Philomela story; the "tongueless vigil" is that of Procne's sister, Philomela
bows bent Artemis as huntress
most fleet Artemis was swiftest of the gods.

that loses short days of winter
oat shepherd's pipe made of oat straws
Bassarid Maenad and Bassarid are alternative names for female followers of Dionysus.

The ivy falls with the Bacchanal's° hair
  Over her eyebrows hiding her eyes;
The wild vine slipping down leaves bare
  Her bright breast shortening into sighs;
The wild vine slips with the weight of its leaves,
But the berried ivy catches and cleaves
To the limbs that glitter, the feet that scare
120   The wolf that follows, the fawn that flies.

. . .

CHORUS

Who hath given man speech? or who hath set therein
A thorn for peril and a snare for sin?
1040 For in the word his life is and his breath,
  And in the word his death,
That madness and the infatuate heart may breed
  From the word's womb the deed
And life bring one thing forth ere all pass by,
Even one thing which is ours yet cannot die—
Death. Hast thou seen him ever anywhere,
Time's twin-born brother, imperishable as he
Is perishable and plaintive, clothed with care
  And mutable as sand,
1050 But death is strong and full of blood and fair
And perdurable and like a lord of land?
Nay, time thou seest not, death thou wilt not see
Till life's right hand be loosened from thine hand
  And thy life-days from thee.

For the gods very subtly fashion
  Madness with sadness upon earth:
Not knowing in any wise compassion,
  Nor holding pity on any worth;
And many things they have given and taken,
1060 And wrought and ruined many things;
The firm land have they loosed and shaken,
  And sealed the sea with all her springs;
They have wearied time with heavy burdens
  And vexed the lips of life with breath:
Set men to labour and given them guerdons,°
  Death, and great darkness after death:
Put moans into the bridal measure
  And on the bridal wools a stain;
And circled pain about with pleasure,
1070 And girdled pleasure about with pain;

Bacchanal's another name for Maenad or Bas-   guerdons rewards
sarid, based on Bacchus, alternate name of
Dionysus

And strewed one marriage-bed with tears and fire
For extreme loathing and supreme desire.

What shall be done with all these tears of ours?
    Shall they make watersprings in the fair heaven
To bathe the brows of morning? or like flowers
Be shed and shine before the starriest hours,
    Or made the raiment of the weeping Seven?°
Or rather, O our masters, shall they be
Food for the famine of the grievous sea,
1080   A great well-head of lamentation
Satiating the sad gods? or fall and flow
Among the years and seasons to and fro,
    And wash their feet with tribulation
And fill them full with grieving ere they go?
    Alas, our lords, and yet alas again,
Seeing all your iron heaven is gilt as gold
    But all we smite thereat in vain;
Smite the gates barred with groanings manifold,
    But all the floors are paven with our pain.
1090   Yea, and with weariness of lips and eyes,
With breaking of the bosom, and with sighs,
    We labour, and are clad and fed with grief
And filled with days we would not fain behold
And nights we would not hear of; we wax old,
    All we wax old and wither like a leaf.
We are outcast, strayed between bright sun and moon;
    Our light and darkness are as leaves of flowers,
Black flowers and white, that perish; and the noon
    As midnight, and the night as daylight hours.
1100   A little fruit a little while is ours,
    And the worm finds it soon.

But up in heaven the high gods one by one
    Lay hands upon the draught that quickeneth,
Fulfilled with all tears shed and all things done,
    And stir with soft imperishable breath
    The bubbling bitterness of life and death,
And hold it to our lips and laugh; but they
Preserve their lips from tasting night or day,
    Lest they too change and sleep, the fates that spun,
1110   The lips that made us and the hands that slay;
    Lest all these change, and heaven bow down to none,
Change and be subject to the secular sway
    And terrene° revolution of the sun.

weeping Seven The Pleiades, group of seven
stars in constellation Taurus, though only six
are usually visible; in Greek mythology the
Pleiades were the seven daughters of Atlas and
Pleione. The eldest is the lost Pleiad, or star
that cannot be seen. The sisters weep for being
separated.
terrene earthly

Therefore they thrust it from them, putting time away.
I would the wine of time, made sharp and sweet
  With multitudinous days and nights and tears
  And many mixing savours of strange years,
Were no more trodden of them under feet,
  Cast out and spilt about their holy places:
1120 That life were given them as a fruit to eat
And death to drink as water; that the light
Might ebb, drawn backward from their eyes, and night
  Hide for one hour the imperishable faces.
That they might rise up sad in heaven, and know
Sorrow and sleep, one paler than young snow,
  One cold as blight of dew and ruinous rain;
Rise up and rest and suffer a little, and be
Awhile as all things born with us and we,
  And grieve as men, and like slain men be slain.

1130 For now we know not of them; but one saith
  The gods are gracious, praising God; and one,
When hast thou seen? or hast thou felt his breath
  Touch, nor consume thine eyelids as the sun,
Nor fill thee to the lips with fiery death?
  None hath beheld him, none
Seen above other gods and shapes of things,
Swift without feet and flying without wings,
Intolerable, not clad with death or life,
  Insatiable, not known of night or day,
1140 The lord of love and loathing and of strife
  Who gives a star and takes a sun away;
Who shapes the soul, and makes her a barren wife
  To the earthly body and grievous growth of clay;
Who turns the large limbs to a little flame
  And binds the great sea with a little sand;
Who makes desire, and slays desire with shame;
  Who shakes the heaven as ashes in his hand;
Who, seeing the light and shadow for the same,
  Bids day waste night as fire devours a brand,
1150 Smites without sword, and scourges without rod;
  The supreme evil, God.°
Yea, with thine hate, O God, thou hast covered us,
  One saith, and hidden our eyes away from sight,
And made us transitory and hazardous,
  Light things and slight;
Yet have men praised thee, saying, He hath made man thus,
  And he doeth right.
Thou hast kissed us, and hast smitten; thou hast laid

The supreme evil, God Swinburne's most notorious line

Upon us with thy left hand life, and said,
1160 Live: and again thou hast said, Yield up your breath,
And with thy right hand laid upon us death.
Thou hast sent us sleep, and stricken sleep with dreams,
    Saying, Joy is not, but love of joy shall be;
Thou hast made sweet springs for all the pleasant streams,
    In the end thou hast made them bitter with the sea.
Thou hast fed one rose with dust of many men;
    Thou hast marred one face with fire of many tears;
Thou hast taken love, and given us sorrow again;
    With pain thou hast filled us full to the eyes and ears.
1170 Therefore because thou art strong, our father, and we
    Feeble; and thou art against us, and thine hand
Constrains us in the shallows of the sea
    And breaks us at the limits of the land;
Because thou hast bent thy lightnings as a bow,
    And loosed the hours like arrows; and let fall
Sins and wild words and many a wingèd woe
    And wars among us, and one end of all;
Because thou hast made the thunder, and thy feet
    Are as a rushing water when the skies
1180 Break, but thy face as an exceeding heat
    And flames of fire the eyelids of thine eyes;
Because thou art over all who are over us;
    Because thy name is life and our name death;
Because thou art cruel and men are piteous,
    And our hands labour and thine hand scattereth;
Lo, with hearts rent and knees made tremulous,
    Lo, with ephemeral lips and casual breath,
        At least we witness of thee ere we die
That these things are not otherwise, but thus;
1190   That each man in his heart sigheth, and saith,
        That all men even as I,
All we are against thee, against thee, O God most high.

        But ye, keep ye on earth
        Your lips from over-speech,
Loud words and longing are so little worth;
        And the end is hard to reach.
For silence after grievous things is good,
    And reverence, and the fear that makes men whole,
And shame, and righteous governance of blood,
1200   And lordship of the soul.
But from sharp words and wits men pluck no fruit,
And gathering thorns they shake the tree at rest;
    For words divide and rend;
But silence is most noble till the end.
                    1865

Hymn to Proserpine°

After the Proclamation in Rome of the Christian Faith
Vicisti, Galilaee°

I have lived long enough, having seen one thing, that love hath an end;
Goddess and maiden and queen, be near me now and befriend.
Thou art more than the day or the morrow, the seasons that laugh or that weep;
For these give joy and sorrow; but thou, Prosperpina, sleep.
Sweet is the treading of wine,° and sweet the feet of the dove;°
But a goodlier gift is thine than foam of the grapes or love.
Yea, is not even Apollo, with hair and harpstring of gold,
A bitter God to follow, a beautiful God to behold?
I am sick of singing: the bays° burn deep and chafe: I am fain
10 To rest a little from praise and grievous pleasure and pain.
For the Gods we know not of, who give us our daily breath,
We know they are cruel as love or life, and lovely as death.
O Gods dethroned and deceased, cast forth, wiped out in a day!
From your wrath is the world released, redeemed from your chains, men say.
New Gods are crowned in the city; their flowers have broken your rods;
They are merciful, clothed with pity, the young compassionate Gods.
But for me their new device is barren, the days are bare;
Things long past over suffice, and men forgotten that were.
Time and the Gods are at strife; ye dwell in the midst thereof,
20 Draining a little life from the barren breasts of love.
I say to you, cease, take rest; yea, I say to you all, be at peace,
Till the bitter milk of her breast and the barren bosom shall cease.
Wilt thou yet take all, Galilean? but these thou shalt not take,
The laurel, the palms and the paean, the breasts of the nymphs in the brake;
Breasts more soft than a dove's, that tremble with tenderer breath;
And all the wings of the Loves, and all the joy before death;
All the feet of the hours that sound as a single lyre,
Dropped and deep in the flowers, with strings that flicker like fire.
More than these wilt thou give, things fairer than all these things?
30 Nay, for a little we live, and life hath mutable wings.
A little while and we die; shall life not thrive as it may?
For no man under the sky lives twice, outliving his day.
And grief is a grievous thing, and a man hath enough of his tears:

Hymn to Proserpine The chanter of this hymn is a 4th-century Roman poet, a follower of the ancient pagan faith, who foresees the rapid disappearance of the old religion after the Edict of Milan (313) has granted Christianity equal status in the Empire. Though there is deep spiritual defeat throughout the poem, it does not yield to Christianity so much as to the Heraclitean flux, i.e., the necessity for endless change, and to the speaker's overwhelming desire for oblivion, of which he makes Proserpine the goddess. Proserpine was the Queen of the dead; she was stolen from her mother, Ceres, by Pluto, the ruler of Hades, to be his bride.

Vicisti, Galilaee "You have conquered, Galilean"; supposedly said by the philosophic emperor Julian (331–63 A.D., called "the Apostate" by Christian chroniclers), after he received his death wound from a Christian. Julian, raised as a Christian, renounced Christianity for the old religion upon assuming the throne.

treading of wine worship of Bacchus
dove sacred to Venus
bays laurels, emblems of poetic achievement

Why should he labour, and bring fresh grief to blacken his years?
Thou hast conquered, O pale Galilean; the world has grown grey from thy breath;
We have drunken of things Lethean, and fed on the fullness of death.
Laurel is green for a season, and love is sweet for a day;
But love grows bitter with treason, and laurel outlives not May.
Sleep, shall we sleep after all? for the world is not sweet in the end;
40   For the old faiths loosen and fall, the new years ruin and rend.
Fate is a sea without shore, and the soul is a rock that abides;
But her ears are vexed with the roar and her face with the foam of the tides.
O lips that the live blood faints in, the leavings of racks and rods!
O ghastly glories of saints, dead limbs of gibbeted Gods!
Though all men abase them before you in spirit, and all knees bend,
I kneel not neither adore you, but standing, look to the end.
All delicate days and pleasant, all spirits and sorrows are cast
Far out with the foam of the present that sweeps to the surf of the past:
Waste water washes, and tall ships founder, and deep death waits:
50   Where beyond the extreme sea-wall, and between the remote sea-gates
Where, mighty with deepening sides, clad about with the seas as with wings,
And impelled of invisible tides, and fulfilled of unspeakable things,
White-eyed and poisonous-finned, shark-toothed and serpentine-curled
Rolls, under the whitening wind of the future, the wave of the world.
The depths stand naked in sunder behind it, the storms flee away;
In the hollow before it the thunder is taken and snared as a prey;
In its sides is the north-wind bound; and its salt is of all men's tears;
With light of ruin, and sound of changes, and pulse of years:
With travail of day after day, and with trouble of hour upon hour;
60   And bitter as blood is the spray; and the crests are as fangs that devour:
And its vapour and storm of its steam as the sighing of spirits to be;
And its noise as the noise in a dream; and its depth as the roots of the sea;
And the height of its heads as the height of the utmost stars of the air:
And the ends of the earth at the might thereof tremble, and time is made bare.
Will ye bridle the deep sea with reins, will ye chasten the high sea with rods?
Will ye take her to chain her with chains, who is older than all ye Gods?
All ye as a wind shall go by, as a fire shall ye pass and be past;
Ye are Gods, and behold, ye shall die, and the waves be upon you at last.
In the darkness of time, in the deeps of the years, in the changes of things,
70   Ye shall sleep as a slain man sleeps, and the world shall forget you for kings.
Though the feet of thine high priests tread where thy lords and our forefathers
    trod,
Though these that were Gods are dead, and thou being dead art a God,
Though before thee the throned Cytherean° be fallen, and hidden her head,
Yet thy kingdom shall pass, Galilean, thy dead shall go down to thee dead.
Of the maiden thy mother° men sing as a goddess with grace clad around;
Thou art crowned where another was king; where another was queen she is
    crowned.
Yea, once we had sight of another; but now she is queen, say these.

Cytherean Venus   **maiden thy mother** the Virgin Mary

Not as thine, not as thine was our mother,° a blossom of flowering seas,
Clothed round with the world's desire as with raiment, and fair as the foam.
80 And fleeter than kindled fire, and a goddess, and mother of Rome.°
For thine came pale and a maiden, and sister to sorrow; but ours,
Her deep hair heavily laden with odour and colour of flowers,
White rose of the rose-white water, a silver splendour, a flame,
Bent down unto us that besought her, and earth grew sweet with her name.
For thine came weeping, a slave among slaves, and rejected; but she
Came flushed from the full-flushed wave, and imperial, her foot on the sea.
And the wonderful waters knew her, the winds and the viewless ways,
And the roses grew rosier, and bluer the sea-blue stream of the bays.
Ye are fallen, our lords, by what token? we wist° that ye should not fall.
90 Ye were all so fair that are broken; and one more fair than ye all.
But I turn to her still, having seen she shall surely abide in the end;
Goddess and maiden and queen, be near me now and befriend.
O daughter of earth, of my mother, her crown and blossom of birth,
I am also, I also, thy brother; I go as I came unto earth.°
In the night where thine eyes are as moons are in heaven, the night where thou
    art,
Where the silence is more than all tunes, where sleep overflows from the heart,
Where the poppies° are sweet as the rose in our world, and the red rose is white,°
And the wind falls faint as it blows with the fume of the flowers of the night,
And the murmur of spirits that sleep in the shadow of Gods from afar
100 Grows dim in thine ears and deep as the deep dim soul of a star,
In the sweet low light of thy face, under heavens untrod by the sun.
Let my soul with their souls find place, and forget what is done and undone.
Thou art more than the Gods who number the days of our temporal breath;
For these give labour and slumber; but thou, Proserpina, death.
Therefore now at thy feet I abide for a season in silence. I know
I shall die as my fathers died, and sleep as they sleep; even so.
For the glass of the years is brittle wherein we gaze for a span;
A little soul for a little bears up this corpse which is man.°
So long I endure, no longer; and laugh not again, neither weep.
110 For there is no God found stronger than death; and death is a sleep.
1862   1866

our mother Venus
mother of Rome through her son, Aeneas
wist thought
earth Ceres, mother of Proserpine, was goddess
of earth and its fertility.
poppies sacred to Proserpine, because they
give a narcotic that brings forgetfulness

white the exhaustion of sexual passion
A little soul . . . man Swinburne observed
that here he echoed Epictetus, Stoic philosopher
(55–135 A.D.), who urged an ultimate indifference: "Thou art a little soul bearing up
a corpse."

Hertha°

I am° that which began;
Out of me the years roll;
Out of me God and man;
I am equal and whole;
God changes, and man, and the form of them bodily; I am the soul.

Before ever land was,
Before ever the sea,
Or soft hair of the grass,
Or fair limbs of the tree,
10   Or the flesh-coloured fruits of my branches, I was, and thy soul was in me.

First life on my sources
First drifted and swam;
Out of me are the forces
That save it or damn;
Out of me man and woman, and wild-beast and bird; before God was, I am.

Beside or above me
Nought is there to go;
Love or unlove me,
Unknow me or know,
20   I am that which unloves me and loves; I am stricken, and I am the blow.°

I the mark that is missed
And the arrows that miss,
I the mouth that is kissed
And the breath in the kiss,
The search, and the sought, and the seeker, the soul and the body that is.

I am that thing which blesses
My spirit elate;
That which caresses
With hands uncreate
30   My limbs unbegotten that measure the length of the measure of fate.

But what thing dost thou now,
Looking Godward, to cry

Hertha This is Swinburne's central, doctrinal poem, in which the ancient northern earth goddess, patroness of fertility and growth, attempts to define her own nature. Highly eclectic in its sources (the principal ones are Blake, Emerson, Whitman, Victor Hugo, and even—alas—Sade), *Hertha* is a genuinely mythopoeic poem, and perhaps one in which Swinburne created something surprising even to himself. His working ideas in the poem are typical of a late 19th-century naturalistic world view, positivistic and evolutionary, but the emergent mythology is darker in its implications as to what lies beyond the pleasure principle, which Hertha nevertheless urges upon mankind. One critic, Cecil Lang, usefully describes *Hertha* as a deliberately static poem about growth, and Swinburne himself rated it first among his poems, "finding in it the most of lyric force and music combined with the most of condensed and clarified thought."
I am See the statement of Jesus in John 8:58: "Before Abraham was, I am" with its backward reference to Exodus 3:14: "And God said unto Moses, 'I AM THAT I AM'."
I am the blow Ll. 20–40 are very close to Emerson's *Brahma*.

'I am I, thou art thou,
   I am low, thou art high'?
I am thou, whom thou seekest to find him; find thou but thyself, thou art I.

I the grain and the furrow,
   The plough-cloven clod
And the ploughshare drawn thorough,
   The germ and the sod,
40 The deed and the doer, the seed and the sower, the dust which is God.

Hast thou known° how I fashioned thee,
   Child, underground?
Fire that impassioned thee,
   Iron that bound,
Dim changes of water, what thing of all these hast thou known of or found?

Canst thou say in thine heart
   Thou hast seen with thine eyes
With what cunning of art
   Thou wast wrought in what wise,
50 By what force of what stuff thou wast shapen, and shown on my breast to the
   skies?

Who hath given, who hath sold it thee,
   Knowledge of me?
Hath the wilderness told it thee?
   Hast thou learnt of the sea?
Hast thou communed in spirit with night? have the winds taken counsel with
   thee?

Have I set such a star
   To show light on thy brow
That thou sawest from afar
   What I show to thee now?
60 Have ye spoken as brethren together, the sun and the mountains and thou?

What is here, dost thou know it?
   What was, hast thou known?
Prophet nor poet
   Nor tripod° nor throne
Nor spirit nor flesh can make answer, but only thy mother alone.

Mother, not maker,
   Born, and not made;°
Though her children forsake her,
   Allured or afraid,

Hast thou known . . . Ll. 41–62 echo God's
Voice out of the whirlwind with its unanswerable questions, in Job 38–39.
tripod three-legged stool sat upon by the

priestess of the oracle at Delphi; hence priesthood in general
not made Nature evolves, and so there was no
single act of creation, as Judaism and Christianity insisted.

70   Praying prayers to the God of their fashion,° she stirs not for all that have
      prayed.

                    A creed is a rod,°
                    And a crown is of night;°
                    But this thing is God,°
                    To be man with thy might,
      To grow straight in the strength of thy spirit, and live out thy life as the light.

                    I am in thee to save thee,°
                    As my soul in thee saith;
                    Give thou as I gave thee,
                    Thy life-blood and breath,
80   Green leaves of thy labour, white flowers of thy thought, and red fruit° of thy
      death.

                    Be the ways of thy giving
                    As mine were to thee;
                    The free life of thy living,
                    Be the gift of it free;
      Not as servant to lord, nor as master to slave, shalt thou give thee to me.

                    O children of banishment,
                    Souls overcast,
                    Were the lights° ye see vanish meant
                    Always to last,
90   Ye would know not the sun overshining the shadows and stars overpast.

                    I that saw where ye trod
                    The dim paths of the night
                    Set the shadow called God
                    In your skies to give light;
      But the morning of manhood is risen, and the shadowless soul is in sight.

                    The tree many-rooted°
                    That swells to the sky
                    With frondage red-fruited,
                    The life-tree am I;
100   In the buds of your lives is the sap of my leaves: ye shall live and not die.

                    But the Gods of your fashion
                    That take and that give,
                    In their pity and passion
                    That scourge and forgive,
      They are worms that are bred in the back that falls off; they shall die and not
      live.

fashion made by men's fears
rod instrument of chastisement
And a crown is of night ignorance begets kingship
God a humanist Godhead
save thee from religions and patriotisms
Green leaves . . . red fruit The green, white,
and red colors are a salute to the Italian flag,
and to Swinburne's hero Mazzini.
lights religions, particularly the varieties of
Christianity
many-rooted Yggdrasil, the ash world-tree of
northern myth

My own blood is what stanches
The wounds in my bark;
Stars° caught in my branches
Make day of the dark,
110 And are worshipped as suns till the sunrise shall tread out their fires as a spark.

Where dead ages hide under
The live roots of the tree,
In my darkness the thunder
Makes utterance of me;
In the clash of my boughs with each other ye hear the waves sound of the sea.

That noise is of Time,
As his feathers are spread
And his feet set to climb
Through the boughs overhead,
120 And my foliage rings round him and rustles, and branches are bent with his
tread.

The storm-winds of ages
Blow through me and cease,
The war-wind that rages,
The spring-wind of peace,
Ere the breath of them roughen my tresses, ere one of my blossoms increase.

All sounds of all changes,
All shadows and lights
On the world's mountain-ranges
And stream-riven heights,
130 Whose tongue is the wind's tongue and language of storm-clouds on earth-
shaking mights;

All forms of all faces,
All works of all hands
In unsearchable places
Of time-stricken lands,
All death and all life, and all reigns and all ruins, drop through me as sands.

Though sore be my burden
And more than ye know,
And my growth have no guerdon°
But only to grow,
140 Yet I fail not of growing for lightnings above me or death-worms below.

These too have their part in me,
As I too in these;
Such fire is at heart in me,
Such sap is this tree's,
Which hath in it all sounds and all secrets of infinite lands and of seas.

Stars false religions again   **guerdon** reward

In the spring-coloured hours
When my mind was as May's,
There brake forth of me flowers
By centuries of days,
150 Strong blossoms with perfume of manhood, shot out from my spirit as rays.

And the sound of them springing
And smell of their shoots
Were as warmth and sweet singing
And strength to my roots;
And the lives of my children made perfect with freedom of soul were my fruits.

I bid you but be;
I have need not of prayer;
I have need of you free°
As your mouths of mine air;
160 That my heart may be greater within me, beholding the fruits of me fair.

More fair than strange fruit is
Of faiths ye espouse;
In me only the root is
That blooms in your boughs;
Behold now your God that ye made you, to feed him with faith of your vows.

In the darkening and whitening
Abysses adored,
With dayspring and lightning
For lamp and for sword,
170 God thunders in heaven, and his angels are red with the wrath of the Lord.

O my sons, O too dutiful
Toward Gods not of me,
Was not I enough beautiful?
Was it hard to be free?
For behold, I am with you, am in you and of you; look forth now and see.

Lo, winged with world's wonders,
With miracles shod,
With the fires of his thunders
For raiment and rod,
180 God trembles in heaven, and his angels are white with the terror of God.

For his twilight° is come on him,
His anguish is here;
And his spirits gaze dumb on him,
Grown grey from his fear;
And his hour taketh hold on him stricken, the last of his infinite year.

Thought made him and breaks him,
Truth slays and forgives;

free but only of superstitions, not of Necessity   prophecy of the twilght of the gods by passing
twilight Christianity will fulfill the northern   away.

But to you, as time takes him,
This new thing it gives,
190   Even love, the beloved Republic, that feeds upon freedom and lives.

For truth only is living,
Truth only is whole,
And the love of his giving
Man's polestar and pole;
Man, pulse of my centre, and fruit of my body, and seed of my soul.

One birth of my bosom;
One beam of mine eye;
One topmost blossom
That scales the sky;
200   Man, equal and one with me, man that is made of me, man that is I.

1871

Ave Atque Vale°

In Memory of Charles Baudelaire

Nous devrions pourtant lui porter quelques fleurs;
Les morts, les pauvres morts, ont de grandes douleurs,
Et quand Octobre souffle, émondeur des vieux arbres,
Son vent mélancolique à l'entour de leurs marbres,
Certe, ils doivent trouver les vivants bien ingrats.°
Les Fleurs du Mal.

I

Shall I strew on thee rose or rue or laurel,°
Brother, on this that was the veil° of thee?
Or quiet sea-flower moulded by the sea,
Or simplest growth of meadow-sweet or sorrel,
Such as the summer-sleepy Dryads° weave,
Waked up by snow-soft sudden rains at eve?
Or wilt thou rather, as on earth before,
Half-faded fiery blossoms, pale with heat
And full of bitter summer, but more sweet

Ave Atque Vale Swinburne never met Charles Baudelaire, the poet of *Les Fleurs du mal* (Flowers of Evil) who died, aged 46, in 1867, but he admired him most among modern French poets, after his demi-god, Victor Hugo. *Ave Atque Vale*, though it deliberately echoes Baudelaire, is very much a poem in the tradition of English pastoral elegies, from Spenser's *Astrophel* on through Milton's *Lycidas* and their Romantic descendants in Shelley's *Adonais* and Arnold's *Thyrsis*. Swinburne is necessarily closest to Shelley's agnostic lament, but tries to go beyond Shelley by offering even less consolation, as in the immensely noble and stoic final stanza.
The title, *Ave Atque Vale*, is taken from the last line of Catullus' lament for his brother (*Carmen* 101): *Atque in perpetuum, frater, ave atque vale* (and now forever, brother, hail and farewell).
Nous . . . ingrats "Still, we ought to bring him some flowers. The dead, the unhappy dead, are very sorrowful, and when October blows its melancholy breath, pruning the old trees, around their tombs, surely they must discover that the living are truly ungrateful."
rose . . . laurel the rose is emblematic of love, rue of memory, the laurel of poetry
veil the body as covering, as in Shelley's poetry
Dryads wood nymphs

10   To thee than gleanings of a northern shore
    Trod by no tropic feet?

        II

For always thee the fervid languid glories
    Allured of heavier suns in mightier skies;
    Thine ears knew all the wandering watery sighs
Where the sea sobs round Lesbian promontories,
    The barren kiss of piteous wave to wave
    That knows not where is that Leucadian grave
Which hides too deep the supreme head of song.°
    Ah, salt and sterile as her kisses were,
20   The wild sea winds her and the green gulfs bear
Hither and thither, and vex and work her wrong,
    Blind gods that cannot spare.

        III

Thou sawest, in thine old singing season, brother,
    Secrets and sorrows unbeheld of us:
    Fierce loves, and lovely leaf-buds poisonous,
Bare to thy subtler eye, but for none other
    Blowing by night in some unbreathed-in clime;
    The hidden harvest of luxurious time,
Sin without shape, and pleasure without speech;
30   And where strange dreams in a tumultuous sleep
    Make the shut eyes of stricken spirits weep;
And with each face thou sawest the shadow on each,
    Seeing as men sow men reap.°

        IV

O sleepless heart and sombre soul unsleeping,
    That were athirst for sleep and no more life
    And no more love, for peace and no more strife!
Now the dim gods of death have in their keeping
    Spirit and body and all the springs of song,
    Is it well now where love can do no wrong,
40   Where stingless pleasure has no foam or fang
    Behind the unopening closure of her lips?
    Is it not well where soul from body slips
And flesh from bone divides without a pang
    As dew from flower-bell drips?

        V

It is enough; the end and the beginning
    Are one thing to thee, who art past the end.

---

supreme head of song the great poetess Sappho
of Lesbos, 7th century B.C., who according to
one tradition drowned herself by leaping from
the heights of the Ionian island Leucas
as men . . . reap Galatians 6:7

O hand unclasped of unbeholden friend,
For thee no fruits to pluck, no palms for willing,
No triumph and no labour and no lust,
50   Only dead yew-leaves and a little dust.
O quiet eyes wherein the light saith nought,
Whereto the day is dumb, nor any night
With obscure finger silences your sight,
Nor in your speech the sudden soul speaks thought,
Sleep, and have sleep for light.

VI

Now all strange hours and all strange loves are over,
Dreams and desires and sombre songs and sweet,
Hast thou found place at the great knees and feet
Of some pale Titan-woman° like a lover,
60   Such as thy vision here solicited,
Under the shadow of her fair vast head,
The deep division of prodigious breasts,
The solemn slope of mighty limbs asleep,
The weight of awful tresses that still keep
The savour and shade of old-world pine-forests
Where the wet hill-winds weep?

VII

Hast thou found any likeness for thy vision?
O gardener of strange flowers, what bud, what bloom,
Hast thou found sown, what gathered in the gloom?
70   What of despair, of rapture, of derision.
What of life is there, what of ill or good?
Are the fruits grey like dust or bright like blood?
Does the dim ground grow any seed of ours,
The faint fields quicken any terrene° root,
In low lands where the sun and moon are mute
And all the stars keep silence? Are there flowers
At all, or any fruit?

VIII

Alas, but though my flying song flies after,
O sweet strange elder singer, thy more fleet
80   Singing, and footprints of thy fleeter feet,
Some dim derision of mysterious laughter
From the blind tongueless warders of the dead,
Some gainless glimpse of Proserpine's veiled head,
Some little sound of unregarded tears
Wept by effaced unprofitable eyes,
And from pale mouths some cadence of dead sighs—

Titan-woman See Baudelaire's poem *La Géante*
(The Giantess).
terrene of the earth

These only, these the hearkening spirit hears,
  Sees only such things rise.

IX

Thou art far too far for wings of words to follow,
90   Far too far off for thought or any prayer.
  What ails us with thee, who art wind and air?
What ails us gazing where all seen is hollow?
  Yet with some fancy, yet with some desire,
  Dreams pursue death as winds a flying fire,
Our dreams pursue our dead and do not find.
  Still, and more swift than they, the thin flame flies,
  The low light fails us in elusive skies,
Still the foiled earnest ear is deaf, and blind
  Are still the eluded eyes.

X

100 Not thee, O never thee, in all time's changes,
  Not thee, but this the sound of thy sad soul,
  The shadow of thy swift spirit, this shut scroll
I lay my hand on, and not death estranges
  My spirit from communion of thy song—
  These memories and these melodies that throng
Veiled porches of a Muse funereal—
  These I salute, these touch, these clasp and fold
  As though a hand were in my hand to hold,
Or through mine ears a mourning musical
110   Of many mourners rolled.

XI

I among these, I also, in such station
  As when the pyre was charred, and piled the sods,
  And offering to the dead made, and their gods,
The old mourners had, standing to make libation,
  I stand, and to the gods and to the dead
  Do reverence without prayer or praise, and shed
Offering to these unknown, the gods of gloom,
  And what of honey and spice my seedlands bear,
  And what I may of fruits in this chilled air,
120 And lay, Orestes-like,° across the tomb
  A curl of severed hair.

XII

But by no hand nor any treason stricken,
  Not like the low-lying head of Him, the King,°

Orestes-like Orestes, Agamemnon's son, gives a tress of his hair in sacrifice to his dead father in the first scene of *The Choëphoroe* (The Liba-tion-Bearers) of Aeschylus.
King Agamemnon

The flame that made of Troy a ruinous thing,
Thou liest, and on this dust no tears could quicken
   There fall no tears like theirs that all men hear
   Fall tear by sweet imperishable tear
Down the opening leaves of holy poets' pages.
   Thee not Orestes, not Electra° mourns;
130   But bending us-ward with memorial urns
The most high Muses that fulfil all ages
   Weep, and our God's heart yearns.

XIII

For, sparing of his sacred strength, not often
   Among us darkling here the lord of light°
   Makes manifest his music and his might
In hearts that open and in lips that soften
   With the soft flame and heat of songs that shine.
   Thy lips indeed he touched with bitter wine,
And nourished them indeed with bitter bread;
140   Yet surely from his hand thy soul's food came,
   The fire that scarred thy spirit at his flame
Was lighted, and thine hungering heart he fed
   Who feeds our hearts with fame.

XIV

Therefore be too now at thy soul's sunsetting,
   God of all suns and songs, he too bends down
   To mix his laurel with the cypress° crown,
And save thy dust from blame and from forgetting.
   Therefore he too, seeing all thou wert and art,
   Compassionate, with sad and sacred heart,
150 Mourns thee of many his children the last dead,
   And hallows with strange tears and alien sighs
   Thine unmelodious mouth and sunless eyes,
And over thine irrevocable head
   Sheds light from the under skies.

XV

And one weeps with him in the ways Lethean,°
   And stains with tears her changing bosom chill:
   That obscure Venus of the hollow hill,°
That thing transformed which was the Cytherean,°
   With lips that lost their Grecian laugh divine
160   Long since, and face no more called Erycine;°
A ghost, a bitter and luxurious god.

Electra sister of Orestes, daughter of Agamemnon
lord of light Apollo
cypress tree of mourning
Lethean Lethe was the river of forgetfulness
in the underworld.
hollow hill the mountain of Venus where as an

enchantress she collects her victims in the
medieval story of the knight Tannhäuser
Cytherean Venus, who rose from the foam near
the island Cythera
Erycine another title of Venus, from Mt. Eryx
in Sicily, one of her several places of worship

Thee also with fair flesh and singing spell
   Did she, a sad and second prey, compel
Into the footless places once more trod,
   And shadows hot from hell.

XVI

And now no sacred staff shall break in blossom,°
   No choral salutation lure to light
   A spirit sick with perfume and sweet night
And love's tired eyes and hands and barren bosom.
170   There is no help for these things; none to mend
    And none to mar; not all our songs, O friend,
Will make death clear or make life durable.
   Howbeit with rose and ivy and wild vine
   And with wild notes about this dust of thine
At least I fill the place where white dreams dwell
   And wreathe an unseen shrine.

XVII

Sleep; and if life was bitter to thee, pardon,
   If sweet, give thanks; thou hast no more to live;
   And to give thanks is good, and to forgive.
180 Out of the mystic and the mournful garden
    Where all day through thine hands in barren braid
    Wove the sick flowers of secrecy and shade,
Green buds of sorrow and sin, and remnants grey,
   Sweet-smelling, pale with poison, sanguine-hearted,
   Passions that sprang from sleep and thoughts that started,
Shall death not bring us all as thee one day
   Among the days departed?

XVIII

For thee, O now a silent soul, my brother,
   Take at my hands this garland, and farewell.
190   Thin is the leaf, and chill and wintry smell,
And chill the solemn earth, a fatal mother,
   With sadder than the Niobean° womb,
   And in the hollow of her breasts a tomb.
Content thee, howsoe'er, whose days are done;
   There lies not any troublous thing before,
   Nor sight nor sound to war against thee more,
For whom all winds are quiet as the sun,
   All waters as the shore.
   1868   1878

And now . . . blossom The miracle which almost saved Tannhäuser is not available for Baudelaire; Tannhäuser, after a year as the lover of Venus, quested for penance to Rome, but absolution was refused by the pope until the papal staff should burst into bloom. Soon after Tannhäuser returned to Venus, the staff began to flower.
Niobean All Niobe's children were slain by Artemis and Apollo, to satisfy their jealous mother, Leto, who resented Niobe's boast of having had more children than Leto.

A Forsaken Garden°

In a coign° of the cliff between lowland and highland,
  At the sea-down's° edge between windward and lee,
Walled round with rocks as an inland island,
  The ghost of a garden fronts the sea.
A girdle of brushwood and thorn encloses
  The steep square slope of the blossomless bed
Where the weeds that grew green from the graves of its roses°
    Now lie dead.

The fields fall southward, abrupt and broken,
10 To the low last edge of the long lone land.
If a step should sound or a word be spoken,
  Would a ghost not rise at the strange guest's hand?
So long have the grey bare walks lain guestless,
  Through branches and briars if a man make way,
He shall find no life but the sea-wind's, restless
    Night and day.

The dense hard passage is blind and stifled
  That crawls by a track none turn to climb
To the strait waste place that the years have rifled
20 Of all but the thorns that are touched not of time.
The thorns he° spares when the rose is taken;
  The rocks are left when he wastes the plain.
The wind that wanders, the weeds wind-shaken,
    These remain.

Not a flower to be pressed of the foot that falls not;
  As the heart of a dead man the seed-plots are dry;
From the thicket of thorns whence the nightingale calls not,
  Could she call, there were never a rose to reply.
Over the meadows that blossom and wither
30 Rings but the note of a sea-bird's song;
Only the sun and the rain come hither
    All year long.

The sun burns sere and the rain dishevels
  One gaunt bleak blossom of scentless breath.
Only the wind here hovers and revels
  In a round where life seems barren as death.
Here there was laughing of old, there was weeping,
  Haply, of lovers none ever will know,
Whose eyes went seaward a hundred sleeping
40   Years ago.

A Forsaken Garden a memory of a garden on
the Isle of Wight, where Swinburne lived as a
boy; the coast is sinking into the sea, which
now makes the garden a desolation; the vision
of absolute entropy and hopelessness here is
central to Swinburne

coign corner
sea-down's seashore dune of sand
roses sea-flowers
he presumably time

Heart handfast in heart as they stood, 'Look thither,'
    Did he whisper? 'look forth from the flowers to the sea;
For the foam-flowers endure when the rose-blossoms wither,
    And men that love lightly may die—but we?'
And the same wind sang and the same waves whitened,
    And or ever the garden's last petals were shed,
In the lips that had whispered, the eyes that had lightened,
        Love was dead.

Or they loved their life through, and then went whither?
50   And were one to the end—but what end who knows?
Love deep as the sea as a rose must wither,
    As the rose-red seaweed that mocks the rose.
Shall the dead take thought for the dead to love them?
    What love was ever as deep as a grave?
They are loveless now as the grass above them
        Or the wave.

All are at one now, roses and lovers,
    Not known of the cliffs and the fields and the sea.
Not a breath of the time that has been hovers
60   In the air now soft with a summer to be.
Not a breath shall there sweeten the seasons hereafter
    Of the flowers or the lovers that laugh now or weep,
When as they that are free now of weeping and laughter
        We shall sleep.

Here death may deal not again for ever;
    Here change may come not till all change end.
From the graves they have made they shall rise up never,
    Who have left nought living to ravage and rend.
Earth, stones, and thorns of the wild ground growing,
70   While the sun and the rain live, these shall be;
Till a last wind's breath upon all these blowing
        Roll the sea.

Till the slow sea rise and the sheer cliff crumble,
    Till terrace and meadow the deep gulfs drink,
Till the strength of the waves of the high tides humble
    The fields that lessen, the rocks that shrink,
Here now in his triumph where all things falter,
    Stretched out on the spoils that his own hand spread,
As a god self-slain on his own strange altar,
80   Death lies dead.
        1876   1878

Sonnet for a Picture°

That nose is out of drawing. With a gasp,
  She pants upon the passionate lips that ache
  With the red drain of her own mouth, and make
A monochord of colour. Like an asp,
One lithe lock wriggles in his rutilant° grasp.
  Her bosom is an oven of myrrh,° to bake
  Love's white warm shewbread° to a browner cake.
The lock his fingers clench has burst its hasp.
The legs are absolutely abominable.
10   Ah! what keen overgust of wild-eyed woes
  Flags in that bosom, flushes in that nose?
Nay! Death sets riddles for desire to spell,
  Responsive. What red hem earth's passion sews,
But may be ravenously unripped in hell?

                    1880

Poeta Loquitur°

If a person conceives an opinion
  That my verses are stuff that will wash,
Or my Muse has one plume on her pinion,
  That person's opinion is bosh.
My philosophy, politics, free-thought!
  Are worth not three skips of a flea,
And the emptiest of thoughts that can be thought
  Are mine on the sea.

In a maze of monotonous murmur
10   Where reason roves ruined by rhyme,
In a voice neither graver nor firmer
  Than the bells on a fool's cap chime,
A party pretentiously pensive,
  With a Muse that deserves to be skinned,
Makes language and metre offensive
  With rhymes on the wind.

A perennial procession of phrases
  Pranked primly, though pruriently prime,
Precipitates preachings on praises
20   In a ruffianly riot of rhyme

Sonnet for a Picture from Swinburne's anonymous volume *The Heptalogia, or the Seven
Against Sense* . . . (1880). This is an un-
sparing parody of D. G. Rossetti's sonnets for
pictures in *The House of Life.*
rutilant glowing or shining, with reddish or
golden light
myrrh gum resin used in perfume and incense

shewbread 12 loaves placed every Sabbath before Jehovah, to be eaten by the priests alone
at the end of the week
Poeta Loquitur "The Poet Speaks"; the greatest *deliberate* self-parody in the language, not
published until after Swinburne's death. The
last two (extra) stanzas were transcribed by
Cecil Lang.

Through the pressure of print on my pages:
   But reckless the reader must be
Who imagines me one of the sages
   That steer through Time's sea.

Mad mixtures of Frenchified offal
   With insults to Christendom's creed,
Blind blasphemy, schoolboylike scoff, all
   These blazon me blockhead indeed.
I conceive myself obviously some one
30   Whose audience will never be thinned,
But the pupil must needs be a rum one
   Whose teacher is wind.

In my poems, with ravishing rapture
   Storm strikes me and strokes me and stings:
But I'm scarcely the bird you might capture
   Out of doors in the thick of such things.
I prefer to be well out of harm's way
   When tempest makes tremble the tree,
And the wind with omnipotent arm-sway
40   Makes soap of the sea.

Hanging hard on the rent rags of others,
   Who before me did better, I try
To believe them my sisters and brothers,
   Though I know what a low lot am I.
The mere sight of a church sets me yelping
   Like a boy that at football is shinned!
But the cause must indeed be past helping
   Whose gospel is wind!

All the pale past's red record of history
50   Is dusty with damnable deeds;
But the future's mild motherly mystery
   Peers pure of all crowns and all creeds.
Truth dawns on time's resonant ruin,
   Frank, fulminant,° fragrant, and free:
And apparently this is the doing
   Of wind on the sea.

Fame flutters in front of pretension
   Whose flagstaff is flagrantly fine:
And it cannot be needful to mention
60   That such beyond question is mine.
Some singers indulging in curses,
   Though sinful, have splendidly sinned:
But my would-be maleficent verses
   Are nothing but wind.

fulminant explosive, thundering

[For freedom to swagger and scribble,
   In a style that's too silly for school,
At the heels of his betters to nibble,
   While flaunting the flag of a fool,
May to me seem the part of a poet,
70   But where out of Bedlam is he
Who can think that in struggling to show it
   I am not at sea?]

[I may think to get honour and glory at
   The rate of a comet of star,
By maligning the Muse of a Laureate,
   Or denouncing the deeds of a Czar.
But such rollicking rhymsters get duly
   (As schoolboys at football say) shinned,
When their Muse, as such trollops will truly,
80   Sails too near the wind.]
             1918

The Lake of Gaube°

    The sun is lord and god, sublime, serene,
        And sovereign on the mountains: earth and air
    Lie prone in passion, blind with bliss unseen
        By force of sight and might of rapture, fair
        As dreams that die and know not what they were.
    The lawns,° the gorges, and the peaks, are one
    Glad glory, thrilled with sense of unison
    In strong compulsive silence of the sun.

    Flowers dense and keen as midnight stars aflame
10   And living things° of light like flames in flower
    That glance and flash as though no hand might tame
       Lightnings whose life outshone their stormlit hour
       And played and laughed on earth, with all their power
    Gone, and with all their joy of life made long
    And harmless as the lightning life of song,
    Shine sweet like stars when darkness feels them strong.

    The deep mild purple flaked with moonbright gold
       That makes the scales seem flowers of hardened light,
    The flamelike tongue, the feet that noon leaves cold,
20   The kindly trust in man, when once the sight
       Grew less than strange, and faith bade fear take flight,

The Lake of Gaube This end-of-the-century poem recalls Swinburne's experience of the *Lac de Gaube*, in the Pyrenees, near Cauterets, nearly 40 years before. In his *Notes of Travel* (1894), Swinburne vividly described the experience: ". . . the deliciously keen and exquisite shock of a first plunge under its tempting and threatening surface . . .", the temptation being that of the ultimate masochism of suicide.
lawns opens spaces
living things salamanders, which in alchemical tradition could live in fire

Outlive the little harmless life that shone
And gladdened eyes that loved it, and was gone
Ere love might fear that fear had looked thereon.

Fear held the bright thing hateful, even as fear,
   Whose name is one with hate and horror, saith
That heaven, the dark deep heaven of water near,
   Is deadly deep as hell and dark as death.°
   The rapturous plunge that quickens blood and breath
30   With pause more sweet than passion, ere they strive
To raise again the limbs that yet would dive
Deeper, should there have slain the soul alive.

As the bright salamander in fire of the noonshine exults and is glad his day,
The spirit that quickens my body rejoices to pass from the sunlight away,
To pass from the glow of the mountainous flowerage, the high multitudinous
   bloom,
Far down through the fathomless night of the water, the gladness of silence
   and gloom.
Death-dark and delicious as death in the dream of a lover and dreamer may be,
It clasps and encompasses body and soul with delight to be living and free:
Free utterly now, though the freedom endure but the space of a perilous breath,
40 And living, though girdled about with the darkness and coldness and strangeness
   of death:
Each limb and each pulse of the body rejoicing, each nerve of the spirit at rest,
All sense of the soul's life rapture, a passionate peace in its blindness blest.
So plunges the downward swimmer, embraced of the water unfathomed of man,
The darkness unplummeted, icier than seas in midwinter, for blessing or ban;
And swiftly and sweetly, when strength and breath fall short, and the dive is
   done,
Shoots up as a shaft from the dark depth shot, sped straight into sight of the sun;
And sheer through the snow-soft water, more dark than the roof of the pines
   above,
Strikes forth, and is glad as a bird whose flight is impelled and sustained of love.
As a sea-mew's love of the sea-wind breasted and ridden for rapture's sake
50 Is the love of his body and soul for the darkling delight of the soundless lake:
As the silent speed of a dream too living to live for a thought's space more
Is the flight of his limbs through the still strong chill of the darkness from shore
   to shore.
Might life be as this is and death be as life that casts off time as a robe,
The likeness of infinite heaven were a symbol revealed of the lake of Gaube.

      Whose thought has fathomed and measured
         The darkness of life and of death,
      The secret within them treasured,
         The spirit that is not breath?
      Whose vision has yet beholden
60   The splendour of death and of life?

death There was a local tradition that to bathe
in the lake of Gaube was certain to bring death.

Though sunset as dawn be golden,
   Is the word of them peace, not strife?
Deep silence answers: the glory
   We dream of may be but a dream,
And the sun of the soul wax hoary
   As ashes that show not a gleam.
But well shall it be with us ever
   Who drive through the darkness here,
If the soul that we live by never,
   For aught that a lie saith, fear.
1899   1904

COVENTRY PATMORE

To the Body°

Creation's and Creator's crowning good;
Wall of infinitude;
Foundation of the sky,
In Heaven forecast
And longed for from eternity,
Though laid the last;
Reverberating dome,
Of music cunningly built home
Against the void and indolent disgrace
10 Of unresponsive space;
Little, sequestered pleasure-house
For God and for His Spouse;
Elaborately, yea, past conceiving, fair,
Since, from the graced decorum of the hair,
Even to the tingling, sweet
Soles of the simple, earth-confiding feet,
And from the inmost heart
Outwards unto the thin
Silk curtains of the skin,
20 Every least part
Astonished hears
And sweet replies to some like region of the spheres;
Formed for a dignity prophets but darkly name,
Lest shameless men cry 'Shame!'
So rich with wealth concealed
That Heaven and Hell fight chiefly for this field;
Clinging to everything that pleases thee
With indefectible fidelity;

To the Body is an ode from Patmore's *The Unknown Eros.*

Alas, so true
30   To all thy friendships that no grace
Thee from thy sin can wholly disembrace;
Which thus 'bides with thee as the Jebusite,°
That, maugre° all God's promises could do,
The chosen People never conquered quite,
Who therefore lived with them,
And that by formal truce and as of right,
In metropolitan Jerusalem.
For which false fealty
Thou needs must, for a season, lie
40   In the grave's arms, foul and unshriven,
Albeit, in Heaven,
Thy crimson-throbbing Glow
Into its old abode aye pants to go,
And does with envy see
Enoch, Elijah, and the Lady,° she
Who left the lilies in her body's lieu.
Or, if the pleasure I have known in thee
But my poor faith's poor first-fruits be,
What quintessential, keen, ethereal bliss
50   Then shall be his
Who has thy birth-time's consecrating dew
For death's sweet chrism° retained,
Quick, tender, virginal, and unprofaned!

                                                    1877

GERARD MANLEY HOPKINS

1844–1889

Of all Victorian poets, Hopkins has been the most misrepresented and overpraised by modern critics. He has been discussed as though his closest affinities were with Donne on the one side, and T. S. Eliot on the other. Yet his poetry stems directly from Keats and the Pre-Raphaelites, and the dominant influences upon his literary thought came from Ruskin and Pater. A disciple of Newman, he is as High Romantic as his master, and his best poetry, with all its peculiarities of diction and metric, is less of a departure from the Victorian norm than Browning's, or Swinburne's, or even Patmore's. His case is analogous to Emily Dickinson's. Published out of their own century, they became for a time pseudo-contemporaries of twentieth-century poets, but perspectives later became corrected, and we learned to read both poets as very much involved in the literature and thought of their own generation. Hopkins was,

Jebusite See Joshua 15:63.
maugre in spite of
the Lady Like Enoch and Elijah, Mary the Mother was translated (carried over) soul and

body into Heaven; as the next line says, her tomb held lilies instead of her body.
chrism oil mixed with balm to anoint the dead

in many of his attitudes, a representative Victorian gentleman; indeed he was as much a nationalistic jingo as Tennyson or Kipling, and his religious anguish is clearly related to a characteristic sorrow of his age. His more properly poetic anguish is wholly Romantic, like Arnold's, for it derives both from baffled or repressed sexual passion (possibly homosexual, in Hopkins) and from an incurably Romantic sensibility desperately striving not to be Romantic, but to make a return to a lost tradition. Hopkins quested for ideas of order that were not available to his poetic mind, and as a poet he ended in bitterness, convinced that he had failed his genius.

Hopkins was born on July 28, 1844, at Stratford in Essex, the eldest of nine children, into a very religious High Anglican family, of comfortable means. He did not enjoy his early school years, but flowered at Balliol College, Oxford, where he studied Classics from 1863 to 1867, and became a student of Walter Pater, who corrected his essays. In the atmosphere of the continuing Oxford Movement, Hopkins underwent a crisis, which came in March 1865 and resulted from meeting an enthusiastic, very young, and beautiful religious poet, Digby Dolben, who was to drown in June 1867 at the age of nineteen.

In 1866, under Newman's sponsorship, Hopkins was received into the Roman Catholic Church. Two years later, he began his Jesuit novitiate, and continued faithful to the Order until he died. Ordained a priest in 1877, he preached in Liverpool, taught at Stonyhurst, a Jesuit seminary, and from 1884 until his death in 1889 served as Professor of Greek at the Catholic University in Dublin. Though perfectly free to write poems and paint pictures, so far as his superiors in the Society of Jesus were concerned, Hopkins was a congenital self-torturer, and so much a Romantic that he found the professions of priest and poet to be mutually exclusive.

Much fuss has been made over Hopkins's poetic ideas, but in fact they were commonplaces of his century, and are surprising only in vocabulary, just as his poems are original only in diction and rhythm, but never in imagery or vision, or indeed in any observations upon the human condition. Austin Warren, one of Hopkins' best and most sympathetic critics, justly remarked that in Hopkins's most ambitious poems there is "a discrepancy between texture and structure: the copious, violent detail is matched by no corresponding intellectual or mythic vigor." Following Keats's advice to Shelley, that an artist must serve Mammon by loading every rift of his poem with ore, Hopkins sometimes went too far, and even a sympathetic reader can decide that the poems are overloaded. Some of the accusations made by modern criticism against Swinburne might be directed more accurately against Hopkins.

What then is Hopkins's achievement as poet? It remains considerable, for all the reservations that this editor has expressed, which are not so much directed at Hopkins as they are at an absurd critical tradition that has fastened to him. The original, almost incredible, accomplishment of Hopkins is to have made Keatsian poetry into a devotional mode, however strained. In the "Subtle Doctor," the Scottish Franciscan philosopher Duns Scotus (1265–1308), also an Oxonian, Hopkins found doctrine to reconcile a concern for individual form, for the "thisness" of people and natural things, with the universal truths of the church. Following his own understanding of Scotus, Hopkins coined the word "inscape" for every natural pattern he apprehended. "Instress," another coinage, meant for him the effect of each pattern upon his own imagination. Taken together, the terms are an attempt at scholasticizing Keats's fundamental approach to perception: detachment, the poet's recourse to nonidentity, Negative Capability.

Hopkins's accomplishment as an innovator is almost entirely technical, and no longer excites poets as it did some decades ago. Hopkins remained unpublished until his friend, the poet Robert Bridges, brought out a first edition of the poems in 1918, nearly thirty years after Hopkins's death. By chance, this first publication almost coincided with the start of the aggressive literary modernism that dominated British and American poetry until the 1950's, and Hopkins was acclaimed by poets and critics as the true continuator of English poetry in the otherwise benighted 19th century, and as a precursor who could help justify modern experiments in diction, metrics, and imagistic procedure. This produced some quaint interpretations of English literary history, and exaggerated the nature and importance of Hopkins's technical innovations.

Hopkins's diction adds to its Keatsian and Pre-Raphaelite base a large stock of language derived from his study of Welsh and Old English, and from an amorphous group of Victorian philologists who sought a "pure English," less contaminated by the Latin and French elements that are incurably part of the language. Hopkins's metric is best left to the specialists who delight in such matters, but simply it was based, as he said, upon nursery rhymes, the choruses of Milton's *Samson Agonistes,* and Welsh poetry. Against what he called the "running" or "common" rhythm of 19th-century poetry, Hopkins espoused "sprung rhythm," which he insisted was inherent in the English language, the older, purely accentual meter of Anglo-Saxon verse. Evidently, Hopkins read Keats's odes as having this rhythm, despite Keats's Spenserian smoothness.

Though Hopkins came to the study of Old English late, his essential metrical achievement was to revive the schemes of Old English poetry. But the main traditions of English poetic rhythm go from Chaucer to Spenser and Milton and on to the major Romantics, and Hopkins's archaizing return to Cynewulf and Langland, though influential for a time, now seems an honorable eccentricity. Nevertheless, its expressive effectiveness is undeniable. The metrical basis of many of Hopkins's poems is a fixed number of primary-stressed syllables, surrounded by a variable number of unstressed ones, or "outrides" as he called them. The alliterations of early Germanic poetry also work powerfully to recast the poetic line into a chain of rhythmic bursts. Thus, in "The Windhover," the first two lines each have five of Hopkins's beats (as opposed to five regularized, alternating, accentual-syllabic ones):

> I caúght this mórning mórning's minión, kíng-
> dom of dáylight's daúphin, dapple-dáwn-drawn Fálcon, in his ríding . . .

But the first line has ten syllables, and might be mistaken for an iambic pentameter, while the second has sixteen; and we realize as we read through the poem that what is common to them, their *meter* rather than their individual rhythms, is the sequence of five major stresses. Moreover, the phrase "dapple-*dawn*-drawn" is so accented as to preserve the meaning "drawn by dappled dawn" through its interior rhyme and alliterative clusters. Hopkins's own invented metrical terminology is, like his other philosophical vocabulary, highly figurative: "hangers" or "outrides," "sprung rhythm," "counterpointing" (or superposition of rhythmic schemes), even the blended emotive-linguistic meanings of "stress" itself, all invoke the imagery of his poems, and are as subjective, in their interpretation of what was, after all, a fairly obvious neo-accentual technique, as are his metaphysical concepts.

God's Grandeur

The world is charged with the grandeur of God.°
   It will flame out, like shining from shook foil;°
   It gathers to a greatness, like the ooze of oil°
Crushed. Why do men then now not reck his rod?°
Generations have trod, have trod, have trod;
   And all is seared with trade; bleared, smeared with toil;
   And wears man's smudge and shares man's smell: the soil
Is bare now, nor can foot feel, being shod.

And for all this, nature is never spent;
10   There lives the dearest freshness deep down things;
And though the last lights off the black West went
   Oh, morning, at the brown brink eastward, springs—
Because the Holy Ghost over the bent
   World broods with warm breast and with ah! bright wings.°
1877   1918

Spring

Nothing is so beautiful as Spring—
   When weeds, in wheels, shoot long and lovely and lush;
   Thrush's eggs look little low heavens, and thrush
Through the echoing timber does so rinse and wring
The ear, it strikes like lightnings to hear him sing;
   The glassy peartree leaves and blooms, they brush
   The descending blue; that blue is all in a rush
With richness; the racing lambs too have fair their fling.

What is all this juice and all this joy?
10   A strain of the earth's sweet being in the beginning
In Eden garden.—Have, get,° before it cloy,
   Before it cloud, Christ, lord, and sour with sinning,
Innocent mind and Mayday in girl and boy,
   Most, O maid's child,° thy choice and worthy the winning.
1877   1918

grandeur of God "All things therefore are charged with love, are charged with God and if we know how to touch them give off sparks and take fire, yield drops and flow, ring and tell of him." Hopkins, *Sermons and Devotional Writings*, ed. Devlin, p. 195.
shook foil In a letter to Bridges, January 4, 1883, Hopkins explained: "I mean foil in its sense of leaf or tinsel . . . Shaken goldfoil

gives off broad glares like sheet lightning . . .".
ooze of oil as in the process of crushing olives
Why do . . . rod Why do men now not recognize God's discipline?
bright wings See Luke 3:22, Genesis 1:2, and Milton, *Paradise Lost* I.19–22.
Have, get a plea to Christ to secure young minds before they "sour with sinning"
O maid's child Christ, as son of Mary

The Windhover:°

To Christ our Lord°

I caught° this morning morning's minion,° king-
    dom of daylight's dauphin,° dapple-dawn-drawn°Falcon, in his riding
    Of the rolling level underneath him steady air, and striding
High there, how he rung upon the rein° of a wimpling° wing
In his ecstasy! then off, off forth on swing,
    As a skate's heel sweeps smooth on a bow-bend: the hurl and gliding
    Rebuffed the big wind. My heart in hiding
Stirred for a bird,—the achieve of, the mastery of the thing!

Brute beauty and valour and act, oh, air, pride, plume, here
10   Buckle!° AND° the fire that breaks from thee° then, a billion
Times told lovelier, more dangerous, O my chevalier!

No wonder of it: shéer plód makes plough down sillion°
Shine, and blue-bleak embers, ah my dear,°
    Fall, gall themselves, and gash gold-vermilion.
1877   1918

Pied Beauty°

Glory be to God for dappled things—
    For skies of couple-colour as a brinded° cow;
      For rose-moles all in stipple° upon trout that swim;
Fresh-firecoal chestnut-falls; finches' wings;
    Landscape plotted and pieced—fold, fallow, and plough;
      And áll trádes, their gear and tackle and trim.

All things counter, original, spare, strange;
    Whatever is fickle, freckled (who knows how?)
      With swift, slow; sweet, sour; adazzle, dim;
10   He fathers-forth whose beauty is past change:
                      Praise him.
1877   1918

The Windhover Hopkins thought this his best poem. The sparrow-hawk or kestrel can hover in the wind, even head-on.
To Christ our Lord a unique dedication in Hopkins; see "my chevalier" in line 11; there as here we are given a suggestion of chivalric, medieval service
I caught as in falconry
minion beloved
dauphin heir to the throne
dapple-dawn-drawn drawn out by the dappled dawns
rung upon the rein to check at rein's end, as in horse training
wimpling rippling
Buckle! a much-disputed word here; it may

mean "to give way as if under stress," or it may mean "buckle on! fasten!," or even "get ready to fight!," or it may be some combination of these
AND Presumably the capitals here indicate an epiphany, or moment of breakthrough.
thee Christ our Lord
sillion furrow
ah my dear See George Herbert's "Love," II: "I the unkinde, ungratefull? Ah my deare, / I cannot look on thee," where "my dear" is Christ, as it is here.
Pied Beauty particolored or variegated beauty
brinded streaked
stipple colored dots

Inversnaid°

This darksome burn,° horseback brown,
His rollrock highroad roaring down,
In coop° and in comb° the fleece of his foam
Flutes and low to the lake falls home.

A windpuff-bonnet of fáwn-fróth
Turns and twindles° over the broth
Of a pool so pitchblack, féll-frówning,
It rounds and rounds Despair to drowning.

10 Degged° with dew, dappled with dew
Are the groins of the braes° that the brook treads through,
Wiry heathpacks,° flitches° of fern,
And the beadbonny ash° that sits over the burn.

What would the world be, once bereft
Of wet and of wildness? Let them be left,
O let them be left, wildness and wet;
Long live the weeds and the wilderness yet.
1881   1918

Spelt from Sibyl's Leaves°

Earnest, earthless, equal, attuneable,° | vaulty, voluminous, . . . stupendous
Evening strains° to be tíme's vást, | womb-of-all, home-of-all, hearse-of-all night.
Her fond yellow hornlight° wound° to the west, | her wild hollow hoarlight°
    hung to the height
Waste;° her earliest stars, earlstars, | stárs principal, overbend us,
Fíre-féaturing heaven. For earth | her being has unbound; her dapple° is at an
    end, as-
tray or aswarm, all throughther,° in throngs; | self ín self steepèd and páshed°—
    qúite
Disremembering,° dísmémbering | áll now. Heart, you round° me right

Inversnaid town in Scottish Highlands
burn Scots for stream
coop a hollow, an enclosed spot
comb crest of the water
twindles W. H. Gardner reads this as a portmanteau coinage combining "twists," "twitches,"
and "dwindles"; but it may mean "dwindling
into twins," dividing exactly in half.
Degged sprinkled
braes Scots for deep banks of river valley
heathpacks heather clumps
flitches bunches
beadbonny ash ash trees clustered like lovely
beads
Spelt from Sibyl's Leaves One of Hopkins's
darkest poems, this is technically a vision of
Apocalypse; the title tells us that the poet is
spelling out our condition by reading the leaves
scattered in the wind by the seeress or Sibyl at
Cumae, leaves upon which she has written her
prophecies. Gardner suggests, as hints Hopkins

took up, the *Aeneid* VI.11–12, 268–72, 539–
43, and the medieval Latin hymn by Thomas
of Celano, *Dies irae* ("Day of wrath, that
fearful day, / When all the earth shall pass
away, / as David and the Sibyl say").
attuneable harmonious, unlike more various daylight
strains seeks to become
hornlight either moonlight, or the light of the
setting sun
wound either "is wound up" or else "blown"
as in the "winding" or blowing of a horn
hoarlight bleak light, like hoar-frost
Waste wasteland of sky at night
dapple here a noun, evidently meaning a variety
of colors
throughther through-other
pashed fallen apart into formlessness
Disremembering forgetting
round whisper to, warn against

With:° Óur évening is over us; óur night | whélms, whélms, ánd will end us.
Only the beakleaved boughs dragonish | damask° the tool-smooth bleak light;
black,°
10 Ever so black on it. Óur tale,° O óur oracle!° | Lét life, wáned, ah lét life wind
Off hér once skéined stained véined varíety | upon, áll on twó spools; párt, pen,
páck°
Now her áll in twó flocks, twó folds—black, white; | right, wrong; reckon but,
reck but, mind
But thése two: wáre° of a wórld where bút these | twó tell,° each off the óther;
of a rack°
Where, selfwrung, selfstrung,° sheathe- and shelterless, | thóughts agaínst
thoughts ín groans grínd.
1885   1918

(Carrion Comfort)°

Not, I'll not, carrion comfort, Despair, not feast on thee;
Not untwist—slack they may be—these last strands of man
In me ór, most weary, cry I can no more, I can;°
Can something, hope, wish day come, not choose not to be.

But ah, but O thou terrible,° why wouldst thou rude° on me
Thy wring-world° right foot rock?° lay a lionlimb against me? scan
With darksome devouring eyes my bruisèd bones? and fan,
O in turns of tempest, me heaped there; me frantic to avoid thee and flee?

Why? That my chaff might fly; my grain lie, sheer and clear.
10 Nay in all that toil, that coil, since (seems) I kissed the rod,
Hand rather,° my heart lo! lapped strength, stole joy, would laugh, chéer.
Cheer whom though? The hero° whose heaven-handling flung me, fóot tród
Me? or me° that fought him? O which one? is it each one? That night, that year
Of now done darkness I wretch lay wrestling° with (my God!)° my God.
1885   1918

With the heart speaks, and gives the warning that follows
damask to make a complex pattern
black this may be a verb, to blacken
tale story, but it may be "tally," our sins numbered up
oracle presumably the Cumaen Sibyl
pack the parable of sheep and goats; let life part us into two groups, pen us down as one or the other, and then pack us into one of the two folds
ware be wary of, be aware of, beware of both this world and the one to come
tell add up
rack our world, but also perhaps a Hell to come, both seen as a rack or instrument of torture
selfstrung we string ourselves upon the rack, here and hereafter
(Carrion Comfort) Bridges gave the poem this title; the phrase defines religious despair, or feeding upon the corpse of one's own soul; Bridges thought this to be the sonnet of which Hopkins said: "If ever anything was written in blood, one of these was."
I can I can do more
O thou terrible not despair but Christ the Wrestler
rude violently
wring-world powerful enough to wring all the world
rock wouldst rock
Hand rather God's hand chastising Hopkins
hero Christ
Me? or me the first "me" passively accepts; the second wrestles
wrestling The great original is certainly Jacob wrestling with the Angel of God, Genesis 32: 24–30, in order to secure the blessing of the name "Israel."
(my God!) a horrified whisper at his own daring

No Worst, There Is None

No worst, there is none.° Pitched past pitch° of grief,
More pangs will, schooled at forepangs,° wilder wring.
Comforter,° where, where is your comforting?
Mary, mother of us, where is your relief?
My cries heave, herds-long;° huddle in a main,° a chief-
woe, world-sorrow; on an age-old anvil wince and sing°—
Then lull, then leave off. Fury had shrieked 'No ling-
ering! Let me be fell:° force I must be brief.'
O the mind, mind has mountains; cliffs of fall
10 Frightful, sheer, no-man-fathomed. Hold them cheap
May who ne'er hung there. Nor does long our small
Durance° deal with that steep or deep. Here! creep,
Wretch, under a comfort serves in a whirlwind:° all
Life death does end and each day dies with sleep.
1885   1918

I Wake and Feel the Fell of Dark

I wake and feel the fell° of dark, not day.
What hours, O what black hoürs we have spent
This night! what sights you, heart, saw; ways you went!
And more must, in yet longer light's delay.

With witness I speak this. But where I say
Hours I mean years, mean life. And my lament
Is cries countless, cries like dead letters sent
To dearest him that lives alas! away.

I am gall, I am heartburn. God's most deep decree
10 Bitter would have me taste: my taste was me;
Bones built in me, flesh filled, blood brimmed the curse.

Selfyeast of spirit a dull dough sours.° I see
The lost are like this, and their scourge to be
As I am mine, their sweating selves; but worse.°
1885   1918

there is none no greater agony than religious
despair, like Satan on Mt. Niphates, at the
opening of *Paradise Lost* IV
Pitched past pitch Made blacker than black?
Thrown farther than grief can throw? Pitched
as high in consciousness of self as to be beyond
measurable pitch? Or perhaps all of these at
once?
schooled at forepangs educated by earlier pangs
Comforter the Paraclete, the Holy Spirit
herds-long like a procession of abandoned sheep;
the forsaken pastoral image is crucial in this
context
huddle in a main bunch themselves together
like terrified sheep
wince and sing like the keening of metal beaten
out upon an anvil

fell savage, even malevolent
Durance strength, our capacity to endure
whirlwind the comfort that serves here as the
sin of suicidal despair. It cannot hope to serve
in this whirlwind (the poem's final terrible
irony) for out of the whirlwind, as in the Book
of Job, will come the voice of God demanding
that Hopkins (Job) confront him.
fell evidently both adjective and noun; as
adjective it means "evil," as non "hairy skin"
sours The subject of "sours" is "selfyeast"
rather than "dough."
but worse He believes that the lost in Hell are
in a worse condition than he is, but he just
barely believes it.

That Nature Is a Heraclitean Fire and of the Comfort of the Resurrection°

Cloud-puffball,° torn tufts, tossed pillows° | flaunt forth, then chevy° on an air-
built thoroughfare: heaven-roysterers, in gay-gangs° | they throng; they glitter
   in marches.
Down roughcast, down dazzling whitewash,° | wherever an elm arches.
Shivelights° and shadowtackle° in long | lashes lace, lance, and pair.
Delightfully the bright wind boisterous | ropes, wrestles, beats° earth bare
Of yestertempest's creases; | in pool and rutpeel parches
Squandering ooze to squeezed | dough, crust, dust; stanches, starches
Squadroned masks° and manmarks | treadmire toil there
Footfretted in it. Million-fuelèd, | nature's bonfire° burns on.
10   But quench her bonniest, dearest | to her, her clearest-selvèd spark
Man, how fast his firedint,° | his mark on mind, is gone!
Both are in an unfathomable, all is in an enormous dark
Drowned. O pity and indig | nation! Manshape, that shone
Sheer off, disseveral,° a star, | death blots black out; nor mark
         Is any of him at all so stark
But vastness blurs and time | beats level. Enough! the Resurrection,
A heart's-clarion! Away grief's gasping, | joyless days, dejection.
         Across my foundering deck shone
A beacon, an eternal beam. | Flesh fade, and mortal trash
20   Fall to the residuary worm; | world's wildfire, leave but ash:
         In a flash, at a trumpet crash,
I am all at once what Christ is, | since he was what I am, and
This Jack,° joke, poor potsherd,° | patch,° matchwood, immortal diamond,
         Is immortal diamond.°
        1888   1918

That nature . . . the Resurrection The poem's
title contrasts an ancient but still prevalent
metaphysical materialism with the most spiritual
of events, Christ's Resurrection and the promised resurrection of mankind. Heraclitus (535–
475 B.C.) made fire the first element, and proclaimed that no single thing abides, but all
things flow, since all things are distinguished
from fire only through incessant strife which
divides them out of the fire.
Cloud-puffball reminding us of air and water,
and the instability of those elements
tossed pillows clouds
chevy scamper
gay-gangs See Whitman's "The Sleepers," 3:
"Onward we move! a gay gang of blackguards";
the influence of Walt Whitman was conceded
by Hopkins himself. Hopkins admired but
dreaded Whitman's poetry.
whitewash rain falling on leaves of the arching
elms

Shivelights splinters of light
shadowtackle trees outlined against the sky's
light, throwing a shadow like a ship's tackle
beats the wind's power striking the earth into
changes
masks impressions, as in plaster casts
bonfire original meaning: funeral pyre, or fire
of bones
firedint a coinage: fire-mark, the stamp of the
fire on man
disseveral another coinage: both disseveral and
several
Jack Everyman
potsherd broken pot, shard; see Isaiah 64:8:
". . . we are the clay, and thou our potter;
and we are all the work of thy hand."
patch fool
diamond the hardest substance made by the
Heraclitean fire that is Nature

Thou Art Indeed Just, Lord°

Justus quidem tu es, Domine, si disputem tecum; verumtamen
justa loquar ad te: Quare via impiorum prosperatur? &c.°

Thou art indeed just, Lord, if I contend
With thee; but, sir, so what I plead is just.
Why do sinners' ways prosper? and why must
Disappointment all I endeavour end?

Wert thou my enemy, O thou my friend,
How wouldst thou worse, I wonder, than thou dost
Defeat, thwart me? Oh, the sots and thralls of lust
Do in spare hours more thrive than I that spend,

Sir, life upon thy cause. See, banks and brakes°
10   Now, leavèd how thick! lacèd they are again
With fretty chervil,° look, and fresh wind shakes

Them; birds build—but not I build; no, but strain,
Time's eunuch, and not breed one work that wakes.
Mine, O thou lord of life, send my roots rain.
1889   1918

To R.B.°

The fine delight that fathers° thought; the strong
Spur, live and lancing like the blowpipe flame,
Breathes once and, quenchèd faster than it came,
Leaves yet the mind a mother of immortal song.

Nine months she then, nay years, nine years she long
Within her wears, bears, cares and combs° the same:
The widow of an insight lost she lives,° with aim
Now known and hand at work now never wrong.

Sweet fire the sire of muse, my soul needs this;
10   I want the one rapture of an inspiration
O then if in my lagging lines you miss

Thou Art Indeed Just, Lord a poem of creative
despair, written in the last year of the poet's
life
Justus quidem . . . prosperatur? &c. the Vulgate or Latin translation of Jeremiah 12:1. As
the "&c" indicates, later parts of chap. 12 are
employed in the rest of the sonnet; the poem's
first three lines translate this epigraph.
brakes thickets
fretty chervil wild parsley with fringed (fretted)
leaves

R.B. Robert Bridges, his close friend, later Poet
Laureate, and first editor of Hopkins's poems.
More than the other poems, this is Hopkins's
lament for the waste and loss of his poetic gift.
fathers begets
combs the mind is a mother caring for the child
she lives close to Shelley's "the mind in creation is like a fading coal"; the inspiration goes,
but the mind brings forth what the insight
fathered

The roll, the rise, the carol, the creation,
My winter world, that scarcely breathes that bliss
Now, yields you, with some sighs, our explanation.
1889   1918

OTHER VICTORIAN POETS

These half-dozen poets are united only in being Victorian, having no Pre-Raphaelite connections, and in being significant without achieving major status, at least for their poetry alone. Mrs. Browning had an enormous contemporary reputation, and now survives only in her husband's work and in a handful of lyrics, of which "A Musical Instrument" is the best. Edward Lear is the greatest master of nonsense verse in the language, and Lewis Carroll and Emily Brontë are remembered for their very different prose fictions. Clough, a fine satirical poet and moving skeptical consciousness still receives little recognition for his talents. Finally, the second James Thomson (not to be confused with his 18th-century namesake) carries the poetic passion for affirmation of what might be called Christian unbelief rather farther even than Swinburne could manage.

Elizabeth Barrett Browning (1806–61) was born in Durham. Her unfortunate father, who has been immortalized as the villain in the most famous literary love affair of the 19th century, carries the stigma in addition of having derived his income from West Indian slave plantations. Educated at home, Miss Barrett became an invalid (for still mysterious reasons) from 1838 to 1846 when, Andromeda to Browning's Perseus, she eloped with the best poet of the age. Her long poem *Aurora Leigh* (1856) was much admired, even by Ruskin, but is very bad. Quite bad too are the famous *Sonnets from the Portuguese*, dedicated to Browning (who thought she looked Portuguese). Though the Brownings' married life was reasonably happy, Mrs. Browning's enthusiasms for Napoleon III, spiritualism, and dressing her only child, a son, as though he were a toy, all gave her husband much pain. She died in Florence, June 29, 1861, to her husband's great grief.

Edward Lear (1812–88), a delightful personality, was primarily a landscape painter who traveled to exotic climes (Sinai, Albania) to find subjects for his work. His first *A Book of Nonsense* (1864) was his best, featuring his marvelous limericks and his curious visionary nonsense lyrics which combine Shelley and Tennyson to produce mysterious, uneasy quest-poems of lost love that can be read as utterly cheerful madness. He died happy at San Remo in Italy, while at work illustrating the poems of his good friend Tennyson.

Emily Brontë (1818–48), born and raised at Haworth in Yorkshire, wrote only one novel, but that was *Wuthering Heights* (1847). She published her poems in a joint volume in 1846 with her novelist sisters, as *Poems by Currer, Ellis and Acton Bell* (Emily was Ellis). Many of those poems, as well as some published posthumously, were written for the Gondal Saga, a childlike vision of Byronic passion, that Emily Brontë never quite gave up. She died in 1848 of tuberculosis, aged only thirty.

Arthur Hugh Clough (1819–61) was born January 1, 1819, into a family of cotton merchants and bankers, in Liverpool. He spent five years of his childhood in South Carolina, and then attended Rugby and Balliol College, Oxford, becoming Matthew Arnold's close friend. In 1848, Clough resigned his Fellowship at Oriel College, Oxford, because he refused to subscribe to the Thirty-Nine Articles of the Church of England. He went to Paris to observe the 1848 revolution, with which he sympathized, and began to write his longer poems, of which the best are *Dipsychus* (finished in 1850, but not published in his lifetime) and *Amours de Voyage* (1858). A man of enormous talents, even larger doubts, and engaging personality, he was the close friend not only of Arnold and Thackeray, but of the Boston and Concord literary men of America— Emerson, Charles Eliot Norton, Longfellow, and Lowell—all of whom burdened him with excessive expectations (he had been Dr. Thomas Arnold's prize pupil). Clough's sardonic temper rebelled against these expectations, against the Arnoldian High Seriousness, and against all the pieties of the age. But the effort was too great for Clough; a broken man, and a self-accused failure, he subsided (in 1854) into a marriage with a cousin of the formidable Florence Nightingale, for whom he became a kind of glorified errand-boy. He died on November 13, 1861, in Florence, where he had gone for his health, and was mourned by Arnold in the pastoral elegy *Thyrsis*.

Lewis Carroll (1832–98) (pen-name of the mathematician Charles Lutwidge Dodgson), spent his life lecturing at Oxford. As a solitary eccentric, he was much given to the company of little girls, and to these Muses he wrote *Alice's Adventures in Wonderland* (1865), *Through the Looking-Glass* (1871), *The Hunting of the Snark* (1876), and *Silvie and Bruno* (1889–93), all of which have survived his *Symbolic Logic* (1896).

James Thomson (1834–82), who led the most miserable life of any Victorian poet, wrote his poems under the dark initials of "B.V.," for "Bysshe Vanolis," to signify his allegiance to two great Romantic poets, Shelley and Novalis, the pen-name of the German Romantic poet Friedrich Leopold von Hardenberg (1772–1801). Orphaned at eight, and desperately poor throughout his youth, Thomson was enrolled by his guardians as an army schoolmaster. Serving in Ireland, he fell in love with a Miss Matilda Weller, but her early death augmented his already intense melancholia. A sad but pungent atheist, suffering from alcoholism and depression mania, he kept himself going by courage and will. In 1874, he wrote his best but bleakest poem, *The City of Dreadful Night*, which was published in 1880. Despite George Meredith's kind encouragement, Thomson could restrain neither his depressions nor his drinking, and he died a street vagrant in London, in 1882, when he was forty-eight. Despite its unrelieved gloom, *The City of Dreadful Night* maintains a fine negative exuberance, and is a superb period-piece.

ELIZABETH BARRETT BROWNING

A Musical Instrument

What was he doing, the great god Pan,°
  Down in the reeds by the river?
Spreading ruin and scattering ban,°
Splashing and paddling with hoofs of a goat,
And breaking the golden lilies afloat
  With the dragon-fly on the river.

He tore out a reed, the great god Pan,
  From the deep cool bed of the river;
The limpid water turbidly ran,
10 And the broken lilies a-dying lay,
And the dragon-fly had fled away,
  Ere he brought it out of the river.

High on the shore sat the great god Pan
  While turbidly flowed the river;
And hacked and hewed as a great god can,
With his hard bleak steel at the patient reed,
Till there was not a sign of the leaf indeed
  To prove it fresh from the river.

He cut it short, did the great god Pan
20   (How tall it stood in the river!),
Then drew the pith, like the heart of a man.
Steadily from the outside ring,
And notched the poor dry empty thing
  In holes, as he sat by the river.

'This is the way,' laughed the great god Pan
  (Laughed while he sat by the river),
'The only way, since gods began
To make a sweet music, they could succeed.'
Then, dropping his mouth to a hole in the reed,
30   He blew in power by the river.

Sweet, sweet, sweet, O Pan!
  Piercing sweet by the river!
Blinding sweet, O great god Pan!
The sun on the hill forgot to die,
And the lilies revived, and the dragon-fly
  Came back to dream on the river.

Yet half a beast is the great god Pan,
  To laugh as he sits by the river,

the great god Pan Pan was the god of forest
life and pastoral life; a man from the waist up,
but a goat in his lower half; his name means

"all" and essentially he represented everything
that is vital.
ban ruin, destruction

Making a poet out of a man;
40 The true gods sigh for the cost and pain
For the reed which grows nevermore again
    As a reed with the reeds in the river.

                    1860

EDWARD LEAR

Incidents in the Life
of My Uncle Arly°

I

O my agèd Uncle Arly!
Sitting on a heap of Barley
    Through the silent hours of night,—
Close beside a leafy thicket:—
On his nose there was a Cricket,—
In his hat a Railway-Ticket;—
    (But his shoes were far too tight.)

II

Long ago, in youth, he squandered
All his goods away, and wandered
    To the Tiniskoop-hills afar.
There on golden sunsets blazing,
Every evening found him gazing,—
Singing,—'Orb! you're quite amazing!
    How I wonder what you are!'

III

Like the ancient Medes and Persians,
Always by his own exertions
    He subsisted on those hills;—
Whiles,—by teaching children spelling,—
Or at times by merely yelling,—
Or at intervals by selling
    'Propter's Nicodemus Pills.'

IV

Later in his morning rambles
He perceived the moving brambles—
    Something square and white disclose;—
'Twas a First-Class Railway-Ticket;

Incidents . . . Uncle Arly a parody of Wordsworth's "Resolution and Independence"; cf.
below Lewis Carroll's "The White Knight's
Song" for a rival parody of the same indomitable leech-gatherer and his poetic questioner
who does not listen to any replies

But, on stooping down to pick it
Off the ground,—a pea-green Cricket
    Settled on my uncle's Nose.

V

Never—never more,—oh! never,
Did that Cricket leave him ever,—
    Dawn or evening, day or night;—
Clinging as a constant treasure,—
Chirping with a cheerious measure,—
Wholly to my uncle's pleasure,—
    (Though his shoes were far too tight.)

VI

So for three-and-forty winters,
Till his shoes were worn to splinters,
    All those hills he wandered o'er,—
Sometimes silent;—sometimes yelling;—
Till he came to Borley-Melling,
Near his old ancestral dwelling;—
    (But his shoes were far too tight.)

VII

On a little heap of Barley
Died my agèd uncle Arly,
    And they buried him one night;—
Close beside the leafy thicket;—
There,—his hat and Railway-Ticket;—
There,—his ever-faithful Cricket;—
    (But his shoes were far too tight.)
              1895

The Courtship of
the Yonghy-Bonghy-Bò

I

On the Coast of Coromandel
Where the early pumpkins blow,
In the middle of the woods
    Lived the Yonghy-Bonghy-Bò.
Two old chairs, and half a candle,—
One old jug without a handle,—
    These were all the worldly goods,
    In the middle of the woods,
    These were all the worldly goods,
Of the Yonghy-Bonghy-Bò,
Of the Yonghy-Bonghy-Bò.

II

Once, among the Bong-trees walking
　　Where the early pumpkins blow,
　　　To a little heap of stones
　　　Came the Yonghy-Bonghy-Bò.
There he heard a Lady talking,
　　To some milk-white Hens of Dorking,—
　　　' 'Tis the Lady Jingly Jones!
　　　On that little heap of stones
　　　Sits the Lady Jingly Jones!'
Said the Yonghy-Bonghy-Bò,
Said the Yonghy-Bonghy-Bò.

III

'Lady Jingly! Lady Jingly!
　　Sitting where the pumpkins blow,
　　　Will you come and be my wife?'
　　　Said the Yonghy-Bonghy-Bò.
'I am tired of living singly,—
On this coast so wild and shingly,—
　　　I'm a-weary of my life:
　　　If you'll come and be my wife,
　　　Quite serene would be my life!'—
Said the Yonghy-Bonghy-Bò,
Said the Yonghy-Bonghy-Bò.

IV

'On this Coast of Coromandel,
　　Shrimps and watercresses grow,
　　　Prawns are plentiful and cheap,'
　　　Said the Yonghy-Bonghy-Bò.
'You shall have my chairs and candle,
And my jug without a handle!—
　　　Gaze upon the rolling deep
　　　(Fish is plentiful and cheap)
　　　As the sea, my love is deep!'
Said the Yonghy-Bonghy-Bò,
Said the Yonghy-Bonghy-Bò.

V

Lady Jingly answered sadly,
　　And her tears began to flow,—
　　　'Your proposal comes too late,
　　　Mr. Yonghy-Bonghy-Bò!
I would be your wife most gladly!'
(Here she twirled her fingers madly,)
　　　'But in England I've a mate!
　　　Yes! you've asked me far too late,
　　　For in England I've a mate,

Mr. Yonghy-Bonghy-Bò!
Mr. Yonghy-Bonghy-Bò!'

VI

'Mr. Jones—(his name is Handel,—
Handel Jones, Esquire, & Co.)
    Dorking fowls delights to send,
Mr. Yonghy-Bonghy-Bò!
Keep, oh! keep your chairs and candle,
And your jug without a handle,—
    I can merely be your friend!
    —Should my Jones more Dorkings send,
    I will give you three, my friend!
Mr. Yonghy-Bonghy-Bò!
Mr. Yonghy-Bonghy-Bò!'

VII

'Though you've such a tiny body,
    And your head so large doth grow,—
    Though your hat may blow away,
Mr. Yonghy-Bonghy-Bò!
Though you're such a Hoddy Doddy—
Yet I wish that I could modi-
    fy the words I needs must say!
    Will you please to go away?
    That is all I have to say—
Mr. Yonghy-Bonghy-Bò!
Mr. Yonghy-Bonghy-Bò!'

VIII

Down the slippery slopes of Myrtle,
    Where the early pumpkins blow,
    To the calm and silent sea
Fled the Yonghy-Bonghy-Bò.
There, beyond the Bay of Gurtle,
Lay a large and lively Turtle;—
    'You're the Cove,' he said, 'for me
    On your back beyond the sea,
    Turtle, you shall carry me!'
Said the Yonghy-Bonghy-Bò,
Said the Yonghy-Bonghy-Bò.

IX

Through the silent-roaring ocean
    Did the Turtle swiftly go;
    Holding fast upon his shell
Rode the Yonghy-Bonghy-Bò.
With a sad primæval motion
Towards the sunset isles of Boshen

Still the Turtle bore him well.
Holding fast upon his shell,
'Lady Jingly Jones, farewell!'
Sang the Yonghy-Bonghy-Bò,
Sang the Yonghy-Bonghy-Bò.

      x

From the Coast of Coromandel,
  Did that Lady never go;
    On that heap of stones she mourns
    For the Yonghy-Bonghy-Bò.
On that Coast of Coromandel,
In his jug without a handle
    Still she weeps, and daily moans;
    On that little heap of stones
    To her Dorking Hens she moans,
  For the Yonghy-Bonghy-Bò,
  For the Yonghy-Bonghy-Bò.

       1877

EMILY BRONTË

Stanzas

Often rebuked, yet always back returning
  To those first feelings that were born with me,
And leaving busy chase of wealth and learning
  For idle dreams of things which cannot be:

Today, I will seek not the shadowy region;
  Its unsustaining vastness waxes drear;
And visions rising, legion after legion,
  Bring the unreal world too strangely near.

I'll walk, but not in old heroic traces,
10 And not in paths of high morality,
And not among the half-distinguished faces,
  The clouded forms of long-past history.

I'll walk where my own nature would be leading—
  It vexes me to choose another guide—
Where the grey flocks in ferny glens are feeding,
  Where the wild wind blows on the mountainside.

What have those lonely mountains worth revealing?
  More glory and more grief than I can tell:
The earth that wakes one human heart to feeling
20 Can centre both the worlds of Heaven and Hell.

       1850

Last Lines

No coward soul is mine,
No trembler in the world's storm-troubled sphere;
I see Heaven's glories shine,
And faith shines equal, arming me from fear.

O God within my breast,
Almighty, ever-present Deity!
Life—that in me has rest,
As I—undying Life—have power in Thee!

Vain are the thousand creeds
10 That move men's hearts—unutterably vain;
Worthless as withered weeds,
Or idlest froth amid the boundless main,

To waken doubt in one
Holding so fast by Thine infinity;
So surely anchored on
The steadfast rock of immortality.

With wide-embracing love
Thy spirit animates eternal years,
Pervades and broods above,
20 Changes, sustains, dissolves, creates, and rears.

Though earth and man were gone,
And suns and universes ceased to be,
And Thou were left alone,
Every existence would exist in Thee.

There is not room for Death,
Nor atom that his might could render void;
Thou—Thou art Being and Breath,
And what that Thou art may never be destroyed.
1846   1850

ARTHUR HUGH CLOUGH

The Latest Decalogue°

Thou shalt have one God only; who
Would be at the expense of two?
No graven images may be
Worshipped, except the currency:
Swear not at all; for for thy curse
Thine enemy is none the worse:

The Latest Decalogue the Ten Commandments
as Clough saw them lived by his contemporaries

At church on Sunday to attend
Will serve to keep the world thy friend:
Honour thy parents; that is, all
From whom advancement may befall:

Thou shalt not kill; but needst not strive
Officiously to keep alive:
Do not adultery commit;
Advantage rarely comes of it:
Thou shalt not steal; an empty feat,
When it's so lucrative to cheat:
Bear not false witness; let the lie
Have time on its own wings to fly:
Thou shalt not covet; but tradition
Approves all forms of competition.

The sum of all is, thou shalt love,
If any body, God above:
At any rate shall never labour
More than thyself to love thy neighbour.
1847   1862

Say Not the Struggle Nought Availeth

Say not the struggle° nought availeth,
  The labour and the wounds are vain,
The enemy faints not, nor faileth,
  And as things have been, things remain.

If hopes were dupes, fears may be liars;
  It may be, in yon smoke concealed,
Your comrades chase e'en now the fliers,
  And, but for you, possess the field.

For while the tired waves, vainly breaking,
  Seem here no painful inch to gain,
Far back through creeks and inlets making
  Came, silent, flooding in, the main,

And not by eastern windows only,
  When daylight comes, comes in the light,
In front the sun climbs slow, how slowly,
  But westward, look, the land is bright.
1849   1862

struggle Clough had supported the European
revolutions of 1848; he wrote this poem after
they had been defeated.

From Dipsychus°

[SPIRIT'S SONG]

130   As I sat at the café, I said to myself,
They may talk as they please about what they call pelf,°
They may sneer as they like about eating and drinking,
But help it I cannot, I cannot help thinking
    How pleasant it is to have money, heigh ho!
    How pleasant it is to have money.

I sit at my table *en grand seigneur,*°
And when I have done, throw a crust to the poor;
Not only the pleasure, one's self, of good living,
But also the pleasure of now and then giving.
140   So pleasant it is to have money, heigh ho!
    So pleasant it is to have money.

It was but last winter I came up to Town,
But already I'm getting a little renown;
I make new acquaintance where'er I appear;
I am not too shy, and have nothing to fear.
    So pleasant it is to have money, heigh ho!
    So pleasant it is to have money.

I drive through the streets, and I care not a d—mn;
The people they stare, and they ask who I am;
150   And if I should chance to run over a cad,
I can pay for the damage if ever so bad.
    So pleasant it is to have money, heigh ho!
    So pleasant it is to have money.

We stroll to our box and look down on the pit,
And if it weren't low should be tempted to spit;
We loll and we talk until people look up,
And when it's half over we go out and sup.
    So pleasant it is to have money, heigh ho!
    So pleasant it is to have money.

160   The best of the tables and best of the fare—
And as for the others, the devil may care;
It isn't our fault if they dare not afford
To sup like a prince and be drunk as a lord.
    So pleasant it is to have money, heigh ho!
    So pleasant it is to have money.

Dipsychus This is Clough's sardonic version of *Faust* and consists of dialogues between "Dipsychus" (his Faust), whose name means "doubleminded" or "of two minds," and a Spirit like Mephistopheles. The poem's high point is the following Spirit's song, which expresses a universal truth, and hits hard at Ruskin's *The Stones of Venice.*
pelf derogatory term for wealth
en grand seigneur as a noble lord

We sit at our tables and tipple champagne;
Ere one bottle goes, comes another again;
The waiters they skip and they scuttle about,
And the landlord attends us so civilly out.
170   So pleasant it is to have money, heigh ho!
      So pleasant it is to have money.

It was but last winter I came up to town,
But already I'm getting a little renown;
I get to good houses without much ado,
Am beginning to see the nobility too.
      So pleasant it is to have money, heigh ho!
      So pleasant it is to have money.

O dear! what a pity they ever should lose it!
For they are the gentry that know how to use it;
180   So grand and so graceful, such manners, such dinners,
But yet, after all, it is we are the winners.
      So pleasant it is to have money, heigh ho!
      So pleasant it is to have money.

Thus I sat at my table *en grand seigneur,*
And when I had done threw a crust to the poor;
Not only the pleasure, one's self, of good eating,
But also the pleasure of now and then treating.
      So pleasant it is to have money, heigh ho!
      So pleasant it is to have money.

190   They may talk as they please about what they call pelf,
And how one ought never to think of one's self,
And how pleasures of thought surpass eating and drinking—
My pleasure of thought is the pleasure of thinking
      How pleasant it is to have money, heigh ho!
      How pleasant it is to have money.

(Written in Venice, but for all parts true,
'Twas not a crust I gave him, but a sou.°)

A gondola here, and a gondola there,
'Tis the pleasantest fashion of taking the air.
200   To right and to left; stop, turn, and go yonder,
And let us repeat, o'er the tide as we wander,
      How pleasant it is to have money, heigh ho!
      How pleasant it is to have money.

      Come, leave your Gothic, worn-out story,
      San Giorgio and the Redemptore;°
      I from no building, gay or solemn,

sou French penny
San Giorgio and the Redemptore Against Ruskin, the Spirit denounces not only Gothic architecture, but the Italian classic or Palladian style, as exemplified by two great Renaissance Venetian churches, San Giorgio Maggiore and Redentore.

Can spare the shapely Grecian column.
'Tis not, these centuries four,° for nought
Our European world of thought
210 Hath made familiar to its home
The classic mind of Greece and Rome;
In all new work that would look forth
To more than antiquarian worth,
Palladio's° pediments and bases,
Or something such, will find their places:
Maturer optics don't delight,
In childish dim religious light,°
In evanescent vague effects
That shirk, not face, one's intellects;
220 They love not fancies fast betrayed,
And artful tricks of light and shade,
But pure form nakedly displayed,
And all things absolutely made.
The Doge's palace° though, from hence,
In spite of Ruskin's d——d pretence,
The tide now level with the quay,
Is certainly a thing to see.
We'll turn to the Rialto° soon;
One's told to see it by the moon.

230 A gondola here, and a gondola there,
'Tis the pleasantest fashion of taking the air.
To right and to left; stop, turn, and go yonder,
And let us repeat, o'er the flood as we wander,
How pleasant it is to have money, heigh ho!
How pleasant it is to have money.
1850–51   1865

centuries four since the Renaissance began
Palladio's Andrea Palladio, greatest architect
of the Italian 16th century

dim religious light a smack at Milton's *Il Pense-roso*, l. 160
Doge's palace where Venice's rulers governed
Rialto bridge over Venice's Grand Canal

LEWIS CARROLL
(Charles Lutwidge Dodgson)

Songs from Through the Looking-Glass

Jabberwocky°

'Twas brillig,° and the slithy° toves°
  Did gyre° and gimble° in the wabe;°
All mimsy° were the borogoves,°
  And the mome° raths° outgrabe.°

'Beware the Jabberwock, my son!
  The jaws that bite, the claws that catch!
Beware the Jubjub bird, and shun
  The frumious° Bandersnatch!'

10 He took his vorpal sword in hand;
  Long time the manxome foe he sought—
So rested he by the Tumtum tree,
  And stood awhile in thought.

And, as in uffish thought he stood,
  The Jabberwock, with eyes of flame,
Came whiffling through the tulgey wood,
  And burbled as it came!

One, two! One, two! And through and through
  The vorpal blade went snicker-snack!
He left it dead, and with its head
20   He went galumphing back.

'And hast thou slain the Jabberwock?
  Come to my arms, my beamish boy
O frabjous day! Callooh! Callay!'
  He chortled in his joy.

'Twas brillig, and the slithy toves
  Did gyre and gimble in the wabe;

Jabberwocky The definitions following are those given by Humpty Dumpty in *Through the Looking-Glass*, except for the last, which comes from the "Preface" to *The Hunting of the Snark*.
brillig ". . . four o'clock in the afternoon . . . when you begin *broiling* things for dinner"
slithy ". . . 'Lithe and slimy.' 'Lithe' is the same as 'active'. . . like a portmanteau . . . two meanings packed up into one word"
toves ". . . something like badgers—they're something like lizards—and they're something like corkscrews . . . they make their nests under sundials—also they live on cheese."
gyre ". . . to go round and round like a gyroscope. . . ."
gimble ". . . to make holes like a gimlet."
wabe "the grass plot round a sundial . . . be-

cause it goes a long way before it, and a long way behind it——" "And a long way beyond it on each side. . . ."
mimsy ". . .'flimsy and miserable'. . . ."
borogove ". . . a thin, shabby-looking bird with its feathers sticking out all round—something like a live mop."
mome Here Humpty Dumpty said: " 'mome' I'm not certain about. I think it's short for 'from home'—meaning that they'd lost their way. . . ."
raths ". . . a sort of green pig. . . ."
outgrabe (past tense of "outgribe") ". . . 'outgribing' is something between bellowing and whistling, with a kind of sneeze in the middle. . . ."
frumious ". . . fuming" and "furious'. . . ."

1488

All mimsy were the borogoves,
    And the mome raths outgrabe.
            1872

The White Knight's Song°

Haddock's Eyes or *The Aged Aged Man*
or *Ways and Means* or *A-Sitting On A Gate*

I'll tell thee everything I can;
    There's little to relate.
I saw an aged, aged man,
    A-sitting on a gate.
'Who are you, aged man?' I said.
    'And how is it you live?'
And his answer trickled through my head
    Like water through a sieve.

He said 'I look for butterflies
10   That sleep among the wheat;
I make them into mutton-pies,
    And sell them in the street.
I sell them unto men,' he said,
    'Who sail on stormy seas;
And that's the way I get my bread—
    A trifle, if you please.'

But I was thinking of a plan
    To dye one's whiskers green,
And always use so large a fan
20   That it could not be seen.
So, having no reply to give
    To what the old man said,
I cried, 'Come, tell me how you live!'
    And thumped him on the head.

His accents mild took up the tale;
    He said, 'I go my ways,
And when I find a mountain-rill,
    I set it in a blaze;
And thence they make a stuff they call
30   Rowland's Macassar Oil—
Yet twopence-halfpenny is all
    They give me for my toil.'

But I was thinking of a way
    To feed oneself on batter,

The White Knight's Son Like Edward Lear's "Incidents in the Life of My Uncle Arly," this is a parody of Wordsworth's "Resolution and Independence."

And so go on from day to day
   Getting a little fatter.
I shook him well from side to side,
   Until his face was blue;
'Come, tell me how you live,' I cried
40   'And what it is you do!'

He said, 'I hunt for haddocks' eyes
   Among the heather bright,
And work them into waistcoat-buttons
   In the silent night.
And these I do not sell for gold
   Or coin of silvery shine,
But for a copper halfpenny,
   And that will purchase nine.

'I sometimes dig for buttered rolls,
50   Or set limed twigs for crabs;
I sometimes search the grassy knolls
   For wheels of hansom-cabs.
And that's the way' (he gave a wink)
   'By which I get my wealth—
And very gladly will I drink
   Your Honour's noble health.'

I heard him then, for I had just
   Completed my design
To keep the Menai bridge from rust
60   By boiling it in wine.
I thanked him much for telling me
   The way he got his wealth,
But chiefly for his wish that he
   Might drink my noble health.

And now, if e'er by chance I put
   My fingers into glue,
Or madly squeeze a right-hand foot
   Into a left-hand shoe,
Or if I drop upon my toe
70   A very heavy weight,
I weep, for it reminds me so
   Of that old man I used to know—
Whose look was mild, whose speech was slow,
Whose hair was whiter than the snow,
Whose face was very like a crow,
With eyes, like cinders, all aglow,
Who seemed distracted with his woe,
Who rocked his body to and fro,

80 And mutttered mumblingly and low,
As if his mouth were full of dough,
Who snorted like a buffalo—
That summer evening long ago
A-sitting on a gate.
1872

JAMES THOMSON

From The City of Dreadful Night

XIV

Large glooms were gathered in the mighty fane,°
With tinted moongleams slanting here and there;
And all was hush—no swelling organ-strain,
No chant, no voice or murmuring of prayer;
690 No priests came forth, no tinkling censers fumed,
And the high altar space was unillumed.

Around the pillars and against the walls
Leaned men and shadows; others seemed to brood,
Bent or recumbent, in secluded stalls.
Perchance they were not a great multitude
Save in that city of so lonely streets
Where one may count up every face he meets.

All patiently awaited the event
Without a stir or sound, as if no less
700 Self-occupied, doomstricken, while attent.
And then we heard a voice of solemn stress
From the dark pulpit, and our gaze there met
Two eyes which burned as never eyes burned yet—

Two steadfast and intolerable eyes
Burning beneath a broad and rugged brow;
The head behind it of enormous size.
And as black fir-groves in a large wind bow,
Our rooted congregation, gloom-arrayed,
By that great sad voice deep and full were swayed:

710 'O melancholy Brothers, dark, dark, dark!°
O battling in black floods without an ark!

fane temple, here a cathedral, but given over
to a very different kind of sermon than is
customary

dark, dark, dark See Milton's *Samson Agonistes,*
l. 80.

O spectral wanderers of unholy Night!
My soul hath bled for you these sunless years,
With bitter blood-drops running down like tears;
    Oh, dark, dark, dark, withdrawn from joy and light!

'My heart is sick with anguish for your bale;°
Your woe hath been my anguish; yea, I quail
    And perish in your perishing unblest.
And I have searched the heights and depths, the scope
720   Of all our universe, with desperate hope
    To find some solace for your wild unrest.

'And now at last authentic word I bring,
Witnessed by every dead and living thing;
    Good tidings of great joy for you, for all;
There is no God; no Fiend with names divine
Made us and tortures us; if we must pine,
    It is to satiate no Being's gall.

'It was the dark delusion of a dream,
That living Person conscious and surpreme,
730   Whom we must curse for cursing us with life;
Whom we must curse because the life He gave
Could not be buried in the quiet grave,
    Could not be killed by poison or by knife.

'This little life is all we must endure,
The grave's most holy peace is ever sure,
    We fall asleep and never wake again;
Nothing is of us but the moldering flesh,
Whose elements dissolve and merge afresh
    In earth, air, water, plants, and other men.

740   'We finish thus; and all our wretched race
Shall finish with its cycle, and give place
    To other beings, with their own time-doom;
Infinite æons ere our kind began;
Infinite æons after the last man
    Has joined the mammoth° in earth's tomb and womb.

'We bow down to the universal laws,
Which never had for man a special clause
    Of cruelty or kindness, love or hate;
If toads and vultures are obscene to sight,
750   If tigers burn with beauty and with might,°
    Is it by favour or by wrath of fate?

---

bale torment
mammoth prehistoric beast

If tigers . . . with might an allusion to Blake's
"The Tyger"

'All substance lives and struggles evermore
Through countless shapes continually at war,
    By countless interactions interknit;
If one is born a certain day on earth,
All times and forces tended to that birth,
    Not all the world could change or hinder it.

'I find no hint throughout the Universe
Of good or ill, of blessing or of curse;
760   I find alone Necessity Supreme;
With infinite Mystery, abysmal, dark,
Unlighted ever by the faintest spark
    For us the flitting shadows of a dream.

'O Brothers of sad lives; they are so brief;
A few short years must bring us all relief—
    Can we not bear these years of labouring breath?
But if you would not this poor life fulfill,
Lo, you are free to end it when you will,
    Without the fear of waking after death.'

770   The organ-like vibrations of his voice
    Thrilled through the vaulted aisles and died away;
    The yearning of the tones which bade rejoice
    Was sad and tender as a requiem lay;
Our shadowy congregation rested still
As brooding on that 'End it when you will.'
1870–74   1874

POETRY OF THE 'NINETIES

Yeats named the poets of the 'Nineties, who were the friends of his youth, the "Tragic Generation." In his cosmological book, *A Vision,* Yeats said of the phase of the moon which, he claimed, characterized the poet Ernest Dowson and the artist Aubrey Beardsley that in it self-hatred reached a height, and through this hatred there came the slow liberation of intellectual love. In his beautiful *Autobiographies,* Yeats gave the best account of the 'Nineties, as an apocalyptic time when the young aesthetes lived as though time must have a stop. The decade ended with Yeats's fine volume of lyrics *The Wind Among the Reeds,* which catches the irrational intensity of the moment at the end of a turbulent century.

This intensity is the particular mark of the doomed poets of the 'Nineties. The Aesthetic Movement in England began with Swinburne and Pater and the American expatriate painter James Whistler, and reached its height in the 'Nineties with the work of the novelist George Moore, with Oscar Wilde as playwright, critic, and conversationalist, with Beardsley the illustrator in such periodicals as *The Savoy* and *The*

Yellow Book, and with the work of what seemed a hopeful school of new poets that met as the Rhymers' Club. They included Dowson, Yeats, Arthur Symons, whose translations from the French Symbolists were influential, and Lionel Johnson, who was to write the best poem of the 'Nineties in his tragic "The Dark Angel." John Davidson, a Nietzschean Scots poet, hovered at the edges of this group. Except for one great ballad by Davidson, the powerfully proletarian "Thirty Bob a Week," and a few fine lyrics by Dowson and Johnson, only Yeats's early poetry seems today to have survived, of all the intensities of the 'Nineties. Wilde was a poor poet, though a superb critic and dazzling dramatist, and the other men of talent wasted themselves in dissipation, self-hatred, or sudden conversions to a Catholicism they could not hope to sustain. But this tragic decade retains a peculiar fascination, and is now inseparable from Yeats's heightening vision of it.

This section begins with **W. S. Gilbert**'s (1836–1911) parody of Wilde as the Aesthetic poetaster Bunthorne in the comic opera *Patience* (1881). Gilbert, besides his light operas with Sir Arthur Sullivan, wrote the *Bab Ballads* (1869), a rather nasty volume of light verse. Though his parodic portrait of Wilde in his glory precedes the 'Nineties by a decade, it sets the scene.

A short biography of **Oscar Wilde** (1856–1900) is given elsewhere in this volume. His first volume, *Poems* (1881), was worthy of Gilbert's parody. As a writer of verse, Wilde was overwhelmed by influences of very nearly the whole Romantic tradition. Even *The Ballad of Reading Gaol,* given here in curtailed (and thus improved) form, his best poem, is altogether too haunted by Coleridge's *Ancient Mariner.* The prose poem "The Disciple," bitterly charming in itself, is given as one of the rare instances of a successful English domestication of a French literary form.

John Davidson (1857–1909), the son of a Scottish minister, came to London in 1889, where he led a life of fierce dreams and terrible poverty. His best volume was *Ballads and Songs,* from which "Thirty Bob a Week" is taken. He killed himself before completing a series of "Testaments," hortatory works proclaiming a new gospel of evolutionary selfishness.

Ernest Dowson (1867–1900), largely remembered now, like Lionel Johnson, because of Yeats's descriptions of him, was raised mostly in France. He left Oxford without a degree in 1887, and lived poorly as a translator, frequently drunk or drugged. He died in Paris, aged thirty-three, as the century ended. His best work is in *Verses* (1896), but there are excellent Horatian lyrics scattered throughout his books.

Lionel Johnson (1867–1902), the epitome of his generation, associated himself with the Irish literary movement though he was an Englishman. He came from a family with a long military tradition, and he could not come to terms with his own homosexuality, though he sought solace in the Roman Catholic Church in 1891. Although he was an excellent critic, whose book on Thomas Hardy (1894) is still useful, his overwhelming ambitions were poetic, but only "The Dark Angel" fully realizes his gifts.

WILLIAM SCHWENK GILBERT

Bunthorne's Song: The Aesthete°

If you're anxious for to shine in the high aesthetic line as a man of culture rare,
You must get up all the germs of the transcendental terms, and plant them
   everywhere.
You must lie upon the daisies, and discourse in novel phrases of your compli-
   cated state of mind
(The meaning doesn't matter if it's only idle chatter of a transcendental kind).
          And everyone will say,
          As you walk your mystic way,
'If this young man expresses himself in terms too deep for *me*,
Why, what a very singularly deep young man this deep young man must be!'

Be eloquent in praise of the very dull old days which have long since passed
   away.
10 And convince 'em, if you can, that the reign of good Queen Anne° was Culture's
   palmiest day.
Of course you will pooh-pooh whatever's fresh and new, and declare it's crude
   and mean.
For Art stopped short in the cultivated court of the Empress Josephine.°
          And everyone will say,
          As you walk your mystic way,
'If that's not good enough for him which is good enough for *me*,
Why, what a very cultivated kind of youth this kind of youth must be!'

Then a sentimental passion of a vegetable fashion must excite your languid
   spleen,
An attachment *à la* Plato for a bashful young potato, or a not-too-French French
   bean!
Though the Philistines° may jostle, you will rank as an apostle in the high
   aesthetic band,
20 If you walk down Piccadilly with a poppy or a lily in your medieval hand.
          And everyone will say,
          As you walk your flowery way,
'If he's content with a vegetable love, which would certainly not suit *me*,
Why, what a most particularly pure young man this pure young man must be!'
1881   1881

Bunthorne's . . . Aesthete from *Patience*
good Queen Anne daughter of James II; born
1665, Queen of Great Britain 1702–14, patroness of the Tory writers
Empress Josephine Empress of the French
(1804–9) as wife of Napoleon
Philistines Biblical enemies of the Hebrews;
popularized by Arnold as a term for middle-class
hostility to high culture

OSCAR WILDE

The Disciple

When Narcissus° died the pool of his pleasure changed from a cup of sweet waters into a cup of salt tears, and the Oreads° came weeping through the woodland that they might sing to the pool and give it comfort.

And when they saw that the pool had changed from a cup of sweet waters into a cup of salt tears, they loosened the green tresses of their hair and cried to the pool and said, 'We do not wonder that you should mourn in this manner for Narcissus, so beautiful was he.'

'But was Narcissus beautiful?' said the pool.

'Who should know better than you?' answered the Oreads. 'Us did he ever pass by, but you he sought for, and would lie on your banks and look down at you, and in the mirror of your waters he would mirror his own beauty.'

And the pool answered, 'But I loved Narcissus because, as he lay on my banks and looked down at me, in the mirror of his eyes I saw ever my own beauty mirrored.'

1893

From The Ballad of Reading Gaol°

I

He did not wear his scarlet coat,
   For blood and wine are red,
And blood and wine were on his hands
   When they found him with the dead,
The poor dead woman whom he loved,
   And murdered in her bed.

He walked amongst the Trial Men°
   In a suit of shabby grey;
A cricket cap was on his head,
   And his step seemed light and gay;
But I never saw a man who looked
   So wistfully at the day.

I never saw a man who looked
   With such a wistful eye
Upon that little tent of blue
   Which prisoners call the sky,
And at every drifting cloud that went
   With sails of silver by.

10

Narcissus beautiful youth who spurned the nymph Echo and fell in love with the reflection of his own face in a forest pool; as he could not satisfy this love, he pined away and changed into the flower named for him
Oreads mountain nymphs

Reading Gaol where Wilde was imprisoned in 1896–97. A soldier was executed there, for murder, on July 7, 1896; Wilde wrote the poem in France after his release.
Trial Men men who had been sentenced but whose verdict still might be appealed

I walked, with other souls in pain,
20   Within another ring,
And was wondering if the man had done
      A great or little thing,
When a voice behind me whispered low,
      'That fellow's got to swing.'

          .   .   .

          II

For oak and elm have pleasant leaves
      That in the spring-time shoot:
But grim to see is the gallows-tree,
      With its adder-bitten root,
And, green or dry, a man must die
      Before it bears its fruit!

The loftiest place is that seat of grace
      For which all worldlings try:
140   But who would stand in hempen band
      Upon a scaffold high,
And through a murderer's collar take
      His last look at the sky?

It is sweet to dance to violins
      When Love and Life are fair:
To dance to flutes, to dance to lutes
      Is delicate and rare:
But it is not sweet with nimble feet
      To dance upon the air!

150   So with curious eyes and sick surmise
      We watched him day by day,
And wondered if each one of us
      Would end the self-same way,
For none can tell to what red Hell
      His sightless soul may stray.

At last the dead man walked no more
      Amongst the Trial Men,
And I knew that he was standing up
      In the black dock's dreadful pen,
160   And that never would I see his face
      In God's sweet world again.

Like two doomed ships that pass in storm
      We had crossed each other's way:
But we made no sign, we said no word,
      We had no word to say;
For we did not meet in the holy night,
      But in the shameful day.

A prison wall was round us both,
   Two outcast men we were:
170 The world had thrust us from its heart,
   And God from out His care:
And the iron gin° that waits for Sin
   Had caught us in its snare.

III

In Debtors' Yard° the stones are hard,
   And the dripping wall is high,
So it was there he look the air
   Beneath the leaden sky,
And by each side a Warder walked,
   For fear the man might die.

180 Or else he sat with those who watched
   His anguish night and day;
Who watched him when he rose to weep,
   And when he crouched to pray;
Who watched him lest himself should rob
   Their scaffold of its prey.

   .   .   .

And twice a day he smoked his pipe,
   And drank his quart of beer:
His soul was resolute, and held
   No hiding-place for fear;
He often said that he was glad
   The hangman's hands were near.

But why he said so strange a thing
   No Warder dared to ask:
200 For he to whom a watcher's doom
   Is given as his task,
Must set a lock upon his lips,
   And make his face a mask.

Or else he might be moved, and try
   To comfort or console:
And what should Human Pity do
   Pent up in Murderers' Hole?
What word of grace in such a place
   Could help a brother's soul?

   .   .   .

We tore the tarry rope to shreds°
   With blunt and bleeding nails;

gin trap
Debtors' Yard part of the exercise ground in
Reading Gaol, once used for debtors

rope to shreds Wilde was condemned to hard
labor; he tore ropes to shreds to produce oakum
used in calking vessels.

We rubbed the doors, and scrubbed the floors,
   And cleaned the shining rails:
220   And, rank by rank, we soaped the plank,
   And clattered with the pails.

We sewed the sacks, we broke the stones,
   We turned the dusty drill:
We banged the tins, and bawled the hymns,
   And sweated on the mill:
But in the heart of every man
   Terror was lying still.

So still it lay that every day
   Crawled like a weed-clogged wave:
230   And we forgot the bitter lot
   That waits for fool and knave,
Till once, as we tramped in from work,
   We passed an open grave.

With yawning mouth the yellow hole
   Gaped for a living thing;
The very mud cried out for blood
   To the thirsty asphalte ring:
And we knew that ere one dawn grew fair
   Some prisoner had to swing.

240   Right in we went, with soul intent
   On Death and Dread and Doom:
The hangman, with his little bag,
   Went shuffling through the gloom:
And each man trembled as he crept
   Into his numbered tomb.

That night the empty corridors
   Were full of forms of Fear,
And up and down the iron town
   Stole feet we could not hear,
250   And through the bars that hide the stars
   White faces seemed to peer.

He lay as one who lies and dreams
   In a pleasant meadow-land,
The watchers watched him as he slept,
   And could not understand
How one could sleep so sweet a sleep
   With a hangman close at hand.

But there is no sleep when men must weep
   Who never yet have wept:
260   So we—the fool, the fraud, the knave—
   That endless vigil kept,

And through each brain on hands of pain
  Another's terror crept.

     .   .   .

       IV

There is no chapel on the day
  On which they hang a man:
The Chaplain's heart is far too sick,
  Or his face is far too wan,
280 Or there is that written in his eyes
  Which none should look upon.

So they kept us close till nigh on noon,
  And then they rang the bell,
And the Warders with their jingling keys
  Opened each listening cell,
And down the iron stair we tramped,
  Each from his separate Hell.

Out into God's sweet air we went,
  But not in wonted way,
290 For this man's face was white with fear,
  And that man's face was gray,
And I never saw sad men who looked
  So wistfully at the day.

I never saw sad men who looked
  With such a wistful eye
Upon that little tent of blue
  We prisoners called the sky,
And at every careless cloud that passed
  In happy freedom by.

     .   .   .

The Warders strutted up and down,
  And kept their herd of brutes,
Their uniforms were spick and span,
  And they wore their Sunday suits,
But we knew the work they had been at,
  By the quicklime on their boots.

330 For where a grave had opened wide,
  There was no grave at all:
Only a stretch of mud and sand
  By the hideous prison-wall,
And a little heap of burning lime,
  That the man should have his pall.

     .   .   .

For three long years they will not sow
  Or root or seedling there:

350   For three long years the unblessed spot
     Will sterile be and bare,
  And look upon the wondering sky
     With unreproachful stare.

They think a murderer's heart would taint
     Each simple seed they sow.
It is not true! God's kindly earth
     Is kindlier than men know,
And the red rose would but blow more red,
     The white rose whiter blow.
    1897   1898

JOHN DAVIDSON

Thirty Bob° a Week

I couldn't touch a stop and turn a screw,
    And set the blooming world a-work for me
Like such as cut their teeth—I hope, like you—
    On the handle of a skeleton gold key;
I cut mine on a leek, which I eat it every week:
    I'm a clerk at thirty bob as you can see.

But I don't allow it's luck and all a toss;
    There's no such thing as being starred and crossed;
It's just the power of some to be a boss,
10   And the bally° power of others to be bossed:
I face the music, sir; you bet I ain't a cur;
    Strike me lucky if I don't believe I'm lost!

For like a mole I journey in the dark,
    A-travelling along the underground
From my Pillared Halls and broad Suburbean Park,
    To come the daily dull official round;
And home again at night with my pipe all alight,
    A-scheming how to count° ten bob a pound.

And it's often very cold and very wet,
20   And my missis stitches towels for a hunks;°
And the Pillared Halls is half of it to let—
    Three rooms about the size of travelling trunks.
And we cough, my wife and I, to dislocate a sigh,
    When the noisy little kids are in their bunks.

But you never hear her do a growl or whine,
    For she's made of flint and roses, very odd;
And I've got to cut my meaning rather fine,

Bob shilling   **count** make it count for
bally euphemism for "bloody"   **hunks** stingy old fellow

Or I'd blubber, for I'm made of greens and sod:
So p'r'aps we are in Hell for all that I can tell,
30   And lost and damn'd and served up hot to God.

I ain't blaspheming, Mr. Silver-tongue;
    I'm saying things a bit beyond your art:
Of all the rummy starts you ever sprung,
    Thirty bob a week's the rummiest start!
With your science and your books and your the'ries about spooks,
    Did you ever hear of looking in your heart?

I didn't mean your pocket, Mr., no:
    I mean that having children and a wife,
With thirty bob on which to come and go,
40   Isn't dancing to the tabor and the fife:
When it doesn't make you drink, by Heaven! it makes you think,
    And notice curious items about life.

I step into my heart and there I meet
    A god-almighty devil singing small,
Who would like to shout and whistle in the street,
    And squelch the passers flat against the wall;
If the whole world was a cake he had the power to take,
    He would take it, ask for more, and eat it all.

And I meet a sort of simpleton beside,
50   The kind that life is always giving beans;
With thirty bob a week to keep a bride
    He fell in love and married in his teens:
At thirty bob he stuck; but he knows it isn't luck:
    He knows the seas are deeper than tureens.

And the god-almighty devil and the fool
    That meet me in the High Street on the strike,
When I walk about my heart a-gathering wool,
    Are my good and evil angels if you like.
And both of them together in every kind of weather
60   Ride me like a double-seated bike.

That's rough a bit and needs its meaning curled.
    But I have a high old hot un in my mind—
A most engrugious° notion of the world,
    That leaves your lightning 'rithmetic behind—
I give it a glance when I say 'There ain't no chance,
    Nor nothing of the lucky-lottery kind.'

And it's this way that I make it out to be:
    No fathers, mothers, countries, climates—none;
Not Adam was responsible for me,
70   Nor society, not systems, nary one:

engrugious egregious, shocking

A little sleeping seed, I woke—I did, indeed—
  A million years before the blooming sun.

I woke because I thought the time had come;
  Beyond my will there was no other cause;
And everywhere I found myself at home,
  Because I chose to be the thing I was;
And in whatever shape of mollusc or of ape
  I always went according to the laws.

I was the love that chose my mother out;
80   I joined two lives and from the union burst;
My weakness and my strength without a doubt
  Are mine alone for ever from the first:
It's just the very same with a difference in the name
  As 'Thy will be done.' You say it if you durst!

They say it daily up and down the land
  As easy as you take a drink, it's true;
But the difficultest go to understand,
  And the difficultest job a man can do,
Is to come it brave and meek with thirty bob a week,
90   And feel that that's the proper thing for you.

It's a naked child against a hungry wolf;
  It's playing bowls upon a splitting wreck;
It's walking on a string across a gulf
  With millstones fore-and-aft about your neck;
But the thing is daily done by many and many a one;
  And we fall, face forward, fighting, on the deck.

1894

ERNEST DOWSON

Non sum qualis eram bonae sub regno Cynarae°

Last night, ah, yesternight, betwixt her lips and mine
There fell thy shadow, Cynara! thy breath was shed
Upon my soul between the kisses and the wine;
And I was desolate and sick of an old passion,
  Yea, I was desolate and bowed my head:
I have been faithful to thee, Cynara! in my fashion.

All night upon mine heart I felt her warm heart beat,
Night-long within mine arms in love and sleep she lay;
Surely the kisses of her bought red mouth were sweet;
10 But I was desolate and sick of an old passion,

Non sum. . . Cynarae "I am not what once
I was under the reign of the kind Cynara"
Horace, *Odes* IV.i.3–4. Dowson's use of this as
title is a bitter irony.

When I awoke and found the dawn was gray:
I have been faithful to thee, Cynara! in my fashion.

I have forgot much, Cynara! gone with the wind,
Flung roses, roses riotously with the throng,
Dancing, to put thy pale, lost lilies out of mind;
But I was desolate and sick of an old passion,
    Yea, all the time, because the dance was long:
I have been faithful to thee, Cynara! in my fashion.

I cried for madder music and for stronger wine,
20   But when the feast is finished and the lamps expire,
Then falls thy shadow, Cynara! the night is thine;
And I am desolate and sick of an old passion,
    Yea, hungry for the lips of my desire:
I have been faithful to thee, Cynara! in my fashion.

                                                    1896

Extreme Unction°

Upon the eyes, the lips, the feet,
    On all the passages of sense,
The atoning oil is spread with sweet
    Renewal of lost innocence.

The feet, that lately ran so fast
    To meet desire, are soothly sealed;
The eyes, that were so often cast
    On vanity, are touched and healed.

From troublous sights and sounds set free;
10   In such a twilight hour of breath,
Shall one retrace his life, or see,
    Through shadows, the true face of death?

Vials of mercy! Sacring° oils!
    I know not where nor when I come,
Nor through what wanderings and toils,
    To crave of you Viaticum.°

Yet, when the walls of flesh grow weak,
    In such an hour, it well may be,
Through mist and darkness, light will break,
20   And each anointed sense will see.

                                                    1899

Extreme Unction Roman Catholic sacrament in
which the sick in danger of dying is anointed
by a priest, who employs a set form of words;
(now called the Anointing of the Sick)

Sacring consecrating for service of the Mass,
usually refers to the bread and the wine
Viaticum the Eucharist when received by someone dying or in danger of death

LIONEL JOHNSON°

The Church of a Dream

Sadly the dead leaves rustle in the whistling wind,
Around the weather-worn, grey church, low down the vale:
The Saints in golden vesture shake before the gale;
The glorious windows shake, where still they dwell enshrined;
Old Saints by long-dead, shrivelled hands, long since designed:
There still, although the world autumnal be, and pale,
Still in their golden vesture the old Saints prevail;
Alone with Christ, desolate else, left by mankind.
Only one ancient Priest offers the Sacrifice,
10 Murmuring holy Latin immemorial:
Swaying with tremulous hands the old censer full of spice,
In grey, sweet incense clouds; blue, sweet clouds mystical:
To him, in place of men, for he is old, suffice
    Melancholy remembrances and vesperal.°

                                        1890

To Morfydd°

A voice on the winds,
A voice by the waters,
    Wanders and cries:
Oh! what are the winds?
And what are the waters?
    Mine are your eyes!

Western the winds are,
And western the waters,
    Where the light lies:
10 *Oh! what are the winds?*
And what are the waters?
    Mine are your eyes!

Cold, cold, grow the winds,
And wild grow the waters,
    Where the sun dies:
Oh! what are the winds?
And what are the waters?
    Mine are your eyes!

The Church of a Dream Another of Yeats's favorites, this is echoed in "Sailing to Byzantium" and more crucially in Yeats's last poem, "The Black Tower."
vesperal a little book or antiphonary containing the chants used at vespers (evening prayers)

To Morfydd Yeats thought this almost disembodied love lyric, to a probably imaginary Welsh girl, an "incomparable" poem. It is a deliberately knowing narcist's self-confrontation (see the refrain) and might have been written by Beddoes, like Johnson a homosexual struggling against his condition.

And down the night winds,
20 And down the night waters,
    The music flies:
Oh! what are the winds?
And what are the waters?
Cold be the winds,
And wild be the waters,
    So mine be your eyes!
                            1891

The Dark Angel°

Dark Angel, with thine aching lust
To rid the world of penitence:°
Malicious Angel, who still dost
My soul such subtile violence!

Because of thee, no thought, no thing
Abides for me undesecrate:
Dark Angel, ever on the wing,
Who never reachest me too late!

When music sounds, then changest thou
10 Its silvery to a sultry fire:
Nor will thine envious heart allow
Delight untortured by desire.

Through thee, the gracious Muses turn
To Furies, O mine Enemy!
And all the things of beauty burn
With flames of evil ecstasy.°

Because of thee, the land of dreams
Becomes a gathering-place of fears:
Until tormented slumber seems
20 One vehemence of useless tears.

When sunlight glows upon the flowers,
Or ripples down the dancing sea:
Thou, with thy troop of passionate powers,
Beleaguerest, bewilderest me.

Within the breath of autumn woods,
Within the winter silences:

The Dark Angel Johnson's masterpiece, both
the most representative and the best poem of
the 'Nineties; the Dark Angel is a composite of
Satan, Johnson's shadow self, his homosexuality,
his idol Shelley, who had so passionately argued
against remorse, and also his other idol, Pater,
who had urged an intensity of aesthetic experience that Johnson could not sustain.

To rid . . . penitence Johnson's Shelleyan heritage; see Shelley's *The Revolt of Islam*, where
remorse is denounced repeatedly, as being only
"the dark idolatry of self"
flames of evil ecstasy Pater's "gem-like flame,"
but here found morally unacceptable

Thy venomous spirit stirs and broods,
O master of impieties!

The ardour of red flame is thine,
30   And thine the steely soul of ice:
Thou poisonest the fair design
Of nature, with unfair device.

Apples of ashes, golden bright;
Waters of bitterness, how sweet!
O banquet of a foul delight,
Prepared by thee, dark Paraclete.°

Thou art the whisper in the gloom,
The hinting tone, the haunting laugh:
Thou art the adorner of my tomb,
40   The minstrel of mine epitaph.

I fight thee, in the Holy Name!
Yet, what thou dost, is what God saith:°
Tempter! should I escape thy flame,
Thou wilt have helped my soul from Death:

The second Death, that never dies,°
That cannot die, when time is dead:
Live Death, wherein the lost soul cries,
Eternally uncomforted.

Dark Angel, with thine aching lust!
50   Of two defeats, of two despairs:°
Less dread, a change to drifting dust,
Than thine eternity of cares.

Do what thou wilt, thou shalt not so,
Dark Angel! triumph over me:
Lonely, unto the Lone I go;
Divine, to the Divinity.°
1893

dark Paraclete a parody of the Holy Spirit as comforter
God saith Like the Satan of Job, the Dark Angel is sanctioned by God to try Johnson.
never dies spiritual death, damnation
two despairs the first defeat and despair is the death-in-life of giving up homosexual love; the second is the Dark Angel's

Lonely . . . Divinity Ian Fletcher notes the source in Plotinus, *Enneads* VI. ix: "This, therefore, is the life of the Gods, and of divine and happy men, a liberation from all terrene concerns, a life unaccompanied with human pleasures, and a flight of the alone to the alone."

Modern British Literature

Modern British Literature

AT THE TURN OF THE CENTURY

When Queen Victoria died in 1901 people found it easy to think that an age had ended, but the Edwardians nevertheless preserved much of their heritage intact. It included the consequences of the great spiritual and intellectual discoveries of the Victorians, and capitalized their material gains. English society was as firmly as ever dominated by class; English wealth was still in a few hands, despite a growing suspicion that it was unfairly gained at the expense of the industrial workers; the British Empire was firm, well serviced, showing some respect for the rights of "lesser breeds without the law"; it was powerfully represented in literature by Kipling. Life, for the rich, was full of possibilities but also of restrictions; the early novels of Galsworthy and E. M. Forster well document the latter. Since the Education Act of 1870 the poor were literate or semi-literate, but they remained poor, and the new cheap papers were preparing them for the age of full democracy and advertising.

The legacy of Darwin, and of the whole complex Victorian loss of Christian faith, grew more troublesome, and so did the different versions of Socialism that had grown up during the century, whether native or Marxist. The Fabian Society, which stood for reformist, not revolutionary, socialism, was an important intellectual focus. The position of women, their lack of freedom and lack of votes, became an urgent question. There was a growing awareness of external threats to England's wealth and security, especially threats emanating from Germany. The Boer War, in the opening years of the century, had something of the effect of the Vietnam War in the American Sixties: the forces of the most powerful country on earth had great difficulty in defeating the small and ill-equipped Boer forces. There was much talk of decadence, and it could be substantiated by pointing to such figures as those which proved a rapid rise in the insanity rate, and those which indicated that half the volunteers for military service in South Africa were unfit. The arts were impeded by prudery and censorship, yet the decade saw the production of some of Shaw's best plays and the publication of the best novels of Conrad. The Irish Yeats had made of the Abbey a great playhouse, and was about to come into his full strength as an artist, while in England the artists of this "tragic generation" were dying.

Edward VII, symbol of the self-indulgence but also of the peace of his period, died in 1910; the war with Germany, which seemed preventable but was not prevented, began on August 4, 1914. Some would give that as the true date for the ending of the old world; others say 1916, when the better part of a generation of Englishmen died on the Somme. The Great War produced a few good books, and some good resolutions, quickly abandoned. Politically, it broke Europe into pieces and gave rise to the first Communist state.

NEW IDEAS

The first decade of the century saw several crucial developments in the field of ideas, so new and so far-reaching in their implications that we may think the new world was born after all in 1901. In December of the previous year the foundations of quantum theory were laid; in 1905 Einstein published his Special Theory of Relativity. Freud's *Interpretation of Dreams,* in some ways his fundamental work, appeared in 1900, and *The Psychopathology of Everyday Life* in 1901. Edmund Husserl was preparing one revolution in philosophy—a very modern one, involving an entirely new way of considering the relation between the mind and phenomena; and Bertrand Russell was preparing another, in the field of logic, which would also change the whole course of twentieth-century philosophical thought and make possible the further revolutions brought about by Ludwig Wittgenstein.

In the visual arts perhaps the greatest single crisis in the history of the subject—the introduction of Cubism in 1907—preceded by three years the first showing in England of the paintings of its forerunner, Post-Impressionist movement. Changes were pending also in music; the arts were preparing for some huge alteration, some decisive break with the past. Marinetti (1876–1944) issued his Futurist Manifesto in 1909, calling the arts to a recognition of modern technology, speed, noise; demanding the abolition of syntax in poetry and of the representation of movement in painting, as the Russian Futurists demanded the abolition of the past. In Paris Guillaume Apollinaire, publicist of poetry and painting alike, propagated scorn for all that was *passéiste.* In London T. E. Hulme sketched, with Wyndham Lewis and Ezra Pound, a movement called Vortex, which had some of the aims of Futurism; but it was cut off, like its magazine BLAST, by the war, which brought also the death of its most gifted visual artist, Henri Gaudier-Brzeska. With the war at its most terrible stage in 1916, Tristan Tzara and others in neutral Switzerland founded the most radical and influential of all these "abolitionist" movements, and called it "Dada," denying progress, knowledge, morality, the family, logic, memory, the past, all that is not "the immediate product of spontaneity," all that is not "indifferent" in a Buddhist sense, that does not reflect the fact that "everything happens in a completely idiotic way"; and affirming that the emotion we need most of, the Dada emotion, is disgust.

MODERNISM: TOWARD A DEFINITION

There is a danger of making "Modernism" too inclusive; and it must be said that many good writers—some represented in this anthology—were largely unaffected by these turbulences. Nevertheless the "revolution" of the Modern did occur, and we may understand it better if we isolate a few of its recurrent themes. One such theme, obviously, is the demand for an open breach with the past, or even the abolition of the past. This professes to be more than a simple reaction against the art of the preceding generation: it is a whole new thing. Such, at any rate, is the case with such extreme positions as Dada, and others more recent which are sometimes called Neo-Dada. This may be seen—in part at any rate—as a reaction against the crushing weight of an artistic past which cannot be surveyed any longer by any one person, which may be thought tainted by the cruelty and injustice of the civilizations which produced it, or which is simply handed down with the uncritical approval of the establishment. But it is rather more than that; it is the extreme statement of a view which derives from genuine discontinuities discovered in the world, of which the quantum theory is an example. New conceptions of the operations of the human mind were coming to birth; like other instruments, it was beginning to be seen as other than had been supposed, and as having a different relation to objective reality.

The Modern *was* so different from the past that one could fairly easily think it discontinuous with the past. One measure of that difference, more obvious than phenomenology or quantum theory, is technology. The technology of the first decade of the century was much more advanced than might be thought; as Buckminster Fuller says, if you can throw a missile weighing a ton from one platform moving forward at twenty-five miles an hour and also rolling and pitching, and hit another sixteen miles away and moving in a different direction, you have already solved most of the real problems of a moonshot; and this could be done in 1907. Such technology was, whether desirable or not, *modern;* so was the increasingly rapid supersession, especially in weaponry, of one model by another. In some degree the arts imitated the technology—not with the same rapidity of obsolescence that obtains in our time, but one can see it beginning. The New had always played some part in aesthetic appreciation—even classical artists do not exactly repeat the performances of their classical predecessors—but newness now become essential. So the language of the arts changed more and more rapidly in this new age; and to change rapidly, and to abolish the precedents, became a program for artists.

But this is a very partial view of the Modern, because full discontinuity is never achieved by anything that remains recognizably part of the constantly changing language of art; this is true of Cubism and of twelve-tone music as well as of poetry. There is a continuity of languages; and there is also a continuity of ideologies. Baudelaire in the 1850's already spoke of going to the depths of the unknown to find the New. Many of the ideas and techniques of "abolitionism" were invented by Rimbaud in the Seventies. The whole French Symbolist movement underprops Modernism, as Romanticism underprops Symbolism. If you follow the Modern to its roots you go back to the seventeenth century and beyond. Equally, if you believe that reality is not something given, but something imposed on the world by human fictions, you go back to Nietzsche at least, for an authoritative expression of the theory. If you interpret the Modern as that which has the power to make an impressive engagement with the finest minds of your own time, you will find it throughout history, as Matthew Arnold found it in Athens, and others in Byzantine painting, African statues, Dante, or the seventeenth-century poets. The Modern soon acquires a Tradition of its own. It is related to the sense of the artists of the early part of the century that certain apparent laws were merely arbitrary conventions, to be overthrown as the religious and ethical establishment had been overthrown; but this does not and cannot entail a breach with the past, or even with all conventions, unless one can believe in a wholly random art. This situation accounts for the number of different dates given for the birth of Modernism: 1857, Baudelaire's *Les*

Fleurs du mal (Flowers of Evil) and Flaubert's *Madame Bovary*; 1859, Darwin's *Origin of Species*, and so on. As good a date as any, for English literature, would be 1899, the year Arthur Symons's *The Symbolist Movement in France* was published.

This particular Modernism has historical limits, for it may be said to have ended in the middle Twenties. If we look at the great works of those years we will be struck not only by their novelty but also by their respect for the past they had chosen out of all possible pasts. They include the great novels of Joseph Conrad, D. H. Lawrence, E. M. Forster, Ford Madox Ford, and James Joyce, together with much of the best poetry of W. B. Yeats and Ezra Pound. In French literature there was Marcel Proust. In American Gertrude Stein was characteristically more extreme. In the visual arts there were Pablo Picasso, a great ransacker of the past, and Wassily Kandinsky, the theorist of abstraction but no abolitionist; in music Igor Stravinsky was a classicist innovator. As Richard Ellmann and Charles Feidelson, collecting the relevant documents (and going back two centuries to do so) remark: "Modernism strongly implies some sort of historical discontinuity, either a liberation from inherited patterns or, at another extreme, deprivation and disinheritance"; but then they have to add that the "modernists have been as much imbued with a feeling for their historical role, their relation to the past, as with a feeling of historical discontinuity" (*The Modern Tradition*, 1965).

MYTHOLOGY AND PSYCHOLOGY

But there is another recurrent theme, one that involved a return, if not to the past, then to the primitive.

The poets of the Renaissance commanded easily a large syncretic body of myth, which, in combination with the teaching of the church and the whole range of Christian learning, gave them a remarkably rich and flexible body of materials. By the middle of the seventeenth century this had lost elasticity. Truth, identified either with revealed religion or with discoveries of natural science or empirical thinking, was divorced from myth; the epic poets of the 1650's tried to get along without myth, and later poets tended to use it only decoratively. The difference can be measured by looking at Bacon's use of myth at the beginning of the new science, and the handbook *Polymetis* of Joseph Spence (1699–1768), which is a relatively undynamic and decorative handling of the material. Romantic poets rebelled against this; and myth—in various new formulations—came back as the substance of poetry in Blake, Shelley, Keats. The nineteenth century, especially in France, accumulated a great deal of occultist mythological study which was important to poets partly in its own right and partly as an instrument of their fervent anti-rationalism; the great example in English is Yeats. By the turn of the century the need for a mythological repository was strongly felt; and it was supplied in various ways characteristic of a time when much more was known about societies outside Europe, about the ancient world, and above all about the human mind.

There are, broadly speaking, three main sources of modern mythology: exotic societies, classical scholarship, and psychiatry. Cubism, which broke up the conventional European picture surface, owed a debt to African primitive carving, which, at the turn of the century, suddenly became of great interest to eyes which had formerly ignored it or regarded it as simply curious. The primitive quite suddenly became a concern of the civilized, and in a wholly new way. It was also of increasing interest to scholars who sought behind the classical texts the origins of Greek poetry in religion. Of this "Cambridge School of Anthropology" Sir James G. Frazer (1854–1941) had the most powerful effect on literature. His huge composite book *The Golden Bough*—completed in twelve volumes, 1911–15, and abridged in 1922—is important not only because of the use Eliot made of it, but also because it gave a coherent ritual pattern to a huge mass of disparate mythical material. It became, as it were, the *Metamorphoses* of the twentieth century, because it appeared to indicate possibilities of a new commerce between the primitive and the civilized. Further, Frazer seemed to show that the Christian myth of a dying and resurrected god was merely one of an enormous class of such myths, invented everywhere by the primitive mind. So he strengthened the sense that underneath our own skeptical and rationalizing intellects there are remnants of such mythical thinking; that the primitive affects our conduct insofar as it is not, for good or ill, repressed by our civilization; and this, in other hands, became almost the most important single idea of the new century.

Not that it originated then; magicians of the kind cultivated by Yeats and other poets had assumed a primordial shared body of "archetypes" some time before C. G. Jung, with whom we usually associate the idea. Nevertheless, it was in this century that it became important to scientists, namely doctors, and therefore validated for others. Here the key name is Sigmund Freud (1856–1938). Freud quarreled with the Jungian position that in dream and neurosis we re-create or remember the primitive myths and cosmogonies, but he did believe that primitive myth afforded the best explanations for much of our behavior. The antiquity with which we each live is in the first place our own individual, our private childhood; but as that childhood is an abbreviated version of the development of the human race, we are, whether we remember or forget it, behaving in accordance with universal patterns. Here the two theories converge, but that of Freud has been more successful.

Freud elaborated his theory and terminology over many years, and he was not always well understood; but the general proposition that there are hidden layers of the mind which exert an enormous effect on human conduct certainly got through, and has had a profound influence not only on our views of human motive and the operation of the mind but also on the production and interpretation of works of art. In the process such a myth as that of Oedipus becomes a universal explanation of certain aspects of human behavior, both "normal" and "abnormal." Our views of the operation of time are changed, since the id, the deepest instinctual level of our personality, has nothing to do with concepts of time or space. Our views of authority are changed, since our egos (that part of the id which has been modified to deal with the external world and exhibits reason and circumspection) are supervised by a severe super-ego, the agent of external authority and repression. "Goaded on by the id, hemmed in by the super-ego, and rebuffed by reality, the ego struggles to cope with its economic task of reducing the forces and influences which work in it and upon it to some kind of harmony; and we may well understand how it is that we so often cannot repress the cry: 'Life is not easy' " (*New Introductory Lecture on Psychoanalysis*, 1933).

Dreams allow us to sleep by dealing with the problem that arises when the powers that normally repress unwelcome impulses are no longer alert; the "dream-work" entertains and modifies these impulses and makes them acceptable images. They are "censored," they are "condensed" and "displaced"—"dream-distortion" makes them tolerable, but uses means of combining and rendering unintelligible the subjects of the dream that have nothing to do with logic, and can be explained rationally only by a long process of interpretation which will recover the primitive material. The implications of all this, and of Freud's clinical techniques—such as free-association—for literature, are immense. They are not confined to Surrealism—a movement descended partly from Dada and proclaimed in 1924—which is expressly Freudian, seeking truth by the suspension of reason and by making works of art conform to a logic only of dreams. The Freudian movement restored to Modernism in general a confidence in the reasonableness of irrationality, a mistrust of what had formerly seemed the artistic equivalents of logical thinking.

Freud is not the whole story, but he is an index of this important change; he knew that some of his roots were in literature, and that literature (Dostoevsky, for example) also exerted a direct influence on later writers. It is possible that the alogical structure of The Waste Land or of Pound's Cantos, or the "stream-of-consciousness" techniques of Ulysses could not have been achieved without him; though there are the precedents of Symbolism and even earlier works. The point is not to establish Freud's direct influence but his symptomatic quality. In different ways the influence of Freud and other students of the primitive has continued to affect later kinds of Modernism. They provide us with a necessary past but one that is very different from that of the Victorians or any society before them. They have also created for twentieth-century art the possibility of a diversity of theme and treatment never before imaginable, and this is one of the most obvious and least mentioned aspects of the subject. A walk around a gallery that is arranged historically, or a glance at an anthology of twentieth-century literature, or a moment's thought about the varieties of modern philosophy, or indeed theology, will sufficiently confirm that it exists.

SOCIETY AND THE ARTS

Socially the twenties was an age of relaxation following the war. At the level of manners there were changes; the quest for a self-conscious modernity affected even the most trivial aspects of behavior. The implications of the Russian Revolution, and the Fascist revolution in Italy, were naturally of concern. Yet in England there was no profound change. The early twenties saw great industrial unrest, especially in the mines, but the General Strike of 1926 lasted only a few days, and the upper-class fear that the British worker was ripe for revolution was certainly exaggerated. Britain had its first brief spells of Labour Government, frustrated from the outset by economic crises; but the general political tone of the years was set by Stanley Baldwin, the amazingly dull Conservative politician who was Prime Minister, with intervals, from 1924 up to 1937, when Neville Chamberlain began his inglorious administration. Baldwin is associated with Britain's settling down into tranquility; he handled the General Strike; but he could not control the plunge Britain took, with the rest of the world, into the financial crisis, war, unemployment—in short, into the Great Depression. There had been no revolution, but conservatism was not working either.

In the arts, however, there was revolutionary activity. The great years of literary Modernism (anni mirabiles, as the critic R. P. Blackmur called them) were 1922–25. It is important to remember that there is only a negative correlation between this movement and any idea of political revolution. The politics of its leaders was of the right; they saw the world of the modern city and the democratic state with its half-literate population with the same horror that Yeats expressed for it. Indeed, reactionary politics is one important characteristic of the great early Modernists, Pound, Eliot, Wyndham Lewis; and not only Yeats but also D. H. Lawrence was with them in this. Their views were naturally not identical. Yeats believed in an Irish aristocracy to which he himself, in his opinion, belonged, and although he flirted with European dictatorship, the focus of his politics was Ireland. Lawrence talked about the need for aristocracy and a leader, the submission of women and the threat of Jews, but shared almost none of the ideas of Eliot, which in the end crystallized as Tory and Anglo-Catholic, or of Pound, who identified himself with the cause of Italian Fascism, or of Lewis, whose aesthetic was as abhorrent to Lawrence as Lawrence's to him. Still, a strenuous anti-egalitarianism, coupled with a powerful sense that the true politics as well as the true poetic were to be sought *in the past,* formed part of all their attitudes.

One important center of English Modernism, though dissolved by the war of 1914, continued to exert influence later. This was the group which had T. E. Hulme as its philosopher, Wyndham Lewis as its publicist and painter, Pound as its poet, and which developed the aesthetic of Vortex in prewar London. Hulme, who was killed in France in 1917 (b. 1883), was a disciple of Albert Sorel, the philosopher of anti-Liberalism, and of Henri Bergson and Wilhelm Worringer. Hulme's aesthetic, which he thought anti-Romantic, derives from Bergson the notion of an image out of the flux of time (which is, fundamentally, Romantic). From Worringer's *Abstraction and Empathy* he borrowed the idea that periods which place a low value on the individual person and imagine a universe authoritatively ordered, produce an art of "abstraction" (formal, geometric, impersonal), while others, which overvalue the human, an art of "empathy." Archaic Greek, art, Byzantine art, exemplify the abstract; the Renaissance and all that has followed it—the decay of dogmatic, ritualistic religion, the rise of individualism and democracy, the history of painting—exemplify empathy. Romanticism—"spilt religion"—Hulme especially abhorred. Out of this mix he produced an extremely influential aesthetic; the art object must be dry, hard, clearly defined, unique, and discontinuous with ordinary space and time. It must lack any facile humanity or "life." Such were the teachings enshrined at first in Imagism—"An 'Image' is that which presents an intellectual and emotional complex in an instant of time" is Pound's definition—and later, in a more dynamic form, in Vorticism. Hulme's essays were published after his death as *Speculations* (1924), and his thought resumed its influential career; but most of his ideas had long been affecting Pound and, through him, Eliot. The presentation of *The Waste Land* (1922) as a non-temporal set of interrelated images owes something therefore to the aesthetic of Hulme. The practical recommendations of Imagism—to avoid sloppy diction and Romantic "feeling," to achieve "the exact curve of the thing" and not a ready-made approximation to it—had an astringent effect on the diction of the new poetry. As Ford Madox Ford liked to say, it should be "at least as well written as prose."

Ford's point was that in the early years of the century, before Imagism, most of the radical thinking about literature had been done in relation to the novel. He was remembering the late Henry James, and his own passionate researches into the novel form, sometimes in collaboration with Conrad. And it is true that if we think of the latest work of James, of Conrad's extraordinary inventions in his great novels of the first decade (e.g. *Nostromo* and *Under Western Eyes*), and of Ford's superb *The Good Soldier* (1916), we must agree that this is where thinking was productively in progress.

Lawrence published *The Rainbow* in 1915 and finished *Women in Love* in 1916, and these works have an originality of form within the native tradition far in excess of anything the poets were achieving. It was only in the twenties that there seemed at last to be a Modernism that belonged to all literature: *Ulysses*, which was well known to Eliot and others long before its publication, and *The Waste Land* appeared in the same year, 1922. Nor was this efflorescence confined to members of a group. Other works, less strikingly novel in manner but original in conception, also belong to these years. They produced some remarkable books: Yeats's *The Trembling of the Veil* (1922), Arnold Bennett's *Riceyman Steps* (1923), Lawrence's *Studies in Classic American Literature* (1923), Ford's *Some Do Not*, Forster's *A Passage to India*, as well as Hulme's *Speculations* and I. A. Richards's *Principles of Literary Criticism* (1924). That year also saw the publication of Thomas Mann's *Magic Mountain*, and André Breton's *Surrealist Manifesto*. 1925 was the year of F. Scott Fitzgerald's *The Great Gatsby*, André Gide's *Counterfeiters*, Franz Kafka's *The Trial*, of Lawrence's *St. Mawr*, Virginia Woolf's *Mrs. Dalloway*, Sean O'Casey's *Juno and the Paycock*, and Pound's first *Cantos*. In these *anni mirabiles* Modern literature as we know it was fully launched. The twenties became one of the epochal moments of literary development; one could list more works by Yeats and Lawrence and Eliot, by Robert Graves and Wyndham Lewis and Pound, by Hart Crane and Robert Musil, Ernest Hemingway, Christopher Isherwood and Evelyn Waugh, Kafka and Virginia Woolf. And the explosion in a sense ended with the Twenties; many of the writers went on writing in their own ways (some had always kept to them), but the sense of a great moment, when literature had as it were caught up with the Modern in the other arts, faded. The Twenties themselves ended with the business slump and the beginning of the age of depression.

THE THIRTIES

Mass unemployment, the rise of the Nazis, rearmament, the threat of war everywhere from Japan to Western Europe, and finally world war, the fall of France, and the battle of Britain: this was the world of the thirties. Something can be learned from the success of Victor Gollancz's Left Book Club, a highly successful operation which circulated cheap editions of left-wing publications to its members, and for which Orwell wrote *The Road to Wigan Pier* (1937). The intelligentsia was, on the whole, moving rapidly leftward. The Depression and the Spanish Civil War, which looked like a straight confrontation between the government of the Left, and the Fascist insurgents, rapidly polarized political opinion. Marxism made some way, but not in terms of political power; England was governed by a government made by coalition between the two chief parties, non-Marxist Labour and Conservative, but mostly Conservative. But reports from Spain, and from the new Germany, sent young men into or near the Communist Party and the campaign for a popular front against Fascism. The group of poets which was for a time dominated by W. H. Auden took this line, though without losing their respect for their Tory seniors such as Eliot, who was also incidentally their publisher. But the moment represented by Auden's *Spain*—a pamphlet poem of 1936 which with poster-like stridency directed everybody's attention to Spain as the center of the world crisis—and by poems about derelict industry and the poor, soon passed; the poets went their own ways, Auden into Christianity, Stephen Spender into editorship and anti-Communism, Louis MacNeice into broadcasting.

The Thirties was not a barren period; but people did go their own ways, and the sense of a politico-poetic movement was soon lost. Waugh, Graham Greene, the remarkable and neglected novelist Henry Green, Ivy Compton-Burnett, Hugh Mac-Diarmid, Isherwood (Catholics, Communists, traditionalists, experimenters) were publishing books; Elizabeth Bowen's *The Death of the Heart,* Greene's *Brighton Rock,* Richard Hughes's *In Hazard,* Isherwood's *Lions and Shadows,* Waugh's *Scoop,* Cyril Connolly's *Enemies of Promise,* Samuel Beckett's *Murphy,* and Orwell's *Homage to Catalonia,* all appeared in one year, 1938. It was certainly not a slump; but it was not a movement.

THE SECOND WORLD WAR AND AFTER

The war years 1939–45 were in one sense marked by a great interest in literature, as indicated by the success of literary magazines and the great demand for books—paper was scarce, huge stocks were destroyed by bombing, and at the time when people most wanted them books were not to be had; nor, though people wanted them also, and there was no shortage of volunteers, were there any very important war poets. The great poetry of the second war is "Little Gidding," written in 1941; there are other poems by Dylan Thomas, for example and other minor poets—Keith Douglas, Sidney Keyes, Alun Lewis—but the terrible experience did not yield poets or poems. A barren movement of Neo-Apocalyptics rose and fell; it was not a time for movements. Thousands recorded their wartime experiences, some competently; few had the time, whether in the service or not, to concentrate on writing. The best novel of the war is Virginia Woolf's *Between the Acts,* a still underestimated masterpiece which came direct out of her reaction to the crisis of 1940 after which she killed herself.

On the condition of post-war English literature a note and examples are found at the end of the book. In spite of the "Movement" of the fifties—which was hardly more than association-by-journalism of a few writers who never pretended to be a school—it does appear that in poetry and the novel English writers have continued to go their own way. The major post-war novelists—we may name Iris Murdoch, Muriel Spark, William Golding, Anthony Powell, and Henry Green, with contributions from Graham Greene, Anthony Burgess, Ivy Compton-Burnett, Joyce Cary, Evelyn Waugh, and Angus Wilson—have very little in common; perhaps if they had, their impact would be greater, our valuation of them higher. The second wave of Modernism, the Neo-Dada of the Sixties, has had little effect. English poets became more conscious of American literature than of French, their traditional source; they grew susceptible to the influence of Wallace Stevens, then of William Carlos Williams, then of Louis Zukofsky and the American Black Mountain school. There has been a strong vogue of spoken poetry, a return to those looser, more allusive or more rhetorical forms deplored by the Movement and especially its best poet, Philip Larkin. A few novelists have tried to learn from the French *nouveau roman,* but this has led to no fierce conflict, no forming of schools, no manifestos. The ferment of modern Paris has no parallel in London. Only in the drama has any sort of Modern movement occurred, partly inspired by Antonin Artaud in France and Bertolt Brecht in Germany, and more directly by Samuel Beckett.

The "new" psychiatry of R. D. Laing, the "new" cultural history of Marshall McLuhan, the "new" anthropology of Claude Lévi-Strauss, have been much discussed in the last few years, but seem to bring about no great change in the literary arts, though music and the visual arts have responded more readily, as they usually do, to the challenge of this new New. The truth is that insofar as Modernism is a matter of concerted programs and manifestos, it hardly exists in contemporary Britain. It can and should be argued that most of the neo-Modernisms—aleatory techniques, concrete poetry, and the rest—are in fact only belated developments of the old. In England, where literary history has never centered itself on a manifesto or a literary line-up of party against party, this seems to be taken for granted. We had Modernism in the twenties, as we had Romanticism at the turn of the eighteenth century; and we are not quite ready for another Copernican revolution. The history of French literature since the war is vastly more involved in creeds and manifestos than British, and modern American literature is certainly more adventurous, readier to realize theory, grasp new thought. In England there is even a feeling that the last Modernism was only a transient import —none of its practitioners were really English anyway. That this view is wrong is clear from the relation between the Tradition and the individual talents outlined above. But meanwhile English literature takes its unpredictable course, depending, as Matthew Arnold complained it did, more on the individual genius than any corporate intellectual and artistic effort. And ours is not the first period in which, with genius in short supply, it has contented itself with a reasonable abundance of scattered talents.

THOMAS HARDY
1840–1928

Thomas Hardy was born in Dorchester, the country town of Dorset, on June 12, 1840. His early education was in the classics and in architecture, and it was as an architect that he left his native Wessex—the name he gave in his fiction to an area of the West Country—for London in 1862. He worked and studied there and published his first novel, *Desperate Remedies,* in 1871. From then on for more than twenty years he produced prose fiction and was recognized as one of the greatest Victorian novelists. Among the major novels are: *Far from the Madding Crowd* (1874), *The Return of the Native* (1878), *The Mayor of Casterbridge* (1887), and *Tess of the D'Urbervilles* (1891). By the time (1896) of the hostile reception of his great, unrelentingly gloomy last novel *Jude the Obscure* (a crafty, stupid woman reviewing it for a New York newspaper called it "Jude the Obscene") he had started to devote himself exclusively to the corpus of over nine hundred poems which occupied the rest of his long creative life.

Hardy's career as a poet lies mainly within the first quarter of the twentieth century, and his qualified and peculiar modernism makes him one of the most problematic of the truly major poets of our age. He had written verse since his middle twenties and had begun to absorb the English Romantic poetic tradition, reading Keats, Shelley, Browning, and later, Swinburne, allowing their worlds to enter an inner landscape of his own. His first book of verse, *Wessex Poems,* was published in 1898; and in 1904, 1906, and 1908, the three parts of *The Dynasts*—a huge, visionary treatment in unperformable dramatic form (deriving from *Prometheus Unbound* more than from actual Greek tragedy) of the Napoleonic Wars, a project toward which Hardy had been working for forty years. *The Dynasts* is one of those works which, like Browning's *The Ring and the Book,* newer fashions of changing response to literary surface and format (a novel in verse; a historical mythology in an unsingable, non-musical opera) have caused to be unfairly neglected.

It is in Hardy's short lyrics that his greatness lies, however, and it is just here that he seems such an anomaly in the history of twentieth-century poetry. His poems range widely over so many genres: narratives; dramatic lyrics; imitations of folksong and of regional balladry; brilliant, tough short stories condensed into carefully polished verse; satirical epigrams couched in unexpectedly intricate and seemingly irrelevant stanza forms; starkly personal evocations of sorrow or bitterness; occasional poems celebrating and distrusting local and international events—these and many more defy the challenge of the age to the poetic imagination to produce a *sui generis* mode, a total kind of all-encompassing lyric, approaching the condition of music in its avoidance of exposition, argument, and prosaic truth. Hardy is often expository. His poetic language seems far less experimental than that of a genuinely Victorian poet like Gerard Manley Hopkins; the latter's highly personalized revision of accentual-syllabic meter in his "sprung rhythm," the highly poetic language in which he talked about his formal inventions—these all would be taken by a later age as prophetic marks, or even as those of premature membership in that age.

Hardy's verse is traditional in almost every sense of the word: his experiments are with arrays of forms and patterns, and with the intensifications of language which come from an archaized vocabulary employed in advanced ways. He was much influenced by the Dorchester poet William Barnes (1800–1886), who wrote both in standard English and in the dialect of Dorset. Wessex usage abounds in his poems, but so do Elizabethanisms, biblical echoes, reflections of Latin and Greek and slightly strange coinages out of existing words. Spenser in *The Faerie Queene* had to invent a poetic language, one component of which would be Chaucerian, in order to root his imaginative project in an English, as well as a classical, antiquity; the young Milton deliberately used Spenserian and Shakespearan words; the Elizabethan elements in Keats's vocabulary are mirrored by the Keatsian ones in Tennyson's. This process of classicizing the language of the English poetic past has gone on for centuries, and if T. S. Eliot would find his resonating language in Jacobean English, in Dante's Italian, and in Baudelaire's French, Hardy's tongue was a composite of other sorts. The West Country landscape is full of suggestions of history—many ruins and relics of Roman Britain are there, and the Celtic presence has always been stronger in the western parts of the island toward which Roman and Saxon conquerors drove the native Britons. It is also the country of Hardy's childhood (to which he permanently returned to live in 1883), and it is the world of his novels. In his poems the local landscape, like the unique vocabulary, forms a mediating screen between the interior, private, even autobiographical references and occasions of most of these poems, and the vastly general human rhythms that lie beyond, and around, them.

Many of Hardy's poems were written during, and about, World War I; the profound skepticism which marks the world of his novels and which late Victorian readers, still anxious for their ebbing faith, dismissed as "pessimistic," seems to some readers of today almost benign. It marks many of his poems, particularly the episodic pieces and condensed narratives fixed in a moment of time. It is when the past—a personal one, England's, the planet's—wells up in what Hardy himself calls a "moment of vision," that the poems develop another dimension. And it is in this dimension that their unpredictable, sometimes arbitrary-seeming, use of the intricate verse forms more usually associated with tripping "society-verse," or their constant echoing of the stanzas of church hymns and old songs, becomes most effective. Hardy's short poems are often highly patterned in ways that are immediately apparent: seasonal or daily rhythms will be disposed among stanzas, or the two halves of a poem will embody two opposed principles in a bald and even brutal dialectic; sestet will correct octave in a sonnet like "Hap," where the anti-providential assertion of its conclusion paradoxically has a strong Miltonic resonance. Old forms of verse provide Hardy with old tunes on which to brood, and with schematic patterns upon which to drape those ironies whose patterns are not contrived (the poet will always insist), but are the work of some great Neatener who keeps making life look so much, so much like tragic art.

Hap°

If but some vengeful god would call to me
From up the sky, and laugh: 'Thou suffering thing,
Know that thy sorrow is my ecstasy,
That thy love's loss is my hate's profiting!'

Hap chance (the title of the poem in Hardy's manuscript), thought of as the guiding principle, or the substitute for one, of Darwin's "natural selection." Unlike Tennyson in *In Memoriam*, Hardy accepts it and contemplates its ironies.

Then would I bear it, clench myself, and die,
Steeled by the sense of ire unmerited;
Half-eased in that a Powerfuller than I
Had willed and meted me the tears I shed.

10 But not so. How arrives it joy lies slain,
And why unblooms the best hope ever sown?
—Crass Casualty° obstructs the sun and rain,
And dicing Time for gladness casts a moan. . . .
These purblind Doomsters had as readily strown
Blisses about my pilgrimage as pain.
1866   1898

Neutral Tones°

We stood by a pond that winter day,
And the sun was white, as though chidden of God,
And a few leaves lay on the starving sod;
    —They had fallen from an ash, and were grey.

Your eyes on me were as eyes that rove
Over tedious riddles of years ago;
And some words played between us to and fro
        On which lost the more by our love.

The smile on your mouth was the deadest thing
10 Alive enough to have strength to die;
And a grin of bitterness swept thereby
        Like an ominous bird a-wing. . . .

Since then, keen lessons that love deceives,
And wrings with wrong, have shaped to me
Your face, and the God-curst sun, and a tree,
        And a pond edged with greyish leaves.
1867   1898

The Subalterns°

I

'Poor wanderer,' said the leaden sky,
    'I fain would lighten thee,

Crass Casualty unthinking, or insensible (not coarse or brutal) contingency or circumstance; along with "dicing Time," the "Doomsters" whose carelessness is even less consoling to consider than a malicious, but at least purposeful, demonic deity might be
Neutral Tones not the grays of photography, but of etching or wood engraving. The scene of souring love drains everything of color, and even the green ash leaves are ashen as well, as the tree's name, in the poem, takes on a new significance.
The Subalterns "Subalterns" (accent on *sub*) are junior officers (lieutenants); here, various types of force upon which human misery can be blamed, all profess to be acting under orders, from general earth, or fallen nature (as a Christian would see it), or reality. Hardy might have spoken of earth, itself subject to Will. Note the ironic use of the common meter of hymns here.

But there are laws in force on high
    Which say it must not be.'

II

—'I would not freeze thee, shorn one,' cried
    The North, 'knew I but how
To warm my breath, to slack my stride;
    But I am ruled as thou.'

III

—'To-morrow I attack thee, wight,'°
10   Said Sickness. 'Yet I swear
I bear thy little ark no spite,
    But am bid enter there.'

IV

—'Come hither, Son,' I heard Death say;
    'I did not will a grave
Should end thy pilgrimage to-day,
    But I, too, am a slave!'

V

We smiled upon each other then,
    And life to me had less
Of that fell look it wore ere when
20   They owned their passiveness.

                1902

The Darkling Thrush°

I leant upon a coppice gate°
    When Frost was spectre-grey,
And Winter's dregs made desolate
    The weakening eye of day.
The tangled bine-stems scored the sky
    Like strings of broken lyres.
And all mankind that haunted nigh
    Had sought their household fires.

---

wight archaic for "person"
The Darkling Thrush originally entitled "By the Century's Death-bed," published before the date of December 31, 1900, affixed to the final version. This is a secular ode, a celebration of the onset of a 20th century which can bring no cause for rejoicing, save for the cylic moment itself, the continuance of nature which cannot, eventually, go uncelebrated. "Darkling" is a word derived through Keats from Milton ("Ode to a Nightingale"; *Paradise Lost* III. 39), who both used it for their nightingale myths, singing out of the darkness and thereby releasing a kind of light. In "Dover Beach" Matthew Arnold uses it simply to mean "darkened." Here, the scruffy, unprepossessing thrush is a version of the poetic nightbird, but a demythologized one.
coppice gate gate to a copse, or wooded grove

10 The land's sharp features seemed to be
        The Century's corpse outleant,
    His crypt the cloudy canopy,
        The wind his death-lament.
    The ancient pulse of germ and birth
        Was shrunken hard and dry,
    And every spirit upon earth
        Seemed fervourless as I.

    At once a voice arose among
        The bleak twigs overhead
    In a full-hearted evensong
20   Of joy illimited;
    An agèd thrush, frail, gaunt, and small,
        In blast-beruffled plume,
    Had chosen thus to fling his soul
        Upon the growing gloom.

    So little cause for carolings
        Of such ecstatic sound
    Was written on terrestrial things
        Afar or nigh around,
    That I could think there trembled through
30   His happy good-night air
    Some blessèd Hope, whereof he knew
        And I was unaware.
        1900   1902

In Tenebris° (I)

'Percussus sum sicut foenum, et aruit cor meum.'—
                                    Ps. ci

    Wintertime nighs;
But my bereavement-pain
It cannot bring again:
    Twice no one dies.

    Flower-petals flee;
But, since it once hath been,
No more that severing scene
    Can harrow me.

    Birds faint in dread:
10 I shall not lose old strength
In the lone frost's black length:
    Strength long since fled!

In Tenebris "In Darkness"; one of three poems
originally entitled "De Profundis" ("out of the
depths"). The epigraph is from the Vulgate
Bible: "I am smitten like dry grass, and my
heart is dry" (in the King James version, Psalms
102:4).

Leaves freeze to dun;
But friends can not turn cold
This season as of old
    For him with none.

Tempests may scath;
But love can not make smart
Again this year his heart
20   Who no heart hath.

Black is night's cope;°
But death will not appal
One who, past doubtings all,
    Waits in unhope.
1896   1902

In Tenebris (III)

'Heu mihi, quia incolatus meus prolongatus est! Habitavi cum habitantibus
Cedar; multum incola fuit anima mea.'°—
                                    Ps. cxix.

There have been times when I well might have passed and the ending have
    come—
Points in my path when the dark might have stolen on me, artless, unrueing—
Ere I had learnt that the world was a welter of futile doing:
Such had been times when I well might have passed, and the ending have come!
Say, on the noon when the half-sunny hours told that April was nigh,
And I upgathered and cast forth the snow from the crocus-border,
Fashioned and furbished the soil into a summer-seeming order,
Glowing in gladsome faith that I quickened the year thereby.
Or on that loneliest of eves when afar and benighted we stood,
10 She who upheld me and I, in the midmost of Egdon° together,
Confident I in her watching and ward through the blackening heather,
Deeming her matchless in might and with measureless scope endued.
Or on that winter-wild night when, reclined by the chimney-nook quoin,°
Slowly a drowse overgat me, the smallest and feeblest of folk there,
Weak from my baptism of pain; when at times and anon I awoke there—
Heard of a world wheeling on, with no listing or longing to join.
Even then! while unweeting that vision could vex or that knowledge could numb,
That sweets to the mouth in the belly are bitter, and tart, and untoward,°
Then, on some dim-coloured scene should my briefly raised curtain have lowered,
20 Then might the Voice that is law have said 'Cease!' and the ending have come.
1896   1902

cope ecclesiastical cape
Heu . . . mea "Woe to me that my habitation
is prolonged! I have dwelt with the dwellers of
Cedar; my soul has been a longtime inhabitant"
from the Vulgate Bible (Psalms 120:5–6 of
the King James version).
Egdon "Egdon Heath" is the fictional name,
in Hardy's novels, for a whole area of rolling

land, wild and sparse, in Dorset (described
with power in the first chapter of *The Return
of the Native*).
quoin exterior corner
That sweets . . . untoward See Revelation
10:9–10; what was sweet to eat once was the
books, read with hope when he was young.

The Schreckhorn°

(With thoughts of Leslie Stephen)

(June 1897)
Aloof, as if a thing of mood and whim;
Now that its spare and desolate figure gleams
Upon my nearing vision, less it seems
A looming Alp-height than a guise of him
Who scaled its horn with ventured life and limb,
Drawn on by vague imaginings, maybe,
Of semblance to his personality
In its quaint glooms, keen lights, and rugged trim.
At his last change, when Life's dull coils unwind,
10 Will he, in old love, hitherward escape,
And the eternal essence of his mind
Enter this silent adamantine shape,
And his low voicing haunt its slipping snows
When dawn that calls the climber dyes them rose?

                                          1906

From The Dynasts°

[Chorus on the Eve of Waterloo]
            Fires begin to shine up from the English bivouacs. Camp
            kettles are slung, and the men pile arms and stand
            round the blaze to dry themselves. The French opposite
            lie down like dead men in the dripping green wheat and
            rye, without supper and without fire.
                  By and by the English army also lies down, the men
            huddling together on the ploughed mud in their wet
            blankets, while some sleep sitting round the dying fires.

      Chorus of the Years (aerial music)
      The eyelids of eve fall together at last,
      And the forms so foreign to plain and tree
      Lie down as though native, and slumber fast!

      Chorus of the Pities
      Sore are the thrills of misgiving we see
      In the artless champaign at this harlequinade,
      Distracting a vigil where calm should be!

Schreckhorn A 13,000-foot peak in the Swiss Alps, first climbed by Leslie Stephen (1832–1904), ex-clergyman, writer, and editor whose more famous daughter was Virginia Woolf. The poem was written after Stephen's death, the date on the epigraph recording Hardy's moment of vision while visiting the environs of the mountain, a reduced and particularized version of Shelley's perception of the interaction of mind and object in "Mont Blanc."

The Dynasts This selection is from Pt. III, vi, 8. In *The Dynasts*, a visionary pageantry covers all of Europe, and the characters are historical ones, save for various Spirits, whose expository and lyrical comments interpret the significance of the Napoleonic wars on a cosmic scale, particularly as the manifestations of an Immanent Will. The Spirits of the Years are a kind of voice of reason, and those of the Pities, of human sympathy.

The trees seem opprest, and the Plain afraid
Of a Something to come, whereof these are the proofs,—
Neither earthquake, nor storm, nor eclipse's shade!

      Chorus of the Years
Yea, the coneys° are scared by the thud of hoofs,
And their white scuts flash at their vanishing heels,
And swallows abandon the hamlet-roofs.

The mole's tunnelled chambers are crushed by wheels,
The lark's eggs scattered, their owners fled,
And the hare's hid litter the sapper unseals.

The snail draws in at the terrible tread,
But in vain; he is crushed by the felloe-rim;°
The worm asks what can be overhead,

And wriggles deep from a scene so grim,
And guesses him safe; for he does not know
What a foul red flood will soak down to him!

Beaten about by the heel and the toe
Are butterflies, sick of the day's long rheum,
To die of a worse than the weather-foe.

Trodden and bruised to a miry tomb
Are ears that have greened but will never be gold,
And flowers in the bud that will never bloom.

      Chorus of the Pities
So the season's intent, ere its fruit unfold,
Is frustrate, and mangled, and made succumb,°
Like a youth of promise struck stark and cold! . . .

And what of these who to-night have come?

      Chorus of the Years
The young sleep sound; but the weather awakes
In the veteran, pains from the past that numb;

Old stabs of Ind., old Peninsular aches,
Old Friedland chills, haunt his moist mud bed,
Cramps from Austerlitz; till his slumber breaks.

      Chorus of Sinister Spirits
And each soul shivers as sinks his head
On the loam he's to lease with the other dead
From to-morrow's mist-fall till Time be sped!

The fires of the English go out, and silence prevails,
save for the soft hiss of the rain that falls impartially on
both the sleeping armies.

(1882–1908)   1908

---

coneys rabbits
felloe-rim wheel rim

succumb used adjectivally; "dead" (or elliptically, "made to succumb")

The Convergence of the Twain

(Lines on the loss of the 'Titanic'°)

I

In a solitude of the sea
Deep from human vanity,
And the Pride of Life that planned her, stilly couches she.

II

Steel chambers, late the pyres
Of her salamandrine° fires,
Cold currents thrid,° and turn to rhythmic tidal lyres.

III

Over the mirrors meant
To glass the opulent
The sea-worm crawls—grotesque, slimed, dumb, indifferent.

IV

10   Jewels in joy designed
To ravish the sensuous mind
Lie lightless, all their sparkles bleared and black and blind.

V

Dim moon-eyed fishes near
Gaze at the gilded gear
And query: 'What does this vaingloriousness down here?' . . .

VI

Well: while was fashioning
This creature of cleaving wing,
The Immanent Will that stirs and urges everything

VII

Prepared a sinister mate
20   For her—so gaily great—
A Shape of Ice, for the time far and dissociate.

VIII

And as the smart ship grew
In stature, grace, and hue,
In shadowy silent distance grew the Iceberg too.

'Titanic' the famous luxury liner, touted as un-
sinkable, which hit an iceberg and sank on
her maiden voyage, with more than 1500 persons aboard (fewer than half of that number
were rescued) on April 15, 1912

salamandrine "Salamanders" were mythical
dragon-like spirits that inhabited flames.
thrid threaded themselves among

IX

Alien they seemed to be:
No mortal eye could see
The intimate welding of their later history.

X

Or sign that they were bent
By paths coincident
30   On being anon twin halves of one august event,

XI

Till the Spinner of the Years
Said 'Now!' And each one hears,
And consummation comes, and jars two hemispheres.
(1912)   1912

Wessex Heights

There are some heights in Wessex, shaped as if by a kindly hand
For thinking, dreaming, dying on, and at crises when I stand,
Say, on Ingpen Beacon° eastward, or on Wylls-Neck westwardly,
I seem where I was before my birth, and after death may be.

In the lowlands I have no comrade, not even the lone man's friend—
Her who suffereth long and is kind; accepts what he is too weak to mend:
Down there they are dubious and askance; there nobody thinks as I,
But mind-chains do not clank where one's next neighbour is the sky.

In the towns I am tracked by phantoms having weird detective ways—
Shadows of beings who fellowed with myself of earlier days:
They hang about at places, and they say harsh heavy things—
Men with a wintry sneer, and women with tart disparagings.

Down there I seem to be false to myself, my simple self that was,
And is not now, and I see him watching, wondering what crass cause
Can have merged him into such a strange continuator as this,
Who yet has something in common with himself, my chrysalis.°

I cannot go to the great grey Plain;° there's a figure against the moon,
Nobody sees it but I, and it makes my breast beat out of tune;
I cannot go to the tall-spired town,° being barred by the forms now passed
For everybody but me, in whose long vision they stand there fast.

There's a ghost at Yell'ham Bottom chiding loud at the fall of the night,
There's a ghost in Froom-side Vale, thin lipped and vague, in a shroud of white,

Ingpen Beacon All the high places named in
the poem are in Hardy's Wessex—in Wiltshire,
Hampshire, Dorset, Somerset—associated with
high moments in youth.
chrysalis The cocoon-spinning stage of metamorphosis, whose "continuator" he is. Avoiding
the ghosts of his women, he meets those of
himself.
Plain possibly Salisbury Plain; possibly Egdon
Heath
town Salisbury, with its great, tall, cathedral
spire

There is one in the railway train whenever I do not want it near,
I see its profile against the pane, saying what I would not hear.

As for one rare fair woman, I am now but a thought of hers,
I enter her mind and another thought succeeds me that she prefers;
Yet my love for her in its fulness she herself even did not know;
Well, time cures hearts of tenderness, and now I can let her go.

So I am found on Ingpen Beacon, or on Wylls-Neck to the west,
Or else on homely Bulbarrow, or little Pilsdon Crest,
Where men have never cared to haunt, nor women have walked with me,
And ghosts then keep their distance; and I know some liberty.

1896   1914

'I Found Her Out There'°

I found her out there
On a slope few see,
That falls westwardly
To the salt-edged air,
Where the ocean breaks
On the purple strand,
And the hurricane shakes
The solid land.

10 I brought her here,
And have laid her to rest
In a noiseless nest
No sea beats near.
She will never be stirred
In her loamy cell
By the waves long heard
And loved so well.

So she does not sleep
By those haunted heights
The Atlantic smites
20 And the blind gales sweep,
Whence she often would gaze
At Dundagel's famed head,°
While the dipping blaze
Dyed her face fire-red;

'I Found Her Out There' This and the following
poem are part of the group, published in *Poems
of 1912–13*, which confronts the sudden death,
in November 1912, of Hardy's first wife, Emma
Gifford; here, as in many other poems, he remembers visiting her in her native Cornwall
in 1870. The epigraph to the whole group of
poems is the Virgilian *Veteris vestigia flammae*:
"relics of the old flame" (*Aeneid* IV.23).
Dundagel's . . . head Tintagel Head, site of
the ruins today called King Arthur's Castle;
Arthur is supposed to have been born there.

And would sigh at the tale
Of sunk Lyonnesse,°
As a wind-tugged tress
Flapped her cheek like a flail;
Or listen at whiles
30   With a thought-bound brow
To the murmuring miles
She is far from now.

Yet her shade, maybe,
Will creep underground
Till it catch the sound
Of that western sea

As it swells and sobs
Where she once domiciled,
And joy in its throbs
40   With the heart of a child.
1912   1912

The Voice°

Woman much missed, how you call to me, call to me,
Saying that now you are not as you were
When you had changed from the one who was all to me,
But as at first, when our day was fair.

Can it be you that I hear? Let me view you, then,
Standing as when I drew near to the town
Where you would wait for me: yes, as I knew you then,
Even to the original air-blue gown!

Or is it only the breeze, in its listlessness
10   Travelling across the wet mead° to me here,
Your being ever dissolved to wan wistlessness,°
Heard no more again far and near?

    Thus I; faltering forward,
    Leaves around me falling,
Wind oozing thin through the thorn from norward,°
    And the woman calling.
                    1913

sunk Lyonnesse A local Cornish tradition has
it that the southern coast was once Arthur's
Lyonnesse; all the losses in this poem, Emma's
lost childhood of myth, that western sea remembered from further inland, seem to center on
this historical missing past.
The Voice again, a memory of an 1870 meeting
with Emma Gifford, the dactyllic lines and

triple rhymes deliberately evoking old songs
mead meadow
wistlessness heedlessness
norward northward; the north wind blows death.
Notice the return, in the penultimate line of
the poem, to the jingly rhythm of the first
eight, after the rhythmic hardening just before.

Channel Firing

That night your great guns, unawares,
Shook all our coffins as we lay,°
And broke the chancel window-squares,
We thought it was the Judgment-day

And sat upright. While drearisome
Arose the howl of wakened hounds:
The mouse let fall the altar-crumb,
The worms drew back into the mounds,

The glebe° cow drooled. Till God called, 'No;
10 It's gunnery practice out at sea
Just as before you went below;
The world is as it used to be:

All nations striving strong to make
Red war yet redder. Mad as hatters
They do no more for Christés sake
Than you who are helpless in such matters.

That this is not the judgment-hour
For some of them's a blessed thing,
For if it were they'd have to scour
20 Hell's floor for so much threatening. . . .

Ha, ha. It will be warmer when
I blow the trumpet if indeed
I ever do; for you are men,
And rest eternal sorely need).'

So down we lay again. 'I wonder,
Will the world ever saner be,'
Said one, 'than when He sent us under
In our indifferent century!'

And many a skeleton shook his head.
30 'Instead of preaching forty year,'
My neighbour Parson Thirdly said,
'I wish I had stuck to pipes and beer.'

Again the guns disturbed the hour,
Roaring their readiness to avenge,
As far inland as Stourton Tower,
And Camelot, and starlit Stonehenge.°

April 1914   1914

we lay The narrator is a corpse, "wakened
from the dead," as the saying goes, by the
English warships' gunnery practice in the English Channel.
glebe a parson's field
Stourton . . . Stonehenge The resonances of
warfare over the Channel reach a tower com-
memorating Alfred the Great's repulsion of a
Danish invasion (879), King Arthur's Camelot
(thought to be in or near Glastonbury), and
finally, the earlier, pre-Celtic, mysterious Stonehenge.

The Oxen°

Christmas Eve, and twelve of the clock.
  'Now they are all on their knees,'
An elder said as we sat in a flock
  By the embers in hearthside ease.

We pictured the meek mild creatures where
  They dwelt in their strawy pen,
Nor did it occur to one of us there
  To doubt they were kneeling then.

So fair a fancy few would weave
  In these years! Yet, I feel,
If someone said on Christmas Eve,
  'Come; see the oxen kneel,

In the lonely barton° by yonder coomb°
  Our childhood used to know,'
I should go with him in the gloom,
  Hoping it might be so.
1915   1915

During Wind and Rain°

  They sing their dearest songs—
  He, she, all of them—yea,
  Treble and tenor and bass,
    And one to play;°
  With the candles mooning each face. . .
    Ah, no; the years O!
How the sick leaves reel down in throngs!

  They clear the creeping moss—
  Elders and juniors—aye,
  Making the pathways neat
    And the garden gay;
  And they build a shady seat. . . .
    Ah, no; the years, the years;
See, the white storm-birds wing across!

  They are blithely breakfasting all—
  Men and maidens—yea,
  Under the summer tree,
    With a glimpse of the bay,

10

The Oxen invoking an old legend that oxen will
kneel in their stables at midnight on Christmas
Eve
barton farmyard
coomb valley
During Wind and Rain a bleak, contemplative

November, a miserable human season intruding
in the last two lines of each stanza, the beginning of which will present, in turn, a natural
and social cycle from winter to autumn
play the piano (this is family music indoors)

While pet fowl come to the knee. . . .
20   Ah, no; the years O!
And the rotten rose is ript from the wall.

They change to a high new house,
He, she, all of them—aye,
Clocks and carpets and chairs
    On the lawn all day,
And brightest things that are theirs. . . .
    Ah, no; the years, the years;
Down their carved names the rain-drop ploughs.
                    1917

In Time of 'The Breaking of Nations'°

I

Only a man harrowing clods
    In a slow silent walk
With an old horse that stumbles and nods
    Half asleep as they stalk.

II

Only thin smoke without flame
    From the heaps of couch-grass;
Yet this will go onward the same
    Though Dynasties pass.

III

Yonder a maid and her wight°
10   Come whispering by:
War's annals will fade into night
    Ere their story die.
    1915   1916

Moments of Vision

    That mirror
Which makes of men a transparency,
    Who holds that mirror
And bids us such a breast-bare spectacle see
    Of you and me?

    That mirror
Whose magic penetrates like a dart,

In Time of . . . Nations "Thou art my battle axe and weapons of war: for with thee will I break in pieces the nations, and with thee will I destroy kingdoms" (Jeremiah 51:20); a poem of World War I, based on a memory of a moment in 1870, during the Franco-Prussian War
wight man

Who lifts that mirror
And throws our mind back on us, and our heart,
10   Until we start?

That mirror
Works well in these night hours of ache;
    Why in that mirror
Are tincts° we never see ourselves once take
    When the world is awake?

That mirror
Can test each mortal when unaware;
    Yea, that strange mirror
May catch his last thoughts, whole life foul or fair,
20   Glassing° it—where?

Afterwards°

When the Present has latched its postern° behind my tremulous stay,
    And the May month flaps its glad green leaves like wings,
Delicate-filmed as new-spun silk, will the neighbours say,
    'He was a man who used to notice such things'?

If it be in the dusk when, like an eyelid's soundless blink,
    The dewfall-hawk comes crossing the shades to alight
Upon the wind-warped upland thorn, a gazer may think,
    'To him this must have been a familiar sight.'

If I pass during some nocturnal blackness, mothy and warm,
10   When the hedgehog travels furtively over the lawn,
One may say, 'He strove that such innocent creatures should come to no harm,
    But he could do little for them; and now he is gone.'

If, when hearing that I have been stilled at last, they stand at the door,
    Watching the full-starred heavens that winter sees,
Will this thought rise on those who will meet my face no more,
    'He was one who had an eye for such mysteries'?

And will any say when my bell of quittance° is heard in the gloom,
    And a crossing breeze cuts a pause in its outrollings,
Till they rise again, as they were a new bell's boom,
20   'He hears it not now, but used to notice such things?'
1917   1917

tincts shades of color   volume entitled *Moments of Vision* (1917)
Glassing mirroring   postern a backyard gate
Afterwards written as a closing poem for the   quittance departure

'And There Was a Great Calm'°

(On the Signing of the Armistice, Nov. 11, 1918)

I

There had been years of Passion—scorching, cold,
And much Despair, and Anger heaving high,
Care whitely watching, Sorrows manifold,
Among the young, among the weak and old,
And the pensive Spirit of Pity whispered, 'Why?'

II

Men had not paused to answer. Foes distraught
Pierced the thinned peoples in a brute-like blindness,
Philosophies that sages long had taught,
And Selflessness, were as an unknown thought,
10   And 'Hell!' and 'Shell!' were yapped at Lovingkindness.

III

The feeble folk at home had grown full-used
To 'dug-outs,' 'snipers,' 'Huns,' from the war-adept
In the mornings heard, and at evetides perused;
To day-dreamt men in millions, when they mused—
To nightmare-men in millions when they slept.

IV

Waking to wish existence timeless, null,
Sirius° they watched above where armies fell;
He seemed to check his flapping when, in the lull
Of night a boom came thencewise, like the dull
20   Plunge of a stone dropped into some deep well.

V

So, when old hopes that earth was bettering slowly
Were dead and damned, there sounded 'War is done!'
One morrow. Said the bereft, and meek, and lowly,
'Will men some day be given to grace? yea, wholly,
And in good sooth, as our dreams used to run?'

VI

Breathless they paused. Out there men raised their glance
To where had stood those poplars lank and lopped,
As they had raised it through the four years' dance
Of Death in the now familiar flats of France;
30   And murmured, 'Strange, this! How? All firing stopped?'

Great Calm "And he arose and rebuked the
wind, and said unto the sea, Peace, be still.
And the wind ceased, and there was a great
calm" (Matthew 8:26).

Sirius the Dog Star, rising after Orion, early on
late-autumn evenings

VII

Aye; all was hushed. The about-to-fire fired not,
The aimed-at moved away in trance-lipped song.
One checkless regiment slung a clinching shot
And turned. The Spirit of Irony smirked out, 'What?
Spoil peradventures° woven of Rage and Wrong?'

VIII

Thenceforth no flying fires inflamed the grey,
No hurtlings shook the dewdrop from the thorn,
No moan perplexed the mute bird on the spray;
Worn horses mused: 'We are not whipped to-day';
40 No weft-winged engines blurred the moon's thin horn.

IX

Calm fell. From Heaven distilled a clemency;
There was peace on earth, and silence in the sky;
Some could, some could not, shake off misery:
The Sinister Spirit sneered: 'It had to be!'
And again the Spirit of Pity whispered, 'Why?'
1920   1920

Snow in the Suburbs

Every branch big with it,
Bent every twig with it;
Every fork like a white web-foot;
Every street and pavement mute;
Some flakes have lost their way, and grope back upward, when
Meeting those meandering down they turn and descend again.
The palings are glued together like a wall,
And there is no waft of wind with the fleecy fall.

A sparrow enters the tree,
10 Whereon immediately
A snow-lump thrice his own slight size
Descends on him and showers his head and eyes,
And overturns him,
And near inurns him,
And lights on a nether twig, when its brush
Starts off a volley of other lodging lumps with a rush.

The steps are a blanched slope,
Up which, with feeble hope,
A black cat comes, wide-eyed and thin;
And we take him in.
1925

peradventures used in an archaic sense: per-
haps-es, what might have been

GEORGE BERNARD SHAW
1856–1950

The twentieth century is now old enough so that the brightness of some who had looked to be its eternal sages has somewhat paled. Shaw was one of the great Irish writers—Wilde, Yeats, Joyce, and perhaps Samuel Beckett being the others—who contributed so much to English wisdom, vision, and eloquence in the first half of the century, and for young people growing up after World War I, he was for many decades a kind of absentee schoolmaster. His plays, the prefaces to them, and some of his writing on music and theater were for a whole intellectual generation part of an introduction both to the life of the mind and to a vision of what civilization might possibly be said to mean. His kind of wit, and his approach to dialectic may have receded from a position of what looked to be moral centrality into a more totally stagey existence, but it remains true that, short of the imminence of apocalypse, he had something to teach the old and the young about each other.

Shaw left his native Dublin, as he wrote, "at the age of twenty; and forty years later [I] have learned from the books of Mr. Joyce that Dublin is still what it was, and young men are still drivelling in slackjawed blackguardism just as they were in 1870." Shaw's mother was a singer—his early education was more musical than literary—and she went with her children to study in London. There, Shaw read widely in the British Museum, tried unsuccessfully for many years to make himself into a novelist, and did some reviewing—his musical criticism published under the pseudonym of Corno di Bassetto remains some of the finest writing on musical performance that we possess. It was not until 1893 that the first of his plays, *Widowers' Houses,* was published, two years after his long, programmatic study *The Quintessence of Ibsenism* had appeared in its first form.

For the next thirty years, his plays and tracts appeared with great frequency, the former purportedly being written in aid of, and to publicize and explicate, the latter. One of the founders of the Fabian Society, with Beatrice and Sidney Webb, in 1884, Shaw was committed to evolutionary socialism brought about by legal and democratic means, to the right sort of rationalistic education, and to both the liberation of women and the liberation of men from unliberated females. His political views, in short, remained a not unpleasant amalgam of John Stuart Mill, William Morris (whom he knew personally), and a residue of Romantic hopefulness. Shaw's moral vision was more revolutionary: he was a Nietzschean, and a champion of Wagner when that still meant taking a moral as well as an aesthetic stance. In *The Perfect Wagnerite* of 1898 he gives a Marxist reading of the significance of *The Ring of the Niebelungs,* too reductive to be totally serious, too brilliant to be totally frivolous. Yet he was more concerned with the continuing operation of Will in the individual and collective psyche than with any Marxist Historical Process in the individual and collective action. Suspended somewhere between describing the world (to use the terms by which Marx had criticized philosophy for its historical inertness) and changing it, Shaw became in his major plays a unique kind of satirical explainer, his secular sermonizing and aphoristic mode deriving in some measure from Samuel Butler, and occasionally resembling Oscar Wilde's.

It is not merely that the sorts of hero and heroine Shaw invented were refreshing combinations of candor, ironic perception, and energy—Ibsenian figures of Resolution but less crippled by a slightly more southern moral climate and not totally humorless.

That Shaw should turn to the London stage of Sir Arthur Wing Pinero and Arthur Henry Jones, manipulators of the surface of stagecraft, and to the realm of the so-called "well-made play" was strange enough: his perception of the dramatic, after all, could be typified by Mozart's *Don Giovanni,* a cult masterpiece of the romantic tradition, and by Wagner's *Ring* cycle. But starting with his *Plays Pleasant and Unpleasant* (1898), he evolved a use of stage comedy as a framework for the demonstration of ideas in the only kind of action ideas can have—the dialectic of confrontation, revision, and self-criticism of a position. At the same time, his dramatic types—handsome, candid girls, clever older men, industrialists who turn out to be more revolutionary and humane than the would-be redistributors of their wealth, working-class snobs, and in general, open minds where the open mind in his audience would expect closed ones—began to take shape, and to lend form in turn to a kind of comedy all their own. Just as the action in major opera may truly be said to be taking place in the music itself, so, in one tradition of English stage comedy, the action is in the language. From Ben Jonson's *Epicoene,* through Congreve and Sheridan to Oscar Wilde and Shaw (and, ultimately, to Samuel Beckett), there stretches a line of drama in which the forward motion consists not in the unrolling of plot (which is often virtually held in contempt) but in a far less mechanical operation of the spirit of discourse. One sits on the edge of one's seat, as a member of the audience of such theater, waiting to hear what will be said next, in response to what has just been uttered. In Wilde, such dialogue is often made of a succession of aphorisms; in Shaw, character and argument are always inter-twined.

In his earlier plays, he was intent on revealing the flaws, hypocrisies, traps, inner horrors, and ailments of society in the way a true Ibsenite should: prostitution was not evil for official Christian reasons, nor even only because its practitioners were largely wretched, but because their misery was so hugely profitable to proper entre-preneurs whose respectability would not countenance the production of plays like *Mrs. Warren's Profession* (1898) which exposed it. His plays needed no structural appa-ratus for the playing of ideas off each other when keeping to the mode of the social problem drama. But beginning with *Caesar and Cleopatra* (published 1901), a new, quizzical direction opens up. It is not merely the second-guessing of history in re-workings of famous themes and episodes of the past that were treated so tediously by nineteenth-century historical stage pageantry. It is also the way in which Shaw starts to pit his own ideas against each other, to surprise himself not with the soundness, but even with the imagination and generosity behind a position which he is in the process of showing to be wrong. This is not the mere technological cynicism of the debating team's view of argument, but something as close to a sense of humanity as Shaw's celebrated coldness seemed ever to allow.

Major Barbara, Pygmalion, and *Man and Superman* are all triumphs in this mode. *Heartbreak House* (1919) is puzzlingly Chekhovian, a lyrical meditation on the breaking-up of nineteenth-century Europe mirrored in a single weird household. *Saint Joan* is a masterpiece of another sort. Joan of Arc was finally canonized in 1920, culminating a lengthy process of rehabilitation which had started in 1455, and Shaw's play is in some measure a response not to the historical figure but to the historical process of mythol-ogizing heroes. Joan is his greatest hero, a saint in his own non-Christian sense of an embodiment of Genius, not so much crudely super-human as quintessentially so. The opening of his own Preface to the play puts the historical matter as he saw it:

Joan the Original and Presumptuous

Joan of Arc, a village girl from the Vosges, was born about 1412; burnt for heresy, witchcraft, and sorcery in 1431; rehabilitated after a fashion in 1456; designated Venerable in 1904; declared Blessed in 1908; and finally canonized in 1920. She is the most notable Warrior Saint in the Christian calendar, and the queerest fish among the eccentric worthies of the Middle Ages. Though a professed and most pious Catholic, and the projector of a Crusade against the Husites, she was in fact one of the first Protestant martyrs. She was also one of the first apostles of Nationalism, and the first French practitioner of Napoleonic realism in warfare as distinguished from the sporting ransom-gambling chivalry of her time. She was the pioneer of rational dressing for women, and, like Queen Christina of Sweden two centuries later, to say nothing of Catalina de Erauso and innumerable obscure heroines who have disguised themselves as men to serve as soldiers and sailors, she refused to accept the specific woman's lot, and dressed and fought and lived as men did.

As she contrived to assert herself in all these ways with such force that she was famous throughout western Europe before she was out of her teens (indeed she never got out of them), it is hardly surprising that she was judicially burnt, ostensibly for a number of capital crimes which we no longer punish as such, but essentially for what we call unwomanly and insufferable presumption. At eighteen Joan's pretensions were beyond those of the proudest Pope or the haughtiest emperor. She claimed to be the ambassador and plenipotentiary of God, and to be, in effect, a member of the Church Triumphant whilst still in the flesh on earth. She patronized her own king, and summoned the English king to repentance and obedience to her commands. She lectured, talked down, and overruled statesmen and prelates. She pooh-poohed the plans of generals, leading their troops to victory on plans of her own. She had an unbounded and quite unconcealed contempt for official opinion, judgment, and authority, and for War Office tactics and strategy. Had she been a sage and monarch in whom the most venerable hierarchy and the most illustrious dynasty converged, her pretensions and proceedings would have been as trying to the official mind as the pretensions of Caesar were to Cassius. As her actual condition was pure upstart, there were only two opinions about her. One was that she was miraculous: the other that she was unbearable.

Joan of Arc had been given a variety of literary treatments in the past. She was a hypocritical and treacherous whore in British tradition (see, for example, the partly Shakespearean I *King Henry VI*); Voltaire took a high irreverent glee in reducing her to a lewd hoyden, the daughter of a priest, no less; Schiller, in *Die Jungfrau von Orleans*, had made her a pious heroine; various later nineteenth-century writers had attempted historical portraits of some accuracy. Even after Shaw's play, one can have the serious proposal of an anthropological scholar like Margaret Murray that Joan (as well as Gilles de Rais, the "Bluebeard" of fact and fairy-tale fiction) was in fact a witch, and the member of a powerful coven. Shaw is not so much interested in the history lesson he so amusingly works out as in the ironies of the human response to an instance of what humanity might itself generally be. He is playing throughout against his English audience's expectations of how the play will take sides in the Hundred Years' War. In the Middle Ages and Renaissance, the English reader would identify totally with the Trojans rather than the Greeks (because the story was read through Virgil, rather than through Homer, whom no one knew); an audience reared on Shakespeare's history plays might expect to know where to look for good sense and where for folly.

One of the great successes of the play is the way in which Joan's major antagonists —the Earl of Warwick, totally political, distantly hedonistic, and scrupulously amoral;

the Bishop of Beauvais; Peter Cauchon; and the Inquisitor at her trial, whose long speech is more magnificent than any single utterance of Joan's—are shown to be right about almost everything. If the crudest kind of hero is great in direct proportion to the size of the dragon he kills, another stage of heroism (as the Danish philosopher Søren Kierkegaard defined it), that of the moral hero, would be evaluated by the correctness, consistency, and all but ultimate truth of the position it resisted. Joan has her straw men (like the wretched English chaplain, De Stogumber, who knows that archangels must speak English), but they are there to test our characters, our prior dispositions to think along conventional and unheroic lines. It is the De Stogumber in every sincere person whom Cauchon rebukes in the Epilogue, when, after the chaplain has just confessed that seeing Joan actually burned changed his life, made him see how moralistic and narrow he had been ("But I have been a different man ever since . . ."), he produces that most resonant line of the play, perhaps: "Must then a Christ perish in torment in every age to save those that have no imagination?"

Saint Joan is, ultimately, a comedy of the historical processes which themselves can never wither away. The double catastrophe of her trial scene, the redemptive ending of the Epilogue, are both put in a final perspective by the schematic rejection of the responsibilities that accepting her sainthood would, for each of the penitents in the scene, entail. In a series of moments that surely must have influenced T. S. Eliot in the speeches of the assassins in *Murder in the Cathedral*, practical reason kneels to what transcends it, then finally slips away, in each of its aspects, one by one. Only brute human feeling, unable to make its own decisions, would just as soon remain, in the person of the soldier. But it has no choice.

Saint Joan

Scene I

A fine spring morning on the river Meuse, between Lorraine and Champagne, in the year 1429 A.D., in the castle of Vaucouleurs.

Captain Robert de Baudricourt, a military squire, handsome and physically energetic, but with no will of his own, is disguising that defect in his usual fashion by storming terribly at his steward, a trodden worm, scanty of flesh, scanty of hair, who might be any age from 18 to 55, being the sort of man whom age cannot wither because he has never bloomed.

The two are in a sunny stone chamber on the first floor of the castle. At a plain strong oak table, seated in chair to match, the captain presents his left profile. The steward stands facing him at the other side of the table, if so deprecatory a stance as his can be called standing. The mullioned thirteenth-century window is open behind him. Near it in the corner is a turret with a narrow arched doorway leading to a winding stair which descends to the courtyard. There is a stout fourlegged stool under the table, and a wooden chest under the window.

ROBERT   No eggs! No eggs!! Thousand thunders, man, what do you mean by
        no eggs?

STEWARD   Sir: it is not my fault. It is the act of God.

ROBERT   Blasphemy. You tell me there are no eggs; and you blame your Maker for it.

STEWARD   Sir: what can I do? I cannot lay eggs.

ROBERT [*sarcastic*]   Ha! You jest about it.

STEWARD   No, sir, God knows. We all have to go without eggs just as you have, sir. The hens will not lay.

ROBERT   Indeed! [*rising*] Now listen to me, you.

STEWARD [*humbly*]   Yes, sir.

ROBERT   What am I?

STEWARD   What are you, sir?

ROBERT [*coming at him*]   Yes: what am I? Am I Robert, squire of Baudricourt and captain of this castle of Vaucouleurs; or am I a cowboy?

STEWARD   Oh, sir, you know you are a greater man here than the king himself.

ROBERT   Precisely. And now, do you know what you are?

STEWARD   I am nobody, sir, except that I have the honor to be your steward.

ROBERT [*driving him to the wall, adjective by adjective*]   You have not only the honor of being my steward, but the privilege of being the worst, most incompetent, drivelling snivelling jibbering jabbering idiot of a steward in France. [*He strides back to the table.*]

STEWARD [*cowering on the chest*]   Yes, sir: to a great man like you I must seem like that.

ROBERT [*turning*]   My fault, I suppose. Eh?

STEWARD [*coming to him deprecatingly*]   Oh, sir: you always give my most innocent words such a turn!

ROBERT   I will give your neck a turn if you dare tell me when I ask you how many eggs there are that you cannot lay any.

STEWARD [*protesting*]   Oh sir, oh sir—

ROBERT   No: not oh sir, oh sir, but no sir, no sir. My three Barbary hens and the black are the best layers in Champagne. And you come and tell me that there are no eggs! Who stole them? Tell me that, before I kick you out through the castle gate for a liar and a seller of my goods to thieves. The milk was short yesterday, too: do not forget that.

STEWARD [*desperate*]   I know, sir. I know only too well. There is no milk: there are no eggs: tomorrow there will be nothing.

ROBERT   Nothing! You will steal the lot: eh?

STEWARD   No, sir: nobody will steal anything. But there is a spell on us: we are bewitched.

ROBERT   That story is not good enough for me. Robert de Baudricourt burns witches and hangs thieves. Go. Bring me four dozen eggs and two gallons of milk here in this room before noon, or Heaven have mercy on your bones! I will teach you to make a fool of me. [*He resumes his seat with an air of finality.*]

STEWARD   Sir: I tell you there are no eggs. There will be none—not if you were to kill me for it—as long as The Maid is at the door.

ROBERT   The Maid! What maid? What are you talking about?

STEWARD   The girl from Lorraine, sir. From Domrémy.

ROBERT [*rising in fearful wrath*]   Thirty thousand thunders! Fifty thousand devils! Do you mean to say that that girl, who had the impudence to ask to see me two days ago, and whom I told you to send back to her father with my orders that he was to give her a good hiding, is here still?

STEWARD   I have told her to go, sir. She wont.

ROBERT   I did not tell you to tell her to go: I told you to throw her out. You have fifty men-at-arms and a dozen lumps of able-bodied servants to carry out my orders. Are they afraid of her?

STEWARD   She is so positive, sir.

ROBERT [*seizing him by the scruff of the neck*]   Positive! Now see here. I am going to throw you downstairs.

STEWARD   No, sir. Please.

ROBERT   Well, stop me by being positive. It's quite easy: any slut of a girl can do it.

STEWARD [*hanging limp in his hands*]   Sir, sir: you cannot get rid of her by throwing me out. [*Robert has to let him drop. He squats on his knees on the floor, contemplating his master resignedly.*] You see, sir, you are much more positive than I am. But so is she.

ROBERT   I am stronger than you are, you fool.

STEWARD   No, sir: it isnt that: it's your strong character, sir. She is weaker than we are: she is only a slip of a girl; but we cannot make her go.

ROBERT   You parcel of curs: you are afraid of her.

STEWARD [*rising cautiously*]   No sir: we are afraid of you; but she puts courage into us. She really doesnt seem to be afraid of anything. Perhaps you could frighten her, sir.

ROBERT [*grimly*]   Perhaps. Where is she now?

STEWARD   Down in the courtyard, sir, talking to the soldiers as usual. She is always talking to the soldiers except when she is praying.

ROBERT   Praying! Ha! You believe she prays, you idiot. I know the sort of girl that is always talking to soldiers. She shall talk to me a bit. [*He goes to the window and shouts fiercely through it.*] Hallo, you there!

A GIRL'S VOICE [*bright, strong and rough*]   Is it me, sir?

ROBERT   Yes, you.

THE VOICE   Be you captain?

ROBERT   Yes, damn your impudence, I be captain. Come up here. [*to the soldiers in the yard*] Shew her the way, you. And shove her along quick. [*He leaves the window, and returns to his place at the table, where he sits magisterially.*]

STEWARD [*whispering*]   She wants to go and be a soldier herself. She wants you to give her soldier's clothes. Armor, sir! And a sword! Actually! [*He steals behind Robert.*]

Joan appears in the turret doorway. She is an ablebodied country girl of 17 or 18, respectably dressed in red, with an uncommon face; eyes very wide apart and bulging as they often do in very imaginative people, a long well-shaped nose with wide nostrils, a short upper lip, resolute but full-lipped mouth, and handsome fighting chin. She comes eagerly to the table, delighted at having penetrated to Baudricourt's presence at last, and full of hope as to the results. His scowl does not *check or frighten her in the least. Her voice is normally a hearty coax-ing voice, very confident, very appealing, very hard to resist.*

JOAN [*bobbing a curtsey*] Good morning, captain squire. Captain: you are to give me a horse and armor and some soldiers, and send me to the Dauphin. Those are your orders from my Lord.

ROBERT [*outraged*] Orders from your lord! And who the devil may your lord be? Go back to him, and tell him that I am neither duke nor peer at his orders: I am squire of Baudricourt; and I take no orders except from the king.

JOAN [*reassuringly*] Yes, squire: that is all right. My Lord is the King of Heaven.

ROBERT Why, the girl's mad. [*to the steward*] Why didnt you tell me so, you blockhead?

STEWARD Sir: do not anger her: give her what she wants.

JOAN [*impatient, but friendly*] They all say I am mad until I talk to them, squire. But you see that it is the will of God that you are to do what He has put into my mind.

ROBERT It is the will of God that I shall send you back to your father with orders to put you under lock and key and thrash the madness out of you. What have you to say to that?

JOAN You think you will, squire; but you will find it all coming quite different. You said you would not see me; but here I am.

STEWARD [*appealing*] Yes, sir. You see, sir.

ROBERT Hold your tongue, you.

STEWARD [*abjectly*] Yes, sir.

ROBERT [*to Joan, with a sour loss of confidence*] So you are presuming on my seeing you, are you?

JOAN [*sweetly*] Yes, squire.

ROBERT [*feeling that he has lost ground, brings down his two fists squarely on the table, and inflates his chest imposingly to cure the unwelcome and only too familiar sensation*] Now listen to me. I am going to assert myself.

JOAN [*busily*] Please do, squire. The horse will cost sixteen francs. It is a good deal of money: but I can save it on the armor. I can find a soldier's armor that will fit me well enough: I am very hardy; and I do not need beautiful armor made to my measure like you wear. I shall not want many soldiers: the Dauphin will give me all I need to raise the siege of Orleans.

ROBERT [*flabbergasted*] To raise the siege of Orleans!

JOAN [*simply*] Yes, squire: that is what God is sending me to do. Three men will be enough for you to send with me if they are good men and gentle to me. They have promised to come with me. Polly and Jack and —

ROBERT Polly!! You impudent baggage, do you dare call squire Bertrand de Poulengey Polly to my face?

JOAN His friends call him so, squire: I did not know he had any other name. Jack—

ROBERT   That is Monsieur John of Metz, I suppose?

JOAN   Yes, squire. Jack will come willingly: he is a very kind gentleman, and
gives me money to give to the poor. I think John Godsave will come,
and Dick the Archer, and their servants John of Honecourt and Julian.
There will be no trouble for you, squire: I have arranged it all: you
have only to give the order.

ROBERT   [contemplating her in a stupor of amazement]   Well, I am damned!

JOAN   [with unruffled sweetness]   No, squire: God is very merciful; and the
blessed saints Catherine and Margaret, who speak to me every day
[he gapes], will intercede for you. You will go to paradise; and your
name will be remembered for ever as my first helper.

ROBERT   [to the steward, still much bothered, but changing his tone as he
pursues a new clue]   Is this true about Monsieur de Poulengey?

STEWARD   [eagerly]   Yes, sir, and about Monsieur de Metz too. They both
want to go with her.

ROBERT   [thoughtful]   Mf! [He goes to the window, and shouts into the courtyard.] Hallo! You there: send Monsieur de Poulengey to me, will you?
[He turns to Joan] Get out; and wait in the yard.

JOAN   [smiling brightly at him]   Right, squire. [She goes out.]

ROBERT   [to the steward]   Go with her, you, you dithering imbecile. Stay
within call; and keep your eye on her. I shall have her up here again.

STEWARD   Do so in God's name, sir. Think of those hens, the best layers in
Champagne; and—

ROBERT   Think of my boot; and take your backside out of reach of it.

The steward retreats hastily and finds himself confronted in the doorway by Bertrand de Poulengey, a lymphatic[1] French gentleman-at-arms,
aged 36 or thereabout, employed in the department of the provost-
marshal, dreamily absent-minded, seldom speaking unless spoken to,
and then slow and obstinate in reply; altogether in contrast to the self-
assertive, loud-mouthed, superficially energetic, fundamentally will-less
Robert. The steward makes way for him, and vanishes.

Poulengey salutes, and stands awaiting orders.

ROBERT   [genially]   It isnt service, Polly. A friendly talk. Sit down. [He hooks
the stool from under the table with his instep.]

Poulengey, relaxing, comes into the room: places the stool between
the table and the window: and sits down ruminatively. Robert, half
sitting on the end of the table, begins the friendly talk.

ROBERT   Now listen to me, Polly. I must talk to you like a father.

Poulengey looks up at him gravely for a moment, but says nothing.

ROBERT   It's about this girl you are interested in. Now, I have seen her. I
have talked to her. First, she's mad. That doesnt matter. Second, she's
not a farm wench. She's a bourgeoise. That matters a good deal. I know
her class exactly. Her father came here last year to represent his village in
a lawsuit: he is one of their notables. A farmer. Not a gentleman farmer:
he makes money by it, and lives by it. Still, not a laborer. Not a
mechanic. He might have a cousin a lawyer, or in the Church. People
of this sort may be of no account socially; but they can give a lot of

1. Sluggish.

bother to the authorities. That is to say, to me. Now no doubt it seems to you a very simple thing to take this girl away, humbugging her into the belief that you are taking her to the Dauphin. But if you get her into trouble, you may get me into no end of a mess, as I am her father's lord, and responsible for her protection. So friends or no friends, Polly, hands off her.

POULENGEY [*with deliberate impressiveness*] I should as soon think of the Blessed Virgin herself in that way, as of this girl.

ROBERT [*coming off the table*] But she says you and Jack and Dick have offered to go with her. What for? You are not going to tell me that you take her crazy notion of going to the Dauphin seriously, are you?

POULENGEY [*slowly*] There is something about her. They are pretty foulmouthed and foulminded down there in the guardroom, some of them. But there hasnt been a word that has anything to do with her being a woman. They have stopped swearing before her. There is something. Something. It may be worth trying.

ROBERT Oh, come, Polly! pull yourself together. Commonsense was never your strong point; but this is a little too much. [*He retreats disgustedly.*]

POULENGEY [*unmoved*] What is the good of commonsense? If we had any commonsense we should join the Duke of Burgundy and the English king. They hold half the country, right down to the Loire. They have Paris. They have this castle: you know very well that we had to surrender it to the Duke of Bedford, and that you are only holding it on parole. The Dauphin is in Chinon, like a rat in a corner, except that he wont fight. We dont even know that he is the Dauphin: his mother says he isnt; and she ought to know. Think of that! the queen denying the legitimacy of her own son!

ROBERT Well, she married her daughter to the English king. Can you blame the woman?

POULENGEY I blame nobody. But thanks to her, the Dauphin is down and out; and we may as well face it. The English will take Orleans: the Bastard [2] will not be able to stop them.

ROBERT He beat the English the year before last at Montargis. I was with him.

POULENGEY No mattter: his men are cowed now; and he cant work miracles. And I tell you that nothing can save our side now but a miracle.

ROBERT Miracles are all right, Polly. The only difficulty about them is that they dont happen nowadays.

POULENGEY I used to think so. I am not so sure now. [*rising, and moving ruminatively towards the window*] At all events this is not a time to leave any stone unturned. There is something about the girl.

ROBERT Oh! You think the girl can work miracles, do you?

POULENGEY I think the girl herself is a bit of a miracle. Anyhow, she is the last card left in our hand. Better play her than throw up the game. [*He wanders to the turret.*]

ROBERT [*wavering*] You really think that?

POULENGEY [*turning*] Is there anything else left for us to think?

2. Jean Dunois (1403–68), military leader, bastard son of the Duc d'Orleans; throughout the play, his status is never referred to as a reproach, but as a proper title. After Joan's death he went on to take Paris (1536) and to liberate Normandy from the English.

ROBERT [*going to him*]   Look here, Polly. If you were in my place would you let a girl like that do you out of sixteen francs for a horse?

POULENGEY   I will pay for the horse.

ROBERT   You will!

POULENGEY   Yes: I will back my opinion.

ROBERT   You will really gamble on a forlorn hope to the tune of sixteen francs?

POULENGEY   It is not a gamble.

ROBERT   What else is it?

POULENGEY   It is a certainty. Her words and her ardent faith in God have put fire into me.

ROBERT [*giving him up*]   Whew! You are as mad as she is.

POULENGEY [*obstinately*]   We want a few mad people now. See where the sane ones have landed us!

ROBERT [*his irresoluteness now openly swamping his affected decisiveness*]   I shall feel like a precious fool. Still, if you feel sure—?

POULENGEY   I feel sure enough to take her to Chinon—unless you stop me.

ROBERT   This is not fair. You are putting the responsibility on me.

POULENGEY   It is on you whichever way you decide.

ROBERT   Yes: thats just it. Which way am I to decide? You dont see how awkward this is for me. [*snatching at a dilatory step with an unconscious hope that Joan will make up his mind for him*]   Do you think I ought to have another talk to her?

POULENGEY [*rising*]   Yes. [*He goes to the window and calls.*] Joan!

JOAN'S VOICE   Will he let us go, Polly?

POULENGEY   Come up. Come in. [*turning to Robert*] Shall I leave you with her?

ROBERT   No: stay here; and back me up.

Poulengey sits down on the chest. Robert goes back to his magisterial chair, but remains standing to inflate himself more imposingly. Joan comes in, full of good news.

JOAN   Jack will go halves for the horse.

ROBERT   Well!! [*He sits, deflated.*]

POULENGEY [*gravely*]   Sit down, Joan.

JOAN [*checked a little, and looking to Robert*]   May I?

ROBERT   Do what you are told.

Joan curtsies and sits down on the stool between them. Robert outfaces his perplexity with his most peremptory air.

ROBERT   What is your name?

JOAN [*chattily*]   They always call me Jenny in Lorraine. Here in France I am Joan. The soldiers call me The Maid.

ROBERT   What is your surname?

JOAN   Surname? What is that? My father sometimes calls himself d'Arc; but I know nothing about it. You met my father. He—

ROBERT   Yes, yes; I remember. You come from Domrémy in Lorraine, I think.

JOAN   Yes; but what does it matter? we all speak French.

ROBERT   Don't ask questions: answer them. How old are you?

JOAN   Seventeen: so they tell me. It might be nineteen. I dont remember.

ROBERT   What did you mean when you said that St Catherine and St Margaret talked to you every day?

JOAN   They do.

ROBERT   What are they like?

JOAN   [*suddenly obstinate*]   I will tell you nothing about that: they have not given me leave.

ROBERT   But you actually see them; and they talk to you just as I am talking to you?

JOAN   No: it is quite different. I cannot tell you: you must not talk to me about my voices.

ROBERT   How do you mean? voices?

JOAN   I hear voices telling me what to do. They come from God.

ROBERT   They come from your imagination.

JOAN   Of course. That is how the messages of God come to us.

POULENGEY.   Checkmate.

ROBERT   No fear! [*to Joan*] So God says you are to raise the siege of Orleans?

JOAN   And to crown the Dauphin in Rheims Cathedral.

ROBERT [*gasping*]   Crown the D—! Gosh!

JOAN   And to make the English leave France.

ROBERT [*sarcastic*]   Anything else?

JOAN [*charming*]   Not just at present, thank you, squire.

ROBERT   I suppose you think raising a siege is as easy as chasing a cow out of a meadow. You think soldiering is anybody's job?

JOAN   I do not think it can be very difficult if God is on your side, and you are willing to put your life in His hand. But many soldiers are very simple.

ROBERT [*grimly*]   Simple! Did you ever see English soldiers fighting?

JOAN   They are only men. God made them just like us; but He gave them their own country and their own language; and it is not His will that they should come into our country and try to speak our language.

ROBERT   Who has been putting such nonsense into your head? Dont you know that soldiers are subject to their feudal lord, and that it is nothing to them or to you whether he is the duke of Burgundy or the king of England or the king of France? What has their language to do with it?

JOAN   I do not understand that a bit. We are all subject to the King of Heaven; and He gave us our countries and our languages, and meant us to keep them. If it were not so it would be murder to kill an Englishman in battle; and you, squire, would be in great danger of hell fire. You must not think about your duty to your feudal lord, but about your duty to God.

POULENGEY   It's no use, Robert: she can choke you like that every time.

ROBERT   Can she, by Saint Dennis! We shall see. [*to Joan*] We are not talking about God: we are talking about practical affairs. I ask you again, girl, have you ever seen English soldiers fighting? Have you ever seen them plundering, burning, turning the countryside into a desert? Have you heard no tales of their Black Prince [3] who was blacker than the devil himself, or of the English king's father?

JOAN   You must not be afraid, Robert—

3. Edward, Prince of Wales (1330–76), son of Edward III, famed as a soldier, and ruler of parts of the south of France, captured in behalf of his father's claim to the French crown.

ROBERT   Damn you, I am not afraid. And who gave you leave to call me Robert?

JOAN   You were called so in church in the name of our Lord. All the other names are your father's or your brother's or anybody's.

ROBERT   Tcha!

JOAN   Listen to me, squire. At Domrémy we had to fly to the next village to escape from the English soldiers. Three of them were left behind, wounded. I came to know these three poor goddams quite well. They had not half my strength.

ROBERT   Do you know why they are called goddams?

JOAN   No. Everyone calls them goddams.

ROBERT   It is because they are always calling on their God to condemn their souls to perdition. That is what goddam means in their language. How do you like it?

JOAN   God will be merciful to them; and they will act like His good children when they go back to the country He made for them, and made them for. I have heard the tales of the Black Prince. The moment he touched the soil of our country the devil entered into him, and made him a black fiend. But at home, in the place made for him by God, he was good. It is always so. If I went into England against the will of God to conquer England, and tried to live there and speak its language, the devil would enter into me; and when I was old I should shudder to remember the wickedness I did.

ROBERT   Perhaps. But the more devil you were the better you might fight. That is why the goddams will take Orleans. And you cannot stop them, nor ten thousand like you.

JOAN   One thousand like me can stop them. Ten like me can stop them with God on our side. [*She rises impetuously, and goes at him, unable to sit quiet any longer.*] You do not understand, squire. Our soldiers are always beaten because they are fighting only to save their skins; and the shortest way to save your skin is to run away. Our knights are thinking only of the money they will make in ransoms: it is not kill or be killed with them, but pay or be paid. But I will teach them all to fight that the will of God may be done in France; and then they will drive the poor goddams before them like sheep. You and Polly will live to see the day when there will not be an English soldier on the soil of France; and there will be but one king there: not the feudal English king, but God's French one.

ROBERT   [*to Poulengey*]   This may be all rot, Polly; but the troops might swallow it, though nothing that we can say seems able to put any fight into them. Even the Dauphin might swallow it. And if she can put fight into him, she can put it into anybody.

POULENGEY   I can see no harm in trying. Can you? And there is something about the girl—

ROBERT   [*turning to Joan*]   Now listen you to me; and [*desperately*] dont cut in before I have time to think.

JOAN   [*plumping down on the stool again, like an obedient schoolgirl*]   Yes, squire.

ROBERT   Your orders are, that you are to go to Chinon under the escort of this gentleman and three of his friends.

JOAN [*radiant, clasping her hands*]   Oh, squire! Your head is all circled with light, like a saint's.

POULENGEY   How is she to get into the royal presence?

ROBERT [*who has looked up for his halo rather apprehensively*]   I dont know: how did she get into my presence? If the Dauphin can keep her out he is a better man than I take him for. [*rising*] I will send her to Chinon; and she can say I sent her. Then let come what may: I can do no more.

JOAN   And the dress? I may have a soldier's dress, maynt I, squire?

ROBERT   Have what you please. I wash my hands of it.

JOAN [*wildly excited by her success*]   Come, Polly. [*She dashes out.*]

ROBERT [*shaking Poulengey's hand*]   Goodbye, old man, I am taking a big chance. Few other men would have done it. But as you say, there is something about her.

POULENGEY   Yes: there is something about her. Goodbye. [*He goes out.*]
Robert, still very doubtful whether he has not been made a fool of by a crazy female, and a social inferior to boot, scratches his head and slowly comes back from the door.
The steward runs in with a basket.

STEWARD   Sir, sir—

ROBERT   What now?

STEWARD   The hens are laying like mad, sir. Five dozen eggs!

ROBERT [*stiffens convulsively: crosses himself: and forms with his pale lips the words*]   Christ in heaven! [*aloud but breathless*] She did come from God.

Scene II

Chinon, in Touraine. An end of the throne room in the castle, curtained off to make an antechamber. The Archbishop of Rheims, close on 50, a full-fed prelate with nothing of the ecclesiastic about him except his imposing bearing, and the Lord Chamberlain, Monseigneur de la Trémouille, a monstrous arrogant wineskin of a man, are waiting for the Dauphin. There is a door in the wall to the right of the two men. It is late in the afternoon on the 8th of March, 1429. The Archbishop stands with dignity whilst the Chamberlain, on his left, fumes about in the worst of tempers.

LA TRÉMOUILLE   What the devil does the Dauphin mean by keeping us waiting like this? I dont know how you have the patience to stand there like a stone idol.

THE ARCHBISHOP   You see, I am an archbishop; and an archbishop is a sort of idol. At any rate he has to learn to keep still and suffer fools patiently. Besides, my dear Lord Chamberlain, it is the Dauphin's royal privilege to keep you waiting, is it not?

LA TRÉMOUILLE   Dauphin be damned! saving your reverence. Do you know how much money he owes me?

THE ARCHBISHOP   Much more than he owes me, I have no doubt, because you are a much richer man. But I take it he owes you all you could afford to lend him. That is what he owes me.

LA TRÉMOUILLE   Twenty-seven thousand: that was his last haul. A cool twenty-seven thousand!

THE ARCHBISHOP   What becomes of it all? He never has a suit of clothes that I would throw to a curate.

LA TRÉMOUILLE   He dines on a chicken or a scrap of mutton. He borrows my last penny; and there is nothing to shew for it. [*A page appears in the doorway.*] At last!

THE PAGE   No, my lord: it is not His Majesty. Monsieur de Rais is approaching.

LA TRÉMOUILLE   Young Bluebeard! Why announce him?

THE PAGE   Captain La Hire is with him. Something has happened, I think.

Gilles de Rais, a young man of 25, very smart and self-possessed, and sporting the extravagance of a little curled beard dyed blue at a clean-shaven court, comes in. He is determined to make himself agreeable, but lacks natural joyousness, and is not really pleasant. In fact when he defies the Church some eleven years later he is accused of trying to extract pleasure from horrible cruelties, and hanged. So far, however, there is no shadow of the gallows on him. He advances gaily to the Archbishop. The page withdraws.

BLUEBEARD   Your faithful lamb, Archbishop. Good day, my lord. Do you know what has happened to La Hire?

LA TRÉMOUILLE   He has sworn himself into a fit, perhaps.

BLUEBEARD   No: just the opposite. Foul Mouthed Frank, the only man in Touraine who could beat him at swearing, was told by a soldier that he shouldnt use such language when he was at the point of death.

THE ARCHBISHOP   Nor at any other point. But was Foul Mouthed Frank on the point of death?

BLUEBEARD   Yes: he has just fallen into a well and been drowned. La Hire is frightened out of his wits.

Captain La Hire comes in: a war dog with no court manners and pronounced camp ones.

BLUEBEARD   I have just been telling the Chamberlain and the Archbishop. The Archbishop says you are a lost man.

LA HIRE   [*striding past Bluebeard, and planting himself between the Archbishop and La Trémouille*]   This is nothing to joke about. It is worse than we thought. It was not a soldier, but an angel dressed as a soldier.

THE ARCHBISHOP
THE CHAMBERLAIN   } [*exclaiming all together*] An angel!
BLUEBEARD

LA HIRE   Yes, an angel. She has made her way from Champagne with half a dozen men through the thick of everything: Burgundians, Goddams, deserters, robbers, and Lord knows who; and they never met a soul except the country folk. I know one of them: de Poulengey. He says she's an angel. If ever I utter an oath again may my soul be blasted to eternal damnation!

THE ARCHBISHOP   A very pious beginning, Captain.

Bluebeard and La Trémouille laugh at him. The page returns.

THE PAGE   His Majesty.

> *They stand perfunctorily at court attention. The Dauphin, aged 26, really King Charles the Seventh since the death of his father, but as yet uncrowned, comes in through the curtains with a paper in his hands. He is a poor creature physically; and the current fashion of shaving closely, and hiding every scrap of hair under the headcovering or head-dress, both by women and men, makes the worst of his appearance. He has little narrow eyes, near together, a long pendulous nose that droops over his thick short upper lip, and the expression of a young dog accustomed to be kicked, yet incorrigible and irrepressible. But he is neither vulgar nor stupid; and he has a cheeky humor which enables him to hold his own in conversation. Just at present he is excited, like a child with a new toy. He comes to the Archbishop's left hand. Bluebeard and La Hire retire towards the curtains.*

CHARLES   Oh, Archbishop, do you know what Robert de Baudricourt is sending me from Vaucouleurs?

THE ARCHBISHOP [*contemptuously*]   I am not interested in the newest toys.

CHARLES [*indignantly*]   It isnt a toy. [*sulkily*] However, I can get on very well without your interest.

THE ARCHBISHOP   Your Highness is taking offence very unnecessarily.

CHARLES   Thank you. You are always ready with a lecture, arent you?

LA TRÉMOUILLE [*roughly*]   Enough grumbling. What have you got there?

CHARLES   What is that to you?

LA TRÉMOUILLE   It is my business to know what is passing between you and the garrison at Vaucouleurs. [*He snatches the paper from the Dauphin's hand, and begins reading it with some difficulty, following the words with his finger and spelling them out syllable by syllable.*]

CHARLES [*mortified*]   You all think you can treat me as you please because I owe you money, and because I am no good at fighting. But I have the blood royal in my veins.

THE ARCHBISHOP   Even that has been questioned, your Highness. One hardly recognizes in you the grandson of Charles the Wise.

CHARLES   I want to hear no more of my grandfather. He was so wise that he used up the whole family stock of wisdom for five generations and left me the poor fool I am, bullied and insulted by all of you.

THE ARCHBISHOP   Control yourself, sir. These outbursts of petulance are not seemly.

CHARLES   Another lecture! Thank you. What a pity it is that though you are an archbishop saints and angels dont come to see you!

THE ARCHBISHOP   What do you mean?

CHARLES   Aha! Ask that bully there [*pointing to La Trémouille*].

LA TRÉMOUILLE [*furious*]   Hold your tongue. Do you hear?

CHARLES   Oh, I hear. You neednt shout. The whole castle can hear. Why dont you go and shout at the English, and beat them for me?

LA TRÉMOUILLE [*raising his fist*]   You young—

CHARLES [*running behind the Archbishop*]   Dont you raise your hand to me. It's high treason.

LA HIRE   Steady, Duke! Steady!

THE ARCHBISHOP [*resolutely*]   Come, come! this will not do. My Lord Chamberlain: please! please! we must keep some sort of order. [*to the Dauphin*] And you, sir: if you cannot rule your kingdom, at least try to rule yourself.

CHARLES   Another lecture! Thank you.

LA TRÉMOUILLE [*handing over the paper to the Archbishop*]   Here: read the accursed thing for me. He has sent the blood boiling into my head: I cant distinguish the letters.

CHARLES [*coming back and peering round La Trémouille's left shoulder*]   I will read it for you if you like. I can read, you know.

LA TRÉMOUILLE [*with intense contempt, not at all stung by the taunt*]   Yes: reading is about all you are fit for. Can you make it out, Archbishop?

THE ARCHBISHOP   I should have expected more commonsense from De Baudricourt. He is sending some cracked country lass here—

CHARLES [*interrupting*]   No: he is sending a saint: an angel. And she is coming to me: to me, the king, and not to you, Archbishop, holy as you are. She knows the blood royal if you dont. [*He struts up to the curtains between Bluebeard and La Hire.*]

THE ARCHBISHOP   You cannot be allowed to see this crazy wench.

CHARLES [*turning*]   But I am the king; and I will.

LA TRÉMOUILLE [*brutally*]   Then she cannot be allowed to see you. Now!

CHARLES   I tell you I will. I am going to put my foot down—

BLUEBEARD [*laughing at him*]   Naughty! What would your wise grandfather say?

CHARLES   That just shews your ignorance, Bluebeard. My grandfather had a saint who used to float in the air when she was praying, and told him everything he wanted to know. My poor father had two saints, Marie de Maillé and the Gasque of Avignon. It is in our family; and I dont care what you say: I will have my saint too.

THE ARCHBISHOP   This creature is not a saint. She is not even a respectable woman. She does not wear women's clothes. She is dressed like a soldier, and rides round the country with soldiers. Do you suppose such a person can be admitted to your Highness's court?

LA HIRE   Stop. [*going to the Archbishop*] Did you say a girl in armor, like a soldier?

THE ARCHBISHOP   So De Baudricourt describes her.

LA HIRE   But by all the devils in hell—Oh, God forgive me, what am I saying?—by Our Lady and all the saints, this must be the angel that struck Foul Mouthed Frank dead for swearing.

CHARLES [*triumphant*]   You see! A miracle!

LA HIRE   She may strike the lot of us dead if we cross her. For Heaven's sake, Archbishop, be careful what you are doing.

THE ARCHBISHOP [*severely*]   Rubbish! Nobody has been struck dead. A drunken blackguard who has been rebuked a hundred times for swearing has fallen into a well, and been drowned. A mere coincidence.

LA HIRE   I do not know what a coincidence is. I do know that the man is dead, and that she told him he was going to die.

THE ARCHBISHOP   We are all going to die, Captain.

LA HIRE [*crossing himself*] I hope not. [*He backs out of the conversation.*]

BLUEBEARD We can easily find out whether she is an angel or not. Let us arrange when she comes that I shall be the Dauphin, and see whether she will find me out.

CHARLES Yes: I agree to that. If she cannot find the blood royal I will have nothing to do with her.

THE ARCHBISHOP It is for the Church to make saints: let De Baudricourt mind his own business, and not dare usurp the function of his priest. I say the girl shall not be admitted.

BLUEBEARD But, Archbishop—

THE ARCHBISHOP [*sternly*] I speak in the Church's name. [*to the Dauphin*] Do you dare say she shall?

CHARLES [*intimidated but sulky*] Oh, if you make it an excommunication matter, I have nothing more to say, of course. But you havnt read the end of the letter. De Baudricourt says she will raise the siege of Orleans, and beat the English for us.

LA TRÉMOUILLE Rot!

CHARLES Well, will you save Orleans for us, with all your bullying?

LA TRÉMOUILLE [*savagely*] Do not throw that in my face again: do you hear? I have done more fighting than you ever did or ever will. But I cannot be everywhere.

THE DAUPHIN Well, thats something.

BLUEBEARD [*coming between the Archbishop and Charles*] You have Jack Dunois at the head of your troops in Orleans: the brave Dunois, the handsome Dunois, the wonderful invincible Dunois, the darling of all the ladies, the beautiful bastard.[1] Is it likely that the country lass can do what he cannot do?

CHARLES Why doesnt he raise the siege, then?

LA HIRE The wind is against him.

BLUEBEARD How can the wind hurt him at Orleans? It is not on the Channel.

LA HIRE It is on the river Loire; and the English hold the bridgehead. He must ship his men across the river and upstream, if he is to take them in the rear. Well, he cannot, because there is a devil of a wind blowing the other way. He is tired of paying the priests to pray for a west wind. What he needs is a miracle. You tell me that what the girl did to Foul Mouthed Frank was no miracle. No matter: it finished Frank. If she changes the wind for Dunois, that may not be a miracle either; but it may finish the English. What harm is there in trying?

THE ARCHBISHOP [*who has read the end of the letter and become more thoughtful*] It is true that De Baudricourt seems extraordinarily impressed.

LA HIRE De Baudricourt is a blazing ass; but he is a soldier; and if he thinks she can beat the English, all the rest of the army will think so too.

LA TRÉMOUILLE [*to the Archbishop, who is hesitating*] Oh, let them have their way. Dunois' men will give up the town in spite of him if somebody does not put some fresh spunk into them.

THE ARCHBISHOP The Church must examine the girl before anything decisive

1. See Scene I, n. 2.

is done about her. However, since his Highness desires it, let her attend the Court.

LA HIRE   I will find her and tell her. [*He goes out.*]

CHARLES   Come with me, Bluebeard; and let us arrange so that she will not know who I am. You will pretend to be me. [*He goes out through the curtains.*]

BLUEBEARD   Pretend to be that thing! Holy Michael! [*He follows the Dauphin.*]

LA TRÉMOUILLE   I wonder will she pick him out!

THE ARCHBISHOP   Of course she will.

LA TRÉMOUILLE   Why? How is she to know?

THE ARCHBISHOP   She will know what everybody in Chinon knows: that the Dauphin is the meanest-looking and worst-dressed figure in the Court, and that the man with the blue beard is Gilles de Rais.

LA TRÉMOUILLE   I never thought of that.

THE ARCHBISHOP   You are not so accustomed to miracles as I am. It is part of my profession.

LA TRÉMOUILLE   [*puzzled and a little scandalized*]   But that would not be a miracle at all.

THE ARCHBISHOP   [*calmy*]   Why not?

LA TRÉMOUILLE   Well, come! what is a miracle?

THE ARCHBISHOP   A miracle, my friend, is an event which creates faith. That is the purpose and nature of miracles. They may seem very wonderful to the people who witness them, and very simple to those who perform them. That does not matter: if they confirm or create faith they are true miracles.

LA TRÉMOUILLE   Even when they are frauds, do you mean?

THE ARCHBISHOP   Frauds deceive. An event which creates faith does not deceive: therefore it is not a fraud, but a miracle.

LA TRÉMOUILLE   [*scratching his neck in his perplexity*]   Well, I suppose as you are an archbishop you must be right. It seems a bit fishy to me. But I am no churchman, and dont understand these matters.

THE ARCHBISHOP   You are not a churchman; but you are a diplomatist and a soldier. Could you make our citizens pay war taxes, or our soldiers sacrifice their lives, if they knew what is really happening instead of what seems to them to be happening?

LA TRÉMOUILLE   No, by Saint Dennis: the fat would be in the fire before sundown.

THE ARCHBISHOP   Would it not be quite easy to tell them the truth?

LA TRÉMOUILLE   Man alive, they wouldnt believe it.

THE ARCHBISHOP   Just so. Well, the Church has to rule men for the good of their souls as you have to rule them for the good of their bodies. To do that, the Church must do as you do: nourish their faith by poetry.

LA TRÉMOUILLE   Poetry! I should call it humbug.

THE ARCHBISHOP   You would be wrong, my friend. Parables are not lies because they describe events that have never happened. Miracles are not frauds because they are often—I do not say always—very simple and innocent contrivances by which the priest fortifies the faith of his flock. When this girl picks out the Dauphin among his courtiers, it will not be a miracle for me, because I shall know how it has been done, and my faith will not be increased. But as for the others, if they feel the thrill of the supernatural, and forget their sinful clay in a sudden sense of the glory of God, it will be a miracle and a blessed one. And you will find that the girl herself will be more affected than anyone else. She will forget how she really picked him out. So, perhaps, will you.

LA TRÉMOUILLE   Well, I wish I were clever enough to know how much of you is God's archbishop and how much the most artful fox in Touraine. Come on, or we shall be late for the fun; and I want to see it, miracle or no miracle.

THE ARCHBISHOP [*detaining him a moment*]   Do not think that I am a lover of crooked ways. There is a new spirit rising in men: we are at the dawning of a wider epoch. If I were a simple monk, and had not to rule men, I should seek peace for my spirit with Aristotle and Pythagoras rather than with the saints and their miracles.

LA TRÉMOUILLE   And who the deuce was Pythagoras?

THE ARCHBISHOP   A sage who held that the earth is round, and that it moves round the sun.

LA TRÉMOUILLE   What an utter fool! Couldnt he use his eyes?

They go out together through the curtains, which are presently withdrawn, revealing the full depth of the throne room with the Court assembled. On the right are two Chairs of State on a dais. Bluebeard is standing theatrically on the dais, playing the king, and, like the courtiers, enjoying the joke rather obviously. There is a curtained arch in the wall behind the dais; but the main door, guarded by men-at-arms, is at the other side of the room; and a clear path across is kept and lined by the courtiers. Charles is in this path in the middle of the room. La Hire is on his right. The Archbishop, on his left, has taken his place by the dais: La Trémouille at the other side of it. The Duchess de la Trémouille, pretending to be the Queen, sits in the Consort's chair, with a group of ladies in waiting close by, behind the Archbishop.

The chatter of the courtiers makes such a noise that nobody notices the appearance of the page at the door.

THE PAGE   The Duke of—[*Nobody listens.*] The Duke of—[*The chatter continues. Indignant at his failure to command a hearing, he snatches the halberd of the nearest man-at-arms, and thumps the floor with it. The chatter ceases; and everybody looks at him in silence.*] Attention! [*He restores the halberd to the man-at-arms.*] The Duke of Vendôme presents Joan the Maid to his Majesty.

CHARLES [*putting his finger on his lip*]   Ssh! [*He hides behind the nearest courtier, peering out to see what happens.*]

BLUEBEARD [*majestically*]   Let her approach the throne.

Joan, dressed as a soldier, with her hair bobbed and hanging thickly round her face, is led in by a bashful and speechless nobleman, from whom she detaches herself to stop and look round eagerly for the Dauphin.

THE DUCHESS [*to the nearest lady in waiting*]   My dear! her hair!

All the ladies explode in uncontrollable laughter.

BLUEBEARD [*trying not to laugh, and waving his hand in deprecation of their merriment*]   Ssh—ssh! Ladies! Ladies!!

JOAN [*not at all embarrassed*]   I wear it like this because I am a soldier. Where be Dauphin?

A titter runs through the Court as she walks to the dais.

BLUEBEARD [*condescendingly*]   You are in the presence of the Dauphin.

Joan looks at him sceptically for a moment, scanning him hard up and down to make sure. Dead silence, all watching her. Fun dawns in her face.

JOAN   Coom,[2] Bluebeard! Thou canst not fool me. Where be Dauphin?

A roar of laughter breaks out as Gilles, with a gesture of surrender, joins in the laugh, and jumps down from the dais beside La Trémouille. Joan, also on the broad grin, turns back, searching along the row of courtiers, and presently makes a dive and drags out Charles by the arm.

JOAN [*releasing him and bobbing him a little curtsey*]   Gentle little Dauphin, I am sent to you to drive the English away from Orleans and from France, and to crown you king in the cathedral at Rheims, where all true kings of France are crowned.

CHARLES [*triumphant, to the Court*]   You see, all of you: she knew the blood royal. Who dare say now that I am not my father's son? [*To Joan*] But if you want me to be crowned at Rheims you must talk to the Archbishop, not to me. There he is [*He is standing behind her.*]!

JOAN [*turning quickly, overwhelmed with emotion*]   Oh, my lord! [*She falls on both knees before him, with bowed head, not daring to look up.*] My lord: I am only a poor country girl; and you are filled with the blessedness and glory of God Himself; but you will touch me with your hands, and give me your blessing, wont you?

BLUEBEARD [*whispering to La Trémouille*]   The old fox blushes.

LA TRÉMOUILLE   Another miracle!

THE ARCHBISHOP [*touched, putting his hand on her head*]   Child: you are in love with religion.

JOAN [*startled: looking up at him*]   Am I? I never thought of that. Is there any harm in it?

THE ARCHBISHOP   There is no harm in it, my child. But there is danger.

JOAN [*rising, with a sunflush of reckless happiness irradiating her face*]   There is always danger, except in heaven.[3] Oh, my lord, you have given me such strength, such courage. It must be a most wonderful thing to be Archbishop.

The Court smiles broadly: even titters a little.

THE ARCHBISHOP [*drawing himself up sensitively*]   Gentlemen: your levity is rebuked by this maid's faith. I am, God help me, all unworthy; but your mirth is a deadly sin.

Their faces fall. Dead silence.

BLUEBEARD   My lord: we were laughing at her, not at you.

THE ARCHBISHOP   What? Not at my unworthiness but at her faith! Gilles de

---

2. With "oo" sounded as in "book"; one of several Northern usages given to Joan to establish her dialect as being provincial.
3. This is an echo of Nietzsche's famous aphorism, "Live dangerously."

Rais: this maid prophesied that the blasphemer should be drowned in his sin—

JOAN [*distressed*] No!

THE ARCHBISHOP [*silencing her by a gesture*] I prophesy now that you will be hanged in yours if you do not learn when to laugh and when to pray.

BLUEBEARD My lord: I stand rebuked. I am sorry: I can say no more. But if you prophesy that I shall be hanged, I shall never be able to resist temptation, because I shall always be telling myself that I may as well be hanged for a sheep as a lamb.

The courtiers take heart at this. There is more tittering.

JOAN [*scandalized*] You are an idle fellow, Bluebeard; and you have great impudence to answer the Archbishop.

LA HIRE [*with a huge chuckle*] Well said, lass! Well said!

JOAN [*impatiently to the Archbishop*] Oh, my lord, will you send all these silly folks away so that I may speak to the Dauphin alone?

LA HIRE [*goodhumoredly*] I can take a hint. [*He salutes; turns on his heel; and goes out.*]

THE ARCHBISHOP Come, gentlemen. The Maid comes with God's blessing, and must be obeyed.

The courtiers withdraw, some through the arch, others at the opposite side. The Archbishop marches across to the door, followed by the Duchess and La Trémouille. As the Archbishop passes Joan, she falls on her knees, and kisses the hem of his robe fervently. He shakes his head in instinctive remonstrance; gathers the robe from her; and goes out. She is left kneeling directly in the Duchess's way.

THE DUCHESS [*coldly*] Will you allow me to pass, please?

JOAN [*hastily rising, and standing back*] Beg pardon, maam, I am sure.

The Duchess passes on. Joan stares after her; then whispers to the Dauphin.

JOAN Be that Queen?

CHARLES No. She thinks she is.

JOAN [*again staring after the Duchess*] Oo-oo-oooh! [*Her awestruck amazement at the figure cut by the magnificently dressed lady is not wholly complimentary.*]

LA TRÉMOUILLE [*very surly*] I'll trouble your Highness not to gibe at my wife. [*He goes out. The others have already gone.*]

JOAN [*to the Dauphin*] Who be old Gruff-and-Grum?

CHARLES He is the Duke de la Trémouille.

JOAN What be his job?

CHARLES He pretends to command the army. And whenever I find a friend I can care for, he kills him.

JOAN Why dost let him?

CHARLES [*petulantly moving to the throne side of the room to escape from her magnetic field*] How can I prevent him? He bullies me. They all bully me.

JOAN Art afraid?

CHARLES Yes: I am afraid. It's no use preaching to me about it. It's all very well for these big men with their armor that is too heavy for me, and their swords that I can hardly lift, and their muscle and their shouting and their bad tempers. They like fighting: most of them are making fools of themselves all the time they are not fighting; but I am quiet and sensible; and I dont want to kill people: I only want to be left alone to enjoy myself in my own way. I never asked to be a king: it was pushed on me. So if you are going to say 'Son of St Louis: gird on the sword of your ancestors, and lead us to victory' you may spare your breath to cool your porridge; for I cannot do it. I am not built that way; and there is an end of it.

JOAN [*trenchant and masterful*]   Blethers![4] We are all like that to begin with. I shall put courage into thee.

CHARLES   But I dont want to have courage put into me. I want to sleep in a comfortable bed, and not live in continual terror of being killed or wounded. Put courage into the others, and let them have their bellyful of fighting; but let me alone.

JOAN   It's no use, Charlie: thou must face what God puts on thee. If thou fail to make thyself king, thoult be a beggar: what else art fit for? Come! Let me see thee sitting on the throne. I have looked forward to that.

CHARLES   What is the good of sitting on the throne when the other fellows give all the orders? However! [*he sits enthroned, a piteous figure*] here is the king for you! Look your fill at the poor devil.

JOAN   Thourt not king yet, lad: thourt but Dauphin. Be not led away by them around thee. Dressing up dont fill empty noddle. I know the people: the real people that make thy bread for thee; and I tell thee they count no man king of France until the holy oil has been poured on his hair, and himself consecrated and crowned in Rheims Cathedral. And thou needs new clothes, Charlie. Why does not Queen look after thee properly?

CHARLES   We're poor. She wants all the money we can spare to put on her own back. Besides, I like to see her beautifully dressed; and I dont care what I wear myself: I should look ugly anyhow.

JOAN   There is some good in thee, Charlie; but it is not yet a king's good.

CHARLES   We shall see. I am not such a fool as I look. I have my eyes open; and I can tell you that one good treaty is worth ten good fights. These fighting fellows lose all on the treaties that they gain on the fights. If we can only have a treaty, the English are sure to have the worst of it, because they are better at fighting than at thinking.

JOAN   If the English win, it is they that will make the treaty: and then God help poor France! Thou must fight, Charlie, whether thou will or no. I will go first to hearten thee. We must take our courage in both hands: aye, and pray for it with both hands too.

CHARLES   [*descending from his throne and again crossing the room to escape from her dominating urgency*]   Oh do stop talking about God and praying. I cant bear people who are always praying. Isnt it bad enough to have to do it at the proper times?

4. Scots for "blather" or "nonsense."

JOAN [*pitying him*]   Thou poor child, thou hast never prayed in thy life. I must teach thee from the beginning.

CHARLES   I am not a child: I am a grown man and a father; and I will not be taught any more.

JOAN   Aye, you have a little son. He that will be Louis the Eleventh when you die. Would you not fight for him?

CHARLES   No: a horrid boy. He hates me. He hates everybody, selfish little beast! I dont want to be bothered with children. I dont want to be a father; and I dont want to be a son: especially a son of St. Louis. I dont want to be any of these fine things you all have your heads full of: I want to be just what I am. Why cant you mind your own business, and let me mind mine?

JOAN [*again contemptuous*]   Minding your own business is like minding your own body; it's the shortest way to make yourself sick. What is my business? Helping mother at home. What is thine? Petting lapdogs and sucking sugar-sticks. I call that muck. I tell thee it is God's business we are here to do: not our own. I have a message to thee from God; and thou must listen to it, though thy heart break with the terror of it.

CHARLES   I dont want a message; but can you tell me any secrets? Can you do any cures? Can you turned lead into gold, or anything of that sort?

JOAN   I can turn thee into a king, in Rheims Cathedral; and that is a miracle that will take some doing, it seems.

CHARLES   If we go to Rheims, and have a coronation, Anne will want new dresses. We cant afford them. I am all right as I am.

JOAN   As you are! And what is that? Less than my father's poorest shepherd. Thou'rt not lawful owner of thy own land of France till thou be consecrated.

CHARLES   But I shall not be lawful owner of my own land anyhow. Will the consecration pay off my mortgages? I have pledged my last acre to the Archbishop and that fat bully. I owe money even to Bluebeard.

JOAN [*earnestly*]   Charlie: I come from the land, and have gotten my strength working on the land; and I tell thee that the land is thine to rule righteously and keep God's peace in, and not to pledge at the pawnshop as a drunken woman pledges her children's clothes. And I come from God to tell thee to kneel in the cathedral and solemnly give thy kingdom to Him for ever and ever, and become the greatest king in the world as His steward and His bailiff, His soldier and His servant. The very clay of France will become holy: her soldiers will be the soldiers of God: the rebel dukes will be rebels against God: the English will fall on their knees and beg thee let them return to their lawful homes in peace. Wilt be a poor little Judas, and betray me and Him that sent me?

CHARLES [*tempted at last*]   Oh, if I only dare!

JOAN   I shall dare, dare, and dare again, in God's name! Art for or against me?

CHARLES [*excited*]   I'll risk it, I warn you I shant be able to keep it up; but I'll risk it. You shall see. [*running to the main door and shouting*] Hallo! Come back, everybody. [*to Joan, as he runs back to the arch opposite*] Mind you stand by and dont let me be bullied. [*through the arch*]

Come along, will you: the whole Court. [*He sits down in the royal chair as they all hurry in to their former places, chattering and wondering.*] Now I'm in for it; but no matter: here goes! [*to the page*] Call for silence, you little beast, will you?

THE PAGE [*snatching a halberd as before and thumping with it repeatedly*] Silence for His Majesty the King. The King speaks. [*peremptorily*] Will you be silent there? [*Silence*].

CHARLES [*rising*]   I have given the command of the army to The Maid. The Maid is to do as she likes with it. [*He descends from the dais*].

   General amazement. La Hire, delighted, slaps his steel thighpiece with his gauntlet.

LA TRÉMOUILLE [*turning threateningly towards Charles*]   What is this? I command the army.

   Joan quickly puts her hand on Charles's shoulder as he instinctively recoils. Charles, with a grotesque effort culminating in an extravagant gesture, snaps his fingers in the Chamberlain's face.

JOAN   Thourt answered, old Gruff-and-Grum. [*suddenly flashing out her sword as she divines that her moment has come*] Who is for God and His Maid? Who is for Orleans with me?

LA HIRE [*carried away, drawing also*]   For God and His Maid! To Orleans!

ALL THE KNIGHTS [*following his lead with enthusiasm*]   To Orleans!

   Joan, radiant, falls on her knees in thanksgiving to God. They all kneel, except the Archbishop, who gives his benediction with a sigh, and La Trémouille, who collapses, cursing.

   Scene III

Orleans, April 29th, 1429. Dunois, aged 26, is pacing up and down a patch of ground on the south bank of the silver Loire, commanding a long view of the river in both directions. He has had his lance stuck up with a pennon, which streams in a strong east wind. His shield with its bend sinister [1] *lies beside it. He has his commander's baton in his hand. He is well built, carrying his armor easily. His broad brow and pointed chin give him an equilaterally triangular face, already marked by active service and responsibility, with the expression of a good-natured and capable man who has no affectations and no foolish illusions. His page is sitting on the ground, elbows on knees, cheeks on fists, idly watching the water. It is evening; and both man and boy are affected by the loveliness of the Loire.*

DUNOIS [*halting for a moment to glance up at the streaming pennon and shake his head wearily before he resumes his pacing*]   West wind, west wind, west wind. Strumpet: steadfast when you should be wanton, wanton when you should be steadfast. West wind on the silver Loire: what rhymes to Loire? [*He looks again at the pennon, and shakes his fist at it.*] Change, curse you, change, English harlot of a wind, change. West, west, I tell you. [*With a growl he resumes his march in silence, but soon begins again.*] West wind, wanton wind, wilful wind, womanish wind, wind from over the water, will you never blow again?

---

1. A heraldic device (diagonal stripe like that in the letter "N"), denoting illegitimacy.

THE PAGE [*bounding to his feet*]   See! There! There she goes!

DUNOIS [*startled from his reverie: eagerly*]   Where? Who? The Maid?

THE PAGE   No: the kingfisher. Like blue lightning. She went into that bush.

DUNOIS [*furiously disappointed*]   Is that all? You infernal young idiot: I have a mind to pitch you into the river.

THE PAGE [*not afraid, knowing his man*]   It looked frightfully jolly, that flash of blue. Look! There goes the other!

DUNOIS [*running eagerly to the river brim*]   Where? Where?

THE PAGE [*pointing*]   Passing the reeds.

DUNOIS [*delighted*]   I see.

They follow the flight till the bird takes cover.

THE PAGE   You blew me up because you were not in time to see them yesterday.

DUNOIS   You knew I was expecting The Maid when you set up your yelping. I will give you something to yelp for next time.

THE PAGE   Arnt they lovely? I wish I could catch them.

DUNOIS   Let me catch you trying to trap them, and I will put you in the iron cage for a month to teach you what a cage feels like. You are an abominable boy.

THE PAGE [*laughs, and squats down as before*]

DUNOIS [*pacing*]   Blue bird, blue bird, since I am friend to thee, change thou the wind for me. No: it does not rhyme. He who has sinned for thee: thats better. No sense in it, though. [*He finds himself close to the page.*] You abominable boy! [*He turns away from him*] Mary in the blue snood,[2] kingfisher color: will you grudge me a west wind?

A SENTRY'S VOICE WESTWARD   Halt! Who goes there?

JOAN'S VOICE   The Maid.

DUNOIS   Let her pass. Hither, Maid! To me!

Joan, in splendid armor, rushes in in a blazing rage. The wind drops; and the pennon flaps idly down the lance; but Dunois is too much occupied with Joan to notice it.

JOAN [*bluntly*]   Be you Bastard of Orleans?

DUNOIS [*cool and stern, pointing to his shield*]   You see the bend sinister. Are you Joan the Maid?

JOAN   Sure.

DUNOIS   Where are your troops?

JOAN   Miles behind. They have cheated me. They have brought me to the wrong side of the river.

DUNOIS   I told them to.

JOAN   Why did you? The English are on the other side!

DUNOIS   The English are on both sides.

JOAN   But Orleans is on the other side. We must fight the English there. How can we cross the river?

DUNOIS [*grimly*]   There is a bridge.

JOAN   In God's name, then, let us cross the bridge, and fall on them.

DUNOIS   It seems simple; but it cannot be done.

JOAN   Who says so?

2. Her hair band, proper to a virgin.

DUNOIS   I say so; and older and wiser heads than mine are of the same opinion.

JOAN   [*roundly*]   Then your older and wiser heads are fatheads: they have made a fool of you; and now they want to make a fool of me too, bringing me to the wrong side of the river. Do you not know that I bring you better help than ever came to any general or any town?

DUNOIS   [*smiling patiently*]   Your own?

JOAN   No: the help and counsel of the King of Heaven. Which is the way to the bridge?

DUNOIS   You are impatient, Maid.

JOAN   Is this a time for patience? Our enemy is at our gates; and here we stand doing nothing. Oh, why are you not fighting? Listen to me: I will deliver you from fear. I—

DUNOIS   [*laughing heartily, and waving her off*]   No, no, my girl: if you delivered me from fear I should be a good knight for a story book, but a very bad commander of the army. Come! let me begin to make a soldier of you. [*He takes her to the water's edge.*] Do you see those two forts at this end of the bridge? the big ones?

JOAN   Yes. Are they ours or the goddams'?

DUNOIS   Be quiet, and listen to me. If I were in either of those forts with only ten men I could hold it against an army. The English have more than ten times ten goddams in those forts to hold them against us.

JOAN   They cannot hold them against God. God did not give them the land under those forts: they stole it from Him. He gave it to us. I will take those forts.

DUNOIS   Single-handed?

JOAN   Our men will take them. I will lead them.

DUNOIS   Not a man will follow you.

JOAN   I will not look back to see whether anyone is following me.

DUNOIS   [*recognizing her mettle, and clapping her heartily on the shoulder*]   Good. You have the makings of a soldier in you. You are in love with war.

JOAN   [*startled*]   Oh! And the Archbishop said I was in love with religion.

DUNOIS   I, God forgive me, am a little in love with war myself, the ugly devil! I am like a man with two wives. Do you want to be like a woman with two husbands?

JOAN   [*matter-of-fact*]   I will never take a husband. A man in Toul took an action against me for breach of promise; but I never promised him. I am a soldier: I do not want to be thought of as a woman. I will not dress as a woman. I do not care for the things women care for. They dream of lovers, and of money. I dream of leading a charge, and of placing the big guns. You soldiers do not know how to use the big guns: you think you can win battles with a great noise and smoke.

DUNOIS   [*with a shrug*]   True. Half the time the artillery is more trouble than it is worth.

JOAN   Aye, lad; but you cannot fight stone walls with horses: you must have guns, and much bigger guns too.

DUNOIS   [*grinning at her familiarity, and echoing it*]   Aye, lass; but a good heart and a stout ladder will get over the stoniest wall.

JOAN   I will be first up the ladder when we reach the fort, Bastard. I dare you to follow me.

DUNOIS   You must not dare a staff officer, Joan: only company officers are allowed to indulge in displays of personal courage. Besides, you must know that I welcome you as a saint, not as a soldier. I have daredevils enough at my call, if they could help me.

JOAN   I am not a daredevil: I am a servant of God. My sword is sacred: I found it behind the altar in the church of St Catherine, where God hid it for me; and I may not strike a blow with it. My heart is full of courage, not of anger. I will lead; and your men will follow: that is all I can do. But I must do it: you shall not stop me.

DUNOIS   All in good time. Our men cannot take those forts by a sally across the bridge. They must come by water, and take the English in the rear on this side.

JOAN   [*her military sense asserting itself*]   Then make rafts and put big guns on them; and let your men cross to us.

DUNOIS   The rafts are ready; and the men are embarked. But they must wait for God.

JOAN   What do you mean? God is waiting for them.

DUNOIS   Let Him send us a wind then. My boats are downstream: they cannot come up against both wind and current. We must wait until God changes the wind. Come: let me take you to the church.

JOAN   No. I love church; but the English will not yield to prayers: they understand nothing but hard knocks and slashes. I will not go to church until we have beaten them.

DUNOIS   You must: I have business for you there.

JOAN   What business?

DUNOIS   To pray for a west wind. I have prayed; and I have given two silver candlesticks; but my prayers are not answered. Yours may be: you are young and innocent.

JOAN   Oh yes: you are right. I will pray: I will tell St Catherine: she will make God give me a west wind. Quick: shew me the way to the church.

THE PAGE   [*sneezes violently*]   At-cha!!!

JOAN   God bless you, child! Coom, Bastard.

> *They go out. The page rises to follow. He picks up the shield, and is taking the spear as well when he notices the pennon, which is now streaming eastward.*

THE PAGE   [*dropping the shield and calling excitedly after them*]   Seigneur! Seigneur! Mademoiselle!

DUNOIS   [*running back*]   What is it? The kingfisher? [*He looks eagerly for it up the river.*]

JOAN   [*joining them*]   Oh, a kingfisher! Where?

THE PAGE   No: the wind, the wind, the wind [*pointing to the pennon*]: that is what made me sneeze.

DUNOIS   [*looking at the pennon*]   The wind has changed. [*He crosses himself.*] God has spoken. [*kneeling and handing his baton to Joan*]   You command the king's army. I am your soldier.

THE PAGE [*looking down the river*]   The boats have put off. They are ripping upstream like anything.

DUNOIS [*rising*]   Now for the forts. You dared me to follow. Dare you lead?

JOAN [*bursting into tears and flinging her arms round Dunois, kissing him on both cheeks*]   Dunois, dear comrade in arms, help me. My eyes are blinded with tears. Set my foot on the ladder, and say 'Up, Joan.'

DUNOIS [*dragging her out*]   Never mind the tears: make for the flash of the guns.

JOAN [*in a blaze of courage*]   Ah!

DUNOIS [*dragging her along with him*]   For God and Saint Dennis!

THE PAGE [*shrilly*]   The Maid! The Maid! God and The Maid! Hurray-ay-ay!
[*He snatches up the shield and lance, and capers out after them, mad with excitement.*]

Scene IV

A tent in the English camp. A bullnecked English chaplain of 50 is sitting on a stool at a table, hard at work writing. At the other side of the table an imposing nobleman, aged 46, is seated in a handsome chair turning over the leaves of an illuminated Book of Hours.[1] *The nobleman is enjoying himself: the chaplain is struggling with suppressed wrath. There is an unoccupied leather stool on the nobleman's left. The table is on his right.*

THE NOBLEMAN   Now this is what I call workmanship. There is nothing on earth more exquisite than a bonny book, with well-placed columns of rich black writing in beautiful borders, and illuminated pictures cunningly inset. But nowadays, instead of looking at books, people read them. A book might as well be one of those orders for bacon and bran that you are scribbling.

THE CHAPLAIN   I must say, my lord, you take our situation very coolly. Very coolly indeed.

THE NOBLEMAN [*supercilious*]   What is the matter?

THE CHAPLAIN   The matter, my lord, is that we English have been defeated.

THE NOBLEMAN   That happens, you know. It is only in history books and ballads that the enemy is always defeated.

THE CHAPLAIN   But we are being defeated over and over again. First, Orleans—

THE NOBLEMAN [*poohpoohing*]   Oh, Orleans!

THE CHAPLAIN   I know what you are going to say, my lord: that was a clear case of witchcraft and sorcery. But we are still being defeated. Jargeau, Meung, Beaugency, just like Orleans. And now we have been butchered at Patay, and Sir John Talbot [2] taken prisoner. [*He throws down his pen, almost in tears.*] I feel it, my lord: I feel it very deeply. I cannot bear to see my countrymen defeated by a parcel of foreigners.

THE NOBLEMAN   Oh! you are an Englishman, are you?

---

1. A manuscript book containing the prayers and offices to be said at the canonical hours of the day (prime, terce, sext, none, compline); they were often illuminated with brilliantly colored miniatures of calendrical subjects and scenes of daily life.
2. First Earl of Shrewsbury (1388–1453), fought in 40 battles before being stopped at Orléans, and taken prisoner by Joan's forces at Patay in 1429.

THE CHAPLAIN Certainly not, my lord: I am a gentleman. Still, like your lordship, I was born in England; and it makes a difference.

THE NOBLEMAN You are attached to the soil, eh?

THE CHAPLAIN It pleases your lordship to be satirical at my expense: your
greatness privileges you to be so with impunity. But your lordship knows
very well that I am not attached to the soil in a vulgar manner, like a
serf. Still, I have a feeling about it; [*with growing agitation*] and I am
not ashamed of it; and [*rising wildly*] by God, if this goes on any longer
I will fling my cassock to the devil, and take arms myself, and strangle
the accursed witch with my own hands.

THE NOBLEMAN [*laughing at him good naturedly*] So you shall, chaplain: so
you shall, if we can do nothing better. But not yet, not quite yet.

   The Chaplain resumes his seat very sulkily.

THE NOBLEMAN [*airily*] I should not care very much about the witch—you
see, I have made my pilgrimage to the Holy Land; and the Heavenly
Powers, for their own credit, can hardly allow me to be worsted by a
village sorceress—but the Bastard of Orleans is a harder nut to crack;
and as he has been to the Holy Land too, honors are easy between us
as far as that goes.

THE CHAPLAIN He is only a Frenchman, my lord.

THE NOBLEMAN A Frenchman! Where did you pick up that expression? Are
these Burgundians and Bretons and Picards and Gascons beginning to
call themselves Frenchmen, just as our fellows are beginning to call themselves Englishmen? They actually talk of France and England as their
countries. Theirs, if you please! What is to become of me and you if that
way of thinking comes into fashion?

THE CHAPLAIN Why, my lord? Can it hurt us?

THE NOBLEMAN Men cannot serve two masters. If this cant of serving their
country once takes hold of them, goodbye to the authority of their feudal
lords, and goodbye to the authority of the Church. That is, goodbye to
you and me.

THE CHAPLAIN I hope I am a faithful servant of the Church; and there are
only six cousins between me and the barony of Stogumber, which was
created by the Conqueror. But is that any reason why I should stand by
and see Englishmen beaten by a French bastard and a witch from
Lousy Champagne?

THE NOBLEMAN Easy, man, easy: we shall burn the witch and beat the bastard
all in good time. Indeed I am waiting at present for the Bishop of
Beauvais, to arrange the burning with him. He has been turned out of
his diocese by her faction.

THE CHAPLAIN You have first to catch her, my lord.

THE NOBLEMAN Or buy her. I will offer a king's ransom.

THE CHAPLAIN A king's ransom! For that slut!

THE NOBLEMAN One has to leave a margin. Some of Charles's people will sell
her to the Burgundians; the Burgundians will sell her to us; and there
will probably be three or four middlemen who will expect their little
commissions.

THE CHAPLAIN Monstrous. It is all those scoundrels of Jews: they get in every time money changes hands.[3] I would not leave a Jew alive in Christendom if I had my way.

THE NOBLEMAN   Why not? The Jews generally give value. They make you pay; but they deliver the goods. In my experience the men who want something for nothing are invariably Christians.

A page appears.

THE PAGE   The Right Reverend the Bishop of Beauvais: Monseigneur Cauchon.
Cauchon, aged about 60, comes in. The page withdraws. The two Englishmen rise.

THE NOBLEMAN [*with effusive courtesy*]   My dear Bishop, how good of you to come! Allow me to introduce myself: Richard de Beauchamp, Earl of Warwick, at your service.

CAUCHON   Your lordship's fame is well known to me.

WARWICK   This reverend cleric is Master John de Stogumber.

THE CHAPLAIN [*glibly*]   John Bowyer Spenser Neville de Stogumber, at your service, my lord: Bachelor of Theology, and Keeper of the Private Seal to His Eminence the Cardinal of Winchester.

WARWICK [*to Cauchon*]   You call him the Cardinal of England, I believe. Our king's uncle.

CAUCHON   Messire John de Stogumber: I am always the very good friend of His Eminence. [*He extends his hand to the chaplain, who kisses his ring.*]

WARWICK   Do me the honor to be seated. [*He gives Cauchon his chair, placing it at the head of the table.*]

Cauchon accepts the place of honor with a grave inclination. Warwick fetches the leather stool carelessly, and sits in his former place. The chaplain goes back to his chair.

Though Warwick has taken second place in calculated deference to the Bishop, he assumes the lead in opening the proceedings as a matter of course. He is still cordial and expansive; but there is a new note in his voice which means that he is coming to business.

WARWICK   Well, my Lord Bishop, you find us in one of our unlucky moments. Charles is to be crowned at Rheims, practically by the young woman from Lorraine; and—I must not deceive you, nor flatter your hopes—we cannot prevent it. I suppose it will make a great difference to Charles's position.

CAUCHON   Undoubtedly. It is a masterstroke of The Maid's.

THE CHAPLAIN [*again agitated*]   We were not fairly beaten, my lord. No Englishman is ever fairly beaten.

Cauchon raises his eybrow slightly, then quickly composes his face.

WARWICK   Our friend here takes the view that the young woman is a sorceress. It would, I presume, be the duty of your reverend lordship to denounce her to the Inquisition, and have her burnt for that offence.

CAUCHON   If she were captured in my diocese: yes.

WARWICK [*feeling that they are getting on capitally*]   Just so. Now I suppose there can be no reasonable doubt that she is a sorceress.

---

3. In the Middle Ages in Europe, Jews were forbidden by law to engage in any other business than money-lending at interest, usury being forbidden by the Church, and money borrowed at interest being constantly in demand.

THE CHAPLAIN   Not the least. An arrant witch.

WARWICK [*gently reproving the interruption*]   We are asking for the Bishop's opinion, Messire John.

CAUCHON   We shall have to consider not merely our own opinions here, but the opinions—the prejudices, if you like—of a French court.

WARWICK [*correcting*]   A Catholic court, my lord.

CAUCHON   Catholic courts are composed of mortal men, like other courts, however sacred their function and inspiration may be. And if the men are Frenchmen, as the modern fashion calls them, I am afraid the bare fact that an English army has been defeated by a French one will not convince them that there is any sorcery in the matter.

THE CHAPLAIN   What! Not when the famous Sir Talbot himself has been defeated and actually taken prisoner by a drab from the ditches of Lorraine!

CAUCHON   Sir John Talbot, we all know, is a fierce and formidable soldier, Messire; but I have yet to learn that he is an able general. And though it pleases you to say that he has been defeated by this girl, some of us may be disposed to give a little of the credit to Dunois.

THE CHAPLAIN [*contemptuously*]   The Bastard of Orleans!

CAUCHON   Let me remind—

WARWICK [*interposing*]   I know what you are going to say, my lord. Dunois defeated me at Montargis.

CAUCHON [*bowing*]   I take that as evidence that the Seigneur Dunois is a very able commander indeed.

WARWICK   Your lordship is the flower of courtesy. I admit, on our side, that Talbot is a mere fighting animal, and that it probably served him right to be taken at Patay.

THE CHAPLAIN [*chafing*]   My lord: at Orleans this woman had her throat pierced by an English arrow, and was seen to cry like a child from the pain of it. It was a death wound; yet she fought all day; and when our men had repulsed all her attacks like true Englishmen, she walked alone to the wall of our fort with a white banner in her hand; and our men were paralyzed, and could neither shoot nor strike whilst the French fell on them and drove them on to the bridge, which immediately burst into flames and crumbled under them, letting them down into the river, where they were drowned in heaps. Was this your bastard's generalship? or were those flames the flames of hell, conjured up by witchcraft?

WARWICK   You will forgive Messire John's vehemence, my lord; but he has put our case. Dunois is a great captain, we admit; but why could he do nothing until the witch came?

CAUCHON   I do not say that there were no supernatural powers on her side. But the names on that white banner were not the names of Satan and Beelzebub, but the blessed names of our Lord and His holy mother. And your commander who was drowned—Clahz-da I think you call him—

WARWICK   Glasdale. Sir William Glasdale.

CAUCHON   Glass-dell, thank you. He was no saint; and many of our people think that he was drowned for his blasphemies against The Maid.

WARWICK [*beginning to look very dubious*]   Well, what are we to infer from all this, my lord? Has The Maid converted you?

CAUCHON   If she had, my lord, I should have known better than to have trusted myself here within your grasp.

WARWICK [*blandly deprecating*]   Oh! oh! My lord!

CAUCHON   If the devil is making use of this girl—and I believe he is—

WARWICK [*reassured*]   Ah! You hear, Messire John? I knew your lordship would not fail us. Pardon my interruption. Proceed.

CAUCHON   If it be so, the devil has longer views than you give him credit for.

WARWICK   Indeed? In what way? Listen to this, Messire John.

CAUCHON   If the devil wanted to damn a country girl, do you think so easy a task would cost him the winning of half a dozen battles? No, my lord: any trumpery imp could do that much if the girl could be damned at all. The Prince of Darkness does not condescend to such cheap drudgery. When he strikes, he strikes at the Catholic Church, whose realm is the whole spiritual world. When he damns, he damns the souls of the entire human race. Against that dreadful design The Church stands ever on guard. And it is as one of the instruments of that design that I see this girl. She is inspired, but diabolically inspired.

THE CHAPLAIN   I told you she was a witch.

CAUCHON [*fiercely*]   She is not a witch. She is a heretic.

THE CHAPLAIN   What difference does that make?

CAUCHON   You, a priest, ask me that! You English are strangely blunt in the mind. All these things that you call witchcraft are capable of a natural explanation. The woman's miracles would not impose on a rabbit: she does not claim them as miracles herself. What do her victories prove but that she has a better head on her shoulders than your swearing Glassdells and mad bull Talbots, and that the courage of faith, even though it be a false faith, will always outstay the courage of wrath?

THE CHAPLAIN [*hardly able to believe his ears*]   Does your lordship compare Sir John Talbot, three times Governor of Ireland, to a mad bull?!!!

WARWICK   It would not be seemly for you to do so, Messire John, as you are still six removes from a barony. But as I am an earl, and Talbot is only a knight, I may make bold to accept the comparison. [*to the Bishop*] My lord: I wipe the slate as far as the witchcraft goes. None the less, we must burn the woman.

CAUCHON   I cannot burn her. The Church cannot take life. And my first duty is to seek this girl's salvation.

WARWICK   No doubt. But you do burn people occasionally.

CAUCHON   No. When The Church cuts off an obstinate heretic as a dead branch from the tree of life, the heretic is handed over to the secular arm. The Church has no part in what the secular arm may see fit to do.

WARWICK   Precisely. And I shall be the secular arm in this case. Well, my lord, hand over your dead branch; and I will see that the fire is ready for it. If you will answer for The Church's part, I will answer for the secular part.

CAUCHON [*with smouldering anger*]   I can answer for nothing. You great lords are too prone to treat The Church as a mere political convenience.

WARWICK [*smiling and propitiatory*]   Not in England, I assure you.

CAUCHON   In England more than anywhere else. No, my lord: the soul of this village girl is of equal value with yours or your king's before the throne of God; and my first duty is to save it. I will not suffer your lordship to smile at me as if I were repeating a meaningless form of words, and it were well understood between us that I should betray the girl to you. I am no mere political bishop: my faith is to me what your honor is to you; and if there be a loophole through which this baptized child of God can creep to her salvation, I shall guide her to it.

THE CHAPLAIN [*rising in a fury*]   You are a traitor.

CAUCHON [*springing up*]   You lie, priest. [*trembling with rage*]   If you dare do what this woman has done—set your country above the holy Catholic Church—you shall go to the fire with her.

THE CHAPLAIN   My lord: I—Iwent too far. I—[*He sits down with a submissive gesture.*]

WARWICK [*who has risen apprehensively*]   My lord: I apologize to you for the word used by Messire John de Stogumber. It does not mean in England what it does in France. In your language traitor means betrayer: one who is perfidious, treacherous, unfaithful, disloyal. In our country it means simply one who is not wholly devoted to our English interests.

CAUCHON   I am sorry: I did not understand. [*He subsides into his chair with dignity.*]

WARWICK [*resuming his seat, much relieved*]   I must apologize on my own account if I have seemed to take the burning of this poor girl too lightly. When one has seen whole countrysides burnt over and over again as mere items in military routine, one has to grow a very thick skin. Otherwise one might go mad: at all events, I should. May I venture to assume that your lordship also, having to see so many heretics burned from time to time, is compelled to take—shall I say a professional view of what would otherwise be a very horrible incident?

CAUCHON   Yes: it is a painful duty: even, as you say, a horrible one. But in comparison with the horror of heresy it is less than nothing. I am not thinking of this girl's body, which will suffer for a few moments only, and which must in any event die in some more or less painful manner, but of her soul, which may suffer to all eternity.

WARWICK   Just so; and God grant that her soul may be saved! But the practical problem would seem to be how to save her soul without saving her body. For we must face it, my lord: if this cult of The Maid goes on, our cause is lost.

THE CHAPLAIN [*his voice broken like that of a man who has been crying*]   May I speak, my lord?

WARWICK   Really, Messire John, I had rather you did not, unless you can keep your temper.

THE CHAPLAIN   It is only this. I speak under correction; but The Maid is full of deceit: she pretends to be devout. Her prayers and confessions are endless. How can she be accused of heresy when she neglects no observance of a faithful daughter of The Church?

CAUCHON [*flaming up*]   A faithful daughter of The Church! The Pope himself at his proudest dare not presume as this woman presumes. She acts as if she herself were The Church. She brings the message of God to

Charles; and The Church must stand aside. She will crown him in the cathedral of Rheims: she, not The Church! She sends letters to the king of England giving him God's command through her to return to his island on pain of God's vengeance, which she will execute. Let me tell you that the writing of such letters was the practice of the accursed Mahomet, the anti-Christ. Has she ever in all her utterances said one word of The Church? Never. It is always God and herself.

WARWICK   What can you expect? A beggar on horseback! Her head is turned.

CAUCHON   Who has turned it? The devil. And for a mighty purpose. He is spreading this heresy everywhere. The man Hus,[4] burnt only thirteen years ago at Constance, infected all Bohemia with it. A man named WcLeef,[5] himself an anointed priest, spread the pestilence in England; and to your shame you let him die in his bed. We have such people here in France too: I know the breed. It is cancerous: if it be not cut out, stamped out, burnt out, it will not stop until it has brought the whole body of human society into sin and corruption, into waste and ruin. By it an Arab camel driver [6] drove Christ and His Church out of Jerusalem, and ravaged his way west like a wild beast until at last there stood only the Pyrenees and God's mercy between France and damnation. Yet what did the camel driver do at the beginning more than this shepherd girl is doing? He had his voices from the angel Gabriel: she has her voices from St Catherine and St Margaret and the Blessed Michael. He declared himself the messenger of God, and wrote in God's name to the kings of the earth. Her letters to them are going forth daily. It is not the Mother of God now to whom we must look for intercession, but to Joan the Maid. What will the world be like when The Church's accumulated wisdom and knowledge and experience, its councils of learned, venerable, pious men, are thrust into the kennel by every ignorant laborer or dairymaid whom the devil can puff up with the monstrous self-conceit of being directly inspired from heaven? It will be a world of blood, of fury, of devastation, of each man striving for his own hand: in the end a world wrecked back into barbarism. For now you have only Mahomet and his dupes, and the Maid and her dupes; but what will it be when every girl thinks herself a Joan and every man a Mahomet? I shudder to the very marrow of my bones when I think of it. I have fought it all my life; and I will fight it to the end. Let all this woman's sins be forgiven her except only this sin; for it is the sin against the Holy Ghost; and if she does not recant in the dust before the world, and submit herself to the last inch of her soul to her Church, to the fire she shall go if she once falls into my hand.

WARWICK [unimpressed]   You feel strongly about it, naturally.

CAUCHON   Do not you?

WARWICK   I am a soldier, not a churchman. As a pilgrim I saw something of the Mahometans. They were not so ill-bred as I had been led to believe. In some respects their conduct compared favorably with ours.

4. Jan Hus (1373–1415), Bohemian church reformer, burned at the stake.
5. John Wyclif (1320–84), English church reformer and heretic; Hus was one of his followers.
6. Mohammed (570–632).

CAUCHON [*displeased*]   I have noticed this before. Men go to the East to convert the infidels. And the infidels pervert them. The Crusader comes back more than half a Saracen. Not to mention that all Englishmen are born heretics.

THE CHAPLAIN   Englishmen heretics!!! [*appealing to Warwick*] My lord: must we endure this? His lordship is beside himself. How can what an Englishman believes be heresy? It is a contradiction in terms.

CAUCHON   I absolve you, Messire de Stogumber, on the ground of invincible ignorance. The thick air of your country does not breed theologians.

WARWICK   You would not say so if you heard us quarrelling about religion, my lord! I am sorry you think I must be either a heretic or a blockhead because, as a travelled man, I know that the followers of Mahomet profess great respect for our Lord, and are more ready to forgive St Peter for being a fisherman than your lordship is to forgive Mahomet for being a camel driver. But at least we can proceed in this matter without bigotry.

CAUCHON   When men call the zeal of the Christian Church bigotry I know what to think.

WARWICK   They are only east and west views of the same thing.

CAUCHON [*bitterly ironical*]   Only east and west! Only!!

WARWICK   Oh, my Lord Bishop, I am not gainsaying you. You will carry The Church with you; but you have to carry the nobles also. To my mind there is a stronger case against The Maid than the one you have so forcibly put. Frankly, I am not afraid of this girl becoming another Mahomet, and superseding The Church by a great heresy. I think you exaggerate that risk. But have you noticed that in these letters of hers, she proposes to all the kings of Europe, as she has already pressed on Charles, a transaction which would wreck the whole social structure of Christendom?

CAUCHON   Wreck The Church. I tell you so.

WARWICK [*whose patience is wearing out*]   My lord: pray get The Church out of your head for a moment; and remember that there are temporal institutions in the world as well as spiritual ones. I and my peers represent the feudal aristocracy as you represent The Church. We are the temporal power. Well, do you not see how this girl's idea strikes at us?

CAUCHON   How does her idea strike at you, except as it strikes at all of us, through The Church?

WARWICK   Her idea is that the kings should give their realms to God, and then reign as God's bailiffs.

CAUCHON [*not interested*]   Quite sound theologically, my lord. But the king will hardly care, provided he reign. It is an abstract idea: a mere form of words.

WARWICK   By no means. It is a cunning device to supersede the aristocracy, and make the king sole and absolute autocrat. Instead of the king being merely the first among his peers, he becomes their master. That we cannot suffer: we call no man master. Nominally we hold our lands and dignities from the king, because there must be a keystone to the arch of human society; but we hold our lands in our own hands, and defend them with our own swords and those of our own tenants. Now by The Maid's doctrine the king will take our lands—our lands!—and make them a present to God; and God will then vest them wholly in the king.

CAUCHON   Need you fear that? You are the makers of kings after all. York or Lancaster in England, Lancaster or Valois in France: they reign according to your pleasure.

WARWICK   Yes; but only as long as the people follow their feudal lords, and know the king only as a travelling show, owning nothing but the highway that belongs to everybody. If the people's thoughts and hearts were turned to the king, and their lords became only the king's servants in their eyes, the king could break us across his knee one by one; and then what should we be but liveried courtiers in his halls?

CAUCHON   Still you need not fear, my lord. Some men are born kings; and some are born statesmen. The two are seldom the same. Where would the king find counsellors to plan and carry out such a policy for him?

WARWICK   [with a not too friendly smile]   Perhaps in the Church, my lord.
    Cauchon, with an equally sour smile, shrugs his shoulders, and does not contradict him.

WARWICK   Strike down the barons; and the cardinals will have it all their own way.

CAUCHON   [conciliatory, dropping his polemical tone]   My lord: we shall not defeat The Maid if we strive against one another. I know well that there is a Will to Power [7] in the world. I know that while it lasts there will be a struggle between the Emperor and the Pope, between the dukes and the political cardinals, between the barons and the kings. The devil divides us and governs. I see you are no friend to The Church: you are an earl first and last, as I am a churchman first and last. But can we not sink our differences in the face of a common enemy? I see now that what is in your mind is not that this girl has never once mentioned The Church, and thinks only of God and herself, but that she has never once mentioned the peerage, and thinks only of the king and herself.

WARWICK   Quite so. These two ideas of hers are the same idea at bottom. It goes deep, my lord. It is the protest of the individual soul against the interference of priest or peer between the private man and his God. I should call it Protestantism if I had to find a name for it.

CAUCHON   [looking hard at him]   You understand it wonderfully well, my lord. Scratch an Englishman, and find a Protestant.

WARWICK   [playing the pink of courtesy]   I think you are not entirely void of sympathy with The Maid's secular heresy, my lord. I leave you to find a name for it.

CAUCHON   You mistake me, my lord. I have no sympathy with her political presumptions. But as a priest I have gained a knowledge of the minds of the common people; and there you will find yet another most dangerous idea. I can express it only by such phrases as France for the French, England for the English, Italy for the Italians, Spain for the

---

7. The phrase is Friedrich Wilhelm Nietzsche's (1844–1900); *Der Wille zur Macht* was the title of an unfinished work, a vast collection of aphorisms. The invocation to "live dangerously," quoted above, comes from one of these passages beginning "I am writing for a race of men not yet in existence."

Spanish, and so forth. It is sometimes so narrow and bitter in country folk that it surprises me that this country girl can rise above the idea of her village for its villagers. But she can. She does. When she threatens to drive the English from the soil of France she is undoubtedly thinking of the whole extent of country in which French is spoken. To her the French-speaking people are what the Holy Scriptures describe as a nation. Call this side of her heresy Nationalism if you will: I can find you no better name for it. I can only tell you that it is essentially anti-Catholic and anti-Christian; for the Catholic Church knows only one realm, and that is the realm of Christ's kingdom. Divide that kingdom into nations, and you dethrone Christ. Dethrone Christ, and who will stand between our throats and the sword? The world will perish in a welter of war.

WARWICK Well, if you will burn the Protestant, I will burn the Nationalist, though perhaps I shall not carry Messire John with me there. England for the English will appeal to him.

THE CHAPLAIN Certainly England for the English goes without saying: it is the simple law of nature. But this woman denies to England her legitimate conquests, given her by God because of her peculiar fitness to rule over less civilized races for their own good. I do not understand what your lordships mean by Protestant and Nationalist: you are too learned and subtle for a poor clerk like myself. But I know as a matter of plain commonsense that the woman is a rebel; and that is enough for me. She rebels against Nature by wearing man's clothes, and fighting. She rebels against The Church by usurping the divine authority of the Pope. She rebels against God by her damnable league with Satan and his evil spirits against our army. And all these rebellions are only excuses for her great rebellion against England. That is not to be endured. Let her perish. Let her burn. Let her not infect the whole flock. It is expedient that one woman die for the people.

WARWICK [rising] My lord: we seem to be agreed.

CAUCHON [rising also, but in protest] I will not imperil my soul. I will uphold the justice of the Church. I will strive to the utmost for this woman's salvation.

WARWICK I am sorry for the poor girl. I hate these severities. I will spare her if I can.

THE CHAPLAIN [implacably] I would burn her with my own hands.

CAUCHON [blessing him] Sancta simplicitas! [8]

Scene V

The ambulatory [1] *in the cathedral of Rheims, near the door of the vestry. A pillar bears one of the stations of the cross.* [2] *The organ is playing the people*

8. "Holy simplicity!" A legendary anecdote about the burning of the Protestant martyr Jan Hus (see note 4) tells that, while he was tied to the stake, "a little old woman was bearing not merely one, but two fagots to the fire. On seeing her, Hus is said to have exclaimed 'Sancta simplicitas'" (quoted from the life of Hus by Benito Mussolini). It is hard to believe that Shaw did not have Hus's irony in mind.

1. The semi-circular aisle behind the apse of a Norman church, with chapels opening off it.
2. One of 14 carved or painted representations of stages in Christ's passion and death.

out of the nave after the coronation. Joan is kneeling in prayer before the station. She is beautifully dressed, but still in male attire. The organ ceases as Dunois, also splendidly arrayed, comes into the ambulatory from the vestry.

DUNOIS   Come, Joan! you have had enough praying. After that fit of crying you will catch a chill if you stay here any longer. It is all over: the cathedral is empty; and the streets are full. They are calling for The Maid. We have told them you are staying here alone to pray; but they want to see you again.

JOAN   No: let the king have all the glory.

DUNOIS   He only spoils the show, poor devil. No, Joan: you have crowned him; and you must go through with it.

JOAN [*shakes her head reluctantly.*]

DUNOIS [*raising her*]   Come, come! it will be over in a couple of hours. It's better than the bridge at Orleans: eh?

JOAN   Oh, dear Dunois, how I wish it were the bridge at Orleans again! We lived at that bridge.

DUNOIS   Yes, faith, and died too: some of us.

JOAN   Isnt it strange, Jack? I am such a coward: I am frightened beyond words before a battle; but it is so dull afterwards when there is no danger: oh, so dull! dull! dull!

DUNOIS   You must learn to be abstemious in war, just as you are in your food and drink, my little saint.

JOAN   Dear Jack: I think you like me as a soldier likes his comrade.

DUNOIS   You need it, poor innocent child of God. You have not many friends at court.

JOAN   Why do all these courtiers and knights and churchmen hate me? What have I done to them? I have asked nothing for myself except that my village shall not be taxed; for we cannot afford war taxes. I have brought them luck and victory: I have set them right when they were doing all sorts of stupid things: I have crowned Charles and made him a real king; and all the honors he is handing out have gone to them. Then why do they not love me?

DUNOIS [*rallying her*]   Sim-ple-ton! Do you expect stupid people to love you for shewing them up? Do blundering old military dug-outs love the successful young captains who supersede them? Do ambitious politicians love the climbers who take the front seats from them? Do archbishops enjoy being played off their own altars, even by saints? Why, I should be jealous of you myself if I were ambitious enough.

JOAN   You are the pick of the basket here, Jack: the only friend I have among all these nobles. I'll wager your mother was from the country. I will go back to the farm when I have taken Paris.

DUNOIS   I am not so sure that they will let you take Paris.

JOAN [*startled*]   What!

DUNOIS   I should have taken it myself before this if they had all been sound about it. Some of them would rather Paris took you, I think. So take care.

JOAN   Jack: the world is too wicked for me. If the goddams and the Burgundians do not make an end of me, the French will. Only for my voices I should lose all heart. That is why I had to steal away to pray here alone after the coronation. I'll tell you something, Jack. It is in the bells I hear my voices. Not to-day, when they all rang: that was nothing but jangling. But here in this corner, where the bells come down from heaven, and the echoes linger, or in the fields, where they come from a distance through the quiet of the countryside, my voices are in them. [*The cathedral clock chimes the quarter.*] Hark! [*She becomes rapt.*] Do you hear? 'Dear-child-of-God': just what you said. At the half-hour they will say 'Be-brave-go-on.' At the three-quarters they will say 'I-am-thy-Help.' But it is at the hour, when the great bell goes after 'God-will-save-France': it is then that St Margaret and St Catherine and sometimes even the blessed Michael will say things that I cannot tell beforehand. Then, oh then—

DUNOIS [*interrupting her kindly but not sympathetically*]   Then, Joan, we shall hear whatever we fancy in the booming of the bell. You make me uneasy when you talk about your voices: I should think you were a bit cracked if I hadnt noticed that you give me very sensible reasons for what you do, though I hear you tell others you are only obeying Madame Saint Catherine.

JOAN [*crossly*]   Well, I have to find reasons for you, because you do not believe in my voices. But the voices come first; and I find the reasons after: whatever you may choose to believe.

DUNOIS   Are you angry, Joan?

JOAN   Yes. [*Smiling*] No: not with you. I wish you were one of the village babies.

DUNOIS   Why?

JOAN   I could nurse you for awhile.

DUNOIS   You are a bit of a woman after all.

JOAN   No: not a bit: I am a soldier and nothing else. Soldiers always nurse children when they get a chance.

DUNOIS   That is true. [*He laughs.*]

> *King Charles, with Bluebeard on his left and La Hire on his right, comes from the vestry, where he has been disrobing. Joan shrinks away behind the pillar. Dunois is left between Charles and La Hire.*

DUNOIS   Well, your Majesty is an anointed king at last. How do you like it?

CHARLES   I would not go through it again to be emperor of the sun and moon. The weight of those robes! I thought I should have dropped when they loaded that crown on to me. And the famous holy oil they talked so much about was rancid: phew! The Archbishop must be nearly dead: his robes must have weighed a ton: they are stripping him still in the vestry.

DUNOIS [*drily*]   Your Majesty should wear armor oftener. That would accustom you to heavy dressing.

CHARLES   Yes: the old jibe! Well, I am not going to wear armor: fighting is not my job. Where is The Maid?

JOAN [*coming forward between Charles and Bluebeard, and falling on her knee*]   Sire: I have made you king: my work is done. I am going back to my father's farm.

CHARLES [*surprised, but relieved*]   Oh, are you? Well, that will be very nice. *Joan rises, deeply discouraged.*

CHARLES [*continuing heedlessly*]   A healthy life, you know.

DUNOIS   But a dull one.

BLUEBEARD   You will find the petticoats tripping you up after leaving them off for so long.

LA HIRE   You will miss the fighting. It's a bad habit, but a grand one, and the hardest of all to break yourself of.

CHARLES [*anxiously*]   Still, we dont want you to stay if you would really rather go home.

JOAN [*bitterly*]   I know well that none of you will be sorry to see me go. [*She turns her shoulder to Charles and walks past him to the more congenial neighborhood of Dunois and La Hire.*]

LA HIRE   Well, I shall be able to swear when I want to. But I shall miss you at times.

JOAN   La Hire: in spite of all your sins and swears we shall meet in heaven; for I love you as I love Pitou, my old sheep dog. Pitou could kill a wolf. You will kill the English wolves until they go back to their country and become good dogs of God, will you not?

LA HIRE   You and I together: yes.

JOAN   No: I shall last only a year from the beginning.

ALL THE OTHERS   What!

JOAN   I know it somehow.

DUNOIS   Nonsense!

JOAN   Jack: do you think you will be able to drive them out?

DUNOIS [*with quiet conviction*]   Yes: I shall drive them out. They beat us because we thought battles were tournaments and ransom markets. We played the fool while the goddams took war seriously. But I have learnt my lesson, and taken their measure. They have no roots here. I have beaten them before; and I shall beat them again.

JOAN   You will not be cruel to them, Jack?

DUNOIS   The goddams will not yield to tender handling. We did not begin it.

JOAN [*suddenly*]   Jack: before I go home, let us take Paris.

CHARLES [*terrified*]   Oh no no. We shall lose everything we have gained. Oh dont let us have any more fighting. We can make a very good treaty with the Duke of Burgundy.

JOAN   Treaty! [*She stamps with impatience.*]

CHARLES   Well, why not, now that I am crowned and anointed? Oh, that oil! *The Archbishop comes from the vestry, and joins the group between Charles and Bluebeard.*

CHARLES   Archbishop: The Maid wants to start fighting again.

THE ARCHBISHOP   Have we ceased fighting, then? Are we at peace?

CHARLES   No: I suppose not; but let us be content with what we have done. Let us make a treaty. Our luck is too good to last; and now is our chance to stop before it turns.

JOAN   Luck! God has fought for us; and you call it luck! And you would stop while there are still Englishmen on this holy earth of dear France!

THE ARCHBISHOP [*sternly*]   Maid: the king addressed himself to me, not to you. You forget yourself. You very often forget yourself.

JOAN [*unabashed, and rather roughly*]   Then speak, you; and tell him that it is not God's will that he should take his hand from the plough.

THE ARCHBISHOP   If I am not so glib with the name of God as you are, it is because I interpret His will with the authority of the Church and of my sacred office. When you first came you respected it, and would not have dared to speak as you are now speaking. You came clothed with the virtue of humility; and because God blessed your enterprises accordingly, you have stained yourself with the sin of pride. The old Greek tragedy is rising among us. It is the chastisement of hubris.[3]

CHARLES   Yes: she thinks she knows better than everyone else.

JOAN   [distressed, but naïvely incapable of seeing the effect she is producing] But I do know better than any of you seem to. And I am not proud: I never speak unless I know I am right.

BLUEBEARD   Ha ha!
                        [exclaiming together]
CHARLES   Just so.

THE ARCHBISHOP   How do you know you are right?

JOAN   I always know. My voices—

CHARLES   Oh, your voices, your voices. Why dont the voices come to me? I am king, not you.

JOAN   They do come to you; but you do not hear them. You have not sat in the field in the evening listening for them. When the angelus rings you cross yourself and have done with it; but if you prayed from your heart, and listened to the thrilling of the bells in the air after they stop ringing, you would hear the voices as well as I do. [turning brusquely from him] But what voices do you need to tell you what the blacksmith can tell you: that you must strike while the iron is hot? I tell you we must make a dash at Compiègne and relieve it as we relieved Orleans. Then Paris will open its gates; or if not, we will break through them. What is your crown worth without your capital?

LA HIRE   That is what I say too. We shall go through them like a red hot shot through a pound of butter. What do you say, Bastard?

DUNOIS   If our cannon balls were all as hot as your head, and we had enough of them, we should conquer the earth, no doubt. Pluck and impetuousity are good servants in war, but bad masters: they have delivered us into the hands of the English every time we have trusted to them. We never know when we are beaten: that is our great fault.

JOAN   You never know when you are victorious: that is a worse fault. I shall have to make you carry looking-glasses in battle to convince you that the English have not cut off all your noses. You would have been besieged in Orleans still, you and your councils of war, if I had not made you attack. You should always attack; and if you only hold on long enough the enemy will stop first. You dont know how to begin a battle; and you dont know how to use your cannons. And I do.

    She squats down on the flags with crossed ankles, pouting.

DUNOIS   I know what you think of us, General Joan.

JOAN   Never mind that, Jack. Tell them what you think of me.

DUNOIS   I think that God was on your side; for I have not forgotten how the wind changed, and how our hearts changed when you came; and by

3. The particular kind of noble pride associated with the hamartia or flaw in the Greek tragic hero. Needless to say, it is a comic anachronism on Shaw's part, as the archbishop would have known no Greek, nor anything of its tragedy.

my faith I shall never deny that it was in your sign that we conquered. But I tell you as a soldier that God is no man's daily drudge, and no maid's either. If you are worthy of it He will sometimes snatch you out of the jaws of death and set you on your feet again; but that is all: once on your feet you must fight with all your might and all your craft. For He has to be fair to your enemy too: dont forget that. Well, He set us on our feet through you at Orleans; and the glory of it has carried us through a few good battles here to the coronation. But if we presume on it further, and trust to God to do the work we should do ourselves, we shall be defeated; and serve us right!

JOAN   But—

DUNOIS   Sh! I have not finished. Do not think, any of you, that these victories of ours were won without generalship. King Charles: you have said no word in your proclamations of my part in this campaign; and I make no complaint of that; for the people will run after The Maid and her miracles and not after the Bastard's hard work finding troops for her and feeding them. But I know exactly how much God did for us through The Maid, and how much He left me to do by my own wits; and I tell you that your little hour of miracles is over, and that from this time on he who plays the war game best will win—if the luck is on his side.

JOAN   Ah! if, if if, if! If ifs and ands were pots and pans there'd be no need of tinkers. [rising impetuously] I tell you, Bastard, your art of war is no use, because your knights are no good for real fighting. War is only a game to them, like tennis and all their other games: they make rules as to what is fair and what is not fair, and heap armor on themselves and on their poor horses to keep out the arrows; and when they fall they cant get up, and have to wait for their squires to come and lift them to arrange about the ransom with the man that has poked them off their horse. Cant you see that all the like of that is gone by and done with? What use is armor against gunpowder? And if it was, do you think men that are fighting for France and for God will stop to bargain about ransoms, as half your knights live by doing? No: they will fight to win; and they will give up their lives out of their own hand into the hand of God when they go into battle, as I do. Common folks understand this. They cannot afford armor and cannot pay ransoms; but they followed me half naked into the moat and up the ladder and over the wall. With them it is my life or thine, and God defend the right! You may shake your head, Jack; and Bluebeard may twirl his billygoat's beard and cock his nose at me; but remember the day your knights and captains refused to follow me to attack the English at Orleans! You locked the gates to keep me in; and it was the townsfolk and the common people that followed me, and forced the gate, and shewed you the way to fight in earnest.

BLUEBEARD   [offended]   Not content with being Pope Joan,[4] you must be Caesar and Alexander as well.

4. A widely believed medieval legend held that, about the year 1100, a woman in male disguise, after a career as a scholar, became pope; after reigning for two years, she gave birth to a child during a procession and died immediately thereafter.

THE ARCHBISHOP   Pride will have a fall, Joan.

JOAN   Oh, never mind whether it is pride or not: is it true? is it commonsense?

LA HIRE   It is true. Half of us are afraid of having our handsome noses broken; and the other half are out for paying off their mortgages. Let her have her way, Dunois: she does not know everything; but she has got hold of the right end of the stick. Fighting is not what it was; and those who know least about it often make the best job of it.

DUNOIS   I know all that. I do not fight in the old way: I have learnt the lesson of Agincourt, of Poitiers and Crecy.[5] I know how many lives any move of mine will cost; and if the move is worth the cost I make it and pay the cost. But Joan never counts the cost at all: she goes ahead and trusts to God: she thinks she has God in her pocket. Up to now she has had the numbers on her side; and she has won. But I know Joan; and I see that some day she will go ahead when she has only ten men to do the work of a hundred. And then she will find that God is on the side of the big battalions. She will be taken by the enemy. And the lucky man that makes the capture will receive sixteen thousand pounds from the Earl of Ouareek.[6]

JOAN [*flattered*]   Sixteen thousand pounds! Eh, laddie, have they offered that for me? There cannot be so much money in the world.

DUNOIS   There is, in England. And now tell me, all of you, which of you will lift a finger to save Joan once the English have got her? I speak first, for the army. The day after she has been dragged from her horse by a goddam or a Burgundian, and he is not struck dead: the day after she is locked in a dungeon, and the bars and bolts do not fly open at the touch of St Peter's angel: the day when the enemy finds out that she is as vulnerable as I am and not a bit more invincible, she will not be worth the life of a single soldier to us; and I will not risk that life, much as I cherish her as a companion-in-arms.

JOAN   I dont blame you, Jack: you are right. I am not worth one soldier's life if God lets me be beaten; but France may think me worth my ransom after what God has done for her through me.

CHARLES   I tell you I have no money; and this coronation, which is all your fault, has cost me the last farthing I can borrow.

JOAN   The Church is richer than you. I put my trust in the Church.

THE ARCHBISHOP   Woman: they will drag you through the streets, and burn you as a witch.

JOAN [*running to him*]   Oh, my lord, do not say that. It is impossible. I a witch!

THE ARCHBISHOP   Peter Cauchon knows his business. The University of Paris has burnt a woman for saying that what you have done was well done, and according to God.

JOAN [*bewildered*]   But why? What sense is there in it? What I have done is according to God. They could not burn a woman for speaking the truth.

THE ARCHBISHOP   They did.

5. Major English victories in the Hundred Years' War.
6. An unnecessary French phonetic representation of "Warwick"; since Dunois is presumably speaking standard stage British, this is almost silly. But Shaw was a spelling crank, and this may be in the background.

JOAN   But you know that she was speaking the truth. You would not let them burn me.

THE ARCHBISHOP   How could I prevent them?

JOAN   You would speak in the name of the Church. You are a great prince of the Church. I would go anywhere with your blessing to protect me.

THE ARCHBISHOP   I have no blessing for you while you are proud and disobedient.

JOAN   Oh, why will you go on saying things like that? I am not proud and disobedient. I am a poor girl, and so ignorant that I do not know A from B. How could I be proud? And how can you say that I am disobedient when I always obey my voices, because they come from God.

THE ARCHBISHOP   The voice of God on earth is the voice of the Church Militant; and all the voices that come to you are the echoes of your own wilfulness.

JOAN   It is not true.

THE ARCHBISHOP   [*flushing angrily*]   You tell the Archbishop in his cathedral that he lies; and yet you say you are not proud and disobedient.

JOAN   I never said you lied. It was you that as good as said my voices lied. When have they ever lied? If you will not believe in them: even if they are only the echoes of my own commonsense, are they not always right? and are not your earthly counsels always wrong?

THE ARCHBISHOP   [*indignantly*]   It is a waste of time admonishing you.

CHARLES   It always comes back to the same thing. She is right; and everyone else is wrong.

THE ARCHBISHOP   Take this as your last warning. If you perish through setting your private judgment above the instructions of your spiritual directors, the Church disowns you, and leaves you to whatever fate your presumption may bring upon you. The Bastard has told you that if you persist in setting up your military conceit above the counsels of your commanders—

DUNOIS   [*interposing*]   To put it quite exactly, if you attempt to relieve the garrison in Compiègne without the same superiority in numbers you had at Orleans—

THE ARCHBISHOP   The army will disown you, and will not rescue you. And His Majesty the King has told you that the throne has not the means of ransoming you.

CHARLES   Not a penny.

THE ARCHBISHOP   You stand alone: absolutely alone, trusting to your own conceit, your own ignorance, your own headstrong presumption, your own impiety in hiding all these sins under the cloak of a trust in God. When you pass through these doors into the sunlight, the crowd will cheer you. They will bring you their little children and their invalids to heal: they will kiss your hands and feet, and do what they can, poor simple souls, to turn your head, and madden you with the self-confidence that is leading you to your destruction. But you will be none the less alone: they cannot save you. We and we only can stand between you and the stake at which our enemies have burnt that wretched woman in Paris.

JOAN   [*her eyes skyward*]   I have better friends and better counsel than yours.

THE ARCHBISHOP I see that I am speaking in vain to a hardened heart. You reject our protection, and are determined to turn us all against you. In future, then, fend for yourself; and if you fail, God have mercy on your soul.

DUNOIS That is the truth, Joan. Heed it.

JOAN Where would you all have been now if I had heeded that sort of truth? There is no help, no counsel, in any of you. Yes: I am alone on earth: I have always been alone. My father told my brothers to drown me if I would not stay to mind his sheep while France was bleeding to death: France might perish if only our lambs were safe. I thought France would have friends at the court of the king of France; and I find only wolves fighting for pieces of her poor torn body. I thought God would have friends everywhere, because He is the friend of everyone; and in my innocence I believed that you who now cast me out would be like strong towers to keep harm from me. But I am wiser now; and nobody is any the worse for being wiser. Do not think you can frighten me by telling me that I am alone. France is alone; and God is alone; and what is my loneliness before the loneliness of my country and my God? I see now that the loneliness of God is His strength: what would He be if He listened to your jealous little counsels? Well, my loneliness shall be my strength too; it is better to be alone with God; His friendship will not fail me, nor His counsel, nor His love. In His strength I will dare, and dare, and dare, until I die. I will go out now to the common people, and let the love in their eyes comfort me for the hate in yours. You will all be glad to see me burnt; but if I go through the fire I shall go through it to their hearts for ever and ever. And so, God be with me!

She goes from them. They stare after her in glum silence for a moment. Then Gilles de Rais twirls his beard.

BLUEBEARD You know, the woman is quite impossible. I dont dislike her, really; but what are you to do with such a character?

DUNOIS As God is my judge, if she fell into the Loire I would jump in in full armor to fish her out. But if she plays the fool at Compiègne, and gets caught, I must leave her to her doom.

LA HIRE Then you had better chain me up; for I could follow her to hell when the spirit rises in her like that.

THE ARCHBISHOP She disturbs my judgment too: there is a dangerous power in her outbursts. But the pit is open at her feet; and for good or evil we cannot turn her from it.

CHARLES If only she would keep quiet, or go home!

They follow her dispiritedly.

Scene VI

Rouen, 30th May 1431. A great stone hall in the castle, arranged for a trial-at-law, but not a trial-by-jury, the court being the Bishop's court with the Inquisition participating: hence there are two raised chairs side by side for the Bishop and the Inquisitor as judges. Rows of chairs radiating from them at an obtuse angle are for the canons, the doctors of law and theology, and the Dominican monks, who act as assessors. In the angle is a table for the scribes, with stools.

There is also a heavy rough wooden stool for the prisoner. All these are at the inner end of the hall. The further end is open to the courtyard through a row of arches. The court is shielded from the weather by screens and curtains.

Looking down the great hall from the middle of the inner end, the judicial chairs and scribes' table are to the right. The prisoner's stool is to the left. There are arched doors right and left. It is a fine sunshiny May morning.

Warwick comes in through the arched doorway on the judges' side, followed by his page.

THE PAGE [*pertly*]   I suppose your lordship is aware that we have no business here. This is an ecclesiastical court; and we are only the secular arm.

WARWICK   I am aware of that fact. Will it please your impudence to find the Bishop of Beauvais for me, and give him a hint that he can have a word with me here before the trial, if he wishes?

THE PAGE [*going*]   Yes, my lord.

WARWICK   And mind you behave yourself. Do not address him as Pious Peter.

THE PAGE   No, my lord. I shall be kind to him, because, when The Maid is brought in, Pious Peter will have to pick a peck of pickled pepper.

> *Cauchon enters through the same door with a Dominican monk and a canon, the latter carrying a brief.*

THE PAGE   The Right Reverend his lordship the Bishop of Beauvais. And two other reverend gentlemen.

WARWICK   Get out; and see that we are not interrupted.

THE PAGE   Right, my lord [*He vanishes airily.*]

CAUCHON   I wish your lordship good-morrow.

WARWICK   Good-morrow to your lordship. Have I had the pleasure of meeting your friends before? I think not.

CAUCHON [*introducing the monk, who is on his right*]   This, my lord, is Brother John Lemaître, of the order of St Dominic. He is acting as deputy for the Chief Inquisitor into the evil of heresy in France. Brother John: the Earl of Warwick.

WARWICK   Your Reverence is most welcome. We have no Inquisitor in England, unfortunately; though we miss him greatly, especially on occasions like the present.

> *The Inquisitor smiles patiently, and bows. He is a mild elderly gentleman, but has evident reserves of authority and firmness.*

CAUCHON [*introducing the canon, who is on his left*]   This gentleman is Canon John D'Estivet, of the Chapter of Bayeux. He is acting as Promoter.

WARWICK   Promoter?

CAUCHON   Prosecutor, you would call him in civil law.

WARWICK   Ah! prosecutor. Quite, quite. I am very glad to make your acquaintance, Canon D'Estivet.

> *D'Estivet bows. [He is on the young side of middle age, well mannered, but vulpine beneath his veneer.]*

WARWICK   May I ask what stage the proceedings have reached? It is now more than nine months since The Maid was captured at Compiègne by the Burgundians. It is fully four months since I bought her from the Burgundians for a very handsome sum, solely that she might be brought to justice. It is very nearly three months since I delivered her up to you, my Lord Bishop, as a person suspected of heresy. May I suggest that you are taking a rather unconscionable time to make up your minds about a very plain case? Is this trial never going to end?

THE INQUISITOR [*smiling*]   It has not yet begun, my lord.

WARWICK   Not yet begun! Why, you have been at it eleven weeks!

CAUCHON   We have not been idle, my lord. We have held fifteen examinations of The Maid: six public and nine private.

THE INQUISITOR [*always patiently smiling*]   You see, my lord, I have been present at only two of these examinations. They were proceedings of the Bishop's court solely, and not of the Holy Office. I have only just decided to associate myself—that is, to associate the Holy Inquisition —with the Bishop's court. I did not at first think that this was a case of heresy at all. I regarded it as a political case, and The Maid as a prisoner of war. But having now been present at two of the examinations, I must admit that this seems to be one of the gravest cases of heresy within my experience. Therefore everything is now in order, and we proceed to trial this morning. [*He moves towards the judicial chairs.*]

CAUCHON   This moment, if your lordship's convenience allows.

WARWICK [*graciously*]   Well, that is good news, gentlemen. I will not attempt to conceal from you that our patience was becoming strained.

CAUCHON   So I gathered from the threats of your soldiers to drown those of our people who favor The Maid.

WARWICK   Dear me! At all events their intentions were friendly to you, my lord.

CAUCHON [*sternly*]   I hope not. I am determined that the woman shall have a fair hearing. The justice of the Church is not a mockery, my lord.

THE INQUISITOR [*returning*]   Never has there been a fairer examination within my experience, my lord. The Maid needs no lawyers to take her part: she will be tried by her most faithful friends, all ardently desirous to save her soul from perdition.

D'ESTIVET   Sir: I am the Promoter; and it has been my painful duty to present the case against the girl; but believe me, I would throw up my case today and hasten to her defence if I did not know that men far my superiors in learning and piety, in eloquence and persuasiveness, have been sent to reason with her, to explain to her the danger she is running, and the ease with which she may avoid it. [*suddenly bursting into forensic eloquence, to the disgust of Cauchon and the Inquisitor, who have listened to him so far with patronizing approval*] men have dared to say that we are acting from hate; but God is our witness that they lie. Have we tortured her? No. Have we ceased to exhort her; to implore her to have pity on herself; to come to the bosom of her Church as an erring but beloved child? Have we—

CAUCHON [*interrupting drily*]   Take care, Canon. All that you say is true; but if you make his lordship believe it I will not answer for your life, and hardly for my own.

WARWICK [*deprecating, but by no means denying*]   Oh, my lord, you are very hard on us poor English. But we certainly do not share your pious desire to save The Maid: in fact I tell you now plainly that her death is a political necessity which I regret but cannot help. If the Church lets her go—

CAUCHON [*with fierce and menacing pride*] If the Church lets her go, woe to the man, were he the Emperor himself, who dares lay a finger on her! The Church is not subject to political necessity, my lord.

THE INQUISITOR [*interposing smoothly*] You need have no anxiety about the result, my lord. You have an invincible ally in the matter: one who is far more determined than you that she shall burn.

WARWICK   And who is this very convenient partisan, may I ask?

THE INQUISITOR   The Maid herself. Unless you put a gag in her mouth you cannot prevent her from convicting herself ten times over every time she opens it.

D'ESTIVET   That is perfectly true, my lord. My hair bristles on my head when I hear so young a creature utter such blasphemies.

WARWICK   Well, by all means do your best for her if you are quite sure it will be of no avail. [*looking hard at Cauchon*] I should be sorry to have to act without the blessing of the Church.

CAUCHON [*with a mixture of cynical admiration and contempt*] And yet they say Englishmen are hypocrites! You play for your side, my lord, even at the peril of your soul. I cannot but admire such devotion; but I dare not go so far myself. I fear damnation.

WARWICK   If we feared anything we could never govern England, my lord. Shall I send your people in to you?

CAUCHON   Yes: it will be very good of your lordship to withdraw and allow the court to assemble.

   Warwick turns on his heel, and goes out through the courtyard. Cauchon takes one of the judicial seats; and D'Estivet sits at the scribes' table, studying his brief.

CAUCHON [*casually, as he makes himself comfortable*] What scoundrels these English nobles are!

THE INQUISITOR [*taking the other judicial chair on Cauchon's left*] All secular power makes men scoundrels. They are not trained for the work; and they have not the Apostolic Succession. Our own nobles are just as bad.

   The Bishop's assessors hurry into the hall, headed by Chaplain de Stogumber and Canon de Courcelles, a young priest of 30. The scribes sit at the table, leaving a chair vacant opposite D'Estivet. Some of the assessors take their seats: other stand chatting, waiting for the proceedings to begin formally. De Stogumber, aggrieved and obstinate, will not take his seat: neither will the Canon, who stands on his right.

CAUCHON   Good morning, Master de Stogumber. [*to the Inquisitor*] Chaplain to the Cardinal of England.

THE CHAPLAIN [*correcting him*] Of Winchester, my lord. I have to make a protest, my lord.

CAUCHON   You make a great many.

THE CHAPLAIN   I am not without support, my lord. Here is Master de Courcelles, Canon of Paris, who associates himself with me in my protest.

CAUCHON   Well, what is the matter?

THE CHAPLAIN [*sulkily*]   Speak you, Master de Courcelles, since I do not seem to enjoy his lordship's confidence. [*He sits down in dudgeon next to Cauchon, on his right.*]

COURCELLES   My lord: we have been at great pains to draw up an indictment of The Maid on sixty-four counts. We are now told that they have been reduced, without consulting us.

THE INQUISITOR   Master de Courcelles: I am the culprit. I am overwhelmed with admiration for the zeal displayed in your sixty-four counts; but in accusing a heretic, as in other things, enough is enough. Also you must remember that all the members of the court are not so subtle and profound as you, and that some of your very great learning might appear to them to be very great nonsense. Therefore I have thought it well to have your sixty-four articles cut down to twelve—

COURCELLES [*thunderstruck*]   Twelve!!!

THE INQUISITOR   Twelve will, believe me, be quite enough for your purpose.

THE CHAPLAIN   But some of the most important points have been reduced almost to nothing. For instance, The Maid has actually declared that the blessed saints Margaret and Catherine, and the holy Archangel Michael, spoke to her in French. That is a vital point.

THE INQUISITOR   You think, doubtless, that they should have spoken in Latin?

CAUCHON   No: he thinks they should have spoken in English.

THE CHAPLAIN   Naturally, my lord.

THE INQUISITOR   Well, as we are all here agreed, I think, that these voices of The Maid are the voices of evil spirits tempting her to her damnation, it would not be very courteous to you, Master de Stogumber, or to the King of England, to assume that English is the devil's native language. So let it pass. The matter is not wholly omitted from the twelve articles. Pray take your places, gentlemen; and let us proceed to business.

All who have not taken their seats, do so.

THE CHAPLAIN   Well, I protest. That is all.

COURCELLES   I think it hard that all our work should go for nothing. It is only another example of the diabolical influence which this woman exercises over the court. [*He takes his chair, which is on the Chaplain's right.*]

CAUCHON   Do you suggest that I am under diabolical influence?

COURCELLES   I suggest nothing, my lord. But it seems to me that there is a conspiracy here to hush up the fact that The Maid stole the Bishop of Senlis's horse.

CAUCHON [*keeping his temper with difficulty*]   This is not a police court. Are we to waste our time on such rubbish?

COURCELLES [*rising, shocked*]   My lord: do you call the Bishop's horse rubbish?

THE INQUISITOR [*blandly*]   Master de Courcelles: The Maid alleges that she paid handsomely for the Bishop's horse, and that if he did not get the money the fault was not hers. As that may be true, the point is one on which The Maid may well be acquitted.

COURCELLES   Yes, if it were an ordinary horse. But the Bishop's horse! how can she be acquitted for that? [*He sits down again, bewildered and discouraged.*]

THE INQUISITOR   I submit to you, with great respect, that if we persist in trying The Maid on trumpery issues on which we may have to declare her innocent, she may escape us on the great main issue of heresy, on which she seems so far to insist on her own guilt. I will ask you, therefore, to say nothing, when The Maid is brought before us, of these stealings of horses, and dancings round fairy trees with the village children, and prayings at haunted wells, and a dozen other things which you were diligently inquiring into until my arrival. There is not a village girl in France against whom you could not prove such things: they all dance around haunted trees, and pray at magic wells. Some of them would steal the Pope's horse if they got the chance. Heresy, gentlemen, heresy is the charge we have to try. The detection and suppression of heresy is my peculiar business: I am here as an inquisitor, not as an ordinary magistrate. Stick to the heresy, gentlemen; and leave the other matters alone.

CAUCHON   I may say that we have sent to the girl's village to make inquiries about her, and there is practically nothing serious against her.

THE CHAPLAIN   [rising and clamoring together]   Nothing serious, my lord—
COURCELLES   What! The fairy tree not—

CAUCHON [out of patience]   Be silent, gentlemen; or speak one at a time. *Courcelles collapses into his chair, intimidated.*

THE CHAPLAIN [sulkily resuming his seat]   That is what The Maid said to us last Friday.

CAUCHON   I wish you had followed her counsel, sir. When I say nothing serious, I mean nothing that men of sufficiently large mind to conduct an inquiry like this would consider serious. I agree with my colleague the Inquisitor that it is on the count of heresy that we must proceed.

LADVENU [a young but ascetically fine-drawn Dominican who is sitting next Courcelles, on his right]   But is there any great harm in the girl's heresy? Is it not merely her simplicity? Many saints have said as much as Joan.

THE INQUISITOR [dropping his blandness and speaking very gravely]   Brother Martin: if you had seen what I have seen of heresy, you would not think it a light thing even in its most apparently harmless and even lovable and pious origins. Heresy begins with people who are to all appearance better than their neighbors. A gentle and pious girl, or a young man who has obeyed the command of our Lord by giving all his riches to the poor, and putting on the garb of poverty, the life of austerity, and the rule of humility and charity, may be the founder of a heresy that will wreck both Church and Empire if not ruthlessly stamped out in time. The records of the Holy Inquisition are full of histories we dare not give to the world, because they are beyond the belief of honest men and innocent women; yet they all began with saintly simpletons. I have seen this again and again. Mark what I say: the woman who quarrels with her clothes, and puts on the dress of a man, is like the man who throws off his fur gown and dresses like John the Baptist: they are followed, as surely as the night follows the day, by bands of wild women and men who refuse to wear any clothes at all. When maids will neither marry nor take regular vows, and men reject marriage and exalt their lusts into divine inspirations, then, as surely as the summer follows the spring, they begin with polygamy, and end by incest. Heresy at first seems innocent and even laudable; but it ends in such a monstrous horror of unnatural wickedness that the most tender-hearted among you, if you saw it at work as I have seen it, would clamor against the mercy of the Church in dealing with it. For two hundred years the Holy Office has striven with these diabolical madnesses; and it knows that they begin always by vain and ignorant persons setting up their own judgment against the Church, and taking it upon themselves to be the interpreters of God's will. You must not fall into the common error of mistaking these simpletons for liars and hypocrites. They believe honestly and sincerely that their diabolical inspiration is divine. Therefore you must be on your guard against your natural compassion. You are all, I hope, merciful men: how else could you have devoted your lives to the service of our gentle Savior? You are going to see before you a young girl, pious and chaste; for I must tell you, gentlemen, that the things said of her by our English friends are supported by no evidence, whilst there is abundant testimony that her excesses have been excesses of religion and charity and not of worldliness and wantonness. This girl is not one of those whose hard features are the sign of hard hearts, and whose brazen looks and lewd demeanor condemn them before they are accused. The devilish pride that has led her into her present peril has left no mark on her countenance. Strange as it may seem to you, it has even left no mark on her character outside those special matters in which she is proud; so that you will see a diabolical pride and a natural humility seated side by side in the selfsame soul. Therefore be on your guard. God forbid that I should tell you to harden your hearts; for her punishment if we condemn her will be so cruel that we should forfeit our own hope of divine mercy were there one grain of malice against her in our hearts. But if you hate cruelty—and if any man here does not hate it I command him on his soul's salvation to quit this holy court— I say, if you hate cruelty, remember that nothing is so cruel in its consequences as the toleration of heresy. Remember also that no court of law can be so cruel as the common people are to those whom they suspect of heresy. The heretic in the hands of the Holy Office is safe from violence, is assured of a fair trial, and cannot suffer death, even when guilty, if repentance follows sin. Innumerable lives of heretics have been saved because the Holy Office has taken them out of the hands of the people, and because the people have yielded them up, knowing that the Holy Office would deal with them. Before the Holy Inquisition existed, and even now when its officers are not within reach, the unfortunate wretch suspected of heresy, perhaps quite ignorantly and unjustly, is stoned, torn in pieces, drowned, burned in his house with all his innocent children, without a trial, unshriven, unburied save as a dog is buried: all of them deeds hateful to God and most cruel to man. Gentlemen: I am compassionate by nature as well as by my profession; and though the work I have to do may seem cruel to those who do not know how much more cruel it would be to leave it undone, I would go to the stake myself sooner than do it if I did not know its righteousness, its necessity, its essential mercy. I ask you to address yourself to this trial in that conviction. Anger is a bad counsellor: cast out anger. Pity is sometimes worse: cast out pity. But do not cast out mercy. Remember only that justice comes first. Have you anything to say, my lord, before we proceed to trial?

CAUCHON You have spoken for me, and spoken better than I could. I do not see how any sane man could disagree with a word that has fallen from you. But this I will add. The crude heresies of which you have told us are horrible; but their horror is like that of the black death: they rage for a while and then die out, because sound and sensible men will not under any incitement be reconciled to nakedness and incest and polygamy and the like. But we are confronted today throughout Europe with a heresy that is spreading among men not weak in mind nor diseased in brain: nay, the stronger the mind, the more obstinate the heretic. It is neither discredited by fantastic extremes nor corrupted by the common lusts of the flesh; but it, too, sets up the private judgment of the single erring mortal against the considered wisdom and experience of the Church. The mighty structure of Catholic Christendom will never be shaken by naked madmen or by the sins of Moab and Ammon.[1] But it may be betrayed from within, and brought to barbarous ruin and desolation, by this arch heresy which the English Commander calls Protestantism.[2]

THE ASSESSORS [whispering] Protestantism! What was that? What does the Bishop mean? Is it a new heresy? The English Commander, he said. Did you ever hear of Protestantism? etc., etc.

CAUCHON [continuing] And that reminds me. What provision has the Earl of Warwick made for the defence of the secular arm should The Maid prove obdurate, and the people be moved to pity her?

THE CHAPLAIN Have no fear on that score, my lord. The noble earl has eight hundred men-at-arms at the gates. She will not slip through our English fingers even if the whole city be on her side.

CAUCHON [revolted] Will you not add, God grant that she repent and purge her sin?

THE CHAPLAIN That does not seem to me to be consistent; but of course I agree with your lordship.

CAUCHON [giving him up with a shrug of contempt] The court sits.

THE INQUISITOR Let the accused be brought in.

LADVENU [calling] The accused. Let her be brought in.

Joan, chained by the ankles, is brought in through the arched door behind the prisoner's stool by a guard of English soldiers. With them

---

1. Pride and carnality, for which their destruction is elaborately prophesied in Jeremiah 48 and 49, among other places.

2. For the effect of this mild, anachronistic joke, the word should be pronounced "Protéstant-ism."

*is the Executioner and his assistants. They lead her to the prisoner's
stool, and place themselves behind it after taking off her chain. She
wears a page's black suit. Her long imprisonment and the strain of the
examinations which have preceded the trial have left their mark on
her; but her vitality still holds; she confronts the court unabashed,
without a trace of the awe which their formal solemnity seems to require
for the complete success of its impressiveness.*

THE INQUISITOR [*kindly*] Sit down, Joan. [*She sits on the prisoner's stool.*]
You look very pale today. Are you not well?

JOAN Thank you kindly: I am well enough. But the Bishop sent me some
carp; and it made me ill.

CAUCHON I am sorry. I told them to see that it was fresh.

JOAN You meant to be good to me, I know; but it is a fish that does not
agree with me. The English thought you were trying to poison me—

CAUCHON   What!
THE CHAPLAIN [*together*] No, my lord.

JOAN [*continuing*] They are determined that I shall be burnt as a witch;
and they sent their doctor to cure me; but he was forbidden to bleed
me because the silly people believe that a witch's witchery leaves her
if she is bled; so he only called me filthy names. Why do you leave
me in the hands of the English? I should be in the hands of the Church.
And why must I be chained by the feet to a log of wood? Are you
afraid I will fly away?

D'ESTIVET [*harshly*] Woman: it is not for you to question the court: it is for
us to question you.

COURCELLES When you were left unchained, did you not try to escape by
jumping from a tower sixty feet high? [3] If you cannot fly like a witch,
how is it that you are still alive?

JOAN I suppose because the tower was not so high then. It has grown higher
every day since you began asking me questions about it.

D'ESTIVET Why did you jump from the tower?

JOAN How do you know that I jumped?

D'ESTIVET You were found lying in the moat. Why did you leave the tower?

JOAN Why would anybody leave a prison if they could get out?

D'ESTIVET You tried to escape?

JOAN Of course I did; and not for the first time either. If you leave the door
of the cage open the bird will fly out.

D'ESTIVET [*rising*] That is a confessioin of heresy. I call the attention of the
court to it.

JOAN Heresy, he calls it! Am I a heretic because I try to escape from prison?

D'ESTIVET Assuredly, if you are in the hands of the Church, and you wilfully
take yourself out of its hands, you are deserting the Church; and that
is heresy.

JOAN It is great nonsense. Nobody could be such a fool as to think that.

D'ESTIVET You hear, my lord, how I am reviled in the execution of my duty
by this woman. [*He sits down indignantly.*]

3. At Beaurevoir Castle, when she heard that Compiègne (where she had been captured by
the Duke of Burgundy and sold to the English) would fall.

CAUCHON   I have warned you before, Joan, that you are doing yourself no good by these pert answers.

JOAN   But you will not talk sense to me. I am reasonable if you will be reasonable.

THE INQUISITOR [*interposing*]   This is not yet in order. You forget, Master Promoter, that the proceedings have not been formally opened. The time for questions is after she has sworn on the Gospels to tell us the whole truth.

JOAN   You say this to me every time. I have said again and again that I will tell you all that concerns this trial. But I cannot tell you the whole truth: God does not allow the whole truth to be told. You do not understand it when I tell it. It is an old saying that he who tells too much truth is sure to be hanged. I am weary of this argument: we have been over it nine times already. I have sworn as much as I will swear; and I will swear no more.

COURCELLES   My lord: she should be put to the torture.

THE INQUISITOR   You hear, Joan? That is what happens to the obdurate. Think before you answer. Has she been shewn the instruments?

THE EXECUTIONER   They are ready, my lord. She has seen them.

JOAN   If you tear me limb from limb until you separate my soul from my body you will get nothing out of me beyond what I have told you. What more is there to tell that you could understand? Besides, I cannot bear to be hurt; and if you hurt me I will say anything you like to stop the pain. But I will take it all back afterwards; so what is the use of it?

LADVENU   There is much in that. We should proceed mercifully.

COURCELLES   But the torture is customary.

THE INQUISITOR   It must not be applied wantonly. If the accused will confess voluntarily, then its use cannot be justified.

COURCELLES   But this is unusual and irregular. She refuses to take the oath.

LADVENU [*disgusted*]   Do you want to torture the girl for the mere pleasure of it?

COURCELLES [*bewildered*] [4]   But it is not a pleasure. It is the law. It is customary. It is always done.

THE INQUISITOR   That is not so, Master, except when the inquiries are carried on by people who do not know their legal business.

COURCELLES   But the woman is a heretic. I assure you it is always done.

CAUCHON [*decisively*]   It will not be done today if it is not necessary. Let there be an end of this. I will not have it said that we proceeded on forced confessions. We have sent our best preachers and doctors to this woman to exhort and implore her to save her soul and body from the fire: we shall not now send the executioner to thrust her into it.

COURCELLES   Your lordship is merciful, of course. But it is a great responsibility to depart from the usual practice.

JOAN   Thou art a rare noodle, Master. Do what was done last time is thy rule, eh?

---

4. He is truly bewildered, and not in the least hypocritical; only a writer of cheap propaganda would have distorted Joan's trial, or her accusers, into caricatures. The ironies of history are played out, Shaw has been saying, by everyone acting in good faith; if everyone were pragmatically hypocritical, nobody would ever have been burned for anything.

COURCELLES [*rising*]   Thou wanton: dost thou dare call me noodle?

THE INQUISITOR   Patience, Master, patience: I fear you will soon be only too terribly avenged.

COURCELLES [*mutters*]   Noodle indeed! [*He sits down, much discontented.*]

THE INQUISITOR   Meanwhile, let us not be moved by the rough side of a shepherd lass's tongue.

JOAN   Nay: I am no shepherd lass, though I have helped with the sheep like anyone else. I will do a lady's work in the house—spin or weave—against any woman in Rouen.

THE INQUISITOR   This is not a time for vanity, Joan. You stand in great peril.

JOAN   I know it: have I not been punished for my vanity? If I had not worn my cloth of gold surcoat in battle like a fool, that Burgundian soldier would never have pulled me backwards off my horse; and I should not have been here.

THE CHAPLAIN   If you are so clever at woman's work why do you not stay at home and do it?

JOAN   There are plenty of other women to do it; but there is nobody to do my work.

CAUCHON   Come! we are wasting time on trifles. Joan: I am going to put a most solemn question to you. Take care how you answer; for your life and salvation are at stake on it. Will you for all you have said and done, be it good or bad, accept the judgment of God's Church on earth? More especially as to the acts and words that are imputed to you in this trial by the Promoter here, will you submit your case to the inspired interpretation of the Church Militant?

JOAN   I am a faithful child of the Church. I will obey the Church—

CAUCHON [*hopefully leaning forward*]   You will?

JOAN   —provided it does not command anything impossible.

    Cauchon sinks back in his chair with a heavy sigh. The Inquisitor purses his lips and frowns. Ladvenu shakes his head pitifully.

D'ESTIVET   She imputes to the Church the error and folly of commanding the impossible.

JOAN   If you command me to declare that all that I have done and said, and all the visions and revelations I have had, were not from God, then that is impossible: I will not declare it for anything in the world. What God made me do I will never go back on; and what He has commanded or shall command I will not fail to do in spite of any man alive. That is what I mean by impossible. And in case the Church should bid me do anything contrary to the command I have from God, I will not consent to it, no matter what it may be.

THE ASSESSORS [*shocked and indignant*]   Oh! The Church contrary to God! What do you say now? Flat heresy. This is beyond everything, etc., etc.

D'ESTIVET [*throwing down his brief*]   My lord: do you need anything more than this?

CAUCHON   Woman: you have said enough to burn ten heretics. Will you not be warned? Will you not understand?

THE INQUISITOR   If the Church Militant tells you that your revelations and visions are sent by the devil to tempt you to your damnation, will you not believe that the Church is wiser than you?

JOAN   I believe that God is wiser than I; and it is His commands that I will do. All the things that you call my crimes have come to me by the command of God. I say that I have done them by the order of God: it is impossible for me to say anything else. If any Churchman says the contrary I shall not mind him: I shall mind God alone, whose command I always follow.

LADVENU [*pleading with her urgently*]   You do not know what you are saying, child. Do you want to kill yourself? Listen. Do you not believe that you are subject to the Church of God on earth?

JOAN   Yes. When have I ever denied it?

LADVENU   Good. That means, does it not, that you are subject to our Lord the Pope, to the cardinals, the archbishops, and the bishops for whom his lordship stands here today?

JOAN   God must be served first.

D'ESTIVET   Then your voices command you not to submit yourself to the Church Militant?

JOAN   My voices do not tell me to disobey the Church; but God must be served first.

CAUCHON   And you, and not the Church, are to be the judge?

JOAN   What other judgment can I judge by but my own?

THE ASSESSORS [*scandalized*]   Oh! [*They cannot find words.*]

CAUCHON   Out of your own mouth you have condemned yourself. We have striven for your salvation to the verge of sinning ourselves: we have opened the door to you again and again; and you have shut it in our faces and in the face of God. Dare you pretend, after what you have said, that you are in a state of grace?

JOAN   If I am not, may God bring me to it: if I am, may God keep me in it!

LADVENU   That is a very good reply, my lord.

COURCELLES   Were you in a state of grace when you stole the Bishop's horse?

CAUCHON [*rising in a fury*]   Oh, devil take the Bishop's horse and you too! We are here to try a case of heresy; and no sooner do we come to the root of the matter than we are thrown back by idiots who understand nothing but horses. [*Trembling with rage, he forces himself to sit down.*]

THE INQUISITOR   Gentlemen, gentlemen: in clinging to these small issues you are The Maid's best advocates. I am not surprised that his lordship has lost patience with you. What does the Promoter say? Does he press these trumpery matters?

D'ESTIVET   I am bound by my office to press everything; but when the woman confesses a heresy that must bring upon her the doom of excommunication, of what consequence is it that she has been guilty also of offences which expose her to minor penances? I share the impatience of his lordship as to these minor charges. Only, with great respect, I must emphasize the gravity of two very horrible and blasphemous crimes which she does not deny. First, she has intercourse with evil spirits, and is therefore a sorceress. Second, she wears men's clothes, which is indecent, unnatural, and abominable; and in spite of our most earnest remonstrances and entreaties, she will not change them even to receive the sacrament.

JOAN   Is the blessed St Catherine an evil spirit? Is St Margaret? Is Michael
the Archangel?

COURCELLES   How do you know that the spirit which appears to you is an
archangel? Does he not appear to you as a naked man?

JOAN   Do you think God cannot afford clothes for him?

*The assessors cannot help smiling, especially as the joke is against
Courcelles.*

LADVENU   Well answered, Joan.

THE INQUISITOR   It is, in effect, well answered. But no evil spirit would be
so simple as to appear to a young girl in a guise that would scandalize
her when he meant her to take him for a messenger from the Most
High. Joan: the Church instructs you that these apparitions are demons
seeking your soul's perdition. Do you accept the instruction of the
Church?

JOAN   I accept the messenger of God. How could any faithful believer in the
Church refuse him?

CAUCHON   Wretched woman: again I ask you, do you know what you are
saying?

THE INQUISITOR   You wrestle in vain with the devil for her soul, my lord: she
will not be saved. Now as to this matter of the man's dress. For the
last time, will you put off that impudent attire, and dress as becomes
your sex?

JOAN   I will not.

D'ESTIVET [*pouncing*]   The sin of disobedience, my lord.

JOAN [*distressed*]   But my voices tell me I must dress as a soldier.

LADVENU   Joan, Joan: does not that prove to you that the voices are the voices
of evil spirits? Can you suggest to us one good reason why an angel
of God should give you such shameless advice?

JOAN   Why, yes: what can be plainer commonsense? I was a soldier living
among soldiers. I am a prisoner guarded by soldiers. If I were to dress
as a woman they would think of me as a woman; and then what would
become of me? If I dress as a soldier they think of me as a soldier, and
I can live with them as I do at home with my brothers. That is why
St Catherine tells me I must not dress as a woman until she gives me
leave.

COURCELLES   When will she give you leave?

JOAN   When you take me out of the hands of the English soldiers. I have told
you that I should be in the hands of the Church, and not left night and
day with four soldiers of the Earl of Warwick. Do you want me to live
with them in petticoats?

LADVENU   My lord: what she says is, God knows, very wrong and shocking;
but there is a grain of worldly sense in it such as might impose on a
simple village maiden.

JOAN   If we were as simple in the village as you are in your courts and palaces,
there would soon be no wheat to make bread for you.

CAUCHON   That is the thanks you get for trying to save her, Brother Martin.

LADVENU   Joan: we are all trying to save you. His lordship is trying to save
you. The Inquisitor could not be more just to you if you were his own
daughter. But you are blinded by a terrible pride and self-sufficiency.

JOAN   Why do you say that? I have said nothing wrong. I cannot understand.

THE INQUISITOR   The blessed St Athanasius has laid it down in his creed [5] that those who cannot understand are damned. It is not enough to be simple. It is not enough even to be what simple people call good. The simplicity of a darkened mind is no better than the simplicity of a beast.

JOAN   There is great wisdom in the simplicity of a beast, let me tell you; and sometimes great foolishness in the wisdom of scholars.

LADVENU   We know that, Joan: we are not so foolish as you think us. Try to resist the temptation to make pert replies to us. Do you see that man who stands behind you [*He indicates the Executioner.*]?

JOAN   [*turning and looking at the man*]   Your torturer? But the Bishop said I was not to be tortured.

LADVENU   You are not to be tortured because you have confessed everything that is necessary to your condemnation. That man is not only the torturer: he is also the Executioner. Executioner: let The Maid hear your answers to my questions. Are you prepared for the burning of a heretic this day?

THE EXECUTIONER   Yes, Master.

LADVENU   Is the stake ready?

THE EXECUTIONER   It is. In the market-place. The English have built it too high for me to get near her and make the death easier. It will be a cruel death.

JOAN   [*horrified*]   But you are not going to burn me now?

THE INQUISITOR   You realize it at last.

LADVENU   There are eight hundred English soldiers waiting to take you to the market-place the moment the sentence of excommunication has passed the lips of your judges. You are within a few short moments of that doom.

JOAN   [*looking round desperately for rescue*]   Oh God!

LADVENU   Do not despair, Joan. The Church is merciful. You can save yourself.

JOAN   [*hopefully*]   Yes: my voices promised me I should not be burnt. St Catherine bade me be bold.

CAUCHON   Woman: are you quite mad? Do you not yet see that your voices have deceived you?

JOAN   Oh no: that is impossible.

CAUCHON   Impossible! They have led you straight to your excommunication, and to the stake which is there waiting for you.

LADVENU   [*pressing the point hard*]   Have they kept a single promise to you since you were taken at Compiègne? The devil has betrayed you. The Church holds out its arms to you.

JOAN   [*despairing*]   Oh, it is true: it is true: my voices have deceived me. I have been mocked by devils: my faith is broken. I have dared and dared; but only a fool will walk into a fire: God, who gave me my commonsense, cannot will me to do that.

5. St. Athanasius (296–373), Bishop of Alexandria, was probably not the author of the so-called Athanasian Creed, used only secondarily, in the Western churches, to the Apostles' and Nicene Creeds as professions of faith.

LADVENU   Now God be praised that He has saved you at the eleventh hour! [*He hurries to the vacant seat at the scribes' table, and snatches a sheet of paper, on which he sets to work writing eagerly.*]

CAUCHON   Amen!

JOAN   What must I do?

CAUCHON   You must sign a solemn recantation of your heresy.

JOAN   Sign? That means to write my name. I cannot write.

CAUCHON   You have signed many letters before.

JOAN   Yes; but someone held my hand and guided the pen. I can make my mark.

THE CHAPLAIN   [*who has been listening with growing alarm and indignation*] My lord: do you mean that you are going to allow this woman to escape us?

THE INQUISITOR   The law must take its course, Master de Stogumber. And you know the law.

THE CHAPLAIN   [*rising, purple with fury*]   I know that there is no faith in a Frenchman. [*tumult, which he shouts down*] I know what my lord the Cardinal of Winchester will say when he hears of this. I know what the Earl of Warwick will do when he learns that you intend to betray him. There are eight hundred men at the gate who will see that this abominable witch is burnt in spite of your teeth.

THE ASSESSORS   [*meanwhile*]   What is this? What did he say? He accuses us of treachery! This is past bearing. No faith in a Frenchman! Did you hear that? This is an intolerable fellow. Who is he? Is this what English Churchmen are like? He must be mad or drunk, etc., etc.

THE INQUISITOR   [*rising*]   Silence, pray! Gentlemen: pray silence! Master Chaplain: bethink you a moment of your holy office: of what you are, and where you are. I direct you to sit down.

THE CHAPLAIN   [*folding his arms doggedly, his face working convulsively*]   I will NOT sit down.

CAUCHON   Master Inquisitor: this man has called me a traitor to my face before now.

THE CHAPLAIN   So you are a traitor. You are all traitors. You have been doing nothing but begging this damnable witch on your knees to recant all through this trial.

THE INQUISITOR   [*placidly resuming his seat*]   If you will not sit, you must stand: that is all.

THE CHAPLAIN   I will NOT stand [*He flings himself back into his chair.*]

LADVENU   [*rising with the paper in his hand*]   My lord: here is the form of recantation for The Maid to sign.

CAUCHON   Read it to her.

JOAN   Do not trouble. I will sign it.

THE INQUISITOR   Woman: you must know what you are putting your hand to. Read it to her, Brother Martin. And let all be silent.

LADVENU   [*reading quietly*]   'I, Joan, commonly called The Maid, a miserable sinner, do confess that I have most grievously sinned in the following articles. I have pretended to have revelations from God and the angels and the blessed saints, and perversely rejected the Church's warnings that these were temptations by demons. I have blasphemed abominably by wearing an immodest dress, contrary to the Holy Scripture and the canons of the Church. Also I have clipped my hair in the style of a man, and, against all the duties which have made my sex specially acceptable in heaven, have taken up the sword, even to the shedding of human blood, inciting men to slay each other, invoking evil spirits to delude them, and stubbornly and most blasphemously imputing these sins to Almighty God. I confess to the sin of sedition, to the sin of idolatry, to the sin of disobedience, to the sin of pride, and to the sin of heresy. All of which sins I now renounce and abjure and depart from, humbly thanking you Doctors and Masters who have brought me back to the truth and into the grace of our Lord. And I will never return to my errors, but will remain in communion with our Holy Church and in obedience to our Holy Father the Pope of Rome. All this I swear by God Almighty and the Holy Gospels, in witness whereto I sign my name to this recantation.'

THE INQUISITOR   You understand this, Joan?

JOAN [*listless*]   It is plain enough, sir.

THE INQUISITOR   And it is true?

JOAN   It may be true. If it were not true, the fire would not be ready for me in the market-place.

LADVENU [*taking up his pen and a book, and going to her quickly lest she should compromise herself again*]   Come, child: let me guide your hand. Take the pen. [*She does so; and they begin to write, using the book as a desk*] J.E.H.A.N.E. So. Now make your mark by yourself.

JOAN [*makes her mark, and gives him back the pen, tormented by the rebellion of her soul against her mind and body*]   There!

LADVENU [*replacing the pen on the table, and handing the recantation to Cauchon with a reverence*]   Praise be to God, my brothers, the lamb has returned to the flock; and the shepherd rejoices in her more than in ninety and nine just persons. [*He returns to his seat*].

THE INQUISITOR [*taking the paper from Cauchon*]   We declare thee by this act set free from the danger of excommunication in which thou stoodest. [*He throws the paper down to the table.*]

JOAN   I thank you.

THE INQUISITOR   But because thou has sinned most presumptuously against God and the Holy Church, and that thou mayst repent thy errors in solitary contemplation, and be shielded from all temptation to return to them, we, for the good of thy soul, and for a penance that may wipe out thy sins and bring thee finally unspotted to the throne of grace, do condemn thee to eat the bread of sorrow and drink the water of affliction to the end of thy earthly days in perpetual imprisonment.

JOAN [*rising in consternation and terrible anger*]   Perpetual imprisonment! Am I not then to be set free?

LADVENU [*mildly shocked*]   Set free, child, after such wickedness as yours! What are you dreaming of?

JOAN   Give me that writing. [*She rushes to the table; snatches up the paper; and tears it into fragments.*] Light your fire: do you think I dread it as much as the life of a rat in a hole? My voices were right.

LADVENU   Joan! Joan!

JOAN   Yes: they told me you were fools [*the word gives great offence*], and that I was not to listen to your fine words nor trust to your charity. You promised me my life; but you lied [*indignant exclamations*]. You think that life is nothing but not being stone dead. It is not the bread and water I fear: I can live on bread: when have I asked for more? It is no hardship to drink water if the water be clean. Bread has no sorrow for me, and water no affliction. But to shut me from the light of the sky and the sight of the fields and flowers; to chain my feet so that I can never again ride with the soldiers nor climb the hills; to make me breathe foul damp darkness, and keep from me everything that brings me back to the love of God when your wickedness and foolishness tempt me to hate Him: all this is worse than the furnace in the Bible that was heated seven times. I could do without my warhorse; I could drag about in a skirt; I could let the banners and the trumpets and the knights and soldiers pass me and leave me behind as they leave the other women, if only I could still hear the wind in the trees, the larks in the sunshine, the young lambs crying through the healthy frost, and the blessed blessed church bells that send my angel voices floating to me on the wind. But without these things I cannot live; and by your wanting to take them away from me, or from any human creature, I know that your counsel is of the devil, and that mine is of God.

THE ASSESSORS [*in great commotion*]   Blasphemy! blasphemy! She is possessed. She said our counsel was of the devil. And hers of God. Monstrous! The devil is in our midst, etc., etc.

D'ESTIVET [*shouting above the din*]   She is a relapsed heretic, obstinate, incorrigible, and altogether unworthy of the mercy we have shewn her. I call for her excommunication.

THE CHAPLAIN [*to the Executioner*]   Light your fire, man. To the stake with her.

The Executioner and his assistants hurry out through the courtyard.

LADVENU   You wicked girl: if your counsel were of God would He not deliver you?

JOAN   His ways are not your ways. He wills that I go through the fire to His bosom; for I am His child, and you are not fit that I should live among you. That is my last word to you.

The soldiers seize her.

CAUCHON [*rising*]   Not yet.

They wait. There is a dead silence. Cauchon turns to the Inquisitor with an inquiring look. The Inquisitor nods affirmatively. They rise solemnly, and intone the sentence antiphonally.

CAUCHON   We decree that thou art a relapsed heretic.

THE INQUISITOR   Cast out from the unity of the Church.

CAUCHON   Sundered from her body.

THE INQUISITOR   Infected with the leprosy of heresy.

CAUCHON   A member of Satan.

THE INQUISITOR   We declare that thou must be excommunicate.

CAUCHON   And now we do cast thee out, segregate thee, and abandon thee to the secular power.

THE INQUISITOR   Admonishing the same secular power that it moderate its judgment of thee in respect of death and division of the limbs. [*He resumes his seat.*]

CAUCHON   And if any true sign of penitence appear in thee, to permit our Brother Martin to administer to thee the sacrament of penance.

THE CHAPLAIN   Into the fire with the witch [*He rushes at her, and helps the soldiers to push her out.*]

> *Joan is taken away through the courtyard. The assessors rise in disorder, and follow the soldiers, except Ladvenu, who has hidden his face in his hands.*

CAUCHON   [*rising again in the act of sitting down*]   No, no: this is irregular. The representative of the secular arm should be here to receive her from us.

THE INQUISITOR   [*also on his feet again*]   That man is an incorrigible fool.

CAUCHON   Brother Martin: see that everything is done in order.

LADVENU   My place is at her side, my lord. You must exercise your own authority. [*He hurries out.*]

CAUCHON   These English are impossible: they will thrust her straight into the fire. Look!

> *He points to the courtyard, in which the glow and flicker of fire can now be seen reddening the May daylight. Only the Bishop and the Inquisitor are left in the court.*

CAUCHON   [*turning to go*]   We must stop that.

THE INQUISITOR   [*calmly*]   Yes; but not too fast, my lord.

CAUCHON   [*halting*]   But there is not a moment to lose.

THE INQUISITOR   We have proceeded in perfect order. If the English choose to put themselves in the wrong, it is not our business to put them in the right. A flaw in the procedure may be useful later on: one never knows. And the sooner it is over, the better for that poor girl.

CAUCHON   [*relaxing*]   That is true. But I suppose we must see this dreadful thing through.

THE INQUISITOR   One gets used to it. Habit is everything. I am accustomed to the fire: it is soon over. But it is a terrible thing to see a young and innocent creature crushed between these mighty forces, the Church and the Law.

CAUCHON   You call her innocent!

THE INQUISITOR   Oh, quite innocent. What does she know of the Church and the Law? She did not understand a word we were saying. It is the ignorant who suffer. Come, or we shall be late for the end.

CAUCHON   [*going with him*]   I shall not be sorry if we are: I am not so accustomed as you.

> *They are going out when Warwick comes in, meeting them.*

WARWICK   Oh, I am intruding. I thought it was all over. [*He makes a feint of retiring.*]

CAUCHON   Do not go, my lord. It is all over.

THE INQUISITOR   The execution is not in our hands, my lord; but it is desirable that we should witness the end. So by your leave—[*He bows, and goes out through the courtyard.*]

CAUCHON There is some doubt whether your people have observed the forms of law, my lord.

WARWICK I am told that there is some doubt whether your authority runs in this city, my lord. It is not in your diocese. However, if you will answer for that I will answer for the rest.

CAUCHON It is to God that we both must answer. Good morning, my lord.

WARWICK My lord: good morning.

They look at one another for a moment with unconcealed hostility. Then Cauchon follows the Inquisitor out. Warwick looks round. Finding himself alone, he calls for attendance.

WARWICK Hallo: some attendance here! [*Silence*]. Hallo, there! [*Silence*]. Hallo! Brian, you young blackguard, where are you? [*Silence*]. Guard! [*Silence*]. They have all gone to see the burning: even that child.

The silence is broken by someone frantically howling and sobbing.

WARWICK What in the devil's name—?

The Chaplain staggers in from the courtyard like a demented creature, his face streaming with tears, making the piteous sounds that Warwick has heard. He stumbles to the prisoner's stool, and throws himself upon it with heartrending sobs.

WARWICK [*going to him and patting him on the shoulder*] What is it, Master John? What is the matter?

THE CHAPLAIN [*clutching at his hand*] My lord, my lord: for Christ's sake pray for my wretched guilty soul.

WARWICK [*soothing him*] Yes, yes: of course I will. Calmly, gently—

THE CHAPLAIN [*blubbering miserably*] I am not a bad man, my lord.

WARWICK No, no: not at all.

THE CHAPLAIN I meant no harm. I did not know what it would be like.

WARWICK [*hardening*] Oh! You saw it, then?

THE CHAPLAIN I did not know what I was doing. I am a hotheaded fool; and I shall be damned to all eternity for it.

WARWICK Nonsense! Very distressing, no doubt; but it was not your doing.

THE CHAPLAIN [*lamentably*] I let them do it. If I had known, I would have torn her from their hands. You dont know: you havnt seen: it is so easy to talk when you dont know. You madden yourself with words: you damn yourself because it feels grand to throw oil on the flaming hell of your own temper. But when it is brought home to you; when you see the thing you have done; when it is blinding your eyes, stifling your nostrils, tearing your heart, then—then—[*Falling on his knees*] O God, take away this sight from me! O Christ, deliver me from this fire that is consuming me! She cried to Thee in the midst of it: Jesus! Jesus! Jesus! She is in Thy bosom; and I am in hell for evermore.

WARWICK [*summarily hauling him to his feet*] Come come, man! you must pull yourself together. We shall have the whole town talking of this. [*He throws him not too gently into a chair at the table.*] If you have not the nerve to see these things, why do you not do as I do, and stay away?

THE CHAPLAIN [*bewildered and submissive*] She asked for a cross. A soldier gave her two sticks tied together. Thank God he was an Englishman!

I might have done it; but I did not: I am a coward, a mad dog, a fool. But he was an Englishman too.

WARWICK   The fool! they will burn him too if the priests get hold of him.

THE CHAPLAIN [*shaken with a convulsion*]   Some of the people laughed at her. They would have laughed at Christ. They were French people, my lord: I know they were French.

WARWICK   Hush! someone is coming. Control yourself.

Ladvenu comes back through the courtyard to Warwick's right hand, carrying a bishop's cross which he has taken from a church. He is very grave and composed.

WARWICK   I am informed that it is all over, Brother Martin.

LADVENU [*enigmatically*]   We do not know, my lord. It may have only just begun.

WARWICK   What does that mean, exactly?

LADVENU   I took this cross from the church for her that she might see it to the last: she had only two sticks that she put into her bosom. When the fire crept round us, and she saw that if I held the cross before her I should be burnt myself, she warned me to get down and save myself. My lord: a girl who could think of another's danger in such a moment was not inspired by the devil. When I had to snatch the cross from her sight, she looked up to heaven. And I do not believe that the heavens were empty. I firmly believe that her Savior appeared to her then in His tenderest glory. She called to Him and died. This is not the end for her, but the beginning.

WARWICK   I am afraid it will have a bad effect on the people.

LADVENU   It had, my lord, on some of them. I heard laughter. Forgive me for saying that I hope and believe it was English laughter.

THE CHAPLAIN [*rising frantically*]   No: it was not. There was only one Englishman there that disgraced his country; and that was the mad dog, de Stogumber. [*He rushes wildly out, shrieking*] Let them torture him. Let them burn him. I will go pray among her ashes. I am no better than Judas: I will hang myself.

WARWICK   Quick, Brother Martin: follow him: he will do himself some mischief. After him, quick.

Ladvenu hurries out, Warwick urging him. The Executioner comes in by the door behind the judges' chairs; and Warwick, returning, finds himself face to face with him.

WARWICK   Well, fellow: who are you?

THE EXECUTIONER [*with dignity*]   I am not addressed as fellow, my lord. I am the Master Executioner of Rouen: it is a highly skilled mystery. I am come to tell your lordship that your orders have been obeyed.

WARWICK   I crave your pardon, Master Executioner; and I will see that you lose nothing by having no relics to sell. I have your word, have I, that nothing remains, not a bone, not a nail, not a hair?

THE EXECUTIONER   Her heart would not burn, my lord; but everything that was left is at the bottom of the river. You have heard the last of her.

WARWICK [*with a wry smile, thinking of what Ladvenu said*]   The last of her? Hm! I wonder!

Epilogue

A restless fitfully windy night in June 1456, full of summer lightning after many days of heat. King Charles the Seventh of France, formerly Joan's Dauphin, now Charles the Victorious, aged 51, is in bed in one of his royal chateaux. The bed, raised on a dais of two steps, is towards the side of the room so as to avoid blocking a tall lancet window in the middle. Its canopy bears the royal arms in embroidery. Except for the canopy and the huge down pillows there is nothing to distinguish it from a broad settee with bed-clothes and a valance. Thus its occupant is in full view from the foot.

Charles is not asleep: he is reading in bed, or rather looking at the pictures in Fouquet's Boccaccio [1] *with his knees doubled up to make a reading-desk. Beside the bed on his left is a little table with a picture of the Virgin, lighted by candles of painted wax. The walls are hung from ceiling to floor with painted curtains which stir at times in the draughts. At first glance the prevailing yellow and red in these hanging pictures is somewhat flamelike when the folds breathe in the wind.*

The door is on Charles's left, but in front of him close to the corner farthest from him. A large watchman's rattle, handsomely designed and gaily painted, is in the bed under his hand.

Charles turns a leaf. A distant clock strikes the half-hour softly. Charles shuts the book with a clap; throws it aside; snatches up the rattle; and whirls it energetically, making a deafening clatter. Ladvenu enters, 25 years older, strange and stark in bearing, and still carrying the cross from Rouen. Charles evidently does not expect him; for he springs out of bed on the farther side from the door.

CHARLES   Who are you? Where is my gentleman of the bedchamber? What do you want?

LADVENU [*solemnly*]   I bring you glad tidings of great joy. Rejoice, O king; for the taint is removed from your blood, and the stain from your crown. Justice, long delayed, is at last triumphant.

CHARLES   What are you talking about? Who are you?

LADVENU   I am Brother Martin.

CHARLES   And who, saving your reverence, may Brother Martin be?

LADVENU   I held this cross when The Maid perished in the fire. Twenty-five years have passed since then: nearly ten thousand days. And on every one of those days I have prayed to God to justify His daughter on earth as she is justified in heaven.

CHARLES [*reassured, sitting down on the foot of the bed*]   Oh, I remember now. I have heard of you. You have a bee in your bonnet about The Maid. Have you been at the inquiry?

LADVENU   I have given my testimony.

CHARLES   Is it over?

LADVENU   It is over.

CHARLES   Satisfactorily?

1. A magnificent manuscript of the works of Giovanni Boccaccio (1313–75) with miniatures possibly by Jean Fouquet (1416–80), still extant. Fouquet was painter to the French court, and Shaw probably mentions him because he painted Agnes Sorel, Charles's mistress, as the Virgin in a famous altarpiece.

LADVENU   The ways of God are very strange.

CHARLES   How so?

LADVENU   At the trial which sent a saint to the stake as a heretic and a sorceress, the truth was told; the law was upheld; mercy was shewn beyond all custom; no wrong was done but the final and dreadful wrong of the lying sentence and the pitiless fire. At this inquiry from which I have just come, there was shameless perjury, courtly corruption, calumny of the dead who did their duty according to their lights, cowardly evasion of the issue, testimony made of idle tales that could not impose on a ploughboy. Yet out of this insult to justice, this defamation of the Church, this orgy of lying and foolishness, the truth is set in the noonday sun on the hilltop; the white robe of innocence is cleansed from the smirch of the burning faggots; the holy life is sanctified; the true heart that lived through the flame is consecrated; a great lie is silenced for ever; and a great wrong is set right before all men.

CHARLES   My friend: provided they can no longer say that I was crowned by a witch and a heretic, I shall not fuss about how the trick has been done. Joan would not have fussed about it if it came all right in the end: she was not that sort: I knew her. Is her rehabilitation complete? I made it pretty clear that there was to be no nonsense about it.

LADVENU   It is solemnly declared that her judges were full of corruption, cozenage, fraud, and malice. Four falsehoods.

CHARLES   Never mind the falsehoods: her judges are dead.

LADVENU   The sentence on her is broken, annulled, annihilated, set aside as non-existent, without value or effect.

CHARLES   Good. Nobody can challenge my consecration now, can they?

LADVENU   Not Charlemagne nor King David himself was more sacredly crowned.

CHARLES [rising]   Excellent. Think of what that means to me!

LADVENUE   I think of what it means to her!

CHARLES   You cannot. None of us ever knew what anything meant to her. She was like nobody else; and she must take care of herself wherever she is; for I cannot take care of her; and neither can you, whatever you may think: you are not big enough. But I will tell you this about her. If you could bring her back to life, they would burn her again within six months, for all their present adoration of her. And you would hold up the cross, too, just the same. So [crossing himself] let her rest; and let you and I mind our own business, and not meddle with hers.

LADVENU   God forbid that I should have no share in her, nor she in me! [He turns and strides out as he came, saying] Henceforth my path will not lie through palaces, nor my conversation be with kings.

CHARLES [following him towards the door, and shouting after him]   Much good may it do you, holy man! [He returns to the middle of the chamber, where he halts, and says quizzically to himself] That was a funny chap. How did he get in? Where are my people? [He goes impatiently to the bed, and swings the rattle. A rush of wind through the open door sets the walls swaying agitatedly. The candles go out. He calls in the darkness.] Hallo! Someone come and shut the windows: everything is being blown all over the place. [A flash of summer lightning shews up the *lancet window. A figure is seen in silhouette against it.*] Who is there? Who is that? Help! Murder! [*Thunder. He jumps into bed, and hides under the clothes.*]

JOAN'S VOICE   Easy, Charlie, easy. What art making all that noise for? No one can hear thee. Thourt asleep. [*She is dimly seen in a pallid greenish light by the bedside.*]

CHARLES [*peeping out*]   Joan! Are you a ghost, Joan?

JOAN   Hardly even that, lad. Can a poor burnt-up lass have a ghost? I am but a dream that thourt dreaming. [*The light increases: they become plainly visible as he sits up.*] Thou looks older, lad.

CHARLES   I am older. Am I really asleep?

JOAN   Fallen asleep over thy silly book.

CHARLES   That's funny.

JOAN   Not so funny as that I am dead, is it?

CHARLES   Are you really dead?

JOAN   As dead as anybody ever is, laddie. I am out of the body.

CHARLES   Just fancy! Did it hurt much?

JOAN   Did what hurt much?

CHARLES   Being burnt.

JOAN   Oh, that! I cannot remember very well. I think it did at first; but then it all got mixed up; and I was not in my right mind until I was free of the body. But do not thou go handling fire and thinking it will not hurt thee. How hast been ever since?

CHARLES   Oh, not so bad. Do you know, I actually lead my army out and win battles? Down into the moat up to my waist in mud and blood. Up the ladders with the stones and hot pitch raining down. Like you.

JOAN   No! Did I make a man of thee after all, Charlie?

CHARLES   I am Charles the Victorious now. I had to be brave because you were. Agnes put a little pluck into me too.

JOAN   Agnes! Who was Agnes?

CHARLES   Agnes Sorel. A woman I fell in love with. I dream of her often. I never dreamed of you before.

JOAN   Is she dead, like me?

CHARLES   Yes. But she was not like you. She was very beautiful.

JOAN [*laughing heartily*]   Ha ha! I was no beauty: I was always a rough one: a regular soldier. I might almost as well have been a man. Pity I wasnt: I should not have bothered you all so much then. But my head was in the skies; and the glory of God was upon me; and, man or woman, I should have bothered you as long as your noses were in the mud. Now tell me what has happened since you wise men knew no better than to make a heap of cinders of me?

CHARLES   Your mother and brothers have sued the courts to have your case tried over again. And the courts have declared that your judges were full of corruption and cozenage, fraud and malice.

JOAN   Not they. They were as honest a lot of poor fools as ever burned their betters.

CHARLES   The sentence on you is broken, annihilated, annulled: null, non-existent, without value or effect.

JOAN   I was burned, all the same. Can they unburn me?

CHARLES   If they could, they would think twice before they did it. But they have decreed that a beautiful cross be placed where the stake stood, for your perpetual memory and for your salvation.

JOAN   It is the memory and the salvation that sanctify the cross, not the cross that sanctifies the memory and the salvation. [*She turns away, forgetting him.*] I shall outlast that cross. I shall be remembered when men will have forgotten where Rouen stood.

CHARLES   There you go with your self-conceit, the same as ever! I think you might say a word of thanks to me for having had justice done at last.

CAUCHON   [*appearing at the window between them*]   Liar!

CHARLES   Thank you.

JOAN   Why, if it isnt Peter Cauchon! How are you, Peter? What luck have you had since you burned me?

CAUCHON   None. I arraign the justice of Man. It is not the justice of God.

JOAN   Still dreaming of justice, Peter? See what justice came to with me! But what has happened to thee? Art dead or alive?

CAUCHON   Dead. Dishonored. They pursued me beyond the grave. They excommunicated my dead body: they dug it up and flung it into the common sewer.

JOAN   Your dead body did not feel the spade and the sewer as my live body felt the fire.

CAUCHON   But this thing that they have done against me hurts justice; destroys faith; saps the foundation of the Church. The solid earth sways like the treacherous sea beneath the feet of men and spirits alike when the innocent are slain in the name of law, and their wrongs are undone by slandering the pure of heart.

JOAN   Well, well, Peter, I hope men will be the better for remembering me; and they would not remember me so well if you had not burned me.

CAUCHON   They will be the worse for remembering me: they will see in me evil triumphing over good, falsehood over truth, cruelty over mercy, hell over heaven. Their courage will rise as they think of you, only to faint as they think of me. Yet God is my witness I was just: I was merciful: I was faithful to my light: I could do no other than I did.

CHARLES   [*scrambling out of the sheets and enthroning himself on the side of the bed*]   Yes: it is always you good men that do the big mischiefs. Look at me! I am not Charles the Good, nor Charles the Wise, nor Charles the Bold. Joan's worshippers may even call me Charles the Coward because I did not pull her out of the fire. But I have done less harm than any of you. You people with your heads in the sky spend all your time trying to turn the world upside down; but I take the world as it is, and say that top-side-up is right-side-up; and I keep my nose pretty close to the ground. And I ask you, what king of France has done better, or been a better fellow in his little way?

JOAN   Art really king of France, Charlie? Be the English gone?

DUNOIS   [*coming through the tapestry on Joan's left, the candles relighting themselves at the same moment, and illuminating his armor and surcoat cheerfully*]   I have kept my word: the English are gone.

JOAN   Praised be God! now is fair France a province in heaven. Tell me all about the fighting, Jack. Was it thou that led them? Wert thou God's captain to thy death?

DUNOIS I am not dead. My body is very comfortably asleep in my bed at Chateaudun; but my spirit is called here by yours.

JOAN And you fought them my way, Jack: eh? Not the old way, chaffering for ransoms; but The Maid's way: staking life against death, with the heart high and humble and void of malice, and nothing counting under God but France free and French. Was it my way, Jack?

DUNOIS Faith, it was any way that would win. But the way that won was always your way. I give you best, lassie. I wrote a fine letter to set you right at the new trial. Perhaps I should never have let the priests burn you; but I was busy fighting; and it was the Church's business, not mine. There was no use in both of us being burned, was there?

CAUCHON Ay! put the blame on the priests. But I, who am beyond praise and blame, tell you that the world is saved neither by its priests nor its soldiers, but by God and His Saints. The Church Militant sent this woman to the fire; but even as she burned, the flames whitened into the radiance of the Church Triumphant.

The clock strikes the third quarter. A rough male voice is heard trolling an improvised tune.

Rum tum trumpledum,
Bacon fat and rumpledum,
Old Saint mumpledum,
Pull his tail and stumpledum
    O my Ma—ry Ann!

A ruffianly English soldier comes through the curtains and marches between Dunois and Joan.

DUNOIS What villainous troubadour taught you that doggrel?

THE SOLDIER No troubadour. We made it up ourselves as we marched. We were not gentlefolks and troubadours. Music straight out of the heart of the people, as you might say. Rum tum trumpledum, Bacon fat and rumpledum, Old Saint mumpledum, Pull his tail and stumpledum: that dont mean anything, you know; but it keeps you marching. Your servant, ladies and gentlemen. Who asked for a saint?

JOAN Be you a saint?

THE SOLDIER Yes, lady, straight from hell.

DUNOIS A saint, and from hell!

THE SOLDIER Yes, noble captain: I have a day off. Every year, you know. Thats my allowance for my one good action.

CAUCHON Wretch! In all the years of your life did you do only one good action?

THE SOLDIER I never thought about it: it came natural like. But they scored it up for me.

CHARLES What was it?

THE SOLDIER Why, the silliest thing you ever heard of. I—

JOAN [*interrupting him by strolling across to the bed, where she sits beside Charles*] He tied two sticks together, and gave them to a poor lass that was going to be burned.

THE SOLDIER Right. Who told you that?

JOAN   Never mind. Would you know her if you saw her again?

THE SOLDIER   Not I. There are so many girls! and they all expect you to re-member them as if there was only one in the world. This one must have been a prime sort; for I have a day off every year for her; and so, until twelve o'clock punctually, I am a saint, at your service, noble lords and lovely ladies.

CHARLES   And after twelve?

THE SOLDIER   After twelve, back to the only place fit for the likes of me.

JOAN [rising]   Back there! You! that gave the lass the cross!

THE SOLDIER [excusing his unsoldierly conduct]   Well, she asked for it; and they were going to burn her. She had as good a right to a cross as they had; and they had dozens of them. It was her funeral, not theirs. Where was the harm in it?

JOAN   Man: I am not reproaching you. But I cannot bear to think of you in torment.

THE SOLDIER [cheerfully]   No great torment, lady. You see I was used to worse.

CHARLES   What! worse than hell?

THE SOLDIER   Fifteen years' service in the French wars. Hell was a treat after that.

> Joan throws up her arms, and takes refuge from despair of humanity before the picture of the Virgin.

THE SOLDIER [continuing]—   Suits me somehow. The day off was dull at first, like a wet Sunday. I dont mind it so much now. They tell me I can have as many as I like as soon as I want them.

CHARLES   What is hell like?

THE SOLDIER   You wont find it so bad, sir. Jolly. Like as if you were always drunk without the trouble and expense of drinking. Tip top company too: emperors and popes and kings and all sorts. They chip me about giving that young judy the cross; but I dont care: I stand up to them proper, and tell them that if she hadnt a better right to it than they, she'd be where they are. That dumbfounds them, that does. All they can do is gnash their teeth, hell fashion; and I just laugh, and go off singing the old chanty: Rum tum trumple—Hullo! Who's that knocking at the door?

> They listen. A long gentle knocking is heard.

CHARLES   Come in.

> The door opens; and an old priest, white-haired, bent, with a silly but benevolent smile, comes in and trots over to Joan.

THE NEWCOMER   Excuse me, gentle lords and ladies. Do not let me disturb you. Only a poor old harmless English rector. Formerly chaplain to the cardinal: to my lord of Winchester. John de Stogumber, at your service. [He looks at them inquiringly.] Did you say anything? I am a little deaf, unfortunately. Also a little—well, not always in my right mind, perhaps; but still, it is a small village with a few simple people. I suffice: I suffice: they love me there; and I am able to do a little good. I am well con-nected, you see; and they indulge me.

JOAN   Poor old John! What brought thee to this state?

DE STOGUMBER   I tell my folks they must be very careful. I say to them, 'If you only saw what you think about you would think quite differently about it. It would give you a great shock. Oh, a great shock.' And they all say 'Yes, parson: we all know you are a kind man, and would not harm a fly.' That is a great comfort to me. For I am not cruel by nature, you know.

THE SOLDIER   Who said you were?

DE STOGUMBER   Well, you see, I did a very cruel thing once because I did not know what cruelty was like. I had not seen it, you know. That is the great thing: you must see it. And then you are redeemed and saved.

CAUCHON   Were not the sufferings of our Lord Christ enough for you?

DE STOGUMBER   No. Oh no: not at all. I had seen them in pictures, and read of them in books, and been greatly moved by them, as I thought. But it was no use: it was not our Lord that redeemed me, but a young woman whom I saw actually burned to death. It was dreadful: oh, most dreadful. But it saved me. I have been a different man ever since, though a little astray in my wits sometimes.

CAUCHON   Must then a Christ perish in torment in every age to save those that have no imagination?

JOAN   Well, if I saved all those he would have been cruel to if he had not been cruel to me, I was not burnt for nothing, was I?

DE STOGUMBER   Oh no; it was not you. My sight is bad: I cannot distinguish your features: but you are not she: oh no: she was burned to a cinder: dead and gone, dead and gone.

THE EXECUTIONER   [*stepping from behind the bed curtains on Charles's right, the bed being between them*]   She is more alive than you, old man. Her heart would not burn; and it would not drown. I was a master at my craft: better than the master of Paris, better than the master of Toulouse; but I could not kill The Maid. She is up and alive everywhere.

THE EARL OF WARWICK   [*sallying from the bed curtains on the other side, and coming to Joan's left hand*]   Madam: my congratulations on your rehabilitation. I feel that I owe you an apology.

JOAN   Oh, please don't mention it.

WARWICK   [*pleasantly*]   The burning was purely political. There was no personal feeling against you, I assure you.

JOAN   I bear no malice, my lord.

WARWICK   Just so. Very kind of you to meet me in that way: a touch of true breeding. But I must insist on apologizing very amply. The truth is, these political necessities sometimes turn out to be political mistakes; and this one was a veritable howler; for your spirit conquered us, madam, in spite of our faggots. History will remember me for your sake, though the incidents of the connection were perhaps a little unfortunate.

JOAN   Ay, perhaps just a little, you funny man.

WARWICK   Still, when they make you a saint, you will owe your halo to me, just as this lucky monarch owes his crown to you.

JOAN   [*turning from him*]   I shall owe nothing to any man: I owe everything to the spirit of God that was within me. But fancy me a saint! What would St Catherine and St Margaret say if the farm girl was cocked up [2] beside them!

2. Celebrated and venerated.

A clerical-looking gentleman in black frockcoat and trousers, and tall hat, in the fashion of the year 1920, suddenly appears before them in the corner on their right. They all stare at him. Then they burst into uncontrollable laughter.

THE GENTLEMAN   Why this mirth, gentlemen?

WARWICK   I congratulate you on having invented a most extraordinarily comic dress.

THE GENTLEMAN   I do not understand. You are all in fancy dress: I am properly dressed.

DUNOIS   All dress is fancy dress, is it not, except our natural skins?

THE GENTLEMAN   Pardon me: I am here on serious business, and cannot engage in frivolous discussions. [*He takes out a paper, and assumes a dry official manner.*] I am sent to announce to you that Joan of Arc, formerly know as The Maid, having been the subject of an inquiry instituted by the Bishop of Orleans—

JOAN [*interrupting*]   Ah! They remember me still in Orleans.

THE GENTLEMAN [*emphatically, to mark his indignation at the interruption*]— by the Bishop of Orleans into the claim of the said Joan of Arc to be canonized as a saint—

JOAN [*again interrupting*]   But I never made any such claim.

THE GENTLEMAN [*as before*]—   the Church has examined the claim exhaustively in the usual course, and, having admitted the said Joan successively to the ranks of Venerable and Blessed,—

JOAN [*chuckling*]   Me venerable!

THE GENTLEMAN—   has finally declared her to have been endowed with heroic virtues and favored with private revelations, and calls the said Venerable and Blessed Joan to the communion of the Church Triumphant as Saint Joan.

JOAN [*rapt*]   Saint Joan!

THE GENTLEMAN   On every thirtieth day of May, being the anniversary of the death of the said most blessed daughter of God, there shall in every Catholic church to the end of time be celebrated a special office in commemoration of her; and it shall be lawful to dedicate a special chapel to her, and to place her image on its altar in every such church. And it shall be lawful and laudable for the faithful to kneel and address their prayers through her to the Mercy Seat.

JOAN   Oh no. It is for the saint to kneel. [*She falls on her knees, still rapt.*]

THE GENTLEMAN [*putting up his paper, and retiring beside the Executioner*] In Basilica Vaticana, the sixteenth day of May, nineteen hundred and twenty.

DUNOIS [*raising Joan*]   Half an hour to burn you, dear Saint, and four centuries to find out the truth about you!

DE STOGUMBER   Sir: I was chaplain to the Cardinal of Winchester once. They always would call him the Cardinal of England. It would be a great comfort to me and to my master to see a fair statue of The Maid in Winchester Cathedral. Will they put one there, do you think?

THE GENTLEMAN   As the building is temporarily in the hands of the Anglican heresy, I cannot answer for that.

A vision of the statue in Winchester Cathedral is seen through the window.

DE STOGUMBER   Oh look! look! that is Winchester.

JOAN   Is that meant to be me? I was stiffer on my feet.

The vision fades.

THE GENTLEMAN   I have been requested by the temporal authorities of France to mention that the multiplication of public statues to The Maid threatens to become an obstruction to traffic. I do so as a matter of courtesy to the said authorities, but most point out on behalf of the Church that The Maid's horse is no greater obstruction to traffic than any other horse.

JOAN   Eh! I am glad they have not forgotten my horse.

A vision of the statue before Rheims Cathedral appears.

JOAN   Is that funny little thing me too?

CHARLES   That is Rheims Cathedral where you had me crowned. It must be you.

JOAN   Who has broken my sword? My sword was never broken. It is the sword of France.

DUNOIS   Never mind. Swords can be mended. Your soul is unbroken; and you are the soul of France.

The vision fades. The Archbishop and the Inquisitor are now seen on the right and left of Cauchon.

JOAN   My sword shall conquer yet: the sword that never struck a blow. Though men destroyed my body, yet in my soul I have seen God.

CAUCHON [*kneeling to her*]   The girls in the field praise thee; for thou hast raised their eyes; and they see that there is nothing between them and heaven.

DUNOIS [*kneeling to her*]   The dying soldiers praise thee, because thou art a shield of glory between them and the judgment.

THE ARCHBISHOP [*kneeling to her*]   The princes of the Church praise thee, because thou hast redeemed the faith their worldlinesses have dragged through the mire.

WARWICK [*kneeling to her*]   The cunning counsellors praise thee, because thou hast cut the knots in which they have tied their own souls.

DE STOGUMBER [*kneeling to her*]   The foolish old men on their deathbeds praise thee, because their sins against thee are turned into blessings.

THE INQUISITOR [*kneeling to her*]   The judges in the blindness and bondage of the law praise thee, because thou hast vindicated the vision and the freedom of the living soul.

THE SOLDIER [*kneeling to her*]   The wicked out of hell praise thee, because thou hast shewn them that the fire that is not quenched is a holy fire.

THE EXECUTIONER [*kneeling to her*]   The tormentors and executioners praise thee, because thou hast shewn that their hands are guiltless of the death of the soul.

CHARLES [*kneeling to her*]   The unpretending praise thee, because thou hast taken upon thyself the heroic burdens that are too heavy for them.

JOAN   Woe unto me when all men praise me! I bid you remember that I am a saint, and that saints can work miracles. And now tell me: shall I rise from the dead, and come back to you a living woman?

A sudden darkness blots out the walls of the room as they all spring to their feet in consternation. Only the figures and the bed remain visible.

JOAN   What! Must I burn again? Are none of you ready to receive me?

CAUCHON   The heretic is always better dead. And mortal eyes cannot distinguish the saint from the heretic. Spare them. [*He goes out as he came.*]

DUNOIS   Forgive us, Joan: we are not yet good enough for you. I shall go back to my bed. [*He also goes.*]

WARWICK   We sincerely regret our little mistake; but political necessities, though occasionally erroneous, are still imperative; so if you will be good enough to excuse me—[*He steals discreetly away.*]

THE ARCHBISHOP   Your return would not make me the man you once thought me. The utmost I can say is that though I dare not bless you, I hope I may one day enter into your blessedness. Meanwhile, however—[*He goes.*]

THE INQUISITOR   I who am of the dead, testified that day that you were innocent. But I do not see how The Inquisition could possibly be dispensed with under existing circumstances. Therefore—[*He goes.*]

DE STOGUMBER   Oh, do not come back: you must not come back. I must die in peace. Give us peace in our time, O Lord! [*He goes.*]

THE GENTLEMAN   The possibility of your resurrection was not contemplated in the recent proceedings for your canonization. I must return to Rome for fresh instructions. [*He bows formally, and withdraws.*]

THE EXECUTIONER   As a master in my profession I have to consider its interests. And, after all, my first duty is to my wife and children. I must have time to think over this. [*He goes.*]

CHARLES   Poor old Joan! They have all run away from you except this blackguard who has to go back to hell at twelve o'clock. And what can I do but follow Jack Dunois' example, and go back to bed too? [*He does so.*]

JOAN [*sadly*]   Goodnight, Charlie.

CHARLES [*mumbling in his pillows*]   Goo ni. [*He sleeps. The darkness envelops the bed.*]

JOAN [*to the soldier*]   And you, my one faithful? What comfort have you for Saint Joan?

THE SOLDIER   Well, what do they all amount to, these kings and captains and bishops and lawyers and such like? They just leave you in the ditch to bleed to death; and the next thing is, you meet them down there, for all the airs they give themselves. What I say is, you have as good a right to your notions as they have to theirs, and perhaps better. [*settling himself for a lecture on the subject*] You see, it's like this. If—[*The first stroke of midnight is heard softly from a distant bell.*] Excuse me: a pressing appointment—[*He goes on tiptoe.*]

The last remaining rays of light gather into a white radiance descending on Joan. The hour continues to strike.

JOAN   O God that madest this beautiful earth, when will it be ready to receive Thy saints? How long, O Lord, how long? [3]

3. "How long, O Lord" is a formula used in Psalms and by the prophets, and echoed in Revelation.

JOSEPH CONRAD
1857–1924

Conrad was born Teodor Josef Konrad Korzeniowski in the Ukraine. His father, Appollo Korzeniowski, was a man of letters and a leader of the Polish revolt against Russia in 1863; after a period of exile he died in Cracow in 1869. The young Conrad had early expressed interest in travel, and would in any case probably have had to emigrate to make his way in the world; but his family did not approve of his taking to the sea. This he did in 1874, when he went to Marseille and helped in a gun-running operation in behalf of the Carlists (supporters of the claim of Don Carlos of Spain to the Spanish throne). Here he had an almost fatal adventure, and fell in love, gambled, and attempted suicide. Thenceforth he followed a more normal seafaring life. In 1878 he joined an English merchant vessel, and followed the sea for sixteen years, rising to command his own ship.

In 1889, in his thirty-second year, he began to write the novel *Almayer's Folly;* in the following year he undertook the Congo trip which is the source of *Heart of Darkness.* He gave up the sea only in 1894, and began his career as a novelist, using a language he had not learned till in his twenties. A painful writer, he nevertheless produced thirty-one books and a vast number of letters. He married in 1896, and settled to a life of drudgery and poverty, lightened only by a distinguished circle of friends, notably H. G. Wells, Henry James, John Galsworthy, Stephen Crane, and his collaborator Ford Madox Hueffer (later and better known as Ford Madox Ford). Suffering and complaining almost ceaselessly, Conrad struggled with a novel (*The Rescuer,* later *The Rescue*) which would not come right, and then turned away from it to write his great early stories *The Nigger of the "Narcissus"* (1897), *Heart of Darkness* (1899), and the first of the major novels, *Lord Jim* (1900). While the importance of all of these in the development of the artist is enormous, he reached his full stature in the years of the three great novels *Nostromo* (1904), *The Secret Agent* (1906), and *Under Western Eyes* (1910). Somewhat surprisingly, a very complicated and on the whole inferior novel, *Chance* (1912), brought him the income which had eluded him as his fame grew. *Victory,* the last of the first-rate books, followed in 1914.

This account omits comment on some of the remarkable shorter works—early and late—such as *The End of the Tether* and *The Shadow Line;* and some relatively unsuccessful novels—*The Rescue, The Outcast of the Islands, The Arrow of Gold* (an autobiographical work about his Carlist period)—and *The Rover.* So large a body of work makes generalization difficult; but two things at least may be said. First, Conrad's fiction is related with unusual closeness to his own experience; and second, he was from the outset an artist, never accepting conventional forms or conventional judgments. The closeness of the novels to Conrad's own experience is something that scholarship increasingly confirms, but in the writing process this experience is developed, transfigured, and shaped in extraordinary ways. No writer did more to establish in the English novel the strict necessity to find new forms for every undertaking. This may seem strange when we consider that Conrad used to be thought of as a master of exotic scenes and narratives, the South Seas and romantic adventure; yet it was a habit of brooding creatively on such adventures that produced *Lord Jim, The End of the Tether, Heart of Darkness*—all closely related to Conrad's own biography and all "good stories" of the kind the narrator is talking about when, in *Heart of Darkness,* he says to Marlow that "the meaning of an episode was not inside like a kernel but outside, enveloping the tale which brought it out only as a glow brings out a haze, in the likeness of one of those misty halos that sometimes are made visible by the spectral illumination of moonshine."

Although the shorter pieces have not, as a rule, the structural complexity of the major novels, they share their fidelity to art and experience. This was to Conrad a moral issue; he is concerned with the truth, the truth as it appeared to his somber imagination. In some famous lines in the Preface to The Nigger of the "Narcissus" he expresses thus the peculiar adventure of the artist, and its purpose:

A work that aspires, however humbly, to the condition of art should carry its justification in every line. And art itself may be defined as a single-minded attempt to render the highest kind of justice to the visible universe, by bringing to light the truth, manifold and one, underlying its every aspect. It is an attempt to find in its forms, in its colours, in its light, in its shadows, in the aspects of matter and in the facts of life what of each is fundamental, what is enduring and essential—their one illuminating and convincing quality—the very truth of their existence. The artist, then, like the thinker or the scientist, seeks the truth and makes his appeal. Impressed by the aspect of the world the thinker plunges into ideas, the scientist into facts—whence, presently, emerging they make their appeal to those qualities of our being that fit us best for the hazardous enterprise of living. They speak authoritatively to our common-sense, to our intelligence, to our desire of peace or to our desire of unrest; not seldom to our prejudices, sometimes to our fears, often to our egoism—but always to our credulity. And their words are heard with reverence, for their concern is with weighty matters: with the cultivation of our minds and the proper care of our bodies, with the attainment of our ambitions, with the perfection of the means and the glorification of our precious aims.

It is otherwise with the artist.

Confronted by the same enigmatical spectacle the artist descends within himself, and in that lonely region of stress and strife, if he be deserving and fortunate, he finds the terms of his appeal. His appeal is made to our less obvious capacities: to that part of our nature which, because of the warlike conditions of existence, is necessarily kept out of sight within the more resisting and hard qualities—like the vulnerable body within a steel armour. His appeal is less loud, more profound, less distinct, more stirring—and sooner forgotten. Yet its effect endures forever. The changing wisdom of successive generations discards ideas, questions facts, demolishes theories. But the artist appeals to that part of our being which is not dependent on wisdom; to that in us which is a gift and not an acquisition—and, therefore, more permanently enduring. He speaks to our capacity for delight and wonder, to the sense of mystery surrounding our lives; to our sense of pity, and beauty, and pain; to the latent feeling of fellowship with all creation—and to the subtle but invincible conviction of solidarity that knits together the loneliness of innumerable hearts, to the solidarity in dreams, in joy, in sorrow, in aspirations, in illusions, in hope, in fear, which binds men to each other, which binds together all humanity—the dead to the living and the living to the unborn.

In the rhetoric of this opening manifesto there are one or two very characteristic phrases: the emphasis on truth, the artist's descent "within himself," the appeal to human nature as it exists universally but concealed by "the warlike conditions of [our] existence." Conrad goes on to argue that fiction achieves this end by its appeal to the senses.

All art . . . appeals primarily to the senses, and the artistic aim when expressing itself in written words must also make its appeal through the senses, if its high desire is to reach the secret spring of responsive emotions. It must strenuously aspire to the plasticity of sculpture, to the colour of painting, and to the magic suggestiveness of music—which is the art of arts. And it is only through complete, unswerving devotion to the perfect blending of form and substance; it is only through an unremitting never-discouraged care for the shape and ring of sentences that an approach can be made to plasticity, to colour, and that the light of magic suggestiveness may be brought to play for an evanescent instant over the commonplace surface of words: of the old, old words, worn thin, defaced by ages of careless usage.

The sincere endeavour to accomplish that creative task, to go as far on that road as his strength will carry him, to go undeterred by faltering, weariness or reproach, is the only valid justification for the worker in prose. And if his conscience is clear, his answer to those who in the fulness of a wisdom which looks for immediate profit, demand specifically to be edified, consoled, amused; who demand to be promptly improved, or encouraged, or frightened, or shocked, or charmed, must run thus:—My task which I am trying to achieve is, by the power of the written word to make you hear, to make you feel—it is, before all, to make you *see*. That—and no more, and it is everything. If I succeed, you shall find there according to your deserts: encouragement, consolation, fear, charm—all you demand—and, perhaps, also that glimpse of truth for which you have forgotten to ask.

To snatch in a moment of courage, from the remorseless rush of time, a passing phase of life, is only the beginning of the task. The task approached in tenderness and faith is to hold up unquestioningly, without choice and without fear, the rescued fragment before all eyes in the light of a sincere mood. It is to show its vibration, its colour, its form; and through its movement, its form, and its colour, reveal the substance of its truth—disclose its inspiring secret: the stress and passion within the core of each convincing moment. In a single-minded attempt of that kind, if one be deserving and fortunate, one may perchance attain to such clearness of sincerity that at last the presented vision of regret or pity, of terror or mirth, shall awaken in the hearts of the beholders that feeling of unavoidable solidarity; of the solidarity in mysterious origin, in toil, in joy, in hope, in uncertain fate, which binds men to each other and all mankind to the visible world.

It is evident that he who, rightly or wrongly, holds by the convictions expressed above cannot be faithful to any one of the temporary formulas of his craft. The enduring part of them—the truth which each only imperfectly veils —should abide with him as the most precious of his possessions, but they all: Realism, Romanticism, Naturalism, even the unofficial sentimentalism (which like the poor, is exceedingly difficult to get rid of), all these gods must, after a short period of fellowship, abandon him—even on the very threshold of the temple—to the stammerings of his conscience and to the outspoken consciousness of the difficulties of his work.

This is not merely the familiar late-nineteenth-century aspiration to the condition of music; it is a declaration of the immense formal difficulty of the novelist's task. Fiction is a mode of truth-telling but also an art: "Fiction is history, human history, or it is nothing," said Conrad elsewhere, but added, "it is also more than that . . . being based on the reality of forms." The art lies in "perfect blending of form and substance." This is why Conrad studied Flaubert and Maupassant, and why he and Ford Madox Ford labored to work out a whole new practice as well as a new aesthetic of the novel, one that required the most intense study of the form. The result is in a new sense "to make you *see*." What you "see" may be that "glimpse of the truth for which you have forgotten to ask," and it will certainly be what you could not have seen at all without the aid of the novel, which Conrad, like Lawrence, regarded as one of the great instruments of knowledge.

This explains not only Conrad's unremitting experiment but also the suffering and labor he complained of. He was always looking, not for some startling novelty, but for the light that plays "over the commonplace surface of words." His own life contained incidents to which imagination gave ambiguous meanings that a man of his sensibility might spend the rest of it exploring: his attempted suicide as a youth, his behavior in certain emergencies at sea, his relation to Poland. All life was made up of such incidents, of solitude and fear relieved, for some, by society, and for some by the simple and difficult virtues, such as fidelity. By the time Conrad's opinions and attitudes have been changed under the pressure of his constructive imagination, they are not as they appear in his straightforward expressions of opinion: the view of Russia in *Under Western Eyes* is not that held by the "waking" Conrad; *The Secret Agent* is not "a simple tale"—whatever the subtitle says—about a police trick played on anarchists, but an ironic, tragic meditation on the darkness at the heart of the world. The technical devices he invents are instruments devised "to make you see" more than you bargained for. *Heart of Darkness* shows him using such devices quite early in his career.

Heart of Darkness

First written to appear as a three-part serial in *Blackwood's Magazine*, *Heart of Darkness* was published in book form with *Youth* and *The End of the Tether* in 1902. Its material derives from Conrad's time in the Congo in 1890, a brief period rightly thought of as the turning point of his career. Conrad had wanted to visit the blank on the map since he was a child; now, thanks to the good offices of an aunt who lived in Brussels, he was able to do so. As a consequence his health suffered badly, but—after "the descent into the self" which the visit entailed—he was transformed into a great writer. He himself says he was "a perfect animal" till that time.

The entire Congo area—nearly one million square miles—belonged personally, by a freak of European diplomacy, to Leopold II, King of the Belgians. The King spoke of opening it to civilization, and of bringing in Christianity to "pierce the darkness which envelops the entire population," but this was merely a cover for ruthless exploitation. The fine talk of high purposes was accompanied by a barbarous labor policy, savage punishments (from flogging to amputation), and a rankling contempt for the savages supposedly to be saved. This was the Congo Conrad found himself in after the long sea trip from England. Later he called it "the vilest scramble for loot that ever disfigured the history of human conscience," but at the time he probably expected something quite different. The period of his stay in Africa is by now well researched, most notably and recently by Norman Sherry in *Conrad's Western World* (1971). So small a detail as the death of Captain Fresleven, which gave Marlow his command, is based on the murder of a real Captain Freisleben, and so is the detail of the grass growing up through his ribs. Conrad himself left a diary covering part of the voyage and revealing, among other things, that he omitted some of the more agreeable early encounters that befell him; and in general he departs from the facts, or stays close to them, as best suits his purposes. The steamer he was sent to had been wrecked like Marlow's; but unlike Marlow he did not stay to repair it. There *was* a brickmaker, but he managed to make bricks. Kurtz is based on a man named

A. E. C. Hodister (though not in minute detail), and the Harlequin, on Hodister's champion Jacques Doré. And the settlement at Stanley Falls was a large one, quite unlike Kurtz's.

None of this is essential to the study of *Heart of Darkness*, though the ironic contrast between the professions of colonists and missionaries, and the actual conduct of the "explorers" and "pilgrims" and "managers" are of course part of the conception. Mr. Sherry even finds that the opening sequence, in which the Thames in Roman times is compared to the modern Congo, owes something to a speech of the famous explorer and journalist Henry Morton Stanley—a speech quoting in turn the question raised by Prime Minister Pitt in 1792, as to whether a Roman senator might not have said of ancient Britain what men now said about Africa (that it was incapable of civilization, and so on): "Sir, we were once as obscure among the nations of the earth, as debased in our morals, as savage in our manners, as degraded in our understandings as these unhappy Africans are at present." Further, the *Nellie* was an actual yawl, and Conrad knew what he was doing when he set Marlow's tale aboard it, and in the salt water of the estuary; for Conrad's primary image of the ordered society, of fidelity, of courage and endurance in human crisis, was a well-found sailing ship in salt water. To explore the heart of darkness both Conrad and Marlow sailed up a river into the heart of a continent.

Marlow is not a mere mouthpiece. Neither is he a veil between author and reader. He contributes, here and everywhere, to Conrad's object, which is to make one see; see more, perhaps, than Marlow. Does he, for instance, see Kurtz as we are made to? He has limitations which, at important points, make his narrative suggestive rather than explicit. He provides the commonplace words over which the haze of meanings develops. What Marlow does is to alter the perspectives in the way which Conrad described as that "wherein almost all my 'art' consists." The setting does the same thing: the yawl with its head to the open sea, and dark London—"devourer of the world's light," he called it in the Preface to *The Secret Agent*—behind; and when Marlow has finished his account of a trip to the edge of the heart of darkness, the tide has turned and the Thames flows out into a darkness of which we have now learned something. It is an alteration of perspectives, and, like the acuteness and limitations of Marlow, it is an instrument to make us see.

The mass of interpretive and critical comment on *Heart of Darkness* cannot be reviewed here. The chief complaint is that Conrad overdoes the "unspeakable," "monstrous," "atrocious," "inconceivable" in his rendering of the story: "adjectival and worse than supererogatory insistence," says F. R. Leavis. Others explain this as a consequence of Conrad's need to keep the heart of the meaning dark; he himself claimed "an inalienable right to the use of all my epithets." In a sense all these views are defensible. Where the story proceeds by means of bizarre colonial vignettes— the doctor, the ship shelling a continent, the objectless dynamiting, the hole, the flogging, the admirable correctness of the accountant's dress, the lack of rivets, the beautiful dull order of the manual of seamanship—such language is not called for. It is needed when Marlow is not equal to the experience described.

Marlow, who feels his affinity with Kurtz, nevertheless contents himself with the lie, "the great and saving illusion." To do otherwise would have been "too dark altogether." And yet, says Marlow ambiguously to the girl, "His words will remain"; these words are "the horror, the horror." We see, in all the anxiety and terror of this, why the narrator entrusts the story to Marlow, who for all his virtues cannot quite tell all, and how we are made to work for our glimpse of a truth we have perhaps not bargained for. It is an instance of how Conrad thought truth may be told in fiction: by "unswerving devotion to the perfect blending of form and substance."

Heart of Darkness

I

The *Nellie*, a cruising yawl, swung to her anchor without a flutter of the sails, and was at rest. The flood had made, the wind was nearly calm, and being bound down the river, the only thing for it was to come to and wait for the turn of the tide.

The sea-reach of the Thames stretched before us like the beginning of an interminable waterway. In the offing the sea and the sky were welded together without a joint, and in the luminous space the tanned sails of the barges drifting up with the tide seemed to stand still in red clusters of canvas sharply peaked, with gleams of varnished spirits. A haze rested on the low shores that ran out to sea in vanishing flatness. The air was dark above Gravesend,[1] and farther back still seemed condensed into a mournful gloom, brooding motionless over the biggest, and the greatest, town on earth.

The Director of Companies was our captain and our host. We four affectionately watched his back as he stood in the bows looking to seaward. On the whole river there was nothing that looked half so nautical. He resembled a pilot, which to a seaman is trustworthiness personified. It was difficult to realise his work was not out there in the luminous estuary, but behind him, within the brooding gloom.

Between us there was, as I have already said somewhere, the bond of the sea. Besides holding our hearts together through long periods of separation, it had the effect of making us tolerant of each other's yarns—and even convictions. The Lawyer—the best of old fellows—had, because of his many years and many virtues, the only cushion on deck, and was lying on the only rug. The Accountant had brought out already a box of dominoes, and was toying architecturally with the bones. Marlow sat cross-legged right aft, leaning against the mizzen-mast. He had sunken cheeks, a yellow complexion, a straight back, an ascetic aspect, and, with his arms dropped, the palms of hands outwards, resembled an idol. The Director, satisfied the anchor had good hold, made his way aft and sat down amongst us. We exchanged a few words lazily. Afterwards there was silence on board the yacht. For some reason or other we did not begin that game of dominoes. We felt meditative, and fit for nothing but placid staring. The day was ending in a serenity of still and exquisite brilliance. The water shone pacifically; the sky, without a speck, was a benign immensity of unstained light; the very mist on the Essex marshes was like a gauzy and radiant fabric, hung from the wooded rises inland, and draping the low shores in diaphanous folds. Only the gloom to the west, brooding over the upper reaches, became more sombre every minute, as if angered by the approach of the sun.

1. Town on the Kent (south) bank of the Thames, 26 miles east of London.

And at last, in its curved and imperceptible fall, the sun sank low, and from glowing white changed to a dull red without rays and without heat, as if about to go out suddenly, stricken to death by the touch of that gloom brooding over a crowd of men.

Forthwith a change came over the waters, and the serenity became less brilliant but more profound. The old river in its broad reach rested unruffled at the decline of day, after ages of good service done to the race that peopled its banks, spread out in the tranquil dignity of a waterway leading to the uttermost ends of the earth. We looked at the venerable stream not in the vivid flush of a short day that comes and departs for ever, but in the august light of abiding memories. And indeed nothing is easier for a man who has, as the phrase goes, 'followed the sea' with reverence and affection, than to evoke the great spirit of the past upon the lower reaches of the Thames. The tidal current runs to and fro in its unceasing service, crowded with memories of men and ships it has borne to the rest of home or to the battles of the sea. It had known and served all the men of whom the nation is proud, from Sir Francis Drake [2] to Sir John Franklin,[3] knights all, titled and untitled—the great knights-errant of the sea. It had borne all the ships whose names are like jewels flashing in the night of time, from the *Golden Hind* returning with her round flanks full of treasure, to be visited by the Queen's Highness and thus pass out of the gigantic tale, to the *Erebus* and *Terror,* bound on other conquests—and that never returned. It had known the ships and the men. They had sailed from Deptford, from Greenwich, from Erith [4]—the adventurers and the settlers; kings' ships and the ships of men on 'Change; [5] captains, admirals, the dark 'interlopers' of the Eastern trade, and the commissioned 'generals' of East India fleets.[6] Hunters for gold or pursuers of fame, they all had gone out on that stream, bearing the sword, and often the torch,[7] messengers of the might within the land, bearers of a spark from the sacred fire. What greatness had not floated on the ebb of that river into the mystery of an unknown earth! . . . The dreams of men, the seed of commonwealths, the germs of empires.

The sun set; the dusk fell on the stream, and lights began to appear along the shore. The Chapman lighthouse, a three-legged thing erect on a mud-flat, shone strongly. Lights of ships moved in the fairway—a great stir of lights going up and going down. And farther west on the upper reaches the place of the monstrous town was still marked ominously on the sky, a brooding gloom in sunshine, a lurid glare under the stars.

'And this also,' said Marlow suddenly, 'has been one of the dark places of the earth.'

2. Sir Francis Drake (*c.* 1540–96) in 1577 sailed *The Golden Hind* around the world, made enormous profits for shareholders, and was knighted by the Queen at Deptford on his return.
3. Sir John Franklin (1786–1847) set out with the *Erebus* and the *Terror* to find a northwest passage, and died in the ice of Victoria Strait.
4. Estuary ports east of London.
5. 'Change Alley was the scene of 18th-century speculation in Eastern trade.
6. The East India Company, founded by royal charter in 1600, was by the 18th century the ruler of India; only in 1858 did the British government take over.
7. Conrad often allowed some disinterested motives to British imperialists; hence they bear not only the "sword" but "often the torch."

He was the only man of us who still 'followed the sea.' The worst that could be said of him was that he did not represent his class. He was a seaman, but he was a wanderer too, while most seamen lead, if one may so express it, a sedentary life. Their minds are of the stay-at-home order, and their home is always with them—the ship; and so is their country—the sea. One ship is very much like another, and the sea is always the same. In the immutability of their surroundings the foreign shores, the foreign faces, the changing immensity of life, glide past, veiled not by a sense of mystery but by a slightly disdainful ignorance; for there is nothing mysterious to a seaman unless it be the sea itself, which is the mistress of his existence and as inscrutable as Destiny. For the rest, after his hours of work, a casual stroll or a casual spree on shore suffices to unfold for him the secret of a whole continent, and generally he finds the secret not worth knowing. The yarns of seamen have a direct simplicity, the whole meaning of which lies within the shell of a cracked nut. But Marlow was not typical (if his propensity to spin yarns be excepted), and to him the meaning of an episode was not inside like a kernel but outside,[8] enveloping the tale which brought it out only as a glow brings out a haze, in the likeness of one of those misty halos that sometimes are made visible by the spectral illumination of moonshine.

His remark did not seem at all surprising. It was just like Marlow. It was accepted in silence. No one took the trouble to grunt even; and presently he said, very slow:

'I was thinking of very old times, when the Romans first came here, nineteen hundred years ago—the other day. . . . Light came out of this river since—you say Knights? Yes; but it is like a running blaze on a plain, like a flash of lightning in the clouds. We live in the flicker—may it last as long as the old earth keeps rolling! But darkness was here yesterday. Imagine the feelings of a commander of a fine—what d'ye call 'em?—trireme[9] in the Mediterranean, ordered suddenly to the north; run overland across the Gauls in a hurry; put in charge of one of these craft the legionaries—a wonderful lot of handy men they must have been too—used to build, apparently by the hundred, in a month or two, if we may believe what we read. Imagine him here—the very end of the world, a sea the colour of lead, a sky the colour of smoke, a kind of ship about as rigid as a concertina—and going up this river with stores, or orders, or what you like. Sandbanks, marshes, forests, savages—precious little to eat fit for a civilised man, nothing but Thames water to drink. No Falernian wine[10] here, no going ashore. Here and there a military camp lost in a wilderness, like a needle in a bundle of hay—cold, fog, tempests, disease, exile, and death —death skulking in the air, in the water, in the bush. They must have been dying like flies here. Oh yes—he did it. Did it very well, too, no doubt, and without thinking much about it either, except afterwards to brag of what he had gone through in his time, perhaps. They were men enough to face the darkness. And perhaps he was cheered by keeping his eye on a chance of

8. A useful account of Conrad's technique in such stories as this, which make a straightforward narrative suggestive.
9. Galley with three banks of oars.
10. A wine celebrated by the Latin poets.

promotion to the fleet at Ravenna [11] by and by, if he had good friends in Rome and survived the awful climate. Or think of a decent young citizen in a toga—perhaps too much dice, you know—coming out here in the train of some prefect, or tax-gatherer, or trader, even, to mend his fortunes. Land in a swamp, march through the woods, and in some inland post feel the savagery, the utter savagery, had closed round him—all that mysterious life of the wilderness that stirs in the forest, in the jungles, in the hearts of wild men. There's no initiation either into such mysteries. He has to live in the midst of the incomprehensible, which is also detestable. And it has a fascination, too, that goes to work upon him. The fascination of the abomination [12]—you know. Imagine the growing regrets, the longing to escape, the powerless disgust, the surrender, the hate.'

He paused.

'Mind,' he began again, lifting one arm from the elbow, the palm of the hand outwards, so that, with his legs folded before him, he had the pose of a Buddha preaching in European clothes and without a lotus-flower—'Mind, none of us would feel exactly like this. What saves us is efficiency—the devotion to efficiency. But these chaps were not much account, really. They were no colonists; their administration was merely a squeeze,[13] and nothing more, I suspect. They were conquerors, and for that you want only brute force—nothing to boast of, when you have it, since your strength is just an accident arising from the weakness of others. They grabbed what they could get for the sake of what was to be got. It was just robbery with violence, aggravated murder on a great scale, and men going at it blind—as is very proper for those who tackle a darkness. The conquest of the earth, which mostly means the taking it away from those who have a different complexion or slightly flatter noses than ourselves, is not a pretty thing when you look into it too much. What redeems it is the idea only. An idea at the back of it; not a sentimental pretence but an idea; and an unselfish belief in the idea—something you can set up, and bow down before, and offer a sacrifice to. . . .'

He broke off. Flames glided in the river, small green flames, red flames, white flames, pursuing, overtaking, joining, crossing each other—then separating slowly or hastily. The traffic of the great city went on in the deepening night upon the sleepless river. We looked on, waiting patiently—there was nothing else to do till the end of the flood; but it was only after a long silence, when he said, in a hesitating voice, 'I suppose you fellows remember I did once turn fresh-water sailor for a bit,' that we knew we were fated, before the ebb began to run, to hear about one of Marlow's inconclusive experiences.

'I don't want to bother you much with what happened to me personally,' he began, showing in this remark the weakness of many tellers of tales who seem so often unaware of what their audience would best like to hear; 'yet to understand the effect of it on me you ought to know how I got out there, what I saw, how I went up that river to the place where I first met the poor chap. It was the farthest point of navigation and the culminating point of my

11. Ravenna, on the Adriatic, then a port.
12. "When ye therefore shall see the abomination of desolation, spoken of by Daniel the prophet, stand in the holy place (whoso readeth, let him understand) . . ."(Matthew 24:15).
13. A means of exploitation.

experience.[14] It seemed somehow to throw a kind of light on everything about me—and into my thoughts. It was sombre enough too—and pitiful—not extraordinary in any way—not very clear either. No, not very clear. And yet it seemed to throw a kind of light.

'I had then, as you remember, just returned to London after a lot of Indian Ocean, Pacific, China Seas—a regular dose of the East—six years or so, and I was loafing about, hindering you fellows in your work and invading your homes, just as though I had got a heavenly mission to civilise you. It was very fine for a time, but after a bit I did get tired of resting. Then I began to look for a ship—I should think the hardest work on earth. But the ships wouldn't even look at me. And I got tired of that game too.

'Now when I was a little chap I had a passion for maps. I would look for hours at South America, or Africa, or Australia, and lose myself in all the glories of exploration. At that time there were many blank spaces on the earth, and when I saw one that looked particularly inviting on a map (but they all look that) I would put my finger on it and say, When I grow up I will go there. The North Pole was one of these places, I remember. Well, I haven't been there yet, and shall not try now. The glamour's off. Other places were scattered about the Equator, and in every sort of latitude all over the two hemispheres. I have been in some of them, and . . . well, we won't talk about that. But there was one yet—the biggest, the most blank,[15] so to speak —that I had a hankering after.

'True, by this time it was not a blank space any more. It had got filled since my boyhood with rivers and lakes and names. It had ceased to be a blank space of delightful mystery—a white patch for a boy to dream gloriously over. It had become a place of darkness. But there was in it one river especially, a mighty big river, that you could see on the map, resembling an immense snake uncoiled, with its head in the sea, its body at rest curving afar over a vast country, and its tail lost in the depths of the land. And as I looked at the map of it in a shop-window, it fascinated me as a snake would a bird—a silly little bird. Then I remembered there was a big concern, a Company for trade on that river. Dash it all! I thought to myself, they can't trade without using some kind of craft on that lot of fresh water—steamboats! Why shouldn't I try to get charge of one? I went on along Fleet Street,[16] but could not shake off the idea. The snake had charmed me.

'You understand it was a Continental concern, that Trading Society; but I have a lot of relations living on the Continent, because it's cheap and not so nasty as it looks, they say.

'I am sorry to own I began to worry them. This was already a fresh departure for me. I was not used to get things that way, you know. I always went my own road and on my own legs where I had a mind to go. I wouldn't have believed it of myself; but, then—you see—I felt somehow I must get there by

14. An important indication of the multiple sense Conrad intends to impose on the simple narrative.

15. The "white space" in the middle of maps of Africa before the exploration of the Congo; see Headnote.

16. Runs from the western limit of the City of London eastward towards St. Paul's and the docks; it is the center of newspaper publishing.

hook or by crook. So I worried them. The men said, "My dear fellow," and did nothing. Then—would you believe it?—I tried the women. I, Charlie Marlow, set the women to work—to get a job. Heavens! Well, you see, the notion drove me. I had an aunt, a dear enthusiastic soul. She wrote: "It will be delightful. I am ready to do anything, anything for you. It is a glorious idea. I know the wife of a very high personage in the Administration, and also a man who has lots of influence with," etc. etc. She was determined to make no end of fuss to get me appointed skipper of a river steamboat, if such was my fancy.

'I got my appointment—of course; and I got it very quick. It appears the Company had received news that one of their captains had been killed in a scuffle with the natives. This was my chance, and it made me the more anxious to go. It was only months and months afterwards, when I made the attempt to recover what was left of the body, that I heard the original quarrel arose from a misunderstanding about some hens. Yes, two black hens. Fresleven [17]— that was the fellow's name, a Dane—thought himself wronged somehow in the bargain, so he went ashore and started to hammer the chief of the village with a stick. Oh, it didn't surprise me in the least to hear this, and at the same time to be told that Fresleven was the gentlest, quietest creature that ever walked on two legs. No doubt he was; but he had been a couple of years already out there engaged in the noble cause, you know, and he probably felt the need at last of asserting his self-respect in some way. Therefore he whacked the old nigger mercilessly, while a big crowd of his people watched him, thunderstruck, till some man—I was told the chief's son—in desperation at hearing the old chap yell, made a tentative jab with a spear at the white man —and of course it went quite easy between the shoulder-blades. Then the whole population cleared into the forest, expecting all kinds of calamities to happen, while, on the other hand, the steamer Fresleven commanded left also in a bad panic, in charge of the engineer, I believe. Afterwards nobody seemed to trouble much about Fresleven's remains, till I got out and stepped into his shoes. I couldn't let it rest, though; but when an opportunity offered at last to meet my predecessor, the grass growing through his ribs was tall enough to hide his bones. They were all there. The supernatural being had not been touched after he fell. And the village was deserted, the huts gaped black, rotting, all askew within the fallen enclosures. A calamity had come to it, sure enough. The people had vanished. Mad terror had scattered them, men, women, and children, through the bush, and they had never returned. What became of the hens I don't know either. I should think the cause of progress got them, anyhow. However, through this glorious affair I got my appointment, before I had fairly begun to hope for it.

'I flew around like mad to get ready, and before forty-eight hours I was crossing the Channel to show myself to my employers, and sign the contract. In a very few hours I arrived in a city that always makes me think of a whited sepulchre. [18] Prejudice no doubt. I had no difficulty in finding the Com-

---

17. For details of origin see Headnote.
18. Christ said the scribes and Pharisees were "like unto whited sepulchres, which indeed appear beautiful outward, but are within full of dead men's bones, and of all uncleanness" (Matthew 23:27). Conrad uses the expression of Brussels, center of the colonial administration.

pany's offices. It was the biggest thing in the town, and everybody I met was full of it. They were going to run an oversea empire, and make no end of coin by trade.

'A narrow and deserted street in deep shadow, high houses, innumerable windows with venetian blinds, a dead silence, grass sprouting between the stones, imposing carriage archways right and left, immense double doors standing ponderously ajar. I slipped through one of these cracks, went up a swept and ungarnished staircase, as arid as a desert, and opened the first door I came to. Two women, one fat and the other slim, sat on straw-bottomed chairs, knitting black wool. The slim one got up and walked straight at me—still knitting with downcast eyes—and only just as I began to think of getting out of her way, as you would for a somnambulist, stood still, and looked up. Her dress was as plain as an umbrella-cover, and she turned round without a word and preceded me into a waiting-room. I gave my name, and looked about. Deal table in the middle, plain chairs all round the walls, on one end a large shining map, marked with all the colours of a rainbow. There was a vast amount of red—good to see at any time, because one knows that some real work is done in there, a deuce of a lot of blue, a little green, smears of orange, and, on the East Coast, a purple patch, to show where the jolly pioneers of progress drink the jolly lager-beer. However, I wasn't going into any of these. I was going into the yellow. Dead in the centre. And the river was there—fascinating—deadly—like a snake. Ough! A door opened, a white-haired secretarial head, but wearing a compassionate expression, appeared, and a skinny forefinger beckoned me into the sanctuary. Its light was dim, and a heavy writing-desk squatted in the middle. From behind that structure came out an impression of pale plumpness in a frock-coat. The great man himself. He was five feet six, I should judge, and had his grip on the handle-end of ever so many millions. He shook hands, I fancy, murmured vaguely, was satisfied with my French. *Bon voyage*.

'In about forty-five seconds I found myself again in the waiting-room with the compassionate secretary, who, full of desolation and sympathy, made me sign some document. I believe I undertook amongst other things not to disclose any trade secrets. Well, I am not going to.

'I began to feel slightly uneasy. You know I am not used to such ceremonies, and there was something ominous in the atmosphere. It was just as though I had been let into some conspiracy—I don't know—something not quite right; and I was glad to get out. In the outer room the two women knitted black wool feverishly. People were arriving, and the younger one was walking back and forth introducing them. The old one sat on her chair. Her flat cloth slippers were propped up on a foot-warmer, and a cat reposed on her lap. She wore a starched white affair on her head, had a wart on one cheek, and silver-rimmed spectacles hung on the tip of her nose. She glanced at me above the glasses. The swift and indifferent placidity of that look troubled me. Two youths with foolish and cheery countenances were being piloted over, and she threw at them the same quick glance of unconcerned wisdom. She seemed to know all about them and about me too. An eerie feeling came over me. She seemed uncanny and fateful. Often far away there I thought of these two, guarding the door of Darkness, knitting black wool as for a warm pall, one introducing,

introducing continuously to the unknown, the other scrutinising the cheery and foolish faces with unconcerned old eyes. *Ave!* Old knitter of black wool. *Morituri te salutant.*[19] Not many of those she looked at ever saw her again—not half, by a long way.

'There was yet a visit to the doctor. "A simple formality," assured me the secretary, with an air of taking an immense part in all my sorrows. Accordingly a young chap wearing his hat over the left eyebrow, some clerk I suppose—there must have been clerks in the business, though the house was as still as a house in a city of the dead—came from somewhere upstairs, and led me forth. He was shabby and careless, with ink-stains on the sleeves of his jacket, and his cravat was large and billowy, under a chin shaped like the toe of an old boot. It was a little too early for the doctor, so I proposed a drink, and thereupon he developed a vein of joviality. As we sat over our vermouths he glorified the Company's business, and by and by I expressed casually my surprise at him not going out there. He became very cool and collected all at once. "I am not such a fool as I look, quoth Plato to his disciples," he said sententiously, emptied his glass with great resolution, and we rose.

'The old doctor felt my pulse, evidently thinking of something else the while. "Good, good for there," he mumbled, and then with a certain eagerness asked me whether I would let him measure my head. Rather surprised, I said Yes, when he produced a thing like callipers and got the dimensions back and front and every way, taking notes carefully. He was an unshaven little man in a thread-bare coat like a gaberdine, with his feet in slippers, and I thought him a harmless fool. "I always ask leave, in the interests of science, to measure the crania of those going out there," he said. "And when they come back too?" I asked. "Oh, I never see them," he remarked; "and, moreover, the changes take place inside, you know." He smiled, as if at some quiet joke. "So you are going out there. Famous. Interesting too." He gave me a searching glance, and made another note. "Ever any madness in your family?" he asked, in a matter-of-fact tone. I felt very annoyed. "Is that question in the interests of science too?" "It would be," he said, without taking notice of my irritation, "interesting for science to watch the mental changes of individuals, on the spot, but . . ." "Are you an alienist?"[20] I interrupted. "Every doctor should be—a little," answered that original imperturbably. "I have a little theory which you Messieurs who go out there must help me to prove. This is my share in the advantages my country shall reap from the possession of such a magnificent dependency. The mere wealth I leave to others. Pardon my questions, but you are the first Englishman coming under my observation . . ." I hastened to assure him I was not in the least typical. "If I were," said I, "I wouldn't be talking like this with you." "What you say is rather profound, and probably erroneous," he said, with a laugh. "Avoid irritation more than exposure to the sun. Adieu. How do you English say, eh? Good-bye. Ah! Good-bye. Adieu. In the tropics one must before everything keep calm.". . . He lifted a warning forefinger. . . . "*Du calme, du calme. Adieu.*"

'One thing more remained to do—say good-bye to my excellent aunt. I found

19. "Those who are about to die salute you" (the greeting of Roman gladiators at the games).
20. Specialist in mental illness.

her triumphant. I had a cup of tea—the last decent cup of tea for many days —and in a room that most soothingly looked just as you would expect a lady's drawing-room to look, we had a long quiet chat by the fireside. In the course of these confidences it became quite plain to me I had been represented to the wife of the high dignitary, and goodness knows to how many more people besides, as an exceptional and gifted creature—a piece of good fortune for the Company—a man you don't get hold of every day. Good Heavens! and I was going to take charge of a two-penny-half-penny river-steamboat with a penny whistle attached! It appeared, however, I was also one of the Workers, with a capital—you know. Something like an emissary of light, something like a lower sort of apostle. There had been a lot of such rot let loose in print and talk just about that time, and the excellent woman, living right in the rush of all that humbug, got carried off her feet. She talked about "weaning those ignorant millions from their horrid ways," till, upon my word, she made me quite uncomfortable. I ventured to hint that the Company was run for profit.

'"You forget, dear Charlie, that the labourer is worthy of his hire," she said brightly. It's queer how out of touch with truth women are. They live in a world of their own, and there had never been anything like it, and never can be. It is too beautiful altogether, and if they were to set it up it would go to pieces before the first sunset. Some confounded fact we men have been living contentedly with ever since the day of creation would start up and knock the whole thing over.

'After this I got embraced, told to wear flannel, be sure to write often, and so on—and I left. In the street—I don't know why—a queer feeling came to me that I was an impostor. Odd thing that I, who used to clear out for any part of the world at twenty-four hours' notice, with less thought than most men give to the crossing of a street, had a moment—I won't say of hesitation, but of startled pause, before this commonplace affair. The best way I can explain it to you is by saying that, for a second or two, I felt as though, instead of going to the centre of a continent, I were about to set off for the centre of the earth.

'I left in a French steamer, and she called in every blamed port they have out there, for, as far as I could see, the sole purpose of landing soldiers and custom-house officers. I watched the coast. Watching a coast as it slips by the ship is like thinking about an enigma. There it is before you—smiling, frowning, inviting, grand, mean, insipid, or savage, and always mute with an air of whispering, Come and find out. This one was almost featureless, as if still in the making, with an aspect of monotonous grimness. The edge of a colossal jungle, so dark green as to be almost black, fringed with white surf, ran straight, like a ruled line, far, far away along a blue sea whose glitter was blurred by a creeping mist. The sun was fierce, the land seemed to glisten and drip with steam. Here and there greyish-whitish specks showed up clustered inside the white surf, with a flag flying above them perhaps—settlements some centuries old, and still no bigger than pin-heads on the untouched expanse of their background. We pounded along, stopped, landed soldiers; went on, landed custom-house clerks to levy toll in what looked like a God-forsaken wilderness, with a tin shed and a flag-pole lost in it; landed more soldiers—to take care of the custom-house clerks presumably. Some, I heard, got drowned in the surf; but whether they did or not, nobody seemed particularly to care. They were just flung out there, and on we went. Every day the coast looked the same, as though we had not moved; but we passed various places—trading places—with names like Gran' Bassam, Little Popo; names that seemed to belong to some sordid farce acted in front of a sinister back-cloth. The idleness of a passenger, my isolation amongst all these men with whom I had no point of contact, the oily and languid sea, the uniform sombreness of the coast, seemed to keep me away from the truth of things, within the toil of a mournful and senseless delusion. The voice of the surf heard now and then was a positive pleasure, like the speech of a brother. It was something natural, that had its reason, that had a meaning. Now and then a boat from the shore gave one a momentary contact with reality. It was paddled by black fellows. You could see from afar the white of their eyeballs glistening. They shouted, sang; their bodies streamed with perspiration; they had faces like grotesque masks—these chaps; but they had bone, muscle, a wild vitality, an intense energy of movement, that was as natural and true as the surf along their coast. They wanted no excuse for being there. They were a great comfort to look at. For a time I would feel I belonged still to a world of straightforward facts; but the feeling would not last long. Something would turn up to scare it away. Once, I remember, we came upon a man-of-war anchored off the coast. There wasn't even a shed there, and she was shelling the bush. It appears the French had one of their wars going on thereabouts. Her ensign dropped limp like a rag; the muzzles of the long six-inch guns stuck out all over the low hull; the greasy, slimy swell swung her up lazily and let her down, swaying her thin masts. In the empty immensity of earth, sky, and water, there she was, incomprehensible, firing into a continent. Pop, would go one of the six-inch guns; a small flame would dart and vanish, a little white smoke would disappear, a tiny projectile would give a feeble screech—and nothing happened. Nothing could happen. There was a touch of insanity in the proceeding, a sense of lugubrious drollery in the sight; and it was not dissipated by somebody on board assuring me earnestly there was a camp of natives—he called them enemies!—hidden out of sight somewhere.

'We gave her her letters (I heard the men in that lonely ship were dying of fever at the rate of three a day) and went on. We called at some more places with farcical names, where the merry dance of death and trade goes on in a still and earthy atmosphere as of an overheated catacomb; all along the formless coast bordered by dangerous surf, as if Nature herself had tried to ward off intruders; in and out of rivers, streams of death in life, whose banks were rotting into mud, whose waters, thickened into slime, invaded the contorted mangroves, that seemed to writhe at us in the extremity of an impotent despair. Nowhere did we stop long enough to get a particularised impression, but the general sense of vague and oppressive wonder grew upon me. It was like a weary pilgrimage amongst hints for nightmares.

'It was upward of thirty days before I saw the mouth of the big river. We anchored off the seat of the government. But my work would not begin till some two hundred miles farther on. So as soon as I could I made a start for a place thirty miles higher up.

'I had my passage on a little sea-going steamer. Her captain was a Swede, and knowing me for a seaman, invited me on the bridge. He was a young man, lean, fair, and morose, with lanky hair and a shuffling gait. As we left the miserable little wharf, he tossed his head contemptuously at the shore. "Been living there?" he asked. I said, "Yes." "Fine lot these government chaps—are they not?" he went on, speaking English with great precision and considerable bitterness. "It is funny what some people will do for a few francs a month. I wonder what becomes of that kind when it goes up country?" I said to him I expected to see that soon. "So-o-o!" he exclaimed. He shuffled athwart, keeping one eye ahead vigilantly. "Don't be too sure," he continued. "The other day I took up a man who hanged himself on the road. He was a Swede, too." "Hanged himself! Why, in God's name?" I cried. He kept on looking out watchfully. "Who knows? The sun too much for him, or the country perhaps."

'At last we opened a reach. A rocky cliff appeared, mounds of turned-up earth by the shore, houses on a hill, others with iron roofs, amongst a waste of excavations, or hanging to the declivity. A continuous noise of the rapids above hovered over this scene of inhabited devastation. A lot of people, mostly black and naked, moved about like ants. A jetty projected into the river. A blinding sunlight drowned all this at times in a sudden recrudescence of glare. "There's your Company's station," said the Swede, pointing to three wooden barrack-like structures on the rocky slope. "I will send your things up. Four boxes did you say? So. Farewell."

'I came upon a boiler wallowing in the grass, then found a path leading up the hill. It turned aside for the boulders, and also for an undersized railway truck lying there on its back with its wheels in the air. One was off. The thing looked as dead as the carcass of some animal. I came upon more pieces of decaying machinery, a stack of rusty rails. To the left a clump of trees made a shady spot, where dark things seemed to stir feebly. I blinked, the path was steep. A horn tooted to the right, and I saw the black people run. A heavy and dull detonation shook the ground, a puff of smoke came out of the cliff, and that was all. No change appeared on the face of the rock. They were building a railway. The cliff was not in the way or anything; but this objectless blasting was all the work going on.

'A slight clinking behind me made me turn my head. Six black men advanced in a file, toiling up the path. They walked erect and slow, balancing small baskets full of earth on their heads, and the clink kept time with their footsteps. Black rags were wound round their loins, and the short ends behind waggled to and fro like tails. I could see every rib, the joints of their limbs were like knots in a rope; each had an iron collar on his neck, and all were connected together with a chain whose bights swung between them, rhythmically clinking. Another report from the cliff made me think suddenly of that ship of war I had seen firing into a continent. It was the same kind of ominous voice; but these men could by no stretch of imagination be called enemies. They were called criminals, and the outraged law, like the bursting shells, had come to them, an insoluble mystery from the sea. All their meagre breasts panted together, the violently dilated nostrils quivered, the eyes stared stonily uphill. They passed me within six inches, without a glance, with that complete, deathlike indifference of unhappy savages. Behind this raw matter one of the reclaimed, the product of the new forces at work, strolled despondently, carrying a rifle by its middle. He had a uniform jacket with one button off, and seeing a white man on the path, hoisted his weapon to his shoulder with alacrity. This was simple prudence, white men being so much alike at a distance that he could not tell who I might be. He was speedily reassured, and with a large, white, rascally grin, and a glance at his charge, seemed to take me into partnership in his exalted trust. After all, I also was a part of the great cause of these high and just proceedings.

'Instead of going up, I turned and descended to the left. My idea was to let that chain-gang get out of sight before I climbed the hill. You know I am not particularly tender; I've had to strike and to fend off. I've had to resist and to attack sometimes—that's only one way of resisting—without counting the exact cost, according to the demands of such sort of life as I had blundered into. I've seen the devil of violence, and the devil of greed, and the devil of hot desire; but, by all the stars! these were strong, lusty, red-eyed devils, that swayed and drove men—men, I tell you. But as I stood on this hillside, I foresaw that in the blinding sunshine of that land I would become acquainted with a flabby, pretending, weak-eyed devil of a rapacious and pitiless folly. How insidious he could be, too, I was only to find out several months later and a thousand miles farther. For a moment I stood appalled, as though by a warning. Finally I descended the hill, obliquely, towards the trees I had seen.

'I avoided a vast artificial hole somebody had been digging on the slope, the purpose of which I found it impossible to divine. It wasn't a quarry or a sandpit, anyhow. It was just a hole. It might have been connected with the philanthropic desire of giving the criminals something to do. I don't know. Then I nearly fell into a very narrow ravine, almost no more than a scar in the hillside. I discovered that a lot of imported drainage-pipes for the settlement had been tumbled in there. There wasn't one that was not broken. It was a wanton smash-up. At last I got under the trees. My purpose was to stroll into the shade for a moment; but no sooner within than it seemed to me I had stepped into the gloomy circle of some Inferno. The rapids were near, and an uninterrupted, uniform, headlong, rushing noise filled the mournful stillness of the grove, where not a breath stirred, not a leaf moved, with a mysterious sound—as though the tearing pace of the launched earth had suddenly become audible.

'Black shapes crouched, lay, sat between the trees, leaning against the trunks, clinging to the earth, half coming out, half effaced within the dim light, in all the attitudes of pain, abandonment, and despair. Another mine [21] on the cliff went off, followed by a slight shudder of the soil under my feet. The work was going on. The work! And this was the place where some of the helpers had withdrawn to die.

'They were dying slowly—it was very clear. They were not enemies, they were not criminals, they were nothing earthly now—nothing but black shadows of disease and starvation, lying confusedly in the greenish gloom. Brought from all the recesses of the coast in all the legality of time contracts, lost in uncongenial surroundings, fed on unfamiliar food, they sickened, became inefficient, and were then allowed to crawl away and rest. These moribund shapes were free as air—and nearly as thin. I began to distinguish the gleam of the eyes under the trees. Then, glancing down, I saw a face near my hand. The black

21. Explosive charge.

bones reclined at full length with one shoulder against the tree, and slowly the eyelids rose and the sunken eyes looked up at me, enormous and vacant, a kind of blind, white flicker in the depths of the orbs, which died out slowly. The man seemed young—almost a boy—but you know with them it's hard to tell. I found nothing else to do but to offer him one of my good Swede's ship's biscuits I had in my pocket. The fingers closed slowly on it and held—there was no other movement and no other glance. He had tied a bit of white worsted round his neck—Why? Where did he get it? Was it a badge—an ornament—a charm—a propitiatory act? Was there any idea at all connected with it? It looked startling round his black neck, this bit of white thread from beyond the seas.

'Near the same tree two more bundles of acute angles sat with their legs drawn up. One, with his chin propped on his knees, stared at nothing, in an intolerable and appalling manner: his brother phantom rested its forehead, as if overcome with a great weariness; and all about others were scattered in every pose of contorted collapse, as in some picture of a massacre or a pestilence. While I stood horror-struck, one of these creature rose to his hands and knees, and went off on all-fours towards the river to drink. He lapped out of his hand, then sat up in the sunlight, crossing his shins in front of him, and after a time let his woolly head fall on his breastbone.

'I didn't want any more loitering in the shade, and I made haste towards the station. When near the buildings I met a white man, in such an unexpected elegance of get-up that in the first moment I took him for a sort of vision. I saw a high starched collar, white cuffs, a light alpaca jacket, snowy trousers, a clean necktie, and varnished boots. No hat. Hair parted, brushed, oiled, under a green-lined parasol held in a big white hand. He was amazing, and had a pen-holder behind his ear.

'I shook hands with this miracle, and I learned he was the Company's chief accountant, and that all the book-keeping was done at this station. He had come out for a moment, he said, "to get a breath of fresh air." The expression sounded wonderfully odd, with its suggestion of sedentary desk-life. I wouldn't have mentioned the fellow to you at all, only it was from his lips that I first heard the name of the man who is so indissolubly connected with the memories of that time. Moreover, I respected the fellow. Yes; I respected his collars, his vast cuffs, his brushed hair. His appearance was certainly that of a hair-dresser's dummy; but in the great demoralisation of the land he kept up his appearance. That's backbone. His starched collars and got-up shirt-fronts were achievements of character. He had been out nearly three years; and, later, I could not help asking him how he managed to sport such linen. He had just the faintest blush, and said modestly, "I've been teaching one of the native women about the station. It was difficult. She had a distaste for the work." Thus this man had verily accomplished something. And he was devoted to his books, which were in apple-pie order.

'Everything else in the station was in a muddle,—heads, things, buildings. Strings of dusty niggers with splay feet arrived and departed; a stream of manu-factured goods, rubbishy cottons, beads, and brass-wire set into the depths of darkness, and in return came a precious trickle of ivory.

'I had to wait in the station for ten days—an eternity. I lived in a hut in the yard, but to be out of the chaos I would sometimes get into the accountant's office. It was built of horizontal planks, and so badly put together that, as he bent over his high desk, he was barred from neck to heels with narrow strips of sunlight. There was no need to open the big shutter to see. It was hot there too; big flies buzzed fiendishly, and did not sting, but stabbed. I sat generally on the floor, while, of faultless appearance (and even slightly scented), perching on a high stool, he wrote, he wrote. Sometimes he stood up for exercise. When a truckle-bed with a sick man (some invalided agent from up-country) was put in there, he exhibited a gentle annoyance. "The groans of this sick person," he said, "distract my attention. And without that it is extremely difficult to guard against clerical errors in this climate."

'One day he remarked, without lifting his head, "In the interior you will no doubt meet Mr. Kurtz." On my asking who Mr. Kurtz was, he said he was a first-class agent; and seeing my disappointment at this information, he added slowly, laying down his pen, "He is a very remarkable person." Further questions elicited from him that Mr. Kurtz was at present in charge of a trading-post, a very important one, in the true ivory-country, at "the very bottom of there. Sends in as much ivory as all the others put together . . ." He began to write again. The sick man was too ill to groan. The flies buzzed in a great peace.

'Suddenly there was a growing murmur of voices and a great tramping of feet. A caravan had come in. A violent babble of uncouth sounds burst out on the other side of the planks. All the carriers were speaking together, and in the midst of the uproar the lamentable voice of the chief agent was heard "giving it up" tearfully for the twentieth time that day. . . . He rose slowly. "What a frightful row," he said. He crossed the room gently to look at the sick man, and returning, said to me, "He does not hear." "What! Dead?" I asked, startled. "No, not yet," he answered, with great composure. Then, alluding with a toss of the head to the tumult in the station-yard, "When one has got to make correct entries, one comes to hate those savages—hate them to the death." He remained thoughtful for a moment. "When you see Mr. Kurtz," he went on, "tell him from me that everything here"—he glanced at the desk—"is very satisfactory. I don't like to write to him—with those messengers of ours you never know who may get hold of your lettter—at that Central Station." He stared at me for a moment with his mild, bulging eyes. "Oh, he will go far, very far," he began again. "He will be a somebody in the Administration before long. They, above—the Council in Europe, you know —mean him to be."

'He turned to his work. The noise outside had ceased, and presently in going out I stopped at the door. In the steady buzz of flies the homeward-bound agent was lying flushed and insensible; the other, bent over his books, was making correct entries of perfectly correct transactions; and fifty feet below the doorstep I could see the still tree-tops of the grove of death.

'Next day I left that station at last, with a caravan of sixty men, for a two-hundred-mile tramp.

'No use telling you much about that. Paths, paths, everywhere; a stamped-in network of paths spreading over the empty land, through long grass, through burnt grass, through thickets, down and up chilly ravines, up and down stony hills ablaze with heat; and a solitude, a solitude, nobody, not a hut. The population had cleared out a long time ago. Well, if a lot of mysterious niggers armed with all kinds of fearful weapons suddenly took to travelling on the road between Deal and Gravesend, catching the yokels right and left to carry heavy loads for them, I fancy every farm and cottage thereabouts would get empty very soon. Only here the dwellings were gone too. Still, I passed through several abandoned villages. There's something pathetically childish in the ruins of grass walls. Day after day, with the stamp and shuffle of sixty pair of bare feet behind me, each pair under a 60-lb. load. Camp, cook, sleep; strike camp, march. Now and then a carrier dead in harness, at rest in the long grass near the path, with an empty water-gourd and his long staff lying by his side. A great silence around and above. Perhaps on some quiet night the tremor of far-off drums, sinking, swelling, a tremor vast, faint; a sound weird, appealing, suggestive, and wild—and perhaps with as profound a meaning as the sound of bells in a Christian country. Once a white man in an unbuttoned uniform, camping on the path with an armed escort of lank Zanzibaris,[22] very hospitable and festive—not to say drunk. Was looking after the upkeep of the road, he declared. Can't say I saw any road or any upkeep, unless the body of a middle-aged negro, with a bullet-hole in the forehead, upon which I absolutely stumbled three miles farther on,[23] may be considered as a permanent improvement. I had a white companion too, not a bad chap, but rather too fleshy and with the exasperating habit of fainting on the hot hillsides, miles away from the least bit of shade and water. Annoying, you know, to hold your own coat like a parasol over a man's head while he is coming to. I couldn't help asking him once what he meant by coming there at all. "To make money, of course. What do you think?" he said scornfully. Then he got fever, and had to be carried in a hammock slung under a pole. As he weighed sixteen stone[24] I had no end of rows with the carriers. They jibbed, ran away, sneaked off with their loads in the night—quite a mutiny. So, one evening, I made a speech in English with gestures, not one of which was lost to the sixty pairs of eyes before me, and the next morning I started the hammock off in front all right. An hour afterwards I came upon the whole concern wrecked in a bush—man, hammock, groans, blankets, horrors. The heavy pole had skinned his poor nose. He was very anxious for me to kill somebody, but there wasn't the shadow of a carrier near. I remembered the old doctor—"It would be interesting for science to watch the mental changes of individuals, on the spot." I felt I was becoming scientifically interesting. However, all that is to no purpose. On the fifteenth day I came in sight of the big river again, and hobbled into the Central Station. It was on a back water surrounded by scrub and forest, with a pretty border of smelly mud on one side, and on the three others enclosed by a crazy fence of rushes. A neglected gap was all the gate it had, and the first glance at the place was enough to let you see the flabby devil was running that show. White men with long staves[25] in their

22. Natives of Zanzibar used as mercenaries.
23. Modified from an actual experience of Conrad's; see Headnote.
24. 224 pounds.
25. It was the custom for white men to carry these staves, which gave rise to Conrad's ironical description of them as "pilgrims."

hands appeared languidly from amongst the buildings, strolling up to take a look at me, and then retired out of sight somewhere. One of them, a stout, excitable chap with black moustaches, informed me with great volubility and many digressions, as soon as I told him who I was, that my steamer was at the bottom of the river. I was thunderstruck. What, how, why? Oh, it was "all right." The "manager himself" was there. All quite correct. "Everybody had behaved splendidly! splendidly!"—"You must," he said in agitation, "go and see the general manager at once. He is waiting."

"I did not see the real significance of that wreck at once. I fancy I see it now, but I am not sure—not at all. Certainly the affair was too stupid—when I think of it—to be altogether natural. Still . . . But at the moment it presented itself simply as a confounded nuisance. The steamer was sunk. They had started two days before in a sudden hurry up the river with the manager on board, in charge of some volunteer skipper, and before they had been out three hours they tore the bottom out of her on stones, and she sank near the south bank. I asked myself what I was to do there, now my boat was lost. As a matter of fact, I had plenty to do in fishing my command out of the river. I had to set about it the very next day. That, and the repairs when I brought the pieces to the station, took some months.

'My first interview with the manager was curious. He did not ask me to sit down after my twenty-mile walk that morning. He was commonplace in complexion, in feature, in manners, and in voice. He was of middle size and of ordinary build. His eyes, of the usual blue, were perhaps remarkably cold, and he certainly could make his glance fall on one as trenchant and heavy as an axe. But even at these times the rest of his person seemed to disclaim the intention. Otherwise there was only an indefinable, faint expression of his lips, something stealthy—a smile—not a smile—I remember it, but I can't explain. It was unconscious, this smile was, though just after he had said something it got intensified for an instant. It came at the end of his speeches like a seal applied on the words to make the meaning of the commonest phrase appear absolutely inscrutable. He was a common trader, from his youth up employed in these parts—nothing more. He was obeyed, yet he inspired neither love nor fear, nor even respect. He inspired uneasiness. That was it! Uneasiness. Not a definite mistrust—just uneasiness—nothing more. You have no idea how effective such a . . . a . . . faculty can be. He had no genius for organising, for initiative, or for order even. That was evident in such things as the deplorable state of the station. He had no learning, and no intelligence. His position had come to him—why? Perhaps because he was never ill . . . He had served three terms of three years out there . . . Because triumphant health in the general rout of constitutions is a kind of power in itself. When he went home on leave he rioted on a large scale—pompously. Jack ashore—with a difference—in externals only. This one could gather from his casual talk. He originated nothing, he could keep the routine going—that's all. But he was great. He was great by this little thing that it was impossible to tell what could control such a man. He never gave that secret away. Perhaps there was nothing within him. Such a suspicion made one pause—for out there there were no external checks. Once when various tropical diseases had laid low almost every "agent" in the station, he was heard to say, "Men who come out here should have no entrails." He sealed the utterance with that smile of his, as though it had been a door opening into a darkness he had in his keeping. You fancied you had seen things—but the seal was on. When annoyed at meal-times by the constant quarrels of the white men about precedence, he ordered an immense round table to be made, for which a special house had to be built. This was the station's mess-room. Where he sat was the first place —the rest were nowhere. One felt this to be his unalterable conviction. He was neither civil or uncivil. He was quiet. He allowed his "boy"—an overfed young negro from the coast—to treat the white men, under his very eyes, with provoking insolence.

'He began to speak as soon as he saw me. I had been very long on the road. He could not wait. Had to start without me. The up-river stations had to be relieved. There had been so many delays already that he did not know who was dead and who was alive, and how they got on—and so on, and so on. He paid no attention to my explanations, and, playing with a stick of sealing-wax, repeated several times that the situation was "very grave, very grave." There were rumours that a very important station was in jeopardy, and its chief, Mr. Kurtz, was ill. Hoped it was not true. Mr. Kurtz was . . . I felt weary and irritable. Hang Kurtz, I thought. I interrupted him by saying I had heard of Mr. Kurtz on the coast, "Ah! So they talk of him down there," he murmured to himself. Then he began again, assuring me Mr. Kurtz was the best agent he had, an exceptional man, of the greatest importance to the Company; therefore I could understand his anxiety. He was, he said, "very, very uneasy." Certainly he fidgeted on his chair a good deal, exclaimed, "Ah, Mr. Kurtz!" broke the stick of sealing-wax and seemed dumbfounded by the accident. Next thing he wanted to know "how long it would take to". . . I interrupted him again. Being hungry, you know, and kept on my feet too, I was getting savage. "How can I tell?" I said. "I haven't even seen the wreck yet—some months, no doubt." All this talk seemed to me so futile. "Some months," he said. "Well, let us say three months before we can make a start. Yes. That ought to do the affair." I flung out of his hut (he lived all alone in a clay hut with a sort of verandah) muttering to myself my opinion of him. He was a chattering idiot. Afterwards I took it back when it was borne in upon me startlingly with what extreme nicety he had estimated the time requisite for the "affair."

'I went to work the next day, turning, so to speak, my back on that station. In that way only it seemed to me I could keep my hold on the redeeming facts of life. Still, one must look about sometimes; and then I saw this station, these men strolling aimlessly about in the sunshine of the yard. I asked myself sometimes what it all meant. They wandered here and there with their absurd long staves in their hands, like a lot of faithless pilgrims bewitched inside a rotten fence. The word "ivory" rang in the air, was whispered, was sighed. You would think they were praying to it. A taint of imbecile rapacity blew through it all, like a whiff from some corpse. By Jove! I've never seen anything so unreal in my life. And outside, the silent wilderness surrounding this cleared speck on the earth struck me as something great and invincible, like evil or truth, waiting patiently for the passing away of this fantastic invasion.

'Oh, those months! Well, never mind. Various things happened. One evening a grass shed full of calico, cotton prints, beads, and I don't know what else, burst into a blaze so suddenly that you would have thought the earth had opened to let an avenging fire consume all that trash. I was smoking my pipe quietly by my dismantled steamer, and saw them all cutting capers in the light, with their arms lifted high, when the stout man with moustaches came tearing down to the river, a tin pail in his hand, assured me that everybody was "behaving splendidly, splendidly," dipped about a quart of water and tore back again. I noticed there was a hole in the bottom of his pail.

'I strolled up. There was no hurry. You see the thing had gone off like a box of matches. It had been hopeless from the very first. The flame had leaped high, driven everybody back, lighted up everything—and collapsed. The shed was already a heap of embers glowing fiercely. A nigger was being beaten near by. They said he had caused the fire in some way; be that as it may, he was screeching most horribly. I saw him, later, for several days, sitting in a bit of shade looking very sick and trying to recover himself: afterwards he arose and went out—and the wilderness without a sound took him into its bosom again. As I approached the glow from the dark I found myself at the back of two men, talking. I heard the name of Kurtz pronounced, then the words, "take advantage of this unfortunate accident." One of the men was the manager. I wished him a good evening. "Did you ever see anything like it—eh? it is incredible." he said, and walked off. The other man remained. He was a first-class agent, young, gentlemanly, a bit reserved, with a forked little beard and a hooked nose. He was stand-offish with the other agents, and they on their side said he was the manager's spy upon them. As to me, I had hardly ever spoken to him before. We got into talk, and by and by we strolled away from the hissing ruins. Then he asked me to his room, which was in the main building of the station. He struck a match, and I perceived that this young aristocrat had not only a silver-mounted dressing-case but also a whole candle all to himself. Just at that time the manager was the only man supposed to have any right to candles. Native mats covered the clay walls; a collection of spears, assegais,[26] shields, knives, was hung up in trophies. The business entrusted to this fellow was the making of bricks—so I had been informed; but there wasn't a fragment of a brick anywhere in the station, and he had been there more than a year—waiting. It seems he could not make bricks without something, I don't know what—straw maybe. Anyway, it could not be found there, and as it was not likely to be sent from Europe, it did not appear clear to me what he was waiting for. An act of special creation [27] perhaps. However, they were all waiting—all the sixteen or twenty pilgrims of them—for something; and upon my word it did not seem an uncongenial occupation, from the way they took it, though the only thing that ever came to them was disease—as far as I could see. They beguiled the time by back-biting and intriguing against each other in a foolish kind of way. There was an air of plotting about that station, but nothing came of it, of course. It was as unreal as everything else—as the philanthropic pretence of the whole concern, as their talk, as their government, as their show of work. The only real

26. Zulu throwing-spears.
27. The doctrine that God created all things according to their kinds ("special creation") was overthrown by 19th-century evolutionism. Here the use is facetious.

feeling was a desire to get appointed to a trading-post where ivory was to be had, so that they could earn percentages. They intrigued and slandered and hated each other only on that account—but as to effectually lifting a little finger—oh no. By Heavens! there is something after all in the world allowing one man to steal a horse while another must not look at a halter. Steal a horse straight out. Very well. He has done it. Perhaps he can ride. But there is a way of looking at a halter that would provoke the most charitable of saints into a kick.

'I had no idea why he wanted to be sociable, but as we chatted in there it suddenly occurred to me the fellow was trying to get at something—in fact, pumping me. He alluded constantly to Europe, to the people I was supposed to know there—putting leading questions as to my acquaintances in the sepulchral city, and so on. His little eyes glittered like mica discs—with curiosity—though he tried to keep up a bit of superciliousness. At first I was astonished, but very soon I became awfully curious to see what he would find out from me. I couldn't possibly imagine what I had in me to make it worth his while. It was very pretty to see how he baffled himself, for in truth my body was full only of chills, and my head had nothing in it but that wretched steamboat business. It was evident he took me for a perfectly shameless prevaricator. At last he got angry, and, to conceal a movement of furious annoyance, he yawned. I rose. Then I noticed a small sketch in oils, on a panel, representing a woman, draped and blindfolded, carrying a lighted torch. The background was sombre—almost black. The movement of the woman was stately, and the effect of the torchlight on the face was sinister.

'It arrested me, and he stood by civilly, holding an empty half-pint champagne bottle (medical comforts) with the candle stuck in it. To my question he said Mr. Kurtz had painted this—in this very station more than a year ago— while waiting for means to go to his trading-post. "Tell me, pray," said I, "who is this Mr. Kurtz?"

' "The chief of the Inner Station," he answered in a short tone, looking away. "Much obliged," I said, laughing. "And you are the brickmaster of the Central Station. Every one knows that." He was silent for a while. "He is a prodigy," he said at last. "He is an emissary of pity, and science, and progress, and devil knows what else. We want," he began to declaim suddenly, "for the guidance of the cause entrusted to us by Europe, so to speak, higher intelligence, wide sympathies, a singleness of purpose." "Who says that?" I asked. "Lots of them," he replied. "Some even write that; and so *he* comes here, a special being, as you ought to know." "Why ought I to know?" I interrupted, really surprised. He paid no attention. "Yes. To-day he is chief of the best station, next year he will be assistant-manager, two years more and . . . but I daresay you know what he will be in two years' time. You are of the new gang—the gang of virtue. The same people who sent him specially also recommended you. Oh, don't say no. I've my own eyes to trust." Light dawned upon me. My dear aunt's influential acquaintances were producing an unexpected effect upon that young man. I nearly burst into a laugh. "Do you read the Company's confidential correspondence?" I asked. He hadn't a word to say. It was great fun. "When Mr. Kurtz," I continued severely, "is General Manager, you won't have the opportunity."

'He blew the candle out suddenly, and we went outside. The moon had risen. Black figures strolled about listlessly, pouring water on the glow, whence proceeded a sound of hissing; steam ascended in the moonlight; the beaten nigger groaned somewhere. "What a row the brute makes!" said the inde-fatigable man with the moustaches, appearing near us. "Serve him right. Trans-gression—punishment—bang! Pitiless, pitiless. That's the only way. This will prevent all conflagrations for the future. I was just telling the manager . . ." He noticed my companion, and became crestfallen all at once. "Not in bed yet," he said, with a kind of servile heartiness; "It's so natural. Ha! Danger—agitation." He vanished. I went on to the river-side, and the other followed me. I heard a scathing murmur at my ear, "Heaps of muffs—go to." The pilgrims could be seen in knots gesticulating, discussing. Several had still their staves in their hands. I verily believe they took these sticks to bed with them. Beyond the fence the forest stood up spectrally in the moonlight, and through the dim stir, through the faint sounds of that lamentable courtyard, the silence of the land went home to one's very heart—its mystery, its greatness, the amazing reality of its concealed life. The hurt nigger moaned feebly somewhere near by, and then fetched a deep sigh that made me mend my pace away from there. I felt a hand introducing itself under my arm. "My dear sir," said the fellow, "I don't want to be misunderstood, and especially by you, who will see Mr. Kurtz long before I can have that pleasure. I wouldn't like him to get a false idea of my disposition. . . ."

'I let him run on, this papier-mâché Mephistopheles, and it seemed to me that if I tried I could poke my forefinger through him, and would find nothing inside but a little loose dirt, maybe. He, don't you see, had been planning to be assistant-manager by and by under the present man, and I could see that the coming of that Kurtz had upset them both not a little. He talked precipitately, and I did not try to stop him. I had my shoulders against the wreck of my steamer, hauled up on the slope like a carcass of some big river animal. The smell of mud, of primeval mud, by Jove! was in my nostrils, the high stillness of primeval forest was before my eyes; there were shiny patches on the black creek. The moon had spread over everything a thin layer of silver—over the rank grass, over the mud, upon the wall of matted vegetation standing higher than the wall of a temple, over the great river I could see through a sombre gap glittering, glittering, as it flowed broadly by without a murmur. All this was great, expectant, mute, while the man jabbered about himself. I wondered whether the stillness on the face of the immensity looking at us two were meant as an appeal or as a menace. What were we who had strayed in here? Could we handle that dumb thing, or would it handle us? I felt how big, how con-foundedly big, was that thing that couldn't talk and perhaps was deaf as well. What was in there? I could see a little ivory coming out from there, and I had heard Mr. Kurtz was in there. I had heard enough about it too—God knows! Yet somehow it didn't bring any image with it—no more than if I had been told an angel or a fiend was in there. I believed it in the same way one of you might believe there are inhabitants in the planet Mars. I knew once a Scotch sailmaker who was certain, dead sure, there were people in Mars. If you asked him for some idea how they looked and behaved, he would get shy and mutter something about "walking on all-fours." If you as much as smiled, he would

—though a man of sixty—offer to fight you. I would not have gone so far as to fight for Kurtz, but I went for him near enough to a lie. You know I hate, detest, and can't bear a lie, not because I am straighter than the rest of us, but simply because it appals me. There is a taint of death, a flavour of mortality in lies—which is exactly what I hate and detest in the world—what I want to forget. It makes me miserable and sick, like biting something rotten would do. Temperament, I suppose. Well, I went near enough to it by letting the young fool there believe anything he liked to imagine as to my influence in Europe. I became in an instant as much of a pretence as the rest of the bewitched pilgrims. This simply because I had a notion it somehow would be of help to that Kurtz whom at the time I did not see—you understand. He was just a word for me. I did not see the man in the name any more than you do. Do you see him? Do you see the story? Do you see anything? It seems to me I am trying to tell you a dream—making a vain attempt, because no relation of a dream can convey the dream-sensation, that commingling of absurdity, surprise, and bewilderment in a tremor of struggling revolt, that notion of being captured by the incredible which is of the very essence of dreams. . . .'

He was silent for a while.

'. . . No, it is impossible; it is impossible to convey the life-sensation of any given epoch of one's existence—that which makes its truth, its meaning —its subtle and penetrating essence. It is impossible. We live, as we dream— alone. . . .'

He paused again as if reflecting, then added:

'Of course in this you fellows see more than I could then. You see me, whom you know. . . .'

It had become so pitch dark that we listeners could hardly see one another. For a long time already he, sitting apart, had been no more to us than a voice. There was not a word from anybody. The others might have been asleep, but I was awake. I listened, I listened on the watch for the sentence, for the word, that would give me the clue to the faint uneasiness inspired by this narrative that seemed to shape itself without human lips in the heavy night-air of the river.

'. . . Yes—I let him run on,' Marlow began again, 'and think what he pleased about the powers that were behind me. I did! And there was nothing behind me! There was nothing but that wretched, old, mangled steamboat I was leaning against, while he talked fluently about "the necessity for every man to get on." "And when one comes out here, you conceive, it is not to gaze at the moon." Mr. Kurtz was a "universal genius," but even a genius would find it easier to work with "adequate tools—intelligent men." He did not make bricks—why, there was a physical impossibility in the way—as I was well aware; and if he did secretarial work for the manager, it was because "no sensible man rejects wantonly the confidence of his superiors." Did I see it? I saw it. What more did I want? What I really wanted was rivets, by Heaven! Rivets. To get on with the work—to stop the hole. Rivets I wanted. There were cases of them down at the coast—cases—piled up—burst—split! You kicked a loose rivet at every second step in that station yard on the hillside. Rivets had rolled into the grove of death. You could fill your pockets with rivets for the trouble of stooping down—and there wasn't one rivet to be found where it was wanted. We had plates that would do, but nothing to fasten them with. And every week the messenger, a lone negro, letter-bag on shoulder and staff in hand, left our station for the coast. And several times a week a coast caravan came in with trade goods—ghastly glazed calico that made you shudder only to look at it, glass beads value about a penny a quart, confounded spotted cotton handkerchiefs. And no rivets. Three carriers could have brought all that was wanted to set that steamboat afloat.

'He was becoming confidential now, but I fancy my unresponsive attitude must have exasperated him at last, for he judged it necessary to inform me he feared neither God nor devil, let alone any mere man. I said I could see that very well, but what I wanted was a certain quantity of rivets—and rivets were what really Mr. Kurtz wanted, if he had only known it. Now letters went to the coast every week. . . . "My dear sir," he cried, "I write from dictation." I demanded rivets. There was a way—for an intelligent man. He changed his manner; became very cold, and suddenly began to talk about a hippopotamus; wondered whether sleeping on board the steamer (I stuck to my salvage night and day) I wasn't disturbed. There was an old hippo that had the bad habit of getting out on the bank and roaming at night over the station grounds. The pilgrims used to turn out in a body and empty every rifle they could lay hands on at him. Some even had sat up o' nights for him. All this energy was wasted, though. "That animal has a charmed life," he said; "but you can say this only of brutes in this country. No man—you apprehend me? —no man here bears a charmed life." He stood there for a moment in the moonlight with his delicate hooked nose set a little askew, and his mica eyes glittering without a wink, then, with a curt Good-night, he strode off. I could see he was disturbed and considerably puzzled, which made me feel more hopeful than I had been for days. It was a great comfort to turn from that chap to my influential friend, the battered, twisted, ruined, tin-pot steamboat. I clambered on board. She rang under my feet like an empty Huntley & Palmer biscuit-tin kicked along a gutter; she was nothing so solid in make, and rather less pretty in shape, but I had expended enough hard work on her to make me love her. No influential friend would have served me better. She had given me a chance to come out a bit—to find out what I could do. No, I don't like work. I had rather laze about and think of all the fine things that can be done. I don't like work—no man does—but I like what is in the work—the chance to find yourself. Your own reality—for yourself, not for others—what no other man can ever know. They can only see the mere show, and never can tell what it really means.

'I was not surprised to see somebody sitting aft, on the deck, with his legs dangling over the mud. You see I rather chummed with the few mechanics there were in that station, whom the other pilgrims naturally despised—on account of their imperfect manners, I suppose. This was the foreman—a boiler-maker by trade—a good worker. He was a lank, bony, yellow-faced man, with big intense eyes. His aspect was worried, and his head was as bald as the palm of my hand; but his hair in falling seemed to have stuck to his chin, and had prospered in the new locality, for his beard hung down to his waist. He was a widower with six young children (he had left them in charge of a sister of his to come out there), and the passion of his life was pigeon-flying. He was an enthusiast and a connoisseur. He would rave about pigeons. After work hours he used sometimes to come over from his hut for a talk about his children and his pigeons; at work, when he had to crawl in the mud under the bottom of the steamboat, he would tie up that beard of his in a kind of white serviette [28] he brought for the purpose. It had loops to go over his ears. In the evening he could be seen squatted on the bank rinsing that wrapper in the creek with great care, then spreading it solemnly on a bush to dry.

'I slapped him on the back and shouted "We shall have rivets!" He scrambled to his feet exclaiming "No! Rivets!" as though he couldn't believe his ears. Then in a low voice, "You . . . eh?" I don't know why we behaved like lunatics. I put my finger to the side of my nose and nodded mysteriously. "Good for you!" he cried, snapped his fingers above his head, lifting one foot. I tried a jig. We capered on the iron deck. A frightful clatter came out of that hulk, and the virgin forest on the other bank of the creek sent it back in a thundering roll upon the sleeping station. It must have made some of the pilgrims sit up in their hovels. A dark figure obscured the lighted doorway of the manager's hut, vanished, then, a second or so after, the doorway itself vanished too. We stopped, and the silence driven away by the stamping of our feet flowed back again from the recesses of the land. The great wall of vegetation, an exuberant and entangled mass of trunks, branches, leaves, boughs, festoons, motionless in the moonlight, was like a rioting invasion of soundless life, a rolling wave of plants, piled up, crested, ready to topple over the creek, to sweep every little man of us out of his little existence. And it moved not. A deadened burst of mighty splashes and snorts reached us from afar, as though an ichthyosaurus [29] had been taking a bath of glitter in the great river. "After all," said the boiler-maker in a reasonable tone, "why shouldn't we get the rivets?" Why not, indeed! I did not know of any reason why we shouldn't. "They'll come in three weeks," I said confidently.

'But they didn't. Instead of rivets there came an invasion, an infliction, a visitation. It came in sections during the next three weeks, each section headed by a donkey carrying a white man in new clothes and tan shoes, bowing from that elevation right and left to the impressed pilgrims. A quarrelsome band of footsore sulky niggers trod on the heels of the donkey; a lot of tents, camp-stools, tin boxes, white cases, brown bales would be shot down in the court-yard, and the air of mystery would deepen a little over the muddle of the station. Five such instalments came, with their absurd air of disorderly flight with the loot of innumerable outfit shops and provision stores, that, one would think, they were lugging, after a raid, into the wilderness for equitable divi-sion. It was an inextricable mess of things decent in themselves but that human folly made look like the spoils of thieving.

'This devoted band called itself the Eldorado Exploring Expedition, and I believe they were sworn to secrecy. Their talk, however, was the talk of sordid buccaneers: it was reckless without hardihood, greedy without audacity, and cruel without courage; there was not an atom of foresight or of serious inten-

28. Napkin.
29. Extinct marine reptile.

tion in the whole batch of them, and they did not seem aware these things are wanted for the work of the world. To tear treasure out of the bowels of the land was their desire, with no more moral purpose at the back of it than there is in burglars breaking into a safe. Who paid the expenses of the noble enterprise I don't know; but the uncle of our manager was leader of that lot.

'In exterior he resembled a butcher in a poor neighbourhood, and his eyes had a look of sleepy cunning. He carried his fat paunch with ostentation on his short legs, and during the time his gang infested the station spoke to no one but his nephew. You could see these two roaming about all day long with their heads close together in an everlasting confab.

'I had given up worrying myself about the rivets. One's capacity for that kind of folly is more limited than you would suppose. I said Hang!—and let things slide. I had plenty of time for meditation, and now and then I would give some thought to Kurtz. I wasn't very interested in him. No. Still, I was curious to see whether this man, who had come out equipped with moral ideas of some sort, would climb to the top after all, and how he would set about his work when there.'

II

'One evening as I was lying flat on the deck of my steamboat, I heard voices approaching—and there were the nephew and the uncle strolling along the bank. I laid my head on my arm again, and had nearly lost myself in a doze, when somebody said in my ear, as it were: "I am as harmless as a little child, but I don't like to be dictated to. Am I the manager—or am I not? I was ordered to send him there. It's incredible.". . . I became aware that the two were standing on the shore alongside the forepart of the steamboat, just below my head. I did not move; it did not occur to me to move: I was sleepy. "It *is* unpleasant," grunted the uncle. "He has asked the Administration to be sent there," said the other, "with the idea of showing what he could do; and I was instructed accordingly. Look at the influence that man must have. Is it not frightful?" They both agreed it was frightful, then made several bizarre remarks: "Make rain and fine weather—one man—the Council—by the nose" —bits of absurd sentences that got the better of my drowsiness, so that I had pretty near the whole of my wits about me when the uncle said, "The climate may do away with this difficulty for you. Is he alone there?" "Yes," answered the manager; "he sent his assistant down the river with a note to me in these terms: 'Clear this poor devil out of the country, and don't bother sending more of that sort. I had rather be alone than have the kind of men you can dispose of with me.' It was more than a year ago. Can you imagine such impudence?" "Anything since then?" asked the other hoarsely. "Ivory," jerked the nephew; "lots of it—prime sort—lots—most annoying, from him." "And with that?" questioned the heavy rumble. "Invoice," was the reply fired out, so to speak. Then silence. They had been talking about Kurtz.

'I was broad awake by this time, but, lying perfectly at ease, remained still, having no inducement to change my position. "How did that ivory come all this way?" growled the elder man, who seemed very vexed. The other explained that it had come with a fleet of canoes in charge of an English half-caste clerk Kurtz had with him; that Kurtz had apparently intended to return himself, the station being by that time bare of goods and stores, but after coming three hundred miles, had suddenly decided to go back, which he started to do alone in a small dugout with four paddlers, leaving the half-caste to continue down the river with the ivory. The two fellows there seemed astounded at anybody attempting such a thing. They were at a loss for an adequate motive. As for me, I seemed to see Kurtz for the first time. It was a distinct glimpse: the dugout, four paddling savages, and the lone white man turning his back suddenly on the headquarters, on relief, on thoughts of home—perhaps; setting his face towards the depths of the wilderness, towards his empty and desolate station. I did not know the motive. Perhaps he was just simply a fine fellow who stuck to his work for its own sake. His name, you understand, had not been pronounced once. He was "that man." The half-caste, who, as far as I could see, had conducted a difficult trip with great prudence and pluck, was invariably alluded to as "that scoundrel." The "scoundrel" had reported that the "man" had been very ill—had recovered imperfectly. . . . The two below me moved away then a few paces, and strolled back and forth at some little distance. I heard: "Military post—doctor—two hundred miles—quite alone now—unavoidable delays—nine months—no news—strange rumours." They approached again, just as the manager was saying, "No one, as far as I know, unless a species of wandering trader—a pestilential fellow, snapping ivory from the natives." Who was it they were talking about now? I gathered in snatches that this was some man supposed to be in Kurtz's district, and of whom the manager did not approve. "We will not be free from unfair competition till one of these fellows is hanged for an example," he said. "Certainly," grunted the other; "get him hanged! Why not? Anything—anything can be done in this country. That's what I say; nobody here, you understand, *here*, can endanger your position. And why? You stand the climate—you outlast them all. The danger is in Europe; but there before I left I took care to——" They moved off and whispered, then their voices rose again. "The extraordinary series of delays is not my fault. I did my possible." The fat man sighed, "Very sad." "And the pestiferous absurdity of his talk," continued the other; "he bothered me enough when he was here. 'Each station should be like a beacon on the road towards better things, a centre for trade of course, but also for humanising, improving, instructing.' Conceive you—that ass! And he wants to be manager! No, it's——" Here he got choked by excessive indignation, and I lifted my head the least bit. I was surprised to see how near they were—right under me. I could have spat upon their hats. They were looking on the ground, absorbed in thought. The manager was switching his leg with a slender twig: his sagacious relative lifted his head. "You have been well since you came out this time?" he asked. The other gave a start. "Who? I? Oh! Like a charm—like a charm. But the rest—oh, my goodness! All sick. They die so quick, too, that I haven't the time to send them out of the country —it's incredible!" "H'm. Just so," grunted the uncle. "Ah! my boy, trust to this —I say, trust to this." I saw him extend his short flipper of an arm for a gesture that took in the forest, the creek, the mud, the river—seemed to beckon with a dishonouring flourish before the sunlit face of the land a treacherous appeal to the lurking death, to the hidden evil, to the profound darkness of its heart. It was so startling that I leaped to my feet and looked back at the edge of the forest, as though I had expected an answer of some sort to that black display of confidence. You know the foolish notions that come to one sometimes. The high stillness confronted these two figures with its ominous patience, waiting for the passing away of a fantastic invasion.

'They swore aloud together—out of sheer fright, I believe—then, pretending not to know anything of my existence, turned back to the station. The sun was low; and leaning forward side by side, they seemed to be tugging painfully uphill their two ridiculous shadows of unequal length, that trailed behind them slowly over the tall grass without bending a single blade.

'In a few days the Eldorado Expedition went into the patient wilderness, that closed upon it as the sea closes over a diver. Long afterwards the news came that all the donkeys were dead. I know nothing as to the fate of the less valuable animals. They, no doubt, like the rest of us, found what they deserved. I did not inquire. I was then rather excited at the prospect of meeting Kurtz very soon. When I say very soon I mean it comparatively. It was just two months from the day we left the creek when we came to the bank below Kurtz's station.

'Going up that river was like travelling back to the earliest beginnings of the world, when vegetation rioted on the earth and the big trees were kings. An empty stream, a great silence, an impenetrable forest. The air was warm, thick, heavy, sluggish. There was no joy in the brilliance of sunshine. The long stretches of the waterway ran on, deserted, into the gloom of over-shadowed distances. On silvery sandbanks hippos and alligators sunned themselves side by side. The broadening waters flowed through a mob of wooded islands; you lost your way on that river as you would in a desert, and butted all day long against shoals, trying to find the channel, till you thought yourself bewitched and cut off for ever from everything you had known once—somewhere—far away—in another existence perhaps. There were moments when one's past came back to one, as it will sometimes when you have not a moment to spare to yourself; but it came in the shape of an unrestful and noisy dream, remembered with wonder amongst the overwhelming realities of this strange world of plants, and water, and silence. And this stillness of life did not in the least resemble a peace. It was the stillness of an implacable force brooding over an inscrutable intention. It looked at you with a vengeful aspect. I got used to it afterwards; I did not see it any more; I had no time. I had to keep guessing at the channel; I had to discern, mostly by inspiration, the signs of hidden banks; I watched for sunken stones; I was learning to clap my teeth smartly before my heart flew out, when I shaved by a fluke some infernal sly old snag that would have ripped the life out of the tin-pot steamboat and drowned all the pilgrims; I had to keep a look-out for the signs of dead wood we could cut up in the night for next day's steaming.[30] When you have to attend to things of that sort, to the mere incidents of the surface, the reality—the reality, I tell you—fades. The inner truth is hidden —luckily, luckily. But I felt it all the same; I felt often its mysterious stillness watching me at my monkey tricks, just as it watches you fellows performing on your respective tight-ropes for—what it is? half a crown a tumble——'

30. A detail based on Conrad's Congo experience.

'Try to be civil, Marlow,' growled a voice, and I knew there was at least one listener awake besides myself.

'I beg your pardon. I forgot the heartache which makes up the rest of the price. And indeed what does the price matter, if the trick be well done? You do your tricks very well. And I didn't do badly either, since I managed not to sink that steamboat on my first trip. It's a wonder to me yet. Imagine a blindfolded man set to drive a van over a bad road. I sweated and shivered over that business considerably, I can tell you. After all, for a seaman, to scrape the bottom of the thing that's supposed to float all the time under his care is the unpardonable sin. No one may know of it, but you never forget the thump—eh? A blow on the very heart. You remember it, you dream of it, you wake up at night and think of it—years after—and go hot and cold all over. I don't pretend to say that steamboat floated all the time. More than once she had to wade for a bit, with twenty cannibals splashing around and pushing. We had enlisted some of these chaps on the way for a crew. Fine fellows—cannibals—in their place. They were men one could work with, and I am grateful to them. And, after all, they did not eat each other before my face: they had brought along a provision of hippo-meat which went rotten, and made the mystery of the wilderness stink in my nostrils. Phoo! I can sniff it now. I had the manager on board and three or four pilgrims with their staves—all complete. Sometimes we came upon a station close by the bank, clinging to the skirts of the unknown, and the white men rushing out of a tumble-down hovel, with great gestures of joy and surprise and welcome, seemed very strange—had the appearance of being held there captive by a spell. The word "ivory" would ring in the air for a while—and on we went again into the silence, along empty reaches, round the still bends, between the high walls of our winding way, reverberating in hollow claps the ponderous beat of the stern-wheel. Trees, trees, millions of trees, massive, immense, running up high; and at their foot, hugging the bank against the stream, crept the little begrimed steamboat, like a sluggish beetle crawling on the floor of a lofty portico. It made you feel very small, very lost, and yet it was not altogether depressing, that feeling. After all, if you were small, the grimy beetle crawled on—which was just what you wanted it to do. Where the pilgrims imagined it crawled to I don't know. To some place where they expected to get something, I bet! For me it crawled towards Kurtz—exclusively; but when the steam-pipes started leaking we crawled very slow. The reaches opened before us and closed behind, as if the forest had stepped leisurely across the water to bar the way for our return. We penetrated deeper and deeper into the heart of darkness. It was very quiet there. At night sometimes the roll of drums behind the curtain of trees would run up the river and remain sustained faintly, as if hovering in the air high over our heads, till the first break of day. Whether it meant war, peace, or prayer we could not tell. The dawns were heralded by the descent of a chill stillness; the woodcutters slept, their fires burned low; the snapping of a twig would make you start. We were wanderers on a prehistoric earth, on an earth that wore the aspect of an unknown planet. We could have fancied ourselves the first of men taking possession of an accursed inheritance, to be subdued at the cost of profound anguish and of excessive toil. But suddenly, as we struggled round a bend, there would be a glimpse of rush walls, of peaked grass-roofs, a burst of yells, a whirl of black limbs, a mass of hands clapping, of feet stamping, of bodies swaying, of eyes rolling, under the droop of heavy and motionless foliage. The steamer toiled along slowly on the edge of a black and incomprehensible frenzy. The prehistoric man was cursing us, praying to us, welcoming us—who could tell? We were cut off from the comprehension of our surroundings; we glided past like phantoms, wondering and secretly appalled, as sane men would be before an enthusiastic [31] outbreak in a madhouse. We could not understand because we were too far and could not remember, because we were travelling in the night of first ages, of those ages that are gone, leaving hardly a sign—and no memories.

'The earth seemed unearthly. We are accustomed to look upon the shackled form of a conquered monster, but there—there you could look at a thing monstrous and free. It was unearthly, and the men were—— No, they were not inhuman. Well, you know, that was the worst of it—this suspicion of their not being inhuman. It would come slowly to one. They howled and leaped, and spun, and made horrid faces; but what thrilled you was just the thought of their humanity—like yours—the thought of your remote kinship with this wild and passionate uproar. Ugly. Yes, it was ugly enough; but if you were man enough you would admit to yourself that there was in you just the faintest trace of a response to the terrible frankness of that noise, a dim suspicion of there being a meaning in it which you—you so remote from the night of first ages—could comprehend. And why not? The mind of man is capable of anything—because everything is in it, all the past as well as all the future. What was there after all? Joy, fear, sorrow, devotion, valour, rage—who can tell?—but truth—truth stripped of its cloak of time. Let the fool gape and shudder—the man knows, and can look on without a wink. But he must at least be as much of a man as these on the shore. He must meet that truth with his own true stuff—with his own inborn strength. Principles? Principles won't do. Acquisitions, clothes, pretty rags—rags that would fly off at the first good shake. No; you want a deliberate belief. An appeal to me in this fiendish row—is there? Very well; I hear; I admit, but I have a voice too, and for good or evil mine is the speech that cannot be silenced. Of course, a fool, what with sheer fright and fine sentiments, is always safe. Who's that grunting? You wonder I didn't go ashore for a howl and a dance? Well, no— I didn't. Fine sentiments, you say? Fine sentiments be hanged! I had no time. I had to mess about with white-lead and strips of woollen blanket helping to put bandages on those leaky steam-pipes—I tell you. I had to watch the steering, and circumvent those snags, and get the tin-pot along by hook or by crook. There was surface-truth enough in these things to save a wiser man. And between whiles I had to look after the savage who was fireman. He was an improved specimen; he could fire up a vertical boiler. He was there below me, and, upon my word, to look at him was as edifying as seeing a dog in a parody of breeches and a feather hat, walking on his hind legs. A few months of training had done for that really fine chap. He squinted at the steam-gauge and at the water-gauge with an evident effort of intrepidity—and he had filed

31. In the older sense of "fanatical," suffering from religious mania.

teeth too, the poor devil, and the wool of his pate shaved into queer patterns, and three ornamental scars on each of his cheeks. He ought to have been clapping his hands and stamping his feet on the bank, instead of which he was hard at work, a thrall to strange witchcraft, full of improving knowledge. He was useful because he had been instructed; and what he knew was this—that should the water in that transparent thing disappear, the evil spirit inside the boiler would get angry through the greatness of his thirst, and take a terrible vengeance. So he sweated and fired up and watched the glass fearfully (with an impromptu charm, made of rags, tied to his arm, and a piece of polished bone, as big as a watch, stuck flatways through his lower lip), while the wooded banks slipped past us slowly, the short noise was left behind, the interminable miles of silence—and we crept on, towards Kurtz. But the snags were thick, the water was treacherous and shallow, the boiler seemed indeed to have a sulky devil in it, and thus neither that fireman nor I had any time to peer into our creepy thoughts.

'Some fifty miles below the Inner Station we came upon a hut of reeds, an inclined and melancholy pole, with the unrecognisable tatters of what had been a flag of some sort flying from it, and a neatly stacked wood-pile. This was unexpected. We came to the bank, and on the stack of firewood found a flat piece of board with some faded pencil-writing on it. When deciphered it said: "Wood for you. Hurry up. Approach cautiously." There was a signature, but it was illegible—not Kurtz—a much longer word. "Hurry up." Where? Up the river? "Approach cautiously." We had not done so. But the warning could not have been meant for the place where it could be only found after approach. Something was wrong above. But what—and how much? That was the question. We commented adversely upon the imbecility of that telegraphic style. The bush around said nothing, and would not let us look very far, either. A torn curtain of red twill hung in the doorway of the hut, and flapped sadly in our faces. The dwelling was dismantled; but we could see a white man had lived there not very long ago. There remained a rude table—a plank on two posts; a heap of rubbish reposed in a dark corner, and by the door I picked up a book. It had lost its covers, and the pages had been thumbed into a state of extremely dirty softness; but the back had been lovingly stitched afresh with white cotton thread, which looked clean yet. It was an extraordinary find. Its title was, *An Inquiry into some Points of Seamanship,* by a man Towser, Towson—some such name—Master in His Majesty's Navy. The matter looked dreary reading enough, with illustrative diagrams and repulsive tables of figures, and the copy was sixty years old. I handled this amazing antiquity with the greatest possible tenderness, lest it should dissolve in my hands. Within, Towson or Towser was inquiring earnestly into the breaking strain of ships' chains and tackle, and other such matters. Not a very enthralling book; but at the first glance you could see there a singleness of intention, an honest concern for the right way of going to work, which made these humble pages, thought out so many years ago, luminous with another than a professional light. The simple old sailor, with his talk of chains and purchases, made me forget the jungle and the pilgrims in a delicious sensation of having come upon something unmistakably real. Such a book being there was wonderful enough; but still more astounding were the notes pencilled in the margin, and plainly referring to the text. I couldn't believe my eyes! They were in cipher! Yes, it looked like cipher. Fancy a man lugging with him a book of that description into this nowhere and studying it—and making notes —in cipher at that! It was an extravagant mystery.

'I had been dimly aware for some time of a worrying noise, and when I lifted my eyes I saw the wood-pile was gone, and the manager, aided by all the pilgrims, was shouting at me from the river-side. I slipped the book into my pocket. I assure you to leave off reading was like tearing myself away from the shelter of an old and solid friendship.

'I started the lame engine ahead. "It must be this miserable trader—this intruder," exclaimed the manager, looking back malevolently at the place we had left. "He must be English," I said. "It will not save him from getting into trouble if he is not careful," muttered the manager darkly. I observed with assumed innocence that no man was safe from trouble in this world.

'The current was more rapid now, the steamer seemed at her last gasp, the stern-wheel flopped languidly, and I caught myself listening on tiptoe for the next beat of the float,[32] for in sober truth I expected the wretched thing to give up every moment. It was like watching the last flickers of a life. But still we crawled. Sometimes I would pick out a tree a little way ahead to measure our progress towards Kurtz by, but I lost it invariably before we got abreast. To keep the eyes so long on one thing was too much for human patience. The manager displayed a beautiful resignation. I fretted and fumed and took to arguing with myself whether or no I would talk openly with Kurtz; but before I could come to any conclusion it occurred to me that my speech or my silence, indeed any action of mine, would be a mere futility. What did it matter what any one knew or ignored? What did it matter who was manager? One gets sometimes such a flash of insight. The essentials of this affair lay deep under the surface, beyond my reach, and beyond my power of meddling.

'Towards the evening of the second day we judged ourselves about eight miles from Kurtz's station. I wanted to push on; but the manager looked grave, and told me the navigation up there was so dangerous that it would be advisable, the sun being very low already, to wait where we were till next morning. Moreover, he pointed out that if the warning to approach cautiously were to be followed, we must approach in daylight—not at dusk, or in the dark. This was sensible enough. Eight miles meant nearly three hours' steaming for us, and I could also see suspicious ripples at the upper end of the reach. Nevertheless, I was annoyed beyond expression at the delay, and most unreasonably too, since one night more could not matter much after so many months. As we had plenty of wood, and caution was the word, I brought up in the middle of the stream. The reach was narrow, straight, with high sides like a railway cutting. The dusk came gliding into it long before the sun had set. The current ran smooth and swift, but a dumb immobility sat on the banks. The living trees, lashed together by the creepers and every living bush of the undergrowth, might have been changed into stone, even to the slenderest twig, to the lightest leaf. It was not sleep—it seemed unnatural, like a state of trance. Not the faintest sound of any kind could be heard. You looked on

32. Floating device to keep water level steady.

amazed, and began to suspect yourself of being deaf—then the night came suddenly, and struck you blind as well. About three in the morning some large fish leaped, and the loud splash made me jump as though a gun had been fired. When the sun rose there was a white fog, very warm and clammy, and more blinding than the night. It did not shift or drive; it was just there, standing all round you like something solid. At eight or nine, perhaps, it lifted as a shutter lifts. We had a glimpse of the towering multitude of trees, of the immense matted jungle, with the blazing little ball of the sun hanging over it—all perfectly still—and then the white shutter came down again, smoothly, as if sliding in greased grooves. I ordered the chain, which we had begun to heave in, to be paid out again. Before it stopped running with a muffled rattle, a cry, a very loud cry, as of infinite desolation, soared slowly in the opaque air. It ceased. A complaining clamour, modulated in savage discords, filled our ears. The sheer unexpectedness of it made my hair stir under my cap. I don't know how it struck the others: to me it seemed as though the mist itself had screamed, so suddenly, and apparently from all sides at once, did this tumultuous and mournful uproar arise. It culminated in a hurried outbreak of almost intolerably excessive shrieking, which stopped short, leaving us stiffened in a variety of silly attitudes, and obstinately listening to the nearly as appalling and excessive silence. "Good God! What is the meaning——?" stammered at my elbow one of the pilgrims—a little fat man, with sandy hair and red whiskers, who wore side-spring boots, and pink pyjamas tucked into his socks. Two others remained open-mouthed a whole minute, then dashed into the little cabin, to rush out incontinently and stand darting scared glances, with Winchesters at "ready" in their hands. What we could see was just the steamer we were on, her outlines blurred as though she had been on the point of dissolving, and a misty strip of water, perhaps two feet broad, around her—and that was all. The rest of the world was nowhere, as far as our eyes and ears were concerned. Just nowhere. Gone, disappeared; swept off without leaving a whisper or a shadow behind.

'I went forward, and ordered the chain to be hauled in short, so as to be ready to trip the anchor and move the steamboat at once if necessary. "Will they attack?" whispered an awed voice. "We will all be butchered in this fog," murmured another. The faces twitched with the strain, the hands trembled slightly, the eyes forgot to wink. It was very curious to see the contrast of expressions of the white men and of the black fellows of our crew, who were as much strangers to that part of the river as we, though their homes were only eight hundred miles away. The whites, of course greatly discomposed, had besides a curious look of being painfully shocked by such an outrageous row. The others had an alert, naturally interested expression; but their faces were essentially quiet, even those of the one or two who grinned as they hauled at the chain. Several exchanged short, grunting phrases, which seemed to settle the matter to their satisfaction. Their head-man, a young, broad-chested black, severely draped in dark-blue fringed cloths, with fierce nostrils and his hair all done up artfully in oily ringlets, stood near me. "Aha!" I said, just for good fellowship's sake. "Catch 'im," he snapped, with a bloodshot widening of his eyes and a flash of sharp teeth—"catch 'im. Give 'im to us." "To you, eh?" I asked; "what would you do with them?" "Eat 'im!" he said curtly, and, leaning his elbow on the rail, looked out into the fog in a dignified and profoundly pensive attitude. I would no doubt have been properly horrified, had it not occurred to me that he and his chaps must be very hungry: that they must have been growing increasingly hungry for at least this month past. They had been engaged for six months (I don't think a single one of them had any clear idea of time, as we at the end of countless ages have. They still belonged to the beginnings of time—had no inherited experience to teach them, as it were), and of course, as long as there was a piece of paper written over in accordance with some farcical law or other made down the river, it didn't enter anybody's head to trouble how they would live. Certainly they had brought with them some rotten hippo-meat, which couldn't have lasted very long, anyway, even if the pilgrims hadn't, in the midst of a shocking hullabaloo, thrown a considerable quantity of it overboard. It looked like a high-handed proceeding; but it was really a case of legitimate self-defence. You can't breathe dead hippo waking, sleeping, and eating, and at the same time keep your precarious grip on existence. Besides that, they had given them every week three pieces of brass wire,[33] each about nine inches long; and the theory was they were to buy their provisions with that currency in river-side villages. You can see how *that* worked. There were either no villages, or the people were hostile, or the director, who like the rest of us fed out of tins, with an occasional old he-goat thrown in, didn't want to stop the steamer for some more or less recondite reason. So, unless they swallowed the wire itself, or made loops of it to snare the fishes with, I don't see what good their extravagant salary could be to them. I must say it was paid with a regularity worthy of a large and honourable trading company. For the rest, the only thing to eat—though it didn't look eatable in the least—I saw in their possession was a few lumps of some stuff like half-cooked dough, of a dirty lavender colour, they kept wrapped in leaves, and now and then swallowed a piece of, but so small that it seemed done more for the look of the thing than for any serious purpose of sustenance.[34] Why in the name of all the gnawing devils of hunger they didn't go for us— they were thirty to five—and have a good tuck-in for once, amazes me now when I think of it. They were big powerful men, with not much capacity to weigh the consequences, with courage, with strength, even yet, though their skins were no longer glossy and their muscles no longer hard. And I saw that something restraining, one of those human secrets that baffle probability, had come into play there. I looked at them with a swift quickening of interest— not because it occurred to me I might be eaten by them before very long, though I own to you that just then I perceived—in a new light, as it were— how unwholesome the pilgrims looked, and I hoped, yes, I positively hoped, that my aspect was not so—what shall I say?—so—unappetising: a touch of fantastic vanity which fitted well with the dream-sensation that pervaded all my days at that time. Perhaps I had a little fever too. One can't live with one's finger everlastingly on one's pulse. I had often "a little fever," or a little touch of other things—the playful paw-strokes of the wilderness, the preliminary trifling before the more serious onslaught which came in due course. Yes; I

33. Such wire was used as currency in the Congo at the time.
34. Cassava, manioc root ground to flour, mixed into a dough, and wrapped in banana leaves (not, as has been suggested, human flesh).

looked at them as you would on any human being, with a curiosity of their impulses, motives, capacities, weaknesses, when brought to the test of an inexorable physical necessity. Restraint! What possible restraint? Was it superstition, disgust, patience, fear—or some kind of primitive honour? No fear can stand up to hunger, no patience can wear it out, disgust simply does not exist where hunger is; and as to superstition, beliefs, and what you may call principles, they are less than chaff in a breeze. Don't you know the devilry of lingering starvation, its exasperating torment, its black thoughts, its sombre and brooding ferocity? Well, I do. It takes a man all his inborn strength to fight hunger properly. It's really easier to face bereavement, dishonour, and the perdition of one's soul—than this kind of prolonged hunger. Sad, but true. And these chaps too had no earthly reason for any kind of scruple. Restraint! I would just as soon have expected restraint from a hyena prowling amongst the corpses of a battlefield. But there was the fact facing me—the fact dazzling, to be seen, like the foam on the depths of the sea, like a ripple on an unfathomable enigma, a mystery greater—when I thought of it—than the curious. inexplicable note of desperate grief in this savage clamour that had swept by us on the river-bank, behind the blind whiteness of the fog.

Two pilgrims were quarrelling in hurried whispers as to which bank. "Left." "No, no; how can you? Right, right, of course." "It is very serious," said the manager's voice behind me; "I would be desolated if anything should happen to Mr. Kurtz before we came up." I looked at him, and had not the slightest doubt he was sincere. He was just the kind of man who would wish to preserve appearances. That was his restraint. But when he muttered something about going on at once, I did not even take the trouble to answer him. I knew, and he knew, that it was impossible. Were we to let go our hold of the bottom, we would be absolutely in the air—in space. We wouldn't be able to tell where we were going to—whether up or down stream, or across—till we fetched against one bank or the other—and then we wouldn't know at first which it was. Of course I made no move. I had no mind for a smash-up. You couldn't imagine a more deadly place for a shipwreck. Whether drowned at once or not, we were sure to perish speedily in one way or another. "I authorise you to take all the risks," he said, after a short silence. "I refuse to take any," I said shortly; which was just the answer he expected, though its tone might have surprised him. "Well, I must defer to your judgment. You are captain," he said, with marked civility. I turned my shoulder to him in sign of my appreciation, and looked into the fog. How long would it last? It was the most hopeless look-out. The approach to this Kurtz grubbing for ivory in the wretched bush was beset by as many dangers as though he had been an enchanted princess sleeping in a fabulous castle. "Will they attack, do you think?" asked the manager, in a confidential tone.

I did not think they would attack, for several obvious reasons. The thick fog was one. If they left the bank in their canoes they would get lost in it, as we would be if we attempted to move. Still, I had also judged the jungle of both banks quite impenetrable—and yet eyes were in it, eyes that had seen us. The river-side bushes were certainly very thick; but the undergrowth behind was evidently penetrable. However, during the short lift I had seen no canoes anywhere in the reach—certainly not abreast of the steamer. But what made the idea of attack inconceivable to me was the nature of the noise—of the cries we had heard. They had not the fierce character boding of immediate hostile intention. Unexpected, wild, and violent as they had been, they had given me an irresistible impression of sorrow. The glimpse of the steamboat had for some reason filled those savages with unrestrained grief. The danger, if any, I expounded, was from our proximity to a great human passion let loose. Even extreme grief may ultimately vent itself in violence—but more generally takes the form of apathy. . . .

'You should have seen the pilgrims stare! They had no heart to grin, or even to revile me; but I believe they thought me gone mad—with fright, maybe. I delivered a regular lecture. My dear boys, it was no good bothering. Keep a look-out? Well, you may guess I watched the fog for the signs of lifting as a cat watches a mouse; but for anything else our eyes were of no more use to us than if we had been buried miles deep in a heap of cotton-wool. It felt like it too—choking, warm, stifling. Besides, all I said, though it sounded extravagant, was absolutely true to fact. What we afterwards alluded to as an attack was really an attempt at repulse. The action was very far from being aggressive— it was not even defensive, in the usual sense: it was undertaken under the stress of desperation, and in its essence was purely protective.

'It developed itself, I should say, two hours after the fog lifted, and its commencement was at a spot, roughly speaking, about a mile and a half below Kurtz's station. We had just floundered and flopped round a bend, when I saw an islet, a mere grassy hummock of bright green, in the middle of the stream. It was the only thing of the kind; but as we opened the reach more, I perceived it was the head of a long sandbank, or rather of a chain of shallow patches stretching down the middle of the river. They were discoloured, just awash, and the whole lot was seen just under the water, exactly as a man's backbone is seen running down the middle of his back under the skin. Now, as far as I did see, I could go to the right or to the left of this. I didn't know either channel, of course. The banks looked pretty well alike, the depth appeared the same; but as I had been informed the station was on the west side, I naturally headed for the western passage.

'No sooner had we fairly entered it than I became aware it was much narrower than I had supposed. To the left of us there was the long uninterrupted shoal, and to the right a high steep bank heavily overgrown with bushes. Above the bush the trees stood in serried ranks. The twigs overhung the current thickly, and from distance to distance a large limb of some tree projected rigidly over the stream. It was then well on in the afternoon, the face of the forest was gloomy, and a broad strip of shadow had already fallen on the water. In this shadow we steamed up—very slowly, as you may imagine. I sheered her well inshore—the water being deepest near the bank, as the sounding-pole informed me.

'One of my hungry and forbearing friends was sounding in the bows just below me. This steamboat was exactly like a decked scow. On the deck there were two little teak-wook houses, with doors and windows. The boiler was in the fore-end, and the machinery right astern. Over the whole there was a light roof, supported on stanchions. The funnel projected through that roof, and in front of the funnel a small cabin built of light planks served for a pilot-house.

It contained a couch, two camp-stools, a loaded Martini-Henry [35] leaning in one corner, a tiny table, and the steering-wheel. It had a wide door in front and a broad shutter at each side. All these were always thrown open, of course. I spent my days perched up there on the extreme fore-end of that roof, before the door. At night I slept, or tried to, on the couch. An athletic black belonging to some coast tribe, and educated by my poor predecessor, was the helmsman. He sported a pair of brass earrings, wore a blue cloth wrapper from the waist to the ankles, and thought all the world of himself. He was the most unstable kind of fool I had ever seen. He steered with no end of a swagger while you were by; but if he lost sight of you, he became instantly the prey of an abject funk, and would let that cripple of a steamboat get the upper hand of him in a minute.

'I was looking down at the sounding-pole, and feeling much annoyed to see at each try a little more of it stick out of that river, when I saw my poleman give up the business suddenly, and stretch himself flat on the deck, without even taking the trouble to haul his pole in. He kept hold on it though, and it trailed in the water. At the same time the fireman, whom I could also see below me, sat down abruptly before his furnace and ducked his head. I was amazed. Then I had to look at the river mighty quick, because there was a snag in the fairway. Sticks, little sticks, were flying about—thick: they were whizzing before my nose, dropping below me, striking behind me against my pilot-house. All this time the river, the shore, the woods, were very quiet—perfectly quiet. I could only hear the heavy splashing thump of the stern-wheel and the patter of these things. We cleared the snag clumsily. Arrows, by Jove! We were being shot at! I stepped in quickly to close the shutter on the land-side. That fool-helmsman, his hands on the spokes, was lifting his knees high, stamping his feet, champing his mouth, like a reined-in horse. Confound him! And we were staggering within ten feet of the bank. I had to lean right out to swing the heavy shutter, and I saw a face amongst the leaves on the level with my own, looking at me very fierce and steady; and then suddenly, as though a veil had been removed from my eyes, I made out, deep in the tangled gloom, naked breasts, arms, legs, glaring eyes—the bush was swarming with human limbs in movement, glistening, of bronze colour. The twigs shook, swayed, and rustled, the arrows flew out of them, and then the shutter came to. "Steer her straight," I said to the helmsman. He held his head rigid, face forward; but his eyes rolled, he kept on lifting and setting down his feet gently, his mouth foamed a little. "Keep quiet!" I said in a fury. I might just as well have ordered a tree not to sway in the wind. I darted out. Below me there was a great scuffle of feet on the iron deck; confused exclamations; a voice screamed, "Can you turn back?" I caught sight of a V-shaped ripple on the water ahead. What? Another snag! A fusillade burst out under my feet. The pilgrims had opened with their Winchesters, and were simply squirting lead into that bush.[36] A deuce of a lot of smoke came up and drove slowly forward. I swore at it. Now I couldn't see the ripple or the snag either. I stood in the doorway, peering, and the arrows came in swarms. They might have been poisoned, but they looked as though

35. Rifle (more powerful than a Winchester).
36. Repeats the image of the gunboat shelling a continent.

they wouldn't kill a cat. The bush began to howl. Our wood-cutters raised a war-like whoop; the report of a rifle just at my back deafened me. I glanced over my shoulder, and the pilot-house was yet full of noise and smoke when I made a dash at the wheel. The fool-nigger had dropped everything, to throw the shutter open and let off that Martini-Henry. He stood before the wide opening, glaring, and I yelled at him to come back, while I straightened the sudden twist out of that steamboat. There was no room to turn even if I had wanted to, the snag was somewhere very near ahead in that confounded smoke, there was no time to lose, so I just crowded her into the bank—right into the bank, where I knew the water was deep.

'We tore slowly along the overhanging bushes in a whirl of broken twigs and flying leaves. The fusillade below stopped short, as I had foreseen it would when the squirts got empty. I threw my head back to a glinting whiz that traversed the pilot-house, in at one shutter-hole and out at the other. Looking past that mad helmsman, who was shaking the empty rifle and yelling at the shore, I saw vague forms of men running bent double, leaping, gliding, distinct, incomplete, evanescent. Something big appeared in the air before the shutter, the rifle went overboard, and the man stepped back swiftly, looked at me over his shoulder in an extraordinary, profound, familiar manner, and fell upon my feet. The side of his head hit the wheel twice, and the end of what appeared a long cane clattered round and knocked over a little camp-stool. It looked as though after wrenching that thing from somebody ashore he had lost his balance in the effort. The thin smoke had blown away, we were clear of the snag, and looking ahead I could see that in another hundred yards or so I would be free to sheer off, away from the bank; but my feet felt so very warm and wet that I had to look down. The man had rolled on his back and stared straight up at me; both his hands clutched that cane. It was the shaft of a spear that, either thrown or lunged through the opening, had caught him in the side just below the ribs; the blade had gone in out of sight, after making a frightful gash; my shoes were full; a pool of blood lay very still, gleaming dark-red under the wheel; his eyes shone with an amazing lustre. The fusillade burst out again. He looked at me anxiously, gripping the spear like something precious, with an air of being afraid I would try to take it away from him. I had to make an effort to free my eyes from his gaze and attend to the steering. With one hand I felt above my head for the line of the steam whistle, and jerked out screech after screech hurriedly. The tumult of angry and warlike yells was checked instantly, and then from the depths of the woods went out such a tremulous and prolonged wail of mournful fear and utter despair as may be imagined to follow the flight of the last hope from the earth. There was a great commotion in the bush; the shower of arrows stopped, a few dropping shots rang out sharply—then silence, in which the languid beat of the stern-wheel came plainly to my ears. I put the helm hard a-starboard at the moment when the pilgrim in pink pyjamas, very hot and agitated, appeared in the dorway. "The manager sends me——" he began in an official tone, and stopped short. "Good God!" he said, glaring at the wounded man.

'We two whites stood over him, and his lustrous and inquiring glance enveloped us both. I declare it looked as though he would presently put to us some question in an understandable language; but he died without uttering a sound, without moving a limb, without twitching a muscle. Only in the very last moment, as though in response to some sign we could not see, to some whisper we could not hear, he frowned heavily, and that frown gave to his black death-mask an inconceivably sombre, brooding, and menacing expression. The lustre of inquiring glance faded swiftly into vacant glassiness. "Can you steer?" I asked the agent eagerly. He looked very dubious; but I made a grab at his arm, and he understood at once I meant him to steer whether or no. To tell you the truth, I was morbidly anxious to change my shoes and socks. "He is dead," murmured the fellow, immensely impressed. "No doubt about it," said I, tugging like mad at the shoe-laces. "And by the way, I suppose Mr. Kurtz is dead as well by this time."

'For the moment that was the dominant thought. There was a sense of extreme disappointment, as though I had found out I had been striving after something altogether without a substance. I couldn't have been more disgusted if I had travelled all this way for the sole purpose of talking with Mr. Kurtz. Talking with . . . I flung one shoe overboard, and became aware that that was exactly what I had been looking forward to—a talk with Kurtz. I made the strange discovery that I had never imagined him as doing, you know, but as discoursing. I didn't say to myself, "Now I will never see him," or "Now I will never shake him by the hand," but, "Now I will never hear him." The man presented himself as a voice. Not of course that I did not connect him with some sort of action. Hadn't I been told in all the tones of jealousy and admiration that he had collected, bartered, swindled, or stolen more ivory than all the other agents together? That was not the point. The point was in his being a gifted creature, and that of all his gifts the one that stood out pre-eminently, that carried with it a sense of real presence, was his ability to talk, his words— the gift of expression, the bewildering, the illuminating, the most exalted and the most contemptible, the pulsating stream of light, or the deceitful flow from the heart of an impenetrable darkness.

'The other shoe went flying unto the devil-god of that river. I thought, By Jove! it's all over. We are too late; he has vanished—the gift has vanished, by means of some spear, arrow, or club. I will never hear that chap speak after all —and my sorrow had a startling extravagance of emotion, even such as I had noticed in the howling sorrow of these savages in the bush. I couldn't have felt more of lonely desolation somehow, had I been robbed of a belief or had missed my destiny in life. . . . Why do you sigh in this beastly way, somebody? Absurd? Well, absurd. Good Lord! mustn't a man ever——Here, give me some tobacco.' [37] . . .

There was a pause of profound stillness, then a match flared, and Marlow's lean face appeared, worn, hollow, with downward folds and dropped eyelids, with an aspect of concentrated attention; and as he took vigorous draws at his pipe, it seemed to retreat and advance out of the night in the regular flicker of the tiny flame. The match went out.

'Absurd!' he cried. 'This is the worst of trying to tell . . . Here you all are, each moored with two good addresses, like a hulk with two anchors, a butcher

---

37. Here Conrad, who in other works has a much less straightforward time-scheme than in *Heart of Darkness*, breaks off the story and allows Marlow to anticipate what has not yet been described.

round one corner, a policeman round another, excellent appetites, and temperature normal—you hear—normal from year's end to year's end. And you say, Absurd! Absurd be—exploded! Absurd! My dear boys, what can you expect from a man who out of sheer nervousness had just flung overboard a pair of new shoes? Now I think of it, it is amazing I did not shed tears. I am, upon the whole, proud of my fortitude. I was cut to the quick at the idea of having lost the inestimable privilege of listening to the gifted Kurtz. Of course I was wrong. The privilege was waiting for me. Oh yes, I heard more than enough. And I was right, too. A voice. He was very little more than a voice. And I heard—him— it—this voice—other voices—all of them were so little more than voices—and the memory of that time itself lingers around me, impalpable, like a dying vibration of one immense jabber, silly, atrocious, sordid, savage, or simply mean, without any kind of sense. Voices, voices—even the girl herself—now—'

He was silent for a long time.

'I laid the ghost of his gifts at last with a lie,' he began suddenly. 'Girl! What? Did I mention a girl? Oh, she is out of it—completely. They—the women I mean—are out of it—should be out of it. We must help them to stay in that beautiful world of their own, lest ours gets worse. Oh, she had to be out of it. You should have heard the disinterred body of Mr. Kurtz saying, "My Intended." You would have perceived directly then how completely she was out of it. And the lofty frontal bone of Mr. Kurtz! They say the hair goes on growing sometimes, but this—ah—specimen was impressively bald. The wilderness had patted him on the head, and, behold, it was like a ball—an ivory ball; it had caressed him, and—lo!—he had withered; it had taken him, loved him, embraced him, got into his veins, consumed his flesh, and sealed his soul to its own by the inconceivable ceremonies of some devilish initiation. He was its spoiled and pampered favourite. Ivory? I should think so. Heaps of it, stacks of it. The old mud shanty was bursting with it. You would think there was not a single tusk left either above or below the ground in the whole country. "Mostly fossil," the manager had remarked disparagingly. It was no more fossil than I am; but they call it fossil when it is dug up. It appears these niggers do bury the tusks sometimes—but evidently they couldn't bury this parcel deep enough to save the gifted Mr. Kurtz from his fate. We filled the steamboat with it, and had to pile a lot on the deck. Thus he could see and enjoy as long as he could see, because the appreciation of this favour had remained with him to the last. You should have heard him say, "My ivory." Oh yes, I heard him. "My Intended, my ivory, my station, my river, my——" everything belonged to him. It made me hold my breath in expectation of hearing the wilderness burst into a prodigious peal of laughter that would shake the fixed stars in their places. Everything belonged to him—but that was a trifle. The thing was to know what he belonged to, how many powers of darkness claimed him for their own. That was the reflection that made you creepy all over. It was impossible—it was not good for one either—trying to imagine. He had taken a high seat amongst the devils of the land—I mean literally. You can't understand. How could you?— with solid pavement under your feet, surrounded by kind neighbours ready to cheer you or to fall on you, stepping delicately between the butcher and the policeman, in the holy terror of scandal and gallows and lunatic asylums—how can you imagine what particular region of the first ages a man's untrammelled

feet may take him into by the way of solitude—utter solitude without a policeman—by the way of silence—utter silence, where no warning voice of a kind
neighbour can be heard whispering of public opinion? These little things make
all the great difference. When they are gone you must fall back upon your own
innate strength, upon your own capacity for faithfulness.[38] Of course you may
be too much of a fool to go wrong—too dull even to know you are being as-
saulted by the powers of darkness. I take it, no fool ever made a bargain for
his soul with the devil: the fool is too much of a fool, or the devil too much of
a devil—I don't know which. Or you may be such a thunderingly exalted creature as to be altogether deaf and blind to anything but heavenly sights and
sounds. Then the earth for you is only a standing place—and whether to be
like this is your loss or your gain I won't pretend to say. But most of us are
neither one nor the other. The earth for us is a place to live in, where we must
put up with sights, with sounds, with smells, too, by Jove!—breathe dead hippo,
so to speak, and not be contaminated. And there, don't you see? your strength
comes in, the faith in your ability for the digging of unostentatious holes to bury
the stuff in—your power of devotion, not to yourself, but to an obscure, back-
breaking business. And that's difficult enough. Mind, I am not trying to excuse
or even explain—I am trying to account to myself for—for—Mr. Kurtz—for
the shade of Mr. Kurtz. This initiated wraith from the back of Nowhere honoured me with its amazing confidence before it vanished altogether. This was
because it could speak English to me. The original Kurtz had been educated
partly in England, and—as he was good enough to say himself—his sympathies
were in the right place. His mother was half-English, his father was half-French.
All Europe contributed to the making of Kurtz; and by and by I learned that,
most appropriately, the International Society for the Suppression of Savage
Customs had entrusted him with the making of a report, for its future guidance.
And he had written it too. I've seen it. I've read it. It was eloquent, vibrating
with eloquence, but too high-strung, I think. Seventeen pages of close writing
he had found time for! But this must have been before his—let us say—nerves
went wrong, and caused him to preside at certain midnight dances ending with
unspeakable rites,[39] which—as far as I reluctantly gathered from what I heard
at various times—were offered up to him—do you understand?—to Mr. Kurtz
himself. But it was a beautiful piece of writing. The opening paragraph, however, in the light of later information, strikes me now as ominous. He began
with the argument that we whites, from the point of development we had
arrived at, "must necessarily appear to them [savages] in the nature of supernatural beings—we approach them with the might as of a deity," and so on,
and so on. "By the simple exercise of our will we can exert a power for good
practically unbounded," etc. etc. From that point he soared and took me with
him. The peroration was magnificent, though difficult to remember, you know.
It gave me the notion of an exotic Immensity ruled by an august Benevolence.
It made me tingle with enthusiasm. This was the unbounded power of eloquence—of words—of burning noble words. There were no practical hints to

38. However Marlow comes out of this story, he is here stating the essence of Conrad's
ethic, and continues to do so in condemning those who are too spiritually inert to "go
wrong," and in praising work.
39. For speculation on these rites see Headnote.

interrupt the magic current of phrases, unless a kind of note at the foot of the last page, scrawled evidently much later, in an unsteady hand, may be regarded as the exposition of a method. It was very simple, and at the end of that moving appeal to every altruistic sentiment it blazed at you, luminous and terrifying, like a flash of lightning in a serene sky: "Exterminate all the brutes!" The curious part was that he had apparently forgotten all about that valuable post-scriptum, because, later on, when he in a sense came to himself, he repeatedly entreated me to take good care of "my pamphlet" (he called it), as it was sure to have in the future a good influence upon his career. I had full information about all these things, and, besides, as it turned out, I was to have the care of his memory. I've done enough for it to give me the indisputable right to lay it, if I choose, for an everlasting rest in the dust-bin of progress, amongst all the sweepings and, figuratively speaking, all the dead cats of civilisation. But then, you see, I can't choose. He won't be forgotten. Whatever he was, he was not common. He had the power to charm or frighten rudimentary souls into an aggravated witch-dance in his honour; he could also fill the small souls of the pilgrims with bitter misgivings: he had one devoted friend at least, and he had conquered one soul in the world that was neither rudimentary nor tainted with self-seeking. No; I can't forget him, though I am not prepared to affirm the fellow was exactly worth the life we lost in getting to him. I missed my late helmsman awfully—I missed him even while his body was still lying in the pilot-house. Perhaps you will think it passing strange this regret for a savage who was no more account than a grain of sand in a black Sahara. Well, don't you see, he had done something, he had steered; for months I had him at my back—a help—an instrument. It was a kind of partnership. He steered for me— I had to look after him, I worried about his deficiencies, and thus a subtle bond had been created, of which I only became aware when it was suddenly broken. And the intimate profundity of that look he gave me when he received his hurt remains to this day in my memory—like a claim of distant kinship affirmed in a supreme moment.

'Poor fool! If he had only left that shutter alone. He had no restraint, no restraint—just like Kurtz—a tree swayed by the wind. As soon as I had put on a dry pair of slippers, I dragged him out, after first jerking the spear out of his side, which operation I confess I performed with my eyes shut tight. His heels leaped together over the little door-step; his shoulders were pressed to my breast; I hugged him from behind desperately. Oh! he was heavy, heavy; heavier than any man on earth, I should imagine. Then without more ado I tipped him overboard. The current snatched him as though he had been a wisp of grass, and I saw the body roll over twice before I lost sight of it for ever. All the pilgrims and the manager were then congregated on the awning-deck about the pilot-house, chattering at each other like a flock of excited magpies, and there was a scandalised murmur at my heartless promptitude. What they wanted to keep that body hanging about for I can't guess. Embalm it, maybe. But I had also heard another, and a very ominous, murmur on the deck below. My friends the wood-cutters were likewise scandalised, and with a better show of reason—though I admit that the reason itself was quite inadmissible. Oh, quite! I had made up my mind that if my late helmsman was to be eaten, the fishes alone should have him. He had been a very second-rate helmsman while alive, but now he was dead he might have become a first-class temptation, and possibly cause some startling trouble. Besides, I was anxious to take the wheel, the man in pink pyjamas showing himself a hopeless duffer at the business.

'This I did directly the simple funeral was over. We were going half-speed, keeping right in the middle of the stream, and I listened to the talk about me. They had given up Kurtz, they had given up the station; Kurtz was dead, and the station had been burnt—and so on, and so on. The red-haired pilgrim was beside himself with the thought that at least this poor Kurtz had been properly revenged. "Say! We must have made a glorious slaughter of them in the bush. Eh? What do you think? Say?" He positively danced, the bloodthirsty little gingery beggar. And he had nearly fainted when he saw the wounded man! I could not help saying, "You made a glorious lot of smoke, anyhow." I had seen, from the way the tops of the bushes rustled and flew, that almost all the shots had gone too high. You can't hit anything unless you take aim and fire from the shoulder; but these chaps fired from the hip with their eyes shut. The retreat, I maintained—and I was right—was caused by the screeching of the steam-whistle. Upon this they forgot Kurtz, and began to howl at me with indignant protests.

'The manager stood by the wheel murmuring confidentially about the necessity of getting well away down the river before dark at all events, when I saw in the distance a clearing on the river-side and the outlines of some sort of building. "What's this?" I asked. He clapped his hands in wonder. "The station!" he cried. I edged in at once, still going half-speed.

'Through my glasses I saw the slope of a hill interspersed with rare trees and perfectly free from undergrowth. A long decaying building on the summit was half buried in the high grass; the large holes in the peaked roof gaped black from afar; the jungle and the woods made a background. There was no enclosure or fence of any kind; but there had been one apparently, for near the house half a dozen slim posts remained in a row, roughly trimmed, and with their upper ends ornamented with round carved balls. The rails, or whatever there had been between, had disappeared. Of course the forest surrounded all that. The river-bank was clear, and on the water side I saw a white man under a hat like a cart-wheel beckoning persistently with his whole arm. Examining the edge of the forest above and below, I was almost certain I could see movements—human forms gliding here and there. I steamed past prudently, then stopped the engines and let her drift down. The man on the shore began to shout, urging us to land. "We have been attacked," screamed the manager. "I know—I know. It's all right," yelled back the other, as cheerful as you please. "Come along. It's all right. I am glad."

'His aspect reminded me of something I had seen—something funny I had seen somewhere. As I manœuvred to get alongside, I was asking myself, "What does this fellow look like?" Suddenly I got it. He looked like a harlequin. His clothes had been made of some stuff that was brown holland probably, but it was covered with patches all over, with bright patches, blue, red, and yellow—patches on the back, patches on the front, patches on elbows, on knees; coloured binding round his jacket, scarlet edging at the bottom of his trousers; and the sunshine made him look extremely gay and wonderfully neat withal, because you could see how beautifully all this patching had been done. A beardless, boyish face, very fair, no features to speak of, nose peeling, little blue eyes, smiles and frowns chasing each other over that open countenance like sunshine and shadow on a wind-swept plain. "Look out, captain!" he cried; "there's a snag lodged in here last night." What! Another snag? I confess I swore shamefully. I had nearly holed my cripple, to finish off that charming trip. The harlequin on the bank turned his little pug-nose up to me. "You English?" he asked, all smiles. "Are you?" I shouted from the wheel. The smiles vanished, and he shook his head as if sorry for my disappointment. Then he brightened up. "Never mind!" he cried encouragingly. "Are we in time?" I asked. "He is up there," he replied, with a toss of the head up the hill, and becoming gloomy all of a sudden. His face was like the autumn sky, overcast one moment and bright the next.

'When the manager, escorted by the pilgrims, all of them armed to the teeth, had gone to the house, this chap came on board. "I say, I don't like this. These natives are in the bush," I said. He assured me earnestly it was all right. "They are simple people," he added; "well, I am glad you came. It took me all my time to keep them off." "But you said it was all right," I cried. "Oh, they meant no harm," he said; and as I stared he corrected himself, "Not exactly." Then vivaciously, "My faith, your pilot-house wants a clean-up!" In the next breath he advised me to keep enough steam on the boiler to blow the whistle in case of any trouble. "One good screech will do more for you than all your rifles. They are simple people," he repeated. He rattled away at such a rate he quite overwhelmed me. He seemed to be trying to make up for lots of silence, and actually hinted, laughing, that such was the case. "Don't you talk with Mr. Kurtz?" I said. "You don't talk with that man—you listen to him," he exclaimed with severe exaltation. "But now——" He waved his arm, and in the twinkling of an eye was in the uttermost depths of despondency. In a moment he came up again with a jump, possessed himself of both my hands, shook them continuously, while he gabbled: "Brother sailor . . . honour . . . pleasure . . . delight . . . introduce myself . . . Russian . . . son of an arch-priest . . . Government of Tambov . . . What? Tobacco! English tobacco; the excellent English tobacco! Now, that's brotherly. Smoke? Where's a sailor that does not smoke?"

'The pipe soothed him, and gradually I made out he had run away from school, had gone to sea in a Russian ship; ran away again; served some time in English ships; was now reconciled with the arch-priest. He made a point of that. "But when one is young one must see things, gather experience, ideas; enlarge the mind." "Here!" I interrupted. "You can never tell! Here I met Mr. Kurtz," he said, youthfully solemn and reproachful. I held my tongue after that. It appears he had persuaded a Dutch trading-house on the coast to fit him out with stores and goods, and had started for the interior with a light heart, and no more idea of what would happen to him than a baby. He had been wandering about that river for nearly two years alone, cut off from everybody and everything. "I am not so young as I look. I am twenty-five," he said. "At first old Van Shuyten would tell me to go to the devil," he narrated with keen enjoyment; "but I stuck to him, and talked and talked, till at last he got afraid I would talk the hind-leg off his favourite dog, so he gave me some cheap things and a few guns, and told me he hoped he would never see my face again. Good old Dutchman, Van Shuyten. I sent him one small lot of ivory a year ago, so that he can't call me a little thief when I get back. I hope he got it. And for the rest, I don't care. I had some wood stacked for you. That was my old house. Did you see?"

'I gave him Towson's book. He made as though he would kiss me, but restrained himself. "The only book I had left, and I thought I had lost it," he said, looking at it ecstatically. "So many accidents happen to a man going about alone, you know. Canoes get upset sometimes—and sometimes you've got to clear out so quick when the people get angry." He thumbed the pages. "You made notes in Russian?" I asked. He nodded. "I thought they were written in cipher," I said. He laughed, then became serious. "I had lots of trouble to keep these people off," he said. "Did they want to kill you?" I asked. "Oh no!" he cried, and checked himself. "Why did they attack us?" I pursued. He hesitated, then said shamefacedly, "They don't want him to go." "Don't they?" I said curiously. He nodded a nod full of mystery and wisdom. "I tell you," he cried, "this man has enlarged my mind." He opened his arms wide, staring at me with his little blue eyes that were perfectly round.'

III

'I looked at him, lost in astonishment. There he was before me, in motley, as though he had absconded from a troupe of mimes, enthusiastic, fabulous. His very existence was improbable, inexplicable, and altogether bewildering. He was an insoluble problem. It was inconceivable how he had existed, how he had succeeded in getting so far, how he had managed to remain—why he did not instantly disappear. "I went a little farther," he said, "then still a little farther—till I had gone so far that I don't know how I'll ever get back. Never mind. Plenty time. I can manage. You take Kurtz away quick—quick—I tell you." The glamour of youth enveloped his parti-coloured rags, his destitution, his loneliness, the essential desolation of his futile wanderings. For months— for years—his life hadn't been worth a day's purchase; and there he was gallantly, thoughtlessly alive, to all appearance indestructible solely by the virtue of his few years and of his unreflecting audacity. I was seduced into something like admiration—like envy. Glamour urged him on, glamour kept him unscathed. He surely wanted nothing from the wilderness but space to breathe in and to push on through. His need was to exist, and to move onwards at the greatest possible risk, and with a maximum of privation. If the abso- lutely pure, uncalculating, unpractical spirit of adventure had ever ruled a human being, it ruled this be-patched youth. I almost envied him the posses- sion of this modest and clear flame. It seemed to have consumed all thought of self so completely, that, even while he was talking to you, you forget that it was he—the man before your eyes—who had gone through these things. I did not envy him his devotion to Kurtz, though. He had not meditated over it. It came to him, and he accepted it with a sort of eager fatalism. I must say that to me it appeared about the most dangerous thing in every way he had come upon so far.

'They had come together unavoidably, like two ships becalmed near each other, and lay rubbing sides at last. I suppose Kurtz wanted an audience, because on a certain occasion, when encamped in the forest, they had talked all night, or more probably Kurtz had talked. "We talked of everything," he said, quite transported at the recollection. "I forgot there was such a thing as sleep. The night did not seem to last an hour. Everything! Everything! . . . Of love too." "Ah, he talked to you of love!" I said, much amused. "It isn't what you think," he cried, almost passionately. "It was in general. He made me see things—things."

'He threw his arms up. We were on deck at the time, and the head-man of my wood-cutters, lounging near by, turned upon him his heavy and glittering eyes. I looked around, and I don't know why, but I assure you that never, never before, did this land, this river, this jungle, the very arch of this blazing sky, appear to me so hopeless and so dark, so impenetrable to human thought, so pitiless to human weakness. "And, ever since, you have been with him, of course?" I said.

'On the contrary. It appears their intercourse had been very much broken by various causes. He had, as he informed me proudly, managed to nurse Kurtz through two illnesses (he alluded to it as you would to some risky feat), but as a rule Kurtz wandered alone, far in the depths of the forest. "Very often coming to this station, I had to wait days and days before he would turn up," he said. "Ah, it was worth waiting for!—sometimes." "What was he doing? exploring or what?" I asked. "Oh yes, of course"; he had discovered lots of villages, a lake too—he did not know exactly in what direction; it was dangerous to inquire too much—but mostly his expeditions had been for ivory. "But he had no goods to trade with by that time," I objected. "There's a good lot of cartridges left even yet," he answered, looking away. "To speak plainly, he raided the country," I said. He nodded. "Not alone, surely!" He muttered something about the villages round that lake. "Kurtz got the tribe to follow him, did he?" I suggested. He fidgeted a little. "They adored him," he said. The tone of these words was so extraordinary that I looked at him searchingly. It was curious to see his mingled eagerness and reluctance to speak of Kurtz. The man filled his life, occupied his thoughts, swayed his emotions. "What can you expect?" he burst out; "he came to them with thunder and lightning, you know—and they had never seen anything like it—and very terrible. He could be very terrible. You can't judge Mr. Kurtz as you would an ordinary man. No, no, no! Now—just to give you an idea—I don't mind telling you, he wanted to shoot me too one day—but I don't judge him." "Shoot you!" I cried. "What for?" "Well, I had a small lot of ivory the chief of that village near my house gave me. You see I used to shoot game for them. Well, he wanted it, and wouldn't hear reason. He declared he would shoot me unless I gave him the ivory and then cleared out of the country, because he could do so, and had a fancy for it, and there was nothing on earth to prevent him killing whom he jolly well pleased. And it was true too. I gave him the ivory. What did I care! But I didn't clear out. No, no. I couldn't leave him. I had to be careful, of course, till we got friendly again for a time. He had his second illness then. Afterwards I had to keep out of the way; but I didn't mind. He was living for the most part in those villages on the lake. When he came down to the river, sometimes he would take to me, and sometimes it was better for me to be careful. This man suffered too much. He hated all this, and somehow he couldn't get away. When

I had a chance I begged him to try and leave while there was time: I offered to go back with him. And he would say yes, and then he would remain; go off on another ivory hunt; disappear for weeks; forget himself amongst these people—forget himself—you know." "Why! he's mad," I said. He protested indignantly. Mr. Kurtz couldn't be mad. If I had heard him talk, only two days ago, I wouldn't dare hint at such a thing. . . . I had taken up my binoculars while we talked, and was looking at the shore, sweeping the limit of the forest at each side and at the back of the house. The consciousness of there being people in that bush, so silent, so quiet—as silent and quiet as the ruined house on the hill—made me uneasy. There was no sign on the face of nature of this amazing tale that was not so much told as suggested to me in desolate exclamations, completed by shrugs, in interrupted phrases, in hints ending in deep sighs. The woods were unmoved, like a mask—heavy, like the closed door of a prison—they looked with their air of hidden knowledge, of patient expectation, of unapproachable silence. The Russian was explaining to me that it was only lately that Mr. Kurtz had come down to the river, bringing along with him all the fighting men of that lake tribe. He had been absent for several months—getting himself adored, I suppose—and had come down unexpectedly, with the intention to all appearance of making a raid either across the river or down stream. Evidently the appetite for more ivory had got the better of the—what shall I say?—less material aspirations. However, he had got much worse suddenly. "I heard he was lying helpless, and so I came up—took my chance," said the Russian. "Oh, he is bad, very bad." I directed my glass to the house. There were no signs of life, but there were the ruined roof, the long mud wall peeping above the grass, with three little square window-holes, no two of the same size; all this brought within reach of my hand, as it were. And then I made a brusque movement, and one of the remaining posts of that vanished fence leaped up in the field of my glass. You remember I told you I had been struck at the distance by certain attempts at ornamentation, rather remarkable in the ruinous aspect of the place. Now I had suddenly a nearer view, and its first result was to make me throw my head back as if before a blow. Then I went carefully from post to post with my glass, and I saw my mistake. These round knobs were not ornamental but symbolic; they were expressive and puzzling, striking and disturbing—food for thought and also for vultures if there had been any looking down from the sky; but at all events for such ants as were industrious enough to ascend the pole. They would have been even more impressive, those heads on the stakes, if their faces had not been turned to the house. Only one, the first I had made out, was facing my way. I was not so shocked as you may think. The start back I had given was really nothing but a movement of surprise. I had expected to see a knob of wood there, you know. I returned deliberately to the first I had seen— and there it was, black, dried, sunken, with closed eyelids—a head that seemed to sleep at the top of that pole, and, with the shrunken dry lips showing a narrow white line of the teeth, was smiling too, smiling continuously at some endless and jocose dream of that eternal slumber.

'I am not disclosing any trade secrets. In fact the manager said afterwards that Mr. Kurtz's methods had ruined the district. I have no opinion on that point, but I want you clearly to understand that there was nothing exactly profitable in these heads being there. They only showed that Mr. Kurtz lacked restraint in the gratification of his various lusts, that there was something wanting in him—some small matter which, when the pressing need arose, could not be found under his magnificent eloquence. Whether he knew of this deficiency himself I can't say. I think the knowledge came to him at last—only at the very last. But the wilderness had found him out early, and had taken on him a terrible vengeance for the fantastic invasion. I think it had whispered to him things about himself which he did not know, things of which he had no conception till he took counsel with this great solitude—and the whisper had proved irresistibly fascinating. It echoed loudly within him because he was hollow at the core. . . . I put down the glass, and the head that had appeared near enough to be spoken to seemed at once to have leaped away from me into inaccessible distance.

'The admirer of Mr. Kurtz was a bit crestfallen. In a hurried, indistinct voice he began to assure me he had not dared to take these—say, symbols—down. He was not afraid of the natives; they would not stir till Mr. Kurtz gave the word. His ascendancy was extraordinary. The camps of these people surrounded the place, and the chiefs came every day to see him. They would crawl . . . "I don't want to know anything of the ceremonies used when approaching Mr. Kurtz," I shouted. Curious, this feeling that came over me that such details would be more intolerable than those heads drying on the stakes under Mr. Kurtz's windows. After all, that was only a savage sight, while I seemed at one bound to have been transported into some lightless region of subtle horrors, where pure, uncomplicated savagery was a positive relief, being something that had a right to exist—obviously—in the sunshine. The young man looked at me with surprise. I suppose it did not occur to him that Mr. Kurtz was no idol of mine. He forgot I hadn't heard any of these splendid monologues on, what was it? on love, justice, conduct of life—or what not. If it had come to crawling before Mr. Kurtz, he crawled as much as the veriest savage of them all. I had no idea of the conditions, he said: these heads were the heads of rebels. I shocked him excessively by laughing. Rebels! What would be the next definition I was to hear? There had been enemies, criminals, workers—and these were rebels. Those rebellious heads looked very subdued to me on their sticks. "You don't know how such a life tries a man like Kurtz," cried Kurtz's last disciple. "Well, and you?" I said. "I! I! I am a simple man. I have no great thoughts. I want nothing from anybody. How can you compare me to . . .?" His feelings were too much for speech, and suddenly he broke down. "I don't understand," he groaned. "I've been doing my best to keep him alive, and that's enough. I had no hand in all this. I have no abilities. There hasn't been a drop of medicine or a mouthful of invalid food for months here. He was shamefully abandoned. A man like this, with such ideas. Shamefully! Shamefully! I—I—haven't slept for the last ten nights. . . ."

'His voice lost itself in the calm of the evening. The long shadows of the forest had slipped downhill while we talked, had gone far beyond the ruined hovel, beyond the symbolic row of stakes. All this was in the gloom, while we down there were yet in the sunshine, and the stretch of the river abreast of the clearing glittered in a still and dazzling splendour, with a murky and overshadowed bend above and below. Not a living soul was seen on the shore. The bushes did not rustle.

'Suddenly round the corner of the house a group of men appeared, as though they had come up from the ground. They waded waist-deep in the grass, in a compact body, bearing an improvised stretcher in their midst. Instantly, in the emptiness of the landscape, a cry arose whose shrillness pierced the still air like a sharp arrow flying straight to the very heart of the land; and, as if by enchantment, streams of human beings—of naked human beings—with spears in their hands, with bows, with shields, with wild glances and savage movements, were poured into the clearing by the dark-faced and pensive forest. The bushes shook, the grass swayed for a time, and then everything stood still in attentive immobility.

' "Now, if he does not say the right thing to them we are all done for," said the Russian at my elbow. The knot of men with the stretcher had stopped too, half-way to the steamer, as if petrified. I saw the man on the stretcher sit up, lank and with an uplifted arm, above the shoulders of the bearers. "Let us hope that the man who can talk so well of love in general will find some particular reason to spare us this time," I said. I resented bitterly the absurd danger of our situation, as if to be at the mercy of that atrocious phantom had been a dishonouring necessity. I could not hear a sound, but through my glasses I saw the thin arm extended commandingly, the lower jaw moving, the eyes of that apparition shining darkly far in its bony head that nodded with grotesque jerks. Kurtz—Kurtz—that means "short" in German—don't it? Well, the name was as true as everything else in his life— and death. He looked at least seven feet long. His covering had fallen off, and his body emerged from it pitiful and appalling as from a winding-sheet. I could see the cage of his ribs all astir, the bones of his arm waving. It was as though an animated image of death carved out of old ivory had been shaking its hand with menaces at a motionless crowd of men made of dark and glittering bronze. I saw him open his mouth wide—it gave him a weirdly voracious aspect, as though he had wanted to swallow all the air, all the earth, all the men before him. A deep voice reached me faintly. He must have been shouting. He fell back suddenly. The stretcher shook as the bearers staggered forward again, and almost at the same time I noticed that the crowd of savages was vanishing without any perceptible movement of retreat, as if the forest that had ejected these beings so suddenly had drawn them in again as the breath is drawn in a long aspiration.

'Some of the pilgrims behind the stretcher carried his arms—two shot-guns, a heavy rifle, and a light revolver-carbine—the thunderbolts of that pitiful Jupiter. The manager bent over him murmuring as he walked beside his head. They laid him down in one of the little cabins—just a room for a bed-place and a camp-stool or two, you know. We had brought his belated correspondence, and a lot of torn envelopes and open letters littered his bed. His hand roamed feebly amongst these papers. I was struck by the fire of his eyes and the composed languor of his expression. It was not so much the exhaustion of disease. He did not seem in pain. This shadow looked satiated and calm, as though for the moment it had had its fill of all the emotions.

'He rustled one of the letters, and looking straight in my face said, "I am glad." Somebody had been writing to him about me. These special recommendations were turning up again. The volume of tone he emitted without effort, almost without the trouble of moving his lips, amazed me. A voice! a voice! It was grave, profound, vibrating, while the man did not seem capable of a whisper. However, he had enough strength in him—factitious no doubt—to very nearly make an end of us, as you shall hear directly.

'The manager appeared silently in the doorway; I stepped out at once and he drew the curtain after me. The Russian, eyed curiously by the pilgrims, was staring at the shore. I followed the direction of his glance.

'Dark human shapes could be made out in the distance, flitting indistinctly against the gloomy border of the forest, and near the river two bronze figures, leaning on tall spears, stood in the sunlight under fantastic head-dresses of spotted skins, warlike and still in statuesque repose. And from right to left along the lighted shore moved a wild and gorgeous apparition of a woman.

'She walked with measured steps, draped in striped and fringed cloths, treading the earth proudly, with a slight jingle and flash of barbarous ornaments. She carried her head high; her hair was done in the shape of a helmet; she had brass leggings to the knees, brass wire gauntlets to the elbow, a crimson spot on her tawny cheek, innumerable necklaces of glass beads on her neck; bizarre things, charms, gifts of witch-men, that hung about her, glittered and trembled at every step. She must have had the value of several elephant tusks upon her. She was savage and superb, wild-eyed and magnificent; there was something ominous and stately in her deliberate progress. And in the hush that had fallen suddenly upon the whole sorrowful land, the immense wilderness, the colossal body of the fecund and mysterious life seemed to look at her, pensive, as though it had been looking at the image of its own tenebrous and passionate soul.

'She came abreast of the steamer, stood still, and faced us. Her long shadow fell to the water's edge. Her face had a tragic and fierce aspect of wild sorrow and of dumb pain mingled with the fear of some struggling, half-shaped resolve. She stood looking at us without a stir, and like the wilderness itself, with an air of brooding over an inscrutable purpose. A whole minute passed, and then she made a step forward. There was a low jingle, a glint of yellow metal, a sway of fringed draperies, and she stopped as if her heart had failed her. The young fellow by my side growled. The pilgrims murmured at my back. She looked at us all as if her life had depended upon the unswerving steadiness of her glance. Suddenly she opened her bared arms and threw them up rigid above her head, as though in an uncontrollable desire to touch the sky, and at the same time the swift shadows darted out on the earth, swept around on the river, gathering the steamer in a shadowy embrace. A formidable silence hung over the scene.

'She turned away slowly, walked on, following the bank, and passed into the bushes to the left. Once only her eyes gleamed back at us in the dusk of the thickets before she disappeared.

' "If she had offered to come aboard I really think I would have tried to shoot her," said the man of patches nervously. "I had been risking my life every day for the last fortnight to keep her out of the house. She got in one day and kicked up a row about those miserable rags I picked up in the storeroom to mend my clothes with. I wasn't decent. At least it must have been that, for she talked like a fury to Kurtz for an hour, pointing at me now and then. I don't understand the dialect of this tribe. Luckily for me, I fancy Kurtz felt too ill that day to care, or there would have been mischief. I don't understand. . . . No—it's too much for me. Ah, well, it's all over now."

'At this moment I heard Kurtz's deep voice behind the curtain: "Save me!—save the ivory, you mean. Don't tell me. Save *me!* Why, I've had to save you. You are interrupting my plans now. Sick! Sick! Not so sick as you would like to believe. Never mind. I'll carry my ideas out yet—I will return. I'll show you what can be done. You with your little peddling notions—you are interfering with me. I will return. I . . . ."

The manager came out. He did me the honour to take me under the arm and lead me aside. "He is very low, very low," he said. He considered it necessary to sigh, but neglected to be consistently sorrowful. "We have done all we could for him—haven't we? But there is no disguising the fact, Mr. Kurtz has done more harm than good to the Company. He did not see the time was not ripe for vigorous action. Cautiously, cautiously—that's my principle. We must be cautious yet. The district is closed to us for a time. Deplorable! Upon the whole, the trade will suffer. I don't deny there is a remarkable quantity of ivory—mostly fossil. We must save it, at all events—but look how precarious the position is—and why? Because the method is unsound." "Do you," said I, looking at the shore, "call it 'unsound method'?" "Without doubt," he exclaimed hotly. "Don't you?" . . . "No method at all," I murmured after a while. "Exactly," he exulted. "I anticipated this. Shows a complete want of judgment. It is my duty to point it out in the proper quarter." "Oh," said I, "that fellow—what's his name?—the brickmaker, will make a readable report for you." He appeared confounded for a moment. It seemed to me I had never breathed an atmosphere so vile, and I turned mentally to Kurtz for relief—positively for relief. "Nevertheless, I think Mr. Kurtz is a remarkable man," I said with emphasis. He started, dropped on me a cold heavy glance, said very quietly, "He *was*," and turned his back on me. My hour of favour was over; I found myself lumped along with Kurtz as a partisan of methods for which the time was not ripe: I was unsound! Ah! but it was something to have at least a choice of nightmares.

'I had turned to the wilderness really, not to Mr. Kurtz, who, I was ready to admit, was as good as buried. And for a moment it seemed to me as if I also [40] were buried in a vast grave full of unspeakable secrets. I felt an intolerable weight oppressing my breast, the smell of the damp earth, the unseen presence of victorious corruption, the darkness of an impenetrable night. . . . The Russian tapped me on the shoulder. I heard him mumbling and stammering something about "brother seaman—couldn't conceal—knowledge of matters that would affect Mr. Kurtz's reputation." I waited. For him evidently Mr. Kurtz was not in his grave; I suspect that for him Mr. Kurtz was one of the immortals. "Well!" said I at last, "speak out. As it happens, I am Mr. Kurtz's friend—in a way."

'He stated with a good deal of formality that had we not been "of the same

40. Again suggesting the "double" theme.

profession," he would have kept the matter to himself without regard to consequences. He suspected "there was an active ill-will towards him on the part of these white men that——" "You are right," I said, remembering a certain conversation I had overheard. "The manager thinks you ought to be hanged." He showed a concern at this intelligence which amused me at first. "I had better get out of the way quietly," he said earnestly. "I can do no more for Kurtz now, and they would soon find some excuse. What's to stop them? There's a military post three hundred miles from here." "Well, upon my word," said I, "perhaps you had better go if you have any friends amongst the savages near by." "Plenty," he said. "They are simple people—and I want nothing, you know." He stood biting his lip, then: "I don't want any harm to happen to these whites here, but of course I was thinking of Mr. Kurtz's reputation—but you are a brother seaman and——" "All right," said I, after a time. "Mr. Kurtz's reputation is safe with me." I did not know how truly I spoke.

'He informed me, lowering his voice, that it was Kurtz who had ordered the attack to be made on the steamer. "He hated sometimes the idea of being taken away—and then again . . . But I don't understand these matters. I am a simple man. He thought it would scare you away—that you would give it up, thinking him dead. I could not stop him. Oh, I had an awful time of it this last month." "Very well," I said. "He is all right now." "Ye-e-es," he muttered, not very convinced apparently. "Thanks," said I; "I shall keep my eyes open." "But quiet—eh?" he urged anxiously. "It would be awful for his reputation if anybody here——" I promised a complete discretion with great gravity. "I have a canoe and three black fellows waiting not very far. I am off. Could you give me a few Martini-Henry cartridges?" I could, and did, with proper secrecy. He helped himself, with a wink at me, to a handful of my tobacco. "Between sailors—you know—good English tobacco." At the door of the pilot-house he turned round—"I say, haven't you a pair of shoes you could spare?" He raised one leg. "Look." The soles were tied with knotted strings sandal-wise under his bare feet. I rooted out an old pair, at which he looked with admiration before tucking it under his left arm. One of his pockets (bright red) was bulging with cartridges, from the other (dark blue) peeped "Towson's Inquiry," etc. etc. He seemed to think himself excellently well equipped for a renewed encounter with the wilderness. "Ah! I'll never, never meet such a man again. You ought to have heard him recite poetry—his own too it was, he told me. Poetry!" He rolled his eyes at the recollection of these delights. "Oh, he enlarged my mind! "Good-bye," said I. He shook hands and vanished in the night. Sometimes I ask myself whether I had ever really seen him—whether it was possible to meet such a phenomenon! . . .

'When I woke up shortly after midnight his warning came to my mind with its hint of danger that seemed, in the starred darkness, real enough to make me get up for the purpose of having a look round. On the hill a big fire burned, illuminating fitfully a crooked corner of the station-house. One of the agents with a picket of a few of our blacks, armed for the purpose, was keeping guard over the ivory; but deep within the forest, red gleams that wavered, that seemed to sink and rise from the ground amongst confused columnar shapes of intense blackness, showed the exact position of the camp where Mr. Kurtz's adorers were keeping their uneasy vigil. The monotonous beating of a big drum filled the air with muffled shocks and a lingering vibration. A steady droning sound of many men chanting each to himself some weird incantation came out from the black, flat wall of the woods as the humming of bees comes out of a hive, and had a strange narcotic effect upon my half-awake senses. I believe I dozed off leaning over the rail, till an abrupt burst of yells, an overwhelming outbreak of a pent-up and mysterious frenzy, woke me up in a bewildered wonder. It was cut short all at once, and the low droning went on with an effect of audible and soothing silence. I glanced casually into the little cabin. A light was burning within, but Mr. Kurtz was not there.

'I think I would have raised an outcry if I had believed my eyes. But I didn't believe them at first—the thing seemed so impossible. The fact is, I was completely unnerved by a sheer blank fright, pure abstract terror, unconnected with any distinct shape of physical danger. What made this emotion so overpowering was—how shall I define it?—the moral shock I received, as if something altogether monstrous, intolerable to thought and odious to the soul, had been thrust upon me unexpectedly. This lasted of course the merest fraction of a second, and then the usual sense of commonplace, deadly danger, the possibility of a sudden onslaught and massacre, or something of the kind, which I saw impending, was positively welcome and composing. It pacified me, in fact, so much, that I did not raise an alarm.

'There was an agent buttoned up inside an ulster and sleeping on a chair on deck within three feet of me. The yells had not awakened him; he snored very slightly; I left him to his slumbers and leaped ashore. I did not betray Mr. Kurtz—it was ordered I should never betray him—it was written I should be loyal to the nightmare of my choice. I was anxious to deal with this shadow by myself alone—and to this day I don't know why I was so jealous of sharing with any one the peculiar blackness of that experience.

'As soon as I got on the bank I saw a trail—a broad trail through the grass. I remember the exultation with which I said to myself, "He can't walk—he is crawling on all-fours—I've got him." The grass was wet with dew. I strode rapidly with clenched fists. I fancy I had some vague notion of falling upon him and giving him a drubbing. I don't know. I had some imbecile thoughts. The knitting old woman with the cat obtruded herself upon my memory as a most improper person to be sitting at the other end of such an affair. I saw a row of pilgrims squirting lead in the air out of Winchesters held to the hip. I thought I would never get back to the steamer, and imagined myself living alone and unarmed in the woods to an advanced age. Such silly things—you know. And I remember I confounded the beat of the drum with the beating of my heart, and was pleased at its calm regularity.

'I kept to the track though—then stopped to listen. The night was very clear; a dark blue space, sparkling with dew and starlight, in which black things stood very still. I thought I could see a kind of motion ahead of me. I was strangely cocksure of everything that night. I actually left the track and ran in a wide semicircle (I verily believe chuckling to myself) so as to get in front of that stir, of that motion I had seen—if indeed I had seen anything. I was circumventing Kurtz as though it had been a boyish game.

'I came upon him, and, if he had not heard me coming, I would have fallen over him too, but he got up in time. He rose, unsteady, long, pale, indistinct, like a vapour exhaled by the earth, and swayed slightly, misty and silent before me; while at my back the fires loomed between the trees, and the murmur of many voices issued from the forest. I had cut him off cleverly; but when actually confronting him I seemed to come to my senses, I saw the danger in its right proportion. It was by no means over yet. Suppose he began to shout? Though he could hardly stand, there was still plenty of vigour in his voice. "Go away—hide yourself," he said, in that profound tone. It was very awful. I glanced back. We were within thirty yards from the nearest fire. A black figure stood up, strode on long black legs, waving long black arms, across the glow. It had horns—antelope horns, I think—on its head. Some sorcerer, some witch-man, no doubt: it looked fiend-like enough. "Do you know what you are doing?" I whispered. "Perfectly," he answered, raising his voice for that single word: it sounded to me far off and yet loud, like a hail through a speaking-trumpet. If he makes a row we are lost, I thought to myself. This clearly was not a case for fisticuffs, even apart from the very natural aversion I had to beat that Shadow—this wandering and tormented thing. "You will be lost," I said—"utterly lost." One gets sometimes such a flash of inspiration, you know. I did say the right thing, though indeed he could not have been more irretrievably lost than he was at this very moment, when the foundations of our intimacy were being laid—to endure—to endure— even to the end—even beyond.

' "I had immense plans," he muttered irresolutely. "Yes," said I; "but if you try to shout I'll smash your head with——" There was not a stick or a stone near. "I will throttle you for good," I corrected myself. "I was on the threshold of great things," he pleaded, in a voice of longing, with a wistfulness of tone that made my blood run cold. "And now for this stupid scoundrel——" "Your success in Europe is assured in any case," I affirmed steadily. I did not want to have the throttling of him, you understand—and indeed it would have been very little use for any practical purpose. I tried to break the spell—the heavy, mute spell of the wilderness—that seemed to draw him to its pitiless breast by the awakening of forgotten and brutal instincts, by the memory of gratified and monstrous passions. This alone, I was convinced, had driven him out to the edge of the forest, to the bush, towards the gleam of fires, the throb of drums, the drone of weird incantations; this alone had beguiled his unlawful soul beyond the bounds of permitted aspirations. And, don't you see, the terror of the position was not in being knocked on the head—though I had a very lively sense of that danger too—but in this, that I had to deal with a being to whom I could not appeal in the name of anything high or low. I had, even like the niggers, to invoke him—himself—his own exalted and incredible degradation. There was nothing either above or below him, and I knew it. He had kicked himself loose of the earth. Confound the man! he had kicked the very earth to pieces. He was alone, and I before him did not know whether I stood on the ground or floated in the air. I've been telling you what we said—repeating the phrases we pronounced—but what's the good? They were common everyday words—the familiar, vague sounds exchanged on every waking day of life. But what of that? They had behind them, to my mind, the terrific suggestiveness of words heard in dreams, of phrases spoken in nightmares. Soul! If anybody had ever struggled with a soul, I am the man. And I wasn't arguing with a lunatic either. Believe me or not, his intelligence was perfectly clear—concentrated, it is true, upon himself with horrible intensity, yet clear; and therein was my only chance—barring, of course, the killing him there and then, which wasn't so good, on account of unavoidable noise. But his soul was mad. Being alone in the wilderness, it had looked within itself, and, by Heavens! I tell you, it had gone mad. I had—for my sins, I suppose, to go through the ordeal of looking into it myself. No eloquence could have been so withering to one's belief in mankind as his final burst of sincerity. He struggled with himself too. I saw it— I heard it. I saw the inconceivable mystery of a soul that knew no restraint, no faith, and no fear, yet struggling blindly with itself. I kept my head pretty well; but when I had him at last stretched on the couch, I wiped my forehead, while my legs shook under me as though I had carried half a ton on my back down that hill. And yet I had only supported him, his bony arm clasped round my neck—and he was not much heavier than a child.

'When next day we left at noon, the crowd, of whose presence behind the curtain of trees I had been acutely conscious all the time, flowed out of the woods again, filled the clearing, covered the slope with a mass of naked, breathing, quivering, bronze bodies. I steamed up a bit, then swung downstream, and two thousand eyes followed the evolutions of the splashing, thumping, fierce river-demon beating the water with its terrible tail and breathing black smoke into the air. In front of the first rank, along the river, three men, plastered with bright red earth from head to foot, strutted to and fro restlessly. When we came abreast again, they faced the river, stamped their feet, nodded their horned heads, swayed their scarlet bodies; they shook towards the fierce river-demon a bunch of black feathers, a mangy skin with a pendent tail—something that looked like a dried gourd; they shouted periodically together strings of amazing words that resembled no sounds of human language; and the deep murmurs of the crowd, interrupted suddenly, were like the responses of some satanic litany.

'We had carried Kurtz into the pilot-house: there was more air there. Lying on the couch, he stared through the open shutter. There was an eddy in the mass of human bodies, and the woman with helmeted head and tawny cheeks rushed out to the very brink of the stream. She put out her hands, shouted something, and all that wild mob took up the shout in a roaring chorus of articulated, rapid, breathless utterance.

'"Do you understand this?" I asked.

'He kept on looking out past me with fiery, longing eyes, with a mingled expression of wistfulness and hate. He made no answer, but I saw a smile, a smile of indefinable meaning, appear on his colourless lips that a moment after twitched convulsively. "Do I not?" he said slowly, gasping, as if the words had been torn out of him by a supernatural power.

'I pulled the string of the whistle, and I did this because I saw the pilgrims on deck getting out their rifles with an air of anticipating a jolly lark. At the sudden screech there was a movement of abject terror through that wedged mass of bodies. "Don't! don't you frighten them away," cried some one on deck disconsolately. I pulled the string time after time. They broke and ran, they leaped, they crouched, they swerved, they dodged the flying terror of the sound. The three red chaps had fallen flat, face down on the shore, as though they had been shot dead. Only the barbarous and superb woman did not so much as flinch, and stretched tragically her bare arms after us over the sombre and glittering river.

'And then that imbecile crowd down on the deck started their little fun, and I could see nothing more for smoke.

'The brown current ran swiftly out of the heart of darkness, bearing us down towards the sea with twice the speed of our upward progress; and Kurtz's life was running swiftly too, ebbing, ebbing out of his heart into the sea of inexorable time. The manager was very placid, he had no vital anxieties now, he took us both in with a comprehensive and satisfied glance: the "affair" had come off as well as could be wished. I saw the time approaching when I would be left alone of the party of "unsound method." The pilgrims looked upon me with disfavour. I was, so to speak, numbered with the dead. It is strange how I accepted this unforeseen partnership, this choice of nightmares forced upon me in the tenebrous land invaded by these mean and greedy phantoms.

'Kurtz discoursed. A voice! a voice! It rang deep to the very last. It survived his strength to hide in the magnificent folds of eloquence the barren darkness of his heart. Oh, he struggled! he struggled! The wastes of his weary brain were haunted by shadowy images now—images of wealth and fame revolving obsequiously round his unextinguishable gift of noble and lofty expression. My Intended, my station, my career, my ideas—these were the subjects for the occasional utterances of elevated sentiments. The shade of the original Kurtz frequented the bedside of the hollow sham, whose fate it was to be buried presently in the mould of primeval earth. But both the diabolic love and the unearthly hate of the mysteries it had penetrated fought for the possession of that soul satiated with primitive emotions, avid of lying fame, of sham distinction, of all the appearances of success and power.

'Sometimes he was contemptibly childish. He desired to have kings meet him at railway stations on his return from some ghastly Nowhere, where he intended to accomplish great things. "You show them you have in you something that is really profitable, and then there will be no limits to the recognition of your ability," he would say. "Of course you must take care of the motives—right motives—always." The long reaches that were like one and the same reach, monotonous bends that were exactly alike, slipped past the steamer with their multitude of secular [41] trees looking patiently after this grimy fragment of another world, the forerunner of change, of conquest, of trade, of massacres, of blessings. I looked ahead—piloting. "Close the shutter," said Kurtz suddenly one day; "I can't bear to look at this." I did so. There was a silence. "Oh, but I will wring your heart yet!" he cried at the invisible wilderness.

'We broke down—as I had expected—and had to lie up for repairs at the head of an island. This delay was the first thing that shook Kurtz's confidence.

41. Living through ages.

One morning he gave me a packet of papers and a photograph—the lot tied together with a shoe-string. "Keep this for me," he said. "This noxious fool" (meaning the manager) "is capable of prying into my boxes when I am not looking." In the afternoon I saw him. He was lying on his back with closed eyes, and I withdrew quietly, but I heard him mutter, "Live rightly, die, die . . ." I listened. There was nothing more. Was he rehearsing some speech in his sleep, or was it a fragment of a phrase from some newspaper article? He had been writing for the papers and meant to do so again, "for the furthering of my ideas. It's a duty."

'His was an impenetrable darkness. I looked at him as you peer down at a man who is lying at the bottom of a precipice where the sun never shines. But I had not much time to give him, because I was helping the engine-driver to take to pieces the leaky cylinders, to straighten a bent connecting-rod, and in other such matters. I lived in an infernal mess of rust, filings, nuts, bolts, spanners, hammers, ratchet-drills—things I abominate, because I don't get on with them. I tended the little forge we fortunately had aboard; I toiled wearily in a wretched scrap-heap—unless I had the shakes too bad to stand.

'One evening coming in with a candle I was startled to hear him say a little tremulously, "I am lying here in the dark waiting for death." The light was within a foot of his eyes. I forced myself to murmur, "Oh, nonsense!" and stood over him as if transfixed.

'Anything approaching the change that came over his features I have never seen before, and hope never to see again. Oh, I wasn't touched. I was fascinated. It was as though a veil had been rent. I saw on that ivory face the expression of sombre pride, of ruthless power, of craven terror—of an intense and hopeless despair. Did he live his life again in every detail of desire, temptation, and surrender during that supreme moment of complete knowledge? He cried in a whisper at some image, at some vision—he cried out twice, a cry that was no more than a breath:

' "The horror! The horror!" [42]

'I blew the candle out and left the cabin. The pilgrims were dining in the mess-room, and I took my place opposite the manager, who lifted his eyes to give me a questioning glance, which I successfully ignored. He leaned back, serene, with that peculiar smile of his sealing the unexpressed depths of his meanness. A continuous shower of small flies streamed upon the lamp, upon the cloth, upon our hands and faces. Suddenly the manager's boy put his insolent black head in the doorway, and said in a tone of scathing contempt:

' "Mistah Kurtz—he dead."

'All the pilgrims rushed out to see. I remained, and went on with my dinner. I believe I was considered brutally callous. However, I did not eat much. There was a lamp in there—light, don't you know—and outside it was so beastly, beastly dark. I went no more near the remarkable man who had pronounced a judgment upon the adventures of his soul on this earth. The voice was gone. What else had been there? But I am of course aware that next day the pilgrims buried something in a muddy hole.

42. The expression Eliot had wished to use as epigraph to *The Waste Land*. Later he used "Mistah Kurtz—he dead" as epigraph to "The Hollow Men," a poem imbued with the atmosphere of *Heart of Darkness*.

'And then they very nearly buried me.

'However, as you see, I did not go to join Kurtz there and then.[43] I did not. I remained to dream the nightmare out to the end, and to show my loyalty to Kurtz once more. Destiny. My destiny! Droll thing life is—that mysterious arrangement of merciless logic for a futile purpose. The most you can hope from it is some knowledge of yourself—that comes too late—a crop of unextinguishable regrets. I have wrestled with death. It is the most unexciting contest you can imagine. It takes place in an impalpable greyness, with nothing underfoot, with nothing around, without spectators, without clamour, without glory, without the great desire of victory, without the great fear of defeat, in a sickly atmosphere of tepid scepticism, without much belief in your own right, and still less in that of your adversary. If such is the form of ultimate wisdom, then life is a greater riddle than some of us think it to be. I was within a hair's-breadth of the last opportunity for pronouncement, and I found with humiliation that probably I would have nothing to say. This is the reason why I affirm that Kurtz was a remarkable man. He had something to say. He said it. Since I had peeped over the edge myself, I understand better the meaning of his stare, that could not see the flame of the candle, but was wide enough to embrace the whole universe, piercing enough to penetrate all the hearts that beat in the darkness. He had summed up—he had judged. "The horror!" He was a remarkable man. After all, this was the expression of some sort of belief; it had candour, it had conviction, it had a vibrating note of revolt in its whisper, it had the appalling face of a glimpsed truth—the strange commingling of desire and hate. And it is not my own extremity I remember best—a vision of greyness without form filled with physical pain, and a careless contempt for the evanescence of all things—even of this pain itself. No! It is his extremity that I seem to have lived through. True, he had made that last stride, he had stepped over the edge, while I had been permitted to draw back my hesitating foot. And perhaps in this is the whole difference; perhaps all the wisdom, and all truth, and all sincerity, are just compressed into that inappreciable moment of time in which we step over the threshold of the invisible. Perhaps! I like to think my summing-up would not have been a word of careless contempt. Better his cry—much better. It was an affirmation, a moral victory paid for by innumerable defeats, by abominable terrors, by abominable satisfactions. But it was a victory! That is why I have remained[44] loyal to Kurtz to the last, and even beyond, when a long time after I heard once more, not his own voice, but the echo of his magnificent eloquence thrown to me from a soul as translucently pure as a cliff of crystal.

'No, they did not bury me, though there is a period of time which I remember mistily, with a shuddering wonder, like a passage through some inconceivable world that had no hope in it and no desire. I found myself back in the sepulchral city resenting the sight of people hurrying through the streets to filch a little money from each other, to devour their infamous cookery, to gulp their unwholesome beer, to dream their insignificant and silly dreams. They trespassed upon my thoughts. They were intruders whose knowledge

43. With the odd implication that later he will.
44. "I remained" (one of Conrad's slight confusions of English tense).

of life was to me an irritating pretence, because I felt so sure they could not possibly know the things I knew. Their bearing, which was simply the bearing of commonplace individuals going about their business in the assurance of perfect safety, was offensive to me like the outrageous flauntings of folly in the face of a danger it is unable to comprehend. I had no particular desire to enlighten them, but I had some difficulty in restraining myself from laughing in their faces, so full of stupid importance. I daresay I was not very well at that time. I tottered about the streets—there were various affairs to settle—grinning bitterly at perfectly respectable persons. I admit my behaviour was inexcusable, but then my temperature was seldom normal in these days. My dear aunt's endeavours to "nurse up my strength" seemed altogether beside the mark. It was not my strength that wanted nursing, it was my imagination that wanted soothing. I kept the bundle of papers given me by Kurtz, not knowing exactly what to do with it. His mother had died lately, watched over, as I was told, by his Intended. A clean-shaved man, with an official manner and wearing gold-rimmed spectacles, called on me one day and made inquiries, at first circuitous, afterwards suavely pressing, about what he was pleased to denominate certain "documents." I was not surprised, because I had had two rows with the manager on the subject out there. I had refused to give up the smallest scrap out of that package, and I took the same attitude with the spectacled man. He became darkly menacing at last, and with much heat argued that the Company had the right to every bit of information about its "territories." And, said he, "Mr. Kurtz's knowledge of unexplored regions must have been necessarily extensive and peculiar—owing to his great abilities and to the deplorable circumstances in which he had been placed: therefore——" I assured him Mr. Kurtz's knowledge, however extensive, did not bear upon the problems of commerce or administration. He invoked then the name of science. "It would be an incalculable loss if," etc. etc. I offered him the report on the "Suppression of Savage Customs," with the postscriptum torn off. He took it up eagerly, but ended by sniffing at it with an air of contempt. "This is not what we had a right to expect," he remarked. "Expect nothing else," I said. "There are only private letters." He withdrew upon some threat of legal proceedings, and I saw him no more; but another fellow, calling himself Kurtz's cousin, appeared two days later, and was anxious to hear all the details about his dear relative's last moments. Incidentally he gave me to understand that Kurtz had been essentially a great musician. "There was the making of an immense success," said the man, who was an organist, I believe, with lank grey hair flowing over a greasy coat-collar. I had no reason to doubt his statement; and to this day I am unable to say what was Kurtz's profession, whether he ever had any—which was the greatest of his talents. I had taken him for a painter who wrote for the papers, or else for a journalist who could paint—but even the cousin (who took snuff during the interview) could not tell me what he had been—exactly. He was a universal genius—on that point I agreed with the old chap, who thereupon blew his nose noisily into a large cotton handkerchief and withdrew in senile agitation, bearing off some family letters and memoranda without importance. Ultimately a journalist anxious to know something of the fate of his "dear colleague" turned up. This visitor informed me Kurtz's proper sphere ought to have been politics "on the popular side." He had furry straight eyebrows, bristly hair cropped short, an eyeglass on a broad ribbon, and, becoming expansive, confessed his opinion that Kurtz really couldn't write a bit—"but Heavens! how that man could talk! He electrified large meetings. He had faith —don't you see?—he had the faith. He could get himself to believe anything— anything. He would have been a splendid leader of an extreme party." "What party?" I asked. "Any party," answered the other. "He was an—an—extremist." Did I not think so? I assented. Did I know, he asked, with a sudden flash of curiosity, "what it was that had induced him to go out there?" "Yes," said I, and forthwith handed him the famous Report for publication, if he thought fit. He glanced through it hurriedly, mumbling all the time, judged "it would do," and took himself off with this plunder.

'Thus I was left at last with a slim packet of letters and the girl's portrait. She struck me as beautiful—I mean she had a beautiful expression. I know that the sunlight can be made to lie too, yet one felt that no manipulation of light and pose could have conveyed the delicate shade of truthfulness upon those features. She seemed ready to listen without mental reservation, without suspicion, without a thought for herself. I concluded I would go and give her back her portrait and those letters myself. Curiosity? Yes; and also some other feeling perhaps. All that had been Kurtz's had passed out of my hands: his soul, his body, his station, his plans, his ivory, his career. There remained only his memory and his Intended—and I wanted to give that up too to the past, in a way—to surrender personally all that remained of him with me to that oblivion which is the last word of our common fate. I don't defend myself. I had no clear perception of what it was I really wanted. Perhaps it was an impulse of unconscious loyalty, or the fulfilment of one of those ironic necessities that lurk in the facts of human existence. I don't know. I can't tell. But I went.

'I thought his memory was like the other memories of the dead that accumulate in every man's life—a vague impress on the brain of shadows that had fallen on it in their swift and final passage; but before the high and ponderous door, between the tall houses of a street as still and decorous as a well-kept alley in a cemetery, I had a vision of him on the stretcher, opening his mouth voraciously, as if to devour all the earth with all its mankind. He lived then before me; he lived as much as he had ever lived—a shadow insatiable of splendid appearances, of frightful realities; a shadow darker than the shadow of the night, and draped nobly in the folds of a gorgeous eloquence. The vision seemed to enter the house with me—the stretcher, the phantom-bearers, the wild crowd of obedient worshippers, the gloom of the forests, the glitter of the reach between the murky bends, the beat of the drum, regular and muffled like the beating of a heart—the heart of a conquering darkness. It was a moment of triumph for the wilderness, an invading and vengeful rush which, it seemed to me, I would have to keep back alone for the salvation of another soul. And the memory of what I had heard him say afar there, with the horned shapes stirring at my back, in the glow of fires, within the patient woods, those broken phrases came back to me, were heard again in their ominous and terrifying simplicity. I remembered his abject pleading, his abject threats, the colossal scale of his vile desires, the meanness, the torment, the tempestuous anguish of his soul. And later on I seemed to see his collected languid manner, when he said one day, "This lot of ivory now is really mine. The Company did not pay for it. I collected it myself at a very great personal risk. I am afraid they will try to claim it as theirs though. H'm. It is a difficult case. What do you think I ought to do—resist? Eh? I want no more than justice.". . . He wanted no more than justice—no more than justice. I rang the bell before a mahogany door on the first floor, and while I waited he seemed to stare at me out of the glassy panel—stare with that wide and immense stare embracing, condemning, loathing all the universe. I seemed to hear the whispered cry, "The horror! The horror!"

'The dusk was falling. I had to wait in a lofty drawing-room with three long windows from floor to ceiling that were like three luminous and bedraped columns. The bent gilt legs and backs of the furniture shone in indistinct curves. The tall marble fireplace had a cold and monumental whiteness. A grand piano stood massively in a corner; with dark gleams on the flat surfaces like a sombre and polished sarcophagus. A high door opened—closed. I rose.

'She came forward, all in black, with a pale head, floating towards me in the dusk. She was in mourning. It was more than a year since his death, more than a year since the news came; she seemed as though she would remember and mourn for ever. She took both my hands in hers and murmured, "I had heard you were coming." I noticed she was not very young—I mean not girlish. She had a mature capacity for fidelity, for belief, for suffering. The room seemed to have grown darker, as if all the sad light of the cloudy evening had taken refuge on her forehead. This fair hair, this pale visage, this pure brow, seemed surrounded by an ashy halo from which the dark eyes looked out at me. Their glance was guileless, profound, confident, and trustful. She carried her sorrowful head as though she were proud of that sorrow, as though she would say, I—I alone know how to mourn for him as he deserves. But while we were still shaking hands, such a look of awful desolation came upon her face that I perceived she was one of those creatures that are not the playthings of Time. For her he had died only yesterday. And, by Jove! the impression was so powerful that for me too he seemed to have died only yesterday—nay, this very minute. I saw her and him in the same instant of time—his death and her sorrow—I saw her sorrow in the very moment of his death. Do you understand? I saw them together—I heard them together. She had said, with a deep catch of the breath, "I have survived"; while my strained ears seemed to hear distinctly, mingled with her tone of despairing regret, the summing-up whisper of his eternal condemnation. I asked myself what I was doing there, with a sensation of panic in my heart as though I had blundered into a place of cruel and absurd mysteries not fit for a human being to behold. She motioned me to a chair. We sat down. I laid the packet gently on the little table, and she put her hand over it. . . . "You knew him well," she murmured, after a moment of mourning silence.

'"Intimacy grows quickly out there," I said. "I knew him as well as it is possible for one man to know another."

'"And you admired him," she said. "It was impossible to know him and not to admire him. Was it?"

' "He was a remarkable man," I said unsteadily. Then before the appealing fixity of her gaze, that seemed to watch for more words on my lips, I went on, "It was impossible not to——"

' "Love him," she finished eagerly, silencing me into an appalled dumbness. "How true! how true! But when you think that no one knew him so well as I! I had all his noble confidence. I knew him best."

' "You knew him best," I repeated. And perhaps she did. But with every word spoken the room was growing darker, and only her forehead, smooth and white, remained illumined by the unextinguishable light of belief and love.

' "You were his friend," she went on. "His friend," she repeated, a little louder. "You must have been, if he had given you this, and sent you to me. I feel I can speak to you—and oh! I must speak. I want you—you who have heard his last words—to know I have been worthy of him. . . . It is not pride. . . . Yes! I am proud to know I understood him better than any one on earth—he told me so himself. And since his mother died I have had no one—no one—to—to——"

'I listened. The darkness deepened. I was not even sure whether he had given me the right bundle. I rather suspect he wanted me to take care of another batch of his papers which, after his death, I saw the manager examining under the lamp. And the girl talked, easing her pain in the certitude of my sympathy; she talked as thirsty men drink. I had heard that her engagement with Kurtz had been disapproved by her people. He wasn't rich enough or something. And indeed I don't know whether he had not been a pauper all his life. He had given me some reason to infer that it was his impatience of comparative poverty that drove him out there.

' ". . . Who was not his friend who had heard him speak once?" she was saying. "He drew men towards him by what was best in them." She looked at me with intensity. "It is the gift of the great," she went on, and the sound of her low voice seemed to have the accompaniment of all the other sounds, full of mystery, desolation, and sorrow, I had ever heard—the ripple of the river, the soughing of the trees swayed by the wind, the murmurs of the crowds, the faint ring of incomprehensible words cried from afar, the whisper of a voice speaking from beyond the threshold of an eternal darkness. "But you have heard him! You know!" she cried.

' "Yes, I know," I said with something like despair in my heart, but bowing my head before the faith that was in her, before that great and saving illusion that shone with an unearthly glow in the darkness, in the triumphant darkness from which I could not have defended her—from which I could not even defend myself.

' "What a loss to me—to us!"—she corrected herself with beautiful generosity; then added in a murmur, "To the world." By the last gleams of twilight I could see the glitter of her eyes, full of tears—of tears that would not fall.

' "I have been very happy—very fortunate—very proud," she went on. "Too fortunate. Too happy for a little while. And now I am unhappy for—for life."

'She stood up; her fair hair seemed to catch all the remaining light in a glimmer of gold. I rose too.

' "And of all this," she went on mournfully, "of all his promise, and of all his greatness, of his generous mind, of his noble heart, nothing remains—nothing but a memory. You and I——"

' "We shall always remember him," I said hastily.

' "No!" she cried. "It is impossible that all this should be lost—that such a life should be sacrificed to leave nothing—but sorrow. You know what vast plans he had. I knew of them too—I could not perhaps understand—but others knew of them. Something must remain. His words, at least, have not died."

' "His words will remain," I said.

' "And his example," she whispered to herself. "Men looked up to him—his goodness shone in every act. His example——"

' "True," I said; "his example too. Yes, his example. I forgot that."

' "But I do not. I cannot—I cannot believe—not yet. I cannot believe that I shall never see him again, that nobody will see him again, never, never, never."

'She put out her arms as if after a retreating figure, stretching them back and with clasped pale hands across the fading and narrow sheen of the window. Never see him! I saw him clearly enough then. I shall see this eloquent phantom as long as I live, and I shall see her too, a tragic and familiar Shade, resembling in this gesture another one, tragic also, and bedecked with powerless charms, stretching bare brown arms over the glitter of the infernal stream, the stream of darkness. She said suddenly very low, "He died as he lived."

' "His end," said I, with dull anger stirring in me, "was in every way worthy of his life."

' "And I was not with him," she murmured. My anger subsided before a feeling of infinite pity.

' "Everything that could be done——" I mumbled.

' "Ah, but I believed in him more than any one on earth—more than his own mother, more than—himself. He needed me! Me! I would have treasured every sigh, every word, every sign, every glance."

'I felt like a chill grip on my chest. "Don't," I said, in a muffled voice.

' "Forgive me. I—I—have mourned so long in silence—in silence. . . . You were with him—to the last? I think of his loneliness. Nobody near to understand him as I would have understood. Perhaps no one to hear . . . ."

' "To the very end," I said shakily. "I heard his very last words. . . ." I stopped in a fright.

' "Repeat them," she murmured in a heart-broken tone. "I want—I want—something—something—to—to live with."

'I was on the point of crying at her, "Don't you hear them?" The dusk was repeating them in a persistent whisper all around us, in a whisper that seemed to swell menacingly like the first whisper of a rising wind. "The horror! The horror!"

' "His last word—to live with," she insisted. "Don't you understand I loved him—I loved him—I loved him!"

'I pulled myself together and spoke slowly.

' "The last word he pronounced was—your name."

'I heard a light sigh and then my heart stood still, stopped dead short by an exulting and terrible cry, by the cry of inconceivable triumph and of unspeakable pain. "I knew it—I was sure!". . . She knew. She was sure. I heard her weeping; she had hidden her face in her hands. It seemed to me that the house would collapse before I could escape, that the heavens would fall upon my head. But nothing happened. The heavens do not fall for such a trifle. Would they have fallen, I wonder, if I had rendered Kurtz that justice which was his due? Hadn't he said he wanted only justice? But I couldn't. I could not tell her. It would have been too dark—too dark altogether. . . .'

Marlow ceased, and sat apart, indistinct and silent, in the pose of a meditating Buddha. Nobody moved for a time. 'We have lost the first of the ebb,' said the Director suddenly. I raised my head. The offing was barred by a black bank of clouds, and the tranquil waterway leading to the uttermost ends of the earth flowed sombre under an overcast sky—seemed to lead into the heart of an immense darkness.

1899   1902

WILLIAM BUTLER YEATS
1865–1939

William Butler Yeats, eldest child of the painter John Butler Yeats, was born in Dublin on June 13, 1865. Two years later the Yeatses moved to London, but frequently visited County Sligo, where lived the family of the poet's mother, the Pollexfens. Yeats went to school first in London and, from 1880 to 1883, in Dublin. He then entered the Dublin School of Art, grew interested in the occult and, through the patriot John O'Leary, in the cause of Irish independence. Back in London in 1887, he made the acquaintance of William Morris, Oscar Wilde, and others, including Edwin J. Ellis, with whom he began work on an edition of William Blake. In 1889 appeared hs book *The Wanderings of Oisin;* and in the same year he met and fell in love with Maud Gonne, who was to figure so prominently in his poetry. In 1890 he joined the Order of the Golden Dawn, a secret society in which he held important office. The Rhymers' Club—a group of poets meeting in inns (of whom Yeats made the famous remark, "The one thing certain is that we are too many")—was founded in 1891, and Yeats became the friend of fellow members Lionel Johnson and Ernest Dowson (see Headnote to *Autobiographies). The Countess Cathleen,* a verse play for Maud Gonne (who in the previous year had issued the first of her many refusals to marry Yeats), appeared in 1892, and the essays called *The Celtic Twilight,* with the Blake edition, in the following year. In 1894 he visited Paris, and grew acquainted with some modern French poetry; the Symbolist aesthetic was explained to him by the poet-critic Arthur Symons, with whom he shared rooms for a time in 1895. This new interest was not inconsistent either with an interest in Blake or continuing research into the occult. *Poems* (1895) collected the lyrics of the early years. In 1896 he met Lady Augusta Gregory and John Millington Synge, both to have a profound effect on his life; in the following year he paid the first of his many visits to Lady Gregory's house at Coole in County Galway. He now had political and theatrical interests, and was writing a good deal of prose, but produced another volume of lyrics, *The Wind Among the Reeds,* in 1899. The theatrical interest resulted in his becoming president of the Irish National Dramatic Society and eventually, in 1904, opening, with Lady Gregory, the Abbey Theatre.

Poems 1895–1905 appeared in 1906, but this was mainly a period of "theatre business, management of men," of box-office takings and training actors, of handling many crises, notably the disturbances at the performance of Synge's *Playboy of the Western World* in 1907. In 1908 Bullen's eight-volume edition of the *Collected Works* was published, though Yeats had as yet written none of the poetry that established him as a major author. His father, who settled permanently in New York in that year, had always urged his son to interest himself in the concrete, for which, he said, Willie had a special gift that Celtic-twilight abstractions tended to conceal. Yeats was aware of this; as a poet he had always understood the need for concreteness, freshness, and flexibility, however tempted into fashionable vagueness. His involvement in the heated day-to-day business of the Dublin theater and politics, though he complained that it interfered with his poetry, may have helped him finally to approach his own and his father's ideal.

A new note is audible in *The Green Helmet and Other Poems* (1910); and, after an American tour with the Abbey troupe in 1911, he met another poet who would influence him decisively, Ezra Pound. Their relation is the nearest in literature to that of Haydn and Mozart in music, for the influence went both ways, and Pound's was perhaps the stronger, although he was twenty years Yeats's junior. In 1914 Pound married the daughter of Olivia Shakespear, Yeats's old friend; and Yeats, at the time working on the first part of his *Autobiographies,* published his most important volume of poetry so far, *Responsibilities.* Pound introduced him to the Japanese Nōh plays, and Yeats began to produce his plays for dancers, the first being *At the Hawk's Well* (1916). This was also the year of the Easter Rising in Dublin, and of Yeats's poem on the subject; he was to write many more about the troubles of Ireland. In 1917 he bought (for £35) an old Norman tower at Ballylee in Galway, near Lady Gregory's house. Again he proposed marriage to Maud Gonne, whose husband, Major Mac-Bride, had been executed by the British for his part in the Rising. Turned down, he proposed to Maud's daughter Iseult; turned down again, he proposed to and was accepted by Georgie Hyde-Lees, October 21, 1917.

This same year of 1917 marked the publication of the collection *The Wild Swans at Coole,* which is headed by the great elegy for Lady Gregory's son Robert and which contains a number of "system" poems: he was "hammering his thoughts into unity," working out an all-inclusive system of personality and history, as a means to realizing himself as an artist. A daughter was born in 1919, and a son in 1921, the year of the volumes *Michael Robartes and the Dancer* and *Four Plays for Dancers.* In 1922 Yeats bought a house in Dublin, but continued to spend his summers at the Tower in Ballylee. He became a senator of the new Irish Free State. Now he published a collection, *Later Poems,* and the part of his autobiography dealing with his life in the Nineties, *The Trembling of the Veil.* In 1923 he was awarded a Nobel Prize. At this time he was working on the first version of *A Vision,* his systematic world-philosophy, and reading widely if eccentrically in history and philosophy. After a winter in Sicily and Italy he returned to Ballylee and Dublin, and made a bold speech to the Senate in favor of divorce. The prose work *A Vision* appeared in January 1926. Though his health was now poor he produced what is probably his greatest single volume, *The Tower* (1928). He spent some time at Coole with the dying Lady Gregory, and wrote the poems that appeared in *The Winding Stair* (1933). In 1934 he underwent a Steinach operation for rejuvenation; it had certainly some such effect.

Yeats now produced an abundance of verse, prose, and plays, and in 1936 published the *Oxford Book of Modern Verse,* an idiosyncratic but fascinating anthology, and the dance-play *A Full Moon in March*. He formed new friendships, notably with the poet Dorothy Wellesley, began the extraordinary "Rabelaisian" verse-play *The Herne's Egg*, and gave a radio lecture on modern poetry; his correspondence is especially rich at this time. Adoption of a new "mask," that of the wild old man, recruited his physical energy, and he gave exciting broadcasts of his poetry. The fuller revised version of *A Vision* appeared in 1937. In 1938 he moved to the south of France, and wrote the pamphlet *On the Boiler*, a miscellany of opinions reflecting his flirtation with fascism and with eugenics. He wrote the play *Purgatory*, performed in his presence at the Abbey in August 1938, and at the end of the year began his last play, *The Death of Cuchulain*, in which a wild old man like Yeats himself speaks an excited prologue. He fell ill at the beginning of 1939 and died on January 28. He was buried at Roquebrune; the body was taken to Drumcliffe Churchyard near Sligo in September 1948.

There are many aspects of Yeats's work that cannot be represented in a selection of thirty-odd poems and a few short prose extracts—a whole corpus of plays of many kinds, a lifework of speculation on politics, verse, the occult. And it is in the hammered unity of all this that his greatness lies. Nevertheless his poems—even when they are not expressly "system" poems—refer to his occult beliefs, as well as to his personal life and the politics of Ireland. The notes explain particular allusions, but a general word of introduction may be useful.

Yeats needed a system not because he needed abstract and systematic thought, but because he saw that the *oeuvre* of a writer is fragmentary and multiple unless one poem "lights up another"—unless all refer, somehow, to an integral whole, namely, the poet; so that the poet needs also to be possessed of some arrangement of beliefs that suggests and promotes the sense of his unity. The world itself, at the period of history he found himself in, was "but a bundle of fragments," and the establishment of some fiction of integrity that would serve a poet in such a world was his own responsibility: it could not, he felt, be done by a church, or by science. It would be achieved at great cost, and as the *Autobiographies* and other works demonstrate, Yeats was so keenly aware of this cost that he judged his own life, and those of his friends, by asking how they paid the cost as well as how near they came to their goal. What was needed in the poet was something the world had lost: confidence in that universal humanity represented by the stored images of the unconscious, the complementary dreams of noble and beggarman that had been destroyed, like all the fine things of traditional civilization, by the rise of the middle classes, the "shopkeeping logicians." Yeats made a remarkably clear statement of what he was after in the opening sentences of an essay on magic, written as early as 1901.

> I believe in the practice and the philosophy of what we have agreed to call magic . . . in the vision of truth in the depths of the mind when the eyes are closed; and I believe in three doctrines, which have, as I think, been handed down from early times, and been the foundation of nearly all magical practices. These doctrines are:
>   (1) That the borders of the mind are ever shifting, and that many minds can flow into one another, as it were, and create or reveal a single mind, a single energy.
>   (2) That the borders of our memories are a part of one great memory, the memory of Nature herself.
>   (3) That this great mind and great memory can be evoked by symbols. . . .
> *Essays and Introductions*, 1961, p. 28

Yeats first thought to reach down to this Great Memory through Irish folktale and, in ever more sophisticated forms, continued to do so, as we see for example from the late poem "The Statues," the last play, *The Death of Cuchulain,* and the last poem, "Cuchulain Comforted." But he also extended his interest far beyond any national boundary, and—although he was not a learned man in the usual sense—sought to include in one package an interpretation of the whole of history and the whole range of human personality. Steeped in the symbolism of Shelley and Blake—he had edited Blake, and knew what a poet's "system" might involve—he had also before him the example of many occult traditions, all seeking some unitary explanation of the world and the soul.

One such system was that of Mme. H. P. Blavatsky (1831–91) and the Theosophical Society, which Yeats had joined in 1887. Madame Blavatsky's elaborate system (expounded in *Isis Unveiled,* 1877) was adapted from Indian philosophy and involved cyclical time and reincarnation, among other things. Although Yeats later broke with the Theosophists, their influence on his thought was considerable. Another system was that of the Cabbalist and ritualist MacGregor Mathers, who introduced Yeats to the society of the Hermetic Students of the Order of the Golden Dawn. With symbol and system Yeats sought access to a place he later called simply, after Plotinus, "There," some center where everything came together. What he was trying to get together, for the sake of major poetry, was himself. He was convinced that his was the age of "the trembling of the veil" (see notes on *Autobiographies*)—that in a disintegrating world, a world near some terrible apocalypse, the way to stand up to the terrors, to resist the appeals of the decadence, was to renew oneself. Hence his system of belief, thought necessary to the avoidance of "multiplicity" in the personality, grew ever more elaborate; and there was a decisive development when it emerged that his new wife, married in 1917, had the gift of automatic writing.

Yeats had been melancholy; now he had "Instructors," who elaborated his thought for him in communications from the spirit world, from "There." These communications led to the doctrinal poems of *Michael Robartes and the Dancer* (1921) and eventually to the system explained in the first and second versions of *A Vision* (1925, 1937). These books assume that *everything* is interrelated, all history, theology, biography; and so all poetry, and in particular all Yeats's poetry, may be. Of the elements of this system the primary and antithetical gyres, the Great Wheel, the Mask, and the Daimon, there is no need to say anything here. Yeats called it his "lunar parable." "Some will ask whether I believe in the actual existence of my circuits of the sun and moon," he wrote, evidently aware that all this raised a problem of belief.

> To such a question I can but answer that if sometimes, overwhelmed by miracle as all men must be when in the midst of it, I have taken such periods literally, my reason has soon recovered; and now that the system stands out clearly in my imagination I regard them as stylistic arrangements of experience comparable to the cubes in the drawings of Wyndham Lewis and to the ovoids in the sculpture of Brancusi. They have helped me to hold in a single thought reality and justice.

The system gave point to Yeats's profound belief in the apocalyptic character of his time, and in his own role and that of the artist in general. That is its justification; it gave him, as he said of his spirit "Instructors," "metaphors for poetry," and for a poetry that should be founded on a single intelligible world in his mind. In this world, as Yeats said in that most memorable sentence, reality and justice constitute but a single thought. Elsewhere they are perpetually at odds. So *A Vision* makes great poetry a project the visionary can sustain; it is, as Yeats said, "a last defence against the chaos of the world."

What is the direct effect on the poetry? There are some poems—"The Phases of the Moon" and "Ego Dominus Tuus" are examples, both written in the first flush of the new "instructions" mediated by his wife—in which Yeats is frankly doctrinal; yet in spite of that they are still, and primarily, poems; the doctrines give Yeats some memorable metaphors and sonorities. He was, even in these extremities, an artist first. There are other poems—"Leda and the Swan," for instance, or "The Second Coming" —which have established themselves as memorable with readers who know and care nothing about the doctrines they certainly do contain. It may be said that in some others—e.g., "Byzantium" with its "Hades' bobbin," or "The Statues," where some very unfamiliar cultural propositions are presented only elliptically—Yeats's allusions to doctrine are too curt, too idiosyncratic, and that the casual technicality of the references damages the poem. It may be so; it grew more probable that such things should happen when Yeats, in old age, deliberately cultivated a dashing, nonchalant attitude toward the reader. His *Last Poems,* which struck everybody dumb with admiration when they appeared (1940), now seem to fall too often into intellectual or rhetorical posturing; the precision of his work in the 1920's is a world ill lost if the reward is the self-indulgent rant of "Under Ben Bulben." And by the same token it may be that at times, in the late poems, the system mastered its master. But how rarely this occurred!

Yeats's passion for making and remaking himself led him to revise his early work; it might contain elements of later thought, and be made, by a few touches, to conform to a later pattern. These revisions are sometimes substantial, when an old essay or story is integrated into a pattern later evolved; sometimes they are matters of detail, the artist in search of the concrete, the flexible, hating the tired or conventional rhythm. Some instances of revision are mentioned in the notes. The process was not always, in the opinions of other readers than its author, successful. But it was part of the process of making oneself whole from moment to moment. The need for stylistic changes in the early poetry is thus part of the same process that led Yeats to revise and expand his system. What developed—perhaps at the cost of a few spoiled poems—was the extraordinary certainty and range of the mature Yeatsian style. This style became an instrument equal to the demands of a great variety of themes— personal, political, doctrinal—and of kinds—song, ballad, romantic meditation, elegy, tragedy—without the loss of what Yeats himself regarded as essential: the powerful and true impression of the whole poet at work behind it.

The Sorrow of Love

The quarrel of the sparrows in the eaves,
The full round moon and the star-laden sky,
And the loud song of the ever-singing leaves
Had hid away earth's old and weary cry.

And then you came with those red mournful lips,
And with you came the whole of the world's tears,

And all the sorrows of her labouring ships,
And all the burden of her myriad years.

And now the sparrows warring in the eaves,
10 The crumbling moon, the white stars in the sky,
And the loud chanting of the unquiet leaves,
Are shaken with earth's old and weary cry.
1891   1892

[This version of "The Sorrow of Love" was written in 1891 and went through several revisions before it appeared in its final form—given below—in *Early Poems and Stories* (1927). Yeats mentions it as an instance of a new poem produced by rewriting an old one. In the revision he was avoiding what came to strike him as inert diction (*star-laden, ever-singing, weary*) and evidently thought *brawling* tougher than *quarrel*. He gave up the gentle, relaxed anaphora of the second stanza; the moon, which had been *crumbling* and then *curd-pale*, was set in action. Yeats liked to use *famous* in a semi-journalistic way from the 1920's on, and does so in line 3. Some florid alliterations are introduced. The last line is so changed as to give the poem a different and obscurer sense. Yeats's search for a harsher and more modern diction went on through these years, and these versions are a slight indication of its direction.]

The Sorrow of Love

The brawling of a sparrow in the eaves,
The brilliant moon and all the milky sky,
And all that famous harmony of leaves,
Had blotted out man's image and his cry.

A girl° arose that had red mournful lips
And seemed the greatness of the world in tears,
Doomed like Odysseus° and the labouring ships
And proud as Priam° murdered with his peers;

Arose, and on the instant clamorous eaves,
10 A climbing moon upon an empty sky,
And all that lamentation of the leaves,
Could but compose man's image and his cry.
1922   1927

The Two Trees

"The Two Trees" was much altered between its first appearance in 1892 and the definitive version, which was established in *Selected Poems* (1929): e.g., lines 13–16:

girl Helen of Troy, who often occurs in Yeat's poetry, usually standing for Maud Gonne
Odysseus After successfully planning the capture of Troy Odysseus (Ulysses) spent ten years wandering about the Mediterranean on his way home to Thrace.
Priam king of Troy killed by Neoptolemus, the son of Achilles

"There, through bewildered branches, go / Winged Loves borne on in gentle strife, / Tossing and tossing to and fro / The flaming circle of our life." The revisions emphasize the difference between the anti-intellectual tree of life and the dead rottenness of the other tree. Yeats had in mind one of Blake's *Poetical Sketches:* "Love and harmony combine, / And around our souls entwine, / While thy branches meet with mine, / And our roots together join. / Joys upon our branches sit, / Chirping loud and singing sweet; / Like gentle streams beneath our feet / Innocence and virtue meet. . . ." He remembered also Blake's later comment: "Art is the Tree of Life . . . Science is the Tree of Death" (*The Laocoon Group*).

His second tree is introspection, thought, the ruin of the body by the abstract mind which Yeats especially deplored in women (see "Michael Robartes and the Dancer," "In Memory of Eva Gore-Booth . . . ," "Easter 1916," as examples). In *Ideas of Good and Evil,* a Blakean book with a Blakean title, he asserts that "men who sought their food among the green leaves of the Tree of Life condemned none but the unimaginative and the idle, and those who forget that even love and death and old age are an imaginative art." Another source is the Cabbala, in which the Sephirotic Tree has two aspects, one benign, one malign. Yeats records in an essay on magic that he found in MacGregor Mathers's book *The Kabbalah Unveiled* this passage: "The Tree . . . is the Tree of the Knowledge of Good and Evil . . . in its branches the birds lodge and build their nests. . . ." He may have remembered Milton's Satan, who "on the tree of Life, . . . / Sat like a cormorant" (*Paradise Lost* IV.194–96).

The Two Trees

Belovèd, gaze in thine own heart,
The holy tree is growing there;
From joy the holy branches start,
And all the trembling flowers they bear.
The changing colours of its fruit
Have dowered the stars with merry light;
The surety of its hidden root
Has planted quiet in the night;
The shaking of its leafy head
10 Has given the waves their melody,
And made my lips and music wed,
Murmuring a wizard song for thee.
There the Loves a circle go,
The flaming circle of our days,
Gyring, spiring to and fro
In those great ignorant° leafy ways;
Remembering all that shaken hair
And how the wingèd sandals dart,
Thine eyes grow full of tender care:
20 Belovèd, gaze in thine own heart.

ignorant This revision enables Yeats to emphasize the vital absence of abstraction and intellect in the good tree.

Gaze no more in the bitter glass
The demons, with their subtle guile,
Lift up before us when they pass,
Or only gaze a little while;
For there a fatal image grows
That the stormy night receives,
Roots half hidden under snows,
Broken boughs and blackened leaves.
For all things turn to barrenness
30 In the dim glass the demons hold,
The glass of outer weariness,
Made when God slept in times of old.
There, through the broken branches, go
The ravens of unresting thought;
Flying, crying, to and fro,
Cruel claw and hungry throat,
Or else they stand and sniff the wind,
And shake their ragged wings; alas!
Thy tender eyes grow all unkind:
40 Gaze no more in the bitter glass.

1929

Adam's Curse°

We sat together at one summer's end,
That beautiful mild woman, your close friend,
And you and I, and talked of poetry.
I said, 'A line will take us hours maybe;
Yet if it does not seem a moment's thought,
Our stitching and unstitching has been naught.

Better go down upon your marrow-bones
And scrub a kitchen pavement, or break stones
Like an old pauper, in all kinds of weather;
10 For to articulate sweet sounds together
Is to work harder than all these, and yet
Be thought an idler by the noisy set
Of bankers, schoolmasters, and clergymen
The martyrs call the world.'

                    And thereupon
That beautiful mild woman for whose sake
There's many a one shall find out all heartache
On finding that her voice is sweet and low
Replied, 'To be born woman is to know—

Adam's Curse Adam's curse is the need to labor (Genesis 3:19). The poem is for Maud Gonne, who recounts in her autobiography (A Servant of the Queen, 1938) the occasion commemorated; the friend had remarked that it "was hard work being beautiful."

Although they do not talk of it at school°—
20   That we must labour to be beautiful.'°

I said, 'It's certain there is no fine thing
Since Adam's fall but needs much labouring.
There have been lovers who thought love should be
So much compounded of high courtesy
That they would sigh and quote with learned looks
Precedents out of beautiful old books;°
Yet now it seems an idle trade enough.'

We sat grown quiet at the name of love;
We saw the last embers of daylight die,
30   And in the trembling blue-green of the sky
A moon, worn as if it had been a shell
Washed by time's waters as they rose and fell
About the stars and broke in days and years.

I had a thought for no one's but your ears:
That you were beautiful, and that I strove
To love you in the old high way of love;
That it had all seemed happy, and yet we'd grown
As weary-hearted as that hollow moon.
1902?   1902

No Second Troy°

Why should I blame her that she filled my days
With misery, or that she would of late
Have taught to ignorant men most violent ways,
Or hurled the little streets upon the great,°
Had they but courage equal to desire?°
What could have made her peaceful with a mind
That nobleness made simple as a fire,
With beauty like a tightened bow, a kind
That is not natural in an age like this,
10   Being high and solitary and most stern?°

at school See concluding line of "Michael
Robartes and the Dancer."
labour . . . beautiful In *Discoveries* (1907)
Yeats has a passage called "The Looking Glass,"
telling of a girl fresh from school, where she has
had her memory, but not her imagination,
cultivated; hence her awkward movements
and monotonous voice. She should have been
taught "the heroic discipline of the looking-
glass."
So much . . . books Yeats is thinking of the
elaborate Renaissance cult of love and courtesy,
which we now associate chiefly with Castiglione,
a writer Yeats was to grow more interested in
later on.
No Second Troy From Yeats's diary; the second
Helen is Maud Gonne.

hurled . . . great called out the mob against
its aristocratic betters
Had . . . desire Reference is to Maud Gonne's
revolutionary activities. In various ways she
stirred up the Irish against the English, though
in Yeats's view of the Catholic middle class and
urban poor (often expressed) the Irish lacked
the nerve to carry out this violence. When they
did Yeats recanted ("Easter 1916" and elsewhere).
high . . . stern One of several such allusions
to Maud Gonne; see the mention of her in
Autobiographies: ". . . great stature . . . solitary . . . her face, like the face of some
Greek statue, showed little thought" (p. 364).

Why, what could she have done, being what she is?
Was there another Troy for her to burn?
1908   1910

A Drinking Song°

Wine comes in at the mouth
And love comes in at the eye;
That's all we shall know for truth
Before we grow old and die.
I lift the glass to my mouth,
I look at you, and I sigh.
1910   1910

To a Friend Whose Work Has Come to Nothing°

Now all the truth is out,
Be secret and take defeat
From any brazen throat,
For how can you compete,
Being honour bred, with one°
Who, were it proved he lies,
Were neither shamed in his own
Nor in his neighbours' eyes?
Bred to a harder thing
10   Than Triumph, turn away
And like a laughing string
Whereon mad fingers play
Amid a place of stone,
Be secret and exult,
Because of all things known
That is most difficult.
1913   1914

A Drinking Song translation of a song in the
play La Locandiera by the Venetian playwright
Carlo Goldoni (1707–93); prepared for Lady
Gregory's Abbey Theatre version
To . . . Nothing Sir Hugh Lane (1874–1915),
a nephew of Lady Gregory, offered his fine
collection of French paintings to the Dublin
Municipal Gallery on condition that a gallery
should be built for them by public subscription.
Lady Gregory worked hard to this end, but
failed; there was fierce opposition in the press
and much bad feeling. Lane, disgusted, placed
his pictures in the National Gallery, London,
and changed his will, leaving them to that
institution. Shortly before leaving for the United
States on board the Lusitania (to be torpedoed
by a German submarine in 1915), he added a
codicil to his will, bequeathing the pictures to
Dublin. Lane was drowned; the codicil was not
witnessed, and the National Gallery was able,
amid much rancor, to keep the pictures. In
1959 a compromise was achieved, and the paintings are now shared.
one William M. Murphy owned the two newspapers which supported the refusal to finance
a gallery.

The Cold Heaven°

Suddenly I saw the cold and rook-delighting heaven
That seemed as though ice burned and was but the more ice,
And thereupon imagination and heart were driven
So wild that every casual thought of that and this
Vanished, and left but memories, that should be out of season
With the hot blood of youth, of love crossed long ago;
And I took all the blame out of all sense and reason,
Until I cried and trembled and rocked to and fro,
Riddled with light. Ah! when the ghost begins to quicken,
Confusion of the death-bed over, is it sent
Out naked on the roads, as the books say, and stricken
By the injustice of the skies for punishment?

10

1910   1910

The Magi°

Now as at all times I can see in the mind's eye,
In their stiff, painted clothes, the pale unsatisfied ones
Appear and disappear in the blue depth of the sky
With all their ancient faces like rain-beaten stones,
And all their helms of silver hovering side by side,
And all their eyes still fixed, hoping to find once more,
Being by Calvary's turbulence unsatisfied,
The uncontrollable mystery on the bestial floor.

1913   1914

In Memory of Major Robert Gregory

Yeats admired Lady Gregory's son Robert (1881–1918) as scholar, horseman, and painter, and when he was killed fighting with the English on the Italian front as a Royal Flying Corps major (January 23, 1918) the poet sought to make a fitting elegy. Preparations were going forward to make the Tower habitable for Yeats and his wife, and its associations with the Gregory family and Coole brought it into his thoughts. It took half a year to produce the poem we now have. Yeats wrote about Gregory in his diary and in letters, and also composed, for the London *Observer*, an obituary containing many of the germs of the poem he eventually produced: it celebrates the

The Cold Heaven A poem partly about Yeats's lost love Maud Gonne, and partly on the theme (to which he returns later) that at death we live our lives again backward (the "dreaming back") and so "live it all again"—all the indignities and suffering; in this moment he seems to be enduring again the pains of his youth, as the dead must.
The Magi The new life found by the Magi at the Epiphany (see Matthew 2:9), with its sequel, the Crucifixion, is not the annunciation of a new cycle of time which will end only with the end of the world; there will be more such "uncontrollable mysteries" because time is cyclical (a notion that later grew very important to Yeats). The Magi, therefore, are perpetually seeking a recurrence. Contrast Eliot's "Journey of the Magi," where what disconcerts the wise men is precisely the finality of what they have witnessed. See the second of "Two Songs from a Play" (below) for further associations of violence with the birth of Christ.

young man's courage and athletic prowess, and discusses his genius as a painter in the line of "visionary landscape" which, according to Yeats, originated with Blake. He sees Gregory as using action to escape from contemplation, from "the growing absorption of his dream."

Yeats heard the news of Gregory's death when he was in Oxford working on Palmer and Calvert, the heirs of Blake and continuators of the tradition of visionary landscape; but he did not at once build a poem on this foundation. First he tried—struck by a resemblance between Gregory and Sir Philip Sidney—to write a pastoral elegy on the pattern of Spenser's *Astrophel,* which mourns Sidney's death in action. This version, which includes a passage on the doctrine of "dreaming-back" at death, stands in Yeats's *Collected Poems,* but is not a success. Yeats then wrote "An Irish Airman Foresees His Death," a short poem about Gregory's delight in action, even on behalf of an alien power. In the present poem, finished by June 14, Yeats moved on from Spenser to Cowley's "Ode on the Death of Mr. William Harvey," the stanza of which he exactly imitates (he uses it again in "A Prayer for My Daughter" and the second poem of *The Tower* sequence).

Yeats's poem is basically about an artist who broke out of that dream into a brief life of action. The eighth stanza was inserted at the request of Gregory's widow, who thought the poem said too little about her husband's physical courage; and it is arguable that the poem is better without it, since the seventh and ninth stanzas are obviously related. Gregory is refined into a symbolic artist, breaking out of the horror of the artist's isolation into activity and death, achieving the condition Yeats called Unity of Being, something more easily achieved in the period 1450–1550 A.D. than in the collapsing modern world. Other artists and contemplatives appear in the poem as a means of measuring the plight and the achievement of its hero. And as is usual in such elegies, the hero is as it were a mask of the poet himself; this poem is as much about Yeats as *Lycidas* is about Milton.

In Memory of Major Robert Gregory

I

Now that we're almost settled in our house°
I'll name the friends that cannot sup with us
Beside a fire of turf° in th' ancient tower,
And having talked to some late hour
Climb up the narrow winding stair to bed:
Discoverers of forgotten truth°
Or mere companions of my youth,
All, all are in my thoughts to-night being dead.

II

Always we'd have the new friend meet the old
10   And we are hurt if either friend seem cold,

---

house the Tower (Thoor Ballylee)
turf peat (commonly cut from the bogs as fuel in Ireland)

Discoverers . . . truth the occultist friends of his youth

And there is salt to lengthen out the smart
In the affections of our heart,
And quarrels are blown up upon that head;
But not a friend that I would bring
This night can set us quarrelling,
For all that come into my mind are dead.

III

Lionel Johnson comes the first to mind,
That loved his learning better than mankind,
Though courteous to the worst; much falling he
20 Brooded upon sanctity
Till all his Greek and Latin learning seemed
A long blast upon the horn that brought
A little nearer to his thought
A measureless consummation that he dreamed.°

IV

And that enquiring man John Synge comes next,
That dying chose the living world for text
And never could have rested in the tomb
But that, long travelling, he had come
Towards nightfall upon certain set apart
30 In a most desolate stony place,
Towards nightfall upon a race
Passionate and simple like his heart.°

V

And then I think of old George Pollexfen,
In muscular youth well known to Mayo men
For horsemanship at meets or at racecourses,
That could have shown how pure-bred horses
And solid men, for all their passion, live
But as the outrageous stars incline
By opposition, square and trine;
40 Having grown sluggish and contemplative.°

Lionel . . . dreamed Lionel Johnson (1867–
1902), learned poet, member of the Rhymers'
Club, devout Catholic, and believer in the poet
as the third order of priesthood (with priest
and deacon). He drank heavily and often fell
down stairs; he died by falling off a barstool.
But he also wrote, in "Mystic and Cavalier," "Go
from me: I am one of those who fall."
And that . . . heart (ll.25–32) Yeats met
Synge (1871–1909) in Paris in 1896, and
persuaded him to go to the Aran Islands off
the west coast of Ireland, having recently been
there himself. Synge went, and listened to the
talk of the islanders; one of the results was
The Playboy of the Western World (1907),
which caused riots when Yeats staged it at the
Abbey; Yeats defended it fiercely. Placing Synge

in the Twenty-third Phase of his lunar division
of personalities, Yeats observed that he was
one of those "who must not pursue an image,
but fly from it. . . . He had to take the first
plunge into the world beyond himself" (Autobiographies, p. 344).
And then . . . contemplative (ll. 33–40)
George Pollexfen, Yeats's maternal uncle, lived
near Sligo, and as a boy Yeats had discussed
occult and folk beliefs with him. He was a
gloomy man, yet he kept himself fit with
Indian clubs when he gave up riding, and
became interested in astrology (incline, opposition, square, trine are technical terms in that
discipline). The first two friends escape the
contemplative by excessive action; Pollexfen
does not.

VI

They were my close companions many a year,
A portion of my mind and life, as it were,
And now their breathless faces seem to look
Out of some old picture-book;
I am accustomed to their lack of breath,
But not that my dear friend's dear son,
Our Sidney and our perfect man,
Could share in that discourtesy of death.

VII

For all things the delighted eye now sees
50   Were loved by him:° the old storm-broken trees
That cast their shadows upon road and bridge;
The tower set on the stream's edge;
The ford where drinking cattle make a stir
Nightly, and startled by that sound
The water-hen must change her ground;
He might have been your heartiest welcomer.

VIII

When with the Galway foxhounds he would ride
From Castle Taylor to the Roxborough side
Or Esserkelly plain, few kept his pace;
60   At Mooneen he had leaped a place
So perilous that half the astonished meet
Had shut their eyes; and where was it
He rode a race without a bit?
And yet his mind outran the horses' feet.

IX

We dreamed that a great painter had been born
To cold Clare rock and Galway rock and thorn,
To that stern colour and that delicate line
That are our secret discipline
Wherein the gazing heart doubles her might.
70   Soldier, scholar, horseman, he,
And yet he had the intensity
To have published all to be a world's delight.

X

What other could so well have counselled us
In all lovely intricacies of a house
As he that practised or that understood
All work in metal or in wood,

loved by him Gregory, who studied at the
Slade, a London art school, made some drawings of the Tower and its surroundings.

In moulded plaster or in carven stone?
Soldier, scholar, horseman, he,
And all he did done perfectly,
80   As though he had but that one trade alone.

XI

Some burn damp faggots, others may consume
The entire combustible world in one small room
As though dried straw, and if we turn about
The bare chimney is gone black out
Because the work had finished in that flare.
Soldier, scholar, horseman, he,
As 'twere all life's epitome.
What made us dream that he could comb grey hair?

XII

I had thought, seeing how bitter is that wind
90   That shakes the shutter, to have brought to mind
All those that manhood tried, or childhood loved
Or boyish intellect approved,
With some appropriate commentary on each;
Until imagination brought
A fitter welcome; but a thought
Of that late death took all my heart for speech.
1918   1919

The Scholars

Bald heads forgetful of their sins,
Old, learned, respectable bald heads
Edit and annotate the lines
That young men, tossing on their beds,
Rhymed out in love's despair
To flatter beauty's ignorant ear.

All shuffle there; all cough in ink;
All wear the carpet with their shoes;
All think what other people think;
10   All know the man their neighbour knows.
Lord, what would they say
Did their Catullus° walk that way?
1914–1915   1919

Catullus Gaius Valerius Catullus (84–54 B.C.),   obscene love poetry addressed to "Lesbia"
Roman anthor of passionate and sometimes   (Clodia, wife of a consul)

A Thought from Propertius°

She might, so noble from head
To great shapely knees
The long flowing line,
Have walked to the altar
Through the holy images
At Pallas Athene's° side,
Or been fit spoil for a centaur
Drunk with the unmixed wine.°
1915   1919

A Deep-Sworn Vow°

Others because you did not keep
That deep-sworn vow have been friends of mine;
Yet always when I look death in the face,
When I clamber to the heights of sleep,
Or when I grow excited with wine,
Suddenly I meet your face.
1915   1919

Michael Robartes and the Dancer°

HE   Opinion° is not worth a rush;
        In this altar-piece° the knight,
        Who grips his long spear so to push
        That dragon through the fading light,
        Loved the lady; and it's plain
        The half-dead dragon was her thought,
        That every morning rose again
        And dug its claws and shrieked and fought.
        Could the impossible come to pass
        She would have time to turn her eyes,
        Her lover thought, upon the glass
        And on the instant would grow wise.°

10

A Thought from Propertius developed from
scattered phrases in *Elegies* II.2 of Sextus
Propertius (50–16 B.C.), a Roman love poet
Pallas Athene goddess born of the head of
Zeus; patroness of Athens; represented as a
woman of stern beauty, and for Yeats an image
of Maud Gonne
fit . . . wine The Centaurs (horse-shaped, with
a man's torso replacing the neck) broke up
the wedding feast of Pirithous and tried to
carry off the women.
A Deep-Sworn Vow to Maud Gonne
Michael Robartes and the Dancer Mrs. Yeats
is recorded as saying that the girl was Iseult
Gonne. *He* certainly represents the views of
Yeats.

Opinion almost in the obsolete sense of knowledge of something less than the truth
altar-piece Of several possible representations
of St. George killing the dragon the most likely
one for Yeats to have had in mind is that by
Paris Bordone (1500–1571) in the National
Gallery, Dublin; but it is not an altar-piece,
as is one that Yeats saw in Ferrara in 1907
(by Cosimo Tura, 1430–95).
the knight . . . wise (ll. 2–12) *He* makes an
allegory of the painting. The knight is trying to
kill the abstract thought that interferes with
the lady's beauty and prevents her studying
herself in a looking-glass (see note on "Adam's
Curse").

SHE   You mean they argued.

HE   Put it so;
       But bear in mind your lover's wage
       Is what your looking-glass can show,
       And that he will turn green with rage
       At all that is not pictured there.

SHE   May I not put myself to college?

HE   Go pluck Athene by the hair;°
20   For what mere book can grant a knowledge
       With an impassioned gravity
       Appropriate to that beating breast,
       That vigorous thigh, that dreaming eye?
       And may the Devil take the rest.

SHE   And must no beautiful woman be
       Learned like a man?

HE   Paul Veronese°
       And all his sacred company
       Imagined bodies all their days
       By the lagoon you love so much,
30   For proud, soft, ceremonious proof
       That all must come to sight and touch;
       While Michael Angelo's Sistine roof,
       His 'Morning' and his 'Night'° disclose
       How sinew that has been pulled tight,
       Or it may be loosened in repose,
       Can rule by supernatural right
       Yet be but sinew.

SHE   I have heard said
       There is great danger in the body.

HE   Did God in portioning wine and bread
40   Give man His thought or His mere body?°

SHE   My wretched dragon° is perplexed.

HE   I have principles to prove me right.
       It follows from this Latin text

Go . . . hair Seize (the goddess of) wisdom
by violence. Yeats was opposed to orthodox education for girls, believing that it caused a separation of body and mind.
Veronese (1525–88), last of the great Venetian
painters. Here he is commended (as Yeats
always commended the High Renaissance
artists) for his power to combine thought and
feeling, sense and intellect.
Michael Angelo's . . . 'Night' Michelangelo
Buonarroti (1475–1564) painted the Sistine
ceiling (1508–12) for Pope Julius II; Yeats
may be thinking of the figure of Adam touched

into life by God. "Morning" and "Night" are
statues in the Medici chapel in Florence:
"Morning" a male figure, awakening and angry;
"Night" a female in uneasy sleep—hence the
"sinews pulled tight" and "loosened."
Did . . . body A reference to the Eucharist, the
blood and body of Christ present in the wine
and bread. This sacramental defense of the
argument gives it a surprising seriousness. Mere
is used almost in the old sense of pure (uncontaminated by thought)—as Queen Elizabeth
claimed to be "mere English."
dragon her intellect

That blest souls are not composite,°
And that all beautiful women may
Live in uncomposite blessedness,
And lead us to the like—if they
Will banish every thought, unless
The lineaments that please their view
50   When the long looking-glass is full,
Even from the foot-sole think it too.°

SHE   They say such different things at school.°
1916   1921

Easter 1916°

I have met them° at close of day
Coming with vivid faces
From counter or desk among grey
Eighteenth-century houses.°
I have passed with a nod of the head
Or polite meaningless words,
Or have lingered awhile and said
Polite meaningless words,
And thought before I had done
10   Of a mocking tale or a gibe
To please a companion
Around the fire at the club,
Being certain that they and I
But lived where motley° is worn:
All changed, changed utterly:
A terrible beauty is born.

That woman's° days were spent
In ignorant good-will,

not composite One soul is diffused throughout the body; there are not separate compartments for body and mind.
unless . . . too That is, no thought is allowed unless the *body* thinks it; as in Donne's famous lines, which Yeats knew and admired: ". . . her pure and eloquent blood / Spoke in her cheeks, and so distinctly wrought / That one might almost say, her body thought" (*The Second Anniversary*, ll. 243–45).
They . . . school See note on "Adam's Curse." Yeats's condemnation of education for girls was perfectly serious.
Easter 1916 On April 24, 1916, the Irish Republican Brotherhood organized a rebellion against the English. They proclaimed an Irish Republic and, after much fighting, occupied central Dublin. The rebellion collapsed on April 29 and its leaders were subsequently executed. One of them was Major John MacBride, estranged husband of Maud Gonne. Another military commander was Constance Markiewicz (née Gore-Booth), daughter of the great house at Lissadell near Sligo, whom Yeats had known

since 1894; she was sentenced to penal servitude for life but was later released. The Rising, though fundamentally a miscalculation, gave a new aura of heroism to the cause of Irish freedom. Yeats was with Maud Gonne in France when he heard the news, and felt at first "that all the work of the years has been overturned." But Maud Gonne told him that "tragic dignity has returned to Ireland." And he was moved as never before by a public event. The poem is dated September 25, 1916, in the manuscript, and appeared both in a periodical and in a privately printed edition before publication in *Michael Robartes and the Dancer*. In the interim it was greatly improved by revision.
them the revolutionary leaders
Eighteenth-century houses Central Dublin was largely an 18th-century city, and is still strongly Georgian in appearance.
motley parti-colored dress of the fool
woman's Constance Markiewicz (1868–1927), the daughter of the Gore-Booths and wife of a Polish count. See also "On a Political Prisoner" and "In Memory of Eva Gore-Booth and Con

Her nights in argument
20 Until her voice grew shrill.
What voice more sweet than hers
When, young and beautiful,
She rode to harriers?
This man° had kept a school
And rode our wingèd horse;
This other° his helper and friend
Was coming into his force;
He might have won fame in the end,
So sensitive his nature seemed,
30 So daring and sweet his thought.
This other man I had dreamed
A drunken, vainglorious lout.°
He had done most bitter wrong
To some who are near my heart,
Yet I number him in the song;
He, too, has resigned his part
In the casual comedy;
He, too, has been changed in his turn,
Transformed utterly:
40 A terrible beauty is born.

Hearts with one purpose alone
Through summer and winter seem
Enchanted to a stone
To trouble the living stream.
The horse that comes from the road,
The rider, the birds that range
From cloud to tumbling cloud,
Minute by minute they change;
A shadow of cloud on the stream
50 Changes minute by minute;
A horse-hoof slides on the brim,
And a horse plashes within it;
The long-legged moor-hens dive,
And hens to moor-cocks call;
Minute by minute they live:
The stone's in the midst of all.°

Markiewicz." She was an officer in the Volunteers of the Irish Republican Brotherhood. Yeats dwelt on the loss of beauty involved in her conversion to fanatical politics.
This man Patrick Pearse (1879–1916), schoolmaster, lawyer, poet in Gaelic and English, and President of the Republic for the few days leading up to his capture by British troops in the Dublin Post Office. Shot as a leader of the Rising, as were those mentioned below.
This other Thomas MacDonagh (1878–1916), poet, dramatist, and critic, English professor at University College Dublin

This . . . lout Major John MacBride, husband of Maud Gonne
Hearts . . . all (ll. 41–56) In this bold metaphor Yeats suggests the rigidity and lack of feeling imposed upon people who dedicate themselves exclusively to some intellectual or political end, their stoniness contrasting with the perpetual change observable in life and nature. This, for him, is the sacrifice made by these people who fought steadfastly for Ireland. As we see in other poems, he had especially in mind the militant women, Constance Markiewicz and Maud Gonne.

Too long a sacrifice
Can make a stone of the heart.
O when may it suffice?
60　That is Heaven's part, our part
To murmur name upon name,
As a mother names her child
When sleep at last has come
On limbs that had run wild.
What is it but nightfall?
No, no, not night but death;
Was it needless death° after all?
For England may keep faith°
For all that is done and said.
70　We know their dream; enough
To know they dreamed and are dead;
And what if excess of love
Bewildered them till they died?
I write it out in a verse—
MacDonagh and MacBride
And Connolly° and Pearse
Now and in time to be,
Wherever green is worn,
Are changed, changed utterly:
80　A terrible beauty is born.
1916　　　　　　　　1921

On a Political Prisoner°

She that but little patience knew,
From childhood on, had now so much
A grey gull lost its fear and flew
Down to her cell and there alit,
And there endured her fingers' touch
And from her fingers ate its bit.

Did she in touching that lone wing
Recall the years before her mind
Became a bitter, an abstract thing,°
10　Her thought some popular enmity:

---

needless death Many Irishmen thought the
Rebellion a terrible mistake, but it had the
value, which Yeats's poem helps to promote,
of endowing the cause with martyrs.
England . . . faith The English Parliament had
passed an act for Home Rule in Ireland in 1913;
it was shelved at the beginning of World War I,
and rumors that the British government meant
to rescind it were partly responsible for the
Rising.
Connolly James Connolly (1870–1916), the
great Irish Labor leader, who organized the Citizen Army. He led the forces in the Post Office,
was wounded, and had to be allowed to recover
sufficiently for the death sentence to be carried
out.
On . . . Prisoner Countess Markiewicz was in
Holloway, a woman's prison in London, serving
a life sentence for her part in the Easter Rising.
bitter . . . thing a recurrence of this preoccupation of Yeats's, often expressed with special
reference to the Countess and Maud Gonne

Blind and leader of the blind
Drinking the foul ditch where they lie?

When long ago I saw her ride
Under Ben Bulben° to the meet,
The beauty of her country-side
With all youth's lonely wildness stirred,
She seemed to have grown clean and sweet
Like any rock-bred, sea-borne bird:

20   Sea-borne, or balanced on the air
When first it sprang out of the nest
Upon some lofty rock to stare
Upon the cloudy canopy,
While under its storm-beaten breast
Cried out the hollows of the sea.°
1919   1921

The Second Coming

The title of this poem is derived from the Christian belief in the second coming of
Christ (see Matthew 24), but the god to be born in the second Bethlehem is a beast,
and not a beast like that in Revelation, for it will not be subdued. As in "The Magi"
there is a succession of "uncontrollable mysteries," and this is antithetical to that of
the Christian Nativity. A new age is to be born, a reversal of the last. Some of Yeats's
poems are rendered very obscure by the presence of allusions to his developing
system of occult beliefs, which came to systematize all his thinking about history, civilization, and personality. There are several such poems in *Michael Robartes;* but "The
Second Coming" is not one of them. For all its occult freight, it is lucid. Yeats believed that the relation between objectivity and subjectivity in personality could be
represented by a figure of two cones, one with its apex on the other's base, so that
a personality envisaged as nearing one or other apex would be confronted with the
breadth of the antithetical base. So with historical epochs:

> The end of an age, which always receives the revelation of the character of the
> next age, is represented by the coming of one gyre [the circling around the
> surfaces of the cones] to its place of greatest expansion and of the other to
> that of its greatest contraction. At the present moment the life gyre is sweeping
> outward, unlike that before the birth of Christ which was narrowing, and has
> almost reached its greatest expansion. The revelation which approaches will,
> however, take its character from the contrary movement of the interior gyre.
> All our scientific, democratic, fact-accumulating, heterogeneous civilization
> belongs to the outward gyre and prepares not the continuance of itself but
> the revelation as in a lightning flash. . . .

Ben Bulben A mountain near Sligo and Lissadell, the Gore-Booth house; Constance Gore-
Booth was reckoned, in youth, the finest horsewoman in Ireland.
Like any . . . sea (ll. 18–24) A beautifully
elaborate and successful example of the mature

Yeatsian use of images; the seabird not only
represents lost youth and physical grace but
also rides over an image of terror and destruction; so that the coming together of woman and
gull at the opening is fully exploited.

So Yeats in his own note, in *Michael Robartes*. Later, when he developed this approach in more detail, Yeats said that it, or the "instructors" who communicated it to him, gave him "metaphors for poetry." This is true of the present case. In general the poem meets an understanding response not because we accept its peculiar doctrine but because its apocalyptic feeling—the terror and decadence of the last days of an epoch—is widely shared.

The Second Coming

Turning and turning in the widening gyre
The falcon cannot hear the falconer;°
Things fall apart; the centre cannot hold;
Mere anarchy is loosed upon the world,
The blood-dimmed tide is loosed,° and everywhere
The ceremony of innocence° is drowned;
The best lack all conviction, while the worst
Are full of passionate intensity.

Surely some revelation is at hand;
10   Surely the Second Coming is at hand.
The Second Coming! Hardly are those words out
When a vast image out of *Spiritus Mundi*°
Troubles my sight: somewhere in sands of the desert
A shape with lion body and the head of a man,°
A gaze blank and pitiless as the sun,
Is moving its slow thighs, while all about it
Reel shadows of the indignant desert birds.
The darkness drops again; but now I know
That twenty centuries of stony sleep°
20   Were vexed to nightmare by a rocking cradle,
And what rough beast, its hour come round at last,
Slouches towards Bethlehem to be born?
1919   1921

Turning . . . falconer The falcon circles in such wide sweeps that it no longer answers its master's call; at the same time this is a figure for the widening base of the cone at the end of an age.
the . . . loosed thinking perhaps of the recent war and the Russian revolution as well as the Irish Troubles
ceremony of innocence Ceremony here, as in "A Prayer for My Daughter," is an image of order and obedience.
Spiritus Mundi "A general storehouse of images which have ceased to be the property of any personality or spirit" (Yeats's words in a note on "An Image from Past Life," also in *Michael Robartes*). He had long believed in a Great

Memory, a reservoir of images on which we all draw.
A shape . . . man This Sphinx-like creature derives from an early magical experiment in which Yeats held an occult symbol and when he closed his eyes had these mental images: "a desert, and a black Titan raising himself up by his hands from the middle of a heap of ancient ruins" (*Autobiographies*, p. 186). Later (*Explorations*, 1962, p. 393) he spoke of an image "at my left side just out of the range of sight, a brazen winged beast that I associated with laughing destruction," and added that he had described it in "The Second Coming."
twenty . . . sleep i.e. before Christ was born

Sailing to Byzantium°

I

That° is no country for old men. The young
In one another's arms, birds in the trees
—Those dying generations—at their song,
The salmon-falls, the mackerel-crowded seas,
Fish, flesh, or fowl, commend all summer long
Whatever is begotten, born, and dies.
Caught in that sensual music all neglect
Monuments of unageing intellect.°

II

An aged man is but a paltry thing,
10   A tattered coat upon a stick, unless
Soul clap its hands and sing, and louder sing
For every tatter in its mortal dress,
Nor is there singing school but studying
Monuments of its own magnificence;
And therefore I have sailed the seas and come
To the holy city of Byzantium.

III

O sages standing in God's holy fire°
As in the gold mosaic of a wall,
Come from the holy fire, perne in a gyre,°
20   And be the singing-masters of my soul.
Consume my heart away; sick with desire
And fastened to a dying animal
It knows not what it is; and gather me
Into the artifice of eternity.

IV

Once out of nature I shall never take
My bodily form from any natural thing,

Sailing to Byzantium In his 63rd year Yeats felt great power and bitterness; the volume *The Tower*, of which this is the first poem, deals with war, old age, the Anglo-Irish inheritance, the decay of the world. Byzantium, the modern Istanbul, housed the Platonic Academy until the 15th century, and was the capital of Eastern (Greek) Christianity. Yeats makes it an image of eternity, a paradise without the growth and change which are the sorrow and the delight of life. Here the artist, free of the distortions wrought by age and labor, finds his place; whereas the young, caught up in natural generation, belong to another country. Yeats says in *A Vision* that if he could choose to spend time in antiquity he would go to Byzantium in the 6th century. When he was in Sicily in 1924 he saw the Byzantine mosaics, and long before he had visited St. Apollinare Nuovo at Ravenna and seen the sages and saints in its walls. In early drafts Yeats describes the voyage to Byzantium, and the title reflects the pre-history of the poem.
That Ireland, and the natural world
sensual . . . intellect The basic opposition of the poem, which contains more than a celebration of spirit and art; Yeats always resented the loss of youth and natural beauty of the body.
sages . . . fire remembered from Ravenna
perne in a gyre A *perne* is a spool, a *gyre* a spiral: he asks them to spiral down the cone to him.

But such a form as Grecian goldsmiths make°
Of hammered gold and gold enamelling
To keep a drowsy Emperor awake;
30 Or set upon a golden bough to sing
To lords and ladies of Byzantium
Of what is past, or passing, or to come.
1926   1928

Ancestral Houses°

Surely among a rich man's flowering lawns,
Amid the rustle of his planted hills,
Life overflows without ambitious pains;
And rains down life until the basin spills,
And mounts more dizzy high the more it rains
As though to choose whatever shape it wills
And never stoop to a mechanical
Or servile shape, at others' beck and call.

Mere dreams, mere dreams! Yet Homer had not sung
10 Had he not found it certain beyond dreams
That out of life's own self-delight° had sprung
The abounding glittering jet; though now it seems
As if some marvellous empty sea-shell flung
Out of the obscure dark of the rich streams,
And not a fountain, were the symbol which
Shadows the inherited glory of the rich.

Some violent bitter man, some powerful man
Called architect and artist in, that they,
Bitter and violent men, might rear in stone
20 The sweetness that all longed for night and day,
The gentleness none there had ever known;

such . . . make Yeats, in a note, writes, "I have read somewhere that in the Emperor's palace at Byzantium was a tree made of gold and silver, and artificial birds that sang." One suggested explanation is that he was thinking of Hans Christian Andersen's story *The Emperor's Nightingale.*
Ancestral Houses This is the first poem of the sequence *Meditations in Time of Civil War.* It is one of those meditations on the decline of the aristocracy that fed Yeats's own aristocratic pretensions and at the same time supported his view that "leveling" was a symptom of the rapid collapse of the good society, in which aristocrat and peasant each knew his place. He believed that sweetness, gentleness, art and courtesy, were possible only where power and violence had made them so; that the inheritors of sweetness and gentleness, art and courtesy, might lack the vigor or violence to preserve these qualities, so that their creation undermined the class that made them possible, by in-

capacitating the heirs from defending them against a new and baser exercise of violence. Later in the sequence he speaks of his own powerlessness against the soldiers who would blow up his bridge; of the breeding-out of aristocratic violence; of his envy: "We are closed in, and the key is turned / On our uncertainty."
self-delight Yeats was fond of such compounds as this: *self-delighting, self-appeasing, self-begotten, self-born.* They all suggest what the fountain symbolizes: a continual supply of energy and vitality without recourse to abstract systems that have nothing to do with the life of the body. The basin of a fountain, perpetually brimming, was for him an image of Unity of Being, the perfection of life, when thought and sensation were one. The seashell is an image of what has been wrought in the past, no longer changing, and fished up by others from the depths of the past.

But when the master's buried mice can play,
And maybe the great-grandson of that house,
For all its bronze and marble,° 's but a mouse.

O what if gardens where the peacock strays
With delicate feet upon old terraces,
Or else all Juno from an urn displays
Before the indifferent garden deities;
O what if levelled lawns and gravelled ways
30   Where slippered Contemplation finds his ease
And Childhood a delight for every sense,
But take our greatness with our violence?

What if the glory of escutcheoned doors,
And buildings that a haughtier age designed,
The pacing to and fro on polished floors
Amid great chambers and long galleries, lined
With famous portraits of our ancestors;
What if those things the greatest of mankind
Consider most to magnify, or to bless,
40   But take our greatness with our bitterness?
1921   1928

Two Songs from a Play°

I

I saw a staring virgin stand
Where holy Dionysus° died,
And tear the heart out of his side,
And lay the heart upon her hand
And bear that beating heart away;
And then did all the Muses sing
Of Magnus Annus° at the spring,
As though God's death were but a play.

Another Troy must rise and set,
10   Another lineage feed the crow,

bronze and marble a favored image of the completeness and lack of change in works of art: see "Among School Children" (below) and also "The Living Beauty"
Two Songs . . . Play Sung by the Chorus of Musicians in the play, Resurrection. The figure of Christ appears, and a Greek, sure that it is a phantom, is horrified to find that it has a beating heart. This is what the musicians presage in their first song, which opens the play. The Syrian character is more like Yeats, asking "What if the irrational return? What if the circle begin again?" —and that is the theme of the second stanza. The first stanza of the second and closing song more or less restates this, and the second states another Yeatsian theme: "Our love-letters

wear out our love . . . every stroke of the brush exhausts the impulse," he says in Autobiographies, and, in A Vision: "Exhausted by the cry that it can never end, my love ends."
Dionysus When he was torn to pieces by the Titans, Athene, the virgin goddess, snatched his heart and bore it to Zeus, who swallowed it and then re-begot Dionysus on Semele, daughter of Cadmus.
Magnus Annus The Great Year; when all the heavenly bodies return to their original places this year is complete (a notion as old as Plato's Timaeus). The values vary from 18,000 to 36,000 years. The Muses sing because, given this cyclical time, the god will be killed and reborn as if in a play often repeated.

Another Argo's painted prow
Drive to a flashier bauble yet.
The Roman Empire stood appalled:
It dropped the reigns of peace and war
When that fierce virgin and her Star
Out of the fabulous darkness called.°

II

In pity for man's darkening thought
He walked that room and issued thence
In Galilean turbulence;°
20 The Babylonian starlight brought
A fabulous, formless darkness in;°
Odour of blood when Christ was slain
Made all Platonic tolerance° vain
And vain all Doric° discipline.

Everything that man esteems
Endures a moment or a day.
Love's pleasure drives his love away,
The painter's brush consumes his dreams;
The herald's cry, the soldier's tread
30 Exhaust his glory and his might:
Whatever flames upon the night
Man's own resinous heart has fed.°
1927   1931

Leda and the Swan°

A sudden blow: the great wings beating still
Above the staggering girl, her thighs caressed

Another Troy . . . called (ll. 9–16) Virgil's
Fourth Eclogue, long regarded as a prophecy
of the birth of Christ, speaks of the return of
Astraea, goddess of Justice, who was last to
leave earth at the end of the Golden Age, and
will inaugurate a new one. Virgil speaks of
another voyage of the *Argo*, another fall of
Troy, in the new cycle of time. Yeats must
also have recalled Shelley's drama *Hellas*,
ll. 1060–79. *Fabulous* is a word that was in
Yeats's head at the time of the *Tower* poems;
it occurs four times in that volume, out of six
in his whole work. Here Yeats adapts a description of Christianity by a fourth-century
Neoplatonist and anti-Christian philosopher,
Proclus, whom Yeats knew in Thomas Taylor's
version of his *Six Books . . . on the Theology
of Plato* (1816). The Roman Empire is appalled because Christianity will be its ruin.
turbulence Yeats sees the arrival of the Christian
age as a deep disturbance of the old world.
fabulous . . . darkness The Babylonian astron-
omers foretold a world in which man would
be as nothing compared with God.

Platonic tolerance A god actually killed by
violence (not merely a myth) ends the free
philosophical speculation of the Greek Academy.
Doric Greek
Whatever . . . fed That is, he consumes himself; he is the fuel of his own splendid conceptions.
Leda and the Swan Yeats may have had in
mind the painting of the subject by Michelangelo,
or some other version. Leda had by Zeus the
twins Castor and Pollux, and also Helen and
Clytemnestra. So her eggs produced the cause
of the fall of Troy and the death of Agamemnon.
Yeats saw the rape of Leda as a "violent annunciation" such as might be expected in our own
day; an annunciation parallel to the Christian,
and involving the union of a god and a woman
as the Christian does. The outcome is terror, but
the poem dwells on the strangeness of Leda's
experience, feeling "the strange heart," and the
question whether such a visitation of the divine
means an access only of power or also of the
knowledge of a new cycle of history which it
inaugurates.

By the dark webs, her nape caught in his bill,
He holds her helpless breast upon his breast.

How can those terrified vague fingers push
The feathered glory from her loosening thighs?
And how can body, laid in that white rush,
But feel the strange heart beating where it lies?

A shudder in the loins engenders there
10 The broken wall, the burning roof and tower°
And Agamemnon dead.°
                        Being so caught up,
So mastered by the brute blood of the air,
Did she put on his knowledge with his power
Before the indifferent beak could let her drop?
1923   1928

Among School Children

In his capacity as senator, Yeats visited a Montessori school in February 1926. In March of that year he noted in his diary as a topic for a poet, "school children and the thought that life will waste them, perhaps that no possible life can fulfill their own dreams or even their teacher's hope. Bring in the old thought that life prepares for what never happens." Later he sent a version of stanza VI to Olivia Shakespear with the comment: ". . . a fragment of my last curse on old age. It means that even the greatest men are owls, scarecrows, by the time their fame has come. Aristotle, remember, was Alexander's tutor, hence the taws [a leather strap used for whipping]. . . . Pythagoras made some measurement of the intervals between notes on a stretched string" (Letters, ed. Wade, 1954). The development of this poem from a form in which there was nothing to suggest "the rhapsodic resolution" of stanza VIII is memorably studied in T. R. Parkinson, W. B. Yeats, The Later Poetry (1964). The topic, and even the account of it sent to Mrs. Shakespear, is transcended, but the labor involved, as Parkinson shows by a study of the drafts, is extraordinary: "puzzlement, self-analysis, revelation, lurching mistake, refinement, recovery, and ultimately, triumph" (p. 113).

Among School Children

I

I walk through the long schoolroom questioning;
A kind old nun in a white hood replies;
The children learn to cipher° and to sing,
To study reading-books and histories,
To cut and sew, be neat in everything

The broken . . . tower the sack of Troy   cipher do arithmetic
Agamemnon dead murdered by his wife Cly-
temnestra on his return from Troy

In the best modern way—the children's eyes
In momentary wonder stare upon
A sixty-year-old smiling public man.

II

I dream of a Ledaean° body, bent
10   Above a sinking fire, a tale that she
Told of a harsh reproof, or trivial event
That changed some childish day to tragedy—
Told, and it seemed that our two natures blent
Into a sphere from youthful sympathy,
Or else, to alter Plato's parable,°
Into the yolk and white of the one shell.

III

And thinking of that fit of grief or rage
I look upon one child or t'other there
And wonder if she stood so at that age—
20   For even daughters of the swan can share
Something of every paddler's heritage—
And had that colour upon cheek or hair,
And thereupon my heart is driven wild:
She stands before me as a living child.

IV

Her present image° floats into the mind—
Did Quattrocento° finger fashion it
Hollow of cheek as though it drank the wind
And took a mess of shadows for its meat?
And I though never of Ledaean kind
30   Had pretty plumage once—enough of that,
Better to smile on all that smile, and show
There is a comfortable kind of old scarecrow.°

V

What youthful mother, a shape upon her lap
Honey of generation° had betrayed,

Ledaean Helen-like, referring to Helen the
daughter of Leda. The reverie is of Maud
Gonne.
Plato's parable In *Symposium* 190, Plato has
Aristophanes suggest that man was originally
double, with two faces, four hands, and so on,
and that after the halves were divided they
strive toward one another in love.
Her present image the woman as she now was,
in her sixties
Quattrocento 15th-century. Among earlier versions there is the nonexistent *quinto-cento* and
also *Da Vinci' finger;* so Yeats was perhaps
thinking of Leonardo da Vinci (1452–1519)
as painter.

scarecrow See "Sailing to Byzantium," l. 9 ff.
Honey of generation taken from *On the Cave of
the Nymphs* by Porphyry, 3rd-century Neoplatonist, a commentary on the cave in *Odyssey*
XIII. There were bowls of honey, allegorized as
"the pleasure which draws souls downward to
generation." Yeats, in a note, suggests that he
meant a drug that destroyed the recollection
of prenatal freedom, but adds that he found
no warrant for this in Porphyry. Certainly
honey of generation has betrayed applies in the
poem to the child, not the mother. It will either
recollect its prenatal state or it will not, depending on whether the drug works.

And that must sleep, shriek, struggle to escape
As recollection or the drug decide,
Would think her son, did she but see that shape
With sixty or more winters on its head,
A compensation for the pang of his birth,°
40   Or the uncertainty of his setting forth?

VI

Plato thought nature but a spume that plays
Upon a ghostly paradigm of things;°
Solider Aristotle played the taws
Upon the bottom of a king of kings;°
World-famous golden-thighed Pythagoras
Fingered upon a fiddle-stick or strings
What a star sang and careless Muses heard:°
Old clothes upon old sticks to scare a bird.°

VII

Both nuns and mothers worship images,
50   But those the candles light are not as those
That animate a mother's reveries,
But keep a marble or a bronze repose.°
And yet they too break hearts—O Presences
That passion, piety or affection knows,
And that all heavenly glory symbolise—
O self-born° mockers of man's enterprise;

VIII

Labour is blossoming or dancing where
The body is not bruised to pleasure soul,
Nor beauty born out of its own despair,
60   Nor blear-eyed wisdom out of midnight oil.
O chestnut-tree, great-rooted blossomer,
Are you the leaf, the blossom or the bole?

A compensation . . . birth See At The Hawk's
Well: "A mother that saw her son / Doubled
over a speckled shin, / Cross-grained with ninety
years, / Would cry, 'How little worth / Were
all my hopes and fears / And the hard pain
of his birth'."
Plato . . . things Plato thought the world of
appearance a mere veil over the real mathematical structure of the forms.
Solider . . . kings Aristotle was Alexander's
tutor.
World-famous . . . heard In working out the
ratios of the notes of the scale Pythagoras discovered the music of the spheres, the harmony
of the cosmos. Pythagoras (late 6th to early
5th century B.C.) was an important precursor
of Plato; Iamblichus, a 4th-century A.D. Neoplatonist who wrote a life of Pythagoras, credits
him with a golden thigh.
Old . . . bird These great thinkers are still
mere scarecrows.
marble . . . repose This points up the distinction so frequent in Yeats between the
natural body that ages and warps, and the
perpetual work of art. But at this point the
poem takes off in a new, unexpected, and
somewhat obscure direction; and Yeats ends
with an image of the natural body as having—
in some paradise out of time—identity with
the permanent work of art.
self-born See note on "Ancestral Houses."

O body swayed to music, O brightening glance,
How can we know the dancer from the dance?°
1926   1928

In Memory of Eva Gore-Booth and Con Markiewicz°

The light of evening, Lissadell,°
Great windows open to the south,
Two girls in silk kimonos, both
Beautiful, one a gazelle.
But a raving autumn shears
Blossom from the summer's wreath;
The older° is condemned to death,
Pardoned, drags out lonely years
Conspiring among the ignorant.°
10 I know not what the younger dreams—
Some vague Utopia—and she seems,
When withered old and skeleton-gaunt,
An image of such politics.
Many a time I think to seek
One or the other out and speak
Of that old Georgian mansion, mix
Pictures of the mind, recall
That table and the talk of youth,
Two girls in silk kimonos, both
20 Beautiful, one a gazelle.
Dear shadows, now you know it all,
All the folly of a fight
With a common wrong or right.
The innocent and the beautiful
Have no enemy but time;
Arise and bid me strike a match
And strike another till time catch;

Labour . . . dance? (ll. 57–64) *Labour* in both senses: physical work and childbirth. In an ideal world where there is no division between soul and body, where it is untrue that "whatever flames upon the night / Man's own resinous heart has fed," labor is identified with product. The *blossoming* and *dancing* look forward to the chestnut tree and the dancer later in the stanza. Goethe, in *Wilhelm Meister,* compares the unity of *Hamlet* to that of a tree: "It is a trunk with boughs, leaves, buds, blossoms and fruit. Are they not all one, and thereby means of one another?" One part of the tree does not precede, or produce, another. The dancer is a favorite image of Yeats; here her labor *is* her dance, the movement of her body is dancing, not labor. Mallarmé, the Symbolist poet (1842–98) whom Yeats studied years before, says that a dancer "is not a woman who dances, for these related reasons: she *is not a woman* but a metaphor summing up elemental aspects of our form, sword, bowl, flower; and *she does not dance,* suggesting [what can be summed up as] *the poem freed of all the apparatus of the writer.*"

In Memory . . . Markiewicz This poem heads Yeats's 1933 collection, *The Winding Stair,* named for the staircase in the Tower. Eva Gore-Booth (b. 1870) died in 1926, Constance (b. 1868) in 1927. See note on "Easter 1916."

Lissadell early 19th-century mansion near Sligo, home of the Gore-Booths; first visited by Yeats in 1894

The older Constance (see note on "Easter 1916")

Conspiring . . . ignorant She returned to revolutionary politics after her release and fought in the Irish Civil War.

Should the conflagration climb,
Run till all the sages know.
30 We the great gazebo° built,
They convicted us of guilt;
Bid me strike a match and blow.
1927   1933

Coole Park, 1929°

I meditate upon a swallow's flight,
Upon an agèd woman° and her house,
A sycamore and lime-tree lost in night
Although that western cloud is luminous,
Great works constructed there in nature's spite
For scholars and for poets after us,
Thoughts long knitted into a single thought,
A dance-like glory that those walls begot.

There Hyde° before he had beaten into prose
10 That noble blade the Muses buckled on,
There one° that ruffled in a manly pose
For all his timid heart, there that slow man,
That meditative man, John Synge,° and those
Impetuous men, Shawe-Taylor° and Hugh Lane°
Found pride established in humility,
A scene well set and excellent company.

They came like swallows and like swallows went,
And yet a woman's powerful character
Could keep a swallow to its first intent;
20 And half a dozen in formation there,
That seemed to whirl upon a compass-point,
Found certainty upon the dreaming air,

gazebo A summer house on the grounds of a mansion, such as the one at Lissadell. In Irish slang "to make a gazebo of yourself" is to make yourself look ridiculous. The sense seems to be of an aristocratic, elegant structure that time and politics have made anachronistic.
Coole Park, 1929 A prose draft survives: "Here Synge came, Hugh Lane, Shawe-Taylor, many names. I too in my timid youth. Coming and going like migratory birds. Then address the swallows fluttering in their dream like circles. Speak of the rarity of the circumstances that bring together such concords of men. Each man more than himself through whom an unknown life speaks. A circle ever returning into itself." This is of interest because it illustrates Yeats's habit of beginning poems with a prose draft, and also because of the transformation of the idea in the writing of the poem, studied by T. R. Parkinson (*W. B. Yeats, The Later Poetry*, (1964), pp. 80–81).

agèd woman Lady Augusta Gregory (1852–1932), close friend of Yeats for almost 40 years, mother of Robert Gregory (see "In Memory of Major Robert Gregory") and aunt of Hugh Lane and John Shawe-Taylor. She translated from the Gaelic, wrote plays, and was co-founder of the Abbey Theatre with Yeats, who believed that this was their role in the liberation of Ireland.
Hyde Dr. Douglas Hyde (1860–1949), Gaelic poet, scholar, first president of Eire (1938–45). He gave up writing poetry because it affected his health.
one Yeats himself
John Synge See note on "In Memory of Major Robert Gregory."
Shawe-Taylor (1866–1911) Anglo-Irish politician
Hugh Lane (1874–1915) See note on "To a Friend Whose Work Has Come to Nothing."

The intellectual sweetness of those lines
That cut through time or cross it withershins.°

Here, traveller, scholar, poet, take your stand
When all those rooms and passages are gone,°
When nettles wave upon a shapeless mound
And saplings root among the broken stone,
And dedicate—eyes bent upon the ground,
30   Back turned upon the brightness of the sun
And all the sensuality of the shade—
A moment's memory to that laurelled head.
1928–29   1933

Byzantium

A poem written in 1930 and included in the collections *Words for Music Perhaps* (1932) and *The Winding Stair* (1933). Yeats had intended to title *The Winding Stair* volume *Byzantium,* and asked the artist T. Sturge Moore (1870–1944), who designed the symbolic covers of several of his later books, for an appropriate drawing. Moore had said in a letter that "Sailing to Byzantium" "let him down" at the end since "such a goldsmith's bird is as much nature as man's body" and Yeats told him that "Byzantium" originated in this criticism, which proved that "the idea needed exposition." Moore had also sent Yeats a poem by James Elroy Flecker (1884–1915), "A Queen's Song," about magically turning living beauty into gold in order to preserve it.

The bird in this second Byzantium poem is contrasted with "common bird or petal" more explicitly than before. Byzantium itself has been developed and made obscure as a symbol, but is essentially the same as in the earlier poem: the completed image of art liberated from all connection with human labor and intellect. The focus is no longer on the poignant contrast between the vigor and beauty of the living and the still permanence of art; nature is now "mere complexities, / The fury and the mire," and is converted into art which though dead has more life and being than the living— echoing Blake's "This World of Imagination is Infinite & Eternal, whereas the world of Generation, or Vegetation, is Finite and Temporal . . . The Human Imagination . . . appear'd to Me . . . throwing off the Temporal that the Eternal might be Establish'd." There is a surviving prose draft: "Describe Byzantium as it is in the system [Yeats's *A Vision*] toward the end of the first Christian millennium. A walking mummy. Flames at the street corners where the soul is purified, birds of hammered gold singing in the golden trees, in the harbour [dolphins] offering their backs to the wailing dead that they may carry them to Paradise."

---

withershins counterclockwise, backward

rooms . . . gone Coole was demolished some years later, after the death of Lady Gregory.

Byzantium

The unpurged images of day recede;
The Emperor's drunken soldiery are abed;
Night resonance recedes, night-walkers' song°
After great cathedral gong;°
A starlit or a moonlit dome° disdains
All that man is,
All mere complexities,
The fury and the mire of human veins.

Before me floats an image, man or shade,
10 Shade more than man, more image than a shade;
For Hades' bobbin bound in mummy-cloth
May unwind the winding path;°
A mouth that has no moisture and no breath
Breathless mouths may summon;
I hail the superhuman;
I call it death-in-life and life-in-death.

Miracle, bird or golden handiwork,
More miracle than bird or handiwork,°
Planted on the star-lit golden bough,°
20 Can like the cocks of Hades° crow,
Or, by the moon embittered, scorn aloud
In glory of changeless metal
Common bird or petal
And all complexities of mire or blood.

At midnight on the Emperor's pavement° flit
Flames that no faggot feeds, nor steel has lit,
Nor storm disturbs, flames begotten of flame,
Where blood-begotten spirits° come
And all complexities of fury leave,
30 Dying into a dance,

---

night-walkers' song the call of the prostitutes
gong suspended in Byzantine church porches
and struck with mallets
dome that of the cathedral of St. Sophia, begun
in 532 A.D.; a mosque after the Turkish conquest (1453); now a museum of Byzantine
art
Before . . . path This is the mummy of the
draft. Yeats imagines it as wound around like
wool on a perne or "bobbin" (see "The Second
Coming" and "Sailing to Byzantinm"). The
man has become a shade, "dreaming back" or
unwinding his natural life, and so an image
of the passage from life into eternity, representing the point that is both life in death and
death in life.
Miracle . . . handiwork removing the bird
from the human context it still had in "Sailing
to Byzantium"

golden bough The tree is artificial. Yeats may
be looking back to his Cabbalistic tree (see
"The Two Trees") and also remembering that
the golden bough was used to achieve entry
into the underworld.
cocks of Hades These do not signal the continuity of existence or, as in some occult writing
earthly cocks do, the Resurrection, but rather
despise those commonplace heralds of life and
rebirth.
Emperor's pavement mosaic pavement in the
Forum of Constantine
blood-begotten spirits The spirits of the recently
dead, they are *blood-begotten* in contrast to
the self-begotten flames of Byzantium which
will purge them of their *complexities of fury,*
the *mire of human veins.*

An agony of trance,
An agony of flame that cannot singe a sleeve.°

Astraddle on the dolphin's mire and blood,°
Spirit after spirit! The smithies break the flood,°
The golden smithies of the Emperor!
Marbles of the dancing floor
Break bitter furies of complexity,
Those images that yet
Fresh images beget,
40   That dolphin-torn, that gong-tormented sea.
1930   1933

Crazy Jane Talks with the Bishop°

I met the Bishop on the road
And much said he and I.
'Those breasts are flat and fallen now,
Those veins must soon be dry;
Live in a heavenly mansion,
Not in some foul sty.'

'Fair and foul are near of kin,
And fair needs foul,' I cried.
'My friends are gone, but that's a truth
10   Nor grave nor bed denied,
Learned in bodily lowliness
And in the heart's pride.

'A woman can be proud and stiff
When on love intent;
But love has pitched his mansion in
The place of excrement;
For nothing can be sole or whole
That has not been rent.'
1929   1932, 1933

An agony . . . sleeve This figure was suggested
to Yeats by a Japanese Nōh play, *Motomezuka*,
in which a girl dances the agony of her burning
in flames that are the subjective creation of
her guilt and have no reality. He also knew
the famous Fire Dance of Loie Fuller, in which,
by means of underfloor electric lighting and
other devices, she seemed to be dancing in
flames that did not burn her.
dolphin's mire and blood Yeats here and elsewhere follows a tradition that the dead are
conveyed to the afterlife on the backs of
dolphins; being themselves natural—having *mire
and blood*—they are another image of the transition from life to death.
smithies . . . flood The Emperor's workshops
convert the natural into the eternal, like the
mosaic pavement or dancing floor.
Crazy Jane Talks with the Bishop Yeats wrote

the poems in *Words for Music Perhaps and
Other Poems* (1932), in a burst of creative
energy after a serious illness, during the spring
of 1929. Among them is the sequence first
called the Cracked Mary, later the Crazy
Jane, poems. The original Crazy Jane was an
old woman who lived at Gort, near Lady
Gregory's estate, and was much admired for
her audacity of speech. This is the sixth of the
poems and the second involving the Bishop.
They belong to a period when Yeats, "full of
desire" as he said, was engaged in giving a
strong sexual dimension to his occult thinking.
Crazy Jane did as Yeats thought he should:
she cast out remorse, and in old age did not
turn against the sensuality of youth but embraced and defended it against the orthodox
advice of the Bishop.

After Long Silence°

Speech after long silence; it is right,
All other lovers being estranged or dead,
Unfriendly lamplight hid under its shade,
The curtains drawn upon unfriendly night,
That we descant and yet again descant
Upon the supreme theme of Art and Song:
Bodily decrepitude is wisdom; young
We loved each other and were ignorant.
1929   1933

A Last Confession°

What lively lad most pleasured me
Of all that with me lay?
I answer that I gave my soul
And loved in misery,
But had great pleasure with a lad
That I loved bodily.

Flinging from his arms I laughed
To think his passion such,
He fancied that I gave a soul
10   Did but our bodies touch,
And laughed upon his breast to think
Beast gave beast as much.

I gave what other women gave
That stepped out of their clothes,
But when this soul, its body off,
Naked to naked goes,
He it has found shall find therein
What none other knows,

And give his own and take his own
20   And rule in his own right;
And though it loved in misery
Close and cling so tight,
There's not a bird of day° that dare
Extinguish that delight.
1926   1933

After Long Silence This is number XVII of
Words for Music Perhaps. The last lines memo-
rably repeat what the reader will now recognize
as a leading theme of Yeats's poetry.
A Last Confession from the sequence *A Woman
Young and Old*

bird of day the bird song at dawn that ends
lovemaking in the ancient type of poem called
the *aubade*

Meru°

Civilisation is hooped together, brought
Under a rule, under the semblance of peace
By manifold illusion; but man's life is thought,
And he, despite his terror, cannot cease
Ravening through century after century,
Ravening, raging, and uprooting that he may come
Into the desolation of reality:
Egypt and Greece, good-bye, and good-bye, Rome!
Hermits upon Mount Meru° or Everest,
10 Caverned in night under the drifted snow,
Or where that snow and winter's dreadful blast
Beat down upon their naked bodies, know
That day brings round the night, that before dawn
His glory and his monuments are gone.
1933–34   1935

Lapis Lazuli

This poem was included in the posthumous *Last Poems and Plays* (1940). In July 1935 Yeats wrote to Dorothy Wellesley that "people much occupied with morality always lose heroic ecstasy" and quoted Dowson's lines "Wine and women and song, / To us they belong / To us the bitter and gay," adding " 'Bitter and gay,' that is the heroic mood." The Dowson poem, "Villanelle of the Poet's Road," was included by Yeats in *The Oxford Book of Modern Verse* (1936), his anthology. He also mentioned in the letter Harry Clifton's gift to him of a carved piece of lapis lazuli (a stone of deep blue color): it was "carved by some Chinese sculptor into the semblance of a mountain with temple, trees, paths and an ascetic and pupil about to climb the mountain. Ascetic, pupil, hard stone, eternal theme of the sensual east. The heroic cry in the midst of despair. But no, I am wrong, the east has its solutions always and therefore knows nothing of tragedy. It is we, not the east, that must raise the heroic cry." He had recently received a letter from his friend the artist Edmund Dulac expressing terror as to the consequences if London were to be bombed from the air. There is a study of the manuscript drafts in Jon Stallworthy, *Vision and Revision in Yeats's Last Poems* (1969).

Meru This sonnet is the twelfth and last in the sequence *Supernatural Songs*, which first appeared in *The King of the Great Clock Tower* (1934, limited edition) and *A Full Moon in March* (1935). There the songs are accompanied by a note explaining the relevance to the sequence of certain affinities between Oriental religion and Irish Christianity; he invents a character Ribh who is critical of St. Patrick ("An abstract Greek absurdity has crazed the man— / Recall that masculine Trinity"). The sequence represents a theological phase of Yeats's thought, and ends with "Meru," which he mentions in the note as a "legendary" place of pilgrimage for Indian holy men. He was interested in a book called *The Holy Mountain* (1934) by his friend Shri Purohit Swami, and prepared his introduction to it at about the time of the poem.

Mount Meru Shri Purohit Swami speaks of advanced meditation by ascetics on Mount Kailas, Yeats's "legendary Meru."

Lapis Lazuli

(*For Harry Clifton*)

I have heard that hysterical women say
They are sick of the palette and fiddle-bow,
Of poets that are always gay,
For everybody knows or else should know
That if nothing drastic is done
Aeroplane and Zeppelin° will come out,
Pitch like King Billy bomb-balls in°
Until the town lie beaten flat.

10 All perform their tragic play,
There struts Hamlet, there is Lear,
That's Ophelia, that Cordelia;
Yet they, should the last scene be there,
The great stage curtain about to drop,
If worthy their prominent part in the play,
Do not break up their lines to weep.
They know that Hamlet and Lear are gay;°
Gaiety transfiguring all that dread.
All men have aimed at, found and lost;
Black out; Heaven blazing into the head:
20 Tragedy wrought to its uttermost.
Though Hamlet rambles and Lear rages,
And all the drop-scenes drop at once
Upon a hundred thousand stages,
It° cannot grow by an inch or an ounce.

On their own feet they came, or on shipboard,
Camel-back, horse-back, ass-back, mule-back,
Old civilisations put to the sword.
Then they and their wisdom went to rack:
No handiwork of Callimachus,°
30 Who handled marble as if it were bronze,
Made draperies that seemed to rise
When sea-wind swept the corner, stands;
His long lamp-chimney shaped like the stem
Of a slender palm, stood but a day;

Zeppelin a World War I lighter-than-air bomber, obsolete by the time of writing
Pitch . . . in Recalls an Irish ballad about the Battle of the Boyne, during which "King William threw his bomb-balls in." William III, who was married to James II's daughter Mary, became joint sovereign with her by invitation of Parliament in 1689, after the flight of James II, king from 1685. William decisively defeated James at the Battle of the Boyne in Ireland, July 1, 1690.
Hamlet . . . gay In "A General Introduction for My Work" (*Essays and Introductions*, 1961, p. 522) Yeats writes: "The heroes of Shakespeare convey to us through their looks, or through the metaphorical patterns of their speech, the sudden enlargement of their vision, their ecstasy at the approach of death"; and he quotes Lady Gregory's remark, "Tragedy must be a joy to the man who dies."
It presumably tragedy
Callimachus Sculptor of 5th century B.C. who is said to have invented the Corinthian column and a method of sculpting the folds of drapery with a rolling drill. Yeats uses him as one who tried to keep up the formal purity of earlier Greek sculpture when Greece was being submerged in Asiatic influences; the lamp he found mentioned in Pausanias' *Description of Greece* (a 2nd-century A.D. tourist guide).

All things fall and are built again,
And those that build them again are gay.

Two Chinamen, behind them a third,
Are carved in lapis lazuli,
Over them flies a long-legged bird,
40   A symbol of longevity;
The third, doubtless a serving-man,
Carries a musical instrument.

Every discoloration of the stone,
Every accidental crack or dent,
Seems a water-course or an avalanche,
Or lofty slope where it still snows
Though doubtless plum or cherry-branch
Sweetens the little half-way house
Those Chinamen climb towards, and I
50   Delight to imagine them seated there;
There, on the mountain and the sky,
On all the tragic scene they stare.
One asks for mournful melodies;
Accomplished fingers begin to play.
Their eyes mid many wrinkles, their eyes,
Their ancient, glittering eyes, are gay.
1936   1940

The Statues

In early prose drafts Yeats is already contrasting the mathematical proportions of Greek sculpture, based on Pythagoras, with the formlessness of the Asiatic, the flood temporarily stemmed at Salamis (the Athenian naval victory over the Persians in 480 B.C.). Yeats says that "Apollo forgot Pythagoras and took the name of Buddha" and that Apollo should return under the name of Cuchulain to give us back Pythagorean number in the formless chaos of the modern world. In his topical pamphlet *On the Boiler* (1939) Yeats has this passage:

> There are moments when I am certain that art must once again accept those Greek proportions which carry into plastic art the Pythagorean numbers, those faces which are divine because all there is empty and measured. Europe was not born when Greek galleys defeated the Persian hordes at Salamis; but when the Doric studios sent out those broad-backed marble statues against the multiform, vague, expressive Asiatic sea, they gave to the sexual instinct of Europe its goal, its fixed type.

Elsewhere in the same booklet he advises that Greek and mathematics be taught in Irish schools, the latter "because being certainty without reality it is the modern key to power. . . ." Yeats's elevation of the Greek statue to a European physical norm is not unrelated to his interest, also expressed in *On the Boiler*, in eugenics, which in turn was, in the formulations then current, related to his interest in the European dictatorships.

The Statues

Pythagoras planned it. Why did the people stare?
His numbers, though they moved or seemed to move
In marble or in bronze,° lacked character.°
But boys and girls, pale from the imagined love
Of solitary beds, knew what they were,
That passion could bring character enough,
And pressed at midnight in some public place
Live lips upon a plummet-measured face.

No! Greater than Pythagoras,° for the men
That with a mallet or a chisel modelled these
Calculations that look but casual flesh, put down
All Asiatic vague immensities,
And not the banks of oars that swam upon
The many-headed foam at Salamis.
Europe put off that foam when Phidias
Gave women dreams and dreams their looking-glass.

One image crossed the many-headed,° sat
Under the tropic shade, grew round and slow,
No Hamlet thin from eating flies,° a fat
Dreamer of the Middle Ages. Empty eyeballs knew
That knowledge increases unreality, that
Mirror on mirror mirrored is all the show.
When gong and conch declare the hour to bless
Grimalkin crawls to Buddha's emptiness.°

When Pearse summoned Cuchulain to his side,
What stalked through the Post Office?° What intellect,
What calculation, number, measurement, replied?
We Irish, born into that ancient sect

marble . . . bronze See note on "Among School
Children."
lacked character For Yeats *character* was un-
desirable, a sign of old age, growing "like the
ash of a burning stick" (essay, "The Tragic
Theatre," 1910); the valuable possession was
personality, more vital, less uselessly differentiated; thus in art personal emotion is expressed not by quirks of character but by "a
mask from whose eyes the disembodied looks."
No . . . Pythagoras On second thought, the
sculptors are greater than the mathematician
who made their measurements possible; for they
rather than the warships at Salamis kept the
Persians out, making the sexual ideal that of
proportions discovered or created by man, not
natural formlessness.
One . . . many-headed Refers to the effect on
Persian and Indian art of Greek influence
brought in by Alexander the Great when he
invaded those regions (4th century B.C.); the
Ghandara (Pakistan) Buddhas of the North West
frontier are Greek in style; *many-headed* from a
Greek epithet for the sea.
Hamlet . . . flies Hamlet says he eats "the

air, promise-crammed" like the chameleon,
thought to live on air (*Hamlet* III.ii.91). Yeats
substitutes flies; cats that eat flies are said to
grow thin, hence perhaps Grimalkin in the
last line of the stanza.
Empty . . . emptiness The eyeballs of the
statues, which the Greeks painted, are now
empty; even in India there is a coming together
of the European and the Asiatic spirit. Here
the wilder, more wantonly allusive manner of
Yeats's later poetry has obscured the meaning
almost completely, except that it is plain there
is a call for Greek proportion in the modern
version of the Asiatic tide.
When . . . Office? Pearse, according to Yeats
himself, "had a cult" of Cuchulain, the ancient
Irish hero, and called on him during the siege
of the Post Office at Easter 1916. (There is
a statue of Cuchulain in the Dublin Post Office
to commemorate this.) Yeats, imagining the
Irish as belonging to a world earlier than the
Christian dispensation now coming to an end,
reads Cuchulain as Apollo and imagines him
bringing back the principles of measurement
implicit in the Greek statues.

But thrown upon this filthy modern tide
30 And by its formless spawning fury wrecked,
Climb to our proper dark, that we may trace
The lineaments of a plummet-measured face.
1938   1940

John Kinsella's Lament for Mrs. Mary Moore°

A bloody and a sudden end,
     Gunshot or a noose,
For Death who takes what man would keep,
     Leaves what man would lose.
He might have had my sister,
     My cousins by the score,
But nothing satisfied the fool
     But my dear Mary Moore,
None other knows what pleasures man
10   At table or in bed.
What shall I do for pretty girls
     Now my old bawd is dead?°

Though stiff to strike a bargain,
     Like an old Jew man,
Her bargain struck we laughed and talked
     And emptied many a can;
And O! but she had stories,
     Though not for the priest's ear,
To keep the soul of man alive,
20   Banish age and care,
And being old she put a skin
     On everything she said.
What shall I do for pretty girls
     Now my old bawd is dead?

The priests have got a book that says
     But for Adam's sin
Eden's Garden would be there
     And I there within.
No expectation fails there,
30   No pleasing habit ends,
No man grows old, no girl grows cold,
     But friends walk by friends.
Who quarrels over halfpennies
     That plucks the trees for bread?

John . . . Moore written July 1938 as "A
Strong Farmer's Complaint about Death"
What . . . dead "I have just thought of a
chorus for a ballad. A strong farmer is mourning over the shortness of life and changing
times, and every stanza ends "What . . .
dead?" (letter of July 1938).

> *What shall I do for pretty girls*
> *Now my old bawd is dead?*
>   1938   1940

The Circus Animals' Desertion°

I

I sought a theme and sought for it in vain,
I sought it daily for six weeks or so.
Maybe at last, being but a broken man,
I must be satisfied with my heart, although
Winter and summer till old age began
My circus animals were all on show,
Those stilted boys, that burnished chariot,
Lion and woman° and the Lord knows what.

II

What can I but enumerate old themes?
10 First that sea-rider Oisin° led by the nose
Through three enchanted islands, allegorical dreams,
Vain gaiety, vain battle, vain repose,
Themes of the embittered heart, or so it seems,
That might adore old songs or courtly shows;
But what cared I that set him on to ride,
I, starved for the bosom of his faery bride?

And then a counter-truth filled out its play,
The Countess Cathleen° was the name I gave it;
She, pity-crazed, had given her soul away,
20 But masterful Heaven had intervened to save it.
I thought my dear must her own soul destroy,
So did fanaticism and hate enslave it,
And this brought forth a dream and soon enough
This dream itself had all my thought and love.°

And when the Fool and Blind Man stole the bread
Cuchulain fought the ungovernable sea;°

The Circus . . . Desertion This is a poem
somewhat like Coleridge's "Dejection" ode,
a poem about no longer being able to write
poems. The "Circus Animals" are his usual
themes.
Lion and woman In a visionary poem, "The
Double Vision of Michael Robartes," Yeats
sees "A Sphinx with woman breast and lion
paw" and a Buddha, with a girl dancing between, symbolizing the Fifteenth Phase of his
system, or Unity of Being.
Oisin (pronounced Usheen) was carried off
to fairyland by Niamh on her horse (see Yeats's
early long poem in three parts, *The Wanderings
of Oisin*).
The Countess Cathleen This is a play (first

version 1889) written for Maud Gonne in
which the devil's agents tempt starving peasants
to sell their souls for gold. The Countess
sacrifices her wealth and then her soul to save
them, but in the end is herself saved. Yeats
thought this an allegory of Maud Gonne's ruining herself for the sake of politics.
This . . love The poetic invention takes possession of its creator and cuts him off from the
pain of his own being.
And when . . . sea In Yeats's play *On Baile's
Strand* (pronounced Bala) Cuchulain dies fighting the waves, and the Fool and Blind Man steal
bread from the full ovens of the empty houses
nearby.

Heart-mysteries there,° and yet when all is said
It was the dream itself enchanted me:
Character isolated by a deed
30 To engross the present and dominate memory.
Players and painted stage took all my love,
And not those things that they were emblems of.°

III

Those masterful images because complete
Grew in pure mind, but out of what began?
A mound of refuse or the sweepings of a street,
Old kettles, old bottles, and a broken can,
Old iron, old bones, old rags, that raving slut
Who keeps the till. Now that my ladder's gone,
I must lie down where all the ladders start,
40 In the foul rag-and-bone shop of the heart.°
1938?   1940

Cuchulain Comforted

This is probably Yeats's last work. From *On Baile's Strand* (1903) Cuchulain (pronounced Cohullan) is a recurring feature in Yeats's plays, of which five include him. In *The Green Helmet* he is a figure of fearless creative joy; in *On Baile's Strand* his integrity is impaired through lamentation for the lack of a son. In Yeats's first adaptation of a Japanese Nōh play, *At the Hawk's Well,* he returns as part of a "system" allegory, lured away from the fountain that represents Unity of Being; and in another dance play, *The Only Jealousy of Emer,* an evil spirit occupies his body (wears his mask) and Cuchulain is redeemed from death (after fighting the waves) by Emer's self-sacrifice. Cuchulain appears once again in the very late dance play, *The Death of Cuchulain* (1938), a remarkable work in which Cuchulain is finally killed by the Fool, and has a vision of his departing soul as "a soft feathery shape." The last poem is closely related to the final Cuchulain play; Yeats called it "a kind of sequel—strange, too, something new." On January 7 he dictated a prose draft, which is close to the resulting poem. Yeats uses Dante's *terza rima* (see Glossary, *Meter: versification*) and also imitates his diction and imagery with unparalleled closeness; he means the poem to sound like an encounter in the *Inferno*.

Heart-mysteries there Again Yeats apparently finds this story allegorical of his own life.
Players . . . emblems of Yeats managed the Abbey Theatre, and wrote much for it, between 1902 and 1910, neglecting (he implies) the personal life of which the stage and the plays were emblems.

Those . . . heart (ll. 33–40) The images he speaks of belonged to the mind, but started in the heart; now, with no access to them, he is left lying in the "mire" of his experience, unredeemed by dream.

Cuchulain Comforted

A man that had six mortal wounds, a man
Violent and famous, strode among the dead;
Eyes stared out of the branches and were gone.

Then certain Shrouds that muttered head to head
Came and were gone. He leant upon a tree
As though to meditate on wounds and blood.

A Shroud that seemed to have authority
Among those bird-like things came, and let fall
A bundle of linen. Shrouds by two and three

10 Came creeping up because the man was still.
And thereupon that linen-carrier said:
'Your life can grow much sweeter if you will

Obey our ancient rule and make a shroud;
Mainly because of what we only know
The rattle of those arms makes us afraid.

We thread the needles' eyes, and all we do
All must together do.' That done, the man
Took up the nearest and began to sew.°

'Now must we sing and sing the best we can,
20 But first you must be told our character:
Convicted cowards all, by kindred slain

Or driven from home and left to die in fear.'
They sang, but had nor human tunes nor words,
Though all was done in common as before,

They had changed their throats and had the throats of birds.
1938–39   1940

Autobiographies

Yeats's output of prose was very large, ranging from journalism of small importance to the long excogitated and central document of his thought, *A Vision*, of which the final revision appeared in 1937. Few, however, would disagree that his most impressive work of art in prose is the accumulation of autobiographical material which, over the years, he shaped into a strange unity and called *Autobiographies* (later *The Autobiography*). This work reflects his intense and continuous effort to shape himself as man and poet; to escape from the destructive "multiplicity" of his youth and give his life and work the power and authority that come only from relatedness and unity. In a lecture of 1910 Yeats defended the position that knowledge of a poet's life is

We thread . . . sew (ll. 16–18) recalling a   *nella cruna* ("and knitted their brows at us
famous passage in *Inferno* XV: *e si ver noi*   like an old tailor peering at his needle")
aguzzavan le ciglia / come vecchio sartor fa

relevant to his work, for the reader ought to see the work as "no rootless flower but the speech of a man." The life and the poetry will have the same symbolic patterns.

Yeats labored over the successive sections of the work (concealing their sources in letters and diaries), and making them conform to the state of his thought and poetry at the time of writing. The first section, *Reveries over Childhood and Youth*, was written in 1914. *The Trembling of the Veil*, the second section, came out in 1922, and included some reworked earlier material. *Dramatis Personae*, covering Yeats's life from 1896 to 1902, and including *Estrangement* (from a diary of 1909), *The Death of Synge*, and *The Bounty of Sweden*, also earlier pieces, the last inspired by his Nobel Prize, appeared in 1936. These were added to *Reveries* and *Trembling* (which were revised in 1926), and the whole was published as *Autobiographies* (1938). There are accordingly six autobiographies, all in different ways what Yeats called "stylistic arrangements of experience." The first, *Reveries*, is about childhood in Ireland and London, youthful dealings with his occultist uncle George Pollexfen, and early reading —the abandonment of conventional knowledge for "psychical research and mystical philosophy." This takes him up to the period described in the first section (Four Years, 1887–91) of *The Trembling of the Veil*. The title he explains thus: "I have found in an old diary a saying from Stéphane Mallarmé, that his epoch was troubled by the trembling of the veil of the Temple" (the allusion is to Matthew 27:51, the rending of the Temple veil at the time of the Crucifixion). The figure is apocalyptic; during the years covered in the book, says Yeats, Mallarmé's words were still true. The beginning of the end was at hand, the change to a new historical epoch that Yeats predicted for 1927.

The selections below are from the third and fourth of the five sections of *The Trembling of the Veil*. At the time described Yeats had a full life; he was deep in occult studies and practices, and in 1891 helped to found the Rhymers' Club, which included Lionel Johnson, Ernest Dowson, John Davidson, Arthur Symons, and others. He was still unhappily in love with Maud Gonne, and this obsession survived love affairs with other women as well as her marriage to John MacBride in 1903. Yet during these years he was, with that marvelous energy which underlies all the affectations of languor in life and work, "hammering his thoughts into unity" (see the essay "If I Were Four and Twenty" in *Explorations* (1962), p. 263).

As in the theoretical elaborations of *A Vision*, Yeats's purpose was "getting one's mind into order," so enabling it to be creative. Lost on the "Path of the Cameleon" it could not free itself of useless multiplicity, or "choose from among [generalizations] those that belonged" to his life. So too with his friends: they also had to be set in order, even, in the end, distributed among the Twenty-eight Phases of the Moon in his system. In this system the Fifteenth Phase represents a Unity of Being toward which artists aspire, though they never attain it. Subjective types, including artists, belong to phases Nine to Twenty-one, and seek fulfillment in an inner self, called a mask; objective types seek fulfillment in the outside world. In *Trembling* he considers his friends in the light of such preoccupations.

The first selection is part of a discussion of the reservoir of souls and images, the Platonic *anima mundi* to which poets, like others, have access ("I know now that revelation is from the self, but from that age-long memoried self, that shapes the elaborate shell of the mollusc and the child in the womb, that teaches the birds to make their nests"). Poets achieve it by crises of despair. "What portion in the world can the artist have, / Who has awakened from the common dream, / But dissipation and despair?"—asks Yeats, quoting his own "Ego Dominus Tuus" (written 1915). And in the fourth section of *Trembling* he considers those artist friends who "had to face their ends when young" (*The Grey Rock*, 1913). Yeats himself was not given to drugs, drink, or harlots; yet around him were men who seemed to reflect in their personalities the disaster of the artist in a world hurrying on to an apocalypse of the objective era. They are his "Tragic Generation," and Lionel Johnson was the most characteristic. Johnson and Dowson alike lacked any objective relation with the world. They, together with the more objective Symons, the victimized Beardsley, and Verlaine, are all systematically placed, all organized in relation to the image of poetry and revelation. This Yeats called the Fifteenth Phase; its image was a Salome-like dancer calling for the head of the victim. Yet Yeats, in his account of these men's struggle for vision, is not solemn or unduly schematic; the strength and conviction of what he says do not preclude humor, or stifle his acute sense of anecdote. When that Unity of Being which he admired in the Renaissance (1450 A.D. and somewhat later, he says) was no longer possible because of the widening gyre of the age, when soul and body began to fall apart, and the quest for the Image required secret study and difficult poetry, men could still be fascinating and even funny. Wilde's tragic life did not prevent his being a great comedian; and the last mention of him in Yeats's book is the ribald story about his exploit with Dowson in Dieppe. This blend of high seriousness and a sense of the comic is one of the many attributes that place Yeats's among the greatest of all autobiographies.

From The Trembling of the Veil: III

Hodos Chameliontos

III

At Sligo we walked twice every day, once after lunch and once after dinner, to the same gate on the road to Knocknarea;[1] and at Rosses Point, to the same rock upon the shore; and as we walked we exchanged those thoughts that never rise before me now without bringing some sight of mountain or of shore. Considering that Mary Battle [2] received our thoughts in sleep, though coarsened or turned to caricature, do not the thoughts of the scholar or the hermit, though they speak no word, or something of their shape and impulse, pass into the general mind? Does not the emotion of some woman of fashion, caught in the subtle torture of self-analysing passion, pass down, although she speak no word, to Joan with her Pot, Jill with her Pail and, it may be, with one knows not what nightmare melancholy to Tom the Fool?

Seeing that a vision could divide itself in divers complementary portions, might not the thought of philosopher or poet or mathematician depend at every moment of its progress upon some complementary thought in minds perhaps at a great distance? Is there nation-wide multiform reverie, every mind passing through a stream of suggestion, and all streams acting and reacting upon one another no matter how distant the minds, how dumb the

---

1. Mountain near Sligo.
2. Servant of Yeats's uncle, George Pollexfen; she had "second sight."

lips? A man walked, as it were, casting a shadow, and yet one could never say which was man and which was shadow, or how many the shadows that he cast. Was not a nation, as distinguished from a crowd of chance comers, bound together by this interchange among streams or shadows; that Unity of Image, which I sought in national literature, being but an originating symbol?

From the moment when these speculations grew vivid, I had created for myself an intellectual solitude, most arguments that could influence action had lost something of their meaning. How could I judge any scheme of education, or of social reform, when I could not measure what the different classes and occupations contributed to that invisible commerce of reverie and of sleep: and what is luxury and what necessity when a fragment of gold braid, or a flower in the wallpaper may be an originating impulse to revolution or to philosophy? I began to feel myself not only solitary but helpless.

IV

I had not taken up these subjects wilfully, nor through love of strangeness, nor love of excitement, nor because I found myself in some experimental circle, but because unaccountable things had happened even in my childhood, and because of an ungovernable craving. When supernatural events begin, a man first doubts his own testimony, but when they repeat themselves again and again, he doubts all human testimony. At least he knows his own bias, and may perhaps allow for it, but how trust historian and psychologist that have for some three hundred years ignored in writing of the history of the world, or of the human mind, so momentous a part of human experience? What else had they ignored and distorted? When Mesmerists[3] first travelled about as public entertainers, a favourite trick was to tell a mesmerised man that some letter of the alphabet had ceased to exist, and after that to make him write his name upon the blackboard. Brown, or Jones, or Robinson would become upon the instant, and without any surprise or hesitation, Rown, or Ones, or Obinson.

Was modern civilisation a conspiracy of the subconscious? Did we turn away from certain thoughts and things because the Middle Ages lived in terror of the dark, or had some seminal illusion been imposed upon us by beings greater than ourselves for an unknown purpose? Even when no facts of experience were denied, might not what had seemed logical proof be but a mechanism of change, an automatic impulse? Once in London, at a dinner party, where all the guests were intimate friends, I had written upon a piece of paper, 'In five minutes York Powell[4] will talk of a burning house,' thrust the paper under my neighbour's plate, and imagined my fire symbol, and waited in silence. Powell shifted conversation from topic to topic and within the five minutes was describing a fire he had seen as a young man. When Locke's French translator Coste[5] asked him how, if there were no 'innate ideas,' he could explain the skill shown by a bird in making its nest, Locke replied,

3. Franz Anton Mesmer (1734?–1815), an Austrian physician, developed a theory of animal magnetism and gave his name to hypnotists.
4. Frederick York Powell (1850–1904), historian and Icelandic scholar.
5. Pierre Coste (1668–1747) translated Locke's *Reasonableness of Christianity* (1696) and his *Essay on Human Understanding* (1700).

'I did not write to explain the actions of dumb creatures,' and his translator thought the answer 'very good, seeing that he had named his book *A Philosophical Essay upon Human Understanding.*' Henry More,[6] upon the other hand, considered that the bird's instinct proved the existence of the Anima Mundi,[7] with its ideas and memories. Did modern enlightenment think with Coste that Locke had the better logic, because it was not free to think otherwise?

V

I ceased to read modern books that were not books of imagination, and if some philosophic idea interested me, I tried to trace it back to its earliest use, believing that there must be a tradition of belief older than any European Church, and founded upon the experience of the world before the modern bias. It was this search for a tradition that urged George Pollexfen[8] and myself to study the visions and thoughts of the country people, and some country conversation, repeated by one or the other, often gave us a day's discussion. These visions, we soon discovered, were very like those we called up by symbol. Mary Battle, looking out of the window at Rosses Point, saw coming from Knocknarea, where Queen Maeve, according to local folklore, is buried under a great heap of stones, 'the finest woman you ever saw travelling right across from the mountains and straight to here.'—I quote a record written at the time. 'She looked very strong, but not wicked' (that is to say, not cruel). 'I have seen the Irish Giant' (some big man shown at a fair). 'And though he was a fine man he was nothing to her, for he was round and could not have stepped out so soldierly . . . she had no stomach on her but was slight and broad in the shoulders, and was handsomer than any one you ever saw; she looked about thirty.' And when I asked if she had seen others like her, she said, 'Some of them have their hair down, but they look quite different, more like the sleepy-looking ladies one sees in the papers. Those with their hair up are like this one. The others have long white dresses, but those with their hair up have short dresses, so that you can see their legs right up to the calf.' And when I questioned her, I found that they wore what might well be some kind of buskin. 'They are fine and dashing-looking, like the men one sees riding their horses in twos and threes on the slopes of the mountains with their swords swinging. There is no such race living now, none so finely proportioned. . . . When I think of her and the ladies now they are like little children running about not knowing how to put their clothes on right . . . why, I would not call them women at all.'

Not at this time, but some three or four years later, when the visions came without any conscious use of symbol for a short time, and with much greater vividness, I saw two or three forms of this incredible beauty, one especially that must always haunt my memory. Then, too, the Master Pilot told us of meeting at night close to the Pilot House a procession of women in what seemed the costume of another age. Were they really people of the past, revisiting, perhaps, the places where they lived, or must I explain them, as

6. English Platonist (1614–87).
7. The Platonists' World Soul, provider of principle of growth in the creation, and reservoir of unconscious images.
8. See note on "In Memory of Major Robert Gregory."

I explained that vision of Eden as a mountain garden, by some memory of the race, as distinct from living memory? Certainly these Spirits, as the country people called them, seemed full of personality; were they not capricious, generous, spiteful, anxious, angry, and yet did that prove them more than images and symbols? When I used a combined earth and fire and lunar symbol my seer, a girl of twenty-five, saw an obvious Diana and her dogs, about a fire in a cavern. Presently, judging from her closed eyes, and from the tone of her voice, that she was in trance, not in reverie, I wished to lighten the trance a little, and made through carelessness or hasty thinking a symbol of dismissal; and at once she started and cried out, 'She says you are driving her away too quickly. You have made her angry.' Then, too, if my visions had a subjective element, so had Mary Battle's, for her fairies had but one tune, *The Distant Waterfall*, and she never heard anything described in a sermon at the Cathedral that she did not 'see it after,' and spoke of seeing in this way the gates of Purgatory.

Furthermore, if my images could affect her dreams, the folk-images could affect mine in turn, for one night I saw between sleeping and waking a strange long-bodied pair of dogs, one black and one white, that I found presently in some country tale. How, too, could one separate the dogs of the country tale from those my uncle heard bay in his pillow? In order to keep myself from nightmare, I had formed the habit of imagining four watch-dogs, one at each corner of my room, and, though I had not told him or anybody, he said, 'Here is a very curious thing; most nights now, when I lay my head upon the pillow, I hear a sound of dogs baying—the sound seems to come up out of the pillow.' A friend of Strindberg's,[9] in *delirium tremens*,[10] was haunted by mice, and a friend in the next room heard the squealing of the mice.

VI

I have much evidence that these images, or the symbols that call them up, can influence the bodily health. My uncle told me one evening that there were cases of smallpox—it turned out to be untrue—somewhere under Knocknarea, and that the doctor was coming to vaccinate him. Vaccination, probably from some infection in the lymph, brought on a very serious illness, bloodpoisoning I heard it called, and presently he was delirious and a second doctor called in consultation. Between eleven and twelve one night when the delirium was at its height, I sat down beside his bed and said, 'What do you see, George?' He said, 'Red dancing figures,' and without commenting, I imagined the cabalistic symbol of water and almost at once he said, 'There is a river running through the room,' and a little later, 'I can sleep now.' I told him what I had done and that, if the dancing figures came again, he was to bid them go in the name of the Archangel Gabriel. Gabriel is angel of the Moon in the Cabala and might, I considered, command the waters at a pinch. The doctor found him much better and heard that I had driven the delirium away and given him such a word of command that when the red men came again in the middle of the night, they looked greatly startled, and fled.

9. August Strindberg (1849–1912), Swedish playwright.
10. A pathological condition resulting from excessive use of alcohol.

The doctor came, questioned, and said, 'Well, I suppose it is a kind of hypnotism, but it is very strange, very strange.' The delirium did not return.

VII

To that multiplicity of interest and opinion, of arts and sciences, which had driven me to conceive a Unity of Culture defined and evoked by Unity of Image, I had but added a multiplicity of images, and I was the more troubled because, the first excitement over, I had done nothing to rouse George Pollexfen from the gloom and hypochondria always thickening about him. I asked no help of books, for I believed that the truth I sought would come to me like the subject of a poem, from some moment of passionate experience, and that if I filled my exposition with other men's thought, other men's investigation, I would sink into all that multiplicity of interest and opinion. That passionate experience could never come—of that I was certain—until I had found the right image or right images. From what but the image of Apollo, fixed always in memory and passion, did his priesthood get that occasional power, a classical historian has described, of lifting great stones and snapping great branches; and did not Gemma Galgani,[11] like many others that had gone before, in 1889 cause deep wounds to appear in her body by contemplating her crucifix? In the essay that Wilde read to me one Christmas Day, occurred these words —'What does not the world owe to the imitation of Christ, what to the imitation of Caesar?' and I had seen Macgregor Mathers [12] paint little pictures combining the forms of men, animals, and birds, according to a rule which provided a combination for every possible mental condition, and I had heard him say, upon what authority I do not remember, that citizens of ancient Egypt assumed, when in contemplation, the images of their gods.

But now image called up image in an endless procession, and I could not always choose among them with any confidence; and when I did choose, the image lost its intensity, or changed into some other image. I had but exchanged the temptation of Flaubert's Bouvard et Pecuchet for that of his St. Anthony,[13] and I was lost in that region a cabalistic manuscript, shown me by Macgregor Mathers, had warned me of; astray upon the Path of the Cameleon, upon Hodos Chameliontos.[14]

11. 1878–1903; modern Christian mystic and canonized saint of the Catholic Church. The phenomenon mentioned by Yeats is known as the *stigmata*.
12. 1854–1918; occultist, Freemason, member of the Magical Order of the Golden Dawn, which Yeats joined; he introduced Yeats to symbol-induced trances.
13. Gustave Flaubert (1821–80), French novelist, author of *Madame Bovary* (1857). His *Temptation of Saint Anthony* (1874) is a highly wrought and symbolic account of the sensual temptations besetting the ascetic saint, founder of Christian monasticism; *Bouvard et Pécuchet* (published posthumously and unfinished, 1881) is the story of two clerks who experiment absurdly in various branches of human knowledge—an expression of disgust at human stupidity.
14. The chameleon, which changes color to match its environment, is here a symbol of intellectual instability and multiplicity.

From The Trembling of the Veil: IV

The Tragic Generation

III

Somewhere about 1450, though later in some parts of Europe by a hundred years or so, and in some earlier, men attained to personality in great numbers, 'Unity of Being,' and became like a 'perfectly proportioned human body,' and as men so fashioned held places of power, their nations had it too, prince and ploughman sharing that thought and feeling. What afterwards showed for rifts and cracks were there already, but imperious impulse held all together. Then the scattering came, the seeding of the poppy, bursting of pea-pod, and for a time personality seemed but the stronger for it. Shakespeare's people make all things serve their passion, and that passion is for the moment the whole energy of their being—birds, beasts, men, women, landscape, society, are but symbols, and metaphors, nothing is studied in itself, the mind is a dark well, no surface, depth only. The men that Titian [1] painted, the men that Jongsen [2] painted, even the men of Van Dyck,[3] seemed at moments like great hawks at rest. In the Dublin National Gallery there hung, perhaps there still hang, upon the same wall, a portrait of some Venetian gentleman by Strozzi [4] and Mr. Sargent's [5] painting of President Wilson. Whatever thought broods in the dark eyes of that Venetian gentleman, has drawn its life from his whole body; it feeds upon it as the flame feeds upon the candle—and should that thought be changed, his pose would change, his very cloak would rustle for his whole body thinks. President Wilson lives only in the eyes, which are steady and intent; the flesh about the mouth is dead, and the hands are dead, and the clothes suggest no movement of his body, nor any movement but that of the valet, who has brushed and folded in mechanical routine. There, all was an energy flowing outward from the nature itself; here, all is the anxious study and slight deflection of external force; there man's mind and body were predominantly subjective; here all is objective, using those words not as philosophy uses them, but as we use them in conversation.

The bright part of the moon's disk, to adopt the symbolism of a certain poem, is subjective mind, and the dark, objective mind, and we have eight and twenty Phases for our classification of mankind, and of the movement

1. Tiziano Vecelli (1477?–1576) greatest of the Venetian painters.
2. In all editions of the work this name appears as *Jongsen*, but there was no such painter. A check of the manuscripts in Dublin, kindly made for us by Professor Denis Donoghue, reveals that in one Yeats has left a blank, and in the other written an indecipherable name beginning with J. (Yeats had some uncertainty about which painters to put in, and at first wrote "Velasquez" instead of Van Dyke.) The likeliest conjecture (J. B. Trapp's) is *Jonson*. Cornelius Jonson or Johnson van Ceulen (1593–1661), born in London of Dutch parents, was a portrait painter who, like Van Dyke, worked for Charles I and for other English patrons before settling in Holland in 1643. Possibly Yeats was uncertain about the spelling of the name, but Professor Donoghue says he cannot see how anybody could have read it as *Jongsen*.
3. Sir Anthony Vandyke or Van Dyck (1599–1641), Flemish artist, court painter to Charles I of England.
4. Bernardo Strozzi ("Il Cappucino"; 1581–1644), painter of the Venetian school, and a Capuchin friar.
5. John Singer Sargent (1856–1925), American painter celebrated for his portraits.

of its thought. At the first Phase—the night where there is no moonlight—all is objective, while when, upon the fifteenth night, the moon comes to the full, there is only subjective mind. The mid-renaissance could but approximate to the full moon 'For there's no human life at the full or the dark,'[6] but we may attribute to the next three nights of the moon the men of Shakespeare, of Titian, of Strozzi, and of Van Dyck, and watch them grow more reasonable, more orderly, less turbulent, as the nights pass; and it is well to find before the fourth—the nineteenth moon counting from the start—a sudden change, as when a cloud becomes rain, or water freezes, for the great transitions are sudden; popular, typical men have grown more ugly and more argumentative; the face that Van Dyck called a fatal face[7] has faded before Cromwell's warty opinionated head. Henceforth no mind made like 'a perfectly proportionated human body' shall sway the public, for great men must live in a portion of themselves, become professional and abstract; but seeing that the moon's third quarter is scarce passed; that abstraction has attained but not passed its climax; that a half, as I affirm it, of the twenty-second night still lingers, they may subdue and conquer, cherish even some Utopian dream, spread abstraction ever further till thought is but a film, and there is no dark depth any more, surface only. But men who belong by nature to the nights near to the full are still born, a tragic minority, and how shall they do their work when too ambitious for a private station, except as Wilde[8] of the nineteenth Phase, as my symbolism has it, did his work? He understood his weakness, true personality was impossible, for that is born in solitude, and at his moon one is not solitary; he must project himself before the eyes of others, and, having great ambition, before some great crowd of eyes; but there is no longer any great crowd that cares for his true thought. He must humour and cajole and pose, take worn-out stage situations, for he knows that he may be as romantic as he please, so long as he does not believe in his romance, and all that he may get their ears for a few strokes of contemptuous wit in which he does believe.

We Rhymers did not humour and cajole; but it was not wholly from demerit, it was in part because of different merit, that he refused our exile. Shaw, as I understand him, has no true quarrel with his time, its moon and his almost exactly coincide. He is quite content to exchange Narcissus and his Pool for the signal-box at a railway junction, where goods and travellers pass perpetually upon their logical glittering road. Wilde was a monarchist, though content that monarchy should turn demagogue for its own safety, and he held a theatre by the means whereby he held a London dinner-table. 'He who can dominate a London dinner-table,' he had boasted, 'can dominate the world.' While Shaw has but carried his street-corner socialist eloquence on to the stage, and in him one discovers, in his writing and his public speech, as once —before their outline had been softened by prosperity or the passage of the years—in his clothes and in his stiff joints, the civilisation that Sargent's

6. Yeats is quoting his own "system" poem, *The Phases of the Moon*, written 1918.
7. That of Charles I.
8. Oscar Wilde (1854–1900), flamboyant wit, dramatist, novelist, poet, and essayist, whose tragic life (convicted of sodomy, he was in prison 1895–97 and lived in exile thereafter) made a deep impression on his friend Yeats.

picture has explored. Neither his crowd nor he have yet made a discovery that brought President Wilson so near his death, that the moon draws to its fourth quarter. But what happens to the individual man whose moon has come to that fourth quarter, and what to the civilisation . . . ?

I can but remember pipe music to-night, though I can half hear beyond it in the memory a weightier music, but this much at any rate is certain—the dream of my early manhood, that a modern nation can return to Unity of Culture, is false; though it may be we can achieve it for some small circle of men and women, and there leave it till the moon bring round its century. . . .

XI

Gradually Arthur Symons [9] came to replace in my intimate friendship, Lionel Johnson [10] from who I was slowly separated by a scruple of conscience. If he came to see me he sat tongue-tied unless I gave him the drink that seemed necessary to bring his vitality to but its normal pitch, and if I called upon him he drank so much that I became his confederate. Once, when a friend and I had sat long after our proper bed-time at his constantly repeated and most earnest entreaty, knowing what black melancholy would descend upon him at our departure, and with the unexpressed hope of getting him to his bed, he fixed upon us a laughing and whimsical look, and said:—'I want you two men to understand that you are merely two men that I am drinking with.' That was the only time that I was to hear from him an imaginary conversation that had not an air of the most scrupulous accuracy. He gave two accounts of a conversation with Wilde in prison; in one Wilde wore his hair long, and in the other it had been cropped by the prison barber. He was gradually losing, too, the faculty of experience, and in his prose and verse repeated the old ideas and emotions, but faintly, as though with fading interest. I am certain that he prayed much, and on those rare days that I came upon him dressed and active before mid-day or but little after, I concluded that he had been to morning Mass at Farm Street.[11]

When with Johnson I had tuned myself to his mood, but Arthur Symons, more than any man I have ever known, could slip as it were into the mind of another, and my thoughts gained in richness and in clearness from his sympathy, nor shall I ever know how much my practice and my theory owe to the passages that he read me from Catullus and from Verlaine and Mallarmé.[12] I had read Axel [13] to myself or was still reading it, so slowly, and with

9. Arthur Symons (1865–1946), a prolific poet and writer on poetry; a dramatist, exponent of Wagner, the dance, and French Symbolist poetry, which he virtually introduced into England and the United States. His strong influence on Yeats is recorded here. He suffered a serious breakdown in middle life; he recovered his sanity but not his vigor or influence.
10. See note on "In Memory of Major Robert Gregory."
11. Immaculate Conception church, London, where artists and intellectuals forgathered.
12. Paul Verlaine (1844–95), Symbolist and Decadent poet; his disorderly life and subtle verse fascinated Yeats, who had met him in Paris and London. Stéphane Mallarmé (1842–98), the greatest of the Symbolist poets in France; Yeats attended some of his Tuesday salons.
13. Comte Philippe Auguste Mathias de Villiers de l'Isle-Adam (1838–89), pioneer Symbolist, whose drama Axël (1890) provided Yeats with his early motto: "As to living, our servants will do that for us."

so much difficulty, that certain passages had an exaggerated importance, while all remained so obscure that I could without much effort imagine that here at last was the Sacred Book I longed for. An Irish friend of mine lives in a house where beside a little old tower rises a great new Gothic hall and stair, and I have sometimes got him to extinguish all light but a little Roman lamp, and in that faint light and among great vague shadows, blotting away the unmeaning ornament, have imagined myself partaking in some incredible romance. Half-a-dozen times, beginning in boyhood with Shelley's *Prometheus Unbound*, I have in that mood possessed for certain hours or months the book that I long for; and Symons, without ever being false to his own impressionist view of art and of life, deepened as I think my longing.

It seems to me, looking backward, that we always discussed life at its most intense moment, that moment which gives a common sacredness to the Song of Songs, and to the Sermon on the Mount, and in which one discovers something supernatural, a stirring as it were of the roots of the hair. He was making those translations from Mallarmé and from Verlaine, from Calderon,[14] from St. John of the Cross,[15] which are the most accomplished metrical translations of our time, and I think that those from Mallarmé may have given elaborate form to my verses of those years, to the latter poems of *The Wind Among the Reeds*, to *The Shadowy Waters*, while Villiers de L'Isle Adam had shaped whatever in my *Rosa Alchemica* [16] Pater [17] had not shaped. I can remember the day in Fountain Court when he first read me Herodiade's address to some Sibyl who is her nurse and it may be the moon also:

> The horror of my virginity
> Delights me, and I would envelope me
> In the terror of my tresses, that, by night,
> Inviolate reptile, I might feel the white
> And glimmering radiance of thy frozen fire,
> Thou that art chaste and diest of desire,
> White night of ice and of the cruel snow!
> Eternal sister, my lone sister, lo
> My dreams uplifted before thee! now, apart,
> So rare a crystal is my dreaming heart,
> And all about me lives but in mine own
> Image, the idolatrous mirror of my pride,
> Mirroring this Herodiade diamond-eyed.

Yet I am certain that there was something in myself compelling me to attempt creation of an art as separate from everything heterogeneous and casual, from all character and circumstance, as some Herodiade [18] of our

14. Pedro Caldéron de la Barca (1600–81), Spanish dramatist and poet.
15. San Juan de la Cruz (1542–91), Spanish mystic and author of a poem called *The Dark Night of the Soul*, of which Symons had made a good translation.
16. An essay included in *The Secret Rose* (1897).
17. Walter Horatio Pater (1839–94), Oxford don whose writings on the Renaissance and aesthetics, and especially his *Marius the Epicurean* (1885), powerfully affected the thought and prose of the young Yeats and his contemporaries.
18. Hérodiade (Salome) recurs frequently in late 19th-century poetry after Mallarmé; Yeats made her a complicated symbol of art.

theatre, dancing seemingly alone in her narrow moving luminous circle. Certainly I had gone a great distance from my first poems, from all that I had copied from the folk-art of Ireland, as from the statue of Mausolus [19] and his Queen, where the luminous circle is motionless and contains the entire popular life; and yet why am I so certain? I can imagine an Aran Islander who had strayed into the Luxembourg Gallery, turning bewildered from Impressionist or Post-Impressionist, but lingering at Moreau's 'Jason,' [20] to study in mute astonishment the elaborate background, where there are so many jewels, so much wrought stone and moulded bronze. Had not lover promised mistress in his own island song, 'A ship with a gold and silver mast, gloves of the skin of a fish, and shoes of the skin of a bird, and a suit of the dearest silk in Ireland'?

XII

Hitherto when in London I had stayed with my family in Bedford Park,[21] but now I was to live for some twelve months in chambers in the Temple [22] that opened through a little passage into those of Arthur Symons. If anybody rang at either door, one or other would look through a window in the connecting passage, and report. We would then decide whether one or both should receive the visitor, whether his door or mine should be opened, or whether both doors were to remain closed. I have never liked London, but London seemed less disagreeable when one could walk in quiet, empty places after dark, and upon a Sunday morning sit upon the margin of a fountain almost as alone as if in the country. I was already settled there, I imagine, when a publisher called and proposed that Symons should edit a Review [23] or Magazine, and Symons consented on the condition that Beardsley [24] were Art Editor—and I was delighted at his condition, as I think were all his other proposed contributors. Aubrey Beardsley had been dismissed from the Art editorship of *The Yellow Book* [25] under circumstances that had made us indignant. He had illustrated Wilde's *Salome*,[26] his strange satiric art had raised the popular press to fury, and at the height of the excitement aroused by Wilde's condemnation, a popular novelist, a woman who had great influence among the most conventional part of the British public, had written demanding his dismissal. 'She owed it to her position before the British people,' she had said. Beardsley was not even a friend of Wilde's—they even disliked each

19. 4th-century B.C. king in Asia Minor, enemy of Athens; his tomb at Halicarnassus is called the Mausoleum.
20. Gustave Moreau (1826–98), French artist much admired by the Yeats circle; he painted Hérodiade.
21. Bedford Park, a section near Chiswick in London, laid out by its architect, Norman Shaw, as a sort of Pre-Raphaelite village for people who wanted to escape Victorian taste. The Yeats family moved there in 1876.
22. The Temple (consisting of the Inner and Middle Temples) lies between Fleet Street and the Thames; accommodation is primarily for lawyers.
23. *The Savoy* was first issued in January 1896, and ceased publication in December 1896.
24. Aubrey Vincent Beardsley (1872–98), artist who worked in black and white; his book illustrations are inseparably associated with the Nineties.
25. In 1894 Beardsley was art editor of *The Yellow Book* (1894–97), which represented the Modernism checked by Wilde's trial.
26. Play, originally in French (1894), on which the libretto of Richard Strauss's opera (1905) was based.

other—he had no sexual abnormality, but he was certainly unpopular, and the moment had come to get rid of unpopular persons. The public at once concluded—they could hardly conclude otherwise, he was dismissed by tele-gram—that there was evidence against him, and Beardsley, who was some twenty-three years old, being embittered and miserable, plunged into dissipa-tion. We knew that we must face an infuriated press and public, but being all young we delighted in enemies and in everything that had an heroic air.

XIII

We might have survived but for our association with Beardsley; perhaps, but for his *Under the Hill*,[27] a Rabelaisian fragment promising a literary genius as great maybe as his artistic genius; and for the refusal of the bookseller who controlled the railway bookstalls to display our wares. The bookseller's man-ager, no doubt looking for a design of Beardsley's, pitched upon Blake's *Anteus setting Virgil and Dante upon the verge of Cocytus* as the ground of refusal, and when Arthur Symons pointed out that Blake was considered 'a very spiritual artist,' replied, 'O, Mr. Symons, you must remember that we have an audience of young ladies as well as an audience of agnostics.' However, he called Arthur Symons back from the door to say, 'If contrary to our expecta-tions the *Savoy* should have a large sale, we should be very glad to see you again.' As Blake's design illustrated an article of mine, I wrote a letter upon that remarkable saying to a principal daily newspaper. But I had mentioned Beardsley, and I was told that the editor had made it a rule that his paper was never to mention Beardsley's name. I said upon meeting him later, 'Would you have made the same rule in the case of Hogarth?'[28] against whom much the same objection could be taken, and he replied with what seemed to me a dreamy look, as though suddenly reminded of a lost opportunity—'Ah, there was no popular press in Hogarth's day.' We were not allowed to forget that in our own day there was a popular press, and its opinions began to affect our casual acquaintance, and even our comfort in public places. At some well-known house, an elderly man to whom I had just been introduced, got up from my side and walked to the other end of the room; but it was as much my reputation as an Irish rebel as the evil company that I was supposed to keep, that excited some young men in a railway carriage to comment upon my general career in voices raised that they might catch my attention. I discovered, however, one evening that we were perhaps envied as well as despised. I was in the pit at some theatre, and had just noticed Arthur Symons a little in front of me, when I heard a young man, who looked like a shop-assistant or clerk, say, 'There is Arthur Symons. If he can't get an order, why can't he pay for a stall?' Clearly we were supposed to prosper upon iniquity, and to go to the pit added a sordid parsimony. At another theatre I caught sight of a woman that I once liked, the widow of some friend of my father's youth, and tried to attract her attention, but she had no eyes for anything but the stage curtain; and at some house where I met no hostility to myself, a popular novelist snatched out of my hand a copy of the *Savoy*, and opening it at Beardsley's

27. A comic erotic fantasy first published in extracts in *The Savoy*, and with other writings in a volume of 1904.
28. William Hogarth (1697–1764), painter, engraver, pictorial satirist.

drawing, called *The Barber*, expounded what he called its bad drawing and wound up with, 'Now if you want to admire really great black and white art, admire the *Punch*[29] Cartoons of Mr. Lindley Sambourne.' Our hostess, after making peace between us, said, 'O, Mr. Yeats, why do you not send your poems to the *Spectator*[30] instead of to the *Savoy*?' The answer, 'My friends read the *Savoy* and they do not read the *Spectator*,' called up a puzzled, disapproving look.

Yet, even apart from Beardsley, we were a sufficiently distinguished body: Max Beerbohm,[31] Bernard Shaw, Ernest Dowson, Lionel Johnson, Arthur Symons, Charles Conder,[32] Charles Shannon,[33] Havelock Ellis,[34] Selwyn Image,[35] Joseph Conrad; but nothing counted but the one hated name. I think that had we been challenged we might have argued something after this fashion: 'Science through much ridicule and some persecution has won its right to explore whatever passes before its corporeal eye, and merely because it passes: to set as it were upon an equality the beetle and the whale though Ben Jonson could find no justification for the entomologist in *The New Inn*,[36] but that he had been crossed in love. Literature now demands the same right of exploration of all that passes before the mind's eye, and merely because it passes.' Not a complete defence, for it substitutes a spiritual for a physical objectivity, but sufficient it may be for the moment, and to settle our place in the historical process.

The critic might well reply that certain of my generation delighted in writing with an unscientific partiality for subjects long forbidden. Yet is it not most important to explore especially what has been long forbidden, and to do this not only 'with the highest moral purpose,' like the followers of Ibsen,[37] but gaily, out of sheer mischief, or sheer delight in that play of the mind? Donne could be as metaphysical as he pleased, and yet never seemed unhuman and hysterical as Shelley often does, because he could be as physical as he pleased; and besides who will thirst for the metaphysical, who have a parched tongue, if we cannot recover the Vision of Evil?

I have felt in certain early works of my own which I have long abandoned, and here and there in the work of others of my generation, a slight, sentimental sensuality which is disagreeable, and does not exist in the work of Donne, let us say, because he, being permitted to say what he pleased, was never tempted to linger, or rather to pretend that we can linger, between spirit and sense.[38] How often had I heard men of my time talk of the meeting of spirit

29. British weekly, very roughly equivalent to *The New Yorker*, founded 1841 and originally radical.

30. British Conservative weekly, founded 1828.

31. Sir Max Beerbohm (1872–1956), caricaturist, novelist, critic.

32. Charles Conder (1868–1909), fan painter.

33. Charles Shannon (1863–1937), painter and lithographer.

34. Henry Havelock Ellis (1859–1939), author of the famous *Studies in the Psychology of Sex* (1897–1928).

35. Selwyn Image, illustrator and designer (1849–1930).

36. A play of 1629.

37. Henrik Ibsen (1828–1906), greatest Norwegian playwright; his work was admired by Shaw and Joyce but not by Wilde and Yeats.

38. Despite the priority attributed to Eliot's essay *The Metaphysical Poets* (see below), it was quite common to speak thus of Donne in Yeats's youth.

and sense, yet there is no meeting but only change upon the instant, and it is by the perception of a change, like the sudden 'blacking out' of the lights of the stage, that passion creates its most violent sensation.[39]

XIV

Dowson was now at Dieppe, now at a Normandy village. Wilde, too, was at Dieppe; and Symons, Beardsley, and others would cross and recross, returning with many tales, and there were letters and telegrams. Dowson wrote a protest against some friend's too vivid essay upon the disorder of his life, and explained that in reality he was living a life of industry in a little country village; but before the letter arrived that friend received a wire, 'arrested, sell watch and send proceeds.' Dowson's watch had been left in London—and then another wire, 'Am free.' Dowson, or so ran the tale as I heard it ten years after, had got drunk and fought the baker, and a deputation of villagers had gone to the magistrate and pointed out that Monsieur Dowson was one of the most illustrious of English poets. 'Quite right to remind me,' said the magistrate, 'I will imprison the baker.'

A Rhymer had seen Dowson at some café in Dieppe with a particularly common harlot, and as he passed, Dowson, who was half drunk, caught him by the sleeve and whispered, 'She writes poetry—it is like Browning and Mrs. Browning.' Then there came a wonderful tale, repeated by Dowson himself, whether by word of mouth or by letter I do not remember. Wilde had arrived in Dieppe, and Dowson pressed upon him the necessity of acquiring 'a more wholesome taste.' They emptied their pockets on to the café table, and though there was not much, there was enough if both heaps were put into one. Meanwhile the news had spread, and they set out accompanied by a cheering crowd. Arrived at their destination, Dowson and the crowd remained outside, and presently Wilde returned. He said in a low voice to Dowson, 'The first these ten years, and it will be the last. It was like cold mutton'—always, as Henley had said, 'a scholar and a gentleman' he now remembered that the Elizabethan dramatists used the words 'Cold mutton' [40]—and then aloud so that the crowd might hear him, 'But tell it in England, for it will entirely restore my character.'

1922, 1926, 1938

JAMES JOYCE
1882–1941

Like Yeats, another truly great writer of our age, Joyce was an Irishman who had to escape from Ireland in order that his imagination might be able to cope with it. Both his life, and the literary career which that life produced and which fed back into it, were directed toward an escape from isolation into universality: in the first instance, an escape from Ireland into Europe, which in his youthful reading and studies had been an earthly paradise within, but hemmed in on all sides by narrowness, bigotry, puritanism, and gray despair. In the second instance, the journey of his imaginative life was from small forms to large, from lyric to epic, from literature to myth. His life

39. See "Lapis Lazuli."
40. Mutton was Elizabethan slang for "prostitute."

and art were so programmatically intertwined that it is hard to comment on his biography without referring to his books, particularly the earlier two, *Dubliners,* and *A Portrait of the Artist as a Young Man.* This is as he might have wished.

Joyce was born to a middle-class Dublin family somewhat come down in the world; his father, as reflected in Simon Daedalus of the autobiographical *A Portrait of the Artist as a Young Man* (1916), had been and done many things but was, like Joyce's own vision of Ireland itself, "at present a praiser of his own past." Joyce attended two Jesuit schools, Clongowes Wood School and, thereafter, Belvedere College, and at sixteen started studying at University College, Dublin, the institution for which John Henry Newman wrote *The Idea of a University.* He had rejected the possibility of entering the Jesuit order, and experienced an early vocation of another sort, a Paterian call to self-fulfillment in art. He read modern languages in college and in 1900 wrote an essay on Ibsen which earned him a certain amount of notoriety (he had learned Norwegian in order to read and correspond with this writer, who spoke so directly to the condition of an artistic temperament struggling to break free from an oppressive society).

Like Stephen Daedalus, Joyce chose "silence, exile and cunning" as his mode of action. After graduating from the university in 1902, he went to Paris, returned briefly to Dublin at his mother's death, and then left Ireland for ever. Nora Barnacle, his girl, went with him. They went to Trieste, where he taught English in a Berlitz school, and then to Zurich, where they remained until 1920. Then they moved to Paris and lived there until the fall of France in 1940, when they returned to Zurich. Although Joyce and Nora had several children, they were married only in 1931, maintaining their irregular alliance with a kind of religious devotion. From about 1917 on, Joyce was the recipient of various kinds and amounts of patronage, both in Zurich and in Paris; and his cause, as an uncommercial writer and as a kind of saint of modernism in literature, was taken up by Ezra Pound, by T. S. Eliot, and by a close and adoring circle of friends in Paris, who made of him and his work something of a cult.

Dubliners, published in 1914, was his second finished book (*Chamber Music,* early lyric poems, had appeared in 1907). It is a collection of fifteen stories, each representing some instance of a failure of self-realization on the part of an inhabitant of the city. "My intention was to write a chapter of the moral history of my country," wrote Joyce to his publisher about this book, "and I chose Dublin for the scene because the city seemed to me to be the centre of paralysis." Indeed, the opening story of the book, about a failing priest, centers on a sensitive boy's apprehension without understanding of the magical sounds of the polysyllabic "paralysis." *Dubliners* starts out in the first person, and moves into the third person narration as though to carry out in miniature Joyce's plan for developing from lyrical art through dramatic to epic —an example of the hard-edged, neo-Aristotelian conceptualizing that his Thomistic education had led him to. And yet *Dubliners* ends, ironically, in lyric: the last story, "The Dead," a summation and concentration of all that has gone before, dissolves into magnificently resonant lyric in its last paragraph.

The "Dead" of the title are all the Dubliners of the preceding stories, and they are the ghosts of the past, sharing present moments with living consciousness. Gabriel Conroy, the story's hero, is the epitome of all the failed Dubliners in that he is aware of his predicament, knows where its solution lies (in journeys eastward, toward Europe, toward all that he holds civilization to be). He is what Joyce would have been had he remained, and the story is all the more powerful for being able to reveal his sensitivity and spiritual generosity.

But Joyce did transcend the condition of his characters in *Dubliners,* and he was able, from the spiritual safety of the Continent, to write of them in a manner both brilliantly and delicately naturalistic (the actual geography and business directory of Dublin pervades these stories), but seeded with symbolic germ everywhere. Whether or not a registering consciousness is present in the story (and often, it must be the reader or even the narrator himself), the resonances of words and phrases, clichés taken literally to reveal unavowed ironies, universal themes transubstantial in the ordinary, all flare up into prominence after more than a casual reading. Joyce himself theorized about this kind of poetic revelation; like the moments of intensification Walter Pater describes, or like the revelations of the "inscapes" in Gerard Manley Hopkins, the "epiphanies" of Stephen Daedalus—Joyce's youthful self in his fiction— are like momentary rips in a gray curtain of hopelessness. In an early manuscript called *Stephen Hero* and, later, more subtly worked out in *A Portrait of the Artist as a Young Man,* Joyce led Stephen, his Gabriel Conroy, his artist-intellectual who could fly out of the labyrinth of insularity on wings of language, through his crucial years. These are years of education, and of renunciation of the status of Dubliner for that of artist.

A Portrait (published in 1916) starts out lyrically and subjectively, and its longish sections cover discontinuous tableaus in Stephen's life. Joyce named him for St. Stephen the Deacon, the first martyr, and for St. Stephen's Green, the park outside University College. Daedalus was the master craftsman of Greek myth who built the famous labyrinth for King Minos; and, to escape it, fashioned wax wings for himself and for his son, Icarus, who came to an unfortunate end when he flew too near the sun. But Stephen is not Icarus, and Simon Daedalus is not Stephen's true father, but merely his biological one. It is his quest for a true, rather than merely an actual, familial identity, which occupies the book. It moves through a youthful sentimental amour, a refusal to become a Jesuit, and a remarkable perception—at twilight along a beach where a girl is standing in the water—of the possibilities of art for transcending the narrowness and spiritual suffocation that religion has become for him and (he feels) for his country.

Yet *A Portrait* still belonged to a known genre of the novel of adolescent awakening. With the exception of his Ibsenish play, *Exiles,* and some later lyric and satiric verses, his mature work would elude easy classification. *Ulysses* and *Finnegans Wake* are both monuments of comprehensiveness; and both books, centering totally on the Dublin Joyce had fled, make of their city an *omphalos,* as Joyce called it, a navel of the world, an oracular pit from which more than Delphic prophecies emerge. Both works, purged of the relentless bitterness of Stephen's self-protectiveness, achieve grandeur through comedy, and through the kind of complexity into which Joyce's early use of symbolic and mythological association (woven into the naturalistic fabric of *Dubliners*) had expanded. In the first of these works the very boundary between naturalism and epic poetry is redrawn at every moment, as is, in the second, that between languages, ages, cultures, and identities. And both works are quintessential examples of their age in that they absorb into themselves the annotations and footnotes on what they are: glosses that, in older books, lie ranged about their texts like borders.

Ulysses is not only Joyce's masterpiece but one of the major works in the entire epic tradition as well. Its germ lay in a possible story idea for *Dubliners,* of a day in the life of a Dublin citizen, but it was put aside until after *A Portrait* was completed. *Ulysses* plants that germ in the great cyclic epic of the *Odyssey,* the Homeric poem of wandering and return, of the hero's movements through different realms and distractions back to his native land and his wife. Even in classical times the *Odyssey* had begun to be read allegorically as a vision of the journey of every man: "Man," indeed, is its opening word. And for Joyce's "man" he chose an embodied joke, an Irish Jew named Leopold Bloom. *Ulysses* is a day in his life (specifically, June 16, 1904) and in the life of Dublin, itself a provincial island city standing for the world. Just as Stephen Daedalus's mythical father, rather than Simon Daedalus, his real one, assumes importance at the end of *A Portrait,* so Bloom's own dead infant son, Rudy, is symbolically supplanted in the novel by Stephen, now returned to Ireland from abroad, as Telemachus to Bloom's Odysseus. The Penelope is an unfaithful wife, Marion Tweedy Bloom ("Molly"), and there is a daughter named Milly.

The events of the day are banal, and universal. Bloom gets up, goes to a Turkish bath, then to the funeral of a friend, Paddy Dignam, shows up at his newspaper office (where he works selling advertising), has lunch, wanders about, goes to a library, makes some purchases, encounters other people, hears some singing, goes to a pub (where he is insulted), sits at twilight along a beach (where he stares up the skirts of a girl he does not know), masturbates, visits a lying-in hospital to inquire about the birth of a friend's baby, ends up in Nighttown, in a whorehouse where at midnight he meets up with Stephen Daedalus and takes him home with him. Meanwhile his wife Molly (with whom he has not slept since Rudy's death) has been cuckolding him with one Blazes Boylan, her concert manager. Molly is a singer; and singing—and particularly opera—plays a complex and vital role in *Ulysses:* an aria from Mozart's *Don Giovanni* and a popular late-nineteenth-century song by J. L. Molloy, "Love's Old Sweet Song," run throughout the book in various ways.

The most audacious element of Joyce's triumph is the style and construction of his comic masterpiece. Each section of the book parallels an incident in Homer, and the relation of each scene to its parallel is slightly different, in a variety of parodistic ways. The first three sections involve Telemachus, and are about Stephen's morning: getting up, teaching a history class at a boys' school (parallel to Nestor's advice in Homer), and walking along the beach, wrestling in his mind with the sea and a sea of thoughts that constantly change (as with Proteus, the old man of the sea) under the grip of intellect. Bloom's day moves through other sorts of parodies: thus Circe, who transforms men into beasts, is seen as Bella Cohen, the owner of a brothel, in a great scene of transformations in which all the events of the day become actualized in forms they might have taken, as well as in those they did.

The section of *Ulysses* given below is the episode Joyce referred to as *Nausicaa,* inasmuch as it parallels the Homeric scene in which the shipwrecked Odysseus is washed up on the strand of Phaeacia, an idyllic kingdom, and is discovered by Nausicaa, the king's daughter, who has gone down to the sea with her handmaidens to wash linen and (unofficially) to play ball. Joyce's episode occurs at dusk. Its style is a hilarious parody of sentimental fiction that is, in its own nastily evasive way, pornographic; in it, the world is seen through the horrendous clichés and coy rhetoric of the bad novels that its Nausicaa, a girl named Gerty MacDowell, would have read and absorbed. Gerty has gone to the beach with her friends Cissy and Edy and their assorted infant brothers; she sees Bloom and romanticizes his tired presence. Halfway through the chapter, an amazing reversal occurs, and we are given a deflating, debunking reduction of the sentimentality in the first part by shifting to the stream-of-consciousness technique with which Bloom's thoughts have been presented to us all along. Joyce referred, half-jokingly, to the technique of the chapter as "tumescencedetumescence," by which he meant not only the literal sexual event in it (Bloom's voyeuristic excitement and his orgasm) but the inflating-deflating of the language in the two halves. It typifies the comic brilliance of the book, which consists in some measure in never totally reducing its classical prototype by comparing it with the modern, and by never showing up the modern as sleazy in comparison with the original (it is not, in fact, mock- or anti-heroic like *The Waste Land*). Throughout *Nausicaa*, the reader is probably to think of the words of the chorus of "Love's Old Sweet Song," for the whole section is, jokingly, "Just a song at twilight / When the lamps are low." If its words are the comic deflation of sentimentally conceived, vulgarized romantic love, its melody unveils Bloom's sexual and domestic loneliness —estranged from Molly, separated from Milly, not actually linked even to Martha, with whom he has been trying to start an affair—embedded in his intellectual and mythological universality.

From Dubliners

The Dead

Lily, the caretaker's daughter, was literally run off her feet. Hardly had she brought one gentleman into the little pantry behind the office on the ground floor and helped him off with his overcoat than the wheezy hall-door bell clanged again and she had to scamper along the bare hallway to let in another guest. It was well for her she had not to attend to the ladies also. But Miss Kate and Miss Julia had thought of that and had converted the bathroom upstairs into a ladies' dressing-room. Miss Kate and Miss Julia were there, gossiping and laughing and fussing, walking after each other to the head of the stairs, peering down over the banisters and calling down to Lily to ask her who had come.

It was always a great affair, the Misses Morkan's annual dance. Everybody who knew them came to it, members of the family, old friends of the family, the members of Julia's choir, any of Kate's pupils that were grown up enough and even some of Mary Jane's pupils too. Never once had it fallen flat. For years and years it had gone off in splendid style as long as anyone could remember; ever since Kate and Julia, after the death of their brother Pat, had left the house in Stoney Batter and taken Mary Jane, their only niece, to live with them in the dark gaunt house on Usher's Island,[1] the upper part of which they had rented from Mr Fulham, the corn-factor[2] on the ground floor. That was a good thirty years ago if it was a day. Mary Jane, who was then a little girl in short clothes, was now the main prop of the household for she had the organ[3] in Haddington Road. She had been through the Academy and gave a pupils' concert every year in the upper room of the Antient Concert Rooms. Many of her pupils belonged to better-class families on the Kingstown and

1. One of the banks of the Liffey, in the city itself.
2. Grain merchant.
3. Was the organist.

Dalkey line. Old as they were, her aunts also did their share. Julia, though she was quite grey, was still the leading soprano in Adam and Eve's,[4] and Kate, being too feeble to go about much, gave music lessons to beginners on the old square piano in the back room. Lily, the caretaker's daughter, did housemaid's work for them. Though their life was modest they believed in eating well; the best of everything: diamond-bone sirloins, three-shilling tea and the best bottled stout. But Lily seldom made a mistake in the orders so that she got on well with her three mistresses. They were fussy, that was all. But the only thing they would not stand was back answers.

Of course they had good reason to be fussy on such a night. And then it was long after ten o'clock and yet there was no sign of Gabriel and his wife. Besides they were dreadfully afraid that Freddy Malins might turn up screwed.[5] They would not wish for worlds that any of Mary Jane's pupils should see him under the influence; and when he was like that it was sometimes very hard to manage him. Freddy Malins always came late but they wondered what could be keeping Gabriel: and that was what brought them every two minutes to the banisters to ask Lily had Gabriel or Freddy come.

—O, Mr Conroy, said Lily to Gabriel when she opened the door for him, Miss Kate and Miss Julia thought you were never coming. Good-night, Mrs Conroy.

—I'll engage they did, said Gabriel, but they forget that my wife here takes three mortal hours to dress herself.

He stood on the mat, scraping the snow from his goloshes, while Lily led his wife to the foot of the stairs and called out:

—Miss Kate, here's Mrs Conroy.

Kate and Julia came toddling down the dark stairs at once. Both of them kissed Gabriel's wife, said she must be perished alive and asked was Gabriel with her.

—Here I am as right as the mail, Aunt Kate! Go on up. I'll follow, called out Gabriel from the dark.

He continued scraping his feet vigorously while the the three women went upstairs, laughing, to the ladies' dressing-room. A light fringe of snow lay like a cape on the shoulders of his overcoat and like toecaps on the toes of his goloshes; and, as the buttons of his overcoat slipped with a squeaking noise through the snow-stiffened frieze, a cold fragrant air from out-of-doors escaped from crevices and folds.

—Is it snowing again, Mr Conroy? asked Lily.

She had preceded him into the pantry to help him off with his overcoat. Gabriel smiled at the three syllables she had given his surname and glanced at her. She was a slim, growing girl, pale in complexion and with hay-coloured hair. The gas in the pantry made her look still paler. Gabriel had known her when she was a child and used to sit on the lowest step nursing a rag doll.

—Yes, Lily, he answered, and I think we're in for a night of it.

He looked up at the pantry ceiling, which was shaking with the stamping and shuffling of feet on the floor above, listened for a moment to the piano

4. A parish church in Dublin.
5. Drunk.

and then glanced at the girl, who was folding his overcoat carefully at the end of a shelf.

—Tell me, Lily, he said in a friendly tone, do you still go to school?

—O no, sir, she answered. I'm done schooling this year and more.

—O, then, said Gabriel gaily, I suppose we'll be going to your wedding one of these fine days with your young man, eh?

The girl glanced back at him over her shoulder and said with great bitterness:

—The men that is now is only all palaver and what they can get out of you.

Gabriel coloured as if he felt he had made a mistake and, without looking at her, kicked off his goloshes and flicked actively with his muffler at his patent-leather shoes.

He was a stout tallish young man. The high colour of his cheeks pushed upwards even to his forehead where it scattered itself in a few formless patches of pale red; and on his hairless face there scintillated restlessly the polished lenses and the bright gilt rims of the glasses which screened his delicate and restless eyes. His glossy black hair was parted in the middle and brushed in a long curve behind his ears where it curled slightly beneath the groove left by his hat.

When he had flicked lustre into his shoes he stood up and pulled his waistcoat down more tightly on his plump body. Then he took a coin rapidly from his pocket.

—O Lily, he said, thrusting it into her hands, it's Christmastime, isn't it? Just . . . here's a little. . . .

He walked rapidly towards the door.

—O no, sir! cried the girl, following him. Really, sir, I wouldn't take it.

—Christmas-time! Christmas-time! said Gabriel, almost trotting to the stairs and waving his hand to her in deprecation.

The girl, seeing that he had gained the stairs, called out after him:

—Well, thank you, sir.

He waited outside the drawing-room door until the waltz should finish, listening to the skirts that swept against it and to the shuffling of feet. He was still discomposed by the girl's bitter and sudden retort. It had cast a gloom over him which he tried to dispel by arranging his cuffs and the bows of his tie. Then he took from his waistcoat pocket a little paper and glanced at the headings he had made for his speech. He was undecided about the lines from Robert Browning for he feared they would be above the heads of his hearers. Some quotation that they could recognise from Shakespeare or from the Melodies [6] would be better. The indelicate clacking of the men's heels and the shuffling of their soles reminded him that their grade of culture differed from his. He would only make himself ridiculous by quoting poetry to them which they could not understand. They would think that he was airing his superior education. He would fail with them just as he had failed with the girl in the

6. The *Irish Melodies* of Thomas Moore (1779–1852), romantic lyrics sung throughout the 19th century ("Believe me, if all those endearing young charms," for one, is still popular today). One of them, "O Ye Dead," begins "It is true, it is true, we are shadows cold and wan; / And the fair and the brave whom we loved on earth are gone." Joyce had it in mind while writing the story.

pantry. He had taken up a wrong tone. His whole speech was a mistake from first to last, an utter failure.

Just then his aunts and his wife came out of the ladies' dressing-room. His aunts were two small plainly dressed old women. Aunt Julia was an inch or so the taller. Her hair, drawn low over the tops of her ears, was grey; and grey also, with darker shadows, was her large flaccid face. Though she was stout in build and stood erect her slow eyes and parted lips gave her the appearance of a woman who did not know where she was or where she was going. Aunt Kate was more vivacious. Her face, healthier than her sister's, was all puckers and creases, like a shrivelled red apple, and her hair, braided in the same old-fashioned way, had not lost its ripe nut colour.

They both kissed Gabriel frankly. He was their favourite nephew, the son of their dead elder sister, Ellen, who had married T. J. Conroy of the Port and Docks.

—Gretta tells me you're not going to take a cab back to Monkstown to-night, Gabriel, said Aunt Kate.

—No, said Gabriel, turning to his wife, we had quite enough of that last year, hadn't we? Don't you remember, Aunt Kate, what a cold Gretta got out of it? Cab windows rattling all the way, and the east wind blowing in after we passed Merrion. Very jolly it was. Gretta caught a dreadful cold.

Aunt Kate frowned severely and nodded her head at every word.

—Quite right, Gabriel, quite right, she said. You can't be too careful.

—But as for Gretta there, said Gabriel, she'd walk home in the snow if she were let.

Mrs Conroy laughed.

—Don't mind him, Aunt Kate, she said. He's really an awful bother, what with green shades for Tom's eyes at night and making him do the dumb-bells, and forcing Eva to eat the stirabout.[7] The poor child! And she simply hates the sight of it! . . . . O, but you'll never guess what he makes me wear now!

She broke out into a peal of laughter and glanced at her husband, whose admiring and happy eyes had been wandering from her dress to her face and hair. The two aunts laughed heartily too, for Gabriel's solicitude was a standing joke with them.

—Goloshes! said Mrs Conroy. That's the latest. Whenever it's wet underfoot I must put on my goloshes. Tonight even he wanted me to put them on, but I wouldn't. The next thing he'll buy me will be a diving suit.

Gabriel laughed nervously and patted his tie reassuringly while Aunt Kate nearly doubled herself, so heartily did she enjoy the joke. The smile soon faded from Aunt Julia's face and her mirthless eyes were directed towards her nephew's face. After a pause she asked:

—And what are goloshes, Gabriel?

—Goloshes, Julia! exclaimed her sister. Goodness me, don't you know what goloshes are? You wear them over your . . . over your boots, Gretta, isn't it?

—Yes, said Mrs Conroy. Guttapercha things. We both have a pair now. Gabriel says everyone wears them on the continent.

—O, on the continent, murmured Aunt Julia, nodding her head slowly.

7. Porridge.

Gabriel knitted his brows and said, as if he were slightly angered:

—It's nothing very wonderful but Gretta thinks it very funny because she says the word reminds her of Christy Minstrels.[8]

—But tell me, Gabriel, said Aunt Kate, with brisk tact. Of course, you've seen about the room. Gretta was saying . . .

—O, the room is all right, replied Gabriel. I've taken one in the Gresham.[9]

—To be sure, said Aunt Kate, by far the best thing to do. And the children, Gretta, you're not anxious about them?

—O, for one night, said Mrs Conroy. Besides, Bessie will look after them.

—To be sure, said Aunt Kate again. What a comfort it is to have a girl like that, one you can depend on! There's that Lily, I'm sure I don't know what has come over her lately. She's not the girl she was at all.

Gabriel was about to ask his aunt some questions on this point but she broke off suddenly to gaze after her sister who had wandered down the stairs and was craning her neck over the banisters.

—Now, I ask you, she said, almost testily, where is Julia going? Julia! Julia! Where are you going?

Julia, who had gone halfway down one flight, came back and announced blandly:

—Here's Freddy.

At the same moment a clapping of hands and a final flourish of the pianist told that the waltz had ended. The drawing-room door was opened from within and some couples came out. Aunt Kate drew Gabriel aside hurriedly and whispered into his ear:

—Slip down, Gabriel, like a good fellow and see if he's all right, and don't let him up if he's screwed. I'm sure he's screwed. I'm sure he is.

Gabriel went to the stairs and listened over the banisters. He could hear two persons talking in the pantry. Then he recognised Freddy Malins' laugh. He went down the stairs noisily.

—It's such a relief, said Aunt Kate to Mrs Conroy, that Gabriel is here. I always feel easier in my mind when he's here. . . . . Julia, there's Miss Daly and Miss Power will take some refreshment. Thanks for your beautiful waltz, Miss Daly. It made lovely time.

A tall wizen-faced man, with a stiff grizzled moustache and swarthy skin, who was passing out with his partner said:

—And may we have some refreshment, too, Miss Morkan?

—Julia, said Aunt Kate summarily, and here's Mr Browne and Miss Furlong. Take them in, Julia, with Miss Daly and Miss Power.

—I'm the man for the ladies, said Mr Browne, pursing his lips until his moustache bristled and smiling in all his wrinkles. You know, Miss Morkan, the reason they are so fond of me is—

He did not finish his sentence, but, seeing that Aunt Kate was out of earshot, at once led the three young ladies into the back room. The middle of the room was occupied by two square tables placed end to end, and on these Aunt Julia and the caretaker were straightening and smoothing a large cloth.

8. A famous blackface minstrel show troupe.
9. Not the most elegant hotel in Dublin, but comfortable and respectable.

On the sideboard were arrayed dishes and plates, and glasses and bundles of knives and forks and spoons. The top of the closed square piano served also as a sideboard for viands and sweets. At a smaller sideboard in one corner two young men were standing, drinking hop-bitters.[10]

Mr Browne led his charges thither and invited them all, in jest, to some ladies' punch, hot, strong and sweet. As they said they never took anything strong he opened three bottles of lemonade for them. Then he asked one of the young men to move aside, and, taking hold of the decanter, filled out for himself a goodly measure of whisky. The young men eyed him respectfully while he took a trial sip.

—God help me, he said, smiling, it's the doctor's orders.

His wizened face broke into a broader smile, and the three young ladies laughed in musical echo to his pleasantry, swaying their bodies to and fro, with nervous jerks of their shoulders. The boldest said:

—O, now, Mr Browne, I'm sure the doctor never ordered anything of the kind.

Mr Browne took another sip of his whisky and said, with sidling mimicry:

—Well, you see, I'm like the famous Mrs Cassidy, who is reported to have said: *Now, Mary Grimes, if I don't take it, make me take it, for I feel I want it.*

His hot face had leaned forward a little too confidentially and he had assumed a very low Dublin accent so that the young ladies, with one instinct, received his speech in silence. Miss Furlong, who was one of Mary Jane's pupils, asked Miss Daly what was the name of the pretty waltz she had played; and Mr Browne, seeing that he was ignored, turned promptly to the two young men who were more appreciative.

A red-face young woman, dressed in pansy, came into the room, excitedly clapping her hands and crying:

—Quadrilles! Quadrilles![11]

Close on her heels came Aunt Kate, crying:

—Two gentlemen and three ladies, Mary Jane!

—O, here's Mr Bergin and Mr Kerrigan, said Mary Jane. Mr Kerrigan, will you take Miss Power? Miss Furlong, may I get you a partner, Mr Bergin. O, that'll just do now.

—Three ladies, Mary Jane, said Aunt Kate.

The two young gentlemen asked the ladies if they might have the pleasure, and Mary Jane turned to Miss Daly.

—O, Miss Daly, you're really awfully good, after playing for the last two dances, but really we're so short of ladies to-night.

—I don't mind in the least, Miss Morkan.

—But I've a nice partner for you, Mr Bartell D'Arcy, the tenor. I'll get him to sing later on. All Dublin is raving about him.

—Lovely voice, lovely voice! said Aunt Kate.

As the piano had twice begun the prelude to the first figure Mary Jane led

10. A soft drink flavored with hops.

11. One of many kinds of figured dances, like reels, in which dancers pair off only temporarily, partners change, and complex groupings emerge. The "lancers" mentioned farther on is another. Square dances are country versions of the more elegant 19th-century ballroom forms.

her recruits quickly from the room. They had hardly gone when Aunt Julia wandered slowly into the room, looking behind her at something.

—What is the matter, Julia? asked Aunt Kate anxiously. Who is it?

Julia, who was carrying in a column of table-napkins, turned to her sister and said, simply, as if the question had surprised her:

—It's only Freddy, Kate, and Gabriel with him.

In fact right behind her Gabriel could be seen piloting Freddy Malins across the landing. The latter, a young man of about forty, was of Gabriel's size and build, with very round shoulders. His face was fleshy and pallid, touched with colour only at the thick hanging lobes of his ears and at the wide wings of his nose. He had coarse features, a blunt nose, a convex and receding brow, tumid and protruded lips. His heavy-lidded eyes and the disorder of his scanty hair made him look sleepy. He was laughing heartily in a high key at a story which he had been telling Gabriel on the stairs and at the same time rubbing the knuckles of his left fist backwards and forwards into his left eye.

—Good-evening, Freddy, said Aunt Julia.

Freddy Malins bade the Misses Morkan good-evening in what seemed an offhand fashion by reason of the habitual catch in his voice and then, seeing that Mr Browne was grinning at him from the sideboard, crossed the room on rather shaky legs and began to repeat in an undertone the story he had just told to Gabriel.

—He's not so bad, is he? said Aunt Kate to Gabriel.

Gabriel's brows were dark but he raised them quickly and answered:

—O no, hardly noticeable.

—Now, isn't he a terrible fellow! she said. And his poor mother made him take the pledge [12] on New Year's Eve. But come on, Gabriel, into the drawing-room.

Before leaving the room with Gabriel she signalled to Mr Browne by frowning and shaking her forefinger in warning to and fro. Mr Browne nodded in answer and, when she had gone, said to Freddy Malins:

—Now, then, Teddy, I'm going to fill you out a good glass of lemonade just to buck you up.

Freddy Malins, who was nearing the climax of his story, waved the offer aside impatiently but Mr Browne, having first called Freddy Malins' attention to a disarray in his dress, filled out and handed him a full glass of lemonade. Freddy Malins' left hand accepted the glass mechanically, his right hand being engaged in the mechanical readjustment of his dress. Mr Browne, whose face was once more wrinkling with mirth, poured out for himself a glass of whisky while Freddy Malins exploded, before he had well reached the climax of his story, in a kink of high-pitched bronchitic laughter and, setting down his untasted and overflowing glass, began to rub the knuckles of his left fist backwards and forwards into his left eye, repeating words of his last phrase as well as his fit of laughter would allow him.

Gabriel could not listen while Mary Jane was playing her Academy piece,[13] full of runs and difficult passages, to the hushed drawing-room. He liked music

12. A temperance pledge, taken by one who solemnly "swears off" drink.
13. A difficult display piece, learned as a qualifying exercise in a musical conservatory.

but the piece she was playing had no melody for him and he doubted whether it had any melody for the other listeners, though they had begged Mary Jane to play something. Four young men, who had come from the refreshment-room to stand in the doorway at the sound of the piano, had gone away quietly in couples after a few minutes. The only persons who seemed to follow the music were Mary Jane herself, her hands racing along the keyboard or lifted from it at the pauses like those of a priestess in momentary imprecation, and Aunt Kate standing at her elbow to turn the page.

Gabriel's eyes, irritated by the floor, which glittered with beeswax under the heavy chandelier, wandered to the wall above the piano. A picture of the balcony scene in *Romeo and Juliet* hung there and beside it was a picture of the two murdered princes in the Tower which Aunt Julia had worked in red, blue and brown wools when she was a girl. Probably in the school they had gone to as girls that kind of work had been taught, for one year his mother had worked for him as a birthday present a waistcoat of purple tabinet,[14] with little foxes' heads upon it, lined with brown satin and having round mulberry buttons. It was strange that his mother had had no musical talent though Aunt Kate used to call her the brains carrier of the Morkan family. Both she and Julia had always seemed a little proud of their serious and matronly sister. Her photograph stood before the pierglass.[15] She held an open book on her knees and was pointing out something in it to Constantine who, dressed in a man-o'-war suit, lay at her feet. It was she who had chosen the names for her sons for she was very sensible of the dignity of family life. Thanks to her, Constantine was now senior curate in Balbriggan and, thanks to her, Gabriel himself had taken his degree in the Royal University. A shadow passed over his face as he remembered her sullen opposition to his marriage. Some slighting phrases she had used still rankled in his memory; she had once spoken of Gretta as being country cute and that was not true of Gretta at all. It was Gretta who had nursed her during all her last long illness in their house at Monkstown.

He knew that Mary Jane must be near the end of her piece for she was playing again the opening melody with runs of scales after every bar and while he waited for the end the resentment died down in his heart. The piece ended with a trill of octaves in the treble and a final deep octave in the bass. Great applause greeted Mary Jane as, blushing and rolling up her music nervously, she escaped from the room. The most vigorous clapping came from the four young men in the doorway who had gone away to the refreshment-room at the beginning of the piece but had come back when the piano had stopped.

Lancers[16] were arranged. Gabriel found himself partnered with Miss Ivors. She was a frank-mannered talkative young lady, with a freckled face and prominent brown eyes. She did not wear a low-cut bodice and the large brooch which was fixed in the front of her collar bore on it an Irish device.

When they had taken their places she said abruptly:

—I have a crow to pluck [17] with you.

14. A kind of Irish cotton cloth, a poplin with a watered surface.
15. Tall vertical mirror, set along a wall.
16. See note 11 above.
17. The American expression would be "a bone to pick."

—With me? said Gabriel.

She nodded her head gravely.

—What is it? asked Gabriel, smiling at her solemn manner.

—Who is G. C.? answered Miss Ivors, turning her eyes upon him.

Gabriel coloured and was about to knit his brows, as if he did not understand, when she said bluntly:

—O, innocent Amy! I have found out that you write for *The Daily Express.* Now, aren't you ashamed of yourself?

—Why should I be ashamed of myself? asked Gabriel, blinking his eyes and trying to smile.

—Well, I'm ashamed of you, said Miss Ivors frankly. To say you'd write for a rag like that. I didn't think you were a West Briton.[18]

A look of perplexity appeared on Gabriel's face. It was true that he wrote a literary column every Wednesday in *The Daily Express,* for which he was paid fifteen shillings. But that did not make him a West Briton surely. The books he received for review were almost more welcome than the paltry cheque. He loved to feel the covers and turn over the pages of newly printed books. Nearly every day when his teaching in the college was ended he used to wander down the quays to the second-hand booksellers, to Hickey's on Bachelor's Walk, to Webb's or Massey's on Aston's Quay, or to O'Clohissey's in the by-street. He did not know how to meet her charge. He wanted to say that literature was above politics. But they were friends of many years' standing and their careers had been parallel, first at the University and then as teachers: he could not risk a grandiose phrase with her. He continued blinking his eyes and trying to smile and murmured lamely that he saw nothing political in writing reviews of books.

When their turn to cross had come he was still perplexed and inattentive. Miss Ivors promptly took his hand in a warm grasp and said in a soft friendly tone:

—Of course, I was only joking. Come, we cross now.

When they were together again she spoke of the University question and Gabriel felt more at ease. A friend of hers had shown her his review of Browning's poems. That was how she had found out the secret: but she liked the review immensely. Then she said suddenly:

—O, Mr Conroy, will you come for an excursion to the Aran Isles [19] this summer? We're going to stay there a whole month. It will be splendid out in the Atlantic. You ought to come. Mr Clancy is coming, and Mr Kilkelly and Kathleen Kearney. It would be splendid for Gretta too if she'd come. She's from Connacht, isn't she?

—Her people are, said Gabriel shortly.

—But you will come, won't you? said Miss Ivors, laying her warm hand eagerly on his arm.

—The fact is, said Gabriel, I have already arranged to go—

18. Meaning one whose "Irish consciousness" had not been sufficiently "raised"—*i.e.* an Irishman who still thought of himself as a subject of the United Kingdom of England and Ireland, rather than as an Irish nationalist. Miss Ivors is a tough and humorless ideologue.
19. Islands off the Galway coast, one of the few places where Gaelic was still spoken. A militant nationalist like Miss Ivors would, in her dedicated way, want to go there.

—Go where? asked Miss Ivors.

—Well, you know, every year I go for a cycling tour with some fellows and so—

—But where? asked Miss Ivors.

—Well, we usually go to France or Belgium or perhaps Germany, said Gabriel awkwardly.

—And why do you go to France and Belgium, said Miss Ivors, instead of visiting your own land?

—Well, said Gabriel, it's partly to keep in touch with the languages and partly for a change.

—And haven't you your own language to keep in touch with—Irish? asked Miss Ivors.

—Well, said Gabriel, if it comes to that, you know, Irish is not my language.

Their neighbours had turned to listen to the cross-examination. Gabriel glanced right and left nervously and tried to keep his good humour under the ordeal which was making a blush invade his forehead.

—And haven't you your own land to visit, continued Miss Ivors, that you know nothing of, your own people, and your own country?

—O, to tell you the truth, retorted Gabriel suddenly, I'm sick of my own country, sick of it!

—Why? asked Miss Ivors.

Gabriel did not answer for his retort had heated him.

—Why? repeated Miss Ivors.

They had to go visiting together and, as he had not answered her, Miss Ivors said warmly:

—Of course, you've no answer.

Gabriel tried to cover his agitation by taking part in the dance with great energy. He avoided her eyes for he had seen a sour expression on her face. But when they met in the long chain he was surprised to feel his hand firmly pressed. She looked at him from under her brows for a moment quizzically until he smiled. Then, just as the chain was about to start again, she stood on tiptoe and whispered into his ear:

—West Briton!

When the lancers were over Gabriel went away to a remote corner of the room where Freddy Malins' mother was sitting. She was a stout feeble old woman with white hair. Her voice had a catch in it like her son's and she stuttered slightly. She had been told that Freddy had come and that he was nearly all right. Gabriel asked her whether she had had a good crossing. She lived with her married daughter in Glasgow and came to Dublin on a visit once a year. She answered placidly that she had had a beautiful crossing and that the captain had been most attentive to her. She spoke also of the beautiful house her daughter kept in Glasgow, and of all the nice friends they had there. While her tongue rambled on Gabriel tried to banish from his mind all memory of the unpleasant incident with Miss Ivors. Of course the girl or woman, or whatever she was, was an enthusiast but there was a time for all things. Perhaps he ought not to have answered her like that. But she had no right to call him a West Briton before people, even in joke. She had tried to make him ridiculous before people, heckling him and staring at him with her rabbit's eyes.

He saw his wife making her way towards him through the waltzing couples. When she reached him she said into his ear:

—Gabriel, Aunt Kate wants to know won't you carve the goose as usual. Miss Daly will carve the ham and I'll do the pudding.

—All right, said Gabriel.

—She's sending in the younger ones first as soon as this waltz is over so that we'll have the table to ourselves.

—Were you dancing? asked Gabriel.

—Of course I was. Didn't you see me? What words had you with Molly Ivors?

—No words. Why? Did she say so?

—Something like that. I'm trying to get that Mr D'Arcy to sing. He's full of conceit, I think.

—There were no words, said Gabriel moodily, only she wanted me to go for a trip to the west of Ireland and I said I wouldn't.

His wife clasped her hands excitedly and gave a little jump.

—O, do go, Gabriel, she cried. I'd love to see Galway again.

—You can go if you like, said Gabriel coldly.

She looked at him for a moment, then turned to Mrs Malins and said:

—There's a nice husband for you, Mrs Malins.

While she was threading her way back across the room Mrs Malins, without adverting to the interruption, went on to tell Gabriel what beautiful places there were in Scotland and beautiful scenery. Her son-in-law brought them every year to the lakes and they used to go fishing. Her son-in-law was a splendid fisher. One day he caught a fish, a beautiful big big fish, and the man in the hotel boiled it for their dinner.

Gabriel hardly heard what she said. Now that supper was coming near he began to think again about his speech and about the quotation. When he saw Freddy Malins coming across the room to visit his mother Gabriel left the chair free for him and retired into the embrasure of the window. The room had already cleared and from the back room came the clatter of plates and knives. Those who still remained in the drawing-room seemed tired of dancing and were conversing quietly in little groups. Gabriel's warm trembling fingers tapped the cold pane of the window. How cool it must be outside! How pleasant it would be to walk out alone, first along by the river and then through the park! The snow would be lying on the branches of the trees and forming a bright cap on the top of the Wellington Monument. How much more pleasant it would be there than at the supper-table!

He ran over the headings of his speech: Irish hospitality, sad memories, the Three Graces, Paris, the quotation from Browning. He repeated to himself a phrase he had written in his review: *One feels that one is listening to a thought-tormented music.* Miss Ivors had praised the review. Was she sincere? Had she really any life of her own behind all her propagandism? There had never been any ill-feeling between them until that night. It unnerved him to think that she would be at the supper-table, looking up at him while he spoke with her critical quizzing eyes. Perhaps she would not be sorry to see him fail in his speech. An idea came into his mind and gave him courage. He would say, alluding to Aunt Kate and Aunt Julia: *Ladies and Gentlemen, the generation which is now on the wane among us may have had its faults but for my part I think it had certain qualities of hospitality, of humour, of humanity, which the new and very serious and hypereducated generation that is growing up around us seems to me to lack.* Very good: that was one for Miss Ivors. What did he care that his aunts were only two ignorant old women?

A murmur in the room attracted his attention. Mr Browne was advancing from the door, gallantly escorting Aunt Julia, who leaned upon his arm, smiling and hanging her head. An irregular musketry of applause escorted her also as far as the piano and then, as Mary Jane seated herself on the stool, and Aunt Julia, no longer smiling, half turned so as to pitch her voice fairly into the room, gradually ceased. Gabriel recognised the prelude. It was that of an old song of Aunt Julia's—*Arrayed for the Bridal.* Her voice, strong and clear in tone, attacked with great spirit the runs which embellish the air and though she sang very rapidly she did not miss even the smallest of the grace notes. To follow the voice, without looking at the singer's face, was to feel and share the excitement of swift and secure flight. Gabriel applauded loudly with all the others at the close of the song and loud applause was borne in from the invisible supper-table. It sounded so genuine that a little colour struggled into Aunt Julia's face as she bent to replace in the music-stand the old leather-bound songbook that had her initials on the cover. Freddy Malins, who had listened with his head perched sideways to hear her better, was still applauding when everyone else had ceased and talking animatedly to his mother who nodded her head gravely and slowly in acquiescence. At last, when he could clap no more, he stood up suddenly and hurried across the room to Aunt Julia whose hand he seized and held in both his hands, shaking it when words failed him or the catch in his voice proved too much for him.

—I was just telling my mother, he said, I never heard you sing so well, never. No, I never heard your voice so good as it is to-night. Now! Would you believe that now? That's the truth. Upon my word and honour that's the truth. I never heard your voice sound so fresh and so . . . so clear and fresh, never.

Aunt Julia smiled broadly and murmured something about compliments as she released her hand from his grasp. Mr Browne extended his open hand towards her and said to those who were near him in the manner of a showman introducing a prodigy to an audience:

—Miss Julia Morkan, my latest discovery!

He was laughing very heartily at this himself when Freddy Malins turned to him and said:

—Well, Browne, if you're serious you might make a worse discovery. All I can say is I never heard her sing half so well as long as I am coming here. And that's the honest truth.

—Neither did I, said Mr Browne. I think her voice has greatly improved.

Aunt Julia shrugged her shoulders and said with meek pride:

—Thirty years ago I hadn't a bad voice as voices go.

—I often told Julia, said Aunt Kate emphatically, that she was simply thrown away in that choir. But she never would be said by me.

She turned as if to appeal to the good sense of the others against a refractory child while Aunt Julia gazed in front of her, a vague smile of reminiscence playing on her face.

—No, continued Aunt Kate, she wouldn't be said or led by anyone, slaving there in that choir night and day, night and day. Six o'clock on Christmas morning! And all for what?

—Well, isn't it for the honour of God, Aunt Kate? asked Mary Jane, twisting round on the piano-stool and smiling.

Aunt Kate turned fiercely on her niece and said:

—I know all about the honour of God, Mary Jane, but I think it's not at all honourable for the pope to turn out the women out of the choirs that have slaved there all their lives and put little whipper-snappers of boys over their heads. I suppose it is for the good of the Church if the pope does it. But it's not just, Mary Jane, and it's not right.

She had worked herself into a passion and would have continued in defence of her sister for it was a sore subject with her but Mary Jane, seeing that all the dancers had come back, intervened pacifically:

—Now, Aunt Kate, you're giving scandal to Mr Browne who is of the other persuasion.[20]

Aunt Kate turned to Mr Browne, who was grinning at this allusion to his religion, and said hastily:

—O, I don't question the pope's being right. I'm only a stupid old woman and I wouldn't presume to do such a thing. But there's such a thing as common everyday politeness and gratitude. And if I were in Julia's place I'd tell that Father Healy straight up to his face . . .

—And besides, Aunt Kate, said Mary Jane, we really are all hungry and when we are hungry we are all very quarrelsome.

—And when we are thirsty we are also quarrelsome, added Mr Browne.

—So that we had better go to supper, said Mary Jane, and finish the discussion afterwards.

On the landing outside the drawing-room Gabriel found his wife and Mary Jane trying to persuade Miss Ivors to stay for supper. But Miss Ivors, who had put on her hat and was buttoning her cloak, would not stay. She did not feel in the least hungry and she had already overstayed her time.

—But only for ten minutes, Molly, said Mrs Conroy. That won't delay you.

—To take a pick itself, said Mary Jane, after all your dancing.

—I really couldn't, said Miss Ivors.

—I am afraid you didn't enjoy yourself at all, said Mary Jane hopelessly.

—Ever so much, I assure you, said Miss Ivors, but you really must let me run off now.

—But how can you get home? asked Mrs Conroy.

—O, it's only two steps up the quay.

Gabriel hesitated a moment and said:

—If you will allow me, Miss Ivors, I'll see you home if you really are obliged to go.

But Miss Ivors broke away from them.

—I won't hear of it, she cried. For goodness sake go in to your suppers and don't mind me. I'm quite well able to take care of myself.

—Well, you're the comical girl, Molly, said Mrs Conroy frankly.

20. She is saying, delicately, that he is a Protestant.

—*Beannacht libh,*[21] cried Miss Ivors, with a laugh, as she ran down the staircase.

Mary Jane gazed after her, a moody puzzled expression on her face, while Mrs Conroy leaned over the banisters to listen for the hall-door. Gabriel asked himself was he the cause of her abrupt departure. But she did not seem to be in ill humour: she had gone away laughing. He stared blankly down the staircase.

At that moment Aunt Kate came toddling out of the supper-room, almost wringing her hands in despair.

—Where is Gabriel? she cried. Where on earth is Gabriel? There's everyone waiting in there, stage to let, and nobody to carve the goose!

—Here I am, Aunt Kate! cried Gabriel, with sudden animation, ready to carve a flock of geese, if necessary.

A fat brown goose lay at one end of the table and at the other end, on a bed of creased paper strewn with sprigs of parsley, lay a great ham, stripped of its outer skin and peppered over with crust crumbs, a neat paper frill round its shin; and beside this was a round of spiced beef. Between these rival ends ran parallel lines of side-dishes: two little minsters of jelly, red and yellow; a shallow dish full of blocks of blancmange and red jam, a large green leaf-shaped dish with a stalk-shaped handle, on which lay bunches of purple raisins and peeled almonds, a companion dish on which lay a solid rectangle of Smyrna figs, a dish of custard topped with grated nutmeg, a small bowl full of chocolates and sweets wrapped in gold and silver papers and a glass vase in which stood some tall celery stalks. In the centre of the table there stood, as sentries to a fruit-stand which upheld a pyramid of oranges and American apples, two squat old-fashioned decanters of cut glass, one containing port and the other dark sherry. On the closed square piano a pudding in a huge yellow dish lay in waiting and behind it were three squads of bottles of stout and ale and minerals, drawn up according to the colours of their uniforms, the first two black, with brown and red labels, the third and smallest squad white, with transverse green sashes.

Gabriel took his seat boldly at the head of the table and, having looked to the edge of the carver, plunged his fork firmly into the goose. He felt quite at ease now for he was an expert carver and liked nothing better than to find himself at the head of a well-laden table.

—Miss Furlong, what shall I send you? he asked. A wing or a slice of the breast?

—Just a small slice of the breast.

—Miss Higgins, what for you?

—O, anything at all, Mr Conroy.

While Gabriel and Miss Daly exchanged plates of goose and plates of ham and spiced beef Lily went from guest to guest with a dish of hot floury potatoes wrapped in a white napkin. This was Mary Jane's idea and she had also suggested apple sauce for the goose but Aunt Kate had said that plain roast goose without apple sauce had always been good enough for her and she hoped she might never eat worse. Mary Jane waited on her pupils and saw that they got the best slices and Aunt Kate and Aunt Julia opened and carried across from

21. "A blessing on you" (Gaelic).

the piano bottles of stout and ale for the gentlemen and bottles of minerals for the ladies. There was a great deal of confusion and laughter and noise, the noise of orders and counter-orders, of knives and forks, of corks and glass-stoppers. Gabriel began to carve second helpings as soon as he had finished the first round without serving himself. Everyone protested loudly so that he compromised by taking a long draught of stout for he had found the carving hot work. Mary Jane settled down quietly to her supper but Aunt Kate and Aunt Julia were still toddling round the table, walking on each other's heels, getting in each other's way and giving each other unheeded orders. Mr Browne begged of them to sit down and eat their suppers and so did Gabriel but they said there was time enough so that, at last, Freddy Malins stood up and, capturing Aunt Kate, plumped her down on her chair amid general laughter.

When everyone had been well served Gabriel said, smiling:

—Now, if anyone wants a little more of what vulgar people call stuffing let him or her speak.

A chorus of voices invited him to begin his own supper and Lily came forward with three potatoes which she had reserved for him.

—Very well, said Gabriel amiably, as he took another preparatory draught, kindly forget my existence, ladies and gentlemen, for a few minutes.

He set to his supper and took no part in the conversation with which the table covered Lily's removal of the plates. The subject of talk was the opera company which was then at the Theatre Royal. Mr Bartell D'Arcy, the tenor, a dark-complexioned young man with a smart moustache, praised very highly the leading contralto of the company but Miss Furlong thought she had a rather vulgar style of production. Freddy Malins said there was a negro chieftain singing in the second part of the Gaiety pantomime [22] who had one of the finest tenor voices he had ever heard.

—Have you heard him? he asked Mr Bartell D'Arcy across the table.

—No, answered Mr Bartell D'Arcy carelessly.

—Because, Freddy Malins explained, now I'd be curious to hear your opinion of him. I think he has a grand voice.

—It takes Teddy to find out the really good things, said Mr Browne familiarly to the table.

—And why couldn't he have a voice too? asked Freddy Malins sharply. Is it because he's only a black?

Nobody answered this question and Mary Jane led the table back to the legitimate opera. One of her pupils had given her a pass for *Mignon*. Of course it was very fine, she said, but it made her think of poor Georgina Burns. Mr Browne could go back farther still, to the old Italian companies that used to come to Dublin—Tietjens, Ilma de Murzka, Campanini, the great Trebelli, Giuglini, Ravelli, Aramburo. Those were the days, he said, when there was something like singing to be heard in Dublin. He told too of how the top gallery of the old Royal used to be packed night after night, of how one night an Italian tenor had sung five encores to *Let Me Like a Soldier Fall*, introducing a high C every time, and of how the gallery boys would sometimes in their

22. In England and Ireland, a kind of formalized musical comedy, using fairy-tale plots such as that of Aladdin but with new song-and-dance routines.

enthusiasm unyoke the horses from the carriage of some great *prima donna* and pull her themselves through the streets to her hotel. Why did they never play the grand old operas now, he asked, *Dinorah, Lucrezia Borgia?* Because they could not get the voices to sing them: that was why.

—O, well, said Mr Bartell D'Arcy, I presume there are as good singers to-day as there were then.

—Where are they? asked Mr Browne defiantly.

—In London, Paris, Milan, said Mr Bartell D'Arcy warmly. I suppose Caruso, for example, is quite as good, if not better than any of the men you have mentioned.

—Maybe so, said Mr Browne. But I may tell you I doubt it strongly.

—O, I'd give anything to hear Caruso sing, said Mary Jane.

—For me, said Aunt Kate, who had been picking a bone, there was only one tenor. To please me, I mean. But I suppose none of you ever heard of him.

—Who was he, Miss Morkan? asked Mr Bartell D'Arcy politely.

—His name, said Aunt Kate, was Parkinson. I heard him when he was in his prime and I think he had then the purest tenor voice that was ever put into a man's throat.

—Strange, said Mr Bartell D'Arcy. I never even heard of him.

—Yes, yes, Miss Morkan is right, said Mr Browne. I remember hearing of old Parkinson but he's too far back for me.

—A beautiful pure sweet mellow English tenor, said Aunt Kate with enthusiasm.

Gabriel having finished, the huge pudding was transferred to the table. The clatter of forks and spoons began again. Gabriel's wife served out spoonfuls of the pudding and passed the plates down the table. Midway down they were held up by Mary Jane, who replenished them with raspberry or orange jelly or with blancmange and jam. The pudding was of Aunt Julia's making and she received praises for it from all quarters. She herself said that it was not quite brown enough.

—Well, I hope, Miss Morkan, said Mr Browne, that I'm brown enough for you because, you know, I'm all brown.

All the gentlemen, except Gabriel, ate some of the pudding out of compliment to Aunt Julia. As Gabriel never ate sweets the celery had been left for him. Freddy Malins also took a stalk of celery and ate it with his pudding. He had been told that celery was a capital thing for the blood and he was just then under doctor's care. Mrs Malins, who had been silent all through the supper, said that her son was going down to Mount Melleray in a week or so. The table then spoke of Mount Melleray, how bracing the air was down there, how hospitable the monks were and how they never asked for a penny-piece from their guests.

—And do you mean to say, asked Mr Browne incredulously, that a chap can go down there and put up there as if it were a hotel and live on the fat of the land and then come away without paying a farthing?

—O, most people give some donation to the monastery when they leave, said Mary Jane.

—I wish we had an institution like that in our Church, said Mr. Browne candidly.

He was astonished to hear that the monks never spoke, got up at two in the morning and slept in their coffins. He asked what they did it for.

—That's the rule of the order, said Aunt Kate firmly.

—Yes, but why? asked Mr Browne.

Aunt Kate repeated that it was the rule, that was all. Mr Browne still seemed not to understand. Freddy Malins explained to him, as best he could, that the monks were trying to make up for the sins committed by all the sinners in the outside world. The explanation was not very clear for Mr Browne grinned and said:

—I like that idea very much but wouldn't a comfortable spring bed do them as well as a coffin?

—The coffin, said Mary Jane, is to remind them of their last end.[23]

As the subject had grown lugubrious it was buried in a silence of the table during which Mrs Malins could be heard saying to her neighbour in an indistinct undertone:

—They are very good men, the monks, very pious men.

The raisins and almonds and figs and apples and oranges and chocolates and sweets were now passed about the table and Aunt Julia invited all the guests to have either port or sherry. At first Mr Bartell D'Arcy refused to take either but one of his neighbours nudged him and whispered something to him upon which he allowed his glass to be filled. Gradually as the last glasses were being filled the conversation ceased. A pause followed, broken only by the noise of the wine and by unsettlings of chairs. The Misses Morkan, all three, looked down at the tablecloth. Someone coughed once or twice and then a few gentlemen patted the table gently as a signal for silence. The silence came and Gabriel pushed back his chair and stood up.

The patting at once grew louder in encouragement and then ceased altogether. Gabriel leaned his ten trembling fingers on the tablecloth and smiled nervously at the company. Meeting a row of upturned faces he raised his eyes to the chandelier. The piano was playing a waltz tune and he could hear the skirts sweeping against the drawing-room door. People, perhaps, were standing in the snow on the quay outside, gazing up at the lighted windows and listening to the waltz music. The air was pure there. In the distance lay the park where the trees were weighted with snow. The Wellington Monument [24] wore a gleaming cap of snow that flashed westward over the white field of Fifteen Acres.

He began:

—Ladies and Gentlemen.

—It has fallen to my lot this evening, as in years past, to perform a very pleasing task but a task for which I am afraid my poor powers as a speaker are all too inadequate.

—No, no! said Mr Browne.

—But, however that may be, I can only ask you tonight to take the will for the deed and to lend me your attention for a few moments while I endeavour to express to you in words what my feelings are on this occasion.

23. The strangeness and resonance of the phrase ("last end" sounds either archaic or awkwardly redundant) are not lost on Gabriel: see the final paragraph of the story.

24. A tall obelisk in Phoenix Park, Dublin, unavowedly but commandingly phallic. Here it is only visualized by Gabriel; later on, we see it.

—Ladies and Gentlemen. It is not the first time that we have gathered together under this hospitable roof, around this hospitable board. It is not the
first time that we have been the recipients—or perhaps, I had better say, the
victims—of the hospitality of certain good ladies.

He made a circle in the air with his arm and paused. Everyone laughed or
smiled at Aunt Kate and Aunt Julia and Mary Jane who all turned crimson
with pleasure. Gabriel went on more boldly:

—I feel more strongly with every recurring year that our country has no
tradition which does it so much honour and which it should guard so jealously
as that of its hospitality. It is a tradition that is unique as far as my experience
goes (and I have visited not a few places abroad) among the modern nations.
Some would say, perhaps, that with us it is rather a failing than anything to
be boasted of. But granted even that, it is, to my mind, a princely failing, and
one that I trust will long be cultivated among us. Of one thing, at least, I am
sure. As long as this one roof shelters the good ladies aforesaid—and I wish
from my heart it may do so for many and many a long year to come—the tradition of genuine warm-hearted courteous Irish hospitality, which our forefathers have handed down to us and which we in turn must hand down to our
descendants, is still alive among us.

A hearty murmur of assent ran round the table. It shot through Gabriel's
mind that Miss Ivors was not there and that she had gone away discourteously:
and he said with confidence in himself:

—Ladies and Gentlemen.

—A new generation is growing up in our midst, a generation actuated by
new ideas and new principles. It is serious and enthusiastic for these new ideas
and its enthusiasm, even when it is misdirected, is, I believe, in the main sincere.
But we are living in a sceptical and, if I may use the phrase, a thought-tormented
age: and sometimes I fear that this new generation, educated or hypereducated
as it is, will lack those qualities of humanity, of hospitality, of kindly humour
which belonged to an older day. Listening to-night to the names of all those
great singers of the past it seemed to me, I must confess, that we were living
in a less spacious age. Those days might, without exaggeration, be called spacious days: and if they are gone beyond recall let us hope, at least, that in
gatherings such as this we shall still speak of them with pride and affection, still
cherish in our hearts the memory of those dead and gone great ones whose
fame the world will not willingly let die.

—Hear, hear! said Mr Browne loudly.

—But yet, continued Gabriel, his voice falling into a softer inflection, there
are always in gatherings such as this sadder thoughts that will recur to our
minds: thoughts of the past, of youth, of changes, of absent faces that we miss
here to-night. Our path through life is strewn with many such sad memories:
and were we to brood upon them always we could not find the heart to go on
bravely with our work among the living. We have all of us living duties and
living affections which claim, and rightly claim, our strenuous endeavours.

—Therefore, I will not linger on the past. I will not let any gloomy moralising
intrude upon us here to-night. Here we are gathered together for a brief moment
from the bustle and rush of our everyday routine. We are met here as friends,
in the spirit of good-fellowship, as colleagues also to a certain extent, in the true

spirit of *camaraderie*,[25] and as the guests of—what shall I call them?—the Three Graces of the Dublin musical world.

The table burst into applause and laughter at this sally. Aunt Julia vainly asked each of her neighbours in turn to tell her what Gabriel had said.

—He says we are the Three Graces, Aunt Julia, said Mary Jane.

Aunt Julia did not understand but she looked up, smiling, at Gabriel, who continued in the same vein:

—Ladies and Gentlemen.

—I will not attempt to play to-night the part that Paris played on another occasion. I will not attempt to choose between them. The task would be an invidious one and one beyond my poor powers. For when I view them in turn, whether it be our chief hostess herself, whose good heart, whose too good heart, has become a byword with all who know her, or her sister, who seems to be gifted with perennial youth and whose singing must have been a surprise and a revelation to us all to-night, or, last but not least, when I consider our youngest hostess, talented, cheerful, hard-working and the best of nieces, I confess, Ladies and Gentlemen, that I do not know to which of them I should award the prize.

Gabriel glanced down at his aunts and, seeing the large smile on Aunt Julia's face and the tears which had risen to Aunt Kate's eyes, hastened to his close. He raised his glass of port gallantly, while every member of the company fingered a glass expectantly, and said loudly:

—Let us toast them all three together. Let us drink to their health, wealth, long life, happiness and prosperity and may they long continue to hold the proud and self-won position which they hold in their profession and the position of honour and affection which they hold in our hearts.

All the guests stood up, glass in hand, and, turning towards the three seated ladies, sang in unison, with Mr Browne as leader:

> *For they are jolly gay fellows,*
> *For they are jolly gay fellows,*
> *For they are jolly gay fellows,*
> *Which nobody can deny.*

Aunt Kate was making frank use of her handkerchief and even Aunt Julia seemed moved. Freddy Malins beat time with his pudding-fork and the singers turned towards one another, as if in melodious conference, while they sang, with emphasis:

> *Unless he tells a lie,*
> *Unless he tells a lie.*

Then, turning once more towards their hostesses, they sang:

> *For they are jolly gay fellows,*
> *For they are jolly gay fellows,*
> *For they are jolly gay fellows,*
> *Which nobody can deny.*

25. Good fellowship.

The acclamation which followed was taken up beyond the door of the supper-room by many of the other guests and renewed time after time, Freddy Malins acting as officer with his fork on high.

The piercing morning air came into the hall where they were standing so that Aunt Kate said:

—Close the door, somebody. Mrs Malins will get her death of cold.

—Browne is out there, Aunt Kate, said Mary Jane.

—Browne is everywhere, said Aunt Kate, lowering her voice.

Mary Jane laughed at her tone.

—Really, she said archly, he is very attentive.

—He has been laid on here like the gas, said Aunt Kate in the same tone, all during the Christmas.

She laughed herself this time good-humouredly and then added quickly:

—But tell him to come in, Mary Jane, and close the door. I hope to goodness he didn't hear me.

At that moment the hall-door was opened and Mr Browne came in from the doorstep, laughing as if his heart would break. He was dressed in a long green overcoat with mock astrakhan cuffs and collar and wore on his head an oval fur cap. He pointed down the snow-covered quay from where the sound of shrill prolonged whistling was borne in.

—Teddy will have all the cabs in Dublin out, he said.

Gabriel advanced from the little pantry behind the office, struggling into his overcoat and, looking round the hall, said:

—Gretta not down yet?

—She's getting on her things, Gabriel, said Aunt Kate.

—Who's playing up there? asked Gabriel.

—Nobody. They're all gone.

—O no, Aunt Kate, said Mary Jane. Bartell D'Arcy and Miss O'Callaghan aren't gone yet.

—Someone is strumming at the piano, anyhow, said Gabriel.

Mary Jane glanced at Gabriel and Mr Browne and said with a shiver:

—It makes me feel cold to look at you two gentlemen muffled up like that. I wouldn't like to face your journey home at this hour.

—I'd like nothing better this minute, said Mr Browne stoutly, than a rattling fine walk in the country or a fast drive with a good spanking goer between the shafts.

—We used to have a very good horse and trap at home, said Aunt Julia sadly.

—The never-to-be-forgotten Johnny, said Mary Jane, laughing.

Aunt Kate and Gabriel laughed too.

—Why, what was wonderful about Johnny? asked Mr Browne.

—The late lamented Patrick Morkan, our grandfather, that is, explained Gabriel, commonly known in his later years as the old gentleman, was a glue-boiler.

—O, now, Gabriel, said Aunt Kate, laughing, he had a starch mill.

—Well, glue or starch, said Gabriel, the old gentleman had a horse by the name of Johnny. And Johnny used to work in the old gentleman's mill, walking round and round in order to drive the mill. That was all very well; but now comes the tragic part about Johnny. One fine day the old gentleman thought he'd like to drive out with the quality to a military review in the park.

—The Lord have mercy on his soul, said Aunt Kate compassionately.

—Amen, said Gabriel. So the old gentleman, as I said, harnessed Johnny and put on his very best tall hat and his very best stock collar and drove out in grand style from his ancestral mansion somewhere near Back Lane, I think.

Everyone laughed, even Mrs Malins, at Gabriel's manner and Aunt Kate said:

—O now, Gabriel, he didn't live in Back Lane, really. Only the mill was there.

—Out from the mansion of his forefathers, continued Gabriel, he drove with Johnny. And everything went on beautifully until Johnny came in sight of King Billy's statue: [26] and whether he fell in love with the horse King Billy sits on or whether he thought he was back again in the mill, anyhow he began to walk round the statue.

Gabriel paced in a circle round the hall in his goloshes amid the laughter of the others.

—Round and round he went, said Gabriel, and the old gentleman, who was a very pompous old gentleman, was highly indignant. *Go on, sir! What do you mean, sir? Johnny! Johnny! Most extraordinary conduct! Can't understand the horse!*

The peals of laughter which followed Gabriel's imitation of the incident were interrupted by a resounding knock at the hall-door. Mary Jane ran to open it and let in Freddy Malins. Freddy Malins, with his hat well back on his head and his shoulders humped with cold, was puffing and steaming after his exertions.

—I could only get one cab, he said.

—O, we'll find another along the quay, said Gabriel.

—Yes, said Aunt Kate. Better not keep Mrs Malins standing in the draught.

Mrs Malins was helped down the front steps by her son and Mr Browne and, after many manœuvres, hoisted into the cab. Freddy Malins clambered in after her and spent a long time settling her on the seat, Mr Browne helping him with advice. At last she was settled comfortably and Freddy Malins invited Mr Browne into the cab. There was a good deal of confused talk, and then Mr Browne got into the cab. The cabman settled his rug over his knees, and bent down for the address. The confusion grew greater and the cabman was directed differently by Freddy Malins and Mr Browne, each of whom had his head out through a window of the cab. The difficulty was to know where to drop Mr Browne along the route and Aunt Kate, Aunt Julia and Mary Jane helped the discussion from the doorstep with cross-directions and contradictions and abundance of laughter. As for Freddy Malins he was speechless with laughter. He popped his head in and out of the window every moment, to the great danger of his hat, and told his mother how the discussion was progressing till at last Mr

26. King William III (1650–1700), following Cromwell, conquered Ireland for the English for the last time at the end of the 17th century. In 1701 an equestrian statue of the King was erected in front of Trinity College. From then on, it was systematically defaced, daubed, smeared, wrecked, rebuilt, protected, and finally, in 1929, blown up, as an emblem of oppression.

Browne shouted to the bewildered cabman above the din of everybody's laughter:

—Do you know Trinity College?

—Yes, sir, said the cabman.

—Well, drive bang up against Trinity College gates, said Mr Browne, and then we'll tell you where to go. You understand now?

—Yes, sir, said the cabman.

—Make like a bird for Trinity College.

—Right, sir, cried the cabman.

The horse was whipped up and the cab rattled off along the quay amid a chorus of laughter and adieus.

Gabriel had not gone to the door with the others. He was in a dark part of the hall gazing up the staircase. A woman was standing near the top of the first flight, in the shadow also. He could not see her face but he could see the terracotta and salmonpink panels of her skirt which the shadow made appear black and white. It was his wife. She was leaning on the banisters, listening to something. Gabriel was surprised at her stillness and strained his ear to listen also. But he could hear little save the noise of laughter and dispute on the front steps, a few chords struck on the piano and a few notes of a man's voice singing.

He stood still in the gloom of the hall, trying to catch the air that the voice was singing and gazing up at his wife. There was grace and mystery in her attitude as if she were a symbol of something. He asked himself what is a woman standing on the stairs in the shadow, listening to distant music, a symbol of. If he were a painter he would paint her in that attitude. Her blue felt hat would show off the bronze of her hair against the darkness and the dark panels of her skirt would show off the light ones. *Distant Music* he would call the picture if he were a painter.[27]

The hall-door was closed; and Aunt Kate, Aunt Julia and Mary Jane came down the hall, still laughing.

—Well, isn't Freddy terrible? said Mary Jane. He's really terrible.

Gabriel said nothing but pointed up the stairs towards where his wife was standing. Now that the hall-door was closed the voice and the piano could be heard more clearly. Gabriel held up his hand for them to be silent. The song seemed to be in the old Irish tonality and the singer seemed uncertain both of his words and of his voice. The voice, made plaintive by distance and by the singer's hoarseness, faintly illuminated the cadence of the air with words expressing grief:

> *O, the rain falls on my heavy locks*
> *And the dew wets my skin,*
> *My babe lies cold . . .*

—O, exclaimed Mary Jane. It's Bartell D'Arcy singing and he wouldn't sing all the night. O, I'll get him to sing a song before he goes.

—O do, Mary Jane, said Aunt Kate.

27. This title is strikingly resonant. Not only will "The Lass of Aughrim" be that distant music (see below), but it will stand also for the general voice of the dead calling the living. Gabriel's question as to what the woman listening to the distant music symbolizes may, of course, be answered "Ireland."

Mary Jane brushed past the others and ran to the staircase but before she reached it the singing stopped and the piano was closed abruptly.

—O, what a pity! she cried. Is he coming down, Gretta?

Gabriel heard his wife answer yes and saw her come down towards them. A few steps behind her were Mr Bartell D'Arcy and Miss O'Callaghan.

—O, Mr D'Arcy, cried Mary Jane, it's downright mean of you to break off like that when we were all in raptures listening to you.

—I have been at him all the evening, said Miss O'Callaghan, and Mrs Conroy too and he told us he had a dreadful cold and couldn't sing.

—O, Mr D'Arcy, said Aunt Kate, now that was a great fib to tell.

—Can't you see that I'm as hoarse as a crow? said Mr D'Arcy roughly.

He went into the pantry hastily and put on his overcoat. The others, taken aback by his rude speech, could find nothing to say. Aunt Kate wrinkled her brows and made signs to the others to drop the subject. Mr D'Arcy stood swathing his neck carefully and frowning.

—It's the weather, said Aunt Julia, after a pause.

—Yes, everybody has colds, said Aunt Kate readily, everybody.

—They say, said Mary Jane, we haven't had snow like it for thirty years; and I read this morning in the newspapers that the snow is general all over Ireland.[28]

—I love the look of snow, said Aunt Julia sadly.

—So do I, said Miss O'Callaghan. I think Christmas is never really Christmas unless we have the snow on the ground.

—But poor Mr D'Arcy doesn't like the snow, said Aunt Kate, smiling.

Mr D'Arcy came from the pantry, fully swathed and buttoned, and in a repentant tone told them the history of his cold. Everyone gave him advice and said it was a great pity and urged him to be very careful of his throat in the night air. Gabriel watched his wife who did not join in the conversation. She was standing right under the dusty fanlight and the flame of the gas lit up the rich bronze of her hair which he had seen her drying at the fire a few days before. She was in the same attitude and seemed unaware of the talk about her. At last she turned towards them and Gabriel saw that there was colour on her cheeks and that her eyes were shining. A sudden tide of joy went leaping out of his heart.

—Mr D'Arcy, she said, what is the name of that song you were singing?

—It's called *The Lass of Aughrim*, said Mr D'Arcy, but I couldn't remember it properly. Why? Do you know it?

—*The Lass of Aughrim*, she repeated. I couldn't think of the name.

—It's a very nice air, said Mary Jane. I'm sorry you were not in voice to-night.

—Now, Mary Jane, said Aunt Kate, don't annoy Mr D'Arcy. I won't have him annoyed.

Seeing that all were ready to start she shepherded them to the door where good-night was said:

—Well, good-night, Aunt Kate, and thanks for the pleasant evening.

—Good-night, Gabriel. Good-night, Gretta!

—Good-night, Aunt Kate, and thanks ever so much. Good-night, Aunt Julia.

28. Gabriel has noticed this phrase of Mary Jane's as well: see final paragraph of story.

—O, good-night, Gretta, I didn't see you.

—Good-night, Mr D'Arcy. Good-night, Miss O'Callaghan.

—Good-night, Miss Morkan.

—Good-night, again.

—Good night, all. Safe home.

—Good-night. Good-night.

The morning was still dark. A dull yellow light brooded over the houses and the river; and the sky seemed to be descending. It was slushy underfoot; and only streaks and patches of snow lay on the roofs, on the parapets of the quay and on the area railings. The lamps were still burning redly in the murky air and, across the river, the palace of the Four Courts stood out menacingly against the heavy sky.

She was walking on before him with Mr Bartell D'Arcy, her shoes in a brown parcel tucked under one arm and her hands holding her skirt up from the slush. She had no longer any grace of attitude but Gabriel's eyes were still bright with happiness. The blood went bounding along his veins; and the thoughts went rioting through his brain, proud, joyful, tender, valorous.

She was walking on before him so lightly and so erect that he longed to run after her noiselessly, catch her by the shoulders and say something foolish and affectionate into her ear. She seemed to him so frail that he longed to defend her against something and then to be alone with her. Moments of their secret life together burst like stars upon his memory. A heliotrope envelope was lying beside his breakfast-cup and he was caressing it with his hand. Birds were twittering in the ivy and the sunny web of the curtain was shimmering along the floor: he could not eat for happiness. They were standing on the crowded platform and he was placing a ticket inside the warm palm of her glove. He was standing with her in the cold, looking in through a grated window at a man making bottles in a roaring furnace. It was very cold. Her face, fragrant in the cold air, was quite close to his; and suddenly she called out to the man at the furnace:

—Is the fire hot, sir?

But the man could not hear her with the noise of the furnace. It was just as well. He might have answered rudely.

A wave of yet more tender joy escaped from his heart and went coursing in warm flood along his arteries. Like the tender fires of stars moments of their life together, that no one knew of or would ever know of, broke upon and illumined his memory. He longed to recall to her those moments, to make her forget the years of their dull existence together and remember only their moments of ecstasy. For the years, he felt, had not quenched his soul or hers. Their children, his writing, her household cares had not quenched all their souls' tender fire. In one letter that he had written to her then he had said: *Why is it that words like these seem to me so dull and cold? Is it because there is no word tender enough to be your name?*

Like distant music these words that he had written years before were borne towards him from the past. He longed to be alone with her. When the others had gone away, when he and she were in their room in the hotel, then they would be alone together. He would call her softly:

—Gretta!

Perhaps she would not hear at once: she would be undressing. Then something in his voice would strike her. She would turn and look at him. . . .

At the corner of Winetavern Street they met a cab. He was glad of its rattling noise as it saved him from conversation. She was looking out of the window and seemed tired. The others spoke only a few words, pointing out some building or street. The horse galloped along wearily under the murky morning sky, dragging his old rattling box after his heels, and Gabriel was again in a cab with her, galloping to catch the boat, galloping to their honeymoon.

As the cab drove across O'Connell Bridge Miss O'Callaghan said:

—They say you never cross O'Connell Bridge without seeing a white horse.

—I see a white man this time, said Gabriel.

—Where? asked Mr Bartell D'Arcy.

Gabriel pointed to the statue, on which lay patches of snow. Then he nodded familiarly to it and waved his hand.

—Good-night, Dan, he said gaily.

When the cab drew up before the hotel Gabriel jumped out and, in spite of Mr Bartell D'Arcy's protest, paid the driver. He gave the man a shilling over his fare. The man saluted and said:

—A prosperous New Year to you, sir.

—The same to you, said Gabriel cordially.

She leaned for a moment on his arm in getting out of the cab and while standing at the curbstone, bidding the others good-night. She leaned lightly on his arm, as lightly as when she had danced with him a few hours before. He had felt proud and happy then, happy that she was his, proud of her grace and wifely carriage. But now, after the kindling again of so many memories, the first touch of her body, musical and strange and perfumed, sent through him a keen pang of lust. Under cover of her silence he pressed her arm closely to his side; and, as they stood at the hotel door, he felt that they had escaped from their lives and duties, escaped from home and friends and run away together with wild and radiant hearts to a new adventure.

An old man was dozing in a great hooded chair in the hall. He lit a candle in the office and went before them to the stairs. They followed him in silence, their feet falling in soft thuds on the thickly carpeted stairs. She mounted the stairs behind the porter, her head bowed in the ascent, her frail shoulders curved as with a burden, her skirt girt tightly about her. He could have flung his arms about her hips and held her still for his arms were trembling with desire to seize her and only the stress of his nails against the palms of his hands held the wild impulse of his body in check. The porter halted on the stairs to settle his guttering candle. They halted too on the steps below him. In the silence Gabriel could hear the falling of the molten wax into the tray and the thumping of his own heart against his ribs.

The porter led them along a corridor and opened a door. Then he set his unstable candle down on a toilet-table and asked at what hour they were to be called in the morning.

—Eight, said Gabriel.

The porter pointed to the tap of the electric-light and began a muttered apology but Gabriel cut him short.

—We don't want any light. We have light enough from the street. And

I say, he added, pointing to the candle, you might remove that handsome article, like a good man.

The porter took up his candle again, but slowly for he was surprised by such a novel idea. Then he mumbled good-night and went out. Gabriel shot the lock to.

A ghostly light from the street lamp lay in a long shaft from one window to the door. Gabriel threw his overcoat and hat on a couch and crossed the room towards the window. He looked down into the street in order that his emotion might calm a little. Then he turned and leaned against a chest of drawers with his back to the light. She had taken off her hat and cloak and was standing before a large swinging mirror, unhooking her waist.[29] Gabriel paused for a few moments, watching her, and then said:

—Gretta!

She turned away from the mirror slowly and walked along the shaft of light towards him. Her face looked so serious and weary that the words would not pass Gabriel's lips. No, it was not the moment yet.

—You looked tired, he said.

—I am a little, she answered.

—You don't feel ill or weak?

—No, tired: that's all.

She went on to the window and stood there, looking out. Gabriel waited again and then, fearing that diffidence was about to conquer him, he said abruptly:

—By the way, Gretta!

—What is it?

—You know that poor fellow Malins? he said quickly.

—Yes. What about him?

—Well, poor fellow, he's a decent sort of chap after all, continued Gabriel in a false voice. He gave me back that sovereign I lent him and I didn't expect it really. It's a pity he wouldn't keep away from that Browne, because he's not a bad fellow at heart.

He was trembling now with annoyance. Why did she seem so abstracted? He did not know how he could begin. Was she annoyed, too, about something? If she would only turn to him or come to him of her own accord! To take her as she was would be brutal. No, he must see some ardour in her eyes first. He longed to be master of her strange mood.

—When did you lend him the pound? she asked, after a pause.

Gabriel strove to restrain himself from breaking out into brutal language about the sottish Malins and his pound. He longed to cry to her from his soul, to crush her body against his, to overmaster her. But he said:

—O, at Christmas, when he opened that little Christmas-card shop in Henry Street.

He was in such a fever of rage and desire that he did not hear her come from the window. She stood before him for an instant, looking at him strangely. Then, suddenly raising herself on tiptoe and resting her hands lightly on his shoulders, she kissed him.

29. Shirtwaist, or blouse.

—You are a very generous person, Gabriel, she said.

Gabriel, trembling with delight at her sudden kiss and at the quaintness of her phrase, put his hands on her hair and began smoothing it back, scarcely touching it with his fingers. The washing had made it fine and brilliant. His heart was brimming over with happiness. Just when he was wishing for it she had come to him of her own accord. Perhaps her thoughts had been running with his. Perhaps she had felt the impetuous desire that was in him and then the yielding mood had come upon her. Now that she had fallen to him so easily he wondered why he had been so diffident.

He stood, holding her head between his hands. Then, slipping one arm swiftly about her body and drawing her towards him, he said softly:

—Gretta dear, what are you thinking about?

She did not answer nor yield wholly to his arm. He said again, softly:

—Tell me what it is, Gretta. I think I know what is the matter. Do I know?

She did not answer at once. Then she said in an outburst of tears:

—O, I am thinking about that song, *The Lass of Aughrim.*

She broke loose from him and ran to the bed and, throwing her arms across the bed-rail, hid her face. Gabriel stood stock-still for a moment in astonishment and then followed her. As he passed in the way of the cheval-glass [30] he caught sight of himself in full length, his broad, well-filled shirt-front, the face whose expression always puzzled him when he saw it in a mirror and his glimmering gilt-rimmed eyeglasses. He halted a few paces from her and said:

—What about the song? Why does that make you cry?

She raised her head from her arms and dried her eyes with the back of her hand like a child. A kinder note than he had intended went into his voice.

—Why, Gretta? he asked.

—I am thinking about a person long ago who used to sing that song.

—And who was the person long ago? asked Gabriel, smiling.

—It was a person I used to know in Galway when I was living with my grandmother, she said.

The smile passed away from Gabriel's face. A dull anger began to gather again at the back of his mind and the dull fires of his lust began to glow angrily in his veins.

—Someone you were in love with? he asked ironically.

—It was a young boy I used to know, she answered, named Michael Furey. He used to sing that song, *The Lass of Aughrim.*[31] He was very delicate.

Gabriel was silent. He did not wish her to think that he was interested in this delicate boy.

—I can see him so plainly, she said after a moment. Such eyes as he had: big dark eyes! And such an expression in them—an expression!

—O then, you were in love with him? said Gabriel.

—I used to go out walking with him, she said, when I was in Galway.

A thought flew across Gabriel's mind.

30. A long mirror framed so that it can tilt.
31. The song is gaining in significance. Aughrim is a village near Galway, in the west of Ireland from which Gretta comes, and away from which, spiritually, Gabriel would like to be able to move. The ballad is about a girl who drowns herself after her betrayal by one Lord Gregory who will not admit her to his house.

—Perhaps that was why you wanted to go to Galway with that Ivors girl? he said coldly.

She looked at him and asked in surprise:

—What for?

Her eyes made Gabriel feel awkward. He shrugged his shoulders and said:

—How do I know? To see him perhaps.

She looked away from him along the shaft of light towards the window in silence.

—He is dead, she said at length. He died when he was only seventeen. Isn't it a terrible thing to die so young as that?

—What was he? asked Gabriel, still ironically.

—He was in the gasworks, she said.

Gabriel felt humiliated by the failure of his irony and by the evocation of this figure from the dead, a boy in the gasworks. While he had been full of memories of their secret life together, full of tenderness and joy and desire, she had been comparing him in her mind with another. A shameful consciousness of his own person assailed him. He saw himself as a ludicrous figure, acting as a pennyboy [32] for his aunts, a nervous well-meaning sentimentalist, orating to vulgarians and idealising his own clownish lusts, the pitiable fatuous fellow he had caught a glimpse of in the mirror. Instinctively he turned his back more to the light lest she might see the shame that burned upon his forehead.

He tried to keep up his tone of cold interrogation but his voice when he spoke was humble and indifferent.

—I suppose you were in love with this Michael Furey, Gretta, he said.

—I was great with him at that time, she said.

Her voice was veiled and sad. Gabriel, feeling now how vain it would be to try to lead her whither he had purposed, caressed one of her hands and said, also sadly:

—And what did he die of so young, Gretta? Consumption, was it?

—I think he died for me, [33] she answered.

A vague terror seized Gabriel at this answer as if, at that hour when he had hoped to triumph, some impalpable and vindictive being was coming against him, gathering forces against him in its vague world. But he shook himself free of it with an effort of reason and continued to caress her hand. He did not question her again for he felt that she would tell him of herself. Her hand was warm and moist: it did not respond to his touch but he continued to caress it just as he had caressed her first letter to him that spring morning.

—It was in the winter, she said, about the beginning of the winter when I was going to leave my grandmother's and come up here to the convent. And he was ill at the time in his lodgings in Galway and wouldn't be let out and his people in Oughterard were written to. He was in decline, they said, or something like that. I never knew rightly.

She paused for a moment and sighed.

32. Toady.

33. It has already been established that he was consumptive. Joyce may be letting Gretta echo a phrase from Yeats's play *Cathleen ni Houlihan* (1902): "He died for love of me; many a man has died for love of me," in which the spirit of Ireland is speaking.

—Poor fellow, she said. He was very fond of me and he was such a gentle boy. We used to go out together, walking, you know, Gabriel, like the way they do in the country. He was going to study singing only for his health. He had a very good voice, poor Michael Furey.

—Well; and then? asked Gabriel.

—And then when it came to the time for me to leave Galway and come up to the convent he was much worse and I wouldn't be let see him so I wrote a letter saying I was going up to Dublin and would be back in the summer and hoping he would be better then.

She paused for a moment to get her voice under control and then went on:

—Then the night before I left I was in my grandmother's house in Nuns' Island, packing up, and I heard gravel thrown up against the window. The window was so wet I couldn't see so I ran downstairs as I was and slipped out the back into the garden and there was the poor fellow at the end of the garden, shivering.

—And did you not tell him to go back? asked Gabriel.

—I implored of him to go home at once and told him he would get his death in the rain. But he said he did not want to live. I can see his eyes as well as well! He was standing at the end of the wall where there was a tree.

—And did he go home? asked Gabriel.

—Yes, he went home. And when I was only a week in the convent he died and he was buried in Oughterard where his people came from. O, the day I heard that, that he was dead!

She stopped, choking with sobs, and, overcome by emotion, flung herself face downward on the bed, sobbing in the quilt. Gabriel held her hand for a moment longer, irresolutely, and then, shy of intruding on her grief, let it fall gently and walked quietly to the window.

She was fast asleep.

Gabriel, leaning on his elbow, looked for a few moments unresentfully on her tangled hair and half-open mouth, listening to her deep-drawn breath. So she had had that romance in her life: a man had died for her sake. It hardly pained him now to think how poor a part he, her husband, had played in her life. He watched her while she slept as though he and she had never lived together as man and wife. His curious eyes rested long upon her face and on her hair: and, as he thought of what she must have been then, in that time of her first girlish beauty, a strange friendly pity for her entered his soul. He did not like to say even to himself that her face was no longer beautiful but he knew that it was no longer the face for which Michael Furey had braved death.

Perhaps she had not told him all the story.[34] His eyes moved to the chair over which she had thrown some of her clothes. A petticoat string dangled to the floor. One boot stood upright, its limp upper fallen down: the fellow of it lay upon its side. He wondered at his riot of emotions of an hour before. From what had it proceeded? From his aunt's supper, from his own foolish speech, from the wine and dancing, the merry-making when saying good-night in the hall, the pleasure of the walk along the river in the snow. Poor Aunt

34. With almost a cinematic technique, the transition from this feeling of jealous doubt (had Gretta ever slept with Michael Furey?) dissolves into an erotic image of underclothes flung across a chair, an empty boot, and such items.

Julia! She too, would soon be a shade with the shade of Patrick Morkan and his horse. He had caught that haggard look upon her face for a moment when she was singing *Arrayed for the Bridal*.[35] Soon, perhaps, he would be sitting in that same drawing-room, dressed in black, his silk hat on his knees. The blinds would be drawn down and Aunt Kate would be sitting beside him, crying and blowing her nose and telling him how Julia had died. He would cast about in his mind for some words that might console her, and would find only lame and useless ones. Yes, yes: that would happen very soon.

The air of the room chilled his shoulders. He stretched himself cautiously along under the sheets and lay down beside his wife. One by one they were all becoming shades. Better pass boldly into that other world, in the full glory of some passion, than fade and wither dismally with age. He thought of how she who lay beside him had locked in her heart for so many years that image of her lover's eyes when he had told her that he did not wish to live.

Generous tears filled Gabriel's eyes. He had never felt like that himself towards any woman but he knew that such a feeling must be love. The tears gathered more thickly in his eyes and in the partial darkness he imagined he saw the form of a young man standing under a dripping tree. Other forms were near. His soul had approached that region where dwell the vast hosts of the dead. He was conscious of, but could not apprehend, their wayward and flickering existence. His own identity was fading out into a grey impalpable world: the solid world itself which these dead had one time reared and lived in was dissolving and dwindling.

A few light taps upon the pane made him turn to the window. It had begun to snow again. He watched sleepily the flakes, silver and dark, falling obliquely against the lamplight. The time had come for him to set out on his journey westward.[36] Yes, the newspapers were right: snow was general all over Ireland. It was falling on every part of the dark central plain, on the treeless hills, falling softly upon the Bog of Allen and, farther westward, softly falling into the dark mutinous Shannon waves. It was falling, too, upon every part of the lonely churchyard on the hill where Michael Furey lay buried. It lay thickly drifted on the crooked crosses and headstones, on the spears of the little gate, on the barren thorns. His soul swooned slowly as he heard the snow falling faintly through the universe and faintly falling, like the descent of their last end, upon all the living and the dead.

1906–7　　　　　　　　　　　　　　　　　　　　　　　　　　　1914

---

35. What is unstated involves his perception of how Aunt Julia was never arrayed for any bridal, and of how the phrase modulates into "arrayed for the burial."
36. To Connaught, to Gretta's home town. But more than that, a journey of renewal in his insularity, of affiliation with the dead around him, both literal and figurative dead who, in this last great paragraph of lyrical dissolution, are becoming each other. The snow that has lurked in the corners of the story now emerges openly and symbolically. Mary Jane's remembered phrases are now recomposed into their true meanings, and lyric permutations of phrase and syntax bring the story to a close in a moment of compensatory beauty and expansion of feeling.

From A Portrait of the Artist as a Young Man

[Stephen's Epiphany]

He turned seaward [1] from the road at Dollymount and as he passed on to the thin wooden bridge he felt the planks shaking with the tramp of heavily shod feet. A squad of christian brothers was on its way back from the Bull and had begun to pass, two by two, across the bridge. Soon the whole bridge was trembling and resounding. The uncouth faces passed him two by two, stained yellow or red or livid by the sea, and as he strove to look at them with ease and indifference, a faint stain of personal shame and commiseration rose to his own face. Angry with himself he tried to hide his face from their eyes by gazing down sideways into the shallow swirling water under the bridge but he still saw a reflection therein of their topheavy silk hats, and humble tapelike collars and loosely hanging clerical clothes.

—Brother Hickey.

Brother Quaid.

Brother MacArdle.

Brother Keogh.

Their piety would be like their names, like their faces, like their clothes, and it was idle for him to tell himself that their humble and contrite hearts,[2] it might be, paid a far richer tribute of devotion than his had ever been, a gift tenfold more acceptable than his elaborate adoration. It was idle for him to move himself to be generous towards them, to tell himself that if he ever came to their gates, stripped of his pride, beaten and in beggar's weeds, that they would be generous towards him, loving him as themselves. Idle and embittering, finally, to argue, against his own dispassionate certitude, that the commandment of love bade us not to love our neighbour as ourselves with the same amount and intensity of love but to love him as ourselves with the same kind of love.

He drew forth a phrase from his treasure and spoke it softly to himself:

—A day of dappled seaborne clouds.

The phrase and the day and the scene harmonised in a chord. Words. Was it their colours? He allowed them to glow and fade, hue after hue: sunrise gold, the russet and green of apple orchards, azure of waves, the greyfringed fleece of clouds. No, it was not their colours: it was the poise and balance of the period itself. Did he then love the rhythmic rise and fall of words better than their associations of legend and colour? Or was it that, being as weak of sight as he was shy of mind, he drew less pleasure from the reflection of the glowing sensible world through the prism of a language manycoloured and richly storied than from the contemplation of an inner world of individual emotions mirrored perfectly in a lucid supple periodic prose?

1. In the previous section Stephen Daedalus has just declined an invitation to prepare himself to enter the Jesuit community. Still asking himself why he had refused, he sets out on a walk along a seawall on Dublin Bay. "The Bull" is the spit of land along which that wall is built.

2. The reference may be to the priest's prayer "In a humble spirit and contrite heart," in the Offertory of the mass, or to its source in Isaiah 57:15: ". . . to revive the spirit of the humble, and to revive the heart of the contrite ones"; or, possibly and more ironically, to its echo in Kipling's "Recessional" (1897): "Still stands Thine ancient sacrifice, / An humble and a contrite heart."

He passed from the trembling bridge on to firm land again. At that instant, as it seemed to him, the air was chilled and looking askance towards the water he saw a flying squall darkening and crisping suddenly the tide. A faint click at his heart, a faint throb in his throat told him once more of how his flesh dreaded the cold infrahuman odour of the sea: yet he did not strike across the downs on his left but held straight on along the spine of rocks that pointed against the river's mouth.

A veiled sunlight lit up faintly the grey sheet of water where the river was embayed. In the distance along the course of the slowflowing Liffey [3] slender masts flecked the sky and, more distant still, the dim fabric of the city lay prone in haze. Like a scene on some vague arras, old as man's weariness, the image of the seventh city of christendom [4] was visible to him across the timeless air, no older nor more weary nor less patient of subjection than in the days of the thingmote.[5]

Disheartened, he raised his eyes towards the slowdrifting clouds, dappled and seaborne. They were voyaging across the deserts of the sky, a host of nomads on the march, voyaging high over Ireland, westward bound. The Europe they had come from lay out there beyond the Irish Sea, Europe of strange tongues and valleyed and woodbegirt and citadelled and of entrenched and marshalled races. He heard a confused music within him as of memories and names which he was almost conscious of but could not capture even for an instant; then the music seemed to recede, to recede, to recede: and from each receding trail of nebulous music there fell always one longdrawn calling note, piercing like a star the dusk of silence. Again! Again! Again! A voice from beyond the world was calling.

—Hello, Stephanos!

—Here comes The Dedalus!

—Ao! . . . Eh, give it over, Dwyer, I'm telling you or I'll give you a stuff in the kisser for yourself. . . . Ao!

—Good man, Towser! Duck him!

—Come along, Dedalus! Bous Stephanoumenos! Bous Stephaneforos! [6]

—Duck him! Guzzle him now, Towser!

—Help! Help! . . . Ao!

He recognised their speech collectively before he distinguished their faces. The mere sight of that medley of wet nakedness chilled him to the bone. Their bodies, corpsewhite or suffused with a pallid golden light or rawly tanned by the suns, gleamed with the wet of the sea. Their divingstone, poised on its rude supports and rocking under their plunges, and the roughhewn stones of the sloping breakwater over which they scrambled in their horseplay, gleamed with cold wet lustre. The towels with which they smacked their bodies were heavy with cold seawater: and drenched with cold brine was their matted hair.

He stood still in deference to their calls and parried their banter with easy

3. The river flowing through Dublin, its Thames, its Tiber. Joyce mythologizes the Liffey in *Finnegans Wake* as the great mothering entity.

4. Dublin.

5. Ancient Danish governmental council; in the 9th and 10th centuries parts of Ireland as well as of England were under Danish occupation.

6. In Greek, *stephanos* means "crown," and *bous,* "ox"; the phrases mean "garlanded ox" —*i.e.* crowned for a sacrifice.

words. How characterless they looked: Shuley without his deep unbuttoned collar, Ennis without his scarlet belt with the snaky clasp, and Connolly without his Norfolk coat [7] with the flapless sidepockets! It was a pain to see them and a swordlike pain to see the signs of adolescence that made repellent their pitiable nakedness. Perhaps they had taken refuge in number and noise from the secret dread in their souls. But he, apart from them and in silence, remembered in what dread he stood of the mystery of his own body.

—Stephanos Dedalos! Bous Stephanoumenos! Bous Stephaneforos!

Their banter was not new to him and now it flattered his mild proud sovereignty. Now, as never before, his strange name seemed to him a prophecy.[8] So timeless seemed the grey warm air, so fluid and impersonal his own mood, that all ages were as one to him. A moment before the ghost of the ancient kingdom of the Danes had looked forth through the vesture of the hazewrapped city. Now, at the name of the fabulous artificer,[9] he seemed to hear the noise of dim waves and to see a winged form flying above the waves and slowly climbing the air. What did it mean? Was it a quaint device opening a page of some medieval book of prophecies and symbols, a hawklike man flying sunward above the sea, a prophecy of the end he had been born to serve and had been following through the mists of childhood and boyhood, a symbol of the artist forging anew in his workshop out of the sluggish matter of the earth a new soaring impalpable imperishable being?

His heart trembled; his breath came faster and a wild spirit passed over his limbs as though he were soaring sunward. His heart trembled in an ecstasy of fear and his soul was in flight. His soul was soaring in an air beyond the world and the body he knew was purified in a breath and delivered of incertitude and made radiant and commingled with the element of the spirit. An ecstasy of flight made radiant his eyes and wild his breath and tremulous and wild and radiant his windswept limbs.

—One! Two! . . . Look out!

—O, cripes, I'm drownded!

—One! Two! Three and away!

—Me next! Me next!

—One! . . . Uk!

—Stephaneforos!

His throat ached with a desire to cry aloud, the cry of a hawk or eagle on high, to cry piercingly of his deliverance to the winds. This was the call of

7. A fashionable jacket, belted in back.

8. Throughout this book the strangeness of Stephen's name has passed without comment (as, in the earlier pages, has that of an aunt named "Dante"). Here, at the point where Stephen is struck by the possible hidden significance of his name, Joyce tacitly alludes to a great heroic tradition, in which the hero receives a new name, or discovers his actual one. Thus, Jacob wrestles with an angel and becomes "Israel"; John Little fights with Robin Hood and becomes "Little John"; Redcross fights with a dragon in Book I of *The Faerie Queene* and becomes St. George.

9. Stephen's true father, he feels, is not his actual father, Simon Daedalus, but the more real mythological figure, the Daedalus of antiquity. This phrase comes up again at the very end of the book, when, in one of the most famous passages of dedicated resolve in modern literature, Stephen notes in his journal as he sets off for Europe and freedom: "I go to encounter for the millionth time the reality of experience and to forge in the smithy of my soul the uncreated conscience of my race. . . . Old father, old artificer, stand me now and ever in good stead."

life to his soul not the dull gross voice of the world of duties and despair, not the inhuman voice that had called him to the pale service of the altar. An instant of wild flight had delivered him and the cry of triumph which his lips withheld cleft his brain.

—Stephaneforos!

What were they now but cerements [10] shaken from the body of death—the fear he had walked in night and day, the incertitude that had ringed him round, the shame that had abased him within and without—cerements, the linens of the grave?

His soul had arisen from the grave of boyhood, spurning her graveclothes. Yes! Yes! Yes! He would create proudly out of the freedom and power of his soul, as the great artificer whose name he bore, a living thing, new and soaring and beautiful, impalpable, imperishable.

He started up nervously from the stoneblock for he could no longer quench the flame in his blood. He felt his cheeks aflame and his throat throbbing with song. There was a lust of wandering in his feet that burned to set out for the ends of the earth. On! On! his heart seemed to cry. Evening would deepen above the, sea, night fall upon the plains, dawn glimmer before the wanderer and show him strange fields and hills and faces. Where?

He looked northward towards Howth. The sea had fallen below the line of seawrack on the shallow side of the breakwater and already the tide was running out fast along the foreshore. Already one long oval bank of sand lay warm and dry amid the wavelets. Here and there warm isles of sand gleamed above the shallow tide, and about the isles and around the long bank and amid the shallow currents of the beach were lightclad gayclad figures, wading and delving.

In a few moments he was barefoot, his stockings folded in his pockets and his canvas shoes dangling by their knotted laces over his shoulders: and, picking a pointed salteaten stick out of the jetsam among the rocks, he clambered down the slope of the breakwater.

There was a long rivulet in the strand: and, as he waded slowly up its course, he wondered at the endless drift of seaweed. Emerald and black and russet and olive, it moved beneath the current, swaying and turning. The water of the rivulet was dark with endless drift and mirrored the high-drifting clouds. The clouds were drifting above him silently and silently the seatangle was drifting below him; and the grey warm air was still: and a new wild life was singing in his veins.

Where was his boyhood now? Where was the soul that had hung back from her destiny, to brood alone upon the shame of her wounds and in her house of squalor and subterfuge to queen it in faded cerements and in wreaths that withered at the touch? Or where was he?

He was alone. He was unheeded, happy and near to the wild heart of life. He was alone and young and wilful and wildhearted, alone amid a waste of wild air and brackish waters and the seaharvest of shells and tangle and veiled grey sunlight and gayclad lightclad figures, of children and girls and voices childish and girlish in the air.

10. Waxed cloth used for wrapping corpses.

A girl stood before him in midstream, alone and still, gazing out to sea. She seemed like one whom magic had changed into the likeness of a strange and beautiful seabird. Her long slender bare legs were delicate as a crane's and pure save where an emerald trail of seaweed had fashioned itself as a sign upon the flesh. Her thighs, fuller and softhued as ivory, were bared almost to the hips where the white fringes of her drawers were like featherings of soft white down. Her slateblue skirts were kilted boldly about her waist and dovetailed behind her. Her bosom was as a bird's soft and slight, slight and soft as the breast of some darkplumaged dove. But her long fair hair was girlish: and girlish, and touched with the wonder mortal beauty, her face.

She was alone and still, gazing out to sea; and when she felt his presence and the worship of his eyes her eyes turned to him in quiet sufferance of his gaze, without shame or wantonness. Long, long she suffered his gaze and then quietly withdrew her eyes from his and bent them towards the stream, gently stirring the water with her foot hither and thither. The first faint noise of gently moving water broke the silence, low and faint and whispering, faint as the bells of sleep; hither and thither, hither and thither: and a faint flame trembled on her cheek.

—Heavenly God! cried Stephen's soul, in an outburst of profane joy.

He turned away from her suddenly and set off across the strand. His cheeks were aflame; his body was aglow; his limbs were trembling. On and on and on and on he strode, far out over the sands, singing wildly to the sea, crying to greet the advent of the life that had cried to him.

Her image had passed into his soul for ever and no word had broken the holy silence of his ecstasy. Her eyes had called him and his soul had leaped at the call. To live, to err, to fall, to triumph, to recreate life out of life! A wild angel had appeared to him, the angel of mortal youth and beauty, an envoy from the fair courts of life, to throw open before him in an instant of ecstasy the gates of all the ways of error and glory. On and on and on and on!

He halted suddenly and heard his heart in the silence. How far had he walked? What hour was it?

There was no human figure near him nor any sound borne to him over the air. But the tide was near the turn and already the day was on the wane. He turned landward and ran towards the shore and, running up the sloping beach, reckless of the sharp shingle, found a sandy nook amid a ring of tufted sand-knolls and lay down there that the peace and silence of the evening might still the riot of his blood.

He felt above him the vast indifferent dome and the calm processes of the heavenly bodies; and the earth beneath him, the earth that had borne him, had taken him to her breast.

He closed his eyes in the languor of sleep. His eyelids trembled as if they felt the vast cyclic movement of the earth and her watchers, trembled as if they felt the strange light of some new world. His soul was swooning into some new world,[11] fantastic, dim, uncertain as under sea, traversed by cloudy

11. At the peak of this visual epiphany of the girl in the water, which complements the aural epiphany of his own name, Stephen "swoons" very much as Gabriel Conroy does, in an overwhelming surge of spiritual generosity, in which subject and object merge, out-lines are blurred by feeling, and a total spiritual fulfillment is glimpsed.

shapes and beings. A world, a glimmer, or a flower? Glimmering and trembling, trembling and unfolding, a breaking light, an opening flower, it spread in endless succession to itself, breaking in full crimson and unfolding and fading to palest rose, leaf by leaf and wave of light by wave of light, flooding all the heavens with its soft flushes, every flush deeper than other.

Evening had fallen when he woke and the sand and arid grasses of his bed glowed no longer. He rose slowly and, recalling the rapture of his sleep, sighed at its joy.

He climbed to the crest of the sandhill and gazed about him. Evening had fallen. A rim of the young moon cleft the pale waste of sky like the rim of a silver hoop embedded in grey sand; and the tide was flowing in fast to the land with a low whisper of her waves, islanding a few last figures in distant pools.

[Stephen's Poem [12]]

Towards dawn he awoke. O what sweet music! His soul was all dewy wet. Over his limbs in sleep pale cool waves of light had passed. He lay still, as if his soul lay amid cool waters, conscious of faint sweet music. His mind was waking slowly to a tremulous morning knowledge, a morning inspiration. A spirit filled him, pure as the purest water, sweet as dew, moving as music. But how faintly it was inbreathed, how passionlessly, as if the seraphim themselves were breathing upon him! His soul was waking slowly, fearing to awake wholly. It was that windless hour of dawn when madness wakes and strange plants open to the light and the moth flies forth silently.

An enchantment of the heart! The night had been enchanted. In a dream or vision he had known the ecstasy of seraphic life. Was it an instant of enchantment only or long hours and days and years and ages?

The instant of inspiration seemed now to be reflected from all sides at once from a multitude of cloudy circumstance of what had happened or of what might have happened. The instant flashed forth like a point of light and now from cloud on cloud of vague circumstance confused form was veiling softly its afterglow. O! In the virgin womb of the imagination the word was made flesh. Gabriel the seraph had come to the virgin's chamber. An afterglow deepened within his spirit, whence the white flame had passed, deepening to a rose and ardent light. That rose and ardent light was her strange wilful heart, strange that no man had known or would know, wilful from before the beginning of the world: and lured by that ardent roselike glow the choirs of the seraphim were falling from heaven.

> *Are you not weary of ardent ways,*
> *Lure of the fallen seraphim?*
> *Tell no more of enchanted days.*

The verses passed from his mind to his lips and, murmuring them over, he felt the rhythmic movement of a villanelle [13] pass through them. The roselike

---

12. In this section we observe and overhear the inner creative processes as Stephen writes a lyric and observes himself as he is writing.
13. The originally French lyric form (featuring repeated refrain lines), as exemplified by Stephen's poem, was used by Victorian poets for easy sentimental effects. But see the way William Empson and Dylan Thomas manipulate the form (below).

glow sent forth its rays of rhyme; ways, days, blaze, praise, raise. Its rays burned up the world, consumed the hearts of men and angels: the rays from the rose that was her wilful heart.

> *Your eyes have set man's heart ablaze*
> *And you have had your will of him.*
> *Are you not weary of ardent ways?*

And then? The rhythm died away, ceased, began again to move and beat. And then? Smoke, incense ascending from the altar of the world.

> *Above the flame the smoke of praise*
> *Goes up from ocean rim to rim.*
> *Tell no more of enchanted days.*

Smoke went up from the whole earth, from the vapoury oceans, smoke of her praise. The earth was like a swinging smoking swaying censer, a ball of incense, an ellipsoidal ball. The rhythm died out at once; the cry of his heart was broken. His lips began to murmur the first verses over and over; then went on stumbling through half verses, stammering and baffled; then stopped. The heart's cry was broken.

The veiled windless hour had passed and behind the panes of the naked window the morning light was gathering. A bell beat faintly very far away. A bird twittered; two birds, three. The bell and the bird ceased: and the dull white light spread itself east and west, covering the world, covering the rose-light in his heart.

Fearing to lose all, he raised himself suddenly on his elbow to look for paper and pencil. There was neither on the table; only the soupplate he had eaten the rice from for supper and the candlestick with its tendrils of tallow and its paper socket, singed by the last flame. He stretched his arm wearily towards the foot of the bed, groping with his hand in the pockets of the coat that hung there. His fingers found a pencil and then a cigarette packet. He lay back and, tearing open the packet, placed the last cigarette on the windowledge and began to write out the stanzas of the villanelle in small neat letters on the rough cardboard surface.

Having written them out he lay back on the lumpy pillow, murmuring them again. The lumps of knotted flock under his head reminded him of the lumps of knotted horsehair in the sofa of her parlour on which he used to sit, smiling or serious, asking himself why he had come, displeased with her and with himself, confounded by the print of the Sacred Heart above the untenanted sideboard. He saw her approach him in a lull of the talk and beg him to sing one of his curious songs. Then he saw himself sitting at the old piano, striking chords softly from its speckled keys and singing, amid the talk which had risen again in the room, to her who leaned beside the mantlepiece a dainty song of the Elizabethans, a sad and sweet loth to depart,[14] the victory chant of Agincourt, the happy air of Greensleeves. While he sang and she listened,

14. A "Loth to Depart" was a kind of Elizabethan keyboard piece based on a song form. All the pieces mentioned might be found in some late 19th-century collection of musical antiquities arranged for piano.

or feigned to listen, his heart was at rest but when the quaint old songs had ended and he heard again the voices in the room he remembered his own sarcasm: the house where young men are called by their christian names a little too soon.

At certain instants her eyes seemed about to trust him but he had waited in vain. She passed now dancing lightly across his memory as she had been that night at the carnival ball, her white dress a little lifted, a white spray nodding in her hair. She danced lightly in the round. She was dancing towards him and, as she came, her eyes were a little averted and a faint glow was on her cheek. At the pause in the chain of hands her hand had lain in his an instant, a soft merchandise.

—You are a great stranger now.

—Yes. I was born to be a monk.

—I am afraid you are a heretic.

—Are you much afraid?

For answer she had danced away from him along the chain of hands, dancing lightly and discreetly, giving herself to none. The white spray nodded to her dancing and when she was in shadow the glow was deeper on her cheek.

A monk! His own image started forth a profaner of the cloister, a heretic Franciscan, willing and willing not to serve, spinning like Gherardino da Borgo San Donnino,[15] a lithe web of sophistry and whispering in her ear.

No, it was not his image. It was like the image of the young priest in whose company he had seen her last, looking at him out of dove's eyes, toying with the pages of her Irish phrase-book.

—Yes, yes, the ladies are coming round to us. I can see it every day. The ladies are with us. The best helpers the language has.

—And the church, Father Moran?

—The church too. Coming round too. The work is going ahead there too. Don't fret about the church.

Bah! he had done well to leave the room in disdain. He had done well not to salute her on the steps of the library. He had done well to leave her to flirt with her priest, to toy with a church which was the scullerymaid of christendom.

Rude brutal anger routed the last lingering instant of ecstasy from his soul. It broke up violently her fair image and flung the fragments on all sides. On all sides distorted reflections of her image started from his memory: the flower-girl in the ragged dress with damp coarse hair and a hoyden's face who had called herself his own girl and begged his handsel,[16] the kitchengirl in the next house who sang over the clatter of her plates with the drawl of a country singer the first bars of *By Killarney's Lakes and Fells*, a girl who had laughed gaily to see him stumble when the iron grating in the footpath near Cork Hill had caught the broken sole of his shoe, a girl he had glanced at, attracted by her small ripe mouth as she passed out of Jacob's biscuit factory, who had cried to him over her shoulder:

15. A 13th-century Franciscan spiritual, follower of the Cistercian Joachim of Fiore (1132–1202) who had founded a group whose views of the absolute poverty of Christ were later declared heretical. Gherardino published Joachim's writings and developed his doctrines, which Stephen would have been taught to distrust.

16. Gift (price paid for a girl).

—Do you like what you seen of me, straight hair and curly eyebrows?

And yet he felt that, however he might revile and mock her image, his anger was also a form of homage. He had left the classroom in disdain that was not wholly sincere, feeling that perhaps the secret of her race lay behind those dark eyes upon which her long lashes flung a quick shadow. He had told himself bitterly as he walked through the streets that she was a figure of the womanhood of her country, a batlike soul waking to the consciousness of itself in darkness and secrecy and loneliness, tarrying awhile, loveless and sinless, with her mild lover and leaving him to whisper of innocent transgressions in the latticed ear of a priest.[17] His anger against her found vent in coarse railing at her paramour, whose name and voice and features offended his baffled pride: a priested peasant, with a brother a policeman in Dublin and a brother a potboy in Moycullen. To him she would unveil her soul's shy nakedness, to one who was but schooled in the discharging of a formal rite rather than to him, a priest of eternal imagination, transmuting the daily bread of experience into the radiant body of everliving life.

The radiant image of the eucharist united again in an instant his bitter and despairing thoughts, their cries arising unbroken in a hymn of thanksgiving.

> *Our broken cries and mournful lays*
> *Rise in one eucharistic hymn.*
> *Are you not weary of ardent ways?*

> *While sacrificing hands upraise*
> *The chalice flowing to the brim,*
> *Tell no more of enchanted days.*

He spoke the verses aloud from the first lines till the music and rhythm suffused his mind, turning it to quiet indulgence; then copied them painfully to feel them the better by seeing them; then lay back on his bolster.

The full morning light had come. No sound was to be heard: but he knew that all around him life was about to awaken in common noises, hoarse voices, sleepy prayers. Shrinking from that life he turned towards the wall, making a cowl of the blanket and staring at the great overblown scarlet flowers of the tattered wallpaper. He tried to warm his perishing joy in their scarlet glow, imagining a roseway from where he lay upwards to heaven all strewn with scarlet flowers. Weary! Weary! He too was weary of ardent ways.

A gradual warmth, a languorous weariness passed over him, descending along his spine from his closely cowled head. He felt it descend and, seeing himself as he lay, smiled. Soon he would sleep.

He had written verses for her again after ten years. Ten years before she had worn her shawl cowlwise about her head, sending sprays of her warm breath into the night air, tapping her foot upon the glassy road. It was the last tram; the lank brown horses knew it and shook their bells to the clear night in admonition. The conductor talked with the driver, both nodding often in the green light of the lamp. They stood on the steps of the tram, he on the upper, she on the lower. She came up to his step many times between their phrases

17. I.e. in the confessional, in which a curtained grille separates priest from penitent to preserve penitent's anonymity.

and went down again and once or twice remained beside him forgetting to go down and then went down. Let be! Let be!

Ten years from that wisdom of children to his folly. If he sent her the verses? They would be read out at breakfast amid the tapping of eggshells. Folly indeed! The brothers would laugh and try to wrest the page from each other with their strong hard fingers. The suave priest, her uncle, seated in his armchair, would hold the page at arm's length, read it smiling and approve of the literary form.

No, no: that was folly. Even if he sent her the verses she would not show them to others. No, no: she could not.

He began to feel that he had wronged her. A sense of her innocence moved him almost to pity her, an innocence he had never understood till he had come to the knowledge of it through sin, an innocence which she too had not understood while she was innocent or before the strange humiliation of her nature had first come upon her. Then first her soul had begun to live as his soul had when he had first sinned: and a tender compassion filled his heart as he remembered her frail pallor and her eyes, humbled and saddened by the dark shame of womanhood.

While his soul had passed from ecstasy to languor where had she been? Might it be, in the mysterious ways of spiritual life, that her soul at those same moments had been conscious of his homage? It might be.

A glow of desire kindled again his soul and fired and fulfilled all his body. Conscious of his desire she was waking from odorous sleep, the temptress of his villanelle. Her eyes, dark and with a look of languor, were opening to his eyes. Her nakedness yielded to him, radiant, warm, odorous and lavish-limbed, enfolded him like a shining cloud, enfolded him like water with a liquid life: and like a cloud of vapour or like waters circumfluent in space the liquid letters of speech, symbols of the element of mystery, flowed forth over his brain.

Are you not weary of ardent ways,
Lure of the fallen seraphim?
Tell no more of enchanted days.

Your eyes have set man's heart ablaze
And you have had your will of him.
Are you not weary of ardent ways?

Above the flame the smoke of praise
Goes up from ocean rim to rim.
Tell no more of enchanted days.

Our broken cries and mournful lays
Rise in one eucharistic hymn.
Are you not weary of ardent ways?

While sacrificing hands upraise
The chalice flowing to the brim,
Tell no more of enchanted days.

And still you hold our longing gaze
With languorous look and lavish limb!

Are you not weary of ardent ways?
Tell no more of enchanted days.
❖   ❖   ❖

What birds were they? He stood on the steps of the library to look at them, leaning wearily on his ashplant. They flew round and round the jutting shoulder of a house in Molesworth Street. The air of the late March evening made clear their flight, their dark darting quivering bodies flying clearly against the sky as against a limphung cloth of smoky tenuous blue.

He watched their flight; bird after bird: a dark flash, a swerve, a flash again, a dart aside, a curve, a flutter of wings. He tried to count them before all their darting quivering bodies passed: six, ten, eleven: and wondered were they odd or even in number. Twelve, thirteen: for two came wheeling down from the upper sky. They were flying high and low but ever round and round in straight and curving lines and ever flying from left to right, circling about a temple of air.

He listened to the cries: like the squeak of mice behind the wainscot: a shrill twofold note. But the notes were long and shrill and whirring, unlike the cry of vermin, falling a third or a fourth and trilled as the flying beaks clove the air. Their cry was shrill and clear and fine and falling like threads of silken light unwound from whirring spools.

The inhuman clamour soothed his ears in which his mother's sobs and reproaches murmured insistently and the dark frail quivering bodies wheeling and fluttering and swerving round an airy temple of the tenuous sky soothed his eyes which still saw the image of his mother's face.

Why was he gazing upwards from the steps of the porch, hearing their shrill twofold cry, watching their flight? For an augury of good or evil? A phrase of Cornelius Agrippa[18] flew through his mind and then there flew hither and thither shapeless thoughts from Swedenborg[19] on the correspondence of birds to things of the intellect and of how the creatures of the air have their knowledge and know their times and seasons because they, unlike man, are in the order of their life and have not perverted that order by reason.

And for ages man had gazed upward as he was gazing at birds in flight. The colonnade above him made him think vaguely of an ancient temple and the ashplant on which he leaned wearily of the curved stick of an augur. A sense of fear of the unknown moved in the heart of his weariness, a fear of symbols and portents, of the hawklike man whose name he bore soaring out of his captivity on osierwoven wings, of Thoth,[20] the god of writers, writing with a reed upon a tablet and bearing on his narrow ibis head the cusped moon.

He smiled as he thought of the god's image for it made him think of a bottlenosed judge in a wig, putting commas into a document which he held at arm's length and he knew that he would not have remembered the god's name but that it was like an Irish oath. It was folly. But was it for this folly that he was about to leave for ever the house of prayer and prudence into which he had been born and the order of life out of which he had come?

18. Cornelius Agrippa von Nettesheim (1486–1535), German alchemist and philosopher.
19. Emanuel Swedenborg (1688–1722), Swedish theologian and philosopher.
20. The Egyptian god who served as scribe to the other gods, and was later identified with the Greek Hermes (founder of "hermetic" knowledge). Thoth was represented as having the head of an ibis.

They came back with shrill cries over the jutting shoulder of the house, flying darkly against the fading air. What birds were they? He thought that they must be swallows who had come back from the south. Then he was to go away for they were birds ever going and coming, building ever an unlasting home under the eaves of men's houses and ever leaving the homes they had built to wander.

> Bend down your faces, Oona and Aleel,
> I gaze upon them as the swallow gazes
> Upon the nest under the eave before
> He wander the loud waters.[21]

A soft liquid joy like the noise of many waters flowed over his memory and he felt in his heart the soft peace of silent spaces of fading tenuous sky above the waters, of oceanic silence, of swallows flying through the seadusk over the flowing waters.

A soft liquid joy flowed through the words[22] where the soft long vowels hurtled noiselessly and fell away, lapping and flowing back and ever shaking the white bells of their waves in mute chime and mute peal and soft low swooning cry; and he felt that the augury he had sought in the wheeling darting birds and in the pale space of sky above him had come forth from his heart like a bird from a turret quietly and swiftly.

Symbol of departure or of loneliness? The verses crooned in the ear of his memory composed slowly before his remembering eyes the scene of the hall on the night of the opening of the national theatre. He was alone at the side of the balcony, looking out of jaded eyes at the culture of Dublin in the stalls and at the tawdry scenecloths and human dolls framed by the garish lamps of the stage. A burly policeman sweated behind him and seemed at every moment about to act. The catcalls and hisses and mocking cries ran in rude gusts round the hall from his scattered fellowstudents.

—A libel on Ireland!
—Made in Germany!
—Blasphemy!
—We never sold our faith!
—No Irish woman ever did it!
—We want no amateur atheists.
—We want no budding buddhists.

A sudden swift hiss fell from the windows above him and he knew that the electric lamps had been switched on in the reader's room. He turned into the pillared hall, now calmly lit, went up the staircase and passed in through the clicking turnstile.

1904–1914   1916

21. Lines from Yeats's play *The Countess Cathleen* (1895).
22. The very words he had just uttered internally to describe the scene. This response to the physical actuality of words, their meanings aside, is part of the Joycean sensibility, and occupies his world from the very first study of *Dubliners* on through *Finnegans Wake*'s world of words. In this scene Stephen is reading the swallows for their symbolic meaning; compare this twilight moment with that in D. H. Lawrence's poem "Bat."

From Ulysses

[Nausicaa]

The summer evening had begun to fold the world in its mysterious embrace. Far away in the west the sun was setting and the last glow of all too fleeting day lingered lovingly on sea and strand, on the proud promontory of dear old Howth guarding as ever the waters of the bay, on the weedgrown rocks along Sandymount [1] shore and, last but not least, on the quiet church whence there streamed forth at times upon the stillness the voice of prayer to her who is in her pure radiance a beacon ever to the storm-tossed heart of man, Mary, star of the sea. [2]

The three girl friends were seated on the rocks, enjoying the evening scene and the air which was fresh but not too chilly. Many a time and oft were they wont to come there to that favourite nook to have a cosy chat beside the sparkling waves and discuss matters feminine, Cissy Caffrey and Edy Boardman with the baby in the pushcar and Tommy and Jacky Caffrey, two little curly-headed boys, dressed in sailor suits with caps to match and the name H.M.S. Belleisle printed on both. For Tommy and Jacky Caffrey were twins, scarce four years old and very noisy and spoiled twins sometimes but for all that darling little fellows with bright merry faces and endearing ways about them. They were dabbling in the sand with their spades and buckets, building castles as children do, or playing with their big coloured ball, happy as the day was long. And Edy Boardman was rocking the chubby baby to and fro in the pushcar while that young gentleman fairly chuckled with delight. He was but eleven months and nine days old and, though still a tiny toddler, was just beginning to lisp his first babyish words. Cissy Caffrey bent over him to tease his fat little plucks and the dainty dimple in his chin.

—Now, baby, Cissy Caffrey said. Say out big, big. I want a drink of water. And baby prattled after her:

—A jink a jink a jawbo.

Cissy Caffrey cuddled the wee chap for she was awfully fond of children, so patient with little sufferers and Tommy Caffrey could never be got to take his castor oil unless it was Cissy Caffrey that held his nose and promised him the scatty heel of the loaf of brown bread with golden syrup on. What a persuasive power that girl had! But to be sure baby was as good as gold, a perfect little dote in his new fancy bib. None of your spoilt beauties, Flora MacFlimsy sort, was Cissy Caffrey. A truerhearted lass never drew the breath of life, always with a laugh in her gipsylike eyes and a frolicsome word on her cherryripe red lips, a girl lovable in the extreme. And Edy Boardman laughed too at the quaint language of little brother.

But just then there was a slight altercation between Master Tommy and

1. Near the beginning of the book, Stephen Daedalus had taken a solitary and introspective morning walk here on the beach along Dublin Bay. Now, at 8 P.M., the evening falling, near Leahy's Terrace and the church of St. Mary's Star of the Sea, the absurd, sentimental narration of the *Nausicaa* episode begins.

2. The parish church, incidentally, of the dead Paddy Dignam, as well as of Gerty Mac-Dowell, the transformed Nausicaa.

Master Jacky. Boys will be boys and our two twins were no exception to this golden rule. The apple of discord [3] was a certain castle of sand which Master Jacky had built and Master Tommy would have it right go wrong that it was to be architecturally improved by a frontdoor like the Martello tower had. But if Master Tommy was headstrong Master Jacky was selfwilled too and, true to the maxim that every little Irishman's house is his castle, he fell upon his hated rival and to such purpose that the wouldbe assailant came to grief and (alas to relate!) the coveted castle too. Needless to say the cries of discomfited Master Tommy drew the attention of the girl friends.

—Come here, Tommy, his sister called imperatively, at once! And you, Jacky, for shame to throw poor Tommy in the dirty sand. Wait till I catch you for that.

His eyes misty with unshed tears Master Tommy came at her call for their big sister's word was law with the twins. And in a sad plight he was after his misadventure. His little man-o'-war top and unmentionables [4] were full of sand but Cissy was a past mistress in the art of smoothing over life's tiny troubles and very quickly not one speck of sand was to be seen on his smart little suit. Still the blue eyes were glistening with hot tears that would well up so she kissed away the hurtness and shook her hand at Master Jacky the culprit and said if she was near him she wouldn't be far from him, her eyes dancing in admonition.

—Nasty bold Jacky! she cried.

She put an arm round the little mariner and coaxed winningly:

—What's your name? Butter and cream?

—Tell us who is your sweetheart, spoke Edy Boardman. Is Cissy your sweetheart?

—Nao, tearful Tommy said.

—Is Edy Boardman your sweetheart? Cissy queried.

—Nao, Tommy said.

—I know, Edy Boardman said none too amiably with an arch glance from her shortsighted eyes. I know who is Tommy's sweetheart, Gerty is Tommy's sweetheart.

—Nao, Tommy said on the verge of tears.

Cissy's quick motherwit guessed what was amiss and she whispered to Edy Boardman to take him there behind the pushcar where the gentlemen couldn't see and to mind he didn't wet his new tan shoes.

But who was Gerty?

Gerty MacDowell who was seated near her companions, lost in thought, gazing far away into the distance, was in very truth as fair a specimen of winsome Irish girlhood as one could wish to see. She was pronounced beautiful by all who knew her though, as folks often said, she was more a Giltrap than a MacDowell. Her figure was slight and graceful, inclining even to fragility but those iron jelloids she had been taking of late had done her a world of good much better than the Widow Welch's female pills and she was much better of those discharges she used to get and that tired feeling. The waxen pallor of her face was almost spiritual in its ivorylike purity though her rosebud mouth

3. A mechanical literary reference to the apple Paris awarded to Venus (in exchange for being given Helen of Troy)—thus precipitating the Trojan War.

4. Underpants. This introduces the attention paid to underwear (mostly Gerty's) throughout the episode and connected to the *Odyssey* through the fact that Nausicaa and her handmaidens were out washing dirty linen on the rocks when they saw Odysseus.

was a genuine Cupid's bow, Greekly perfect. Her hands were of finely veined alabaster with tapering fingers and as white as lemon juice and queen of ointments could make them though it was not true that she used to wear kid gloves in bed or take a milk footbath either. Bertha Supple told that once to Edy Boardman, a deliberate lie, when she was black out at daggers drawn with Gerty (the girl chums had of course their little tiffs from time to time like the rest of mortals) and she told her not let on whatever she did that it was her that told her or she'd never speak to her again. No. Honour where honour is due. There was an innate refinement, a languid queenly *hauteur*[5] about Gerty which was unmistakably evidenced in her delicate hands and higharched instep. Had kind fate but willed her to be born a gentlewoman of high degree in her own right and had she only received the benefit of a good education Gerty MacDowell might easily have held her own beside any lady in the land and have seen herself exquisitely gowned with jewels on her brow and patrician suitors at her feet vying with one another to pay their devoirs to her. Mayhap it was this, the love that might have been, that lent to her softlyfeatured face at whiles a look, tense with suppressed meaning, that imparted a strange yearning tendency to the beautiful eyes a charm few could resist. Why have women such eyes of witchery? Gerty's were of the bluest Irish blue, set off by lustrous lashes and dark expressive brows. Time was when those brows were not so silkilyseductive. It was Madame Vera Verity, directress of the Woman Beautiful page of the Princess novelette, who had first advised her to try eyebrowleine which gave that haunting expression to the eyes, so becoming in leaders of fashion, and she had never regretted it. Then there was blushing scientifically cured and how to be tall increase your height and you have a beautiful face but your nose? That would suit Mrs Dignam[6] because she had a button one. But Gerty's crowning glory was her wealth of wonderful hair. It was dark brown with a natural wave in it. She had cut it that very morning on account of the new moon and it nestled about her pretty head in a profusion of luxuriant clusters and pared her nails too, Thursday for wealth. And just now at Edy's words as a telltale flush, delicate as the faintest rosebloom, crept into her cheeks she looked so lovely in her sweet girlish shyness that of a surety God's fair land of Ireland did not hold her equal.

For an instant she was silent with rather sad downcast eyes. She was about to retort but something checked the words on her tongue. Inclination prompted her to speak out: dignity told her to be silent. The pretty lips pouted a while but then she glanced up and broke out into a joyous little laugh which had in it all the freshness of a young May morning. She knew right well, no-one better, what made squinty Edy say that because of him cooling in his attentions when it was simply a lovers' quarrel. As per usual somebody's nose was out of joint about the boy that had the bicycle always riding up and down in front of her window. Only now his father kept him in the evenings studying hard to get an exhibition[7] in the intermediate that was on and he was going to Trinity college[8] to study for a doctor when he left the high school like his brother W. E. Wylie

5. Lofty manner; haughtiness.
6. The widow of Paddy Dignam.
7. A fellowship.
8. Trinity College (Dublin), founded for, and at that time still attended largely by, Anglo-Irish (Protestant) "gentry."

who was racing in the bicycle races in Trinity college university. Little recked
he perhaps for what she felt, that dull aching void in her heart sometimes,
piercing to the core. Yet he was young and perchance he might learn to love
her in time. They were protestants in his family and of course Gerty knew Who
came first and after Him the blessed Virgin and then Saint Joseph. But he was
undeniably handsome with an exquisite nose and he was what he looked, every
inch a gentleman, the shape of his head too at the back without his cap on that
she would know anywhere something off the common and the way he turned
the bicycle at the lamp with his hands off the bars and also the nice perfume of
those good cigarettes and besides they were both of a size and that was why
Edy Boardman thought she was so frightfully clever because he didn't go and
ride up and down in front of her bit of a garden.

Gerty was dressed simply but with the instinctive taste of a votary of Dame
Fashion for she felt that there was just a might that he might be out. A neat
blouse of electric blue, selftinted by dolly dyes (because it was expected in the
Lady's Pictorial that electric blue would be worn), with a smart vee opening
down to the division and kerchief pocket (in which she always kept a piece of
cottonwool scented with her favourite perfume because the handkerchief spoiled
the sit) and a navy threequarter skirt cut to the stride showed off her slim
graceful figure to perfection. She wore a coquettish little love of a hat of wide-
leaved nigger straw contrast trimmed with an underbrim of eggblue chenille and
at the side a butterfly bow to tone. All Tuesday week afternoon she was hunting to match that chenille but at last she found what she wanted at Clery's
summer sales, the very it, slightly shopsoiled but you would never notice, seven
fingers two and a penny. She did it up all by herself and what joy was hers
when she tried it on then, smiling at the lovely reflection which the mirror gave
back to her! And when she put it on the waterjug to keep the shape she knew
that that would take the shine out of some people she knew. Her shoes were
the newest thing in footwear (Edy Boardman prided herself that she was very
petite but she never had a foot like Gerty MacDowell, a five, and never would
ash, oak or elm) with patent toecaps and just one smart buckle at her high-
arched instep. Her wellturned ankle displayed its perfect proportions beneath
her skirt and just the proper amount and no more of her shapely limbs encased
in finespun hose with high spliced heels and wide garter tops. As for undies
they were Gerty's chief care and who that knows the fluttering hopes and fears
of sweet seventeen (though Gerty would never see seventeen again) can find
it in his heart to blame her? She had four dinky [9] sets, with awfully pretty
stichery, three garments and nighties extra, and each set slotted with different
coloured ribbons, rosepink, pale blue, mauve and peagreen and she aired them
herself and blued them when they came home from the wash and ironed them
and she had a brickbat to keep the iron on because she wouldn't trust those
washerwomen as far as she'd see them scorching the things. She was wearing
the blue for luck, hoping against hope, her own colour and the lucky colour
too for a bride to have a bit of blue somewhere on her because the green she
wore that day week brought grief because his father brought him in to study
for the intermediate exhibition and because she thought perhaps he might be

9. Nifty.

out because when she was dressing that morning she nearly slipped up the old pair on her inside out and that was for luck and lovers' meetings if you put those things on inside out so long as it wasn't on a Friday.

And yet and yet! That strained look on her face! A gnawing sorrow is there all the time. Her very soul is in her eyes and she would give worlds to be in the privacy of her own familiar chamber where, giving way to tears, she could have a good cry and relieve her pentup feelings. Though not too much because she knew how to cry nicely before the mirror. You are lovely, Gerty, it said. The paly light of evening falls upon a face infinitely sad and wistful. Gerty Mac-Dowell yearns in vain. Yes, she had known from the first that her daydream of a marriage has been arranged and the weddingbells ringing for Mrs Reggy Wylie T. C. D.[10] (because the one who married the elder brother would be Mrs Wylie) and in the fashionable intelligence Mrs Gertrude Wylie was wearing a sumptuous confection of grey trimmed with expensive blue fox was not to be. He was too young to understand. He would not believe in love, a woman's birthright. The night of the party long ago in Stoers' (he was still in short trousers) when they were alone and he stole an arm round her waist she went white to the very lips. He called her little one in a strangely husky voice and snatched a half kiss (the first!) but it was only the end of her nose and then he hastened from the room with a remark about refreshments. Impetuous fellow! Strength of character had never been Reggy Wylie's strong point and he who would woo and win Gerty MacDowell must be a man among men. But waiting, always waiting to be asked and it was leap year too and would soon be over. No prince charming is her beau ideal to lay a rare and wondrous love at her feet but rather a manly man with a strong quiet face who had not found his ideal, perhaps his hair slightly flecked with grey, and who would understand, take her in his sheltering arms, strain her to him in all the strength of his deep passionate nature and comfort her with a long long kiss. It would be like heaven. For such a one she yearns this balmy summer eve. With all the heart of her she longs to be his only, his affianced bride for riches for poor,[11] in sickness in health, till death us two part, from this to this day forward.

And while Edy Boardman was with little Tommy behind the pushcar she was just thinking would the day ever come when she could call herself his little wife to be. Then they could talk about her till they went blue in the face, Bertha Supple too, and Edy, the spitfire, because she would be twenty-two in November. She would care for him with creature comforts too for Gerty was womanly wise and knew that a mere man liked that feeling of hominess. Her griddlecakes done to a golden-brown hue and queen Ann's pudding of delightful creaminess had won golden opinions from all because she had a lucky hand also for lighting a fire, dredge in the fine selfraising flour and always stir in the same direction then cream the milk and sugar and whisk well the white of eggs though she didn't like the eating part when there were any people that made her shy and often she wondered why you couldn't eat something poetical like violets or roses and they would have a beautifully appointed drawingroom with pictures and engravings and the photograph of grandpapa

10. Trinity College, Dublin.
11. "For richer, for poorer," which she has garbled, as from the marriage ceremony, "till death us do part."

Giltrap's lovely dog Garryowen that almost talked, it was so human, and chintz covers for the chairs and that silver toastrack in Clery's summer jumble sales [13] like they have in rich houses. He would be tall with broad shoulders (she had always admired tall men for a husband) with glistening white teeth under his carefully trimmed sweeping moustache and they would go on the continent for their honeymoon (three wonderful weeks!) and then, when they settled down in a nice snug and cosy little homely house, every morning they would both have brekky, simple but perfectly served, for their own two selves and before he went out to business he would give his dear little wifey a good hearty hug and gaze for a moment deep down into her eyes.

Edy Boardman asked Tommy Caffrey was he done and he said yes, so then she buttoned up his little knickerbockers for him and told him to run off and play with Jacky and to be good now and not to fight. But Tommy said he wanted the ball and Edy told him no that baby was playing with the ball and if he took it there'd be wigs on the green [13] but Tommy said it was his ball and he wanted his ball and he pranced on the ground, if you please. The temper of him! O, he was a man already was little Tommy Caffrey since he was out of pinnies.[14] Edy told him no, no and to be off now with him and she told Cissy Caffrey not to give in to him.

—You're not my sister, naughty Tommy said. It's my ball.

But Cissy Caffrey told baby Boardman to look up, look up high at her finger and she snatched the ball quickly and threw it along the sand and Tommy after it in full career, having won the day.

—Anything for a quiet life, laughed Ciss.

And she tickled tiny tot's two cheeks to make him forget and played here's the lord mayor, here's his two horses, here's his gingerbread carriage and here he walks in, chinchopper, chinchopper, chinchopper chin. But Edy got as cross as two sticks about him getting his own way like that from everyone always petting him.

—I'd like to give him something, she said, so I would, where I won't say.

—On the beetoteetom, laughed Cissy merrily.

Gerty MacDowell bent down her head and crimsoned at the idea of Cissy saying an unladylike thing like that out loud she'd be ashamed of her life to say, flushing a deep rosy red, and Edy Boardman said she was sure the gentleman opposite heard what she said. But not a pin cared Ciss.

—Let him! she said with a pert toss of her head and a piquant tilt of her nose. Give it to him too on the same place as quick as I'd look at him.

Madcap Ciss with her golliwog [15] curls. You had to laugh at her sometimes. For instance when she asked you would you have some more Chinese tea and jaspberry ram and when she drew the jugs too and the men's faces on her nails with red ink make you split your sides or when she wanted to go where you know she said she wanted to run and pay a visit to the Miss White. That was just like Cissycums. O, and will you ever forget the evening she dressed up in her father's suit and hat and the burned cork moustache and

12. Clearance sales.
13. There'd be trouble, a row.
14. Pinafore. At this date very young boys were still dressed in girls' clothes.
15. A grotesque black doll.

walked down Tritonville road, smoking a cigarette? There was none to come up to her for fun. But she was sincerity itself, one of the bravest and truest hearts heaven ever made, not one of your twofaced things, too sweet to be wholesome.

And then there came out upon the air the sound of voices and the pealing anthem of the organ. It was the men's temperance retreat conducted by the missioner, the reverend John Hughes S.J., rosary, sermon and benediction of the Most Blessed Sacrament. They were there gathered together without distinction of social class (and a most edifying spectacle it was to see) in that simple fane beside the waves, after the storms of this weary world, kneeling before the feet of the immaculate, reciting the litany of Our Lady of Loreto,[16] beseeching her to intercede for them, the old familiar words, holy Mary, holy virgin of virgins. How sad to poor Gerty's ears! Had her father only avoided the clutches of the demon drink, by taking the pledge or those powders the drink habit cured in Pearson's Weekly, she might now be rolling in her carriage, second to none. Over and over had she told herself that as she mused by the dying embers in a brown study without the lamp because she hated two lights or oftentimes gazing out of the window dreamily by the hour at the rain falling on the rusty bucket, thinking. But that vile decoction which has ruined so many hearts and homes had cast its shadow over her childhood days. Nay, she had even witnessed in the home circle deeds of violence caused by intemperance and had seen her own father, a prey to the fumes of intoxication, forget himself completely for if there was one thing of all things that Gerty knew it was the man who lifts his hand to a woman save in the way of kindness deserves to be branded as the lowest of the low.

And still the voices sang in supplication to the Virgin most powerful, Virgin most merciful. And Gerty, wrapt in thought, scarce saw or heard her companions or the twins at their boyish gambols or the gentleman off Sandymount green that Cissy Caffrey called the man that was so like himself passing along the strand taking a short walk. You never saw him anyway screwed but still and for all that she would not like him for a father because he was too old or something or on account of his face (it was a palpable case of doctor Fell[17]) or his carbuncly nose with the pimples on it and his sandy moustache a bit white under his nose. Poor father! With all his faults she loved him still when he sang *Tell me, Mary, how to woo thee* or *My love and cottage near Rochelle* and they had stewed cockles and lettuce with Lazenby's salad dressing for supper and when he sang *The moon hath raised* with Mr Dignam that died suddenly and was buried, God have mercy on him, from a stroke. Her mother's birthday that was and Charley was home on his holidays and Tom and Mr Dignam and Mrs and Patsy and Freddy Dignam and they were to have had a

16. The Litany of the Virgin, which will be sung in the course of the service, is intercut with the gooey narration throughout, to underline the relation between the primary and parodied forms of the Virgin. Also, the sermon on temperance ironically reverses a Homeric event: Alcinous, Nausicaa's father, overdrank.

17. From the nursery rhyme: "I do not like thee, Doctor Fell, / The reason why I cannot tell; / But this I know, and know full well, / I do not like thee Doctor Fell," originally improvised by the 18th-century satirist Tom Brown when the Dr. Fell in question, the dean of his Oxford college, demanded that he translate an epigram of Martial saying much the same thing.

group taken. No-one would have thought the end was so near. Now he was laid to rest. And her mother said to him to let that be a warning to him for the rest of his days and he couldn't even go to the funeral on account of the gout and she had to go into town to bring him the letters and samples from his office about Catesby's cork lino, artistic standard designs, fit for a palace, gives tiptop wear and always bright and cheery in the home.

A sterling good daughter was Gerty just like a second mother in the house, a ministering angel too with a little heart worth its weight in gold. And when her mother had those raging splitting headaches who was it rubbed on the menthol cone on her forehead but Gerty though she didn't like her mother taking pinches of snuff and that was the only single thing they ever had words about, taking snuff. Everyone thought the world of her for her gentle ways. It was Gerty who turned off the gas at the main every night and it was Gerty who tacked up on the wall of that place where she never forgot every fortnight the chlorate of lime Mr Tunney the grocer's christmas almanac the picture of halcyon days where a young gentleman in the costume they used to wear then with a three-cornered hat was offering a bunch of flowers to his ladylove with oldtime chivalry through her lattice window. You could see there was a story behind it. The colours were done something lovely. She was in a soft clinging white in a studied attitude and the gentleman was in chocolate and he looked a thorough aristocrat. She often looked at them dreamily when there for a certain purpose and felt her own arms that were white and soft just like hers with the sleeves back and thought about those times because she had found out in Walker's pronouncing dictionary that belonged to grandpapa Giltrap about the halcyon days what they meant.

The twins were now playing in the most approved brotherly fashion, till at last Master Jacky who was really as bold as brass there was no getting behind that deliberately kicked the ball as hard as ever he could down towards the seaweedy rocks. Needless to say poor Tommy was not slow to voice his dismay but luckily the gentleman in black who was sitting there by himself [18] came gallantly to the rescue and intercepted the ball. Our two champions claimed their plaything with lusty cries and to avoid trouble Cissy Caffrey called to the gentleman to throw it to her please. The gentleman aimed the ball once or twice and then threw it up the strand towards Cissy Caffrey but it rolled down the slope and stopped right under Gerty's skirt near the little pool by the rock. The twins clamoured again for it and Cissy told her to kick it away and let them fight for it so Gerty drew back her foot but she wished their stupid ball hadn't come rolling down to her and she gave a kick but she missed and Edy and Cissy laughed.

—If you fail try again, Edy Boardman said.

Gerty smiled assent and bit her lip. A delicate pink crept into her pretty cheek but she was determined to let them see so she just lifted her skirt a little but just enough and took good aim and gave the ball a jolly good kick and it went ever so far and the two twins after it down towards the shingle. Pure jealousy of course it was nothing else to draw attention on account of the gentleman opposite looking. She felt the warm flush, a danger signal always

18. Leopold Bloom, our hero.

with Gerty MacDowell, surging and flaming into her cheeks. Till then they had only exchanged glances of the most casual but now under the brim of her new hat she ventured a look at him and the face that met her gaze there in the twilight, wan and strangely drawn, seemed to her the saddest she had ever seen.

Through the open window of the church the fragrant incense was wafted and with it the fragrant names of her who was conceived without stain of original sin,[19] spiritual vessel, pray for us, honourable vessel, pray for us, vessel of singular devotion, pray for us, mystical rose. And careworn hearts were there and toilers for their daily bread and many who had erred and wandered, their eyes wet with contrition but for all that bright with hope for the reverend father Hughes had told them what the great saint Bernard said in his famous prayer of Mary, the most pious Virgin's intercessory power that it was not recorded in any age that those who implored her powerful protection were ever abandoned by her.

The twins were now playing again right merrily for the troubles of childhood are but as fleeting summer showers. Cissy played with baby Boardman till he crowed with glee, clapping baby hands in air. Peep she cried behind the hood of the pushcar and Edy asked where was Cissy gone and then Cissy popped up her head and cried ah! and, my word, didn't the little chap enjoy that! And then she told him to say papa.

—Say papa, baby. Say pa pa pa pa pa pa pa.

And baby did his level best to say it for he was very intelligent for eleven months everyone said and big for his age and the picture of health, a perfect little bunch of love, and he would certainly turn out to be something great, they said.

—Haja ja ja haja.

Cissy wiped his little mouth with the dribbling bib and wanted him to sit up properly, and say pa pa pa but when she undid the strap she cried out, holy saint Denis, that he was possing[20] wet and to double the half blanket the other way under him. Of course his infant majesty was most obstreperous at such toilet formalities and he let everyone know it:

—Habaa baaaahabaaa baaaa.

And two great big lovely big tears coursing down his cheeks. It was all no use soothering him with no, nono, baby, no and telling him about the geegee and where was the puffpuff but Ciss, always readywitted, gave him in his mouth the teat of the suckingbottle and the young heathen was quickly appeased.

Gerty wished to goodness they would take their squalling baby home out of that and not get on her nerves no hour to be out and the little brats of twins. She gazed out towards the distant sea. It was like the paintings that man used to do on the pavement with all the coloured chalks and such a pity too leaving

19. "Fragrant names . . . ," further invocations in the litany. "Conceived without stain of original sin" is a reference to the dogma of the Immaculate Conception of the Blessed Virgin Mary, who is here a kind of parody on Gerty, the other virgin of the story. They are both associated with blue, both "stars of the sea" (the latter, for Bloom). The litany is being sung in Gerty's parish church. The "famous prayer" mentioned below is known as the "Memorare."
20. From the same word "poss-tub," in which the washing is churned with a stick.

them there to be all blotted out, the evening and the clouds coming out and the Bailey light on Howth and to hear the music like that and the perfume of those incense they burned in the church like a kind of waft. And while she gazed her heart went pitapat. Yes, it was her he was looking at and there was meaning in his look. His eyes burned into her as though they would search her through and through, read her very soul. Wonderful eyes they were, superbly expressive, but could you trust them? People were so queer. She could see at once by his dark eyes and his pale intellectual face that he was a foreigner, the image of the photo she had of Martin Harvey, the matinée idol, only for the moustache which she preferred because she wasn't stagestruck like Winny Rippingham that wanted they two to always dress the same on account of a play but she could not see whether he had an aquiline nose or a slightly *retroussé* from where [s]he was sitting. He was in deep mourning, she could see that, and the story of a haunting sorrow was written on his face. She would have given worlds to know what it was. He was looking up so intently, so still and he saw her kick the ball and perhaps he could see the bright steel buckles of her shoes if she swung them like that thoughtfully with the toes down. She was glad that something told her to put on the transparent stockings thinking Reggy Wylie might be out but that was far away. Here was that of which she had so often dreamed. It was he who mattered and there was joy on her face because she wanted him because she felt instinctively that he was like no-one else. The very heart of the girlwoman went out to him, her dream-husband, because she knew on the instant it was him. If he had suffered, more sinned against than sinning, or even, even, if he had been himself a sinner, a wicked man, she cared not. Even if he was a protestant or methodist she could convert him easily if he truly loved her. There were wounds that wanted healing with heartbalm. She was a womanly woman not like other flighty girls, unfeminine, he had known, those cyclists showing off what they hadn't got and she just yearned to know all, to forgive all if she could make him fall in love with her, make him forget the memory of the past. Then mayhap he would embrace her gently, like a real man, crushing her soft body to him, and love her, his ownest girlie, for herself alone.

Refuge of sinners. Comfortress of the afflicted. *Ora pro nobis.*[21] Well has it been said that whosoever prays to her with faith and constancy can never be lost or cast away: and fitly is she too a haven of refuge for the afflicted because of the seven dolours which transpierced her own heart. Gerty could picture the whole scene in the church, the stained glass windows lighted up, the candles, the flowers and the blue banners of the blessed Virgin's sodality and Father Conroy was helping Canon O'Hanlon at the altar, carrying things in and out with his eyes cast down. He looked almost a saint and his confession-box was so quiet and clean and dark and his hands were just like white wax and if ever she became a Dominican nun in their white habit perhaps he might come to the convent for the novena of Saint Dominic. He told her that time when she told him about that in confession crimsoning up to the roots of her hair for fear he could see, not to be troubled because that was only the voice of nature and we were all subject to nature's laws, he said, in this life and that

---

21. "Pray for us," the response said after each invocation of the litany.

that was no sin because that came from the nature of woman instituted by God, he said, and that Our Blessed Lady herself said to the archangel Gabriel be it done unto me according to Thy Word. He was so kind and holy and often and often she thought and thought could she work a ruched teacosy with embroidered floral design for him as a present or a clock but they had a clock she noticed on the mantlepiece white and gold with a canary bird that came out of a little house to tell the time the day she went there about the flowers for the forty hours' adoration because it was hard to know what sort of a present to give or perhaps a album of illuminated views of Dublin or some place.

The exasperating little brats of twins began to quarrel again and Jacky threw the ball out towards the sea and they both ran after it. Little monkeys common as ditchwater. Someone ought to take them and give them a good hiding for themselves to keep them in their places, the both of them. And Cissy and Edy shouted after them to come back because they were afraid the tide might come in on them and be drowned.

—Jacky! Tommy!

Not they! What a great notion they had! So Cissy said it was the very last time she'd ever bring them out. She jumped up and called them and she ran down the slope past him, tossing her hair behind her which had a good enough colour if there had been more of it but with all the thingamerry she was always rubbing into it she couldn't get it to grow long because it wasn't natural so she could just go and throw her hat at it. She ran with long gandery strides it was a wonder she didn't rip up her skirt at the side that was too tight on her because there was a lot of the tomboy about Cissy Caffrey and she was a forward piece whenever she thought she had a good opportunity to show off and just because she was a good runner she ran like that so that he could see all the end of her petticoat running and her skinny shanks up as far as possible. It would have served her just right if she had tripped up over something accidentally on purpose with her high crooked French heels on her to make her look tall and got a fine tumble. *Tableau!* [22] That would have been a very charming exposé for a gentleman like that to witness.

Queen of angels, queen of patriarchs, queen of prophets, of all saints, they prayed, queen of the most holy rosary and then Father Conroy handed the thurible to Canon O'Hanlon and he put in the incense and censed the Blessed Sacrament and Cissy Caffrey caught the two twins and she was itching to give them a ringing good clip on the ear but she didn't because she thought he might be watching but she never made a bigger mistake in all her life because Gerty could see without looking that he never took his eyes off of her and then Canon O'Hanlon handed the thurible back to Father Conroy and knelt down looking up at the Blessed Sacrament and the choir began to sing *Tantum ergo* and she just swung her foot in and out in time as the music rose and fell to the *Tantumer gosa cramen tum.* [23] Three and eleven she paid for those stockings in Sparrow's of George's street on the Tuesday, no the Monday

22. Stage direction to indicate a frozen pictured group at the opening or end of a scene. Today one might make the same joke by saying "Cut!" or "Print that!"

23. Gerty's fractured version of *Tantum ergo sacramentum* (literally, "So great a sacrament, therefore . . ."), opening line of a Benediction hymn by St. Thomas Aquinas (actually the last two stanzas of the *Pange Lingua* he composed for the feast of Corpus Christi).

before Easter and there wasn't a brack[24] on them and that was what he was looking at, transparent, and not at her insignificant ones that had neither shape nor form (the cheek of her!) because he had eyes in his head to see the difference for himself.

Cissy came up along the strand with the two twins and their ball with her hat anyhow on her to one side after her run and she did look a streel[25] tugging the two kids along with the flimsy blouse she bought only a fortnight before like a rag on her back and bit of her petticoat hanging like a caricature. Gerty just took off her hat for a moment to settle her hair and a prettier, a daintier head of nutbrown tresses was never seen on a girl's shoulders, a radiant little vision, in sooth, almost maddening in its sweetness. You would have to travel many a long mile before you found a head of hair the like of that. She could almost see the swift answering flush of admiration in his eyes that set her tingling in every nerve. She put on her hat so that she could see from underneath the brim and swung her buckled shoe faster for her breath caught as she caught the expression in his eyes. He was eyeing her as a snake eyes its prey. Her woman's instinct told her that she had raised the devil in him and at the thought a burning scarlet swept from throat to brow till the lovely colour of her face became a glorious rose.

Edy Boardman was noticing it too because she was squinting at Gerty, half smiling, with her specs, like an old maid, pretending to nurse[26] the baby. Irritable little gnat she was and always would be and that was why no-one could get on with her, poking her nose into what was no concern of hers. And she said to Gerty:

—A penny for your thoughts.

—What? replied Gerty with a smile reinforced by the whitest of teeth. I was only wondering was it late.

Because she wished to goodness they'd take the snottynosed twins and their baby home to the mischief out of that so that was why she just gave a gentle hint about its being late. And when Cissy came up Edy asked her the time and Miss Cissy, as glib as you like, said it was half past kissing time, time to kiss again. But Edy wanted to know because they were told to be in early.

—Wait, said Cissy, I'll ask my uncle Peter over there what's the time by his conundrum.

So over she went and when he saw her coming she could see him take his hand out of his pocket, getting nervous, and beginning to play with his watch-chain, looking at the church. Passionate nature though he was Gerty could see that he had enormous control over himself. One moment he had been there, fascinated by a loveliness that made him gaze, and the next moment it was the quiet gravefaced gentleman, selfcontrol expressed in every line of his distin-guishedlooking figure.

Cissy said to excuse her would he mind telling her what was the right time and Gerty could see him taking out his watch, listening to it and looking up and clearing his throat and he said he was very sorry his watch was stopped but he thought it must be after eight because the sun was set. His voice had a

24. A run or, in Ireland, a "ladder."
25. Slattern.
26. Dandle, not give suck.

cultured ring in it and though he spoke in measured accents there was a suspicion of a quiver in the mellow tones. Cissy said thanks and came back with her tongue out and said uncle said his waterworks were out of order.

Then they sang the second verse of the *Tantum ergo* and Canon O'Hanlon got up again and censed the Blessed Sacrament and knelt down and he told Father Conroy that one of the candles was just going to set fire to the flowers and Father Conroy got up and settled it all right and she could see the gentleman winding his watch and listening to the works and she swung her leg more in and out in time. It was getting darker but he could see and he was looking all the time that he was winding the watch or whatever he was doing to it and then he put it back and put his hands back into his pockets. She felt a kind of a sensation rushing all over her and she knew by the feel of her scalp and that irritation against her stays that that thing must be coming on because the last time too was when she clipped her hair on account of the moon. His dark eyes fixed themselves on her again drinking in her every contour, literally worshipping at her shrine. If ever there was undisguised admiration in a man's passionate gaze it was there plain to be seen on that man's face. It is for you, Gertrude MacDowell, and you know it.

Edy began to get ready to go and it was high time for her and Gerty noticed that that little hint she gave had the desired effect because it was a long way along the strand to where there was the place to push up the pushcar and Cissy took off the twins' caps and tidied their hair to make herself attractive of course and Canon O'Hanlon stood up with his cope poking up at his neck and Father Conroy handed him the card to read off and he read out *Panem de cœlo præstitisti eis* [27] and Edy and Cissy were talking about the time all the time and asking her but Gerty could pay them back in their own coin and she just answered with scathing politeness when Edy asked her was she heartbroken about her best boy throwing her over. Gerty winced sharply. A brief cold blaze shone from her eyes that spoke volumes of scorn immeasurable. It hurt. O yes, it cut deep because Edy had her own quiet way of saying things like that she knew would wound like the confounded little cat she was. Gerty's lips parted swiftly to frame the word but she fought back the sob that rose to her throat, so slim, so flawless, so beautifully moulded it seemed one an artist might have dreamed of. She had loved him better than he knew. Lighthearted deceiver and fickle like all his sex he would never understand what he had meant to her and for an instant there was in the blue eyes a quick stinging of tears. Their eyes were probing her mercilessly but with a brave effort she sparkled back in sympathy as she glanced at her new conquest for them to see.

—O, responded Gerty, quick as lightning, laughing, and the proud head flashed up, I can throw my cap at who I like because it's leap year.

Her words rang out crystalclear, more musical than the cooing of the ringdove, but they cut the silence icily. There was that in her young voice that told that she was not a one to be lightly trifled with. As for Mr Reggy with his swank and his bit of money she could just chuck him aside as if he was so much filth and never again would she cast as much as a second thought

27. "You have given them bread from heaven," versicle chanted by celebrant after the *Tantum ergo.*

on him and tear his silly postcard into a dozen pieces. And if ever after he dared to presume she could give him one look of measured scorn that would make him shrivel up on the spot. Miss puny little Edy's countenance fell to no slight extent and Gerty could see by her looking as black as thunder that she was simply in a towering rage though she hid it, the little kinnatt,[28] because that shaft had struck home for her petty jealousy and they both knew that she was something aloof, apart in another sphere, that she was not of them and there was somebody else too that knew it and saw it so they could put that in their pipe and smoke it.

Edy straightened up baby Boardman to get ready to go and Cissy tucked in the ball and the spades and buckets and it was high time too because the sandman was on his way for Master Boardman junior and Cissy told him too that Billy Winks was coming and that baby was to go deedaw and baby looked just too ducky, laughing up out of his gleeful eyes, and Cissy poked him like that out of fun in his wee fat tummy and baby, without as much as by your leave, sent up his compliments on to his brandnew dribbling bib.

—O my! Puddeny pie! protested Ciss. He has his bib destroyed.

The slight *contretemps* claimed her attention but in two twos she set that little matter to rights.

Gerty stifled a smothered exclamation and gave a nervous cough and Edy asked what and she was just going to tell her to catch it while it was flying but she was ever ladylike in her deportment so she simply passed it off with consummate tact by saying that that was the benediction because just then the bell rang out from the steeple over the quiet seashore because Canon O'Hanlon was up on the altar with the veil that Father Conroy put round him round his shoulders giving the benediction with the blessed Sacrament in his hands.

How moving the scene there in the gathering twilight, the last glimpse of Erin, the touching chime of those evening bells and at the same time a bat flew forth from the ivied belfry through the dusk, hither, thither, with a tiny lost cry. And she could see far away the lights of the lighthouses so picturesque she would have loved to do with a box of paints because it was easier than to make a man and soon the lamplighter would be going his rounds past the presbyterian church grounds and along by shady Tritonville avenue where the couples walked and lighting the lamp near her window where Reggy Wylie used to turn his freewheel like she read in that book *The Lamplighter* [29] by Miss Cummins, author of *Mabel Vaughan* and other tales. For Gerty had her dreams that no-one knew of. She loved to read poetry and when she got a keepsake from Bertha Supple of that lovely confession album with the coralpink cover to write her thoughts in she laid it in the drawer of her toilettable which, though it did not err on the side of luxury, was scrupulously neat and clean. It was there she kept her girlish treasures trove, the tortoiseshell combs, her

---

28. Probably Joyce's transcription of the way "gnat" is pronounced in Ireland.
29. A sentimental American bestseller by Maria S. Cummins, first published in 1854. A sample of its style suggests that Joyce was using it, among other texts, as the basis of his parody: "It was a stormy evening. Gerty was standing at the window, watching for True's return from his lamplighting. She was neatly and comfortably dressed, her hair smooth, her face and hands clean. She was now quite well—better than for years before her sickness. . . ."

child of Mary badge, the whiterose scent, the eyebrowleine, her alabaster pouncetbox and the ribbons to change when her things came home from the wash and there were some beautiful thoughts written in it in violet ink that she bought in Hely's of Dame Street for she felt that she too could write poetry if she could only express herself like that poem that appealed to her so deeply that she had copied out of the newspaper she found one evening round the potherbs. *Art thou real, my ideal?* it was called by Louis J. Walsh, Magherafelt, and after there was something about *twilight, wilt thou ever?* and ofttimes the beauty of poetry, so sad in its transient loveliness, had misted her eyes with silent tears that the years were slipping by for her, one by one, and but for that one shortcoming she knew she need fear no competition and and that was an accident coming down Dalkey hill and she always tried to conceal it. But it must end she felt. If she saw that magic lure in his eyes there would be no holding back for her. Love laughs at locksmiths. She would make the great sacrifice. Her every effort would be to share his thoughts. Dearer than the whole world would she be to him and gild his days with happiness. There was the allimportant question and she was dying to know was he a married man or a widower who had lost his wife or some tragedy like the nobleman with the foreign name from the land of song had to have her put into a madhouse, cruel only to be kind. But even if—what then? Would it make a very great difference? From everything in the least indelicate her finebred nature instinctively recoiled. She loathed that sort of person, the fallen women off the accommodation walk beside the Dodder [30] that went with the soldiers and coarse men, with no respect for a girl's honour, degrading the sex and being taken up to the police station. No, no: not that. They would be just good friends like a big brother and sister without all that other in spite of the conventions of Society with a big ess. Perhaps it was an old flame he was in mourning for from the days beyond recall. She thought she understood. She would try to understand him because men were so different. The old love was waiting, waiting with little white hands stretched out, with blue appealing eyes. Heart of mine! She would follow her dream of love, the dictates of her heart that told her he was her all in all, the only man in all the world for her for love was the master guide. Nothing else mattered. Come what might she would be wild, untrammelled, free.

Canon O'Hanlon put the Blessed Sacrament back into the tabernacle and the choir sang *Laudate Dominum omnes gentes* [31] and then he locked the tabernacle door because the benediction was over and Father Conroy handed him his hat to put on and crosscat Edy asked wasn't she coming but Jacky Caffrey called out:

—O, look, Cissy!

And they all looked was it sheet lightning but Tommy saw it too over the trees beside the church, blue, and then green and purple.

—It's fireworks, Cissy Caffrey said.

And they all ran down the strand to see over the houses and the church, helterskelter, Edy with the pushcar with baby Boardman in it and Cissy holding Tommy and Jacky by the hand so they wouldn't fall running.

30. Another Dublin river, flowing into the Bay from the south.
31. "Praise the Lord, all ye people," Psalm 116, sung at the end of Benediction.

—Come on, Gerty, Cissy called. It's the bazaar fireworks.

But Gerty was adamant. She had no intention of being at their beck and call. If they could run like rossies she could sit so she said she could see from where she was. The eyes that were fastened upon her set her pulses tingling. She looked at him a moment, meeting his glance, and a light broke in upon her. Whitehot passion was in that face, passion silent as the grave, and it had made her his. At last they were left alone without the others to pry and pass remarks and she knew he could be trusted to the death, steadfast, a sterling man, a man of inflexible honour to his fingertips. His hands and face were working and a tremor went over her. She leaned back far to look up where the fireworks were and she caught her knee in her hands so as not to fall back looking up and there was no one to see only him and her when she revealed all her graceful beautifully shaped legs like that, supply soft and delicately rounded, and she seemed to hear the panting of his heart, his hoarse breathing, because she knew about the passion of men like that, hot-blooded, because Bertha Supple told her once in dead secret and made her swear she'd never about the gentleman lodger that was staying with them out of the Congested Districts Board that had pictures cut out of papers of those skirtdancers and highkickers and she said he used to do something not very nice that you could imagine sometimes in the bed. But this was altogether different from a thing like that because there was all the difference because she could almost feel him draw her face to his and the first quick hot touch of his handsome lips. Besides there was absolution so long as you didn't do the other thing before being married and there ought to be women priests that would understand without your telling out and Cissy Caffrey too sometimes had that dreamy kind of dreamy look in her eyes so that she too, my dear, and Winny Rippingham so mad about actors' photographs and besides it was on account of that other thing coming on the way it did.

And Jack Caffrey shouted to look, there was another and she leaned back and the garters were blue to match on account of the transparent and they all saw it and shouted to look, look there it was and she leaned back ever so far to see the fireworks and something queer was flying about through the air, a soft thing to and fro, dark. And she saw a long Roman candle going up over the trees up, up, and, in the tense hush, they were all breathless with excitement as it went higher and higher and she had to lean back more and more to look up after it, high, high, almost out of sight, and her face was suffused with a divine, an entrancing blush from straining back and he could see her other things too, nainsook [32] knickers, the fabric that caresses the skin, better than those other pettiwidth, the green, four and eleven, on account of being white and she let him and she saw that he saw and then it went so high it went out of sight a moment and she was trembling in every limb from being bent so far back he had a full view high up above her knee no-one ever not even on the swing or wading and she wasn't ashamed and he wasn't either to look in that immodest way like that because he couldn't resist the sight of the wondrous revealment half offered like those skirtdancers behaving so immodest before gentlemen looking and he kept on looking, looking. She would fain have cried to him chokingly, held out her snowy slender arms to him to come, to

---

32. A fine white cotton, used for underwear.

feel his lips laid on her white brow the cry of a young girl's love, a little strangled cry, wrung from her, that cry that has rung through the ages. And then a rocket sprang and bang shot blind and O! then the Roman candle burst and it was like a sigh of O! and everyone cried O! O! in raptures and it gushed out of it a stream of rain gold hair threads and they shed and ah! they were all greeny dewy stars falling with golden, O so lively! O so soft, sweet, soft! [33]

Then all melted away dewily in the grey air: all was silent. Ah! She glanced at him as she bent forward quickly, a pathetic little glance of piteous protest, of shy reproach under which he coloured like a girl. He was leaning back against the rock behind. Leopold Bloom (for it is he) stands silent, with bowed head before those young guileless eyes. What a brute he had been! At it again? A fair unsullied soul had called to him and, wretch that he was, how had he answered? An utter cad he had been. He of all men! But there was an infinite store of mercy in those eyes, for him too a word of pardon even though he had erred and sinned and wandered. Should a girl tell? No, a thousand times no. That was their secret, only theirs, alone in the hiding twilight and there was none to know or tell save the little bat that flew so softly through the evening to and fro and little bats don't tell.

Cissy Caffrey whistled, imitating the boys in the football field to show what a great person she was: and then she cried:

—Gerty! Gerty! We're going. Come on. We can see from farther up.

Gerty had an idea, one of love's little ruses. She slipped a hand into her kerchief pocket and took out the wadding and waved in reply of course without letting him and then slipped it back. Wonder if he's too far to. She rose. Was it goodbye? No. She had to go but they would meet again, there, and she would dream of that till then, tomorrow, of her dream of yester eve. She drew herself up to her full height. Their souls met in a last lingering glance and the eyes that reached her heart, full of a strange shining, hung enraptured on her sweet flowerlike face. She half smiled at him wanly, a sweet forgiving smile, a smile that verged on tears, and then they parted.

Slowly without looking back she went down the uneven strand to Cissy, to Edy, to Jacky and Tommy Caffrey, to little baby Boardman. It was darker now and there were stones and bits of wood on the strand and slippy seaweed. She walked with a certain quiet dignity characteristic of her but with care and very slowly because Gerty MacDowell was . . . .

Tight boots? No. She's lame! O! [34]

Mr Bloom watched her as she limped away. Poor girl! That's why she's left on the shelf and the others did a sprint. Thought something was wrong by the cut of her jib. Jilted beauty. A defect is ten times worse in a woman. But makes them polite. Glad I didn't know it when she was on show. Hot little devil all the same. Wouldn't mind. Curiosity like a nun or a negress or a girl

33. The softness is of the visionary lights of the fireworks, and of Gerty's own underclothing and flesh. It is at this point in the story that the sentimental evasions of the directly sexual will give way, in the very image of the exploding Roman candle that is a counterpart of Bloom's sexual climax. The "outer" explosion in the world of Gerty's rhetoric is matched by an inner one, and the chapter now moves into that world, undercutting the parody of the first part.

34. The introduction of Bloom's interior monologue is characteristic of him; his practical, even (within its means) scientific, curiosity is always at work, Sherlock Holmes-like, on the phenomena he observes. And so is his memory.

with glasses. That squinty one is delicate. Near her monthlies, I expect, makes them feel ticklish. I have such a bad headache today. Where did I put the letter?[35] Yes, all right. All kinds of crazy longings. Licking pennies. Girl in Tranquilla convent that nun told me liked to smell rock oil. Virgins go mad in the end I suppose. Sister? How many women in Dublin have it today? Martha, she. Something in the air. That's the moon. But then why don't all women menstruate at the same time with same moon, I mean? Depends on the time they were born, I suppose. Or all start scratch then get out of step. Sometimes Molly and Milly together. Anyhow I got the best of that. Damned glad I didn't do it in the bath this morning over her silly I will punish you letter. Made up for that tramdriver this morning. That gouger M'Coy stopping me to say nothing.[36] And his wife engagement in the country valise, voice like a pickaxe. Thankful for small mercies. Cheap too. Yours for the asking. Because they want it themselves. Their natural craving. Shoals of them every evening poured out of offices. Reserve better. Don't want it they throw it at you. Catch em alive, O. Pity they can't see themselves. A dream of wellfilled hose. Where was that? Ah, yes. Mutoscope pictures in Capel street: for men only. Peeping Tom. Willy's hat and what the girls did with it. Do they snapshot those girls or is it all a fake? *Lingerie* does it. Felt for the curves inside her *deshabillé*. Excites them also when they're. I'm all clean come and dirty me. And they like dressing one another for the sacrifice. Milly delighted with Molly's new blouse. At first. Put them all on to take them all off. Molly. Why I bought her the violet garters. Us too: the tie he wore, his lovely socks and turnedup trousers. He wore a pair of gaiters the night that first we met. His lovely shirt was shining beneath his what? of jet. Say a woman loses a charm with every pin she takes out. Pinned together. O Mairy lost the pin of her. Dressed up to the nines for somebody. Fashion part of their charm. Just changes when you're on the track of the secret. Except the east: Mary, Martha: now as then. No reasonable offer refused. She wasn't in a hurry either. Always off to a fellow when they are. They never forget an appointment. Out on spec probably. They believe in chance because like themselves. And the others inclined to give her an odd dig. Girl friends at school, arms round each other's neck or with ten fingers locked, kissing and whispering secrets about nothing in the convent garden. Nuns with whitewashed faces, cool coif and their rosaries going up and down, vindictive too for what they can't get. Barbed wire. Be sure now and write to me. And I'll write to you. Now won't you? Molly and Josie Powell. Till Mr Right comes along then meet once in a blue moon. *Tableau!*[37] O, look who it is for the love of God! How are you at all? What have you been doing with yourself? Kiss and delighted to, kiss, to see you. Picking holes in each other's appearance. You're looking splendid. Sister souls showing their teeth at one another. How many have you left? Wouldn't lend each other a pinch of salt.

    Ah!

35. From Martha Clifford, a typist with whom he is corresponding, under the pseudonym "Henry Flower." In his brooding about menstruation he will revert to Martha a few lines farther along.

36. A bore who had stopped Bloom earlier in the day to cadge a suitcase from him.

37. This reciprocates Gerty's identical joke earlier. See note 22.

Devils they are when that's coming on them.[38] Dark devilish appearance. Molly often told me feel things a ton weight. Scratch the sole of my foot. O that way! O, that's exquisite! Feel it myself too. Good to rest once in a way. Wonder if it's bad to go with them then. Safe in one way. Turns milk, makes fiddlestrings snap. Something about withering plants I read in a garden. Besides they say if the flower withers she wears she's a flirt. All are. Daresay she felt I. When you feel like that you often meet what you feel. Liked me or what? Dress they look at. Always know a fellow courting: collars and cuffs. Well cocks and lions do the same and stags. Same time might prefer a tie undone or something. Trousers? Suppose I when I was? No. Gently does it. Dislike rough and tumble. Kiss in the dark and never tell. Saw something in me. Wonder what. Sooner have me as I am than some poet chap with bearsgrease, plastery hair lovelock over his dexter optic.[39] To aid gentleman in literary. Ought to attend to my appearance my age. Didn't let her see me in profile. Still, you never know. Pretty girls and ugly men marrying. Beauty and the beast. Besides I can't be so if Molly. Took off her hat to show her hair. Wide brim bought to hide her face, meeting someone might know her, bend down or carry a bunch of flowers to smell. Hair strong in rut. Ten bob I got for Molly's combings when we were on the rocks in Holles street. Why not? Suppose he gave her money. Why not? All a prejudice. She's worth ten, fifteen, more a pound. All that for nothing. Bold hand. Mrs Marion. Did I forget to write address on that lettter like the postcard I sent to Flynn? And the day I went to Drimmie's without a necktie. Wrangle with Molly it was put me off. No, I remember. Richie Goulding.[40] He's another. Weighs on his mind. Funny my watch stopped at half past four.[41] Dust. Shark liver oil they use to clean could do it myself. Save. Was that just when he, she?

O, he did. Into her. She did. Done.

Ah! [42]

Mr. Bloom with careful hand recomposed his wet shirt. O Lord, that little limping devil. Begins to feel cold and clammy. Aftereffect not pleasant. Still you have to get rid of it someway. They don't care. Complimented perhaps. Go home to nicey bread and milky and say night prayers with the kiddies. Well, aren't they. See her as she is spoil all. Must have the stage setting, the rouge, costume, position, music. The name too. *Amours* of actresses. Nell Gwynn, Mrs Bracegirdle, Maud Branscombe.[43] Curtain up. Moonlight silver effulgence. Maiden discovered with pensive bosom. Little sweetheart come and kiss me. Still I feel. The strength it gives a man. That's the secret of it. Good job I let off there behind coming out of Dignam's. Cider that was. Otherwise I couldn't have. Makes you want to sing after. *Lacaus esant taratara.*[44] Suppose I spoke to her. What about? Bad plan however if you don't

---

38. Again, menstruation, and remembered superstitions about it.
39. Right eye.
40. Stephen Daedalus's uncle, brother of his dead mother.
41. The moment of Molly Bloom's adultery with Blazes Boylan, her concert manager. Bloom is almost aware of this.
42. The moment of his ejaculation.
43. Famous actresses of the Restoration stage.
44. Bloom is garbling the words (*"La causa è santa"*) of an aria from Meyerbeer's *The*

know how to end the conversation. Ask them a question they ask you another. Good idea if you're in a cart. Wonderful of course if you say: good evening, and you see she's on for it: good evening. O but the dark evening in the Appian way I nearly spoke to Mrs Clinch O thinking she was. Whew! Girl in Meath street that night. All the dirty things I made her say all wrong of course. My arks she called it. It's so hard to find one who. Aho! If you don't answer when they solicit must be horrible for them till they harden. And kissed my hand when I gave her the extra two shillings. Parrots. Press the button and the bird will squeak. Wish she hadn't called me sir. Oh, her mouth in the dark! And you a married man with a single girl! That's what they enjoy. Taking a man from another woman. Or even hear of it. Different with me. Glad to get away from other chap's wife. Eating off his cold plate. Chap in the Burton [45] today spitting back gumchewed gristle. French letter [46] still in my pocketbook. Cause of half the trouble. But might happen sometime, I don't think. Come in. All is prepared. I dreamt. What? [47] Worst is beginning. How they change the venue [48] when it's not what they like. Ask you do you like mushrooms because she once knew a gentleman who. Or ask you what someone was going to say when he changed his mind and stopped. Yet if I went the whole hog, say: I want to, something like that. Because I did. She too. Offend her. Then make it up. Pretend to want something awfully, then cry off for her sake. Flatters them. She must have been thinking of someone else all the time. What harm? Must since she came to the use of reason, he, he and he. First kiss does the trick. The propitious moment. Something inside them goes pop. Mushy like, tell by their eye, on the sly. First thoughts are best. Remember that till their dying day. Molly, lieutenant Mulvey that kissed her under the Moorish wall beside the gardens. [49] Fifteen she told me. But her breasts were developed. Fell asleep then. After Gencree dinner that was when we drove home the featherbed mountain. Gnashing her teeth in sleep. Lord mayor had his eye on her too. Val Dillon. [50] Apoplectic.

There she is with them down there for the fireworks. My fireworks. Up like a rocket, down like a stick. And the children, twins they must be, waiting for something to happen. Want to be grownups. Dressing in mother's clothes. Time enough, understand all the ways of the world. And the dark one with the mop head and the nigger mouth. I knew she could whistle. Mouth made for that. Like Molly. Why that high class whore in Jammet's wore her veil only to her nose. Would you mind, please, telling me the right time? I'll tell you the right time up a dark lane. Say prunes and prisms forty times every morning, cure for fat lips. Caressing the little boy too. Onlookers see most of the game. Of course they understand birds, animals, babies. In their line.

Huguenots: La cause est juste et sainte, through an Italian translation; the "taratara" may be Bloom's version of the famous "Rataplan Chorus" from that opera, although Tara is the name of a hill where the Irish kings were crowned.

45. A restaurant Bloom had entered at lunchtime, only to be revolted by the sight of men eating meat (in the Laestrygonians episode); he went elsewhere for a cheese sandwich.

46. A condom.

47. He is aware of a dream that he does not remember until the end of this episode.

48. In court cases, a change of venue brings about a removal of the trial to another court.

49. Bloom is thinking of an early erotic incident in Molly Bloom's life, in Gibraltar (where she grew up) with an early lover, Lieut. Henry Mulvey.

50. The mayor of Dublin.

Didn't look back when she was going down the strand. Wouldn't give that satisfaction. Those girls, those girls, those lovely seaside girls. Fine eyes she had, clear. It's the white of the eye brings that out not so much the pupil. Did she know what I? Course. Like a cat sitting beyond a dog's jump. Women never meet one like that Wilkins in the high school drawing a picture of Venus with all his belongings on show. Call that innocence? Poor idiot! His wife has her work cut out for her. Never see them sit on a bench marked *Wet Paint*. Eyes all over them. Look under the bed for what's not there. Longing to get the fright of their lives. Sharp as needles they are. When I said to Molly the man at the corner of Cuffe street was goodlooking, thought she might like, twigged at once he had a false arm. Had too. Where do they get that? Typist going up Roger Greene's stairs two at a time to show her understandings. Handed down from father to mother to daughter, I mean. Bred in the bone. Milly for example drying her handkerchief on the mirror to save the ironing. Best place for an ad to catch a woman's eye on a mirror. And when I sent her [51] for Molly's Paisley shawl to Prescott's, by the way that ad I must, carrying home the change in her stocking. Clever little minx! I never told her. Neat way she carried parcels too. Attract men, small thing like that. Holding up her hand, shaking it, to let the blood flow back when it was red. Who did you learn that from? Nobody. Something the nurse taught me. O, don't they know? Three years old she was in front of Molly's dressingtable just before we left Lombard street west. Me have a nice face. Mullingar.[52] Who knows? Ways of the world. Young student. Straight on her pins anyway not like the other. Still she was game. Lord, I am wet. Devil you are. Swell of her calf. Transparent stockings, stretched to breaking point. Not like that frump today. A. E.[53] Rumpled stockings. Or the one in Grafton street. White. Wow! Beef to the heel.

A monkey puzzle rocket burst, spluttering in darting crackles. Zrads and zrads, zrads, zrads. And Cissy and Tommy ran out to see and Edy after with the pushcar and then Gerty beyond the curve of the rocks. Will she? Watch! Watch! See! Looked round. She smelt an onion. Darling, I saw your. I saw all. Lord!

Did me good all the same. Off colour after Kiernan's, Dignam's. For this relief much thanks.[54] In *Hamlet*, that is. Lord! It was all things combined. Excitement. When she leaned back felt an ache at the butt of my tongue. Your head it simply swirls. He's right. Might have made a worse fool of myself however. Instead of talking about nothing. Then I will tell you all. Still it was a kind of language between us. It couldn't be? No, Gerty they called her. Might be false name however like my and the address Dolphin's barn a blind.

> *Her maiden name was Jemina Brown*
> *And she lived with her mother in Irishtown.*

Place made me think of that I suppose. All tarred with the same brush. Wiping pens in their stockings. But the ball rolled down to her as if it under-

---

51. He goes on thinking of Milly.
52. Where Milly is currently working for a photographer.
53. Earlier in the day, Bloom had encountered the poet "A.E." (George Russell, 1867–1935) talking to a woman ("Her stockings are loose over her ankles. I detest that: so tasteless"), and then goes on to brood on Russell's vegetarian habits (in the *Laestrygonians* chapter). Here he remembers this and another incident.
54. *Hamlet* I.i.8.

stood. Every bullet has its billet. Course I never could throw anything straight at school. Crooked as a ram's horn. Sad however because it lasts only a few years till they settle down to potwalloping and papa's pants will soon fit Willy and fullers' earth [55] for the baby when they hold him out to do ah ah. No soft job. Saves them. Keeps them out of harm's way. Nature. Washing child, washing corpse. Dignam. Children's hands always round them. Cocoanut skulls, monkeys, not even closed at first, sour milk in their swaddles and tainted curds. Oughtn't to have given that child an empty teat to suck. Fill it up with wind. Mrs Beaufoy, Purefoy.[56] Must call to the hospital. Wonder is nurse Callan there still. She used to look over some nights when Molly was in the Coffee Palace. That young doctor O'Hare I noticed her brushing his coat. And, Mrs Breen and Mrs Dignam once like that too, marriageable. Worst of all at night Mrs Duggan told me in the City Arms.[57] Husband rolling in drunk, stink of pub off him like a polecat. Have that in your nose in the dark, whiff of stale boose. Then ask in the morning: was I drunk last night? Bad policy however to fault the husband. Chickens come home to roost. They stick by one another like glue. Maybe the women's fault also. That's where Molly can knock spots off them. It is the blood of the south. Moorish.[58] Also the form, the figure. Hands felt for the opulent. Just compare for instance those others. Wife locked up at home, skeleton in the cupboard. Allow me to introduce my. Then they trot you out some kind of a nondescript, wouldn't know what to call her. Always see a fellow's weak point in his wife. Still there's destiny in it, falling in love. Have their own secrets between them. Chaps that would go to the dogs if some woman didn't take them in hand. Then little chits of girls, height of a shilling in coppers, with little hubbies. As God made them He matched them. Sometimes children turn out well enough. Twice nought makes one. Or old rich chap of seventy and blushing bride. Marry in May and repent in December. This wet is very unpleasant. Stuck. Well the foreskin is not back. Better detach.

Ow!

Other hand a sixfooter with a wifey up to his watchpocket. Long and the short of it. Big he and little she. Very strange about my watch.[59] Wristwatches are always going wrong. Wonder is there any magnetic influence between the person because that was about the time he. Yes, I suppose at once. Cat's away the mice will play. I remember looking in Pill lane. Also that now is magnetism. Back of everything magnetism. Earth for instance pulling this and being pulled. That causes movement. And time? Well that's the time the movement takes. Then if one thing stopped the whole ghesabo [60] would stop bit by bit. Because it's arranged. Magnetic needle tells you what's going on in

---

55. Talc, so named for its use in cleaning clothes, but here used as baby powder. "Papa's pants will soon fit Willy"—a well-known music-hall song.
56. Philip Beaufoy was the author of a story Bloom had read that morning in the privy. In the next chapter Mrs. Purefoy, a friend of Bloom's, will be delivered of a baby in the Lying-in Hospital in Holles Street. Earlier in the day, Bloom, in chatting with Mrs. Breen, a youthful flame, got the names mixed up in a Freudian slip, as he does again here.
57. A pub.
58. The Moorish wall in Gibraltar, scene of Molly's early love.
59. It had stopped at 4:30.
60. Contraption.

the sun, the stars. Little piece of steel iron. When you hold out the fork. Come. Come. Tip. Woman and man that is. Fork and steel. Molly, he. Dress up and look and suggest and let you see and see more and defy you if you're a man to see that and, like a sneeze coming, legs, look, look and if you have any guts in you. Tip. Have to let fly.

Wonder how is she feeling in that region. Shame all put on before third person. More put out about a hole in her stocking. Molly, her underjaw stuck out head back, about the farmer in the ridingboots and spurs at the horse show. And when the painters were in Lombard street west. Fine voice that fellow had. How Giuglini [61] began. Smell that I did, like flowers. It was too. Violets. Came from the turpentine probably in the paint. Make their own use of everything. Same time doing it scraped her slipper on the floor so they wouldn't hear. But lots of them can't kick the beam, I think. Keep that thing up for hours. Kind of a general all round over me and half down my back.

Wait. Hm. Hm. Yes. That's her perfume. Why she waved her hand. I leave you this to think of me when I'm far away on the pillow. What is it? Heliotrope? No, Hyacinth? Hm. Roses, I think. She'd like scent of that kind. Sweet and cheap: soon sour. Why Molly likes opoponax.[62] Suits her with a little jessamine mixed. Her high notes and her low notes. At the dance night she met him, dance of the hours. Heat brought it out. She was wearing her black and it had the perfume of the time before. Good conductor, is it? Or bad? Light too. Suppose there's some connection. For instance if you go into a cellar where it's dark. Mysterious thing too. Why did I smell it only now? Took its time in coming like herself, slow but sure. Suppose it's ever so many millions of tiny grains blown across. Yes, it is. Because those spice islands, Cinghalese this morning,[63] smell them leagues off. Tell you what it is. It's like a fine veil or web they have all over the skin, fine like what do you call it gossamer and they're always spinning it out of them, fine as anything, rainbow colours without knowing it. Clings to everything she takes off. Vamp of her stockings. Warm shoe. Stays.[64] Drawers: little kick, taking them off. Byby till next time. Also the cat likes to sniff in her shift on the bed. Know her smell in a thousand. Bathwater too. Reminds me of strawberries and cream. Wonder where it is really. There or the armpits or under the neck. Because you get it out of all holes and corners. Hyacinth perfume made of oil or ether or something. Muskrat. Bag under their tails one grain pour off odour for years. Dogs at each other behind. Good evening. Evening. How do you sniff? Hm. Hm. Very well, thank you. Animals go by that. Yes now, look at it that way. We're the same. Some women for instance warn you off when they have their period. Come near. Then get a hogo [65] you could hang your hat on. Like what? Potted herrings gone stale or. Boof! Please keep off the grass.

61. Antonio Giuglini (1827–65), opera tenor.
62. Resin used in perfumes.
63. At about 10 A.M. Bloom had passed a shop with "finest Ceylon" tea advertised; it sent him into a reverie of the exotic, erotic, spice-laden, mysterious East: "Those Cinghalese lobbing around the sun in *dolce far niente*. Not doing a hand's turn all day. Sleep six months out of the twelve. Too hot to quarrel. Influence of the climate. Lethargy. Flowers of idleness. . . ."
64. Corsets.
65. A stink.

Perhaps they get a man smell off us. What though? Cigary gloves Long John had on his desk the other. Breath? What you eat and drink gives that. No. Mansmell, I mean. Must be connected with that because priests that are supposed to be are different. Women buzz round it like flies round treacle. Railed off the altar get on to it at any cost. The tree of forbidden priest. O father, will you? Let me be the first to. That diffuses itself all through the body, permeates. Source of life and it's extremely curious the smell. Celery sauce. Let me.

Mr Bloom inserted his nose. Hm. Into the. Hm. Opening of his waistcoat. Almonds or. No. Lemons it is. Ah, no, that's the soap.[66]

O by the by that lotion. I knew there was something on my mind. Never went back and the soap not paid. Dislike carrying bottles like that hag this morning. Hynes might have paid me [67] that three shillings. I could mention Meagher's just to remind him. Still if he works that paragraph. Two and nine. Bad opinion of me he'll have. Call tomorrow. How much do I owe you? Three and nine? Two and nine, sir. Ah. Might stop him giving credit another time. Lose your customers that way. Pubs do. Fellow run up a bill on the slate and then slinking around the back streets into somewhere else.

Here's this nobleman passed before. Blown in from the bay. Just went as far as turn back. Always at home at dinnertime. Looks mangled out: had a good tuck in. Enjoying nature now. Grace after meals. After supper walk a mile. Sure he has a small bank balance somewhere, government sit. Walk after him now make him awkward like those newsboys me today. Still you learn something. See ourselves as others see us. So long as women don't mock what matter? That's the way to find out. Ask yourself who is he now. *The Mystery Man on the Beach*,[68] prize titbit story by Mr Leopold Bloom. Payment at the rate of one guinea per column. And that fellow today at the graveside in the brown macintosh. Corns on his kismet [69] however. Healthy perhaps absorb all the. Whistle brings rain they say. Must be some somewhere. Salt in the Ormond [70] damp. The body feels the atmosphere. Old Betty's joints are on the rack. Mother Shipton's [71] prophecy that is about ships around they fly in the twinkling. No. Signs of rain it is. The royal reader. And distant hills seem coming nigh.

Howth.[72] Bailey light. Two, four, six, eight, nine. See. Has to change or they

---

66. Bloom had bought a bar of "sweet lemony" soap at a chemist's (pharmacy), forgetting to pay for it (he had gone in originally to buy some lotion for Molly). He carries the soap about in his pocket all day.

67. A newspaper reporter who owes Bloom a small sum. Bloom has encountered him several times during the day.

68. The "titbit story" was the one by Beaufoy that Bloom had read earlier; the man in the brown macintosh at Dignam's funeral is the "mystery man" of *Ulysses:* we never learn who he is.

69. "Fate," derived from the Turkish.

70. The Ormond Hotel, where all the singing takes place in *Sirens.*

71. A 17th-century prophetess, credited, in an 1862 book about her, with having prophesied the steam engine, telegraphy, and other scientific marvels, as well as the end of the world (to occur in 1881).

72. Bloom is looking across Dublin Bay at the Hill of Howth (mentioned in the epening sentences) and its lighthouse.

might think it a house. Wreckers. Grace Darling.[73] People afraid of the dark. Also glowworms, cyclists: lightingup time. Jewels diamonds flash better. Light is a kind of reassuring. Not going to hurt you. Better now of course than long ago. Country roads. Run you through the small guts for nothing. Still two types there are you bob against. Scowl or smile. Pardon! Not at all. Best time to spray plants too in the shade after the sun. Some light still. Red rays are longest. Roygbiv Vance taught us: red, orange, yellow, green, blue, indigo, violet. A star I see. Venus? Can't tell yet. Two, when three it's night.[74] Were those nightclouds there all the time? Looks like a phantom ship. No. Wait. Trees are they. An optical illusion. Mirage. Land of the setting sun this. Homerule[75] sun setting in the southeast. My native land, goodnight.

Dew falling. Bad for you, dear, to sit on that stone. Brings on white fluxions.[76] Never have little baby then less he was big strong fight his way up through. Might get piles myself. Sticks too like a summer cold, sore on the mouth. Cut with grass or paper worst. Friction of the position. Like to be that rock she sat on. O sweet little, you don't know how nice you looked. I begin to like them at that age. Green apples. Grab at all that offer. Suppose it's the only time we cross legs, seated. Also the library today: those girl graduates. Happy chairs under them. But it's the evening influence. They feel all that. Open like flowers, know their hours, sunflowers, Jerusalem artichokes, in ballrooms, chandeliers, avenues under the lamps. Nightstock[77] in Mat Dillon's garden where I kissed her shoulder. Wish I had a full length oil-painting of her then. June that was too I wooed. The year returns. History repeats itself. Ye crags and peaks I'm with you once again. Life, love, voyage round your own little world. And now? Sad about her lame of course but must be on your guard not to feel too much pity. They take advantage.

All quiet on Howth now. The distant hills seem. Where we. The rhododendrons. I am a fool perhaps. He gets the plums and I the plumstones. Where I come in. All that old hill has seen. Names change: that's all. Lovers: yum yum.

Tired I feel now. Will I get up? O wait. Drained all the manhood out of me, little wretch. She kissed me. My youth. Never again. Only once it comes. Or hers. Take the train there tomorrow. No. Returning not the same. Like kids your second visit to a house. The new I want. Nothing new under the sun. Care of P. O. Dolphin's barn. Are you not happy in your? Naughty darling. At Dolphin's barn charades in Luke Doyle's house. Mat Dillon and his bevy of daughters: Tiny, Atty, Floey, Maimy, Louy, Hetty. Molly too. Eightyseven that was. Year before we. And the old major partial to his drop of spirits. Curious she an only child, I an only child. So it returns. Think you're escaping and run into yourself. Longest way round is the shortest way home. And just when he and she. Circus horse walking in a ring. Rip van Winkle we played. Rip: tear

73. Heroine (1815–42), daughter of a lighthouse keeper who saved people from drowning. Wordsworth wrote a poem about her.

74. According to canonical Jewish law, night (and, thus, the next day) starts when three stars are visible. The evening star that Bloom sees, along with the starry fireworks, is yet another *stella maris*, "star of the sea."

75. Southeast of Dublin is London, and Parliament, which refused to grant Ireland home rule.

76. Discharges.

77. A plant also called garden rocket. Bloom is thinking of his first meeting with Molly.

in Henny Doyle's overcoat. Van: breadvan delivering. Winkle: cockles and peri-
winkles. Then I did Rip van Winkle coming back. She leaned on the sideboard
watching. Moorish eyes. Twenty years asleep in Sleepy Hollow. All changed.
Forgotten. The young are old. His gun rusty from the dew.

Ba. What is that flying about? Swallow? Bat probably.[78] Thinks I'm a tree,
so blind. Have birds no smell? Metempsychosis.[79] They believed you could be
changed into a tree from grief. Weeping willow. Ba. There he goes. Funny
little beggar. Wonder where he lives. Belfry up there. Very likely. Hanging by
his heels in the odour of sanctity. Bell scared him out, I suppose. Mass seems
to be over. Could hear them all at it. Pray for us. And pray for us. And pray
for us. Good idea the repetition. Same thing with ads. Buy from us. And buy
from us. Yes, there's the light in the priest's house. Their frugal meal. Remember
about the mistake in the valuation when I was in Thom's. Twentyeight it is.
Two houses they have. Gabriel Conroy's brother is curate.[80] Ba. Again. Wonder
why they come out at night like mice. They're a mixed breed. Birds are like
hopping mice. What frightens them, light or noise? Better sit still. All instinct
like the bird in drouth got water out of the end of a jar by throwing in pebbles.
Like a little man in a cloak he is with tiny hands. Weeny bones. Almost see
them shimmering, kind of a bluey white. Colours depend on the light you see.
Stare the sun for example like the eagle then look at a shoe see a blotch blob
yellowish. Wants to stamp his trademark on everything. Instance, that cat this
morning on the staircase. Colour of brown turf. Say you never see them with
three colours. Not true. That half tabbywhite tortoiseshell in the *City Arms*
with the letter em on her forehead. Body fifty different colours. Howth a while
ago amethyst. Glass flashing. That's how that wise man what's his name with
the burning glass. Then the heather goes on fire. It can't be tourists' matches.
What? Perhaps the sticks dry rub together in the wind and light. Or broken
bottles in the furze act as a burning glass in the sun. Archimedes. I have it! [81]
My memory's not so bad.

Ba. Who knows what they're always flying for. Insects? That bee last week
got into the room playing with his shadow on the ceiling. Might be the one bit
me, come back to see. Birds too never find out what they say. Like our small
talk. And says she and says he. Nerve? they have to fly over the ocean and
back. Lot must be killed in storms, telegraph wires. Dreadful life sailors have
too. Big brutes of ocean-going steamers floundering along in the dark, lowing
out like seacows. *Faugh a ballagh.*[82] Out of that, bloody curse to you. Others in
vessels, bit of a handkerchief sail, pitched about like snuff at a wake when the
stormy winds do blow. Married too. Sometimes away for years at the ends of
the earth somewhere. No ends really because it's round. Wife in every port they
say. She has a good job if she minds it till Johnny comes marching home again.

78. Compare a similar moment of twilight for the young Stephen Daedalus at the end of
our excerpt from *A Portrait of the Artist as a Young Man,* and the D. H. Lawrence "Bat" poem
referred to there; compare its protagonist's reaction with the same discovery Bloom is making.
79. The word means the transmigration of souls, the doctrine of reincarnation. The word,
and the concept (connected as it is with historical repetition; see "History repeats itself,"
above), have been thematic in *Ulysses.*
80. That is, the Father Conroy referred to in Gerty's half of the chapter; see *The Dead.*
81. "Eureka!" the famous cry of Archimedes on discovering how to measure weight by
water displacement.
82. A worthless person (Gaelic).

If ever he does. Smelling the tail end of ports. How can they like the sea? Yet they do. The anchor's weighed. Off he sails with a scapular or a medal on him for luck. Well? And the tephilim [83] no what's this they call it poor papa's father had on his door to touch. That brought us out of the land of Egypt and into the house of bondage.[84] Something in all those superstitions because when you go out never know what dangers. Hanging on to a plank or astride of a beam for grim life, lifebelt round round him, gulping salt water, and that's the last of his nibs till the sharks catch hold of him. Do fish ever get seasick?

Then you have a beautiful calm without a cloud, smooth sea, placid, crew and cargo in smithereens, Davy Jones' locker. Moon looking down. Not my fault, old cockalorum.

A lost long candle wandered up the sky from Mirus bazaar in search of funds for Mercer's hospital and broke, drooping, and shed a cluster of violet but one white stars. They floated, fell: they faded. The shepherd's hour: the hour of holding: hour of tryst. From house to house, giving his everwelcome double knock, went the nine o'clock postman, the glowworm's lamp at his belt gleaming here and there through the laurel hedges. And among the five young trees a hoisted lintstock lit the lamp at Leahy's terrace.[85] By screens of lighted windows, by equal gardens a shrill voice went crying, wailing: *Evening Telegraph, stop press edition! Result of the Gold Cup race!* [86] and from the door of Dignam's house a boy ran out and called. Twittering the bat flew here, flew there. Far out over the sands the coming surf crept, grey. Howth settled for slumber tired of long days, of yumyum rhododendrons (he was old) and felt gladly the night breeze lift, ruffle his fell of ferns. He lay but opened a red eye unsleeping, deep and slowly breathing, slumberous but awake. And far on Kish bank [87] the anchored lightship twinkled, winked at Mr Bloom.

Life those chaps out there must have, stuck in the same spot. Irish Lights board. Penance for their sins. Coastguards too. Rocket and breeches buoy and lifeboat. Day we went out for the pleasure cruise in the Erin's King, throwing them the sack of old papers. Bears in the zoo. Filthy trip. Drunkards out to shake up their livers. Puking overboard to feed the herrings. Nausea. And the women, fear of God in their faces. Milly, no sign of funk. Her blue scarf loose, laughing. Don't know what death is at that age. And then their stomachs clean. But being lost they fear. When we hid behind the tree at Crumlin. I didn't want to. Mamma! Mamma! Babes in the wood. Frightening them with masks too. Throwing them up in the air to catch them. I'll murder you. Is it only half fun? Or children playing battle. Whole earnest. How can people aim guns at each other? Sometimes they go off. Poor kids. Only troubles wildfire and nettle-rash. Calomel [88] purge I got her for that. After getting better asleep with Molly. Very same teeth she has. What do they love? Another themselves? But the

83. *Tefillin,* phylacteries, small containers of written prayers wrapped around the head and hands of orthodox Jews during daily prayers. Bloom confuses these with a *mezuzzah,* an analogous container of the same text put up on the doorposts of one's house and upon one's gates.

84. He deliberately misquotes the text of the First Commandment: ". . . out of the land of Egypt, out of the house of bondage" (Exodus 20:2).

85. Behind the beach along which he has been sitting.

86. This race has figured prominently in the book.

87. Out across the bay.

88. Mercury salts formerly used in laxatives.

morning she chased her with the umbrella. Perhaps so as not to hurt. I felt her pulse. Ticking. Little hand it was: now big. Dearest Papli.[89] All that the hand says when you touch. Loved to count my waistcoat buttons. Her first stays I remember. Made me laugh to see. Little paps to begin with. Left one is more sensitive, I think. Mine too. Nearer the heart. Padding themselves out if fat is in fashion. Her growing pains at night, calling, wakening me. Frightened she was when her nature came on her first.[90] Poor child! Strange moment for the mother too. Brings back her girlhood. Gibraltar. Looking from Buena Vista. O'Hara's tower. The seabirds screaming. Old Barbary ape that gobbled all his family. Sundown, gunfire for the men to cross the lines. Looking out over the sea she told me. Evening like this, but clear, no clouds. I always thought I'd marry a lord or a gentleman with a private yacht. *Buenas noches, señorita. El hombre ama la muchacha hermosa.*[91] Why me? Because you were so foreign from the others.

Better not stick here all night like a limpet. This weather makes you dull. Must be getting on for nine by the light. Go home. Too late for *Leah, Lily of Killarney.*[92] No. Might be still up. Call to the hospital to see. Hope she's over. Long day I've had. Martha,[93] the bath,[94] funeral,[95] house of keys,[96] museum with those goddesses,[97] Dedalus' song.[98] Then that bawler in Barney Kiernan's.[99] Got my own back there. Drunken ranters. What I said about his God made him wince. Mistake to hit back. Or? No. Ought to go home and laugh at themselves. Always want to be swilling in company. Afraid to be alone like a child of two. Suppose he hit me. Look at it other way round. Not so bad then. Perhaps not to hurt he meant. Three cheers for Israel. Three cheers for the sister-in-law he hawked about, three fangs in her mouth. Same style of beauty. Particularly nice old party for a cup of tea. The sister of the wife of the wild man of Borneo has just come to town. Imagine that in the early morning at close range. Everyone to his taste as Morris said when he kissed the cow. But Dignam's put the boots on it. Houses of mourning so depressing because you never know. Anyhow she wants the money. Must call to those Scottish widows[100] as I promised. Strange name. Takes it for granted we're going to pop off first.

89. Milly had written her father like this.
90. Again, thinking of Milly's first menstruation.
91. "Good evening, Miss. The man loves the pretty girl" (Spanish).
92. Earlier, Bloom had wondered whether to see a play called *Leah, or the Jewish Maiden,* by the American playwright T. A. Daly, that evening, or an operetta called *Lily of Killarney.*
93. Bloom now goes through a résumé of his day, summing up the previous chapters in which he has appeared; Martha Clifford, his secret correspondent (see note 35).
94. The Turkish bath in which Bloom had reclined, in the *Lotus-Eaters* episode.
95. Paddy Dignam's funeral, the *Hades* chapter.
96. At the newspaper office, thinking of an advertisement for the House of Keys. The House of Keys is the legislature of the Isle of Man, the name of which, in the context of *Ulysses,* cannot help but resonate symbolically for us.
97. The museum stands next to the National Library, in which the *Scylla and Charybdis* scene occurs.
98. The *Sirens* episode at the Ormond Hotel, where Simon Daedalus, Stephen's father, sings an aria from Flotow's opera *Martha.*
99. In Barney Kiernan's pub (*Cyclops*), Bloom has suffered rhetorically elaborate anti-Semitic abuse. In a later recapitulation of the episodes of *Ulysses* the present *Nausicaa* section is called "rite of Onan," centering on Bloom's masturbation.
100. A well-known life-insurance company.

That widow on Monday was it outside Cramer's that looked at me. Buried the poor husband but progressing favourably on the premium. Her widow's mite. Well? What do you expect her to do? Must wheedle her way along. Widower I hate to see. Looks so forlorn. Poor man O'Connor wife and five children poisoned by mussels here. The sewage. Hopeless. Some good matronly woman in a porkpie hat to mother him. Take him in tow, platter face and a large apron. Ladies' grey flannelette bloomers, three shillings a pair, astonishing bargain. Plain and loved, loved for ever, they say. Ugly: no woman thinks she is. Love, lie and be handsome for tomorrow we die. See him sometimes walking about trying to find out who played the trick. U. p.: up.[101] Fate that is. He, not me. Also a shop often noticed. Curse seems to dog it. Dream last night?[102] Wait. Something confused. She had red slippers on. Turkish. Wore the breeches. Suppose she does. Would I like her in pyjamas? Damned hard to answer. Nannetti's gone. Mailboat. Near Holyhead[103] by now. Must nail that ad of Keyes's.[104] Work Hynes and Crawford. Petticoats for Molly.[105] She has something to put in them. What's that? Might be money.

Mr Bloom stooped and turned over a piece of paper on the strand. He brought it near his eyes and peered. Letter? No. Can't read. Better go. Better. I'm tired to move. Page of an old copybook. All those holes and pebbles. Who could count them? Never know what you find. Bottle with story of a treasure in it thrown from a wreck. Parcels post. Children always want to throw things in the sea. Trust? Bread cast on the waters. What's this? Bit of stick.

O! Exhausted that female has me. Not so young now. Will she come here tomorrow? Wait for her somewhere for ever. Must come back. Murderers do. Will I?

Mr Bloom with his stick gently vexed the thick sand at his foot. Write a message for her. Might remain. What?

I.

Some flatfoot tramp on it in the morning. Useless. Washed away. Tide comes here a pool near her foot. Bend, see my face there, dark mirror, breathe on it, stirs. All these rocks with lines and scars and letters. O, those transparent! Besides they don't know. What is the meaning of that other world. I called you naughty boy because I do not like.

AM. A[106]

No room. Let it go.

Mr Bloom effaced the letters with his slow boot. Hopeless thing sand. Nothing grows in it. All fades. No fear of big vessels coming up here. Except Guinness's barges. Round the Kish in eighty days. Done half by design.

He flung his wooden pen away. The stick fell in silted sand, stuck. Now if you were trying to do that for a week on end you couldn't. Chance. We'll never

101. An anonymous postcard sent to an acquaintance of Bloom contained this crude pun on the spelling of "up" as "You pee up."
102. Bloom is remembering his dream of Molly in Turkish trousers.
103. Holyhead, across the Irish Sea in Wales. Bloom's longest voyage ended there.
104. The House of Keys, from which Bloom had been trying to solicit an advertisement.
105. Here again, the underwear that has been thematic, in Bloom's thoughts, in the Victorian erotic imagination, and in this *Nausicaa* episode.
106. A what? Was Bloom going to write "Jew"? "cuckold"?

meet again. But it was lovely. Goodbye, dear. Thanks. Made me feel so young.

Short snooze now if I had. Must be near nine. Liverpool boat long gone. Not even the smoke. And she can do the other. Did too. And Belfast. I won't go. Race there, race back to Ennis. Let him. Just close my eyes a moment. Won't sleep though. Half dream. It never comes the same. Bat again. No harm in him. Just a few.

O sweety all your little girlwhite up I saw dirty bracegirdle made me do love sticky we two naughty Grace darling she him half past the bed met him pike hoses[107] frillies for Raoul[108] to perfume your wife black hair heave under embon[109] *señorita* young eyes Mulvey[110] plump years dreams return tail end Agendath[111] swoony love showed me her next year[112] in drawers return next in her next her next.[113]

A bat flew. Here. There. Here. Far in the grey a bell chimed. Mr Bloom with open mouth, his left boot sanded sideways, leaned, breathed. Just for a few.

> *Cuckoo*[113]
> *Cuckoo*
> *Cuckoo*

The clock on the mantelpiece in the priest's house cooed where Canon O'Hanlon and Father Conroy and the reverend John Hughes S. J. were taking tea and sodabread and butter and fried mutton chops with catsup and talking about

> *Cuckoo*
> *Cuckoo*
> *Cuckoo*

Because it was a little canarybird bird that came out of its little house to tell the time that Gerty MacDowell noticed the time she was there because she was as quick as anything about a thing like that, was Gerty MacDowell, and she noticed at once that that foreign gentleman that was sitting on the rocks looking was

> *Cuckoo*
> *Cuckoo*
> *Cuckoo*

1920   1922

---

107. Molly had thus mispronounced the word "metempsychosis" earlier in the day; now, the "hose" part of her word leads to more underwear thoughts.

108. Raoul was a character in *Sweets of Sin,* a cheap, semi-pornographic book Bloom had bought for Molly. In it, the heroine thought of "costliest frillies. For him. For Raoul!" Throughout, Bloom associates Raoul with Boylan.

109. For *embonpoint,* round belly (French).

110. Lieut. Mulvey, Molly's lover in Gibraltar.

111. *"Agendath Netaim"* (Joyce's mistaken Hebrew for *Agudath Netaim*), a Zionist planters' association whose advertisement Bloom had noticed earlier in the day. Its address was on the actual but inadvertently symbolic *Bleibtreustrasse* ("Keep Faithful Street") in Berlin.

112. "Next year in Jerusalem"—a formula at the Passover Seder feast.

113. The cuckoo's cry ("Oh word of fear/ Unpleasing to a married ear," in the spring song in *Love's Labour's Lost*) has been associated, along with the emblem of horns, with a cuckold.

Finnegans Wake

Finnegans Wake, the last and most problematic of Joyce's works, belongs to a genre of mythological anatomies, of handbooks for the ordering of a poet's fictions, that includes Burton's *Anatomy of Melancholy* in the seventeenth century and, in the twentieth, Yeats's *A Vision* and Robert Grave's *The White Goddess.* It is a greater, more important, and yet less available work than the last two mentioned, containing such visions in its totality of story, pattern, and relation.

Renaissance poetic imagination had its mythology in a number of related works, along with instructions known by everyone about how to connect them. Thus, the Old and New Testaments were related typologically, and Ovid's *Metamorphoses* and Homer and other cycles of classic myth were related to Scripture in a complex figural way, foreshadowing in a distorted but retrievable form the truths of Christian biblical narrative. William Blake created a mythological world of his own (rather than being "enslaved by another man's") in his long poems. His system is not easy to grasp, in part because the instructions for putting patterns together, widely known though unstated within the Renaissance fictions themselves, became with Blake elements of the narrative and descriptive material. Dialectical process, that Enlightenment vision of how, in human history, institutions and actions and principles could in time become their own opposites, the cycle of youth and age, the warfare of moral and other contraries—all became thematic for Blake.

Every major modern author has had to do something like this. For a great novelist like Balzac or Dickens or Proust, his fictional world becomes the map of everything: London or Paris is a rich micro-macrocosm. Dublin became, in *Ulysses,* one of these cities. But event and thought and name—the elements of Bloom's and Stephen's world in the book—were finally for Joyce to seem too secondary, too molecular; he wanted to get to the atoms of poetry, and he did so by trying to articulate the pattern out of which all conceptual patterns themselves evolved. That pattern was, on the one hand, historical repetition: the way in which, for the mythological imagination as influenced by the cyclic theory of history of the eighteenth-century thinker Giambattista Vico, everything is a version of something else. In space rather than in time, on the other hand, that pattern was the Freudian one of family romance: ultimately, the oppositions of father-mother, father-son, and son-rival brother, with a peculiarly ancillary father-daughter one, could be used to generate a map of all relations, all events.

Joyce's family is that of an innkeeper named Humphrey Chimpden Earwicker, in Chapelizod (named for Isolde), his wife Anna Livia Plurabella (Ana Liffey is the river Liffey in Irish), their sons Shem and Shaun, and their daughter, Issy. Earwicker (referred to as H.C.E.) is, however, identified with the great sleeping giant Finn MacCool, supposedly buried (as many heroes and kings are buried all over Europe) under the city of Dublin, his head under the Hill of Howth and his feet in Phoenix Park. His wife is the river Liffey, and all women, as he is all men. Shem and Shaun—James and John—are the dialectical pair of Dionysian and Apollonian, organized and lyrical, beloved of mother and of father, antithetical and primary; their rivalry is also an eternal process.

Joyce, delighting in universalizing what was most provincial and peculiar, took his title from an Irish-American ballad that tells how a hodcarrier named Finnegan fell from a ladder to his death, and how everyone became so drunk as his wake that the corpse himself was resurrected. Joyce called his book a "funferal" (made up out of *funeral* and *fun for all,* like the "portmanteau" words of Humpty Dumpty in *Alice in Wonderland*). Finn's awakening, throughout history, at every moment of reality, *is* the book, as well as its subject. The format allows for a total compendium of all the truths and lies and languages Joyce had ever heard of. If the epic style of *Ulysses* involves parodies of all styles, the encyclopedic style of *Finnegans Wake* contains all lists and catalogues, all languages simultaneously. It has the "form" of Earwicker's dream, during which certain Bloomsday-like events appear to happen (such as accusations about sexual transgression); and there are clearly defined sections in which various characters take over in various modes, from learned lecture to parable to song to radio script. Joyce put into the work everything he could think of or find out about; its layers of significance are such that, whenever the surface is scratched, something ironically and comically significant emerges.

A few small excerpts have been given below, in order that the student may realize that Joyce's intention was to create a quasi-scriptural work, one whose reading would have to be a continuing historical process (as it has been a cooperative one among scholars, a kind of rabbinical or patristic continuum). First, there is the opening of Shaun's fable of the *Ondt and the Gracehoper,* adapted from Aesop's ant and grasshopper, the one a diligent and hard-working puritan, the other a carefree (and careless) musician who fiddles all summer long and dies of hunger in the winter. Shaun is an ant, and tells the parable in praise of ant-hood. Joyce intends the opposition to stand also for space (Shaun, *ondt*) and time (Shem, also the artist "Jim the Penman," *gracehoper*). *Ondt* is also an anagram for "don't." The section quoted is the beginning of a description of the grasshopper. The whole tale is full of references to insects and bugs of all sorts: what is sometimes called "entymology" (from *etym-* + *entom-ology*).

From Finnegans Wake

—I apologuise,[1] Shaun began, but I would rather spinooze [2] you one from the grimm gests [3] of Jacko and Esaup,[4] fable one, feeble too. Let us here consider the casus,[5] my dear little cousis (husstenhasstencaffincoffintussemtossemda-mandamnacosaghcusaghhobixhatouxpeswchbechoscashlcarcarcaract) [6] of the Ondt [7] and the Gracehoper.

The Gracehoper was always jigging ajog, hoppy on akkant [8] of his joyicity, (he had a partner pair of findlestilts [9] to supplant him), or, if not, he was always

1. Shaun, the tight, crafty son, would indeed always "guise" an apology.
2. Spinoza is the first philosopher of time and space, good and evil, to be mentioned; also *spin* + *ooze* a tale.
3. Grimm's fairy tales + *geste* (story).
4. *Jacob* and *Esau,* instances of Shem and Shaun + Jacob (Grimm) + *Aesop* of the fables.
5. In Latin, "fall;" also "case."
6. One of ten occurrences in *Finnegans Wake* of a hundred-letter word, this one indicating the voice of thunder, and marking a cyclical progression in the vision of phased history.
7. In Danish, "evil" (Shaun, *vs.* the gracehoping Shem) + *ont-* (pertaining to being).
8. *Account* + *Kant* (another philosopher).
9. The grasshopper's legs are indeed fiddlesticks.

making ungraceful overtures [10] to Floh and Luse and Bienie and Vespatilla [11] to play pupa-pupa [12] and pulicy-pulicy [13] and langtennas and pushpygyddyum and to commence insects with him, there mouthparts to his orefice [14] and his gambills [15] to there airy processes, even if only in chaste, ameng [16] the everlistings, behold a waspering pot. He would of curse melissciously,[17] by his fore feelhers. flexors, contractors, depressors and extensors, lamely, harry me, marry me, bury me, bind me, till she was puce [18] for shame and allso fourmish [19] her in Spinner's housery [20] at the earthsbest schoppinhour [21] so summery as his cottage, which was cald fourmillierly [22] Tingsomingenting,[23] groped up. Or, if he was always striking up funny funereels [24] with Besterfarther Zeuts,[25] the Aged One, with all his wigeared corollas, albedinous [26] and oldbuoyant, inscythe his elytrical [27] wormcasket and Dehlia and Peonia,[28] his druping [29] nymphs, bewheedling him, compound eyes [30] on hornitosehead,[31] and Auld Letty Plussiboots [32] to scratch his cacumen and cackle his tramsitus,[33] diva deborah [34] . . .

[Next follows a part of the *Anna Livia Plurabelle* section, one of the titled parts previously published in separate form. It is the last paragraph of the remarkable dialogue of two washerwomen on the banks of the Liffey, "washing the dirty linen" of the Earwicker family in public, gossiping until darkness falls and their voices become as indistinguishable from the sound of the river herself as objects from each other in the darkness.]

Can't hear with the waters of. The chittering waters of. Flittering bats, field-mice bawk talk. Ho! Are you not gone ahome? What Thom Malone? [35] Can't

10. In a musical sense. The grasshopper as happy fiddler, as artist, is thematic here as in Aesop; he is also sexually joyful.
11. *Flea* and *Louse* and *Bee* and *Wasp*.
12. From insect pupal stage of development.
13. *Policy* + Latin *pulex* (flea).
14. *Orifice* + *ore* + *ora-* (pray, say) + *-fice* (doing, making).
15. *Gambols* + *gams* (legs) + *bills*.
16. *Among* + German *Mengen* (crowds, collections), "*waspering*" (*wasp* + whispering).
17. *Maliciously* + Greek *melissa,* (bee).
18. French for "flea" + the color purple.
19. *Furnish* + *fourmi* (French), "ant."
20. Also *hosiery*.
21. *Shopping hour* + *Schopenhauer* (still another philosopher).
22. *Familiarly* + *fourmi* (ant).
23. "A thing like no thing" (Danish).
24. *Funerals* + *reels* (dances) + *reels* (of movie film).
25. Grandfather Zeus, an instance of H.C.E. (note the "earwig" immediately following.
26. *All-being* + *libidinous*.
27. *Electrical* + *elytron* (beetle's hard wing-covering).
28. *Dahlia* and *Peony* + *Delia* (Artemis, from Delos) and *Peona*, a shepherdess in Keats's *Endymion*.
29. Drupes are fruits of the peach, cherry, plum family.
30. Flies have compound eyes.
31. From *hornito* (Spanish): oven-shaped hill.
32. An instance of A.L.P., with Puss-in-Boots.
33. "Cacumen" is "tip" in Latin. "Tramsitus" is *transit* + *trama* + *site* (*trama* being Latin for the weft of a spider web).
34. Hebrew for "bee."
35. A character in one of the *Dubliners* stories.

hear with bawk of bats, all thim liffeying waters of. Ho,[36] talk save us! My foos [37] won't moos.[38] I feel as old as yonder elm. A tale told of Shaun or Shem? All Livia's daughtersons. Dark hawks hear us. Night! Night! My ho head halls. I feel as heavy as yonder stone. Tell me of John or Shaun? Who were Shem and Shaun the living sons or daughters of? Night now! Tell me, tell me, tell me, elm! Night night! Telmetale of stem or stone.[39] Beside the rivering waters of, hitherandthithering waters of. Night!

[This final quotation is from the very end of the book, when A.L.P. (now totally submerged into her identity as the river of life, of flow and process, moving about the fixity of the land-mass of H.C.E.) forsakes husband, sons, and daughter, and all the past as well, and flows down to meet the sea, her father. To maintain the total circularity of the book itself, her last sentence breaks off, to be completed only by the fragmentary opening sentence of *Finnegans Wake*. The whole passage is one of singular lyrical beauty, suggesting the final paragraph of *The Dead* in its lyrical purification of the complexities of the earlier part of the work in each case, as well as being reminiscent of Molly Bloom's final long soliloquy at the end of *Ulysses*, a flow of more than 45 pages of scarcely broken stream-of-consciousness.]

Try not to part. Be happy, dear ones! May I be wrong! For she'll be sweet for you as I was sweet when I came down out of me mother. My great blue bedroom, the air so quiet, scarce a cloud. In peace and silence. I could have stayed up there for always only. It's something fails us. First we feel. Then we fall. And let her rain now if she likes. Gently or strongly as she likes. Anyway let her rain for my time is come. I done me best when I was let. Thinking always if I go all goes. A hundred cares, a tithe of troubles and is there one who understands me? One in a thousand of years of the nights? All me life I have been lived among them but now they are becoming lothed to me. And I am lothing their little warm tricks. And lothing their mean cosy turns. And all the greedy gushes out through their small souls. And all the lazy leaks down over their brash bodies. How small it's all! And me letting on to meself always. And lilting on all the time. I thought you were all glittering with the noblest of carriage. You're only a bumpkin. I thought you the great in all things, in guilt and in glory. You're but a puny. Home! My people were not their sort out beyond there so far as I can. For all the bold and bad and bleary they are blamed, the seahags. No! Nor for all our wild dances in all their wild din. I can seen meself among them, allaniuvia pulchrabelled.[40] How she was handsome, the wild Amazia,[41] when she would seize to my other breast! And what is she weird, haughty

36. Chinese for "river."
37. In German, "foot."
38. *Move* + *moss* (her foot is turning to moss).
39. Thematically, a stone and an elm tree have been an important dyad of fixity and process; here they merge with Shaun and Shem.
40. The last version of her name, Anna Livia Plurabella, in the book: A.L.P. + *all new via* (way) + *alluvial* (the soil of her bed) + (Latin) *pulchra* (beautiful) + *bella* + *bell*.
41. *Amazon* + *amaze* + etymological, "breastless"; Amazon and Nile are the two rivers, attendant nymphs of Anna Livia.

Niluna,[42] that she will snatch from my ownest hair! For 'tis they are the stormies. Ho hang! Hang ho! [43] And the clash of our cries till we spring to be free. Auravoles,[44] they says, never heed of your name! But I'm loothing them that's here and all I lothe. Loonely in me loneness. For all their faults. I am passing out. O bitter ending! I'll slip away before they're up. They'll never see. Nor know. Nor miss me. And it's old and old it's sad and old it's sad and weary I go back to you, my cold father, my cold mad father, my cold mad feary father, till the near sight of the mere [45] size of him, the moyles [46] and moyles of it, moananoaning, makes me seasilt saltsick and I rush, my only, into your arms. I see them rising! Save me from those therrble prongs! Two more. Onetwo moremens more. So. Avelaval.[47] My leaves have drifted from me. All. But one clings still. I'll bear it on me. To remind me of. Lff! [48] So soft this morning ours. Yes. Carry me along, taddy, like you done through the toy fair. If I seen him bearing down on me now under whitespread wings like he'd come from Arkangels,[49] I sink I'd die down over his feet, humbly dumbly, only to washup. Yes, tid. There's where. First. We pass through grass behush the bush to. Whish! A gull. Gulls. Far calls. Coming, far! End here. Us then. Finn, again! [50] Take. Bussoftlhee, mememormee! Till thousendsthee. Lps. The keys to. Given! A way a lone a last a loved a long the [51]

[The opening sentence of Finnegans Wake]

riverrun, past Eve and Adam's,[52] from swerve of shore to bend of bay, brings us by a commodious [53] vicus [54] of recirculation back to Howth Castle and Environs.[55]

42. *Nile + Luna* (moon); another etymology of "Amazon" was also from a Circassian word for "moon."

43. *Hwang Ho,* the Yellow River of China.

44. *Au revoir* (as "goodbye" and, more literally in the eternally cyclic context, "to the seeing again") + *aureole* (halo) + "thou desirest gold" (Latin) + *volare* (flying or moving rapidly).

45. With pun on German *Meer* (sea) + Latin *mare* + French *mère* (mother).

46. Miles, spelled phonetically for Irish pronunciation + *Magh* (pronounced "moy"), "life."

47. Latin *Ave* (farewell) + *lava* (derived from the meaning "sliding down") + *lave* (wash) + *lave* (the past) (from Germanic, cognate "leave") + *Livia* (Liffey).

48. Liffey.

49. *Archangel* + *angel of the ark* + Russian northern port of *Archangelsk.*

50. Finally, the name of the ever-living, repeatedly resurrected form of H.C.E., as the giant Finn, again, Finnegan has awakened.

51. The sentence ends only with the opening sentence of *Finnegans Wake,* which follows below.

52. A Dublin parish church, but also the first parents. The Liffey flows past this church into Dublin Bay, and back past the Hill of Howth, where the sleeping giant Finn lies buried.

53. "Spacious" + *commode* (chamber pot), into which a city river empties, also called a "Jordan," hence another river; also the Christian name of Giordano Bruno, the Renaissance philosopher of dialectical synthesis of polar opposites, one of the two basic patterns of *Finnegans Wake.* ("A terrible heretic," Stephen Daedalus is told in *A Portrait;* "He was terribly burned," Stephen answers.)

54. Latin for "lane," "vicinity" + Vico Way, the shore road along Dublin Bay + Giambattista Vico, the other philosopher of the cyclic theory of history.

55. The first given instance of H.C.E. Later ones include "Haveth Childers Everywhere" and "Heinz cans everywhere."

D. H. LAWRENCE
1885–1930

David Herbert Lawrence was born at Eastwood, Nottinghamshire, on September 11, 1885. His father was a miner, his mother of somewhat higher class; and her social regrets and aspirations affected the children, especially this son, who, after the death of an elder brother, became her favorite. The conflict between the earthy, careless, often drunk and dirty father and the refined mother was crucial for Lawrence, and he records it, and his escape from his mother, in *Sons and Lovers* (1913). Later he turned against her, and also against the girl represented as Miriam, persuaded that such women were particularly responsible for the prevalence of a consciousness divorced from the life of the body; and he railed furiously against mother-love.

A somewhat sickly child, Lawrence was a little cut off from other boys, and thus early acquired his intimacy with the countryside and with books. But the background life of the mining town, with its blend of the sinister and the genial, stamped him permanently, and emerges throughout his work. Life in such an area was, however, less limited than might be thought. Lawrence and "Miriam" (Jessie Chambers) read very seriously and adventurously; Lawrence knew personally some quite important political thinkers, mostly radical; and after some preliminary teaching he was able to go to what was then Nottingham University College (1906). He had already produced his first poems, and was working on his first novel, *The White Peacock* (finished in 1910 and published in 1911), and on several stories. In 1908 he taught in Croydon (an outer suburb of London), made new friends, and enjoyed something of metropolitan entertainment, including the operas of Wagner; his Croydon novel, *The Trespasser* (1912), is a strangely Wagnerian work.

The year 1910 was a turning point; he broke his engagement with Jessie Chambers, became engaged to Louie Burrows, began the first version of *Sons and Lovers,* and saw his mother die. When a serious illness forced him to give up teaching he returned to Eastwood in 1912, and met Frieda von Richthofen Weekley, the wife of a former professor of his. Eloping in May 1912, they lived first in Germany and then in Italy. At this time Lawrence finished *Sons and Lovers,* and wrote the poems called *Look! We Have Come Through* (a poetic record of the early days with Frieda) and the play *The Widowing of Mrs. Holroyd,* only recently (and successfully) produced on the stage. He began the novel called *The Lost Girl* (completed after the war), wrote the travel sketches later revised for *Twilight in Italy* (1916), and took the first tentative steps toward his major work, a novel called *The Sisters,* which later split into *The Rainbow* (1915) and *Women in Love* (1921). He also produced short stories, of which *The Prussian Officer* is the best.

Lawrence returned to England with Frieda in June 1914, in time for what he was to call the "nightmare" of the war. Struggling against poverty and sickness, taken for a German spy in Cornwall, in profound trouble with the draft, and, above all, hating the hideous decadence typified by the war, with its bogus emotions and universal ugliness, Lawrence nevertheless worked at his writing—philosophical essays, his novel *The Sisters,* short stories—and made and broke friendships with, among others, Bertrand Russell and Lady Ottoline Morell, the original of Hermione in *Women in Love.* He passionately wanted to leave England, preferably for the United States; and his wide reading in American literature at this time came to fruition in 1923 with the publication of his major critical work, *Studies in Classic American Literature.* He also turned out a school history of Europe (under a pseudonym), the novel *Aaron's Rod* (1922), and the important novella *The Fox*. At last, in November 1919, he was able to leave England; and he never again returned for more than visits.

In Italy and Sicily between 1919 and 1922 he wrote his reply to Freud, *Psychoanalysis and the Unconscious* and *Fantasia of the Unconscious* (1921, 1922); he translated the Sicilian novelist Verga, wrote some of the poems in *Birds, Beasts and Flowers,* and finished two more novellas, *The Captain's Doll* and *The Ladybird*. In 1922 the Lawrences went to Ceylon, and then to Australia for a few months during which Lawrence wrote a long novel, *Kangaroo* (1923), and eventually another, *The Boy in the Bush* (1924)—Lawrence's revision of an original by the Australian writer Molly Skinner. In 1923 he accepted the invitation of Mabel Dodge Luhan (an American admirer of his work) to live near her ranch in Taos, New Mexico; and there he stayed, off and on, until February 1925. While visiting Mexico he was almost fatally ill; yet these years in America produced a long novel, *The Plumed Serpent,* the sketches that became *Mornings in Mexico,* the stories called *The Princess* and *The Woman Who Rode Away,* and the greatest of his short novels, *St. Mawr*. He returned to Europe in September 1925. The last years were also prolific of what he called "metaphysical" work, such as the study of the Book of Revelation called *Apocalypse,* published incomplete and posthumously. But there were also more stories, and his best novel after *Women in Love,* namely, *Lady Chatterley's Lover*. Many poems, mostly epigrammatic and satirical, a number of paintings, the brilliant defense of *Lady Chatterley's Lover* called first *My Skirmish with Jolly Roger* and later *A Propos of Lady Chatterley's Lover,* and the pamphlet *Pornography and Obscenity* (1929) also belong to this period. Lawrence died in the south of France on March 2, 1930, aged forty-four, of the tuberculosis that had dogged him through his life.

Such a summary says little about this tempestuous and controversial writer and prophet, albeit a prophet partly unarmed by his own talent; that is, a man given to working out in extraordinary detail his apocalyptic images and predictions, but— because he was a writer of fiction who believed in fiction as a method of achieving truth—allowing the fiction to qualify what he called the "metaphysic." Many times he praised the novel as "the one bright book of life," as the best means to restore some quality of livingness—"quickness" as he called it—to the disastrous modern world. What he said in his famous comment on Hawthorne is equally true of his own work: "Never trust the artist, trust the tale." Lawrence held astonishing opinions—on the strength of his non-fictional writings you might take him to be an anti-Semitic, childbeating, woman-hating fascist; yet these opinions are transfigured when they appear in his fictions. Again and again it is the character in the novel closest in ideas to the author who is put down by another character, usually a woman. But his disgust with the modern world—especially after the war had shown it in its true colors—is very deep, and affects his fiction.

Lawrence had a slightly fearful admiration for miners, with their underground life and distorted bodies, the instruments of rich men and yet their own men, gay and without greed, dedicated to pleasure, until the blight that industry brought to the countryside struck them also. And this admiration for people whose life was not conducted wholly from the head accounts for his use of other primitive figures: game-keepers, gypsies, Italian peasants. He thought that the illness which divorced our minds and bodies, though originating in male shame, was now inflicted on men by women as mothers and lovers; and, especially when entertaining fantasies about his own role as a political or spiritual leader, he usually wanted to put women in a place subordinate to men.

Just as he wanted an educational system which would make society a rigid aristocracy of merit, he called for permanent stable marriages with dominant men. (This is to simplify opinions which changed over the years.) In a full sexual relation, achievable only in marriage, he saw the only means of redemption, a reversal of the death-flow of the modern world. He worked up these views to a level of great complexity; and as qualified by other pressures in his greatest book, *Women in Love,* they become both serious and mysterious. And though we must trust the tale, we cannot but remember that the artist was a man of powerful ideas and violent temperament. The fact is that Lawrence thinks, and also thinks with his story—which is a different matter and a richer, because he was a great artist. In *The Rainbow* and *Women in Love,* especially the latter, he invented a new kind of novel and a new way of treating human personality. He was a poet—some say a great one—and alive in all his senses; his travel writings, especially the remarkable *Etruscan Places* and *The Sea and Sardinia,* are strong testimony to the union of his mind and his eye. His literary criticism is notably creative, and even in his driest "metaphysical" work he is an exciting writer.

After his death Lawrence's reputation sank low for many years. Its revival, helped in part by the eventual publication—openly and legally—of *Lady Chatterley's Lover,* is now complete. Lawrence is an acknowledged master, and not only in the literary sense. There is controversy about his views on women, politics, and writing; he provides texts for those who think him extravagantly repressive, and also for their opponents. Lawrence lived through the years when many modern attitudes were being formed on a basis which made them less easily distinguished from one another than they have later become. Some of the roots of modern left-wing radicalism and those of Fascism were largely the same; the other ideas of Lawrence, though developed in a different way, have enough in common with Freud's to have made him anxious to emphasize the differences. Lawrence would have abhorred the more sharply sexually oriented revision of Freud by Wilhelm Reich ((1897–1957), and yet he resembled Reich strongly, if fleetingly.

In these and many other ways Lawrence belongs to early modernism. A newcomer to his work, expecting it to look "modern," may be surprised to observe that it has no obvious marks of modernism: his poems are not like Eliot's, he knew but did not imitate the Futurists, he largely ignored the kind of experiments with presentation and time-sequence found in Conrad, and he hated Joyce. The revolutionary tactics of Dada and the dream images of Surrealism had no effect on him. He made his own innovations, and discovered his own tradition. For all their novelty, *The Rainbow* and *Women in Love* are closer to George Eliot and Hardy than to the other great experimental fiction of the time—Joyce's, Proust's, Kafka's. He is more prolific, more untidy, more spontaneous than any of these; he has much more design on the reader, and, despite his exiles and wanderings, he gave himself a more urgent social role. Given that our notions of modernism were formed on the evidence of quite different writers, we have here an explanation of why it took so long for Lawrence to achieve his place as a master of the modern. But it is now, though not beyond discussion, beyond denial.

The Prussian Officer

Lawrence saw something of the Prussian military caste when he went to Germany in 1912; he disliked Metz, a garrison town where he stayed, and was aware that Frieda's family was aristocratic and military. It was in the following year, in Bavaria (which he also disliked), that he wrote this story. He called it *Honour and Arms,* and wrote to his publisher Edward Garnett that it was his best story so far. Garnett, to Lawrence's annoyance, changed the title to *The Prussian Officer.* By the time it appeared, in a volume of the same title, England was at war with Germany, and the change was doubtless made to appeal to anti-Prussian sentiment. Lawrence already believed that soldiers, herded together in all-male company, "men without women, never being satisfied by a woman, as a man never is from a street affair, get their surplus sex and their frustration and dissatisfaction into the blood, and *love* cruelty. It is sex lust fermented makes atrocity." Another story, somewhat similar but inferior, which Garnett entitled *The Thorn in the Flesh,* appeared in the same 1914 volume. Lawrence's strong reaction to German militarism was not merely a matter of disliking Germans; his portraits of English military men, particularly the ones he met when under suspicion of spying in Cornwall and in the course of his short visits to barracks for physical examinations, are equally hostile and more contemptuous. In any case, the virtues of *The Prussian Officer* are independent of these circumstances.

The Prussian Officer

They had marched more than thirty kilometres since dawn, along the white, hot road where occasional thickets of trees threw a moment of shade, then out into the glare again. On either hand, the valley, wide and shallow, glittered with heat; dark green patches of rye, pale young corn, fallow and meadow and black pine woods spread in a dull, hot diagram under a glistening sky. But right in front the mountains ranged across, pale blue and very still, snow gleaming gently out of the deep atmosphere. And towards the mountains, on and on, the regiment marched between the rye fields and the meadows, between the scraggy fruit trees set regularly on either side the high road. The burnished, dark green rye threw off a suffocating heat, the mountains drew gradually nearer and more distinct. While the feet of the soldiers grew hotter, sweat ran through their hair under their helmets, and their knapsacks could burn no more in contact with their shoulders, but seemed instead to give off a cold, prickly sensation.

He walked on and on in silence, staring at the mountains ahead, that rose sheer out of the land and stood fold behind fold, half earth, half heaven, the heaven, the barrier with slits of soft snow, in the pale, bluish peaks.

He could now walk almost without pain. At the start, he had determined not to limp. It had made him sick to take the first steps, and during the first mile or so, he had compressed his breath, and the cold drops of sweat had stood on his forehead. But he had walked it off. What were they after all but bruises! He had looked at them, as he was getting up: deep bruises on the backs of his thighs. And since he had made his first step in the morning, he had been conscious of them, till now he had a tight, hot place in his chest, with suppressing the pain, and holding himself in. There seemed no air when he breathed. But he walked almost lightly.

The Captain's hand had trembled at taking his coffee at dawn: his orderly saw it again. And he saw the fine figure of the Captain wheeling on horseback at the farm-house ahead, a handsome figure in pale blue uniform with facings of scarlet, and the metal gleaming on the black helmet and the sword-scabbard, and dark streaks of sweat coming on the silky bay horse. The orderly felt he was connected with that figure moving so suddenly on horseback: he followed it like a shadow, mute and inevitable and damned by it. And the officer was always aware of the tramp of the company behind, the march of his orderly among the men.

The Captain was a tall man of about forty, grey at the temples. He had a handsome, finely knit figure, and was one of the best horsemen in the West. His orderly, having to rub him down, admired the amazing riding-muscles of his loins.

For the rest, the orderly scarcely noticed the officer any more than he noticed himself. It was rarely he saw his master's face: he did not look at it. The Captain had reddish-brown, stiff hair that he wore short upon his skull. His moustache was also cut short and bristly over a full, brutal mouth. His face was rather rugged, the cheeks thin. Perhaps the man was the more handsome for the deep lines in his face, the irritable tension of his brow, which gave him the look of a man who fights with life. His fair eyebrows stood bushy over light blue eyes that were always flashing with cold fire.

He was a Prussian aristocrat, haughty and overbearing. But his mother had been a Polish Countess. Having made too many gambling debts when he was young, he had ruined his prospects in the Army, and remained an infantry captain. He had never married: his position did not allow of it, and no woman had ever moved him to it. His time he spent riding—occasionally he rode one of his own horses at the races—and at the officers' club. Now and then he took himself a mistress. But after such an event, he returned to duty with his brow still more tense, his eyes still more hostile and irritable. With the men, however, he was merely impersonal, though a devil when roused; so that, on the whole, they feared him, but had no great aversion from him. They accepted him as the inevitable.

To his orderly he was at first cold and just and indifferent: he did not fuss over trifles. So that his servant knew practically nothing about him, except just what orders he would give, and how he wanted them obeyed. That was quite simple. Then the change gradually came.

The orderly was a youth of about twenty-two, of medium height, and well built. He had strong, heavy limbs, was swarthy, with a soft, black, young moustache. There was something altogether warm and young about him. He had firmly marked eyebrows over dark, expressionless eyes that seemed never to have thought, only to have received life direct through his senses, and acted straight from instinct.[1]

1. This distinction—between the instinctual integrity of the boy and the officer's divided mind and body—is important not only in Lawrence but in the general thought of artists in the period. Later we hear of the boy's "unmeaning dark eyes" and the officer's head-centered power lust; of the boy's sexual satisfaction and the officer's frustration in his liai-

Gradually the officer had become aware of his servant's young, vigorous, unconscious presence about him. He could not get away from the sense of the youth's person, while he was in attendance. It was like a warm flame upon the older man's tense, rigid body, that had become almost unliving, fixed. There was something so free and self-contained about him, and something in the young fellow's movement, that made the officer aware of him. And this irritated the Prussian. He did not choose to be touched into life by his servant. He might easily have changed his man, but he did not. He now very rarely looked direct at his orderly, but kept his face averted, as if to avoid seeing him. And yet as the young soldier moved unthinking about the apartment, the elder watched him, and would notice the movement of his strong young shoulders under the blue cloth, the bend of his neck. And it irritated him. To see the soldier's young, brown, shapely peasant's hand grasp the loaf or the wine-bottle sent a flash of hate or of anger through the elder man's blood. It was not that the youth was clumsy: it was rather the blind, instinctive sureness of movement of an unhampered young animal that irritated the officer to such a degree.

Once, when a bottle of wine had gone over, and the red gushed out on to the tablecloth, the officer had started up with an oath, and his eyes, bluey like fire, had held those of the confused youth for a moment. It was a shock for the young soldier. He felt something sink deeper, deeper into his soul, where nothing had ever gone before. It left him rather blank and wondering. Some of his natural completeness in himself was gone, a little uneasiness took its place. And from that time an undiscovered feeling had held between the two men.

Henceforward the orderly was afraid of really meeting his master. His subconsciousness remembered those steely blue eyes and the harsh brows, and did not intend to meet them again. So he always stared past his master and avoided him. Also, in a little anxiety, he waited for the three months to have gone, when his time would be up. He began to feel a constraint in the Captain's presence, and the soldier even more than the officer wanted to be left alone, in his neutrality as servant.

He had served the Captain for more than a year, and knew his duty. This he performed easily, as if it were natural to him. The officer and his commands he took for granted, as he took the sun and the rain, and he served as a matter of course. It did not implicate him personally.

But now if he were going to be forced into a personal interchange with his master he would be like a wild thing caught, he felt he must get away.

But the influence of the young soldier's being had penetrated through the officer's stiffened discipline, and perturbed the man in him. He, however, was a gentleman, with long, fine hands and cultivated movements, and was not going to allow such a thing as the stirring of his innate self. He was a man of passionate temper, who had always kept himself suppressed. Occasionally

---

son. Even the boy's revulsions—e.g. from creeping birds—are instinctive, whereas the officer's revulsion from the boy is a kind of love corrupted by his will. Lawrence's emphasis on stimuli such as scent and color reinforces the orderly's, not the officer's, natural acquiescence in the world of sense.

there had been a duel, an outburst before the soldiers. He knew himself to be always on the point of breaking out. But he kept himself hard to the idea of the Service. Whereas the young soldier seemed to live out his warm, full nature, to give it off in his very movements, which had a certain zest, such as wild animals have in free movement. And this irritated the officer more and more.

In spite of himself, the Captain could not regain his neutrality of feeling towards his orderly. Nor could he leave the man alone. In spite of himself, he watched him, gave him sharp orders, tried to take up as much of his time as possible. Sometimes he flew into a rage with the young soldier, and bullied him. Then the orderly shut himself off, as it were out of earshot, and waited, with sullen, flushed face, for the end of the noise. The words never pierced to his intelligence, he made himself, protectively, impervious to the feelings of his master.

He had a scar on his left thumb, a deep seam going across the knuckle. The officer had long suffered from it, and wanted to do something to it. Still it was there, ugly and brutal on the young, brown hand. At last the Captain's reserve gave way. One day, as the orderly was smoothing out the tablecloth, the officer pinned down his thumb with a pencil, asking:

'How did you come by that?'

The young man winced and drew back at attention.

'A wood axe, Herr Hauptmann,'[2] he answered.

The officer waited for further explanation. None came. The orderly went about his duties. The elder man was sullenly angry. His servant avoided him. And the next day he had to use all his will-power to avoid seeing the scarred thumb. He wanted to get hold of it and——A hot flame ran in his blood.

He knew his servant would soon be free, and would be glad. As yet, the soldier had held himself off from the elder man. The Captain grew madly irritable. He could not rest when the soldier was away, and when he was present, he glared at him with tormented eyes. He hated those fine black brows over the unmeaning dark eyes, he was infuriated by the free movement of the handsome limbs, which no military discipline could make stiff. And he became harsh and cruelly bullying, using contempt and satire. The young soldier only grew more mute and expressionless.

'What cattle were you bred by, that you can't keep straight eyes? Look me in the eyes when I speak to you.'

And the soldier turned his dark eyes to the other's face, but there was no sight in them: he stared with the slightest possible cast, holding back his sight, perceiving the blue of his master's eyes, but receiving no look from them. And the elder man went pale, and his reddish eyebrows twitched. He gave his order, barrenly.

Once he flung a heavy military glove into the young soldier's face. Then he had the satisfaction of seeing the black eyes flare up into his own, like a blaze when straw is thrown on a fire. And he had laughed with a little tremor and a sneer.

But there were only two months more. The youth instinctively tried to keep

2. Captain.

himself intact: he tried to serve the officer as if the latter were an abstract authority and not a man. All his instinct was to avoid personal contact, even definite hate. But in spite of himself the hate grew, responsive to the officer's passion. However, he put it in the background. When he had left the Army he could dare acknowledge it. By nature he was active, and had many friends. He thought what amazing good fellows they were. But, without knowing it, he was alone. Now this solitariness was intensified. It would carry him through his term. But the officer seemed to be going irritably insane, and the youth was deeply frightened.

The soldier had a sweetheart, a girl from the mountains, independent and primitive. The two walked together, rather silently. He went with her, not to talk, but to have his arm round her, and for the physical contact. This eased him, made it easier for him to ignore the Captain; for he could rest with her held fast against his chest. And she, in some unspoken fashion, was there for him. They loved each other.

The Captain perceived it, and was mad with irritation. He kept the young man engaged all the evenings long, and took pleasure in the dark look that came on his face. Occasionally, the eyes of the two men met, those of the younger sullen and dark, doggedly unalterable, those of the elder sneering with restless contempt.

The officer tried hard not to admit the passion that had got hold of him. He would not know that his feeling for his orderly was anything but that of a man incensed by his stupid, perverse servant. So, keeping quite justified and conventional in his consciousness, he let the other thing run on. His nerves, however, were suffering. At last he slung the end of a belt in his servant's face. When he saw the youth start back, the pain-tears in his eyes and the blood on his mouth, he had felt at once a thrill of deep pleasure and of shame.

But this, he acknowledged to himself, was a thing he had never done before. The fellow was too exasperating. His own nerves must be going to pieces. He went away for some days with a woman.

It was a mockery of pleasure. He simply did not want the woman. But he stayed on for his time. At the end of it, he came back in an agony of irritation, torment, and misery. He rode all the evening, then came straight in to supper. His orderly was out. The officer sat with his long, fine hands lying on the table, perfectly still, and all his blood seemed to be corroding.

At last his servant entered. He watched the strong, easy young figure, the fine eyebrows, the thick black hair. In a week's time the youth had got back his old well-being. The hands of the officer twitched and seemed to be full of mad flame. The young man stood at attention, unmoving, shut off.

The meal went in silence. But the orderly seemed eager. He made a clatter with the dishes.

'Are you in a hurry?' asked the officer, watching the intent, warm face of his servant. The other did not reply.

'Will you answer my question?' said the Captain.

'Yes, sir,' replied the orderly, standing with his pile of deep Army plates. The Captain waited, looked at him, then asked again:

'Are you in a hurry?'

'Yes, sir,' came the answer, that sent a flash through the listener.

'For what?'

'I was going out, sir.'

'I want you this evening.'

There was a moment's hesitation. The officer had a curious stiffness of countenance.

'Yes, sir,' replied the servant, in his throat.

'I want you tomorrow evening also—in fact, you may consider your evenings occupied, unless I give you leave.'

The mouth with the young mustache set close.

'Yes, sir,' answered the orderly, loosening his lips for a moment.

He again turned to the door.

'And why have you a piece of pencil in your ear?'

The orderly hesitated, then continued on his way without answering. He set the plates in a pile outside the door, took the stump of pencil from his ear, and put it in his pocket. He had been copying a verse for his sweetheart's birthday card. He returned to finish clearing the table. The officer's eyes were dancing, he had a little, eager smile.

'Why have you a piece of pencil in your ear?' he asked.

The orderly took his hands full of dishes. His master was standing near the great green stove, a little smile on his face, his chin thrust forward. When the young soldier saw him his heart suddenly ran hot. He felt blind. Instead of answering, he turned dazedly to the door. As he was crouching to set down the dishes, he was pitched forward by a kick from behind. The pots went in a stream down the stairs, he clung to the pillar of the banisters. And as he was rising he was kicked heavily again, and again, so that he clung sickly to the post for some moments. His master had gone swiftly into the room and closed the door. The maid-servant downstairs looked up the staircase and made a mocking face at the crockery disaster.

The officer's heart was plunging. He poured himself a glass of wine, part of which he spilled on the floor, and gulped the remainder, leaning against the cool, green stove. He heard his man collecting the dishes from the stairs. Pale, as if intoxicated, he waited. The servant entered again. The Captain's heart gave a pang, as of pleasure, seeing the young fellow bewildered and uncertain on his feet, with pain.

'Schöner!'[3] he said.

The soldier was a little slower in coming to attention.

'Yes, sir!'

The youth stood before him, with pathetic young moustache, and fine eyebrows very distinct on his forehead of dark marble.

'I asked you a question.'

'Yes, sir.'

The officer's tone bit like acid.

'Why had you a pencil in your ear?'

Again the servant's heart ran hot, and he could not breathe. With dark, strained eyes, he looked at the officer, as if fascinated. And he stood there sturdily planted, unconscious. The withering smile came into the Captain's eyes, and he lifted his foot.

3. The orderly's name (recalling with some irony the German meaning, "beautiful one").

1. Thomas Hardy in 1923, a portrait by R. G. Eves (1876–1941).
National Portrait Gallery, London.

2. Joseph Conrad, a drawing by Sir William Rothenstein (1872–1945).
National Portrait Gallery.

3. "Central Station"—Kinshassa Station in the Belgian Congo. From H. M. Stanley, *The Congo, Founding of Its Free State* (1885).

HEART OF DARKNESS

4. "Inner Station"—The settlement at Stanley Falls photographed during a Governor-General's inspection. From Albert Chapaux, *Le Congo* (1894).

5. G. B. Shaw, a drawing by Sir Bernard Partridge.
National Portrait Gallery, © *Punch,* London 1925.

6. William Butler Yeats in 1900, a portrait by his father, John B. Yeats.
The National Gallery of Ireland, Dublin.

7. "Was there another Troy for her to burn?" (from "No Second Troy"). Maud Gonne, in a portrait by Sarah Purser. *The Granger Collection.*

8. "Human, superhuman, a bird's round eye, / Everything else withered and mummy-dead . . . " (from "A Bronze Head"). Maud Gonne, by Lawrence Campbell. *The Municipal Gallery,* Dublin *(Photo Barry Mason).*

9. "An image of such politics . . . " (from "In Memory of Constance Markiewicz and Eva Gore-Booth"). Constance (Gore-Booth) Markiewicz in uniform of the Citizens' Army, c. 1914. *Photograph Keogh.*

0. "The innocent and the beautiful / Have no enemy but time . . . " (from "In Memory . . . "). Constance Gore-Booth in her first ball-gown, c. 1886. From the Gore-Booth family album; *courtesy the Gore-Booth family.*

11. Bernardo Strozzi (1581–1644), *Portrait of a Gentleman*.

"In the Dublin National Gallery there hung, perhaps there still hang, upon the same wall, a portrait of some Venetian gentleman by Strozzi, and Mr. Sargent's painting of President Wilson. Whatever thought broods in the dark eyes of that Venetian gentleman has drawn its life from his whole body; it feeds upon it as the flame feeds upon the candle —and should that thought be changed, his pose would change, his very cloak would rustle, for his whole body thinks. President Wilson lives only in the eyes, which are steady and intent; the flesh about the mouth is dead, and the hands are dead, and the clothes suggest no movement of his body, nor any movement but that of the valet, who has brushed and folded in mechanical routine." (From Yeats, *The Trembling of the Veil*).

12. John Singer Sargent (1856–1925), *Portrait of Woodrow Wilson.*
The National Gallery of Ireland.

13. Yeats, as drawn by the noted portraitist
Augustus John (1878–1961).
The Tate Gallery, London, *courtesy of Romilly John.*

14. William Butler Yeats broadcasting in 1937. *BBC Copyright Photograph.*

15. James Joyce, c. 1917.
The Croessman James Joyce Collection,
Southern Illinois University at Carbondale.

JOYCE'S DUBLIN

16. Usher's Island, the bank of the Liffey where Kate and Julia Morkan's house was situated (see "The Dead"). W. Y. Tindall, from his work *The Joyce Country, Pennsylvania State University Press* (1960).

17. Clongowes Wood College, Stephen's—and Joyce's—school (see *A Portrait of the Artist as a Young Man*). Irish Tourist Board.

JOYCE'S DUBLIN

18. The Wellington Monument
(see "The Dead").
W. Y. Tindall, from *The Joyce Country*.

19. "There was no human figure near him, nor any sound borne to him over the air. But the tide was near the turn and already the day was on the wave." Looking across the bay towards the Hill of Howth (see *A Portrait of the Artist*). W. Y. Tindall, from *The Joyce Country*.

20. St. Mary's Star of the Sea (see the "Nausicaa" section of *Ulysses*). W. Y. Tindall, from *The Joyce Country*.

JOYCE'S DUBLIN

21. 7 Eccles Street (Bloom's house),
by Nora Mitchell.
*The Croessman James Joyce Collection,
Southern Illinois University.*

22. ALP, the river Liffey (see *Finnegans Wake*). W. Y. Tindall, from *The Joyce Country.*

23. One of Lawrence's paintings:
Resurrection.
Humanities Research Center
The University of Texas
at Austin.

24. D. H. Lawrence.
George Eastman House,
Rochester (New York).

25. T. S. Eliot, painted in 1938 by Wyndham Lewis, novelist and painter (Eliot described him as the best contemporary writer of English prose). This portrait caused some controversy, but Eliot admired it. (See also Lewis's portrait of Edith Sitwell, Fig. 38.)
Fogg Art Museum, Harvard University Portrait Collection, Gift Mrs. Stanley B. Resor.

26. *Ennui*, the famous image of quiet desperation; Camden Town, London 1913, by Walter Sickert, R.A. (1860–1942).
The Tate Gallery.

TOWARD THE WASTE LAND

27. A crowd flowed over London Bridge, so many,
     I had not thought death had undone so many.

    From *The Waste Land*, ll. 62f. *Radio Times-Hulton Picture Library.*

. . . where the walls
Of Magnus Martyr hold
Inexplicable splendour of Ionian white and gold.

    From *The Waste Land*, ll. 263–65.

28. The Church of St. Magnus Martyr,
Lower Thames St., London.
A. F. Kersting.

After the dark dove with the flickering tongue
Had passed below the horizon of his homing . . .

From "Little Gidding," ll. 83f.

29. Bomb damage surrounding St. Paul's Cathedral, 1940, photographed by Cecil Beaton, photographer and designer best known for his portraits of celebrities.

30. Rudyard Kipling in 1899. Portrait by Philip Burne-Jones.
National Portrait Gallery.

31. Wilfred Owen in 1917.
Oxford University Press, London.

32. The Somme Battlefield, 1916.
Imperial War Museum, London.

33. A Daylight Raid near Arras, 1917.
Imperial War Museum.

34. Front-line Trench, the Battle of the Somme, 1916.
Imperial War Museum, London.

> Why do you lie with your legs ungainly huddled,
> And one arm bent across your sullen, cold
> Exhausted face? It hurts my heart to watch you,
> Deep-shadowed from the candle's guttering gold;
> And you wonder why I shove you by the shoulder;
> Drowsy, you mumble and sigh and turn your head . . .
> *You are too young to fall asleep for ever;*
> *And when you sleep you remind me of the dead.*

From Siegfried Sassoon (1886–1968), "The Dug-Out."

35. David Jones Vision: *Guenever* (1940), an illustration of Arthurian Legend.
The Tate Gallery.

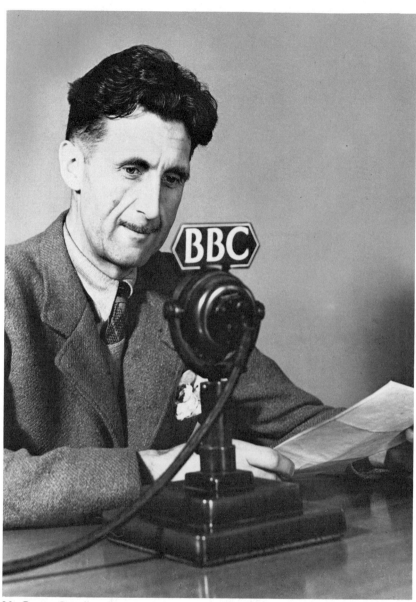

36. George Orwell in 1943.
BBC Copyright Photograph.

37. W. H. Auden, a recent photograph.
Jill Krementz.

38. Edith Sitwell, a portrait by Wyndham Lewis, c. 1926.
The Tate Gallery, courtesy of Ann Wyndham Lewis.

39. Dylan Thomas in 1938, by Augustus John.
The National Museum of Wales, Cardiff.

40. E. M. Forster, by Cecil Beaton (1904–   ).

41. *Shelter Scene* (1941). *Marlborough Gallery,* New York.

Henry Moore (1898–   ), one of the greatest sculptors of the twentieth century, has developed some of his major abstract forms from what Blake called, in another context, "the human form divine." In 1941 he did some remarkable drawings, in combined chalk, crayon, pen and brush, of London Underground areas in use as air-raid shelters. These drawings capture both the historical moment—patience amid horror—and the power to transcend it of visual forms themselves (here so closely related to those of his sculpture) and the eternal life they lead.

42. Francis Bacon (1909–   ), in his post-World War II painting, represents a recent kind of expressionism in his rigid control over modes of distortion. This *Study after Velasquez's Portrait of Pope Innocent X* (1953) transforms the masterful force of the seventeenth-century original into a horrific scream of the atomic age, a scream shared by wielders of power and their victims alike, the whole picture suggesting the qualities of a rubbed, scuffed news photograph.
Collection Carter Burden, New York.

'I—I forgot it—sir,' panted the soldier, his dark eyes fixed on the other man's dancing blue ones.

'What was it doing there?'

He saw the young man's breast heaving as he made an effort for words.

'I had been writing.'

'Writing what?'

Again the soldier looked him up and down. The officer could hear him panting. The smile came into the blue eyes. The soldier worked his dry throat, but could not speak. Suddenly the smile lit like a flame on the officer's face, and a kick came heavily against the orderly's thigh. The youth moved a pace sideways. His face went dead, with two black, staring eyes.

'Well?' said the officer.

The orderly's mouth had gone dry, and his tongue rubbed in it as on dry brown-paper. He worked his throat. The officer raised his foot. The servant went stiff.

'Some poetry, sir,' came the crackling, unrecognizable sound of his voice.

'Poetry, what poetry?' asked the Captain, with a sickly smile.

Again there was the working in the throat. The Captain's heart had suddenly gone down heavily, and he stood sick and tired.

'For my girl, sir,' he heard the dry, inhuman sound.

'Oh!' he said, turning away. 'Clear the table.'

'Click!' went the soldier's throat; then again, 'Click!' and then the half-articulate:

'Yes, sir.'

The young soldier was gone, looking old, and walking heavily.

The officer, left alone, held himself rigid, to prevent himself from thinking. His instinct warned him that he must not think. Deep inside him was the intense gratification of his passion, still working powerfully. Then there was a counter-action, a horrible breaking down of something inside him, a whole agony of reaction. He stood there for an hour motionless, a chaos of sensations, but rigid with a will to keep blank his consciousness, to prevent his mind grasping. And he held himself so until the worst of the stress had passed, when he began to drink, drank himself to an intoxication, till he slept obliterated. When he woke in the morning he was shaken to the base of his nature. But he had fought off the realization of what he had done. He had prevented his mind from taking it in, had suppressed it along with his instincts, and the conscious man had nothing to do with it. He felt only as after a bout of intoxication, weak, but the affair itself all dim and not to be recovered. Of the drunkenness of his passion he successfully refused remembrance. And when his orderly appeared with coffee, the officer assumed the same self he had had the morning before. He refused the event of the past night—denied it had ever been—and was successful in his denial. He had not done any such thing—not he himself. Whatever blame there might be, lay at the door of a stupid, insubordinate servant.

The orderly had gone about in a stupor all the evening. He drank some beer because he was parched, but not much, the alcohol made his feeling come back, and he could not bear it. He was dulled, as if nine-tenths of the ordinary man in him were inert. He crawled about disfigured. Still, when he thought of the kicks, he went sick, and when he thought of the threat of more kicking, in the room afterwards, his heart went hot and faint, and he panted, remembering the one that had come. He had been forced to say, 'For my girl.' He was much too done even to want to cry. His mouth hung slightly open, like an idiot's. He felt vacant, and wasted. So, he wandered at his work, painfully, and very slowly and clumsily, fumbling blindly with the brushes, and finding it difficult, when he sat down, to summon the energy to move again. His limbs, his jaw, were slack and nerveless. But he was very tired. He got to bed at last, and slept inert, relaxed, in a sleep that was rather stupor than slumber, a dead night of stupefaction shot through with gleams of anguish.

In the morning were the manœuvres. But he woke even before the bugle sounded. The painful ache in his chest, the dryness of his throat, the awful steady feeling of misery made his eyes come awake and dreary at once. He knew, without thinking, what had happened. And he knew that the day had come again, when he must go on with his round. The last bit of darkness was being pushed out of the room. He would have to move his inert body and go on. He was so young, and had known so little trouble, that he was bewildered. He only wished it would stay night, so that he could lie still, covered up by the darkness. And yet nothing would prevent the day from coming, nothing would save him from having to get up and saddle the Captain's horse, and make the Captain's coffee. It was there, inevitable. And then, he thought, it was impossible. Yet they would not leave him free. He must go and take the coffee to the Captain. He was too stunned to understand it. He only knew it was inevitable—inevitable, however long he lay inert.

At last, after heaving at himself, for he seemed to be a mass of inertia, he got up. But he had to force every one of his movements from behind, with his will. He felt lost, and dazed, and helpless. Then he clutched hold of the bed, the pain was so keen. And looking at his thighs, he saw the darker bruises on his swarthy flesh and he knew that, if he pressed one of his fingers on one of the bruises, he should faint. But he did not want to faint—he did not want anybody to know. No one should ever know. It was between him and the Captain. There were only the two people in the world now—himself and the Captain.

Slowly, economically, he got dressed and forced himself to walk. Everything was obscure, except just what he had his hands on. But he managed to get through his work. The very pain revived his dull senses. The worst remained yet. He took the tray and went up to the Captain's room. The officer, pale and heavy, sat at the table. The orderly, as he saluted, felt himself put out of existence. He stood still for a moment submitting to his own nullification—then he gathered himself, seemed to regain himself, and then the Captain began to grow vague, unreal, and the younger soldier's heart beat up. He clung to this situation—that the Captain did not exist—so that he himself might live. But when he saw his officer's hand tremble as he took the coffee, he felt everything falling shattered. And he went away, feeling as if he himself were coming to pieces, disintegrated. And when the Captain was there on horseback, giving orders, while he himself stood, with rifle and knapsack, sick with pain, he felt as if he must shut his eyes—as if he must shut his eyes on everything. It was only the long agony of marching with a parched throat that filled him with one single, sleep-heavy intention: to save himself.

II

He was getting used even to his parched throat. That the snowy peaks were radiant among the sky, that the whity-green glacier-river twisted through its pale shoals in the valley below, seemed almost supernatural. But he was going mad with fever and thirst. He plodded on uncomplaining. He did not want to speak, not to anybody. There were two gulls, like flakes of water and snow, over the river. The scent of green rye soaked in sunshine came like a sickness. And the march continued, monotonously, almost like a bad sleep.

At the next farm-house, which stood low and broad near the high road, tubs of water had been put out. The soldiers clustered round to drink. They took off their helmets, and the steam mounted from their wet hair. The Captain sat on horseback, watching. He needed to see his orderly. His helmet threw a dark shadow over his light, fierce eyes, but his moustache and mouth and chin were distinct in the sunshine. The orderly must move under the presence of the figure of the horseman. It was not that he was afraid, or cowed. It was as if he was disembowelled, made empty, like an empty shell. He felt himself as nothing, a shadow creeping under the sunshine. And, thirsty as he was, he could scarcely drink, feeling the Captain near him. He would not take off his helmet to wipe his wet hair. He wanted to stay in shadow, not to be forced into consciousness. Starting, he saw the light heel of the officer prick the belly of the horse; the Captain cantered away, and he himself could relapse into vacancy.

Nothing, however, could give him back his living place in the hot, bright morning. He felt like a gap among it all. Whereas the Captain was prouder, overriding. A hot flash went through the young servant's body. The Captain was firmer and prouder with life, he himself was empty as a shadow. Again the flash went through him, dazing him out. But his heart ran a little firmer.

The company turned up the hill, to make a loop for the return. Below, from among the trees, the farm-bell clanged. He saw the labourers, mowing bare-foot at the thick grass, leave off their work and go downhill, their scythes hanging over their shoulders, like long, bright claws curving down behind them. They seemed like dream-people, as if they had no relation to himself. He felt as in a blackish dream: as if all the other things were there and had form, but he himself was only a consciousness, a gap that could think and perceive.

The soldiers were tramping silently up the glaring hillside. Gradually his head began to revolve, slowly, rhythmically. Sometimes it was dark before his eyes, as if he saw this world through a smoked glass, frail shadows and unreal. It gave him a pain in his head to walk.

The air was too scented, it gave no breath. All the lush green-stuff seemed to be issuing its sap, till the air was deathly, sickly with the smell of greenness. There was the perfume of clover, like pure honey and bees. Then there grew a faint acrid tang—they were near the beeches; and then a queer clattering noise, and a suffocating, hideous smell; they were passing a flock of sheep, a shepherd in a black smock, holding his crook. Why should the sheep huddle together under this fierce sun? He felt that the shepherd would not see him, though he could see the shepherd.

At last there was the halt. They stacked rifles in a conical stack, put down their kit in a scattered circle around it, and dispersed a little, sitting on a small knoll high on the hillside. The chatter began. The soldiers were steaming with heat, but were lively. He sat still, seeing the blue mountains rising upon the land, twenty kilometres away. There was a blue fold in the ranges, then out of that, at the foot, the broad, pale bed of the river, stretches of whity-green water between pinkish-grey shoals among the dark pine woods. There it was, spread out a long way off. And it seemed to come downhill, the river. There was a raft being steered, a mile away. It was a strange country. Nearer, a red-roofed, broad farm with white base and square dots of windows crouched beside the wall of beech foliage on the wood's edge. There were long strips of rye and clover and pale green corn. And just at his feet, below the knoll, was a darkish bog, where globe flowers stood breathless still on their slim stalks. And some of the pale gold bubbles were burst, and a broken fragment hung in the air. He thought he was going to sleep.

Suddenly something moved into this coloured mirage before his eyes. The Captain, a small, light-blue and scarlet figure, was trotting evenly between the strips of corn, along the level brow of the hill. And the man making flag-signals was coming on. Proud and sure moved the horseman's figure, the quick, bright thing, in which was concentrated all the light of this morning, which for the rest lay a fragile, shining shadow. Submissive, apathetic, the young soldier sat and stared. But as the horse slowed to a walk, coming up the last steep path, the great flash flared over the body and soul of the orderly. He sat waiting. The back of his head felt as if it were weighted with a heavy piece of fire. He did not want to eat. His hands trembled slightly as he moved them. Meanwhile the officer on horseback was approaching slowly and proudly. The tension grew in the orderly's soul. Then again, seeing the Captain ease himself on the saddle, the flash blazed through him.

The Captain looked at the patch of light blue and scarlet, and dark heads, scattered closely on the hill-side. It pleased him. The command pleased him. And he was feeling proud. His orderly was among them in common subjection. The officer rose a little on his stirrups to look. The young soldier sat with averted, dumb face. The Captain relaxed on his seat. His slim-legged, beautiful horse, brown as a beech nut, walked proudly uphill. The Captain passed into the zone of the company's atmosphere: a hot smell of men, of sweat, of leather. He knew it very well. After a word with the lieutenant, he went a few paces higher, and sat there, a dominant figure, his sweat-marked horse swishing its tail, while he looked down on his men, on his orderly, a nonentity among the crowd.

The young soldier's heart was like fire in his chest, and he breathed with difficulty. The officer, looking downhill, saw three of the young soldiers, two pails of water between them, staggering across a sunny green field. A table had been set up under a tree, and there the slim lieutenant stood, importantly busy. Then the Captain summoned himself to an act of courage. He called his orderly.

The flame leapt into the young soldier's throat as he heard the command, and he rose blindly, stifled. He saluted, standing below the officer. He did not look up. But there was the flicker in the Captain's voice.

'Go to the inn and fetch me . . .' the officer gave his commands. 'Quick!' he added.

At the last word, the heart of the servant leapt with a flash, and he felt the strength come over his body. But he turned in mechanical obedience, and set off at a heavy run downhill, looking almost like a bear, his trousers bagging over his military boots. And the officer watched this blind, plunging run all the way.

But it was only the outside of the orderly's body that was obeying so humbly and mechanically. Inside had gradually accumulated a core into which all the energy of that young life was compact and concentrated. He executed his commission, and plodded quickly back uphill. There was a pain in his head, as he walked, that made him twist his features unknowingly. But hard there in the centre of his chest was himself, himself, firm, and not to be plucked to pieces.

The Captain had gone up into the wood. The orderly plodded through the hot, powerfully smelling zone of the company's atmosphere. He had a curious mass of energy inside him now. The Captain was less real than himself. He approached the green entrance to the wood. There, in the half-shade, he saw the horse standing, the sunshine and the flickering shadow of leaves dancing over his brown body. There was a clearing where timber had lately been felled. Here, in the gold-green shade beside the brilliant cup of sunshine, stood two figures, blue and pink, the bits of pink showing out plainly. The Captain was talking to his lieutenant.

The orderly stood on the edge of the bright clearing, where great trunks of trees, stripped and glistening, lay stretched like naked, brown-skinned bodies. Chips of wood littered the trampled floor, like splashed light, and the bases of the felled trees stood here and there, with their raw, level tops. Beyond was the brilliant, sunlit green of a beech.

'Then I will ride forward,' the orderly heard his Captain say. The lieutenant saluted and strode away. He himself went forward. A hot flash passed through his belly, as he tramped towards his officer.

The Captain watched the rather heavy figure of the young soldier stumble forward, and his veins, too, ran hot. This was to be man to man between them. He yielded before the solid, stumbling figure with bent head. The orderly stooped and put the food on a level-sawn tree-base. The Captain watched the glistening, sun-inflamed, naked hands. He wanted to speak to the young soldier but could not. The servant propped a bottle against his thigh, pressed open the cork, and poured out the beer into the mug. He kept his head bent. The Captain accepted the mug.

'Hot!' he said, as if amiably.

The flame sprang out of the orderly's heart, nearly suffocating him.

'Yes, sir,' he replied, between shut teeth.

And he heard the sound of the Captain's drinking, and he clenched his fists, such a strong torment came into his wrists. Then came the faint clang of the closing of the pot-lid. He looked up. The Captain was watching him. He glanced swiftly away. Then he saw the officer stoop and take a piece of bread from the tree-base. Again the flash of flame went through the young soldier, seeing the stiff body stoop beneath him, and his hands jerked. He looked away. He could feel the officer was nervous. The bread fell as it was being broken. The officer ate the other piece. The two men stood tense and still, the master laboriously chewing his bread, the servant staring with averted face, his fist clenched.

Then the young soldier started. The officer had pressed open the lid of the mug again. The orderly watched the lid of the mug, and the white hand that clenched the handle, as if he were fascinated. It was raised. The youth followed it with his eyes. And then he saw the thin, strong throat of the elder man moving up and down as he drank, the strong jaw working. And the instinct which had been jerking at the young man's wrists suddenly jerked free. He jumped, feeling as if it were rent in two by a strong flame.

The spur of the officer caught in a tree-root, he went down backwards with a crash, the middle of his back thudding sickeningly against a sharp-edged tree-base, the pot flying away. And in a second the orderly, with serious, earnest young face, and underlip between his teeth, had got his knee in the officer's chest and was pressing the chin backward over the farther edge of the tree-stump, pressing, with all his heart behind in a passion of relief, the tension of his wrists exquisite with relief. And with the base of his palms he shoved at the chin, with all his might. And it was pleasant, too, to have that chin, that hard jaw already slightly rough with beard, in his hands. He did not relax one hair's breadth, but, all the force of all his blood exulting in his thrust, he shoved back the head of the other man, till there was a little 'cluck' and a crunching sensation. Then he felt as if his head went to vapour. Heavy convulsions shook the body of the officer, frightening and horrifying the young soldier. Yet it pleased him, too, to repress them. It pleased him to keep his hands pressing back the chin, to feel the chest of the other man yield in expiration to the weight of his strong, young knees, to feel the hard twitchings of the prostrate body jerking his own whole frame, which was pressed down on it.

But it went still. He could look into the nostrils of the other man, the eyes he could scarcely see. How curiously the mouth was pushed out, exaggerating the full lips, and the moustache bristling up from them. Then, with a start, he noticed the nostrils gradually filled with blood. The red brimmed, hesitated, ran over, and went in a thin trickle down the face to the eyes.

It shocked and distressed him. Slowly, he got up. The body twitched and sprawled there, inert. He stood and looked at it in silence. It was a pity *it* was broken. It represented more than the thing which had kicked and bullied him. He was afraid to look at the eyes. They were hideous now, only the whites showing, and the blood running to them. The face of the orderly was drawn with horror at the sight. Well, it was so. In his heart he was satisfied. He had hated the face of the Captain. It was extinguished now. There was a heavy relief in the orderly's soul. That was as it should be. But he could not bear to see the long, military body lying broken over the tree-base, the fine fingers crisped. He wanted to hide it away.

Quickly, busily, he gathered it up and pushed it under the felled tree-trunks, which rested their beautiful, smooth length either end on logs. The face was horrible with blood. He covered it with the helmet. Then he pushed the limbs straight and decent, and brushed the dead leaves off the fine cloth of the uniform. So, it lay quite still in the shadow under there. A little strip of sunshine ran along the breast, from a chink between the logs. The orderly sat by it for a few moments. Here his own life also ended.

Then, through his daze, he heard the lieutenant, in a loud voice, explaining to the men outside the wood, that they were to suppose the bridge on the river below was held by the enemy. Now they were to march to the attack in such and such a manner. The lieutenant had no gift of expression. The orderly, listening from habit, got muddled. And when the lieutenant began it all again he ceased to hear.

He knew he must go. He stood up. It surprised him that the leaves were glittering in the sun, and the chips of wood reflecting white from the ground. For him a change had come over the world. But for the rest it had not—all seemed the same. Only he had left it. And he could not go back. It was his duty to return with the beer-pot and bottle. He could not. He had left all that. The lieutenant was still hoarsely explaining. He must go, or they would overtake him. And he could not bear contact with anyone now.

He drew his fingers over his eyes, trying to find out where he was. Then he turned away. He saw the horse standing in the path. He went up to it and mounted. It hurt him to sit in the saddle. The pain of keeping his seat occupied him as they cantered through the wood. He would not have minded anything, but he could not get away from the sense of being divided from the others. The path led out of the trees. On the edge of the wood he pulled up and stood watching. There in the spacious sunshine of the valley soldiers were moving in a little swarm. Every now and then, a man harrowing on a strip of fallow shouted to his oxen, at the turn. The village and the white-towered church was small in the sunshine. And he no longer belonged to it— he sat there, beyond, like a man outside in the dark. He had gone out from everyday life into the unknown, and he could not, he even did not want to go back.

Turning from the sun-blazing valley, he rode deep into the wood. Tree-trunks, like people standing grey and still, took no notice as he went. A doe, herself a moving bit of sunshine and shadow, went running through the flecked shade. There were bright green rents in the foliage. Then it was all pine wood, dark and cool. And he was sick with pain, he had an intolerable great pulse in his head, and he was sick. He had never been ill in his life. He felt lost, quite dazed with all this.

Trying to get down from the horse, he fell, astonished at the pain and his lack of balance. The horse shifted uneasily. He jerked its bridle and sent it cantering jerkily away. It was his last connection with the rest of things.

But he only wanted to lie down and not be disturbed. Stumbling through the trees, he came on a quiet place where beeches and pine trees grew on a slope. Immediately he had lain down and closed his eyes, his consciousness went racing on without him. A big pulse of sickness beat in him as if it throbbed through the whole earth. He was burning with dry heat. But he was too busy, too tearingly active in the incoherent race of delirium to observe.

III

He came to with a start. His mouth was dry and hard, his heart beat heavily, but he had not the energy to get up. His heart beat heavily. Where was he? —the barracks—at home? There was something knocking. And, making an effort, he looked round—trees, and litter of greenery, and reddish, bright, still pieces of sunshine on the floor. He did not believe he was himself, he did not believe what he saw. Something was knocking. He made a struggle towards consciousness, but relapsed. Then he struggled again. And gradually his surroundings fell into relationship with himself. He knew, and a great pang of fear went through his heart. Somebody was knocking. He could see the heavy, black rags of a fir tree overhead. Then everything went black. Yet he did not believe he had closed his eyes. He had not. Out of the blackness sight slowly emerged again. And someone was knocking. Quickly, he saw the blood-disfigured face of his Captain, which he hated. And he held himself still with horror. Yet, deep inside him, he knew that it was so, the Captain should be dead. But the physical delirium got hold of him. Someone was knocking. He lay perfectly still, as if dead, with fear. And he went unconscious.

When he opened his eyes again, he started, seeing something creeping swiftly up a tree-trunk. It was a little bird. And the bird was whistling overhead. Tap-tap-tap—it was the small, quick bird rapping the tree-trunk with its beak, as if its head were a little round hammer. He watched it curiously. It shifted sharply, in its creeping fashion. Then, like a mouse, it slid down the bare trunk. Its swift creeping sent a flash of revulsion through him. He raised his head. It felt a great weight. Then, the little bird ran out of the shadow across a still patch of sunshine, its little head bobbing swiftly, its white legs twinkling brightly for a moment. How neat it was in its build, so compact, with pieces of white on its wings. There were several of them. They were so pretty—but they crept like swift, erratic mice, running here and there among the beech-mast.

He lay down again exhausted, and his consciousness lapsed. He had a horror of the little creeping birds. All his blood seemed to be darting and creeping in his head. And yet he could not move.

He came to with a further ache of exhaustion. There was the pain in his head, and the horrible sickness, and his inability to move. He had never been ill in his life. He did not know where he was or what he was. Probably he had got sunstroke. Or what else?—he had silenced the Captain for ever—some time ago—oh, a long time ago. There had been blood on his face, and his eyes had turned upwards. It was all right, somehow. It was peace. But now he had got beyond himself. He had never been here before. Was it life, or not life? He was by himself. They were in a big, bright place, those others, and he was outside. The town, all the country, a big bright place of light: and he was outside, here, in the darkened open beyond, where each thing existed alone. But they would all have to come out there sometime, those others. Little, and left behind him, they all were. There had been father and mother and sweetheart. What did they all matter? This was the open land.

He sat up. Something scuffled. It was a little brown squirrel running in lovely, undulating bounds over the floor, its red tail completing the undulation of its body—and then, as it sat up, furling and unfurling. He watched it, pleased. It ran on again, friskily, enjoying itself. It flew wildly at another squirrel, and they were chasing each other, and making little scolding, chattering noises. The soldier wanted to speak to them. But only a hoarse sound came out of his throat. The squirrels burst away—they flew up the trees. And then he saw the one peeping round at him, half-way up a tree-trunk. A start of fear went through him, though, in so far as he was conscious, he was amused. It still stayed, its little, keen face staring at him half-way up the tree-trunk, its little ears pricked up, its clawey little hands clinging to the bark, its white breast reared. He started from it in panic.

Struggling to his feet, he lurched away. He went on walking, walking, looking for something—for a drink. His brain felt hot and inflamed for want of water. He stumbled on. Then he did not know anything. He went unconscious as he walked. Yet he stumbled on, his mouth open.

When, to his dumb wonder, he opened his eyes on the world again, he no longer tried to remember what it was. There was thick, golden light behind golden-green glitterings, and tall, grey-purple shafts, and darknesses further off, surrounding him, growing deeper. He was conscious of a sense of arrival. He was amid the reality, on the real, dark bottom. But there was the thirst burning in his brain. He felt lighter, not so heavy. He supposed it was newness. The air was muttering with thunder. He thought he was walking wonderfully swiftly and was coming straight to relief—or was it to water?

Suddenly he stood still with fear. There was a tremendous flare of gold, immense—just a few dark trunks like bars between him and it. All the young level wheat was burnished gold glaring on its silky green. A woman, full-skirted, a black cloth on her head for head-dress, was passing like a block of shadow through the glistening green corn, into the full glare. There was a farm, too, pale blue in shadow, and the timber black. And there was a church spire, nearly fused away in the gold. The woman moved on, away from him. He had no language with which to speak to her. She was the bright, solid unreality. She would make a noise of words that would confuse him, and her eyes would look at him without seeing him. She was crossing there to the other side. He stood against a tree.

When at last he turned, looking down the long, bare grove whose flat bed was already filling dark, he saw the mountains in a wonder-light, not far away, and radiant. Behind the soft, grey ridge of the nearest range the further mountains stood golden and pale grey, the snow all radiant like pure, soft gold. So still, gleaming in the sky, fashioned pure out of the ore of the sky, they shone in their silence. He stood and looked at them, his face illuminated. And like the golden, lustrous gleaming of the snow he felt his own thirst bright in him. He stood and gazed, leaning against a tree. And then everything slid away into space.

During the night the lightning fluttered perpetually, making the whole sky white. He must have walked again. The world hung livid round him for moments, fields a level sheen of grey-green light, trees in dark bulk, and the range of clouds black across a white sky. Then the darkness fell like a shutter, and the night was whole. A faint flutter of a half-revealed world, that could not quite leap out of the darkness!—Then there again stood a sweep of pallor for the land, dark shapes looming, a range of clouds hanging overhead. The world was a ghostly shadow, thrown for a moment upon the pure darkness, which returned ever whole and complete.

And the mere delirium of sickness and fever went on inside him—his brain opening and shutting like the night—then sometimes convulsions of terror from something with great eyes that stared round a tree—then the long agony of the march, and the sun decomposing his blood—then the pang of hate for the Captain, followed by a pang of tenderness and ease. But everything was distorted, born of an ache and resolving into an ache.

In the morning he came definitely awake. Then his brain flamed with the sole horror of thirstiness! The sun was on his face, the dew was steaming from his wet clothes. Like one possessed, he got up. There, straight in front of him, blue and cool and tender, the mountains ranged across the pale edge of the morning sky. He wanted them—he wanted them alone—he wanted to leave himself and be identified with them. They did not move, they were still and soft, with white, gentle markings of snow. He stool still, mad with suffering, his hands crisping and clutching. Then he was twisting in a paroxysm on the grass.

He lay still, in a kind of dream of anguish. His thirst seemed to have separated itself from him, and to stand apart, a single demand. Then the pain he felt was another single self. Then there was the clog of his body, another separate thing. He was divided among all kinds of separate beings. There was some strange, agonized connection between them, but they were drawing further apart. Then they would all split. The sun, drilling down on him, was drilling through the bond. Then they would all fall, fall through the everlasting lapse of space. Then again, his consciousness reasserted itself. He roused on to his elbow and stared at the gleaming mountains. There they ranked, all still and wonderful between earth and heaven. He stared till his eyes went black, and the mountains, as they stood in their beauty, so clean and cool, seemed to have it, that which was lost in him.

IV

When the soldiers found him, three hours later, he was lying with his face over his arm, his black hair giving off heat under the sun. But he was still alive. Seeing the open, black mouth, the young soldiers dropped him in horror.

He died in the hospital at night, without having seen again.

The doctors saw the bruises on his legs, behind, and were silent.

The bodies of the two men lay together, side by side, in the mortuary, the one white and slender, but laid rigidly at rest, the other looking as if every moment it must rouse into life again, so young and unused, from a slumber.

1913   1914

St. Mawr

Lawrence wrote St. Mawr on the ranch described in its closing pages. It had been given to Frieda by Mabel Dodge Luhan, and during the summer of 1924 he worked on the property and on the book. The five hundred goats, whose smell still lingered, the horses struck by lightning—these and other details are from life. Earlier in the year he had been in England, and had gone to Pontesbury in Shropshire to visit his correspondent Frederick Carter. Carter makes a brief appearance in *St. Mawr*, thinly disguised as Cartwright, the Pan-like figure with an interest in the occult. He and Lawrence discussed "a certain line of research in symbolism . . . and . . . the problem of the last end of the world."

Lawrence had always been interested in the symbolism of Apocalypse, and this interest grew in his last years. He had read Carter's manuscript, *The Dragon of the Alchemists* (published in 1926), with its astrological interpretation of the Book of Revelation, and used it in writing *The Plumed Serpent* in the following year. Later he wrote a preface, posthumously published, to Carter's book, and worked on his own *Apocalypse*, which remained unfinished and was also published posthumously. Carter himself noted that from Lawrence's visit to Shropshire came not only the landscape of that section of the "little novel" (as Lawrence called it) but also the red horse, an apocalyptic symbol. Thus *St. Mawr*, like *Women in Love, The Plumed Serpent*, and *Lady Chatterley's Lover*, reflects Lawrence's concern with the apocalyptic symbols and patterns; they are all, in a sense, about the end of the world, and the possibility of regeneration. Since Lawrence believed that the modern world was a betrayal of true life, he often set against it an image of the regenerate; he took St. John's Apocalypse to be a corrupt account of an ancient ritual of rebirth. Thus Lawrence's treatment of the theme, like much of his thought, has a strong but not exclusive sexual connotation. What he contrives to do in this, the masterpiece among his shorter fictions, is to establish, in his account of the modern world of death, images of a primeval and somehow still accessible life.

An instance of the indirectness with which Lawrence could use apocalyptic symbolism occurs in the description of the night journey of Mrs. Witt and Lewis; a star falls in heaven, and though Mrs. Witt offers the rational explanation—this is a frequent occurrence in August when the earth passes through a certain region—Lewis sticks to a different one: *There's movement in the sky. The world is going to change again.* This is based on Revelation: "And the stars of heaven fell unto the earth" (6:13) at the time of the opening of the Sixth Seal, when men cower in caves and dens—"For the great day of his wrath is come; and who shall be able to stand?" (6:17) Lawrence associates this with other primitive beliefs of Lewis, and emphasizes the Welshness of the groom: an ancient Briton, he belongs to an earlier time, before the modern sophistication of religion, astronomy, technology. He is closer to the world of St. Mawr, symbol of the world of Pan. Elsewhere—in *Apocalypse*, for example—he also gave horses this role.

In this book Lawrence has to represent both the wasteland of modern life, its joyless gaiety, its dissociation of mind and body, its death wish, and also the true dark integral life by which its fatuity can be measured. Civilization and the flight from it—London, Havana; Rico and his friends—are his subject. He had himself felt this disgust and made this flight. What is remarkable is the skill and varied emphasis with which he renders it. Mrs. Witt, anxious for the experience of death, Lou deciding that love and sex in such a world are to be given up (chastity as preferable to all but true sexuality is also a theme of *Lady Chatterley's Lover*)—all this is given a sort of unemphatic, *actual* quality. Even the great concluding set piece, the totally unsentimental account of the ranch and its New Mexican setting, is rooted in fact. Yet this does not prevent Lawrence's bold symbolic flights, and it does not prevent his directly expressing his own view of the world in a manner which the context makes perfectly acceptable. Both Lewis and the half-Indian Phoenix reflect Lawrence's opinions on race—but not aggressively, qualified as they are by the narrative. In themselves these views are often offensive. "Trust the tale." The long condemnation of the world that follows Lou's recognition of the adder which made first St. Mawr and then her own mare rear is not intrusive. It belongs to the same narrative that, a moment earlier, showed St. Mawr on his back and thrashing his legs, a vision of panic and evil. Lou's vision is of the true evil, the "break," the loosing of the uncontrollable tide which Lawrence saw happening in his own time, correctly predicting worse for the near future; while Rico and his friends in their nervous, brittle way, devoted themselves to illusions of art, pleasure, and thought.

St Mawr is not about the need for a return to the primitive, but about the need for an end to human ignobility, for a new civilization that remembers the body and relates men to the rest of the creation. That is what is hinted at in the end, despite Mrs. Witt's acid comments. The story of the ranch is the story of a genuine human effort to make a life in nature; it is not a wishing away of the sordid and terrible that nature includes. The flight to it—across the world to the American Southwest—was Lawrence's own; he had looked to America as the country where he might find it. It was there, in part; it was also—and rapidly—being ruined, like Phoenix. But Lawrence's passion for a true America still existing under the false was important; it animates his studies in American fiction, and, as developed by others, has had a profound effect on later American thought and art. If the first claim of the "little novel" on our attention is, as Leavis rightly says, that it treats the theme of the waste land with "a creative and technical originality more remarkable" than Eliot's, its second may be that it reflects, more directly than any other work of the period, the thought and the imagery of a later generation of moderns. As a narrative achievement, and as a portent, it is more than worthy to compare with those two other seminal works of the modern mind, Eliot's poem and Conrad's *Heart of Darkness*.

St. Mawr

Lou Witt had had her own way so long that by the age of twenty-five she didn't know where she was. Having one's own way landed one completely at sea.

To be sure, for a while she had failed in her grand love affair with Rico. And then she had had something really to despair about. But even that had worked out as she wanted. Rico had come back to her, and was dutifully married to her. And now, when she was twenty-five and he was three months older, they were a charming married couple. He flirted with other women still, to be sure. He wouldn't be the handsome Rico if he didn't. But she had 'got' him. Oh, yes! You had only to see the uneasy backward glance at her, from his big blue eyes: just like a horse that is edging away from its master: to know how completely he was mastered.

She, with her odd little *museau*,[1] not exactly pretty, but very attractive; and her quaint air of playing at being well-bred, in a sort of charade game;

1. Literally "muzzle," face.

and her queer familiarity with foreign cities and foreign languages; and the lurking sense of being an outsider everywhere, like a sort of gipsy, who is at home anywhere and nowhere: all this made up her charm and her failure. She didn't quite belong.

Of course she was American: Louisiana family, moved down to Texas. And she was moderately rich, with no close relation except her mother. But she had been sent to school in France when she was twelve, and since she had finished school, she had drifted from Paris to Palermo, Biarritz to Vienna and back via Munich to London, then down again to Rome. Only fleeting trips to her America.

So what sort of American was she, after all?

And what sort of European was she either? She didn't 'belong' anywhere. Perhaps most of all in Rome, among the artists and the Embassy people.

It was in Rome she had met Rico. He was an Australian, son of a government official in Melbourne, who had been made a baronet.[2] So one day Rico would be Sir Henry, as he was the only son. Meanwhile he floated around Europe on a very small allowance—his father wasn't rich in capital—and was being an artist.

They met in Rome when they were twenty-two, and had a love affair in Capri. Rico was handsome, elegant, but mostly he had spots of paint on his trousers and he ruined a necktie pulling it off. He behaved in a most floridly elegant fashion, fascinating to the Italians. But at the same time he was canny and shrewd and sensible as any young poser could be, and, on principle, goodhearted, anxious. He was anxious for his future, and anxious for his place in the world, he was poor, and suddenly wasteful in spite of all his tension of economy, and suddenly spiteful in spite of all his ingratiating efforts, and suddenly ungrateful in spite of all his burden of gratitude, and suddenly rude in spite of all his good manners, and suddenly detestable in spite of all his suave, courtier-like amiability.

He was fascinated by Lou's quaint aplomb, her experiences, her 'knowledge,' her *gamine*[3] knowingness, her aloneness, her pretty clothes that were sometimes an utter failure, and her southern 'drawl' that was sometimes so irritating. That sing-song which was so American. Yet she used no Americanisms at all, except when she lapsed into her odd spasms of acid irony, when she was very American indeed!

And she was fascinated by Rico. They played to each other like two butterflies at one flower. They pretended to be very poor in Rome—he *was* poor: and very rich in Naples. Everybody stared their eyes out at them. And they had that love affair in Capri.

But they reacted badly on each other's nerves. She became ill. Her mother appeared. He couldn't stand Mrs. Witt, and Mrs. Witt couldn't stand him. There was a terrible fortnight. Then Lou was popped into a convent nursing-home in Umbria, and Rico dashed off to Paris. Nothing would stop him. He must go back to Australia.

He went to Melbourne, and while there his father died, leaving him a

2. Rank between knight and baron, the lowest hereditary honor.
3. Urchin, waif.

baronet's title and an income still very moderate. Lou visited America once more, as the strangest of strange lands to her. She came aways disheartened, panting for Europe, and, of course, doomed to meet Rico again.

They couldn't get away from one another, even though in the course of their rather restrained correspondence he informed her that he was 'probably' marrying a very dear girl, friend of his childhood, only daughter of one of the oldest families in Victoria.[4] Not saying much.

He didn't commit the probability, but reappeared in Paris, wanting to paint his head off, terribly inspired by Cézanne and by old Renoir. He dined at the Rotonde with Lou and Mrs. Witt, who, with her queer democratic New Orleans sort of conceit, looked round the drinking-hall with savage contempt, and at Rico as part of the show. Certainly, she said, 'when these people here have got any money, they fall in love on a full stomach. And when they've got no money, they fall in love with a full pocket. I never was in a more disgusting place. They take their love like some people take after-dinner pills.'

She would watch with her arching, full, strong grey eyes, sitting there erect and silent in her well-bought American clothes. And then she would deliver some such charge of grape-shot. Rico always writhed.

Mrs. Witt hated Paris: 'this sordid, unlucky city,' she called it. 'Something unlucky is bound to happen to me in this sinister, unclean town,' she said. 'I feel *contagion* in the air of this place. For heaven's sake, Louise, let us go to Morocco or somewhere.'

'No, mother dear, I can't now. Rico has proposed to me, and I have accepted him. Let us think about a wedding, shall we?'

'There!' said Mrs. Witt. 'I said it was an unlucky city!'

And the peculiar look of extreme New Orleans annoyance came round her sharp nose. But Lou and Rico were both twenty-four years old, and beyond management. And anyhow, Lou would be Lady Carrington. But Mrs. Witt was exasperated beyond exasperation. She would almost rather have preferred Lou to elope with one of the great, evil porters at Les Halles.[5] Mrs. Witt was at the age when the malevolent male in man, the old Adam, begins to loom above all the social tailoring. And yet—and yet—it was better to have Lady Carrington for a daughter, seeing Lou was that sort.

There was a marriage, after which Mrs. Witt departed to America. Lou and Rico leased a little old house in Westminster, and began to settle into a certain layer of English society. Rico was becoming an almost fashionable portrait-painter. At least, *he* was almost fashionable, whether his portraits were or not. And Lou too was almost fashionable: almost a hit. There was some flaw somewhere. In spite of their appearances, both Rico and she would never quite go down in any society. They were the drifting artist sort. Yet neither of them was content to be of the drifting artist sort. They wanted to fit in, to make good.

Hence the little house in Westminster, the portraits, the dinners, the friends, and the visits. Mrs. Witt came and sardonically established herself in a suite in a quiet but good-class hotel not far off. Being on the spot. And her terrible grey eyes with the touch of a leer looked on at the hollow mockery of things. As if *she* knew of anything better!

4. Australian state, capital Melbourne.
5. Central Paris market (demolished in the 1970's).

Lou and Rico had a curious exhausting effect on one another: neither knew why. They were fond of one another. Some inscrutable bond held them together. But it was a strange vibration of the nerves, rather than of the blood. A nervous attachment, rather than a sexual love. A curious tension of will, rather than a spontaneous passion. Each was curiously under the domination of the other. They were a pair—they had to be together. Yet quite soon they shrank from one another. This attachment of the will and the nerves was destructive. As soon as one felt strong, the other felt ill. As soon as the ill one recovered strength, down went the one who had been well.

And soon, tacitly, the marriage became more like a friendship, Platonic. It was a marriage, but without sex. Sex was shattering and exhausting, they shrank from it, and became like brother and sister. But still they were husband and wife. And the lack of physical relation was a secret source of uneasiness and chagrin to both of them. They would neither of them accept it. Rico looked with contemplative, anxious eyes at other women.

Mrs. Witt kept track of everything, watching, as it were, from outside the fence, like a potent well-dressed demon, full of uncanny energy and a shattering sort of sense. She said little: but her small, occasionally biting remarks revealed her attitude of contempt for the *ménage*.[6]

Rico entertained clever and well-known people. Mrs. Witt would appear, in her New York gowns and few good jewels. She was handsome, with her vigorous grey hair. But her heavy-lidded grey eyes were the despair of any hostess. They looked too many shattering things. And it was but too obvious that these clever, well-known English people got on her nerves terribly, with their finickiness and their fine-drawn discriminations. She wanted to put her foot through all these fine-drawn distinctions. She thought continually of the house of her girlhood, the plantation, the Negroes, the planters: the sardonic grimness that underlay all the big, shiftless life. And she wanted to cleave with some of this grimness of the big, dangerous America, into the safe, finicky drawing-rooms of London. So naturally she was not popular.

But being a woman of energy, she had to do *something*. During the latter part of the war she had worked with the American Red Cross in France, nursing. She loved men—real men. But, on close contact, it was difficult to define what she meant by 'real' men. She never met any.

Out of the debacle of the war she had emerged with an odd piece of debris, in the shape of Geronimo Trujillo. He was an American, son of a Mexican father and a Navajo Indian mother, from Arizona. When you knew him well, you recognized the real half-breed, though at a glance he might pass as a sunburnt citizen of any nation, particularly of France. He looked like a certain sort of Frenchman, with his curiously set dark eyes, his straight black hair, his thin black moustache, his rather long cheeks, and his almost slouching, diffident, sardonic bearing. Only when you knew him, and looked right into his eyes, you saw that unforgettable glint of the Indian.

He had been badly shell-shocked, and was for a time a wreck. Mrs. Witt, having nursed him into convalescence, asked him where he was going next. He didn't know. His father and mother were dead, and he had nothing to take him back to Phoenix, Arizona. Having had an education in one of the Indian high

6. Establishment, domestic arrangements.

schools, the unhappy fellow had now no place in life at all. Another of the many misfits.

There was something of the Paris *Apache* [7] in his appearance: but he was all the time withheld, and nervously shut inside himself. Mrs. Witt was intrigued by him.

'Very well, Phœnix,' she said, refusing to adopt his Spanish name, 'I'll see what I can do.'

What she did was to get him a place on a sort of manor farm, with some acquaintances of hers. He was very good with horses, and had a curious success with turkeys and geese and fowls.

Some time after Lou's marriage, Mrs. Witt reappeared in London, from the country, with Phœnix in tow, and a couple of horses. She had decided that she would ride in the Park in the morning, and see the world that way. Phœnix was to be her groom.

So, to the great misgiving of Rico, behold Mrs. Witt in splendidly tailored habit and perfect boots, a smart black hat on her smart grey hair, riding a grey gelding as smart as she was, and looking down her conceited, inquisitive, scornful, aristocratic-democratic Louisiana nose at the people in Piccadilly, as she crossed to the Row, [8] followed by the taciturn shadow of Phœnix, who sat on a chestnut with three white feet as if he had grown there.

Mrs. Witt, like many other people, always expected to find the real *beau monde* and the real *grand monde* [9] somewhere or other. She didn't quite give in to what she saw in the Bois de Boulogne, [10] or in Monte Carlo, or on the Pincio; [11] all a bit shoddy, and not very *beau* and not at all *grand*. There she was, with her grey eagle eye, her splendid complexion and her weapon-like health of a woman of fifty, dropping her eyelids a little, very slightly nervous, but completely prepared to despise the *monde* she was entering in Rotten Row.

In she sailed, and up and down that regatta-canal of horsemen and horsewomen under the trees of the Park. And yes, there were lovely girls with fair hair down their backs, on happy ponies. And awfully well-groomed papas, and tight mammas who looked as if they were going to pour tea between the ears of their horses, and converse with banal skill, one eye on the teapot, one on the visitor with whom she was talking, and all the rest of her hostess' argus-eyes [12] upon everybody in sight. That alert argus capability of the English matron was startling and a bit horrifying. Mrs. Witt would at once think of the old Negro mammies, away in Louisiana. And her eyes became dagger-like as she watched the clipped, shorn, mincing young Englishmen. She refused to look at the prosperous Jews.

It was still the days before motor-cars were allowed in the Park, but Rico and Lou, sliding round Hyde Park Corner and up Park Lane in their car, would

7. Hooligan, tough.
8. Rotten Row, track in Hyde Park set aside for riding.
9. Fashionable society, high society.
10. Park on outskirts of Paris.
11. Terrace overlooking Rome, favorite walking place.
12. Argus, in Greek myth, had eyes all over his body; Juno transferred them at his death to the peacock's tail.

watch the steely horsewoman and the saturnine groom with a sort of dismay. Mrs. Witt seemed to be pointing a pistol at the bosom of every other horseman or horsewoman, and announcing: *Your virility or your life! Your femininity or your life!* She didn't know herself what she really wanted them to be: but it was something as democratic as Abraham Lincoln, and as aristocratic as a Russian Czar, as highbrow as Arthur Balfour,[13] and as taciturn and unideal as Phœnix. Everything at once.

There was nothing for it: Lou had to buy herself a horse and ride at her mother's side, for very decency's sake. Mrs. Witt was *so* like a smooth, levelled, gun-metal pistol, Lou had to be a sort of sheath. And she really looked pretty, with her clusters of dark, curly, New Orleans hair, like grapes, and her quaint brown eyes that didn't quite match, and that looked a bit sleepy and vague, and at the same time quick as a squirrel's. She was slight and elegant, and a tiny bit rakish, and somebody suggested she might be in the movies.

Nevertheless, they were in the society columns next morning—*two new and striking figures in the Row this morning were Lady Henry Carrington*[14] *and her mother Mrs. Witt*, etc. And Mrs. Witt liked it, let her say what she might. So did Lou. Lou liked it immensely. She simply luxuriated in the sun of publicity.

'Rico dear, you must get a horse.'

The tone was soft and southern and drawling, but the overtone had a decisive finality. In vain Rico squirmed—he had a way of writhing and squirming which perhaps he had caught at Oxford. In vain he protested that he couldn't ride, and that he didn't care for riding. He got quite angry, and his handsome arched nose tilted and his upper lip lifted from his teeth, like a dog that is going to bite. Yet daren't quite bite.

And that was Rico. He daren't quite bite. Not that he was really afraid of the others. He was afraid of himself, once he let himself go. He might rip up in an eruption of lifelong anger all this pretty-pretty picture of a charming young wife and a delightful little home and a fascinating success as a painter of fashionable and, at the same time, 'great' portraits: with colour, wonderful colour, and, at the same time, form, marvellous form. He had composed this little *tableau vivant*[15] with great effort. He didn't want to erupt like some suddenly wicked horse—Rico was really more like a horse than a dog, a horse that might go nasty any moment. For the time, he was good, very good, dangerously good.

'Why, Rico dear, I thought you used to ride so much, in Australia, when you were young? Didn't you tell me all about it, hm?'—and as she ended on that slow, singing *hm?* which acted on him like an irritant and a drug, he knew he was beaten.

Lou kept the sorrel mare in a mews just behind the house in Westminster and she was always slipping round to the stables. She had a funny little nostalgia for the place: something that really surprised her. She had never had the

13. Arthur James, 1st Earl of Balfour (1848–1930), British philosopher and statesman, prime minister 1902–6, associated with Balfour Declaration (1917), which promised the Jews a national home in Palestine.
14. A slip for which Lawrence is sometimes castigated: Lou, as the wife of a baronet, would be known as Lady Carrington.
15. Living picture.

faintest notion that she cared for horses and stables and grooms. But she did. She was fascinated. Perhaps it was her childhood's Texas associations come back. Whatever it was, her life with Rico in the elegant little house, and all her social engagements, seemed like a dream, the substantial reality of which was those mews in Westminster, her sorrel mare, the owner of the mews, Mr. Saintsbury, and the grooms he employed. Mr. Saintsbury was a horsy elderly man like an old maid, and he loved the sound of titles.

'Lady Carrington!—well, I never! You've come to us for a bit of company again, I see. I don't know whatever we shall do if you go away, we shall be that lonely!' and he flashed his old-maid's smile at her. 'No matter how grey the morning, your Ladyship would make a beam of sunshine. Poppy is all right, I think . . .'

Poppy was the sorrel mare with the three white feet and the startled eye, and she was all right. And Mr. Saintsbury was smiling with his old-maid's mouth, and showing all his teeth.

'Come across with me, Lady Carrington, and look at a new horse just up from the country? I think he's worth a look, and I believe you have a moment to spare, your Ladyship.'

Her Ladyship had too many moments to spare. She followed the sprightly, elderly, clean-shaven man across the yard to a loose box, and waited while he opened the door.

In the inner dark she saw a handsome bay horse with his clean ears pricked like daggers from his naked head as he swung handsomely round to stare at the open doorway. He had big, black, brilliant eyes, with a sharp questioning glint, and that air of tense, alert quietness which betrays an animal that can be dangerous.

'Is he quiet?' Lou asked.

'Why—yes—my Lady! He's quiet, with those that know how to handle him. *Cup! my boy! Cup my beauty! Cup then! St. Mawr!*'

Loquacious even with the animals, he went softly forward and laid his hand on the horse's shoulder, soft and quiet as a fly settling. Lou saw the brilliant skin of the horse crinkle a little in apprehensive anticipation, like the shadow of the descending hand on a bright red-gold liquid. But then the animal relaxed again.

'Quiet with those that know how to handle him, and a bit of a ruffian with those that don't. Isn't that the ticket, eh, St. Mawr?'

'What is his name?' Lou asked.

The man repeated it, with a slight Welsh twist. 'He's from the Welsh borders, belonging to a Welsh gentleman, Mr. Griffith Edwards. But they're wanting to sell him.'

'How old is he?' asked Lou.

'About seven years—seven years and five months,' said Mr. Saintsbury, dropping his voice as if it were a secret.

'Could one ride him in the Park?'

'Well—yes! I should say a gentleman who knew how to handle him could ride him very well and make a very handsome figure in the Park.'

Lou at once decided that this handsome figure should be Rico's. For she was already half in love with St. Mawr. He was of such a lovely red-gold colour, and a dark, invisible fire seemed to come out of him. But in his big black eyes there was a lurking afterthought. Something told her that the horse was not quite happy: that somewhere deep in his animal consciousness lived a danger-ous, half-revealed resentment, a diffused sense of hostility. She realized that he was sensitive, in spite of his flaming, healthy strength, and nervous with a touchy uneasiness that might make him vindictive.

'Has he got any tricks?' she asked.

'Not that I know of, my Lady: not tricks exactly. But he's one of these tem-peramental creatures, as they say. Though I say, every horse is temperamental, when you come down to it. But this one, it is as if he was a trifle raw some-where. Touch this raw spot, and there's no answering for him.'

'Where is he raw?' asked Lou, somewhat mystified. She thought he might really have some physical sore.

'Why, that's hard to say, my Lady. If he was a human being, you'd say something had gone wrong in his life. But with a horse, it's not that, exactly. A highbred animal like St. Mawr needs understanding, and I don't know as any-body has quite got the hang of him. I confess I haven't myself. But I do realize that he is a special animal and needs a special sort of touch, and I'm willing he should have it, did I but know exactly what it is.'

She looked at the glowing bay horse that stood there with his ears back, his face averted, but attending as if he were some lightning-conductor. He was a stallion. When she realized this, she became more afraid of him.

'Why does Mr. Griffith Edwards want to sell him?' she asked.

'Well—my Lady—they raised him for stud purposes—but he didn't answer. There are horses like that: don't seem to fancy the mares, for some reason. Well, anyway, they couldn't keep him for the stud. And as you see, he's a powerful, beautiful hackney, clean as a whistle, and eaten up with his own power. But there's no putting him between the shafts. He won't stand it. He's a fine saddle-horse, beautiful action, and lovely to ride. But he's got to be handled, and there you are.'

Lou felt there was something behind the man's reticence.

'Has he ever made a break?' she asked, apprehensive.

'Made a break?' replied the man. 'Well, if I must admit it, he's had two acci-dents. Mr. Griffith Edwards' son rode him a bit wild, away there in the forest of Deane,[16] and the young fellow had his skull smashed in, against a low oak bough. Last autumn, that was. And some time back, he crushed a groom against the side of the stall—injured him fatally. But they were both accidents, my Lady. Things will happen.'

The man spoke in a melancholy, fatalistic way. The horse, with his ears laid back, seemed to be listening tensely, his face averted. He looked like something finely bred and passionate, that has been judged and condemned.

'May I say *how do you do?*' she said to the horse, drawing a little nearer in her white, summery dress, and lifting her hand that glittered with emeralds and diamonds.

He drifted away from her, as if some wind blew him. Then he ducked his head, and looked sideways at her, from his black, full eye.

'I think I'm all right,' she said, edging nearer, while he watched her.

She laid her hand on his side, and gently stroked him. Then she stroked his

16. On the border of Wales and Gloucestershire.

shoulder, and then the hard, tense arch of his neck. And she was startled to feel the vivid heat of his life come through to her, through the lacquer of red-gold gloss. So slippery with vivid, hot life!

She paused, as if thinking, while her hand rested on the horse's sun-arched neck. Dimly, in her weary young-woman's soul, an ancient understanding seemed to flood in.

She wanted to buy St. Mawr.

'I think,' she said to Saintsbury, 'if I can, I will buy him.'

The man looked at her long and shrewdly.

'Well, my Lady,' he said at last, 'there shall be nothing kept from you. But what would your Ladyship do with him, if I may make so bold?'

'I don't know,' she replied, vaguely. 'I might take him to America.'

The man paused once more, then said:

'They say it's been the making of some horses, to take them over the water, to Australia or such places. It might repay you—you never know.'

She wanted to buy St. Mawr. She wanted him to belong to her. For some reason the sight of him, his power, his alive, alert intensity, his unyieldingness, made her want to cry.

She never did cry: except sometimes with vexation, or to get her own way. As far as weeping went, her heart felt as dry as a Christmas walnut. What was the good of tears, anyhow? You had to keep on holding on, in this life, never give way, and never give in. Tears only left one weakened and ragged.

But now, as if that mysterious fire of the horse's body had split some rock in her, she went home and hid herself in her room, and just cried. The wild, brilliant, alert head of St. Mawr seemed to look at her out of another world. It was as if she had had a vision, as if the walls of her own world had suddenly melted away, leaving her in a great darkness, in the midst of which the large, brilliant eyes of that horse looked at her with demonish question, while his naked ears stood up like daggers from the naked lines of his inhuman head, and his great body glowed red with power.

What was it? Almost like a god looking at her terribly out of the everlasting dark, she had felt the eyes of that horse; great, glowing, fearsome eyes, arched with a question, and containing a white blade of light like a threat. What was his non-human question, and his uncanny threat? She didn't know. He was some splendid demon, and she must worship him.

She hid herself away from Rico. She could not bear the triviality and superficiality of her human relationships. Looming like some god out of the darkness was the head of that horse, with the wide, terrible, questioning eyes. And she felt that it forbade her to be her ordinary, commonplace self. It forbade her to be just Rico's wife, young Lady Carrington, and all that.

It haunted her, the horse. It had looked at her as she had never been looked at before: terrible, gleaming, questioning eyes arching out of darkness, and backed by all the fire of that great ruddy body. What did it mean, and what ban did it put upon her? She felt it put a ban on her heart: wielded some uncanny authority over her, that she dared not, could not understand.

No matter where she was, what she was doing, at the back of her consciousness loomed a great, over-aweing figure out of a dark background: St. Mawr, looking at her without really seeing her, yet gleaming a question at her, from his wide terrible eyes, and gleaming a sort of menace, doom. Master of doom, he seemed to be!

'You are thinking about something, Lou dear!' Rico said to her that evening.

He was so quick and sensitive to detect her moods—so exciting in this respect. And his big, slightly prominent blue eyes, with the whites a little bloodshot, glanced at her quickly, with searching, and anxiety, and a touch of fear, as if his conscience were always uneasy. He, too, was rather like a horse—but forever quivering with a sort of cold, dangerous mistrust, which he covered with anxious love.

At the middle of his eyes was a central powerlessness, that left him anxious. It used to touch her to pity, that central look of powerlessness in him. But now, since she had seen the full, dark, passionate blaze of power and of different life in the eyes of the thwarted horse, the anxious powerlessness of the man drove her mad. Rico was so handsome, and he was so self-controlled, he had a gallant sort of kindness and a real worldly shrewdness. One had to admire him: at least *she* had to.

But after all, and after all, it was a bluff, an attitude. He kept it all working in himself, deliberately. It was an attitude. She read psychologists who said that everything was an attitude. Even the best of everything. But now she realized that, with men and women, everything is an attitude only when something else is lacking. Something is lacking and they are thrown back on their own devices. That black fiery flow in the eyes of the horse was not 'attitude.' It was something much more terrifying, and real, the only thing that was real. Gushing from the darkness in menace and question, and blazing out in the splendid body of the horse.

'Was I thinking about something?' she replied, in her slow, amused, casual fashion. As if everything was so casual and easy to her. And so it was, from the hard, polished side of herself. But that wasn't the whole story.

'I think you were, Loulina. May we offer the penny?'

'Don't trouble,' she said. 'I was thinking, if I was thinking of anything, about a bay horse called St. Mawr.'—Her secret *almost* crept into her eyes.

'The name is awfully attractive,' he said with a laugh.

'Not so attractive as the creature himself. I'm going to buy him.'

'Not really!' he said. 'But why?'

'He *is* so attractive. I'm going to buy him for you.'

'For *me! Darling!* how you do take me for granted! He may not be in the least attractive to me. As you know, I have hardly any feeling for horses at all. — Besides, how much does he cost?'

'That I don't know, Rico dear. But I'm sure you'll love him, for my sake.'— She felt, now, she was merely playing for her own ends.

'Lou dearest, *don't* spend a fortune on a horse for me, which I *don't* want. Honestly, I prefer a car.'

'Won't you ride with me in the Park, Rico?'

'Honestly, dear Lou, I don't want to.'

'Why not, dear boy? You'd look so beautiful. I wish you would.—And anyhow, come with me to look at St. Mawr.'

Rico was divided. He had a certain uneasy feeling about horses. At the same time, he *would* like to cut a handsome figure in the Park.

They went across to the mews. A little Welsh groom was watering the brilliant horse.

'Yes, dear, he certainly *is* beautiful: such a marvellous colour! Almost orange! But rather large, I should say, to ride in the Park.'

'No, for you he's perfect. You are so tall.'

'He'd be marvellous in a composition. That colour!'

And all Rico could do was to gaze with the artist's eye at the horse, with a glance at the groom.

'Don't you think the man is rather fascinating too?' he said, nursing his chin artistically and penetratingly.

The groom, Lewis, was a little, quick, rather bow-legged, loosely built fellow of indeterminate age, with a mop of black hair and little black beard. He was grooming the brilliant St. Mawr, out in the open. The horse was really glorious: like a marigold, with a pure golden sheen, a shimmer of green-gold lacquer, upon a burning red-orange. There on the shoulder you saw the yellow lacquer glisten. Lewis, a little scrub of a fellow, worked absorbedly, unheedingly, at the horse, with an absorption that was almost ritualistic. He seemed the attendant shadow of the ruddy animal.

'He goes with the horse,' said Lou. 'If we buy St. Mawr, we get the man thrown in.'

'They'd be *so* amusing to paint: such an extraordinary contrast! But, darling, I *hope* you won't insist on buying the horse. It's so frightfully expensive.'

'Mother will help me. —You'd look so well on him, Rico.'

'If ever I dared take the liberty of getting on his back—!'

'Why not?' She went quickly across the cobbled yard.

'Good morning, Lewis. How is St. Mawr?'

Lewis straightened himself and looked at her from under the falling mop of his black hair.

'All right,' he said.

He peered straight at her from under his overhanging black hair. He had pale-grey eyes, that looked phosphorescent, and suggested the eyes of a wildcat peering intent from under the darkness of some bush where it lies unseen. Lou, with her brown, unmatched, oddly perplexed eyes, felt herself found out.— 'He's a common little fellow,' she thought to herself. 'But he knows a woman and a horse, at sight.'—Aloud she said, in her southern drawl:

'How do you think he'd be with Sir Henry?'

Lewis turned his remote, coldly watchful eyes on the young baronet. Rico was tall and handsome and balanced on his hips. His face was long and well-defined, and with the hair taken straight back from the brow. It seemed as well-made as his clothing, and as perpetually presentable. You could not imagine his face dirty, or scrubby and unshaven, or bearded, or even moustached. It was perfectly prepared for social purposes. If his head had been cut off, like John the Baptist's, it would have been a thing complete in itself, would not have missed the body in the least.[17] The body was perfectly tailored. The head was one of the famous 'talking heads' of modern youth, with eyebrows

17. A recurrent figure in Lawrence, and also in Yeats and other contemporaries, for the modern divorce of mind and body.

a trifle Mephistophelian, large blue eyes a trifle bold, and curved mouth thrilling to death to kiss.

Lewis, the groom, staring from between his bush of hair and his beard, watched like an animal from the underbrush. And Rico was still sufficiently a colonial to be uneasily aware of the underbrush, uneasy under the watchfulness of the pale-grey eyes, and uneasy in that man-to-man exposure which is characteristic of the democratic colonies and of America. He knew he must ultimately be judged on his merits as a man, alone without a background: an ungarnished colonial.

This lack of background, this defenceless man-to-man business which left him at the mercy of every servant, was bad for his nerves. For he was *also* an artist. He bore up against it in a kind of desperation, and was easily moved to rancorous resentment. At the same time he was free of the Englishman's watertight *suffisance*.[18] He really was aware that he would have to hold his own all alone, thrown alone on his own defences in the universe. The extreme democracy of the colonies had taught him this.

And this the little aboriginal Lewis recognized in him. He recognized also Rico's curious hollow misgiving, fear of some deficiency in himself, beneath all his handsome, young-hero appearance.

'He'd be all right with anybody as would meet him half-way,' said Lewis, in the quick Welsh manner of speech, impersonal.

'You hear, Rico!' said Lou in her sing-song, turning to her husband.

'Perfectly, darling.'

'Would you be willing to meet St. Mawr half-way, hmm?'

'All the way, darling! Mahomet would go *all* the way to that mountain.[19] Who would dare to do otherwise?'

He spoke with a laughing, yet piqued sarcasm.

'Why, I think St. Mawr would understand perfectly,' she said in the soft voice of a woman haunted by love. And she went and laid her hand on the slippery, life-smooth shoulder of the horse. He, with his strange equine head lowered, its exquisite fine lines reaching a little snake-like forward, and his ears a little back, was watching her sideways, from the corner of his eye. He was in a state of absolute mistrust, like a cat crouching to spring.

'St. Mawr!' she said. 'St. Mawr! What is the matter? Surely you and I are all right!'

And she spoke softly, dreamily stroked the animal's neck. She could feel a response gradually coming from him. But he would not lift up his head. And when Rico suddenly moved nearer, he sprang with a sudden jerk backwards, as if lightning exploded in his four hoofs.

The groom spoke a few low words in Welsh. Lou, frightened, stood with lifted hand arrested. She had been going to stroke him.

'Why did he do that?' she said.

'They gave him a beating once or twice,' said the groom in a neutral voice, 'and he doesn't forget.'

18. Self-sufficiency, conceit.
19. Mahomet, asked for a miracle, summoned a mountain to him; when it did not come he thanked God for sparing the people the destruction such a move would have brought, and went to it.

She could hear a neutral sort of judgment in Lewis' voice. And she thought of the 'raw spot.'

Not any raw spot at all. A battle between two worlds. She realized that St. Mawr drew his hot breaths in another world from Rico's, from our world. Perhaps the old Greek horses had lived in St. Mawr's world. And the old Greek heroes, even Hippolytus,[20] had known it.

With their strangely naked equine heads, and something of a snake in their way of looking round, and lifting their sensitive, dangerous muzzles, they moved in a prehistoric twilight where all things loomed phantasmagoric, all on one plane, sudden presences suddenly jutting out of the matrix. It was another world, an older, heavily potent world. And in this world the horse was swift and fierce and supreme, undominated and unsurpassed.—'Meet him half-way,' Lewis said. But half-way across from our human world to that terrific equine twilight was not a small step. It was a step, she knew, that Rico could never take. She knew it. But she was prepared to sacrifice Rico.

St. Mawr was bought, and Lewis was hired along with him. At first, Lewis rode him behind Lou, in the Row,[21] to get him going. He behaved perfectly.

Phœnix, the half-Indian, was very jealous when he saw the black-bearded Welsh groom on St. Mawr.

'What horse you got there?' he asked, looking at the other man with the curious unseeing stare in his hard, Navajo eyes, in which the Indian glint moved like a spark upon a dark chaos. In Phœnix's high-boned face there was all the race-misery of the dispossessed Indian, with an added blankness left by shell-shock. But at the same time, there was that unyielding, save to death, which is characteristic of his tribe: his mother's tribe. Difficult to say what subtle thread bound him to the Navajo, and made his destiny a Red Man's destiny still.

They were a curious pair of grooms, following the correct, and yet extraordinary, pair of American mistresses. Mrs. Witt and Phœnix both rode with long stirrups and straight leg, sitting close to the saddle, without posting. Phœnix looked as if he and the horse were all one piece, he never seemed to rise in the saddle at all, neither trotting nor galloping, but sat like a man riding bareback. And all the time he stared around, at the riders in the Row, at the people grouped outside the rail, chatting, at the children walking with their nurses, as if he were looking at a mirage, in whose actuality he never believed for a moment. London was all a sort of dark mirage to him. His wide, nervous-looking brown eyes, with a smallish brown pupil that showed the white all round, seemed to be focused on the far distance, as if he could not see things too near. He was watching the pale deserts of Arizona shimmer with moving light, the long mirage of a shallow lake ripple, the great pallid concave of earth and sky expanding with interchanged light. And a horse-shape loom large and portentous in the mirage, like some prehistoric beast.

20. Son of Theseus and the Amazon Hippolyta; devoted to chastity, he rejected the advances of Phaedra, his stepmother, who then charged him with seducing her; Theseus invoked the vengeance of Poseidon (Neptune) on his son; Poseidon sent a monster who terrified Hippolytus's horses as he drove his chariot along the beach, so that he was thrown and killed.

21. Another mistake: stallions are not permitted in Rotten Row.

That was real to him: the phantasm of Arizona. But this London was something his eye passed over, as a false mirage.

He looked too smart in his well-tailored groom's clothes, so smart, he might have been one of the satirized new-rich. Perhaps it was a sort of half-breed physical assertion that came through his clothing, the savage's physical assertion of himself. Anyhow, he looked 'common,' rather horsy and loud.

Except his face. In the golden suavity of his high-boned Indian face, that was hairless, with hardly any eyebrows, there was a blank, lost look that was almost touching. The same startled blank look was in his eyes. But in the smallish dark pupils the dagger-point of light still gleamed unbroken.

He was a good groom, watchful, quick, and on the spot in an instant if anything went wrong. He had a curious, quiet power over the horses, unemotional, unsympathetic, but silently potent. In the same way, watching the traffic of Piccadilly with his blank, glinting eye, he would calculate everything instinctively, as if it were an enemy, and pilot Mrs. Witt by the strength of his silent will. He threw around her the tense watchfulness of her own America, and made her feel at home.

'Phœnix,' she said, turning abruptly in her saddle as they walked the horses past the sheltering policeman at Hyde Park Corner, 'I can't tell you how glad I am to have something a hundred per cent American at the back of me, when I go through these gates.'

She looked at him from dangerous grey eyes as if she meant it indeed, in vindictive earnest. A ghost of a smile went up to his high cheek-bones, but he did not answer.

'Why, mother?' said Lou, sing-song. 'It feels to me so friendly—!'

'Yes, Louise, it does. So friendly! That's why I mistrust it so entirely—'

And she set off at a canter up the Row, under the green trees, her face like the face of Medusa [22] at fifty, a weapon in itself. She stared at everything and everybody, with that stare of cold dynamite waiting to explode them all. Lou posted trotting at her side, graceful and elegant, and faintly amused. Behind came Phœnix, like a shadow, with his yellowish, high-boned face still looking sick. And at his side, on the big brilliant bay horse, the smallish, black-bearded Welshman.

Between Phœnix and Lewis there was a latent but unspoken and wary sympathy. Phœnix was terribly impressed by St. Mawr, he could not leave off staring at him. And Lewis rode the brilliant, handsome-moving stallion so very quietly, like an insinuation.

Of the two men, Lewis looked the darker, with his black beard coming up to his thick black eyebrows. He was swarthy, with a rather short nose, and the uncanny pale-green eyes that watched everything and cared about nothing. He cared about nothing in the world, except, at the present, St. Mawr. People did not matter to him. He rode his horse and watched the world from the vantage-ground of St. Mawr, with a final indifference.

'You have been with that horse long?' asked Phœnix.

'Since he was born.'

---

22. One of the three Gorgons, with faces so hideous that the sight of them turned the beholder to stone.

Phœnix watched the action of St. Mawr as they went. The bay moved proud and springy, but with perfect good sense, among the stream of riders. It was a beautiful June morning, the leaves overhead were thick and green; there came the first whiff of lime-tree scent. To Phœnix, however, the city was a sort of nightmare mirage, and to Lewis it was a sort of prison. The presence of people he felt as a prison around him.

Mrs. Witt and Lou were turning, at the end of the Row, bowing to some acquaintances. The grooms pulled aside. Mrs. Witt looked at Lewis with a cold eye.

'It seems an extraordinary thing to me, Louise,' she said, 'to see a groom with a beard.'

'It isn't usual, mother,' said Lou. 'Do you mind?'

'Not at all. At least, I think I don't. I get very tired of modern bare-faced young men, *very!* The clean, pure boy, don't you know! Doesn't it make you tired?—No, I think a groom with a beard is quite attractive.'

She gazed into the crowd defiantly, perching her finely shod toe with warlike firmness on the stirrup-iron. Then suddenly she reined in, and turned her horse towards the grooms.

'Lewis!' she said. 'I want to ask you a question. Supposing, now, that Lady Carrington wanted you to shave off that beard, what should you say?'

Lewis instinctively put up his hand to the said beard.

'They've wanted me to shave it off, Mam,' he said. 'But I've never done it.'

'But why? Tell me why.'

'It's part of me, Mam.'

Mrs. Witt pulled on again.

'Isn't that extraordinary, Louise?' she said. 'Don't you like the way he says *Mam?* It sounds so impossible to me. Could any woman think of herself as Mam? Never, since Queen Victoria! But—do you know?—it hadn't occurred to me that a man's beard was really part of him. It always seemed to me that men wore their beards, like they wear their neckties, for show. I shall always remember Lewis for saying his beard was part of him. Isn't it curious, the way he rides? He seems to sink himself in the horse. When I speak to him, I'm not sure whether I'm speaking to a man or to a horse.'

A few days later, Rico himself appeared on St. Mawr, for the morning ride. He rode self-consciously, as he did everything, and he was just a little nervous. But his mother-in-law was benevolent. She made him ride between her and Lou, like three ships slowly sailing abreast.

And that very day, who should come driving in an open carriage through the Park but the Queen Mother! Dear old Queen Alexandra, there was a flutter everywhere. And she bowed expressly to Rico, mistaking him, no doubt, for somebody else.

'Do you know,' said Rico as they sat at lunch, he and Lou and Mrs. Witt, in Mrs. Witt's sitting-room in the dark, quiet hotel in Mayfair, 'I really like riding St. Mawr *so* much. He really is a noble animal.—If ever I am made a Lord—which heaven forbid!—I shall be Lord St. Mawr.'

'You mean,' said Mrs. Witt, 'his real lordship would be the horse?'

'Very possible, I admit,' said Rico, with a curl of his long upper lip.

'Don't you think, mother,' said Lou, 'there *is* something quite noble about St. Mawr? He strikes me as the first noble thing I have ever seen.'

'Certainly I've not seen any *man* that could compare with him. Because these English noblemen—well! I'd rather look at a Negro Pullman-boy, if I was looking for what *I* call nobility.'

Poor Rico was getting crosser and crosser. There was a devil in Mrs. Witt. She had a hard, bright devil inside her, that she seemed to be able to let loose at will.

She let it loose the next day, when Rico and Lou joined her in the Row. She was silent but deadly with the horses, balking them in every way. She suddenly crowded over against the rail, in front of St. Mawr, so that the stallion had to rear to pull himself up. Then, having a clear track, she suddenly set off at a gallop, like an explosion, and the stallion, all on edge, set off after her.

It seemed as if the whole Park, that morning, were in a state of nervous tension. Perhaps there was thunder in the air. But St. Mawr kept on dancing and pulling at the bit, and wheeling sideways up against the railing, to the terror of the children and the onlookers, who squealed and jumped back suddenly, sending the nerves of the stallion into a rush like rockets. He reared and fought as Rico pulled him round.

Then he went on: dancing, pulling, springily progressing sideways, possessed with all the demons of perversity. Poor Rico's face grew longer and angrier. A fury rose in him, which he could hardly control. He hated his horse, and viciously tried to force him to a quiet, straight trot. Up went St. Mawr on his hind legs, to the terror of the Row. He got the bit in his teeth, and began to fight.

But Phœnix, cleverly, was in front of him.

'You get off, Rico!' called Mrs. Witt's voice, with all the calm of her wicked exultance.

And almost before he knew what he was doing, Rico had sprung lightly to the ground, and was hanging on to the bridle of the rearing stallion.

Phœnix also lightly jumped down, and ran to St. Mawr, handing his bridle to Rico. Then began a dancing and a splashing, a rearing and a plunging. St. Mawr was being wicked. But Phœnix, the indifference of conflict in his face, sat tight and immovable, without any emotion, only the heaviness of his impersonal will settling down like a weight, all the time, on the horse. There was, perhaps, a curious barbaric exultance in bare, dark will devoid of emotion or personal feeling.

So they had a little display in the Row for almost five minutes, the brilliant horse rearing and fighting. Rico, with a stiff long face, scrambled on to Phœnix's horse, and withdrew to a safe distance. Policemen came, and an officious mounted police rode up to save the situation. But it was obvious that Phœnix, detached and apparently unconcerned, but barbarically potent in his will, would bring the horse to order.

Which he did, and rode the creature home. Rico was requested not to ride St. Mawr in the Row any more, as the stallion was dangerous to public safety. The authorities knew all about him.

Where ended the first fiasco of St. Mawr.

'We didn't get on very well with his lordship this morning,' said Mrs. Witt triumphantly.

'No, he didn't like his company *at all!*' Rico snarled back.

He wanted Lou to sell the horse again.

'I doubt if anyone would buy him, dear,' she said. 'He's a known character.'

'Then make a gift of him—to your mother,' said Rico with venom.

'Why to mother?' asked Lou innocently.

'She might be able to cope with him—or he with her!' The last phrase was deadly. Having delivered it, Rico departed.

Lou remained at a loss. She felt almost always a little bit dazed, as if she could not see clear nor feel clear. A curious deadness upon her, like the first touch of death. And through this cloud of numbness, or deadness, came all her muted experiences.

Why was it? She did not know. But she felt that in some way it came from a battle of wills. Her mother, Rico, herself, it was always an unspoken, unconscious battle of wills, which was gradually numbing and paralysing her. She knew Rico meant nothing but kindness by her. She knew her mother only wanted to watch over her. Yet always there was this tension of will, that was so numbing. As if at the depths of him, Rico were always angry, though he seemed so 'happy' on the top. And Mrs. Witt was organically angry. So they were like a couple of bombs, timed to explode some day, but ticking on like two ordinary timepieces in the meanwhile.

She had come definitely to realize this: that Rico's anger was wound up tight at the bottom of him, like a steel spring that kept his works going, while he himself was 'charming,' like a bomb-clock with Sèvres paintings or Dresden figures on the outside. But his very charm was a sort of anger, and his love was a destruction in itself. He just couldn't help it.

And she? Perhaps she was a good deal the same herself. Wound up tight inside, and enjoying herself being 'lovely.' But wound up tight on some tension that, she realized now with wonder, was really a sort of anger. This, the mainspring that drove her on the round of 'joys.'

She used really to enjoy the tension, and the _élan_ [23] it gave her. While she knew nothing about it. So long as she felt it really was life and happiness, this _élan_, this tension and excitement of 'enjoying oneself.'

Now suddenly she doubted the whole show. She attributed to it the curious numbness that was overcoming her, as if she couldn't feel any more.

She wanted to come unwound. She wanted to escape this battle of wills.

Only St. Mawr gave her some hint of the possibility. He was so powerful, and so dangerous. But in his dark eye, that looked, with its cloudy brown pupil, a cloud within a dark fire, like a world beyond our world, there was a dark vitality glowing, and within the fire, another sort of wisdom. She felt sure of it: even when he put his ears back, and bared his teeth, and his great eyes came bolting out of his naked horse's head, and she saw demons upon demons in the chaos of his horrid eyes.

Why did he seem to her like some living background, into which she wanted to retreat? When he reared his head and neighed from his deep chest, like deep wind-bells resounding, she seemed to hear the echoes of another darker, more spacious, more dangerous, more splendid world than ours, that was beyond her. And there she wanted to go.

23. Drive, lift.

Mrs W.tt

She kept it utterly a secret, to herself. Because Rico would just have lifted his long upper lip, in his bare face, in a condescending sort of 'understanding.' And her mother would, as usual, have suspected her of sidestepping. People, all the people she knew, seemed so entirely contained within their cardboard let's-be-happy world. Their wills were fixed like machines on happiness, or fun, or the-best-ever. This ghastly cheery-o! touch, that made all her blood go numb.

Since she had really seen St. Mawr looming fiery and terrible in an outer darkness, she could not believe the world she lived in. She could not believe it was actually happening, when she was dancing in the afternoon at Claridge's, or in the evening at the Carlton, sliding about with some suave young man who wasn't like a man at all to her. Or down in Sussex for the week-end with the Enderleys: the talk, the eating and drinking, the flirtation, the endless dancing: it all seemed far more bodiless and, in a strange way, wraith-like, than any fairy-story. She seemed to be eating Barmecide[24] food, that had been conjured up out of thin air, by the power of words. She seemed to be talking to handsome young bare-faced unrealities, not men at all: as she slid about with them, in the perpetual dance, they too seemed to have been conjured up out of air, merely for this soaring, slithering dance-business. And she could not believe that, when the lights went out, they wouldn't melt back into thin air again, and complete nonentity. The strange nonentity of it all! Everything just conjured up, and nothing real. '*Isn't this the best ever!*' they would beamingly assert, like the wraiths of enjoyment, without any genuine substance. And she would beam back: '*Lots of fun!*'

She was thankful the season was over and everybody was leaving London. She and Rico were due to go to Scotland, but not till August. In the meantime they would go to her mother.

Mrs. Witt had taken a cottage in Shropshire, on the Welsh border, and had moved down there with Phœnix and her horses. The open, heather-and-bilberry-covered hills were splendid for riding.

Rico consented to spend the month in Shropshire, because for near neighbours Mrs. Witt had the Manbys, at Corrabach Hall. The Manbys were rich Australians returned to the old country and set up as Squires, all in full blow. Rico had known them in Victoria: they were of good family: and the girls made a great fuss of him.

So down went Lou and Rico, Lewis, Poppy and St. Mawr, to Shrewsbury, then out into the country. Mrs. Witt's 'cottage' was a tall red-brick Georgian house looking straight on to the churchyard, and the dark, looming big church.

'I never knew what a comfort it would be,' said Mrs. Witt, 'to have gravestones under my drawing-room windows, and funerals for lunch.'

She really did take a strange pleasure in sitting in her panelled room, that was painted grey, and watching the Dean or one of the curates officiating at the graveside, among a group of black country mourners with black-bordered handkerchiefs luxuriantly in use.

'Mother!' said Lou. 'I think it's gruesome!'

24. An illusory banquet served by a prince of the Barmecide family to a poor man (*Arabian Nights*).

She had a room at the back, looking over the walled garden and the stables. Nevertheless there was the *boom! boom!* of the passing-bell, and the chiming and pealing on Sundays. The shadow of the church, indeed! A very audible shadow, making itself heard insistently.

The Dean was a big, burly fat man with a pleasant manner. He was a gentleman, and a man of learning in his own line. But he let Mrs. Witt know that he looked down on her just a trifle—as a parvenu American, a Yankee—though she never was a Yankee: and at the same time he had a sincere respect for her, as a rich woman. Yes, a sincere respect for her, as a rich woman.

Lou knew that every Englishman, especially of the upper classes, has a wholesome respect for riches. But then, who hasn't?

The Dean was more *impressed* by Mrs. Witt than by little Lou. But to Lady Carrington he was charming: she was *almost* 'one of us,' you know. And he was very gracious to Rico: 'your father's splendid colonial service.'

Mrs. Witt had now a new pantomime to amuse her: the Georgian house, her own pew in church—it went with the old house: a village of thatched cottages—some of them with corrugated iron over the thatch: the cottage people, farm labourers and their families, with a few, very few, outsiders: the wicked little group of cottages down at Mile End, famous for ill living. The Mile-Enders were all Allisons and Jephsons, and inbred, the Dean said: result of working through the centuries at the quarry, and living isolated there at Mile End.

Isolated! Imagine it! A mile and a half from the railway station, ten miles from Shrewsbury. Mrs. Witt thought of Texas, and said:

'Yes, they are *very* isolated, away down there!'

And the Dean never for a moment suspected sarcasm.

But there she had the whole thing staged complete for her: English village life. Even miners breaking in to shatter the rather stuffy, unwholesome harmony.—All the men touched their caps to her, all the women did a bit of a reverence, the children stood aside for her, if she appeared in the street.

They were all poor again: the labourers could no longer afford even a glass of beer in the evenings, since the Glorious War.

'Now I think that *is* terrible,' said Mrs. Witt. 'Not to be able to get away from those stuffy, squalid, picturesque cottages for an hour in the evening, to drink a glass of beer.'

'It's a pity, I do agree with you, Mrs. Witt. But Mr. Watson has organized a men's reading-room, where the men can smoke and play dominoes, and read if they wish.'

'But that,' said Mrs. Witt, 'is not the same as that cosy parlour in the "Moon and Stars".'

'I quite agree,' said the Dean. 'It isn't.'

Mrs. Witt marched to the landlord of the 'Moon and Stars,' and asked for a glass of cider.

'I want,' she said, in her American accent, 'these poor labourers to have their glass of beer in the evenings.'

'They want it themselves,' said Harvey.

'Then they must have it—'

The upshot was, she decided to supply one large barrel of beer per week and the landlord was to sell it to the labourers at a penny a glass.

'My own country has gone dry,' she asserted. 'But not because we can't *afford* it.'

By the time Lou and Rico appeared, she was deep in. She actually interfered very little: the barrel of beer was her one public act. But she *did* know everybody by sight, already, and she *did* know everybody's circumstances. And she had attended one prayer-meeting, one mother's meeting, one sewing-bee, one 'social,' one Sunday School meeting, one Band of Hope meeting, and one Sunday School treat. She ignored the poky little Wesleyan and Baptist chapels, and was true-blue Episcopalian.

'How strange these picturesque old villages are, Louise!' she said, with a duskiness around her sharp, well-bred nose. 'How *easy* it all seems, all on a definite pattern. And how false! And underneath, *how corrupt!*'

She gave that queer, triumphant leer from her grey eyes, and queer demonish wrinkles seemed to twitter on her face.

Lou shrank away. She was beginning to be afraid of her mother's insatiable curiosity, that always looked for the snake under the flowers. Or rather, for the maggots.

Always this same morbid interest in other people and their doings, their privacies, their dirty linen. Always this air of alertness for personal happenings, personalities, personalities, personalities. Always this subtle criticism and appraisal of other people, this analysis of other people's motives. If anatomy presupposes a corpse, then psychology presupposes a world of corpses. Personalities, which means personal criticism and analysis, presupposes a whole world-laboratory of human psyches waiting to be vivisected. If you cut a thing up, of course it will smell. Hence, nothing raises such an infernal stink, at last, as human psychology.

Mrs. Witt was a pure psychologist, a fiendish psychologist. And Rico, in his way, was a psychologist too. But he had a formula. 'Let's *know* the worst, dear! But let's look on the bright side, and believe the best.'

'Isn't the Dean a priceless old darling!' said Rico at breakfast.

And it had begun. Work had started in the psychic vivisection laboratory.

'Isn't he wonderful!' said Lou vaguely.

'So delightfully worldly!—*Some of us are not born to make money, dear boy. Luckily for us, we can marry it.*'—Rico made a priceless face.

'Is Mrs. Vyner so rich?' asked Lou.

'She is, quite a wealthy woman—in coal,' replied Mrs. Witt. 'But the Dean is surely worth his weight, even in gold. And he's a massive figure. I can imagine there would be great satisfaction in having him for a husband.'

'Why, mother?' asked Lou.

'Oh, such a presence! One of these old Englishmen, that nobody can put in their pocket. You can't imagine his wife asking him to thread her needle. Something, after all, so *robust!* So different from *young* Englishmen, who all seem to me like ladies, perfect ladies.'

'*Somebody* has to keep up the tradition of the perfect lady,' said Rico.

'I know it,' said Mrs. Witt. 'And if the women won't do it, the young gentlemen take on the burden. They bear it very well.'

It was in full swing, the cut and thrust. And poor Lou, who had reached the point of stupefaction in the game, felt she did not know what to do with herself.

Rico and Mrs. Witt were deadly enemies, yet neither could keep clear of the other. It might have been they who were married to one another, their duel and their duet were so relentless.

But Rico immediately started the social round: first the Manbys: then motor twenty miles to luncheon at Lady Tewkesbury's: then young Mr. Burns came flying down in his aeroplane from Chester: then they must motor to the sea, to Sir Edward Edwards' place, where there was a moonlight bathing-party. Everything intensely thrilling, and so innerly wearisome, Lou felt.

But back of it all was St. Mawr, looming like a bonfire in the dark. He really was a tiresome horse to own. He worried the mares, if they were in the same paddock with him, always driving them round. And with any other horse he just fought with definite intent to kill. So he had to stay alone.

'That St. Mawr, he's a bad horse,' said Phœnix.

'Maybe!' said Lewis.

'You don't like quiet horses?' said Phœnix.

'Most horses is quiet,' said Lewis. 'St. Mawr, he's different.'

'Why don't he never get any foals?'

'Doesn't want to, I should think. Same as me.'

'What good is a horse like that? Better shoot him, before he kill somebody.'

'What good'll they get, shooting St. Mawr?' said Lewis.

'If he kills somebody!' said Phœnix.

But there was no answer.

The two grooms both lived over the stables, and Lou, from her window, saw a good deal of them. They were two quiet men, yet she was very much aware of their presence, aware of Phœnix's rather high square shoulders and his fine, straight, vigorous black hair that tended to stand up assertively on his head, as he went quietly drifting about his various jobs. He was not lazy, but he did everything with a sort of diffidence, as if from a distance, and handled his horses carefully, cautiously, and cleverly, but without sympathy. He seemed to be holding something back, all the time, unconsciously, as if in his very being there was some secret. But it was a secret of *will*. His quiet, reluctant movements, as if he never really wanted to do anything; his long flat-stepping stride; the permanent challenge in his high cheek-bones, the Indian glint in his eyes, and his peculiar stare, watchful and yet unseeing, made him unpopular with the women servants.

Nevertheless, women had a certain fascination for him: he would stare at the pretty young maids with an intent blank stare, when they were not looking. Yet he was rather overbearing, domineering with them, and they resented him. It was evident to Lou that he looked upon himself as belonging to the Master, not to the servant class. When he flirted with the maids, as he very often did, for he had a certain crude ostentatiousness, he seemed to let them feel that he despised them as inferiors, servants, while he admired their pretty charms, as fresh country maids.

'I'm fair nervous of that Phœnix,' said Fanny, the fair-haired maid. 'He makes you feel what he'd do to you if he could.'

'He'd better not try with me,' said Mabel. 'I'd scratch his cheeky eyes out. Cheek!—for it's nothing else! He's nobody—common as they're made!'

'He makes you feel you was there for him to trample on,' said Fanny.

'Mercy, you *are* soft! If anybody's that, it's him. Oh, my, Fanny, you've no right to let a fellow make you feel like *that!* Make *them* feel that *they're* dirt, for *you* to trample on: which they are!'

Fanny, however, being a shy little blond thing, wasn't good at assuming the trampling rôle. She was definitely nervous of Phœnix. And he enjoyed it. An invisible smile seemed to creep up his cheek-bones, and the glint moved in his eyes as he teased her. He tormented her by his very presence, as he knew.

He would come silently up when she was busy, and stand behind her perfectly still, so that she was unaware of his presence. Then, silently, he would *make* her aware. Till she glanced nervously round and, with a scream, saw him.

One day Lou watched this little play. Fanny had been picking over a bowl of black currants, sitting on the bench under the maple tree in a corner of the yard. She didn't look round till she had picked up her bowl to go to the kitchen. Then there was a scream and a crash.

When Lou came out, Phœnix was crouching down silently gathering up the currants, which the little maid, scarlet and trembling, was collecting into another bowl. Phœnix seemed to be smiling down his back.

'Phœnix!' said Lou. 'I wish you wouldn't startle Fanny!'

He looked up, and she saw the glint of ridicule in his eyes.

'Who, me?' he said.

'Yes, you. You go up behind Fanny, to startle her. You're not to do it.'

He slowly stood erect, and lapsed into his peculiar invisible silence. Only for a second his eyes glanced at Lou's, and then she saw the cold anger, the gleam of malevolence and contempt. He could not bear being commanded, or reprimanded, by a woman.

Yet it was even worse with a man.

'What's that, Lou?' said Rico, appearing all handsome and in the picture, in white flannels with an apricot silk shirt.

'I'm telling Phœnix he's not to torment Fanny!'

'Oh!' and Rico's voice immediately became his father's, the important government official's. 'Certainly *not!* Most certainly *not!*' He looked at the scattered currants and the broken bowl. Fanny melted into tears. 'This, I suppose, is some of the results! Now look here, Phœnix, you're to leave the maids strictly alone. I shall ask them to report to me whenever, or *if* ever, you interfere with them. But I hope you *won't* interfere with them—in any way. You understand?'

As Rico became more and more Sir Henry and the government official, Lou's bones melted more and more into discomfort. Phœnix stood in his peculiar silence, the invisible smile on his cheek-bones.

'You understand what I'm saying to you?' Rico demanded, in intensified acid tones.

But Phœnix only stood there, as it were behind a cover of his own will, and looked back at Rico with a faint smile on his face and the glint moving in his eyes.

'Do you intend to answer?' Rico's upper lip lifted nastily.

'Mrs. Witt is my boss,' came from Phœnix.

The scarlet flew up Rico's throat and flushed his face, his eyes went glaucous. Then quickly his face turned yellow.

Lou looked at the two men: her husband, whose rages, over-controlled, were organically terrible; the half-breed, whose dark-coloured lips were widened in a faint smile of derision, but in whose eyes caution and hate were playing against one another. She realized that Phœnix would accept *her* reprimand, or her mother's, because he could despise the two of them as mere women. But Rico's bossiness aroused murder pure and simple.

She took her husband's arm.

'Come, dear!' she said, in her half-plaintive way. 'I'm sure Phœnix understands. We all understand. Go to the kitchen, Fanny, never mind the currants. There are plenty more in the garden.'

Rico was always thankful to be drawn quickly, submissively away from his own rage. He was afraid of it. He was afraid lest he should fly at the groom in some horrible fashion. The very thought horrified him. But in actuality he came very near to it.

He walked stiffly, feeling paralysed by his own fury. And those words, *Mrs. Witt is my boss*, were like hot acid in his brain. An insult!

'By the way, Belle-Mère!' [25] he said when they joined Mrs. Witt—she hated being called Belle-Mère, and once said: 'If I'm the bell-mare, are you one of the colts?'—she also hated his voice of smothered fury—'I had to speak to Phœnix about persecuting the maids. He took the liberty of informing me that you were his boss, so perhaps you had better speak to him.'

'I certainly will. I believe they're my maids, and nobody else's, so it's my duty to look after them. Who was he persecuting?'

'I'm the responsible one, mother,' said Lou—

Rico disappeared in a moment. He must get out: get away from the house. How? Something was wrong with the car. Yet he must get away, away. He would go over to Corrabach. He would ride St. Mawr. He had been talking about the horse, and Flora Manby was dying to see him. She had said: 'Oh, I can't *wait* to see that marvellous horse of yours.'

He would ride him over. It was only seven miles. He found Lou's maid Flena, and sent her to tell Lewis. Meanwhile, to soothe himself, he dressed himself most carefully in white riding-breeches and a shirt of purple silk crêpe, with a flowing black tie spotted red like a ladybird, and black riding-boots. Then he took a *chic* little white hat with a black band.

St. Mawr was saddled and waiting, and Lewis had saddled a second horse.

'Thanks, Lewis, I'm going alone!' said Rico.

This was the first time he had ridden St. Mawr in the country, and he was nervous. But he was also in the hell of a smothered fury. All his careful dressing had not really soothed him. So his fury consumed his nervousness.

He mounted with a swing, blind and rough. St. Mawr reared.

'Stop that!' snarled Rico, and put him to the gate.

Once out in the village street, the horse went dancing sideways. He insisted on dancing at the sidewalk, to the exaggerated terror of the children. Rico, exasperated, pulled him across. But no, he wouldn't go down the centre of the village street. He began dancing and edging on to the other sidewalk, so the foot-passengers fled into the shops in terror.

The devil was in him. He would turn down every turning where he was not

25. Mother-in-law.

meant to go. He reared with panic at a furniture van. He *insisted* on going down the wrong side of the road. Rico was riding him with a martingale, and he could see the rolling, bloodshot eye.

'Damn you, *go!*' said Rico, giving him a dig with the spurs.

And away they went, down the high road, in a thunderbolt. It was a hot day, with thunder threatening, so Rico was soon in a flame of heat. He held on tight, with fixed eyes, trying all the time to rein in the horse. What he really was afraid of was that the brute would shy suddenly, as he galloped. Watching for this, he didn't care when they sailed past the turning to Corrabach.

St. Mawr flew on, in a sort of *élan*. Marvellous, the power and life in the creature! There was really a great joy in the motion. If only he wouldn't take the corners at a gallop, nearly swerving Rico off! Luckily the road was clear. To ride, to ride at this terrific gallop, on into eternity!

After several miles, the horse slowed down, and Rico managed to pull him into a lane that might lead to Corrabach. When all was said and done, it was a wonderful ride. St. Mawr could go like the wind, but with that luxurious heavy ripple of life which is like nothing else on earth. It seemed to carry one at once into another world, away from the life of the nerves.

So Rico arrived after all something of a conqueror at Corrabach. To be sure, he was perspiring, and so was his horse. But he was a hero from another, heroic world.

'Oh, such a hot ride!' he said, as he walked on to the lawn at Corrabach Hall. 'Between the sun and the horse, really!—between two fires!'

'Don't you trouble, you're looking dandy, a bit hot and flushed like,' said Flora Manby. 'Let's go and see your horse.'

And her exclamation was: 'Oh, he's *lovely!* He's *fine!* I'd love to try him once—'

Rico decided to accept the invitation to stay overnight at Corrabach. Usually he was very careful, and refused to stay, unless Lou was with him. But they telephoned to the post office at Chomesbury, would Mr. Jones please send a message to Lady Carrington that Sir Henry was staying the night at Corrabach Hall, but would be home next day? Mr. Jones received the request with unction, and said he would go over himself to give the message to Lady Carrington.

Lady Carrington was in the walled garden. The peculiarity of Mrs. Witt's house was that, for grounds proper, it had the churchyard.

'I never thought, Louise, that one day I should have an old English churchyard for my lawns and shrubbery and park, and funeral mourners for my herds of deer. It's curious. For the first time in my life a funeral has become a real thing to me. I feel I could write a book on them.'

But Louise only felt intimidated.

At the back of the house was a flagged court-yard, with stables and a maple tree in a corner, and big doors opening on to the village street. But at the side was a walled garden, with fruit trees and currant bushes and a great bed of rhubarb, and some tufts of flowers, peonies, pink roses, sweet-williams. Phœnix, who had a certain taste for gardening, would be out there thinning the carrots or tying up the lettuce. He was not lazy. Only he would not take work seriously, as a job. He would be quite amused tying up lettuce, and would tie up head after head, quite prettily. Then, becoming bored, he would abandon his task, light a cigarette, and go and stand on the threshold of the big doors, in full view of the street, watching, and yet completely indifferent.

After Rico's departure on St. Mawr, Lou went into the garden. And there she saw Phœnix working in the onion-bed. He was bending over, in his own silence, busy with nimble, amused fingers among the grassy young onions. She thought he had not seen her, so she went down another path to where a swing bed hung under the apple trees. There she sat with a book and a bundle of magazines. But she did not read.

She was musing vaguely. Vaguely, she was glad that Rico was away for a while. Vaguely, she felt a sense of bitterness, of complete futility: the complete futility of her living. This left her drifting in a sea of utter chagrin. And Rico seemed to her the symbol of the futility. Vaguely, she was aware that something else existed, but she didn't know where it was or what it was.

In the distance she could see Phœnix's dark, rather tall-built head, with its black, fine, intensely living hair tending to stand on end, like a brush with long, very fine black bristles. His hair, she thought, betrayed him as an animal of a different species. He was growing a little bored by weeding onions: that also she could tell. Soon he would want some other amusement.

Presently Lewis appeared. He was small, energetic, a little bit bow-legged, and he walked with a slight strut. He wore khaki riding-breeches, leather gaiters, and a blue shirt. And, like Phœnix, he rarely had any cap or hat on his head. His thick black hair was parted at the side and brushed over heavily sideways, dropping on his forehead at the right. It was very long, a real mop, under which his eyebrows were dark and steady.

'Seen Lady Carrington?' he asked of Phœnix.

'Yes, she's sitting on that swing over there—she's been there quite a while.' The wretch—he had seen her from the very first!

Lewis came striding over, looking towards her with his pale-grey eyes, from under his mop of hair.

'Mr. Jones from the post office wants to see you, my Lady, with a message from Sir Henry.'

Instantly alarm took possession of Lou's soul.

'Oh!—Does he want to see me personally?—What message? Is anything wrong?'—And her voice trailed out over the last word, with a sort of anxious nonchalance.

'I don't think it's anything amiss,' said Lewis reassuringly.

'Oh! You don't'—the relief came into her voice. Then she looked at Lewis with a slight, winning smile in her unmatched eyes. 'I'm so afraid of St. Mawr, you know.' Her voice was soft and cajoling. Phœnix was listening in the distance.

'St. Mawr's all right, if you don't do nothing to him,' Lewis replied.

'I'm sure he is!—But how is one to know when one is doing something to him?—Tell Mr. Jones to come here, please,' she concluded, on a changed tone.

Mr. Jones, a man of forty-five, thickset, with a fresh complexion and rather foolish brown eyes, and a big brown moustache, came prancing down the path, smiling rather fatuously, and doffing his straw hat with a gorgeous bow the moment he saw Lou sitting in her slim white frock on the coloured swing bed under the trees with their hard green apples.

'Good morning, Mr. Jones!'

'Good morning, Lady Carrington.—If I may say so, what a picture you make —a beautiful picture—'

He beamed under his big brown moustache like the greatest lady-killer.

'Do I! Did Sir Henry say he was all right?'

'He didn't *say* exactly, but I should expect he is all right—' and Mr. Jones delivered his message, in the mayonnaise of his own unction.

'Thank you so much, Mr. Jones. It's awfully good of you to come and tell me. Now I shan't worry about Sir Henry *at all.*'

'It's a great pleasure to come and deliver a satisfactory message to Lady Carrington. But it won't be kind to Sir Henry if you don't worry about him *at all* in his absence. We all enjoy being worried about by those we love—so long as there is nothing to worry about of course!'

'Quite!' said Lou. 'Now won't you take a glass of port and a biscuit, or a whisky and soda? And thank you ever so much.'

'Thank *you*, my Lady. I might drink a whisky and soda, since you are so good.'

And he beamed fatuously.

'Let Mr. Jones mix himself a whisky and soda, Lewis,' said Lou.

'Heavens!' she thought, as the postmaster retreated a little uncomfortably down the garden path, his bald spot passing in and out of the sun, under the trees. 'How ridiculous everything is, how ridiculous, ridiculous!' Yet she didn't really dislike Mr. Jones and his interlude.

Phœnix was melting away out of the garden. He had to follow the fun.

'Phœnix!' Lou called. 'Bring me a glass of water, will you? Or send somebody with it.'

He stood in the path looking round at her.

'All right!' he said.

And he turned away again.

She did not like being alone in the garden. She liked to have the men working somewhere near. Curious how pleasant it was to sit there in the garden when Phœnix was about, or Lewis. It made her feel she could never be lonely or jumpy. But when Rico was there, she was all aching nerve.

Phœnix came back with a glass of water, lemon juice, sugar, and a small bottle of brandy. He knew Lou liked a spoonful of brandy in her iced lemonade.

'How thoughtful of you, Phœnix!' she said. 'Did Mr. Jones get his whisky?'

'He was just getting it.'

'That's right.—By the way, Phœnix, I wish you wouldn't get mad if Sir Henry speaks to you. He is *really* so kind.'

She looked up at the man. He stood there watching her in silence, the invisible smile on his face, and the inscrutable Indian glint moving in his eyes. What was he thinking? There was something passive and almost submissive about him, but, underneath this, an unyielding resistance and cruelty: yes, even cruelty. She felt that, on top, he was submissive and attentive, bringing her her lemonade as she liked it, without being told: thinking for her quite subtly. But underneath there was an unchanging hatred. He submitted circumstantially, he worked for a wage. And, even circumstantially, he *liked* his mistress—*la patrona*—and her daughter. But much deeper than any circumstance, or any circumstantial liking, was the categorical hatred upon which he was founded, and with which he was powerless. His liking for Lou and for Mrs. Witt, his serving them and working for a wage, was all side-tracking his own nature, which was grounded on hatred of their very existence. But what was he to do? He had to live. Therefore he had to serve, to work for a wage, and even to be faithful.

And yet *their* existence made his own existence negative. If he was to exist, positively, they would have to cease to exist. At the same time, a fatal sort of tolerance made him serve these women, and go on serving.

'Sir Henry is *so* kind to everybody,' Lou insisted.

The half-breed met her eyes, and smiled uncomfortably.

'Yes, he's a kind man,' he replied, as if sincerely.

'Then why do you mind if he speaks to you?'

'I don't mind,' said Phœnix glibly.

'But you do. Or else you wouldn't make him so angry.'

'Was he angry?—I don't know,' said Phœnix.

'He was very angry. And you *do* know.'

'No, I don't know if he's angry. I don't know,' the fellow persisted. And there was a glib sort of satisfaction in his tone.

'That's awfully unkind of you, Phœnix,' she said, growing offended in her turn.

'No, I don't know if he's angry. I don't want to make him angry. I don't know—'

He had taken on a tone of naïve ignorance, which at once gratified her pride as a woman, and deceived her.

'Well, you believe me when I tell you you *did* make him angry, don't you?'

'Yes, I believe when you tell me.'

'And you promise me, won't you, not to do it again? It's *so* bad for him— so bad for his nerves, and for his eyes. It makes them inflamed, and injures his eyesight. And you know, as an artist, it's terrible if anything happens to his eyesight—'

Phœnix was watching her closely, to take it in. He still was not good at understanding continuous, logical statement. Logical connection in speech seemed to stupefy him, make him stupid. He understood in disconnected assertions of fact. But he had gathered what she said. 'He gets mad at you. When he gets mad, it hurts his eyes. His eyes hurt him. He can't see, because his eyes hurt him. He want to paint a picture, he can't. He can't paint a picture, he can't see clear—'

Yes, he had understood. She saw he had understood. The bright glint of satisfaction moved in his eyes.

'So now promise me, won't you, you won't make him mad again: you won't make him angry?'

'No, I won't make him angry. I don't do anything to make him angry,' Phœnix answered, rather glibly.

'And you do understand, don't you? You do know how kind he is: how he'd do a good turn to anybody?'

'Yes, he's a kind man,' said Phœnix.

'I'm so glad you realize.—There, that's luncheon! How nice it is to sit here in the garden, when everybody is nice to you! No, I can carry the tray, don't you bother.'

But he took the tray from her hand, and followed her to the house. And as he walked behind her, he watched the slim white nape of her neck, beneath the clustering of her bobbed hair, something as a stoat watches a rabbit he is following.

In the afternoon Lou retreated once more to her place in the garden. There she lay, sitting with a bunch of pillows behind her, neither reading nor working, just musing. She had learned the new joy: to do absolutely nothing, but to lie and let the sunshine filter through the leaves, to see the bunch of red-hot-poker flowers pierce scarlet into the afternoon, beside the comparative neutrality of some foxgloves. The mere colour of hard red, like the big oriental poppies that had fallen, and these poker flowers, lingered in her consciousness like a communication.

Into this peaceful indolence, when even the big, dark-grey tower of the church beyond the wall and the yew trees was keeping its bells in silence, advanced Mrs. Witt, in a broad panama hat and the white dress.

'Don't you want to ride, or do something, Louise?' she asked ominously.

'Don't you want to be peaceful, mother?' retorted Louise.

'Yes—an *active* peace.—I can't *believe* that my daughter can be content to lie on a hammock and do *nothing*, not even read or improve her mind, the greater part of the day.'

'Well, your daughter *is* content to do that. It's her greatest pleasure.'

'I know it. I can see it. And it surprises me *very* much. When I was your age, I was never still. I had so much *go*—'

> *"Those maids, thank God,*
> *Are 'neath the sod,*
> *And all their generation."* [26]

'No, but mother, I only take life differently. Perhaps you used up that sort of *go*. I'm the harem type, mother: only I never want the men inside the lattice.'

'Are you really my daughter?—Well! A woman never knows what will happen to her.—I'm an *American* woman, and I suppose I've got to remain one, no matter where I am.—What did you want, Lewis?'

The groom had approached down the path.

'If I am to saddle Poppy?' said Lewis.

'No, apparently *not!*' replied Mrs. Witt. 'Your mistress prefers the hammock to the saddle.'

'Thank you, Lewis. What mother says is true this afternoon, at least.' And she gave him a peculiar little cross-eyed smile.

'Who,' said Mrs. Witt to the man, 'has been cutting at your hair?'

There was a moment of silent resentment.

'I did it myself, Mam! Sir Henry said it was too long.'

'He certainly spoke the truth.—But I believe there's a barber in the village on Saturdays—or you could ride over to Shrewsbury.—Just turn round, and let me look at the back. Is it the money?'

'No, Mam. I don't like these fellows touching my head.'

He spoke coldly, with a certain hostile reserve that at once piqued Mrs. Witt.

26. From an early lyric by William Carlos Williams (1883–1963).

Lawrence

'Don't you really!' she said. 'But it's quite *impossible* for you to go about as you are. It gives you a half-witted appearance. Go now into the yard, and get a chair and dust-sheet. I'll cut your hair.'

The man hesitated, hostile.

'Don't be afraid, I know how it's done. I've cut the hair of many a poor wounded boy in hospital: and shaved them too. *You've got such a touch, nurse!* Poor fellow, he was dying, though none of us knew it.—Those are compliments I value, Louise.—Get that chair now, and a dust-sheet. I'll borrow your hair-scissors from Elena, Louise.'

Mrs. Witt, happily on the war path, was herself again. She didn't care for work, actual work. But she loved trimming. She loved arranging unnatural and pretty salads, devising new and piquant-looking ice-creams, having a turkey stuffed exactly as she knew a stuffed turkey in Louisiana, with chestnuts and butter and stuff, or showing a servant how to turn waffles on a waffle-iron, or to bake a ham with brown sugar and cloves and a moistening of rum. She liked pruning rose trees, or beginning to cut a yew-hedge into shape. She liked ordering her own and Louise's shoes, with an exactitude and a knowledge of shoemaking that sent the salesmen crazy. She was a demon in shoes. Reappearing from America, she would pounce on her daughter. 'Louise, throw those shoes away. Give them to one of the maids.'—'But, mother, they are some of the best French shoes. I like them.'—'Throw them away. A shoe has only two excuses for existing: perfect comfort or perfect appearance. Those have neither. I have brought you some shoes.'—Yes, she had brought ten pairs of shoes from New York. She knew her daughter's foot as she knew her own.

So now she was in her element, looming behind Lewis as he sat in the middle of the yard swathed in a dust-sheet. She had on an overall and a pair of wash-leather gloves, and she poised a pair of long scissors like one of the Fates.[27] In her big hat she looked curiously young, but with the youth of a bygone generation. Her heavy-lidded, laconic grey eyes were alert, studying the groom's black mop of hair. Her eyebrows made thin, uptilting black arches on her brow. Her fresh skin was slightly powdered, and she was really handsome, in a bold, bygone, eighteenth-century style. Some of the curious, adventurous stoicism of the eighteenth century: and then a certain blatant American efficiency.

Lou, who had strayed into the yard to see, looked so much younger and so many thousands of years older than her mother, as she stood in her wisp-like diffidence, the clusters of grape-like bobbed hair hanging beside her face, with its fresh colouring and its ancient weariness, her slightly squinting eyes, that were so disillusioned they were becoming faun-like.

'Not too short, mother, not too short,' she remonstrated, as Mrs. Witt, with a terrific flourish of efficiency, darted at the man's black hair, and the thick flakes fell like black snow.

'Now, Louise, I'm right in this job, please don't interfere.—Two things I hate to see: a man with his wool in his neck and ears: and a bare-faced young man who looks as if he'd bought his face as well as his hair from a men's beauty-specialist.'

27. Of the three Fates Clotho held the distaff, Lachesis drew off the thread, and Atropos cut it; in this way they controlled each human life. One of the many passages associating Mrs. Witt with death.

And efficiently she bent down, clip—clip—clipping! while Lewis sat utterly immobile, with sunken head, in a sort of despair.

Phoenix stood against the stable door, with his restless, eternal cigarette. And in the kitchen doorway the maids appeared and fled, appeared and fled in delight. The old gardener, a fixture who went with the house, creaked in and stood with his legs apart, silent in intense condemnation.

'First time I ever see such a thing!' he muttered to himself, as he creaked on into the garden. He was a bad-tempered old soul, who thoroughly disapproved of the household, and would have given notice, but that he knew which side his bread was buttered: and there was butter unstinted on his bread, in Mrs. Witt's kitchen.

Mrs. Witt stood back to survey her handiwork, holding those terrifying shears with their beak erect. Lewis lifted his head and looked stealthily round, like a creature in a trap.

'Keep still!' she said. 'I haven't finished.'

And she went for his front hair, with vigour, lifting up long layers and snipping off the ends artistically: till at last he sat with a black aureole upon the floor, and his ears standing out with curious new alertness from the sides of his clean-clipped head.

'Stand up,' she said, 'and let me look.'

He stood up, looking absurdly young, with the hair all cut away from his neck and ears, left thick only on top. She surveyed her work with satisfaction.

'You look so much younger,' she said, 'you would be surprised. Sit down again.'

She clipped the back of his neck with the shears, and then, with a very slight hesitation, she said:

'Now about the beard!'

But the man rose suddenly from the chair, pulling the dust-cloth from his neck with desperation.

'No, I'll do that myself,' he said, looking her in the eyes with a cold light in his pale-grey, uncanny eyes.

She hesitated in a kind of wonder at his queer male rebellion.

'Now, listen, I shall do it much better than you—and besides,' she added hurriedly, snatching at the dust-cloth he was flinging on the chair, 'I haven't quite finished round the ears.'

'I think I shall do,' he said, again looking her in the eyes, with a cold, white gleam of finality. 'Thank you for what you've done.'

And he walked away to the stable.

'You'd better sweep up here,' Mrs. Witt called.

'Yes, Mam,' he replied, looking round at her again with an odd resentment, but continuing to walk away.

'However!' said Mrs. Witt. 'I suppose he'll do.'

And she divested herself of gloves and overall, and walked indoors to wash and to change. Lou went indoors too.

'It is extraordinary what hair that man has!' said Mrs. Witt. 'Did I tell you when I was in Paris I saw a woman's face in the hotel that I thought I knew? I couldn't place her, till she was coming towards me. *Aren't you Rachel Fannière?* she said. *Aren't you Janette Leroy?* We hadn't seen each other since we were girls of twelve and thirteen, at school in New Orleans. *Oh!* she said to me. *Is every illusion doomed to perish? You had such wonderful golden curls! All my life I've said: Oh, if only I had such lovely hair as Rachel Fannière! I've seen those beautiful golden curls of yours all my life. And now I meet you, you're grey!* Wasn't that terrible, Louise? Well, that man's hair made me think of it—so thick and curious. It's strange what a difference there is in hair, I suppose it's because he's just an animal—no mind! There's nothing I admire in a man like a good *mind*. Your father was a very clever man, and all the men I've admired have been clever. But isn't it curious now, I've never cared much to touch their hair. How strange life is! If it gives one thing, it takes away another.—And even those poor boys in hospital: I have shaved them, or cut their hair, like a mother, never thinking anything of it. Lovely, intelligent, clean boys most of them were. Yet it never did anything to me. I never knew before that something could happen to one from a person's *hair!* Like to Janette Leroy from my curls when I was a child. And now I'm grey, as she says.—I wonder how old a man Lewis is, Louise! Didn't he look absurdly young, with his ears pricking up?'

'I think Rico said he was forty or forty-one.'

'And never been married?'

'No—not as far as I know.'

'Isn't that curious now!—just an animal! no mind! A man with no mind! I've always thought that the *most* despicable thing. Yet such wonderful hair to touch. Your Henry has quite a good mind, yet I would simply shrink from touching his hair.—I suppose one likes stroking a cat's fur, just the same. Just the animal in man. Curious that I never seem to have met it, Louise. Now I come to think of it, he has the eyes of a human cat: a human tom-cat. Would you call him stupid? Yes, he's very stupid.'

'No, mother, he's not stupid. He only doesn't care about our sort of things.'

'Like an animal! But what a strange look he has in his eyes! a strange sort of intelligence! and a confidence in himself. Isn't that curious, Louise, in a man with as little mind as he has? Do you know, I should say he could see through a woman pretty well.'

'Why, mother!' said Lou impatiently. 'I think one gets so tired of your men with mind, as you call it. There are so many of that sort of clever men. And there are lots of men who aren't very clever, but are rather nice: and lots are stupid. It seems to me there's something else besides mind and cleverness, or niceness or cleanness. Perhaps it is the animal. Just think of St. Mawr! I've thought so much about him. We call him an animal, but we never know what it means. He seems a far greater mystery to me than a clever man. He's a horse. Why can't one say in the same way, of a man: *He's a man?* There seems no mystery in being a man. But there's a terrible mystery in St. Mawr.'

Mrs. Witt watched her daughter quizzically.

'Louise,' she said, 'you won't tell me that the mere animal is all that counts in a man. I will never believe it. Man is wonderful because he is able to *think*.'

'But is he?' cried Lou, with sudden exasperation. 'Their thinking seems to me all so childish: like stringing the same beads over and over again. Ah, men! They and their thinking are all so *paltry*. How can you be impressed?'

Mrs. Witt raised her eyebrows sardonically.

'Perhaps I'm not—any more,' she said with grim smile.

'But,' she added, 'I still can't see that I am to be impressed by the mere animal in man. The animals are the same as we are. It seems to me they have the same feelings and wants as we do, in a commonplace way. The only difference is that they have no minds: no human minds, at least. And no matter what you say, Louise, lack of mind makes the commonplace.'

Lou knitted her brows nervously.

'I suppose it does, mother.—But men's minds *are* so commonplace: look at Dean Vyner and his mind! Or look at Arthur Balfour, as a shining example. Isn't *that* commonplace, that cleverness? I would hate St. Mawr to be spoilt by such a mind.'

'Yes, Louise, so would I. Because the men you mention are really old women, knitting the same pattern over and over again. Nevertheless, I shall never alter my belief that real mind is all that matters in a man, and it's *that* that we women love.'

'Yes, mother!—But what *is* real mind? The old woman who knits the most complicated pattern? Oh, I can hear all their needles clicking, the clever men! As a matter of fact, mother, I believe Lewis has far more real mind than Dean Vyner or any of the clever ones. He has a good intuitive mind, he knows things without thinking them.'

'That may be, Louise! But he is a servant. He is *under*. A real man should never be under. And then you could never be intimate with a man like Lewis.'

'I don't want intimacy, mother. I'm too tired of it all. I love St. Mawr because he isn't intimate. He stands where one can't get at him. And he burns with life. And where does his life come from, to him? That's the mystery. That great burning life in him, which never is dead. Most men have a deadness in them that frightens me so, because of my own deadness. Why can't men get their life straight, like St. Mawr, and then think? Why can't they think quick, mother: quick as a woman: only farther than we do? Why isn't men's thinking quick like fire, mother? Why is it so slow, so dead, so deadly dull?'

'I can't tell you, Louise. My own opinion of the men of to-day has grown very small. But I can live in spite of it.'

'No, mother. We seem to be living off old fuel, like the camel when he lives off his hump. Life doesn't rush into us, as it does even into St. Mawr, and he's a dependent animal. I can't live, mother. I just can't.'

'I don't see why not. *I'm* full of life.'

'I know you are, mother. But I'm not, and I'm your daughter.—And don't misunderstand me, mother. I don't want to be an animal like a horse or a cat or a lioness, though they all fascinate me, the way they get their life *straight*, not from a lot of old tanks, as we do. I don't admire the cave-man, and that sort of thing. But think, mother, if we could get our lives straight from the source, as the animals do, and still be ourselves. You don't like men yourself. But you've no idea how men just tire me out: even the very thought of them. You say they are too animal. But they're not, mother. It's the animal in them has gone perverse, or cringing, or humble, or domesticated, like dogs. I don't know one single man who is a proud living animal. I know they've left off really thinking. But then men always do leave off really thinking, when the last bit of wild animal dies in them.'

'Because we have minds—'

'We have no minds once we are tame, mother. Men are all women, knitting and crocheting words together.'

'I can't altogether agree, you know, Louise.'

'I know you don't.—You like clever men. But clever men are mostly such unpleasant *animals*. As animals, so very unpleasant. And in men like Rico, the animal has gone queer and wrong. And in those nice clean boys you liked so much in the war, there is no wild animal left in them. They're all tame dogs, even when they're brave and well-bred. They're all tame dogs, mother, with human masters. There's no mystery in them.'

'What do you want, Louise? You *do* want the cave-man who'll knock you on the head with a club.'

'Don't be silly, mother. That's much more your subconscious line, you admirer of Mind.—I don't consider the cave-man is a real human animal at all. He's a brute, a degenerate. A pure animal man would be as lovely as a deer or a leopard, burning like a flame fed straight from underneath. And he'd be part of the unseen, like a mouse is, even. And he'd never cease to wonder, he'd breathe silence and unseen wonder, as the partridges do, running in the stubble. He'd be all the animals in turn, instead of one fixed, automatic thing, which he is now, grinding on the nerves.—Ah, no, mother, I want the wonder back again, or I shall die. I don't want to be like you, just criticizing and annihilating these dreary people, and enjoying it.'

'My dear daughter, whatever else the human animal might be, he'd be a dangerous commodity.'

'I wish he would, mother. I'm dying of these empty, dangerless men, who are only sentimental and spiteful.'

'Nonsense, you're not dying.'

'I am, mother. And I should be dead if there weren't St. Mawr and Phœnix and Lewis in the world.'

'St. Mawr and Phœnix and Lewis! I thought you said they were servants!'

'That's the worst of it. If only they were masters! If only there were some men with as much natural life as they have, and their brave, quick minds that commanded instead of serving!'

'There are no such men,' said Mrs. Witt, with a certain grim satisfaction.

'I know it. But I'm young, and I've got to live. And the thing that is offered me as life just starves me, starves me to death, mother. What am I to do? You enjoy shattering people like Dean Vyner. But I am young, I can't live that way.'

'That may be.'

It had long ago struck Lou how much more her mother realized and understood than ever Rico did. Rico was afraid, always afraid of realizing. Rico, with his good manners and his habitual kindness, and that peculiar imprisoned sneer of his.

He arrived home next morning on St. Mawr, rather flushed and gaudy, and over-kind, with an *empressé* [28] anxiety about Lou's welfare which spoke too many volumes. Especially as he was accompanied by Flora Manby, and by Flora's sister Elsie, and Elsie's husband, Frederick Edwards. They all came on horseback.

28. Urgent, forced.

'Such awful ages since I saw you!' said Flora to Lou. 'Sorry if we burst in on you. We're only just saying *How do you do?* and going on to the inn. They've got rooms all ready for us there. We thought we'd stay just one night over here, and ride to-morrow to the Devil's Chair. Won't you come? Lots of fun! Isn't Mrs. Witt at home?'

Mrs. Witt was out for the moment. When she returned she had on her curious stiff face, yet she greeted the new-comers with a certain cordiality: she felt it would be diplomatic, no doubt.

'There *are* two rooms here,' she said, 'and if you care to poke into them, why, we shall be *delighted* to have you. But I'll show them to you first, because they are poor, inconvenient rooms, with no running water and *miles* from the baths.'

Flora and Elsie declared that they were 'perfectly darling sweet rooms—not overcrowded.'

'Well,' said Mrs. Witt, 'the conveniences certainly don't fill up much space. But if you like to take them for what they are—'

'Why, we feel absolutely overwhelmed, don't we, Elsie!—But we've no clothes—!'

Suddenly the silence had turned into a house-party. The Manby girls appeared to lunch in fine muslin dresses, bought in Paris, fresh as daisies. Women's clothing takes up so little space, especially in summer! Fred Edwards was one of those blond Englishmen with a little brush moustache and those strong blue eyes which were always attempting the sentimental, but which Lou, in her prejudice, considered cruel: upon what grounds, she never analysed. However, he took a gallant tone with her at once, and she had to seem to simper. Rico, watching her, was so relieved when he saw the simper coming.

It had begun again, the whole clockwork of 'lots of fun!'

'Isn't Fred flirting perfectly outrageously with Lady Carrington!—She looks so *sweet!*' cried Flora, over her coffee-cup. 'Don't you mind, Harry!'

They called Rico 'Harry'! His boy-name.

'Only a very little,' said Harry. *'L'uomo è cacciatore.'*

'Oh, now, what does that mean?' cried Flora, who always thrilled to Rico's bits of affectation.

'It means,' said Mrs. Witt, leaning forward and speaking in her most suave voice, 'that man is a hunter.'

Even Flora shrank under the smooth acid of the irony.

'Oh, well now!' she cried. 'If he is, then what is woman?'

'The hunted,' said Mrs. Witt, in a still smoother acid.

'At least,' said Rico, 'she is always *game!*'

'Ah, is she though!' came Fred's manly, well-bred tones. 'I'm not so sure.'

Mrs. Witt looked from one man to the other, as if she were dropping them down the bottomless pit.

Lou escaped to look at St. Mawr. He was still moist where the saddle had been. And he seemed a little bit extinguished, as if virtue had gone out of him.

But when he lifted his lovely naked head, like a bunch of flames, to see who it was had entered, she saw he was still himself. Forever sensitive and alert, his head lifted like the summit of a fountain. And within him the clean bones striking to the earth, his hoofs intervening between him and the ground like lesser jewels.

He knew her and did not resent her. But he took no notice of her. He would

Pan

never 'respond.' At first she had resented it. Now she was glad. He would never be intimate, thank heaven.

She hid herself away till tea-time, but she could not hide from the sound of voices. Dinner was early, at seven. Dean Vyner came—Mrs. Vyner was an invalid—and also an artist who had a studio in the village and did etchings. He was a man of about thirty-eight, and poor, just beginning to accept himself as a failure, as far as making money goes. But he worked at his etchings and studied esoteric matters like astrology and alchemy.[29] Rico patronized him, and was a little afraid of him. Lou could not quite make him out. After knocking about Paris and London and Munich, he was trying to become staid, and to persuade himself that English village life, with squire and dean in the background, humble artist in the middle, and labourer in the common foreground, was a genuine life. His self-persuasion was only moderately successful. This was betrayed by the curious arrest in his body: he seemed to have to force himself into movement: and by the curious duplicity in his yellow-grey, twinkling eyes, that twinkled and expanded like a goat's; with mockery, irony, and frustration.

'Your face is curiously like Pan's,' said Lou to him at dinner.

It was true, in a commonplace sense. He had the tilted eyebrows, the twinkling goaty look, and the pointed ears of a goat-Pan.

'People have said so,' he replied. 'But I'm afraid it's not the face of the Great God Pan. Isn't it rather the Great Goat Pan!'

'I say, that's good!' cried Rico. 'The Great Goat Pan!'

'I have always found it difficult,' said the Dean, 'to see the Great God Pan in that goat-legged old father of satyrs. He may have a good deal of influence— the world will always be full of goaty old satyrs. But we find them somewhat vulgar. Even our late King Edward. The goaty old satyrs are too comprehensible to me to be venerable, and I fail to see a Great God in the father of them all.'

'Your ears should be getting red,' said Lou to Cartwright. She, too, had an odd squinting smile that suggested nymphs, so irresponsible and unbelieving.

'Oh, no, nothing personal!' cried the Dean.

'I am not sure,' said Cartwright, with a small smile. 'But don't you imagine Pan once *was* a Great God, before the anthropomorphic Greeks turned him into half a man?'

'Ah!—maybe. That is very possible. But—I have noticed the limitation in myself—my mind has no grasp whatsoever of Europe before the Greeks arose. Mr. Wells' Outline [30] does not help me there, either,' the Dean added with a smile.

'But what was Pan before he was a man with goat legs?' asked Lou.

'Before he looked like me?' said Cartwright, with a faint grin. 'I should say he was the God that is hidden in everything. In those days you saw the thing, you never saw the God in it: I mean in the tree or the fountain or the animal. If you ever saw the God instead of the thing, you died. If you saw it with the naked eye, that is. But in the night you might see the God. And you knew it was there.'

29. This character is drawn directly from Frederick Carter.
30. H. G. Wells (1866–1946), *Outline of History* (1920), a famous book at the time.

'The modern pantheist not only sees the God in everything, he takes photographs of it,' said the Dean.

'Oh, and the divine pictures he paints!' cried Rico.

'Quite!' said Cartwright.

'But if they never *saw* the God in the thing, the old ones, how did they know he was there? How did they have any Pan at all?' said Lou.

'Pan was the hidden mystery—the hidden cause. That's how it was a Great God. Pan wasn't *he* at all: not even a Great God. He was Pan. All: what you see when you see in full. In the daytime you see the thing. But if your third eye is open, which sees only the things that can't be seen, you may see Pan within the thing, hidden: you may see with your third eye, which is darkness.' [31]

'Do you think I might see Pan in a horse, for example?'

'Easily. In St. Mawr!'—Cartwright gave her a knowing look.

'But,' said Mrs. Witt, 'it would be difficult, I should say, to open the third eye and see Pan in a man.'

'Probably,' said Cartwright, smiling. 'In man he is over-visible: the old satyr: the fallen Pan.'

'Exactly!' said Mrs. Witt. And she fell into a muse. 'The fallen Pan!' she re-echoed. 'Wouldn't a man be wonderful in whom Pan hadn't fallen!'

Over the coffee in the grey drawing-room she suddenly asked:

'Supposing, Mr. Cartwright, one *did* open the third eye and see Pan in an actual man—I wonder what it would be like.'

She half lowered her eyelids and tilted her face in a strange way, as if she were tasting something, and not quite sure.

'I wonder!' he said, smiling his enigmatic smile. But she could see he did not understand.

'Louise!' said Mrs. Witt at bedtime. 'Come into my room for a moment, I want to ask you something.'

'What is it, mother?'

'You, you *get* something from what Mr. Cartwright said, about seeing Pan with the third eye? Seeing Pan in something?'

Mrs. Witt came rather close, and tilted her face with strange insinuating question at her daughter.

'I think I do, mother.'

'In what?'—The question came as a pistol-shot.

'I think, mother,' said Lou reluctantly, 'in St. Mawr.'

'In a horse!'—Mrs. Witt contracted her eyes slightly. 'Yes, I can see that. I know what you mean. It *is* in St. Mawr. It *is*! But in St. Mawr it makes me *afraid*—' she dragged out the word. Then she came a step closer. 'But, Louise, did you ever see it in a man?'

'What, mother?'

'Pan. Did you ever see Pan in a man, as you see Pan in St. Mawr?'

Louise hesitated.

'No, mother, I don't think I did. When I look at men with my third eye, as

---

31. The Greek *pan* means "all" and mythologists frequently argued that Pan was the spirit of all nature before he became a goatish god. He caused panic (of which there are examples in this novel). A *pantheist* believes that God and the universe are one.

you call it—I think I see—mostly—a sort of—pancake.' She uttered the last word with a despairing grin, not knowing quite what to say.

'Oh, Louise, isn't that it! Doesn't one always see a pancake!—Now listen, Louise. Have you ever been in love?'

'Yes, as far as I understand it.'

'Listen now. Did you ever see Pan in the man you loved? Tell me if you did.'

'As I see Pan in St. Mawr?—no, mother.' And suddenly her lips began to tremble and the tears came to her eyes.

'Listen, Louise.—I've been in love innumerable times—and *really* in love twice. Twice!—yet for fifteen years I've left off wanting to have anything to do with a man, really. For fifteen years! And why?—Do you know?—Because I couldn't see that peculiar hidden Pan in any of them. And I became that I needed to. I needed it. But it wasn't there. Not in any man. Even when I was in love with a man, it was for other things: because I *understood* him so well, or he understood me, or we had such sympathy. Never the hidden Pan.—Do you understand what I mean? Unfallen Pan!'

'More or less, mother.'

'But now my third eye is coming open, I believe. I am tired of all these men like breakfast cakes, with a teaspoonful of mind or a teaspoonful of spirit in them, for baking-powder. Isn't it extraordinary that young man Cartwright talks about Pan, but he knows nothing of it all? He knows nothing of the unfallen Pan: only the fallen Pan with goat legs and a leer—and that sort of power, don't you know—'

'But what do you know of the unfallen Pan, mother?'

'Don't ask me, Louise! I feel all of a tremble, as if I was just on the verge.'
She flashed a little look of incipient triumph, and said good night.

An excursion on horseback had been arranged for the next day, to two old groups of rocks, called the Angel's Chair and the Devil's Chair, which crowned the moor-like hills looking into Wales, ten miles away. Everybody was going—they were to start early in the morning, and Lewis would be the guide, since no one exactly knew the way.

Lou got up soon after sunrise. There was a summer scent in the trees of early morning, and monkshood flowers stood up dark and tall, with shadows. She dressed in the green linen riding-skirt her maid had put ready for her, with a close bluish smock.

'Are you going out already, dear?' called Rico from his room.

'Just to smell the roses before we start, Rico.'

He appeared in the doorway in his yellow silk pyjamas. His large blue eyes had that rolling irritable look and the slightly bloodshot whites which made her want to escape.

'Booted and spurred!—the *energy!*' he cried.

'It's a lovely day to ride,' she said.

'A lovely day to do anything *except* ride!' he said. 'Why spoil the day riding!'
—A curious bitter-acid escaped into his tone. It was evident he hated the excursion.

'Why, we needn't go if you don't want to, Rico.'

'Oh, I'm sure I shall love it, once I get started. It's all this business of *starting*, with horses and paraphernalia—'

Lou went into the yard. The horses were drinking at the trough under the pump, their colours strong and rich in the shadow of the tree.

'You're not coming with us, Phœnix?' she said.

'Lewis, he's riding my horse.'

She could tell Phœnix did not like being left behind.

By half past seven everybody was ready. The sun was in the yard, the horses were saddled. They came swishing their tails. Lewis brought out St. Mawr from his separate box, speaking to him very quietly in Welsh: a murmuring, soothing little speech. Lou, alert, could see that he was uneasy.

'How is St. Mawr this morning?' she asked.

'He's all right. He doesn't like so many people. He'll be all right once he's started.'

The strangers were in the saddle: they moved out to the deep shade of the village road outside. Rico came to his horse to mount. St. Mawr jumped away as if he had seen the devil.

'Steady, fool!' cried Rico.

The bay stood with his four feet spread, his neck arched, his big dark eye glancing sideways with that watchful, frightening look.

'You shouldn't be irritable with him, Rico!' said Lou. 'Steady then, St. Mawr! Be steady.'

But a certain anger rose also in her. The creature was so big, so brilliant, and so stupid, standing there with his hind legs spread, ready to jump aside or to rear terrifically, and his great eye glancing with a sort of suspicious frenzy. What was there to be suspicious of, after all?—Rico would do him no harm.

'No one will harm you, St. Mawr,' she reasoned, a bit exasperated.

The groom was talking quietly, murmuringly, in Welsh. Rico was slowly advancing again, to put his foot in the stirrup. The stallion was watching from the corner of his eye, a strange glare of suspicious frenzy burning stupidly. Any moment his immense physical force might be let loose in a frenzy of panic— or malice. He was really very irritating.

'Probably he doesn't like that apricot shirt,' said Mrs. Witt, 'although it tones into him wonderfully well.'

She pronounced it *ap*-ricot,[32] and it irritated Rico terribly.

'Ought we to have *asked* him before we put it on?' he flashed, his upper lip lifting venomously.

'I should say you should,' replied Mrs. Witt coolly.

Rico turned with a sudden rush to the horse. Back went the great animal, with a sudden splashing crash of hoofs on the cobble-stones, and Lewis hanging on like a shadow. Up went the forefeet, showing the belly.

'The thing is accursed,' said Rico, who had dropped the reins in sudden shock, and stood marooned. His rage overwhelmed him like a black flood.

'Nothing in the world is so irritating as a horse that is acting up,' thought Lou.

'Say, Harry!' called Flora from the road. 'Come out here into the road to mount him.'

Lewis looked at Rico and nodded. Then, soothing the big, quivering animal, he led him springily out to the road under the trees, where the three friends

32. The usual British pronunciation is *ape-ricot*.

were waiting. Lou and her mother got quickly into the saddle to follow. And in another moment Rico was mounted and bouncing down the road in the wrong direction, Lewis following on the chestnut. It was some time before Rico could get St. Mawr round. Watching him from behind, those waiting could judge how the young Baronet hated it.

But at last they set off—Rico ahead, unevenly but quietly, with the two Manby girls, Lou following with the fair young man who had been in a cavalry regiment and who kept looking round for Mrs. Witt.

'Don't look round for me,' she called. 'I'm riding behind, out of the dust.'

Just behind Mrs. Witt came Lewis. It was a whole cavalcade trotting in the morning sun past the cottages and the cottage gardens, round the field that was the recreation ground, into the deep hedges of the lane.

'Why is St. Mawr so bad at starting? Can't you get him into better shape?' she asked over her shoulder.

'Beg your pardon, Mam!'

Lewis trotted a little nearer. She glanced over her shoulder at him, at his dark, unmoved face, his cool little figure.

'I think *Mam!* is so ugly. Why not leave it out!' she said. Then she repeated her question.

'St. Mawr doesn't trust anybody,' Lewis replied.

'Not you?'

'Yes, he trusts me—mostly.'

'Then why not other people?'

'They're different.'

'All of them?'

'About all of them.'

'How are they different?'

He looked at her with his remote, uncanny grey eyes.

'Different,' he said, not knowing how else to put it.

They rode on slowly, up the steep rise of the wood, then down into a glade where ran a little railway built for hauling some mysterious mineral out of the hill, in war-time, and now already abandoned. Even on this country-side the dead hand of the war lay like a corpse decomposing.

They rode up again, past the foxgloves under the trees. Ahead the brilliant St. Mawr and the sorrel and grey horses were swimming like butterflies through the sea of bracken, glittering from sun to shade, shade to sun. Then once more they were on a crest, and through the thinning trees could see the slopes of the moors beyond the next dip.

Soon they were in the open, rolling hills, golden in the morning and empty save for a couple of distant bilberry-pickers, whitish figures pick—pick—picking with curious, rather disgusting assiduity. The horses were on an old trail which climbed through the pinky tips of heather and ling, across patches of green bilberry. Here and there were tufts of harebells blue as bubbles.

They were out, high on the hills. And there to west lay Wales, folded in crumpled folds, goldish in the morning light, with its moor-like slopes and patches of corn uncannily distinct. Between was a hollow, wide valley of sum-mer haze, showing white farms among trees, and grey slate roofs.

'Ride beside me,' she said to Lewis. 'Nothing makes me want to go back to

America like the old look of these little villages.—You have never been to America?'

'No, Mam.'

'Don't you ever want to go?'

'I wouldn't mind going.'

'But you're not just crazy to go?'

'No, Mam.'

'Quite content as you are?'

He looked at her, and his pale, remote eyes met hers.

'I don't fret myself,' he replied.

'Not about anything at all—ever?'

His eyes glanced ahead, at the other riders.

'No, Mam!' he replied, without looking at her.

She rode a few moments in silence.

'What is that over there?' she asked, pointing across the valley. 'What is it called?'

'Yon's Montgomery.'

'Montgomery! And is that *Wales*—?' She trailed the ending curiously.

'Yes, Mam.'

'Where you come from?'

'No, Mam! I come from Merioneth.'

'Not from Wales? I thought you were Welsh?'

'Yes, Mam. Merioneth *is* Wales.'

'And you are Welsh?'

'Yes, Mam.'

'I had a Welsh grandmother. But I come from Louisiana, and when I go back home, the Negroes still call me Miss Rachel. *Oh, my, it's little Miss Rachel come back home. Why, ain't I mighty glad to see you—u, Miss Rachel!* That gives me such a strange feeling, you know.'

The man glanced at her curiously, especially when she imitated the Negroes.

'Do you feel strange when you go home?' she asked.

'I was brought up by an aunt and uncle,' he said. 'I never go to see them.'

'And you don't have any home?'

'No, Mam.'

'No wife nor anything?'

'No, Mam.'

'But what do you do with your life?'

'I keep to myself.'

'And care about nothing?'

'I mind St. Mawr.'

'But you've not always had St. Mawr—and you won't always have him.— Were you in the war?'

'Yes, Mam.'

'At the front?'

'Yes, Mam—but I was a groom.'

'And you came out all right?'

'I lost my little finger from a bullet.'

He held up his small, dark left hand, from which the little finger was missing.

'And did you like the war—or didn't you?'

'I didn't like it.'

Again his pale-grey eyes met hers, and they looked so non-human and uncommunicative, so without connection, and inaccessible, she was troubled.

'Tell me,' she said. 'Did you never want a wife and a home and children, like other men?'

'No, Mam. I never wanted a home of my own.'

'Nor a wife of your own?'

'No, Mam.'

'Nor children of your own?'

'No, Mam.'

She reined in her horse.

'Now wait a minute,' she said. 'Now tell me why.'

His horse came to standstill, and the two riders faced one another.

'Tell me why—I must know why you never wanted a wife and children and a home. I must know why you're not like other men.'

'I never felt like it,' he said. 'I made my life with horses.'

'Did you hate people very much? Did you have a very unhappy time as a child?'

'My aunt and uncle didn't like me, and I didn't like them.'

'So you've never liked anybody?'

'Maybe not,' he said. 'Not to get as far as marrying them.'

She touched her horse and moved on.

'Isn't that curious!' she said. 'I've loved people, at various times. But I don't believe *I've* ever liked anybody, except a few of our Negroes. I don't like Louise, though she's my daughter and I love her. But I don't really *like* her.— I think you're the first person I've ever liked since I was on our plantation, and we had some *very fine* Negroes.—And I think that's very curious.—Now I want to know if you like *me*.'

She looked at him searchingly, but he did not answer.

'Tell me,' she said. 'I don't mind if you say no. But tell me if you like me. I feel I must know.'

The flicker of a smile went over his face—a very rare thing with him.

'Maybe I do,' he said. He was thinking that she put him on a level with a Negro slave on a plantation: in his idea, Negroes were still slaves. But he did not care where she put him.

'Well, I'm glad—I'm glad if you like me. Because you *don't* like most people, I know that.'

They had passed the hollow where the old Aldecar Chapel hid in damp isolation, beside the ruined mill, over the stream that came down from the moors. Climbing the sharp slope, they saw the folded hills like great shut fingers, with steep, deep clefts between. On the near sky-line was a bunch of rocks; and away to the right another bunch.

'Yon's the Angel's Chair,' said Lewis, pointing to the nearer rocks. 'And yon's the Devil's Chair, where we're going.'

'Oh!' said Mrs. Witt. 'And aren't we going to the Angel's Chair?'

'No, Mam.'

'Why not?'

'There's nothing to see there. The other's higher, and bigger, and that's where folks mostly go.'

'Is that so!—They give the Devil the higher seat in this country, do they? I think they're right.'—And as she got no answer, she added: 'You believe in the Devil, don't you?'

'I never met him,' he answered, evasively.

Ahead, they could see the other horses twinkling in a cavalcade up the slope, the black, the bay, the two greys and the sorrel, sometimes bunching, sometimes straggling. At a gate all waited for Mrs. Witt. The fair young man fell in beside her, and talked hunting at her. He had hunted the fox over these hills, and was vigorously excited locating the spot where the hounds gave the first cry, etc.

'Really!' said Mrs. Witt. '*Really! Is that so!*'

If irony could have been condensed to prussic acid, the fair young man would have ended his life's history with his reminiscences.

They came at last, trotting in file along a narrow track between heather, along the saddle of a hill, to where the knot of pale granite suddenly cropped out. It was one of those places where the spirit of aboriginal England still lingers, the old savage England, whose last blood flows still in a few Englishmen, Welshmen, Cornishmen. The rocks, whitish with weather of all the ages, jutted against the blue August sky, heavy with age-moulded roundnesses.

Lewis stayed below with the horses, the party scrambled rather awkwardly, in their riding-boots, up the foot-worn boulders. At length they stood in the place called the Chair, looking west, west towards Wales, that rolled in golden folds upwards. It was neither impressive nor a very picturesque landscape: the hollow valley with farms, and then the rather bare upheaval of hills, slopes with corn and moor and pasture, rising like a barricade, seemingly high, slantingly. Yet it had a strange effect on the imagination.

'Oh, mother,' said Lou, 'doesn't it make you feel old, old, older than anything ever was?'

'It certainly does seem aged,' said Mrs. Witt.

'It makes me want to die,' said Lou. 'I feel we've lasted almost too long.'

'Don't say that, Lady Carrington. Why, you're a spring chicken yet: or shall I say an unopened rosebud?' remarked the fair young man.

'No,' said Lou. 'All these millions of ancestors have used all the life up. We're not really alive, in the sense that they were alive.'

'But who?' said Rico. 'Who are *they*?'

'The people who lived on these hills, in the days gone by.'

'But the same people still live on the hills, darling. It's just the same stock.'

'No, Rico. That old fighting stock that worshipped devils among these stones —I'm sure they did—'

'But look here, do you mean they were any better than we are?' asked the fair young man.

Lou looked at him quizzically.

'We don't exist,' she said, squinting at him oddly.

'I jolly well know I do,' said the fair young man.

'I consider these days are the best ever, especially for girls,' said Flora

Manby. 'And anyhow they're our own days, so I don't jolly well see the use of crying them down.'

They were all silent, with the last echoes of emphatic *joie de vivre* trumpeting on the air, across the hills of Wales.

'Spoken like a brick, Flora,' said Rico. 'Say it again, we may not have the Devil's Chair for a pulpit next time.'

'I do,' reiterated Flora. 'I think this is the best age there ever was for a girl to have a good time in. I read all through H. G. Wells' history, and I shut it up and thanked my stars I live in nineteen-twenty odd, not in some other beastly date when a woman had to cringe before mouldy domineering men.'

After this they turned to scramble to another part of the rocks, to the famous Needle's Eye.

'Thank you so much, I am really better without help,' said Mrs. Witt to the fair young man, as she slid downwards till a piece of grey silk stocking showed above her tall boot. But she got her toe in a safe place, and in a moment stood beside him, while he caught her arm protectingly. He might as well have caught the paw of a mountain lion protectingly.

'I should like *so* much to know,' she said suavely, looking into his eyes with a demonish straight look, 'what makes you so certain that you exist.'

He looked back at her, and his jaunty blue eyes went baffled. Then a slow, hot, salmon-coloured flush stole over his face, and he turned abruptly round.

The Needle's Eye was a hole in the ancient grey rock, like a window, looking to England: England at the moment in shadow. A stream wound and glinted in the flat shadow, and beyond that the flat, insignificant hills leaped in mounds of shade. Cloud was coming—the English side was in shadow. Wales was still in the sun, but the shadow was spreading. The day was going to disappoint them. Lou was a tiny bit chilled already.

Luncheon was still several miles away. The party hastened down to the horses. Lou picked a few sprigs of ling, and some harebells, and some straggling yellow flowers: not because she wanted them, but to distract herself. The atmosphere of 'enjoying ourselves' was becoming cruel to her: it sapped all the life out of her. 'Oh, if only I needn't enjoy myself,' she moaned inwardly. But the Manby girls were enjoying themselves so much. 'I think it's frantically lovely up here,' said the other one—not Flora—Elsie.

'It *is* beautiful, isn't it! I'm *so* glad you like it,' replied Rico. And he was really relieved and gratified, because the other one said she was enjoying it so frightfully. He dared not say to Lou, as he wanted to: 'I'm afraid, Lou darling, you don't love it as much as we do.'—He was afraid of her answer: 'No, dear, I don't love it at all! I want to be away from these people.'

Slightly piqued, he rode on with the Manby group, and Lou came behind with her mother. Cloud was covering the sky with grey. There was a cold wind. Everybody was anxious to get to the farm for luncheon, and be safely home before rain came.

They were riding along one of the narrow little foot-tracks, mere grooves of grass between heather and bright green bilberry. The blond young man was ahead, then his wife, then Flora, then Rico. Lou, from a little distance, watched the glossy, powerful haunches of St. Mawr swaying with life, always too much life, like a menace. The fair young man was whistling a new dance tune.

St Mawr backwards

'That's an awfully attractive tune,' Rico called. 'Do whistle it again, Fred, I should like to memorize it.'

Fred began to whistle it again.

At that moment St. Mawr exploded again, shied sideways as if a bomb had gone off, and kept backing through the heather.

'Fool!' cried Rico, thoroughly unnerved: he had been terribly sideways in the saddle, Lou had feared he was going to fall. But he got his seat, and pulled the reins viciously, to bring the horse to order, and put him on the track again. St. Mawr began to rear: his favourite trick. Rico got him forward a few yards, when up he went again.

'Fool!' yelled Rico, hanging in the air.

He pulled the horse over backwards on top of him.

Lou gave a loud, unnatural, horrible scream: she heard it herself, at the same time as she heard the crash of the falling horse. Then she saw a pale gold belly, and hoofs that worked and flashed in the air, and St. Mawr writhing, straining his head terrifically upwards, his great eyes starting from the naked lines of his nose. With a great neck arching cruelly from the ground, he was pulling frantically at the reins, which Rico still held tight.—Yes, Rico, lying strangely sideways, his eyes also starting from his yellow-white face, among the heather, still clutched the reins.

Young Edwards was rushing forward, and circling round the writhing, immense horse, whose pale-gold, inverted bulk seemed to fill the universe.

'Let him get up, Carrington! Let him get up!' he was yelling, darting warily near, to get the reins.—Another spasmodic convulsion of the horse.

Horror! The young man reeled backwards with his face in his hands. He had got a kick in the face. Red blood running down his chin!

Lewis was there, on the ground, getting the reins out of Rico's hands. St. Mawr gave a great curve like a fish, spread his forefeet on the earth and reared his head, looking round in a ghastly fashion. His eyes were arched, his nostrils wide, his face ghastly in a sort of panic. He rested thus, seated with his forefeet planted and his face in panic, almost like some terrible lizard, for several moments. Then he heaved sickeningly to his feet, and stood convulsed, trembling.

There lay Rico, crumpled and rather sideways, staring at the heavens from a yellow, dead-looking face. Lewis, glancing round in a sort of horror, looked in dread at St. Mawr again. Flora had been hovering.—She now rushed screeching to the prostrate Rico:

'Harry! Harry! you're not dead! Oh, Harry! Harry! Harry!'

Lou had dismounted.—She didn't know when. She stood a little way off, as if spellbound, while Flora cried *Harry! Harry! Harry!*

Suddenly Rico sat up.

'Where is the horse?' he said.

At the same time an added whiteness came on his face, and he bit his lip with pain, and he fell prostrate again in a faint. Flora rushed to put her arm round him.

Where was the horse? He had backed slowly away, in an agony of suspicion, while Lewis murmured to him in vain. His head was raised again, the eyes still starting from their sockets, and a terrible guilty, ghostlike look on his face.

When Lewis drew a little nearer, he twitched and shrank like a shaken steel spring, away—not to be touched. He seemed to be seeing legions of ghosts, down the dark avenues of all the centuries that have lapsed since the horse became subject to man.

And the other young man? He was still standing, at a little distance, with his face in his hands, motionless, the blood falling on his white shirt, and his wife at his side, pleading, distracted.

Mrs. Witt too was there, as if cast in steel, watching. She made no sound and did not move, only, from a fixed, impassive face, watched each thing.

'Do tell me what you think is the matter?' Lou pleaded, distracted, to Flora, who was supporting Rico and weeping torrents of unknown tears.

Then Mrs. Witt came forward and began in a very practical manner to unclose the shirt-neck and feel the young man's heart. Rico opened his eyes again, said *'Really!'* and closed his eyes once more.

'It's fainting!' said Mrs. Witt. 'We have no brandy.'

Lou, too weary to be able to feel anything, said:

'I'll go and get some.'

She went to her alarmed horse, who stood among the others with her head down, in suspense. Almost unconsciously Lou mounted, set her face ahead, and was riding away.

Then Poppy shied too, with a sudden start, and Lou pulled up. 'Why?' she said to her horse. 'Why did you do that?'

She looked round, and saw in the heather a glimpse of yellow and black.

'A snake!' she said wonderingly.

And she looked closer.

It was a dead adder that had been drinking at a reedy pool in a little depression just off the road, and had been killed with stones. There it lay, also crumpled, its head crushed, its gold-and-yellow back still glittering dully, and a bit of pale-blue belly showing, killed that morning.

Lou rode on, her face set towards the farm. An unspeakable weariness had overcome her. She could not even suffer. Weariness of spirit left her in a sort of apathy.

And she had a vision, a vision of evil. Or not strictly a vision. She became aware of evil, evil, evil, rolling in great waves over the earth. Always she had thought there was no such thing—only a mere negation of good. Now, like an ocean to whose surface she had risen, she saw the dark-grey waves of evil rearing in a great tide.

And it had swept mankind away without mankind's knowing. It had caught up the nations as the rising ocean might lift the fishes, and was sweeping them on in a great tide of evil. They did not know. The people did not know. They did not even wish it. They wanted to be good and to have everything joyful and enjoyable. Everything joyful and enjoyable: for everybody. This was what they wanted, if you asked them.

But at the same time, they had fallen under the spell of evil. It was a soft, subtle thing, soft as water, and its motion was soft and imperceptible, as the running of a tide is invisible to one who is out on the ocean. And they were all out on the ocean, being borne along in the current of the mysterious evil, creatures of the evil principle, as fishes are creatures of the sea.

There was no relief. The whole world was enveloped in one great flood. All the nations, the white, the brown, the black, the yellow, all were immersed in the strange tide of evil that was subtly, irresistibly rising. No one, perhaps, deliberately wished it. Nearly every individual wanted peace and a good time all round: everybody to have a good time.

But some strange thing had happened, and the vast, mysterious force of positive evil was let loose. She felt that from the core of Asia the evil welled up, as from some strange pole, and slowly was drowning earth.

It was something horrifying, something you could not escape from. It had come to her as in a vision, when she saw the pale-gold belly of the stallion upturned, the hoofs working wildly, the wicked curved hams of the horse, and then the evil straining of that arched, fish-like neck, with the dilated eyes of the head. Thrown backwards, and working its hoofs in the air. Reversed, and purely evil.

She saw the same in people. They were thrown backwards, and writhing with evil. And the rider, crushed, was still reining them down.

What did it mean? Evil, evil, and a rapid return to the sordid chaos. Which was wrong, the horse or the rider? Or both?

She thought with horror of St. Mawr, and of the look on his face. But she thought with horror, a colder horror, of Rico's face as he snarled *Fool!* His fear, his impotence as a master, as a rider, his presumption. And she thought with horror of those other people, so glib, so glibly evil.

What did they want to do, those Manby girls? Undermine, undermine, undermine. They wanted to undermine Rico, just as that fair young man would have liked to undermine her. Believe in nothing, care about nothing: but keep the surface easy, and have a good time. *Let us undermine one another. There is nothing to believe in, so let us undermine everything. But look out! No scenes, no spoiling the game. Stick to the rules of the game. Be sporting, and don't do anything that would make a commotion. Keep the game going smooth and jolly, and bear your bit like a sport. Never, by any chance, injure your fellow man openly. But always injure him secretly. Make a fool of him, and undermine his nature. Break him up by undermining him, if you can. It's good sport.*

The evil! The mysterious potency of evil. She could see it all the time, in individuals, in society, in the press. There it was in socialism and Bolshevism: the same evil. But Bolshevism made a mess of the outside of life, so turn it down. Try Fascism. Fascism would keep the surface of life intact, and carry on the undermining business all the better. All the better sport. Never draw blood. Keep the hæmorrhage internal, invisible.

And as soon as Fascism makes a break—which it is bound to, because all evil works up to a break—then turn it down. With gusto, turn it down.

Mankind, like a horse, ridden by a stranger, smooth-faced, evil rider. Evil himself, smooth-faced and pseudo-handsome, riding mankind past the dead snake, to the last break.

Mankind no longer its own master. Ridden by this pseudo-handsome ghoul of outward loyalty, inward treachery, in a game of betrayal, betrayal, betrayal. The last of the gods of our era, Judas supreme!

People performing outward acts of loyalty, piety, self-sacrifice. But inwardly bent on undermining, betraying. Directing all their subtle evil will against any positive living thing. Masquerading as the ideal, in order to poison the real.

Creation destroys as it goes, throws down one tree for the rise of another. But ideal mankind would abolish death, multiply itself million upon million, rear up city upon city, save every parasite alive, until the accumulation of mere existence is swollen to a horror. But go on saving life, the ghastly salvation army of ideal mankind. At the same time secretly, viciously, potently undermine the natural creation, betray it with kiss after kiss, destroy it from the inside, till you have the swollen rottenness of our teeming existence.—But keep the game going. Nobody's going to make another bad break, such as Germany and Russia made.

Two bad breaks the secret evil has made: in Germany and in Russia. Watch it! Let evil keep a policeman's eye on evil! The surface of life must remain unruptured. Production must be heaped upon production. And the natural creation must be betrayed by many more kisses, yet. Judas is the last God, and, by heaven, the most potent.

But even Judas made a break: hanged himself, and his bowels gushed out. Not long after his triumph.

Man must destroy as he goes, as trees fall for trees to rise. The accumulation of life and things means rottenness. Life must destroy life, in the unfolding of creation. We save up life at the expense of the unfolding, till all is full of rottenness. Then at last, we make a break.

What's to be done? Generally speaking, nothing. The dead will have to bury their dead, while the earth stinks of corpses. The individual can but depart from the mass, and try to cleanse himself. Try to hold fast to the living thing, which destroys as it goes, but remains sweet. And in his soul fight, fight, fight to preserve that which is life in him from the ghastly kisses and poison-bites of the myriad evil ones. Retreat to the desert, and fight. But in his soul adhere to that which is life itself, creatively destroying as it goes: destroying the stiff old thing to let the new bud come through. The one passionate principle of creative being, which recognizes the natural good, and has a sword for the swarms of evil. Fights, fights, fights to protect itself. But with itself, is strong and at peace.

Lou came to the farm, and got brandy, and asked the men to come out to carry in the injured.

It turned out that the kick in the face had knocked a couple of young Edwards' teeth out, and would disfigure him a little.

'To go through the war, and then get this!' he mumbled, with a vindictive glance at St. Mawr.

And it turned out that Rico had two broken ribs and a crushed ankle. Poor Rico, he would limp for life.

'I want St. Mawr *shot!*' was almost his first word, when he was in bed at the farm and Lou was sitting beside him.

'What good would that do, dear?' she said.

'The brute is evil. I want him *shot!*'

Rico could make the last word sound like the spitting of a bullet.

'Do you want to shoot him yourself?'

'No. But I want to have him shot. I shall never be easy till I know he has a bullet through him. He's got a wicked character. I don't feel you are safe, with him down there. I shall get one of the Manbys' gamekeepers to shoot him. You might tell Flora—or I'll tell her myself, when she comes.'

'Don't talk about it now, dear. You've got a temperature.'

Was it true, St. Mawr was evil? She would never forget him writhing and lunging on the ground, nor his awful face when he reared up. But then that noble look of his: surely he was not mean? Whereas all evil had an inner meanness, mean! Was he mean? Was he meanly treacherous? Did he know he could kill, and meanly wait his opportunity?

She was afraid. And if this were true, then he *should* be shot. Perhaps he ought to be shot.

This thought haunted her. Was there something mean and treacherous in St. Mawr's spirit, the vulgar evil? If so, then have him shot. At moments, an anger would rise in her, as she thought of his frenzied rearing, and his mad, hideous writhing on the ground, and in the heat of her anger she would want to hurry down to her mother's house and have the creature shot at once. It would be a satisfaction, and a vindication of human rights. Because, after all, Rico was considerate of the brutal horse. But not a spark of consideration did the stallion have for Rico. No, it was the slavish malevolence of a domesticated creature that kept cropping up in St. Mawr. The slave, taking his slavish vengeance, then dropping back into subservience.

All the slaves of this world, accumulating their preparations for slavish vengeance, and then, when they have taken it, ready to drop back into servility. Freedom! Most slaves can't be freed, no matter how you let them loose. Like domestic animals, they are, in the long run, more afraid of freedom than of masters: and freed by some generous master, they will at last crawl back to some mean boss, who will have no scruples about kicking them. Because, for them, far better kicks and servility than the hard, lonely responsibility of real freedom.

The wild animal is at every moment intensely self-disciplined, poised in the tension of self-defence, self-preservation, and self-assertion. The moments of relaxation are rare and most carefully chosen. Even sleep is watchful, guarded, unrelaxing, the wild courage pitched one degree higher than the wild fear. Courage, the wild thing's courage to maintain itself alone and living in the midst of a diverse universe.

Did St. Mawr have this courage?

And did Rico?

Ah, Rico! He was one of mankind's myriad conspirators, who conspire to live in absolute physical safety, whilst willing the minor disintegration of all positive living.

But St. Mawr? Was it the natural wild thing in him which caused these disasters? Or was it the slave, asserting himself for vengeance?

If the latter, let him be shot. It would be a great satisfaction to see him dead.

But if the former—

When she could leave Rico with the nurse, she motored down to her mother for a couple of days. Rico lay in bed at the farm.

Everything seemed curiously changed. There was a new silence about the place, a new coolness. Summer had passed with several thunderstorms, and the blue, cool touch of autumn was about the house. Dahlias and perennial yellow sunflowers were out, the yellow of ending summer, the red coals of early autumn. First mauve tips of Michaelmas daisies were showing. Something suddenly carried her away to the great bare spaces of Texas, the blue sky, the flat, burnt earth, the miles of sunflowers. Another sky, another silence, towards the setting sun.

And suddenly, she craved again for the more absolute silence of America. English stillness was so soft, like an inaudible murmur of voices, of presences. But the silence in the empty spaces of America was still unutterable, almost cruel.

St. Mawr was in a small field by himself: she could not bear that he should be always in stable. Slowly she went through the gate towards him. And he stood there looking at her, the bright bay creature.

She could tell he was feeling somewhat subdued, after his late escapade. He was aware of the general human condemnation: the human damning. But something obstinate and uncanny in him made him not relent.

'Hello! St. Mawr!' she said, as she drew near, and he stood watching her, his ears pricked, his big eyes glancing sideways at her.

But he moved away when she wanted to touch him.

'Don't trouble,' she said. 'I don't want to catch you or do anything to you.'

He stood still, listening to the sound of her voice, and giving quick, small glances at her. His underlip trembled. But he did not blink. His eyes remained wide and unrelenting. There was a curious malicious obstinacy in him which aroused her anger.

'I don't want to touch you,' she said. 'I only want to look at you, and even you can't prevent that.'

She stood gazing hard at him, wanting to know, to settle the question of his meanness or his spirit. A thing with a brave spirit is not mean.

He was uneasy as she watched him. He pretended to hear something, the mares two fields away, and he lifted his head and neighed. She knew the powerful, splendid sound so well: like bells made of living membrane. And he looked so noble again, with his head tilted up, listening, and his male eyes looking proudly over the distance, eagerly.

But it was all a bluff.

He knew, and became silent again. And as he stood there a few yards away from her, his head lifted and wary, his body full of power and tension, his face slightly averted from her, she felt a great animal sadness come from him. A strange animal atmosphere of sadness, that was vague and disseminated through the air, and made her feel as though she breathed grief. She breathed it into her breast, as if it were a great sigh down the ages, that passed into her breast. And she felt a great woe: the woe of human unworthiness. The race of men judged in the consciousness of the animals they have subdued, and there found unworthy, ignoble.

Ignoble men, unworthy of the animals they have subjugated, bred the woe in the spirit of their creatures. St. Mawr, that bright horse, one of the kings of creation in the order below man, it had been a fulfilment for him to serve the brave, reckless, perhaps cruel men of the past, who had a flickering, rising flame of nobility in them. To serve that flame of mysterious further nobility.

Nothing matters but that strange flame, of inborn nobility that obliges men to be brave, and onward plunging. And the horse will bear him on.

But now where is the flame of dangerous, forward-pressing nobility in men? Dead, dead, guttering out in a stink of self-sacrifice whose feeble light is a light of exhaustion and *laissez-faire*.

And the horse, is he to go on carrying man forward into this?—this gutter?

No! Man wisely invents motor-cars and other machines, automobile and locomotive. The horse is superannuated, for man.

But alas, man is even more superannuated, for the horse.

Dimly in a woman's muse, Lou realized this, as she breathed the horse's sadness, his accumulated vague woe from the generations of latter-day igno-bility. And a grief and a sympathy flooded her, for the horse. She realized now how his sadness recoiled into these frenzies of obstinacy and malevolence. Underneath it all was grief, an unconscious, vague, pervading animal grief, which perhaps only Lewis understood, because he felt the same. The grief of the generous creature which sees all ends turning to the morass of ignoble living.

She did not want to say any more to the horse: she did not want to look at him any more. The grief flooded her soul, that made her want to be alone. She knew now what it all amounted to. She knew that the horse, born to serve nobly, had waited in vain for someone noble to serve. His spirit knew that nobility had gone out of men. And this left him high and dry, in a sort of despair.

As she walked away from him, towards the gate, slowly he began to walk after her.

Phœnix came striding through the gate towards her. 'You not afraid of that horse?' he asked sardonically, in his quiet, subtle voice.

'Not at the present moment,' she replied, even more quietly, looking direct at him. She was not in any mood to be jeered at.

And instantly the sardonic grimace left his face, followed by the sudden blankness, and the look of race-misery in the keen eyes.

'Do you want me to be afraid?' she said, continuing to the gate.

'No, I don't want it,' he replied, dejected.

'Are you afraid of him yourself?' she said, glancing round. St. Mawr had stopped, seeing Phœnix, and had turned away again.

'I'm not afraid of no horses,' said Phœnix.

Lou went on quietly. At the gate, she asked him:

'Don't you like St. Mawr, Phœnix?'

'I like him. He's a very good horse.'

'Even after what he's done to Sir Henry?'

'That don't make no difference to him being a good horse.'

'But suppose he'd done it to you?'

'I don't care. I say it my own fault.'

'Don't you think he is wicked?'

'I don't think so. He don't kick anybody. He don't bite anybody. He don't pitch, he don't buck, he don't do nothing.'

'He rears,' said Lou.

'Well, what is rearing!' said the man, with a slow, contemptuous smile.

'A good deal, when a horse falls back on you.'

'That horse don't want to fall back on you, if you don't make him. If you know how to ride him.—That horse want his own way sometime. If you don't let him, you got to fight him. Then look out!'

'Look out he doesn't kill you, you mean!'

'Look out you don't let him,' said Phœnix, with his slow, grim, sardonic smile.

Lou watched the smooth, golden face with its thin line of moustache and its sad eyes with the glint in them. Cruel—there was something cruel in him, right down in the abyss of him. But at the same time, there was an aloneness, and a grim little satisfaction in a fight, and the peculiar courage of an inherited despair. People who inherit despair may at last turn it into greater heroism. It was almost so with Phœnix. Three quarters of his blood was probably Indian and the remaining quarter, that came through the Mexican father, had the Spanish-American despair to add to the Indian. It was almost complete enough to leave him free to be heroic.

'What are we going to do with him, though?' she asked.

'Why don't you and Mrs. Witt go back to America—you never been West. You go West.'

'Where, to California?'

'No. To Arizona or New Mexico or Colorado or Wyoming, anywhere. Not to California.'

Phœnix looked at her keenly, and she saw the desire dark in him. He wanted to go back. But he was afraid to go back alone, empty-handed, as it were. He had suffered too much, and in that country his sufferings would overcome him, unless he had some other background. He had been too much in contact with the white world, and his own world was too dejected, in a sense, too hopeless for his own hopelessness. He needed an alien contact to give him relief.

But he wanted to go back. His necessity to go back was becoming too strong for him.

'What is it like in Arizona?' she asked. 'Isn't it all pale-coloured sand and alkali, and a few cactuses, and terribly hot and deathly?'

'No!' he cried. 'I don't take you there. I take you to the mountains—trees—' he lifted up his hand and looked at the sky—'big trees—pine! *Pino—real* and *pinovetes*, smell good. And then you come down, *piñon*, not very tall, and *cedro*, cedar, smell good in the fire. And then you see the desert, away below, go miles and miles, and where the canyon go, the crack where it look red! I know, I been there, working a cattle ranch.'

He looked at her with a haunted glow in his dark eyes. The poor fellow was suffering from nostalgia. And as he glowed at her in that queer mystical way, she too seemed to see that country, with its dark, heavy mountains holding in their lap the great stretches of pale, creased, silent desert that still is virgin of idea, its word unspoken.

Phœnix was watching her closely and subtly. He wanted something of her. He wanted it intensely, heavily, and he watched her as if he could force her to give it him. He wanted her to take him back to America, because, rudderless, he was afraid to go back alone. He wanted her to take him back: avidly he wanted it. She was to be the means to his end.

Why shouldn't he go back by himself? Why should he crave for her to go too? Why should he want her there?

There was no answer, except that he did.

'Why, Phœnix,' she said, 'I might possibly go back to America. But you know, Sir Henry would never go there. He doesn't like America, though he's never been. But I'm sure he'd never go there to live.'

'Let him stay here,' said Phœnix abruptly, the sardonic look on his face as he watched her face. 'You come, and let him stay here.'

'Ah, that's a whole story!' she said, and moved away.

As she went, he looked after her, standing silent and arrested and watching as an Indian watches.—It was not love. Personal love counts so little when the greater griefs, the greater hopes, the great despairs and the great resolutions come upon us.

She found Mrs. Witt rather more silent, more firmly closed within herself, than usual. Her mouth was shut tight, her brows were arched rather more imperiously than ever, she was revolving some inward problem about which Lou was far too wise to enquire.

In the afternoon Dean Vyner and Mrs. Vyner came to call on Lady Carrington.

'What bad luck this is, Lady Carrington!' said the Dean. 'Knocks Scotland on the head for you this year, I'm afraid. How did you leave your husband?'

'He seems to be doing as well as he could do!' said Lou.

'But how *very* unfortunate!' murmured the invalid Mrs. Vyner. 'Such a handsome young man, in the bloom of youth! Does he suffer much pain?'

'Chiefly his foot,' said Lou.

'Oh, I *do* so hope they'll be able to restore the ankle. Oh, how dreadful to be lamed at his age!'

'The doctor doesn't know. There *may* be a limp,' said Lou.

'That horse has certainly left his mark on two good-looking young fellows,' said the Dean. 'If you don't mind my saying so, Lady Carrington, I think he's a bad egg.'

'Who, St. Mawr?' said Lou, in her American sing-song.

'Yes, Lady Carrington,' murmured Mrs. Vyner, in her invalid's low tone. 'Don't you think he ought to be put away? He seems to me the incarnation of cruelty. His neigh. It goes through me like knives. Cruel! Cruel! Oh, I think he should be put away.'

'How put away?' murmured Lou, taking on an invalid's low tone herself.

'Shot, I suppose,' said the Dean.

'It is quite painless. He'll know nothing,' murmured Mrs. Vyner hastily. 'And think of the harm he has done already! Horrible! Horrible!' she shuddered. 'Poor Sir Henry lame for life, and Eddy Edwards disfigured. Besides all that has gone before. Ah, no, such a creature ought not to live!'

'To live, and have a groom to look after him and feed him,' said the Dean. 'It's a bit thick, while he's smashing up the very people that give him bread— or oats, since he's a horse. But I suppose you'll be wanting to get rid of him?'

'Rico does,' murmured Lou.

'Very naturally. So should I. A vicious horse is worse than a vicious man— except that you are free to put him six feet underground, and end his vice finally, by your own act.'

'Do you think St. Mawr is vicious?' said Lou.

'Well, of course—if we're driven to definitions!—I *know* he's dangerous.'

'And do you think we ought to shoot everything that is dangerous?' asked Lou, her colour rising.

'But, Lady Carrington, have you consulted your husband? Surely his wish should be law, in a matter of this sort! And on such an occasion! For *you*, who are a woman, it is enough that horse is cruel, cruel, evil! I felt it long before anything happened. That evil male cruelty! Ah!' and she clasped her hands convulsively.

'I suppose,' said Lou slowly, 'that St. Mawr is really Rico's horse: I gave him to him, I suppose. But I don't believe I could let him shoot him, for all that.'

'Ah, Lady Carrington,' said the Dean breezily, 'you can shift the respon-sibility. The horse is a public menace, put it at that. We can get an order to have him done away with, at the public expense. And among ourselves we can find some suitable compensation for you, as a mark of sympathy. Which, believe me, is very sincere! One hates to have to destroy a fine-looking animal. But I would sacrifice a dozen rather than have our Rico limping.'

'Yes, indeed,' murmured Mrs. Vyner.

'Will you excuse me one moment, while I see about tea?' said Lou, rising and leaving the room. Her colour was high, and there was a glint in her eye. These people almost roused her to hatred. Oh, these awful, house-bred, house-inbred human beings, how repulsive they were!

She hurried to her mother's dressing-room. Mrs. Witt was very carefully putting a touch of red on her lips.

'Mother, they want to shoot St. Mawr,' she said.

'I know,' said Mrs. Witt, as calmly as if Lou had said tea was ready.

'Well—' stammered Lou, rather put out, 'don't you think it cheek?'

'It depends, I suppose, on the point of view,' said Mrs. Witt dispassionately, looking closely at her lips. 'I don't think the English climate agrees with me. I need something to stand up against, no matter whether it's great heat or great cold. This climate, like the food and the people, is most always luke-warm or tepid, one or the other. And the tepid and the lukewarm are not really my line.' She spoke with a slow drawl.

'But they're in the drawing-room, mother, trying to force me to have St. Mawr killed.'

'What about tea?' said Mrs. Witt.

'I don't care,' said Lou.

Mrs. Witt worked the bell-handle.

'I suppose, Louise,' she said, in her most beaming eighteenth-century man-ner, 'that these are your guests, so you will preside over the ceremony of pouring out.'

'No, mother, you do it. I can't smile to-day.'

'I can,' said Mrs. Witt.

And she bowed her head slowly, with a faint, ceremoniously effusive smile, as if handing a cup of tea.

Lou's face flickered to a smile.

'Then you pour out for them. You can stand them better than I can.'

'Yes,' said Mrs. Witt. 'I saw Mrs. Vyner's hat coming across the churchyard. It looks so like a crumpled cup and saucer, that I have been saying to myself ever since: *Dear Mrs. Vyner, can't I fill your cup?*—and then pouring tea into that hat. And I hear the Dean responding: *My head is covered with cream, my cup runneth over.*—That is the way they make *me* feel.'

They marched downstairs, and Mrs. Witt poured tea with that devastating correctness which made Mrs. Vyner, who was utterly impervious to sarcasm, pronounce her 'indecipherably vulgar.'

But the Dean was the old bulldog, and he had set his teeth in a subject.

'I was talking to Lady Carrington about that stallion, Mrs. Witt.'

'Did you say stallion?' asked Mrs. Witt, with perfect neutrality.

'Why, yes, I presume that's what he is.'

'I presume so,' said Mrs. Witt colourlessly.

'I'm afraid Lady Carrington is a little sensitive on the wrong score,' said the Dean.

'I beg your pardon,' said Mrs. Witt, leaning forward in her most colourless polite manner. 'You mean stallion's score?'

'Yes,' said the Dean testily. 'The horse St. Mawr.'

'The stallion St. Mawr,' echoed Mrs. Witt, with utmost mild vagueness. She completely ignored Mrs. Vyner, who felt plunged like a specimen into methylated spirit. There was a moment's full stop.

'Yes?' said Mrs. Witt naïvely.

'You agree that we can't have any more of these accidents to your young men?' said the Dean rather hastily.

'I certainly do!' Mrs. Witt spoke very slowly, and the Dean's lady began to look up. She might find a loophole through which to wriggle into the contest. 'You know, Dean, that my son-in-law calls me, for preference, *belle-mère!* It sounds so awfully English when he says it; I always see myself as an old grey mare with a bell round her neck, leading a bunch of horses.' She smiled a prim little smile, *very* conversationally. 'Well!' and she pulled herself up from the aside. 'Now, as the bell-mare of the bunch of horses, I shall see to it that my son-in-law doesn't go too near that stallion again. That stallion won't stand mischief.'

She spoke so earnestly that the Dean looked at her with round wide eyes, completely taken aback.

'We all know, Mrs. Witt, that the author of the mischief is St. Mawr himself,' he said, in a loud tone.

'Really! you think *that?*' Her voice went up in American surprise. 'Why, how *strange*—!' and she lingered over the last word.

'Strange, eh?—After what's just happened?' said the Dean, with a deadly little smile.

'Why, yes! Most strange! I saw with my own eyes my son-in-law pull that stallion over backwards, and hold him down with the reins as tight as he could hold them; pull St. Mawr's head backwards on to the ground, till the groom had to crawl up and force the reins out of my son-in-law's hands. Don't you think that was mischievous on Sir Henry's part?'

The Dean was growing purple. He made an apoplectic movement with his hand. Mrs. Vyner was turned to a seated pillar of salt, strangely dressed up.

'Mrs. Witt, you are playing on words.'

'No, Dean Vyner, I am not. My son-in-law pulled that horse over backwards and pinned him down with the reins.'

'I am sorry for the horse,' said the Dean, with heavy sarcasm.

'I am *very*,' said Mrs. Witt, 'sorry for that stallion: *very!*'

Here Mrs. Vyner rose as if a chair-spring had suddenly propelled her to her feet. She was streaky pink in the face.

'Mrs. Witt,' she panted, 'you misdirect your sympathies. That poor young man—in the beauty of youth!'

'Isn't he *beautiful*—' murmured Mrs. Witt, extravagantly in sympathy. 'He is my daughter's husband!' And she looked at the petrified Lou.

'Certainly!' panted the Dean's wife. 'And you can defend that—that—'

'That stallion,' said Mrs. Witt. 'But you see, Mrs. Vyner,' she added, leaning forward female and confidential, 'if the old grey mare doesn't defend the stallion, who will? All the blooming young ladies will defend my beautiful son-in-law. You feel so *warmly* for him yourself! I'm an American woman, and I always have to stand up for the accused. And I stand up for that stallion. I say it is not right. He was pulled over backwards and then pinned down by my son-in-law—who may have meant to do it, or may not. And now people abuse him.—Just tell everybody, Mrs. Vyner and Dean Vyner'—she looked round at the Dean—'that the *belle-mère's* sympathies are with the stallion.'

She looked from one to the other with a faint and gracious little bow, her black eyebrows arching in her eighteenth-century face like black rainbows, and her full, bold grey eyes absolutely incomprehensible.

'Well, it's a peculiar message to have to hand round, Mrs. Witt,' the Dean began to boom, when she interrupted him by laying her hand on his arm and leaning forward, looking up into his face like a clinging, pleading female.

'Oh, but *do* hand it, Dean, *do* hand it,' she pleaded, gazing intently into his face.

He backed uncomfortably from that gaze.

'Since you wish it,' he said, in a chest voice.

'I most certainly *do*—' she said, as if she were wishing the sweetest wish on earth. Then, turning to Mrs. Vyner:

'Good-bye, Mrs. Vyner. We *do* appreciate your coming, my daughter and I.'

'I came out of kindness—' said Mrs. Vyner.

'Oh, I know it, I know it,' said Mrs. Witt. 'Thank you *so* much. Good-bye! Good-bye, Dean! Who is taking the morning service on Sunday? I hope it is you, because I want to come.'

'It *is* me,' said the Dean. 'Good-bye! Well, good-bye, Lady Carrington. I shall be going over to see our young man to-morrow, and will gladly take you or any thing you have to send.'

'Perhaps mother would like to go,' said Lou, softly, plaintively.

'Well, we shall see,' said the Dean. 'Good-bye for the present!'

Mother and daughter stood at the window watching the two cross the churchyard. Dean and wife knew it, but daren't look round, and daren't admit the fact to one another.

Lou was grinning with a complete grin that gave her an odd, dryad or faun look, intensified.

'It was almost as good as pouring tea into her hat,' said Mrs. Witt serenely. 'People like that tire me out. I shall take a glass of sherry.'

'So will I, mother.—It was even better than pouring tea in her hat.—You meant, didn't you, if you poured tea in her hat, to put cream and sugar in first?'

'I did,' said Mrs. Witt.

But after the excitement of the encounter had passed away, Lou felt as if her life had passed away too. She went to bed, feeling she could stand no more.

In the morning she found her mother sitting at a window watching a funeral. It was raining heavily, so that some of the mourners even wore mackintosh coats. The funeral was in the poorer corner of the churchyard, where another new grave was covered with wreaths of sodden, shrivelling flowers.—The yellowish coffin stood on the wet earth, in the rain: the curate held his hat, in a sort of permanent salute, above his head like a little umbrella, as he hastened on with the service. The people seemed too wet to weep more wet.

It was a long coffin.

'Mother, do you really *like* watching?' asked Lou irritably, as Mrs. Witt sat in complete absorption.

'I do, Louise, I really enjoy it.'

'Enjoy, mother!'—Lou was almost disgusted.

'I'll tell you why. I imagine I'm the one in the coffin—this is a girl of eighteen, who died of consumption—and those are my relatives, and I'm watching them put me away. And you know, Louise, I've come to the conclusion that hardly anybody in the world really lives, and so hardly anybody really dies. They may well say: *O Death, where is thy sting-a-ling-a-ling?* [33] Even Death can't sting those that have never really lived.—I always used to want that—to die without death stinging me.—And I'm sure the girl in the coffin is saying to herself: *Fancy Aunt Emma putting on a drab slicker, and wearing it while they bury me. Doesn't show much respect. But then my mother's family always were common!* I feel there should be a solemn burial of a roll of newspapers containing the account of the death and funeral, next week. It would be just as serious: the grave of all the world's remarks—'

'I don't want to think about it, mother. One ought to be able to laugh at it. I want to laugh at it.'

'Well, Louise, I think it's just as great a mistake to laugh at everything as to cry at everything. Laughter's not the one panacea, either. I should *really* like, before I do come to be buried in a box, to know where I am. That young girl in that coffin never was anywhere—any more than the newspaper remarks on her death and burial. And I begin to wonder if I've ever been anywhere. I seem to have been a daily sequence of newspaper remarks, myself. I'm sure I never really conceived you and gave you birth. It all happened in newspaper notices. It's a newspaper fact that you are my child, and that's about all there is to it.'

Lou smiled as she listened.

'I always knew you were philosophic, mother. But I never dreamed it would come to elegies in a country churchyard, written to your motherhood.'

'*Exactly*, Louise! Here I sit and sing the elegy to my own motherhood. I never had any motherhood, except in newspaper fact. I never was a wife, except in newspaper notices. I never was a young girl, except in newspaper

33. From a revivalist hymn ("The bells of hell go ting-aling-aling . . .").

remarks. Bury everything I ever said or that was said about me, and you've buried *me*. But since Kind Words Can Never Die, I can't be buried, and death has no sting-a-ling-a-ling for *me!*—Now listen to me, Louise: I want death to be real to me—not as it was to that young girl. I *want* it to hurt me, Louise. If it hurts me enough, I shall know I was alive.'

She set her face and gazed under half-dropped lids at the funeral, stoic, fate-like, and yet, for the first time, with a certain pure wistfulness of a young, virgin girl. This frightened Lou very much. She was so used to the matchless Amazon in her mother, that when she saw her sit there still, wistful, virginal, tender as a girl who has never taken armour, wistful at the window that only looked on graves, a serious terror took hold of the young woman. The terror of *too late!*

Lou felt years, centuries older than her mother, at that moment, with the tiresome responsibility of youth to protect and guide their elders.

'What can we do about it, mother?' she asked protectively.

'Do nothing, Louise. I'm not going to have anybody wisely steering my canoe, now I feel the rapids are near. I shall go with the river. Don't you pretend to do anything for me. I've done enough mischief myself, that way. I'm going down the stream, at last.'

There was a pause.

'But in actuality, what?' asked Lou, a little ironically.

'I don't quite know. Wait awhile.'

'Go back to America?'

'That is possible.'

'I may come too.'

'I've always waited for you to go back of your own will.'

Lou went away, wandering round the house. She was so unutterably tired of everything—weary of the house, the graveyard, weary of the thought of Rico. She would have to go back to him to-morrow, to nurse him. Poor old Rico, going on like an amiable machine from day to day. It wasn't his fault. But his life was a rattling nullity, and her life rattled in null correspondence. She had hardly strength enough to stop rattling and be still. Perhaps she had not strength enough.

She did not know. She felt so weak that unless something carried her away, she would go on rattling her bit in the great machine of human life till she collapsed, and her rattle rattled itself out, and there was a sort of barren silence where the sound of her had been.

She wandered out in the rain, to the coach-house where Lewis and Phœnix were sitting facing one another, one on a bin, the other on the inner door-step.

'Well,' she said, smiling oddly. 'What's to be done?'

The two men stood up. Outside, the rain fell steadily on the flagstones of the yard, past the leaves of trees. Lou sat down on the little iron step of the dogcart.

'That's cold,' said Phœnix. 'You sit here.' And he threw a yellow horse-blanket on the box where he had been sitting.

'I don't want to take your seat,' she said.

'All right, you take it.'

He moved across and sat gingerly on the shaft of the dogcart.—Lou seated herself, and loosened her soft tartan shawl. Her face was pink and fresh, and her dark hair curled almost merrily in the damp. But under her eyes were the finger-prints of deadly weariness.

She looked up at the two men, again smiling in her odd fashion.

'What are we going to do?' she asked.

They looked at her closely, seeking her meaning.

'What about?' said Phœnix, a faint smile reflecting on his face, merely because she smiled.

'Oh, everything,' she said, hugging her shawl again. 'You know what they want? They want to shoot St. Mawr.'

The two men exchanged glances.

'Who want it?' said Phœnix.

'Why—all our *friends!*' she made a little *moue*.[34] 'Dean Vyner does.'

Again the men exchanged glances. There was a pause. Then Phœnix said, looking aside:

'The boss is selling him.'

'Who?'

'Sir Henry.'—The half-breed always spoke the title with difficulty, and with a sort of sneer. 'He sell him to Miss Manby.'

'How do you know?'

'The man from Corrabach told me last night. Flora, she say it.' Lou's eyes met the sardonic, empty-seeing eyes of Phœnix direct. There was too much sarcastic understanding. She looked aside.

'What else did he say?' she asked.

'I don't know,' said Phœnix, evasively. 'He say they cut him—else shoot him. Think they cut him—and if he die, he die.'

Lou understood. He meant they would geld St. Mawr—at his age.

She looked at Lewis. He sat with his head down, so she could not see his face.

'Do you think it is true?' she asked. 'Lewis? Do you think they would try to geld St. Mawr—to make him a gelding?'

Lewis looked up at her. There was a faint deadly glimmer of contempt on his face.

'Very likely, Mam,' he said.

She was afraid of his cold, uncanny pale eyes, with their uneasy grey dawn of contempt. These two men, with their silent, deadly inner purpose, were not like other men. They seemed like two silent enemies of all the other men she knew. Enemies in the great white camp, disguised as servants, waiting the incalculable opportunity. What the opportunity might be, none knew.

'Sir Henry hasn't mentioned anything to me about selling St. Mawr to Miss Manby,' she said.

The derisive flicker of a smile came on Phœnix's face.

'He sell him first, and tell you then,' he said, with his deadly impassive manner.

'But do you really think so?' she asked.

It was extraordinary how much corrosive contempt Phœnix could convey, saying nothing. She felt it almost as an insult. Yet it was a relief to her.

34. Pout.

'You know, I can't believe it. I can't believe Sir Henry would want to have St. Mawr mutilated. I believe he'd rather shoot him.'

'You think so?' said Phœnix, with a faint grin.

Lou turned to Lewis.

'Lewis, will you tell me what you truly think?'

Lewis looked at her with a hard, straight, fearless British [35] stare.

'That man Philips was in the "Moon and Stars" last night. He said Miss Manby told him she was buying St. Mawr, and she asked him if he thought it would be safe to cut him, and make a horse of him. He said it would be better, take some of the nonsense out of him. He's no good for a sire, anyhow—'

Lewis dropped his head again, and tapped a tattoo with the toe of his rather small foot.

'And what do you think?' said Lou.—It occurred to her how sensible and practicable Miss Manby was, so much more so than the Dean.

Lewis looked up at her with his pale eyes.

'It won't have anything to do with me,' he said. 'I shan't go to Corrabach Hall.'

'What will you do, then?'

Lewis did not answer. He looked at Phœnix.

'Maybe him and me go to America,' said Phœnix, looking at the void.

'Can he get in?' said Lou.

'Yes, he can. I know how,' said Phœnix.

'And the money?' she said.

'We got money.'

There was a silence, after which she asked of Lewis:

'You'd leave St. Mawr to his fate?'

'I can't help his fate,' said Lewis. 'There's too many people in the world for me to help anything.'

'Poor St. Mawr!'

She went indoors again, and up to her room: then higher, to the top rooms of the tall Georgian house. From one window she could see the fields in the rain. She could see St. Mawr himself, alone as usual, standing with his head up, looking across the fences. He was streaked dark with rain. Beautiful, with his poised head and massive neck, and his supple hindquarters. He was neighing to Poppy. Clear on the wet wind came the sound of his bell-like, stallion's calling, that Mrs. Vyner called cruel. It was a strange noise, with a splendour that belonged to another world-age. The mean cruelty of Mrs. Vyner's humanitarianism, the barren cruelty of Flora Manby, the eunuch cruelty of Rico. Our whole eunuch civilization, nasty-minded as eunuchs are, with their kind of sneaking, sterilizing cruelty.

Yet even she herself, seeing St. Mawr's conceited march along the fence, could not help addressing him:

'Yes, my boy! If you knew what Miss Flora Manby was preparing for you! *She'll* sharpen a knife that will settle you.'

And Lou called her mother.

The two American women stood high at the window, overlooking the wet,

35. Here meaning "Celtic," "ancient British."

close, hedged-and-fenced English landscape. Everything enclosed, enclosed, to stifling. The very apples on the trees looked so shut in, it was impossible to imagine any speck of 'Knowledge' lurking inside them. Good to eat, good to cook, good even for show. But the wild sap of untamable and inexhaustible knowledge—no! Bred out of them. Geldings, even the apples.

Mrs. Witt listened to Lou's half-humorous statements.

'You must admit, mother, Flora is a sensible girl,' she said.

'I admit it, Louise.'

'She goes straight to the root of the matter.'

'And eradicates the root. Wise girl! And what is your answer?'

'I don't know, mother. What would you say?'

'I know what *I* should say.'

'Tell me.'

'I should say: *Miss Manby, you may have my husband, but not my horse. My husband won't need emasculating, and my horse I won't have you meddle with. I'll preserve one last male thing in the museum of this world, if I can.*'

Lou, listened, smiling faintly.

'That's what I will say,' she replied at length. 'The funny thing is, mother, they think all their men with their bare faces or their little quotation-marks moustaches *are* so tremendously male. That foxhunting one!'

'I know it. Like little male motor-cars. Give him a little gas, and start him on the low gear, and away he goes: all his male gear rattling, like a cheap motor-car.'

'I'm afraid I dislike men altogether, mother.'

'You may, Louise. Think of Flora Manby, and how you love the fair sex.'

'After all. St. Mawr is better. And I'm glad if he gives them a kick in the face.'

'Ah, Louise!' Mrs. Witt suddenly clasped her hands with wicked passion. '*Ay, que gozo!* [36] as our Juan used to say, on your father's ranch in Texas.' She gazed in a sort of wicked ecstasy out of the window.

They heard Lou's maid softly calling Lady Carrington from below. Lou went to the stairs.

'What is it?'

'Lewis wants to speak to you, my Lady.'

'Send him into the sitting-room.'

The two women went down.

'What is it, Lewis?' asked Lou.

'Am I to bring in St. Mawr, in case they send for him from Corrabach?'

'No,' said Lou swiftly.

'Wait a minute,' put in Mrs. Witt. 'What makes you think they will send for St. Mawr from Corrabach, Lewis?' she asked, suave as a grey leopard cat.

'Miss Manby went up to Flints Farm with Dean Vyner this morning, and they've just come back. They stopped the car, and Miss Manby got out at the field gate, to look at St. Mawr. I'm thinking if she made the bargain with Sir Henry, she'll be sending a man over this afternoon, and if I'd better brush St. Mawr down a bit, in case.'

36. "What joy!"

The man stood strangely still, and the words came like shadows of his real meaning. It was a challenge.

'I see,' said Mrs. Witt slowly.

Lou's face darkened. She too saw.

'So that is her game,' she said. 'That is why they got me down here.'

'Never mind, Louise,' said Mrs. Witt. Then to Lewis: 'Yes, please bring in St. Mawr. You wish it, don't you, Louise?'

'Yes,' hesitated Lou. She saw by Mrs. Witt's closed face that a counter-move was prepared.

'And, Lewis,' said Mrs. Witt, 'my daughter may wish you to ride St. Mawr this afternoon—not to Corrabach Hall.'

'Very good, Madam.'

Mrs. Witt sat silent for some time, after Lewis had gone, gathering inspiration from the wet, grisly gravestones.

'Don't you think it's time we made a move, daughter?' she asked.

'Any move,' said Lou desperately.

'Very well then.—My dearest friends, and my *only* friends, in this country, are in Oxfordshire. I will set off to *ride* to Merriton this afternoon, and Lewis will ride with me on St. Mawr.'

'But you can't ride to Merriton in an afternoon,' said Lou.

'I know it. I shall ride across country. I shall *enjoy* it, Louise.—Yes.—I shall consider I am on my way back to America. I am most deadly tired of this country. From Merriton I shall make my arrangements to go to America, and take Lewis and Phœnix and St. Mawr along with me. I think they want to go.—You will decide for yourself.'

'Yes, I'll come too,' said Lou casually.

'Very well. I'll start immediately after lunch, for I can't *breathe* in this place any longer. Where are Henry's automobile maps?'

Afternoon saw Mrs. Witt, in a large waterproof cape, mounted on her horse, Lewis, in another cape, mounted on St. Mawr, trotting through the rain, splashing in the puddles, moving slowly southwards. They took the open country, and would pass quite near to Flints Farm. But Mrs. Witt did not care. With great difficulty she had managed to fasten a small waterproof roll behind her, containing her night things. She seemed to breathe the first breath of freedom.

And sure enough, an hour or so after Mrs. Witt's departure, arrived Flora Manby in a splashed-up motor-car, accompanied by her sister, and bringing a groom and a saddle.

'Do you know, Harry sold me St. Mawr,' she said. 'I'm just wild to get that horse in hand.'

'How?' said Lou.

'Oh, I don't know. There are ways. Do you mind if Philips rides him over now, to Corrabach?—Oh, I forgot, Harry sent you a note.'

DEAREST LOULINA: *Have you been gone from here two days or two years? It seems the latter. You are terribly missed. Flora wanted so much to buy St. Mawr, to save us further trouble, that I have sold him to her. She is giving me what we paid: rather, what you paid; so of course the money is yours. I am thankful we are rid of the animal, and*

*that he falls into competent hands—I asked her please to remove him
from your charge to-day. And I can't tell how much easier I am in my
mind, to think of him gone. You are coming back to me to-morrow, aren't
you? I shall think of nothing else but you, till I see you. A rivederti,[37]
darling dear! R.*

'I'm so sorry,' said Lou. 'Mother went on horseback to see some friends, and
Lewis went with her on St. Mawr. He knows the road.'

'She'll be back this evening?' said Flora.

'I don't know. Mother is so uncertain. She may be away a day or two.'

'Well, here's the cheque for St. Mawr.'

'No, I won't take it now—no, thank you—not till mother comes back with
the goods.'

Flora was chagrined. The two women knew they hated one another. The visit
was a brief one.

Mrs. Witt rode on in the rain, which abated as the afternoon wore down, and
the evening came without rain, and with a suffusion of pale yellow light. All the
time she had trotted in silence, with Lewis just behind her. And she scarcely
saw the heather-covered hills with the deep clefts between them, nor the oak-
woods, nor the lingering foxgloves, nor the earth at all. Inside herself she felt a
profound repugnance for the English country: she preferred even the crudeness
of Central Park in New York.

And she felt an almost savage desire to get away from Europe, from everything European. Now she was really *en route*, she cared not a straw for St.
Mawr or for Lewis or anything. Something just writhed inside her, all the time,
against Europe. That closeness, that sense of cohesion, that sense of being fused
into a lump with all the rest—no matter how much distance you kept—this
drove her mad. In America the cohesion was a matter of choice and will. But
in Europe it was organic, like the helpless particles of one sprawling body. And
the great body in a state of incipient decay.

She was a woman of fifty-one: and she seemed hardly to have lived a day.
She looked behind her—the thin trees and swamps of Louisiana, the sultry,
sub-tropical excitement of decaying New Orleans, the vast bare dryness of
Texas, with mobs of cattle in an illumined dust! The half-European thrills of
New York! The false stability of Boston! A clever husband, who was a brilliant
lawyer, but who was far more thrilled by his cattle ranch than by his law: and
who drank heavily and died. The years of first widowhood in Boston, consoled
by a self-satisfied sort of intellectual courtship from clever men.—For curiously
enough, while she wanted it, she had always been able to compel men to pay
court to her. All kinds of men.—Then a rather dashing time in New York—
when she was in her early forties. Then the long *visual* philandering in Europe.
She left off 'loving,' save through the eye, when she came to Europe. And when
she made her trips to America, she found it was finished there also, her 'loving.'

What was the matter? Examining herself, she had long ago decided that her
nature was a destructive force. But then, she justified herself, she had only destroyed that which was destructible. If she could have found something inde-

37. Italian equivalent of *Au revoir* (more commonly *Arrivederci*).

structible, especially in men, though she would have fought against it, she would have been glad at last to be defeated by it.

That was the point. She really wanted to be defeated, in her own eyes. And nobody had ever defeated her. Men were never really her match. A woman of terrible strong health, she felt even that in her strong limbs there was far more electric power than in the limbs of any man she had met. That curious fluid electric force, that could make any man kiss her hand, if she so willed it. A queen, as far as she wished. And not having been very clever at school, she always had the greatest respect for the mental powers. Her own were not mental powers. Rather electric, as of some strange physical dynamo within her. So she had been ready to bow before Mind.

But alas! After a brief time, she had found Mind, at least the man who was supposed to have the mind, bowing before her. Her own peculiar dynamic force was stronger than the force of Mind. She could make Mind kiss her hand.

And not by any sensual tricks. She did not really care about sensualities, especially as a younger woman. Sex was a mere adjunct. She cared about the mysterious, intense, dynamic sympathy that could flow between her and some 'live' man—a man who was highly conscious, a real live wire. That she cared about.

But she had never rested until she had made the man she admired: and admiration was the root of her attraction to any man: made him kiss her hand. In both senses, actual and metaphorical. Physical and metaphysical. Conquered his country.

She had always succeeded. And she believed that, if she cared, she always *would* succeed. In the world of living men. Because of the power that was in her, in her arms, in her strong, shapely, but terrible hands, in all the great dynamo of her body.

For this reason she had been so terribly contemptuous of Rico, and of Lou's infatuation. Ye Gods! what was Rico in the scale of men!

Perhaps she despised the younger generation too easily. Because she did not see its sources of power, she concluded it was powerless. Whereas perhaps the power of accommodating oneself to any circumstance and committing oneself to no circumstance is the last triumph of mankind.

Her generation had had its day. She had had her day. The world of her men had sunk into a sort of insignificance. And with a great contempt she despised the world that had come into place instead: the world of Rico and Flora Manby, the world represented, to her, by the Prince of Wales.[38]

In such a world there was nothing even to conquer. It gave everything and gave nothing to everybody and anybody all the time. *Dio benedetto!* as Rico would say. A great complicated tangle of nonentities ravelled in nothingness. So it seemed to her.

Great God! This was the generation she had helped to bring into the world.

She had had her day. And, as far as the mysterious battle of life went, she had won all the way. Just as Cleopatra, in the mysterious business of a woman's life, won all the way.

38. Edward, Prince of Wales (1894–1972), for a scant year (1936) King Edward VIII, famous during the post-war years for his world tours and leadership of the smart set.

Though that bald tough Cæsar had drawn his iron from the fire without losing much of its temper. And he had gone his way. And Antony surely was splendid to die with.

In her life there had been no tough Cæsar to go his way in cold blood, away from her. Her men had gone from her like dogs on three legs, into the crowd. And certainly there was no gorgeous Antony to die for and with.

Almost she was tempted in her heart to cry: 'Conquer me, O God, before I die!'—But then she had a terrible contempt for the God that was supposed to rule this universe. She felt she could make *Him* kiss her hand. Here she was, a woman of fifty-one, past the change of life. And her great dread was to die an empty, barren death. Oh, if only Death might open dark wings of mystery and consolation! To die an easy, barren death. To pass out as she had passed in, without mystery or the rustling of darkness! That was her last, final, ashy dread.

'Old!' she said to herself. 'I am not *old!* I have lived many years, that is all. But I am as timeless as an hour-glass that turns morning and night, and spills the hours of sleep one way, the hours of consciousness the other way, without itself being affected. Nothing in all my life has ever truly affected me.—I believe Cleopatra only tried the asp, as she tried her pearls in wine, to see if it would really, really have any effect on her. Nothing had ever really had any effect on her, neither Cæsar nor Antony nor any of them. Never once had she really been lost, lost to herself. Then try death, see if that trick would work. If she would lose herself to herself that way.—Ah, death—!'

But Mrs. Witt mistrusted death too. She felt she might pass out as a bed of asters passes out in autumn, to mere nothingness.—And something in her longed to die, at least, *positively:* to be folded then at last into throbbing wings of mystery, like a hawk that goes to sleep. Not like a thing made into a parcel and put into the last rubbish-heap.

So she rode trotting across the hills, mile after mile, in silence. Avoiding the roads, avoiding everything, avoiding everybody, just trotting forwards, towards night.

And by nightfall they had travelled twenty-five miles. She had motored around this country, and knew the little towns and the inns. She knew where she would sleep.

The morning came beautiful and sunny. A woman so strong in health, why should she ride with the fact of death before her eyes? But she did.

Yet in sunny morning she must do something about it.

'Lewis!' she said. 'Come here and tell me something, please! Tell me,' she said, 'do you believe in God?'

'In God!' he said, wondering. 'I never think about it.'

'But do you say your prayers?'

'No, Mam!'

'Why don't you?'

He thought about it for some minutes.

'I don't like religion. My aunt and uncle were religious.'

'You don't like religion,' she repeated. 'And you don't believe in God.—Well, then—'

'Nay!' he hesitated. 'I never said I didn't believe in God.—Only I'm sure I'm not a Methodist. And I feel a fool in a proper church. And I feel a fool saying my prayers.—And I feel a fool when ministers and parsons come getting at me. —I never think about God, if folks don't try to make me.' He had a small, sly smile, almost gay.

'And you don't like feeling a fool?' She smiled rather patronizingly.

'No, Mam.'

'Do I make you feel a fool?' she asked, dryly.

He looked at her without answering.

'Why don't you answer?' she said, pressing.

'I think you'd like to make a fool of me sometimes,' he said.

'Now?' she pressed.

He looked at her with that slow, distant look.

'Maybe!' he said, rather unconcernedly.

Curiously, she couldn't touch him. He always seemed to be watching her from a distance, as if from another country. Even if she made a fool of him, something in him would all the time be far away from her, not implicated.

She caught herself up in the personal game, and returned to her own isolated question. A vicious habit made her start the personal tricks. She didn't want to, really.

There was something about this little man—sometimes, to herself, she called him *Little Jack Horner, Sat in a corner*—that irritated her and made her want to taunt him. His peculiar little inaccessibility, that was so tight and easy.

Then again, there was something, his way of looking at her as if he looked from out of another country, a country of which he was an inhabitant, and where she had never been: this touched her strangely. Perhaps behind this little man was the mystery. In spite of the fact that in actual life, in her world, he was only a groom, almost *chétif*,[39] with his legs a little bit horsy and bowed; and of no education, saying *Yes, Mam!* and *No, Mam!* and accomplishing nothing, simply nothing at all on the face of the earth. Strictly a nonentity.

And yet, what made him perhaps the only real entity to her, his seeming to inhabit another world than hers. A world dark and still, where language never ruffled the growing leaves, and seared their edges like a bad wind.

Was it an illusion, however? Sometimes she thought it was. Just bunkum, which she had faked up, in order to have something to mystify about.

But then, when she saw Phœnix and Lewis silently together, she knew there *was* another communion, silent, excluding her. And sometimes when Lewis was alone with St. Mawr: and once, when she saw him pick up a bird that had stunned itself against a wire: she had realized another world, silent, where each creature is alone in its own aura of silence, the mystery of power: as Lewis had power with St. Mawr, and even with Phœnix.

The visible world, and the invisible. Or rather, the audible and the inaudible. She had lived so long, and so completely, in the visible, audible world. She would not easily admit that other, inaudible. She always wanted to jeer, as she approached the brink of it.

Even now, she wanted to jeer at the little fellow, because of his holding himself inaccessible within the inaudible, silent world. And she knew he knew it.

39. Puny.

'Did you never want to be rich, and be a gentleman, like Sir Henry?' she asked.

'I would many times have liked to be rich. But I never exactly wanted to be a gentleman,' he said.

'Why not?'

'I can't exactly say. I should be uncomfortable if I was like they are.'

'And are you comfortable now?'

'When I'm let alone.'

'And do they let you alone? Does the world let you alone?'

'No, they don't.'

'Well, then—!'

'I keep to myself all I can.'

'And are you comfortable, as you call it, when you keep to yourself?'

'Yes, I am.'

'But when you keep to yourself, what do you keep to? What precious treasure have you to keep to?'

He looked, and saw she was jeering.

'None,' he said. 'I've got nothing of that sort.'

She rode impatiently on ahead.

And the moment she had done so, she regretted it. She might put the little fellow, with contempt, out of her reckoning. But no, she would not do it.

She had put so much out of her reckoning: soon she would be left in an empty circle, with her empty self at the centre.

She reined in again.

'Lewis!' she said. 'I don't want you to take offence at anything I say.'

'No, Mam.'

'I don't want you to say just *No, Mam!* all the time!' she cried impulsively. 'Promise me.'

'Yes, Mam!'

'But really! Promise me you won't be offended at whatever I say.'

'Yes, Mam!'

She looked at him searchingly. To her surprise, she was almost in tears. A woman of her years! And with a servant!

But his face was blank and stony, with a stony, distant look of pride that made him inaccessible to her emotions. He met her eyes again: with that cold, distant look, looking straight into her hot, confused, pained self. So cold and as if merely refuting her. He didn't believe her, nor trust her, nor like her even. She was an attacking enemy to him. Only he stayed really far away from her, looking down at her from a sort of distant hill where her weapons could not reach: not quite.

And at the same time, it hurt him in a dumb, living way, that she made these attacks on him. She could see the cloud of hurt in his eyes, no matter how distantly he looked at her.

They bought food in a village shop, and sat under a tree near a field where men were already cutting oats, in a warm valley. Lewis had stabled the horses for a couple of hours, to feed and rest. But he came to join her under the tree, to eat.—He sat at a little distance from her, with the bread and cheese in his small brown hands, eating silently, and watching the harvesters. She was cross with him, and therefore she was stingy, would give him nothing to eat but dry bread and cheese. Herself, she was not hungry.—So all the time he kept his face a little averted from her. As a matter of fact, he kept his whole being averted from her, away from her. He did not want to touch her, nor to be touched by her. He kept his spirit there, alert, on its guard, but out of contact. It was as if he had unconsciously accepted the battle, the old battle. He was her target, the old object of her deadly weapons. But he refused to shoot back. It was as if he caught all her missiles in full flight, before they touched him, and silently threw them on the ground behind him. And in some essential part of himself he ignored her, staying in another world.

That other world! Mere male armour of artificial imperviousness! It angered her.

Yet she knew, by the way he watched the harvesters, and the grasshoppers popping into notice, that it was another world. And when a girl went by, carrying food to the field, it was at him she glanced. And he gave that quick, animal little smile that came from him unawares. Another world!

Yet also, there was a sort of meanness about him: a *suffisance!* [40] A keep-yourself-for-yourself, and don't give yourself away.

Well!—she rose impatiently.

It was hot in the afternoon, and she was rather tired. She went to the inn and slept, and did not start again till tea-time.

Then they had to ride rather late. The sun sank, among a smell of cornfields, clear and yellow-red behind motionless dark trees. Pale smoke rose from cottage chimneys. Not a cloud was in the sky, which held the upward-floating like a bowl inverted on purpose. A new moon sparkled and was gone. It was beginning of night.

Away in the distance, they saw a curious pinkish glare of fire, probably furnaces. And Mrs. Witt thought she could detect the scent of furnace smoke, or factory smoke. But then she always said that of the English air: it was never quite free of the smell of smoke, coal-smoke.

They were riding slowly on a path through fields, down a long slope. Away below was a puther [41] of lights. All the darkness seemed full of half-spent crossing lights, a curious uneasiness. High in the sky a star seemed to be walking. It was an aeroplane with a light. Its buzz rattled above. Not a space, not a speck of this country that wasn't humanized, occupied by the human claim. Not even the sky.

They descended slowly through a dark wood, which they had entered through a gate. Lewis was all the time dismounting and opening gates, letting her pass, shutting the gate and mounting again.

So, in a while she came to the edge of the wood's darkness, and saw the open pale concave of the world beyond. The darkness was never dark. It shook with the concussion of many invisible lights, lights of towns, villages, mines, factories, furnaces, squatting in the valleys and behind all the hills.

Yet, as Rachel Witt drew rein at the gate emerging from the wood, a very big, soft star fell in heaven, cleaving the hubbub of this human night with a gleam from the greater world.

40. Self-sufficiency, conceit.
41. Muddle, disturbance.

'See! a star falling!' said Lewis, as he opened the gate.

'I saw it,' said Mrs. Witt, walking her horse past him.

There was a curious excitement of wonder, or magic, in the little man's voice. Even in this night something strange had stirred awake in him.

'You ask me about God,' he said to her, walking his horse alongside in the shadow of the wood's edge, the darkness of the old Pan, that kept our artificially lit world at bay. 'I don't know about God. But when I see a star fall like that out of long-distance places in the sky: and the moon sinking saying Good-bye! Good-bye! Good-bye! and nobody listening: I think I hear something, though I wouldn't call it God.'

'What then?' said Rachel Witt.

'And you smell the smell of oak-leaves now,' he said, 'now the air is cold. They smell to me more alive than people. The trees hold their bodies hard and still, but they watch and listen with their leaves. And I think they say to me: *Is that you passing there, Morgan Lewis? All right, you pass quickly, we shan't do anything to you. You are like a holly bush.*'

'Yes,' said Rachel Witt, dryly. '*Why?*'

'All the time, the trees grow, and listen. And if you cut a tree down without asking pardon, trees will hurt you some time in your life, in the night-time.'

'I suppose,' said Rachel Witt, 'that's an old superstition.'

'They say that ash trees don't like people. When the other people were most in the country—I mean like what they call fairies, that have all gone now—they liked ash trees best. And you know the little green things with little small nuts in them, that come flying down from ash trees—*pigeons*, we call them—they're the seeds—the other people used to catch them and eat them before they fell to the ground. And that made the people so they could hear trees living and feeling things.—But when all these people that there are now came to England, they liked the oak trees best, because their pigs ate the acorns. So now you can tell the ash trees are mad, they want to kill all these people. But the oak trees are many more than the ash trees.'

'And do you eat the ash-tree seeds?' she asked.

'I always ate them when I was little. Then I wasn't frightened of ash trees, like most of the others. And I wasn't frightened of the moon. If you didn't go near the fire all day, and if you didn't eat any cooked food nor anything that had been in the sun, but only things like turnips or radishes or pig-nuts, and then went without any clothes on, in the full moon, then you could see the people in the moon, and go with them. They never have fire, and they never speak, and their bodies are clear almost like jelly. They die in a minute if there's a bit of fire near them. But they know more than we. Because unless fire touches them, they never die. They see people live and they see people perish, and they say people are only like twigs on a tree, you break them off the tree, and kindle with them. You made a fire of them, and they are gone, the fire is gone, everything is gone. But the people of the moon don't die, and fire is nothing to them. They look at it from the distance of the sky, and see it burning things up, people all appearing and disappearing like twigs that come in spring and you cut them in autumn and make a fire of them and they are gone. And they say: what do people matter? If you want to matter, you must become a moon-boy. Then, all your life, fire can't blind you and people can't hurt you. Because at full moon you can join the moon people, and go through the air and pass any cool places, pass through rocks and through the trunks of trees, and when you come to people lying warm in bed, you punish them.'

'How?'

'You sit on the pillow where they breathe, and you put a web across their mouth, so they can't breathe the fresh air that comes from the moon. So they go on breathing the same air again and again, and that makes them more and more stupefied. The sun gives out heat, but the moon gives out fresh air. That's what the moon people do: they wash the air clean with moonlight.'

He was talking with a strange eager naïveté that amused Rachel Witt, and made her a little uncomfortable in her skin. Was he after all no more than a sort of imbecile?

'Who told you all this stuff?' she asked abruptly.

And, as abruptly, he pulled himself up.

'We used to say it, when we were children.'

'But you don't believe it? It *is* only childishness, after all.'

He paused a moment or two.

'No,' he said, in his ironical little day-voice. 'I know I shan't make anything but a fool of myself, with that talk. But all sorts of things go through our heads, and some seem to linger, and some don't. But you asking me about God put it into my mind, I suppose. I don't know what sort of things I believe in: only I know it's not what the chapel-folks believe in. We, none of us believe in them when it comes to earning a living, or, with you people, when it comes to spending your fortune. Then we know that bread costs money, and even your sleep you have to pay for.—That's work. Or, with you people, it's just owning property and seeing you get your value for your money.—But a man's mind is always full of things. And some people's mind's like my aunt and uncle, are full of religion and hell for everybody except themselves. And some people's minds are all money, money, money, and how to get hold of something they haven't got hold of yet. And some people, like you, are always curious about what everybody else in the world is after. And some people are all for enjoying themselves and being thought much of, and some, like Lady Carrington, don't know what to do with themselves. Myself, I don't want to have in my mind the things other people have in their minds. I'm one that likes my own things best. And if, when I see a bright star fall, like to-night, I think to myself: *There's movement in the sky. The world is going to change again. They're throwing something to us from the distance, and we've got to have it, whether we want it or not. To-morrow there will be a difference for everybody, thrown out of the sky upon us, whether we want it or not:* then that's how I want to think, so let me please myself.'

'You know what a shooting star actually is, I suppose?—and that there are always many in August, because we pass through a region of them?'

'Yes, Mam, I've been told. But stones don't come at us from the sky for nothing. Either it's like when a man tosses an apple to you out of his orchard, as you go by, or it's like when somebody shies a stone at you, to cut your head open. You'll never make me believe the sky is like an empty house with a slate falling from the roof. The world has its own life, the sky has a life of its own, and never is it like stones rolling down a rubbish-heap and falling into a pond.

Many things twitch and twitter within the sky, and many things happen beyond us. My own way of thinking is my own way.'

'I never knew you talk so much.'

'No, Mam. It's your asking me that about God. Or else it's the night-time. I don't believe in God and being good and going to heaven. Neither do I worship idols, so I'm not a heathen, as my aunt called me. Never from a boy did I want to believe the things they kept grinding in their guts at home, and at Sunday School, and at school. A man's mind has to be full of something, so I keep to what we used to think as lads. It's childish nonsense, I know it. But it suits me. Better than other people's stuff. Your man Phœnix is about the same, when he lets on.—Anyhow, it's my own stuff, that we believed as lads, and I like it better than other people's stuff.—You asking about God made me let on. But I would never belong to any club, or trades-union, and God's the same to my mind.'

With this he gave me a little kick to his horse, and St. Mawr went dancing excitedly along the highway they now entered, leaving Mrs. Witt to trot after as rapidly as she could.

When she came to the hotel, to which she had telegraphed for rooms, Lewis disappeared, and she was left thinking hard.

It was not till they were twenty miles from Merriton, riding through a slow morning mist, and she had a rather far-away, wistful look on her face, unusual for her, that she turned to him in the saddle and said:

'Now don't be surprised, Lewis, at what I am going to say. I am going to ask you, now, supposing I wanted to marry you, what should you say?'

He looked at her quickly, and was at once on his guard.

'That you didn't mean it,' he replied hastily.

'Yes,'—she hesitated, and her face looked wistful and tired.—'Supposing I *did* mean it. Supposing I did *really*, from my heart, want to marry you and be a wife to you—' she looked away across the fields—'then what should you say?'

Her voice sounded sad, a little broken.

'Why, Mam!' he replied, knitting his brow and shaking his head a little. 'I should say you didn't mean it, you know. Something would have come over you.'

'But supposing I *wanted* something to come over me?'

He shook his head.

'It would never do, Mam! Some people's flesh and blood is kneaded like bread: and that's me. And some are rolled like fine pastry, like Lady Carrington. And some are mixed with gun-powder. They're like a cartridge you put in a gun, Mam.'

She listened impatiently.

'Don't talk,' she said, 'about bread and cakes and pastry, it all means nothing. You used to answer short enough, Yes, Mam! No, Mam! That will do now. Do you mean *Yes!* or *No?*'

His eyes met hers. She was again hectoring.

'No, Mam!' he said, quite neutral.

'Why?'

As she waited for his answer, she saw the foundations of his loquacity dry up, his face go distant and mute again, as it always used to be, till these last two days, when it had had a funny touch of inconsequential merriness.

He looked steadily into her eyes, and his look was neutral, sombre, and hurt. He looked at her as if infinite seas, infinite spaces divided him and her. And his eyes seemed to put her away beyond some sort of fence. An anger congealed cold like lava, set impassive against her and all her sort.

'No, Mam. I couldn't give my body to any woman who didn't respect it.'

'But I do respect it, I do!'—she flushed hot like a girl.

'No, Mam. Not as I mean it,' he replied.

There was a touch of anger against her in his voice, and a distance of distaste.

'And how do you mean it?' she replied, the full sarcasm coming back into her tones. She could see that as a woman to touch and fondle he saw her as repellent: only repellent.

'I have to be a servant to women now,' he said, 'even to earn my wage. I could never touch with my body a woman whose servant I was.'

'You're not my servant: my daughter pays your wages.—And all that is beside the point, between a man and a woman.'

'No woman who I touched with my body should ever speak to me as you speak to me, or think of me as you think of me,' he said.

'But—' she stammered, 'I think of you—with love. And can you be so unkind as to notice the way I speak? You know it's only my way.'

'You, as a woman,' he said, 'you have no respect for a man.'

'Respect! Respect!' she cried. 'I'm likely to lose what respect I have left. I know I can love a man. But whether a man can love a woman—'

'No,' said Lewis. 'I never could, and I think I never shall. Because I don't want to. The thought of it makes me feel shame.'

'What do you mean?' she cried.

'Nothing in the world,' he said, 'would make me feel such shame as to have a woman shouting at me, or mocking at me, as I see women mocking and despising the men they marry. No woman shall touch my body, and mock me or despise me. No woman.'

'But men must be mocked, or despised even, sometimes.'

'No. Not this man. Not by the woman I touch with my body.'

'Are you perfect?'

'I don't know. But if I touch a woman with my body, it must put a lock on her, to respect what I will never have despised: never!'

'What will you never have despised?'

'My body! And my touch upon the woman.'

'Why insist so on your body?'—And she looked at him with a touch of contemptuous mockery, raillery.

He looked her in the eyes, steadily, and coldly, putting her away from him, and himself far away from her.

'Do you expect that any woman will stay your humble slave to-day?' she asked cuttingly.

But he only watched her, coldly, distant, refusing any connection.

'Between men and women, it's a question of give and take. A man can't expect always to be humbly adored.'

He watched her still, cold, rather pale, putting her far from him. Then he turned his horse and set off rapidly along the road, leaving her to follow.

She walked her horse and let him go, thinking to herself:

'There's a little bantam cock. And a groom! Imagine it! Thinking he can dictate to a woman!'

She was in love with him. And he, in an odd way, was in love with her. She had known it by the odd, uncanny merriment in him, and his unexpected loquacity. But he would not have her come physically near him. Unapproachable there as a cactus, guarding his 'body' from her contact. As if contact with her would be mortal insult and fatal injury to his marvellous 'body.'

What a little cock-sparrow!

Let him ride ahead. He would have to wait for her somewhere.

She found him at the entrance to the next village. His face was pallid and set. She could tell he felt he had been insulted, so he had congealed into stiff insentience.

'At the bottom of all men is the same,' she said to herself: 'an empty, male conceit of themselves.'

She too rode up with a face like a mask, and straight on to the hotel.

'Can you serve dinner to myself and my servant?' she asked at the inn: which, fortunately for her, accommodated motorists, otherwise they would have said *No!*

'I think,' said Lewis as they came in sight of Merriton, 'I'd better give Lady Carrington a week's notice.'

A complete little stranger! And an impudent one.

'Exactly as you please,' she said.

She found several letters from her daughter at Marshall Place.

DEAR MOTHER: *No sooner had you gone off than Flora appeared, not at all in the bud, but rather in full blow. She demanded her victim: Shylock demanding the pound of flesh: and wanted to hand over the shekels.*

Joyfully I refused them. She said 'Harry' was much better, and invited him and me to stay at Corrabach Hall till he was quite well: it would be less strain on your household while he was still in bed and helpless. So the plan is that he shall be brought down on Friday, if he is really fit for the journey, and we drive straight to Corrabach. I am packing his bags and mine, clearing up our traces: his trunks to go to Corrabach, mine to stay here and make up their minds.—I am going to Flints Farm again to-morrow, dutifully, though I am no flower for the bedside.—I do so want to know if Rico has already called her Fiorita: or perhaps Florecita.[42] *It reminds me of old William's joke: Now yuh tell me, little Missy: which is the best posy that grow? And the hushed whisper in which he said the answer: The Collyposy! Oh, dear, I am so tired of feeling spiteful, but how else is one to feel?*

You looked most prosaically romantic, setting off in a rubber cape, followed by Lewis. Hope the roads were not very slippery, and that you had a good time, à la Mademoiselle de Maupin.[43] *Do remember, dear, not to devour little Lewis before you have got half-way—*

42. Italian and Spanish diminutives.
43. In *Mademoiselle de Maupin* (1835), a novel of somewhat risqué character by Théophile Gautier (1811–72), the heroine, dressed as a boy, travels with a young man.

DEAR MOTHER: *I half expected word from you before I left, but nothing came. Forrester drove me up here just before lunch. Rico seems much better, almost himself, and a little more than that. He broached our staying at Corrabach very tactfully. I told him Flora had asked me, and it seemed a good plan. Then I told him about St. Mawr.* He was a little piqued, and there was a pause of very disapproving silence. Then he said: Very well, darling. If you wish to keep the animal, do so by all means. I make a present of him again. *Me:* That's so good of you, Rico. Because I know revenge is sweet. *Rico:* Revenge, Loulina! I don't think I was selling him for vengeance! Merely to get rid of him to Flora, who can keep better hold over him. *Me:* But you know, dear, she was going to geld him! *Rico:* I don't think anybody knew it. We only wondered if it were possible, to make him more amenable. Did she tell you? *Me:* No—Phœnix did. He had it from a groom. *Rico:* Dear me! A concatenation of grooms! So your mother rode off with Lewis, and carried St. Mawr out of danger! I understand! Let us hope worse won't befall. *Me:* Whom? *Rico:* Never mind, dear! It's so lovely to see you. You are looking rested. I thought those Countess of Witton roses the most marvellous things in the world, till you came, now they're quite in the background. *He had some very lovely red roses, in a crystal bowl: the room smelled of roses. Me:* Where did they come from? *Rico:* Oh, Flora brought them! *Me:* Bowl and all? *Rico:* Bowl and all! Wasn't it dear of her? *Me:* Why, yes! But then she's the goddess of flowers, isn't she? *Poor darling, he was offended that I should twit him while he is ill, so I relented. He has had a couple of marvellous invalid's bed-jackets sent from London: one a pinkish yellow, with rose-arabesque facings: this one in fine cloth. But unfortunately he has already dropped soup on it. The other is a lovely silvery and blue and green soft brocade. He had that one on to receive me, and I at once complimented him on it. He has got a new ring too: sent by Aspasia Weingartner, a rather lovely intaglio of Priapus* [44] *under an apple bough, at least so he says it is. He made a naughty face, and said:* The Priapus stage is rather advanced for poor me. *I asked what the Priapus stage was, but he said:* Oh, nothing! *Then nurse said:* There's a big classical dictionary that Miss Manby brought up, if you wish to see it. *So I have been studying the Classical Gods. The world always was a queer place. It's a very queer one when Rico is the god Priapus. He would go round the orchard painting lifelike apples on the trees, and inviting nymphs to come and eat them. And the nymphs would pretend they were real:* Why, Sir Prippy, what stunningly naughty apples! *There's nothing so artificial as sinning nowadays. I suppose it once was real.*

I'm bored here: wish I had my horse.

DEAR MOTHER: *I'm so glad you are enjoying your ride. I'm sure it is like riding into history, like the Yankee at the Court of King Arthur,* [45] *in those old by-lanes and Roman roads. They still fascinate me: at least, more before I get there than when I am actually there. I begin to feel*

---

44. God of gardens and fertility, represented with a large phallus.
45. *A Connecticut Yankee at King Arthur's Court* (1889), by Mark Twain.

real American and resent the past. Why doesn't the past decently bury itself, instead of sitting waiting to be admired by the present?

Phœnix brought Poppy. I am so fond of her: rode for five hours yesterday. I was glad to get away from this farm. The doctor came, and said Rico would be able to go down to Corrabach to-morrow. Flora came to hear the bulletin, and sailed back full of zest. Apparently Rico is going to do a portrait of her, sitting up in bed. What a mercy the bed-clothes won't be mine when Priapus wields his pallette from the pillow.

Phœnix thinks you intend to go to America with St. Mawr, and that I am coming too, leaving Rico this side.—I wonder. I feel so unreal, nowadays, as if I too were nothing more than a painting by Rico on a millboard. I feel almost too unreal even to make up my mind to anything. It is terrible when the life-flow dies out of one, and everything is like cardboard, and oneself is like cardboard. I'm sure it is worse than being dead. I realized it yesterday when Phœnix and I had a picnic lunch by a stream. You see I must imitate you in all things. He found me some watercresses, and they tasted so damp and alive, I knew how deadened I was. Phœnix wants us to go and have a ranch in Arizona, and raise horses, with St. Mawr, if willing, for Father Abraham. I wonder if it matters what one does: if it isn't all the same thing over again. Only Phœnix, his funny blank face, makes my heart melt and go sad. But I believe he'd be cruel too. I saw it in his face when he didn't know I was looking. Anything though, rather than this deadness and this paint-Priapus business. Au revoir, mother dear! Keep on having a good time—

DEAR MOTHER: *I had your letter from Merriton: am so glad you arrived safe and sound in body and temper. There was such a funny letter from Lewis, too: I enclose it. What makes him take this extraordinary line? But I'm writing to tell him to take St. Mawr to London, and wait for me there. I have telegraphed Mrs. Squire to get the house ready for me. I shall go straight there.*

Things developed here as they were bound to. I just couldn't bear it. No sooner was Rico put in the automobile than a self-conscious importance came over him, like when the wounded hero is carried into the middle of the stage. Why so solemn, Rico dear? I asked him, trying to laugh him out of it. Not solemn, dear, only a feeling a little transient. I don't think he knew himself what he meant. Flora was on the steps as the car drew up, dressed in severe white. She only needed an apron, to become a nurse: or a veil, to become a bride. Between the two, she had an unbearable air of a woman in seduced circumstances, as the Times *said.*[46] *She ordered two menservants about in subdued, you would have said hushed, but competent tones. And then I saw there was a touch of the priestess about her as well: Cassandra preparing for her violation:* [47] *Iphigenia, with Rico for Orestes, on a stretcher:* [48] *he looking*

---

46. A joke attributed apocryphally to a London *Times* misprint ("in reduced circumstances").
47. Cassandra, daughter of Priam, king of Troy, was violated by Ajax at the fall of the city.
48. Iphigenia saved her brother Orestes from execution, and fled with him.

like Adonis,[49] *fully prepared to be an unconscionable time in dying. They had given him a lovely room, downstairs, with doors opening on to a little garden all of its own. I believe it was Flora's boudoir. I left nurse and the men to put him to bed. Flora was hovering anxiously in the passage outside.* Oh, what a marvellous room! Oh, how colourful, how beautiful! *came Rico's tones, the hero behind the scenes. I must say, it was like a harvest festival, with roses and gaillardias in the shadow, and cornflowers in the light, and a bowl of grapes, and nectarines among leaves.* I'm so anxious that he should be happy, *Flora said to me in the passage.* You know him best. Is there anything else I could do for him? *Me:* Why, if you went to the piano and sang, I'm sure he'd love it. Couldn't you sing: Oh, my love is like a rred, rred rrose! [50]—*You know how Rico imitates Scotch!*

Thank goodness I have a bedroom upstairs: nurse sleeps in a little antechamber to Rico's room. The Edwards are still here, the blond young man with some very futuristic plaster on his face. Awfully good of you to come! *he said to me, looking at me out of one eye, and holding my hand fervently.* How's that for cheek? *It's awfully good of Miss Manby to let me come, said I. He:* Ah, but Flora is always a sport, a topping good sport!

I don't know what's the matter, but it just all put me into a fiendish temper. I felt I couldn't sit there at luncheon with that bright, youthful company, and hear about their tennis and their polo and their hunting and have their flirtatiousness making me sick. So I asked for a tray in my room. Do as I might, I couldn't help being horrid.

Oh, and Rico! He really is too awful. Lying there in bed with every ear open, like Adonis waiting to be persuaded not to die. Seizing a hushed moment to take Flora's hand and press it to his lips, murmuring: How awfully good you are to me, dear Flora! *And Flora:* I'd be better if I knew how, Harry! *So cheerful with it all! No, it's too much. My sense of humour is leaving me: which means, I'm getting into too bad a temper to be able to ridicule it all. I suppose I feel in the minority. It's an awful thought, to think that most all the young people in the world are like this: so bright and cheerful, and* sporting, *and so brimming with* libido.[51] *How awful!*

I said to Rico: You're very comfortable here, aren't you? *He:* Comfortable! It's comparative heaven. *Me:* Would you mind if I went away? *A deadly pause. He is deadly afraid of being left alone with Flora. He feels safe so long as I am about, and he can take refuge in his marriage ties. He:* Where do you want to go, dear? *Me:* To mother. To London. Mother is planning to go to America, and she wants me to go. *Rico:*

---

49. Adonis was beloved of Venus, but a boar killed him while hunting. King Charles II is said to have remarked on his deathbed that he was an unconscionable time a-dying.
50. From the song "A Red, Red Rose" by Robert Burns.
51. Instinctual energy deriving, in Freud's psychoanalytic theory, from the Id. Lawrence had been reading Freud and attacking him in *Psychoanalysis and the Unconscious* (1921) and *Fantasia of the Unconscious* (1922). This is an early use of the word in nontechnical writing.

But you don't want to go t—he—e—re—e! *You know, mother, how Rico can put a venomous emphasis on a word, till it suggests pure poison. It nettled me.* I'm not sure, I said. Rico: Oh, but you can't stand that awful America. *Me:* I want to try again. *Rico:* But, Lou dear, it will be winter before you get there. And this is absolutely the wrong moment for me to go over there. I am only just making headway over here. When I am absolutely sure of a position in England, then we nip across the Atlantic and scoop in a few dollars, if you like. Just now, even when I am well, would be fatal. I've only just sketched in the outline of my success in London, and one ought to arrive in New York ready-made as a famous and important Artist. *Me:* But mother and I didn't think of going to New York. We thought we'd sail straight to New Orleans—if we could: or to Havana. And then go West to Arizona. *The poor boy looked at me in such distress.* But, Loulina darling, do you mean you want to leave me in the lurch for the winter season? You can't mean it. We're just getting on so splendidly, really!—*I was surprised at the depth of feeling in his voice: how tremendously his career as an artist—a popular artist—matters to him. I can never believe it. —You know, mother, you and I feel alike about daubing paint on canvas: every possible daub that can be daubed has already been done, so people ought to leave off. Rico is so shrewd. I always think he's got his tongue in his cheek, and I'm always staggered once more to find that he takes it absolutely seriously. His career! The Modern British Society of Painters: perhaps even the Royal Academy! Those people we see in London, and those portraits Rico does! He may even be a second Laslow,*[52] *or a thirteenth Orpen,*[53] *and die happy! Oh! mother! How can it really matter to* anybody!

But I was really rather upset, when I realized how his heart was fixed on his career, and that I might be spoiling everything for him. So I went away to think about it. And then I realized how unpopular you are, and how unpopular I shall be myself, in a little while. A sort of hatred for people has come over me. I hate their ways and their bunk, and I feel like kicking them in the face, as St. Mawr did that young man. Not that I should ever do it. And I don't think I should ever have made my final announcement to Rico, if he hadn't been such a beautiful pig in clover, here at Corrabach Hall. He has known the Manbys all his life; they and he are sections of one engine. He would be far happier with Flora: or I won't say happier, because there is something in him which rebels: but he would on the whole fit much better. I myself am at the end of my limit, and beyond it. I can't 'mix' any more, and I refuse to. I feel like a bit of eggshell in the mayonnaise: the only thing is to take it out, you can't beat it in. I know I shall cause a fiasco, even in Rico's career, if I stay. I shall go on being rude and hateful to people as I am at Corrabach, and Rico will lose all his nerve.

So I have told him. I said this evening, when no one was about: Rico

52. Sir Philip László (1869–1937), Hungarian-born British portrait painter.
53. Sir William Orpen (1878–1931), portrait painter, official war artist, and painter at the Peace Conference.

dear, listen to me seriously. I can't stand these people. If you ask me to endure another week of them, I shall either become ill or insult them, as mother does. And I don't want to do either. *Rico:* But, darling, isn't everybody perfect to you! *Me:* I tell you, I shall just make a break, like St. Mawr, if I don't get out. I simply can't stand people.—*The poor darling, his face goes so blank and anxious. He knows what I mean, because, except that they tickle his vanity all the time, he hates them as much as I do. But his vanity is the chief thing to him. He:* Lou darling, can't you wait till I get up, and we can go away to the Tyrol or some-where for a spell? *Me:* Won't you come with me to America, to the South-west? I believe it's marvellous country.—*I saw his face switch into hostility; quite vicious. He:* Are you so keen on spoiling everything for me? Is that what I married you for? Do you do it deliberately? *Me:* Everything is already spoilt for me. I tell you I can't stand people, your Floras and your Aspasias, and your forthcoming young Englishmen. After all, I am an American, like mother, and I've got to go back. *He:* Really! And am I to come along as part of the luggage, labelled cabin! *Me:* You do as you wish, Rico. *He:* I wish to God you did as you wished, Lou dear. I'm afraid you do as Mrs. Witt wishes. I've always heard that the holiest thing in the world was a mother. *Me:* No, dear, it's just that I can't stand people. *He (with a snarl):* And I suppose I'm lumped in as PEOPLE! *And when he'd said it, it was true. We neither of us said anything for a time. Then he said, calculating:* Very well, dear! You take a trip to the land of stars and stripes, and I'll stay here and go on with my work. And when you've seen enough of their stars and tasted enough of their stripes, you can come back and take your place again with me.—*We left it at that.*

You and I are supposed to have important business connected with our estates in Texas—it sounds so well—so we are making a hurried trip to the States, as they call them. I shall leave for London early next week—

Mrs. Witt read this long letter with satisfaction. She herself had one strange craving: to get back to America. It was not that she idealized her native country: she was a tartar of restlessness there, quite as much as in Europe. It was not that she expected to arrive at any blessed abiding-place. No, in America she would go on fuming and chafing the same. But at least she would be in America, in her own country. And that was what she wanted.

She picked up the sheet of poor paper, that had been folded in Lou's letter. It was the letter from Lewis, quite nicely written.

Lady Carrington, I write to tell you and Sir Henry that I think I had better quit your service, as it would be more comfortable all round. If you will write and tell me what you want me to do with St. Mawr, I will do whatever you tell me. With kind regards to Lady Carrington and Sir Henry, I remain, Your obedient servant, MORGAN LEWIS.

Mrs. Witt put the letter aside, and sat looking out of the window. She felt, strangely, as if already her soul had gone away from her actual surroundings.

She was there, in Oxfordshire, in the body, but her spirit had departed elsewhere. A listlessness was upon her. It was with an effort she roused herself, to write to her lawyer in London, to get her release from her English obligations. Then she wrote to the London hotel.

For the first time in her life she wished she had a maid, to do little things for her. All her life, she had had too much energy to endure anyone hanging round her, personally. Now she gave up. Her wrists seemed numb, as if the power in her were switched off.

When she went down, they said Lewis had asked to speak to her. She had hardly seen him since they had arrived at Merriton.

'I've had a letter from Lady Carrington, Mam. She says will I take St. Mawr to London and wait for her there. But she says I am to come to you, Mam, for definite orders.'

'Very well, Lewis. I shall be going to London in a few days' time. You arrange for St. Mawr to go up one day this week, and you will take him to the Mews. Come to me for anything you want. And don't talk of leaving my daughter. We want you to go with St. Mawr to America, with us and Phœnix.'

'And your horse, Mam?'

'I shall leave him here at Merriton. I shall give him to Miss Atherton.'

'Very good, Mam!'

DEAR DAUGHTER: *I shall be in my old quarters in Mayfair next Saturday, calling the same day at your house to see if everything is ready for you. Lewis has fixed up with the railway: he goes to town to-morrow. The reason of his letter was that I had asked him if he would care to marry me, and he turned me down with emphasis. But I will tell you about it. You and I are the scribe and the Pharisee; I never could write a letter, and you could never leave off—*

DEAREST MOTHER: *I smelt something rash, but I know it's no use saying: How could you? I only wonder, though, that you should think of marriage. You know, dear, I ache in every fibre to be left alone, from all that sort of thing. I feel all bruises, like one who has been assassinated. I do so understand why Jesus said: Noli me tangere.[54] Touch me not, I am not yet ascended unto the Father. Everything had hurt him so much, wearied him so beyond endurance, he felt he could not bear one little human touch on his body. I am like that. I can hardly bear even Elena to hand me a dress. As for a man—and marriage—ah, no! Noli me tangere, homo! I am not yet ascended unto the Father. Oh, leave me alone, leave me alone! That is all my cry to all the world.*

Curiously, I feel that Phœnix understands what I feel. He leaves me so understandingly alone, he almost gives me my sheath of aloneness: or at least, he protects me in my sheath. I am grateful for him.

Whereas Rico feels my aloneness as a sort of shame to himself. He wants at least a blinding pretence *of intimacy. Ah, intimacy! The thought of it fills me with aches, and the pretence of it exhausts me beyond myself.*

54. John 20:17; a quotation Lawrence was particularly prone to use, especially in his later years.

> *Yes, I long to go away to the West, to be away from the world like one dead and in another life, in a valley that life has not yet entered.*
>
> *Rico asked me: What are you doing with St. Mawr? When I said we were taking him with us, he said: Oh, the corpus delicti!* [55] *Whether that means anything I don't know. But he has grown sarcastic beyond my depth.*
>
> *I shall see you to-morrow—*

Lou arrived in town, at the dead end of August, with her maid and Phœnix. How wonderful it seemed to have London empty of all her set: her own little house to herself, with just the housekeeper and her own maid. The fact of being alone in those surroundings was so wonderful. It made the surroundings themselves seem all the more ghostly. Everything that had been actual to her was turning ghostly: even her little drawing-room was the ghost of a room, belonging to the dead people who had known it, or to all the dead generations that had brought such a room into being, evolved it out of their quaint domestic desires. And now, in herself, those desires were suddenly spent: gone out like a lamp that suddenly dies. And then she saw her pale, delicate room with its little green agate bowl and its two little porcelain birds and its soft, roundish chairs, turned into something ghostly, like a room set out in a museum. She felt like fastening little labels on the furniture: *Lady Louise Carrington Lounge Chair, Last used August, 1923.* Not for the benefit of posterity: but to remove her own self into another world, another realm of existence.

'My house, my house, my house, how can I ever have taken so much pains about it!' she kept saying to herself. It was like one of her old hats, suddenly discovered neatly put away in an old hatbox. And what a horror: an old 'fashionable' hat!

Lewis came to see her, and he sat there in one of her delicate mauve chairs, with his feet on a delicate old carpet from Turkestan, and she just wondered. He wore his leather gaiters and khaki breeches as usual, and a faded blue shirt. But his beard and hair were trimmed, he was tidy. There was a certain fineness of contour about him, a certain subtle gleam, which made him seem, apart from his rough boots, not at all gross, or coarse, in that setting of rather silky, Oriental furnishings. Rather he made the Asiatic, sensuous exquisiteness of her old rugs and her old white Chinese figures seem a weariness. Beauty! What was beauty, she asked herself? The Oriental exquisiteness seemed to her all like dead flowers whose hour had come, to be thrown away.

Lou could understand her mother's wanting, for a moment, to marry him. His detachedness and his acceptance of something in destiny which people cannot accept. Right in the middle of him he accepted something from destiny, that gave him a quality of eternity. He did not care about persons, people, even events. In his own odd way, he was an aristocrat, inaccessible in his aristocracy. But it was the aristocracy of the invisible powers, the greater influences, nothing to do with human society.

'You don't really want to leave St. Mawr, do you?' Lou asked him. 'You don't really want to quit, as you said?'

---

55. The material thing in respect of which a crime has been committed, whether a body or a stolen object; he means that they are removing the evidence of a crime.

He looked at her steadily, from his pale-grey eyes, without answering, not knowing what to say.

'Mother told me what she said to you.—But she doesn't mind, she says you are entirely within your rights. She has a real regard for you. But we mustn't let our regards run us into actions which are beyond our scope, must we? That makes everything unreal. But you will come with us to America with St. Mawr, won't you? We depend on you.'

'I don't want to be uncomfortable,' he said.

'Don't be,' she smiled. 'I myself hate unreal situations—I feel I can't stand them any more. And most marriages are unreal situations. But apart from anything exaggerated, you like being with mother and me, don't you?'

'Yes, I do. I like Mrs. Witt as well. But not—'

'I know. There won't be any more of that—'

'You see, Lady Carrington,' he said, with a little heat, 'I'm not by nature a marrying man. And I should feel I was selling myself.'

'Quite!—Why do you think you are not a marrying man, though?'

'Me! I don't feel myself after I've been with women.' He spoke in a low tone, looking down at his hands. 'I feel messed up. I'm better to keep to myself.—Because—' and here he looked up with a flare in his eyes—'women—they only want to make you give in to them, so that they feel almighty, and you feel small.'

'Don't you like feeling small?' Lou smiled. 'And don't you want to make them give in to you?'

'Not me,' he said. 'I don't want nothing. Nothing, I want.'

'Poor mother!' said Lou. 'She thinks if she feels moved by a man, it must result in marriage—or that kind of thing. Surely she makes a mistake. I think you and Phœnix and mother and I might live somewhere in a far-away wild place, and make a good life: so long as we didn't begin to mix up marriage, or love or that sort of thing, into it. It seems to me men and women have really hurt one another so much, nowadays, that they had better stay apart till they have learned to be gentle with one another again. Not all this forced passion and destructive philandering. Men and women should stay apart, till their hearts grow gentle towards one another again. Now, it's only each one fighting for his own—or her own—underneath the cover of tenderness.'

'*Dear!—darling!—Yes, my love!*' mocked Lewis, with a faint smile of amused contempt.

'Exactly. People always say *dearest!* when they hate each other most.'

Lewis nodded, looking at her with a sudden sombre gloom in his eyes. A queer bitterness showed on his mouth. But even then, he was so still and remote.

The housekeeper came and announced The Honourable Laura Ridley. This was like a blow in the face to Lou. She rose hurriedly—and Lewis rose, moving to the door.

'Don't go, please, Lewis,' said Lou—and then Laura Ridley appeared in the doorway. She was a woman a few years older than Lou, but she looked younger. She might have been a shy girl of twenty-two, with her fresh complexion, her hesitant manner, her round, startled brown eyes, her bobbed hair.

'Hello!' said the new-comer. 'Imagine your being back! I saw you in Paddington.'

Those sharp eyes would see everything.

'I thought everyone was out of town,' said Lou. 'This is Mr. Lewis.'

Laura gave him a little nod, then sat on the edge of her chair.

'No,' she said. 'I did go to Ireland to my people, but I came back. I prefer London when I can be more or less alone in it. I though I'd just run in for a moment, before you're gone again.—Scotland, isn't it?'

'No, mother and I are going to America.'

'America! Oh, I thought it was Scotland.'

'It was. But we have suddenly to go to America.'

'I see!—And what about Rico?'

'He is staying on in Shropshire. Didn't you hear of his accident?'

Lou told about it briefly.

'But how awful!' said Laura. 'But there! I knew it! I had a premonition when I saw that horse. We had a horse that killed a man. Then my father got rid of it. But ours was a mare, that one. Yours is a boy.'

'A full-grown man, I'm afraid.'

'Yes, of course, I remember.—But how awful! I suppose you won't ride in the Row. The awful people that ride there nowadays, anyhow! Oh, aren't they awful! Aren't people monstrous, really! My word, when I see the horses crossing Hyde Park corner, on a wet day, and coming down smash on those slippery stones, giving their riders a fractured skull!—No joke!'

She enquired details of Rico.

'Oh, I suppose I shall see him when he gets back,' she said. 'But I'm sorry you are going. I shall miss you, I'm afraid. Though you won't be staying long in America. No one stays there longer than they can help.'

'I think the winter through, at least,' said Lou.

'Oh, all the winter! So long? I'm sorry to hear *that*. You're one of the few, very few people one can talk *really* simply with. Extraordinary, isn't it, how few really simple people there are! And they get fewer and fewer. I stayed a fortnight with my people, and a week of that I was in bed. It was really horrible. They really try to take the life out of one, *really!* Just because one won't be as they are, and play their game. I simply refused, and came away.'

'But you can't cut yourself off altogether,' said Lou.

'No, I suppose not. One has to see somebody. Luckily one has a few artists for friends. They're the only real people, anyhow—' She glanced round inquisitively at Lewis, and said, with a slight, impertinent elvish smile on her virgin face:

'Are you an artist?'

'No, Mam!' he said. 'I'm a groom.'

'Oh, I see!' She looked him up and down.

'Lewis is St. Mawr's master,' said Lou.

'Oh, the horse! the terrible horse!' She paused a moment. Then again she turned to Lewis with that faint smile, slightly condescending, slightly impertinent, slightly flirtatious.

'Aren't you afraid of him?' she asked.

'No, Mam.'

'Aren't you *really!*—And can you always master him?'

'Mostly. He knows me.'

'Yes! I suppose that's it.'—She looked him up and down again, then turned away to Lou.

'What have you been painting lately?' said Lou. Laura was not a bad painter.

'Oh, hardly anything. I haven't been able to get on at all. This is one of my bad intervals.'

Here Lewis rose, and looked at Lou.

'All right,' she said. 'Come in after lunch, and we'll finish those arrangements.'

Laura gazed after the man, as he dived out of the room, as if her eyes were gimlets that could bore into his secret.

In the course of the conversation she said:

'What a curious little man that was!'

'Which?'

'The groom who was here just now. Very curious! Such peculiar eyes. I shouldn't wonder if he had psychic powers.'

'What sort of psychic powers?' said Lou.

'Could see things.—And hypnotic too. He might have hypnotic powers.'

'What makes you think so?'

'He gives me that sort of feeling. Very curious! Probably he hypnotizes the horse.—Are you leaving the horse here, by the way, in stable?'

'No, taking him to America.'

'Taking him to America! How extraordinary!'

'It's mother's idea. She thinks he might be valuable as a stock horse on a ranch. You know we still have interest in a ranch in Texas.'

'Oh, I see! Yes, probably he'd be very valuable, to improve the breed of the horses over there.—My father has some very lovely hunters. Isn't it disgraceful, he would never let me ride!'

'Why?'

'Because we girls weren't important, in his opinion.—So you're taking the horse to America! With the little man?'

'Yes, St. Mawr will hardly behave without him.'

'I see!—I see—ee—ee! Just you and Mrs. Witt and the little man. I'm sure you'll find he has psychic powers.'

'I'm afraid I'm not so good at finding things out,' said Lou.

'Aren't you? No, I suppose not. I am. I have a flair. I sort of smell things.— Then the horse is already here, is he? When do you think you'll sail?'

'Mother is finding a merchant-boat that will go to Galveston, Texas, and take us along with the horse. She knows people who will find the right thing. But it takes time.'

'What a much nicer way to travel than on one of those great liners! Oh, how awful they are! So vulgar! Floating palaces they call them! My word, the people inside the palaces!—Yes, I should say that would be a much pleasanter way of travelling: on a cargo-boat.'

Laura wanted to go down to the Mews to see St. Mawr. The two women went together.

St. Mawr stood in his box, bright and tense as usual.

'Yes!' said Laura Ridley, with a slight hiss. 'Yes! Isn't he beautiful! Such very perfect legs!'—She eyed him round with those gimlet, sharp eyes of hers.

'Almost a pity to let him go out of England. We need some of his perfect *bone,* I feel.—But his eye! Hasn't he got a look in it, my word!'

'I can never see that he looks wicked,' said Lou.

'Can't you!'—Laura had a slight hiss in her speech, a sort of aristocratic decision in her enunciation, that got on Lou's nerves.—'He looks wicked to me!'

'He's not *mean,*' said Lou. 'He'd never do anything mean to you.'

'Oh, mean! I dare say not. No! I'll grant him that, he gives fair warning. His eye says *Beware!*—But isn't he a beauty, *isn't* he!' Lou could feel the peculiar reverence for St. Mawr's breeding, his show qualities. Herself, all she cared about was the horse himself, his real nature. 'Isn't it extraordinary,' Laura continued, 'that you never get a *really,* perfectly satisfactory animal! There's always something wrong. And in men too. Isn't it curious? there's always something—something wrong—or something missing. Why is it?'

'I don't know,' said Lou. She felt unable to cope with any more. And she was glad when Laura left her.

The days passed slowly, quietly, London almost empty of Lou's acquaintances. Mrs. Witt was busy getting all sorts of papers and permits: such a fuss! The battle light was still in her eye. But about her nose was a dusky, pinched look that made Lou wonder.

Both women wanted to be gone: they felt they had already flown in spirit, and it was weary having the body left behind.

At last all was ready: they only awaited the telegram to say when their cargo-boat would sail. Trunks stood there packed, like great stones locked forever. The Westminster house seemed already a shell. Rico wrote and telegraphed, tenderly, but there was a sense of relentless effort in it all, rather than of any real tenderness. He had taken his position.

Then the telegram came, the boat was ready to sail.

'There now!' said Mrs. Witt, as if it had been a sentence of death.

'Why do you look like that, mother?'

'I feel I haven't an ounce of energy left in my body.'

'But how queer, for you, mother. Do you think you are ill?'

'No, Louise. I just feel that way: as if I hadn't an ounce of energy left in my body.'

'You'll feel yourself again, once you are away.'

'Maybe I shall.'

After all, it was only a matter of telephoning. The hotel and the railway porters and taxi-men would do the rest.

It was a grey, cloudy day, cold even. Mother and daughter sat in a cold first-class carriage and watched the little Hampshire country-side go past: little, old, unreal it seemed to them both, and passing away like a dream whose edges only are in consciousness. Autumn! Was this autumn? Were these trees, fields, villages? It seemed but the dim, dissolving edges of a dream, without inward substance.

At Southampton it was raining: and just a chaos, till they stepped on to a clean boat, and were received by a clean young captain, quite sympathetic, and quite a gentleman. Mrs. Witt, however, hardly looked at him, but went down to her cabin and lay down in her bunk.

There, lying concealed, she felt the engines start, she knew the voyage had begun. But she lay still. She saw the clouds and the rain, and refused to be disturbed.

Lou had lunch with the young captain, and she felt she ought to be flirty. The young man was so polite and attentive. And she wished so much she were alone.

Afterwards, she sat on deck and saw the Isle of Wight pass shadowy, in a misty rain. She didn't know it was the Isle of Wight. To her, it was just the lowest bit of the British Isles. She saw it fading away: and with it, her life, going like a clot of shadow in a mist of nothingness. She had no feelings about it, none: neither about Rico, nor her London house, nor anything. All passing in a grey curtain of rainy drizzle, like a death, and she with not a feeling left.

They entered the Channel, and felt the slow heave of the sea. And soon the clouds broke in a little wind. The sky began to clear. By mid-afternoon it was blue summer, on the blue, running waters of the Channel. And soon, the ship steering for Santander, there was the coast of France, the rock twinkling like some magic world.

The magic world! And back of it, that post-war Paris which Lou knew only too well, and which depressed her so thoroughly. Or that post-war Monte Carlo, the Riviera still more depressing even than Paris. No, one must not land, even on magic coasts. Else you found yourself in a railway station and a 'centre of civilization' in five minutes.

Mrs. Witt hated the sea, and stayed, as a rule, practically the whole time of the crossing, in her bunk. There she was now, silent, shut up like a steel trap, as in her tomb. She did not even read. Just lay and stared at the passing sky. And the only thing to do was to leave her alone.

Lewis and Phœnix hung on the rail, and watched everything. Or they went down to see St. Mawr. Or they stood talking in the doorway of the wireless operator's cabin. Lou begged the captain to give them jobs to do.

The queer, transitory, unreal feeling, as the ship crossed the great, heavy Atlantic. It was rather bad weather. And Lou felt, as she had felt before, that this grey, wolf-like, cold-blooded Ocean hated men and their ships and their smoky passage. Heavy grey waves, a low-sagging sky: rain: yellow, weird evenings with snatches of sun: so it went on. Till they got way South, into the westward-running stream. Then they began to get blue weather and blue water.

To go South! Always to go South, away from the arctic horror as far as possible! That was Lou's instinct. To go out of the clutch of greyness and low skies, of sweeping rain, and of slow, blanketing snow. Never again to see the mud and rain and snow of a northern winter, nor to feel the idealistic, Christianized tension of the now irreligious North.

As they neared Havana, and the water sparkled at night with phosphorus, and the flying-fishes came like drops of bright water, sailing out of the massive-slippery waves, Mrs. Witt emerged once more. She still had that shut-up, deathly look on her face. But she prowled round the deck, and manifested at least a little interest in affairs not her own. Here at sea, she hardly remembered the existence of St. Mawr or Lewis or Phœnix. She was not very deeply aware even of Lou's existence.—But, of course, it would all come back, once they were on land.

They sailed in hot sunshine out of a blue, blue sea, past the castle into the harbour at Havana. There was a lot of shipping: and this was already America. Mrs. Witt had herself and Lou put ashore immediately. They took a motor-car and drove at once to the great boulevard that is the centre of Havana. Here they saw a long rank of motor-cars, all drawn up ready to take a couple of hundred American tourists for one more tour. There were the tourists, all with badges in their coats, lest they should get lost.

'They get so drunk by night,' said the driver in Spanish, 'that the policemen find them lying in the road—turn them over, see the badge—and, hup!—carry them to their hotel.' He grinned sardonically.

Lou and her mother lunched at the Hotel d'Angleterre, and Mrs. Witt watched transfixed while a couple of her countrymen, a stout successful man and his wife, lunched abroad. They had cocktails—then lobster—and a bottle of hock—then a bottle of champagne—then a half-bottle of port.—And Mrs. Witt rose in haste as the liqueurs came. For that successful man and his wife had gone on imbibing with a sort of fixed and deliberate will, apparently tasting nothing, but saying to themselves: Now we're drinking Rhine wine! Now we're drinking 1912 champagne. Yah, Prohibition! Thou canst not put it over me.—Their complexions became more and more lurid. Mrs. Witt fled, fearing a Havana debacle. But she said nothing.

In the afternoon, they motored into the country, to see the great brewery gardens, the new villa suburb, and through the lanes past the old, decaying plantations with palm trees. In one lane they met the fifty motor-cars with the two hundred tourists all with badges on their chests and self-satisfaction on their faces. Mrs. Witt watched in grim silence.

'Plus ça change, plus c'est la même chose,' said Lou, with a wicked little smile. 'On n'est pas mieux ici,[56] mother.'

'I know it,' said Mrs. Witt.

The hotels by the sea were all shut up: it was not yet the 'season.' Not till November. And then!—Why, then Havana would be an American city, in full leaf of green dollar bills. The green leaf of American prosperity shedding itself recklessly, from every roaming sprig of a tourist, over this city of sunshine and alcohol. Green leaves unfolded in Pittsburgh and Chicago, showering in winter downfall in Havana.

Mother and daughter drank tea in a corner of the Hotel d'Angleterre once more, and returned to the ferry.

The Gulf of Mexico was blue and rippling, with the phantom of islands on the south. Great porpoises rolled and leaped, running in front of the ship in the clear water, diving, travelling in perfect motion, straight, with the tip of the ship touching the tip of their tails, then rolling over, corkscrewing, and showing their bellies as they went. Marvellous! The marvellous beauty and fascination of natural wild things! The horror of man's unnatural life, his heaped-up civilization!

The flying-fishes burst out of the sea in clouds of silvery, transparent motion. Blue above and below, the Gulf seemed a silent, empty, timeless place where

56. "The more it changes the more it stays the same"; "things are no better here."

man did not really reach. And Lou was again fascinated by the glamour of the universe.

But bump! She and her mother were in a first-class hotel again, calling down the telephone for the bell-boy and ice-water. And soon they were in a Pullman, off towards San Antonio.

It was America, it was Texas. They were at their ranch, on the great level of yellow autumn, with the vast sky above. And after all, from the hot wide sky, and the hot, wide, red earth, there *did* come something new, something not used up. Lou *did* feel exhilarated.

The Texans were there, tall blond people, ingenuously cheerful, ingenuously, childishly intimate, as if the fact that you had never seen them before was as nothing compared to the fact that you'd all been living in one room together all your lives, so that nothing was hidden from either of you. The one room being the mere shanty of the world in which we all live. Strange, uninspired cheerfulness, filling, as it were, the blank of complete incomprehension.

And off they set in their motor-cars, chiefly high-legged Fords, rattling away down the red trails between yellow sunflowers or sere grass or dry cotton, away, away into great distances, cheerfully raising the dust of haste. It left Lou in a sort of blank amazement. But it left her amused, not depressed. The old screws of emotion and intimacy that had been screwed down so tightly upon her fell out of their holes, here. The Texan intimacy weighed no more on her than a postage stamp, even if, for the moment, it stuck as close. And there was a certain underneath recklessness, even a stoicism, in all the apparently childish people, which left one free. They might appear childish: but they stoically depended on themselves alone, in reality. Not as in England, where every man waited to pour the burden of himself upon you.

St. Mawr arrived safely, a bit bewildered. The Texans eyed him closely, struck silent, as ever, by anything pure-bred and beautiful. He was somehow too beautiful, too perfected, in this great open country. The long-legged Texan horses, with their elaborate saddles, seemed somehow more natural.

Even St. Mawr felt himself strange, as it were naked and singled out, in this rough place. Like a jewel among stones, a pearl before swine, maybe. But the swine were no fools. They knew a pearl from a grain of maize, and a grain of maize from a pearl. And they knew what they wanted. When it was pearls, it was pearls; though chiefly it was maize. Which shows good sense. They could see St. Mawr's points. Only he needn't draw the point too fine, or it would just not pierce the tough skin of this country.

The ranch-man mounted him—just threw a soft skin over his back, jumped on, and away down the red trail, raising the dust among the tall wild yellow of sunflowers, in the hot wild sun. Then back again in a fume, and the man slipped off.

'He's got the stuff in him, he sure has,' said the man.

And the horse seemed pleased with this rough handling. Lewis looked on in wonder, and a little envy.

Lou and her mother stayed a fortnight on the ranch. It was all so queer: so crude, so rough, so easy, so artificially civilized, and so meaningless. Lou could not get over the feeling that it all meant nothing. There were no roots of reality at all. No consciousness below the surface, no meaning in anything save the obvious, the blatantly obvious. It was like life enacted in a mirror. Visually, it was wildly vital. But there was nothing behind it. Or like a cinematograph: flat shapes, exactly like men, but without any substance of reality, rapidly rattling away with talk, emotions, activity, all in the flat, nothing behind it. No deeper consciousness at all.—So it seemed to her.

One moved from dream to dream, from phantasm to phantasm.

But at least this Texan life, if it had no bowels, no vitals, at least it could not prey on one's own vitals. It was this much better than Europe.

Lewis was silent, and rather piqued. St. Mawr had already made advances to the boss' long-legged, arched-necked, glossy-maned Texan mare. And the boss was pleased.

What a world!

Mrs. Witt eyed it all shrewdly. But she failed to participate. Lou was a bit scared at the emptiness of it all, and the queer, phantasmal self-consciousness. Cowboys just as self-conscious as Rico, far more sentimental, inwardly vague and unreal. Cowboys that went after their cows in black Ford motor-cars: and who self-consciously saw Lady Carrington falling to them, as elegant young ladies from the East fall to the noble cowboy of the films, or in Zane Grey. It was all film-psychology.

And at the same time, these boys led a hard, hard life, often dangerous and gruesome. Nevertheless, inwardly they were self-conscious film-heroes. The boss himself, a man over forty, long and lean and with a great deal of stringy energy, showed off before her in a strong silent manner, existing for the time being purely in his imagination of the sort of picture he made to her, the sort of impression he made on her.

So they all were, coloured up like a Zane Grey book-jacket, all of them living in the mirror. The kind of picture they made to somebody else.

And at the same time, with energy, courage, and a stoical grit getting their work done, and putting through what they had to put through.

It left Lou blank with wonder. And in the face of this strange, cheerful living in the mirror—a rather cheap mirror at that—England began to seem real to her again.

Then she had to remember herself back in England. And no, O God, England was not real either, except poisonously.

What was real? What under heaven was real?

Her mother had gone dumb and, as it were, out of range. Phœnix was a bit assured and bouncy, back more or less in his own conditions. Lewis was a bit impressed by the emptiness of everything, the *lack* of concentration. And St. Mawr followed at the heels of the boss' long-legged black Texan mare, almost slavishly.

What, in heaven's name, was one to make of it all?

Soon, she could not stand this sort of living in a film-setting, with the mechanical energy of 'making good,' that is, making money, to keep the show going. The mystic duty to 'make good,' meaning to make the ranch pay a laudable interest on the 'owners'' investment. Lou herself being one of the owners. And the interest that came to her, from her father's will, being the money she spent to buy St. Mawr and to fit up that house in Westminster. Then also the mystic duty to 'feel good.' Everybody had to *feel good, fine!* 'How are you this morning, Mr. Latham?'—'*Fine!* Eh! Don't you feel good out here, eh, Lady Carrington?' —'*Fine!*'—Lou pronounced it with the same ringing conviction. It was Coué [57] all the time!

'Shall we stay here long, mother?' she asked.

'Not a day longer than you want to, Louise. I stay entirely for your sake.'

'Then let us go, mother.'

They left St. Mawr and Lewis. But Phœnix wanted to come along. So they motored to San Antonio, got into the Pullman, and travelled as far as El Paso. Then they changed to go north. Santa Fe would be at least 'easy.' And Mrs. Witt had acquaintances there.

They found the fiesta over in Santa Fe: Indians, Mexicans, artists had finished their great effort to amuse and attract the tourists. *Welcome, Mr. Tourist,* said a great board on one side of the high road. And on the other side, a little nearer to town: *Thank You, Mr. Tourist.*

'*Plus ça change—*' Lou began.

'*Ca ne change jamais* [58]—except for the worse!' said Mrs. Witt, like a pistol going off. And Lou held her peace, after she had sighed to herself, and said in her own mind: '*Welcome Also Mrs. and Miss Tourist!*'

There was no getting a word out of Mrs. Witt, these days. Whereas Phœnix was becoming almost loquacious.

They stayed awhile in Sante Fe, in the clean, comfortable, 'homely' hotel, where 'every room had its bath': a spotless white bath, with very hot water night and day. The tourists and commercial travellers sat in the big hall down below, everybody living in the mirror! And, of course, they knew Lady Carrington down to her shoe-soles. And they all expected her to know them down to their shoe-soles. For the only object of the mirror is to reflect images.

For two days mother and daughter ate in the salad-bowl intimacy of the dining-room. Then Mrs. Witt struck, and telephoned down, every meal-time, for her meal in her room. She got to staying in bed later and later, as on the ship. Lou became uneasy. This was worse than Europe.

Phœnix was still there, as a sort of half-friend, half-servant retainer. He was perfectly happy, roving round among the Mexicans and Indians, talking Spanish all day, and telling about England and his two mistresses, rolling the ball of his own importance.

'I'm afraid we've got Phœnix for life,' said Lou.

'Not unless we wish,' said Mrs. Witt indifferently. And she picked up a novel which she didn't want to read, but which she was going to read.

'What shall we do next, mother?' Lou asked.

'As far as I am concerned, there is no next,' said Mrs. Witt.

'Come, mother! Let's go back to Italy or somewhere, if it's as bad as that.'

'Never again, Louise, shall I cross that water. I have come home to die.'

'I don't see much home about it—the Gonzales Hotel in Santa Fe.'

'Indeed not! But as good as anywhere else, to die in.'

---

57. Emile Coué (1857–1926), famous for his "autosuggestion"—the patient recites "Every day and in every way I'm getting better and better."
58. "It never changes."

'Oh, mother, don't be silly! Shall we look for somewhere where we can be by ourselves?'

'I leave it to you, Louise. I have made my last decision.'

'What is that, mother?'

'Never, never to make another decision.'

'Not even to decide to die?'

'No, not even that.'

'Or *not* to die?'

'Not that either.'

Mrs. Witt shut up like a trap. She refused to rise from her bed that day.

Lou went to consult Phœnix. The result was, the two set out to look at a little ranch that was for sale.

It was autumn, and the loveliest time in the South-west, where there is no spring, snow blowing into the hot lap of summer; and no real summer, hail falling in thick ice, from the thunderstorms: and even no very definite winter, hot sun melting the snow and giving an impression of spring at any time. But autumn there is, when the winds of the desert are almost still, and the mountains fume no clouds. But morning comes cold and delicate, upon the wild sunflowers and the puffing, yellow-flowered greasewood.[59] For the desert blooms in autumn. In spring it is grey ash all the time, and only the strong breath of the summer sun, and the heavy splashing of thunder-rain, succeed at last, by September, in blowing it into soft, puffy yellow fire.

It was such a delicate morning when Lou drove out with Phœnix towards the mountains, to look at this ranch that a Mexican wanted to sell. For the brief moment the high mountains had lost their snow: it would be back again in a fortnight: and stood dim and delicate with autumn haze. The desert stretched away pale, as pale as the sky, but silvery and sere, with hummock-mounds of shadow, and long wings of shadow, like the reflection of some great bird. The same eagle-shadows came like rude paintings of the outstretched bird, upon the mountains, where the aspens were turning yellow. For the moment, the brief moment, the great desert-and-mountain landscape had lost its certain cruelty, and looked tender, dreamy. And many, many birds were flickering around.

Lou and Phœnix bumped and hesitated over a long trail: then wound down into a deep canyon: and then the car began to climb, climb, climb, in steep rushes, and in long heart-breaking, uneven pulls. The road was bad, and driving was no joke. But it was the sort of road Phœnix was used to. He sat impassive and watchful, and kept on, till his engine boiled. He was *himself* in this country: impassive, detached, self-satisfied, and silently assertive. Guarding himself at every moment, but on his guard, sure of himself. Seeing no difference at all between Lou or Mrs. Witt and himself, except that they had money and he had none, while he had a native importance which they lacked. He depended on them for money, they on him for the power to live out here in the West. Intimately, he was as good as they. Money was their only advantage.

As Lou sat beside him in the front seat of the car, where it bumped less than behind, she felt this. She felt a peculiar tough-necked arrogance in him, as if he

59. Low shrub common in the West of the United States.

were asserting himself to put something over her. He wanted her to allow him to make advances to her, to allow him to suggest that he should be her lover. And then, finally, she would marry him, and he would be on the same footing as she and her mother.

In return, he would look after her, and give her his support and countenance, as a man, and stand between her and the world. In this sense, he would be faithful to her, and loyal. But as far as other women went, Mexican women or Indian women: why, that was none of her business. His marrying her would be a pact between two aliens, on behalf of one another, and he would keep his part of it all right. But himself, as a private man and a predative alien-blooded male, this had nothing to do with her. It didn't enter into her scope and count. She was one of these nervous white women with lots of money. She was very nice too. But as a *squaw*—as a real woman in a shawl whom a man went after for the pleasure of the night—why, she hardly counted. One of these white women who talk clever and know things like a man. She could hardly expect a half-savage male to acknowledge her as his female counterpart.—No! She had the bucks! And she had all the paraphernalia of the white man's civilization, which a savage can play with and so escape his own hollow boredom. But his own real female counterpart?—Phœnix would just have shrugged his shoulders, and thought the question not worth answering. How could there be any answer in *her* to the phallic male in him? Couldn't! Yet it would flatter his vanity and his self-esteem immensely, to possess her. That would be possessing the very clue to the white man's overwhelming world. And if she would let him possess her, he would be absolutely loyal to her, as far as affairs and appearances went. Only, the aboriginal phallic male in him simply couldn't recognize her as a woman at all. In this respect, she didn't exist. It needed the shawled Indian or Mexican women, with their squeaky, plaintive voices, their shuffling, watery humility, and the dark glances of their big, knowing eyes. When an Indian woman looked at him from under her black fringe, with dark, half-secretive suggestion in her big eyes: and when she stood before him hugged in her shawl, in such apparently complete quiescent humility: and when she spoke to him in her mousy squeak of a high, plaintive voice, as if it were difficult for her female bashfulness even to emit so much sound: and when she shuffled away with her legs wide apart, because of her wide-topped, white, high buckskin boots with tiny white feet, and her dark-knotted hair so full of hard, yet subtle lure: and when he remembered the almost watery softness of the Indian woman's dark, warm flesh: then he was a male, an old, secretive, rat-like male. But before Lou's straightforwardness and utter sexual incompetence, he just stood in contempt. And to him, even a French *cocotte* was utterly devoid of the right sort of sex. She couldn't really move him. She couldn't satisfy the furtiveness in him. He needed this plaintive, squeaky, dark-fringed Indian quality. Something furtive and soft and rat-like, really to rouse him.

Nevertheless he was ready to trade his sex, which, in his opinion, every white woman was secretly pining for, for the white woman's money and social privileges. In the daytime, all the thrill and excitement of the white man's motor-cars and moving pictures and ice-cream sodas and so forth. In the night, the soft, watery-soft warmth of an Indian or half-Indian woman. This was Phœnix's idea of life for himself.

Meanwhile, if a white woman gave him the privileges of the white man's world, he would do his duty by her as far as all that went.

Lou, sitting very, very still beside him as he drove the car: he was not a very good driver, not quick and marvellous as some white men are, particularly some French chauffeurs she had known, but usually a little behindhand in his movements: she knew more or less all that he felt. More or less she divined as a woman does. Even from a certain rather assured stupidity of his shoulders, and a certain rather stupid assertiveness of his knees, she knew him.

But she did not judge him too harshly. Somewhere deep, deep in herself she knew she too was at fault. And this made her sometimes inclined to humble herself, as a woman, before the furtive assertiveness of this underground, 'knowing' savage. He was so different from Rico.

Yet, after all, *was* he? In his rootlessness, his drifting, his real meaninglessness, was he different from Rico? And his childish, spellbound absorption in the motor-car, or in the moving pictures, or in an ice-cream soda—was it very different from Rico? Anyhow, was it really any better? Pleasanter, perhaps, to a woman, because of the childishness of it.

The same with his opinion of himself as a sexual male! So childish, really, it was almost thrilling to a woman. But then, so stupid also, with that furtive lurking in holes and imagining it could not be detected. He imagined he kept himself dark, in his sexual rat-holes. He imagined he was not detected!

No, no, Lou was not such a fool as she looked, in his eyes anyhow. She knew what she wanted. She wanted relief from the nervous tension and irritation of her life, she wanted to escape from the friction [60] which is the whole stimulus in modern social life. She wanted to be still: only that, to be very, very still, and recover her own soul.

When Phœnix presumed she was looking for some secretly sexual male such as himself, he was ridiculously mistaken. Even the illusion of the beautiful St. Mawr was gone. And Phœnix, roaming round like a sexual rat in promiscuous back yards!—*Merci, mon cher!* For that was all he was: a sexual rat in the great barn-yard of man's habitat, looking for female rats!

Merci, mon cher! You are had.

Nevertheless, in his very mistakenness, he was a relief to her. His mistake was amusing rather than impressive. And the fact that one-half of his intelligence was a complete dark blank, that too was a relief.

Strictly, and perhaps in the best sense, he was a servant. His very unconsciousness and his very limitation served as a shelter, as one shelters within the limitations of four walls. The very decided limits to his intelligence were a shelter to her. They made her feel safe.

But that feeling of safety did not deceive her. It was the feeling one derived from having a *true* servant attached to one, a man whose psychic limitations left him incapable of anything but service, and whose strong flow of natural life, at the same time, made him need to serve.

And Lou, sitting there so very still and frail, yet self-contained, had not lived for nothing. She no longer wanted to fool herself. She had no desire at all to fool herself into thinking that a Phœnix might be a husband and a mate. No desire

60. Another key-word of Lawrence's, used of bad, mechanical sex, and so on.

that way at all. His obtuseness was a servant's obtuseness. She was grateful to him for serving, and she paid him a wage. Moreover, she provided him with something to do, to occupy his life. In a sense, she gave him his life, and rescued him from his own boredom. It was a balance.

He did not know what she was thinking. There was a certain physical sympathy between them. His obtuseness made him think it was also a sexual sympathy.

'It's a nice trip, you and me,' he said suddenly, turning and looking her in the eyes with an excited look, and ending on a foolish little laugh.

She realized that she should have sat in the back seat.

'But it's a bad road,' she said. 'Hadn't you better stop and put the sides of the hood up? your engine is boiling.'

He looked away with a quick switch of interest to the red thermometer in front of his machine.

'She's boiling,' he said, stopping, and getting out with a quick alacrity to go to look at the engine.

Lou got out also, and went to the back seat, shutting the door decisively.

'I think I'll ride at the back,' she said; 'it gets so frightfully hot in front, when the engine heats up.—Do you think she needs some water? Have you got some in the canteen?'

'She's full,' he said, peering into the steaming valve.

'You can run a bit out, if you think there's any need. I wonder if it's much further!'

'*Quién sabe?*' [61] said he, slightly impertinent.

She relapsed in her own stillness. She realized how careful, how very careful she must be of relaxing into sympathy, and reposing, as it were, on Phœnix. He would read it as a sexual appeal. Perhaps he couldn't help it. She had only herself to blame. He was obtuse, as a man and a savage. He had only one interpretation, sex, for any woman's approach to him.

And she knew, with the last clear knowledge of weary disillusion, that she did not want to be mixed up in Phœnix's sexual promiscuities. The very thought was an insult to her. The crude, clumsy servant-male: no, no, not that. He was a good fellow, a very good fellow, as far as he went. But he fell far short of physical intimacy.

'No, no,' she said to herself, 'I was wrong to ride in the front seat with him. I must sit alone, just alone. Because sex, mere sex, is repellent to me. I will never prostitute myself again. Unless something touches my very spirit, the very quick of me, I will stay alone, just alone. Alone, and give myself only to the unseen presences, serve only the other, unseen presences.'

She understood now the meaning of the Vestal Virgins, the Virgins of the holy fire in the old temples. They were symbolic of herself, of woman weary of the embrace of incompetent men, weary, weary, weary of all that, turning to the unseen gods, the unseen spirits, the hidden fire, and devoting herself to that, and that alone. Receiving thence her pacification and her fulfilment.

Not these little, incompetent, childish, self-opionated men! Not these to touch her. She watched Phœnix's rather stupid shoulders, as he drove the car on be-

61. "Who knows?"

tween the piñon trees and the cedars of the narrow mesa ridge, to the mountain foot. He was a good fellow. But let him run among women of his own sort. Something was beyond him. And this something must remain beyond him, never allow itself to come within his reach. Otherwise he would paw it and mess it up, and be as miserable as a child that has broken its father's watch.

No, no! She had loved an American, and lived with him for a fortnight. She had had a long, intimate friendship with an Italian. Perhaps it was love on his part. And she had yielded to him. Then her love and marriage to Rico.

And what of it all? Nothing. It was almost nothing. It was as if only the outside of herself, her top layers, were human. This inveigled her into intimacies. As soon as the inimacy penetrated, or attempted to penetrate, inside her, it was a disaster. Just a humiliation and a breaking down.

Within these outer layers of herself lay the successive inner sanctuaries of herself. And these were inviolable. She accepted it.

'I am not a marrying woman,' she said to herself. 'I am not a lover nor a mistress nor a wife. It is no good. Love can't really come into me from the outside, and I can never, never mate with any man, since the mystic new man will never come to me. No, no, let me know myself and my rôle. I am one of the eternal Virgins, serving the eternal fire. My dealings with men have only broken my stillness and messed up my doorways. It has been my own fault. I ought to stay virgin, and still, very, very still, and serve the most perfect service. I want my temple and my loneliness and my Apollo mystery of the inner fire. And with men, only the delicate, subtler, more remote relations. No coming near. A coming near only breaks the delicate veils, and broken veils, like broken flowers, only lead to rottenness.'

She felt a great peace inside herself as she made this realization. And a thankfulness. Because, after all, it seemed to her that the hidden fire was alive and burning in this sky, over the desert, in the mountains. She felt a certain latent holiness in the very atmosphere, a young spring-fire of latent holiness, such as she had never felt in Europe, or in the East. 'For me,' she said, as she looked away at the mountains in shadow and the pale-warm desert beneath, with wings of shadow upon it: 'For me, this place is sacred. It is blessed.'

But as she watched Phœnix: as she remembered the motor-cars and tourists, and the rather dreary Mexicans of Santa Fe, and the lurking, invidious Indians, with something of a rat-like secretiveness and defeatedness in their bearing, she realized that the latent fire of the vast landscape struggled under a great weight of dirt-like inertia. She had to mind the dirt, most carefully and vividly avoid it and keep it away from her, here in this place that at least seemed sacred to her.

The motor-car climbed up, past the tall pine trees, to the foot of the mountains, and came at last to a wire gate, where nothing was to be expected. Phœnix opened the gate, and they drove on, through more trees, into a clearing where dried-up bean-plants were yellow.

'This man got no water for his beans,' said Phœnix. 'Not got much beans this year.'

They climbed slowly up the incline, through more pine trees, and out into another clearing, where a couple of horses were grazing. And there they saw the ranch itself, little low cabins with patched roofs, under a few pine trees, and facing the long twelve-acre clearing, or field, where the Michaelmas daisies were purple mist, and spangled with clumps of yellow flowers.

'Not got no alfalfa here neither!' said Phœnix, as the car waded past the flowers. 'Must be a dry place up here. Got no water, sure they haven't.'

Yet it was the place Lou wanted. In an instant, her heart sprang to it. The instant the car stopped, and she saw the two cabins inside the rickety fence, the rather broken corral beyond, and, behind all, tall, blue balsam pines, the round hills, the solid uprise of the mountain flank: and, getting down, she looked across the purple and gold of the clearing, downwards at the ring of pine trees standing so still, so crude and untamable, the motionless desert beyond the bristles of the pine crests, a thousand feet below: and, beyond the desert, blue mountains, and far, far-off blue mountains in Arizona: '*This is the place*,' she said to herself.

This little tumble-down ranch, only a homestead of a hundred and sixty acres, was, as it were, man's last effort towards the wild heart of the Rockies, at this point. Sixty years before, a restless schoolmaster had wandered out from the East, looking for gold among the mountains. He found a very little, then no more. But the mountains had got hold of him, he could not go back.

There was a little trickling spring of pure water, a thread of treasure perhaps better than gold. So the schoolmaster took up a homestead on the lot where this little spring arose. He struggled, and got himself his log cabin erected, his fence put up, sloping at the mountain-side through the pine trees and dropping into the hollows where the ghost-white mariposa lilies stood leafless and naked in flower, in spring, on tall invisible stems. He made the long clearing for alfalfa.

And fell so into debt, that he had to trade his homestead away, to clear his debt. Then he made a tiny living teaching the children of the few American prospectors who had squatted in the valleys, beside the Mexicans.

The trader who got the ranch tackled it with a will. He built another log cabin, and a big corral, and brought water from the canyon two miles and more across the mountain-slope, in a little runnel ditch, and more water, piped a mile or more down the little canyon immediately above the cabins. He got a flow of water for his houses: for, being a true American, he felt he could not *really* say he had conquered his environment till he had got running water, taps, and wash-hand basins inside his house.

Taps, running water, and wash-hand basins he accomplished. And, un-daunted through the years, he prepared the basin for a fountain in the little fenced-in enclosure, and he built a little bath-house. After a number of years, he sent up the enamelled bath-tub to be put in the little log bath-house on the little wild ranch hung right against the savage Rockies, above the desert.

But here the mountains finished him. He was a trader down below, in the Mexican village. This little ranch was, as it were, his hobby, his ideal. He and his New England wife spent their summers there: and turned on the taps in the cabins and turned them off again, and felt really that civilization had con-quered.

All this plumbing from the savage ravines of the canyons—one of them name-less to this day—cost, however, money. In fact, the ranch cost a great deal of money. But it was all to be got back. The big clearing was to be irrigated for alfalfa, the little clearing for beans, and the third clearing, under the corral, for potatoes. All these things the trader could trade to the Mexicans, very advantageously.

And, moreover, since somebody had started a praise of the famous goat's cheese made by Mexican peasants in New Mexico, goats there should be.

Goats there were: five hundred of them, eventually. And they fed chiefly in the wild mountain hollows, the no-man's-land. The Mexicans call them firemouths, because everything they nibble dies. Not because of their flaming mouths, really, but because they nibble a live plant down, down to the quick, till it can put forth no more.

So, the energetic trader, in the course of five or six years, had got the ranch ready. The long three-roomed cabin was for him and his New England wife. In the two-roomed cabin lived the Mexican family who really had charge of the ranch. For the trader was mostly fixed to his store, seventeen miles away, down in the Mexican village.

The ranch lay over eight thousand feet up, the snows of winter came deep, and the white goats, looking dirty yellow, swam in snow with their poor curved horns poking out like dead sticks. But the corral had a long, cosy, shut-in goatshed all down one side, and into this crowded the five hundred, their acrid goatsmell rising like hot acid over the snow. And the thin, pock-marked Mexican threw them alfalfa out of the log barn. Until the hot sun sank the snow again, and froze the surface, when patter-patter went the two thousand little goathoofs, over the silver-frozen snow, up at the mountain. Nibble, nibble, nibble, the fire-mouths, at every tender twig. And the goat-bell climbed, and the baaing came from among the dense and shaggy pine trees. And sometimes, in a soft drift under the trees, a goat, or several goats, went through, into the white depths, and some were lost thus, to reappear dead and frozen at the thaw.

By evening, they were driven down again, like a dirty yellowish-white stream carrying dark sticks on its yeasty surface, tripping and bleating over the frozen snow, past the bustling dark-green pine trees, down to the trampled mess of the corral. And everywhere, everywhere over the snow, yellow stains and dark pills of goat-droppings melting into the surface crystal. On still, glittering nights, when the frost was hard, the smell of goats came up like some uncanny acid fire, and great stars sitting on the mountain's edge seemed to be watching like the eyes of a mountain lion, brought by the scent. Then the coyotes in the near canyon howled and sobbed, and ran like shadows over the snow. But the goat corral had been built tight.

In the course of years the goat-herd had grown from fifty to five hundred, and surely that was increase. The goat-milk cheeses sat drying on their little racks. In spring, there was a great flowing and skipping of kids. In summer and early autumn, there was a pest of flies, rising from all that goat-smell and that cast-out whey of goats'-milk, after the cheese-making. The rats came, and the pack-rats, swarming.

And, after all, it was difficult to sell or trade the cheeses, and little profit to be made. And, in dry summers, no water came down in the narrow ditchchannel, that straddled in wooden runnels over the deep clefts in the mountainside. No water meant no alfalfa. In winter the goats scarcely drank at all. In summer they could be watered at the little spring. But the thirsty land was not so easy to accommodate.

Five hundred fine white Angora goats, with their massive handsome padres! They were beautiful enough. And the trader made all he could of them. Come summer, they were run down into the narrow tank filled with the fiery dipping fluid. Then their lovely white wool was clipped. It was beautiful, and valuable, but comparatively little of it.

And it all cost, cost, cost. And a man was always let down. At one time no water. At another a poison-weed. Then a sickness. Always, some mysterious malevolence fighting, fighting against the will of man. A strange invisible influence coming out of the livid rock-fastnesses in the bowels of those uncreated Rocky Mountains, preying upon the will of man, and slowly wearing down his resistance, his onward-pushing spirit. The curious, subtle thing, like a mountain fever, got into the blood, so that the men at the ranch, and the animals with them, had bursts of queer, violent, half-frenzied energy, in which, however, they were wont to lose their wariness. And then, damage of some sort. The horses ripped and cut themselves, or they were struck by lightning, the men had great hurts, or sickness. A curious disintegration working all the time, a sort of malevolent breath, like a stupefying, irritant gas, coming out of the unfathomed mountains.

The pack-rats with their bushy tails and big ears came down out of the hills, and were jumping and bouncing about: symbols of the curious debasing malevolence that was in the spirit of the place. The Mexicans in charge, good honest men, worked all they could. But they were like most of the Mexicans in the South-west, as if they had been pithed, to use one of Kipling's words. As if the invidious malevolence of the country itself had slowly taken all the pith of manhood from them, leaving a hopeless sort of corpus of a man.

And the same happened to the white men, exposed to the open country. Slowly, they were pithed. The energy went out of them. And, more than that, the interest. An inertia of indifference invading the soul, leaving the body healthy and active, but wasting the soul, the living interest, quite away.

It was the New England wife of the trader who put most energy into the ranch. She looked on it as her home. She had a little white fence put all round the two cabins: the bright brass water-taps she kept shining in the two kitchens: outside the kitchen door she had a little kitchen garden and nasturtiums, after a great fight with invading animals, that nibbled everything away. And she got so far as the preparation of the round concrete basin which was to be a little pool, under the few enclosed pine trees between the two cabins, a pool with a tiny fountain jet.

But this, with the bath-tub, was her limit, as the five hundred goats were her man's limit. Out of the mountains came two breaths of influence: the breath of the curious, frenzied energy, that took away one's intelligence as alcohol or any other stimulus does: and then the most strange invidiousness that ate away the soul. The woman loved her ranch, almost with passion. It was she who felt the stimulus, more than the men. It seemed to enter her like a sort of sex passion, intensifying her ego, making her full of violence and of blind female energy. The energy, and the blindness of it! A strange blind frenzy, like an intoxication while it lasted. And the sense of beauty that thrilled her New England woman's soul.

Her cabin faced the slow down-slope of the clearing, the alfalfa field: her long, low cabin, crouching under the great pine tree that threw up its trunk sheer in front of the house, in the yard. That pine tree was the guardian of the place. But a bristling, almost demonish guardian, from the far-off crude ages of the world. Its great pillar of pale, flaky-ribbed copper rose there in strange callous indifference, and the grim permanence, which is in pine trees. A passionless, non-phallic column, rising in the shadows of the pre-sexual world, before the hot-blooded ithyphallic column ever erected itself. A cold, blossomless, resinous sap surging and oozing gum, from that pallid brownish bark. And the wind hissing in the needles, like a vast nest of serpents. And the pine cones falling plumb as the hail hit them. Then lying all over the yard, open in the sun like wooden roses, but hard, sexless, rigid with a blind will.

Past the column of that pine tree, the alfalfa field sloped gently down, to the circling guard of pine trees, from which silent, living barrier isolated pines rose to ragged heights at intervals, in blind assertiveness. Strange, those pine trees! In some lights all their needles glistened like polished steel, all subtly glittering with a whitish glitter among darkness, like real needles. Then again, at evening, the trunks would flare up orange-red, and the tufts would be dark, alert tufts like a wolf's tail touching the air. Again, in the morning sunlight they would be soft and still, hardly noticeable. But all the same, present, and watchful. Never sympathetic, always watchfully on their guard, and resistant, they hedged one in with the aroma and the power and the slight horror of the pre-sexual primeval world. The world where each creature was crudely limited to its own ego, crude and bristling and cold, and then crowding in packs like pine trees and wolves.

But beyond the pine trees, ah, there beyond, there was beauty for the spirit to soar in. The circle of pines, with the loose trees rising high and ragged at intervals, this was the barrier, the fence to the foreground. Beyond was only distance, the desert a thousand feet below, and beyond.

The desert swept its great fawn-coloured circle around, away beyond and below like a beach, with a long mountain-side of pure blue shadow closing in the near corner, and strange bluish hummocks of mountains rising like wet rock from a vast strand, away in the middle distance, and beyond, in the farthest distance, pale-blue crests of mountains looking over the horizon, from the west, as if peering in from another world altogether.

Ah, that was beauty!—perhaps the most beautiful thing in the world. It was pure beauty, *absolute* beauty! There! That was it. To the little woman from New England, with her tense, fierce soul and her egoistic passion of service, this beauty was absolute, a *ne plus ultra*.[62] From her doorway, from her porch, she could watch the vast, eagle-like wheeling of the daylight, that turned as the eagles which lived in the near rocks turned overhead in the blue, turning their luminous, dark-edged-patterned bellies and under-wings upon the pure air, like winged orbs. So the daylight made the vast turn upon the desert, brushing the farthest outwatching mountains. And sometimes the vast strand of the desert would float with curious undulations and exhalations amid the blue fragility of mountains, whose upper edges were harder than the floating bases. And sometimes she would see the little brown adobe houses of the village

62. "Nothing further"—the most perfect state anything can be brought to.

Mexicans, twenty miles away, like little cube crystals of insect-houses dotting upon the desert, very distinct, with a cottonwood tree or two rising near. And sometimes she would see the far-off rocks, thirty miles away, where the canyon made a gateway between the mountains. Quite clear, like an open gateway out of a vast yard, she would see the cut-out bit of the canyon-passage. And on the desert itself curious puckered folds of mesa-sides. And a blackish crack which in places revealed the otherwise invisible canyon of the Rio Grande. And beyond everything, the mountains like icebergs showing up from an outer sea. Then later, the sun would go down blazing above the shallow cauldron of simmering darkness, and the round mountain of Colorado would lump up into uncanny significance, northwards. That was always rather frightening. But morning came again, with the sun peeping over the mountain-slopes and lighting the desert away in the distance long, long before it lighted on her yard. And then she would see another valley, like magic and very lovely, with green fields and long tufts of cottonwood trees, and a few long-cubical adobe houses, lying floating in shallow light below, like a vision.

Ah! It was beauty, beauty absolute, at any hour of the day: whether the perfect clarity of morning, or the mountains beyond the simmering desert at noon, or the purple lumping of northern mounds under a red sun at night. Or whether the dust whirled in tall columns, travelling across the desert far away, like pillars of cloud by day, tall, leaning pillars of dust hastening with ghostly haste: or whether, in the early part of the year, suddenly in the morning a whole sea of solid white would rise rolling below, a solid mist from melted snow, ghost-white under the mountain sun, the world below blotted out: or whether the black rain and cloud streaked down, far across the desert, and lightning stung down with sharp white stings on the horizon: or the cloud travelled and burst overhead, with rivers of fluid blue fire running out of heaven and exploding on earth, and hail coming down like a world of ice shattered above: or the hot sun rode in again: or snow fell in heavy silence: or the world was blinding white under a blue sky, and one must hurry under the pine trees for shelter against that vast, white, back-beating light which rushed up at one and made one almost unconscious, amid the snow.

It was always beauty, *always!* It was always great, and splendid, and, for some reason, natural. It was never grandiose or theatrical. Always, for some reason, perfect. And quite simple, in spite of it all.

So it was, when you watched the vast and living landscape. The landscape lived, and lived as the world of the gods, unsullied and unconcerned. The great circling landscape lived its own life, sumptuous and uncaring. Man did not exist for it.

And if it had been a question simply of living through the eyes, into the *distance*, then this would have been Paradise, and the little New England woman on her ranch would have found what she was always looking for, the earthly paradise of the spirit.

But even a woman cannot live only into the distance, the beyond. Willy-nilly she finds herself juxtaposed to the near things, the thing in itself. And willy-nilly she is caught up into the fight with the immediate object.

The New England woman had fought to make the nearness as perfect as the distance: for the distance was absolute beauty. She had been confident of success. She had felt quite assured, when the water came running out of her bright brass taps, the wild water of the hills caught, tricked into the narrow iron pipes, and led tamely to her kitchen, to jump out over her sink, into her wash-basin, at her service. *There!* she said. I have tamed the waters of the mountain to my service.

So she had, for the moment.

At the same time, the invisible attack was being made upon her. While she revelled in the beauty of the luminous world that wheeled around and below her, the grey, rat-like spirit of the inner mountains was attacking her from behind. She could not keep her attention. And, curiously, she could not keep even her speech. When she was saying something, suddenly the next word would be gone out of her, as if a pack-rat had carried it off. And she sat blank, stuttering, staring in the empty cupboard of her mind, like Mother Hubbard, and seeing the cupboard bare. And this irritated her husband intensely.

Her chickens, of which she was so proud, were carried away. Or they strayed. Or they fell sick. At first she could cope with their circumstances. But after a while, she couldn't. She couldn't care. A drug-like numbness possessed her spirit, and at the very middle of her, she couldn't care what happened to her chickens.

The same when a couple of horses were struck by lightning. It frightened her. The rivers of fluid fire that suddenly fell out of the sky and exploded on the earth near by, as if the whole earth had burst like a bomb, frightened her from the very core of her, and made her know, secretly and with cynical certainty, *that there was no merciful God in the heavens.* A very tall, elegant pine tree just above her cabin took the lightning, and stood tall and elegant as before, but with a white seam spiralling from its crest, all down its tall trunk, to earth. The perfect scar, white and long as lightning itself. And every time she looked at it, she said to herself, in spite of herself: *There is no Almighty loving God. The God there is shaggy as the pine trees, and horrible as the lightning.* Outwardly, she never confessed this. Openly, she thought of her dear New England Church as usual. But in the violent undercurrent of her woman's soul, after the storms, she would look at that living seamed tree, and the voice would say in her, almost savagely: *What nonsense about Jesus and a God of Love, in a place like this! This is more awful and more splendid. I like it better.* The very chipmunks, in their jerky helter-skelter, the blue jays wrangling in the pine tree in the dawn, the grey squirrel undulating to the tree-trunk, then pausing to chatter at her and scold her, with a shrewd fearlessness, as if she were the alien, the outsider, the creature that should not be permitted among the trees, all destroyed the illusion she cherished, of love, universal love. There was no love on this ranch. There was life, intense, bristling life, full of energy, but also with an undertone of savage sordidness.

The black ants in her cupboard, the pack-rats bouncing on her ceiling like hippopotamuses in the night, the two sick goats: there was a peculiar undercurrent of squalor, flowing under the curious *tussle* of wild life. That was it. The wild life, even the life of the trees and flowers, seemed one bristling, hair-raising tussle. The very flowers came up bristly, and many of them were fang-mouthed, like the dead-nettle: and none had any real scent. But they were very fascinating, too, in their very fierceness. In May, the curious columbines of the stream-beds, columbines scarlet outside and yellow in, like the red and yellow of a herald's uniform: farther from the dove nothing could be: then the beautiful rosy-blue of the great tufts of the flower they called bluebell, but which was really a flower of the snapdragon family: these grew in powerful beauty in the little clearing of the pine trees, followed by the flower the settlers had mysteriously called herb honeysuckle: a tangle of long drops of pure fire-red, hanging from slim invisible stalks of smoke-colour. The purest, most perfect vermilion scarlet, cleanest fire-colour, hanging in long drops like a shower of fire-rain that is just going to strike the earth. A little later, more in the open, there came another sheer fire-red flower, sparking, fierce red stars running up a bristly grey ladder, as if earth's fire-centre had blown out some red sparks, white-speckled and deadly inside, puffing for a moment in the day air.

So it was! The alfalfa field was one raging, seething conflict of plants trying to get hold. One dry year, and the bristly wild things had got hold: the spiky, blue-leaved thistle-poppy with its moon-white flowers, the low clumps of blue nettle-flower, the later rush, after the sereness of June and July, the rush of red sparks and Michaelmas daisies, and the tough wild sunflowers, strangling and choking the dark, tender green of the clover-like alfalfa! A battle, a battle, with banners of bright scarlet and yellow.

When a really defenceless flower did issue, like the moth-still, ghost-centered mariposa lily, with its inner moth-dust of yellow, it came invisible. There was nothing to be seen but a hair of greyish grass near the oak-scrub. Behold, this invisible long stalk was balancing a white, ghostly, three-petalled flower, naked out of nothingness. A mariposa lily!

Only the pink wild roses smelled sweet, like the Old World. They were sweet brier-roses. And the dark-blue harebells among the oak-scrub, like the ice-dark bubbles of the mountain flowers in the Alps, the Alpenglocken.

The roses of the desert are the cactus flowers, crystal of translucent yellow or of rose-colour. But set among spines the devil himself must have conceived in a moment of sheer ecstasy.

Nay, it was a world before and after the God of Love. Even the very humming-birds hanging about the flowering squawberry bushes, when the snow had gone, in May, they were before and after the God of Love. And the blue jays were crested dark with challenge, and the yellow-and-dark woodpecker was fearless like a warrior in war-paint, as he struck the wood. While on the fence the hawks sat motionless, like dark fists clenched under heaven, ignoring man and his ways.

Summer, it was true, unfolded the tender cottonwood leaves, and the tender aspen. But what a tangle and a ghostly aloofness in the aspen thickets high up on the mountains, the coldness that is in the eyes and the long cornelian talons of the bear.

Summer brought the little wild strawberries, with their savage aroma, and the late summer brought the rose-jewel raspberries in the valley cleft. But how lonely, how harsh-lonely and menacing it was, to be alone in that shadowy, steep cleft of a canyon just above the cabins, picking raspberries, while the thunder gathered thick and blue-purple at the mountain-tops. The many wild raspberries hanging rose-red in the thickets. But the stream-bed below all silent, waterless. And the trees all bristling in silence, and waiting like warriors at an outpost. And the berries waiting for the sharp-eyed, cold, long-snouted bear to come rambling and shaking his heavy sharp fur. The berries grew for the bears, and the little New England woman, with her uncanny sensitiveness to underlying influences, felt all the time she was stealing. Stealing the wild raspberries in the secret little canyon behind her home. And when she had made them into jam, she could almost taste the theft in her preserves.

She confessed nothing of this. She tried even to confess nothing of her dread. But she was afraid. Especially she was conscious of the prowling, intense aerial electricity all the summer, after June. The air was thick with wandering currents of fierce electric fluid, waiting to discharge themselves. And almost every day there was the rage and battle of thunder. But the air was never cleared. There was no relief. However the thunder raged, and spent itself, yet, afterwards, among the sunshine was the strange lurking and wandering of the electric currents, moving invisible, with strange menace, between the atoms of the air. She knew. Oh, she knew!

And her love for her ranch turned sometimes into a certain repulsion. The underlying rat-dirt, the everlasting bristling tussle of the wild life, with the tangle and the bones strewing. Bones of horses struck by lightning, bones of dead cattle, skulls of goats with little horns: bleached, unburied bones. Then the cruel electricity of the mountains. And then, most mysterious but worst of all, the animosity of the spirit of place: the crude, half-created spirit of place, like some serpent-bird forever attacking man, in a hatred of man's onward-struggle towards further creation.

The seething cauldron of lower life, seething on the very tissue of the higher life, seething the soul away, seething at the marrow. The vast and unrelenting will of the swarming lower life, working forever against man's attempt at a higher life, a further created being.

At last, after many years, the little woman admitted to herself that she was glad to go down from the ranch when November came with snows. She was glad to come to a more human home, her house in the village. And as winter passed by, and spring came again, she knew she did not want to go up to the ranch again. It had broken something in her. It had hurt her terribly. It had maimed her forever in her hope, her belief in paradise on earth. Now, she hid from herself her own corpse, the corpse of her New England belief in a world ultimately all for love. The belief, and herself with it, was a corpse. The gods of those inner mountains were grim and invidious and relentless, huger than man, and lower than man. Yet man could never master them.

The little woman in her flower-garden away below, by the stream-irrigated village, hid away from the thought of it all. She would not go to the ranch any more.

The Mexicans stayed in charge, looking after the goats. But the place didn't pay. It didn't pay, not quite. It had paid. It might pay. But the effort, the effort! And as the marrow is eaten out of a man's bones and the soul out of his belly, contending with the strange rapacity of savage life, the lower stage of creation, he cannot make the effort any more.

Then also, the war came, making many men give up their enterprises at civilization.

Every new stroke of civilization has cost the lives of countless brave men, who have fallen defeated by the 'dragon,' in their efforts to win the apples of the Hesperides, or the fleece of gold.[63] Fallen in their efforts to overcome the old, half-sordid savagery of the lower stages of creation, and win to the next stage.

For all savagery is half sordid. And man is only himself when he is fighting on and on, to overcome the sordidness.

And every civilization, when it loses its inward vision and its cleaner energy, falls into a new sort of sordidness, more vast and more stupendous than the old savage sort. An Augean stable of metallic filth.

And all the time, man has to rouse himself afresh, to cleanse the new accumulations of refuse. To win from the crude wild nature the victory and the power to make another start, and to cleanse behind him the century-deep deposits of layer upon layer of refuse: even of tin cans.

The ranch dwindled. The flock of goats declined. The water ceased to flow. And at length the trader gave it up.

He rented the place to a Mexican, who lived on the handful of beans he raised, and who was being slowly driven out by the vermin.

And now arrived Lou, new blood to the attack. She went back to Santa Fe, saw the trader and a lawyer, and bought the ranch for twelve hundred dollars. She was so pleased with herself.

She went upstairs to tell her mother.

'Mother, I've bought a ranch.'

'It is just as well, for I can't stand the noise of automobiles outside here another week.'

'It is quiet on my ranch, mother: the stillness simply speaks.'

'I had rather it held its tongue. I am simply drugged with all the bad novels I have read. I feel as if the sky was a big cracked bell and a million clappers were hammering human speech out of it.'

'Aren't you interested in my ranch, mother?'

'I hope I may be, by and by.'

Mrs. Witt actually got up the next morning, and accompanied her daughter in the hired motor-car, driven by Phœnix, to the ranch: which was called Las Chivas.[64] She sat like a pillar of salt, her face looking what the Indians call a False Face, meaning a mask. She seemed to have crystallized into neutrality. She watched the desert with its tufts of yellow greasewood go lurching past: she saw the fallen apples on the ground in the orchards near the adobe cottages: she looked down into the deep arroyo, and at the stream they forded in the car, and at the mountains blocking up the sky ahead, all with indifference. High on the mountains was snow: lower, blue-grey livid rock: and below the livid rock the aspens were expiring their daffodil-yellow, this year, and the oak-scrub was dark and reddish, like gore. She saw it all with a sort of stony indifference.

'Don't you think it's lovely?' said Lou.

'I can *see* it is lovely,' replied her mother.

The Michaelmas daisies in the clearing as they drove up to the ranch were sharp-rayed with purple, like a coming night.

Mrs. Witt eyed the two log cabins, one of which was dilapidated and prac-

63. The apples of the Hesperides, which Hercules was sent to pick, were protected by a dragon; Jason, to win the Golden Fleece, had to sow dragon's teeth from which armed men arose to combat him.

64. The She Goats (Spanish).

tically abandoned. She looked at the rather rickety corral, whose long planks had silvered and warped in the fierce sun. On one of the roof-planks a pack-rat was sitting erect like an old Indian keeping watch on a pueblo roof. He showed his white belly, and folded his hands and lifted his big ears, for all the world like an old immobile Indian.

'Isn't it for all the world as if *he* were the real boss of the place, Louise?' she said cynically.

And, turning to the Mexican, who was a rag of a man but a pleasant, courteous fellow, she asked him why he didn't shoot the rat.

'Not worth a shell!' said the Mexican, with a faint hopeless smile.

Mrs. Witt paced round and saw everything: it did not take long. She gazed in silence at the water of the spring, trickling out of an iron pipe into a barrel, under the cottonwood tree in an arroyo.

'Well, Louise,' she said, 'I am glad you feel competent to cope with so much hopelessness and so many rats.'

'But, mother, you must admit it is beautiful.'

'Yes, I suppose it is. But, to use one of your Henry's phrases, beauty is a cold egg,[65] as far as I am concerned.'

'Rico never would have said that beauty was a cold egg to him.'

'No, he wouldn't. He sits on it like a broody old hen on a china imitation.— Are you going to bring him here?'

'*Bring* him!—No. But he can come if he likes,' stammered Lou.

'*Oh—h!* won't it be beau—ti—ful!' cried Mrs. Witt, rolling her head and lifting her shoulders in savage imitation of her son-in-law.

'Perhaps he won't come, mother,' said Lou, hurt.

'He will most certainly come, Louise, to see what's doing: unless you tell him you don't want him.'

'Anyhow, I needn't think about it till spring,' said Lou, anxiously pushing the matter aside.

Mrs. Witt climbed the steep slope above the cabins, to the mouth of the little canyon. There she sat on a fallen tree, and surveyed the world beyond: a world not of men. She could not fail to be roused.

'What is your idea in coming here, daughter?' she asked.

'I love it here, mother.'

'But what do you expect to achieve by it?'

'I was rather hoping, mother, to escape achievement. I'll tell you—and you mustn't get cross if it sounds silly. As far as people go, my heart is quite broken. As far as people go, I don't want any more. I can't stand any more. What heart I ever had for it—for life with people—is quite broken. I want to be alone, mother: with you here, and Phœnix perhaps to look after horses and drive a car. But I want to be by myself, really.'

'With Phœnix in the background! Are you sure he won't be coming into the foreground before long?'

'No, mother, no more of that. If I've got to say it, Phœnix is a servant: he's really placed, as far as I can see. Always the same, playing about in the old back yard. I can't take those men seriously. I can't fool round with them, or

65. See "The Mess of Love," l. 8.

fool myself about them. I can't and I won't fool myself any more, mother, especially about men. They don't count. So why should you want them to pay me out?'

For the moment, this silenced Mrs. Witt. Then she said:

'Why, *I* don't want it. Why should I? But after all you've got to live. You've never *lived* yet: not in my opinion.'

'Neither, mother, in my opinion, have you,' said Lou dryly.

And this silenced Mrs. Witt altogether. She had to be silent, or angrily on the defensive. And the latter she wouldn't be. She couldn't, really, in honesty.

'What do you call life?' Lou continued. 'Wriggling half naked at a public show, and going off in a taxi to sleep with some half-drunken fool who thinks he's a man because—oh, mother, I don't even want to think of it. I know you have a lurking idea that *that is life*. Let it be so then. But leave me out. Men in that aspect simply nauseate me: so grovelling and ratty. Life in that aspect simply drains all my life away. I tell you, for all that sort of thing, I'm broken, absolutely broken: if I wasn't broken to start with.'

'Well, Louise,' said Mrs. Witt after a pause, 'I'm convinced that ever since men and women were men and women, people who took things seriously, and had time for it, got their hearts broken. Haven't I had mine broken? It's as sure as having your virginity broken: and it amounts to about as much. It's a beginning rather than an end.'

'So it is, mother. It's the beginning of something else, and the end of something that's done with. I *know*, and there's no altering it, that I've got to live differently. It sounds silly, but I don't know how else to put it. I've got to live for something that matters, way, way down in me. And I think sex would matter, to my very soul, if it was really sacred. But cheap sex kills me.'

'You have had a fancy for rather cheap men, perhaps.'

'Perhaps I have. Perhaps I should always be a fool, where people are concerned. Now I want to leave off that kind of foolery. There's something else, mother, that I want to give myself to. I know it. I know it absolutely. Why should I let myself be shouted down any more?'

Mrs. Witt sat staring at the distance, her face a cynical mask.

'What is the something bigger? And *pray*, what is it bigger than?' she asked, in that tone of honeyed suavity which was her deadliest poison. 'I want to learn. I am out to know. I'm terribly intrigued by it. Something bigger! Girls in my generation occasionally entered convents, for *something bigger*. I always wondered if they found it. They seemed to me inclined in the imbecile direction, but perhaps that was because I was *something less*—'

There was a definite pause between the mother and daughter, a silence that was a pure breach. Then Lou said:

'You know quite well I'm not conventy, mother, whatever else I am—even a bit of an imbecile. But that kind of religion seems to me the other half of men. Instead of running after them, you run away from them, and get the thrill that way. I don't hate men *because* they're men, as nuns do. I dislike them because they're not men enough: babies, and playboys, and poor things showing off all the time, even to themselves. I don't say I'm any better. I only wish, with all my soul, that some men *were* bigger and stronger and *deeper* than I am . . .'

'How do you know they're not?' asked Mrs. Witt.

'How *do* I know?—' said Lou mockingly.

And the pause that was a breach resumed itself. Mrs. Witt was teasing with a little stick the bewildered black ants among the fir-needles.

'And no doubt you are right about men,' she said at length. 'But at your age, the only sensible thing is to try and keep up the illusion. After all, as you say, you may be no better.'

'I may be no better. But keeping up the illusion means fooling myself. And I won't do it. When I see a man who is even a bit attractive to me—even as much as Phœnix—I say to myself: *Would you care for him afterwards? Does he really mean anything to you, except just a sensation?*—And I know he doesn't. No, mother, of this I am convinced: either my taking a man shall have a meaning and a mystery that penetrates my very soul, or I will keep to myself.—And what I *know* is that the time has come for me to keep to myself. No more messing about.'

'Very well, daughter. You will probably spend your life keeping to yourself.'

'Do you think I mind! There's something else for me, mother. There's something else even that loves me and wants me. I can't tell you what it is. It's a spirit. And it's here, on this ranch. It's here, in this landscape. It's something more real to me than men are, and it soothes me, and it holds me up. I don't know what it is, definitely. It's something wild, that will hurt me sometimes and will wear me down sometimes. I know it. But it's something big, bigger than men, bigger than people, bigger than religion. It's something to do with wild America. And it's something to do with me. It's a mission, if you like. I am imbecile enough for that!—But it's my mission to keep myself for the spirit that is wild, and has waited so long here: even waited for such as me. Now I've come! Now I'm here. Now I am where I want to be: with the spirit that wants me.—And that's how it is. And neither Rico nor Phœnix nor anybody else really matters to me. They are in the world's back yard. And I am here, right deep in America, where there's a wild spirit wants me, a wild spirit more than men. And it doesn't want to save me either. It needs me. It craves for me. And to it, my sex is deep and sacred, deeper than I am, with a deep nature aware deep down of my sex. It saves me from cheapness, mother. And even you could never do that for me.'

Mrs. Witt rose to her feet, and stood looking far, far away, at the turquoise ridge of mountains half sunk under the horizon.

'How much did you say you paid for Las Chivas?' she asked.

'Twelve hundred dollars,' said Lou, surprised.

'Then I call it cheap, considering all there is to it: even the name.'

1924   1925

Poems

Like Thomas Hardy, Lawrence produced, aside from his fiction, a body of major poetry. Unlike the older writer who was, indeed, his master in many ways, Lawrence did not turn to poems when the impulse to write fiction was stifled by the institutions of literary life, but kept writing verse throughout his career. His early *Love Poems* and Others (1913) showed a good bit of Hardy's influence, but it was not until the free-verse poetry of *Look, We Have Come Through!* (1917) that he was able to come to terms with the demands that his reading of Walt Whitman and, through him, earlier Romantic poetic tradition, was making upon him. Although at first purporting to share in the Imagist (see Glossary) revision of Victorian formal modes, Lawrence soon developed a range of keys of his own, in a verse derived from Whitman and ultimately from the English Bible. But like all programmatic and self-conscious formal choices in the history of English poetry, the form claimed to come either from on high or—its later equivalent—from within. ". . . Free verse is, or should be, direct utterance from the instant, whole man. It is the soul and the mind and the body surging at once, nothing left out," wrote Lawrence in a preface to the American edition of his *New Poems* (1918); and the arguments of Whitman, who likened his own lines to the wave motions of the sea, are not far away.

Characteristically, Lawrence does not discuss *per se* the mythopoetic quality which is so central to his greatest poetry. Much of his verse is a vehicle for a certain kind of hard, relentless ironic epigram he made his own; the volume entitled *Pansies* (1929), not for conventional floral reasons but because of the origin of the name in the French *pensée* ("thought"), is composed of these, and they constitute an impressive and subsequently influential body of what Yeats would have called "rhetoric," made out of a writer's quarrel with other men. But the larger Lawrentian poetry appears in early love poems and glimpses of childhood, and fully emerges in the great emblematic readings of *Birds, Beasts, and Flowers* (1923). The presence of life other than human evokes visions of temporarily buried human visions of the earth and its depths (as in "Snake"). Sometimes the poem's meditation drives a wedge between two aspects of a phenomenon which ordinary plain speech blurs: thus the difference between fig as fruit and apple as fruit in "Figs"; the difference between the gently sad twilight of approaching darkness seen through the swallows of Keats's "to Autumn," and a horrid, fearful bat-twilight of imminent death in "Bat."

Piano

Softly, in the dusk, a woman is singing to me;
Taking me back down the vista of years, till I see
A child sitting under the piano, in the boom of the tingling strings
And pressing the small, poised feet of a mother who smiles as she sings.

In spite of myself, the insidious mastery of song
Betrays me back, till the heart of me weeps to belong
To the old Sunday evenings at home, with winter outside
And hymns in the cozy parlour, the tinkling piano our guide.

So now it is vain for the singer to burst into clamour
10   With the great black piano appassionato.° The glamour
Of childish days is upon me, my manhood is cast
Down in the flood of remembrance, I weep like a child for the past.

                                                                                    1913

appassionato impassioned

River Roses°

By the Isar, in the twilight
We were wandering and singing,
By the Isar, in the evening
We climbed the huntsman's ladder and sat swinging
In the fir-tree overlooking the marshes,
While river met with river, and the ringing
Of their pale-green glacier water filled the evening.

By the Isar, in the twilight
We found the dark wild roses
10 Hanging red at the river; and simmering
Frogs were singing, and over the river closes
Was savour of ice and of roses; and glimmering
Fear was abroad. We whispered: 'No one knows us.
Let it be as the snake disposes
Here in this simmering marsh.'

1917

Medlars and Sorb-Apples°

I love you, rotten,
Delicious rottenness.

I love to suck you out from your skins
So brown and soft and coming suave,
So morbid,° as the Italians say.

What a rare, powerful, reminiscent flavour
Comes out of your falling through the stages of decay:
Stream within stream.

Something of the same flavour as Syracusan muscat wine
10 Or vulgar Marsala.°

Though even the word Marsala will smack of preciosity
Soon in the pussyfoot West.°

What is it?
What is it, in the grape turning raisin,
In the medlar, in the sorb-apple,

River Roses This scene in the Bavarian Tyrol became more highly mythologized, with its Edenic overtones and its serpent, in a second version; it is instructive to compare the original second stanza from the poem's first publication in *Poetry* in 1914: "By the Isar, in the twilight / We found our warm wild roses / Hanging red at the river; and simmering / Frogs were singing, and over the river closes / Was scent of roses, and glimmering / In the twilight, our kisses across the roses / Met, and her face, and my face were roses."

Medlars and Sorb-Apples Medlars are a fruit of the apple-pear-quince family, edible only when they have started to rot; the sorb, likewise. The poem begins with a meditation on decay as promise, a reversal of the normal cycles in which spring promises, autumn fulfills.
morbid Italian *morbido* means soft (of fruit, "ripe"), although the original Latin "diseased" supplies the English meaning.
Marsala the sweet fortified wine of Sicily
pussyfoot West presumably because of the onset of Prohibition in the United States in 1920

Wineskins of brown morbidity,
Autumnal excrementa;
What is it that reminds us of white gods?

Gods nude as blanched nut-kernels,
20 Strangely, half-sinisterly flesh-fragrant
As if with sweat,
And drenched with mystery.

Sorb-apples, medlars with dead crowns.

I say, wonderful are the hellish experiences,
Orphic,° delicate
Dionysos of the Underworld.

A kiss, and a spasm of farewell, a moment's orgasm of rupture,
Then along the damp road alone, till the next turning.
And there, a new partner, a new parting, a new unfusing into twain,
30 A new gasp of further isolation,
A new intoxication of loneliness, among decaying, frost-cold leaves.

Going down the strange lanes of hell, more and more intensely alone,
The fibres of the heart parting one after the other
And yet the soul continuing, naked-footed, ever more vividly embodied
Like a flame blown whiter and whiter
In a deeper and deeper darkness
Ever more exquisite, distilled in separation.

So, in the strange retorts of medlars and sorb-apples
The distilled essence of hell.
40 The exquisite odour of leave-taking.
    Jamque vale!°
Orpheus, and the winding, leaf-clogged, silent lanes of hell.

Each soul departing with its own isolation,
Strangest of all strange companions,
And best.

Medlars, sorb-apples,
More than sweet
Flux of autumn
Sucked out of your empty bladders
50 And sipped down, perhaps, with a sip of Marsala
So that the rambling, sky-dropped grape can add its savour to yours,
Orphic farewell, and farewell, and farewell
And the *ego sum*° of Dionysos
The *sono io*° of perfect drunkenness
Intoxication of final loneliness.

1921

Orphic pertaining to the Orphic mysteries celebrated in late Greek times, which assimilated the Orpheus legend to the worship of Dionysus as underworld god, and one of whose doctrines was that of *metempsychosis*, the transmigration of souls after death
Jamque vale "and now, farewell"
ego sum "I am"
sono io "I am" (Italian)

Bat

At evening, sitting on this terrace,°
When the sun from the west, beyond Pisa, beyond the mountains of Carrara
Departs, and the world is taken by surprise . . .

When the tired flower of Florence is in gloom beneath the glowing
Brown hills surrounding . . .

When under the arches of the Ponte Vecchio
A green light enters against the stream, flush from the west,
Against the current of obscure Arno . . .

Look up, and you see things flying
10   Between the day and the night;
Swallows with spools of dark thread sewing the shadows together.

A circle swoop, and a quick parabola under the bridge arches
Where light pushes through;
A sudden turning upon itself of a thing in the air.
A dip to the water.

And you think:
'The swallows are flying so late!'

Swallows?

Dark air-life looping
20   Yet missing the pure loop . . .
A twitch, a twitter, an elastic shudder in flight
And serrated wings against the sky,
Like a glove, a black glove thrown up at the light,
And falling back.

Never swallows!
Bats!
The swallows are gone.

At a wavering instant the swallows give way to bats
By the Ponte Vecchio . . .
30   Changing guard.

Bats, and an uneasy creeping in one's scalp
As the bats swoop overhead!
Flying madly.

Pipistrello!°
Black piper on an infinitesimal pipe.
Little lumps that fly in air and have voices indefinite, wildly vindictive;
Wings like bits of umbrella.

---

terrace The poet is looking out over the river   bridge") crosses the river near a central square.
Arno in Florence; the Ponte Vecchio ("old   **Pipistrello** "bat" in Italian

1944

Bats!

Creatures that hang themselves up like an old rag to sleep;
40   And disgustingly upside down.
Hanging upside down like rows of disgusting old rags
And grinning in their sleep.
Bats!

In China the bat is symbol of happiness.

Not for me!
1921   1923

Snake

A snake came to my water-trough
On a hot, hot day, and I in pyjamas for the heat,
To drink there.

In the deep, strange-scented shade of the great dark carob tree
I came down the steps with my pitcher
And must wait, must stand and wait, for there he was at the trough before me.

He reached down from a fissure in the earth-wall in the gloom
And trailed his yellow-brown slackness soft-bellied down, over the edge of the
       stone trough

And rested his throat upon the stone bottom,
10   And where the water had dripped from the tap, in a small clearness,
He sipped with his straight mouth,
Softly drank through his straight gums, into his slack long body,
Silently.

Someone was before me at my water-trough,
And I, like a second comer, waiting.

He lifted his head from his drinking, like cattle do,
And looked at me vaguely, as drinking cattle do,
And flickered his two-forked tongue from his lips, and mused a moment,
And stooped and drank a little more,
20   Being earth-brown, earth-golden from the burning bowels of the earth
On the day of Sicilian July, with Etna° smoking.

The voice of my education said to me
He must be killed,
For in Sicily the black, black snakes are innocent, the gold are venomous.

And voices in me said, if you were a man
You would take a stick and break him now, and finish him off.

Etna the great Sicilian volcano, still active

But I must confess how I liked him,
How glad I was he had come like a guest in quiet, to drink at my water-trough
And depart peaceful, pacified, and thankless,
30   Into the burning bowels of this earth.

Was it cowardice, that I dared not kill him?
Was it perversity, that I longed to talk to him?
Was it humility, to feel so honoured?
I felt so honoured.

And yet those voices:
If you were not afraid, you would kill him!

And truly I was afraid, I was most afraid,
But even so, honoured still more
That he should seek my hospitality
40   From out the dark door of the secret earth.

He drank enough
And lifted his head, dreamily, as one who has drunken,
And flickered his tongue like a forked night on the air, so black,
Seeming to lick his lips,
And looking around like a god, unseeing, into the air,
And slowly turned his head,
And slowly, very slowly, as if thrice adream,
Proceeded to draw his slow length curving round
And climb again the broken bank of my wall-face.

50   And as he put his head into that dreadful hole,
And as he slowly drew up, snake-easing his shoulders, and entered farther,
A sort of horror, a sort of protest against his withdrawing into that horrid black
        hole,
Deliberately going into the blackness, and slowly drawing himself after,
Overcame me now his back was turned.

I looked around, I put down my pitcher,
I picked up a clumsy log
And threw it at the water-trough with a clatter.

I think I did not hit him,
But suddenly that part of him that was left behind convulsed in undignified
        haste,
60   Writhed like lightning, and was gone
Into the black hole, the earth-lipped fissure in the wall-front,
At which, in the intense still noon, I stared with fascination.

And immediately I regretted it.
I thought how paltry, how vulgar, what a mean act!
I despised myself and the voices of my accursed human education.
And I thought of the albatross,
And I wished he would come back, my snake.

For he seemed to me again like a king,
Like a king in exile, uncrowned in the underworld,
70   Now due to be crowned again.

And so, I missed my chance with one of the lords
Of life.
And I have something to expiate;
A pettiness.

1923

Tortoise Shell

The Cross, the Cross
Goes deeper in than we know,
Deeper into life;
Right into the marrow
And through the bone.

Along the back of the baby tortoise
The scales are locked in an arch like a bridge,
Scale-lapping, like a lobster's sections
Or a bee's.

10   Then crossways down his sides
Tiger-stripes and wasp-bands.

Five, and five again, and five again,
And round the edges twenty-five little ones,
The sections of the baby tortoise shell.

Four, and a keystone;
Four, and a keystone;
Four, and a keystone;
Then twenty-four, and a tiny little keystone.

It needed Pythagoras° to see life playing with counters on the living back
20   Of the baby tortoise;
Life establishing the first eternal mathematical tablet,
Not in stone, like the Judean Lord,° or bronze, but in life-clouded, life-rosy
      tortoise shell.

The first little mathematical gentleman
Stepping, wee mite, in his loose trousers
Under all the eternal dome of mathematical law.

Fives, and tens,
Threes and fours and twelves,
All the *volte face*° of decimals,
The whirligig of dozens and the pinnacle of seven.

Pythagoras the Greek philosopher of the 6th century B.C. who was associated with numerical and geometric mysteries

Judean Lord who gave Moses stone tablets
volte face turnabout (Italian)

30　Turn him on his back,
　　The kicking little beetle,
　　And there again, on his shell-tender, earth-touching belly,
　　The long cleavage of division, upright of the eternal cross
　　And on either side count five,
　　On each side, two above, on each side, two below
　　The dark bar horizontal.

　　The Cross!
　　It goes right through him, the sprottling insect,
　　Through his cross-wise cloven psyche,
40　Through his five-fold complex-nature.

　　So turn him over on his toes again;
　　Four pin-point toes, and a problematical thumb-piece,
　　Four rowing limbs, and one wedge-balancing head,
　　Four and one makes five, which is the clue to all mathematics.

　　The Lord wrote it all down on the little slate
　　Of the baby tortoise.
　　Outward and visible indication of the plan within,
　　The complex, manifold involvedness of an individual creature
　　Plotted out
50　On this small bird, this rudiment,
　　This little dome, this pediment
　　Of all creation,
　　This slow one.
　　1921　　　　　　　　　　　　　　　　　　　　　　　　1923

Figs

　　The proper way to eat a fig, in society,
　　Is to split it in four, holding it by the stump,
　　And open it, so that it is a glittering, rosy, moist, honied, heavy-petalled four-
　　　　petalled flower.

　　Then you throw away the skin
　　Which is just like a four-sepalled calyx,°
　　After you have taken off the blossom with your lips.

　　But the vulgar way
　　Is just to put your mouth to the crack, and take out the flesh in one bite.

　　Every fruit has its secret.

10　The fig is a very secretive fruit.
　　As you see it standing growing, you feel at once it is symbolic:

---

four-sepalled calyx a cup-like section behind the
petals of a flower

And it seems male.
But when you come to know it better, you agree with the Romans, it is female.

The Italians vulgarly say, it stands for the female part; the fig-fruit:
The fissure, the yoni,°
The wonderful moist conductivity towards the centre.

Involved,
Inturned,
The flowering all inward and womb-fibrilled;
20 And but one orifice.

The fig, the horse-shoe, the squash-blossom.
Symbols.

There was a flower that flowered inward, womb-ward;
Now there is a fruit like a ripe womb.

It was always a secret.
That's how it should be, the female should always be secret.

There never was any standing aloft and unfolded on a bough
Like other flowers, in a revelation of petals;

Silver-pink peach, venetian green glass of medlars and sorb-apples,
30 Shallow wine-cups on short, bulging stems
Openly pledging heaven:
Here's to the thorn in flower! Here is to Utterance!
The brave, adventurous rosaceae.

Folded upon itself, and secret unutterable,
And milky-sapped, sap that curdles milk and makes *ricotta,*°
Sap that smells strange on your fingers, that even goats won't taste it;
Folded upon itself, enclosed like any Mohammedan woman,
Its nakedness all within-walls, its flowering forever unseen,
One small way of access only, and this close-curtained from the light;
40 Fig, fruit of the female mystery, covert and inward,
Mediterranean fruit, with your covert nakedness,
Where everything happens invisible, flowering and fertilisation, and fruiting
In the inwardness of your you, that eye will never see
Till it's finished, and you're over-ripe, and you burst to give up your ghost.

Till the drop of ripeness exudes,
And the year is over.

And then the fig has kept her secret long enough.
So it explodes, and you see through the fissure the scarlet.
And the fig is finished, the year is over.

50 That's how the fig dies, showing her crimson through the purple slit
Like a wound, the exposure of her secret, on the open day.
Like a prostitute, the bursten fig, making a show of her secret.

yoni Sanskrit for vagina   **ricotta** a white pot cheese

That's how women die too.

The year is fallen over-ripe,
The year of our women.
The year of our women is fallen over-ripe.
The secret is laid bare.
And rottenness soon sets in.
The year of our women is fallen over-ripe.

60 When Eve once knew *in her mind* that she was naked
She quickly sewed fig-leaves, and sewed the same for the man.
She'd been naked all her days before,
But till then, till that apple of knowledge, she hadn't had the fact on her mind.

She got the fact on her mind, and quickly sewed fig-leaves.
And women have been sewing ever since.
But now they stitch to adorn the bursten fig, not to cover it.
They have their nakedness more than ever on their mind,
And they won't let us forget it.

Now, the secret
70 Becomes an affirmation through moist, scarlet lips
That laugh at the Lord's indignation.

What then, good Lord! cry the women.
We have kept our secret long enough.
We are a ripe fig.
Let us burst into affirmation.

They forget, ripe figs won't keep.
Ripe figs won't keep.
Honey-white figs of the north, black figs with scarlet inside, of the south.
Ripe figs won't keep, won't keep in any clime.
80 What then, when women the world over have all bursten into self-assertion?
And bursten figs won't keep?
                    1923

The American Eagle

The dove of Liberty sat on an egg
And hatched another eagle.

But didn't disown the bird.

Down with all eagles! cooed the Dove.
And down all eagles began to flutter, reeling from their perches:
Eagles with two heads, eagles with one, presently eagles with none
Fell from the hooks and were dead.

Till the American Eagle was the only eagle left in the world.

Then it began to fidget, shifting from one leg to the other,
10   Trying to look like a pelican,
And plucking out of his plumage a few loose feathers to feather the nest of all
The new naked little republics come into the world.

But the feathers were, comparatively, a mere flea-bite.
And the bub-eagle that Liberty had hatched was growing a startling big bird
On the roof of the world;
A bit awkward, and with a funny squawk in his voice,
His mother Liberty trying always to teach him to coo
And him always ending with a yawp°
Coo! Coo! Coo! Coo-ark! Coo-ark! Quark!! Quark!!
20   YAWP!!!

So he clears his throat, the young Cock-eagle!

Now if the lilies of France lick Solomon in all his glory;°
And the leopard cannot change his spots;
Nor the British lion his appetite;
Neither can a young Cock-eagle sit simpering
With an olive-sprig in his mouth.

It's not his nature.

The big bird of the Amerindian being the eagle,
Red Men still stick themselves over with bits of his fluff,
30   And feel absolutely IT.

So better make up your mind, American Eagle,
Whether you're a sucking dove, *Roo—coo—ooo! Quark! Yawp!!*
Or a pelican
Handing out a few loose golden breast-feathers, at moulting time;
Or a sort of prosperity-gander
Fathering endless ten-dollar golden eggs.

Or whether it actually is an eagle you are,
With a Roman nose
And claws not made to shake hands with,
40   And a Me-Almighty eye.

The new Proud Republic
Based on the mystery of pride.
Overweening men, full of power of life, commanding a teeming obedience.

Eagle of the Rockies, bird of men that are masters,
Lifting the rabbit-blood of the myriads up into something splendid,
Leaving a few bones;
Opening great wings in the face of the sheep-faced ewe

yawp "Barbaric yawp" is Walt Whitman's phrase: "I sound my barbaric yawp over the roofs of the world" ("Song of Myself"). **Now . . . glory** "Consider the lilies of the field, how they grow; they toil not, neither do they spin: And yet I say unto you, That even Solomon in all his glory was not arrayed like one of these" (Matthew 6:28–29).

Who is losing her lamb,
Drinking a little blood, and loosing another royalty unto the world.

50   Is that you, American Eagle?

Or are you the goose that lays the golden egg?
Which is just a stone to anyone asking for meat.
And are you going to go on for ever
Laying that golden egg,
That addled golden egg?
                    1923

The Mess of Love

We've made a great mess of love
Since we made an ideal of it.

The moment I swear to love a woman, a certain woman, all my life
That moment I begin to hate her.

The moment I even say to a woman: I love you!—
My love dies down considerably.

The moment love is an understood thing between us, we are sure of it,
It's a cold egg,° it isn't love any more.

Love is like a flower, it must flower and fade;
10   If it doesn't fade, it is not a flower,
It's either an artificial rag blossom, or an immortelle, for the cemetery.

The moment the mind interferes with love, or the will fixes on it,
Or the personality assumes it as an attribute, or the ego takes possession of it,
It is not love any more, it's just a mess.
And we've made a great mess of love, mind-perverted, will-perverted, ego-
    perverted love.
                                                    1929

The Ship of Death

                    I
Now it is autumn and the falling fruit
and the long journey towards oblivion.

The apples falling like great drops of dew
to bruise themselves an exit from themselves.

And it is time to go, to bid farewell
to one's own self, and find an exit
from the fallen self.

cold egg See "beauty is a cold egg" in St.
Mawr, n. 65.

II

Have you built your ship of death,° O have you?
O build your ship of death, for you will need it.

10   The grim forest is at hand, when the apples will fall
thick, almost thunderous, on the hardened earth.

And death is on the air like a smell of ashes!
Ah! can't you smell it?

And in the bruised body, the frightened soul
finds itself shrinking, wincing from the cold
that blows upon it through the orifices.

III

And can a man his own quietus make
with a bare bodkin?°

With daggers, bodkins, bullets, man can make
20   a bruise or break of exit for his life;
but is that a quietus, O tell me, is it quietus?

Surely not so! for how could murder, even self-murder
ever a quietus make?

IV

O let us talk of quiet that we know,
that we can know, the deep and lovely quiet
of a strong heart at peace!

How can we this, our own quietus, make?

V

Build then the ship of death, for you must take
the longest journey, to oblivion.

30   And die the death, the long and painful death
that lies between the old self and the new.

Already our bodies are fallen, bruised, badly bruised,
already our souls are oozing through the exit
of the cruel bruise.

Already the dark and endless ocean of the end
is washing in through the breaches of our wounds,
already the flood is upon us.

O build your ship of death, your little ark
and furnish it with food, with little cakes, and wine
40   for the dark flight down oblivion.

---

ship of death Lawrence is thinking of the ship
models, with all their crew and fully supplied,
put into Etruscan and Egyptian tombs to ferry
the dead across final waters.

his own . . . bare bodkin "quietus," a release
from life; "bodkin," here, a sword. This phrase
is quoted from Hamlet's soliloquy on suicide
(*Hamlet* III.i.75–76).

VI

Piecemeal the body dies, and the timid soul
has her footing washed away, as the dark flood rises.

We are dying, we are dying, we are all of us dying
and nothing will stay the death-flood rising within us
and soon it will rise on the world, on the outside world.

We are dying, we are dying, piecemeal our bodies are dying
and our strength leaves us,
and our soul cowers naked in the dark rain over the flood,
cowering in the last branches of the tree of our life.

VII

50   We are dying, we are dying, so all we can do
is now to be willing to die, and to build the ship
of death to carry the soul on the longest journey.

A little ship, with oars and food
and little dishes, and all accoutrements
fitting and ready for the departed soul.

Now launch the small ship, now as the body dies
and life departs, launch out, the fragile soul
in the fragile ship of courage, the ark of faith
with its store of food and little cooking pans
60   and change of clothes,
upon the flood's black waste
upon the waters of the end
upon the sea of death, where still we sail
darkly, for we cannot steer, and have no port.

There is no port, there is nowhere to go
only the deepening blackness darkening still
blacker upon the soundless, ungurgling flood
darkness at one with darkness, up and down
and sideways utterly dark, so there is no direction any more.
70   and the little ship is there; yet she is gone.
She is not seen, for there is nothing to see her by.
She is gone! gone! and yet
somewhere she is there.

Nowhere!

VIII

And everything is gone, the body is gone
completely under, gone, entirely gone.
The upper darkness is heavy as the lower,
between them the little ship
is gone
80   she is gone

It is the end, it is oblivion.

IX

And yet out of eternity a thread
separates itself on the blackness,
a horizontal thread
that fumes a little with pallor upon the dark.

Is it illusion? or does the pallor fume
a little higher?
Ah wait, wait, for there's the dawn,
the cruel dawn of coming back to life
90 out of oblivion.

Wait, wait, the little ship
drifting, beneath the deadly ashy grey
of a flood-dawn.

Wait, wait! even so, a flush of yellow
and strangely, O chilled wan soul, a flush of rose.

A flush of rose, and the whole thing starts again.

X

The flood subsides, and the body, like a worn sea-shell
emerges strange and lovely.
And the little ship wings home, faltering and lapsing
on the pink flood,
100 and the frail soul steps out, into her house again
filling the heart with peace.

Swings the heart renewed with peace
even of oblivion.

Oh build your ship of death. Oh build it!
for you will need it.
For the voyage of oblivion awaits you.
1929–30   1932

Bavarian Gentians°

(version of Manuscript "A")

Not every man has gentians in his house
In soft September, at slow, sad Michaelmas.

Bavarian Gentians This is the manuscript version of one of Lawrence's greatest last poems, a reading of the intensely dark blue-violet of the autumnal flowers as the color of the "darkness visible," in Milton's phase, of the underworld. The story of Persephone, daughter of Demeter (Ceres), carried off to be queen of Hades by Pluto (Dis), was a myth of the seasons: because Persephone ate some pomegranate seeds while in the underworld, she had to remain there part of each year, during which time Demeter, the grain goddess (our word "cereal" comes from her Latin name) grieves. The revised version is appended.

Bavarian gentians, tall and dark, but dark
darkening the day-time torch-like with the smoking blueness of Pluto's gloom,
ribbed hellish flowers erect, with their blaze of darkness spread blue
Blown into points, by the heavy white draught of the day.

Torch-flowers of the blue-smoking darkness, Pluto's dark-blue blaze
black lamps from the halls of Dis, smoking dark blue
giving off darkness, blue darkness, upon Demeter's yellow-pale day
Whom have you come for, here in the white-cast day?

Reach me a gentian, give me a torch!
let me guide myself with the blue, forked torch of a flower
down the darker and darker stairs, where blue is darkened on blueness
down the way Persephone goes, just now, in first-frosted September
to the sightless realm where darkness is married to dark
and Persephone herself is but a voice, as a bride,
a gloom invisible enfolded in the deeper dark
of the arms of Pluto as he ravishes her once again
and pierces her once more with his passion of the utter dark.
among the splendour of black-blue torches, shedding fathomless darkness on the
    nuptials.

Give me a flower on a tall stem, and three dark flames,
For I will go to the wedding, and be wedding-guest
At the marriage of the living dark.

Bavarian Gentians

(*final version*)

Not every man has gentians in his house
In Soft September, at slow, Sad Michaelmas.

Bavarian gentians, big and dark, only dark
Darkening the day-time torch-like with the smoking blueness of Pluto's gloom,
Ribbed and torch-like with their blaze of darkness spread blue
Down flattening into points, flattened under the sweep of white day
Torch-flower of the blue-smoking darkness, Pluto's dark-blue daze,
Black lamps from the halls of Dis, burning dark blue,
Giving off darkness, blue darkness, as Demeter's pale lamps give off light,
Lead me then, lead me the way.

Reach me a gentian, give me a torch
Let me guide myself with the blue, forked torch of this flower
Down the darker and darker stairs, where blue is darkened on blueness,
Even where Persephone goes, just now, from the frosted September
To the sightless realm where darkness is awake upon the dark
And Persephone herself is but a voice
Or a darkness invisible enfolded in the deeper dark

Of the arms Plutonic, and pierced with the passion of dense gloom,
Among the splendour of torches of darkness, shedding darkness on the lost bride
   and her groom.
1929   1932

Pornography and Obscenity

Lawrence had first-hand experience of those he called the "censor-morons." *The Rainbow* was prosecuted and withdrawn from circulation in 1915, to the great detriment of his income in the following years. *Lady Chatterley's Lover,* with its deliberate use of "shocking" words, ran head-on into censorship, and was not published in an openly available unexpurgated edition until 1959. In his last years Lawrence painted, and when his paintings were shown in London they were seized by the police. He wrote the present essay in 1929, and it was published by Faber and Faber in the same series of pamphlets as Lord Brentford's defense of censorship. William Joynson-Hicks, 1st Viscount Brentford (1865–1932), unpopularly known as Jix, was Home Secretary (with responsibilities that in the United States are assumed partly by the Attorney General and partly by the Secretary of the Interior), and a symbol of all that was most repressive and sanctimonious in the administration of the laws relating to censorship. While in his pamphlet Lawrence ridicules Jix, he has more important matters in hand —partly the defense of his own shock tactic in *Lady Chatterley,* a tactic intended to liberate the "four-letter words" from their bondage to dirt and secrecy, and even more importantly to emphasize one of his main preoccupations—the need for a revolutionary change in sexual attitudes. He distinguishes between works which deal cleanly with sex, and those which "do dirt on it"; then, having defined pornography, he explains the harm it does, relating it to a diseased—and very widespread—attitude toward sex, an attitude exemplified by the puritans themselves.

    Lawrence over the years developed a vigorous journalistic and polemical manner; occasionally it sank into a kind of tabloid shouting, but this selection shows it at its best. For many years he had speculated, sometimes in a rather highflown way, on the consequences for human conduct of the juxtaposition of sexual and excremental functions; here he returns to this topic in the context of his argument against puritanism, and it does not sound at all cranky, but reinforces what he is saying. He believed that since the Renaissance we have gone badly wrong about sex, partly from fear of disease, partly because of a dissociation of mind and bodily function which has made for the wrong kind of secrecy. The abolition of the "dirty little secret" is necessary to human freedom and the redevelopment of the whole man. Thus, in this lively and lucid polemic, Lawrence attacks a specific target but also gives expression to some of his most deeply held convictions about the modern world. That sex is degraded was for him a catastrophe in itself, and also a symptom of the whole disease of modern life.

From Pornography and Obscenity

. . . The reaction to any word may be, in any individual, either a mob-reaction or an individual reaction. It is up to the individual to ask himself: Is my reaction individual, or am I merely reacting from my mob-self?

When it comes to the so-called obscene words, I should say that hardly one person in a million escapes mob-reaction. The first reaction is almost sure to be mob-reaction, mob-indignation, mob-condemnation. And the' mob gets no further. But the real individual has second thoughts and says: Am I really shocked? Do I *really* feel outraged and indignant? And the answer of any individual is bound to be: No, I am not shocked, not outraged, nor indignant. I know the word, and take it for what it is, and I am not going to be jockeyed into making a mountain out of a mole-hill, not for all the law in the world.

Now if the use of a few so-called obscene words will startle man or woman out of a mob-habit into an individual state, well and good. And word prudery is so universal a mob-habit that it is time we were startled out of it.

But still we have only tackled obscenity, and the problem of pornography goes even deeper. When a man is startled into his individual self, he still may not be able to know, inside himself, whether Rabelais [1] is or is not pornographic: and over Aretino or even Boccaccio [2] he may perhaps puzzle in vain, torn between different emotions.

One essay on pornography, I remember, comes to the conclusion that pornography in art is that which is calculated to arouse sexual desire, or sexual excitement. And stress is laid on the fact, whether the author or artist *intended* to arouse sexual feelings. It is the old vexed question of intention, become so so dull today, when we know how strong and influential our unconscious intentions are. And why a man should be held guilty of his conscious intentions, and innocent of his unconscious intentions, I don't know, since every man is more made up of unconscious intentions than of conscious ones. I am what I am, not merely what I think I am.

However! We take it, I assume, that *pornography* is something base, something unpleasant. In short, we don't like it. And why don't we like it? Because it arouses sexual feelings?

I think not. No matter how hard we may pretend otherwise, most of us rather like a moderate rousing of our sex. It warms us, stimulates us like sunshine on a grey day. After a century or two of Puritanism, this is still true of most people. Only the mob-habit of condemning any form of sex is too strong to let us admit it naturally. And there are, of course, many people who are genuinely repelled by the simplest and most natural stirrings of sexual feeling. But these people are perverts who have fallen into hatred of their fellow men: thwarted, disappointed, unfulfilled people, of whom, alas, our civilization contains so many. And they nearly always enjoy some unsimple and unnatural form of sex excitement, secretly.

Even quite advanced art critics would try to make us believe that any picture or book which had 'sex appeal' was ipso facto a bad book or picture. This is just canting hypocrisy. Half the great poems, pictures, music, stories of the whole

---

1. François Rabelais (1495–1553), French humanist and satirist, author of *Gargantua* and *Pantagruel* (1546–64); he was against asceticism, in favor of obeying the dictates of experience rather than authority, and frequently obscene.
2. Pietro Aretino (1492–1556), humanist and poet, famous for erotic and obscene verses, for which appropriate illustrations were provided. Giovanni Boccaccio (1313–75), whose hundred tales called the *Decameron* (Greek: "10 days") include some that are indecent.

world are great by virtue of the beauty of their sex appeal. Titian [3] or Renoir,[4] the Song of Solomon or *Jane Eyre*,[5] Mozart or 'Annie Laurie,' [6] the loveliness is all interwoven with sex appeal, sex stimulus, call it what you will. Even Michelangelo,[7] who rather hated sex, can't help filling the Cornucopia with phallic acorns. Sex is a very powerful, beneficial and necessary stimulus in human life, and we are all grateful when we feel its warm, natural flow through us, like a form of sunshine.

So we can dismiss the idea that sex appeal in art is pornography. It may be so to the grey Puritan, but the grey Puritan is a sick man, soul and body sick, so why should we bother about his hallucinations? Sex appeal, of course, varies enormously. There are endless different kinds, and endless degrees of each kind. Perhaps it may be argued that a mild degree of sex appeal is not pornographical, whereas a high degree is. But this is a fallacy. Boccaccio at his hottest seems to me less pornographical than *Pamela* or *Clarissa Harlowe* [8] or even *Jane Eyre*, or a host of modern books or films which pass uncensored. At the same time Wagner's *Tristan and Isolde* [9] seems to me very near to pornography, and so, even, do some quite popular Christian hymns.

What is it, then? It isn't a question of sex appeal, merely: nor even a question of deliberate intention on the part of the author or artist to arouse sexual excitement. Rabelais sometimes had a deliberate intention, so, in a different way, did Boccaccio. And I'm sure poor Charlotte Brontë, or the authoress of *The Sheik*,[10] did not have any deliberate intention to stimulate sex feelings in the reader. Yet I find *Jane Eyre* verging towards pornography and Boccaccio seems to me always fresh and wholesome.

The late British Home Secretary,[11] who prides himself on being a very sincere Puritan, grey, grey in every fibre, said with indignant sorrow in one of his outbursts on improper books: '—and these two young people, who had been perfectly pure up till that time, after reading this book went and had sexual intercourse together!!!' *One up to them!* is all we can answer. But the grey Guardian of British Morals seemed to think that if they had murdered one another, or worn each other to rags of nervous prostration, it would have been much better. The grey disease!

3. Tiziano Vercelli (1490?–1576), one of the greatest Venetian painters.

4. Pierre Auguste Renoir (1841–1919), French painter celebrated for sensuous rendering of women.

5. Novel (1847) by Charlotte Brontë (1816–55), in which the passion of Mr. Rochester, who has a mad wife, remains unrequited until her death and his disfigurement in a fire.

6. Famous love song by William Douglas (1672–1748).

7. Michelangelo Buonarroti (1475–1564), greatest of the Florentine Renaissance artists; architect, sculptor, poet, and painter of the Sistine ceiling in the Vatican, in which this cornucopia and its contents appear (under the figure of Adam).

8. Samuel Richardson (1689–1761) wrote *Pamela* (1741), about the resistance of a virtuous servant-girl to her master and their subsequent marriage; and *Clarissa Harlowe* (1748), about the seduction of a virtuous woman by a rake and her subsequent noble death.

9. Richard Wagner (1813–83), after many difficulties, had his *Tristan and Isolde* performed in 1865. It is the story of a consuming erotic passion between the two, and its tragic end.

10. A bestseller of 1921, by Edith Maud Hull; later a famous film starring Rudolph Valentino.

11. See Headnote.

Then what is pornography, after all this? It isn't sex appeal or sex stimulus in art. It isn't even a deliberate intention on the part of the artist to arouse or excite sexual feelings. There's nothing wrong with sexual feelings in themselves, so long as they are straightforward and not sneaking or sly. The right sort of sex stimulus is invaluable to human daily life. Without it the world grows grey. I would give everybody the gay Renaissance stories to read, they would help to shake off a lot of grey self-importance, which is our modern civilized disease.

But even I would censor genuine pornography, rigorously. It would not be very difficult. In the first place, genuine pornography is almost always underworld, it doesn't come into the open. In the second, you can recognize it by the insult it offers, invariably, to sex, and to the human spirit.

Pornography is the attempt to insult sex, to do dirt on it. This is unpardonable. Take the very lowest instance, the picture post-card sold under hand, by the underworld, in most cities. What I have seen of them have been of an ugliness to make you cry. The insult to the human body, the insult to a vital human relationship! Ugly and cheap they make the human nudity, ugly and degraded they make the sexual act, trivial and cheap and nasty.

It is the same with the books they sell in the underworld. They are either so ugly they make you ill, or so fatuous you can't imagine anybody but a cretin or a moron reading them, or writing them.

It is the same with the dirty limericks that people tell after dinner, or the dirty stories one hears commercial travellers telling each other in a smoke-room. Occasionally there is a really funny one, that redeems a great deal. But usually they are just ugly and repellent, and the so-called 'humour' is just a trick of doing dirt on sex.

Now the human nudity of a great many modern people is just ugly and degraded, and the sexual act between modern people is just the same, merely ugly and degrading. But this is nothing to be proud of. It is the catastrophe of our civilization. I am sure no other civilization, not even the Roman, has showed such a vast proportion of ignominious and degraded nudity, and ugly, squalid, dirty sex. Because no other civilization has driven sex into the underworld, and nudity to the w.c.

The intelligent young, thank heaven, seem determined to alter in these two respects. They are rescuing their young nudity from the stuffy, pornographical, hole-and-corner underworld of their elders, and they refuse to sneak about the sexual relation. This is a change the elderly grey ones of course deplore, but it is in fact a very great change for the better, and a real revolution.

But it is amazing how strong is the will in ordinary, vulgar people to do dirt on sex. It was one of my fond illusions, when I was young, that the ordinary healthy-seeming sort of men, in railway carriages, or the smoke-room of an hotel or a pullman, were healthy in their feelings and had a wholesome rough devil-may-care attitude towards sex. All wrong! All wrong! Experience teaches that common individuals of this sort have a disgusting attitude towards sex, a disgusting contempt of it, a disgusting desire to insult it. If such fellows have intercourse with a woman, they triumphantly feel that they have done her dirt, and now she is lower, cheaper, more contemptible than she was before.

It is individuals of this sort that tell dirty stories, carry indecent picture post-cards, and know the indecent books. This is the great pornographical class—

the really common men-in-the-street and women-in-the-street. They have as great a hate and contempt of sex as the greyest Puritan, and when an appeal is made to them, they are always on the side of the angels. They insist that a film-heroine shall be a neuter, a sexless thing of washed-out purity. They insist that real sex-feeling shall only be shown by the villain or villainess, low lust. They find a Titian or a Renoir really indecent, and they don't want their wives and daughters to see it.

Why? Because they have the grey disease of sex-hatred, coupled with the yellow disease of dirt-lust. The sex functions and the excrementory functions in the human body work so close together, yet they are, so to speak, utterly differ-ent in direction. Sex is a creative flow, the excrementory flow is towards dissolu-tion, de-creation, if we may use such a word. In the really healthy human being the distinction between the two is instant, our profoundest instincts are perhaps our instincts of opposition between the two flows.

But in the degraded human being the deep instincts have gone dead, and then the two flows become identical. *This* is the secret of really vulgar and of pornographical people: the sex flow and the excrement flow is the same to them. It happens when the psyche deteriorates, and the profound controlling instincts collapse. Then sex is dirt and dirt is sex, and sexual excitement becomes a playing with dirt, and any sign of sex in a woman becomes a show of her dirt. This is the condition of the common, vulgar human being whose name is legion, and who lifts his voice and it is the *Vox populi, vox Dei*.[12] And this is the source of all pornography.

And for this reason we must admit that *Jane Eyre* or Wagner's *Tristan* are much nearer to pornography than is Boccaccio. Wagner and Charlotte Brontë were both in the state where the strongest instincts have collapsed, and sex has become something slightly obscene, to be wallowed in, but despised. Mr. Rochester's sex passion is not 'respectable' till Mr. Rochester is burned, blinded, disfigured, and reduced to helpless dependence. Then, thoroughly humbled and humiliated, it may be merely admitted. All the previous titillations are slightly indecent, as in *Pamela* or *The Mill on the Floss*[13] or *Anna Karenina*.[14] As soon as there is sex excitement with a desire to spite the sexual feeling, to humiliate it and degrade it, the element of pornography enters.

For this reason, there is an element of pornography in nearly all nineteenth century literature and very many so-called pure people have a nasty porno-graphical side to them, and never was the pornographical appetite stronger than it is today. It is a sign of a diseased condition of the body politic. But the way to treat the disease is to come out into the open with sex and sex stimulus. The real pornographer truly dislikes Boccaccio, because the fresh healthy naturalness of the Italian story-teller makes the modern pornographical shrimp feel the dirty worm he is. Today Boccaccio should be given to everybody, young or old, to

12. "The voice of the people is the voice of God," advice contained in a letter to Charle-magne (*c*. 800 A.D.) from his English theological consultant, Alcuin.
13. Novel (1860) by George Eliot (Mary Ann Evans; 1819–80). Lawrence is thinking of a scene in which the heroine drifts down river with a handsome young man.
14. Novel (1874–76) by Leo Tolstoy (1828–1910). Lawrence often expressed his dis-agreement with the conventional judgment that it is one of the greatest of novels, or perhaps even the greatest; he thought it sexually repressive.

read if they like. Only a natural fresh openness about sex will do any good, now we are being swamped by secret or semi-secret pornography. And perhaps the Renaissance story-tellers, Boccaccio, Lasca,[15] and the rest, are the best antidote we can find now, just as more plasters of Puritanism are the most harmful remedy we can resort to.

The whole question of pornography seems to me a question of secrecy. Without secrecy there would be no pornography. But secrecy and modesty are two utterly different things. Secrecy has always an element of fear in it, amounting very often to hate. Modesty is gentle and reserved. Today, modesty is thrown to the winds, even in the presence of the grey guardians. But secrecy is hugged, being a vice in itself. And the attitude of the grey ones is: Dear young ladies, you may abandon all modesty, so long as you hug your dirty little secret.

This 'dirty little secret' has become infinitely precious to the mob of people today. It is a kind of hidden sore or inflammation which, when rubbed or scratched, gives off sharp thrills that seem delicious. So the dirty little secret is rubbed and scratched more and more, till it becomes more and more secretly inflamed, and the nervous and psychic health of the individual is more and more impaired. One might easily say that half the love novels and half the love films today depend entirely for their success on the secret rubbing of the dirty little secret. You can call this sex excitement if you like, but it is sex excitement of a secretive, furtive sort, quite special. The plain and simple excitement, quite open and wholesome, which you find in some Boccaccio stories is not for a minute to be confused with the furtive excitement aroused by rubbing the dirty little secret in all secrecy in modern best-sellers. This furtive, sneaking, cunning rubbing of an inflamed spot in the imagination is the very quick of modern pornography, and it is a beastly and very dangerous thing. You can't so easily expose it, because of its very furtiveness and its sneaking cunning. So the cheap and popular modern love novel and love film flourishes and is even praised by moral guardians, because you get the sneaking thrill fumbling under all the purity of dainty underclothes, without one single gross word to let you know what is happening.

Without secrecy there would be no pornography. But if pornography is the result of sneaking secrecy, what is the result of pornography? What is the effect on the individual?

The effect on the individual is manifold, and always pernicious. But one effect is perhaps inevitable. The pornography of today, whether it be the pornography of the rubber-goods shop or the pornography of the popular novel, film, and play, is an invariable stimulant to the vice of self-abuse, onanism, masturbation, call it what you will. In young or old, man or woman, boy or girl, modern pornography is a direct provocative of masturbation. It cannot be otherwise. When the grey ones wail that the young man and the young woman went and had sexual intercourse, they are bewailing the fact that the young man and the young woman didn't go separately and masturbate. Sex must go somewhere, especially in young people. So, in our glorious civilization, it goes in masturbation. And the mass of our popular literature, the bulk of our popular amuse-

---

15. Anton Francesco Grazzini (1503–84), a Florentine satirist and academician, was called *Il Lasca*, "The Roach."

ments just exists to provoke masturbation. Masturbation is the one thoroughly secret act of the human being, more secret even than excrementation. It is the one functional result of sex-secrecy, and it is stimulated and provoked by our glorious popular literature of pretty pornography, which rubs on the dirty secret without letting you know what is happening.

Now I have heard men, teachers and clergymen, commend masturbation as the solution of an otherwise insoluble sex problem. This at least is honest. The sex problem is there, and you can't just will it away. There it is, and under the ban of secrecy and taboo in mother and father, teacher, friend, and foe, it has found its own solution, the solution of masturbation.

But what about the solution? Do we accept it? Do all the grey ones of this world accept it? If so, they must now accept it openly. We can none of us pretend any longer to be blind to the fact of masturbation, in young and old, man and woman. The moral guardians who are prepared to censor all open and plain portrayal of sex must now be made to give their only justification: We prefer that the people shall masturbate. If this preference is open and declared, then the existing forms of censorship are justified. If the moral guardians prefer that the people shall masturbate, then their present behaviour is correct, and popular amusements are as they should be. If sexual intercourse is deadly sin, and masturbation is comparatively pure and harmless, then all is well. Let things continue as they now are.

Is masturbation so harmless, though? Is it even comparatively pure and harmless? Not to my thinking. In the young, a certain amount of masturbation is inevitable, but not therefore natural. I think, there is no boy or girl who masturbates without feeling a sense of shame, anger, and futility. Following the excitement comes the shame, anger, humiliation, and the sense of futility. This sense of futility and humiliation deepens as the years go on, into a suppressed rage, because of the impossibility of escape. The one thing that it seems impossible to escape from, once the habit is formed, is masturbation. It goes on and on, on into old age, in spite of marriage or love affairs or anything else. And it always carries this secret feeling of futility and humiliation, futility and humiliation. And this is, perhaps, the deepest and most dangerous cancer of our civilization. Instead of being a comparatively pure and harmless vice, masturbation is certainly the most dangerous sexual vice that a society can be afflicted with, in the long run. Comparatively pure it may be—purity being what it is. But harmless!!!

The great danger of masturbation lies in its merely exhaustive nature. In sexual intercourse, there is a give and take. A new stimulus enters as the native stimulus departs. Something quite new is added as the old surcharge is removed. And this is so in all sexual intercourse where two creatures are concerned, even in the homosexual intercourse. But in masturbation there is nothing but loss. There is no reciprocity. There is merely the spending away of a certain force, and no return. The body remains, in a sense, a corpse, after the act of self-abuse. There is no change, only deadening. There is what we call dead loss. And this is not the case in any act of sexual intercourse between two people. Two people may destroy one another in sex. But they cannot just produce the null effect of masturbation.

The only positive effect of masturbation is that it seems to release a certain mental energy, in some people. But it is mental energy which manifests itself always in the same way, in a vicious circle of analysis and impotent criticism, or else a vicious circle of false and easy sympathy, sentimentalities. The sentimentalism and the niggling analysis, often self-analysis, of most of our modern literature, is a sign of self-abuse. It is the manifestation of masturbation, the sort of conscious activity stimulated by masturbation, whether male or female. The outstanding feature of such consciousness is that there is no real object, there is only subject. That is just the same whether it be a novel or a work of science. The author never escapes from himself, he pads along within the vicious circle of himself. There is hardly a writer living who gets out of the vicious circle of himself—or a painter either. Hence the lack of creation, and the stupendous amount of production. It is a masturbation result, within the vicious circle of the self. It is self-absorption made public.

And of course the process is exhaustive. The real masturbation of Englishmen began only in the nineteenth century. It has continued with an increasing emptying of the real vitality and the real *being* of men, till now people are little more than shells of people. Most of the responses are dead, most of the awareness is dead, nearly all the constructive activity is dead, and all that remains is a sort of shell, a half-empty creature fatally self-preoccupied and incapable of either giving or taking. Incapable either of giving or taking, in the vital self. And this is masturbation's result. Enclosed within the vicious circle of the self, with no vital contacts outside, the self becomes emptier and emptier, till it is almost a nullus, a nothingness.

But null or nothing as it may be, it still hangs on to the dirty little secret, which it must still secretly rub and inflame. For ever the vicious circle. And it has a weird, blind will of its own.

One of my most sympathetic critics wrote: 'If Mr. Lawrence's attitude to sex were adopted, then two things would disappear, the love lyric and the smoking-room story.' And this, I think, is true. But it depends on which love lyric he means. If it is the: *Who is Sylvia, what is she?* [16]—then it may just as well disappear. All that pure and noble and heaven-blessed stuff is only the counterpart to the smoking-room story. *Du bist wie eine Blume!* [17] Jawohl! One can see the elderly gentleman laying his hands on the head of the pure maiden and praying God to keep her for ever so pure, so clean and beautiful. Very nice for him! Just pornography! Tickling the dirty little secret and rolling his eyes to heaven! He knows perfectly well that if God keeps the maiden so clean and pure and beautiful—in his vulgar sense of clean and pure—for a few more years, then she'll be an unhappy old maid, and not pure nor beautiful at all, only stale and pathetic. Sentimentality is a sure sign of pornography. Why should 'sadness strike through the heart' of the old gentleman, because the maid was pure and beautiful? Anybody but a masturbator would have been glad and would have thought: What a lovely bride for some lucky man!—But no, not the self-enclosed, pornographic masturbator. Sadness has to strike into his beastly heart!—Away with such love lyrics, we've had too much of their pornographic poison, tickling the dirty little secret and rolling the eyes to heaven.

16. Song from Shakespeare's *Two Gentlemen of Verona;* it has a famous setting by Schubert.
17. Song by Heinrich Heine (1799–1856): "Thou art like a flower, so chaste and pure, . . ." "Yes, indeed!" adds Lawrence in German.

But if it is a question of the sound love lyric, *My love is like a red, red rose*—! [18] then we are on other ground. My love is like a red, red rose only when she's *not* like a pure, pure lily. And nowadays the pure, pure lilies are mostly festering, anyhow. Away with them and their lyrics. Away with the pure, pure lily lyric, along with the smoking-room story. They are counterparts, and the one is as pornographic as the other. *Du bist wie eine Blume* is really as pornographic as a dirty story: tickling the dirty little secret and rolling the eyes to heaven. But oh, if only Robert Burns had been accepted for what he is, then love might still have been like a red, red rose.

The vicious circle, the vicious circle! The vicious circle of masturbation! The vicious circle of self-consciousness that is never *fully* self-conscious, never fully and openly conscious, but always harping on the dirty little secret. The vicious circle of secrecy, in parents, teachers, friends—everybody. The specially vicious circle of family. The vast conspiracy of secrecy in the press, and, at the same time, the endless tickling of the dirty little secret. The needless masturbation! and the endless purity! The vicious circle!

How to get out of it? There is only one way: Away with the secret! No more secrecy! The only way to stop the terrible mental itch about sex is to come out quite simply and naturally into the open with it. It is terribly difficult, for the secret is cunning as a crab. Yet the thing to do is to make a beginning. The man who said to his exasperating daughter: 'My child, the only pleasure I ever had out of you was the pleasure I had in begetting you' has already done a great deal to release both himself and her from the dirty little secret.

How to get out of the dirty little secret! It is, as a matter of fact, extremely difficult for us secretive moderns. You can't do it by being wise and scientific about it, like Dr. Marie Stopes: [19] though to be wise and scientific like Dr. Marie Stopes is better than to be utterly hypocritical, like the grey ones. But by being wise and scientific in the serious and earnest manner you only tend to disinfect the dirty little secret, and either kill sex altogether with too much seriousness and intellect, or else leave it a miserable disinfected secret. The unhappy 'free and pure' love of so many people who have taken out the dirty little secret and thoroughly disinfected it with scientific words is apt to be more pathetic even than the common run of dirty-little-secret love. The danger is, that in killing the dirty little secret, you kill dynamic sex altogether, and leave only the scientific and deliberate mechanism.

This is what happens to many of those who become seriously 'free' in their sex, free and pure. They have mentalized sex till it is nothing at all, nothing at all but a mental quantity. And the final result is disaster, every time.

The same is true, in an even greater proportion, of the emancipated bohemians: and very many of the young are bohemian today, whether they ever set foot in Bohemia or not. But the bohemian is 'sex free.' The dirty little secret is no secret either to him or her. It is, indeed, a most blatantly open question. There is nothing they don't say: everything that can be revealed is revealed. And they do as they wish.

And then what? They have apparently killed the dirty little secret, but

---

18. Song by Robert Burns (1759–96). Lawrence admired Burns and even, at one stage, began a novel based on his life.

19. Marie Carmichael Stopes (1880–1958), pioneer birth control clinician and author of early sex manuals.

somehow, they have killed everything else too. Some of the dirt still sticks, perhaps; sex remains still dirty. But the thrill of secrecy is gone. Hence the terrible dreariness and depression of modern Bohemia, and the inward dreariness and emptiness of so many young people of today. They have killed, they imagine, the dirty little secret. The thrill of secrecy is gone. Some of the dirt remains. And for the rest, depression, inertia, lack of life. For sex is the fountainhead of our energetic life, and now the fountain ceases to flow.

Why? For two reasons. The idealists along the Marie Stopes line, and the young bohemians of today, have killed the dirty little secret as far as their personal self goes. But they are still under its dominion socially. In the social world, in the press, in literature, film, theatre, wireless, everywhere purity and the dirty little secret reign supreme. At home, at the dinner table, it is just the same. It is the same wherever you go. The young girl and the young woman is by tacit assumption pure, virgin, sexless. *Du bist wie eine Blume.* She, poor thing, knows quite well that flowers, even lilies, have tippling yellow anthers and a sticky stigma, sex, rolling sex. But to the popular mind flowers are sexless things, and when a girl is told she is like a flower, it means she is sexless and ought to be sexless. She herself knows quite well she isn't sexless and she isn't merely like a flower. But how bear up against the great social life forced on her? She can't! She succumbs, and the dirty little secret triumphs. She loses her interest in sex, as far as men are concerned, but the vicious circle of masturbation and self-consciousness encloses her even still faster.

This is one of the disasters of young life today. Personally, and among themselves, a great many, perhaps a majority, of the young people of today have come out into the open with sex and laid salt on the tail of the dirty little secret. And this is a very good thing. But in public, in the social world, the young are still entirely under the shadow of the grey elderly ones. The grey elderly ones belong to the last century, the eunuch century, the century of the mealy-mouthed lie, the century that has tried to destroy humanity, the nineteenth century. All our grey ones are left over from this century. And they rule us. They rule us with the grey, mealy-mouthed, canting lie of that great century of lies which, thank God, we are drifting away from. But they rule us still with the lie, for the lie, in the name of the lie. And they are too heavy and too numerous, the grey ones. It doesn't matter what government it is. They are all grey ones, left over from the last century, the century of mealy-mouthed liars, the century of purity and the dirty little secret.

So there is one cause for the depression of the young: the public reign of the mealy-mouthed lie, purity and the dirty little secret, which they themselves have privately overthrown. Having killed a good deal of the lie in their own private lives, the young are still enclosed and imprisoned within the great public lie of the grey ones. Hence the excess, the extravagance, the hysteria, and then the weakness, the feebleness, the pathetic silliness of the modern youth. They are all in a sort of prison, the prison of a great lie and a society of elderly liars. And this is one of the reasons, perhaps the main reason why the sex-flow is dying out of the young, the real energy is dying away. They are enclosed within a lie, and the sex won't flow. For the length of a complete lie is never more than three generations, and the young are the fourth generation of the nineteenth century lie.

The second reason why the sex-flow is dying is of course, that the young, in spite of their emancipation, are still enclosed within the vicious circle of self-conscious masturbation. They are thrown back into it, when they try to escape, by the enclosure of the vast public lie of purity and the dirty little secret. The most emancipated bohemians, who swank most about sex, are still utterly self-conscious and enclosed within the narcissus-masturbation circle. They have perhaps less sex even than the grey ones. The whole thing has been driven up into their heads. There isn't even the lurking hole of a dirty little secret. Their sex is more mental than their arithmetic; and as vital physical creatures they are more non-existent than ghosts. The modern bohemian is indeed a kind of ghost, not even narcissus, only the image of narcissus reflected on the face of the audience. The dirty little secret is most difficult to kill. You may put it to death publicly a thousand times, and still it reappears, like a crab, stealthily from under the submerged rocks of the personality. The French, who are supposed to be so open about sex, will perhaps be the last to kill the dirty little secret. Perhaps they don't want to. Anyhow, mere publicity won't do it.

You may parade sex abroad, but you will not kill the dirty little secret. You may read all the novels of Marcel Proust, with everything there in all detail. Yet you will not kill the dirty little secret. You will perhaps only make it more cunning. You may even bring about a state of utter indifference and sex-inertia, still without killing the dirty little secret. Or you may be the most wispy and enamoured little Don Juan of modern days, and still the core of your spirit merely be the dirty little secret. That is to say, you will still be in the narcissus-masturbation circle, the vicious circle of self-enclosure. For whenever the dirty little secret exists, it exists as the centre of the vicious circle of masturbation self-enclosure. And whenever you have the vicious circle of masturbation self-enclosure, you have at the core the dirty little secret. And the most high-flown sex-emancipated young people today are perhaps the most fatally and nervously enclosed within the masturbation self-enclosure. Nor do they want to get out of it, for there would be nothing left to come out.

But some people surely do want to come out of the awful self-enclosure. Today, practically everybody is self-conscious and imprisoned in self-consciousness. It is the joyful result of the dirty little secret. Vast numbers of people don't want to come out of the prison of their self-consciousness: they have so little left to come out with. But some people, surely, want to escape this doom of self-enclosure which is the doom of our civilization. There is surely a proud minority that wants once and for all to be free of the dirty little secret.

And the way to do it is, first, to fight the sentimental lie of purity and the dirty little secret wherever you meet it, inside yourself or in the world outside. Fight the great lie of the nineteenth century, which has soaked through our sex and our bones. It means fighting with almost every breath, for the lie is ubiquitous.

Then secondly, in his adventure of self-consciousness a man must come to the limits of himself and become aware of something beyond him. A man must be self-conscious enough to know his own limits, and to be aware of that which surpasses him. What surpasses me is the very urge of life that is within me, and this life urges me to forget myself and to yield to the stirring half-born impulse to smash up the vast lie of the world, and make a new world. If my life is merely to go on in a vicious circle of self-enclosure, masturbating self-consciousness, it is worth nothing to me. If my individual life is to be enclosed within the huge corrupt lie of society today, purity and the dirty little secret, then it is worth not much to me. Freedom is a very great reality. But it means, above all things, freedom from lies. It is, first, freedom from myself, from the lie of myself, from the lie of my all-importance, even to myself; it is freedom from the self-conscious masturbating thing I am, self-enclosed. And second, freedom from the vast lie of the social world, the lie of purity and the dirty little secret. All the other monstrous lies lurk under the cloak of this one primary lie. The monstrous lie of money lurks under the cloak of purity. Kill the purity-lie, and the money-lie will be defenceless.

We have to be sufficiently conscious, and self-conscious, to know our own limits and to be aware of the greater urge within us and beyond us. Then we cease to be primarily interested in ourselves. Then we learn to leave ourselves alone, in all the affective centres: not to force our feelings in any way, and never to force our sex. Then we make the great onslaught on to the outside lie, the inside lie being settled. And that is freedom and the fight for freedom. . . .

1929   1929

Apocalypse

Lawrence's interest in this subject was of long standing, and it occupied him a good deal during the last years of his life. He came to believe that the Book of Revelation was a distorted version of an older myth, itself an account of the ritual of a mystery religion such as that associated with Eleusis. This primitive text, he proposes, had been corrupted first by Jewish and then by Christian scribes. His intention is to recover the original, and use it as testimony of that condition of vital correspondence with the cosmos which has disappeared from our lives "in a time of the long slow death of the human being." In his theory the first part of the biblical text relates to the ritual directly; the rest is more a reflection of Christian power lust, the desire of the underdog for revenge. He finds in the recovered ritual a process of self-purgation very congenial to him in these years (witness the asceticism of his long late story *The Man Who Died*): a ritual death from which emerges "a new whole cloven flame of a new-bodied man with golden thighs and a face of glory," a man equipped with a third eye.

In the Bible, Lawrence feels, the imagery is corrupted; the Dragon (originally the Logos, wisdom) is now debased and becomes the insane acquisitive consciousness which entraps us all, especially women. The lurid prophecies and allegories of the later part of Revelation do not concern him; but in his final pages (among the last things Lawrence wrote) he considers the implication, religious and political, of this cult of the underdog, attacking the curse of power-seeking democracy and individualism, and asserting the need for a new collective consciousness of our relation to the universe, such as the original Apocalypse-myth embodies.

From Apocalypse

. . . Let us give up our false position as Christians, as individuals, as democrats. Let us find some conception of ourselves that will allow us to be peaceful and happy, instead of tormented and unhappy.

The Apocalypse shows us what we are resisting, unnaturally. We are unnaturally resisting our connection with the cosmos, with the world, with mankind, with the nation, with the family. All these connections are, in the Apocalypse, anathema, and they are anathema to us. We *cannot bear connection*. That is our malady. We *must* break away, and be isolate. We call that being free, being individual. Beyond a certain point, which we have reached, it is suicide. Perhaps we have chosen suicide. Well and good. The Apocalypse too chose suicide, with subsequent self-glorification.

But the Apocalypse shows, by its very resistance, the things that the human heart secretly yearns after. By the very frenzy with which the Apocalypse destroys the sun and the stars, the world, and all kings and all rulers, all scarlet and purple and cinnamon, all harlots, finally all men altogether who are not 'sealed,' we can see how deeply the apocalyptists are yearning for the sun and the stars and the earth and the waters of the earth, for nobility and lordship and might, and scarlet and gold splendour, for passionate love, and a proper unison with men, apart from this sealing business. What man most passionately wants is his living wholeness and his living unison, not his own isolate salvation of his 'soul.' Man wants his physical fulfilment first and foremost, since now, once and once only, he is in the flesh and potent. For man, the vast marvel is to be alive. For man, as for flower and beast and bird, the supreme triumph is to be most vividly, most perfectly alive. Whatever the unborn and the dead may know, they cannot know the beauty, the marvel of being alive in the flesh. The dead may look after the afterwards. But the magnificent here and now of life in the flesh is ours, and ours alone, and ours only for a time. We ought to dance with rapture that we should be alive and in the flesh, and part of the living, incarnate cosmos. I am part of the sun as my eye is part of me. That I am part of the earth my feet know perfectly, and my blood is part of the sea. My soul knows that I am part of the human race, my soul is an organic part of the great human soul, as my spirit is part of my nation. In my own very self, I am part of my family. There is nothing of me that is alone and absolute except my mind, and we shall find that the mind has no existence by itself, it is only the glitter of the sun on the surface of the waters.

So that my individualism is really an illusion. I am a part of the great whole, and I can never escape. But I *can* deny my connections, break them, and become a fragment. Then I am wretched.

What we want is to destroy our false, inorganic connections, especially those related to money, and re-establish the living organic connections, with the cosmos, the sun and earth, with mankind and nation and family. Start with the sun, and the rest will slowly, slowly happen.

1929   1931

T. S. ELIOT
1888–1965

Thomas Stearns Eliot was born in St. Louis, Missouri, on September 26, 1888. The family, Unitarian in religion, was descended from one Andrew Eliot who left East Coke, Somerset, England, in the mid-seventeenth century and settled in Massachusetts. His earliest writings appeared in the magazine of Smith Academy, St. Louis, in 1905. In the following year he entered Harvard, where he edited and contributed poems to *The Advocate*. While still in college he wrote several of the poems, including the title work, published in *Prufrock and Other Observations* (1917). *Prufrock* was written in 1910–11, by which time his early taste for such poetry as the *Rubáiyát* had been qualified by the anti-Romantic teachings of Irving Babbitt. His main academic interest was philosophy, and in 1910, armed with a Harvard M.A., Eliot went to Paris for a year and studied the philosophy of Henri Bergson (1859–1941), whose theory of time and intuition—distinguishing between clock time and a duration of a different order, and between orders of experience which one analyzes with the intelligence and those which one intuits as "intensive manifolds"—left its traces on the poetry. In 1911 he was a graduate assistant in philosophy at Harvard, and in 1914 went to Germany with the intention of studying philosophy at Marburg; in September 1914, the war having begun, he went instead to Oxford, where he worked on his thesis, a study of the Oxford philosopher F. H. Bradley.

In 1915 Eliot married, and taught for some time before joining a bank, where he was to work for eight years. During this period he was an editor of *The Egoist*, a London literary magazine, and reviewed for several journals. He was writing poetry, still influenced by the French Symbolist poets and especially Jules Laforgue, of whom he had learned in 1908 from Arthur Symons's influential book, *The Symbolist Movement in Literature* (1899); he was also studying the "metaphysical" poets and the Jacobean drama. In poor health, he obtained three months' leave from his bank and, first at Margate (a seaside resort near London) and then at a clinic in Lausanne, made *The Waste Land* ready for publication. In January 1922 he stopped at Paris on his way home to consult Ezra Pound about the poem. Later in that year he founded *The Criterion*, the influential right-wing literary journal which he continued until 1939; *The Waste Land* appeared in the first number. In 1925 he became a director of Faber and Gwyer (now Faber and Faber), the publishers. Already a celebrated London critic and lecturer, he took British citizenship in 1927, and was received into the Church of England. In 1930 he published *Ash Wednesday*.

It was only after an interval of four years that Eliot's poetry appeared again, with the choruses written for a church charity pageant, *The Rock*; this was followed in 1935 by his first play, *Murder in the Cathedral*. Unused material from this work went into the making of the poem "Burnt Norton" (1936), which was to be the first of the *Four Quartets*. A second play, *The Family Reunion*, appeared in 1939, and the remaining quartets were written in 1940–42. "Little Gidding," written twenty-three years before his death, was Eliot's last important poem. In 1948 he was awarded the Nobel Prize for literature. Three more plays, *The Cocktail Party*, *The Confidential Clerk*, and *The Elder Statesman*, belong to 1950, 1954, and 1959. Eliot's wife, from whom he had been separated for many years, died after a long illness in 1947; he married Valerie Fletcher in 1957. Eliot died in London on January 4, 1965.

1970

Eliot's poetry and its historical background are discussed in the Headnotes to the individual poems; the principal critical works are treated in connection with the prose selections.

The Love Song of J. Alfred Prufrock

Eliot began *Prufrock* at Harvard in 1910 and finished it in Munich in the following year. It has something in common with earlier Harvard poems, but is much more ambitious and elaborate. At this time he was much under the influence of the French poet Jules Laforgue (1860–87), whose methods of fantastic irony, free association, and deliberate bathos are here adopted. *Prufrock* is a dramatic monologue, and owes an obvious debt to Browning also, but has developed a new obliquity and reticence; there is no attempt to give the *persona* of Prufrock the interiority or solidity of a Browning *persona*. This is in part due to Eliot's current study of the philosopher F. H. Bradley (1846–1924), who treated personality as a delusion, holding that the "finite center" of the perceiving person is unknowable by other such centers. Prufrock is, it has been said, a name with a voice; the relations between his remarks are bound to seem arbitrary. It becomes a characteristic of all Eliot's poetry that it will not offer generally acceptable endorsements of its internal logic.

At the time of this poem Eliot had learned something about the Symbolist movement in literature from Arthur Symons's ground-breaking book of that title. This introduced the young poet to the bizarre alternations of cynicism and sentiment in Laforgue but also to other recent French poets, notably Mallarmé and Verlaine, who were to become important to him. The effect of Symons is in fact hard to exaggerate; this friend, contemporary, and instructor of Yeats also shaped the interests of the younger man at Harvard. Symons wrote some verse that faintly resembles *Prufrock;* but, more importantly, he handed on to Eliot a mixture of interests—in the Jacobean drama and Donne, in Wagner and the Symbolists—which, though we think it characteristic of Eliot, was a fashionable blend of the concerns of the avant-garde in the generation immediately preceding his. (The affinity between modernist and Metaphysical poetry, as Eliot saw it, is expressed in his essay "The Metaphysical Poets.")

This does not detract from the modernist virtuosity of Eliot's poem, which was first recognized by Ezra Pound. Pound was responsible for its publication in the magazine *Poetry* (Chicago) in 1915, by which time Eliot was living in London and had formed his mutually admiring and fruitful relationship with Pound. He developed his own interests in Donne, the Jacobean drama, and the French poets; they were not identical with Pound's, but the poets had much in common: Eliot's belief (stated in the essay "Tradition and the Individual Talent") that poetry involved an extinction of the personality of the author, justified the use of an inscrutable *persona;* and his other famous theory, expressed briefly in the essay on *Hamlet* (1921), of the *objective correlative,* implied that the work in its objective existence called for a collaborative effort which would be different for different readers so that it would suggest no agreed story or interpretation; its relationship to what went on in the poet's mind is impenetrably obscure and irrelevant. Since *Prufrock* is written quite expressly to exemplify this kind of poetry, it is a mistake to try to extract from it a concealed narrative, even to assert that it is the story of what is going on in the mind of a man who may or may not be on the point of issuing a marriage proposal; or at any rate to do this at the expense of all the other possibilities inherent in the impenetrable reverie.

The strength of the poem lies in its apparently random transitions, its rhetorical and poetic flights, interrupted by bathos or irrelevance; its echoes of other poems. The image of the fog is *too* playful and elaborate, and the point lies partly in its being so. The indecorum of "butt-ends" tells us nothing about a character, but only helps to constitute a poem. The slight movement of disappointed erotic feeling (lines 62 ff., and at the end) like the comic inflation of "Do I dare / Disturb the universe," the Salome and Lazarus figures incongruously irrupting into an atmosphere of coffee-spoon life, all contribute to the substance of a poem, not of a personality; and the way to read it is to move with its movement, ride its little shocks, and, in a sense, live along its lines. The point is worth dwelling on here, since that is also the way to handle the much tougher poems that follow *Prufrock*.

The Love Song of J. Alfred Prufrock°

S'io credesse che mia risposta fosse
A persona che mai tornasse al mondo,
Questa fiamma staria senza più scosse.
Ma perciocché giammai di questo fondo
Non tornò vivo alcun, s'i'odo il vero,
Senza tema d'infamia ti rispondo.°

Let us go then, you and I,
When the evening is spread out against the sky
Like a patient etherised° upon a table;
Let us go, through certain half-deserted streets,
The muttering retreats
Of restless nights in one-night cheap hotels
And sawdust restaurants with oyster-shells:
Streets that follow like a tedious argument
Of insidious intent
To lead you to an overwhelming question . . .
Oh, do not ask, 'What is it?'
Let us go and make our visit.

In the room the women come and go
Talking of Michelangelo.

10

Prufrock Eliot apparently noted this name on a shopfront in the St. Louis of his youth.
S'io . . . rispondo "If I thought that my answer were being made to someone who would ever return to earth, this flame would remain without further movement; but since no one has ever returned alive from this depth, if what I hear is true, I answer you without fear of infamy" (Dante, *Inferno* XXVII.61–66). The speaker is Guido de Montefeltro, placed in the eighth circle of hell for giving evil counsel to a pope. He is wrapped in a flame and speaks from its trembling tip. The *persona* of the poem also tries to speak—though of a much less dramatic life—with a similar candor, on the assumption that whatever hell he is in, the reader is there also; or expecting (ll. 95 ff.) that to give such importance to his plight would simply gain him a rebuff.
etherised anesthetized

The yellow fog that rubs its back upon the window-panes,
The yellow smoke that rubs its muzzle on the window-panes,
Licked its tongue into the corners of the evening,
Lingered upon the pools that stand in drains,
Let fall upon its back the soot that falls from chimneys,
20   Slipped by the terrace, made a sudden leap,
And seeing that it was a soft October night,
Curled once about the house, and fell asleep.

And indeed there will be time°
For the yellow smoke that slides along the street,
Rubbing its back upon the window-panes;
There will be time, there will be time
To prepare a face to meet the faces that you meet;
There will be time to murder and create,
And time for all the works and days° of hands
30   That lift and drop a question on your plate;
Time for you and time for me,°
And time yet for a hundred indecisions,
And for a hundred visions and revisions,
Before the taking of a toast and tea.

In the room the women come and go
Talking of Michelangelo.

And indeed there will be time
To wonder, 'Do I dare?' and, 'Do I dare?'
Time to turn back and descend the stair,
40   With a bald spot in the middle of my hair—
(They will say: 'How his hair is growing thin!')
My morning coat, my collar mounting firmly to the chin,
My necktie rich and modest, but asserted by a simple pin—
(They will say: 'But how his arms and legs are thin!')
Do I dare
Disturb the universe?°
In a minute there is time
For decisions and revisions which a minute will reverse.

For I have known them all already, known them all—
50   Have known the evenings, mornings, afternoons,
I have measured out my life with coffee spoons;

there . . . time Here and in the subsequent
uses of the word "time" we hear a tired
allusion to Ecclesiastes 3:1–8: "To everything
there is a season, and a time to every purpose
under heaven: A time to be born, and a time
to die; a time to plant, and a time to pluck up
that which is planted; a time to kill, and a time
to heal; . . . a time to weep, and a time to
laugh; a time to mourn, and a time to dance;
. . . a time to keep silence, and a time to speak."
works and days title of didactic poem by the
early Greek poet Hesiod (8th century B.C.)
concerning rural labor
Time . . . me The theme and the rhythm drop
together into pure banality. In the fogbound
drawing room all the trivial issues seem important enough for solemn language, but only
momentarily; their futility declares itself in
various ways, this being one.
Do . . . universe? one of the poem's ironical
overstatements

I know the voices dying with a dying fall°
Beneath the music from a farther room.
    So how should I presume?

    And I have known the eyes already, known them all—
The eyes that fix you in a formulated phrase,
And when I am formulated, sprawling on a pin,
When I am pinned and wriggling on the wall,
Then how should I begin
60   To spit out all the butt-ends of my days and ways?
    And how should I presume?

    And I have known the arms already, known them all—
Arms that are braceleted and white and bare
(But in the lamplight, downed with light brown hair!)
Is it perfume from a dress
That makes me so digress?
Arms that lie along a table, or wrap about a shawl.
    And should I then presume?
    And how should I begin?

          ✸   ✸   ✸

70   Shall I say, I have gone at dusk through narrow streets
And watched the smoke that rises from the pipes
Of lonely men in shirt-sleeves, leaning out of windows? . . .

    I should have been a pair of ragged claws°
Scuttling across the floors of silent seas.

          ✸   ✸   ✸

    And the afternoon, the evening, sleeps so peacefully!
Smoothed by long fingers,
Asleep . . . tired . . . or it malingers,
Stretched on the floor, here beside you and me.
Should I, after tea and cakes and ices,
80   Have the strength to force the moment to its crisis?°
But though I have wept and fasted, wept and prayed,
Though I have seen my head (grown slightly bald) brought in upon a platter,
I am no prophet°—and here's no great-matter;
I have seen the moment of my greatness flicker,
And I have seen the eternal Footman hold my coat, and snicker,
And in short, I was afraid.

    And would it have been worth it, after all,
After the cups, the marmalade, the tea,
Among the porcelain, among some talk of you and me,

---

dying fall "That strain again! It had a dying
fall," *Twelfth Night* I.i.4, where the lovesick
Duke commends the music; here applied to
affected upperclass accents
pair . . . claws A crab; thus, it would be a
relief to lead a merely instinctual life, involving
no moral decisions and revisions.

ices . . . crisis The comic rhyme is another
deflationary device.
Though . . . prophet Salome asked the head of
John the Baptist on a platter as a reward for
her dance before Herod (Mark 6, Matthew
14). The story was one much used by poets as
an image of the sacrifices required by art.
Laforgue wrote an ironic *Salome*.

90   Would it have been worth while,
To have bitten off the matter with a smile,
To have squeezed the universe into a ball°
To roll it toward some overwhelming question,
To say: 'I am Lazarus,° come from the dead,
Come back to tell you all, I shall tell you all'—
If one, settling a pillow by her head,
    Should say: 'That is not what I meant at all;
    That is not it, at all.'

    And would it have been worth it, after all,
100 Would it have been worth while,
After the sunsets and the dooryards and the sprinkled streets,
After the novels, after the teacups, after the skirts that trail along the
    floor—
And this, and so much more?—
It is impossible to say just what I mean!
But as if a magic lantern threw the nerves in patterns on a screen:°
Would it have been worth while
If one, settling a pillow or throwing off a shawl,
And turning toward the window, should say:
    'That is not it at all,
110   That is not what I meant, at all.'

         ❋   ❋   ❋

No! I am not Prince Hamlet, nor was meant to be;
Am an attendant lord, one that will do
To swell a progress,° start a scene or two,
Advise the prince; no doubt, an easy tool,
Deferential, glad to be of use,
Politic, cautious, and meticulous;
Full of high sentence,° but a bit obtuse;
At times, indeed, almost ridiculous—
Almost, at times, the Fool.°

120   I grow old . . . I grow old . . .
I shall wear the bottoms of my trousers rolled.°

    Shall I part my hair behind?° Do I dare to eat a peach?
I shall wear white flannel trousers, and walk upon the beach.
I have heard the mermaids singing,° each to each.

squeezed . . . ball "Let us roll all our strength and all / Our sweetness up into one ball," Marvell, "To His Coy Mistress"—a seduction poem in which the lover *wants* something to happen
Lazarus See John 11:1–44.
as if . . . screen the equivalent of "telling all"
swell a progress A progress was a ceremonial royal journey; here he sees himself as an "extra" in a progress in a play.
Full . . . sentence expressing worthly sentiments (see Chaucer, the General Prologue, l. 306)
the Fool the Fool of Elizabethan drama, li-

censed not only to clown but to quibble with his betters
wear . . . rolled presumably, adopt the new fashion of trouser cuffs
part . . . behind a daring new hair style. He seems to contemplate a series of faintly daring gestures in defiance of advancing age, but soon gives up; the white trousers suggest the beach, the beach the mermaids, and the mermaids the myth of drowning which ends the work.
mermaids singing See Donne's "Go and Catch a Falling Star": "Teach me to hear mermaids singing" (l. 5), considered an impossibility.

I do not think that they will sing to me.

I have seen them riding seaward on the waves
Combing the white hair of the waves blown back
When the wind blows the water white and black.

130   We have lingered in the chambers of the sea
By sea-girls wreathed with seaweed red and brown
Till human voices wake us, and we drown.

1911   1917

Gerontion

This poem, which Eliot at one time wished to use as the prelude to *The Waste Land*, heads his *Poems, 1920* and represents his mature middle style. The method is not greatly different from *Prufrock*, but the tone of *vers de société* has been eliminated; the stylistic transitions and imitations are even more abrupt, the allusions and pastiche still more private and unsusceptible to "public" explanation. In the arbitrariness of the poem there are a few forces that make for cohesion. A past is exposed and contemplated in a reverie; the reverie is proper to the fractured, spiritually moribund world of Europe immediately after the Great War. Eliot's preoccupation with the spiritual sterility of this world, which he saw as involved in a great doomed experiment in heresy, a suicidal separation from the past and from religion, achieves an expression which is as far as possible *not* an expression but a statement of all these things in a mysterious and arbitrary image. Eliot believed that the man who suffers should be kept separate from the artist who creates, and by the same token divorced his "thought" from his poetry; the "thought" is nevertheless there, though in extraordinary disguises; and naturally it is the thought he had in his head at the time. Hence the echoes of his recent reading, the imitations of Jacobean dramatic verse, the use of Lancelot Andrewes's sermons, the presentation of the past as instantaneously there in the present, which is a condition expounded by Eliot in his essay "Tradition and the Individual Talent." The modern idea of history as meaningless chaos, related to the view that all nature is a chaos on which only the mind of man imposes fictions of order, Eliot derived from *The Education of Henry Adams* (1918).

Gerontion, "little old man," is obviously in some ways the image of a moribund civilization. He is near death, like Cardinal Newman's protagonist in *The Dream of Gerontius*, and, it has rightly been said, shares some attributes with another modern man to whom Eliot gave his careful attention, the Kurtz of Conrad's *Heart of Darkness*, who said he was "lying here in the dark waiting for death." The corruption of European religion, culture, and sex are the topics here as in *The Waste Land*, the method of which derives from "Gerontion." Eliot's prose deliberations, in his journal *The Criterion* and in many essays and lectures, are reflections in a different mode on the same subject.

Gerontion°

> *Thou hast nor youth nor age*
> *But as it were an after dinner sleep*
> *Dreaming of both.°*

Here I am, an old man in a dry month,
Being read to by a boy, waiting for rain.°
I was neither at the hot gates°
Nor fought in the warm rain
Nor knee deep in the salt marsh, heaving a cutlass,
Bitten by flies, fought.
My house is a decayed house,
And the Jew° squats on the window sill, the owner,
Spawned in some estaminet° of Antwerp,

10   Blistered in Brussels, patched and peeled in London.
The goat coughs at night in the field overhead;
Rocks, moss, stonecrop, iron, merds.°
The woman keeps the kitchen,° makes tea,
Sneezes at evening, poking the peevish gutter.°
                    I an old man,

A dull head among windy spaces.

  Signs are taken for wonders. 'We would see a sign!'°
The word within a word, unable to speak a word,
Swaddled with darkness.° In the juvescence° of the year

Gerontion "little old man"

Thou . . . both Shakespeare, *Measure for Measure* III.i.32–34. The Duke is counseling Claudio to accept his death sentence calmly. Later his sister Isabella explains to him that she could have had him reprieved by sleeping with his judge, Angelo, and he allows his fear of death and its consequences to overcome him. In expressing these fears he speaks of the guilty spirit after death: "imprisoned in the viewless winds / And blown with restless violence round about / The pendent world"—a speech based on the same passage in Cicero's *Somnium Scipionis* that is at the root of "Gerontion," ll. 67–69. The poem is in part a contemplation, in a dry season, of death and judgment.

in . . . rain A. C. Benson, in his biography (1905) of Edward FitzGerald, the translator of Omar Khayyam, summarizes a letter describing the poet as sitting "in a dry month, old and blind, being read to by a country boy, longing for rain."

hot gates literal translation of "Thermopylae," the pass which was the scene of the famous battle in 480 B.C. between Persians and Greeks, crucial to the history of Europe

Jew In earlier texts, this was *jew*; the word, in association with great European commercial centers, suggests perhaps the decay of culture through corrupt love of money.

estaminet cheap café

merds turds

woman . . . kitchen reminiscence of another FitzGerald letter

gutter drain

Signs . . . sign When the Scribes and Pharisees said, "Master, we would see a sign from thee,"

Christ answered, "An evil and adulterous generation seeketh after a sign" (Matthew 12:38–39). In John 4:48 Jesus says "Except ye see signs and wonders, ye will not believe"; the two words often go together in the Bible but Eliot dissociates them, quoting Andrewes (see next note).

The word . . . darkness Lancelot Andrewes (1555–1626) in a Nativity Sermon of 1618 on the text "And this shall be a sign unto you . . ." (Luke 2:12): "Signs are taken for wonders. 'Master, we would fain see a sign,' that is a miracle. And in this sense it is a sign to wonder at . . . *Verbum infans*, the Word without a word; the eternal Word not able to speak a word . . . a wonder sure. And the *sparganismos*, 'swaddled' [Luke 2:12], and that a wonder too. 'He,' that (as in the thirty-eighth of Job he saith) 'taketh the vast body of the main sea, turns it to and fro, as a little child, and rolls it about with the swaddling bands of darkness;'—He to come thus in clouts, Himself!" Eliot's admiration for Andrewes, and this passage in particular, is expressed in his essay on the preacher. Andrewes says "the Word without a word," a literal translation of the Latin *verbum infans;* Eliot says "The word within a word," and that this is an odd mistake rather than a deliberate alteration is suggested by the fact that in the essay (1926) he gives the same wrong version, quoting his poem rather than Andrewes (see *Selected Essays*, 1932, p. 307; *For Lancelot Andrewes*, 1928, p. 18).

juvescence presumably a mistake for *juvenescence*—youth, spring

1977

20   Came Christ the tiger°

    In depraved May, dogwood and chestnut, flowering judas,°
To be eaten, to be divided, to be drunk
Among whispers; by Mr. Silvero
With caressing hands, at Limoges°
Who walked all night in the next room;

    By Hakagawa, bowing among the Titians;
By Madame de Tornquist, in the dark room
Shifting the candles; Fräulein von Kulp
Who turned in the hall, one hand on the door. Vacant shuttles
30 Weave the wind.° I have no ghosts,
An old man in a draughty house
Under a windy knob.

    After such knowledge, what forgiveness? Think now
History has many cunning passages, contrived corridors
And issues, deceives with whispering ambitions,
Guides us by vanities. Think now
She gives when our attention is distracted
And what she gives, gives with such supple confusions
That the giving famishes the craving. Gives too late
40 What's not believed in, or if still believed,
In memory only, reconsidered passion. Gives too soon
Into weak hands, what's thought can be dispensed with
Till the refusal propagates a fear. Think
Neither fear nor courage saves us. Unnatural vices
Are fathered by our heroism. Virtues
Are forced upon us by our impudent crimes.
These tears are shaken from the wrath-bearing tree.°

    The tiger springs in the new year. Us he devours. Think at last
50 We have not reached conclusion, when I
Stiffen in a rented house.° Think at last
I have not made this show purposelessly

Christ the tiger In Andrewes's Nativity Sermon of 1622 he has the people who will not hurry (as the Magi did) to see the newborn Christ, exclaim, "Christ is no wild-cat. . . . What needs such haste?" Eliot admired this passage (see *Selected Essays*, p. 307). Insofar as these people were wrong, Christ *can* be called a wildcat. In the bestiaries a panther is sometimes an emblem of Christ.
In . . . judas alluding to *The Education of Henry Adams*, a description of the Maryland spring: "the . . . intermixture of delicate grace and passionate depravity that marked the Maryland May"
Limoges French town producing fine china. Silvero and the other names appear to have no significance beyond their cosmopolitanism; all are enacting rituals which are not those of the Mass.
Vacant . . . wind "My days are swifter than a weaver's shuttle, and are spent without hope. O remember that my life is wind: mine eye shall no more see good" (Job 7:6–7).
After . . . tree (ll. 33–47) a meditation on history and the moral confusion of the times written in the manner of some Jacobean dramatic poets. Henry Adams's *Education* furnished the hint for the material. The excited ellipses of the passionate argument are Jacobean in origin. Given the confusion that disorderly knowledge has brought, the past cannot be understood with any immediacy, as is necessary to a healthy culture. Hence an ethical confusion pointed up by the vices and virtues demonstrated, for example, in war.
wrath-bearing tree Compare Blake's *Poison Tree,* where wrath produces a tree, watered by tears.
We . . . house Simply: the death of the body is not the end of the matter.

And it is not by any concitation°
Of the backward devils.
I would meet you° upon this honestly.
I that was near your heart was removed therefrom°
To lose beauty in terror, terror in inquisition.
I have lost my passion: why should I need to keep it
Since what is kept must be adulterated?
60   I have lost my sight, smell, hearing, taste, and touch:
How should I use them for your closer contact?

These° with a thousand small deliberations
Protract the profit of their chilled delirium,°
Excite the membrane, when the sense has cooled,
With pungent sauces, multiply variety
In a wilderness of mirrors.° What will the spider do,
Suspend its operations, will the weevil
Delay? De Bailhache, Fresca, Mrs. Cammel,° whirled
Beyond the circuit of the shuddering Bear°
In fractured atoms. Gull against the wind,° in the windy straits
70   Of Belle Isle,° or running on the Horn,°
White feathers in the snow, the Gulf° claims,
And an old man driven by the Trades°
To a sleepy corner.

                                          Tenants of the house,
Thoughts of a dry brain in a dry season.
1919   1920

concitation conjuring, exciting
you He now seems to address a lover, perhaps
simply the world of sense.
I . . . therefrom Middleton, *The Changeling*
V.111: "I am that of" [or, "I that am of" in
that inferior reading used by Eliot] "your blood
was taken from you / For your better health":
quoted with admiration by Eliot in the essay
on Middleton (*Selected Essays*, pp. 140–48)
These these people (as though pointing to
others who will not abandon the sensual life)
Protract . . . delirium See "Little Gidding"
II.
multiply . . . mirrors remembering the voluptuous Sir Epicure Mammon in Jonson's *The
Alchemist:* "my glasses / Cut in more subtle
angles, to disperse / And multiply the figures
as I walk / Naked among my succubae" (II.i),
but thinking also of brothels that specialize in
mirrors
De Bailhache . . . Cammel More random cosmopolitan names, as if from a society paper;
these are the rootless, the dissociated from the
past, who, after death, suffer the fate foreseen
by Claudio. Fresca appears again as the central
figure of the pseudo-Popean section of "The

Fire Sermon" in *The Waste Land*, which Eliot
canceled on Pound's advice.
whirled . . . Bear This version uses the language of George Chapman's dying superhero in
Bussy D'Ambois V.iv: "fly where men feel / The
burning axletree, and those that suffer / Beneath
the chariot of the snowy Bear"—a passage
commended by Eliot, who remarks that what the
image meant to Seneca, to Chapman, and to
himself would in each case be "too obscure"
for any of them quite to understand. (*The
Use of Poetry and the Use of Criticism*, pp.
46–47). The Great Bear belongs to the northern hemisphere, hence "shuddering."
Gull . . . wind The picture of the whirling
souls dissolves associatively into that of the
gull and the white feathers; so to the trade
winds and back to the beginning. The new
poetry anticipates later cinema.
Belle Isle island in North Atlantic
Horn Cape Horn, the southern tip of the South
American continent
Gulf the warmer water of the Gulf Stream
Trades trade winds, blowing constantly from
the northeast in the northern tropics

The Waste Land

The poem was originally a longer sequence, composed for the most part in the fall of 1921, when Eliot, on the verge of a nervous breakdown, obtained paid leave from his City of London bank and went to recuperate first in Margate and then in Lausanne, Switzerland. He was in continuous correspondence with Pound, and on the way back to London early in 1922 took the manuscript to him in Paris. Pound made extensive cuts and changes, and a few more were made later at the suggestion of the first Mrs. Eliot. The poem was published in 1922 and in the same year the manuscript was sold to the New York collector John Quinn. It was then thought to have been lost, but it is now in the Berg Collection of the New York Public Library, and an edition of the uncut poem, by Mrs. Valerie Eliot, appeared in 1971. From it we learn more of the personal crisis that Eliot underwent during the time leading up to the composition of the poem. He was exhausted by overwork and by the stress of his marriage to a brilliant but mentally unstable woman; and the writing of the poem represented both an assessment of the world as he felt it to be, and a creative transformation of it, which culminates in the final section, "What the Thunder Said." This, we now know, was as it were "given" to the poet, without the long processes of trial and error, cancellation and rewriting, that were necessary for all the others. The entire effort to find the true shape of the work was suddenly rewarded, and this section was "right" from the first draft, and written in a condition of exaltation. It formed, of course, but a small proportion of the original thousand-line manuscript he took to Pound in Paris; in helping to reduce the work to 433 lines Pound left the last section alone.

Elsewhere Pound recommended many changes of detail. He diminished, without destroying, the dependence of the poem on a basic iambic pentameter measure; he deleted what was rhythmically inert; he cut passages that seemed to belong to an earlier stage of the poet's development—lines reminiscent, for example, of *Prufrock*. Pound, as Eliot several times acknowledged, had an incalculably beneficial effect on the poem, simply in his sense of Eliot's true quality and voice. His changes are all of detail and have no direct bearing on the mythic structure and allusions. One or two instances must serve. Where Eliot wrote:

> Unreal City, I have sometimes seen and see
> Under the brown fog of a winter dawn—

Pound simply reduced it to

> Unreal City,
> Under the brown fog of a winter dawn—

cutting out, without replacement, an inert piece of filling, and economically eliminating the somewhat mannered invocation to the City (the first line does all that). In the seduction scene in "The Fire Sermon" Pound canceled lines and part-lines of the regular quatrains in which it was originally written; Eliot did not reconstitute them, but left them in their cut state. Some quatrains remain intact; the whole movement has grown more flexible without the slightest loss of weight, and the gain in authenticity and authority of tone is quite extraordinary.

There are minor changes, too many to mention; an example is the substitution by Pound of *demotic* for "abominable" in the account of Mr. Eugenides's French— the superior sharpness of the word is matched by an increase in rhythmic force.

Eliot did not by any means accept all of Pound's cuts and changes, and he preserved some fine things that were marked for deletion. But few fine things were lost by his attending to Pound's advice, and it is hard to think of any comparable instance of a great poem that owes so much to the counsel of another poet.

Eliot showed his gratitude to Pound not only in the dedication of the poem but also by remarking later that his friend's skill had "done so much to turn The Waste Land from a jumble of good and bad passages into a poem"; and in 1946 he paid further tribute to the man who reduced to about half its size the "sprawling, chaotic poem."

It is important to remember that however interesting we may find the original as deciphered from the Quinn manuscript, the poem we have to deal with is the one published in 1922; the other is simply a draft in which it had not found its own shape. What kind of shape did it find? In spite of the labors of the commentators, The Waste Land remains, and will always remain, an obscure poem. It is not a matter of cracking a code or reconstructing a suppressed narrative. When Eliot in 1956 professed to regret the inclusion of his own notes with the poem, he had in mind the fact that it is very easy to avoid the difficulties of such a poem as this by pretending that it is something other than it is.

Speaking of a French poet, Eliot once remarked that poetry uses the logic of the imagination, not the logic of concepts. "People who do not appreciate poetry always find it difficult to distinguish between order and chaos in the arrangement of images; and even those who are capable of appreciating poetry cannot depend upon first impressions. I was not convinced of Mr. Perse's imaginative order until I had read the poem five or six times" (Preface to Anabasis: A poem by St. John Perse, with a translation into English by T. S. Eliot, 1930, p. 8). There is no doubt that he would have said the same thing about his own poem. It is offered as an arrangement of images; their order is not expository or narrative, and one is required not to extract that order but to enter the poem and inhabit it.

This might be thought a tall order, and recently there have been critics willing to say that it is not so much imaginative as imaginary; that The Waste Land is simply a sequence of poems more or less arbitrarily brought together, and having a number of internal cross references not in excess of what might be expected of any such sequence, though the Notes, later ridiculed by Eliot himself, suggest otherwise. These same critics tend also to stress the Americanism of Eliot's culture and imagination, pointing out, for example, that his cosmopolitan range of reference, the sense he gives of inventing a cultural tradition, add up to a modernism that belongs to the New World, not the Old, or even to a characteristic American rejection of the New. Nor is this an entirely English reaction; William Carlos Williams regarded The Waste Land as a disaster for American poetry: "Eliot had turned his back on the possibility of reviving my world. And being an accomplished craftsman, better skilled in some ways than I could ever hope to be, I had to watch him carry my world off with him, the fool, to the enemy" (Autobiography, 1951, p. 174).

Yet the fact of the matter is that The Waste Land, for whatever reasons, is the central English poem of the twentieth century. This means that many readers have, by reading it six times, somehow intuited its order, so that it is useless to insist on the nonexistence, or the cultural instability, of that order. There can be no doubt that the best way to read it is any way that enables one to intuit its order. For some readers this may mean ignoring Eliot's notes, ignoring the supplementary notes of his commentators, and letting the poem do its own work. Others will need help. Even if the background of myth and ritual to which the poem alludes is perfunctory or unnecessary or mere scaffolding, even if the network of allusions to occult materials and other poets is inessential, there is some comfort in having them pointed out. These things are at worst useful fictions, instruments which can be thrown away once a true encounter with the poem itself is achieved.

The myth to which the title refers us, but which asserts itself powerfully only in the last section of the poem, is that of the country which shares the infertility of its ruler, whose cure can only be brought about by a knight who will ask the right questions at a ritual. Eliot refers us to Jessie L. Weston's *From Ritual to Romance* (1920), a book in the tradition of the Cambridge school of anthropology of which the best-known product is Sir James Frazer's vast work *The Golden Bough* (1890–1915); Eliot also refers to this in his notes, and frequently elsewhere. In the poem he uses Frazer's account of ancient vegetation ceremonies in the cults of Adonis, Attis, and Osiris. Commenting on Stravinsky's *Rite of Spring* he spoke of the *Golden Bough* as "a revelation of that vanished mind of which our mind is a continuum" (in *Dial*, October 1921). Eliot's own notes say: "Not only the title, but a good deal of the incidental symbolism of the poem were suggested by [Jessie L. Weston] . . . Indeed, so deeply am I indebted, Miss Weston's notes will elucidate the difficulties of the poem much better than my notes can do. . . ." He goes on to acknowledge the debt to Frazer. "Anyone who is acquainted with these works will immediately recognize in the poem certain references to vegetation ceremonies."

Weston's book argues that the medieval romances of the Grail derive from primitive religious rituals and vegetation ceremonies, the Grail being a female, and the Lance a male symbol. The Fisher King, the impotent ruler, is a romance manifestation of another primitive myth. (See Headnote to David Jones for more discussion.) Miss Weston's book is not well thought of by modern students of romance, and it is doubtful whether the Waste Land theme is one of the more primitive parts of the romance cycle; but it does not matter. The basic notion of sexual sterility or the dissociation of sexuality from the cultural and religious health of a society is in Eliot's mind, and the anthropological material enabled him to perform for himself the act he found so admirable in Joyce, namely the application of myth to a modern world lacking the order of myth. The pressure of these and many related ideas on his mind and imagination is undoubted; he was interested in the origins of Catholic ritual, in religious dancing, and in Wagner.

That *The Waste Land* is a Wagnerian work is so obvious that only the dip in Wagner's reputation between the 1920's and the 1960's can explain the relative neglect of the fact. Eliot, like George Moore, Shaw, Forster, and Lawrence, was a Wagnerite. It was hard to avoid it; Wagner was venerated by the Symbolists and by all who valued his concept of the great work which not only employed all the arts but projected a universal myth onto the chaos of modern life. If Eliot had not been reading Miss Weston's new book—Miss Weston herself was a Wagner expert, and saw her material *through* Wagner—he could as easily have referred us to *Parsifal*, with its wounded impotent king, its questing knight, its Chapel Perilous and Grail ritual. He does in fact allude briefly to the close of the opera when he quotes Verlaine's Sonnet "Parsifal" at line 202. He also refers to *Tristan and Isolde*, the type-myth of romantic love and its frustration, and to *The Ring*, especially to its opening section, the *Rhinegold*, and to its last, the *Twilight of the Gods*. The body of myth is very similar to that treated by Wagner; Eliot goes behind the German treatment, but also evokes it with great deliberation, as the notes indicate. There are other hints of Wagner, as in the reference to the Starnbergersee, powerfully associated with Wagner and also with his extraordinary patron (possibly even his lover), King Ludwig II of Bavaria, who drowned in the lake.

Eliot is, in a sense, attempting to achieve in heroic poetry (or mock-heroic: the genres are now indistinguishable) what Wagner did in music; he even imitates Wagner's verse. Above all, the effect is intended to be musical, suggestive as the interplay of leitmotifs, a complex image of a mythic integrity against a background of actual sterility and decadence. This is a better way of stating the case than to call Eliot's poem a poem *about* spiritual dryness or decadence. He himself denied that it was "melancholy"; later he would argue that the structures of truth persist throughout the tumults of heresy, and here he is neither merely stating decadence nor proposing remedies for it, but providing an image of an accessible integrity that somehow persists; just as the right questions exist to be asked, the right conduct is knowable, even if the questions are not asked and the knowledge not applied. This is the sense in which the past interpenetrates the present, "quick, now, here, always"; the poem is a kind of Mass, itself the image of an eternal truth in the midst of flux or chaos.

Eliot's theory of poetry, and ultimately his theories of everything, support this view; he was in 1928 to announce himself "classicist in literature, royalist in politics, and Anglo-Catholic in religion" (Preface to *For Lancelot Andrewes*)—all positions depending on the coexistence of modernity with truths existing in a different order of time. Such views are consistent with the opinion that modern poetry must be "difficult," since the poetry stemming from them must reflect both the ancient order and the modern disorder which normally conceals it. Of that difficulty, as of that order, *The Waste Land* is Eliot's supreme expression; as Eliot said of Baudelaire, it is not merely a matter of "the imagery of the sordid life of a great metropolis, but . . . the elevation of such imagery to the *first intensity*—presenting it as it is, and yet making it represent something much more than itself" (*Selected Essays*, p. 377).

It remains to be said that poetry of this kind will often in its allusions be private; nothing except the poetry itself really causes all the bric-à-brac to cohere, and the poet can use the materials that he has in his head. That the myth finds its expression in whatever material happens to be available is consistent with the teaching of a later mythographer than Frazer, namely Claude Lévi-Strauss. He calls this random material, momentarily integrated in a restatement of a myth, *bricolage,* and that is what we are examining when we track down the bits and pieces of Eliot's material in our notes.

The Waste Land

Nam Sibyllam quidem Cumis ego ipse oculis meis vidi
in ampulla pendere, et cum illi pueri dicerent Σίβυλλα
τί θέλεις; respondebat illa: ἀποθανεῖν θέλω. °

Nam . . . thélo "For once I saw with my own eyes the Sibyl at Cumae hanging in a cage, and when the boys asked her, 'Sibyl, what do you want?' she answered, 'I want to die.'" That this is part of a drunken boast in the *Satyricon* of Petronius Arbiter (1st century A.D.) has no apparent relevance. The Cumaean Sibyl, who conducted Aeneas through the underworld (Virgil, *Aeneid VI*) was granted immortality but not youth.

For Ezra Pound
il miglior fabbro.°

1. *The Burial of the Dead*°
April is the cruellest month,° breeding
Lilacs out of the dead land, mixing
Memory and desire, stirring
Dull roots with spring rain.
Winter kept us warm, covering
Earth in forgetful snow, feeding
A little life with dried tubers.
Summer surprised us, coming over the Starnbergersee°
With a shower of rain; we stopped in the colonnade,
10   And went on in sunlight, into the Hofgarten,°
And drank coffee, and talked for an hour.
Bin gar keine Russin, stamm' aus Litauen, echt deutsch.°
And when we were children, staying at the archduke's,
My cousin's, he took me out on a sled,
And I was frightened. He said, Marie,
Marie, hold on tight. And down we went.
In the mountains, there you feel free.
I read, much of the night, and go south in the winter.

What are the roots that clutch, what branches grow
20   Out of this stony rubbish?° Son of man,°
You cannot say, or guess, for you know only
A heap of broken images,° where the sun beats,
And the dead tree gives no shelter, the cricket° no relief,
And the dry stone no sound of water. Only
There is shadow under this red rock,
(Come in under the shadow of this red rock),

---

il miglior fabbro "The better workman";
Dante, *Purgatorio* XXVI.117, pays this tribute
to the Provençal poet Arnaut Daniel, and Eliot
turns it into a graceful tribute to Pound.
The . . . Dead The funeral service in the
English Book of Common Prayer is called
"The Order for the Burial of the Dead."
April . . . month usually of Easter, the month
of remembered but no longer wanted divine
resurrections
Starnbergersee Lake near Munich, which Eliot
visited in 1911. It was then a fashionable
resort, and also the site of King Ludwig's
castle, Schloss Berg; in escaping from imprisonment there he drowned in the lake. The following lines to 17 borrow from *My Past*, a volume
of recollections published in 1913 by Countess
Marie Larisch, a kinswoman of the king who
had a vision of him after his death, believed
in fortune-telling by cards, and was assassinated
at Lake Leman (see l. 182). Ludwig was mad
and sick; Wagner, who had once called him
Parsifal, later called him Amfortas, the sick
king whom Parsifal (Wagner himself) will relieve with the Grail. Many further suggestions

of the importance of Countess Marie's memoirs
and other Wagnerian and Bavarian parallels
are proposed by Herbert Knust, *Wagner, The
King, and The Waste Land* (1967), a book
over-enthusiastically argued but establishing that
the Countess's memoirs provided Eliot with
more than a picture of frivolous and rootless
high society. (In the original version Eliot wrote
Königsee.)
Hofgarten public park in Munich
Bin . . . deutsch "I'm not Russian at all, I
come from Lithuania, a pure German." This, we
now learn from Mrs. Eliot, directly reports a
remark of Countess Marie Larisch to Eliot when
he met her, presumably, at Munich.
What . . . rubbish Note this unmotivated
transition, more abrupt than that at l. 8; for
the language see Job 8.
Son of man "See Ezekiel 2:1" (T.S.E.); Ezekiel
is told to preach the coming of the Messiah
to an incredulous people.
broken images Ezekiel 6:6
Cricket "Cf. Ecclesiastes 12:5" (T.S.E.): "the
grasshopper shall be a burden, and desire shall
fail. . . ."

And I will show you something different from either
Your shadow at morning striding behind you
Or your shadow at evening rising to meet you;°
30 I will show you fear in a handful of dust.°

      Frisch weht der Wind
      Der Heimat zu
      Mein Irisch Kind,
      Wo weilest du?°
'You gave me hyacinths° first a year ago;
They called me the hyacinth girl.'
—Yet when we came back, late, from the Hyacinth garden,
Your arms full, and your hair wet, I could not
Speak, and my eyes failed, I was neither
40 Living nor dead, and I knew nothing,
Looking into the heart of light, the silence.°
Oed' und leer das Meer.°

    Madame Sosostris,° famous clairvoyante,
Had a bad cold, nevertheless
Is known to be the wisest woman in Europe,
With a wicked pack of cards.° Here, said she,
Is your card, the drowned Phoenician Sailor,°
(Those are pearls that were his eyes.° Look!)
Here is Belladonna,° the Lady of the Rocks,°
50 The lady° of situations.

Come . . . you based on Eliot's *The Death of Saint Narcissus*, c. 1912, a poem printed but never published until it appeared, with other rejected material, in Mrs. Eliot's edition.
handful of dust "consumes himself to a handful of dust" (Donne, *Devotions*, 1624, Meditation 4)
Frisch . . . du Sailor's song which opens Wagner's *Tristan and Isolde:* he is sailing away from Ireland and singing, "Fresh blows the wind to the homeland—my Irish child, where do you wait?"
hyacinths symbols of resurrection
Yet . . . silence (ll. 37–41) This describes a moment of mystical love-recognition like that at the end of Act I of Wagner's *Tristan*, when the lovers, having drunk the potion, gaze silently at each other for a long time. This is sometimes taken to be the crucial moment; the quester meets the Grail-bearer and fails to ask the right question, so losing his chance of success. Pound tried to change this, but Eliot kept it intact.
Oed' . . . Meer At the beginning of the third and last act of *Tristan* the hero lies sick with a deadly wound, waiting for Isolde's ship; the shepherd lookout reports no sign: "Waste and empty the sea." Isolde's arrival is followed instantly by Tristan's virtually self-inflicted death. Eliot must mean some reference to the fact that passionate sexual love is not the answer to the wound and the waste.
Sosostris Eliot thinks he unconsciously borrowed the name from the fake fortune-teller Madame Sesostris in Aldous Huxley's novel *Crome Yellow* (1921).
cards Eliot's note says that he was not familiar "with the exact constitution of the Tarot pack of cards. . . . The Hanged Man, a member of the traditional pack, fits my purpose in two ways: because he is associated in my mind with the Hanged God of Frazer, and because I associate him with the hooded figure in the passage of the disciples to Emmaus in Part V. The Phoenician Sailor and the Merchant appear later; also the 'crowds of people,' and Death by Water is executed in Part IV. The Man with Three Staves (an authentic member of the Tarot pack) I associate, quite arbitrarily, with the Fisher King himself." The Tarot pack of 78 cards is thought (e.g. by Jessie Weston) to use symbols of ancient ritual origin, and is used for fortune-telling.
Phoenician Sailor See Part IV.
Those . . . eyes *The Tempest* I.ii.398: Ariel's song tells Ferdinand that the king his father is drowned and transfigured.
Belladonna Italian, "beautiful lady"; also the flower Deadly Nightshade, and the poison extracted from it
Lady of the Rocks The reference to a painting of Leonardo da Vinci (Madonna of the Rocks) is ironical; these are wasteland rocks.
lady reducing the word in its new vulgar context by substituting lower-case *l*

Here is the man with three staves, and here the Wheel,°
And here is the one-eyed merchant, and this card,
Which is blank, is something he carries on his back,
Which I am forbidden to see. I do not find
The Hanged Man. Fear death by water.
I see crowds of people, walking round in a ring.
Thank you. If you see dear Mrs. Equitone,
Tell her I bring the horoscope myself:
One must be so careful these days.

60   Unreal City,°
Under the brown fog of a winter dawn,
A crowd flowed over London Bridge, so many,
I had not thought death had undone so many.°
Sighs, short and infrequent, were exhaled,°
And each man fixed his eyes before his feet.
Flowed up the hill and down King William Street,
To where Saint Mary Woolnoth° kept the hours
With a dead sound on the final stroke of nine.°
There I saw one I knew, and stopped him, crying: 'Stetson!
70   You who were with me in the ships at Mylae!°
That corpse you planted last year in your garden,
Has it begun to sprout?° Will it bloom this year?
Or has the sudden frost disturbed its bed?
Oh keep the Dog far hence, that's friend to men,
Or with his nails he'll dig it up again!°
You! hypocrite lecteur!—mon semblable,—mon frère!'°

Wheel of Fortune
Unreal City This passage begins, without transition, a City of London scene; see Headnote remarks about Baudelaire's use of metropolitan imagery. "Cf. Baudelaire: *Fourmillante cité, cité pleine de rêves, / Où le spectre en plein jour raccroche le passant*" (T.S.E.): "Swarming city, city full of dreams, where the ghost stops the passer-by in full daylight."
so many "Cf. *Inferno* III.55–57: *sì lunga tratta / di gente, ch'io non avrei mai creduto / che morte tanta n'avesse disfatta*" (T.S.E.): "so long a stream of people that I should never have believed that death had undone so many." They are the spirits who in life knew neither good nor evil; see Eliot's essay on Baudelaire for a striking condemnation of such lives.
Sighs . . . exhaled "Cf. *Inferno* IV.25–27: *Quivi, secondo che per ascoltare, / non avea pianto, ma' che di sospiri, / che l'aura eterna facevan tremare*" (T.S.E.): "Here, to my hearing, there was no lamentation except sighs, which caused the eternal air to tremble." Dante is in the Limbo of the unbaptised.
St. Mary Woolnoth one of the many fine churches, mostly by Wren, in the City of London (the financial district) in which these people are going to work. Eliot joined the campaign to save these churches from destruction.

dead . . . nine "A phenomenon which I have often noticed" (T.S.E.). Nine was the hour when office work began.
Mylae a battle in the First Punic War (260 B.C.) between the Romans and the Carthaginians, fought for control of Mediterranean trade
That . . . sprout Stetson, some veteran of the Great War perhaps, has buried its memories as formerly people buried images of the dead god, but unlike them does not wish it to sprout; he is like all the others in the City procession, indifferent to the central images of religion.
Oh . . . again "Cf. the Dirge in Webster's *White Devil*" (T.S.E.). In that play, IV.iv, Cornelia, referring to "the friendless bodies of unburied men," sings: "But keep the wolf far hence that's foe to men, / For with his nails he'll dig them up again." In the tame life of Stetson there are friendly dogs, not hostile wolves; a milieu unsuited to the rising of a god. There were originally more allusions to Webster in the poem.
hypocrite . . . frère "V. Baudelaire, Preface to *Fleurs du Mal*" (T.S.E.): "Hypocrite reader! my likeness, my brother!" Baudelaire says the reader shares with him the sin of *ennui*, which, under some more modern formulation such as *anomie*, is the sin of the city-workers and of us all.

II. *A Game of Chess*°

The Chair she sat in, like a burnished throne,°
Glowed on the marble, where the glass
Held up by standards wrought with fruited vines
80   From which a golden Cupidon peeped out
(Another hid his eyes behind his wing)
Doubled the flames of sevenbranched candelabra
Reflecting light upon the table as
The glitter of her jewels rose to meet it,
From satin cases poured in rich profusion;
In vials of ivory and coloured glass
Unstoppered, lurked her strange synthetic perfumes,
Unguent, powdered, or liquid—troubled, confused
And drowned the sense in odours; stirred by the air
90   That freshened from the window, these ascended
In fattening the prolonged candle-flames,
Flung their smoke into the laquearia,°
Stirring the pattern on the coffered ceiling.
Huge sea-wood fed with copper
Burned green and orange, framed by the coloured stone,
In which sad light a carvèd dolphin swam.
Above the antique mantel was displayed
As though a window gave upon the sylvan scene°
The change of Philomel,° by the barbarous king
100   So rudely forced; yet there the nightingale°
Filled all the desert with inviolable voice
And still she cried, and still the world pursues,°
'Jug Jug'° to dirty ears.
And other withered stumps of time
Were told upon the walls; staring forms
Leaned out, leaning, hushing the room enclosed.
Footsteps shuffled on the stair.
Under the firelight, under the brush, her hair

A **Game of Chess** Referring not to Middleton's *A Game at Chess* but to his *Women Beware Women*, one of the great Jacobean tragedies. In one scene the Duke's procuress plays chess with a girl's mother while the Duke is seducing the girl upstairs; the chess moves are made to correspond to the progress of the seduction. **The Chair . . . throne** "Cf. *Antony and Cleopatra* II.ii.90" (T.S.E.). This is the description by Enobarbus of Cleopatra's barge at her first meeting with Antony: "The barge she sat in, like a burnished throne, / Burned on the water. . . ." Eliot is perhaps thinking also of the bedchamber in *Cymbeline* II.ii and iv, and possibly of Keats's banquet scene in *Lamia*. The luxury is an ironical setting for ennui and hysteria in a loveless marriage; later we switch to a proletarian version of the same horror.
laquearia Eliot's note refers to Virgil, *Aeneid*

I.726: ". . . flaming torches hang from the golden paneled ceiling, and the torches conquer the night with flames." This is at a banquet given by Dido to Aeneas, who makes love to her but deserts her at the call of duty.
sylvan scene "V. Milton, *Paradise Lost* IV.140" (T.S.E.). Satan sees it when he arrives in Eden.
The . . . Philomel "V. Ovid, *Metamorphoses* VI, Philomela" (T.S.E.). In Ovid Philomel is raped by the husband of her sister Procne, King Tereus, who also cut out her tongue; she was changed into the nightingale.
yet . . . nightingale "Cf. Part III, 204" (T.S.E.).
cried . . . pursues Note change of tense.
Jug Jug the nightingale's sound in Elizabethan poetry; also sexual slang, and so a dirty story to "dirty ears"

Spread out in fiery points
110   Glowed into words, then would be savagely still.

'My nerves are bad to-night. Yes, bad. Stay with me.
Speak to me. Why do you never speak. Speak.
What are you thinking of? What thinking? What?
I never know what you are thinking. Think.'

I think we are in rats' alley°
Where the dead men lost their bones.

'What is that noise?'

                    The wind under the door.°
'What is that noise now? What is the wind doing?'
120   Nothing again nothing.
                                        'Do
You know nothing? Do you see nothing? Do you remember
Nothing?'

I remember
Those are pearls that were his eyes.°
'Are you alive, or not? Is there nothing in your head?'

                                        But
O O O O that Shakespeherian Rag—
It's so elegant
So intelligent°
130   'What shall I do now? What shall I do?'
'I shall rush out as I am, and walk the street
With my hair down, so. What shall we do to-morrow?
What shall we ever do?'
                    The hot water at ten.
And if it rains, a closed car at four.
And we shall play a game of chess,°
Pressing lidless eyes and waiting for a knock upon the door.

When Lil's husband got demobbed,° I said—
140   I didn't mince my words, I said to her myself,
HURRY UP PLEASE ITS TIME°
Now Albert's coming back, make yourself a bit smart.
He'll want to know what you done with that money he gave you
To get yourself some teeth. He did, I was there.

I . . . alley "Cf. Part III, 195" (T.S.E.).
wind . . . door "Cf. Webster; "Is the wind in
that door still?" (T.S.E.) (The Devil's Law
Case, III.ii).
Those . . . eyes "Cf. Part I. 37, 48" (T.S.E.).
The reference to 37 is mysterious; the other is
to Ariel's song in The Tempest I.ii, a leitmotif
partly explicated in "Death by Water."
O . . . intelligent A burst of contemporary
ragtime, with a sophisticated 'twenties lyric,
momentarily varies the atmosphere of tense
ennui.

a game of chess "Cf. the game of chess in
Middleton's Women Beware Woman" (T.S.E.):
here presumably a substitute for sexual activity,
just as the rape of Tereus only figuratively
represents the civilized cruelty of this marriage
demobbed Slang for "demobilized," released
from the army. Eliot tries here to catch the
tone of proletarian conversation.
Hurry . . . time signifying that the closing
time set by the licensing laws has come, so
that everybody must drink up and leave the
pub

You have them all out, Lil, and get a nice set,
He said, I swear, I can't bear to look at you.
And no more can't I, I said, and think of poor Albert,
He's been in the army four years, he wants a good time,
And if you don't give it him, there's others will, I said.
150   Oh is there, she said. Something o' that, I said.
Then I'll know who to thank, she said, and give me a straight look.
HURRY UP PLEASE ITS TIME
If you don't like it you can get on with it,° I said.
Others can pick and choose if you can't.
But if Albert makes off, it won't be for lack of telling.
You ought to be ashamed, I said, to look so antique.
(And her only thirty-one.)
I can't help it, she said, pulling a long face,
It's them pills I took, to bring it off,° she said.
160   (She's had five already, and nearly died of young George.)
The chemist° said it would be all right, but I've never been the same.
You *are* a proper fool, I said.
Well, if Albert won't leave you alone, there it is, I said,
What you get married for if you don't want children?
HURRY UP PLEASE ITS TIME
Well, that Sunday Albert was home, they had a hot gammon,°
And they asked me in to dinner, to get the beauty of it hot—
HURRY UP PLEASE ITS TIME
HURRY UP PLEASE ITS TIME
170   Goonight Bill. Goonight Lou. Goonight May. Goonight.
Ta ta. Goonight. Goonight.
Good night, ladies, good night, sweet ladies, good night, good night.°

    III. *The Fire Sermon*°
The river's tent is broken: the last fingers of leaf
Clutch and sink into the wet bank. The wind
Crosses the brown land, unheard. The nymphs are departed.
Sweet Thames, run softly, till I end my song.°
The river bears no empty bottles, sandwich papers,
Silk handkerchiefs, cardboard boxes, cigarette ends
Or other testimony of summer nights. The nymphs are departed.
180   And their friends, the loitering heirs of City directors,
Departed, have left no addresses.
By the waters of Leman° I sat down and wept . . .

Sweet Thames, run softly till I end my song,
Sweet Thames, run softly, for I speak not loud or long.
But at my back in a cold blast I hear
The rattle of the bones, and chuckle spread from ear to ear.°
A rat crept softly through the vegetation
Dragging its slimy belly on the bank
While I was fishing° in the dull canal
190   On a winter evening round behind the gashouse
Musing upon the king my brother's wreck°
And on the king my father's death before him.
White bodies naked on the low damp ground
And bones cast in a little low dry garret,
Rattled by the rat's foot only, year to year.
But at my back from time to time I hear°
The sound of horns and motors, which shall bring
Sweeney to Mrs. Porter in the spring.°
O the moon shone bright on Mrs. Porter
200   And on her daughter
They wash their feet in soda water°
Et O ces voix d'enfants, chantant dans la coupole!°

Twit twit twit
Jug jug jug jug jug jug°
So rudely forc'd.
Tereu°

Unreal City°
Under the brown fog of a winter noon
Mr. Eugenides, the Smyrna merchant°

But . . . ear parodying "But at my back I always hear / Time's winged chariot hurrying near" (Marvell, "To His Coy Mistress")
fishing The notion of polluted water is even stronger when we come to the figure of the desolate Fisher.
Musing . . . wreck "Cf. *The Tempest* I.ii" (T.S.E.). Ferdinand: "Sitting upon a bank, Weeping again the king my father's wrack, / This music crept by me upon the waters, / Allaying both their fury and my passion . . ." (I.ii.389–92). Eliot reserves the last regenerative, calming line until 257. Eliot's changes have not been satisfactorily explained, least of all by his note on l. 218.
But . . . hear "Cf. Marvell, 'To His Coy Mistress' " (T.S.E.).
The sound . . . spring "Cf. Day, *Parliament of Bees:* When of the sudden, listening, you shall hear, / A noise of horns and hunting, which shall bring / Actaeon to Diana in the spring, / Where all shall see her naked skin . . . " (T.S.E.). Actaeon surprised Diana bathing, and as a punishment was turned into a stag and killed by his own hounds; usually regarded as an allegory of how men are destroyed by their own intemperate desires. Sweeney is Eliot's natural man, and his leman Mrs. Porter is so named for the sake of the ballad. Again the effect is to take a stately mythical representation of disordered passion

and juxtapose it with a modern banality.
O . . . water "I do not know the origin of the ballad from which these lines are taken: it was reported to me from Sydney, Australia" (T.S.E.). The ballad, usually more obscene, is well known in Australia and was sung by Australian troops in World War I.
Et . . . coupole A line of the sonnet *Parsifal* by Paul Verlaine (1844–96): "And O those children's voices singing in the dome!" Verlaine refers to the choir of children in Wagner's opera near the close, when Parsifal's feet are ceremonially washed before he proceeds to the worship of the Grail.
Jug . . . jug See l. 103; the purity of Parsifal, quester, now juxtaposed with the story of rape and violence.
Tereu O Tereus!, but also the nightingale's song, as in John Lyly (1554–1606), *Alexander and Campaspe:* " 'Tis the ravished nightingale; / Jug, jug, jug, jug, tereu, she cries."
Unreal City Back in the commercial scene, Eliot describes an encounter which, he later revealed, happened to him personally.
Eugenides . . . merchant The name ironically suggests that the merchant comes of good family. Smyrna is in Turkey and a source of currants, which some take to be symbolic of the shriveling up of fruit in the hands of the modern descendants of those early Levantine merchants who spread the Grail cult.

210　Unshaven, with a pocket full of currants
　　　C.i.f.° London: documents at sight,
　　　Asked me in demotic° French
　　　To luncheon at the Cannon Street Hotel°
　　　Followed by a weekend at the Metropole.°

　　　　　At the violet hour,° when the eyes and back
　　　Turn upward from the desk, when the human engine waits
　　　Like a taxi throbbing waiting,
　　　I Tiresias,° though blind, throbbing between two lives,
　　　Old man with wrinkled female breasts, can see
220　At the violet hour, the evening hour that strives
　　　Homeward, and brings the sailor home from sea,°
　　　The typist home at teatime, clears her breakfast, lights
　　　Her stove, and lays out food in tins.
　　　Out of the window perilously spread
　　　Her drying combinations touched by the sun's last rays,
　　　On the divan are piled (at night her bed)
　　　Stockings, slippers, camisoles, and stays.
　　　I Tiresias, old man with wrinkled dugs
　　　Perceived the scene, and foretold the rest—
230　I too awaited the expected guest.
　　　He, the young man carbuncular, arrives,
　　　A small house agent's clerk, with one bold stare,
　　　One of the low on whom assurance sits
　　　As a silk hat on a Bradford° millionaire.
　　　The time is now propitious, as he guesses,
　　　The meal is ended, she is bored and tired,
　　　Endeavours to engage her in caresses

C.i.f. "The currants were quoted at a price 'cost insurance and freight to London'; and the Bill of Lading, etc., were to be handed to the buyer upon payment of the sight draft" (T.S.E.).
demotic vulgar
Cannon Street Hotel hotel in the City (at which Wagner was banqueted when he came to London with the libretto of *Parsifal*)
Metropole Luxury hotel at Brighton, one hour from London on the south coast; the invitation seems to be sexual.
At . . . hour The hint of sexual temptation in the city will give way to this scene of loveless sex between clerks at the end of the work day.
Tiresias "Tiresias, although a mere spectator and not indeed a 'character,' is yet the most important personage in the poem, uniting all the rest. Just as the one-eyed merchant, seller of currants, melts into the Phoenician Sailor, and the latter is not wholly distinct from Ferdinand Prince of Naples [in *The Tempest*], so all the women are one woman, and the two sexes meet in Tiresias. What Tiresias *sees*, in fact, is the substance of the poem. The whole passage from Ovid is of great anthropological interest. . . ." (T.S.E.) Eliot then quotes in Latin Ovid's account of the sex change of Tiresias: Jupiter tells Juno that he believes women to have more pleasure in sex than men do; she disagrees, and they

decide to consult Tiresias, who has been both man and woman. He took Jupiter's view, and Juno, in anger, blinded him. Jupiter, to compensate him, gave him the gift of prophecy. In this note Eliot identifies Tiresias with the Bradleyan finite center of consciousness that is the *persona* of his poems; he is merely saying that Tiresias has a role similar to that of Gerontion. He is *not* saying that we must construct out of the discrete episodes a continuous narrative in which Tiresias, under various disguises, has a central part. In a sense Tiresias is the poem itself, informed of, yet detached from, the life of the sexes as it discovers that life to be, bringing together all the female characters, and all the male, and eventually uniting them in one poem, one center.
sailor . . . sea "This may not appear as exact as Sappho's lines, but I had in mind the 'longshore' or 'dory' fisherman, who returns home at nightfall" (T.S.E.). Sappho (Greek poetess of the 7th century B.C.), in Fragment 149, prays to the Evening Star, which brings "the sheep, the goat, and the child back to the mother." Eliot is more directly remembering Robert Louis Stevenson's "Requiem": "Home is the sailor, home from sea. . . ."
Bradford Yorkshire wool town with many manufacturers who were said to have made fortunes out of the war.

Which still are unreproved, if undesired.
Flushed and decided, he assaults at once;
240   Exploring hands encounter no defence;
His vanity requires no response,
And makes a welcome of indifference.
(And I Tiresias have foresuffered all
Enacted on this same divan or bed;
I who have sat by Thebes° below the wall
And walked among the lowest of the dead.°)
Bestows one final patronising kiss,
And gropes his way, finding the stairs unlit . . .

    She turns and looks a moment in the glass,
250   Hardly aware of her departed lover;
Her brain allows one half-formed thought to pass:
'Well now that's done: and I'm glad it's over.'
When lovely woman stoops to folly° and
Paces about her room again, alone,
She smooths her hair with automatic hand,
And puts a record on the gramophone.

    'This music crept by me upon the waters'°
And along the Strand, up Queen Victoria Street.
O City city, I can sometimes hear
260   Beside a public bar in Lower Thames Street,
The pleasant whining of a mandoline
And a clatter and a chatter from within
Where fishmen° lounge at noon: where the walls
Of Magnus Martyr hold
Inexplicable splendour of Ionian white and gold.°

        The river sweats°
        Oil and tar
        The barges drift
        With the turning tide

Thebes Tiresias (who has "foresuffered" love-less sex in both ways) is also the blind seer who knows that the curse which makes Thebes a waste land stems from the unwitting incest of Oedipus and his mother Jocasta; in Sophocles (495–406 B.C.), *Oedipus the King.*
walked . . . dead In Homer's *Odyssey* XI Odysseus meets Tiresias in the underworld.
When . . . folly "V. Goldsmith, the song in *The Vicar of Wakefield*" (T.S.E.): "When lovely woman stoops to folly, / And finds too late that men betray, / What charm can soothe her melancholy, / What art can wash her guilt away? / The only art her guilt to cover, / To hide her shame from every eye, / To give repentance to her lover / And wring his bosom—is to die."
This . . . waters "V. *The Tempest,* as above" (T.S.E.); see ll. 48 and 125.
fishmen workers from the nearby Billingsgate fishmarket

Magnus Martyr . . . gold. "The interior of St. Magnus Martyr is to my mind one of the finest among Wren interiors . . . " (T.S.E.).
The river sweats "The Song of the (three) Thames-daughters begins here. From line 292 to 306 they speak in turn. V. *Götterdämmerung* III.i: the Rhine-daughters" (T.S.E.). Wagner's Rhinemaidens in the last opera of *The Ring* flirt with Siegfried but also lament the theft of the gold of the Nibelungs and the destruction of the old world of the gods. Eliot imitates Wagner's verse, and at the end of each section the wordless cries of the Rhinemaidens' refrains. The picture of the Thames may owe something to the beginning of Conrad's *Heart of Darkness,* a work we know Eliot had in mind during the writing of *The Waste Land;* the original epigraph (vetoed by Pound) was Kurtz's exclamation *"The horror! The horror!"*

270   Red sails
       Wide
       To leeward, swing on the heavy spar.
       The barges wash
       Drifting logs
       Down Greenwich reach°
       Past the Isle of Dogs.°
                Weialala leia
                Wallala leialala

       Elizabeth and Leicester°
280   Beating oars
       The stern was formed
       A gilded shell
       Red and gold
       The brisk swell
       Rippled both shores
       Southwest wind
       Carried down stream
       The peal of bells
       White towers
290   Weialala leia
                Wallala leialala

       'Trams and dusty trees.°
       Highbury bore me. Richmond and Kew
       Undid me.° By Richmond I raised my knees
       Supine on the floor of a narrow canoe.'

       'My feet are at Moorgate,° and my heart
       Under my feet. After the event
       He wept. He promised "a new start."
       I made no comment. What should I resent?'

300   'On Margate Sands.°
       I can connect
       Nothing with nothing.
       The broken fingernails of dirty hands.
       My people humble people who expect

Greenwich reach the river at Greenwich, east of London
Isle of Dogs riverbank opposite Greenwich
Elizabeth and Leicester "V. Froude, *Elizabeth*, Vol. I, ch. iv, letter of De Quadra to Philip of Spain: 'In the afternoon we were in a barge, watching the games on the river. (The queen) was alone with Lord Robert and myself on the poop, when they began to talk nonsense, and went so far that Lord Robert at last said, as I was on the spot there was no reason why they should not be married if the queen pleased" (T.S.E.) (J. A. Froude, *History of England* Vol. VII, p. 349; Lord Robert Dudley, Earl of Leicester; Elizabeth had a palace at Greenwich). Elizabeth's failure to marry Leicester, or anybody, meant that she was a sterile queen.
Trams . . . trees back to the modern river and the lament of the Thames-daughters
Highbury . . . me "Cf. *Purgatorio* V.133: *Ricorditi di mi, che son la Pia; / Siena mi fe', disfecemi Maremma*" (T.S.E.): "Remember me, who am La Pia; Siena made me, Maremma unmade me." La Pia, the lady of Siena, was murdered by her husband at Maremma. Highbury is an inner suburb of North London; Richmond and Kew are on the river to the west, popular boating places.
Moorgate City area of East London
Margate seaside resort near London

Nothing.'
la la

To Carthage then I came°

Burning burning burning burning°
O Lord Thou pluckest me out°
310   O Lord Thou pluckest

burning

iv.   *Death by Water*°
Phlebas the Phoenician, a fortnight dead,
Forgot the cry of gulls, and the deep sea swell
And the profit and loss.
                    A current under sea
Picked his bones in whispers. As he rose and fell
He passed the stages of his age and youth°
Entering the whirlpool.
                    Gentile or Jew
320   O you who turn the wheel and look to windward,
Consider Phlebas, who was once handsome and tall as you.

v.   *What the Thunder Said*°
After the torchlight red on sweaty faces
After the frosty silence in the gardens
After the agony in stony places
The shouting and the crying
Prison and palace and reverberation

To . . . came "V. St. Augustine's *Confessions:* "to Carthage then I came, where a cauldron of unholy loves sang all about mine ears" (T.S.E.); *Confessions* III.1, on the temptations of sense that assailed the young Augustine.
Burning . . . burning Eliot refers to "the Buddha's Fire Sermon (which corresponds in importance to the Sermon on the Mount)." The Buddha condemns all the senses, which, he maintains, introduce the soul to a world of fire and prevent its becoming free of desire.
O Lord . . . out "From St. Augustine's *Confessions* again. The collocation of these two representatives of eastern and western asceticism, as the culmination of his part of the poem, is not an accident" (T.S.E.): "I entangle my steps with these outward beauties, but thou pluckest me out, O Lord, thou pluckest me out!" (*Confessions* X.34). The asceticism here celebrated is related to that required of the quester Parsifal; the poem intends it to be an abstention from the desolating indulgences of the world in general, though in the context it is easy to see it as a specific sexual disgust.
Death by Water See l. 55. These lines are adapted from the last seven of Eliot's poem in French, *Dans le Restaurant* (1916–17), here translated: "Phlebas the Phoenician, two weeks drowned, forgot the cries of gulls, and the profit and the loss, and the cargo of tin: an undersea current carried him very far, taking him back through

the stages of his former life. Think of it, it was a hard fate; he was after all once handsome and tall." The main part of the poem is about an old waiter who remembers a moment of power and delight with a young girl when he was a child, a moment that ended when he ran away, in fear of a dog. He is now a dirty, frustrated old man. The Phlebas lines follow. Pound was insistent on the retention of these lines in *The Waste Land*. Their connection with the poem is obscure, though the sailor is related to Mr. Eugenides and death by water is a recurring theme, related to the *Tempest* quotations. The manuscript includes a long nautical poem of which these remaining lines form the brief conclusion.
He . . . youth This is what Yeats calls the "dreaming-back" that follows death, a return to the source.
What the Thunder Said "In the first part of Part V three themes are employed: the journey to Emmaus, the approach to the Chapel Perilous (see Miss Weston's book) and the present decay of Eastern Europe" (T.S.E.). For the Emmaus journey see Luke 24:13–31, in which the resurrected Jesus joins two disciples on the road to Emmaus and they do not recognize him; the Chapel Perilous is the critical final stage of the Grail quest; by "the present decay" Eliot means the chaos of Eastern Europe after World War I, and the success of the Bolsheviks.

Of thunder of spring over distant mountains
He who was living is now dead°
We who were living are now dying
330   With a little patience

　　Here is no water but only rock
Rock and no water and the sandy road
The road winding above among the mountains
Which are mountains of rock without water
If there were water we should stop and drink
Amongst the rock one cannot stop or think
Sweat is dry and feet are in the sand
If there were only water amongst the rock
Dead mountain mouth of carious teeth that cannot spit
340   Here one can neither stand nor lie nor sit
There is not even silence in the mountains
But dry sterile thunder without rain
There is not even solitude in the mountains
But red sullen faces sneer and snarl
From doors of mudcracked houses
　　　　　　　　　　　　If there were water

　　And no rock
　　If there were rock
　　And also water
350   And water
　　A spring
　　A pool among the rock
　　If there were the sound of water only
　　Not the cicada°
　　And dry grass singing
　　But sound of water over a rock
　　Where the hermit-thrush° sings in the pine trees
　　Drip drop drip drop drop drop drop
　　But there is no water

360   Who is the third who walks always beside you?°
When I count, there are only you and I together
But when I look ahead up the white road
There is always another one walking beside you
Gliding wrapt in a brown mantle, hooded
I do not know whether a man or a woman
—But who is that on the other side of you?

　　What is that sound high in the air

Murmur of maternal lamentation
Who are those hooded hordes swarming
370 Over endless plains, stumbling in cracked earth
Ringed by the flat horizon only
What is the city over the mountains
Cracks and reforms and bursts in the violet air
Falling towers
Jerusalem Athens Alexandria
Vienna London
Unreal°

A woman° drew her long black hair out tight
And fiddled whisper music on those strings
380 And bats with baby faces in the violet light
Whistled, and beat their wings
And crawled head downward down a blackened wall
And upside down in air were towers
Tolling reminiscent bells, that kept the hours
And voices singing out of empty cisterns° and exhausted wells.

In this decayed hole among the mountains
In the faint moonlight, the grass is singing
Over the tumbled graves, about the chapel
There is the empty chapel, only the wind's home.°
390 It has no windows, and the door swings,
Dry bones can harm no one.
Only a cock stood on the rooftree
Co co rico co co rico°
In a flash of lightning. Then a damp gust
Bringing rain

Ganga° was sunken, and the limp leaves
Waited for rain, while the black clouds
Gathered far distant, over Himavant.°
The jungle crouched, humped in silence.
400 Then spoke the thunder

What . . . Unreal (ll. 367–77) Eliot quotes Hermann Hesse's *Glimpse into Chaos* (1920): "Already half of Europe, already at least half of Eastern Europe, on the way to chaos, drives drunkenly in spiritual frenzy along the edge of the abyss, sings drunkenly, as though singing hymns, as Dmitri Karamazov sang. The offended bourgeois laughs at the songs; the saint and the seer hear them with tears." The reference is to Dostoevsky's *The Brothers Karamazov* (1880). The apocalyptic quality of the lines, reinforced by the repetition "Unreal" which suggests the contrast between the earthly and the heavenly city, recalls the scenes of destruction at the end of Wagner's *Götterdämmerung*.
A woman This phantasmagorical interlude (ll. 378–85) owing something to Surrealism and to the painter Hieronymous Bosch (b. 1450) con-

tinues the note of apocalyptic fantasy and horror, and looks forward to the terrifying illusions of Chapel Perilous.
And . . . cisterns In Richard Strauss's opera *Salome* John the Baptist sings out of the empty cistern in which he is imprisoned.
empty . . . home *Empty* echoes l. 385; the quester will have to give the right answers under inauspicious conditions, as St. John did. The Chapel Perilous, in medieval romance, was surrounded by deterrent horrors.
cock . . . rico The cock is a symbol of Christ and, as *Hamlet* I.i., heralds the return of light and the departure of ghosts and evil spirits; here it announces a rainstorm, but in the next section the rain has not materialized.
Ganga Ganges, the sacred river of India
Himavant holy mountain in the Himalayas

DA

Datta:° what have we given?
My friend, blood shaking my heart
The awful daring of a moment's surrender
Which an age of prudence can never retract°
By this, and this only, we have existed
Which is not to be found in our obituaries
Or in memories draped by the beneficent spider°
Or under seals broken by the lean solicitor
410   In our empty rooms
DA
Dayadhvam: I have heard the key°
Turn in the door once and turn once only
We think of the key, each in his prison
Thinking of the key, each confirms a prison
Only at nightfall, aethereal rumours
Revive for a moment a broken Coriolanus°
DA
Damyata: The boat responded
420   Gaily, to the hand expert with sail and oar
The sea was calm, your heart would have responded
Gaily, when invited, beating obedient
To controlling hands°

                I sat upon the shore
Fishing,° with the arid plain behind me
Shall I at least set my lands in order?°
London Bridge is falling down falling down falling down°

Datta "Datta, dayadhvam, damyata (Give, sympathize, control). The fable of the meaning of the Thunder is found in the *Brihadaranyaka-Upanishad* 5.1" (T.S.E.). In that fable gods, demons, and men ask the Creator to speak to them; he replies DA, and each group interprets the answer differently, using the three words employed by Eliot. *Datta* means "give" in Sanskrit, which Eliot had studied at Harvard.
The awful . . . retract presumably a sexual surrender, not the kind of giving proposed by the Thunder
spider "Cf. Webster, *The White Devil* V.vi: " . . . they'll remarry / Ere the worm pierce your winding-sheet, ere the spider / Make a thin curtain for your epitaphs" (T.S.E.). *They* are women.
the key "Cf. *Inferno* XXXIII.46: *ed io sentii chiavar l'uscio di sotto / all'orribile torre*" (T.S.E.): "and from below I heard the door of the horrible tower being locked." The words of Ugolino, who devoured his children when starving in captivity; the key of the tower was thrown into the river. Eliot adds in his note to this image of suffering isolation a quotation from F. H. Bradley's *Appearance and Reality* (1893), p. 346: "My external sensations are no less private to myself than are my thoughts

and feelings. In either case my experience falls within my own circle, a circle closed on the outside; and, with all its elements alike, every sphere is opaque to the others which surround it. . . . In brief, regarded as an existence which appears in the soul, the whole world for each is peculiar and private to that soul." This is an important testimony to what Eliot is doing in such poems as "Gerontion" and *The Waste Land.*
Coriolanus broken and exiled through his own pride; reviving only momentarily, as when Coriolanus is revived by the chance of fighting against Rome
controlling hands The picture provided for *control* is first a well-managed sailing boat, secondly, some moment when control could have assured a personal relation, now lost.
Fishing "V. Weston: *From Ritual to Romance;* chapter on the Fisher King" (T.S.E.). The land is still "arid."
set . . . order Isaiah to Hezekiah, the sick king whose lands lie waste: "Thus saith the Lord, Set thine house in order: for thou shalt die and not live" (Isaiah 38:1). The Fisher King contemplates death; no successful quest is recorded in the poem.
London . . . down an English nursery rhyme

Poi s'ascose nel foco che gli affina°
Quando fiam uti chelidon°—O swallow swallow
Le Prince d'Aquitaine à la tour abolie°
These fragments I have shored against my ruins°
Why then Ile fit you. Hieronymo's mad againe.°
Datta. Dayadhvam. Damyata.
　　　Shantih shantih shantih°
　　　1921　　　　　　1922

The Hollow Men

Eliot said in an interview that "The Hollow Men", "originated out of separate poems.
. . . That's one way in which my mind does seem to have evolved through the years
poetically—doing things separately and then seeing the possibility of focusing them
together, altering them, making a kind of whole of them." The first four sections
had all appeared separately before the publication of the whole, in 1925. Some of
the material was originally in *The Waste Land*. The Hollow Men are like the city
crowds of *The Waste Land,* the damned who are so because of a lack of spiritual
reality, even their sins lacking violence and conviction. The first references are, then,
Dantean. There is a contrast with the blessed; their "direct eyes" are avoided in II,
where the hollowness of the Hollow Men begets scarecrow imagery. The landscape is
a stony desert of privation; despair and a consciousness of the necessary imperfection
of a life which resembles that of the faint-hearted damned are the other themes
developed. For the title see *Julius Caesar* IV.ii.23, where the word means "insincere";
Conrad uses "hollow" several times in *Heart of Darkness*.

Poi . . . affina "V. *Purgatorio* XXVI.148: 'Ara
vos prec, per aquella valor / que vos guida al
som de l'escalina, / sovegna vos a temps de ma
dolor.' / Poi s'ascose nel foco che gli affina"
(T.S.E.): " 'Now I pray you, by that virtue
which leads you to the top of the stair, think
of me in my time of pain.' Then he hid himself
in the fire that refines them." The speaker in
purgatory is the Provençal poet Arnaut Daniel,
speaking his own language. The passage was
especially dear to Eliot, who comments on
it in his remarkable essay *"Dante"* / (*Selected
Essays*, 1932, pp. 199–237), that the suffering
of purgatory is embraced voluntarily, and is so
distinguished from that of hell, where it is of
"the very nature of the damned themselves,
expresses their essence"; this reflects Eliot's
views in the Baudelaire essay, and the stress
in *The Waste Land* on the difference between
sin actively and boldly committed and the
anomie of the modern scene.
Quando . . . chelidon "V. *Pervigilium Veneris.*
Cf. Philomela in Parts II and III" (T.S.E.):
"When shall I be like the swallow?"—from *The
Vigil of Venus*, an anonymous late Latin poem
about Venus and the spring. The other references
are to Philomel's sister Procne, wife of Tereus,
who became a swallow.
Le Prince . . . abolie "The Prince of Aquitaine

in the ruined tower"—from Gérard de Nerval's
sonnet "El Deschidado" (The Disinherited).
Nerval (1808–55) refers to himself as the disinherited prince; the troubadour poets were
associated with the castles of Aquitaine in
southern France. A Tarot card shows a tower
struck by lightning.
These . . . ruins meaning these disjointed but
obliquely relevant scraps which render the situation of the unrelieved Fisher King and support
him in his isolation and loneliness
Why . . . againe "V. Kyd's *Spanish Tragedy*"
(T.S.E.). In this play of Thomas Kyd (1557?–
95), which is subtitled *Hieronymo's Mad Again,*
Hieronymo, seeking revenge for the murder
of his son, takes the opportunity offered by an
invitation to stage a court entertainment, saying,
"Why then, I'll fit you," meaning both "I'll
give you what you want" and "I'll give you
your due"; he contrives the murder of the
guilty in a play made up of bits in various
languages.
Shantih . . . shantih "Repeated as here, a
formal ending to an Upanishad. 'The Peace
which passeth understanding' is our equivalent
to this word" (T.S.E.). The Upanishads are
poetic dialogues commenting on the Hindu
scriptures or Vedas.

The Hollow Men

Mistah Kurtz—he dead.°
A penny for the Old Guy°

I

We are the hollow men
We are the stuffed men
Leaning together
Headpiece filled with straw. Alas!
Our dried voices, when
We whisper together
Are quiet and meaningless
As wind in dry grass
Or rats' feet over broken glass
10 In our dry cellar°

Shape without form, shade without colour,
Paralysed force, gesture without motion;°

Those who have crossed
With direct eyes, to death's other Kingdom°
Remember us—if at all—not as lost
Violent souls, but only
As the hollow men
The stuffed men.

II

Eyes I dare not meet in dreams
20 In death's dream kingdom
These do not appear:
There, the eyes are
Sunlight on a broken column
There, is a tree swinging
And voices are
In the wind's singing
More distant and more solemn
Than a fading star.

Mistah . . . dead the boy's announcement of Kurtz's death in *Heart of Darkness.* The whole passage, from Marlow's visit to Kurtz, to the paragraph about Marlow's own contest with death, is relevant to "The Hollow Men"; indeed, the whole work is.
A penny . . . Guy Every year on November 5, English children burn a scarecrow effigy of the traitor Guy Fawkes, who tried to blow up the Parliament buildings in 1605; on preceding days they carry their "guys" around begging pennies for fireworks.
rats' . . . cellar See *The Waste Land,* ll. 115, 195.
Shape . . . motion These distinctions between near-synonyms (shape-form, shade-colour) and near oxymorons (paralysed force, gesture without motion) constitute a theme to be developed differently in the final section. See Conrad's "A vision of grayness without form" (*Heart of Darkness*).
death's . . . Kingdom The habitation of the hollow men is one, the other is a heaven for those who have passed into a condition in which eyes look directly, and beyond the acquaintance of lost souls—lost not for their strong sinning but for spiritual incapacity. At the end of the *Purgatorio* and in *Paradiso* IV Dante cannot meet the gaze of Beatrice (see Eliot's essay "Dante").

Let me be no nearer°
In death's dream kingdom
Let me also wear
Such deliberate disguises
Rat's coat, crowskin, crossed staves
In a field°
Behaving as the wind behaves
No nearer—

Not that final meeting
In the twilight kingdom°

III

This is the dead land
This is the cactus land
Here the stone images°
Are raised, here they receive
The supplication of a dead man's hand
Under the twinkle of a fading star.
Is it like this
In death's other kingdom
Waking alone
At the hour when we are
Trembling with tenderness°
Lips that would kiss
Form prayers to broken stone.

IV

The eyes are not here
There are no eyes here
In this valley of dying stars
In this hollow valley
This broken jaw of our lost kingdoms

In this last of meeting places
We grope together
And avoid speech
Gathered on this beach of the tumid river°

Sightless, unless
The eyes reappear
As the perpetual star

(line numbers: 30, 40, 50, 60 in margin)

Let . . . nearer He wants to have only a distant view of such eyes, and himself to remain without decision or volition, like a scarecrow.
Rat's . . . field a typical English scarecrow, with dead birds and animals attached to it
final . . . kingdom Referring perhaps to the meeting of Dante with Beatrice after he has crossed the Lethe; he is reminded of his sin and disloyalty, but without the confrontation cannot go on to Paradise (*Purgatorio* XXX).
stone images See *The Waste Land*, l. 22.
Waking . . . tenderness In this condition the true recognition of love (as in *The Waste Land*, ll. 39 ff. and 418 ff.) is frustrated.
Gathered . . . river Dante's Acheron, encircling hell, and Conrad's Congo; they are in the "heart of darkness" unless they cross.

Multifoliate rose°
Of death's twilight kingdom
The hope only
Of empty men.

        V

Here we go round the prickly pear
Prickly pear prickly pear
70   *Here we go round the prickly pear*
At five o'clock in the morning.°

    Between the idea
And the reality°
Between the motion
And the act
Falls the Shadow°
        For Thine is the Kingdom°

    Between the conception
And the creation
80   Between the emotion
And the response
Falls the Shadow
        Life is very long

    Between the desire
And the spasm
Between the potency
And the existence°
Between the essence
And the descent°
90   Falls the Shadow
        For Thine is the Kingdom

    For Thine is
Life is
For Thine is the

Multifoliate rose Dante's image of heaven (*Paradiso* XXXII)

Here . . . morning parodying the children's rhyme "Here we go round the mulberry bush on a cold frosty morning"

Between . . . reality See ll. 11–12n; developed from *Julius Caesar* II.i.63 ff.: "Between the acting of a dreadful thing / And the first motion, all the interim is / Like a phantasma or a hideous dream."

Falls the Shadow Eliot agreed that this expression probably came to him from Dowson's *Non sum qualis eram . . .* : "There fell thy shadow . . .". The Shadow divides concepts increasingly difficult to divide as the section continues.

For . . . Kingdom from the Lord's Prayer, but echoing the other uses of the word *kingdom* earlier

potency . . . existence ultimately Aristotelian philosophical terms, e.g. matter has only potency till form gives it existence (the actual possession of being)

essence . . . descent Unlike the former example, this is a false pair, brought together by serious punning. *Essence* is that which constitutes the being of a thing, that by which it is what it is; it is converted by assonance into *ascent* for the purposes of the poem. *Descent* accordingly has overtones of loss of being.

This is the way the world ends°
This is the way the world ends
This is the way the world ends
Not with a bang but a whimper.°
1924–25   1925

Little Gidding

Eliot's most notable work after "The Hollow Men" was *Ash Wednesday,* a sequence of allusive religious meditations assembled, as usual, piecemeal, and published in 1930. In 1934, he wrote choruses for *The Rock,* a church pageant; and this led to the commissioning of *Murder in the Cathedral* (1935), a verse play, for Canterbury Cathedral. He has attributed to the exercise afforded by *The Rock* the revival of his "numbed powers": he was now able to proceed to "the second half of his creative life" (H. Howarth, *Notes on Some Figures Behind T. S. Eliot,* 1965). Out of some lines left over from *Murder in the Cathedral* he developed the long sequence, meditating on time and eternity, called "Burnt Norton" (1935). This work stood alone until 1940, when an obviously parallel poem, "East Coker," appeared. In the meantime Eliot had written a second play, the highly wrought *Family Reunion* (1939), which shows some of the same preoccupations. While writing "East Coker" he conceived the notion of a set of four related works, and added "The Dry Salvages" (1941) and "Little Gidding" (1941). The *Four Quartets* were first published together in 1943.

Each of the poems is named for a place of special significance to the author; they are parallel in structure; and there is a great deal of cross reference. Eliot wrote the first two in the London borough of Kensington and first wanted to call the work *Kensington Quartets.* Mrs. Eliot says that the "place of disaffection" in "Burnt Norton" is the Gloucester Road Underground station in Kensington, and the pavement they "trod . . . in a dead patrol" in "Little Gidding" is Cromwell Road, a main artery of the borough.

Eliot dropped this idea but kept to his original intention of giving the work a musical title. He rejected "sonata" and, while admitting that there were "general objections to these musical analogies," chose *Quartets.* "I should like to indicate that these poems are all in a particular set from which I have elaborated, and the word 'quartet' does seem to me to start people on the right tack for understanding them. . . . It suggests to me the notion of making a poem by weaving in together three or four superficially unrelated themes: the 'poem' being the degree of success in making a new whole out of them" (letter to John Hayward, September 3, 1942, quoted by Valerie Eliot in a letter to the (London) *Times Literary Supplement,* July 16, 1971). Eliot also had in mind the late quartets of Beethoven (Opp. 127, 130–32, 135), with their strange transitions, intermingling of conventional and original forms, internal references and unpredicted sonorities.

This . . . ends partly from the same children's game and rhyme as ll. 68–71: "This is the way we clap our hands . . . "; mixed with the end of the *Gloria,* "as it was in the beginning, is now and ever shall be, world without end, Amen"
whimper Eliot, in his *Choice of Kipling's Verse,*

commended Kipling's choice of this word in "Danny Deever" as "exactly right": Deever is executed for killing a comrade and this dialogue occurs: " 'What's that that whimpers over'ead?' said Files-on-Parade, / 'It's Danny's soul that's passin' now,' the Colour-Sergeant said."

In his lecture "The Music of Poetry" (1942, see *On Poetry and Poets*, 1957), in which he must have had his recent poems in mind, he asserts that music in poetry is not a matter of "beautiful words" but of the whole structure and does not preclude the prosaic: in fact "no poet can write a poem of amplitude unless he is a master of the prosaic." Speaking of structural music, he says that it will depend on interlinked allusions, recurrent themes. The poet should not work "too closely to musical analogies"; yet "there are possibilities for verse which bear some analogy to the development of a theme by different groups of instruments; there are possibilities of transitions in a poem comparable to the different movements of a symphony or a quartet; there are possibilities of contrapuntal arrangement of subject matter. It is in the concert room, rather than in the opera house, that the germ of a poem may be quickened." This is farewell to Wagner, welcome to Beethoven.

The four poems have strong structural similarities. The first movements are divided into three parts, like sonata form in the opening movements of classical music. The second movement varies from lyric stanzas to a "prosaic" section ("Little Gidding" is a slight exception); the third is a discursive exploration of stated themes; the fourth is lyrical and usually in stanzas, and its themes are usually explicitly Christian; the fifth (itself anomalous in the classical quartet except for Beethoven) is in two sections and recapitulates the whole.

The four poems share preoccupations most clearly enunciated in the first, and "Little Gidding," coming last, is full of references to the earlier poems. Since we have but one of the four we can do little to indicate these references. All that needs to be said on this score is that the poems are all concerned with time and eternity, history and the present, the intervention of the divine in human life. They are thus philosophical poems, and their philosophy is Christian; Eliot's acceptance into the church, predictable enough on the evidence of his early work, had happened years before. Yet the poems are *not* doctrinal and do not depend upon religious or intellectual assent from the reader. The "set" from which Eliot says they are elaborated is not the Thirty-nine Articles of his church. Its images are sometimes those private ones, inexplicably meaningful, mentioned in the notes to "The Journey of the Magi"; others—the garden, the wounded god, the sea and death by water, the chapel and the refining fire—are familiar to readers of *The Waste Land*. The *Quartets* comprise a complex poem of great transparency, virtuosity, and originality; and quite obviously they are colored by the mind of a poet, not a philosopher or theologian.

Each of the four poems has its own season and its own element; "Little Gidding" is winter and fire. Its title is the name of a village in Huntingdonshire, off the Great North Road out of London, where, in 1625, Nicholas Ferrar established the Anglican community described by Izaak Walton in his *Life of Herbert* (the description is reprinted in the Renaissance section of this anthology). The community had one, perhaps two, visits from King Charles I; it was eventually broken up by Parliamentary troops. Eliot visited it in 1936. It had not for him the personal associations of East Coker, the Somerset village from which his ancestors had set out for New England, nor of the Dry Salvages—rocks off the coast of Cape Ann, Massachusetts—where he spent boyhood summers; but its attractions, as the site of a rare experiment in Anglican piety in the days of the seventeenth-century Anglican preachers and poets he venerated, and as a spot associated with the Royal Martyr, were great. The blend of monasticism and family life, ruined by that Civil War to which Eliot in a sense attributed the "dissociation of sensibility" (see "Milton" in *On Poetry and Poets*, and

"The Metaphysical Poets," below) gave him a locus for his meditation on conflicts resolved by divine intervention.

Eliot wrote "Little Gidding" in the darkest time of the war for the British; and just as in the other poems he suggests his London, its crowds and "tubes" (subways), here he incorporates into the texture of the poem the heavy night bombing and fire raids of the winter of 1940–41. "Little Gidding" is a poem of fire, and not only Pentecostal fire but also the conflagration of cities, of St. Paul's ringed by flame as it was in December 1940 (see Fig. 29). One of the epigraphs to "Burnt Norton" is a fragment of Heraclitus: "The way up and the way down are one and the same." One is "redeemed from fire by fire." The image of a purgatorial London, set against both history and the timeless that intersects history and the present moment, is essential to the feeling of the poem.

From The Four Quartets

Little Gidding

1°

Midwinter spring is its own season
Sempiternal though sodden towards sundown,
Suspended in time, between pole and tropic.
When the short day is brightest, with frost and fire,
The brief sun flames the ice, on pond and ditches,
In windless cold that is the heart's heat,
Reflecting in a watery mirror
A glare that is blindness in the early afternoon.
And glow more intense than blaze of branch, or brazier,
10 Stirs the dumb spirit: no wind, but pentecostal fire°
In the dark time of the year. Between melting and freezing
The soul's sap quivers.° There is no earth smell
Or smell of living thing. This is the spring time
But not in time's covenant.° Now the hedgerow
Is blanched for an hour with transitory blossom
Of snow, a bloom more sudden
Than that of summer, neither budding nor fading,
Not in the scheme of generation.°

1 The opening movement begins with an evocation of season and place. The season is the illusory spring of midwinter, sun reflected in ice, a moment of reconciled opposites, *sempiternal*—having some characteristics of the intemporal or eternal—and holding together as in an image heat and cold, pole and tropic, ice and fire, winter and summer.
pentecostal fire At Pentecost, commemorated on the seventh Sunday after Easter, the Holy Ghost descended on the apostles: "And there appeared unto them cloven tongues like as of fire" (Acts 2:3). The symbol for this is the Dove. These

figures, here introduced, become very important in the poem.
soul's sap quivers caught in this uncanonical season between the seasons of the sap's rise and fall
There is . . . covenant (ll. 12–14) The absence of these smells establishes a difference from normal spring, the one "in time's covenant."
Not . . . generation (ll. 15–19) The blossoms of this spring are not those of the season which plays a part in the generative cycle.

Where is the summer, the unimaginable
20 Zero summer?°

                    If you came this way,
Taking the route you would be likely to take
From the place you would be likely to come from,
If you came this way in may time,° you would find the hedges
White again, in May, with voluptuary sweetness.
It would be the same at the end of the journey,
If you came at night like a broken king,°
If you came by day not knowing what you came for,
It would be the same, when you leave the rough road
30 And turn behind the pig-sty to the dull façade
And the tombstone. And what you thought you came for
Is only a shell, a husk of meaning
From which the purpose breaks only when it is fulfilled
If at all. Either you had no purpose
Or the purpose is beyond the end you figured
And is altered in fulfilment. There are other places
Which also are the world's end,° some at the sea jaws,
Or over a dark lake, in a desert or a city—
But this is the nearest, in place and time,
40 Now and in England.

                    If you came this way,
Taking any route, starting from anywhere,
At any time or at any season,
It would always be the same: you would have to put off
Sense and notion.° You are not here to verify,
Instruct yourself, or inform curiosity
Or carry report. You are here to kneel
Where prayer has been valid. And prayer is more
Than an order of words, the conscious occupation
50 Of the praying mind, or the sound of the voice praying.
And what the dead had no speech for, when living,
They can tell you, being dead: the communication
Of the dead is tongued with fire° beyond the language of the living.
Here, the intersection of the timeless moment°
Is England and nowhere. Never and always.

Zero summer A summer complementary to this
winter would have to appear cold as this appears
warm; but this is unimaginable. The uniqueness
of this moment is reinforced.
may time the time when the hawthorn blossoms
broken king Charles I is said to have visited
Little Gidding after his defeat at the Battle of
Naseby (1645).
the world's end This is not the only spot where
one can meet one's transfigured purpose, one's
true meaning realized only in this end, as the
result of a prayer.

Sense and notion modifying the more usual
"sense and motion"—the use of the senses
for trivial purposes, commonplace notional ideas
tongued with fire The Holy Ghost gave the
apostles the gift of tongues (Acts 2:4); by
the same gift the dead can now communicate
with the living.
intersection . . . moment As the midwinter
spring is a timeless moment, so is the place;
eternity crosses time, space and time are both
present and not present.

II°

Ash on an old man's sleeve
Is all the ash the burnt roses leave.
Dust in the air suspended
Marks the place where a story ended.
60   Dust inbreathed was a house—
The wall, the wainscot and the mouse.
The death of hope and despair,
        This is the death of air.

There are flood and drouth
Over the eyes and in the mouth,
Dead water and dead sand
Contending for the upper hand.
The parched eviscerate soil
Gapes at the vanity of toil,
70   Laughs without mirth.
        This is the death of earth.

Water and fire succeed
The town, the pasture and the weed.
Water and fire deride
The sacrifice that we denied.
Water and fire shall rot
The marred foundations we forgot,
Of sanctuary and choir.
        This is the death of water and fire.

80   In the uncertain hour before the morning
        Near the ending of interminable night
        At the recurrent end of the unending°
After the dark dove with the flickering tongue
        Had passed below the horizon of his homing°
        While the dead leaves still rattled on like tin
Over the asphalt where no other sound was
        Between three districts whence the smoke arose
        I met one walking, loitering and hurried
As if blown towards me like the metal leaves
90   Before the urban dawn wind unresisting.
        And as I fixed upon the down-turned face
        That pointed scrutiny with which we challenge

II A lyric recapitulation of the elements, with reminiscences of the three other poems associated with them, opens the movement. The third stanza refers to the damage by fire and water in London, as well as to the desecration of Little Gidding; in the bombing of the City many churches were damaged or destroyed. This is the link with the second section, a totally original imitation, without rhyme, of Dante's *terza rima*—"the nearest equivalent to a canto of the *Inferno* or *Purgatorio*" Eliot could achieve, and "a parallel . . . between the *Inferno* and the *Purgatorio* . . . and a hallucinated scene after an air-raid" (*To Criticize the Critic*, 1965). Eliot transfers the conditions of hell and purgatory, as Dante treats them, to the streets of London in the early morning after a raid has ended.

recurrent . . . unending The short daylight of winter days provided only brief respite between night raids that began with the onset of dark.

dark dove . . . homing The *dark* dove is the German warplanes, of which exhaust flames might be visible, returning to base.

The first-met stranger in the waning dusk
I caught the sudden look of some dead master
Whom I had known, forgotten, half recalled
　　Both one and many; in the brown baked features
　　The eyes of a familiar compound ghost°
Both intimate and unidentifiable.
　　So I assumed a double part, and cried
100　　And heard another's voice cry: 'What! are *you* here?'
Although we were not. I was still the same,
　　Knowing myself yet being someone other—
　　And he a face still forming; yet the words sufficed
To compel the recognition they preceded.
　　And so, compliant to the common wind,
　　Too strange to each other for misunderstanding,
In concord at this intersection time°
Of meeting nowhere, no before and after,
　　We trod the pavement in a dead patrol.
110　I said: 'The wonder that I feel is easy,
　　Yet ease is cause of wonder. Therefore speak:
　　I may not comprehend, may not remember.'
And he: 'I am not eager to rehearse
　　My thought and theory which you have forgotten.
　　These things have served their purpose: let them be.
So with your own, and pray they be forgiven
　　By others, as I pray you to forgive
　　Both bad and good. Last season's fruit is eaten
And the fullfed beast shall kick the empty pail.
120　For last year's words belong to last year's language°
　　And next year's words await another voice.
But, as the passage now presents no hindrance
　　To the spirit unappeased and peregrine
　　Between two worlds become much like each other,
So I find words I never thought to speak
　　In streets I never thought I should revisit
　　When I left my body on a distant shore.°
Since our concern was speech, and speech impelled us
　　To purify the dialect of the tribe°

familiar compound ghost recalling Shake-speare, Sonnet LXXXVI: "affable familiar ghost." Eliot said that a major element in the compound "master" was Yeats, who died in France in 1939 and whose body could not be brought back to Ireland till after the war; but in the nature of the passage there are other masters present also, including perhaps Dante himself and Arnaut Daniel, recalled in l. 147 by an allusion to the passage in the *Purgatorio* Eliot used in *The Waste Land*, l. 427. The ghost is finally a double of the speaker himself. The root is in Dante's encounter (*Inferno* XV) with his damned teacher Brunetto Latini, who provides the facial type.

intersection time neither night nor morning, a moment when place and time are abolished by the simultaneity of past and present

last year's language An important preoccupation of the *Quartets* is the difficulty of finding language, or cleansing it to make it adequate to its task.

left . . . shore Palinurus, the helmsman who fell overboard, tells Aeneas in the underworld that his body was buried on a foreign shore (*Aeneid* VI.325 ff.).

To purify . . . tribe *Donner un sens plus pur aux mots de la tribu*, Mallarmé, "Le Tombeau d'Edgar Poe" (Poe's Tomb).

130   And urge the mind to aftersight and foresight,°
      Let me disclose the gifts reserved for age
          To set a crown upon your lifetime's effort.
          First, the cold friction of expiring sense
      Without enchantment, offering no promise
          But bitter tastelessness of shadow fruit°
          As body and soul begin to fall asunder.
      Second, the conscious impotence of rage
          At human folly, and the laceration°
          Of laughter at what ceases to amuse.
140   And last, the rending pain of re-enactment
          Of all that you have done, and been;° the shame
          Of motives late revealed, and the awareness
      Of things ill done and done to others' harm
          Which once you took for exercise of virtue.°
          Then fools' approval stings, and honour stains.°
      From wrong to wrong the exasperated spirit
          Proceeds, unless restored by that refining fire°
          Where you must move in measure, like a dancer.'°
      The day was breaking. In the disfigured street
150   He left me, with a kind of valediction,
          And faded on the blowing of the horn.°

              III°

      There are three conditions which often look alike
      Yet differ completely, flourish in the same hedgerow:
      Attachment to self and to things and to persons, detachment
      From self and from things and from persons; and, growing between
              them, indifference
      Which resembles the others as death resembles life,
      Being between two lives—unflowering, between

aftersight and foresight "He that made us with such large discourse / Stretching before and after, gave us not / That capability and god-like reason / To rust in us unused" (*Hamlet* IV.iv. 36–39).
bitter . . . fruit See the Sodom apples in Milton, *Paradise Lost* X.565–66.
laceration remembering Swift's epitaph in St. Patrick's Cathedral (Dublin), *Ubi saeva indignatio ulterius cor lacerare nequit*, of which Eliot knew Yeats's translation: "Savage indignation there / Cannot lacerate his breast" ("Swift's Epitaph," *Collected Poems*, 1951)
re-enactment . . . been See Yeat's "Dialogue of Self and Soul."
shame . . . virtue See Yeats's, "Vacillation" V and the opening of "The Man and the Echo."
Then . . . stains See Samuel Johnson, *The Vanity of Human Wishes*, l. 117: "Grief aids disease, remembered folly stings."
refining fire See *The Waste Land*, l. 427n.
like a dancer remembering Yeats's "Byzantium," stanza 4
faded . . . horn "It faded on the crowing of the cock"—the departure of the Ghost in

Hamlet I.i.157; the "horn" is the air-raid siren sounding the all-clear. This episode has occurred in the interval between the end of the raid and the blowing of the siren. Eliot, who served as a civilian firewatcher, must often have experienced such moments.
III Opens with a discursive but difficult passage. As usual the "trimmers" are condemned; attachment to the world may lead to something better, in a larger pattern of eternal detachment. The intermediate condition, neither attachment nor detachment, is deadly. The second strophe quotes from the *Shewings* of Dame Julian of Norwich, one of the 14th-century English mystics, who heard a divine voice telling her that sin is necessary but that all shall be well; the "happy sin" of Adam was the cause of the Incarnation that saved us; attachment is a stage on the way to detachment. He thinks of the people at Little Gidding, and of those on the other side of the political and religious dispute. In honoring them we do not neglect men who are now dying in war; they are that attachment which, by the action of Christ, produces detachment.

The live and the dead nettle. This is the use of memory:
For liberation—not less of love but expanding
60 Of love beyond desire, and so liberation
From the future as well as the past. Thus, love of a country
Begins as attachment to our own field of action
And comes to find that action of little importance
Though never indifferent. History may be servitude,
History may be freedom. See, now they vanish,
The faces and places, with the self which, as it could, loved them,
To become renewed, transfigured, in another pattern.

Sin is Behovely, but
All shall be well, and
70 All manner of thing shall be well.°
If I think, again, of this place,
And of people, not wholly commendable,
Of no immediate kin or kindness,°
But some of peculiar genius,
All touched by a common genius,°
United in the strife which divided them;
If I think of a king at nightfall,
Of three men, and more, on the scaffold
And a few who died forgotten
80 In other places, here and abroad,°
And of one who died blind and quiet,°
Why should we celebrate
These dead men more than the dying?
It is not to ring the bell backward
Nor is it an incantation
To summon the spectre of a Rose.°
We cannot revive old factions
We cannot restore old policies
Or follow an antique drum.
90 These men, and those who opposed them
And those whom they opposed
Accept the constitution of silence
And are folded in a single party.
Whatever we inherit from the fortunate
We have taken from the defeated
What they had to leave us—a symbol:
A symbol perfected in death.
And all shall be well and

Sin . . . well "Sin is behovable, but all shall
be well & all shall be well & all manner of
thing shall be well."
kin or kindness "A little more than kin and less
than kind" (Hamlet I.ii.65)
peculiar . . . genius the peculiar genius of such
as Herbert, the common genius of the unique
institution

a few . . . abroad perhaps Richard Crashaw
(1613–49), convert Catholic poet who knew
Ferrar and died in Loreto
blind and quiet Milton, the opponent of king,
bishop, and the Anglican Church
spectre of a Rose referring to title of a Nijinsky
ballet

200 All manner of thing shall be well
By the purification of the motive
In the ground of our beseeching.°

    IV°

The dove descending breaks the air
With flame of incandescent terror
Of which the tongues declare
The one discharge from sin and error.
The only hope, or else despair
    Lies in the choice of pyre or pyre—
    To be redeemed from fire by fire.
Who then devised the torment? Love.
210 Love is the unfamiliar Name
Behind the hands that wove
The intolerable shirt of flame
Which human power cannot remove.
    We only live, only suspire
    Consumed by either fire or fire.

    V°

What we call the beginning is often the end
And to make an end is to make a beginning.
The end is where we start from. And every phrase
And sentence that is right (where every word is at home,
220 Taking its place to support the others,
The word neither diffident nor ostentatious,
An easy commerce of the old and the new,
The common word exact without vulgarity,
The formal word precise but not pedantic,
The complete consort dancing together)
Every phrase and every sentence is an end and a beginning,
Every poem an epitaph. And any action
Is a step to the block, to the fire, down the sea's throat

In . . . beseeching The voice said to Dame Julian: "I am the Ground of thy beseeching; first it is my will that thou have it; and after, I make thee to will it."
IV a gnomic lyric on the themes of the first three movements. The dove is the Holy Spirit proclaiming that only suffering—the fire that refines—can release us from sin, from attachment to the world (the fires of London, properly understood, might be an emblem of that refining fire). The tormentor is love; the torment is compared to that of the shirt of Nessus which Deianira gave her husband Hercules to wear, believing it to have the power to make him love her; the torment of the poisoned shirt was such that in order to escape it he burnt himself on a pyre and ascended to heaven.
V In this conclusion of the whole work Eliot echoes themes of all the *Quartets;* thus the opening line refers to the first and last lines of

"East Coker": "In my beginning is my end. . . . In my end is my beginning" (referring to the motto of Mary Queen of Scots, "In my end is my beginning"). The poem stresses the contemporaneity of the past, dismissing the illusion that the present is separated from it by time; a well-written poem, any confrontation with death, confronts the past in an order out of time. So, the first section ends, with this moment in time, in the fading light of a winter afternoon at Little Gidding, the meaningful past is present and actual. The link to the second and final section is another line from a 14th-century mystic. Then the theme of all journeying as a return to origins is restated; the children in the tree were there at the beginning of "Burnt Norton." "Quick now, here, now, always" is the timeless experience they represent at the end of that opening poem.

Or to an illegible stone: and that is where we start.
230 We die with the dying:
See, they depart, and we go with them.
We are born with the dead:
See, they return, and bring us with them.
The moment of the rose and the moment of the yew-tree
Are of equal duration. A people without history
Is not redeemed from time, for history is a pattern
Of timeless moments. So, while the light fails
On a winter's afternoon, in a secluded chapel
History is now and England.

240 With the drawing of this Love and the voice of this Calling°

We shall not cease from exploration
And the end of all our exploring
Will be to arrive where we started
And know the place for the first time.
Through the unknown, remembered gate
When the last of earth left to discover
Is that which was the beginning;
At the source of the longest river
250 The voice of the hidden waterfall
And the children in the apple-tree
Not known, because not looked for
But heard, half-heard, in the stillness
Between two waves of the sea.
Quick now, here, now, always—
A condition of complete simplicity
(Costing not less than everything)
And all shall be well and
All manner of thing shall be well
When the tongues of flame are in-folded
260 Into the crowned knot of fire
And the fire and the rose° are one.
1941   1943

Prose

Eliot was a distinguished and prolific prosewriter, editor of an important journal, *The Criterion*, which ran from 1922 to 1939. In the first number he spoke up for "the application, in literature, of principles which have their consequences also in politics and in private conduct," and this is an indication of the surprising, if not always pleasing, homogeneity of Eliot's prose, over the whole wide range of criticism, sociol-

With . . . Calling from The Cloud of *Unknowing*, an anonymous mystical work of the 14th century
rose The Dantean symbol of the Host of the Blessed (*Paradiso* XXXI ff.); the union is of the   heavenly order of the purged spirit and the fire that purges it. There are here, as throughout the movement, internal allusions of much complexity.

ogy, theology, and economics which he attempted. His first published book, *The Sacred Wood* (1920), is criticism of high historical importance which is yet closely allied to the poet's own practice. Of the considerable volume of criticism he wrote in periodicals and elsewhere some was collected, some not, in *Selected Essays* (1932), *On Poetry and Poets* (1957), and *To Criticize the Critic* (1965). His Norton lectures at Harvard appeared as *The Use of Poetry and the Use of Criticism* (1933). Of his other writing the most important are: *After Strange Gods* (1934), lectures delivered at the University of Virginia, and expressing, together with an admiration for the American writers known as the Southern Agrarians, opinions so far to the right (in those days of polarized political opinions) that he later suppressed it; *The Idea of a Christian Society* (1939); and *Notes Toward a Definition of Culture* (1948).

It is not within the scope of this note to provide more than the most general idea of all this prose; all the selections are critical essays, and a word must serve by way of explanation as to how the whole thing hangs together. We have seen from the poetry that Eliot's chief horror was of life and society divorced from the stresses and torments of genuine spiritual engagement; one of his mottos might have been, though it was not, the Lutheran *pecca fortiter* (sin strongly)—rather than merely exist like the crowd flowing over London Bridge, the Hollow Men by the tumid river, the inhabitants of Baudelaire's *fourmillante cité*. There is a strong sense of *election*, of the superiority of men who are in conscious engagement with sin and reality, over those unaware of law and sunk in a bestial hedonism like Sweeney's. Speaking of Communism, which he hated but saw as a rival religion to Christianity, he says that the young who "would like to grow up and believe in something" find it a godsend, and "have joined that bitter fraternity which lives on a higher level of doubt"; and Christians live on that level also (*Criterion*, vol. 12). Feelings of this kind animate Eliot's famous choice of conservatism and a hierarchical society, his insistence on the need for *élites*, his acceptance of the authority of an established Catholic Church (the Church of England), and his interest, during the years of political crisis in Europe, in the virtually fascist, but also Catholic and Royalist, French organization called *Action Française*.

There is in Eliot a persistent requirement of *authority*—in the state, the church, the arts. The source of authority in the arts is the art of the past. He was fond of such expressions as "the mind of Europe" and "the mind of England"; he had an imperial imagination, which was fed by the notion of a continuous transmission of authority, such as what the Roman empire, duly associated with Christianity, may be said to have achieved in Europe. Politically, the consequences may strike one as having a provincial air, since the time and the place—now and England—called for acceptance of the English reformed church, the English post-Stuart royal house, and an English general culture—soccer, cheese, music hall—not his own. And in much of this the student of poetry may not be directly interested. It is the reflection of these doctrines in the sphere of literature that most concerns him. Eliot's "imperialism" led him to undertake a profound and delicate study of Dante, and to respect him and Virgil (in this second admiration he differed from his associates in the poetic revolution) as transmitters of a literary *imperium*. But of more direct importance, it led him to a consideration of the meaning of tradition in the light of the further and apparently contradictory truth that all good art is in various ways *new*, and apparently a departure from tradition. It led him further to a consideration of how the individual artist, the new sufferer and creator, stands in relation to the authority of the tradition. The answer lies in a necessary and difficult *impersonality*.

In addition to this whole complex problem of the relations of new to old, and of the individual talent to the past on which it operates, there was the further difficulty that people habitually thought of a poem as the *expression* of an individual, and as having some kind of *message*. Eliot had also to deal with this, to redefine not only the role of the artist but the mode of existence of the poem itself; and also to explain how these and other mistaken notions of poetry had grown up since—when? Since the seventeenth century; and this introduces the historical problem, of how and when all this came about. A new history of poetry was required, and Eliot sketched it; later it was filled out by others. The practical problem, of putting things right, he tackled as a poet; there were of course others—political, cultural, economic—on which he said his say in prose. But the radical diagnosis is really to be sought in a few pages of his early critical essays.

These have a "pontifical solemnity" he later came to disown, but the tone of authority is right for the material. That there are many things wrong with the arguments of the essays goes without saying and has often been said; but rarely has a powerful—and what is more, effective—poetic, aesthetic, and historical conjecture been so clearly and forcefully expressed in so few pages.

Tradition and the Individual Talent [1]

I

In English writing we seldom speak of tradition,[2] though we occasionally apply its name in deploring its absence. We cannot refer to 'the tradition' or to 'a tradition'; at most, we employ the adjective in saying that the poetry of So-and-so is 'traditional' or even 'too traditional.' Seldom, perhaps, does the word appear except in a phrase of censure. If otherwise, it is vaguely approbative, with the implication, as to the work approved, of some pleasing archaeological reconstruction. You can hardly make the word agreeable to English ears without this comfortable reference to the reassuring science of archaeology.

Certainly the word is not likely to appear in our appreciations of living or dead writers. Every nation, every race, has not only its own creative, but its own critical turn of mind; and is even more oblivious of the shortcomings and limitations of its critical habits than of those of its creative genius. We know, or think we know, from the enormous mass of critical writing that has appeared

---

1. "Tradition and the Individual Talent" appeared in the *Egoist*, 1919, and was reprinted in *The Sacred Wood* (1920). The essay re-values the idea of tradition: in the mature poet past poetry is part of his individuality; the past is part of the present, and is modified by it. Thus what is genuinely new is to be aware of, and a part of, the ever-changing "mind of Europe." To achieve this integral relation with the body of European poetry a poet must aim at the extinction of his personality. He must be not a personality but a medium for the digestion and transmutation of his material. The result is its own kind of thing; its complexity is not that of the emotions represented or suffered by the man who wrote the poem. Consequently the Romantic doctrines are rejected as too personal, too crudely related to the emotions of the poet. There is, further, a distinction between poetic value and anything "semi-ethical"; it is not the good things said, but the good saying, that marks mature poetry. The business of the poem is "emotion which has its life in the poem," not the poet's emotions or his opinions. That is why he must strive for Impersonality.
2. That this is now palpably untrue is directly attributable to the influence of Eliot's essay.

in the French language the critical method or habit of the French; we only conclude (we are such unconscious people) that the French are 'more critical' than we, and sometimes even plume ourselves a little with the fact, as if the French were the less spontaneous. Perhaps they are; but we might remind ourselves that criticism is as inevitable as breathing, and that we should be none the worse for articulating what passes in our minds when we read a book and feel an emotion about it, for criticizing our own minds in their work of criticism. One of the facts that might come to light in this process is our tendency to insist, when we praise a poet, upon those aspects of his work in which he least resembles anyone else. In these aspects or parts of his work we pretend to find what is individual, what is the peculiar essence of the man. We dwell with satisfaction upon the poet's difference from his predecessors, especially his immediate predecessors; we endeavour to find something that can be isolated in order to be enjoyed. Whereas if we approach a poet without this prejudice we shall often find that not only the best, but the most individual parts of his work may be those in which the dead poets, his ancestors, assert their immortality most vigorously. And I do not mean the impressionable period of adolescence, but the period of full maturity.

Yet if the only form of tradition, of handing down, consisted in following the ways of the immediate generation before us in a blind or timid adherence to its successes, 'tradition' should positively be discouraged. We have seen many such simple currents soon lost in the sand; and novelty is better than repetition. Tradition is a matter of much wider significance. It cannot be inherited, and if you want it you must obtain it by great labour.[3] It involves, in the first place, the historical sense, which we may call nearly indispensable to any one who would continue to be a poet beyond his twenty-fifth year; and the historical sense involves a perception, not only of the pastness of the past, but of its presence; the historical sense compels a man to write not merely with his own generation in his bones, but with a feeling that the whole of the literature of Europe from Homer and within it the whole of the literature of his own country has a simultaneous existence and composes a simultaneous order. This historical sense, which is a sense of the timeless as well as of the temporal and of the timeless and of the temporal together, is what makes a writer traditional. And it is at the same time what makes a writer most acutely conscious of his place in time, of his own contemporaneity.

No poet, no artist of any art, has his complete meaning alone. His significance, his appreciation is the appreciation of his relation to the dead poets and artists. You cannot value him alone; you must set him, for contrast and comparison, among the dead. I mean this as a principle of aesthetic, not merely historical, criticism. The necessity that he shall conform, that he shall cohere, is not one-sided; what happens when a new work of art is created is something that happens simultaneously to all the works of art which preceded it. The existing monuments form an ideal order among themselves, which is modified by the introduction of the new (the really new) work of art among them. The existing order is complete before the new work arrives; for order to persist after the supervention of novelty, the *whole* existing order must be, if ever so slightly,

3. There is a paradox in stating that what is "handed down" cannot be inherited.

altered; and so the relations, proportions, values of each work of art toward the whole are readjusted; and this is conformity between the old and the new. Whoever has approved this idea of order, of the form of European, of English literature will not find it preposterous that the past should be altered by the present as much as the present is directed by the past. And the poet who is aware of this will be aware of great difficulties and responsibilities.

In a peculiar sense he will be aware also that he must inevitably be judged by the standards of the past. I say judged, not amputated, by them; not judged to be as good as, or worse or better than, the dead; and certainly not judged by the canons of dead critics. It is a judgment, a comparison, in which two things are measured by each other. To conform merely would be for the new work not really to conform at all; it would not be new, and would therefore not be a work of art. And we do not quite say that the new is more valuable because it fits in; but its fitting in is a test of its value—a test, it is true, which can only be slowly and cautiously applied, for we are none of us infallible judges of conformity. We say: it appears to conform, and is perhaps individual, or it appears individual, and may conform; but we are hardly likely to find that it is one and not the other.

To proceed to a more intelligible exposition of the relation of the poet to the past: he can neither take the past as a lump, an indiscriminate bolus,[4] nor can he form himself wholly on one or two private admirations, nor can he form himself wholly upon one preferred period. The first course is inadmissible, the second is an important experience of youth, and the third is a pleasant and highly desirable supplement. The poet must be very conscious of the main current, which does not at all flow invariably through the most distinguished reputations.[5] He must be quite aware of the obvious fact that art never improves, but that the material of art is never quite the same. He must be aware that the mind of Europe—the mind of his own country—a mind which he learns in time to be much more important than his own private mind—is a mind which changes, and that this change is a development which abandons nothing en route, which does not superannuate either Shakespeare, or Homer, or the rock drawing of the Magdalenian [6] draughtsmen. That this development, refinement perhaps, complication certainly,[7] is not, from the point of view of the artist, any improvement. Perhaps not even an improvement from the point of view of the psychologist or not to the extent which we imagine; perhaps only in the end based upon a complication in economics and machinery. But the difference between the present and the past is that the conscious present is an awareness of the past in a way and to an extent which the past's awareness of itself cannot show.

Someone said: 'The dead writers are remote from us because we *know* so much more than they did.' Precisely, and they are that which we know.

4. A large pill.
5. Related to Eliot's current preoccupation with the Metaphysical poets, minor Jacobean drama, and such poets as Laforgue; the implication for criticism is that the map of literary history needs redrawing; see "The Metaphysical Poets."
6. Paleolithic drawings at La Madeleine, France, gave the draftsmen this name; later the caves at Lascaux became more famous.
7. Because Eliot also held the view that modern poetry, because of the character of our civilization, must be difficult, and supported it in his verse.

I am alive to a usual objection to what is clearly part of my programme for the *métier* of poetry. The objection is that the doctrine requires a ridiculous amount of erudition (pedantry), a claim which can be rejected by appeal to the lives of poets in any pantheon. It will even be affirmed that much learning deadens or perverts poetic sensibility. While, however, we persist in believing that a poet ought to know as much as will not encroach upon his necessary receptivity and necessary laziness, it is not desirable to confine knowledge to whatever can be put into a useful shape for examinations, drawing rooms, or the still more pretentious modes of publicity. Some can absorb knowledge, the more tardy must sweat for it. Shakespeare acquired more essential history from Plutarch [8] than most men could from the whole British Museum. What is to be insisted upon is that the poet must develop or procure the consciousness of the past and that he should continue to develop this consciousness throughout his career.

What happens is a continual surrender of himself as he is at the moment to something which is more valuable. The progress of an artist is a continual self-sacrifice, a continual extinction of personality.[9]

There remains to define this process of depersonalization and its relation to the sense of tradition. It is in this depersonalization that art may be said to approach the condition of science. I, therefore, invite you to consider, as a suggestive analogy, the action which takes place when a bit of finely filiated [10] platinum is introduced into a chamber containing oxygen and sulphur dioxide.

II

Honest criticism and sensitive appreciation are directed not upon the poet but upon the poetry.[11] If we attend to the confused cries of the newspaper critics and the *susurrus* [12] of popular repetition that follows, we shall hear the names of poets in great numbers; if we seek not Blue-book [13] knowledge but the enjoyment of poetry, and ask for a poem, we shall seldom find it. I have tried to point out the importance of the relation of the poem to other poems by other authors, and suggested the conception of poetry as a living whole of all the poetry that has ever been written. The other aspect of this Impersonal theory of poetry *is* the relation of the poem to its author. And I hinted, by an analogy, that the mind of the mature poet differs from that of the immature one not precisely in any valuation of 'personality,' not being necessarily more interesting, or having 'more to say,' but rather by being a more finely perfected medium in which special, or very varied, feelings are at liberty to enter into new combinations.

The analogy was that of the catalyst.[14] When the two gases previously mentioned are mixed in the presence of a filament of platinum, they form sulphurous acid. This combination takes place only if the platinum is present; nevertheless

8. First-century A.D. Greek philosopher and biographer, whose *Lives* contain the source material of Shakespeare's Roman plays.
9. This central doctrine involves an asceticism which links it to Eliot's religious interests, and to much in *The Waste Land* and *Four Quartets*.
10. Drawn out into a fine wire.
11. Another doctrine with intensely important implications for 20th-century criticism.
12. Murmuring.
13. Official government publication.
14. Substance causing a chemical reaction in which it plays no direct part.

the newly formed acid contains no trace of platinum, and the platinum itself is apparently unaffected; has remained inert, neutral, and unchanged. The mind of the poet is the shred of platinum. It may partly or exclusively operate upon the experience of the man himself; but, the more perfect the artist, the more completely separate in him will be the man who suffers and the mind which creates; the more perfectly will the mind digest and transmute the passions which are its material.

The experience, you will notice, the elements which enter the presence of the transforming catalyst, are of two kinds: emotions and feelings. The effect of a work of art upon the person who enjoys it is an experience different in kind from any experience not of art. It may be formed out of one emotion, or may be a combination of several; and various feelings, inhering for the writer in particular words or phrases or images, may be added to compose the final result.[15] Or great poetry may be made without the direct use of any emotion whatever: composed out of feelings solely. Canto XV of the *Inferno* (Brunetto Latini [16]) is a working up of the emotion evident in the situation; but the effect, though single as that of any work of art, is obtained by considerable complexity of detail. The last quatrain gives an image, a feeling attaching to an image, which 'came,' which did not develop simply out of what precedes, but which was probably in suspension in the poet's mind until the proper combination arrived for it to add itself to. The poet's mind is in fact a receptacle for seizing and storing up numberless feelings, phrases, images, which remain there until all the particles which can unite to form a new compound are present together.[17]

If you compare several representative passages of the greatest poetry you see how great is the variety of types of combination, and also how completely any semi-ethical criterion of 'sublimity' misses the mark.[18] For it is not the 'greatness,' the intensity, of the emotions, the components, but the intensity of the artistic process, the pressure, so to speak, under which the fusion takes place, that counts. The episode of Paolo and Francesca [19] employs a definite emotion, but the intensity of the poetry is something quite different from whatever intensity in the supposed experience it may give the impression of. It is no more intense, furthermore, than Canto XXVI, the voyage of Ulysses,[20] which has not the direct dependence upon an emotion. Great variety is possible in the process of transmutation of emotion: the murder of Agamemnon,[21] or the agony of Othello, gives an artistic effect apparently closer to a possible original than the scenes from Dante. In the *Agamemnon*, the artistic emotion approximates to the

15. This has a direct relation to the method of "Gerontion" and *The Waste Land*. Critics have objected to the imprecision with which Eliot, in this passage and later, uses the words *emotion* and *feeling*.

16. This is the scene closely imitated by Eliot in "Little Gidding" II (see l. 98n.).

17. In representing the poet's mind as "medium" or "receptacle" Eliot provokes the criticism, e. g. of F. R. Leavis, that the connnection of the poem with a real and intense life is something we value very highly.

18. An attempt to dissociate himself from the criticism of Arnold, which in some ways his own resembles; Eliot was always shocked by the idea that poetry could be a sort of religion-substitute.

19. The illicit lovers of *Inferno* V; an episode famous for its pathos though the lovers are in hell.

20. Ulysses is in hell as a false counselor, and tells Dante the story of his final voyage.

21. By his wife, Clytemnestra, in Aeschylus' *Agamemnon*.

emotion of an actual spectator; in *Othello* to the emotion of the protagonist himself. But the difference between art and the event is always absolute; the combination which is the murder of Agamemnon is probably as complex as that which is the voyage of Ulysses. In either case there has been a fusion of elements. The ode of Keats contains a number of feelings which have nothing particular to do with the nightingale, but which the nightingale, partly, perhaps, because of its attractive name, and partly because of its reputation, served to bring together.

The point of view which I am struggling to attack is perhaps related to the metaphysical theory of the substantial unity of the soul: for my meaning is, that the poet has, not a 'personality' to express, but a particular medium, which is only a medium and not a personality, in which impressions and experiences combine in peculiar and unexpected ways. Impressions and experiences which are important for the man may take no place in the poetry, and those which become important in the poetry may play quite a negligible part in the man, the personality.

I will quote a passage which is unfamiliar enough to be regarded with fresh attention in the light—or darkness—of these observations:

> And now methinks I could e'en chide myself
> For doting on her beauty, though her death
> Shall be revenged after no common action.
> Does the silkworm expend her yellow labours
> For thee? For thee does she undo herself?
> Are lordships sold to maintain ladyships
> For the poor benefit of a bewildering minute?
> Why does yon fellow falsify highways,
> And put his life between the judge's lips,
> To refine such a thing—keeps horse and men
> To beat their valours for her? . . .[22]

In this passage (as is evident if it is taken in its context) there is a combination of positive and negative emotions: an intensely strong attraction toward beauty and an equally intense fascination by the ugliness which is contrasted with it and which destroys it. This balance of contrasted emotion is in the dramatic situation to which the speech is pertinent, but that situation alone is inadequate to it. This is, so to speak, the structural emotion, provided by the drama. But the whole effect, the dominant tone, is due to the fact that a number of floating feelings, having an affinity to this emotion by no means superficially evident, have combined with it to give us a new art emotion.

It is not in his personal emotions, the emotions provoked by particular events in his life, that the poet is in any way remarkable or interesting. His particular emotions may be simple, or crude, or flat. The emotion in his poetry will be a very complex thing, but not with the complexity of the emotions of people who have very complex or unusual emotions in life. One error, in fact, of eccentricity

---

22. Cyril Tourneur, *The Revenger's Tragedy* (1607) III.v.67–78; *bewitching* is probably the true reading in l. 73, though Eliot in his essay "Tourneur" (*Selected Essays*, p. 192) says that "*bewildering* is much the richer word here."

in poetry is to seek for new human emotions to express; and in this search for novelty in the wrong place it discovers the perverse.[23] The business of the poet is not to find new emotions, but to use the ordinary ones and, in working them up into poetry, to express feelings which are not in actual emotions at all. And emotions which he has never experienced will serve his turn as well as those familiar to him. Consequently, we must believe that 'emotion recollected in tranquillity'[24] is an inexact formula. For it is neither emotion, nor recollection, nor, without distortion of meaning, tranquillity. It is a concentration, and a new thing resulting from the concentration, of a very great number of experiences which to the practical and active person would not seem to be experiences at all; it is a concentration which does not happen consciously or of deliberation. These experiences are not 'recollected,' and they finally unite in an atmosphere which is 'tranquil' only in that it is a passive attending upon the event. Of course this is not quite the whole story. There is a great deal, in the writing of poetry, which must be conscious and deliberate. In fact, the bad poet is usually unconscious where he ought to be conscious, and conscious where he ought to be unconscious. Both errors tend to make him 'personal.' Poetry is not a turning loose of emotion, but an escape from emotion; it is not the expression of personality, but an escape from personality. But, of course, only those who have personality and emotions know what it means to want to escape from these things.[25]

III

ὁ δὲ νοῦς ἴσως Θειότερόν τι χαὶ ἀπαθές ἐστιν.[26]

This essay proposes to halt at the frontier of metaphysics or mysticism, and confine itself to such practical conclusions as can be applied by the responsible person interested in poetry. To divert interest from the poet to the poetry is a laudable aim: for it would conduce to a juster estimation of actual poetry, good and bad. There are many people who appreciate the expression of sincere emotion in verse, and there is a smaller number of people who can appreciate technical excellence. But very few know when there is an expression of *significant* emotion, emotion which has its life in the poem and not in the history of the poet. The emotion of art is impersonal. And the poet cannot reach this impersonality without surrendering himself wholly to the work to be done. And he is not likely to know what is to be done unless he lives in what is not merely the present, but the present moment of the past, unless he is conscious, not of what is dead, but of what is already living.

1920

23. Perhaps a complaint against the Dada movement which developed into Surrealism and was strong at this time; Eliot has occasional affinities with it but of course did not share its disavowal of the past.

24. Wordsworth in the Preface to the second edition of *Lyrical Ballads* (1800) said that poetry "takes its origin in emotion recollected in tranquillity," which is not quite the same thing.

25. A touch of the familiar contempt for the half-life of the non-elect.

26. "The mind is doubtless more divine and less subject to passion," Aristotle, *De Anima* (On the Soul) I.4.

The Metaphysical Poets [1]

By collecting these poems [2] from the work of a generation more often named than read, and more often read than profitably studied, Professor Grierson has rendered a service of some importance. Certainly the reader will meet with many poems already preserved in other anthologies, at the same time that he discovers poems such as those of Aurelian Townshend or Lord Herbert of Cherbury here included. But the function of such an anthology as this is neither that of Professor Saintsbury's admirable edition of Caroline poets nor that of the *Oxford Book of English Verse*. Mr. Grierson's book is in itself a piece of criticism and a provocation of criticism; and we think that he was right in including so many poems of Donne, elsewhere (though not in many editions) accessible, as documents in the case of 'metaphysical poetry.' The phrase has long done duty as a term of abuse or as the label of a quaint and pleasant taste. [3] The question is to what extent the so-called metaphysicals formed a school (in our own time we should say a 'movement'), and how far this so-called school or movement is a digression from the main current.

Not only is it extremely difficult to define metaphysical poetry, but difficult to decide what poets practise it and in which of their verses. The poetry of Donne (to whom Marvell and Bishop King are sometimes nearer than any of the other authors) is late Elizabethan, its feeling often very close to that of Chapman. The 'courtly' poetry is derivative from Jonson, who borrowed liberally from the Latin; it expires in the next century with the sentiment and witticism of Prior. There is finally the devotional verse of Herbert, Vaughan, and Crashaw (echoed long after by Christina Rossetti and Francis Thompson); Crashaw, sometimes more profound and less sectarian than the others, has a quality which returns through the Elizabethan period to the early Italians. It is difficult to find any precise use of metaphor, simile, or other conceit, which is common to all the poets and at the same time important enough as an element of style to isolate these poets as a group. Donne, and often Cowley, employ a device which is sometimes considered characteristically 'metaphysical'; the elaboration (contrasted with the condensation) of a figure of speech to the farthest stage to which ingenuity can carry it. Thus Cowley develops the commonplace comparison of the world to a chessboard through long stanzas (*To Destiny*), and Donne, with more grace, in *A Valediction*,[4] the comparison of two lovers to a pair of compasses. But elsewhere we find, instead of the mere explication of the content of a comparison, a development by rapid association of thought which requires considerable agility on the part of the reader.

1. "The Metaphysical Poets" was originally a book review in the (London) *Times Literary Supplement* in 1921. This essay bears the marks of its origin, but is very important as the central statement of the doctrine of "dissociation of sensibility" and the sketch of a new history of English poetry which acceptance of such a doctrine (and, it appeared, of the validity of Eliot's own current poetry) entailed.
2. Eliot was reviewing H. J. C. Grierson's anthology, *Metaphysical Lyrics and Poems of the Seventeenth Century* (1921).
3. This and some later passages in the essay underestimate the degree to which the Metaphysicals had already been rescued from such criticism in the late 19th century and the years leading up to Grierson's edition of Donne (1912).
4. "A Valediction: Forbidding Mourning."

> On a round ball
> A workman that hath copies by, can lay
> An Europe, Afrique, and an Asia,
> And quickly make that which was nothing, all;
>> So doth each tear,
>> Which thee doth wear,
> A globe, yea world, by that impression grow,
> Till thy tears mixed with mine do overflow
> This world; by waters sent from thee, my heaven dissolvèd so.[5]

Here we find at least two connections which are not implicit in the first figure, but are forced upon it by the poet: from the geographer's globe to the tear, and the tear to the deluge. On the other hand, some of Donne's most successful and characteristic effects are secured by brief words and sudden contrasts:

> A bracelet of bright hair about the bone,[6]

where the most powerful effect is produced by the sudden contrast of associations of 'bright hair' and of 'bone.' This telescoping of images and multiplied associations is characteristic of the phrase of some of the dramatists of the period which Donne knew: not to mention Shakespeare, it is frequent in Middleton, Webster, and Tourneur, and is one of the sources of the vitality of their language.[7]

Johnson, who employed the term 'metaphysical poets,' apparently having Donne, Cleveland, and Cowley chiefly in mind, remarks of them that 'the most heterogeneous ideas are yoked by violence together.'[8] The force of this impeachment lies in the failure of the conjunction, the fact that often the ideas are yoked but not united; and if we are to judge of styles of poetry by their abuse, enough examples may be found in Cleveland to justify Johnson's condemnation. But a degree of heterogeneity of material compelled into unity by the operation of the poet's mind is omnipresent in poetry. We need not select for illustration such a line as:

> *Notre âme est un trois-mâts cherchant son Icarie;*[9]

we may find it in some of the best lines of Johnson himself (*The Vanity of Human Wishes*):

> His fate was destined to a barren strand,
> A petty fortress, and a dubious hand;
> He left a name at which the world grew pale,
> To point a moral, or adorn a tale.

where the effect is due to a contrast of ideas, different in degree but the same in principle, as that which Johnson mildly reprehended. And in one of the finest

---

5. "A Valediction: Of Weeping," ll. 10–18.
6. "The Relic," l. 6.
7. Here Eliot brings together two bodies of "minor" poetry to which he himself was heavily indebted.
8. In the *Life of Cowley.*
9. "Our soul is a three-master seeking its Icarie" (Baudelaire, "Le Voyage"). Icarie is a utopia.

poems of the age (a poem which could not have been written in any other age), the *Exequy* of Bishop King, the extended comparison is used with perfect success: the idea and the simile become one, in the passage in which the Bishop illustrates his impatience to see his dead wife, under the figure of a journey:

> Stay for me there; I will not fail
> To meet thee in that hollow Vale.
> And think not much of my delay;
> I am already on the way,
> And follow thee with all the speed
> Desire can make, or sorrows breed.
> Each minute is a short degree,
> And ev'ry hour a step towards thee.
> At night when I betake to rest,
> Next morn I rise nearer my West
> Of life, almost by eight hours sail,
> Then when sleep breathed his drowsy gale. . . .
> But hark! My pulse, like a soft drum
> Beats my approach, tells Thee I come;
> And slow howe'er my marches be,
> I shall at last sit down by Thee.

(In the last few lines there is that effect of terror which is several times attained by one of Bishop King's admirers, Edgar Poe.) Again, we may justly take these quatrains from Lord Herbert's Ode,[10] stanzas which would, we think, be immediately pronounced to be of the metaphysical school:

> So when from hence we shall be gone,
>   And be no more, nor you, nor I,
>   As one another's mystery,
> Each shall be both, yet both but one.
>
> This said, in her uplifted face,
>   Her eyes, which did that beauty crown,
>   Were like two stars, that having faln down,
> Look up again to find their place:
>
> While such a moveless silent peace
>   Did seize on their becalmèd sense,
>   One would have thought some influence
> Their ravished spirits did possess.

There is nothing in these lines (with the possible exception of the stars, a simile not at once grasped, but lovely and justified) which fits Johnson's general observations on the metaphysical poets in his essay on Cowley. A good deal resides in the richness of association which is at the same time borrowed from and given to the word 'becalmed'; but the meaning is clear, the language simple and elegant. It is to be observed that the language of these poets is as a rule simple and pure; in the verse of George Herbert this simplicity is carried as far as it

10. "Ode upon a Question Moved, Whether Love Should Continue for Ever," by Lord Herbert of Cherbury (1583–1648).

can go—a simplicity emulated without success by numerous modern poets. The *structure* of the sentences, on the other hand, is sometimes far from simple, but this is not a vice; it is a fidelity to thought and feeling.[11] The effect, at its best, is far less artificial than that of an ode by Gray. And as this fidelity induces variety of thought and feeling, so it induces variety of music. We doubt whether, in the eighteenth century, could be found two poems in nominally the same metre, so dissimilar as Marvell's *Coy Mistress* and Crashaw's *Saint Teresa;* the one producing an effect of great speed by the use of short syllables, and the other an ecclesiastical solemnity by the use of long ones:

> Love, thou art absolute sole lord
> Of life and death.

If so shrewd and sensitive (though so limited) a critic as Johnson failed to define metaphysical poetry by its faults, it is worth while to inquire whether we may not have more success by adopting the opposite method: by assuming that the poets of the seventeenth century (up to the Revolution [12]) were the direct and normal development of the precedent age; and, without prejudicing their case by the adjective 'metaphysical,' consider whether their virtue was not something permanently valuable, which subsequently disappeared, but ought not to have disappeared. Johnson has hit, perhaps by accident, on one of their peculiarities, when he observes that 'their attempts were always analytic'; he would not agree that, after the dissociation, they put the material together again in a new unity.

It is certain that the dramatic verse of the later Elizabethan and early Jacobean poets expresses a degree of development of sensibility which is not found in any of the prose, good as it often is. If we except Marlowe, a man of prodigious intelligence, these dramatists were directly or indirectly (it is at least a tenable theory) affected by Montaigne. Even if we except also Jonson and Chapman, these two were probably erudite, and were notably men who incorporated their erudition into their sensibility: their mode of feeling was directly and freshly altered by their reading and thought. In Chapman especially there is a direct sensuous apprehension of thought, or a recreation of thought into feeling,[13] which is exactly what we find in Donne:

> in this one thing, all the discipline
> Of manners and of manhood is contained;
> A man to join himself with th' Universe
> In his main sway, and make in all things fit
> One with that All, and go on, round as it;
> Not plucking from the whole his wretched part,

11. Here *thought* and *feeling* are brought together; later in the essay their dissociation will be discussed.

12. The Civil War, which for Eliot brought the great and continuing change in "the mind of England." Ordinarily "Revolution" would refer to the Glorious Revolution of 1688, which established a constitutional monarchy; but Eliot attached special importance to the Civil War, which, in his Marvell essay, he calls "The Great Rebellion." See "Milton II" in *On Poetry and Poets* for Eliot's later reflections on the Civil War and the "dissociation of sensibility."

13. This terminology derives from the French Symbolist writer Rémy de Gourmont (1858–1915), who uses it in a different context.

> And into straits, or into nought revert,
> Wishing the complete Universe might be
> Subject to such a rag of it as he;
> But to consider great Necessity.[14]

We compare this with some modern passage:

> No, when the fight begins within himself,
> A man's worth something. God stoops o'er his head,
> Satan looks up between his feet—both tug—
> He's left, himself, i' the middle; the soul wakes
> And grows. Prolong that battle through his life! [15]

It is perhaps somewhat less fair, though very tempting (as both poets are concerned with the perpetuation of love by offspring), to compare with the stanzas already quoted from Lord Herbert's Ode the following from Tennyson:

> One walked between his wife and child,
> With measured footfall firm and mild,
> And now and then he gravely smiled.
>   The prudent partner of his blood
>   Leaned on him, faithful, gentle, good,
>   Wearing the rose of womanhood.
> And in their double love secure,
> The little maiden walked demure,
> Pacing with downward eyelids pure.
>   These three made unity so sweet,
>   My frozen heart began to beat,
>   Remembering its ancient heat.[16]

The difference is not a simple difference of degree between poets. It is something which had happened to the mind of England between the time of Donne or Lord Herbert of Cherbury and the time of Tennyson and Browning; [17] it is the difference between the intellectual poet and the reflective poet. Tennyson and Browning are poets, and they think; but they do not feel their thought as immediately as the odor of a rose. A thought to Donne was an experience; it modified his sensibility. When a poet's mind is perfectly equipped for its work, it is constantly amalgamating disparate experience; the ordinary man's experience is chaotic, irregular, fragmentary. The latter falls in love, or reads Spinoza, and these two experiences have nothing to do with each other, or with the noise of the typewriter or the smell of cooking; in the mind of the poet these experiences are always forming new wholes.[18]

We may express the difference by the following theory: The poets of the

14. George Chapman (1559?–1634), *The Revenge of Bussy d'Ambois* IV.i.137 ff.
15. Robert Browning (1812–89), *Bishop Blougram's Apology*, ll. 693–97.
16. *The Two Voices*, ll. 412–23.
17. The heart of Eliot's doctrine, historically considered. Are the examples chosen fairly? Is this the right way to project a modern, post-Symbolist doctrine of the poem as non-discursive image onto the past? These and other questions have been cogently raised by subsequent critics.
18. As in the passage in "Tradition and the Individual Talent" on the "medium . . . in which impressions and experiences combine in peculiar and unexpected ways."

seventeenth century, the successors of the dramatists of the sixteenth, possessed a mechanism of sensibility which could devour any kind of experience. They are simple, artificial, difficult, or fantastic, as their predecessors were; no less nor more than Dante, Guido Cavalcanti, Guinicelli, or Cino.[19] In the seventeenth century a dissociation of sensibility [20] set in, from which we have never recovered; and this dissociation, as is natural, was aggravated by the influence of the two most powerful poets of the century, Milton and Dryden. Each of these men performed certain poetic functions so magnificently well that the magnitude of the effect concealed the absence of others. The language went on and in some respects improved; the best verse of Collins, Gray, Johnson, and even Goldsmith satisfies some of our fastidious demands better than that of Donne or Marvell or King. But while the language became more refined, the feeling became more crude. The feeling, the sensibility, expressed in the *Country Churchyard* (to say nothing of Tennyson and Browning) is cruder than that in the *Coy Mistress*.

The second effect of the influence of Milton and Dryden followed from the first, and was therefore slow in manifestation. The sentimental age began early in the eighteenth century, and continued. The poets revolted against the ratiocinative, the descriptive; they thought and felt by fits, unbalanced; they reflected. In one or two passages of Shelley's *Triumph of Life*, in the second *Hyperion*, there are traces of a struggle toward unification of sensibility. But Keats and Shelley died, and Tennyson and Browning ruminated.

After this brief exposition of a theory—too brief, perhaps, to carry conviction —we may ask, what would have been the fate of the 'metaphysical' had the current of poetry descended in a direct line from them, as it descended in a direct line to them? They would not, certainly, be classified as metaphysical. The possible interests of a poet are unlimited; the more intelligent he is the better; the more intelligent he is the more likely that he will have interests: our only condition is that he turn them into poetry, and not merely meditate on them poetically. A philosophical theory which has entered into poetry is established, for its truth or falsity in one sense ceases to matter, and its truth in another sense is proved. The poets in question have, like other poets, various faults. But they were, at best, engaged in the task of trying to find the verbal equivalent for states of mind and feeling. And this means both that they are more mature, and that they wear better, than later poets of certainly not less literary ability.

It is not a permanent necessity that poets should be interested in philosophy, or in any other subject. We can only say that it appears likely that poets in our civilization, as it exists at present, must be *difficult*. Our civilization comprehends great variety and complexity, and this variety and complexity, playing upon a refined sensibility, must produce various and complex results. The poet must become more and more comprehensive, more allusive, more indirect, in order to force, to dislocate if necessary, language into his meaning.[21] (A brilliant and

---

19. Cavalcanti, Guinicelli, and Cino da Pistoia were poets of the *dolce stil nuovo* ("sweet new style"), predecessors and contemporaries of Dante (late 13th, early 14th century). Pound sets his date for the "dissociation of sensibility" between them and Petrarch (1304–74).

20. The first use of the phrase in English (borrowed from De Gourmont).

21. An influential idea, later labeled by the American critic Yvor Winters "the fallacy of imitative form."

extreme statement of this view, with which it is not requisite to associate oneself, is that of M. Jean Epstein, *La Poésie d' aujourd'hui*.[22]) Hence we get something which looks very much like the conceit—we get, in fact, a method curiously similar to that of the 'metaphysical poets,' similar also in its use of obscure
words and of simple phrasing.

> *O géraniums diaphanes, guerroyeurs sortilèges,*
> *Sacrilèges monomanes!*
> *Emballages, dévergondages, douches! O pressoirs*
> *Des vendanges des grands soirs!*
> *Layettes aux abois,*
> *Thyrses au fond des bois!*
> *Transfusions, représailles,*
> *Relevailles, compresses et l'éternal potion,*
> *Angélus! n'en pouvoir plus*
> *De débâcles nuptiales! de débâcles nuptiales!* [23]

The same poet could write also simply:

> *Elle est bien loin, elle pleure,*
> *Le grand vent se lamente aussi . . .* [24]

Jules Laforgue, and Tristan Corbière [25] in many of his poems, are nearer to the
'school of Donne' than any modern English poet. But poets more classical than
they have the same essential quality of transmuting ideas into sensations, of
transforming an observation into a state of mind.

> *Pour l'enfant, amoureux de cartes et d'estampes,*
> *L'univers est égal à son vaste appétit.*
> *Ah, que le monde est grand à la clarté des lampes!*
> *Aux yeux du souvenir que le monde est petit!* [26]

In French literature the great master of the seventeenth century—Racine—and
the great master of the nineteenth—Baudelaire—are in some ways more like
each other than they are like any one else. The greatest two masters of diction
are also the greatest two psychologists, the most curious explorers of the soul.
It is interesting to speculate whether it is not a misfortune that two of the

---

22. *The Poetry of Today.*

23. Jules Laforgue (1860–87) at his most chaotic: "O transparent geraniums, warrior
spells, / monomaniac sacrileges! / Packing materials, shamelessness, showers! O wine-
presses / Of the vintages of evening parties! / Baby-clothes under siege, / Thyrsis in the
depths of the woods! / Transfusions, reprisals, / Churchings, compresses and the eternal
potion, / Angelus! no more are possible / Nuptial disasters! Nuptial disasters!" From *Derniers Vers* (Last Poems), 1890.

24. "She is far away, she weeps, / The great wind laments also." From "Sur un Défunte"
(On a Dead Woman), in *Derniers Vers.*

25. Tristan Corbière (1845–75), French poet and early Symbolist; Eliot wanted to think
Corbière and Laforgue into a special affinity with the English Metaphysicals and Jacobean
dramatists.

26. From Baudelaire's "Le Voyage": "For the child, in love with maps and prints, / The
universe is equal to his vast appetite. / Ah, how big the world is by lamplight! / And how
small the world is to the eyes of memory!"

greatest masters of diction in our language, Milton and Dryden, triumph with a dazzling disregard of the soul. If we continued to produce Miltons and Drydens it might not so much matter, but as things are it is a pity that English poetry has remained so incomplete. Those who object to the 'artificiality' of Milton or Dryden sometimes tell us to 'look into our hearts and write.' But that is not looking deep enough; Racine or Donne looked into a good deal more than the heart. One must look into the cerebral cortex, the nervous system, and the digestive tracts.

May we not conclude, then, that Donne, Crashaw, Vaughan, Herbert and Lord Herbert, Marvell, King, Cowley at his best, are in the direct current of English poetry,[27] and that their faults should be reprimanded by this standard rather than coddled by antiquarian affection? They have been enough praised in terms which are implicit limitations because they are 'metaphysical' or 'witty,' 'quaint' or 'obscure,' though at their best they have not these attributes more than other serious poets. On the other hand, we must not reject the criticism of Johnson (a dangerous person to disagree with) without having mastered it, without having assimilated the Johnsonian canons of taste. In reading the celebrated passage in his essay on Cowley we must remember that by wit he clearly means something more serious than we usually mean today; in his criticism of their versification we must remember in what a narrow discipline he was trained, but also how well trained; we must remember that Johnson tortures chiefly the chief offenders, Cowley and Cleveland. It would be a fruitful work, and one requiring a substantial book, to break up the classification of Johnson (for there has been none since) and exhibit these poets in all their difference of kind and of degree, from the massive music of Donne to the faint, pleasing tinkle of Aurelian Townshend—whose *Dialogue Between a Pilgrim and Time* is one of the few regrettable omissions from the excellent anthology of Professor Grierson.

1921

ROBERT BRIDGES
1844–1930

Born in Kent, educated at Eton and Corpus Christi College, Oxford, Robert Bridges went on to study medicine at St. Bartholomew's Hospital, where he took a degree in 1874. Although he continued to practice for seven years thereafter, a poetic career, which he had always planned, claimed the remainder of a very long life. Temporary ill health, combined with the possession of sufficient money to do so, allowed him to give up medical work, move to Berkshire, and devote his life to musical and literary studies and to poetry. Always interested in prosodic theory, he wrote a small but important book, *Milton's Prosody* (1921), championed the poetry of Gerard Manley Hopkins, whom he had known well, and eventually, at the age of eighty-five, published a long philosophical poem in a somewhat cranky, purportedly quantitative meter, *The Testament of Beauty*. His finest poetry remains in his lyrics, however, and in the loose accentual meters with which he tempered impulses toward a late Vic-

27. A theme later developed by F. R. Leavis in his theory of a "Line of Wit."

torian smoothness. The sense of a true classical learning, too, pervades Bridges's best work. He succeeded, in 1913, the unbelievably undistinguished Alfred Austin as Poet Laureate. Bridges published his first volume of poems in 1873; many volumes appeared thereafter, and he lived on, writing, through the dawn of the modern age in literature, not always pleased (if his late "Poor Poll" is indeed the attack on *The Waste Land* it appears to be) with its monuments.

A Passer-by

Whither, O splendid ship, thy white sails crowding,
   Leaning across the bosom of the urgent West,
That fearest nor sea rising, nor sky clouding,
   Whither away, fair rover, and what thy quest?
   Ah! soon, when Winter has all our vales opprest,
When skies are cold and misty, and hail is hurling,
   Wilt thou glide on the blue Pacific, or rest
In a summer haven asleep, thy white sails furling.

I there before thee, in the country that well thou knowest,
10   Already arrived am inhaling the odorous air:
I watch thee enter unerringly where thou goest,
   And anchor queen of the strange shipping there,
   Thy sails for awnings spread, thy masts bare;
Nor is aught from the foaming reef to the snow-capped, grandest
   Peak, that is over the feathery palms more fair
Than thou, so upright, so stately, and still thou standest.

And yet, O splendid ship, unhailed and nameless,
   I know not if, aiming a fancy, I rightly divine
That thou hast a purpose joyful, a courage blameless,
20   Thy port assured in a happier land than mine.
   But for all I have given thee, beauty enough is thine,
As thou, aslant with trim tackle and shrouding,
   From the proud nostril curve of a prow's line
In the offing scatterest foam, thy white sails crowding.

                                1879

London Snow°

When men were all asleep the snow came flying,
In large white flakes falling on the city brown,
Stealthily and perpetually settling and loosely lying,

London Snow Bridges wrote this poem in what he took to be a version of Gerard Manley Hopkins's "sprung rhythm". Hopkins' comments on Bridges' effort can be found on pp. 122–3 of *Letters of Gerard Manley Hopkins to Robert Bridges*, ed. C. C. Abbott (1935).

Hushing the latest traffic of the drowsy town;
Deadening, muffling, stifling its murmurs failing;
Lazily and incessantly floating down and down:
    Silently sifting and veiling road, roof and railing;
Hiding difference, making unevenness even,
Into angles and crevices softly drifting and sailing.
10   All night it fell, and when full inches seven
It lay in the depth of its uncompacted lightness,
The clouds blew off from a high and frosty heaven;
    And all woke earlier for the unaccustomed brightness
Of the winter dawning, the strange unheavenly glare:
The eye marvelled—marvelled at the dazzling whiteness;
    The ear hearkened to the stillness of the solemn air;
No sound of wheel rumbling nor of foot falling,
And the busy morning cries came thin and spare.
    Then boys I heard, as they went to school, calling,
20   They gathered up the crystal manna to freeze
Their tongues with tasting, their hands with snowballing;
    Or rioted in a drift, plunging up to the knees;
Or peering up from under the white-mossed wonder,
'O look at the trees!' they cried, 'O look at the trees!'
    With lessened load a few carts creak and blunder,
Following along the white deserted way,
A country company long dispersed asunder:
    When now already the sun, in pale display
Standing by Paul's° high dome, spread forth below
30   His sparkling beams, and awoke the stir of the day.
    For now doors open, and war is waged with the snow;
And trains of somber men, past tale of number,
Tread long brown paths, as toward their toil they go:
    But even for them awhile no cares encumber
Their minds diverted; the daily word is unspoken,
The daily thoughts of labour and sorrow slumber
At the sight of the beauty that greets them, for the charm they have broken.

                                1880

Nightingales

  Beautiful must be the mountains whence ye come,
    And bright in the fruitful valleys the streams, wherefrom
      Ye learn your song:
Where are those starry woods? O might I wander there,
    Among the flowers, which in that heavenly air
      Bloom the year long!

Paul's   St. Paul's Cathedral, until recently one
of the highest points on the London skyline.

Nay, barren are those mountains and spent the streams:°
Our song is the voice of desire, that haunts our dreams,
        A throe of the heart,
10 Whose pining visions dim, forbidden hopes profound,
    No dying cadence nor long sigh can sound,
            For all our art.

    Alone, aloud in the raptured ear of men
    We pour our dark nocturnal secret; and then,
            As night is withdrawn
From these sweet-springing meads° and bursting boughs of May,
    Dream, while the innumerable choir of day
            Welcome the dawn.
                            1893

A. E. HOUSMAN
1859–1936

Alfred Edward Housman was born in Fockbury, Worcestershire, on March 26, 1859. He went to Oxford in 1887, and surprisingly failed in his Honors degree examination. In 1892 he took a job in the Patent Office in London, and in his leisure time established a reputation for classical scholarship which served him well, for ten years later he was appointed Professor of Latin at University College, London. His fame as a scholar grew, and by 1911, when he became Professor of Latin at Cambridge, he was recognized as the greatest English classicist since Bentley in the eighteenth century, and among the handful of scholars with unchallenged world reputations. He published his first book of poems, *A Shropshire Lad,* in 1896. Between 1911 and 1936 his work was that of an editor, and his five-volume edition of the difficult Latin astronomical poet Manilius is regarded as his masterpiece. In 1922 he published *Last Poems,* and after his death on April 30, 1936, his writer-brother Laurence brought out another small volume, *More Poems,* and included a few more for the *Additional Poems* in his book, *My Brother, A. E. Housman* (1939).

Housman was a bachelor and something of a recluse, a man of melancholic though excitable temperament. He wanted fame, but had a "horror of being known to like being known"; he sought pleasure in male friendship, but avoided love; he understood food and wine and yet condemned himself for the most part to a life of stoic repression. Among scholars he is famous for the bitter epigrammatic insults he carefully sharpened and used on his enemies and "inferiors." As a poet he sought no fellowship with other poets. Despite many reminiscences of the Greek Anthology and of such Latin poets as Propertius, whom he had edited, the connection in Housman between scholar and poet is not obvious on the surface. He said himself, "The Shropshire Lad is an imaginary figure, with something of my temperament and view of life. . . . I did not begin to write poetry in earnest until the really emotional part of my life was over; and my poetry, as far as I could make out, sprang chiefly from

---

streams In this and the following stanza, the nightingales answer; their "dark nocturnal secret" may or may not be the Ovidian myth of the transformation of the raped, muted

Philomel into the eloquent, tragic singer of night.
meads fields

physical conditions, such as a relaxed sore throat during my most prolific period, the first five months of 1895." He was then thirty-six; the "emotional part of his life" was his Oxford friendship with Moses Jackson, long since married and emigrated. In this "most prolific period," immediately following the death of his father, he wrote *A Shropshire Lad*.

Some of his feeling about this book can be guessed at from the fact that he refused to accept any royalties from its sale. The book combines a sort of idiosyncratically gloomy urgency about the life of the senses with a dramatically simplified acceptance of fate, the darkness which encloses a life; there is also the notion that to yield to the dark is the right proud thing to do. To make statements of that kind was itself for Housman a sensual experience. In his lecture *The Name and Nature of Poetry* (1933) he speaks of the physical tremor by which he recognizes true poetry, his own or another's. Writing poetry was a quite different experience from writing prose, which he claims to have done with great labor; the poems "came into [his] head" half done, and he had only to finish them (though it often took a long time to do so). Into them went not only the landscapes of Worcestershire and Shropshire but also the poetry in his head—Heine, Arnold, Shakespeare's songs, the "border" ballads, Milton.

There is no marked difference of style between *A Shropshire Lad* and *Last Poems* published twenty-six years later, in the year of *Ulysses* and *The Waste Land*. He prefaced the later volume thus: "I publish these poems, few though they are, because it is not likely that I shall ever be impelled to write any more. I can no longer expect to be revisited by the continuous excitement under which in the early months of 1895 I wrote the greater part of my other book, nor indeed could I well sustain it if it came. . . . About a quarter of this matter belongs to the April of the present year, but most of it dates between 1895 and 1910." The posthumous poetry consists mostly of poems rejected from the two volumes Housman published. Housman produced some good comic verse as well—parodies and nonsense poetry in the tradition of Lewis Carroll and Edward Lear.

From A Shropshire Lad

II

Loveliest of trees, the cherry now
Is hung with bloom along the bough,
And stands about the woodland ride
Wearing white for Eastertide.

Now, of my threescore years and ten,
Twenty will not come again,
And take from seventy springs a score,
It only leaves me fifty more.

And since to look at things in bloom
Fifty springs are little room,
About the woodlands I will go
To see the cherry hung with snow.

XXXV

On the idle hill of summer,
    Sleepy with the flow of streams,
Far I hear the steady drummer
    Drumming like a noise in dreams.

Far and near and low and louder
    On the roads of earth go by,
Dear to friends and food for powder,°
    Soldiers marching, all to die.

East and west on fields forgotten
10   Bleach the bones of comrades slain,
Lovely lads and dead and rotten;
    None that go return again.

Far the calling bugles hollo,
    High the screaming fife replies,
Gay the files of scarlet follow:
    Woman bore me, I will rise.

XL

Into my heart an air that kills
    From yon far country blows:
What are those blue remembered hills,
    What spires, what farms are those?

That is the land of lost content,
    I see it shining plain,
The happy highways where I went
    And cannot come again.

XLVIII

Be still, my soul, be still; the arms you bear are brittle,
    Earth and high heaven are fixt of old and founded strong.
Think rather,—call to thought, if now you grieve a little,
    The days when we had rest, O soul, for they were long.

Men loved unkindness then, but lightless in the quarry
    I slept and saw not; tears fell down, I did not mourn;
Sweat ran and blood sprang out and I was never sorry:
    Then it was very well with me, in days ere I was born.

Now, and I muse for why and never find the reason,
10   I pace the earth, and drink the air, and feel the sun.
Be still, be still, my soul; it is but for a season:
    Let us endure an hour and see injustice done.

food for power Falstaff's description of his
conscripts in 1 *Henry IV* IV.ii.56

Ay, look: high heaven and earth ail from the prime foundation;
    All thoughts to rive the heart are here, and all are vain:
Horror and scorn and hate and fear and indignation—
    Oh why did I awake? when shall I sleep again?
                    1896

We'll to the Woods No More°

We'll to the woods no more,
The laurels all are cut,
The bowers are bare of bay
That once the Muses wore;
The year draws in the day
And soon will evening shut:
The laurels all are cut,
We'll to the woods no more.
Oh we'll no more, no more
10 To the leafy woods away,
To the high wild woods of laurel
And the bowers of bay no more.
                    1922

Her Strong Enchantments Failing

Her strong enchantments failing,
  Her towers of fear in wreck,
Her limbecks° dried of poisons
  And the knife at her neck,

The Queen of air and darkness
  Begins to shrill and cry,
'O young man, O my slayer,
  To-morrow you shall die.'

O Queen of air and darkness,
10 I think 'tis truth you say,
And I shall die to-morrow;
  But you will die to-day.
                    1922

In Valleys Green and Still

In valleys green and still
  Where lovers wander maying

We'll . . . more These prefatory verses to
Last Poems are translated from a poem by
Théodore de Banville (1823–91): Nous n'irons
plus aux bois, / Les lauriers sont coupés.
limbecks alchemical retorts, for distillation

They hear from over hill
   A music playing.

Behind the drum and fife,
   Past hawthornwood and hollow,
Through earth and out of life
   The soldiers follow.

The soldier's is the trade:
10   In any wind or weather
He steals the heart of maid
   And man together.

The lover and his lass
   Beneath the hawthorn lying
Have heard the soldiers pass,
   And both are sighing.
            1922

When the Eye of Day Is Shut

When the eye of day is shut,
   And the stars deny their beams,
And about the forest hut
   Blows the roaring wood of dreams,

From deep clay, from desert rock,
   From the sunk sands of the main,
Come not at my door to knock,
   Hearts that loved me not again.

Sleep, be still, turn to your rest
10   In the lands where you are laid;
In far lodgings east and west
   Lie down on the beds you made.

In gross marl,° in blowing dust,
   In the drowned ooze of the sea,
Where you would not, lie you must,
   Lie you must, and not with me.
            1922

Tell Me Not Here, It Needs Not Saying

Tell me not here, it needs not saying,
   What tune the enchantress plays
In aftermaths of soft September

marl clayey soil

Or under blanching mays,
For she and I were long acquainted
    And I knew all her ways.

On russet floors, by waters idle,
    The pine lets fall its cone;
The cuckoo shouts all day at nothing
10   In leafy dells alone;
And traveller's joy beguiles in autumn
    Hearts that have lost their own.

On acres of the seeded grasses
    The changing burnish heaves;
Or marshalled under moons of harvest
    Stand still all night the sheaves;
Or beeches strip in storms for winter
    And stain the wind with leaves.

Possess, as I possessed a season,
20   The countries I resign,°
Where over elmy plains the highway
    Would mount the hills and shine,
And full of shade the pillared forest
    Would murmur and be mine.

For nature, heartless, witless nature,
    Will neither care nor know
What stranger's feet may find the meadow
    And trespass there and go,
Nor ask amid the dews of morning
30   If they are mine or no.
                1922

Ho, Everyone That Thirsteth°

Ho, everyone that thirsteth
    And hath the price to give,
Come to the stolen waters,
    Drink and your soul shall live.

Come to the stolen waters
    And leap the guarded pale,
And pull the flower in season
    Before desire shall fail.°

It shall not last for ever,
10   No more than earth and skies;

Ho, Everyone . . . Thirsteth This poem combines the *carpe diem* theme with biblical texts.

"If any man thirst, let him come unto me, and drink" (John 7:37).
desire . . . fail Ecclesiastes 12:5

But he that drinks in season
   Shall live before he dies.

June suns, you cannot store them
   To warm the winter's cold,
The lad that hopes for heaven
   Shall fill his mouth with mould.

                   1936

To Stand Up Straight

To stand up straight and tread the turning mill,
To lie flat and know nothing and be still,
   Are the two trades of man; and which is worse
I know not, but I know that both are ill.

                   1936

Here Dead Lie We

Here dead lie we because we did not choose
   To live and shame the land from which we sprung.
Life, to be sure, is nothing much to lose;
   But young men think it is, and we were young.

                   1936

WALTER DE LA MARE
1873–1956

A poetry in, but not of, the period of the reign of modernism, de la Mare's work has been admired chiefly by poets themselves. They have always prized his unfailing skill, his pointed ability to intensify a lyrical moment, and his access to the mythologies which the modern movement would either ignore, or enlist in its program of rhetorical debunking of the late nineteenth century. Born in Kent (related to Browning on his mother's side), educated in London, he worked as a clerk for Standard Oil Company there until, in 1908, a pension and government grants enabled him to write all the time. His earliest works were strange evocations of childhood, in poems written for both children and adults. From 1902 until his death he published eighteen volumes of verse—in addition to his fiction (including the remarkable and strangely neglected *Memoirs of a Midget* in 1921) and the anthologies he edited. His mastery of the detail of image forever fixing a moment of transformation—or, more usually, transformation just missed—is as keen as that of the Imagist poets who would have scorned the narratives and dramatic lyrics in which he framed those images, and the lyrical forms in whose chambers they resounded.

Winter

Clouded with snow
The cold winds blow,
And shrill on leafless bough
The robin with its burning breast
Alone sings now.

The rayless sun,
Day's journey done,
Sheds its last ebbing light
On fields in leagues of beauty spread
10   Unearthly white.

Thick draws the dark,
And spark by spark,
The frost-fires kindle, and soon
Over that sea of frozen foam
Floats the white moon.

1912

All That's Past

Very old are the woods;
And the buds that break
Out of the brier's boughs,
When March winds wake,
So old with their beauty are—
Oh, no man knows
Through what wild centuries
Roves back the rose.°

Very old are the brooks;
10   And the rills that rise
Where snow sleeps cold beneath
The azure skies
Sing such a history
Of come and gone,
Their every drop is as wise
As Solomon.

Very old are we men;
Our dreams are tales
Told in dim Eden
20   By Eve's nightingales;
We wake and whisper awhile,
But, the day gone by,

Through . . . rose an observation one might find
in early Yeats, who, in fact, admired these lines

Silence and sleep like fields
  Of amaranth° lie.
      1912

The Ghost

'Who knocks?' 'I, who was beautiful,
  Beyond all dreams to restore,
I, from the roots of the dark thorn am hither,
  And knock on the door.'

'Who speaks?' 'I—once was my speech
  Sweet as the bird's on the air,
When echo lurks by the waters to heed;
  'Tis I speak thee fair.'

'Dark is the hour!' 'Ay, and cold.'
  'Lone is my house.' 'Ah, but mine?'
'Sight, touch, lips, eyes yearned in vain.'
  'Long dead these to thine . . .'

Silence. Still faint on the porch
  Brake the flames of the stars.
In gloom groped a hope-wearied hand
  Over keys, bolts, and bars.

A face peered. All the grey night
  In chaos of vacancy shone;
Nought but vast sorrow was there—
  The sweet cheat gone.°
      1918

(line number 10 in margin)

RUDYARD KIPLING
1865–1936

Joseph Rudyard Kipling was born in Bombay, the son of the principal of Lahore Art School. He was extremely happy during his early childhood, but his life became a nightmare when he was sent to school in England (at age 6), and the beatings and humiliations of those six years—though he sometimes spoke of them as a good preparation for life—left a permanent mark on him. Many of his stories are about subtle and horrible revenges, and the one here included is a masterly example of the kind. Upon his return to India in 1882 he quickly achieved success as a journalist, and as a writer of verse and stories (notably *Plain Tales from the Hills*, 1888). During his second visit to England in 1889 he wrote his first novel, *The Light That Failed* (1890), not a great success. He married an American and lived for some years in Vermont,

---

amaranth a mythical undying flower
The sweet cheat gone This phrase may resonate for the reader because of its use, by C. K.

Scott-Moncrieff, to translate the title (*Albertine Disparue*) of one of the volumes of Proust's *Remembrance of Things Past*.

but the marriage did not work out and he returned once more to England in 1899.

Meanwhile with such verse as *Barrack Room Ballads* (1892), the two *Jungle Books* (1894, 1895), and the stories in *Many Inventions* and *The Day's Work* (1893, 1899) he had become one of the most famous English writers of his time, and one who steadfastly preferred action and machinery to the prevalent Art for Art's Sake. *Stalky & Co.*, a series of school stories often thought brutal, appeared in 1899. His work continued until there was enough of it to fill the thirty-five volumes of the Collected Edition; he was awarded the Nobel Prize in 1907. His (unfinished) autobiography, *Something of Myself*, was published posthumously in 1937.

Some of the finest and strangest of Kipling's stories are late ones. *Mary Postgate* was published in 1915. England was full of atrocity stories—some true and some not —about the Germans, and Mary Postgate was evidently one who believed them. The power of the tale lies in the way in which she is established as an obedient, patient, passionless woman, already old at forty-four, hardly capable of reacting to a snub, yet concealing, unknown to herself, an appalling ferocity which the destruction of the dead young man's property, the death of the child, and the lie of the doctor somehow bring to the surface. The consequences of this surfacing become a sensual act, leading to the unheard-of break with such routines as that of the hot bath, and the compliments of her employer on her appearance. An act of cruelty and revenge has rejuvenated her, almost as though it were a sexual fulfillment. She even represents it to herself as woman's work. In the later stories it is the richness of ambiguous implications and a kind of masked horror that make them, for some readers, Kipling's best, most disquieting, and most permanent work. Certainly this one appears appropriately in an anthology that contains so much writing about the great and crucial war of 1914–18.

Mary Postgate

Of Miss Mary Postgate, Lady McCausland wrote that she was 'thoroughly conscientious, tidy, companionable, and ladylike. I am very sorry to part with her, and shall always be interested in her welfare.'

Miss Fowler engaged her on this recommendation, and to her surprise, for she had had experience of companions, found that it was true. Miss Fowler was nearer sixty than fifty at the time, but though she needed care she did not exhaust her attendant's vitality. On the contrary, she gave out, stimulatingly and with reminiscences. Her father had been a minor Court official in the days when the Great Exhibition of 1851 [1] had just set its seal on Civilisation made perfect. Some of Miss Fowler's tales, none the less, were not always for the young. Mary was not young, and though her speech was as colourless as her eyes or her hair, she was never shocked. She listened unflinchingly to every one; said at the end, 'How interesting!' or 'How shocking!' as the case might be, and never again referred to it, for she prided herself on a trained mind, which 'did not dwell on these things.' She was, too, a treasure at domestic accounts,

1. The first international exposition, celebrating British art, industry, and empire. The Crystal Palace was built for it.

for which the village tradesmen, with their weekly books, loved her not. Otherwise she had no enemies; provoked no jealousy even among the plainest; neither gossip nor slander had ever been traced to her; she supplied the odd place at the Rector's or the Doctor's table at half an hour's notice; she was a sort of public aunt to very many small children of the village street, whose parents, while accepting everything, would have been swift to resent what they called 'patronage'; she served on the Village Nursing Committee as Miss Fowler's nominee when Miss Fowler was crippled by rheumatoid arthritis, and came out of six months' fort-nightly meetings equally respected by all the cliques.

And when Fate threw Miss Fowler's nephew, an unlovely orphan of eleven, on Miss Fowler's hands, Mary Postgate stood to her share of the business of education as practised in private and public schools. She checked printed clothes-lists, and unitemised bills of extras; wrote to Head and House masters, matrons, nurses and doctors, and grieved or rejoiced over half-term reports. Young Wyndham Fowler repaid her in his holidays by calling her 'Gatepost,' 'Postey,' or 'Packthread,' by thumping her between her narrow shoulders, or by chasing her bleating, round the garden, her large mouth open, her large nose high in air, at a stiff-necked shamble very like a camel's. Later on he filled the house with clamour, argument, and harangues as to his personal needs, likes and dislikes, and the limitations of 'you women,' reducing Mary to tears of physical fatigue, or, when he chose to be humorous, of helpless laughter. At crises, which multiplied as he grew older, she was his ambassadress and his interpretress to Miss Fowler, who had no large sympathy with the young; a vote in his interest at the councils on his future; his sewing-woman, strictly accountable for mislaid boots and garments; always his butt and his slave.

And when he decided to become a solicitor, and had entered an office in London; when his greeting had changed from 'Hullo, Postey, you old beast,' to 'Mornin' Packthread,' there came a war which, unlike all wars that Mary could remember, did not stay decently outside England and in the newspapers, but intruded on the lives of people whom she knew. As she said to Miss Fowler, it was 'most vexatious.' It took the Rector's son who was going into business with his elder brother; it took the Colonel's nephew on the eve of fruit-farming in Canada; it took Mrs. Grant's son who, his mother said, was devoted to the ministry; and, very early indeed, it took Wynn Fowler, who announced on a postcard that he had joined the Flying Corps[2] and wanted a cardigan waistcoat.

'He must go, and he must have the waistcoat,' said Miss Fowler. So Mary got the proper-sized needles and wool, while Miss Fowler told the men of her establishment—two gardeners and an odd man, aged sixty—that those who could join the Army had better do so. The gardeners left. Cheape, the odd man, stayed on, and was promoted to the gardener's cottage. The cook, scorning to be limited in luxuries, also left, after a spirited scene with Miss Fowler, and took the house-maid with her. Miss Fowler gazetted Nellie, Cheape's seventeen-year-old daughter, to the vacant post; Mrs. Cheape to the rank of cook with occasional cleaning bouts; and the reduced establishment moved forward smoothly.

2. Royal Flying Corps (later, Royal Air Force).

Wynn demanded an increase in his allowance. Miss Fowler, who always looked facts in the face, said, 'He must have it. The chances are he won't live long to draw it, and if three hundred makes him happy——'

Wynn was grateful, and came over, in his tight-buttoned uniform, to say so. His training centre was not thirty miles away, and his talk was so technical that it had to be explained by charts of the various types of machines. He gave Mary such a chart.

'And you'd better study it, Postey,' he said. 'You'll be seeing a lot of 'em soon.' So Mary studied the chart, but when Wynn next arrived to swell and exalt himself before his womenfolk, she failed badly in cross-examination, and he rated her as in the old days.

'You *look* more or less like a human being,' he said in his new Service voice. 'You *must* have had a brain at some time in your past. What have you done with it? Where d'you keep it? A sheep would know more than you do, Postey. You're lamentable. You are less use than an empty tin can, you dowey old cassowary.'

'I suppose that's how your superior officer talks to *you?*' said Miss Fowler from her chair.

'But Postey doesn't mind,' Wynn replied. 'Do you, Packthread?'

'Why? Was Wynn saying anything? I shall get this right next time you come,' she muttered, and knitted her pale brows again over the diagrams of Taubes, Farmans, and Zeppelins.[3]

In a few weeks the mere land and sea battles which she read to Miss Fowler after breakfast passed her like idle breath. Her heart and her interest were high in the air with Wynn, who had finished 'rolling' (whatever that might be) and had gone on from a 'taxi' to a machine more or less his own. One morning it circled over their very chimneys, alighted on Vegg's Heath, almost outside the garden gate, and Wynn came in, blue with cold, shouting for food. He and she drew Miss Fowler's bath-chair,[4] as they had often done, along the Heath foot-path to look at the biplane. Mary observed that 'it smelt very badly.'

'Postey, I believe you think with your nose,' said Wynn. 'I know you don't with your mind. Now, what type's that?'

'I'll go and get the chart,' said Mary.

'You're hopeless! You haven't the mental capacity of a white mouse,' he cried, and explained the dials and the sockets for bomb-dropping till it was time to mount and ride the wet clouds once more.

'Ah!' said Mary, as the stinking thing flared upward. 'Wait till our Flying Corps gets to work! Wynn says it's much safer than in the trenches.'

'I wonder,' said Miss Fowler. 'Tell Cheape to come and tow me home again.'

'It's all downhill. I can do it,' said Mary, 'if you put the brake on.' She laid her lean self against the pushing-bar and home they trundled.

'Now, be careful you aren't heated and catch a chill,' said overdressed Miss Fowler.

'Nothing makes me perspire,' said Mary. As she bumped the chair under the porch she straightened her long back. The exertion had given her a colour, and

3. Fighting airplanes and lighter-than-air craft of World War I.
4. Wheelchair.

the wind had loosened a wisp of hair across her forehead. Miss Fowler glanced at her.

'What do you ever think of, Mary?' she demanded suddenly.

'Oh, Wynn says he wants another three pairs of stockings—as thick as we can make them.'

'Yes. But I mean the things that women think about. Here you are, more than forty——'

'Forty-four,' said truthful Mary.

'Well?'

'Well?' Mary offered Miss Fowler her shoulder as usual.

'And you've been with me ten years now.'

'Let's see,' said Mary. 'Wynn was eleven when he came. He's twenty now, and I came two years before that. It must be eleven.'

'Eleven! And you've never told me anything that matters in all that while. Looking back, it seems to me that *I've* done all the talking.'

'I'm afraid I'm not much of a conversationalist. As Wynn says, I haven't the mind. Let me take your hat.'

Miss Fowler, moving stiffly from the hip, stamped her rubber-tipped stick on the tiled hall floor. 'Mary, aren't you *anything* except a companion? Would you *ever* have been anything except a companion?'

Mary hung up the garden hat on its proper peg. 'No,' she said after consideration. 'I don't imagine I ever should. But I've no imagination, I'm afraid.'

She fetched Miss Fowler her eleven-o'clock glass of Contrexeville.[5]

That was the wet December when it rained six inches to the month, and the women went abroad as little as might be. Wynn's flying chariot visited them several times, and for two mornings (he had warned her by postcard) Mary heard the thresh of his propellers at dawn. The second time she ran to the window, and stared at the whitening sky. A little blur passed overhead. She lifted her lean arms towards it.

That evening at six o'clock there came an announcement in an official envelope that Second Lieutenant W. Fowler had been killed during a trial flight. Death was instantaneous. She read it and carried it to Miss Fowler.

'I never expected anything else,' said Miss Fowler; 'but I'm sorry it happened before he had done anything.'

The room was whirling round Mary Postgate, but she found herself quite steady in the midst of it.

'Yes,' she said. 'It's a great pity he didn't die in action after he had killed somebody.'

'He was killed instantly. That's one comfort,' Miss Fowler went on.

'But Wynn says the shock of a fall kills a man at once—whatever happens to the tanks,' quoted Mary.

The room was coming to rest now. She heard Miss Fowler say impatiently, 'But why can't we cry, Mary?' and herself replying, 'There's nothing to cry for. He has done his duty as much as Mrs. Grant's son did.'

'And when he died, *she* came and cried all the morning,' said Miss Fowler.

5. Mineral water from a French spa.

'This only makes me feel tired—terribly tired. Will you help me to bed, please, Mary?—And I think I'd like the hot-water bottle.'

So Mary helped her and sat beside, talking of Wynn in his riotous youth.

'I believe,' said Miss Fowler suddenly, 'that old people and young people slip from under a stroke like this. The middle-aged feel it most.'

'I expect that's true,' said Mary, rising. 'I'm going to put away the things in his room now. Shall we wear mourning?'

'Certainly not,' said Miss Fowler. 'Except, of course, at the funeral. I can't go. You will. I want you to arrange about his being buried here. What a blessing it didn't happen at Salisbury!'

Every one, from the Authorities of the Flying Corps to the Rector, was most kind and sympathetic. Mary found herself for the moment in a world where bodies were in the habit of being despatched by all sorts of conveyances to all sorts of places. And at the funeral two young men in buttoned-up uniforms stood beside the grave and spoke to her afterwards.

'You're Miss Postgate, aren't you?' said one. 'Fowler told me about you. He was a good chap—a first-class fellow—a great loss.'

'Great loss!' growled his companion. 'We're all awfully sorry.'

'How high did he fall from?' Mary whispered.

'Pretty nearly four thousand feet, I should think, didn't he? You were up that day, Monkey?'

'All of that,' the other child replied. 'My bar [6] made three thousand, and I wasn't as high as him by a lot.'

'Then *that's* all right,' said Mary. 'Thank you very much.'

They moved away as Mrs. Grant flung herself weeping on Mary's flat chest, under the lych-gate, and cried, '*I* know how it feels! *I* know how it feels!'

'But both his parents are dead,' Mary returned, as she fended her off. 'Perhaps they've all met by now,' she added vaguely as she escaped towards the coach.

'I've thought of that too,' wailed Mrs. Grant; 'but then he'll be practically a stranger to them. Quite embarrassing!'

Mary faithfully reported every detail of the ceremony to Miss Fowler, who, when she described Mrs. Grant's outburst, laughed aloud.

'Oh, how Wynn would have enjoyed it! He was always utterly unreliable at funerals. D'you remember——' And they talked of him again, each piecing out the other's gaps. 'And now,' said Miss Fowler, 'we'll pull up the blinds and we'll have a general tidy. That always does us good. Have you seen to Wynn's things?'

'Everything—since he first came,' said Mary, 'He was never destructive —even with his toys.'

They faced that neat room.

'It can't be natural not to cry,' Mary said at last. 'I'm *so* afraid you'll have a reaction.'

'As I told you, we old people slip from under the stroke. It's you I'm afraid for. Have you cried yet?'

'I can't. It only makes me angry with the Germans.'

6. Altimeter (works by barometric pressure).

'That's sheer waste of vitality,' said Miss Fowler. 'We must live till the war's finished.' She opened a full wardrobe. 'Now, I've been thinking things over. This is my plan. All his civilian clothes can be given away—Belgian refugees, and so on.'

Mary nodded. 'Boots, collars, and gloves?'

'Yes. We don't need to keep anything except his cap and belt.'

'They came back yesterday with his Flying Corps clothes'—Mary pointed to a roll on the little iron bed.

'Ah, but keep his Service things. Some one may be glad of them later. Do you remember his sizes?'

'Five feet eight and a half; thirty-six inches round the chest. But he told me he's just put on an inch and a half. I'll mark it on a label and tie it on his sleeping-bag.'

'So that disposes of *that*,' said Miss Fowler, tapping the palm of one hand with the ringed third finger of the other. 'What waste it all is! We'll get his old school trunk to-morrow and pack his civilian clothes.'

'And the rest?' said Mary. 'His books and pictures and the games and the toys—and—and the rest?'

'My plan is to burn every single thing,' said Miss Fowler. 'Then we shall know where they are and no one can handle them afterwards. What do you think?'

'I think that would be much the best,' said Mary. 'But there's such a lot of them.'

'We'll burn them in the destructor,' said Miss Fowler.

This was an open-air furnace for the consumption of refuse; a little circular four-foot tower of pierced brick over an iron grating. Miss Fowler had noticed the design in a gardening journal years ago, and had had it built at the bottom of the garden. It suited her tidy soul, for it saved unsightly rubbish-heaps, and the ashes lightened the stiff clay soil.

Mary considered for a moment, saw her way clear, and nodded again. They spent the evening putting away well-remembered civilian suits, underclothes that Mary had marked, and the regiments of very gaudy socks and ties. A second trunk was needed, and, after that, a little packing-case, and it was late next day when Cheape and the local carrier [7] lifted them to the cart. The Rector luckily knew of a friend's son, about five feet eight and a half inches high, to whom a complete Flying Corps outfit would be most acceptable, and sent his gardener's son down with a barrow to take delivery of it. The cap was hung up in Miss Fowler's bedroom, the belt in Miss Postgate's; for, as Miss Fowler said, they had no desire to make tea-party talk of them.

'That disposes of *that*,' said Miss Fowler. 'I'll leave the rest to you, Mary. I can't run up and down the garden. You'd better take the big clothes-basket and get Nellie to help you.'

'I shall take the wheel-barrow and do it myself,' said Mary, and for once in her life closed her mouth.

Miss Fowler, in moments of irritation, had called Mary deadly methodical. She put on her oldest water-proof and gardening-hat and her ever-slipping

7. Small trucker.

goloshes, for the weather was on the edge of more rain. She gathered fire-lighters from the kitchen, a half-scuttle of coals, and a faggot of brushwood. These she wheeled in the barrow down the mossed paths to the dank little laurel shrubbery where the destructor stood under the drip of three oaks. She climbed the wire fence into the Rector's glebe [8] just behind, and from his tenant's rick pulled two large armfuls of good hay, which she spread neatly on the fire-bars. Next, journey by journey, passing Miss Fowler's white face at the morning-room window each time, she brought down in the towel-covered clothes-basket, on the wheel-barrow, thumbed and used Hentys, Marryats, Levers, Stevensons, Baroness Orczys, Garvices,[9] schoolbooks, and atlases, unrelated piles of the *Motor Cyclist,* the *Light Car,* and catalogues of Olympia Exhibitions; [10] the remnants of a fleet of sailing-ships from nine-penny cutters to a three-guinea yacht; a prep.-school dressing-gown; bats from three-and-sixpence to twenty-four shillings; cricket and tennis balls; disintegrated steam and clockwork locomotives with their twisted rails; a grey and red tin model of a submarine; a dumb gramophone and cracked records; golf-clubs that had to be broken across the knee, like his walking-sticks, and an assegai; [11] photographs of private and public school cricket and football elevens, and his O.T.C.[12] on the line of march; kodaks, and film-rolls; some pewters, and one real silver cup, for boxing competitions and Junior Hurdles; sheaves of school photographs; Miss Fowler's photograph; her own which he had borne off in fun and (good care she took not to ask!) had never returned; a playbox with a secret drawer; a load of flannels, belts, and jerseys, and a pair of spiked shoes unearthed in the attic; a packet of all the letters that Miss Fowler and she had ever written to him, kept for some absurd reason through all these years; a five-day attempt at a diary; framed pictures of racing motors in full Brooklands career, and load upon load of undistinguishable wreckage of tool-boxes, rabbit-hutches, electric batteries, tin soldiers, fret-saw outfits, and jig-saw puzzles.

Miss Fowler at the window watched her come and go, and said to herself, 'Mary's an old woman. I never realised it before.'

After lunch she recommended her to rest.

'I'm not in the least tired,' said Mary. 'I've got it all arranged. I'm going to the village at two o'clock for some paraffin.[13] Nellie hasn't enough, and the walk will do me good.'

She made one last quest round the house before she started, and found that she had overlooked nothing. It began to mist as soon as she had skirted Vegg's Heath, where Wynn used to descend—it seemed to her that she could almost hear the beat of his propellers overhead, but there was nothing to see. She hoisted her umbrella and lunged into the blind wet till she had reached the shelter of the empty village. As she came out of Mr. Kidd's shop with a bottle full of paraffin in her string shopping-bag, she met Nurse Eden, the village nurse, and fell into talk with her, as usual, about the village children. They

8. Cultivable field belonging to a vicarage.
9. Books (chiefly for boys) by adventure novelists.
10. Exhibitions of all kinds held in a large building in West London.
11. Zulu throwing spear (relic of the 19-century Zulu wars).
12. Officers Training Corps.
13. Kerosene.

were just parting opposite the 'Royal Oak' when a gun, they fancied, was fired immediately behind the house. It was followed by a child's shriek dying into a wail.

'Accident!' said Nurse Eden promptly, and dashed through the empty bar, followed by Mary. They found Mrs. Gerritt, the publican's wife, who could only gasp and point to the yard, where a little cart-lodge was sliding sideways amid a clatter of tiles. Nurse Eden snatched up a sheet drying before the fire, ran out, lifted something from the ground, and flung the sheet round it. The sheet turned scarlet and half her uniform too, as she bore the load into the kitchen. It was little Edna Gerritt, aged nine, whom Mary had known since her perambulator days.

'Am I hurted bad?' Edna asked, and died between Nurse Eden's dripping hands. The sheet fell aside and for an instant, before she could shut her eyes, Mary saw the ripped and shredded body.

'It's a wonder she spoke at all,' said Nurse Eden. 'What in God's name was it?'

'A bomb,' said Mary.

'One o' the Zeppelins?'

'No. An aeroplane. I thought I heard it on the Heath but I fancied it was one of ours. It must have shut off its engines as it came down. That's why we didn't notice it.'

'The filthy pigs!' said Nurse Eden, all white and shaken. 'See the pickle I'm in! Go and tell Dr. Hennis, Miss Postgate.' Nurse looked at the mother, who had dropped face down on the floor. 'She's only in a fit. Turn her over.'

Mary heaved Mrs. Gerritt right side up, and hurried off for the doctor. When she told her tale, he asked her to sit down in the surgery till he got her something.

'But I don't need it, I assure you,' said she. 'I don't think it would be wise to tell Miss Fowler about it, do you? Her heart is so irritable in this weather.'

Dr. Hennis looked at her admiringly as he packed up his bag.

'No. Don't tell anybody till we're sure,' he said, and hastened to the 'Royal Oak,' while Mary went on with the paraffin. The village behind her was as quiet as usual, for the news had not yet spread. She frowned a little to herself, her large nostrils expanded uglily and from time to time she muttered a phrase which Wynn who never restrained himself before his women-folk, had applied to the enemy. 'Bloody pagans! They *are* bloody pagans. But,' she continued, falling back on the teaching that had made her what she was, 'one mustn't let one's mind dwell on these things.'

Before she reached the house Dr. Hennis, who was also a special constable, overtook her in his car.

'Oh, Miss Postgate,' he said, 'I wanted to tell you that that accident at the "Royal Oak" was due to Gerritt's stable tumbling down. It's been dangerous for a long time. It ought to have been condemned.'

'I thought I heard an explosion too,' said Mary.

'You might have been misled by the beams snapping. I've been looking at 'em. They were dry-rotted through and through. Of course, as they broke, they would make a noise just like a gun.'

'Yes?' said Mary politely.

'Poor little Edna was playing underneath it,' he went on, still holding her with his eyes, 'and that and the tiles cut her to pieces, you see?'

'I saw it,' said Mary, shaking her head. 'I heard it too.'

'Well, we cannot be sure.' Dr. Hennis changed his tone completely. 'I know both you and Nurse Eden (I've been speaking to her) are perfectly trustworthy, and I can relay on you not to say anything—yet at least. It is no good to stir up people unless——'

'Oh, I never do—anyhow,' said Mary, and Dr. Hennis went on to the country town.

After all, she told herself, it might, just possibly, have been the collapse of the old stable that had done all those things to poor little Edna. She was sorry she had even hinted at other things, but Nurse Eden was discretion itself. By the time she reached home the affair seemed increasingly remote by its very monstrosity. As she came in, Miss Fowler told her that a couple of aeroplanes had passed half an hour ago.

'I thought I heard them,' she replied, 'I'm going down to the garden now. I've got the paraffin.'

'Yes, but—what *have* you got on your boots? They're soaking wet. Change them at once.'

Not only did Mary obey but she wrapped the boots in a newspaper, and put them into the string bag with the bottle. So, armed with the longest kitchen poker, she left.

'It's raining again,' was Miss Fowler's last word, 'but—I know you won't be happy till that's disposed of.'

'It won't take long. I've got everything down there, and I've put the lid on the destructor to keep the wet out.'

The shrubbery was filling with twilight by the time she had completed her arrangements and sprinkled the sacrificial oil. As she lit the match that would burn her heart to ashes, she heard a groan or a grunt behind the dense Portugal laurels.

'Cheape?' she called impatiently, but Cheape, with his ancient lumbago, in his comfortable cottage would be the last man to profane the sanctuary. 'Sheep,' she concluded, and threw in the fusee. The pyre went up in a roar, and the immediate flame hastened night around her.

'How Wynn would have loved this!' she thought, stepping back from the blaze.

By its light she saw, half hidden behind a laurel not five paces away, a bare-headed man sittting very stiffly at the foot of one of the oaks. A broken branch lay across his lap—one booted leg protruding from beneath it. His head moved ceaselessly from side to side, but his body was as still as the tree's trunk. He was dressed—she moved sideways to look more closely—in a uniform something like Wynn's, with a flap buttoned across the chest. For an instant she had some idea that it might be one of the young flying men she had met at the funeral. But their heads were dark and glossy. This man's was as pale as a baby's, and so closely cropped that she could see the disgusting pinky skin beneath. His lips moved.

'What do you say?' Mary moved towards him and stooped.

'Laty! Laty! Laty!' he muttered, while his hands picked at the dead wet leaves. There was no doubt as to his nationality. It made her so angry that she strode back to the destructor, though it was still too hot to use the poker there. Wynn's books seemed to be catching well. She looked up at the oak behind the man; several of the light upper and two or three rotten lower branches had broken and scattered their rubbish on the shrubbery path. On the lowest fork a helmet with dependent strings, showed like a bird's-nest in the light of a long-tongued flame. Evidently this person had fallen through the tree. Wynn had told her that it was quite possible for people to fall out of aeroplanes. Wynn told her too, that trees were useful things to break an aviator's fall, but in this case the aviator must have been broken or he would have moved from his queer position. He seemed helpless except for his horrible rolling head. On the other hand, she could see a pistol case at his belt—and Mary loathed pistols. Months ago, after reading certain Belgian reports together, she and Miss Fowler had had dealings with one—a huge revolver with flat-nosed bullets, which latter, Wynn said, were forbidden by the rules of war to be used against civilised enemies. 'They're good enough for us,' Miss Fowler had replied. 'Show Mary how it works.' And Wynn, laughing at the mere possibility of any such need, had led the craven winking Mary into the Rector's disused quarry, and had shown her how to fire the terrible machine. It lay now in the top-left-hand drawer of her toilet-table—a memento not included in the burning. Wynn would be pleased to see how she was not afraid.

She slipped up to the house to get it. When she came through the rain, the eyes in the head were alive with expectation. The mouth even tried to smile. But at sight of the revolver its corners went down just like Edna Gerritt's. A tear trickled from one eye, and the head rolled from shoulder to shoulder as though trying to point out something.

'Cassée. Tout cassée,[14] it whimpered.

'What do you say?' said Mary disgustedly, keeping well to one side, though only the head moved.

'Cassée,' it repeated. 'Che me rends.[15] Le médicin! Toctor!'

'Nein!' said she, bringing all her small German to bear with the big pistol. 'Ich haben der todt Kinder gesehn.'[16]

The head was still. Mary's hand dropped. She had been careful to keep her finger off the trigger for fear of accidents. After a few moments' waiting, she returned to the destructor, where the flames were falling, and churned up Wynn's charring books with the poker. Again the head groaned for the doctor.

'Stop that!' said Mary, and stamped her foot. 'Stop that, you bloody pagan!'

The words came quite smoothly and naturally. They were Wynn's own words, and Wynn was a gentleman who for no consideration on earth would have torn little Edna into those vividly coloured strips and strings. But this thing hunched under the oak-tree had done that thing. It was no question of reading horrors out of newspapers to Miss Fowler. Mary had seen it with her own eyes on the 'Royal Oak' kitchen table. She must not allow her mind to dwell upon it. Now Wynn was dead, and everything connected with him was lumping and rustling and tinkling under her busy poker into red black dust and grey leaves of ash. The thing beneath the oak would die too. Mary had seen death more than once. She came of a family that had a knack of dying

---

14. "Broken. All broken."
15. "I giff up. Doctor!"
16. "I've seen the dead child" (quite ungrammatically said).

under, as she told Miss Fowler, 'most distressing circumstances.' She would stay where she was till she was entirely satisfied that It was dead—dead as dear papa in the late 'eighties; aunt Mary in 'eighty-nine; mamma in 'ninety-one; cousin Dick in 'ninety-five; Lady McCausland's housemaid in 'ninety-nine; Lady McCausland's sister in nineteen hundred and one; Wynn buried five days ago; and Edna Gerritt still waiting for decent earth to hide her. As she thought—her underlip caught up by one faded canine, brows knit and nostrils wide—she wielded the poker with lunges that jarred the grating at the bottom, and careful scrapes round the brick-work above. She looked at her wrist-watch. It was getting on to half-past four, and the rain was coming down in earnest. Tea would be at five. If It did not die before that time, she would be soaked and would have to change. Meantime, and this occupied her, Wynn's things were burning well in spite of the hissing wet though now and again a book-back with a quite distinguishable title would be heaved up out of the mass. The exercise of stoking had given her a glow which seemed to reach to the marrow of her bones. She hummed—Mary never had a voice—to herself. She had never believed in all those advanced views—though Miss Fowler herself leaned a little that way—of woman's work in the world; but now she saw there was much to be said for them. This, for instance, was *her* work—work which no man, least of all Dr. Hennis, would ever have done. A man, at such a crisis, would be what Wynn called a 'sportsman'; would leave everything to fetch help, and would certainly bring It into the house. Now a woman's business was to make a happy home for—for a husband and children. Failing these—it was not a thing one should allow one's mind to dwell upon—but——

'Stop it!' Mary cried once more across the shadows. 'Nein, I tell you! Ich haben der todt Kinder gesehn.'

But it was a fact. A woman who had missed these things could still be useful—more useful than a man in certain respects. She thumped like a paviour [17] through the settling ashes at the secret thrill of it. The rain was damping the fire, but she could feel—it was too dark to see—that her work was done. There was a dull red glow at the bottom of the destructor, not enough to char the wooden lid if she slipped it half over against the driving wet. This arranged, she leaned on the poker and waited, while an increasing rapture laid hold on her. She ceased to think. She gave herself up to feel. Her long pleasure was broken by a sound that she had waited for in agony several times in her life. She leaned forward and listened, smiling. There could be no mistake. She closed her eyes and drank it in. Once it ceased abruptly.

'Go on,' she murmured, half aloud. 'That isn't the end.'

Then the end came very distinctly in a lull between two rain-gusts. Mary Postgate drew her breath short between her teeth and shivered from head to foot. 'That's all right,' said she contentedly, and went up to the house, where she scandalised the whole routine by taking a luxurious hot bath before tea, and came down looking, as Miss Fowler said when she saw her lying all relaxed on the other sofa, 'quite handsome!'

1915   1915

---

17. Street paver, ramming down cobblestones.

WILFRED OWEN
1893–1918

It is hard for Americans to realize the extent and significance of the toll taken by World War I of the middle classes which had contributed so much to English culture. Such previous wars as those against Napoleon, and those fought all over the globe to maintain "Dominion over palm and pine," as Kipling half-ironically described the Empire, had been paid for with the blood of working-class and rural laboring enlisted men and often aristocratic career officers (the Navy had always drawn its officers from a broader social base). But the publication of the casualty lists of the Battle of the Somme (1916), with their record of decimation of a whole generation of young men of promise, fell across England like the shadow of a scythe. Many talented and brilliant young people who had not yet produced evidence of their gifts enlisted and perished. It is rare to find a young painter or musician who leaves behind, in his twenties, a body of work mature enough to constitute a recognizable though truncated career. It is easier for young mathematicians and poets to bequeath creative work that is more than merely promising.

Wilfred Owen was one such poet. While the popular verses and celebrated physical beauty of Rupert Brooke (1887–1915) were the subject of much patriotic piety, Owen's poems not only provided the protoype for subsequent visions of modern warfare but also came up with some technical developments (such as the off-rhymes of "Strange Meeting") which would influence even the British poetry of the thirties, which was manifestly opposed to Georgian poetry and its stylistic and moral norms. Owen's poetry reveals an ironic distrust of all the traditional ideologies which have kept soldiers fighting, but it informs that distrust with a passion of personal engagement with the direct experience of pain, apocalyptically violent death, and the other sophisticated horrors of a new technology of warfare which the conventional literary language and ethic of battle could not embody. Owen's war poems range from an expression of a private, even an erotic, sense of the being of other men in combat to the most distantly classical of formulations.

Wilfred Owen was born in Shropshire, studied at London University, taught school and tutored privately in France, and enlisted in the army in 1915. He was commissioned in 1916, wounded early the next year, convalesced in Scotland and in England, returned to combat in 1918, and was killed in action exactly one week before the Armistice. His *Collected Poems* was published in 1920; the texts printed below are all from C. Day Lewis's edition of 1963.

Dulce et Decorum Est°

Bent double, like old beggars under sacks,
Knock-kneed, coughing like hags, we cursed through sludge,
Till on the haunting flares we turned our backs
And towards our distant rest began to trudge.

Dulce et Decorum Est a tag from Horace (*Odes* III.2.13), well known to British schoolboys: *Dulce et decorum est pro patria mori*—It is sweet and honorable to die for your country"

Men marched asleep. Many had lost their boots
But limped on, blood-shod. All went lame; all blind;
Drunk with fatigue; deaf even to the hoots
Of tired, outstripped Five-Nines° that dropped behind.

Gas! Gas! Quick, boys!—An ecstasy of fumbling,
10   Fitting the clumsy helmets just in time;
But someone still was yelling out and stumbling
And flound'ring like a man in fire or lime . . .
Dim, through the misty panes and thick green light,
As under a green sea, I saw him drowning.

In all my dreams, before my helpless sight,
He plunges at me, guttering, choking, drowning.

If in some smothering dreams you too could pace
Behind the wagon that we flung him in,
And watch the white eyes writhing in his face,
20   His hanging face, like a devil's sick of sin;
If you could hear, at every jolt, the blood
Come gargling from the froth-corrupted lungs,
Obscene as cancer, bitter as the cud
Of vile, incurable sores on innocent tongues,—
My friend, you would not tell with such high zest
To children ardent for some desperate glory,
The old Lie: Dulce et decorum est
Pro patria mori.
1917   1920

Strange Meeting

It seemed that out of battle I escaped
Down some profound dull tunnel, long since scooped
Through granites which titanic wars had groined.°
Yet also there encumbered sleepers groaned,
Too fast in thought or death to be bestirred.
Then, as I probed them, one sprang up, and stared
With piteous recognition in fixed eyes,
Lifting distressful hands as if to bless.
And by his smile, I knew that sullen hall,
10   By his dead smile I knew we stood in Hell.
With a thousand pains that vision's face was grained;
Yet no blood reached there from the upper ground,
And no guns thumped, or down the flues made moan.
'Strange friend,' I said, 'here is no cause to mourn.'

Five-Nines Shells containing poison gas. This whole poem is about a gas attack, gas being the World War I weapon which raised moral problems (like atomic weapons, or napalm, thereafter).
groined carved out into arches

'None,' said that other, 'save the undone years,
The hopelessness. Whatever hope is yours,
Was my life also; I went hunting wild
After the wildest beauty in the world,
Which lies not calm in eyes, or braided hair,
20 But mocks the steady running of the hour,
And if it grieves, grieves richlier than here.
For of my glee might many men have laughed,
And of my weeping something had been left,
Which must die now. I mean the truth untold,
The pity of war, the pity war distilled.
Now men will go content with what we spoiled,
Or, discontent, boil bloody, and be spilled.
They will be swift with swiftness of the tigress.
None will break ranks, though nations trek from progress.
30 Courage was mine, and I had mystery,
Wisdom was mine, and I had mastery:
To miss the march of this retreating world
Into vain citadels that are not walled.
Then, when much blood had clogged their chariot-wheels,
I would go up and wash them from sweet wells,
Even with truths that lie too deep for taint.
I would have poured my spirit without stint
But not through wounds; not on the cess° of war.
Foreheads of men have bled where no wounds were.
40 I am the enemy you killed, my friend.
I knew you in this dark: for so you frowned
Yesterday through me as you jabbed and killed.
I parried; but my hands were loath and cold.
Let us sleep now. . . .'
1918   1920

Arms and the Boy°

Let the boy try along this bayonet-blade
How cold steel is, and keen with hunger of blood;
Blue with all malice, like a madman's flash;
And thinly drawn with famishing for flesh.

Lend him to stroke these blind, blunt bullet-leads
Which long to nuzzle in the hearts of lads,
Or give him cartridges of fine zinc teeth,
Sharp with the sharpness of grief and death.

For his teeth seem for laughing round an apple.
10 There lurk no claws behind his fingers supple;

---

cess garbage, refuse
Arms and the Boy a parodic twist on the opening phrase of Virgil's *Aeneid*, "Arms and the
man I sing . . ." (*Arma virumque cano . . .*)

And God will grow no talons at his heels,
Nor antlers through the thickness of his curls.
1918   1920

Fragment: I Saw His Round Mouth's Crimson . . .

I saw his round mouth's crimson deepen as it fell,
   Like a Sun, in his last deep hour;
Watched the magnificent recession of farewell,
   Clouding, half gleam, half glower,
And a last splendour burn the heavens of his cheek.
   And in his eyes
The cold stars lighting, very old and bleak,
   In different skies.
        1963

Anthem for Doomed Youth

What passing-bells for these who die as cattle?
   Only the monstrous anger of the guns.
   Only the stuttering rifles' rapid rattle
Can patter out their hasty orisons.°
No mockeries now for them; no prayers nor bells,
   Nor any voice of mourning save the choirs,—
The shrill, demented choirs of wailing shells;
   And bugles calling for them from sad shires.

What candles may be held to speed them all?
10   Not in the hands of boys, but in their eyes
Shall shine the holy glimmers of good-byes.
   The pallor of girls' brows shall be their pall;
Their flowers the tenderness of patient minds,
And each slow dusk of drawing-down of blinds.
1917   1920

EDWARD THOMAS
1878–1917

Along with Wilfred Owen and Isaac Rosenberg, a third poet of the highest gifts to be killed in World War I was Edward Thomas. Unlike Owen and Rosenberg, however, he had been well known since the early years of the century as an essayist, literary critic, and particularly as a writer about nature and country life. Born in London of Welsh parents, he read History at Oxford, married while still an undergraduate, and took to writing essays and commissioned books, of which he published

orisons prayers

some thirty. It was not until 1914, when he met the American poet Robert Frost, then living in England, that he began writing poems, and these he first submitted to magazines under an assumed name, so hesitant was he about possible presumption in an area for which he had so much respect.

His first published poems appeared, under the pseudonym of "Edward Eastaway", in an anthology he had edited in 1915; volumes appeared in 1917 and (posthumously) 1918, and a *Collected Poems* in 1920. It is possible to detect, here and there, the influence of Frost upon Thomas's verse, particularly in its cadences; but along with Frost, he had read John Clare and other nineteenth-century English poetry which flamed with awareness of nature; and his ability to make the English countryside stand for so much in human life generally parallels, rather than follows, Frost's use of New England. Thomas enlisted in the army in 1915, and was killed fighting at Arras two years later.

The Owl

Downhill I came, hungry, and yet not starved;
Cold, yet had heat within me that was proof
Against the North wind; tired, yet so that rest
Had seemed the sweetest thing under a roof.

Then at the inn I had food, fire, and rest,
Knowing how hungry, cold, and tired was I.
All of the night was quite barred out except
An owl's cry, a most melancholy cry

Shaken out long and clear upon the hill,
10   No merry note,° nor cause of merriment,
But one telling me plain what I escaped
And others could not, that night, as in I went.

And salted was my food, and my repose,
Salted and sobered, too, by the bird's voice
Speaking for all who lay under the stars,
Soldiers and poor, unable to rejoice.

1917

Swedes°

They have taken the gable from the roof of clay
On the long swede pile. They have let in the sun
To the white and gold and purple of curled fronds
Unsunned. It is a sight more tender-gorgeous
At the wood-corner where Winter moans and drips

merry note In the great "Winter" song at the   owl's cry is "Tu-whit, Tu-whoo, a merry note."
end of Shakespeare's *Love's Labour's Lost* the   Swedes rutabagas, Swedish turnips

Than when, in the Valley of the Tombs of Kings,
A boy crawls down into a Pharaoh's tomb
And, first of Christian men, beholds the mummy,
God and monkey, chariot and throne and vase,
10   Blue pottery, alabaster, and gold.

But dreamless long-dead Amen-hotep° lies.
This is a dream of Winter, sweet as Spring.

                              1917

Liberty

The last light has gone out of the world, except
This moonlight lying on the grass like frost
Beyond the brink of the tall elm's shadow.
It is as if everything else had slept
Many an age, unforgotten and lost—
The men that were, the things done, long ago,
All I have thought; and but the moon and I
Live yet and here stand idle over a grave
Where all is buried. Both have liberty
10   To dream what we could do if we were free
To do some thing we had desired long,
The moon and I. There's none less free than who
Does nothing and has nothing else to do,
Being free only for what is not to his mind,
And nothing is to his mind. If every hour
Like this one passing that I have spent among
The wiser others when I have forgot
To wonder whether I was free or not,
Were piled before me, and not lost behind,
20   And I could take and carry them away
I should be rich; or if I had the power
To wipe out every one and not again
Regret, I should be rich to be so poor.
And yet I still am half in love with pain,°
With what is imperfect, with both tears and mirth,
With things that have an end, with life and earth,
And this moon that leaves me dark within the door.

                              1917

Amen-hotep the Pharaoh Amenhotep IV, called
Ikhnaton (reigned 1375?–1357 B.C.), founder
of a monotheistic worship that vanished with his
death

half . . . pain a deliberate Keatsian echo: "I
have been half in love with easeful Death"
("Ode to a Nightingale" l. 52)

The Brook

Seated once by a brook, watching a child
Chiefly that paddled, I was thus beguiled.
Mellow the blackbird sang and sharp the thrush
Not far off in the oak and hazel brush,
Unseen. There was a scent like honeycomb
From mugwort dull. And down upon the dome
Of the stone the cart-horse kicks against so oft
A butterfly alighted. From aloft
He took the heat of the sun, and from below.
10 On the hot stone he perched contented so,
As if never a cart would pass again
That way; as if I were the last of men
And he the first of insects to have earth
And sun together and to know their worth.
I was divided between him and the gleam,
The motion, and the voices, of the stream,
The waters running frizzled over gravel,
That never vanish and for ever travel.
A grey flycatcher° silent on a fence
20 And I sat as if we had been there since
The horseman and the horse lying beneath
The fir-tree-covered barrow on the heath,
The horseman and the horse with silver shoes,
Galloped the downs last. All that I could lose
I lost. And then the child's voice raised the dead.
'No one's been here before' was what she said
And what I felt, yet never should have found
A word for, while I gathered sight and sound.

1918

ISAAC ROSENBERG
1890–1918

Born in Bristol, moved to the East End of London in childhood, educated in local schools, Rosenberg showed an artistic talent and an interest in poetry while still at school. Working by day, he took art classes at night at Birkbeck College and finally, with the help of some patrons, attended the Slade School from 1911 through 1914. He sold a few pictures and published poems here and there (in 1912 a pamphlet of early poems; *Youth* in 1915; his verse drama *Moses* the following year). Never in the best of health, he traveled to South Africa in 1914–15, and upon his return enlisted in the army. In April of 1918 he was killed in France. A selection of his poems was published in 1922, and a *Collected Works* appeared in 1937.

Rosenberg's was an amazingly promising talent, and it is hard to say in what direc-

---

flycatcher a bird that catches insects in mid-air

tion it might have developed had he lived. Certainly he had a remarkable ear, a thoroughly modern economy of setting for his extraordinarily evocative images, and a control of tone of voice which, like Owen's, seemed to be lost to so many of the Georgian poets.

Break of Day in the Trenches

The darkness crumbles away—
It is the same old druid Time as ever.
Only a live thing leaps my hand—
A queer sardonic rat—
As I pull the parapet's poppy
To stick behind my ear.
Droll rat, they would shoot you if they knew
Your cosmopolitan sympathies
(And God knows what antipathies).
10   Now you have touched this English hand
You will do the same to a German—
Soon, no doubt, if it be your pleasure
To cross the sleeping green between.
It seems you inwardly grin as you pass
Strong eyes, fine limbs, haughty athletes
Less chanced than you for life,
Bonds to the whims of murder,
Sprawled in the bowels of the earth,
The torn fields of France.
20   What do you see in our eyes
At the shrieking iron and flame
Hurled through still heavens?
What quaver—what heart aghast?
Poppies whose roots are in man's veins
Drop, and are ever dropping;
But mine in my ear is safe,
Just a little white with the dust.

                    1922

Returning, We Hear the Larks

Sombre the night is:
And, though we have our lives, we know
What sinister threat lurks there.

Dragging these anguished limbs, we only know
This poison-blasted track opens on our camp—
On a little safe sleep.

But hark! Joy—joy—strange joy.
Lo! Heights of night ringing with unseen larks:
Music showering on our upturned listening faces.

10   Death could drop from the dark
As easily as song—
But song only dropped,
Like a blind man's dreams on the sand
By dangerous tides;
Like a girl's dark hair, for she dreams no ruin lies there,
Or her kisses where a serpent hides.

1922

A Worm Fed on the Heart of Corinth

A worm° fed on the heart of Corinth,
Babylon and Rome:
Not Paris raped tall Helen,
But this incestuous worm,
Who lured her vivid beauty
To his amorphous sleep.
England! famous as Helen
Is thy betrothal° sung
To him the shadowless,
More amorous than Solomon.
1917   1922

DAVID JONES
1895–

The most remarkable writing about the trench warfare during World War I is *In Parenthesis*. It was done in retrospect, in a strange kind of brief epic that covered not the whole scope of the war, like some later version of Hardy's *The Dynasts*, but one small corner of it. The Richebourg sector of the Western Front is the place, and the time from December of 1915 until July of 1916, when the Battle of the Somme with its astonishing casualty lists brought the whole war, and the twentieth century itself, into new focus.

David Jones, born of Welsh parents in Kent in 1895, was trained as an artist, and served in the trenches until wounded in the Battle of the Somme. He returned to the trenches until demobilization in 1919, and then resumed art studies. After his conversion to Catholicism in 1921, he spent some fruitful years with the community of artists and craftsmen founded at Ditchling (Sussex) by sculptor-essayist Eric Gill and hand-printer-poet Hilary Pepler. In 1929 he began work on *In Parenthesis*, which was published only in 1937, as the clouds of World War II were gathering. Jones

---

worm Satan, in his attributes of being "shadowless", "amorphous" and, half-echoingly, "amorous"; part-biblical, part-Blakean, this prophecy of the fall of empire ranks perhaps highest among Rosenberg's visionary fragments.

betrothal with the implication that England's marriage to Satan and historically inevitable downfall is not yet consummated, with time yet for moral redemption and escape created this unique mixture of prose and free verse, held together with collages of quotations, and effecting transitions that would become normal only in film later on, ostensibly to describe the war as he felt it had been. The title referred, he said, to the parenthetical time of life and history in which it was written, and also to the fact that human life on earth is, for an orthodox Christian, parenthetical as well. But other intentions governed the genesis of the work; and although the naturalistic reportage, the fragmentary and intimate glimpses of day-to-day life in the trenches in the months before they had become slaughterhouses, is splendid indeed, the work reaches beyond topical history. A huge body of myth, primarily Welsh but read through subsequent poetic history, is as much a part of the material of the work as its descriptive language.

Arthurian legend, a mainstay of the British imagination, is everywhere. Also, throughout the poem (for such, despite its prose, it is) Jones keeps the reader in mind of *Y Gododdin*, the sixth-century Welsh epic (attributed to Aneirin) describing the raid of three hundred Welsh from a part of what is now Scotland upon an English kingdom, and the destruction of that raiding force, which left only three survivors, including the poet. Jones invokes the poem in many places and is particularly interested in the relation of Roman Britain to the whole of the European Roman empire, and the implicit contrasts with the split and warring European continent in his own time.

The episode given below is from Part IV, and is entitled "King Pellam's Launde." The name refers to the land laid waste by the dolorous spear-stroke given to King Pellam by Sir Balin in Malory's *Morte Darthur*. According to the legend, the spear was the one that had pierced the side of Christ, brought to England, with the Holy Grail, by Joseph of Arimathea. Pellam's wound would not heal, and he lay maimed until Galahad, Lancelot's son, eventually cured him as he came by on his quest of the Grail. When Pellam was wounded, "the castle broke roof and walls and fell down to the earth"; later on, Balin "rode forth through the fair countries and cities and found the people dead slain on every side." T. S. Eliot in *The Waste Land* uses this same story, and Jones follows him in connecting the wounded king with the desolation and dead waste of his kingdom. But this kingdom, the trenches of 1915–16, and the moral life of Europe are connected in a more logical as well as a more mythological way in Jones's work than they are in the more symbolic linking of the Arthurian legend to Eliot's private wasteland of sexual inadequacy.

Jones's own notes to the poem are copious and sometimes digressive; they lead into the mythology (like Eliot, Jones connects his wasteland story with myths of regeneration, such as those of Attis and Adonis). Sometimes they are really part of the work itself, as in this commentary on the phrase "stand to" toward the beginning of the section below:

> Shortly before daybreak all troops in the line stood in their appointed places, their rifles in their hands, or immediately convenient, with bayonets fixed, ready for any dawn action on the part of the enemy. When it was fully day and the dangerous half-light past, the order would come to 'stand-down and clean rifles.' This procedure was strict and binding anywhere in the forward zone, under any circumstances whatever. The same routine was observed at dusk. So that that hour occurring twice in the twenty-four, of 'stand-to,' was one of peculiar significance and there was attaching to it a degree of solemnity, in that one was conscious that from the sea dunes to the mountains, everywhere, on the whole front the two opposing lines stood alertly, waiting any eventuality.

Jones's technique in *In Parenthesis* forms an interesting parallel to the growingly fragmentary assemblages of Ezra Pound's *Cantos*, which Jones had not read. In a later work composed during World War II and titled *The Anathémata* (1952), Jones moved more toward a lyric montage, and toward a total absorption of myth by inner vision. In the earlier war book, the interpenetration of remembered impression and photographic detail with the cadences, however archaic, of old songs of war and peace generate the general truth of its "account" of battle.

From In Parenthesis

King Pellam's Launde

Like an home-reared animal° in a quiet nook, before his day came . . . before entering into the prison of earth . . . around the contest, active and defensive, around the fort, around the steep-piled sods.

So thus he sorrowed till it was day and heard the foules sing, then somewhat he was comforted.°

Stand-to.
Stand-to-arms.

Stealthly, imperceptibly stript back, thinning
night wraps
unshrouding, unsheafing—
and insubstantial barriers dissolve.
This blind night-negative° yields uncertain flux.
At your wrist the phosphorescent dial describes the equal seconds.
   The flux yields up a measurable body; bleached forms emerge and stand.
   Where their faces turned, grey wealed earth bared almost of last clung weeds
of night-weft°—

behind them the stars still shined.

   Her fractured contours dun where soon his ray would show more clear her dereliction.
   Already before him low atmospheres harbingered° his bright influence.
   The filtering irradiance spread, you could begin to know that thing from this; this nearer from that away over.
   There at ten o'clock from that leaning picket-iron,° where the horizon most invented its character to their eyes straining, a changing dark, variant-textured, shaped to their very watching a wooded gradient.
   Skin off those comforters—to catch with their
cocked ears
the early bird,

Like . . . animal This is quoted from *Y Gododd-din* (see Headnote).
So thus . . . comforted quoted from Malory (XIII.19) about Lancelot, lamenting that his adultery with Guinevere prevents him from taking further part in "adventures to seek of holy things," the Grail quest

night-negative The image is of a photographic negative.
night-weft as if the darkness of night were a fabric woven by dark threads (weft) onto the transverse gray warp
harbingered heralded
picket-iron a vertical boundry stake

and meagre chattering of
December's prime
shrill over from
Biez wood.

Biez wood fog pillowed, by low mist isled, a play of hide and seek arboreal for the white diaphane.°

To their eyes seeming a wood moving,

> a moving grove advisioned.
>
> Stand-to.
>
> Stand-to.
>
> Stand-to-arms.

Out there,
get out there
get into that fire trench.

Pass it along to Stand-to.

To peel back those eider-ducks me slumberin' lovelies—Prince Charming presents his compliments. Who's this John Moores in his martial cloak—get off it, wontcher—come away counterfeiting death—cantcher—hear the bird o' dawnin'—roll up—it's tomorrow alright.

Sergeant Charming's through your thorny slumbers, who bends over sweet Robin's rose cheek.

Morning sergeant—kiss me sergeant.

Whose toe porrects° the ritual instrument to
break the spell to
resurrect the traverses.°

Fog refracted, losing articulation in the cloying damp, the word of command unmade in its passage, mischiefed of the opaque air, mutated, bereaved of content, become an incoherent uttering, a curious bent cry out of the smarting drift, lost altogether—yet making rise again the grey bundles where they lie.

Sodden night-bones vivify, wet bones live.

With unfathomed passion—this stark stir and waking—contort the comic mask of these tragic japers.

With a great complaining, bay by bay, the furrowed traverses whiten and agitate.

In 'P' sap, in 'Q' post,
in the fire-trench,
in Moggs Hole and Cats Post.°

An eastward alignment of troubled, ashen faces; delicate mechanisms of nerve and sinew, grapple afresh, deal for another day; ill-matched contesting, handicapped out of reason, spirits at the ebb bare up; strung taut—by what volition keyed—as best they may.

As grievous invalids watch the returning light pale-bright the ruckled counter-

---

diaphane transparency
porrects tenders, presents (an ecclesiatical usage)
traverses the embankments projecting above the

trench as a protection against shell bursts or rifle fire (pronounced "tráverses")
Moggs . . . Post parts of the battlefield; "Mogg," slang for "cat"

pane,° see their uneased bodies only newly clear; fearful to know afresh their ill condition; yet made glad for that rising, yet strain ears to the earliest note—should some prevenient° bird make his kindly cry.

Chance modulations in the fluxing mist, retro-fold° roll, banked up—shield again the waking arborage.°

With the gaining spread grey proto-light,
Morning-star pallid,
with the freshing day,
billowed damp more thickly hung yet whitened marvellously.

Nothing was defined beyond where the ground steepened just in front, where the trip-wire° graced its snare-barbs with tinselled moistnesses.

Cloying drift-damp cupped in every concave place.

It hurts you in the bloody eyes, it grips chill and harmfully and rasps the sensed membrane of the throat; it's raw cold, it makes you sneeze—christ how cold it is.

With each moment passing—the opaque creeping into every crevice creeping, whiter—thick whitened, through-white, argent wall nebulous, took on, gave back, wholly reflected—till transfigured bright in each drenched dew particle—and the last Night-Sentry fidgets expectantly.

Keep on that fire-step.

Keep a sharp look out.

Sights down—watch the wire.

Keep your eyes skinned—it's a likely morning.

Behind them, beyond the brumous° piling the last stars paled and twinkled fitfully, then faded altogether; knowing the mastery and their visitation; this beautiful one, his cloud garments dyed, ruddy-flecked, fleecy stoled; the bright healer, climbing certainly the exact degrees to his meridian. Yet the brume° holds, defiantly, and with winter confident, to shroud the low places.

Even now you couldn't see his line, but it was much lighter. The wire-tangle hanging, the rank grass-tangle drenched, tousled, and the broken-tin glint showed quite clearly. Left and right in the fire-bays you could see: soft service-caps wet-moulded to their heads moving—their drawn upward cloth flaps like home-spun angler-heads—moving in the morning reaches.

Very slowly the dissipating mist reveals saturate green-grey flats, and dark up-jutting things; and pollard boles° by more than timely wood-craftsman's cunning pruning dockt,—these weeping willows shorn.

And the limber-wheel, whose fractured spokes search upward vainly for the rent-off mortised-rim.°

Now his wire thickets were visible as dark surf, before a strand rising to bleached wall of bags in neat layers. The light of day is fully master now, and all along, and from beyond the glistering wall, at irregular intervals, thin blue smoke rises straight, like robber-fire,° to thin-out amber against the eastern bright.

---

ruckled counterpane rumpled bedspread
prevenient anticipatory
retro-fold folded back on itself
arborage foliage
trip-wire set at shin-height, often in tall grass
brumous misty
brume mist
pollard boles trunks of trees that have been

pollarded, or cut back to produce foliage close to the trunk
mortised-rim showing the holes wherein the spokes would be set
robber-fire an allusion to a story in Welsh folklore about a column of smoke unbending in the highest wind in the world, described by one of the protagonists as the fire of a robber

Over Biez Copse, as nainsook,° low vapours yet could draw out tenuous parallels.

Head inclined to head in the bay to the left.

They call from round the traverse wall.

Pass it along to Stand-down.

Stand-down and clean rifles.

Post day-sentries—pass it along.

They stood miserably.

They stretched encumbered limbs to take their rifles, listless, bemused, to slowly scrape away the thicker mire caked, with deadness in their eyes and hands as each to each they spoke—like damned-corpse-gossiping, of hopeless bleedin' dawns—then laught to see themselves so straitened, tricked out in mudded stiffening.

They beat against the padded walls to flow again the ebbing blood. They kicked the oozing sacks above the water surface till their toe-joints ached.

A lean lance-jack,° grey faced with his one night's vicarious office, called over the revetment.°

Get on those rifles at once—get on with it.

Orl right Corp—got any gauze.

Wot we want is gauze.

Wot we want is boiling water,°

boiling bleedin' water.

Got any boiling water?

Then was great to-do and business, then were butt-heel-irons opened, and splintering of thumb nails with the jammed metal, and jack-knife blades shivered.

Got any oil.

Why don't you go to Sergeant and get for yourselves.

Why didn't you ask the Quarter-bloke back there.

Only a drop, china, just for the bolt—just a spot—be a kind virgin—he's coming round the bend—he's doing No. 5°—just a spot.

Then was a pulling through of barrels and searching of minute vents and under-facets with pins, and borrowing of small necessaries to do with this care of arms. Then began prudent men to use their stored-up oil freely on bolt and back-sight-flange. And harassed men, and men ill-furnished, complained bitterly. And men improvising and adventurous slipped away along the traverses, to fetch back brimming mess-tin lids, or salvaged jam tins steaming.

How do you get hot water in this place of all water—all cold water up to the knees. These poured quickly lest it should cool off, and eyed their barrels' bright rifling with a great confidence, and boasted to their envious fellows, and offered

---

nainsook a striped cotton fabric
lance-jack an acting lance corporal (with private's pay)
revetment a retaining wall
boiling water for cleaning fouled rifle barrels,

the fine wire gauze mentioned before being expensive and hard to come by
No. 5 "Field Punishment No. 5," presumably for some minor offense

them the luke-warm left over. So that one way and another they cleaned their rifles—anyway the oil softened the open cracks in your finger-tips.

While these things were being done, while they were at this oiling and tearing off of closely rationed 'four by two,'° conserving carefully each flannel slip, plumbing dexterously with weighted cords, scraping and making their complaint, a message reached them from the right for the Lewis Team with No. 8: to get at once on their day-target, to send a man for S.A.A.° to Pioneer Keep; further, to furnish a report of their night firing. They stood unhappily, and believed themselves to be ill-fortuned above the common lot, for they had barely slept—and a great cold to gnaw them. Their wet-weighted gear pulled irksomely, soaking cloth impeded all their action, adhered in saturate layers when they stood still.

Night-begotten fear yet left them frail, nor was the waking day much cheer for them. They felt with each moment's more ample light, but a measuring, a nearing only, of the noonday hour—when the nescient trouble comes walking.° Their vitality seemed not to extend to the finger-tips nor to enable any precise act; so that to do an exact thing, competently to clean a rifle, to examine and search out intricate parts, seemed to them an enormity and beyond endurance; as one, who, clumsied with fear or unnerved by some grief, seeks to thread needle or turn an exact phrase; for they were unseasoned, nor inured, not knowing this to be much less than the beginning of sorrows. They stood as a lost child stands in his fatigue, and gape-eyed, where tall Guardsmen, their initiators and instructors, moved leisurely about, well pleased with the quiet of the sector.

Presently Mr. Jenkins came with Sergeant Snell and they ported arms for inspection.

He neither blames nor praises,
he whistles low,
he whistles *Dixieland*,
he passes on to Section 4: but
Sergeant Snell checks Jac Jones, checks Jack Float at the ease springs.° Sergeant Snell turns on this going; pokes this right-middle finger at this lance-jack—instructs him:
Have ready two on 'em—section's rations.
Sergeant Snell gobs in the trench drain; comes to Mr. Jenkins's heel.

It was yet quite early in the morning, at the time of Saturnalia, when men properly are in winter quarters, lighting His birthday candles—
all a green-o.°

'four by two' "Slips of flannelette 4 in. wide cut in lengths of 2 in. from a roll—oiled and drawn through barrel on pull-through to clean bore" (Jones)
S.A.A. "Small Arms Ammunition. Ball cartridge" (Jones)
nescient . . . walking the unknowing (and perhaps, unbelieving) trouble; from Psalm 90 (in the Vulgate), a passage quoted and expounded in Sir Thomas More's *Dialogue of Comfort*, which Jones may have known. The Authorized Version reads: "Thou shalt not be afraid for the terror by night, nor for the arrow that flieth by day, Nor for the pestilence that walketh in darkness, nor for the destruction that wasteth at noonday" (Psalms 91:5–6).

The Vulgate text reads: . . . *A sagitta volante in die, a negotio perambulante in tenebris, ab incursu a demonio meridiano"* ("nor of the arrow flying in the day, nor of the business walking about in the darknesses, nor of the incursion of the devil in the midday," in the Douay-Rheims translation). More is interested in connecting the devil that is called "business" with the devil at noon (the time of the Fall).
ease springs a command at rifle inspection
green-o Jones notes the source as "Two, two, the lily-white boys / Clothèd all in green-o," from "Green Grow the Rushes-o," the well-known counting song, and identifies "boys" as "Our Lord and St. John Baptist."

When children look with serious eyes on brand-new miracles, and red berry sheen makes a Moses-bush,° to mirror in multiplicity the hearth-stones creature of fire.

But John Ball, posted as 1st Day Sentry, sat on the fire-step; and looking upward, sees in a cunning glass the image of: his morning parapets, his breakfast-fire smoke, the twisted wood beyond.

Across the very quiet of no-man's-land came still some twittering. He found the wood, visually so near, yet for the feet forbidden by a great fixed gulf, a sight somehow to powerfully hold his mind. To the woods of all the world is this potency—to move the bowels of us.

To groves always men come both to their joys and their undoing. Come lightfoot in heart's ease and school-free; walk on a leafy holiday with kindred and kind; come perplexedly with first loves—to tread the tangle frustrated, striking—bruising the green.

Come on night's fall for ambuscade.

Find harbour with a remnant.

Share with the prescribed their unleavened cake.

Come for sweet princes by malignant interests deprived.

Wait, wait long for—

with the broken men, nest with badger and the martin-cat till such time as he come again, crying the waste for his chosen.

Or come in gathering nuts and may;°

or run want-wit° in a shirt for the queen's unreason.

Beat boys-bush for Robin and Bobin.°

Come with Merlin in his madness,° for the pity of it; for

the young men reaped like green barley,

for the folly of it.

Seek a way separate and more strait.

Keep date with the genius of the place—come with a weapon or effectual branch—and here this winter copse might well be special to Diana's Jack, for none might attempt it, but by perilous bough-plucking.°

Draughtsman at Army° made note on a blue-print of the significance of that grove as one of his strong-points; this wooded rise as the gate of their enemies, a door at whose splintered posts, Janus-wise° emplacements shield an automatic fire.

Moses-bush a burning yet unconsumed bush in which God appeared to Moses (Exodus 3:2)
nuts and may from "Here we go gathering nuts and may / On a cold and frosty morning," children's song; "may," hawthorne
want-wit in madness, like that of Sir Lancelot driven insane by Guinevere's magic (after he had, under another spell and hence unwittingly, slept with Elaine, daughter of the wounded fisher-king Pelles and granddaughter of King Pellam). See Malory XI.3.
Robin and Bobin Welsh version of "The Cutty Wren," a folk song for St. Stephen's Day (December 26), when all over northern Europe a wren was hunted: "We hunted the wren for Robin and Bobin, / We hunted the wren for everyman."

Merlin . . . madness In one story, Merlin, the Arthurian wizard, went mad at a battle and ran wild in the woods.
bough-plucking This refers to the description in Sir James Frazer's *The Golden Bough* of the priest of Diana at Nemi, who became so by killing his predecessor and cutting off the branch of a sacred tree, that branch being identified with the Golden Bough plucked by Aeneas before descending to the Underworld (Virgil, *Aeneid* VI).
Army Army headquarters; the man who drew the maps there, safe and remote from the trenches
Janus-wise looking out backward and forward, like the two heads of Janus, the Roman god of doorways and beginnings

2066   DAVID JONES

In the mirror: below the wood, his undulating breastworks all along, he sees
and loses, thinks he sees again, grey movement for the grey stillness, where the
sand-bag wall dipped a little.

He noted that movement as with half a mind—at two o'clock from the petrol-
tin.° He is indeterminate of what should be his necessary action. Leave him be
on a winter's morning—let him bide. And the long-echoing sniper-shot from
down by 'Q' Post alone disturbed his two hours' watching.

His eyes turned again to where the wood thinned to separate broken trees; to
where great strippings-off hanged from tenuous fibres swaying, whitened to
decay—as swung
immolations
for the northern Cybele.°
The hanged, the offerant:
        himself to himself
        on the tree.
Whose own,
whose grey war-band, beyond the stapled war-net—
(as grey-banded rodents for a shelving warren—cooped in
their complex runnels, where the sea-fret percolates).
Come from outlandish places,
from beyond the world,
from the Hercynian°—
they were at breakfast and were cold as he, they too made
their dole.°
        And one played on an accordion:
                Es ist ein' Ros' entsprungen
                Aus einer Wurzel zart.°
Since Boniface° once walked in Odin's wood.
Two men in the traverse mouth-organ'd;
four men took up that song.
                Casey Jones mounted on his engine°
                Casey Jones with his orders in his hand.

petrol-tin gasoline can used to take a bearing
from
Cybele Originally an Asiatic nature goddess,
identified in the west with Rhea, worshiped in
wild rites by followers called Corybantes, one
of whom would assume the name of her son,
Attis (who castrated himself at the foot of a
pine when driven mad by a goddess he had
spurned); the worshipers would inflict this
same, as well as other, wounds on themselves,
and Attis was worshiped by an effigy hung on a
pine. In Norse mythology human victims were
dedicated to Odin, strung up on a tree, and
wounded with a spear; and indeed, says Frazer
in The Golden Bough, "he is said to have been
sacrificed to himself in the ordinary way."
Frazer, and Jones in a note, quote an Icelandic
poem: "I know that I hung on the windy
tree / For nine whole nights, / Wounded myself with the spear, dedicated to Odin, / Myself
to myself."

Hercynian forested mountains in south Germany
(Caesar's term in his Gallic Wars)
dole See Jones's note on this whole passage:
"The German field-grey seemed to us more than
a mere colour. It seemed always to call up
the grey wolf of Nordic literature. To watch
these grey shapes moving elusively among the
bleached breast works or emerging from between
broken tree-stumps was a sight to powerfully
impress us. . . . It would be interesting to
know what myth-conception our own ochre
coats and saucer hats suggested to our antagonists."
Es ist . . . zart from the German carol usually
sung in English as "Lo, how a rose ere blooming" (literally, "It is a rose sprung up from a
tender root")
Boniface English missionary (680–754) called
the "Apostle to Germany"
Casey . . . engine Jones actually misquotes the
line, "Casey Jones mounted to the cabin."

Which nearer,
which so rarely insular,
unmade his harmonies,
honouring
this rare and indivisible
New Light
for us,
over the still morning honouring.
This concertina'd
Good news
of these
barbarians,
them
bastard square-heads.°
    Put the fluence on,°
Rotherhithe°—
drownd the bastards on
Christmass Day in the Morning. Wot's this—
wot type's this of bloody waits°
wot's this he's striking up—
wot type's this of universall Peace
through Sea and Land.°
1929   1937

EDWIN MUIR
1887–1959

A poet of the remote Orkney Islands rather than of the Scottish mainland, Muir
founded his imaginative life more and more on transcendent and on inward realms
—of myth generalized across civilizations, of the repetitions of myth in dream,
and of visions of an integration of life and vision in a lost bucolic world. He moved to
industrial Glasgow at fourteen, educated himself, became a literary journalist, lived
in Europe, and, with his wife Willa, translated Kafka's novels into English. The Muirs
lived in Prague, where he was head of the British Council, from the end of World
War II until the overthrow of the democratic socialist government of Czechoslovakia
(1948). His posthumous Collected Poems, appearing in 1960, took by surprise many
readers who had previously undervalued his accomplishments as a poet. Muir never
became as committed to Scottish literary nationalism as did Hugh MacDiarmid (see
below), and differed with him about the role of dialect in poetry; his sense of place is
located far more in the imagery of his poems, which move from landscape to fable
in a smooth, unmediated way, without the intellectualizations of, for example, W. H.
Auden's equally strong and deeply felt visions of the landscape of the north of England.

square-heads "Term used of the Germans, not
perhaps so commonly as Jerry" (Jones)
Put . . . on cast a spell over
Rotherhithe district of London's dockland
waits carol singers

striking . . . Land (ll. 323–25) quoted from
Milton's "Hymn on the Morning of Christ's
Nativity," l. 52: "She strikes a universal peace
through sea and land."

Muir wrote an *Autobiography* (1954; a revision of the earlier *The Story and the Fable)* and a number of essays on literature and politics. T. S. Eliot in an introduction to a reissue of Muir's *Collected Poems* tried to place Muir's poetic world in a biographical framework. As Eliot wrote, "There is the sensibility of the remote islander, the boy from a primitive offshore community who was then plunged into the sordid horror of industrialism in Glasgow, who struggled to understand the modern world of the metropolis in London and finally the realities of central Europe in Prague. . . ." This is perhaps a bit schematic and a touch condescending, but it will serve to suggest to the reader the kind of imaginative modulations which must have resulted in the difference between the first and last of the poems given below, ostensibly on the same "subject."

Horses

Those lumbering horses in the steady plough,
On the bare field—I wonder why, just now,
They seemed terrible, so wild and strange,
Like magic power on the stony grange.

Perhaps some childish hour has come again,
When I watched fearful, through the blackening rain,
Their hooves like pistons in an ancient mill
Move up and down, yet seem as standing still.

Their conquering hooves which trod the stubble down
10   Were ritual that turned the field to brown,
And their great hulks were seraphim of gold,
Or mute ecstatic monsters on the mould.

And oh the rapture, when, one furrow done,
They marched broad-breasted to the sinking sun!
The light flowed off their bossy sides in flakes;
The furrows rolled behind like struggling snakes.

But when at dusk with steaming nostrils home
They came, they seemed gigantic in the gloam,
And warm and glowing with mysterious fire
20   That lit their smouldering bodies in the mire.

Their eyes as brilliant and as wide as night
Gleamed with a cruel apocalyptic light.
Their manes the leaping ire of the wind
Lifted with rage invisible and blind.

Ah, now it fades! it fades! and I must pine
Again for that dread country crystalline,
Where the blank field and the still-standing tree
Were bright and fearful presences to me.

1925

The Island

Your arms will clasp the gathered grain
For your good time, and wield the flail
In merry fire and summer hail.
There stand the golden hills of corn
Which all the heroic clans have borne,
And bear the herdsmen of the plain,
The horseman in the mountain pass,
The archaic goat with silver horn,
Man, dog and flock and fruitful hearth.
10   Harvests of men to men give birth.
These the ancestral faces bred
And show as through a golden glass
Dances and temples of the dead.
Here speak through the transmuted tongue
The full grape bursting in the press,
The barley seething in the vat,
Which earth and man as one confess,
Babbling of what both would be at
In garrulous story and drunken song.
20   Though come a different destiny,
Though fall a universal wrong
More stern than simple savagery,
Men are made of what is made,
The meat, the drink, the life, the corn,
Laid up by them, in them reborn.
And self-begotten cycles close
About our way; indigenous art
And simple spells make unafraid
The haunted labyrinths of the heart,
30   And with our wild succession braid
The resurrection of the rose.

                    1956

The Horses

Barely a twelvemonth after
The seven days war that put the world to sleep,
Late in the evening the strange horses came.
By then we had made our covenant with silence,
But in the first few days it was so still
We listened to our breathing and were afraid.
On the second day
The radios failed; we turned the knobs; no answer.
On the third day a warship passed us, heading north,
10   Dead bodies piled on the deck. On the sixth day

A plane plunged over us into the sea. Thereafter
Nothing. The radios dumb;
And still they stand in corners of our kitchens,
And stand, perhaps, turned on, in a million rooms
All over the world. But now if they should speak,
If on a sudden they should speak again,
If on the stroke of noon a voice should speak,
We would not listen, we would not let it bring
That old bad world that swallowed its children quick
20   At one great gulp. We would not have it again.
Sometimes we think of the nations lying asleep,
Curled blindly in impenetrable sorrow,
And then the thought confounds us with its strangeness.
The tractors lie about our fields; at evening
They look like dank sea-monsters couched and waiting.
We leave them where they are and let them rust:
'They'll moulder away and be like other loam.'
We make our oxen drag our rusty ploughs,
Long laid aside. We have gone back
30   Far past our fathers' land.
                    And then, that evening
Late in the summer the strange horses came.
We heard a distant tapping on the road,
A deepening drumming; it stopped, went on again
And at the corner changed to hollow thunder.
We saw the heads
Like a wild wave charging and were afraid.
We had sold our horses in our fathers' time
To buy new tractors. Now they were strange to us
As fabulous steeds set on an ancient shield
40   Or illustrations in a book of knights.
We did not dare go near them. Yet they waited,
Stubborn and shy, as if they had been sent
By an old command to find our whereabouts
And that long-lost archaic companionship.
In the first moment we had never a thought
That they were creatures to be owned and used.
Among them were some half-a-dozen colts
Dropped in some wilderness of the broken world,
Yet new as if they had come from their own Eden.
50   Since then they have pulled our ploughs and borne our loads,
But that free servitude still can pierce our hearts.
Our life is changed; their coming our beginning.
                                    1956

HUGH MACDIARMID

1892–

Hugh MacDiarmid (Christopher Murray Grieve) was born in Dumfries, worked as a journalist, and in the mid-nineteen-twenties began to publish the books of verse with which he attempted to create a Scottish literary Renaissance. Writing both in English and in an artificial literary language of his own which he called "Lallans," he spoke through a complex *persona* derived in some measure from Robert Burns (the language of whose poetry was similarly an artificial one) and from a broader vision of Scottish nationality as representing a version of a "complex fate"—as Henry James described the predicament of being American with respect to British culture.

As with his fifteenth-century forebears, who were closer to France and more in touch with a main line of poetic culture than their English contemporaries, Mac-Diarmid's poetic world and literary program for Scottish poetry were far from pro-vincial or parochial; his work is marked by a cosmopolitanism that rages beneath the relative inaccessibility of some of the language. A very peculiar, personal sort of communism marks his work, as well; it has ranged from a Stalinist orthodoxy on some political matters, to the broad, human revisionism of the end of his *Second Hymn to Lenin,* which is something of a complex self-rebuke for having chosen what Yeats called *rhetoric* (what men make from quarrels with others), as opposed to poetry (which they make from quarrels with themselves). The poet rejects, in effect, the injunctions of "socialist realism" to celebrate the Revolution in verse. The strength of MacDiarmid's language often lies in conflict; he has revived the Scots tradition, as exemplified in poets like Dunbar in the Renaissance, of "flyting" or poetic dispute. And he has contributed to that major movement of the modern in literature, which makes of a regional or private milieu an aspect of a more general condition.

MacDiarmid's early poems hid a lot of Hardy in their heather and thistle gar-ments; his later poems owe something to Lawrence, something to French and German Romantic and modern verse. His "Lallans," made up of Burns's dialect words—both those used in speech and those sleeping in dictionaries—and phonetic spellings, is nev-ertheless a powerful poetic language, modulating in different poems from the more to the less arcane. Most important, it allows the poet in the closing stanzas of the *Second Hymn to Lenin* to achieve a ruggedness and simplicity, an almost biblical force, which, if attempted in modern, colloquial English, might sound only like propagandistic rant.

Moonlight Among the Pines°

Thraw oot your shaddaws
Owre the heich hillsides,
A' ye lang trees
Quhair the white mune rides.

Moonlight Among the Pines A translation of this early poem in "Lallans" may be helpful: "Threw out your shadows / Over the high hill-sides, / All ye tall trees / Where the white moon rides. / My spirit would darken / The sun in the East / For ever, if my love / Laid bare her white breast. / O shadow that hides / In my heart till a sight / Of Love sends it plung-ing / All else into night!"

My spirit 'ud darken
The sun in the East
For aye, gin my luve
Laid bare her white breist.

O shaddaw that derns
10 In my hert till a sicht
O'Luve sends it plungin'
A' else into nicht! . . . .

                    1925

From Second Hymn to Lenin°

Ah, Lenin, you were richt. But I'm a poet
(And you c'ud mak allowances for that!)
Aimin' at mair than you aimed at
Tho' yours comes first, I know it.

An unexamined life is no' worth ha'in'.°
Yet Burke was richt; owre muckle° concern
Wi' Life's foundations is a sure
Sign o' decay; tho' Joyce in turn

Is richt, and the principal question
10 Aboot a work o' art is frae° hoo deep
A life it springs—and syne° hoo faur
Up frae't it has the poo'er° to leap.

And hoo muckle it lifts up wi' it
Into the sunlight like a saumon there,
Universal Spring! For Morand's richt°—
It s'ud be like licht in the air—

Are my poems spoken in the factories and fields,
    In the streets o' the toon?°
Gin° *they're no', then I'm failin' to dae*°
20   *What I ocht to ha' dune.*°

Gin I canna win through to the man in the street,
    The wife by the hearth,
A' the cleverness on earth'll no' mak' up
    For the damnable dearth.

Lenin V. I. Lenin (1870–1924), father of the
Soviet Union, Russian communist in whose
tradition and in whose name a repressive policy
against individual creative imagination in the
arts flourished in opposition to the more humane
one of his exiled follower Leon Trotsky. Mac-
Diarmid, for an orthodox communist, comes
dangerously close to a Trotskyite position in
this poem.
An . . . ha'in' "The unexamined life is not
worth living"—Socrates, in Plato's *Apology*

muckle great
frae from
syne thereafter
poo'er power
Morand's richt "Morand's right:" Paul Morand
(b. 1888), French writer and diplomat
toon town
Gin if
dae do
dune done

'Haud on haud on; what poet's dune that?
   Is Shakespeare read,
Or Dante or Milton or Goethe or Burns?'
   —You heard what I said.

—A means o' world locomotion,
30 The maist perfected and aerial o' a'.°
Lenin's name's gane owre the haill earth,
But the names o' the ithers?—Ha!

What hidie-hole o' the vineyard d'they scart
Wi' minds like the look on a hen's face,
Morand, Joyce, Burke, and the rest
That e'er wrote; me noo in like case?

Great poets hardly onybody kens o'?
Geniuses like a man talkin' t'm sel'?
Nonsense! They're nocht o' the sort
40 Their character's easy to tell.

They're nocht but romantic rebels
Strikin' dilettante poses;
Trotsky—Christ, no' wi' a croon o' thorns
But a wreath o' paper roses.

A' that's great is free and expansive.
What ha' they expanded tae?
They've affected nocht but a fringe
O' mankind in ony way.

Barbarian saviour o' civilization
50 Hoo weel ye kent (we're owre dull witted)
Naething is dune save as we ha'e
Means to en's° transparently fitted.

Poetry like politics maun° cut
The cackle and pursue real ends,
Unerringly as Lenin, and to that
Its nature better tends.

Wi' Lenin's vision equal poet's gift
And what unparalleled force was there!
Nocht in a' literature wi' that
60 Begins to compare.

Nae simple rhymes for silly folk
But the haill art, as Lenin gied
Nae Marx-without-tears to workin' men
But the fu' course insteed.

o' a'. of all   maun must
ens ends

Organic constructional work,
Practicality, and work by degrees;
First things first; and poetry in turn
'll be built by these.°

.   .   .

Freend, foe; past, present, future;
Success, failure; joy, fear;
Life, Death; and a'thing else,
For us, are equal here.

Male, female; quick or deid,
Let us fike° nae mair;
The deep line o'cleavage
Disna lie there.

150 *Black in the pit the miner is,*
The shepherd reid° on the hill,
And I'm wi' them baith° until
The end of mankind, I wis.

Whatever their jobs a' men are ane
In life, and syne in daith
(Tho' it's sma' patience I can ha'e
Wi' life's ideas o' that by the way)
And he's nae poet but kens it, faith,
And ony job but the hardest's ta'en.

160 *The sailor gangs owre the curve o' the sea,*
The hoosewife's thrang° in the wash-tub,
And whatna rhyme can I find but hub,
And what else can poetry be?

The core o' a' activity,
Changin't in accordance wi'
Its inward necessity
And mede o' integrity.

Unremittin', relentless,
Organized to the last degree,
170 Ah, Lenin, politics is bairns'° play
To what this maun be!

                1935

---

these Eighteen stanzas are omitted here, in   reid red
which the poet rejects by degrees the easy   baith both
formulation just given.   thrang strain of hard work
fike fuss   bairns' children's

Bagpipe Music°

Let me play to you tunes without measure or end,
Tunes that are born to die without a herald,
As a flight of storks rises from a marsh, circles,
And alights on the spot from which it rose.

Flowers. A flower-bed like hearing the bagpipes.
The fine black earth has clotted into sharp masses
As if the frost and not the sun had come.
It holds many lines of flowers.
First faint rose peonies, then peonies blushing,
Then again red peonies, and, behind them,
Massive, apoplectic peonies, some of which are so red
And so violent as to seem almost black; behind these
Stands a low hedge of larkspur, whose tender apologetic blossoms
Appear by contrast pale, though some, vivid as the sky above them,
Stand out from their fellows iridescent and slaty as a pigeon's breast,
The bagpipes—they are screaming and they are sorrowful.
There is a wail in their merriment, and cruelty in their triumph.
They rise and they fall like a weight swung in the air at the end of a string.
They are like the red blood of those peonies.
And like the melancholy of those blue flowers.
They are like a human voice—no! for the human voice lies!
They are like human life that flows under the words.
That flower-bed is like the true life that wants to express itself
And does . . . while we human beings lie cramped and fearful.

1962

ROBERT GRAVES
1895–

Graves's literary career is fascinatingly problematic, although as his earlier works begin to be reread in the light of his later ones a consistency may emerge which he himself, up to now, has tended to obscure. He is a poet whose major poetic work may not be in his poems at all, but rather in a strange, disparate corpus of mythographic writings in various forms—historical novels, reworkings of classical story, criticism, and purportedly anthropological studies of mythology and imagination. And yet he has been insisting for more than forty years that these works of his left hand were simply day-labor to enable him to support himself for the writing of verse. Were that verse to exist on its own and without the larger corpus, however, it might have fewer claims to major importance, representing as it does a continuation of the tradition of the Georgians. Still, read in context, it is an impressive body of poetry.

Bagpipe Music It is instructive to compare this beautiful poem, which seems indebted to D. H. Lawrence, with Louis MacNeice's satirical piece of the same title; MacDiarmid was the more conmmitted Communist, and yet there is not a trace, in this poem touching his deep Scottish pieties, of the propagandistic writing known throughout international Communism as "agitprop."

Born in London, educated at Charterhouse, Robert von Ranke Graves did not go up to Oxford until after World War I. In *Goodbye to All That* (1929) he vividly describes his war service in the Royal Welch Fusiliers; he suffered combat neurosis, and ultimately achieved psychic integration through poetry. Graves taught briefly in Cairo, but in 1929 settled in Majorca where, with the exception of the World War II years, he has lived ever since. His historical novels—*I, Claudius* (1934), *Claudius the God* (1934), *King Jesus* (1946), and many more—are based on vast classical and biblical scholarship; but from the outset (as in his strange, profound, but neglected little biblical fiction, *My Head, My Head,* 1925) he began to weave tendentious interpretations into his treatment of ancient subjects. His two-volume *The Greek Myths* (1955) organizes an encyclopedic body of material around a series of patterns that had only fully emerged in his monumental study, *The White Goddess* (1948).

The thrust of Graves's whole mythographic career has been to build up a great if fragmented vision of The Muse. In an age when such fictions as the Petrarchan Sonnet-Lady were long past possibility, when the romantic feminine demons had been forced to dissolve, as far as their role in a theory of the Imagination was concerned, into systems like Yeats's, Graves began an intense study of what he called the Triple Goddess who had once reigned supreme in a matriarchal culture, until smashed into her components. (These appear in the Greek pantheon, in the phased aspects of, say, Diana the virgin moon goddess, and Hecate, her underground witch-like form.) And yet all mythologies retain the visionary fragments of the original goddess, broken by the encounter with a patriarchy which, in one phase of Graves's hypothesis, invaded the Aegean and brought with it a male sun-god. Throughout his writings, Graves uses historical conjecture, backed up with anthropological data, in the way that other mytho-poetic writers of the past have used a central fiction; he even goes so far, in *The Nazarene Gospel Restored,* as to reconstruct a supposed pre-Pauline Aramaic gospel of a non-divine Jesus, as if to lend truth to his earlier novel, *King Jesus*. His major study of the Feminine as Muse is fascinating; tendentious as historical mythology, it cannot be faulted as a coherent, cyclical vision of the relation between life process and imaginative existence. Along with certain other mythological works of Graves, it will remain (like Yeats's *A Vision* with its attendant doctrinal poems, and Joyce's *Finnegans Wake*) a monument of the imagination.

Graves's poems are many and various; his favorite writers of the past, like Catullus and Skelton (he loathes Milton), were masters of voice and tone, and his whole commitment to lyric poetry would appear to avoid the romantic and the visionary elements so enshrined in his mythical system. His love poems are among the best heterosexual erotic lyrics in modern English, and some of the poems written around the mythology are compellingly direct in a way not chosen by many of his younger contemporaries. As a critic Graves has often been cranky and perverse but never bland, and the primary failure of his essays and lectures, whether in influential early studies or as Professor of Poetry at Oxford, has been a refusal to acknowledge in some of the major traditions of English poetry forces to which his own work has been responsive.

Love Without Hope

Love without hope, as when the young bird-catcher
Swept off his tall hat to the Squire's own daughter,
So let the imprisoned larks escape and fly
Singing about her head, as she rode by.

1920

The Succubus°

Thus will despair
In ecstasy of nightmare
Fetch you a devil-woman through the air,
   To slide below the sweated sheet
And kiss your lips in answer to your prayer
   And lock her hands with yours and your feet with her feet.

Yet why does she
Come never as longed-for beauty
Slender and cool, with limbs lovely to see,
10   (The bedside candle guttering high)
And toss her head so the thick curls fall free
   Of halo'd breast, firm belly and long, slender thigh?

Why with hot face,
With paunched and uddered carcase,
Sudden and greedily does she embrace,
   Gulping away your soul, she lies so close,
Fathering you with brats of her own race?
   Yet is the fancy grosser than your lusts were gross?

1930

Sick Love°

O Love, be fed with apples while you may,
And feel the sun and go in royal array,
A smiling innocent on the heavenly causeway,

Though in what listening horror for the cry
That soars in outer blackness dismally,
The dumb blind beast, the paranoiac fury:

Be warm, enjoy the season, lift your head,
Exquisite in the pulse of tainted blood,
That shivering glory not to be despised.

10 Take your delight in momentariness,

Succubus a demon who assumes a female form in order to have sexual intercourse with sleeping men
Sick Love The title refers to the Song of Songs

2:5 ("Stay me with flagons, comfort me with apples: for I am sick of love"), quoted in the first line. (Originally titled "O Love in Me".)

Walk between dark and dark—a shining space
With the grave's narrowness, though not its peace.

1930

Warning to Children

Children, if you dare to think
Of the greatness, rareness, muchness,
Fewness of this precious only
Endless world in which you say
You live, you think of things like this:
Blocks of slate enclosing dappled
Red and green, enclosing tawny
Yellow nets, enclosing white
And black acres of dominoes,
Where a neat brown paper parcel°
Tempts you to untie the string.
In the parcel a small island,
On the island a large tree,
On the tree a husky fruit.
Strip the husk and pare the rind off:
In the kernel you will see
Blocks of slate enclosed by dappled
Red and green, enclosed by tawny
Yellow nets, enclosed by white
And black acres of dominoes,
Where the same brown paper parcel—
Children, leave the string untied!
For who dares undo the parcel
Finds himself at once inside it,
On the island, in the fruit,
Blocks of slate about his head,
Finds himself enclosed by dappled
Green and red, enclosed by yellow
Tawny nets, enclosed by black
And white acres of dominoes,
With the same brown paper parcel
Still untied upon his knee.
And, if he then should dare to think
Of the fewness, muchness, rareness,
Greatness of this endless only
Precious world in which he says
He lives—he then unties the string.

1930

parcel The image of attempting to discover truth as opening a set of Chinese boxes, one inside another, or as a Russian doll, is almost a cliché in modern literature; in André Gide's *The Counterfeiters,* Aldous Huxley's *Point Counter Point,* and other novels, the infinite regression has symbolized the ultimate horror of the intellect's failure to grasp experience. Most recently this has been seen in the works of Jorge Luis Borges.

Down, Wanton, Down!

Down, wanton, down!° Have you no shame
That at the whisper of Love's name,
Or Beauty's, presto! up you raise
Your angry head and stand at gaze?

Poor bombard°-captain, sworn to reach
The ravelin° and effect a breach—
Indifferent what you storm or why,
So be that in the breach you die!

Love may be blind, but Love at least
10 Knows what is man and what mere beast;
Or Beauty wayward, but requires
More delicacy from her squires.

Tell me, my witless, whose one boast
Could be your staunchness at the post,
When were you made a man of parts°
To think fine and profess the arts?

Will many-gifted Beauty come
Bowing to your bald rule of thumb,
Or Love swear loyalty to your crown?
20 Be gone, have done! Down, wanton, down!

                1933

Recalling War

Entrance and exit wounds are silvered clean,
The track aches only when the rain reminds.
The one-legged man forgets his leg of wood,
The one-armed man his jointed wooden arm.
The blinded man sees with his ears and hands
As much or more than once with both his eyes.
Their war was fought these twenty years ago
And now assumes the nature-look of time,
As when the morning traveller turns and views
10 His wild night-stumbling carved into a hill.

What, then, was war? No mere discord of flags
But an infection of the common sky
That sagged ominously upon the earth
Even when the season was the airiest May.
Down pressed the sky, and we, oppressed, thrust out

---

down The notion that the male sexual organ has a will or mind of its own is an ancient one, perhaps present even in the etymology of the Latin colloquialism *mentula* (a favorite word of the poet Catullus, in whose mood this poem is written) as derived from *mens*: "mind."
bombard a primitive cannon
ravelin a V-shaped fortification
parts punning on "private parts" and worldliness

Boastful tongue, clenched fist and valiant yard.
Natural infirmities were out of mode,
For Death was young again: patron alone
Of healthy dying, premature fate-spasm.

20   Fear made fine bed-fellows. Sick with delight
At life's discovered transitoriness,
Our youth became all-flesh and waived the mind.
Never was such antiqueness of romance,
Such tasty honey oozing from the heart.
And old importances came swimming back—
Wine, meat, log-fires, a roof over the head,
A weapon at the thigh, surgeons at call.
Even there was a use again for God—
A word of rage in lack of meat, wine, fire,
30   In ache of wounds beyond all surgeoning.

War was return of earth to ugly earth,
War was foundering of sublimities,
Extinction of each happy art and faith
By which the world had still kept head in air.
Protesting logic or protesting love,
Until the unendurable moment struck—
The inward scream, the duty to run mad.

And we recall the merry ways of guns—
Nibbling the walls of factory and church
40   Like a child, piecrust; felling groves of trees
Like a child, dandelions with a switch!
Machine-guns rattle toy-like from a hill,
Down in a row the brave tin-soldiers fall:
A sight to be recalled in elder days
When learnedly the future we devote
To yet more boastful visions of despair.

                              1938

The Thieves

Lovers in the act dispense
With such meum-teum° sense
As might warningly reveal
What they must not pick or steal,°
And their nostrum° is to say:
'I and you are both away.'

---

meum-teum "mine-yours" (Latin)
pick or steal In the Catechism of the Church
of England there is an injunction to keep one's
hands from "picking and stealing"; Hamlet

alludes to it when he calls his fingers "pickers
and stealers" (III.ii.320).
nostrum "ours" (Latin), with a pun on "nostrum" meaning "remedy"

After, when they disentwine
You from me and yours from mine,
Neither can be certain who
Was that I whose mine was you.
To the act again they go
More completely not to know.

Theft is theft and raid is raid
Though reciprocally made.
Lovers, the conclusion is
Doubled sighs and jealousies
In a single heart that grieves
For lost honour among thieves.

1946

To Juan° at the Winter Solstice

There is one story and one story only
That will prove worth your telling,
Whether as learned bard or gifted child;
To it all lines or lesser gauds belong
That startle with their shining
Such common stories as they stray into.

Is it of trees you tell, their months and virtues,
Or strange beasts that beset you,
Of birds that croak at you the Triple will?°
Or of the Zodiac and how slow it turns
Below the Boreal Crown,
Prison of all true kings that ever reigned?

Water to water, ark again to ark,
From woman back to woman:°
So each new victim treads unfalteringly
The never altered circuit of his fate,
Bringing twelve peers° as witness
Both to his starry rise and starry fall.

Or is it of the Virgin's° silver beauty,
All fish below the thighs?

Juan Graves's young son; the winter solstice
was a nodal point in the life and death cycles
of many primitive vegetation and sun gods.
The sun dies on the shortest day, and is reborn
in a new guise or person, as when one of
his young priests kills off the older one or
one king supplants another. In Graves's mythology, the young poetic acolyte or ephebe must
risk this cycle as well, and he chooses the
occasion, like an orthodox Jew explaining the
story of the Exodus to his sons on Passover, to
tell of the Muse who controls these cycles.
Triple will The White Goddess is the triple

queen of female role: mother, bride, and
killer-hag. Until Graves revealed her mysteries
they were hidden in primitive alphabets made
of tree-twigs, in birds' omens, in the constellations.
From . . . woman Born of woman biologically,
man returns to woman mythologically (to
mother earth, now as the hag of the grave).
twelve peers an archetypal number of companions (Apostles, etc.)
Virgin's Aphrodite's; some of these attributes
are obscure (e.g., the sexual quince held before her, as depicted on Cretan seals).

20   She in her left hand bears a leafy quince;
When, with her right she crooks a finger smiling,
How may the King hold back?
Royally then he barters life for love.

Or of the undying snake from chaos hatched,°
Whose coils contain the ocean,
Into whose chops with naked sword he springs,
Then in black water, tangled by the reeds,
Battles three days and nights,
30   To be spewed up beside her scalloped shore?

Much snow is falling, winds roar hollowly,
The owl hoots from the elder,
Fear in your heart cries to the loving-cup:
Sorrow to sorrow as the sparks fly upward.
The log groans and confesses
There is one story and one story only.

Dwell on her graciousness, dwell on her smiling,
Do not forget what flowers
The great boar trampled down in ivy time.
40   Her brow was creamy as the crested wave,
Her sea-blue eyes were wild
But nothing promised that is not performed.

            1946

The White Goddess°

All saints revile her, and all sober men
Ruled by the God Apollo's golden mean—
In scorn of which we sailed to find her°
In distant regions likeliest to hold her
Whom we desired above all things to know,
Sister of the mirage and echo.°

It was a virtue not to stay,
To go our headstrong and heroic way
Seeking her out at the volcano's head,
Among pack ice, or where the track had faded
Beyond the cavern of the seven sleepers:°

snake . . . hatched Ophion, the serpent created
out of chaos by Eurynome, dead and reborn
like Osiris, Adonis, Blake's Orc (though in
simpler form)
The White Goddess See notes on "To Juan
at the Winter Solstice"; this poem was originally
an epigraph to *The White Goddess*.
sailed to find her primarily the Argonauts, sailing
under Jason in the *Argo* for the Golden Fleece,
a relic of the earlier, pre-Hellenic, matriarchal
cult of the Triple Goddess. Graves began ad-

vancing this notion in his prose fiction *Hercules
My Shipmate* (1945).
mirage and echo thus the elusiveness of all
fictions
cavern . . . sleepers the old myth of the Seven
Sleepers of Ephesus, who took to a cave in the
year 250 to escape a persecution of Christians,
and slept for 230 years. Like most other bits
of famous folklore, Graves has an explanation
of it in *The White Goddess*, but even the
archetypal character of the "seven" of their
number will be obvious.

Whose broad high brow was white as any leper's,
Whose eyes were blue, with rowan-berry° lips,
With hair curled honey-coloured to white hips.

The sap of Spring in the young wood a-stir
Will celebrate with green the Mother,
And every song-bird shout awhile for her;
But we are gifted, even in November
Rawest of seasons, with so huge a sense
Of her nakedly worn magnificence
We forget cruelty and past betrayal,
Heedless of where the next bright bolt may fall.

1948

ALDOUS HUXLEY
1894–1963

Grandson of Thomas Henry Huxley, the great Victorian scientific theorist, great-nephew of Matthew Arnold, nephew of Mrs. Humphry Ward, the reformer and novelist, brother of the scientist Julian Huxley, and son of the editor of the *Cornhill Magazine*, Aldous Leonard Huxley might have pursued any one of a number of non-literary careers; but since he did not, his entire intellectual inheritance was, it seems, simultaneously available to him.

Born in Surrey in 1894, Huxley went to Eton and to Balliol, the most serious of Oxford colleges, from which he took his degree in 1915. He returned to Eton to teach for a while, flirted with the idea of studying medicine (he read literature rather than biology because of poor vision), wrote a good many poems (his first book of verse was published in Oxford in 1916), and by 1921 had published *Crome Yellow*, the first of a series of clever and brittle novels. Like the much more recherché and weird novels of Ronald Firbank, and like the satirical theatrical pieces and songs of Noel Coward, Huxley's glittering novels later came to represent the historical period they were so committed to denouncing from within. Starting out from a largely aesthetic critique of life style and of ideology in books like *Antic Hay* (1923—perhaps his best novel) and *Those Barren Leaves* (1925), he went on to write the more experimental *Point Counter Point* (1928), which is famous for its fictionalized portraits of the critic John Middleton Murry and D. H. Lawrence, with whom Huxley and his wife maintained a devoted and trusting friendship, particularly toward the end of Lawrence's life. Huxley's equally famous, half-satiric Utopia (or Dystopia), *Brave New World*, appeared in 1932; it is interesting not so much for its anticipation of a drug culture and an erotic life totally divorced from reproduction, as for the remarkable ambivalence felt toward the vision by its author. Huxley, who had struggled since the age of sixteen with near blindness (he was to recover a good portion of his sight in 1939, by a discipline of exercise), was evolving a complex kind of synthetic religion, first to emerge in his *The Perennial Philosophy* (1945) and resulting, after his move to Southern California in 1937, in an attachment to Indian Vedantic thought. At times influenced by Lawrence

rowan-berry again, because the rowan or mountain ash is sacred to her mysteries, involving such realms of fable as are dealt with in Sir James Frazer's *The Golden Bough* (1890) himself, Huxley moved in his later novels and meditative writings beyond skepticism to a kind of humanism open to Eastern influence, but still maintaining a critical relation with Western rationalism.

It may be in his large number of familiar and literary essays that Huxley is at his most profound, elegant, and moving. In such collections as *On the Margin* (1923), *Proper Studies* (1927), *Do What You Will* (1929), from which the essay given below is taken, and *Music at Night and Other Essays* (1931), Huxley demonstrated suppleness and fluency in the handling of a form that we tend to think of as having vanished with the nineteenth century, leaving our day with the philosophical novelist, the post-Symbolist poet, and perhaps, at best, the brilliant aphorist to find forms for wisdom. Without being informed by any particular technical expertise, an essay like "Wordsworth in the Tropics" derives from a widely read, ironically tested humane intelligence.

Wordsworth in the Tropics

In the neighbourhood of latitude fifty north, and for the last hundred years or thereabouts, it has been an axiom that Nature is divine and morally uplifting. For good Wordsworthians—and most serious-minded people are now Wordsworthians, either by direct inspiration or at second hand—a walk in the country is the equivalent of going to church, a tour through Westmorland [1] is as good as a pilgrimage to Jerusalem. To commune with the fields and waters, the woodlands and the hills, is to commune, according to our modern and northern ideas, with the visible manifestations of the 'Wisdom and Spirit of the Universe.'

The Wordsworthian who exports this pantheistic worship of Nature to the tropics is liable to have his religious convictions somewhat rudely disturbed. Nature, under a vertical sun, and nourished by the equatorial rains, is not at all like that chaste, mild deity who presides over the *Gemütlichkeit*,[2] the prettiness, the cozy sublimities of the Lake District. The worst that Wordsworth's goddess ever did to him was to make him hear

> Low breathings coming after me, and sounds
> Of undistinguishable motion, steps
> Almost as silent as the turf they trod; [3]

was to make him realize, in the shape of 'a huge peak, black and huge,' the existence of 'unknown modes of being.' He seems to have imagined that this was the worst Nature *could* do. A few weeks in Malaya or Borneo would have undeceived him. Wandering in the hothouse darkness of the jungle, he would not have felt so serenely certain of those 'Presences of Nature,' those 'Souls of Lonely Places,' which he was in the habit of worshipping on the shores of Windermere and Rydal.[4] The sparse inhabitants of the equatorial forest are all believers in devils. When one has visited, in even the most superficial

---

1. The northern county which, together with Cumberland, contains the Lake District, Wordsworth's actual and visionary home.
2. German for a kind of spiritual coziness.
3. From Wordsworth's *The Prelude* I.323–25.
4. Two of Wordsworth's lakes.

manner, the places where they live, it is difficult not to share their faith. The jungle is marvelous, fantastic, beautiful; but it is also terrifying, it is also profoundly sinister. There is something in what, for lack of a better word, we must call the character of great forests—even in those of temperate lands—which is foreign, appalling, fundamentally and utterly inimical to intruding man. The life of those vast masses of swarming vegetation is alien to the human spirit and hostile to it. Meredith, in his 'Woods of Westermaine,' [5] has tried reassuringly to persuade us that our terrors are unnecessary, that the hostility of these vegetable forces is more apparent than real, and that if we will but trust Nature we shall find our fears transformed into serenity, joy, and rapture. This may be sound philosophy in the neighbourhood of Dorking; [6] but it begins to be dubious even in the forests of Germany—there is too much of them for a human being to feel himself at ease within their enormous glooms; and when the woods of Borneo are substituted for those of Westermaine, Meredith's comforting doctrine becomes frankly ridiculous.

It is not the sense of solitude that distresses the wanderer in equatorial jungles. Loneliness is bearable enough—for a time, at any rate. There is something actually rather stimulating and exciting about being in an empty place where there is no life but one's own. Taken in reasonably small doses, the Sahara exhilarates, like alcohol. Too much of it, however (I speak, at any rate, for myself), has the depressing effect of the second bottle of Burgundy. But in any case it is not loneliness that oppresses the equatorial traveller: it is too much company; it is the uneasy feeling that he is an alien in the midst of an innumerable throng of hostile beings. To us who live beneath a temperate sky and in the age of Henry Ford,[7] the worship of Nature comes almost naturally. It is easy to love a feeble and already conquered enemy. But an enemy with whom one is still at war, an unconquered, unconquerable, ceaselessly active enemy—no; one does not, one should not, love him. One respects him, perhaps; one has a salutary fear of him; and one goes on fighting. In our latitudes the hosts of Nature have mostly been vanquished and enslaved. Some few detachments, it is true, still hold the field against us. There are wild woods and mountains, marshes and heaths, even in England. But they are there only on sufferance, because we have chosen, out of our good pleasure, to leave them their freedom. It has not been worth our while to reduce them to slavery. We love them because we are the masters, because we know that at any moment we can overcome them as we overcame their fellows. The inhabitants of the tropics have no such comforting reasons for adoring the sinister forces which hem them in on every side. For us, the notion 'river' implies (how obviously!) the notion 'bridge.' When we think of a plain, we think of agriculture, towns, and good roads. The corollary of mountain is tunnel; of swamp, an embankment; of distance, a railway. At latitude zero, however, the obvious is not the same as with us. Rivers imply wading, swimming, alligators. Plains mean swamps, forests, fevers. Mountains are either dangerous or impassable. To travel is to hack one's way laboriously through a tangled, prickly, and venomous

5. A poem by George Meredith (1828–1909) which seeks an almost providential operation in biological phases and cycles.

6. A comfortable town in Surrey, near London.

7. Here taken as the inventor of the assembly line and of mass production.

darkness. 'God made the country,' said Cowper, in his rather too blank verse.[8] In New Guinea he would have had his doubts; he would have longed for the man-made town.

The Wordsworthian adoration of Nature has two principal defects. The first, as we have seen, is that it is only possible in a country where Nature has been nearly or quite enslaved to man. The second is that it is only possible for those who are prepared to falsify their immediate intuitions of Nature. For Nature, even in the temperate zone, is always alien and inhuman, and occasionally diabolic. Meredith explicitly invites us to explain any unpleasant experiences away. We are to interpret them, Pangloss[9] fashion, in terms of a preconceived philosophy; after which, all will surely be for the best in the best of all possible Westermaines. Less openly, Wordsworth asks us to make the same falsification of immediate experience. It is only very occasionally that he admits the existence in the world around him of those 'unknown modes of being' of which our immediate intuitions of things make us so disquietingly aware. Normally what he does is to pump the dangerous Unknown out of Nature and refill the emptied forms of hills and woods, flowers and waters, with something more reassuringly familiar—with humanity, with Anglicanism. He will not admit that a yellow primrose is simply a yellow primrose—beautiful, but essentially strange, having its own alien life apart. He wants it to possess some sort of soul, to exist humanly, not simply flowerily. He wants the earth to be more than earthy, to be a divine person. But the life of vegetation is radically unlike the life of man: the earth has a mode of being that is certainly not the mode of being of a person. 'Let Nature be your teacher,' says Wordsworth. The advice is excellent. But how strangely he himself puts it into practice! Instead of listening humbly to what the teacher says, he shuts his ears and himself dictates the lesson he desires to hear. The pupil knows better than his master; the worshipper substitutes his own oracles for those of the god. Instead of accepting the lesson as it is given to his immediate intuitions, he distorts it rationalistically into the likeness of a parson's sermon or a professorial lecture. Our direct intuitions of Nature tell us that the world is bottomlessly strange: alien, even when it is kind and beautiful; having innumerable modes of being that are not our modes; always mysteriously not personal, not conscious, not moral; often hostile and sinister; sometimes even unimaginably, because inhumanly, evil. In his youth, it would seem, Wordsworth left his direct intuitions of the world unwarped.

> The sounding cataract
> Haunted me like a passion: the tall rock,
> The mountain, and the deep and gloomy wood,
> Their colours and their forms, were then to me
> An appetite; a feeling and a love,
> That had no need of a remoter charm,
> By thought supplied, nor any interest
> Unborrowed from the eye.[10]

8. William Cowper (1731–1800); the quotation is from *The Task* I.749: "God made the country, and man made the town."

9. Dr. Pangloss, Voltaire's optimistic philosopher in *Candide,* who held that this is "the best of all possible worlds," despite much evidence to the contrary.

10. From "Lines Composed a Few Miles Above Tintern Abbey," ll. 76–83.

As the years passed, however, he began to interpret them in terms of a precon-ceived philosophy. Procrustes-like,[11] he tortured his feelings and perceptions until they fitted his system. By the time he was thirty,

> The immeasurable height
> Of woods decaying, never to be decayed,
> The stationary blasts of waterfalls—
> The torrents shooting from the clear blue sky,
> The rocks that muttered close upon our ears,
> Black drizzling crags that spake by the wayside
> As if a voice were in them, the sick sight
> And giddy prospect of the raving stream,
> The unfettered clouds and regions of the heavens,
> Tumult and peace, the darkness and the light—
> Were all like workings of one mind, the features
> Of the same face, blossoms upon one tree,
> Characters of the great Apocalypse,
> The types and symbols of eternity,
> Of first, and last, and midst, and without end.[12]

'Something far more deeply interfused' had made its appearance on the Wordsworthian scene. The god of Anglicanism had crept under the skin of things, and all the stimulatingly inhuman strangeness of Nature had become as flatly familiar as a page from a textbook of metaphysics or theology. As familiar and as safely simple. Pantheistically[13] interpreted, our intuitions of Nature's endless varieties of impersonal mysteriousness lose all their exciting and dis-turbing quality. It makes the world seem delightfully cozy, if you can pretend that all the many alien things about you are really only manifestations of one person. It is fear of the labyrinthine flux and complexity of phenomena that has driven men to philosophy, to science, to theology—fear of the complex reality driving them to invent a simpler, more manageable, and, therefore, consoling fiction. For simple, in comparison with the external reality of which we have direct intuitions, childishly simple is even the most elaborate and subtle system devised by the human mind. Most of the philosophical systems hitherto popular have not been subtle and elaborate even by human standards. Even by human standards they have been crude, bald, preposterously straightforward. Hence their popularity. Their simplicity has rendered them instantly comprehensible. Weary with much wandering in the maze of phenomena, frightened by the inhospitable strangeness of the world, men have rushed into the systems pre-pared for them by philosophers and founders of religions, as they would rush from a dark jungle into the haven of a well-lit, commodious house. With a sigh of relief and a thankful feeling that here at last is their true home, they settle down in their snug metaphysical villa and go to sleep. And how furious they are when any one comes rudely knocking at the door to tell them that their

11. A giant of Greek myth, who chopped his guests down to, or stretched them out to, the size of his bed.
12. From *The Prelude* VI.624–40; this is a passage about crossing the Alps. Ll. 627–28: "And in the narrow rent at every turn / Winds thwarting winds, bewildered and forlorn" are omitted.
13. Pantheism finds that God is everything everywhere.

villa is jerry-built, dilapidated, unfit for human habitation, even non-existent! Men have been burnt at the stake for even venturing to criticize the colour of the front door or the shape of the third-floor windows.

That man must build himself some sort of metaphysical shelter in the midst of the jungle of immediately apprehended reality is obvious. No practical activity, no scientific research, no speculation is possible without some preliminary hypothesis about the nature and the purpose of things. The human mind cannot deal with the universe directly, nor even with its own immediate intuitions of the universe. Whenever it is a question of thinking about the world or of practically modifying it, men can only work on a symbolic plan of the universe, only a simplified, two-dimensional map of things abstracted by the mind out of the complex and multifarious reality of immediate intuition. History shows that these hypotheses about the nature of things are valuable even when, as later experience reveals, they are false. Man approaches the unattainable truth through a succession of errors. Confronted by the strange complexity of things, he invents, quite arbitrarily, a simple hypothesis to explain and justify the world. Having invented, he proceeds to act and think in terms of this hypothesis, as though it were correct. Experience gradually shows him where his hypothesis is unsatisfactory and how it should be modified. Thus, great scientific discoveries have been made by men seeking to verify quite erroneous theories about the nature of things. The discoveries have necessitated a modification of the original hypotheses, and further discoveries have been made in the effort to verify the modifications—discoveries which, in their turn, have led to yet further modifications. And so on, indefinitely. Philosophical and religious hypotheses, being less susceptible of experimental verification than the hypotheses of science, have undergone far less modification. For example, the pantheistic hypothesis of Wordsworth is an ancient doctrine, which human experience has hardly modified throughout history. And rightly, no doubt. For it is obvious that there must be some sort of unity underlying the diversity of phenomena; for if there were not, the world would be quite unknowable. Indeed, it is precisely in the knowableness of things, in the very fact that they are known, that their fundamental unity consists. The world which we know, and which our minds have fabricated out of goodness knows what mysterious things in themselves, possesses the unity which our minds have imposed upon it. It is part of our thought, hence fundamentally homogeneous. Yes, the world is obviously one. But at the same time it is no less obviously diverse. For if the world were absolutely one, it would no longer be knowable, it would cease to exist. Thought must be divided against itself before it can come to any knowledge of itself. Absolute oneness is absolute nothingness: homogeneous perfection, as the Hindus perceived and courageously recognized, is equivalent to non-existence, is nirvana.[14] The Christian idea of a perfect heaven that is something other than a non-existence is a contradiction in terms. The world in which we live may be fundamentally one, but it is a unity divided up into a great many diverse fragments. A tree, a table, a newspaper, a piece of artificial silk are all made of wood. But

---

14. In Hindu thought, a total merging of an inner presence with one totally beyond (Atman and Brahman); in Buddhism, a state of total disengagement from the turning wheel of process. Huxley probably means the first of these.

they are, none the less, distinct and separate objects. It is the same with the world at large. Our immediate intuitions are of diversity. We have only to open our eyes to recognize a multitude of different phenomena. These intuitions of diversity are as correct, as well justified, as is our intellectual conviction of the fundamental homogeneity of the various parts of the world with one another and with ourselves. Circumstances have led humanity to set an ever-increasing premium on the conscious and intellectual comprehension of things. Modern man's besetting temptation is to sacrifice his direct perceptions and spontaneous feelings to his reasoned reflections; to prefer in all circumstances the verdict of his intellect to that of his immediate intuitions. '*L'homme est visiblement fait pour penser,*' says Pascal; '*c'est toute sa dignité et tout son mérite; et tout son devoir est de penser comme il faut.*[15] Noble words; but do they happen to be true? Pascal seems to forget that man has something else to do besides think: he must live. Living may not be so dignified or meritorious as thinking (particularly when you happen to be, like Pascal, a chronic invalid); but it is, perhaps unfortunately, a necessary process. If one would live well, one must live completely, with the whole being—with the body and the instincts, as well as with the conscious mind. A life lived, as far as may be, exclusively from the consciousness and in accordance with the considered judgments of the intellect, is a stunted life, a half-dead life. This is a fact that can be confirmed by daily observation. But consciousness, the intellect, the spirit, have acquired an inordinate prestige; and such is men's snobbish respect for authority, such is their pedantic desire to be consistent, that they go on doing their best to lead the exclusively conscious, spiritual, and intellectual life, in spite of its manifest disadvantages. To know is pleasant; it is exciting to be conscious; the intellect is a valuable instrument, and for certain purposes the hypotheses which it fabricates are of great practical value. Quite true. But, therefore, say the moralists and men of science, drawing conclusions only justified by their desire for consistency, therefore *all* life should be lived from the head, consciously, *all* phenomena should at *all* times be interpreted in terms of the intellect's hypotheses. The religious teachers are of a slightly different opinion. All life, according to them, should be lived spiritually, not intellectually. Why? On the grounds, as we discover when we push our analysis far enough, that certain occasional psychological states, currently called spiritual, are extremely agreeable and have valuable consequences in the realm of social behaviour. The unprejudiced observer finds it hard to understand why these people should set such store by consistency of thought and action. Because oysters are occasionally pleasant, it does not follow that one should make of oysters one's exclusive diet. Nor should one take castor-oil every day because castor-oil is occasionally good for one. Too much consistency is as bad for the mind as it is for the body. Consistency is contrary to nature, contrary to life. The only completely consistent people are the dead. Consistent intellectualism and spirituality may be socially valuable, up to a point; but they make, gradually, for individual death. And individual death, when the slow murder has been consummated, is finally social death. So that the social utility of pure intellectualism and pure spirituality is only apparent

15. "Man is patently made for thinking; it is his entire dignity and his entire virtue, and his only duty is to think correctly." Blaise Pascal (1623–62), *Pensées.*

and temporary. What is needed is, as ever, a compromise. Life must be lived in different ways at different moments. The only satisfactory way of existing in the modern, highly specialized world is to live with two personalities. A Dr. Jekyll [16] that does the metaphysical and scientific thinking, that transacts business in the city, adds up figures, designs machines, and so forth. And a natural, spontaneous Mr. Hyde to do the physical, instinctive living in the intervals of work. The two personalities should lead their unconnected lives apart, without poaching on one another's preserves or inquiring too closely into one another's activities. Only by living discretely and inconsistently can we preserve both the man and the citizen, both the intellectual and the spontaneous animal being, alive within us. The solution may not be very satisfactory; but it is, I believe now (though once I thought differently), the best that, in the modern circumstances, can be devised.

The poet's place, it seems to me, is with the Mr. Hydes of human nature. He should be, as Blake [17] remarked of Milton, 'of the devil's party without knowing it'—or preferably with the full consciousness of being of the devil's party. There are so many intellectual and moral angels battling for rationalism, good citizenship, and pure spirituality; so many and such eminent ones, so very vocal and authoritative! The poor devil in man needs all the support and advocacy he can get. The artist is his natural champion. When an artist deserts to the side of the angels, it is the most odious of treasons. How unforgivable, for example, is Tolstoy! Tolstoy, the perfect Mr. Hyde, the complete embodiment, if ever there was one, of non-intellectual, non-moral, instinctive life—Tolstoy, who betrayed his own nature, betrayed his art, betrayed life itself, in order to fight against the devil's party of his earlier allegiances, under the standard of Dr. Jesus-Jekyll. Wordsworth's betrayal was not so spectacular: he was never so wholly of the devil's party as Tolstoy. Still, it was bad enough. It is difficult to forgive him for so utterly repenting his youthful passions and enthusiasms, and becoming, personally as well as politically, the anglican tory. One remembers B. R. Haydon's [18] account of the poet's reactions to that charming classical sculpture of Cupid and Psyche. 'The devils!' he said malignantly, after a long-drawn contemplation of their marble embrace. 'The devils!' And he was not using the word in the complimentary sense in which I have employed it here: he was expressing his hatred of passion and life, he was damning the young man he had himself been—the young man who had hailed the French Revolution with delight and begotten an illegitimate child. From being an ardent lover of the nymphs, he had become one of those all too numerous

> woodmen who expel
> Love's gentle dryads from the haunts of life,
> And vex the nightingales in every dell.[19]

Yes, even the nightingales he vexed. Even the nightingales, though the poor birds can never, like those all too human dryads, have led him into sexual

16. "Dr. Jekyll and Mr. Hyde" is Robert Louis Stevenson's story of a benign scientist who, under the influence of a drug, metamorphoses into his bestial *alter ego*.
17. This famous remark is from *The Marriage of Heaven and Hell.*
18. Benjamin Robert Haydon (1786–1846), painter, friend of Wordsworth and other poets.
19. Shelley, "The Woodman and the Nightingale," ll. 68–70.

temptation. Even the innocuous nightingales were moralised, spiritualised, turned into citizens and anglicans—and along with the nightingales, the whole of animate and inanimate Nature.

The change in Wordsworth's attitude toward Nature is symptomatic of his general apostasy. Beginning as what I may call a natural aesthete, he transformed himself, in the course of years, into a moralist, a thinker. He used his intellect to distort his exquisitely acute and subtle intuitions of the world, to explain away their often disquieting strangeness, to simplify them into a comfortable metaphysical unreality. Nature had endowed him with the poet's gift of seeing more than ordinarily far into the brick walls of external reality, of intuitively comprehending the character of the bricks, of feeling the quality of their being, and establishing the appropriate relationship with them. But he preferred to think his gifts away. He preferred, in the interests of a preconceived religious theory, to ignore the disquieting strangeness of things, to interpret the impersonal diversity of Nature in terms of a divine, anglican unity. He chose, in a word, to be a philosopher, comfortably at home with a man-made and, therefore, thoroughly comprehensible system, rather than a poet adventuring for adventure's sake through the mysterious world revealed by his direct and undistorted intuitions.

It is a pity that he never travelled beyond the boundaries of Europe. A voyage through the tropics would have cured him of his too easy and comfortable pantheism. A few months in the jungle would have convinced him that the diversity and utter strangeness of Nature are at least as real and significant as its intellectually discovered unity. Nor would he have felt so certain, in the damp and stifling darkness, among the leeches and the malevolently tangled rattans,[20] of the divinely anglican character of that fundamental unity. He would have learned once more to treat Nature naturally, as he treated it in his youth; to react to it spontaneously, loving where love was the appropriate emotion, fearing, hating, fighting whenever Nature presented itself to his intuition as being, not merely strange, but hostile, inhumanly evil. A voyage would have taught him this. But Wordsworth never left his native continent. Europe is so well gardened that it resembles a work of art, a scientific theory, a neat metaphysical system. Man has re-created Europe in his own image. Its tamed and temperate Nature confirmed Wordsworth in his philosophizings. The poet, the devil's partisan were doomed; the angels triumphed. Alas!

1929

W. H. AUDEN
1907–

The major English poet and man of letters to follow Eliot has been a strange sort of representative of the second generation of modernism. A socialist; a Freudian; a student and transmitter of Germanic rather than Romance Continental literary traditions; a temperament that has always felt a kinship with the scientific imagination, finding itself more at home with Goethe than with Baudelaire; a poetic voice

20. Tropical reed-like palms with pliable stems.

which, no matter how devoted to strategic *personae* and disguises, mastered an expository mode and the art of verse essay at a moment in literary history when these had become most discredited; a devoted composer of occasional poems; a Marxist of sorts who became a Christian; a creator of opera libretti and translator-adapter of opera; a devotee and author of light verse—all of these would seem divergent enough from any career we might have projected for a modern writer of such importance.

Wystan Hugh Auden has been all these and more. He emigrated to the United States in 1934 and became an American citizen, reciprocating in an ironic way the transatlantic displacements of T. S. Eliot and, before him, Henry James. There is a very real sense in which the work of Auden's later years can be called American poetry (language alone, for example: in "The Fall of Rome" he rhymes "clerk" with "work" instead of with "dark"); it is nevertheless part of that same quintessentially English poetic career that started among the members of a particularly self-conscious generation at Oxford in the mid–1920's.

Auden's early work is often spoken of in the context of his literary friendships—with Stephen Spender, Christopher Isherwood, Louis MacNeice, and others; his early poems and, in particular, his remarkable little book called *The Orators* (1930), are full of the almost conspiratorial sense of a strange avant-garde group. Perhaps something should be said of the new spirit that gave this post-World War I generation its sense of itself. Actually, various fashions in generation gaps have succeeded each other ever since the Romantic period invented the condition of adolescence and put a premium on its chronological and moral in-betweenness. Changes of style in the relation of one generation's attitudes toward those of its predecessor have been accompanied by changes of style in the expression of expressing those relations. The French Romantic poet Alfred de Musset had characterized his own generation as played-out and spiritually weakened. The concept of the *poète maudit,* the accursed, alienated artist, had pervaded nineteenth-century French literature before being imported into English tradition first by the writers of the 1890's, then by Eliot. Yet the basic healthiness of society itself, or at least of those principles its institutions were designed, however badly, to embody, had remained an English theme; the Victorian imagination continues to amaze us in the ways it could accompany that theme with both high vision and tough moral perception.

World War I finally ended the possibility of such a view; but even before the war, instances of new versions of a Byronic, ironic youth had begun to appear. The actualities of the life and works of an Aubrey Beardsley were matched by the fictional brilliancies of fierce young gilded youths like Saki's (H. H. Munro's) Clovis or Reginald in his turn-of-the-century sketches. The latter of these young men is reminded by an interlocutor "Some one who Must Not be Contradicted said that a man must be a success by the time he's thirty, or never." "To have reached thirty," said Reginald, "is to have failed in life." Saki built the bridge between the comedy of Oscar Wilde and the post-World War I satiric hilarities of the fiction of Evelyn Waugh, Aldous Huxley, and Ronald Firbank. The role of the pranking doomster, only faintly sinister in the unassailable world of country houses, Continental travel, and aristocratic connections of Saki's stories, took on a new meaning for the intellectual and moral life of young men at Oxford in the 1920's. Many of the cleverest of them became communists, and even those who wished to maintain something of an older, aestheticist tradition, were either revising it along Eliot's lines or adapting it to some fresh social vision. Unlike Eliot, whose conversion to Anglo-Catholicism was accompanied by professions of commitment to royalism in politics and classicism in literature, Auden's later reversion to the homely Anglicanism of his boyhood household was influenced along the way by Søren Kierkegaard's critique of philosophy and by the "crisis theology" of Paul Tillich and Reinhold Niebuhr.

Auden's personal sense of generation was always more of an antithetical cycle, in some general sense, against an older primary state, than merely a Marxist or an aestheticist engagement against the bourgeois. Auden was born in York, the son of a doctor, and showed an early interest in matters mechanical and geological. Prepared at Gresham's School in Cheshire, he went to Christ Church, Oxford, taught school, lived in the pre-Hitler Berlin of the Brecht-Weill operas and entertainments, took literary journeys to Iceland and China, collaborated with Louis MacNeice on a book about their Iceland trip and with Christopher Isherwood on plays, and then went to Spain. The Spanish Civil War (1936–38) resulted from the counter-insurgency of the Spanish Republican government to the military coup of General Francisco Franco, who was backed in the struggle by weapons and men supplied by Hitler and Mussolini, and moral support supplied by the Vatican. A whole range of political viewpoints supported the Loyalist or Republican cause: those with a distaste for fascism saw the Spanish war as a testing ground for a far more general European conflict, while direct Soviet intervention on the Loyalist side produced some very nasty political results (such as the murder of anarchists and other factions supposedly allied with them) which the Stalinist, or official Soviet-communist-sympathizing adherents of the Spanish cause, refused to admit. It would take the self-searching candor of the socialist George Orwell to reveal, in *Homage to Catalonia* (1938), some of the unpleasant realities which even the committed would have to face. But whether one's will was to "build the Just City" or to find "the suicide pact, the romantic / Death," as Auden wrote in a poem in 1937, commitment was obligatory: "I accept, for / I am your choice, your decision: yes, I am Spain." But the inconclusiveness of such decisions, save in the death of many young English intellectuals who went to fight there, was typified by Auden's return to England and then, as the inevitable conflict of World War II drew nearer, by his emigration to the United States in 1939, a private response to what seemed increasing social hopelessness.

Auden's earlier poetry was shocking and immediately famous. He drew on many sources—Anglo-Saxon alliterative verse and its puzzling kennings, balladry, cabaret and music-hall lyrics, many traditions of complex verse form—and coupled these with an amazing range of diction—slang, technical, scientific, and philosophical vocabularies of all sorts, and even eighteenth-century personifications. From the beginning he always used a wide array of metrical forms, rhyme schemes, and structural patterns, as if to suggest that each kind of form had a different sort of modality, a different tone. His long poems have included the strange mixed-prose-and-verse of *The Orators*, the varied forms of *The Sea and the Mirror* (a verse commentary on *The Tempest* of Shakespeare, published in 1944), *The Age of Anxiety* (1947)—an eclogue in a Third Avenue bar, projected in unrhymed alliterative verse—and the tight, highly allusive name-dropping couplets of his 1941 *New Year Letter*.

Auden's occasional poetry and his earlier political poems have given way, in later years, to an almost sermonizing meditative style, but many of the elements that made him so popular as a young modernist are still present in his imaginative world. He still admires Byron and dislikes Shelley. His neoclassicism has become more and more apparent. He has produced an impressive body of prose criticism, *The Enchafèd Flood* of 1950 being perhaps the most remarkable. If his early poems typified the New in England between-the-wars, his reasonable and knowing voice had a strong influence on American poetry of the 1940's and '50's.

Auden has continually revised and rewritten his poems for successive collected editions, and even deleted certain earlier poems (such as his "September 1, 1939," which the editors would like to have reprinted). Auden did this not so much for ideological reasons but because of an awareness that topical or momentarily "relevant" verse always produces what subsequent assessment will see as dated. But what is important throughout his work is the constancy of his major themes: the sanctity of the private heart and the necessity for protecting it even when, to protect the hearts of others, one must act publicly; the natural providence of body and landscape; and the belief in the possibility—especially by a mind technically skilled in the apprehension of the phony—of wisdom.

The Watershed

Who stands, the crux left of the watershed,
On the wet road between the chafing grass
Below him sees dismantled washing-floors,
Snatches of tramline° running to a wood,
An industry already comatose,
Yet sparsely living. A ramshackle engine
At Cashwell raises water; for ten years
It lay in flooded workings° until this,
Its latter office, grudgingly performed.
10 And, further, here and there, though many dead
Lie under the poor soil, some acts are chosen
Taken from recent winters; two there were
Cleaned out a damaged shaft by hand, clutching
The winch a gale would tear them from; one died
During a storm, the fells° impassable,
Not at his village, but in wooden shape
Through long abandoned levels nosed his way
And in his final valley went to ground.
Go home, now, stranger, proud of your young stock,
20 Stranger, turn back again, frustrate and vexed:
This land, cut off, will not communicate,
Be no accessory content to one
Aimless for faces rather there than here.
Beams from your car may cross a bedroom wall,
They wake no sleeper; you may hear the wind
Arriving driven from the ignorant sea

tramline rail lines   fells high hills, and the fields along their sides
workings excavations; here, for a quarry

To hurt itself on pane, on bark of elm
Where sap unbaffled rises, being spring;
But seldom this. Near you, taller than grass,
Ears poise before decision, scenting danger.

1928

Song°

'O where are you going?' said reader to rider,
'That valley is fatal when furnaces burn,
Yonder's the midden° whose odours will madden,
That gap is the grave where the tall return.'

'O do you imagine,' said fearer to farer,
'That dusk will delay on your path to the pass,
Your diligent looking discover the lacking
Your footsteps feel from granite to grass?'

10 'O what was that bird,' said horror to hearer,
'Did you see that shape in the twisted trees?
Behind you swiftly the figure comes softly,
The spot on your skin is a shocking disease?'

'Out of this house'—said rider to reader,
'Yours never will'—said farer to fearer,
'They're looking for you'—said hearer to horror,
As he° left them there, as he left them there.

1932   1932

Letter to a Wound°

The maid has just cleared away tea and I shall not be disturbed until supper.
I shall be quite alone in this room, free to think of you if I choose, and believe
me, my dear, I do choose. For a long time now I have been aware that you are
taking up more of my life every day, but I am always being surprised to find
how far this has gone. Why, it was only yesterday, I took down all those photographs from my mantelpiece—Gabriel, Olive, Mrs. Marshall, Molim, and the

---

Song This poem is based on the folk song
called "The Cutty Wren" (see note to "Robin
and Bobin" in David Jones, *In Parenthesis*),
beginning " 'O where are you going?' said
Milder to Malder / 'Where are you going?'
said Festel to Fose.' " It concludes *The Orators*
with rapid instances of escape from one's pre-

dicament (social, economic, sexual, imaginative).
midden dungheap
he "Rider," "farer," and "hearer" are all the
same person, the resolved hero. His questioners
are rather like the people called "They" in the
limericks of Edward Lear, the warning father
in Lewis Carroll's "Jabberwocky," and the uncle
in same author's "The Hunting of the Snark."

Wound Manifestly, a cancer; beyond that, the kind of interior "wound," like homosexuality, or even more significantly, an artist's calling, whose discovery demands a reassessment
of priorities; beyond that, the condition of sinfulness that a Christian would equate with
his very humanity. On this prose poem's first publication in *The Orators*, Auden did not
give his own text the last of these readings.

others. How could I have left them there like that so long, memorials to my days of boasting? As it is, I've still far too many letters. (Vow. To have a grand clearance this week—hotel bills—bus tickets from Damascus, presentation pocket-mirrors, foreign envelopes, etc.)

Looking back now to that time before I lost my 'health' (Was that really only last February?) I can't recognize myself. The discontinuity seems absolute. But of course the change was really gradual. Over and over again in the early days when I was in the middle of writing a newsy letter to M., or doing tricks in the garden to startle R. and C., you showed your resentment by a sudden bout of pain. I had outbursts, wept even, at what seemed to me then your insane jealousy, your bad manners, your passion for spoiling things. What a little idiot I was not to trust your more exquisite judgment, which declined absolutely to let me go on behaving like a child. People would have tried to explain it all. You would not insult me with pity. I think I've learned my lesson now. Thank you, my dear. I'll try my hardest not to let you down again.

Do you realize we have been together now for almost a year? Eighteen months ago, if anyone had foretold this to me I should have asked him to leave the house. Haven't I ever told you about my first interview with the surgeon? He kept me waiting three-quarters of an hour. It was raining outside. Cars passed or drew up squeaking by the curb. I sat in my overcoat, restlessly turning over the pages of back numbers of illustrated papers, accounts of the Battle of Jutland,° jokes about special constables and conscientious objectors. A lady came down with a little girl. They put on their hats, speaking in whispers, tight-lipped. Mr. Gangle° would see me. A nurse was just coming out as I entered, carrying a white-enamelled bowl containing a pair of scissors, some instruments, soiled swabs of cotton wool. Mr. Gangle was washing his hands. The examination on the hard leather couch under the brilliant light was soon over. Washing again as I dressed he said nothing. Then reaching for a towel turned, 'I'm afraid,' he said. . . .

Outside I saw nothing, walked, not daring to think. I've lost everything, I've failed. I wish I was dead. And now, here we are, together, intimate, mature.

Later. At dinner Mrs. T. announced that she'd accepted an invitation for me to a whist-drive° at the Stewarts' on Wednesday. 'It's so good for you to get out in the evenings sometimes. You're as bad as Mr. Bedder.' She babbled on, secretly disappointed, I think, that I did not make more protest. Certainly six months ago she couldn't have brought it off, which makes me think what a great change has come over us recently. In what I might call our honeymoon stage, when we had both realized what we meant to each other (how slow I was, wasn't I?) and that this would always be so, I was obsessed (You too a little? No?) by what seemed my extraordinary fortune. I pitied everybody. Little do you know, I said to myself, looking at my neighbour on the bus, what has happened to the little man in the black hat sitting next to you. I was always smiling. I mortally offended Mrs. Hunter, I remember, when she was describing

Battle of Jutland major naval battle of World War I, the question of who actually won it being always and tiresomely in dispute
Mr. Gangle Surgeons in England are called "Mr." (not "Dr.").
whist-drive card party

her son's career at Cambridge. She thought I was laughing at her. In restaurants I found myself drawing pictures of you on the bottom of the table mats. 'Who'll ever guess what that is?' Once, when a whore accosted me, I bowed, 'I deeply regret it, Madam, but I have a friend.' Once I carved on a seat in the park 'We have sat here. You'd better not.'

Now I see that all that sort of thing is juvenile and silly, merely a reaction against insecurity and shame. You as usual of course were the first to realize this, making yourself felt whenever I had been particularly rude or insincere.

Thanks to you, I have come to see a profound significance in relations I never dreamt of considering before, an old lady's affection for a small boy, the Waterhouses and their retriever, the curious bond between Offal and Snig, the partners in the hardware shop on the front. Even the close-ups on the films no longer disgust nor amuse me. On the contrary they sometimes make me cry; knowing you has made me understand.

It's getting late and I have to be up betimes in the morning. You are so quiet these days that I get quite nervous, remove the dressing. No I am safe, you are still there. The wireless says that the frost is coming. When it does, we know what to expect, don't we? But I am calm. I can wait. The surgeon was dead right. Nothing will ever part us. Good-night and God bless you, my dear.

Better burn this.°

1932

Paysage Moralisé°

Hearing of harvests rotting in the valleys,
Seeing at end of street the barren mountains,
Round corners coming suddenly on water,
Knowing them shipwrecked who were launched for islands,
We honour founders of these starving cities
Whose honour is the image of our sorrow,

Which cannot see its likeness in their sorrow
That brought them desperate to the brink of valleys;
Dreaming of evening walks through learned cities
They reined their violent horses on the mountains,
Those fields like ships to castaways on islands,
Visions of green to them who craved for water.

They built by rivers and at night the water
Running past windows comforted their sorrow;
Each in his little bed conceived of islands
Where every day was dancing in the valleys
And all the green trees blossomed on the mountains,
Where love was innocent, being far from cities.

10

Better burn this the usual prudent postscript to a clandestine love-letter

Paysage Moralisé "Moralized landscape"—the interpretation of pictorial scenes in ethical and psychological ways, as in 17th- and 18th-century painting. This sestina (see Glossary) develops the latent meanings in its terminal words in a way like that of Sir Philip Sidney's double sestina, "Ye Goatherd Gods."

But dawn came back and they were still in cities;
20 No marvellous creature rose up from the water;
There was still gold and silver in the mountains
But hunger was a more immediate sorrow,
Although to moping villages in valleys
Some waving pilgrims were describing islands . . .

'The gods,' they promised, 'visit us from islands,
Are stalking, head-up, lovely, through our cities;
Now is the time to leave your wretched valleys
And sail with them across the lime-green water,
Sitting at their white sides, forget your sorrow,
30 The shadow cast across your lives by mountains.'

So many, doubtful, perished in the mountains,
Climbing up crags to get a view of islands,
So many, fearful, took with them their sorrow
Which stayed them when they reached unhappy cities,
So many, careless, dived and drowned in water,
So many, wretched, would not leave their valleys.

It is our sorrow. Shall it melt? Then water
Would gush, flush, green these mountains and these valleys,
And we rebuild our cities, not dream of islands.
1933   1933

Lullaby

Lay your sleeping head, my love,
Human on my faithless arm;
Time and fevers burn away
Individual beauty from
Thoughtful children, and the grave
Proves the child ephemeral:
But in my arms till break of day
Let the living creature lie,
Mortal, guilty, but to me
10 The entirely beautiful.

Soul and body have no bounds:
To lovers as they lie upon
Her tolerant enchanted slope
In their ordinary swoon,
Grave the vision Venus sends
Of supernatural sympathy,
Universal love and hope;
While an abstract insight wakes

20 Among the glaciers and the rocks
The hermit's carnal° ecstasy.

Certainty, fidelity
On the stroke of midnight pass
Like vibrations of a bell
And fashionable madmen raise
Their pedantic boring cry:
Every farthing° of the cost,
All the dreaded cards foretell,
Shall be paid, but from this night
Not a whisper, not a thought,
30 Not a kiss nor look be lost.

Beauty, midnight, vision dies:
Let the winds of dawn that blow
Softly round your dreaming head
Such a day of welcome show
Eye and knocking heart may bless,
Find our mortal world enough;
Noons of dryness find you fed
By the involuntary powers,
Nights of insult let you pass
40 Watched by every human love.
1937   1937

Song

As I walked out one evening,
    Walking down Bristol Street,
The crowds upon the pavement
    Were fields of harvest wheat.

And down by the brimming river
    I heard a lover sing
Under an arch of the railway:
    'Love has no ending.

I'll love you, dear, I'll love you
10   Till China and Africa meet
And the river jumps over the mountain
    And the salmon sing in the street.

I'll love you till the ocean
    Is folded and hung up to dry

---

carnal All printed versions of this poem before 1967 had "sensual."

farthing smallest English coin, worth one-quarter penny (now obsolete)

And the seven stars° go squawking
    Like geese about the sky.

The years shall run like rabbits
    For in my arms I hold
The Flower of the Ages
20   And the first love of the world.'

But all the clocks in the city
    Began to whirr and chime:
'O let not Time deceive you,
    You cannot conquer Time.

In the burrows of the Nightmare
    Where Justice naked is,
Time watches from the shadow
    And coughs when you would kiss.

In headaches and in worry
30   Vaguely life leaks away,
And Time will have his fancy
    To-morrow or to-day.

Into many a green valley
    Drifts the appalling snow;
Time breaks the threaded dances
    And the diver's brilliant bow.

O plunge your hands in water,
    Plunge them in up to the wrist;
Stare, stare in the basin
40   And wonder what you've missed.

The glacier knocks in the cupboard,
    The desert sighs in the bed,
And the crack in the tea-cup opens
    A lane to the land of the dead.

Where the beggars raffle the banknotes
    And the Giant is enchanting to Jack,°
And the Lily-white Boy is a Roarer°
    And Jill goes down on her back.°

O look, look in the mirror,
50   O look in your distress;
Life remains a blessing
    Although you cannot bless.

---

seven stars the Pleiades, referred to through the
ancient and mysterious counting song, "Green
Grow the Rushes-O": "Seven for the seven
stars in the sky and six for the six proud
walkers. . . ."
Jack of the folk tale of Jack the Giant-Killer
Roarer "Roaring boy" meant a kind of Elizabethan criminal, hell-raising youth; from the
same song as above: "Two, two the lily-white
boys, clothèd all in green-o" (in Christian
reading, they are Christ and John the Baptist).
Jill . . . back for Jack, on the hill, with the
pail of water

O stand, stand at the window
    As the tears scald and start;
You shall love your crooked neighbour
    With your crooked heart.'

It was late, late in the evening,
    The lovers they were gone;
The clocks had ceased their chiming
60   And the deep river ran on.
    1938   1940

In Memory of Sigmund Freud°
(d. Sept. 1939)

When there are so many we shall have to mourn,
when grief has been made so public, and exposed
    to the critique of a whole epoch
    the frailty of our conscience and anguish,

of whom shall we speak? For every day they die
among us, those who were doing us some good,
    who knew it was never enough but
    hoped to improve a little by living.

Such was this doctor: still at eighty he wished
10 to think of our life from whose unruliness
    so many plausible young futures
    with threats or flattery ask obedience,

but his wish was denied him: he closed his eyes
upon that last picture, common to us all,
    of problems like relatives gathered
    puzzled and jealous about our dying.

For about him till the very end were still
those he had studied, the fauna of the night,
    and shades that still waited to enter
20   the bright circle of his recognition

turned elsewhere with their disappointment as he
was taken away from his life interest
    to go back to the earth in London,
    an important Jew who died in exile.

Freud One of the greatest thinkers of our age (b. 1856), he started his career as a neurologist in Vienna treating girls with hysterical symptoms. From the attempt to understand certain local psychopathologies he moved to a general theory of the human psyche and its development. He died a refugee from Nazism in London, having altered most of the moral and psychological concepts of his time. Auden's ode celebrates Freud as a humane moralist; it deliberately introduces antique personifications ("Hate," "Impulse") and speaks to the general significance of such notions as the relation between instinct and the internalized mechanisms of civilization, and the maintenance of the hidden past in the present inner life. The poem is in syllabic verse, with stanzas of lines of 11–11–9–10 syllables, indented and arranged so as to suggest Horatian odes and German Romantic poets' adaptations of Greek lyric meters.

Only Hate was happy, hoping to augment
his practice now, and his dingy clientele
　　who think they can be cured by killing
　　and covering the gardens with ashes.

They are still alive, but in a world he changed
30　simply by looking back with no false regrets;
　　all he did was to remember
　　like the old and be honest like children.

He wasn't clever at all: he merely told
the unhappy Present to recite the Past
　　like a poetry lesson till sooner
　　or later it faltered at the line where

long ago the accusations had begun,
and suddenly knew by whom it had been judged,
　　how rich life had been and how silly,
40　and was life-forgiven and more humble,

able to approach the Future as a friend
without a wardrobe of excuses, without
　　a set mask of rectitude or an
　　embarrassing over-familiar gesture.

No wonder the ancient cultures of conceit°
in his technique of unsettlement foresaw
　　the fall of princes, the collapse of
　　their lucrative patterns of frustration:

if he succeeded, why, the Generalised Life
50　would become impossible, the monolith
　　of State be broken and prevented
　　the co-operation of avengers.

Of course they called on God, but he went his way
down among the lost people like Dante, down
　　to the stinking fosse° where the injured
　　lead the ugly life of the rejected,

and showed us what evil is, not, as we thought,
deeds that must be punished, but our lack of faith,
　　our dishonest mood of denial,
60　the concupiscence of the oppressor.

If some traces of the autocratic pose,
the paternal strictness he distrusted, still
　　clung to his utterance and features,
　　it was a protective coloration

---

cultures of conceit He means not only Western
political and economic structures but also their
bureaucracies and markets internalized in the
psyche of every person living among them.
fosse ditch; the pit of hell, here seen as a
state of crippling neurosis

for one who'd lived among enemies so long:
if often he was wrong and, at times, absurd,
    to us he is no more a person
    now but a whole climate of opinion°

under whom we conduct our different lives:
70 Like weather he can only hinder or help,
    the proud can still be proud but find it
    a little harder, the tyrant tries to

make do with him but doesn't care for him much:
he quietly surrounds all our habits of growth
    and extends, till the tired in even
    the remotest miserable duchy

have felt the change in their bones and are cheered,
till the child, unlucky in his little State,
    some hearth where freedom is excluded,
80   a hive whose honey is fear and worry,

feels calmer now and somehow assured of escape,
while, as they lie in the grass of our neglect,
    so many long-forgotten objects
    revealed by his undiscouraged shining

are returned to us and made precious again;
games we had thought we must drop as we grew up,
    little noises we dared not laugh at,
    faces we made when no one was looking.

But he wishes us more than this. To be free
90 is often to be lonely. He would unite
    the unequal moieties° fractured
    by our own well-meaning sense of justice,

would restore to the larger the wit and will
the smaller possesses but can only use
    for arid disputes, would give back to
    the son the mother's richness of feeling:

but he would have us remember most of all
to be enthusiastic over the night,
    not only for the sense of wonder
100   it alone has to offer, but also

because it needs our love. With large sad eyes
its delectable creatures look up and beg
    us dumbly to ask them to follow:
    they are exiles who long for the future

climate of opinion the phrase of the American
philosopher Alfred North Whitehead (1861–
1947)

moieties halved parts of the human whole

that lies in our power, they too would rejoice
if allowed to serve enlightenment like him,
    even to bear our cry of 'Judas,'
  as he did and all must bear who serve it.

One rational voice is dumb. Over his grave
110 the household of Impulse mourns one dearly loved:
    sad is Eros, builder of cities,
  and weeping anarchic Aphrodite.°
  1939   1940

In Memory of W. B. Yeats
    (*d. Jan. 1939*)

      I

He disappeared in the dead of winter:
The brooks were frozen, the airports almost deserted,
And snow disfigured the public statues;
The mercury sank in the mouth of the dying day.
O all the instruments agree°
The day of his death was a dark cold day.

Far from his illness
The wolves ran on through the evergreen forests,
The peasant river was untempted by the fashionable quays;
10 By mourning tongues
The death of the poet was kept from his poems.

But for him it was his last afternoon as himself,
An afternoon of nurses and rumours;
The provinces of his body revolted,
The squares of his mind were empty,
Silence invaded the suburbs,
The current of his feeling failed: he became his admirers.

Now he is scattered among a hundred cities
And wholly given over to unfamiliar affections;
20 To find his happiness in another kind of wood
And be punished under a foreign code of conscience.
The words of a dead man
Are modified in the guts of the living.

One rational . . . Aphrodite (ll. 109–12) Ultimately, Auden acknowledges that Freud, like
Blake and other great Romantic visionaries,
were fulfillments of the rationalist tradition
of the Enlightenment, rather than destroyers
of it. "Eros" here is the Freudian sexual force
which in its sublimated form is all creative
power (like Venus in Lucretius's *Of the Nature
of Things*); "Aphrodite," the destructive but
complementary force of Romantic love. Both lament the death of a visionary who knew their
relation as no one else in his age did.
O . . . agree In revising this ode for his
Collected Shorter Poems (1950), Auden qualified the tone of this almost Dryden-like evocation of formal ceremonial diction; the rewritten
form, "What instruments we have agree" is used
also at l. 30.

But in the importance and noise of tomorrow
When the brokers are roaring like beasts on the floor of the Bourse,°
And the poor have the sufferings to which they are fairly accustomed,
And each in the cell of himself is almost convinced of his freedom;
A few thousand will think of this day
As one thinks of a day when one did something slightly unusual.
30 O all the instruments agree
The day of his death was a dark cold day.

II

You were silly like us: your gift survived it all;
The parish of rich women, physical decay,
Yourself; mad Ireland hurt you into poetry.
Now Ireland has her madness and her weather still,
For poetry makes nothing happen: it survives
In the valley of its saying where executives
Would never want to tamper; it flows south
From ranches of isolation and the busy griefs,
40 Raw towns that we believe and die in; it survives,
A way of happening, a mouth.

III

Earth, receive an honoured guest;
William Yeats is laid to rest:
Let the Irish vessel lie
Emptied of its poetry.

Time that is intolerant
Of the brave and innocent,
And indifferent in a week
To a beautiful physique,

50 Worships language and forgives
Everyone by whom it lives;
Pardons cowardice, conceit,
Lays its honours at their feet.

Time that with this strange excuse
Pardoned Kipling and his views,°
And will pardon Paul Claudel,
Pardons him for writing well.

In the nightmare of the dark
All the dogs of Europe bark,

Bourse the Paris stock exchange, probably used for its alliterative value rather than for any specific quality not shared by, say, Wall Street **Pardoned . . . views** In 1940, Auden shared the fashionable left-wing view of Kipling as an apologist for imperialism; actually, Kipling's position was far more complex. Paul Claudel (1868–1955), French Catholic poet, was more unambiguously right-wing politically. Both examples are given in acknowledgment that Yeats's flirtations with fascism in the 1930's needed some apology. Auden canceled the three stanzas concluding with this one (ll. 46–57) in the *Collected Shorter Poems*.

60   And the living nations wait,
          Each sequestered in its hate;

          Intellectual disgrace
          Stares from every human face,
          And the seas of pity lie
          Locked and frozen in each eye.

          Follow, poet, follow right
          To the bottom of the night,
          With your unconstraining voice
          Still persuade us to rejoice;

70   With the farming of a verse
          Make a vineyard of the curse,
          Sing of human unsuccess
          In a rapture of distress;

          In the deserts of the heart
          Let the healing fountain start,
          In the prison of his days
          Teach the free man how to praise.

                              1940

From For the Time Being°

NARRATOR

Well, so that is that. Now we must dismantle the tree,
Putting the decorations back into their cardboard boxes—
Some have got broken—and carrying them up to the attic.
The holly and the mistletoe must be taken down and burnt,
And the children got ready for school. There are enough
Left-overs to do, warmed-up, for the rest of the week—
Not that we have much appetite, having drunk such a lot,
Stayed up so late, attempted—quite unsuccessfully—
To love all of our relatives, and in general

10   Grossly overestimated our powers. Once again
As in previous years we have seen the actual Vision and failed
To do more than entertain it as an agreeable
Possibility, once again we have sent Him away,
Begging though to remain His disobedient servant,
The promising child who cannot keep His word for long.
The Christmas Feast is already a fading memory,
And already the mind begins to be vaguely aware
Of an unpleasant whiff of apprehension at the thought

For the Time Being This is the closing speech of a Christmas oratorio. In a blend of easy, colloquial language and theological reference, it outlines the concept of the period between Christmas and Easter, two festivals representing events that transcended ordinariness, as a temporary return to that ordinariness again, as though the human significance of religious experience were almost held in abeyance.

Of Lent and Good Friday which cannot, after all, now
20 Be very far off. But, for the time being, here we all are,
Back in the moderate Aristotelian city°
Of darning and the Eight-Fifteen, where Euclid's geometry
And Newton's mechanics would account for our experience,
And the kitchen table exists because I scrub it.
It seems to have shrunk during the holidays. The streets
Are much narrower than we remembered; we had forgotten
The office was as depressing as this. To those who have seen
The Child, however dimly, however incredulously,
The Time Being is, in a sense, the most trying time of all.
30 For the innocent children who whispered so excitedly
Outside the locked door where they knew the presents to be
Grew up when it opened. Now, recollecting that moment
We can repress the joy, but the guilt remains conscious;
Remembering the stable where for once in our lives
Everything became a You and nothing was an It.°
And craving the sensation but ignoring the cause,
We look round for something, no matter what, to inhibit
Our self-reflection, and the obvious thing for that purpose
Would be some great suffering. So, once we have met the Son,
40 We are tempted ever after to pray to the Father;
'Lead us into temptation and evil for our sake.'
They will come, all right, don't worry; probably in a form
That we do not expect, and certainly with a force
More dreadful than we can imagine. In the meantime
There are bills to be paid, machines to keep in repair,
Irregular verbs to learn, the Time Being to redeem
From insignificance. The happy morning is over,
The night of agony still to come; the time is noon:
When the Spirit must practise his scales of rejoicing
50 Without even a hostile audience, and the Soul endure
A silence that is neither for nor against her faith
That God's Will will be done, that, in spite of her prayers,
God will cheat no one, not even the world of its triumph.
1942   1944

In Praise of Limestone

If it form the one landscape that we the inconstant ones
      Are consistently homesick for, this is chiefly
Because it dissolves in water. Mark these rounded slopes

Aristotelian city the city of Aristotle's golden mean—the world to which reason, reasonableness, and scientific explanation apply, as opposed to the spiritual extremes of "the happy morning" and "the night of agony," to which they do not

You . . . It the difference between the relation of man to God (called "I-Thou") and others (called "I-It"), crucial in the theology of Martin Buber (1878–1965), Jewish existentialist philosopher and scholar

With their surface fragrance of thyme and beneath
A secret system of caves and conduits; hear these springs
   That spurt out everywhere with a chuckle
Each filling a private pool for its fish and carving
   Its own little ravine whose cliffs entertain
The butterfly and the lizard; examine this region
10   Of short distances and definite places:
What could be more like Mother or a fitter background
   For her son, for the nude young male who lounges
Against a rock displaying his dildo,° never doubting
   That for all his faults he is loved, whose works are but
Extensions of his power to charm? From weathered outcrop
   To hill-top temple, from appearing waters to
Conspicuous fountains, from a wild to a formal vineyard,
   Are ingenious but short steps that a child's wish
To receive more attention than his brothers, whether
20   By pleasing or teasing, can easily take.

Watch, then, the band of rivals as they climb up and down
   Their steep stone gennels° in twos and threes, sometimes
Arm in arm, but never, thank God, in step; or engaged
   On the shady side of a square at midday in
Voluble discourse, knowing each other too well to think
   There are any important secrets, unable
To conceive a god whose temper-tantrums are moral
   And not to be pacified by a clever line
Or a good lay: for, accustomed to a stone that responds,
30   They have never had to veil their faces in awe
Of a crater whose blazing fury could not be fixed;
   Adjusted to the local needs of valleys
Where everything can be touched or reached by walking,
   Their eyes have never looked into infinite space
Through the lattice-work of a nomad's comb;° born lucky,
   Their legs have never encountered the fungi
And insects of the jungle, the monstrous forms and lives
   With which we have nothing, we like to hope, in common.
So, when one of them goes to the bad, the way his mind works
40   Remains comprehensible: to become a pimp
Or deal in fake jewelry or ruin a fine tenor voice
   For effects that bring down the house could happen to all
But the best and the worst of us . . .
                    That is why, I suppose,
The best and worst never stayed here long but sought
Immoderate soils where the beauty was not so external,
   The light less public and the meaning of life

---

dildo literally, an artificial phallus; here, his own real one
gennels ordinarily, "channels," but in Yorkshire dialect, "alley-ways"

nomad's comb simply his hair comb, but considered an important possession

Something more than a mad camp.° 'Come!' cried the granite wastes,
   'How evasive is your humour, how accidental
Your kindest kiss, how permanent is death.' (Saints-to-be
50   Slipped away sighing.) 'Come!' purred the clays and gravels.
'On our plains there is room for armies to drill; rivers
   Wait to be tamed and slaves to construct you a tomb
In the grand manner: soft as the earth is mankind and both
   Need to be altered.' (Intendant Caesars rose and
Left, slamming the door.) But the really reckless were fetched
   By an older colder voice, the oceanic whisper:
'I am the solitude that asks and promises nothing;
   That is how I shall set you free. There is no love;
There are only the various envies, all of them sad.'

60   They were right, my dear, all those voices were right
And still are; this land is not the sweet home that it looks,
   Nor its peace the historical calm of a site
Where something was settled once and for all: A backward
   And delapidated province, connected
To the big busy world by a tunnel, with a certain
   Seedy appeal, is that all it is now? Not quite:
It has a worldly duty which in spite of itself
   It does not neglect, but calls into question
All the Great Powers assume; it disturbs our rights. The poet,
70   Admired for his earnest habit of calling
The sun the sun, his mind Puzzle, is made uneasy
   By these solid statues which so obviously doubt
His antimythological myth; and these gamins,
   Pursuing the scientist down the tiled colonnade
With such lively offers,° rebuke his concern for Nature's
   Remotest aspects: I, too, am reproached, for what
And how much you know. Not to lose time, not to get caught,
   Not to be left behind, not, please! to resemble
The beasts who repeat themselves, or a thing like water
80   Or stone whose conduct can be predicted, these
Are our Common Prayer, whose greatest comfort is music
   Which can be made anywhere, is invisible,
And does not smell. In so far as we have to look forward
   To death as a fact, no doubt we are right: But if
Sins can be forgiven, if bodies rise from the dead,
   These modifications of matter into
Innocent athletes and gesticulating fountains,
   Made solely for pleasure, make a further point:
The blessed will not care what angle they are regarded from,

---

mad camp When this poem was written, "camp" was exclusively a homosexual coterie word to designate overelaborate displays of parodied effeminacy, and, at a higher level, being friv-olous about what meant most to one, being solemn about what mattered least. The term then became general theatrical usage.
lively offers sexual offers of various sorts

90   Having nothing to hide. Dear, I know nothing of
Either, but when I try to imagine a faultless love
      Or the life to come, what I hear is the murmur
Of underground streams, what I see is a limestone landscape.
1948   1951

The Fall of Rome

[*For Cyril Connolly*]

The piers are pummelled by the waves;
In a lonely field the rain
Lashes an abandoned train;
Outlaws fill the mountain caves.

Fantastic grow the evening gowns;
Agents of the Fisc° pursue
Absconding tax-defaulters through
The sewers of provincial towns.

Private rites of magic send
10   The temple prostitutes to sleep;
All the literati keep
An imaginary friend.

Cerebrotonic Cato° may
Extoll the Ancient Disciplines,
But the muscle-bound Marines
Mutiny for food and pay.

Caesar's double-bed is warm
As an unimportant clerk
Writes I DO NOT LIKE MY WORK
20   On a pink official form.

Unendowed with wealth or pity,
Little birds with scarlet legs,
Sitting on their speckled eggs,.
Eye each flu-infected city.

Altogether elsewhere, vast
Herds of reindeer move across
Miles and miles of golden moss,
Silently and very fast.
                              1951

Fisc the state treasury
Cerebrotonic Cato "Cato the Censor," Marcus Porcius Cato (234–139 B.C.), used here as the type of those who confront social problems with rigid solutions. The word "cerebrotonic" comes from Dr. W. H. Sheldon's theory of the relation between type of physique and personality: according to him, the cerebrotonic type is "an 'introvert' . . . he is not at home at social gatherings and he shrinks from crowds."

The Proof°

'When rites and melodies begin
   To alter modes and times,
And timid bar-flies° boast aloud
   Of uncommitted crimes,
And leading families are proud
   To dine with their black sheep,
What promises, what discipline,
   If any, will Love keep?'
     So roared Fire on their right:
10   But Tamino and Pamina
        Walked past its rage,
     Sighing O, sighing O,
In timeless fermatas° of awe and delight
     (Innocent? Yes. Ignorant? No.)
        Down the grim passage.

'When stinking Chaos lifts the latch,°
   And Grotte° backward spins,
And Helen's nose° becomes a beak,
   And cats and dogs grow chins,
20 And daisies claw and pebbles shriek,
   And Form and Colour part,
What swarming hatreds then will hatch
   Out of Love's riven heart.'
     So hissed Water on their left:
        But Pamina and Tamino
        Opposed its spite,
With his worship, with her sweetness—
O look now! See how they emerge from the cleft
     (Frightened? No. Happy? Yes.)
30   Out into sunlight.
            1955

Marginalia

Auden has always been interested in the wisdom of aphorism; his wide reading in German literature had acquainted him early on with the writings of Georg Christoph Lichtenberg (1742–99), that great aphorist of the Enlightenment, and the major

The Proof refers to the testing, in Mozart's *The Magic Flute*, of Prince Tamino and his beloved, Pamina (daughter of an enchantress Queen of the Night named Astrafiammante— "flaming star"), by Priests of Isis, the trials being by the two elements of fire and water.
bar-flies harmless solitary drinkers
fermatas held, extended notes in music
latch that keeps disorder from reclaiming the world again
Grotte or, more properly, Grotti, was a magic

mill belonging to Mägde and turned, at the command of a king, by the two giantesses Fenja and Menja; it ground out Joy, Riches, and Freedom. But to avenge an injury done them they ground it backward to produce bloody warlike weapons, fiery destruction, and a monstrous army that undid the king's realm (from *The Song of the Mill*, in the Old Norse Poetic Edda).
Helen's nose that of Helen of Troy, supposedly perfect

Austrian journalist Karl Kraus; and the epigraph to *The Orators* was an observation of powerful relevance to more than the private jokes of that volume: "*Private faces in public places / Are wiser and nicer / Than public faces in private places.*" In Auden's most recent book he has turned to aphorism himself, combining prose observation with line structures adapted from the Japanese forms called *haiku* and *tanka* (of 17 and 31 syllables, respectively). The first group is a connected sequence; the very last poem refers to the poet himself.

From Marginalia

A dead man
who never caused others to die
seldom rates a statue.

The last king
of a fallen dynasty
is seldom well spoken of.

Few even wish they could read
the lost annals
of a cudgeled people.

The tyrant's device:
Whatever Is Possible
Is Necessary.

Small tyrants, threatened by big,
sincerely believe
they love Liberty.

No tyrant ever fears
his geologists or his engineers.

Tyrants may get slain,
but their hangmen usually
die in their beds.

Patriots? Little boys,
obsessed by Bigness,
Big Pricks, Big Money, Big Bangs.

In States unable
to alleviate Distress,
Discontent is hanged.

In semiliterate countries
demagogues pay
court to teen-agers.

When Chiefs of State
prefer to work at night,
let the citizens beware.

The palm extended in welcome:
*Look! for you
I have unclenched my fist.*

The class whose vices
he pilloried was his own,
now extinct, except
for lone survivors like him
who remember its virtues.

                                      1970

LOUIS MACNEICE
1907–1965

Born in Belfast, educated at boarding school (Marlborough College) and Oxford, Mac-
Neice studied classics and taught them for a while, before becoming a writer for the
British Broadcasting Corporation. In 1936 he went with his friend and fellow poet
W. H. Auden on a journey to Iceland which resulted in their joint volume, *Letters from
Iceland* (1937). MacNeice's poetry and politics were never as doctrinaire in their commitment to the reform of society as those of other poets of the Left, and attempts to
limit his accomplishment by bracketing him with such very different writers as Auden,
Stephen Spender, C. Day Lewis, and that much underrated poet Roy Fuller are useful
only in pointing toward a kind of shared mode of topical poetry—witty, sardonic,
and ironically self-aware of the dangers to poetry, and to the world, of poets' involvement with political causes they may only half-understand. A poem like "Bagpipe
Music" represents that moment in English poetry between the two World Wars when
a parallel emerges with some of the didactic lyric verse of Bertolt Brecht. It is certainly
a moment which political poetry in English has not reached since.

Bagpipe Music°

It's no go the merrygoround, it's no go the rickshaw,°
All we want is a limousine and a ticket for the peepshow.
Their knickers° are made of crêpe-de-chine, their shoes are made of python,
Their halls are lined with tiger rugs and their walls with heads of bison.

John MacDonald found a corpse, put it under the sofa,
Waited till it came to life and hit it with a poker,

Bagpipe Music To a revolutionary socialist the
extremely depressed state of the Scottish economy in the thirties would demand radical solutions, not retreats into a whole range of "opiates"
aside from official religion, including the traditionalism symbolized in the title—which also
characterizes the clever squealing of the poem's
off-rhymes.
rickshaw one in an amusement park
knickers panties (the China silk ones of the
rich)

Sold its eyes for souvenirs, sold its blood for whisky,
Kept its bones for dumb-bells to use when he was fifty.
It's no go the Yogi-Man, it's no go Blavatsky,°
10   All we want is a bank balance and a bit of skirt in a taxi.

Annie MacDougall went to milk, caught her foot in the heather,
Woke to hear a dance record playing of Old Vienna.
It's no go your maidenheads, it's no go your culture,
All we want is a Dunlop tyre° and the devil mend the puncture.

The Laird o' Phelps spent Hogmanay° declaring he was sober,
Counted his feet to prove the fact and found he had one foot over.
Mrs. Carmichael had her fifth, looked at the job with repulsion,
Said to the midwife 'Take it away; I'm through with overproduction.

It's no go the gossip column, it's no go the ceilidh,°
20   All we want is a mother's help and a sugar-stick for the baby.

Willie Murray cut his thumb, couldn't count the damage,
Took the hide of an Ayrshire cow and used it for a bandage.
His brother caught three hundred cran° when the seas were lavish,
Threw the bleeders back in the sea and went upon the parish.°

It's no go the Herring Board,° it's no go the Bible,
All we want is a packet of fags when our hands are idle.

It's no go the picture palace, it's no go the stadium,
It's no go the country cot° with a pot of pink geraniums,
It's no go the Government grants, it's no go the elections,
30   Sit on your arse for fifty years and hang your hat on a pension.

It's no go my honey love, it's no go my poppet;
Work your hands from day to day, the winds will blow the profit.
The glass is falling hour by hour, the glass will fall for ever,
But if you break the bloody glass you won't hold up the weather.

                                                        1937

Whit Monday°

Their feet on London, their heads in the grey clouds,
The Bank (if you call it a holiday) Holiday crowds
Stroll from street to street, cocking an eye

Yogi-Man . . . Blavatsky rejecting the fake solutions of Eastern religions and pseudo-religions: a swami and Madame H. P. Blavatsky, the Russian theosophist (1831–91), stand here for the lot.
Dunlop tyre a bicycle tire
Hogmanay New Year's Eve (Scots)
ceilidh in Scotland, an evening of songs and story telling (pronounced "kay-lee")—a more homely distraction

cran the volume of a herring catch (approximately 750 fish)
upon the parish on welfare
Herring Board national agency set up to aid the failing herring-fishing industry
cot small farm cottage
Whit Monday The Monday after the seventh Sunday following Easter (Whitsuntide) was at the time a bank holiday in England, and a national holiday weekend. But this is London at war.

For where the angel used to be in the sky;
But the Happy Future is a thing of the past and the street
Echoes to nothing but their dawdling feet.
The Lord's my shepherd°—familiar words of myth
Stand up better to bombs than a granite monolith,
Perhaps there is something in them. *I'll not want*—
10   Not when I'm dead. *He makes me down to lie*—
Death my christening and fire my font—
The quiet (Thames, or Don's or Salween's)° *waters by.*

1941

STEPHEN SPENDER
1909–

Born in London of a literary family, educated at Oxford, Spender was one of the generation of left-wing writers for whom the Spanish Civil War was an important confrontation with aspects of the self, as well as what was seen by so many people as simply a struggle against fascism (see the Headnote to W. H. Auden). More interested in German poetry than in the French Symbolists that Eliot and his generation had admired, Spender, like some of his other contemporaries who went to Spain, published poems in both a public and a spiritually private mode, the latter emerging as the dominant one. Spender has been active in the literary life of London, co-editing two important periodicals of the pre- and post-World War II periods, *Horizon* and *Encounter,* and is currently Professor of English Literature at University College, London.

I Think Continually of Those Who Were Truly Great

I think continually of those who were truly great.
Who, from the womb, remembered the soul's history
Through corridors of light where the hours are suns,
Endless and singing. Whose lovely ambition
Was that their lips, still touched with fire,
Should tell of the Spirit, clothed from head to foot in song.
And who hoarded from the Spring branches
The desires falling across their bodies like blossoms.

What is precious, is never to forget
10   The essential delight of the blood drawn from ageless springs
Breaking through rocks in worlds before our earth.
Never to deny its pleasure in the morning simple light
Nor its grave evening demand for love.

---

shepherd The italicized words are from a metrical paraphrase of the 23rd Psalm.
Don's . . . Salween's The Don, in central Rus-   sia, and the Salween, flowing through Tibet, China and Burma. Both, like the Thames, were the scenes of battles in 1941.

Never to allow gradually the traffic to smother
With noise and fog the flowering of the Spirit.

Near the snow, near the sun, in the highest fields,
See how these names are fêted by the waving grass
And by the streamers of white cloud
And whispers of wind in the listening sky.
20 The names of those who in their lives fought for life,
Who wore at their hearts the fire's centre.
Born of the sun, they travelled a short while toward the sun,
And left the vivid air signed with their honor.

                              1933

Ultima Ratio Regum°

The guns spell money's ultimate reason
In letters of lead on the Spring hillside.
But the boy lying dead under the olive trees
Was too young and too silly
To have been notable to their important eye.
He was a better target for a kiss.

When he lived, tall factory hooters never summoned him
Nor did restaurant plate-glass doors revolve to wave him in.
His name never appeared in the papers.
10 The world maintained its traditional wall
Round the dead with their gold sunk deep as a well,
Whilst his life, intangible as a Stock Exchange rumour, drifted outside.

O too lightly he threw down his cap
One day when the breeze threw petals from the trees.
The unflowering wall sprouted with guns,
Machine-gun anger quickly scythed the grasses;
Flags and leaves fell from hands and branches;
The tweed cap rotted in the nettles.

Consider his life which was valueless
20 In terms of employment, hotel ledgers, news files.
Consider. One bullet in ten thousand kills a man.
Ask. Was so much expenditure justified
On the death of one so young, and so silly
Lying under the olive trees, O world, O death?

                              1939

Ultima Ratio Regum "The Ultimate Argument of Kings," a phrase referring to (and engraved on) cannon, by order of Louis XIV; also found on Prussian artillery as late as the early 20th century. This poem refers to the fragile comprehension of the moral and political realities embedded in the violence of the Spanish Civil War that marked the idealistic young Englishmen who enlisted in the Loyalist cause, as well as their Spanish counterparts (the young soldier in the poem might be either). See also the Headnote to W. H. Auden.

EDITH SITWELL

1887–1964

A picturesque and flamboyant literary personage, Edith Sitwell was born at the seaside house of her father, Sir George Sitwell, Baronet, and brought up there and on her family's six-hundred-year-old estate, Renishaw, near Sheffield. Educated privately at home, she and her younger brothers, Osbert and Sacheverell, formed even in their youth a literary community of their own. In 1915 she published her first book of verse, and during the following year began editing, with her brothers, an annual anthology called *Wheels*. With the public performance of *Façade* in London in 1923 her fame was assured; this remarkable suite of poems, spoken rhythmically to amusing musical accompaniments composed by Sir William Walton for chamber orchestra, evidenced all the marks of her subsequent literary and personal style. The influence of French Symbolist poets (Rimbaud, in his *Les Illuminations*; Verlaine's famous dictum about poetry, *De la musique avant toute chose*—"Music before anything else"), the elevation of the brilliant free associations of Victorian nonsense verse (Lewis Carroll's and Edward Lear's) into poetic solemnities, the play with sounds and rhymes and assonances, the vast and curious learning, the fascination with stagey decor, dress, and gesture—all of these mark her poetic and critical works. She was given to eccentric dress, and in many of her portraits, particularly in some of the later photographs by Cecil Beaton, she apparently arranged to look dead. She wrote a novel based on material from the life of Swift (*I Live under a Black Sun*, 1937), a strange biography of Alexander Pope (1930), and a posthumously published autobiography, *Taken Care Of* (1965). She was made Dame Commander of the British Empire in 1953.

The poem from *Façade* given below reflects the satirical turn of many of the nautical poems in the collection; it is as though the archly social world of Victorian seaside resorts fed one half of the poet's childhood imagination, while the richer, dreamier side of her imagination subsisted on the house and books of Renishaw Park, where poetry, to alter Marianne Moore's expression, was a real garden with imaginary toads in it.

Hornpipe°

    Sailors come
    To the drum
    Out of Babylon;
        Hobby-horses
    Foam, the dumb
    Sky rhinoceros-glum

Watched the courses of the breakers' rocking-horses and with Glaucis°
Lady Venus on the settee of the horsehair sea!°

Hornpipe the traditional sailor's dance. As usual, Walton's score quotes from popular tunes, and the well-known hornpipe theme sounds against the opening sections of the text. This text, incidentally, was written to be recited at breakneck speed, thus ensuring that the internal rhymes all come out clearly.

Glaucis presumably a sea nymph, *glaukos* ("shining," "blue-gray") being used of the sea in Greek literature

horsehair sea Victorian settees were frequently covered with and / or stuffed with horsehair.

Where Lord Tennyson in laurels° wrote a gloria free,
In a borealic iceberg came Victoria; she
Knew Prince Albert's tall memorial° took the colours of the floreal
And the borealic iceberg; floating on they see
New-arisen Madam Venus for whose sake from far
Came the fat and zebra'd emperor from Zanzibar
Where like golden bouquets lay far Asia, Africa, Cathay,
All laid before that shady lady by the fibroid Shah.
Captain Fracasse° stout as any water-butt came, stood
With Sir Bacchus both a-drinking the black tarr'd grapes' blood
Plucked among the tartan leafage
By the furry wind whose grief age
Could not wither°—like a squirrel with a gold star-nut.
Queen Victoria sitting shocked upon the rocking-horse
Of a wave said to the Laureate, 'This minx of course
Is as sharp as any lynx and blacker-deeper than the drinks and quite as
Hot as any hottentot, without remorse!
    For the minx,'
        Said she,
   'And the drinks,
      You can see,
Are hot as any hottentot and not the goods for me!'
                     1922

WILLIAM EMPSON
1906–

Although famous when still young for his brilliant and erratic critical work *Seven Types of Ambiguity* (1930), Empson had to await the post-World War II generation of younger poets before his verse achieved wide critical acclaim and influence. It did so not only because of its clean, hard diction, rhetorical directness, and aphoristic knottiness, but also because, apprehended in connection with Empson's own way of reading English literature as expounded in his critical works, it could become a rallying point for the young, clever writers who were to form a new community of university wits. Empson's poetic corpus is quite small (his 1955 *Collected Poems* contained only fifty-six) but it is never diffuse; philosophical and playful by turns and at once, their syntax more elliptically puzzling than their diction, these poems became models of poetic deportment for the fifties generation, which admired D. H. Lawrence's novels and remained unaffected by his poems.

Empson was born in Yorkshire, and educated at Magdalene College, Cambridge, where he was an early student of I. A. Richards, one of the founders of modern

Lord Tennyson in laurels that is, as poet laureate. The scene in the poem obliquely invokes Tennyson's reading of *his* 'tall memorial" (*In Memoriam*) to Queen Victoria, also treated comically in Max Beerbohm's drawing from *The Poet's Corner*.
memorial an ornate and rhetorical structure

erected by Queen Victoria in Kensington Gardens in 1863.
Fracasse named coined from "fracas" ("uproar")
age . . . wither "Age cannot wither her, nor custom stale / Her infinite variety": proverbially famous description of Cleopatra from Shakespeare, *Antony and Cleopatra*

criticism. Rather more sophisticated in the sciences than most critics of poetry in England, he produced a number of seminal critical works. After the *Seven Types* came *English Pastoral Poetry* (1935), *The Structure of Complex Words* (1951), and *Milton's God* (1961), all of which reflected his pioneering insights into the language of poetry and the interpretive questions raised by the very act of serious reading. He published two collections of verse, *Poems* (1935) and *The Gathering Storm* (1940), many of them written while he was teaching in the Orient—in Japan from 1931 to 1934, and in Peking thereafter. In 1952 he returned to England and held the Chair of English at the University of Sheffield until 1971.

This Last Pain

This last pain for the damned the Fathers° found:
'They knew the bliss with which they were not crowned.'
    Such, but on earth, let me foretell,
    Is all, of heaven or of hell.

Man, as the prying housemaid of the soul,
May know her happiness° by eye to hole:
    He's safe; the key is lost; he knows
    Door will not open, nor hole close.

'What is conceivable can happen too,'
10   Said Wittgenstein,° who had not dreamt of you;
    But wisely; if we worked it long
    We should forget where it was wrong.

Those thorns are crowns which, woven into knots,
Crackle under and soon boil fool's pots;°
    And no man's watching, wise and long,
    Would ever stare them into song.

Thorns burn to a consistent ash, like man;
A splendid cleanser for the frying-pan:
    And those who leap from pan to fire°
20   Should this brave opposite admire.

Fathers The Church Fathers (early Christian theologians), perfecting the idea of hell for use on earth, framed statements like this one; Satan, in *Paradise Lost*, was keenly aware of their meaning.
her happiness The soul's. The soul is the mistress, and philosophical and scientific man is the housemaid peering at her secrets and joys through holes in bodies (like keyholes), the only access available to him.
Wittgenstein A rewriting of several propositions such as "What is thinkable is also possible" in the *Tractatus Logico-Philosophicus* (1921–22) of Ludwig Wittgenstein (1889–1951), one of the philosophical giants of our age but, when Empson was writing this, still primarily a local

Cambridge presence. In the *Tractatus* Wittgenstein was concerned with, among other things, elementary propositions embodying facts alone; the idea of Empson's poem is, in his own words, "that human nature can conceive of divine states which it cannot attain."
fool's pots Combining (1) Christ's crown of thorns; (2) "As the crackling of thorns under a pot, so is the laughter of a fool" (Ecclesiastes 7:6); (3) "A watched pot never boils" (proverbial). "The folly which has the courage to maintain careless self-deceit is compared to the mock-regal crown of thorns" (Empson).
pan to fire "Out of the frying pan into the fire" is proverbial.

All those large dreams by which men long live well
Are magic-lanterned on the smoke of hell;°
   This then is real, I have implied,
   A painted, small, transparent slide.

These the inventive can hand-paint at leisure,
Or most emporia would stock our measure;
   And feasting in their dappled shade
   We should forget how they were made.

Feign then what's by a decent tact believed
30   And act that state is only so conceived,
   And build an edifice of form
   For house where phantoms may keep warm.

Imagine, then, by miracle, with me,
(Ambiguous gifts, as what gods give must be)
   What could not possibly be there,
   And learn a style from a despair.

1935

Villanelle°

It is the pain, it is the pain, endures.
Your chemic beauty burned my muscles through.
Poise° of my hands reminded me of yours.

What later purge from this deep toxin cures?
What kindness now could the old salve renew?
It is the pain, it is the pain, endures.

The infection slept (custom or change inures)
And when pain's secondary phase was due
Poise of my hands reminded me of yours.

10   How safe I felt, whom memory assures,
Rich that your grace safely by heart I knew.
It is the pain, it is the pain, endures.

My stare drank deep beauty that still allures.
My heart pumps yet the poison draught of you.
Poise of my hands reminded me of yours.

You are still kind whom the same shape immures.
Kind and beyond adieu. We miss our cue.
It is the pain, it is the pain, endures.
Poise of my hands reminded me of yours.

1935

hell "It was done somewhere by missionaries onto a pagan bonfire" (Empson).
Villanelle For a note on this difficult form see the Glossary; notice how subtly the meaning of

the refrain is modulated through its repetitions, rather than with bald puns or divided syntax.
Poise weight, balance, posture, and the way in which parts of our bodies feel their own presence

Missing Dates

Slowly the poison the whole blood stream fills.
It is not the effort nor the failure tires.
The waste remains, the waste remains and kills.°

It is not your system or clear sight that mills
Down small to the consequence a life requires;
Slowly the poison the whole blood stream fills.

They bled an old dog dry yet the exchange rills°
Of young dog blood gave but a month's desires;
The waste remains, the waste remains and kills.

10   It is the Chinese tombs and the slag hills
Usurp the soil, and not the soil retires.
Slowly the poison the whole blood stream fills.

Not to have fire is to be a skin that shrills.
The complete fire is death. From partial fires
The waste remains, the waste remains and kills.

It is the poems you have lost, the ills
From missing dates, at which the heart expires.
Slowly the poison the whole blood stream fills.
The waste remains, the waste remains and kills.

1940

DYLAN THOMAS
1914–1953

Drawing on a Welsh bardic tradition that still manifests itself in poetry competitions in the Welsh language, Dylan Thomas also assimilated in his small but remarkably personal and intense body of work a number of European modernist poetic influences. Always remaining close to an oral poetry (witness his unique attentiveness to sound patterning), he nonetheless manifests in his early poems perhaps more than any other English poet of his stature the effects of Continental surrealism. Gerard Manley Hopkins; the complex cadences and structures of Welsh verse; T. S. Eliot's poems and, in response to the directions of Eliot's criticism, the English devotional poets of the seventeenth century (Donne, Herbert, Vaughan, Crashaw); Joyce's *A Portrait of the Artist as a Young Man* and *Ulysses;* a visionary Welsh religious tradition that informed the Catholicism of his countryman David Jones, and became in Thomas the basis for a kind of pagan use of Christian mythology—elements of all these are present in his poems and in his few moving and intimate prose works.

The . . . kills I. A. Richards suggested that Empson was echoing, in this refrain, the opening line of another marvelous villanelle, the opening line of Tennyson's "Tithonus": "The woods decay, the woods decay and fall."

rills Brooks, streams; "It is true about the old dog, at least I saw it reported somewhere, but the legend that a fifth or some such part of the soil of China is given up to ancestral tombs is (by the way) not true" (Empson).

Thomas was born in Swansea in Wales and educated at the grammar school there; he then worked as a newspaper reporter, and attracted notice when still quite young for his dense, brilliant, and difficult poetry. Concealed in the meshes of his early verse —the *Eighteen Poems* (1934), *The Map of Love* (1939), and *Deaths and Entrances* (1946; with its title taken from John Donne's last sermon, "Death's Duel")—were an intense sexuality, a linking of sexual themes to religious mythology, and a programmatic modernist obliqueness of reference that use epithet and puzzling kenning (see Glossary) to stand for the object mentioned, and depended upon puns at times almost in the manner of difficult British crossword puzzles. In his poetry published after World War II, and particularly during the last years of his life, when he toured the United States giving flamboyant and resonant readings from his work, a more genial and publicly available mode dominated his work.

Thomas was at home, metrically, both in the iambic rhythms of the seventeenth-century poets he admired, and in a loose accentual "sprung rhythm" (Hopkins's phrase) involving a good deal of internal rhyming and alliterating of phrases. His long *Vision and Prayer* even adopts for its stanzas two graphic patterns in the manner of Herbert. He would let his images evolve through strange and anomalous grammatical constructions—the kind that E. E. Cummings had made familiar in American verse, but which Auden and his followers had never wholeheartedly adopted—ranging from the simple phrase "a grief ago" to all sorts of powerful, but wrenched, verbing of nouns and compoundings. The later pieces in his 1957 *Collected Poems*, his radio play *Under Milk Wood* and some late prose pieces, e.g *A Child's Christmas in Wales* (1955), gained a wide audience for themselves, but not for his earlier and perhaps more interesting work.

When, Like a Running Grave°

When, like a running grave, time tracks you down,
Your calm and cuddled is a scythe of hairs,°
Love in her gear° is slowly through the house,
Up naked stairs, a turtle° in a hearse,
Hauled to the dome,

Comes, like a scissors stalking, tailor age,°
Deliver me who, timid in my tribe,
Of love am barer than Cadaver's° trap
Robbed of the foxy tongue, his footed tape
Of the bone inch,

Deliver me, my masters, head and heart,
Heart of Cadaver's candle waxes thin,

10

When . . . Grave a meditation on love and death, on how each act of love is a death (Thomas is aware of the 17th-century pun on "die," meaning sexual orgasm—as a modern pun would turn on "come")
scythe of hairs both "made of hairs" (pubic)

and "mowing down hairs" (like grass, and the sign of old age)
gear costume
turtle turtledove, emblem of true love
tailor age Age, the shroud tailor
Cadaver's the protagonist of the poem—man, his body, his penis

When blood, spade-handed, and the logic time
Drive children up like bruises to the thumb,
From maid and head,°

For, sunday faced, with dusters° in my glove,
Chaste and the chaser, man with the cockshut° eye,
I, that time's jacket or the coat of ice
20   May fail to fasten° with a virgin o
In the straight grave,

Stride through Cadaver's country in my force,
My pickbrain masters morsing° on the stone
Despair of blood, faith in the maiden's slime,
Halt among eunuchs, and the nitric stain
On fork° and face.

Time is a foolish fancy, time and fool.
No, no, you lover skull, descending hammer
Descends, my masters, on the entered honour.°
You hero skull, Cadaver in the hangar
30   Tells the stick,° 'fail.'

Joy is no knocking nation, sir and madam,
The cancer's fusion, or the summer feather
Lit on the cuddled tree, the cross of fever,
Nor city tar and subway bored to foster
Man through macadam.°

I damp the waxlights in your tower dome.
Joy is the knock of dust, Cadaver's shoot°
Of bud of Adam through his boxy shift,
Love's twilit nation and the skull of state,
40   Sir, is your doom.

Everything ends, the tower ending° and,
(Have with the house of wind), the leaning scene,
Ball of the foot depending from the sun,
(Give, summer, over), the cemented skin,
The actions' end.

All, men my madmen, the unwholesome wind
With whistler's cough contages,° time on track

maid and head maidenhead, and thus all young
girls
dusters "knuckledusters" (brass knuckles)
cockshut literally, "sunset," the end of day; also
with sense of "cocksure" and "cock" in the
phallic, slang sense
fasten as with a buttonhole
morsing tapping out Morse code; also "mossing"
fork crotch
honour as Andrew Marvell used "quaint honour"
in "To His Coy Mistress" to mean not only
chastity but also the sexual organ it protects
stick The aeronautical images in the poem all
cluster around the term "joystick," meaning
the basic altitude and banking control on older,
single-engined planes, and here, of course, the
lover's erection.
macadam blacktop paving material named for
its inventor; also, literally, "son of Adam"
shoot Words like this and "bud," "boxy," and
"country" (in l. 21) are all used with sexual
overtones.
tower ending This stanza meditates on detu-
mescence.
contages verb coined from "contagion"

Shapes in a cinder death; love for his trick,
Happy Cadaver's hunger as you take
50   The kissproof° world.

                    1934

Sonnet°

Let the tale's sailor° from a Christian voyage
Atlaswise° hold half-way off the dummy bay
Time's ship-racked gospel on the globe I balance:
So shall winged harbours through the rockbirds' eyes
Spot the blown word, and on the seas I imagine
December's thorn screwed in a brow of holly.°
Let the first Peter from a rainbow's quayrail°
Ask the tall fish° swept from the bible east,
What rhubarb° man peeled in her foam-blue channel
10   Has sown a flying garden round that sea-ghost?
Green as beginning, let the garden diving
Soar, with its two bark towers,° to that Day°
When the worm° builds with the gold straws of venom
My nest of mercies in the rude, red tree.°

                    1936

After the Funeral

In memory of Ann Jones°

After the funeral, mule praises, brays,
Windshake of sailshaped ears, muffle-toed tap
Tap happily of one peg in the thick
Grave's foot, blinds down the lids, the teeth in black,
The spittled eyes, the salt ponds in the sleeves,

kissproof probably an ironic adoption of a recently introduced advertising term for a lipstick that would not come off

Sonnet This is one of Thomas's very difficult earlier poems, the last of a sequence of ten loosely connected poems all moving "Altarwise by owl light" (as the first poem begins)—through Christian imagery in a starry night-world—toward a vision of apocalypse implied in this last poem. In the background of this poem are sexual and religious images, frequently superimposed (as in "tall fish"), a vision from an implied shipboard, Crucifixion, St. Peter the fisherman fishing for the fish Christ, and others.

tale's sailor Sinbad, in the *Arabian Nights*, with Christian puns on the two syllables of his name

Atlaswise because the poet-sailor-pilgrim may be holding a celestial globe and turning it (like Atlas bearing the globe of the world), looking at its "seas" of darkness, contemplating the constellations

December's . . . holly a holly wreath for Christ-

mas seen as a Good Friday crown of thorns

quayrail railing on a dock (but "quay," pronounced "key," puns on St. Peter's keys)

fish The Greek acronym for Christ's name and epithet was *ichthus,* "fish," which was an early Christian symbol.

rhubarb perhaps because rhubarb is grown from old roots of its plant, or because its tops are poisonous; also because its stem is red like the flesh of man and his phallus

two bark towers the two trees, in Paradise, of Life and Knowledge

Day Apocalypse

worm the serpent, identified in Revelation with Satan

rude, red tree The pun on "rood" as meaning Christ's cross associates it with the fatal Tree of Knowledge in the manner of old biblical interpretation, picks up the rhubarb phallic image, and closes the poem and the sequence with a vision of first and last things brought together.

Ann Jones Thomas's aunt

Morning smack of the spade that wakes up sleep,
Shakes a desolate boy who slits his throat
In the dark of the coffin and sheds dry leaves,
That breaks one bone to light with a judgment clout,
10 After the feast of tear-stuffed time and thistles
In a room with a stuffed fox and a stale fern,
I stand, for this memorial's sake, alone
In the snivelling hours with dead, humped Ann
Whose hooded, fountain heart once fell in puddles
Round the parched worlds of Wales and drowned each sun
(Though this for her is a monstrous image blindly
Magnified out of praise; her death was a still drop;
She would not have me sinking in the holy
Flood of her heart's fame; she would lie dumb and deep
20 And need no druid° of her broken body).
But I, Ann's bard on a raised hearth, call all
The seas to service that her wood-tongued virtue
Babble like a bellbuoy over the hymning heads,
Bow down the walls of the ferned and foxy woods
That her love sing and swing through a brown chapel,
Bless her bent spirit with four, crossing birds.
Her flesh was meek as milk, but this skyward statue
With the wild breast and blessed and giant skull
Is carved from her in a room with a wet window
30 In a fiercely mourning house in a crooked year.
I know her scrubbed and sour humble hands
Lie with religion in their cramp, her threadbare
Whisper in a damp word, her wits drilled hollow,
Her fist of a face died clenched on a round pain;
And sculptured Ann is seventy years of stone.
These cloud-sopped, marble hands, this monumental
Argument of the hewn voice, gesture and psalm,
Storm me forever over her grave until
The stuffed lung of the fox twitch and cry Love
And the strutting fern lay seeds on the black sill.

1938

A Refusal To Mourn the Death, by Fire, of a Child in London

Never until the mankind making
Bird beast and flower
Fathering and all humbling darkness°
Tells with silence the last light breaking
And the still hour
Is come of the sea tumbling in harness

---

druid priest of an ancient British nature-religion
darkness Read all the foregoing phrases as
epithets of darkness: "mankind-making"; "bird-
beast-and-flower-fathering"; "all-humbling."

And I must enter again the round
Zion of the water bead
And the synagogue of the ear of corn
Shall I let pray the shadow of a sound
Or sow my salt seed
In the least valley of sackcloth to mourn

The majesty and burning of the child's death.
I shall not murder
The mankind of her going with a grave truth
Nor blaspheme down the stations of the breath°
With any further
Elegy of innocence and youth.

Deep with the first dead lies London's daughter,
Robed in the long friends,
The grains beyond age, the dark veins of her mother,
Secret by the unmourning water
Of the riding Thames.
After the first death, there is no other.

1946

Fern Hill°

Now as I was young and easy under the apple boughs
About the lilting house and happy as the grass was green,
    The night above the dingle° starry,
        Time let me hail and climb
      Golden in the heydays of his eyes,
And honoured among wagons I was prince of the apple towns
And once below a time I lordly had the trees and leaves
        Trail with daisies and barley
      Down the rivers of the windfall light.

10   And as I was green and carefree, famous among the barns
About the happy yard and singing as the farm was home,
    In the sun that is young once only,
        Time let me play and be
      Golden in the mercy of his means,
And green and golden I was huntsman and herdsman, the calves
Sang to my horn, the foxes on the hills barked clear and cold,
        And the sabbath rang slowly
      In the pebbles of the holy streams.

All the sun long it was running, it was lovely, the hay
20   Fields high as the house, the tunes from the chimneys, it was air

And playing, lovely and watery
  And fire green as grass.
And nightly under the simple stars
As I rode to sleep the owls were bearing the farm away,
All the moon long I heard, blessed among stables, the nightjars°
  Flying with the ricks,° and the horses
    Flashing into the dark.

And then to awake, and the farm, like a wanderer white
With the dew, come back, the cock on his shoulder: it was all
30 Shining, it was Adam and maiden,
    The sky gathered again
  And the sun grew round that very day.
So it must have been after the birth of the simple light
In the first, spinning place, the spellbound horses walking warm
  Out of the whinnying green stable
    On to the fields of praise.

And honoured among foxes and pheasants by the gay house
Under the new made° clouds and happy as the heart was long,
40 In the sun born over and over,
    I ran my heedless ways,
  My wishes raced through the house high hay
And nothing I cared, at my sky blue trades, that time allows
In all his tuneful turning so few and such morning songs
  Before the children green and golden
    Follow him out of grace.

Nothing I cared, in the lamb white days, that time would take me
Up to the swallow thronged loft by the shadow of my hand,
  In the moon that is always rising,
50   Nor that riding to sleep
  I should hear him fly with the high fields
And wake to the farm forever fled from the childless land.
Oh as I was young and easy in the mercy of his means,
    Time held me green and dying
  Though I sang in my chains like the sea.

       1946

'Do Not Go Gentle into That Good Night'°

Do not go gentle into that good night,
Old age should burn and rave at close of day;
Rage, rage against the dying of the light.

nightjars harsh-voiced birds
ricks haystacks
new made as frequently in Thomas, "new-made"
Do Not . . . Night In form this poem is a
villanelle (see the two by William Empson given
above, and the one composed by Stephen Daedalus in Joyce's *A Portrait of the Artist as a
Young Man,* given earlier). This was written for
Thomas' dying father.

Though wise men at their end know dark is right,
Because their words had forked no lightning they
Do not go gentle into that good night.

Good men, the last wave by, crying how bright
Their frail deeds might have danced in a green bay,
Rage, rage against the dying of the light.

10   Wild men who caught and sang the sun in flight,
And learn, too late, they grieved it on its way,
Do not go gentle into that good night.

Grave men, near death, who see with blinding sight
Blind eyes could blaze like meteors and be gay,
Rage, rage against the dying of the light.

And you, my father, there on the sad height,
Curse, bless, me now with your fierce tears, I pray .
Do not go gentle into that good night.
Rage, rage against the dying of the light.

1951   1957

E. M. FORSTER
1879–1970

Edward Morgan Forster was born in London on January 1, 1879. He was the great-grandson of Henry Thornton, the central figure of the Clapham Sect, a Victorian Evangelical group of strong ethical cast and dedicated to reform and philanthropy. Though he was not a Christian, Forster inherited many of their concerns, but he criticized them for their indifference to the evils inherent in the system which produced their wealth, as well as for their lack of "mysticism, a sense of the unseen." He attended Tonbridge, a public school he remembers in his novels—especially in the second, The Longest Journey (1907)—as a center of stupidity, false morality, and unspirituality. Cambridge was different; King's College, also celebrated in The Longest Journey, was a sort of paradise where friendship and Hellenism ruled.

Forster became a member of the "Apostles," a group founded in 1825 and dedicated to candor, gaiety, and self-effacing honesty. Their sense of the need for these ingredients of true friendship in a very stuffy and hypocritical world was given formal expression by the Cambridge philosopher G. E. Moore (1873–1958) in his Principia Ethica (1903). Moore argued, among other things, that the good cannot be identified with anything existent—with evolution, say, or with what benefits the greatest number; rather, it is something in one's head, by which he evaluated the world. He believed also that the "complex wholes" of consciousness in relation to beautiful objects and personal relations are the most valuable things we can know. His followers, translated to London, came to be known as the Bloomsbury group, from the district where most of them lived.

Forster was probably not interested in the technicalities of the Principia. He had already acquired, in part from another and very different Cambridge philosopher, J. M. E. McTaggart (1866–1925), a sense of the almost mystical virtues of friendship.

From his friend Goldsworthy Lowes Dickinson he made similar acquisitions, and like Dickinson he especially associated the cult of friendship, candor, and liberty with Greece. On his return after almost two years in Italy and Greece, however, Forster became associated with the so-called Bloomsbury group of Moore's followers, though he was never one of the central figures.

After the death of their father Sir Leslie Stephen (1832–1924), a distinguished man of letters and historian of thought, his children moved to Bloomsbury. It was Sir Leslie's son Thoby who brought the Cambridge ethos to London; but he died young in 1906, and the focus of the group was thenceforth the houses of Thoby's sisters Vanessa (who married the art critic Clive Bell in 1906) and Virginia (later married to Leonard Woolf). The best-known members (Forster apart) are the biographer Lytton Strachey (1880–1932), the economist J. M. Keynes (1883–1946), Leonard Woolf (1880–1969), Roger Fry (1866–1934), and Desmond MacCarthy (1878–1952). The eccentric hostess Lady Ottoline Morrell (1873–1938)—Lawrence's Hermione in *Women in Love*—was also important. Bertrand Russell (1872–1969) was an associate. All these people were extremely talented, and one or two were geniuses. Virginia Woolf (1882–1941) was an important experimental novelist, Keynes transformed twentieth-century economics, and Fry organized the Post-Impressionist exhibition of 1910, one of the most important dates in the history of art in England; Virginia Woolf said that it changed human nature.

Meanwhile the Bloomsbury group, cutting itself off from "good society," made its own rules, talked its own dialect (imitating perhaps the squeaky voice of Lytton Strachey), and attracted dislike and obloquy for many reasons—social, religious, ethical, artistic. Its members believed in freedom: for women, for homosexuals, for the subject races, even for the poor. They saw themselves—much in the manner of that Clapham Sect which lay far behind not only Forster but others of the group—as a sort of elect; and they put personal relations above all else, which is why Forster could make his famous remark (see below) about betraying his country before he would betray his friend, and why Orwell (see below) took great exception to such statements.

Forster has to be understood with reference to this Edwardian development of the old Victorian liberalism; yet he remained very much his own man, with his own voice and his own preoccupations. Between 1905 and 1910 he published four novels, *Where Angels Fear to Tread* (1905), *The Longest Journey* (1907), *A Room with a View* (1908, begun in 1903), and *Howards End* (1910). Though launching himself in a decade of modernism, Forster was not particularly experimental; his modern masters were Wagner, Samuel Butler, Meredith, Hardy, not the late James, Conrad, and Joyce. His novels are, as he said of Meredith's, "contrived": they are very carefully put together, and always mean more than they seem to say, but they are rooted in the contemporary problems of class, and in the difficulties it creates for men and women who are trying to find their true personalities and establish good relations with others and with the world, surrounded as they are by temptations to "sin against passion and truth." Structurally these books have considerable complexity, but nowadays they seem preoccupied with problems one cannot profoundly care about.

In 1912–13 Forster went to India with Lowes Dickinson, and on his return began work on the novel that was to be *A Passage to India*. He broke off, however, to write another novel, *Maurice*, about the happy outcome of a homosexual's search for truth and happiness (which outcome, incidentally, involves the destruction of class barriers). This book he did not publish, though he later revised it; he dedicated it "to a Happier Year," meaning some future, in which he did not really believe, when homosexual relations between men would no longer be forbidden by English law. Although the law was changed during Forster's life, the book did not appear until 1971, after his death. Part of its interest (which is admittedly rather limited) lies in the fact that this was in some ways Forster's true early subject, that in the sinning heroes and heroines of his earlier work he was using substitutes for the homosexual hero, and that now the whole subject of Hellenist freedom and friendship is more clearly defined.

After spending most of World War I as a Red Cross worker in Egypt, Forster returned to journalism. But he returned also to India, and to *A Passage to India,* which was to appear in 1924. *Passage* is an enormous advance on the earlier books—indeed, it is one of the great modern novels. While ostensibly about the relations of the British with the native populations of India, it is fundamentally a highly organized work of art, a limited world commenting on the tragedies and mitigations of the larger one. In 1927 Forster gave the lectures—characteristically whimsical, sly, evasive, unassertive —which were published as *Aspects of the Novel,* one of the most stimulating books ever written on the theory of fiction. In the years between 1927 and his death other books of various kinds appeared: a biography of Lowes Dickinson (1934), and one of Forster's aunt Marianne Thornton (1956), collections of essays—*Abinger Harvest* (1936) and *Two Cheers for Democracy* (1951); but he wrote no more novels.

Forster's reputation has risen and fallen and risen again. But one great book is enough to prove a writer's greatness, and that he wrote in *A Passage to India.* As a more general influence he is harder to assess. His opinions are precisely and characteristically stated in the famous essay given below; and they are not fashionable opinions, though they will always be listened to by intelligent liberals. He spent most of the last years of his life at King's College, Cambridge, and he died there among friends. His private influence on the young has been, within that small circle, considerable, and he has spoken out again and again for the victims of oppression, always in the same mild yet penetrating tones. In a sense he was an Edwardian version of a Victorian sage; but he held a different view of morality, and was also an artist of great strength and delicacy. This last is the attribute that saves him from obsolescence; in him, as in his great book, it is only the surface that looks old-fashioned.

What I Believe, first published in 1939, contains references to the threat of war, which then preoccupied everybody and which was realized in September of the same year. The essay's argument is lucid and unforced, and states Forster's own version of what is recognizably a Bloomsbury position: intelligent skepticism, the supremacy of personal relations over such external loyalties as may be demanded of one. A qualified cheer for democracy as being better than the alternatives is followed by an expression, paralleled elsewhere, of Forster's view that creative work goes on in spite of the "ultimate reality" of force, and that the best we can hope for is that that reality can sometimes, more or less by accident, be overlooked long enough for the work to continue, though hardly at such a moment as the time of writing. Forster's belief in aristocracy—not of birth but of "the sensitive, the considerate and the plucky"—is in the line of the Clapham Sect as well as the secularized Bloomsbury version of vocation and election. These people recognize one another, flash their signal lights through the surrounding dark. The imagery was borrowed soon after by W. H. Auden in his poem "September 1, 1939" (now forbidden the press by its author): "Ironic points of light / Flash out wherever the just / Exchange their messages"; and in 1951 Forster responded, in a review of Auden's *The Enchaféd Flood,* with the words "Because he once wrote 'We must love one another or die' he can command me to follow him."

What I Believe

I do not believe in Belief. But this is an age of faith, and there are so many militant creeds that, in self-defence, one has to formulate a creed of one's own. Tolerance, good temper and sympathy are no longer enough in a world which is rent by religious and racial persecution, in a world where ignorance rules, and science, who ought to have ruled, plays the subservient pimp. Tolerance, good temper and sympathy—they are what matter really, and if the human race is not to collapse they must come to the front before long. But for the moment they are not enough, their action is no stronger than a flower,[1] battered beneath a military jack-boot. They want stiffening, even if the process coarsens them. Faith, to my mind, is a stiffening process, a sort of mental starch, which ought to be applied as sparingly as possible. I dislike the stuff. I do not believe in it, for its own sake, at all. Herein I probably differ from most people, who believe in Belief, and are only sorry they cannot swallow even more than they do. My law-givers are Erasmus [2] and Montaigne,[3] not Moses and St. Paul. My temple stands not upon Mount Moriah [4] but in that Elysian Field where even the immoral are admitted. My motto is: 'Lord, I disbelieve—help thou my unbelief.' [5]

I have, however, to live in an Age of Faith—the sort of epoch I used to hear praised when I was a boy. It is extremely unpleasant really. It is bloody in every sense of the word. And I have to keep my end up in it. Where do I start?

With personal relationships. Here is something comparatively solid in a world full of violence and cruelty. Not absolutely solid, for Psychology has split and shattered the idea of a 'Person,' and has shown that there is something incalculable in each of us, which may at any moment rise to the surface and destroy our normal balance. We don't know what we are like. We can't know

1. "How with this rage shall beauty hold a plea, / Whose action is no stronger than a flower?" Shakespeare, Sonnet LXV.
2. Desiderius Erasmus (*c.* 1466–1536), humanist famous for his learning, his satire on pendantry, and his defense of the freedom of the will and of the right to doubt and inquire.
3. Michel Eyquem de Montaigne (1533–92), author of *Essays,* written over many years and progressing from a stoical attitude to skepticism (a conviction of the fallibility of the human mind) and thence to the notion of the desirability of free and harmonious use of the human faculties.
4. The hill on which Abraham tried to sacrifice Isaac (Genesis 22) was held to be that on which the Temple later stood.
5. In Mark 9 the father of a sick child asks Jesus to cure him, and when Jesus replies that "all things are possible to him that believeth" the man cries out, "Lord, I believe; help thou mine unbelief" (*help* in the obsolete sense of *cure*). In Forster's parody *help* of course has its modern sense.

what other people are like. How, then, can we put any trust in personal relationships, or cling to them in the gathering political storm? In theory we cannot. But in practice we can and do. Though A is not unchangeably A or B unchangeably B, there can still be love and loyalty between the two. For the purpose of living one has to assume that the personality is solid, and the 'self' is an entity, and to ignore all contrary evidence. And since to ignore evidence is one of the characteristics of faith, I certainly can proclaim that I believe in personal relationships.

Starting from them, I get a little order into the contemporary chaos. One must be fond of people and trust them if one is not to make a mess of life, and it is therefore essential that they should not let one down. They often do. The moral of which is that I must, myself, be as reliable as possible, and this I try to be. But reliability is not a matter of contract—that is the main difference between the world of personal relationships and the world of business relationships. It is a matter for the heart, which signs no documents. In other words, reliability is impossible unless there is a natural warmth. Most men possess this warmth, though they often have bad luck and get chilled. Most of them, even when they are politicians, *want* to keep faith. And one can, at all events, show one's own little light here, one's own poor little trembling flame, with the knowledge that it is not the only light that is shining in the darkness, and not the only one which the darkness does not comprehend. Personal relations are despised today. They are regarded as bourgeois luxuries, as products of a time of fair weather which is now past, and we are urged to get rid of them, and to dedicate ourselves to some movement or cause instead. I hate the idea of causes, and if I had to choose between betraying my country and betraying my friend, I hope I should have the guts to betray my country. Such a choice may scandalise the modern reader, and he may stretch out his patriotic hand to the telephone at once and ring up the police. It would not have shocked Dante, though. Dante places Brutus and Cassius in the lowest circle of Hell because they had chosen to betray their friend Julius Caesar rather than their country Rome. Probably one will not be asked to make such an agonising choice. Still, there lies at the back of every creed something terrible and hard for which the worshipper may one day be required to suffer, and there is even a terror and a hardness in this creed of personal relationships, urbane and mild though it sounds. Love and loyalty to an individual can run counter to the claims of the State. When they do—down with the State, say I, which means that the State would down me.

This brings me along to Democracy, 'even Love, the Beloved Republic, which feeds upon Freedom and lives.' [6] Democracy is not a Beloved Republic really, and never will be. But it is less hateful than other contemporary forms of government, and to that extent it deserves our support. It does start from the assumption that the individual is important, and that all types are needed to make a civilisation. It does not divide its citizens into the bossers and the bossed—as an efficiency-regime tends to do. The people I admire most are those who are sensitive and want to create something or discover something,

6. Fifth line of stanza 38 of *Hertha*, by A. C. Swinburne (1837–1909).

and do not see life in terms of power, and such people get more of a chance under a democracy than elsewhere. They found religions, great or small, or they produce literature and art, or they do disinterested scientific research, or they may be what is called 'ordinary people,' who are creative in their private lives, bring up their children decently, for instance, or help their neighbours. All these people need to express themselves; they cannot do so unless society allows them liberty to do so, and the society which allows them most liberty is a democracy.

Democracy has another merit. It allows criticism, and if there is not public criticism there are bound to be hushed-up scandals. That is why I believe in the Press, despite all its lies and vulgarity, and why I believe in Parliament. Parliament is often sneered at because it is a Talking Shop.[7] I believe in it *because* it is a talking shop. I believe in the Private Member who makes himself a nuisance. He gets snubbed and is told that he is cranky or ill-informed, but he does expose abuses which would otherwise never have been mentioned, and very often an abuse gets put right just by being mentioned. Occasionally, too, a well-meaning public official starts losing his head in the cause of efficiency, and thinks himself God Almighty. Such officials are particularly frequent in the Home Office.[8] Well, there will be questions about them in Parliament sooner or later, and then they will have to mind their steps. Whether Parliament is either a representative body or an efficient one is questionable, but I value it because it criticises and talks, and because its chatter gets widely reported.

So Two Cheers for Democracy: one because it admits variety and two because it permits criticism. Two cheers are quite enough: there is no occasion to give three. Only Love the Beloved Republic deserves that.

What about Force, though? While we are trying to be sensitive and advanced and affectionate and tolerant, an unpleasant question pops up: does not all society rest upon force? If a government cannot count upon the police and the army, how can it hope to rule? And if an individual gets knocked on the head or sent to a labour camp, of what significance are his opinions?

This dilemma does not worry me as much as it does some. I realise that all society rests upon force. But all the great creative actions, all the decent human relations, occur during the intervals when force has not managed to come to the front. These intervals are what matter. I want them to be as frequent and as lengthy as possible, and I call them 'civilisation.' Some people idealise force and pull it into the foreground and worship it, instead of keeping it in the background as long as possible. I think they make a mistake, and I think that their opposites, the mystics, err even more when they declare that force does not exist. I believe that it exists, and that one of our jobs is to prevent it from getting out of its box. It gets out sooner or later, and then it destroys us and all the lovely things which we have made. But it is not out all the time, for the fortunate reason that the strong are so stupid. Consider their conduct

7. The description of Dickens at the time when he was a stenographic reporter in Parliament.
8. See note on Sir William Joynson-Hicks under D. H. Lawrence, *Pornography and Obscenity*.

for a moment in the Niebelung's Ring.[9] The giants there have the guns, or in other words the gold; but they do nothing with it, they do not realise that they are all-powerful, with the result that the catastrophe is delayed and the castle of Walhalla, insecure but glorious, fronts the storms. Fafnir, coiled round his hoard, grumbles and grunts; we can hear him under Europe today; the leaves of the wood already tremble, and the Bird calls its warnings uselessly. Fafnir will destroy us, but by a blessed dispensation he is stupid and slow, and creation goes on just outside the poisonous blast of his breath. The Nietzschean [10] would hurry the monster up, the mystic would say he did not exist, but Wotan, wiser than either, hastens to create warriors before doom declares itself. The Valkyries are symbols not only of courage but of intelligence; they represent the human spirit snatching its opportunity while the going is good, and one of them even finds time to love. Brünnhilde's last song hymns the recurrence of love, and since it is the privilege of art to exaggerate, she goes even further, and proclaims the love which is eternally triumphant and feeds upon freedom, and lives.

So that is what I feel about force and violence. It is, alas! the ultimate reality on this earth, but it does not always get to the front. Some people call its absences 'decadence'; I call them 'civilisation' and find in such interludes the chief justification for the human experiment. I look the other way until fate strikes me. Whether this is due to courage or to cowardice in my own case I cannot be sure. But I know that if men had not looked the other way in the past, nothing of any value would survive. The people I respect most behave as if they were immortal and as if society was eternal. Both assumptions are false: both of them must be accepted as true if we are to go on eating and

---

9. In the libretto he composed for his four-opera cycle *The Ring of the Nibelung* (first performances 1869–76), Richard Wagner (1813–83) tells the story of how Alberich steals the gold of the Nibelung and fashions a ring of it. The gods have built a new home named Valhalla, and plan to avoid paying the promised price to the giant builders—Freia, the goddess of youth—by stealing the gold from Alberich and offering that instead. Alberich puts a curse on the stolen ring, but Wotan, king of the gods, gives it to the giants, and Valhalla is occupied. Fafnir, the giant who has the ring, turns himself into a dragon to guard it, but Wotan needs it, lest the race of gods become extinct. The task of recovering the ring falls to Siegfried, son of Siegmund and Sieglinde, the mortal children of Wotan. Siegfried kills the dragon Fafnir, and, because he accidentally tastes his blood, can understand what the birds are saying. He goes to the rescue of the Valkyrie Brunnhilde, who was imprisoned by fire on a rock as a punishment for disobeying Wotan; he passes through the fire, awakes her, and places the ring on her finger. Wotan understands that he cannot save the race of gods, ruined by the immorality brought on by the ring; and Valhalla must be destroyed before the curse of the ring can end. This happens in the last opera, *The Twilight of the Gods*. Brunnhilde will not give up the ring (now a pledge of Siegfried's love) to the Rhinemaidens who originally owned it. Nor will Siegfried relinquish it. When he is killed by treachery the ring cannot be taken from his finger. But after her last song over Siegfried's corpse Brunnhilde rides her horse into his funeral pyre; and as the Rhine rises to extinguish the flames the Rhinemaidens seize back the ring. Valhalla is seen in the distance in flames.

Forster's private reading involves him in admiring Wotan for carrying on with Valhalla under threat; and in the last sentence of the paragraph he attributes to Brunnhilde the sentiments of his favorite quotation from Swinburne.

10. Friedrich Wilhelm Nietzsche (1844–1900), German philosopher, was at first a fervent Wagnerite but later attacked the composer. Forster is referring to Nietzsche's doctrine of the Superman, beyond good and evil, which came to be identified with the rule of force in Europe.

working and loving, and are to keep open a few breathing holes for the human spirit. No millennium seems likely to descend upon humanity; no better and stronger League of Nations will be instituted; no form of Christianity and no alternative to Christianity will bring peace to the world or integrity to the individual; no 'change of heart' will occur. And yet we need not despair, indeed, we cannot despair; the evidence of history shows us that men have always insisted on behaving creatively under the shadow of the sword; that they have done their artistic and scientific and domestic stuff for the sake of doing it, and that we had better follow their example under the shadow of the aeroplanes. Others, with more vision or courage than myself, see the salvation of humanity ahead, and will dismiss my conception of civilisation as paltry, a sort of tip-and-run game. Certainly it is presumptuous to say that we *cannot* improve, and that Man, who has only been in power for a few thousand years, will never learn to make use of his power. All I mean is that, if people continue to kill one another as they do, the world cannot get better than it is, and that since there are more people than formerly, and their means for destroying one another superior, the world may well get worse. What is good in people— and consequently in the world—is their insistence on creation, their belief in friendship and loyalty for their own sakes; and though Violence remains and is, indeed, the major partner in this muddled establishment, I believe that creativeness remains too, and will always assume direction when violence sleeps. So, though I am not an optimist, I cannot agree with Sophocles that it were better never to have been born.[11] And although, like Horace,[12] I see no evidence that each batch of births is superior to the last, I leave the field open for the more complacent view. This is such a difficult moment to live in, one cannot help getting gloomy and also a bit rattled, and perhaps short-sighted.

In search of a refuge, we may perhaps turn to hero-worship. But here we shall get no help, in my opinion. Hero-worship is a dangerous vice, and one of the minor merits of a democracy is that it does not encourage it, or produce that unmanageable type of citizen known as the Great Man. It produces instead different kinds of small men—a much finer achievement. But people who cannot get interested in the variety of life, and cannot make up their own minds, get discontented over this, and they long for a hero to bow down before and to follow blindly. It is significant that a hero is an integral part of the authoritarian stock-in-trade today. An efficiency-regime cannot be run without a few heroes stuck about it to carry off the dullness—much as plums have be put into a bad pudding to make it palatable. One hero at the top and a smaller one each side of him is a favourite arrangement, and the timid and the bored are comforted by the trinity, and, bowing down, feel exalted and strengthened.

No, I distrust Great Men. They produce a desert of uniformity around them and often a pool of blood too, and I always feel a little man's pleasure when they come a cropper. Every now and then one reads in the newspapers some such statement as: 'The coup d'état appears to have failed, and Admiral Toma's whereabouts is at present unknown.' Admiral Toma had probably every

11. Refers to the closing chorus of *Oedipus the King*.
12. Refers to *Odes* III.vi.46.

qualification for being a Great Man—an iron will, personal magnetism, dash, flair, sexlessness—but fate was against him, so he retires to unknown whereabouts instead of parading history with his peers. He fails with a completeness which no artist and no lover can experience, because with them the process of creation is itself an achievement, whereas with him the only possible achievement is success.

I believe in aristocracy, though [13]—if that is the right word, and if a democrat may use it. Not an aristocracy of power, based upon rank and influence; but an aristocracy of the sensitive, the considerate and the plucky. Its members are to be found in all nations and classes, and all through the ages, and there is a secret understanding between them when they meet. They represent the true human tradition, the one permanent victory of our queer race over cruelty and chaos.[14] Thousands of them perish in obscurity, a few are great names. They are sensitive for others as well as for themselves, they are considerate without being fussy, their pluck is not swankiness but the power to endure, and they can take a joke. I give no examples—it is risky to do that— but the reader may as well consider whether this is the type of person he would like to meet and to be, and whether (going farther with me) he would prefer that this type should *not* be an ascetic one. I am against asceticism myself. I am with the old Scotsman who wanted less chastity and more delicacy. I do not feel that my aristocrats are a real aristocracy if they thwart their bodies, since bodies are the instruments through which we register and enjoy the world. Still, I do not insist. This is not a major point. It is clearly possible to be sensitive, considerate and plucky and yet be an ascetic too; if anyone possesses the first three qualities, I will let him in! On they go—an invincible army, yet not a victorious one. The aristocrats, the elect, the chosen, the Best People—all the words that describe them are false, and all attempts to organise them fail. Again and again Authority, seeing their value, has tried to net them and to utilise them as the Egyptian Priesthood or the Christian Church or the Chinese Civil Service or the Group Movement,[15] or some other worthy stunt. But they slip through the net and are gone; when the door is shut, they are no longer in the room; their temple, as one of them [16] remarked, is the Holiness of the Heart's Affection, and their kingdom, though they never possess it, is the wide-open world.

With this type of person knocking about, and constantly crossing one's path if one has eyes to see or hands to feel, the experiment of earthly life cannot be dismissed as a failure. But it may well be hailed as a tragedy, the tragedy being that no device has been found by which these private decencies can be transmitted to public affairs. As soon as people have power they go crooked and sometimes dotty as well, because the possession of power lifts them into a region

13. This passage is famous as a summary of the Bloomsbury attitude toward personality.
14. In another essay, *Art for Art's Sake* (1949), Forster says of art that it is "the one orderly product that our muddling race has produced". There is no contradiction here, since it was a Bloomsbury doctrine, formulated in the *Principia Ethica* of G. E. Moore (see Headnote) that personal relations were a form of art.
15. The Oxford Group, founded in 1921 by the American Frank Buchman (1878–1961); the purpose was to "change" people's lives by a sort of up-to-date Christian revivalism. Moral Re-Armament is another name for it.
16. Keats.

where normal honesty never pays. For instance, the man who is selling news-papers outside the Houses of Parliament can safely leave his papers to go for a drink and his cap beside them: anyone who takes a paper is sure to drop a copper into the cap. But the men who are inside the Houses of Parliament—they cannot trust one another like that, still less can the Government they com-pose trust other governments. No caps upon the pavement here, but suspicion, treachery and armaments. The more highly public life is organised the lower does its morality sink; the nations of today behave to each other worse than they ever did in the past, they cheat, rob, bully and bluff, make war without notice, and kill as many women and children as possible; whereas primitive tribes were at all events restrained by taboos. It is a humiliating outlook—though the greater the darkness, the brighter shine the little lights, reassuring one another, signalling: 'Well, at all events, I'm still here. I don't like it very much, but how are you?' Unquenchable lights of my aristocracy! Signals of the invincible army! 'Come along—anyway, let's have a good time while we can.' I think they signal that too.

The Saviour of the future—if ever he comes—will not preach a new Gospel. He will merely utilise my aristocracy, he will make effective the good will and the good temper which are already existing. In other words, he will introduce a new technique. In economics, we are told that if there was a new technique of distribution, there need be no poverty, and people would not starve in one place while crops were being ploughed under in another. A similar change is needed in the sphere of morals and politics. The desire for it is by no means new; it was expressed, for example, in theological terms by Jacopone da Todi [17] over six hundred years ago. '*Ordina questo amore, O tu che m'ami,*' he said; 'O thou who lovest me—set this love in order.' His prayer was not granted, and I do not myself believe that it ever will be, but here, and not through a change of heart, is our probable route. Not by becoming better, but by ordering and distributing his native goodness, will Man shut up Force into its box, and so gain time to explore the universe and to set his mark upon it worthily. At pres-ent he only explores it at odd moments, when Force is looking the other way, and his divine creativeness appears as a trivial by-product, to be scrapped as soon as the drums beat and the bombers hum.

Such a change, claim the orthodox, can only be made by Christianity, and will be made by it in God's good time: man always has failed and always will fail to organise his own goodness, and it is presumptuous of him to try. This claim—solemn as it is—leaves me cold. I cannot believe that Christianity will ever cope with the present world-wide mess, and I think that such influence as it retains in modern society is due to the money behind it, rather than to its spiritual appeal. It was a spiritual force once, but the indwelling spirit will have to be restated if it is to calm the waters again, and probably restated in a non-Christian form. Naturally a lot of people, and people who are not only good but able and intelligent, will disagree here; they will vehemently deny that Christianity has failed, or they will argue that its failure proceeds from the wickedness of men, and really proves its ultimate success. They have Faith, with a large F. My faith has a very small one, and I only intrude it because

17. Italian Franciscan poet (*c.*1230–1306); Forster quotes this line several times.

these are strenuous and serious days, and one likes to say what one thinks while speech is comparatively free: it may not be free much longer.

The above are the reflections of an individualist and a liberal who has found liberalism crumbling beneath him and at first felt ashamed. Then, looking around, he decided there was no special reason for shame, since other people, whatever they felt, were equally insecure. And as for individualism—there seems no way of getting off this, even if one wanted to. The dictator-hero can grind down his citizens till they are all alike, but he cannot melt them into a single man. That is beyond his power. He can order them to merge, he can incite them to mass-antics, but they are obliged to be born separately, and to die separately, and, owing to these unavoidable termini, will always be running off the totalitarian rails. The memory of birth and the expectation of death always lurk within the human being, making him separate from his fellows and consequently capable of intercourse with them. Naked I came into the world, naked I shall go out of it! And a very good thing too, for it reminds me that I am naked under my shirt, whatever its colour.

1939

JOHN BETJEMAN
1906–

Modern England's finest exponent of the tradition of "serious" light verse, Betjeman was educated, like Louis MacNeice, at Marlborough and Oxford. He is an authority on Victorian and Edwardian architecture, and has interested himself in the preservation and restoration of ecclesiastical buildings all over England. His verse is frequently satiric, as in the poem given below, which chides the unaltered commitments of a rich London lady at the onset of the Blitz in World War II. He frequently uses that same verse for nostalgic, only vaguely ironic celebrations of the platitudes of upper-middle-class English life. The result is that in certain of his poems, such as the well-known "Subaltern's Love Song" in praise of an athletic "Miss Joan Hunter Dunn," it is difficult to tell whether the transparently cool verse is gently mocking its subject or speaker, or unwittingly, by taking their part, revealing a self-betrayal. In 1972 Betjeman was appointed Poet Laureate, in succession to Cecil Day Lewis.

In Westminster Abbey

Let me take this other glove off
    As the *vox humana*° swells,
And the beauteous fields of Eden
    Bask beneath the Abbey bells.
Here, where England's statesmen lie,°
Listen to a lady's cry.

vox humana a particularly throbbing organ stop   **statesmen lie** in part of the cathedral, under stained-glass windows of biblical scenes

Gracious Lord, oh bomb the Germans.
    Spare their women for Thy Sake,
And if that is not too easy
10   We will pardon Thy Mistake.
But, gracious Lord, whate'er shall be,
Don't let anyone bomb me.

Keep our Empire undismembered
    Guide our Forces by Thy Hand,
Gallant blacks from far Jamaica,
    Honduras and Togoland;
Protect them Lord in all their fights,
And, even more, protect the whites.

Think of what our Nation stands for,
20   Books from Boots'° and country lanes,
Free speech, free passes, class distinction,
    Democracy and proper drains.°
Lord, put beneath Thy special care
One-eighty-nine Cadogan Square.°

Although dear Lord I am a sinner,
    I have done no major crime;
Now I'll come to Evening Service
    Whensoever I have the time.
So, Lord, reserve for me a crown,
30 And do not let my shares° go down.

I will labour for Thy Kingdom,
    Help our lads to win the war,
Send white feathers to the cowards
    Join the Women's Army Corps,
Then wash the Steps around Thy Throne
In the Eternal Safety Zone.

Now I feel a little better,
    What a treat to hear Thy Word,
Where the bones of leading statesmen,
40   Have so often been interr'd.
And now, dear Lord, I cannot wait
Because I have a luncheon date.

1940

Boots' a chain of drugstores with circulating libraries
proper drains real indoor plumbing (England has always lagged behind Western Europe in the technology of comfort)

Cadogan Square an expensive, fashionable address
shares stock

GEORGE ORWELL
1903–1950

Orwell was born Eric Arthur Blair in 1903, in British India. He was brought to England in 1907 and was educated at a private preparatory school and at Eton. On leaving school he joined the Imperial Indian Police and, after serving for five years in Burma, resigned in 1928. He then made his first attempt to explore the life of the English poor, and also worked as a dishwasher in Paris. These experiences formed the subject of his first book, *Down and Out in Paris and London* (1933), for which he chose the pseudonym George Orwell. Three novels followed: *Burmese Days* (1934)—based on his police experience, *A Clergyman's Daughter* (1935), and *Keep the Aspidistra Flying* (1936).

In 1936 he took over a village store, married, and at about the same time was commissioned to write about life among the English unemployed. The result was *The Road to Wigan Pier* (1937), in which he not only produced the kind of reportage he was already well known for, but also developed his own kind of politics: anti-imperialist, anti-capitalist, but not identified with any socialist institution. By January 1937 he was fighting with POUM—an anarchist unit supporting the legal government—in Spain. He was wounded and left Spain that June to write *Homage to Catalonia* (1938), perhaps his best book, certainly one of the best books about the Spanish Civil War, and a clear statement of his independent political position. He developed tuberculosis, and while recovering in Morocco wrote the novel *Coming up for Air* (1939).

Upon returning to England he wrote several now-famous essays on popular culture —on boy's weeklies, seaside postcards, and the like—and critical essays on Dickens, Tolstoy, and Henry Miller. When World War II began he abandoned his view that the Left should not fight, and supported the cause, working for the British Broadcasting Corporation and serving as a Home Guard, but had to relinquish these duties when he became ill again. He became literary editor of the left-wing *Tribune,* and wrote *Animal Farm* (finished by February 1944 but not published till August 1945), an allegory of the failure of Russian socialism under Stalin. In 1945, when his wife died, he settled on the island of Jura off the Scottish coast. His own health grew worse while he was composing *Nineteen-Eighty-Four* (1948). He remarried in October 1949 and died of tuberculosis in January 1950.

Orwell stands in a tradition of English upper-class eccentrics, but also in the more important tradition of plain prose. His behavior and his opinions are individualistic, but they tell because he can always say exactly what he means; a sort of honest completeness of statement characterizes his writing, and that is why, apart from the last two political allegories, his fiction is less effective than his discursive prose. Thus he conveys with rare force the sense of his country as "two nations" (or more than two) but also as one; he sensed this solidarity most strongly at the time of immense national danger, when he wrote "England Your England." This essay has been criticized for mythologizing the English "family" situation—for stressing the tolerance and mildness that coexist with all the social injustice—on the ground that it is not merely superficial class differences that set certain members of the family apart from others, but also the fact that a few of them own almost everything, while most of them own nothing. He makes it easy to laugh at the "ruling class" as comic and inefficient, instead of emphasizing that they are certainly efficient enough to hold on and run the show more or less their way. His images hide the truth. That is the New Left complaint against Orwell; yet he saw the poor, as he saw the population of the colonies, as exploited. On the other hand, he knew the importance of ownership; and when he wrote this essay he saw also that in 1940 the country had been saved by some kind of family solidarity, that the conservatism of rich and poor came together usefully and enabled Britain to hold out. It is by no means clear that the nation would have been better off if this had not happened, and Orwell was too honest and also too patriotic not to realize this and say so.

England Your England

As I write, highly civilised human beings are flying overhead, trying to kill me.[1]

They do not feel any enmity against me as an individual, nor I against them. They are 'only doing their duty,' as the saying goes. Most of them, I have no doubt, are kind-hearted law-abiding men who would never dream of committing murder in private life. On the other hand, if one of them succeeds in blowing me to pieces with a well-placed bomb, he will never sleep any the worse for it. He is serving his country, which has the power to absolve him from evil.

One cannot see the modern world as it is unless one recognises the overwhelming strength of patriotism, national loyalty. In certain circumstances it can break down, at certain levels of civilisation it does not exist, but as a *positive* force there is nothing to set beside it. Christianity and international socialism are as weak as straw in comparison with it. Hitler and Mussolini rose to power in their own countries very largely because they could grasp this fact and their opponents could not.

Also, one must admit that the divisions between nation and nation are founded on real differences of outlook. Till recently it was thought proper to pretend that all human beings are very much alike, but in fact anyone able to use his eyes knows that the average of human behaviour differs enormously from country to country. Things that could happen in one country could not happen in another. Hitler's June Purge,[2] for instance, could not have happened in England. And, as Western peoples go, the English are very highly differentiated. There is a sort of backhanded admission of this in the dislike which nearly all foreigners feel for our national way of life. Few Europeans can endure living in England, and even Americans often feel more at home in Europe.

When you come back to England from any foreign country, you have immediately the sensation of breathing a different air. Even in the first few minutes dozens of small things conspire to give you this feeling. The beer is bitterer, the coins are heavier, the grass is greener, the advertisements are more blatant. The crowds in the big towns, with their mild knobby faces, their bad teeth and gentle manners, are different from a European crowd. Then the vast-

1. After the fall of France in mid-June 1940 German aircraft made daylight raids on England: first on ports and airfields, then, in September, on London. Enemy losses were too heavy for daylight bombing to continue, and from mid-September to the spring of 1941 the Germans bombed English cities, especially London, almost nightly. Civilians killed numbered over 30,000, more than half of them in London; and 3,500,000 houses were damaged or destroyed.

2. The murder of Ernst Röhm and his stormtroopers in June 1934.

ness of England swallows you up, and you lose for a while your feeling that the whole nation has a single identifiable character. Are there really such things as nations? Are we not 46 million individuals, all different? And the diversity of it, the chaos! The clatter of clogs in the Lancashire mill towns, the to-and-fro of the lorries on the Great North Road, the queues outside the Labour Exchanges, the rattle of pin-tables in the Soho pubs, the old maids biking to Holy Communion through the mists of the autumn mornings—all these are not only fragments, but *characteristic* fragments, of the English scene. How can one make a pattern out of this muddle?

But talk to foreigners, read foreign books or newspapers, and you are brought back to the same thought. Yes, there *is* something distinctive and recognisable in English civilisation. It is a culture as individual as that of Spain. It is some-how bound up with solid breakfasts and gloomy Sundays, smoky towns and winding roads, green fields and red pillar-boxes.[3] It has a flavour of its own. Moreover it is continuous, it stretches into the future and the past, there is some-thing in it that persists, as in a living creature. What can the England of 1940 have in common with the England of 1840? But then, what have you in com-mon with the child of five whose photograph your mother keeps on the mantel-piece? Nothing, except that you happen to be the same person.

And above all, it is *your* civilisation, it is *you*. However much you hate it or laugh at it, you will never be happy away from it for any length of time. The suet puddings and the red pillar-boxes have entered into your soul. Good or evil, it is yours, you belong to it, and this side the grave you will never get away from the marks that it has given you.

Meanwhile England, together with the rest of the world, is changing. And like everything else it can change only in certain directions, which up to a point can be foreseen. That is not to say that the future is fixed, merely that certain alternatives are possible and others not. A seed may grow or not grow, but at any rate a turnip seed never grows into a parsnip. It is therefore of the deepest importance to try and determine what England *is*, before guessing what part England *can play* in the huge events that are happening.

II

National characteristics are not easy to pin down, and when pinned down they often turn out to be trivialities or seem to have no connection with one another. Spaniards are cruel to animals, Italians can do nothing without making a deaf-ening noise, the Chinese are addicted to gambling. Obviously such things don't matter in themselves. Nevertheless, nothing is causeless, and even the fact that Englishmen have bad teeth can tell one something about the realities of English life.

Here are a couple of generalisations about England that would be accepted by almost all observers. One is that the English are not gifted artistically. They are not as musical as the Germans or Italians, painting and sculpture have never flourished in England as they have in France. Another is that, as Europeans go, the English are not intellectual. They have a horror of abstract thought, they

3. Pillar-shaped red mailboxes in the streets.

feel no need for any philosophy or systematic 'world-view.' Nor is this because they are 'practical,' as they are so fond of claiming for themselves. One has only to look at their methods of town-planning and water-supply, their obstinate clinging to everything that is out of date and a nuisance, a spelling system that defies analysis and a system of weights and measures that is intelligible only to the compilers of arithmetic books, to see how little they care about mere efficiency. But they have a certain power of acting without taking thought. Their world-famed hypocrisy—their double-faced attitude towards the Empire, for instance—is bound up with this. Also, in moments of supreme crisis the whole nation can suddenly draw together and act upon a species of instinct, really a code of conduct which is understood by almost everyone, though never formulated. The phrase that Hitler coined for the Germans, 'a sleepwalking people,' would have been better applied to the English. Not that there is anything to be proud of in being a sleepwalker.

But here it is worth noticing a minor English trait which is extremely well marked though not often commented on, and that is a love of flowers. This is one of the first things that one notices when one reaches England from abroad, especially if one is coming from southern Europe. Does it not contradict the English indifference to the arts? Not really, because it is found in people who have no esthetic feelings whatever. What it does link up with, however, is another English characteristic which is so much a part of us that we barely notice it, and that is the addiction to hobbies and spare-time occupations, the *privateness* of English life. We are a nation of flower-lovers, but also a nation of stamp-collectors, pigeon-fanciers, amateur carpenters, coupon-snippers, darts-players, crossword-puzzle fans. All the culture that is most truly native centres round things which even when they are communal are not official—the pub, the football match, the back garden, the fireside and the 'nice cup of tea.' The liberty of the individual is still believed in, almost as in the nineteenth century. But this has nothing to do with economic liberty, the right to exploit others for profit. It is the liberty to have a home of your own, to do what you like in your spare time, to choose your own amusements instead of having them chosen for you from above. The most hateful of all names in an English ear is Nosey Parker. It is obvious, of course, that even this purely private liberty is a lost cause. Like all other modern peoples, the English are in process of being numbered, labelled, conscripted, 'coordinated.' But the pull of their impulses is in the other direction, and the kind of regimentation that can be imposed on them will be modified in consequence. No party rallies, no Youth Movements, no coloured shirts, no Jew-baiting or 'spontaneous' demonstrations. No Gestapo either, in all probability.

But in all societies the common people must live to some extent *against* the existing order. The genuinely popular culture of England is something that goes on beneath the surface, unofficially and more or less frowned on by the authorities. One thing one notices if one looks directly at the common people, especially in the big towns, is that they are not puritanical. They are inveterate gamblers, drink as much beer as their wages will permit, are devoted to bawdy jokes, and use probably the foulest language in the world. They have to satisfy these tastes in the face of astonishing, hypocritical laws (licensing laws, lottery acts,[4] etc., etc.) which are designed to interfere with everybody but in practice allow everything to happen. Also, the common people are without definite religious belief, and have been so for centuries. The Anglican Church never had a real hold on them, it was simply a preserve of the landed gentry, and the Nonconformist sects only influenced minorities. And yet they have retained a deep tinge of Christian feeling, while almost forgetting the name of Christ. The power-worship which is the new religion of Europe, and which has infected the English intelligentsia, has never touched the common people. They have never caught up with power politics. The 'realism' which is preached in Japanese and Italian newspapers would horrify them. One can learn a good deal about the spirit of England from the comic coloured postcards that you see in the windows of cheap stationers' shops. These things are a sort of diary upon which the English people have unconsciously recorded themselves. Their old-fashioned outlook, their graded snobberies, their mixture of bawdiness and hypocrisy, their extreme gentleness, their deeply moral attitude to life, are all mirrored there.

The gentleness of the English civilisation is perhaps its most marked characteristic. You notice it the instant you set foot on English soil. It is a land where the bus conductors are good-tempered and the policemen carry no revolvers. In no country inhabited by white men is it easier to shove people off the pavement. And with this goes something that is always written off by European observers as 'decadence' or hypocrisy, the English hatred of war and militarism. It is rooted deep in history, and it is strong in the lower-middle class as well as the working class. Successive wars have shaken it but not destroyed it. Well within living memory it was common for 'the redcoats' to be booed at in the street and for the landlords of respectable public-houses to refuse to allow soldiers on the premises. In peace-time, even when there are two million unemployed, it is difficult to fill the ranks of the tiny standing army, which is officered by the county gentry and a specialized stratum of the middle class, and manned by farm labourers and slum proletarians. The mass of the people are without military knowledge or tradition, and their attitude towards war is invariably defensive. No politician could rise to power by promising them conquests or military 'glory,' no Hymn of Hate[5] has ever made any appeal to them. In the 1914–18 war the songs which the soldiers made up and sang of their own accord were not vengeful but humorous and mock-defeatist.[6] The only enemy they ever named was the sergeant-major.

In England all the boasting and flag-wagging, the 'Rule Britannia' stuff, is done by small minorities. The patriotism of the common people is not vocal or even conscious. They do not retain among their historical memories the name of a single military victory. English literature, like other literatures, is full of

4. The English licensing laws prescribe opening and closing hours for public houses (saloons) but not for private clubs. The lottery acts were full of loopholes and did not prevent enormous expenditure on the football pools.

5. The *Hassgesang*, a poem by Ernst Lissauer (1882–1937) which was popular in Germany during World War I; its refrain, *Gott strafe England*, is said to have been used as a greeting, and gave English the verb "to strafe."

6. "For example: 'I don't want to join the bloody Army. / I don't want to go into the war; / I want no more to roam. / I'd rather stay at home / Living on the earnings of a whore.' But it was not in that spirit that they fought." (Orwell)

battle-poems, but it is worth noticing that the ones that have won for themselves a kind of popularity are always a tale of disasters and retreats. There is no popular poem about Trafalgar or Waterloo, for instance. Sir John Moore's army at Corunna, fighting a desperate rear-guard action before escaping overseas (just like Dunkirk! [7]) has more appeal than a brilliant victory. The most stirring battle-poem in English is about a brigade of cavalry which charged in the wrong direction.[8] And of the last war, the four names which have really engraved themselves on the popular memory are Mons, Ypres, Gallipoli, and Passchendaele,[9] every time a disaster. The names of the great battles that finally broke the German armies are simply unknown to the general public.

The reason why the English anti-militarism disgusts foreign observers is that it ignores the existence of the British Empire. It looks like sheer hypocrisy. After all, the English absorbed a quarter of the earth and held on to it by means of a huge navy. How dare they then turn round and say that war is wicked?

It is quite true that the English are hypocritical about their Empire. In the working class this hypocrisy takes the form of not knowing that the Empire exists. But their dislike of standing armies is a perfectly sound instinct. A navy employs comparatively few people, and it is an external weapon which cannot affect home politics directly. Military dictatorships exist everywhere, but there is no such thing as a naval dictatorship. What English people of nearly all classes loathe from the bottom of their hearts is the swaggering officer type, the jingle of spurs and the crash of boots. Decades before Hitler was ever heard of, the word 'Prussian' had much the same significance in England as 'Nazi' has today. So deep does this feeling go that for a hundred years past the officers of the British Army, in peace-time, have always worn civilian clothes when off duty.

One rapid but fairly sure guide to the social atmosphere of a country is the parade-step of its army. A military parade is really a kind of ritual dance, something like a ballet, expressing a certain philosophy of life. The goose-step, for instance, is one of the most horrible sights in the world, far more terrifying than a dive-bomber. It is simply an affirmation of naked power; contained in it,

7. Sir John Moore (1761–1809) led the British retreat to Corunna in the winter of 1808–1809 during the Peninsula War. He began evacuating the troops and repulsed a French attack, but was fatally wounded. The poem on his death is by Charles Wolfe (1791–1823), published 1817. Dunkirk was the scene (from May 26 to June 4, 1940) of the evacuation —in almost a thousand vessels of all kinds—of the main part of the British Expeditionary Force, which had been cut off in northern France by the German advance through the Low Countries.

8. Although they knew they had received wrong orders, the Light Cavalry Brigade charged the Russian guns at Balaclava on September 20, 1854, during the Crimean War. Their heroism was celebrated in the famous poem "The Charge of the Light Brigade," by the Poet Laureate Tennyson, completed during the same year.

9. Mons was the scene of a battle in August 1914. Ypres was a stalemated battle later in the same year and another battle (in which poison gas was used for the first time) in March 1915. Passchendaele was the third and most disastrous Ypres campaign, a stubborn attempt to advance through mud; between June and November 1917 the British suffered, by drowning as well as by enemy action, a quarter-million casualties. Gallipoli was an attempt to open a new front by forcing the Dardanelles and capturing Constantinople. The campaign began well in February 1915 but was a failure by the end of the year.

quite consciously and intentionally, is the vision of a boot crashing down on a face. Its ugliness is part of its essence, for what it is saying is 'Yes, I *am* ugly, and you daren't laugh at me,' like the bully who makes faces at his victim. Why is the goose-step not used in England? There are, heaven knows, plenty of army officers who would be only too glad to introduce some such thing. It is not used because the people in the street would laugh. Beyond a certain point, military display is only possible in countries where the common people dare not laugh at the army. The Italians adopted the goose-step at about the time when Italy passed definitely under German control, and, as one would expect, they do it less well than the Germans. The Vichy government,[10] had it survived, was bound to introduce a stiffer parade-ground discipline into what was left of the French army. In the British army the drill is rigid and complicated, full of memories of the eighteenth century, but without definite swagger; the march is merely a formalised walk. It belongs to a society which is ruled by the sword, no doubt, but a sword which must never be taken out of the scabbard.

And yet the gentleness of English civilisation is mixed up with barbarities and anachronisms. Our criminal law is as out of date as the muskets in the Tower. Over against the Nazi Storm Trooper you have got to set that typically English figure, the hanging judge, some gouty old bully with his mind rooted in the nineteenth century, handing out savage sentences. In England until recently people were still hanged by the neck and flogged with the cat o' nine tails. Both of these punishments are obscene as well as cruel, but there has never been any genuinely popular outcry against them. People accept them (and Dartmoor,[11] and Borstal[12]) almost as they accept the weather. They are part of 'the law,' which is assumed to be unalterable.

Here one comes upon an all-important English trait: the respect for constitutionalism and legality, the belief in 'the law' as something above the State and above the individual, something which is cruel and stupid, of course, but at any rate *incorruptible*.

It is not that anyone imagines the law to be just. Everyone knows that there is one law for the rich and another for the poor. But no one accepts the implications of this, everyone takes it for granted that the law, such as it is, will be respected, and feels a sense of outrage when it is not. Remarks like 'They can't run me in; I haven't done anything wrong,' or 'They can't do that; it's against the law,' are part of the atmosphere of England. The professed enemies of society have this feeling as strongly as anyone else. One sees it in prison-books like Wilfred Macartney's *Walls Have Mouths*[13] or Jim Phelan's *Jail Journey*,[14] in the solemn idiocies that take place at the trials of Conscientious Objectors,[15] in letters to the papers from eminent Marxist professors, pointing out that this

10. After the fall of France the Germans set up a puppet government under Marshal Pétain at Vichy in the unoccupied part of the country.
11. Prison on the Devonshire moors.
12. Generic name for English schools for delinquent boys.
13. Subtitled "A Record of Ten Years Penal Servitude" (1936).
14. Published in 1940.
15. Conscientious objectors to the draft had the right to appear before a tribunal usually consisting of a judge and distinguished local laymen. They pleaded their case of conscience and answered questions such as, "What would you do if you saw a German trying to rape your sister?"

or that is a 'miscarriage of British justice.' Everyone believes in his heart that the law can be, ought to be, and, on the whole, will be impartially administered. The totalitarian idea that there is no such thing as law, there is only power, has never taken root. Even the intelligentsia have only accepted it in theory.

An illusion can become a half-truth, a mask can alter the expression of a face. The familiar arguments to the effect that democracy is 'just the same as' or 'just as bad as' totalitarianism never take account of this fact. All such arguments boil down to saying that half a loaf is the same as no bread. In England such concepts as justice, liberty, and objective truth are still believed in. They may be illusions, but they are very powerful illusions. The belief in them influences conduct, national life is different because of them. In proof of which, look about you. Where are the rubber truncheons, where is the castor oil? [16] The sword is still in the scabbard, and while it stays there corruption cannot go beyond a certain point. The English electoral system, for instance, is an all but open fraud. In a dozen obvious ways it is gerrymandered [17] in the interest of the monied class. But until some deep change has occurred in the public mind, it cannot become *completely* corrupt. You do not arrive at the polling booth to find men with revolvers telling you which way to vote, nor are the votes miscounted, nor is there any direct bribery. Even hypocrisy is a powerful safeguard. The hanging judge, that evil old man in scarlet robe and horsehair wig, whom nothing short of dynamite will ever teach what century he is living in, but who will at any rate interpret the law according to the books and will in no circumstances take a money bribe, is one of the symbolic figures of England. He is a symbol of the strange mixture of reality and illusion, democracy and privilege, humbug and decency, the subtle network of compromises, by which the nation keeps itself in its familiar shape.

III

I have spoken all the while of 'the nation,' 'England,' 'Britain,' as though 45 million souls could somehow be treated as a unit. But is not England notoriously two nations, the rich and the poor? Dare one pretend that there is anything in common between people with £ 100,000 a year and people with £ 1 a week? And even Welsh and Scottish readers are likely to have been offended because I have used the word 'England' oftener than 'Britain,' as though the whole population dwelt in London and the Home Counties and neither north nor west possessed a culture of its own.

One gets a better view of this question if one considers the minor point first. It is quite true that the so-called races of Britain feel themselves to be very different from one another. A Scotsman, for instance, does not thank you if you call him an Englishman. You can see the hesitation we feel on this point by the fact that we call our islands by no less than six different names, England, Britain, Great Britain, the British Isles, the United Kingdom, and, in very exalted moments, Albion. [18] Even the differences between north and south England loom large in our own eyes. But somehow these differences fade away

16. Huge overdoses of castor oil were used by interrogators.
17. To gerrymander is to rig the constituencies for the benefit of one's own party.
18. Ancient poetic name for Great Britain.

the moment that any two Britons are confronted by a European. It is very rare
to meet a foreigner, other than an American, who can distinguish between
English and Scots or even English and Irish. To a Frenchman, the Breton and
the Auvergnat [19] seem very different beings, and the accent of Marseilles is a
stock joke in Paris. Yet we speak of 'France' and 'the French,' recognising
France as an entity, a single civilisation, which in fact it is. So also with ourselves. Looked at from the outside, even the cockney and the Yorkshireman
have a strong family resemblance.

And even the distinction between rich and poor dwindles somewhat when
one regards the nation from the outside. There is no question about the inequality of wealth in England. It is grosser than in any European country, and
you have only to look down the nearest street to see it. Economically, England
is certainly two nations, if not three or four. But at the same time the vast majority of the people *feel* themselves to be a single nation and are conscious of
resembling one another more than they resemble foreigners. Patriotism is usually
stronger than class-hatred, and always stronger than any kind of internationalism. Except for a brief moment in 1920 (the 'Hands off Russia' [20] movement)
the British working class have never thought or acted internationally. For two
and a half years they watched their comrades in Spain slowly strangled, and
never aided them by even a single strike.[21] But when their own country (the
country of Lord Nuffield [22] and Mr. Montagu Norman [23]) was in danger, their
attitude was very different. At the moment when it seemed likely that England
might be invaded, Anthony Eden appealed over the radio for Local Defence
Volunteers.[24] He got a quarter of a million men in the first twenty-four hours,
and another million in the subsequent month. One has only to compare these
figures with, for instance, the number of Conscientious Objectors to see how
vast is the strength of traditional loyalties compared with new ones.

In England patriotism takes different forms in different classes, but it runs
like a connecting thread through nearly all of them. Only the Europeanised
intelligentsia are really immune to it. As a positive emotion it is stronger in the
middle class than in the upper class—the cheap public schools,[25] for instance,
are more given to patriotic demonstrations than the expensive ones—but the

19. Frenchmen from Brittany and from the Auvergne region.
20. In 1920, when there was thought to be some danger of Britain's involving itself with
Poland against Soviet Russia, there were demonstrations against intervention. London dock-
ers refused to load a munition ship, and the Trade Unions resolved to take industrial action
if necessary.
21. "It is true that they aided them to a certain extent with money. Still, the sums raised for
the various aid-Spain funds would not equal 5 per cent of the turnover of the Football Pools
during the same period." (Orwell)
22. William Morris, 1st Viscount Nuffield, pioneer British automobile manufacturer—the
English Henry Ford.
23. Governor of the Bank of England 1920–44.
24. Eden resigned the office of Foreign Secretary in 1938 as a protest against Chamberlain's
appeasement, and became Churchill's War Minister in 1940. In the early summer of 1940,
under threat of immediate German invasion, Eden broadcast an appeal for an emergency
civilian army, first called the Local Defence Volunteers, later the Home Guard. Eden was
prime minister 1955–57.
25. Private, fee-charging schools.

number of definitely treacherous rich men, the Laval-Quisling [26] type, is probably very small. In the working class patriotism is profound, but it is unconscious. The working man's heart does not leap when he sees a Union Jack.[27] But the famous 'insularity' and 'xenophobia' [28] of the English is far stronger in the working class than in the bourgeoisie. In all countries the poor are more national than the rich, but the English working class are outstanding in their abhorrence of foreign habits. Even when they are obliged to live abroad for years they refuse either to accustom themselves to foreign food or to learn foreign languages. Nearly every Englishman of working-class origin considers it effeminate to pronounce a foreign word correctly. During the war of 1914–18 the English working class were in contact with foreigners to an extent that is rarely possible. The sole result was that they brought back a hatred of all Europeans, except the Germans, whose courage they admired. In four years on French soil they did not even acquire a liking for wine. The insularity of the English, their refusal to take foreigners seriously, is a folly that has to be paid for very heavily from time to time. But it plays its part in the English *mystique*, and the intellectuals who have tried to break it down have generally done more harm than good. At bottom it is the same quality in the English character that repels the tourist and keeps out the invader.

Here one comes back to two English characteristics that I pointed out, seemingly rather at random, at the beginning of the last chapter. One is the lack of artistic ability. This is perhaps another way of saying that the English are outside the European culture. For there is one art in which they have shown plenty of talent, namely literature. But this is also the only art that cannot cross frontiers. Literature, especially poetry, and lyric poetry most of all, is a kind of family joke, with little or no value outside its own language-group. Except for Shakespeare, the best English poets are barely known in Europe, even as names. The only poets who are widely read are Byron, who is admired for the wrong reasons, and Oscar Wilde, who is pitied as a victim of English hypocrisy. And linked up with this, though not very obviously, is the lack of philosophical faculty, the absence in nearly all Englishmen of any need for an ordered system of thought or even for the use of logic.

Up to a point, the sense of national unity is a substitute for a 'world-view.' Just because patriotism is all but universal and not even the rich are uninfluenced by it, there can come moments when the whole nation suddenly swings together and does the same thing, like a herd of cattle facing a wolf. There was such a moment, unmistakably, at the time of the disaster in France.[29] After eight months of vaguely wondering what the war was about, the people suddenly knew what they had got to do: first, to get the army away from Dunkirk, and secondly to prevent invasion. It was like the awakening of a giant. Quick!

26. Pierre Laval, right-wing French politician, Pétain's prime minister 1942–44, shot as Nazi collaborator in 1945; Vidkin Quisling, Norwegian Nazi collaborator whose name became the generic term for such traitors.
27. British national flag, incorporating the crosses of St. George (England), St. David (Wales), and St. Andrew (Scotland).
28. Hatred of foreigners.
29. During May and June, 1940.

Danger! The Philistines be upon thee, Samson! And then the swift unanimous action—and then, alas, the prompt relapse into sleep. In a divided nation that would have been exactly the moment for a big peace movement to arise. But does this mean that the instinct of the English will always tell them to do the right thing? Not at all, merely that it will tell them to do the same thing. In the 1931 General Election,[30] for instance, we all did the wrong thing in perfect unison. We were as single-minded as the Gadarene swine.[31] But I honestly doubt whether we can say that we were shoved down the slope against our will.

It follows that British democracy is less of a fraud than it sometimes appears. A foreign observer sees only the huge inequality of wealth, the unfair electoral system, the governing-class control over the Press, the radio, and education, and concludes that democracy is simply a polite name for dictatorship. But this ignores the considerable agreement that does unfortunately exist between the leaders and the led. However much one may hate to admit it, it is almost certain that between 1931 and 1940 the National Government represented the will of the mass of the people. It tolerated slums, unemployment, and a cowardly foreign policy. Yes, but so did public opinion. It was a stagnant period, and its natural leaders were mediocrities.

In spite of the campaigns of a few thousand left-wingers, it is fairly certain that the bulk of the English people were behind Chamberlain's foreign policy.[32] More, it is fairly certain that the same struggle was going on in Chamberlain's mind as in the minds of ordinary people. His opponents professed to see in him a dark and wily schemer, plotting to sell England to Hitler, but it is far likelier that he was merely a stupid old man doing his best according to his very dim lights. It is difficult otherwise to explain the contradictions of his policy, his failure to grasp any of the courses that were open to him. Like the mass of the people, he did not want to pay the price either of peace or of war. And public opinion was behind him all the while, in policies that were completely incompatible with one another. It was behind him when he went to Munich,[33] when he tried to come to an understanding with Russia, when he gave the guarantee

30. The fall of the Labor government as a result of the economic crisis of 1931 was followed by the establishment of a "National" government with representatives of all parties and no effective opposition. This arrangement was overwhelmingly endorsed by a general election. The administration was dominated by the Conservative Party, though Ramsay MacDonald, the Labor leader, was prime minister. He was succeeded by a Tory, Stanley Baldwin, in June 1935, and another general election ensured the continuance of coalition government until the end of the war. Throughout the 'thirties, despite the efforts of Churchill (who held no office) this government delayed rearmament and followed the policy of appeasing the European dictators.

31. When Jesus exorcised the unclean spirits from a madman, he allowed these spirits to pass into the swine of Gadara, which then "ran violently down a steep place into the sea . . . and were choked in the sea" (Mark 5:13).

32. Arthur Neville Chamberlain (1869–1940), who succeeded Baldwin as prime minister in 1937, continued the policy of appeasement culminating in the Munich Agreement of 1938, which sacrificed part of Czechoslovakia to Germany in return for a promise (broken six months later) to make no further demands on that or any other country.

33. Chamberlain's flight to Munich was his third visit to Hitler during September 1938. The agreement was signed on September 29 by Hitler, Mussolini, Chamberlain, and French Premier Daladier.

to Poland,[34] when he honoured it, and when he prosecuted the war half-heartedly. Only when the results of his policy became apparent did it turn against him; which is to say that it turned against its own lethargy of the past seven years. Thereupon the people picked a leader nearer to their mood, Churchill, who was at any rate able to grasp that wars are not won without fighting. Later, perhaps, they will pick another leader who can grasp that only socialist nations can fight effectively.

Do I mean by all this that England is a genuine democracy? No, not even a reader of the *Daily Telegraph* [35] could quite swallow that.

England is the most class-ridden country under the sun. It is a land of snobbery and privilege, ruled largely by the old and silly. But in any calculation about it one has got to take into account its emotional unity, the tendency of nearly all its inhabitants to feel alike and act together in moments of supreme crisis. It is the only great country in Europe that is not obliged to drive hundreds of thousands of its nationals into exile or the concentration camp. At this moment, after a year of war, newspapers and pamphlets abusing the Government, praising the enemy and clamouring for surrender are being sold on the streets, almost without interference. And this is less from a respect for freedom of speech than from a simple perception that these things don't matter. It is safe to let a paper like *Peace News* [36] be sold, because it is certain that 95 per cent of the population will never want to read it. The nation is bound together by an invisible chain. At any normal time the ruling class will rob, mismanage, sabotage, lead us into the muck; but let popular opinion really make itself heard, let them get a tug from below that they cannot avoid feeling, and it is difficult for them not to respond. The left-wing writers who denounce the whole of the ruling class as 'pro-fascist' are grossly oversimplifying. Even among the inner clique of politicians who brought us to our present pass, it is doubtful whether there were any *conscious* traitors. The corruption that happens in England is seldom of that kind. Nearly always it is more in the nature of self-deception, of the right hand not knowing what the left hand doeth. And being unconscious, it is limited. One sees this at its most obvious in the English press. Is the English press honest or dishonest? At normal times it is deeply dishonest. All the papers that matter live off their advertisements, and the advertisers exercise an indirect censorship over news. Yet I do not suppose there is one paper in England that can be straightforwardly bribed with hard cash. In the France of the Third Republic [37] all but a very few of the newspapers could notoriously be bought over the counter like so many pounds of cheese. Public life in England has never been *openly* scandalous. It has not reached the pitch of disintegration at which humbug can be dropped.

England is not the jewelled isle of Shakespeare's much-quoted passage, nor

34. In March 1939 German troops marched into Prague and took over the rest of Czechoslovakia. When there were rumors of an imminent attack on Poland in the same month, Chamberlain, stung by Hitler's Munich treachery, offered Poland British support; an Anglo-Polish Agreement was signed on April 6.

35. Conservative newspaper.

36. Newspaper of the Peace Pledge Union, the principal pacifist organization.

37. 1871–1946.

is it the inferno depicted by Dr. Goebbels.[38] More than either it resembles a family, a rather stuffy Victorian family, with not many black sheep in it but with all its cupboards bursting with skeletons. It has rich relations who have to be kow-towed to and poor relations who are horribly sat upon, and there is a deep conspiracy of silence about the source of the family income. It is a family in which the young are generally thwarted and most of the power is in the hands of irresponsible uncles and bedridden aunts. Still, it is a family. It has its private language and its common memories, and at the approach of an enemy it closes its ranks. A family with the wrong members in control—that, perhaps, is as near as one can come to describing England in a phrase.

IV

Probably the battle of Waterloo *was* won on the playing-fields of Eton,[39] but the opening battles of all subsequent wars have been lost there. One of the dominant facts in English life during the past three-quarters of a century has been the decay of ability in the ruling class.

In the years between 1920 and 1940 it was happening with the speed of a chemical reaction. Yet at the moment of writing it is still possible to speak of a ruling class. Like the knife which has had two new blades and three new handles, the upper fringe of English society is still almost what it was in the mid-nineteenth century. After 1832 [40] the old landowning aristocracy steadily lost power, but instead of disappearing or becoming a fossil they simply inter-married with the merchants, manufacturers, and financiers who had replaced them, and soon turned them into accurate copies of themselves. The wealthy ship-owner or cotton-miller set up for himself an alibi as a country gentleman, while his sons learned the right mannerisms at public schools which had been designed for just that purpose. England was ruled by an aristocracy constantly recruited from parvenus.[41] And considering what energy the self-made men possessed, and considering that they were buying their way into a class which at any rate had a tradition of public service, one might have expected that able rulers could be produced in some such way.

And yet somehow the ruling class decayed, lost its ability, its daring, finally even its ruthlessness, until a time came when stuffed shirts like Eden or Halifax [42] could stand out as men of exceptional talent. As for Baldwin,[43] one could not even dignify him with the name of stuffed shirt. He was simply a hole in the air. The mishandling of England's domestic problems during the nineteen-twenties had been bad enough, but British foreign policy between 1931 and 1939 is one of the wonders of the world. Why? What had happened? What was it that at every decisive moment made every British statesman do the wrong thing with so unerring an instinct?

38. Hitler's Minister of Propaganda.
39. Remark attributed to the Duke of Wellington.
40. The First Reform Bill, extending the franchise, was passed that year.
41. Upstarts; newly wealthy or important people.
42. Lord Halifax was Viceroy of India and Foreign Secretary in Chamberlain's adminis-tration.
43. Stanley Baldwin was prime minister 1923–24, 1924–29, 1935–37; responsible for British nonintervention in the Spanish Civil War and held to represent the quietist mood of England between the world wars.

The underlying fact was that the whole position of the monied class had long ceased to be justifiable. There they sat, at the centre of a vast empire and a world-wide financial network, drawing interest and profits and spending them—on what? It was fair to say that life within the British Empire was in many ways better than life outside it. Still, the Empire was undeveloped, India slept in the Middle Ages, the Dominions lay empty, with foreigners jealously barred out, and even England was full of slums and unemployment. Only half a million people, the people in the country houses, definitely benefited from the existing system. Moreover, the tendency of small businesses to merge together into large ones robbed more and more of the monied class of their function and turned them into mere *owners,* their work being done for them by salaried managers and technicians. For long past there had been in England an entirely functionless class, living on money that was invested they hardly knew where, the 'idle rich,' the people whose photographs you can look at in the *Tatler* and the *Bystander,*[44] always supposing that you want to. The existence of these people was by any standard unjustifiable. They were simply parasites, less useful to society than his fleas are to a dog.

By 1920 there were many people who were aware of all this. By 1930 millions were aware of it. But the British ruling class obviously could not admit to themselves that their usefulness was at an end. Had they done that they would have had to abdicate. For it was not possible for them to turn themselves into mere bandits, like the American millionaires, consciously clinging to unjust privileges and beating down opposition by bribery and tear-gas bombs. After all, they belonged to a class with a certain tradition, they had been to public schools where the duty of dying for your country, if necessary, is laid down as the first and greatest of the Commandments. They had to *feel* themselves true patriots, even while they plundered their countrymen. Clearly there was only one escape for them—into stupidity. They could keep society in its existing shape only by being *unable* to grasp that any improvement was possible. Difficult though this was, they achieved it, largely by fixing their eyes on the past and refusing to notice the changes that were going on round them.

There is much in England that this explains. It explains the decay of country life, due to the keeping-up of a sham feudalism which drives the more spirited workers off the land. It explains the immobility of the public schools, which have barely altered since the 'eighties of the last century. It explains the military incompetence which has again and again startled the world. Since the 'fifties every war in which England has engaged has started off with a series of disasters, after which the situation has been saved by people comparatively low in the social scale. The higher commanders, drawn from the aristocracy, could never prepare for modern war, because in order to do so they would have had to admit to themselves that the world was changing. They have always clung to obsolete methods and weapons, because they inevitably saw each war as a repetition of the last. Before the Boer War they prepared for the Zulu War,[45] before 1914 for the Boer War, and before the present war for 1914. Even at this moment hundreds of thousands of men in England are being trained with

44. Papers devoted to "society" gossip.
45. 1879.

the bayonet, a weapon entirely useless except for opening tins. It is worth noticing that the navy and, latterly, the Air Force, have always been more efficient than the regular army. But the navy is only partially, and the Air Force hardly at all, within the ruling-class orbit.

It must be admitted that so long as things were peaceful the methods of the British ruling class served them well enough. Their own people manifestly tolerated them. However unjustly England might be organised, it was at any rate not torn by class warfare or haunted by secret police. The Empire was peaceful as no area of comparable size has ever been. Throughout its vast extent, nearly a quarter of the earth, there were fewer armed men than would be found necessary by a minor Balkan state. As people to live under, and looking at them merely from a liberal, *negative* standpoint, the British ruling class had their points. They were preferable to the truly modern men, the Nazis and Fascists. But it had long been obvious that they would be helpless against any serious attack from the outside.

They could not struggle against Nazism or Fascism, because they could not understand them. Neither could they have struggled against Communism, if Communism had been a serious force in Western Europe. To understand Fascism they would have had to study the theory of socialism, which would have forced them to realise that the economic system by which they lived was unjust, inefficient, and out of date. But it was exactly this fact that they had trained themselves never to face. They dealt with Fascism as the cavalry generals of 1914 dealt with the machine gun—by ignoring it. After years of aggression and massacres, they had grasped only one fact, that Hitler and Mussolini were hostile to Communism. Therefore, it was argued, they *must* be friendly to the British dividend-drawer. Hence the truly frightening spectacle of Conservative M.P.s wildly cheering the news that British ships, bringing food to the Spanish Republican government, had been bombed by Italian aeroplanes.[46] Even when they had begun to grasp that Fascism was dangerous, its essentially revolutionary nature, the huge military effort it was capable of making, the sort of tactics it would use, were quite beyond their comprehension. At the time of the Spanish civil war, anyone with as much political knowledge as can be acquired from a sixpenny pamphlet on socialism knew that if Franco [47] won, the result would be strategically disastrous for England; and yet generals and admirals who had given their lives to the study of war were unable to grasp this fact. This vein of political ignorance runs right through English official life, through Cabinet ministers, ambassadors, consuls, judges, magistrates, policemen. The policeman who arrests the 'Red' does not understand the theories the 'Red' is preaching; if he did, his own position as bodyguard of the monied class might seem less pleasant to him. There is reason to think that even military espionage is hopelessly hampered by ignorance of the new economic doctrines and the ramifications of the underground parties.

The British ruling class were not altogether wrong in thinking that Fascism

46. The rejoicing of the Conservative members of Parliament arose from their conviction that a Fascist victory in Spain was preferable to a Republican-Socialist one achieved with Soviet aid.

47. Francisco Franco (b. 1892), leader of the Spanish rebellion.

was on their side. It is a fact that any rich man, unless he is a Jew, has less to fear from Fascism than from either Communism or democratic socialism. One ought never to forget this, for nearly the whole of German and Italian propaganda is designed to cover it up. The natural instinct of men like Simon,[48] Hoare,[49] Chamberlain, etc., was to come to an agreement with Hitler. But— and here the peculiar feature of English life that I have spoken of, the deep sense of national solidarity, comes in—they could only do so by breaking up the Empire and selling their own people into semi-slavery. A truly corrupt class would have done this without hesitation, as in France. But things had not gone that distance in England. Politicians who would make cringing speeches about 'the duty of loyalty to our conquerors' are hardly to be found in English public life. Tossed to and fro between their incomes and their principles, it was impossible that men like Chamberlain should do anything but make the worst of both worlds.

One thing that has always shown that the English ruling class are *morally* fairly sound, is that in time of war they are ready enough to get themselves killed. Several dukes, earls and what-not were killed in the recent campaign in Flanders. That could not happen if these people were the cynical scoundrels that they are sometimes declared to be. It is important not to misunderstand their motives, or one cannot predict their actions. What is to be expected of them is not treachery or physical cowardice, but stupidity, unconscious sabotage, an infallible instinct for doing the wrong thing. They are not wicked, or not altogether wicked; they are merely unteachable. Only when their money and power are gone will the younger among them begin to grasp what century they are living in.

The stagnation of the Empire in the between-war years affected everyone in England, but it had an especially direct effect upon two important sub-sections of the middle class. One was the military and imperialist middle class, generally nicknamed the Blimps,[50] and the other the left-wing intelligentsia. These two seemingly hostile types, symbolic opposites—the half-pay colonel with his bull neck and diminutive brain, like a dinosaur, the highbrow with his domed forehead and stalk-like neck—are mentally linked together and constantly interact upon one another; in any case they are born to a considerable extent into the same families.

Thirty years ago the Blimp class was already losing its vitality. The middle-class families celebrated by Kipling, the prolific lowbrow families whose sons officered the army and navy and swarmed over all the waste places of the earth from the Yukon to the Irrawaddy,[51] were dwindling before 1914. The thing that had killed them was the telegraph. In a narrowing world, more and more

48. John Allsebrook Simon held many high offices and was Lord Chancellor in Churchill's wartime administration.
49. Samuel Hoare, Conservative politician and appeaser, was Foreign Secretary at the time of the Ethiopian crisis of 1935, and British diplomatic representative in Madrid during the Civil War.
50. Colonel Blimp was invented by the cartoonist David Low to ridicule Conservative upper-class "stupidity."
51. Principal river of Burma.

governed from Whitehall, there was every year less room for individual initiative. Men like Clive, Nelson, Nicholson, Gordon [52] would find no place for themselves in the modern British Empire. By 1920 nearly every inch of the colonial empire was in the grip of Whitehall. Well-meaning, overcivilized men, in dark suits and black felt hats, with neatly rolled umbrellas crooked over the left forearm, were imposing their constipated view of life on Malaya and Nigeria, Mombasa and Mandalay. The one-time empire-builders were reduced to the status of clerks, buried deeper and deeper under mounds of paper and red tape. In the early 'twenties one could see, all over the Empire, the older officials, who had known more spacious days, writhing impotently under the changes that were happening. From that time onwards it has been next door to impossible to induce young men of spirit to take any part in imperial administration. And what was true of the official world was true also of the commercial. The great monopoly companies swallowed up hosts of petty traders. Instead of going out to trade adventurously in the Indies one went to an office stool in Bombay or Singapore. And life in Bombay or Singapore was actually duller and safer than life in London. Imperialist sentiment remained strong in the middle class, chiefly owing to family tradition, but the job of administering the Empire had ceased to appeal. Few able men went east of Suez if there was any way of avoiding it.

But the general weakening of imperialism, and to some extent of the whole British morale, that took place during the nineteen-thirties, was partly the work of the left-wing intelligentsia, itself a kind of growth that had sprouted from the stagnation of the Empire.

It should be noted that there is now no intelligentsia that is not in some sense 'Left.' Perhaps the last right-wing intellectual was T. E. Lawrence.[53] Since about 1930 everyone describable as an 'intellectual' has lived in a state of chronic discontent with the existing order. Necessarily so, because society as it was constituted had no room for him. In an Empire that was simply stagnant, neither being developed nor falling to pieces, and in an England ruled by people whose chief asset was their stupidity, to be 'clever' was to be suspect. If you had the kind of brain that could understand the poems of T. S. Eliot or the theories of Karl Marx, the higher-ups would see to it that you were kept out of any important job. The intellectuals could find a function for themselves only in the literary reviews and the left-wing political parties.

The mentality of the English left-wing intelligentsia can be studied in half a dozen weekly and monthly papers. The immediately striking thing about all these papers is their generally negative, querulous attitude, their complete

52. Robert Clive (1725–74) rose in the East India Company to become its leading general; for a time virtual ruler of Bengal. Horatio Viscount Nelson (1758–1805), greatest British admiral, victor and victim of Trafalgar. John Nicholson (1822–57), soldier, administrator in India, killed at siege of Delhi. Charles George Gordon (1833–85) took part in capture of Peking (1860), hence known as "Chinese Gordon." Later, as governor of the Sudan, he was besieged in Khartoum in 1884 and murdered two days before the arrival of Kitchener's relief force.
53. Known as "Lawrence of Arabia" (1888–1935) for his part in stimulating Arab revolt against the Turks during World War I.

lack at all times of any constructive suggestion. There is little in them except the irresponsible carping of people who have never been and never expect to be in a position of power. Another marked characteristic is the emotional shallow-ness of people who live in a world of ideas and have little contact with physical reality. Many intellectuals of the Left were flabbily pacifist up to 1935, shrieked for war against Germany in the years 1935–39, and then promptly cooled off when the war started. It is broadly though not precisely true that the people who were most 'anti-Fascist' during the Spanish civil war are most defeatist now. And underlying this is the really important fact about so many of the English intelligentsia—their severance from the common culture of the country.

In intention, at any rate, the English intelligentsia are Europeanised. They take their cookery from Paris and their opinions from Moscow. In the general patriotism of the country they form a sort of island of dissident thought. England is perhaps the only great country whose intellectuals are ashamed of their own nationality. In left-wing circles it is always felt that there is something slightly disgraceful in being an Englishman and that it is a duty to snigger at every English institution, from horse-racing to suet puddings. It is a strange fact, but it is unquestionably true, that almost any English intellectual would feel more ashamed of standing to attention during 'God save the King' than of stealing from a poor box. All through the critical years many left-wingers were chipping away at English morale, trying to spread an outlook that was some-times squashily pacifist, sometimes violently pro-Russian, but always anti-British. It is questionable how much effect this had, but it certainly had some. If the English people suffered for several years a real weakening of morale, so that the Fascist nations judged that they were 'decadent' and that it was safe to plunge into war, the intellectual sabotage from the Left was partly responsible. Both the *New Statesman* and the *News-Chronicle*[54] cried out against the Munich settlement, but even they had done something to make it possible. Ten years of systematic Blimp-baiting affected even the Blimps themselves and made it harder than it had been before to get intelligent young men to enter the armed forces. Given the stagnation of the Empire the military middle class must have decayed in any case, but the spread of a shallow Leftism hastened the process.

It is clear that the special position of the English intellectuals during the past ten years as purely *negative* creatures, mere anti-Blimps, was a by-product of ruling-class stupidity. Society could not use them, and they had not got it in them to see that devotion to one's country implies 'for better, for worse.' Both Blimps and highbrows took for granted, as though it were a law of nature, the divorce between patriotism and intelligence. If you were a patriot you read *Blackwood's Magazine*[55] and publicly thanked God that you were 'not brainy.' If you were an intellectual you sniggered at the Union Jack and regarded physical courage as barbarous. It is obvious that this preposterous convention

54. *The New Statesman* was launched in 1913 as the journal of the Fabian Society (social-ism by reform) and still represents the viewpoint of intellectual socialism in England; the *News Chronicle,* a daily of liberal opinions, is now defunct.
55. Edinburgh-based literary journal of conservative cast, founded 1817.

cannot continue. The Bloomsbury highbrow,[56] with his mechanical snigger, is as out of date as the cavalry colonel. A modern nation cannot afford either of them. Patriotism and intelligence will have to come together again. It is the fact that we are fighting a war, and a very peculiar kind of war, that may make this possible.

VI

One of the most important developments in England during the past twenty years has been the upward and downward extension of the middle class. It has happened on such a scale as to make the old classification of society into capitalists, proletarians, and petit-bourgeois (small property-owners) almost obsolete.

England is a country in which property and financial power are concentrated in very few hands. Few people in modern England *own* anything at all, except clothes, furniture, and possibly a house. The peasantry have long since disappeared, the independent shopkeeper is being destroyed, the small businessman is diminishing in numbers. But at the same time modern industry is so complicated that it cannot get along without great numbers of managers, salesmen, engineers, chemists, and technicians of all kinds, drawing fairly large salaries. And these in turn call into being a professional class of doctors, lawyers, teachers, artists, etc., etc. The tendency of advanced capitalism has therefore been to enlarge the middle class and not to wipe it out as it once seemed likely to do.

But much more important than this is the spread of middle-class ideas and habits among the working class. The British working class are now better off in almost all ways than they were thirty years ago. This is partly due to the efforts of the Trade Unions, but partly to the mere advance of physical science. It is not always realised that within rather narrow limits the standard of life of a country can rise without a corresponding rise in real wages. Up to a point, civilisation can lift itself up by its boot-tags. However unjustly society is organised, certain technical advances are bound to benefit the whole community, because certain kinds of goods are necessarily held in common. A millionaire cannot, for example, light the streets for himself while darkening them for other people. Nearly all citizens of civilised countries now enjoy the use of good roads, germ-free water, police protection, free libraries and probably free education of a kind. Public education in England has been meanly starved of money, but it has nevertheless improved, largely owing to the devoted efforts of the teachers, and the habit of reading has become enormously more widespread. To an increasing extent the rich and the poor read the same books, and they also see the same films and listen to the same radio programmes. And the differences in their way of life have been diminished by the mass-production of cheap clothes and improvements in housing. So far as outward

56. A type of intellectual associated with King's College and Trinity College Cambridge, and the Bloomsbury district of London, where Leonard and Virginia Woolf, Lytton Strachey, J. M. Keynes, and others congregated (see E. M. Forster Headnote, above). Their mannerisms and cliquishness, as well as their dissociation from popular thought and practical politics, made them odious to such as Lawrence and Orwell; the designation "highbrow" belonged to them from the start.

appearance goes, the clothes of rich and poor, especially in the case of women, differ far less than they did thirty or even fifteen years ago. As to housing, England still has slums which are a blot on civilisation, but much building has been done during the past ten years, largely by the local authorities. The modern Council house,[57] with its bathroom and electric light, is smaller than the stockbroker's villa, but it is recognisably the same kind of house, which the farm labourer's cottage is not. A person who has grown up in a Council housing estate is likely to be—indeed, visibly *is*—more middle class in outlook than a person who has grown up in a slum.

The effect of all this is a general softening of manners. It is enhanced by the fact that modern industrial methods tend always to demand less muscular effort and therefore to leave people with more energy when their day's work is done. Many workers in the light industries are less truly manual labourers than is a doctor or a grocer. In tastes, habits, manners, and outlook the working class and the middle class are drawing together. The unjust distinctions remain, but the real differences diminish. The old-style 'proletarian'—collarless, unshaven and with muscles warped by heavy labour—still exists, but he is constantly decreasing in numbers; he only predominates in the heavy-industry areas of the north of England.

After 1918 there began to appear something that had never existed in England before: people of indeterminate social class. In 1910 every human being in these islands could be 'placed' in an instant by his clothes, manners and accent. That is no longer the case. Above all, it is not the case in the new townships that have developed as a result of cheap motor cars and the south-ward shift of industry. The place to look for the germs of the future England is in the light-industry areas and along the arterial roads. In Slough, Dagenham, Barnet, Letchworth, Hayes[58]—everywhere, indeed, on the outskirts of great towns—the old pattern is gradually changing into something new. In those vast new wildernesses of glass and brick the sharp distinctions of the older kind of town, with its slums and mansions, or of the country, with its manor-houses and squalid cottages, no longer exist. There are wide gradations of income, but it is the same kind of life that is being lived at different levels, in labour-saving flats or Council houses, along the concrete roads and in the naked democracy of the swimming-pools. It is a rather restless, cultureless life, cen-tering round tinned food, *Picture Post*,[59] the radio and the internal combustion engine. It is a civilisation in which children grow up with an intimate knowl-edge of magnetoes and in complete ignorance of the Bible. To that civilisation belong the people who are most at home in and most definitely *of* the modern world, the technicians and the higher-paid skilled workers, the airmen and their mechanics, the radio experts, film producers, popular journalists, and industrial chemists. They are the indeterminate stratum at which the older class distinc-tions are beginning to break down.

This war, unless we are defeated, will wipe out most of the existing class privileges. There are every day fewer people who wish them to continue. Nor

57. Low-cost housing unit rented from local town council.
58. Towns now virtually absorbed in Greater London.
59. Popular (and intelligent) picture paper, 1938–57.

need we fear that as the pattern changes life in England will lose its peculiar flavour. The new red cities of Greater London are crude enough, but these things are only the rash that accompanies a change. In whatever shape England emerges from the war, it will be deeply tinged with the characteristics that I have spoken of earlier. The intellectuals who hope to see it Russianised or Germanised will be disappointed. The gentleness, the hypocrisy, the thought-lessness, the reverence for law and the hatred of uniforms will remain, along with the suet puddings and the misty skies. It needs some very great disaster, such as prolonged subjugation by a foreign enemy, to destroy a national culture. The Stock Exchange will be pulled down, the horse plough will give way to the tractor, the country houses will be turned into children's holiday camps, the Eton and Harrow match[60] will be forgotten, but England will still be England, an everlasting animal stretching into the future and the past, and, like all living things, having the power to change out of recognition and yet remain the same.

1940   1941

SAMUEL BECKETT
1906–

Perhaps the greatest living writer in English, and certainly the direct follower of James Joyce in many ways, Beckett was born in Dublin, to a family of middle-class Protes-tants. He attended the same school as Oscar Wilde, and took a prize degree in Modern Languages at Trinity College, Dublin, in 1927. Thereafter he took a post, in Paris, as a visiting lecturer in English at the *Ecole Normale Supérieure*. In Paris he met Joyce and became part of his circle—indeed, in 1929 he published an essay on Joyce's *Work in Progress* (which was to become part of *Finnegans Wake*). Returning in 1930 to a Lectureship in French at Trinity College, he completed a master's degree in the philosophy of Descartes and his followers; but he abandoned the post in 1931 and wandered about Europe, living in London, France, and Germany. In 1937 he settled in Paris, where he has remained, save for trips abroad, ever since.

Beckett started to publish stories and poems while teaching in Paris; his poem *Whoroscope*, replete with notes that seem to parody those of Eliot's *The Waste Land*, won a prize for a poem on Time in 1930 (it concerned Descartes staring meditatively at his breakfast egg). He brought out a brilliant short book on Marcel Proust in 1931. A collection of short stories, *More Pricks than Kicks*, published in London in 1937, introduced a strange, involuted, meditative protagonist named Belacqua Shuah, whose Christian name comes from that of a slothful figure in Dante's *Purgatorio*. *Murphy*, a hilarious and profoundly philosophical novel, appeared the next year. Its milieu is London, and its anti-hero, Murphy (the first of several Beckettian protagonists whose names begin with a letter from the middle of the alphabet, the 13th one), starts out by literally and figuratively going off his rocker (a rocking chair, and his mind), ending in an insane asylum (as does the central figure in *Watt*). *Murphy* is concerned in good measure with the philosophical problem of the relation of mind and body, and

60. The annual cricket match between these two aristocratic public schools played in London, and the occasion of much upperclass display.

with Beckett's lifelong humorous fascination with the reductions, diagrams, schematiza-
tions, and generalities of human thought. This is evident from its opening sentence,
with its almost cosmic shrug about determinism ("The sun rose, having no alternative,
on the nothing new"), to its penultimate episode in which the hero's ashes, after his
cremation, are mixed with the detritus and dirt on the floor of a pub (a scene Joyce
is reputed to have loved). His next novel, *Watt*, is more abstract than *Murphy*, less
Joycean in its prose and in the nature of its jokes. It was Beckett's last fictional work
written in English, for after World War II he began to compose in French, and
during an incredibly creative period between 1945 and 1951 he produced a trilogy
of novels, which he himself subsequently translated into English under the titles of
Molloy, *Malone Dies*, and *The Unnamable* (French, 1951–53; English, 1955–58), and
the play for which he is perhaps most famous, *En Attendant Godot* (*Waiting for Godot*,
1954). *Fin de partie* (tr. as *Endgame*, 1958) is easily as great a play: *Krapp's Last Tape*
(1959), *Embers* (1959), and *Happy Days* (1961) are all plays originally written in English.

Beckett's later prose comes more and more to seem like parts of an eternal meditative lyrical monologue. In more problematic works like *How it Is* (1961) the writing becomes fragmentary, elusive, and occasionally opaque. *Watt*, despite its strangeness, is a
thoroughly comprehensible work, and shows none of the abstruseness of the *récits*, or
fictional monologues, which Beckett started writing in French. It was composed during
the years 1942–44 when Beckett was in hiding, doing menial work like the hero of
Watt, in the village of Rousillon in the Vaucluse, in the south of France (he had been
a member of a Resistance group in Paris, most of whose members the Gestapo had
arrested). *Watt* concerns a meditative hero of that questioning name about whom
we know very little (he is first seen getting off a streetcar by a minor character who
is not sure whether what he sees is a man or a woman, not sure "that it was not a
parcel, a carpet for example, or a roll of tarpaulin, wrapped up in dark paper and
tied about the middle with a cord"). But we do know a lot of what Watt thinks. In
the almost plotless story, he goes to work for a mysterious householder named Mr.
Knott (if Watt is *What?*, then his employer's name suggests *Not* and *Naught* and *Knot*
and the German word *Not* meaning "need") who, like the famous Godot, never
appears. Watt goes to work on the ground floor of Mr. Knott's house, and the bulk
of the middle part of the story concerns his acutely, often hilariously detailed consideration of the not very much that goes on while he works there. Here again is
Beckett joking about the schematic, about what the world resembles when stripped
to essentials (here, a thinker; something that can be known; and something that can't
or, at any rate, isn't). Certainly there is more than a suggestion of the theological
parable of Franz Kafka's *The Castle* here, and Mr. Knott is certainly very like the object
that results, however unintentionally, from much theological thought. The book employs an array of comic discursive devices; they range from what one critic has called
the misplaced literalness which is so basic to the dialogue of the plays ("Poor woman,
God forgive her, said Tetty. Faith I wouldn't put it past him, said Mr Hackett") to
intense and flamboyant parodies of analysis and philosophical argument. Finally we
learn that most of it has been told by Watt to Sam, his fellow inmate in a mental
hospital, and at the very end of the book, its by now universalized hero climbs on a
tramcar again to go to the end of the line, out of the world of our fiction.

The episode given below, from the beginning of Part II, contains a sort of parody
of an event. A piano tuner and his son come to tune Mr. Knott's piano; they have a
riotously gloomy conversation and go home, but the event lingers, grows, develops,

crystallizes, dissolves, changes, and becomes something else in Watt's mind. In the quasi-theological milieu of Mr. Knott's house (in which Watt is a not-really-suffering servant) we come to feel more and more that the incident of the Galls has many dimensions: event, happening, symbol, myth—indeed, by the end of the section, the blind father and his son seem to have been biblical. The reader should be prepared, throughout *Watt*, for all manner of unexpected meanings, generated by punning and word-play. And if he has followed the devout attempts in this episode, to wring Truth from what can be known, he will realize that despite all that Watt can try to comprehend of the Galls, father and son, he is brought no closer to final knowledge—that, in fact, what Watt knows is not Knott. Nor ever can be.

From Watt

[*The Incident of the Galls, Father and Son*]

Mr Knott never left the grounds, as far as Watt could judge. Watt thought it unlikely that Mr Knott could leave the grounds, without it's coming to his notice. But he did not reject the possibility of Mr Knott's leaving the grounds, without his being any the wiser. But the unlikelihood, on the one hand of Mr Knott's leaving the grounds, and on the other of his doing so without exciting the general comment, seemed very great, to Watt.

On only one occasion, during Watt's period of service on the ground floor, was the threshold crossed by a stranger, by other feet that is than Mr Knott's, or Erskine's,[1] or Watt's, for all were strangers to Mr Knott's establishment, as far as Watt could see, with the exception of Mr Knott himself, and his personnel at any given moment.

This fugitive penetration took place shortly after Watt's arrival. On his answering the door, as his habit was, when there was a knock at the door, he found standing before it, or so he realized later, arm in arm, an old man and a middleaged man.[2] The latter said:

We are the Galls, father and son, and we are come, what is more, all the way from town, to choon the piano.

They were two, and they stood, arm in arm, in this way, because the father was blind, like so many members of his profession. For if the father had not been blind, then he would not have needed his son to hold his arm, and guide him on his rounds, no, but he would have set his son free, to go about his own business. So Watt supposed, though there was nothing in the father's face to show that he was blind, nor in his attitude either, except that he leaned on his son in a way expressive of a great need of support. But he might have done this, if he had been halt, or merely tired, on account of his great age. There

---

1. Erskine is the servant who worked on the ground floor before Watt, and now works on the first one.
2. A master-servant pair, representing a schematic relation between people. Variations of this type are frequent in Beckett's works. Notice how, in this passage, the relation is itself qualified into a step-relation, calling into question even the father-son relation that links the pair.

was no family likeness between the two, as far as Watt could make out, and nevertheless he knew that he was in the presence of a father and son, for had he not just been told so. Or were they not perhaps merely stepfather and stepson. We are the Galls, stepfather and stepson—those were perhaps the words that should have been spoken. But it was natural to prefer the others. Not that they could not very well be a true father and son, without resembling each other in the very least, for they could.

How very fortunate for Mr Gall, said Watt, that he has his son at his command, whose manner is all devotion and whose mere presence, when he might obviously be earning an honest penny elsewhere, attests an affliction characteristic of the best tuners, and justifies emoluments rather higher than the usual.

When he had led them to the music-room, and left them there, Watt wondered if he had done right. He felt he had done right, but he was not sure. Should he not perhaps rather have sent them flying about their business? Watt's feeling was that anyone who demanded, with such tranquil assurance, to be admitted to Mr Knott's house, deserved to be admitted, in the absence of precise instructions to the contrary.

The music-room was a large bare white room. The piano was in the window. The head, and neck, in plaster, very white, of Buxtehude,[3] was on the mantelpiece. A ravanastron[4] hung, on the wall, from a nail, like a plover.

After a short time Watt returned to the music-room, with a tray, of refreshments.

Not Mr Gall Senior, but Mr Gall Junior, was tuning the piano, to Watt's great surprise. Mr Gall Senior was standing in the middle of the room, perhaps listening. Watt did not take this to mean that Mr Gall Junior was the true piano-tuner, and Mr Gall Senior simply a poor blind old man, hired for the occasion, no. But he took it rather to mean that Mr Gall Senior, feeling his end at hand, and anxious that his son should follow in his footsteps, was putting the finishing touches to a hasty instruction, before it was too late.

While Watt looked round, for a place to set down his tray, Mr Gall Junior brought his work to a close. He reassembled the piano case, put back his tools in their bag, and stood up.

The mice have returned, he said.

The elder said nothing. Watt wondered if he had heard.

Nine dampers[5] remain, said the younger, and an equal number of hammers.

Not corresponding, I hope, said the elder.

In one case, said the younger.

The elder had nothing to say to this.

The strings are in flitters, said the younger.

The elder had nothing to say to this either.

The piano is doomed, in my opinion, said the younger.

The piano-tuner also, said the elder.

The pianist also, said the younger.

This was perhaps the principal incident of Watt's early days in Mr Knott's house.

3. Dietrich Buxtehude (1637–1707), Danish baroque composer.
4. A long-necked, single-stringed banjo-like instrument, used in India for thousands of years.
5. Dampers and hammers are part of the internal workings, or "action," of a piano.

In a sense it resembled all the incidents of note proposed to Watt during his stay in Mr Knott's house, and of which a certain number will be recorded in this place, without addition, or subtraction, and in a sense not.

It resembled them in the sense that it was not ended, when it was past, but continued to unfold, in Watt's head, from beginning to end, over and over again, the complex connexions of its lights and shadows, the passing from silence to sound and from sound to silence, the stillness before the movement and the stillness after, the quickenings and retardings, the approaches and the separations, all the shifting detail of its march and ordinance, according to the irrevocable caprice of its taking place. It resembled them in the vigour with which it developed a purely plastic content, and gradually lost, in the nice processes of its light, its sound, its impacts and its rhythm, all meaning, even the most literal.

Thus the scene in the music-room, with the two Galls, ceased very soon to signify for Watt a piano tuned, an obscure family and professional relation, an exchange of judgments more or less intelligible, and so on, if indeed it had ever signified such things, and became a mere example of light commenting bodies, and stillness motion, and silence sound, and comment comment.

This fragility of the outer meaning had a bad effect on Watt, for it caused him to seek for another, for some meaning of what had passed, in the image of how it had passed.

The most meagre, the least plausible, would have satisfied Watt, who had not seen a symbol, nor executed an interpretation, since the age of fourteen, or fifteen, and who had lived, miserably it is true, among face values all his adult life, face values at least for him. Some see the flesh before the bones, and some see the bones before the flesh, and some never see the bones at all, and some never see the flesh at all, never never see the flesh at all. But whatever it was Watt saw, with the first look, that was enough for Watt, that had always been enough for Watt, more than enough for Watt. And he had experienced literally nothing, since the age of fourteen, or fifteen, of which in retrospect he was not content to say, That is what happened then. He could recall, not indeed with any satisfaction, but as ordinary occasions, the time when his dead father appeared to him in a wood, with his trousers rolled up over his knees and his shoes and socks in his hand; or the time when in his surprise at hearing a voice urging him, in terms of unusual coarseness, to do away with himself, he narrowly escaped being knocked down, by a dray [6]; or the time when alone in a rowing-boat, far from land, he suddenly smelt flowering currant; or the time when an old lady of delicate upbringing, and advantageous person, for she was amputated well above the knee, whom he had pursued with his assiduities on no fewer than three distinct occasions, unstrapped her wooden leg, and laid aside her crutch. Here no tendency appeared, on the part of his father's trousers, for example, to break up into an arrangement of appearances, grey, flaccid and probably fistular, or of his father's legs to vanish in the farce of their properties, no, but his father's legs and trousers, as then seen, in the wood, and subsequently brought to mind, remained legs and trousers, and not only legs and trousers, but his father's legs and trousers, that is to say quite different from any of the legs and trousers that Watt had ever seen, and he had

6. A horse-drawn cart for carrying heavy loads.

seen a great quantity, both of legs and of trousers, in his time. The incident of the Galls, on the contrary, ceased so rapidly to have even the paltry significance of two men, come to tune a piano, and tuning it, and exchanging a few words, as men will do, and going, that this seemed rather to belong to some story heard long before, an instant in the life of another, ill told, ill heard, and more than half forgotten.

So Watt did not know what had happened. He did not care, to do him justice, what had happened. But he felt the need to think that such and such a thing had happened then, the need to be able to say, when the scene began to unroll its sequences, Yes, I remember, that is what happened then.

This need remained with Watt, this need not always satisfied, during the greater part of his stay in Mr Knott's house. For the incident of the Galls father and son was followed by others of a similar kind, incidents that is to say of great formal brilliance and indeterminable purport.

Watt's stay in Mr Knott's house was less agreeable, on this account, than it would have been, if such incidents had been unknown, or his attitude towards them less anxious, that is to say, if Mr Knott's house had been another house, or Watt another man. For outside Mr Knott's house, and of course grounds, such incidents were unknown, or so Watt supposed. And Watt could not accept them for what they perhaps were, the simple games that time plays with space, now with these toys, and now with those, but was obliged, because of his peculiar character, to enquire into what they meant, oh not into what they really meant, his character was not so peculiar as all that, but into what they might be induced to mean, with the help of a little patience, a little ingenuity.

But what was this pursuit of meaning, in this indifference to meaning? And to what did it tend? These are delicate questions. For when Watt at last spoke of this time, it was a time long past, and of which his recollections were, in a sense, perhaps less clear than he would have wished, though too clear for his liking, in another. Add to this the notorious difficulty of recapturing, at will, modes of feeling peculiar to a certain time, and to a certain place, and perhaps also to a certain state of the health, when the time is past, and the place left, and the body struggling with quite a new situation. Add to this the obscurity of Watt's communications, the rapidity of his utterance and the eccentricities of his syntax, as elsewhere recorded. Add to this the material conditions in which these communications were made. Add to this the scant aptitude to receive of him to whom they were proposed. Add to this the scant aptitude to give of him to whom they were committed. And some idea will perhaps be obtained of the difficulties experienced in formulating, not only such matters as those here in question, but the entire body of Watt's experience, from the moment of his entering Mr Knott's establishment to the moment of his leaving it.

But before passing from the Galls father and son to matters less litigious,[7] or less tediously litigious, it seems advisable that the little that is known, on this subject, should be said. For the incident of the Galls father and son was the first and type [8] of many. And the little that is known about it has not yet all been said. Much has been said, but not all.

7. Here, in the sense of problematic, or argumentative.
8. "Type" is probably being used in both a general sense, and in the technical one of biblical interpretation (see Glossary).

Not that many things remain to be said, on the subject of the Galls father and son, for they do not. For only three or four things remain to be said in this connexion. And three or four things are not really many, in comparison with the number of things that might have been known, and said, on this subject, and now never shall.

What distressed Watt in this incident of the Galls father and son, and in subsequent similar incidents, was not so much that he did not know what had happened, for he did not care what had happened, as that nothing had happened, that a thing that was nothing had happened, with the utmost formal distinctness, and that it continued to happen, in his mind, he supposed, though he did not know exactly what that meant, and though it seemed to be outside him, before him, about him, and so on, inexorably to unroll its phases, beginning with the first (the knock that was not a knock) and ending with the last (the door closing that was not a door closing), and omitting none, uninvoked, at the most unexpected moments, and the most inopportune. Yes, Watt could not accept, as no doubt Erskine could not accept, and as no doubt Arsene and Walter and Vincent [9] and the others had been unable to accept, that nothing had happened, with all the clarity and solidity of something, and that it revisited him in such a way that he was forced to submit to it all over again, to hear the same sounds, see the same lights, touch the same surfaces, and so on, as when they had first involved him in their unintelligible intricacies. If he had been able to accept it, then perhaps it would not have revisited him, and this would have been a great saving of vexation, to put it mildly. But he could not accept it, could not bear it. One wonders sometimes where Watt thought he was. In a culture-park?

But if he could say, when the knock came, the knock become a knock, or the door become a door, in his mind, presumably in his mind, whatever that might mean, Yes, I remember, that is what happened then, if then he could say that, then he thought that then the scene would end, and trouble him no more, as the appearance of his father with his trousers rolled up and his shoes and socks in his hands troubled him no more, because he could say, when it began, Yes, yes, I remember, that was when my father appeared to me, in the wood, dressed for wading. But to elicit something from nothing requires a certain skill and Watt was not always successful, in his efforts to do so. Not that he was always unsuccessful either, for he was not. For if he had been always unsuccessful, how would it have been possible for him to speak of the Galls father and son, and of the piano they had come all the way from town to tune, and of their tuning it, and of their passing the remarks they had passed, the one to the other, in the way he did? No, he could never have spoken at all of these things, if all had continued to mean nothing, as some continued to mean nothing, that is to say, right up to the end. For the only way one can speak of nothing is to speak of it as though it were something, just as the only way one can speak of God is to speak of him as though he were a man, which to be sure he was, in a sense, for a time, and as the only way one can speak of man, even our anthropologists have realised that, is to speak of him as though he were a termite. But if Watt was sometimes unsuccessful, and sometimes successful, as in the affair

9. Watt's predecessors on the ground floor at Mr. Knott's.

of the Galls father and son, in foisting a meaning there where no meaning appeared, he was most often neither the one, nor the other. For Watt considered, with reason, that he was successful, in this enterprise, when he could evolve, from the meticulous phantoms that beset him, a hypothesis proper to disperse them, as often as this might be found necessary. There was nothing, in this operation, at variance with Watt's habits of mind. For to explain had always been to exorcize, for Watt. And he considered that he was unsuccessful, when he failed to do so. And he considered that he was neither wholly successful, nor wholly unsuccessful, when the hypothesis evolved lost its virtue, after one or two applications, and had to be replaced by another, which in its turn had to be replaced by another, which in due course ceased to be of the least assistance, and so on. And that is what happened, in the majority of cases. Now to give examples of Watt's failures, and of Watt's successes, and of Watt's partial successes, in this connexion, is so to speak impossible. For when he speaks, for example, of the incident of the Galls father and son, does he speak of it in terms of the unique hypothesis that was required, to deal with it, and render it innocuous, or in terms of the latest, or in terms of some other of the series? For when Watt spoke of an incident of this kind, he did not necessarily do so in terms of the unique hypothesis, or of the latest, though this at first sight seems the only possible alternative, and the reason why he did not, why it is not, is this, that when one of the series of hypotheses, with which Watt laboured to preserve his peace of mind, lost its virtue, and had to be laid aside, and another set up in its place, then it sometimes happened that the hypothesis in question, after a sufficient period of rest, recovered its virtue and could be made to serve again, in the place of another, whose usefulness had come to an end, for the time being at least. To such an extent is this true, that one is sometimes tempted to wonder, with reference to two or even three incidents related by Watt as separate and distinct, if they are not in reality the same incident, variously interpreted. As to giving an example of the second event, namely the failure, that is clearly quite out of the question. For there we have to do with events that resisted all Watt's efforts to saddle them with meaning, and a formula, so that he could neither think of them, nor speak of them, but only suffer them, when they recurred, though it seems probable that they recurred no more, at the period of Watt's revelation, to me, but were as though they had never been.

Finally, to return to the incident of the Galls father and son, as related by Watt, did it have that meaning for Watt at the time of its taking place, and then lose that meaning, and then recover it? Or did it have some quite different meaning for Watt at the time of its taking place, and then lose that meaning, and then receive that, alone or among others, which it exhibited, in Watt's relation? Or did it have no meaning whatever for Watt at the moment of its taking place, were there neither Galls nor piano then, but only an unintelligible succession of changes, from which Watt finally extracted the Galls and the piano, in self-defence? These are most delicate questions. Watt spoke of it as involving, in the original, the Galls and the piano, but he was obliged to do this, even if the original had nothing to do with the Galls and the piano. For even if the Galls and the piano were long posterior to the phenomena destined to become them, Watt was obliged to think, and speak, of the incident, even at the moment of its taking place, as the incident of the Galls and the piano, if he was to think and speak of it at all, and it may be assumed that Watt would never have thought or spoken of such incidents, if he had not been under the absolute necessity of doing so. But generally speaking it seems probable that the meaning attributed to this particular type of incident, by Watt, in his relations, was now the initial meaning that had been lost and then recovered, and now a meaning quite distinct from the initial meaning, and now a meaning evolved, after a delay of varying length, and with greater or less pains, from the initial absence of meaning.

ENGLISH LITERARY HISTORY IN PROCESS

The history of English poetry since World War II has been marked by the absence of anything like a traceable line of development, however broadly one might draw it. The literature of the past twenty-five years belongs to the realm of the contemporary, rather than specifically to the historical period we can now call Modern; from within the perspective of the contemporary age it is as difficult to agree on the selection of monuments, and to delineate continuities, as it is in any other mode of current experience. Because of the dynamics of literary influence, the ways in which early promise may crystallize, mature, or fizzle out, and the often bewildering spotlight of current fashion, the anthologist of the contemporary cannot attempt to extend the canon of the Modern age down to recent years. He can only remark upon what has seemed prominent, and commend what he thinks excellent.

But a somewhat self-conscious sense of its historical moment by a post-war literary generation in Britain was accompanied by a number of sharply defined intentions on the part of groups of writers who thought of themselves perhaps as analogues rather than descendants of groups like the Auden circle in the nineteen-thirties. Auden himself had gone to the United States at the beginning of World War II and become an American. The new generation of poets was emerging from the universities, where their training had been primarily in literature and literary criticism, and it is not surprising that for several of them the poetry of William Empson should have been as influential as Auden's might otherwise have been. Some of the older of the post-war poets had, indeed, started publishing in the 'thirties, and it is among these that an eclectic range of individual manners and styles can still be observed. Such poets as Vernon Watkins (1906–67), Roy Fuller (b. 1912), Lawrence Durrell (b. 1912), better known for his fiction but author of a group of promising, somewhat surrealist early poems, and others of their generation seem to represent no particular association of interests.

BASIL BUNTING
1900–

The oldest and most anomalous of such poets is Basil Bunting. A professional music critic after World War I, later an associate and follower of Ezra Pound, who published some of his early work in an anthology, he was for a while a diplomat, and after World War II became a journalist, first in Persia, then in his native county of Northumberland. He started publishing obscurely in 1950, but it was not until 1966, when his long autobiographical and mythological poem *Briggflatts* appeared, that he achieved recognition. Championed in a climate which was beginning to encourage the influence of American poetry styles developed by the followers of Pound and William Carlos Williams, *Briggflatts* brought together local Northumbrian allusions and legendary material, astronomical imagery, details of personal narrative, and gnomic aphorism, all informed by an intense, lyrical compression that marks him off strongly from the more expository styles of other post-war poets. The section given below, from the close of Part V, represents the moment of contemplation upon its own completion and upon the life that has both produced and been reflected in it.

Briggflatts

From *Part V*

Light lifts from the water.
Frost has put rowan° down,
a russet blotch of bracken
tousled about the trunk.
Bleached sky. Cirrus
reflects sun that has left
nothing to badger eyes.

Young flutes, harps touched by a breeze,
drums and horns escort
70   Aldebaran,° low in the clear east,
beckoning boats to the fishing.
Capella° floats from the north
with shields hung on his gunwale.
That is no dinghy's lantern
occulted by the swell—Betelgeuse,°
calling behind him to Rigel.
Starlight is almost flesh.

Great strings next the post of the harp
clang, the horn has majesty,
80   flutes flicker in the draft and flare.
Orion strides over Farne.°
Seals shuffle and bark,
terns shift on their ledges,

rowan the mountain-ash or service-tree
Aldebaran the first-magnitude orange star in the constellation Taurus, the Bull; followed by Orion, which in turn is followed by the dogs, Canis Minor and Canis Major. Taurus, with the bright Pleiades, leads the magnificent procession of stars across the winter sky.
Capella the fifth or sixth brightest star in the sky, in Auriga, the Chariot

Betelgeuse "Sailors pronounce *Betelgeuse* 'Beetle juice' and so do I. His companion is 'Ridgel,' not 'Rhy-ghel'" (Bunting). This star is the first-magnitude red giant in Orion's shoulder. Rigel is in his left foot.
Farne an island in the North Sea, lying off the English-Scottish border

watching Capella steer for the zenith,
and Procyon° starts his climb.

Furthest, fairest things, stars, free of our humbug,
each his own, the longer known the more alone,
wrapt in emphatic fire roaring out to a black flue.
Each spark trills on a tone beyond chronological compass,
90 yet in a sextant's bubble present and firm
places a surveyor's stone or steadies a tiller.
Then is Now. The star you steer by is gone,
its tremulous thread spun in the hurricane
spider floss on my cheek; light from the zenith
spun when the slowworm° lay in her lap
fifty years ago.

The sheets are gathered and bound,
the volume indexed and shelved,
dust on its marbled leaves.
00 Lofty, an empty combe,°
silent but for bees.
Finger tips touched and were still
fifty years ago.
Sirius° is too young to remember.

Sirius glows in the wind. Sparks on ripples
mark his line, lures for spent fish.

Fifty years a letter unanswered;
a visit postponed for fifty years.

She has been with me fifty years.

10 Starlight quivers. I had day enough.
For love uninterrupted night.
       1966

Coda

A strong song tows
us, long earsick.
Blind, we follow
rain slant, spray flick
to fields we do not know.

Night, float us.
Offshore wind, shout,

Procyon the first-magnitude star in Canis Minor, rising just before the dog star, Sirius
slowworm the blindworm, a kind of limbless lizard whose stirring in May opens the cyclic vision of Part I of *Briggflatts*
combe a narrow valley

Sirius "Sirius is too young to remember because the light we call by his name left its star only eight years ago; but the light from *Capella*, now in the zenith, set out 45 years ago—as near fifty as makes no difference to a poet" (Bunting). Sirius is the brightest star in the heavens.

ask the sea
what's lost, what's left,
10   what horn sunk,
what crown adrift.

Where we are who knows
of kings who sup
while day fails? Who,
swinging his axe
to fell kings, guesses
where we go?
       1965

STEVIE SMITH
1902–1970

Although the first work of Stevie Smith (Florence Margaret Smith) was published in the late 1930's, she became best known in the post-war period. She was a writer of an almost proverbial eccentricity. Her weighty casualness, apparently haphazard verse forms, and mastery in providing a resonant context for the flat and colloquial, constitute an intense yet improvisatory tone, a blend of the ceremonious and the grotesque.

Not Waving but Drowning

Nobody heard him, the dead man,
But still he lay moaning:
I was much farther out than you thought
And not waving but drowning.

Poor chap, he always loved larking
And now he's dead
It must have been too cold for him his heart gave way,
They said.

Oh, no no no, it was too cold always
(Still the dead one lay moaning)
I was much too far out all my life
And not waving but drowning.
       1957

JOHN HEATH-STUBBS
1918–

John Heath-Stubbs was born in London in 1918, studied at Oxford with C. S. Lewis, and took his B.A. in 1942. Despite encroaching blindness he has continued, throughout a career as schoolmaster, free-lance writer, and college teacher, to perfect his intense and elegant poetry, with a voice that has managed to keep faith with an earlier Romantic tradition while speaking in its own accents. With a Byronic urbanity contrasting strongly in tone with that occasionally adopted by W. H. Auden, Heath-Stubbs has avowed a moral commitment to speak out not as a political or theological conscience but as the votary of another muse—sometimes neo-Hellenic, sometimes at her home in the English countryside. "Permit not," he says to her in the epilogue to his The Triumph of the Muse (1958), "We should allow the things your wings had taught us, / As in a dream's shame, utterly to vanish, / Through keeping silence."

The Dark Planet

There is a dark planet striking against us. Invisible,
Its venomed arrows whisk through the purple air.
It is the masked dancer, shifting among
The beneficent choir, deflecting
All dulcet influence of Aphrodite the gay,
Ingenious Mercury with his legerdemain,
And Artemis on her silver-sandalled way.

It is because the dark planet decrees,
That the rose discards to the dust her flush-fire mantle.
10   It is the dark planet's malice that has choked
The song of the bird in its throat, and grinds desire
Down to the bitter ashes, the gritty cinders of time,
Where, with the brazen monument, crumbles the rhyme.

Where the dark planet strikes, nothing is innocent;
My boyhood impulses it caught in a net of fear.
My friends it suborns from me. Now you, my dear,
The dark planet has hit in the thick of the night.
It has turned you away from us all, and away from the light,
And the times we in common possessed, that went by like dreams—
20   With the unquiet speed of all dreams—must likewise fade,
As memory fades, your image becomes a shade.

In the web of things we perceive, there is nothing the dark planet spares;
For not to our condition is granted ever
Perfection of beauty, intellect, power. They fade like those cold
Prismatic garlands, the abstract blossoms of snow,
In the beams of that black sun, whose visage we may not know.
For it is an envious star. Not one, in their hierarchies,
But must bend to its importunate, to its absolute demands.
Though we turn, in our rage, and upbraid, through our tears, its assaults,
30   It will yield no retrograde motion, no slackening of its bands.

The dark planet swings through its ebony kingdom above.
Listen, do you not hear the whoosh-whoosh of its wings?
No, it will not cease fire, till every image is emptied

Of all significance, saving only its own.
Ah my dear, has your parting this hypothesis taught me?
Implacable, that sky-wanderer. Its name is Love.

1958

During the early 1950's a number of tendencies began to coalesce among some of the younger poets who had commenced publishing only after the end of the war. A reaction against the complexities engendered in modernist poetry by the influence of French Symbolism combined with a newly rediscovered sense of a native English poetic tradition which had been abandoned since the Georgians. When interwoven with a distrust of gesture and posture, and a revival of concern with the speaking voice, these impulses led to new stylistic directions—certainly not the directions one might expect, say, from poets following Dylan Thomas. A loose affiliation of a number of poets known as "The Movement" was evident in an anthology called *New Lines* edited by Robert Conquest in 1956. Among them were Philip Larkin (b. 1922), Donald Davie (b. 1922), Kingsley Amis (b. 1922), and Thom Gunn (b. 1929).

These poets all spoke in distinctly individual voices, but what they seemed at the beginning to have in common was this new kind of clarity. Metrically iambic and orderly, their poetry generally eschewed experimentation and the cultivation of stylistic idiosyncrasy. Rhetorically smooth even when most intense, the new stylistic trend showed some affinities with eighteenth-century poetic traditions, particularly in that these poets were quite unafraid of writing a poetry of statement, of working in the expository and even essayistic modes which the roots of modernist theory had associated with scientific discourse as the negation of true poetry's irrational music. In the following decade these poets developed in divergent directions, but in many ways Philip Larkin's poetry seems to remain prototypical of its moment, as well as influential.

PHILIP LARKIN
1922–

Philip Larkin, born in Coventry and currently Librarian of the University of Hull, published *The North Ship* in 1945, but it was in *The Less Deceived,* ten years later (and in *The Whitsun Weddings* in 1964), that his exchange (as he later put it) of the influence of Yeats for that of Hardy was confirmed. "Church Going," given below, depicts in an almost completely exemplary way the skeptical and witty terrain, almost bare of metaphor and with low rhetorical contours, that the newer poetry of "The Movement" would inhabit.

Church Going

Once I am sure there's nothing going on
I step inside, letting the door thud shut.
Another church: matting, seats, and stone,
And little books; sprawlings of flowers, cut
For Sunday, brownish now; some brass and stuff
Up at the holy end; the small neat organ;
And a tense, musty, unignorable silence,
Brewed God knows how long. Hatless, I take off
My cycle-clips in awkward reverence,

10 Move forward, run my hand around the font.
From where I stand, the roof looks almost new—
Cleaned, or restored? Someone would know: I don't.
Mounting the lectern, I peruse a few
Hectoring large-scale verses, and pronounce
'Here endeth'° much more loudly than I'd meant.
The echoes snigger briefly. Back at the door
I sign the book, donate an Irish sixpence,
Reflect the place was not worth stopping for.

Yet stop I did: in fact I often do,
20 And always end much at a loss like this,
Wondering what to look for; wondering, too,
When churches fall completely out of use
What we shall turn them into, if we shall keep
A few cathedrals chronically on show,
Their parchment, plate and pyx° in locked cases,
And let the rest rent-free to rain and sheep.
Shall we avoid them as unlucky places?

Or, after dark, will dubious women come
To make their children touch a particular stone;
30 Pick simples° for a cancer; or on some
Advised night see walking a dead one?
Power of some sort or other will go on
In games, in riddles, seemingly at random;
But superstition, like belief, must die
And what remains when disbelief has gone?
Grass, weedy pavement, brambles, buttress, sky,

A shape less recognizable each week,
A purpose more obscure. I wonder who
Will be the last, the very last, to seek
40 This place for what it was; one of the crew
That tap and jot and know what rood-lofts° were?

'Here endeth' The complete phrase is "Here endeth the Lesson," pronounced after each reading from Sacred Scripture in the Church of England services.
pyx case containing Communion wafer

simples herbs; so called because they were used uncompounded
rood-lofts galleries forming the head of the screens which separate the nave from the choir of a church

Some ruin-bibber, randy for antique,
Or Christmas-addict, counting on a whiff
Of gown-and-bands and organ-pipes and myrrh?
Or will he be my representative,

Bored, uninformed, knowing the ghostly silt
Dispersed, yet tending to this cross of ground
Through suburb scrub because it held unspilt
So long and equably what since is found
50 Only in separation—marriage, and birth,
And death, and thoughts of these—for whom was built
This special shell? For, though I've no idea
What this accoutred frowsty° barn is worth,
It pleases me to stand in silence here;

A serious house on serious earth it is,
In whose blent air all our compulsions meet,
Are recognized, and robed as destinies.
And that much never can be obsolete,
Since someone will forever be surprising
60 A hunger in himself to be more serious,
And gravitating with it to this ground,
Which, he once heard, was proper to grow wise in,
If only that so many dead lie round.

                                1955

Lines on a Young Lady's
Photograph Album

At last you yielded up the album, which,
Once open, sent me distracted. All your ages
Matt and glossy on the thick black pages!
Too much confectionary, too rich:
I choke on such nutritious images.

My swivel eye hungers from pose to pose—
In pigtails, clutching a reluctant cat;
Or furred yourself, a sweet girl-graduate;
Or lifting a heavy-headed rose
10 Beneath a trellis, or in a trilby hat°

(Faintly disturbing, that, in several ways)—
From every side you strike at my control,
Not least through these disquieting chaps who loll
At ease about your earlier days:
Not quite your class, I'd say, dear, on the whole.

---

frowsty dowdy   **trilby hat** ordinary soft men's felt hat

But o, photography! as no art is,
Faithful and disappointing! that records
Dull days as dull, and hold-it smiles as frauds,
And will not censor blemishes
20   Like washing-lines, and Hall's-Distemper° boards,

But shows the cat as disinclined, and shades
A chin as doubled when it is, what grace
Your candour thus confers upon her face!
How overwhelmingly persuades
That this is a real girl in a real place,

In every sense empirically true!
Or is it just *the past?* Those flowers, that gate,
These misty parks and motors,° lacerate
Simply by being over; you
30   Contract my heart by looking out of date.

Yes, true; but in the end, surely, we cry
Not only at exclusion, but because
It leaves us free to cry. We know *what was*
Won't call on us to justify
Our grief, however hard we yowl across

The gap from eye to page. So I am left
To mourn (without a chance of consequence)
You, balanced on a bike against a fence;
To wonder if you'd spot the theft
40   Of this one of you bathing; to condense,

In short, a past that no one now can share,
No matter whose your future; calm and dry,
It holds you like a heaven, and you lie
Unvariably lovely there,
Smaller and clearer as the years go by.

                                            1955

DONALD DAVIE
1922–

Donald Davie, who comes from Yorkshire and was educated at Cambridge, is a literary critic of importance as well as a poet, and his sequence of critical writings reflects in some degree the development of his own poetic concerns. *Purity of Diction in English Verse* (1952) was as influential among his poetic contemporaries as it was upon his academic colleagues. *Articulate Energy* (1955) gave new impetus to the study of syntax in English poetry, which a modernist interest in metaphor and image had largely neglected, and his *Ezra Pound: Poet as Sculptor* (1964), marked his developing involvement in American poetic tradition. After having taught in Dublin, Cam-

Hall's-Distemper an interior wall paint   **motors** cars bridge, and Essex, Davie moved to the United States, where he now teaches at Stanford University. Most recently, his *Thomas Hardy and British Poetry* (1972) reaffirmed in a more historical way the commitment that Larkin had acknowledged personally two decades earlier. A *Collected Poems* was published in the same year. He is also a student of Slavic languages, and has translated Russian and Polish poetry.

A Winter Talent

Lighting a spill° late in the afternoon,
I am that coal whose heat it should unfix;
Winter is come again, and none too soon
For meditation on its raft of sticks.

Some quick bright talents can dispense with coals
And burn their boats continually, command
An unreflecting brightness that unrolls
Out of whatever firings come to hand.

What though less sunny spirits never turn
10   The dry detritus° of an August hill
To dangerous glory? Better still to burn
Upon that gloom where all have felt a chill.

                                        1957

Gardens No Emblems

Man with a scythe: the torrent of his swing
Finds its own level; and is not hauled back
But gathers fluently, like water rising
Behind the watergates that close a lock.

The gardener eased his foot into a boot;
Which action like the mower's had its mould,
Being itself a sort of taking root,
Feeling for lodgment in the leather's fold.

But forms of thought move in another plane
10   Whose matrices no natural forms afford
Unless subjected to prodigious strain:
Say, light proceeding edgewise, like a sword.

                                        1957

spill a twist of paper or splinter of wood   **detritus** debris

KINGSLEY AMIS
1922–

Kingsley Amis, a Londoner, is better known as a comic novelist than as a poet. The influence of American humorists like S. J. Perelman, and of the films of the Marx Brothers, on his fiction was replaced in his poems by a mode of rueful wit more philosophically studious than learned or allusive in its manner. Amis has published many novels and several books of verse, the most recent being *A Case of Samples* (1957) and *A Look Round the Estate* (1967).

A Dream of Fair Women°

The door still swinging to, and girls revive,
Aeronauts in the utmost altitudes
   Of boredom fainting, dive
Into the bright oxygen of my nod;
Angels as well, a squadron of draped nudes,
   They roar towards their god.

Militant all, they fight to take my hat,
No more as yet; the other men retire
   Insulted, gestured at;
10 Each girl presses on me her share of what
Makes up the barn-door target of desire:
   And I am a crack shot.

Speech fails them, amorous, but each one's look,
Endorsed in other ways, begs me to sign
   Her body's autograph-book;
'Me first, Kingsley; I'm cleverest' each declares,
But no gourmet races downstairs to dine,
   Nor will I race upstairs.

Feigning aplomb, perhaps for half an hour,
20 I hover, and am shown by each princess
   The entrance to her tower;
Open, in that its tenant throws the key
At once to anyone, but not unless
   The anyone is me.

Now from the corridor their fathers cheer,
Their brothers, their young men; the cheers increase
   As soon as I appear;
From each I win a handshake and sincere
Congratulations; from the chief of police
30   A nod, a wink, a leer.

A Dream of Fair Women an ironic reference
to Tennyson's vastly chaste poem of the same
title

This over, all delay is over too;
The first eight girls (the roster now agreed)
    Leap on me, and undo . . .
But honesty impels me to confess
That this is 'all a dream,' which was, indeed,
    Not difficult to guess.

But wait; not 'just a dream,' because, though good
And beautiful, it is also true, and hence
    Is rarely understood;
40 Who would choose any feasible ideal
In here and now's giant circumference,
    If that small room were real?

Only the best; the others find, have found
Love's ordinary distances too great,
    And eager, stand their ground;
Map-drunk explorers, dry-land sailors, they
See no arrival that can compensate
    For boredom on the way;

And, seeming doctrinaire, but really weak,
50 Limelighted dolls guttering in their brain,
    They come with me, to seek
The halls of theoretical delight,
The women of that ever-fresh terrain,
    The night after to-night.
                            1957

THOM GUNN
1929–

The youngest poet of "The Movement" was Thom Gunn. Born in London, educated at Cambridge, he has lived in the United States for the past fifteen years, mostly in California. His *Fighting Terms* (1954) was an early success; *The Sense of Movement* (1957) began to reveal a more idiosyncratic involvement with the American scene. Gunn may have been influenced by some of the ideas of the American critic Yvor Winters (whom he knew at Stanford University), particularly in regard to Winters's notions of clarity and power in the short poem. In his later work Gunn has written in the purely syllabic meters passed on by Auden to many contemporary American poets, but used by hardly anyone in England. The scene of "On the Move," with its colloquial American epigraph and its black-jacketed motorcyclists, contrasts sharply with the almost pious Englishness of Larkin's British bicyclist in "Church Going"; the two poems nevertheless can be heard speaking a common tongue.

On the Move

Man, you gotta Go.

The blue jay scuffling in the bushes follows
Some hidden purpose, and the gust of birds
That spurts across the field, the wheeling swallows,
Have nested in the trees and undergrowth.
Seeking their instinct, or their poise, or both,
One moves with an uncertain violence
Under the dust thrown by a baffled sense
Or the dull thunder of approximate words.

On motorcycles, up the road, they come:
10 Small, black, as flies hanging in heat, the Boys,
Until the distance throws them forth, their hum
Bulges to thunder held by calf and thigh.
In goggles, donned impersonality,
In gleaming jackets trophied with the dust,
They strap in doubt—by hiding it, robust—
And almost hear a meaning in their noise.

Exact conclusion of their hardiness
Has no shape yet, but from known whereabouts
They ride, direction where the tyres press.
20 They scare a flight of birds across the field:
Much that is natural, to the will must yield.
Men manufacture both machine and soul,
And use what they imperfectly control
To dare a future from the taken routes.

It is a part solution, after all.
One is not necessarily discord
On earth; or damned because, half animal,
One lacks direct instinct, because one wakes
Afloat on movement that divides and breaks.
30 One joins the movement in a valueless world,
Choosing it, till, both hurler and the hurled,
One moves as well, always toward, toward.

A minute holds them, who have come to go:
The self-defined, astride the created will
They burst away; the towns they travel through
Are home for neither bird nor holiness,
For birds and saints complete their purposes.
At worst, one is in motion; and at best,
Reaching no absolute, in which to rest,
40 One is always nearer by not keeping still.

1957

"The Movement," tentative as its thematic and stylistic boundaries were, did seem to characterize something of the spirit of the nineteen-fifties in English poetry. But such literary groupings are often misleading and seldom central. Three of the most impressive and interesting of post-war British poets could not be thought of as associated with the tradition of the new, plain style.

CHARLES TOMLINSON
1927–

Charles Tomlinson was born in Staffordshire in 1927, studied at Cambridge and London universities, and teaches at the University of Bristol. He is a poet of considerable stature whose work was marked by a particular openness, at first, to French Symbolist poetry and, later on, to the tradition of American verse stemming from William Carlos Williams. Tomlinson represents more of a continuation of the modernist tradition than do many of his contemporaries, even though the internationalism is in this instance transatlantic in the reverse direction. "Through Binoculars" shows his affinity with Williams (particularly in the earlier Williams), as well as a concern for breaking new formal ground in his use of free verse.

Through Binoculars

In their congealed light
We discover that what we had taken for a face
Has neither eyes nor mouth,
But only the impersonality of anatomy.

Silencing movement,
They withdraw life.

Definition grows clear-cut, but bodiless,
Withering by a dimension.

To see thus
10 Is to ignore the revenge of light on shadow,
To confound both in a brittle and false union.

This fictive extension into madness
Has a kind of bracing effect:
That normality is, after all, desirable
One can no longer doubt having experienced its opposite.

Binoculars are the last phase in a romanticism:
The starkly mad vision, not mortal,
But dangling one in a vicarious, momentary idiocy.

To dispense with them
20 Is to make audible the steady roar of evening,
Withdrawing in slow ripples of orange,
Like the retreat of water from sea-caves.

1955

TED HUGHES
1930–

Ted Hughes was at Cambridge with Thom Gunn, but his poetry, from the very outset,
moved in a rather different direction. Emerging from various kinds of influence—the
poems of D. H. Lawrence, Robert Graves, Edward Thomas—Hughes developed in his
emblematic nature poems and in his mythological liturgies a powerful sense of communion with his almost totemic subjects. He has lived in the United States and was
married to an American poet, the late Sylvia Plath, with whose expressionistic verse
his own later poetry shares some characteristics. His recent poems in Crow (1971)
center on a demonic sort of protagonist, a figure of blackness and negation who
cackles and groans throughout the poems' exploration of horror and misery, and
through their grotesque reworkings of traditional myth, as in "A Childish Prank."

Pibroch°

The sea cries with its meaningless voice,
Treating alike its dead and its living,
Probably bored with the appearance of heaven
After so many millions of nights without sleep,
Without purpose, without self-deception.

Stone likewise. Stone is imprisoned
Like nothing in the Universe.
Created for black sleep. Or growing
Conscious of the sun's red spot occasionally,
10 Then dreaming it is the foetus of God.

Over the stone rushes the wind,
Able to mingle with nothing,
Like the hearing of the blind stone itself.
Or turns, as if the stone's mind came feeling
A fantasy of directions.

Drinking the sea and eating the rock
A tree struggles to make leaves—
An old woman fallen from space

Pibroch a Scottish bagpipe composition consisting of ornamented variations on a theme

Unprepared for these conditions.
20   She hangs on, because her mind's gone completely.

Minute after minute, aeon after aeon,
Nothing lets up or develops.
And this is neither a bad variant nor a tryout.
This is where the staring angels go through.
This is where all the stars bow down.

                    1961

A Childish Prank

Man's and woman's bodies lay without souls,
Dully gaping, foolishly staring, inert
On the flowers of Eden.
God pondered.

The problem was so great, it dragged him asleep.

Crow laughed.
He bit the Worm, God's only son,
Into two writhing halves.

He stuffed into man the tail half
With the wounded end hanging out.

He stuffed the head half headfirst into woman
And it crept in deeper and up
To peer out through her eyes
Calling its tail-half to join up quickly, quickly
Because O it was painful.

Man awoke being dragged across the grass.
Woman awoke to see him coming.
Neither knew what had happened.

God went on sleeping.

Crow went on laughing.

                    1971

GEOFFREY HILL
1932–

Geoffrey Hill, born in Worcestershire in 1932 and educated at Oxford, may be the most original poet of his generation; certainly his poems are among the most difficult that have appeared in England since the post-war renunciation of the density and obliqueness which modern poetry of previous decades had felt to be almost mandatory for poetic truth. His poems are compressed in their structure and argument, and intense in their visionary, mythological mode. Even a relatively accessible work like "Genesis" is exceedingly problematic in its Blakean sense of the simultaneity of the Fall and Creation, of the impossibility of visualizing an unfallen nature.

Genesis

I

Against the burly air I strode,
Where the tight ocean heaves its load,
Crying the miracles of God.

And first I brought the sea to bear
Upon the dead weight of the land;
And the waves flourished at my prayer,
The rivers spawned their sand.

And where the streams were salt and full
The tough pig-headed salmon strove,
10   Curbing the ebb and the tide's pull,
To reach the steady hills above.

II

The second day I stood and saw
The osprey plunge with triggered claw,
Feathering blood along the shore,
To lay the living sinew bare.

And the third day I cried: 'Beware
The soft-voiced owl, the ferret's smile,
The hawk's deliberate stoop in air,
Cold eyes, and bodies hooped in steel,
20   Forever bent upon the kill.'

III

And I renounced, on the fourth day,
This fierce and unregenerate clay,

Building as a huge myth for man
The watery Leviathan,
And made the glove-winged albatross
Scour the ashes of the sea
Where Capricorn and Zero cross,°
A brooding immortality—
Such as the charmèd phoenix has
30   In the unwithering tree.

Where . . . cross where the tropic of Capricorn
crosses the zero degree of longitude

IV

The phoenix burns as cold as frost;
And, like a legendary ghost,
The phantom-bird goes wild and lost,
Upon a pointless ocean tossed.

So, the fifth day, I turned again
To flesh and blood and the blood's pain.

V

On the sixth day, as I rode
In haste about the works of God,
With spurs I plucked the horse's blood.

40   By blood we live, the hot, the cold,
To ravage and redeem the world:
There is no bloodless myth will hold.

And by Christ's blood are men made free
Though in close shrouds their bodies lie
Under the rough pelt of the sea;

Though Earth has rolled beneath her weight
The bones that cannot bear the light.

1959

Despite the transitory viability of "The Movement" as a way of classifying writers, it is obvious that modern English literary history, unlike that of France, only rarely lends itself to treatment in terms of schools and movements. The post-war French novel may be studied in terms of successive new waves, but there is nothing closely resembling them in England: novelists are more private and self-cultivated. Lists of the most important will of course vary, but few would omit the names—here set out variously, and covering three generations—of Henry Green, Grahame Greene, Ivy Compton-Burnett, Evelyn Waugh, Kingsley Amis, Anthony Powell, Iris Murdoch, Muriel Spark, William Golding, and Angus Wilson; and some would add C. P. Snow, Anthony Burgess, Richard Hughes, and Sibylle Bedford.

Of these the one who has suffered the most neglect may be the best: Henry Green, author of Living (1929), perhaps the best proletarian novel in English, and Loving (1945), a unique poetic-prosaic masterpiece. Amis's best book is his first, the irreverent Lucky Jim (1954), which, of several rather similar novels published about the same time, best struck the note of change in the attitude of the young toward authority, especially toward the absurdly institutionalized authority in the expanding universities. Iris Murdoch's first novel, Under the Net (1953), is a uniquely gay philosopher's novel; but bringing to her work one of the best minds to engage with English fiction since George Eliot's, she seems not, in the long list of titles that follow the first, ever to have performed the promised wonders. Green is silent, Greene has written no major book for many years, Golding has had a period of seclusion—though The Scorpion God

(1971) reminds us of his extraordinarily original gifts. Powell's long sequence *The Music of Time* has a devoted but restricted following, and for all his elegant humor offers a rather cultish kind of interest. The original blend of the humane and the viciously satirical which made Angus Wilson's early work uniquely valuable in the post-war period survives in the latest novel of this vigorous and inquiring writer, *No Laughing Matter* (1967); but by now he can scarcely do much to surprise us. The virtuosos are Muriel Spark, probably the most gifted English novelist alive, and Anthony Burgess; and of these much more—and that very likely surprising—may be looked for.

It is in the theater that England has a genuine modern movement. One might take 1952, the year of the first London performance of Samuel Beckett's *Waiting for Godot,* as the date when things began to happen; since then a whole new theater has developed. This has its physical center, as such movements tend to, in one theater, the Royal Court, where the English Stage Company still continues its aggressive, experimental way; but it is important to realize that much larger areas of English theater are involved. The first production of *Godot* was by Peter Hall, later director of the Royal Shakespeare Company; and it is in that company that Peter Brook, a director of genius, has shaped his greatest works—the *King Lear* and *A Midsummer Night's Dream,* but also *Marat-Sade,* under the influence of Antonin Artaud. The next historic date, however, had nothing to do with Beckett or Artaud; it was the success of John Osborne's *Look Back in Anger* at the Royal Court in 1956. This play, with its forceful, unconventional, uneuphemistic presentation of modern speech and behavior, created new theatrical standards and exploited new subjects. Osborne has written many more plays, some of them better, but none of such historical importance. The English Stage Company continued its adventures with new playwrights; and important work was going on to the east, where, in a poor district, Joan Littlewood discovered and performed the plays of Shelagh Delaney and Brendan Behan.

The most important of the new writers in this wave is certainly Harold Pinter (b. 1930), whose first major play was *The Birthday Party* (1957) and whose latest and best is *Old Times* (1971). Pinter has studied Brecht and Beckett, but his work is intensely individual, with the appearance of domestic realism, always qualified by imaginative presences, by silence, by the sudden long, broken speech. He is pure playwright; his imagination uses the theater as a painter uses paint, and his work is virtually indescribable. Among his juniors Tom Stoppard, whose *Rosencrantz and Guildenstern Are Dead* was performed by the National Theater Company, comes closest in theatrical genius.

The connections between this theatrical revival and the names of Brecht, Beckett, and Artaud may not be clear. Beckett's work showed how the prose theater could become the medium of a strange new poetry that is much more than merely a doctrinaire Theater of the Absurd; Brecht finally destroyed all obligations to the old illusionist theater; Artaud taught Peter Brook how to realize such a work as Peter Weiss's *Marat-Sade* (1964) in a manner so far transcending any notion of a doctrinaire Theater of Cruelty that the work of the Royal Shakespeare Company, and of serious British writers for the theater, has never been the same since. Experimental theater of all kinds flourishes in England. Some of it may be affected by the American Living Theater; but its health depends on its close association with the major state-subsidized theaters, and the adventurousness of their directors. If the center of the modern literature of contemporary Britain lies so close to the theater, it is perhaps because of English eloquence; manifesting itself in talk, mimetic language, and a national consciousness of the energy and joy of speech, this eloquence continues to provide both a great tradition of stage acting and a love for the theater which affects writers in other genres as well. No matter how experimental Beckett's plays may seem, despite their having been written and produced initially for the French stage, they belong in the line of great English—and Anglo-Irish—prose comedy running from Ben Jonson's *Epicoene* and Congreve's *The Way of the World* through Sheridan, Oscar Wilde, and Shaw. In theater as in poetry, the strands of tradition and innovation are tightly interwoven.

Glossary

A Commentary on Selected Literary and Historical Terms

Allegory Literally, "other reading"; originally a way of interpreting a narrative or other text in order to extract a more general, or a less literal, meaning from it, e.g. reading Homer's *Odyssey* as the universal voyage of human life—with Odysseus standing for all men—which must be made toward a final goal. In the Middle Ages allegory came to be associated with ways of reading the Bible, particularly the Old Testament in relation to the New. In addition, stories came to be written with the intention of being interpreted symbolically; thus e.g. the *Psychomachia* or "battle for the soul" of Prudentius (b. 348 A.D.) figured the virtues and vices as contending soldiers in a battle (see *Personification*). There is allegorical lyric poetry and allegorical drama as well as allegorical narrative. In works such as Spenser's *The Faerie Queene* and Bunyan's *Pilgrim's Progress* allegory becomes a dominant literary form. See also *Figure,* under *Rhetoric; Type, Typology.*

Alliteration A repeated initial consonant in successive words. In Old English verse, any vowel alliterates with any other, and alliteration is not an unusual or expressive phenomenon but a regularly recurring structural feature of the verse, occurring on the first and third, and often on the first, second, and third, primary-stressed syllables of the four-stressed line. Thus, from "The Seafarer":

> hréran mid hóndum hrímcælde sæ
> ("to stir with his hand the rime-cold sea")

In later English verse tradition, alliteration becomes expressive in a variety of ways. Spenser uses it decoratively, or to link adjective and noun, verb and object, as in the line: "Much daunted with that dint, her sense was dazed." In the 18th and 19th centuries it becomes even less systematic and more "musical."

Assonance A repeated vowel sound, a part-rhyme, which has great expressive effect when used internally (within lines), e.g. "An old, mad, blind, despised and dying king,—" (Shelley, "Sonnet: England in 1819").

Baroque (1) Originally (and still), an oddly shaped rather than a spherical pearl, and hence something twisted, contorted, involuted. (2) By a complicated analogy, a term designating stylistic periods in art, music, and literature during the 16th and 17th centuries in Europe. The analogies among the arts are frequently strained, and the stylistic periods by no means completely coincide. But the relation between the poetry of Richard Crashaw in English and Latin, and the sculpture and architecture of Gianlorenzo Bernini (1598–1680), is frequently taken to typify the spirit of the baroque. (See Wylie Sypher, *Four Stages of Renaissance Style,* 1955.)

Balade, Ballade   The dominant lyric form in French poetry of the 14th and 15th centuries; a strict form consisting of three stanzas of eight lines each, with an *envoi* (*q.v.*), or four-line conclusion, addressing either a person of importance or a personification. Each stanza, including the *envoi,* ends in a refrain.

Ballad Meter   Or *common meter;* four-lined stanzas, rhyming *abab,* the first and third lines in iambic tetrameter (four beats), and the second and fourth lines in iambic trimeter (three beats). See *Meter.*

Courtly Love   Modern scholarship has coined this name for a set of conventions around which medieval love-poetry was written. It was essentially chivalric and a product of 12th-century France, especially of the troubadours. This poetry involves an idealization of the beloved woman, whose love, like all love, refines and ennobles the lover so that the union of their minds and/or bodies—a union that ought not to be apparent to others—allows them to attain excellence of character.

Dada   A satirical, anti-literary movement in European art and literature, 1916–21, its name having been selected to connote *nothing* (the movement's founders are in dispute over its method of selection). Dadaists engaged in a systematic nullification of reason, religion, and art itself, producing pictures and poems out of the random and the absurd, sculpture out of ordinary objects, and entertainments out of elaborately staged exhibitions that must have been alternately hilarious and tedious. Founded in Zurich by Tristan Tzara, Hans Arp, Hugo Ball, and Richard Huelsenbeck, Dada moved to Paris in 1919, took on a more international character, and was embraced by many young writers who would thereafter become attached to Surrealism (*q.v.*).

Decorum   Propriety of discourse; what is becoming in action, character, and style; the avoidance of impossibilities and incongruities in action, style, and character: "the good grace of everything after his kind" and the "great masterpiece to observe." More formally, a neoclassical doctrine maintaining that literary style—grand, or high, middle, and low—be appropriate to the subject, occasion, and genre. Thus Milton, in *Paradise Lost* (I.13–14), invokes his "adventurous song, / That with no middle flight intends to soar. . . ." See also *Rhetoric.*

Dissenters   In England, members of Protestant churches and sects that do not conform to the doctrines of the established Church of England; from the 16th century on, this would include Baptists, Puritans of various sorts within the Anglican Church, Presbyterians, Congregationalists, and (in the 18th century) Methodists. Another term, more current in the 19th century, is *Nonconformist.*

Elegy   Originally, in Greek and Latin poetry, a poem composed not in the hexameter lines of epic (*q.v.*) and, later, of pastoral, but in the elegiac couplets consisting of one hexameter line followed by a pentameter. Elegiac poetry was amatory, epigrammatic. By the end of the 16th century, English poets were using heroic couplets (q.v.), to stand for both hexameters and elegiacs; and an elegiac poem was any serious meditative piece. Perhaps because of the tradition of the pastoral elegy (q.v.), the general term "elegy" came to be reserved, in modern terminology, for an elaborate and formal lament, longer than a *dirge* or *threnody*, for a dead person. By extension, "elegiac" has come to mean, in general speech, broodingly sad.

Enjambment The "straddling" of a clause or sentence across two lines of verse, as opposed to closed, or end-stopped, lines. Thus, in the opening lines of Shakespeare's *Twelfth Night:*

> If music be the food of love, play on!
> Give me excess of it, that, surfeiting
> The appetite may sicken and so die . . .

the first line is stopped, the second enjambed. When enjambment becomes strong or violent, it may have an ironic or comic effect.

The Enlightenment A term used very generally, to refer to the late 17th and the 18th century in Europe, a period characterized by a programmatic rationalism—i.e. a belief in the ability of human reason to understand the world and thereby to transform whatever in it needed transforming; an age in which ideas of science and progress accompanied the rise of new philosophies of the relation of man to the state, an age which saw many of its hopes for human betterment fulfilled in the French Revolution.

Envoi, Envoy Short concluding stanza found in certain French poetic forms and their English imitations, e.g. the *ballade* (q.v.). It serves as a dedicatory postscript, and a summing up of the poem of which it repeats the refrain.

Epic Or, *heroic poetry;* originally, oral narrative delivered in a style different from that of normal discourse by reason of verse, music, and heightened diction, and concerning the great deeds of a central heroic figure, or group of figures, usually having to do with a crisis in the history of a race or culture. Its setting lies in this earlier "heroic" period, and it will often have been written down only after a long period of oral transmission. The Greek *Iliad* and *Odyssey* and the Old English *Beowulf* are examples of this, in their narration mixing details from both the heroic period described and the actual time of their own composition and narration. What is called *secondary* or *literary* epic is a long, ambitious poem, composed by a single poet on the model of the older, primary forms, and of necessity being more allusive and figurative than its predecessors. Homer's poems lead to Virgil's *Aeneid,* which leads to Milton's *Paradise Lost,* in a chain of literary dependency. Spenser's *Faerie Queene* might be called *romantic epic* of the secondary sort, and Dante's *Divine Comedy* might also be assimilated to post-Virgilian epic tradition.

Epic Simile An extended comparison, in Homeric and subsequently in Virgilian and later epic poetry, between an event in the story (the *fable*) and something in the experience of the epic audience, to the effect of making the fabulous comprehensible in terms of the familiar. From the Renaissance on, additional complications have emerged from the fact that what is the familiar for the classical audience becomes, because of historical change, itself fabled (usually, pastoral) for the modern audience. Epic similes compare the fabled with the familiar usually with respect to one property or element; thus, in the *Odyssey*, when the stalwart forward motion of a ship in high winds is described, the simile goes:

> And as amids a fair field four brave horse
> Before a chariot, stung into their course
> With fervent lashes of the smarting scourge
> That all their fire blows high, and makes them rise
> To utmost speed the measure of their ground:
> So bore the ship aloft her fiery bound
> About whom rushed the billows, black and vast
> In which the sea-roars burst . . .
>   (*Chapman translation*)

Notice the formal order of presentation: "even as . . .": *the familiar event, often described in detail;* "just so . . .": *the fabled one.*

Epicureanism   A system of philosophy founded by the Greek Epicurus (342–270 B.C.), who taught that the five senses are the sole source of ideas and sole criterion of truth, and that the goal of human life is pleasure (i.e. hedonism), though this can be achieved only by practicing moderation. Later the term came to connote bestial self-indulgence, which Epicurus had clearly rejected.

Figurative Language   In a general sense, any shift away from a literal meaning of words, brought about by the use of tropes (*q.v.*) or other rhetorical devices. See *Rhetoric*.

Free Verse, Vers Libre   Generally, any English verse form whose lines are measured neither by the number of 1) stressed syllables (see *Meter* §3, accentual verse), 2) alternations of stressed and unstressed syllables (§4, accentual-syllabic verse), nor syllables alone (§2, syllabic verse). The earliest English free verse —that of Christopher Smart in *Jubilate Agno* (18th century)—imitates the prosody of Hebrew poetry (reflected also in the translation of the English Bible), in maintaining unmeasured units marked by syntactic parallelism. While many free-verse traditions (e.g. that of Walt Whitman) remain close to the impulses of this biblical poetry, yet others, in the 20th century, have developed new *ad hoc* patterns of their own. *Vers libre* usually refers to the experimental, frequently very short unmeasured lines favored by poets of the World War I period, although the term, rather than the form, was adopted from French poetry of the 19th century.

Gothic   Term (originally pejorative, as alluding to the Teutonic barbarians) designating the architectural style of the Middle Ages. The revival of interest in medieval architecture in the later 18th century produced not only pseudo-Gothic castles like Horace Walpole's "Strawberry Hill", and more modest artificial ruins on modern estates, but also a vogue for atmospheric prose romances set in medieval surroundings and involving improbable terrors, and known as Gothic novels. The taste for the Gothic, arising during the Age of Sensibility (*q.v.*), is another reflection of a reaction against earlier 18th-century neoclassicism (*q.v*).

Heroic Couplet   In English prosody, a pair of rhyming, iambic pentameter lines, used at first for closure—as at the end of the Shakespearean sonnet (*q.v.*)— or to terminate a scene in blank-verse drama; later adapted to correspond in English poetry to the elegiac couplet of classical verse as well as to the heroic, unrhymed, Greek and Latin hexameter. Octosyllabic couplets, with four stresses (eight syllables) to the line, are a minor, shorter, jumpier form, used satirically unless in implicit allusion to the form of Milton's "Il Penseroso," in which they develop great lyrical power. (See *Meter*.)

Irony   Generally, a mode of saying one thing to mean another. *Sarcasm*, in which one means exactly the opposite of what one says, is the easiest and cheapest form; thus, e.g. "Yeah, it's a *nice day–*" when one means that it's a miserable one. But serious literature produces ironies of a much more complex and revealing sort. *Dramatic irony* occurs when a character in a play or story asserts something whose meaning the audience or reader knows will change in time. Thus, in Genesis when Abraham assures his son Isaac (whom he is about to sacrifice) that "God will provide his own lamb," the statement is lighted with dramatic irony when a sacrificial ram is actually provided at the last minute to save Isaac. Or, in the case of Sophocles' *Oedipus*, when almost everything the protagonist says about the predicament of his city is hideously ironic in view of the fact (which he does not know) that he is responsible therefor. The ironies generated by the acknowledged use of non-literal language (see *Rhetoric*) and fictions in drama, song, and narrative are at the core of imaginative literature.

Kenning   An Old Norse form designating, strictly, a condensed simile or metaphor of the kind frequently used in Old Germanic poetry; a figurative circumlocution for a thing not actually named—e.g. "swan's path" for sea; "world-candle" or "sky-candle" for sun. More loosely, often used to mean also a metaphorical compound word or phrase such as "ring-necked" or "foamy-necked" for a ship, these being descriptive rather than figurative in character.

Macaronic   Verse in which two languages are mingled, usually for burlesque purposes.

Meter   Verse may be made to differ from prose and from ordinary speech in a number of ways, and in various languages these ways may be very different. Broadly speaking, lines of verse may be marked out by the following regularities of pattern:

  1. *Quantitative Verse*, used in ancient Greek poetry and adopted by the Romans, used a fixed number of what were almost musical measures, called *feet;* they were built up of long and short syllables (like half- and quarter-notes in music), which depended on the vowel and consonants in them. *Stress accent* (the *word* stress which, when accompanied by vowel reduction, distinguishes the English noun "*content*" from the adjective "*content*") did not exist in ancient Greek, and played no part in the rhythm of the poetic line. Thus, the first line of the *Odyssey: Andra moi ennepe mousa, polytropon hos mala polla* ("Sing me, O muse, of that man of many resources who, after great hardship . . .") is composed in *dactyls* of one long syllable followed by two shorts (but, as in musical rhythm, replaceable by two longs, a *spondee*).

With six dactyls to a line, the resulting meter is called *dactylic hexameter* (*hexameter,* for short), the standard form for epic poetry. Other kinds of foot or measure were: the *anapest* ($\cup \cup -$); the *iamb* ($\cup -$); the *trochee* ($- \cup$); and a host of complex patterns used in lyric poetry. Because of substitutions, however, the number of syllables in a classical line was not fixed, only the number of measures.

2. *Syllabic Verse,* used in French, Japanese, and many other languages, and in English poetry of the mid-20th century, measures only the *number* of syllables per line with no regard to considerations of *quantity* or *stress.* Because of the prominence of stress in the English language, two lines of the same purely syllabic length may not necessarily sound at all as though they were in the same meter, e.g.:

> These two incommensurably sounding
> Lines are both written with ten syllables.

3. *Accentual Verse,* used in early Germanic poetry, and thus in Old English poetry, depended upon the number of strong *stress accents* per line. These accents were four in number, with no fixed number of unstressed. Folk poetry and nursery rhymes often preserve this accentual verse, e.g.:

> Sing, sing, what shall I sing?
> The cat's run away with the pudding-bag string

The first line has six syllables, the second, eleven, but they sound more alike (and not merely by reason of their rhyme) than the two syllabic lines quoted above.

4. *Accentual-Syllabic Verse,* the traditional meter of English poetry from Chaucer on, depends upon both numbered *stresses* and numbered *syllables,* a standard form consisting of ten syllables alternately stressed and unstressed, and having five stresses; thus it may be said to consist of five syllable pairs.

For complex historical reasons, accentual-syllabic groups of stressed and unstressed syllables came to be known by the names used for Greek and Latin feet—which can be very confusing. The analogy was made between *long* syllables in the classical languages, and *stressed* syllables in English. Thus, the pair of syllables in the adjective "*content*" is called an *iamb,* and in the noun "*content,*" a *trochee;* the word "classical" is a *dactyll,* and the phrase "of the best," an *anapest.* When English poetry is being discussed, these terms are always used in their adapted, accentual-syllabic meanings, and hence the ten-syllable line mentioned earlier is called "iambic pentameter" in English. The phrase "high-tide" would be a *spondee* (as would, in general, two monosyllables comprising a proper name, e.g. "John Smith"); whereas compound nouns like "highway" would be *trochaic.* In this adaptation of classical nomenclature, the terms *dimeter, trimeter, tetrameter, pentameter, hexameter* refer not to the number of quantitative feet but to the number of syllable-groups (pairs or triplets, from one to six) composing the line. Iambic pentameter and tetrameter lines are frequently also called *decasyllabic* and *octosyllabic* respectively.

5. *Versification.* In verse, lines may be arranged in patterns called *stichic*

or *strophic*, that is, the same linear form (say, iambic pentameter) repeated without grouping by rhyme or interlarded lines of another form, or varied in just such a way into *stanzas* or *strophes* ("turns"). Unrhymed iambic pentameter, called *blank verse*, is the English stichic form that Milton thought most similar to classic hexameter or *heroic* verse. But in the Augustan period iambic pentameter rhymed pairs, called heroic couplets (*q.v.*), came to stand for this ancient form as well as for the classical elegiac verse (*q.v.*). Taking couplets as the simplest strophic unit, we may proceed to *tercets* (groups of three lines) and to *quatrains* (groups of four), rhymed *abab* or *abcb*, and with equal or unequal line lengths. Other stanzaic forms: *ottava rima*, an eight-line, iambic pentameter stanza, rhyming *abababcc*; *Spenserian stanza*, rhyming *ababbcbcc*, all pentameter save for the last line, an iambic hexameter, or *alexandrine*. There have been adaptations in English (by Shelley, notably, and without rhyme by T. S. Eliot) of the Italian *terza rima* used by Dante in *The Divine Comedy*, interlocking tercets rhyming *aba bcb cdc ded*, etc. More elaborate stanza forms developed in the texts of some Elizabethan songs and in connection with the ode (*q.v.*).

Myth A primitive story explaining the origins of certain phenomena in the world and in human life, and usually embodying gods or other supernatural forces, heroes (men who are either part human and part divine, or are placed between an ordinary mortal and a divine being), men, and animals. Literature continues to incorporate myths long after the mythology (the system of stories containing them) ceases to be a matter of actual belief. Moreover, discarded beliefs of all sorts tend to become myths when they are remembered but no longer literally clung to, and are used in literature in a similar way. The classical mythology of the Greeks and Romans was apprehended in this literary, or interpreted, way, even in ancient times. The gods and heroes and their deeds came to be read as allegory (*q.v.*). During the Renaissance, *mythography*—the interpretation of myths in order to make them reveal a moral or historical significance (rather than merely remaining entertaining but insignificant stories)—was extremely important, both for literature and for painting and sculpture. In modern criticism, mythical or *archetypal* situations and personages have been interpreted as being central objects of the work of the imagination.

Neoclassicism (1) In general the term refers to Renaissance and post-Renaissance attempts to model enterprises in the various arts on Roman and Greek originals—or as much as was known of them. Thus, in the late Renaissance, the architectural innovations of Andrea Palladio may be called "neoclassic," as may Ben Jonson's relation, and Alexander Pope's as well, to the Roman poet Horace. The whole Augustan period in English literary history (1660–1740) was a deliberately neoclassical one.

(2) More specifically, neoclassicism refers to that period in the history of all European art spanning the very late 18th and early 19th century, which period may be seen as accompanying the fulfillment, and the termination, of the Enlightenment (*q.v.*). In England such neoclassic artists as Henry Fuseli, John Flaxman, George Romney, and even, in some measure, William Blake, are close to the origins of pictorial and literary Romanticism itself.

Neoplatonism   See *Platonism.*
Nonconformist   See *Dissenters.*

Octosyllabic Couplet   See *Heroic Couplet; Meter.*

Ode   A basic poetic form, originating in Greek antiquity. The *choral ode* was a public event, sung and danced, at a large ceremony, or as part of the tragic and comic drama. Often called *Pindaric ode,* after a great Greek poet, the form consisted of *triads* (groups of three sections each). These were units of song and dance, and had the form *aab*—that is, a *strophe* (or "turn"), an *antistrophe* (or "counter-turn"), and an *epode* (or "stand"), the first two being identical musically and metrically, the third different. In English poetry, the Pindaric ode form, only in its metrical aspects, became in the 17th century a mode for almost essayistic poetic comment, and was often used also as a kind of cantata libretto, in praise of music and poetry (the so-called *musical ode*). By the 18th century the ode became the form for a certain kind of personal, visionary poem, and it is this form that Wordsworth and Coleridge transmitted to Romantic tradition. A second English form, known as *Horatian ode,* was based on the lyric (not choral) poems of Horace, and is written in *aabb* quatrains, with the last two lines shorter than the first two by a pair of syllables or more.

Paradox   In logic, a self-contradictory statement, hence meaningless (or a situation producing one), with an indication that something is wrong with the language in which such a situation can occur, e.g. the famous paradox of Epimenedes the Cretan, who held that all Cretans are liars (and thus could be lying if— and only if—he wasn't), or that of Zeno, of the arrow in flight: since at any instant of time the point of the arrow can always be said to be at one precise point, therefore it is continually at rest at a continuous sequence of such points, and therefore never moves. In literature, however, particularly in the language of lyric poetry, paradox plays another role. From the beginnings of lyric poetry, paradox has been deemed necessary to express feelings and other aspects of human inner states, e.g. Sappho's invention of the Greek word *glykypikron* ("bittersweet") to describe love, or her assertion that she was freezing and burning at the same time. So too the Latin poet Catullus, in his famous couplet

> I'm in hate and I'm in love; why do I? you may ask.
> Well, I don't know, but I feel it, and I'm in agony.

may be declaring thereby that true love poetry must be illogical.

In Elizabethan poetry, paradoxes were frequently baldly laid out in the rhetorical form called *oxymoron* (see *Rhetoric*), as in "the victor-victim," or across a fairly mechanical sentence structure, as in "My feast of joy is but a dish of pain." In the highest poetic art, however, the seeming self-contradiction is removed when one realizes that either, or both, of the conflicting terms is to be taken figuratively, rather than literally. The apparent absurdity, or strangeness, thus gives rhetorical power to the utterance. Elaborate and sophisticated paradoxes, insisting on their own absurdity, typify the poetic idiom of the tradition of John Donne.

Pastoral   A literary mode in which the lives of simple country people are celebrated, described, and used allegorically by sophisticated urban poets and writers. The *idylls* of Sicilian poet Theocritus (3rd century B.C.) were imitated and made more symbolic in Virgil's *eclogues;* shepherds in an Arcadian landscape stood for literary and political personages, and the Renaissance adapted these narrative and lyric pieces for moral and aesthetic discussion. Spenser's *Shepheardes Calendar* is an experimental collection of eclogues involving an array of forms and subjects. In subsequent literary tradition, the pastoral imagery of both Old and New Testaments (Psalms, Song of Songs, priest as *pastor* or shepherd of his flock, and so on) joins with the classical mode. Modern critics, William Empson in particular, have seen the continuation of pastoral tradition in other versions of the country-city confrontation, such as child-adult and criminal-businessman. See *Pastoral Elegy.*

Pastoral Elegy   A form of lament for the death of a poet, originating in Greek bucolic tradition (Bion's lament for Adonis, a lament for Bion by a fellow poet, Theocritus' first idyll, Virgil's tenth eclogue) and continued in use by Renaissance poets as a public mode for the presentation of private, inner, and even coterie matters affecting poets and their lives, while conventionally treating questions of general human importance. At a death one is moved to ask, "Why this death? Why now?" and funeral elegy must always confront these questions, avoiding easy resignation as an answer. Pastoral elegy handled these questions with formal mythological apparatus, such as the Muses, who should have protected their dead poet, local spirits, and other presences appropriate to the circumstances of the life and death, and perhaps figures of more general mythological power. The end of such poems is the eternalization of the dead poet in a monument of myth, stronger than stone or bronze: Spenser's *Astrophel,* a lament for Sir Philip Sidney, concludes with an Ovidian change—the dead poet's harp, like Orpheus' lyre, becomes the constellation Lyra. Milton's *Lycidas* both exemplifies and transforms the convention. Later examples include Shelley's *Adonais* (for Keats), Arnold's *Thyrsis* (for Clough), and Swinburne's *Ave Atque Vale* (for Baudelaire).

Pathetic Fallacy   John Ruskin's term (used in *Modern Painters,* 1856) for the projection of human emotions onto the world in such a way as to personify inanimate things ineptly or falsely.

Personification   Treating a thing or, more properly, an abstract quality, as though it were a person. Thus, "Surely *goodness* and *mercy* shall follow me all the days of my life" tends to personify the italicized terms by reason of the metaphoric use of "follow me." On the other hand, a conventional, complete personification, like *Justice* (whom we recognize by her *attributes*—she is blindfolded, she has scales and a sword) might also be called an *allegorical figure* in her own right, and her attributes *symbols* (blindness = impartiality; scales = justly deciding; sword = power to mete out what is deserved). Often the term "personification" applies to momentary, or *ad hoc,* humanizations.

Platonism   The legacy of Plato (429–347 B.C.) is virtually the history of philosophy. His *Timaeus* was an important source of later cosmology; his doctrine of ideas is central to Platonic tradition. His doctrine of love (especially in the *Symposium*) had enormous influence in the Renaissance, at which time its applicability was shifted to heterosexual love specifically. The *Republic* and the *Laws* underlie a vast amount of political thought, and the *Republic* contains also a philosophical attack on poetry (fiction) which defenders of the arts have always had to answer. Neoplatonism—a synthesis of Platonism, Pythagoreanism, and Aristotelianism—was dominant in the 3rd century A.D.; and the whole tradition was revived in the 15th and 16th centuries. The medieval Plato was Latinized, largely at second-hand; the revival of Greek learning in the 15th century led to another Neoplatonism: a synthesis of Platonism, the medieval Christian Aristotle, and Christian doctrine. Out of this came the doctrines of love we associate with some Renaissance poetry; a sophisticated version of older systems of allegory and symbol; and notions of the relation of spirit and matter reflected in Marvell and many other poets.

Rhetoric   In classical times, rhetoric was the art of persuading through the use of language. The major treatises on style and structure of discourse—Aristotle's *Rhetoric*, Quintilian's *Institutes of Oratory*, the *Rhetorica ad Herrenium* ascribed for centuries to Cicero—were concerned with the "arts" of language in the older sense of "skills." In the Middle Ages the *trivium* (*q.v.*), or program that led to the degree of Bachelor of Arts, consisted of grammar, logic, and rhetoric, but it was an abstract study, based on the Roman tradition. In the Renaissance, classical rhetorical study became a matter of the first importance, and it led to the study of literary stylistics and the application of principles and concepts of the production and structure of eloquence to the higher eloquence of poetry.

Rhetoricians distinguished three stages in the production of discourse: *inventio* (finding or discovery), *dispositio* (arranging), and *elocutio* (style). Since the classical discipline aimed always at practical oratory (e.g. winning a case in court, or making a point effectively in council), *memoria* (memory) and *pronuntiatio* (delivery) were added. For the Renaissance, however, rhetoric became the art of writing. Under the heading of *elocutio*, style became stratified into three levels, *elevated* or high, *elegant* or middle, and *plain* or low. The proper fitting of these styles to the subject of discourse comprised the subject of decorum (*q.v.*).

Another area of rhetorical theory was concerned with classification of devices of language into *schemes, tropes,* and *figures.* A basic but somewhat confused distinction between figures of speech and figures of thought need not concern us here, but we may roughly distinguish between schemes (or patterns) of words, and tropes as manipulations of meanings, and of making words non-literal.

Common Schemes

anadiplosis   repeating the terminal word in a clause as the start of the next one: "Pleasure might cause her read; reading might cause her know; / Knowledge might pity win, and pity grace obtain" (Sidney, *Astrophel and Stella*).

anaphora   the repetition of a word or phrase at the openings of successive clauses, e.g. "The Lord sitteth above the water floods. The Lord remaineth King forever. The Lord shall give strength unto his people. The Lord shall give his people the blessing of peace."

chiasmus   a pattern of criss-crossing a syntactic structure, whether of noun and adjective, e.g. "Empty his bottle, and his girlfriend gone," or of a reversal of normal syntax with similar effect, e.g. "A fop her passion, and her prize, a sot," reinforced by assonance (*q.v.*). Chiasmus may even extend to assonance, as in Coleridge's line "In Xanadu did Kubla Khan."

Common Tropes

metaphor and simile both involve comparison of one thing to another, the difference being that the *simile* will actually compare, using the words "like" or "as," while the metaphor identifies one with the other, thus producing a non-literal use of a word or attribution. Thus, Robert Burns's "O, my love is like a red, red rose / That's newly sprung in June" is a simile; had Burns written, "My love, thou art a red, red rose . . .", it would have been a metaphor—and indeed, it would not mean that the lady had acquired petals. In modern critical theory, *metaphor* has come to stand for various non-expository kinds of evocative signification. I. A. Richards, the modern critic most interested in a general theory of metaphor in this sense, has contributed the terms *tenor* (as in the case above, the girl) and *vehicle* (the rose) to designate the components. See also *Epic Simile*.

metonymy a trope in which the vehicle is closely and conventionally associated with the tenor, e.g. "crown" and "king," "pen" and "writing," "pencil" and "drawing," "sword" and "warfare."

synecdoche a trope in which the part stands for the whole, e.g. "sail" for "ship."

hyperbole intensifying exaggeration, e.g. the combined synecdoche and hyperbole in which Christopher Marlowe's Faustus asks of Helen of Troy "Is this the face that launched a thousand ships / And burned the topless towers of Ilium?"

oxymoron literally, sharp-dull; a figure of speech involving a witty paradox, e.g. "sweet harm"; "darkness visible" (Milton, *Paradise Lost* I.63).

Satire A literary mode painting a distorted verbal picture of part of the world in order to show its true moral, as opposed merely to its physical, nature. In this sense, Circe, the enchantress in Homer's *Odyssey* who changed Odysseus' men into pigs (because they made pigs of themselves while eating) and would have changed Odysseus into a fox (for he was indeed foxy), was the first satirist. Originally the Latin word *satura* meant a kind of literary grab bag, or medley, and a satire was a fanciful kind of tale in mixed prose and verse; but later a false etymology connected the word with *satyr* and thus with the grotesque. Satire may be in verse or in prose; in the 16th and 17th centuries, the Roman poets Horace and Juvenal were imitated and expanded upon by writers of satiric moral verse, the tone of the verse being wise, smooth, skeptical, and urbane, that of the prose, sharp, harsh, and sometimes nasty. A tradition of English verse satire runs through Donne, Jonson, Dryden, Pope, and Samuel Johnson; of prose satire, Addison, Swift, and Fielding.

Seneca Lucius Annaeus Seneca (4 B.C.–65 A.D.) was an important source of Renaissance stoicism (*q.v.*), a model for the "closet" drama of the period, and an exemplar for the kind of prose that shunned the Ciceronian loquacity of early humanism and cultivated terseness. He was Nero's tutor; in 62 A.D. he retired from public life, and in 65 was compelled to commit suicide for taking part in a political conspiracy. He produced writings on ethics and physics, as well as ten tragedies often imitated in the Renaissance.

Sensibility (1) In the mid-18th century, the term came to be used in a literary context to refer to a susceptibility to fine or tender feelings, particularly involving the feelings and sorrows of others. This became a quality to be cultivated in despite of stoical rejections of unreasonable emotion which the neoclassicism (*q.v.*) of the earlier Augustan age had prized. The meaning of the word blended easily into "sentimentality"; but the literary period in England characterized by the work of writers such as Sterne, Goldsmith, Gray, Collins, and Cowper is often called the Age of Sensibility.

(2) A meaning more important for modern literature is that of a special kind of total awareness, an ability to make the finest discriminations in its perception of the world, and yet at the same time not lacking in a kind of force by the very virtue of its own receptive power. The varieties of awareness celebrated in French literature from Baudelaire through Marcel Proust have been adapted by modernist English critics, notably T. S. Eliot, for a fuller extension of the meaning of *sensibility*. By the term "dissociation of sensibility," Eliot implied the split between the sensuous and the intellectual faculties which he thought characterized English poetry after the Restoration (1660).

Sententia A wise, fruitful saying, functioning as a guide to morally correct thought or action.

Sestina Originally a Provençal lyric form supposedly invented by Arnaut Daniel in the 12th century, and one of the most complex of those structures. It has six stanzas of six lines each, followed by an *envoi* (*q.v.*) or *tornada* of three lines. Instead of rhyming, the end-words of the lines of the first stanza are all repeated in the following stanzas, but in a constant set of permutations. The *envoi* contains all six words, three in the middle of each line. D. G. Rossetti, Swinburne, Pound, Auden, and other modern poets have used the form, and Sir Philip Sidney composed a magnificent double-sestina, "Ye Goat-herd Gods."

Skepticism A philosophy that denies the possibility of certain knowledge, and, although opposed to Stoicism and Epicureanism (*q.v.*), advocated *ataraxy*, imperturbability of mind. Skepticism originated with Pyrrhon (*c.* 360–270 B.C.), and its chief transmitter was Sextus Empiricus (*c.* 200 B.C.). In the Renaissance, skepticism had importance as questioning the power of the human mind to know truly (for a classic exposition see Donne's *Second Anniversary*, ll. 254–300), and became a powerful influence in morals and religion through the advocacy of Montaigne.

Sonnet A basic lyric form, consisting of fourteen lines of iambic pentameter rhymed in various patterns. The *Italian* or *Petrarchan* sonnet is divided clearly into *octave* and *sestet*, the first rhyming *abba abba* and the second in a pattern such as *cdc dcd*. The *Shakespearean* sonnet consists of three quatrains followed by a couplet: *abab cdcd efef gg*. In the late 16th century in England, sonnets were written either independently as short epigrammatic forms, or grouped in sonnet sequences, i.e. collections of upwards of a hundred poems, in imitation of Petrarch, purportedly addressed to one central figure or muse—a lady usually with a symbolic name like "Stella" or "Idea." Milton made a new kind of use of the Petrarchan form, and the Romantic poets continued in the Miltonic tradition. Several variations have been devised, including the addition of "tails" or extra lines, or the recasting into sixteen lines, instead of fourteen.

Stoicism, Stoics Philosophy founded by Zeno (335–263 B.C.), and opposing the hedonistic tendencies of Epicureanism (*q.v.*). The Stoics' world-view was pantheistic: God was the energy that formed and maintained the world, and wisdom lay in obedience to this law of nature as revealed by the conscience. Moreover, every man is free because the life according to nature and conscience is available to all; so too is suicide—a natural right. Certain Stoics saw the end of the world as caused by fire. In the Renaissance, Latin Stoicism, especially that of Seneca (*q.v.*), had a revival of influence and was Christianized in various ways.

Stream of Consciousness A literary technique of modern fiction which attempts to imitate or duplicate, in patterns other than those of discourse, the flow of thoughts, impressions, memories, meditations, musings, and other products of an individual character's consciousness. It can result either in the fragmentation of sentence structure, or the overwhelming of it in long strings of eloquence. In James Joyce's *Ulysses*, where it is called "interior monologue," it operates in different styles to represent the thoughts of different characters, but its most celebrated use is in Molly Bloom's forty-two page soliloquy that concludes the book.

Style See *Decorum*.

Sublime "Lofty"; as a literary idea, originally the basic concept of a Greek treatise (by the so-called "Longinus") on style. In the 18th century, however, the *sublime* came to mean a loftiness perceivable in nature, and sometimes in art—a loftiness different from the composed vision of landscape known as the *picturesque*, because of the element of wildness, power, and even terror. The *beautiful*, the picturesque, and the sublime became three modes for the perception of nature.

Surrealism (1) A literary and artistic movement, predominantly French but with vast international influence; initiated after World War I by André Breton and others, and enshrining the irrational as the best mode of perceiving and representing reality. Pathological forms of vision, hallucination, psychotic utterance, automatic writing, free association, and other means of nullifying even the structures of Symbolist poetic tradition were celebrated. Poetic form was abandoned as though it were as inauthentic as bookkeeping or scientific language, and the surrealistic "texts" are neither prose nor verse. The unconscious, the impulsive, and particularly the erotic are the domains of the surrealistic imagination, which occupied many European painters including Pablo Picasso at a phase in his career, and particularly and with greatest success, René Magritte. Among French writers associated with the movement were Paul Eluard, Louis Aragon, Philippe Soupault, Antonin Artaud, René Char, and Raymond Queneau.

(2) In a looser sense, "surrealist" has been commonly (and misleadingly) used to describe representations in modern literature of the visionary, the dreamlike, the fantastic in any of its forms.

Symbolism (1) Broadly, the process by which one phenomenon, in literature, stands for another, or group of others, and usually of a different sort. Clearcut cases of this in medieval and Renaissance literature are *emblems* or *attributes* (see *Personification; Allegory*). Sometimes conventional symbols may be used in more than one way, e.g. a mirror betokening both truth and vanity. See also *Figure*, under *Rhetoric*.

(2) In a specific sense (and often given in its French form, *symbolisme*), an important esthetic concept for modern literature, formulated by French poets and critics of the later 19th century following Baudelaire. In this view, the literary symbol becomes something closer to a kind of commanding, central metaphor, taking precedence over any more discursive linguistic mode for poetic communication. The effects of this concept on literature in English have been immense; and some version of the concept survives in modern notions of the poetic *image*, or *fiction*.

Trope (1) See *Rhetoric*. (2) In the liturgy of the Catholic Church, a phrase, sentence, or verse with its musical setting, introduced to amplify or embellish some part of the text of the mass or the office (i.e. the prayers and Scripture readings recited daily by priests, religious, and even laymen) when chanted in choir. Tropes of this second kind were discontinued in 1570 by the authority of Pope Pius V. Troping new material into older or conventional patterns seems to have been, in a general way, a basic device of medieval literature, and was the genesis of modern drama.

Type, Typology (1) Strictly, in medieval biblical interpretation, the prefiguration of the persons and events of the New Testament by persons and events of the Old, the Old Testament being fulfilled in, but not entirely superseded by, the New. Thus, the Temptation and Fall of Man were held to prefigure the first Temptation of Christ, pride in each case being the root of the temptation, and a warning against gluttony the moral lesson to be drawn from both. The Brazen Serpent raised up by Moses was held to prefigure the crucifixion of Christ; Isaac, as a sacrificial victim ("God will provide his own Lamb," says Abraham to him) is a *type* of Christ. The forty days and nights of the Deluge, the forty years of Israel's wandering in the desert, Moses' forty days in the desert are all typologically related.

(2) In a looser sense, a person or event seen as a model or paradigm. See also *Figure*, under *Rhetoric*.

Villanelle A lyric form originally used in French Renaissance poetry for pastoral subjects, adopted by 19th-century English writers of light verse, and eventually taken up again by poets such as James Joyce, William Empson, and Dylan Thomas for more than trivial effects. The form consists of five (see *Meter* §5) tercets rhyming *aba*, followed by a quatrain rhyming *abaa*. The first and last line of the first tercet are alternately repeated as refrains at the end of each following tercet. Thus, in Edward Arlington Robinson's famous villanelle beginning

> They are all gone away,
> > The house is shut and still,
> There is nothing more to say.

the first and third line are alternated, finally to follow each other in the last tercet. Modern use of the form depends upon subtle variations of the meaning of the refrain lines at each repetition.

Suggestions for Further Reading

ROMANTIC POETRY AND PROSE
The Period in General

Political and Social Backgrounds The most useful single study remains Alfred Cobban's *Edmund Burke and the Revolt Against the Eighteenth Century*, 1929, which emphasizes Burke's influence on the later thought of Wordsworth and Coleridge. G. M. Trevelyan's *English Social History*, 1942, sketches the period with great vividness. Supplemental detail may be sought in R. J. White's *From Waterloo to Peterloo*, 1957, and in Kenneth MacLean's *Agrarian Age*, 1951. Still valuable is Edward Dowden's *The French Revolution and English Literature*, 1897, which can be filled out by Carl Woodring's *Politics in English Romantic Poetry*, 1970. The relevant pages in Raymond Williams's *Culture and Society, 1780–1950*, 1960, provide a vigorous instance of a modern radical view.

Literary History Douglas Bush, *Mythology and the Romantic Tradition in English Poetry*, 1937, remains the classical study of a crucial element in Romantic poetry, though its bias is firmly anti-Romantic. The best literary history is the superbly informed work of Oliver Elton, *A Survey of English Literature*, two vols., 1928. The two relevant volumes in the Oxford History of English Literature are rather inadequate, but much useful information may be derived from Ian Jack, *English Literature, 1815–1832*, 1963, and W. L. Renwick, *English Literature, 1789–1815*, 1963.

Collections of Critical Essays *English Romantic Poets*, ed. M. H. Abrams, 1960, balances a variety of viewpoints on the major poets. *Romanticism Reconsidered*, ed. N. Frye, 1963, sums up leading critical attitudes of the period. *Romanticism and Consciousness*, ed. H. Bloom, 1970, collects essays on the major poets and essays investigating the central Romantic ideas of Nature, literary form, and political revolution. *From Sensibility to Romanticism*, ed. F. W. Hilles and H. Bloom, 1965, gathers essays on the main continuity of English poetry from Pope to Keats.

General Studies Two works by M. H. Abrams, *The Mirror and the Lamp*, 1953, and *Natural Supernaturalism*, 1971, are distinguished and sympathetic studies respectively of Romantic critical theory and Romantic poetry. W. J. Bate, *From Classic to Romantic*, 1946, remains a highly useful account of the development of Romantic attitudes. The most comprehensive volume giving readings of individual Romantic poems is *The Visionary Company* by H. Bloom, rev. ed., 1971. More advanced studies are offered in H. Bloom, *The Ringers in the Tower*, 1971; N. Frye, *A Study of English*

Romanticism, 1968; and G. Hartman, *Beyond Formalism*, 1970. D. G. James, *Scepticism and Poetry*, 1937, is still a useful account of Romantic theories of imagination. F. Kermode, *Romantic Image*, 1957, was a pioneer exploration of the continuity of Romantic and Modern poetry.

Bibliography   R. H. Fogle, *Romantic Poets and Prose Writers*, 1967. T. M. Raysor, *The English Romantic Poets*, 1956; C. W. and L. H. Houtchens, *The English Romantic Poets and Essayists*, 1966.

Poetry
WILLIAM BLAKE

Editions   *Poetry and Prose,* ed. D. V. Erdman, with commentary by H. Bloom, 1965.

Critical Studies   Hazard Adams, *William Blake*, 1963. H. Bloom, *Blake's Apocalypse*, 1963. S. Foster Damon, *William Blake*, 1924, and *A Blake Dictionary*, 1965. D. V. Erdman, *Blake, Prophet against Empire*, 1954. P. F. Fisher, *The Valley of Vision*, 1961. *Blake*, ed. N. Frye, 1966. N. Frye, *Fearful Symmetry*, 1947. *Discussions of Blake*, ed. J. Grant, 1961. J. M. Murry, *William Blake*, 1933. Milton Percival, *Blake's Circle of Destiny*, 1938. *Blake's Visionary Forms Dramatic*, ed. D. V. Erdman and J. Grant, 1970.

Biography   The best continues to be Alexander Gilchrist, *Life of William Blake*, 1863, in the edition of Ruthven Todd, 1945.

WILLIAM WORDSWORTH

Editions   *Poetical Works*, ed. E. de Selincourt and H. Darbishire, five vols., 1940–49. *The Prelude*, 1805 and 1850 facing texts, ed. E. de Selincourt and H. Darbishire, 1959. Best one-volume edition, ed. T. Hutchinson and E. de Selincourt, 1950.

Critical Studies   *Wordsworth*, ed. M. H. Abrams, 1971. L. Abercrombie, *The Art of Wordsworth*, 1952. Matthew Arnold, *Essays in Criticism*, 2nd series, 1888. A. C. Bradley, *Oxford Lectures on Poetry*, 1909. *Wordsworth*, ed. J. Davis, 1963. *Wordsworth*, ed. G. T. Dunklin, 1951. D. Ferry, *The Limits of Mortality*, 1959. G. Hartman, *Wordsworth's Poetry, 1787–1814*, 1965. E. D. Hirsch, *Wordsworth and Schelling*, 1960. J. Jones, *The Egotistical Sublime*, 1953. W. L. Sperry, *Wordsworth's Anti-Climax*, 1935. C. Woodring, *Wordsworth*, 1965.

Biography   The best is Mary Moorman's *Wordsworth, A Biography*, two vols., 1957 (corrected 1968) and 1965, respectively.

SAMUEL TAYLOR COLERIDGE

Editions   Complete edition at this date in progress, ed. Kathleen Coburn, who is editing the *Notebooks* also (first two vols., 1957–61). *Complete Poetical Works*, ed. E. H. Coleridge, two vols., 1912. *Biographia Literaria*, ed. J. Shawcross, two vols., 1907. *Collected Letters* (through 1819), ed. E. L. Griggs, four vols. 1956–59. *Inquiring Spirit*, ed. K. Coburn, 1951: miscellaneous prose.

Critical Studies   W. J. Bate, *Coleridge*, 1967. J. B. Beer, *Coleridge, the Visionary*, 1959. *Coleridge*, ed. K. Coburn, 1967. *New Perspectives on Coleridge and Words-worth*, ed. G. Hartman, 1972. Humphry House, *Coleridge*, 1953. J. L. Lowes, *The Road to Xanadu*, 1927. I. A. Richards, *Coleridge on Imagination*, 1960.

LORD BYRON

Editions   *Works*, 13 vols., ed. E. H. Coleridge and R. E. Prothero, 1898–1904; one-volume ed. of *Poetical Works*, ed. E. H. Coleridge, 1905. *Byron: A Self-Portrait*, ed. P. Quennell, two vols., 1950, gives diaries and selected letters.

Critical Studies   M. G. Cooke, *The Blind Man Traces the Circle*, 1969. G. W. Knight, *The Burning Oracle*, 1939. J. J. McGann, *Fiery Dust*, 1968. G. Ridenour, *The Style of "Don Juan,"* 1960. A. Rutherford, *Byron*, 1961. *Byron*, ed. P. West, 1963.

Biography   The most comprehensive is L. A. Marchand, *Byron*, three vols., 1957.

PERCY BYSSHE SHELLEY

Editions   *Complete Works*, ten vols., ed. R. Ingpen and W. E. Peck, 1926–30. *Complete Poetical Works*, ed. T. Hutchinson, 1904. *Shelley's Prose*, ed. D. L. Clarke, 1954. *Letters*, ed. F. L. Jones, two vols., 1964.

Critical Studies   Carlos Baker, *Shelley's Major Poetry*, 1948. H. Bloom, *Shelley's Mythmaking*, 1959. A. M. D. Hughes, *The Nascent Mind of Shelley*, 1947. C. E. Pulos, *The Deep Truth*, 1954. *Shelley*, ed. G. M. Ridenour, 1965. J. Todhunter, *A Study of Shelley*, 1880. E. Wasserman, *Shelley*, 1971. M. Wilson, *Shelley's Later Poetry*, 1959. For *The Triumph of Life* see D. H. Reiman, ed., 1965.

Biography   The best are E. Blunden, *Shelley, A Life Story*, 1946 (repr. 1965), and N. I. White, *Shelley*, two vols., 1940.

JOHN KEATS

Editions   *Poetical Works*, ed. H. W. Garrod, 1958. *Letters*, ed. H. E. Rollins, two vols., 1958.

Critical Studies   W. J. Bate, *Negative Capability*, 1939. *Keats*, ed. W. J. Bate, 1964. J. R. Caldwell, *John Keats' Fancy*, 1945. J. M. Murry, *Keats*, 1955, and *Keats and Shakespeare*, 1926. C. D. Thorpe, *The Mind of Keats*, 1926. M. Dickstein, *Keats and His Poetry*, 1971. E. Wasserman, *The Finer Tone*, 1953.

Biography   The best is W. J. Bate, *John Keats*, 1963.

OTHER ROMANTIC POETS

William Lisle Bowles   *Poetical Works*, ed. G. Gilfillan, two vols., 1855. S. T. Coleridge, *Biographia Literaria*, Vol. I, chap. 1. A. Symons, *Romantic Movement in English Poetry*, 1909.

Sir Walter Scott *Poetical Works,* ed. J. L. Robertson, 1904. See Scott chapter in H. J. C. Grierson and J. C. Smith, *A Critical Survey of English Poetry,* 1944.

Walter Savage Landor *Poetical Works,* ed. S. Wheeler, three vols., 1937. Donald Davie, "The Shorter Poems of Walter Savage Landor," *Essays in Criticism,* ed. F. W. Bateson, Vol. I, 1951. R. Pinsky, *Landor's Poetry,* 1968.

Thomas Love Peacock *Works,* ed. H. F. B. Brett-Smith and C. E. Jones, ten vols., 1928, and *Poems,* ed. B. Johnson, 1906. O. W. Campbell, *Peacock,* 1953.

John Clare *Poems,* ed. J. W. Tibble, two vols., 1935; *Poems of John Clare's Madness,* ed. G. Grigson, 1949; *The Later Poems,* ed. E. Robinson and G. Summerfield, 1964. J. M. Murry, *John Clare and Other Studies,* 1950.

George Darley *Complete Poetical Works,* ed. R. Colles, 1908. C. C. Abbott, *Life and Letters of George Darley,* 1928. J. Heath-Stubbs, *The Darkling Plain,* 1950.

Hartley Coleridge *Complete Poetical Works,* ed. R. Colles, 1908. E. Blunden, *Votive Tablets,* 1931.

Thomas Hood *Complete Poetical Works,* ed. W. C. Jerrold, 1911. George Saintsbury, *Collected Essays,* Vol. II, 1923.

Thomas Lovell Beddoes *Works,* ed. H. W. Donner, 1935. H. W. Donner, *Beddoes: The Making of a Poet,* 1935. N. Frye, *A Study of English Romanticism,* 1968.

Samuel Palmer G. Grigson, *Samuel Palmer's Valley of Vision,* 1960.

Thomas Wade H. B. Forman, "Wade: The Poet and His Surroundings," in *Literary Anecdotes of the Nineteenth Century,* ed. W. R. Nicoll and T. J. Wise, Vol. I, 1895.

Prose
THOMAS DE QUINCEY

Editions *The Collected Writings,* ed. David Masson, 14 vols., 1889–90. *Uncollected Writings,* ed. James Hogg, two vols., 1890. *Posthumous Writings,* ed. A. H. Japp, two vols., 1891–93. *A Diary of Thomas De Quincey for 1803,* ed. H. A. Eaton, 1927. *De Quincey's Literary Criticism,* ed. Helen Darbishire, 1909.

Critical Studies Albert Goldman, *The Mine and the Mint: Sources for the Writings of De Quincey,* 1965. D. Grant, "Thomas De Quincey," in *Some British Romantics,* ed. J. V. Logan and others, 1966. John E. Jordan, *Thomas De Quincey, Literary Critic,* 1952. J. Hillis Miller, *The Disappearance of God: Five Nineteenth-Century Writers,* 1963. S. Kobayashi, *Rhythm in the Prose of Thomas De Quincey,* 1956. René Wellek, *History of Modern Criticism, 1750–1950,* Vol. II, 1955.

Biography There is as yet no definitive biography of De Quincey, understandably enough, for the difficulties he puts in the way of a biographer are enormous. The following works are variously useful. M. H. Abrams, *The Milk of Paradise,* 1934, 1970, on De Quincey's use of opium. H. S. Davies, *Thomas De Quincey,* 1964. *De Quincey and His Friends: Personal Recollections, Souvenirs and Anecdotes,* ed. James Hogg, 1895. Horace A. Eaton, *Thomas De Quincey: A Biography,* 1936, the most reliable of the lives. Malcolm Elwin, *Thomas De Quincey*, 1935. Alethea Hayter, *Opium and the Romantic Imagination*, 1968, 1971, on De Quincey's use of opium. John E. Jordan, *De Quincey to Wordsworth: A Biography of a Relationship*, 1962. Edward Sackville-West, *A Flame in Sunlight*, 1936.

WILLIAM HAZLITT

Editions   *The Complete Works*, ed. P. P. Howe, 1930–34. *Selected Essays*, ed. Geoffrey Keynes, 1930. *Hazlitt Painted by Himself and Presented by Catherine Macdonald Maclean*, 1949.

Critical Studies   W. P. Albrecht, *Hazlitt and the Creative Imagination*, 1965. David Cecil, "Hazlitt's Occasional Essays," *The Fine Art of Reading*, 1957. Herschel Baker, *William Hazlitt*, 1962, the most thorough account of Hazlitt's ideas. K. Coburn, "Hazlitt on the Disinterested Imagination," *Some British Romantics*, ed. J. V. Logan and others, 1966. H. W. Garrod, "The Place of Hazlitt in English Criticism," *The Profession of Poetry*, 1929. J. B. Priestley, *Hazlitt*, 1960. Elizabeth Schneider, *The Aesthetics of William Hazlitt*, 1933, 1952. H. M. Sikes, "The Infernal Hazlitt," *Essays Presented to Stanley Pargellis*, ed. H. Bluhm, 1965. René Wellek, *History of Modern Criticism, 1750–1950*, Vol. II, 1955. Stewart C. Wilcox, *Hazlitt in the Workshop*, 1943.

Biography   P. P. Howe, *Life of William Hazlitt*, 1922 (new ed. 1947). Although spoken of as the standard biography, this is both less detailed and less perceptive than Catherine Macdonald Maclean's *Born Under Saturn*, 1944, which is the best biography.

CHARLES LAMB

Editions   *Works of Charles and Mary Lamb*, ed. E. V. Lucas, 1903–05; *Letters*, 1935. *The Letters of Charles Manning to Charles Lamb*, ed. G. A. Anderson, 1925.

Critical Studies   G. L. Barnett, "The Evolution of Elia," Princeton dissertation, 1942. *Lamb's Criticism*, ed. E. M. W. Tillyard, 1923; Tillyard's introductory essay, "Lamb as a Literary Critic," is a useful study. Walter Pater, *Appreciations*, 1889. Mario Praz, *The Hero in Eclipse in Victorian Literature*, 1956. S. M. Rich, *The Elian Miscellany*, 1931. Denys Thompson, "Our Debt to Lamb," *Determinations*, ed. F. R. Leavis, 1934. Geoffrey Tillotson, "The Historical Importance of Certain Essays of Elia," *Some British Romantics*, ed. J. V. Logan and others, 1966. René Wellek, *History of Modern Criticism, 1750–1950*, Vol. II, 1955.

Biography   E. V. Lucas, *Life of Charles Lamb*, 1921; the best biography. Edmund Blunden, *Charles Lamb: His Life Recorded by His Contemporaries*, 1934. W. C. Hazlitt, *The Lambs: Their Lives, Their Friends, and Their Correspondence*, 1897; *Lamb and Hazlitt*, 1900.

VICTORIAN PROSE AND POETRY

The Period in General

Political and Social Backgrounds Asa Briggs, *The Making of Modern England: The Age of Improvement, 1783–1867*, 1959; *Victorian Cities*, 1965; and *Victorian People*, 1954 (rev. 1965). Friedrich Engels, *The Condition of the Working Class in England*, 1844. The W. O. Henderson and W. H. Chaloner translation (1958) is the best and most complete. Despite Engels's errors of detail, which the translators are at pains to remark, this work is still of great authority and importance. Norman Gash, *Politics in the Age of Peel*, 1953. Elie Halévy, *History of the English People in the Nineteenth Century*, Vols. III–IV, 1949–52. This classic work by an eminent French scholar has had a decisive influence on all later historians of 19th-century England. E. P. Thompson's *The Making of the English Working Class*, 1963, is the authoritative account of that subject. R. K. Webb's *Modern England: From the Eighteenth Century to the Present*, 1968, is an excellent summary account. Ernest L. Woodward, *The Age of Reform, 1815–1870*, 1939. G. M. Young's *Victorian England: Portrait of an Age*, 1936, is a classic work but often difficult by reason of its brilliant allusiveness. Young also edited two useful collections of essays: *Victorian Essays*, 1962, and *Early Victorian England, 1830–1865*, 1934.

Cultural and Literary History Crane Brinton, *English Political Thought in the Nineteenth Century*, 1933. Jerome H. Buckley's *The Victorian Temper*, 1951, is an excellent summary introduction to the culture of the period. W. L. Burn, *The Age of Equipoise*, 1964. Owen Chadwick, *The Victorian Church*, Vol. I, 1966. G. K. Chesterton's *The Victorian Age in Literature*, 1913, is a classic work, brilliant and willful in its judgments. A useful survey is S. C. Chew's *The Nineteenth Century and After* (Vol. IV of *A Literary History of England*, ed. A. C. Baugh), 1948. John W. Dodds, *The Age of Paradox: A Biography of England, 1841–1851*, 1952, provides an engaging summary account. L. E. Elliott-Binns, *Religion in the Victorian Era*, 1936. Oliver Elton, *A Survey of English Literature*, Vol. II, 1928, is basic. An excellent summary introduction to Victorian thought and culture is Walter Houghton's *The Victorian Frame of Mind*, 1957. J. Hillis Miller, *The Disappearance of God: Five Nineteenth-Century Writers*, 1963. Raymond Williams, *Culture and Society, 1780–1950*, 1958. Basil Willey's *Nineteenth Century Studies*, 1949, and *More Nineteenth Century Studies*, 1956, bring together notable essays on the influential writers of the period.

Bibliography "Victorian Bibliography for 1970," ed. R. E. Freeman, in *Victorian Studies*, XIV, 4 (June 1971). E. C. Batho and B. Dobrée, *The Victorians and After*, 1938.

Prose

MATTHEW ARNOLD

Editions *Complete Prose Works*, ed. R. H. Super, seven vols. to date, 1960–70, is the authoritative edition. *The Prose Works*, 1903 (incomplete). *The Portable Matthew Arnold*, ed. Lionel Trilling, 1949, is a selection of the poetry and the prose. *Letters of Matthew Arnold, 1848–1888*, ed. G. W. E. Russell, 1895. *Letters of*

Matthew Arnold to Arthur Hugh Clough, ed. H. F. Lowry, 1932, is an excellent edition of the young Arnold's vivacious and revealing letters to his closest friend. *The Note-books of Matthew Arnold,* ed. H. F. Lowry, Karl Young, and W. H. Dunn, 1952.

Critical Studies   Edward Alexander, *Arnold and John Stuart Mill,* 1965. Warren D. Anderson, *Matthew Arnold and the Classical Tradition,* 1965. R. Bromwich, *Arnold and Celtic Literature: A Retrospect 1865-1965,* 1965. Edward K. Brown, *Matthew Arnold: A Study in Conflict,* 1948. Dwight Culler, *Imaginative Reason,* 1966. T. S. Eliot, "Arnold and Pater," *Selected Essays,* 1932, a famous essay, and his "Matthew Arnold," *The Use of Poetry and the Use of Criticism,* 1932. Leon Gottfried, *Matthew Arnold and the Romantics,* 1963. W. Stacey Johnson, *The Voices of Matthew Arnold,* 1961. F. R. Leavis, "Arnold as Critic," *The Importance of Scrutiny,* ed. Eric Bentley, 1948, an essay by one of the most notable modern critics defining Arnold's continuing importance. P. J. McCarthy's *Arnold and the Three Classes,* 1964, is a cogent discussion of Arnold's social and political thought. William Robbins, *The Ethical Idealism of Matthew Arnold,* 1959. G. Robert Stange, *Matthew Arnold: The Poet as Humanist,* 1967. C. D. Wright, *Arnold's Response to German Culture,* 1965.

Biography   Arnold expressed the wish that no biography of him be written, and as as yet none has been. The most recent approach is Lionel Trilling, *Matthew Arnold* (1939, 1949, 1955), of which its author observes that "it may be thought of as a biography of Arnold's mind."

SAMUEL BUTLER

Editions   *The Shrewsbury Edition,* ed. Henry Festing Jones and A. T. Bartholomew, 1923-26. *The Note-books . . . Selections* arr. and ed. H. F. Jones, 1915. *Further Extracts from the Note-Books,* ed. A. T. Bartholomew, 1934. *Samuel Butler's Note Books,* ed. Geoffrey Keynes and Brian Hill, 1951. *Butleriana,* ed. A. T. Bartholomew, 1932. *The Family Letters of Samuel Butler,* ed. Arnold Silver, 1962. *The Correspondence of Samuel Butler and His Sister May,* ed. Daniel F. Howard, 1962.

Critical Studies   Walter Allen, *The English Novel, A Short Critical History,* 1954. Clyde T. Bissell, "A Study in *The Way of All Flesh,*" *Nineteenth-Century Studies,* ed. Herbert J. Davis, 1940. G. D. H. Cole, *Samuel Butler and "The Way of All Flesh,*" 1947. P. N. Furbank, *Samuel Butler, 1835-1902,* 1948. Arnold Kettle, *An Introduction to the English Novel,* 1953. Basil Willey's *Darwin and Butler—Two Versions of Evolution,* 1960, is a useful study of Butler's views on evolution. Edmund Wilson, *The Triple Thinkers: Ten Essays in Literature,* 1945. M. D. Zabel, "Butler, the Victorian Insolvency," *Craft and Character,* 1957.

Biography
Philip Henderson's *Samuel Butler, the Incarnate Bachelor,* 1953, is an adequate account of Butler's life, although it takes but little notice of his ideas. Lee E. Holt's *Samuel Butler,* 1964, is an excellent biography and quite the best introduction to Butler's ideas.

Bibliography   Stanley B. Harkness, *The Career of Samuel Butler, 1835-1902: A Bibliography,* 1956, is the definitive bibliography.

THOMAS CARLYLE

Editions *The Works of Thomas Carlyle,* Centenary Edition, in 34 volumes, ed. H. D. Traill, 1896–1901. Carlyle was an indefatigable correspondent; several volumes of his letters have been published, among the most important being Charles Eliot Norton's edition of *Correspondence of Carlyle and Emerson,* two vols., 1883; of *Correspondence between Goethe and Carlyle,* two vols., 1886; *Letters of Thomas Carlyle: 1826–1836,* two vols., 1888; and the following collections edited by Alexander Carlyle: *New Letters of Thomas Carlyle,* two vols., 1904; *Love Letters of Thomas Carlyle and Jane Welsh Carlyle,* two vols., 1909; *Letters of Thomas Carlyle to John Stuart Mill, John Sterling, and Robert Browning,* 1923; *Letters of Thomas Carlyle to His Brother Alexander,* 1968. There is also a *Selected Works, Reminiscences and Letters,* ed. Julian Symons, 1957. The Duke-Edinburgh edition of the letters of Thomas and Jane Welsh Carlyle, under the general editorship of C. R. Sanders, will be definitive upon completion. The first four volumes were published in 1970.

Critical Studies Eric Bentley, *A Century of Hero-Worship,* 1944. Louis Cazamian, *Carlyle,* trans. E. K. Brown, 1932. C. F. Harrold, *Carlyle and German Thought, 1819–1834,* 1934. John Holloway, *The Victorian Sage,* 1953. Albert J. La Valley, *Carlyle and the Idea of the Modern,* 1968. Emery Neff, *Carlyle and Mill: Mystic and Utilitarian,* 1924. G. B. Tennyson, *Sartor Called Resartus,* 1965.

Biography There is as yet no satisfactory modern biography of Carlyle, although J. H. Froude's *Thomas Carlyle: A History of the First Forty Years of His Life,* two vols., 1882, and *Thomas Carlyle: A History of His Life in London,* two vols., 1884, are interesting and valuable. Even more compendious is D. A. Wilson's *Life of Thomas Carlyle,* six vols., 1923–34. Emery Neff's *Carlyle,* 1934, based on these works, is a useful short account emphasizing Carlyle's intellectual rather than his emotional life.

THOMAS HENRY HUXLEY

Editions *Collected Essays,* nine vols., 1893–94. *The Scientific Memoirs of Thomas Henry Huxley,* ed. Michael Foster and E. Roy Lankester, four vols., 1898–1902; suppl. vol., 1903. *Religion Without Revelation,* ed. Julian Huxley (his grandson), 1957. Huxley's *Diary of the Voyage of HMS Rattlesnake,* ed. Julian Huxley, 1935.

Critical Studies C. E. Ayres, *Huxley,* 1932. Aldous Huxley, *Huxley as a Man of Letters,* 1932. H. Peterson, *Huxley: A Prophet of Science,* 1932. J. S. Huxley and D. Cleverdon, *Julian Huxley on T. H. Huxley: A New Judgment,* 1945. Walter Houghton, "The Rhetoric of Huxley," *University of Toronto Quarterly,* XVIII (1949). William Irvine, "Carlyle and T. H. Huxley," *Booker Memorial Studies,* ed. H. Shine, 1950. William Irvine, *Apes, Angels, and the Victorians: The Story of Darwin, Huxley, and Evolution,* 1955; and *Huxley,* 1960. C. Bibby, *Huxley: Scientist, Humanist, and Educator,* 1959. A. O. J. Cockshut, "Huxley: The Scientific Sage," *Unbelievers: English Agnostic Thought, 1840–90,* 1964. Philip Appleman, W. A. Madden, and M. Wolff, eds., *1859: Entering an Age of Crisis,* 1959.

Biography The biography by Huxley's son Leonard Huxley, *The Life and Letters of Thomas Henry Huxley,* two vols., 1900, is still standard.

JOHN STUART MILL

Editions   *Collected Works of John Stuart Mill*, gen. ed., F. E. L. Priestley; assoc. ed., J. M. Robson, 1963, six vols. to date; when completed this will be the definitive edition. *The Earlier Letters of John Stuart Mill, 1812–1848*, ed. Francis E. Mineka (Vols. XII and XIII of the *Collected Works*), 1963. *The Early Draft of John Stuart Mill's Autobiography*, ed. Jack Stillinger, 1961. *John Stuart Mill: Literary Essays*, ed. Edward Alexander, 1967. *Mill's Essays on Literature and Society*, 1965, and *Mill: A Collection of Critical Essays*, 1968, both ed. Jerome Schneewind. *Essays on Politics and Culture*, ed. Gertrude Himmelfarb, 1962. *The Spirit of the Age*, ed. Frederick A. von Hayek, 1942, is a series of articles published by Mill in the *Examiner* in 1831.

Critical Studies   Edward Alexander, *Matthew Arnold and John Stuart Mill*, 1965. R. P. Anschutz, *The Philosophy of John Stuart Mill*, 1953. Karl Britton, *John Stuart Mill*, 1953. Joseph Hamburger, *Intellectuals in Politics: John Stuart Mill and the Philosophical Radicals*, 1965. Emery Neff, *Carlyle and Mill: Mystic and Utilitarian*, 1926. Dorothea Krook, *Three Traditions of Moral Thought*, 1959. F. R. Leavis, Introduction to *Mill on Bentham and Coleridge*, 1950. John M. Robson, *The Improvement of Mankind: The Social and Political Thought of John Stuart Mill*, 1968. Basil Willey, *Nineteenth Century Studies*, 1949. Raymond Williams, *Culture and Society, 1780–1950*, 1958.

Biography   Michael St. John Packe, *The Life of John Stuart Mill* (1954), is the best biography.

WILLIAM MORRIS

Editions   *Collected Works*, edited in 24 volumes by his daughter May Morris, 1910–15 (repr. 1966); two suppl. vols., *William Morris, Artist, Writer, Socialist*, published in 1936 (repr. 1966). *The Letters of William Morris*, ed. Philip Henderson, 1950. *William Morris, Selected Writings and Designs*, ed. Asa Briggs, 1962.

Critical Studies   E. P. Thompson, *William Morris, Romantic to Revolutionary*, 1955. George Bernard Shaw, *William Morris As I Knew Him*, 1936. Graham Hough, *The Last Romantics*, 1949. W. B. Yeats, "Happiest of the Poets," in *Essays and Introductions*, 1961.

Biography   Philip Henderson's *William Morris, His Life, Work, and Friends*, 1967, is the best biography. R. P. Arnot, *Morris: The Man and the Myth*, 1964. J. W. Mackail, *The Life of William Morris*, 1899 (repr. 1950), still excellent, although its treatment of Morris's personal life is limited by piety and convention.

JOHN HENRY CARDINAL NEWMAN

Editions   [*Works*] 41 vols., 1874–1921: "Uniform Edition of Dr. Newman's Works." *Letters and Diaries of John Henry Newman*, ed. C. Stephen Dessain, 1961. *Letters and Correspondence of John Henry Newman During His Life in the English Church*, ed. Anne Mozley, 1891. *John Henry Newman: Autobiographical Writings*, ed. Henry Tristram, 1957.

Critical Studies   R. W. Church, *The Oxford Movement 1833–1845*, 1891. A. Dwight Culler, *The Imperial Intellect: A Study of Cardinal Newman's Educational Ideal*, 1955. C. F. Harrold, *John Henry Newman: An Expository and Critical Study of His Mind, Thought, and Art*. 1945. John Holloway, *The Victorian Sage*, 1953. Walter Houghton, *The Art of Newman's Apologia*, 1945. Meriol Trevor, *Newman;* Vol. I: *The Pillar of Cloud*, 1962; Vol. II: *Light in Winter*, 1963. Thomas Vargish, *Newman: The Contemplation of Mind*, 1970. J. H. Walgrave, *Newman the Theologian*, 1960.

Biography   The best introduction to Newman's life and thought is the brief and lucid work of C. Stephen Dessain, *John Henry Newman*, 1966. Louis Bouyer, *Newman: His Life and Spirituality*, 1958. Wilfrid Ward, *Life of John Henry Cardinal Newman*, two vols., 1912.

WALTER PATER

Editions   *Works*, ten vols., 1910 (reissued 1971). *Letters of Walter Pater*, ed. Lawrence Evans, 1970. *Selected Writings*, ed. H. Bloom, 1973.

Critical Studies   P. Appleman, "Darwin, Pater and a Crisis in Classicism," *1859: Entering a Year of Crisis*, ed. P. Appleman and others, 1959. C. M. Bowra, "Walter Pater," *Inspiration and Poetry*, 1957. David Cecil, *Pater: The Scholar-Artist*, 1955. B. Charlesworth, *Dark Passages: The Decadent Consciousness in Victorian Literature*, 1965. T. S. Eliot, "Arnold and Pater," *Selected Essays*, 1932. Graham Hough, *The Last Romantics*, 1949. R. V. Johnson, *Pater as Critic: His Critical Practices Considered in Relation to His Theories of Life and Art*, 1962. U. C. Knoepflmacher, *Religious Humanism and the Victorian Novel*, 1965. Mario Praz, *The Romantic Agony*, 1933. Ruth Z. Temple, "The Ivory Tower as Lighthouse," *Edwardians and Late Victorians*, ed. Richard Ellmann, 1960. Geoffrey Tillotson, "Arnold and Pater," *Criticism of the Nineteenth Century*, 1951. René Wellek, "Pater's Literary Theory and Criticism," in *History of Modern Criticism, 1750–1950*, Vol. III, 1958. The most comprehensive study is the monograph *Walter Pater*, by Ian Fletcher, rev. ed., 1972.

Biography   The only extensive biography is that by Thomas Wright, *The Life of Walter Pater*, two vols., 1907.

JOHN RUSKIN

Editions   *The Works of John Ruskin*, ed. E. T. Cook and Alexander Wedderburn, 1903–12. *Diaries of John Ruskin*, ed. Joan Evans and J. H. Whitehouse, 1956. *Brantwood Diary* (1878), ed. Helen Wilhuen, 1971.

Critical Studies   George Landow, *Aesthetic and Cultural Theories of Ruskin*, 1971. Frederick W. Roe, *Social Philosophy of Carlyle and Ruskin*, 1921. John Rosenberg's *The Darkening Glass: A Portrait of John Ruskin's Genius*, 1961, is the fullest account of Ruskin's intellectual life. George Bernard Shaw, *Ruskin's Politics*, 1921. R. H. Wilenski, *John Ruskin*, 1933.

Biography   Joan Evans, *John Ruskin*, 1952. John Holloway, *The Victorian Sage*, 1953. Graham Hough, *The Last Romantics*, 1949.

OSCAR WILDE

Editions *Complete Works*, ed. G. F. Maine, first collected ed., 1948 (rev. ed., P. Drake, 1966). *The Artist as Critic: Critical Writings of Oscar Wilde*, ed. Richard Ellmann, 1969, *The Letters of Oscar Wilde*, ed. Rupert Hart-Davis, 1962, contains the full text of the famous letter from prison, previously published in various curtailed versions under the title *De Profundis*.

Critical Studies *Oscar Wilde: The Critical Heritage*, ed. Karl Beckson, 1970, a collection of early critical responses to Wilde. St. John Ervine, *Oscar Wilde: A Present Time Appraisal*, 1951. André Gide, *Oscar Wilde: A Study*, 1905. Holbrook Jackson, *The Eighteen-Nineties*, 1913 (revised 1922). G. Wilson Knight, *Christian Renaissance*, 1962. Edouard Roditi, *Oscar Wilde*, 1947. Arthur Symons, *A Study of Oscar Wilde*, 1930. Frances Winwar, *Oscar Wilde and the Yellow Nineties*, 1940.

Biography There is to date no satisfactory biography of Wilde and presumably there will be none until Richard Ellmann completes the one he is engaged on. The following works are useful in one way or another: Rupert Croft-Cooke, *The Unrecorded Life of Oscar Wilde,* 1972. André Gide, *Oscar Wilde: In Memoriam*, 1949. Frank Harris's *The Life and Confessions of Oscar Wilde*, 1918 (repr. 1960), is notoriously unreliable but of some interest. Vyvyan Holland's *Oscar Wilde, a Pictorial Biography*, 1960, is an attractive and engaging book; the pictorial method is most appropriate to Wilde. H. Montgomery Hyde has edited *The Trials of Oscar Wilde*, 1950, 1960, and also written *Oscar Wilde in Prison*, 1956, and *The Three Trials of Oscar Wilde*, 1956. Hesketh Pearson's *Oscar Wilde, His Life and Wit*, 1946, is the fullest account. Robert H. Sherard, *Bernard Shaw, Frank Harris, and Oscar Wilde*, 1937.

Poetry

In addition to the general references to Victorian Literature cited in the Prose section above, the reader may consult the following works having more specifically to do with Victorian Poetry.

Bibliography F. E. Faverty, ed., *The Victorian Poets: A Guide to Research*, 1968.

Critical Studies J. W. Beach, *The Concept of Nature in Nineteenth-Century English Poetry*, 1936. G. H. Ford, *Keats and the Victorians*, 1944. E. D. H. Johnson, *The Alien Vision of Victorian Poetry*, 1952. Robert Langbaum, *The Poetry of Experience*, 1957, and *The Modern Spirit*, 1970. F. L. Lucas, *Ten Victorian Poets*, 1940. **Collections of Essays** *The Major Victorian Poets: Reconsiderations*, ed. I. Armstrong, 1969. *Victorian Literature*, ed. R. O. Preyer, 1966. *The Victorian Age*, ed. R. Langbaum, 1967. *Victorian Literature*, ed. Austin Wright, 1961.

ALFRED, LORD TENNYSON

Editions *The Poems of Tennyson*, ed. C. Ricks, 1969.

Critical Studies *Critical Essays*, ed. J. Killham, 1960. J. H. Buckley, *Tennyson*, 1961. *Tennyson*, ed. A. D. Culler, 1973. On *In Memoriam*: the *Commentary* by A. C. Bradley, 1901.

Biography   Hallam Tennyson, *Alfred Lord Tennyson: A Memoir,* 1897. Sir Charles Tennyson, *Alfred Tennyson,* 1949. C. Ricks, *Tennyson,* 1972.

ROBERT BROWNING

Editions   A modern edition, by R. A. King and others, is in progress; to date the *Complete Poetical Works,* ed. Augustine Birrell, 1915, remains the best edition. The *Letters* of Browning and Elizabeth Barrett, ed. E. Kintner, two vols., 1969. *Essay on Shelley,* ed. H. F. B. Brett-Smith, 1921.

Critical Studies   The best critical work by a single hand remains G. K. Chesterton, *Robert Browning,* 1903. **Collections of Essays**   *The Browning Critics,* ed. B. Litzinger and K. L. Knickerbocker, 1967. *Robert Browning,* ed. Philip Drew, 1966. *Browning,* ed. Harold Bloom, 1973. W. C. DeVane, *A Browning Handbook,* 1955, is crucial.

Biography   W. Hall Griffin and H. C. Minchin, *Life,* 1938. Betty Miller, *Portrait,* 1952.

MATTHEW ARNOLD

Editions   *Poetical Works,* ed. C. B. Tinker and H. F. Lowry, 1950. *Poems of Arnold,* ed. K. Allott, 1965. See also Arnold references in Victorian Prose bibliography above.

THE PRE-RAPHAELITES

Bibliography   W. E. Fredeman, *Pre-Raphaelitism; A Bibliocritical Study,* 1965.

Critical Studies   (Benjamin) Ifor Evans, *English Poetry in the Later Nineteenth Century,* 2nd ed. rev., 1966. *Pre-Raphaelite Painters,* ed. Robin Ironside, 1948. *The Pre-Raphaelites and Their Circle,* ed. C. Y. Lang, 1968.

Dante Gabriel Rossetti   *Works,* ed. W. M. Rossetti, 1911. Oswald Doughty, *A Victorian Romantic,* 1960.

George Meredith   *Poetical Works,* ed. G. M. Trevelyan, 1928. Norman Kelvin, *A Troubled Eden,* 1961.

Christina Rossetti   *Poetical Works,* ed. W. M. Rossetti, 1904. L. M. Packer, *Christina Rossetti,* 1963.

William Morris   See Morris references in Victorian Prose bibliography above, and the following: Paul Thompson, *The Work of William Morris,* 1967.

Algernon Charles Swinburne   *Collected Poetical Works,* two vols., 1924. *The Swinburne Letters,* ed. C. Y. Lang, six vols., 1959–62. Georges Lafourcade, *Swinburne: A Literary Biography,* 1932. J. J. McGann, *Swinburne,* 1972.

Coventry Patmore   *Poems,* ed. F. Page, 1949. D. Patmore, *Life and Times of Coventry Patmore,* 1950.

GERARD MANLEY HOPKINS

Poems, ed. W. H. Gardner and N. H. MacKenzie, 1970. *Hopkins,* ed. G. Hartman, 1966. W. H. Gardner, *Hopkins,* two vols., 1949. J. Pick, *Hopkins,* 1966.

OTHER VICTORIAN POETS

Elizabeth Barrett Browning *Poetical Works,* 1951. G. B. Taplin, *Life,* 1957.

Edward Lear *Complete Nonsense,* ed. H. Jackson, 1947. Angus Davidson, *Edward Lear,* 1938.

Emily Brontë *Complete Poems,* ed. C. W. Hatfield, 1941. *Gondal's Queen,* arranged by F. E. Ratchford, 1955.

Arthur Hugh Clough *Poems,* ed. A. L. Norrington, 1968. Walter Houghton, *The Poetry of Clough,* 1963.

Lewis Carroll *Complete Works,* 1949. Derek Hudson, *Lewis Carroll,* 1954.

James Thomson *Poetical Works.* two vols., ed. Bertram Dobell, 1895. Arthur Symons, *Studies in Two Literatures,* 1924.

THE 'NINETIES

General Backgrounds O. Burdett, *The Beardsley Period,* 1925. R. Le Gallienne, *The Romantic '90s,* 1926. H. Jackson, *The Eighteen Nineties,* 1913. W. B. Yeats, *Auto-biographies,* 1926. Relevant also are some of the essays in *Romantic Mythologies,* ed. Ian Fletcher, 1967.

Editions The best anthology of 'Nineties verse is still Donald Davidson, ed., *British Poetry of the Eighteen-nineties,* 1937.

William Schwenk Gilbert, *Bab Ballads,* 1924. *The Savoy Operas,* 1926. H. Pearson, *Gilbert and Sullivan,* 1935.

Oscar Wilde See Wilde references in Victorian Prose bibliography above. The defini-tive study, by Richard Ellmann, is in progress. Criticism is gathered in *Oscar Wilde: Collection of Critical Essays,* ed. R. Ellmann, 1969.

John Davidson *Poems and Ballads,* ed. R. D. MacLeod, 1959.

Ernest Dowson *Poetical Works,* ed. D. Flower, 1967.

Lionel Johnson *Complete Poems,* ed. Ian Fletcher, 1953.

MODERN BRITISH LITERATURE
The Period in General

Historical Backgrounds The liveliest survey of the period is A. J. P. Taylor's *English History 1914–1945,* 1965 (final volume of the Oxford History of England). See also John A. Lester, Jr., *Journey Through Despair* (1968); Samuel Hynes, *The Edwardian Turn of Mind,* 1969; Julian Symons, *The Thirties,* 1960; Robert Graves and Alan Hodge, *The Long Week-End,* 1940; and the autobiographies of Stephen Spender (*World Within a World,* 1951) and John Lehmann (*In My Own Time,* 1969). Taylor's *Illustrated History of the First World War,* 1964, and Angus Calder's *The People's War,* 1969, give vivid impressions of the two great wars of the period. A. Hamilton,

The Appeal of Fascism, 1971, studies the record of intellectuals in relation to various forms of Fascism. Useful short histories are L. C. B. Seaman's *Post-Victorian Britain, 1902–51*, 1966, and Arthur Marwick's *Britain in an Age of Total War*, 1968.

Literary Backgrounds Among the many literary surveys of and introductions to modernism are: R. Ellmann and C. Feidelson, Jr., *The Modern Tradition*, 1965, which collects the documents; Stephen Spender, *The Struggle of the Modern*, 1963; Irving Howe, *The Idea of the Modern*, 1968; F. Kermode, *Romantic Image*, 1957, and *Continuities*, 1968; Monroe K. Spears, *Dionysus and the City*, 1971. M. L. Rosenthal's *The New Modern Poetry* (1967), William Y. Tindall's *Forces in Modern British Literature*, 1947, C. K. Stead's *The New Poetic* (1964), A. Alvarez's *Stewards of Excellence*, 1958, Graham Hough's *Image and Experience*, 1960 (seventh and last volume of The Pelican Guide to English Literature), *The Modern Age*, ed. Boris Ford, and J. I. M. Stewart's *Eight Modern Writers*, 1963 (Vol. XII of the Oxford History of English Literature), are introductions and discussions with various perspectives. F. R. Leavis's *New Bearings in English Poetry*, 1932 (repr. 1950), is an important document in itself. See also the essay "On the Modern Element in Modern Literature," in Lionel Trilling's *Beyond Culture*, 1965.

THOMAS HARDY

Editions The collected "Mellstock" (English) edition in 37 volumes includes prose and verse; standard in America is the "Anniversary Edition" of *The Writings of Thomas Hardy*, 1920. The standard edition of the poetry is the *Collected Poems* of 1926 (repr. 1961) exclusive of a posthumous *Winter Words in Various Moods and Metres*, 1928. There are also *Letters*, ed. C. J. Weber, 1954; *Notebooks*, ed. Evelyn Hardy, 1955; and *A Choice of Thomas Hardy's Poems* by Geoffrey Grigson, 1969.

Critical Studies The indispensable consideration of the poems, containing a great wealth of biographical and bibliographical information, is by J. O. Bailey, *The Poetry of Thomas Hardy: A Handbook and Commentary*, 1970; *Thomas Hardy and the Cosmic Mind*, 1956, by the same author, offers a reading of *The Dynasts*, as does Walter F. Wright, in *The Shaping of The Dynasts*, 1967. Samuel Hynes's *The Pattern of Hardy's Poetry*, 1961, is a brief general study. Chapters on the poetry in Irving Howe's critical study entitled *Thomas Hardy*, 1967, and in *Thomas Hardy: Distance and Desire* by J. Hillis Miller, 1970, are both good, and the Hardy Centennial Number of *The Southern Review*, VI (1940), contains essays by a number of American critics. Donald Davie's *Thomas Hardy and British Poetry*, 1972, is a fine study of Hardy's influence on poetry down to the present moment. Richard L. Purdy's *Thomas Hardy: A Bibliographical Study*, 1954, is authoritative.

GEORGE BERNARD SHAW

Editions Publication of the 30-volume Ayot St. Lawrence edition was initiated in 1930; in addition, there are editions of *Nine Plays*, 1931; *Seven Plays*, 1951; a four-volume *Selected Plays*, 1948–57; a *Complete Plays, with Prefaces*, 1962; and a *Selected Prose*, ed. Diarmuid Russell, 1952. Eric Bentley has edited a selection of *Shaw* *on Music* (1955); and Dan H. Laurence, a *Collected Letters of Bernard Shaw 1874–97*, 1965, and *Collected Letters 1898–1910*, 1972.

Critical Studies   Eric Bentley's *Bernard Shaw, A Reconsideration*, rev. ed., 1955, is very good, as is Richard M. Ohmann, *The Style and the Man*, 1962. Donald P. Costello's *Serpent's Eye* (1965) deals with the filming of Shaw's plays, and Bernard F. Dukore has edited the screenplay of *St. Joan* (1968). Harold Fromm, *Bernard Shaw and the Theatre of the Nineties*, 1967, and Frederick Mayne, *Wit and Satire of George Bernard Shaw*, 1967, represent different critical approaches.

Biography   Hesketh Pearson's *George Bernard Shaw: His Life and Personality*, 1963, may be supplemented by Stanley Weintraub's *Private Shaw and Public Shaw*, 1962, and *Journey to Heartbreak*, 1971.

JOSEPH CONRAD

Editions   The New Collected Edition in 22 volumes, 1946, is standard in England; in America the individual works have been published in careful critical editions. There are also several volumes of correspondence, among them *Letters from Joseph Conrad, 1895–1924*, ed. with introduction and notes by E. Garnett, 1928 (1962). *Last Essays*, 1926, has been reprinted with an introduction by R. Curle, 1970.

Critical Studies   Of many studies the best is Albert J. Guérard's *Conrad the Novelist*, 1958. See also Frederick Karl's *Reader's Guide to Conrad*, 1960, and F. R. Leavis's essays in *The Great Tradition*, 1948. Conrad's voracious use of his own experience in his stories is illuminated by Norman Sherry in *Conrad's Eastern World*, 1966, and *Conrad's Western World*, 1971.

Biography   The standard is Jocelyn Baines's *Joseph Conrad: A Critical Biography*, 1960 (repr. 1967). The autobiographical works of Ford Madox Ford, *Memories and Impressions*, 1911, and Bertrand Russell, *Autobiography*, 1968, 1969, are important sources of information.

WILLIAM BUTLER YEATS

Editions   The unusually complex bibliography is simplified by the posthumous publication of most of Yeats's output in large groupings: for the poetry, *Collected Poems*, 1950; and *Variorum Edition of the Poems of W. B. Yeats*, ed. P. Allt, 1957; for the plays, *Collected Plays*, 1952, and *Variorum Edition of the Plays of W. B. Yeats*, ed. R. K. Alspach, 1966; for the correspondence, *The Letters of W. B. Yeats*, ed. Allan Wade, 1954. For the prose, there are the subject's collections entitled *Autobiographies*, 1938; *Mythologies*, 1959; *Essays and Introductions*, 1961; and *Explorations*, 1962.

Critical Studies   The pioneer analytical introduction is P. Ure's *Towards a Mythology: Studies in the Poetry of W. B. Yeats*, 1946 (repr. 1947). See also his *W. B. Yeats*, 1968, *Yeats the Playwright*, 1963. Of dozens of critical or critico-biographical writings, see L. MacNeice's *Poetry of W. B. Yeats*, 1941; A. N. Jeffare's *W. B. Yeats: Man and Poet*, 1949, and his valuable *Commentary on the Collected Poems*, 1968; T. R. Henn's *The Lonely Tower*, 1950; R. Ellmann's *Yeats: The Man and the Masks*, 1948 (repr. 1962), and *The Identity of Yeats*, 1954; T. R. Parkinson's *W. B. Yeats, Self-Critic*,

1951, and *W. B. Yeats: The Later Poetry*, 1964, both investigating Yeats's revisions, as do Curtis Bradford's *Yeats at Work*, 1965, and Jon Stallworthy's *Between the Lines*, 1963, and *Vision and Revision in Yeats's Poetry*, 1969. Further works are J. Unterecker's *Reader's Guide to William Butler Yeats*, 1959; Virginia Moore's *The Unicorn*, 1954; Giorgio Melchiori's *The Whole Mystery of Art*, 1960; *Images of a Poet*, ed. D. J. Gordon, 1961; T. Whitaker's *Swan and Shadow*, 1964; and Harold Bloom's *William Butler Yeats*, 1970. There is a *Bibliography of the Writings*, by Allan Wade, 1951 (2nd ed. rev., 1958).

Biography   The standard life, *W. B. Yeats*, by J. M. Hone, 1942 (2nd ed., 1962), will be superseded by that of D. Donoghue when it is completed.

JAMES JOYCE

Editions   The early *Stephen Hero* was first published (ed. Theodore Spencer) in 1944, and republished with new material (ed. John J. Slocum and Herbert Cahoon) in 1955. The MS. fragments of *Epiphanies* were edited by O. A. Silverman, 1956. The major works appeared as follows: *Dubliners*, 1914; *A Portrait of the Artist as a Young Man*, 1914; *Ulysses*, 1922; and *Finnegans Wake*, 1939. A *Collected Poems* was published in 1937, and all Joyce's verse is reproduced, together with *Dubliners*, *A Portrait*, and the play *Exiles*, in Harry Levin's comprehensive *Portable James Joyce* of 1947. *The Critical Writings of James Joyce*, 1959, was edited by Ellsworth Mason and Richard Ellmann; the *Letters*, Vol. I (ed. Stuart Gilbert) appeared in 1957, Vols. II and III (ed. Richard Ellmann), in 1966.

Critical Studies   There are three useful short introductory studies: Harry Levin's *James Joyce: A Critical Introduction* (rev. ed., 1960), still the best; and those of S. L. Goldberg, 1962, and John Gross, 1970, both entitled *James Joyce* and both excellent also. Marvin Magalaner and Richard M. Kain, *Joyce: The Man, the Work, the Reputation*, 1956, is standard, and A. Walton Litz, *James Joyce*, 1966, is very fine. Anthologies of criticism are Seon Givens (Manley), ed., *James Joyce: Two Decades of Criticism*, rev. ed., 1963; and the two volumes of Robert Deming, ed., *James Joyce, the Critical Heritage*, 1970. Clive Hart edited a collections of essays on *Dubliners*, 1969. Particularly good longer studies on *Ulysses* and *Finnegans Wake* are: Stuart Gilbert, *James Joyce's Ulysses*, 1952; S. L. Goldberg, *The Classical Temper*, 1961; Robert Martin Adams, *Surface and Symbol*, 1962; Clive Hart, *Structure and Motif in Finnegans Wake*, 1962; A. Walton Litz, *The Art of James Joyce*, 1961; Bernard Benstock, *Joyce-Again's Wake*, 1965. Weldon Thornton compiled a handbook of *Allusions in Ulysses*, 1968, and William York Tindall, *A Reader's Guide to Finnegans Wake*, 1969. Richard Ellmann, in *Ulysses on the Liffey*, 1972, presents some fascinating and amusing new insights.

Biography   The great biography is the *James Joyce* of Richard Ellmann, 1959; Stanislaus Joyce's *My Brother's Keeper: James Joyce's Early Years*, 1958, and Frank Budgen's *James Joyce and the Making of "Ulysses,"* rev. ed., 1960, are both of great value.

D. H. LAWRENCE

Editions   *Collected Poems*, two vols., ed. V. de S. Pinto and F. W. Roberts, 1964; *Complete Plays*, 1966. The novels are accessible in many formats, as is much of the discursive prose: *Phoenix I*, 1936 (repr. 1961), and *Phoenix II*, 1968, contain generous quantities. Selections are available also in *The Portable D. H. Lawrence*, ed. D. Trilling, 1947; and *Selected Literary Criticism*, ed. A. Beale, 1955. The complete edition of the correspondence is *Collected Letters*, ed. H. T. Moore, two vols., 1961. Lawrence's early versions of *Studies in Classical Literature* (in many ways superior to the later) are included in *The Symbolic Meaning*, ed. A. Arnold, 1962.

Critical Studies   A small selection from a vast output: *Son of Woman*, by Lawrence's onetime friend, J. Middleton Murry, 1931; F. R. Leavis, *D. H. Lawrence*, 1930, and *D. H. Lawrence: Novelist*, 1955; Graham Hough, *The Dark Sun*, 1956; George Ford, *Double Measure*, 1965; H. M. Dalewski, *The Forked Flame*, 1965; Keith Sagar, *The Art of D. H. Lawrence*, 1966; Frank Kermode, *D. H. Lawrence*, 1973: a brief introduction. An important article is M. Kinkhead-Weekes's "The Marble and the Statue," in *Imagined Worlds*, ed. M. Mack and Ian Gregor, 1968. R. Draper's *The Critical Heritage of D. H. Lawrence*, 1970, describes the early reception of his work. A. Alvarez, *Stewards of Excellence*, 1958, deals with the poetry, as does an essay in Harold Bloom's *The Ringers in the Tower*, 1971.

Biography   There are several works of personal reminiscence, the most revelatory being that of "E.T." (Jessie Chambers, the "Miriam" of *Sons and Lovers*), *D. H. Lawrence: A Personal Record*, 1935; and Frieda Lawrence's *Not I but the Wind*, 1934. Biographical material is reproduced or résuméd in *D. H. Lawrence: A Composite Biography*, ed. E. Nehls, three vols., 1957–59. The best life is H. T. Moore's *The Intelligent Heart*, 1955 (repr. 1960).

T. S. ELIOT

Editions   All the canonical verse is collected in *The Complete Poems and Plays*, 1952; the original *Waste Land* text, ed. Valerie Eliot, appeared in 1971. Most but by no means all of the more permanent prose is found in *Selected Essays*, 1932; *The Use of Poetry and the Use of Criticism*, 1934; *Notes Toward the Definition of Culture*, 1949; *On Poetry and Poets*, 1957; and *To Criticize the Critic*, 1965.

Critical Studies   A few of the critical works are F. O. Matthiessen, *The Achievement of T. S. Eliot*, 3rd ed., 1958; *T. S. Eliot*, essays ed. B. Rajan, 1947 (repr. 1966); Helen Gardner, *The Art of T. S. Eliot*, 1950; George Williamson, *A Reader's Guide to T. S. Eliot*, 1953; Grover Smith, *T. S. Eliot's Poetry and Plays*, 1956 (rev. ed., 1962); Hugh Kenner, *The Invisible Poet*, 1959; *The Pound Era*, 1972; and ed. *T. S. Eliot* in (Twentieth Century Views), 1962; Kristian Smidt, *Poetry and Belief in the Work of T. S. Eliot*, 2nd rev. ed., 1961; Northrop Frye, *T. S. Eliot*, 1963; Herbert Howarth, *Notes on Some Figures Behind T. S. Eliot*, 1965; Allen Tate, ed., *T. S. Eliot: The Man and His Work*, 1966; B. C. Southam, *A Student's Guide to the Selected Poems of T. S. Eliot*; Graham Martin, ed., *Eliot in Perspective*, 1970.

ROBERT BRIDGES

Editions   *The Poetical Works of Robert Bridges* in six volumes, 1920, must be supplemented by *New Verse*, 1925, as well as by *The Testament of Beauty*, 1929. There is an enlarged edition of *The Shorter Poems*, 1931, and a selection of poetry and prose edited by John Sparrow, 1955.

Critical Studies   Albert J. Guérard, *Robert Bridges: A Study of Traditionalism in Poetry*, 1942; E. J. Thompson, *Robert Bridges, 1844–1930*, 1945, and G. S. Gordon, *Robert Bridges* (Rede Lecture), 1946. Yvor Winters's essay "Traditional Mastery: The Lyrics of Robert Bridges" was published in *Hound and Horn* in 1932. E. C. Wright's *Metaphor, Sound and Meaning in Bridges' The Testament of Beauty* appeared in 1951.

A. E. HOUSMAN

Editions   There are three volumes of verse: *A Shropshire Lad*, 1896; *Last Poems*, 1922; and the posthumous *More Poems*, 1936; plus a little new material in Laurence Housman's *My Brother, A. E. Housman*, 1938 (repr. 1969). *The Collected Poems*, 1939, was revised in 1953. *Selected Prose*, ed. J. Carter, appeared in 1961; the *Letters*, ed. H. Maas, in 1971.

Critico-biographical Studies   Norman Marlow, *A. E. Housman*, 1958; G. L. Watson, *A. E. Housman: A Divided Life*, 1957; B. J. Leggett, *Housman's Land of Lost Content: A Critical Study of a Shropshire Lad*, 1970; and *A. E. Housman: A Collection of Critical Essays*, ed. C. B. Ricks, 1968, in the series Twentieth Century Views.

WALTER DE LA MARE

There is the massive *Complete Poems*, 1970; an excellent *Selected Poems* chosen by R. N. Green-Armytage, 1954; and *A Choice of De la Mare's Verse*, ed. with introduction by W. H. Auden, 1963. Prose works include *Pleasures and Speculations*, 1940; *Private View*, 1953; and the novel *Memoirs of a Midget*, 1921. There are critical studies—all entitled *Walter de la Mare* with appropriate subtitles—by Forrest Reid, 1929; H. C. Duffin, 1949; and Kenneth Hopkins, 1953.

RUDYARD KIPLING

Editions   The definitive collection in England is the Sussex Edition, in 35 vols., 1937–39. For the poetry see T. S. Eliot, ed., *A Choice of Kipling's Verse*, 1941. Randall Jarrell's *Best Short Stories of Rudyard Kipling*, 1961, contains the important briefer fiction.

Critical Studies   There are good essays by Edmund Wilson in *The Wound and the Bow*, 1941; George Orwell in *Critical Essays*, 1946; and Lionel Trilling in *The Liberal Imagination*, 1950. J. M. S. Tompkins, *The Art of Rudyard Kipling*, 1959; C. A. Bodelsen, *Aspects of Kipling's Art*, 1964; and Bonamy Dobrée, *Rudyard Kipling, Realist and Fabulist*, 1967, are the leading books; a collection of essays entitled *Kipling's Mind and Art* is edited by Andrew Rutherford, 1964.

Biography   Charles Carrington, *Life of Rudyard Kipling*, 1955. Richard Faber's *The Vision and the Need* (1966) is useful on Kipling's imperialism, as are, in their way, studies by J. I. M. Stewart, *Rudyard Kipling*, 1966, and T. R. Henn, *Kipling*, 1968. R. L. Green compiled *The Reader's Guide to Kipling's Works*, 1961.

WILFRED OWEN

Poems, with an Introduction by Siegfried Sassoon, appeared in 1920; a later edition carried commentary by Edmund Blunden, 1931. The best edition is the scholarly text entitled *The Collected Poems of Wilfred Owen*, 1964, with introductory notes by C. Day Lewis and a memoir by Edmund Blunden. Owen's *Letters*, ed. Harold Owen and John Bell, 1967, complements the three-volume biography by Harold Owen, *Journey into Obscurity: Wilfred Owen 1893–1918*, 1963–65. D. S. R. Welland's *Wilfred Owen: A Critical Study*, was published in 1960.

EDWARD THOMAS

The *Collected Poems* was published in 1936, with a foreword by Walter de la Mare; from 1949 on, reprintings have contained one additional poem. John Moore's *The Life and Letters of Edward Thomas*, 1939, is a biographical study; it may be supplemented with memoirs by the poet's widow, Helen Thomas, *As It Was*, 1926, and *World Without End*, 1931. There are critical studies by H. Coombes, 1956, and Vernon Scannell, 1963, both entitled *Edward Thomas*.

ISAAC ROSENBERG

Collected Works, ed. Gordon Bottomley and Denys Harding, 1937, is abridged in a *Collected Poems* of 1949. The *Poems* of 1922 has a prefatory memoir by Laurence Binyon, and the *Collected Works*, an essay on Rosenberg by Siegfried Sassoon. John H. Johnston, *English Poetry of the First World War*, 1964, includes valuable background material for the study of Rosenberg, Wilfred Owen, and Edward Thomas.

DAVID JONES

In Parenthesis, published in 1937, was reprinted, with an introductory note by T. S. Eliot, in 1961; *The Anathémata*, his remarkable long poem, was first published in 1952. A collection of his prose writing, entitled *Epoch and Artist*, was edited by Harman Grisewood in 1959. Subsequent poetry includes *The Fatigue*, 1965, and *The Tribune's Visitation*, 1969. There is a good chapter on *In Parenthesis* in John H. Johnston, *English Poetry of the First World War*, 1964. Robin Ironside edited and introduced the Jones volume of the Penguin Modern Painters, 1949. David Balmires's *David Jones: Artist and Writer*, 1972, is a full-view study.

EDWIN MUIR

Editions available are *Collected Poems*, 2nd ed., 1965, with a preface by T. S. Eliot; *Essays on Literature and Society*, 2nd ed., 1965; *The Estate of Poetry*, 1962. *An Autobiography*, 1964, continues and expands *The Story and the Fable*, 1940. P. H. Butter's *Edwin Muir, Man and Poet*, 1966, is biographical; the same author's critical study appeared in 1962 (repr. 1967). Other recent works include D. G. Hoffman, *Barbarous Knowledge*, 1967; and E. Huberman, *The Poetry of Edwin Muir*, 1971.

HUGH MACDIARMID
(*Christopher Murray Grieve*)

Collected Poems was published in 1962, and a second edition, with an expanded glossary, appeared in 1967. An autobiography, *The Company I've Kept,* 1966, and *Selected Essays,* ed. Duncan Glen, 1970, comprise his published prose. A volume of essays in his honor, *Hugh MacDiarmid: A Festschrift,* ed. K. Duval and S. G. Smith, appeared in 1962, and, in 1964, studies by Kenneth Buthlay (*Hugh MacDiarmid*), and by Duncan Glen, entitled *Hugh MacDiarmid and the Scottish Renaissance.*

ROBERT GRAVES

Editions   Since Graves has published more than 120 books, and has been regathering his verse into *Collected Poems* volumes since 1926, the bibliographical problems are immense. The 1959 *Collected Poems* was followed by another in 1965; then a *Poems, 1965–1968,* appeared in 1969. *The White Goddess* originally appeared in 1948, but was expanded in 1952. The memoir of World War I, *Goodbye to All That,* 1929, was revised and extended in 1957. Of the novels the most remarkable are *I, Claudius,* 1934, *Claudius The God,* 1934, *Antigua, Penny, Puce,* 1936, and *Hercules My Shipmate,* 1944. His (frequently annoying) essays on poetry are included in *The Common Asphodel,* 1948, *The Crowning Privilege,* 1955, and a *Collected Talks and Essays,* 1969.

Critical Studies   There are critical studies—all entitled *Robert Graves*—by Martin Seymour-Smith, 1956 (rev. ed., 1965); J. M. Cohen, 1960; George Stade, 1967; and Michael Kirkham, *The Poetry of Robert Graves,* 1969; Lionel Trilling has an excellent essay on Graves in *A Gathering of Fugitives,* 1956. Douglas Day's *Swifter Than Reason,* 1963, deals with the critical writings as well. F. H. Higginson brought out his *Bibliography of the Works of Robert Graves* in 1966.

ALDOUS HUXLEY

The most important novels are *Crome Yellow,* 1921; *Antic Hay,* 1923; *Brave New World,* 1932; *Eyeless in Gaza,* 1936; *After Many a Summer,* 1939; *Time Must Have a Stop,* 1944; *Ape and Essence,* 1948 (a horrific antithetical alternative to *Brave New World*); *Collected Essays,* 1959, a selection; *Collected Letters,* ed. Grover Smith, 1969; *Collected Poetry,* 1971. Useful studies, all entitled *Aldous Huxley,* are by Jocelyn Brooke, 1954; J. A. Atkins, 1956; and Peter Bowering, 1969. See also George Woodcock, *Dawn and the Darkest Hour,* 1971.

W. H. AUDEN

Editions   From the *Collected Poems* of 1945 onward, the poet has revised and re-written his selections from past books. Subsequent volumes were *The Age of Anxiety,* 1947; *Nones,* 1951; *The Shield of Achilles,* 1955; *Homage to Clio,* 1960; *About the House,* 1965; and *City Without Walls,* 1969. A new *Collected Shorter Poems* in 1966 was followed by a *Collected Longer Poems,* 1969; a shorter *Selected Poetry* was published in 1959. *The Enchafèd Flood*, 1951, is a long essay on "the romantic iconography of the sea"; and *The Dyer's Hand*, 1962, a generous selection of critical essays. Auden's commonplace book, entitled *A Certain World*, appeared in 1970. Of his many collaborations, two plays written with Christopher Isherwood are available, *The Ascent of F6* and *On the Frontier*, new ed. 1958; with Chester Kallmann, a translation of *The Magic Flute*, 1957; and narration for *The Play of Daniel*, ed. Noah Greenberg, 1959. The opera libretti with Kallmann, for *The Rake's Progress* (Stravinsky), *Elegy for Young Lovers* and *The Bassarids* (Hans Werner Henze) are not published as books. A co-translation with Paul B. Taylor of a selection from *The Elder Edda*, 1970, is to be followed by further versions of Icelandic poetry.

Critical Studies   The best comprehensive critique is by Monroe K. Spears, *The Poetry of W. H. Auden*, 1963. Appearing earlier were Richard Hoggart's *Auden: An Introductory Essay*, 1951; and a somewhat tendentious bibliographical study by Joseph Warren Beach, *The Making of the Auden Canon*, 1957. Current studies include J. G. Blair, *The Poetic Art of W. H. Auden*, 1965; George W. Bahlke, *The Later Auden*, 1970; John Fuller, *A Reader's Guide to W. H. Auden*, 1970; and a (forthcoming) study of the early poetry, by Frederick Buell.

LOUIS MACNIECE

The complete poetry canon is contained in *Collected Poems*, ed. E. R. Dodds, 1967. Prose works include *Modern Poetry: A Personal Essay*, 1938; *The Poetry of William Butler Yeats*, 1941; *Varieties of Parable*, 1965; and the unfinished, posthumously published autobiographical *The Strings Are False*, 1966. There are critical studies (both under the subject as title) by John Press, 1965 (2nd ed. 1967); and Elton E. Smith, 1970. An essay on MacNeice appears in F. O. Matthiessen's *The Responsibilities of the Critic*, 1952.

STEPHEN SPENDER

Collected Poems, 1928–1953, 1955, actually a carefully pruned selection; there are also *Selected Poems*, 1964, and *The Generous Days*, 1971. Prose works include *The Destructive Element*, 1934; the autobiographical *World Within World*, 1953; *The Creative Element*, 1954; *The Making of a Poem*, 1955; *The Struggle of the Modern*, 1963; and *Year of the Young Rebels*, 1969. There is material on Spender in Derek Stanford's monograph, *Pylon Poets*, 1969.

EDITH SITWELL

The basic work is contained in *Collected Poems*, 1930; an enlarged *Collected Poems*, 1954, contains explanatory and introductory notes by the poet herself. *The Outcasts*, 1962, and its slightly expanded U.S. version, *Music and Ceremonies*, 1963, prints poems not in the collected edition. Of the prose works, her *Alexander Pope* appeared in 1930, *The English Eccentrics* in 1933, and an autobiography, *Taken Care of*, after her death in 1965. There is a brief study by John Lehmann, 1952, and a longer one by Ralph J. Mills, Jr., 1966, both entitled *Edith Sitwell*. John Lehmann's *A Nest of Tigers*, 1968, concerns the Sitwell family.

WILLIAM EMPSON

The *Collected Poems,* 1955, contains slightly more material than the previous collection of 1949. Of his critical works, *Seven Types of Ambiguity* appeared in 1930 (rev. ed., 1947); *Some Versions of Pastoral* (also known as *English Pastoral Poetry*) in 1935; and *The Structure of Complex Words* in 1951. Essays on Empson's poetry are included in John Wain's *Preliminary Essays,* 1957, and A. Alvarez, *Stewards of Excellence,* 1958. In June 1963 *The Review* devoted a double number (Nos. 6–7) to Empson.

DYLAN THOMAS

Editions The expanded edition of the 1952 *Collected Poems,* published in 1957, is the standard. Prose works include *Portrait of the Artist as a Young Dog,* 1940; *Adventures in the Skin Trade,* 1955; and *Quite Early One Morning,* 1954. Thomas's popular radio play, *Under Milk Wood,* was published also in 1954; and his *Notebooks* were edited by Ralph N. Maud in 1967.

Critical Studies Interpretive works range from the early one by Henry Treece, *Dylan Thomas: Dog Among the Fairies,* 1949 (revised 1956), to those by Elder Olson, *The Poetry of Dylan Thomas,* and Derek Stanford, *Dylan Thomas: A Literary Study,* both in 1954; and G. S. Fraser, *Dylan Thomas,* 3rd ed., 1965; and William T. Moynihan, *The Craft and Art of Dylan Thomas,* 1966. Ralph N. Maud's *Entrances to Dylan Thomas's Poetry* (1963) is probably the best of these.

Biography The standard is Constantine FitzGibbon's *The Life of Dylan Thomas,* 1965, which was preceded by John Malcolm Brinnin's *Dylan Thomas in America,* 1955. Bill Read's *The Days of Dylan Thomas,* 1964, contains valuable photographs.

E. M. FORSTER

Editions Apart from the novels the most important books are *Aspects of the Novel,* 1927, and the two collections of essays *Abinger Harvest,* 1936, and *Two Cheers for Democracy,* 1951. There is also the book on his second Indian visit, *The Hill of Devi,* 1953.

Critical Studies Of several full-length essays the best are by Lionel Trilling, 1943; (2nd ed. rev., 1965); F. C. Crews, *E. M. Forster: The Perils of Humanism,* 1962; and Wilfred Stone, *The Cave and the Mountain,* 1966. There is an extensive survey (under his subject's name) by Laurence Brander, 1968; and *Forster: A Collection of Critical Essays,* ed. Malcolm Bradbury, in the series Twentieth Century Views. See also J. K. Johnstone's *The Bloomsbury Group,* 1954; and Quentin Bell's *Bloomsbury,* 1968. At this writing, P. N. Furbank is at work on an authorized biography.

JOHN BETJEMAN

A *Collected Poems* (rev. ed., 1970) preserve all that the poet wishes to keep from earlier volumes; its first publication was followed by *High and Low* in 1966. A previous *Selected Poems,* 1948, and *A Few Late Chrysanthemums,* 1953, are still in print. *Slick But Not Streamlined,* 1947, an earlier selection, had an introduction by W. H.

Auden. *Summoned by Bells*, 1960, is a verse autobiography. Among his architectural prose works are *The American's Guide to English Parish Churches*, 1959, and *Ghastly Good Taste*, 1933. There are analyses by Derek Stanford, *John Betjeman: A Study*, 1961, and Jocelyn Brooke, *Ronald Firbank and John Betjeman*, 1962.

GEORGE ORWELL

The novels are published in various editions; the nonfiction titles, *The Road to Wigan Pier, Homage to Catalonia*, and *Down and Out in London and Paris*, are supplemented by the standard collection of his shorter pieces, *Collected Essays, Journalism and Letters*, ed. S. Orwell and I. Angus, four vols., 1968. There is a useful *Orwell Reader*, ed. R. Rovere, 1956. Studies include George Woodcock, *The Crystal Spirit*, 1966; and Raymond Williams's briefer *George Orwell*, 1971.

SAMUEL BECKETT

There is a *Collected Works* published in 16 vols., 1970, and available in America. The past fifteen years have seen the accumulation of a vast amount of criticism of Beckett; among the best of the critiques are Hugh Kenner, *Samuel Beckett, A Critical Study*, 1961; Ruby Cohn, *Samuel Beckett*, 1962; John Fletcher, *The Novels of Samuel Beckett*, 1964; Raymond Federman, *Journey into Chaos*, 1965, on Beckett's earlier fiction. Stanley Cavell's "Ending the Waiting Game," in *Must We Mean What We Say?*, 1969, is a brilliant study of *Endgame* by a philosopher whose techniques are analytic rather than existential. Lawrence E. Harvey's *Samuel Beckett: Poet and Critic* (1970) is thoroughly detailed in documenting the background to the poems. Martin Esslin edited *Samuel Beckett: A Collection of Critical Essays* in 1965.

THE CONTEMPORARY PERIOD

Critical Essays and Anthologies   For the study of post-war poetry: G. S. Fraser, *Vision and Rhetoric*, 1959; John Press, *Rule and Energy*, 1963; Robert Conquest, ed., *New Lines*, 1956, and *New Lines* II, 1963; and A. Alvarez, *The New Poetry*, 1966. Perhaps the most useful volumes are John Press, *A Map of Modern English Verse*, 1969, with extensive quotation of entire poems, and the tasteful and broadly inclusive anthology of Edward Lucie-Smith, *British Poetry Since 1945*, 1970. A good general treatment of developments in the theatre is John Russell Taylor, *The Angry Theatre: New British Drama*, 1969.

Basil Bunting   *Poems*, 1950; *Briggflatts*, 1966; *Collected Poems*, 1968.

Stevie Smith   *Selected Poems*, 1962; *The Frog Prince*, 1966; *The Best Beast*, 1969; among her novels are *Novel on Yellow Paper*, 1937, and *Harold's Leap*, 1950.

John Heath-Stubbs   *The Charity of the Stars*, 1944; *The Triumph of the Muse*, 1958; *Selected Poems*, 1966; *Satires and Epigrams*, 1968.

Donald Davie   *New and Selected Poems*, 1961; *Essex Poems*, 1969; *Collected Poems*, 1972. Criticism: *Purity of Diction in English Verse*, 1952; *Articulate Energy*, 1955 (repr. 1971).

Philip Larkin   *The North Ship*, 1945 (rev. ed., 1966); *The Less Deceived*, 1955; *The Whitsun Weddings*, 1964.

Kingsley Amis   *A Case of Samples*, 1957; *A Look Round the Estate*, 1967. Novels: *Lucky Jim* (1954); *The Anti-Death League*, 1967; *The Green Man*, 1970 (among several fictional titles); the critical piece *What Became of Jane Austen?* 1971.

Charles Tomlinson   *The Necklace*, 1955; *Seeing is Believing*, 1960; *A Peopled Landscape*, 1963; *American Scenes*, 1966; *The Way of a World*, 1969.

Thom Gunn   *Fighting Terms*, 1954 (rev. ed., 1962); *The Sense of Movement*, 1957; *My Sad Captains*, 1961; *Positives*, 1966; *Touch*, 1967. Gunn also edited and introduced a selection of Fulke Greville poetry in 1969.

Ted Hughes *The Hawk in the Rain*, 1957; *Lupercal*, 1960; *Wodwo*, 1967; *Crow*, 1970.

Geoffrey Hill   *For the Unfallen*, 1959; *King Log*, 1968; *Mercian Hymns*, 1971.

Other poets working during the post-World War II period are **Roy Fuller,** with a *Collected Poems*, 1962, and a subsequent *New Poems*, 1968; **George Barker,** *Collected Poems*, 1957, and *The True Confessions of George Barker*, 1965. **Keith Douglas** (killed in the war) had a posthumous *Collected Poems*, 1966, ed. J. Waller, G. S. Fraser and J. C. Hall.

Author and Title Index

First-Line Index

2233